HARRAP'S

MINI

French-English

DICTIONARY
DICTIONNAIRE

Anglais-Français

Michael Janes

HARRAP

EDINBURGH
NEW YORK TORONTO

Distributed in the United States by
PRENTICE HALL
New York

French Consultant
Fabrice Antoine

English Consultants
Hazel Curties   Stuart Fortey

First published in Great Britain 1988
by HARRAP BOOKS Ltd
43–45 Annandale Street, Edinburgh EH7 4AZ

Reprinted 1989 (twice), 1990 (five times), 1991 (twice), 1992

In the United States, ISBN 0-13-383142-6

Library of Congress Cataloguing-in-Publication Data

Harrap's mini French–English dictionary = dictionnaire Anglais–
Français/[edited by] Michael Janes.
p.   cm.
"First published in Great Britain, 1988". T.p. verso.
ISBN 0-13-383142-6 : $4.00 (U.S.:est.)
1. French language – Dictionaries – English.
2. English language – Dictionaries – French.
I. Janes, Michael. II. Mini French–English dictionary. III. Title:
Dictionnaire Anglais–Français.
PC2640.H277 1990   89-26637
443′.21 – dc20   CIP

Dépôt légal pour cette édition : avril 1988

Printed in England by Clays Ltd, St Ives plc

Contents/Table des matières

TRADEMARKS

Words considered to be trademarks have been designated in this dictionary by the symbol ®. However, no judgment is implied concerning the legal status of any trademark by virtue of the presence or absence of such a symbol.

MARQUES DÉPOSÉES

Les termes considérés comme des marques déposées sont signalés dans ce dictionnaire par le symbole ®. Cependant, la présence ou l'absence de ce symbole ne constitue nullement une indication quant à la valeur juridique de ces termes.

Preface

This dictionary is an entirely new publication designed to provide an up-to-date, practical and concise work of reference giving translations of the most useful French and English vocabulary.

The aim has been to achieve a work of great clarity of equal value to French and to English speakers, whether students, tourists, businessmen or -women or general readers, and to produce a text offering the maximum amount of guidance in pinpointing and understanding translations. Equal importance has been given to the presentation of French and English. Different translations of the same word or phrase are clearly labelled by means of bracketed context indicators and/or style and field labels. A single translation of a word is also often labelled as an additional aid to the user (e.g. **hedgehog** n (*animal*) hérisson m; **ungainly** a (*clumsy*) gauche; **béotien, -ienne** nmf (*inculte*) philistine). The user is helped by having indicators and labels in French in the French section and in English in the English section of the dictionary.

Style and field labels follow bracketed indicators (e.g. **grid** n . . . (*system*) El réseau m; **bidule** nm (*chose*) Fam thingummy). In the event that more than one translation within a grammatical category being qualified by the same style or field label, the label may then precede (see **calé, liquidizer, trucker**).

The user will find in the text important abbreviations, useful geographical information such as names of countries, and a wide coverage of American words and usage. The vocabulary treated includes French and English colloquialisms and slang, and important technical jargon. Comparatives and superlatives of English adjectives are also indicated.

In order to save space, derived words are usually included within the entry of a headword. All such words are highlighted by means of a lozenge. Derivatives may be written in full or abbreviated, as is usually the case for important derived forms (such as English **-ly** or French **-ment**).

An oblique stroke in bold is used to mark the stem of a headword at which point the derived ending is added. A bold dash stands for a headword or the portion of a headword to the left of the oblique stroke (e.g. **awkward** a . . . ◆**—ly** adv . . . ◆**—ness** n . . . ; **boulevers/er** vt . . . ◆**—ant** a . . . ◆**—ement** nm).

An oblique stroke within an entry is another space-saving device. It is used to separate non equivalent alternative parts of a phrase or expression matched exactly in French and English (e.g. **les basses/hautes classes** the lower/upper classes is to be understood as: **les basses classes** the lower classes and **les hautes classes** the upper classes; **to give s.o./sth a push** pousser qn/qch as: **to give s.o. a push** pousser qn and **to give sth a push** pousser qch).

A further typographical device, a filled square, may be used to introduce a string of English phrasal verbs (see **come, take**).

In common with other Harrap dictionaries, when a headword appears in an example in the same form, it is represented by its initial letter. This applies whether the headword starts a new line (e.g. **advance** n **in a. of s.o.** avant qn) or appears within an entry, either in full form (e.g. ◆**arterial** a **a. road** route f principale), or in abbreviated form (e.g. (where ◆**—ed** stands for **advanced**) ◆**—ed** a **a. in years** âgé).

The pronunciation of both English and French is shown using the latest symbols of the International Phonetic Alphabet. Pronunciation is given for headwords at the start of an entry, and, as an additional help to the user, for a word within an entry where the correct pronunciation may be difficult to derive from the form of the word (e.g. ◆**aristocratie** [-asi]; ◆**aoûtien, -ienne** [ausje, -jen]; ◆**rabid** ['ræbid]; ◆**prayer** [preər]).

Stress in English is indicated for headwords and for derived words in which stress differs from that of a headword (e.g. **civilize** ['sɪvɪlaɪz] and ◆**civili'zation**). American English pronunciation is listed wherever it is considered to differ substantially from that of British English (e.g. **aristocrat** ['ærɪstəkræt, Am ə'rɪstəkræt], **quinine** ['kwɪniɪn, Am 'kwaɪnaɪn]). American spelling is also given if considered sufficiently different (e.g. **tire** and **tyre, plow** and **plough**).

An original feature of this dictionary is its semantic approach to the order and arrangement of entries. An approach whereby the meaning of words is allowed to influence the structure of entries is felt to be of particular benefit to the user in his or her understanding of language.

Important semantic categories have been indicated by bold Arabic numerals within an entry (see **bolt, tail, général**) or have been entered as separate headwords (see **bug¹** and **bug²**, **draw¹** and **draw²**, **start¹** and **start²**). Note that grammatical categories, apart from the first, have been marked by a dash.

Words are entered under the headword from which they are considered to derive (e.g. **approfondi**, abbreviated as ◆**─i** follows **approfond/ir**; ◆**astronomer** and ◆**astro'nom-ical** follow **astronomy**). Present and past participles (used adjectivally) are felt to be closely associated in meaning and form with the infinitive from which they derive. They are entered, usually in abbreviated form, within an entry immediately after the infinitive, any other derivatives there may be following in alphabetical order (e.g. **exalt/er** *vt* . . . ◆**─ant** *a* . . . ◆**─é** *a* . . . ◆**exaltation** *nf*: **accommodat/e** *vt* . . . ◆**─ing** *a* . . . ◆**accommo'dation** *n*; **accommodat/e** *vi* . . . ◆**─ed** *a* . . . ◆**expi'ration** *n* . . . ◆**expiry** *n*).

Derived words and compounds are felt to be semantically distinct and are, wherever possible, grouped together alphabetically and listed separately from each other (e.g. **base** *n* . . . ◆**─less** *a* . . . ◆**─ness** *n* . . . ◆**baseball** *n* . . . ◆**baseboard** *n*; **bouton** *nm* . . . ◆**b.-d'or** *nm* . . . ◆**b.-pression** *nm* . . . ◆**boutonner** *vt* . . . ◆**boutonneux. -euse** *a* . . . ◆**boutonnière** *nf*). Compounds may be listed in the place within an entry where they are felt best to belong by virtue of meaning.

The author wishes to express his gratitude to Monsieur F. Antoine, Mrs H. Curties and Mr S. Fortey for their advice and help, to Mrs R. Hillmore for her assistance with proofreading, and to Mr J.-L. Barbanneau for his support and encouragement.

M. Janes
London, 1988

Préface

Ce dictionnaire entièrement nouveau a pour ambition d'être un ouvrage de référence moderne, pratique et compact, offrant les traductions des termes les plus courants du français comme de l'anglais.

Il veut être un ouvrage qui, par sa grande clarté, soit utile autant au francophone qu'à l'anglophone, pour les études, le tourisme, les affaires aussi bien que pour l'usage courant: il tente de fournir le plus d'indications possible pour aider l'utilisateur à cerner et à comprendre les traductions proposées. On a accordé la même importance à la présentation du français qu'à celle de l'anglais. Les différentes traductions d'un même mot ou d'une même expression sont clairement définies à l'aide d'indications de contexte entre parenthèses et/ou de symboles indiquant le niveau de langue et le domaine d'utilisation. Lorsqu'un mot est accompagné d'une seule traduction, celle-ci est également souvent précédée d'une indication destinée à fournir à l'utilisateur une aide supplémentaire (par exemple **hedgehog** *n* (*animal*) hérisson *m*; **ungainly** *a* (*clumsy*) gauche; **béotien, -ienne** *nmf* (*inculte*) philistine). L'accès à cet ouvrage est facilité par l'utilisation d'indications en français dans la partie français-anglais et en anglais dans la partie anglais-français.

Les indications de niveau de langue et de domaine d'utilisation viennent à la suite de celles entre parenthèses (par exemple **grid** *n* . . . (*system*) *El* réseau *m*; **bidule** *nm* (*chose*) *Fam* thingummy). Lorsque plusieurs traductions dans la même catégorie grammaticale sont définies par la même indication, celle-ci peut alors venir en tête (voir **calé, liquidizer, trucker**).

L'utilisateur trouvera dans cet ouvrage des abréviations importantes, de précieux éléments de géographie tels que des noms de pays, ainsi qu'une large sélection d'américanismes. Le lexique retenu comprend des mots et des expressions familiers et argotiques, tant en français qu'en anglais, et des termes techniques courants. De plus, les comparatifs et superlatifs des adjectifs anglais sont donnés.

Par souci de concision, les mots dérivés sont généralement donnés dans le corps des articles. Tous ces mots sont repérés par un losange. Les dérivés sont donnés soit sous leur forme complète, soit en abrégé, ce qui est généralement le cas pour les formes dérivées courantes (telles que celles en **-ly** en anglais ou en **-ment** en français).

On utilise une barre oblique pour indiquer le radical d'une entrée à la suite duquel la terminaison d'un dérivé sera ajoutée. Un tiret en gras remplace le mot d'entrée ou la partie de ce mot qui précède la barre oblique (par exemple **awkward** *a* . . . **—ly** *adv* . . . **◆—ness** *n* . . . ; **boulevers/er** *vt* . . . **◆—ement** *nm*).

Toujours par souci de concision, une barre oblique est utilisée dans un article pour éviter la répétition d'un même élément de phrase (par exemple **les basses/hautes classes** the lower/upper classes se lira: **les basses classes** the lower classes et **les hautes classes** the upper classes; **to give s.o./sth a push** pousser qn/qch se lira: **to give s.o. a push** pousser qn et **to give sth a push** pousser qch).

Enfin, un carré plein peut être utilisé pour introduire une série de verbes à particule en anglais (voir **come**, **take**).

Comme il est d'usage dans les autres dictionnaires Harrap, lorsqu'un mot d'entrée est repris sous la même forme dans un exemple, il est remplacé par sa première lettre. Cela est le cas aussi bien lorsque le mot est au début d'un article (par exemple **advance** *n* in a. of s.o. avant qn) qu'il apparaît dans un article, sous forme complète (par exemple **◆arterial** *a* **a. road** route *f* principale) ou en abrégé (par exemple **◆—ed** remplaçant **advanced**) **◆—ed a a. in years** âgé).

La prononciation de l'anglais comme du français est fournie; elle utilise la notation la plus moderne de l'Alphabet Phonétique International. La phonétique est donnée pour les mots d'entrée au début de l'article et, pour aider l'utilisateur, pour tout mot dans un article dont il pourrait être difficile de déduire la prononciation à partir de l'orthographe (par exemple **◆aristocratie** [-asi]; **◆aoûtien, -ienne** [ausjɛ̃, -jɛn]; **◆rabid** [ˈræbid]; **◆prayer** [preər]).

En anglais, l'accent tonique est indiqué pour les mots d'entrée et pour les dérivés chaque fois que l'accentuation diffère de celle de l'entrée (par exemple **civilize** et **◆civili'zation**). Les prononciations américaines sont indiquées chaque fois qu'elles diffèrent de façon substantielle de celles de l'anglais britannique (par exemple **aristocrat** [ˈærɪstəkræt, *Am* əˈrɪstəkræt], **quinine** [ˈkwɪniːn, *Am* ˈkwaɪnaɪn]). On indique également l'orthographe américaine lorsqu'elle est suffisamment différente de celle de l'anglais britannique (par exemple **tire** et **tyre**, **plow** et **plough**).

Une des caractéristiques originales de ce dictionnaire est son approche sémantique du classement et de l'organisation des articles. On a considéré que cette approche, où le sens des mots détermine pour une part l'organisation des articles, serait d'un grand secours à l'utilisateur en ce qui concerne sa compréhension de la langue.

Les catégories sémantiques importantes sont indiquées dans un article par des chiffres arabes en gras (voir **bolt**, **tail**, **général**) ou sont présentées comme des mots distincts (voir **bug**[1] et **bug**[2], **draw**[1] et **draw**[2], **start**[1] et **start**[2]). Les catégories grammaticales autres que la première traitée sont indiquées par un tiret.

Les mots apparaissent sous les mots d'entrée dont ils sont dérivés (par exemple **approfondi**, abrégé en **◆—i** suit **approfond/ir**; **◆astronomer** et **◆astro'nomical** suivent **astronomy**). Les participes présents et passés (utilisés comme adjectifs) sont considérés comme étant étroitement associés par le sens et par la forme à l'infinitif dont ils sont dérivés. Ils sont placés dans l'article, généralement en abrégé, immédiatement après l'infinitif; tous les autres dérivés éventuels apparaissent ensuite par ordre alphabétique (par exemple **exalt/er** *vt* . . . **◆—ant** *a* . . . **◆é** *a* . . . **◆exaltation** *nf*; **accommodat/e** *vt* . . . **◆—ing** *a* . . . **◆accommo'dation** *n*; **expir/e** *vi* . . . **◆—ed** *a* . . . **◆expi'ration** *n* . . . **◆expiry** *n*).

Les mots dérivés et les mots composés sont considérés comme étant distincts, du point de vue du sens, et sont, chaque fois que possible, regroupés séparément (par exemple **base** *n* . . . **◆—less** *a* . . . **◆—ness** *n* . . . **◆baseball** *n* . . . **◆baseboard** *n*; **bouton** *nm* . . . **◆b.-d'or** *nm* . . . **◆b.-pression** *nm* . . . **◆boutonner** *vt* . . . **◆boutonneux, -euse** *a* . . . **◆boutonnière** *nf*). Les composés se trouvent placés dans les articles là où leur sens a semblé devoir les appeler.

L'auteur tient à exprimer sa gratitude à Monsieur F. Antoine, à Mrs H. Curties et à Mr S. Fortey pour leurs conseils et leur collaboration, à Mrs R. Hillmore qui a bien voulu nous aider à relire les épreuves, et à Monsieur J.-L. Barbanneau pour son soutien et ses encouragements.

M. Janes
Londres, 1988

Grammar notes

In French, the feminine of an adjective is formed as a rule by adding **e** to the masculine form (e.g. grand, grande; carré, carrée; chevalin, chevaline). If the masculine already ends in **e**, the feminine is the same as the masculine (e.g. utile). Irregular feminine forms of adjectives (e.g. généreux, généreuse; léger, légère; doux; douce) are given in the French-English side of the dictionary. In the English-French side, French adjectives are shown in the masculine form only. Irregular feminines of adjectives are listed in the following way: généreux, -euse; léger, -ère; doux, douce.

To form the plural of a French noun or adjective **s** is usually added to the singular (e.g. arbre, arbres; taxi, taxis; petit, petits). The plural form of a noun ending in **s**, **x** or **z** (e.g. pois, croix, nez) is the same as that of the singular. Plurals of nouns and adjectives which do not follow these general rules are listed in the French section, including the plurals of French compounds, where the formation of the plural involves a change other than the addition of final **s** (e.g. arc-en-ciel, arcs-en-ciel). Those nouns and adjectives where **x** or **aux** is added in the plural are shown in the following way: cerveau, -x; général, -aux.

In English also, **s** is added to form the plural of a noun (e.g. cat, cats; taxi, taxis) but a noun ending in **ch**, **s**, **sh**, **x** or **z** forms its plural by the addition of **es** (e.g. glass, glasses; match, matches). (Note that when **ch** is pronounced [k], the plural is in **s**, e.g. monarch, monarchs.) When a noun ends in **y** preceded by a consonant, **y** is changed to **ies** to form the plural (e.g. army, armies). Irregular English plurals are given in the English-French side, including the plurals of English compounds where the formation of the plural involves a change other than the addition of final **s** (e.g. brother-in-law, brothers-in-law).

English nouns may be used as adjectives. When a French adjective is translated in this way, this use is made clear by the addition of a hyphen following the noun translation (e.g. farm- as a translation of **agricole**).

Most French verbs have regular conjugations though some display spelling anomalies (see French verb conjugations on p (i)). In the French section an asterisk is used to mark an irregular verb, and refers the user to the table of irregular verbs on p (ii).

Most English verbs form their past tense and past participle by adding **ed** to the infinitive (e.g. look, looked) or **d** to an infinitive already ending in **e** (e.g. love, loved). When a verb ends in **y** preceded by a consonant, **y** becomes **ied** (e.g. satisfy, satisfied). To form the third person singular of a verb in the present tense **s** is added to the infinitive (e.g. know, knows) but an infinitive in **ch**, **s**, **sh**, **x** or **z** forms its third person singular by the addition of **es** (e.g. dash, dashes). When an infinitive ends in **y** preceded by a consonant, **y** is changed to **ies** to form the third person singular (e.g. satisfy, satisfies).

The English present participle is formed by the addition of **ing** to the infinitive (e.g. look, looking) but final **e** is omitted when an infinitive ends in **e** (e.g. love, loving). When the infinitive ends in a single consonant preceded by a vowel (e.g. tug), the final consonant is usually doubled in the past tense, past and present participles (e.g. tug, tugged, tugging).

Irregular English verb conjugations are given in the English headword list, and a summary of the most important irregular verbs may also be found on p (vii). The doubling of consonants in English verbs is indicated in the text. The latter is shown in the following way: **tug** . . . *vt* (**-gg-**).

Notes sur la grammaire

En français, le féminin d'un adjectif se forme en général en ajoutant **e** au masculin (par exemple grand, grande; carré, carrée; chevalin, chevaline). Lorsque le masculin se termine déjà par **e**, le féminin est identique (par exemple utile). Les féminins d'adjectifs qui ne se conforment pas à ces règles (par exemple généreux, généreuse; léger, légère; doux, douce) sont donnés dans la partie français-anglais où ils sont notés comme suit: généreux, -euse; léger, -ère; doux, douce. Dans la partie anglais-français, on ne donne que la forme masculine des adjectifs.

On forme en général le pluriel d'un nom ou d'un adjectif français en ajoutant **s** au singulier (par exemple arbre, arbres; taxi, taxis; petit, petits). Le pluriel d'un nom se terminant par **s**, **x** ou **z** (par exemple pois, croix, nez) est identique au singulier. Les pluriels des noms et adjectifs qui font exception à ces règles générales sont signalés dans la partie français-anglais, de même que les pluriels des mots composés français dont le passage au pluriel appelle une modification autre que le simple ajout d'un **s** final (par exemple arc-en-ciel, arcs-en-ciel). Les noms et adjectifs dont le pluriel se forme à l'aide d'un **x** ou de **aux** sont notés comme suit: cerveau, -x; général, -aux.

De la même façon, en anglais, on forme le pluriel des noms en ajoutant **s** (par exemple cat, cats; taxi, taxis) mais on ajoutera **es** aux noms qui se terminent par **ch**, **s**, **sh**, **x** ou **z** (par exemple glass, glasses; match, matches). (Noter cependant que lorsque **ch** se prononce [k], le pluriel est en **s**, comme dans monarch, monarchs.) Lorsqu'un nom se termine par un **y** précédé d'une consonne, ce **y** devient **ies** au pluriel (par exemple army, armies). Les pluriels irréguliers de l'anglais sont signalés dans la partie anglais-français, de même que les pluriels des mots composés anglais dont le passage au pluriel entraîne une modification autre que le simple ajout d'un **s** final (par exemple brother-in-law, brothers-in-law).

Les noms anglais peuvent s'utiliser comme adjectifs. Lorsqu'un adjectif français est traduit par un nom, cela est signalé par l'ajout d'un trait d'union à la suite de ce nom (par exemple farm- comme traduction de **agricole**).

La plupart des verbes ont des conjugaisons régulières; cependant, certains subissent des variations orthographiques (voir: Conjugaisons des verbes français à la page (i)) Dans la partie français-anglais, un astérisque signale un verbe irrégulier et renvoie à la table des verbes irréguliers donnée en page (ii).

En anglais, le passé et le participe passé des verbes se forment dans la plupart des cas en ajoutant **ed** à l'infinitif (par exemple look, looked) ou seulement **d** lorsque l'infinitif se termine par un **e** (par exemple love, loved). Lorsqu'un verbe se termine par un **y** précédé d'une consonne, ce **y** devient **ied** (par exemple satisfy, satisfied). La troisième personne du singulier d'un verbe au présent se forme en ajoutant **s** à l'infinitif (par exemple know, knows), mais on ajoutera **es** aux infinitifs qui se terminent par **ch**, **s**, **sh**, **x** ou **z** (par exemple dash, dashes). Enfin, lorsqu'un verbe se termine par un **y** précédé d'une consonne, ce **y** devient **ies** à la troisième personne du singulier (par exemple satisfy, satisfies).

Le participe présent en anglais se forme en ajoutant la désinence **ing** à l'infinitif (par exemple look, looking); lorsqu'un infinitif comporte un **e** final, celui-ci disparaît (par exemple love, loving). Lorsque l'infinitif se termine par une seule consonne précédée d'une voyelle (par exemple tug), la consonne finale est souvent doublée au passé et aux participes passé et présent (par exemple tug, tugged, tugging).

Les formes des verbes irréguliers anglais sont données dans la partie anglais-français et une liste récapitulative des verbes irréguliers usuels figure en page (vii). Le doublement des consonnes dans les verbes anglais est signalé dans le corps de l'ouvrage; il est noté comme suit: **tug** . . . *vt* (**-gg-**).

Abbreviations

Abréviations

adjective	*a*	adjectif
abbreviation	*abbr, abrév*	abréviation
adverb	*adv*	adverbe
agriculture	*Agr*	agriculture
American	*Am*	américain
anatomy	*Anat*	anatomie
architecture	*Archit*	architecture
slang	*Arg*	argot
article	*art*	article
cars, motoring	*Aut*	automobile
auxiliary	*aux*	auxiliaire
aviation, aircraft	*Av*	aviation
biology	*Biol*	biologie
botany	*Bot*	botanique
British	*Br*	britannique
Canadian	*Can*	canadien
carpentry	*Carp*	menuiserie
chemistry	*Ch*	chimie
cinema	*Cin*	cinéma
commerce	*Com*	commerce
conjunction	*conj*	conjonction
cookery	*Culin*	cuisine
definite	*def, déf*	défini
demonstrative	*dem, dém*	démonstratif
economics	*Econ, Écon*	économie
electricity	*El, Él*	électricité
et cetera	*etc*	et cetera
feminine	*f*	féminin
familiar	*Fam*	familier
football	*Fb*	football
figurative	*Fig*	figuré
finance	*Fin*	finance
feminine plural	*fpl*	féminin pluriel
French	*Fr*	français
geography	*Geog, Géog*	géographie
geology	*Geol, Géol*	géologie
geometry	*Geom, Géom*	géométrie
grammar	*Gram*	grammaire
history	*Hist*	histoire
humorous	*Hum*	humoristique
indefinite	*indef, indéf*	indéfini
indicative	*indic*	indicatif
infinitive	*inf*	infinitif
interjection	*int*	interjection
invariable	*inv*	invariable
ironic	*Iron*	ironique
journalism	*Journ*	journalisme
legal, law	*Jur*	juridique
linguistics	*Ling*	linguistique
literary	*Lit, Litt*	littéraire
literature	*Liter, Littér*	littérature

masculine	*m*	masculin
mathematics	*Math*	mathématique
medicine	*Med, Méd*	médecine
carpentry	*Menuis*	menuiserie
meteorology	*Met, Mét*	météorologie
military	*Mil*	militaire
masculine plural	*mpl*	masculin pluriel
music	*Mus*	musique
noun	*n*	nom
nautical	*Nau*	nautique
noun feminine	*nf*	nom féminin
noun masculine	*nm*	nom masculin
noun masculine and feminine	*nmf*	nom masculin et féminin
pejorative	*Pej, Péj*	péjoratif
philosophy	*Phil*	philosophie
photography	*Phot*	photographie
physics	*Phys*	physique
plural	*pl*	pluriel
politics	*Pol*	politique
possessive	*poss*	possessif
past participle	*pp*	participe passé
prefix	*pref, préf*	préfixe
preposition	*prep, prép*	préposition
present participle	*pres p*	participe présent
present tense	*pres t*	temps présent
pronoun	*pron*	pronom
psychology	*Psy*	psychologie
past tense	*pt*	prétérit
	qch	quelque chose
	qn	quelqu'un
registered trademark	®	marque déposée
radio	*Rad*	radio
railway, *Am* railroad	*Rail*	chemin de fer
relative	*rel*	relatif
religion	*Rel*	religion
school	*Sch, Scol*	école
singular	*sing*	singulier
slang	*Sl*	argot
someone	*s.o.*	
sport	*Sp*	sport
something	*sth*	
subjunctive	*sub*	subjonctif
technical	*Tech*	technique
telephone	*Tel, Tél*	téléphone
textiles	*Tex*	industrie textile
theatre	*Th*	théâtre
television	*TV*	télévision
typography, printing	*Typ*	typographie
university	*Univ*	université
United States	*US*	États-Unis
auxiliary verb	*v aux*	verbe auxiliaire
intransitive verb	*vi*	verbe intransitif
impersonal verb	*v imp*	verbe impersonnel
pronominal verb	*vpr*	verbe pronominal
transitive verb	*vt*	verbe transitif
transitive and intransitive verb	*vti*	verbe transitif et intransitif

Pronunciation of French

TABLE OF PHONETIC SYMBOLS

Vowels

[i]	vite, cygne	[y]	cru, sûr
[e]	été, donner	[ø]	feu, meule
[ɛ]	elle, mais	[œ]	œuf, jeune
[a]	chat, fameux	[ə]	le, refaire
[ɑ]	pas, âgé	[ɛ̃]	vin, plein, faim
[ɔ]	donne, fort	[ɑ̃]	enfant, temps
[o]	dos, chaud, peau	[ɔ̃]	mon, nombre
[u]	tout, cour	[œ̃]	lundi, humble

Consonants

[p]	pain, absolu	[z]	cousin, zéro
[b]	beau, abbé	[ʃ]	chose, schéma
[t]	table, nette	[ʒ]	gilet, jeter
[d]	donner, sud	[l]	lait, facile
[k]	camp, képi	[r]	rare, rhume
[g]	garde, second	[m]	mon, flamme
[f]	feu, phrase	[n]	né, canne
[v]	voir, wagon	[ɲ]	campagne
[s]	sou, cire	[ŋ]	jogging
		[']	hanche (*i.e. no liaison or elision*)

Semi-consonants

[j]	piano, voyage
[w]	ouest, noir
[ɥ]	muet, lui

Prononciation de l'anglais

TABLEAU DES SIGNES PHONÉTIQUES

Voyelles et diphtongues

[iː]	bee, police	[ɒ]	lot, what
[ɪə]	beer, real	[ɔː]	all, saw
[ɪ]	bit, added	[ɔɪ]	boil, toy
[e]	bet, said	[əʊ]	low, soap
[eɪ]	date, nail	[ʊ]	put, wool
[eə]	bear, air	[uː]	shoe, too
[æ]	bat, plan	[ʊə]	poor, sure
[aɪ]	fly, life	[ʌ]	cut, some
[ɑː]	art, ask	[ɜː]	burn, learn
[aʊ]	fowl, house	[ə]	china, annoy
		[(ə)]	relation

Consonnes

[p]	pat, top	[ð]	that, breathe
[b]	but, tab	[h]	hat, rehearse
[t]	tap, patter	[l]	lad, all
[d]	dab, sadder	[r]	red, barring
[k]	cat, kite	[r]	better, here (*représente un r*
[g]	go, rogue		*final qui se prononce en*
[f]	fat, phrase		*liaison devant une voyelle,*
[v]	veal, rave		*par exemple* 'here is' [hɪərɪz])
[s]	sat, ace	[m]	mat, hammer
[z]	zero, houses	[n]	no, banner
[ʃ]	dish, pressure	[ŋ]	singing, link
[ʒ]	pleasure	[j]	yet, onion
[tʃ]	charm, rich	[w]	wall, quite
[dʒ]	judge, rage	[']	*marque l'accent tonique;*
[θ]	thatch, breath		*précède la syllable accentuée*

A

A, a [ɑ] *nm* A, a.

a [a] *voir* avoir.

à [a] *prép* (à + le = au [o], à + les = aux [o]) **1** (*direction: lieu*) to; (*temps*) till, to; **aller à Paris** to go to Paris; **de 3 à 4 h** from 3 till *ou* to 4 (o'clock). **2** (*position: lieu*) at, in; (*surface*) on; (*temps*) at; **être au bureau/à la ferme/au jardin/à Paris** to be at *ou* in the office/on *ou* at the farm/in the garden/in Paris; **à la maison** at home; **à l'horizon** on the horizon; **à 8 h** at 8 (o'clock); **à mon arrivée** on (my) arrival; **à lundi!** see you (on) Monday! **3** (*description*) **l'homme à la barbe** the man with the beard; **verre à liqueur** liqueur glass. **4** (*attribution*) **donner qch à qn** to give sth to s.o., give s.o. sth. **5** (*devant inf*) **apprendre à lire** to learn to read; **travail à faire** work to do; **maison à vendre** house for sale; **prêt à partir** ready to leave. **6** (*appartenance*) **c'est son** (*livre*) **à lui** it's his (book); **c'est à vous de** (*décider, protester etc*) it's up to you to; (*lire, jouer etc*) it's your turn to. **7** (*prix*) for; **pain à 2F** loaf for 2F. **8** (*poids*) by; **vendre au kilo** to sell by the kilo. **9** (*moyen, manière*) **à bicyclette** by bicycle; **à la main** by hand; **à pied** on foot; **au crayon** with a pencil, in pencil; **au galop** at a gallop; **à la française** in the French style *ou* way; **deux à deux** two by two. **10** (*appel*) **au voleur!** (stop) thief!

abaiss/er [abese] *vt* to lower; **a. qn** to humiliate s.o.; **— s'a.** (*barrière*) to lower; (*température*) to drop; **s'a. à faire** to stoop to doing. ◆**—ement** [-esmɑ̃] *nm* (*chute*) drop.

abandon [abɑ̃dɔ̃] *nm* abandonment; surrender; desertion; *Sp* withdrawal; (*naturel*) abandon; (*confiance*) lack of restraint; **à l'a.** in a neglected state. ◆**abandonner** *vt* (*renoncer à*) to give up, abandon; (*droit*) to surrender; (*quitter*) to desert, abandon; **— vi** to give up; *Sp* to withdraw; **— s'a.** *vpr* (*se détendre*) to let oneself go; (*se confier*) to open up; **s'a. à** to give oneself up to, abandon oneself to.

abasourdir [abazurdir] *vt* to stun, astound.

abat-jour [abaʒur] *nm inv* lampshade.

abats [aba] *nmpl* offal; (*de volaille*) giblets.

abattant [abatɑ̃] *nm* leaf, flap.

abattis [abati] *nmpl* giblets.

abatt/re [abatr] *vt* (*mur*) to knock down; (*arbre*) to cut down, fell; (*animal etc*) to slaughter; (*avion*) to shoot down; (*déprimer*) to demoralize; (*épuiser*) to exhaust; **— s'a.** *vpr* (*tomber*) to collapse; (*oiseau*) to swoop down; (*pluie*) to pour down. ◆**—u** (*triste*) dejected, demoralized; (*faible*) at a low ebb. ◆**—age** *nm* felling; slaughter(ing). ◆**—ement** *nm* (*faiblesse*) exhaustion; (*désespoir*) dejection. ◆**abattoir** *nm* slaughterhouse.

abbaye [abei] *nf* abbey.

abbé [abe] *nm* (*chef d'abbaye*) abbot; (*prêtre*) priest. ◆**abbesse** *nf* abbess.

abcès [apsɛ] *nm* abscess.

abdiquer [abdike] *vti* to abdicate. ◆**abdication** *nf* abdication.

abdomen [abdɔmɛn] *nm* abdomen. ◆**abdominal, -aux** *a* abdominal.

abeille [abɛj] *nf* bee.

aberrant [aberɑ̃] *a* (*idée etc*) ludicrous, absurd. ◆**aberration** *nf* (*égarement*) aberration; (*idée*) ludicrous idea; **dire des aberrations** to talk sheer nonsense.

abhorrer [abɔre] *vt* to abhor, loathe.

abîme [abim] *nm* abyss, chasm, gulf.

abîmer [abime] *vt* to spoil, damage; **— s'a.** *vpr* to get spoilt; **s'a. dans ses pensées** *Litt* to lose oneself in one's thoughts.

abject [abʒɛkt] *a* abject, despicable.

abjurer [abʒyre] *vti* to abjure.

ablation [ablasjɔ̃] *nf* (*d'organe*) removal.

ablutions [ablysjɔ̃] *nfpl* ablutions.

abnégation [abnegasjɔ̃] *nf* self-sacrifice, abnegation.

abois (aux) [ozabwa] *adv* at bay.

abolir [abɔlir] *vt* to abolish. ◆**abolition** *nf* abolition.

abominable [abɔminabl] *a* abominable, obnoxious. ◆**abomination** *nf* abomination.

abondant [abɔ̃dɑ̃] *a* abundant, plentiful. ◆**abondamment** *adv* abundantly. ◆**abondance** *nf* abundance (**de** of); **en a.** in abundance; **années d'a.** years of plenty. ◆**abonder** *vi* to abound (**en** in).

abonné, -ée [abɔne] *nmf* (*à un journal, au téléphone*) subscriber; *Rail Sp Th* season ticket holder; (*du gaz etc*) consumer.

◆**abonnement** *nm* subscription; (**carte d'**)a. season ticket. ◆**s'abonner** *vpr* to subscribe (**à** to); to buy a season ticket.

abord [abɔr] **1** *nm* (*accès*) **d'un a. facile** easy to approach. **2** *nm* (*vue*) **au premier a.** at first sight. **3** *nmpl* (*environs*) surroundings; **aux abords de** around, nearby. ◆**abordable** *a* (*personne*) approachable; (*prix, marchandises*) affordable.

abord (d') [dabɔr] *adv* (*avant tout*) first; (*au début*) at first.

aborder [abɔrde] *vi* to land; — *vt* (*personne*) to approach, accost; (*lieu*) to approach, reach; (*problème*) to tackle, approach; (*attaquer*) Nau to board; (*heurter*) Nau to run foul of. ◆**abordage** *nm* (*assaut*) Nau boarding; (*accident*) Nau collision.

aborigène [abɔriʒɛn] *a & nm* aboriginal.

about/ir [abutir] *vi* to succeed; **a. à** to end at, lead to, end up in; **n'a. à rien** to come to nothing. ◆**—issants** *nmpl voir* **tenants.** ◆**—issement** *nm* (*résultat*) outcome; (*succès*) success.

aboyer [abwaje] *vi* to bark. ◆**aboiement** *nm* bark; *pl* barking.

abrasif, -ive [abrazif, -iv] *a & nm* abrasive.

abrég/er [abreʒe] *vt* (*récit*) to shorten, abridge; (*mot*) to abbreviate. ◆**-é** *nm* summary; **en a.** (*phrase*) in shortened form; (*mot*) in abbreviated form.

abreuver [abrœve] *vt* (*cheval*) to water; — **s'a.** *vpr* to drink. ◆**abreuvoir** *nm* (*récipient*) drinking trough; (*lieu*) watering place.

abréviation [abrevjasjɔ̃] *nf* abbreviation.

abri [abri] *nm* shelter; **à l'a. de** (*vent*) sheltered from; (*besoin*) safe from; **sans a.** homeless. ◆**abriter** *vt* (*protéger*) to shelter; (*loger*) to house; — **s'a.** *vpr* to (take) shelter.

abricot [abriko] *nm* apricot. ◆**abricotier** *nm* apricot tree.

abroger [abrɔʒe] *vt* to abrogate.

abrupt [abrypt] *a* (*versant*) sheer; (*sentier*) steep, abrupt; (*personne*) abrupt.

abrut/ir [abrytir] *vt* (*alcool*) to stupefy (*s.o.*); (*propagande*) to brutalize (*s.o.*); (*travail*) to leave (*s.o.*) dazed, wear (*s.o.*) out. ◆**-i, -ie** *nmf* idiot; — *a* idiotic.

absence [apsɑ̃s] *nf* absence. ◆**absent, -e** *a* (*personne*) absent, away; (*chose*) missing; **air a.** faraway look; — *nmf* absentee. ◆**absentéisme** *nm* absenteeism. ◆**s'absenter** *vpr* to go away.

abside [apsid] *nf* (*d'une église*) apse.

absolu [apsɔly] *a & nm* absolute. ◆**—ment** *adv* absolutely.

absolution [apsɔlysjɔ̃] *nf* absolution.

absorb/er [apsɔrbe] *vt* to absorb. ◆**—ant** *a* absorbent; **travail a.** absorbing job. ◆**absorption** *nf* absorption.

absoudre* [apsudr] *vt* to absolve.

absten/ir* (s') [sapstənir] *vpr* to abstain; **s'a. de** to refrain *ou* abstain from. ◆**abstention** *nf* abstention.

abstinence [apstinɑ̃s] *nf* abstinence.

abstraire* [apstrɛr] *vt* to abstract. ◆**abstrait** *a & nm* abstract. ◆**abstraction** *nf* abstraction; **faire a. de** to disregard, leave aside.

absurde [apsyrd] *a & nm* absurd. ◆**absurdité** *nf* absurdity; **dire des absurdités** to talk nonsense.

abus [aby] *nm* abuse, misuse; over-indulgence; (*injustice*) abuse. ◆**abuser 1** *vi* to go too far; **a. de** (*situation, personne*) to take unfair advantage of; (*autorité*) to abuse, misuse; (*friandises*) to over-indulge in. **2 s'a.** *vpr* to be mistaken.

abusi/f, -ive [abyzif, -iv] *a* excessive; **emploi a.** Ling improper use, misuse. ◆**—vement** *adv* Ling improperly.

acabit [akabi] *nm* **de cet a.** Péj of that ilk *ou* sort.

acacia [akasja] *nm* (*arbre*) acacia.

académie [akademi] *nf* academy; Univ = (regional) education authority. ◆**académicien, -ienne** *nmf* academician. ◆**académique** *a* academic.

acajou [akaʒu] *nm* mahogany; **cheveux a.** auburn hair.

acariâtre [akarjɑtr] *a* cantankerous.

accabl/er [akable] *vt* to overwhelm, overcome; **a. d'injures** to heap insults upon; **accablé de dettes** (over)burdened with debt. ◆**—ement** *nm* dejection.

accalmie [akalmi] *nf* lull.

accaparer [akapare] *vt* to monopolize; (*personne*) Fam to take up all the time of.

accéd/er [aksede] *vi* **a. à** (*lieu*) to have access to, reach; (*pouvoir, trône, demande*) to accede to.

accélérer [akselere] *vi* Aut to accelerate; — *vt* (*travaux etc*) to speed up; (*allure, pas*) to quicken, speed up; — **s'a.** *vpr* to speed up. ◆**accélérateur** *nm* Aut accelerator. ◆**accélération** *nf* acceleration; speeding up.

accent [aksɑ̃] *nm* accent; (*sur une syllabe*) stress; **mettre l'a. sur** to stress. ◆**accentuation** *nf* accentuation. ◆**accentuer** *vt* to emphasize, accentuate, stress; — **s'a.** *vpr* to become more pronounced.

accepter [aksɛpte] *vt* to accept; **a. de faire**

to agree to do. ◆**acceptable** a acceptable. ◆**acceptation** nf acceptance.

acception [aksɛpsjɔ̃] nf sense, meaning.

accès [aksɛ] nm access (à to); (de folie, colère, toux) fit; (de fièvre) attack, bout; pl (routes) approaches. ◆**accessible** a accessible; (personne) approachable. ◆**accession** nf accession (à to); (à un traité) adherence; a. à la propriété home ownership.

accessoire [akseswar] a secondary; – nmpl Th props; (de voiture etc) accessories; **accessoires de toilette** toilet requisites.

accident [aksidɑ̃] nm accident; a. d'avion/de train plane/train crash; par a. by accident, by chance. ◆**accidenté, -ée** a (terrain) uneven; (région) hilly; (voiture) damaged (in an accident); – nmf accident victim, casualty. ◆**accidentel, -elle** a accidental. ◆**accidentellement** adv accidentally, unintentionally.

acclamer [aklame] vt to cheer, acclaim. ◆**acclamations** nfpl cheers, acclamations.

acclimater [aklimate] vt, – **s'a.** vpr to acclimatize, Am acclimate. ◆**acclimatation** nf acclimatization, Am acclimation.

accointances [akwɛ̃tɑ̃s] nfpl Péj contacts.

accolade [akɔlad] nf (embrassade) embrace; Typ brace, bracket.

accoler [akɔle] vt to place (side by side) (à against).

accommoder [akɔmɔde] vt to adapt; Culin to prepare; **s'a.** à to adapt (oneself) to; **s'a.** de to make the best of. ◆—**ant** a accommodating, easy to please. ◆—**ement** nm arrangement, compromise.

accompagner [akɔ̃paɲe] vt (personne) to accompany, go ou come with, escort; (chose) & Mus to accompany; **s'a. de** to be accompanied by, go with. ◆**accompagnateur, -trice** nmf Mus accompanist; (d'un groupe) guide. ◆**accompagnement** nm Mus accompaniment.

accomplir [akɔ̃plir] vt to carry out, fulfil, accomplish. ◆—**i** a accomplished. ◆—**issement** nm fulfilment.

accord [akɔr] nm agreement; (harmonie) harmony; Mus chord; être d'a. to agree, be in agreement (avec with); **d'a.!** all right! ◆**accorder** vt (donner) to grant; Mus to tune; Gram to make agree; – **s'a.** vpr to agree; (s'entendre) to get along.

accordéon [akɔrdeɔ̃] nm accordion; **en a.** (chaussette etc) wrinkled.

accoster [akɔste] vt to accost; Nau to come alongside; – vi Nau to berth.

accotement [akɔtmɑ̃] nm roadside, verge.

accoucher [akuʃe] vi to give birth (de to); – vt (enfant) to deliver. ◆—**ement** nm delivery. ◆—**eur** nm (médecin) a. obstetrician.

accouder (s') [sakude] vpr **s'a.** à ou sur to lean on (with one's elbows). ◆**accoudoir** nm armrest.

accoupler [akuple] vt to couple; – **s'a.** vpr (animaux) to mate (à with). ◆—**ement** nm coupling; mating.

accourir* [akurir] vi to come running, run over.

accoutrement [akutrəmɑ̃] nm Péj garb, dress.

accoutumer [akutyme] vt to accustom; – **s'a.** vpr to get accustomed (à to); **comme à l'accoutumée** as usual. ◆**accoutumance** nf familiarization (à with); Méd addiction.

accréditer [akredite] vt (ambassadeur) to accredit; (rumeur) to lend credence to.

accroc [akro] nm (déchirure) tear; (difficulté) hitch, snag.

accrocher [akrɔʃe] vt (déchirer) to catch; (fixer) to hook; (suspendre) to hang up (on a hook); (heurter) to hit, knock; – vi (affiche etc) to grab one's attention; – **s'a.** vpr (ne pas céder) to persevere; (se disputer) Fam to clash; **s'a.** à (se cramponner etc) to cling to; (s'écorcher) to catch oneself on. ◆—**age** nm Aut knock, slight hit; (friction) Fam clash. ◆—**eur, -euse** a (personne) tenacious; (affiche etc) eyecatching, catchy.

accroître* [akrwatr] vt to increase; – **s'a.** vpr to increase, grow. ◆**accroissement** nm increase; growth.

accroupir (s') [sakrupir] vpr to squat ou crouch (down). ◆—**i** a squatting, crouching.

accueil [akœj] nm reception, welcome. ◆**accueillir*** vt to receive, welcome, greet. ◆—**ant** a welcoming.

acculer [akyle] vt a. qn à qch to drive s.o. to ou against sth.

accumuler [akymyle] vt, – **s'a.** vpr to pile up, accumulate. ◆**accumulateur** nm accumulator, battery. ◆**accumulation** nf accumulation.

accuser [akyze] vt (dénoncer) to accuse; (rendre responsable) to blame (de for); (révéler) to show; (faire ressortir) to bring out; a. réception to acknowledge receipt (de of); a. le coup to stagger under the blow. ◆—**é, -ée** 1 nmf accused; (cour d'assises) defendant. 2 a prominent. ◆**accusateur, -trice** a (regard) accusing;

(*document*) incriminating; — *nmf* accuser. ◆**accusation** *nf* accusation; *Jur* charge.

acerbe [aserb] *a* bitter, caustic.

acéré [asere] *a* sharp.

acétate [asetat] *nm* acetate. ◆**acétique** *a* acetic.

achalandé [aʃalɑ̃de] *a* **bien a.** (*magasin*) well-stocked.

acharn/er (s') [saʃarne] *vpr* **s'a. sur** (*attaquer*) to set upon, lay into; **s'a. contre** (*poursuivre*) to pursue (relentlessly); **s'a. à faire** to struggle to do, try desperately to do. ◆—**é, -ée** *a* relentless; — *nmf* (*du jeu etc*) fanatic. ◆—**ement** *nm* relentlessness.

achat [aʃa] *nm* purchase; *pl* shopping.

acheminer [aʃmine] *vt* to dispatch; — **s'a.** *vpr* to proceed (**vers** towards).

achet/er [aʃte] *vti* to buy, purchase; **a. à qn** (*vendeur*) to buy from s.o.; (*pour qn*) to buy for s.o. ◆—**eur, -euse** *nmf* buyer, purchaser; (*dans un magasin*) shopper.

achever [aʃve] *vt* to finish (off); **a. de faire qch** (*personne*) to finish doing sth; **a. qn** (*tuer*) to finish s.o. off; — **s'a.** *vpr* to end, finish. ◆**achèvement** *nm* completion.

achoppement [aʃɔpmɑ̃] *nm* **pierre d'a.** stumbling block.

acide [asid] *a* acid, sour; — *nm* acid. ◆**acidité** *nf* acidity.

acier [asje] *nm* steel. ◆**aciérie** *nf* steelworks.

acné [akne] *nf* acne.

acolyte [akɔlit] *nm* *Péj* confederate, associate.

acompte [akɔ̃t] *nm* part payment, deposit.

à-côté [akote] *nm* (*d'une question*) side issue; *pl* (*gains*) little extras.

à-coup [aku] *nm* jerk, jolt; **sans à-coups** smoothly; **par à-coups** in fits and starts.

acoustique [akustik] *a* acoustic; — *nf* acoustics.

acquérir* [akerir] *vt* to acquire, gain; (*par achat*) to purchase; **a. une réputation**/*etc* to win a reputation/*etc*; **être acquis à** (*idée, parti*) to be a supporter of. ◆**acquéreur** *nm* purchaser. ◆**acquis** *nm* experience. ◆**acquisition** *nf* acquisition; purchase.

acquiesc/er [akjese] *vi* to acquiesce (**à** to). ◆—**ement** *nm* acquiescence.

acquit [aki] *nm* receipt; **'pour a.'** 'paid'; **par a. de conscience** for conscience sake. ◆**acquitt/er** *vt* (*dette*) to clear, pay; (*accusé*) to acquit; **s'a. de** (*devoir, promesse*) to discharge; **s'a. envers qn** to repay s.o. ◆—**ement** *nm* payment; acquittal; discharge.

âcre [akr] *a* bitter, acrid, pungent.

acrobate [akrɔbat] *nmf* acrobat. ◆**acrobatie(s)** *nf(pl)* acrobatics. ◆**acrobatique** *a* acrobatic.

acrylique [akrilik] *a* & *nm* acrylic.

acte [akt] *nm* act, deed; *Th* act; **un a. de** an act of; **a. de naissance** birth certificate; **prendre a. de** to take note of.

acteur, -trice [aktœr, -tris] *nmf* actor, actress.

actif, -ive [aktif, -iv] *a* active; — *nm* *Fin* assets; **à son a.** to one's credit; (*vols, meurtres*) *Hum* to one's name.

action [aksjɔ̃] *nf* action; *Fin* share. ◆**actionnaire** *nmf* shareholder. ◆**actionner** *vt* to set in motion, activate, actuate.

activer [aktive] *vt* to speed up; (*feu*) to boost; — **s'a.** *vpr* to bustle about; (*se dépêcher*) *Fam* to get a move on.

activiste [aktivist] *nmf* activist.

activité [aktivite] *nf* activity; **en a.** (*personne*) fully active; (*volcan*) active.

actuaire [aktɥɛr] *nmf* actuary.

actualité [aktyalite] *nf* (*d'un problème*) topicality; (*événements*) current events; *pl* *TV* *Cin* news; **d'a.** topical.

actuel, -elle [aktɥɛl] *a* (*présent*) present; (*contemporain*) topical. ◆**actuellement** *adv* at present, at the present time.

acuité [akɥite] *nf* (*de douleur*) acuteness; (*de vision*) keenness.

acupuncture [akypɔ̃ktyr] *nf* acupuncture. ◆**acupuncteur, -trice** *nmf* acupuncturist.

adage [adaʒ] *nm* (*maxime*) adage.

adapter [adapte] *vt* to adapt; (*ajuster*) to fit (**à** to); **s'a. à** (*s'habituer*) to adapt to; (*tuyau etc*) to fit. ◆**adaptable** *a* adaptable. ◆**adaptateur, -trice** *nmf* adapter. ◆**adaptation** *nf* adaptation.

additif [aditif] *nm* additive.

addition [adisjɔ̃] *nf* addition; (*au restaurant*) bill, *Am* check. ◆**additionnel, -elle** *a* additional. ◆**additionner** *vt* to add (**à** to); (*nombres*) to add up.

adepte [adept] *nmf* follower.

adéquat [adekwa] *a* appropriate.

adhérer [adere] *vi* **a. à** (*coller*) to adhere or stick to; (*s'inscrire*) to join; (*pneu*) to grip. ◆**adhérence** *nf* (*de pneu*) grip. ◆**adhérent, -ente** *nmf* member.

adhésif, -ive [adezif, -iv] *a* & *nm* adhesive. ◆**adhésion** *nf* membership; (*accord*) support.

adieu, -x [adjø] *int* & *nm* farewell, goodbye.

adipeux, -euse [adipø, -øz] *a* (*tissu*) fatty; (*visage*) fat.

adjacent [adʒasã] a (contigu) & Géom adjacent.

adjectif [adʒɛktif] nm adjective.

adjoindre* [adʒwɛ̃dr] vt (associer) to appoint (s.o.) as an assistant (à to); (ajouter) to add; **s'a. qn** to appoint s.o. ◆**adjoint, -ointe** nmf & a assistant; **a. au maire** deputy mayor.

adjudant [adʒydã] nm warrant officer.

adjuger [adʒyʒe] vt (accorder) to award; **s'a. qch** Fam to grab sth for oneself.

adjurer [adʒyre] vt to beseech, entreat.

admettre* [admɛtr] vt (laisser entrer, accueillir, reconnaître) to admit; (autoriser, tolérer) to allow; (supposer) to admit, grant; (candidat) to pass; **être admis à** (examen) to have passed.

administrer [administre] vt (gérer, donner) to administer. ◆**administrateur, -trice** nmf administrator. ◆**administratif, -ive** a administrative. ◆**administration** nf administration; **l'A.** (service public) government service, the Civil Service.

admirer [admire] vt to admire. ◆**admirable** a admirable. ◆**admirateur, -trice** nmf admirer. ◆**admiratif, -ive** a admiring. ◆**admiration** nf admiration.

admissible [admisibl] a acceptable, admissible; (après un concours) eligible (à for). ◆**admission** nf admission.

adolescent, -ente [adɔlesã, -ãt] nmf adolescent, teenager; − a teenage. ◆**adolescence** nf adolescence.

adonner (s') [sadɔne] vpr **s'a. à** (boisson) to take to; (étude) to devote oneself to.

adopter [adɔpte] vt to adopt. ◆**adoptif, -ive** a (fils, patrie) adopted. ◆**adoption** nf adoption; **suisse d'a.** Swiss by adoption.

adorer [adɔre] vt (personne) & Rel to worship, adore; (chose) Fam to adore, love; **a. faire** to adore ou love doing. ◆**adorable** a adorable. ◆**adoration** nf adoration, worship.

adosser [adose] vt **a. qch à** to lean sth back against; **s'a. à** to lean back against.

adouc/ir [adusir] vt (voix, traits etc) to soften; (boisson) to sweeten; (chagrin) to mitigate, ease; − **s'a.** vpr (temps) to turn milder; (caractère) to mellow. ◆**—issement** nm **a. de la température** milder weather.

adrénaline [adrenalin] nf adrenalin(e).

adresse [adrɛs] nf 1 (domicile) address. 2 (habileté) skill. ◆**adresser** vt (lettre) to send; (compliment, remarque etc) to address; (coup) to direct, aim; (personne) to direct (à to); **a. la parole à** to speak to;

s'a. à to speak to; (aller trouver) to go and see; (bureau) to enquire at; (être destiné à) to be aimed at.

Adriatique [adriatik] nf **l'A.** the Adriatic.

adroit [adrwa] a skilful, clever.

adulation [adylasjɔ̃] nf adulation.

adulte [adylt] a & nmf adult, grown-up.

adultère [adyltɛr] a adulterous; − nm adultery.

advenir [advənir] v imp to occur; **a. de** (devenir) to become of; **advienne que pourra** come what may.

adverbe [advɛrb] nm adverb. ◆**adverbial, -aux** a adverbial.

adversaire [advɛrsɛr] nmf opponent, adversary. ◆**adverse** a opposing.

adversité [advɛrsite] nf adversity.

aérer [aere] vt (chambre) to air (out), ventilate; (lit) to air (out); − **s'a.** vpr Fam to get some air. ◆**aéré** a airy. ◆**aération** nf ventilation. ◆**aérien, -ienne** a (ligne, attaque etc) air-; (photo) aerial; (câble) overhead; (léger) airy.

aérobic [aerɔbik] nf aerobics.

aéro-club [aerɔklœb] nm flying club. ◆**aérodrome** nm aerodrome. ◆**aérodynamique** a streamlined, aerodynamic. ◆**aérogare** nf air terminal. ◆**aéroglisseur** nm hovercraft. ◆**aérogramme** nm air letter. ◆**aéromodélisme** nm model aircraft building and flying. ◆**aéronautique** nf aeronautics. ◆**aéronavale** nf = Br Fleet Air Arm, = Am Naval Air Force. ◆**aéroport** nm airport. ◆**aéroporté** a airborne. ◆**aérosol** nm aerosol.

affable [afabl] a affable.

affaibl/ir [afeblir] vt, − **s'a.** vpr to weaken.

affaire [afɛr] nf (question) matter, affair; (marché) deal; (firme) concern, business; (scandale) affair; (procès) Jur case; pl Com business; (d'intérêt public, personnel) affairs; (effets) belongings, things; **avoir a. à** to have to deal with; **c'est mon a.** that's my business ou affair ou concern; **faire une bonne a.** to get a good deal, get a bargain; **ça fera l'a.** that will do nicely; **toute une a.** (histoire) quite a business.

affair/er (s') [safere] vpr to busy oneself, run ou bustle about. ◆**—é** a busy. ◆**affairiste** nm (political) racketeer.

affaiss/er (s') [safese] vpr (personne) to collapse; (plancher) to cave in, give way; (sol) to subside, sink. ◆**—ement** [afesmã] nm (du sol) subsidence.

affaler (s') [safale] vpr to flop down, collapse.

affamé [afame] *a* starving; **a. de** *Fig* hungry for.

affect/er [afɛkte] *vt* (*destiner*) to earmark, assign; (*nommer à un poste*) to post; (*feindre, émouvoir*) to affect. ◆**—é a** (*manières, personne*) affected. ◆**affectation** *nf* assignment; posting; (*simulation*) affectation.

affectif, -ive [afɛktif, -iv] *a* emotional.

affection [afɛksjɔ̃] *nf* (*attachement*) affection; (*maladie*) ailment. ◆**affectionner** *vt* to be fond of. ◆**—é a** loving. ◆**affectueux, -euse** *a* affectionate.

affermir [afɛrmir] *vt* (*autorité*) to strengthen; (*muscles*) to tone up; (*voix*) to steady.

affiche [afiʃ] *nf* poster; *Th* bill. ◆**affich/er** *vt* (*affiche etc*) to post *ou* stick up; *Th* to bill; (*sentiment*) *Péj* to display; **a. qn** *Péj* to parade s.o., flaunt s.o. ◆**—age** *nm* (bill-)posting; **panneau d'a.** hoarding, *Am* billboard.

affilée (d') [dafile] *adv* (*à la suite*) in a row, at a stretch.

affiler [afile] *vt* to sharpen.

affilier (s') [safilje] *vpr* **s'a. à** to join, become affiliated to. ◆**affiliation** *nf* affiliation.

affiner [afine] *vt* to refine.

affinité [afinite] *nf* affinity.

affirmatif, -ive [afirmatif, -iv] *a* (*ton*) assertive, positive; (*proposition*) affirmative; **il a été a.** he was quite positive; **—** *nf* **répondre par l'affirmative** to reply in the affirmative.

affirmer [afirme] *vt* to assert; (*proclamer solennellement*) to affirm. ◆**affirmation** *nf* assertion.

affleurer [aflœre] *vi* to appear on the surface.

affliger [afliʒe] *vt* to distress; **affligé de** stricken *ou* afflicted with.

affluence [aflyɑ̃s] *nf* crowd; **heures d'a.** rush hours.

affluent [aflyɑ̃] *nm* tributary.

affluer [aflye] *vi* (*sang*) to flow, rush; (*gens*) to flock. ◆**afflux** *nm* flow; (*arrivée*) influx.

affol/er [afɔle] *vt* to drive out of one's mind; (*effrayer*) to terrify; **— s'a.** *vpr* to panic. ◆**—ement** *nm* panic.

affranch/ir [afrɑ̃ʃir] *vt* (*timbrer*) to stamp; (*émanciper*) to free. ◆**—issement** *nm* **tarifs d'a.** postage.

affréter [afrete] *vt* (*avion*) to charter; (*navire*) to freight.

affreux, -euse [afrø, -øz] *a* hideous, dreadful, ghastly. ◆**affreusement** *adv* dreadfully.

affriolant [afriɔlɑ̃] *a* enticing.

affront [afrɔ̃] *nm* insult, affront; **faire un a. à** to insult.

affront/er [afrɔ̃te] *vt* to confront, face; (*mauvais temps, difficultés etc*) to brave. ◆**—ement** *nm* confrontation.

affubler [afyble] *vt* *Péj* to dress, rig out (**de** in).

affût [afy] *nm* **à l'a. de** *Fig* on the look-out for.

affûter [afyte] *vt* (*outil*) to sharpen, grind.

Afghanistan [afganistɑ̃] *nm* Afghanistan.

afin [afɛ̃] *prép* **a. de** (+ *inf*) in order to; **—** *conj* **a. que** (+ *sub*) so that.

Afrique [afrik] *nf* Africa. ◆**africain, -aine** *a* & *nmf* African.

agac/er [agase] *vt* (*personne*) to irritate, annoy. ◆**—ement** *nm* irritation.

âge [ɑʒ] *nm* age; **quel â. as-tu?** how old are you?; **avant l'â.** before one's time; **d'un certain â.** middle-aged; **l'â. adulte** adulthood; **la force de l'â.** the prime of life; **le moyen â.** the Middle Ages. ◆**âgé** *a* elderly; **â. de six ans** six years old; **un enfant â. de six ans** a six-year-old child.

agence [aʒɑ̃s] *nf* agency; (*succursale*) branch office; **a. immobilière** estate agent's office, *Am* real estate office.

agenc/er [aʒɑ̃se] *vt* to arrange; **bien agencé** (*maison etc*) well laid-out; (*phrase*) well put-together. ◆**—ement** *nm* (*de maison etc*) lay-out.

agenda [aʒɛ̃da] *nm* diary, *Am* datebook.

agenouiller (s') [saʒnuje] *vpr* to kneel (down); **être agenouillé** to be kneeling (down).

agent [aʒɑ̃] *nm* agent; **a. (de police)** policeman; **a. de change** stockbroker; **a. immobilier** estate agent, *Am* real estate agent.

aggloméré [aglɔmere] *nm* & *a* (*bois*) chipboard, fibreboard.

agglomérer (s') [saglɔmere] *vpr* (*s'entasser*) to conglomerate. ◆**agglomération** *nf* conglomeration; (*habitations*) built-up area; (*ville*) town.

aggraver [agrave] *vt* to worsen, aggravate; **— s'a.** *vpr* to worsen. ◆**aggravation** *nf* worsening.

agile [aʒil] *a* agile, nimble. ◆**agilité** *nf* agility, nimbleness.

agir [aʒir] **1** *vi* to act; **a. auprès de** to intercede with. **2 s'agir** *v imp* **il s'agit d'argent**/*etc* it's a question *ou* matter of money/*etc*, it concerns money/*etc*; **de quoi s'agit-il?** what is it?, what's it about?; **il s'agit de se dépêcher**/*etc* we have to hurry/*etc.* ◆**agissant** *a* active, effective. ◆**agissements** *nmpl Péj* dealings.

agit/er [aʒite] *vt* (*remuer*) to stir; (*secouer*) to shake; (*brandir*) to wave; (*troubler*) to agitate; (*discuter*) to debate; — **s'a.** *vpr* (*enfant*) to fidget; (*peuple*) to stir. ◆**—é** *a* (*mer*) rough; (*malade*) restless, agitated; (*enfant*) fidgety, restless. ◆**agitateur, -trice** *nmf* (*political*) agitator. ◆**agitation** *nf* (*de la mer*) roughness; (*d'un malade etc*) restlessness; (*nervosité*) agitation; (*de la rue*) bustle; *Pol* unrest.

agneau, -x [aɲo] *nm* lamb.

agonie [agɔni] *nf* death throes; **être à l'a.** to be suffering the pangs of death. ◆**agoniser** *vi* to be dying.

agrafe [agraf] *nf* hook; (*pour papiers*) staple. ◆**agrafer** *vt* to fasten, hook, do up; (*papiers*) to staple. ◆**agrafeuse** *nf* stapler.

agrand/ir [agrɑ̃dir] *vt* to enlarge; (*grossir*) to magnify; — **s'a.** *vpr* to expand, grow. ◆**—issement** *nm* (*de ville*) expansion; (*de maison*) extension; (*de photo*) enlargement.

agréable [agreabl] *a* pleasant, agreeable, nice. ◆**—ment** [-əmɑ̃] *adv* pleasantly.

agré/er [agree] *vt* to accept; **veuillez a. mes salutations distinguées** (*dans une lettre*) yours faithfully. ◆**—é** *a* (*fournisseur, centre*) approved.

agrégation [agregasjɔ̃] *nf* competitive examination for recruitment of *lycée* teachers. ◆**agrégé, -ée** *nmf* teacher who has passed the *agrégation*.

agrément [agremɑ̃] *nm* (*attrait*) charm; (*accord*) assent; **voyage d'a.** pleasure trip. ◆**agrémenter** *vt* to embellish; **a. un récit d'anecdotes** to pepper a story with anecdotes.

agrès [agrɛ] *nmpl Nau* tackle, rigging; (*de gymnastique*) apparatus.

agress/er [agrese] *vt* to attack. ◆**agresseur** *nm* attacker; (*dans la rue*) mugger; (*dans un conflit*) aggressor. ◆**agressif, -ive** *a* aggressive. ◆**agression** *nf* (*d'un État*) aggression; (*d'un individu*) attack. ◆**agressivité** *nf* aggressiveness.

agricole [agrikɔl] *a* (*peuple*) agricultural, farming; (*ouvrier, machine*) farm-. ◆**agriculteur** [agrikyltœr] *nm* farmer. ◆**agriculture** *nf* agriculture, farming.

agripper [agripe] *vt* to clutch, grip; **s'a.** à to cling to, clutch, grip.

agronomie [agrɔnɔmi] *nf* agronomics.

agrumes [agrym] *nmpl* citrus fruit(s).

aguerri [ageri] *a* seasoned, hardened.

aguets (aux) [ozagɛ] *adv* on the look-out.

aguich/er [agiʃe] *vt* to tease, excite. ◆**—ant** *a* enticing.

ah! [a] *int* ah!, oh!

ahur/ir [ayrir] *vt* to astound, bewilder. ◆**—i, -ie** *nmf* idiot.

ai [e] *voir* avoir.

aide [ɛd] *nf* help, assistance, aid; — *nmf* (*personne*) assistant; **à l'a. de** with the help ou aid of. ◆**a.-électricien** *nm* electrician's mate. ◆**a.-familiale** *nf* home help. ◆**a.-mémoire** *nm inv Scol* handbook (*of facts etc*).

aider [ede] *vt* to help, assist, aid (**à faire** to do); **s'a. de** to make use of.

aïe! [aj] *int* ouch!, ow!

aïeul, -e [ajœl] *nmf* grandfather, grandmother.

aïeux [ajø] *nmpl* forefathers, forebears.

aigle [ɛgl] *nmf* eagle. ◆**aiglon** *nm* eaglet.

aiglefin [ɛgləfɛ̃] *nm* haddock.

aigre [ɛgr] *a* (*acide*) sour; (*voix, vent, parole*) sharp, cutting. ◆**a.-doux, -douce** *a* bitter-sweet. ◆**aigreur** *nf* sourness; (*de ton*) sharpness; *pl* heartburn.

aigrette [ɛgrɛt] *nf* (*de plumes*) tuft.

aigr/ir (s') [segrir] *vpr* (*vin*) to turn sour; (*caractère*) to sour. ◆**—i** [egri] *a* (*personne*) embittered, bitter.

aigu, -uë [egy] *a* (*crise etc*) acute; (*dents*) pointed; (*voix*) shrill.

aiguille [egɥij] *nf* (*à coudre, de pin*) needle; (*de montre*) hand; (*de balance*) pointer; **a.** (**rocheuse**) peak.

aiguill/er [egɥije] *vt* (*train*) to shunt, *Am* switch; *Fig* to steer, direct. ◆**—age** *nm* (*appareil*) *Rail* points, *Am* switches. ◆**—eur** *nm Rail* signalman, *Am* switchman; **a. du ciel** air traffic controller.

aiguillon [egɥijɔ̃] *nm* (*dard*) sting; (*stimulant*) spur. ◆**aiguillonner** *vt* to spur (on), goad.

aiguiser [eg(ɥ)ize] *vt* (*affiler*) to sharpen; (*appétit*) to whet.

ail [aj] *nm* garlic.

aile [ɛl] *nf* wing; (*de moulin à vent*) sail; *Aut* wing, *Am* fender; **battre de l'a.** to be in a bad way; **d'un coup d'a.** (*avion*) in continuous flight. ◆**ailé** [ele] *a* winged. ◆**aileron** *nm* (*de requin*) fin; (*d'avion*) aileron; (*d'oiseau*) pinion. ◆**ailier** [elje] *nm Fb* wing(er).

ailleurs [ajœr] *adv* somewhere else, elsewhere; **partout a.** everywhere else; **d'a.** (*du reste*) besides, anyway; **par a.** (*en outre*) moreover; (*autrement*) otherwise.

ailloli [ajɔli] *nm* garlic mayonnaise.

aimable [ɛmabl] *a* (*complaisant*) kind;

(*sympathique*) likeable, amiable; (*agréable*) pleasant. ◆**-ment** [-əma] *adv* kindly.

aimant [emɑ̃] **1** *nm* magnet. **2** *a* loving. ◆**aimanter** *vt* to magnetize.

aimer [eme] *vt* (*chérir*) to love; **a. (bien)** (*apprécier*) to like, be fond of; **a. faire** to like doing *ou* to do; **a. mieux** to prefer; **ils s'aiment** they're in love.

aine [ɛn] *nf* groin.

aîné, -e [ene] *a* (*de deux frères etc*) elder, older; (*de plus de deux*) eldest, oldest; — *nmf* (*enfant*) elder *ou* older (child); eldest *ou* oldest (child); **c'est mon a.** he's my senior.

ainsi [ɛ̃si] *adv* (*comme ça*) (in) this *ou* that way, thus; (*alors*) so; **a. que** as well as; **et a. de suite** and so on; **pour a. dire** so to speak.

air [ɛr] *nm* **1** air; **en plein a.** in the open (air), outdoors; **ficher** *ou* **flanquer en l'a.** *Fam* (*jeter*) to chuck away; (*gâcher*) to mess up, upset; **en l'a.** (*jeter*) (up) in the air; (*paroles, menaces*) empty; (*projets*) uncertain, (up) in the air; **dans l'a.** (*grippe, idées*) about, around. **2** (*expression*) look, appearance; **avoir l'a.** to look, seem; **avoir l'a. de** to look like; **a. de famille** family likeness. **3** (*mélodie*) tune; **a. d'opéra** aria.

aire [ɛr] *nf* (*de stationnement etc*) & *Math* area; (*d'oiseau*) eyrie; **a. de lancement** launching site.

airelle [ɛrɛl] *nf* bilberry, *Am* blueberry.

aisance [ɛzɑ̃s] *nf* (*facilité*) ease; (*prospérité*) easy circumstances, affluence.

aise [ɛz] *nf* **à l'a.** (*dans un vêtement etc*) comfortable; (*dans une situation*) at ease; (*fortuné*) comfortably off; **aimer ses aises** to like one's comforts; **mal à l'a.** uncomfortable, ill at ease. ◆**aisé** [eze] *a* (*fortuné*) comfortably off; (*naturel*) free and easy; (*facile*) easy. ◆**aisément** *adv* easily.

aisselle [ɛsɛl] *nf* armpit.

ait [ɛ] *voir* **avoir**.

ajonc(s) [aʒɔ̃] *nm(pl)* gorse, furze.

ajouré [aʒure] *a* (*dentelle etc*) openwork.

ajourn/er [aʒurne] *vt* to postpone, adjourn. ◆**-ement** *nm* postponement, adjournment.

ajout [aʒu] *nm* addition. ◆**ajouter** *vti* to add (à to); **s'a. à** to add to.

ajust/er [aʒyste] *vt* (*pièce, salaires*) to adjust; (*coiffure*) to arrange; (*coup*) to aim; **a. à** (*adapter*) to fit to. ◆**-é** *a* (*serré*) close-fitting. ◆**-ement** *nm* adjustment. ◆**-eur** *nm* (*ouvrier*) fitter.

alaise [alɛz] *nf* (*waterproof*) undersheet.

alambic [alɑ̃bik] *nm* still.

alambiqué [alɑ̃bike] *a* convoluted, over-subtle.

alanguir [alɑ̃gir] *vt* to make languid.

alarme [alarm] *nf* (*signal, inquiétude*) alarm; **jeter l'a.** to cause alarm. ◆**alarmer** *vt* to alarm; **s'a. de** to become alarmed at.

Albanie [albani] *nf* Albania. ◆**albanais, -aise** *a* & *nmf* Albanian.

albâtre [albɑtr] *nm* alabaster.

albatros [albatros] *nm* albatross.

albinos [albinos] *nmf* & *a inv* albino.

album [albɔm] *nm* (*de timbres etc*) album; (*de dessins*) sketchbook.

alcali [alkali] *nm* alkali. ◆**alcalin** *a* alkaline.

alchimie [alʃimi] *nf* alchemy.

alcool [alkɔl] *nm* alcohol; (*spiritueux*) spirits; **a. à brûler** methylated spirit(s); **lampe à a.** spirit lamp. ◆**alcoolique** *a* & *nmf* alcoholic. ◆**alcoolisé** *a* (*boisson*) alcoholic. ◆**alcoolisme** *nm* alcoholism. ◆**alcootest**® *nm* breath test; (*appareil*) breathalyzer.

alcôve [alkov] *nf* alcove.

aléas [alea] *nmpl* hazards, risks. ◆**aléatoire** *a* chancy, uncertain; (*sélection*) random.

alentour [alɑ̃tur] *adv* round about, around; **d'a.** surrounding; — *nmpl* surroundings, vicinity; **aux alentours de** in the vicinity of.

alerte [alɛrt] **1** *a* (*leste*) agile, spry; (*éveillé*) alert. **2** *nf* alarm; **en état d'a.** on the alert; **a. aérienne** air-raid warning. ◆**alerter** *vt* to warn, alert.

alezan, -ane [alzɑ̃ -an] *a* & *nmf* (*cheval*) chestnut.

algarade [algarad] *nf* (*dispute*) altercation.

algèbre [alʒɛbr] *nf* algebra. ◆**algébrique** *a* algebraic.

Alger [alʒe] *nm ou f* Algiers.

Algérie [alʒeri] *nf* Algeria. ◆**algérien, -ienne** *a* & *nmf* Algerian.

algue(s) [alg] *nf(pl)* seaweed.

alias [aljɑs] *adv* alias.

alibi [alibi] *nm* alibi.

alién/er [aljene] *vt* to alienate; **s'a. qn** to alienate s.o. ◆**-é, -ée** *nmf* insane person; *Péj* lunatic. ◆**-ation** *nf* alienation; *Méd* derangement.

align/er [aline] *vt* to align, line up; **les a.** *Arg* to fork out, pay up; — **s'a.** (*personnes*) to fall into line, line up; *Pol* to align oneself (**sur** with). ◆**-ement** *nm* alignment.

aliment [alimɑ̃] *nm* food. ◆**alimentaire** *a* (*industrie, produit etc*) food-. ◆**alimentation** *nf* feeding; supply(ing); (*régime*) diet, nutrition; (*nourriture*) food; **magasin d'a.** grocer's, grocery store. ◆**alimenter** *vt* (*nourrir*) to feed; (*fournir*) to supply (**en** with); (*débat, feu*) to fuel.

alinéa [alinea] *nm* paragraph.

alité [alite] *a* bedridden.

allaiter [alete] *vti* to (breast)feed.

allant [alɑ̃] *nm* drive, energy, zest.

allécher [aleʃe] *vt* to tempt, entice.

allée [ale] *nf* path, walk, lane; (*de cinéma*) aisle; **allées et venues** comings and goings, running about.

allégation [alegasjɔ̃] *nf* allegation.

alléger [aleʒe] *vt* to alleviate, lighten.

allégorie [alegɔri] *nf* allegory.

allègre [alɛgr] *a* gay, lively, cheerful. ◆**allégresse** *nf* gladness, rejoicing.

alléguer [alege] *vt* (*excuser etc*) to put forward.

alléluia [aleluja] *nm* hallelujah.

Allemagne [alman] *nf* Germany. ◆**allemand, -ande** *a & nmf* German; – *nm* (*langue*) German.

aller° [ale] **1** *vi* (*aux être*) to go; (*montre etc*) to work; (*convenir à*) to suit; **a. avec** (*vêtement*) to go with, match; **a. bien/mieux** (*personne*) to be well/better; **il va savoir/venir**/*etc* he'll know/come/*etc*, he's going to know/come/*etc*; **il va partir** he's about to leave, he's going to leave; **va voir!** go and see!; **comment vas-tu?**, (**comment**) **ça va?** how are you?; **ça va!** all right!, fine!; **ça va** (**comme ça**)! that's enough!; **allez-y** go on, go ahead; **j'y vais** I'm coming; **allons** (**donc**)! come on!, come off it!; **allez!** au lit! come on *ou* go on to bed!; **ça va de soi** that's obvious; – **s'en aller** *vpr* to go away; (*tache*) to come out. **2** *nm* outward journey; **a.** (**simple**) single (ticket); **a.** (**et**) **retour** return (ticket), *Am* round-trip (ticket).

allergie [alɛrʒi] *nf* allergy. ◆**allergique** *a* allergic (**à** to).

alliage [aljaʒ] *nm* alloy.

alliance [aljɑ̃s] *nf* (*anneau*) wedding ring; *Pol* alliance; *Rel* covenant; (*mariage*) marriage.

alli/er [alje] *vt* (*associer*) to combine (**à** with); (*pays*) to ally (**à** with); – **s'a.** *vpr* (*couleurs*) to combine; (*pays*) to become allied (**à** with, to); **s'a. à** (*famille*) to ally oneself with. ◆**-é, -ée** *nmf* ally.

alligator [aligatɔr] *nm* alligator.

allô! [alo] *int Tél* hullo!, hallo!, hello!

allocation [alɔkasjɔ̃] *nf* (*somme*) allowance; **a.** (**de**) **chômage** unemployment benefit. ◆**allocataire** *nmf* claimant.

allocution [alɔkysjɔ̃] *nf* (short) speech, address.

allong/er [alɔ̃ʒe] *vt* (*bras*) to stretch out; (*jupe*) to lengthen; (*sauce*) to thin; – *vi* (*jours*) to get longer; – **s'a.** *vpr* to stretch out. ◆**-é** *a* (*oblong*) elongated.

allouer [alwe] *vt* to allocate.

allum/er [alyme] *vt* (*feu, pipe etc*) to light; (*électricité*) to turn *ou* switch on; (*désir, colère*) *Fig* to kindle; – **s'a.** *vpr* to light up; (*feu, guerre*) to flare up. ◆**-age** *nm* lighting; *Aut* ignition. ◆**allume-gaz** *nm inv* gas lighter. ◆**allumeuse** *nf* (*femme*) teaser.

allumette [alymet] *nf* match.

allure [alyr] *nf* (*vitesse*) pace; (*de véhicule*) speed; (*démarche*) gait; walk; (*maintien*) bearing; (*air*) look; *pl* (*conduite*) ways.

allusion [alyzjɔ̃] *nf* allusion; (*voilée*) hint; **faire a. à** to refer *ou* allude to; to hint at.

almanach [almana] *nm* almanac.

aloi [alwa] *nm* **de bon a.** genuine, worthy.

alors [alɔr] *adv* (*en ce temps-là*) then; (*en ce cas-là*) so, then; **a. que** (*lorsque*) when; (*tandis que*) whereas.

alouette [alwɛt] *nf* (sky)lark.

alourd/ir [alurdir] *vt* to weigh down; – **s'a.** *vpr* to become heavy *ou* heavier. ◆**-i** *a* heavy.

aloyau [alwajo] *nm* sirloin.

alpaga [alpaga] *nm* (*tissu*) alpaca.

alpage [alpaʒ] *nm* mountain pasture. ◆**Alpes** *nfpl* **les A.** the Alps. ◆**alpestre** *a*, ◆**alpin** *a* alpine. ◆**alpinisme** *nm* mountaineering. ◆**alpiniste** *nmf* mountaineer.

alphabet [alfabe] *nm* alphabet. ◆**alphabétique** *a* alphabetic(al). ◆**alphabétiser** *vt* to teach to read and write.

altercation [alterkasjɔ̃] *nf* altercation.

altér/er [altere] *vt* (*denrée, santé*) to impair, spoil; (*voix, vérité*) to distort; (*monnaie, texte*) to falsify; (*donner soif à*) to make thirsty; – **s'a.** *vpr* (*santé, relations*) to deteriorate. ◆**-ation** *nf* deterioration, change (**de** in); (*de visage*) distortion.

alternatif, -ive [alternatif, -iv] *a* alternating. ◆**alternative** *nf* alternative; *pl* alternate periods. ◆**alternativement** *adv* alternately.

altern/er [alterne] *vti* to alternate. ◆**-é** *a* alternate. ◆**alternance** *nf* alternation.

altesse [altes] *nf* (*titre*) Highness.

altier, -ière [altje, -jɛr] *a* haughty.

altitude [altityd] *nf* altitude, height.

alto [alto] *nm* (*instrument*) viola.

aluminium [alyminjɔm] *nm* aluminium, *Am*

aluminum; papier a., Fam papier alu tin foil.

alunir [alynir] vi to land on the moon.

alvéole [alveɔl] nf (de ruche) cell; (dentaire) socket. ◆alvéolé a honeycombed.

amabilité [amabilite] nf kindness; faire des amabilités à to show kindness to.

amadouer [amadwe] vt to coax, persuade.

amaigrir [amegrir] vt to make thin(ner). ◆—i a thin(ner). ◆—issant a (régime) slimming.

amalgame [amalgam] nm amalgam, mixture. ◆amalgamer vt, — s'a. vpr to blend, mix, amalgamate.

amande [amɑ̃d] nf almond.

amant [amɑ̃] nm lover.

amarre [amar] nf (mooring) rope, hawser; pl moorings. ◆amarrer vt to moor; Fig to tie down, make fast.

amas [amɑ] nm heap, pile. ◆amasser vt to pile up; (richesse, preuves) to amass, gather; — s'a. vpr to pile up; (gens) to gather.

amateur [amatœr] nm (d'art etc) lover; Sp amateur; (acheteur) Fam taker; d'a. (talent) amateur; (travail) Péj amateurish; une équipe a. an amateur team. ◆amateurisme nm Sp amateurism; Péj amateurishness.

amazone [amazon] nf horsewoman; monter en a. to ride sidesaddle.

ambages (sans) [sɑ̃zɑ̃baʒ] adv to the point, in plain language.

ambassade [ɑ̃basad] nf embassy. ◆ambassadeur, -drice nmf ambassador.

ambiance [ɑ̃bjɑ̃s] nf atmosphere. ◆ambiant a surrounding.

ambigu, -guë [ɑ̃bigy] a ambiguous. ◆ambiguïté [-gɥite] nf ambiguity.

ambitieux, -euse [ɑ̃bisjø, -øz] a ambitious. ◆ambition nf ambition. ◆ambitionner vt to aspire to; il ambitionne de his ambition is to.

ambre [ɑ̃br] nm (jaune) amber; (gris) ambergris.

ambulance [ɑ̃bylɑ̃s] nf ambulance. ◆ambulancier, -ière nmf ambulance driver.

ambulant [ɑ̃bylɑ̃] a itinerant, travelling.

âme [ɑm] nf soul; â. qui vive a living soul; état d'â. state of mind; â. sœur soul mate; â. damnée evil genius, henchman; avoir charge d'âmes to be responsible for human life.

améliorer [ameljɔre] vt, — s'a. vpr to

improve. ◆amélioration nf improvement.

amen [amɛn] adv amen.

aménag/er [amenaʒe] vt (arranger, installer) to fit up, fit out (en as); (bateau) to fit out; (transformer) to convert (en into); (construire) to set up; (ajuster) to adjust. ◆—ement nm fitting up; fitting out; conversion; setting up; adjustment.

amende [amɑ̃d] nf fine; frapper d'une a. to impose a fine on; faire a. honorable to make an apology.

amender [amɑ̃de] vt Pol to amend; (terre) to improve; — s'a. vpr to mend ou improve one's ways.

amener [amne] vt to bring; (causer) to bring about; — s'a. vpr Fam to come along, turn up.

amenuiser (s') [samənɥize] vpr to grow smaller, dwindle.

amer, -ère [amɛr] a bitter. ◆amèrement adv bitterly.

Amérique [amerik] nf America; A. du Nord/du Sud North/South America. ◆américain, -aine a & nmf American.

amerrir [amerir] vi to make a sea landing; (cabine spatiale) to splash down.

amertume [amɛrtym] nf bitterness.

améthyste [ametist] nf amethyst.

ameublement [amœblamɑ̃] nm furniture.

ameuter [amøte] vt (soulever) to stir up; (attrouper) to gather, muster; (voisins) to bring out; — s'a. vpr to gather, muster.

ami, -e [ami] nmf friend; (des livres, de la nature etc) lover (de of); petit a. boyfriend; petite amie girlfriend; – a friendly.

amiable (à l') [alamjabl] a amicable; – adv amicably.

amiante [amjɑ̃t] nm asbestos.

amical, -aux [amikal, -o] a friendly. ◆—ement adv in a friendly manner.

amicale [amikal] nf association.

amidon [amidɔ̃] nm starch. ◆amidonner vt to starch.

amincir [amɛ̃sir] vt to make thin(ner); – vi (personne) to slim; — s'a. vpr to become thinner.

amiral, -aux [amiral, -o] nm admiral. ◆amirauté nf admiralty.

amitié [amitje] nf friendship; (amabilité) kindness; pl kind regrds; prendre en a. to take a liking to.

ammoniac [amɔnjak] nm (gaz) ammonia. ◆ammoniaque nf (liquide) ammonia.

amnésie [amnezi] nf amnesia.

amnistie [amnisti] nf amnesty.

amocher [amɔʃe] vt Arg to mess up, bash.

amoindrir [amwɛ̃drir] vt, **— s'a.** vpr to decrease, diminish.

amoll/ir [amolir] vt to soften; (affaiblir) to weaken. **◆—issant** a enervating.

amonceler [amɔ̃sle] vt, **— s'a.** vpr to pile up. **◆amoncellement** nm heap, pile.

amont (en) [ɑ̃namɔ̃] adv upstream.

amoral, -aux [amoral, -o] a amoral.

amorce [amɔrs] nf (début) start; Pêche bait; (détonateur) fuse, detonator; (de pistolet d'enfant) cap. **◆amorcer** vt to start; (hameçon) to bait; (pompe) to prime; **— s'a.** vpr to begin.

amorphe [amɔrf] a listless, apathetic.

amort/ir [amɔrtir] vt (coup) to cushion, absorb; (bruit) to deaden; (dette) to pay off; **il a vite amorti sa voiture** his car has been made to pay for itself quickly. **◆—issement** nm Fin redemption. **◆—isseur** nm shock absorber.

amour [amur] nm love; (liaison) romance, love; (Cupidon) Cupid; **pour l'a. de** for the sake of; **mon a.** my darling, my love. **◆a.-propre** nm self-respect, self-esteem. **◆s'amouracher** vpr Péj to become infatuated (de with). **◆amoureux, -euse** nmf lover; — a amorous, loving; a. de (personne) in love with; (gloire) Fig enamoured of.

amovible [amovibl] a removable, detachable.

ampère [ɑ̃pɛr] nm Él amp(ere).

amphi [ɑ̃fi] nm Univ Fam lecture hall.

amphibie [ɑ̃fibi] a amphibious; — nm amphibian.

amphithéâtre [ɑ̃fiteatr] nm Hist amphitheatre; Univ lecture hall.

ample [ɑ̃pl] a (vêtement) ample, roomy; (provision) full; (vues) broad. **◆amplement** adv amply, fully; **a. suffisant** ample. **◆ampleur** nf (de robe) fullness; (importance, étendue) scale, extent; **prendre de l'a.** to grow.

amplifier [ɑ̃plifje] vt (accroître) to develop; (exagérer) to magnify; (son, courant) to amplify; **— s'a.** vpr to increase. **◆amplificateur** nm amplifier. **◆amplification** nf (extension) increase.

amplitude [ɑ̃plityd] nf Fig magnitude.

ampoule [ɑ̃pul] nf (électrique) (light) bulb; (aux pieds etc) blister; (de médicament) phial.

ampoulé [ɑ̃pule] a turgid.

amputer [ɑ̃pyte] vt **1** (membre) to amputate; **a. qn de la jambe** to amputate s.o.'s leg. **2** (texte) to curtail, cut (de by). **◆amputation** nf amputation; curtailment.

amuse-gueule [amyzgœl] nm inv cocktail snack, appetizer.

amus/er [amyze] vt (divertir) to amuse, entertain; (occuper) to divert the attention of; **— s'a.** vpr to enjoy oneself, have fun; (en chemin) to dawdle, loiter; **s'a. avec** to play with; **s'a. à faire** to amuse oneself doing. **◆—ant** a amusing. **◆—ement** nm amusement; (jeu) game. **◆amusette** nf frivolous pursuit.

amygdale [amidal] nf tonsil.

an [ɑ̃] nm year; **il a dix ans** he's ten (years old); **par a.** per annum, per year; **bon a., mal a.** putting the good years and the bad together; **Nouvel A.** New Year.

anachronisme [anakronism] nm anachronism.

anagramme [anagram] nf anagram.

analogie [analɔʒi] nf analogy. **◆analogue** a similar; — nm analogue.

analphabète [analfabɛt] a & nmf illiterate. **◆analphabétisme** nm illiteracy.

analyse [analiz] nf analysis; **a. grammaticale** parsing. **◆analyser** vt to analyse; (phrase) to parse. **◆analytique** a analytic(al).

ananas [anana(s)] nm pineapple.

anarchie [anarʃi] nf anarchy. **◆anarchique** a anarchic. **◆anarchiste** nmf anarchist; — a anarchistic.

anathème [anatɛm] nm Rel anathema.

anatomie [anatɔmi] nf anatomy. **◆anatomique** a anatomical.

ancestral, -aux [ɑ̃sɛstral, -o] a ancestral.

ancêtre [ɑ̃sɛtr] nm ancestor.

anche [ɑ̃ʃ] nf Mus reed.

anchois [ɑ̃ʃwa] nm anchovy.

ancien, -ienne [ɑ̃sjɛ̃, -jɛn] a (vieux) old; (meuble) antique; (qui n'est plus) former, ex-, old; (antique) ancient; (dans une fonction) senior; **a. élève old boy,** Am alumnus; — nmf (par l'âge) elder; (dans une fonction) senior; **les anciens** (auteurs, peuples) the ancients. **◆anciennement** adv formerly. **◆ancienneté** nf age; (dans une fonction) seniority.

ancre [ɑ̃kr] nf anchor; **jeter l'a.** to (cast) anchor; **lever l'a.** to weigh anchor. **◆ancrer** vt Nau to anchor; (idée) Fig to root, fix; **ancré dans** rooted in.

andouille [ɑ̃duj] nf sausage (made from chitterlings); **espèce d'a.!** Fam (you) nitwit!

âne [ɑn] nm (animal) donkey, ass; (personne) Péj ass; **bonnet d'â.** dunce's cap; **dos d'â.** (*d'une route*) hump; **pont en dos d'â.** humpback bridge.

anéant/ir [aneɑtir] *vt* to annihilate, wipe out, destroy; — **s'a.** *vpr* to vanish. ◆**—i** *a* (*épuisé*) exhausted; (*stupéfait*) dismayed; (*accablé*) overwhelmed. ◆**—issement** *nm* annihilation; (*abattement*) dejection.

anecdote [anɛkdɔt] *nf* anecdote. ◆**anecdotique** *a* anecdotal.

anémie [anemi] *nf* an(a)emia. ◆**anémique** *a* an(a)emic. ◆**s'anémier** *vpr* to become an(a)emic.

anémone [anemɔn] *nf* anemone.

ânerie [ɑnri] *nf* stupidity; (*action etc*) stupid thing. ◆**ânesse** *nf* she-ass.

anesthésie [anɛstezi] *nf* an(a)esthesia; **a. générale/locale** general/local an(a)esthetic. ◆**anesthésier** *vt* to an(a)esthetize. ◆**anesthésique** *nm* an(a)esthetic.

anfractuosité [ɑfraktyɔzite] *nf* crevice, cleft.

ange [ɑ̃ʒ] *nm* angel; **aux anges** in seventh heaven. ◆**angélique** *a* angelic.

angélus [ɑʒelys] *nm Rel* angelus.

angine [ɑʒin] *nf* sore throat; **a. de poitrine** angina (pectoris).

anglais, -aise [ɑ̃glɛ, -ɛz] *a* English; — *nmf* Englishman, Englishwoman; — *nm* (*langue*) English; **filer à l'anglaise** to take French leave.

angle [ɑ̃gl] *nm* (*point de vue*) & *Géom* angle; (*coin*) corner.

Angleterre [ɑ̃glətɛr] *nf* England.

anglican, -ane [ɑ̃glikɑ̃, -an] *a* & *nmf* Anglican.

anglicisme [ɑ̃glisism] *nm* Anglicism. ◆**angliciste** *nmf* English specialist.

anglo- [ɑ̃glo] *préf* Anglo-. ◆**anglo-normand** *a* Anglo-Norman; **îles a.-normandes** Channel Islands. ◆**anglophile** *a* & *nmf* anglophile. ◆**anglophone** *a* English-speaking; — *nmf* English speaker. ◆**anglo-saxon, -onne** *a* & *nmf* Anglo-Saxon.

angoisse [ɑ̃gwas] *nf* anguish. ◆**angoissant** *a* distressing. ◆**angoissé** *a* (*personne*) in anguish; (*geste, cri*) anguished.

angora [ɑ̃gɔra] *nm* (*laine*) angora.

anguille [ɑ̃gij] *nf* eel.

angulaire [ɑ̃gylɛr] *a* **pierre a.** cornerstone. ◆**anguleux, -euse** *a* (*visage*) angular.

anicroche [anikrɔʃ] *nf* hitch, snag.

animal, -aux [animal, -o] *nm* animal; (*personne*) *Péj* brute; — *a* animal.

animer [anime] *vt* (*inspirer*) to animate; (*encourager*) to spur on; (*débat, groupe*) to

lead; (*soirée*) to enliven; (*regard*) to light up, brighten up; (*mécanisme*) to actuate, drive; **a. la course** *Sp* to set the pace; **animé de** (*sentiment*) prompted by; — **s'a.** *vpr* (*rue etc*) to come to life; (*yeux*) to light up, brighten up. ◆**animé** *a* (*rue*) lively; (*conversation*) animated, lively; (*doué de vie*) animate. ◆**animateur, -trice** *nmf TV* compere, *Am* master of ceremonies, emcee; (*de club*) leader, organizer; (*d'entreprise*) driving force, spirit. ◆**animation** *nf* (*des rues*) activity; (*de réunion*) liveliness; (*de visage*) brightness; *Cin* animation.

animosité [animozite] *nf* animosity.

anis [ani(s)] *nm* (*boisson, parfum*) aniseed. ◆**anisette** *nf* (*liqueur*) anisette.

ankylose [ɑ̃kiloz] *nf* stiffening. ◆**s'ankylos/er** *vpr* to stiffen up. ◆**—é** *a* stiff.

annales [anal] *nfpl* annals.

anneau, -x [ano] *nm* ring; (*de chaîne*) link.

année [ane] *nf* year; **bonne a.!** Happy New Year!

annexe [anɛks] *nf* (*bâtiment*) annex(e); — *a* (*pièces*) appended; **bâtiment a.** annex(e). ◆**annexer** *vt* (*pays*) to annex; (*document*) to append. ◆**annexion** *nf* annexation.

annihiler [aniile] *vt* to destroy, annihilate.

anniversaire [anivɛrsɛr] *nm* (*d'événement*) anniversary; (*de naissance*) birthday; — *a* anniversary.

annonce [anɔ̃s] *nf* (*avis*) announcement; (*publicitaire*) advertisement; (*indice*) sign; **petites annonces** classified advertisements, small ads. ◆**annoncer** *vt* (*signaler*) to announce, report; (*être l'indice de*) to indicate; (*vente*) to advertise; **a. le printemps** to herald spring; **s'a. pluvieux/difficile/etc** to look like being rainy/difficult/etc. ◆**annonceur** *nm* advertiser; *Rad TV* announcer.

annonciation [anɔ̃sjasjɔ̃] *nf* Annunciation.

annoter [anɔte] *vt* to annotate. ◆**annotation** *nf* annotation.

annuaire [anɥɛr] *nm* yearbook; (*téléphonique*) directory, phone book.

annuel, -elle [anɥɛl] *a* annual, yearly. ◆**annuellement** *adv* annually. ◆**annuité** *nf* annual instalment.

annulaire [anɥlɛr] *nm* ring or third finger.

annuler [anɥle] *vt* (*visite etc*) to cancel; (*mariage*) to annul; (*jugement*) to quash; — **s'a.** *vpr* to cancel each other out. ◆**annulation** *nf* cancellation; annulment; quashing.

anoblir [anɔblir] *vt* to ennoble.

anodin [anɔdɛ̃] a harmless; (remède) ineffectual.

anomalie [anɔmali] nf (irrégularité) anomaly; (difformité) abnormality.

ânonner [ɑnɔne] vt (en hésitant) to stumble through; (d'une voix monotone) to drone out.

anonymat [anɔnima] nm anonymity; garder l'a. to remain anonymous. ◆anonyme a & nmf anonymous (person).

anorak [anɔrak] nm anorak.

anorexie [anɔrɛksi] nf anorexia.

anormal, -aux [anɔrmal, -o] a abnormal; (enfant) educationally subnormal.

anse [ɑ̃s] nf (de tasse etc) handle; (baie) cove.

antagonisme [ɑ̃tagɔnism] nm antagonism. ◆antagoniste a antagonistic; – nmf antagonist.

antan (d') [dɑ̃tɑ̃] a Litt of yesteryear.

antarctique [ɑ̃tarktik] a antarctic; – nm l'A. the Antarctic, Antarctica.

antécédent [ɑ̃tesedɑ̃] nm Gram antecedent; pl past history, antecedents.

antenne [ɑ̃tɛn] nf TV Rad aerial, Am antenna; (station) station; (d'insecte) antenna, feeler; a. chirurgicale surgical outpost; Aut emergency unit; sur ou à l'a. on the air.

antérieur [ɑ̃terjœr] a (précédent) former, previous, earlier; (placé devant) front; membre a. forelimb; a. à prior to. ◆antérieurement adv previously. ◆antériorité nf precedence.

anthologie [ɑ̃tɔlɔʒi] nf anthology.

anthropologie [ɑ̃trɔpɔlɔʒi] nf anthropology.

anthropophage [ɑ̃trɔpɔfaʒ] nm cannibal. ◆anthropophagie nf cannibalism.

antiaérien, -ienne [ɑ̃tiaerjɛ̃, -jɛn] a (canon) antiaircraft; (abri) air-raid.

antiatomique [ɑ̃tiatɔmik] a abri a. fallout shelter.

antibiotique [ɑ̃tibjɔtik] a & nm antibiotic.

antibrouillard [ɑ̃tibrujar] a & nm (phare) a. fog lamp.

anticancéreux, -euse [ɑ̃tikɑ̃serø, -øz] a centre a. cancer hospital.

antichambre [ɑ̃tiʃɑ̃br] nf antechamber, anteroom.

antichoc [ɑ̃tiʃɔk] a inv shockproof.

anticip/er [ɑ̃tisipe] vti a. (sur) to anticipate. ◆–é a (retraite etc) early; (paiement) advance; avec mes remerciements anticipés thanking you in advance. ◆anticipation nf anticipation; par a. in advance; d'a. (roman etc) science-fiction.

anticlérical, -aux [ɑ̃tiklerikal, -o] a anticlerical.

anticonformiste [ɑ̃tikɔ̃fɔrmist] a & nmf nonconformist.

anticonstitutionnel, -elle [ɑ̃tikɔ̃stitysjɔnɛl] a unconstitutional.

anticorps [ɑ̃tikɔr] nm antibody.

anticyclone [ɑ̃tisiklɔn] nm anticyclone.

antidater [ɑ̃tidate] vt to backdate, antedate.

antidémocratique [ɑ̃tidemɔkratik] a undemocratic.

antidérapant [ɑ̃tiderapɑ̃] a non-skid.

antidote [ɑ̃tidɔt] nm antidote.

antigel [ɑ̃tiʒɛl] nm antifreeze.

Antilles [ɑ̃tij] nfpl les A. the West Indies. ◆antillais, -aise a & nmf West Indian.

antilope [ɑ̃tilɔp] nf antelope.

antimite [ɑ̃timit] a mothproof; – nm mothproofing agent.

antiparasite [ɑ̃tiparazit] a dispositif a. Rad suppressor.

antipathie [ɑ̃tipati] nf antipathy. ◆antipathique a disagreeable.

antipodes [ɑ̃tipɔd] nmpl aux a. (partir) to the antipodes; aux a. de at the opposite end of the world from; Fig poles apart from.

antique [ɑ̃tik] a ancient. ◆antiquaire nmf antique dealer. ◆antiquité nf (temps, ancienneté) antiquity; (objet ancien) antique; pl (monuments etc) antiquities.

antirabique [ɑ̃tirabik] a (anti-)rabies.

antisémite [ɑ̃tisemit] a anti-Semitic. ◆antisémitisme nm anti-Semitism.

antiseptique [ɑ̃tisɛptik] a & nm antiseptic.

antisudoral, -aux [ɑ̃tisydɔral, -o] nm antiperspirant.

antithèse [ɑ̃titɛz] nf antithesis.

antivol [ɑ̃tivɔl] nm anti-theft lock ou device.

antonyme [ɑ̃tɔnim] nm antonym.

antre [ɑ̃tr] nm (de lion etc) den.

anus [anys] nm anus.

Anvers [ɑ̃vɛr(s)] nm ou f Antwerp.

anxiété [ɑ̃ksjete] nf anxiety. ◆anxieux, -euse a anxious; – nmf worrier.

août [u(t)] nm August. ◆aoûtien, -ienne [ausjɛ̃, -jɛn] nmf August holidaymaker ou Am vacationer.

apais/er [apeze] vt (personne) to appease, calm; (scrupules, faim) to appease; (douleur) to allay; – s'a. vpr (personne) to calm down. ◆–ant a soothing. ◆–ements nmpl reassurances.

apanage [apanaʒ] nm privilege, monopoly (de of).

aparté [aparte] nm Th aside; (dans une réunion) private exchange; en a. in private.

apartheid [aparted] nm apartheid.

apathie [apati] *nf* apathy. ◆**apathique** *a* apathetic, listless.

apatride [apatrid] *nmf* stateless person.

apercevoir* [apɛrsəvwar] *vt* to see, perceive; (*brièvement*) to catch a glimpse of; **s'a. de** to notice, realize. ◆**aperçu** *nm* overall view, general outline; (*intuition*) insight.

apéritif [aperitif] *nm* aperitif. ◆**apéro** *nm Fam* aperitif.

apesanteur [apəzɑ̃tœr] *nf* weightlessness.

à-peu-près [apøprɛ] *nm inv* vague approximation.

apeuré [apœre] *a* frightened, scared.

aphone [afɔn] *a* voiceless.

aphorisme [afɔrism] *nm* aphorism.

aphrodisiaque [afrɔdizjak] *a & nm* aphrodisiac.

aphte [aft] *nm* mouth ulcer. ◆**aphteuse** *af* **fièvre a.** foot-and-mouth disease.

apiculture [apikyltyr] *nf* beekeeping.

apit/oyer [apitwaje] *vt* to move (to pity); **s'a. sur** to pity. ◆**-oiement** *nm* pity, commiseration.

aplanir [aplanir] *vt* (*terrain*) to level; (*difficulté*) to iron out, smooth out.

aplat/ir [aplatir] *vt* to flatten (out); — **s'a.** *vpr* (*s'étendre*) to lie flat; (*s'humilier*) to grovel; (*tomber*) *Fam* to fall flat on one's face; **s'a. contre** to flatten oneself against. ◆**-i a flat.** ◆**-issement** *nm* (*état*) flatness.

aplomb [aplɔ̃] *nm* self-possession, self-assurance; *Péj* impudence; **d'a.** (*équilibré*) well-balanced; (*sur ses jambes*) steady; (*bien portant*) in good shape; **tomber d'a.** (*soleil*) to beat down.

apocalypse [apokalips] *nf* apocalypse; **d'a.** (*vision etc*) apocalyptic. ◆**apocalyptique** *a* apocalyptic.

apogée [apɔʒe] *nm* apogee; *Fig* peak, apogee.

apolitique [apɔlitik] *a* apolitical.

Apollon [apɔlɔ̃] *nm* Apollo.

apologie [apɔlɔʒi] *nf* defence, vindication. ◆**apologiste** *nmf* apologist.

apoplexie [apɔplɛksi] *nf* apoplexy. ◆**apoplectique** *a* apoplectic.

apostolat [apɔstɔla] *nm* (*prosélytisme*) proselytism; (*mission*) *Fig* calling. ◆**apostolique** *a* apostolic.

apostrophe [apɔstrɔf] *nf* **1** (*signe*) apostrophe. **2** (*interpellation*) sharp *ou* rude remark. ◆**apostropher** *vt* to shout at.

apothéose [apɔteoz] *nf* final triumph, apotheosis.

apôtre [apotr] *nm* apostle.

apparaître* [aparɛtr] *vi* (*se montrer, sembler*) to appear.

apparat [apara] *nm* pomp; **d'a.** (*tenue etc*) ceremonial, formal.

appareil [aparɛj] *nm* (*instrument etc*) apparatus; (*électrique*) appliance; *Anat* system; *Tél* telephone; (*avion*) aircraft; (*législatif etc*) *Fig* machinery; **a.** (**photo**) camera; **a.** (**auditif**) hearing aid; **a.** (**dentier**) brace; **qui est à l'a.?** *Tél* who's speaking?

appareiller [apareje] **1** *vi Nau* to get under way. **2** *vt* (*assortir*) to match (up).

apparence [aparɑ̃s] *nf* appearance; (*vestige*) semblance; **en a.** outwardly; **sous l'a. de** under the guise of; **sauver les apparences** to keep up appearances. ◆**apparemment** [-amɑ̃] *adv* apparently. ◆**apparent** *a* apparent; (*ostensible*) conspicuous.

apparent/er (s') [saparɑ̃te] *vpr* (*ressembler*) to be similar *ou* akin (à to). ◆**-é a** (*allié*) related; (*semblable*) similar.

appariteur [aparitœr] *nm Univ* porter.

apparition [aparisjɔ̃] *nf* appearance; (*spectre*) apparition.

appartement [apartəmɑ̃] *nm* flat, *Am* apartment.

appartenir* [apartənir] **1** *vi* to belong (à to); **il vous appartient de** it's your responsibility to. **2 s'a.** *vpr* to be one's own master. ◆**appartenance** *nf* membership (à to).

appât [apɑ] *nm* (*amorce*) bait; (*attrait*) lure. ◆**appâter** *vt* (*attirer*) to lure.

appauvrir [apovrir] *vt* to impoverish; — **s'a.** *vpr* to become impoverished *ou* poorer.

appel [apɛl] *nm* (*cri, attrait etc*) call; (*demande pressante*) & *Jur* appeal; *Mil* call-up; **faire l'a.** *Scol* to take the register; *Mil* to have a roll call; **faire a.** à to appeal to, call upon; (*requérir*) to call for.

appel/er [aple] *vt* (*personne, nom etc*) to call; (*en criant*) to call out to; *Mil* to call up; (*nécessiter*) to call for; **a. à l'aide** to call for help; **en a. à** to appeal to; **il est appelé à** (*de hautes fonctions*) he is marked out for; (*témoigner etc*) he is called upon to; — **s'a.** *vpr* to be called; **il s'appelle Paul** his name is Paul. ◆**-é** *nm Mil* conscript. ◆**appellation** *nf* (*nom*) term; **a. contrôlée** trade name guaranteeing quality of wine.

appendice [apɛ̃dis] *nm* appendix; (*d'animal*) appendage. ◆**appendicite** *nf* appendicitis.

appentis [apɑ̃ti] *nm* (*bâtiment*) lean-to.

appesantir (s') [sapəzɑ̃tir] *vpr* to become heavier; **s'a. sur** (*sujet*) to dwell upon.

appétit [apeti] *nm* appetite (de for); **mettre**

qn en a. to whet s.o.'s appetite; **bon a.!** enjoy your meal! ◆**appétissant** a appetizing.

applaud/ir [aplodir] vti to applaud, clap; a. à (approuver) to applaud. ◆**—issements** nmpl applause.

applique [aplik] nf wall lamp.

appliqu/er [aplike] vt to apply (à to); (surnom, baiser, gifle) to give; (loi, décision) to put into effect; **s'a. à** (un travail) to apply oneself to; (concerner) to apply to; **s'a. à faire** to take pains to do. ◆**—é** a (travailleur) painstaking; (sciences) applied. ◆**applicable** a applicable. ◆**application** nf application.

appoint [apwɛ̃] nm contribution; **faire l'a.** to give the correct money ou change.

appointements [apwɛ̃tmɑ̃] nmpl salary.

appontement [apɔ̃tmɑ̃] nm landing stage.

apport [apɔr] nm contribution.

apporter [apɔrte] vt to bring.

apposer [apoze] vt Jur to affix. ◆**apposition** nf Gram apposition.

apprécier [apresje] vt (évaluer) to appraise; (aimer, percevoir) to appreciate. ◆**appréciable** a appreciable. ◆**appréciation** nf appraisal; appreciation.

appréhender [apreɑ̃de] vt (craindre) to fear; (arrêter) to apprehend. ◆**appréhension** nf apprehension.

apprendre* [aprɑ̃dr] vti (étudier) to learn; (événement, fait) to hear of, learn of; (nouvelle) to hear; **a. à faire** to learn to do; **a. qch à qn** (enseigner) to teach s.o. sth; (informer) to tell s.o. sth; **a. à qn à faire** to teach s.o. to do; **a. que** to learn that; (être informé) to hear that.

apprenti, -ie [aprɑ̃ti] nmf apprentice; (débutant) novice. ◆**apprentissage** nm apprenticeship; **faire l'a. de** Fig to learn the experience of.

apprêt/er [aprete] vt, — **s'a.** vpr to prepare. ◆**—é** a Fig affected.

apprivois/er [aprivwaze] vt to tame; — **s'a.** vpr to become tame. ◆**—é** a tame.

approbation [aprɔbasjɔ̃] nf approval. ◆**approbateur, -trice** a approving.

approche [aprɔʃ] nf approach. ◆**approch/er** vt (chaise etc) to bring up, draw up (de to, close to); (personne) to approach, come close to; — vi to approach, draw near(er); **a. de, s'a. de** to approach, come close(r) ou near(er) to. ◆**—ant** a similar. ◆**—é** a approximate. ◆**—able** a approachable.

approfond/ir [aprɔfɔ̃dir] vt (trou etc) to deepen; (question) to go into thoroughly;

(mystère) to plumb the depths of. ◆**—i** a thorough. ◆**—issement** nm deepening; (examen) thorough examination.

approprié [apropije] a appropriate.

approprier (s') [saproprije] vpr **s'a. qch** to appropriate sth.

approuver [apruve] vt (autoriser) to approve; (apprécier) to approve of.

approvisionn/er [aprovizjɔne] vt (ville etc) to supply (with provisions); (magasin) to stock; — **s'a.** vpr to stock up (de with), get one's supplies (de of). ◆**—ements** nmpl stocks, supplies.

approximat/if, -ive [aprɔksimatif, -iv] a approximate. ◆**—ivement** adv approximately. ◆**approximation** nf approximation.

appui [apɥi] nm support; (pour coude etc) rest; (de fenêtre) sill; **à hauteur d'a.** breast-high. ◆**appuie-tête** nm inv headrest. ◆**appuyer** vt (soutenir) to support; (accentuer) to stress; **a. qch sur** (poser) to lean ou rest sth on; (presser) to press sth on; — vi **a. sur** to rest on; (bouton etc) to press (on); (mot, élément etc) to stress; **s'a.** sur to lean on, rest on; (compter) to rely on; (se baser) to base oneself on.

âpre [ɑpr] a harsh, rough; **a. au gain** grasping.

après [aprɛ] prép (temps) after; (espace) beyond; **a. un an** after a year; **a. le pont** beyond the bridge; **a. coup** after the event; **a. avoir mangé** after eating; **a. qu'il t'a vu** after he saw you; **d'a.** (selon) according to, from; — adv after(wards); **l'année d'a.** the following year; **et a.?** and then what?

après-demain [aprɛdmɛ̃] adv the day after tomorrow. ◆**a.-guerre** nm inv post-war period; **d'a.-guerre** post-war. ◆**a.-midi** nm ou f inv afternoon. ◆**a.-shampooing** nm (hair) conditioner. ◆**a.-ski** nm ankle boot, snow boot.

a priori [aprijɔri] adv at the very outset, without going into the matter; — nm inv premiss.

à-propos [apropo] nm timeliness, aptness.

apte [apt] a suited (à to), capable (à of). ◆**aptitude** nf aptitude, capacity (à, pour for).

aquarelle [akwarɛl] nf watercolour, aquarelle.

aquarium [akwarjɔm] nm aquarium.

aquatique [akwatik] a aquatic.

aqueduc [akdyk] nm aqueduct.

aquilin [akilɛ̃] a aquiline.

arabe [arab] a & nmf Arab; — a & nm (langue) Arabic; **chiffres arabes** Arabic

numerals; **désert** a. Arabian desert.
◆**Arable** nf Arabia; **A. Séoudite** Saudi
Arabia.

arabesque [arabesk] nf arabesque.

arable [arabl] a arable.

arachide [araʃid] nf peanut, groundnut.

araignée [areɲe] nf spider.

arbalète [arbalɛt] nf crossbow.

arbitraire [arbitrɛr] a arbitrary.

arbitre [arbitr] nm Jur arbitrator; (maître
absolu) arbiter; Fb referee; Tennis umpire;
libre a. free will. ◆**arbitr/er** vt to arbitrate; to referee; to umpire. ◆**—age** nm
arbitration; refereeing; umpiring.

arborer [arbɔre] vt (insigne, vêtement) to
sport, display.

arbre [arbr] nm tree; Aut shaft, axle.
◆**arbrisseau, -x** nm shrub. ◆**arbuste**
nm (small) shrub, bush.

arc [ark] nm (arme) bow; (voûte) arch; Math
arc; **tir à l'a.** archery. ◆**arcade** nf
arch(way); pl arcade.

arc-boutant [arkbutã] nm (pl
arcs-boutants) flying buttress.
◆**s'arc-bouter** vpr s'a. à ou contre to
brace oneself against.

arceau, -x [arso] nm (de voûte) arch.

arc-en-ciel [arkãsjɛl] nm (pl arcs-en-ciel)
rainbow.

archaïque [arkaik] a archaic.

archange [arkãʒ] nm archangel.

arche [arʃ] nf (voûte) arch; **l'a. de Noé**
Noah's ark.

archéologie [arkeɔlɔʒi] nf arch(a)eology.
◆**archéologue** nmf arch(a)eologist.

archer [arʃe] nm archer, bowman.

archet [arʃe] nm Mus bow.

archétype [arketip] nm archetype.

archevêque [arʃəvɛk] nm archbishop.

archicomble [arʃikɔ̃bl] a jam-packed.

archipel [arʃipɛl] nm archipelago.

archiplein [arʃiplɛ̃] a chock-full,
chock-a-block.

architecte [arʃitɛkt] nm architect.
◆**architecture** nf architecture.

archives [arʃiv] nfpl archives, records.
◆**archiviste** nmf archivist.

arctique [arktik] a arctic; – nm **l'A.** the
Arctic.

ardent [ardã] a (chaud) burning, scorching;
(actif, passionné) ardent, fervent;
(empressé) eager. ◆**ardemment** [-amã]
adv eagerly, fervently. ◆**ardeur** nf heat;
(énergie) ardour, fervour.

ardoise [ardwaz] nf slate.

ardu [ardy] a arduous, difficult.

are [ar] nm (mesure) 100 square metres.

arène [arɛn] nf Hist arena; (pour taureaux)
bullring; pl Hist amphitheatre; bullring.

arête [arɛt] nf (de poisson) bone; (de cube
etc) & Géog ridge.

argent [arʒã] nm (métal) silver; (monnaie)
money; **a. comptant** cash. ◆**argenté** a
(plaqué) silver-plated; (couleur) silvery.
◆**argenterie** nf silverware.

Argentine [arʒãtin] nf Argentina. ◆**argentin, -ine** a & nmf Argentinian.

argile [arʒil] nf clay. ◆**argileux, -euse** a
clayey.

argot [argo] nm slang. ◆**argotique** a
(terme) slang.

arguer [argɥe] vi **a. de qch** to put forward
sth as an argument; **a. que** (protester) to
protest that. ◆**argumentation** nf argumentation, arguments. ◆**argumenter** vi
to argue.

argument [argymã] nm argument.

argus [argys] nm guide to secondhand cars.

argutie [argysi] nf specious argument, quibble.

aride [arid] a arid, barren.

aristocrate [aristɔkrat] nmf aristocrat.
◆**aristocratie** [-asi] nf aristocracy.
◆**aristocratique** a aristocratic.

arithmétique [aritmetik] nf arithmetic; – a
arithmetical.

arlequin [arləkɛ̃] nm harlequin.

armateur [armatœr] nm shipowner.

armature [armatyr] nf (charpente) framework; (de lunettes, tente) frame.

arme [arm] nf arm, weapon; **a. à feu** firearm; **carrière des armes** military career.
◆**arm/er** vt (personne etc) to arm (de
with); (fusil) to cock; (appareil photo) to
wind on; (navire) to equip; (béton) to reinforce; **— s'a.** vpr to arm oneself (de with).
◆**—ement(s)** nm(pl) arms.

armée [arme] nf army; **a. active/de métier**
regular/professional army; **a. de l'air** air
force.

armistice [armistis] nm armistice.

armoire [armwar] nf cupboard, Am closet;
(penderie) wardrobe, Am closet; **a. à
pharmacie** medicine cabinet.

armoiries [armwari] nfpl (coat of) arms.

armure [armyr] nf armour.

armurier [armyrje] nm gunsmith.

arôme [arom] nm aroma. ◆**aromate** nm
spice. ◆**aromatique** a aromatic.

arpent/er [arpãte] vt (terrain) to survey;
(trottoir etc) to pace up and down. ◆**—eur**
nm (land) surveyor.

arqué [arke] a arched, curved; (jambes)
bandy.

arrache-pied (d') [daraʃpje] adv unceasingly, relentlessly.

arrach/er [araʃe] vt (clou, dent etc) to pull out; (cheveux, page) to tear out, pull out; (plante) to pull up; (masque) to tear off, pull off; **a. qch à qn** to snatch sth from s.o.; (aveu, argent) to force sth out of s.o.; **a. un bras à qn** (obus etc) to blow s.o.'s arm off; **a. qn de son lit** to drag s.o. out of bed. ◆**—age** nm (de plante) pulling up.

arraisonner [arezɔne] vt (navire) to board and examine.

arrang/er [arɑ̃ʒe] vt (chambre, visite etc) to arrange, fix up; (voiture, texte) to put right; (différend) to settle; **a. qn** (maltraiter) Fam to fix s.o.; **ça m'arrange** that suits me fine; **— s'a.** vpr (se réparer) to be put right; (se mettre d'accord) to come to an agreement ou arrangement; (finir bien) to turn out fine; **s'a. pour faire** to arrange to do, manage to do. ◆**—eant** a accommodating. ◆**—ement** nm arrangement.

arrestation [arɛstɑsjɔ̃] nf arrest.

arrêt [arɛ] nm (halte, endroit) stop; (action) stopping; Jur decree; **temps d'a.** pause; **à l'a.** stationary; **a. de travail** (grève) stoppage; (congé) sick leave; **sans a.** constantly, non-stop.

arrêté [arete] nm order, decision.

arrêt/er [arete] vt to stop; (appréhender) to arrest; (regard, jour) to fix; (plan) to draw up; **— vi** to stop; **il n'arrête pas de critiquer/etc** he doesn't stop criticizing/etc, he's always criticizing/etc; **— s'a.** vpr to stop; **s'a. de faire** to stop doing. ◆**—é** a (projet) fixed; (volonté) firm.

arrhes [ar] nfpl Fin deposit.

arrière [arjɛr] adv en a. (marcher) backwards; (rester) behind; (regarder) back; **en a. de qn/qch** behind s.o./sth; **— nm & a** inv rear, back; (nm Fb (full) back; **faire marche a.** to reverse, back.

arrière-boutique [arjɛrbutik] nm back room (of a shop). ◆**a.-garde** nf rearguard. ◆**a.-goût** nm aftertaste. ◆**a.-grand-mère** nf great-grandmother. ◆**a.-grand-père** nm (pl **arrière-grands-pères**) great-grand-father. ◆**a.-pays** nm hinterland. ◆**a.-pensée** nf ulterior motive. ◆**a.-plan** nm background. ◆**a.-saison** nf end of season, (late) autumn. ◆**a.-train** nm hindquarters.

arriéré [arjere] **1** a (enfant) (mentally) retarded; (idée) backward. **2** nm (dette) arrears.

arrimer [arime] vt (fixer) to rope down, secure.

arriv/er [arive] vi (aux être) (venir) to arrive, come; (réussir) to succeed; (survenir) to happen; **a. à** (atteindre) to reach; **a. à faire** to manage to do, succeed in doing; **a. à qn** to happen to s.o.; **il m'arrive d'oublier/etc** I happen (sometimes) to forget/etc, I (sometimes) forget/etc; **en a. à faire** to get to the point of doing. ◆**—ant, -ante** nmf new arrival. ◆**—ée** nf arrival; Sp (winning) post. ◆**—age** nm consignment. ◆**arriviste** nmf Péj social climber, self-seeker.

arrogant [arɔgɑ̃] a arrogant. ◆**arrogance** nf arrogance.

arroger (s') [sarɔʒe] vpr (droit etc) to assume (falsely).

arrond/ir [arɔ̃dir] vt to make round; (somme, chiffre) to round off. ◆**—i** a rounded.

arrondissement [arɔ̃dismɑ̃] nm (d'une ville) district.

arros/er [aroze] vt (terre) to water; (repas) to wash down; (succès) to drink to. ◆**—age** nm watering; Fam booze-up, celebration. ◆**arrosoir** nm watering can.

arsenal, -aux [arsənal, -o] nm Nau dockyard; Mil arsenal.

arsenic [arsənik] nm arsenic.

art [ar] nm art; **film/critique d'a.** film/critic; **arts ménagers** domestic science.

artère [artɛr] nf Anat artery; Aut main road. ◆**artériel, -elle** a arterial.

artichaut [artiʃo] nm artichoke.

article [artikl] nm (de presse, de commerce) & Gram article; (dans un contrat, catalogue) item; **a. de fond** feature (article); **articles de toilette/de voyage** toilet/travel requisites; **à l'a. de la mort** at death's door.

articuler [artikyle] vt (mot etc) to articulate; **— s'a.** vpr Anat to articulate; Fig to connect. ◆**articulation** nf Ling articulation; Anat joint; **a. du doigt** knuckle.

artifice [artifis] nm trick, contrivance; **feu d'a.** (spectacle) fireworks, firework display.

artificiel, -elle [artifisjɛl] a artificial. ◆**artificiellement** adv artificially.

artillerie [artijri] nf artillery. ◆**artilleur** nm gunner.

artisan [artizɑ̃] nm craftsman, artisan. ◆**artisanal, -aux** a (métier) craftsman's. ◆**artisanat** nm (métier) craftsman's trade; (classe) artisan class.

artiste [artist] nmf artist; Th Mus Cin performer, artist. ◆**artistique** a artistic.

as [as] nm (carte, champion) ace; **a. du volant** crack driver.

ascendant [asɑ̃dɑ̃] *a* ascending, upward; — *nm* ascendancy, power; *pl* ancestors. ◆**ascendance** *nf* ancestry.

ascenseur [asɑ̃sœr] *nm* lift, *Am* elevator.

ascension [asɑ̃sjɔ̃] *nf* ascent; l'A. Ascension Day.

ascète [aset] *nmf* ascetic. ◆**ascétique** *a* ascetic. ◆**ascétisme** *nm* asceticism.

Asie [azi] *nf* Asia. ◆**Asiate** *nmf* Asian. ◆**asiatique** *a* & *nmf* Asian, Asiatic.

asile [azil] *nm* (*abri*) refuge, shelter; (*pour vieillards*) home; *Pol* asylum; **a.** (**d'aliénés**) *Péj* (lunatic) asylum; **a. de paix** haven of peace.

aspect [aspɛ] *nm* (*vue*) appearance; (*perspective*) & *Gram* aspect.

asperge [aspɛrʒ] *nf* asparagus.

asperger [aspɛrʒe] *vt* to spray, sprinkle (**de** with).

aspérité [asperite] *nf* rugged edge, bump.

asphalte [asfalt] *nm* asphalt.

asphyxie [asfiksi] *nf* suffocation. ◆**asphyxier** *vt* to suffocate, asphyxiate.

aspic [aspik] *nm* (*vipère*) asp.

aspirant [aspirɑ̃] *nm* (*candidat*) candidate.

aspirateur [aspiratœr] *nm* vacuum cleaner, hoover®; **passer l'a.** to vacuum, hoover.

aspir/er [aspire] *vt* (*respirer*) to breathe in, inhale; (*liquide*) to suck up; **a.** à to aspire to. ◆**-é** *a Ling* aspirate(d). ◆**aspiration** *nf* inhaling; suction; (*ambition*) aspiration.

aspirine [aspirin] *nf* aspirin.

assagir (s') [sasaʒir] *vpr* to sober (down), settle down.

assaill/ir [asajir] *vt* to assault, attack; **a. de** (*questions etc*) to assail with. ◆**-ant** *nm* assailant, attacker.

assainir [asenir] *vt* (*purifier*) to clean up; *Fin* to stabilize.

assaisonn/er [asɛzɔne] *vt* to season. ◆**-ement** *nm* seasoning.

assassin [asasɛ̃] *nm* murderer; assassin. ◆**assassinat** *nm* murder; assassination. ◆**assassiner** *vt* to murder; (*homme politique etc*) to assassinate.

assaut [aso] *nm* assault, onslaught; **prendre d'a.** to (take by) storm.

assécher [aseʃe] *vt* to drain.

assemblée [asɑ̃ble] *nf* (*personnes réunies*) gathering; (*réunion*) meeting; *Pol Jur* assembly; (*de fidèles*) *Rel* congregation.

assembl/er [asɑ̃ble] *vt* to assemble, put together; — **s'a.** *vpr* to assemble, gather. ◆**-age** *nm* (*montage*) assembly; (*réunion d'objets*) collection.

asséner [asene] *vt* (*coup*) to deal, strike.

assentiment [asɑ̃timɑ̃] *nm* assent, consent.

asseoir* [aswar] *vt* (*personne*) to sit (down), seat (**sur** on); (*fondations*) to lay; (*autorité, réputation*) to establish; **a. sur** (*théorie etc*) to base on; — **s'a.** *vpr* to sit (down).

assermenté [asɛrmɑ̃te] *a* sworn.

assertion [asɛrsjɔ̃] *nf* assertion.

asserv/ir [asɛrvir] *vt* to enslave. ◆**-issement** *nm* enslavement.

assez [ase] *adv* enough; **a. de pain/de gens** enough bread/people; **j'en ai a.** I've had enough; **a. grand/intelligent/etc** (*suffisamment*) big/clever/etc enough (**pour** to); **a. fatigué/etc** (*plutôt*) fairly *ou* rather *ou* quite tired/etc.

assidu [asidy] *a* (*appliqué*) assiduous, diligent; **a. auprès de** attentive to. ◆**assiduité** *nf* assiduousness, diligence; *pl* (*empressement*) attentiveness. ◆**assidûment** *adv* assiduously.

assiég/er [asjeʒe] *vt* (*ville*) to besiege; (*guichet*) to mob, crowd round; (*importuner*) to pester, harry; **assiégé de** (*demandes*) besieged with; (*maux*) beset by. ◆**-eant, -eante** *nmf* besieger.

assiette [asjɛt] *nf* 1 (*récipient*) plate; **a. anglaise** *Culin* (assorted) cold meats, *Am* cold cuts. 2 (*à cheval*) seat; **il n'est pas dans son a.** he's feeling out of sorts.

assigner [asiɲe] *vt* (*attribuer*) to assign; (*à comparaître*) *Jur* to summon, subpoena. ◆**assignation** *nf Jur* subpoena, summons.

assimiler [asimile] *vt* to assimilate; — **s'a.** *vpr* (*immigrants*) to assimilate, become assimilated (**à** with). ◆**assimilation** *nf* assimilation.

assis [asi] *a* (*sitting* (down), seated; (*caractère*) settled; (*situation*) stable, secure.

assise [asiz] *nf* (*base*) *Fig* foundation; *pl* Jur assizes; *Pol* congress; **cour d'assises** court of assizes.

assistance [asistɑ̃s] *nf* 1 (*assemblée*) audience; (*nombre de personnes présentes*) attendance, turn-out. 2 (*aide*) assistance; **l'A. (publique)** the child care service; **enfant de l'A.** child in care. ◆**assist/er** 1 *vt* (*aider*) to assist, help. 2 *vi* **a.** à (*réunion, cours etc*) to attend, be present at; (*accident*) to witness. ◆**-ant, -ante** *nmf* assistant; — *nmpl* (*spectateurs*) members of the audience; (*témoins*) those present; **assistante sociale** social worker; **assistante maternelle** mother's help.

associ/er [asɔsje] *vt* to associate (**à** with); **a. qn à** (*ses travaux, profits*) to involve s.o. in; **s'a. à** (*collaborer*) to associate with, become associated with; (*aux vues ou au chagrin de qn*) to share; (*s'harmoniser*) to combine

with. ◆—é, -ée *nmf* partner, associate; −
a associate. ◆**association** *nf* association;
(*amitié, alliance*) partnership, association.

assoiffé [aswafe] *a* thirsty (**de** for).

assombrir [asɔbrir] *vt* (*obscurcir*) to darken;
(*attrister*) to cast a cloud over, fill with
gloom; **— s'a.** *vpr* to darken; to cloud over.

assomm/er [asɔme] *vt* (*animal*) to stun,
brain; (*personne*) to knock unconscious;
(*ennuyer*) to bore stiff. ◆**—ant** *a* tiresome,
boring.

assomption [asɔpsjɔ] *nf* Rel Assumption.

assort/ir [asɔrtir] *vt*, **— s'a.** (*objet*) to match.
◆**—i** *a* **bien a.** (*magasin*) well-stocked; −
apl (*objets semblables*) matching;
(*fromages etc variés*) assorted; **époux bien
assortis** well-matched couple. ◆**—iment**
nm assortment.

assoup/ir [asupir] *vt* (*personne*) to make
drowsy; (*douleur, sentiment etc*) Fig to dull;
— s'a. *vpr* to doze off; Fig to subside. ◆**—i**
a (*personne*) drowsy. ◆**—issement** *nm*
drowsiness.

assoupl/ir [asuplir] *vt* (*étoffe, muscles*) to
make supple; (*corps*) to limber up; (*caractère*) to soften; (*règles*) to ease, relax.
◆**—issement** **un exercices d'a.** limbering
up exercises.

assourd/ir [asurdir] *vt* (*personne*) to
deafen; (*son*) to muffle. ◆**—issant** *a* deafening.

assouvir [asuvir] *vt* to appease, satisfy.

assujett/ir [asyʒetir] *vt* (*soumettre*) to
subject (**à** to); (*peuple*) to subjugate; (*fixer*)
to secure; **s'a. à** to subject oneself to,
submit to. ◆**—issant** *a* (*travail*)
constraining. ◆**—issement** *nm* subjec-
tion; (*contrainte*) constraint.

assumer [asyme] *vt* (*tâche, rôle*) to assume,
take on; (*emploi*) to take up, assume;
(*remplir*) to fill, hold.

assurance [asyrɑs] *nf* (*aplomb*)
(self-)assurance; (*promesse*) assurance;
(*contrat*) insurance; **a. au tiers/tous risques**
third-party/comprehensive insurance;
assurances sociales = national insurance,
Am = social security.

assur/er [asyre] *vt* (*rendre sûr*) to ensure,
Am insure; (*par un contrat*) to insure;
(*travail etc*) to carry out; (*fixer*) to secure;
a. à qn que to assure s.o. that; **a. qn de qch,
a. qch à qn** to assure s.o. of sth; **— s'a.** *vpr*
(*se procurer*) to ensure, secure; (*par un
contrat*) to insure oneself, get insured
(**contre** against); **s'a. que/de** to make sure
that/of. ◆**—é, -ée** *a* (*succès*) assured,
certain; (*pas*) firm, secure; (*air*)

(self-)assured, (self-)confident; **— nmf** poli-
cyholder, insured person. ◆**—ément** *adv*
certainly, assuredly. ◆**assureur** *nm*
insurer.

astérisque [asterisk] *nm* asterisk.

asthme [asm] *nm* asthma. ◆**asthmatique**
a & *nmf* asthmatic.

asticot [astiko] *nm* maggot, worm.

astiquer [astike] *vt* to polish.

astre [astr] *nm* star.

astreindre★ [astrɛdr] *vt* **a.** à (*discipline*) to
compel to accept; **a. à faire** to compel to
do. ◆**astreignant** *a* exacting ◆**astreinte**
nf constraint.

astrologie [astrɔlɔʒi] *nf* astrology. ◆**astrologue** *nm* astrologer.

astronaute [astronot] *nmf* astronaut.
◆**astronautique** *nf* space travel.

astronomie [astronomi] *nf* astronomy.
◆**astronome** *nm* astronomer. ◆**astronomique** *a* astronomical.

astuce [astys] *nf* (*pour faire qch*) knack,
trick; (*invention*) gadget; (*plaisanterie*)
clever joke, wisecrack; (*finesse*) astuteness;
les astuces du métier the tricks of the trade.
◆**astucieux, -euse** *a* clever, astute.

atelier [atəlje] *nm* (*d'ouvrier*) workshop; (*de
peintre*) studio.

atermoyer [atɛrmwaje] *vi* to procrastinate.

athée [ate] *a* atheistic; **— nmf** atheist.
◆**athéisme** *nm* atheism.

Athènes [atɛn] *nm ou f* Athens.

athlète [atlɛt] *nmf* athlete. ◆**athlétique** *a*
athletic. ◆**athlétisme** *nm* athletics.

atlantique [atlɑ̃tik] *a* Atlantic; **− nm l'A.**
the Atlantic.

atlas [atlas] *nm* atlas.

atmosphère [atmɔsfɛr] *nf* atmosphere.
◆**atmosphérique** *a* atmospheric.

atome [atom] *nm* atom. ◆**atomique**
[atɔmik] *a* atomic; **bombe a.** atom ou
atomic bomb.

atomis/er [atɔmize] *vt* (*liquide*) to spray;
(*région*) to destroy (*by atomic weapons*).
◆**—eur** *nm* spray.

atone [atɔn] *a* (*personne*) lifeless; (*regard*)
vacant.

atours [atur] *nmpl* Hum finery.

atout [atu] *nm* trump (card); (*avantage*) Fig
trump card, asset; **l'a. est cœur** hearts are
trumps.

âtre [atr] *nm* (*foyer*) hearth.

atroce [atrɔs] *a* atrocious; (*crime*) heinous,
atrocious. ◆**atrocité** *nf* atrociousness; *pl*
(*actes*) atrocities.

atrophie [atrɔfi] *nf* atrophy. ◆**atrophié** *a*
atrophied.

attabl/er (s') [satable] *vpr* to sit down at the table. ◆**—é** *a* (seated) at the table.

attache [ataʃ] *nf* (*objet*) attachment, fastening; *pl* (*liens*) links.

attach/er [ataʃe] *vt* (*lier*) to tie (up), attach (à to); (*boucler, fixer*) to fasten; **a. du prix/un sens à qch** to attach great value/a meaning to sth; **cette obligation m'attache à lui** this obligation binds me to him; **s'a. à** (*adhérer*) to stick to; (*se lier*) to become attached to; (*se consacrer*) to apply oneself to. ◆**—ant** *a* (*enfant etc*) engaging, appealing. ◆**—é, -ée** *nmf* (*personne*) Pol Mil attaché. ◆**—ement** *nm* attachment, affection.

attaque [atak] *nf* attack; **a. aérienne** air raid; **d'a.** in tip-top shape, on top form. ◆**attaqu/er** *vt*, **s'a. à** to attack; (*difficulté, sujet*) to tackle; *– vi* to attack. ◆**—ant, —ante** *nmf* attacker.

attard/er (s') [atarde] *vpr* (*chez qn*) to linger (on), stay on; (*en chemin*) to loiter, dawdle; **s'a. sur** *ou* **à** (*détails etc*) to linger over; **s'a. derrière qn** to lag behind s.o. ◆**—é** *a* (*enfant etc*) backward; (*passant*) late.

atteindre* [atɛ̃dr] *vt* (*parvenir à*) to reach; (*idéal*) to attain; (*blesser*) to hit, wound; (*toucher*) to affect; (*offenser*) to hurt, wound; **être atteint de** (*maladie*) to be suffering from.

atteinte [atɛ̃t] *nf* attack; **porter a.** à to attack, undermine; **a. à** (*honneur*) slur on; **hors d'a.** (*objet, personne*) out of reach; (*réputation*) unassailable.

attel/er [atle] *vt* (*bêtes*) to harness, hitch up; (*remorque*) to couple; **s'a. à** (*travail etc*) to apply oneself to. ◆**—age** *nm* harnessing; coupling; (*bêtes*) team.

attenant [atnã] *a a.* (**à**) adjoining.

attend/re [atɑ̃dr] *vt* to wait for, await; (*escompter*) to expect (**de** of, from); **elle attend un bébé** she's expecting a baby; *– vi* to wait; **s'a. à** to expect; **a. d'être informé** to wait to be informed; **a. que qn vienne** to wait for s.o. to come, wait until s.o. comes; **faire a. qn** to keep s.o. waiting; **se faire a.** (*réponse, personne etc*) to be a long time coming; **attends voir** *Fam* let me see; **en attendant** meanwhile; **en attendant que** (*+ sub*) until. ◆**—u** *a* (*avec joie*) eagerly-awaited; (*prévu*) expected; *– prép* considering; **a. que** considering that.

attendr/ir [atɑ̃drir] *vt* (*émouvoir*) to move (to compassion); (*viande*) to tenderize; *– s'a.* *vpr* to be moved (**sur** by). ◆**—i** *a*

compassionate. ◆**—issant** *a* moving. ◆**—issement** *nm* compassion.

attentat [atɑ̃ta] *nm* attempt (*on s.o.'s life*), murder attempt; *Fig* crime, outrage (**à** against); **a. (à la bombe)** (bomb) attack. ◆**attenter** *vi* **a.** à (*la vie de qn*) to make an attempt on; *Fig* to attack.

attente [atɑ̃t] *nf* (*temps*) wait(ing); (*espérance*) expectation(s); **une a. prolongée** a long wait; **être dans l'a. de** to be waiting for; **salle d'a.** waiting room.

attentif, -ive [atɑ̃tif, -iv] *a* (*personne*) attentive; (*travail, examen*) careful; **a. à** (*plaire etc*) anxious to; (*ses devoirs etc*) mindful of. ◆**attentivement** *adv* attentively.

attention [atɑ̃sjɔ̃] *nf* attention; *pl* (*égards*) consideration; **faire** *ou* **prêter a. à** (*écouter, remarquer*) to pay attention to; **faire a. à/que** (*prendre garde*) to be careful of/that; **a.! look out!, be careful!; a. à la voiture!** mind *ou* watch the car! ◆**attentionné** *a* considerate.

atténu/er [atenɥe] *vt* to attenuate, mitigate; *– s'a. vpr* to subside. ◆**—antes** *afpl* **circonstances** a. extenuating circumstances.

atterrer [atere] *vt* to dismay.

atterr/ir [aterir] *vi* *Av* to land. ◆**—issage** *nm* *Av* landing; **a. forcé** crash *ou* emergency landing.

attester [ateste] *vt* to testify to; **a. que** to testify that. ◆**attestation** *nf* (*document*) declaration, certificate.

attifer [atife] *vt* *Fam* *Péj* to dress up, rig out.

attirail [atiraj] *nm* (*équipement*) *Fam* gear.

attir/er [atire] *vt* (*faire venir*) to attract, draw; (*plaire à*) to attract; (*attention*) to draw (**sur** on); **a. qch à qn** (*causer*) to bring s.o. sth; (*gloire etc*) to win *ou* earn s.o. sth; **a. dans** (*coin, guet-apens*) to draw into; *– s'a. vpr* (*ennuis etc*) to bring upon oneself; (*sympathie de qn*) to win; **a. sur soi** (*colère de qn*) to bring down upon oneself. ◆**—ant** *a* attractive. ◆**attirance** *nf* attraction.

attiser [atize] *vt* (*feu*) to poke; (*sentiment*) *Fig* to rouse.

attitré [atitre] *a* (*représentant*) appointed; (*marchand*) regular.

attitude [atityd] *nf* attitude; (*maintien*) bearing.

attraction [atraksjɔ̃] *nf* attraction.

attrait [atrɛ] *nm* attraction.

attrape [atrap] *nf* trick. ◆**a.-nigaud** *nm* con, trick.

attraper [atrape] *vt* (*ballon, maladie, voleur, train etc*) to catch; (*accent, contravention etc*) to pick up; **se laisser a.** (*duper*) to get taken in *ou* tricked; **se faire a.** (*gronder*) *Fam* to get a telling off. ◆**attrapade** *nf* (*gronderie*) *Fam* telling off.

attrayant [atrɛjɑ̃] *a* attractive.

attribuer [atribɥe] *vt* (*donner*) to assign, allot (à to); (*imputer, reconnaître*) to attribute, ascribe (à to); (*décerner*) to grant, award (à to). ◆**attribuable** *a* attributable. ◆**attribution** *nf* assignment; attribution; (*de prix*) awarding; *pl* (*compétence*) powers.

attribut [atriby] *nm* attribute.

attrister [atriste] *vt* to sadden.

attroup/er [atrupe] *vt*, **— s'a.** *vpr* to gather. ◆**—ement** *nm* gathering, (disorderly) crowd.

au [o] *voir* à.

aubaine [obɛn] *nf* (**bonne**) **a.** stroke of good luck, godsend.

aube [ob] *nf* dawn; **dès l'a.** at the crack of dawn.

aubépine [obepin] *nf* hawthorn.

auberge [obɛrʒ] *nf* inn; **a. de jeunesse** youth hostel. ◆**aubergiste** *nmf* innkeeper.

aubergine [obɛrʒin] *nf* aubergine, eggplant.

aucun, -une [okœ̃, -yn] *a* no, not any; **il n'a a. talent** he has no talent, he doesn't have any talent; **a. professeur n'est venu** no teacher has come; **— pron** none, not any; **il n'en a a.** he has none (at all), he doesn't have any (at all); **plus qu'a.** more than any(one); **d'aucuns** some (people). ◆**aucunement** *adv* not at all.

audace [odas] *nf* (*courage*) daring, boldness; (*impudence*) audacity; *pl* daring innovations. ◆**audacieux, -euse** *a* daring, bold.

au-dedans, au-dehors, au-delà *voir* dedans *etc*.

au-dessous [odsu] *adv* (*en bas*) below, underneath; (*moins*) below, under; (*à l'étage inférieur*) downstairs; **— prép au-d. de** (*arbre etc*) below, under, beneath; (*âge, prix*) under; (*température*) below; **au-d. de sa tâche** not up to *ou* unequal to one's task.

au-dessus [odsy] *adv* above; over; on top; (*à l'étage supérieur*) upstairs; **— prép au-d. de** above; (*âge, température, prix*) over; (*posé sur*) on top of.

au-devant de [odvɑ̃də] *prép* **aller au-d. de** (*personne*) to go to meet; (*danger*) to court; (*désirs de qn*) to anticipate.

audible [odibl] *a* audible.

audience [odjɑ̃s] *nf* *Jur* hearing; (*entretien*) audience.

audio [odjo] *a inv* (*cassette etc*) audio.

◆**audiophone** *nm* hearing aid. ◆**audio-visuel, -elle** *a* audio-visual.

auditeur, -trice [oditœr, -tris] *nmf* *Rad* listener; **les auditeurs** the audience; **a. libre** *Univ* auditor, student allowed to attend classes but not to sit examinations. ◆**auditif, -ive** *a* (*nerf*) auditory. ◆**audition** *nf* (*ouïe*) hearing; (*séance d'essai*) *Th* audition; (*séance musicale*) recital. ◆**auditionner** *vti* to audition. ◆**auditoire** *nm* audience. ◆**auditorium** *nm* *Rad* recording studio (*for recitals*).

auge [oʒ] *nf* (*feeding*) trough.

augmenter [ogmɑ̃te] *vt* to increase (**de** by); (*salaire, prix, impôt*) to raise, increase; **a. qn** to give s.o. a rise *ou Am* raise; **— vi** to increase (**de** by); (*prix, population*) to rise, go up. ◆**augmentation** *nf* increase (**de** in, of); **a. de salaire** (pay) rise, *Am* raise; **a. de prix** price rise *ou* increase.

augure [ogyr] *nm* (*présage*) omen; (*devin*) oracle; **être de bon/mauvais a.** to be a good/bad omen. ◆**augurer** *vt* to augur, predict.

auguste [ogyst] *a* august.

aujourd'hui [oʒurdɥi] *adv* today; (*actuellement*) nowadays, today; **a. en quinze** two weeks today.

aumône [omon] *nf* alms.

aumônier [omonje] *nm* chaplain.

auparavant [oparavɑ̃] *adv* (*avant*) before(hand); (*d'abord*) first.

auprès de [oprɛdə] *prép* (*assis, situé etc*) by, close to, next to; (*en comparaison de*) compared to; **agir a. de** (*ministre etc*) to use one's influence with; **accès a. de qn** access to s.o.

auquel [okɛl] *voir* lequel.

aura, aurait [ora, orɛ] *voir* avoir.

auréole [oreɔl] *nf* (*de saint etc*) halo; (*trace*) ring.

auriculaire [orikyler] *nm* **l'a.** the little finger.

aurore [orɔr] *nf* dawn, daybreak.

ausculter [oskylte] *vt* (*malade*) to examine (*with a stethoscope*); (*cœur*) to listen to. ◆**auscultation** *nf* *Méd* auscultation.

auspices [ospis] *nmpl* **sous les a. de** under the auspices of.

aussi [osi] *adv* **1** (*comparaison*) as; **a. sage que** as wise as. **2** (*également*) too, also, as well; **moi a.** so do, can, am *etc* I; **a. bien que** as well as. **3** (*tellement*) so; **un repas a. délicieux** so delicious a meal, such a delicious meal. **4** *conj* (*donc*) therefore.

aussitôt [osito] *adv* immediately, at once; **a. que** as soon as; **a. levé, il partit** as soon as he was up, he left; **a. dit, a. fait** no sooner said than done.

austère [ɔster] *a* austere. ◆**austérité** *nf* austerity.

austral, *mpl* **-als** [ɔstral] *a* southern.

Australie [ɔstrali] *nf* Australia. ◆**australien, -ienne** *a* & *nmf* Australian.

autant [otɑ̃] *adv* **1 a. de ... que** (*quantité*) as much ... as; (*nombre*) as many ... as; **il a a. d'argent/de pommes que vous** he has as much money/as many apples as you. **2 a. de** (*tant de*) so much; (*nombre*) so many; **je n'ai jamais vu a. d'argent/de pommes** I've never seen so much money/so many apples; **pourquoi manges-tu a.?** why are you eating so much? **3 a. que** (*souffrir, lire etc*) as much as; **il lit a. que vous/que possible** he reads as much as you/as possible; **il n'a jamais souffert a.** he's never suffered as *ou* so much; **a. que je sache** as far as I know; **d'a. (plus) que** all the more (so) since; **d'a. moins que** even less since; **a. avouer/etc** we, *etc* might as well confess/*etc*; **en faire/dire a.** to do/say the same; **j'aimerais a. aller au cinéma** I'd just as soon go to the cinema.

autel [otɛl] *nm* altar.

auteur [otœr] *nm* (*de livre*) author, writer; (*de chanson*) composer; (*de procédé*) originator; (*de crime*) perpetrator; (*d'accident*) cause; **droit d'a.** copyright; **droits d'a.** royalties.

authenticité [otɑ̃tisite] *nf* authenticity. ◆**authentifier** *vt* to authenticate. ◆**authentique** *a* genuine, authentic.

autiste [otist] *a*, **autistique** *a* autistic.

auto [oto] *nf* car; **autos tamponneuses** bumper cars, dodgems.

auto- [oto] *préf* self-.

autobiographie [otobjɔgrafi] *nf* autobiography.

autobus [otobys] *nm* bus.

autocar [otokar] *nm* coach, bus.

autochtone [otɔktɔn] *a* & *nmf* native.

autocollant [otokɔlɑ̃] *nm* sticker.

autocrate [otokrat] *nm* autocrat. ◆**autocratique** *a* autocratic.

autocuiseur [otokɥizœr] *nm* pressure cooker.

autodéfense [otodefɑ̃s] *nf* self-defence.

autodestruction [otodestryksjɔ̃] *nf* self-destruction.

autodidacte [otodidakt] *a* & *nmf* self-taught (person).

autodrome [otodrom] *nm* motor-racing track.

auto-école [otoekɔl] *nf* driving school, school of motoring.

autographe [otograf] *nm* autograph.

automate [otomat] *nm* automaton. ◆**automation** *nf* automation. ◆**automatisation** *nf* automation. ◆**automatiser** *vt* to automate.

automatique [otomatik] *a* automatic; *– nm* **l'a. Tél** direct dialling. ◆**-ment** *adv* automatically.

automne [otɔn] *nm* autumn, *Am* fall. ◆**automnal, -aux** *a* autumnal.

automobile [otɔmɔbil] *nf* & *a* (motor) car, *Am* automobile; **l'a. Sp** motoring; **Salon de l'a.** Motor Show; **canot a.** motor boat. ◆**automobiliste** *nmf* motorist.

autonome [otonɔm] *a* (*région etc*) autonomous, self-governing; (*personne*) *Fig* independent. ◆**autonomie** *nf* autonomy.

autopsie [otɔpsi] *nf* autopsy, post-mortem.

autoradio [otoradjo] *nm* car radio.

autorail [otoraj] *nm* railcar.

autoris/er [otorize] *vt* (*habiliter*) to authorize (**à faire** to do); (*permettre*) to permit (**à faire** to do). ◆**-é** *a* (*qualifié*) authoritative. ◆**autorisation** *nf* authorization; permission.

autorité [otorite] *nf* authority. ◆**autoritaire** *a* authoritarian; (*homme, ton*) authoritative.

autoroute [otorut] *nf* motorway, *Am* highway, freeway.

auto-stop [otostɔp] *nm* hitchhiking; **faire de l'a.** to hitchhike. ◆**autostoppeur, -euse** *nmf* hitchhiker.

autour [otur] *adv* around; *– prép* **a. de** around.

autre [otr] *a* & *pron* other; **un a. livre** another book; **un a.** another (one); **d'autres** others; **as-tu d'autres questions?** have you any other *ou* further questions?; **qn/personne/rien d'a.** s.o./no one/nothing else; **a. chose/part** sth/somewhere else; **qui/quoi d'a.?** who/what else?; **l'un l'a., les uns les autres** each other; **l'un et l'a.** both (of them); **l'un ou l'a.** either (of them); **ni l'un ni l'a.** neither (of them); **les uns ... les autres** some ... others; **nous/vous autres Anglais** we/you English; **d'un moment à l'a.** any moment (now); **... et autres ...** and so on. ◆**autrement** *adv* (*différemment*) differently; (*sinon*) otherwise; (*plus*) far more (**que** than); **pas a. satisfait/etc** not particularly satisfied/*etc*.

autrefois [otrəfwa] *adv* in the past, in days gone by.

Autriche [otriʃ] *nf* Austria. ◆**autrichien, -ienne** *a & nmf* Austrian.

autruche [otryʃ] *nf* ostrich.

autrui [otrɥi] *pron* others, other people.

auvent [ovɑ̃] *nm* awning, canopy.

aux [o] *voir* à.

auxiliaire [ɔksiljɛr] *a* auxiliary; – *nm* Gram auxiliary; – *nmf* (aide) helper, auxiliary.

auxquels, -elles [okɛl] *voir* lequel.

avachir (s') [savaʃir] *vpr* (soulier, personne) to become flabby *ou* limp.

avait [avɛ] *voir* avoir.

aval (en) [ɑ̃naval] *adv* downstream (de from).

avalanche [avalɑ̃ʃ] *nf* avalanche, Fig flood, avalanche.

avaler [avale] *vt* to swallow; (livre) to devour; (mots) to mumble; – *vi* to swallow.

avance [avɑ̃s] *nf* (marche, acompte) advance; (de coureur, chercheur etc) lead; *pl* (galantes) advances; **à l'a., d'a., par a.** in advance; **en a.** (arriver, partir) early; (avant l'horaire prévu) ahead of (time); (dans son développement) ahead, in advance; (montre etc) fast; **en a. sur** (qn, son époque etc) ahead of, in advance of; **avoir une heure d'a.** (train etc) to be an hour early.

avanc/er [avɑ̃se] *vt* (thèse, argent) to advance; (date) to bring forward; (main, chaise) to move forward; (travail) to speed up; – *vi* to advance, move forward; (montre) to be fast; (faire saillie) to jut out (sur over); **a. en âge** to be getting on (in years); – **s'a.** *vpr* to advance, move forward; (faire saillie) to jut out. ◆**—é** *a* advanced; (saison) well advanced. ◆**—ée** *nf* projection, overhang. ◆**—ement** *nm* advancement.

avanie [avani] *nf* affront, insult.

avant [avɑ̃] *prép* before; **a. de voir** before seeing; **a. qu'il (ne) parte** before he leaves; **a. huit jours** within a week; **a. tout** above all; **a. toute chose** first and foremost; **a. peu** before long; – *adv* before; **en a.** (mouvement) forward; (en tête) ahead; **en a. de** in front of; **bien a. dans** (creuser etc) very deep(ly) into; **la nuit d'a.** the night before; – *nm & a inv* front; – *nm* (joueur) Sp forward.

avantage [avɑ̃taʒ] *nm* advantage; (bénéfice) Fin benefit; **tu as a. à le faire** it's worth your while to do it; **tirer a. de** to benefit from. ◆**avantager** *vt* (favoriser) to favour; (faire valoir) to show off to advantage. ◆**avantageux, -euse** *a* worthwhile, attractive; (flatteur) flattering; Péj conceited; **a. pour qn** advantageous to s.o.

avant-bras [avɑ̃bra] *nm inv* forearm. ◆**a.-centre** *nm* Sp centre-forward. ◆**a.-coureur** *am* Sp-coureur de (signe) heralding. ◆**a.-dernier, -ière** *a & nmf* last but one. ◆**a.-garde** *nf* Mil advance guard; **d'a.-garde** (idée, film etc) avant-garde. ◆**a.-goût** *nm* foretaste. ◆**a.-guerre** *nm ou f* pre-war period; **d'a.-guerre** pre-war. ◆**a.-hier** [avɑ̃tjɛr] *adv* the day before yesterday. ◆**a.-poste** *nm* outpost. ◆**a.-première** *nf* preview. ◆**a.-propos** *nm inv* foreword. ◆**a.-veille** *nf* **l'a.-veille (de)** two days before.

avare [avar] *a* miserly; **a. de** (compliments etc) sparing of; – *nmf* miser. ◆**avarice** *nf* avarice.

avarie(s) [avari] *nf(pl)* damage. ◆**avarié** *a* (aliment) spoiled, rotting.

avatar [avatar] *nm* Péj misadventure.

avec [avɛk] *prép* with; (envers) to(wards); et **a. ça?** (dans un magasin) Fam anything else?; – *adv* **il est venu a.** (son chapeau etc) Fam he came with it.

avenant [avnɑ̃] *a* pleasing, attractive; **à l'a.** in keeping (de with).

avènement [avɛnmɑ̃] *nm* **l'a. de** the coming *ou* advent of; (roi) the accession of.

avenir [avnir] *nm* future; **d'a.** (personne, métier) with future prospects; **à l'a.** (désormais) in future.

aventure [avɑ̃tyr] *nf* adventure; (en amour) affair; **à l'a.** (marcher etc) aimlessly; **dire la bonne a. à qn** to tell s.o.'s fortune. ◆**aventur/er** *vt* to risk; (remarque) to venture; (réputation) to risk; – **s'a.** *vpr* to venture (sur on to, **à faire** to do). ◆**—é** *a* risky. ◆**aventureux, -euse** *a* (personne, vie) adventurous; (risqué) risky. ◆**aventurier, -ière** *nmf* Péj adventurer.

avenue [avny] *nf* avenue.

avér/er (s') [savere] *vpr* (juste etc) to prove (to be); **il s'avère que** it turns out that. ◆**—é** *a* established.

averse [avɛrs] *nf* shower, downpour.

aversion [avɛrsjɔ̃] *nf* aversion (pour to).

avert/ir [avɛrtir] *vt* (mettre en garde, menacer) to warn; (informer) to notify, inform. ◆**—i** *a* informed. ◆**—issement** *nm* warning; notification; (dans un livre) foreword. ◆**—isseur** *nm* Aut horn; **a. d'incendie** fire alarm.

aveu, -x [avø] *nm* confession; **de l'a. de** by the admission of.

aveugle [avœgl] *a* blind; – *nmf* blind man, blind woman; **les aveugles** the blind. ◆**aveuglément** [-emɑ̃] *adv* blindly.

◆**aveugl/er** vt to blind. ◆**—ement** [-əmã] nm (égarement) blindness.

aveuglette (à l') [alavœglɛt] adv blindly; **chercher qch à l'a.** to grope for sth.

aviateur, -trice [avjatœr, -tris] nmf airman, airwoman. ◆**aviation** nf (industrie, science) aviation; (armée de l'air) air force; (avions) aircraft; **l'a.** Sp flying; **d'a.** (terrain, base) air-.

avide [avid] a (rapace) greedy (**de** for); **a. d'apprendre/etc** (désireux) eager to learn/etc. ◆**—ment** adv greedily. ◆**avidité** nf greed.

avilir [avilir] vt to degrade, debase.

avion [avjɔ̃] nm aircraft, (aero)plane, Am airplane; **a. à réaction** jet; **a. de ligne** airliner; **par a.** (lettre) airmail; **en a., par a.** (voyager) by plane, by air; **aller en a.** to fly.

aviron [avirɔ̃] nm oar; **faire de l'a.** to row, practise rowing.

avis [avi] nm opinion; Pol Jur judgement; (communiqué) notice; (conseil) & Fin advice; **à mon a.** in my opinion, to my mind; **changer d'a.** to change one's mind. ◆**avis/er** vt to advise, inform; (voir) to notice; **s'a. de qch** to realize sth suddenly; **s'a. de faire** to venture to do. ◆**—é** a prudent, wise; **bien/mal a.** well-/ill-advised.

aviver [avive] vt (couleur) to bring out; (douleur) to sharpen.

avocat, -ate [avɔka, -at] 1 nmf barrister, counsel, Am attorney, counselor; (d'une cause) Fig advocate. 2 nm (fruit) avocado (pear).

avoine [avwan] nf oats; **farine d'a.** oatmeal.

avoir* [avwar] 1 v aux to have; **je l'ai vu** I've seen him. 2 vt (posséder) to have; (obtenir) to get; (tromper) Fam to take for a ride; **il a** he has, he's got; **qu'est-ce que tu as?** what's the matter with you?, what's wrong with you?; **j'ai à lui parler** I have to speak

to her; **il n'a qu'à essayer** he only has to try; **a. faim/chaud/etc** to be ou feel hungry/hot/etc; **a. cinq ans/etc** to be five (years old)/etc; **en a. pour longtemps** to be busy for quite a while; **j'en ai pour dix minutes** this will take me ten minutes; (ne bouge pas) I'll be with you in ten minutes; **en a. pour son argent** to get ou have one's money's worth; **en a. après** ou **contre** to have a grudge against. 3 v imp **il y a** there is, pl there are; **il y a six ans** six years ago; **il n'y a pas de quoi!** don't mention it!; **qu'est-ce qu'il y a?** what's the matter?, what's wrong? 4 nm assets, property; (d'un compte) Fin credit.

avoisin/er [avwazine] vt to border on. ◆**—ant** a neighbouring, nearby.

avort/er [avɔrte] vi (projet etc) Fig to miscarry, fail; (se faire) **a.** (femme) to have ou get an abortion. ◆**—ement** nm abortion; Fig failure. ◆**avorton** nm Péj runt, puny shrimp.

avou/er [avwe] vt to confess, admit (**que** that); **s'a. vaincu** to admit defeat; — vi (coupable) to confess. ◆**—é** a (ennemi, but) avowed; — nm solicitor, Am attorney.

avril [avril] nm April; **un poisson d'a.** (farce) an April fool joke.

axe [aks] nm Math axis; (essieu) axle; (d'une politique) broad direction; **grands axes** (routes) main roads. ◆**axer** vt to centre; **il est axé sur** his mind is drawn towards.

axiome [aksjom] nm axiom.

ayant [ɛjã] voir avoir.

azalée [azale] nf (plante) azalea.

azimuts [azimyt] nmpl **dans tous les a.** Fam all over the place, here there and everywhere; **tous a.** (guerre, publicité etc) all-out.

azote [azɔt] nm nitrogen.

azur [azyr] nm azure, (sky) blue; **la Côte d'A.** the (French) Riviera.

azyme [azim] a (pain) unleavened.

B

B, b [be] nm B, b.

babeurre [babœr] nm buttermilk.

babill/er [babije] vi to prattle, babble. ◆**—age** nm prattle, babble.

babines [babin] nfpl (lèvres) chops, chaps.

babiole [babjɔl] nf (objet) knick-knack; (futilité) trifle.

bâbord [babɔr] nm Nau Av port (side).

babouin [babwɛ̃] nm baboon.

baby-foot [babifut] nm inv table ou miniature football.

bac [bak] nm 1 (bateau) ferry(boat). 2 (cuve) tank; **b. à glace** ice tray; **b. à laver** washtub. 3 abrév = baccalauréat.

baccalauréat [bakalɔrea] nm school leaving certificate.

bâche [bɑʃ] nf (toile) tarpaulin. ◆**bâcher** vt to cover over (with a tarpaulin).

bachelier, -ière [baʃəlje, -jɛr] nmf holder of the baccalauréat.

bachot [baʃo] nm abrév = **baccalauréat.** ◆**bachoter** vi to cram (for an exam).

bacille [basil] nm bacillus, germ.

bâcler [bɑkle] vt (travail) to dash off carelessly, botch (up).

bactéries [bakteri] nfpl bacteria. ◆**bactériologique** a bacteriological; **la guerre b.** germ warfare.

badaud, -aude [bado, -od] nmf (inquisitive) onlooker, bystander.

baderne [badɛrn] nf **vieille b.** Péj old fogey, old fuddy-duddy.

badigeon [badiʒɔ̃] nm whitewash. ◆**badigeonner** vt (mur) to whitewash, distemper; (écorchure) Méd to paint, coat.

badin [badɛ̃] a (peu sérieux) light-hearted, playful. ◆**badiner** vi to jest, joke; **b. avec** (prendre à la légère) to trifle with. ◆**—age** nm banter, jesting.

badine [badin] nf cane, switch.

bafouer [bafwe] vt to mock ou scoff at.

bafouiller [bafuje] vti to stammer, splutter.

bâfrer [bɑfre] vi Fam to stuff oneself (with food).

bagage [bagaʒ] nm (valise etc) piece of luggage ou baggage; (connaissances) Fig (fund of) knowledge; pl (ensemble des valises) luggage, baggage. ◆**bagagiste** nm baggage handler.

bagarre [bagar] nf brawl. ◆**bagarrer** vi Fam to fight, struggle; — **se b.** vpr to fight, brawl; (se disputer) to fight, quarrel.

bagatelle [bagatɛl] nf trifle, mere bagatelle; **la b. de** Iron the trifling sum of.

bagne [baɲ] nm convict prison; **c'est le b. ici** Fig this place is a real hell hole ou workhouse. ◆**bagnard** nm convict.

bagnole [baɲɔl] nf Fam car; **vieille b.** Fam old banger.

bagou(t) [bagu] nm Fam glibness; **avoir du b.** to have the gift of the gab.

bague [bag] nf (anneau) ring; (de cigare) band. ◆**bagué** a (doigt) ringed.

baguenauder [bagnode] vi, — **se b.** vpr to loaf around, saunter.

baguette [bagɛt] nf (canne) stick; (de chef d'orchestre) baton; (pain) (long thin) loaf, stick of bread; pl (de tambour) drumsticks; (pour manger) chopsticks; **b. (magique)** (magic) wand; **mener à la b.** to rule with an iron hand.

bah! [bɑ] int really!, bah!

bahut [bay] nm (meuble) chest, cabinet; (lycée) Fam school.

baie [bɛ] nf 1 Géog bay. 2 Bot berry. 3 (fenêtre) picture window.

baignade [bɛɲad] nf (bain) bathe, bathing; (endroit) bathing place. ◆**baign/er** vt (immerger) to bathe; (enfant) to bath, Am bathe; **b. les rivages** (mer) to wash the shores; **baigné de** (sueur, lumière) bathed in; (sang) soaked in; — vi **b. dans** (tremper) to soak in; (être imprégné de) to be steeped in; — **se b.** vpr to go swimming ou bathing; (dans une baignoire) to have ou take a bath. ◆**—eur, -euse** 1 nmf bather. 2 nm (poupée) baby doll. ◆**baignoire** nf bath (tub).

bail, pl **baux** [baj, bo] nm lease. ◆**bailleur** nm Jur lessor; **b. de fonds** financial backer.

bâill/er [bɑje] vi to yawn; (chemise etc) to gape; (porte) to stand ajar. ◆**—ement** nm yawn; gaping.

bâillon [bɑjɔ̃] nm gag. ◆**bâillonner** vt (victime, presse etc) to gag.

bain [bɛ̃] nm (de mer) swim, bathe; **salle de bain(s)** bathroom; **être dans le b.** (au courant) Fam to have got into the swing of things; **petit/grand b.** (piscine) shallow/deep end; **b. de bouche** mouthwash. ◆**b.-marie** nm (pl **bains-marie**) Culin double boiler.

baïonnette [bajɔnɛt] nf bayonet.

baiser [beze] **1** vt **b. au front/sur la joue** to kiss on the forehead/cheek; — nm kiss; **bons baisers** (dans une lettre) (with) love. **2** vt (duper) Fam to con.

baisse [bɛs] nf fall, drop (de in); **en b.** (température) falling.

baisser [bese] vt (voix, prix etc) to lower, drop; (tête) to bend; (radio, chauffage) to turn down; — vi (prix, niveau etc) to drop, go down; (soleil) to go down, sink; (marée) to go out, ebb; (santé, popularité) to decline; — **se b.** vpr to bend down, stoop.

bajoues [baʒu] nfpl (d'animal, de personne) chops.

bal, pl **bals** [bal] nm (réunion de grand apparat) ball; (populaire) dance; (lieu) dance hall.

balade [balad] nf Fam walk; (en auto) drive; (excursion) tour. ◆**balader** vt (enfant etc) to take for a walk ou drive; (objet) to trail around; — **se b.** vpr (à pied) to go for a walk; (excursionner) to tour (around); **se b. (en voiture)** to go for a drive. ◆**baladeur** nm Walkman®. ◆**baladeuse** nf inspection lamp.

balafre [balafr] nf (blessure) gash, slash;

(*cicatrice*) scar. ◆**balafrer** *vt* to gash, slash; to scar.

balai [bale] *nm* broom; **b. mécanique** carpet sweeper; **manche à b.** broomstick; *Av* joystick. ◆**b.-brosse** *nm* (*pl* **balais-brosses**) garden brush *ou* broom (*for scrubbing paving stones*).

balance [balɑ̃s] *nf* (*instrument*) (pair of) scales; (*équilibre*) *Pol Fin* balance; **la B.** (*signe*) Libra; **mettre en b.** to balance, weigh up.

balanc/er [balɑ̃se] *vt* (*bras*) to swing; (*hanches, tête, branches*) to sway; (*lancer*) *Fam* to chuck; (*se débarrasser de*) *Fam* to chuck out; **un compte** *Fin* to balance an account; **— se b.** *vpr* (*personne*) to swing (from side to side); (*arbre, bateau etc*) to sway; **je m'en balance!** I couldn't care less! ◆**—é** *a* **bien b.** (*phrase*) well-balanced; (*personne*) *Fam* well-built. ◆**—ement** *nm* swinging; swaying. ◆**balancier** *nm* (*d'horloge*) pendulum; (*de montre*) balance wheel. ◆**balançoire** *nf* (*escarpolette*) swing; (*bascule*) seesaw.

balayer [baleje] *vt* (*chambre, rue*) to sweep (out *ou* up); (*enlever, chasser*) to sweep away; **le vent balayait la plaine** the wind swept the plain. ◆**balayette** *nf* (*hand*) brush; (*à poils*) short-handled broom. ◆**balayeur, -euse** [balɛjœr, -øz] *nmf* roadsweeper.

balbutier [balbysje] *vti* to stammer.

balcon [balkɔ̃] *nm* balcony; *Th Cin* dress circle.

baldaquin [baldakɛ̃] *nm* (*de lit etc*) canopy.

baleine [balɛn] *nf* (*animal*) whale; (*fanon*) whalebone; (*de parapluie*) rib. ◆**baleinier** *nm* (*navire*) whaler. ◆**baleinière** *nf* whaleboat.

balise [baliz] *nf* *Nau* beacon; *Av* (*ground*) light; *Aut* road sign. ◆**balis/er** *vt* to mark with beacons *ou* lights; (*route*) to signpost. ◆**—age** *nm* *Nau* beacons; *Av* lighting; *Aut* signposting.

balistique [balistik] *a* ballistic.

balivernes [balivɛrn] *nfpl* balderdash, nonsense.

ballade [balad] *nf* (*légende*) ballad; (*poème court*) &-*Mus* ballade.

ballant [balɑ̃] *a* (*bras, jambes*) dangling.

ballast [balast] *nm* ballast.

balle [bal] *nf* (*de tennis, golf etc*) ball; (*projectile*) bullet; (*paquet*) bale; *pl* (*francs*) *Fam* francs; **se renvoyer la b.** to pass the buck (to each other).

ballet [balɛ] *nm* ballet. ◆**ballerine** *nf* ballerina.

ballon [balɔ̃] *nm* (*jouet d'enfant*) & *Av* balloon; (*sport*) ball; **b. de football** football; **lancer un b. d'essai** *Fig* to put out a feeler. ◆**ballonné** *a* (*ventre*) bloated, swollen. ◆**ballot** *nm* (*paquet*) bundle; (*imbécile*) *Fam* idiot.

ballottage [balɔtaʒ] *nm* (*scrutin*) second ballot (*no candidate having achieved the required number of votes*).

ballotter [balɔte] *vti* to shake (about); **ballotté entre** (*sentiments contraires*) torn between.

balnéaire [balneɛr] *a* **station b.** seaside resort.

balourd, -ourde [balur, -urd] *nmf* (clumsy) oaf. ◆**balourdise** *nf* clumsiness, oafishness; (*gaffe*) blunder.

Baltique [baltik] *nf* **la B.** the Baltic.

balustrade [balystrad] *nf* (hand)rail, railing(s).

bambin [bɑ̃bɛ̃] *nm* tiny tot, toddler.

bambou [bɑ̃bu] *nm* bamboo.

ban [bɑ̃] *nm* (*de tambour*) roll; (*applaudissements*) round of applause; *pl* (*de mariage*) banns; **mettre qn au b. de** to cast s.o. out from, outlaw s.o. from; **un b. pour . . .** three cheers for . . . .

banal, mpl -als [banal] *a* (*fait, accident etc*) commonplace, banal; (*idée, propos*) banal, trite. ◆**banalisé** *a* (*voiture de police*) unmarked. ◆**banalité** *nf* banality; *pl* (*propos*) banalities.

banane [banan] *nf* banana.

banc [bɑ̃] *nm* (*siège, établi*) bench; (*de poissons*) shoal; **b. d'église** pew; **b. d'essai** *Fig* testing ground; **b. de sable** sandbank; **des accusés** *Jur* dock.

bancaire [bɑ̃kɛr] *a* (*opération*) banking-; (*chèque*) bank-.

bancal, mpl -als [bɑ̃kal] *a* (*personne*) bandy, bow-legged; (*meuble*) wobbly; (*idée*) shaky.

bande [bɑ̃d] *nf* **1** (*de terrain, papier etc*) strip; (*de film*) reel; (*de journal*) wrapper; (*rayure*) stripe; (*de fréquences*) *Rad* band; (*pansement*) bandage; (*sur la chaussée*) line; **b.** (*magnétique*) tape; **b. vidéo** videotape; **b. sonore** sound track; **b. dessinée** comic strip, strip cartoon; **par la b.** indirectly. **2** (*groupe*) gang, troop, band; (*de chiens*) pack; (*d'oiseaux*) flock; **on a fait b. à part** we split into our own group; **b. d'idiots!** you load of idiots! ◆**bandeau, -x** *nm* (*sur les yeux*) blindfold; (*pour la tête*) headband; (*pansement*) head bandage.

◆**band/er** *vt* (*blessure etc*) to bandage; (*yeux*) to blindfold; (*arc*) to bend; (*muscle*) to tense. ◆**—age** nm (pansement) bandage.

banderole [bãdrɔl] nf (sur mât) pennant, streamer; (sur montants) banner.

bandit [bãdi] nm robber, bandit; (enfant) Fam rascal. ◆**banditisme** nm crime.

bandoulière [bãduljɛr] nf shoulder strap; **en b.** slung across the shoulder.

banjo [bã(d)ʒo] nm Mus banjo.

banlieue [bãljø] nf suburbs, outskirts; **la grande b.** the outer suburbs; **de b.** (magasin etc) suburban; (train) commuter-. ◆**banlieusard, -arde** nmf (habitant) suburbanite; (voyageur) commuter.

banne [ban] nf (de magasin) awning.

bannière [banjɛr] nf banner.

bann/ir [banir] vt (exiler) to banish; (supprimer) to ban, outlaw. ◆**—issement** nm banishment.

banque [bãk] nf bank; (activité) banking.

banqueroute [bãkrut] nf (fraudulent) bankruptcy.

banquet [bãkɛ] nm banquet.

banquette [bãkɛt] nf (de bench) seat.

banquier [bãkje] nm banker.

banquise [bãkiz] nf ice floe ou field.

baptême [batɛm] nm christening, baptism; **b. du feu** baptism of fire; **b. de l'air** first flight. ◆**baptiser** vt (enfant) to christen, baptize; (appeler) Fig to christen.

baquet [bakɛ] nm tub, basin.

bar [bar] nm **1** (lieu, comptoir, meuble) bar. **2** (poisson marin) bass.

baragouin [baragwɛ̃] nm gibberish, gabble. ◆**baragouiner** vt (langue) to gabble (a few words of); — vi to gabble away.

baraque [barak] nf hut, shack; (maison) Fam house, place; Péj hovel; (de forain) stall. ◆**—ment** nm (makeshift) huts.

baratin [baratɛ̃] nm Fam sweet talk; Com patter. ◆**baratiner** vt to chat up; Am sweet-talk.

barbare [barbar] a (manières, crime) barbaric; (peuple, invasions) barbarian; — nmf barbarian. ◆**barbarie** nf (cruauté) barbarity. ◆**barbarisme** nm Gram barbarism.

barbe [barb] nf beard; **une b. de trois jours** three days' growth of beard; **se faire la b.** to shave; **à la b. de** under the nose(s) of; **rire dans sa b.** to laugh up one's sleeve; **la b.!** enough!; **quelle b.!** what a drag!; **b. à papa** candyfloss, Am cotton candy.

barbecue [barbəkju] nm barbecue.

barbelé [barbəle] a barbed; — nmpl barbed wire.

barb/er [barbe] vt Fam to bore (stiff); — **se** **b.** vpr to be ou get bored (stiff). ◆**—ant** a Fam boring.

barbiche [barbiʃ] nf goatee (beard).

barbiturique [barbityrik] nm barbiturate.

barbot/er [barbɔte] **1** vi (s'agiter) to splash about, paddle. **2** vt (voler) Fam to filch. ◆**—euse** nf (de bébé) rompers.

barbouill/er [barbuje] vt (salir) to smear; (peindre) to daub; (gribouiller) to scribble; **avoir l'estomac barbouillé** Fam to feel queasy. ◆**—age** nm smear; daub; scribble.

barbu [barby] a bearded.

barda [barda] nm Fam gear; (de soldat) kit.

bardé [barde] a **b. de** (décorations etc) covered with.

barder [barde] v imp **ça va b.!** Fam there'll be fireworks!

barème [barɛm] nm (des tarifs) table; (des salaires) scale; (livre de comptes) ready reckoner.

baril [bari(l)] nm barrel; **b. de poudre** powder keg.

bariolé [barjɔle] a brightly-coloured.

barman, pl **-men** ou **-mans** [barman, -mɛn] nm barman, Am bartender.

baromètre [barɔmɛtr] nm barometer.

baron, -onne [barɔ̃, -ɔn] nm baron; — nf baroness.

baroque [barɔk] **1** a (idée etc) bizarre, weird. **2** a & nm Archit Mus etc baroque.

baroud [barud] nm **b. d'honneur** Arg gallant last fight.

barque [bark] nf (small) boat.

barre [bar] nf bar; (trait) line, stroke; Nau helm; **b. de soustraction** minus sign; **b.** Sp horizontal bar. ◆**barreau, -x** nm (de fenêtre etc) & Jur bar; (d'échelle) rung.

barr/er [bare] **1** vt (route etc) to block (off), close (off); (porte) to bar; (chèque) to cross; (phrase) to cross out; Nau to steer; **la route à qn, b. qn** to bar s.o.'s way; **'rue barrée'** 'road closed'. **2 se b.** vpr Arg to hop it, make off. ◆**—age** nm (sur une route) roadblock; (barrière) barrier; (ouvrage hydraulique) dam; (de petite rivière) weir; **le b. d'une rue** the closure of a street; **tir de b.** barrage fire; **b. d'agents** cordon of police. ◆**—eur** nm Sp Nau cox.

barrette [barɛt] nf (pince) (hair)slide, Am barrette.

barricade [barikad] nf barricade. ◆**barricader** vt to barricade; — **se b.** vpr to barricade oneself.

barrière [barjɛr] nf (porte) gate; (clôture) fence; (obstacle, mur) barrier.

barrique [barik] nf (large) barrel.

baryton [baritɔ̃] *nm* baritone.

bas¹, basse [bɑ, bɑs] *a* (*table, prix etc*) low; (*âme, action*) base, mean; (*partie de ville etc*) lower; (*origine*) lowly; **au b. mot** at the very least; **enfant en b. âge** young child; **avoir la vue basse** to be short-sighted; **le peuple** *Péj* the lower orders; **coup b.** *Boxe* blow below the belt; *– adv* low; (*parler*) in a whisper, softly; (*mettre b.*) (*animal*) to give birth; **mettre b. les armes** to lay down one's arms; **jeter b.** to overthrow; **plus b.** further *ou* lower down; **en b.** down (below); (*par l'escalier*) downstairs, down below; **en** *ou* **au b. de** at the foot *ou* bottom of; **de haut en b.** from top to bottom; **sauter à b. du lit** to jump out of bed; **à b. les dictateurs/etc!** down with dictators/etc!; *– nm* (*de côte, page etc*) bottom, foot; **du b.** (*tiroir, étagère*) bottom.

bas² [bɑ] *nm* (*chaussette*) stocking; **b. de laine** *Fig* nest egg.

basané [bazane] *a* (*visage etc*) tanned.

bas-bleu [bablø] *nm Péj* bluestocking.

bas-côté [bakote] *nm* (*de route*) roadside, shoulder.

bascule [baskyl] *nf* (*jeu de*) **b.** (game of) seesaw; (*balance à*) **b.** weighing machine; **cheval/fauteuil à b.** rocking horse/chair. ◆**basculer** *vti* (*personne*) to topple over; (*benne*) to tip up.

base [bɑz] *nf* base; (*principe fondamental*) basis, foundation; **de b.** (*salaire etc*) basic; **produit à b. de lait** milk-based product; **militant de b.** rank-and-file militant. ◆**baser** *vt* to base; **se b. sur** to base oneself on.

bas-fond [bafɔ̃] *nm* (*eau*) shallows; (*terrain*) low ground; *pl* (*population*) *Péj* dregs.

basilic [bazilik] *nm Bot Culin* basil.

basilique [bazilik] *nf* basilica.

basket(-ball) [basket(bɔl)] *nm* basketball.

basque [bask] **1** *a & nmf* Basque. **2** *nfpl* (*pans de veste*) skirts.

basse [bɑs] **1** *voir* **bas¹. 2** *nf Mus* bass.

basse-cour [baskur] *nf* (*pl* **basses-cours**) farmyard.

bassement [basmɑ̃] *adv* basely, meanly. ◆**bassesse** *nf* baseness, meanness; (*action*) base *ou* mean act.

bassin [basɛ̃] *nm* (*pièce d'eau*) pond; (*piscine*) pool; (*cuvette*) bowl, basin; (*rade*) dock; *Anat* pelvis; *Géog* basin; **b. houiller** coalfield. ◆**bassine** *nf* bowl.

basson [basɔ̃] *nm* (*instrument*) bassoon; (*musicien*) bassoonist.

bastingage [bastɛ̃gaʒ] *nm Nau* bulwarks, rail.

bastion [bastjɔ̃] *nm* bastion.

bastringue [bastrɛ̃g] *nm* (*bal*) *Fam* popular dance hall; (*tapage*) *Arg* shindig, din; (*attirail*) *Arg* paraphernalia.

bas-ventre [bavɑ̃tr] *nm* lower abdomen.

bat [ba] *voir* **battre.**

bât [ba] *nm* packsaddle.

bataclan [bataklɑ̃] *nm Fam* paraphernalia; **et tout le b.** *Fam* and the whole caboodle.

bataille [bataj] *nf* battle; *Cartes* beggar-my-neighbour. ◆**–eur, -euse** *nmf* fighter; *a* belligerent. ◆**bataillon** *nm* battalion.

bâtard, -arde [batar, -ard] *a & nmf* bastard; **chien b.** mongrel; **œuvre bâtarde** hybrid work.

bateau, -x [bato] *nm* boat; (*grand*) ship. ◆**b.-citerne** *nm* (*pl* **bateaux-citernes**) tanker. ◆**b.-mouche** *nm* (*pl* **bateaux-mouches**) (*sur la Seine*) pleasure boat.

batifoler [batifole] *vi Hum* to fool *ou* lark about.

bâtiment [batimɑ̃] *nm* (*édifice*) building; (*navire*) vessel; **le b., l'industrie du b.** the building trade; **ouvrier du b.** building worker. ◆**bât/ir** *vt* (*construire*) to build; (*coudre*) to baste, tack; **terrain à b.** building site. ◆**–i** **a bien b.** well-built; *– nm Menuis* frame, support. ◆**bâtisse** *nf Péj* building. ◆**bâtisseur, -euse** *nmf* builder (*de*).

bâton [batɔ̃] *nm* (*canne*) stick; (*de maréchal, d'agent*) baton; **b. de rouge** lipstick; **donner des coups de b. à qn** to beat s.o. (with a stick); **parler à bâtons rompus** to ramble from one subject to another; **mettre des bâtons dans les roues à qn** to put obstacles in s.o.'s way.

batterie [batri] *nf Mil Aut* battery; **la b.** *Mus* the drums; **b. de cuisine** set of kitchen utensils.

batt/re [batr] **1** *vt* (*frapper, vaincre*) to beat; (*blé*) to thresh; (*cartes*) to shuffle; (*pays, chemins*) to scour; (*à coups redoublés*) to batter, pound; **b. la mesure** to beat time; **b. à mort** to batter *ou* beat to death; **b. pavillon** to fly a flag; *– vi* to beat; (*porte*) to bang; **b. des mains** to clap (one's hands); **b. des paupières** to blink; **b. des ailes** (*oiseau*) to flap its wings; **le vent fait b. la porte** the wind bangs the door. **2 se b.** *vpr* to fight. ◆**–ant 1** *a* (*pluie*) driving; (*porte*) swing-. **2** *nm* (*de cloche*) tongue; (*vantail de porte etc*) flap; **porte à deux battants** double door. **3** *nm* (*personne*) fighter. ◆**–u a chemin** *ou* **sentier b.** beaten track. ◆**–age** *nm* (*du blé*) threshing; (*publicité*) *Fam* publicity, hype, ballyhoo. ◆**—ement** *nm* (*de cœur, de tambour*) beat; (*délai*) interval; **battements de cœur** palpitations. ◆**—eur** *nm* (*musicien*) percussionist; **b. à œufs** egg beater.

baudet [bodɛ] *nm* donkey.

baume [bom] *nm* (*résine*) & *Fig* balm.

baux [bo] *voir* bail.

bavard, -arde [bavar, -ard] *a* (*loquace*) talk-ative; (*cancanier*) gossipy; − *nmf* chatter-box; gossip. ◆**bavard/er** *vi* to chat, chat-ter; (*papoter*) to gossip; (*divulguer*) to blab. ◆**—age** *nm* chatting, chatter(ing); gossip(ing).

bave [bav] *nf* dribble, slobber; foam; (*de limace*) slime. ◆**baver** *vi* to dribble, slob-ber; (*chien enragé*) to foam; (*encre*) to smudge; **en b.** *Fam* to have a rough time of it. ◆**bavette** *nf* bib. ◆**baveux, -euse** *a* (*bouche*) slobbery; (*omelette*) runny. ◆**bavoir** *nm* bib. ◆**bavure** *nf* smudge; (*erreur*) blunder; **sans b.** perfect(ly), flaw-less(ly).

bazar [bazar] *nm* (*magasin, marché*) bazaar; (*désordre*) mess, clutter; (*attirail*) *Fam* stuff, gear. ◆**bazarder** *vt* *Fam* to sell off, get rid of.

bazooka [bazuka] *nm* bazooka.

béant [beɑ̃] *a* (*plaie*) gaping; (*gouffre*) yawning.

béat [bea] *a Péj* smug; (*heureux*) *Hum* bliss-ful. ◆**béatitude** [-tityd] *nf Hum* bliss.

beau (*or* **bel** *before vowel or mute h*), **belle**, *pl* **beaux, belles** [bo, bɛl] *a* (*femme, fleur etc*) beautiful, attractive; (*homme*) hand-some, good-looking; (*voyage, temps etc*) fine, lovely; **au b. milieu** right in the middle; **j'ai b. crier/essayer/***etc* it's no use (my) shouting/trying/*etc*; **un b. morceau** a good *or* sizeable bit; **de plus belle** (*recom-mencer etc*) worse than ever; **bel et bien** really; − *nm* **le b.** the beautiful; **faire le b.** (*chien*) to sit up and beg; **le plus b. de l'histoire** the best part of the story; − *nf* (*femme*) beauty; *Sp* deciding game.

beaucoup [boku] *adv* (*lire etc*) a lot, a great deal; **aimer b.** to like very much; **s'intéresser b. à** to be very interested in; **b. de** (*livres etc*) many, a lot *ou* a great deal of; (*courage etc*) a lot *ou* a great deal of, much; **pas b. d'argent/***etc* not much money/*etc*; **j'en ai b.** (*quantité*) I have a lot; (*nombre*) I have many; **b. plus/moins** much more/less; many more/fewer; **b. trop** much too much; much too many; **de b.** by far; **b. sont . . .** many are . . . .

beau-fils [bofis] *nm* (*pl* **beaux-fils**) (*d'un*

précédent *mariage*) stepson; (*gendre*) son-in-law. ◆**b.-frère** *nm* (*pl* **beaux-frères**) brother-in-law. ◆**b.-père** *nm* (*pl* **beaux-pères**) father-in-law; (*parâ-tre*) stepfather.

beauté [bote] *nf* beauty; **institut** *ou* **salon de b.** beauty parlour; **en b.** (*gagner etc*) magnificently; **être en b.** to look one's very best; **de toute b.** beautiful.

beaux-arts [bozar] *nmpl* fine arts. ◆**b.-parents** *nmpl* parents-in-law.

bébé [bebe] *nm* baby; **b.-lion/***etc* (*pl* **bébés-lions/***etc*) baby lion/*etc*.

bébête [bebɛt] *a Fam* silly.

bec [bɛk] *nm* (*d'oiseau*) beak, bill; (*de cruche*) lip, spout; (*de plume*) nib; (*bouche*) *Fam* mouth; *Mus* mouthpiece; **coup de b.** peck; **b. de gaz** gas lamp; **clouer le b. à** *Fam* to shut s.o. up; **tomber sur un b.** *Fam* to come up against a serious snag. ◆**b.-de-cane** *nm* (*pl* **becs-de-cane**) door handle.

bécane [bekan] *nf Fam* bike.

bécarre [bekar] *nm Mus* natural.

bécasse [bekas] *nf* (*oiseau*) woodcock; (*personne*) *Fam* simpleton.

bêche [bɛʃ] *nf* spade. ◆**bêcher** *vt* **1** (*cultiver*) to dig. **2** *Fig* to criticize; (*snober*) to snub. ◆**bêcheur, -euse** *nmf* snob.

bécot [beko] *nm Fam* kiss. ◆**bécoter** *vt*, − **se b.** *vpr Fam* to kiss.

becquée [beke] *nf* beakful; **donner la b. à** (*oiseau, enfant*) to feed. ◆**becqueter** *vt* (*picorer*) to peck (at); (*manger*) *Fam* to eat.

bedaine [bədɛn] *nf Fam* paunch, potbelly.

bedeau, -x [bədo] *nm* beadle, verger.

bedon [bədɔ̃] *nm Fam* paunch. ◆**bedon-nant** *a* paunchy, potbellied.

bée [be] *a* **bouche b.** open-mouthed.

beffroi [befrwa] *nm* belfry.

bégayer [begeje] *vi* to stutter, stammer. ◆**bègue** [bɛg] *nmf* stutterer, stammerer; − *a* **être b.** to stutter, stammer.

bégueule [begœl] *a* a prudish; − *nf* prude.

béguin [begɛ̃] *nm* **avoir le b. pour qn** *Fam* to have taken a fancy to s.o.

beige [bɛʒ] *a & nm* beige.

beignet [bɛɲɛ] *nm Culin* fritter.

bel [bɛl] *voir* beau.

bêler [bele] *vi* to bleat.

belette [bəlɛt] *nf* weasel.

Belgique [bɛlʒik] *nf* Belgium. ◆**belge** *a & nmf* Belgian.

bélier [belje] *nm* (*animal, machine*) ram; **le B.** (*signe*) Aries.

belle [bɛl] *voir* beau.

belle-fille [bɛlfij] *nf* (*pl* **belles-filles**) (*d'un* *précédent mariage)* stepdaughter; *(bru)* daughter-in-law. ◆**b.-mère** *nf (pl* **belles-mères)** mother-in-law; *(marâtre)* stepmother. ◆**b.-sœur** *nf (pl* **belles-sœurs)** sister-in-law.

belligérant [beliʒerã] *a & nm* belligerent.

belliqueux, -euse [belikø, -øz] *a* warlike; *Fig* aggressive.

belvédère [belveder] *nm (sur une route)* viewpoint.

bémol [bemɔl] *nm Mus* flat.

bénédiction [benediksjɔ̃] *nf* blessing, benediction.

bénéfice [benefis] *nm (gain)* profit; *(avantage)* benefit; **b.** *(ecclésiastique)* living, benefice. ◆**bénéficiaire** *nmf* beneficiary; *– a (marge, solde)* profit-. ◆**bénéficier** *vi* **b.** de to benefit from, have the benefit of. ◆**bénéfique** *a* beneficial.

Bénélux [benelyks] *nm* Benelux.

benêt [bənɛ] *nm* simpleton; *– am* simple-minded.

bénévole [benevɔl] *a* voluntary, unpaid.

bénin, -igne [benɛ̃, -iɲ] *a (tumeur, critique)* benign; *(accident)* minor.

bénir [benir] *vt* to bless; *(exalter, remercier)* to give thanks to. ◆**bénit** *a (pain)* consecrated; **eau bénite** holy water. ◆**bénitier** [-itje] *nm (holy-water)* stoup.

benjamin, -ine [bɛ̃ʒamɛ̃, -in] *nmf* youngest child; *Sp* young junior.

benne [bɛn] *nf (de grue)* scoop; *(à charbon)* tub, skip; *(de téléphérique)* cable car; **camion à b. basculante** dump truck; **b. à ordures** skip.

béotien, -ienne [beɔsjɛ̃, -jɛn] *nmf (inculte)* philistine.

béquille [bekij] *nf (canne)* crutch; *(de moto)* stand.

bercail [berkaj] *nm (famille etc) Hum* fold.

berceau, -x [berso] *nm* cradle.

berc/er [berse] *vt (balancer)* to rock; *(apaiser)* to lull; *(leurrer)* to delude **(de** with); **se b. d'illusions** to delude oneself. ◆**—euse** *nf* lullaby.

béret [bere] *nm* beret.

berge [berʒ] *nf (rivage)* (raised) bank.

berger, -ère [berʒe, -er] **1** *nm* shepherd; **chien (de) b.** sheepdog; *– nf* shepherdess. **2** *nm* **b. allemand** Alsatian (dog), *Am* German shepherd. ◆**bergerie** *nf* sheepfold.

berline [berlin] *nf Aut* (four-door) saloon, *Am* sedan.

berlingot [berlɛ̃go] *nm (bonbon aux fruits)* boiled sweet; *(à la menthe)* mint; *(emballage)* (milk) carton.

berlue [berly] *nf* **avoir la b.** to be seeing things.

berne (en) [ãbern] *adv* at half-mast.

berner [berne] *vt* to fool, hoodwink.

besogne [bəzɔɲ] *nf* work, job, task. ◆**besogneux, -euse** *a* needy.

besoin [bəzwɛ̃] *nm* need; **avoir b. de** to need; **au b.** if necessary, if need(s) be; **dans le b.** in need, needy.

bestial, -aux [bestjal, -o] *a* bestial, brutish. ◆**bestiaux** *nmpl* livestock; *(bovins)* cattle. ◆**bestiole** *nf (insecte)* creepy-crawly, bug.

bétail [betaj] *nm* livestock; *(bovins)* cattle.

bête[1] [bɛt] *nf* animal; *(bestiole)* bug, creature; **b. de somme** beast of burden; **b. à bon dieu** ladybird, *Am* ladybug; **b. noire** pet hate, pet peeve; **chercher la petite b.** *(critiquer)* to pick holes.

bête[2] [bɛt] *a* silly, stupid. ◆**bêtement** *adv* stupidly; **tout b.** quite simply. ◆**bêtise** [betiz] *nf* silliness, stupidity; *(action, parole)* silly *ou* stupid thing; *(bagatelle)* mere trifle.

béton [betɔ̃] *nm* concrete; **en b.** concrete-; **b. armé** reinforced concrete. ◆**bétonnière** *nf,* ◆**bétonneuse** *nf* cement *ou* concrete mixer.

betterave [betrav] *nf Culin* beetroot, *Am* beet; **b. sucrière** *ou* **à sucre** sugar beet.

beugler [bøgle] *vi (taureau)* to bellow; *(vache)* to moo; *(radio)* to blare (out).

beurre [bœr] *nm* butter; **b. d'anchois** anchovy paste. ◆**beurrer** *vt* to butter. ◆**beurrier** *nm* butter dish.

beuverie [bøvri] *nf* drinking session, booze-up.

bévue [bevy] *nf* blunder, mistake.

biais [bjɛ] *nm (moyen détourné)* device, expedient; *(aspect)* angle; **regarder de b.** to look at sidelong; **traverser en b.** to cross at an angle. ◆**biaiser** [bjeze] *vi* to prevaricate, hedge.

bibelot [biblo] *nm* curio, trinket.

biberon [bibrɔ̃] *nm* feeding bottle.

bible [bibl] *nf* bible; **la B.** the Bible. ◆**biblique** *a* biblical.

bibliobus [biblijobys] *nm* mobile library.

bibliographie [biblijɔgrafi] *nf* bibliography.

bibliothèque [biblijɔtɛk] *nf* library; *(meuble)* bookcase; *(à la gare)* bookstall. ◆**bibliothécaire** *nmf* librarian.

bic® [bik] *nm* ballpoint, biro®.

bicarbonate [bikarbɔnat] *nm* bicarbonate.

bicentenaire [bisãtner] *nm* bicentenary, bicentennial.

biceps [bisɛps] *nm Anat* biceps.

biche [biʃ] *nf* doe, hind; **ma b.** *Fig* my pet.

bichonner [biʃɔne] *vt* to doll up.

bicoque [bikɔk] *nf Péj* shack, hovel.

bicyclette [bisiklɛt] *nf* bicycle, cycle; **la b.** *Sp* cycling; **aller à b.** to cycle.

bide [bid] *nm* (*ventre*) *Fam* belly; **faire un b.** *Arg* to flop.

bidet [bidɛ] *nm* (*cuvette*) bidet.

bidon [bidɔ̃] **1** *nm* (*d'essence*) can; (*pour boissons*) canteen; (*ventre*) *Fam* belly. **2** *nm* **du b.** *Fam* rubbish, bluff; – *a inv* (*simulé*) *Fam* fake, phoney. ◆**se bidonner** *vpr Fam* to have a good laugh.

bidonville [bidɔ̃vil] *nf* shantytown.

bidule [bidyl] *nm* (*chose*) *Fam* thingummy, whatsit.

bielle [bjɛl] *nf Aut* connecting rod.

bien [bjɛ̃] *adv* well; **il joue b.** he plays well; **je vais b.** I'm fine *ou* well; **b. fatigué/souvent/etc** (*très*) very tired/often/*etc*; **merci b.!** thanks very much!; **b.! fine!, right!; b. du courage/etc** a lot of courage/*etc*; **b. des fois/des gens/etc** lots of *ou* many times/people/*etc*; **je l'ai b. dit** (*intensif*) I *did* say so; **c'est b. compris?** is that quite understood?; **c'est b. toi?** is it really you?; **tu as b. fait** you did right; **c'est b. fait (pour lui)** it serves him right; – *a inv* (*convenable*) all right, fine; (*agréable*) nice, fine; (*compétent, bon*) good, fine; (*à l'aise*) comfortable, fine; (*beau*) attractive; (*en forme*) well; (*moralement*) nice; **une fille à** a nice *ou* respectable girl; – *nm* (*avantage*) good; (*capital*) possession; **ça te fera du b.** it will do you good; **le b. et le mal** good and evil; **biens de consommation** consumer goods. ◆**b.-aimé, -ée** *a & nmf* beloved. ◆**b.-être** *nm* wellbeing. ◆**b.-fondé** *nm* validity, soundness.

bienfaisance [bjɛ̃fəzɑ̃s] *nf* benevolence, charity; **de b.** (*société etc*) benevolent, charitable. ◆**bienfaisant** *a* beneficial.

bienfait [bjɛ̃fɛ] *nm* (*générosité*) favour; *pl* benefits, blessings. ◆**bienfaiteur, -trice** *nmf* benefactor, benefactress.

bienheureux, -euse [bjɛ̃nœrø, -øz] *a* blessed, blissful.

biennal, -aux [bjenal, -o] *a* biennial.

bien que [bjɛ̃k(ə)] *conj* although.

bienséant [bjɛ̃seɑ̃] *a* proper. ◆**bienséance** *nf* propriety.

bientôt [bjɛ̃to] *adv* soon; **à b.! see you soon!; il est b. dix heures/etc** it's nearly ten o'clock/*etc*.

bienveillant [bjɛ̃vɛjɑ̃] *a* kindly. ◆**bienveillance** *nf* kindliness.

bienvenu, -ue [bjɛ̃vny] *a* welcome; – *nmf*

soyez b.! welcome!; – *nf* welcome; **souhaiter la bienvenue à** to welcome.

bière [bjɛr] *nf* **1** (*boisson*) beer; **b. pression** draught beer. **2** (*cercueil*) coffin.

biffer [bife] *vt* to cross *ou* strike out.

bifteck [biftɛk] *nm* steak; **gagner son b.** *Fam* to earn one's (daily) bread.

bifurquer [bifyrke] *vi* to branch off, fork. ◆**bifurcation** *nf* fork, junction.

bigame [bigam] *a* bigamous; – *nmf* bigamist. ◆**bigamie** *nf* bigamy.

bigarré [bigare] *a* (*bariolé*) mottled; (*hétéroclite*) motley, mixed.

bigler [bigle] *vi* (*loucher*) *Fam* to squint; – *vti* **b. (sur)** (*lorgner*) *Fam* to leer at. ◆**bigleux, -euse** *a Fam* cock-eyed.

bigorneau, -x [bigɔrno] *nm* (*coquillage*) winkle.

bigot, -ote [bigo, -ɔt] *nmf Péj* religious bigot; – *a* over-devout, fanatical.

bigoudi [bigudi] *nm* (hair)curler *ou* roller.

bigrement [bigrəmɑ̃] *adv Fam* awfully.

bijou, -x [biʒu] *nm* jewel; (*ouvrage élégant*) *Fig* gem. ◆**bijouterie** *nf* (*commerce*) jeweller's shop; (*bijoux*) jewellery. ◆**bijoutier, -ière** *nmf* jeweller.

bikini [bikini] *nm* bikini.

bilan [bilɑ̃] *nm Fin* balance sheet; (*résultat*) outcome; (*d'un accident*) (casualty) toll; **b. de santé** checkup; **faire le b.** to make an assessment (**de** of).

bilboquet [bilbɔkɛ] *nm* cup-and-ball (game).

bile [bil] *nf* bile; **se faire de la b.** *Fam* to worry, fret. ◆**bilieux, -euse** *a* bilious.

bilingue [bilɛ̃g] *a* bilingual.

billard [bijar] *nm* (*jeu*) billiards; (*table*) billiard table; *Méd Fam* operating table; **c'est du b.** it's a cinch.

bille [bij] *nf* (*d'un enfant*) marble; (*de billard*) billiard ball; **stylo à b.** ballpoint pen, biro®.

billet [bijɛ] *nm* ticket; **b. (de banque)** (bank)note, *Am* bill; **b. aller, b. simple** single ticket, *Am* one-way ticket; **b. (d')aller et retour** return ticket, *Am* round trip ticket; **b. doux** love letter.

billion [biljɔ̃] *nm* billion, *Am* trillion.

billot [bijo] *nm* (*de bois*) block.

bimensuel, -elle [bimɑ̃sɥɛl] *a* bimonthly, fortnightly.

bimoteur [bimɔtœr] *a* twin-engined.

binaire [binɛr] *a* binary.

biner [bine] *vt* to hoe. ◆**binette** *nf* hoe; (*visage*) *Arg* mug, face.

biochimie [bjɔʃimi] *nf* biochemistry.

biodégradable [bjɔdegradabl] *a* biodegradable.

biographie [bjɔgrafi] *nf* biography. ◆**biographe** *nmf* biographer.

biologie [bjɔlɔʒi] *nf* biology. ◆**biologique** *a* biological.

bip-bip [bipbip] *nm* bleeper.

bipède [biped] *nm* biped.

bique [bik] *nf Fam* nanny-goat.

Birmanie [birmani] *nf* Burma. ◆**birman, -ane** *a & nmf* Burmese.

bis¹ [bis] *adv* (cri) Th encore; *Mus* repeat; **4 bis** (numéro) 4A; – *nm* Th encore.

bis², bise [bi, biz] *a* greyish-brown.

bisbille [bisbij] *nf* squabble; **en b. avec** *Fam* at loggerheads with.

biscornu [biskɔrny] *a* (objet) distorted, misshapen; (idée) cranky.

biscotte [biskɔt] *nf* (pain) Melba toast; (biscuit) rusk, *Am* zwieback.

biscuit [biskɥi] *nm* (salé) biscuit, *Am* cracker; (sucré) biscuit, *Am* cookie; **b. de Savoie** sponge (cake). ◆**biscuiterie** *nf* biscuit factory.

bise [biz] *nf* **1** (vent) north wind. **2** (baiser) *Fam* kiss.

biseau, -x [bizo] *nm* bevel.

bison [bizõ] *nm* bison, (American) buffalo.

bisou [bizu] *nm Fam* kiss.

bisser [bise] *vt* (musicien, acteur) to encore.

bissextile [bisɛkstil] *af* **année b.** leap year.

bistouri [bisturi] *nm* scalpel, lancet.

bistre [bistr] *a inv* bistre, dark-brown.

bistro(t) [bistro] *nm* bar, café.

bitume [bitym] *nm* (revêtement) asphalt.

bivouac [bivwak] *nm Mil* bivouac.

bizarre [bizar] *a* peculiar, odd, bizarre. ◆—**ment** *adv* oddly. ◆**bizarrerie** *nf* peculiarity.

blabla(bla) [blabla(bla)] *nm* claptrap, bunkum.

blafard [blafar] *a* pale, pallid.

blague [blag] *nf* **1** (à tabac) pouch. **2** (plaisanterie, farce) *Fam* joke; *pl* (absurdités) *Fam* nonsense; **sans b.!** you're joking! ◆**blaguer** *vi* to be joking; – *vt* to tease. ◆—**eur, -euse** *nmf* joker.

blair [blɛr] *nm* (nez) *Arg* snout, conk. ◆**blairer** *vt Arg* to stomach.

blaireau, -x [blero] *nm* **1** (animal) badger. **2** (brosse) (shaving) brush.

blâme [blɑm] *nm* (réprimande) rebuke; (reproche) blame. ◆**blâmable** *a* blameworthy. ◆**blâmer** *vt* to rebuke; to blame.

blanc, blanche [blɑ̃, blɑ̃ʃ] **1** *a* white; (page etc) blank; **nuit blanche** sleepless night; **voix blanche** expressionless voice; – *nmf* (personne) white (man *ou* woman); – *nm* (couleur) white; (de poulet) white meat, breast; (espace, interligne) blank; **b. (d'œuf)** (egg) white; **le b.** (linge) whites; **magasin de b.** linen shop; **laisser en b.** to leave blank; **chèque en b.** blank cheque; **cartouche à b.** blank (cartridge); **saigner à b.** to bleed white. **2** *nf Mus* minim, *Am* half-note. ◆**blanchâtre** *a* whitish. ◆**blancheur** *nf* whiteness.

blanchir [blɑ̃ʃir] *vt* to whiten; (draps) to launder; (mur) to whitewash; *Culin* to blanch; (argent) *Fig* to launder; **b. qn** (disculper) to clear s.o.; – *vi* to turn white, whiten. **2** *nf* **blanchissage** *nm* laundering. ◆**blanchisserie** *nf* (lieu) laundry. ◆**blanchisseur, -euse** *nmf* laundryman, laundrywoman.

blanquette [blɑ̃kɛt] *nf* **b. de veau** veal stew in white sauce.

blasé [blaze] *a* blasé.

blason [blazõ] *nm* (écu) coat of arms; (science) heraldry.

blasphème [blasfɛm] *nm* blasphemy. ◆**blasphématoire** *a* (propos) blasphemous. ◆**blasphémer** *vti* to blaspheme.

blatte [blat] *nf* cockroach.

blazer [blazœr] *nm* blazer.

blé [ble] *nm* wheat; (argent) *Arg* bread.

bled [blɛd] *nm Péj Fam* (dump of a) village.

blême [blɛm] *a* sickly pale, wan; **b. de colère** livid with anger.

bless/er [blese] *vt* to injure, hurt; (avec un couteau, une balle etc) to wound; (offenser) to hurt, offend, wound; **se b. la** *ou* **au bras**/etc to hurt one's arm/etc. ◆—**ant** [blɛsɑ̃] *a* (parole, personne) hurtful. ◆—**é, -ée** *nmf* casualty, injured *ou* wounded person. ◆**blessure** *nf* injury; wound.

blet, blette [blɛ, blɛt] *a* (fruit) overripe.

bleu [blø] *a* **b. de colère** blue in the face; **steak b.** *Culin* very rare steak; – *nm* (couleur) blue; (contusion) bruise; (vêtement) overalls; (conscrit) raw recruit; **bleus de travail** overalls. ◆**bleuir** *vti* to turn blue.

bleuet [bløɛ] *nm* cornflower.

blind/er [blɛ̃de] *vt Mil* to armour(-plate). ◆—**é** *a* (train etc) *Mil* armoured; **porte blindée** reinforced steel door; – *nm Mil* armoured vehicle.

bloc [blɔk] *nm* block; (de pierre) lump, block; (de papier) pad; (masse compacte) unit; *Pol* bloc; **en b.** all together; **b.** (serrer etc) tight, hard; **travailler à b.** *Fam* to work flat out. ◆**b.-notes** *nm* (*pl* **blocs-notes**) writing pad.

blocage [blɔkaʒ] *nm* (*des roues*) locking; *Psy* mental block; **b. des prix** price freeze.

blocus [blɔkys] *nm* blockade.

blond, -onde [blɔ̃, -ɔ̃d] *a* fair(-haired), blond; — *nm* fair-haired man; (*couleur*) blond; — *nf* fair-haired woman, blonde; (*bière*) **blonde** lager, pale *ou* light ale. ◆**blondeur** *nf* fairness, blondness.

bloquer [blɔke] *vt* (*obstruer*) to block; (*coincer*) to jam; (*grouper*) to group together; (*ville*) to blockade; (*freins*) to slam *ou* jam on; (*roue*) to lock; (*salaires, prix*) to freeze; **bloqué par la neige/la glace** snowbound/icebound; — **se b.** *vpr* to stick, jam; (*roue*) to lock.

blottir (se) [səblɔtir] *vpr* (*dans un coin etc*) to crouch; (*dans son lit*) to snuggle down; **se b. contre** to huddle up to, snuggle up to.

blouse [bluz] *nf* (*tablier*) overall, smock; (*corsage*) blouse. ◆**blouson** *nm* (waist-length) jacket.

blue-jean [bludʒin] *nm* jeans, denims.

bluff [blœf] *nm* bluff. ◆**bluffer** *vti* to bluff.

boa [bɔa] *nm* (*serpent, tour de cou*) boa.

bobard [bɔbar] *nm* Fam fib, yarn, tall story.

bobine [bɔbin] *nf* (*de fil, film etc*) reel, spool; (*pour machine à coudre*) bobbin, spool.

bobo [bɔbo] *nm* (*langage enfantin*) pain; **j'ai b., ça fait b.** it hurts.

bocage [bɔkaʒ] *nm* copse.

bocal, -aux [bɔkal, -o] *nm* glass jar; (*à poissons*) bowl.

bock [bɔk] *nm* (*récipient*) beer glass; (*contenu*) glass of beer.

bœuf, *pl* -**fs** [bœf, bø] *nm* (*animal*) ox (*pl* oxen), bullock; (*viande*) beef.

bohème [bɔɛm] *a* & *nmf* bohemian. ◆**bohémien, -ienne** *a* & *nmf* gipsy.

boire* [bwar] *vt* to drink; (*absorber*) to soak up; (*paroles*) *Fig* to take *ou* drink in; **un coup** to have a drink; **offrir à b. à qn** to offer s.o. a drink; **b. à petits coups** to sip; — *vi* to drink.

bois¹ [bwa] *voir* boire.

bois² [bwa] *nm* (*matière, forêt*) wood; (*de construction*) timber; (*gravure*) woodcut; (*de cerf*) antlers; *Mus* woodwind instruments; **en ou de b.** wooden; **b. de chauffage** firewood; **b. de lit** bedstead. ◆**boisé** *a* wooded. ◆**boiserie(s)** *nf*(*pl*) panelling.

boisson [bwasɔ̃] *nf* drink, beverage.

boit [bwa] *voir* boire.

boîte [bwat] *nf* box; (*de conserve*) tin, *Am* can; (*lieu de travail*) *Fam* firm; **b. aux ou à lettres** letterbox; **b. de nuit** nightclub; **mettre qn en b.** *Fam* to pull s.o.'s leg. ◆**boîtier** *nm* (*de montre etc*) case.

boiter [bwate] *vi* (*personne*) to limp. ◆**boiteux, -euse** *a* lame; (*meuble*) wobbly; (*projet etc*) *Fig* shaky.

bol [bɔl] *nm* (*récipient*) bowl; **prendre un b. d'air** to get a breath of fresh air; **avoir du b.** *Fam* to be lucky.

bolide [bɔlid] *nm* (*véhicule*) racing car.

Bolivie [bɔlivi] *nf* Bolivia. ◆**bolivien, -ienne** *a* & *nmf* Bolivian.

bombard/er [bɔ̃barde] *vt* (*ville etc*) to bomb; (*avec des obus*) to shell; **b. qn** *Fam* (*nommer*) to pitchfork s.o. (**à un poste** into a job); (*objets*) to pelt with; **b. de** (*questions*) to bombard with; ◆**-ement** *nm* bombing; shelling. ◆**bombardier** *nm* (*avion*) bomber.

bombe [bɔ̃b] *nf* (*projectile*) bomb; (*atomiseur*) spray; **tomber comme une b.** *Fig* to be a bombshell, be quite unexpected; **faire la b.** *Fam* to have a binge.

bomb/er [bɔ̃be] **1** *vi* (*gonfler*) to bulge; — *vt* **b. la poitrine** to throw out one's chest. **2** *vi* (*véhicule etc*) *Fam* to bomb *ou* belt along. ◆**-é** *a* (*verre etc*) rounded; (*route*) cambered.

bon¹, bonne¹ [bɔ̃, bɔn] *a* **1** (*satisfaisant etc*) good. **2** (*charitable*) kind, good. **3** (*agréable*) nice, good; **il fait b. se reposer** it's nice *ou* good to rest; **b. anniversaire!** happy birthday! **4** (*qui convient*) right; **c'est le b. clou** it's the right nail. **5** (*approprié, apte*) fit; **b. à manger** fit to eat; **b. pour le service** fit for service; **ce n'est b. à rien** it's useless; **comme b. te semble** as you think fit *ou* best; **c'est b. à savoir** it's worth knowing. **6** (*prudent*) wise, good; **croire b.** to think it wise *ou* good to do; **b. en français** good at French. **8** (*valable*) good; **ce billet est encore b.** this ticket's still good. **9** (*intensif*) **un b. moment** a good while. **10** **à quoi b.?** what's the use *ou* point *ou* good; **pour de b.** in earnest; **tenir b.** to stand firm; **ah b.?** is that so? **11** *nm* **du b.** some good; **les bons** the good.

bon² [bɔ̃] *nm* (*billet*) coupon, voucher; (*titre*) *Fin* bond; (*formulaire*) slip.

bonbon [bɔ̃bɔ̃] *nm* sweet, *Am* candy. ◆**bonbonnière** *nf* sweet box, *Am* candy box.

bonbonne [bɔ̃bɔn] *nf* (*récipient*) demijohn.

bond [bɔ̃] *nm* leap, bound; (*de balle*) bounce; **faire faux b. à qn** to stand s.o. up, let s.o. down (*by not turning up*). ◆**bondir** *vi* to leap, bound.

bonde [bɔ̃d] *nf* (*bouchon*) plug; (*trou*) plughole.

bondé [bɔ̃de] *a* packed, crammed.

bonheur [bɔnœr] *nm* (*chance*) good luck, good fortune; (*félicité*) happiness; **par b.** luckily; **au petit b.** haphazardly.

bonhomie [bɔnɔmi] *nf* good-heartedness.

bonhomme, pl bonshommes [bɔnɔm, bɔ̃zɔm] **1** *nm* fellow, guy; **b. de neige** snowman; **aller son petit b. de chemin** to go in one's own sweet way. **2** *a inv* good-hearted.

boniment(s) [bɔnimɑ̃] *nm(pl)* (*bobard*) claptrap; (*baratin*) patter.

bonjour [bɔ̃ʒur] *nm & int* good morning; (*après-midi*) good afternoon; **donner le b. à**, **dire b. à** to say hello to.

bonne² [bɔn] *nf* (*domestique*) maid; **b. d'enfants** nanny.

bonnement [bɔnmɑ̃] *adv* **tout b.** simply.

bonnet [bɔne] *nm* cap; (*de femme, d'enfant*) bonnet; (*de soutien-gorge*) cup; **gros b.** *Fam* bigshot, bigwig. **◆bonneterie** *nf* hosiery.

bonsoir [bɔ̃swar] *nm & int* (*en rencontrant qn*) good evening; (*en quittant qn*) goodbye; (*au coucher*) good night.

bonté [bɔ̃te] *nf* kindness, goodness.

bonus [bɔnys] *nm* no claims bonus.

bonze [bɔ̃z] *nm Péj* bigwig.

boom [bum] *nm Écon* boom.

bord [bɔr] *nm* (*rebord*) edge; (*rive*) bank; (*de vêtement*) border; (*de chapeau*) brim; (*de verre*) rim, brim, edge; **au b. de la mer/route** at *ou* by the seaside/roadside; **b. du trottoir** kerb, *Am* curb; **au b. de** (*précipice*) on the brink of; **au b. des larmes** on the verge of tears; **à bord (de)** *Nau Av* on board; **jeter par-dessus b.** to throw overboard. **◆border** *vt* (*vêtement*) to border, edge; (*lit, personne*) to tuck in; **b. la rue/etc** (*maisons, arbres etc*) to line the street/*etc*. **◆bordure** *nf* border; **en b. de** bordering on.

bordeaux [bɔrdo] *a inv* maroon.

bordée [bɔrde] *nf* (*salve*) *Nau* broadside; (*d'injures*) *Fig* torrent, volley.

bordel [bɔrdɛl] *nm* **1** *Fam* brothel. **2** (*désordre*) *Fam* mess.

bordereau, -x [bɔrdəro] *nm* (*relevé*) docket, statement; (*formulaire*) note.

borgne [bɔrɲ] *a* (*personne*) one-eyed, blind in one eye; (*hôtel etc*) *Fig* shady.

borne [bɔrn] *nf* (*pierre*) boundary mark; *Él* terminal; *pl* (*limites*) *Fig* bounds. **b. kilométrique** = milestone; **dépasser** *ou* **franchir les bornes** to go too far. **◆born/er** *vt* (*limiter*) to confine; **se b. à** to confine oneself to. **◆—é** *a* (*personne*) narrow-minded; (*intelligence*) narrow, limited.

bosquet [bɔskɛ] *nm* grove, thicket, copse.

bosse [bɔs] *nf* (*grosseur dorsale*) hump; (*enflure*) bump, lump; (*de terrain*) bump; **avoir la b. de** *Fam* to have a flair for; **rouler sa b.** *Fam* to knock about the world. **◆bossu, -ue** *a* hunchbacked; **dos b.** hunchback; – *nmf* (*personne*) hunchback.

bosseler [bɔsle] *vt* (*orfèvrerie*) to emboss; (*déformer*) to dent.

bosser [bɔse] *vi Fam* to work (hard).

bot [bo] *am* **pied b.** club foot.

botanique [bɔtanik] *a* botanical; – *nf* botany.

botte [bɔt] *nf* (*chaussure*) boot; (*faisceau*) bunch, bundle. **◆botter** *vt* (*ballon etc*) *Fam* to boot. **◆bottier** *nm* bootmaker. **◆bottillon** *nm*, **◆bottine** *nf* (*ankle*) boot.

Bottin® [bɔtɛ̃] *nm* telephone book.

bouc [buk] *nm* billy goat; (*barbe*) goatee; **b. émissaire** scapegoat.

boucan [bukɑ̃] *nm Fam* din, row, racket.

bouche [buʃ] *nf* mouth; **faire la petite** *ou* **fine b.** *Péj* to turn up one's nose; **une fine b.** a gourmet; **b. de métro** métro entrance; **b. d'égout** drain opening, manhole; **b. d'incendie** fire hydrant; **le b.-à-b.** the kiss of life. **◆bouchée** *nf* mouthful.

bouch/er¹ [buʃe] **1** *vt* (*évier, nez etc*) to block (up), stop up; (*bouteille*) to close, cork; (*vue, rue etc*) to block; **se b. le nez** to hold one's nose. **◆—é** *a* (*vin*) bottled; (*temps*) overcast; (*personne*) *Fig* stupid, dense. **◆bouche-trou** *nm* stopgap. **◆bouchon** *nm* stopper, top; (*de liège*) cork; (*de tube, bidon*) cap, top; *Pêche* float; (*embouteillage*) *Fig* traffic jam.

boucher² [buʃe] *nm* butcher. **◆boucherie** *nf* butcher's (shop); (*carnage*) butchery.

boucle [bukl] *nf* **1** (*de ceinture*) buckle; (*de fleuve etc*) & *Av* loop; (*de ruban*) bow; **b. d'oreille** earring. **2 b.** (*de cheveux*) curl. **◆boucl/er** *vt* to fasten, buckle; (*travail etc*) to finish off; (*enfermer, fermer*) *Fam* to lock up; (*budget*) to balance; (*circuit*) to lap; (*encercler*) to surround, cordon off; **b. la boucle** *Av* to loop the loop; **la b.** *Fam* to shut up. **2** *vt* (*cheveux*) to curl; – *vi* to be curly. **◆—é** *a* (*cheveux*) curly.

bouclier [buklije] *nm* shield.

bouddhiste [budist] *a & nmf* Buddhist.

bouder [bude] *vi* to sulk; – *vt* (*personne, plaisirs etc*) to steer clear of. **◆bouderie** *nf* sulkiness. **◆boudeur, -euse** *a* sulky, moody.

boudin [budɛ̃] *nm* black pudding, *Am* blood pudding.

boue [bu] *nf* mud. **◆boueux, -euse 1** *a*

muddy. **2** *nm* dustman, *Am* garbage collector.

bouée [bwe] *nf* buoy; **b. de sauvetage** lifebuoy.

bouffe [buf] *nf Fam* food, grub, nosh.

bouffée [bufe] *nf (de fumée)* puff; *(de parfum)* whiff; *(d'orgueil)* fit; **b. de chaleur** *Méd* hot flush. ◆**bouff/er 1** *vi* to puff out. **2** *vti (manger) Fam* to eat. ◆**—ant** *a (manche)* puff(ed). ◆**bouffi** *a* puffy, bloated.

bouffon, -onne [bufɔ̃, -ɔn] *a* farcical; – *nm* buffoon. ◆**bouffonneries** *nfpl* antics, buffoonery.

bouge [buʒ] *nm (bar)* dive; *(taudis)* hovel.

bougeotte [buʒɔt] *nf* **avoir la b.** *Fam* to have the fidgets.

bouger [buʒe] *vi* to move; *(agir)* to stir; *(rétrécir)* to shrink; – *vt* to move; – **se b.** *vpr Fam* to move.

bougie [buʒi] *nf* candle; *Aut* spark(ing) plug. ◆**bougeoir** *nm* candlestick.

bougon, -onne [bugɔ̃, -ɔn] *a Fam* grumpy; – *nmf* grumbler, grouch. ◆**bougonner** *vi Fam* to grumble, grouch.

bougre [bugr] *nm* fellow, bloke; *(enfant) Péj* (little) devil. ◆**bougrement** *adv Arg* damned.

bouillabaisse [bujabɛs] *nf* fish soup.

bouillie [buji] *nf* porridge; **en b.** in a mush, mushy.

bouill/ir [bujir] *vi* to boil; **b. à gros bouillons** to bubble, boil hard; **faire b. qch** to boil sth. ◆**—ant** *a* boiling; **b. de colère/**etc seething with anger/etc. ◆**bouilloire** *nf* kettle. ◆**bouillon** *nm (eau)* broth, stock; *(bulle)* bubble. ◆**bouillonner** *vi* to bubble. ◆**bouillotte** *nf* hot water bottle.

boulanger, -ère [bulɑ̃ʒe, -er] *nmf* baker. ◆**boulangerie** *nf* baker's (shop).

boule [bul] *nf (sphère)* ball; *pl (jeu)* bowls; **b. de neige** snowball; **faire b. de neige** to snowball; **perdre la b.** *Fam* to go out of one's mind; **se mettre en b.** *(chat etc)* to curl up into a ball; **boules Quiès®** earplugs. ◆**boulet** *nm (de forçat)* ball and chain; **b. de canon** cannonball. ◆**boulette** *nf (de papier)* pellet; *(de viande)* meatball; *(gaffe) Fam* blunder.

bouleau, -x [bulo] *nm* (silver) birch.

bouledogue [buldɔg] *nm* bulldog.

boulevard [bulvar] *nm* boulevard.

boulevers/er [bulverse] *vt (déranger)* to turn upside down; *(émouvoir)* to upset deeply, distress; *(vie de qn, pays)* to disrupt. ◆**—ant** *a* upsetting, distressing. ◆**—ement** *nm* upheaval.

boulon [bulɔ̃] *nm* bolt.

boulot, -otte [bulo, -ɔt] **1** *a* dumpy. **2** *nm (travail) Fam* work.

boum [bum] **1** *int & nm* bang. **2** *nf (surprise-partie) Fam* party.

bouquet [buke] *nm (de fleurs)* bunch, bouquet; *(d'arbres)* clump; *(de vin)* bouquet; *(crevette)* prawn; **c'est le b.!** that's the last straw!

bouquin [bukɛ̃] *nm Fam* book. ◆**bouquiner** *vti Fam* to read. ◆**bouquiniste** *nmf* second-hand bookseller.

bourbeux, -euse [burbø, -øz] *a* muddy. ◆**bourbier** *nm (lieu, situation)* quagmire, morass.

bourde [burd] *nf* blunder, bloomer.

bourdon [burdɔ̃] *nm (insecte)* bumblebee. ◆**bourdonn/er** *vi* to buzz, hum. ◆**—ement** *nm* buzzing, humming.

bourg [bur] *nm* (small) market town. ◆**bourgade** *nf* (large) village.

bourgeois, -oise [burʒwa, -waz] *a & nmf* middle-class (person); *Péj* bourgeois. ◆**bourgeoisie** *nf* middle class, bourgeoisie.

bourgeon [burʒɔ̃] *nm* bud. ◆**bourgeonner** *vi* to bud; *(nez) Fam* to be pimply.

bourgmestre [burgmestr] *nm (en Belgique, Suisse)* burgomaster.

bourgogne [burgɔɲ] *nm (vin)* Burgundy.

bourlinguer [burlɛ̃ge] *vi (voyager) Fam* to knock about.

bourrade [burad] *nf (du coude)* poke.

bourrasque [burask] *nf* squall.

bourratif, -ive [buratif, -iv] *a (aliment) Fam* filling, stodgy.

bourreau, -x [buro] *nm* executioner; **b. d'enfants** child batterer; **b. de travail** workaholic.

bourrelet [burlɛ] *nm* weather strip; **b. de graisse** roll of fat, spare tyre.

bourr/er [bure] *vt* **1** to stuff, cram (full) (de with); *(pipe, coussin)* to fill; **b. de coups** to thrash; **b. le crâne à qn** to brainwash s.o. **2 se b.** *vpr (s'enivrer) Fam* to get plastered. ◆**—age** *nm* **b. de crâne** brainwashing.

bourrique [burik] *nf* ass.

bourru [bury] *a* surly, rough.

bourse [burs] *nf (sac)* purse; *Scol Univ* grant, scholarship; **la B.** the Stock Exchange; **sans b. délier** without spending a penny. ◆**boursier, -ière 1** *a* Stock Exchange-. **2** *nmf Scol Univ* grant holder, scholar.

boursouflé [bursufle] *a (visage etc)* puffy; *(style) Fig* inflated.

bousculer [buskyle] *vt (heurter, pousser)* to

jostle; (*presser*) to rush, push; **b. qch** (*renverser*) to knock sth over; **b. les habitudes**/*etc* to turn one's habits/*etc* upside down. ◆**bousculade** *nf* rush, jostling.

bouse [buz] *nf* **b. de vache** cow dung.

bousiller [buzije] *vt Fam* to mess up, wreck.

boussole [busl] *nf* compass.

bout [bu] *nm* end; (*de langue, canne, doigt*) tip; (*de papier, pain, ficelle*) bit; **un b. de temps/chemin** a little while/way; **au b. d'un moment** after a moment; **à b. exhausted; **à b. de souffle** out of breath; **à b. de bras** at arm's length; **venir à b. de** (*travail*) to get through; (*adversaire*) to get the better of; **à tout b. de champ** at every turn, every minute; **à b. portant** point-blank.

boutade [butad] *nf* (*plaisanterie*) quip, witticism.

boute-en-train [butɑ̃trɛ̃] *nm inv* (*personne*) live wire.

bouteille [butɛj] *nf* bottle; (*de gaz*) cylinder.

bouteur [butœr] *nm* bulldozer.

boutique [butik] *nf* shop; (*d'un grand couturier*) boutique. ◆**boutiquier, -ière** *nmf Péj* shopkeeper.

boutoir [butwar] *nm* **coup de b.** staggering blow.

bouton [butɔ̃] *nm* (*bourgeon*) bud; (*pustule*) pimple, spot; (*de vêtement*) button; (*poussoir*) (push-)button; (*de porte, de télévision*) knob; **b. de manchette** cuff link. ◆**b.-d'or** *nm* (*pl* **boutons-d'or**) buttercup. ◆**b.-pression** *nm* (*pl* **boutons-pression**) press-stud, *Am* snap. ◆**boutonner** *vt*, **— se b.** *vpr* to button (up). ◆**boutonneux, -euse** *a* pimply, spotty. ◆**boutonnière** *nf* buttonhole.

bouture [butyr] *nf* (*plante*) cutting.

bouvreuil [buvrœj] *nm* (*oiseau*) bullfinch.

bovin [bɔvɛ̃] *a* bovine; – *nmpl* cattle.

bowling [bolin] *nm* (*tenpin*) bowling; (*lieu*) bowling alley.

box, *pl* **boxes** [bɔks, bɔksiz] *nm* (*d'écurie*) (loose) box; (*de dortoir*) cubicle; *Jur* dock; *Aut* lockup *ou* individual garage.

boxe [bɔks] *nf* boxing. ◆**boxer** *vi Sp* to box; – *vt Fam* to whack, punch. ◆**boxeur** *nm* boxer.

boyau, -x [bwajo] *nm Anat* gut; (*corde*) catgut; (*de bicyclette*) (racing) tyre *ou Am* tire.

boycott [bɔjkɔt] *vt* to boycott. ◆**—age** *nm* boycott.

BP [bepe] *abrév* (*boîte postale*) PO Box.

bracelet [brasle] *nm* bracelet, bangle; (*de montre*) strap.

braconner [brakɔne] *vi* to poach. ◆**braconnier** *nm* poacher.

brader [brade] *vt* to sell off cheaply. ◆**braderie** *nf* open-air (clearance) sale.

braguette [bragɛt] *nf* (*de pantalon*) fly, flies.

braille [brɑj] *nm* Braille.

brailler [brɑje] *vti* to bawl. ◆**braillard** *a* bawling.

braire[e] [brɛr] *vi* (*âne*) to bray.

braise(s) [brɛz] *nf(pl)* embers, live coals. ◆**braiser** [brɛze] *vt Culin* to braise.

brancard [brɑ̃kar] *nm* (*civière*) stretcher; (*de charrette*) shaft. ◆**brancardier** *nm* stretcher-bearer.

branche [brɑ̃ʃ] *nf* (*d'un arbre, d'une science etc*) branch; (*de compas*) leg; (*de lunettes*) side piece. ◆**branchages** *nmpl* (cut *ou* fallen) branches.

branch/er [brɑ̃ʃe] *vt El* to plug in; (*installer*) to connect. ◆**—é** *a* (*informé*) *Fam* with it. ◆**—ement** *nm El* connection.

brandir [brɑ̃dir] *vt* to brandish, flourish.

brandon [brɑ̃dɔ̃] *nm* (*paille, bois*) firebrand.

branle [brɑ̃l] *nm* impetus; **mettre en b.** to set in motion. ◆**b.-bas** *nm inv* turmoil. ◆**branl/er** *vi* to be shaky, shake. ◆**—ant** *a* shaky.

braqu/er [brake] **1** *vt* (*arme etc*) to point, aim; (*yeux*) to fix; **b. qn contre qn** to set *ou* turn s.o. against s.o. **2** *vti Aut* to steer, turn. ◆**—age** *nm Aut* steering; **rayon de b.** turning circle.

bras [bra] *nm* arm; **en b. de chemise** in one's shirtsleeves; **b. dessus b. dessous** arm in arm; **sur les b.** Fig on one's hands; **son b. droit** Fig his right-hand man; **à b. ouverts** with open arms; **à tour de b.** with all one's might; **faire le b. d'honneur** *Fam* to make an obscene gesture; **à b.-le-corps** round the waist. ◆**brassard** *nm* armband. ◆**brassée** *nf* armful. ◆**brassière** *nf* (*de bébé*) vest, *Am* undershirt.

brasier [brazje] *nm* inferno, blaze.

brasse [bras] *nf* (*nage*) breaststroke; (*mesure*) fathom; **b. papillon** butterfly stroke.

brasser [brase] *vt* to mix; (*bière*) to brew. ◆**brassage** *nm* mixture; brewing. ◆**brasserie** *nf* (*usine*) brewery; (*café*) brasserie. ◆**brasseur** *nm* **b. d'affaires** *Péj* big businessman.

bravache [bravaʃ] *nm* braggart.

bravade [bravad] *nf* **par b.** out of bravado.

brave [brav] *a* & *nm* (*hardi*) brave (man); (*honnête*) good (man). ◆**bravement** *adv* bravely. ◆**braver** *vt* to defy; (*danger*) to brave. ◆**bravoure** *nf* bravery.

bravo [bravo] *int* well done, bravo, good show; – *nm* cheer.

break [brɛk] *nm* estate car, *Am* station wagon.

brebis [brəbi] *nf* ewe; **b. galeuse** black sheep.

brèche [brɛʃ] *nf* breach, gap; **battre en b.** (*attaquer*) to attack (mercilessly).

bredouille [brəduj] *a* **rentrer b.** to come back empty-handed.

bredouiller [brəduje] *vti* to mumble.

bref, brève [brɛf, brɛv] *a* brief, short; – *adv* (*enfin*) **b.** in a word.

breloque [brəlɔk] *nf* charm, trinket.

Brésil [brezil] *nm* Brazil. ◆**brésilien, -ienne** *a* & *nmf* Brazilian.

Bretagne [brətaɲ] *nf* Brittany. ◆**breton, -onne** *a* & *nmf* Breton.

bretelle [brətɛl] *nf* strap; (*voie de raccordement*) *Aut* access road; *pl* (*pour pantalon*) braces, *Am* suspenders.

breuvage [brœvaʒ] *nm* drink, brew.

brève [brɛv] *voir* bref.

brevet [brəvɛ] *nm* diploma; **b.** (**d'invention**) patent. ◆**brevet/er** *vt* to patent. ◆**-é** *a* (*technicien*) qualified.

bréviaire [brevjɛr] *nm* breviary.

bribes [brib] *nfpl* scraps, bits.

bric-à-brac [brikabrak] *nm inv* bric-à-brac, jumble, junk.

brick [brik] *nm* (*de lait, jus d'orange etc*) carton.

bricole [brikɔl] *nf* (*objet, futilité*) trifle. ◆**bricol/er** *vi* to do odd jobs; – *vt* (*réparer*) to patch up; (*fabriquer*) to put together. ◆**-age** *nm* (*petits travaux*) odd jobs; (*passe-temps*) do-it-yourself; **salon/rayon du b.** do-it-yourself exhibition/department. ◆**-eur, -euse** *nmf* handyman, handywoman.

bride [brid] *nf* (*de cheval*) bridle; **à b. abattue** at full gallop. ◆**brider** *vt* (*cheval*) to bridle; (*personne, désir*) to curb; *Culin* to truss; **avoir les yeux bridés** to have slit eyes.

bridge [bridʒ] *nm* (*jeu*) bridge.

brièvement [brievmɑ̃] *adv* briefly. ◆**brièveté** *nf* brevity.

brigade [brigad] *nf* (*de gendarmerie*) squad; *Mil* brigade; **b. des mœurs** vice squad. ◆**brigadier** *nm* police sergeant; *Mil* corporal.

brigand [brigɑ̃] *nm* robber; (*enfant*) rascal.

briguer [brige] *vt* to covet; (*faveurs, suffrages*) to court.

brillant [brijɑ̃] *a* (*luisant*) shining; (*astiqué*) shiny; (*couleur*) bright; (*magnifique*) *Fig* brilliant; – *nm* shine; brightness; *Fig* bril-

liance; (*diamant*) diamond. ◆**brillamment** *adv* brilliantly.

briller [brije] *vi* to shine; **faire b.** (*meuble*) to polish (up).

brimer [brime] *vt* to bully. ◆**brimade** *nf* *Scol* bullying, ragging, *Am* hazing; *Fig* vexation.

brin [brɛ̃] *nm* (*d'herbe*) blade; (*de corde, fil*) strand; (*de muguet*) spray; **un b. de** *Fig* a bit of.

brindille [brɛ̃dij] *nf* twig.

bringue [brɛ̃g] *nf* **faire la b.** *Fam* to have a binge.

bringuebaler [brɛ̃gbale] *vi* to wobble about.

brio [brijo] *nm* (*virtuosité*) brilliance.

brioche [brijɔʃ] *nf* **1** brioche (*light sweet bun*). **2** (*ventre*) *Fam* paunch.

brique [brik] *nf* brick. ◆**briquette** *nf* (*aggloméré*) breezeblock.

briquer [brike] *vt* to polish (up).

briquet [brikɛ] *nm* (*cigarette*) lighter.

brise [briz] *nf* breeze.

bris/er [brize] *vt* to break; (*en morceaux*) to smash, break; (*espoir, carrière*) to shatter; (*fatiguer*) to exhaust; – **se b.** *vpr* to break. ◆**-ants** *nmpl* reefs. ◆**brise-lames** *nm inv* breakwater.

britannique [britanik] *a* British; – *nmf* Briton; **les Britanniques** the British.

broc [bro] *nm* pitcher, jug.

brocanteur, -euse [brɔkɑ̃tœr, -øz] *nmf* secondhand dealer (*in furniture etc*).

broche [brɔʃ] *nf* *Culin* spit; (*bijou*) brooch; *Méd* pin. ◆**brochette** *nf* (*tige*) skewer; (*plat*) kebab.

broché [brɔʃe] *a* **livre b.** paperback.

brochet [brɔʃɛ] *nm* (*poisson*) pike.

brochure [brɔʃyr] *nf* brochure, booklet, pamphlet.

broder [brɔde] *vt* to embroider (**de** with). ◆**broderie** *nf* embroidery.

broncher [brɔ̃ʃe] *vi* (*bouger*) to budge; (*reculer*) to flinch; (*regimber*) to balk.

bronches [brɔ̃ʃ] *nfpl* bronchial tubes. ◆**bronchite** *nf* bronchitis.

bronze [brɔ̃z] *nm* bronze.

bronz/er [brɔ̃ze] *vt* to tan; – *vi*, – **se b.** *vpr* to get (sun)tanned; **se b.** to sunbathe. ◆**-age** *nm* (sun)tan, sunburn.

brosse [brɔs] *nf* brush; **b. à dents** tooth-brush; **cheveux en b.** crew cut. ◆**brosser** *vt* to brush; **b. un tableau de** to give an outline of; – **se b. les dents/les cheveux** to brush one's teeth/one's hair.

brouette [bruɛt] *nf* wheelbarrow.

brouhaha [bruaa] *nm* hubbub.

brouillard [brujar] *nm* fog; **il fait du b.** it's foggy.

brouille [bruj] *nf* disagreement, quarrel. ◆**brouiller 1** *vt* (*papiers, idées etc*) to mix up; (*vue*) to blur; (*œufs*) to scramble; *Rad* to jam; — **se b.** *vpr* (*idées*) to be ou get confused; (*temps*) to cloud over; (*vue*) to blur. **2** *vt* (*amis*) to cause a split between; — **se b.** *vpr* to fall out (**avec** with). ◆**brouillon, -onne 1** *a* confused. **2** *nm* rough draft.

broussailles [brusaj] *nfpl* brushwood.

brousse [brus] *nf* **la b.** the bush.

brouter [brute] *vti* to graze.

broyer [brwaje] *vt* to grind; (*doigt, bras*) to crush; **b. du noir** to be (down) in the dumps.

bru [bry] *nf* daughter-in-law.

brugnon [bryɲɔ̃] *nm* (*fruit*) nectarine.

bruine [brɥin] *nf* drizzle. ◆**bruiner** *v imp* to drizzle.

bruissement [brɥismɑ̃] *nm* (*de feuilles*) rustle, rustling.

bruit [brɥi] *nm* noise, sound; (*nouvelle*) rumour; **faire du b.** to be noisy, make a noise. ◆**bruitage** *nm Cin* sound effects.

brûle-pourpoint (à) [abrylpurpwɛ̃] *adv* point-blank.

brûl/er [bryle] *vt* to burn; (*consommer*) to use up, burn; (*signal, station*) to go through (*without stopping*); **b. un feu (rouge)** to jump ou go through the lights; **ce désir le brûlait** this desire consumed him; — *vi* to burn; **b. d'envie de faire** to be burning to do; **ça brûle** (*temps*) it's baking ou scorching; — **se b.** *vpr* to burn oneself. ◆**—ant** *a* (*objet, soleil*) burning (hot); (*sujet*) *Fig* red-hot. ◆**—é 1** *nm* **odeur de b.** smell of burning. **2** *a* **cerveau b.**, **tête brûlée** hothead. ◆**brûlure** *nf* burn; **brûlures d'estomac** heartburn.

brume [brym] *nf* mist, haze. ◆**brumeux, -euse** *a* misty, hazy; (*obscur*) *Fig* hazy.

brun, brune [brœ̃, bryn] *a* brown; (*cheveux*) dark, brown; (*personne*) dark-haired; — *nm* (*couleur*) brown; — *nmf* dark-haired person. ◆**brunette** *nf* brunette. ◆**brunir** *vt* (*peau*) to tan; — *vi* to turn brown; (*cheveux*) to go darker.

brushing [brœʃiŋ] *nm* blow-dry.

brusque [brysk] *a* (*manière etc*) abrupt, blunt; (*subit*) sudden, abrupt. ◆**brusquement** *adv* suddenly, abruptly. ◆**brusquer** *vt* to rush. ◆**brusquerie** *nf* abruptness, bluntness.

brut [bryt] *a* (*pétrole*) crude; (*diamant*) rough; (*sucre*) unrefined; (*soie*) raw; (*poids*) & *Fin* gross.

brutal, -aux [brytal, -o] *a* (*violent*) savage, brutal; (*franchise, réponse*) crude, blunt; (*fait*) stark. ◆**brutaliser** *vt* to ill-treat. ◆**brutalité** *nf* (*violence, acte*) brutality. ◆**brute** *nf* brute.

Bruxelles [brysɛl] *nm ou f* Brussels.

bruyant [brɥijɑ̃] *a* noisy. ◆**bruyamment** *adv* noisily.

bruyère [brɥijɛr] *nf* (*plante*) heather; (*terrain*) heath.

bu [by] *voir* **boire**.

buanderie [bɥɑ̃dri] *nf* (*lieu*) laundry.

bûche [byʃ] *nf* log; **ramasser une b.** *Fam* to come a cropper, *Am* take a spill. ◆**bûcher 1** *nm* (*local*) woodshed; (*supplice*) stake. **2** *vt* (*étudier*) *Fam* to slog away at. ◆**bûcheron** *nm* woodcutter, lumberjack.

budget [bydʒɛ] *nm* budget. ◆**budgétaire** *a* budgetary; (*année*) financial.

buée [bɥe] *nf* condensation, mist.

buffet [byfɛ] *nm* (*armoire*) sideboard; (*table, restaurant, repas*) buffet.

buffle [byfl] *nm* buffalo.

buis [bɥi] *nm* (*arbre*) box; (*bois*) boxwood.

buisson [bɥisɔ̃] *nm* bush.

buissonnière [bɥisɔnjɛr] *af* **faire l'école b.** to play truant ou *Am* hookey.

bulbe [bylb] *nm* bulb. ◆**bulbeux, -euse** *a* bulbous.

Bulgarie [bylgari] *nf* Bulgaria. ◆**bulgare** *a* & *nmf* Bulgarian.

bulldozer [byldozɛr] *nm* bulldozer.

bulle [byl] *nf* **1** bubble; (*de bande dessinée*) balloon. **2** (*décret du pape*) bull.

bulletin [byltɛ̃] *nm* (*communiqué, revue*) bulletin; (*de la météo*) & *Scol* report; (*de bagages*) ticket, *Am* check; **b. de paie** pay slip; **b. de vote** ballot paper.

buraliste [byralist] *nmf* (*à la poste*) clerk; (*au tabac*) tobacconist.

bureau, -x [byro] *nm* **1** (*table*) desk. **2** (*lieu*) office; (*comité*) board; **b. de change** bureau de change; **b. de location** *Th Cin* box office; **b. de tabac** tobacconist's (shop). ◆**bureaucrate** *nmf* bureaucrat. ◆**bureaucratie** [-asi] *nf* bureaucracy. ◆**bureautique** *nf* office automation.

burette [byrɛt] *nf* oilcan; *Culin* cruet.

burlesque [byrlɛsk] *a* (*idée etc*) ludicrous; (*genre*) burlesque.

bus [bys] *nm Fam* bus.

bus [by] *voir* **boire**.

busqué [byske] *a* (*nez*) hooked.

buste [byst] *nm* (*torse, sculpture*) bust. ◆**bustier** *nm* long-line bra(ssiere).

but [by(t)] *nm* (*dessein, objectif*) aim, goal;

(*cible*) target; Fb goal; **de b. en blanc** point-blank; **aller droit au b.** to go straight to the point; **j'ai pour b. de . . .** my aim is to . . . .

but² [by] *voir* **boire**.

butane [bytan] *nm* (*gaz*) butane.

but/er [byte] **1** *vi* **b. contre** to stumble over; (*difficulté*) Fig to come up against. **2 se b.** *vpr* (*s'entêter*) to get obstinate. ◆**—é** *a* obstinate.

butin [bytɛ̃] *nm* loot, booty.

butiner [bytine] *vi* (*abeille*) to gather nectar.

butoir [bytwar] *nm* Rail buffer; (*de porte*) stop(per).

butor [bytɔr] *nm* Péj lout, oaf, boor.

butte [byt] *nf* hillock, mound; **en b. à** (*calomnie etc*) exposed to.

buvable [byvabl] *a* drinkable. ◆**buveur, -euse** *nmf* drinker.

buvard [byvar] *a & nm* (*papier*) **b.** blotting paper.

buvette [byvet] *nf* refreshment bar.

C

C, c [se] *nm* C, c

c *abrév* centime.

c' [s] *voir* **ce¹**.

ça [sa] *pron dém* (*abrév de* **cela**) (*pour désigner*) that; (*plus près*) this; (*sujet indéfini*) it, that; **ça m'amuse que . . .** it amuses me that . . . ; **où/quand/ comment/etc** where?/when?/how?/ *etc*; **ça va (bien)?** how's it going?; **ça va!** fine!, OK!; **ça alors!** (*surprise, indignation*) well I never!, how about that!; **c'est ça** that's right; **et avec ça?** (*dans un magasin*) anything else?

çà [sa] *adv* **çà et là** here and there.

caban [kabã] *nm* (*veste*) reefer.

cabane [kaban] *nf* hut, cabin; (*à outils*) shed; (*à lapins*) hutch.

cabaret [kabarɛ] *nm* night club, cabaret.

cabas [kaba] *nm* shopping bag.

cabillaud [kabijo] *nm* (fresh) cod.

cabine [kabin] *nf* Nau Av cabin; Tél phone booth, phone box; (*de camion*) cab; (*d'ascenseur*) car, cage; **c. (de bain)** beach hut; (*à la piscine*) cubicle; **c. (de pilotage)** cockpit; (*d'un grand avion*) flight deck; **c. d'essayage** fitting room; **c. d'aiguillage** signal box.

cabinet [kabine] *nm* (*local*) Méd surgery, Am office; (*d'avocat*) office, chambers; (*clientèle de médecin ou d'avocat*) practice; Pol cabinet; *pl* (*toilettes*) toilet; **c. de toilette** bathroom, toilet; **c. de travail** study.

câble [kabl] *nm* cable; (*cordage*) rope; **la télévision par c.** cable television; **le c.** TV cable. ◆**câbler** *vt* (*message*) to cable; **être câblé** TV to have cable.

caboche [kabɔʃ] *nf* (*tête*) Fam nut, noddle.

cabosser [kabɔse] *vt* to dent.

caboteur [kabɔtœr] *nm* (*bateau*) coaster.

cabotin, -ine [kabɔtɛ̃, -in] *nmf* Th ham actor, ham actress; Fig play-actor. ◆**cabotinage** *nm* histrionics, play-acting.

cabrer (se) [səkabre] *vpr* (*cheval*) to rear (up); (*personne*) to rebel.

cabri [kabri] *nm* (*chevreau*) kid.

cabrioles [kabriɔl] *nfpl* **faire des c.** (*sauts*) to cavort, caper.

cabriolet [kabriɔlɛ] *nm* Aut convertible.

cacah(o)uète [kakawɛt] *nf* peanut.

cacao [kakao] *nm* (*boisson*) cocoa.

cacatoès [kakatɔɛs] *nm* cockatoo.

cachalot [kaʃalo] *nm* sperm whale.

cache-cache [kaʃkaʃ] *nm inv* hide-and-seek. ◆**c.-col** *nm inv*, ◆**c.-nez** *nm inv* scarf, muffler. ◆**c.-sexe** *nm inv* G-string.

cachemire [kaʃmir] *nm* (*tissu*) cashmere.

cacher [kaʃe] *vt* to hide, conceal (à from); **je ne cache pas que . . .** I don't hide the fact that . . . ; **c. la lumière à qn** to stand in s.o.'s light; **— se c.** *vpr* to hide. ◆**cachette** *nf* hiding place; **en c.** in secret; **en c. de qn** without s.o. knowing.

cachet [kaʃe] *nm* (*sceau*) seal; (*de la poste*) postmark; (*comprimé*) tablet; (*d'acteur etc*) fee; Fig distinctive character. ◆**cacheter** *vt* to seal.

cachot [kaʃo] *nm* dungeon.

cachotteries [kaʃɔtri] *nfpl* secretiveness; (*petits secrets*) little mysteries. ◆**cachottier, -ière** *a & nmf* secretive (person).

cacophonie [kakɔfɔni] *nf* cacophony.

cactus [kaktys] *nm* cactus.

cadastre [kadastr] *nm* (*registre*) land register.

cadavre [kadavr] *nm* corpse. ◆**cadavéri-**

que a (teint etc) cadaverous; **rigidité c.** rigor mortis.

caddie® [kadi] nm supermarket trolly ou Am cart.

cadeau, -x [kado] nm present, gift.

cadenas [kadna] nm padlock. ◆**cadenasser** vt to padlock.

cadence [kadɑ̃s] nf rhythm; Mus cadence; (taux, vitesse) rate; **en c.** in time. ◆**cadencé** a rhythmical.

cadet, -ette [kadɛ, -ɛt] a (de deux frères etc) younger; (de plus de deux) youngest; – nmf (enfant) younger (child); youngest (child); Sp junior; **c'est mon c.** he's my junior.

cadran [kadrɑ̃] nm (de téléphone etc) dial; (de montre) face; **c. solaire** sundial; **faire le tour du c.** to sleep round the clock.

cadre [kadr] nm **1** (de photo, vélo etc) frame; (décor) setting; (sur un imprimé) box; **dans le c. de** (limites, contexte) within the framework ou scope of, as part of. **2** (chef) Com executive, manager; pl (personnel) Mil officers; Com management, managers.

cadr/er [kadre] vi to tally (avec with); – vt (image) Cin Phot to centre. ◆**—eur** nm cameraman.

caduc, -uque [kadyk] a (usage) obsolete; Bot deciduous; Jur null and void.

cafard, -arde [kafar, -ard] **1** nmf (espion) sneak. **2** nm (insecte) cockroach; **avoir le c.** to be in the dumps; **ça me donne le c.** it depresses me. ◆**cafardeux, -euse** a (personne) in the dumps; (qui donne le cafard) depressing.

café [kafe] nm coffee; (bar) café; **c. au lait, c. crème** white coffee, coffee with milk; **c. noir, c. nature** black coffee; **tasse de c.** cup of black coffee. ◆**caféine** nf caffeine. ◆**cafétéria** nf cafeteria. ◆**cafetier** nm café owner. ◆**cafetière** nf percolator, coffeepot.

cafouiller [kafuje] vi Fam to make a mess (of things). ◆**cafouillage** nm Fam mess, muddle, snafu.

cage [kaʒ] nf cage; (d'escalier) well; (d'ascenseur) shaft; **c. des buts** Fb goal (area).

cageot [kaʒo] nm crate.

cagibi [kaʒibi] nm (storage) room, cubbyhole.

cagneux, -euse [kaɲø, -øz] a knock-kneed.

cagnotte [kaɲɔt] nf (tirelire) kitty.

cagoule [kagul] nf (de bandit, pénitent) hood.

cahier [kaje] nm (carnet) (note)book; Scol exercise book.

cahin-caha [kaɛ̃kaa] adv **aller c.-caha** to jog along (with ups and downs).

cahot [kao] nm jolt, bump. ◆**cahot/er** vt to jolt, bump; – vi (véhicule) to jolt along. ◆**—ant** a, ◆**cahoteux, -euse** a bumpy.

caïd [kaid] nm Fam big shot, leader.

caille [kaj] nf (oiseau) quail.

cailler [kaje] vti, **— se c.** vpr (sang) to clot, congeal; (lait) to curdle; **faire c.** (lait) to curdle; **ça caille** Fam it's freezing cold. ◆**caillot** (blood) clot.

caillou, -x [kaju] nm stone; (galet) pebble. ◆**caillouté** a gravelled. ◆**caillouteux, -euse** a stony.

caisse [kɛs] nf (boîte) case, box; (cageot) crate; (guichet) cash desk, pay desk; (de supermarché) checkout; (fonds) fund; (bureau) (paying-in) office; Mus drum; Aut body; **c. (enregistreuse)** cash register, till; **c. d'épargne** savings bank; **de c.** (livre, recettes) cash-. ◆**caissier, -ière** nmf cashier; (de supermarché) checkout assistant.

caisson [kɛsɔ̃] nm (de plongeur) & Mil caisson.

cajoler [kaʒole] vt (câliner) to pamper, pet, cosset. ◆**cajolerie(s)** nf(pl) pampering.

cajou [kaʒu] nm (noix) cashew.

cake [kɛk] nm fruit cake.

calamité [kalamite] nf calamity.

calandre [kalɑ̃dr] nf Aut radiator grille.

calcaire [kalkɛr] a (terrain) chalky; (eau) hard; – nm Géol limestone.

calciné [kalsine] a charred, burnt to a cinder.

calcium [kalsjɔm] nm calcium.

calcul [kalkyl] nm **1** calculation; (estimation) calculation, reckoning; (discipline) arithmetic; (différentiel) calculus. **2** Méd stone. ◆**calcul/er** vt (compter) to calculate, reckon; (évaluer, combiner) to calculate. ◆**—é** a (risque etc) calculated. ◆**calculateur** nm calculator, computer. ◆**calculatrice** nf (ordinateur) calculator.

cale [kal] nf **1** (pour maintenir) wedge. **2** Nau hold; **c. sèche** dry dock.

calé [kale] a Fam (instruit) clever (**en qch** at sth); (difficile) tough.

caleçon [kalsɔ̃] nm underpants; **c. de bain** bathing trunks.

caleṁbour [kalɑ̃bur] nm pun.

calendrier [kalɑ̃drije] nm (mois et jours) calendar; (programme) timetable.

cale-pied [kalpje] nm (de bicyclette) toeclip.

calepin [kalpɛ̃] nm (pocket) notebook.

caler [kale] **1** vt (meuble etc) to wedge (up); (appuyer) to prop (up). **2** vt (moteur) to stall; − *vi* to stall; (*abandonner*) *Fam* give up.

calfeutrer [kalføtre] *vt* (*avec du bourrelet*) to draughtproof; **se c.** (*chez soi*) to shut oneself away, hole up.

calibre [kalibr] *nm* (*diamètre*) calibre; (*d'œuf*) grade; **de ce c.** (*bêtise etc*) of this degree. ◆**calibrer** *vt* (*œufs*) to grade.

calice [kalis] *nm* (*vase*) *Rel* chalice.

calicot [kaliko] *nm* (*tissu*) calico.

califourchon (à) [kalifurʃɔ̃] *adv* astride; **se mettre à c. sur** to straddle.

câlin [kalɛ̃] *a* endearing, cuddly. ◆**câliner** *vt* (*cajoler*) to make a fuss of; (*caresser*) to cuddle. ◆**câlineries** *nfpl* endearing ways.

calleux, -euse [kalø, -øz] *a* callous, horny.

calligraphie [kaligrafi] *nf* calligraphy.

calme [kalm] *a* calm; (*flegmatique*) calm, cool; (*journée etc*) quiet, calm; − *nm* calm(ness); **du c.!** keep quiet!; (*pas de panique*) keep calm!; **dans le c.** (*travailler, étudier*) in peace and quiet. ◆**calmer** *vt* (*douleur*) to soothe; (*inquiétude*) to calm; (*ardeur*) to damp(en); **c. qn** to calm s.o. (down); − **se c.** *vpr* to calm down. ◆**-ant** *nm* sedative; **sous calmants** under sedation.

calomnie [kalɔmni] *nf* slander; (*par écrit*) libel. ◆**calomnier** *vt* to slander; to libel. ◆**calomnieux, -euse** *a* slanderous, libellous.

calorie [kalɔri] *nf* calorie.

calorifère [kalɔrifɛr] *nm* stove.

calorifuge [kalɔrifyʒ] *a* (*heat-*)insulating. ◆**calorifuger** *vt* to lag.

calot [kalo] *nm* *Mil* forage cap.

calotte [kalɔt] *nf* *Rel* skull cap; (*gifle*) *Fam* slap; **c. glaciaire** icecap.

calque [kalk] *nm* (*dessin*) tracing; (*imitation*) (exact *ou* carbon) copy; (**papier-)c.** tracing paper. ◆**calquer** *vt* to trace; to copy; **c. sur** to model on.

calumet [kalymɛ] *nm* **c. de la paix** peace pipe.

calvaire [kalvɛr] *nm* *Rel* calvary; *Fig* agony.

calvitie [kalvisi] *nf* baldness.

camarade [kamarad] *nmf* friend, chum; *Pol* comrade; **c. de jeu** playmate; **c. d'atelier** workmate. ◆**camaraderie** *nf* friendship, companionship.

cambouis [kãbwi] *nm* grease, (engine) oil.

cambrer [kãbre] *vt* to arch; **c. les reins** *ou* **la buste** to throw out one's chest; − **se c.** *vpr* to throw back one's shoulders. ◆**cambrure** *nf* curve; (*de pied*) arch.

cambriol/er [kãbrijɔle] *vt* to burgle, *Am* burglarize. ◆**-age** *nm* burglary. ◆**-eur, -euse** *nmf* burglar.

came [kam] *nf* *Tech* cam; **arbre à cames** camshaft.

camée [kame] *nm* (*pierre*) cameo.

caméléon [kameleɔ̃] *nm* (*reptile*) chameleon.

camélia [kamelja] *nm* *Bot* camellia.

camelot [kamlo] *nm* street hawker. ◆**camelote** *nf* cheap goods, junk.

camembert [kamãber] *nm* Camembert (cheese).

camer (se) [səkame] *vpr* *Fam* to get high (on drugs).

caméra [kamera] *nf* (TV *ou* film) camera. ◆**caméraman** *nm.* (*pl* **-mans** *ou* **-men**) cameraman.

camion [kamjɔ̃] *nm* lorry, *Am* truck. ◆**c.-benne** *nm* (*pl* **camions-bennes**) dustcart, *Am* garbage truck. ◆**c.-citerne** *nm* (*pl* **camions-citernes**) tanker, *Am* tank truck. ◆**camionnage** *nm* (road) haulage, *Am* trucking. ◆**camionnette** *nf* van. ◆**camionneur** *nm* (*entrepreneur*) haulage contractor, *Am* trucker; (*conducteur*) lorry *ou Am* truck driver.

camisole [kamizɔl] *nf* **c. de force** straitjacket.

camomille [kamɔmij] *nf* *Bot* camomile; (*tisane*) camomile tea.

camoufl/er [kamufle] *vt* to camouflage. ◆**-age** *nm* camouflage.

camp [kã] *nm* camp; **feu de c.** campfire; **lit de c.** camp bed; **c. de concentration** concentration camp; **dans mon c.** (*jeu*) on my side; **ficher** *ou* **foutre le c.** *Arg* to clear off. ◆**camp/er** *vi* to camp; − *vt* (*personnage*) to portray (boldly); (*chapeau etc*) to plant boldly; − **se c.** *vpr* to plant oneself (boldly) (**devant** in front of). ◆**-ement** *nm* encampment, camp. ◆**-eur, -euse** *nmf* camper. ◆**camping** *nm* camping; (*terrain*) camp(ing) site. ◆**camping-car** *nm* camper.

campagne [kãpaɲ] *nf* **1** country(side); **à la c.** in the country. **2** (*électorale, militaire etc*) campaign. ◆**campagnard, -arde** *a* country-y; − *nm* countryman; *nf* countrywoman.

campanile [kãpanil] *nm* belltower.

camphre [kãfr] *nm* camphor.

campus [kãpys] *nm* *Univ* campus.

camus [kamy] *a* (*personne*) snub-nosed; **nez c.** snub nose.

Canada [kanada] *nm* Canada. ◆**canadien, -ienne** *a* & *nmf* Canadian; − *nf* fur-lined jacket.

canaille [kanaj] *nf* rogue, scoundrel; − *a* vulgar, cheap.

canal, -aux [kanal, -o] *nm* (*artificiel*) canal; (*bras de mer*) & *TV* channel; (*conduite*) & *Anat* duct; **par le c. de** via, through. ◆**canalisation** *nf* (*de gaz etc*) mains. ◆**canaliser** *vt* (*rivière etc*) to canalize; (*diriger*) *Fig* to channel.

canapé [kanape] *nm* **1** (*siège*) sofa, couch, settee. **2** (*tranche de pain*) canapé.

canard [kanar] *nm* **1** duck; (*mâle*) drake. **2** *Mus* false note. **3** (*journal*) *Péj* rag. ◆**canarder** *vt* (*faire feu sur*) to fire at *ou* on.

canari [kanari] *nm* canary.

cancans [kɑ̃kɑ̃] *nmpl* (malicious) gossip. ◆**cancaner** *vi* to gossip. ◆**cancanier, -ière** *a* gossipy.

cancer [kɑ̃sɛr] *nm* cancer; **le C.** (*signe*) Cancer. ◆**cancéreux, -euse** *a* cancerous; – *nmf* cancer patient. ◆**cancérigène** *a* carcinogenic. ◆**cancérologue** *nmf* cancer specialist.

cancre [kɑ̃kr] *nm* *Scol* *Péj* dunce.

cancrelat [kɑ̃krəla] *nm* cockroach.

candélabre [kɑ̃delɑbr] *nm* candelabra.

candeur [kɑ̃dœr] *nf* innocence, artlessness. ◆**candide** *a* artless, innocent.

candidat, -ate [kɑ̃dida, -at] *nmf* candidate; (*à un poste*) applicant, candidate; **être** *ou* **se porter c. à** to apply for. ◆**candidature** *nf* application; *Pol* candidacy; **poser sa c.** to apply (**à** for).

cane [kan] *nf* (female) duck. ◆**caneton** *nm* duckling.

canette [kanɛt] *nf* **1** (*de bière*) (small) bottle. **2** (*bobine*) spool.

canevas [kanva] *nm* (*toile*) canvas; (*ébauche*) framework, outline.

caniche [kaniʃ] *nm* poodle.

canicule [kanikyl] *nf* scorching heat; (*période*) dog days.

canif [kanif] *nm* penknife.

canine [kanin] **1** *af* (*espèce, race*) canine; **exposition c.** dog show. **2** *nf* (*dent*) canine.

caniveau, -x [kanivo] *nm* gutter (*in street*).

canne [kan] *nf* (*walking*) stick; (*à sucre, de bambou*) cane; (*de roseau*) reed; **c. à pêche** fishing rod.

cannelle [kanɛl] *nf* *Bot Culin* cinnamon.

cannelure [kanlyr] *nf* groove; *Archit* flute.

cannette [kanɛt] *nf* = **canette**.

◆**cannibale** [kanibal] *nmf* & *a* cannibal. ◆**cannibalisme** *nm* cannibalism.

canoë [kanɔe] *nm* canoe; *Sp* canoeing. ◆**canoéiste** *nmf* canoeist.

canon [kanɔ̃] *nm* **1** (big) gun; *Hist* cannon; (*de fusil etc*) barrel; **c. lisse** smooth bore; **chair à c.** cannon fodder. **2** (*règle*) canon.

◆**canoniser** *vt* to canonize. ◆**canonnade** *nf* gunfire. ◆**canonnier** *nm* gunner.

cañon [kanjɔ̃] *nm* canyon.

canot [kano] *nm* boat; **c. de sauvetage** lifeboat; **c. pneumatique** rubber dinghy. ◆**canot/er** *vi* to boat, go boating. ◆**—age** *nm* boating.

cantaloup [kɑ̃talu] *nm* (*melon*) cantaloup(e).

cantate [kɑ̃tat] *nf* *Mus* cantata.

cantatrice [kɑ̃tatris] *nf* opera singer.

cantine [kɑ̃tin] *nf* **1** (*réfectoire*) canteen; **manger à la c.** *Scol* to have school dinners. **2** (*coffre*) tin trunk.

cantique [kɑ̃tik] *nm* hymn.

canton [kɑ̃tɔ̃] *nm* (*en France*) district (*division of arrondissement*); (*en Suisse*) canton. ◆**cantonal, -aux** *a* divisional; cantonal.

cantonade (à la) [alakɑ̃tɔnad] *adv* (*parler etc*) to all and sundry, to everyone in general.

cantonn/er [kɑ̃tɔne] *vt* *Mil* to billet; (*confiner*) to confine; – *vi* *Mil* to be billeted; — **se c.** *vpr* to confine oneself (**dans** to). ◆**—ement** *nm* (*lieu*) billet, quarters.

cantonnier [kɑ̃tɔnje] *nm* road mender.

canular [kanylar] *nm* practical joke, hoax.

canyon [kanjɔ̃] *nm* canyon.

caoutchouc [kautʃu] *nm* rubber; (*élastique*) rubber band; *pl* (*chaussures*) galoshes; **en c.** (*balle etc*) rubber-; **c. mousse** foam. ◆**caoutchouter** *vt* to rubberize. ◆**caoutchouteux, -euse** *a* rubbery.

CAP [seape] *nm abrév* (*certificat d'aptitude professionnelle*) technical and vocational diploma.

cap [kap] *nm* *Géog* cape, headland; *Nau* course; **mettre le c. sur** to steer a course for; **franchir** *ou* **doubler le c. de** (*difficulté*) to get over the worst of; **franchir** *ou* **doubler le c. de la trentaine**/*etc* to turn thirty/*etc*.

capable [kapabl] *a* capable, able; **c. de faire** able to do, capable of doing. ◆**capacité** *nf* ability, capacity; (*contenance*) capacity.

cape [kap] *nf* cape; (*grande*) cloak.

CAPES [kapɛs] *nm abrév* (*certificat d'aptitude professionnelle à l'enseignement secondaire*) teaching diploma.

capillaire [kapilɛr] *a* (*huile, lotion*) hair-.

capitaine [kapitɛn] *nm* captain.

capital, -ale, -aux [kapital, -o] **1** *a* major, fundamental, capital; (*peine*) capital; (*péché*) deadly. **2** *a* (*lettre*) capital; – *nf* (*lettre, ville*) capital. **3** *nm* & *nmpl* *Fin* capital. ◆**capitaliser** *vt* (*accumuler*) to build up; – *vi* to save up. ◆**capitalisme** *nm*

capitalism. ◆**capitaliste** *a & nmf* capitalist.

capiteux, -euse [kapitø, -øz] *a* (vin, parfum) heady.

capitonn/er [kapitɔne] *vt* to pad, upholster. ◆**—age** *nm* (garniture) padding, upholstery.

capituler [kapityle] *vi* to surrender, capitulate. ◆**capitulation** *nf* surrender, capitulation.

caporal, -aux [kapɔral, -o] *nm* corporal.

capot [kapo] *nm Aut* bonnet, *Am* hood.

capote [kapɔt] *nf Aut* hood, *Am* (convertible) top; *Mil* greatcoat; **c. (anglaise)** (préservatif) *Fam* condom. ◆**capoter** *vi Aut Av* to overturn.

câpre [kɑpr] *nf Bot Culin* caper.

caprice [kapris] *nm* (passing) whim, caprice. ◆**capricieux, -euse** *a* capricious.

Capricorne [kaprikɔrn] *nm* **le C.** (signe) Capricorn.

capsule [kapsyl] *nf* (spatiale) & Méd etc capsule; (de bouteille, pistolet d'enfant) cap.

capter [kapte] *vt* (faveur etc) to win; (attention) to capture, win; (eau) to draw off; Rad to pick up.

captif, -ive [kaptif, -iv] *a & nmf* captive. ◆**captiver** *vt* to captivate, fascinate. ◆**captivité** *nf* captivity.

capture [kaptyr] *nf* capture; catch. ◆**capturer** *vt* (criminel, navire) to capture; (animal) to catch, capture.

capuche [kapyʃ] *nf* hood. ◆**capuchon** *nm* hood; (de moine) cowl; (pèlerine) hooded (rain)coat; (de stylo) cap, top.

capucine [kapysin] *nf* (plante) nasturtium.

caquet [kakɛ] *nm* (bavardage) cackle. ◆**caquet/er** *vi* (poule, personne) to cackle. ◆**—age** *nm* cackle.

car [kar] **1** *conj* because, for. **2** *nm* coach, bus, *Am* bus; **c. de police** police van.

carabine [karabin] *nf* rifle, carbine; **c. à air comprimé** airgun.

carabiné [karabine] *a Fam* violent; (punition, amende) very stiff.

caracoler [karakɔle] *vi* to prance, caper.

caractère [karaktɛr] *nm* **1** (lettre) Typ character; **en petits caractères** in small print; **caractères d'imprimerie** block capitals *ou* letters; **caractères gras** bold type *ou* characters. **2** (tempérament, nature) character, nature; (attribut) characteristic; **aucun c. de gravité** no serious element; **son c. inégal** his *ou* her uneven temper; **avoir bon c.** to be good-natured. ◆**caractériel, -ielle** *a* (trait, troubles) character-; – *a & nmf*

disturbed (child). ◆**caractériser** *vt* to characterize; **se c. par** to be characterized by. ◆**caractéristique** *a & nf* characteristic.

carafe [karaf] *nf* decanter, carafe.

carambol/er [karɑ̃bɔle] *vt Aut* to smash into. ◆**—age** *nm* pileup, multiple smashup.

caramel [karamɛl] *nm* caramel; (bonbon dur) toffee.

carapace [karapas] *nf* (de tortue etc) & Fig shell.

carat [kara] *nm* carat.

caravane [karavan] *nf* (dans le désert) caravan; *Aut* caravan, *Am* trailer; **c. publicitaire** publicity convoy. ◆**caravaning** *n*, ◆**caravanage** *n* caravanning.

carbone [karbɔn] *nm* carbon; **(papier) c.** carbon (paper). ◆**carboniser** *vt* to burn (to ashes), char; (substance) *Ch* to carbonize; **être mort carbonisé** to be burned to death.

carburant [karbyrɑ̃] *nm Aut* fuel. ◆**carburateur** *nm* carburettor, *Am* carburetor.

carcan [karkɑ̃] *nm Hist* iron collar; (contrainte) *Fig* yoke.

carcasse [karkas] *nf Anat* carcass; (d'immeuble etc) frame, shell.

cardiaque [kardjak] *a* (trouble etc) heart-; **crise c.** heart attack; **arrêt c.** cardiac arrest; – *nmf* heart patient.

cardinal, -aux [kardinal, -o] **1** *a* (nombre, point) cardinal. **2** *nm Rel* cardinal.

Carême [karɛm] *nm* Lent.

carence [karɑ̃s] *nf* inadequacy, incompetence; *Méd* deficiency.

carène [karɛn] *nf Nau* hull. ◆**caréné** *a Aut Av* streamlined.

caresse [karɛs] *nf* caress. ◆**caress/er** [karese] *vt* (animal, enfant etc) to stroke, pat, fondle; (femme, homme) to caress; (espoir) to cherish. ◆**—ant** *a* endearing, loving.

cargaison [kargɛzɔ̃] *nf* cargo, freight. ◆**cargo** *nm* freighter, cargo boat.

caricature [karikatyr] *nf* caricature. ◆**caricatural, -aux** *a* ludicrous; **portrait c.** portrait in caricature. ◆**caricaturer** *vt* to caricature.

carie [kari] *nf* **la c.** (dentaire) tooth decay; **une c.** a cavity. ◆**carié** *a* (dent) decayed, bad.

carillon [karijɔ̃] *nm* (cloches) chimes, peal; (horloge) chiming clock. ◆**carillonner** *vi* to chime, peal.

carlingue [karlɛ̃g] *nf* (fuselage) *Av* cabin.

carnage [karnaʒ] nm carnage.

carnassier, -ière [karnasje, -jɛr] a carnivorous; — nm carnivore.

carnaval [karnaval] nm (pl -als) carnival.

carné [karne] a (régime) meat-.

carnet [karnɛ] nm notebook; (de timbres, chèques, adresses etc) book; **c. de notes** school report; **c. de route** logbook; **c. de vol** Av logbook.

carnivore [karnivɔr] a carnivorous; — nm carnivore.

carotte [karɔt] nf carrot.

carotter [karɔte] vt Arg to wangle, cadge (à qn from s.o.).

carpe [karp] nf carp.

carpette [karpɛt] nf rug.

carquois [karkwa] nm (étui) quiver.

carré [kare] a square; (en affaires) Fig plain-dealing; — nm square; (de jardin) patch; Nau messroom; **c. de soie** (square) silk scarf.

carreau, -x [karo] nm (vitre) (window) pane; (pavé) tile; (sol) tiled floor; Cartes diamonds; **à carreaux** (nappe etc) check(ed); **se tenir à c.** to watch one's step; **rester sur le c.** to be left for dead; (candidat) to be left out in the cold. ◆**carrel/er** vt to tile. ◆**-age** nm (sol) tiled floor; (action) tiling.

carrefour [karfur] nm crossroads.

carrelet [karlɛ] nm (poisson) plaice, Am flounder.

carrément [karemɑ̃] adv (dire etc) straight out, bluntly; (complètement) downright, well and truly.

carrer (se) [səkare] vpr to settle down firmly.

carrière [karjɛr] nf 1 (terrain) quarry. 2 (métier) career.

carrosse [karɔs] nm Hist (horse-drawn) carriage. ◆**carrossable** a suitable for vehicles. ◆**carrosserie** nf Aut body(work).

carrousel [karuzɛl] nm (tourbillon) Fig whirl, merry-go-round.

carrure [karyr] nf breadth of shoulders, build; Fig calibre.

cartable [kartabl] nm Scol satchel.

carte [kart] nf card; (de lecteur) ticket; Géog map; Nau Mét chart; Culin menu; (de jeu) cards; **c. (postale)** (post)card; **c. à jouer** playing card; **c. de crédit** credit card; **c. des vins** wine list; **c. grise** Aut vehicle registration; **c. blanche** Fig free hand.

cartel [kartɛl] nm Écon Pol cartel.

carter [kartɛr] nm (de moteur) Aut crankcase; (de bicyclette) chain guard.

cartilage [kartilaʒ] nm cartilage.

carton [kartɔ̃] nm cardboard; (boîte) cardboard box, carton; **c. à dessin** portfolio; **en c.-pâte** (faux) Péj pasteboard; **faire un c. sur** Fam to take a potshot at. ◆**cartonn/er** vt (livre) to case; **livre cartonné** hardback. ◆**-age** nm (emballage) cardboard package.

cartouche [kartuʃ] nf cartridge; (de cigarettes) carton; Phot cassette. ◆**cartouchière** nf (ceinture) cartridge belt.

cas [kɑ] nm case; **en tout c.** in any case ou event; **en aucun c.** on no account; **en c. de besoin** if need(s) be; **en c. d'accident** in the event of an accident; **en c. d'urgence** in (case of) an emergency; **faire c. de/peu de c.** de to set great/little store by; **au c. où elle tomberait** if she should fall; **pour le c. où il pleuvrait** in case it rains.

casanier, -ière [kazanje, -jɛr] a & nmf home-loving (person); (pantouflard) Péj stay-at-home (person).

casaque [kazak] nf (de jockey) shirt, blouse.

cascade [kaskad] nf 1 waterfall; (série) Fig spate; **en c.** in succession. 2 Cin stunt. ◆**cascadeur, -euse** nmf Cin stunt man, stunt woman.

case [kaz] nf 1 pigeonhole; (de tiroir) compartment; (d'échiquier etc) square; (de formulaire) box. 2 (hutte) hut, cabin.

caser [kaze] vt Fam (ranger) to park, place; **c. qn** (dans un logement ou un travail) to find a place for s.o.; (marier) to marry s.o. off; — **se c.** vpr to settle down.

caserne [kazɛrn] nf Mil barracks; **c. de pompiers** fire station.

casier [kazje] nm pigeonhole, compartment; (meuble à tiroirs) filing cabinet; (fermant à clef, à consigne automatique) locker; **c. à bouteilles/à disques** bottle/record rack; **c. judiciaire** criminal record.

casino [kazino] nm casino.

casque [kask] nm helmet; (pour cheveux) (hair) dryer; **c. (à écouteurs)** headphones; **les Casques bleus** the UN peace-keeping force. ◆**casqué** a helmeted, wearing a helmet.

casquer [kaske] vi Fam to pay up, cough up.

casquette [kaskɛt] nf (coiffure) cap.

cassation [kasasjɔ̃] nf Cour de c. supreme court of appeal.

casse¹ [kas] nf 1 (action) breakage; (objets) breakages; (grabuge) Fam trouble; **mettre à la c.** to scrap; **vendre à la c.** to sell for scrap. **2** *Typ* case; **bas/haut de c.** lower/upper case.

casse² [kɑs] *nm* (*cambriolage*) *Arg* break-in.

casse-cou [kasku] *nmf inv* (*personne*) *Fam* daredevil. ◆**c.-croûte** *nm inv Fam* snack. ◆**c.-gueule** *nm inv Fam* death trap; **- a c. perilous. ◆c.-noisettes** *nm inv,* ◆**c.-noix** *nm inv* nut-cracker(s). ◆**c.-pieds** *nmf inv* (*personne*) *Fam* pain in the neck. ◆**c.-tête** *nm inv* **1** (*massue*) club. **2** (*problème*) headache; (*jeu*) puzzle, brain teaser.

cass/er [kɑse] *vt* to break; (*noix*) to crack; (*annuler*) *Jur* to annul; (*dégrader*) *Mil* to cashier; **- vi, - se c.** *vpr* to break; **il me casse la tête** *Fam* he's giving me a headache; **elle me casse les pieds** *Fam* she's getting on my nerves; **se c. la tête** *Fam* to rack one's brains; **c. la figure à qn** *Fam* to smash s.o.'s face in; **se c. la figure** (*tomber*) *Fam* to come a cropper, *Am* take a spill; **ça ne casse rien** *Fam* it's nothing special; **ça vaut 50F à tout c.** *Fam* it's worth 50F at the very most; **il ne s'est pas cassé** *Iron Fam* he didn't bother himself *ou* exhaust himself. ◆**-ant** *a* (*fragile*) brittle; (*brusque*) curt, imperious; (*fatigant*) *Fam* exhausting. ◆**-eur** *nm Aut* breaker, scrap merchant; (*manifestant*) demonstrator who damages property.

casserole [kɑsrɔl] *nf* (sauce)pan.

cassette [kaset] *nf* (*pour magnétophone ou magnétoscope*) cassette; **sur c.** (*film*) on video; **faire une c. de** (*film*) to make a video of.

cassis 1 [kasis] *nm Bot* blackcurrant; (*boisson*) blackcurrant liqueur. **2** [kasi] *nm Aut* dip (across road).

cassoulet [kasule] *nm* stew (of meat and beans).

cassure [kɑsyr] *nf* (*fissure, rupture*) break; *Géol* fault.

castagnettes [kastaɲet] *nfpl* castanets.

caste [kast] *nf* caste; **esprit de c.** class consciousness.

castor [kastɔr] *nm* beaver.

castrer [kɑstre] *vt* to castrate. ◆**castration** *nf* castration.

cataclysme [kataklism] *nm* cataclysm.

catacombes [katakɔ̃b] *nfpl* catacombs.

catalogue [katalɔg] *nm* catalogue. ◆**cataloguer** *vt* (*livres etc*) to catalogue; **c. qn** *Péj* to categorize s.o.

catalyseur [katalizœr] *nm Ch* & *Fig* catalyst.

cataphote® [katafɔt] *nm Aut* reflector.

cataplasme [kataplasm] *nm Méd* poultice.

catapulte [katapylt] *nf Hist Av* catapult. ◆**catapulter** *vt* to catapult.

cataracte [katarakt] *nf* **1** *Méd* cataract. **2** (*cascade*) falls, cataract.

catastrophe [katastrɔf] *nf* disaster, catastrophe; **atterrir en c.** to make an emergency landing. ◆**catastrophique** *a* disastrous, catastrophic.

catch [katʃ] *nm* (all-in) wrestling. ◆**catcheur, -euse** *nmf* wrestler.

catéchisme [kateʃism] *nm Rel* catechism.

catégorie [kategɔri] *nf* category. ◆**catégorique** *a* categorical.

cathédrale [katedral] *nf* cathedral.

catholicisme [katɔlisism] *nm* Catholicism. ◆**catholique** *a* & *nmf* Catholic; **pas (très) c.** (*affaire, personne*) *Fig* shady, doubtful.

catimini (en) [ɑ̃katimini] *adv* on the sly.

cauchemar [koʃmar] *nm* nightmare.

cause [koz] *nf* cause; *Jur* case; **à c. de** because of, on account of; **et pour c.!** for a very good reason!; **pour c. de** on account of; **en connaissance de c.** in full knowledge of the facts; **mettre en c.** (*la bonne foi de qn etc*) to (call into) question; (*personne*) to implicate; **en c.** involved, in question.

caus/er 1 [koze] *vt* (*provoquer*) to cause. **2** *vi* (*bavarder*) to chat (**de** about); (*discourir*) to talk; (*jaser*) to blab. ◆**-ant** *a Fam* chatty, talkative. ◆**causerie** *nf* talk. ◆**causette** *nf* **faire la c.** *Fam* to have a little chat.

caustique [kostik] *a* (*substance, esprit*) caustic.

cauteleux, -euse [kotlø, -øz] *a* wily, sly.

cautériser [koterize] *vt Méd* to cauterize.

caution [kosjɔ̃] *nf* surety; (*pour libérer qn*) *Jur* bail; **sous c.** on bail; **sujet à c.** (*nouvelle etc*) very doubtful. ◆**cautionner** *vt* (*approuver*) to sanction. ◆**-ement** *nm* (*garantie*) surety.

cavalcade [kavalkad] *nf Fam* stampede; (*défilé*) cavalcade. ◆**cavale** *nf* **en c.** *Arg* on the run. ◆**cavaler** *vi Fam* to run, rush.

cavalerie [kavalri] *nf Mil* cavalry; (*de cirque*) horses. ◆**cavalier, -ière** *nmf* rider; **- nm** *Mil* trooper, cavalryman; *Échecs* knight; **- a** *fille cavalière* bridle path. **2** *nmf* (*pour danser*) partner, escort. **3** *a* (*insolent*) offhand.

cave [kav] **1** *nf* cellar, vault. **2** *a* sunken, hollow. ◆**caveau, -x** *nm* (*sépulture*) (burial) vault.

caverne [kavern] *nf* cave, cavern; **homme**

des **cavernes** caveman. ◆**caverneux, -euse** a (voix, rire) hollow, deep-sounding.

caviar [kavjar] nm caviar(e).

cavité [kavite] nf cavity.

CCP [sesepe] nm abrév (Compte chèque postal) PO Giro account, Am Post Office checking account.

ce[1] [s(ə)] (c' before e and é) pron dém 1 it, that; **c'est toi/bon/demain**/etc it's you/good/tomorrow/etc; **c'est mon médecin** he's my doctor; **ce sont eux qui ...** they are the ones who ...; **c'est à elle de jouer** it's her turn to play; **est-ce que tu viens?** are you coming?; **sur ce** at this point, thereupon. **2 ce que, ce qui** what; **je sais ce qui est bon**/**ce que tu veux** I know what is good/what you want; **ce que c'est beau!** how beautiful it is!

ce[2], **cette**, pl **ces** [s(ə), sɛt, se] (ce becomes **cet** before a vowel or mute h) a dém this, that; (+ -ci) this, pl these; (+ -là) that, pl those; **cet homme** this ou that man; **cet homme-ci** this man; **cet homme-là** that man.

ceci [səsi] pron dém this; **écoutez bien c.** listen to this.

cécité [sesite] nf blindness.

céder [sede] vt to give up (à to); Jur to transfer; **c. le pas à** to give way ou precedence to; – vi (personne) to give way, give in, yield (à to); (branche, chaise etc) to give way.

cédille [sedij] nf Gram cedilla.

cèdre [sɛdr] nm (arbre, bois) cedar.

CEE [seøø] nf abrév (Communauté économique européenne) EEC.

ceindre [sɛ̃dr] vt (épée) Lit to gird on.

ceinture [sɛ̃tyr] nf belt; (de robe de chambre) cord; (taille) Anat waist; (de remparts) Hist girdle; **petite**/**grande c.** Rail inner/outer circle; **c. de sécurité** Aut Av seatbelt; **c. de sauvetage** lifebelt. ◆**ceinturer** vt to seize round the waist; Rugby to tackle; (ville) to girdle, surround.

cela [s(ə)la] pron dém (pour désigner) that; (sujet indéfini) it, that; **c. m'attriste que ...** it saddens me that ...; **quand/comment**/etc **c.?** when?/how?/etc; **c'est c.** that is so.

célèbre [selɛbr] a famous. ◆**célébrité** nf fame; (personne) celebrity.

célébrer [selebre] vt to celebrate. ◆**célébration** nf celebration (de of).

céleri [sɛlri] nm (en branches) celery.

céleste [selɛst] a celestial, heavenly.

célibat [seliba] nm celibacy. ◆**célibataire** a (non marié) single, unmarried; (chaste)

celibate; – nm bachelor; – nf unmarried woman, spinster.

celle voir celui.

cellier [selje] nm storeroom (for wine etc).

cellophane® [selɔfan] nf cellophane®.

cellule [selyl] nf cell. ◆**cellulaire** a (tissu etc) Biol cell-; **voiture c.** prison van.

celluloïd [selylɔid] nm celluloid.

cellulose [selyloz] nf cellulose.

celtique ou **celte** [sɛltik, sɛlt] a Celtic.

celui, celle, pl **ceux, celles** [səlɥi, sɛl, sø, sɛl] pron dém 1 the one, pl those, the ones; **c. de Jean** John's (one); **ceux de Jean** John's (ones), those of John. **2** (+ -ci) this one, pl these (ones); (dont on vient de parler) the latter; (+ -là) that one, pl those (ones); the former; **ceux-ci sont gros** these (ones) are big.

cendre [sɑ̃dr] nf ash. ◆**cendré** a ash(-coloured), ashen. ◆**cendrée** nf Sp cinder track.

Cendrillon [sɑ̃drijɔ̃] nm Cinderella.

censé [sɑ̃se] a supposed; **il n'est pas c. le savoir** he's not supposed to know.

censeur [sɑ̃sœr] nm censor; Scol assistant headmaster, vice-principal. ◆**censure** nf **la c.** (examen) censorship; (comité, service) the censor; **motion de c.** Pol censure motion. ◆**censurer** vt (film etc) to censor; (critiquer) & Pol to censure.

cent [sɑ̃] ([sɑ̃t] pl [sɑ̃z] before vowel and mute h except un and onze) a & nm hundred; **c. pages** a ou one hundred pages; **deux cents pages** two hundred pages; **deux c. trois pages** two hundred and three pages; **cinq pour c.** five per cent. ◆**centaine** nf **une c.** a hundred (or so); **des centaines de** hundreds of. ◆**centenaire** a & nmf centenarian; – nm (anniversaire) centenary. ◆**centième** a & nmf hundredth; **un c.** a hundredth. ◆**centigrade** a centigrade. ◆**centime** nm centime. ◆**centimètre** nm centimetre; (ruban) tape measure.

central, -aux [sɑ̃tral, -o] **1** a central; **pouvoir c.** (power of) central government. **2** nm **c.** (téléphonique) (telephone) exchange. ◆**centrale** nf (usine) power station. ◆**centraliser** vto centralize. ◆**centre** nm centre; **c. commercial** shopping centre. ◆**c.-ville** nm inv city ou town centre. ◆**centrer** vt to centre. ◆**centrifuge** a centrifugal. ◆**centrifugeuse** nf liquidizer, juice extractor.

centuple [sɑ̃typl] nm hundredfold; **au c.** a hundredfold. ◆**centupler** vti to increase a hundredfold.

cep [sep] nm vine stock. ◆**cépage** nm vine (plant).

cependant [səpɑ̃dɑ̃] conj however, yet.

céramique [seramik] nf (art) ceramics; (matière) ceramic; **de** ou **en c.** ceramic.

cerceau, -x [serso] nm hoop.

cercle [serkl] nm (forme, groupe, étendue) circle; **c. vicieux** vicious circle.

cercueil [serkœj] nm coffin.

céréale [sereal] nf cereal.

cérébral, -aux [serebral, -o] a cerebral.

cérémonie [seremoni] nf ceremony; **de c.** (tenue etc) ceremonial; **sans c.** (inviter, manger) informally; **faire des cérémonies** Fam to make a lot of fuss. ◆**cérémonial,** pl **-als** nm ceremonial. ◆**cérémonieux, -euse** a ceremonious.

cerf [ser] nm deer; (mâle) stag. ◆**cerf-volant** nm (pl **cerfs-volants**) (jouet) kite.

cerise [s(ə)riz] nf cherry. ◆**cerisier** nm cherry tree.

cerne [sern] nm (cercle, marque) ring. ◆**cerner** vt to surround; (problème) to define; **les yeux cernés** with rings under one's eyes.

certain [sertɛ̃] **1** a (sûr) certain, sure; **il est** ou **c'est c. que tu réussiras** you're certain ou sure to succeed; **je suis c. de réussir** I'm certain ou sure I'll succeed; **être c. de qch** to be certain ou sure of sth. **2** a (imprécis, difficile à fixer) certain; pl certain, some; **un c. temps** a certain (amount of) time; — pron pl some (people), certain people; (choses) some. ◆**certainement** adv certainly. ◆**certes** adv indeed.

certificat [sertifika] nm certificate. ◆**certifi/er** vt to certify; **je vous certifie que** I assure you that. ◆**-é** a (professeur) qualified.

certitude [sertityd] nf certainty; **avoir la c. que** to be certain that.

cerveau, -x [servo] nm (organe) brain; (intelligence) mind, brain(s); **rhume de c.** head cold; **fuite des cerveaux** brain drain.

cervelas [servəla] nm saveloy.

cervelle [servɛl] nf (substance) brain; Culin brains; **tête sans c.** scatterbrain.

ces voir **ce**².

CES [seəs] nm abrév (collège d'enseignement secondaire) comprehensive school, Am high school.

césarienne [sezarjɛn] nf Méd Caesarean (section).

cessation [sesasjɔ̃] nf (arrêt, fin) suspension.

cesse [ses] nf **sans c.** incessantly; **elle n'a**

(pas) eu de c. que je fasse ... she had no rest until I did ....

cesser [sese] vti to stop; **faire c.** to put a stop ou halt to; **il ne cesse (pas) de parler** he doesn't stop talking. ◆**cessez-le-feu** nm inv ceasefire.

cession [sesjɔ̃] nf Jur transfer.

c'est-à-dire [setadir] conj that is (to say), in other words.

cet, cette voir **ce**².

ceux voir **celui**.

chacal, -als [ʃakal] nm jackal.

chacun, -une [ʃakœ̃, -yn] pron each (one), every one; (tout le monde) everyone.

chagrin [ʃagrɛ̃] **1** nm sorrow, grief; **avoir du c.** to be very upset. **2** a Lit doleful. ◆**chagriner** vt to upset, distress.

chahut [ʃay] nm racket, noisy disturbance. ◆**chahut/er** vi to create a racket ou a noisy disturbance; — vt (professeur) to be rowdy with, play up. ◆**-eur, -euse** nmf rowdy.

chai [ʃe] nm wine and spirits storehouse.

chaîne [ʃen] nf chain; TV channel, network; Géog chain, range; Nau cable; Tex warp; pl (liens) Fig shackles, chains; **c. de montage** assembly line; **travail à la c.** production-line work; **c. haute fidélité, hi-fi** hi-fi system; **c. de magasins** chain of shops ou Am stores; **collision en c.** Aut multiple collision; **réaction en c.** chain reaction. ◆**chaînette** nf (small) chain. ◆**chaînon** nm (anneau, lien) link.

chair [ʃer] nf flesh; (couleur) **c.** flesh-coloured; **en c. et en os** in the flesh; **la c. de poule** goose pimples, gooseflesh; **bien en c.** plump; **c. à saucisses** sausage meat.

chaire [ʃer] nf Univ chair; Rel pulpit.

chaise [ʃez] nf chair, seat; **c. longue** (siège pliant) deckchair; **c. d'enfant, c. haute** high-chair.

chaland [ʃalɑ̃] nm barge, lighter.

châle [ʃal] nm shawl.

chalet [ʃale] nm chalet.

chaleur [ʃalœr] nf heat; (douce) warmth; (d'un accueil, d'une voix etc) warmth; (des convictions) ardour; (d'une discussion) heat. ◆**chaleureux, -euse** a warm.

challenge [ʃalɑ̃ʒ] nm Sp contest.

chaloupe [ʃalup] nf launch, long boat.

chalumeau, -x [ʃalymo] nm blowlamp, Am blowtorch; Mus pipe.

chalut [ʃaly] nm trawl net, drag net. ◆**chalutier** nm (bateau) trawler.

chamailler (se) [səʃamɑje] vpr to squabble, bicker. ◆**chamailleries** nfpl squabbling, bickering.

chamarré [ʃamare] *a* (*robe etc*) richly coloured; **c. de** (*décorations etc*) *Péj* bedecked with.

chambard [ʃãbar] *nm Fam* (*tapage*) rumpus, row. **◆chambarder** *vt Fam* to turn upside down; **il a tout chambardé dans** he's turned everything upside down.

chambouler [ʃãbule] *vt Fam* to make topsy-turvy, turn upside down.

chambre [ʃãbr] *nf* (*bed*)*room*; *Pol Jur Tech Anat* chamber; **c. à coucher** bedroom; (*mobilier*) bedroom suite; **c. à air** (*de pneu*) inner tube; **C. des Communes** *Pol* House of Commons; **c. d'ami** guest *ou* spare room; **c. forte** strongroom; **c. noire** *Phot* darkroom; **garder la c.** to stay indoors. **◆chambrée** *nf Mil* barrack room. **◆chambrer** *vt* (*vin*) to bring to room temperature.

chameau, -x [ʃamo] *nm* camel.

chamois [ʃamwa] **1** *nm* (*animal*) chamois; **peau de c.** chamois (leather), shammy. **2** *a inv* buff(-coloured).

champ [ʃã] *nm* field; (*domaine*) *Fig* scope, range; **c. de bataille** battlefield; **c. de courses** racecourse, racetrack; **c. de foire** fairground; **c. de tir** (*terrain*) rifle range; **laisser le c. libre à qn** to leave the field open for s.o. **◆champêtre** *a* rustic, rural.

champagne [ʃãpaɲ] *nm* champagne; **c. brut** extra-dry champagne.

champignon [ʃãpiɲ5] *nm* **1** *Bot* mushroom; **c. vénéneux** toadstool, poisonous mushroom; **c. atomique** mushroom cloud. **2** *Aut Fam* accelerator pedal.

champion [ʃãpj5] *nm* champion. **◆championnat** *nm* championship.

chance [ʃãs] *nf* luck; (*probabilité de réussir, occasion*) chance; **avoir de la c.** to be lucky; **tenter** *ou* **courir sa c.** to try one's luck; **c'est une c. que ...** it's a stroke of luck that ...; **mes chances de succès** my chances of success. **◆chanceux, -euse** *a* lucky.

chancel/er [ʃãsle] *vi* to stagger, totter; (*courage*) *Fig* to falter. **◆—ant** *a* (*pas, santé*) faltering, shaky.

chancelier [ʃãsəlje] *nm* chancellor. **◆chancellerie** *nf* chancellery.

chancre [ʃãkr] *nm Méd & Fig* canker.

chandail [ʃãdaj] *nm* (thick) sweater, jersey.

chandelier [ʃãdəlje] *nm* candlestick.

chandelle [ʃãdɛl] *nf* candle; **voir trente-six chandelles** *Fig* to see stars; **en c.** *Av Sp* straight into the air.

change [ʃãʒ] *nm Fin* exchange; **le contrôle des changes** exchange control; **donner le c. à qn** to deceive s.o. **◆chang/er** *vt* (*modifier, remplacer, échanger*) to change; **c. qn**

en to change s.o. into; **ça la changera de ne pas travailler** it'll be a change for her not to be working; **– vi** to change; **c. de voiture/d'adresse/**etc to change one's car/address/etc; **c. de train/de place** to change trains/places; **c. de vitesse/de cap** to change gear/course; **c. de sujet** to change the subject; **– se c.** *vpr* to change (one's clothes). **◆—eant** *a* (*temps*) changeable; (*humeur*) fickle; (*couleurs*) changing. **◆—ement** *nm* change; **aimer le c.** to like change. **◆—eur** *nm* moneychanger; **c. de monnaie** change machine.

chanoine [ʃanwan] *nm* (*personne*) *Rel* canon.

chanson [ʃãs5] *nf* song. **◆chant** *nm* singing; (*chanson*) song; (*hymne*) hymn; **c. de Noël** Christmas carol. **◆chant/er** *vi* to sing; (*psalmodier*) to chant; (*coq*) to crow; **si ça te chante** *Fam* if you feel like it; **faire c. qn** to blackmail s.o.; **– vt** to sing; (*glorifier*) to sing of; (*dire*) *Fam* to say. **◆—ant** *a* (*air, voix*) melodious. **◆—age** *nm* blackmail. **◆—eur, -euse** *nm* singer.

chantier [ʃãtje] *nm* (*building*) site; (*entrepôt*) builder's yard; **c. naval** shipyard; **mettre un travail en c.** to get a task under way.

chantonner [ʃãtɔne] *vti* to hum.

chantre [ʃãtr] *nm Rel* cantor.

chanvre [ʃãvr] *nm* hemp; **c. indien** (*plante*) cannabis.

chaos [kao] *nm* chaos. **◆chaotique** *a* chaotic.

chaparder [ʃaparde] *vt Fam* to filch, pinch (à from).

chapeau, -x [ʃapo] *nm* hat; (*de champignon, roue*) cap; **c.!** well done!; **donner un coup de c.** (*pour saluer etc*) to raise one's hat; **c. mou** trilby, *Am* fedora. **◆chapelier** *nm* hatter.

chapelet [ʃaplɛ] *nm* rosary; **dire son c.** to tell one's beads; **un c. de** (*saucisses, injures etc*) a string of.

chapelle [ʃapɛl] *nf* chapel; **c. ardente** chapel of rest.

chaperon [ʃapr5] *nm* chaperon(e). **◆chaperonner** *vt* to chaperon(e).

chapiteau, -x [ʃapito] *nm* (*de cirque*) big top; (*pour expositions etc*) marquee, tent; (*de colonne*) *Archit* capital.

chapitre [ʃapitr] *nm* chapter; **sur le c. de** on the subject of. **◆chapitrer** *vt* to scold, lecture.

chaque [ʃak] *a* each, every.

char [ʃar] *nm Hist* chariot; (*de carnaval*)

float; *Can Fam* car; **c. à bœufs** oxcart; **c. (d'assaut)** *Mil* tank.

charabia [ʃarabja] *nm Fam* gibberish.

charade [ʃarad] *nf (énigme)* riddle; *(mimée)* charade.

charbon [ʃarbɔ̃] *nm (poids)* coal; *(fusain)* charcoal; **c. de bois** charcoal; **sur des charbons ardents** like a cat on hot bricks. ◆**charbonnages** *nmpl* coalmines, collieries. ◆**charbonnier, -ière** *a* coal-; *— nm* coal merchant.

charcuter [ʃarkyte] *vt (opérer) Fam Péj* to cut up (badly).

charcuterie [ʃarkytri] *nf* pork butcher's shop; *(aliment)* cooked (pork) meats. ◆**charcutier, -ière** *nmf* pork butcher.

chardon [ʃardɔ̃] *nm Bot* thistle.

chardonneret [ʃardɔnrɛ] *nm (oiseau)* goldfinch.

charge [ʃarʒ] *nf (poids)* load; *(fardeau)* burden; *Jur Él Mil* charge; *(fonction)* office; *pl Fin* financial obligations; *(dépenses)* expenses; *(de locataire)* (maintenance) charges; **charges sociales** national insurance contributions, *Am* Social Security contributions; **à c.** *(enfant, parent)* dependent; **être à c. à qn** to be a burden to s.o.; **à la c. de qn** *(personne)* dependent on s.o.; *(frais)* payable by s.o.; **prendre en c.** to take charge of, take responsibility for.

charg/er [ʃarʒe] *vt* to load; *Él Mil* to charge; *(passager) Fam* to pick up; **se c. de** *(enfant, tâche etc)* to take charge of; **c. qn de** *(impôts etc)* to burden s.o. with; *(paquets etc)* to load s.o. with; *(tâche etc)* to entrust s.o. with; **c. qn de faire** to instruct s.o. to do. ◆**-é, -ée** *a (personne, véhicule, arme etc)* loaded; *(journée etc)* heavy, busy; *(langue)* coated; **c. de** *(arbre, navire etc)* laden with; *— nm* **c. de cours** *Univ* (temporary) lecturer. ◆**-ement** *nm (action)* loading; *(objet)* load. ◆**-eur** *nm (de piles)* charger.

chariot [ʃarjo] *nm (à bagages etc)* trolley, *Am* cart; *(de ferme)* waggon; *(de machine à écrire)* carriage.

charité [ʃarite] *nf (vertu, secours)* charity; *(acte)* act of charity; **faire la c.** to give to charity; **faire la c. à** *(mendiant)* to give to. ◆**charitable** *a* charitable.

charivari [ʃarivari] *nm Fam* hubbub, hullabaloo.

charlatan [ʃarlatɑ̃] *nm* charlatan, quack.

charme [ʃarm] *nm* **1** charm; *(magie)* spell. **2** *(arbre)* hornbeam. ◆**charm/er** *vt* to charm; **je suis charmé de vous voir** I'm delighted to see you. ◆**-ant** *a* charming.

◆**-eur, -euse** *nmf* charmer; *— a* engaging.

charnel, -elle [ʃarnɛl] *a* carnal.

charnier [ʃarnje] *nm* mass grave.

charnière [ʃarnjɛr] *nf* hinge; *Fig* meeting point (**de** between).

charnu [ʃarny] *a* fleshy.

charogne [ʃarɔɲ] *nf* carrion.

charpente [ʃarpɑ̃t] *nf* frame(work); *(de personne)* build. ◆**charpenté** **à bien c.** solidly built. ◆**charpenterie** *nf* carpentry. ◆**charpentier** *nm* carpenter.

charpie [ʃarpi] *nf* **mettre en c.** *(déchirer)* & *Fig* to tear to shreds.

charrette [ʃarɛt] *nf* cart. ◆**charretier** *nm* carter. ◆**charrier 1** *vt (transporter)* to cart; *(rivière)* to carry along, wash down *(sand etc)*. **2** *vti (taquiner) Fam* to tease.

charrue [ʃary] *nf* plough, *Am* plow.

charte [ʃart] *nf Pol* charter.

charter [ʃartɛr] *nm Av* charter (flight).

chas [ʃa] *nm* eye *(of a needle)*.

chasse [ʃas] *nf* **1** hunting, hunt; *(poursuite)* chase; *Av* fighter forces; **de c.** *(pilote, avion)* fighter-; **c. sous-marine** underwater (harpoon) fishing; **c. à courre** hunting; **tableau de c.** *(animaux abattus)* bag; **faire la c. à** to hunt down, hunt for; **donner la c. à** to give chase to; **c. à l'homme** manhunt. **2** **c. d'eau** toilet flush; **tirer la c.** to flush the toilet.

châsse [ʃas] *nf* shrine.

chassé-croisé [ʃasekwaze] *nm (pl* **chassés-croisés)** *Fig* confused coming(s) and going(s).

chass/er [ʃase] *vt (animal)* to hunt; *(papillon)* to chase; *(faire partir)* to drive out ou off; *(employé)* to dismiss; *(mouche)* to brush away; *(odeur)* to get rid of; *— vi* to hunt; *Aut* to skid. ◆**-eur, -euse** *nmf* hunter; *— nm (domestique)* pageboy, bellboy; *Av* fighter; **c. à pied** infantryman. ◆**chasse-neige** *nm inv* snowplough, *Am* snowplow.

châssis [ʃasi] *nm* frame; *Aut* chassis.

chaste [ʃast] *a* chaste, pure. ◆**chasteté** *nf* chastity.

chat, chatte [ʃa, ʃat] *nmf* cat; **un c. dans la gorge** a frog in one's throat; **d'autres chats à fouetter** other fish to fry; **pas un c.** not a soul; **ma (petite) chatte** my darling; **c. perché** *(jeu)* tig.

châtaigne [ʃatɛɲ] *nf* chestnut. ◆**châtaignier** *nm* chestnut tree. ◆**châtain** *a m (inv)* (chestnut) brown.

château, -x [ʃato] *nm (forteresse)* castle; *(palais)* palace, stately home; **c. fort** fortified castle; **châteaux en Espagne** *Fig* castles in the air; **c. d'eau** water tower; **c. de cartes** house of cards. ◆**châtelain, -aine** *nmf* lord of the manor, lady of the manor.

châtier [ʃɑtje] *vt Litt* to chastise, castigate; *(style)* to refine.

châtiment [ʃɑtimɑ̃] *nm* punishment.

chaton [ʃatɔ̃] *nm* 1 *(chat)* kitten. 2 *(de bague)* setting, mounting. 3 *Bot* catkin.

chatouiller [ʃatuje] *vt (pour faire rire)* to tickle; *(exciter, plaire à) Fig* to titillate. ◆**—ement** *nm* tickle; *(action)* tickling. ◆**chatouilleux, -euse** *a* ticklish; *(irritable)* touchy.

chatoyer [ʃatwaje] *vi* to glitter, sparkle.

châtrer [ʃɑtre] *vt* to castrate.

chatte [ʃat] *voir* **chat**.

chatteries [ʃatri] *nfpl* cuddles; *(friandises)* delicacies.

chatterton [ʃatertɔn] *nm* adhesive insulating tape.

chaud [ʃo] *a* hot; *(doux)* warm; *(fervent) Fig* warm; **pleurer à chaudes larmes** to cry bitterly; **—** *nm* heat; warmth; **avoir c.** to be hot; **to be warm**; **il fait c.** it's hot; it's warm; **être au c.** to be in the warm(th); **ça ne me fait ni c. ni froid** it leaves me indifferent. ◆**chaudement** *adv* warmly; *(avec passion)* hotly.

chaudière [ʃodjɛr] *nf* boiler.

chaudron [ʃodrɔ̃] *nm* cauldron.

chauffard [ʃofar] *nm* road hog, reckless driver.

chauff/er [ʃofe] *vt* to heat up, warm up; *(métal etc) Tech* to heat; **—** *vi* to heat up, warm up; *Aut* to overheat; **ça va c.** *Fam* things are going to hot up; **— se c.** *vpr* to warm oneself up. ◆**—ant** *a (couverture)* electric; *(plaque)* hot-; *(surface)* heating. ◆**—age** *nm* heating. ◆**—eur** *nm* 1 *(de chaudière)* stoker. 2 *Aut* driver; *(employé, domestique)* chauffeur. ◆**chauffe-bain** *nm*, ◆**chauffe-eau** *nm inv* water heater. ◆**chauffe-plats** *nm inv* hotplate.

chaume [ʃom] *nm (tiges coupées)* stubble, straw; *(pour toiture)* thatch; **toit de c.** thatched roof. ◆**chaumière** *nf* thatched cottage.

chaussée [ʃose] *nf* road(way).

chausser [ʃose] *vt (chaussures)* to put on; *(fournir)* to supply in footwear; **c. qn** to put shoes on (to) s.o.; **c. du 40** to take a size 40 shoe; **ce soulier te chausse bien** this shoe fits (you) well; **— se c.** *vpr* to put on one's shoes. ◆**chausse-pied** *nm* shoehorn. ◆**chausson** *nm* slipper; *(de danse)* shoe; **c. (aux pommes)** apple turnover. ◆**chaus-**

sure *nf* shoe; *pl* shoes, footwear; **chaussures à semelles compensées** platform shoes.

chaussette [ʃosɛt] *nf* sock.

chauve [ʃov] *a* & *nmf* bald (person).

chauve-souris [ʃovsuri] *nf (pl* **chauves-souris)** *(animal)* bat.

chauvin, -ine [ʃovɛ̃, -in] *a* & *nmf* chauvinist.

chaux [ʃo] *nf* lime; **blanc de c.** whitewash.

chavirer [ʃavire] *vti Nau* to capsize.

chef [ʃɛf] *nm* 1 **de son propre c.** on one's own authority. 2 leader, head; *(de tribu)* chief; *Culin* chef; **en c.** *(commandant, rédacteur)* in chief; **c'est un c.!** *(personne remarquable)* he's an ace!; **c. d'atelier** *(shop)* foreman; **c. de bande** ringleader, gang leader; **c. d'entreprise** company head; **c. d'équipe** foreman; **c. d'État** head of state; **c. d'état-major** chief of staff; **c. de famille** head of the family; **c. de file** leader; **c. de gare** stationmaster; **c. d'orchestre** conductor. ◆**chef-lieu** *nm (pl* **chefs-lieux)** chief town *(of a département)*.

chef-d'œuvre [ʃɛdœvr] *nm (pl* **chefs-d'œuvre)** masterpiece.

chemin [ʃ(ə)mɛ̃] *nm* 1 road, path; *(trajet, direction)* way; **beaucoup de c. à faire** a long way to go; **dix minutes de c.** ten minutes' walk; **se mettre en c.** to start out, set out; **faire du c.** to come a long way; *(idée)* to make considerable headway; **c. faisant** on the way; **à mi-c.** half-way. 2 **c. de fer** railway, *Am* railroad. ◆**chemin/er** *vi* to proceed; *(péniblement)* to trudge (along) on foot; *(évoluer) Fig* to progress. ◆**—ement** *nm Fig* progress. ◆**cheminot** *nm* railway *ou Am* railroad employee.

cheminée [ʃ(ə)mine] *nf (sur le toit)* chimney; *(de navire)* funnel; *(être)* fireplace; *(encadrement)* mantelpiece.

chemise [ʃ(ə)miz] *nf* shirt; *(couverture cartonnée)* folder; **c. de nuit** nightdress. ◆**chemiserie** *nf* men's shirt and (underwear) shop. ◆**chemisette** *nf* short-sleeved shirt. ◆**chemisier** *nm (vêtement)* blouse.

chenal, -aux [ʃənal, -o] *nm* channel.

chenapan [ʃ(ə)napɑ̃] *nm Hum* rogue, scoundrel.

chêne [ʃɛn] *nm (arbre, bois)* oak.

chenet [ʃ(ə)nɛ] *nm* firedog, andiron.

chenil [ʃ(ə)ni(l)] *nm* kennels.

chenille [ʃ(ə)nij] *nf* caterpillar; *(de char) Mil* caterpillar track.

cheptel [ʃɛptɛl] *nm* livestock.

chèque [ʃɛk] *nm* cheque, *Am* check; **c. de voyage** traveller's cheque, *Am* traveler's check. ◆c.-repas *nm* (*pl* chèques-repas) luncheon voucher. ◆chéquier *nm* cheque book, *Am* checkbook.

cher, chère [ʃɛr] 1 *a* (aimé) dear (à to); – *nmf* mon c. my dear fellow; ma chère my dear (woman). 2 *a* (coûteux) dear, expensive; (quartier, hôtel etc) expensive; la vie chère the high cost of living; payer c. (objet) to pay a lot for; (erreur etc) *Fig* to pay dearly for. ◆chèrement *adv* dearly.

cherch/er [ʃɛrʃe] *vt* to look for, search for; (du secours, la paix etc) to seek; (dans un dictionnaire) to look up; c. ses mots to fumble for one's words; aller c. to (go and) fetch ou get; c. à faire to attempt to do; tu l'as bien cherché! it's your own fault!, you asked for it! ◆—eur, -euse *nmf* research worker; c. d'or gold-digger.

chér/ir [ʃerir] *vt* to cherish. ◆—i, -ie *a* dearly loved, beloved; – *nmf* darling.

chérot [ʃero] *am* *Fam* pricey.

cherté [ʃɛrte] *nf* high cost, expensiveness.

chétif, -ive [ʃetif, -iv] *a* puny; (dérisoire) wretched.

cheval, -aux [ʃ(ə)val, -o] *nm* horse; c. (vapeur) *Aut* horsepower; à c. on horse-back; faire du c. to go horse riding; à c. sur straddling; à c. sur les principes a stickler for principle; monter sur ses grands chevaux to get excited; c. à bascule rocking horse; c. d'arçons *Sp* vaulting horse; c. de bataille (dada) hobbyhorse; chevaux de bois (manège) merry-go-round. ◆chevaleresque *a* chivalrous. ◆chevalier *nm* knight. ◆chevalin *a* equine; (boucherie) horse-.

chevalet [ʃ(ə)valɛ] *nm* easel; *Menuis* trestle.

chevalière [ʃ(ə)valjɛr] *nf* signet ring.

chevauchée [ʃ(ə)voʃe] *nf* (horse) ride.

chevaucher [ʃ(ə)voʃe] *vt* to straddle; – *vi*, – se c. *vpr* to overlap.

chevet [ʃ(ə)vɛ] *nm* bedhead; table/livre de c. bedside table/book; au c. de at the bedside of.

cheveu, -x [ʃ(ə)vø] *nm* un c. a hair; les cheveux hair; couper les cheveux en quatre *Fig* to split hairs; tiré par les cheveux (argument) far-fetched. ◆chevelu *a* hairy. ◆chevelure *nf* (head of) hair.

cheville [ʃ(ə)vij] *nf* *Anat* ankle; *Menuis* peg, pin; (pour vis) (wall)plug; c. ouvrière *Aut* & *Fig* linchpin; en c. avec *Fam* in cahoots with. ◆cheviller *vt* *Menuis* to pin, peg.

chèvre [ʃɛvr] *nf* goat; (femelle) nanny-goat. ◆chevreau, -x *nm* kid.

chèvrefeuille [ʃɛvrəfœj] *nm* honeysuckle.

chevreuil [ʃəvrœj] *nm* roe deer; *Culin* venison.

chevron [ʃəvrɔ̃] *nm* (poutre) rafter; *Mil* stripe, chevron; à chevrons (tissu, veste etc) herringbone.

chevronné [ʃəvrɔne] *a* seasoned, experienced.

chevroter [ʃəvrɔte] *vi* to quaver, tremble.

chez [ʃe] *prép* c. qn at s.o.'s house, flat etc; il est c. Jean/c. l'épicier he's at John's (place)/at the grocer's; il va c. Jean/c. l'épicier he's going to John's (place)/to the grocer's; c. moi, c. nous at home; je vais c. moi I'm going home; c. les Suisses/les jeunes among the Swiss/the young; c. Camus in Camus; c. l'homme in man; une habitude c. elle a habit with her; c. Mme Dupont (adresse) care of ou c/o Mme Dupont. ◆c.-soi *nm inv* un c.-soi a home (of one's own).

chialer [ʃjale] *vi* (pleurer) *Fam* to cry.

chic [ʃik] 1 *a inv* stylish, smart; (gentil) *Fam* decent, nice; – *int* c. (alors)! great!; – *nm* style, elegance. 2 *nm* avoir le c. pour faire to have the knack of doing.

chicane [ʃikan] 1 *nf* (querelle) quibble. 2 *nfpl* (obstacles) zigzag barriers. ◆chicaner *vt* to quibble with (s.o.); – *vi* to quibble.

chiche [ʃiʃ] 1 *a* mean, niggardly; c. de sparing of. 2 *int* (défi) *Fam* I bet you!; c. que je parte sans lui I bet I leave without him.

chichis [ʃiʃi] *nmpl* faire des c. to make a lot of fuss.

chicorée [ʃikɔre] *nf* (à café) chicory; (pour salade) endive.

chien [ʃjɛ̃] *nm* dog; c. d'arrêt pointer, retriever; un mal de c. a hell of a job; temps de c. filthy weather; vie de c. *Fig* dog's life; entre c. et loup at dusk, in the gloaming. ◆c.-loup *nm* (*pl* chiens-loups) wolf-hound. ◆chienne *nf* dog, bitch.

chiendent [ʃjɛ̃dɑ̃] *nm* *Bot* couch grass.

chiffon [ʃifɔ̃] *nm* rag; (à poussière) duster. ◆chiffonner *vt* to crumple; (ennuyer) *Fig* to bother, distress. ◆chiffonnier *nm* ragman.

chiffre [ʃifr] *nm* figure, number; (romain, arabe) numeral; (code) cipher; c. d'affaires *Fin* turnover. ◆chiffrer *vt* (montant) to assess, work out; (message) to cipher, code; – *vi* to mount up; se c. à to amount to, work out at.

chignon [ʃiɲɔ̃] *nm* bun, chignon.

Chili [ʃili] *nm* Chile. ◆chilien, -ienne *a* & *nmf* Chilean.

chimère [ʃimɛr] *nf* fantasy, (wild) dream. ◆**chimérique** *a* fanciful.

chimie [ʃimi] *nf* chemistry. ◆**chimique** *a* chemical. ◆**chimiste** *nmf* (research) chemist.

chimpanzé [ʃɛ̃pɑ̃ze] *nm* chimpanzee.

Chine [ʃin] *nf* China. ◆**chinois, -oise** *a & nmf* Chinese; — *nm* (*langue*) Chinese. ◆**chinoiser** *vi* to quibble. ◆**chinoiserie** *nf* (*objet*) Chinese curio; *pl* (*bizarreries*) *Fig* weird complications.

chiner [ʃine] *vi* (*brocanteur etc*) to hunt for bargains.

chiot [ʃjo] *nm* pup(py).

chiper [ʃipe] *vt Fam* to swipe, pinch (à from).

chipie [ʃipi] *nf* **vieille c.** (*femme*) *Péj* old crab.

chipoter [ʃipɔte] *vi* **1** (*manger*) to nibble. **2** (*chicaner*) to quibble.

chips [ʃips] *nmpl* (potato) crisps, *Am* chips.

chiquenaude [ʃiknod] *nf* flick (of the finger).

chiromancie [kirɔmɑ̃si] *nf* palmistry.

chirurgie [ʃiryrʒi] *nf* surgery. ◆**chirurgical, -aux** *a* surgical. ◆**chirurgien** *nm* surgeon.

chlore [klɔr] *nm* chlorine. ◆**chloroforme** *nm* chloroform. ◆**chlorure** *nm* chloride.

choc [ʃɔk] *nm* (*heurt*) impact, shock; (*émotion*) & *Méd* shock; (*collision*) crash; (*des opinions, entre manifestants etc*) clash.

chocolat [ʃɔkɔla] *nm* chocolate; **c. à croquer** plain *ou Am* bittersweet chocolate; **c. au lait** milk chocolate; **c. glacé** choc-ice; — *a inv* chocolate(-coloured). ◆**chocolaté** *a* chocolate-flavoured.

chœur [kœr] *nm* (*chanteurs, nef*) *Rel* choir; (*composition musicale*) & *Fig* chorus; **en c.** (all) together, in chorus.

choir [ʃwar] *vi* **laisser c. qn** *Fam* to turn one's back on s.o.

chois/ir [ʃwazir] *vt* to choose, pick, select. ◆**-i** *a* (*œuvres*) selected; (*terme, langage*) well-chosen; (*public*) select. ◆**choix** *nm* choice; (*assortiment*) selection; **morceau de c.** choice piece; **au c. du client** according to choice.

choléra [kɔlera] *nm* cholera.

cholestérol [kɔlɛsterɔl] *nm* cholesterol.

chôm/er [ʃome] *vi* (*ouvrier etc*) to be unemployed; **jour chômé** (public) holiday. ◆**-age** *nm* unemployment; **en** *ou* **au c.** unemployed; **mettre en c. technique** to lay off, dismiss.

chope [ʃɔp] *nf* beer mug, tankard; (*contenu*) pint.

choqu/er [ʃɔke] *vt* to offend, shock; (*verres*) to clink; (*commotionner*) to shake up. ◆**-ant** *a* shocking, offensive.

choral, mpl -als [kɔral] *a* choral. ◆**chorale** *nf* choral society. ◆**choriste** *nmf* chorister.

chorégraphe [kɔregraf] *nmf* choreographer. ◆**chorégraphie** *nf* choreography.

chose [ʃoz] *nf* thing; **état de choses** state of affairs; **par la force des choses** through force of circumstance; **dis-lui bien des choses de ma part** remember me to him *ou* her; **ce monsieur C.** that Mr What's-name; **se sentir tout c.** *Fam* (*déconcentré*) to feel all funny; (*malade*) to feel out of sorts.

chou, -x [ʃu] *nm* cabbage; **choux de Bruxelles** Brussels sprouts; **mon c.!** my pet!; **c. à la crème** cream puff. ◆**c.-fleur** *nm* (*pl* **choux-fleurs**) cauliflower.

choucas [ʃuka] *nm* jackdaw.

chouchou, -oute [ʃuʃu, -ut] *nmf* (*favori*) *Fam* pet, darling. ◆**chouchouter** *vt* to pamper.

choucroute [ʃukrut] *nf* sauerkraut.

chouette [ʃwɛt] **1** *nf* (*oiseau*) owl. **2** *a* (*chic*) *Fam* super, great.

choyer [ʃwaye] *vt* to pet, pamper.

chrétien, -ienne [kretjɛ̃, -jɛn] *a & nmf* Christian. ◆**chrétienté** *nf* Christendom. ◆**Christ** [krist] *nm* Christ. ◆**christianisme** *nm* Christianity.

chrome [krom] *nm* chromium, chrome. ◆**chromé** *a* chromium-plated.

chromosome [krɔmozom] *nm* chromosome.

chronique [krɔnik] **1** *a* (*malade, chômage etc*) chronic. **2** *nf* (*annales*) chronicle; *Journ* report, news; (*rubrique*) column. ◆**chroniqueur** *nm* chronicler; *Journ* reporter, columnist.

chronologie [krɔnɔlɔʒi] *nf* chronology. ◆**chronologique** *a* chronological.

chronomètre [krɔnɔmɛtr] *nm* stopwatch. ◆**chronométr/er** *vt Sp* to time. ◆**-eur** *nm Sp* timekeeper.

chrysanthème [krizɑ̃tɛm] *nm* chrysanthemum.

chuchot/er [ʃyʃɔte] *vti* to whisper. ◆**-ement** *nm* whisper(ing). ◆**chuchoteries** *nfpl Fam* whispering.

chuinter [ʃwɛ̃te] *vi* (*vapeur*) to hiss.

chut! [ʃyt] *int* sh!, hush!

chute [ʃyt] *nf* fall; (*défaite*) (down)fall; **c. d'eau** waterfall; **c. de neige** snowfall; **c. de pluie** rainfall; **c. des cheveux** hair loss. ◆**chuter** *vi Fam* to fall.

Chypre [ʃipr] *nf* Cyprus. ◆**chypriote** *a* & *nmf* Cypriot.

ci [si] **1** *adv* par-ci par-là here and there. **2** *pron dém* comme ci comme ça so so. **3** *voir* ce², celui.

ci-après [siapre] *adv* below, hereafter. ◆**ci-contre** *adv* opposite. ◆**ci-dessous** *adv* below. ◆**ci-dessus** *adv* above. ◆**ci-gît** *adv* here lies (*on gravestones*). ◆**ci-inclus** *a*, ◆**ci-joint** *a* (*inv before n*) (*dans une lettre*) enclosed (herewith).

cible [sibl] *nf* target.

ciboulette [sibulɛt] *nf* Culin chives.

cicatrice [sikatris] *nf* scar. ◆**cicatriser** *vt*, − **se c.** *vpr* to heal up (*leaving a scar*).

cidre [sidr] *nm* cider.

Cie *abrév* (*compagnie*) Co.

ciel [sjɛl] *nm* **1** (*pl* ciels) sky; **à c.** ouvert (*piscine etc*) open-air; **c. de lit** canopy. **2** (*pl* cieux [sjø]) *Rel* heaven; **juste c.!** good heavens!; **sous d'autres cieux** *Hum* in other climes.

cierge [sjɛrʒ] *nm* Rel candle.

cigale [sigal] *nf* (*insecte*) cicada.

cigare [sigar] *nm* cigar. ◆**cigarette** *nf* cigarette.

cigogne [sigɔɲ] *nf* stork.

cil [sil] *nm* (eye)lash.

cime [sim] *nf* (*d'un arbre*) top; (*d'une montagne*) & Fig peak.

ciment [simɑ̃] *nm* cement. ◆**cimenter** *vt* to cement.

cimetière [simtjɛr] *nm* cemetery, graveyard; **c. de voitures** scrapyard, breaker's yard, Am auto graveyard.

ciné [sine] *nm* Fam cinema. ◆**c.-club** *nm* film society. ◆**cinéaste** *nm* film maker. ◆**cinéphile** *nmf* film buff.

cinéma [sinema] *nm* cinema; **faire du c.** to make films. ◆**cinémascope** *nm* cinemascope. ◆**cinémathèque** *nf* film library; (*salle*) film theatre. ◆**cinématographique** *a* cinema-.

cinglé [sɛ̃gle] *a* Fam crazy.

cingl/er [sɛ̃gle] *vt* to lash. ◆**−ant** *a* (*vent, remarque*) cutting, biting.

cinoche [sinɔʃ] *nm* Fam cinema.

cinq [sɛ̃k] *nm* five; − *a* ([sɛ̃] *before consonant*) five. ◆**cinquième** *a* & *nmf* fifth; *nm* **c.** a fifth.

cinquante [sɛ̃kɑ̃t] *a* & *nm* fifty. ◆**cinquantaine** *nf* about fifty. ◆**cinquantenaire** *a* & *nmf* fifty-year-old (person); − *nm* fiftieth anniversary. ◆**cinquantième** *a* & *nmf* fiftieth.

cintre [sɛ̃tr] *nm* coathanger; Archit arch.

◆**cintré** *a* arched; (*veste etc*) tailored, slim-fitting.

cirage [siraʒ] *nm* (shoe) polish.

circoncis [sirkɔ̃si] *a* circumcised. ◆**circoncision** *nf* circumcision.

circonférence [sirkɔ̃ferɑ̃s] *nf* circumference.

circonflexe [sirkɔ̃flɛks] *a* Gram circumflex.

circonlocution [sirkɔ̃lɔkysjɔ̃] *nf* circumlocution.

circonscrire [sirkɔ̃skrir] *vt* to circumscribe. ◆**circonscription** *nf* division; **c.** (**électorale**) constituency.

circonspect, -ecte [sirkɔ̃spɛ(kt), -ɛkt] *a* cautious, circumspect. ◆**circonspection** *nf* caution.

circonstance [sirkɔ̃stɑ̃s] *nf* circumstance; **pour/en la c.** for this occasion; **de c.** (*habit, parole etc*) appropriate. ◆**circonstancié** *a* detailed. ◆**circonstanciel, -ielle** *a* Gram adverbial.

circonvenir [sirkɔ̃vnir] *vt* to circumvent.

circuit [sirkɥi] *nm* Sp Él Fin circuit; (*périple*) tour, trip; (*détour*) roundabout way; El circuitry, circuits.

circulaire [sirkylɛr] *a* circular; − *nf* (*lettre*) circular. ◆**circulation** *nf* circulation; Aut traffic. ◆**circuler** *vi* to circulate; (*véhicule, train*) to move, travel; (*passant*) to walk about; (*rumeur*) to go round, circulate; **faire c.** to circulate; (*piétons etc*) to move on; **circulez!** keep moving!

cire [sir] *nf* wax; (*pour meubles*) polish, wax. ◆**cir/er** *vt* to polish, wax. ◆**−é** *nm* (*vêtement*) oilskin(s). ◆**−eur** *nm* bootblack. ◆**−euse** *nf* (*appareil*) floor polisher. ◆**cireux, -euse** *a* waxy.

cirque [sirk] *nm* Th Hist circus.

cirrhose [siroz] *nf* Méd cirrhosis.

cisaille [sizaj] *nf*(*pl*) shears. ◆**ciseau, -x** *nm* chisel; *pl* scissors. ◆**ciseler** *vt* to chisel.

citadelle [sitadɛl] *nf* citadel.

cité [site] *nf* city; **c.** (**ouvrière**) housing estate (*for workers*), Am housing project *ou* development; **c. universitaire** (students') halls of residence. ◆**citadin, -ine** *nmf* city dweller; − *a* city-, urban.

citer [site] *vt* to quote; Jur to summon; Mil to mention, cite. ◆**citation** *nf* quotation; Jur summons; Mil mention, citation.

citerne [sitɛrn] *nf* (*réservoir*) tank.

cithare [sitar] *nf* zither.

citoyen, -enne [sitwajɛ̃, -ɛn] *nmf* citizen. ◆**citoyenneté** *nf* citizenship.

citron [sitrɔ̃] *nm* lemon; **c. pressé** (fresh)

lemon juice. ◆**citronnade** *nf* lemon drink, (still) lemonade.

citrouille [sitruj] *nf* pumpkin.

civet [sivɛ] *nm* stew; **c. de lièvre** jugged hare.

civière [sivjɛr] *nf* stretcher.

civil [sivil] *a* (*droits, guerre, mariage etc*) civil; (*non militaire*) civilian; (*courtois*) civil; **année civile** calendar year. **2** *nm* civilian; **dans le c.** in civilian life; **en c.** (*policier*) in plain clothes; (*soldat*) in civilian clothes. ◆**civilité** *nf* civility.

civiliser [sivilize] *vt* to civilize; — **se c.** *vpr* to become civilized. ◆**civilisation** *nf* civilization.

civique [sivik] *a* civic; **instruction c.** *Scol* civics. ◆**civisme** *nm* civic sense.

clair [klɛr] *a* (*distinct, limpide, évident*) clear; (*éclairé*) light; (*pâle*) light(-coloured); (*sauce, chevelure*) thin; **bleu/vert c.** light blue/green; **il fait c.** it's light (out); — *adv* (*voir*) clearly; — *nm* **c. de lune** moonlight; **le plus c. de** the major ou greater part of; **tirer au c.** (*question etc*) to clear up. ◆—**ement** *adv* clearly. ◆**claire-voie** (*à c.-voie* (*barrière*) lattice-; (*caisse*) openwork; (*porte*) louvre(d).

clairière [klɛrjɛr] *nf* clearing, glade.

clairon [klɛrɔ̃] *nm* bugle; (*soldat*) bugler. ◆**claironner** *vt* (*annoncer*) to trumpet forth.

clairsemé [klɛrsəme] *a* sparse.

clairvoyant [klɛrvwajɑ̃] *a* (*perspicace*) clear-sighted. ◆**clairvoyance** *nf* clear-sightedness.

clam/er [klame] *vt* to cry out. ◆—**eur** *nf* clamour, outcry.

clan [klɑ̃] *nm* clan, clique, set.

clandestin [klɑ̃dɛstɛ̃] *a* secret, clandestine; (*journal, mouvement*) underground; **passager c.** stowaway.

clapet [klapɛ] *nm Tech* valve; (*bouche*) *Arg* trap.

clapier [klapje] *nm* (rabbit) hutch.

clapot/er [klapɔte] *vi* (*vagues*) to lap. ◆—**ement** *nm*, ◆**clapotis** *nm* lap(ping).

claque [klak] *nf* smack, slap. ◆**claquer** *vt* (*porte*) to slam, bang; (*gifler*) to smack, slap; (*fouet*) to crack; (*fatiguer*) *Fam* to tire out; (*dépenser*) *Arg* to blow; **se c. un muscle** to tear a muscle; **faire c.** (*doigts*) to snap; (*langue*) to click; (*fouet*) to crack; — *vi* (*porte*) to slam, bang; (*drapeau*) to flap; (*coup de revolver*) to ring out; (*mourir*) *Fam* to die; (*tomber en panne*) *Fam* to break down; **c. des mains** to clap one's hands; **elle claque des dents** her teeth are chattering.

claquemurer (se) [səklakmyre] *vpr* to shut oneself up, hole up.

claquettes [klakɛt] *nfpl* tap dancing.

clarifier [klarifje] *vt* to clarify. ◆**clarification** *nf* clarification.

clarinette [klarinɛt] *nf* clarinet.

clarté [klarte] *nf* light, brightness; (*précision*) clarity, clearness.

classe [klɑs] *nf* class; **aller en c.** to go to school; **c. ouvrière/moyenne** working/middle class; **avoir de la c.** to have class.

class/er [klɑse] *vt* to classify, class; (*papiers*) to file; (*candidats*) to grade; (*affaire*) to close; **se c. parmi** to rank ou be classed among; **se c. premier** to come first. ◆—**ement** *nm* classification; filing; grading; (*rang*) place; *Sp* placing. ◆—**eur** *nm* (*meuble*) filing cabinet; (*portefeuille*) (loose leaf) file. ◆**classification** *nf* classification. ◆**classifier** *vt* to classify.

classique [klasik] *a* classical; (*typique*) classic; — *nm* (*œuvre, auteur*) classic. ◆**classicisme** *nm* classicism.

clause [kloz] *nf* clause.

claustrophobie [klostrɔfɔbi] *nf* claustrophobia. ◆**claustrophobe** *a* claustrophobic.

clavecin [klavsɛ̃] *nm Mus* harpsichord.

clavicule [klavikyl] *nf* collarbone.

clavier [klavje] *nm* keyboard.

clé, clef [kle] *nf* key; (*outil*) spanner, wrench; *Mus* clef; **fermer à c.** to lock; **sous c.** under lock and key; **c. de contact** ignition key; **c. de voûte** keystone; **poste/industrie c.** key post/industry; **clés en main** (*acheter une maison etc*) ready to move in; **prix clés en main** (*voiture*) on the road price.

clément [klemɑ̃] *a* (*temps*) mild, clement; (*juge*) lenient, clement. ◆**clémence** *nf* mildness; leniency; clemency.

clémentine [klemɑ̃tin] *nf* clementine.

clerc [klɛr] *nm Rel* cleric; (*de notaire*) clerk. ◆**clergé** *nm* clergy. ◆**clérical, -aux** *a Rel* clerical.

cliché [kliʃe] *nm Phot* negative; *Typ* plate; (*idée*) cliché.

client, -ente [klijɑ̃, -ɑ̃t] *nmf* (*de magasin etc*) customer; (*d'un avocat etc*) client; (*d'un médecin*) patient; (*d'hôtel*) guest. ◆**clientèle** *nf* customers, clientele; (*d'un avocat*) practice, clientele; (*d'un médecin*) practice, patients; **accorder sa c. à** to give one's custom to.

cligner [kliɲe] *vi* **c. des yeux** (*ouvrir et fermer*) to blink; (*fermer à demi*) to screw up one's eyes; **c. de l'œil** to wink.

◆clignot/er *vi* to blink; (*lumière*) to flicker; *Aut* to flash; (*étoile*) to twinkle. ◆—ant *nm* *Aut* indicator, *Am* directional signal.

climat [klima] *nm* *Mét* & *Fig* climate. ◆climatique *a* climatic. ◆climatisation *nf* air-conditioning. ◆climatiser *vt* to air-condition.

clin d'œil [klɛ̃dœj] *nm* wink; en un c. d'œil in the twinkling of an eye.

clinique [klinik] *a* clinical; — *nf* (*hôpital*) (private) clinic.

clinquant [klɛ̃kɑ̃] *a* tawdry.

clique [klik] *nf* *Péj* clique; *Mus* *Mil* (drum and bugle) band.

cliqueter [klikte] *vi* to clink. ◆cliquetis *nm* clink(ing).

clivage [klivaʒ] *nm* split, division (de in).

cloaque [klɔak] *nm* cesspool.

clochard, -arde [klɔʃar, -ard] *nmf* tramp, vagrant.

cloche [klɔʃ] *nf* 1 bell; c. à fromage cheese cover. 2 (*personne*) *Fam* idiot, oaf. ◆clocher 1 *nm* bell tower; (*en pointe*) steeple; de c. *Fig* parochial; esprit de c. parochialism. 2 *vi* to be wrong ou amiss. ◆clochette *nf* (small) bell.

cloche-pied (à) [aklɔʃpje] *adv* sauter à c.-pied to hop on one foot.

cloison [klwazɔ̃] *nf* partition; *Fig* barrier. ◆cloisonner *vt* to partition; (*activités etc*) *Fig* to compartmentalize.

cloître [klwatr] *nm* cloister. ◆se cloîtrer *vpr* to shut oneself away, cloister oneself.

clopin-clopant [klɔpɛ̃klɔpɑ̃] *adv* aller c.-clopant to hobble.

cloque [klɔk] *nf* blister.

clore [klɔr] *vt* (*débat, lettre*) to close. ◆clos *a* (*incident etc*) closed; (*espace*) enclosed; — *nm* (enclosed) field. ◆clôture *nf* (*barrière*) enclosure, fence; (*fermeture*) closing. ◆clôturer *vt* to enclose; (*compte, séance etc*) to close.

clou [klu] *nm* nail; (*furoncle*) boil; le c. (du spectacle) *Fam* the star attraction; les clous (*passage*) pedestrian crossing; des clous! *Fam* nothing at all! ◆clouer *vt* to nail; cloué au lit confined to (one's) bed; cloué sur place nailed to the spot; le bec à qn *Fam* to shut s.o. up. ◆clouté *a* (*chaussures*) hobnailed; (*ceinture, pneus*) studded; passage c. pedestrian crossing, *Am* crosswalk.

clown [klun] *nm* clown.

club [klœb] *nm* (*association*) club.

cm *abrév* (*centimètre*) cm.

co- [kɔ] *préf* co-.

coaguler [kɔagyle] *vti*, — se c. *vpr* to coagulate.

coaliser (se) [sɔkɔalize] *vpr* to form a coalition, join forces. ◆coalition *nf* coalition.

coasser [kɔase] *vi* (*grenouille*) to croak.

cobaye [kɔbaj] *nm* (*animal*) & *Fig* guinea pig.

cobra [kɔbra] *nm* (*serpent*) cobra.

coca [kɔka] *nm* (*Coca-Cola®*) coke.

cocagne [kɔkaɲ] *nf* pays de c. dreamland, land of plenty.

cocaïne [kɔkain] *nf* cocain.

cocarde [kɔkard] *nf* rosette, cockade; *Av* roundel. ◆cocardier, -ière *a* *Péj* flag-waving.

cocasse [kɔkas] *a* droll, comical. ◆cocasserie *nf* drollery.

coccinelle [kɔksinɛl] *nf* ladybird, *Am* ladybug.

cocher¹ [kɔʃe] *vt* to tick (off), *Am* to check (off).

cocher² [kɔʃe] *nm* coachman. ◆cochère *af* porte c. main gateway.

cochon, -onne [kɔʃɔ̃, -ɔn] 1 *nm* pig; (*mâle*) hog; c. d'Inde guinea pig. 2 *nmf* (*personne sale*) (dirty) pig; (*salaud*) swine; — *a* (*histoire, film*) dirty, filthy. ◆cochonnerie(s) *nf*(*pl*) (*obscénité(s)*) filth; (*pacotille*) *Fam* rubbish.

cocktail [kɔktɛl] *nm* (*boisson*) cocktail; (*réunion*) cocktail party.

coco [kɔko] *nm* noix de c. coconut. ◆cocotier *nm* coconut palm.

cocon [kɔkɔ̃] *nm* cocoon.

cocorico [kɔkɔriko] *int* & *nm* cock-a-doodle-doo; faire c. (*crier victoire*) *Fam* to give three cheers for France, wave the flag.

cocotte [kɔkɔt] *nf* (*marmite*) casserole; c. minute® pressure cooker.

cocu [kɔky] *nm* *Fam* cuckold.

code [kɔd] *nm* code; codes, phares c. *Aut* dipped headlights, *Am* low beams; C. de la route Highway Code. ◆coder *vt* to code. ◆codifier *vt* to codify.

coefficient [kɔefisjɑ̃] *nm* *Math* coefficient; (*d'erreur, de sécurité*) *Fig* margin.

coéquipier, -ière [kɔekipje, -jɛr] *nmf* team mate.

cœur [kœr] *nm* heart; *Cartes* hearts; au c. de (*ville, hiver etc*) in the heart of; par c. by heart; ça me (sou)lève le c. that turns my stomach; à c. ouvert (*opération*) open-heart; (*parler*) freely; avoir mal au c. to feel sick; avoir le c. gros ou serré to have a heavy heart; ça me tient à c. that's close to my heart; avoir bon c. to be

kind-hearted; **de bon c.** (*offrir*) with a good
heart, willingly; (*rire*) heartily; **si le c. vous
en dit** if you so desire.

coexister [kɔɛgziste] *vi* to coexist.
◆**coexistence** *nf* coexistence.

coffre [kɔfr] *nm* chest; (*de banque*) safe; (*de
voiture*) boot, *Am* trunk; (*d'autocar*)
luggage *ou Am* baggage compartment.
◆**c.-fort** *nm* (*pl* **coffres-forts**) safe. ◆**coffret** *nm* casket, box.

cogiter [kɔʒite] *vi Iron* to cogitate.

cognac [kɔɲak] *nm* cognac.

cogner [kɔɲe] *vti* to knock; **c. qn** *Arg* (*frapper*) to thump s.o.; (*tabasser*) to beat s.o.
up; **se c. la tête/etc** to knock one's
head/*etc*.

cohabiter [kɔabite] *vi* to live together.
◆**cohabitation** *nf* living together; *Pol
Fam* power sharing.

cohérent [kɔerã] *a* coherent. ◆**cohérence**
nf coherence. ◆**cohésion** *nf* cohesion,
cohesiveness.

cohorte [kɔɔrt] *nf* (*groupe*) troop, band,
cohort.

cohue [kɔy] *nf* crowd, mob.

coiffe [kwaf] *nf* headdress.

coiff/er [kwafe] *vt* (*chapeau*) to put on,
wear; (*surmonter*) *Fig* to cap; (*être à la tête
de*) to head; **c. qn** to do s.o.'s hair; **c. qn
d'un chapeau** to put a hat on s.o.; **— se c.**
vpr to do one's hair; **se c. d'un chapeau** to
put on a hat. ◆**-eur, -euse**[1] *nmf* (*pour
hommes*) barber, hairdresser; (*pour dames*)
hairdresser. ◆**-euse**[2] *nf* dressing table.
◆**coiffure** *nf* headgear, hat; (*arrangement*) hairstyle; (*métier*) hairdressing.

coin [kwɛ̃] *nm* (*angle*) corner; (*endroit*) spot;
(*de terre, de ciel*) patch; (*cale*) wedge; **du c.**
(*magasin etc*) local; **dans le c.** in the (local)
area; **au c. du feu** by the fireside; **petit c.**
Fam loo, *Am* john.

coinc/er [kwɛse] *vt* (*mécanisme, tiroir*) to
jam; (*caler*) to wedge; **c. qn** *Fam* to catch
s.o., corner s.o.; **— se c.** *vpr* (*mécanisme
etc*) to get jammed *ou* stuck. ◆**-é** *a* (*tiroir
etc*) stuck, jammed; (*personne*) *Fam* stuck.

coïncider [kɔɛside] *vi* to coincide.
◆**coïncidence** *nf* coincidence.

coin-coin [kwɛkwɛ] *nm inv* (*de canard*)
quack.

coing [kwɛ̃] *nm* (*fruit*) quince.

coke [kɔk] *nm* (*combustible*) coke.

col [kɔl] *nm* (*de chemise*) collar; (*de
bouteille*) & *Anat* neck; *Géog* pass; **c. roulé**
polo neck, *Am* turtleneck.

colère [kɔlɛr] *nf* anger; **une c.** (*accès*) a fit of
anger; **en c.** angry (**contre** with); **se mettre**

en c. to lose one's temper. ◆**coléreux,
-euse** *a*, ◆**colérique** *a* quick-tempered.

colibri [kɔlibri] *nm* hummingbird.

colifichet [kɔlifiʃɛ] *nm* trinket.

colimaçon (en) [ãkɔlimasɔ̃] *adv* **escalier en
c.** spiral staircase.

colin [kɔlɛ̃] *nm* (*poisson*) hake.

colique [kɔlik] *nf* diarrh(o)ea; (*douleur*)
stomach pain, colic.

colis [kɔli] *nm* parcel, package.

collaborer [kɔlabɔre] *vi* collaborate (**avec**
with, à on); **c. à** (*journal*) to contribute to.
◆**collaborateur, -trice** *nmf* collaborator;
contributor. ◆**collaboration** *nf* collaboration; contribution.

collage [kɔlaʒ] *nm* (*œuvre*) collage.

collant [kɔlã] **1** *a* (*papier*) sticky; (*vêtement*)
skin-tight; **être c.** (*importun*) *Fam* to be a
pest. **2** *nm* (pair of) tights; (*de danse*)
leotard.

collation [kɔlasjɔ̃] *nf* (*repas*) light meal.

colle [kɔl] *nf* (*transparente*) glue; (*blanche*)
paste; (*question*) *Fam* poser, teaser; (*interrogation*) *Scol Arg* oral; (*retenue*) *Scol Arg*
detention.

collecte [kɔlɛkt] *nf* (*quête*) collection.
◆**collect/er** *vt* to collect. ◆**-eur** *nm*
collector; (*égout*) **c. main** sewer.

collectif, -ive [kɔlɛktif, -iv] *a* collective;
(*hystérie, démission*) mass-; **billet c.** group
ticket. ◆**collectivement** *adv* collectively.
◆**collectivisme** *nm* collectivism. ◆**col-
lectivité** *nf* community, collectivity.

collection [kɔlɛksjɔ̃] *nf* collection. ◆**col-
lectionn/er** *vt* (*timbres etc*) to collect.
◆**-eur, -euse** *nmf* collector.

collège [kɔlɛʒ] *nm* (secondary) school, *Am*
(high) school; (*électoral, sacré*) college.
◆**collégien** *nm* schoolboy. ◆**col-
légienne** *nf* schoolgirl.

collègue [kɔlɛg] *nmf* colleague.

coller [kɔle] *vt* (*timbre etc*) to stick; (*à la
colle transparente*) to glue; (*à la colle
blanche*) to paste; (*affiche*) to stick up;
(*papier peint*) to hang; (*mettre*) *Fam* to
stick, shove; **c. contre** (*nez, oreille etc*) to
press against; **c. qn** (*embarrasser*) *Fam* to
stump s.o., catch s.o. out; (*consigner*) *Scol*
to keep s.o. in; **être collé à** (*examen*) *Fam* to
fail, flunk; **se c. contre** to cling (close) to; **se
c. qn/qch** *Fam* to get stuck with s.o./sth; **—
vi to stick, cling; **c. à** (*s'adapter*) to fit,
correspond to; **ça colle!** *Fam* everything's
just fine! ◆**colleur, -euse** *nmf* **c.
d'affiches** billsticker.

collet [kɔlɛ] *nm* (*lacet*) snare; **prendre qn au
c.** to grab s.o. by the scruff of the neck; **elle**

est/ils sont c. monté she is/they are prim and proper *ou* straight-laced.

collier [kɔlje] *nm* (*bijou*) necklace; (*de chien, cheval*) & *Tech* collar.

colline [kɔlin] *nf* hill.

collision [kɔlizjɔ̃] *nf* (*de véhicules*) collision; (*bagarre, conflit*) clash; **entrer en c. avec** to collide with.

colloque [kɔlɔk] *nm* symposium.

collusion [kɔlyzjɔ̃] *nf* collusion.

colmater [kɔlmate] *vt* (*fuite, fente*) to seal; (*trou*) to fill in; (*brèche*) *Mil* to close, seal.

colombe [kɔlɔ̃b] *nf* dove.

colon [kɔlɔ̃] *nm* settler, colonist; (*enfant*) child taking part in a holiday camp. ◆**colonial, -aux** *a* colonial. ◆**colonie** *nf* colony; **c. de vacances** (children's) holiday camp *ou Am* vacation camp.

coloniser [kɔlɔnize] *vt Pol* to colonize; (*peupler*) to settle. ◆**colonisateur, -trice** *a* colonizing; – *nmf* colonizer. ◆**colonisation** *nf* colonization.

côlon [kolɔ̃] *nm Anat* colon.

colonel [kɔlɔnɛl] *nm* colonel.

colonne [kɔlɔn] *nf* column; **c. vertébrale** spine. ◆**colonnade** *nf* colonnade.

color/er [kɔlɔre] *vt* to colour. ◆**-ant** *a* & *nm* colouring. ◆**-é** *a* (*verre etc*) coloured; (*teint*) ruddy; (*style, foule*) colourful. ◆**coloration** *nf* colouring, colour. ◆**coloriage** *nm* colouring; (*dessin*) coloured drawing. ◆**colorier** *vt* (*dessin etc*) to colour (in). ◆**coloris** *nm* (*effet*) colouring; (*nuance*) shade.

colosse [kɔlɔs] *nm* giant, colossus. ◆**colossal, -aux** *a* colossal, gigantic.

colporter [kɔlpɔrte] *vt* to peddle, hawk.

coltiner [kɔltine] *vt* (*objet lourd*) *Fam* to lug, haul; **— se c.** *vpr* (*tâche pénible*) *Fam* to take on, tackle.

coma [kɔma] *nm* coma; **dans le c.** in a coma.

combat [kɔ̃ba] *nm* fight; *Mil* combat. ◆**combatif, -ive** *a* (*personne*) eager to fight; (*instinct, esprit*) fighting. ◆**combatt/re** *vt* to fight; (*maladie, inflation etc*) to combat, fight; **— vi** to fight. ◆**-ant** *nm Mil* combattant; (*bagarreur*) *Fam* brawler; **—** *a* (*unité*) fighting.

combien [kɔ̃bjɛ̃] **1** *adv* (*quantité*) how much; (*nombre*) how many; **c. de** (*temps, argent etc*) how much; (*gens, livres etc*) how many. **2** *adv* (*à quel point*) how; **tu verras c. il est bête** you'll see how silly he is. **3** *adv* (*distance*) **c. y a-t-il d'ici à . . . ?** how far is it to . . . ? **4** *nm inv* **le c. sommes-nous?** (*date*) *Fam* what date is it?; **tous les c.?** (*fréquence*) *Fam* how often?

combine [kɔ̃bin] *nf* (*truc, astuce*) *Fam* trick.

combin/er [kɔ̃bine] *vt* (*disposer*) to combine; (*calculer*) to devise, plan (out). ◆**-é** *nm* (*de téléphone*) receiver. ◆**combinaison** *nf* **1** combination; (*manœuvre*) scheme. **2** (*vêtement de femme*) slip; (*de mécanicien*) boiler suit, *Am* overalls; (*de pilote*) flying suit; **c. de ski** ski suit.

comble [kɔ̃bl] **1** *nm* **le c. de** (*la joie etc*) the height of; **pour c.** (*de malheur*) to crown *ou* cap it all; **c'est un** *ou* **le c.!** that's the limit! **2** *nmpl* (*mansarde*) attic, loft; **sous les combles** beneath the roof, in the loft *ou* attic. **3** *a* (*bondé*) packed, full.

combler [kɔ̃ble] *vt* (*trou, lacune etc*) to fill; (*retard, perte*) to make good; (*vœu*) to fulfil; **c. qn de** (*cadeaux etc*) to lavish on s.o.; (*joie*) to fill s.o. with; **je suis comblé** I'm completely satisfied; **vous me comblez!** you're too good to me!

combustible [kɔ̃bystibl] *nm* fuel; **—** *a* combustible. ◆**combustion** *nf* combustion.

comédie [kɔmedi] *nf* comedy; (*complication*) *Fam* fuss, palaver; **c. musicale** musical; **jouer la c.** *Fig* to put on an act, play-act; **c'est de la c.** (*c'est faux*) it's a sham. ◆**comédien** *nm Th & Fig* actor. ◆**comédienne** *nf Th & Fig* actress.

comestible [kɔmɛstibl] *a* edible; **—** *nmpl* foods.

comète [kɔmɛt] *nf* comet.

comique [kɔmik] *a* (*style etc*) *Th* comic; (*amusant*) *Fig* comical, funny; (*auteur*) **c.** comedy writer; **—** *nm* (*acteur*) comic (actor); **le c.** (*genre*) comedy; *Fig* the comical side (*de*).

comité [kɔmite] *nm* committee; **c. de gestion** board of (management); **en petit c.** in a small group.

commande [kɔmãd] **1** *nf* (*achat*) order; **sur c.** to order. **2** *nfpl* **les commandes** *Av Tech* the controls; **tenir les commandes** (*diriger*) *Fig* to have control.

command/er [kɔmãde] **1** *vt* (*diriger, exiger, dominer*) to command; (*faire fonctionner*) to control; **— vi c. à** (*ses passions etc*) to have control over; **c. à qn de faire** to command s.o. to do. **2** *vt* (*acheter*) to order. ◆**-ant** *nm Nau* captain; (*grade*) *Mil* major; (*grade*) *Av* squadron leader; **c. de bord** *Av* captain. ◆**-ement** *nm* (*autorité*) command; *Rel* commandment. ◆**commando** *nm* commando.

commanditaire [kɔmãditɛr] *nm Com* sleeping *ou* limited partner, *Am* silent partner.

comme [kɔm] **1** *adv* & *conj* as, like; **un peu**

c. a bit like; **c. moi** like me; **c. cela** like that; **blanc c. neige** (as) white as snow; **c. si** as if; **c. pour faire** as if to do; **c. par hasard** as if by chance; **joli c. tout** *Fam* ever so pretty; **c. ami** as a friend; **c. c'est gros** (*disant que*) to the effect that; (*ce qui prouve que*) so, which goes to show that; **qu'as-tu c. diplômes?** what do you have in the way of certificates? **2** *adv* (*exclamatif*) **regarde c. il pleut!** look how it's raining!; **c. c'est petit!** isn't it small! **3** *conj* (*temps*) as; (*cause*) as, since; **c. je pars** as I'm leaving; **c. elle entrait** (just) as she was coming in.

commémorer [kɔmemɔre] *vt* to commemorate. ◆**commémoratif, -ive** *a* commemorative. ◆**commémoration** *nf* commemoration.

commenc/er [kɔmɑ̃se] *vti* to begin, start (**à faire** to do, doing; **par** with; **par faire** by doing); **pour c.** to begin with. ◆**-ement** *nm* beginning, start.

comment [kɔmɑ̃] *adv* how; **c. le sais-tu?** how do you know?; **et c.!** and how!; **c.?** (*répétition, surprise*) what?; **c.!** (*indignation*) what!; **c. est-il?** what is he like?; **c. faire?** what's to be done?; **c. t'appelles-tu?** what's your name?; **c. allez-vous?** how are you?

commentaire [kɔmɑ̃tɛr] *nm* (*explications*) commentary; (*remarque*) comment. ◆**commentateur, -trice** *nmf* commentator. ◆**commenter** *vt* to comment (up)on.

commérage(s) [kɔmeraʒ] *nm(pl)* gossip.

commerce [kɔmɛrs] *nm* trade, commerce; (*magasin*) shop, business; **de c.** (*voyageur, maison, tribunal*) commercial; (*navire*) trading; **chambre de c.** chamber of commerce; **faire du c.** to trade; **dans le c.** (*objet*) (on sale) in the shops. ◆**commercer** *vi* to trade. ◆**commerçant, -ante** *nmf* shopkeeper; **c. en gros** wholesale dealer; **–** *a* (*nation*) trading, mercantile; (*rue, quartier*) shopping-; (*personne*) business-minded. ◆**commercial, -aux** *a* commercial, business-. ◆**commercialiser** *vt* to market.

commère [kɔmɛr] *nf* (*femme*) gossip.

commettre* [kɔmɛtr] *vt* (*délit etc*) to commit; (*erreur*) to make.

commis [kɔmi] *nm* (*de magasin*) assistant, *Am* clerk; (*de bureau*) clerk, *Am* clerical worker.

commissaire [kɔmisɛr] *nm* *Sp* steward; **c.** (**de police**) police superintendent *ou Am* chief; **c. aux comptes** auditor; **c. du bord** *Nau* purser. ◆**c.-priseur** *nm* (*pl* commissaires-priseurs) auctioneer. ◆**commis-**

sariat *nm* **c.** (**de police**) (central) police station.

commission [kɔmisjɔ̃] *nf* (*course*) errand; (*message*) message; (*réunion*) commission, committee; (*pourcentage*) *Com* commission (**sur** on); **faire les commissions** to do the shopping. ◆**commissionnaire** *nm* messenger; (*d'hôtel*) commissionaire; *Com* agent.

commod/e [kɔmɔd] **1** *a* (*pratique*) handy; (*simple*) easy; **il n'est pas c.** (*pas aimable*) he's unpleasant; (*difficile*) he's a tough one. **2** *nf* chest of drawers, *Am* dresser. ◆**-ément** *adv* comfortably. ◆**commodité** *nf* convenience.

commotion [kɔmosjɔ̃] *nf* shock; **c.** (**cérébrale**) concussion. ◆**commotionner** *vt* to shake up.

commuer [kɔmɥe] *vt* (*peine*) *Jur* to commute (**en** to).

commun [kɔmœ̃] **1** *a* (*collectif, comparable, habituel*) common; (*frais, cuisine etc*) shared; (*action, démarche etc*) joint; **ami c.** mutual friend; **peu c.** uncommon; **en c.** in common; **transports en c.** public transport; **avoir** *ou* **mettre en c.** to share; **vivre en c.** to live together; **il n'a rien de c. avec** he has nothing in common with. **2** *nm* **le c. des mortels** ordinary mortals. ◆**-ément** [kɔmynemɑ̃] *adv* commonly.

communauté [kɔmynote] *nf* community. ◆**communautaire** *a* community-.

commune [kɔmyn] *nf* (*municipalité française*) commune; **les Communes** *Br Pol* the Commons. ◆**communal, -aux** *a* communal, local, municipal.

communi/er [kɔmynje] *vi* to receive Holy Communion, communicate. ◆**-ant, -ante** *nmf Rel* communicant. ◆**communion** *nf* communion; *Rel* (Holy) Communion.

communiqu/er [kɔmynike] *vt* to communicate, pass on; (*mouvement*) to impart, communicate; **se c. à** (*feu, rire*) to spread to; **–** *vi* (*personne, pièces etc*) to communicate. ◆**-é** *nm* (*avis*) *Pol* communiqué; (*publicitaire*) message; **c. de presse** press release. ◆**communicatif, -ive** *a* communicative; (*contagieux*) infectious. ◆**communication** *nf* communication; **c.** (**téléphonique**) (telephone) call; **mauvaise c.** *Tél* bad line.

communisme [kɔmynism] *nm* communism. ◆**communiste** *a & nmf* communist.

communs [kɔmœ̃] *nmpl* (*bâtiments*) outbuildings.

commutateur [kɔmytatœr] nm (bouton) Él switch.

compact [kɔpakt] a dense; (mécanisme, disque, véhicule) compact.

compagne [kɔpaɲ] nf (camarade) friend; (épouse, maîtresse) companion. ◆**compagnie** nf (présence, société) & Com Mil company; **tenir c. à qn** to keep s.o. company. ◆**compagnon** nm companion; (ouvrier) workman; **c. de route** travelling companion, fellow traveller; **c. de jeu/de travail** playmate/workmate.

comparaître [kɔparetr] vi Jur to appear (in court) (**devant** before).

compar/er [kɔpare] vt to compare; **— se c.** vpr to be compared (**à** to). ◆**—é** a (science etc) comparative. ◆**—able** a comparable. ◆**comparaison** nf comparison; Littér simile. ◆**comparatif, -ive** a (méthode etc) comparative; **—** nm Gram comparative.

comparse [kɔpars] nmf Jur minor accomplice, stooge.

compartiment [kɔpartimā] nm compartment. ◆**compartimenter** vt to compartmentalize, divide up.

comparution [kɔparysjɔ̃] nf Jur appearance (in court).

compas [kɔpa] nm 1 (pour mesurer etc) (pair of) compasses, Am compass. 2 (boussole) Nau compass.

compassé [kɔpase] a (affecté) starchy, stiff.

compassion [kɔpasjɔ̃] nf compassion.

compatible [kɔpatibl] a compatible. ◆**compatibilité** nf compatibility.

compat/ir [kɔpatir] vi to sympathize; **c. à** (la douleur etc de qn) to share in. ◆**—issant** a sympathetic.

compatriote [kɔpatrijɔt] nmf compatriot.

compenser [kɔpāse] vt to make up for, compensate for; **—** vi to compensate. ◆**compensation** nf compensation; **en c.** de in compensation for.

compère [kɔper] nm accomplice.

compétent [kɔpetā] a competent. ◆**compétence** nf competence.

compétition [kɔpetisjɔ̃] nf competition; (épreuve) Sp event; **de c.** (esprit, sport) competitive. ◆**compétitif, -ive** a competitive. ◆**compétitivité** nf competitiveness.

compiler [kɔpile] vt (documents) to compile.

complainte [kɔplēt] nf (chanson) lament.

complaire (se) [səkɔpler] vpr **se c. dans qch/à faire** to delight in sth/in doing.

complaisant [kɔplezā] a kind, obliging; (indulgent) self-indulgent, complacent. ◆**complaisance** nf kindness, obligingness; self-indulgence, complacency.

complément [kɔplemā] nm complement; **le c.** (le reste) the rest; **un c. d'information** additional information. ◆**complémentaire** a complementary; (détails) additional.

complet, -ète [kɔple, -et] 1 a complete; (train, hôtel, examen etc) full; (aliment) whole; **au (grand) c.** in full strength. 2 nm (costume) suit. ◆**complètement** adv completely. ◆**compléter** vt to complete; (ajouter à) to complement; (somme) to make up; **— se c.** vpr (caractères) to complement each other.

complexe [kɔpleks] 1 a complex. 2 nm (sentiment, construction) complex. ◆**complexé** a Fam hung up, inhibited. ◆**complexité** nf complexity.

complication [kɔplikasjɔ̃] nf complication; (complexité) complexity.

complice [kɔplis] nm accomplice; **—** a (regard) knowing; (silence, attitude) conniving; **c. de** Jur a party to. ◆**complicité** nf complicity.

compliment [kɔplimā] nm compliment; (éloges) compliments; (félicitations) congratulations. ◆**complimenter** vt to compliment (**sur, pour** on).

compliqu/er [kɔplike] vt to complicate; **— se c.** vpr (situation) to get complicated. ◆**—é** a complicated; (mécanisme etc) intricate; complicated; (histoire, problème etc) involved, complicated.

complot [kɔplo] nm plot, conspiracy. ◆**comploter** vti to plot (**faire** to do).

comport/er [kɔporte] vt (impliquer) to involve, contain; (comprendre en soi, présenter) to contain, comprise, have. 2 **se c.** vpr to behave; (joueur, voiture) to perform. ◆**—ement** nm behaviour; (de joueur etc) performance.

compos/er [kɔpoze] vt (former, constituer) to compose, make up; (musique, visage) to compose; (numéro) Tél to dial; (texte) Typ to set (up); **se c. de, être composé de** to be composed of; **—** vi Scol to take an examination; **c. avec** to come to terms with. ◆**—ant** nm (chimique, électronique) component. ◆**—ante** nf (d'une idée etc) component. ◆**—é** a & nm compound. ◆**compositeur, -trice** nmf Mus composer; Typ typesetter. ◆**composition** nf (action) composing, making up; Typ typesetting; Mus Littér Ch composition; Scol test, class exam; **c. française** Scol French essay ou composition.

composter [kɔ̃pɔste] vt (billet) to cancel, punch.

compote [kɔ̃pɔt] nf stewed fruit; **c. de pommes** stewed apples, apple sauce. ◆**compotier** nm fruit dish.

compréhensible [kɔ̃preɑ̃sibl] a understandable, comprehensible. ◆**compréhensif, -ive** a (personne) understanding. ◆**compréhension** nf understanding, comprehension.

comprendre* [kɔ̃prɑ̃dr] vt to understand, comprehend; (comporter) to include, comprise; **je n'y comprends rien** I don't understand anything about it; **ça se comprend** that's understandable. ◆**compris** a (inclus) included (dans in); **frais c.** including expenses; **tout c.** (all) inclusive; **y c.** including; **c. entre** (situated) between; (c'est) **c.!** it's agreed!

compresse [kɔ̃pres] nf Méd compress.

compresseur [kɔ̃presœr] a **rouleau c.** steam roller.

comprim/er [kɔ̃prime] vt to compress; (colère etc) to repress; (dépenses) to reduce. ◆**-é** nm Méd tablet. ◆**compression** nf compression; (du personnel etc) reduction.

compromettre* [kɔ̃prɔmetr] vt to compromise. ◆**compromis** nm compromise. ◆**compromission** nf compromising action, compromise.

comptable [kɔ̃tabl] a (règles etc) book-keeping-; – nmf bookkeeper; (expert) accountant. ◆**comptabilité** nf (comptes) accounts; (science) bookkeeping, accountancy; (service) accounts department.

comptant [kɔ̃tɑ̃] a **argent c.** (hard) cash; – adv **payer c.** to pay (in) cash; **(au) c.** (acheter, vendre) for cash.

compte [kɔ̃t] nm (comptabilité) account; (calcul) count; (nombre) (right) number; **avoir un c. en banque** to have a bank(ing) account; **c. chèque** cheque account, Am checking account; **tenir c. de** to take into account; **c. tenu de** considering; **entrer en ligne de c.** to be taken into account; **se rendre c. de** to realize; **rendre c. de** (exposer) to report on; (justifier) to account for; **c. rendu** report; (de livre, film) review; **demander des comptes à** to call to account; **faire le c. de** to count; **à son c.** (travailler) for oneself; (s'installer) on one's own; **pour le c. de** on behalf of; **pour mon c.** for my part; **sur le c. de qn** about s.o.; **en fin de c.** all things considered; **à bon c.** (acheter) cheap(ly); **s'en tirer à bon c.** to get off lightly; **avoir un c. à régler avec qn** to have a score to settle with s.o.; **c. à rebours** countdown. ◆**c.-gouttes** nm inv Méd dropper; **au c.-gouttes** very sparingly. ◆**c.-tours** nm inv Aut rev counter.

compt/er [kɔ̃te] vt (calculer) to count; (prévoir) to reckon, allow; (considérer) to consider; (payer) to pay; **c. faire** to expect to do; (avoir l'intention de) to intend to do; **c. qch à qn** (facturer) to charge s.o. for sth; **il compte deux ans de service** he has two years' service; **ses jours sont comptés** his or her days are numbered; – vi (calculer, avoir de l'importance) to count; **c. sur** to rely on; **c. avec** to reckon with; **c. parmi** to be (numbered) among. ◆**-eur** nm Él meter; **c. de vitesse** Aut speedometer; **c.** (kilométrique) milometer, clock; **c. Geiger** Geiger counter.

comptoir [kɔ̃twar] nm 1 (de magasin) counter; (de café) bar; (de bureau) (reception) desk. 2 Com branch, agency.

compulser [kɔ̃pylse] vt to examine.

comte [kɔ̃t] nm (noble) count; Br earl. ◆**comté** nm county. ◆**comtesse** nf countess.

con, conne [kɔ̃, kɔn] a (idiot) Fam stupid; – nm Fam stupid fool.

concave [kɔ̃kav] a concave.

concéder [kɔ̃sede] vt to concede, grant (à to, que that).

concentr/er [kɔ̃sɑ̃tre] vt to concentrate; (attention etc) to focus, concentrate; — **se c.** vpr (réfléchir) to concentrate. ◆**-é** a (solution) concentrated; (lait) condensed; (attentif) in a state of concentration; – nm Ch concentrate; **c. de tomates** tomato purée. ◆**concentration** nf concentration.

concentrique [kɔ̃sɑ̃trik] a concentric.

concept [kɔ̃sɛpt] nm concept. ◆**conception** nf (idée) & Méd conception.

concern/er [kɔ̃sɛrne] vt to concern; **en ce qui me concerne** as far as I'm concerned. ◆**-ant** prép concerning.

concert [kɔ̃sɛr] nm Mus concert; (de louanges) chorus; **de c.** (agir) together, in concert.

concert/er [kɔ̃sɛrte] vt to arrange, devise (in agreement); — **se c.** vpr to consult together. ◆**-é** a (plan) concerted. ◆**concertation** nf (dialogue) dialogue.

concession [kɔ̃sesjɔ̃] nf concession (à to); (terrain) plot (of land). ◆**concessionnaire** nmf Com (authorized) dealer, agent.

concev/oir* [kɔ̃səvwar] 1 vt (imaginer, éprouver, engendrer) to conceive; (comprendre) to understand; **ainsi conçu** (dépêche etc) worded as follows. 2 vi (femme) to conceive. ◆**-able** a conceivable.

concierge [kɔ̃sjerʒ] *nmf* caretaker, *Am* janitor.

concile [kɔ̃sil] *nm Rel* council.

concili/er [kɔ̃silje] *vt* (*choses*) to reconcile; **se c. l'amitié/***etc* **de qn** to win (over) s.o.'s friendship/*etc.* **◆—ant** *a* conciliatory. **◆conciliateur, -trice** *nmf* conciliator. **◆conciliation** *nf* conciliation.

concis [kɔ̃si] *a* concise, terse. **◆concision** *nf* conciseness.

concitoyen, -enne [kɔ̃sitwajɛ̃, -ɛn] *nmf* fellow citizen.

conclu/re* [kɔ̃klyr] *vt* (*terminer, régler*) to conclude; **c. que** (*déduire*) to conclude that; **–** *vi* (*orateur etc*) to conclude; **c. à** to conclude in favour of. **◆—ant** *a* conclusive. **◆conclusion** *nf* conclusion.

concombre [kɔ̃kɔ̃br] *nm* cucumber.

concorde [kɔ̃kɔrd] *nf* concord, harmony. **◆concord/er** *vi* (*faits etc*) to agree; (*caractères*) to match; **c. avec** to match. **◆—ant** *a* in agreement. **◆concordance** *nf* agreement; (*de situations, résultats*) similarity; **c. des temps** *Gram* sequence of tenses.

concourir* [kɔ̃kurir] *vi* (*candidat*) to compete (**pour** for); (*directions*) to converge; **c. à** (*un but*) to contribute to. **◆concours** *nm Scol Univ* competitive examination; (*jeu*) competition; (*aide*) assistance; (*de circonstances*) combination; **c. hippique** horse show.

concret, -ète [kɔ̃krɛ, -ɛt] *a* concrete. **◆concrétiser** *vt* to give concrete form to; **— se c.** *vpr* to materialize.

conçu [kɔ̃sy] *voir* **concevoir**; **–** *a* **c. pour faire** designed to do; **bien c.** (*maison etc*) well-designed.

concubine [kɔ̃kybin] *nf* (*maîtresse*) concubine. **◆concubinage** *nm* cohabitation; **en c.** as husband and wife.

concurrent, -ente [kɔ̃kyrã, -ãt] *nmf* competitor; *Scol Univ* candidate. **◆concurrence** *nf* competition; **faire c. à** to compete with; **jusqu'à c.** de up to the amount of. **◆concurrencer** *vt* to compete with. **◆concurrentiel, -ielle** *a* (*prix etc*) competitive.

condamn/er [kɔ̃dane] *vt* to condemn; *Jur* to sentence (**à** to); (*porte*) to block up, bar; (*pièce*) to keep locked; **c. à une amende** to fine. **◆—é, -ée** *nmf Jur* condemned man, condemned woman; **être c.** (*malade*) to be doomed, be a hopeless case. **◆condamnation** *nf Jur* sentence; (*censure*) condemnation.

condenser [kɔ̃dãse] *vt*, **— se c.** *vpr* to condense. **◆condensateur** *nm* *Él* condenser. **◆condensation** *nf* condensation.

condescendre [kɔ̃desãdr] *vi* to condescend (**à** to). **◆condescendance** *nf* condescension.

condiment [kɔ̃dimã] *nm* condiment.

condisciple [kɔ̃disipl] *nm Scol* classmate, schoolfellow; *Univ* fellow student.

condition [kɔ̃disjɔ̃] *nf* (*état, stipulation, rang*) condition; *pl* (*clauses, tarifs*) *Com* terms; **à c. de faire, à c. que l'on fasse** providing *ou* provided (that) one does; **mettre en c.** (*endoctriner*) to condition; **sans c.** (*se rendre*) unconditionally. **◆conditionnel, -elle** *a* conditional. **◆conditionn/er** *vt* **1** (*influencer*) to condition. **2** (*article*) *Com* to package. **◆—é** *a* (*réflexe*) conditioned; **à air c.** (*pièce etc*) air-conditioned. **◆—ement** *nm* conditioning; packaging.

condoléances [kɔ̃dɔleãs] *nfpl* condolences.

conducteur, -trice [kɔ̃dyktœr, -tris] **1** *nmf* *Aut Rail* driver. **2** *a* & *nm* (*corps*) *a* . *Él* conductor; (*fil*) **c.** *Él* lead (wire).

conduire* [kɔ̃dyir] *vt* **1** to lead; *Aut* to drive; (*affaire etc*) & *Él* to conduct; (*eau*) to carry; **c. qn à** (*accompagner*) to take s.o. to. **2 se c.** *vpr* to behave. **◆conduit** *nm* duct. **◆conduite** *nf* conduct, behaviour; *Aut* driving (**de** of); (*d'entreprise etc*) conduct; (*d'eau, de gaz*) main; **c. à gauche** (*volant*) left-hand drive; **faire un bout de c. à qn** to go with s.o. part of the way; **sous la c. de** under the guidance of.

cône [kon] *nm* cone.

confection [kɔ̃fɛksjɔ̃] *nf* making (**de** of); **vêtements de c.** ready-made clothes; **magasin de c.** ready-made clothing shop. **◆confectionner** *vt* (*gâteau, robe*) to make.

confédération [kɔ̃federasjɔ̃] *nf* confederation. **◆confédéré** *a* confederate.

conférence [kɔ̃ferãs] *nf* conference; (*exposé*) lecture. **◆conférencier, -ière** *nmf* lecturer. **◆conférer** *vt* (*attribuer, donner*) to confer (**à** on).

confess/er [kɔ̃fɛse] *vt* to confess; **— se c.** *vpr Rel* to confess (**à** to). **◆—eur** *nm* (*prêtre*) confessor. **◆confession** *nf* confession. **◆confessionnal, -aux** *nm Rel* confessional. **◆confessionnel, -elle** *a* (*école*) *Rel* denominational.

confettis [kɔ̃feti] *nmpl* confetti.

confiance [kɔ̃fjãs] *nf* trust, confidence; **faire c. à qn, avoir c. en qn** to trust s.o.; **c. en soi** (self-)confidence; **poste/abus de c.** position/breach of trust; **homme de c.** reliable man; **en toute c.** (*acheter*) quite confidently; **poser la question de c.** *Pol* to ask for a vote of confidence. ◆**confiant** *a* trusting; (*sûr de soi*) confident; **être c. en** *ou* **dans** to have confidence in.

confidence [kɔ̃fidɑ̃s] *nf* (*secret*) confidence; **en c.** in confidence; **il m'a fait une c.** he confided in me. ◆**confident** *nm* confidant. ◆**confidente** *nf* confidante. ◆**confidentiel, -ielle** *a* confidential.

confier [kɔ̃fje] *vt* **c. à qn** (*enfant, objet*) to give s.o. to look after, entrust s.o. with; **c. un secret/etc à qn** to confide a secret/etc to s.o.; — **se c.** *vpr* to confide (**à qn** in s.o.).

configuration [kɔ̃figyrasjɔ̃] *nf* configuration.

confin/er [kɔ̃fine] *vt* to confine; — *vi* **c. à** to border on; — **se c.** *vpr* to confine oneself (**dans** to). ◆**-é** *a* (*atmosphère*) stuffy.

confins [kɔ̃fɛ̃] *nmpl* confines.

confire [kɔ̃fir] *vt* (*cornichon*) to pickle; (*fruit*) to preserve.

confirmer [kɔ̃firme] *vt* to confirm (**que** that); **c. qn dans sa résolution** to confirm s.o.'s resolve. ◆**confirmation** *nf* confirmation.

confiserie [kɔ̃fizri] *nf* (*magasin*) sweet shop, *Am* candy store; *pl* (*produits*) confectionery, sweets, *Am* candy. ◆**confiseur, -euse** *nmf* confectioner.

confisquer [kɔ̃fiske] *vt* to confiscate (**à qn** from s.o.). ◆**confiscation** *nf* confiscation.

confit [kɔ̃fi] *a* **fruits confits** crystallized *ou* candied fruit. ◆**confiture** *nf* jam, preserves.

conflit [kɔ̃fli] *nm* conflict. ◆**conflictuel, -elle** *a* *Psy* conflict-provoking.

confluent [kɔ̃flyɑ̃] *nm* (*jonction*) confluence.

confondre [kɔ̃fɔ̃dr] *vt* (*choses, personnes*) to confuse, mix up; (*consterner, étonner*) to confound; (*amalgamer*) to fuse; **c. avec** to mistake for; — **se c.** *vpr* (*s'unir*) to merge; **se c. en excuses** to be very apologetic.

conforme [kɔ̃fɔrm] *a* **c. à** in accordance with; **c.** (**à l'original**) (*copie*) true (to the original). ◆**conform/er** *vt* to model, adapt; — **se c.** *vpr* to conform (**à** to). ◆**-ément** *adv* **c. à** in accordance with. ◆**conformisme** *nm* conformity, conformism. ◆**conformiste** *a* & *nmf* conformist. ◆**conformité** *nf* conformity.

confort [kɔ̃fɔr] *nm* comfort. ◆**confortable** *a* comfortable.

confrère [kɔ̃frɛr] *nm* colleague. ◆**confrérie** *nf* *Rel* brotherhood.

confronter [kɔ̃frɔ̃te] *vt Jur etc* to confront

(avec with); (*textes*) to collate; **confronté à** confronted with. ◆**confrontation** *nf* confrontation; collation.

confus [kɔ̃fy] *a* (*esprit, situation, bruit*) confused; (*idée, style*) confused, jumbled, hazy; (*gêné*) embarrassed; **je suis c.!** (*désolé*) I'm terribly sorry!; (*comblé de bienfaits*) I'm overwhelmed! ◆**confusément** *adv* indistinctly, vaguely. ◆**confusion** *nf* confusion; (*gêne, honte*) embarrassment.

congé [kɔ̃ʒe] *nm* leave of (absence); (*avis pour locataire*) notice (to quit); (*pour salarié*) notice (of dismissal); (*vacances*) holiday, *Am* vacation; **c. de maladie** sick leave; **congés payés** holidays with pay, paid holidays; **donner son c. à** (*employé, locataire*) to give notice to; **prendre c. de** to take leave of. ◆**congédier** *vt* (*domestique etc*) to dismiss.

congeler [kɔ̃ʒle] *vt* to freeze. ◆**congélateur** *nm* freezer, deep-freeze. ◆**congélation** *nf* freezing.

congénère [kɔ̃ʒenɛr] *nmf* fellow creature. ◆**congénital, -aux** *a* congenital.

congère [kɔ̃ʒɛr] *nf* snowdrift.

congestion [kɔ̃ʒɛstjɔ̃] *nf* congestion; **c. cérébrale** *Méd* stroke. ◆**congestionn/er** *vt* to congest. ◆**-é** *a* (*visage*) flushed.

Congo [kɔ̃go] *nm* Congo. ◆**congolais, -aise** *a* & *nmf* Congolese.

congratuler [kɔ̃gratyle] *vt Iron* to congratulate.

congrégation [kɔ̃gregasjɔ̃] *nf* (*de prêtres etc*) congregation.

congrès [kɔ̃grɛ] *nm* congress. ◆**congressiste** *nmf* delegate (**to a congress**).

conifère [kɔnifɛr] *nm* conifer.

conique [kɔnik] *a* conic(al), cone-shaped.

conjecture [kɔ̃ʒɛktyr] *nf* conjecture. ◆**conjectural, -aux** *a* conjectural. ◆**conjecturer** *vt* to conjecture, surmise.

conjoint [kɔ̃ʒwɛ̃] **1** *a* (*problèmes, action etc*) joint. **2** *nm* spouse; *pl* husband and wife. ◆**conjointement** *adv* jointly.

conjonction [kɔ̃ʒɔ̃ksjɔ̃] *nf Gram* conjunction.

conjoncture [kɔ̃ʒɔ̃ktyr] *nf* circumstances; *Écon* economic situation. ◆**conjoncturel, -elle** *a* (*prévisions etc*) economic.

conjugal, -aux [kɔ̃ʒygal] *a* conjugal.

conjuguer [kɔ̃ʒyge] *vt* (*verbe*) to conjugate; (*efforts*) to combine; — **se c.** *vpr* (*verbe*) to be conjugated. ◆**conjugaison** *nf Gram* conjugation.

conjur/er [kɔ̃ʒyre] *vt* (*danger*) to avert; (*mauvais sort*) to ward off; **c. qn** (*implorer*)

to entreat s.o. (**de faire** to do). ◆**—é, -ée**
nmf conspirator. ◆**conjuration** *nf*
(*complot*) conspiracy.

connaissance [kɔnɛsɑ̃s] *nf* knowledge;
(*personne*) acquaintance; *pl* (*science*)
knowledge (**en** of); **faire la c. de qn, faire c.
avec qn** to make s.o.'s acquaintance, meet
s.o.; (*ami, époux etc*) to get to know s.o.; **à
ma c.** as far as I know; **avoir c. de** to be
aware of; **perdre c.** to lose consciousness,
faint; **sans c.** unconscious. ◆**connaisseur** *nm* connoisseur.

connaître* [kɔnɛtr] *vt* to know; (*rencontrer*)
to meet; (*un succès etc*) to have; (*un
malheur etc*) to experience; **faire c.** to make
known; **— se c.** *vpr* (*amis etc*) to get to
know each other; **nous nous connaissions
déjà** we've met before; **s'y c. à** *ou* **en qch** to
know (all) about sth; **il ne se connaît plus**
he's losing his cool.

connecter [kɔnɛkte] *vt* El to connect.
◆**connexe** *a* (*matières*) allied. ◆**con-
nexion** *nf* El connection.

connerie [kɔnri] *nf Fam* (*bêtise*) stupidity;
(*action*) stupid thing; *pl* (*paroles*) stupid
nonsense.

connivence [kɔnivɑ̃s] *nf* connivance.

connotation [kɔnɔtasjɔ̃] *nf* connotation.

connu *voir* **connaître**; — *a* (*célèbre*)
well-known.

conquér/ir* [kɔ̃kerir] *vt* (*pays, marché etc*)
to conquer. ◆**—ant, -ante** *nmf* conqueror.
◆**conquête** *nf* conquest; **faire la c. de**
(*pays, marché etc*) to conquer.

consacrer [kɔ̃sakre] *vt* (*temps, vie etc*) to
devote (**à** to); (*église etc*) Rel to consecrate;
(*coutume etc*) to establish, sanction, consecrate; **se c. à** to devote oneself to.

conscience [kɔ̃sjɑ̃s] *nf* **1** (*psychologique*)
consciousness; **la c. de qch** the awareness
ou consciousness of sth; **c. de soi** self-
awareness; **avoir**/**prendre c. de** to
be/become aware *ou* conscious of; **perdre
c.** to lose consciousness. **2** (*morale*)
conscience; **avoir mauvaise c.** to have a
guilty conscience; **c. professionnelle**
conscientiousness. ◆**consciemment**
[kɔ̃sjamɑ̃] *adv* consciously. ◆**con-
scientieux, -euse** *a* conscientious.
◆**conscient** *a* conscious; **c. de** aware *ou*
conscious of.

conscrit [kɔ̃skri] *nm Mil* conscript. ◆**conscription** *nf* conscription.

consécration [kɔ̃sekrasjɔ̃] *nf Rel* consecration; (*confirmation*) sanction, consecration.

consécuti/f, -ive [kɔ̃sekytif, -iv] *a* consecu-

tive; **c. à** following upon. ◆**—vement** *adv*
consecutively.

conseil [kɔ̃sɛj] *nm* **1 un c.** a piece of advice,
some advice; **des conseils** advice;
(**expert-**)**c.** consultant. **2** (*assemblée*) council, committee; **c. d'administration** board of
directors; **C. des ministres** Pol Cabinet;
(*réunion*) Cabinet meeting. ◆**conseiller**[1]
vt (*guider, recommander*) to advise; **c. qch à
qn** to recommend sth to s.o.; **c. à qn de faire**
to advise s.o. to do. ◆**conseiller**[2], **-ère**
nmf (*expert*) consultant; (*d'un conseil*)
councillor.

consent/ir* [kɔ̃sɑ̃tir] *vi* **c. à** to consent to;
— *vt* to grant (**à** to). ◆**—ement** *nm*
consent.

conséquence [kɔ̃sekɑ̃s] *nf* consequence;
(*conclusion*) conclusion; **en c.** accordingly;
sans c. (*importance*) of no importance.
◆**conséquent** *a* logical; (*important*) Fam
important; **par c.** consequently.

conservatoire [kɔ̃sɛrvatwar] *nm* academy,
school (*of music, drama*).

conserve [kɔ̃sɛrv] *nf* conserves tinned *ou*
canned food; **de** *ou* **en c.** tinned, canned;
mettre en c. to tin, can.

conserv/er [kɔ̃sɛrve] *vt* (*ne pas perdre*) to
retain, keep; (*fruits, vie etc*) to preserve; **—
se c.** *vpr* (*aliment*) to keep. ◆**—é a bien c.**
(*vieillard*) well-preserved. ◆**conserva-
teur, -trice 1** *a & nmf Pol* Conservative. **2** *nm* (*de musée*) curator; (*de
bibliothèque*) (chief) librarian. **3** *nm*
(*produit*) Culin preservative. ◆**conservation** *nf* preservation; **instinct de c.** survival
instinct. ◆**conservatisme** *nm* conserva-
tism.

considér/er [kɔ̃sidere] *vt* to consider (**que**
that); **c. qn** (*faire cas de*) to respect s.o.; **c.
comme** to consider to be, regard as; **tout
bien considéré** all things considered.
◆**—able** *a* considerable. ◆**considération** *nf* (*motif, examen*) consideration;
(*respect*) regard, esteem; *pl* (*remarques*)
observations; **prendre en c.** to take into
consideration.

consigne [kɔ̃siɲ] *nf* (*instruction*) orders;
Rail left-luggage office, Am baggage checkroom; Scol detention; Mil confinement to
barracks; (*somme*) deposit; **c. automatique**
Rail luggage lockers, Am baggage lockers.
◆**consignation** *nf* (*somme*) deposit.
◆**consigner** *vt* (*écrire*) to record;
(*bouteille etc*) to charge a deposit on;
(*bagages*) to deposit in the left-luggage
office, Am to check; (*élève*) Scol to keep in;

(soldat) Mil to confine (to barracks); *(salle)* to seal off, close.

consistant [kɔ̃sistɑ̃] *a (sauce, bouillie)* thick; *(argument, repas)* solid. ◆**consistance** *nf (de liquide)* consistency; **sans c.** *(rumeur)* unfounded; *(esprit)* irresolute.

consister [kɔ̃siste] *vi* **c. en/dans** to consist of/in; **c. à faire** to consist in doing.

consistoire [kɔ̃sistwar] *nm Rel* council.

console [kɔ̃sɔl] *nf Tech Él* console.

consoler [kɔ̃sɔle] *vt* to console, comfort (**de** for); **se c. de** *(la mort de qn etc)* to get over. ◆**consolation** *nf* consolation, comfort.

consolider [kɔ̃sɔlide] *vt* to strengthen, consolidate. ◆**consolidation** *nf* strengthening, consolidation.

consomm/er [kɔ̃sɔme] *vt (aliment, carburant etc)* to consume; *(crime, œuvre) Litt* to accomplish; — *vi (au café)* to drink; **c. beaucoup/peu** *(véhicule)* to be heavy/light on petrol *ou Am* gas. ◆**—é 1** *a (achevé)* consummate. **2** *nm* clear meat soup, consommé. ◆**consommateur, -trice** *nmf* Com consumer; *(au café)* customer. ◆**consommation** *nf* consumption; drink; **biens/société de c.** consumer goods/society.

consonance [kɔ̃sɔnɑ̃s] *nf Mus* consonance; *pl (sons)* sounds.

consonne [kɔ̃sɔn] *nf* consonant.

consortium [kɔ̃sɔrsjɔm] *nm Com* consortium.

consorts [kɔ̃sɔr] *nmpl* **et c.** *Péj* people of that ilk.

conspirer [kɔ̃spire] *vi* **1** to conspire, plot (**contre** against). **2 c. à faire** *(concourir)* to conspire to do. ◆**conspirateur, -trice** *nmf* conspirator. ◆**conspiration** *nf* conspiracy.

conspuer [kɔ̃spye] *vt (orateur etc)* to boo.

constant, -ante [kɔ̃stɑ̃, -ɑ̃t] *a* constant; — *nf Math* constant. ◆**constamment** *adv* constantly. ◆**constance** *nf* constancy.

constat [kɔ̃sta] *nm* (official) report; **dresser un c. d'échec** to acknowledge one's failure.

constater [kɔ̃state] *vt* to note, observe *(que* that); *(vérifier)* to establish; *(enregistrer)* to record; **je ne fais que c.** I'm merely stating a fact. ◆**constatation** *nf (remarque)* observation.

constellation [kɔ̃stelasjɔ̃] *nf* constellation. ◆**constellé** *a* **c. de** *(étoiles, joyaux)* studded with.

consterner [kɔ̃sterne] *vt* to distress, dismay. ◆**consternation** *nf* distress, (profound) dismay.

constip/er [kɔ̃stipe] *vt* to constipate. ◆**—é**

a constipated; *(gêné) Fam* embarrassed, stiff. ◆**constipation** *nf* constipation.

constitu/er [kɔ̃stitye] *vt (composer)* to make up, constitute; *(être, représenter)* to constitute; *(organiser)* to form; *(instituer) Jur* to appoint; **constitué de** made up of; **se c. prisonnier** to give oneself up. ◆**—ant** *a (éléments)* component, constituent; *(assemblée) Pol* constituent. ◆**constitutif, -ive** *a* constituent. ◆**constitution** *nf (santé)* & *Pol* constitution; *(fondation)* formation *(de* of); *(composition)* composition. ◆**constitutionnel, -elle** *a* constitutional.

constructeur [kɔ̃stryktœr] *nm* builder; *(fabricant)* maker *(de* of). ◆**constructif, -ive** *a* constructive. ◆**construction** *nf (de pont etc)* building, construction *(de* of); *(édifice)* building, structure; *(de théorie etc)* & *Gram* construction; **de c.** *(matériaux, jeu)* building-.

construire* [kɔ̃strɥir] *vt (maison, route etc)* to build, construct; *(phrase, théorie etc)* to construct.

consul [kɔ̃syl] *nm* consul. ◆**consulaire** *a* consular. ◆**consulat** *nm* consulate.

consulter [kɔ̃sylte] **1** *vt* to consult; — **se c.** *vpr* to consult (each other), confer. **2** *vi (médecin)* to hold surgery, *Am* hold office hours. ◆**consultatif, -ive** *a* consultative, advisory. ◆**consultation** *nf* consultation; **cabinet de c.** *Méd* surgery, *Am* office; **heures de c.** *Méd* surgery hours, *Am* office hours.

consumer [kɔ̃syme] *vt (détruire, miner)* to consume.

contact [kɔ̃takt] *nm* contact; *(toucher)* touch; *Aut* ignition; **être en c. avec** to be in touch *ou* contact with; **prendre c.** to get in touch (avec with); **entrer en c. avec** to come into contact with; **prise de c.** first meeting; **mettre/couper le c.** *Aut* to switch on/off the ignition. ◆**contacter** *vt* to contact.

contagieux, -euse [kɔ̃taʒjø, -øz] *a (maladie, rire)* contagious, infectious; **c. est** c. it's catching *ou* contagious. ◆**contagion** *nf Méd* contagion, infection; *(de rire etc)* contagiousness.

contaminer [kɔ̃tamine] *vt* to contaminate. ◆**contamination** *nf* contamination.

conte [kɔ̃t] *nm* tale; **c. de fée** fairy tale.

contempler [kɔ̃tɑ̃ple] *vt* to contemplate, gaze at. ◆**contemplatif, -ive** *a* contemplative. ◆**contemplation** *nf* contemplation.

contemporain, -aine [kɔ̃tɑ̃pɔrɛ̃, -ɛn] *a* & *nmf* contemporary.

contenance [kɔ̃tnɑ̃s] *nf* **1** (*contenu*) capacity. **2** (*allure*) bearing; **perdre c.** to lose one's composure.

conten/ir* [kɔ̃tnir] *vt* (*renfermer*) to contain; (*avoir comme capacité*) to hold; (*contrôler*) to hold back, contain; — **se c.** *vpr* to contain oneself. ◆—**ant** *nm* container. ◆—**eur** *nm* (freight) container.

content [kɔ̃tɑ̃] **1** *a* pleased, happy, glad (**de faire** to do); **c. de qn/qch** pleased *ou* happy with s.o./sth; **c. de soi** self-satisfied; **non c. d'avoir fait** not content with having done. **2** *nm* **avoir son c.** to have had one's fill (**de** of). ◆**content/er** *vt* to satisfy, please; **se c.** **de** to be content with, content oneself with. ◆—**ement** *nm* contentment, satisfaction.

contentieux [kɔ̃tɑ̃sjø] **1** *a* (*affaires*) matters in dispute; (*service*) legal *ou* claims department.

contenu [kɔ̃tny] *nm* (*de récipient*) contents; (*de texte, film etc*) content.

cont/er [kɔ̃te] *vt* (*histoire etc*) to tell, relate. ◆—**eur, -euse** *nmf* storyteller.

conteste (sans) [sɑ̃kɔ̃tɛst] *adv* indisputably.

contest/er [kɔ̃tɛste] **1** *vt* (*fait etc*) to dispute, contest. **2** *vi* (*étudiants etc*) to protest; — *vt* to protest against. ◆—**é** *a* (*théorie etc*) controversial. ◆—**able** *a* debatable. ◆**contestataire** *a* **étudiant/ouvrier c.** student/worker protester; — *nmf* protester. ◆**contestation** *nf* (*discussion*) dispute; **faire de la c.** to protest (against the establishment).

contexte [kɔ̃tɛkst] *nm* context.

contigu, -uë [kɔ̃tigy] *a* **c. (à)** (*maisons etc*) adjoining. ◆**contiguïté** *nf* close proximity.

continent [kɔ̃tinɑ̃] *nm* continent; (*opposé à une île*) mainland. ◆**continental, -aux** *a* continental.

contingent [kɔ̃tɛ̃ʒɑ̃] **1** *a* (*accidentel*) contingent. **2** *nm* Mil contingent; (*part, quota*) quota. ◆**contingences** *nfpl* contingencies.

continu [kɔ̃tiny] *a* continuous. ◆**continuel, -elle** *a* continual, unceasing. ◆**continuellement** *adv* continually.

continuer [kɔ̃tinɥe] *vt* to continue, carry on (**à** *ou* **de faire** doing); (*prolonger*) to continue; — *vi* to continue, go on. ◆**continuation** *nf* continuation; **bonne c.!** *Fam* I hope the rest of it goes well, keep up the good work! ◆**continuité** *nf* continuity.

contondant [kɔ̃tɔ̃dɑ̃] *a* **instrument c.** *Jur* blunt instrument.

contorsion [kɔ̃tɔrsjɔ̃] *nf* contortion. ◆**se**

contorsionner *vpr* to contort oneself. ◆**contorsionniste** *nmf* contortionist.

contour [kɔ̃tur] *nm* outline, contour; *pl* (*de route, rivière*) twists, bends. ◆**contourn/er** *vt* (*colline etc*) to go round, skirt; (*difficulté, loi*) to get round. ◆—**é** *a* (*style*) convoluted, tortuous.

contraception [kɔ̃trasɛpsjɔ̃] *nf* contraception. ◆**contraceptif, -ive** *a* & *nm* contraceptive.

contract/er [kɔ̃trakte] *vt* (*muscle, habitude, dette etc*) to contract; — **se c.** *vpr* (*cœur etc*) to contract. ◆—**é** *a* (*inquiet*) tense. ◆**contraction** *nf* contraction.

contractuel, -elle [kɔ̃traktɥɛl] **1** *nmf* traffic warden; — *nf* *Am* meter maid. **2** *a* contractual.

contradicteur [kɔ̃tradiktœr] *nm* contradictor. ◆**contradiction** *nf* contradiction. ◆**contradictoire** *a* (*propos etc*) contradictory; (*rapports, théories*) conflicting; **débat c.** debate.

contraindre* [kɔ̃trɛ̃dr] *vt* to compel, force (**à faire** to do); — **se c.** *vpr* to compel *ou* force oneself; (*se gêner*) to restrain oneself. ◆**contraignant** *a* constraining, restricting. ◆**contraint** *a* (*air etc*) forced, constrained. ◆**contrainte** *nf* compulsion, constraint; (*gêne*) constraint, restraint.

contraire [kɔ̃trɛr] *a* opposite; (*défavorable*) contrary; **c. à** contrary to; — *nm* opposite; (**bien) au c.** on the contrary. ◆—**ment** *adv* **c. à** contrary to.

contrari/er [kɔ̃trarje] *vt* (*projet, action*) to thwart; (*personne*) to annoy. ◆—**ant** *a* (*action etc*) annoying; (*personne*) difficult, perverse. ◆**contrariété** *nf* annoyance.

contraste [kɔ̃trast] *nm* contrast. ◆**contraster** *vi* to contrast (**avec** with); **faire c.** (*mettre en contraste*) to contrast.

contrat [kɔ̃tra] *nm* contract.

contravention [kɔ̃travɑ̃sjɔ̃] *nf* (*amende*) *Aut* fine; (*pour stationnement interdit*) (parking) ticket; **en c.** contravening the law; **en c. à** in contravention of.

contre [kɔ̃tr] **1** *prép* & *adv* against; (*en échange de*) (in exchange) for; **échanger c.** to exchange for; **fâché c.** angry with; **s'abriter c.** to shelter from; **il va s'appuyer c.** he's going to lean against it; **six voix c. deux** six votes to two; **Nîmes c. Arras** *Sp* Nîmes versus Arras; **un médicament c.** (*toux, grippe etc*) a medicine for; **par c.** on the other hand; **tout c.** close to *ou* by. **2** *nm* (*riposte*) *Sp* counter.

contre- [kɔ̃tr] *préf* counter-.

contre-attaque [kɔ̃tratak] *nf* counterattack. ◆**contre-attaquer** *vt* to counterattack.

contrebalancer [kɔ̃trəbalɑ̃se] *vt* to counterbalance.

contrebande [kɔ̃trəbɑ̃d] *nf* (*fraude*) smuggling, contraband; (*marchandise*) contraband; **de c.** (*tabac etc*) contraband, smuggled; **faire de la c.** to smuggle; **passer qch en c.** to smuggle sth. ◆**contrebandier, -ière** *nmf* smuggler.

contrebas (en) [ɑ̃kɔ̃trəba] *adv & prép* **en c. (de)** down below.

contrebasse [kɔ̃trəbas] *nf* Mus double-bass.

contrecarrer [kɔ̃trəkare] *vt* to thwart, frustrate.

contrecœur (à) [akɔ̃trəkœr] *adv* reluctantly.

contrecoup [kɔ̃trəku] *nm* (indirect) effect *ou* consequence; **par c.** as an indirect consequence.

contre-courant (à) [akɔ̃trəkurɑ̃] *adv* against the current.

contredanse [kɔ̃trədɑ̃s] *nf* (*amende*) Aut Fam ticket.

contredire* [kɔ̃trədir] *vt* to contradict; — **se c.** *vpr* to contradict oneself.

contrée [kɔ̃tre] *nf* region, land.

contre-espionnage [kɔ̃trɛspjɔnaʒ] *nm* counterespionage.

contrefaçon [kɔ̃trəfasɔ̃] *nf* counterfeiting, forgery; (*objet imité*) counterfeit, forgery. ◆**contrefaire** *vt* (*parodier*) to mimic; (*déguiser*) to disguise; (*monnaie etc*) to counterfeit, forge.

contreforts [kɔ̃trəfɔr] *nmpl* Géog foothills.

contre-indiqué [kɔ̃trɛ̃dike] *a* (*médicament*) dangerous, not recommended.

contre-jour (à) [akɔ̃trəʒur] *adv* against the (sun)light.

contremaître [kɔ̃trəmɛtr] *nm* foreman.

contre-offensive [kɔ̃trɔfɑ̃siv] *nf* counteroffensive.

contrepartie [kɔ̃trəparti] *nf* compensation; **en c.** in exchange.

contre-performance [kɔ̃trəperfɔrmɑ̃s] *nf* Sp bad performance.

contre-pied [kɔ̃trəpje] *nm* **le c.-pied d'une opinion/attitude** the (exact) opposite view/attitude; **à c.-pied** Sp on the wrong foot.

contre-plaqué [kɔ̃trəplake] *nm* plywood.

contrepoids [kɔ̃trəpwa] *nm* Tech & Fig counterbalance; **faire c. (à)** to counterbalance.

contrepoint [kɔ̃trəpwɛ̃] *nm* Mus counterpoint.

contrer [kɔ̃tre] *vt* (*personne, attaque*) to counter.

contre-révolution [kɔ̃trərevɔlysjɔ̃] *nf* counter-revolution.

contresens [kɔ̃trəsɑ̃s] *nm* misinterpretation; (*en traduisant*) mistranslation; (*non-sens*) absurdity; **à c.** the wrong way.

contresigner [kɔ̃trəsiɲe] *vt* to countersign.

contretemps [kɔ̃trətɑ̃] *nm* hitch, mishap; **à c.** (*arriver etc*) at the wrong moment.

contre-torpilleur [kɔ̃trətɔrpijœr] *nm* (*navire*) destroyer, torpedo boat.

contrevenir [kɔ̃trəvnir] *vi* **c. à** (*loi etc*) to contravene.

contre-vérité [kɔ̃trəverite] *nf* untruth.

contribu/er [kɔ̃tribɥe] *vi* to contribute (**à** to). ◆**—able** *nmf* taxpayer. ◆**contribution** *nf* contribution; (*impôt*) tax; *pl* (*administration*) tax office; **mettre qn à c.** to use s.o.'s services.

contrit [kɔ̃tri] *a* (*air etc*) contrite. ◆**contrition** *nf* contrition.

contrôle [kɔ̃trol] *nm* (*vérification*) inspection, check(ing) (**de** of); (*des prix, de la qualité*) control; (*maîtrise*) control; (*sur bijou*) hallmark; **un c.** (*examen*) a check (**sur** on); **le c. de soi(-même)** self-control; **le c. des naissances** birth control; **un c. d'identité** an identity check. ◆**contrôl/er** *vt* (*examiner*) to inspect, check; (*maîtriser, surveiller*) to control; — **se c.** *vpr* (*se maîtriser*) to control oneself. ◆**—eur, -euse** *nmf* (*de train*) (ticket) inspector; (*au quai*) ticket collector; (*de bus*) conductor, conductress.

contrordre [kɔ̃trɔrdr] *nm* change of orders.

controverse [kɔ̃trɔvers] *nf* controversy. ◆**controversé** *a* controversial.

contumace (par) [parkɔ̃tymas] *adv* Jur in one's absence, in absentia.

contusion [kɔ̃tyzjɔ̃] *nf* bruise. ◆**contusionner** *vt* to bruise.

convainc/re* [kɔ̃vɛ̃kr] *vt* to convince (**de** of); (*accusé*) to prove guilty (**de** of); **c. qn de faire** to persuade s.o. to do. ◆**—ant** *a* convincing. ◆**—u** *a* (*certain*) convinced (**de** of).

convalescent, -ente [kɔ̃valesɑ̃, -ɑ̃t] *nmf* convalescent; — *a* **être c.** to convalesce. ◆**convalescence** *nf* convalescence; **être en c.** to convalesce; **maison de c.** convalescent home.

conven/ir [kɔ̃vnir] *vi* **c. à** (*être approprié à*) to be suitable for; (*plaire à, aller à*) to suit; **ça convient** (*date etc*) that's suitable; **c. de** (*lieu etc*) to agree upon; (*erreur*) to admit; **c. que** to admit that; **il convient de** it's advisable to; (selon les usages) it is proper ou fitting to. ◆—u a (prix etc) agreed. ◆—able a (approprié, acceptable) suitable; (correct) decent, proper. ◆—ablement adv suitably; decently. ◆convenance nf convenances (usages) convention(s), proprieties; à sa c. to one's satisfaction ou taste.

convention [kɔ̃vɑ̃sjɔ̃] nf (accord) agreement, convention; (règle) & Am Pol convention; c. collective collective bargaining; de c. (sentiment etc) conventional. ◆conventionné a (prix, tarif) regulated (by voluntary agreement); médecin c. = National Health Service doctor (bound by agreement with the State). ◆conventionnel, -elle a conventional.

convergent [kɔ̃vɛrʒɑ̃] a converging, convergent. ◆convergence nf convergence. ◆converger vi to converge.

converser [kɔ̃vɛrse] vi to converse. ◆conversation nf conversation.

conversion [kɔ̃vɛrsjɔ̃] nf conversion. ◆convert/ir vt to convert (à to, en into); — se c. vpr to be converted, convert. ◆—i, -ie nmf convert. ◆convertible a convertible; — nm (canapé) c. bed settee.

convexe [kɔ̃vɛks] a convex.

conviction [kɔ̃viksjɔ̃] nf (certitude, croyance) conviction; pièce à c. Jur exhibit.

convier [kɔ̃vje] vt to invite (à une soirée/etc to a party/etc, à faire to do).

convive [kɔ̃viv] nmf guest (at table).

convoi [kɔ̃vwa] nm (véhicules, personnes etc) convoy; Rail train; c. (funèbre) funeral procession. ◆convoy/er vt to escort. ◆—eur nm Nau escort ship; c. de fonds security guard.

convoiter [kɔ̃vwate] vt to desire, envy, covet. ◆convoitise nf desire, envy.

convoquer [kɔ̃vɔke] vt (candidats, membres etc) to summon ou invite (to attend); (assemblée) to convene, summon; c. à to summon ou invite to. ◆convocation nf (action) summoning; convening; (ordre) summons (to attend); (lettre) (written) notice (to attend).

convulser [kɔ̃vylse] vt to convulse. ◆convulsif, -ive a convulsive. ◆convulsion nf convulsion.

coopérer [kɔɔpere] vi to co-operate (à in, avec with). ◆coopératif, -ive a co-operative; — nf co-operative (society). ◆coopération nf co-operation.

coopter [kɔɔpte] vt to co-opt.

coordonn/er [kɔɔrdɔne] vt to co-ordinate. ◆—ées nfpl Math co-ordinates; (adresse,

téléphone) Fam particulars, details. ◆coordination nf co-ordination.

copain [kɔpɛ̃] nm Fam (camarade) pal; (petit ami) boyfriend; être c. avec to be pals with.

copeau, -x [kɔpo] nm (de bois) shaving.

copie [kɔpi] nf copy; (devoir, examen) Scol paper. ◆copier vti to copy; Scol to copy, crib (sur from). ◆copieur, -euse nmf (élève etc) copycat, copier.

copieux, -euse [kɔpjø, -øz] a copious, plentiful.

copilote [kɔpilɔt] nm co-pilot.

copine [kɔpin] nf Fam (camarade) pal; (petite amie) girlfriend; être c. avec to be pals with.

copropriété [kɔprɔprjete] nf joint ownership; (immeuble en) c. block of flats in joint ownership, Am condominium.

copulation [kɔpylasjɔ̃] nf copulation.

coq [kɔk] nm cock, rooster; c. au vin coq au vin (chicken cooked in wine); passer du c. à l'âne to jump from one subject to another.

coque [kɔk] nf 1 (de navire) hull; (mollusque) cockle; œuf à la c. boiled egg. 2 Nau hull.

coquelicot [kɔkliko] nm poppy.

coqueluche [kɔklyʃ] nf Méd whooping-cough; la c. de Fig the darling of.

coquet, -ette [kɔkɛ, -ɛt] a (chic) smart; (joli) pretty; (provocant) coquettish, flirtatious; (somme) Fam tidy; — nf coquette, flirt. ◆coquetterie nf (élégance) smartness; (goût de la toilette) dress sense; (galanterie) coquetry.

coquetier [kɔktje] nm egg cup.

coquille [kɔkij] nf shell; Typ misprint; c. Saint-Jacques scallop. ◆coquillage nm (mollusque) shellfish; (coquille) shell.

coquin, -ine [kɔkɛ̃, -in] nmf rascal; — a mischievous, rascally; (histoire etc) naughty.

cor [kɔr] nm Mus horn; c. (au pied) corn; réclamer ou demander à c. et à cri to clamour for.

corail, -aux [kɔraj, -o] nm coral.

Coran [kɔrɑ̃] nm le C. the Koran.

corbeau, -x [kɔrbo] nm crow; (grand) c. raven.

corbeille [kɔrbɛj] nf basket; c. à papier waste paper basket.

corbillard [kɔrbijar] nm hearse.

corde [kɔrd] nf rope; (plus mince) (fine) cord; (de raquette, violon etc) string; c. (raide) (d'acrobate) tightrope; instrument à cordes Mus string(ed) instrument; c. à linge (washing ou clothes) line; c. à sauter skipping rope, Am jump rope; usé jusqu'à la c. threadbare; **cordes vocales** vocal cords; **prendre un virage à la c.** *Aut* to hug a bend; **pas dans mes cordes** *Fam* not my line. ◆**cordage** *nm Nau* rope. ◆**cordée** *nf* roped (climbing) party. ◆**cordelette** *nf* (fine) cord. ◆**corder** *vt* (*raquette*) to string. ◆**cordon** *nm* (*de tablier, sac etc*) string; (*de soulier*) lace; (*de rideau*) cord, rope; (*d'agents de police*) cordon; (*décoration*) ribbon, sash; (*ombilical*) *Anat* cord. ◆**c.-bleu** *nm* (*pl* **cordons-bleus**) cordon bleu (cook), first-class cook.

cordial, -aux [kɔrdjal, -o] *a* cordial, warm; – *nm Méd* cordial. ◆**cordialité** *nf* cordiality.

cordonnier [kɔrdɔnje] *nm* shoe repairer, cobbler. ◆**cordonnerie** *nf* shoe repairer's shop.

Corée [kɔre] *nf* Korea. ◆**coréen, -enne** *a* & *nmf* Korean.

coriace [kɔrjas] *a* (*aliment, personne*) tough.

corne [kɔrn] *nf* (*de chèvre etc*) horn; (*de cerf*) antler; (*matière, instrument*) horn; (*angle, pli*) corner.

cornée [kɔrne] *nf Anat* cornea.

corneille [kɔrnɛj] *nf* crow.

cornemuse [kɔrnəmyz] *nf* bagpipes.

corner [kɔrne] **1** *vt* (*page*) to turn down the corner of, dog-ear. **2** *vi* (*véhicule*) to sound its horn. **3** [kɔrnɛr] *nm Fb* corner.

cornet [kɔrnɛ] *nm* **1** c. (**à pistons**) *Mus* cornet. **2** (*de glace*) cornet, cone; **c.** (**de papier**) (paper) cone.

corniaud [kɔrnjo] *nm* (*chien*) mongrel; (*imbécile*) *Fam* drip, twit.

corniche [kɔrnif] *nf Archit* cornice; (*route*) cliff road.

cornichon [kɔrnifɔ̃] *nm* (*concombre*) gherkin; (*niais*) *Fam* clot, twit.

cornu [kɔrny] *a* (*diable etc*) horned.

corollaire [kɔrɔlɛr] *nm* corollary.

corporation [kɔrpɔrasjɔ̃] *nf* trade association, professional body.

corps [kɔr] *nm Anat Ch Fig etc* body; *Mil Pol* corps; **c. électoral** electorate; **c. enseignant** teaching profession; **c. d'armée** army corps; **garde du c.** bodyguard; **un c. de bâtiment** a main building; **c. et âme** body and soul; **lutter c. à c.** to fight hand-to-hand; **à son c. défendant** under protest; **prendre c.** (*projet*) to take shape; **donner c. à** (*rumeur, idée*) to give substance to; **faire c. avec** to form a part of, belong with; **perdu c. et biens** *Nau* lost with all hands; **esprit de c.** corporate spirit. ◆**corporel, -elle** *a* bodily; (*châtiment*) corporal.

corpulent [kɔrpylɑ̃] *a* stout, corpulent. ◆**corpulence** *nf* stoutness, corpulence.

corpus [kɔrpys] *nm Ling* corpus.

correct [kɔrɛkt] *a* (*exact*) correct; (*bienséant, honnête*) proper, correct; (*passable*) adequate. ◆**—ement** *adv* correctly; properly; adequately. ◆**correcteur, -trice 1** *a* (*verres*) corrective. **2** *nmf Scol* examiner; *Typ* proofreader. ◆**correctif, -ive** *a* corrective.

correction [kɔrɛksjɔ̃] *nf* (*rectification etc*) correction; (*punition*) thrashing; (*exactitude, bienséance*) correctness; **la c. de** (*devoirs, examen*) the marking of; **c. d'épreuves** *Typ* proofreading. ◆**correctionnel, -elle** *a* **tribunal c.,** – *nm* magistrates' court, *Am* police court.

corrélation [kɔrelasjɔ̃] *nf* correlation.

correspond/re [kɔrɛspɔ̃dr] **1** *vi* (*s'accorder*) to correspond (à to, with); (*chambres etc*) to communicate; **c. avec** *Rail* to connect with; **— se c.** *vpr* (*idées etc*) to correspond; (*chambres etc*) to communicate. **2** (*écrire*) to correspond (**avec** with). ◆**—ant, -ante** *a* corresponding; – *nmf* correspondent; (*d'un élève, d'un adolescent*) pen friend; *Tél* caller. ◆**correspondance** *nf* correspondence; (*de train, d'autocar*) connection, *Am* transfer.

corrida [kɔrida] *nf* bullfight.

corridor [kɔridɔr] *nm* corridor.

corrig/er [kɔriʒe] *vt* (*texte, injustice etc*) to correct; (*épreuve*) *Typ* to read; (*devoir*) *Scol* to mark, correct; (*châtier*) to beat, punish; **c. qn de** (*défaut*) to cure s.o. of; **se c. de** to cure oneself of. ◆**—é** *nm Scol* model (answer), correct version, key.

corroborer [kɔrɔbɔre] *vt* to corroborate.

corroder [kɔrɔde] *vt* to corrode. ◆**corrosif, -ive** *a* corrosive. ◆**corrosion** *nf* corrosion.

corromp/re [kɔrɔ̃pr] *vt* to corrupt; (*soudoyer*) to bribe; (*aliment, eau*) to taint. ◆**—u** *a* corrupt; (*altéré*) tainted. ◆**corruption** *nf* (*dépravation*) corruption; (*de juge etc*) bribery.

corsage [kɔrsaʒ] *nm* (*chemisier*) blouse; (*de robe*) bodice.

corsaire [kɔrsɛr] *nm* (*marin*) *Hist* privateer.

Corse [kɔrs] *nf* Corsica. ◆**corse** *a* & *nmf* Corsican.

cors/er [kɔrse] *vt* (*récit, action*) to heighten; **l'affaire se corse** things are hotting up. ◆**—é** *a* (*vin*) full-bodied; (*café*) strong; (*sauce, histoire*) spicy; (*problème*) tough; (*addition de restaurant*) steep.

corset [kɔrsɛ] *nm* corset.

cortège [kɔrtɛʒ] *nm* (*défilé*) procession; (*suite*) retinue; **c. officiel** (*automobiles*) motorcade.

corvée [kɔrve] *nf* chore, drudgery; *Mil* fatigue (duty).

cosaque [kɔzak] *nm* Cossack.

cosmopolite [kɔsmɔpɔlit] *a* cosmopolitan.

cosmos [kɔsmɔs] *nm* (*univers*) cosmos; (*espace*) outer space. ◆**cosmique** *a* cosmic. ◆**cosmonaute** *nmf* cosmonaut.

cosse [kɔs] *nf* (*de pois etc*) pod.

cossu [kɔsy] *a* (*personne*) well-to-do; (*maison etc*) opulent.

costaud [kɔsto] *a Fam* brawny, beefy; — *nm Fam* strong man.

costume [kɔstym] *nm* (*pièces d'habillement*) costume, dress; (*complet*) suit. ◆**costum/er** *vt* **c. qn** to dress s.o. up (**en** as). ◆**-é** **a bal c.** fancy-dress ball.

cote [kɔt] *nf* (*marque de classement*) mark, letter, number; (*tableau des valeurs*) (official) listing; (*des valeurs boursières*) quotation; (*évaluation, popularité*) rating; (*de cheval*) odds (**de** on); **c. d'alerte** danger level.

côte [kot] *nf* **1** *Anat* rib; (*de mouton*) chop; (*de veau*) cutlet; **à côtes** (*étoffe*) ribbed; **c. à c.** side by side; **se tenir les côtes** to split one's sides (laughing). **2** (*montée*) hill; (*versant*) hillside. **3** (*littoral*) coast.

côté [kote] *nm* side; (*direction*) way; **de l'autre c.** on the other side (**de** of); (*direction*) the other way; **de ce c.** (*passer*) this way; **du c. de** (*vers, près de*) towards; **de c.** (*se jeter, mettre de l'argent etc*) to one side; (*regarder*) sideways, to one side; **à c.** close by, nearby; (*pièce*) in the other room; (*maison*) next door; **la maison (d')à c.** the house next door; **à c. de** next to, beside; (*comparaison*) compared to; **passer à c.** (*balle*) to fall wide (**de** of); **venir de tous côtés** to come from all directions; **d'un c.** on the one hand; **de mon c.** for my part; **à mes côtés** by my side; **laisser de c.** (*travail*) to neglect; (**du**) **c. argent/etc** *Fam* as regards money/*etc*, moneywise/*etc*; **le bon c.** (*d'une affaire*) the bright side (**de** of).

coteau, -x [kɔto] *nm* (small) hill; (*versant*) hillside.

côtelé [kotle] *a* (*étoffe*) ribbed; **velours c.** cord(uroy).

côtelette [kotlɛt] *nf* (*d'agneau, de porc*) chop; (*de veau*) cutlet.

cot/er [kɔte] *vt* (*valeur boursière*) to quote. ◆**-é a bien c.** highly rated.

coterie [kɔtri] *nf Péj* set, clique.

côtier, -ière [kotje, -jɛr] *a* coastal; (*pêche*) inshore.

cotiser [kɔtize] *vi* to contribute (**à** to, **pour** towards); **c.** (**à**) (*club*) to subscribe (to); — **se c.** *vpr* to club together (**pour acheter** to buy). ◆**cotisation** *nf* (*de club*) dues, subscription; (*de pension etc*) contribution(s).

coton [kɔtɔ̃] *nm* cotton; **c.** (**hydrophile**) cottonwool, *Am* (absorbent) cotton. ◆**cotonnade** *nf* cotton (fabric). ◆**cotonnier, -ière** *a* (*industrie*) cotton-.

côtoyer [kotwaje] *vt* (*route, rivière*) to run along, skirt; (*la misère, la folie etc*) *Fig* to be ou come close to; **c. qn** (*fréquenter*) to rub shoulders with s.o.

cotte [kɔt] *nf* (*de travail*) overalls.

cou [ku] *nm* neck; **sauter au c. de qn** to throw one's arms around s.o.; **jusqu'au c.** *Fig* up to one's eyes ou ears.

couche [kuʃ] *nf* **1** (*épaisseur*) layer; (*de peinture*) coat; *Géol* stratum; **couches sociales** social strata. **2** (*linge de bébé*) nappy, *Am* diaper. **3 faire une fausse c.** *Méd* to have a miscarriage; **les couches** *Méd* confinement.

couch/er [kuʃe] *vt* to put to bed; (*héberger*) to put up; (*allonger*) to lay (down ou out); (*blé*) to flatten; **c.** (**par écrit**) to put down (in writing); **c. qn en joue** to aim at s.o.; — *vi* to sleep (**avec** with); — **se c.** *vpr* to go to bed; (*s'allonger*) to lie flat ou down; (*soleil*) to set, go down; — *nm* (*moment*) bedtime; **c. de soleil** sunset. ◆**-ant** *a* (*soleil*) setting; — *nm* (*aspect*) sunset; **le c.** (*ouest*) west. ◆**-é a être c.** to be in bed; (*étendu*) to be lying (down). ◆**-age** *nm* sleeping (situation); (*matériel*) bedding; **sac de c.** sleeping bag. ◆**couchette** *nf Rail* sleeping berth, couchette; *Nau* bunk.

couci-couça [kusikusa] *adv Fam* so-so.

coucou [kuku] *nm* (*oiseau*) cuckoo; (*pendule*) cuckoo clock; *Bot* cowslip.

coude [kud] *nm* elbow; (*de chemin, rivière*) bend; **se serrer** *ou* **se tenir les coudes** to help one another, stick together; **c. à c.** side by side; **coup de c.** poke ou dig (with one's elbow), nudge; **pousser du c.** to nudge. ◆**coudoyer** *vt* to rub shoulders with.

cou-de-pied [kudpje] *nm* (*pl* **cous-de-pied**) instep.

coudre [kudr] *vti* to sew.

couenne [kwan] *nf* (*pork*) crackling.

couette [kwɛt] *nf* (*édredon*) duvet, continental quilt.

couffin [kufɛ̃] *nm* (*de bébé*) Moses basket, *Am* bassinet.

couic! [kwik] *int* eek!, squeak! ◆**couiner** *vi Fam* to squeal; (*pleurer*) to whine.

couillon [kujɔ̃] *nm* (idiot) *Arg* drip, cretin.

coul/er[1] [kule] *vi* (*liquide*) to flow; (*robinet, nez, sueur*) to run; (*fuir*) to leak; **c. de source** *Fig* to follow naturally; **faire c. le sang** to cause bloodshed; – *vt* (*métal, statue*) to cast; (*vie*) *Fig* to pass, lead; (*glisser*) to slip; **se c. dans** (*passer*) to slip into; **se la c. douce** to have things easy. ◆**—ant** *a* (*style*) flowing; (*caractère*) easygoing. ◆**—ée** *nf* (*de métal*) casting; **c. de lave** lava flow. ◆**—age** *nm* (*de métal, statue*) casting; (*gaspillage*) *Fam* wastage.

couler[2] [kule] *vi* (*bateau, nageur*) to sink; **c. à pic** to sink to the bottom; – *vt* to sink; (*discréditer*) *Fig* to discredit.

couleur [kulœr] *nf* colour; (*colorant*) paint; *Cartes* suit; *pl* (*teint, carnation*) colour; **c. chair** flesh-coloured; **de c.** (*homme, habit etc*) coloured; **en couleurs** (*photo, télévision*) colour-; **téléviseur c.** colour TV set; **haut en c.** colourful; **sous c. de faire** while pretending to do.

couleuvre [kulœvr] *nf* (grass) snake.

coulisse [kulis] *nf* **1** (*de porte*) runner; **à c.** (*porte etc*) sliding. **2 dans les coulisses** *Th* in the wings, backstage; **dans la c.** (*caché*) *Fig* behind the scenes. ◆**coulissant** *a* (*porte etc*) sliding.

couloir [kulwar] *nm* corridor; (*de circulation*) & *Sp* lane; (*dans un bus*) gangway.

coup [ku] *nm* blow, knock; (*léger*) tap, touch; (*choc moral*) blow; (*de fusil etc*) shot; (*de crayon, d'horloge*) & *Sp* stroke; (*aux échecs etc*) move; (*fois*) *Fam* time; **donner des coups à qn** to hit s.o.; **c. de brosse** brush(-up); **c. de chiffon** wipe (with a rag); **c. de sonnette** ring (on a bell); **c. de dents** bite; **c. de chance** stroke of luck; **c. d'État** coup; **c. dur** *Fam* nasty blow; **sale c.** dirty trick; **mauvais c.** piece of mischief; **c. franc** *Fb* free kick; **tenter le c.** *Fam* to have a go *ou* try; **réussir son c.** to bring it off; **faire les quatre cents coups** to get into all kinds of mischief; **tenir le c.** to hold out; **avoir/attraper le c.** *Fam* to have/get the knack; **sous le c. de** (*émotion etc*) under the influence of; **il est dans le c.** *Fam* he's in the know; **après c.** after the event, afterwards; **sur le c. de midi** on the stroke of twelve; **sur le c.** (*alors*) at the time; **tué sur le c.** killed outright; **à c. sûr** for sure; **sur c.** (*à la suite*) one after the other, in quick succession; **tout à c., tout d'un c.** suddenly; **à tout c.** at every go; **d'un seul c.** in one go; **du premier c.** *Fam* (at they first go; **du c.**

suddenly; (*de ce fait*) as a result; **pour le c.** this time. ◆**c.-de-poing** *nm* (*pl* **coups-de-poing**) **c.-de-poing** (**américain**) knuckle-duster.

coupable [kupabl] *a* guilty (**de** of); (*plaisir, désir*) sinful; **déclarer c.** *Jur* to convict; – *nmf* guilty person, culprit.

coupe [kup] *nf* **1** *Sp* cup; (*à fruits*) dish; (*à boire*) goblet, glass. **2** (*de vêtement etc*) cut; *Géom* section; **c. de cheveux** haircut. ◆**coup/er** *vt* to cut; (*arbre*) to cut down; (*vivres etc*) & *Tél* to cut off; (*courant etc*) to switch off; (*voyage*) to break (off); (*faim, souffle etc*) to take away; (*vin*) to water down; (*morceler*) to cut up; (*croiser*) to cut across; **c. la parole à** to cut short; – *vi* to cut; **c. à** (*corvée*) *Fam* to get out of; **ne coupez pas!** *Tél* hold the line!; – **se c.** *vpr* (*routes*) to intersect; (*se trahir*) to give oneself away; **se c. au doigt** to cut one's finger. ◆**—ant** *a* sharp; – *nm* (cutting) edge. ◆**—é** *nm* *Aut* coupé.

coupe-circuit [kupsirkɥi] *nm inv Él* cutout, circuit breaker. ◆**c.-file** *nm inv* (*laissez-passer*) official pass. ◆**c.-gorge** *nm inv* cut-throat alley. ◆**c.-ongles** *nm inv* (finger nail) clippers. ◆**c.-papier** *nm inv* paper knife.

couperet [kupre] *nm* (meat) chopper; (*de guillotine*) blade.

couperosé [kuproze] *a* (*visage*) blotchy.

couple [kupl] *nm* pair, couple. ◆**coupler** *vt* to couple, connect.

couplet [kuplε] *nm* verse.

coupole [kupɔl] *nf* dome.

coupon [kupɔ̃] *nm* (*tissu*) remnant, oddment; (*pour la confection d'un vêtement*) length; (*ticket, titre*) coupon; **c. réponse** reply coupon.

coupure [kupyr] *nf* cut; (*de journal*) cutting, *Am* clipping; (*billet*) banknote.

cour [kur] *nf* **1** court(yard); (*de gare*) forecourt; **c. (de récréation)** *Scol* playground. **2** (*de roi*) & *Jur* court. **3** (*de femme, d'homme*) courtship; **faire la c. à qn** to court s.o., woo s.o.

courage [kuraʒ] *nm* courage; (*zèle*) spirit; **perdre c.** to lose heart *ou* courage; **s'armer de c.** to pluck up courage; **bon c.!** keep your chin up! ◆**courageux, -euse** *a* courageous; (*énergique*) spirited.

couramment [kuramɑ̃] *adv* (*parler*) fluently; (*souvent*) frequently.

courant [kurɑ̃] **1** *a* (*fréquent*) common; (*compte, année, langage*) current; (*eau*) running; (*modèle, taille*) standard; (*affaires*) routine; **le dix/etc c.** *Com* the tenth/etc inst(ant). **2** *nm* (*de l'eau, élec-*

trique) current; **c. d'air** draught; **coupure de c.** *El* power cut; **dans le c. de** (*mois etc*) during the course of; **être/mettre au c.** to know/tell (**de** about); **au c.** (*à jour*) up to date.

courbature [kurbatyr] *nf* (muscular) ache. ◆**courbaturé** *a* aching (all over).

courbe [kurb] *a* curved; — *nf* curve. ◆**courber** *vti* to bend; — **se c.** *vpr* to bend (over).

courge [kur3] *nf* marrow, *Am* squash. ◆**courgette** *nf* courgette, *Am* zucchini.

cour/ir* [kurir] *vi* to run; (*se hâter*) to rush; (*à bicyclette, en auto*) to race; **en courant** (*vite*) in a rush; **le bruit court que . . .** ; there's a rumour going around that . . .; **faire c.** (*nouvelle*) to spread; **il court encore** (*voleur*) he's still at large; — *vt* (*risque*) to run; (*épreuve sportive*) to run (in); (*danger*) to face, court; (*rues, monde*) to roam; (*magasins, cafés*) to go round; (*filles*) to run after. ◆**—eur** *nm Sp etc* runner; (*cycliste*) cyclist; *Aut* racing driver; (*galant*) *Péj* womanizer.

couronne [kuron] *nf* (*de roi, dent*) crown; (*funéraire*) wreath. ◆**couronn/er** *vt* to crown; (*auteur, ouvrage*) to award a prize to. ◆**—é** *a* (*tête*) crowned; (*ouvrage*) prize-. ◆**—ement** *nm* (*sacre*) coronation; *Fig* crowning achievement.

courrier [kurje] *nm* post, mail; (*transport*) postal *ou* mail service; (*article*) *Journ* column; **par retour du c.** by return of post, *Am* by return mail.

courroie [kurwa] *nf* (*attache*) strap; (*de transmission*) *Tech* belt.

courroux [kuru] *nm Litt* wrath.

cours [kur] *nm* **1** (*de maladie, rivière, astre, pensées etc*) course; (*cote*) rate, price; **c. d'eau** river, stream; **suivre son c.** (*déroulement*) to follow its course; **avoir c.** (*monnaie*) to be legal tender; (*théorie*) to be current; **en c.** (*travail*) in progress; (*année*) current; (*affaires*) outstanding; **en c. de route** on the way; **au c. de** during; **donner libre c. à** to give free rein to. **2** (*leçon*) class; (*série de leçons*) course; (*conférence*) lecture; (*établissement*) school; (*manuel*) textbook; **c. magistral** lecture. **3** (*allée*) avenue.

course [kurs] *nf* **1** (*action*) running(in); (*épreuve de vitesse*) & *Fig* race; (*trajet*) journey, run; (*excursion*) hike; (*de projectile etc*) path, flight; *pl* (*de chevaux*) races; **il n'est plus dans la c.** *Fig* he's out of touch; **cheval de c.** racehorse; **voiture de c.** racing car. **2** (*commission*) errand; *pl* (*achats*)

shopping; **faire une c.** to run an errand; **faire les courses** to do the shopping.

coursier, -ière [kursje, -jɛr] *nmf* messenger.

court [kur] **1** *a* short; **c'est un peu c.** *Fam* that's not very much; — *adv* short; **couper c.** (*entretien*) to cut short; **tout c.** quite simply; **à c. de** (*argent etc*) short of; **pris de c.** caught unawares. **2** *nm* Tennis court. ◆**c.-bouillon** *nm* (*pl* **courts-bouillons**) court-bouillon (spiced water for cooking fish). ◆**c.-circuit** *nm* (*pl* **courts-circuits**) *El* short circuit. ◆**c.-circuiter** *vt* to short-circuit.

courtier, -ière [kurtje, -jɛr] *nmf* broker. ◆**courtage** *nm* brokerage.

courtisan [kurtizɑ̃] *nm Hist* courtier. ◆**courtisane** *nf Hist* courtesan. ◆**courtiser** *vt* to court.

courtois [kurtwa] *a* courteous. ◆**courtoisie** *nf* courtesy.

couru [kury] *a* (*spectacle, lieu*) popular; **c'est c.** (*d'avance*) *Fam* it's a sure thing.

couscous [kuskus] *nm Culin* couscous.

cousin, -ine [kuzɛ̃, -in] **1** *nmf* cousin. **2** *nm* (*insecte*) gnat, midge.

coussin [kusɛ̃] *nm* cushion.

cousu [kuzy] *a* sewn; **c. main** handsewn.

coût [ku] *nm* cost. ◆**coût/er** *vti* to cost; **ça coûte combien?** how much is it?, how much does it cost?; **ça lui en coûte de faire** it pains him *ou* her to do; **coûte que coûte** at all costs; **c. les yeux de la tête** to cost the earth. ◆**—ant** *a* **prix c.** cost price. ◆**coûteux, -euse** *a* costly, expensive.

couteau, -x [kuto] *nm* knife; **coup de c.** stab; **à couteaux tirés** at daggers drawn (**avec** with); **visage en lame de c.** hatchet face; **retourner le c. dans la plaie** *Fig* to rub it in.

coutume [kutym] *nf* custom; **avoir c. de faire** to be accustomed to doing; **comme de c.** as usual; **plus que de c.** more than is customary. ◆**coutumier, -ière** *a* customary.

couture [kutyr] *nf* sewing, needlework; (*métier*) dressmaking; (*raccord*) seam; **maison de c.** fashion house. ◆**couturier** *nm* fashion designer. ◆**couturière** *nf* dressmaker.

couvent [kuvɑ̃] *nm* (*pour religieuses*) convent; (*pour moines*) monastery; (*pensionnat*) convent school.

couv/er [kuve] *vt* (*œufs*) to sit on, hatch; (*projet*) to hatch; (*rhume etc*) to be getting; **c. qn** to pamper s.o.; **c. des yeux** (*convoiter*) to look at enviously; — *vi* (*poule*) to brood; (*mal*) to be brewing;

(*feu*) to smoulder. ◆—ée *nf* (*petits*) brood; (*œufs*) clutch. ◆**couveuse** *nf* (*pour nouveaux-nés, œufs*) incubator.

couvercle [kuvɛrkl] *nm* lid, cover.

couvert [kuvɛr] **1** *nm* (*cuiller, fourchette, couteau*) (set of) cutlery; (*au restaurant*) cover charge; **mettre le c.** to lay the table; **table de cinq couverts** table set for five. **2** *nm* **sous** (**le**) **c. de** (*apparence*) under cover of; **se mettre à c.** to take cover. **3** *a* covered (**de** with, in); (*ciel*) overcast. ◆**couverture** *nf* (*de lit*) blanket, cover; (*de livre etc*) & *Fin Mil* cover; (*de toit*) roofing; **c. chauffante** electric blanket; **c. de voyage** travelling rug.

couvre-chef [kuvrəʃɛf] *nm Hum* headgear. ◆**c.-feu** *nm* (*pl* -x) curfew. ◆**c.-lit** *nm* bedspread. ◆**c.-pied** *nm* quilt.

couvr/ir* [kuvrir] *vt* to cover (**de** with); (*voix*) to drown; **— se c.** *vpr* (*se vêtir*) to cover up, wrap up; (*se coiffer*) to cover one's head; (*ciel*) to cloud over. ◆—**eur** *nm* roofer.

cow-boy [kɔbɔj] *nm* cowboy.

crabe [krab] *nm* crab.

crac! [krak] *int* (*rupture*) snap!; (*choc*) bang!, smash!

crach/er [kraʃe] *vi* to spit; (*stylo*) to splutter; (*radio*) to crackle; **—** *vt* to spit (out); **c. sur qch** (*dédaigner*) *Fam* to turn one's nose up at sth. ◆—**é** *a* **c'est son portrait tout c.** *Fam* that's the spitting image of him *ou* her. ◆**crachat** *nm* spit, spittle.

crachin [kraʃɛ̃] *nm* (fine) drizzle.

crack [krak] *nm Fam* ace, wizard, real champ.

craie [krɛ] *nf* chalk.

craindre* [krɛ̃dr] *vt* (*personne, mort, douleur etc*) to be afraid of, fear, dread; (*chaleur etc*) to be sensitive to; **c. de faire** to be afraid of doing, dread doing; **je crains qu'elle ne vienne** I'm afraid (that) she might come; **c. pour qch** to fear for sth; **ne craignez rien** have no fear. ◆**crainte** *nf* fear, dread; **de c. de faire** for fear of doing; **de c. que** (+ *sub*) for fear that. ◆**craintif, -ive** *a* timid.

cramoisi [kramwazi] *a* crimson.

crampe [krɑ̃p] *nf Méd* cramp.

crampon [krɑ̃pɔ̃] **1** *nm* (*personne*) *Fam* leech, hanger-on. **2** *nmpl* (*de chaussures*) studs.

cramponner (se) [səkrɑ̃pɔne] *vpr* **se c. à** to hold on to, cling to.

cran [krɑ̃] *nm* **1** (*entaille*) notch; (*de ceinture*) hole; **c. d'arrêt** catch; **couteau à c. d'arrêt** flick-knife, *Am* switchblade; **c. de**

sûreté safety catch. **2** (*de cheveux*) wave. **3** (*audace*) *Fam* pluck, guts. **4** **à c.** (*excédé*) *Fam* on edge.

crâne [krɑn] *nm* skull; (*tête*) *Fam* head. ◆**crânienne** *af* **boîte c.** cranium, brain pan.

crâner [krɑne] *vi Péj* to show off, swagger.

crapaud [krapo] *nm* toad.

crapule [krapyl] *nf* villain, (filthy) scoundrel. ◆**crapuleux, -euse** *a* vile, sordid.

craqueler [krakle] *vt*, **— se c.** *vpr* to crack.

craqu/er [krake] *vi* (*branche*) to snap; (*chaussure*) to creak; (*bois sec*) to crack; (*sous la dent*) to crunch; (*se déchirer*) to split, rip; (*projet, entreprise etc*) to come apart at the seams, crumble; (*personne*) to break down, reach breaking point; **—** *vt* (**faire**) **c.** (*allumette*) to strike. ◆—**ement** *nm* snapping *ou* creaking *ou* cracking (sound).

crasse [kras] **1** *a* (*ignorance*) crass. **2** *nf* filth. ◆**crasseux, -euse** *a* filthy.

cratère [kratɛr] *nm* crater.

cravache [kravaʃ] *nf* horsewhip, riding crop.

cravate [kravat] *nf* (*autour du cou*) tie. ◆**cravaté** *a* wearing a tie.

crawl [krol] *nm* (*nage*) crawl. ◆**crawlé** *a* **dos c.** backstroke.

crayeux, -euse [krɛjø, -øz] *a* chalky.

crayon [krɛjɔ̃] *nm* (*en bois*) pencil; (*de couleur*) crayon; **c. à bille** ballpoint (pen). ◆**crayonner** *vt* to pencil.

créance [kreɑ̃s] *nf* **1** *Fin Jur* claim (for money). **2** **lettres de c.** *Pol* credentials. ◆**créancier, -ière** *nmf* creditor.

créateur, -trice [kreatœr, -tris] *nmf* creator; **—** *a* creative; **esprit c.** creativeness. ◆**créatif, -ive** *a* creative. ◆**création** *nf* creation. ◆**créativité** *nf* creativity. ◆**créature** *nf* (*être*) creature.

crécelle [kresɛl] *nf* (*de supporter*) rattle.

crèche [krɛʃ] *nf* (*de Noël*) *Rel* crib, manger; *Scol* day nursery, crèche. ◆**crécher** *vi* (*loger*) *Arg* to bed down, hang out.

crédible [kredibl] *a* credible. ◆**crédibilité** *nf* credibility.

crédit [kredi] *nm* (*influence*) & *Fin* credit; *pl* (*sommes*) funds; **à c.** (*acheter*) on credit, on hire purchase; **faire c.** *Fin* to give credit (**à** to). ◆**créditer** *vt Fin* to credit (**de** with). ◆**créditeur, -euse** (*solde, compte*) credit-; **son compte est c.** his account is in credit, he is in credit.

credo [kredo] *nm* creed.

crédule [kredyl] *a* credulous. ◆**crédulité** *nf* credulity.

créer [kree] vt to create.

crémaillère [kremajer] nf **pendre la c.** to have a house-warming (party).

crématoire [krematwar] a **four c.** crematorium. ◆**crémation** nf cremation.

crème [krɛm] nf (dessert) cream; (dessert) cream dessert; **café c.** white coffee, coffee with cream ou milk; **c. Chantilly** whipped cream; **c. glacée** ice cream; **c. à raser** shaving cream; **c. anglaise** custard; – a inv cream(-coloured); – nm (café) white coffee. ◆**crémerie** nf (magasin) dairy (shop). ◆**crémeux, -euse** a creamy. ◆**crémier, -ière** nmf dairyman, dairywoman.

créneau, -x [kreno] nm Hist crenellation; (trou) Fig slot, gap; Écon market opportunity, niche; **faire un c.** Aut to park between two vehicles.

créole [kreɔl] nmf Creole; – nm Ling Creole.

crêpe [krɛp] **1** nf Culin pancake. **2** nm (tissu) crepe; (caoutchouc) crepe (rubber). ◆**crêperie** nf pancake bar.

crépi [krepi] a & nm roughcast.

crépit/er [krepite] vi to crackle. ◆**-ement** nm crackling (sound).

crépu [krepy] a (cheveux, personne) frizzy.

crépuscule [krepyskyl] nm twilight, dusk. ◆**crépusculaire** a (lueur etc) twilight-, dusk-.

crescendo [kreʃɛndo] adv & nm inv crescendo.

cresson [kresɔ̃] nm (water) cress.

crête [krɛt] nf (d'oiseau, de vague, de montagne) crest; **c. de coq** cockscomb.

Crète [krɛt] nf Crete.

crétin, -ine [kretɛ̃, -in] nmf cretin; – a cretinous.

creus/er [krøze] **1** vt (terre, sol) to dig (a hole ou holes in); (trou, puits) to dig; (évider) to hollow (out); (idée) Fig to go deeply into; **c. l'estomac** to whet the appetite. **2** se c.** vpr (joues etc) to become hollow; (abîme) Fig to form; **se c. la tête** ou **la cervelle** to rack one's brains. ◆**-é** a **c. de rides** (visage) furrowed with wrinkles.

creuset [krøze] nm (récipient) crucible; (lieu) Fig melting pot.

creux, -euse [krø, -øz] a (tube, joues, paroles etc) hollow; (estomac) empty; (sans activité) slack; **assiette creuse** soup plate; – nm hollow; (de l'estomac) pit; (moment) slack period; **c. des reins** small of the back.

crevaison [krəvɛzɔ̃] nf puncture.

crevasse [krəvas] nf crevice, crack; (de glacier) crevasse; pl (aux mains) chaps.

crevasser vt, — **se c.** vpr to crack; (peau) to chap.

crève [krɛv] nf (rhume) Fam bad cold.

crev/er [krəve] vi (bulle etc) to burst; (pneu) to puncture, burst; (mourir) Fam to die, drop dead; **c. d'orgueil** to be bursting with pride; **c. de rire** Fam to split one's sides; **c. d'ennui/de froid** Fam to be bored/to freeze to death; **c. de faim** Fam to be starving; – vt to burst; (œil) to put ou knock out; **c. qn** Fam to wear ou knock s.o. out; **ça (vous) crève les yeux** Fam it's staring you in the face; **c. le cœur** to be heartbreaking. ◆**-ant** a (fatigant) Fam exhausting; (drôle) Arg hilarious, killing. ◆**-é** a (fatigué) Fam worn ou knocked out; (mort) Fam dead. ◆**crève-cœur** nm inv heartbreak.

crevette [krəvɛt] nf (grise) shrimp; (rose) prawn.

cri [kri] nm (de joie, surprise) cry, shout; (de peur) scream; (de douleur, d'alarme) cry; (appel) call, cry; **c. de guerre** war cry; **un chapeau/etc dernier c.** the latest hat/etc. ◆**criard** a (enfant) bawling; (son) screeching; (couleur) gaudy, showy.

criant [krijã] a (injustice etc) glaring.

crible [kribl] nm sieve, riddle. ◆**cribler** vt to sift; **criblé de** (balles, dettes etc) riddled with.

cric [krik] nm (instrument) Aut jack.

cricket [krikɛt] nm Sp cricket.

crier [krije] vi to shout (out), cry (out); (de peur) to scream; (oiseau) to chirp; (grincer) to creak, squeak; **c. au scandale/etc** to proclaim sth to be a scandal/etc; **c. après qn** Fam to shout at s.o.; – vt (injure, ordre) to shout (out); (son innocence etc) to proclaim; **c. vengeance** to cry out for vengeance. ◆**crieur, -euse** nmf **c. de journaux** newspaper seller.

crime [krim] nm crime; (assassinat) murder. ◆**criminalité** nf crime (in general), criminal practice. ◆**criminel, -elle** a criminal; – nmf criminal; (assassin) murderer.

crin [krɛ̃] nm horsehair; **c. végétal** vegetable fibre; **à tous crins** (pacifiste etc) out-and-out. ◆**crinière** nf mane.

crique [krik] nf creek, cove.

criquet [krikɛ] nm locust.

crise [kriz] nf crisis; (accès) attack; (de colère etc) fit; (pénurie) shortage; **c. de conscience** (moral) dilemma.

crisp/er [krispe] vt (muscle) to tense; (visage) to make tense; (poing) to clench; **c. qn** Fam to aggravate s.o.; **c. se c.** sur (main) to grip tightly. ◆**-ant** a aggravating. ◆**-é**

a (*personne*) tense. ◆**crispation** *nf* (*agacement*) aggravation.◆

crisser [krise] *vi* (*pneu, roue*) to screech; (*neige*) to crunch.

cristal, -aux [kristal, -o] *nm* crystal; *pl* (*objets*) crystal(ware); (*pour nettoyer*) washing soda. ◆**cristallin** *a* (*eau, son*) crystal-clear. ◆**cristalliser** *vti*, — **se c.** *vpr* to crystallize.

critère [kriter] *nm* criterion.

critérium [kriterjɔm] *nm* (*épreuve*) Sp eliminating heat.

critique [kritik] *a* critical; — *nf* (*reproche*) criticism; (*analyse de film, livre etc*) review; (*de texte*) critique; **faire la c. de** (*film etc*) to review; **affronter la c.** to confront the critics; — *nm* critic. ◆**critiqu/er** *vt* to criticize. ◆—**able** *a* open to criticism.

croasser [krɔase] *vi* (*corbeau*) to caw.

croc [kro] *nm* (*crochet*) hook; (*dent*) fang. ◆**c.-en-jambe** *nm* (*pl crocs-en-jambe*) = **croche-pied**.

croche [krɔʃ] *nf* Mus quaver, Am eighth (note).

croche-pied [krɔʃpje] *nm* **faire un c.-pied à** **qn** to trip s.o. up.

crochet [krɔʃɛ] *nm* (*pour accrocher*) & Boxe hook; (*aiguille*) crochet hook; (*travail*) crochet; (*clef*) picklock; Typ (*square*) bracket; **faire qch au c.** to crochet sth; **faire un c.** (*route*) to make a sudden turn; (*personne*) to make a detour *ou* side trip; (*pour éviter*) to swerve; **vivre aux crochets** **de qn** Fam to sponge off *ou* on s.o. ◆**crocheter** *vt* (*serrure*) to pick. ◆**crochu** *a* (*nez*) hooked.

crocodile [krɔkɔdil] *nm* crocodile.

crocus [krɔkys] *nm* Bot crocus.

croire* [krwar] *vt* to believe; (*estimer*) to think, believe (**que** that); **j'ai cru la voir I** thought I saw her; **je crois que oui I** think *ou* believe so; **je n'en crois pas mes yeux I** can't believe my eyes; **à l'en c.** according to him; **il se croit malin/quelque chose he** thinks he's smart/quite something; — *vi* to believe (**à, en** in).

croisé¹ [krwaze] *nm* Hist crusader. ◆**croisade** *nf* crusade.

crois/er [krwaze] *vt* to cross; (*bras*) to fold, cross; **c. qn** to pass *ou* meet s.o.; — *vi* (*veston*) to fold over; Nau to cruise; — **se c.** *vpr* (*voitures etc*) to pass *ou* meet (each other); (*routes*) to cross, intersect; (*lettres*) to cross in the post. ◆—**é²**, -**ée** *a* (*bras*) folded, crossed; (*veston*) double-breasted; **mots croisés** crossword; **tirs croisés** crossfire; **race croisée** crossbreed; — *nf* (*fenêtre*)

casement; **croisée des chemins** crossroads. ◆—**ement** *nm* (*action*) crossing; (*de routes*) crossroads, intersection; (*de véhicules*) passing. ◆—**eur** *nm* (*navire de guerre*) cruiser. ◆**croisière** *nf* cruise; **vitesse de c.** Nau Av & Fig cruising speed.

croître* [krwatr] *vi* (*plante etc*) to grow; (*augmenter*) to grow, increase; (*lune*) to wax. ◆**croissant 1** *a* (*nombre etc*) growing. **2** *nm* crescent; (*pâtisserie*) croissant. ◆**croissance** *nf* growth.

croix [krwa] *nf* cross.

croque-mitaine [krɔkmiten] *nm* bogeyman. ◆**c.-monsieur** *nm inv* toasted cheese and ham sandwich. ◆**c.-mort** *nm* Fam undertaker's assistant.

croqu/er [krɔke] **1** *vt* (*manger*) to crunch; — *vi* (*fruit etc*) to be crunchy, crunch. **2** *vt* (*peindre*) to sketch; **joli à c.** pretty as a picture. ◆—**ant** *a* (*biscuit etc*) crunchy. ◆**croquette** *nf* Culin croquette.

croquet [krɔke] *nm* Sp croquet.

croquis [krɔki] *nm* sketch.

crosse [krɔs] *nf* (*d'évêque*) crook; (*de fusil*) butt; (*de hockey*) stick.

crotte [krɔt] *nf* (*de lapin etc*) mess, droppings. ◆**crottin** *nm* (*horse*) dung.

crotté [krɔte] *a* (*bottes etc*) muddy.

croul/er [krule] *vi* (*édifice, projet etc*) to crumble, collapse; **c. sous une charge** (*porteur etc*) to totter beneath a burden; **faire c.** (*immeuble etc*) to bring down. ◆—**ant** *a* (*mur etc*) tottering; — *nm* (*vieux*) Fam old-timer.

croupe [krup] *nf* (*de cheval*) rump; **monter** **en c.** (*à cheval*) to ride pillion. ◆**croupion** *nm* (*de poulet*) parson's nose.

croupier [krupje] *nm* (*au casino*) croupier.

croupir [krupir] *vi* (*eau*) to stagnate, become foul; **c. dans** (*le vice etc*) to wallow in; **eau croupie** stagnant water.

croustill/er [krustije] *vi* to be crusty; to be crunchy. ◆—**ant** *a* (*pain*) crusty; (*biscuit*) crunchy; (*histoire*) Fig spicy, juicy.

croûte [krut] *nf* (*de pain etc*) crust; (*de fromage*) rind; (*de plaie*) scab; **casser la c.** Fam to have a snack; **gagner sa c.** Fam to earn one's bread and butter. ◆**croûton** *nm* crust (*at end of loaf*); *pl* (*avec soupe*) croûtons.

croyable [krwajabl] *a* credible, believable. ◆**croyance** *nf* belief (**à, en** in). ◆**croyant, -ante** *a* **être c.** to be a believer; — *nmf* believer.

CRS [seers] *nmpl abrév* (*Compagnies républicaines de sécurité*) French state security police, riot police.

cru[1] [kry] *voir* **croire.**

cru[2] [kry] **1** *a* (*aliment etc*) raw; (*lumière*) glaring; (*propos*) crude; **monter à c.** to ride bareback; **un grand c.** (*vin*) a vintage wine; **vin du c.** local wine. **2** *nm* (*vignoble*) vineyard; (*vin*) wine.

cruauté [kryote] *nf* cruelty (*envers* to).

cruche [kryʃ] *nf* pitcher, jug.

crucial, -aux [krysjal, -o] *a* crucial. **crucifier** [krysifje] *vt* to crucify. ◆**crucifix** [krysifi] *nm* crucifix. ◆**crucifixion** *nf* crucifixion.

crudité [krydite] *nf* (*grossièreté*) crudeness; *pl* Culin assorted raw vegetables.

crue [kry] *nf* (*de cours d'eau*) swelling, flood; **en c.** in spate.

cruel, -elle [kryɛl] *a* cruel (*envers, avec* to). ◆**crûment** [krymɑ̃] *adv* crudely.

crustacés [krystase] *nmpl* shellfish, crustaceans.

crypte [kript] *nf* crypt.

Cuba [kyba] *nm* Cuba. ◆**cubain, -aine** *a* & *nmf* Cuban.

cube [kyb] *nm* cube; *pl* (*jeu*) building blocks; – *a* (*mètre etc*) cubic. ◆**cubique** *a* cubic.

cueillir[*] [kœjir] *vt* to gather, pick; (*baiser*) to snatch; (*voleur*) Fam to pick up, run in. ◆**cueillette** *nf* gathering, picking; (*fruits cueillis*) harvest.

cuiller, cuillère [kɥijɛr] *nf* spoon; **petite c., c. à café** teaspoon; **c. à soupe** table spoon. ◆**cuillerée** *nf* spoonful.

cuir [kɥir] *nm* leather; (*peau épaisse d'un animal vivant*) hide; **c. chevelu** scalp.

cuirasse [kɥiras] *nf* Hist breastplate. ◆**se cuirass/er** *vpr* to steel oneself (*contre* against). ◆**–é** *nm* battleship.

cuire[*] [kɥir] *vt* to cook; (*à l'eau*) to boil; (*porcelaine*) to bake, fire; **c.** (*au four*) to bake; (*viande*) to roast; – *vi* to cook; to boil; to bake; to roast; (*soleil*) to bake, boil; **faire c.** to cook. ◆**cuisant** *a* (*affront, blessure etc*) stinging. ◆**cuisson** *nm* cooking; (*de porcelaine*) baking, firing.

cuisine [kɥizin] *nf* (*pièce*) kitchen; (*art*) cooking, cuisine, cookery; (*aliments*) cooking; (*intrigues*) Péj scheming; **faire la c.** to cook, do the cooking; **livre de c.** cook(ery) book; **haute c.** high-class cooking. ◆**cuisin/er** *vti* to cook; **c. qn** (*interroger*) Fam to grill s.o. ◆**–ier, -ière** *nmf* cook; – *nf* (*appareil*) cooker, stove, Am range.

cuisse [kɥis] *nf* thigh; (*de poulet, mouton*) leg.

cuit [kɥi] **1** *voir* **cuire;** – *a* cooked; **bien c.**

well done *ou* cooked. **2** *a* (*pris*) Fam done for.

cuite [kɥit] *nf* **prendre une c.** Fam to get plastered *ou* drunk.

cuivre [kɥivr] *nm* (*rouge*) copper; (*jaune*) brass; *pl* (*ustensiles*) & Mus brass. ◆**cuivré** *a* copper-coloured, coppery.

cul [ky] *nm* (*derrière*) Fam backside; (*de bouteille etc*) bottom. ◆**c.-de-jatte** *nm* (*pl* **culs-de-jatte**) legless cripple. ◆**c.-de-sac** *nm* (*pl* **culs-de-sac**) dead end, cul-de-sac.

culasse [kylas] *nf* Aut cylinder head; (*d'une arme à feu*) breech.

culbute [kylbyt] *nf* (*cabriole*) sommersault; (*chute*) (*backward*) tumble; **faire une c.** to sommersault; to tumble. ◆**culbuter** *vi* to tumble over (*backwards*); – *vt* (*personne, chaise*) to knock over.

culinaire [kyliner] *a* (*art*) culinary; (*recette*) cooking.

culmin/er [kylmine] *vi* (*montagne*) to reach its highest point, peak (*à* at); (*colère*) Fig to reach a peak. ◆**–ant** *a* **point c.** (*de réussite, montagne etc*) peak.

culot [kylo] *nm* **1** (*aplomb*) Fam nerve, cheek. **2** (*d'ampoule, de lampe etc*) base. ◆**culotté** *a* **être c.** Fam to have plenty of nerve *ou* cheek.

culotte [kylɔt] *nf* Sp (*pair of*) shorts; (*de femme*) (*pair of*) knickers *ou* Am panties; **culottes** (**courtes**) (*de jeune garçon*) short trousers *ou* Am pants; **c. de cheval** riding breeches.

culpabilité [kylpabilite] *nf* guilt.

culte [kylt] *nm* (*hommage*) Rel worship, cult; (*pratique*) Rel religion; (*service protestant*) service; (*admiration*) Fig cult.

cultiv/er [kyltive] *vt* (*terre*) to farm, cultivate; (*plantes*) to grow, cultivate; (*goût, relations etc*) to cultivate; – **se c.** *vpr* to cultivate one's mind. ◆**–é** *a* (*esprit, personne*) cultured, cultivated. ◆**cultivateur, -trice** *nmf* farmer. ◆**culture** *nf* (*action*) farming, cultivation; (*agriculture*) farming; (*horticulture*) growing, cultivation; (*éducation, civilisation*) culture; *pl* (*terres*) fields (under cultivation); (*plantes*) crops; **c. générale** general knowledge. ◆**culturel, -elle** *a* cultural.

cumin [kymɛ̃] *nm* Bot Culin caraway.

cumul [kymyl] *nm* **c. de fonctions** plurality of offices. ◆**cumulatif, -ive** *a* cumulative. ◆**cumuler** *vt* **c. deux fonctions** to hold two offices (at the same time).

cupide [kypid] *a* avaricious. ◆**cupidité** *nf* avarice, cupidity.

Cupidon [kypidɔ̃] *nm* Cupid.

cure [kyr] *nf* **1** (course of) treatment, cure. **2** (*fonction*) office (of a parish priest); (*résidence*) presbytery. ◆**curable** *a* curable. ◆**curatif, -ive** *a* curative. ◆**curé** *nm* (parish) priest.

curer [kyre] *vt* to clean out; **se c. le nez/les dents** to pick one's nose/teeth. ◆**cure-dent** *nm* toothpick. ◆**cure-ongles** *nm inv* nail cleaner. ◆**cure-pipe** *nm* pipe cleaner.

curieux, -euse [kyrjø, -øz] *a* (*bizarre*) curious; (*indiscret*) inquisitive, curious (**de** about); **c. de savoir** curious to know; – *nmf* inquisitive *ou* curious person; (*badaud*) onlooker. ◆**curieusement** *adv* curiously. ◆**curiosité** *nf* (*de personne, forme etc*) curiosity; (*chose*) curiosity; (*spectacle*) unusual sight.

curriculum (vitæ) [kyrikylɔm(vite)] *nm inv* curriculum (vitæ), *Am* résumé.

curseur [kyrsœr] *nm* (*d'un ordinateur*) cursor.

cutané [kytane] *a* (*affection etc*) skin-. ◆**cuti(-réaction)** *nf* skin test.

cuve [kyv] *nf* vat; (*réservoir*) & *Phot* tank. ◆**cuvée** *nf* (*récolte de vin*) vintage.

◆**cuver** *vt* **c. son vin** *Fam* to sleep it off. ◆**cuvette** *nf* (*récipient*) & *Géog* basin, bowl; (*des cabinets*) pan, bowl.

cyanure [sjanyr] *nm* cyanide.

cybernétique [sibernetik] *nf* cybernetics.

cycle [sikl] *nm* **1** (*série, révolution*) cycle. **2** (*bicyclette*) cycle. ◆**cyclable** *a* (*piste*) cycle-. ◆**cyclique** *a* cyclic(al). ◆**cyclisme** *nm* *Sp* cycling. ◆**cycliste** *nmf* cyclist; – *a* (*course*) cycle-; (*champion*) cycling; **coureur c.** racing cyclist. ◆**cyclomoteur** *nm* moped.

cyclone [siklon] *nm* cyclone.

cygne [siɲ] *nm* swan; **chant du c.** *Fig* swan song.

cylindre [silɛ̃dr] *nm* cylinder; (*de rouleau compresseur*) roller. ◆**cylindrée** *nf* (*Aut* (engine) capacity. ◆**cylindrique** *a* cylindrical.

cymbale [sɛ̃bal] *nf* cymbal.

cynique [sinik] *a* cynical; – *nmf* cynic. ◆**cynisme** *nm* cynicism.

cyprès [siprɛ] *nm* (*arbre*) cypress.

cypriote [siprijɔt] *a* & *nmf* Cypriot.

cytise [sitiz] *nm* *Bot* laburnum.

D

D, d [de] *nm* D, d.

d' [d] *voir* **de** [1,2].

d'abord [dabɔr] *adv* (*en premier lieu*) first; (*au début*) at first.

dactylo [daktilo] *nf* (*personne*) typist; (*action*) typing. ◆**dactylographie** *nf* typing. ◆**dactylographier** *vt* to type.

dada [dada] *nm* (*manie*) hobby horse, pet subject.

dadais [dadɛ] *nm* (**grand**) **d.** big oaf.

dahlia [dalja] *nm* dahlia.

daigner [deɲe] *vt* **d. faire** to condescend *ou* deign to do.

daim [dɛ̃] *nm* fallow deer; (*mâle*) buck; (*cuir*) suede.

dais [de] *nm* (*de lit, feuillage etc*) canopy.

dalle [dal] *nf* paving stone; (*funèbre*) (flat) gravestone. ◆**dallage** *nm* (*action, surface*) paving. ◆**dallé** *a* (*pièce, cour etc*) paved.

daltonien, -ienne [daltɔnjɛ̃, -jɛn] *a* & *n* colour-blind (person). ◆**daltonisme** *nm* colour blindness.

dame [dam] *nf* **1** lady; (*mariée*) married lady. **2** *Échecs Cartes* queen; (*au jeu de dames*) king; (*jeu de*) **dames** draughts, *Am*

checkers. ◆**damer** *vt* (*au jeu de dames*) to crown; **d. le pion à qn** to outsmart s.o. ◆**damier** *nm* draughtboard. *Am* checkerboard.

damner [dane] *vt* to damn; **faire d.** *Fam* to torment, drive mad; **— se d.** *vpr* to be damned. ◆**damnation** *nf* damnation.

dancing [dɑ̃siŋ] *nm* dance hall.

dandiner (se) [sədɑ̃dine] *vpr* to waddle.

dandy [dɑ̃di] *nm* dandy.

Danemark [danmark] *nm* Denmark. ◆**danois, -oise** *a* Danish; – *nmf* Dane; – *nm* (*langue*) Danish.

danger [dɑ̃ʒe] *nm* danger; **en d.** in danger *ou* jeopardy; **mettre en d.** to endanger, jeopardize; **en cas de d.** in an emergency; **en d. de mort** in peril of death; **'d. de mort'** (*panneau*) 'danger'; **sans d.** (*se promener etc*) safely; **être sans d.** to be safe; **pas de d.!** *Fam* no way!, no fear! ◆**dangereux, -euse** *a* dangerous (**pour** to). ◆**dangereusement** *adv* dangerously.

dans [dɑ̃] *prép* in; (*changement de lieu*) into; (*à l'intérieur de*) inside, within; **entrer d.** to go in(to); **d. Paris** in Paris, within Paris;

d. un rayon de within (a radius of); **boire/prendre/etc d.** to drink/take/etc from ou out of; **marcher d. les rues** (à travers) to walk through ou about the streets; **d. ces circonstances** under ou in these circumstances; **d. deux jours/etc** (temps futur) in two days/etc, in two days/etc time; **d. les dix francs/etc** (quantité) about ten francs/etc.

danse [dɑ̃s] nf dance; (art) dancing. ◆**dans/er** vti to dance; **faire d. l'anse du panier** (domestique) to fiddle on the shopping money. ◆**—eur, -euse** nmf dancer; **en danseuse** (cycliste) standing on the pedals.

dard [dar] nm (d'abeille etc) sting; (de serpent) tongue. ◆**darder** vt Litt (flèche) to shoot; (regard) to flash, dart; **le soleil dardait ses rayons** the sun cast down its burning rays.

dare-dare [dardar] adv Fam at ou on the double.

date [dat] nf date; **de vieille d.** (amitié etc) (of) long-standing; **faire d.** (événement) to mark an important date, be epoch-making; **en d. du . . .** dated the . . . ; **d. limite** deadline. ◆**datation** nf dating. ◆**dater** vt (lettre etc) to date; – vi (être dépassé) to date, be dated; **à d. de** to date back to, date from; **à d. de** as from. ◆**dateur** nm (de montre) date indicator; – a & nm (tampon) date stamp.

datte [dat] nf (fruit) date. ◆**dattier** nm date palm.

daube [dob] nf bœuf en d. braised beef stew.

dauphin [dofɛ̃] nm (mammifère marin) dolphin.

davantage [davɑ̃taʒ] adv (quantité) more; (temps) longer; **de temps/etc** time/etc/more; **d. que** more than; longer than.

de¹ [d(ə)] (d' before a vowel or mute h; **de + le = du, de + les = des**) prép 1 (complément d'un nom) of; **les rayons du soleil** the rays of the sun, the sun's rays; **la ville de Paris** the town of Paris; **le livre de Paul** Paul's book; **un pont de fer** an iron bridge; **le train de Londres** the London train; **une augmentation/diminution de** an increase/decrease in. 2 (complément d'un adjectif) **digne de** worthy of; **heureux de partir** happy to leave; **content de qch** pleased with sth. 3 (complément d'un verbe) **parler de** to speak of ou about; **se souvenir de** to remember; **décider de faire** to decide to do; **traiter de lâche** to call a coward. 4 (provenance: lieu & temps) from; **venir/dater de** to come/date from; **mes**

amis du village my friends from the village, my village friends; **le train de Londres** the train from London. 5 (agent) **accompagné de** accompanied by. 6 (moyen) **armé de** armed with; **se nourrir de** to live on. 7 (manière) **d'une voix douce** in ou with a gentle voice. 8 (cause) **puni de** punished for; **mourir de faim** to die of hunger. 9 (temps) **travailler de nuit** to work by night; **six heures du matin** six o'clock in the morning. 10 (mesure) **avoir six mètres de haut, être haut de six mètres** to be six metres high; **retarder de deux heures** to delay by two hours; **homme de trente ans** thirty-year-old man; **gagner cent francs de l'heure** to earn one hundred francs an hour.

de² [d(ə)] art partitif some; **elle boit du vin** she drinks (some) wine; **il ne boit pas de vin** (négation) he doesn't drink (any) wine; **des fleurs** (some) flowers; **de jolies fleurs** (some) pretty flowers; **d'agréables soirées** (some) pleasant evenings; **il y en a six de tués** (avec un nombre) there are six killed.

dé [de] nm (à jouer) dice; (à coudre) thimble; **les dés** the dice; (jeu) dice; **les dés sont jetés** Fig the die is cast; **couper en dés** Culin to dice.

déambuler [deɑ̃byle] vi to stroll, saunter.

débâcle [debɑkl] nf Mil rout; (ruine) Fig downfall; (des glaces) Géog breaking up.

déball/er [debale] vt to unpack; (étaler) to display. ◆**—age** nm unpacking; display.

débandade [debɑ̃dad] nf (mad) rush, stampede; Mil rout; **à la d.** in confusion; **tout va à la d.** everything's going to rack and ruin.

débaptiser [debatize] vt (rue) to rename.

débarbouiller [debarbuje] vt **d. qn** to wash s.o.'s face; **se d.** to wash one's face.

débarcadère [debarkader] nm landing stage, quay.

débardeur [debardœr] nm 1 (docker) stevedore. 2 (vêtement) slipover, Am (sweater) vest.

débarqu/er [debarke] vt (passagers) to land; (marchandises) to unload; **d. qn** (congédier) Fam to sack s.o.; – vi (passagers) to disembark, land; (être naïf) Fam not to be quite with it; **d. chez qn** Fam to turn up suddenly at s.o.'s place. ◆**—ement** nm landing; unloading; Mil landing.

débarras [debara] nm lumber room, Am storeroom; **bon d.!** Fam good riddance! ◆**débarrasser** vt (voie, table etc) to clear (de of); **d. qn de** (ennemi, soucis etc) to rid s.o. of; (*manteau etc*) to relieve s.o. of; **se d.** **de** to get rid of, rid oneself of.

débat [deba] *nm* discussion, debate; *pl Pol Jur* proceedings. ◆**débattre*** *vt* to discuss, debate; — **se d.** *vpr* to struggle *ou* fight (to get free), put up a fight.

débauche [deboʃ] *nf* debauchery; **une d. de** *Fig* a wealth *ou* profusion of. ◆**débauch/er*** *vt* **d. qn** (*détourner*) *Fam* to entice s.o. away from his work; (*licencier*) to dismiss s.o., lay s.o. off. ◆**-é, -ée** *a* (*libertin*) debauched, profligate; — *nmf* debauchee, profligate.

débile [debil] *a* (*esprit, enfant etc*) weak, feeble; (*d'esprit*) *Fam* idiotic; — *nmf Péj* *Fam* idiot, moron. ◆**débilité** *nf* debility, weakness; *pl* (*niaiseries*) *Fam* sheer nonsense. ◆**débiliter** *vt* to debilitate, weaken.

débiner [debine] **1** *vt* (*décrier*) *Fam* to run down. **2 se d.** *vpr* (*s'enfuir*) *Arg* to beat it, bolt.

débit [debi] *nm* **1** (*vente*) turnover, sales; (*de fleuve*) (rate of) flow; (*d'un orateur*) delivery; **d. de tabac** tobacconist's shop, *Am* tobacco store; **d. de boissons** bar, café. **2** (*compte*) *Fin* debit. ◆**débiter** *vt* **1** (*découper*) to cut up, slice up (en into); (*vendre*) to sell; (*fournir*) to yield; (*dire*) *Péj* to utter, spout. **2** *Fin* to debit. ◆**débiteur, -trice** *nmf* debtor; — *a* (*solde, compte*) debit-; **son compte est d.** his account is in debit, he is in debit.

déblais [deble] *nmpl* (*terre*) earth; (*décombres*) rubble. ◆**déblayer** *vt* (*terrain, décombres*) to clear.

débloquer [debloke] **1** *vt* (*machine*) to unjam; (*crédits, freins, compte*) to release; (*prix*) to decontrol. **2** *vi* (*divaguer*) *Fam* to talk through one's hat, talk nonsense.

déboires [debwar] *nmpl* disappointments, setbacks.

déboît/er [debwate] **1** *vt* (*tuyau*) to disconnect; (*os*) *Méd* to dislocate. **2** *vi Aut* to pull out, change lanes. ◆**-ement** *nm Méd* dislocation.

débonnaire [deboner] *a* good-natured, easy-going.

débord/er [deborde] *vi* (*fleuve, liquide*) to overflow; (*en bouillant*) to boil over; **d. de** (*vie, joie etc*) *Fig* to be overflowing *ou* bubbling over with; **l'eau déborde du vase** the water is running over the top of the vase *ou* is overflowing the vase; — *vt* (*dépasser*) to go beyond; (*faire saillie*) to stick out from; *Mil Sp* to outflank; **débordé de travail/de visites** snowed under with work/visits.

◆**-ement** *nm* overflowing; (*de joie, activité*) outburst.

débouch/er [debuʃe] **1** *vt* (*bouteille*) to open, uncork; (*lavabo, tuyau*) to clear, unblock. **2** *vi* (*surgir*) to emerge, come out (**de** from); **d. sur** (*rue*) to lead out onto, lead into; *Fig* to lead up to. ◆**-é** *nm* (*carrière* & *Géog*) opening; (*de rue*) exit; (*marché*) *Com* outlet.

débouler [debule] *vi* (*arriver*) *Fam* to burst in, turn up.

déboulonner [debulone] *vt* to unbolt; **d. qn** *Fam* (*renvoyer*) to sack *ou* fire s.o.; (*discréditer*) to bring s.o. down.

débours [debur] *nmpl* expenses. ◆**débourser** *vt* to pay out.

debout [d(ə)bu] *adv* standing (up); **mettre d.** (*planche etc*) to stand up, put upright; **se mettre d.** to stand *ou* get up; **se tenir** *ou* **rester d.** (*personne*) to stand (up), remain standing (up); **rester d.** (*édifice etc*) to remain standing; **être d.** (*levé*) to be up (and about); **d.!** get up!; **ça ne tient pas d.** (*théorie etc*) that doesn't hold water *ou* make sense.

déboutonner [debutone] *vt* to unbutton, undo; — **se d.** *vpr* (*personne*) to undo one's buttons.

débraillé [debraje] *a* (*tenue etc*) slovenly, sloppy; — *nm* slovenliness, sloppiness.

débrancher [debrɑ̃ʃe] *vt El* to unplug, disconnect.

débrayer [debreje] *vi* **1** *Aut* to declutch, release the clutch. **2** (*se mettre en grève*) to stop work. ◆**débrayage** (*grève*) strike, walk-out.

débridé [debride] *a* (*effréné*) unbridled.

débris [debri] *nmpl* fragments, scraps; (*restes*) remains; (*détritus*) rubbish, debris.

débrouiller [debruje] *vt* (*écheveau etc*) to unravel, disentangle; (*affaire*) to sort out. **2 se d.** *vpr* to manage, get by, make out; **se d. pour faire** to manage (somehow) to do. ◆**débrouillard** *a* smart, resourceful. ◆**débrouillardise** *nf* smartness, resourcefulness.

débroussailler [debrusaje] *vt* (*chemin*) to clear (of brushwood); (*problème*) *Fig* to clarify.

débusquer [debyske] *vt* (*gibier, personne*) to drive out, dislodge.

début [deby] *nm* start, beginning; **au d.** at the beginning; **faire ses débuts** (*sur la scène etc*) to make one's debut. ◆**début/er** *vi* to start, begin; (*dans une carrière*) to start out in life; (*sur la scène etc*) to make one's debut. ◆—ant, -ante *nmf* beginner; – a novice.

déca [deka] *nm Fam* decaffeinated coffee.

deçà (en) [ɑ̃d(ə)sa] *adv* (on) this side; – *prép* en d. de (on) this side of; (*succès, prix etc*) Fig short of.

décacheter [dekaʃte] *vt* (*lettre etc*) to open, unseal.

décade [dekad] *nf* (*dix jours*) period of ten days; (*décennie*) decade.

décadent [dekadɑ̃] *a* decadent. ◆**décadence** *nf* decay, decadence.

décaféiné [dekafeine] *a* decaffeinated.

décalaminer [dekalamine] *vt* (*moteur*) Aut to decoke, decarbonize.

décalcomanie [dekalkɔmani] *nf* (*image*) transfer, *Am* decal.

décal/er [dekale] *vt* 1 (*avancer*) to shift; (*départ, repas*) to shift (the time of). 2 (*ôter les cales de*) to unwedge. ◆—**age** *nm* (*écart*) gap, discrepancy; d. horaire time difference.

décalque [dekalk] *nm* tracing. ◆**décalquer** *vt* (*dessin*) to trace.

décamper [dekɑ̃pe] *vi* to make off, clear off.

décanter [dekɑ̃te] *vt* (*liquide*) to settle, clarify; d. ses idées to clarify one's ideas; – se d. *vpr* (*idées, situation*) to become clearer, settle.

décap/er [dekape] *vt* (*métal*) to clean, scrape down; (*surface peinte*) to strip. ◆—**ant** *nm* cleaning agent; (*pour enlever la peinture*) paint stripper. ◆—**eur** *nm* d. thermique hot-air paint stripper.

décapiter [dekapite] *vt* to decapitate, behead.

décapotable [dekapɔtabl] *a* (*voiture*) convertible.

décapsul/er [dekapsyle] *vt* d. une bouteille to take the cap *ou* top off a bottle. ◆—**eur** *nm* bottle-opener.

décarcasser (se) [sədekarkase] *vpr Fam* to flog oneself to death (**pour faire** doing).

décathlon [dekatlɔ̃] *nm Sp* decathlon.

décati [dekati] *a* worn out, decrepit.

décavé [dekave] *a Fam* ruined.

décéd/er [desede] *vi* to die. ◆—**é** *a* deceased.

déceler [desle] *vt* (*trouver*) to detect, uncover; (*révéler*) to reveal.

décembre [desɑ̃br] *nm* December.

décennie [deseni] *nf* decade.

décent [desɑ̃] *a* (*bienséant, acceptable*) decent. ◆**décemment** [-amɑ̃] *adv* decently. ◆**décence** *nf* decency.

décentraliser [desɑ̃tralize] *vt* to decentral-ize. ◆**décentralisation** *nf* decentralization.

déception [desɛpsjɔ̃] *nf* disappointment. ◆**décevoir*** *vt* to disappoint. ◆**décevant** *a* disappointing.

décerner [deserne] *vt* (*prix etc*) to award; (*mandat d'arrêt etc*) Jur to issue.

décès [desɛ] *nm* death.

déchaîn/er [deʃene] *vt* (*colère, violence*) to unleash, let loose; d. l'enthousiasme/les rires to set off wild enthusiasm/a storm of laughter; – se d. *vpr* (*tempête, rires*) to break out; (*foule*) to run amok *ou* riot; (*colère, personne*) to explode. ◆—**é** *a* (*foule, flots*) wild, raging. ◆—**ement** [-ɛnmɑ̃] *nm* (*de rires, de haine etc*) outburst; (*de violence*) outbreak, eruption; le d. de la tempête the raging of the storm.

déchanter [deʃɑ̃te] *vi Fam* to become disillusioned; (*changer de ton*) to change one's tune.

décharge [deʃarʒ] *nf Jur* discharge; d. (**publique**) (rubbish) dump *ou* tip, *Am* (garbage) dump; d. (**électrique**) (electrical) discharge, shock; recevoir une d. (**électrique**) to get a shock; à la d. de qn in s.o.'s defence. ◆**décharg/er** *vt* to unload; (*batterie*) El to discharge; (*accusé*) Jur to discharge, exonerate; d. qn de (*travail etc*) to relieve s.o. of; d. sur qn (*son arme*) to fire at s.o.; (*sa colère*) to vent on s.o.; – se d. *vpr* (*batterie*) to go flat; se d. sur qn du soin de faire qch to unload onto s.o. the job of doing sth. ◆—**ement** *nm* unloading.

décharné [deʃarne] *a* skinny, bony.

déchausser (se) [sədeʃose] *vpr* to take s.o.'s shoes off; se d. to take one's shoes off; (*dent*) to get loose.

dèche [dɛʃ] *nf* être dans la d. *Arg* to be flat broke.

déchéance [deʃeɑ̃s] *nf* (*déclin*) decline, decay, degradation.

déchet [deʃɛ] *nm* des déchets (*résidus*) scraps, waste; il y a du d. there's some waste *ou* wastage.

déchiffrer [deʃifre] *vt* (*message*) to decipher; (*mauvaise écriture*) to make out, decipher.

déchiquet/er [deʃikte] *vt* to tear to shreds, cut to bits. ◆—**é** *a* (*drapeau etc*) (all) in shreds; (*côte*) jagged.

déchir/er [deʃire] *vt* to tear (up), rip (up); (*vêtement*) to tear, rip; (*ouvrir*) to tear *ou* rip open; (*pays, groupe*) to tear apart; d. l'air (*bruit*) to rend the air; ce bruit me déchire les oreilles this noise is ear-splitting; – se d. *vpr* (*robe etc*) to tear, rip. ◆—ant *a* (*navrant*) heart-breaking; (*aigu*) ear-splitting. ◆—ement *nm* (*souffrance*) heartbreak; *pl* (*divisions*) Pol deep rifts. ◆**déchirure** *nf* tear, rip; d. musculaire torn muscle.

déchoir [deʃwar] *vi* to lose prestige. ◆**déchu** *a* (*ange*) fallen; **être d. de** (*ses droits etc*) to have forfeited.

décibel [desibel] *nm* decibel.

décid/er [deside] *vt* (*envoi, opération*) to decide on; d. que to decide that; d. qn à faire to persuade s.o. to do; — *vi* d. de (*destin de qn*) to decide; (*voyage etc*) to decide on; d. de faire to decide to do; — se d. *vpr* (*question*) to be decided; se d. à faire to make up one's mind to do; se d. pour qch to decide on sth *ou* in favour of sth. ◆—é *a* (*air, ton*) determined, decided; (*net, pas douteux*) decided; c'est d. it's settled; être d. à faire to be decided about doing *ou* determined to do. ◆—ément *adv* undoubtedly.

décilitre [desilitr] *nm* decilitre.

décimal, -aux [desimal, -o] *a* decimal. ◆**décimale** *nf* decimal.

décimer [desime] *vt* to decimate.

décimètre [desimetr] *nm* decimetre; double d. ruler.

décisif, -ive [desizif, -iv] *a* decisive; (*moment*) crucial. ◆**décision** *nf* decision; (*fermeté*) determination.

déclamer [deklame] *vt* to declaim; Péj to spout. ◆**déclamatoire** *a* Péj bombastic.

déclarer [deklare] *vt* to declare (que that); (*décès, vol etc*) to notify; d. coupable to convict, find guilty; d. la guerre to declare war (à on); — se d. *vpr* (*s'expliquer*) to declare one's views; (*incendie, maladie*) to break out; se d. contre to come out against. ◆**déclaration** *nf* declaration; (*de décès etc*) notification; (*commentaire*) statement, comment; d. de revenus tax return.

déclasser [deklase] *vt* (*livres etc*) to put out of order; (*hôtel etc*) to downgrade; d. qn Sp to relegate to s.o. (in the placing).

déclench/er [deklɑ̃ʃe] *vt* (*mécanisme*) to set *ou* trigger off, release; (*attaque*) to launch; (*provoquer*) to trigger off, spark off; d. le travail Méd to induce labour; — se d. *vpr* (*sonnerie*) to go off; (*attaque, grève*) to start. ◆—ement *nm* (*d'un appareil*) release.

déclic [deklik] *nm* (*mécanisme*) catch, trigger; (*bruit*) click.

déclin [deklɛ̃] *nm* decline; (*du jour*) close; (*de la lune*) wane. ◆**décliner 1** *vt* (*refuser*) to decline. 2 *vt* (*réciter*) to state. 3 *vi* (*forces*

etc) to decline, wane; (*jour*) to draw to a close.

déclivité [deklivite] *nf* slope.

décocher [dekɔʃe] *vt* (*flèche*) to shoot, fire; (*coup*) to let fly, aim; (*regard*) to flash.

décoder [dekɔde] *vt* (*message*) to decode.

décoiffer [dekwafe] *vt* d. qn to mess up s.o.'s hair.

décoincer [dekwɛ̃se] *vt* (*engrenage*) to unjam.

décoll/er [dekɔle] **1** *vi* (*avion etc*) to take off; elle ne décolle pas d'ici Fam she won't leave *ou* budge. **2** *vt* (*timbre etc*) to unstick; — se d. *vpr* to come unstuck. ◆—age *nm* Av takeoff.

décolleté [dekɔlte] *a* (*robe*) low-cut; — *nm* (*de robe*) low neckline; (*de femme*) bare neck and shoulders.

décoloniser [dekɔlɔnize] *vt* to decolonize. ◆**décolonisation** *nf* decolonization.

décolor/er [dekɔlɔre] *vt* to discolour, fade; (*cheveux*) to bleach. ◆—ant *nm* bleach. ◆**décoloration** *nf* discolo(u)ration; bleaching.

décombres [dekɔ̃br] *nmpl* ruins, rubble, debris.

décommander [dekɔmɑ̃de] *vt* (*marchandises, invitation*) to cancel; (*invités*) to put off; — se d. *vpr* to cancel (one's appointment).

décomposer [dekɔ̃poze] *vt* to decompose; (*visage*) to distort; — se d. *vpr* (*pourrir*) to decompose; (*visage*) to become distorted. ◆**décomposition** *nf* decomposition.

décompresser [dekɔ̃prese] *vi* Psy Fam to unwind.

décompression [dekɔ̃presjɔ̃] *nf* decompression.

décompte [dekɔ̃t] *nm* deduction; (*détail*) breakdown. ◆**décompter** *vt* to deduct.

déconcerter [dekɔ̃serte] *vt* to disconcert.

déconfit [dekɔ̃fi] *a* downcast. ◆**déconfiture** *nf* (*state of*) collapse *ou* defeat; (*faillite*) Fam financial ruin.

décongeler [dekɔ̃ʒle] *vt* (*aliment*) to thaw, defrost.

décongestionner [dekɔ̃ʒɛstjɔne] *vt* (*rue*) & Méd to relieve congestion in.

déconnecter [dekɔnɛkte] *vt* Él & Fig to disconnect.

déconner [dekɔne] *vi* (*divaguer*) Fam to talk nonsense.

déconseiller [dekɔ̃seje] *vt* d. qch à qn to advise s.o. against sth; d. à qn de faire to advise s.o. against doing; c'est déconseillé it is inadvisable.

déconsidérer [dekɔ̃sidere] *vt* to discredit.

décontaminer [dekɔ̃tamine] *vt* to decontaminate.

décontenancer [dekɔ̃tnɑ̃se] *vt* to disconcert; **— se d.** *vpr* to lose one's composure, become flustered.

décontracter [dekɔ̃trakte] *vt*, **— se d.** *vpr* to relax. ◆**décontraction** *nf* relaxation.

déconvenue [dekɔ̃vny] *nf* disappointment.

décor [dekɔr] *nm* Th scenery, decor; Cin set; (*paysage*) scenery; (*d'intérieur*) decoration; (*cadre, ambiance*) setting; **entrer dans le d.** (*véhicule*) Fam to run off the road.

décorer [dekɔre] *vt* (*maison, soldat etc*) to decorate (de with). ◆**décorateur, -trice** *nmf* (interior) decorator; Cin set designer. ◆**décoratif, -ive** *a* decorative. ◆**décoration** *nf* decoration.

décortiquer [dekɔrtike] *vt* (*graine*) to husk; (*homard etc*) to shell; (*texte*) Fam to take to pieces, dissect.

découcher [dekuʃe] *vi* to stay out all night.

découdre [dekudr] *vt* to unstitch; **—** *vi* **en d.** Fam to fight it out; **— se d.** *vpr* to come unstitched.

découler [dekule] *vi* **d. de** to follow from.

découp/er [dekupe] *vt* (*poulet etc*) to carve; (*article etc*) Journ to cut out; **se d. sur** to stand out against. ◆**—é** *a* (*côte*) jagged. ◆**—age** *nm* carving; cutting out; (*image*) cut-out. ◆**découpure** *nf* (*contour*) jagged outline; (*morceau*) piece cut out, cut-out.

découplé [dekuple] *a* **bien d.** (*personne*) well-built, strapping.

décourag/er [dekuraʒe] *vt* (*dissuader*) to discourage (de from); (*démoraliser*) to dishearten, discourage; **— se d.** *vpr* to get discouraged *ou* disheartened. ◆**—ement** *nm* discouragement.

décousu [dekuzy] *a* (*propos, idées*) disconnected.

découvrir* [dekuvrir] *vt* (*trésor, terre etc*) to discover; (*secret, vérité etc*) to find out, discover; (*casserole etc*) to take the lid off; (*dévoiler*) to disclose (à to); (*dénuder*) to uncover, expose; (*voir*) to perceive; **d. que** to discover *ou* find out that; **— se d.** *vpr* (*se dénuder*) to uncover oneself; (*enlever son chapeau*) to take one's hat off; (*ciel*) to clear (up). ◆**découvert 1** *a* (*terrain*) open; (*tête etc*) bare; **à d.** exposed, unprotected; **agir à d.** to act openly. **2** *nm* (*d'un compte*) Fin overdraft. ◆**découverte** *nf* discovery; **partir** *ou* **aller à la d. de** to go in search of.

décrasser [dekrase] *vt* (*éduquer*) to take the rough edges off.

décrépit [dekrepi] *a* (*vieillard*) decrepit.

décrépitude *nf* (*des institutions etc*) decay.

décret [dekre] *nm* decree. ◆**décréter** *vt* to order, decree.

décrier [dekrije] *vt* to run down, disparage.

décrire* [dekrir] *vt* to describe.

décroch/er [dekrɔʃe] *vt* (*détacher*) to unhook; (*tableau*) to take down; (*obtenir*) Fam to get, land; **d. (le téléphone)** to pick up the phone. **2** *vi* Fam (*abandonner*) to give up; (*perdre le fil*) to be unable to follow, lose track. ◆**—é** *a* (*téléphone*) off the hook.

décroître* [dekrwatr] *vi* (*mortalité etc*) to decrease, decline; (*eaux*) to subside; (*jours*) to draw in. ◆**décroissance** *nf* decrease, decline (de in).

décrotter [dekrɔte] *vt* (*chaussures*) to clean *ou* scrape (the mud off). ◆**décrottoir** *nm* shoe scraper.

décrypter [dekripte] *vt* (*message*) to decipher, decode.

déçu [desy] *voir* **décevoir**; **—** *a* disappointed.

déculotter (se) [sədekylɔte] *vpr* to take off one's trousers *ou* Am pants. ◆**déculottée** *nf* Fam thrashing.

décupler [dekyple] *vti* to increase tenfold.

dédaigner [dedɛɲe] *vt* (*personne, richesse etc*) to scorn, despise; (*repas*) to turn up one's nose at; (*offre*) to spurn; (*ne pas tenir compte de*) to disregard. ◆**dédaigneux, -euse** *a* scornful, disdainful (de of). ◆**dédain** *nm* scorn, disdain (pour, de for).

dédale [dedal] *nm* maze, labyrinth.

dedans [d(ə)dɑ̃] *adv* inside; **de d.** from (the) inside, from within; **en d.** on the inside; **au-d. (de), au d. (de)** inside; **au-d.** *ou* **au d. de lui-même** inwardly; **tomber d.** (*trou*) to fall in (it); **donner d.** (*être dupé*) Fam to fall in; **mettre d.** Fam (*en prison*) to put inside; (*tromper*) to take in; **je me suis fait rentrer d.** (*en voiture*) someone went *ou* crashed into me; **—** *nm* **le d.** the inside.

dédicace [dedikas] *nf* dedication, inscription. ◆**dédicacer** *vt* (*livre etc*) to dedicate, inscribe (à to).

dédier [dedje] *vt* to dedicate.

dédire (se) [sədedir] *vpr* to go back on one's word; **se d. de** (*promesse etc*) to go back on. ◆**dédit** *nm* (*somme*) Com forfeit, penalty.

dédommag/er [dedɔmaʒe] *vt* to compensate (de for). ◆**—ement** *nm* compensation.

dédouaner [dedwane] *vt* (*marchandises*) to clear through customs; **d. qn** to restore s.o.'s prestige.

dédoubl/er [deduble] vt (classe etc) to split into two; **d. un train** to run an extra train; **– se d.** vpr to be in two places at once. **◆—ement** nm **d. de la personnalité** Psy split personality.

déduire* [dedɥir] vt (retirer) to deduct (de from); (conclure) to deduce (de from). **◆déductible** a (frais) deductible, allowable. **◆déduction** nf (raisonnement & Com deduction.

déesse [dees] nf goddess.

défaill/ir* [defajir] vi (s'évanouir) to faint; (forces) to fail, flag; **sans d.** without flinching. **◆—ant** a (personne) faint; (témoin) Jur defaulting. **◆—ance** nf (évanouissement) fainting fit; (faiblesse) weakness; (panne) fault; **une d. de mémoire** a lapse of memory.

défaire* [defɛr] vt (nœud etc) to undo, untie; (bagages) to unpack; (installation) to take down; (coiffure) to mess up; **d. qn de** to rid s.o. of; **– se d.** vpr (nœud etc) to come undone ou untied; **se d. de** to get rid of. **◆défait** a (lit) unmade; (visage) drawn; (armée) defeated. **◆défaite** nf defeat. **◆défaitisme** nm defeatism.

défalquer [defalke] vt (frais etc) to deduct (de from).

défaut [defo] nm (faiblesse) fault, shortcoming, failing, defect; (de diamant etc) flaw; (désavantage) drawback; (contumace) Jur default; **le d. de la cuirasse** the chink in the armour; **faire d.** to be lacking; **le temps me fait d.** I lack time; **à d. de** for want of; **en d.** at fault; **prendre qn en d.** to catch s.o. out; **ou, à d. . . .** or, failing that . . . .

défaveur [defavœr] nf disfavour. **◆défavorable** a unfavourable (à to). **◆défavoriser** vt to put at a disadvantage, be unfair to.

défection [defɛksjɔ̃] nf defection, desertion; **faire d.** to desert; (ne pas venir) to fail to turn up.

défectueux, -euse [defɛktɥø, -øz] a faulty, defective. **◆défectuosité** nf defectiveness; (défaut) defect (de in).

défendre [defɑ̃dr] vt (protéger) to defend; **– se d.** vpr to defend oneself; **se d. de** (pluie etc) to protect oneself from; **se d. de faire** (s'empêcher de) to refrain from doing; **je me défends (bien)** Fam I can hold my own. **2** vt **d. à qn de faire** (interdire) to forbid s.o. to do, not allow s.o. to do; **d. qch à qn** to forbid s.o. sth. **◆défendable** a defensible.

défense [defɑ̃s] nf **1** (protection) defence, Am defense; **sans d.** defenceless. **2**

(interdiction) **'d. de fumer'** no smoking'; **'d. d'entrer'** 'no entry', 'no admittance'. **3** (d'éléphant) tusk. **◆défenseur** nm defender; (des faibles) protector, defender. **◆défensif, -ive** a defensive; **– nf sur la** défensive on the defensive.

déférent [deferɑ̃] a deferential. **◆déférence** nf deference.

déférer [defere] **1** vt (coupable) Jur to refer (à to). **2** vi **d. à l'avis de qn** to defer to s.o.'s opinion.

déferler [defɛrle] vi (vagues) to break; (haine etc) to erupt; **d. dans ou sur** (foule) to surge ou sweep into.

défi [defi] nm challenge; **lancer un d. à qn** to challenge s.o.; **mettre qn au d. de faire** to defy ou dare ou challenge s.o. to do.

déficient [defisjɑ̃] a Méd deficient. **◆déficience** nf Méd deficiency.

déficit [defisit] nm deficit. **◆déficitaire** a (budget etc) in deficit; (récolte etc) Fig short, insufficient.

défier¹ [defje] vt (provoquer) to challenge (à to); (braver) to defy; **d. qn de faire** to defy ou challenge s.o. to do.

défier² (se) [sədefje] vpr **se d. de** Litt to distrust. **◆défiance** nf distrust (de of). **◆défiant** a distrustful (à l'égard de of).

défigur/er [defigyre] vt (visage) to disfigure; (vérité etc) to distort. **◆—ement** nm disfigurement; distortion.

défil/er [defile] vi (manifestants) to march (devant past); Mil to march ou file past; (paysage, jours) to pass by; (visiteurs) to keep coming and going, stream in and out; (images) Cin to flash by (on the screen); **– se d.** vpr Fam (s'éloigner) to sneak off; (éviter d'agir) to cop out. **◆—é** nm **1** (cortège) procession; (de manifestants) march; Mil parade, march past; (de visiteurs) stream, succession. **2** Géog gorge, pass.

défin/ir [definir] vt to define. **◆—i** a (article) Gram definite. **◆définition** nf definition; (de mots croisés) clue.

définitif, -ive [definitif, -iv] a final, definitive; **– nf en définitive** in the final analysis, finally. **◆définitivement** adv (partir) permanently, for good; (exclure) definitively.

déflagration [deflagrasjɔ̃] nf explosion.

déflation [deflasjɔ̃] nf Écon deflation.

déflorer [deflɔre] vt (idée, sujet) to spoil the freshness of.

défonc/er [defɔ̃se] vt (porte, mur etc) to smash in ou down; (trottoir, route etc) to dig up, break up. **2 se d.** vpr (drogué) Fam to get high (à on). ◆**-é** a **1** (*route*) full of potholes, bumpy. **2** (*drogué*) *Fam* high.

déform/er [deforme] vt *put ou* knock out of shape; (*doigt, main*) to deform; (*faits, image etc*) to distort; (*goût*) to corrupt; — **se d.** vpr to lose its shape. ◆**-é** a (*objet*) misshapen; (*corps etc*) deformed, misshapen; **chaussée déformée** uneven road surface. ◆**déformation** nf distortion; corruption; (*de membre*) deformity; **c'est la d. professionnelle** it's an occupational hazard, it's a case of being conditioned by one's job.

défouler (se) [səfule] vpr *Fam* to let off steam.

défraîchir (se) [sədefreʃir] vpr (*étoffe etc*) to lose its freshness, become faded.

défrayer [defreje] vt **d. qn** to pay *ou* defray s.o.'s expenses; **d. la chronique** to be the talk of the town.

défricher [defriʃe] vt (*terrain*) to clear (for cultivation); (*sujet etc*) *Fig* to open up.

défriser [defrize] vt (*cheveux*) to straighten; **d. qn** (*contrarier*) *Fam* to ruffle *ou* annoy s.o.

défroisser [defrwase] vt (*papier*) to smooth out.

défroqué [defrɔke] a (*prêtre*) defrocked.

défunt, -unte [defœ̃, -œ̃t] a (*mort*) departed; **son d. mari** her late husband; — nmf **le d., la défunte** the deceased, the departed.

dégag/er [degaʒe] vt (*lieu, table*) to clear (**de** of); (*objet en gage*) to redeem; (*odeur*) to give off; (*chaleur*) to give out; (*responsabilité*) to disclaim; (*idée, conclusion*) to bring out; **d. qn de** (*promesse*) to release s.o. from; (*décombres*) to free s.o. from, pull s.o. out of; **cette robe dégage la taille** this dress leaves the waist free and easy; — vi *Fb* to clear the ball (down the pitch); **d.!** clear the way!; — **se d.** vpr (*rue, ciel*) to clear; **se d. de** (*personne*) to get free from (*promise*); to get free from, free oneself from (*rubble*); **se d. de** (*odeur*) to issue *ou* emanate from; (*vérité, impression*) to emerge from. ◆**-é** a (*ciel*) clear; (*ton, allure*) easy-going, casual; (*vue*) open. ◆**-ement** nm **1** (*action*) clearing; redemption; (*d'odeur*) emanation; (*de chaleur*) emission; release; freeing; *Fb* clearance, kick; **itinéraire de d.** *Aut* relief road. **2** (*espace libre*) clearing; (*de maison*) passage.

dégainer [degene] vti (*arme*) to draw.

dégarn/ir [degarnir] vt to clear, empty; (*arbre, compte*) to strip; — **se d.** vpr (*crâne*) to go bald; (*salle*) to clear, empty. ◆**-i** a

(*salle*) empty, bare; (*tête*) balding; **front d.** receding hairline.

dégâts [dega] nmpl damage; **limiter les d.** *Fig* to prevent matters getting worse.

dégel [deʒɛl] nm thaw. ◆**dégeler** vt to thaw (out); (*crédits*) to unfreeze; — vi to thaw (out); – v imp to thaw; — **se d.** vpr (*personne, situation*) to thaw (out).

dégénér/er [deʒenere] vi to degenerate (**en** into). ◆**-é, -ée** a & nmf degenerate. ◆**dégénérescence** nf degeneration.

dégingandé [deʒɛ̃gɑ̃de] a ungainly, gangling, lanky.

dégivrer [deʒivre] vt *Aut Av* to de-ice; (*réfrigérateur*) to defrost.

déglingu/er (se) [sədeglɛ̃ge] vpr *Fam* to fall to bits. ◆**-é** a falling to bits, in bits.

dégobiller [degɔbije] vt *Fam* to spew up.

dégonfl/er [degɔ̃fle] vt (*pneu etc*) to deflate, let down; — **se d.** vpr (*flancher*) *Fam* to chicken out, get cold feet. ◆**-é, -ée** a (*pneu*) flat; (*lâche*) *Fam* chicken, yellow; – nmf *Fam* yellow belly.

dégorger [degɔrʒe] vi (*se déverser*) to discharge (**dans** into); faire **d.** (*escargots*) *Culin* to cover with salt.

dégot(t)er [degɔte] vt *Fam* to find, turn up.

dégouliner [deguline] vi to trickle, drip, run.

dégourd/ir [degurdir] vt (*doigts etc*) to take the numbness out of; **d. qn** *Fig* to smarten *ou* wise s.o. up, sharpen s.o.'s wits; — **se d.** vpr to smarten up, wise up; **se d. les jambes** to stretch one's legs. ◆**-i** a (*malin*) smart, sharp.

dégoût [degu] nm disgust; **le d. de** (*la vie, les gens etc*) disgust for; **avoir un** *ou* **du d. pour qch** to have a (strong) dislike *ou* distaste for sth. ◆**dégoût/er** vt to disgust; **d. qn de qch** to put s.o. off sth; **se d. de** to take a (strong) dislike to, become disgusted with. ◆**-ant** a disgusting. ◆**-é** a disgusted; **être d. de** to be sick *ou* disgusted with *ou* by *ou* at; **elle est partie dégoûtée** she left in disgust; **il n'est pas d.** (*difficile*) he's not too fussy; **faire le d.** to be fussy.

dégrad/er [degrade] **1** vt (*avilir*) to degrade; (*mur etc*) to deface, damage; — **se d.** vpr (*s'avilir*) to degrade oneself; (*édifice, situation*) to deteriorate. **2** vt (*couleur*) to shade off. ◆**-ant** a degrading. ◆**-é** nm (*de couleur*) shading off, gradation. ◆**dégradation** nf (*de drogué etc*) & *Ch* degradation; (*de situation etc*) deterioration; (*pl dégâts*) damage.

dégrafer [degrafe] vt (*vêtement*) to unfasten, unhook.

dégraisser [degrese] vt **1** (*bœuf*) to take the

fat off; (*bouillon*) to skim. **2** (*entreprise*) *Fam* to slim down, trim down the size of (*by laying off workers*).

degré [dəgre] *nm* **1** degree; **enseignement du premier/second d.** primary/secondary education; **au plus haut d.** (*avare etc*) extremely. **2** (*gradin*) *Litt* step.

dégrever [degrəve] *vt* (*contribuable*) to reduce the tax burden on.

dégriffé [degrife] *a* **vêtement d.** unlabelled designer garment.

dégringoler [degrɛ̃gɔle] *vi* to tumble (down); **faire d. qch** to topple sth over; — *vt* (*escalier*) to rush down. ◆**dégringolade** *nf* tumble.

dégriser [degrize] *vt* **d. qn** to sober s.o. (up).

dégrossir [degrosir] *vt* (*travail*) to rough out; **d. qn** to refine s.o.

déguerpir [degɛrpir] *vi* to clear off *ou* out.

dégueulasse [degœlas] *a Fam* lousy, disgusting.

dégueuler [degœle] *vi* (*vomir*) *Arg* to puke.

déguis/er [degize] *vt* (*pour tromper*) to disguise; **d. qn en** (*costumer*) to dress s.o. up as, disguise s.o. as; — **se d.** *vpr* to dress oneself up, disguise oneself (**en** as). ◆**—ement** *nm* disguise; (*de bal costumé etc*) fancy dress.

déguster [degyste] *vt* **1** (*goûter*) to taste, sample; (*apprécier*) to relish. **2** *vi* (*subir des coups*) *Fam* to cop it, get a good hiding. ◆**dégustation** *nf* tasting, sampling.

déhancher (se) [sədeɑ̃ʃe] *vpr* (*femme etc*) to sway *ou* wiggle one's hips; (*boiteux*) to walk lop-sided.

dehors [dəɔr] *adv* out(side); (*à l'air*) outdoors, outside; **en d.** on the outside; **en d. de** outside; (*excepté*) apart from; **en d. de la ville/fenêtre** out of town/the window; **au-d.** (**de**), **au d.** (**de**) outside; **déjeuner/jeter/etc d.** to lunch/throw/etc out; — *nm* (*extérieur*) outside; *pl* (*aspect*) outward appearance.

déjà [deʒa] *adv* already; **est-il d. parti?** has he left yet *ou* already?; **elle l'a d. vu** she's seen it before, she's already seen it; **c'est d. pas mal** that's not bad at all; **quand partez-vous, d.?** when are you leaving, again?

déjeuner [deʒœne] *vi* (*à midi*) to (have) lunch; (*le matin*) to (have) breakfast; — *nm* lunch; **petit d.** breakfast.

déjouer [deʒwe] *vt* (*intrigue etc*) to thwart, foil.

déjuger (se) [sədeʒyʒe] *vpr* to go back on one's opinion *ou* decision.

delà [d(ə)la] *adv* **au-d.** (**de**), **au d.** (**de**), **par-d.**,

par d. beyond; **au-d. du pont**/*etc* beyond *ou* past the bridge/*etc*; — **nm l'au-d.** the (world) beyond.

délabr/er (se) [sədelabre] *vpr* (*édifice*) to become dilapidated, fall into disrepair; (*santé*) to become impaired. ◆**—ement** *nm* dilapidation, disrepair; impaired state.

délacer [delase] *vt* (*chaussures*) to undo.

délai [dele] *nm* time limit; (*répit, sursis*) extra time, extension; **dans un d. de dix jours** within ten days; **sans d.** without delay; **à bref d.** at short notice; **dans les plus brefs délais** as soon as possible; **dernier d.** final date.

délaisser [delese] *vt* to forsake, desert, abandon; (*négliger*) to neglect.

délass/er [delase] *vt*, — **se d.** *vpr* to relax. ◆**—ement** *nm* relaxation, diversion.

délateur, -trice [delatœr, -tris] *nmf* informer.

délavé [delave] *a* (*tissu, jean*) faded; (*ciel*) watery; (*terre*) waterlogged.

délayer [deleje] *vt* (*mélanger*) to mix (with liquid); (*discours, texte*) *Fig* to pad out, drag out.

delco [dɛlko] *nm Aut* distributor.

délect/er (se) [sədelɛkte] *vpr* **se d. de qch/à faire** to (take) delight in sth/in doing. ◆**—able** *a* delectable. ◆**délectation** *nf* delight.

délégu/er [delege] *vt* to delegate (**à** to). ◆**—é, -ée** *nmf* delegate. ◆**délégation** *nf* delegation.

délest/er [deleste] *vt* *Él* to cut the power from; **d. qn de** (*voler à qn*) *Fam* to relieve s.o. of. ◆**—age** *nm Aut* relief; **itinéraire de d.** alternative route (*to relieve congestion*).

délibér/er [delibere] *vi* to deliberate (**sur** upon); (*se consulter*) to confer, deliberate (**de** about). ◆**—é, -ée** (*résolu*) determined; (*intentionnel*) deliberate; **de propos d.** deliberately. ◆**—ément** *adv* (*à dessein*) deliberately. ◆**délibération** *nf* deliberation.

délicat [delika] *a* (*santé, travail etc*) delicate; (*question*) tricky, delicate; (*geste*) tactful; (*conscience*) scrupulous; (*exigeant*) particular. ◆**délicatement** *adv* delicately; tactfully. ◆**délicatesse** *nf* delicacy; tact(fulness); scrupulousness.

délice [delis] *nm* delight; — *nfpl* delights. ◆**délicieux, -euse** *a* (*mets, fruit etc*) delicious; (*endroit, parfum etc*) delightful.

délié [delje] **1** *a* (*esprit*) sharp; (*doigts*) nimble; (*mince*) slender. **2** *nm* (*d'une lettre*) (thin) upstroke.

délier [delje] *vt* to untie, undo; (*langue*) *Fig*

to loosen; **d. qn de** to release s.o. from; — **se d.** *vpr* (*paquet etc*) to come undone *ou* untied.

délimiter [delimite] *vt* to mark off, delimit; (*définir*) to define. ◆**délimitation** *nf* demarcation, delimitation; definition.

délinquant, -ante [delɛ̃kɑ̃, -ɑ̃t] *a & nmf* delinquent. ◆**délinquance** *nf* delinquency.

délire [delir] *nm* Méd delirium; (*exaltation*) Fig frenzy. ◆**délir/er** *vi* Méd to be delirious; (*dire n'importe quoi*) Fig to rave; **d.** (*de joie etc*) to be wild with. ◆—**ant** *a* (*malade*) delirious; (*joie*) frenzied; wild; (*déraisonnable*) utterly absurd.

délit [deli] *nm* offence, misdemeanour.

délivrer [delivre] *vt* **1** (*prisonnier*) to release, deliver; (*ville*) to deliver; **d. qn de** (*souci etc*) to rid s.o. of. **2** (*billet, diplôme etc*) to issue. ◆**délivrance** *nf* release; deliverance; issue; (*soulagement*) relief.

déloger [deloʒe] *vi* to move out; — *vt* to force *ou* drive out; Mil to dislodge.

déloyal, -aux [delwajal, -o] *a* disloyal; (*concurrence*) unfair. ◆**déloyauté** *nf* disloyalty; unfairness; (*action*) disloyal act.

delta [dɛlta] *nm* (*de fleuve*) delta.

deltaplane® [dɛltaplan] *nm* (*engin*) hang-glider; **faire du d.** to practise hang-gliding.

déluge [delyʒ] *nm* flood; (*de pluie*) downpour; (*de compliments, coups*) shower.

déluré [delyre] *a* (*malin*) smart, sharp; (*fille*) Péj brazen.

démagogie [demagɔʒi] *nf* demagogy. ◆**démagogue** *nmf* demagogue.

demain [d(ə)mɛ̃] *adv* tomorrow; **à d.!** see you tomorrow!; **ce n'est pas d. la veille** Fam that won't happen for a while yet.

demande [d(ə)mɑ̃d] *nf* request; (*d'emploi*) application; (*de renseignements*) inquiry; Écon demand; (*question*) question; **d.** (**en mariage**) proposal (of marriage); **demandes d'emploi** Journ situations wanted. ◆**demander** *vt* to ask for; (*emploi*) to apply for; (*autorisation*) to request, ask for; (*charité*) to beg for; (*prix*) to charge; (*nécessiter, exiger*) to require; **d. un nom/le chemin/l'heure** to ask a name/the way/the time; **d. qch à qn** to ask s.o. for sth; **d. à qn de faire** to ask s.o. to do; **d. si/où** to ask *ou* inquire whether/where; **on te demande!** you're wanted!; **ça demande du temps/une heure** it takes time/an hour; **d. en mariage** to propose (marriage) to; — **se d.** *vpr* to wonder, ask oneself (*pourquoi* why, *si* if).

démanger [demɑ̃ʒe] *vti* to itch; **son bras le**

ou **lui démange** his arm itches; **ça me démange de...** Fig I'm itching to.... ◆**démangeaison** *nf* itch; **avoir des démangeaisons** to be itching; **j'ai une d. au bras** my arm's itching.

démanteler [demɑ̃tle] *vt* (*bâtiment*) to demolish; (*organisation etc*) to break up.

démantibuler [demɑ̃tibyle] *vt* (*meuble etc*) Fam to pull to pieces.

démaquiller (se) [sədemakije] *vpr* to take off one's make-up. ◆—**ant** *nm* make-up remover.

démarcation [demarkasjɔ̃] *nf* demarcation.

démarche [demarʃ] *nf* walk, step, gait; (*de pensée*) process; **faire des démarches** to take the necessary steps (**pour faire** to do).

démarcheur, -euse [demarʃœr, -øz] *nmf* Pol canvasser; Com door-to-door salesman *ou* saleswoman.

démarquer [demarke] *vt* (*prix*) to mark down; **se d. de** Fig to dissociate oneself from.

démarr/er [demare] *vi* (*moteur*) Aut to start (up); (*partir*) Aut to move *ou* drive off; (*entreprise etc*) Fig to get off the ground; — *vt* (*commencer*) Fam to start. ◆—**age** *nm* Aut start; **d. en côte** hill start. ◆—**eur** *nm* Aut starter.

démasquer [demaske] *vt* to unmask.

démêl/er [demele] *vt* to disentangle; (*discerner*) to fathom. ◆—**ê** *nm* (*dispute*) squabble; *pl* (*ennuis*) trouble (**avec** with).

démembrer [demɑ̃bre] *vt* (*pays etc*) to dismember.

déménag/er [demenaʒe] *vi* to move (out), move house; — *vt* (*meubles*) to (re)move. ◆—**ement** *nm* move, moving (house); (*de meubles*) removal, moving (of); **voiture de d.** removal van, Am moving van. ◆—**eur** *nm* removal man, Am (furniture) mover.

démener (se) [sədemene] *vpr* to fling oneself about; **se d. pour faire** to spare no effort to do.

dément, -ente [demɑ̃, -ɑ̃t] *a* insane; (*génial*) Iron fantastic; — *nmf* lunatic. ◆**démence** *nf* insanity. ◆**démentiel, -ielle** *a* insane.

dément/ir [demɑ̃tir] *vt* (*informer*) to belie; (*nouvelle, faits etc*) to deny; **d. qn** to give the lie to s.o. ◆—**i** *nm* denial.

démerder (se) [sədemɛrde] *vpr* (*se débrouiller*) Arg to manage (by oneself).

démesure [deməzyr] *nf* excess. ◆**démesuré** *a* excessive, inordinate.

démettre [demɛtr] *vt* **1** (*os*) to dislocate; **se d. le pied** to dislocate one's foot. **2 d. qn de**

to dismiss s.o. from; **se d. de ses fonctions** to resign one's office.

demeurant (au) [odəmœrɑ̃] adv for all that, after all.

demeure [dəmœr] nf **1** dwelling (place), residence. **2** mettre qn en d. de faire to summon ou instruct s.o. to do. ◆**demeurer/** vi **1** (aux être) (rester) to remain; **en d. là** (affaire etc) to rest there. **2** (aux avoir) (habiter) to live, reside. ◆**—é a** Fam (mentally) retarded.

demi, -ie [d(ə)mi] a half; **d.-journée** half-day; **une heure et demie** an hour and a half; (horloge) half past one; – adv (à) **d. plein** half-full; **à d. nu** half-naked; **ouvrir à d.** to open halfway; **faire les choses à d.** to do things by halves; – nmf (moitié) half; – nm (verre) (half-pint) glass of beer; Fb half-back; – nf (à l'horloge) half-hour.

demi-cercle [d(ə)miserkl] nm semicircle. ◆**d.-douzaine** nf **une d.-douzaine (de)** a half-dozen, half a dozen. ◆**d.-finale** nf Sp semifinal. ◆**d.-frère** nm stepbrother. ◆**d.-heure** nf **une d.-heure a** half-hour, half an hour. ◆**d.-mesure** nf half-measure. ◆**d.-mot** nm **tu comprendras à d.-mot** you'll understand without my having to spell it out. ◆**d.-pension** nf half-board. ◆**d.-pensionnaire** nmf day boarder, Am day student. ◆**d.-saison** nf **de d.-saison** (vêtement) between seasons. ◆**d.-sel** a inv (beurre) slightly salted; (fromage) **d.-sel** cream cheese. ◆**d.-sœur** nf stepsister. ◆**d.-tarif** nm & a inv (billet) (à) **d.-tarif** half-price. ◆**d.-tour** nm about turn, Am about face; Aut U-turn; **faire d.-tour** to turn back.

démission [demisjɔ̃] nf resignation. ◆**démissionnaire** (ministre etc) outgoing. ◆**démissionner** vi to resign.

démobiliser [demɔbilize] vt to demobilize. ◆**démobilisation** nf demobilization.

démocrate [demɔkrat] nmf democrat; – a democratic. ◆**démocratie** [-asi] nf democracy. ◆**démocratique** a democratic.

démod/er (se) [sədemɔde] vpr to go out of fashion. ◆**—é** a old-fashioned.

démographie [demɔgrafi] nf demography.

demoiselle [d(ə)mwazɛl] nf (célibataire) spinster, single woman; (jeune fille) young lady; **d. d'honneur** (à un mariage) bridesmaid; (de reine) maid of honour.

démolir [demɔlir] vt (maison, jouet etc) to demolish; (projet etc) to shatter; **d. qn** (battre, discréditer) Fam to tear s.o. to

pieces. ◆**démolition** nf demolition; **en d.** being demolished.

démon [demɔ̃] nm demon; **petit d.** (enfant) little devil. ◆**démoniaque** a devilish, fiendish.

démonstrateur, -trice [demɔ̃stratœr, -tris] nmf (dans un magasin etc) demonstrator. ◆**démonstratif, -ive** a demonstrative. ◆**démonstration** nf demonstration; **d. de force** show of force.

démonter [demɔ̃te] vt (assemblage) to dismantle, take apart; (installation) to take down; **d. qn** (troubler) Fig to disconcert s.o.; **une mer démontée** a stormy sea; – **se d.** vpr to come apart; (installation) to come down; (personne) to be put out ou disconcerted.

démontrer [demɔ̃tre] vt to demonstrate, show.

démoraliser [demɔralize] vt to demoralize; – **se d.** vpr to become demoralized. ◆**démoralisation** nf demoralization.

démordre [demɔrdr] vi **il ne démordra pas de** (son opinion etc) he won't budge from.

démouler [demule] vt (gâteau) to turn out (from its mould).

démunir [demynir] vt **d. qn de** to deprive s.o. of; **se d. de** to part with.

démystifier [demistifje] vt (public etc) to disabuse; (idée etc) to debunk.

dénationaliser [denasjɔnalize] vt to denationalize.

dénaturer [denatyre] vt (propos, faits etc) to misrepresent, distort. ◆**—é** (goût, père etc) unnatural.

dénégation [denegasjɔ̃] nf denial.

déneiger [deneʒe] vt to clear of snow.

dénicher [denife] vt (trouver) to dig up, turn up; (ennemi, fugitif) to hunt out, flush out.

dénier [denje] vt to deny; (responsabilité) to disclaim, deny; **d. qch à qn** to deny s.o. sth.

dénigr/er [denigre] vt to denigrate, disparage. ◆**—ement** nm denigration, disparagement.

dénivellation [denivelasjɔ̃] nf unevenness; (pente) gradient; pl (accidents) bumps.

dénombrer [denɔ̃bre] vt to count, number.

dénomm/er [denɔme] vt to name. ◆**—é, -ée** nmf **un d. Dupont** a man named Dupont. ◆**dénomination** nf designation, name.

dénonc/er [denɔ̃se] vt (injustice etc) to denounce (à to); **d. qn** to inform on s.o., Scol to tell on s.o. (à to); – **se d.** vpr to give oneself up (à to). ◆**dénonciateur, -trice** nmf informer. ◆**dénonciation** nf denunciation.

dénoter [denɔte] vt to denote.

dénouer [denwe] vt (nœud, corde) to undo, untie; (cheveux) to undo; (situation, intrigue) to unravel; (problème, crise) to clear up; — **se d.** vpr (nœud) to come undone ou untied; (cheveux) to come undone. **◆dénouement** nm outcome, ending; Th dénouement.

dénoyauter [denwajote] vt (prune etc) to stone, to pit.

denrée [dɑ̃re] nf food(stuff); **denrées alimentaires** foodstuffs.

dense [dɑ̃s] a dense. **◆densité** nf density.

dent [dɑ̃] nf tooth; (de roue) cog; (de fourche) prong; (de timbre-poste) perforation; **d. de sagesse** wisdom tooth; **rien à se mettre sous la d.** nothing to eat; **manger à belles dents/du bout des dents** to eat whole-heartedly/half-heartedly; **faire ses dents** (enfant) to be teething; **coup de d.** bite; **sur les dents** (surmené) exhausted; (énervé) on edge; **avoir une d. contre qn** to have it in for s.o. **◆dentaire** a dental. **◆dentée** a **d. de roue d.** cogwheel. **◆dentier** nm denture(s), (set of) false teeth. **◆dentifrice** nm toothpaste. **◆dentiste** n dentist; **chirurgien d.** dental surgeon. **◆dentition** nf (dents) (set of) teeth.

dentelé [dɑ̃tle] a (côte) jagged; (feuille) serrated. **◆dentelure** nf jagged outline ou edge.

dentelle [dɑ̃tɛl] nf lace.

dénud/er [denyde] vt to (lay) bare. **◆—é** a bare.

dénué [denye] a **d.** devoid of, without.

dénuement [denymɑ̃] nm destitution; **dans le d.** poverty-stricken.

déodorant [deɔdɔrɑ̃] nm deodorant.

dépann/er [depane] vt (mécanisme) to get going (again), to repair; **d. qn** Fam to help s.o. out. **◆—age** nm (emergency) repair; **voiture/service de d.** breakdown vehicle/service. **◆—eur** nm repairman; Aut breakdown mechanic. **◆—euse** nf (voiture) Aut breakdown lorry, Am wrecker, tow truck.

dépareillé [depareje] a (chaussure etc) odd, not matching; (collection) incomplete.

déparer [depare] vt to mar, spoil.

départ [depar] nm departure; (début) start, beginning; Sp start; **point/ligne de d.** starting point/post; **au d.** at the outset, at the start; **au d. de Paris/etc** (excursion etc) departing from Paris/etc.

départager [departaʒe] vt (concurrents) to decide between; **d. les votes** to give the casting vote.

département [departəmɑ̃] nm department.

◆départemental, -aux a departmental; **route départementale** secondary road.

départir (se) [sədepartir] vpr se d. de (attitude) to depart from, abandon.

dépass/er [depase] vt (durée, attente etc) to go beyond, exceed; (endroit) to go past, to go beyond; (véhicule, bicyclette etc) to overtake, pass; (pouvoir) to go beyond, overstep; **d. qn** (en hauteur) to be taller than s.o.; (surclasser) to be ahead of s.o.; **ça me dépasse** Fig that's (quite) beyond me; — vi (jupon, clou etc) to stick out, show. **◆—é a** (démodé) outdated; (incapable) unable to cope. **◆—ement** nm Aut overtaking, passing.

dépays/er [depeize] vt to disorientate, Am disorient. **◆—ement** nm disorientation; (changement) change of scenery.

dépecer [depəse] vt (animal) to cut up, carve up.

dépêche [depɛʃ] nf telegram; (diplomatique) dispatch. **◆dépêcher** vt to dispatch; — **se d.** vpr to hurry (up).

dépeigner [depeɲe] vt **d. qn** to make s.o.'s hair untidy. **◆—é a être d.** to have untidy hair; **sortir d.** to go out with untidy hair.

dépeindre* [depɛ̃dr] vt to depict, describe.

dépenaillé [depənaje] a in a tatters ou rags.

dépend/re [depɑ̃dr] **1** vt (appartenir à) to belong to; (être soumis à) to be dependent on; **ça dépend de toi** that depends on you, that's up to you. **2** vt (décrocher) to take down. **◆—ant** a dependent (de on). **◆dépendance 1** nf dependence; **sous la d. de qn** under s.o.'s domination. **2** nfpl (bâtiments) outbuildings.

dépens [depɑ̃] nmpl Jur costs; **aux d. de** at the expense of; **apprendre à ses d.** to learn to one's cost.

dépense [depɑ̃s] nf (action) spending; (frais) expense, expenditure; (d'électricité etc) consumption; (physique) exertion. **◆dépenser** vt (argent) to spend; (électricité etc) to use; (forces) to exert; (énergie) to expend; — **se d.** vpr to exert oneself. **◆dépensier, -ière** a wasteful, extravagant.

déperdition [deperdisjɔ̃] nf (de chaleur etc) loss.

dépér/ir [deperir] vi (personne) to waste away; (plante) to wither; (santé etc) to decline. **◆—issement** nm (baisse) decline.

dépêtrer [depetre] vt to extricate; — **se d.** vpr to extricate oneself (de from).

dépeupl/er [depœple] vt to depopulate. **◆—ement** nm depopulation.

dépilatoire [depilatwar] *nm* hair-remover.

dépist/er [depiste] *vt* (*criminel etc*) to track down; (*maladie, fraude*) to detect. ◆**—age** *nm* Méd detection.

dépit [depi] *nm* resentment, chagrin; **en d.** de in spite of. ◆**dépiter** *vt* to vex, chagrin; **— se d.** *vpr* to feel resentment *ou* chagrin.

déplac/er [deplase] *vt* to shift, move; (*fonctionnaire*) to transfer; **— se d.** *vpr* to move (about); (*voyager*) to get about, travel (about). ◆**—é a** (*mal à propos*) out of place; **personne déplacée** (*réfugié*) displaced person. ◆**—ement** *nm* (*voyage*) (business *ou* professional) trip; (*d'ouragan, de troupes*) movement; **les déplacements** (*voyages*) travel(ling); **frais de d.** travelling expenses.

déplaire* [depler] *vi* **d. à qn** to displease s.o.; **cet aliment lui déplaît** he *ou* she dislikes this food; **n'en déplaise à** *Iron* with all due respect to; *– v imp* **il me déplaît de faire** I dislike doing, it displeases me to do; **— se d.** *vpr* to dislike it. ◆**déplaisant** *a* unpleasant, displeasing. ◆**déplaisir** *nm* displeasure.

dépli/er [deplije] *vt* to open out, unfold. ◆**—ant** *nm* (*prospectus*) leaflet.

déplor/er [deplore] *vt* (*regretter*) to deplore; (*la mort de qn*) to mourn (over), lament (over); **d. qn** to mourn (for) s.o.; **d. que** (+ *sub*) to deplore the fact that, regret that. ◆**—able** *a* deplorable, lamentable.

déployer [deplwaje] *vt* (*ailes*) to spread; (*journal, carte*) to unfold, spread (out); (*objets, courage etc*) to display; (*troupes*) to deploy; **— se d.** *vpr* (*drapeau*) to unfurl. ◆**déploiement** *nm* (*démonstration*) display; Mil deployment.

dépoli [depoli] *a* **verre d.** frosted glass.

déport/er [deporte] *vt* **1** (*exiler*) Hist to deport (to a penal colony); (*dans un camp de concentration*) Hist to send to a concentration camp. **2** (*dévier*) to veer *ou* carry (off course). ◆**—é, —ée** *nmf* deportee; (*concentration camp*) inmate. ◆**déportation** *nf* deportation; internment (in a concentration camp).

dépos/er [depoze] *vt* (*poser*) to put down; (*laisser*) to leave; (*argent, lie*) to deposit; (*plainte*) to lodge; (*armes*) to lay down; (*gerbe*) to lay; (*ordures*) to dump; (*marque de fabrique*) to register; (*projet de loi*) to introduce; (*souverain*) to depose; **d. qn** Aut to drop s.o. (off), put s.o. off; **d. son bilan** Fin to go into liquidation, file for bankruptcy; *– vi* Jur to testify; (*liquide*) to leave a deposit; **— se d.** *vpr* (*poussière, lie*) to

settle. ◆**dépositaire** *nmf* Fin agent; (*de secret*) custodian. ◆**déposition** *nf* Jur statement; (*de souverain*) deposing.

déposséder [deposede] *vt* to deprive, dispossess (*de* of).

dépôt [depo] *nm* (*d'ordures etc*) dumping, (*lieu*) dump; (*de gerbe*) laying; (*d'autobus, de trains*) depot; (*entrepôt*) warehouse; (*argent*) deposit; (*de vin*) deposit, sediment; **d.** (*calcaire*) (*de chaudière etc*) deposit; **laisser qch à qn en d.** to give s.o. sth for safekeeping *ou* in trust.

dépotoir [depotwar] *nm* rubbish dump, Am garbage dump.

dépouille [depuj] *nf* hide, skin; (*de serpent*) slough; *pl* (*butin*) spoils; **d.** (**mortelle**) mortal remains. ◆**dépouill/er** *vt* (*animal*) to skin, flay; (*analyser*) to go through, analyse; **d. de** (*dégarnir*) to strip of; (*déposséder*) to deprive of; **se d. de** to rid *ou* divest oneself of, cast off; **d. un scrutin** to count votes. ◆**—é a** (*arbre*) bare; (*style*) austere, spare; **d.** bereft of. ◆**—ement** *nm* (*de document etc*) analysis; (*privation*) deprivation; (*sobriété*) austerity. **d. du scrutin** counting of the votes.

dépourvu [depurvy] *a* **d.** **de** devoid of; **prendre qn au d.** to catch s.o. unawares *ou* off his guard.

dépraver [deprave] *vt* to deprave. ◆**dépravation** *nf* depravity.

dépréci/er [depresje] *vt* (*dénigrer*) to disparage; (*monnaie, immeuble etc*) to depreciate; **— se d.** *vpr* (*baisser*) to depreciate, lose (its) value. ◆**dépréciation** *nf* depreciation.

déprédations [depredasjɔ̃] *nfpl* damage, ravages.

dépression [depresjɔ̃] *nf* depression; **zone de d.** trough of low pressure; **d.** **nerveuse** nervous breakdown; **d. économique** slump. ◆**dépressif, -ive** *a* depressive. ◆**déprime** *nf* **la d.** (*dépression*) Fam the blues. ◆**déprim/er** *vt* to depress. ◆**—é a** depressed.

depuis [dəpɥi] *prép* since; **d.** **lundi** since Monday; **d. qu'elle est partie** since she left; **j'habite ici d. un mois** I've been living here for a month; **d. quand êtes-vous là?** how long have you been here?; **d. peu/longtemps** for a short/long time; **d. Paris jusqu'à Londres** from Paris to London; *– adv* since (then), ever since.

députation [depytasjɔ̃] *nf* (*groupe*) deputation, delegation; **candidat à la d.** parliamentary candidate. ◆**député** *nm* delegate, deputy; (*au parlement*) deputy, = *Br* MP, = *Am* congressman, congresswoman.

déracin/er [derasine] *vt* (*personne, arbre etc*) to uproot; (*préjugés etc*) to eradicate, root out. ◆**-ement** *nm* uprooting; eradication.

déraill/er [deraje] *vi* 1 (*train*) to jump the rails, be derailed; **faire d.** to derail. 2 (*divaguer*) *Fam* to drivel, talk through one's hat. ◆**-ement** *nm* (*de train*) derailment. ◆**-eur** *nm* (*de bicyclette*) derailleur (gear change).

déraisonnable [derezɔnabl] *a* unreasonable. ◆**déraisonner** *vi* to talk nonsense.

dérang/er [derãʒe] *vt* (*affaires*) to disturb, upset; (*estomac*) to upset; (*projets*) to mess up, upset; (*vêtements*) to mess up; (*cerveau, esprit*) to derange; **d. qn** to disturb *ou* bother *ou* trouble s.o.; **je viendrai si ça ne te dérange pas** I'll come if that doesn't put you out *ou* if that's not imposing; **ça vous dérange si je fume?** do you mind if I smoke?; — **se d.** *vpr* to put oneself to a lot of trouble (**pour faire** to do); (*se déplacer*) to move; **ne te dérange pas!** don't trouble yourself!, don't bother! ◆**-ement** *nm* (*gêne*) bother, inconvenience; (*désordre*) disorder; **en d.** (*téléphone etc*) out of order.

dérap/er [derape] *vi* to skid. ◆**-age** *nm* skid; (*des prix, de l'inflation*) *Fig* loss of control *ou* (over).

dératé [derate] *nm* **courir comme un d.** to run like mad.

dérégl/er [deregle] *vt* (*mécanisme*) to put out of order; (*estomac, habitudes*) to upset; (*esprit*) to unsettle; — **se d.** *vpr* (*montre, appareil*) to go wrong. ◆**-é** *a* out of order; (*vie, mœurs*) dissolute, wild; (*imagination*) wild. ◆**dérèglement** *nm* (*de mécanisme*) breakdown; (*d'esprit*) disorder; (*d'estomac*) upset.

dérider [deride] *vt*, — **se d.** *vpr* to cheer up.

dérision [derizjɔ̃] *nf* derision, mockery; **tourner en d.** to mock, deride; **par d.** derisively; **de d.** derisive. ◆**dérisoire** *a* ridiculous, derisory, derisive.

dérive [deriv] *nf Nau* drift; **partir à la d.** (*navire*) to drift out to sea; **aller à la d.** (*navire*) to go adrift; (*entreprise etc*) *Fig* to drift (towards ruin). ◆**dériv/er** *vi Nau Av* to drift; **d. de** (*venir*) to derive from, be derived from; — *vt* (*cours d'eau*) to divert; *Ling* to derive (**de** from). ◆**-é** *nm Ling Ch* derivative; (*produit*) by-product. ◆**dérivatif** *nm* distraction (**à** from). ◆**dérivation** *nf* (*de cours d'eau*) diversion; *Ling* derivation; (*déviation routière*) bypass.

dermatologie [dɛrmatɔlɔʒi] *nf* dermatology.

dernier -ière [dɛrnje, -jɛr] *a* last; (*nouvelles, mode*) latest; (*étage*) top; (*degré*) highest; (*qualité*) lowest; **le d. rang** the back *ou* last row; **ces derniers mois** these past few months, these last *ou* final months; **de la dernière importance** of (the) utmost importance; **en d.** last; — *nmf* last (person *ou* one); **ce d.** (*de deux*) the latter; (*de plusieurs*) the last-mentioned; **être le d. de la classe** to be (at) the bottom of the class; **le d. des derniers** the lowest of the low; **le d. de mes soucis** the least of my worries. ◆**d.-né**, ◆**dernière-née** *nmf* youngest (child). ◆**dernièrement** *adv* recently.

dérob/er [derɔbe] *vt* (*voler*) to steal (**à** from); (*cacher*) to hide (**à** from); — **se d.** *vpr* to get out of one's obligations; (*s'éloigner*) to slip away; (*éviter de répondre*) to dodge the issue; **se d. à** (*obligations*) to shirk, get out of; (*regards*) to hide from; **ses jambes se sont dérobées sous lui** his legs gave way beneath him. ◆**-é** *a* (*porte etc*) hidden, secret; **à la dérobée** *adv* on the sly, stealthily. ◆**dérobade** *nf* dodge, evasion.

déroger [derɔʒe] *vi* **d. à une règle/etc** to depart from a rule/etc. ◆**dérogation** *nf* exemption, (special) dispensation.

dérouiller [deruje] *vt* **d. qn** (*battre*) *Arg* to thrash *ou* thump s.o.; **se d. les jambes** *Fam* to stretch one's legs.

déroul/er [derule] *vt* (*carte etc*) to unroll; (*film*) to unwind; — **se d.** *vpr* (*événement*) to take place, pass off; (*paysage, souvenirs*) to unfold; (*récit*) to develop. ◆**-ement** *nm* (*d'une action*) unfolding, development; (*cours*) course;

dérouter [derute] *vt* (*avion, navire*) to divert, reroute; (*candidat etc*) to baffle; (*poursuivant*) to throw off the scent.

derrick [derik] *nm* derrick.

derrière [dɛrjɛr] *prép & adv* behind; **d. moi** behind me, *Am* in back of me; **assis d.** (*dans une voiture*) sitting in the back; (*d'une voiture*) sitting in the back; (*de roue*) back, rear; (*pattes*) back; **par d.** (*attaquer*) from behind, from the rear; — *nm* (*de maison etc*) back, rear; (*fesses*) behind, bottom.

des [de] *voir* à [1], [2], le.

dès [dɛ] *prép* from, from then on; **d. cette époque** (as) from that time, from that time on; **d. le début** (right) from the start; **d. son enfance** since *ou* from (his *ou* her) childhood; **d. le**

sixième siècle as early as *ou* as far back as the sixth century; **d. l'aube** at (the crack of) dawn; **d. qu'elle viendra** as soon as she comes.

désabusé [dezabyze] *a* disenchanted, disillusioned.

désaccord [dezakɔr] *nm* disagreement. ◆**désaccordé** *a* Mus out of tune.

désaccoutumer (se) [sədezakutyme] *vpr* **se d. de** to lose the habit of.

désaffecté [dezafɛkte] *a* (école etc) disused.

désaffection [dezafɛksjɔ̃] *nf* loss of affection, disaffection (**pour** for).

désagréable [dezagreabl] *a* unpleasant, disagreeable. ◆—**ment** [-əmɑ̃] *adv* unpleasantly.

désagréger [dezagreʒe] *vt*, **— se d.** *vpr* to disintegrate, break up. ◆**désagrégation** *nf* disintegration.

désagrément [dezagremɑ̃] *nm* annoyance, trouble.

désaltérer [dezaltere] *vt* **d. qn** to quench s.o.'s thirst; **se d.** to quench one's thirst. ◆—**ant** *a* thirst-quenching.

désamorcer [dezamɔrse] *vt* (obus, situation) to defuse.

désappointer [dezapwɛ̃te] *vt* to disappoint.

désapprouver [dezapruve] *vt* to disapprove of; **— vi** to disapprove. ◆**désapprobateur, -trice** *a* disapproving. ◆**désapprobation** *nf* disapproval.

désarçonner [dezarsɔne] *vt* (jockey) to throw, unseat; (déconcerter) Fig to nonpluss, throw.

désarm/er [dezarme] *vt* (émouvoir) & Mil to disarm; **— vi** Mil to disarm; (céder) to let up. ◆—**ant** *a* (charme etc) disarming. ◆—**é** *a* (sans défense) unarmed; Fig helpless. ◆—**ement** *nm* (de nation) disarmament.

désarroi [dezarwa] *nm* (angoisse) distress.

désarticuler [dezartikyle] *vt* (membre) to dislocate.

désastre [dezastr] *nm* disaster. ◆**désastreux, -euse** *a* disastrous.

désavantage [dezavɑ̃taʒ] *nm* disadvantage, handicap; (inconvénient) drawback, disadvantage. ◆**désavantager** *vt* to put at a disadvantage, handicap. ◆**désavantageux, -euse** *a* disadvantageous.

désaveu, -x [dezavø] *nm* repudiation. ◆**désavouer** *vt* (livre, personne etc) to disown, repudiate.

désaxé, -ée [dezakse] *a* & *nmf* unbalanced (person).

desceller [desele] *vt* (pierre etc) to loosen; **— se d.** *vpr* to come loose.

descend/re [desɑ̃dr] *vi* (aux être) to come *ou* go down, descend (**de** from); (d'un train etc) to get off *ou* out, alight (**de** from); (d'un arbre) to climb down (**de** from); (nuit, thermomètre) to fall; (marée) to go out; **d. à** (une bassesse) to stoop to; **d. à l'hôtel** to put up at a hotel; **d. de** (être issu de) to be descended from; **d. de cheval** to dismount; **d. en courant/flânant**/etc to run/stroll/etc down; **— vt** (aux avoir) (escalier) to come *ou* go down, descend; (objets) to bring *ou* take down; (avion) to bring *ou* shoot down; **d. qn** (tuer) Fam to bump s.o. off. ◆—**ant, -ante 1** *a* descending; (marée) outgoing. **2** *nmf* (personne) descendant. ◆**descendance** *nf* (enfants) descendants; (origine) descent.

descente [desɑ̃t] *nf* (action) descent; (irruption) raid (**dans** upon); (en parachute) drop; (pente) slope; **la d. des bagages** bringing *ou* taking down the luggage; **il fut accueilli à sa d. d'avion** he was met as he got off the plane; **d. à skis** downhill run; **d. de lit** (tapis) bedside rug.

descriptif, -ive [dɛskriptif, -iv] *a* descriptive. ◆**description** *nf* description.

déségrégation [desegregasjɔ̃] *nf* desegregation.

désemparé [dezɑ̃pare] *a* distraught, at a loss; (navire) crippled.

désemplir [dezɑ̃plir] *vi* **ce magasin**/etc **ne désemplit pas** this shop/etc is always crowded.

désenchant/er [dezɑ̃ʃɑ̃te] *vt* to disenchant. ◆—**ement** *nm* disenchantment.

désencombrer [dezɑ̃kɔ̃bre] *vt* (passage etc) to clear.

désenfler [dezɑ̃fle] *vi* to go down, become less swollen.

déséquilibre [dezekilibr] *nm* (inégalité) imbalance; (mental) unbalance; **en d.** (meuble etc) unsteady. ◆**déséquilibrer** *vt* to throw off balance; (esprit, personne) Fig to unbalance.

désert [dezɛr] *a* deserted; **île déserte** desert island; **— nm** desert, wilderness. ◆**désertique** *a* (région etc) desert-.

déserter [dezɛrte] *vti* to desert. ◆**déserteur** *nm* Mil deserter. ◆**désertion** *nf* desertion.

désespér/er [dezɛspere] *vi* to despair (**de** of); **— vt** to drive to despair; **— se d.** *vpr* to (be in) despair. ◆—**ant** *a* (enfant etc) that drives one to despair, hopeless. ◆—**é, -ée** *a* (personne) in despair, despairing; (cas, situation) desperate, hopeless; (efforts, cris) desperate; **— nmf** (suicidé) person driven to despair *ou* desperation. ◆**—ément** *adv* desperately. ◆**désespoir** *nm* despair; **au d.** in despair; **en d. de cause** in desperation, as a (desperate) last resort.

déshabiller [dezabije] *vt* to undress, strip; **— se d.** *vpr* to get undressed, undress.

déshabituer [dezabitɥe] *vt* **d. qn de** to break s.o. of the habit of.

désherb/er [dezɛrbe] *vti* to weed. ◆**—ant** *nm* weed killer.

déshérit/er [dezerite] *vt* to disinherit. ◆**—é** *a* (*pauvre*) underprivileged; (*laid*) ill-favoured.

déshonneur [dezɔnœr] *nm* dishonour, disgrace. ◆**déshonor/er** *vt* to disgrace, dishonour. ◆**—ant** *a* dishonourable.

déshydrater [dezidrate] *vt* to dehydrate; **— se d.** *vpr* to become dehydrated.

désigner [dezine] *vt* (*montrer*) to point to, point out; (*élire*) to appoint, designate; (*signifier*) to indicate, designate; **ses qualités le désignent pour** his qualities mark him out for. ◆**désignation** *nf* designation.

désillusion [dezilyzjɔ̃] *nf* disillusion(ment). ◆**désillusionner** *vt* to disillusion.

désincarné [dezɛ̃karne] *a* (*esprit*) disembodied.

désinence [dezinɑ̃s] *nf* *Gram* ending.

désinfect/er [dezɛ̃fɛkte] *vt* to disinfect. ◆**—ant** *nm & a* disinfectant. ◆**désinfection** *nf* disinfection.

désinformation [dezɛ̃fɔrmasjɔ̃] *nf* *Pol* misinformation.

désintégrer (se) [sədezɛ̃tegre] *vpr* to disintegrate. ◆**désintégration** *nf* disintegration.

désintéress/er (se) [sədezɛ̃terese] *vpr* **se d. de** to lose interest in, take no further interest in. ◆**—é** *a* (*altruiste*) disinterested. ◆**—ement** [-ɛsmɑ̃] *nm* (*altruisme*) disinterestedness. ◆**désintérêt** *nm* lack of interest.

désintoxiquer [dezɛ̃tɔksike] *vt* (*alcoolique*, *drogué*) to cure.

désinvolte [dezɛ̃vɔlt] *a* (*dégagé*) easy-going, casual; (*insolent*) offhand, casual. ◆**désinvolture** *nf* casualness; offhandedness.

désir [dezir] *nm* desire, wish. ◆**désirable** *a* desirable. ◆**désirer** *vt* to want, desire; (*convoiter*) to desire; **je désire venir** I would like to come, I wish *ou* want to come; **je désire que tu viennes** I want you to come; **ça laisse à d.** it leaves something *ou* a lot to be desired. ◆**désireux, -euse** *a* **d. de faire** anxious *ou* eager to do, desirous of doing.

désist/er (se) [sədeziste] *vpr* (*candidat etc*) to withdraw. ◆**—ement** *nm* withdrawal.

désobé/ir [dezɔbeir] *vi* to disobey; **d. à qn** to disobey s.o. ◆**—issant** *a* disobedient. ◆**désobéissance** *nf* disobedience (à to).

désobligeant [dezɔbliʒɑ̃] *a* disagreeable, unkind.

désodorisant [dezɔdɔrizɑ̃] *nm* air freshener.

désœuvré [dezœvre] *a* idle, unoccupied. ◆**désœuvrement** *nm* idleness.

désol/er [dezɔle] *vt* to distress, upset (very much); **— se d.** *vpr* to be distressed *ou* upset (**de** at). ◆**—ant** *a* distressing, upsetting. ◆**—é** *a* (*région*) desolate; (*affligé*) distressed; **être d.** (*navré*) to be sorry (**que** (+ *sub*) that, **de faire** to do). ◆**désolation** *nf* (*peine*) distress, grief.

désolidariser (se) [sədesɔlidarize] *vpr* to dissociate oneself (**de** from).

désopilant [dezɔpilɑ̃] *a* hilarious, screamingly funny.

désordre [dezɔrdr] *nm* (*de papiers, affaires, idées*) mess, muddle, disorder; (*de cheveux, pièce*) untidiness; *Méd* disorder; *pl* (*émeutes*) disorder, unrest; **en d.** untidy, messy. ◆**désordonné** *a* (*personne, chambre*) untidy, messy.

désorganiser [dezɔrganize] *vt* to disorganize. ◆**désorganisation** *nf* disorganization.

désorienter [dezɔrjɑ̃te] *vt* **d. qn** to disorientate *ou* *Am* disorient s.o., make s.o. lose his bearings; (*déconcerter*) to bewilder s.o. ◆**désorientation** *nf* disorientation.

désormais [dezɔrmɛ] *adv* from now on, in future, henceforth.

désosser [dezɔse] *vt* (*viande*) to bone.

despote [dɛspɔt] *nm* despot. ◆**despotique** *a* despotic. ◆**despotisme** *nm* despotism.

desquels, desquelles [dekɛl] *voir* **lequel.**

dessaisir (se) [sədesezir] *vpr* **se d. de qch** to part with sth, relinquish sth.

dessaler [desale] *vt* (*poisson etc*) to remove the salt from (*by smoking*).

dessécher [deseʃe] *vt* (*végétation*) to dry up, wither; (*gorge, bouche*) to dry, parch; (*fruits*) to desiccate, dry; (*cœur*) to harden; **— se d.** *vpr* (*plante*) to wither, dry up; (*peau*) to dry (up), get dry; (*maigrir*) to waste away.

dessein [desɛ̃] *nm* aim, design; **dans le d. de faire** with the aim of doing; **à d.** intentionally.

desserrer [desere] *vt* (*ceinture etc*) to loosen, slacken; (*poing*) to open, unclench;

(*frein*) to release; **il n'a pas desserré les dents** he didn't open his mouth; **— se d.** *vpr* to come loose.

dessert [desɛr] *nm* dessert, sweet.

desserte [desɛrt] *nf* **assurer la d. de** (*village etc*) to provide a (bus *ou* train) service to. ◆**desservir** *vt* **1** (*table*) to clear (away). **2 d. qn** to harm s.o., do s.o. a disservice. **3 l'autobus/etc dessert ce village** the bus/*etc* provides a service to *ou* stops at this village; **ce quartier est bien desservi** this district is well served by public transport.

dessin [desɛ̃] *nm* drawing; (*rapide*) sketch; (*motif*) design, pattern; (*contour*) outline; **d. animé** *Cin* cartoon; **d. humoristique** *Journ* cartoon; **école de d.** art school; **planche à d.** drawing board. ◆**dessinateur, -trice** *nmf* drawer; sketcher; **d. humoristique** cartoonist; **d. de modes** dress designer; **d. industriel** draughtsman, *Am* draftsman. ◆**dessiner** *vt* to draw; (*rapidement*) to sketch; (*meuble, robe etc*) to design; (*indiquer*) to outline, trace; **d. (bien) la taille** (*vêtement*) to show off the figure; **— se d.** *vpr* (*colline etc*) to stand out, be outlined; (*projet*) to take shape.

dessoûler [desule] *vti Fam* to sober up.

dessous [d(ə)su] *adv* under(neath), beneath, below; **en d.** (*sous*) under(neath); (*agir*) *Fig* in an underhand way; **vêtement de d.** undergarment; **drap de d.** bottom sheet; **— nm** (*vêtements*) underclothes; **d. de table** backhander, bribe; **les gens du d.** the people downstairs *ou* below; **avoir le d.** to be defeated, get the worst of it. ◆**d.-de-plat** *nm inv* table mat.

dessus [d(ə)sy] *adv* (*marcher, écrire*) on it; (*monter*) on top (of it), on; (*lancer, passer*) over it; **de d. la table** off *ou* from the table; **vêtement de d.** outer garment; **drap de d.** top sheet; **par-d.** (*sauter etc*) over (it); **par-d. tout** above all; **— nm** top; (*de chaussure*) upper; **avoir le d.** to have the upper hand, get the best of it; **les gens du d.** the people upstairs *ou* above. ◆**d.-de-lit** *nm inv* bedspread.

déstabiliser [destabilize] *vt* to destabilize.

destin [destɛ̃] *nm* fate, destiny. ◆**destinée** *nf* fate, destiny (*of an individual*).

destin/er [destine] *vt* **d. qch à qn** to intend *ou* mean sth for s.o.; **d. qn à** (*carrière, fonction*) to intend *ou* destine for; **se d. à** (*carrière etc*) to intend *ou* mean to take up; **destiné à mourir/etc** (*condamné*) destined *ou* fated to die/*etc*. ◆**destinataire** *nmf* addressee. ◆**destination** *nf* (*usage*)

purpose; (*lieu*) destination; **à d. de** (*train etc*) (going) to, (bound) for.

destituer [dɛstitɥe] *vt* (*fonctionnaire etc*) to dismiss (from office). ◆**destitution** *nf* dismissal.

destructeur, -trice [dɛstryktœr, -tris] *a* destructive; — *nmf* (*personne*) destroyer. ◆**destructif, -ive** *a* destructive. ◆**destruction** *nf* destruction.

désuet, -ète [desɥɛ, -ɛt] *a* antiquated, obsolete.

désunir [dezynir] *vt* (*famille etc*) to divide, disunite. ◆**désunion** *nf* disunity, dissension.

détach/er¹ [detaʃe] *vt* (*ceinture, vêtement*) to undo; (*nœud*) to untie, undo; (*personne, mains*) to untie; (*ôter*) to take off, detach; (*mots*) to pronounce clearly; **d. qn** (*libérer*) to let s.o. loose; (*affecter*) to transfer s.o. (on assignment) (**à** to); **d. les yeux de qn/qch** to take one's eyes off s.o./sth; **— se d.** *vpr* (*chien, prisonnier*) to break loose; (*se dénouer*) to come undone; **se d.** (**de qch**) (*fragment*) to break away from; **se d. de** (*amis*) to break away from, grow apart from; **se d.** (**sur**) (*ressortir*) to stand out (against). ◆**-é à 1** (*nœud*) loose, undone. **2** (*air, ton etc*) detached. ◆**-ement** *nm* **1** (*indifférence*) detachment. **2** (*de fonctionnaire*) (temporary) transfer; *Mil* detachment.

détach/er² [detaʃe] *vt* (*linge etc*) to remove the spots *ou* stains from. ◆**-ant** *nm* stain remover.

détail [detaj] *nm* **1** detail; **en d.** in detail; **le d. de** (*dépenses etc*) a detailing *ou* breakdown of. **2 de d.** (*magasin, prix*) retail; **vendre au d.** to sell retail; (*par petites quantités*) to sell separately; **faire le d.** to retail *ou* sell separately; (*au détail*) to (sell) retail. **2** (*énumérer etc*) to detail. ◆**-ant, -ante** *nmf* retailer. ◆**-é à** (*récit etc*) detailed.

détaler [detale] *vi Fam* to run off, make tracks.

détartrer [detartre] *vt* (*chaudière, dents etc*) to scale.

détaxer [detakse] *vt* (*denrée etc*) to reduce the tax on; (*supprimer*) to take the tax off; **produit détaxé** duty-free article.

détecter [detɛkte] *vt* to detect. ◆**détecteur** *nm* (*appareil*) detector. ◆**détection** *nf* detection.

détective [detɛktiv] *nm* **d.** (*privé*) (private) detective.

déteindre* [detɛ̃dr] *vi* (*couleur ou étoffe au lavage*) to run; (*au soleil*) to fade; **ton**

tablier bleu a déteint sur ma chemise the blue of my apron has come off on(to) my shirt; **d. sur qn** (*influencer*) to leave one's mark on s.o.

dételer [detle] *vt* (*chevaux*) to unhitch, unharness.

détend/re [detɑ̃dr] *vt* (*arc etc*) to slacken, relax; (*situation, atmosphère*) to ease; **d. qn** to relax s.o.; **— se d.** *vpr* to slacken, get slack; to ease; (*se reposer*) to relax; (*rapports*) to become less strained. **◆—u** *a* (*visage, atmosphère*) relaxed; (*ressort, câble*) slack. **◆détente** *nf* **1** (*d'arc*) slackening; (*de relations*) easing of tension, *Pol* détente; (*repos*) relaxation; (*saut*) leap, spring. **2** (*gâchette*) trigger.

déten/ir* [detnir] *vt* to hold; (*secret, objet volé*) to be in possession of; (*prisonnier*) to hold, detain. **◆—u, -ue** *nmf* prisoner. **◆détenteur, -trice** *nmf* (*de record etc*) holder. **◆détention** *nf* (*d'armes*) possession; (*captivité*) detention; **d. préventive** *Jur* custody.

détergent [detɛrʒɑ̃] *nm* detergent.

détérior/er [deterjɔre] *vt* (*abîmer*) to damage; **— se d.** *vpr* (*empirer*) to deteriorate. **◆détérioration** *nf* damage (**de** to); (*d'une situation etc*) deterioration (**de** in).

détermin/er [detɛrmine] *vt* (*préciser*) to determine; (*causer*) to bring about; **d. qn à faire** to induce s.o. to do, make s.o. do; **se d. à faire** to resolve ou determine to do. **◆—ant** *a* (*motif*) determining, deciding; (*rôle*) decisive. **◆—é** *a* (*précis*) specific; (*résolu*) determined. **◆détermination** *nf* (*fermeté*) determination; (*résolution*) resolve.

déterrer [detere] *vt* to dig up, unearth.

détest/er [detɛste] *vt* to hate; **d. faire** to hate doing ou to do, detest doing. **◆—able** *a* awful, foul.

détonateur [detɔnatœr] *nm* detonator. **◆détonation** *nf* explosion, blast.

détonner [detɔne] *vi* (*contraster*) to jar, be out of place.

détour [detur] *nm* (*de route etc*) bend, curve; (*crochet*) detour; **sans d.** (*parler*) without beating about the bush; **faire des détours** (*route*) to wind.

détourn/er [deturne] *vt* (*fleuve, convoi etc*) to divert; (*tête*) to turn (away); (*coups*) to ward off; (*conversation, sens*) to change; (*fonds*) to embezzle, misappropriate; (*avion*) to hijack; **d. qn de** (*son devoir, ses amis*) to take ou turn s.o. away from; (*sa route*) to lead s.o. away from; (*projet*) to talk s.o. out of; **d. les yeux** to look away,

avert one's eyes; **— se d.** *vpr* to turn aside ou away; **se d. de** (*chemin*) to wander ou stray from. **◆—é** *a* (*chemin, moyen*) roundabout, indirect. **◆—ement** *nm* (*de cours d'eau*) diversion; **d.** (**d'avion**) hijack(ing); (*de fonds*) embezzlement.

détraqu/er [detrake] *vt* (*mécanisme*) to break, put out of order; **— se d.** *vpr* (*machine*) to go wrong; **se d. l'estomac** to upset one's stomach; **se d. la santé** to ruin one's health. **◆—é, -ée** *a* out of order; (*cerveau*) deranged; **— nmf** crazy ou deranged person.

détremper [detrɑ̃pe] *vt* to soak, saturate.

détresse [detrɛs] *nf* distress; **en d.** (*navire, âme*) in distress; **dans la d.** (*misère*) in (great) distress.

détriment de (au) [odetrimɑ̃də] *prép* to the detriment of.

détritus [detritys] *nmpl* refuse, rubbish.

détroit [detrwa] *nm* *Géog* strait(s), sound.

détromper [detrɔ̃pe] *vt* to undeceive s.o., put s.o. right; **détrompez-vous!** don't you believe it!

détrôner [detrone] *vt* (*souverain*) to dethrone; (*supplanter*) to supersede, oust.

détrousser [detruse] *vt* (*voyageur, tuer*) to rob.

détruire* [detrɥir] *vt* (*ravager, tuer*) to destroy; (*projet, santé*) to ruin, wreck, destroy.

dette [dɛt] *nf* debt; **faire des dettes** to run ou get into debt; **avoir des dettes** to be in debt.

deuil [dœj] *nm* (*affliction, vêtements*) mourning; (*mort de qn*) bereavement; **porter le d., être en d.** to be in mourning.

deux [dø] *a & nm* two; **d. fois** twice, two times; **tous (les) d.** both; **en moins de d.** *Fam* in no time. **◆d.-pièces** *nm inv* (*vêtement*) two-piece; (*appartement*) two-roomed flat ou *Am* apartment. **◆d.-points** *nm inv* *Gram* colon. **◆d.-roues** *nm inv* two-wheeled vehicle. **◆d.-temps** *nm inv* two-stroke (engine).

deuxième [døzjɛm] *a & nmf* second. **◆—ment** *adv* secondly.

dévaler [devale] *vt* (*escalier etc*) to hurtle ou race ou rush down; **— vi** (*tomber*) to tumble down, come tumbling down.

dévaliser [devalize] *vt* (*détrousser*) to clean out, strip, rob (of everything).

dévaloriser [devalɔrize] **1** *vt*, **— se d.** *vpr* (*monnaie*) to depreciate. **2** *vt* (*humilier etc*) to devalue, disparage. **◆dévalorisation** *nf* (*de monnaie*) depreciation.

dévaluer [devalɥe] *vt* (*monnaie*) & *Fig* to devalue. **◆dévaluation** *nf* devaluation.

devancer [d(ə)vɑ̃se] vt to get ou be ahead of; (question etc) to anticipate, forestall; (surpasser) to outstrip; **tu m'as devancé** (action) you did it before me; (lieu) you got there before me. ◆**devancier, -ière** nmf predecessor.

devant [d(ə)vɑ̃] prép & adv in front (of); d. (l'hôtel/etc) in front (of the hotel/etc); **marcher d. (qn)** to walk in front (of s.o.) ou ahead (of s.o.); **passer d. (l'église/etc)** to go past (the church/etc); **assis d.** (dans une voiture) sitting in the front; **l'avenir est d. toi** the future is ahead of you; **loin d.** a long way ahead ou in front; **le d. danger** (confronté à) in the face of danger; **d. mes yeux/la loi** before my eyes/the law; — nm front; **de d.** (roue, porte) front; **patte de d.** foreleg; **par d.** from ou at the front; **prendre les devants** (action) to take the initiative. ◆**devanture** nf (vitrine) shop window; (façade) shop front.

dévaster [devaste] vt (ruiner) to devastate. ◆**dévastation** nf devastation.

déveine [deven] nf Fam tough ou bad luck.

développ/er [devlɔpe] vt to develop; Phot to develop, process; — **se d.** vpr to develop. ◆**—ement** nm development; Phot developing, processing; **les pays en voie de d.** the developing countries.

devenir [dəvnir] vi (aux être) to become; (vieux, difficile etc) to get, grow, become; (rouge, bleu etc) to turn, go, become; **d'un papillon/un homme/etc** to grow into a butterfly/a man/etc; **qu'est-il devenu?** what's become of him ou it?, where's he ou it got to?; **qu'est-ce que tu deviens?** Fam how are you doing?

dévergond/er (se) [sədevɛrgɔ̃de] vpr to fall into dissolute ways. ◆**—é** a dissolute, licentious.

déverser [devɛrse] vt (liquide, rancune) to pour out; (bombes, ordures) to dump; — **se d.** vpr (liquide) to empty, pour out (dans into).

dévêtir [devetir] vt, — **se d.** vpr Litt to undress.

dévier [devje] vt (circulation, conversation) to divert; (coup, rayons) to deflect; — vi (de ses principes etc) to deviate (de from); (de sa route) to veer (off course). ◆**déviation** nf deflection; deviation; (chemin) bypass; (itinéraire provisoire) diversion.

deviner [d(ə)vine] vt to guess (que that); (avenir) to predict; **d. (le jeu de) qn** to see through s.o. ◆**devinette** nf riddle.

devis [d(ə)vi] nm estimate (of cost of work to be done).

dévisager [deviʒaʒe] vt d. qn to stare at s.o.

devise [deviz] nf (légende) motto; pl (monnaie) (foreign) currency.

dévisser [devise] vt to unscrew, undo; — **se d.** vpr (bouchon etc) to come undone.

dévoiler [devwale] vt (révéler) to disclose; (statue) to unveil; — **se d.** vpr (mystère) to come to light.

devoir*¹ [d(ə)vwar] v aux 1 (nécessité) **je dois refuser** I must refuse, I have (got) to refuse; **j'ai dû refuser** I had to refuse. 2 (forte probabilité) **il doit être tard** it must be late; **elle a dû oublier** she must have forgotten; **il ne doit pas être bête** he can't be stupid. 3 (obligation) **tu dois l'aider** you should help her, you ought to help her; **il aurait dû venir** he should have come, he ought to have come; **vous devriez rester** you should stay, you ought to stay. 4 (supposition) **elle doit venir** she should be coming, she's supposed to be coming, she's due to come; **le train devait arriver à midi** the train was due (to arrive) at noon; **je devais le voir** I was (due) to see him.

devoir*² [d(ə)vwar] vt (argent) **d. qch à qn** to owe s.o. sth, owe sth to s.o.; **l'argent qui m'est dû** the money due to ou owing to me, the money owed (to) me; **se d. à** to have to devote oneself to; **comme il se doit** as is proper. 2 nm duty; Scol exercise; **devoir(s)** (travail à faire à la maison) Scol homework; **présenter ses devoirs à qn** to pay one's respects to s.o.

dévolu [devɔly] 1 a d. à qn (pouvoirs, tâche) vested in s.o., allotted to s.o. 2 nm **jeter son d. sur** to set one's heart on.

dévor/er [devɔre] vt (manger) to gobble up, devour; (incendie) to engulf, devour; (tourmenter, lire) to devour. ◆**—ant** a (faim) ravenous; (passion) devouring.

dévot, -ote [devo, -ɔt] a & nmf devout ou pious (person). ◆**dévotion** nf devotion.

dévou/er (se) [sədevwe] vpr (à une tâche) to dedicate oneself, devote oneself (à to); **se d. (pour qn)** (se sacrifier) to sacrifice oneself (for s.o.). ◆**—é** a (ami, femme etc) devoted (à qn to s.o.); (domestique, soldat etc) dedicated. ◆**—ement** [-umɑ̃] nm devotion, dedication; (de héros) devotion to duty.

dévoyé, -ée [devwaje] a & nmf delinquent.

dextérité [deksterite] nf dexterity, skill.

diabète [djabɛt] nm Méd diabetes. ◆**diabétique** a & nmf diabetic.

diable [djabl] nm devil; **d.!** heavens!; **où/pourquoi/que d.?** where/why/what the devil?; **un bruit/vent/etc du d.** the devil of a noise/wind/*etc*; **à la d.** anyhow; **habiter au d.** to live miles from anywhere. ◆**diablerie** *nf* devilment, mischief. ◆**diablesse** *nf* **c'est une d.** *Fam* she's a devil. ◆**diablotin** *nm* (*enfant*) little devil. ◆**diabolique** *a* diabolical, devilish.

diabolo [djabolo] *nm* (*boisson*) lemonade *ou Am* lemon soda flavoured with syrup.

diacre [djakr] *nm Rel* deacon.

diadème [djadɛm] *nm* diadem.

diagnostic [djagnɔstik] *nm* diagnosis. ◆**diagnostiquer** *vt* to diagnose.

diagonal, -aux [djagɔnal, -o] *a* diagonal. ◆**diagonale** *nf* diagonal (line); **en d.** diagonally.

diagramme [djagram] *nm* (*schéma*) diagram; (*courbe*) graph.

dialecte [djalɛkt] *nm* dialect.

dialogue [djalɔg] *nm* conversation; *Pol Cin Th Littér* dialogue. ◆**dialoguer** *vi* to have a conversation *ou* dialogue.

dialyse [djaliz] *nf Méd* dialysis.

diamant [djamã] *nm* diamond.

diamètre [djamɛtr] *nm* diameter. ◆**diamétralement** *adv* **d. opposés** (*avis etc*) diametrically opposed, poles apart.

diapason [djapazɔ̃] *nm Mus* tuning fork; **être/se mettre au d.** de *Fig* to be/get in tune with.

diaphragme [djafragm] *nm* diaphragm.

diapositive, *Fam* **diapo** [djapozitiv, djapo] *nf* (colour) slide, transparency.

diarrhée [djare] *nf* diarrh(o)ea.

diatribe [djatrib] *nf* diatribe.

dictateur [diktatœr] *nm* dictator. ◆**dictatorial, -aux** *a* dictatorial. ◆**dictature** *nf* dictatorship.

dict/er [dikte] *vt* to dictate (**à** to). ◆**-ée** *nf* dictation. ◆**dictaphone**® *nm* dictaphone®.

diction [diksjɔ̃] *nf* diction, elocution.

dictionnaire [diksjɔnɛr] *nm* dictionary.

dicton [diktɔ̃] *nm* saying, adage, dictum.

didactique [didaktik] *a* didactic.

dièse [djɛz] *a* & *nm Mus* sharp.

diesel [djezɛl] *a* & *nm* (**moteur**) **d.** diesel (engine).

diète [djɛt] *nf* (*jeûne*) starvation diet; **à la d.** on a starvation diet. ◆**diététicien, -ienne** *nmf* dietician. ◆**diététique** *nf* dietetics; — *a* (*magasin etc*) health-; **aliment** *ou* **produit d.** health food.

dieu, -x [djø] *nm* god; **D.** God; **D. merci!** thank God!, thank goodness!

diffamer [difame] *vt* (*en paroles*) to slander; (*par écrit*) to libel. ◆**diffamation** *nf* (*en paroles*) slander; (*par écrit*)

libel; **campagne de d.** smear campaign. ◆**diffamatoire** *a* slanderous; libellous.

différent [diferã] *a* different; *pl* (*divers*) different, various; **d. de** different from *ou* to, unlike. ◆**différemment** [-amã] *adv* differently (**de** from, to). ◆**différence** *nf* difference (**de** in); **à la d. de** unlike; **faire la d. entre** to make a distinction between.

différencier [diferãsje] *vt* to differentiate (**de** from); — **se d.** *vpr* to differ (**de** from).

différend [diferã] *nm* difference (of opinion).

différentiel, -ielle [diferãsjɛl] *a* differential.

différ/er [difere] **1** *vi* to differ (**de** from). **2** *vt* (*remettre*) to postpone, defer. ◆**-é** *nm* **en d.** (*émission*) (pre)recorded.

difficile [difisil] *a* difficult; (*exigeant*) fussy, particular, hard to please; **c'est d. à faire** it's hard *ou* difficult to do; **il (nous) est d. de faire ça** it's hard *ou* difficult (for us) to do that. ◆**-ment** *adv* with difficulty; **d. lisible** not easily read. ◆**difficulté** *nf* difficulty (**à faire** in doing); **en d.** in a difficult situation.

difforme [diform] *a* deformed, misshapen. ◆**difformité** *nf* deformity.

diffus [dify] *a* (*lumière, style*) diffuse.

diffuser [difyze] *vt* (*émission, nouvelle etc*) to broadcast; (*lumière, chaleur*) *Phys* to diffuse; (*livre*) to distribute. ◆**diffusion** *nf* broadcasting; (*de connaissances*) & *Phys* diffusion; (*de livre*) distribution.

digérer [diʒere] *vt* to digest; (*endurer*) *Fam* to stomach; — *vi* to digest. ◆**digeste** *a*, ◆**digestible** *a* digestible. ◆**digestif, -ive** *a* digestive; — *nm* after-dinner liqueur. ◆**digestion** *nf* digestion.

digital [diʒital] *a* digital; **empreinte d.** fingerprint.

digne [diɲ] *a* (*fier*) dignified; (*honnête*) worthy; **d. de qn** worthy of s.o.; **d. d'admiration/etc** worthy of *ou* deserving of admiration/etc; **d. de foi** reliable. ◆**dignement** *adv* with dignity. ◆**dignitaire** *nm* dignitary. ◆**dignité** *nf* dignity.

digression [digresjɔ̃] *nf* digression.

digue [dig] *nf* dyke, dike.

dilapider [dilapide] *vt* to squander, waste.

dilater [dilate] *vt*, — **se d.** *vpr* to dilate, expand. ◆**dilatation** *nf* dilation, expansion.

dilatoire [dilatwar] *a* **manœuvre** *ou* **moyen d.** delaying tactic.

dilemme [dilɛm] *nm* dilemma.

dilettante [diletãt] *nmf Péj* dabbler, amateur.

diligent [diliʒã] *a* (*prompt*) speedy and efficient; (soin) diligent. ◆**diligence** nf 1 (célérité) speedy efficiency; **faire d.** to make haste. 2 (véhicule) Hist stagecoach.

diluer [dilɥe] vt to dilute. ◆**dilution** nf dilution.

diluvienne [dilyvjɛn] af **pluie d.** torrential rain.

dimanche [dimɑ̃ʃ] nm Sunday.

dimension [dimɑ̃sjɔ̃] nf dimension; **à deux dimensions** two-dimensional.

diminuer [diminɥe] vt to reduce, decrease; (frais) to cut down (on), reduce; (mérite, forces) to diminish, lessen, reduce; **d. qn** (rabaisser) to diminish s.o., lessen s.o.; – vi (réserves, nombre) to decrease, diminish; (jours) to get shorter, draw in; (prix) to drop, decrease. ◆**diminutif, -ive** a & nm Gram diminutive; – nm (prénom) nickname. ◆**diminution** nf reduction, decrease (**de** in).

dinde [dɛ̃d] nf turkey (hen), Culin turkey. ◆**dindon** nm turkey (cock).

dîner [dine] vi to have dinner, dine; (au Canada, en Belgique etc) to (have) lunch; – nm dinner; lunch; (soirée) dinner party. ◆**dînette** nf (jouet) doll's dinner service; (jeu) doll's dinner party. ◆**dîneur, -euse** nmf diner.

dingue [dɛ̃g] a Fam nuts, screwy, crazy; – nmf Fam nutcase.

dinosaure [dinozɔr] nm dinosaur.

diocèse [djɔsɛz] nm Rel diocese.

diphtérie [difteri] nf diphtheria.

diphtongue [diftɔ̃g] nf Ling diphthong.

diplomate [diplɔmat] nm Pol diplomat; – nmf (négociateur) diplomatist; – a (habile, plein de tact) diplomatic. ◆**diplomatie** [-asi] nf (tact) & Pol diplomacy; (carrière) diplomatic service. ◆**diplomatique** a Pol diplomatic.

diplôme [diplom] nm certificate, diploma; Univ degree. ◆**diplômé, -ée** a & nmf qualified (person); **être d. (de)** Univ to be a graduate (of).

dire* [dir] vt (mot, avis etc) to say; (vérité, secret, heure etc) to tell; (penser) to think (de of, about); **d. des bêtises** to talk nonsense; **elle dit que tu mens** she says (that) you're lying; **d. qch à qn** to tell s.o. sth, say sth to s.o.; **d. à qn que** to tell s.o. that, say to s.o. that; **d. à qn de faire** to tell s.o. to do; **dit-il** he said; **dit-on** they say; **d. que oui/non** to say yes/no; **d. du mal/du bien de** to speak ill/well of; **on dirait un château** it looks like a castle; **on dirait du Mozart** it sounds like Mozart; **on dirait du cabillaud** it tastes like cod; **on dirait que il**

would seem that; **ça ne me dit rien** (envie) I don't feel like ou fancy that; (souvenir) it doesn't ring a bell; **ça vous dit de rester?** do you feel like staying?; **dites donc!** I say!; **ça va sans d.** that goes without saying; **autrement dit** in other words; **c'est beaucoup d.** that's going too far; **à l'heure dite** at the agreed time; **à vrai d.** to tell the truth; **il se dit malade/etc** he says he's ill/etc; **ça ne se dit pas** that's not said; – nm **au d. de** according to; **les dires de** (déclarations) the statements of.

direct [dirɛkt] a direct; (chemin) straight, direct; (manière) straightforward, direct; (train) through train, non-stop train; – nm **en d.** (émission) live; **un d. du gauche** Boxe a straight left. ◆**—ement** adv directly; (immédiatement) straight (away), directly.

directeur, -trice [dirɛktœr, -tris] nmf director; (d'entreprise) manager(ess), director; (de journal) editor; Scol headmaster, headmistress; – a (principe) guiding; **idées** ou **lignes directrices** guidelines.

direction [dirɛksjɔ̃] nf 1 (de société) running, management; (de club) leadership, running; (d'études) supervision; (mécanisme) Aut steering; **avoir la d. de** to be in charge of; **sous la d. de** (orchestre) conducted by; **la d.** (équipe dirigeante) the management; **une d.** (fonction) Com a directorship; Scol a headmastership; Journ an editorship. **2** (sens) direction; **en d. de** (train) (going) to, for.

directive [dirɛktiv] nf directive, instruction.

dirig/er [diriʒe] vt (société) to run, manage, direct; (débat, cheval) to lead; (véhicule) to steer; (orchestre) to conduct; (études) to supervise, direct; (conscience) to guide; (orienter) to turn (**vers** towards); (arme, lumière) to point, direct (**vers** towards); **se d. vers** (lieu, objet) to make one's way towards, head ou make for; (dans une carrière) to turn towards. ◆**—eant** a (classe) ruling; – nm (de pays, club) leader; (d'entreprise) manager. ◆**—é** a (économie) planned. ◆**—eable** a & nm (ballon) **d.** airship. ◆**dirigisme** nm Écon state control.

dis [di] voir **dire**.

discern/er [disɛrne] vt (voir) to make out, discern; (différencier) to distinguish. ◆**—ement** nm discernment, discrimination.

disciple [disipl] nm disciple, follower.

discipline [disiplin] nf (règle, matière) discipline. ◆**disciplinaire** a disciplinary. ◆**disciplin/er** vt (contrôler, éduquer) to

discipline; — **se d.** *vpr* to discipline oneself. ◆**—é** *a* well-disciplined.

disco [disko] *nf Fam* disco; **aller en d.** to go to a disco.

discontinu [diskɔ̃tiny] *a* (*ligne*) discontinuous; (*bruit etc*) intermittent. ◆**discontinuer** *vi* **sans d.** without stopping.

disconvenir [diskɔ̃vnir] *vi* **je n'en disconviens pas** I don't deny it.

discorde [diskɔrd] *nf* discord. ◆**discordance** *nf* (*de caractères*) clash, conflict; (*de son*) discord. ◆**discordant** *a* (*son*) discordant; (*témoignages*) conflicting; (*couleurs*) clashing.

discothèque [diskɔtɛk] *nf* record library; (*club*) discotheque.

discours [diskur] *nm* speech; (*écrit littéraire*) discourse. ◆**discourir** *vi Péj* to speechify, ramble on.

discourtois [diskurtwa] *a* discourteous.

discrédit [diskredi] *nm* disrepute, discredit. ◆**discréditer** *vt* to discredit, bring into disrepute; — **se d.** *vpr* (*personne*) to become discredited.

discret, -ète [diskrɛ, -ɛt] *a* (*personne, manière etc*) discreet; (*vêtement*) simple. ◆**discrètement** *adv* discreetly. ◆**discrétion** *nf* discretion; **vin/etc à d.** as much wine/etc as one wants. ◆**discrétionnaire** *a* discretionary.

discrimination [diskriminasjɔ̃] *nf* (*ségrégation*) discrimination. ◆**discriminatoire** *a* discriminatory.

disculper [diskylpe] *vt* to exonerate (**de** from).

discussion [diskysjɔ̃] *nf* discussion; (*conversation*) talk; (*querelle*) argument; **pas de d.!** no argument! ◆**discuter** *vt* to discuss; (*familièrement*) to talk over; (*contester*) to question; **ça peut se d., ça se discute** that's arguable; — *vi* (*parler*) to talk (**de** about, **avec** with); (*répliquer*) to argue; **d. de** *ou* **sur qch** to discuss sth. ◆**—é** *a* (*auteur*) much discussed *ou* debated; (*théorie, question*) disputed, controversial. ◆**—able** *a* arguable, debatable.

disette [dizɛt] *nf* food shortage.

diseuse [dizœz] *nf* **d. de bonne aventure** fortune-teller.

disgrâce [disgras] *nf* disgrace, disfavour. ◆**disgracier** *vt* to disgrace.

disgracieux, -euse [disgrasjø, -øz] *a* ungainly.

disjoindre [disʒwɛ̃dr] *vt* (*questions*) to treat separately. ◆**disjoint** *a* (*questions*) unconnected, separate. ◆**disjoncteur** *nm Él* circuit breaker.

disloquer [dislɔke] *vt* (*membre*) to dislocate; (*meuble, machine*) to break; — **se d.** *vpr* (*cortège*) to break up; (*meuble etc*) to fall apart; **se d. le bras** to dislocate one's arm. ◆**dislocation** *nf* (*de membre*) dislocation.

dispar/aître* [disparɛtr] *vi* to disappear; (*être porté manquant*) to be missing; (*mourir*) to die; **d. en mer** to be lost at sea; **faire d.** to remove, get rid of. ◆**—u, -ue** *a* (*soldat etc*) missing, lost; — *nmf* (*absent*) missing person; (*mort*) departed; **être porté d.** to be reported missing. ◆**disparition** *nf* disappearance; (*mort*) death.

disparate [disparat] *a* ill-assorted.

disparité [disparite] *nf* disparity (**entre, de** between).

dispendieux, -euse [dispɑ̃djø, -øz] *a* expensive, costly.

dispensaire [dispɑ̃sɛr] *nm* community health centre.

dispense [dispɑ̃s] *nf* exemption; **d. d'âge** waiving of the age limit. ◆**dispenser** *vt* (*soins, bienfaits etc*) to dispense; **d. qn de** (*obligation*) to exempt *ou* excuse s.o. from; **je vous dispense de** (*vos réflexions etc*) I can dispense with; **se d. de faire** to spare oneself the bother of doing.

disperser [disperse] *vt* to disperse, scatter; (*efforts*) to dissipate; — **se d.** *vpr* (*foule*) to disperse; **elle se disperse trop** she tries to do too many things at once. ◆**dispersion** *nf* (*d'une armée etc*) dispersal, dispersion.

disponible [disponibl] *a* available; (*place*) spare, available; (*esprit*) alert. ◆**disponibilité** *nf* availability; *pl Fin* available funds.

dispos [dispo] *a* **fit, in fine fettle; frais et d.** refreshed.

dispos/er [dispoze] *vt* to arrange; (*troupes*) *Mil* to dispose; **d. qn à** (*la bonne humeur etc*) to dispose *ou* incline s.o. towards; **se d. à faire** to prepare to do; — *vi* **d. de qch** to have sth at one's disposal; (*utiliser*) to make use of sth; **d. de qn** *Péj* to take advantage of s.o., abuse s.o. ◆**—é** *a* **bien/mal d.** in a good/bad mood; **bien d. envers** well-disposed towards; **d. à faire** prepared *ou* disposed to do. ◆**disposition** *nf* arrangement; (*de troupes*) disposition; (*de maison, page*) layout; (*humeur*) frame of mind; (*tendance*) tendency, (pre)disposition (**à** to); (*clause*) *Jur* provision; *pl* (*aptitudes*) ability, aptitude (**pour** for); **à la d. de qn** at s.o.'s disposal; **prendre ses** *ou* **des dispositions** (*préparatifs*) to make arrangements, prepare; (*pour l'avenir*) to

make provision; **dans de bonnes disposi-tions à l'égard de** well-disposed towards.
dispositif [dispozitif] nm (mécanisme) device; **d. de défense** Mil defence system; **d. antiparasite** Él suppressor.
disproportion [disprɔpɔrsjɔ̃] nf dispropor-tion. ◆**disproportionné** a disproportion-ate.
dispute [dispyt] nf quarrel. ◆**disputer** vt (match) to play; (terrain, droit etc) to contest, dispute; (rallye) to compete in; **d. qch à qn** (prix, première place etc) to fight with s.o. for ou over sth, contend with s.o. for sth; **d. qn** (gronder) Fam to tell s.o. off; **— se d.** vpr to quarrel (**avec** with); (match) to take place; **se d. qch** to fight over sth.
disqualifier [diskalifje] vt Sp to disqualify; **— se d.** vpr Fig to become discredited. ◆**disqualification** nf Sp disqualification.
disque [disk] nm Mus record; Sp discus; (cercle) disc, Am disk; (pour ordinateur) disk. ◆**disquaire** nmf record dealer. ◆**disquette** nf (pour ordinateur) floppy disk.
dissection [diseksjɔ̃] nf dissection.
dissemblable [disɑ̃mblabl] a dissimilar (à to).
disséminer [disemine] vt (graines, mines etc) to scatter; (idées) Fig to disseminate. ◆**dissémination** nf scattering; (d'idées) Fig dissemination.
dissension [disɑ̃sjɔ̃] nf dissension.
disséquer [diseke] vt to dissect.
disserter [diserte] vi **d. sur** to comment upon, discuss. ◆**dissertation** nf Scol essay.
dissident, -ente [disidɑ̃, -ɑ̃t] a & nmf dissi-dent. ◆**dissidence** nf dissidence.
dissimuler [disimyle] vt (cacher) to conceal, hide (à from); **—** vi (feindre) to pretend; **— se d.** vpr to hide, conceal oneself. ◆**-é** a (enfant) Péj secretive. ◆**dissimulation** nf concealment; (dupli-cité) deceit.
dissiper [disipe] vt (brouillard, craintes) to dispel; (fortune) to squander, dissipate; **d. qn** to lead s.o. astray, distract s.o.; **— se d.** vpr (brume) to clear, lift; (craintes) to disappear; (élève) to misbehave. ◆**-é** a (élève) unruly; (vie) dissipated. ◆**dissipa-tion** nf (de brouillard) clearing; (indis-cipline) misbehaviour; (débauche) Litt dissipation.
dissocier [disɔsje] vt to dissociate (**de** from).
dissolu [disɔly] a (vie etc) dissolute.
dissoudre* [disudr] vt, **— se d.** vpr to

dissolve. ◆**dissolution** nf dissolution. ◆**dissolvant** a & nm solvent; (pour vernis à ongles) nail polish remover.
dissuader [disɥade] vt to dissuade, deter (**de qch** from sth, **de faire** from doing). ◆**dissuasif, -ive** a (effet) deterrent; **être d.** Fig to be a deterrent. ◆**dissuasion** nf dissuasion; **force de d.** Mil deterrent.
distant [distɑ̃] a distant; (personne) aloof, distant; **d. de dix kilomètres** (éloigné) ten kilometres away; (à intervalles) ten kilo-metres apart. ◆**distance** nf distance; **à deux mètres de d.** two metres apart; **à d.** at ou from a distance; **garder ses distances** to keep one's distance. ◆**distancer** vt to leave behind, outstrip.
distendre [distɑ̃dr] vt, **— se d.** vpr to distend.
distiller [distile] vt to distil. ◆**distillation** nf distillation. ◆**distillerie** nf (lieu) distil-lery.
distinct, -incte [distɛ̃, -ɛ̃kt] a (différent) distinct, separate (**de** from); (net) clear, distinct. ◆**distinctement** adv distinctly, clearly. ◆**distinctif, -ive** a distinctive. ◆**distinction** nf (différence, raffinement) distinction.
distinguer [distɛ̃ge] vt (différencier) to distinguish; (voir) to make out; (choisir) to single out; **d. le blé de l'orge** to tell wheat from barley, distinguish between wheat and barley; **— se d.** vpr (s'illustrer) to distinguish oneself; **se d. de** (différer) to be distinguishable from; **se d. par** (sa gaieté, beauté etc) to be conspicuous for. ◆**-é** a (bien élevé, éminent) distinguished; **senti-ments distingués** (formule épistolaire) Com yours faithfully.
distorsion [distɔrsjɔ̃] nf (du corps, d'une image etc) distortion.
distraction [distraksjɔ̃] nf amusement, distraction; (étourderie) (fit of) absent-mindedness. ◆**distraire*** vt (diver-tir) to entertain, amuse; **d. qn** (de) (détourner) to distract s.o. (from); **— se d.** vpr to amuse oneself, enjoy oneself. ◆**dis-trait** a absent-minded. ◆**distraitement** adv absent-mindedly. ◆**distrayant** a entertaining.
distribuer [distribɥe] vt (répartir) to distribute; (donner) to give ou hand out, distribute; (courrier) to deliver; (eau) to supply; (cartes) to deal; **bien distribué** (appartement) well-arranged. ◆**distri-buteur** nm Aut Cin distributor; **d. (automa-tique)** vending machine; **d. de billets** Rail ticket machine; (de billets de banque) cash

dispenser *ou* machine. ◆**distribution** *nf* distribution; (*du courrier*) delivery; (*de l'eau*) supply; (*acteurs*) *Th Cin* cast; d. des prix prize giving.

district [distrikt] *nm* district.

dit [di] *voir* **dire**; – a (*convenu*) agreed; (*surnommé*) called.

dites [dit] *voir* **dire**.

divaguer [divage] *vi* (*dérailler*) to rave, talk drivel. ◆**divagations** *nfpl* ravings.

divan [divã] *nm* divan, couch.

divergent [divergã] *a* diverging, divergent. ◆**divergence** *nf* divergence. ◆**diverger** *vi* to diverge (**de** from).

divers, -erses [diver, -ers] *apl* (*distincts*) varied, diverse; d. groupes (*plusieurs*) various *ou* sundry groups. ◆**diversement** *adv* in various ways. ◆**diversifier** *vt* to diversify; – **se d.** *vpr* Écon to diversify. ◆**diversité** *nf* diversity.

diversion [diversjɔ̃] *nf* diversion.

divert/ir [divertir] *vt* to amuse, entertain; – **se d.** *vpr* to enjoy oneself, amuse oneself. ◆–**issement** *nm* amusement, entertainment.

dividende [dividãd] *nm* Math Fin dividend.

divin [divɛ̃] *a* divine. ◆**divinité** *nf* divinity.

diviser [divize] *vt*, – **se d.** *vpr* to divide (**en** into). ◆**divisible** *a* divisible. ◆**division** *nf* division.

divorce [divɔrs] *nm* divorce. ◆**divorc/er** *vi* to get *ou* to be divorced, divorce; d. d'avec qn to divorce s.o. ◆–**é, -ée** *a* divorced (d'avec from); – *nmf* divorcee.

divulguer [divylge] *vt* to divulge. ◆**divulgation** *nf* divulgence.

dix [dis] ([di] before consonant, [diz] before vowel) *a* & *nm* ten. ◆**dixième** [dizjɛm] *a* & *nmf* tenth; un d. a tenth. ◆**dix-huit** [dizɥit] *a* & *nm* eighteeen. ◆**dix-huitième** *a* & *nmf* eighteenth. ◆**dix-neuf** [diznœf] *a* & *nm* nineteen. ◆**dix-neuvième** *a* & *nmf* nineteenth. ◆**dix-sept** [disset] *a* & *nm* seventeen. ◆**dix-septième** *a* & *nmf* seventeenth.

dizaine [dizen] *nf* about ten.

docile [dɔsil] *a* submissive, docile. ◆**docilité** *nf* submissiveness, docility.

dock [dɔk] *nm* Nau dock. ◆**docker** [dɔker] *nm* docker.

docteur [dɔktœr] *nm* Méd Univ doctor (**ès**, **en** of). ◆**doctorat** *nm* doctorate, = PhD (**ès**, **en** in).

doctrine [dɔktrin] *nf* doctrine. ◆**doctrinaire** *a* & *nmf* Péj doctrinaire.

document [dɔkymã] *nm* document. ◆**documentaire** *a* documentary; – *nm* (*film*) documentary. ◆**documentaliste** *nmf* information officer.

document/er [dɔkymãte] *vt* (*informer*) to document; – **se d.** *vpr* to collect material *ou* information. ◆–**é a** (**bien** *ou* **très**) **d.** (*personne*) well-informed. ◆**documentation** *nf* (*documents*) documentation, Com literature; (*renseignements*) information.

dodeliner [dɔdline] *vi* **d. de la tête** to nod (one's head).

dodo [dɔdo] *nm* (*langage enfantin*) **faire d.** to sleep; **aller au d.** to go to bye-byes.

dodu [dɔdy] *a* chubby, plump.

dogme [dɔgm] *nm* dogma. ◆**dogmatique** *a* dogmatic. ◆**dogmatisme** *nm* dogmatism.

dogue [dɔg] *nm* (*chien*) mastiff.

doigt [dwa] *nm* finger; **d. de pied** toe; **à deux doigts de** within an ace of; **montrer du d.** to point (to); **savoir sur le bout du d.** to have at one's finger tips. ◆**doigté** *nm* Mus fingering, touch; (*savoir-faire*) tact, expertise. ◆**doigtier** *nm* fingerstall.

dois, doit [dwa] *voir* **devoir**[1,2].

doléances [dɔleãs] *nfpl* (*plaintes*) grievances.

dollar [dɔlar] *nm* dollar.

domaine [dɔmen] *nm* (*terres*) estate, domain; (*sphère*) province, domain.

dôme [dom] *nm* dome.

domestique [dɔmestik] *a* (*animal*) domestic(ated); (*de la famille*) family-, domestic; (*ménager*) domestic, household; – *nmf* servant. ◆**domestiquer** *vt* to domesticate.

domicile [dɔmisil] *nm* home; Jur abode; **travailler à d.** to work at home; **livrer à d.** (*pain etc*) to deliver (to the house). ◆**domicilié** *a* resident (**à, chez** at).

domin/er [dɔmine] *vt* to dominate; (*situation, sentiment*) to master, dominate; (*être supérieur à*) to surpass, outclass; (*tour, rocher*) to tower above, dominate; (*valley, building etc*) – *vi* (*être le plus fort*) to be dominant, dominate; (*être le plus important*) to predominate; – **se d.** *vpr* to control oneself. ◆–**ant a** dominant. ◆–**ante** *nf* dominant feature; Mus dominant. ◆**dominateur, -trice** *a* domineering. ◆**domination** *nf* domination.

dominicain, -aine [dɔminikɛ̃, -ɛn] *a* & *nmf* Rel Dominican.

dominical, -aux [dɔminikal, -o] *a* (*repos*) Sunday-.

domino [dɔmino] *nm* domino; *pl* (*jeu*) dominoes.

dommage [dɔmaʒ] *nm* **1** (**c'est**) **d.!** it's a

pity *ou* a shame! (*que* that); **quel d.!** what a pity *ou* a shame! **2** (*tort*) prejudice, harm; *pl* (*dégâts*) damage; **dommages-intérêts** *Jur* damages.

dompt/er [d3te] *vt* (*animal*) to tame; (*passions, rebelles*) to subdue. **◆—eur, -euse** *nmf* (*de lions*) lion tamer.

don [d3] *nm* (*cadeau, aptitude*) gift; (*aumône*) donation; **le d. du sang/etc** the giving of blood/etc; **faire d. de** to give; **avoir le d. de** (*le chic pour*) to have the knack of. **◆donateur, -trice** *nmf Jur* donor. **◆donation** *nf Jur* donation.

donc [d3(k)] *conj* so, then; (*par conséquent*) so, therefore; **asseyez-vous d.!** (*intensif*) will you sit down!, sit down then!; **qui/quoi d.?** who?/what?; **allons d.!** come on!

donjon [d333] *nm* (*de château*) keep.

donne [dɔn] *nf Cartes* deal.

donner [dɔne] *vt* to give; (*récolte, résultat*) to produce; (*sa place*) to give up; (*pièce, film*) to put on; (*cartes*) to deal; **d. un coup à** to hit, give a blow to; **d. le bonjour à qn** to say hello to s.o.; **d. à réparer** to take (in) to be repaired; **d. raison à qn** to say s.o. is right; **ça donne soif/faim** it makes you thirsty/hungry; **je lui donne trente ans** I'd say *ou* guess he *ou* she was thirty; **ça n'a rien donné** (*efforts*) it hasn't got us anywhere; **c'est donné** *Fam* it's dirt cheap; **étant donné** (*la situation etc*) considering, in view of; **étant donné que** seeing (that), considering (that); **à un moment donné** at some stage; *– vi* **d. sur** (*fenêtre*) to look out onto, overlook; (*porte*) to open onto; **d. dans** (*piège*) to fall into; **d. de la tête contre** to hit one's head against; *– se d. vpr* (*se consacrer*) to devote oneself (à to); **se d. du mal** to go to a lot of trouble (*pour faire* to do); **s'en d. à cœur joie** to have a whale of a time, enjoy oneself to the full. **◆données** *nfpl* (*information*) data; (*de problème*) (known) facts; (*d'un roman*) basic elements. **◆donneur, -euse** *nmf* giver; (*de sang, d'organe*) donor; *Cartes* dealer.

dont [d3] *pron rel* (= *de qui, duquel, de quoi etc*) (*personne*) of whom; (*chose*) of which; (*appartenance: personne*) whose, of whom; (*appartenance: chose*) of which, whose; **une mère d. le fils est malade** a mother whose son is ill; **la fille d. il est fier** the daughter he is proud of *ou* of whom he is proud; **les outils d. j'ai besoin** the tools I need; **la façon d. elle joue** the way (in which) she plays; **voici ce d. il s'agit** here's what it's about.

doper [dɔpe] *vt* (*cheval, sportif*) to dope; *–*

se d. *vpr* to dope oneself. **◆doping** *nm* (*action*) doping; (*substance*) dope.

dorénavant [dɔrenavã] *adv* henceforth.

dor/er [dɔre] *vt* (*objet*) to gild; **d. la pilule** *Fig* to sugar the pill; **se (faire) d. au soleil** to bask in the sun; *– vi Culin* to brown. **◆—é** *a* (*objet*) gilt; (*couleur*) golden; *– nm* (*couche*) gilt. **◆dorure** *nf* gilding.

dorloter [dɔrlɔte] *vt* to pamper, coddle.

dormir* [dɔrmir] *vi* to sleep; (*être endormi*) to be asleep; (*argent*) to lie idle; **histoire à d. debout** tall story, cock-and-bull story; **eau dormante** stagnant water. **◆dortoir** *nm* dormitory.

dos [do] *nm* back; (*de nez*) bridge; (*de livre*) spine; **voir qn de d.** to have a back view of s.o.; **à d. de chameau** (riding) on a camel; **'voir au d.'** (*verso*) 'see over'; **j'en ai plein le d.** *Fam* I'm sick of it; **mettre qch sur le d. de qn** (*accusation*) to pin sth on s.o. **◆dossard** *nm Sp* number (*fixed on back*). **◆dossier** *nm* **1** (*de siège*) back. **2** (*papiers, compte rendu*) file, dossier; (*classeur*) folder, file.

dose [doz] *nf* dose; (*quantité administrée*) dosage. **◆dos/er** *vt* (*remède*) to measure out the dose of; (*équilibrer*) to strike the correct balance between. **◆—age** *nm* measuring out (*of dose*); (*équilibre*) balance; **faire le d. de** = **doser**. **◆—eur** *nm* **bouchon d.** measuring cap.

dot [dɔt] *nf* dowry.

doter [dɔte] *vt* (*hôpital etc*) to endow; **d. de** (*matériel*) to equip with; (*qualité*) *Fig* to endow with. **◆dotation** *nf* endowment; equipping.

douane [dwan] *nf* customs. **◆douanier, -ière** *nm* customs officer; *– a* (*union etc*) customs-.

double [dubl] *a* double; (*rôle, avantage etc*) twofold; *– adv* double; *– nm* (*de personne*) double; (*copie*) copy, duplicate; (*de timbre*) swap, duplicate; **le d.** (*de*) (*quantité*) twice as much (as). **◆doublage** *nm* (*de film*) dubbing. **◆doublement** *adv* doubly; *– nm* doubling. **◆doubler 1** *vt* (*augmenter*) to double; (*vêtement*) to line; (*film*) to dub; (*acteur*) to stand in for; (*classe*) *Scol* to repeat; (*cap*) *Nau* to round; **se d. de** to be coupled with; *– vi* (*augmenter*) to double. **2** *vti Aut* to overtake, pass. **◆doublure** *nf* (*étoffe*) lining; *Th* understudy; *Cin* stand-in, double.

douce [dus] *voir* **doux**. **◆doucement** *adv* (*délicatement*) gently; (*à voix basse*) softly; (*sans bruit*) quietly; (*lentement*) slowly; (*sans à-coups*) smoothly; (*assez bien*) *Fam* so-so. ◆**douceur** *nf (de miel etc)* sweetness; *(de personne, pente etc)* gentleness; *(de peau etc)* softness; *(de temps)* mildness; *pl (sucreries)* sweets, *Am* candies; **en d.** *(démarrer etc)* smoothly.

douche [duʃ] *nf* shower. ◆**doucher** *vt* **d. qn** to give s.o. a shower; — **se d.** *vpr* to take *ou* have a shower.

doué [dwe] *a* gifted, talented **(en** at); *(intelligent)* clever; **d. de** gifted with; **il est d. pour** he has a gift *ou* talent for.

douille [duj] *nf (d'ampoule) Él* socket; *(de cartouche)* case.

douillet, -ette [duje, -et] *a (lit etc)* soft, cosy, snug; **il est d.** *(délicat)* Péj he's soft.

douleur [dulœr] *nf (mal)* pain; *(chagrin)* sorrow, grief. ◆**douloureux, -euse** *a (maladie, membre, décision, perte etc)* painful.

doute [dut] *nm* doubt; *pl (méfiance)* doubts, misgivings; **sans d.** no doubt, probably; **sans aucun d.** without (any *ou* a) doubt; **mettre en d.** to cast doubt on; **dans le d.** uncertain, doubtful; **ça ne fait pas de d.** there is no doubt about it. ◆**douter** *vi* to doubt; **d. de qch/qn** to doubt sth/s.o.; **d. que** (+ *sub*) to doubt whether *ou* that; **se d. de qch** to suspect sth; **je m'en doute** I suspect so, I would think so. ◆**douteux, -euse** *a* doubtful; *(louche, médiocre)* dubious; **il est d. que** (+ *sub*) it's doubtful whether *ou* that.

douve(s) [duv] *nf(pl) (de château)* moat.

Douvres [duvr] *nm ou f* Dover.

doux, douce [du, dus] *a (miel, son etc)* sweet; *(personne, pente etc)* gentle; *(peau, lumière, drogue etc)* soft; *(émotion, souvenir etc)* pleasant; *(temps, climat)* mild; **en douce** on the quiet.

douze [duz] *a & nm* twelve. ◆**douzaine** *nf (douze, environ)* about twelve; **une d. d'œufs/etc** a dozen eggs/etc. ◆**douzième** *a & nmf* twelfth; **un d.** a twelfth.

doyen, -enne [dwajɛ̃, -ɛn] *nmf* Rel Univ dean; *(d'âge)* oldest person.

draconien, -ienne [drakɔnjɛ̃, -jɛn] *a (mesures)* drastic.

dragée [draʒe] *nf* sugared almond; **tenir la d. haute à qn** *(tenir tête à qn)* to stand up to s.o.

dragon [dragɔ̃] *nm (animal)* dragon; *Mil Hist* dragoon.

drague [drag] *nf (appareil)* dredge; *(filet)* drag net. ◆**draguer** *vt* **1** *(rivière etc)* to dredge. **2** *Arg (racoler)* to try and pick up;

(faire du baratin à) to chat up, *Am* smooth-talk.

drainer [drene] *vt* to drain.

drame [dram] *nm* drama; *(catastrophe)* tragedy. ◆**dramatique** *a* dramatic; **critique d.** drama critic; **auteur d.** playwright, dramatist; **film d.** drama. ◆**dramatiser** *vt (exagérer)* to dramatize. ◆**dramaturge** *nmf* dramatist.

drap [dra] *nm (de lit)* sheet; *(tissu)* cloth; **dans de beaux draps** *Fig* in a fine mess.

drapeau, -x [drapo] *nm* flag; **être sous les drapeaux** *Mil* to be in the services.

draper [drape] *vt* to drape **(de** with). ◆**draperie** *nf (étoffe)* drapery.

dresser [drese] **1** *vt (échelle, statue)* to put up, erect; *(piège)* to lay, set; *(oreille)* to prick up; *(liste)* to draw up, make out; — **se d.** *vpr (personne)* to stand up; *(statue, montagne)* to rise up, stand; **se d. contre** *(abus)* to stand up against. **2** *vt (animal)* to train; *(personne)* Péj to drill, teach. ◆**dressage** *nm* training. ◆**dresseur, -euse** *nmf* trainer.

dribbler [drible] *vti* Fb to dribble.

drogue [drɔg] *nf (médicament)* Péj drug; **une d.** *(stupéfiant)* a drug; **la d.** drugs, drug. ◆**droguer** *vt (victime)* to drug; *(malade)* to dose up; — **se d.** *vpr* to take drugs, be on drugs; *(malade)* to dose oneself up. ◆**-é, -ée** *nmf* drug addict.

droguerie [drɔgri] *nf* hardware shop *ou Am* store. ◆**droguiste** *nmf* owner of a *droguerie.*

droit¹ [drwa] *nm (privilège)* right; *(d'inscription etc)* fee(s), dues; *pl (de douane)* duty; **le d.** *(science juridique)* law; **avoir d. à** to be entitled to; **avoir le d. de faire** to be entitled to do, have the right to do; **à bon d.** rightly; **d. d'entrée** entrance fee.

droit² [drwa] *a (ligne, route etc)* straight; *(personne, mur etc)* upright, straight; *(angle)* right; *(veston)* single-breasted; *(honnête)* Fig upright; — *adv* straight; **tout d.** straight *ou* right ahead. ◆**droite¹** *nf (ligne)* straight line.

droit³ [drwa] *a (côté, bras etc)* right; — *nm (coup)* Boxe right. ◆**droite²** *nf* **la d.** *(côté)* the right (side); *Pol* the right (wing); **à d.** *(tourner)* (to the) right; *(rouler, se tenir)* on the right(-hand) side; **de d.** *(fenêtre etc)* right-hand; *(politique, candidat)* right-wing; **à d. de** on *ou* to the right of; **à d. et à gauche** *(voyager etc)* here, there and everywhere. ◆**droitier, -ière** *a & nmf* right-handed (person). ◆**droiture** *nf* uprightness.

drôle [drol] a funny; **d. d'air/de type** funny look/fellow. ◆**—ment** adv funnily; (*extrêmement*) *Fam* dreadfully.

dromadaire [dromadɛr] nm dromedary.

dru [dry] a (*herbe etc*) thick, dense; – adv **tomber d.** (*pluie*) to pour down heavily; **pousser d.** to grow thick(ly).

du [dy] = **de + le.**

dû, due [dy] a **d. à** (*accident etc*) due to; – nm due; (*argent*) dues.

dualité [dɥalite] nf duality.

dubitatif, -ive [dybitatif, -iv] a (*regard etc*) dubious.

duc [dyk] nm duke. ◆**duché** nm duchy. ◆**duchesse** nf duchess.

duel [dɥɛl] nm duel.

dûment [dymã] adv duly.

dune [dyn] nf (sand) dune.

duo [dɥo] nm *Mus* duet; (*couple*) *Hum* duo.

dupe [dyp] nf dupe, fool; – a **d. de** duped by, fooled by. ◆**duper** vt to fool, dupe.

duplex [dyplɛks] nm split-level flat, *Am* duplex; (*émission en*) **d.** *Tél* link-up.

duplicata [dyplikata] nm inv duplicate.

duplicateur [dyplikatœr] nm (*machine*) duplicator.

duplicité [dyplisite] nf duplicity, deceit.

dur [dyr] a (*substance*) hard; (*difficile*) hard, tough; (*viande*) tough; (*hiver, leçon, ton*) harsh; (*personne*) hard, harsh; (*brosse, carton*) stiff; (*œuf*) hard-boiled; **d. d'oreille** hard of hearing; **d. à cuire** *Fam* hard-bitten, tough; – adv (*travailler*) hard; – nm *Fam* tough guy. ◆**durement** adv harshly. ◆**dureté** nf hardness; harshness; toughness.

durant [dyrã] prép during.

durc/ir [dyrsir] vti, — **se d.** vpr to harden. ◆**—issement** nm hardening.

durée [dyre] nf (*de film, événement etc*) length; (*période*) duration; (*de pile*) *Él* life; **de longue d.** (*disque*) long-playing. ◆**dur/er** vi to last; **ça dure depuis . . .** it's been going on for . . . . ◆**—able** a durable, lasting.

durillon [dyrijɔ̃] nm callus.

duvet [dyvɛ] nm **1** (*d'oiseau, de visage*) down. **2** (*sac*) sleeping bag. ◆**duveté** a, ◆**duveteux, -euse** a downy.

dynamique [dinamik] a dynamic; – nf (*force*) *Fig* dynamic force, thrust. ◆**dynamisme** nm dynamism.

dynamite [dinamit] nf dynamite. ◆**dyna-miter** vt to dynamite.

dynamo [dinamo] nf dynamo.

dynastie [dinasti] nf dynasty.

dysenterie [disãtri] nf *Méd* dysentery.

dyslexique [disleksik] a & nmf dyslexic.

E

E, e [ə, ø] nm E, e.

eau, -x [o] nf water; **il est tombé beaucoup d'e.** a lot of rain fell; **e. douce** (*non salée*) fresh water; (*du robinet*) soft water; **e. salée** salt water; **e. de Cologne** eau de Cologne; **e. de toilette** toilet water; **grandes eaux** (*d'un parc*) ornamental fountains; **tomber à l'e.** (*projet*) to fall through; **ça lui fait venir l'e. à la bouche** it makes his *ou* her mouth water; **tout en e.** sweating; **pren-dre l'e.** (*chaussure*) to take water, leak. ◆**e.-de-vie** nf (pl **eaux-de-vie**) brandy. ◆**e.-forte** nf (pl **eaux-fortes**) (*gravure*) etching.

ébah/ir [ebair] vt to astound, dumbfound, amaze. ◆**—issement** nm amazement.

ébattre (s') [sebatr] vpr to frolic, frisk about. ◆**ébats** nmpl frolics.

ébauche [ebof] nf (*esquisse*) (rough) outline, (rough) sketch; (*début*) beginnings. ◆**ébaucher** vt (*projet, tableau, œuvre*) to sketch out, outline; **e. un sourire** to give a faint smile; – **s'é.** vpr to take shape.

ébène [ebɛn] nf (*bois*) ebony.

ébéniste [ebenist] nm cabinet-maker. ◆**ébénisterie** nf cabinet-making.

éberlué [ebɛrlɥe] a *Fam* dumbfounded.

éblou/ir [ebluir] vt to dazzle. ◆**—isse-ment** nm (*aveuglement*) dazzling, dazzle; (*émerveillement*) feeling of wonder; (*malaise*) fit of dizziness.

éboueur [ebwœr] nm dustman, *Am* garbage collector.

ébouillanter [ebujɑ̃te] vt to scald; – **s'é.** vpr to scald oneself.

éboul/er (s') [sebule] vpr (*falaise etc*) to crumble; (*terre, roches*) to fall. ◆**—ement** nm landslide. ◆**éboulis** nm (mass of) fallen debris.

ébouriffant [eburifã] a *Fam* astounding.

ébouriffer [eburife] vt (*cheveux*) to dishevel, ruffle, tousle.

ébranl/er [ebrɑ̃le] vt (mur, confiance etc) to shake; (santé) to weaken, affect; (personne) to shake, shatter; — **s'é.** vpr (train, cortège etc) to move off. ◆**—ement** nm (secousse) shaking, shock; (nerveux) shock.

ébrécher [ebreʃe] vt (assiette) to chip; (lame) to nick. ◆**ébréchure** nf chip; nick.

ébriété [ebrijete] nf drunkenness.

ébrouer (s') [sebrue] vpr (cheval) to snort; (personne) to shake oneself (about).

ébruiter [ebrɥite] vt (nouvelle etc) to make known, divulge.

ébullition [ebylisjɔ̃] nf boiling; **être en é.** (eau) to be boiling; (ville) Fig to be in turmoil.

écaille [ekɑj] nf 1 (de poisson) scale; (de tortue, d'huître) shell; (résine synthétique) tortoise-shell. 2 (de peinture) flake. ◆**écailler 1** vt (poisson) to scale; (huître) to shell. **2 s'é.** vpr (peinture) to flake (off), peel.

écarlate [ekarlat] a & nf scarlet.

écarquiller [ekarkije] vt **é. les yeux** to open one's eyes wide.

écart [ekar] nm (intervalle) gap, distance; (mouvement, embardée) swerve; (différence) difference (de in, entre between); **écarts de** (conduite, langage) lapses in; **le grand é.** (de gymnaste) the splits; **à l'é.** out of the way; **tenir qn à l'é.** Fig to keep s.o. out of things; **à l'é. de** away from, clear of. ◆**écart/er** vt (objets) to move away from each other, move apart; (jambes) to spread, open; (rideaux) to draw (aside), open; (crainte, idée) to brush aside, dismiss; (carte) to discard; **é. qch de qch** to move sth away from sth; **é. qn de** (éloigner) to keep ou take s.o. away from; (exclure) to keep s.o. out of; — **s'é.** vpr (s'éloigner) to move away (de from); (se séparer) to move aside (de from); **s'é. de** (sujet, bonne route) to stray ou deviate from. ◆**—é** a (endroit) remote; **les jambes écartées** with legs (wide) apart. ◆**—ement** nm (espace) gap, distance (de between).

ecchymose [ekimoz] nf bruise.

ecclésiastique [eklezjastik] a ecclesiastical; — nm ecclesiastic, clergyman.

écervelé, -ée [eservəle] a scatterbrained; — nmf scatterbrain.

échafaud [eʃafo] nm (pour exécution) scaffold.

échafaudage [eʃafodaʒ] nm (construction) scaffold(ing); (tas) heap; (système) Fig fabric. ◆**échafauder** vi-to put up scaf-

folding ou a scaffold; — vt (projet etc) to put together, think up.

échalas [eʃala] nm **grand é.** tall skinny person.

échalote [eʃalɔt] nf Bot Culin shallot, scallion.

échancré [eʃɑ̃kre] a (encolure) V-shaped, scooped. ◆**échancrure** nf (de robe) opening.

échange [eʃɑ̃ʒ] nm exchange; **en é.** in exchange (de for). ◆**échanger** vt to exchange (contre for). ◆**échangeur** nm (intersection) Aut interchange.

échantillon [eʃɑ̃tijɔ̃] nm sample. ◆**échantillonnage** nm (collection) range (of samples).

échappatoire [eʃapatwar] nf evasion, way out.

échapp/er [eʃape] vi **é. à qn** to escape from s.o.; **é. à la mort/un danger/etc** to escape death/a danger/etc; **ce nom m'échappe** that name escapes me; **ça lui a échappé (des mains)** it slipped out of his ou her hands; **laisser é.** (cri) to let out; (objet, occasion) to let slip; **l'é. belle** to have a close shave; **ça m'a échappé** (je n'ai pas compris) I didn't catch it; — **s'é.** vpr (s'enfuir) to escape (de from); (s'éclipser) to slip away; Sp to break away; (gaz, eau) to escape, come out. ◆**—é, -ée** nmf runaway. ◆**—ée** nf Sp breakaway; (vue) vista. ◆**—ement** nm tuyau d'é. Aut exhaust pipe; **pot d'é.** Aut silencer, Am muffler.

écharde [eʃard] nf (de bois) splinter.

écharpe [eʃarp] nf scarf; (de maire) sash; **en é.** (bras) in a sling; **prendre en é.** Aut to hit sideways.

écharper [eʃarpe] vt **é. qn** to cut s.o. to bits.

échasse [eʃas] nf (bâton) stilt. ◆**échassier** nm wading bird.

échauder [eʃode] vt être échaudé, se faire é. (déçu) Fam to be taught a lesson.

échauffer [eʃofe] vt (moteur) to overheat; (esprit) to excite; — **s'é.** vpr (discussion) & Sp to warm up.

échauffourée [eʃofure] nf (bagarre) clash, brawl, skirmish.

échéance [eʃeɑ̃s] nf Com date (due), expiry ou Am expiration date; (paiement) payment (due); (obligation) commitment; **à brève/longue é.** (projet, emprunt) short-/long-term.

échéant (le cas) [ləkazeʃeɑ̃] adv if the occasion should arise, possibly.

échec [eʃɛk] nm 1 (insuccès) failure; **faire é. à** (inflation etc) to hold in check. 2 **les**

échecs (*jeu*) chess; **en é.** in check; **é.!** check!; **é. et mat!** checkmate!

échelle [eʃɛl] *nf* **1** (*marches*) ladder; **faire la courte é. à qn** to give s.o. a leg up. **2** (*mesure, dimension*) scale; **à l'é. nationale** on a national scale. ◆**échelon** *nm* (*d'échelle*) rung; (*de fonctionnaire*) grade; (*dans une organisation*) echelon; **à l'é. régional/national** on a regional/national level. ◆**échelonner** *vt* (*paiements*) to spread out, space out; **— s'é.** *vpr* to be spread out.

écheveau, -x [eʃvo] *nm* (*de laine*) skein; *Fig* muddle, tangle.

échevelé [eʃəvle] *a* (*ébouriffé*) dishevelled; (*course, danse etc*) *Fig* wild.

échine [eʃin] *nf Anat* backbone, spine.

échiner (s') [seʃine] *vpr* (*s'évertuer*) *Fam* to knock oneself out (à faire doing).

échiquier [eʃikje] *nm* (*tableau*) chessboard.

écho [eko] *nm* (*d'un son etc*) (*réponse*) response; *pl Journ* gossip (items), local news; **avoir des échos de** to hear some news about; **se faire l'é. de** (*opinions etc*) to echo. ◆**échotier, -ière** *nmf Journ* gossip columnist.

échographie [ekɔgrafi] *nf* (ultrasound) scan; **passer une é.** (*femme enceinte*) to have a scan.

échoir* [eʃwar] *vi* (*terme*) to expire; **é. à qn** (*part*) to fall to s.o.

échouer [eʃwe] **1** *vi* to fail; **é. à** (*examen*) to fail. **2** *vi*, **— s'é.** *vpr* (*navire*) to run aground.

éclabousser [eklabuse] *vt* to splash, spatter (**de** with); (*salir*) *Fig* to tarnish the image of. ◆**éclaboussure** *nf* splash, spatter.

éclair [eklɛr] **1** *nm* (*lumière*) flash; **un é.** *Mét* a flash of lightning. **2** *nm* (*gâteau*) éclair. **3** *a inv* (*visite, raid*) lightning.

éclaircir [eklɛrsir] *vt* (*couleur etc*) to lighten, make lighter; (*sauce*) to thin out; (*question, mystère*) to clear up, clarify; **— s'é.** *vpr* (*ciel*) to clear (up); (*idées*) to become clear(er); (*devenir moins dense*) to thin out; **s'é. la voix** to clear one's throat. ◆**—ie** *nf* (*dans le ciel*) clear patch; (*durée*) sunny spell. ◆**—issement** *nm* (*explication*) clarification.

éclairer [eklɛre] *vt* (*pièce etc*) to light (up); (*situation*) *Fig* to throw light on; **é. qn** (*avec une lampe etc*) to give s.o. some light; (*informer*) *Fig* to enlighten s.o.; **— vi** (*lampe*) to give light; **— s'é.** *vpr* (*visage*) to light up, brighten up; (*question, situation*) *Fig* to become clear(er); **s'é. à la bougie** to use candlelight. ◆**—é** *a* (*averti*) enlightened; **bien/mal é.** (*illuminé*) well/badly lit. ◆**—age** *nm* (*de pièce etc*) light(ing); (*point de vue*) *Fig* light.

éclaireur, -euse [eklɛrœr, -øz] *nm Mil* scout; **—** *nmf* (boy) scout, (girl) guide.

éclat [ekla] *nm* **1** (*de la lumière*) brightness; (*de phare*) *Aut* glare; (*du feu*) blaze; (*splendeur*) brilliance, radiance; (*de la jeunesse*) bloom; (*de diamant*) glitter, sparkle. **2** (*fragment de verre ou de bois*) splinter; (*de rire, colère*) (out)burst; **é. d'obus** shrapnel; **éclats de voix** noisy outbursts, shouts. ◆**éclater** *vi* (*pneu, obus etc*) to burst; (*pétard, bombe*) to go off, explode; (*verre*) to shatter, break into pieces; (*guerre, incendie*) to break out; (*orage, scandale*) to break; (*parti*) to break up; **é. de rire** to burst out laughing; **é. en sanglots** to burst into tears. ◆**—ant** *a* (*lumière, couleur, succès*) brilliant; (*bruit*) thunderous; (*vérité*) blinding; (*beauté*) radiant. ◆**—ement** *nm* (*de pneu etc*) bursting; (*de bombe etc*) explosion; (*de parti*) break-up.

éclectique [eklektik] *a* eclectic.

éclipse [eklips] *nf* (*du soleil*) & *Fig* eclipse. ◆**éclipser** *vt* to eclipse; **— s'é.** *vpr* (*soleil*) to be eclipsed; (*partir*) *Fam* to slip away.

éclopé, -ée [eklɔpe] *a* & *nmf* limping ou lame (person).

éclore [eklɔr] *vi* (*œuf*) to hatch; (*fleur*) to open (out), blossom. ◆**éclosion** *nf* hatching; opening, blossoming.

écluse [eklyz] *nf Nau* lock.

écœurer [ekœre] *vt* (*aliment etc*) to make (s.o.) feel sick; (*au moral*) to sicken, nauseate. ◆**—ement** *nm* (*répugnance*) nausea, disgust.

école [ekɔl] *nf* school; (*militaire*) academy; **aller à l'é.** to go to school; **é. de danse/dessin** dancing/art school; **faire é.** to gain a following; **les grandes écoles** *university* establishments offering high-level professional training; **é. normale** teachers' training college. ◆**écolier, -ière** *nmf* schoolboy, schoolgirl.

écologie [ekɔlɔʒi] *nf* ecology. ◆**écologique** *a* ecological. ◆**écologiste** *nmf Pol* environmentalist.

éconduire [ekɔ̃dɥir] *vt* (*repousser*) to reject.

économe [ekɔnɔm] **1** *a* thrifty, economical. **2** *nmf* (*de collège*) bursar, steward. ◆**économie** *nf* (*activité économique, vertu*) economy; *pl* (*pécule*) savings; **une é. de** (*gain*) a saving of; **faire une é. de temps** to save time; **faire des économies** to save (up); **é. politique** economics. ◆**économique** *a* **1** (*doctrine etc*) economic; **science é.** economics. **2** (*bon marché*, *avantageux*) economical. ◆**économiquement** *adv* economically. ◆**économiser** *vt* (*forces, argent, énergie etc*) to save; – *vi* to economize (**sur** on). ◆**économiste** *nmf* economist.

écoper [ekɔpe] **1** *vt* (*bateau*) to bail out, bale out. **2** *vi Fam* to cop it; **é.** (**de**) (*punition*) to cop, get.

écorce [ekɔrs] *nf* (*d'arbre*) bark; (*de fruit*) peel, skin; **l'é. terrestre** the earth's crust.

écorcher [ekɔrʃe] *vt* (*animal*) to skin, flay; (*érafler*) to graze; (*client*) *Fam* to fleece; (*langue étrangère*) *Fam* to murder; **é. les oreilles** to grate on one's ears; – **s'é.** *vpr* to graze oneself. ◆**écorchure** *nf* graze.

Écosse [ekɔs] *nf* Scotland. ◆**écossais, -aise** *a* Scottish; (*tissu*) tartan; (*whisky*) Scotch; – *nmf* Scot.

écosser [ekɔse] *vt* (*pois*) to shell.

écot [eko] *nm* (*quote-part*) share.

écoul/er [ekule] **1** *vt* (*se débarrasser de*) to dispose of; (*produits*) *Com* to sell (off), clear. **2 s'é.** *vpr* (*eau*) to flow out, run out; (*temps*) to pass, elapse; (*foule*) to disperse. ◆**—é** *a* (*années etc*) past. ◆**—ement** *nm* **1** (*de liquide, véhicules*) flow; (*de temps*) passage. **2** (*débit*) *Com* sale, selling.

écourter [ekurte] *vt* (*séjour, discours etc*) to cut short; (*texte, tige etc*) to shorten.

écoute [ekut] *nf* listening; **à l'é.** *Rad* tuned in, listening in (**de** to); **être aux écoutes** (*attentif*) to keep one's ears open (**de** for). ◆**écout/er** *vt* to listen to; (*radio*) to listen (in) to; – *vi* to listen; (*aux portes etc*) to eavesdrop, listen; **si je m'écoutais** if I did what I wanted. ◆**—eur** *nm* (*de téléphone*) earpiece; *pl* (*casque*) headphones, earphones.

écrabouiller [ekrabuje] *vt Fam* to crush to a pulp.

écran [ekrɑ̃] *nm* screen; **le petit é.** television.

écras/er [ekraze] *vt* (*broyer*) to crush; (*fruit, insecte*) to squash, crush; (*cigarette*) to put out; (*tuer*) *Aut* to run over; (*vaincre*) to beat (hollow), crush; (*dominer*) to outstrip; **écrasé de** (*travail, douleur*) overwhelmed with; **se faire é.** *Aut* to get run over; – **s'é.** *vpr* (*avion, voiture*) to crush ou squash into. ◆**—ant** *a* (*victoire, nombre, chaleur*) overwhelming. ◆**—é a** (*nez*) snub. ◆**—ement** *nm* crushing.

écrémer [ekreme] *vt* (*lait*) to skim, cream; (*collection etc*) *Fig* to cream off the best from.

écrevisse [ekrəvis] *nf* (*crustacé*) crayfish.

écrier (s') [ekrije] *vpr* to cry out, exclaim (**que** that).

écrin [ekrɛ̃] *nm* (*jewel*) case.

écrire [ekrir] *vt* to write; (*noter*) to write (down); (*orthographier*) to spell; **é. à la machine** to type; – *vi* to write; – **s'é.** *vpr* (*mot*) to be spelt. ◆**écrit** *nm* written document, paper; (*examen*) *Scol* written paper; *pl* (*œuvres*) writings; **par é.** in writing. ◆**écriteau, -x** *nm* notice, sign. ◆**écriture** *nf* (*système*) writing; (*personnelle*) (hand)writing; *pl Com* accounts; **l'É. Rel** the Scriptures. ◆**écrivain** *nm* author, writer.

écrou [ekru] *nm Tech* nut.

écrouer [ekrue] *vt* to imprison.

écrouler (s') [ekrule] *vpr* (*édifice, projet etc*) to collapse; (*blessé etc*) to slump down, collapse. ◆**—ement** *nm* collapse.

écru [ekry] *a* toile é. unbleached linen; **soie é.** raw silk.

écueil [ekœj] *nm* (*rocher*) reef; (*obstacle*) *Fig* pitfall.

écuelle [ekɥɛl] *nf* (*bol*) bowl.

éculé [ekyle] *a* (*chaussure*) worn out at the heel; *Fig* hackneyed.

écume [ekym] *nf* (*de mer, bave d'animal etc*) foam; *Culin* scum. ◆**écumer** *vt Culin* to skim; (*piller*) to plunder; – *vi* to foam (**de rage** with anger). ◆**écumoire** *nf Culin* skimmer.

écureuil [ekyrœj] *nm* squirrel.

écurie [ekyri] *nf* stable.

écusson [ekysɔ̃] *nm* (*emblème d'étoffe*) badge.

écuyer, -ère [ekɥije, -ɛr] *nmf* (*cavalier*) (horse) rider, equestrian.

eczéma [egzema] *nm Méd* eczema.

édenté [edɑ̃te] *a* toothless.

édicter [edikte] *vt* to enact, decree.

édifice [edifis] *nm* building, edifice; (*ensemble organisé*) *Fig* edifice. ◆**édification** *nf* construction; edification; enlightenment. ◆**édifier** *vt* (*bâtiment*) to construct, erect; (*théorie*) to construct; **é. qn** (*moralement*) to edify s.o.; (*détromper*) *Iron* to enlighten s.o.

Édimbourg [edɛ̃bur] *nm ou f* Edinburgh.

édit [edi] *nm Hist* edict.

éditer [edite] *vt* (*publier*) to publish; (*annoter*) to edit. ◆**éditeur, -trice** *nmf* publisher; editor. ◆**édition** *nf* (*livre, journal*) edition; (*diffusion, métier*) publishing. ◆**éditorial, -aux** *nm* (*article*) editorial.

édredon [edrədɔ̃] *nm* eiderdown.

éducation [edykasjɔ̃] *nf* (*enseignement*) education; (*façon d'élever*) upbringing, education; **avoir de l'é.** to have good manners, be well-bred. ◆**éducateur, -trice** *nmf* educator. ◆**éducatif, -ive** *a* educational. ◆**éduquer** *vt* (*à l'école*) to educate (*s.o.*); (*à la maison*) to bring (*s.o.*) up, educate (*s.o.*) (**à faire** to do); (*esprit*) to educate, train.

effac/er [efase] *vt* (*gommer*) to rub out, erase; (*en lavant*) to wash out; (*avec un chiffon*) to wipe away; (*souvenir*) *Fig* to blot out, erase; — **s'e.** *vpr* (*souvenir, couleur etc*) to fade; (*se placer en retrait*) to step ou draw aside. ◆**—é** *a* (*modeste*) self-effacing. ◆**—ement** *nm* (*modestie*) self-effacement.

effar/er [efare] *vt* to scare, alarm. ◆**—ement** *nm* alarm.

effaroucher [efaruʃe] *vt* to scare away, frighten away.

effectif, -ive [efɛktif, -iv] **1** *a* (*réel*) effective, real. **2** *nm* (*nombre*) (total) strength; (*de classe*) *Scol* size, total number; *pl* (*employés*) & *Mil* manpower. ◆**effectivement** *adv* (*en effet*) actually, effectively, indeed.

effectuer [efɛktɥe] *vt* (*expérience etc*) to carry out; (*paiement, trajet etc*) to make.

efféminé [efemine] *a* effeminate.

effervescent [efɛrvesɑ̃] *a* (*mélange, jeunesse*) effervescent. ◆**effervescence** *nf* (*exaltation*) excitement; effervescence; (*de liquide*) effervescence.

effet [efɛ] *nm* **1** (*résultat*) effect; (*impression*) impression, effect (**sur** on); **faire de l'e.** (*remède etc*) to be effective; **rester sans e.** to have no effect; **à cet e.** to this end, for this purpose; **en e.** indeed, in fact; **il me fait l'e. d'être fatigué** he seems to be tired; **sous l'e. de la colère** (*agir*) in anger, out of anger. **2 e. de commerce** bill, draft.

effets [efɛ] *nmpl* (*vêtements*) clothes, things.

efficace [efikas] *a* (*mesure etc*) effective; (*personne*) efficient. ◆**efficacité** *nf* effectiveness; efficiency.

effigie [efiʒi] *nf* effigy.

effilé [efile] *a* tapering, slender.

effilocher (s') [sefilɔʃe] *vpr* to fray.

efflanqué [eflɑ̃ke] *a* emaciated.

effleurer [eflœre] *vt* (*frôler*) to skim, touch lightly; (*égratigner*) to graze; (*question*) *Fig* to touch on; **e. qn** (*pensée etc*) to cross s.o.'s mind.

effondr/er (s') [sefɔ̃dre] *vpr* (*projet, édifice, personne*) to collapse; (*toit*) to cave in, collapse. ◆**—ement** *nm* collapse; *Com* slump; (*abattement*) dejection.

efforcer (s') [sefɔrse] *vpr* **s'e. de faire** to try (hard) ou endeavour ou strive to do.

effort [efɔr] *nm* effort; **sans e.** (*réussir etc*) effortlessly; (*réussite etc*) effortless.

effraction [efraksjɔ̃] *nf* **pénétrer par e.** (*cambrioleur*) to break in; **vol avec e.** housebreaking.

effranger (s') [sefrɑ̃ʒe] *vpr* to fray.

effray/er [efreje] *vt* to frighten, scare; — **s'e.** *vpr* to be frightened ou scared. ◆**—ant** *a* frightening, scary.

effréné [efrene] *a* unrestrained, wild.

effriter [efrite] *vt*, — **s'e.** *vpr* to crumble (away).

effroi [efrwa] *nm* (*frayeur*) dread. ◆**effroyable** *a* dreadful, appalling. ◆**effroyablement** *adv* dreadfully.

effronté [efrɔ̃te] *a* (*enfant etc*) cheeky, brazen; (*mensonge*) shameless. ◆**effronterie** *nf* effrontery.

effusion [efyzjɔ̃] *nf* **1 e. de sang** bloodshed. **2** (*manifestation*) effusion; **avec e.** effusively.

égailler (s') [segaje] *vpr* to disperse.

égal, -ale, -aux [egal, -o] *a* equal (**à** to); (*uniforme, régulier*) even; **ça m'est é.** I don't care, it's all the same to me; — *nmf* (*personne*) equal; **traiter qn d'é. à é.** ou **en é.** to treat s.c. as an equal; **sans é.** without match. ◆**—ement** *adv* (*au même degré*) equally; (*aussi*) also, as well. ◆**égaler** *vt* to equal, match (**en** in); (*en quantité*) *Math* to equal. ◆**égalisation** *nf* *Sp* equalization; levelling. ◆**égaliser** *vt* to equalize; (*terrain*) to level; — *vi* *Sp* to equalize. ◆**égalitaire** *a* egalitarian. ◆**égalité** *nf* equality; (*régularité*) evenness; **à é. (de score)** *Sp* equal (on points); **signe d'é.** *Math* equals sign.

égard [egar] *nm* **à l'é. de** (*concernant*) with respect ou regard to; (*envers*) towards; **avoir des égards pour** to have respect ou consideration for; **à cet é.** in this respect; **à certains égards** in some respects.

égarer [egare] *vt* (*objet*) to mislay; **é. qn** (*dérouter*) to mislead s.o.; (*aveugler, troubler*) to lead s.o. astray, misguide s.o.; — **s'é.** *vpr* to lose one's way, get lost; (*objet*) to get mislaid, go astray; (*esprit*) to wander.

égayer [egeje] *vt* (*pièce*) to brighten up; **é. qn** (*réconforter, amuser*) to cheer s.o. up; — **s'é.** *vpr* (*par la moquerie*) to be amused.

égide [eʒid] *nf* **sous l'é. de** under the aegis of.

églantier [eglɑ̃tje] *nm* (*arbre*) wild rose. ◆**églantine** *nf* (*fleur*) wild rose.

église [egliz] *nf* church.

égocentrique [egɔsɑ̃trik] *a* egocentric.

égoïne [egɔin] *nf* (scie) é. hand saw.

égoïsme [egɔism] *nm* selfishness, egoism.
◆**égoïste** *a* selfish, egoistic(al); – *nmf* egoist.

égorger [egɔrʒe] *vt* to cut ou slit the throat of.

égosiller (s') [segɔzije] *vpr* to scream one's head off, bawl out.

égotisme [egɔtism] *nm* egotism.

égout [egu] *nm* sewer; **eaux d'é.** sewage.

égoutter [egute] *vt* (vaisselle) to drain; (légumes) to strain, drain; – *vi*, – **s'é.** *vpr* to drain; to strain; (linge) to drip. ◆**égouttoir** *nm* (panier) (dish) drainer.

égratigner [egratiɲe] *vt* to scratch. ◆**égratignure** *nf* scratch.

égrener [egrəne] *vt* (raisins) to pick off; (épis) to shell; **é. son chapelet** *Rel* to count one's beads.

Égypte [eʒipt] *nf* Egypt. ◆**égyptien, -ienne** [-sjɛ̃, -sjɛn] *a & nmf* Egyptian.

eh! [e] *int* hey!; **eh bien!** well!

éhonté [eɔ̃te] *a* shameless; **mensonge é.** barefaced lie.

éjecter [eʒɛkte] *vt* to eject. ◆**éjectable** *a* **siège é.** *Av* ejector seat. ◆**éjection** *nf* ejection.

élaborer [elabɔre] *vt* (système etc) to elaborate. ◆**élaboration** *nf* elaboration.

élaguer [elage] *vt* (arbre, texte etc) to prune.

élan [elɑ̃] *nm* **1** (vitesse) momentum, impetus; (impulsion) impulse; (fougue) fervour, spirit; **prendre son é.** *Sp* to take a run (up); **d'un seul é.** in one bound. **2** (animal) elk.

élanc/er [elɑ̃se] **1** *vt* (dent etc) to give shooting pains. **2 s'é.** *vpr* (bondir) to leap ou rush (forward); **s'é. vers le ciel** (tour) to soar up (high) into the sky. ◆**—é** *a* (personne, taille etc) slender. ◆**—ement** *nm* shooting pain.

élargir [elarʒir] **1** *vt* (chemin) to widen; (esprit, débat) to broaden; – **s'é.** *vpr* (sentier etc) to widen out. **2** *vt* (prisonnier) to free.

élastique [elastik] *a* (objet, caractère) elastic; (règlement, notion) flexible, supple; – *nm* (tissu) elastic; (lien) elastic ou rubber band. ◆**élasticité** *nf* elasticity.

élection [elɛksjɔ̃] *nf* election; **é. partielle** by-election. ◆**électeur, -trice** *nmf* voter, elector. ◆**électoral, -aux** *a* (campagne, réunion) election-; **collège é.** electoral college. ◆**électorat** *nm* (électeurs) electorate, voters.

électricien [elɛktrisjɛ̃] *nm* electrician. ◆**électricité** *nf* electricity; **coupure d'é.** power cut. ◆**électrifier** *vt* Rail to electrify. ◆**électrique** *a* (pendule, décharge) electric; (courant, fil) electric(al); (phénomène, effet) Fig electric. ◆**électriser** *vt* (animer) Fig to electrify. ◆**électrocuter** *vt* to electrocute.

électrode [elɛktrɔd] *nf* Él electrode.

électrogène [elɛktrɔʒɛn] *a* **groupe é.** Él generator.

électroménager [elɛktromenaʒe] *am* **appareil é.** household electrical appliance.

électron [elɛktrɔ̃] *nm* electron. ◆**électronicien, -ienne** *nmf* electronics engineer. ◆**électronique** *a* electronic; (microscope) electron-; – *nf* electronics.

électrophone [elɛktrofɔn] *nm* record player.

élégant [elegɑ̃] *a* (style, mobilier, solution etc) elegant; (bien habillé) smart, elegant. ◆**élégamment** *adv* elegantly; smartly. ◆**élégance** *nf* elegance.

élégie [eleʒi] *nf* elegy.

élément [elemɑ̃] *nm* (composante, personne) & Ch element; (de meuble) unit; (d'ensemble) Math member; *pl* (notions) rudiments, elements; **dans son é.** (milieu) in one's element. ◆**élémentaire** *a* elementary.

éléphant [elefɑ̃] *nm* elephant. ◆**éléphantesque** *a* (énorme) Fam elephantine.

élévateur [elevatœr] *am* **chariot é.** forklift truck.

élévation [elevasjɔ̃] *nf* raising; Géom elevation; **é. de** (hausse) rise in.

élève [elɛv] *nmf* Scol pupil.

élev/er [elve] *vt* (prix, objection, voix etc) to raise; (enfant) to bring up, raise; (animal) to breed, rear; (âme) to uplift, raise; – **s'é.** *vpr* (prix, montagne, ton, avion etc) to rise; **s'é. à** (prix etc) to amount to; **s'é. contre** to rise up against. ◆**—é** *a* (haut) high; (noble) noble; **bien/mal é.** well-/bad-mannered. ◆**—age** *nm* (de bovins) cattle rearing. **l'é. de** the breeding ou rearing of. ◆**—eur, -euse** *nmf* breeder.

élider [elide] *vt* Ling to elide.

éligible [eliʒibl] *a* Pol eligible (à for).

élimé [elime] *a* (tissu) threadbare, worn thin.

éliminer [elimine] *vt* to eliminate. ◆**élimination** *nf* elimination. ◆**éliminatoire** *a & nf* (épreuve) Sp heat, qualifying round.

élire* [elir] *vt* Pol to elect (à to).

élision [elizjɔ̃] *nf* Ling elision.

élite [elit] *nf* elite (**de** of); **d'é.** (chef, sujet etc) top-notch.

elle [ɛl] *pron* **1** (sujet) she; (chose, animal) it;

pl they; **e. est** she is; it is; **elles sont** they are. **2** (*complément*) her; (*chose, animal*) it; (*pl* them; **pour e.** for her; **pour elles** for them; **plus grande qu'e./qu'elles** taller than her/them. ◆**e.-même** *pron* herself; (*chose, animal*) itself; *pl* themselves.

ellipse [elips] *nf Géom* ellipse. ◆**elliptique** *a* elliptical.

élocution [elɔkysjɔ̃] *nf* diction; **défaut d'é.** speech defect.

éloge [elɔʒ] *nm* praise; (*panégyrique*) eulogy; **faire l'é. de** to praise. ◆**élogieux, -euse** *a* laudatory.

éloign/er [elwaɲe] *vt* (*chose, personne*) to move *ou* take away (**de** from); (*clients*) to keep away; (*crainte, idée*) to get rid of, banish; (*date*) to put off; **é. qn de** (*sujet, but*) to take *ou* get s.o. away from; **— s'é.** *vpr* (*partir*) to move *ou* go away (**de** from); (*dans le passé*) to become (more) remote; **s'é. de** (*sujet, but*) to get away from. ◆**-é** *a* far-off, remote, distant; (*parent*) distant; **é. de** (*village, maison etc*) far (away) from; (*très différent*) far removed from. ◆**-ement** *nm* remoteness, distance; (*absence*) separation (**de** from); **avec l'é.** (*avec le recul*) with time.

élongation [elɔ̃gasjɔ̃] *nf Méd* pulled muscle.

éloquent [elɔkɑ̃] *a* eloquent. ◆**éloquence** *nf* eloquence.

élu, -ue [ely] *voir* **élire;** – *nmf Pol* elected member *ou* representative; **les élus** *Rel* the chosen, the elect.

élucider [elyside] *vt* to elucidate. ◆**élucidation** *nf* elucidation.

éluder [elyde] *vt* to elude, evade.

émacié [emasje] *a* emaciated.

émail, -aux [emaj, -o] *nm* enamel; **en é.** enamel-. ◆**émailler** *vt* to enamel.

émaillé [emaje] *a* **é. de fautes/etc** (*texte*) peppered with errors/*etc*.

émanciper [emɑ̃sipe] *vt* (*femmes*) to emancipate; **— s'é.** *vpr* to become emancipated. ◆**émancipation** *nf* emancipation.

émaner [emane] *vi* to emanate. ◆**émanation** *nf* emanation; **une é. de** *Fig* a product of.

emball/er [ɑ̃bale] **1** *vt* (*dans une caisse etc*) to pack; (*dans du papier*) to wrap (up). **2** *vt* (*moteur*) to race; **e. qn** (*passionner*) *Fam* to enthuse s.o., thrill s.o.; **— s'e.** *vpr* (*personne*) *Fam* to get carried away; (*cheval*) to bolt; (*moteur*) to race. ◆**-é** *a Fam* enthusiastic. ◆**-age** *nm* (*action*) ɩ packing; wrapping; (*caisse*) packaging; (*papier*) wrapping (paper). ◆**-ement** *nm Fam* (*sudden*) enthusiasm.

embarcadère [ɑ̃barkader] *nm* landing place, quay.

embarcation [ɑ̃barkasjɔ̃] *nf* (small) boat.

embardée [ɑ̃barde] *nf Aut* (sudden) swerve; **faire une é.** to swerve.

embargo [ɑ̃bargo] *nm* embargo.

embarqu/er [ɑ̃barke] *vt* (*passagers*) to embark, take on board; (*marchandises*) to load (up); (*voler*) *Fam* to walk off with; (*prisonnier*) *Fam* to cart off; **e. qn dans** (*affaire*) *Fam* to involve s.o. in, launch s.o. into; – *vi*, **— s'e.** *vpr* to embark, (go on) board; **s'e. dans** (*aventure etc*) *Fam* to embark on. ◆**-ement** *nm* (*de passagers*) boarding.

embarras [ɑ̃bara] *nm* (*malaise, gêne*) embarrassment; (*difficulté*) difficulty, trouble; (*obstacle*) obstacle; **dans l'e.** in difficulty; **faire des e.** (*chichis*) to make a fuss. ◆**embarrass/er** *vt* (*obstruer*) to clutter, encumber; **e. qn** to be in s.o.'s way; (*déconcerter*) to embarrass s.o., bother s.o.; **s'e. de** to burden oneself with; (*se soucier*) to bother oneself about. ◆**-ant** *a* (*paquet*) cumbersome; (*question*) embarrassing.

embauche [ɑ̃boʃ] *nf* (*action*) hiring; (*travail*) work. ◆**embaucher** *vt* (*ouvrier*) to hire, take on.

embaumer [ɑ̃bome] **1** *vt* (*cadavre*) to embalm. **2** *vt* (*parfumer*) to give a sweet smell to; – *vi* to smell sweet.

embell/ir [ɑ̃belir] *vt* (*texte, vérité*) to embellish; **e. qn** to make s.o. attractive. ◆**-issement** *nm* (*de ville etc*) improvement, embellishment.

embêt/er [ɑ̃bete] *vt Fam* (*contrarier, taquiner*) to annoy, bother; (*raser*) to bore; **— s'e.** *vpr Fam* to get bored. ◆**-ant** *a Fam* annoying; boring. ◆**-ement** *nm* [-etma] *Fam* **un e.** (some) trouble *ou* bother; **des embêtements** trouble(s), bother.

emblée (d') [dɑ̃ble] *adv* right away.

emblème [ɑ̃blɛm] *nm* emblem.

emboîner [ɑ̃bwane] *vt* (*tromper*) *Fam* to hoodwink.

emboîter [ɑ̃bwate] *vt*, **— s'e.** *vpr* (*pièces*) to fit into each other, fit together; **e. le pas à qn** to follow on s.o.'s heels; (*imiter*) *Fig* to follow in s.o.'s footsteps.

embonpoint [ɑ̃bɔ̃pwɛ̃] *nm* plumpness.

embouchure [ɑ̃buʃyr] *nf* (*de cours d'eau*) mouth; *Mus* mouthpiece.

embourber (s') [sɑ̃burbe] *vpr* (*véhicule*) & *Fig* to get bogged down.

embourgeoiser (s') [sɑ̃burʒwaze] *vpr* to become middle-class.

embout [ãbu] nm (de canne) tip, end piece; (de seringue) nozzle.

embouteill/er [ãbuteje] vt Aut to jam, congest. ◆**-age** nm traffic jam.

emboutir [ãbutir] vt (voiture) to bash ou crash into; (métal) to stamp, emboss.

embranch/er (s') [sãbrãʃe] vpr (voie) to branch off. ◆**-ement** nm (de voie) junction, fork; (de règne animal) branch.

embras/er [ãbraze] vt to set ablaze; — **s'e.** vpr (prendre feu) to flare up. ◆**-ement** nm (troubles) flare-up.

embrasser [ãbrase] vt (adopter, contenir) to embrace; **e. qn** to kiss s.o.; (serrer) to embrace ou hug s.o.; — **s'e.** vpr to kiss (each other). ◆**embrassade** nf embrace, hug.

embrasure [ãbrazyr] nf (de fenêtre, porte) opening.

embray/er [ãbreje] vi to let in ou engage the clutch. ◆**-age** nm (mécanisme, pédale) Aut clutch.

embrigader [ãbrigade] vt to recruit.

embrocher [ãbrɔʃe] vt Culin & Fig to skewer.

embrouiller [ãbruje] vt (fils) to tangle (up); (papiers etc) to muddle (up), mix up; **e. qn** to confuse s.o., get s.o. muddled; — **s'e.** vpr to get confused ou muddled (**dans** in, with). ◆**embrouillamini** nm Fam muddle, mix-up. ◆**embrouillement** nm confusion, muddle.

embroussaillé [ãbrusaje] a (barbe, chemin) bushy.

embruns [ãbrœ̃] nmpl (sea) spray.

embryon [ãbrijɔ̃] nm embryo. ◆**embryonnaire** a Méd & Fig embryonic.

embûches [ãbyʃ] nfpl (difficultés) traps, pitfalls.

embuer [ãbɥe] vt (vitre, yeux) to mist up.

embusquer (s') [sãbyske] vpr to lie in ambush. ◆**embuscade** nf ambush.

éméché [emeʃe] a (ivre) Fam tipsy.

émeraude [emrod] nf emerald.

émerger [emerʒe] vi to emerge (**de** from).

émeri [emri] nm **toile (d')é.** emery cloth.

émerveill/er [emerveje] vt to amaze; — **s'é.** vpr to marvel, be filled with wonder (**de** at). ◆**-ement** nm wonder, amazement.

émett/re* [emetr] vt (lumière, son etc) to give out, emit; Rad to transmit, broadcast; (cri) to utter; (opinion, vœu) to express; (timbre-poste, monnaie) to issue; (chèque) to draw; (emprunt Com to float. ◆**-eur** nm (poste) é. Rad transmitter.

émeute [emøt] nf riot. ◆**émeutier, -ière** nm rioter.

émietter [emjete] vt, — **s'é.** vpr (pain etc) to crumble.

émigr/er [emigre] vi (personne) to emigrate. ◆**-ant, -ante** nmf emigrant. ◆**-é, -ée** nmf exile, émigré. ◆**émigration** nf emigration.

éminent [eminã] a eminent. ◆**éminemment** [-amã] adv eminently. ◆**éminence** nf **1** (colline) hillock. **2** son É. Rel his Eminence.

émissaire [emiser] nm emissary.

émission [emisjɔ̃] nf (trouble) TV Rad broadcast; (action) emission (**de** of); (de programme) TV Rad transmission; (de timbre-poste, monnaie) issue.

emmagasiner [ãmagazine] vt to store (up).

emmanchure [ãmɑ̃ʃyr] nf (de vêtement) arm hole.

emmêler [ãmele] vt to tangle (up).

emménag/er [ãmenaʒe] vi (dans un logement) to move in; **e. dans** to move into. ◆**-ement** nm moving in.

emmener [ãmne] vt to take (à to); (prisonnier) to take away; **e. qn faire une promenade** to take s.o. for a walk.

emmerd/er [ãmɛrde] vt Arg to annoy, bug; (raser) to bore stiff; — **s'e.** vpr Arg to get bored stiff. ◆**-ement** nm Arg bother, trouble. ◆**-eur, -euse** nmf (personne) Arg pain in the neck.

emmitoufler (s') [sãmitufle] vpr to wrap (oneself) up.

emmurer [ãmyre] vt (personne) to wall in.

émoi [emwa] nm excitement; **en é.** agog, excited.

émoluments [emɔlymã] nmpl remuneration.

émotion [emosjɔ̃] nf (trouble) excitement; (sentiment) emotion; **une é.** (peur) a scare. ◆**émotif, -ive** a emotional. ◆**émotionné** a Fam upset.

émouss/er [emuse] vt (pointe) to blunt; (sentiment) to dull. ◆**-é** a (pointe) blunt; (sentiment) dulled.

émouv/oir* [emuvwar] vt (affecter) to move, touch; — **s'é.** vpr to be moved ou touched. ◆**-ant** a moving, touching.

empailler [ãpaje] vt (animal) to stuff.

empaler (s') [sãpale] vpr to impale oneself.

empaqueter [ãpakte] vt to pack(age).

emparer (s') [sãpare] vpr **s'e. de** to seize, take hold of.

empât/er (s') [sãpate] vpr to fill out, get fat(ter). ◆**-é** a fleshy, fat.

empêch/er [ãpeʃe] vt to prevent, stop; **e. qn de faire** to prevent ou stop s.o. (from) doing; **n'empêche qu'elle a raison** Fam all the same she's right; **n'empêche!** *Fam* all the same!; **elle ne peut pas s'e. de rire** she can't help laughing. ◆**—ement** [-ɛʃmɑ̃] *nm* difficulty, hitch; **avoir un e.** to be unavoidably detained.

empereur [ɑ̃prœr] *nm* emperor.

empeser [ɑ̃pəze] *vt* to starch.

empester [ɑ̃pɛste] *vt* (*pièce*) to make stink, stink out; (*tabac etc*) to stink of; **e. qn** to stink s.o. out; — *vi* to stink.

empêtrer (s') [sɑ̃pɛtre] *vpr* to get entangled (**dans** in).

emphase [ɑ̃faz] *nf* pomposity. ◆**emphatique** *a* pompous.

empiéter [ɑ̃pjete] *vi* **e. sur** to encroach upon. ◆**empiétement** *nm* encroachment.

empiffrer (s') [sɑ̃pifre] *vpr Fam* to gorge *ou* stuff oneself (**de** with).

empil/er [ɑ̃pile] *vt*, — **s'e.** *vpr* to pile up (**sur** on); **s'e. dans** (*personnes*) to pile into (*building, car etc*). ◆**—ement** *nm* (*tas*) pile.

empire [ɑ̃pir] *nm* (*territoires*) empire; (*autorité*) hold, influence; **sous l'e. de** (*peur etc*) in the grip of.

empirer [ɑ̃pire] *vi* to worsen, get worse.

empirique [ɑ̃pirik] *a* empirical. ◆**empirisme** *nm* empiricism.

emplacement [ɑ̃plasmɑ̃] *nm* site, location; (*de stationnement*) place.

emplâtre [ɑ̃plɑtr] *nm* (*onguent*) *Méd* plaster.

emplette [ɑ̃plɛt] *nf* purchase; *pl* shopping.

emplir [ɑ̃plir] *vt*, — **s'e.** *vpr* to fill (**de** with).

emploi [ɑ̃plwa] *nm* **1** (*usage*) use; **e. du temps** timetable; **mode d'e.** directions (for use). **2** (*travail*) job, position, employment; **l'e.** (*travail*) *Écon Pol* employment; **sans e.** unemployed. ◆**employ/er** *vt* (*utiliser*) to use; (*qn*) to employ s.o.; — **s'e.** *vpr* (*expression*) to be used; **s'e. à faire** to devote oneself to doing. ◆**—é, -ée** *nmf* employee; (*de bureau, banque*) clerk, employee; **e. des postes/etc** postal/*etc* worker; **e. de magasin** shop assistant, *Am* sales clerk. ◆**employeur, -euse** *nmf* employer.

empocher [ɑ̃pɔʃe] *vt* (*argent*) to pocket.

empoigner [ɑ̃pwaɲe] *vt* (*saisir*) to grab, grasp; — **s'e.** *vpr* to come to blows, fight. ◆**empoignade** *nf* (*querelle*) fight.

empoisonn/er [ɑ̃pwazɔne] *vt* (*personne, aliment, atmosphère*) to poison; (*empester*) to stink out; (*gâter, altérer*) to trouble, bedevil; **e. qn** (*embêter*) *Fam* to get on s.o.'s nerves; — **s'e.** *vpr* (*par accident*) to be poisoned; (*volontairement*) to poison oneself. ◆**—ant** *a* (*embêtant*) *Fam* irritating.

◆**—ement** *nm* poisoning; (*ennui*) *Fam* problem, trouble.

emport/er [ɑ̃pɔrte] *vt* (*prendre*) to take (away) (**avec soi** with one); (*enlever*) to take away; (*prix, trophée*) to carry off; (*décision*) to carry; (*entraîner*) to carry along *ou* away; (*par le vent*) to blow off *ou* away; (*par les vagues*) to sweep away; (*par la maladie*) to carry off; **l'e. sur qn** to get the upper hand over s.o.; **se laisser e.** *Fig* to get carried away (**par** by); — **s'e.** *vpr* to lose one's temper (**contre** with). ◆**—é** *a* (*caractère*) hot-tempered. ◆**—ement** *nm* anger; *pl* fits of anger.

empoté [ɑ̃pɔte] *a Fam* clumsy.

empourprer (s') [sɑ̃purpre] *vpr* to turn crimson.

empreint [ɑ̃prɛ̃] *a* **e. de** stamped with, heavy with.

empreinte [ɑ̃prɛ̃t] *nf* (*marque*) & *Fig* mark, stamp; **e. digitale** fingerprint; **e. des pas** footprint.

empress/er (s') [sɑ̃prese] *vpr* **s'e. de faire** to hasten to do; **s'e. auprès de qn** to busy oneself with s.o., be attentive to s.o.; **s'e. autour de qn** to rush around s.o. ◆**—é** *a* eager, attentive; **e. à faire** eager to do. ◆**—ement** [-ɛsmɑ̃] *nm* (*hâte*) eagerness; (*auprès de qn*) attentiveness.

emprise [ɑ̃priz] *nf* ascendancy, hold (**sur** over).

emprisonn/er [ɑ̃prizɔne] *vt Jur* to imprison; (*enfermer*) *Fig* to confine. ◆**—ement** *nm* imprisonment.

emprunt [ɑ̃prœ̃] *nm* (*argent*) *Com* loan; (*mot*) *Ling* borrowed word; **un e. à** *Ling* a borrowing from; **l'e. de qch** the borrowing of sth; **d'e.** borrowed; **nom d'e.** assumed name. ◆**emprunt/er** *vt* (*obtenir*) to borrow (**à qn** from s.o.); (*route etc*) to use; (*nom*) to assume; **e. à** (*tirer de*) to derive *ou* borrow from. ◆**—é** *a* (*gêné*) ill-at-ease.

empuantir [ɑ̃pɥɑ̃tir] *vt* to make stink, stink out.

ému [emy] *voir* **émouvoir**; — *a* (*attendri*) moved; (*apeuré*) nervous; (*attristé*) upset; **une voix émue** a voice charged with emotion.

émulation [emylasjɔ̃] *nf* emulation.

émule [emyl] *nmf* imitator, follower.

en¹ [ɑ̃] *prép* **1** (*lieu*) in; (*direction*) into; **être en ville/en France** to be in town/in France; **aller en ville/en France** to go (in)to town/to France. **2** (*temps*) in; **en été** in summer; **en février** in February; **d'heure en heure** from hour to hour. **3** (*moyen, état etc*) by; in; at; on; **en avion** by plane; **en groupe**

in a group; **en mer** at sea; **en guerre** at war; **en fleur** in flower; **en congé** on leave; **en vain** in vain. **4** (*matière*) in; **en bois** wooden, in wood; **chemise en nylon** nylon shirt; **c'est en or** it's (made of) gold. **5** (*comme*) **en cadeau** as a present; **en ami** as a friend. **6** (+ *participe présent*) **en mangeant/chantant/etc** while eating/singing/etc; **en apprenant que...** on hearing that...; **en souriant** smiling, with a smile; **en ne disant rien** by saying nothing; **sortir en courant** to run out. **7** (*transformation*) into; **traduire en** to translate into.

en² [ɑ̃] *pron & adv* **1** (= *de là*) from there; **j'en viens** I've just come from there. **2** (= *de ça, lui, eux etc*) **il en est content** he's pleased with it *ou* him *ou* them; **en parler** to talk about it; **en mourir** to die of *ou* from it; **elle m'en frappa** she struck me with it. **3** (*partitif*) some; **j'en ai** I have some; **en veux-tu?** do you want some *ou* any?; **je t'en supplie** I beg you (to).

encadr/er [ɑ̃kadre] *vt* (*tableau*) to frame; (*entourer d'un trait*) to box in; (*troupes, étudiants*) to supervise, train; (*prisonnier, accusé*) to flank. ◆**—ement** *nm* (*action*) framing; supervision; (*de porte, photo*) frame; (*décor*) setting; (*personnel*) training and supervisory staff.

encaissé [ɑ̃kese] *a* (*vallée*) deep.

encaiss/er [ɑ̃kese] *vt* (*argent, loyer etc*) to collect; (*effet, chèque*) *Com* to cash; (*coup*) *Fam* to take; **je ne peux pas l'e.** *Fam* I can't stand him *ou* her. ◆**—ement** *nm* (*de loyer etc*) collection; (*de chèque*) cashing.

encapuchonné [ɑ̃kapyʃɔne] *a* hooded.

encart [ɑ̃kar] *nm* (*feuille*) insert. ◆**encarter** *vt* to insert.

en-cas [ɑ̃ka] *nm inv* (*repas*) snack.

encastrer [ɑ̃kastre] *vt* to build in (**dans** to), embed (**dans** into).

encaustique [ɑ̃kostik] *nf* (wax) polish. ◆**encaustiquer** *vt* to wax, polish.

enceinte¹ [ɑ̃sɛ̃t] *a f* (*femme*) pregnant; **e. de six mois/etc** six months/etc pregnant. **2** *nf* (*muraille*) (surrounding) wall; (*espace*) enclosure; **e. acoustique** (loud)speakers.

encens [ɑ̃sɑ̃] *nm* incense. ◆**encensoir** *nm* *Rel* censer.

encercler [ɑ̃sɛrkle] *vt* to surround, encircle.

enchaîner [ɑ̃ʃene] *vt* (*animal*) to chain (up); (*prisonnier*) to put in chains, chain (up); (*assembler*) to link (up), connect; − *vi* (*continuer à parler*) to continue; − **s'e.** *vpr* (*idées etc*) to be linked (up). ◆**enchaînement** *nm* (*succession*) chain, series; (*liaison*) link(ing) (**de** between, of).

enchant/er [ɑ̃ʃɑ̃te] *vt* (*ravir*) to delight, enchant; (*ensorceler*) to bewitch, enchant. ◆**—é** *a* (*ravi*) delighted (**de** with, **que** + *sub*) that); **e. de faire votre connaissance!** pleased to meet you! ◆**—ement** *nm* delight; enchantment; **comme par e.** as if by magic. ◆**—eur** *a* delightful, enchanting; − *nm* (*sorcier*) magician.

enchâsser [ɑ̃ʃɑse] *vt* (*diamant*) to set, embed.

enchère [ɑ̃ʃɛr] *nf* (*offre*) bid; **vente aux enchères** auction; **mettre aux enchères** (to put up for) auction. ◆**enchér/ir** *vi* **e. sur qn** to outbid s.o. ◆**—isseur** *nm* bidder.

enchevêtrer [ɑ̃ʃvetre] *vt* to (en)tangle; − **s'e.** *vpr* to get entangled (**dans** in). ◆**enchevêtrement** *nm* tangle, entanglement.

enclave [ɑ̃klav] *nf* enclave. ◆**enclaver** *vt* to enclose (completely).

enclencher [ɑ̃klɑ̃ʃe] *vt* *Tech* to engage.

enclin [ɑ̃klɛ̃] *am* **e. à** inclined *ou* prone to.

enclore [ɑ̃klɔr] *vt* (*terrain*) to enclose. ◆**enclos** *nm* (*terrain, clôture*) enclosure.

enclume [ɑ̃klym] *nf* anvil.

encoche [ɑ̃kɔʃ] *nf* notch, nick (**à** in).

encoignure [ɑ̃kwaɲyr] *nf* corner.

encoller [ɑ̃kɔle] *vt* to paste.

encolure [ɑ̃kɔlyr] *nf* (*de cheval, vêtement*) neck; (*tour du cou*) collar (size).

encombre (sans) [sɑ̃zɑ̃kɔ̃br] *adv* without a hitch.

encombr/er [ɑ̃kɔ̃bre] *vt* (*couloir, pièce etc*) to clutter up (**de** with); (*rue*) to congest, clog (**de** with); **e. qn** to hamper s.o.; **s'e. de** to burden *ou* saddle oneself with. ◆**—ant** *a* (*paquet*) bulky, cumbersome; (*présence*) awkward. ◆**—é** *a* (*profession, marché*) overcrowded, saturated. ◆**—ement** *nm* (*embarras*) clutter; *Aut* traffic jam; (*volume*) bulk(iness).

encontre de (à l') [alɑ̃kɔ̃trədə] *adv* against; (*contrairement à*) contrary to.

encore [ɑ̃kɔr] *adv* **1** (*toujours*) still; **tu es e. là?** are you still here? **2** (*avec négation*) yet; **pas e.** not yet; **ne pars pas e.** don't go yet; **je ne suis pas e. prêt** I'm not ready yet, I'm still not ready. **3** (*de nouveau*) again; **essaie e.** try again. **4** (*de plus*) **e.** du café another coffee, one more coffee; **e. une fois** (once) again, once more; **e. un** another (one), one more; **e. du pain** (some) more bread; **que veut-il e.?** what else *ou* more does he want?; **e. quelque chose** something else; **qui/quoi e.?** who/what else?; **chante e.** sing some more. **5** (*avec comparatif*) even, still; **e. mieux** even better, better still. **6** (*aussi*) also. **7 si e.** (*si seulement*) if only; **et e.!** (*à peine*) if that!, only just! **8 e. que** (+ *sub*) although.

encourag/er [ākuraʒe] *vt* to encourage (à faire to do). **◆—eant** *a* encouraging. **◆—ement** *nm* encouragement.

encourir* [ākurir] *vt* (*amende etc*) to incur.

encrasser [ākrase] *vt* to clog up (with dirt).

encre [ākr] *nf* ink; **e. de Chine** Indian ink; **e. sympathique** invisible ink. **◆encrier** *nm* inkwell, inkpot.

encroûter (s') [sākrute] *vpr Péj* to get set in one's ways; **s'e. dans** (*habitude*) to get stuck in.

encyclique [āsiklik] *nf Rel* encyclical.

encyclopédie [āsiklɔpedi] *nf* encyclop(a)edia. **◆encyclopédique** *a* encyclop(a)edic.

endémique [ādemik] *a* endemic.

endetter [ādete] *vt* **e. qn** to get s.o. into debt; **— s'e.** *vpr* to get into debt. **◆endettement** *nm* (*dettes*) debts.

endeuiller [ādœje] *vt* to plunge into mourning.

endiablé [ādjable] *a* (*rythme etc*) frantic, wild.

endiguer [ādige] *vt* (*fleuve*) to dam (up); (*réprimer*) *Fig* to stem.

endimanché [ādimāʃe] *a* in one's Sunday best.

endive [ādiv] *nf* chicory, endive.

endoctrin/er [ādɔktrine] *vt* to indoctrinate. **◆—ement** *nm* indoctrination.

endolori [ādɔlɔri] *a* painful, aching.

endommager [ādɔmaʒe] *vt* to damage.

endorm/ir* [ādɔrmir] *vt* (*enfant, patient*) to put to sleep; (*ennuyer*) to send to sleep; (*soupçons etc*) to lull; (*douleur*) to deaden; **— s'e.** *vpr* to fall asleep, go to sleep. **◆—i** *a* asleep, sleeping; (*indolent*) *Fam* sluggish.

endosser [ādose] *vt* (*vêtement*) to put on; don; (*responsabilité*) to assume; (*chèque*) to endorse.

endroit [ādrwa] *nm* **1** place, spot; (*de film, livre*) part, place. **2** (*de tissu*) right side; **à l'e.** (*vêtement*) right side out, the right way round.

enduire* [ādɥir] *vt* to smear, coat (de with). **◆enduit** *nm* coating; (*de mur*) plaster.

endurant [ādyrā] *a* hardy, tough. **◆endurance** *nf* endurance.

endurc/ir [ādyrsir] *vt* to harden; **s'e. à** (*personne*) to become hardened to (*pain etc*). **◆—i** *a* hardened; (*célibataire*) confirmed. **◆—issement** *nm* hardening.

endurer [ādyre] *vt* to endure, bear.

énergie [enɛrʒi] *nf* energy; **avec é.** (*protester*

etc) forcefully. **◆énergétique** *a* (*ressources etc*) energy-. **◆énergique** *a* (*dynamique*) energetic; (*remède*) powerful; (*mesure, ton*) forceful. **◆énergiquement** *adv* (*protester etc*) energetically.

énergumène [enɛrgymen] *nmf Péj* rowdy character.

énerv/er [enɛrve] *vt* **é. qn** (*irriter*) to get on s.o.'s nerves; (*rendre énervé*) to make s.o. nervous; **— s'é.** *vpr* to get worked up. **◆—é** *a* on edge, irritated. **◆—ement** *nm* irritation, nervousness.

enfant [āfā] *nmf* child (*pl* children); **en bas âge** infant; **un e. de** (*originaire*) a native of; **attendre un e.** to expect a baby *ou* a child; **e. trouvé** foundling; **e. de chœur** *Rel* altar boy; **e. prodige** child prodigy; **e. prodigue** prodigal son; **bon e.** (*caractère*) good natured. **◆enfance** *nf* childhood; **première e.** infancy, early childhood; **dans son e.** (*science etc*) in its infancy. **◆enfanter** *vt* to give birth to; **— vi** to give birth. **◆enfantillage** *nm* childishness. **◆enfantin** *a* (*voix, joie*) childlike; (*langage, jeu*) children's; (*puéril*) childish; (*simple*) easy.

enfer [āfɛr] *nm* hell; **feu d'e.** roaring fire; **à un train d'e.** at breakneck speed.

enfermer [āfɛrme] *vt* (*personne etc*) to shut up, lock up; (*objet précieux*) to lock up, shut away; (*jardin*) to enclose; **s'e. dans** (*chambre etc*) to shut *ou* lock oneself (up) in; (*attitude etc*) *Fig* to maintain stubbornly.

enferrer (s') [sāfere] *vpr* **s'e. dans** to get caught up in.

enfiévré [āfjevre] *a* (*surexcité*) feverish.

enfiler [āfile] *vt* (*aiguille*) to thread; (*perles etc*) to string; (*vêtement*) *Fam* to slip on, pull on; (*rue, couloir*) to take. **s'e. dans** (*rue etc*) to take. **◆enfilade** *nf* (*série*) row, string.

enfin [āfɛ̃] *adv* (*à la fin*) finally, at last; (*en dernier lieu*) lastly; (*en somme*) in a word; (*conclusion résignée*) well; **e. bref** (*en somme*) *Fam* in a word; **il est grand, e. pas trop petit** he's tall – well, not too short anyhow; **mais e.** but; (*mais*) **e.!** for heaven's sake!

enflamm/er [āflame] *vt* to set fire to, ignite; (*allumette*) to light; (*irriter*) *Méd* to inflame; (*imagination, colère*) to excite, inflame; **— s'e.** *vpr* to catch fire, ignite; **s'e. de colère** to flare up. **◆—é** *a* (*discours*) fiery.

enfler [ɑ̃fle] vt to swell; (voix) to raise; – vi Méd to swell (up). ◆**enflure** nf swelling.

enfonc/er [ɑ̃fɔ̃se] vt (clou etc) to knock in, drive in; (chapeau) to push ou force down; (porte, voiture) to smash in; **e. dans** (couteau, mains etc) to plunge into; – vi, – **s'e.** vpr (s'enliser) to sink (dans into); **s'e. dans** (pénétrer) to plunge into, disappear (deep) into. ◆**—é** a (yeux) sunken.

enfouir [ɑ̃fwir] vt to bury.

enfourcher [ɑ̃furʃe] vt (cheval etc) to mount, bestride.

enfourner [ɑ̃furne] vt to put in the oven.

enfreindre* [ɑ̃frɛ̃dr] vt to infringe.

enfuir* (s') [sɑ̃fɥir] vpr to run away ou off, flee (de from).

enfumer [ɑ̃fyme] vt (pièce) to fill with smoke; (personne) to smoke out.

engag/er [ɑ̃gaʒe] vt (bijou etc) to pawn; (parole) to pledge; (discussion, combat) to start; (clef etc) to insert (dans into); (capitaux) to tie up, invest; **e. la bataille avec** to join battle with; **e. qn** (lier) to bind s.o., commit s.o.; (embaucher) to hire s.o., engage s.o.; **e. qn dans** (affaire etc) to involve s.o. in; **e. qn à faire** (exhorter) to urge s.o. to do; – **s'e.** vpr (s'inscrire) Mil to enlist; Sp to enter; (au service d'une cause) to commit oneself; (action) to start; **s'e. à faire** to commit oneself to doing, undertake to do; **s'e. dans** (voie) to enter; (affaire etc) to get involved in. ◆**—eant** a engaging, inviting. ◆**—é** a (écrivain etc) committed. ◆**—ement** nm (promesse) commitment; (commencement) start; (de recrues) Mil enlistment; (inscription) Sp entry; (combat) Mil engagement; **prendre l'e. de** to undertake to.

engelure [ɑ̃ʒlyr] nf chilblain.

engendrer [ɑ̃ʒɑ̃dre] vt (procréer) to beget; (causer) to generate, engender.

engin [ɑ̃ʒɛ̃] nm machine, device; (projectile) missile; **e. explosif** explosive device.

englober [ɑ̃glɔbe] vt to include, embrace.

engloutir [ɑ̃glutir] vt (avaler) to wolf (down), gobble (up); (faire sombrer ou disparaître) to engulf.

engorger [ɑ̃gɔrʒe] vt to block up, clog.

engouement [ɑ̃gumɑ̃] nm craze.

engouffrer [ɑ̃gufre] vt (avaler) to wolf (down); (fortune) to consume; **s'e. dans** to sweep ou rush into.

engourd/ir [ɑ̃gurdir] vt (membre) to numb; (esprit) to dull; – **s'e.** vpr to go numb; to become dull. ◆**—issement** nm numbness; dullness.

engrais [ɑ̃grɛ] nm (naturel) manure; (chimique) fertilizer.

engraisser [ɑ̃grese] vt (animal) to fatten (up); – vi, – **s'e.** vpr to get fat, put on weight.

engrenage [ɑ̃grənaʒ] nm Tech gears; Fig mesh, chain, web.

engueuler [ɑ̃gœle] vt **e. qn** Fam to swear at s.o., give s.o. hell. ◆**engueulade** nf Fam (réprimande) dressing-down, severe talking-to; (dispute) slanging match, row.

enhardir [ɑ̃ardir] vt to make bolder; **s'e. à faire** to make bold to do.

énième [enjɛm] a Fam umpteenth, nth.

énigme [enigm] nf enigma, riddle. ◆**énigmatique** a enigmatic.

enivrer [ɑ̃nivre] vt (soûler, troubler) to intoxicate; – **s'e.** vpr to get drunk (de on).

enjamber [ɑ̃ʒɑ̃be] vt to step over; (pont etc) to span (river etc). ◆**enjambée** nf stride.

enjeu, -x [ɑ̃ʒø] nm (mise) stake(s).

enjoindre [ɑ̃ʒwɛ̃dr] vt **e. à qn de faire** Litt to order s.o. to do.

enjôler [ɑ̃ʒole] vt to wheedle, coax.

enjoliv/er [ɑ̃ʒɔlive] vt to embellish. ◆**—eur** nm Aut hubcap.

enjoué [ɑ̃ʒwe] a playful. ◆**enjouement** nm playfulness.

enlacer [ɑ̃lase] vt to entwine; (serrer dans ses bras) to clasp.

enlaidir [ɑ̃ledir] vt to make ugly; – vi to grow ugly.

enlev/er [ɑ̃lve] vt to take away ou off, remove (à qn from s.o.); (ordures) to collect; (vêtement) to take off, remove; (tache) to take out, lift, remove; (enfant etc) to kidnap, abduct; – **s'e.** vpr (tache) to come out; (vernis) to come off. ◆**—é** a (scène, danse etc) well-rendered. ◆**—ement** nm kidnapping, abduction; (d'un objet) removal; (des ordures) collection.

enliser (s') [sɑ̃lize] vpr (véhicule) & Fig to get bogged down (dans in).

enneigé [ɑ̃neʒe] a snow-covered. ◆**enneigement** nm snow coverage; **bulletin d'e.** snow report.

ennemi, -ie [ɛnmi] nmf enemy; – a (personne) hostile (de to); (pays etc) enemy-.

ennui [ɑ̃nɥi] nm boredom; (mélancolie) weariness; **un e.** (tracas) (some) trouble ou bother; **des ennuis** trouble(s), bother; **l'e., c'est que ...** the annoying thing is that ...

ennuy/er [ɑ̃nɥije] vt (agacer) to annoy, bother; (préoccuper) to bother; (fatiguer) to bore; – **s'e.** vpr to get bored. ◆**—é**

a (*air*) bored; **je suis e.** that annoys *ou* bothers me. ◆**ennuyeux, -euse** *a* (*fastidieux*) boring; (*contrariant*) annoying.

énonc/er [enɔse] *vt* to state, express. ◆**—é** *nm* (*de texte*) wording, terms; (*phrase*) Ling utterance.

enorgueillir [ɑnɔrgœjir] *vt* to make proud; **s'e. de** to pride oneself on.

énorme [enɔrm] *a* enormous, huge, tremendous. ◆**énormément** *adv* enormously, tremendously; **e. de** an enormous *ou* tremendous amount of. ◆**énormité** *nf* (*dimension*) enormity; (*faute*) (enormous) blunder.

enquérir (s') [sɑkerir] *vpr* **s'e. de** to inquire about.

enquête [ɑket] *nf* (*de police etc*) investigation; (*judiciaire, administrative*) inquiry; (*sondage*) survey. ◆**enquêter** *vi* (*police etc*) to investigate; (*sur un crime*) to investigate. ◆**enquêteur, -euse** *nmf* investigator.

enquiquiner [ɑkikine] *vt* Fam to annoy, bug.

enraciner (s') [sɑrasine] *vpr* to take root; **enraciné dans** (*personne, souvenir*) rooted in; **bien enraciné** (*préjugé etc*) deep-rooted.

enrag/er [ɑraʒe] *vi* **e. de faire** to be furious about doing; **faire e. qn** to get on s.o.'s nerves. ◆**—eant** *a* infuriating. ◆**—é** *a* (*chien*) rabid, mad; (*joueur etc*) Fam fanatical (*about*); **rendre/devenir e.** (*furieux*) to make/become furious.

enrayer [ɑreje] *vt* **e. qn** to check; — **s'e.** *vpr* (*fusil*) to jam.

enregistr/er [ɑrʒistre] *vt* **1** (*inscrire*) to record; (*sur registre*) to register; (*constater*) to note, register; (*faire*) **e.** (*bagages*) to register, Am check. **2** (*musique, émission etc*) to record. ◆**—ement** *nm* (*des bagages*) registration, Am checking; (*d'un acte*) registration; (*sur bande etc*) recording. ◆**—eur, -euse** *a* (*appareil*) recording-; **caisse enregistreuse** cash register.

enrhumer [ɑryme] *vt* **e. qn** to give s.o. a cold; **être enrhumé** to have a cold; — **s'e.** *vpr* to catch a cold.

enrich/ir [ɑriʃir] *vt* to enrich (**de** with); — **s'e.** *vpr* (*personne*) to get rich. ◆**—issement** *nm* enrichment.

enrober [ɑrɔbe] *vt* to coat (**de** in); **enrobé de chocolat** chocolate-coated.

enrôl/er [ɑrole] *vt*, — **s'e.** *vpr* to enlist. ◆**—ement** *nm* enlistment.

enrou/er (s') [sɑrwe] *vpr* to get hoarse. ◆**—é** *a* hoarse. ◆**—ement** [ɑrumɑ] *nm* hoarseness.

enrouler [ɑrule] *vt* (*fil etc*) to wind; (*tapis, cordage*) to roll up; **s'e.** (*autour de*) to roll *ou* wrap oneself in; **s'e. sur** *ou* **autour de qch** to wind round sth.

ensabler [ɑsɑble] *vt,* — **s'e.** *vpr* (*port*) to silt up.

ensanglanté [ɑsɑglɑte] *a* bloodstained.

enseigne [ɑsεɲ] **1** *nf* (*de magasin etc*) sign; **e. lumineuse** neon sign; **logés à la même e.** Fig in the same boat. **2** *nm* **e. de vaisseau** lieutenant, Am ensign.

enseign/er [ɑsεɲe] *vt* to teach; **e. qch à qn** to teach s.o. sth; — *vi* to teach. ◆**—ant, -ante** [-ɡnɑ, -ɑt] *a* (*corps*) teaching-; — *nmf* teacher. ◆**—ement** [-ɡnmɑ] *nm* education; (*action, métier*) teaching.

ensemble [ɑsɑbl] **1** *adv* together. **2** *nm* (*d'objets*) group, set; Math set; Mus ensemble; (*mobilier*) suite; (*vêtement féminin*) outfit; (*harmonie*) unity; **l'e. du personnel** the whole *ou* all of the staff; **l'e. des enseignants** all (of) the teachers; **dans l'e.** on the whole; **d'e.** (*vue etc*) general; **grand e.** (*quartier*) housing complex *ou* Am development; (*ville*) = new town, = Am planned community. ◆**ensemblier** *nm* (interior) decorator.

ensemencer [ɑsmɑse] *vt* (*terre*) to sow.

ensevelir [ɑsɑvlir] *vt* to bury.

ensoleillé [ɑsɔleje] *a* (*endroit, journée*) sunny.

ensommeillé [ɑsɔmeje] *a* sleepy.

ensorceler [ɑsɔrsale] *vt* (*envoûter, séduire*) to bewitch. ◆**ensorcellement** *nm* (*séduction*) spell.

ensuite [ɑsɥit] *adv* (*puis*) next, then; (*plus tard*) afterwards.

ensuivre* (s') [sɑsɥivr] *vpr* to follow, ensue; — *v imp* **il s'ensuit que** it follows that.

entacher [ɑtaʃe] *vt* (*honneur etc*) to sully, taint.

entaille [ɑtaj] *nf* (*fente*) notch; (*blessure*) gash, slash. ◆**entailler** *vt* to notch; to gash, slash.

entame [ɑtam] *nf* first slice.

entamer [ɑtame] *vt* (*pain, peau etc*) to start (into); (*bouteille, boîte etc*) to start (on); (*négociations etc*) to enter into, start; (*sujet*) to broach; (*capital*) to break *ou* eat into; (*métal, plastique*) to damage; (*résolution, réputation*) to shake.

entass/er [ɑtase] *vt,* — **s'e.** *vpr* (*objets*) to pile up, heap up; (*s'e.* **dans** (*passagers etc*) to crowd *ou* pack *ou* pile into; **ils s'entassaient sur la plage** they were crowded *ou* packed (together) on the beach.

◆—ement nm (tas) pile, heap; (de gens) crowding.

entend/re [ãtãdr] vt to hear; (comprendre) to understand; (vouloir) to intend, mean; e. parler de to hear of; e. dire que to hear (it said) that; e. raison to listen to reason; laisser e. à qn que to give s.o. to understand that; — s'e. vpr (être entendu) to be understood; (être compris) to be understood; s'e. (sur) (être d'accord) to agree (on); s'e. (avec qn) (s'accorder) to get on (with s.o.); on ne s'entend plus! (à cause du bruit etc) we can't hear ourselves speak!; il s'y entend (est expert) he knows all about that. ◆—u a (convenu) agreed; (compris) understood; (sourire, air) knowing; e.! all right!; bien e. of course. ◆—ement nm (faculté) understanding. ◆entente nf (accord) agreement, understanding; (bonne) e. (amitié) good relationship, harmony.

entériner [ãterine] vt to ratify.

enterrer [ãtere] vt (mettre en ou sous terre) to bury; (projet) Fig to scrap. ◆enterrement nm burial; (funérailles) funeral.

entêtant [ãtetã] a (enivrant) heady.

en-tête [ãtɛt] nm (de papier) heading; papier à en-tête headed paper.

entêt/er (s') [sãtete] vpr to persist (à faire in doing). ◆—é a (têtu) stubborn; (persévérant) persistent. ◆—ement [ãtɛtmã] nm stubbornness; (à faire qch) persistence.

enthousiasme [ãtuzjasm] nm enthusiasm. ◆enthousiasmer vt to fill with enthusiasm, enthuse; s'e. pour to be ou get enthusiastic over, enthuse over. ◆enthousiaste a enthusiastic.

enticher (s') [sãtiʃe] vpr s'e. de to become infatuated with.

entier, -ière [ãtje, -jɛr] 1 a (total) whole, entire; (absolu) absolute, complete, entire; (intact) intact; payer place entière to pay full price; le pays tout e. the whole ou entire country; — nm (unité) whole; en e. dans son e. in its entirety, completely. 2 a (caractère, personne) unyielding. ◆entièrement adv entirely.

entité [ãtite] nf entity.

entonner [ãtone] vt (air) to start singing.

entonnoir [ãtonwar] nm (ustensile) funnel.

entorse [ãtors] nf Méd sprain; e. à (règlement) infringement of.

entortill/er [ãtortije] vt e. qch autour de qch (papier etc) to wrap sth around sth; e. qn Fam to dupe s.o., get round s.o.; — s'e. vpr (lierre etc) to wind, twist. ◆—é a (phrase etc) convoluted.

entour [ãtur] vt to surround (de with;

(envelopper) to wrap (de in); e. qn de ses bras to put one's arms round s.o.; s'e. de to surround oneself with. ◆—age nm (proches) circle of family and friends.

entourloupette [ãturlupɛt] nf Fam nasty trick.

entracte [ãtrakt] nm Th interval, Am intermission.

entraide [ãtrɛd] nf mutual aid. ◆s'entraider [sãtrɛde] vpr to help each other.

entrailles [ãtraj] nfpl entrails.

entrain [ãtrɛ̃] nm spirit, liveliness; plein d'e. lively.

entrain/er [ãtrene] 1 vt (charrier) to sweep ou carry away; (roue) Tech to drive; (causer) to bring about; (impliquer) to entail, involve; e. qn (emmener) to lead ou draw s.o. (away); (de force) to lead s.o. (away); (attirer) Péj to lure s.o.; (charmer) to carry s.o. away; e. qn à faire (amener) to lead s.o. to do. 2 vt (athlète, cheval etc) to train (à for); — s'e. vpr to train oneself; Sp to train. ◆—ant [-ɛnã] a (musique) captivating. ◆—ement [-ɛnmã] nm 1 Sp training. 2 Tech drive; (élan) impulse. ◆—eur [-ɛnœr] nm (instructeur) Sp trainer, coach; (de cheval) trainer.

entrave [ãtrav] nf (obstacle) Fig hindrance (à to). ◆entraver vt to hinder, hamper.

entre [ãtr(ə)] prép between; (parmi) among(st); l'un d'e. vous one of you; (soit dit) e. nous between you and me; se dévorer e. eux (réciprocité) to devour each other; e. deux âges middle-aged; e. autres among other things; e. les mains de in the hands of.

entrebâill/er [ãtrəbaje] vt (porte) to open slightly. ◆—é a ajar, slightly open. ◆—eur nm e. (de porte) door chain.

entrechoquer (s') [sãtrəʃɔke] vpr (bouteilles etc) to knock against each other, chink.

entrecôte [ãtrəkot] nf (boned) rib steak.

entrecouper [ãtrəkupe] vt (entremêler) to punctuate (de with), intersperse (de with).

entrecroiser [ãtrəkrwaze] vt, — s'e. vpr (fils) to intersect; (routes) to intersect.

entre-deux-guerres [ãtrədøgɛr] nm inv inter-war period.

entrée [ãtre] nf (action) entry, entrance; (porte) entrance; (accès) entry, admission (de to); (vestibule) entrance hall, entry; (billet) ticket (of admission); Culin first course, entrée; (mot dans un dictionnaire etc) entry; (processus informatique) input; à son e. as he ou she came in; 'e. interdite' 'no entry', 'no admittance'; 'e. libre' 'admission free'; **e. en matière** (*d'un discours*) opening.

entrefaites (sur ces) [syrsezɑ̃trəfɛt] *adv* at that moment.

entrefilet [ɑ̃trəfilɛ] *nm Journ* (news) item.

entrejambes [ɑ̃trəʒɑ̃b] *nm inv* (*de pantalon*) crutch, crotch.

entrelacer [ɑ̃trəlase] *vt*, — **s'e.** *vpr* to intertwine.

entremêler [ɑ̃trəmele] *vt*, — **s'e.** *vpr* to intermingle.

entremets [ɑ̃trəmɛ] *nm* (*plat*) sweet, dessert.

entremetteur, -euse [ɑ̃trəmɛtœr, -øz] *nmf Péj* go-between.

entremise [ɑ̃trəmiz] *nf* intervention; **par l'e. de qn** through s.o.

entreposer [ɑ̃trəpoze] *vt* to store; *Jur* to bond. ◆**entrepôt** *nm* warehouse; (*de la douane*) *Jur* bonded warehouse.

entreprendre* [ɑ̃trəprɑ̃dr] *vt* (*travail, voyage etc*) to start on, undertake; **e. de faire** to undertake to do. ◆**entreprenant** *a* (*galant*) brash, forward. ◆**entrepreneur** *nm* (*en bâtiment*) (building) contractor. ◆**entreprise** *nf* 1 (*opération*) undertaking. 2 (*firme*) company, firm.

entrer [ɑ̃tre] *vi* (*aux être*) (*aller*) to go in, enter; (*venir*) to come in, enter; **e. dans** to go into; (*carrière*) to enter, go into; (*club*) to join, enter; (*détail, question*) to go into; (*pièce*) to come ou go into, enter; (*arbre etc*) *Aut* to crash into; **e. en action** to go ou get into action; **e. en ébullition** to start boiling; **entrez!** come in!; **faire/laisser e. qn** to show/let s.o. in.

entresol [ɑ̃trəsɔl] *nm* mezzanine (floor).

entre-temps [ɑ̃trətɑ̃] *adv* meanwhile.

entreten/ir* [ɑ̃trətnir] *vt* 1 (*voiture, maison etc*) to maintain; (*relations, souvenir*) to keep up; (*famille*) to keep, maintain; (*sentiment*) to entertain; **e. sa forme/sa santé** to keep fit/healthy. 2 **e. qn de** to talk to s.o. about; **s'e. de** to talk about (*avec with*). ◆**-u** (*femme*) kept. ◆**entretien** *nm* 1 (*de route, maison etc*) maintenance, upkeep; (*subsistance*) keep. 2 (*dialogue*) conversation; (*entrevue*) interview.

entre-tuer (s') [sɑ̃trətɥe] *vpr* to kill each other.

entrevoir* [ɑ̃trəvwar] *vt* (*rapidement*) to catch a glimpse of; (*pressentir*) to (fore)see.

entrevue [ɑ̃trəvy] *nf* interview.

entrouvrir* [ɑ̃truvrir] *vt*, — **s'e.** *vpr* to half-open. ◆**entrouvert** *a* (*porte, fenêtre*) ajar, half-open.

énumérer [enymere] *vt* to enumerate, list. ◆**énumération** *nf* enumeration.

envah/ir [ɑ̃vair] *vt* to invade; (*herbe etc*) to overrun; **e. qn** (*doute, peur etc*) to overcome s.o. ◆**-issant** *a* (*voisin etc*) intrusive. ◆**-issement** *nm* invasion. ◆**-isseur** *nm* invader.

enveloppe [ɑ̃vlɔp] *nf* (*pli*) envelope; (*de colis*) wrapping; (*de pneu*) casing; (*d'oreiller*) cover; (*apparence*) *Fig* exterior; **mettre sous e.** to put into an envelope. ◆**envelopp/er** *vt* to wrap (up); **e. la ville** (*brouillard etc*) to envelop the town; **enveloppé de mystère** shrouded ou enveloped in mystery; — **s'e.** *vpr* to wrap oneself (up) (**dans** in). ◆**-ant** *a* (*séduisant*) captivating.

envenimer [ɑ̃vnime] *vt* (*plaie*) to make septic; (*querelle*) *Fig* to envenom; — **s'e.** *vpr* to turn septic; *Fig* to become envenomed.

envergure [ɑ̃vɛrgyr] *nf* 1 (*d'avion, d'oiseau*) wingspan. 2 (*de personne*) calibre; (*ampleur*) scope, importance; **de grande e.** wide-ranging, far-reaching.

envers [ɑ̃vɛr] 1 *prép* towards, *Am* toward(s). 2 *nm* (*de tissu*) wrong side; (*de médaille*) reverse side; **à l'e.** (*chaussette*) inside out; (*pantalon*) back to front; (*à contresens, de travers*) the wrong way; (*en désordre*) upside down.

envie [ɑ̃vi] *nf* 1 (*jalousie*) envy; (*désir*) longing, desire; **avoir e. de qch** to want sth; **j'ai e. de faire** I feel like doing, I would like to do; **elle meurt d'e. de faire** she's dying ou longing to do. 2 (*peau autour des ongles*) hangnail. ◆**envier** *vt* to envy (*qch à qn* s.o. sth). ◆**envieux, -euse** *a & nmf* envious (person); **faire des envieux** to cause envy.

environ [ɑ̃virɔ̃] *adv* (*à peu près*) about; — *nmpl* outskirts, surroundings; **aux environs de** (*Paris, Noël, dix francs etc*) around, in the vicinity of. ◆**environn/er** *vt* to surround. ◆**-ant** *a* surrounding. ◆**-ement** *nm* environment.

envisag/er [ɑ̃vizaʒe] *vt* to consider; (*imaginer comme possible*) to envisage, *Am* envision, consider; **e. de faire** to consider ou contemplate doing. ◆**-eable** *a* thinkable.

envoi [ɑ̃vwa] *nm* (*action*) dispatch, sending; (*paquet*) consignment; **coup d'e.** *Fb* kick-off.

envol [ɑ̃vɔl] *nm* (*d'oiseau*) taking flight; (*d'avion*) take-off; **piste d'e.** *Av* runway. ◆**s'envol/er** *vpr* (*oiseau*) to fly away; (*avion*) to take off; (*emporté par le vent*) to blow away; (*espoir*) *Fig* to vanish. ◆—**ée** *nf* (*élan*) *Fig* flight.

envoût/er [ɑ̃vute] *vt* to bewitch. ◆—**ement** *nm* bewitchment.

envoy/er* [ɑ̃vwaje] *vt* to send; (*pierre*) to throw; (*gifle*) to give; **e. chercher qn** to send for s.o.; — **s'e.** *vpr Fam* (*travail etc*) to take on, do; (*repas etc*) to put *ou* stash away. ◆—**é, -ée** *nmf* envoy; *Journ* correspondent. ◆—**eur** *nm* sender.

épagneul, -eule [epaɲœl] *nmf* spaniel.

épais, -aisse [epɛ, -ɛs] *a* thick; (*personne*) thick-set; (*esprit*) dull. ◆**épaisseur** *nf* thickness; (*dimension*) depth. ◆**épaissir** *vt* to thicken; — *vi*, — **s'é.** *vpr* to thicken; (*grossir*) to fill out; **le mystère s'épaissit** the mystery is deepening.

épanch/er [epɑ̃ʃe] *vt* (*cœur*) *Fig* to pour out; — **s'é.** *vpr* (*parler*) to pour out one's heart, unbosom oneself. ◆—**ement** *nm* (*aveu*) outpouring; *Méd* effusion.

épanou/ir (s') [sepanwir] *vpr* (*fleur*) to open out; (*personne*) *Fig* to fulfil oneself, blossom (out); (*visage*) to beam. ◆—**i** *a* (*fleur, personne*) in full bloom; (*visage*) beaming. ◆—**issement** *nm* (*éclat*) full bloom; (*de la personnalité*) fulfilment.

épargne [eparɲ] *nf* saving (de of); (*qualité, vertu*) thrift; (*sommes d'argent*) savings. ◆**épargn/er** *vt* (*ennemi etc*) to spare; (*denrée rare etc*) to be sparing with; (*argent, temps*) to save; **e. qch à qn** (*ennuis, chagrin etc*) to spare s.o. sth. ◆—**ant, -ante** *nmf* saver.

éparpiller [eparpije] *vt*, — **s'é.** *vpr* to scatter; (*efforts*) to dissipate. ◆**épars** *a* scattered.

épaté [epate] *a* (*nez*) flat. ◆**épatement** *nm* flatness.

épat/er [epate] *vt Fam* to stun, astound. ◆—**ant** *a Fam* stunning, marvellous.

épaule [epol] *nf* shoulder. ◆**épauler** *vt* (*fusil*) to raise (to one's shoulder); **é. qn** (*aider*) to back s.o. up.

épave [epav] *nf* (*bateau, personne*) wreck; *pl* (*débris*) *Nau* (pieces of) wreckage.

épée [epe] *nf* sword; **un coup d'é.** a sword thrust.

épeler [eple] *vt* (*mot*) to spell.

éperdu [eperdy] *a* frantic, wild (de with); (*regard*) distraught. ◆—**ment** *adv* (*aimer*) madly; **elle s'en moque e.** she couldn't care less.

éperon [eprɔ̃] *nm* (de *cavalier, coq*) spur. ◆**éperonner** (*cheval, personne*) to spur (on).

épervier [epɛrvje] *nm* sparrowhawk.

éphémère [efemɛr] *a* a short-lived, ephemeral, transient.

épi [epi] *nm* (de *blé etc*) ear; (*mèche de cheveux*) tuft of hair.

épice [epis] *nf Culin* spice. ◆**épic/er** *vt* to spice. ◆—**é** *a* (*plat, récit etc*) spicy.

épicier, -ière [episje, -jɛr] *nmf* grocer. ◆**épicerie** *nf* (*magasin*) grocer's (shop); (*produits*) groceries.

épidémie [epidemi] *nf* epidemic. ◆**épidémique** *a* epidemic.

épiderme [epidɛrm] *nm Anat* skin.

épier [epje] *vt* (*observer*) to watch closely; (*occasion*) to watch out for; **é. qn** to spy on s.o.

épilepsie [epilɛpsi] *nf* epilepsy. ◆**épileptique** *a* et *nmf* epileptic.

épiler [epile] *vt* (*jambe*) to remove unwanted hair from; (*sourcil*) to pluck.

épilogue [epilɔg] *nm* epilogue.

épinard [epinar] *nm* (*plante*) spinach; *pl* (*feuilles*) *Culin* spinach.

épine [epin] *nf* **1** (de *buisson*) thorn; (*d'animal*) spine, prickle. **2 é. dorsale** *Anat* spine. ◆**épineux, -euse** *a* (*tige, question*) thorny.

épingle [epɛ̃gl] *nf* pin; **é. de nourrice, é. de sûreté** safety pin; **é. à linge** clothes peg, *Am* clothes pin; **virage en é. à cheveux** hairpin bend; **tiré à quatre épingles** very spruce. ◆**épingler** *vt* to pin; **é. qn** (*arrêter*) *Fam* to nab s.o.

épique [epik] *a* epic.

épiscopal, -aux [episkɔpal, -o] *a* episcopal.

épisode [epizɔd] *nm* episode; **film à épisodes** serial. ◆**épisodique** *a* occasional, episodic; (*accessoire*) minor.

épitaphe [epitaf] *nf* epitaph.

épithète [epitɛt] *nf* epithet; *Gram* attribute.

épître [epitr] *nf* epistle.

éploré [eplɔre] *a* (*personne, air*) tearful.

éplucher [eplyʃe] *vt* (*pommes de terre*) to peel; (*salade*) to clean, pare; (*texte*) *Fig* to dissect. ◆**épluchure** *nf* peeling.

éponge [epɔ̃ʒ] *nf* sponge. ◆**éponger** *vt* (*liquide*) to sponge up, mop up; (*carrelage*) to sponge (down), mop; (*dette*) *Fin* to absorb; **s'é. le front** to mop one's brow.

épopée [epɔpe] *nf* epic.

époque [epɔk] *nf* (*date*) time, period; (*historique*) age; **meubles d'é.** period furniture; **à l'é.** at the *ou* that time.

épouse [epuz] *nf* wife, *Jur* spouse.

épouser [epuze] *vt* **1 é. qn** to marry s.o. **2** (*opinion etc*) to espouse; (*forme*) to assume, adopt.

épousseter [epuste] *vt* to dust.

époustoufler [epustufle] *vt Fam* to astound.

épouvantail [epuvɑ̃taj] *nm* (*à oiseaux*) scarecrow.

épouvante [epuvɑ̃t] *nf* (*peur*) terror; (*appréhension*) dread; **d'é.** (*film etc*) horror-. ◆**épouvant/er** *vt* to terrify. ◆**—able** *a* terrifying; (*très mauvais*) appalling.

époux [epu] *nm* husband, *Jur* spouse; *pl* husband and wife.

éprendre* (s') [seprɑ̃dr] *vpr* **s'é. de qn** to fall in love with s.o. ◆**épris** *a* in love (**de** with).

épreuve [eprœv] *nf* (*essai, examen*) test; *Sp* event, heat; *Phot* print; *Typ* proof; (*malheur*) ordeal, trial; **mettre à l'é.** to put to the test. ◆**éprouv/er** [epruve] *vt* to test, try; (*sentiment etc*) to experience, feel; **é. qn** (*mettre à l'épreuve*) to put s.o. to the test; (*faire souffrir*) to distress s.o. ◆**—ant** *a* (*pénible*) trying. ◆**—é** *a* (*sûr*) well-tried.

éprouvette [epruvɛt] *nf* test tube; **bébé é.** test tube baby.

épuis/er [epɥize] *vt* (*personne, provisions, sujet*) to exhaust; **— s'é.** *vpr* (*réserves, patience*) to run out; **s'é. à faire** (*patience*) to exhaust oneself doing. ◆**—ant** *a* exhausting. ◆**—é** *a* exhausted; (*édition*) out of print; (*marchandise*) out of stock. ◆**—ement** *nm* exhaustion.

épuisette [epɥizɛt] *nf* fishing net (*on pole*).

épurer [epyre] *vt* to purify; (*personnel etc*) to purge; (*goût*) to refine. ◆**épuration** *nf* purification; purging; refining.

équateur [ekwatœr] *nm* equator; **sous l'é.** at *ou* on the equator. ◆**équatorial, -aux** *a* equatorial.

équation [ekwasjɔ̃] *nf Math* equation.

équerre [ekɛr] *nf* **é.** (*à dessiner*) setsquare, *Am* triangle; **d'é.** straight, square.

équestre [ekɛstr] *a* (*figure etc*) equestrian; (*exercices etc*) horseriding-.

équilibre [ekilibr] *nm* balance; **tenir** *ou* **mettre en é.** to balance (**sur** on); **se tenir en é.** to keep one's balance; **perdre l'é.** to lose one's balance. ◆**équilibrer** *vt* (*charge, budget etc*) to balance; **— s'é.** *vpr* (*équipes etc*) to (counter)balance each other; (*comptes*) to balance.

équinoxe [ekinɔks] *nm* equinox.

équipage [ekipaʒ] *nm Nau Av* crew.

équipe [ekip] *nf* team; (*d'ouvriers*) gang; **é. de nuit** night shift; **é. de secours** search party; **faire é. avec** to team up with. ◆**équipier, -ière** *nf* team member.

équipée [ekipe] *nf* escapade.

équip/er [ekipe] *vt* to equip (**de** with); **— s'é.** *vpr* to equip oneself. ◆**—ement** *nm* equipment; (*de camping, ski etc*) gear, equipment.

équitation [ekitasjɔ̃] *nf* (horse) riding.

équité [ekite] *nf* fairness. ◆**équitable** *a* fair, equitable. ◆**équitablement** *adv* fairly.

équivalent [ekivalɑ̃] *a* & *nm* equivalent. ◆**équivalence** *nf* equivalence. ◆**équivaloir** *vi* **é. à** to be equivalent to.

équivoque [ekivɔk] *a* (*ambigu*) equivocal; (*douteux*) dubious; **— *nf* ambiguity.

érable [erabl] *nm* (*arbre, bois*) maple.

érafler [erafle] *vt* to graze, scratch. ◆**éraflure** *nf* graze, scratch.

éraillée [eraje] *a* (*voix*) rasping.

ère [ɛr] *nf* era.

érection [erɛksjɔ̃] *nf* (*de monument etc*) erection.

éreinter [erɛ̃te] *vt* (*fatiguer*) to exhaust; (*critiquer*) to tear to pieces, slate, slam.

ergot [ergo] *nm* (*de coq*) spur.

ergoter [ergɔte] *vi* to quibble, cavil.

ériger [eriʒe] *vt* to erect; **s'é.** to set oneself up as.

ermite [ermit] *nm* hermit.

érosion [erozjɔ̃] *nf* erosion. ◆**éroder** *vt* to erode.

érotique [erɔtik] *a* erotic. ◆**érotisme** *nm* eroticism.

err/er [ere] *vi* to wander, roam. ◆**—ant** *a* wandering, roving; (*animal*) stray.

erreur [erœr] *nf* (*faute*) error, mistake; (*action blâmable, opinion fausse*) error; **par e.** by mistake, in error; **dans l'e.** mistaken. ◆**erroné** *a* erroneous.

ersatz [erzats] *nm* substitute.

éructer [erykte] *vi Litt* to belch.

érudit, -ite [erydi, -it] *a* scholarly, erudite; **— *nmf* scholar. ◆**érudition** *nf* scholarship, erudition.

éruption [erypsjɔ̃] *nf* (*de volcan, colère*) eruption (**de** of); *Méd* rash.

ès [ɛs] *prép* of; **licencié/docteur ès lettres** = BA/PhD.

es *voir* **être**.

escabeau, -x [eskabo] *nm* stepladder, (pair of) steps; (*tabouret*) stool.

escadre [eskadr] *nf Nau Av* fleet, squadron. ◆**escadrille** *nf* (*unité*) *Av* flight. ◆**escadron** *nm* squadron.

escalade [eskalad] *nf* climbing; (*de prix*) & *Mil* escalation. ◆**escalader** *vt* to climb, scale.

escale [eskal] *nf Av* stop(over); *Nau* port of call; **faire e. à** *Av* to stop (over) at; *Nau* to put in at; **vol sans e.** non-stop flight.

escalier [eskalje] *nm* staircase, stairs; **e. mé-**

canique *ou* roulant escalator; **e. de secours** fire escape.

escalope [ɛskalɔp] *nf Culin* escalope.

escamot/er [ɛskamɔte] *vt* (*faire disparaître*) to make vanish; (*esquiver*) to dodge. ◆**—able** *a Av Tech* retractable.

escapade [ɛskapad] *nf* (*excursion*) jaunt; **faire une e.** to run off.

escargot [ɛskargo] *nm* snail.

escarmouche [ɛskarmuʃ] *nf* skirmish.

escarpé [ɛskarpe] *a* steep. ◆**escarpement** *nm* (*côte*) steep slope.

escarpin [ɛskarpɛ̃] *nm* (*soulier*) pump, court shoe.

escient [ɛsjã] *nm* **à bon e.** discerningly, wisely.

esclaffer (s') [sɛsklafe] *vpr* to roar with laughter.

esclandre [ɛsklãdr] *nm* (noisy) scene.

esclave [ɛsklav] *nmf* slave; **être l'e. de** to be a slave to. ◆**esclavage** *nm* slavery.

escompte [ɛskɔ̃t] *nm* discount; **taux d'e.** bank rate. ◆**escompter** *vt* **1** (*espérer*) to anticipate (*faire* doing), expect (**faire** to do). **2** *Com* to discount.

escorte [ɛskɔrt] *nf Mil Nau etc* escort. ◆**escorter** *vt* to escort.

escouade [ɛskwad] *nf* (*petite troupe*) squad.

escrime [ɛskrim] *nf Sp* fencing. ◆**escrimeur, -euse** *nmf* fencer.

escrimer (s') [sɛskrime] *vpr* to slave away (**à faire** at doing).

escroc [ɛskro] *nm* swindler, crook. ◆**escroquer** *vt* **e. qn** to swindle s.o.; **e. qch à qn** to swindle s.o. out of sth. ◆**escroquerie** *nf* swindling; **une e.** a swindle.

espace [ɛspas] *nm* space; **e. vert** garden, park. ◆**espacer** *vt* to space out; **espacés d'un mètre** (spaced out) one metre apart; — **s'e.** (*maisons, visites etc*) to become less frequent.

espadon [ɛspadɔ̃] *nm* swordfish.

espadrille [ɛspadrij] *nf* rope-soled sandal.

Espagne [ɛspaɲ] *nf* Spain. ◆**espagnol, -ole** *a* Spanish; — *nmf* Spaniard; — *nm* (*langue*) Spanish.

espèce [ɛspɛs] **1** *nf* (*race*) species; (*genre*) kind, sort; **c'est une e. d'idiot** he's a silly fool; **e. d'idiot!/de maladroit!/***etc* (you) silly fool!/oaf!/*etc.* **2** *nfpl* (*argent*) **en espèces** in cash.

espérance [ɛsperãs] *nf* hope; **avoir des espérances** to have expectations; **e. de vie** life expectancy. ◆**espérer** *vt* to hope for; **e. que** to hope that; **e. faire** to hope to do; — *vi* to hope; **e. en qn/qch** to trust in s.o./sth.

espiègle [ɛspjɛgl] *a* mischievous. ◆**es-**

pièglerie *nf* mischievousness; (*farce*) mischievous trick.

espion, -onne [ɛspjɔ̃, -ɔn] *nmf* spy. ◆**espionnage** *nm* espionage, spying. ◆**espionner** *vt* to spy on; — *vi* to spy.

esplanade [ɛsplanad] *nf* esplanade.

espoir [ɛspwar] *nm* hope; **avoir de l'e.** to have hope(s); **sans e.** (*cas etc*) hopeless.

esprit [ɛspri] *nm* (*attitude, fantôme*) spirit; (*intellect*) mind; (*humour*) wit; (*être humain*) person; **avoir de l'e.** to be witty; **cette idée m'est venue à l'e.** this idea crossed my mind.

esquimau, -aude, -aux [ɛskimo, -od, -o] **1** *a & nmf* Eskimo. **2** *nm* (*glace*) choc-ice (*on a stick*).

esquinter [ɛskɛ̃te] *vt Fam* (*voiture etc*) to damage, bash; (*critiquer*) to slam, pan (*author, film etc*); **s'e. la santé** to damage one's health; **s'e. à faire** (*se fatiguer*) to wear oneself out doing.

esquisse [ɛskis] *nf* (*croquis, plan*) sketch. ◆**esquisser** *vt* to sketch; **e. un geste** to make a (slight) gesture.

esquive [ɛskiv] *nf Boxe* dodge; **e. de** (*question*) dodging of, evasion of. ◆**esquiver** *vt* (*coup, problème*) to dodge; — **s'e.** *vpr* to slip away.

essai [ɛse] *nm* (*épreuve*) test, trial; (*tentative*) try, attempt; *Rugby* try; *Littér* essay; **à l'e.** (*objet*) *Com* on trial, on approval; **pilote d'e.** test pilot; **période d'e.** trial·period.

essaim [ɛsɛ̃] *nm* swarm (*of bees etc*).

essayer [ɛseje] *vt* to try (**de faire** to do); (*vêtement*) to try on; (*méthode*) to try (out); **s'e. à qch/à faire** to try one's hand at sth/at doing. ◆**essayage** *nm* (*de costume*) fitting.

essence [ɛsãs] *nf* **1** (*extrait*) *Ch Culin* essence; *Aut* petrol, *Am* gas; **poste d'e.** filling station. **2** *Phil* essence. **3** (*d'arbres*) species. ◆**essentiel, -ielle** *a* essential (**à, pour** for); — *nm* **l'e.** the main thing *ou* point; (*quantité*) the main part (**de** of). ◆**essentiellement** *adv* essentially.

essieu, -x [ɛsjø] *nm* axle.

essor [ɛsɔr] *nm* (*de pays, d'entreprise etc*) development, rise, expansion; **en plein e.** (*industrie etc*) booming.

essor/er [ɛsɔre] *vt* (*linge*) to wring; (*dans une essoreuse*) to spin-dry; (*dans une machine à laver*) to spin. ◆**—euse** *nf* (*à main*) wringer; (*électrique*) spin dryer.

essouffler [ɛsufle] *vt* to make (*s.o.*) out of breath; — **s'e.** *vpr* to get out of breath.

essuyer [ɛsɥije] **1** *vt* to wipe; — **s'e.** *vpr* to wipe oneself. **2** *vt* (*subir*) to suffer. ◆**es-**

suie-glace nm inv windscreen wiper, Am windshield wiper. ◆**essuie-mains** nm inv (hand) towel.

est¹ [ɛ] voir **être**.

est² [ɛst] nm east; – a inv (côte) east(ern); d'e. (vent) east(erly); de l'e. eastern; Allemagne de l'E. East Germany. ◆**e.-allemand, -ande** a & nmf East German.

estafilade [ɛstafilad] nf gash, slash.

estampe [ɛstɑ̃p] nf (gravure) print.

estamper [ɛstɑ̃pe] vt (rouler) Fam to swindle.

estampille [ɛstɑ̃pij] nf mark, stamp.

esthète [ɛstɛt] nmf aesthete, Am esthete. ◆**esthétique** a aesthetic, Am esthetic.

esthéticienne [ɛstetisjɛn] nf beautician.

estime [ɛstim] nf esteem, regard. ◆**estim/er** vt (objet) to value; (juger) to consider (que that); (calculer) to estimate; (apprécier) to appreciate; **e. qn** to have high regard for s.o.; **s'e. heureux/etc** to consider oneself happy/etc. ◆**-able** a respectable. ◆**estimation** nf (de mobilier etc) valuation; (calcul) estimation.

estival, -aux [ɛstival, -o] a (période etc) summer-. ◆**estivant, -ante** nmf holidaymaker, Am vacationer.

estomac [ɛstɔma] nm stomach.

estomaquer [ɛstɔmake] vt Fam to flabbergast.

estomper [ɛstɔ̃pe] vt (rendre flou) to blur; – **s'e.** vpr to become blurred.

estrade [ɛstrad] nf (tribune) platform.

estropi/er [ɛstrɔpje] vt to cripple, maim. ◆**-é, -ée** nmf cripple.

estuaire [ɛstɥɛr] nm estuary.

esturgeon [ɛstyrʒɔ̃] nm (poisson) sturgeon.

et [e] conj and; **vingt et un/etc** twenty-one/etc.

étable [etabl] nf cowshed.

établi [etabli] nm Menuis (work)bench.

établ/ir [etablir] vt to establish; (installer) to set up; (plan, chèque, liste) to draw up; – **s'é.** vpr (habiter) to settle; (épicier etc) to set up shop as, set (oneself) up as. ◆**-issement** nm (action, bâtiment, institution) establishment; Com firm, establishment; **é. scolaire** school.

étage [etaʒ] nm (d'immeuble) floor, storey, Am story; (de fusée etc) stage; **à l'é.** upstairs; **au premier é.** on the first ou Am second floor. ◆**étager** vt, – **s'é.** vpr (rochers, maisons etc) to range above one another.

étagère [etaʒɛr] nf shelf; (meuble) shelving unit.

étai [etɛ] nm Tech prop, stay.

étain [etɛ̃] nm (métal) tin; (de gobelet etc) pewter.

était [etɛ] voir **être**.

étal, pl étals [etal] nm (au marché) stall.

étalage [etalaʒ] nm display; (vitrine) display window; **faire é. de** to make a show ou display of. ◆**étalagiste** nmf window dresser.

étaler [etale] vt (disposer) to lay out; (luxe etc) & Com to display; (crème, beurre etc) to spread; (vacances) to stagger; – **s'é.** vpr (s'affaler) to sprawl; (tomber) Fam to fall flat; **s'é. sur** (congés, paiements etc) to be spread over.

étalon [etalɔ̃] nm **1** (cheval) stallion. **2** (modèle) standard.

étanche [etɑ̃ʃ] a watertight; (montre) waterproof.

étancher [etɑ̃ʃe] vt (sang) to stop the flow of; (soif) to quench, slake.

étang [etɑ̃] nm pond.

étant [etɑ̃] voir **être**.

étape [etap] nf (de voyage etc) stage; (lieu) stop(over); **faire é. à** to stop off ou over at.

état [eta] nm **1** (condition, manière d'être) state; (registre, liste) statement, list; **en bon é.** in good condition; **en é.** de **faire** in a position to do; **é. d'esprit** state ou frame of mind; **é. d'âme** mood; **é. civil** civil status (birth, marriage, death etc); **é. de choses** situation, state of affairs; **à l'é. brut** in a raw state; **de son é.** (métier) by trade; **faire é. de** (mention) to mention, put forward. **2** É. (nation) State; **homme d'É.** statesman. ◆**étatisé** a a state-controlled, state-owned.

état-major [etamaʒɔr] nm (pl **états-majors**) (d'un parti etc) senior staff.

États-Unis [etazyni] nmpl É.-Unis (d'Amérique) United States (of America).

étau, -x [eto] nm Tech vice, Am vise.

étayer [eteje] vt to prop up, support.

été¹ [ete] nm summer.

été² [ete] voir **être**.

éteindre* [etɛ̃dr] vt (feu, cigarette etc) to put out, extinguish; (lampe etc) to turn ou switch off; (dette, espoir) to extinguish; – vt to switch off; – **s'é.** vpr (feu) to go out; (personne) to pass away; (race) to die out. ◆**éteint** a (feu) out; (volcan, race, amour) extinct; (voix) faint.

étendard [etɑ̃dar] nm (drapeau) standard.

étend/re [etɑ̃dr] vt (nappe) to spread (out); (beurre) to spread; (linge) to hang out; (agrandir) to extend; **é. le bras/etc** to stretch out one's arm/etc; **é. qn** to stretch s.o. out; – **s'é.** vpr (personne) to stretch (oneself) out; (*plaine etc*) to stretch; (*feu*) to spread; (*pouvoir*) to extend; **s'é. sur** (*sujet*) to dwell on. **◆—u** *a* (*forêt, vocabulaire etc*) extensive; (*personne*) stretched out. **◆—ue** *nf* (*importance*) extent; (*surface*) area; (*d'eau*) expanse, stretch.

éternel, -elle [etɛrnɛl] *a* eternal. **◆éternellement** *adv* eternally, for ever. **◆éterniser** *vt* to perpetuate; — **s'é.** *vpr* (*débat etc*) to drag on endlessly; (*visiteur etc*) to stay for ever. **◆éternité** *nf* eternity.

éternu/er [etɛrnɥe] *vi* to sneeze. **◆—ement** [-ymã] *nm* sneeze.

êtes [ɛt] *voir* **être**.

éther [etɛr] *nm* ether.

Éthiopie [etjɔpi] *nf* Ethiopia. **◆éthiopien, -ienne** *a* & *nmf* Ethiopian.

éthique [etik] *a* ethical; — *nf Phil* ethics; **l'é. puritaine** the Puritan ou WASP ethic.

ethnie [ɛtni] *nf* ethnic group. **◆ethnique** *a* ethnic.

étinceler [etɛ̃sle] *vi* to sparkle. **◆étincelle** *nf* spark. **◆étincellement** *nm* sparkle.

étioler (s') [setjɔle] *vpr* to wilt, wither.

étiqueter [etikte] *vt* to label. **◆étiquette** *nf* **1** (*marque*) label. **2** (*protocole*) (diplomatic ou court) etiquette.

étirer [etire] *vt* to stretch; — **s'é.** *vpr* to stretch (oneself).

étoffe [etɔf] *nf* material, cloth, fabric; (*de héros etc*) *Fig* stuff (de of).

étoffer [etɔfe] *vt*, — **s'é.** *vpr* to fill out.

étoile [etwal] *nf* **1** star; **à la belle é.** in the open. **2** é. **de mer** starfish. **◆étoilé** *a* (*ciel, nuit*) starry; (*vitre*) cracked (*star-shaped*); **é. de** (*rubis etc*) studded with; **la bannière étoilée** *Am* the Star-Spangled Banner.

étonn/er [etɔne] *vt* to surprise, astonish; — **s'é.** *vpr* to be surprised ou astonished (de qch at sth, que (+ sub) that). **◆—ant** *a* (*ahurissant*) surprising; (*remarquable*) amazing. **◆—ement** *nm* surprise, astonishment.

étouff/er [etufe] *vt* (*tuer*) to suffocate, smother; (*bruit*) to muffle; (*feu*) to smother; (*révolte, sentiment*) to stifle; (*scandale*) to hush up; **é. qn** (*chaleur*) to choke s.o.; (*aliment, colère*) to choke s.o.; — *vi* to suffocate; **on étouffe!** it's stifling!; **é. de colère** to choke with anger. — **s'é.** *vpr* (*en mangeant*) to choke, gag (**sur, avec** on); (*mourir*) to suffocate. **◆—ant** *a* (*air*) stifling. **◆—ement** *nm Méd* suffocation.

étourd/ir [eturdir] *vt* to stun, daze; (*vertige,*

vin) to make dizzy; (*abrutir*) to deafen. **◆—issant** *a* (*bruit*) deafening; (*remarquable*) stunning. **◆—issement** *nm* dizziness; (*syncope*) dizzy spell.

étourneau, -x [eturno] *nm* starling.

étrange [etrɑ̃ʒ] *a* strange, odd. **◆—ment** *adv* strangely, oddly. **◆étrangeté** *nf* strangeness, oddness.

étranger, -ère [etrɑ̃ʒe, -ɛr] *a* (*d'un autre pays*) foreign; (*non familier*) strange (à to); **il m'est é.** he's unknown to me; — *nmf* foreigner; (*inconnu*) stranger; **à l'é.** abroad; **de l'é.** from abroad.

étrangl/er [etrɑ̃gle] *vt* **é. qn** (*tuer*) to strangle s.o.; (*col, aliment*) to choke s.o.; — **s'é.** *vpr* (*de colère, en mangeant etc*) to choke. **◆—é** *a* (*voix*) choking; (*passage*) constricted. **◆—ement** *nm* (*d'une victime*) strangulation. **◆—eur, -euse** *nmf* strangler.

être* [ɛtr] **1** *vi* to be; **il est tailleur** he's a tailor; **est-ce qu'elle vient?** is she coming?; **il vient, n'est-ce pas?** he's coming, isn't he?; **est-ce qu'il aime le thé?** does he like tea?; **nous sommes dix** there are ten of us; **nous sommes le dix** today is the tenth (of the month); **où en es-tu?** how far have you got?; **il a été à Paris** (*est allé*) he's been to Paris; **elle est de Paris** she's from Paris; **elle est de la famille** she's one of the family; **c'est à faire tout de suite** it must be done straight away; **c'est à lui** it's his; **cela étant** that being so. **2** *v aux* (*avec venir, partir etc*) to have; **elle est déjà arrivée** she has already arrived. **3** *nm* (*personne*) being; **ê. humain** human being; **les êtres chers** the loved ones.

étreindre [etrɛ̃dr] *vt* to grip; (*ami*) to embrace. **◆étreinte** *nf* grip; (*amoureuse etc*) embrace.

étrenner [etrene] *vt* to use ou wear for the first time.

étrennes [etrɛn] *nfpl* New Year gift; (*gratification*) = Christmas box ou tip.

étrier [etrije] *nm* stirrup.

étriper (s') [setripe] *vpr Fam* to fight (each other) to the kill.

étriqué [etrike] *a* (*vêtement*) tight, skimpy; (*esprit, vie*) narrow.

étroit [etrwa] *a* narrow; (*vêtement*) tight; (*parenté, collaboration etc*) close; (*discipline*) strict; **être à l'é.** to be cramped. **◆étroitement** *adv* (*surveiller etc*) closely. **◆étroitesse** *nf* narrowness; closeness; **é. d'esprit** narrow-mindedness.

étude [etyd] *nf* **1** (*action, ouvrage*) study; (*salle*) *Scol* study room; **é.** (*projet*) under consideration; **faire des études de** (*médecine etc*) to study. **2** (*de notaire etc*) office. ◆**étudier** *vti* to study.

étui [etɥi] *nm* (*à lunettes, à cigarettes etc*) case; (*de revolver*) holster.

étymologie [etimɔlɔʒi] *nf* etymology.

eu, eue [y] *voir* **avoir.**

eucalyptus [økaliptys] *nm* (*arbre*) eucalyptus.

Eucharistie [økaristi] *nf Rel* Eucharist.

euh! [ø] *int* hem!, er!, well!

euphémisme [øfemism] *nm* euphemism.

euphorie [øfɔri] *nf* euphoria.

eurent [yr] *voir* **avoir.**

euro- [øro] *préf* Euro-.

Europe [ørɔp] *nf* Europe. ◆**européen, -enne** *a & nmf* European.

eut [y] *voir* **avoir.**

euthanasie [øtanazi] *nf* euthanasia.

eux [ø] *pron* (*sujet*) they; (*complément*) them; (*réfléchi, emphase*) themselves. ◆**eux-mêmes** *pron* themselves.

évacuer [evakɥe] *vt* to evacuate; (*liquide*) to drain off. ◆**évacuation** *nf* evacuation.

évad/er (s') [evade] *vpr* to escape (*de* from). ◆**-é, -ée** *nmf* escaped prisoner.

évaluer [evalɥe] *vt* (*chiffre, foule etc*) to estimate; (*meuble etc*) to value. ◆**évaluation** *nf* estimation; valuation.

évangile [evɑ̃ʒil] *nm* gospel; **É. Gospel.** ◆**évangélique** *a* evangelical.

évanou/ir (s') [evanwir] *vpr Méd* to black out, faint; (*espoir, crainte etc*) to vanish. ◆**-i** *a Méd* unconscious. ◆**-issement** *nm* (*syncope*) blackout, fainting fit; (*disparition*) vanishing.

évaporer (s') [evapore] *vpr Ch* to evaporate; (*disparaître*) *Fam* to vanish into thin air. ◆**évaporation** *nf* evaporation.

évasif, -ive [evazif, -iv] *a* evasive.

évasion [evazjɔ̃] *nf* escape (**d'un lieu** from a place, **devant un danger**/*etc* from a danger/*etc*); (*hors de la réalité*) escapism; **é. fiscale** tax evasion.

évêché [eveʃe] *nm* (*territoire*) bishopric, see.

éveil [evɛj] *nm* awakening; **en é.** on the alert; **donner l'é. à** to alert.

éveill/er [eveje] *vt* (*susciter*) to arouse; **é. qn** to awake(n) s.o.; **— s'é.** *vpr* to awake(n) (*à* to); (*sentiment, idée*) to be aroused. ◆**-é** *a* awake; (*vif*) lively, alert.

événement [evenmɑ̃] *nm* event.

éventail [evɑ̃taj] *nm* **1** (*instrument portatif*) fan; **en é.** (*orteils*) spread out. **2** (*choix*) range.

éventer [evɑ̃te] *vt* **1** (*secret*) to discover. **2**

é. qn to fan s.o. **3 s'é.** *vpr* (*bière, vin etc*) to turn stale. ◆**-é-a** (*bière, vin etc*) stale.

éventrer [evɑ̃tre] *vt* (*animal etc*) to disembowel; (*sac*) to rip open.

éventuel, -elle [evɑ̃tɥɛl] *a* possible. ◆**éventuellement** *adv* possibly. ◆**éventualité** *nf* possibility; **dans l'é. de** in the event of.

évêque [evɛk] *nm* bishop.

évertuer (s') [evertɥe] *vpr* **s'é. à faire** to do one's utmost to do, struggle to do.

éviction [eviksjɔ̃] *nf* (*de concurrent etc*) & *Pol* ousting.

évident [evidɑ̃] *a* obvious, evident (**que** that). ◆**évidemment** [-amɑ̃] *adv* certainly, obviously. ◆**évidence** *nf* obviousness; **une é.** an obvious fact; **nier l'é.** to deny the obvious; **être en é.** to be conspicuous *ou* in evidence; **mettre en é.** (*fait*) to underline.

évider [evide] *vt* to hollow out.

évier [evje] *nm* (*kitchen*) sink.

évincer [evɛ̃se] *vt* (*concurrent etc*) & *Pol* to oust.

éviter [evite] *vt* to avoid (**de faire** doing); **é. qch à qn** to spare *ou* save s.o. sth.

évolu/er [evolɥe] *vi* **1** (*changer*) to develop, change; (*société, idée, situation*) to evolve. **2** (*se déplacer*) to move; *Mil* to manœuvre, *Am* maneuver. ◆**-é-a** (*pays*) advanced; (*personne*) enlightened. ◆**évolution** *nf* **1** (*changement*) development; evolution. **2** (*d'un danseur etc*) & *Mil* movement.

évoquer [evoke] *vt* to evoke, call to mind. ◆**évocateur, -trice** *a* evocative. ◆**évocation** *nf* evocation, recalling.

ex [ɛks] *nmf* (*mari, femme*) *Fam* ex.

ex- [ɛks] *préf* ex-; **ex-mari** ex-husband.

exacerber [ɛgzasɛrbe] *vt* (*douleur etc*) to acerbate.

exact [ɛgzakt] *a* (*précis*) exact, accurate; (*juste, vrai*) correct, exact, right; (*ponctuel*) punctual. ◆**exactement** *adv* exactly. ◆**exactitude** *nf* exactness; accuracy; correctness; punctuality.

exaction [ɛgzaksjɔ̃] *nf* exaction.

ex aequo [ɛgzeko] *adv* **être classés ex ae.** *Sp* to tie, be equally placed.

exagér/er [ɛgzaʒere] *vt* to exaggerate; **– vi** (*parler*) to exaggerate; (*agir*) to overdo it, go too far. ◆**-é-a** excessive. ◆**-ément** *adv* excessively. ◆**exagération** *nf* exaggeration; (*excès*) excessiveness.

exalt/er [ɛgzalte] *vt* (*glorifier*) to exalt; (*animer*) to fire, stir. ◆**-ant** *a* stirring. ◆**-é, -ée** *a* (*sentiment*) impassioned,

wild; – *nmf Péj* fanatic. ◆**exaltation** *nf*
(*délire*) elation, exaltation.

examen [egzamɛ̃] *nm* examination; *Scol* ex-
am(ination); **e. blanc** *Scol* mock ex-
am(ination). ◆**examinateur, -trice** *nmf*
Scol examiner. ◆**examiner** *vt* (*considérer,
regarder*) to examine.

exaspérer [egzaspere] *vt* (*énerver*) to aggravate, exasperate. ◆**exaspération** *nf* exasperation, aggravation.

exaucer [egzose] *vt* (*désir*) to grant; **e. qn** to
grant s.o.'s wish(es).

excavation [ekskavasjɔ̃] *nf* (*trou*) hollow.

excéder [eksede] *vt* **1** (*dépasser*) to exceed. **2**
é. qn (*fatiguer, énerver*) to exasperate s.o.
◆**excédent** *nm* surplus, excess; **e. de**
bagages excess luggage *ou* *Am* baggage.
◆**excédentaire** *a* (*poids etc*) excess-.

excellent [ekselɑ̃] *a* excellent. ◆**excellence** *nf* **1** excellence; **par e.** above all else
ou all others. **2 E.** (*titre*) Excellency.
◆**exceller** *vi* to excel (**en qch** in sth, **à faire**
in doing).

excentrique [eksɑ̃trik] **1** *a & nmf* (*original*)
eccentric. **2** *a* (*quartier*) remote. ◆**excentricité** *nf* (*bizarrerie*) eccentricity.

excepté [eksepte] *prép* except. ◆**excepter**
vt to except. ◆**exception** *nf* exception; **à**
l'e. de except (for), with the exception of;
faire e. to be an exception. ◆**exceptionnel, -elle** *a* exceptional. ◆**exceptionnellement** *adv* exceptionally.

excès [eksɛ] *nm* excess; (*de table*)
over-eating; **e. de vitesse** *Aut* speeding.
◆**excessif, -ive** *a* excessive. ◆**excessivement** *adv* excessively.

excit/er [eksite] *vt* (*faire naître*) to excite,
rouse, stir; **e. qn** (*mettre en colère*) to provoke s.o.; (*agacer*) to annoy s.o.; (*enthousiasmer*) to thrill s.o., excite s.o.; **e. qn à**
faire to incite s.o. to do; **– s'e.** *vpr*
(*nerveux, enthousiaste*) to get excited.
◆**—ant** *a* exciting; – *nm* stimulant. ◆**—é**
a excited. ◆**—able** *a* excitable. ◆**excitation** *nf* (*agitation*) excitement; **e. à** (*haine
etc*) incitement to.

exclamer (s') [seksklame] *vpr* to exclaim.
◆**exclamatif, -ive** *a* exclamatory. ◆**exclamation** *nf* exclamation.

excl/ure* [eksklyr] *vt* (*écarter*) to exclude
(**de** from); (*chasser*) to expel (**de** from); **e.**
qch (*rendre impossible*) to preclude sth.
◆**—u** (*solution etc*) out of the question;
(*avec une date*) excluded. ◆**exclusif, -ive**
a (*droit, modèle, préoccupation*) exclusive.
◆**exclusion** *nf* exclusion. ◆**exclusivement** *adv* exclusively. ◆**exclusivité** *nf*

Com exclusive rights; **en e.** (*film*) having an
exclusive showing (**à** at).

excommunier [ekskɔmynje] *vt* to excommunicate. ◆**excommunication** *nf* excommunication.

excrément(s) [ekskremɑ̃] *nm(pl)* excrement.

excroissance [ekskrwasɑ̃s] *nf* (out)growth.

excursion [ekskyrsjɔ̃] *nf* outing, excursion,
tour; (*à pied*) hike.

excuse [ekskyz] *nf* (*prétexte*) excuse; *pl* (*regrets*) apology; **des excuses** an apology;
faire ses excuses to apologize (**à** to); **toutes**
mes excuses (my) sincere apologies.
◆**excuser** *vt* (*justifier, pardonner*) to excuse (**qn d'avoir fait, qn de faire** s.o. for doing); **– s'e.** *vpr* to apologize (**de** for, **auprès**
de to); **excusez-moi!, je m'excuse!** excuse
me!

exécrer [egzekre] *vt* to loathe. ◆**exécrable**
a atrocious.

exécut/er [egzekyte] *vt* **1** (*projet, tâche etc*)
to carry out, execute; (*statue, broderie etc*)
to produce; (*jouer*) *Mus* to perform. **2 e. qn**
(*tuer*) to execute s.o. **3 s'e.** *vpr* to comply.
◆**—ant, -ante** *nmf* *Mus* performer.
◆**—able** *a* practicable. ◆**exécutif, -ive**
a (*pouvoir*) executive; – *nm* **l'e.** *Pol* the executive. ◆**exécution** *nf* **1** carrying out, execution; production; performance. **2** (*mise
à mort*) execution.

exemple [egzɑ̃pl] *nm* example; **par e.** for example, for instance; (**ça**) **par e.!** *Fam* good
heavens!; **donner l'e.** to set an example (**à**
to). ◆**exemplaire 1** *a* exemplary. **2** *nm*
(*livre etc*) copy.

exempt [egzɑ̃] *a* **e. de** (*dispensé de*) exempt
from; (*sans*) free from. ◆**exempter** *vt* to
exempt (**de** from). ◆**exemption** *nf* exemption.

exercer [egzerse] *vt* (*muscles, droits*) to exercise; (*autorité, influence*) to exert (**sur** over);
(*métier*) to carry on, work at; (*profession*)
to practise; **e. qn à** (*couture etc*) to train s.o.
in; **e. qn à faire** to train s.o. to do; – *vi*
(*médecin*) to practise; **– s'e.** *vpr* (*influence
etc*) to be exerted; (*sportif etc*) **s'e. à qch**
(*sportif etc*) to practise; **s'e. à faire** to
practise doing. ◆**exercice** *nm* (*physique etc*) & *Scol* exercise; *Mil* drill, exercise; (*de métier*) prac-
tice; **l'e. de** (*pouvoir etc*) the exercise of; **en**
e. (*fonctionnaire*) in office; (*médecin*) in
practice; **faire de l'e., prendre de l'e.** to
(take) exercise.

exhaler [egzale] *vt* (*odeur etc*) to give off.

exhaustif, -ive [egzostif, -iv] *a* exhaustive.

exhiber [egzibe] *vt* to exhibit, show.

◆**exhibition** nf exhibition. ◆**exhibition-niste** nmf exhibitionist.

exhorter [εgzɔrte] vt to urge, exhort (à faire to do).

exhumer [εgzyme] vt (cadavre) to exhume; (vestiges) to dig up.

exiger [εgziʒe] vt to demand, require (de from, que (+ sub) that). ◆**exigeant** a demanding, exacting. ◆**exigence** nf demand, requirement; **d'une grande e.** very demanding.

exigu, -uë [εgzigy] a (appartement etc) cramped, tiny. ◆**exiguïté** nf crampedness.

exil [εgzil] nm (expulsion) exile. ◆**exil/er** vt to exile; — **s'e.** vpr to go into exile. ◆**-é, -ée** nmf (personne) exile.

existence [εgzistãs] nf existence. ◆**existentialisme** nm existentialism. ◆**exist/er** vi to exist; – v imp **il existe** ... (sing) there is ... ; (pl) there are ... . ◆**-ant** a existing.

exode [εgzɔd] nm exodus.

exonérer [εgzonere] vt to exempt (de from). ◆**exonération** nf exemption.

exorbitant [εgzɔrbitã] a exorbitant.

exorciser [εgzɔrsize] vt to exorcize. ◆**exorcisme** nm exorcism.

exotique [εgzɔtik] a exotic. ◆**exotisme** nm exoticism.

expansif, -ive [εkspãsif, -iv] a expansive, effusive.

expansion [εkspãsjõ] nf Com Phys Pol expansion; **en (pleine) e.** (fast ou rapidly) expanding.

expatri/er (s') [εkspatrije] vpr to leave one's country. ◆**-é, -ée** a & nmf expatriate.

expectative [εkspεktativ] nf **être dans l'e.** to be waiting to see what happens.

expédient [εkspedjã] nm (moyen) expedient.

expédier [εkspedje] vt **1** (envoyer) to send off. **2** (affaires, client) to dispose of quickly, dispatch. ◆**expéditeur, -trice** nmf sender. ◆**expéditif, -ive** a expeditious, quick. ◆**expédition** nf **1** (envoi) dispatch. **2** (voyage) expedition.

expérience [εksperjãs] nf (pratique, connaissance) experience; (scientifique) experiment; **faire l'e. de qch** to experience sth. ◆**expérimental, -aux** a experimental. ◆**expérimentation** nf experimentation. ◆**expériment/er** vt Phys Ch to try out, experiment with; – vi to experiment. ◆**-é** a experienced.

expert [εkspεr] a expert, skilled (en in); – nm expert; (d'assurances) valuer. ◆**e.-comptable** nm (pl **experts-comptables**) = chartered accountant, = Am certified public accountant. ◆**expertise** nf (évaluation) (expert) appraisal; (compétence) expertise.

expier [εkspje] vt (péchés, crime) to expiate, atone for. ◆**expiation** nf expiation (de of).

expir/er [εkspire] **1** vti to breathe out. **2** vi (mourir) to pass away; (finir, cesser) to expire. ◆**-ant** a dying. ◆**expiration** nf (échéance) expiry, Am expiration.

explicite [εksplisit] a explicit. ◆**-ment** adv explicitly.

expliquer [εksplike] vt to explain (à to); – **s'e.** vpr to explain oneself; (discuter) to talk things over, have it out (avec with); **s'e. qch** (comprendre) to understand sth; **ça s'explique** that is understandable. ◆**explicable** a understandable. ◆**explicatif, -ive** a explanatory. ◆**explication** nf explanation; (mise au point) discussion.

exploit [εksplwa] nm exploit, feat.

exploit/er [εksplwate] vt **1** (champs) to farm; (ferme, entreprise) to run; (mine) to work; (situation) Fig to exploit. **2** (abuser de) Péj to exploit (s.o.). ◆**-ant, -ante** nmf farmer. ◆**exploitation** nf **1** Péj exploitation. **2** farming; running; working; (entreprise) concern; (agricole) farm.

explorer [εksplɔre] vt to explore. ◆**explorateur, -trice** nmf explorer. ◆**exploration** nf exploration.

exploser [εksploze] vi (gaz etc) to explode; (bombe) to blow up, explode; **e. (de colère)** Fam to explode, blow up; **faire e.** (bombe) to explode. ◆**explosif, -ive** a & nm explosive. ◆**explosion** nf explosion; (de colère, joie) outburst.

exporter [εkspɔrte] vt to export (vers to, de from). ◆**exportateur, -trice** nmf exporter; – a exporting. ◆**exportation** nf (produit) export; (action) export(ation), exporting.

expos/er [εkspoze] vt (présenter, soumettre) & Phot to expose (à to); (marchandises) to display; (tableau etc) to exhibit; (idée, théorie) to set out; (vie, réputation) to risk, endanger; **s'e. à** to expose oneself to. ◆**-ant, -ante** nmf exhibitor. ◆**-é 1** a **bien e.** (édifice) having a good exposure; **e. au sud** facing south. **2** nm (compte rendu) account (de of); (discours) talk; Scol paper. ◆**exposition** nf (de marchandises etc) display; (salon) exhibition; (au danger etc) &

Phot exposure (à to); *(de maison etc)* aspect.

exprès¹ [ekspre] *adv* on purpose, intentionally; *(spécialement)* specially.

exprès², **-esse** [ekspres] **1** *a (ordre, condition)* express. **2** *a inv* **lettre/colis e.** express letter/parcel. ◆**expressément** *adv* expressly.

express [ekspres] *a & nm inv (train)* express; *(café)* espresso.

expressif, -ive [ekspresif, -iv] *a* expressive. ◆**expression** *nf (phrase, mine etc)* expression. ◆**exprimer** *vt* to express; **— s'e.** *vpr* to express oneself.

exproprier [eksproprije] *vt* to seize the property of by compulsory purchase.

expulser [ekspylse] *vt* to expel (**de** from); *(joueur)* *Sp* to send off; *(locataire)* to evict. ◆**expulsion** *nf* expulsion; eviction; sending off.

expurger [ekspyrʒe] *vt* to expurgate.

exquis [ekski] *a* exquisite.

extase [ekstaz] *nf* ecstasy, rapture. ◆**s'extasi/er** *vpr* to be in raptures (**sur** over, about). ◆**—é** *a* ecstatic.

extensible [ekstɑ̃sibl] *a* expandable. ◆**extension** *nf* extension; *(essor)* expansion.

exténuer [ekstenɥe] *vt (fatiguer)* to exhaust. ◆**exténuation** *nf* exhaustion.

extérieur [eksterjœr] *a (monde etc)* outside; *(surface)* outer; *(signe)* outward, external; *(politique)* foreign; **e. à** external to; **— nm** outside, exterior; **à l'e. (de)** outside; **à l'e. (match)** away; **en e.** *Cin* on location. ◆**—ement** *adv* externally; *(en apparence)* outwardly. ◆**extérioriser** *vt* to express.

exterminer [ekstermine] *vt* to exterminate, wipe out. ◆**extermination** *nf* extermination.

externe [ekstern] **1** *a* external. **2** *nmf Scol* day pupil; *Méd* non-resident hospital doctor, *Am* extern.

extincteur [ekstɛ̃ktœr] *nm* fire extinguisher. ◆**extinction** *nf (de feu)* extinguishing; *(de voix)* loss; *(de race)* extinction.

extirper [ekstirpe] *vt* to eradicate.

extorquer [ekstorke] *vt* to extort (**à** from). ◆**extorsion** *nf* extortion.

extra [ekstra] **1** *a inv (très bon) Fam* top-quality. **2** *nm inv (repas)* (extra-special) treat; *(serviteur)* extra hand *ou* help.

extra- [ekstra] *préf* extra-. ◆**e.-fin** *a* extra-fine. ◆**e.-fort** *a* extra-strong.

extradition [ekstradisjɔ̃] *nf* extradition. ◆**extrader** *vt* to extradite.

extraire* [ekstrer] *vt* to extract (**de** from); *(charbon)* to mine. ◆**extraction** *nf* extraction. ◆**extrait** *nm* extract; **un e. de naissance** a (copy of one's) birth certificate.

extraordinaire [ekstraordiner] *a* extraordinary. ◆**—ment** *adv* exceptionally; *(très, bizarrement)* extraordinarily.

extravagant [ekstravagɑ̃] *a* extravagant. ◆**extravagance** *nf* extravagance.

extrême [ekstrem] *a* extreme; **— nm** extreme; **pousser à l'e.** to take *ou* carry to extremes. ◆**—ment** *adv* extremely. ◆**extrémiste** *a & nmf* extremist. ◆**extrémité** *nf (bout)* extremity, end; *pl (excès)* extremes.

exubérant [egzyberɑ̃] *a* exuberant. ◆**exubérance** *nf* exuberance.

exulter [egzylte] *vi* to exult, rejoice. ◆**exultation** *nf* exultation.

F

F, f [ef] *nm* F, f.

F *abrév* franc(s).

fable [fɑbl] *nf* fable.

fabrique [fabrik] *nf* factory; **marque de f.** trade mark.

fabriquer [fabrike] *vt (objet)* to make; *(industriellement)* to manufacture; *(récit)* *Péj* to fabricate, make up; **qu'est-ce qu'il fabrique?** *Fam* what's he up to? ◆**fabricant, -ante** *nmf* manufacturer. ◆**fabrication** *nf* manufacture; *(artisanale)* making; **de f. française** of French make.

fabuleux, -euse [fabylø, -øz] *a (légendaire, incroyable)* fabulous.

fac [fak] *nf Univ Fam* = **faculté 2.**

façade [fasad] *nf (de bâtiment)* front, façade; *(apparence)* *Fig* pretence, façade; **de f.** *(luxe etc)* sham.

face [fas] *nf (visage)* face; *(de cube etc)* side; *(de monnaie)* head; **de f.** *(photo)* full-face; *(vue)* front; **faire f. à** *(situation etc)* to face, face up to; **en f.** opposite; **en f. de** opposite, facing; *(en présence de)* in front of; **en f. d'un problème, f. à un problème** in the face of a problem, faced with a problem; **f. à** (*vis-à-vis de*) facing; **regarder qn en f.** to look s.o. in the face; **f. à f.** face to face; **un f. à f.** *TV* a face to face encounter; **sauver/perdre la f.** to save/lose face.

facétie [fasesi] *nf* joke, jest. ◆**facétieux, -euse** [-sjø, -øz] *a* (*personne*) facetious.

facette [faset] *nf* (*de diamant, problème etc*) facet.

fâch/er [faʃe] *vt* to anger; **— se f.** *vpr* to get angry ou annoyed (*contre qn*); **se f. avec qn** (*se brouiller*) to fall out with s.o. ◆**—é** *a* (*air*) angry; (*amis*) on bad terms; **f. avec** *ou* **contre qn** angry ou annoyed with s.o.; **f. de qch** sorry about sth. ◆**fâcherie** *nf* quarrel. ◆**fâcheux, -euse** *a* (*nouvelle etc*) unfortunate.

facho [faʃo] *a & nmf Fam* fascist.

facile [fasil] *a* easy; (*caractère, humeur*) easygoing; (*banal*) *Péj* facile; **c'est f. à faire** it's easy to do; **il est f. de faire ça** it's easy to do that; **f. à vivre** easy to get along with, easygoing. ◆**—ment** *adv* easily. ◆**facilité** *nf* (*simplicité*) easiness; (*aisance*) ease; **facilités de paiement** *Com* easy terms; **avoir de la f.** to be gifted; **avoir toutes facilités pour** to have every facility ou opportunity to. ◆**faciliter** *vt* to facilitate, make easier.

façon [fasɔ̃] *nf* 1 way; **la f. dont elle parle** the way (in which) she talks; **f. (d'agir)** behaviour; **je n'aime pas ses façons** I don't like his *ou* her manners *ou* ways; **une f. de parler** a manner of speaking; **à la f. de** in the fashion of; **de toute f.** anyway, anyhow; **de f.** à so as to; **de f. générale** generally speaking; **à ma f.** my way, (in) my own way; **faire des façons** to make a fuss; **table f. chêne** imitation oak table. 2 (*coupe de vêtement*) cut, style. ◆**façonner** *vt* (*travailler, former*) to fashion, shape; (*fabriquer*) to manufacture.

facteur [faktœr] *nm* 1 postman, *Am* mailman. 2 (*élément*) factor. ◆**factrice** *nf Fam* postwoman.

factice [faktis] *a* false, artificial; (*diamant*) imitation-.

faction [faksjɔ̃] *nf* 1 (*groupe*) *Pol* faction. 2 **de f.** *Mil* on guard (duty), on sentry duty.

facture [faktyr] *nf Com* invoice, bill. ◆**facturer** *vt* to invoice, bill.

facultatif, -ive [fakyltatif, -iv] *a* optional; **arrêt f.** request stop.

faculté [fakylte] *nf* 1 (*aptitude*) faculty; (*possibilité*) freedom (**de faire** to do); **f. de travail** a capacity for work. 2 *Univ* faculty; **à la f.** *Fam* at university, *Am* at school.

fadaises [fadɛz] *nfpl* twaddle, nonsense.

fade [fad] *a* insipid. ◆**fadasse** *a Fam* wishy-washy.

fagot [fago] *nm* bundle (of firewood).

fagoter [fagɔte] *vt Péj* to dress, rig out.

faible [fɛbl] *a* weak, feeble; (*bruit, voix*) faint; (*vent, quantité, chances*) slight; (*revenus*) small; **f. en anglais/etc** poor at English/etc; **— nm** (*personne*) weakling; **les faibles** the weak; **avoir un f. pour** to have a weakness ou a soft spot for. ◆**faiblement** *adv* weakly; (*légèrement*) slightly; (*éclairer, parler*) faintly. ◆**faiblesse** *nf* weakness, feebleness; faintness; slightness; small-ness; (*défaut, syncope*) weakness. ◆**faiblir** *vi* (*forces*) to weaken; (*courage, vue*) to fail; (*vent*) to slacken.

faïence [fajɑ̃s] *nf* (*matière*) earthenware; *pl* (*objets*) crockery, earthenware.

faille [faj] *nf Géol* fault; *Fig* flaw.

faillible [fajibl] *a* fallible.

faillir* [fajir] *vi* **1 il a failli tomber** he almost *ou* nearly fell. **2 f. à** (*devoir*) to fail in.

faillite [fajit] *nf Com* bankruptcy; *Fig* fail-ure; **faire f.** to go bankrupt.

faim [fɛ̃] *nf* hunger; **avoir f.** to be hungry; **donner f. à qn** to make s.o. hungry; **manger à sa f.** to eat one's fill; **mourir de f.** to die of starvation; (*avoir très faim*) *Fig* to be starv-ing.

fainéant, -ante [feneɑ̃, -ɑ̃t] *a* idle; *— nmf* idler. ◆**fainéanter** *vi* to idle. ◆**fainéan-tise** *nf* idleness.

faire* [fɛr] **1** *vt* (*bruit, pain, faute etc*) to make; (*devoir, dégâts, ménage etc*) to do; (*rêve, chute*) to have; (*sourire, grognement*) to give; (*promenade, sieste*) to have; (*guerre*) to wage, make; **ça fait dix mètres de large** (*mesure*) it's ten metres wide; **2 et 2 font 4** 2 and 2 are 4; **ça fait dix francs** *ou* comes to ten francs; **qu'a-t-il fait (de)?** what's he done (with)?; **que f.?** what's to be done?; **f. du tennis/du piano/etc** to play tennis/the piano/etc; **f. l'idiot** to act *ou* play the fool; **ça ne fait rien** that doesn't matter; **comment as-tu fait pour . . . ?** how did you manage to . . . ?; **il ne fait que travailler** he does nothing but work, he keeps on working; **je ne fais que d'arriver** I've just arrived; **oui, fit-elle** yes, she said. **2** *vi* (*agir*) to do; (*paraître*) to look; **il fait vieux** he looks old; **il fera un bon médecin** he'll be *ou* make a good doctor; **elle ferait bien de partir** she'd do well to leave. **3** *v imp* **il fait beau/froid/etc** it's fine/cold/etc; **quel temps fait-il?** what's the weather like?; **ça fait deux ans que je ne l'ai pas vu** I haven't seen him for two years, it's (been) two years since I saw him. **4** *v aux* (+ *inf*): **f. construire une maison** to have *ou* get a house built (à qn, par qn by s.o.); **f. crier/souffrir/etc** qn to make s.o. shout/suffer/etc; **se f. couper les cheveux** to have one's hair cut; **se f. craindre/obéir/etc** to make oneself feared/obeyed/etc; **se f. tuer/renverser/etc** to be killed/knocked down/etc. **5 se f.** *vpr* (*fabrication*) to be made; (*activité*) to be done; **se f. des illusions** to have illusions; **se f. des amis** to make friends; **se f. vieux/etc** (*devenir*) to get old/etc; **il se fait tard** it's getting late; **comment se fait-il que?** how is it that?; **se f. à** to get used to, adjust to; **ne t'en fais pas!** don't worry!

faire-part [fɛrpar] *nm inv* (*de mariage etc*) announcement.

faisable [fəzabl] *a* feasible.

faisan [fəzɑ̃] *nm* (*oiseau*) pheasant.

faisandé [fəzɑ̃de] *a* (*gibier*) high.

faisceau, -x [fɛso] *nm* (*lumineux*) beam; (*de tiges etc*) bundle.

fait [fɛ] **1** *voir* **faire**; – *a* (*fromage*) ripe; (*homme*) grown; (*yeux*) made up; (*ongles*) polished; **tout f.** ready made; **bien f.** (*jambes, corps etc*) shapely; **c'est bien f.!** it serves you right! **2** *nm* event, occurrence; (*donnée, réalité*) fact; **prendre sur le f.** *Jur* to catch in the act; **du f. de** on account of; **f. divers** *Journ* (miscellaneous) news item; **au f.** (*à propos*) by the way; **aller au f.** to get to the point; **faits et gestes** actions; **en f.** in fact; **en f. de** in the matter of.

faîte [fɛt] *nm* (*haut*) top; (*apogée*) *Fig* height.

faites [fɛt] *voir* **faire**.

faitout [fɛtu] *nm* stewing pot, casserole.

falaise [falɛz] *nf* cliff.

falloir [falwar] **1** *v imp* **il faut qch/qn** I, you, we *etc* need sth/s.o.; **il lui faut un stylo** he *ou* she needs a pen; **il faut partir/etc** I, you, we *etc* have to go/etc; **il faut que je parte** I have to go; **il faudrait qu'elle reste** she ought to stay; **il faut un jour** it takes a day (**pour faire**) (to do); **comme il faut** proper(ly); **s'il le faut** if need be. **2 s'en f.** *vpr* **peu s'en est fallu qu'il ne pleure** he almost cried; **tant s'en faut** far from it.

falsifier [falsifje] *vt* (*texte etc*) to falsify. ◆**falsification** *nf* falsification.

famé (mal) [malfame] *a* of ill repute.

famélique [famelik] *a* ill-fed, starving.

fameux, -euse [famø, -øz] *a* famous; (*excellent*) *Fam* first-class; **pas f.** *Fam* not much good.

familial, -aux [familjal, -o] *a* family-.

familier, -ière [familje, -jɛr] *a* (*bien connu*) familiar (à to); (*amical*) friendly, informal; (*locution*) colloquial, familiar; **f. avec qn** (over)familiar with s.o.; – *nm* (*de club etc*) regular visitor. ◆**familiariser** *vt* to familiarize (**avec with**); – **se f.** *vpr* to familiarize oneself (**avec with**). ◆**familiarité** *nf* familiarity; *pl Péj* liberties. ◆**familièrement** *adv* familiarly; (*parler*) informally.

famille [famij] *nf* family; (*dîner etc*) with one's family; **un père de f.** a family man.

famine [famin] *nf* famine.

fan [fã] *nm* (*admirateur*) *Fam* fan.

fana [fana] *nmf Fam* fan; **être f. de** to be crazy about.

fanal, -aux [fanal, -o] *nm* lantern, light.

fanatique [fanatik] *a* fanatical; – *nmf* fanatic. ◆**fanatisme** *nm* fanaticism.

faner (se) [səfane] *vpr* (*fleur, beauté*) to fade. ◆**-é** *a* faded.

fanfare [fãfar] *nf* (*orchestre*) brass band; (*air, musique*) fanfare.

fanfaron, -onne [fãfarɔ̃, -ɔn] *a* boastful; – *nmf* braggart.

fange [fãʒ] *nf Litt* mud, mire.

fanion [fanjɔ̃] *nm* (*drapeau*) pennant.

fantaisie [fãtezi] *nf* (*caprice*) fancy, whim; (*imagination*) imagination, fantasy; (**de**) **f.** (*bouton etc*) fancy. ◆**fantaisiste** *a* (*pas sérieux*) fanciful; (*irrégulier*) unorthodox.

fantasme [fãtasm] *nm Psy* fantasy. ◆**fantasmer** *vi* to fantasize (**sur** about).

fantasque [fãtask] *a* whimsical.

fantassin [fãtasɛ̃] *nm Mil* infantryman.

fantastique [fãtastik] *a* (*imaginaire, excellent*) fantastic.

fantoche [fãtɔʃ] *nm* & *a* puppet.

fantôme [fãtom] *nm* ghost, phantom; – *a* (*ville, train*) ghost-; (*firme*) bogus.

faon [fã] *nm* (*animal*) fawn.

faramineux, -euse [faraminø, -øz] *a Fam* fantastic.

farce¹ [fars] *nf* practical joke, prank; *Th* farce; **magasin de farces et attrapes** joke shop. ◆**farceur, -euse** *nmf* (*blagueur*) wag, joker.

farce² [fars] *nf Culin* stuffing. ◆**farcir** *vt* **1** *Culin* to stuff. **2 se f. qn/qch** *Fam* to put up with s.o./sth.

fard [far] *nm* make-up; ◆**farder** *vt* (*vérité*) to camouflage; – **se f.** *vpr* (*se maquiller*) to make up.

fardeau, -x [fardo] *nm* burden, load.

farfelu, -ue [farfəly] *a Fam* crazy, bizarre; – *nmf Fam* weirdo.

farine [farin] *nf* (*de blé*) flour; **f. d'avoine**

oatmeal. ◆**farineux, -euse** *a Péj* floury, powdery.

farouche [faruʃ] *a* **1** (*timide*) shy, unsociable; (*animal*) easily scared. **2** (*violent, acharné*) fierce. ◆**—ment** *adv* fiercely.

fart [far(t)] *nm* (ski) wax. ◆**farter** *vt* (*skis*) to wax.

fascicule [fasikyl] *nm* volume.

fasciner [fasine] *vt* to fascinate. ◆**fascination** *nf* fascination.

fascisme [faʃism] *nm* fascism. ◆**fasciste** *a* & *nmf* fascist.

fasse(nt) [fas] *voir* faire.

faste [fast] *nm* ostentation, display.

fastidieux, -euse [fastidjø, -øz] *a* tedious, dull.

fatal, mpl -als [fatal] *a* (*mortel*) fatal; (*inévitable*) inevitable; (*moment, ton*) fateful; **c'était f.!** it was bound to happen! ◆**—ement** *adv* inevitably. ◆**fataliste** *a* fatalistic. *— nmf* fatalist. ◆**fatalité** *nf* (*destin*) fate. ◆**fatidique** *a* (*jour, date*) fateful.

fatigue [fatig] *nf* tiredness, fatigue, weariness. ◆**fatigant** *a* (*épuisant*) tiring; (*ennuyeux*) tiresome. ◆**fatigu/er** *vt* to tire, fatigue; (*yeux*) to strain; (*importuner*) to annoy; (*raser*) to bore; *— vi* (*moteur*) to strain; **— se f.** *vpr* (*se lasser*) to get tired, tire (**de** of); (*travailler*) to tire oneself out (**à faire** doing). ◆**—é** *a* tired, weary (**de** of).

fatras [fatra] *nm* jumble, muddle.

faubourg [fobur] *nm* suburb. ◆**faubourien, -ienne** *a* (*accent etc*) suburban, common.

fauché [foʃe] *a* (*sans argent*) *Fam* broke.

fauch/er [foʃe] *vt* **1** (*herbe*) to mow; (*blé*) to reap; (*abattre, renverser*) *Fig* to mow down. **2** (*voler*) *Fam* to snatch, pinch. ◆**—euse** *nf* (*machine*) reaper.

faucille [fosij] *nf* (*instrument*) sickle.

faucon [fokɔ̃] *nm* (*oiseau*) falcon, hawk; (*personne*) *Fig* hawk.

faudra, faudrait [fodra, fodrɛ] *voir* falloir.

faufiler (se) [safofile] *vpr* to edge ou inch one's way (**dans** through; **into**; **entre** between).

faune [fon] *nf* wildlife, fauna; (*gens*) *Péj* set.

faussaire [fosɛr] *nm* (*faux-monnayeur*) forger.

fausse [fos] *voir* faux[1]. ◆**faussement** *adv* falsely.

fausser [fose] *vt* (*sens, réalité etc*) to distort; (*clé etc*) to buckle; **f. compagnie à qn** to give s.o. the slip.

fausseté [foste] *nf* (*d'un raisonnement etc*) falseness; (*hypocrisie*) duplicity.

faut [fo] *voir* falloir.

faute [fot] *nf* (*erreur*) mistake; (*responsabilité*) fault; (*délit*) offence; (*péché*) sin; **Fb** foul; **c'est ta f.** it's your fault, you're to blame; **f. de temps/etc** for lack of time/etc; **f. de mieux** for want of anything better; **en f.** at fault; **sans f.** without fail. ◆**fautif, -ive** *a* (*personne*) at fault; (*erroné*) faulty.

fauteuil [fotœj] *nm* armchair; (*de président*) chair; **f. d'orchestre** *Th* seat in the stalls; **f. roulant** wheelchair; **f. pivotant** swivel chair.

fauteur [fotœr] *nm* **f. de troubles** troublemaker.

fauve [fov] **1** *a* & *nm* (*couleur*) fawn. **2** *nm* wild beast; **chasse aux fauves** big game hunting.

faux[1], fausse [fo, fos] *a* (*inauthentique*) false; (*pas vrai*) untrue, false; (*pas exact*) wrong; (*monnaie*) counterfeit, forged; (*bijou, marbre*) imitation-, fake; (*voix*) out of tune; (*col*) detachable; *— adv* (*chanter*) out of tune; *— nm* (*contrefaçon*) forgery; **le f.** the false, the untrue. ◆**f.-filet** *nm Culin* sirloin. ◆**f.-fuyant** *nm* subterfuge. ◆**f.-monnayeur** *nm* counterfeiter.

faux[2] [fo] *nf* (*instrument*) scythe.

faveur [favœr] *nf* favour; **en f. de** (*au profit de*) in favour of; **de f.** (*billet*) complimentary; (*traitement, régime*) preferential. ◆**favorable** *a* favourable (**à** to). ◆**favori, -ite** *a* & *nmf* favourite. ◆**favoriser** *vt* to favour. ◆**favoritisme** *nm* favouritism.

favoris [favori] *nmpl* sideburns, side whiskers.

fébrile [febril] *a* feverish. ◆**fébrilité** *nf* feverishness.

fécond [fekɔ̃] *a* (*femme, idée etc*) fertile. ◆**féconder** *vt* to fertilize. ◆**fécondité** *nf* fertility.

fécule [fekyl] *nf* starch. ◆**féculents** *nmpl* (*aliments*) carbohydrates.

fédéral, -aux [federal, -o] *a* federal. ◆**fédération** *nf* federation. ◆**fédérer** *vt*

fée [fe] *nf* fairy. ◆**féerie** *nf Th* fantasy extravaganza; *Fig* fairy-like spectacle. ◆**féerique** *a* fairy(-like), magical.

feindre* [fɛ̃dr] *vt* to feign, sham; **f. de faire** to pretend to do. ◆**feint** *a* feigned, sham. ◆**feinte** *nf* sham, pretence; *Boxe Mil* feint.

fêler [fele] *vt*, **— se f.** *vpr* (*tasse*) to crack. ◆**fêlure** *nf* crack.

félicité [felisite] *nf* bliss, felicity.

féliciter [felisite] *vt* to congratulate (**qn de** *ou* **sur** s.o. on); **se f. de** to congratulate oneself on. ◆**félicitations** *nfpl* congratulations (**pour** on).

félin [felẽ] *a & nm* feline.

femelle [fəmɛl] *a & nf* (*animal*) female.

féminin [feminẽ] *a* (*prénom, hormone etc*) female; (*trait, intuition etc*) & *Gram* feminine; (*mode, revue, équipe etc*) women's. ◆**féministe** *a & nmf* feminist. ◆**féminité** *nf* femininity.

femme [fam] *nf* woman; (*épouse*) wife; **f. médecin** woman doctor; **f. de chambre** (chamber)maid; **f. de ménage** cleaning lady, maid; **bonne f.** *Fam* woman.

fémur [femyr] *nm* thighbone, femur.

fendiller (se) [səfɑ̃dije] *vpr* to crack.

fendre [fɑ̃dr] *vt* (*bois etc*) to split; (*foule*) to force one's way through; (*onde, air*) to cleave; (*cœur*) *Fig* to break, rend; **— se f.** *vpr* (*se fissurer*) to crack.

fenêtre [f(ə)nɛtr] *nf* window.

fenouil [fənuj] *nm Bot Culin* fennel.

fente [fɑ̃t] *nf* (*de tirelire, palissade, jupe etc*) slit; (*de rocher*) split, crack.

féodal, -aux [feɔdal, -o] *a* feudal.

fer [fɛr] *nm* iron; (*partie métallique de qch*) metal (part); **de f., en f.** (*outil etc*) iron-; **fil de f.** wire; **f. à cheval** horseshoe; **f.** (**à repasser**) iron; **f. à friser** curling tongs; **f. de lance** *Fig* spearhead; **de f.** (*santé*) *Fig* cast-iron; (*main, volonté*) *Fig* iron-. ◆**fer-blanc** *nm* (*pl* **fers-blancs**) tin(-plate).

fera, ferait [fəra, fərɛ] *voir* **faire**.

férié [ferje] *a* **jour f.** (*public*) holiday.

ferme¹ [fɛrm] *nf* farm; (*maison*) farm(house).

ferme² [fɛrm] *a* (*beurre, décision etc*) firm; (*autoritaire*) firm (**avec with**); (*pas, voix*) steady; (*pâte*) stiff; **— adv** (*travailler, boire*) hard; (*discuter*) keenly; **tenir f.** to stand firm *ou* fast. ◆**—ment** [-əmɑ̃] *adv* firmly.

ferment [fɛrmɑ̃] *nm* ferment. ◆**fermentation** *nf* fermentation. ◆**fermenter** *vi* to ferment.

fermer [fɛrme] *vt* to close, shut; (*gaz, radio etc*) to turn *ou* switch off; (*passage*) to block; (*vêtement*) to do up; **f.** (**à clef**) to lock; **f. la marche** to bring up the rear; **— vi, — se f.** *vpr* to close, shut. ◆**—é** *a* (*porte, magasin etc*) closed, shut; (*route, circuit etc*) closed; (*gaz etc*) off. ◆**fermeture** *nf* closing, closure; (*heure*) closing time; (*mécanisme*) catch; **f. éclair®** zip (fastener), *Am* zipper. ◆**fermoir** *nm* clasp, (snap) fastener.

fermeté [fɛrməte] *nf* firmness; (*de geste, voix*) steadiness.

fermier, -ière [fɛrmje, -jɛr] *nmf* farmer; **— a** (*poulet, produit*) farm-.

féroce [ferɔs] *a* fierce, ferocious. ◆**férocité** *nf* ferocity, fierceness.

ferraille [fɛraj] *nf* scrap-iron; **mettre à la f.** to scrap. ◆**ferrailleur** *nm* scrap-iron merchant.

ferré [fɛre] *a* **1** (*canne*) metal-tipped; **voie ferrée** railway, *Am* railroad; (*rails*) track. **2** (*calé*) *Fam* well up (**en** in, **sur** on).

ferrer [fɛre] *vt* (*cheval*) to shoe.

ferronnerie [fɛrɔnri] *nf* ironwork.

ferroviaire [fɛrɔvjɛr] *a* (*compagnie etc*) railway-, *Am* railroad-.

ferry-boat [feribot] *nm* ferry.

fertile [fɛrtil] *a* (*terre, imagination etc*) fertile; **f. en incidents** eventful. ◆**fertiliser** *vt* to fertilize. ◆**fertilité** *nf* fertility.

fervent, -ente [fɛrvɑ̃, -ɑ̃t] *a* fervent; **— nmf** devotee (**de** of). ◆**ferveur** *nf* fervour.

fesse [fɛs] *nf* buttock; **les fesses** one's behind. ◆**fessée** *nf* spanking.

festin [fɛstẽ] *nm* (*banquet*) feast.

festival, pl -als [fɛstival] *nm Mus Cin* festival.

festivités [fɛstivite] *nfpl* festivities.

festoyer [fɛstwaje] *vi* to feast, carouse.

fête [fɛt] *nf* (*civile*) holiday; *Rel* festival, feast; (*entre amis*) party; **f. du village** village fair *ou* fête; **f. de famille** family celebration; **c'est sa f.** it's his *ou* her saint's day; **f. des Mères** Mother's Day; **jour de f.** (*public*) holiday; **faire la f.** to make merry, revel; **air de f.** festive air. ◆**fêter** *vt* (*événement*) to celebrate.

fétiche [fetiʃ] *nm* (*objet de culte*) fetish; (*mascotte*) *Fig* mascot.

fétide [fetid] *a* fetid, stinking.

feu¹, -x [fø] *nm* fire; (*lumière*) *Aut Nau Av* light; (*de réchaud*) burner; (*de dispute*) *Fig* heat; *pl* (*de signalisation*) traffic lights; **feux de position** *Aut* parking lights; **feux de croisement** *Aut* dipped headlights, *Am* low beams; **f. rouge** *Aut* (*lumière*) red light; (*objet*) traffic lights; **tous feux éteints** *Aut* without lights; **mettre le f. à** to set fire to; **en f.** on fire, ablaze; **avez-vous du f.?** have you got a light?; **donner le f. vert** to give the go-ahead (**à** to); **ne pas faire long f.** not to last very long; **à f. doux** *Culin* on a low light; **au f.!** (there's a) fire!; **f.!** *Mil* fire!; **coup de f.** (*bruit*) gunshot; **feux croisés** *Mil* crossfire.

feu² [fø] *a inv* late; **f. ma tante** my late aunt.

feuille [fœj] *nf* leaf; (*de papier etc*) sheet; (*de température*) chart; *Journ* newssheet; **f. d'impôt** tax form *ou* return; **f. de paye** pay slip. ◆**feuillage** nm foliage. ◆**feuillet** nm (de livre) leaf. ◆**feuilleter** vt (livre) to flip ou leaf through; **pâte feuilletée** puff ou flaky pastry. ◆**feuilleton** nm (roman, film etc) serial. ◆**feuillu** a leafy.

feutre [føtr] nm felt; (chapeau) felt hat; **crayon f.** felt-tip(ped) pen. ◆**feutré** a (bruit) muffled; **à pas feutrés** silently.

fève [fɛv] nf bean.

février [fevrije] nm February.

fiable [fjabl] a reliable. ◆**fiabilité** nf reliability.

fiacre [fjakr] nm Hist hackney carriage.

fianc/er (se) [səfjɑ̃se] vpr to become engaged (avec to). ◆**—é** nm fiancé; pl engaged couple. ◆**—ée** nf fiancée. ◆**fiançailles** nfpl engagement.

fiasco [fjasko] nm fiasco; **faire f.** to be a fiasco.

fibre [fibr] nf fibre; **f.** (alimentaire) roughage, (dietary) fibre; **f. de verre** fibreglass.

ficelle [fisɛl] nf 1 string; **connaître les ficelles** (d'un métier etc) to known the ropes. 2 (pain) long thin loaf. ◆**ficeler** vt to tie up.

fiche [fiʃ] nf 1 (carte) index ou record card; (papier) slip, form; **f. technique** data record. 2 El (broche) pin; (prise) plug. ◆**fichier** nm card index, file.

fiche(r) [fiʃ(e)] vt (pp **fichu**) Fam (faire) to do; (donner) to give; (jeter) to throw; (mettre) to put; **f. le camp** to shove off; **fiche-moi la paix!** leave me alone!; **se f. de qn** to make fun of s.o.; **je m'en fiche!** I don't give a damn!

ficher [fiʃe] vt 1 to drive in. 2 (renseignement, personne) to put on file.

fichu [fiʃy] 1 a Fam (mauvais) lousy, rotten; (capable) able (**de faire** to do); **il est f.** he's had it, he's done for; **mal f.** (malade) not well. 2 nm (head) scarf.

fictif, -ive [fiktif, -iv] a fictitious. ◆**fiction** nf fiction.

fidèle [fidɛl] a faithful (à to); — nmf faithful supporter; (client) regular (customer); **les fidèles** (croyants) the faithful; (à l'église) the congregation. ◆**—ment** adv faithfully. ◆**fidélité** nf fidelity, faithfulness.

fief [fjɛf] nm (spécialité, chasse gardée) domain.

fiel [fjɛl] nm gall.

fier (se) [səfje] vpr **se f.** à to trust.

fier, fière [fjɛr] a proud (**de** of); **un f. culot** Péj a rare cheek. ◆**fièrement** adv proudly. ◆**fierté** nf pride.

fièvre [fjɛvr] nf (maladie) fever; (agitation) frenzy; **avoir de la f.** to have a temperature ou a fever. ◆**fiévreux, -euse** a feverish.

fig/er [fiʒe] vt (sang, sauce etc) to congeal; **f. qn** (paralyser) Fig to freeze s.o.; — vi (liquide) to congeal; — **se f.** vpr (liquide) to congeal; (sourire, personne) Fig to freeze. ◆**—é** a (locution) set, fixed; (regard) frozen; (société) petrified.

fignol/er [fiɲɔle] vt Fam to round off meticulously, refine. ◆**—é** a Fam meticulous.

figue [fig] nf fig; **mi-f., mi-raisin** (accueil etc) neither good nor bad, mixed. ◆**figuier** nm fig tree.

figurant, -ante [figyrɑ̃, -ɑ̃t] nmf Cin Th extra.

figure [figyr] nf 1 (visage) face. 2 (personnage) & Géom figure; (de livre) figure, illustration; **faire f. de riche/d'imbécile**/etc to look rich/a fool/etc. ◆**figurine** nf statuette.

figur/er [figyre] vt to represent; — vi to appear, figure; — **se f.** vpr to imagine; **figurez-vous que...?** would you believe that...? ◆**—é** a (sens) figurative; — nm **au f.** figuratively.

fil [fil] nm 1 (de coton, pensée etc) thread; (lin) linen; **f. dentaire** dental floss; **de f. en aiguille** bit by bit. 2 (métallique) wire; **f. de fer** wire; **f. à plomb** plumbline; **au bout du f.** Tél on the line; **passer un coup de f. à qn** Tél to give s.o. a ring ou a call. 3 (de couteau) edge. 4 **au f. de l'eau/des jours** with the current/the passing of time.

filament [filamɑ̃] nm El filament.

filandreux, -euse [filɑ̃drø, -øz] a (phrase) long-winded.

filant [filɑ̃] a **étoile f.** shooting star.

file [fil] nf line; (couloir) Aut lane; **f. d'attente** queue, Am line; **en f.** (indienne) in single file; **chef de f.** leader; (se) **mettre en f.** to line up.

filer [file] vt 1 (coton etc) to spin. 2 vt **f.** qn (suivre) to shadow s.o., tail s.o. 3 vt Fam **f.** qch à qn (objet) to slip s.o. sth; **f. un coup de pied/etc à qn** to give s.o. a kick/etc. 4 vi (partir) to shoot off, bolt; (aller vite) to speed along; (temps) to fly; (bas, collant) to ladder, run; (liquide) to trickle, run; **filez!** hop it!; **f. entre les doigts de qn** to slip through s.o.'s fingers; **f. doux** to be obedient. ◆**filature** nf 1 (usine) textile mill. 2 (de policiers etc) shadowing; **prendre en f.** to shadow.

filet [filɛ] nm 1 (de pêche) & Sp net; (à bagages) Rail (luggage) rack; **f.** (à provisions) string ou net bag (for shopping). 2 (d'eau) trickle. 3 (de poisson, viande) fillet.

filial, -aux [filjal, -o] a filial.

filiale [filjal] nf subsidiary (company).

filiation [filjasjɔ̃] *nf* relationship.

filière [filjɛr] *nf* (*de drogue*) network; **suivre la f.** (*pour obtenir qch*) to go through the official channels; (*employé*) to work one's way up.

filigrane [filigran] *nm* (*de papier*) watermark.

filin [filɛ̃] *nm* Nau rope.

fille [fij] *nf* **1** girl; **petite f.** (little *ou* young) girl; **jeune f.** girl, young lady; **vieille f.** Péj old maid; **f. (publique)** Péj prostitute. **2** (*parenté*) daughter, girl. ◆**f.-mère** *nf* (*pl* **filles-mères**) Péj unmarried mother. ◆**fillette** *nf* little girl.

filleul [fijœl] *nm* godson. ◆**filleule** *nf* goddaughter.

film [film] *nm* film, movie; (*pellicule*) film; **f. muet/parlant** silent/talking film *ou* movie; **le f. des événements** the sequence of events. ◆**filmer** *vt* (*personne, scène*) to film.

filon [filɔ̃] *nm* Géol seam; **trouver le (bon) f.** to strike it lucky.

filou [filu] *nm* rogue, crook.

fils [fis] *nm* son; **Dupont f.** Dupont junior.

filtre [filtr] *nm* filter; (**à bout**) **f.** (*cigarette*) (filter-)tipped; (**bout**) **f.** filter tip. ◆**filtrer** *vt* to filter; (*personne, nouvelles*) to scrutinize; – *vi* to filter.

fin [fɛ̃] **1** *nf* end; (*but*) end, aim; **mettre f. à** to put an end *ou* a stop to; **prendre f.** to come to an end; **tirer à sa f.** to draw to an end *ou* a close; **sans f.** endless; **à la f.** in the end; **arrêtez, à la f.!** stop, for heaven's sake!; **f. de semaine** weekend; **f. mai** at the end of May; **à cette f.** to this end. **2** *a* (*pointe, travail, tissu etc*) fine; (*taille, tranche*) thin; (*plat*) delicate, choice; (*esprit, oreille*) sharp; (*observation*) sharp, fine; (*gourmet*) discerning; (*rusé*) shrewd; (*intelligent*) clever; **au f. fond de** in the depths of; – *adv* (*couper, moudre*) finely; (*écrire*) small.

final, -aux *ou* **-als** [final, -o] *a* final; – *nm* Mus finale. ◆**finale** *nf* Sp final; Gram final syllable; – *nm* Mus finale. ◆**finalement** *adv* finally; (*en somme*) after all. ◆**finaliste** *nmf* Sp finalist.

finance [finãs] *nf* finance. ◆**financer** *vt* to finance. ◆**—ement** *nm* financing. ◆**financier, -ière** *a* financial; – *nm* financier. ◆**financièrement** *adv* financially.

fine [fin] *nf* liqueur brandy.

finement [finmã] *adv* (*broder, couper etc*) finely; (*agir*) cleverly.

finesse [finɛs] *nf* (*de pointe etc*) fineness; (*de taille etc*) thinness; (*de plat*) delicacy; (*d'esprit, de goût*) finesse; *pl* (*de langue*) niceties.

fin/ir [finir] *vt* to finish; (*discours, vie*) to end, finish; – *vi* to finish, end; **f. de faire** to finish doing; (*cesser*) to stop doing; **f. par faire** to end up *ou* finish up doing; **f. par qch** to finish (up) *ou* end (up) with sth; **en f. avec** to put an end to, finish with; **elle n'en finit pas** there's no end to it, she goes on and on. ◆**—i** *a* (*produit*) finished; (*univers etc*) & Math finite; **c'est f.** it's over *ou* finished; **il est f.** (*fichu*) he's done for *ou* finished; – *nm* (*poli*) finish. ◆**—issant** *a* (*siècle*) declining. ◆**finish** *nm* Sp finish. ◆**finition** *nf* (*action*) Tech finishing; (*résultat*) finish.

Finlande [fɛ̃lɑ̃d] *nf* Finland. ◆**finlandais, -aise** *a* Finnish; – *nmf* Finn. ◆**finnois, -oise** *a* Finnish; – *nmf* Finn; – *nm* (*langue*) Finnish.

fiole [fjɔl] *nf* phial, flask.

firme [firm] *nf* (*entreprise*) Com firm.

fisc [fisk] *nm* tax authorities; = Inland Revenue, = Am Internal Revenue. ◆**fiscal, -aux** *a* fiscal, tax-. ◆**fiscalité** *nf* tax system; (*charges*) taxation.

fission [fisjɔ̃] *nf* Phys fission.

fissure [fisyr] *nf* split, crack, fissure. ◆**se fissurer** *vpr* to split, crack.

fiston [fistɔ̃] *nm* Fam son, sonny.

fixe [fiks] *a* fixed; (*prix, heure*) set, fixed; **idée f.** obsession; **regard f.** stare; **être au beau f.** Mét to be set fair; – *nm* (*paie*) fixed salary. ◆**—ment** [-əmã] *adv* **regarder f.** to stare at. ◆**fixer** *vt* (*attacher*) to fix (**à** to); (*choix*) to settle; (*règle, date etc*) to decide, fix; **f. (du regard)** to stare at; **f. qn sur** to inform s.o. clearly about; **être fixé** (*décidé*) to be decided; **comme ça on est fixé!** (*renseigné*) we've got the picture! — **se f.** *vpr* (*regard*) to become fixed; (*s'établir*) to settle, settle. ◆**fixateur** *nm* Phot fixer; (*pour cheveux*) setting lotion. ◆**fixation** *nf* (*action*) fixing; (*dispositif*) fastening, binding; Psy fixation.

flacon [flakɔ̃] *nm* bottle, flask.

flageoler [flaʒɔle] *vi* to shake, tremble.

flageolet [flaʒɔlɛ] *nm* Bot Culin (dwarf) kidney bean.

flagrant [flagrɑ̃] *a* (*injustice etc*) flagrant, glaring; **pris en f.** (*cesser*) caught in the act *ou* red-handed.

flair [flɛr] *nm* **1** (*d'un chien etc*) (sense of) smell, scent. **2** (*clairvoyance*) intuition, flair. ◆**flairer** *vt* to sniff at, smell; (*discerner*) Fig to smell, sense.

flamand, -ande [flamɑ̃, -ɑ̃d] *a* Flemish; – *nmf* Fleming; – *nm* (*langue*) Flemish.

flamant [flamɑ̃] *nm* (*oiseau*) flamingo.

flambant [flɑ̃bɑ̃] *adv* f. neuf brand new.

flambeau, -x [flɑ̃bo] *nm* torch.

flamb/er [flɑ̃be] **1** *vi* to burn, blaze; – *vt* (*aiguille*) *Méd* to sterilize; (*poulet*) to singe. **2** *vi* (*jouer*) *Fam* to gamble for big money. **◆—é** *a* (*ruiné*) *Fam* done for. **◆—ée** *nf* blaze; (*de colère, des prix etc*) *Fig* surge; (*de violence*) flare-up, eruption. **◆—eur** *nm* *Fam* big gambler. **◆flamboyer** *vi* to blaze, flame.

flamme [flɑm] *nf* flame; (*ardeur*) *Fig* fire; **en flammes** on fire. **◆flammèche** *nf* spark.

flan [flɑ̃] *nm* **1** *Culin* custard tart *ou* pie. **2 au f.** *Fam* on the off chance, on the spur of the moment.

flanc [flɑ̃] *nm* side; (*d'une armée, d'un animal*) flank; **tirer au f.** *Fam* to shirk, idle.

flancher [flɑ̃ʃe] *vi* *Fam* to give in, weaken.

Flandre(s) [flɑ̃dr] *nf*(*pl*) Flanders.

flanelle [flanɛl] *nf* (*tissu*) flannel.

flâner [flɑne] *vi* to stroll, dawdle. **◆flânerie** *nf* (*action*) strolling; (*promenade*) stroll.

flanquer [flɑ̃ke] *vt* **1** to flank (**de** with). **2** *Fam* (*jeter*) to chuck; (*donner*) to give; **f. qn à la porte** to throw s.o. out.

flaque [flak] *nf* puddle, pool.

flash, *pl* **flashes** [flaʃ] *nm* **1** *Phot* (*éclair*) flashlight; (*dispositif*) flash(gun). **2** *TV Rad* (*news*)flash.

flasque [flask] *a* flabby, floppy.

flatt/er [flɑte] *vt* to flatter; **se f. d'être malin/de réussir** to flatter oneself on being smart/on being able to succeed. **◆—é** *a* flattered (**de qch** by sth, **de faire** to do, **que** that). **◆flatterie** *nf* flattery. **◆flatteur, -euse** *nmf* flatterer; – *a* flattering.

fléau, -x [fleo] *nm* **1** (*calamité*) scourge; (*personne, chose*) bane, plague. **2** *Agr* flail.

flèche [flɛʃ] *nf* arrow; (*d'église*) spire; **monter en f.** (*prix*) to (sky)rocket, shoot ahead. **◆flécher** [fleʃe] *vt* to signpost (with arrows). **◆fléchette** *nf* dart; *pl* (*jeu*) darts.

fléchir [fleʃir] *vt* (*membre*) to flex, bend; **f. qn** *Fig* to move s.o., persuade s.o.; – *vi* (*membre*) to bend; (*poutre*) to sag; (*faiblir*) to give way; (*baisser*) to fall off.

flegme [flɛgm] *nm* composure. **◆flegmatique** *a* phlegmatic, stolid.

flemme [flɛm] *nf* *Fam* laziness; **il a la f.** he can't be bothered, he's just too lazy. **◆flemmard, -arde** *a* *Fam* lazy; – *nmf* *Fam* lazybones.

flétrir [fletrir] *vt*, **– se f.** *vpr* to wither. **2** *vt* (*blâmer*) to stigmatize, brand.

fleur [flœr] *nf* flower; (*d'arbre, d'arbuste*) blossom; **en f.** in flower, in bloom; in blos-

som; **à** *ou* **dans la f. de l'âge** in the prime of life; **à f. d'eau** just above the water; **à fleurs** (*tissu*) floral, floral, bloom; (*arbre etc*) to blossom; (*art, commerce etc*) *Fig* to flourish; – *vt* (*table etc*) to decorate with flowers. **◆—i** *a* (*fleur, jardin*) in bloom; (*tissu*) flowered, floral; (*teint*) florid; (*style*) flowery, florid. **◆fleuriste** *nmf* florist.

fleuve [flœv] *nm* river.

flexible [flɛksibl] *a* flexible, pliable. **◆flexibilité** *nf* flexibility.

flexion [flɛksjɔ̃] *nf* **1** *Anat* flexion, flexing. **2** *Gram* inflexion.

flic [flik] *nm* *Fam* cop, policeman.

flinguer [flɛ̃ge] *vt* **f. qn** *Arg* to shoot s.o.

flipper [flipœr] *nm* (*jeu*) pinball.

flirt [flœrt] *nm* (*rapports*) flirtation; (*personne*) flirt. **◆flirter** *vi* to flirt (**avec** with). **◆flirteur, -euse** *a* flirtatious; – *nmf* flirt.

flocon [flɔkɔ̃] *nm* (*de neige*) flake; (*de laine*) flock; **flocons d'avoine** *Culin* porridge oats. **◆floconneux, -euse** *a* fluffy.

floraison [flɔrɛzɔ̃] *nf* flowering; **en pleine f.** in full bloom. **◆floral, -aux** *a* floral. **◆floralies** *nfpl* flower show.

flore [flɔr] *nf* flora.

florissant [flɔrisɑ̃] *a* flourishing.

flot [flo] *nm* (*de souvenirs, larmes*) flood, stream; (*marée*) floodtide; *pl* (*de mer*) waves; (*de lac*) waters; **à flots** in abundance; **à f.** (*bateau, personne*) afloat; **mettre à f.** (*bateau, firme*) to launch; **remettre qn à f.** to restore s.o.'s fortunes.

flotte [flɔt] *nf* **1** *Nau Av* fleet. **2** *Fam* (*pluie*) rain; (*eau*) water. **◆flottille** *nf* *Nau* flotilla.

flott/er [flɔte] *vi* to float; (*drapeau*) to fly; (*cheveux*) to flow; (*pensées*) to drift; (*pleuvoir*) *Fam* to rain. **◆—ant** *a* **1** (*bois, dette etc*) floating; (*vêtement*) flowing, loose. **2** (*esprit*) indecisive. **◆—ement** *nm* (*hésitation*) indecision. **◆—eur** *nm* *Pêche etc* float.

flou [flu] *a* (*photo*) fuzzy, blurred; (*idée*) hazy, fuzzy; – *nm* fuzziness.

fluctuant [flyktɥɑ̃] *a* (*prix, opinions*) fluctuating. **◆fluctuations** *nfpl* fluctuation(s) (**de** in).

fluet, -ette [flɥɛ, -ɛt] *a* thin, slender.

fluide [flɥid] *a* (*liquide*) & *Fig* fluid; – *nm* (*liquide*) fluid. **◆fluidité** *nf* fluidity.

fluorescent [flyɔresɑ̃] *a* fluorescent.

flûte [flyt] **1** *nf* *Mus* flute. **2** *nf* (*verre*) champagne glass. **3** *int* heck!, darn!, dash it! **◆flûté** *a* (*voix*) piping. **◆flûtiste** *nmf* flautist, *Am* flutist.

fluvial, -aux [flyvjal, -o] *a* a river-, fluvial.

flux [fly] *nm* (*abondance*) flow; **f. et reflux** ebb and flow.

focal, -aux [fɔkal, -o] *a* focal. ◆**focaliser** *vt* (*intérêt etc*) to focus.

fœtus [fetys] *nm* foetus, *Am* fetus.

foi [fwa] *nf* faith; **sur la f. de** on the strength of; **agir de bonne/mauvaise f.** to act in good/bad faith; **ma f., oui!** yes, indeed!

foie [fwa] *nm* liver.

foin [fwɛ̃] *nm* hay; **faire du f.** (*scandale*) *Fam* to make a stink.

foire [fwar] *nf* fair; **faire la f.** *Fam* to go on a binge, have a ball.

fois [fwa] *nf* time; **une f.** once; **deux f.** twice, two times; **chaque f. que** each time (that), whenever; **une f. qu'il sera arrivé** (*dès que*) once he has arrived; **à la f.** at the same time, at once; **à la f. riche et heureux** both rich and happy; **une autre f.** (*elle fera attention etc*) next time; **des f.** *Fam* sometimes; **non mais des f.!** *Fam* you must be joking!; **une f. pour toutes, une bonne f.** once and for all.

foison [fwazɔ̃] *nf* **à f.** in plenty. ◆**foisonn/er** *vi* to abound (**de, en** in). ◆**—ement** *nm* abundance.

fol [fɔl] *voir* **fou**.

folâtre [fɔlatr] *a* playful. ◆**folâtrer** *vi* to romp, frolic.

folichon, -onne [fɔliʃɔ̃, -ɔn] *a* **pas f.** not very funny, not much fun.

folie [fɔli] *nf* madness, insanity; **faire une f.** to do a foolish thing; (*dépense*) to be wildly extravagant; **aimer qn à la f.** to be madly in love with s.o.

folklore [fɔlklɔr] *nm* folklore. ◆**folklorique** *a* (*danse etc*) folk-; (*pas sérieux*) *Fam* lightweight, trivial, silly.

folle [fɔl] *voir* **fou**. ◆**follement** *adv* madly.

fomenter [fɔmɑ̃te] *vt* (*révolte etc*) to foment.

foncé [fɔ̃se] *a* (*couleur*) dark.

foncer [fɔ̃se] **1** *vi* (*aller vite*) to tear ou charge along; **f. sur qn** to charge into ou at s.o. **2** *vti* (*couleur*) to darken.

foncier, -ière [fɔ̃sje, -jɛr] *a* **1** fundamental, basic. **2** (*propriété*) landed. ◆**foncièrement** *adv* fundamentally.

fonction [fɔ̃ksjɔ̃] *nf* (*rôle*) & *Math* function; (*emploi*) office, function, duty; **f. publique** civil service; **faire f. de** (*personne*) to act as; (*objet*) to serve ou act as; **en f. de** according to. ◆**fonctionnaire** *nmf* civil servant. ◆**fonctionnel, -elle** *a* functional. ◆**fonctionn/er** *vi* (*machine etc*) to work, operate, function; (*organisation*) to function; **faire f.** to operate, work. ◆**—ement** *nm* working.

fond [fɔ̃] *nm* (*de boîte, jardin, vallée etc*) bottom; (*de salle, armoire etc*) back; (*de culotte*) seat; (*de problème, débat etc*) essence; (*arrière-plan*) background; (*contenu*) content; (*du désespoir*) *Fig* depths; **au f. de** at the bottom of; at the back of; **fonds de verre** dregs; **f. de teint** foundation cream; **f. sonore** background music; **un f. de bon sens** a stock of good sense; **au f.** basically, in essence; **à f.** (*connaître etc*) thoroughly; **de f. en comble** from top to bottom; **de f.** (*course*) long-distance; (*bruit*) background-.

fondamental, -aux [fɔ̃damɑ̃tal, -o] *a* fundamental, basic.

fond/er [fɔ̃de] *vt* (*ville etc*) to found; (*commerce*) to set up; (*famille*) to start; (**se**) **f. sur** to base (oneself) on; **être fondé à croire**/*etc* to be justified in thinking/*etc*; **bien fondé** well-founded. ◆**—ement** *nm* foundation. ◆**fondateur, -trice** *nmf* founder; — *a* (*membre*) founding, founder-. ◆**fondation** *nf* (*création, œuvre*) foundation (**de** of).

fond/re [fɔ̃dr] *vt* to melt; (*métal*) to smelt; (*cloche*) to cast; (*amalgamer*) *Fig* to fuse (**avec** with); **faire f.** (*dissoudre*) to dissolve; — *vi* to melt; (*se dissoudre*) to dissolve; **f. en larmes** to burst into tears; **f. sur** to swoop on; — **se f.** *vpr* to merge, fuse. ◆**—ant** *a* (*fruit*) which melts in the mouth. ◆**—ue** *nf Culin* fondue. ◆**fonderie** *nf* (*usine*) smelting works, foundry.

fonds [fɔ̃] **1** *nm* **un f. de commerce** a business. **2** *nmpl* (*argent*) funds. **3** *nm* (*culturel etc*) *Fig* fund.

font [fɔ̃] *voir* **faire**.

fontaine [fɔ̃tɛn] *nf* (*construction*) fountain; (*source*) spring.

fonte [fɔ̃t] *nf* **1** (*des neiges*) melting; (*d'acier*) smelting. **2** (*fer*) cast iron; **en f.** (*poêle etc*) cast-iron.

fonts [fɔ̃] *nmpl* **f. baptismaux** *Rel* font.

football [futbol] *nm* football, soccer. ◆**footballeur, -euse** *nmf* footballer.

footing [futiŋ] *nm Sp* jogging, jog-trotting.

forage [fɔraʒ] *nm* drilling, boring.

forain [fɔrɛ̃] *a* (*marchand*) itinerant; **fête foraine** (fun)fair.

forçat [fɔrsa] *nm* (*prisonnier*) convict.

force [fɔrs] *nf* force; (*physique, morale*) strength; (*atomique etc*) power; **de toutes ses forces** with all one's strength; **les forces armées** the armed forces; **de f.** by force, forcibly; **en f.** (*attaquer, venir*) in force; **cas de f. majeure** circumstances beyond one's control; **dans la f. de l'âge** in the prime of life; **à f.** de through sheer force of, by dint of. ◆**forc/er** *vt* (*porte, fruits etc*) to force; (*attention*) to force, compel; (*voix*) to strain; (*sens*) to stretch; **f. qn à faire** to force *ou* compel s.o. to do; – *vi* (*y aller trop fort*) to overdo it; – **se f.** *vpr* to force oneself (à faire to do). ◆**–é** *a* forced (**de faire** to do); **un sourire f.** a forced smile; **c'est f.** *Fam* it's inevitable *ou* obvious. ◆**–ément** *adv* inevitably, obviously; **pas f.** not necessarily.

forcené, -ée [fɔrsəne] *a* frantic, frenzied; – *nmf* madman, madwoman.

forceps [fɔrsɛps] *nm* forceps.

forcir [fɔrsir] *vi* (*grossir*) to fill out.

forer [fɔre] *vt* to drill, bore. ◆**foret** *nm* drill.

forêt [fɔrɛ] *nf* forest. ◆**forestier, -ière** *a* forest-; – *nm* (**garde**) **f.** forester, *Am* (forest) ranger.

forfait [fɔrfɛ] *nm* **1** (*prix*) all-inclusive price; **travailler à f.** to work for a lump sum. **2 déclarer f.** *Sp* to withdraw from the game. **3** (*crime*) *Litt* heinous crime. ◆**forfaitaire** *a* **prix f.** all-inclusive price.

forge [fɔrʒ] *nf* forge. ◆**forg/er** *vt* (*métal, liens etc*) to forge; (*inventer*) to make up. ◆**–é** *a* **fer f.** wrought iron. ◆**forgeron** *nm* (black)smith.

formaliser (se) [səfɔrmalize] *vpr* to take offence (**de** at).

formalité [fɔrmalite] *nf* formality.

format [fɔrma] *nm* format, size.

forme [fɔrm] *nf* (*contour*) shape, form; (*manière, genre*) form; *pl* (**de femme, d'homme**) figure; **en f.** in the form of; **en f. d'aiguille/de poire/etc** needle-/pear-/etc shaped; **dans les formes** in due form; **en** (**pleine**) **f.** in good shape *ou* form, on form; **prendre f.** to take shape. ◆**formateur, -trice** *a* formative. ◆**formation** *nf* formation; (*éducation*) education, training. ◆**formel, -elle** *a* (*structure, logique etc*) formal; (*démenti*) categorical, formal; (*preuve*) positive, formal. ◆**formellement** *adv* (*interdire*) strictly. ◆**form/er** *vt* (*groupe, caractère etc*) to form; (*apprenti etc*) to train; – **se f.** *vpr* (*apparaître*) to form; (*institution*) to be formed. ◆**–é** *a* (*personne*) fully-formed.

formidable [fɔrmidabl] *a* tremendous.

formule [fɔrmyl] *nf* **1** formula; (*phrase*) (set) expression; (*méthode*) method; **f. de politesse** polite expression. **2** (*feuille*) form. ◆**formulaire** *nm* (*feuille*) form. ◆**formulation** *nf* formulation. ◆**formuler** *vt* to formulate.

fort¹ [fɔr] *a* strong; (*pluie, mer*) heavy;

(*voix*) loud; (*fièvre*) high; (*femme, homme*) large; (*élève*) bright; (*pente*) steep; (*ville*) fortified; (*chances*) good; **f. en** (*maths etc*) good at; **c'est plus f. qu'elle** she can't help it; **c'est un peu f.** *Fam* that's a bit much; **à plus forte raison** all the more reason; – *adv* **1** (*frapper*) hard; (*pleuvoir*) hard, heavily; (*parler*) loud; (*serrer*) tight; **sentir f.** to have a strong smell. **2** (*très*) *Vieilli* very; (*beaucoup*) *Litt* very much; – *nm* **f.** one's strong point; **les forts** the strong; **au plus f. de** in the thick of. ◆**fortement** *adv* greatly; (*frapper*) hard.

fort² [fɔr] *nm* *Hist* *Mil* fort. ◆**forteresse** *nf* fortress.

fortifi/er [fɔrtifje] *vt* to strengthen, fortify; – **se f.** *vpr* (*malade*) to fortify oneself. ◆**–ant** *nm* *Méd* tonic. ◆**–é** *a* (*ville, camp*) fortified. ◆**fortification** *nf* fortification.

fortuit [fɔrtɥi] *a* (*rencontre etc*) chance-, fortuitous. ◆**fortuitement** *adv* by chance.

fortune [fɔrtyn] *nf* (*argent, hasard*) fortune; **avoir de la f.** to have (private) means; **faire f.** to make one's fortune; **de f.** (*moyens etc*) makeshift; **dîner à la f. du pot** to take pot luck. ◆**fortuné** *a* (*riche*) well-to-do.

forum [fɔrɔm] *nm* forum.

fosse [fos] *nf* (*trou*) pit; (*tombe*) grave; **f. d'aisances** cesspool.

fossé [fose] *nm* ditch; (*douve*) moat; (*dissentiment*) *Fig* gulf, gap.

fossette [fosɛt] *nf* dimple.

fossile [fosil] *nm* & *a* fossil.

fossoyeur [foswajœr] *nm* gravedigger.

fou (*or* **fol** *before vowel or mute* h), **folle** [fu, fɔl] *a* (*personne, projet etc*) mad, insane, crazy; (*envie*) wild, mad; (*espoir*) foolish; (*rire*) uncontrollable; (*cheval, camion*) runaway; (*succès, temps*) tremendous; **f. à lier** raving mad; **f. de** (*musique, personne etc*) mad *ou* wild *ou* crazy about; **f. de joie** wild with joy; – *nmf* madman, madwoman; (*bouffon*) jester; *Échecs* bishop; **faire le f.** to play the fool.

foudre [fudr] *nf* la **f.** lightning; **coup de f.** *Fig* love at first sight. ◆**foudroy/er** *vt* to strike by lightning; *Él* to electrocute; (*malheur etc*) *Fig* to strike (s.o.) down. ◆**–ant** *a* (*succès, vitesse etc*) staggering. ◆**–é** *a* (*stupéfait*) thunderstruck.

fouet [fwɛ] *nm* whip; *Culin* (egg) whisk. ◆**fouetter** *vt* to whip; (*œufs*) to whisk; (*pluie etc*) to lash (*face, windows etc*); **crème fouettée** whipped cream.

fougère [fuʒɛr] *nf* fern.

fougue [fug] *nf* fire, ardour. ◆**fougueux, -euse** *a* fiery, ardent.

fouille [fuj] *nf* **1** (*archéologique*) excavation, dig. **2** (*de personne, bagages etc*) search. ◆**fouiller 1** *vti* (*creuser*) to dig. **2** *vt* (*personne, maison etc*) to search; – *vi* **f. dans** (*tiroir etc*) to rummage *ou* search through.

fouillis [fuji] *nm* jumble.

fouine [fwin] *nf* (*animal*) stone marten.

fouin/er [fwine] *vi Fam* to nose about. ◆**—eur, -euse** *a Fam* nosy; – *nmf Fam* nosy parker.

foulard [fular] *nm* (head) scarf.

foule [ful] *nf* crowd; **en f.** in mass; **une f. de** (*objets etc*) a mass of; **un bain de f.** a walkabout.

foulée [fule] *nf Sp* stride; **dans la f.** *Fam* at one and the same time.

fouler [fule] *vt* to press; (*sol*) to tread; **f. aux pieds** to trample on; **se f. la cheville/etc** to sprain one's ankle/etc; **il ne se foule pas (la rate)** *Fam* he doesn't exactly exert himself. ◆**foulure** *nf* sprain.

four [fur] *nm* **1** oven; (*de potier etc*) kiln. **2 petit f.** (*gâteau*) (small) fancy cake. **3** *Th Cin* flop; **faire un f.** to flop.

fourbe [furb] *a* deceitful; – *nmf* cheat. ◆**fourberie** *nf* deceit.

fourbi [furbi] *nm* (*choses*) *Fam* stuff, gear, rubbish.

fourbu [furby] *a* (*fatigué*) dead beat.

fourche [furʃ] *nf* fork; **f. à foin** pitchfork. ◆**fourchette** *nf* **1** *Culin* fork. **2** (*de salaires etc*) *Écon* bracket. ◆**fourchu** *a* forked.

fourgon [furgɔ̃] *nm* (*camion*) van; (*mortuaire*) hearse; *Rail* luggage van, *Am* baggage car. ◆**fourgonnette** *nf* (small) van.

fourmi [furmi] *nf* **1** (*insecte*) ant. **2 avoir des fourmis** *Méd* to have pins and needles (**dans** in). ◆**fourmilière** *nf* anthill. ◆**fourmiller** *vi* **1** to teem, swarm (**de** with). **2** to tingle.

fournaise [furnɛz] *nf* (*chambre etc*) *Fig* furnace.

fourneau, -x [furno] *nm* (*poêle*) stove; (*four*) furnace; **haut f.** blast furnace.

fournée [furne] *nf* (*de pain, gens*) batch.

fourn/ir [furnir] *vt* to supply, provide; (*effort*) to make; **f. qch à qn** to supply s.o. with sth; – *vi* **f. à** (*besoin etc*) to provide for; — **se f.** *vpr* to get one's supplies (**chez** from), shop (**chez** at). ◆**—l** *a* (*barbe*) bushy; **bien f.** (*boutique*) well-stocked. ◆**fournisseur** *nm* (*commerçant*) supplier. ◆**fourniture** *nf* (*action*) supply(ing) (**de** of); *pl* (*objets*) supplies.

fourrage [furaʒ] *nm* fodder.

fourrager [furaʒe] *vi Fam* to rummage (**dans** in, through).

fourreau, -x [furo] *nm* (*gaine*) sheath.

fourr/er [fure] **1** *vt Culin* to fill, stuff; (*vêtement*) to fur-line. **2** *vt Fam* (*mettre*) to stick; (*flanquer*) to chuck; **f. qch dans la tête de qn** to knock sth into s.o.'s head; **f. son nez dans** to poke one's nose into; — **se f.** *vpr* to put *ou* stick oneself (**dans** in). ◆**—é 1** *a* (*gant etc*) fur-lined; (*gâteau*) jam-*ou* cream-filled; **coup f.** (*traîtrise*) stab in the back. ◆**—eur** *nm* furrier. ◆**fourrure** *nf* (*pour vêtement etc, de chat etc*) fur.

fourre-tout [furtu] *nm inv* (*pièce*) junk room; (*sac*) holdall, *Am* carryall.

fourrière [furjɛr] *nf* (*lieu*) pound.

fourvoyer (se) [səfurvwaje] *vpr* to go astray.

foutre* [futr] *vt Arg* = **fiche(r)**. ◆**foutu** *a Arg* = **fichu 1**. ◆**foutaise** *nf Arg* rubbish, rot.

foyer [fwaje] *nm* (*domicile*) home; (*d'étudiants etc*) hostel; (*âtre*) hearth; (*lieu de réunion*) club; *Th* foyer; *Géom Phys* focus; **f. de** (*maladie etc*) seat of; (*énergie, lumière*) source of; **fonder un f.** to start a family.

fracas [fraka] *nm* din; (*d'un objet qui tombe*) crash. ◆**fracass/er** *vt*, — **se f.** *vpr* to smash. ◆**—ant** *a* (*nouvelle, film etc*) sensational.

fraction [fraksjɔ̃] *nf* fraction. ◆**fractionner** *vt*, — **se f.** *vpr* to split (up).

fracture [fraktyr] *nf* fracture; **se faire une f. au bras/etc** to fracture one's arm/etc. ◆**fracturer** *vt* (*porte etc*) to break (open); **se f. la jambe/etc** to fracture one's leg/etc.

fragile [fraʒil] *a* (*verre, santé etc*) fragile; (*enfant etc*) frail; (*équilibre*) shaky. ◆**fragilité** *nf* fragility; (*d'un enfant etc*) frailty.

fragment [fragmɑ̃] *nm* fragment. ◆**fragmentaire** *a* fragmentary, fragmented. ◆**fragmentation** *nf* fragmentation. ◆**fragmenter** *vt* to fragment, divide.

frais¹, fraîche [frɛ, frɛʃ] *a* (*poisson, souvenir etc*) fresh; (*temps*) cool, fresh, (*plutôt désagréable*) chilly; (*œufs*) new-laid, fresh; (*boisson*) cold, cool; (*peinture*) wet; (*date*) recent; **boire f.** to drink something cold *ou* cool; **servir f.** (*vin etc*) to serve chilled; — *nm* **prendre le f.** to get some fresh air; **il fait f.** it's cool; (*froid*) it's chilly; **mettre au f.** to put in a cool place. ◆**fraîchement** *adv* **1** (*récemment*) freshly. **2** (*accueillir etc*) coolly. ◆**fraîcheur** *nf* freshness; coolness;

chilliness. ◆**fraîchir** vi (temps) to get cooler ou chillier, freshen.

frais² [frɛ] nmpl expenses; (droits) fees; **à mes f.** at my expense; **faire des f.** to go to some expense; **faire les f.** to bear the cost (de of); **j'en ai été pour mes f.** I wasted my time and effort; **faux f.** incidental expenses; **f. généraux** running expenses, overheads.

fraise [frɛz] nf 1 (fruit) strawberry. 2 (de dentiste) drill. ◆**fraisier** nm (plante) strawberry plant.

framboise [frɑ̃bwaz] nf raspberry. ◆**framboisier** nm raspberry cane.

franc¹, franche [frɑ̃, frɑ̃ʃ] a 1 (personne, réponse etc) frank; (visage, gaieté) open; (net) clear; (cassure, coupe) clean; (vrai) Péj downright. 2 (zone) free; **coup f.** Fb free kick; **f. de port** carriage paid. ◆**franchement** adv (honnêtement) frankly; (sans ambiguïté) clearly; (vraiment) really. ◆**franchise** nf 1 frankness; openness; **en toute f.** quite frankly. 2 (exemption) Com exemption; **en f.** (produit) duty-free; **'f. postale'** 'official paid'. 3 (permis de vendre) Com franchise.

franc² [frɑ̃] nm (monnaie) franc.

France [frɑ̃s] nf France. ◆**français, -aise** a French; – nmf Frenchman, Frenchwoman; **les F.** the French; – nm (langue) French.

franch/ir [frɑ̃ʃir] vt (fossé) to jump (over), clear; (frontière, seuil etc) to cross; (porte) to go through; (distance) to cover; (limites) to exceed; (mur du son) to break (through), go through. ◆**-issable** a (rivière, col) passable.

franc-maçon [frɑ̃masɔ̃] nm (pl francs-maçons) Freemason. ◆**franc-maçonnerie** nf Freemasonry.

franco [frɑ̃ko] adv carriage paid.

franco- [frɑ̃ko] préf Franco-.

francophile [frɑ̃kɔfil] a & nmf francophile. ◆**francophone** a French-speaking; – nmf French speaker. ◆**francophonie** nf **la f.** the French-speaking community.

frange [frɑ̃ʒ] nf (de vêtement etc) fringe; (de cheveux) fringe, Am bangs.

frangin [frɑ̃ʒɛ̃] nm Fam brother. ◆**frangine** nf Fam sister.

franquette (à la bonne) [alabɔnfrɑ̃kɛt] adv without ceremony.

frappe [frap] nf 1 (dactylographie) typing; (de dactylo etc) touch; **faute de f.** typing error. 2 **force de f.** Mil strike force. ◆**frapp/er** vt (battre) to strike, hit; (monnaie) to mint; **f. qn** (surprendre, affecter) to

strike s.o.; (impôt, mesure etc) to hit s.o.; **frappé de** (horreur etc) stricken with; **frappé de panique** panic-stricken; – vi (à la porte etc) to knock, bang (à at); **f. du pied** to stamp (one's foot); – **se f.** vpr (se tracasser) to worry. ◆**-ant** a striking. ◆**-é** a (vin) chilled.

frasque [frask] nf prank, escapade.

fraternel, -elle [fraternɛl] a fraternal, brotherly. ◆**fraterniser** vi to fraternize (avec with). ◆**fraternité** nf fraternity, brotherhood.

fraude [frod] nf Jur fraud; (à un examen) cheating; **passer qch en f.** to smuggle sth; **prendre qn en f.** to catch s.o. cheating. ◆**fraud/er** vt to defraud; – vi Jur to commit fraud; (à un examen) to cheat (à in); **f. sur** (poids etc) to cheat on ou over. ◆**-eur, -euse** nmf Jur defrauder. ◆**frauduleux, -euse** a fraudulent.

frayer [freje] vt (voie etc) to clear; **se f. un passage** to clear a way, force one's way (à travers, dans through).

frayeur [frejœr] nf fear, fright.

fredaine [frədɛn] nf prank, escapade.

fredonner [frədɔne] vt to hum.

freezer [frizœr] nm (de réfrigérateur) freezer.

frégate [fregat] nf (navire) frigate.

frein [frɛ̃] nm brake; **donner un coup de f.** to brake; **mettre un f. à** Fig to put a curb on. ◆**frein/er** vi Aut to brake; – vt (gêner) Fig to check, curb. ◆**-age** nm Aut braking.

frelaté [frəlate] a (vin etc) & Fig adulterated.

frêle [frɛl] a frail, fragile.

frelon [frəlɔ̃] nm (guêpe) hornet.

frémir [fremir] vi to shake, shudder (de with); (feuille) to quiver; (eau chaude) to simmer.

frêne [frɛn] nm (arbre, bois) ash.

frénésie [frenezi] nf frenzy. ◆**frénétique** a frenzied, frantic.

fréquent [frekɑ̃] a frequent. ◆**fréquemment** [-amɑ̃] adv frequently. ◆**fréquence** nf frequency.

fréquent/er [frekɑ̃te] vt (lieu) to visit, frequent; (école, église) to attend; **f. qn** to see ou visit s.o.; – **se f.** vpr (fille et garçon) to see each other, go out together; (voisins) to see each other socially. ◆**-é** a très f. (lieu) very busy. ◆**fréquentable** a peu f. (personne, endroit) not very commendable. ◆**fréquentation** nf visiting; pl (personnes) company.

frère [frɛr] nm brother.

fresque [frɛsk] nf (œuvre peinte) fresco.

fret [frɛ] nm freight.

frétiller [fretije] vi (poisson) to wriggle; **f. de** (impatience) to quiver with; **f. de joie** to tingle with excitement.

fretin [frətɛ̃] nm menu **f.** small fry.

friable [frijabl] a crumbly.

friand [frijã] a **f.** de fond of, partial to. ◆**friandises** nfpl sweet stuff, sweets, Am candies.

fric [frik] nm (argent) Fam cash, dough.

fric-frac [frikfrak] nm (cambriolage) Fam break-in.

friche (en) [ãfriʃ] adv fallow.

friction [friksjɔ̃] nf **1** massage, rub(-down); (de cheveux) friction. **2** (désaccord) friction. ◆**frictionner** vt to rub (down).

frigidaire® [friʒidɛr] nm fridge. ◆**frigo** nm Fam fridge. ◆**frigorifié** a (personne) Fam very cold. ◆**frigorifique** a (vitrine) refrigerated; (wagon) refrigerator.

frigide [friʒid] a frigid. ◆**frigidité** nf frigidity.

frileux, -euse [frilø, -øz] a sensitive to cold, chilly.

frime [frim] nf Fam sham, show.

frimousse [frimus] nf Fam little face.

fringale [frɛ̃gal] nf Fam raging appetite.

fringant [frɛ̃gã] a (allure etc) dashing.

fringues [frɛ̃g] nfpl (vêtements) Fam togs, clothes.

trip/er [fripe] vt to crumple; — **se f.** vpr to get crumpled. ◆**-é** a (visage) crumpled, wrinkled.

fripier, -ière [fripje, -jɛr] nmf secondhand clothes dealer.

fripon, -onne [fripɔ̃, -ɔn] nmf rascal; — a rascally.

fripouille [fripuj] nf rogue, scoundrel.

frire* [frir] vti to fry; **faire f.** to fry.

frise [friz] nf Archit frieze.

fris/er [frize] **1** vti (cheveux) to curl, wave; **f. qn** to curl ou wave s.o.'s hair. **2** vt (effleurer) to skim; (accident etc) to be within an ace of; **f. la trentaine** to be close on thirty. ◆**-é** a curly. ◆**frisette** nf ringlet, little curl.

frisquet [friskɛ] am chilly, coldish.

frisson [frisɔ̃] nm shiver; shudder; **donner le f. à qn** to give s.o. the creeps ou shivers. ◆**frissonner** vi (de froid) to shiver; (de peur etc) to shudder (de with).

frit [fri] voir **frire**; — a (poisson etc) fried. ◆**frites** nfpl chips, Am French fries. ◆**friteuse** nf (deep) fryer. ◆**friture** nf (matière) (frying) oil ou fat; (aliment) fried fish; (bruit) Rad Tél crackling.

frivole [frivɔl] a frivolous. ◆**frivolité** nf frivolity.

froid [frwa] a cold; **garder la tête froide** to keep a cool head; — nm cold; **avoir/prendre f.** to be/catch cold; **il fait f.** it's cold; **coup de f.** Méd chill; **jeter un f.** to cast a chill (dans over); **démarrer à f.** Aut to start (from) cold; **être en f.** to be on bad terms (avec with). ◆**froidement** adv coldly. ◆**froideur** nf (de sentiment, personne etc) coldness.

froisser [frwase] **1** vt, — **se f.** vpr (tissu etc) to crumple, rumple; **se f. un muscle** to strain a muscle. **2** vt **f. qn** to offend s.o.; **se f.** to take offence (de at).

frôler [frole] vt (toucher) to brush against, touch lightly; (raser) to skim; (la mort etc) to come within an ace of.

fromage [frɔmaʒ] nm cheese; **f. blanc** soft white cheese. ◆**fromager, -ère** a (industrie) cheese-; — nm (fabricant) cheesemaker. ◆**fromagerie** nf cheese dairy.

froment [frɔmã] nm wheat.

fronce [frɔ̃s] nf (pli dans un tissu) gather, fold. ◆**froncer** vt **1** (étoffe) to gather. **2 f. les sourcils** to frown. ◆**-ement** nm **f.** de sourcils frown.

fronde [frɔ̃d] nf **1** (arme) sling. **2** (sédition) revolt.

front [frɔ̃] nm forehead, brow; Mil Pol front; **de f.** (heurter) head-on; (côte à côte) abreast; (à la fois) (all) at once; **faire f. à** to face.

frontière [frɔ̃tjɛr] nf border, frontier; — a ville/etc **f.** border town/etc. ◆**frontalier, -ière** a border-, frontier-.

fronton [frɔ̃tɔ̃] nm Archit pediment.

frott/er [frɔte] vt to rub; (astiquer) to rub (up), shine; (plancher) to scrub; (allumette) to strike; **se f. à qn** (défier) to meddle with s.o., provoke s.o.; — vi to rub; (nettoyer, laver) to scrub. ◆**-ement** nm rubbing; Tech friction.

froufrou(s) [frufru] nm(pl) (bruit) rustling.

frousse [frus] nf Fam funk, fear; **avoir la f.** to be scared. ◆**froussard, -arde** nmf Fam coward.

fructifier [fryktifje] vi (arbre, capital) to bear fruit. ◆**fructueux, -euse** a (profitable) fruitful.

frugal, -aux [frygal, -o] a frugal. ◆**frugalité** nf frugality.

fruit [frɥi] nm fruit; **des fruits, les fruits** fruit; **porter f.** to bear fruit; **fruits de mer** seafood; **avec f.** fruitfully. ◆**fruité** a fruity. ◆**fruitier, -ière** a (arbre) fruit-; — nmf fruiterer.

frusques [frysk] nfpl (vêtements) Fam togs, clothes.

fruste [fryst] a (personne) rough.

frustr/er [frystre] vt f. qn to frustrate s.o.; f. qn de to deprive s.o. of. ◆—é a frustrated. ◆**frustration** nf frustration.

fuel [fjul] nm (fuel) oil.

fugace [fygas] a fleeting.

fugitif, -ive [fyʒitif, -iv] **1** nmf runaway, fugitive. **2** a (passager) fleeting.

fugue [fyg] nf **1** Mus fugue. **2** (absence) flight; **faire une f.** to run away.

fuir* [fɥir] vi to flee, run away; (temps) to fly; (gaz, robinet, stylo etc) to leak; — vt (éviter) to shun, avoid. ◆**fuite** nf (évasion) flight (de from); (de gaz etc) leak(age); (de documents) leak; **en f.** on the run; **prendre la f.** to take flight; **f. des cerveaux** brain drain; **délit de f.** Aut hit-and-run offence.

fulgurant [fylgyrã] a (regard) flashing; (vitesse) lightning-; (idée) spectacular, striking.

fulminer [fylmine] vi (personne) to thunder forth (contre against).

fumée [fyme] nf smoke; (vapeur) steam, fumes; pl (de vin) fumes. ◆**fum/er** vi to smoke; (liquide brûlant) to steam; (rager) Fam to fume; — vt to smoke. ◆—é a (poisson, verre etc) smoked. ◆—eur, -euse nmf smoker; **compartiment fumeurs** Rail smoking compartment. ◆**fume-cigarette** nm inv cigarette holder.

fumet [fyme] nm aroma, smell.

fumeux, -euse [fymø, -øz] a (idée etc) hazy, woolly.

fumier [fymje] nm manure, dung; (tas) dunghill.

fumigation [fymigɑsjɔ̃] nf fumigation.

fumigène [fymiʒɛn] a (bombe, grenade etc) smoke-.

fumiste [fymist] nmf (étudiant etc) time-waster, good-for-nothing. ◆**fumisterie** nf Fam farce, con.

funambule [fynãbyl] nmf tightrope walker.

funèbre [fynɛbr] a (service, marche etc) funeral-; (lugubre) gloomy. ◆**funérailles** nfpl funeral. ◆**funéraire** a (frais, salon etc) funeral-.

funeste [fynɛst] a (désastreux) catastrophic.

funiculaire [fynikylɛr] nm funicular.

fur et à mesure (au) [ofyreamzyr] adv as one goes along, progressively; **au f. et à m. que** as.

furet [fyrɛ] nm (animal) ferret. ◆**furet/er** vi to pry ou ferret about. ◆—eur, -euse a inquisitive, prying; — nmf inquisitive person.

fureur [fyrœr] nf (violence) fury; (colère) rage, fury; (passion) passion (de for); **en f.** furious; **faire f.** (mode etc) to be all the rage. ◆**furibond** a furious. ◆**furie** nf (colère, mégère) fury. ◆**furieux, -euse** a (violent, en colère) furious (contre with, at); (vent) raging; (coup) Fig tremendous.

furoncle [fyrɔ̃kl] nm Méd boil.

furtif, -ive [fyrtif, -iv] a furtive, stealthy.

fusain [fyzɛ̃] nm **1** (crayon, dessin) charcoal. **2** Bot spindle tree.

fuseau, -x [fyzo] nm **1** Tex spindle; **en f.** (jambes) spindly. **2** f. horaire time zone. **3** (pantalon) ski pants. ◆**fuselé** a slender.

fusée [fyze] nf rocket; (d'obus) fuse; **f. éclairante** flare.

fuselage [fyzlaʒ] nm Av fuselage.

fuser [fyze] vi (rires etc) to burst forth.

fusible [fyzibl] nm Él fuse.

fusil [fyzi] nm rifle, gun; (de chasse) shotgun; **coup de f.** gunshot, report; **un bon f.** (personne) a good shot. ◆**fusillade** nf (tirs) gunfire; (exécution) shooting. ◆**fusiller** vt (exécuter) to shoot; **f. qn du regard** to glare at s.o.

fusion [fyzjɔ̃] nf **1** melting; Phys Biol fusion; **point de f.** melting point; **en f.** (métal) molten. **2** (union) fusion; Com merger. ◆**fusionner** vti Com to merge.

fut [fy] voir être.

fût [fy] nm **1** (tonneau) barrel, cask. **2** (d'arbre) trunk. ◆**futaie** nf timber forest.

futé [fyte] a cunning, smart.

futile [fytil] a (propos, prétexte etc) frivolous, futile; (personne) frivolous; (tentative, action) futile. ◆**futilité** nf futility; pl (bagatelles) trifles.

futur, -ure [fytyr] a future; **future mère** mother-to-be; — nmf **f.** (mari) husband-to-be; **future** (épouse) wife-to-be; — nm future.

fuyant [fɥijã] voir **fuir**; — a (front, ligne) receding; (personne) evasive. ◆**fuyard** nm (soldat) runaway, deserter.

G

G, g [ʒe] *nm* G, g.

gabardine [gabardin] *nf* (*tissu, imperméable*) gabardine.

gabarit [gabari] *nm* (*de véhicule etc*) size, dimension.

gâcher [gɑʃe] *vt* 1 (*gâter*) to spoil; (*occasion, argent*) to waste; (*vie, travail*) to mess up. 2 (*plâtre*) to mix. ◆**gâchis** *nm* (*désordre*) mess; (*gaspillage*) waste.

gâchette [gɑʃɛt] *nf* (*d'arme à feu*) trigger; **une fine g.** (*personne*) *Fig* a marksman.

gadget [gadʒɛt] *nm* gadget.

gadoue [gadu] *nf* (*boue*) dirt, sludge; (*neige*) slush.

gaffe [gaf] *nf* (*bévue*) *Fam* blunder, gaffe. ◆**gaff/er** *vi* to blunder. ◆**-eur, -euse** *nmf* blunderer.

gag [gag] *nm* (*effet comique*) *Cin Th* (*sight*) gag.

gaga [gaga] *a Fam* senile, gaga.

gage [gaʒ] 1 *nm* (*promesse*) pledge; (*témoignage*) proof; (*caution*) security; **mettre en g.** to pawn. 2 *nmpl* (*salaire*) pay; **tueur à gages** hired killer, hitman.

gager [gaʒe] *vt* **g. que** *Litt* to wager that. ◆**gageure** [gaʒyr] *nf* (*impossible*) wager.

gagn/er [gaɲe] 1 *vt* (*par le travail*) to earn; (*mériter*) *Fig* to earn. 2 *vt* (*par le jeu*) to win; (*réputation, estime etc*) *Fig* to win, gain; **g. qn** to win s.o. over (à to); **g. une heure**/*etc* (*économiser*) to save an hour/*etc*; **g. du temps** (*temporiser*) to gain time; **g. du terrain/du poids** to gain ground/weight; – *vi* (*être vainqueur*) to win; **g. à être connu** to be well worth getting to know. 3 *vt* (*atteindre*) to reach; **g. qn** (*sommeil, faim etc*) to overcome s.o.; – *vi* (*incendie etc*) to spread, gain. ◆**-ant, -ante** *a* (*billet, cheval*) winning; – *nmf* winner. ◆**gagne-pain** *nm inv* (*emploi*) job, livelihood.

gai [ge] *a* (*personne, air etc*) cheerful, gay, jolly; (*ivre*) merry, tipsy; (*couleur, pièce*) bright, cheerful. ◆**gaiement** *adv* cheerfully, gaily. ◆**gaieté** *nf* (*de personne etc*) gaiety, cheerfulness, jollity.

gaillard [gajar] *a* vigorous; (*grivois*) coarse; – *nm* (*robuste*) strapping fellow; (*type*) *Fam* fellow. ◆**gaillarde** *nf Péj* brazen wench.

gain [gɛ̃] *nm* (*profit*) gain, profit; (*avantage*) *Fig* advantage; *pl* (*salaire*) earnings; (*au jeu*) winnings; **un g. de temps** a saving of time.

gaine [gɛn] *nf* 1 (*sous-vêtement*) girdle. 2 (*étui*) sheath.

gala [gala] *nm* official reception, gala.

galant [galɑ̃] *a* (*homme*) gallant; (*ton, propos*) *Hum* amorous; – *nm* suitor. ◆**galanterie** *nf* (*courtoisie*) gallantry.

galaxie [galaksi] *nf* galaxy.

galbe [galb] *nm* curve, contour. ◆**galbé** *a* (*jambes*) shapely.

gale [gal] *nf* **la g.** *Méd* the itch, scabies; (*d'un chien*) mange; **une (mauvaise) g.** (*personne*) *Fam* a pest.

galère [galɛr] *nf* (*navire*) *Hist* galley. ◆**galérien** *nm Hist* & *Fig* galley slave.

galerie [galri] *nf* 1 (*passage, magasin etc*) gallery; *Th* balcony. 2 *Aut* roof rack.

galet [galɛ] *nm* pebble, stone; *pl* shingle, pebbles.

galette [galɛt] *nf* 1 round, flat, flaky cake; (*crêpe*) pancake. 2 (*argent*) *Fam* dough, money.

galeux, -euse [galø, -øz] *a* (*chien*) mangy.

galimatias [galimatja] *nm* gibberish.

Galles [gal] *nfpl* **pays de G.** Wales. ◆**gallois, -oise** *a* Welsh; – *nm* (*langue*) Welsh; – *nmf* Welshman, Welshwoman.

gallicisme [galisism] *nm* (*mot etc*) gallicism.

galon [galɔ̃] *nm* (*ruban*) braid; (*signe*) *Mil* stripe; **prendre du g.** *Mil* & *Fig* to get promoted.

galop [galo] *nm* gallop; **aller au g.** to gallop; **g. d'essai** *Fig* trial run. ◆**galopade** *nf* (*ruée*) stampede. ◆**galop/er** *vi* (*cheval*) to gallop; (*personne*) to rush. ◆**-ant** *a* (*inflation etc*) *Fig* galloping.

galopin [galopɛ̃] *nm* urchin, rascal.

galvaniser [galvanize] *vt* (*métal*) & *Fig* to galvanize.

galvauder [galvode] *vt* (*talent, avantage etc*) to debase, misuse.

gambade [gɑ̃bad] *nf* leap, caper. ◆**gambader** *vi* to leap *ou* frisk about.

gambas [gɑ̃bas] *nfpl* scampi.

gamelle [gamɛl] *nf* (*de soldat*) mess tin; (*de campeur*) billy(can).

gamin, -ine [gamɛ̃, -in] *nmf* (*enfant*) *Fam*

kid; – a playful, naughty. ◆**gaminerie** nf
playfulness; (acte) naughty prank.

gamme [gam] nf Mus scale; (série) range.

gammée [game] af croix g. swastika.

gang [gãg] nm (de malfaiteurs) gang.
◆**gangster** nm gangster.

gangrène [gãgrεn] nf gangrene. ◆**se gan-
grener** [sɔgãgrəne] vpr Méd to become
gangrenous.

gangue [gãg] nf (enveloppe) Fig Péj outer
crust.

gant [gã] nm glove; g. de toilette face cloth,
cloth glove (for washing); jeter/relever le
g. Fig to throw down/take up the gauntlet;
boîte à gants glove compartment. ◆**ganté**
a (main) gloved; (personne) wearing gloves.

garage [garaʒ] nm Aut garage; voie de g.
Rail siding; Fig dead end. ◆**garagiste**
nmf garage owner.

garant, -ante [garã, -ãt] nmf (personne) Jur
guarantor; se porter g. de to guarantee,
vouch for; – nm (garantie) guarantee.
◆**garantie** nf guarantee; (caution) security; (protection) Fig safeguard; garantie(s)
(de police d'assurance) cover. ◆**garantir** vt
to guarantee (contre against); g. (à qn) que
to guarantee (s.o.) that; g. de (protéger) to
protect from.

garce [gars] nf Péj Fam bitch.

garçon [garsɔ̃] nm boy, lad; (jeune homme)
young man; (célibataire) bachelor; g. (de
café) waiter; g. d'honneur (d'un mariage)
best man; g. manqué tomboy; g. (comportement) boyish. ◆**garçonnet** nm little
boy. ◆**garçonnière** nf bachelor flat ou
Am apartment.

garde [gard] 1 nm (gardien) guard; Mil
guardsman; g. champêtre rural policeman;
g. du corps bodyguard; G. des Sceaux Fr
Justice Minister. 2 nf (d'enfants, de bagages
etc) care, custody (de of); avoir la g. de to
be in charge of; faire bonne g. to keep a
close watch; prendre g. to pay attention (à
qch to sth), (be careful (à qch of sth); prendre g. de ne pas faire to be careful not to
do; mettre en g. to warn (contre against);
mise en g. warning; de g. on duty; (soldat)
on guard duty; monter la g. to stand ou
mount guard; sur ses gardes on one's
guard; g. à vue (police) custody; chien de g.
watchdog. 3 nf (escorte, soldats) guard.
garde-à-vous [gardavu] nm inv Mil (position of) attention. ◆**g.-boue** nm inv mudguard, Am fender. ◆**g.-chasse** nm (pl
gardes-chasses) gamekeeper. ◆**g.-côte**
nm (personne) coastguard. ◆**g.-fou**
nm railing(s), parapet. ◆**g.-malade** nmf (pl

gardes-malades) nurse. ◆**g.-manger** nm
inv (armoire) food safe; (pièce) larder.
◆**g.-robe** nf (habits, armoire) wardrobe.

garder [garde] vt (maintenir, conserver, mettre de côté) to keep; (vêtement) to keep on;
(surveiller) to watch (over); (défendre) to
guard; (enfant) to look after, watch; (habitude) to keep up; g. qn (retenir) to keep s.o.;
g. la chambre to stay in one's room; g. le lit
to stay in bed; – se g. vpr (aliment) to
keep; se g. de qch (éviter) to beware of sth;
se g. de faire to take care not to do.
◆**garderie** nf day nursery. ◆**gardeuse**
nf g. d'enfants babysitter.

gardien, -ienne [gardjɛ̃, -jɛn] nmf (d'immeuble, d'hôtel) caretaker; (de prison)
(prison) guard, warder; (de zoo, parc) keeper; (de musée) attendant; g. de but Fb goalkeeper; gardienne d'enfants child minder;
g. de nuit night watchman; g. de la paix
policeman; g. de (libertés etc) Fig guardian
of; – am ange g. guardian angel.

gare [gar] 1 nf Rail station; g. routière bus
ou coach station. 2 int g. à watch ou look
out for; g. à toi! watch ou look out!; sans
crier g. without warning.

garer [gare] vt (voiture etc) to keep; (au garage) to garage; – se g. vpr (se protéger) to
get out of the way (de of); Aut to park.

gargariser (se) [səgargarize] vpr to gargle.
◆**gargarisme** nm gargle.

gargote [gargɔt] nf cheap eating house.

gargouille [garguj] nf Archit gargoyle.
gargouiller [garguje] vi (fontaine, eau) to
gurgle; (ventre) to rumble. ◆**gargouillis**
nm gurgling; rumbling.

garnement [garnəmã] nm rascal, urchin.
garn/ir [garnir] vt (équiper) to furnish, fit
out (de with); (magasin) to stock; (tissu) to
line; (orner) to adorn (de with); (enjoliver)
to trim (de with); (couvrir) to cover; Culin
to garnish; – se g. vpr (lieu) to fill (up) (de
with). ◆**—i** a (plat) served with vegetables; bien g. (portefeuille) Fig well-lined.
◆**garniture** nf Culin garnish, trimmings;
pl Aut fittings, upholstery; g. de lit bed
linen.

garnison [garnizɔ̃] nf Mil garrison.

gars [gɑ] nm Fam fellow, guy.

gas-oil [gazwal] nm diesel (oil).

gaspill/er [gaspije] vt to waste. ◆**—age**
nm waste.

gastrique [gastrik] a gastric. ◆**gastro-
nome** nmf gourmet. ◆**gastronomie** nf
gastronomy.

gâteau, -x [gɑto] nm cake; g. de riz rice
pudding; g. sec (sweet) biscuit, Am cookie;

c'était du g. (*facile*) *Fam* it was a piece of cake. **gât/er** [gate] *vt* to spoil; (*plaisir, vue*) to mar, spoil; **— se g.** *vpr* (*aliment, dent*) to go bad; (*temps, situation*) to get worse; (*relations*) to turn sour. ◆**—é** *a* (*dent, fruit etc*) bad. ◆**gâteries** *nfpl* (*cadeaux*) treats.

gâteux, -euse [gatø, -øz] *a* senile, soft in the head.

gauche¹ [goʃ] *a* (*côté, main etc*) left; **— nf** la g. (*côté*) the left (side); *Pol* the left (wing); à g. (*tourner etc*) (to the) left; (*marcher, se tenir*) on the left(-hand) side; de g. (*fenêtre etc*) left-hand; (*parti, politique etc*) left-wing; à g. de *on ou* to the left of. ◆**gaucher, -ère** *a* & *nmf* left-handed (person). ◆**gauchisant** *a Pol* leftish. ◆**gauchiste** *a* & *nmf Pol* (extreme) leftist.

gauche² [goʃ] *a* (*maladroit*) awkward. ◆**—ment** *adv* awkwardly. ◆**gaucherie** *nf* awkwardness; (*acte*) blunder.

gauchir [goʃir] *vti* to warp.

gaufre [gofr] *nf Culin* waffle. ◆**gaufrette** *nf* wafer (biscuit).

gaule [gol] *nf* long pole; *Pêche* fishing rod.

Gaule [gol] *nf* (*pays*) *Hist* Gaul. ◆**gaulois** *a* Gallic; (*propos etc*) *Fig* broad, earthy; **—** *nmpl* les G. *Hist* the Gauls. ◆**gauloiserie** *nf* broad joke.

gausser (se) [səgose] *vpr Litt* to poke fun (de at).

gaver [gave] *vt* (*animal*) to force-feed; (*personne*) *Fig* to cram (de with); **— se g.** *vpr* to gorge *ou* stuff oneself (de with).

gaz [gaz] *nm inv* gas; usine à g. gasworks; chambre/réchaud à g. gas chamber/stove; avoir des g. to have wind *ou* flatulence.

gaze [gaz] *nf* (*tissu*) gauze.

gazelle [gazɛl] *nf* (*animal*) gazelle.

gazer [gaze] **1** *vi Aut Fam* to whizz along; ça gaze! everything's just fine! **2** *vt Mil* to gas.

gazette [gazɛt] *nf Journ* newspaper.

gazeux, -euse [gazø, -øz] *a* (*état*) gaseous; (*boisson, eau*) fizzy. ◆**gazomètre** *nm* gasometer.

gazinière [gazinjɛr] *nf* gas cooker *ou Am* stove.

gazole [gazɔl] *nm* diesel (oil).

gazon [gazɔ̃] *nm* grass, lawn.

gazouiller [gazuje] *vi* (*oiseau*) to chirp; (*bébé, ruisseau*) to babble. ◆**gazouillis** *nm* chirping; babbling.

geai [ʒɛ] *nm* (*oiseau*) jay.

géant, -ante [ʒeɑ̃, -ɑ̃t] *a* & *nmf* giant.

Geiger [ʒeʒɛr] *nm* compteur G. Geiger counter.

geindre [ʒɛ̃dr] *vi* to whine, whimper.

gel [ʒɛl] *nm* **1** (*temps, glace*) frost; (*de crédits*) *Écon* freezing. **2** (*substance*) gel. ◆**gel/er** *vti* to freeze; **on gèle ici** it's freezing here; **— v imp** il **gèle** it's freezing. ◆**—é** *a* frozen; (*doigts*) *Méd* frostbitten. ◆**—ée** *nf* frost; *Culin* jelly, *Am* jello; g. blanche ground frost.

gélatine [ʒelatin] *nf* gelatin(e).

gélule [ʒelyl] *nf* (*médicament*) capsule.

Gémeaux [ʒemo] *nmpl* les G. (*signe*) Gemini.

gém/ir [ʒemir] *vi* to groan, moan. ◆**—issement** *nm* groan, moan.

gencive [ʒɑ̃siv] *nf Anat* gum.

gendarme [ʒɑ̃darm] *nm* gendarme, policeman (*soldier performing police duties*). ◆**gendarmerie** *nf* police force; (*local*) police headquarters.

gendre [ʒɑ̃dr] *nm* son-in-law.

gène [ʒɛn] *nm Biol* gene.

gêne [ʒɛn] *nf* (*trouble physique*) discomfort; (*confusion*) embarrassment; (*dérangement*) bother, trouble; dans la g. *Fin* in financial difficulties. ◆**gên/er** *vt* (*déranger, irriter*) to bother, annoy; (*troubler*) to embarrass; (*mouvement, action*) to hamper, hinder; (*circulation*) *Aut* to hold up, block; g. qn (*vêtement*) to be uncomfortable on s.o.; (*par sa présence*) to be in s.o.'s way; ça me gêne pas I don't mind (si if); **— se g.** *vpr* (*se déranger*) to put oneself out; ne te gêne pas pour moi! don't mind me! ◆**—ant** *a* (*objet*) cumbersome; (*présence, situation*) awkward; (*personne*) annoying. ◆**—é** *a* (*intimidé*) embarrassed; (*mal à l'aise*) uneasy, awkward; (*silence, sourire*) awkward; (*sans argent*) short of money.

généalogie [ʒenealɔʒi] *nf* genealogy. ◆**généalogique** *a* genealogical; arbre g. family tree.

général, -aux [ʒeneral, -o] **1** *a* (*global, commun*) general; en g. in general. **2** *nm* (*officier*) *Mil* general. ◆**générale** *nf Th* dress rehearsal. ◆**généralement** *adv* generally; g. parlant broadly *ou* generally speaking. ◆**généralisation** *nf* generalization. ◆**généraliser** *vti* to generalize; **— se g.** *vpr* to become general *ou* widespread. ◆**généraliste** *nmf Méd* general practitioner, GP. ◆**généralité** *nf* generality; la g. de the majority of.

générateur [ʒeneratœr] *nm*, ◆**génératrice** *nf El* generator.

génération [ʒenerasjɔ̃] *nf* generation.

généreux, -euse [ʒenerø, -øz] *a* generous (de with). ◆**généreusement** *adv* generously. ◆**générosité** *nf* generosity.

générique [ʒenerik] nm Cin credits.

genèse [ʒənɛz] nf genesis.

genêt [ʒənɛ] nm (arbrisseau) broom.

génétique [ʒenetik] nf genetics; – a genet-ic.

Genève [ʒənɛv] nm ou f Geneva.

génie [ʒeni] nm 1 (aptitude, personne) ge-nius; avoir le g. pour faire/de qch to have a genius for doing/for sth. 2 (lutin) genie, spirit. 3 g. civil civil engineering; g. militaire engineering corps. ◆**génial, -aux** a (personne, invention) brilliant; (for-midable) Fam fantastic.

génisse [ʒenis] nf (vache) heifer.

génital, -aux [ʒenital, -o] a genital; organes génitaux genitals.

génocide [ʒenɔsid] nm genocide.

genou, -x [ʒ(ə)nu] nm knee; être à genoux to be kneeling (down); se mettre à genoux to kneel (down); prendre qn sur ses genoux to take s.o. on one's lap ou knee. ◆**ge-nouillère** a nf Fb etc knee pad.

genre [ʒɑ̃r] nm 1 (espèce) kind, sort; (atti-tude) manner, way; g. humain mankind; le g. de vie way of life. 2 Littér Cin genre; Gram gender; Biol genus.

gens [ʒɑ̃] nmpl ou nfpl people; jeunes g. young people; (hommes) young men.

gentil, -ille [ʒɑ̃ti, -ij] a (agréable) nice, pleasant; (aimable) kind, nice; (mignon) pretty; g. avec qn nice ou kind to s.o.; sois g. (sage) be good. ◆**gentillesse** nf kind-ness; avoir la g. de faire to be kind enough to do. ◆**gentiment** adv (aimablement) kindly; (sagement) nicely.

gentilhomme, pl **gentilshommes** [ʒɑ̃tijɔm, ʒɑ̃tizɔm] nm (noble) Hist gen-tleman.

géographie [ʒeɔgrafi] nf geography. ◆**géographique** a geographical.

geôlier, -ière [ʒolje, -jɛr] nmf jailer, gaoler.

géologie [ʒeɔlɔʒi] nf geology. ◆**géo-logique** a geological. ◆**géologue** nmf ge-ologist.

géomètre [ʒeɔmɛtr] nm (arpenteur) sur-veyor.

géométrie [ʒeɔmetri] nf geometry. ◆**géométrique** a geometric(al).

géranium [ʒeranjɔm] nm Bot geranium.

gérant, -ante [ʒerɑ̃, -ɑ̃t] nmf manager, man-ageress; g. d'immeubles landlord's agent. ◆**gérance** nf (gestion) management.

gerbe [ʒɛrb] nf (de blé) sheaf; (de fleurs) bunch; (d'eau) spray; (d'étincelles) shower.

gercer [ʒɛrse] vti, — **se g.** vpr (peau, lèvres) to chap, crack. ◆**gerçure** nf chap, crack.

gérer [ʒere] vt (fonds, commerce etc) to man-age.

germain [ʒɛrmɛ̃] a cousin g. first cousin.

germanique [ʒɛrmanik] a Germanic.

germe [ʒɛrm] nm Méd Biol germ; Bot shoot; (d'une idée) Fig seed, germ. ◆**germer** vi Bot & Fig to germinate.

gésir [ʒezir] vi (être étendu) Litt to be lying; il gît/gisait he is/was lying; ci-gît here lies.

gestation [ʒɛstasjɔ̃] nf gestation.

geste [ʒɛst] nm gesture; ne pas faire un g. (ne pas bouger) not to make a move. ◆**gesticuler** vi to gesticulate.

gestion [ʒɛstjɔ̃] nf (action) management, ad-ministration. ◆**gestionnaire** nmf ad-ministrator.

geyser [ʒezɛr] nm Géol geyser.

ghetto [gɛto] nm ghetto.

gibecière [ʒibsjɛr] nf shoulder bag.

gibier [ʒibje] nm (animaux, oiseaux) game.

giboulée [ʒibule] nf shower, downpour.

gicl/er [ʒikle] vi (liquide) to spurt, squirt; (boue) to splash; faire g. to spurt, squirt. ◆**—ée** nf jet, spurt. ◆**—eur** nm (de carburateur) Aut jet.

gifle [ʒifl] nf slap (in the face). ◆**gifler** vt g. qn to slap s.o., slap s.o.'s face.

gigantesque [ʒigɑ̃tɛsk] a gigantic.

gigogne [ʒigɔɲ] a table g. nest of tables.

gigot [ʒigo] nm leg of mutton ou lamb.

gigoter [ʒigɔte] vi Fam to kick, wriggle.

gilet [ʒile] nm waistcoat, Am vest; (cardi-gan) cardigan, Am vest; (de corps) vest, Am undershirt; g. pare-balles bulletproof jacket ou Am vest; g. de sauvetage life jacket.

gin [dʒin] nm (eau-de-vie) gin.

gingembre [ʒɛ̃ʒɑ̃br] nm Bot Culin ginger.

girafe [ʒiraf] nf giraffe.

giratoire [ʒiratwar] a sens g. Aut round-about, Am traffic circle.

girl [gœrl] nf (danseuse) chorus girl.

girofle [ʒirɔfl] nm clou de g. Bot clove.

giroflée [ʒirɔfle] nf Bot wall flower.

girouette [ʒirwɛt] nf weathercock, weather vane.

gisement [ʒizmɑ̃] nm (de minerai, pétrole) Géol deposit.

gitan, -ane [ʒitɑ̃, -an] nmf (Spanish) gipsy.

gîte [ʒit] nm (abri) resting place.

gîter [ʒite] vi (navire) to list.

givre [ʒivr] nm (hoar)frost. ◆**se givrer** vpr (pare-brise etc) to ice up, frost up. ◆**givré** a frost-covered.

glabre [glabr] a (visage) smooth.

glace [glas] nf 1 (eau gelée) ice; (crème glacée) ice cream. 2 (vitre) window; (miroir) mirror; (verre) plate glass.

glacer [glase] **1** vt (sang) Fig to chill; g. qn (transir, paralyser) to chill s.o.; **— se g.** vpr (eau) to freeze. **2** vt (gâteau) to ice, (au jus) to glaze; (papier) to glaze. **◆glaçant** a (attitude etc) chilling, icy. **◆glacé** a **1** (eau, main, pièce) ice-cold, icy; (vent) freezing, icy; (accueil) Fig icy, chilly. **2** (thé) iced; (fruit, marron) candied; (papier) glazed. **◆glaçage** nm (de gâteau etc) icing. **◆glacial, -aux** a icy. **◆glacier** nm **1** Géol glacier. **2** (vendeur) ice-cream man. **◆glacière** nf (boîte, endroit) icebox. **◆glaçon** nm Culin ice cube; Géol block of ice; (sur le toit) icicle.

glaïeul [glajœl] nm Bot gladiolus.

glaires [glɛr] nfpl Méd phlegm.

glaise [glɛz] nf clay.

gland [glã] nm **1** Bot acorn. **2** (pompon) Tex tassel.

glande [glãd] nf gland.

glander [glãde] vi Arg to fritter away one's time.

glaner [glane] vt (blé, renseignement etc) to glean.

glapir [glapir] vi to yelp, yap.

glas [glã] nm (de cloche) knell.

glauque [glok] a sea-green.

gliss/er [glise] vi (involontairement) to slip; (patiner, coulisser) to slide; (sur l'eau) to glide; g. **sur** (sujet) to slide ou gloss over; ça glisse it's slippery; — vt (introduire) to slip (dans into); (murmurer) to whisper; **se g. dans/sous** to slip into/under. **◆—ant** a slippery. **◆glissade** nf (involontaire) slip; (volontaire) slide. **◆glissement** nm (de sens) Ling shift; g. à gauche Pol swing ou shift to the left; g. de terrain Géol landslide. **◆glissière** nf groove; porte à g. sliding door; fermeture à g. zip (fastener), Am zipper.

global, -aux [glɔbal, -o] a total, global; somme globale lump sum. **◆—ement** adv collectively, as a whole.

globe [glɔb] nm globe; g. de l'œil eyeball.

globule [glɔbyl] nm (du sang) corpuscle.

gloire [glwar] nf (renommée, louange, mérite) glory; (personne célèbre) celebrity; se faire g. de to glory in; à la g. de in praise of. **◆glorieux, -euse** a (plein de gloire) glorious. **◆glorifier** vt to glorify; se g. de to glory in.

glossaire [glɔsɛr] nm glossary.

glouglou [gluglu] nm (de liquide) gurgle. **◆glouglouter** vi to gurgle.

glouss/er [gluse] vi (poule) to cluck; (personne) to chuckle. **◆—ement** nm cluck; chuckle.

glouton, -onne [glutɔ̃, -ɔn] a greedy, gluttonous; — nmf glutton. **◆gloutonnerie** nf gluttony.

gluant [glyã] a sticky.

glucose [glykoz] nm glucose.

glycérine [gliserin] nf glycerin(e).

glycine [glisin] nf Bot wisteria.

gnome [gnom] nm (nain) gnome.

gnon [ɲɔ̃] nm Arg blow, punch.

goal [gol] nm Fb goalkeeper.

gobelet [gɔblɛ] nm tumbler; (de plastique, papier) cup.

gober [gɔbe] vt (œuf, mouche etc) to swallow (whole); (propos) Fig to swallow.

godasse [gɔdas] nf Fam shoe.

godet [gɔdɛ] nm (récipient) pot; (verre) Arg drink.

goéland [gɔelã] nm (sea)gull.

gogo [gogo] nm (homme naïf) Fam sucker.

gogo (à) [agogo] adv Fam galore.

goguenard [gɔgnar] a mocking.

goguette (en) [ãgɔgɛt] adv Fam on the spree.

goinfre [gwɛ̃fr] nm (glouton) Fam pig, guzzler. **◆se goinfrer** vpr Fam to stuff oneself (de with).

golf [gɔlf] nm golf; (terrain) golf course. **◆golfeur, -euse** nmf golfer.

golfe [gɔlf] nm gulf, bay.

gomme [gɔm] nf **1** (substance) gum. **2** (à effacer) rubber, Am eraser. **◆gommé** a (papier) gummed. **◆gommer** vt (effacer) to rub out, erase.

gomme (à la) [alagɔm] adv Fam useless.

gond [gɔ̃] nm (de porte etc) hinge.

gondole [gɔ̃dɔl] nf (bateau) gondola. **◆gondolier** nm gondolier.

gondoler [gɔ̃dɔle] **1** vi **, — se g.** vpr (planche) to warp. **2 se g.** vpr (rire) Fam to split one's sides.

gonfl/er [gɔ̃fle] vt to swell; (pneu) to inflate, pump up; (en soufflant) to blow up; (poitrine) to swell out; (grossir) Fig to inflate; — vi, **— se g.** vpr to swell; se g. de (orgueil, émotion) to swell with. **◆—é** a swollen; être g. Fam (courageux) to have plenty of pluck; (insolent) to have plenty of nerve. **◆—able** a inflatable. **◆—ement** nm swelling. **◆—eur** nm (air) pump.

gong [gɔ̃g] nm gong.

gorge [gɔrʒ] nf **1** throat; (seins) Litt bust. **2** Géog gorge. **◆gorg/er** vt (remplir) to stuff (de with); se g. de to stuff ou gorge oneself with. **◆—ée** nf mouthful; petite g. sip; d'une seule g. in ou at one gulp.

gorille [gɔrij] *nm* **1** (*animal*) gorilla. **2** (*garde du corps*) *Fam* bodyguard.

gosier [gozje] *nm* throat, windpipe.

gosse [gɔs] *nmf* (*enfant*) *Fam* kid, youngster.

gothique [gɔtik] *a & nm* Gothic.

gouache [gwaʃ] *nf* (*peinture*) gouache.

goudron [gudrɔ̃] *nm* tar. ◆**goudronner** *vt* to tar.

gouffre [gufr] *nm* gulf, chasm.

goujat [guʒa] *nm* churl, lout.

goulasch [gulaʃ] *nf* *Culin* goulash.

goulot [gulo] *nm* (*de bouteille*) neck; **boire au g.** to drink from the bottle.

goulu, -ue [guly] *a* greedy; – *nmf* glutton. ◆**goulûment** *adv* greedily.

goupille [gupij] *nf* (*cheville*) pin.

goupiller [gupije] *vt* (*arranger*) *Fam* to work out, arrange.

gourde [gurd] *nf* **1** (*à eau*) water bottle, flask. **2** (*personne*) *Péj* *Fam* chump, oaf.

gourdin [gurdɛ̃] *nm* club, cudgel.

gourer (se) [səgure] *vpr* *Fam* to make a mistake.

gourmand, -ande [gurmã, -ãd] *a* fond of eating, *Péj* greedy; **g. de** fond of; (*de sucreries*) to have a sweet tooth; – *nmf* hearty eater, *Péj* glutton. ◆**gourmandise** *nf* good eating, *Péj* gluttony; *pl* (*mets*) delicacies.

gourmet [gurmɛ] *nm* gourmet, epicure.

gourmette [gurmɛt] *nf* chain *ou* identity bracelet.

gousse [gus] *nf* **g. d'ail** clove of garlic.

goût [gu] *nm* taste; **de bon g.** in good taste; **prendre g. à qch** to take a liking to sth; **par g.** from *ou* by choice; **sans g.** tasteless. ◆**goûter** *vt* (*aliment*) to taste; (*apprécier*) to relish, enjoy; **g. à qch** to taste (a little of) sth; **g. de** (*pour la première fois*) to try out, taste; – *vi* to have a snack, have tea; – *nm* snack, tea.

goutte [gut] *nf* **1** drop. **couler g. à g.** to drip. **2** (*maladie*) gout. ◆**g.-à-goutte** *nm inv* *Méd* drip. ◆**gouttelette** *nf* droplet. ◆**goutter** *vi* (*eau, robinet, nez*) to drip (*de* from).

gouttière [gutjɛr] *nf* (*d'un toit*) gutter.

gouvernail [guvɛrnaj] *nm* (*pale*) rudder; (*barre*) helm.

gouvernante [guvɛrnɑ̃t] *nf* governess.

gouvernement [guvɛrnəmã] *nm* government. ◆**gouvernemental, -aux** *a* (*parti, politique etc*) government-.

gouvern/er [guvɛrne] *vti* *Pol & Fig* to govern, rule. ◆**-ants** *nmpl* rulers. ◆**-eur** *nm* governor.

grabuge [grabyʒ] *nm du g.* (*querelle*) *Fam* a rumpus.

grâce [gras] *nf* **1** (*charme*) & *Rel* grace; (*avantage*) favour; (*miséricorde*) mercy; **crier g.** to cry for mercy; **de bonne/ mauvaise g.** with good/bad grace; **donner le coup de g. à** to finish off; **faire g. de qch à qn** to spare s.o. sth. **2** *prép* **g. à** thanks to. ◆**gracier** *vt* (*condamné*) to pardon.

gracieux, -euse [grasjø, -øz] *a* **1** (*élégant*) graceful; (*aimable*) gracious. **2** (*gratuit*) gratuitous; **à titre g.** free (of charge). ◆**gracieusement** *adv* gracefully; graciously; free (of charge).

gracile [grasil] *a* *Litt* slender.

gradation [gradasjɔ̃] *nf* gradation.

grade [grad] *nm* *Mil* rank; **monter en g.** to be promoted. ◆**gradé** *nm* *Mil* non-commissioned officer.

gradin [gradɛ̃] *nm* *Th* row of seats, tier.

graduel, -elle [graduɛl] *a* gradual.

graduer [gradye] *vt* (*règle*) to graduate; (*exercices*) to grade, make gradually more difficult.

graffiti [grafiti] *nmpl* graffiti.

grain [grɛ̃] *nm* (*de blé etc*) & *Fig* grain; (*de café*) bean; (*de chapelet*) bead; (*de poussière*) speck; (*de céréales*) grain; **le g.** (*de cuir, papier*) the grain; **g. de beauté** mole; (*sur le visage*) beauty spot; **g. de raisin** grape. **2** *Mét* shower.

graine [grɛn] *nf* seed; **mauvaise g.** (*enfant*) *Péj* bad lot, rotten egg.

graisse [grɛs] *nf* fat; (*lubrifiant*) grease. ◆**graissage** *nm* *Aut* lubrication. ◆**graisser** *vt* to grease. ◆**graisseux, -euse** *a* (*vêtement etc*) greasy, oily; (*bourrelets, tissu*) fatty.

grammaire [gramɛr] *nf* grammar. ◆**grammatical, -aux** *a* grammatical.

gramme [gram] *nm* gram(me).

grand, grande [grã, grãd] *a* big, large; (*en hauteur*) tall; (*mérite, âge, chaleur, ami etc*) great; (*bruit*) loud, great; (*différence*) wide, great, big; (*adulte, mûr, plus âgé*) grown up, big; (*officier, maître*) grand; (*âme*) noble; **g. frère/etc** (*plus âgé*) big brother/etc; **le g. air** the open air; **il est g. temps** it's high time (*que* that); – *adv* **g. ouvert** (*yeux, fenêtre*) wide-open; **ouvrir g.** to open wide; **en g.** on a grand *ou* large scale; – *nmf* *Scol* senior; (*adulte*) grown-up; **les quatre Grands** *Pol* the Big Four. ◆**grandement** *adv* (*beaucoup*) greatly; (*généreusement*) grandly; **avoir g. de quoi vivre** to have plenty to live on. ◆**grandeur** *nf* (*importance, gloire*) greatness; (*dimension*) size, magni-

tude; (*majesté, splendeur*) grandeur; **g. na-**
ture life-size; **g. d'âme** generosity.

grand-chose [grãʃoz] *pron* **pas g.-chose** not
much. ◆**g.-mère** *nf* (*pl* **grands-mères**)
grandmother. ◆**grands-parents** *nmpl*
grandparents. ◆**g.-père** *nm* (*pl* **grands-**
pères) grandfather.

Grande-Bretagne [grãdbrǝtaɲ] *nf* Great
Britain.

grandiose [grãdjoz] *a* grandiose, grand.

grandir [grãdir] *vi* to grow; (*bruit*) to grow
louder; – *vt* (*grossir*) to magnify; (*faire*
paraître plus grand) to make s.o.
seem taller.

grange [grãʒ] *nf* barn.

granit(e) [granit] *nm* granite.

graphique [grafik] *a* (*signe, art*) graphic; –
nm graph.

grappe [grap] *nf* (*de fruits etc*) cluster; **g. de**
raisin bunch of grapes.

grappin [grapɛ̃] *nm* **mettre le g. sur** *Fam* to
grab hold of.

gras, grasse [grɑ, grɑs] *a* (*personne, ventre*
etc) fat; (*aliment*) fatty; (*graisseux*) greasy,
oily; (*caractère*) *Typ* bold, heavy; (*plante,*
contour) thick; (*rire*) throaty, deep; (*toux*)
loose, phlegmy; (*récompense*) rich; **matiè-**
res grasses fat; *Culin* foie gras, fatted
goose liver; – *nm* (*de viande*) fat. ◆**gras-**
sement *adv* (*abondamment*) handsomely.
◆**grassouillet, -ette** *a* plump.

gratifier [gratifje] *vt* **g. qn de** to present
ou favour s.o. with. ◆**gratification** *nf* (*prime*) bonus.

gratin [gratɛ̃] *nm* **1** **au g.** *Culin* baked with
breadcrumbs and grated cheese. **2** (*élite*)
Fam upper crust.

gratis [gratis] *adv* *Fam* free (of charge), gratis.

gratitude [gratityd] *nf* gratitude.

gratte-ciel [gratsjɛl] *nm inv* skyscraper.
gratte-papier [gratpapje] *nm* (*employé*) *Péj*
pen-pusher.

gratter [grate] *vt* (*avec un outil etc*) to scrape;
(*avec les ongles, les griffes etc*) to scratch;
(*boue*) to scrape off; (*effacer*) to scratch
out; **ça me gratte** *Fam* it itches, I have an
itch; – *vi* (*à la porte etc*) to scratch; (*tissu*)
to be scratchy; – **se g.** *vpr* to scratch oneself. ◆**grattoir** *nm* scraper.

gratuit [gratɥi] *a* (*billet etc*) free; (*hypothèse,*
acte) gratuitous. ◆**gratuité** *nf* **la g. de**
l'enseignement free education/*etc*.
◆**gratuitement** *adv* free (of charge); gra-
tuitously.

gravats [grava] *nmpl* rubble, debris.

grave [grav] *a* serious; (*juge, visage*) grave,

solemn; (*voix*) deep, low; (*accent*) *Gram*
grave; **ce n'est pas g.!** it's not important!
◆—**ment** *adv* (*malade, menacé*) seriously;
(*dignement*) gravely.

grav/er [grave] *vt* (*sur métal etc*) to engrave;
(*sur bois*) to carve; (*disque*) to cut; (*dans sa*
mémoire) to imprint, engrave. ◆—**eur** *nm*
engraver.

gravier [gravje] *nm* gravel. ◆**gravillon** *nm*
gravel; *pl* gravel, (loose) chippings.

gravir [gravir] *vt* to climb (with effort).

gravité [gravite] *nf* **1** (*de situation etc*) seriousness; (*solennité*) gravity. **2** *Phys* gravity.

graviter [gravite] *vi* to revolve (**autour de**
around). ◆**gravitation** *nf* gravitation.

gravure [gravyr] *nf* (*action, art*) engraving;
(*à l'eau forte*) etching; (*estampe*) print; (*de*
disque) recording; **g. sur bois** (*objet*) woodcut.

gré [gre] *nm* **à son g.** (*goût*) to his *ou* her
taste; (*désir*) as he *ou* she pleases; **de bon g.**
willingly; **contre le g. de** against the will of;
bon g. mal g. willy-nilly; **au g. de** (*vent etc*)
at the mercy of.

Grèce [grɛs] *nf* Greece. ◆**grec, grecque** *a*
& *nmf* Greek; – *nm* (*langue*) Greek.

greffe [grɛf] **1** *nf* (*de peau*) & *Bot* graft;
(*d'organe*) transplant. **2** *nm* *Jur* record office. ◆**greffer** *vt* (*peau etc*) & *Bot* to graft
(**à** on to); (*organe*) to transplant. ◆**gref-**
fier *nm* clerk of the court). ◆**greffon** *nm*
(*de peau*) & *Bot* graft.

grégaire [greger] *a* (*instinct*) gregarious.

grêle [grɛl] **1** *nf* (*Mét* & *Fig* hail. **2** *a* (*fin*)
spindly, (very) slender *ou* thin. ◆**grêler** *v*
imp to hail. ◆**grêlon** *nm* hailstone.

grêlé [grele] *a* (*visage*) pockmarked.

grelot [grǝlo] *nm* (small round) bell.

grelotter [grǝlɔte] *vi* to shiver (**de** with).

grenade [grǝnad] *nf* **1** *Bot* pomegranate. **2**
(*projectile*) *Mil* grenade. ◆**grenadine** *nf*
pomegranate syrup, grenadine.

grenat [grǝna] *a inv* (*couleur*) dark red.

grenier [grǝnje] *nm* attic; *Agr* granary.

grenouille [grǝnuj] *nf* frog.

grès [grɛ] *nm* (*roche*) sandstone; (*poterie*)
stoneware.

grésiller [grezije] *vi Culin* to sizzle; *Rad* to
crackle.

grève [grɛv] *nf* **1** strike; **g. de la faim** hunger
strike; **g. du zèle** work-to-rule, *Am*
rule-book slow-down; **g. perlée** go-slow,
Am slow-down (strike); **g. sauvage/sur le**
tas wildcat/sit-down strike; **g. tournante**
strike by rota. **2** (*de mer*) shore; (*de rivière*)
bank. ◆**gréviste** *nmf* striker.

gribouiller [gribuje] *vti* to scribble. ◆**gribouillis** *nm* scribble.

grief [grijɛf] *nm* (*plainte*) grievance.

grièvement [grijɛvmɑ̃] *adv* g. blessé seriously *ou* badly injured.

griffe [grif] *nf* 1 (*ongle*) claw; **sous la g. de qn** (*pouvoir*) in s.o.'s clutches. 2 (*de couturier*) (designer) label; (*tampon*) printed signature; (*d'auteur*) Fig mark, stamp. ◆**griffé** *a* (*vêtement*) designer-. ◆**griffer** *vt* to scratch, claw.

griffonn/er [grifɔne] *vt* to scrawl, scribble. ◆**—age** *nm* scrawl, scribble.

grignoter [griɲɔte] *vti* to nibble.

gril [gril] *nm* Culin grill, grid(iron). ◆**grillade** [grijad] *nf* (*viande*) grill. ◆**grille-pain** *nm inv* toaster. ◆**griller** *vt* (*viande*) to grill, broil; (*pain*) to toast; (*café*) to roast; (*ampoule*) El to blow; (*brûler*) to scorch; (*cigarette*) Fam to smoke; g. **un feu rouge** Aut Fam to drive through *ou* jump a red light; – *vi* **mettre à g.** to put on the grill; **on grille ici** Fam it's scorching; g. **de faire** to be itching to do.

grille [grij] *nf* (*clôture*) railings; (*porte*) (iron) gate; (*de fourneau, foyer*) grate; (*de radiateur*) Aut grid, grille; (*des salaires*) Fig scale; *pl* (*de fenêtre*) bars, grating; g. (**des horaires**) schedule. ◆**grillage** *nm* wire netting.

grillon [grijɔ̃] *nm* (*insecte*) cricket.

grimace [grimas] *nf* (*pour faire rire*) (funny) face, grimace; (*de dégoût, douleur*) grimace. ◆**grimacer** *vi* to grimace (de with).

grimer [grime] *vt*, – se g. *vpr* (*acteur*) to make up.

grimp/er [grɛ̃pe] *vi* to climb (à qch up sth); (*prix*) Fam to rocket; – *vt* to climb. ◆**—ant** *a* (*plante*) climbing.

grinc/er [grɛ̃se] *vi* to grate, creak; g. **des dents** to grind *ou* gnash one's teeth. ◆**—ement** *nm* grating; grinding.

grincheux, -euse [grɛ̃ʃø, -øz] *a* grumpy, peevish.

gringalet [grɛ̃galɛ] *nm* (*homme*) Péj puny runt, weakling.

grippe [grip] *nf* 1 (*maladie*) flu, influenza. 2 **prendre qch/qn en g.** to take a strong dislike to sth/s.o. ◆**grippé** *a* **être g.** to have (the) flu.

gripper [gripe] *vi*, – se g. *vpr* (*moteur*) to seize up.

grippe-sou [gripsu] *nm* skinflint, miser.

gris [gri] *a* grey, *Am* gray; (*temps*) dull, grey; (*ivre*) tipsy; – *nm* grey. ◆**grisaille** *nf* (*de vie*) dullness, greyness, *Am* grayness. ◆**grisâtre** *a* greyish, *Am* grayish.

◆**griser** *vt* (*vin etc*) to make (s.o.) tipsy, intoxicate (s.o.); (*air vif, succès*) to exhilarate (s.o.). ◆**griserie** *nf* intoxication; exhilaration. ◆**grisonn/er** *vi* (*cheveux, personne*) to go grey. ◆**—ant** *a* greying.

grisou [grizu] *nm* (*gaz*) firedamp.

grive [griv] *nf* (*oiseau*) thrush.

grivois [grivwa] *a* bawdy. ◆**grivoiserie** *nf* (*propos*) bawdy talk.

Groenland [grɔɛnlɑ̃d] *nm* Greenland.

grog [grɔg] *nm* (*boisson*) grog, toddy.

grogn/er [grɔɲe] *vi* to growl, grumble (**contre** at); (*cochon*) to grunt. ◆**—ement** *nm* growl, grumble; grunt. ◆**grognon, -onne** *a* grumpy, peevish.

grommeler [grɔmle] *vti* to grumble, mutter.

gronder [grɔ̃de] *vi* (*chien*) to growl; (*tonnerre*) to rumble; – *vt* (*réprimander*) to scold. ◆**grondement** *nm* growl; rumble. ◆**gronderie** *nf* scolding.

gros, grosse [gro, gros] *a* big; (*gras*) fat; (*épais*) thick; (*effort, progrès*) great; (*fortune, somme*) large; (*bruit*) loud; (*averse, mer, rhume*) heavy; (*faute*) serious, gross; (*traits, laine, fil*) coarse; g. **mot** swear word; – *adv* **gagner g.** to earn big money; **risquer g.** to take a big risk; **en g.** (*globalement*) roughly; (*écrire*) in big letters; (*vendre*) in bulk, wholesale; – *nmf* (*personne*) fat man, fat woman; – *nm* **le g. de** the bulk of; **de g.** (*maison, prix*) wholesale.

groseille [grozɛj] *nf* (white *ou* red) currant; g. **à maquereau** gooseberry.

grossesse [grosɛs] *nf* pregnancy.

grosseur [grosœr] *nf* 1 (*volume*) size; (*obésité*) weight. 2 (*tumeur*) Méd lump.

grossier, -ière [grosje, -jɛr] *a* (*matière, tissu, traits*) coarse, rough; (*idée, solution*) rough, crude; (*instrument*) crude; (*erreur*) gross; (*personne, manières*) coarse, uncouth, rude; **être g. envers** (*insolent*) to be rude to. ◆**grossièrement** *adv* (*calculer*) roughly; (*se tromper*) grossly; (*répondre*) coarsely, rudely. ◆**grossièreté** *nf* coarseness; roughness; (*insolence*) rudeness; (*mot*) rude word.

gross/ir [grosir] *vi* (*personne*) to put on weight; (*fleuve*) to swell; (*nombre, bosse, foule*) to swell, get bigger; (*bruit*) to get louder; – *vt* to swell; (*exagérer*) Fig to magnify; – *vti* (*verre, loupe etc*) to magnify; **verre grossissant** magnifying glass. ◆**—issement** *nm* increase in weight; swelling, increase in size; (*de microscope etc*) magnification.

grossiste [grosist] *nmf* Com wholesaler.

grosso modo [grosomɔdo] *adv* (*en gros*) roughly.

grotesque [grɔtɛsk] *a* (*risible*) ludicrous, grotesque.

grotte [grɔt] *nf* grotto.

grouill/er [gruje] **1** *vi* (*rue, fourmis, foule etc*) to be swarming (**de** with). **2 se g.** *vpr* (*se hâter*) *Arg* to step on it. ◆**—ant** *a* swarming (**de** with).

groupe [grup] *nm* group; **g. scolaire** (*bâtiments*) school block. ◆**groupement** *nm* (*action*) grouping; (*groupe*) group. ◆**grouper** *vt* to group (together); **— se g.** *vpr* to band together, group (together).

grue [gry] *nf* (*machine, oiseau*) crane.

grumeau, -x [grymo] *nm* (*dans une sauce etc*) lump. ◆**grumeleux, -euse** *a* lumpy.

gruyère [gryjɛr] *nm* gruyère (cheese).

gué [ge] *nm* ford; **passer à g.** to ford.

guenilles [gɑnij] *nfpl* rags (and tatters).

guenon [gɑnɔ̃] *nf* female monkey.

guépard [gepar] *nm* cheetah.

guêpe [gɛp] *nf* wasp. ◆**guêpier** *nm* (*nid*) wasp's nest; (*piège*) *Fig* trap.

guère [gɛr] *adv* (**ne**) . . . **g.** hardly, scarcely; **il ne sort g. he** hardly *ou* scarcely goes out.

guéridon [geridɔ̃] *nm* pedestal table.

guérilla [gerija] *nf* guerrilla warfare. ◆**guérillero** *nm* guerrilla.

guér/ir [gerir] *vt* (*personne, maladie*) to cure (**de** of); (*blessure*) to heal; **—** *vi* to recover; (*blessure*) to heal; (*rhume*) to get better; **g. de** (*fièvre etc*) to get over, recover from. ◆**—i** *a* cured, better, well. ◆**guérison** *nf* (*de personne*) recovery; (*de maladie*) cure; (*de blessure*) healing. ◆**guérisseur, -euse** *nmf* faith healer.

guérite [gerit] *nf* *Mil* sentry box.

guerre [gɛr] *nf* war; (*chimique etc*) warfare; **en g.** at war (**avec** with); **faire la g.** to wage *ou* make war (**à** on, against); **g. d'usure** war of attrition; **conseil de g.** court-martial. ◆**guerrier, -ière** *a* (*chant, danse*) war-; (*nation*) war-like; **—** *nmf* warrior. ◆**guerroyer** *vi* *Litt* to war.

guet [gɛ] *nm* **faire le g.** to be on the look-out. ◆**guett/er** *vt* to be on the look-out for,

watch (out) for; (*gibier*) to lie in wait for. ◆**—eur** *nm* (*soldat*) look-out.

guet-apens [gɛtapɑ̃] *nm inv* ambush.

guêtre [gɛtr] *nf* gaiter.

gueule [gœl] *nf* (*d'animal, de canon*) mouth; (*de personne*) *Fam* mouth; (*figure*) *Fam* face; **avoir la g. de bois** *Fam* to have a hangover; **faire la g.** *Fam* to sulk. ◆**gueuler** *vti* to bawl (out). ◆**gueuleton** *nm* (*repas*) *Fam* blow-out, feast.

gui [gi] *nm* *Bot* mistletoe.

guichet [giʃɛ] *nm* (*de gare, cinéma etc*) ticket office; (*de banque etc*) window; *Th* box office, ticket office; **à guichets fermés** *Th Sp* with all tickets sold in advance. ◆**guichetier, -ière** *nmf* (*à la poste etc*) counter clerk; (*à la gare*) ticket office clerk.

guide [gid] **1** *nm* (*personne, livre etc*) guide. **2** *nf* (*éclaireuse*) (girl) guide. **3** *nfpl* (*rênes*) reins. ◆**guider** *vt* to guide; **se g. sur** to guide oneself by.

guidon [gidɔ̃] *nm* (*de bicyclette etc*) handlebar(s).

guigne [giɲ] *nf* (*malchance*) *Fam* bad luck.

guignol [giɲɔl] *nm* (*spectacle*) = Punch and Judy show.

guillemets [gijmɛ] *nmpl* *Typ* inverted commas, quotation marks.

guilleret, -ette [gijrɛ, -ɛt] *a* lively, perky.

guillotine [gijɔtin] *nf* guillotine.

guimauve [gimov] *nf* *Bot Culin* marshmallow.

guimbarde [gɛ̃bard] *nf* (*voiture*) *Fam* old banger, *Am* (old) wreck.

guindé [gɛ̃de] *a* (*affecté*) stiff, stilted, stuck-up.

guingois (de) [dəgɛ̃gwa] *adv* askew.

guirlande [girlɑ̃d] *nf* garland, wreath.

guise [giz] *nf* **n'en faire qu'à sa g.** to do as one pleases; **en g. de** by way of.

guitare [gitar] *nf* guitar. ◆**guitariste** *nmf* guitarist.

guttural, -aux [gytyral, -o] *a* guttural.

gymnase [ʒimnaz] *nm* gymnasium. ◆**gymnaste** *nmf* gymnast. ◆**gymnastique** *nf* gymnastics.

gynécologie [ʒinekɔlɔʒi] *nf* gynaecology, *Am* gynecology. ◆**gynécologue** *nmf* gynaecologist, *Am* gynecologist.

H

H, h [aʃ] *nm* H, h; **l'heure H** zero hour; **bombe H** H-bomb.

ha! [ʼɑ] *int* ah!, oh!; **ha, ha!** (*rire*) ha-ha!

habile [abil] *a* clever, skilful (**à qch** at sth, **à faire** at doing). ◆**habilement** *adv* cleverly, skilfully. ◆**habileté** *nf* skill, ability.

habill/er [abije] *vt* to dress (**de** in); (*fournir en vêtements*) to clothe; (*couvrir*) to cover (**de** with); **h. qn en soldat**/*etc* (*déguiser*) to dress s.o. up as a soldier/*etc*; — **s'h.** *vpr* to dress (oneself), get dressed; (*avec élégance, se déguiser*) to dress up. ◆**—é** *a* dressed (**de** in); (*costume, robe*) smart, dressy. ◆**—ement** *nm* (*vêtements*) clothing, clothes.

habit [abi] *nm* costume, outfit; (*tenue de soirée*) evening dress, tails; *pl* (*vêtements*) clothes.

habit/er [abite] *vi* to live (**à, en, dans** in); — *vt* (*maison, région*) to live in; (*planète*) to inhabit. ◆**—ant, -ante** *nmf* (*de pays etc*) inhabitant; (*de maison*) resident, occupant. ◆**—é** *a* (*région*) inhabited; (*maison*) occupied. ◆**habitat** *nm* (*d'animal, de plante*) habitat; (*conditions*) housing, living conditions. ◆**habitation** *nf* house, dwelling; (*action de résider*) living.

habitude [abityd] *nf* habit; **avoir l'h. de qch** to be used to sth; **avoir l'h. de faire** to be used to doing, be in the habit of doing; **prendre l'h. de faire** to get into the habit of doing; **d'h.** usually; **comme d'h.** as usual. ◆**habituel, -elle** *a* usual, customary. ◆**habituellement** *adv* usually. ◆**habitu/er** *vt* **h. qn à** to accustom s.o. to; **être habitué à** to be used *ou* accustomed to; — **s'h.** *vpr* to get accustomed (**à** to). ◆**—é, -ée** *nmf* regular (customer *ou* visitor).

hache [ʼaʃ] *nf* axe, *Am* ax. ◆**hachette** *nf* hatchet.

hach/er [ʼaʃe] *vt* (*au couteau*) to chop (up); (*avec un appareil*) to mince, *Am* grind; (*déchiqueter*) to cut to pieces. ◆**—é a 1** (*viande*) minced, *Am* ground; chopped. **2** (*style*) staccato, broken. ◆**hachis** *nm* (*viande*) mince, minced *ou Am* ground meat. ◆**hachoir** *nm* (*couteau*) chopper; (*appareil*) mincer, *Am* grinder.

hagard [ʼagar] *a* wild-looking, frantic.

haie [ʼɛ] *nf* (*clôture*) *Bot* hedge; (*rangée*) row; (*de coureur*) *Sp* hurdle; (*de chevaux*) *Sp* fence, hurdle; **course de haies** (*coureurs*) hurdle race; (*chevaux*) steeplechase.

haillons [ʼɑjõ] *nmpl* rags (and tatters).

haine [ʼɛn] *nf* hatred, hate. ◆**haineux, -euse** *a* full of hatred.

haïr* [ʼair] *vt* to hate. ◆**haïssable** *a* hateful, detestable.

hâle [ʼɑl] *nm* suntan. ◆**hâlé** *a* (*par le soleil*) suntanned; (*par l'air*) weather-beaten.

haleine [alɛn] *nf* breath; **hors d'h.** out of breath; **perdre h.** to get out of breath; **reprendre h.** to get one's breath back, catch one's breath; **de longue h.** (*travail*) long-term; **tenir en h.** to hold in suspense.

hal/er [ʼale] *vt Nau* to tow. ◆**—age** *nm* towing; **chemin de h.** towpath.

halet/er [ʼalte] *vi* to pant, gasp. ◆**—ant** *a* panting, gasping.

hall [ʼol] *nm* (*de gare*) main hall, concourse; (*d'hôtel*) lobby, hall; (*de maison*) hall(way).

halle [ʼal] *nf* (*covered*) market; **les halles** *nm* central food market.

hallucination [alysinɑsjõ] *nf* hallucination. ◆**hallucinant** *a* extraordinary.

halo [ʼalo] *nm* (*auréole*) halo.

halte [ʼalt] *nf* (*arrêt*) stop, *Mil* halt; (*lieu*) stopping place, *Mil* halting place; **faire h.** to stop; — *int* stop!, *Mil* halt!

haltère [alter] *nm* (*poids*) *Sp* dumbbell. ◆**haltérophilie** *nf* weight lifting.

hamac [ʼamak] *nm* hammock.

hameau, -x [ʼamo] *nm* hamlet.

hameçon [amsõ] *nm* (*fish*) hook; **mordre à l'h.** *Pêche & Fig* to rise to *ou* swallow the bait.

hamster [ʼamster] *nm* hamster.

hanche [ʼãʃ] *nf Anat* hip.

hand(-)ball [ʼadbal] *nm Sp* handball.

handicap [ʼadikap] *nm* (*désavantage*) & *Sp* handicap. ◆**handicap/er** *vt* to handicap. ◆**—é, -ée** *a & nmf* handicapped (person); **h. moteur** spastic.

hangar [ʼãgar] *nm* (*entrepôt*) shed; (*pour avions*) hangar.

hanneton [ʼantõ] *nm* (*insecte*) cockchafer.

hanter [ʼãte] *vt* to haunt.

hantise [ʼãtiz] *nf* **la h. de** an obsession with

happer ['ape] vt (saisir) to catch, snatch; (par la gueule) to snap up.

haras ['aʀɑ] nm stud farm.

harasser ['aʀase] vt to exhaust.

harceler ['aʀsəle] vt to harass, torment (de with). ◆**harcèlement** nm harassment.

hardi ['aʀdi] a bold, daring. ◆**—ment** adv boldly. ◆**hardiesse** nf (boldness, daring; **une h.** (action) Litt an audacity.

harem ['aʀɛm] nm harem.

hareng ['aʀɑ̃] nm herring.

hargne ['aʀɲ] nf aggressive bad temper. ◆**hargneux, -euse** a bad-tempered, aggressive.

haricot ['aʀiko] nm (blanc) (haricot) bean; (vert) French bean, green bean.

harmonica [aʀmɔnika] nm harmonica, mouthorgan.

harmonie [aʀmɔni] nf harmony. ◆**harmonieux, -euse** a harmonious. ◆**harmonique** a & nm Mus harmonic. ◆**harmoniser** vt, — **s'h.** vpr to harmonize. ◆**harmonium** nm Mus harmonium.

harnacher ['aʀnaʃe] vt (cheval etc) to harness. ◆**harnais** nm (de cheval, bébé) harness.

harpe ['aʀp] nf harp. ◆**harpiste** nmf harpist.

harpon ['aʀpɔ̃] nm harpoon. ◆**harponner** vt (baleine) to harpoon; **h. qn** (arrêter) Fam to waylay s.o.

hasard ['azaʀ] nm **le h.** chance; **un h.** (coïncidence) a coincidence; **un heureux h.** a stroke of luck, some luck; **un malheureux h.** a rotten piece of luck; **par h.** by chance; **si par h.** if by any chance; **au h.** at random, haphazardly; **à tout h.** just in case; **les hasards de** (risques) the hazards of. ◆**hasard/er** vt (remarque, démarche) to venture, hazard; (vie, réputation) to risk; **se h. dans** to venture into; **se h. à faire** to risk doing, venture to do. ◆**—é a**, ◆**hasardeux, -euse** a risky, hazardous.

haschisch ['aʃiʃ] nm hashish.

hâte ['ɑt] nf haste, speed; (impatience) eagerness; **en h., à la h.** hurriedly, in a hurry, in haste; **avoir h. de faire** (désireux) to be eager to do, be in a hurry to do. ◆**hâter** vt (pas, départ etc) to hasten; — **se h.** vpr to hurry, make haste (**de faire** to do). ◆**hâtif, -ive** a hasty, hurried; (développement) precocious; (fruit) early.

hausse ['os] nf rise (**de** in); **en h.** rising. ◆**hausser** vt (prix, voix etc) to raise; (épaules) to shrug; **se h. sur la pointe des pieds** to stand on tip-toe.

haut ['o] a high; (de taille) tall; (classes) up-per, higher; (fonctionnaire etc) high-ranking; **le h. Rhin** the upper Rhine; **la haute couture** high fashion; **à haute voix** aloud, in a loud voice; **h. de 5 mètres** 5 metres high ou tall; — adv (voler, viser etc) high (up); (estimer) highly; (parler) loud, loudly; **tout h.** (lire, penser) aloud, out loud; **h. placé** (personne) in a high position; **plus h.** (dans un texte) above, further back; — nm (partie haute) top; **en h. de** at the top of; **en h.** (loger) upstairs; (regarder) up; (mettre) on (the) top; **d'en h.** (de la partie haute, du ciel etc) from high up, from up above; **avoir 5 mètres de h.** to be 5 metres high ou tall; **des hauts et des bas** Fig ups and downs.

hautain ['otɛ̃] a haughty.

hautbois ['obwa] nm Mus oboe.

haut-de-forme ['odfɔʀm] nm (pl hauts-de-forme) top hat.

hautement ['otmɑ̃] adv (tout à fait, très) highly. ◆**hauteur** nf height; Géog hill; (orgueil) Péj haughtiness; Mus pitch; **la h. de** (objet) level with; (cri) opposite; (situation) Fig equal to; **il n'est pas à la h.** he isn't up to it; **saut en h.** Sp high jump.

haut-le-cœur ['olkœʀ] nm inv **avoir des h.-le-cœur** to retch, gag.

haut-le-corps ['olkɔʀ] nm inv (sursaut) sudden start, jump.

haut-parleur ['oparlœʀ] nm loudspeaker.

hâve ['av] a gaunt, emaciated.

havre ['avʀ] nm (refuge) Litt haven.

Haye (La) [la'ɛ] nf The Hague.

hayon ['ɛjɔ̃] nm (porte) Aut tailgate, hatchback.

hé! [e] int (là) (appel) hey!; **hé! hé!** well, well!

hebdomadaire [ɛbdɔmadɛʀ] a weekly; — nm (publication) weekly.

héberg/er [ebɛʀʒe] vt to put up, accommodate. ◆**—ement** nm accommodation; **centre d'h.** shelter.

hébété [ebete] a dazed, stupefied.

hébreu, -x [ebrø] am Hebrew; — nm (langue) Hebrew. ◆**hébraïque** a Hebrew.

hécatombe [ekatɔ̃b] nf (great) slaughter.

hectare [ɛktaʀ] nm hectare (= 2.47 acres).

hégémonie [eʒemɔni] nf hegemony, supremacy.

hein! [ɛ̃] int (surprise, interrogation etc) eh!

hélas! ['elas] int alas!, unfortunately.

héler ['ele] vt (taxi etc) to hail.

hélice [elis] nf Av Nau propeller.

hélicoptère [elikɔptɛʀ] nm helicopter. ◆**héliport** nm heliport.

hellénique [elenik] a Hellenic, Greek.

helvétique [ɛlvetik] *a* Swiss.

hem! ['ɛm] *int* (a)hem!, hm!

hémicycle [emisikl] *nm* semicircle; *Pol Fig* French National Assembly.

hémisphère [emisfɛr] *nm* hemisphere.

hémorragie [emoraʒi] *nf Méd* h(a)emorrhage; (*de capitaux*) *Com* outflow, drain.

hémorroïdes [emɔrɔid] *nfpl* piles, h(a)emorrhoids.

henn/ir ['enir] *vi* (*cheval*) to neigh. ◆**—issement** *nm* neigh.

hep! ['ɛp] *int* hey!, hey there!

hépatite [epatit] *nf* hepatitis.

herbe [ɛrb] *nf* grass; (*médicinale etc*) herb; **mauvaise h.** weed; **fines herbes** *Culin* herbs; **en h.** (*blés*) green; (*poète etc*) *Fig* budding. ◆**herbage** *nm* grassland. ◆**herbeux, -euse** *a* grassy. ◆**herbicide** *nm* weed killer. ◆**herbivore** *a* grass-eating, herbivorous. ◆**herbu** *a* grassy.

hercule [ɛrkyl] *nm* Hercules, strong man. ◆**herculéen, -enne** *a* herculean.

hérédité [eredite] *nf* heredity. ◆**héréditaire** *a* hereditary. — *nmf* heretic.

hérésie [erezi] *nf* heresy. ◆**hérétique** *a* heretical; — *nmf* heretic.

hériss/er ['erise] *vt* (*poils*) to bristle (up); **h. qn** (*irriter*) to ruffle s.o., ruffle s.o.'s feathers; — **se h.** *vpr* to bristle (up); to get ruffled. ◆**—é** *a* (*cheveux*) bristly; (*cactus*) prickly; **h. de** bristling with.

hérisson ['erisɔ̃] *nm* (*animal*) hedgehog.

hérit/er [erite] *vti* to inherit (**qch de qn sth from s.o.**); **h. de qch** to inherit sth. ◆**—age** *nm* (*biens*) inheritance; (*culturel, politique etc*) *Fig* heritage. ◆**héritier** *nm* heir. ◆**héritière** *nf* heiress.

hermétique [ɛrmetik] *a* hermetically sealed, airtight; (*obscur*) *Fig* impenetrable. ◆**—ment** *adv* hermetically.

hermine [ɛrmin] *nf* (*animal, fourrure*) ermine.

hernie ['erni] *nf Méd* hernia, rupture; (*de pneu*) swelling.

héron ['erɔ̃] *nm* (*oiseau*) heron.

héros ['ero] *nm* hero. ◆**héroïne** [erɔin] *nf* 1 (*femme*) heroine. 2 (*stupéfiant*) heroin. ◆**héroïque** [erɔik] *a* heroic. ◆**héroïsme** [erɔism] *nm* heroism.

hésit/er [ezite] *vi* to hesitate (**sur** over, about; **à faire** to do); (*en parlant*) to falter, hesitate. ◆**—ant** *a* (*personne*) hesitant; (*pas, voix*) faltering, unsteady, wavering. ◆**hésitation** *nf* hesitation; **avec h.** hesitantly.

hétéroclite [eteroklit] *a* (*disparate*) motley.

hétérogène [eterɔʒɛn] *a* heterogeneous.

hêtre ['ɛtr] *nm* (*arbre, bois*) beech.

heu! ['ø] *int* (*hésitation*) er!

heure [œr] *nf* (*mesure*) hour; (*moment*) time; **quelle h. est-il?** what time is it?; **il est six heures** it's six (o'clock); **six heures moins cinq** five to six; **six heures cinq** five past *ou Am* after six; **à l'h.** (*arriver*) on time; (*être payé*) by the hour; **dix kilomètres à l'h.** ten kilometres an hour; **à l'h. qu'il est** (by) now; **de dernière h.** (*nouvelle*) last minute; **de bonne h.** early; **à une h. avancée** at a late hour, late at night; **tout à l'h.** (*futur*) in a few moments, later; (*passé*) a moment ago; **à toute h.** (*continuellement*) at all hours; **faire des heures supplémentaires** to work *ou* do overtime; **heures creuses** off-peak *ou* slack periods; **l'h. d'affluence**, **l'h. de pointe** (*circulation etc*) rush hour; (*dans les magasins*) peak period; **l'h. de pointe** (*électricité etc*) peak period.

heureux, -euse [œrø, -øz] *a* happy (*chanceux*) lucky, fortunate; (*issue, changement*) successful; (*expression*) apt; **h. de qch/de voir qn** (*satisfait*) happy *ou* pleased *ou* glad about sth/to see s.o.; — *adv* (*vivre, mourir*) happily. ◆**heureusement** *adv* (*par chance*) fortunately, luckily, happily (*pour* for); (*avec succès*) successfully; (*exprimer*) aptly.

heurt [œr] *nm* bump, knock; (*d'opinions etc*) *Fig* clash; **sans heurts** smoothly. ◆**heurt/er** *vt* (*cogner*) to knock, bump, hit (*contre* against); (*mur, piéton*) to bump into, hit; **h. qn** (*choquer*) to offend s.o., upset s.o.; — **se h. à** to bump into, hit; (*difficultés*) *Fig* to come up against. ◆**—é** *a* (*couleurs, tons*) clashing; (*style, rythme*) jerky. ◆**heurtoir** *nm* (*door*) knocker.

hexagone [ɛgzagɔn] *nm* hexagon; **l'H.** *Fig* France. ◆**hexagonal, -aux** *a* hexagonal; *Fig Fam* French.

hiatus [jatys] *nm Fig* hiatus, gap.

hiberner [ibɛrne] *vi* to hibernate. ◆**hibernation** *nf* hibernation.

hibou, -x ['ibu] *nm* owl.

hic ['ik] *nm* **voilà le h.** *Fam* that's the snag.

hideux, -euse ['idø, -øz] *a* hideous.

hier [(i)jɛr] *adv* & *nm* yesterday; **h. soir** last *ou* yesterday night, yesterday evening; **elle n'est pas née d'h.** *Fig* she wasn't born yesterday.

hiérarchie ['jerarʃi] *nf* hierarchy. ◆**hiérarchique** *a* (*ordre*) hierarchical; **par la voie h.** through (the) official channels. ◆**hiérarchiser** *vt* (*emploi, valeurs*) to grade.

hi-fi ['ifi] *a inv* & *nf inv Fam* hi-fi.

hilare [ilar] *a* merry. ◆**hilarant** *a* (*drôle*) hilarious. ◆**hilarité** *nf* (sudden) laughter.

hindou, -oue [ɛ̃du] *a* & *nmf* Hindu.

hippie [ipi] *nmf* hippie.

hippique [ipik] *a* **un concours h.** a horse show, a show-jumping event. ◆**hippodrome** *nm* racecourse, racetrack (*for horses*).

hippopotame [ipɔpɔtam] *nm* hippopotamus.

hirondelle [irɔ̃del] *nf* (*oiseau*) swallow.

hirsute [irsyt] *a* (*personne, barbe*) unkempt, shaggy.

hispanique [ispanik] *a* Spanish, Hispanic.

hisser ['ise] *vt* (*voile, fardeau etc*) to hoist, raise; **– se h.** *vpr* to raise oneself (up).

histoire [istwar] *nf* (*science, événements*) history; (*récit, mensonge*) story; (*affaire*) *Fam* business, matter; *pl* (*ennuis*) trouble; (*façons, chichis*) fuss; **toute une h.** (*problème*) quite a lot of trouble; (*chichis*) quite a lot of fuss; **h. de voir/etc** (so as) to see/etc; **h. de rire** for (the sake of) a laugh; **sans histoires** (*voyage etc*) uneventful. ◆**historien, -ienne** *nmf* historian. ◆**historique** *a* historical; (*lieu, événement*) historic; **– nm** **faire l'h. de** to give an historical account of.

hiver [iver] *nm* winter. ◆**hivernal, -aux** *a* (*froid etc*) winter-.

HLM [aʃɛlɛm] *nm ou f abrév* (*habitation à loyer modéré*) = council flats, *Am* = low-rent apartment building (*sponsored by government*).

hoch/er ['ɔʃe] *vt* **h. la tête** (*pour dire oui*) to nod one's head; (*pour dire non*) to shake one's head. ◆**–ement** *nm* **h. de tête** nod; shake of the head.

hochet ['ɔʃe] *nm* (*jouet*) rattle.

hockey ['ɔke] *nm* hockey; **h. sur glace** ice hockey.

holà ['ɔla] *int* (*arrêtez*) hold on!, stop!; (*pour appeler*) hallo!; **– nm inv mettre le h.** à to put a stop to.

hold-up ['ɔldœp] *nm inv* (*attaque*) holdup, stick-up.

Hollande ['ɔlɑ̃d] *nf* Holland. ◆**hollandais, -aise** *a* Dutch; **– nmf** Dutchman, Dutchwoman; **– nm** (*langue*) Dutch.

holocauste [ɔlɔkost] *nm* (*massacre*) holocaust.

homard ['ɔmar] *nm* lobster.

homélie [ɔmeli] *nf* homily.

homéopathie [ɔmeɔpati] *nf* hom(o)eopathy.

homicide [ɔmisid] *nm* murder, homicide; **h. involontaire** manslaughter.

hommage [ɔmaʒ] *nm* tribute, homage (à to); *pl* (*civilités*) respects; **rendre h.** à to pay (a) tribute to, pay homage to.

homme [ɔm] *nm* man; **l'h.** (*espèce*) man(kind); **des vêtements d'h.** men's clothes; **d'h. à h.** man to man; **l'h. de la rue** *Fig* the man in the street; **h. d'affaires** businessman. ◆**h.-grenouille** *nm* (*pl* **hommes-grenouilles**) frogman.

homogène [ɔmɔʒɛn] *a* homogeneous. ◆**homogénéité** *nf* homogeneity.

homologue [ɔmɔlɔg] *a* equivalent (de to); **– nmf** counterpart, opposite number.

homologuer [ɔmɔlɔge] *vt* to approve *ou* recognize officially, validate.

homonyme [ɔmɔnim] *nm* (*personne, lieu*) namesake.

homosexuel, -elle [ɔmɔseksɥel] *a* & *nmf* homosexual. ◆**homosexualité** *nf* homosexuality.

Hongrie ['ɔ̃gri] *nf* Hungary. ◆**hongrois, -oise** *a* & *nmf* Hungarian; **– nm** (*langue*) Hungarian.

honnête [ɔnet] *a* (*intègre*) honest; (*satisfaisant, passable*) decent, fair. ◆**honnêtement** *adv* honestly; decently. ◆**honnêteté** *nf* honesty.

honneur [ɔnœr] *nm* (*dignité, faveur*) honour; (*mérite*) credit; **en l'h. de** in honour of; **faire h.** à (*sa famille etc*) to be a credit to; (*par sa présence*) to do honour to; (*promesse etc*) to honour; (*repas*) to do justice to; **en h.** (*roman etc*) in vogue; **invité d'h.** guest of honour; **membre d'h.** honorary member; **avoir la place d'h.** to have pride of place *ou* the place of honour. ◆**honorabilité** *nf* respectability. ◆**honorable** *a* honourable; (*résultat, salaire etc*) *Fig* respectable. ◆**honoraire** **1** *a* (*membre*) honorary. **2** *nmpl* (*d'avocat etc*) fees. ◆**honorer** *vt* to honour (de with); **h. qn** (*conduite etc*) to do credit to s.o.; **s'h. d'être** to pride oneself *ou* itself on being. ◆**honorifique** *a* (*titre*) honorary.

honte ['ɔ̃t] *nf* shame; **avoir h.** to be *ou* feel ashamed (de qch/de faire of sth/to do, of doing); **faire h.** à to put to shame; **fausse h.** self-consciousness; **– honteux, -euse** *a* (*déshonorant*) shameful; (*penaud*) ashamed, shamefaced; **être h. de** to be ashamed of. ◆**honteusement** *adv* shamefully.

hop! ['ɔp] *int* **allez, h.!** jump!, move!

hôpital, -aux [ɔpital, -o] *nm* hospital; **à l'h.** in hospital, *Am* in the hospital.

hoquet ['ɔke] *nm* hiccup; **le h.** (the) hiccups. ◆**hoqueter** *vi* to hiccup.

horaire [ɔrɛr] a (salaire etc) hourly; (vitesse) per hour; – nm timetable, schedule.

horde [ɔrd] nf (troupe) Péj horde.

horizon [ɔrizɔ̃] nm horizon; (vue, paysage) view; à l'h. on the horizon.

horizontal, -aux [ɔrizɔ̃tal, -o] a horizontal. ◆**—ement** adv horizontally.

horloge [ɔrlɔʒ] nf clock. ◆**horloger, -ère** nmf watchmaker. ◆**horlogerie** nf (magasin) watchmaker's (shop); (industrie) watchmaking.

hormis [ɔrmi] prép Litt save, except (for).

hormone [ɔrmɔn] nf hormone. ◆**hormonal, -aux** a (traitement etc) hormone-.

horoscope [ɔrɔskɔp] nm horoscope.

horreur [ɔrœr] nf horror; pl (propos) horrible things; **faire h. à** to disgust; **avoir h. de** to hate, loathe. ◆**horrible** a horrible, awful. ◆**horriblement** adv horribly. ◆**horrifiant** a horrifying, horrific. ◆**horrifié** a horrified.

horripiler [ɔripile] vt to exasperate.

hors [ɔr] prép **h. de** (maison, boîte etc) outside, out of; (danger, haleine etc) Fig out of; **h. de doute** beyond doubt; **h. de soi** (furieux) beside oneself; **être h. jeu** Fb to be offside. ◆**h.-bord** nm inv speedboat; **moteur h.-bord** outboard motor. ◆**h.-concours** a inv non-competing. ◆**h.-d'œuvre** nm inv Culin starter, hors-d'œuvre. ◆**h.-jeu** nm inv Fb offside. ◆**h.-la-loi** nm inv outlaw. ◆**h.-taxe** a inv (magasin, objet) duty-free.

hortensia [ɔrtɑ̃sja] nm (arbrisseau) hydrangea.

horticole [ɔrtikɔl] a horticultural. ◆**horticulteur, -trice** nmf horticulturalist. ◆**horticulture** nf horticulture.

hospice [ɔspis] nm (pour vieillards) geriatric hospital.

hospitalier, -ère [ɔspitalje, -jɛr] a **1** (accueillant) hospitable. **2** (personnel etc) Méd hospital-. ◆**hospitaliser** vt to hospitalize. ◆**hospitalité** nf hospitality.

hostie [ɔsti] nf (pain) Rel host.

hostile [ɔstil] a hostile (à to, towards). ◆**hostilité** nf hostility (envers to, towards); pl Mil hostilities.

hôte [ot] **1** nm (maître) host. **2** nmf (invité) guest. ◆**hôtesse** nf hostess; **h. (de l'air)** (air) hostess.

hôtel [otɛl] nm hotel; **h. particulier** mansion, town house; **h. de ville** town hall; **h. des ventes** auction rooms. ◆**hôtelier, -ière** nmf hotel-keeper, hotelier; – a (industrie etc) hotel-. ◆**hôtellerie** nf **1** (auberge) inn, hostelry. **2** (métier) hotel trade.

hotte [ɔt] nf **1** (panier) basket (carried on back). **2** (de cheminée etc) hood.

houblon [ublɔ̃] nm le **h.** Bot hops.

houille [uj] nf coal; **h. blanche** hydroelectric power. ◆**houiller, -ère** a (bassin, industrie) coal-; – nf coalmine, colliery.

houle [ul] nf (de mer) swell, surge. ◆**houleux, -euse** a (mer) rough; (réunion etc) Fig stormy.

houppette [upɛt] nf powder puff.

hourra [ura] nm & int hurray, hurrah.

houspiller [uspije] vt to scold, upbraid.

housse [us] nf (protective) cover.

houx [u] nm holly.

hublot [yblo] nm Nau Av porthole.

huche [yʃ] nf **h. à pain** bread box ou chest.

hue! [y] int gee up! (to horse).

huer [ɥe] vt to boo. ◆**huées** nfpl boos.

huile [ɥil] nf **1** oil; **peinture à l'h.** oil painting. **2** (personnage) Fam big shot. ◆**huiler** vt to oil. ◆**huileux, -euse** a oily.

huis [ɥi] nm **à h. clos** Jur in camera.

huissier [ɥisje] nm (introducteur) usher; (officier) Jur bailiff.

huit [ɥit] a (['ɥi] before consonant) eight; **h. jours** a week; – nm eight. ◆**huitaine** nf (about) eight; (semaine) week. ◆**huitième** a & nmf eighth; **un h.** an eighth.

huître [ɥitr] nf oyster.

hululer [ylyle] vi (hibou) to hoot.

humain [ymɛ̃] a a human; (compatissant) humane; – nmpl humans. ◆**humainement** adv (possible etc) humanly; (avec humanité) humanely. ◆**humaniser** vt (prison, ville etc) to humanize, make more humane ◆**humanitaire** a humanitarian. ◆**humanité** nf (genre humain, sentiment) humanity.

humble [œbl] a humble. ◆**humblement** adv humbly.

humecter [ymɛkte] vt to moisten damp(en).

humer [yme] vt (respirer) to breathe in (sentir) to smell.

humeur [ymœr] nf (caprice) mood, humour (caractère) temperament; (irritation) bac temper; **bonne h.** (gaieté) good humour; de **bonne/mauvaise h.** in a good/bad mood ou humour; **égalité d'h.** evenness of temper.

humide [ymid] a damp, wet; (saison, route wet; (main, yeux) moist; (climat/temps h (chaud) humid climate/weather; (froid pluvieux) damp ou wet climate/weather ◆**humidifier** vt to humidify. ◆**humidité** nf humidity; (plutôt froide) damp(ness) (vapeur) moisture.

humili/er [ymilje] vt to humiliate, humble

◆—ant a humiliating. ◆humiliation nf humiliation. ◆humilité nf humility.

humour [ymur] nm humour; avoir de l'h. ou beaucoup d'h. ou le sens de l'h. to have a sense of humour. ◆humoriste nmf humorist. ◆humoristique (a livre, ton etc) humorous.

huppé ['ype] a (riche) Fam high-class, posh.

hurl/er ['yrle] vi (loup, vent) to howl; (personne) to scream, yell; – vt (slogans, injures etc) to scream. ◆—ement nm howl; scream, yell.

hurluberlu [yrlyberly] nm (personne) scatterbrain.

hutte ['yt] nf hut.

hybride [ibrid] a & nm hybrid.

hydrater [idrate] vt (peau) to moisturize; crème hydratante moisturizing cream.

hydraulique [idrolik] a hydraulic.

hydravion [idravjɔ̃] nm seaplane.

hydro-électrique [idroelektrik] a hydroelectric.

hydrogène [idrɔʒɛn] nm Ch hydrogen.

hydrophile [idrɔfil] a coton h. cotton wool, Am (absorbent) cotton.

hyène [jɛn] nf (animal) hyena.

hygiaphone [iʒjafon] nm (hygienic) grill.

hygiène [iʒjɛn] nf hygiene. ◆hygiénique a hygienic; (promenade) healthy; (serviette, conditions) sanitary; papier h. toilet paper.

hymne [imn] nm Rel Littér hymn; h. national national anthem.

hyper- [iper] préf hyper-.

hypermarché [ipermarʃe] nm hypermarket.

hypertension [ipertɑ̃sjɔ̃] nf high blood pressure.

hypnose [ipnoz] nf hypnosis. ◆hypnotique a hypnotic. ◆hypnotiser vt to hypnotize. ◆hypnotiseur nm hypnotist. ◆hypnotisme nm hypnotism.

hypocrisie [ipɔkrizi] nf hypocrisy. ◆hypocrite a hypocritical; – nmf hypocrite.

hypodermique [ipɔdermik] a hypodermic.

hypothèque [ipotɛk] nf mortgage. ◆hypothéquer (maison, avenir) to mortgage.

hypothèse [ipotez] nf assumption; (en sciences) hypothesis; dans l'h. où . . . supposing (that) . . . . ◆hypothétique a hypothetical.

hystérie [isteri] nf hysteria. ◆hystérique a hysterical.

I

I, i [i] nm I, i.

iceberg [isberg] nm iceberg.

ici [isi] adv here; par i. (passer) this way; (habiter) around here, hereabouts; jusqu'i. (temps) up to now; (lieu) as far as this ou here; d'i. à mardi by Tuesday, between now and Tuesday; d'i. à une semaine within a week; d'i. peu before long; i. Dupont Tél this is Dupont, Dupont here; je ne suis pas d'i. I'm a stranger around here; les gens d'i. the people (from) around here, the locals. ◆i.-bas adv on earth.

icône [ikon] nf Rel icon.

idéal, -aux [ideal, -o] a & nm ideal; l'i. (valeurs spirituelles) ideals; c'est l'i. Fam that's the ideal thing. ◆idéalement adv ideally. ◆idéaliser vt to idealize. ◆idéalisme nm idealism. ◆idéaliste a idealistic; – nmf idealist.

idée [ide] nf idea (de of, que that); changer d'i. to change one's mind; il m'est venu à l'i. que it occurred to me that; se faire une i. de (rêve) to imagine; (concept) to get ou have

an idea of; avoir dans l'i. de faire to have it in mind to do; i. fixe obsession.

idem [idem] adv ditto.

identifier [idɑ̃tifje] vt to identify (à, avec with). ◆identification nf identification. ◆identique a identical (à to, with). ◆identité nf identity; carte d'i identity card.

idéologie [ideɔlɔʒi] nf ideology. ◆idéologique a ideological.

idiome [idjom] nm (langue) idiom. ◆idiomatique a idiomatic.

idiot, -ote [idjo, -ɔt] a idiotic, silly; – nmf idiot. ◆idiotement adv idiotically. ◆idiotie [-ɔsi] nf (état) idiocy; une i. an idiotic ou silly thing.

idole [idɔl] nm idol. ◆idolâtrer vt to idolize.

idylle [idil] nf (amourette) romance.

idyllique [idilik] a (merveilleux) idyllic.

if [if] nm yew (tree).

igloo [iglu] nm igloo.

ignare [iɲar] a Péj ignorant; – nmf ignoramus.

ignifugé [iɲifyʒe] a fireproof(ed).
ignoble [iɲɔbl] a vile, revolting.
ignorant [iɲɔrɑ̃] a ignorant (**de** of).
◆**ignorance** nf ignorance. ◆**ignor/er**
vt not to know, be ignorant of; **j'ignore si** I
don't know if; **i. qn** (être indifférent à) to
ignore s.o., cold-shoulder s.o. ◆**—é** a (inconnu) unknown.
il [il] pron (personne) he; (chose, animal) it; **il**
est he is; it is; **il pleut** it's raining; **il est vrai**
que it's true that; **il y a** there is; pl there are;
il y a six ans (temps écoulé) six years ago; **il**
y a une heure qu'il travaille (durée) he's
been working for an hour; **qu'est-ce qu'il y**
a? what's the matter?, what's wrong?; **il n'y**
a pas de quoi! don't mention it!; **il**
doit/peut y avoir there must/may be.
île [il] nf island; **les îles Britanniques** the
British Isles.
illégal, -aux [ilegal, -o] a illegal. ◆**illéga-**
lité nf illegality.
illégitime [ileʒitim] a (enfant, revendication)
illegitimate; (non fondé) unfounded.
illettré, -ée [iletre] a & nmf illiterate.
illicite [ilisit] a unlawful, illicit.
illico [iliko] adv (presto) Fam straight-
away.
illimité [ilimite] a unlimited.
illisible [ilizibl] a (écriture) illegible; (livre)
unreadable.
illogique [ilɔʒik] a illogical.
illumin/er [ilymine] vt to light up, illuminate; — **s'i.** vpr (visage, personne, ciel) to
light up. ◆**—é** a (monument) floodlit, lit
up. ◆**illumination** nf (action, lumière) illumination.
illusion [ilyzjɔ̃] nf illusion (**sur** about); **se**
faire des illusions to delude oneself.
◆**s'illusionner** vpr to delude oneself (**sur**
about). ◆**illusionniste** nmf conjurer.
◆**illusoire** a illusory, illusive.
illustre [ilystr] a famous, illustrious.
illustr/er [ilystre] vt (d'images, par des
exemples) to illustrate (**de** with); — **s'i.** vpr
to become famous. ◆**—é** a (livre, magazine) illustrated; — nm (périodique) comic.
◆**illustration** nf illustration.
îlot [ilo] nm **1** (île) small island. **2** (maisons)
block.
ils [il] pron they; **ils sont** they are.
image [imaʒ] nf picture; (ressemblance,
symbole) image; (dans une glace) reflection;
i. de marque (de firme etc) (public) image.
◆**imagé** a (style) colourful, full of imagery.
imagination [imaʒinasjɔ̃] nf imagination; pl
(chimères) imaginings.

imaginer [imaʒine] vt (envisager, supposer)
to imagine; (inventer) to devise; — **s'i.** vpr
(se figurer) to imagine (**que** that); (voir)
to imagine oneself. ◆**imaginable** a
imaginable. ◆**imaginaire** a imaginary.
◆**imaginatif, -ive** a imaginative.
imbattable [ɛ̃batabl] a unbeatable.
imbécile [ɛ̃besil] a idiotic; — nmf imbecile,
idiot. ◆**imbécillité** nf (état) imbecility;
une **i.** (action, parole) an idiotic thing.
imbiber [ɛ̃bibe] vt to soak (**de** with, in); —
s'i. vpr to become soaked.
imbriquer (s') [sɛ̃brike] vpr (questions etc)
to overlap, be bound up with each other.
imbroglio [ɛ̃brɔljo] nm muddle, foul-up.
imbu [ɛ̃by] a **i. de** imbued with.
imbuvable [ɛ̃byvabl] a undrinkable; (personne) Fig insufferable.
imiter [imite] vt to imitate; (contrefaire) to
forge; **i. qn** (pour rire) to mimic s.o., take
s.o. off; (faire comme) to do the same as
s.o., follow suit. ◆**imitateur, -trice** nmf
imitator; (artiste) Th impersonator, mimic.
◆**imitatif, -ive** a imitative. ◆**imitation** nf
imitation.
immaculé [imakyle] a (sans tache, sans
péché) immaculate.
immangeable [ɛ̃mɑ̃ʒabl] a inedible.
immanquable [ɛ̃mɑ̃kabl] a inevitable.
immatriculer [imatrikyle] vt to register; **se**
faire i. to register. ◆**immatriculation** nf
registration.
immédiat [imedja] a immediate; — nm dans
l'i. for the time being. ◆**immédiatement**
adv immediately.
immense [imɑ̃s] a immense, vast. ◆**im-**
mensément adv immensely. ◆**immen-**
sité nf immensity, vastness.
immerger [imɛrʒe] vt to immerse, put under
water; — **s'i.** vpr (sous-marin) to submerge
◆**immersion** nf immersion; submersion.
immettable [ɛ̃metabl] a (vêtement) unfit to
be worn.
immeuble [imœbl] nm building; (d'habitation) block of flats, Am apartment building; (de bureaux) office block.
immigr/er [imigre] vi to immigrate
◆**—ant, -ante** nmf immigrant. ◆**—é, -ée**
a & nmf immigrant. ◆**immigration** nf immigration.
imminent [iminɑ̃] a imminent. ◆**immi-**
nence nf imminence.
immiscer (s') [simise] vpr to interfere (**dans**
in).
immobile [imɔbil] a still, motionless. ◆**im-**
mobiliser vt to immobilize; (arrêter) to

stop; — **s'i.** vpr to stop, come to a standstill. ◆**immobilité** nf stillness; (inactivité) immobility.

mmobilier, -ière [imɔbilje, -jɛr] a (vente) property-; (société) construction-; **agent i.** estate agent, Am real estate agent.

mmodéré [imɔdere] a immoderate.

mmonde [imɔ̃d] a filthy. ◆**immondices** nfpl refuse, rubbish.

mmoral, -aux [imɔral, -o] a immoral. ◆**immoralité** nf immorality.

mmortel, -elle [imɔrtɛl] a immortal. ◆**immortaliser** vt to immortalize. ◆**immortalité** nf immortality.

mmuable [imɥabl] a immutable, unchanging.

mmuniser [imynize] vt to immunize (contre against); **immunisé contre (à l'abri de)** Méd & Fig immune to ou from. ◆**immunitaire** a (déficience etc) Méd immune. ◆**immunité** nf immunity.

mpact [ɛ̃pakt] nm impact (sur on).

mpair [ɛ̃pɛr] **1** a (nombre) odd, uneven. **2** nm (gaffe) blunder.

mparable [ɛ̃parabl] a (coup etc) unavoidable.

mpardonnable [ɛ̃pardɔnabl] a unforgivable.

mparfait [ɛ̃parfɛ] **1** a (connaissance etc) imperfect. **2** nm (temps) Gram imperfect.

mpartial, -aux [ɛ̃parsjal, -o] a impartial, unbiased. ◆**impartialité** nf impartiality.

mpartir [ɛ̃partir] vt to grant (à to).

mpasse [ɛ̃pas] nf (rue) dead end, blind alley; (situation) Fig impasse; **dans l'i.** (négociations) in deadlock.

mpassible [ɛ̃pasibl] a impassive, unmoved. ◆**impassibilité** nf impassiveness.

mpatient [ɛ̃pasjã] a impatient; **i. de faire** eager ou impatient to do. ◆**impatiemment** [-amã] adv impatiently. ◆**impatience** nf impatience. ◆**impatienter** vt to annoy, make impatient; — **s'i.** vpr to get impatient.

mpayable [ɛ̃pejabl] a (comique) Fam hilarious, priceless.

mpayé [ɛ̃peje] a unpaid.

mpeccable [ɛ̃pekabl] a impeccable, immaculate. ◆**—ment** [-əmã] adv impeccably, immaculately.

mpénétrable [ɛ̃penetrabl] a (forêt, mystère etc) impenetrable.

mpénitent [ɛ̃penitã] a unrepentant.

mpensable [ɛ̃pãsabl] a unthinkable.

mper [ɛ̃pɛr] nm Fam raincoat, mac.

mpératif, -ive [ɛ̃peratif, -iv] a (consigne, ton) imperative; — nm (mode) Gram imperative.

impératrice [ɛ̃peratris] nf empress.

imperceptible [ɛ̃pɛrsɛptibl] a imperceptible (à to).

imperfection [ɛ̃pɛrfɛksjɔ̃] nf imperfection.

impérial, -aux [ɛ̃perjal, -o] a imperial. ◆**impérialisme** nm imperialism.

impériale [ɛ̃perjal] nf (d'autobus) top deck.

impérieux, -euse [ɛ̃perjø, -øz] a (autoritaire) imperious; (besoin) pressing, imperative.

imperméable [ɛ̃pɛrmeabl] **1** a impervious (à to); (manteau, tissu) waterproof. **2** nm raincoat, mackintosh. ◆**imperméabilisé** a waterproof.

impersonnel, -elle [ɛ̃pɛrsɔnɛl] a impersonal.

impertinent [ɛ̃pɛrtinã] a impertinent (envers to). ◆**impertinence** nf impertinence.

imperturbable [ɛ̃pɛrtyrbabl] a unruffled, imperturbable.

impétueux, -euse [ɛ̃petɥø, -øz] a impetuous. ◆**impétuosité** nf impetuosity.

impitoyable [ɛ̃pitwajabl] a ruthless, pitiless, merciless.

implacable [ɛ̃plakabl] a implacable, relentless.

implanter [ɛ̃plãte] vt (industrie, mode etc) to establish; — **s'i.** vpr to become established. ◆**implantation** nf establishment.

implicite [ɛ̃plisit] a implicit. ◆**—ment** adv implicitly.

impliquer [ɛ̃plike] vt (entraîner) to imply; **i. que** (supposer) to imply that; **i. qn** (engager) to implicate s.o. (dans in). ◆**implication** nf (conséquence, participation) implication.

implorer [ɛ̃plɔre] vt to implore (qn de faire s.o. to do).

impoli [ɛ̃pɔli] a impolite, rude. ◆**impolitesse** nf impoliteness; **une i.** an act of rudeness.

impopulaire [ɛ̃pɔpylɛr] a unpopular.

important [ɛ̃pɔrtã] a (personnage, événement etc) important; (quantité, somme etc) considerable, big, great; — nm **l'i., c'est de . . .** the important thing is to . . . . ◆**importance** nf importance, significance; (taille) size; (de dégâts) extent; **ça n'a pas d'i.** it doesn't matter.

importer [ɛ̃pɔrte] **1** v imp to matter, be important (à to); **il importe de faire** it's important to do; **peu importe, n'importe** it doesn't matter; **n'importe qui/quoi/ où/quand/comment** anyone/anything/ anywhere/any time/anyhow. **2** vt (marchandises etc) to import (de from). ◆**im-**

portateur, -trice *nmf* importer; − *a* importing. ◆**importation** *nf* (*objet*) import; (*action*) import(ing), importation; **d'i.** (*article*) imported.

importun, -une [ɛ̃pɔrtœ̃, -yn] *a* troublesome, intrusive; − *nmf* nuisance, intruder. ◆**importuner** *vt* to inconvenience, trouble.

impos/er [ɛ̃poze] **1** *vt* to impose, enforce (**à** on); (*exiger*) to demand; (*respect*) to command; − *vi* **en i. à qn** to impress s.o., command respect from s.o.; − **s'i.** *vpr* (*chez qn*) *Péj* to impose; (*s'affirmer*) to assert oneself, compel recognition; (*aller de soi*) to stand out; (*être nécessaire*) to be essential. **2** *vt* *Fin* to tax. ◆**−ant** *a* imposing. ◆**−able** *a* *Fin* taxable. ◆**imposition** *nf* *Fin* taxation.

impossible [ɛ̃posibl] *a* impossible (**à faire** to do); **il (nous) est i. de faire** it is impossible (for us) to do; **il est i. que** (+ *sub*) it is impossible that; **ça m'est i.** I cannot possibly; − *nm* **faire l'i.** to do the impossible. ◆**impossibilité** *nf* impossibility.

imposteur [ɛ̃pɔstœr] *nm* impostor. ◆**imposture** *nf* deception.

impôt [ɛ̃po] *nm* tax; *pl* (*contributions*) (income) tax, taxes; **i. sur le revenu** income tax.

impotent, -ente [ɛ̃pɔtɑ̃, -ɑ̃t] *a* crippled, disabled; − *nmf* cripple, invalid.

impraticable [ɛ̃pratikabl] *a* (*projet etc*) impracticable; (*chemin etc*) impassable.

imprécis [ɛ̃presi] *a* imprecise. ◆**imprécision** *nf* lack of precision.

imprégner [ɛ̃preɲe] *vt* to saturate, impregnate (**de** with); − **s'i.** *vpr* to become saturated *ou* impregnated (**de** with); **imprégné de** (*idées*) imbued *ou* infused with. ◆**imprégnation** *nf* saturation.

imprenable [ɛ̃prənabl] *a* *Mil* impregnable.

impresario [ɛ̃presarjo] *nm* (business) manager, impresario.

impression [ɛ̃presjɔ̃] *nf* **1** impression; **avoir l'i. que** to have the feeling *ou* impression that, be under the impression that; **faire une bonne i. à qn** to make a good impression on s.o. **2** *Typ* printing. ◆**impressionn/er** [ɛ̃presjɔne] *vt* (*influencer*) to impress; (*émouvoir, troubler*) to make a strong impression on. ◆**−ant** *a* impressive. ◆**−able** *a* impressionable.

imprévisible [ɛ̃previzibl] *a* unforeseeable. ◆**imprévoyance** *nf* lack of foresight. ◆**imprévoyant** *a* shortsighted. ◆**imprévu** *a* unexpected, unforeseen; − *nm* **en cas d'i.** in case of anything unexpected.

imprim/er [ɛ̃prime] *vt* **1** (*livre etc*) to print;

(*trace*) to impress (**dans** in); (*cachet*) to stamp. **2** (*communiquer*) *Tech* to impart (**à** to). ◆**−ante** *nf* (*d'ordinateur*) printer. ◆**−é** *nm* (*formulaire*) printed form; − *nm(pl)* (*par la poste*) printed matter. ◆**imprimerie** *nf* (*technique*) printing; (*lieu*) printing works. ◆**imprimeur** *nm* printer.

improbable [ɛ̃prɔbabl] *a* improbable, unlikely. ◆**improbabilité** *nf* improbability unlikelihood.

impromptu [ɛ̃prɔ̃pty] *a* & *adv* impromptu.

impropre [ɛ̃prɔpr] *a* inappropriate; **i. à qch** unfit for sth. ◆**impropriété** *nf* (*incorrection*) *Ling* impropriety.

improviser [ɛ̃prɔvize] *vti* to improvise. ◆**improvisation** *nf* improvisation.

improviste (à l') [alɛ̃prɔvist] *adv* unexpectedly; **une visite à l'i.** an unexpected visit; **prendre qn à l'i.** to catch s.o. unawares.

imprudent [ɛ̃prydɑ̃] *a* (*personne, action*) careless, rash; **il est i. de** it is unwise to. ◆**imprudemment** [-amɑ̃] *adv* carelessly. ◆**imprudence** *nf* carelessness; **une i.** an act of carelessness.

impudent [ɛ̃pydɑ̃] *a* impudent ◆**impudence** *nf* impudence.

impudique [ɛ̃pydik] *a* lewd.

impuissant [ɛ̃pɥisɑ̃] *a* helpless; *Méd* impotent; **i. à faire** powerless to do. ◆**impuissance** *nf* helplessness; *Méd* impotence.

impulsif, -ive [ɛ̃pylsif, -iv] *a* impulsive. ◆**impulsion** *nf* impulse; **donner une i. à** (*élan*) *Fig* to give an impetus *ou* impulse to.

impunément [ɛ̃pynemɑ̃] *adv* with impunity. ◆**impuni** *a* unpunished.

impur [ɛ̃pyr] *a* impure. ◆**impureté** *nf* impurity.

imputer [ɛ̃pyte] *vt* to attribute, impute (**à** to); (*affecter*) *Fin* to charge (**à** to). ◆**imputable** *a* attributable (**à** to). ◆**imputation** *nf* *Jur* accusation.

inabordable [inabɔrdabl] *a* (*lieu*) inaccessible; (*personne*) unapproachable; (*prix*) prohibitive.

inacceptable [inaksɛptabl] *a* unacceptable.

inaccessible [inaksesibl] *a* inaccessible.

inaccoutumé [inakutyme] *a* unusual, unaccustomed.

inachevé [inaʃve] *a* unfinished.

inactif, -ive [inaktif, -iv] *a* inactive. ◆**inaction** *nf* inactivity, inaction. ◆**inactivité** *nf* inactivity.

inadapté, -ée [inadapte] *a* & *nmf* maladjusted (person). ◆**inadaptation** *nf* maladjustment.

inadmissible [inadmisibl] a unacceptable, inadmissible.

inadvertance (par) [parinadvɛrtɑ̃s] adv inadvertently.

inaltérable [inalterabl] a (couleur) fast; (sentiment) unchanging.

inamical, -aux [inamikal, -o] a unfriendly.

inanimé [inanime] a (mort) lifeless; (évanoui) unconscious; (matière) inanimate.

inanité [inanite] nf (vanité) futility.

inanition [inanisjɔ̃] nf mourir d'i. to die of starvation.

inaperçu [inapɛrsy] a passer i. to go unnoticed.

inapplicable [inaplikabl] a inapplicable (à to).

inappliqué [inaplike] a (élève etc) inattentive.

inappréciable [inapresjabl] a invaluable.

inapte [inapt] a unsuited (à qch to sth), inept (à qch at sth); Mil unfit ◆**inaptitude** nf ineptitude, incapacity.

inarticulé [inartikyle] a (son) inarticulate.

inattaquable [inatakabl] a unassailable.

inattendu [inatɑ̃dy] a unexpected.

inattentif, -ive [inatɑ̃tif, -iv] a inattentive, careless; i. à (soucis, danger etc) heedless of. ◆**inattention** nf lack of attention; dans un moment d'i. in a moment of distraction.

inaudible [inodibl] a inaudible.

inaugurer [inogyre] vt (politique, édifice) to inaugurate; (école, congrès) to open, inaugurate; (statue) to unveil. ◆**inaugural, -aux** a inaugural. ◆**inauguration** nf inauguration; opening; unveiling.

inauthentique [inotɑ̃tik] a not authentic.

inavouable [inavwabl] a shameful.

incalculable [ɛ̃kalkylabl] a incalculable.

incandescent [ɛ̃kɑ̃desɑ̃] a incandescent.

incapable [ɛ̃kapabl] a incapable; i. de faire unable to do, incapable of doing; — nmf (personne) incompetent. ◆**incapacité** nf incapacity, inability (de faire to do); Méd disability, incapacity.

incarcérer [ɛ̃karsere] vt to incarcerate. ◆**incarcération** nf incarceration.

incarné [ɛ̃karne] a (ongle) ingrown.

incarner [ɛ̃karne] vt to embody, incarnate. ◆**incarnation** nf embodiment, incarnation.

incartade [ɛ̃kartad] nf indiscretion, prank.

incassable [ɛ̃kasabl] a unbreakable.

incendie [ɛ̃sɑ̃di] nm fire; (guerre) Fig conflagration. ◆**incendiaire** nf arsonist; — a (bombe) incendiary; (discours) inflammatory. ◆**incendier** vt to set fire to, set on fire.

incertain [ɛ̃sɛrtɛ̃] a uncertain; (temps) unsettled; (entreprise) chancy; (contour) indistinct. ◆**incertitude** nf uncertainty.

incessamment [ɛ̃sesamɑ̃] adv without delay, shortly.

incessant [ɛ̃sesɑ̃] a incessant.

inceste [ɛ̃sɛst] nm incest. ◆**incestueux, -euse** a incestuous.

inchangé [ɛ̃ʃɑ̃ʒe] a unchanged.

incidence [ɛ̃sidɑ̃s] nf (influence) effect.

incident [ɛ̃sidɑ̃] nm incident; (accroc) hitch.

incinérer [ɛ̃sinere] vt (ordures) to incinerate; (cadavre) to cremate. ◆**incinération** nf incineration; cremation.

inciser [ɛ̃size] vt to make an incision in. ◆**incision** nf (entaille) incision.

incisif, -ive[1] [ɛ̃sizif, -iv] a incisive, sharp.

incisive[2] [ɛ̃siziv] nf (dent) incisor.

inciter [ɛ̃site] vt to urge, incite (à faire to do). ◆**incitation** nf incitement (à to).

incliner [ɛ̃kline] vt (courber) to bend; (pencher) to tilt, incline; i. la tête (approuver) to nod one's head; (révérence) to bow (one's head); i. qn à faire to induce s.o. to do; — vi i. à être incliné to be inclined to, incline s.o. to do; — s'i. vpr (se courber) to bow (down); (s'avouer vaincu) to admit defeat; (chemin) to slope down. ◆**inclinaison** nf incline, slope. ◆**inclination** nf (goût) inclination; (de tête) nod, (révérence) bow.

incl/ure* [ɛ̃klyr] vt to include; (enfermer) to enclose. ◆**-us** a inclusive; du quatre jusqu'au dix mai i. from the fourth to the tenth of May inclusive; jusqu'à lundi i. up to and including (next) Monday. ◆**inclusion** nf inclusion. ◆**inclusivement** adv inclusively.

incognito [ɛ̃kɔɲito] adv incognito.

incohérent [ɛ̃kɔerɑ̃] a incoherent. ◆**incohérence** nf incoherence.

incollable [ɛ̃kɔlabl] a Fam infallible, unable to be caught out.

incolore [ɛ̃kɔlɔr] a colourless; (verre, vernis) clear.

incomber [ɛ̃kɔ̃be] vi i. à qn (devoir) to fall to s.o.; il lui incombe de faire it's his ou her duty ou responsiblity to do.

incommode [ɛ̃kɔmɔd] a awkward. ◆**incommodité** nf awkwardness.

incommod/er [ɛ̃kɔmɔde] vt to bother, annoy. ◆**-ant** a annoying.

incomparable [ɛ̃kɔ̃parabl] a incomparable.

incompatible [ɛ̃kɔ̃patibl] a incompatible, inconsistent (avec with). ◆**incompatibilité** nf incompatibility, inconsistency.

incompétent [ɛ̃kɔ̃petɑ̃] a incompetent. ◆**incompétence** nf incompetence.

incomplet, -ète [ɛ̃kɔ̃plɛ, -ɛt] a incomplete; (fragmentaire) scrappy, sketchy.

incompréhensible [ɛ̃kɔ̃preɑ̃sibl] a incomprehensible. ◆**incompréhensif, -ive** a uncomprehending, lacking understanding. ◆**incompréhension** nf lack of understanding. ◆**incompris** a misunderstood.

inconcevable [ɛ̃kɔ̃svabl] a inconceivable.

inconciliable [ɛ̃kɔ̃siljabl] a irreconcilable.

inconditionnel, -elle [ɛ̃kɔ̃disjɔnɛl] a unconditional.

inconfort [ɛ̃kɔ̃fɔr] nm lack of comfort. ◆**inconfortable** a uncomfortable.

incongru [ɛ̃kɔ̃gry] a unseemly, incongruous.

inconnu, -ue [ɛ̃kɔny] a unknown (à to); – nmf (étranger) stranger; (auteur) unknown; – nm l'i. the unknown; – nf Math unknown (quantity).

inconscient [ɛ̃kɔ̃sjɑ̃] a unconscious (de of); (irréfléchi) thoughtless, senseless; – nm l'i. Psy the unconscious. ◆**inconsciemment** [-amɑ̃] adv unconsciously. ◆**inconscience** nf (physique) unconsciousness; (irréflexion) utter thoughtlessness.

inconséquence [ɛ̃kɔ̃sekɑ̃s] nf inconsistency.

inconsidéré [ɛ̃kɔ̃sidere] a thoughtless.

inconsolable [ɛ̃kɔ̃sɔlabl] a inconsolable.

inconstant [ɛ̃kɔ̃stɑ̃] a fickle. ◆**inconstance** nf fickleness.

incontestable [ɛ̃kɔ̃tɛstabl] a undeniable, indisputable. ◆**incontesté** a undisputed.

incontinent [ɛ̃kɔ̃tinɑ̃] a incontinent.

incontrôlé [ɛ̃kɔ̃trole] a unchecked. ◆**incontrôlable** a unverifiable.

inconvenant [ɛ̃kɔ̃vnɑ̃] a improper. ◆**inconvenance** nf impropriety.

inconvénient [ɛ̃kɔ̃venjɑ̃] nm (désavantage) drawback; (risque) risk; (objection) objection.

incorporer [ɛ̃kɔrpɔre] vt (introduire, admettre) to incorporate (dans into); (ingrédient) to blend (à with); Mil to enrol. ◆**incorporation** nf incorporation (de of); Mil enrolment.

incorrect [ɛ̃kɔrɛkt] a (inexact) incorrect; (inconvenant) improper; (grossier) impolite. ◆**incorrection** nf (faute) impropriety, error; (inconvenance) impropriety; une i. (grossièreté) an impolite word ou act.

incorrigible [ɛ̃kɔriʒibl] a incorrigible.

incorruptible [ɛ̃kɔryptibl] a incorruptible.

incrédule [ɛ̃kredyl] a incredulous. ◆**incrédulité** nf disbelief, incredulity.

increvable [ɛ̃krəvabl] a (robuste) Fam tireless.

incriminer [ɛ̃krimine] vt to incriminate.

incroyable [ɛ̃krwajabl] a incredible, unbelievable. ◆**incroyablement** adv incredibly. ◆**incroyant, -ante** a unbelieving; – nmf unbeliever.

incrusté [ɛ̃kryste] a (de tartre) encrusted; i. de (orné) inlaid with. ◆**incrustation** nf (ornement) inlay; (action) inlaying.

incruster (s') [sɛ̃kryste] vpr (chez qn) Fig to dig oneself in, be difficult to get rid of.

incubation [ɛ̃kybasjɔ̃] nf incubation.

inculp/er [ɛ̃kylpe] vt Jur to charge (de with), indict (de for). ◆**-é, -ée** nmf l'i. the accused. ◆**inculpation** nf charge, indictment.

inculquer [ɛ̃kylke] vt to instil (à into).

inculte [ɛ̃kylt] a (terre) uncultivated; (personne) uneducated.

incurable [ɛ̃kyrabl] a incurable.

incursion [ɛ̃kyrsjɔ̃] nf incursion, inroad (dans into).

incurver [ɛ̃kyrve] vt to curve.

Inde [ɛ̃d] nf India.

indécent [ɛ̃desɑ̃] a indecent. ◆**indécemment** [-amɑ̃] adv indecently. ◆**indécence** nf indecency.

indéchiffrable [ɛ̃deʃifrabl] a undecipherable.

indécis [ɛ̃desi] a (victoire, résultat) undecided; (indistinct) vague; être i. (hésiter) to be undecided; (de tempérament) to be indecisive ou irresolute. ◆**indécision** nf indecisiveness, indecision.

indéfectible [ɛ̃defɛktibl] a unfailing.

indéfendable [ɛ̃defɑ̃dabl] a indefensible.

indéfini [ɛ̃defini] a (indéterminé) indefinite; (imprécis) undefined. ◆**indéfiniment** adv indefinitely. ◆**indéfinissable** a indefinable.

indéformable [ɛ̃defɔrmabl] a (vêtement) which keeps its shape.

indélébile [ɛ̃delebil] a (encre, souvenir) indelible.

indélicat [ɛ̃delika] a (grossier) indelicate; (malhonnête) unscrupulous.

indemne [ɛ̃dɛmn] a unhurt, unscathed.

indemniser [ɛ̃dɛmnize] vt to indemnify, compensate (de for). ◆**indemnisation** nf compensation. ◆**indemnité** nf (dédommagement) indemnity; (allocation) allowance.

indémontable [ɛ̃demɔ̃tabl] a that cannot be taken apart.

indéniable [ɛ̃denjabl] a undeniable.

indépendant [ɛ̃depɑ̃dɑ̃] a independent (de

of); (*chambre*) self-contained; (*journaliste*) freelance. ◆**indépendamment** *adv* independently (**de** of); **i. de** (*sans aucun égard à*) apart from. ◆**indépendance** *nf* independence.

indescriptible [ɛ̃dɛskriptibl] *a* indescribable.

indésirable [ɛ̃dezirabl] *a* & *nmf* undesirable.

indestructible [ɛ̃dɛstryktibl] *a* indestructible.

indéterminé [ɛ̃detɛrmine] *a* indeterminate. ◆**indétermination** *nf* (*doute*) indecision.

index [ɛ̃dɛks] *nm* (*liste*) index; *Anat* forefinger, index finger.

indexer [ɛ̃dɛkse] *vt Écon* to index-link, tie (**sur** to).

indicateur, -trice [ɛ̃dikatœr, -tris] **1** *nmf* (*espion*) (police) informer. **2** *nm Rail* guide, timetable; *Tech* indicator, gauge. **3** *a* **poteau i.** signpost. ◆**indicatif, -ive 1** *a* indicative (**de** of); – *nm Mus* signature tune; *Tél* dialling code, *Am* area code. **2** *nm* (*mode*) *Gram* indicative. ◆**indication** *nf* indication (**de** of); (*renseignement*) (piece of) information; (*directive*) instruction.

indice [ɛ̃dis] *nm* (*indication*) sign; (*dans une enquête*) *Jur* clue; (*des prix*) index; (*de salaire*) grade; **i. d'écoute** TV Rad rating.

indien, -ienne [ɛ̃djɛ̃, -jɛn] *a* & *nmf* Indian.

indifférent [ɛ̃diferɑ̃] *a* indifferent (**à** to); **ça m'est i.** that's all the same to me. ◆**indifféremment** [-amɑ̃] *adv* indifferently. ◆**indifférence** *nf* indifference (**à** to).

indigène [ɛ̃diʒɛn] *a* & *nmf* native.

indigent [ɛ̃diʒɑ̃] *a* (very) poor. ◆**indigence** *nf* poverty.

indigeste [ɛ̃diʒɛst] *a* indigestible. ◆**indigestion** *nf* (attack of) indigestion.

indigne [ɛ̃diɲ] *a* (*personne*) unworthy; (*chose*) shameful; **i. de qn/qch** unworthy of s.o./sth. ◆**indignité** *nf* unworthiness; **une i.** (*honte*) an indignity.

indigner [ɛ̃diɲe] *vt* **i. qn** to make s.o. indignant; – **s'i.** *vpr* to be *ou* become indignant (**de** at). ◆**indignation** *nf* indignation.

indigo [ɛ̃digo] *nm* & *a inv* (*couleur*) indigo.

indiqu/er [ɛ̃dike] *vt* (*montrer*) to show, indicate; (*dire*) to point out, tell; (*recommander*) to recommend; **i. du doigt** to point to *ou* at. ◆**-é** *a* (*heure*) appointed; (*conseillé*) recommended; (*adéquat*) appropriate.

indirect [ɛ̃dirɛkt] *a* indirect. ◆**-ement** *adv* indirectly.

indiscipline [ɛ̃disiplin] *nf* lack of discipline. ◆**indiscipliné** *a* unruly.

indiscret, -ète [ɛ̃diskrɛ, -ɛt] *a* (*indélicat*) indiscreet, tactless; (*curieux*) *Péj* inquisitive, prying. ◆**indiscrétion** *nf* indiscretion.

indiscutable [ɛ̃diskytabl] *a* indisputable.

indispensable [ɛ̃dispɑ̃sabl] *a* indispensable, essential.

indispos/er [ɛ̃dispoze] *vt* (*incommoder*) to make unwell, upset; **i. qn** (*contre soi*) (*mécontenter*) to antagonize s.o. ◆**-é** *a* (*malade*) indisposed, unwell. ◆**indisposition** *nf* indisposition.

indissoluble [ɛ̃disolybl] *a* (*liens etc*) solid, indissoluble.

indistinct, -incte [ɛ̃distɛ̃(kt), -ɛ̃kt] *a* indistinct. ◆**-ement** [-ɛ̃ktəmɑ̃] *adv* indistinctly; (*également*) without distinction.

individu [ɛ̃dividy] *nm* individual. ◆**individualiser** *vt* to individualize. ◆**individualiste** *a* individualistic; – *nmf* individualist. ◆**individualité** *nf* (*originalité*) individuality. ◆**individuel, -elle** *a* individual. ◆**individuellement** *adv* individually.

indivisible [ɛ̃divizibl] *a* indivisible.

Indochine [ɛ̃dɔʃin] *nf* Indo-China.

indolent [ɛ̃dɔlɑ̃] *a* indolent. ◆**indolence** *nf* indolence.

indolore [ɛ̃dɔlɔr] *a* painless.

indomptable [ɛ̃dɔ̃tabl] *a* (*énergie, volonté*) indomitable. ◆**indompté** *a* (*animal*) untamed.

Indonésie [ɛ̃dɔnezi] *nf* Indonesia.

indubitable [ɛ̃dybitabl] *a* beyond doubt.

indue [ɛ̃dy] *af* **à une heure i.** at an ungodly hour.

induire* [ɛ̃dɥir] *vt* **i. qn en erreur** to lead s.o. astray.

indulgent [ɛ̃dylʒɑ̃] *a* indulgent (**envers** to, **avec** with). ◆**indulgence** *nf* indulgence.

industrie [ɛ̃dystri] *nf* industry. ◆**industrialisé** *a* industrialized. ◆**industriel, -elle** *a* industrial; – *nmf* industrialist.

inébranlable [inebrɑ̃labl] *a* (*certitude, personne*) unshakeable, unwavering.

inédit [inedi] *a* (*texte*) unpublished; (*nouveau*) *Fig* original.

ineffable [inefabl] *a Litt* inexpressible, ineffable.

inefficace [inefikas] *a* (*mesure, effort etc*) ineffective, ineffectual; (*personne*) inefficient. ◆**inefficacité** *nf* ineffectiveness; inefficiency.

inégal, -aux [inegal, -o] *a* unequal; (*sol, humeur*) uneven. ◆**inégalable** *a* incomparable. ◆**inégalé** *a* unequalled. ◆**inégalité** *nf* (*morale*) inequality; (*physique*) difference; (*irrégularité*) unevenness; *pl* (*bosses*) bumps.

inélégant [inelegã] *a* coarse, inelegant.

inéligible [ineliʒibl] *a* (*candidat*) ineligible.

inéluctable [inelyktabl] *a* inescapable.

inepte [inɛpt] *a* absurd, inept. ◆**ineptie** [-si] *nf* absurdity, ineptitude.

inépuisable [inepɥizabl] *a* inexhaustible.

inerte [inɛrt] *a* inert; (*corps*) lifeless. ◆**inertie** [-si] *nf* inertia.

inespéré [inespere] *a* unhoped-for.

inestimable [inestimabl] *a* priceless.

inévitable [inevitabl] *a* inevitable, unavoidable.

inexact [inɛgzakt] *a* (*erroné*) inaccurate, inexact; **c'est i.!** it's incorrect! ◆**inexactitude** *nf* inaccuracy, inexactitude; (*manque de ponctualité*) lack of punctuality.

inexcusable [inɛkskyzabl] *a* inexcusable.

inexistant [inɛgzistɑ̃] *a* non-existent.

inexorable [inɛgzɔrabl] *a* inexorable.

inexpérience [inɛksperjɑ̃s] *nf* inexperience. ◆**inexpérimenté** *a* (*personne*) inexperienced; (*machine, arme*) untested.

inexplicable [inɛksplikabl] *a* inexplicable. ◆**inexpliqué** *a* unexplained.

inexploré [inɛksplɔre] *a* unexplored.

inexpressif, -ive [inɛkspresif, -iv] *a* expressionless.

inexprimable [inɛksprimabl] *a* inexpressible.

inextricable [inɛkstrikabl] *a* inextricable.

infaillible [ɛ̃fajibl] *a* infallible. ◆**infaillibilité** *nf* infallibility.

infaisable [ɛ̃fəzabl] *a* (*travail etc*) that cannot be done.

infamant [ɛ̃famɑ̃] *a* ignominious.

infâme [ɛ̃fam] *a* (*odieux*) vile, infamous; (*taudis*) squalid. ◆**infamie** *nf* infamy.

infanterie [ɛ̃fɑ̃tri] *nf* infantry.

infantile [ɛ̃fɑ̃til] *a* (*maladie, réaction*) infantile.

infarctus [ɛ̃farktys] *nm* **un i.** *Méd* a coronary.

infatigable [ɛ̃fatigabl] *a* tireless, indefatigable.

infect [ɛ̃fɛkt] *a* (*puant*) foul; (*mauvais*) lousy, vile.

infecter [ɛ̃fɛkte] **1** *vt* (*air*) to contaminate, foul. **2** *vt Méd* to infect; — **s'i.** *vpr* to get infected. ◆**infectieux, -euse** *a* infectious. ◆**infection** *nf* **1** *Méd* infection. **2** (*odeur*) stench.

inférer [ɛ̃fere] *vt* (*conclure*) to infer (**de** from, **que** that).

inférieur, -eure [ɛ̃ferjœr] *a* (*partie*) lower; (*qualité, personne*) inferior; **à l'étage i.** on the floor below; **i. à** inferior to; (*plus petit que*) smaller than; — *nmf* (*personne*) *Péj* inferior. ◆**infériorité** *nf* inferiority.

infernal, -aux [ɛ̃fɛrnal, -o] *a* infernal.

infester [ɛ̃fɛste] *vt* to infest, overrun (**de** with). ◆—**é à i. de** requins/de fourmis/*etc* shark-/ant-/*etc* infested.

infidèle [ɛ̃fidɛl] *a* unfaithful (**à** to). ◆**infidélité** *nf* unfaithfulness; **une i.** (*acte*) an infidelity.

infiltrer (s') [sɛ̃filtre] *vpr* (*liquide*) to seep *ou* percolate (through) (**dans** into); (*lumière*) to filter (through) (**dans** into); **s'i. dans** (*groupe, esprit*) *Fig* to infiltrate. ◆**infiltration** *nf* (*de personne, idée, liquide*) infiltration.

infime [ɛ̃fim] *a* (*très petit*) tiny; (*personne*) *Péj* lowly.

infini [ɛ̃fini] *a* infinite; — *nm Math Phot* infinity; *Phil* infinite; **à l'i.** (*beaucoup*) ad infinitum, endlessly; *Math* to infinity. ◆**infiniment** *adv* infinitely; (*regretter, remercier*) very much. ◆**infinité** *nf* **une i. de** an infinite amount of.

infinitif [ɛ̃finitif] *nm Gram* infinitive.

infirme [ɛ̃firm] *a* disabled, crippled; — *nmf* disabled person. ◆**infirmité** *nf* disability.

infirmer [ɛ̃firme] *vt* to invalidate.

infirmerie [ɛ̃firməri] *nf* infirmary, sickbay. ◆**infirmier** *nm* male nurse. ◆**infirmière** *nf* nurse.

inflammable [ɛ̃flamabl] *a* (in)flammable.

inflammation [ɛ̃flamasjõ] *nf Méd* inflammation.

inflation [ɛ̃flasjõ] *nf Écon* inflation. ◆**inflationniste** *a Écon* inflationary.

infléchir [ɛ̃fleʃir] *vt* (*courber*) to inflect, bend; (*modifier*) to shift. ◆**inflexion** *nf* bend; (*de voix*) tone, inflexion; **une i. de la tête** a nod.

inflexible [ɛ̃flɛksibl] *a* inflexible.

infliger [ɛ̃fliʒe] *vt* to inflict (**à** on); (*amende*) to impose (**à** on).

influence [ɛ̃flyɑ̃s] *nf* influence. ◆**influencer** *vt* to influence. ◆**influençable** *a* easily influenced. ◆**influent** *a* influential. ◆**influer** *vi* **i. sur** to influence.

information [ɛ̃fɔrmasjõ] *nf* information; (*nouvelle*) piece of news; (*enquête*) *Jur* inquiry; *pl* information; *Journ Rad TV* news.

informatique [ɛ̃fɔrmatik] *nf* (*science*) computer science; (*technique*) data processing. ◆**informaticien, -ienne** *nmf* computer scientist. ◆**informatiser** *vt* to computerize.

informe [ɛ̃fɔrm] *a* shapeless.

informer [ɛ̃fɔrme] *vt* to inform (**de** of, about;

que that); **— s'i.** *vpr* to inquire (**de** about; **si** if, whether). ◆**informateur, -trice** *nmf* informant.

infortune [ɛ̃fɔrtyn] *nf* misfortune. ◆**infortuné** *a* ill-fated, hapless.

infraction [ɛ̃fraksjɔ̃] *nf* (*délit*) offence; **i. à** breach of, infringement of.

infranchissable [ɛ̃frɑ̃ʃisabl] *a* (*mur, fleuve*) impassable; (*difficulté*) *Fig* insuperable.

infrarouge [ɛ̃fraruʒ] *a* infrared.

infroissable [ɛ̃frwasabl] *a* a crease-resistant.

infructueux, -euse [ɛ̃fryktɥø, -øz] *a* a fruitless.

infuser [ɛ̃fyze] *vt* (faire) **i.** (*thé*) to infuse. ◆**infusion** *nf* (*tisane*) (herb *ou* herbal) tea, infusion.

ingénier (s') [sɛ̃ʒenje] *vpr* to exercise one's wits (**à faire** in order to do).

ingénieur [ɛ̃ʒenjœr] *nm* engineer. ◆**ingénierie** [-iri] *nf* engineering.

ingénieux, -euse [ɛ̃ʒenjø, -øz] *a* ingenious. ◆**ingéniosité** *nf* ingenuity.

ingénu [ɛ̃ʒeny] *a* artless, naïve.

ingérer (s') [sɛ̃ʒere] *vpr* to interfere (**dans** in). ◆**ingérence** *nf* interference.

ingrat [ɛ̃gra] *a* (*personne*) ungrateful (**envers** to); (*sol*) barren; (*tâche*) thankless; (*visage, physique*) unattractive; (*âge*) awkward. ◆**ingratitude** *nf* ingratitude.

ingrédient [ɛ̃gredjɑ̃] *nm* ingredient.

inguérissable [ɛ̃gerisabl] *a* incurable.

ingurgiter [ɛ̃gyrʒite] *vt* to gulp down.

inhabitable [inabitabl] *a* uninhabitable. ◆**inhabité** *a* uninhabited.

inhabituel, -elle [inabitɥel] *a* unusual.

inhalateur [inalatœr] *nm Méd* inhaler. ◆**inhalation** *nf* inhalation; **faire des inhalations** to inhale.

inhérent [inerɑ̃] *a* inherent (**à** in).

inhibé [inibe] *a* inhibited. ◆**inhibition** *nf* inhibition.

inhospitalier, -ière [inɔspitalje, -jer] *a* inhospitable.

inhumain [inymɛ̃] *a* (*cruel, terrible*) inhuman.

inhumer [inyme] *vt* to bury, inter. ◆**inhumation** *nf* burial.

inimaginable [inimaʒinabl] *a* unimaginable.

inimitable [inimitabl] *a* inimitable.

inimitié [inimitje] *nf* enmity.

ininflammable [inɛ̃flamabl] *a* (*tissu etc*) non-flammable.

inintelligent [inɛ̃teliʒɑ̃] *a* unintelligent.

inintelligible [inɛ̃teliʒibl] *a* unintelligible.

inintéressant [inɛ̃teresɑ̃] *a* uninteresting.

ininterrompu [inɛ̃tɛrɔ̃py] *a* uninterrupted, continuous.

inique [inik] *a* iniquitous. ◆**iniquité** *nf* iniquity.

initial, -aux [inisjal, -o] *a* initial. ◆**initiale** *nf* (*lettre*) initial. ◆**initialement** *adv* initially.

initiative [inisjativ] *nf* **1** initiative. **2** syndicat **d'i.** tourist office.

initi/er [inisje] *vt* to initiate (**à** into); **s'i. à** (*art, science*) to become acquainted with *ou* initiated into. ◆**-é, -ée** *nmf* initiate; **les initiés** the initiated. ◆**initiateur, -trice** *nmf* initiator. ◆**initiation** *nf* initiation.

injecter [ɛ̃ʒekte] *vt* to inject; **injecté de sang** bloodshot. ◆**injection** *nf* injection.

injonction [ɛ̃ʒɔ̃ksjɔ̃] *nf* order, injunction.

injure [ɛ̃ʒyr] *nf* insult; *pl* abuse, insults. ◆**injurier** *vt* to abuse, insult, swear at. ◆**injurieux, -euse** *a* abusive, insulting (**pour** to).

injuste [ɛ̃ʒyst] *a* (*contraire à la justice*) unjust; (*partial*) unfair. ◆**injustice** *nf* injustice.

injustifiable [ɛ̃ʒystifjabl] *a* unjustifiable. ◆**injustifié** *a* unjustified.

inlassable [ɛ̃lɑsabl] *a* untiring.

inné [ine] *a* innate, inborn.

innocent, -ente [inɔsɑ̃, -ɑ̃t] *a* innocent (**de** of); **— nmf** *Jur* innocent person; (*idiot*) simpleton. ◆**innocemment** [-amã] *adv* innocently. ◆**innocence** *nf* innocence. ◆**innocenter** *vt* **qn** to clear s.o. (**de** of).

innombrable [inɔ̃brabl] *a* innumerable.

innommable [inɔmabl] *a* (*dégoûtant*) unspeakable, foul.

innover [inɔve] *vi* to innovate. ◆**innovateur, -trice** *nmf* innovator. ◆**innovation** *nf* innovation.

inoccupé [inɔkype] *a* unoccupied.

inoculer [inɔkyle] *vt* **i. qch à qn** to infect *ou* inoculate s.o. with sth. ◆**inoculation** *nf* (*vaccination*) inoculation.

inodore [inɔdɔr] *a* odourless.

inoffensif, -ive [inɔfɑ̃sif, -iv] *a* harmless, inoffensive.

inonder [inɔ̃de] *vt* to flood, inundate; (*mouiller*) to soak; **inondé de** (*envahi*) inundated with; **inondé de soleil** bathed in sunlight. ◆**inondable** *a* (*chaussée etc*) liable to flooding. ◆**inondation** *nf* flood; (*action*) flooding (**de** of).

inopérant [inɔperɑ̃] *a* inoperative.

inopiné [inɔpine] *a* unexpected.

inopportun [inɔpɔrtœ̃] *a* inopportune.

inoubliable [inublijabl] *a* unforgettable.

inouï [inwi] *a* incredible, extraordinary.

inox [inɔks] nm stainless steel; **en i.** (couteau etc) stainless-steel. ◆**inoxydable** a (couteau etc) stainless-steel; **acier i.** stainless steel.

inqualifiable [ɛ̃kalifjabl] a (indigne) unspeakable.

inquiet, -iète [ɛ̃kjɛ, -jɛt] a anxious, worried (de about). ◆**inquiét/er** vt (préoccuper) to worry; (police) to bother, harass (suspect etc); — **s'i.** vpr to worry (de about). ◆—**ant** a worrying. ◆**inquiétude** nf anxiety, concern, worry.

inquisiteur, -trice [ɛ̃kizitœr, -tris] a (regard) Péj inquisitive. ◆**inquisition** nf inquisition.

insaisissable [ɛ̃sezisabl] a elusive.

insalubre [ɛ̃salybr] a unhealthy, insalubrious.

insanités [ɛ̃sanite] nfpl (idioties) absurdities.

insatiable [ɛ̃sasjabl] a insatiable.

insatisfait [ɛ̃satisfɛ] a unsatisfied, dissatisfied.

inscrire* [ɛ̃skrir] vt to write ou put down; (sur un registre) to register; (graver) to inscribe; i. qn to enrol s.o.; — **s'i.** vpr to enrol (à at); **s'i. à** (parti, club) to join, enrol in; (examen) to enrol ou enrol ou register for; **s'i. dans (le cadre de)** to be part of; **s'i. en faux contre** to deny absolutely. ◆**inscription** nf writing down; enrolment; registration; (de médaille, sur écriteau etc) inscription; **frais d'i.** Univ tuition fees.

insecte [ɛ̃sɛkt] nm insect. ◆**insecticide** nm insecticide.

insécurité [ɛ̃sekyrite] nf insecurity.

insémination [ɛ̃seminasjɔ̃] nf Méd insemination.

insensé [ɛ̃sɑ̃se] a senseless, absurd.

insensible [ɛ̃sɑ̃sibl] a (indifférent) insensitive (à to); (graduel) imperceptible, very slight. ◆**insensiblement** adv imperceptibly. ◆**insensibilité** nf insensitivity.

inséparable [ɛ̃separabl] a inseparable (de from).

insérer [ɛ̃sere] vt to insert (dans into, in); **s'i. dans** (programme etc) to be part of. ◆**insertion** nf insertion.

insidieux, -euse [ɛ̃sidjø, -øz] a insidious.

insigne [ɛ̃siɲ] nm badge, emblem; pl (de maire etc) insignia.

insignifiant [ɛ̃siɲifjɑ̃] a insignificant, unimportant. ◆**insignifiance** nf insignificance.

insinuer [ɛ̃sinɥe] vt Péj to insinuate (que that); — **s'i.** vpr to insinuate oneself (dans into). ◆**insinuation** nf insinuation.

insipide [ɛ̃sipid] a insipid.

insist/er [ɛ̃siste] vi to insist (pour faire on doing); (continuer) Fam to persevere; **i. sur** (détail, syllabe etc) to stress; **i. pour que** (+ sub) to insist that. ◆—**ant** a insistent, persistent. ◆**insistance** nf insistence, persistence.

insolation [ɛ̃sɔlasjɔ̃] nf Méd sunstroke.

insolent [ɛ̃sɔlɑ̃] a (impoli) insolent; (luxe) indecent. ◆**insolence** nf insolence.

insolite [ɛ̃sɔlit] a unusual, strange.

insoluble [ɛ̃sɔlybl] a insoluble.

insolvable [ɛ̃sɔlvabl] a Fin insolvent.

insomnie [ɛ̃sɔmni] nf insomnia; pl (periods of) insomnia; **nuit d'i.** sleepless night. ◆**insomniaque** nmf insomniac.

insondable [ɛ̃sɔ̃dabl] a unfathomable.

insonoriser [ɛ̃sɔnɔrize] vt to soundproof, insulate. ◆**insonorisation** nf soundproofing, insulation.

insouciant [ɛ̃susjɑ̃] a carefree; **i. de** unconcerned about. ◆**insouciance** nf carefree attitude, lack of concern.

insoumis [ɛ̃sumi] a rebellious. ◆**insoumission** nf rebelliousness.

insoupçonnable [ɛ̃supsɔnabl] a beyond suspicion. ◆**insoupçonné** a unsuspected.

insoutenable [ɛ̃sutnabl] a unbearable; (théorie) untenable.

inspecter [ɛ̃spɛkte] vt to inspect. ◆**inspecteur, -trice** nmf inspector. ◆**inspection** nf inspection.

inspir/er [ɛ̃spire] **1** vt to inspire; **i. qch à qn** to inspire s.o. with sth; **s'i. de** to take one's inspiration from. **2** vi Méd to breathe in. ◆—**é** a inspired; **être bien i. de faire** to have the good idea to do. ◆**inspiration** nf **1** inspiration. **2** Méd breathing in.

instable [ɛ̃stabl] a (meuble) unsteady, shaky; (temps) unsettled; (caractère, situation) unstable. ◆**instabilité** nf unsteadiness; instability.

installer [ɛ̃stale] vt (équiper) to fit out, fix up; (appareil, meuble etc) to install, put in; (étagère) to put up; **i. qn** (dans une fonction, un logement) to install s.o. (dans in); — **s'i.** vpr (s'asseoir, s'établir) to settle (down); (médecin etc) to set oneself up; **s'i. dans** (maison, hôtel) to move into. ◆**installateur** nm fitter. ◆**installation** nf fitting out; installation; putting in; moving in; pl (appareils) fittings; (bâtiments) facilities.

instance [ɛ̃stɑ̃s] **1** nf (juridiction, autorité) authority; **tribunal de première i.** = magistrates' court; **en i. de** (divorce, départ) in the process of. **2** *nfpl* (*prières*) insistence, entreaties.

instant [ɛ̃stɑ̃] *nm* moment, instant; **à l'i.** a moment ago; **pour l'i.** for the moment. ◆**instantané** *a* instantaneous; **café i.** instant coffee; — *nm Phot* snapshot.

instaurer [ɛ̃stɔre] *vt* to found, set up.

instigateur, -trice [ɛ̃stigatœr, -tris] *nmf* instigator. ◆**instigation** *nf* instigation.

instinct [ɛ̃stɛ̃] *nm* instinct; **d'i.** instinctively, by instinct. ◆**instinctif, -ive** *a* instinctive.

instituer [ɛ̃stitɥe] *vt* (*règle, régime*) to establish, institute.

institut [ɛ̃stity] *nm* institute; **i. de beauté** beauty salon *ou* parlour; **i. universitaire de technologie** polytechnic, technical college.

instituteur, -trice [ɛ̃stitytœr, -tris] *nmf* primary school teacher.

institution [ɛ̃stitysjɔ̃] *nf* (*règle, organisation, structure etc*) institution; *Scol* private school. ◆**institutionnel, -elle** *a* institutional.

instructif, -ive [ɛ̃stryktif, -iv] *a* instructive.

instruction [ɛ̃stryksjɔ̃] *nf* education, schooling; *Mil* training; *Jur* investigation; (*document*) directive; *pl* (*ordres*) instructions. ◆**instructeur** *nm* (*moniteur* & *Mil* instructor.

instruire* [ɛ̃strɥir] *vt* to teach, educate; *Mil* to train; *Jur* to investigate; **i. qn de** to inform *ou* instruct s.o. of; — **s'i.** *vpr* to educate oneself; **s'i. de** to inquire about. ◆**instruit** *a* educated.

instrument [ɛ̃strymɑ̃] *nm* instrument; (*outil*) implement, tool. ◆**instrumental, -aux** *a* *Mus* instrumental. ◆**instrumentiste** *nmf Mus* instrumentalist.

insu (à l') [alɛ̃syd(ə)] *prép* without the knowledge of.

insuccès [ɛ̃syksɛ] *nm* failure.

insuffisant [ɛ̃syfizɑ̃] *a* (*en qualité*) inadequate; (*en quantité*) insufficient, inadequate. ◆**insuffisance** *nf* inadequacy.

insulaire [ɛ̃syler] *a* insular; — *nmf* islander.

insuline [ɛ̃sylin] *nf Méd* insulin.

insulte [ɛ̃sylt] *nf* insult (à to). ◆**insulter** *vt* to insult.

insupportable [ɛ̃syportabl] *a* unbearable.

insurg/er (s') [sɛ̃syrʒe] *vpr* to rise (up), rebel (**contre** against). ◆**-é, -ée** *a & nmf* insurgent, rebel. ◆**insurrection** *nf* insurrection, uprising.

insurmontable [ɛ̃syrmɔ̃tabl] *a* insurmountable, insuperable.

intact [ɛ̃takt] *a* intact.

intangible [ɛ̃tɑ̃ʒibl] *a* intangible.

intarissable [ɛ̃tarisabl] *a* inexhaustible.

intégral, -aux [ɛ̃tegral, -o] *a* full, complete; (*édition*) unabridged. ◆**intégralement** *adv* in full, fully. ◆**intégralité** *nf* whole (**de** of); **dans son i.** in full.

intègre [ɛ̃tegr] *a* upright, honest. ◆**intégrité** *nf* integrity.

intégr/er [ɛ̃tegre] *vt* to integrate (**dans** in); — **s'i.** *vpr* to become integrated, adapt. ◆**-ante** *af* **faire partie i. de** to be part and parcel of. ◆**intégration** *nf* integration.

intellectuel, -elle [ɛ̃telɛktɥel] *a & nmf* intellectual.

intelligent [ɛ̃teliʒɑ̃] *a* intelligent, clever. ◆**intelligemment** [-amɑ̃] *adv* intelligently. ◆**intelligence** *nf* (*faculté*) intelligence; *pl Mil Pol* secret relations; **avoir l'i. de qch** (*compréhension*) to have an understanding of sth; **d'i. avec qn** in complicity with s.o. ◆**intelligentsia** [-dʒɛntsja] *nf* intelligentsia.

intelligible [ɛ̃teliʒibl] *a* intelligible. ◆**intelligibilité** *nf* intelligibility.

intempérance [ɛ̃tɑ̃perɑ̃s] *nf* intemperance.

intempéries [ɛ̃tɑ̃peri] *nfpl* **les i.** the elements, bad weather.

intempestif, -ive [ɛ̃tɑ̃pestif, -iv] *a* untimely.

intenable [ɛ̃tnabl] *a* (*position*) untenable; (*enfant*) unruly, uncontrollable.

intendant, -ante [ɛ̃tɑ̃dɑ̃, -ɑ̃t] *nmf Scol* bursar. ◆**intendance** *nf Scol* bursar's office.

intense [ɛ̃tɑ̃s] *a* intense; (*circulation, trafic*) heavy. ◆**intensément** *adv* intensely. ◆**intensif, -ive** *a* intensive. ◆**intensifier** *vt*, — **s'i.** *vpr* to intensify. ◆**intensité** *nf* intensity.

intenter [ɛ̃tɑ̃te] *vt* **i. un procès à** *Jur* to institute proceedings against.

intention [ɛ̃tɑ̃sjɔ̃] *nf* intention; *Jur* intent; **avoir l'i. de faire** to intend to do; **à l'i. de qn** for s.o.; **à votre i.** for you. ◆**intentionné** *a* **bien i.** well-intentioned. ◆**intentionnel, -elle** *a* intentional, wilful. ◆**intentionnellement** *adv* intentionally.

inter- [ɛ̃ter] *préf* inter-.

interaction [ɛ̃teraksjɔ̃] *nf* interaction.

intercaler [ɛ̃terkale] *vt* to insert.

intercéder [ɛ̃tersede] *vt* to intercede (**auprès de** with).

intercepter [ɛ̃tersepte] *vt* to intercept. ◆**interception** *nf* interception.

interchangeable [ɛ̃terʃɑ̃ʒabl] *a* interchangeable.

interclasse [ɛ̃terklɑs] *nm Scol* break (between classes).

intercontinental, -aux [ɛ̃terkɔ̃tinɑtal, -o] *a* intercontinental.

interdépendant [ɛ̃tɛrdepɑ̃dɑ̃] *a* interdependent.

interd/ire* [ɛ̃tɛrdir] *vt* to forbid, not to allow (**qch à qn** s.o. sth); (*meeting, film etc*) to ban; **i. à qn de faire** (*médecin, père etc*) not to allow s.o. to do, forbid s.o. to do; (*attitude, santé etc*) to prevent s.o. from doing, not allow s.o. to do. ◆**—it a 1** forbidden, not allowed; **il est i. de** it is forbidden to; **'stationnement i.'** 'no parking'. **2** (*étonné*) nonplussed. ◆**interdiction** *nf* ban (**de** on); **'i. de fumer'** 'no smoking'.

intéress/er [ɛ̃terese] *vt* to interest; (*concerner*) to concern; **s'i. à** to take an interest in, be interested in. ◆**—ant** *a* (*captivant*) interesting; (*affaire, prix etc*) attractive, worthwhile. ◆**—é, -ée** *a* (*avide*) self-interested; (*motif*) selfish; (*concerné*) concerned; – *nmf* **l'i.** the interested party.

intérêt [ɛ̃terɛ] *nm* interest; *Péj* self-interest; *pl Fin* interest; **tu as i. à** it would pay you to do, you'd do well to do; **des intérêts dans** *Com* an interest *ou* stake in.

interface [ɛ̃tɛrfas] *nf Tech* interface.

intérieur [ɛ̃terjœr] *a* (*cour, paroi*) inner, interior; (*poche*) inside; (*vie, sentiment*) inner, inward; (*mer*) inland; (*politique, vol*) internal, domestic; – *nm* (*de boîte etc*) inside (**de** of); (*de maison*) interior, inside; (*de pays*) interior; **à l'i.** (**de**) inside; **d'i.** (*vêtement, jeux*) indoor; **femme d'i.** home-loving woman; **ministère de l'I.** Home Office, *Am* Department of the Interior. ◆**—ement** *adv* (*dans le cœur*) inwardly.

intérim [ɛ̃terim] *nm* **pendant l'i.** in the interim; **assurer l'i.** to deputize (**de** for); **ministre/etc par i.** acting minister/*etc.* ◆**intérimaire** *a* temporary, interim; – *nmf* (*fonctionnaire*) deputy; (*secrétaire*) temporary.

interligne [ɛ̃tɛrliɲ] *nm Typ* space (between the lines).

interlocuteur, -trice [ɛ̃tɛrlɔkytœr, -tris] *nmf Pol* negotiator; **mon i.** the person I am, was *etc* speaking to.

interloqué [ɛ̃tɛrlɔke] *a* dumbfounded.

interlude [ɛ̃tɛrlyd] *nm Mus TV* interlude.

intermède [ɛ̃tɛrmɛd] *nm* (*interruption*) & *Th* interlude.

intermédiaire [ɛ̃tɛrmedjɛr] *a* intermediate; – *nmf* intermediary; **par l'i. de** through (the medium of).

interminable [ɛ̃tɛrminabl] *a* endless, interminable.

intermittent [ɛ̃tɛrmitɑ̃] *a* intermittent. ◆**intermittence** *nf* **par i.** intermittently.

international, -aux [ɛ̃tɛrnasjɔnal, -o] *a* in-

ternational; – *nm* (*joueur*) *Sp* international.

interne [ɛ̃tɛrn] **1** *a* (*douleur etc*) internal; (*oreille*) inner. **2** *nmf Scol* boarder; (*des hôpitaux*) houseman, *Am* intern. ◆**internat** *nm* (*école*) boarding school.

intern/er [ɛ̃tɛrne] *vt* (*réfugié*) to intern; (*aliéné*) to confine. ◆**—ement** *nm* internment; confinement.

interpeller [ɛ̃tɛrpele] *vt* to shout at, address sharply; (*dans une réunion*) to question, (*interrompre*) to heckle; (*arrêter*) *Jur* to take in for questioning. ◆**interpellation** *nf* sharp address; questioning; heckling; (*de police*) arrest.

interphone [ɛ̃tɛrfɔn] *nm* intercom.

interplanétaire [ɛ̃tɛrplanetɛr] *a* interplanetary.

interpoler [ɛ̃tɛrpɔle] *vt* to interpolate.

interposer (s') [sɛ̃tɛrpoze] *vpr* (*dans une dispute etc*) to intervene (**dans** in); **s'i. entre** to come between.

interprète [ɛ̃tɛrprɛt] *nmf Ling* interpreter; (*chanteur*) singer; *Th Mus* performer; (*porte-parole*) spokesman, spokeswoman; **faire l'i.** *Ling* to interpret. ◆**interprétariat** *nm* (*métier*) *Ling* interpreting. ◆**interprétation** *nf* interpretation; *Th Mus* performance. ◆**interpréter** *vt* (*expliquer*) to interpret; (*chanter*) to sing; (*jouer*) *Th* to play, perform; (*exécuter*) *Mus* to perform.

interroger [ɛ̃terɔʒe] *vt* to question; *Jur* to interrogate; (*faits*) to examine. ◆**interrogateur, -trice** *a* (*air*) questioning; – *nmf Scol* examiner. ◆**interrogatif, -ive** *a* & *nm Gram* interrogative. ◆**interrogation** *nf* question; (*action*) questioning; (*épreuve*) *Scol* test. ◆**interrogatoire** *nm Jur* interrogation.

interrompre* [ɛ̃terɔ̃pr] *vt* to interrupt, break off; **i. qn** to interrupt s.o.; – **s'i.** *vpr* (*personne*) to break off, stop. ◆**interrupteur** *nm* (*bouton*) *El* switch. ◆**interruption** *nf* interruption; (*des hostilités, du courant*) break (**de** in).

intersection [ɛ̃tɛrseksjɔ̃] *nf* intersection.

interstice [ɛ̃tɛrstis] *nm* crack, chink.

interurbain [ɛ̃teryrbɛ̃] *a* & *nm* (**téléphone**) **i.** long-distance telephone service.

intervalle [ɛ̃tɛrval] *nm* (*écart*) space, gap; (*temps*) interval; **dans l'i.** (*entretemps*) in the meantime.

intervenir* [ɛ̃tɛrvənir] *vi* (*s'interposer, agir*) to intervene; (*survenir*) to occur; (*opérer*) *Méd* to operate; **être intervenu** (*accord*) to be reached. ◆**intervention** *nf* intervention; **i. (chirurgicale)** operation.

intervertir [ɛ̃tɛrvɛrtir] *vt* to invert. ◆**interversion** *nf* inversion.

interview [ɛ̃tɛrvju] *nf Journ TV* interview. ◆**interviewer** [-vjuve] *vt* to interview.

intestin [ɛ̃tɛstɛ̃] *nm* intestine, bowel. ◆**intestinal, -aux** *a* intestinal, bowel-.

intime [ɛ̃tim] *a* intimate; (*ami*) close, intimate; (*vie, fête, journal*) private; (*pièce, coin*) cosy; (*cérémonie*) quiet; – *nmf* close ou intimate friend. ◆**—ment** *adv* intimately. ◆**intimité** *nf* intimacy; privacy; cosiness; **dans l'i.** (*mariage etc*) in private.

intimider [ɛ̃timide] *vt* to intimidate, frighten. ◆**intimidation** *nf* intimidation.

intituler [ɛ̃tityle] *vt* to entitle; – **s'i.** *vpr* to be entitled.

intolérable [ɛ̃tɔlerabl] *a* intolerable (que that). ◆**intolérance** *nf* intolerance. ◆**intolérant** *a* intolerant (**de** of).

intonation [ɛ̃tɔnasjɔ̃] *nf Ling* intonation; (*ton*) tone.

intoxiqu/er [ɛ̃tɔksike] *vt* (*empoisonner*) to poison; *Psy Pol* to brainwash; – **s'i.** *vpr* to be ou become poisoned. ◆**—é, -ée** *nmf* addict. ◆**intoxication** *nf* poisoning; *Psy Pol* brainwashing.

intra- [ɛ̃tra] *préf* intra-.

intraduisible [ɛ̃tradɥizibl] *a* untranslatable.

intraitable [ɛ̃trɛtabl] *a* uncompromising.

intransigeant [ɛ̃trɑ̃ziʒɑ̃] *a* intransigent. ◆**intransigeance** *nf* intransigence.

intransitif, -ive [ɛ̃trɑ̃zitif, -iv] *a & nm Gram* intransitive.

intraveineux, -euse [ɛ̃travɛnø, -øz] *a Méd* intravenous.

intrépide [ɛ̃trepid] *a* (*courageux*) fearless, intrepid; (*obstiné*) headstrong. ◆**intrépidité** *nf* fearlessness.

intrigue [ɛ̃trig] *nf* intrigue; *Th Cin Littér* plot. ◆**intrigant, -ante** *nmf* schemer. ◆**intriguer 1** *vi* to scheme, intrigue. **2** *v t.* **i. qn** (*intéresser*) to intrigue s.o., puzzle s.o.

intrinsèque [ɛ̃trɛ̃sɛk] *a* intrinsic. ◆**—ment** *adv* intrinsically.

introduire* [ɛ̃trɔdɥir] *vt* (*présenter*) to introduce, bring in; (*insérer*) to insert (**dans** into), put in (**dans** to); (*faire entrer*) to show (*s.o.*) in; **s'i. dans** to get into. ◆**introduction** *nf* (*texte, action*) introduction.

introspectif, -ive [ɛ̃trɔspɛktif, -iv] *a* introspective. ◆**introspection** *nf* introspection.

introuvable [ɛ̃truvabl] *a* that cannot be found anywhere.

introverti, -ie [ɛ̃trɔvɛrti] *nmf* introvert.

intrus, -use [ɛ̃try, -yz] *nmf* intruder. ◆**intrusion** *nf* intrusion (**dans** into).

intuition [ɛ̃tɥisjɔ̃] *nf* intuition. ◆**intuitif, -ive** *a* intuitive.

inusable [inyzabl] *a Fam* hard-wearing.

inusité [inyzite] *a Gram* unused.

inutile [inytil] *a* unnecessary, useless; **c'est i. de crier** it's pointless ou useless to shout. ◆**inutilement** *adv* (*vainement*) needlessly. ◆**inutilité** *nf* uselessness.

inutilisable [inytilizabl] *a* unusable. ◆**inutilisé** *a* unused.

invalider [ɛ̃valide] *vt* to invalidate.

invariable [ɛ̃varjabl] *a* invariable. ◆**—ment** [-əmɑ̃] *adv* invariably.

invasion [ɛ̃vazjɔ̃] *nf* invasion.

invective [ɛ̃vɛktiv] *nf* invective. ◆**invectiver** *vt* to abuse; – *vi* **i. contre** to inveigh against.

invendable [ɛ̃vɑ̃dabl] *a* unsaleable. ◆**invendu** *a* unsold.

inventaire [ɛ̃vɑ̃tɛr] *nm* (*liste*) *Com* inventory; (*étude*) *Fig* survey; **faire l'i.** *Com* to do the stocktaking (**de** of).

inventer [ɛ̃vɑ̃te] *vt* (*découvrir*) to invent; (*imaginer*) to make up. ◆**inventeur, -trice** *nmf* inventor. ◆**inventif, -ive** *a* inventive. ◆**invention** *nf* invention.

inverse [ɛ̃vɛrs] *a* (*sens*) opposite; (*ordre*) reverse; *Math* inverse; – *nm* **l'i.** the reverse, the opposite. ◆**inversement** *adv* conversely. ◆**inverser** *vt* (*ordre*) to reverse. ◆**inversion** *nf Gram Anat etc* inversion.

investigation [ɛ̃vɛstigasjɔ̃] *nf* investigation.

invest/ir [ɛ̃vɛstir] **1** *vti Com* to invest (**dans** in). **2** **i. qn de** (*fonction etc*) to invest s.o. with. ◆**—issement** *nm Com* investment. ◆**investiture** *nf Pol* nomination.

invétéré [ɛ̃vetere] *a* inveterate.

invincible [ɛ̃vɛ̃sibl] *a* invincible.

invisible [ɛ̃vizibl] *a* invisible.

invit/er [ɛ̃vite] *vt* to invite; **i. qn à faire** to invite ou ask s.o. to do; (*inciter*) to tempt s.o. to do. ◆**—é, -ée** *nmf* guest. ◆**invitation** *nf* invitation.

invivable [ɛ̃vivabl] *a* unbearable.

involontaire [ɛ̃vɔlɔ̃tɛr] *a* involuntary. ◆**—ment** *adv* accidentally, involuntarily.

invoquer [ɛ̃vɔke] *vt* (*argument etc*) to put forward; (*appeler*) to invoke, call upon. ◆**invocation** *nf* invocation (**à** to).

invraisemblable [ɛ̃vrɛsɑ̃blabl] *a* incredible; (*improbable*) improbable. ◆**invraisemblance** *nf* improbability.

invulnérable [ɛ̃vylnerabl] *a* invulnerable.

iode [jɔd] *nm* teinture d'i. *Méd* iodine.

ira, irait [ira, irɛ] *voir* **aller 1**.

Irak [irak] *nm* Iraq. ◆**irakien, -ienne** *a & nmf* Iraqi.

Iran [irã] nm Iran. ◆**iranien, -ienne** a & nmf Iranian.

irascible [irasibl] a irascible.

iris [iris] nm Anat Bot iris.

Irlande [irlãd] nf Ireland. ◆**irlandais, -aise** a Irish; – nmf Irishman, Irishwoman; – nm (langue) Irish.

ironie [irɔni] nf irony. ◆**ironique** a ironic(al).

irradier [iradje] vt to irradiate.

irraisonné [irezɔne] a irrational.

irréconciliable [irekɔ̃siljabl] a irreconcilable.

irrécusable [irekyzabl] a irrefutable.

irréel, -elle [ireel] a unreal.

irréfléchi [irefleʃi] a thoughtless, unthinking.

irréfutable [irefytabl] a irrefutable.

irrégulier, -ière [iregylje, -jɛr] a irregular. ◆**irrégularité** nf irregularity.

irrémédiable [iremedjabl] a irreparable.

irremplaçable [irãplasabl] a irreplaceable.

irréparable [ireparabl] a (véhicule etc) beyond repair; (tort, perte) irreparable.

irrépressible [irepresibl] a (rires etc) irrepressible.

irréprochable [ireprɔʃabl] a beyond reproach, irreproachable.

irrésistible [irezistibl] a (personne, charme etc) irresistible.

irrésolu [irezɔly] a irresolute.

irrespirable [irespirabl] a unbreathable; Fig stifling.

irresponsable [irespɔ̃sabl] a (personne) irresponsible.

irrévérencieux, -euse [ireverãsjø, -øz] a irreverent.

irréversible [ireversibl] a irreversible.

irrévocable [irevɔkabl] a irrevocable.

irriguer [irige] vt to irrigate. ◆**irrigation** nf irrigation.

irriter [irite] vt to irritate; – s'i. vpr to get angry (de, contre at). ◆—ant a irritating; – nm irritant. ◆**irritable** a irritable. ◆**irritation** nf (colère) & Méd irritation.

irruption [irypsjɔ̃] nf faire i. dans to burst into.

islam [islam] nm Islam. ◆**islamique** a Islamic.

Islande [islãd] nf Iceland. ◆**islandais, -aise** a Icelandic.

isol/er [izɔle] vt to isolate (de from); (contre le froid etc) & Él to insulate; – s'i. vpr to cut oneself off, isolate oneself. ◆—ant a insulating; – nm insulating material. ◆—é a isolated; (écarté) remote, isolated; i. de cut off ou isolated from. ◆**isolation** nf insulation. ◆**isolement** nm isolation. ◆**isolément** adv in isolation, singly. ◆**isoloir** nm polling booth.

isorel® [izɔrel] nm hardboard.

Israël [israel] nm Israel. ◆**israélien, -ienne** a & nmf Israeli. ◆**israélite** a Jewish; – nm Jew; – nf Jewess.

issu [isy] a être i. de to come from.

issue [isy] nf (sortie) exit, way out; (solution) Fig way out; (résultat) outcome; à l'i. de at the close of; rue etc sans i. dead end; situation etc sans i. Fig dead end.

isthme [ism] nm Géog isthmus.

Italie [itali] nf Italy. ◆**italien, -ienne** a & nmf Italian; – nm (langue) Italian.

italique [italik] a Typ italic; – nm italics.

itinéraire [itinerɛr] nm itinerary, route.

itinérant [itinerã] a itinerant.

IVG [iveʒe] nf abrév (interruption volontaire de grossesse) (voluntary) abortion.

ivoire [ivwar] nm ivory.

ivre [ivr] a drunk (de with). ◆**ivresse** nf drunkenness; en état d'i. under the influence of drink. ◆**ivrogne** nmf drunk(ard).

J

J, j [ʒi] nm J, j; le jour J. D-day.

j' [ʒ] voir je.

jacasser [ʒakase] vi (personne, pie) to chatter.

jachère (en) [ãʒaʃɛr] adv (champ etc) fallow.

jacinthe [ʒasɛ̃t] nf hyacinth.

jacousi [ʒakuzi] nm (baignoire, piscine) jacuzzi.

jade [ʒad] nm (pierre) jade.

jadis [ʒadis] adv at one time, once.

jaguar [ʒagwar] nm (animal) jaguar.

jaill/ir [ʒajir] vi (liquide) to spurt (out), gush (out); (lumière) to flash, stream; (cri) to burst out; (vérité) to burst forth; (étincelle) to fly out. ◆—issement nm (de liquide) gush.

jais [ʒɛ] nm (noir) de j. jet-black.

jalon [ʒalɔ̃] *nm* (*piquet*) marker; **poser les jalons** *Fig* to prepare the way (**de** for). ◆**jalonner** *vt* to mark (out); (*border*) to line.

jaloux, -ouse [ʒalu, -uz] *a* jealous (**de** of). ◆**jalouser** *vt* to envy. ◆**jalousie** *nf* **1** jealousy. **2** (*persienne*) venetian blind.

Jamaïque [ʒamaik] *nf* Jamaica.

jamais [ʒamɛ] *adv* **1** (*négatif*) never; **sans j. sortir** without ever going out; **elle ne sort j.** she never goes out. **2** (*positif*) ever; **à (tout) j.** for ever; **si j.** if ever.

jambe [ʒɑ̃b] *nf* leg; **à toutes jambes** as fast as one can; **prendre ses jambes à son cou** to take to one's heels.

jambon [ʒɑ̃bɔ̃] *nm Culin* ham. ◆**jambonneau, -x** *nm* knuckle of ham.

jante [ʒɑ̃t] *nf* (*de roue*) rim.

janvier [ʒɑ̃vje] *nm* January.

Japon [ʒapɔ̃] *nm* Japan. ◆**japonais, -aise** *a nmf* Japanese; – & *nm* (*langue*) Japanese.

japp/er [ʒape] *vi* (*chien etc*) to yap, yelp. ◆**-ement** *nm* yap, yelp.

jaquette [ʒakɛt] *nf* (*d'homme*) tailcoat, morning coat; (*de femme, livre*) jacket.

jardin [ʒardɛ̃] *nm* garden; **j. d'enfants** kindergarten, playschool; **j. public** park; (*plus petit*) gardens. ◆**jardinage** *nm* gardening. ◆**jardiner** *vi* to do the garden, be gardening. ◆**jardinerie** *nf* garden centre. ◆**jardinier** *nm* gardener. ◆**jardinière** *nf* (*personne*) gardener; (*caisse à fleurs*) window box; **j. (de légumes)** *Culin* mixed vegetable dish; **j. d'enfants** kindergarten teacher.

jargon [ʒargɔ̃] *nm* jargon.

jarret [ʒarɛ] *nm Anat* back of the knee.

jarretelle [ʒartɛl] *nf* (*de gaine*) suspender, *Am* garter. ◆**jarretière** *nf* (*autour de la jambe*) garter.

jaser [ʒaze] *vi* (*bavarder*) to jabber.

jasmin [ʒasmɛ̃] *nm Bot* jasmine.

jatte [ʒat] *nf* (*bol*) bowl.

jauge [ʒoʒ] *nf* **1** (*instrument*) gauge. **2** (*capacité*) capacity; *Nau* tonnage. ◆**jauger** *vt* (*personne*) *Litt* to size up.

jaune [ʒon] **1** *a* yellow; – *nm* (*couleur*) yellow; **j. d'œuf** (egg) yolk. **2** *nm* (*ouvrier*) *Péj* blackleg, scab. ◆**jaunâtre** *a* yellowish. ◆**jaunir** *vti* to (turn) yellow. ◆**jaunisse** *nf Méd* jaundice.

Javel (eau de) [odʒavɛl] *nf* bleach. ◆**javelliser** *vt* to chlorinate.

javelot [ʒavlo] *nm* javelin.

jazz [dʒaz] *nm* jazz.

je [ʒ(ə)] *pron* (**j'** before vowel or mute h) I; **je suis** I am.

jean [dʒin] *nm* (pair of) jeans.

jeep [dʒip] *nf* jeep.

je-m'en-fichisme [ʒmɑ̃fiʃism] *nm Fam* couldn't-care-less attitude.

jérémiades [ʒeremjad] *nfpl Fam* lamentations.

jerrycan [(d)ʒerikan] *nm* jerry can.

jersey [ʒɛrze] *nm* (*tissu*) jersey.

Jersey [ʒɛrze] *nf* Jersey.

jésuite [ʒezɥit] *nm* Jesuit.

Jésus [ʒezy] *nm* Jesus; **J.-Christ** Jesus Christ.

jet [ʒɛ] *nm* throw; (*de vapeur*) burst, gush; (*de lumière*) flash; **j. d'eau** fountain; **premier j.** (*ébauche*) first draft; **d'un seul j.** in one go.

jetée [ʒ(ə)te] *nf* pier, jetty.

jeter [ʒ(ə)te] *vt* to throw (**à** to, **dans** into); (*mettre à la poubelle*) to throw away; (*ancre, regard, sort*) to cast; (*bases*) to lay; (*cri, son*) to let out, utter; (*éclat, lueur*) to throw out, give out; (*noter*) to jot down; **j. un coup d'œil sur** *ou* **à** to have *ou* take a look at; (*rapidement*) to glance at; – **se j.** *vpr* to throw oneself; **se j. sur** to fall on, pounce on; **se j.** (*contre véhicule*) to crash into; **se j. dans** (*fleuve*) to flow into. ◆**jetable** *a* (*rasoir etc*) disposable.

jeton [ʒ(ə)tɔ̃] *nm* (*pièce*) token; (*pour compter*) counter; (*à la roulette*) chip.

jeu, -x [ʒø] *nm* **1** game; (*amusement*) play; (*d'argent*) gambling; *Th* acting; *Mus* playing; **j. de mots** play on words, pun; **jeux de société** parlour *ou* party games; **j. télévisé** television quiz; **maison de jeux** gambling club; **en j.** (*en cause*) at stake; (*forces etc*) at work; **entrer en j.** to come into play. **2** (*série complète*) set; (*de cartes*) pack, deck, *Am* deck; (*cartes en main*) hand; **j. d'échecs** (*boîte, pièces*) chess set. **3** (*de ressort, verrou*) *Tech* play.

jeudi [ʒødi] *nm* Thursday.

jeun (à) [aʒœ̃] *adv* on an empty stomach; **être à j.** to have eaten no food.

jeune [ʒœn] *a* young; (*inexpérimenté*) inexperienced; **Dupont j.** Dupont junior; **d'allure j.** young-looking; **jeunes gens** young people; – *nmf* young person; **les jeunes** young people. ◆**jeunesse** *nf* youth; (*apparence*) youthfulness; **la j.** (*jeunes*) the young, youth.

jeûne [ʒøn] *nm* fast; (*action*) fasting. ◆**jeûner** *vi* to fast.

joaillier, -lère [ʒɔaje, -jɛr] *nmf* jeweller.

◆**joaillerie** *nf* jewellery; (*magasin*) jewellery shop.

jockey [ʒɔkɛ] *nm* jockey.

jogging [dʒɔgiŋ] *nm Sp* jogging; (*chaussure*) running *ou* jogging shoe; **faire du j.** to jog.

joie [ʒwa] *nf* joy, delight; **feu de j.** bonfire.

joindre* [ʒwɛ̃dr] *vt* (*mettre ensemble, relier*) to join; (*efforts*) to combine; (*insérer dans une enveloppe*) to enclose (à with); (*ajouter*) to add (à to); **j. qn** (*contacter*) to get in touch with s.o.; **j. les deux bouts** *Fig* to make ends meet; **se j.** (*se mettre ensemble, participer à*) to join. ◆**joint** *a* (*efforts*) joint, combined; **à pieds joints** with feet together; – *nm Tech* joint; (*de robinet*) washer. ◆**jointure** *nf Anat* joint.

joker [ʒɔkɛr] *nm Cartes* joker.

joli [ʒɔli] *a* nice, lovely; (*femme, enfant*) pretty. ◆—**ment** *adv* nicely; (*très, beaucoup*) awfully.

jonc [ʒɔ̃] *nm Bot* (bul)rush.

joncher [ʒɔ̃ʃe] *vt* to litter (de with); **jonché de** strewn *ou* littered with.

jonction [ʒɔ̃ksjɔ̃] *nf* (*de tubes, routes etc*) junction.

jongl/er [ʒɔ̃gle] *vi* to juggle. ◆—**eur, -euse** *nmf* juggler.

jonquille [ʒɔ̃kij] *nf* daffodil.

Jordanie [ʒɔrdani] *nf* Jordan.

joue [ʒu] *nf Anat* cheek; **coucher qn en j.** to aim (a gun) at s.o.

jouer [ʒwe] *vi* to play; *Th* to act; (*au tiercé etc*) to gamble, bet; (*à la Bourse*) to gamble; (*entrer en jeu*) to come into play; (*être important*) to count; (*fonctionner*) to work; **j. au tennis/aux cartes/***etc* to play tennis/cards/*etc*; **j. du piano/du violon/***etc* to play the piano/violin/*etc*; **j. des coudes** to use one's elbows; – *vt* (*musique, tour, jeu*) to play; (*risquer*) to gamble, bet (**sur** on); (*cheval*) to bet on; (*personnage, rôle*) *Th* to play; (*pièce*) *Th* to perform, put on; (*film*) to show, put on; **j. gros jeu** to play for high stakes; **se j. de** to scoff at; (*difficultés*) to make light of. ◆**jouet** *nm* toy; **le j. de qn** *Fig* s.o.'s plaything. ◆**joueur, -euse** *nmf* player; (*au tiercé etc*) gambler; **beau j., bon j.,** good loser.

joufflu [ʒufly] *a* (*visage*) chubby; (*enfant*) chubby-cheeked.

joug [ʒu] *nm Agr & Fig* yoke.

jouir [ʒwir] *vi* **1 j. de** (*savourer, avoir*) to enjoy. **2** (*éprouver le plaisir sexuel*) to come. ◆**jouissance** *nf* enjoyment; (*usage*) *Jur* use.

joujou, -x [ʒuʒu] *nm Fam* toy.

jour [ʒur] *nm* day; (*lumière*) (day)light; (*ouverture*) gap, opening; (*aspect*) *Fig* light; **il fait j.** it's (day)light; **grand j., plein j.** broad daylight; **de nos jours** nowadays, these days; **au j. le j.** from day to day; **du j. au lendemain** overnight; **mettre à j.** to bring up to date; **mettre au j.** to bring to the open; **se faire j.** to come to light; **donner le j. à** to give birth to; **le j. de l'An** New Year's day. ◆**journalier, -ière** *a* daily. ◆**journée** *nf* day; **pendant la j.** during the day(time); **toute la j.** all day (long). ◆**journellement** *adv* daily.

journal, -aux [ʒurnal, -o] *nm* (news)paper; (*spécialisé*) journal; (*intime*) diary; **j.** (*parlé*) *Rad* news bulletin; **j. de bord** *Nau* logbook. ◆**journalisme** *nm* journalism. ◆**journaliste** *nmf* journalist. ◆**journalistique** *a* (*style etc*) journalistic.

jovial, -aux [ʒɔvjal, -o] *a* jovial, jolly. ◆**jovialité** *nf* jollity.

joyau, -aux [ʒwajo] *nm* jewel.

joyeux, -euse [ʒwajø, -øz] *a* merry, happy, joyful; **j. anniversaire!** happy birthday!; **j. Noël!** merry *ou* happy Christmas!

jubilé [ʒybile] *nm* (golden) jubilee.

jubiler [ʒybile] *vi* to be jubilant. ◆**jubilation** *nf* jubilation.

jucher [ʒyʃe] *vt*, – **se j.** *vpr* to perch (**sur** on).

judaïque [ʒydaik] *a* Jewish. ◆**judaïsme** *nm* Judaism.

judas [ʒyda] *nm* (*de porte*) peephole, spy hole.

judiciaire [ʒydisjɛr] *a* judicial, legal.

judicieux, -euse [ʒydisjø, -øz] *a* sensible, judicious.

judo [ʒydo] *nm* judo. ◆**judoka** *nmf* judo expert.

juge [ʒyʒ] *nm* judge; *Sp* referee, umpire; **j. d'instruction** examining magistrate; **j. de paix** Justice of the Peace; **j. de touche** *Fb* linesman. ◆**juger** *vt* (*personne, question etc*) to judge; (*affaire*) *Jur* to try; (*estimer*) to consider (**que** that); **j. qn** *Jur* to try; – *vi* **j. de** to judge; **jugez de ma surprise/***etc* imagine my surprise/*etc*. ◆**jugement** *nm* judg(e)ment; (*verdict*) *Jur* sentence; **passer en j.** *Jur* to stand trial. ◆**jugeote** *nf Fam* commonsense.

jugé (au) [oʒyʒe] *adv* by guesswork.

juguler [ʒygyle] *vt* to check, suppress.

juif, juive [ʒɥif, ʒɥiv] *a* Jewish; – *nm* Jew; – *nf* Jew(ess).

juillet [ʒɥijɛ] *nm* July.

juin [ʒɥɛ̃] *nm* June.

jumeau, -elle, *pl* **-eaux, -elles** [ʒymo, -ɛl] **1** *a* (*frères, lits etc*) twin; – *nmf* twin. **2** *nfpl* *(longue-vue)* binoculars; **jumelles de théâtre** opera glasses. ◆**jumel/er** *vt (villes)* to twin. ◆**—age** *nm* twinning.

ungle [ʒœgl] *nf* jungle.

unior [ʒynjɔr] *nm & a (inv au sing) Sp* junior.

unte [ʒœt] *nf Pol* junta.

upe [ʒyp] *nf* skirt. ◆**jupon** *nm* petticoat.

urer [ʒyre] **1** *vi (blasphémer)* to swear. **2** *vt (promettre)* to swear (que that, **de faire** to do); — *vi* **j. de qch** to swear to sth. **3** *vi (contraster)* to clash (avec with). ◆**juré** *a (ennemi)* sworn; — *nm Jur* juror. ◆**juron** *nm* swearword, oath.

uridiction [ʒyridiksjɔ̃] *nf* jurisdiction.

uridique [ʒyridik] *a* legal. ◆**juriste** *nmf* legal expert, jurist.

ury [ʒyri] *nm Jur* jury; *(de concours)* panel *(of judges)*, jury.

us [ʒy] *nm (des fruits etc)* juice; *(de viande)* gravy; *(café) Fam* coffee; *(électricité) Fam* power.

usque [ʒysk] *prép* **jusqu'à** *(espace)* as far as, *(right)* up to; *(temps)* until, (up) till, to; *(même)* even; **jusqu'à dix francs**/*etc* up to ten francs/*etc;* **jusqu'en mai**/*etc* until May/*etc;* **jusqu'où?** how far?; **j. dans**/**sous**/*etc* right into/under/*etc;* **j. chez moi** as far as my place; **jusqu'ici** as far as this; *(temps)* up till now; **en avoir j.-là** *Fam* to be fed up; — *conj* **jusqu'à ce qu'il vienne** until he comes.

juste [ʒyst] *a (équitable)* fair, just; *(légitime)* just; *(calcul, heure, réponse)* correct, right, accurate; *(remarque)* sound; *(oreille)* good; *(voix) Mus* true; *(vêtement)* tight; **un peu j.** *(quantité, repas etc)* barely enough; **très j.!** quite so *ou* right!; **à 3 heures j.** on the stroke of 3; — *adv (deviner, compter)* correctly, right, accurately; *(chanter)* in tune; *(exactement, seulement)* just; **au j.** exactly; **tout j.** *(à peine, seulement)* only just; **c'était j.!** *(il était temps)* it was a near thing!; **un peu j.** *(mesurer, compter)* a bit on the short side; — *nm (homme)* just man. ◆**justement** *adv* precisely, exactly, just; *(avec justesse ou justice)* justly. ◆**justesse** *nf (exactitude)* accuracy; **de j.** *(éviter, gagner etc)* just.

justice [ʒystis] *nf* justice; *(organisation, autorités)* law; **en toute j.** in all fairness; **rendre j. à** to do justice to. ◆**justicier, -ière** *nmf* dispenser of justice.

justifier [ʒystifje] *vt* to justify; — *vi* **j. de** to prove; — **se j.** *vpr Jur* to clear oneself (de of); *(attitude etc)* to be justified. ◆**justifiable** *a* justifiable. ◆**justificatif, -ive** *a* document **j.** supporting document, proof. ◆**justification** *nf* justification; *(preuve)* proof.

jute [ʒyt] *nm (fibre)* jute.

juteux, -euse [ʒytø, -øz] *a* juicy.

juvénile [ʒyvenil] *a* youthful.

juxtaposer [ʒykstapoze] *vt* to juxtapose. ◆**juxtaposition** *nf* juxtaposition.

K

K, k [ka] *nm* K, k.

kaki [kaki] *a inv & nm* khaki.

kaléidoscope [kaleidɔskɔp] *nm* kaleidoscope.

kangourou [kɑ̃guru] *nm* **1** *(animal)* kangaroo. **2®** *(porte-bébé)* baby sling.

karaté [karate] *nm Sp* karate.

kart [kart] *nm Sp* (go-)kart, go-cart. ◆**karting** [-iŋ] *nm Sp* (go-)karting.

kascher [kaʃɛr] *a inv Rel* kosher.

kayac [kajak] *nm (bateau) Sp* canoe.

képi [kepi] *nm (coiffure) Mil* kepi.

kermesse [kɛrmɛs] *nf* charity fête; *(en Belgique etc)* village fair.

kérosène [kerozɛn] *nm* kerosene, aviation fuel.

kibboutz [kibuts] *nm* kibbutz.

kidnapp/er [kidnape] *vt* to kidnap. ◆**—eur, -euse** *nmf* kidnapper.

kilo(gramme) [kilo, kilogram] *nm* kilo(gramme).

kilomètre [kilometr] *nm* kilometre. ◆**kilométrage** *nm Aut* = mileage. ◆**kilométrique à borne k.** = milestone.

kilowatt [kilowat] *nm* kilowatt.

kimono [kimono] *nm (tunique)* kimono.

kinésithérapie [kineziterapi] *nf* physiotherapy. ◆**kinésithérapeute** *nmf* physiotherapist.

kiosque [kjɔsk] *nm (à journaux)* kiosk, stall; **k. à musique** bandstand.

kit [kit] *nm (meuble etc prêt à monter)* kit; **en k.** in kit form, ready to assemble.

klaxon® [klaksɔn] *nm Aut* horn. ◆**klaxonner** *vi* to hoot, *Am* honk.

km *abrév (kilomètre)* km.

k.-o. [kao] *a inv* mettre k.-o. *Boxe* to knock out.

kyrielle [kirjɛl] *nf* une k. de a long string of.

kyste [kist] *nm Méd* cyst.

L

L, l [ɛl] *nm* L, l.

l', la [l, la] *voir* le.

là [la] **1** *adv* there; *(chez soi)* in, home; je reste là I'll stay here; c'est là que *ou* où that's where; c'est là ton erreur that's *ou* there's your mistake; là où il est where he is; à cinq mètres de là five metres away; de là son échec *(cause)* hence his *ou* her failure; jusque-là *(lieu)* as far as that; passe par là go that way. **2** *adv (temps)* then; jusque-là up till then. **3** *int* là, là! *(pour rassurer)* there, there!; alors là! well!; oh là là! oh dear! **4** *voir ce²*, celui.

là-bas [laba] *adv* over there.

label [label] *nm Com* label, mark *(of quality, origin etc).*

labeur [labœr] *nm Litt* toil.

labo [labo] *nm Fam* lab. ◆**laboratoire** *nm* laboratory; l. de langues language laboratory.

laborieux, -euse [labɔrjø, -øz] *a (pénible)* laborious; *(personne)* industrious; les classes laborieuses the working classes.

labour [labur] *nm* ploughing, *Am* plowing, digging over. ◆**labour/er** *vt (avec charrue)* to plough, *Am* plow; *(avec bêche)* to dig over; *(visage etc) Fig* to furrow. ◆**—eur** *nm* ploughman, *Am* plowman.

labyrinthe [labirɛ̃t] *nm* maze, labyrinth.

lac [lak] *nm* lake.

lacer [lase] *vt* to lace (up). ◆**lacet** *nm* **1** *(shoe- ou boot-)*lace. **2** *(de route)* twist, zigzag; route en l. winding *ou* zigzag road.

lacérer [lasere] *vt (papier etc)* to tear; *(visage etc)* to lacerate.

lâche [laʃ] **1** *a* a cowardly; — *nmf* coward. **2** *a (détendu)* loose, slack. ◆**lâchement** *adv* in a cowardly manner. ◆**lâcheté** *nf* cowardice; une l. *(action)* a cowardly act.

lâch/er [laʃe] *vt (main, objet etc)* to let go of; *(bombe, pigeon etc)* to release; *(place, études)* to give up; *(juron)* to utter, let slip; *(secret)* to let out; l. qn *(laisser tranquille)* to leave s.o. (alone); *(abandonner) Fam* to drop s.o.; l. prise to let go; — *vi (corde)* to give way; — *nm* release. ◆**—eur, -euse** *nmf Fam* deserter.

laconique [lakɔnik] *a* laconic.

lacrymogène [lakrimɔʒɛn] *a* gaz l. tear gas.

lacté [lakte] *a (régime)* milk-; la Voie lactée the Milky Way.

lacune [lakyn] *nf* gap, deficiency.

lad [lad] *nm* stable boy, groom.

là-dedans [lad(ə)dɑ̃] *adv (lieu)* in there, inside. ◆**là-dessous** *adv* underneath. ◆**là-dessus** *adv* on it, on that; *(monter)* on top; *(alors)* thereupon. ◆**là-haut** *adv* up there; *(à l'étage)* upstairs.

lagon [lagɔ̃] *nm (small)* lagoon. ◆**lagune** *nf* lagoon.

laid [lɛ] *a* ugly; *(ignoble)* wretched. ◆**laideur** *nf* ugliness.

laine [lɛn] *nf* wool; de l., en l. woollen. ◆**lainage** *nm (vêtement)* woollen garment, woolly; *(étoffe)* woollen material; *pl (vêtements, objets fabriqués)* woollens. ◆**laineux, -euse** *a* woolly.

laïque [laik] *a (vie)* secular; *(habit, tribunal)* lay; — *nmf (non-prêtre)* layman, laywoman.

laisse [lɛs] *nf* lead, leash; en l. on a lead *ou* leash.

laisser [lese] *vt* to leave; l. qn partir/entrer/etc *(permettre)* to let s.o. go/come in/*etc*; l. qch à qn *(confier, donner)* to let s.o. have sth, leave sth with s.o.; *(vendre)* to let s.o. have sth; laissez-moi le temps de le faire give me *ou* leave me time to do it; se l. aller/faire to let oneself go/be pushed around. ◆**laissé(e)-pour-compte** *nmf (personne)* misfit, reject. ◆**laisser-aller** *nm inv* carelessness, slovenliness; ◆**laissez-passer** *nm inv (sauf-conduit)* pass.

lait [lɛ] *nm* milk; frère/sœur de l. foster-brother/-sister; dent de l. milk tooth. ◆**laitage** *nm* milk product *ou* food. ◆**laiterie** *nf* dairy. ◆**laiteux, -euse** *a* milky. ◆**laitier, -ière** *a (produits)* dairy-; — *nm (livreur)* milkman; *(vendeur)* dairyman; — *nf* dairywoman.

laiton [lɛtɔ̃] *nm* brass.

altue [lety] *nf* lettuce.

aïus [lajys] *nm Fam* speech.

ama [lama] *nm (animal)* llama.

ambeau, -x [lãbo] *nm* shred, bit; **mettre en lambeaux** to tear to shreds; **tomber en lambeaux** to fall to bits.

ambin, -ine [lãbɛ̃, -in] *nmf* dawdler. ◆**lambiner** *vi* to dawdle.

ambris [lãbri] *nm* panelling. ◆**lambrisser** *vt* to panel.

ame [lam] *nf* **1** *(de couteau, rasoir etc)* blade; *(de métal)* strip, plate; **l. de parquet** floorboard. **2** *(vague)* wave; **l. de fond** ground swell.

amelle [lamɛl] *nf* thin strip; **l. de verre** *(pour microscope)* slide.

amenter (se) [səlamãte] *vpr* to moan, lament; **se l. sur** to lament (over). ◆**lamentable** *a (mauvais)* deplorable; *(voix, cri)* mournful. ◆**lamentation** *nf* lament(ation).

aminé [lamine] *a (métal)* laminated.

ampadaire [lãpadɛr] *nm* standard lamp; *(de rue)* street lamp.

ampe [lãp] *nf* lamp; *(au néon)* light; *(de vieille radio)* valve, *Am* (vacuum) tube; **l. de poche** torch, *Am* flashlight.

ampée [lãpe] *nf Fam* gulp.

ampion [lãpjɔ̃] *nm* Chinese lantern.

ance [lãs] *nf* spear; *(de tournoi) Hist* lance; *(extrémité de tuyau)* nozzle; **l. d'incendie** fire hose.

ance-flammes [lãsflam] *nm inv* flame thrower. ◆**l.-pierres** *nm inv* catapult. ◆**l.-roquettes** *nm inv* rocket launcher.

anc/er [lãse] *vt (jeter)* to throw (à to); *(avec force)* to hurl; *(navire, mode, acteur, idée)* to launch; *(regard)* to cast (à at); *(moteur)* to start; *(ultimatum)* to issue; *(bombe)* to drop; *(gifle)* to give; *(cri)* to utter; **— se l.** *vpr (se précipiter)* to rush; **se l. dans** *(aventure, discussion)* to launch into; **— nm un l.** a throw; **le l. de** the throwing of. ◆**-ée** *nf* momentum. ◆**-ement** *nm Sp* throwing; *(de fusée, navire etc)* launch(ing).

ancinant [lãsinã] *a (douleur)* shooting; *(obsédant)* haunting.

landau [lãdo] *nm (pl -s)* pram, *Am* baby carriage.

lande [lãd] *nf* moor, heath.

langage [lãgaʒ] *nm (système, faculté d'expression)* language; **l. machine** computer language.

lange [lãʒ] *nm* (baby) blanket. ◆**langer** *vt (bébé)* to change.

langouste [lãgust] *nf* (spiny) lobster.

◆**langoustine** *nf* (Dublin) prawn, Norway lobster.

langue [lãg] *nf Anat* tongue; *Ling* language; **de l. anglaise/française** English-/French-speaking; **l. maternelle** mother tongue; **mauvaise l.** *(personne)* gossip. ◆**languette** *nf (patte)* tongue.

langueur [lãgœr] *nf* languor. ◆**langu/ir** *vi* to languish *(après* for, after); *(conversation)* to flag. ◆**-issant** *a* languid; *(conversation)* flagging.

lanière [lanjɛr] *nf* strap; *(d'étoffe)* strip.

lanterne [lãtɛrn] *nf* lantern; *(électrique)* lamp; *pl Aut* sidelights.

lanterner [lãtɛrne] *vi* to loiter.

lapalissade [lapalisad] *nf* statement of the obvious, truism.

laper [lape] *vt (boire)* to lap up; **— vi** to lap.

lapider [lapide] *vt* to stone.

lapin [lapɛ̃] *nm* rabbit; **mon (petit) l.!** my dear!; **poser un l. à qn** *Fam* to stand s.o. up.

laps [laps] *nm* **un l. de temps** a lapse of time.

lapsus [lapsys] *nm* slip (of the tongue).

laquais [lakɛ] *nm Hist & Fig* lackey.

laque [lak] *nf* lacquer; **l. à cheveux** hair spray, (hair) lacquer. ◆**laquer** *vt* to lacquer.

laquelle [lakɛl] *voir* **lequel.**

larbin [larbɛ̃] *nm Fam* flunkey.

lard [lar] *nm (fumé)* bacon; *(gras)* (pig's) fat. ◆**lardon** *nm Culin* strip of bacon *ou* fat.

large [larʒ] *a* wide, broad; *(vêtement)* loose; *(idées, esprit)* broad; *(grand)* large; *(généreux)* liberal; **l. d'esprit** broad-minded; **l. de six mètres** six metres wide; **— adv (calculer)** liberally, broadly; **— nm** breadth, width; **avoir six mètres de l.** to be six metres wide; **le l. (mer)** the open sea; **au l. de Cherbourg** *Nau* off Cherbourg; **être au l.** to have lots of room. ◆**-ment** *adv* widely; *(ouvrir)* wide; *(servir, payer)* liberally; *(au moins)* easily; **avoir l. le temps** to have plenty of time, have ample time. ◆**largesse** *nf* liberality. ◆**largeur** *nf* width, breadth; *(d'esprit)* breadth.

larguer [large] *vt (bombe, parachutiste)* to drop; **l. qn** *(se débarrasser de)* to drop s.o.; **l. les amarres** *Nau* to cast off.

larme [larm] *nf* tear; *(goutte) Fam* drop; **en larmes** in tears; **rire aux larmes** to laugh till one cries. ◆**larmoyer** *vi (yeux)* to water.

larve [larv] *nf (d'insecte)* larva, grub.

larvé [larve] *a* latent, underlying.

larynx [larɛ̃ks] *nm Anat* larynx ◆**laryngite** *nf Méd* laryngitis.

las, lasse [lɑ, lɑs] *a* tired, weary *(de* of).

◆**lasser** vt to tire, weary; **se l. de** to tire of.
◆**lassitude** nf tiredness, weariness.

lascar [laskar] nm Fam (clever) fellow.

lascif, -ive [lasif, -iv] a lascivious.

laser [lazɛr] nm laser.

lasso [laso] nm lasso.

latent [latɑ̃] a latent.

latéral, -aux [lateral, -o] a lateral, side-.

latin, -ine [latɛ̃, -in] a & nmf Latin; — (langue) Latin.

latitude [latityd] nf Géog & Fig latitude.

latrines [latrin] nfpl latrines.

latte [lat] nf slat, lath; (de plancher) board.

lauréat, -ate [lɔrea, -at] nmf (prize)winner; – a prize-winning.

laurier [lɔrje] nm Bot laurel, bay; du l. Culin bay leaves.

lavabo [lavabo] nm washbasin, sink; pl (cabinet) toilet(s), Am washroom.

lavande [lavɑ̃d] nf lavender.

lave [lav] nf Géol lava.

lave-auto [lavoto] nm car wash. ◆**l.-glace** nm windscreen ou Am windshield washer. ◆**l.-linge** nm washing machine. ◆**l.-vaisselle** nm dishwasher.

laver [lave] vt to wash; **l. qn de** (soupçon etc) to clear s.o. of; — **se l.** vpr to wash (oneself), Am wash up; **se l. les mains** to wash one's hands (Fig de of). ◆**lavable** a washable. ◆**lavage** nm washing; **l. de cerveau** Psy brainwashing. ◆**laverie** nf (automatique) launderette, Am laundromat. ◆**lavette** nf dish cloth; (homme) Péj drip. ◆**laveur** nm **l. de carreaux** window cleaner ou Am washer. ◆**lavoir** nm (bâtiment) washhouse.

laxatif, -ive [laksatif, -iv] nm & a Méd laxative.

laxisme [laksism] nm permissiveness, laxity. ◆**laxiste** a permissive, lax.

layette [lɛjɛt] nf baby clothes, layette.

le, la, pl les [l(ə), la, le] (le & la become l' before a vowel or mute h) **1** art déf (à + le = au, à + les = aux; de + le = du, de + les = des) the; **le garçon** the boy; **la fille** the girl; **venez, les enfants!** come children!; **les petits/rouges/etc** the little ones/red ones/etc; **mon ami le plus intime** my closest friend. **2** (généralisation, abstraction) la beauté beauty; **la France** France; **les Français** the French; **les hommes** men; **aimer le café** to like coffee. **3** (possession) **il ouvrit la bouche** he opened his mouth; **se blesser au pied** to hurt one's foot; **avoir les cheveux blonds** to have blond hair. **4** (mesure) **dix francs le kilo** ten francs a kilo. **5** (temps) **elle vient le lundi** she comes on Monday(s);

elle passe le soir she comes over in the evening(s); **l'an prochain** next year; **une fois l'an** once a year. **6** pron (homme) him (femme) her; (chose, animal) pl them; **je la vois** I see her; I see it; **je le vois** I see him I see it; **je les vois** I see them; **es-tu fatigué – je le suis** are you tired? – I am; **je le crois** I think so.

leader [lidœr] nm Pol leader.

lécher [lefe] vt to lick; **se l. les doigts** to lick one's fingers. ◆**lèche-vitrines** nm faire du l.-vitrines to go window-shopping.

leçon [ləsɔ̃] nf lesson; **faire la l. à qn** to lecture s.o.

lecteur, -trice [lɛktœr, -tris] nmf reader Univ (foreign language) assistant; **l. de cas settes** cassette player. ◆**lecture** nf read ing; pl (livres) books; **faire de la l. à qn** t read to s.o.; **de la l.** some reading matter.

légal, -aux [legal, -o] a legal; (médecine) fo rensic. ◆**légalement** adv legally. ◆**léga liser** vt to legalize. ◆**légalité** nf legality (d of); **respecter la l.** to respect the law.

légation [legasjɔ̃] nf Pol legation.

légende [leʒɑ̃d] nf **1** (histoire, fable) legend **2** (de plan, carte) key, legend; (de photo caption. ◆**légendaire** a legendary.

léger, -ère [leʒe, -er] a light; (bruit, faute fièvre etc) slight; (café, thé, argumen weak; (bière, tabac) mild; (frivole) frivo lous; (irréfléchi) careless; **à la légère** (agir rashly. ◆**légèrement** adv lightly; (un peu slightly; (à la légère) rashly. ◆**légèreté** n lightness; frivolity.

légiférer [leʒifere] vi to legislate.

légion [leʒjɔ̃] nf Mil & Fig legion. ◆**lé gionnaire** nm (de la Légion étrangère) le gionnaire.

législatif, -ive [leʒislatif, -iv] a legislative (élections) parliamentary. ◆**législation** n legislation. ◆**législature** nf (période) Po term of office.

légitime [leʒitim] a (action, enfant etc) legit imate; **en état de l. défense** acting in self-defence. ◆**légitimité** nf legitimacy.

legs [lɛg] nm Jur legacy, bequest; (héritage Fig legacy. ◆**léguer** vt to bequeath (à to).

légume [legym] **1** nm vegetable. **2** nf grosse **l.** (personne) Fam bigwig.

lendemain [lɑ̃dmɛ̃] nm **le l.** the next day; (avenir) Fig the future; **le l. de** the day after; **le l. matin** the next morning.

lent [lɑ̃] a slow. ◆**lentement** adv slowly. ◆**lenteur** nf slowness.

lentille [lɑ̃tij] nf **1** Bot Culin lentil. **2** (verre lens.

léopard [leɔpar] nm leopard.

èpre [lɛpr] *nf* leprosy. ◆**lépreux, -euse** *a* – *nmf* leper.

equel, laquelle, *pl* **lesquels, lesquelles** [lɔkɛl, lakɛl, lekɛl] (+ à = **auquel, à laquelle, auxquel(le)s;** + de = **duquel, de laquelle, desquel(le)s**) *pron* (*chose, animal*) which; (*personne*) who, (*indirect*) whom; (*interrogatif*) which (one); **dans l.** in which, **parmi lesquels** (*choses, animaux*) among which; (*personnes*) among whom; **l. préférez-vous?** which (one) do you prefer?

es [le] *voir* **le.**

esbienne [lɛsbjɛn] *nf* & *af* lesbian.

éser [leze] *vt* (*personne*) *Jur* to wrong.

ésiner [lezine] *vi* to be stingy (**sur** on).

ésion [lezjɔ̃] *nf* *Méd* lesion.

essive [lesiv] *nf* (*produit*) washing powder; (*linge*) washing; **faire la l.** to do the washing. ◆**lessiver** *vt* to scrub, wash. ◆**–é** *a* *Fam* (*fatigué*) washed-out; (*battu*) washed-up. ◆**–euse** *nf* (*laundry*) boiler.

est [lɛst] *nm* ballast. ◆**lester** *vt* to ballast, weight down; (*remplir*) *Fam* to overload.

este [lɛst] *a* (*agile*) nimble; (*grivois*) coarse.

éthargie [letarʒi] *nf* lethargy. ◆**léthargique** *a* lethargic.

ettre [lɛtr] *nf* (*missive, caractère*) letter; **en toutes lettres** (*mot*) in full; (*nombre*) in words; **les lettres** (*discipline*) *Univ* arts; **homme de lettres** man of letters. ◆**lettré, -ée** *a* well-read; – *nmf* scholar.

eucémie [løsemi] *nf* leuk(a)emia.

eur [lœr] **1** *a poss* their; **l. chat** their cat; **leurs voitures** their cars; – *pron poss* **le l., la l., les leurs** theirs. **2** *pron inv* (*indirect*) (to) them; **il l. est facile de...** it's easy for them to ....

eurre [lœr] *nm* illusion; (*tromperie*) trickery. ◆**leurrer** *vt* to delude.

ev/er [l(ə)ve] *vt* to lift (up), raise; (*blocus, interdiction*) to lift; (*séance*) to close; (*camp*) to strike; (*plan*) to draw up; (*impôts, armée*) to levy; **l. les yeux** to look up; – *vi* (*pâte*) to rise; (*blé*) to come up; – **se l.** *vpr* to get up; (*soleil, rideau*) to rise; (*jour*) to break; (*brume*) to clear, lift; – *nm* **le l. du soleil** sunrise; **le l. du rideau** *Th* the curtain. ◆**–ant** *a* (*soleil*) rising; – *nm* **le l.** the east. ◆**–é** *a* **être l.** (*debout*) to be up. ◆**–ée** *nf* (*d'interdiction*) lifting; (*d'impôts*) levying; (*du courrier*) collection; **l. de boucliers** public outcry.

evier [ləvje] *nm* lever; (*pour soulever*) crowbar.

èvre [lɛvr] *nf* lip; **du bout des lèvres** half-heartedly, grudgingly.

lévrier [levrije] *nm* greyhound.

levure [ləvyr] *nf* yeast.

lexique [lɛksik] *nm* vocabulary, glossary.

lézard [lezar] *nm* lizard.

lézarde [lezard] *nf* crack, split. ◆**lézarder 1** *vi Fam* to bask in the sun. **2 se l.** *vpr* to crack, split.

liaison [ljɛzɔ̃] *nf* (*rapport*) connection; (*routière etc*) link; *Gram Mil* liaison; **l.** (*amoureuse*) love affair; **en l. avec qn** in contact with s.o.

liane [ljan] *nf Bot* jungle vine.

liant [ljɑ̃] *a* sociable.

liasse [ljas] *nf* bundle.

Liban [libɑ̃] *nm* Lebanon. ◆**libanais, -aise** *a* & *nmf* Lebanese.

libell/er [libele] *vt* (*contrat etc*) to word, draw up; (*chèque*) to make out. ◆**–é** *nm* wording.

libellule [libelyl] *nf* dragonfly.

libéral, -ale, -aux [liberal, -o] *a* & *nmf* liberal. ◆**libéraliser** *vt* to liberalize. ◆**libéralisme** *nm* liberalism. ◆**libéralité** *nf* liberality; (*don*) liberal gift.

libérer [libere] *vt* (*prisonnier etc*) to (set) free, release; (*pays, esprit*) to liberate (**de** from); **l. qn de** to free s.o. from *ou* of; – **se l.** *vpr* to get free, free oneself (**de** of, from). ◆**libérateur, -trice** *a* (*sentiment etc*) liberating; – *nmf* liberator. ◆**libération** *nf* freeing, release; liberation; **l. conditionnelle** *Jur* parole. ◆**liberté** *nf* freedom, liberty; **en l. provisoire** *Jur* on bail; **mettre en l.** to free, release; **mise en l.** release.

libraire [librɛr] *nmf* bookseller. ◆**librairie** *nf* (*magasin*) bookshop.

libre [libr] *a* free (**de qch** from sth, **de faire** to do); (*voie, route*) clear; (*place*) vacant, free; (*école*) private (*and religious*); **l. penseur** freethinker. ◆**l.-échange** *nm Écon* free trade. ◆**l.-service** *nm* (*pl* **libres-services**) (*système, magasin etc*) self-service. ◆**librement** *adv* freely.

Libye [libi] *nf* Libya. ◆**libyen, -enne** *a* & *nmf* Libyan.

licence [lisɑ̃s] *nf Sp Com Littér* licence; *Univ* (bachelor's) degree; **l. ès lettres/sciences** arts/science degree, = BA/BSc, = *Am* BA/BS. ◆**licencié, -ée** *a* & *nmf* graduate; **l. ès lettres/sciences** bachelor of arts/science, = BA/BSc, = *Am* BA/BS.

licencier [lisɑ̃sje] *vt* (*ouvrier*) to lay off, dismiss. ◆**licenciement** *nm* dismissal.

licite [lisit] *a* licit, lawful.

licorne [likɔrn] *nf* unicorn.

lie [li] *nf* dregs.

liège [ljɛʒ] *nm* (*matériau*) cork.

lien [ljɛ̃] *nm* (*rapport*) link, connection; (*de*

parenté) tie, bond; (_attache, ficelle_) tie. ◆**lier** _vt_ (_attacher_) to tie (up), bind; (_relier_) to link (up), connect; (_conversation, amitié_) to strike up; **l. qn** (_unir, engager_) to bind s.o.; **— se l.** _vpr_ (_idées etc_) to connect, link together; **se l. avec qn** to make friends with s.o.; **amis très liés** very close friends.

lierre [ljɛr] _nm_ ivy.

lieu, -x [ljø] _nm_ place; (_d'un accident_) scene; **les lieux** (_locaux_) the premises; **sur les lieux** on the spot; **avoir l.** to take place, be held; **au l. de** instead of; **avoir l. de faire** (_des raisons_) to have good reason to do; **en premier l.** in the first place, firstly; **en dernier l.** lastly; **l. commun** commonplace. ◆**i.-dit** _nm_ (_pl_ **lieux-dits**) _Géog_ locality.

lieue [ljø] _nf_ (_mesure_) _Hist_ league.

lieutenant [ljøtnɑ̃] _nm_ lieutenant.

lièvre [ljɛvr] _nm_ hare.

ligament [ligamɑ̃] _nm_ ligament.

ligne [liɲ] _nf_ (_trait, règle, contour, transport_) line; (_belle silhouette de femme_) figure; (_rangée_) row, line; (**se**) **mettre en l.** to line up; **en l. de compte** in, through; **entrer en l. de compte** to be of consequence, count; **faire entrer en l. de compte** to take into account; **grande l.** _Rail_ main line; **les grandes lignes** _Fig_ the broad outline; **pilote de l.** airline pilot; **à la l.** _Gram_ new paragraph.

lignée [liɲe] _nf_ line, ancestry.

ligoter [ligɔte] _vt_ to tie up.

ligue [lig] _nf_ (_alliance_) league. ◆**se liguer** _vpr_ to join together, gang up (**contre** against).

lilas [lila] _nm_ lilac; _– a inv_ (_couleur_) lilac.

limace [limas] _nf_ (_mollusque_) slug.

limaille [limaj] _nf_ filings.

limande [limɑ̃d] _nf_ (_poisson_) dab.

lime [lim] _nf_ (_outil_) file. ◆**limer** _vt_ to file.

limier [limje] _nm_ (_chien_) bloodhound.

limite [limit] _nf_ limit; (_de propriété, jardin etc_) boundary; _pl_ _Fb_ boundary lines; **dépasser la l.** to go beyond the bounds; _– a_ (_cas_) extreme; (_vitesse, prix, âge etc_) maximum; **date l.** latest date, deadline; **date l. de vente** _Com_ sell-by date. ◆**limitatif, ive** _a_ restrictive. ◆**limitation** _nf_ limitation; (_de vitesse_) limit. ◆**limiter** _vt_ to limit, restrict; (_délimiter_) to border; **se l. à faire** to limit _ou_ restrict oneself to doing.

limoger [limɔʒe] _vt_ (_destituer_) to dismiss.

limonade [limɔnad] _nf_ (_fizzy_) lemonade.

limpide [lɛ̃pid] _a_ (_eau, explication_) (crystal) clear. ◆**limpidité** _nf_ clearness.

lin [lɛ̃] _nm_ _Bot_ flax; (_tissu_) linen; **huile de l.** linseed oil.

linceul [lɛ̃sœl] _nm_ shroud.

linéaire [lineɛr] _a_ linear.

linge [lɛ̃ʒ] _nm_ (_pièces de tissu_) linen; (_à laver_) washing, linen; (_torchon_) cloth; **l.** (**de corps**) underwear. ◆**lingerie** _nf_ (_de femmes_) underwear; (_local_) linen room.

lingot [lɛ̃go] _nm_ ingot.

linguiste [lɛ̃guist] _nmf_ linguist. ◆**linguistique** _a_ linguistic; _– nf_ linguistics.

lino [lino] _nm_ lino. ◆**linoléum** _nm_ linoleum.

linotte [linɔt] _nf_ (_oiseau_) linnet; **tête de l.** _Fig_ scatterbrain.

lion [ljɔ̃] _nm_ lion. ◆**lionceau, -x** _nm_ lion cub. ◆**lionne** _nf_ lioness.

liquéfier [likefje] _vt_, **— se l.** _vpr_ to liquefy.

liqueur [likœr] _nf_ liqueur.

liquide [likid] _a_ liquid; **argent l.** ready cash _– nm_ liquid; **du l.** (_argent_) ready cash.

liquider [likide] _vt_ (_dette, stock etc_) to liquidate; (_affaire, travail_) to wind up, finish off; **l. qn** (_tuer_) _Fam_ to liquidate s.o. ◆**liquidation** _nf_ liquidation; winding up; (_vente_) clearance sale.

lire[1] [lir] _vti_ to read.

lire[2] [lir] _nf_ (_monnaie_) lira.

lis[1] [lis] _nm_ (_plante, fleur_) lily.

lis[2], **lisent** [li, liz] _voir_ **lire**[1].

liseron [lizrɔ̃] _nm_ _Bot_ convolvulus.

lisible [lizibl] _a_ (_écriture_) legible; (_livre_) readable. ◆**lisiblement** _adv_ legibly.

lisière [lizjɛr] _nf_ edge, border.

lisse [lis] _a_ smooth. ◆**lisser** _vt_ to smooth; (_plumes_) to preen.

liste [list] _nf_ list; **l. électorale** register of electors, electoral roll; **sur la l. rouge** _Tél_ ex-directory, _Am_ unlisted.

lit[1] [li] _nm_ bed; **l. d'enfant** cot, _Am_ crib; **lits superposés** bunk beds; **garder le l.** to stay in bed. ◆**literie** _nf_ bedding, bed clothes.

lit[2] [li] _voir_ **lire**[1].

litanie [litani] **1** _nf_ (_énumération_) long list (**de** of). **2** _nfpl_ (_prière_) _Rel_ litany.

litière [litjɛr] _nf_ (_couche de paille_) litter.

litige [litiʒ] _nm_ dispute; _Jur_ litigation. ◆**litigieux, -euse** _a_ contentious.

litre [litr] _nm_ litre.

littéraire [literɛr] _a_ literary. ◆**littérature** _nf_ literature.

littéral, -aux [literal, -o] _a_ literal. ◆**—ement** _adv_ literally.

littoral, -aux [litɔral, -o] _a_ coastal; _– nm_ coast(line).

liturgie [lityrʒi] _nf_ liturgy. ◆**liturgique** _a_ liturgical.

livide [livid] _a_ (_bleuâtre_) livid; (_pâle_) (ghastly) pale, pallid.

livre [livr] **1** _nm_ book; **l. de bord** _Nau_ logbook; **l. de poche** paperback (book); **le l., l'industrie du l.** the book industry. **2** *nf* (*monnaie, poids*) pound. ◆**livresque** *a* (*savoir*) *Péj* bookish. ◆**livret** *nm* (*registre*) book; *Mus* libretto; **l. scolaire** school report book; **l. de famille** family registration book; **l. de caisse d'épargne** bankbook, passbook.

vrée [livre] *nf* (*uniforme*) livery.

vrer [livre] *vt* (*marchandises*) to deliver (à to); (*secret*) to give away; (*qn à la police etc*) to give up *ou* over to; **l.** *qn* **à** (*la police etc*) to do *ou* join battle; — **se l.** *vpr* (*se rendre*) to give oneself up (à to); (*se confier*) to confide (à in); **se l. à** (*habitude, excès etc*) to indulge in; (*tâche*) to devote oneself to; (*désespoir, destin*) to abandon oneself to. ◆**livraison** *nf* delivery. ◆**livreur, -euse** *nmf* delivery man, delivery woman.

obe [lɔb] *nm Anat* lobe.

ocal, -aux [lɔkal, -o] **1** *a* local. — **2** *nm & nmpl* (*pièce, bâtiment*) premises. ◆**localement** *adv* locally. ◆**localiser** *vt* (*déterminer*) to locate; (*limiter*) to localize. ◆**localité** *nf* locality.

ocataire [lɔkatɛr] *nmf* tenant; (*hôte payant*) lodger.

ocation [lɔkasjɔ̃] *nf* (*de maison etc*) renting; (*à bail*) leasing; (*de voiture*) hiring; (*réservation*) booking; (*par propriétaire*) renting (out), letting; leasing (out); hiring (out); (*loyer*) rental; (*bail*) lease; **bureau de l.** booking office; **en l.** on hire.

ock-out [lɔkawt] *nm inv* (*industriel*) lockout.

ocomotion [lɔkɔmɔsjɔ̃] *nf* locomotion. ◆**locomotive** *nf* locomotive, engine.

ocuteur [lɔkytœr] *nm Ling* speaker. ◆**locution** *nf* phrase, idiom; *Gram* phrase.

ogarithme [lɔgaritm] *nm* logarithm.

oge [lɔʒ] *nf* (*de concierge*) lodge; (*d'acteur*) dressing-room; (*de spectateur*) *Th* box.

og/er [lɔʒe] *vt* (*recevoir, mettre*) to accommodate, house; (*héberger*) to put up; **être logé et nourri** to have board and lodging; — *vi* (*à l'hôtel etc*) to put up, lodge; (*habiter*) to live; (*trouver à*) **se l.** to find somewhere to live; (*temporairement*) to find somewhere to stay; **se l. dans** (*balle*) to lodge (itself) in. ◆**—eable** *a* habitable. ◆**—ement** *nm* accommodation, lodging; (*habitat*) housing; (*appartement*) lodgings, flat, *Am* apartment; (*maison*) dwelling. ◆**—eur, -euse** *nmf* landlord, landlady.

ogiciel [lɔʒisjɛl] *nm* (*d'un ordinateur*) software *inv*.

logique [lɔʒik] *a* logical. — *nf* logic. ◆**—ment** *adv* logically.

logistique [lɔʒistik] *nf* logistics.

logo [lɔgo] *nm* logo.

loi [lwa] *nf* law; *Pol* act; **projet de l.** *Pol* bill; **faire la l.** to lay down the law (à to).

loin [lwɛ̃] *adv* far (away *ou* off); **Boston est l.** (**de Paris**) Boston is a long way away (from Paris); **plus l.** further, farther; (*ci-après*) further on; **l. de là** *Fig* far from it; **au l.** in the distance, far away; **de l.** from a distance; (*de beaucoup*) by far; **de l. en l.** every so often. ◆**lointain** *a* distant, far-off; — *nm* **dans le l.** in the distance.

loir [lwar] *nm* (*animal*) dormouse.

loisir [lwazir] *nm* **le l. de faire** the time to do; **moment de l.** moment of leisure; **loisirs** *mpl* (*temps libre*) spare time, leisure (time); (*distractions*) spare-time *ou* leisure activities.

Londres [lɔ̃dr] *nm ou f* London. ◆**londonien, -ienne** *a* London-; — *nmf* Londoner.

long, longue [lɔ̃, lɔ̃g] *a* long; **être l.** (**à faire**) to be a long time *ou* slow (in doing); **l. de deux mètres** two metres long; — *nm* **avoir deux mètres de l.** to be two metres long; **tomber de tout son l.** to fall flat; (*tout*) **le l. de** (*espace*) (all) along; **tout le l. de** (*temps*) throughout; **de l. en large** (*marcher etc*) up and down; **en l. et en large** thoroughly; **en l.** lengthwise; **à la longue** in the long run. ◆**l.-courrier** *nm Av* long-distance airliner. ◆**longue-vue** *nf* (*pl* **longues-vues**) telescope.

longer [lɔ̃ʒe] *vt* to pass *ou* go along; (*forêt, mer*) to skirt; (*mur*) to hug.

longévité [lɔ̃ʒevite] *nf* longevity.

longitude [lɔ̃ʒityd] *nf* longitude.

longtemps [lɔ̃tɑ̃] *adv* (for) a long time; **trop/avant l.** too/before long; **aussi l. que** as long as.

longue [lɔ̃g] *voir* **long**. ◆**longuement** *adv* at length. ◆**longuet, -ette** *a Fam* (fairly) lengthy. ◆**longueur** *nf* length; *pl* (*de texte, film*) over-long passages; **saut en l.** *Sp* long jump; **à l. de journée** all day long; **l. d'onde** *Rad & Fig* wavelength.

lopin [lɔpɛ̃] *nm* **l. de terre** plot *ou* patch of land.

loquace [lɔkas] *a* loquacious.

loque [lɔk] **1** *nfpl* rags. **2** *nf* **l.** (**humaine**) (*personne*) human wreck.

loquet [lɔkɛ] *nm* latch.

lorgner [lɔrɲe] *vt* (*regarder, convoiter*) to eye.

lors [lɔr] *adv* **l. de** at the time of; **depuis l.,**

dès l. from then on; **dès l. que** (*puisque*) since.

losange [lɔzɑ̃ʒ] *nm* Géom diamond, lozenge.

lot [lo] *nm* **1** (*de loterie*) prize; **gros l.** top prize, jackpot. **2** (*portion, destin*) lot. ◆**loterie** *nf* lottery, raffle. ◆**lotir** *vt* (*terrain*) to divide into lots; **bien loti** Fig favoured by fortune. ◆**lotissement** *nm* (*terrain*) building plot; (*habitations*) housing estate ou development.

lotion [losjɔ̃] *nf* lotion.

loto [loto] *nm* (*jeu*) lotto.

louche [luʃ] **1** *a* (*suspect*) shady, fishy. **2** *nf* Culin ladle.

loucher [luʃe] *vi* to squint; **l. sur** Fam to eye.

louer [lwe] *vt* **1** (*prendre en location*) to rent (*house, flat etc*); (*à bail*) to lease; (*voiture*) to hire, rent; (*réserver*) to book; (*donner en location*) to rent (out), let; to lease (out); to hire (out); **maison/chambre à l.** house/room to let. **2** (*exalter*) to praise (**de** for); **se l. de** to be highly satisfied with. ◆**louable** *a* praiseworthy, laudable. ◆**louange** *nf* praise; **à la l. de** in praise of.

loufoque [lufɔk] *a* (*fou*) Fam nutty, crazy.

loukoum [lukum] *nm* Turkish delight.

loup [lu] *nm* wolf; **avoir une faim de l.** to be ravenous. ◆**l.-garou** *nm* (*pl* **loups-garous**) werewolf.

loupe [lup] *nf* magnifying glass.

louper [lupe] *vt* Fam (*train etc*) to miss; (*examen*) to fail; (*travail*) to mess up.

lourd [lur] *a* heavy (Fig **de** with); (*temps, chaleur*) close, sultry; (*faute*) gross; (*tâche*) arduous; (*esprit*) dull; – *adv* **peser l.** (*mâle etc*) to be heavy. ◆**lourdaud, -aude** *a* loutish, oafish; – *nmf* lout, oaf. ◆**lourdement** *adv* heavily. ◆**lourdeur** *nf* heaviness; (*de temps*) closeness; (*d'esprit*) dullness.

loutre [lutr] *nf* otter.

louve [luv] *nf* she-wolf. ◆**louveteau, -x** *nm* (*scout*) cub (scout).

louvoyer [luvwaje] *vi* (*tergiverser*) to hedge, be evasive.

loyal, -aux [lwajal, -o] *a* (*fidèle*) loyal (**envers** to); (*honnête*) honest, fair (**envers** to). ◆**loyalement** *adv* loyally; fairly. ◆**loyauté** *nf* loyalty; honesty, fairness.

loyer [lwaje] *nm* rent.

lu [ly] *voir* **lire** [1].

lubie [lybi] *nf* whim.

lubrifi/er [lybrifje] *vt* to lubricate. ◆—**ant** *nm* lubricant.

lubrique [lybrik] *a* lewd, lustful.

lucarne [lykarn] *nf* (*ouverture*) skylight (*fenêtre*) dormer window.

lucide [lysid] *a* lucid. ◆**lucidité** *nf* lucidity

lucratif, -ive [lykratif, -iv] *a* lucrative.

lueur [lɥœr] *nf* (*lumière*) & Fig glimmer.

luge [lyʒ] *nf* toboggan, sledge.

lugubre [lygybr] *a* gloomy, lugubrious.

lui [lɥi] **1** *pron mf* (*complément indirect*) (to) him; (*femme*) (to) her; (*chose, animal*) (to) it; **je le lui ai montré** I showed it to him *ou* to her, I showed him it *ou* her it; **il lui est facile de** . . . it's easy for him *ou* her to . . . **2** *pron m* (*complément direct*) him; (*chose animal*) it; (*sujet emphatique*) he; **pour lui** for him; **plus grand que lui** taller than him **il ne pense qu'à lui** he only thinks of himself. ◆**lui-même** *pron* himself; (*chose animal*) itself.

luire [lɥir] *vi* to shine, gleam. ◆**luisant** *a* (*métal etc*) shiny.

lumbago [lɔ̃bago] *nm* lumbago.

lumière [lymjɛr] *nf* light; **à la l.** by the light of; (*grâce à*) Fig in the light of; **faire toute la l. sur** Fig to clear up; **mettre en l.** to bring to light. ◆**luminaire** *nm* (*appareil*) lighting appliance. ◆**lumineux, -euse** *a* (*idée, ciel etc*) bright, brilliant; (*ondes, source etc*) light-; (*cadran, corps etc*) Tech luminous.

lunaire [lynɛr] *a* lunar; **clarté l.** light *ou* brightness of the moon.

lunatique [lynatik] *a* temperamental.

lunch [lœ̃ʃ, lœntʃ] *nm* buffet lunch, snack.

lundi [lœ̃di] *nm* Monday.

lune [lyn] *nf* moon; **l. de miel** honeymoon.

lunette [lynɛt] *nf* **1 lunettes** glasses, spectacles; (*de protection, de plongée*) goggles; **lunettes de soleil** sunglasses. **2** (*astronomique*) telescope; **l. arrière** Aut rear window.

lurette [lyrɛt] *nf* **il y a belle l.** a long time ago.

luron [lyrɔ̃] *nm* **gai l.** gay fellow.

lustre [lystr] *nm* (*éclairage*) chandelier; (*éclat*) lustre. ◆**lustré** *a* (*par l'usure*) shiny.

luth [lyt] *nm* Mus lute.

lutin [lytɛ̃] *nm* elf, imp, goblin.

lutte [lyt] *nf* fight, struggle; Sp wrestling; **l. des classes** class warfare *ou* struggle. ◆**lutter** *vi* to fight, struggle; Sp to wrestle. ◆**lutteur, -euse** *nmf* fighter; Sp wrestler.

luxe [lyks] *nm* luxury; **un l. de** a wealth of; **de l.** (*article*) luxury-; (*modèle*) de luxe. ◆**luxueux, -euse** *a* luxurious.

Luxembourg [lyksɑ̃bur] *nm* Luxembourg.

luxure [lyksyr] *nf* lewdness, lust.

luxuriant [lyksyrjɑ̃] *a* luxuriant.

azerne [lyzɛrn] *nf Bot* lucerne, *Am* alfalfa.

cée [lise] *nm* (secondary) school, *Am* high school. ◆**lycéen, -enne** *nmf* pupil (*de lycée*).

ymphatique [lɛ̃fatik] *a* (*apathique*) sluggish.

lynch/er [lɛ̃ʃe] *vt* to lynch. ◆**—age** *nm* lynching.

lynx [lɛ̃ks] *nm* (*animal*) lynx.

lyre [lir] *nf Mus Hist* lyre.

lyrique [lirik] *a* (*poème etc*) lyric; (*passionné*) *Fig* lyrical. ◆**lyrisme** *nm* lyricism.

lys [lis] *nm* (*plante, fleur*) lily.

M

M, m [ɛm] *nm* M, m.

m *abrév* (*mètre*) metre.

M [məsjø] *abrév* = **Monsieur**.

m' [m] *voir* **me**.

ma [ma] *voir* **mon**.

macabre [makabr] *a* macabre, gruesome.

macadam [makadam] *nm* (*goudron*) tarmac.

macaron [makarɔ̃] *nm* (*gâteau*) macaroon; (*insigne*) (round) badge.

macaroni(s) [makaroni] *nm*(*pl*) macaroni.

macédoine [masedwan] *nf* **m. (de légumes)** mixed vegetables; **m. (de fruits)** fruit salad.

macérer [masere] *vti Culin* to soak. ◆**macération** *nf* soaking.

mâcher [mɑʃe] *vt* to chew; **il ne mâche pas ses mots** he doesn't mince matters *ou* his words.

machiavélique [makjavelik] *a* Machiavellian.

machin [maʃɛ̃] *nm Fam* (*chose*) thing, what's-it; (*personne*) what's-his-name.

machinal, -aux [maʃinal, -o] *a* (*involontaire*) unconscious, mechanical. ◆**—ement** *adv* unconsciously, mechanically.

machination [maʃinasjɔ̃] *nf* machination.

machine [maʃin] *nf* (*appareil, avion, système etc*) machine; (*locomotive, moteur*) engine; *pl Tech* machines, (heavy) machinery; **m. à coudre** sewing machine; **m. à écrire** typewriter; **m. à laver** washing machine. ◆**machinerie** *nf Nau* engine room. ◆**machiniste** *nm Th* stage-hand.

macho [matʃo] *nm* macho *m*; – *a* (*f inv*) (*attitude etc*) macho.

mâchoire [mɑʃwar] *nf* jaw.

mâchonner [mɑʃone] *vt* to chew, munch.

maçon [masɔ̃] *nm* builder; bricklayer; mason. ◆**maçonnerie** *nf* (*travaux*) building work; (*ouvrage de briques*) brickwork; (*de pierres*) masonry, stonework.

maculer [makyle] *vt* to stain (**de** with).

Madagascar [madagaskar] *nf* Madagascar.

madame, *pl* **mesdames** [madam, medam] *nf* madam; **oui m.** yes (madam); **bonjour mesdames** good morning (ladies); **Madame *ou* Mme Legras** Mrs Legras; **Madame** (*sur une lettre*) *Com* Dear Madam.

madeleine [madlɛn] *nf* (small) sponge cake.

mademoiselle, *pl* **mesdemoiselles** [madmwazɛl, medmwazɛl] *nf* miss; **oui m.** yes (miss); **bonjour mesdemoiselles** good morning (ladies); **Mademoiselle *ou* Mlle Legras** Miss Legras; **Mademoiselle** (*sur une lettre*) *Com* Dear Madam.

madère [madɛr] *nm* (*vin*) Madeira.

madone [madɔn] *nf Rel* madonna.

madrier [madrije] *nm* (*poutre*) beam.

maestro [maɛstro] *nm Mus* maestro.

maf(f)ia [mafja] *nf* Mafia.

magasin [magazɛ̃] *nm* shop, *Am* store; (*entrepôt*) warehouse; (*d'arme*) & *Phot* magazine; **grand m.** department store. ◆**magasinier** *nm* warehouseman.

magazine [magazin] *nm* (*revue*) magazine.

magie [maʒi] *nf* magic. ◆**magicien, -ienne** *nmf* magician. ◆**magique** *a* (*baguette, mot*) magic; (*mystérieux, enchanteur*) magical.

magistral, -aux [maʒistral, -o] *a* masterly, magnificent. ◆**—ement** *adv* magnificently.

magistrat [maʒistra] *nm* magistrate. ◆**magistrature** *nf* judiciary, magistracy.

magnanime [maɲanim] *a* magnanimous.

magnat [maɲa] *nm* tycoon, magnate.

magner (se) [səmaɲe] *vpr Fam* to hurry up.

magnésium [maɲezjɔm] *nm* magnesium.

magnétique [maɲetik] *a* magnetic. ◆**magnétiser** *vt* to magnetize. ◆**magnétisme** *nm* magnetism.

magnétophone [maɲetɔfɔn] *nm* (*Fam* **magnéto**) tape recorder; **m. à cassettes** cassette recorder. ◆**magnétoscope** *nm* video (cassette) recorder.

magnifique [manifik] *a* magnificent. ◆**magnificence** *nf* magnificence. ◆**magnifiquement** *adv* magnificently.

magnolia [manɔlja] *nm (arbre)* magnolia.

magot [mago] *nm (économies)* nest egg, hoard.

magouille(s) [maguj] *nf(pl) Pol Fam* fiddling, graft.

mai [mɛ] *nm* May.

maigre [mɛgr] *a* thin, lean; *(viande)* lean; *(fromage, yaourt)* low-fat; *(repas, salaire, espoir)* meagre; **faire m.** to abstain from meat ◆**maigrement** *adv (chichement)* meagrely. ◆**maigreur** *nf* thinness; *(de viande)* leanness; *(médiocrité)* Fig meagreness. ◆**maigrichon, -onne** *a* & *nmf* skinny (person). ◆**maigrir** *vi* to get thin(ner); – *vt* to make thin(ner).

maille [maj] *nf (de tricot)* stitch; *(de filet)* mesh; **m. filée** *(de bas)* run, ladder. ◆**maillon** *nm (de chaîne)* link.

maillet [majɛ] *nm (outil)* mallet.

maillot [majo] *nm (de sportif)* jersey; *(de danseur)* leotard, tights; m. *(de corps)* vest, *Am* undershirt; **m. (de bain)** *(de femme)* swimsuit; *(d'homme)* (swimming) trunks.

main [mɛ̃] *nf* hand; **tenir à la m.** to hold in one's hand; **à la m.** *(livrer, faire etc)* by hand; **la m. dans la m.** hand in hand; **haut les mains!** hands up!; **donner un coup de m.** à qn to lend s.o. a (helping) hand; **coup de m.** *(habileté)* knack; **sous la m.** at hand, handy; **en venir aux mains** to come to blows; **avoir la m. heureuse** to be lucky, have a lucky streak; **mettre la dernière m.** à to put the finishing touches to; **en m. propre** *(remettre qch)* in person; **attaque/vol à m. armée** armed attack/robbery; **homme de m.** henchman, hired man; **m. courante** handrail; **prêter m.-forte** à to lend assistance to. ◆**m.-d'œuvre** *nf (pl mains-d'œuvre) (travail)* manpower, labour; *(salariés)* labour *ou* work force.

maint [mɛ̃] *a Litt* many a; **maintes fois, à maintes reprises** many a time.

maintenant [mɛ̃tnã] *adv* now; *(de nos jours)* nowadays; **m. que** now that; **dès m.** from now on.

maintenir* [mɛ̃tnir] *vt (conserver)* to keep, maintain; *(retenir)* to hold, keep; *(affirmer)* to maintain (que that); – **se m.** *vpr (malade, vieillard)* to hold one's own; *(rester)* to keep; *(malade, vieillard)* to hold one's own. ◆**maintien** *nm (action)* maintenance (de); *(allure)* bearing.

maire [mɛr] *nm* mayor. ◆**mairie** *nf* town hall; *(administration)* town council.

mais [mɛ] *conj* but; **m. oui, m. si** yes of course; **m. non** definitely not.

maïs [mais] *nm (céréale)* maize, *Am* corn; **farine de m.** cornflour, *Am* cornstarch.

maison [mɛzɔ̃] *nf (bâtiment)* house; *(immeuble)* building; *(chez-soi, asile)* home; *Com* firm; *(famille)* household; **à la m.** *(être)* at home; *(rentrer, aller)* home; – *a inv (pâté, tartes etc)* homemade; **m. de la culture** arts *ou* cultural centre; **m. d'étudiants** student hostel; **m. des jeunes** youth club; **m. de repos** rest home; **m. de retraite** old people's home. ◆**maisonnée** *nf* household. ◆**maisonnette** *nf* small house.

maître [mɛtr] *nm* master; **se rendre m. de** *(incendie)* to master, control; *(pays)* to conquer; **être m. de** *(situation etc)* to be in control of, be master of; **m. de soi** in control of oneself; **m. d'école** teacher; **m. d'hôtel** *(restaurant)* head waiter; **m. de maison** host; **m. chanteur** blackmailer; **m. nageur (sauveteur)** swimming instructor (and lifeguard). ◆**maîtresse** *nf* mistress; **m. d'école** teacher; **m. de maison** hostess *(ménagère)* housewife; **être m. de** *(situation etc)* to be in control of; – *af (idée, poutre etc)* master.

maîtrise [mɛtriz] *nf (habileté, contrôle)* mastery (de of); *(grade) Univ* master's degree (de in); **m. (de soi)** self-control. ◆**maîtriser** *vt (émotion)* to master, control; *(sujet)* to master; *(incendie)* to (bring under) control; **m. qn** to subdue s.o.; – **se m.** *vpr* to control oneself.

majesté [maʒɛste] *nf* majesty; **Votre M.** *(titre)* Your Majesty. ◆**majestueux, -euse** *a* majestic, stately.

majeur [maʒœr] **1** *a (primordial)* & *Mus* major; **être m.** *Jur* to be of age; **la majeure partie de** most of; **en majeure partie** for the most part. **2** *nm (doigt)* middle finger.

majorer [maʒɔre] *vt* to raise, increase. ◆**majoration** *nf (hausse)* increase (de in).

majorette [maʒɔrɛt] *nf (drum)* majorette.

majorité [maʒɔrite] *nf* majority (de of); *(âge) Jur* coming of age, majority; *(gouvernement)* party in office, government; **en m.** in the *ou* a majority; *(pour la plupart)* in the main. ◆**majoritaire** *a (vote etc)* majority-; **être m.** to be in the *ou* a majority; **être m. aux élections** to win the elections.

Majorque [maʒɔrk] *nf* Majorca.

majuscule [maʒyskyl] *a* capital; – *nf* capital letter.

mal, maux [mal, mo] **1** *nm Phil Rel* evil;

dommage) harm; *(douleur)* pain; *(maladie)* illness; *(malheur)* misfortune; **dire du m. de** to speak ill of; **m. de dents** toothache; **m. de gorge** sore throat; **m. de tête** headache; **m. de ventre** stomachache; **m. de mer** seasickness; **m. du pays** homesickness; **avoir le m. du pays/etc** to be homesick/*etc*; **avoir m. à la tête/à la gorge/etc** to have a headache/sore throat/*etc*; **ça (me) fait m., j'ai m.** it hurts (me); **faire du m. à** to harm, hurt; **avoir du m. à faire** to have trouble (in) doing; **se donner du m. pour faire** to go to a lot of trouble to do. **2** *adv (travailler etc)* badly; *(entendre, comprendre)* not too well; **aller m.** *(projet etc)* to be going badly; *(personne)* Méd to be bad *or* ill; **m. (à l'aise)** uncomfortable; **se trouver m.** to feel faint; **(ce n'est) pas m.** *(mauvais)* (that's) not bad; **pas m.** *Fam* quite a lot *ou (beaucoup)* Fam quite a lot; **c'est m. de jurer/etc** *(moralement)* it's wrong to swear/*etc*; **de m. en pis** from bad to worse; **m. renseigner/interpréter/** *etc* to misinform/misinterpret/*etc*.

malade [malad] *a* ill, sick; *(arbre, dent)* diseased; *(estomac, jambe)* bad; **être m. du foie/cœur** to have a bad liver/heart; − *nmf* sick person; *(à l'hôpital, d'un médecin)* patient; **les malades** the sick. ◆**maladie** *nf* illness, sickness, disease. ◆**maladif, -ive** *a (personne)* sickly; *(morbide)* morbid.

maladroit [maladrwa] *a (malhabile)* clumsy, awkward; *(indélicat)* tactless. ◆**maladresse** *nf* clumsiness, awkwardness; tactlessness; *(bévue)* blunder.

malaise [malɛz] *nm (angoisse)* uneasiness, malaise; *(indisposition)* faintness, dizziness; **avoir un m.** to feel faint *ou* dizzy.

malaisé [malɛze] *a* difficult.

Malaisie [malɛzi] *nf* Malaysia.

malaria [malarja] *nf* malaria.

malavisé [malavize] *a* ill-advised **(de faire** to do).

malax/er [malakse] *vt (pétrir)* to knead; *(mélanger)* to mix. ◆−**eur** *nm Tech* mixer.

malchance [malʃɑ̃s] *nf* bad luck; **une m.** *(mésaventure)* a mishap. ◆**malchanceux, -euse** *a* unlucky.

malcommode [malkɔmɔd] *a* awkward.

mâle [mal] *a* a male; *(viril)* manly; − *nm* male.

malédiction [malediksjɔ̃] *nf* curse.

maléfice [malefis] *nm* evil spell. ◆**maléfique** *a* baleful, evil.

malencontreux, -euse [malɑ̃kɔ̃trø, -øz] *a* unfortunate.

malentendant, -ante [malɑ̃tɑ̃dɑ̃, -ɑ̃t] *nmf* person who is hard of hearing.

malentendu [malɑ̃tɑ̃dy] *nm* misunderstanding.

malfaçon [malfasɔ̃] *nf* defect.

malfaisant [malfəzɑ̃] *a* evil, harmful.

malfaiteur [malfɛtœr] *nm* criminal.

malformation [malfɔrmasjɔ̃] *nf* malformation.

malgré [malgre] *prép* in spite of; **m. tout** for all that, after all; **m. soi** *(à contrecœur)* reluctantly.

malhabile [malabil] *a* clumsy.

malheur [malœr] *nm (événement)* misfortune; *(accident)* mishap; *(malchance)* bad luck, misfortune; **par m.** unfortunately. ◆**malheureusement** *adv* unfortunately. ◆**malheureux, -euse** *a (misérable, insignifiant)* wretched, miserable; *(fâcheux)* unfortunate; *(malchanceux)* unlucky, unfortunate; − *nmf (infortuné)* (poor) wretch; *(indigent)* needy person.

malhonnête [malɔnɛt] *a* dishonest. ◆**malhonnêteté** *nf* dishonesty; **une m.** *(action)* a dishonest act.

malice [malis] *nf* mischievousness. ◆**malicieux, -euse** *a* mischievous.

malin, -igne [malɛ̃, -iɲ] *a (astucieux)* smart, clever; *(plaisir)* malicious; *(tumeur)* Méd malignant. ◆**malignité** *nf (méchanceté)* malignity; Méd malignancy.

malingre [malɛ̃gr] *a* a puny, sickly.

malintentionné [malɛ̃tɑ̃sjɔne] *a* ill-intentioned **(à l'égard de** towards).

malle [mal] *nf (coffre)* trunk; *(de véhicule)* boot, Am trunk. ◆**mallette** *nf* small suitcase; *(pour documents)* attaché case.

malléable [maleabl] *a* malleable.

malmener [malməne] *vt* to manhandle, treat badly.

malodorant [malɔdɔrɑ̃] *a* smelly.

malotru, -ue [malɔtry] *nmf* boor, lout.

malpoli [malpɔli] *a* impolite.

malpropre [malprɔpr] *a (sale)* dirty. ◆**malpropreté** *nf* dirtiness.

malsain [malsɛ̃] *a* unhealthy, unwholesome.

malséant [malseɑ̃] *a* unseemly.

malt [malt] *nm* malt.

Malte [malt] *nf* Malta. ◆**maltais, -aise** *a* & *nmf* Maltese.

maltraiter [maltrete] *vt* to ill-treat.

malveillant [malvejɑ̃] *a* malevolent. ◆**malveillance** *nf* malevolence, ill will.

malvenu [malvəny] *a (déplacé)* uncalled-for.

maman [mamɑ̃] *nf* mum(my), *Am* mom(my).

mamelle [mamɛl] *nf (d'animal)* teat; *(de*

vache) udder. ◆**mamelon** *nm* **1** (*de femme*) nipple. **2** (*colline*) hillock.

mamie [mami] *nf Fam* granny, grandma.

mammifère [mamifɛr] *nm* mammal.

manche [mɑ̃ʃ] **1** *nf* (*de vêtement*) sleeve; *Sp Cartes* round; **la M.** *Géog* the Channel. **2** *nm* (*d'outil etc*) handle; **m. à balai** broomstick; (*d'avion, d'ordinateur*) joystick. ◆**manchette** *nf* **1** (*de chemise etc*) cuff. **2** *Journ* headline. ◆**manchon** *nm* (*fourrure*) muff.

manchot, -ote [mɑ̃ʃo, -ɔt] **1** *a & nmf* one-armed ou one-handed (person). **2** *nm* (*oiseau*) penguin.

mandarin [mɑ̃darɛ̃] *nm* (*lettré influent*) *Univ Péj* mandarin.

mandarine [mɑ̃darin] *nf* (*fruit*) tangerine, mandarin (orange).

mandat [mɑ̃da] *nm* **1** (*postal*) money order. **2** *Pol* mandate; *Jur* power of attorney; **m. d'arrêt** warrant (**contre qn** for s.o.'s arrest). ◆**mandataire** *nmf* (*délégué*) representative, proxy. ◆**mandater** *vt* to delegate; *Pol* to give a mandate to.

manège [manɛʒ] *nm* **1** (*à la foire*) merry-go-round, roundabout; (*lieu*) riding-school; (*piste*) ring, manège; (*exercice*) horsemanship. **2** (*intrigue*) wiles, trickery.

manette [manɛt] *nf* lever, handle.

manger [mɑ̃ʒe] *vt* to eat; (*essence, électricité*) *Fig* to eat up; (*corroder*) to eat into; **donner à m.** à to feed; — *vi* to eat; **on mange bien ici** the food is good here; **m. à sa faim** to have enough to eat; — *nm* food. ◆**mangeable** *a* eatable. ◆**mangeaille** *nf Péj* (bad) food. ◆**mangeoire** *nf* (feeding) trough. ◆**mangeur, -euse** *nmf* eater.

mangue [mɑ̃g] *nf* (*fruit*) mango.

manie [mani] *nf* mania, craze (de for). ◆**maniaque** *a* finicky, fussy; – *nmf* fusspot, *Am* fussbudget; **un m. de la propreté/etc** a maniac for cleanliness/*etc*.

manier [manje] *vt* to handle; **se m. bien** (*véhicule etc*) to handle well. ◆**maniabilité** *nf* (*de véhicule etc*) manoeuvrability. ◆**maniable** *a* easy to handle. ◆**maniement** *nm* handling; **m. d'armes** *Mil* drill.

manière [manjɛr] *nf* way, manner; *pl* (*politesse*) manners; **de toute m.** anyway, anyhow; **de m. à faire** so as to do; **à ma m.** my way, (in) my own way; **de cette m.** (in) this way; **la m. dont elle parle** the way (in which) she talks; **d'une m. générale** generally speaking; **faire des manières** (*chichis*) to make a fuss; (*être affecté*) to put on airs. ◆**maniéré** *a* affected; (*style*) mannered.

manif [manif] *nf Fam* demo.

manifeste [manifɛst] **1** *a* (*évident*) manifest, obvious. **2** *nm Pol* manifesto.

manifester [manifɛste] **1** *vt* to show, manifest; — **se m.** *vpr* (*apparaître*) to appear; (*sentiment, maladie etc*) to show ou manifest itself. **2** *vi Pol* to demonstrate. ◆**manifestant, -ante** *nmf* demonstrator. ◆**manifestation** *nf* **1** (*expression*) expression, manifestation; (*apparition*) appearance. **2** *Pol* demonstration; (*réunion, fête*) event.

manigance [manigɑ̃s] *nf* little scheme. ◆**manigancer** *vt* to plot.

manipuler [manipyle] *vt* (*manier*) to handle; (*faits, électeurs*) *Péj* to manipulate. ◆**manipulation** *nf* handling; *Péj* manipulation (de of); *pl Pol Péj* manipulation.

manivelle [manivɛl] *nf Aut* crank.

mannequin [mankɛ̃] *nm* (*femme, homme*) (fashion) model; (*statue*) dummy.

manœuvre [manœvr] **1** *nm* (*ouvrier*) labourer. **2** *nf* (*opération*) & *Mil* manoeuvre, *Am* maneuver; (*action*) manoeuvring, (*intrigue*) scheme. ◆**manœuvrer** *vt* (*véhicule, personne etc*) to manoeuvre, *Am* to maneuver; (*machine*) to operate; – *vi* to manoeuvre ou *Am* maneuver.

manoir [manwar] *nm* manor house.

manque [mɑ̃k] *nm* lack (de of); (*lacune*) gap; *pl* (*défauts*) shortcomings; **m. à gagner** loss of profit. ◆**manqu/er** *vt* (*chance, cible etc*) to miss; (*ne pas réussir*) to make a mess of, ruin; (*examen*) to fail; – *vi* (*faire défaut*) to be short ou lacking; (*être absent*) to be absent (à from); (*être en moins*) to be missing ou short; (*défaillir, échouer*) to fail; **m. de** (*pain, argent etc*) to be short of; (*attention, cohérence*) to lack; **ça manque de sel/etc** it lacks salt/*etc*, there isn't any salt/*etc*; **il manque/il lui manque** (*sa role*) to break; **le temps lui manque** he's short of time, he has no time; **elle/cela lui manque** he misses her/that; **je ne manquerai pas de venir** I won't fail to come; **ne manquez pas de venir** don't forget to come; **elle a manqué (de) tomber** (*faillir*) she nearly fell; – *v imp* **il manque/il nous manque dix tasses** there are/we are ten cups short. ◆**—ant** *a* missing. ◆**—é** *a* (*médecin, pilote etc*) failed; (*livre*) unsuccessful. ◆**—ement** *nm* breach (à of).

mansarde [mɑ̃sard] *nf* attic.

manteau, -x [mɑ̃to] *nm* coat.

manucure [manykyr] *nmf* manicurist. ◆**manucurer** *vt Fam* to manicure.

manuel, -elle [manɥɛl] **1** *a* (*travail etc*) manual. **2** *nm* (*livre*) handbook, manual.

manufacture [manyfaktyr] *nf* factory. ◆**manufacturé** *a* (*produit*) manufactured.

manuscrit [manyskri] *nm* manuscript; (*tapé à la machine*) typescript.

manutention [manytɑ̃sjɔ̃] *nf* Com handling (*of stores*). ◆**manutentionnaire** *nmf* packer.

mappemonde [mapmɔ̃d] *nf* map of the world; (*sphère*) Fam globe.

maquereau, -x [makro] *nm* (*poisson*) mackerel.

maquette [makɛt] *nf* (scale) model.

maquill/er [makije] *vt* (*visage*) to make up; (*voiture etc*) Péj to tamper with; (*vérité etc*) Péj to fake; **– se m.** to make (oneself) up. ◆**–age** *nm* (*fard*) make-up.

maquis [maki] *nm* Bot scrub, bush; Mil Hist maquis.

maraîcher, -ère [mareʃe, -ɛʃer] *nmf* market gardener, Am truck farmer.

marais [mare] *nm* marsh, bog; **m. salant** saltworks, saltern.

marasme [marasm] *nm* Écon stagnation.

marathon [maratɔ̃] *nm* marathon.

maraudeur, -euse [marodœr, -øz] *nmf* petty thief.

marbre [marbr] *nm* marble. ◆**marbrier** *nm* (*funéraire*) monumental mason.

marc [mar] *nm* (*eau-de-vie*) marc, brandy; **m.** (**de café**) coffee grounds.

marchand, -ande [marʃɑ̃, -ɑ̃d] *nmf* trader, shopkeeper; (*de vins, charbon*) merchant; (*de cycles, meubles*) dealer; **m. de bonbons** confectioner; **m. de couleurs** hardware merchant *ou* dealer; **m. de journaux** (*dans la rue*) newsvendor; (*dans un magasin*) newsagent, Am news dealer; **m. de légumes** greengrocer; **m. de poissons** fishmonger; **– a** (*valeur*) market; (*prix*) trade-. ◆**marchandise(s)** *nf*(*pl*) goods, merchandise.

marchand/er [marʃɑ̃de] *vi* to haggle, bargain; **– vt** (*objet*) to haggle over. ◆**–age** *nm* haggling, bargaining.

marche [marʃ] *nf* **1** (*d'escalier*) step, stair. **2** (*démarche, trajet*) walk; Mil Mus march; (*pas*) pace; (*de train, véhicule*) movement; (*de maladie, d'événement*) progress, course; **la m.** (*action*) Sp walking; **faire m. arrière** Aut to reverse; **la bonne m. de** (*opération, machine*) the smooth running of; **un train/véhicule en m.** a moving train/vehicle; **mettre qch en m.** to start sth (up). ◆**marcher** *vi* (*à pied*) to walk; Mil to

march; (*poser le pied*) to tread, step; (*train, véhicule etc*) to run, go, move; (*fonctionner*) to go, work, run; (*prospérer*) to go well; **faire m.** (*machine*) to work; (*entreprise*) to run; (*personne*) Fam to kid; **ça marche?** Fam how's it going?; **elle va m.** (*accepter*) Fam she'll go along (with it). ◆**marcheur, -euse** *nmf* walker.

marché [marʃe] *nm* (*lieu*) market; (*contrat*) deal; **faire son ou le m.** to do one's shopping (*in the market*); **être bon m.** to be cheap; **voiture(s)/etc bon m.** cheap car(s)/etc; **vendre (à) bon m.** to sell cheap(ly); **c'est meilleur m.** it's cheaper; **par-dessus le m.** Fig into the bargain; **au m. noir** on the black market; **le M. commun** the Common Market.

marchepied [marʃəpje] *nm* (*de train, bus*) step(s); (*de voiture*) running board.

mardi [mardi] *nm* Tuesday; **M. gras** Shrove Tuesday.

mare [mar] *nf* (*flaque*) pool; (*étang*) pond.

marécage [mareka3] *nm* swamp, marsh. ◆**marécageux, -euse** *a* marshy, swampy.

maréchal, -aux [mareʃal, -o] *nm* Fr Mil marshal. ◆**m.-ferrant** *nm* (*pl* maréchaux-ferrants*) blacksmith.

marée [mare] *nf* tide; (*poissons*) fresh (sea) fish; **m. noire** oil slick.

marelle [marɛl] *nf* (*jeu*) hopscotch.

margarine [margarin] *nf* margarine.

marge [mar3] *nf* margin; **en m. de** (*en dehors de*) on the periphery of, on the fringe(s) of; **m. de sécurité** safety margin. ◆**marginal, -ale, -aux** *a* (*secondaire, asocial*) marginal; **– nmf** misfit, dropout; (*bizarre*) weirdo.

marguerite [margərit] *nf* (*fleur*) marguerite, daisy.

mari [mari] *nm* husband.

mariage [marja3] *nm* marriage; (*cérémonie*) wedding; (*mélange*) Fig blend, marriage; **demande en m.** proposal (of marriage). ◆**mari/er** *vt* (*couleurs*) to blend; **m. qn** (*maire, prêtre etc*) to marry s.o.; **m. qn avec** to marry s.o. (off) to; **– se m.** *vpr* to get married, marry; **se m. avec qn** to marry s.o., get married to s.o. ◆**–é** *a* married; **– nm** (bride)groom; **les mariés** the bride and (bride)groom; **les jeunes mariés** the newly-weds. ◆**–ée** *nf* bride.

marijuana [mariʒɥana] *nf* marijuana.

marin [marɛ̃] *a* (*air, sel etc*) sea-; (*flore*) marine; (*mille*) nautical; (*costume*) sailor-; **– nm** seaman, sailor. ◆**marine** *nf* **m.** (*de guerre*) navy; **m. marchande** merchant navy; (*bleu*) **m.** (*couleur*) navy (blue).

marina [marina] nf marina.

mariner [marine] vti Culin to marinate.

marionnette [marjɔnɛt] nf puppet; (à fils) marionette.

maritalement [maritalmã] adv vivre m. to live together (as husband and wife).

maritime [maritim] a (droit, province, climat etc) maritime; (port) sea-; (gare) harbour-; (chantier) naval; (agent) shipping-.

marjolaine [marʒɔlɛn] nf (aromate) marjoram.

mark [mark] nm (monnaie) mark.

marmaille [marmaj] nf (enfants) Fam kids.

marmelade [marmalad] nf en m. (de fruits) stewed fruit; en m. Culin Fig in a mush.

marmite [marmit] nf (cooking) pot.

marmonner [marmɔne] vti to mutter.

marmot [marmo] nm (enfant) Fam kid.

marmotter [marmɔte] vti to mumble.

Maroc [marɔk] nm Morocco. ◆**marocain, -aine** a & nmf Moroccan.

maroquinerie [marɔkinri] nf (magasin) leather goods shop. ◆**maroquinier** nm leather dealer.

marotte [marɔt] nf (dada) Fam fad, craze.

marque [mark] nf (trace, signe) mark; (de fabricant) make, brand; (points) Sp score; m. de fabrique trademark; m. déposée registered trademark; la m. de (preuve) the stamp of; de m. (hôte, visiteur) distinguished; (produit) of quality. ◆**marqu/er** vt (par une marque etc) to mark; (écrire) to note down; (indiquer) to show, mark; (point, but) Sp to score; m. qn Sp to mark s.o.; m. les points Sp to keep (the) score; m. le coup to mark the event; – vi (trace) to leave a mark; (date, événement) to stand out; Sp to score. ◆—**ant** a (remarquable) outstanding. ◆—**é** a (différence, accent etc) marked, pronounced. ◆—**eur** nm (crayon) marker.

marquis [marki] nm marquis. ◆**marquise** nf 1 marchioness. 2 (auvent) glass canopy.

marraine [marɛn] nf godmother.

marre [mar] nf en avoir m. Fam to be fed up (de with).

marr/er (se) [səmare] vpr Fam to have a good laugh. ◆—**ant** a Fam hilarious, funny.

marron¹ [marɔ̃] 1 nm chestnut; (couleur) (chestnut) brown; m. (d'Inde) horse chestnut; – a inv (couleur) (chestnut) brown. 2 nm (coup) Fam punch, clout. ◆**marronnier** nm (horse) chestnut tree.

marron², -onne [marɔ̃, -ɔn] a (médecin etc) bogus.

mars [mars] nm March.

marsouin [marswɛ̃] nm porpoise.

marteau, -x [marto] nm hammer; (de porte) (door)knocker; m. piqueur, m. pneumatique pneumatic drill. ◆**marteler** vt to hammer. ◆**martèlement** nm hammering.

martial, -aux [marsjal, -o] a martial; cour martiale court-martial; loi martiale martial law.

martien, -ienne [marsjɛ̃, -jɛn] nmf & a Martian.

martinet [martinɛ] nm (fouet) (small) whip.

martin-pêcheur [martɛ̃pɛʃœr] nm (pl martins-pêcheurs) (oiseau) kingfisher.

martyr, -yre¹ [martir] nmf (personne) martyr; enfant m. battered child. ◆**martyre²** nm (souffrance) martyrdom. ◆**martyriser** vt to torture; (enfant) to batter.

marxisme [marksism] nm Marxism. ◆**marxiste** a & nmf Marxist.

mascara [maskara] nm mascara.

mascarade [maskarad] nf masquerade.

mascotte [maskɔt] nf mascot.

masculin [maskylɛ̃] a male; (viril) masculine, manly; Gram masculine; (vêtement, équipe) men's; – nm Gram masculine. ◆**masculinité** nf masculinity.

masochisme [mazɔʃism] nm masochism. ◆**masochiste** nmf masochist; – a masochistic.

masque [mask] nm mask. ◆**masquer** vt (dissimuler) to mask (à from); (cacher à la vue) to block off.

massacre [masakr] nm massacre, slaughter. ◆**massacr/er** vt to massacre, slaughter; (abîmer) Fam to ruin. ◆—**ant** a (humeur) excruciating.

massage [masaʒ] nm massage.

masse [mas] nf 1 (volume) mass; (gros morceau, majorité) bulk (de of); en m. (venir, vendre) in large numbers; départ en m. mass ou wholesale departure; manifestation de m. mass demonstration; la m. (foule) the masses; les masses (peuple) the masses; une m. de (tas) a mass of; des masses de Fam masses of. 2 (outil) sledgehammer. 3 Él earth, Am ground. ◆**mass/er** 1 vt, – se m. vpr (gens) to mass. 2 vt (frotter) to massage. ◆—**eur** nm masseur. ◆—**euse** nf masseuse.

massif, -ive [masif, -iv] 1 a massive; (départs etc) mass-; (or, chêne etc) solid. 2 nm (d'arbres, de fleurs) clump; Géog massif. ◆**massivement** adv (en masse) in large numbers.

massue [masy] nf (bâton) club.

mastic [mastik] nm (pour vitres) putty; (pour bois) filler; m. (silicone) mastic.

◆**mastiquer** vt 1 (vitre) to putty; (porte) to mastic; (bois) to fill. 2 (mâcher) to chew, masticate.

mastoc [mastɔk] a inv Péj Fam massive.

mastodonte [mastɔdɔ̃t] nm (personne) Péj monster; (véhicule) juggernaut.

masturber (se) [səmastyrbe] vpr to masturbate. ◆**masturbation** nf masturbation.

masure [mazyr] nf tumbledown house.

mat [mat] 1 a (papier, couleur) mat(t); (bruit) dull. 2 a inv & nm Échecs (check)mate; **faire** ou **mettre m.** to (check)mate.

mât [mɑ] nm (de navire) mast; (poteau) pole.

match [matʃ] nm Sp match, Am game; **m. nul** tie, draw.

matelas [matlɑ] nm mattress; **m. pneumatique** air bed. ◆**matelassé** a (meuble) padded; (tissu) quilted.

matelot [matlo] nm sailor, seaman.

mater [mate] vt (enfant, passion etc) to subdue.

matérialiser [materjalize] vt, **— se m.** vpr to materialize. ◆**matérialisation** nf materialization.

matérialisme [materjalism] nm materialism. ◆**matérialiste** a materialistic; — nmf materialist.

matériaux [materjo] nmpl (building) materials; (de roman, enquête etc) material.

matériel, -ielle [materjel] 1 a (besoin, personne) Péj materialistic; (financier) financial; (pratique) practical. 2 nm equipment, material(s); (d'un ordinateur) hardware inv. ◆**matériellement** adv materially; **m. impossible** physically impossible.

maternel, -elle [maternel] a motherly, maternal; (parenté, réprimande) maternal; — nf (école) **maternelle** nursery school. ◆**materner** vt to mother. ◆**maternité** nf (état) motherhood, maternity; (hôpital) maternity hospital ou unit; (grossesse) pregnancy; **de m.** (congé, allocation) maternity.

mathématique [matematik] a mathematical; — nfpl **mathématiques** mathematics. ◆**mathématicien, -ienne** nmf mathematician. ◆**maths** [mat] nfpl Fam maths, Am math.

matière [matjɛr] nf (sujet) & Scol subject; (de livre) subject matter; **une m., la m., des matières** (substance(s)) matter; **m. première** raw material; **en m. d'art/etc** as regards art/etc, in art/etc; **s'y connaître en m. de** to be experienced in.

matin [matɛ̃] nm morning; **de grand m., de bon m., au petit m.** very early (in the morn-

ing); **le m.** (chaque matin) in the morning; à **sept heures du m.** at seven in the morning; **tous les mardis m.** every Tuesday morning. ◆**matinal, -aux** a (personne) early; (fleur, soleil etc) morning-. ◆**matinée** nf morning; Th **matinée; faire la grasse m.** to sleep late, lie in.

matou [matu] nm tomcat.

matraque [matrak] nf (de policier) truncheon, Am billy (club); (de malfaiteur) cosh, club. ◆**matraqu/er** vt (frapper) to club; (publicité etc) to plug (away) at. ◆**—age** nm **m. (publicitaire)** plugging, publicity build-up.

matrice [matris] nf 1 Anat womb. 2 Tech matrix.

matricule [matrikyl] nm (registration) number; — a (livret, numéro) registration-.

matrimonial, -aux [matrimɔnjal, -o] a matrimonial.

mâture [mɑtyr] nf Nau masts.

maturité [matyrite] nf maturity. ◆**maturation** nf maturing.

maudire* [modir] vt to curse. ◆**maudit** a (sacré) (ac)cursed, damned.

maugréer [mogree] vi to growl, grumble (contre at).

mausolée [mozole] nm mausoleum.

maussade [mosad] a (personne etc) glum, sullen; (temps) gloomy.

mauvais [move] a bad; (méchant, malveillant) evil, wicked; (mal choisi) wrong; (mer) rough; **plus m.** worse; **le plus m.** the worst; **il fait m.** the weather's bad; **ça sent m.** it smells bad; **être m. en** (anglais etc) to be bad at; **mauvaise santé** ill ou bad ou poor health; — nm **le bon et le m.** the good and the bad.

mauve [mov] a & nm (couleur) mauve.

mauviette [movjɛt] nf personne Péj weakling.

maux [mo] voir **mal**.

maxime [maksim] nf maxim.

maximum [maksimɔm] nm maximum; **le m. de** (force etc) the maximum (amount of); **au m.** as mucn as possible; (tout au plus) at most; — a maximum; **la température m.** maximum temperature. ◆**maximal, -aux** a maximum.

mayonnaise [majɔnɛz] nf mayonnaise.

mazout [mazut] nm (fuel) oil.

me [m(ə)] (m' before vowel or mute h) pron 1 (complément direct) me; **il me voit** he sees me. 2 (indirect) (to) me; **elle me parle** she speaks to me; **tu me l'as dit** you told me. 3 (réfléchi) myself; **je me lave** I wash myself.

méandres [meɑ̃dr] nmpl meander(ing)s.

mec [mɛk] nm (individu) Arg guy, bloke.

mécanique [mekanik] a mechanical; (jouet) clockwork-; – nf (science) mechanics; (mécanisme) mechanism. ◆**mécanicien** nm mechanic; Rail train driver. ◆**mécanisme** nm mechanism.

mécaniser [mekanize] vt to mechanize. ◆**mécanisation** nf mechanization.

mécène [mesɛn] nm patron (of the arts).

méchant [meʃɑ̃] a (cruel) malicious, wicked, evil; (désagréable) nasty; (enfant) naughty; (chien) vicious; ce n'est pas m. (grave) Fam it's nothing much. ◆**méchamment** adv (cruellement) maliciously; (très) Fam terribly. ◆**méchanceté** nf malice, wickedness; une m. (acte) a malicious act; (parole) a malicious word.

mèche [mɛʃ] nf 1 (de cheveux) lock; pl (reflets) highlights. 2 (de bougie) wick; (de pétard) fuse; (de perceuse) drill, bit. 3 de m. avec qn (complicité) Fam in collusion ou cahoots with s.o.

méconn/aître° [mekɔnɛtr] vt to ignore; (méjuger) to fail to appreciate. ◆–**u** a unrecognized. ◆–**aissable** a unrecognizable.

mécontent [mekɔ̃tɑ̃] a dissatisfied, discontented (de with). ◆**mécontenter** vt to displease, dissatisfy. ◆–**ement** nm dissatisfaction, discontent.

médaille [medaj] nf (décoration) Sp medal; (pieuse) medallion; (pour chien) name tag; être m. d'or/d'argent Sp to be a gold/silver medallist. ◆**médaillé, -ée** nmf medal holder. ◆**médaillon** nm (bijou) locket, medallion; (ornement) Archit medallion.

médecin [medsɛ̃] nm doctor, physician. ◆**médecine** nf medicine; étudiant en m. medical student. ◆**médical, -aux** a medical. ◆**médicament** nm medicine. ◆**médicinal, -aux** a medicinal. ◆**médico-légal, -aux** a (laboratoire) forensic.

médias [medja] nmpl (mass) media. ◆**médiatique** a media-.

médiateur, -trice [medjatœr, -tris] nmf mediator; – a mediating. ◆**médiation** nf mediation.

médiéval, -aux [medjeval, -o] a medi(a)eval.

médiocre [medjɔkr] a mediocre, second-rate. ◆**médiocrement** adv (pas très) not very; (pas très bien) not very well. ◆**médiocrité** nf mediocrity.

médire° [medir] vi m. de to speak ill of, slander. ◆**médisance(s)** nf(pl) mali-

cious gossip, slander; une m. a piece of malicious gossip.

méditer [medite] vt (conseil etc) to meditate on; m. de faire to consider doing; – vi to meditate (sur on). ◆**méditatif, -ive** a meditative. ◆**méditation** nf meditation.

Méditerranée [mediterane] nf la M. the Mediterranean. ◆**méditerranéen, -enne** a Mediterranean.

médium [medjɔm] nm (spirite) medium.

méduse [medyz] nf jellyfish.

méduser [medyze] vt to stun, dumbfound.

meeting [mitiŋ] nm Pol Sp meeting, rally.

méfait [mefɛ] nm Jur misdeed; pl (dégâts) ravages.

méfi/er (se) [səmefje] vpr se m. de to distrust, mistrust; (faire attention à) to watch out for, beware of; méfie-toi! watch out!, beware!; je me méfie I'm distrustful ou suspicious. ◆–**ant** a distrustful, suspicious. ◆**méfiance** nf distrust, mistrust.

mégalomane [megalɔman] nmf megalomaniac. ◆**mégalomanie** nf megalomania.

mégaphone [megafɔn] nm loudhailer.

mégarde (par) [parmegard] adv inadvertently, by mistake.

mégère [meʒɛr] nf (femme) Péj shrew.

mégot [mego] nm Fam cigarette end ou butt.

meilleur, -eure [mejœr] a better (que than); le m. moment/résultat/etc the best moment/result/etc; – nmf le m., la meilleure the best (one).

mélancolie [melɑ̃kɔli] nf melancholy, gloom. ◆**mélancolique** a melancholy, gloomy.

mélange [melɑ̃ʒ] nm mixture, blend; (opération) mixing. ◆**mélanger** vt (mêler) to mix; (brouiller) to mix (up), muddle; – se m. vpr to mix; (idées etc) to get mixed (up) ou muddled.

mélasse [melas] nf treacle, Am molasses.

mêl/er [mele] vt to mix, mingle (à with); (qualités, thèmes) to combine; (brouiller) to mix (up), muddle; m. qn à (impliquer) to involve s.o. in; – se m. vpr to mix, mingle (à with); se m. à (la foule etc) to join; se m. de (s'ingérer dans) to meddle in; mêle-toi de ce qui te regarde! mind your own business! ◆–**é** a mixed (de with). ◆–**ée** nf (bataille) rough-and-tumble; Rugby scrum(mage).

méli-mélo [melimelo] nm (pl mélis-mélos) Fam muddle.

mélodie [melɔdi] nf melody. ◆**mélodieux, -euse** a melodious. ◆**mélodique** a Mus melodic. ◆**mélomane** nmf music lover.

mélodrame [melodram] *nm* melodrama.
◆**mélodramatique** *a* melodramatic.

melon [m(ə)lɔ̃] *nm* **1** (*fruit*) melon. **2** (*chapeau*) *m.* bowler (hat).

membrane [mãbran] *nf* membrane.

membre [mãbr] *nm* **1** *Anat* limb. **2** (*d'un groupe*) member.

même [mɛm] **1** *a* (*identique*) same; en m. temps at the same time (que as); ce livre/ etc m. (*exact*) this very book/etc; il est la bonté m. he is kindness itself; lui-m./vous-m./etc himself/yourself/etc; − *pron* le, la m. the same (one); j'ai les mêmes I have the same (ones). **2** *adv* (*y compris, aussi*) even; m. si even if; tout de m., quand m. all the same; de m. likewise; de m. que just as; ici m. in this very place; à m. de in a position to; à m. le sol on the ground; à m. la bouteille from the bottle.

mémento [memɛ̃to] *nm* (*aide-mémoire*) handbook; (*agenda*) notebook.

mémoire [memwar] **1** *nf* memory; de m. d'homme in living memory; à la m. de in memory of. **2** *nm* (*requête*) petition; *Univ* memoir; *pl Littér* memoirs. ◆**mémorable** *a* memorable. ◆**mémorandum** [memɔrãdɔm] *nm Pol Com* memorandum. ◆**mémorial, -aux** *nm* (*monument*) memorial.

menace [mənas] *nf* threat, menace. ◆**mena/cer** *vt* to threaten (de faire to do). ◆−**çant** *a* threatening.

ménage [menaʒ] *nm* (*entretien*) housekeeping; (*couple*) couple, household; faire le m. to do the housework; faire bon m. avec to get on happily with. ◆**ménager¹, -ère** *a* (*appareil*) domestic, household-; travaux ménagers housework; − *nf* (*femme*) housewife.

ménag/er² [menaʒe] *vt* (*arranger*) to prepare *ou* arrange (carefully); (*épargner*) to use sparingly, be careful with; (*fenêtre, escalier etc*) to build; m. qn to treat *ou* handle s.o. gently *ou* carefully. ◆−**ement** *nm* (*soin*) care.

ménagerie [menaʒri] *nf* menagerie.

mendier [mãdje] *vi* to beg; − *vt* to beg for. ◆**mendiant, -ante** *nmf* beggar. ◆**mendicité** *nf* begging.

menées [məne] *nfpl* schemings, intrigues.

men/er [məne] *vt* (*personne, vie etc*) to lead; (*lutte, enquête, tâche etc*) to carry out; (*affaires*) to run; (*bateau*) to command; m. qn à (*accompagner, transporter*) to take s.o. to; m. à bien *Fig* to carry through; − *vi Sp* to lead. ◆−**eur, -euse** *nmf* (*de révolte*) (ring)leader.

méningite [menɛ̃ʒit] *nf Méd* meningitis.

ménopause [menɔpoz] *nf* menopause.

menottes [mənɔt] *nfpl* handcuffs.

mensonge [mãsɔ̃ʒ] *nm* lie; (*action*) lying. ◆**mensonger, -ère** *a* untrue, false.

menstruation [mãstryasjɔ̃] *nf* menstruation.

mensuel, -elle [mãsɥɛl] *a* monthly; − (*revue*) monthly. ◆**mensualité** *nf* monthly payment. ◆**mensuellement** *adv* monthly.

mensurations [mãsyrasjɔ̃] *nfpl* measurements.

mental, -aux [mãtal, -o] *a* mental. ◆**mentalité** *nf* mentality.

menthe [mãt] *nf* mint.

mention [mãsjɔ̃] *nf* mention, reference; (*annotation*) comment; m. bien *Scol Univ* distinction; faire m. de to mention. ◆**mentionner** *vt* to mention.

ment/ir* [mãtir] *vi* to lie, tell lies *ou* a lie (à to). ◆−**eur, -euse** *nmf* liar; − *a* lying.

menton [mãtɔ̃] *nm* chin.

menu [məny] **1** *a* (*petit*) tiny; (*mince*) slender, fine; (*peu important*) minor, petty; − *adv* (*hacher*) small, finely; − *nm* par le m. in detail. **2** *nm* (*carte*) *Culin* menu.

menuisier [mənɥizje] *nm* carpenter, joiner. ◆**menuiserie** *nf* carpentry, joinery; (*ouvrage*) woodwork.

méprendre (se) [səmeprãdr] *vpr* se m. sur to be mistaken about. ◆**méprise** *nf* mistake.

mépris [mepri] *nm* contempt (de of, for), scorn (de for); au m. de without regard to. ◆**mépris/er** *vt* to despise, scorn. ◆−**ant** *a* scornful, contemptuous. ◆−**able** *a* despicable.

mer [mɛr] *nf* sea; (*marée*) tide; en m. at sea; par m. by sea; aller à la m. to go to the seaside; un homme à la m.! man overboard!

mercantile [mɛrkãtil] *a Péj* money-grabbing.

mercenaire [mɛrsənɛr] *a & nm* mercenary.

mercerie [mɛrsəri] *nf* (*magasin*) haberdasher's, *Am* notions store. ◆**mercier, -ière** *nmf* haberdasher, *Am* notions merchant.

merci [mɛrsi] **1** *int & nm* thank you, thanks (de, pour for); (*non*) m.! no, thank you! **2** *nf* à la m. de at the mercy of.

mercredi [mɛrkrədi] *nm* Wednesday.

mercure [mɛrkyr] *nm* mercury.

merde! [mɛrd] *int Fam* (bloody) hell!

mère [mɛr] *nf* mother; m. de famille mother (of a family); la m. Dubois *Fam* old Mrs Dubois; maison m. *Com* parent firm.

méridien [meridjɛ̃] *nm* meridian.

méridional, -ale, -aux [meridjɔnal, -o] *a* southern; – *nmf* southerner.

meringue [mərɛ̃g] *nf* (*gâteau*) meringue.

merisier [mərizje] *nm* (*bois*) cherry.

mérite [merit] *nm* merit; **homme de m.** (*valeur*) man of worth. ◆**mérit/er** *vt* (*être digne de*) to deserve; (*valoir*) to be worth; **m. de réussir**/*etc* to deserve to succeed/*etc*. ◆**—ant** *a* deserving. ◆**méritoire** *a* commendable.

merlan [mɛrlɑ̃] *nm* (*poisson*) whiting.

merle [mɛrl] *nm* blackbird.

merveille [mɛrvɛj] *nf* wonder, marvel; **à m.** wonderfully (well). ◆**merveilleusement** *adv* wonderfully. ◆**merveilleux, -euse** *a* wonderful, marvellous; – *nm* **le m.** (*surnaturel*) the supernatural.

mes [me] *voir* **mon.**

mésange [mezɑ̃ʒ] *nf* (*oiseau*) tit.

mésaventure [mezavɑ̃tyr] *nf* misfortune, misadventure.

mesdames [medam] *voir* **madame.**

mesdemoiselles [medmwazɛl] *voir* **mademoiselle.**

mésentente [mezɑ̃tɑ̃t] *nf* misunderstanding.

mesquin [mɛskɛ̃] *a* mean, petty. ◆**mesquinerie** *nf* meanness, pettiness; **une m.** an act of meanness.

mess [mɛs] *nm inv* Mil mess.

message [mesaʒ] *nm* message. ◆**messager, -ère** *nmf* messenger.

messageries [mesaʒri] *nfpl* Com courier service.

messe [mɛs] *nf* Rel mass.

Messie [mesi] *nm* Messiah.

messieurs [mesjø] *voir* **monsieur.**

mesure [məzyr] *nf* (*évaluation, dimension*) measurement; (*quantité, disposition*) measure; (*retenue*) moderation; (*cadence*) Mus time, beat; **fait sur m.** made to measure; **à m. que** as, as soon *ou* as fast as; **dans la m. où** in so far as; **dans une certaine m.** to a certain extent; **en m. de** able to, in a position to; **dépasser la m.** to exceed the bounds. ◆**mesur/er** *vt* to measure; (*juger, estimer*) to calculate, assess, measure; (*argent, temps*) to ration (out); **m. 1 mètre 83** (*personne*) to be six feet tall; (*objet*) to measure six feet; **se m. à** *ou* **avec qn** *Fig* to pit oneself against s.o. ◆**–é** *a* (*pas, ton*) measured; (*personne*) moderate.

met [me] *voir* **mettre.**

métal, -aux [metal, -o] *nm* metal. ◆**métallique** *a* (*objet*) metal-; (*éclat, reflet, couleur*) metallic. ◆**métallisé** *a* (*peinture*) metallic.

métallo [metalo] *nm Fam* steelworker. ◆**métallurgie** *nf* (*industrie*) steel industry; (*science*) metallurgy. ◆**métallurgique** *a* **usine m.** steelworks. ◆**métallurgiste** *a & nm* (*ouvrier*) **m.** steelworker.

métamorphose [metamɔrfoz] *nf* metamorphosis. ◆**métamorphoser** *vt*, – **se m.** *vpr* to transform (**en** into).

métaphore [metafɔr] *nf* metaphor. ◆**métaphorique** *a* metaphorical.

métaphysique [metafizik] *a* metaphysical. '

météo [meteo] *nf* (*bulletin*) weather forecast.

météore [meteɔr] *nm* meteor. ◆**météorite** *nm* meteorite.

météorologie [meteɔrɔlɔʒi] *nf* (*science*) meteorology; (*service*) weather bureau. ◆**météorologique** *a* meteorological; (*bulletin, station, carte*) weather-.

méthode [metɔd] *nf* method; (*livre*) course. ◆**méthodique** *a* methodical.

méticuleux, -euse [metikylø, -øz] *a* meticulous.

métier [metje] *nm* **1** (*travail*) job; (*manuel*) trade; (*intellectuel*) profession; (*habileté*) professional skill; **homme de m.** specialist. **2 m. (à tisser)** loom.

métis, -isse [metis] *a & nmf* half-caste.

mètre [mɛtr] *nm* (*mesure*) metre; (*règle*) (metre) rule; **m. (à ruban)** tape measure. ◆**métr/er** *vt* (*terrain*) to survey. ◆**–age** *nm* **1** surveying. **2** (*tissu*) length; (*de film*) footage; **long m.** (*film*) full length film; **court m.** (*film*) short (film). ◆**–eur** *nm* quantity surveyor. ◆**métrique** *a* metric.

métro [metro] *nm* underground, *Am* subway.

métropole [metrɔpɔl] *nf* (*ville*) metropolis; (*pays*) mother country. ◆**métropolitain** *a* metropolitan.

mets [me] *nm* (*aliment*) dish.

mett/re★ [mɛtr] **1** *vt* to put; (*table*) to lay; (*vêtement, lunettes*) to put on, wear; (*chauffage, radio etc*) to put on, switch on; (*réveil*) to set (à for); (*dépenser*) to spend (**pour une robe**/*etc* on a dress/*etc*); **m. dix heures**/*etc* **à venir** (*consacrer*) to take ten hours/*etc* coming *ou* to come; **m. à l'aise** (*rassurer*) to put *ou* set at ease; (*dans un fauteuil etc*) to make comfortable; **m. en colère** to make angry; **m. en liberté** to free; **m. en bouteille(s)** to bottle; **m. du soin à faire** to take care to do; **mettons que** (+ *sub*) let's suppose that; – **se m.** *vpr* (*se placer*) to put oneself; (*debout*) to stand; (*assis*) to sit; (*objet*) to be put, go; **se m. en short/pyjama/***etc* to get into one's shorts/pyjamas/etc; **se m. en rapport avec** to get in touch with; **se m. à** (endroit) to go to; (travail) to set oneself to, start; **se m. à faire** to start doing; **se m. à table** to sit (down) at the table; **se m. à l'aise** to make oneself comfortable; **se m. au beau/froid** (temps) to turn fine/cold. ◆**—able** a wearable. ◆**—eur** nm m. en scène Th producer; Cin director.

meuble [mœbl] nm piece of furniture; pl furniture. ◆**meubl/er** vt to furnish; (remplir) Fig to fill. ◆**—é** nm furnished flat ou Am apartment.

meugl/er [møgle] vi to moo, low. ◆**—ement(s)** nm(pl) mooing.

meule [møl] nf **1** (de foin) haystack. **2** (pour moudre) millstone.

meunier, -ière [mønje, -jɛr] nmf miller.

meurt [mœr] voir **mourir**.

meurtre [mœrtr] nm murder. ◆**meurtrier, -ière** nmf murderer; – a deadly, murderous.

meurtrir [mœrtrir] vt to bruise. ◆**meurtrissure** nf bruise.

meute [møt] nf (de chiens, de créanciers etc) pack.

Mexique [mɛksik] nm Mexico. ◆**mexicain, -aine** a & nmf Mexican.

mi- [mi] préf la mi-mars/etc mid March/etc; **à mi-distance** mid-distance, midway.

miaou [mjau] nm (cri du chat) miaow.

miaul/er [mjole] vi to miaow, mew. ◆**—ement(s)** nm(pl) miaowing, mewing.

mi-bas [miba] nm inv knee sock.

miche [miʃ] nf round loaf.

mi-chemin (à) [amiʃmɛ̃] adv halfway.

mi-clos [miklo] a half-closed.

micmac [mikmak] nm (manigance) Fam intrigue.

mi-corps (à) [amikɔr] adv (up) to the waist.

mi-côte (à) [amikot] adv halfway up ou down (the hill).

micro [mikro] nm microphone, mike. ◆**microphone** nm microphone.

micro- [mikro] préf micro-.

microbe [mikrɔb] nm germ, microbe.

microcosme [mikrɔkɔsm] nm microcosm.

microfilm [mikrɔfilm] nm microfilm.

micro-onde [mikrɔ̃d] nf microwave; **four à micro-ondes** microwave oven.

microscope [mikrɔskɔp] nm microscope. ◆**microscopique** a microscopic.

midi [midi] nm **1** (heure) midday, noon, twelve o'clock; (heure du déjeuner) lunchtime. **2** (sud) south; **le M.** the south of France.

mie [mi] nf soft bread, crumb.

miel [mjɛl] nm honey. ◆**mielleux, -euse** a (parole, personne) unctuous.

mien, mienne [mjɛ̃, mjɛn] pron poss **le m.**, **la mienne** mine, my one; **les miens**, **les miennes** mine, my ones; **les deux miens** my two; – nmpl **les miens** (amis etc) my (own) people.

miette [mjɛt] nf (de pain, de bon sens etc) crumb; **réduire en miettes** to smash to pieces.

mieux [mjø] adv & a inv better (que than); (plus à l'aise) more comfortable; (plus beau) better-looking; **le m.**, **la m.**, **les m.** (convenir, être etc) the best; (de deux) the better; **le m. serait de...** the best thing would be to...; **de m. en m.** better and better; **tu ferais m. de partir** you had better leave; **je ne demande pas m.** there's nothing I'd like better (que de faire than to do); – nm (amélioration) improvement; **faire de son m.** to do one's best.

mièvre [mjɛvr] a (doucereux) Péj mannered, wishy-washy.

mignon, -onne [miɲɔ̃, -ɔn] a (charmant) cute; (agréable) nice.

migraine [migrɛn] nf headache; Méd migraine.

migration [migrasjɔ̃] nf migration. ◆**migrant, -ante** a & nmf (travailleur) m. migrant worker, migrant.

mijoter [miʒɔte] vt Culin to simmer (lovingly); (lentement) to simmer; (complot) Fig Fam to brew; – vi to simmer.

mil [mil] nm inv (dans les dates) a ou one thousand; **l'an deux m.** the year two thousand.

milice [milis] nf militia. ◆**milicien** nm militiaman.

milieu, -x [miljø] nm (centre) middle; (cadre, groupe social) environment; (entre extrêmes) middle course; (espace) Phys medium; pl (groupes, littéraires etc) circles; **au m. de** in the middle of; **au m. du danger** in the midst of danger; **le juste m.** the happy medium; **le m.** (de malfaiteurs) the underworld.

militaire [militɛr] a military; – nm serviceman; (dans l'armée de terre) soldier.

milit/er [milite] vi (personne) to be a militant; (arguments etc) to militate (**pour** in favour of). ◆**—ant, -ante** a & nmf militant.

mille [mil] **1** a & nm inv thousand; **m. hommes**/etc a ou one thousand men/etc; **deux m.** two thousand; **mettre dans le m.** to hit the bull's-eye. **2** nm (mesure) mile. ◆**m.-pattes** nm inv (insecte) centipede.

◆**millième** a & nmf thousandth; **un m.** a thousandth. ◆**millier** nm thousand; **un m. (de)** a thousand or so.

millefeuille [milfœj] nm (gâteau) cream slice.

millénaire [milenɛr] nm millennium.

millésime [milezim] nm date (on coins, wine etc).

millet [mijɛ] nm Bot millet.

milli- [mili] préf milli-.

milliard [miljar] nm thousand million, Am billion. ◆**milliardaire** a & nmf multimillionaire.

millimètre [milimɛtr] nm millimetre.

million [miljɔ̃] nm million; **un m. de livres/etc** a million pounds/etc; **deux millions** two million. ◆**millionième** a & nmf millionth. ◆**millionnaire** nmf millionaire.

mime [mim] nmf (acteur) mime; **le m.** (art) mime. ◆**mimer** vti to mime. ◆**mimique** nf (mine) (funny) face; (gestes) signs, sign language.

mimosa [mimoza] nm (arbre, fleur) mimosa.

minable [minabl] a (médiocre) pathetic; (lieu, personne) shabby.

minaret [minarɛ] nm (de mosquée) minaret.

minauder [minode] vi to simper, make a show of affectation.

mince [mɛ̃s] 1 a thin; (élancé) slim; (insignifiant) slim, paltry. 2 int **m. (alors)!** oh heck!, blast (it)! ◆**minceur** nf thinness; slimness. ◆**mincir** vi to grow slim.

mine [min] nf 1 appearance; (physionomie) look; **avoir bonne/mauvaise m.** (santé) to look well/ill; **faire m. de faire** to appear to do, make as if to do. 2 (d'or, de charbon etc) & Fig mine; **m. de charbon** coalmine. 3 (de crayon) lead. 4 (engin explosif) mine. ◆**miner** vt 1 (saper) to undermine. 2 (garnir d'explosifs) to mine.

minerai [minrɛ] nm ore.

minéral, -aux [mineral, -o] a & nm mineral. ◆**minéralogique** a **numéro m.** Aut registration ou Am license number.

minet, -ette [minɛ, -ɛt] nmf 1 (chat) puss. 2 (personne) Fam fashion-conscious young man ou woman.

mineur, -eure [minœr] nm 1 (ouvrier) miner. 2 a (jeune, secondaire) & Mus minor; – nmf Jur minor. ◆**minier, -ière** a (industrie) mining-.

mini- [mini] préf mini-.

miniature [minjatyr] nf miniature; – a inv (train etc) miniature-.

minibus [minibys] nm minibus.

minime [minim] a trifling, minor, minimal. ◆**minimiser** vt to minimize.

minimum [minimɔm] nm minimum; **le m. de** (force etc) the minimum (amount of); **au (grand) m.** at the very least; **la température m.** the minimum temperature. ◆**minimal, -aux** a minimum, minimal.

ministre [ministr] nm Pol Rel minister; **m. de l'Intérieur** = Home Secretary, Am Secretary of the Interior. ◆**ministère** nm ministry; (gouvernement) government; **m. de l'Intérieur** = Home Office, Am Department of the Interior. ◆**ministériel, -ielle** a ministerial; (crise, remaniement) cabinet-.

minorer [minɔre] vt to reduce.

minorité [minɔrite] nf minority; **en m.** in the ou a minority. ◆**minoritaire** a (parti etc) minority-; **être m.** to be in the ou a minority.

Minorque [minɔrk] nf Minorca.

minuit [minɥi] nm midnight, twelve o'clock.

minus [minys] nm (individu) Péj Fam moron.

minuscule [minyskyl] 1 a (petit) tiny, minute. 2 a & nf (lettre) m. small letter.

minute [minyt] nf minute; **à la m.** (tout de suite) this (very) minute; **d'une m. à l'autre** any minute (now); – a inv **aliments** ou **plats m.** convenience food(s). ◆**minuter** vt to time. ◆**minuterie** nf time switch.

minutie [minysi] nf meticulousness. ◆**minutieux, -euse** a meticulous.

mioche [mjɔʃ] nmf (enfant) Fam kid, youngster.

miracle [mirakl] nm miracle; **par m.** miraculously. ◆**miraculeux, -euse** a miraculous.

mirador [miradɔr] nm Mil watchtower.

mirage [miraʒ] nm mirage.

mirifique [mirifik] a Hum fabulous.

mirobolant [mirɔbɔlɑ̃] a Fam fantastic.

miroir [mirwar] nm mirror. ◆**miroiter** vi to gleam, shimmer.

mis [mi] voir mettre; – a **bien m.** (vêtu) well dressed.

misanthrope [mizɑ̃trɔp] nmf misanthropist; – a misanthropic.

mise [miz] nf 1 (action de mettre) putting; **m. en service** putting into service; **m. en marche** starting up; **m. à la retraite** pensioning off; **m. à feu** (de fusée) blast-off; **m. en scène** Th production; Cin direction. 2 (argent) stake. 3 (tenue) attire. ◆**miser** vt (argent) to stake (sur on); – vi **m. sur** (cheval) to back; (compter sur) to bank on.

misère [mizɛr] nf (grinding) poverty; (malheur) misery; (bagatelle) trifle. ◆**mi-**

sérable a miserable, wretched; (*indigent*) poor, destitute; (*logement, quartier*) seedy, slummy; – nmf (poor) wretch; (*indigent*) pauper. ◆**miséreux, -euse** a destitute; – nmf pauper.

miséricorde [mizerikɔrd] nf mercy. ◆**miséricordieux, -euse** a merciful.

misogyne [mizɔʒin] nmf misogynist.

missile [misil] nm (*fusée*) missile.

mission [misjɔ̃] nf mission; (*tâche*) task. ◆**missionnaire** nm & a missionary.

missive [misiv] nf (*lettre*) missive.

mistral [mistral] nm inv (*vent*) mistral.

mite [mit] nf (*clothes*) moth; (*du fromage etc*) mite. ◆**mité** a moth-eaten.

mi-temps [mitɑ̃] nf (*pause*) Sp half-time; (*période*) Sp half; **à mi-t.** (*travailler etc*) part-time.

miteux, -euse [mitø, -øz] a shabby.

mitigé [mitiʒe] a (*zèle etc*) moderate, luke-warm; (*mêlé*) Fam mixed.

mitraille [mitraj] nf gunfire. ◆**mitrailler** vt to machinegun; (*photographier*) Fam to click ou snap away at. ◆**mitraillette** nf submachine gun. ◆**mitrailleur** a fusil m. machinegun. ◆**mitrailleuse** nf machine-gun.

mi-voix (à) [amivwa] adv in an undertone.

mixe(u)r [miksœr] nm (*pour mélanger*) (food) mixer.

mixte [mikst] a mixed; (*école*) co-ed-ucational, mixed; (*tribunal*) joint.

mixture [mikstyr] nf (*boisson*) Péj mixture.

Mlle [madmwazɛl] abrév = **Mademoiselle**.

MM [mesjø] abrév = **Messieurs**.

mm abrév (*millimètre*) mm.

Mme [madam] abrév = **Madame**.

mobile [mɔbil] 1 a (*pièce etc*) moving; (*personne*) mobile; (*feuillets*) detachable, loose; (*reflets*) changing; **échelle m.** sliding scale; **fête m.** mov(e)able feast; – nm (*œuvre d'art*) mobile. 2 nm (*motif*) motive (de for). ◆**mobilité** nf mobility.

mobilier [mɔbilje] nm furniture.

mobiliser [mɔbilize] vti to mobilize. ◆**mobilisation** nf mobilization.

mobylette [mɔbilɛt] nf moped.

mocassin [mɔkasɛ̃] nm (*chaussure*) mocca-sin.

moche [mɔʃ] a Fam (*laid*) ugly; (*mauvais, peu gentil*) lousy, rotten.

modalité [mɔdalite] nf method (de of).

mode [mɔd] 1 nf fashion; (*industrie*) fashion trade; **à la m.** in fashion, fashionable; **passé de m.** out of fashion; **à la m. de** in the man-ner of. 2 nm mode, method; **m. d'emploi**

directions (for use); **m. de vie** way of life. **3** nm Gram mood.

modèle [mɔdɛl] nm (*schéma, exemple, personne*) model; **m. (réduit)** (scale) model; – a (*élève etc*) model-. ◆**model/er** vt to model (**sur** on); **se m. sur** to model oneself on. ◆**–age** nm (*de statue etc*) modelling. ◆**modéliste** nmf Tex stylist, designer.

modéré a moderate. ◆**–ment** adv moderately.

modérer [mɔdere] vt to moderate, restrain; (*vitesse, allure*) to reduce; – **se m.** vpr to restrain oneself. ◆**modérateur, -trice** a moderating; – nmf moderator. ◆**modération** nf moderation, restraint; reduction; **avec m.** in moderation.

moderne [mɔdɛrn] a modern; – nm **le m.** (*mobilier*) modern furniture. ◆**modernisation** nf modernization. ◆**moderniser** vt, – **se m.** vpr to modernize. ◆**modernisme** nm modernism.

modeste [mɔdɛst] a modest. ◆**modestement** adv modestly. ◆**modestie** nf modesty.

modifier [mɔdifje] vt to modify, alter; – **se m.** vpr to alter. ◆**modification** nf modification, alteration.

modique [mɔdik] a (*salaire, prix*) modest. ◆**modicité** nf modesty.

module [mɔdyl] nm module.

moduler [mɔdyle] vt to modulate. ◆**modulation** nf modulation.

moelle [mwal] nf Anat marrow; **m. épinière** spinal cord.

moelleux, -euse [mwalø, -øz] a soft; (*voix, vin*) mellow.

mœurs [mœr(s)] nfpl (*morale*) morals; (*habitudes*) habits, customs.

mohair [mɔɛr] nm mohair.

moi [mwa] pron **1** (*complément direct*) me; **laissez-moi** leave me; **pour moi** for me. **2** (*indirect*) (to) me; **montrez-le-moi** show it to me, show me it. **3** (*sujet*) I; **moi, je veux** I want. **4** nm inv Psy self, ego. ◆**moi-même** pron myself.

moignon [mwaɲɔ̃] nm stump.

moindre [mwɛ̃dr] a **être m.** (*moins grand*) to be less; **le m. doute/etc** the slightest ou least doubt/etc; **le m.** (*de mes problèmes etc*) the least (**de** of); (*de deux problèmes etc*) the lesser (**de** of).

moine [mwan] nm monk, friar.

moineau, -x [mwano] nm sparrow.

moins [mwɛ̃] **1** adv (*before vowel*) less (**que** than); **m. de** (*temps, zèle etc*) less (**que** than), not so much (**que** as); (*gens, livres etc*) fewer (**que** than), not so many

(que as); (*cent francs etc*) less than; **m. froid/grand/etc** not as cold/big/*etc* (que as); de **m. en m.** less and less; **le m., la m., les m.** (*travailler etc*) the least; **le m. grand** the smallest; **au m., du m.** at least; de **m., en m.** (*qui manque*) missing; **dix ans/etc** de **m.** ten years/*etc* less; **en m.** (*personne, objet*) less; (*personnes, objets*) fewer; **les m.** de vingt ans those under twenty, the under-twenties; **à m. que** (+ *sub*) unless. **2** *prép Math* minus; **deux heures m.** cinq five to two; **il fait m. dix** (**degrés**) it's minus ten (degrees).

mois [mwa] *nm* month; **au m. de juin**/*etc* in (the month of) June/*etc*.

mois/ir [mwazir] *vi* to go mouldy; (*attendre*) *Fig* to hang about. **◆—i** *a* mouldy; **—nm** mould, mildew; **sentir le m.** to smell musty. **◆moisissure** *nf* mould, mildew.

moisson [mwasɔ̃] *nf* harvest. **◆moissonner** *vt* to harvest. **◆moissonneuse-batteuse** *nf* (*pl* moissonneuses-batteuses) combine-harvester.

moite [mwat] *a* sticky, moist. **◆moiteur** *nf* stickiness, moistness.

moitié [mwatje] *nf* half; **la m. de la pomme**/*etc* half (of) the apple/*etc*; **à m.** (*remplir etc*) halfway; **à m. fermé/cru/etc** half closed/raw/*etc*; **de m.** by half; **à m.-moitié** *Fam* half-price; **de m.** by half; **à m.-moitié** *Fam* so-so; **partager m.-moitié** *Fam* to split fifty-fifty.

moka [mɔka] *nm* (*café*) mocha.

mol [mɔl] *voir* **mou.**

molaire [mɔlɛr] *nf* (*dent*) molar.

molécule [mɔlekyl] *nf* molecule.

moleskine [mɔlɛskin] *nf* imitation leather.

molester [mɔlɛste] *vt* to manhandle.

molette [mɔlɛt] *nf* **clé à m.** adjustable wrench *ou* spanner.

mollasse [mɔlas] *a Péj* flabby.

molle [mɔl] *voir* **mou.** **◆mollement** *adv* feebly; (*paresseusement*) lazily. **◆mollesse** *nf* softness; (*faiblesse*) feebleness. **◆mollir** *vi* to go soft; (*courage*) to flag.

mollet [mɔlɛ] **1** *a* **œuf m.** soft-boiled egg. **2** *nm* (*de jambe*) calf.

mollusque [mɔlysk] *nm* mollusc.

môme [mom] *nmf* (*enfant*) *Fam* kid.

moment [mɔmɑ̃] *nm* (*instant*) moment; (*période*) time; **en ce m.** at the moment; **par moments** at times; **au m. de partir** when just about to leave; **au m. où** when, just as; **du m. que** (*puisque*) seeing that. **◆momentané** *a* momentary. **◆momentanément** *adv* temporarily, for the moment.

momie [mɔmi] *nf* (*cadavre*) mummy.

mon, ma, *pl* **mes** [mɔ̃, ma, me] (**ma** becomes **mon** [mɔ̃n] *before a vowel or mute h*) *a poss* my; **mon père** my father; **ma mère** my mother; **mon ami(e)** my friend.

Monaco [mɔnako] *nf* Monaco.

monarque [mɔnark] *nm* monarch. **◆monarchie** *nf* monarchy. **◆monarchique** *a* monarchic.

monastère [mɔnastɛr] *nm* monastery.

monceau, -x [mɔ̃so] *nm* heap, pile.

monde [mɔ̃d] *nm* world; (*milieu social*) set; **du m.** (*gens*) people; (*beaucoup*) a lot of people; **un m. fou** a tremendous crowd; **le (grand) m.** (high) society; **le m. entier** the whole world; **tout le m.** everybody; **mettre au m.** to give birth to; **pas le moins du m.!** not in the least *ou* slightest! **◆mondain, -aine** *a* (*vie, réunion etc*) society-. **◆mondanités** *nfpl* (*événements*) social events. **◆mondial, -aux** *a* (*renommée etc*) world-; (*crise*) worldwide. **◆mondialement** *adv* the (whole) world over.

monégasque [mɔnegask] *a & nmf* Monegasque.

monétaire [mɔnetɛr] *a* monetary.

mongolien, -ienne [mɔ̃gɔljɛ̃, -jɛn] *a & nmf Méd* mongol.

moniteur, -trice [mɔnitœr, -tris] *nmf* **1** instructor; (*de colonie de vacances*) assistant, *Am* camp counselor. **2** (*écran*) *Tech* monitor.

monnaie [mɔnɛ] *nf* (*devise*) currency, money; (*appoint, pièces*) change; **pièce de m.** coin; (*petite*) **m.** (small) change; **faire de la m.** to get change; **faire de la m. à qn** to give s.o. change (**sur un billet** for a note); **c'est m. courante** it's very frequent; **Hôtel de la M.** mint. **◆monnayer** *vt* (*talent etc*) to cash in on; (*bien, titre*) *Com* to convert into cash.

mono [mɔno] *a inv* (*disque etc*) mono.

mono- [mɔno] *préf* mono-.

monocle [mɔnɔkl] *nm* monocle.

monologue [mɔnɔlɔg] *nm* monologue.

monoplace [mɔnoplas] *a & nmf* (*avion, voiture*) single-seater.

monopole [mɔnɔpɔl] *nm* monopoly. **◆monopoliser** *vt* to monopolize.

monosyllabe [mɔnosilab] *nm* monosyllable. **◆monosyllabique** *a* monosyllabic.

monotone [mɔnɔtɔn] *a* monotonous. **◆monotonie** *nf* monotony.

monseigneur [mɔ̃sɛɲœr] *nm* (*évêque*) His *ou* Your Grace; (*prince*) His *ou* Your Highness.

monsieur, *pl* **messieurs** [məsjø, mesjø] *nm* gentleman; **oui m.** yes; (*avec déférence*) yes sir; **oui messieurs** yes (gentlemen); **M. Legras** Mr Legras; **Messieurs** *ou* **MM Legras** Messrs Legras; **tu vois ce m.?** do you see that man *ou* gentleman?; **Monsieur** (*sur une lettre*) Com Dear Sir.

monstre [mɔ̃str] *nm* monster; – *a* (*énorme*) *Fam* colossal. **◆monstrueux, -euse** *a* (*abominable, énorme*) monstrous. **◆monstruosité** *nf* (*horreur*) monstrosity.

mont [mɔ̃] *nm* (*montagne*) mount.

montagne [mɔ̃taɲ] *nf* mountain; **la m.** (*zone*) the mountains; **montagnes russes** *Fig* roller coaster. **◆montagnard, -arde** *nmf* mountain dweller; – *a* (*peuple*) mountain-. **◆montagneux, -euse** *a* mountainous.

mont-de-piété [mɔ̃dpjete] *nm* (*pl* monts-de-piété*) pawnshop.

monte-charge [mɔ̃tʃarʒ] *nm inv* service lift *ou Am* elevator.

mont/er [mɔ̃te] *vi* (*aux être*) (*personne*) to go *ou* come up; (*s'élever*) to go up; (*grimper*) to climb (up) (*sur* onto); (*prix*) to go up, rise; (*marée*) to come in; (*avion*) to climb; **m. dans un véhicule** to get in(to) a vehicle; **m. dans un train** to get on(to) a train; **m. sur** (*échelle etc*) to climb up; (*trône*) to ascend; **en courant/etc** to run/etc up; **m.** (*à cheval*) *Sp* to ride (a horse); **m. en graine** (*salade etc*) to go to seed; – *vt* (*aux avoir*) (*côte etc*) to climb (up); (*objets*) to bring *ou* take up; (*cheval*) to ride; (*tente, affaire*) to set up; (*machine*) to assemble; (*bijou*) to set, mount; (*complot, démonstration*) to mount; (*pièce*) Th to stage, mount; **m. l'escalier** to go *ou* come upstairs *ou* up the stairs; **faire m.** (*visiteur etc*) to show up; **m. qn contre qn** to set s.o. against s.o.; – **se m.** *vpr* (*s'irriter*) *Fam* to get angry; **se m. à** (*frais*) to amount to. **◆—ant¹** *a* (*chemin*) uphill; (*mouvement*) upward; (*marée*) rising; (*col*) stand-up; (*robe*) high-necked; **chaussure montante** boot. **2** *nm* (*somme*) amount. **3** *nm* (*de barrière*) post; (*d'échelle etc*) upright. **◆—é** *a* (*police*) mounted. **◆—ée** *nf* ascent, climb; (*de prix, des eaux*) rise; (*chemin*) slope. **◆—age** *nm* Tech assembling, assembly; *Cin* editing. **◆—eur, -euse** *nmf* Tech fitter; *Cin* editor.

montre [mɔ̃tr] *nf* **1** watch; **course contre la m.** race against time. **2 faire m. de** to show. **◆m.-bracelet** *nf* (*pl* montres-bracelets) wristwatch.

Montréal [mɔ̃real] *nm ou f* Montreal.

montrer [mɔ̃tre] *vt* to show (**à** to); **m. du doigt** to point to; **m. à qn à faire qch** to

show s.o. how to do sth; – **se m.** *vpr* to show oneself, appear; (*s'avérer*) to turn out to be; **se m. courageux/etc** (*être*) to be courageous/etc.

monture [mɔ̃tyr] *nf* **1** (*cheval*) mount. **2** (*de lunettes*) frame; (*de bijou*) setting.

monument [mɔnymɑ̃] *nm* monument; **m. aux morts** war memorial. **◆monumental, -aux** *a* (*imposant, énorme etc*) monumental.

moquer (se) [səmɔke] *vpr* **se m. de** (*allure etc*) to make fun of; (*personne*) to make a fool of, make fun of; **je m'en moque!** *Fam* I couldn't care less! **◆moquerie** *nf* mockery. **◆moqueur, -euse** *a* mocking.

moquette [mɔkɛt] *nf* fitted carpet(s), wall-to-wall carpeting.

moral, -aux [mɔral, -o] *a* moral; – *nm* **le m.** spirits, morale. **◆morale** *nf* (*principes*) morals; (*code*) moral code; (*d'histoire etc*) moral; **faire la m. à qn** to lecture s.o. **◆moralement** *adv* morally. **◆moraliser** *vi* to moralize. **◆moraliste** *nmf* moralist. **◆moralité** *nf* (*mœurs*) morality; (*de fable, récit etc*) moral.

moratoire [mɔratwar] *nm* moratorium.

morbide [mɔrbid] *a* morbid.

morceau, -x [mɔrso] *nm* piece, bit; (*de sucre*) lump; (*de viande*) Culin cut; (*extrait*) *Littér* extract. **◆morceler** *vt* (*terrain*) to divide up.

mordiller [mɔrdije] *vt* to nibble.

mord/re [mɔrdr] *vti* to bite; **ça mord** *Pêche* I have a bite. **◆—ant¹** *a* (*voix, manière*) scathing; (*froid*) biting; (*personne, ironie*) caustic. **◆—ant²** *nm* (*énergie*) punch. **◆—u, -ue** *nmf* **un m. du jazz/etc** *Fam* a jazz/etc fan.

morfondre (se) [səmɔrfɔ̃dr] *vpr* to get bored (waiting), mope (about).

morgue [mɔrg] *nf* (*lieu*) mortuary, morgue.

moribond, -onde [mɔribɔ̃, -ɔ̃d] *a* & *nmf* dying *ou* moribund (person).

morne [mɔrn] *a* dismal, gloomy, dull.

morose [mɔroz] *a* morose, sullen.

morphine [mɔrfin] *nf* morphine.

mors [mɔr] *nm* (*de harnais*) bit.

morse [mɔrs] *nm* **1** Morse (code). **2** (*animal*) walrus.

morsure [mɔrsyr] *nf* bite.

mort¹ [mɔr] *nf* death; **mettre à m.** to put to death; **silence de m.** dead silence. **◆mortalité** *nf* death rate, mortality. **◆mortel, -elle** *a* (*hommes, ennemi, danger etc*) mortal; (*accident*) fatal; (*chaleur*) deadly; (*pâleur*) deathly; – *nmf* mortal. **◆mortellement** *adv* (*blessé*) fatally.

mort², morte [mɔr, mɔrt] *a* (*personne, plante, ville etc*) dead; **m. de fatigue** dead tired; **m. de froid** numb with cold; **m. de peur** frightened to death; – *nmf* dead man, dead woman; **les morts the dead; de nombreux morts** (*victimes*) many deaths *ou* casualties; **le jour** *ou* **la fête des Morts** All Souls' Day. ◆**morte-saison** *nf* off season. ◆**mort-né** *a* (*enfant*) & *Fig* stillborn.

mortier [mɔrtje] *nm* mortar.

mortifier [mɔrtifje] *vt* to mortify.

mortuaire [mɔrtɥɛr] *a* (*avis, rites etc*) death-, funeral.

morue [mɔry] *nf* cod.

morve [mɔrv] *nf* (*nasal*) mucus. ◆**morveux, -euse** *a* (*enfant*) snotty (-nosed).

mosaïque [mɔzaik] *nf* mosaic.

Moscou [mɔsku] *nm ou f* Moscow.

mosquée [mɔske] *nf* mosque.

mot [mo] *nm* word; **envoyer un m. à** to drop a line to; **m. à** *ou* **pour m.** word for word; **bon m.** witticism; **mots croisés** crossword (puzzle); **m. d'ordre** *Pol* resolution, order; (*slogan*) watchword; **m. de passe** password.

motard [mɔtar] *nm Fam* motorcyclist.

motel [mɔtɛl] *nm* motel.

moteur¹ [mɔtœr] *nm* (*de véhicule etc*) engine, motor; *El* motor.

moteur², -trice [mɔtœr, -tris] *a* (*force*) driving-; (*nerf, muscle*) motor.

motif [mɔtif] *nm* **1** reason, motive. **2** (*dessin*) pattern.

motion [mosjɔ̃] *nf Pol* motion; **on a voté une m. de censure** a vote of no confidence was given.

motiver [mɔtive] *vt* (*inciter, causer*) to motivate; (*justifier*) to justify. ◆**motivation** *nf* motivation.

moto [mɔto] *nf* motorcycle, motorbike. ◆**motocycliste** *nmf* motorcyclist.

motorisé [mɔtɔrize] *a* motorized.

motte [mɔt] *nf* (*de terre*) clod, lump; (*de beurre*) block.

mou (*or* **mol** *before vowel or mute h*), **molle** [mu, mɔl] *a* soft; (*faible, sans énergie*) feeble; – *nm* **avoir du m.** (*cordage*) to be slack.

mouchard, -arde [muʃar, -ard] *nmf Péj* informer. ◆**moucharder** *vt* **m. qn** *Fam* to inform on s.o.

mouche [muʃ] *nf* (*insecte*) fly; **prendre la m.** (*se fâcher*) to go into a huff; **faire m.** to hit the bull's-eye. ◆**moucheron** *nm* (*insecte*) midge.

moucher [muʃe] *vt* **m. qn** to wipe s.o.'s nose; **se m.** to blow one's nose.

moucheté [muʃte] *a* speckled, spotted.

mouchoir [muʃwar] *nm* handkerchief; (*en papier*) tissue.

moudre* [mudr] *vt* (*café, blé*) to grind.

moue [mu] *nf* long face, pout; **faire la m.** to pout, pull a (long) face.

mouette [mwɛt] *nf* (sea)gull.

moufle [mufl] *nf* (*gant*) mitt(en).

mouill/er [muje] **1** *vt* to wet, make wet; **se faire m.** to get wet; – **se m.** *vpr* to get (oneself) wet; (*se compromettre*) *Fam* to get involved (*by taking risks*). **2** *vt* **m. l'ancre** *Nau* to (drop) anchor; – *vi* to anchor. ◆**–é** *a* wet (**de** with). ◆**–age** *nm* (*action*) *Nau* anchoring; (*lieu*) anchorage.

moule¹ [mul] *nm* mould, *Am* mold; **m. à gâteaux** cake tin. ◆**moul/er** *vt* to mould, *Am* mold; (*statue*) to cast; **m. qn** (*vêtement*) to fit s.o. tightly. ◆**–ant** *a* (*vêtement*) tight-fitting. ◆**–age** *nm* moulding; casting; (*objet*) cast. ◆**moulure** *nf Archit* moulding.

moule² [mul] *nf* (*mollusque*) mussel.

moulin [mulɛ̃] *nm* mill; (*moteur*) *Fam* engine; **m. à vent** windmill; **m. à café** coffee-grinder.

moulinet [mulinɛ] *nm* **1** (*de canne à pêche*) reel. **2** (*de bâton*) twirl.

moulu [muly] *voir* **moudre**; – *a* (*café*) ground; (*éreinté*) *Fam* dead tired.

mour/ir* [murir] *vi* (*aux être*) to die (**de**, of, from); **m. de froid** to die of exposure; **m. d'ennui/de fatigue** *Fig* to be dead bored/tired; **m. de peur** *Fig* to be frightened to death; **s'ennuyer à m.** to be bored to death; – **se m.** *vpr* to be dying. ◆**–ant, -ante** *a* dying; (*voix*) faint; – *nmf* dying person.

mousquetaire [muskətɛr] *nm Mil Hist* musketeeer.

mousse [mus] *nf* **1** *Bot* moss. **2** *nf* (*écume*) froth, foam; (*de bière*) froth; (*de savon*) lather; **m. à raser** shaving foam. **3** *nf Culin* mousse. **4** *nm Nau* ship's boy. ◆**mousser** *vi* (*bière etc*) to froth; (*savon*) to lather; (*eau savonneuse*) to foam. ◆**mousseux, -euse** *a* frothy; (*vin*) sparkling; – *nm* sparkling wine. ◆**moussu** *a* mossy.

mousseline [muslin] *nf* (*coton*) muslin.

mousson [musɔ̃] *nf* (*vent*) monsoon.

moustache [mustaʃ] *nf* moustache, *Am* mustache; *pl* (*de chat etc*) whiskers. ◆**moustachu** *a* wearing a moustache.

moustique [mustik] *nm* mosquito. ◆**moustiquaire** *nf* mosquito net; (*en métal*) screen.

moutard [mutar] *nm* (*enfant*) *Arg* kid.

moutarde [mutard] *nf* mustard.

mouton [mutɔ̃] *nm* sheep; (*viande*) mutton;

pl (sur la mer) white horses; *(poussière)* bits of dust; **peau de m.** sheepskin.

mouvement [muvmɑ̃] *nm (geste, déplacement, groupe etc) & Mus* movement; *(de colère)* outburst; *(impulsion)* impulse; **en m.** in motion. ◆**mouvementé** *a (animé)* lively, exciting; *(séance, vie etc)* eventful.

mouv/oir* [muvwar] *vi,* — **se m.** *vpr* to move; **mû par** *(mécanisme)* driven by. ◆**—ant** *a (changeant)* changing; **sables mouvants** quicksands.

moyen¹, -enne [mwajɛ̃, -ɛn] *a* average; *(format, entreprise etc)* medium(-sized); *(solution)* intermediate, middle; — *nf* average; *(dans un examen)* pass mark; *(dans un devoir)* half marks; **la moyenne d'âge** the average age; **en moyenne** on average. ◆**moyennement** *adv* averagely, moderately.

moyen² [mwajɛ̃] *nm (procédé, façon)* means, way *(de faire* of doing, to do); *pl (capacités)* ability, powers; *(argent, ressources)* means; **au m. de** by means of; **il n'y a pas m. de faire** it's not possible to do; **je n'ai pas les moyens** *(argent)* I can't afford it; **par mes propres moyens** under my own steam.

moyennant [mwajɛnɑ̃] *prép (pour)* (in return) for; *(avec)* with.

moyeu, -x [mwajø] *nm (de roue)* hub.

mucosités [mykozite] *nfpl* mucus.

mue [my] *nf* moulting; breaking of the voice. ◆**muer** [mɥe] *vi (animal)* to moult; *(voix)* to break; **se m. en** to become transformed into.

muet, -ette [mɥɛ, -ɛt] *a (infirme)* dumb; *(de surprise etc)* speechless; *(film, reproche etc)* silent; *Gram* mute; — *nmf* dumb person.

mufle [myfl] *nm* **1** *(d'animal)* nose, muzzle. **2** *(individu)* Péj lout.

mug/ir [myʒir] *vi (vache)* to moo; *(bœuf)* to bellow; *(vent)* Fig to roar. ◆**—issement(s)** *nm(pl)* moo(ing); bellow(ing); roar(ing).

muguet [mygɛ] *nm* lily of the valley.

mule [myl] *nf* **1** *(pantoufle)* mule. **2** *(animal)* (she-)mule. ◆**mulet¹** *nm* (he-)mule.

mulet² [mylɛ] *nm (poisson)* mullet.

multi- [mylti] *préf* multi-.

multicolore [myltikɔlɔr] *a* multicoloured.

multinationale [myltinasjɔnal] *nf* multinational.

multiple [myltipl] *a (nombreux)* numerous; *(ayant des formes variées)* multiple; — *nm Math* multiple. ◆**multiplication** *nf* multiplication; *(augmentation)* increase. ◆**multiplicité** *nf* multiplicity. ◆**multiplier** *vt* to

multiply; — **se m.** *vpr* to increase; *(se reproduire)* to multiply.

multitude [myltityd] *nf* multitude.

municipal, -aux [mynisipal, -o] *a* municipal; **conseil m.** town council. ◆**municipalité** *nf (corps)* town council; *(commune)* municipality.

munir [mynir] *vt* **m. de** to provide *ou* equip with; **se m. de** to provide oneself with; **muni de** *(papiers, arme etc)* in possession of.

munitions [mynisjɔ̃] *nfpl* ammunition.

muqueuse [mykøz] *nf* mucous membrane.

mur [myr] *nm* wall; **m. du son** sound barrier; **au pied du m.** Fig with one's back to the wall. ◆**muraille** *nf* (high) wall. ◆**mural, -aux** *a (carte etc)* wall-; **peinture murale** mural (painting). ◆**murer** *vt (porte)* to wall up; **m. qn** to wall s.o. in.

mûr [myr] *a (fruit, projet etc)* ripe; *(âge, homme)* mature. ◆**mûrement** *adv (réfléchir)* carefully. ◆**mûrir** *vti (fruit)* to ripen; *(personne, projet)* to mature.

muret [myrɛ] *nm* low wall.

murmure [myrmyr] *nm* murmur. ◆**murmurer** *vti* to murmur.

musc [mysk] *nm (parfum)* musk.

muscade [myskad] *nf* nutmeg.

muscle [myskl] *nm* muscle. ◆**musclé** *a (bras)* brawny, muscular. ◆**musculaire** *a (tissu, système etc)* muscular. ◆**musculature** *nf* muscles.

museau, -x [myzo] *nm (de chien etc)* muzzle; *(de porc)* snout. ◆**museler** *vt (animal, presse etc)* to muzzle. ◆**muselière** *nf (appareil)* muzzle.

musée [myze] *nm* museum; **m. de peinture** (public) art gallery. ◆**muséum** *nm* (natural history) museum.

musette [myzɛt] *nf (d'ouvrier)* duffel bag, kit bag.

music-hall [myzikol] *nm* variety theatre.

musique [myzik] *nf* music; *(fanfare)* Mil band. ◆**musical, -aux** *a* musical. ◆**musicien, -ienne** *nmf* musician; — *a* **être très/assez m.** to be very/quite musical.

musulman, -ane [myzylmɑ̃, -an] *a & nmf* Moslem, Muslim.

muter [myte] *vt (employé)* to transfer. ◆**mutation** *nf* **1** transfer. **2** *Biol* mutation.

mutil/er [mytile] *vt* to mutilate, maim; **être mutilé** to be disabled. ◆**—é, -ée** *nmf* **m. de guerre/du travail** disabled ex-serviceman/worker. ◆**mutilation** *nf* mutilation.

mutin [mytɛ̃] **1** *a (espiègle)* saucy. **2** *nm (rebelle)* mutineer. ◆**se mutin/er** *vpr* to mutiny. ◆**—é** *a* mutinous. ◆**mutinerie** *nf* mutiny.

mutisme [mytism] *nm* (stubborn) silence.

mutualité [mytɥalite] *nf* mutual insurance. ◆**mutualiste** *nmf* member of a friendly or *Am* benefit society. ◆**mutuelle**[1] *nf* friendly society, *Am* benefit society.

mutuel, -elle[2] [mytɥɛl] *a* (*réciproque*) mutual. ◆**mutuellement** *adv* (*l'un l'autre*) each other (mutually).

myope [mjɔp] *a* & *nmf* shortsighted (person). ◆**myopie** *nf* shortsightedness.

myosotis [mjɔzɔtis] *nm Bot* forget-me-not.

myrtille [mirtij] *nf Bot* bilberry.

mystère [mister] *nm* mystery. ◆**mystérieux, -euse** *a* mysterious.

mystifier [mistifje] *vt* to fool, deceive, hoax. ◆**mystification** *nf* hoax.

mystique [mistik] *a* mystic(al); – *nmf* (*personne*) mystic; – *nf* mystique (**de** of). ◆**mysticisme** *nm* mysticism.

mythe [mit] *nm* myth. ◆**mythique** *a* mythical. ◆**mythologie** *nf* mythology. ◆**mythologique** *a* mythological.

mythomane [mitɔman] *nmf* compulsive liar.

N

N, n [ɛn] *nm* N, n.

n' [n] *voir* ne.

nabot [nabo] *nm Péj* midget.

nacelle [nasɛl] *nf* (*de ballon*) car, gondola; (*de landau*) carriage, carrycot.

nacre [nakr] *nf* mother-of-pearl. ◆**nacré** *a* pearly.

nage [naʒ] *nf* (swimming) stroke; **n. libre** freestyle; **traverser à la n.** to swim across; **en n.** *Fig* sweating. ◆**nager** *vi* to swim; (*flotter*) to float; **je nage dans le bonheur** my happiness knows no bounds; **je nage complètement** (*je suis perdu*) *Fam* I'm all at sea; – *vt* (*crawl etc*) to swim. ◆**nageur, -euse** *nmf* swimmer.

nageoire [naʒwar] *nf* (*de poisson*) fin; (*de phoque*) flipper.

naguère [nagɛr] *adv Litt* not long ago.

naïf, -ïve [naif, -iv] *a* simple, naïve; – *nmf* (*jobard*) simpleton.

nain, naine [nɛ̃, nɛn] *nmf* dwarf; – *a* (*arbre, haricot*) dwarf-.

naissance [nɛsɑ̃s] *nf* birth; (*de bras, cou*) base; **donner n. à** *Fig* to give rise to; **de n.** from birth.

naître° [nɛtr] *vi* to be born; (*jour*) to dawn; (*sentiment, difficulté*) to arise (**de** from); **faire n.** (*soupçon, industrie etc*) to give rise to, create. ◆**naissant** *a* (*amitié etc*) incipient.

naïveté [naivte] *nf* simplicity, naïveté.

nant/ir [nɑ̃tir] *vt* **n. de** to provide with. ◆**—i** *a* & *nmf* (*riche*) affluent.

naphtaline [naftalin] *nf* mothballs.

nappe [nap] *nf* **1** table cloth. **2** (*d'eau*) sheet; (*de gaz, pétrole*) layer; (*de brouillard*) blanket. ◆**napperon** *nm* (soft) table mat; (*pour vase etc*) (soft) mat, cloth.

narcotique [narkɔtik] *a* & *nm* narcotic.

narguer [narge] *vt* to flout, mock.

narine [narin] *nf* nostril.

narquois [narkwa] *a* sneering.

narration [narasjɔ̃] *nf* (*récit, acte, art*) narration. ◆**narrateur, -trice** *nmf* narrator.

nasal, -aux [nazal, -o] *a* nasal.

naseau, -x [nazo] *nm* (*de cheval*) nostril.

nasiller [nazije] *vi* (*personne*) to speak with a twang; (*micro, radio*) to crackle. ◆**nasillard** *a* (*voix*) nasal; (*micro etc*) crackling.

natal, mpl -als [natal] *a* (*pays etc*) native; **sa maison natale** the house where he *ou* she was born. ◆**natalité** *nf* birthrate.

natation [natasjɔ̃] *nf* swimming.

natif, -ive [natif, -iv] *a* & *nmf* native; **être n. de** to be a native of.

nation [nasjɔ̃] *nf* nation; **les Nations Unies** the United Nations. ◆**national, -aux** *a* national; ◆**nationale** *nf* (*route*) trunk road, *Am* highway. ◆**nationaliser** *vt* to nationalize. ◆**nationaliste** *a Péj* nationalistic; – *nmf* nationalist. ◆**nationalité** *nf* nationality.

nativité [nativite] *nf Rel* nativity.

natte [nat] *nf* **1** (*de cheveux*) plait, *Am* braid. **2** (*tapis*) mat, (piece of) matting. ◆**natt/er** *vt* to plait, *Am* braid. ◆**—age** *nm* (*matière*) matting.

naturaliser [natyralize] *vt* (*personne*) *Pol* to naturalize. ◆**naturalisation** *nf* naturalization.

nature [natyr] *nf* (*monde naturel, caractère*) nature; **de toute n.** of every kind; **être de n. à** to be likely to; **payer en n.** *Fin* to pay in kind; **n. morte** (*tableau*) still life; **plus grand que n.** larger than life; – *a inv* (*omelette, yaourt etc*) plain; (*café*) black. ◆**natura-**

liste *nmf* naturalist. ◆**naturiste** *nmf* nudist, naturist.

naturel, -elle [natyrɛl] *a* natural; **mort naturelle** death from natural causes; — *nm* (*caractère*) nature; (*simplicité*) naturalness. ◆**naturellement** *adv* naturally.

naufrage [nofraʒ] *nm* (ship)wreck; (*ruine*) *Litt Fig* ruin; **faire n.** to be (ship)wrecked. ◆**naufragé, -ée** *a & nmf* shipwrecked (person).

nausée [noze] *nf* nausea, sickness. ◆**nauséabond** *a* nauseating, sickening.

nautique [notik] *a* nautical; (*sports, ski*) water-.

naval, mpl -als [naval] *a* naval; **constructions navales** shipbuilding.

navet [navɛ] *nm* **1** *Bot Culin* turnip. **2** (*film etc*) *Péj* flop, dud.

navette [navɛt] *nf* (*transport*) shuttle (service); **faire la n.** (*véhicule, personne etc*) to shuttle back and forth (**entre** between); **n. spatiale** space shuttle.

naviguer [navige] *vi* (*bateau*) to sail; (*piloter, voler*) to navigate. ◆**navigabilité** *nf* (*de bateau*) seaworthiness; (*d'avion*) airworthiness. ◆**navigable** *a* (*fleuve*) navigable. ◆**navigant** *a* **personnel n.** *Av* Nau crew. ◆**navigateur** *nm* *Av* navigator. ◆**navigation** *nf* (*pilotage*) navigation; (*trafic*) *Nau* shipping.

navire [navir] *nm* ship.

navr/er [navre] *vt* to upset (greatly), grieve. ◆**-ant** *a* upsetting. ◆**-é** *a* (*air*) grieved; **je suis n.** I'm (terribly) sorry (**de faire** to do).

nazi, -ie [nazi] *a & nmf* *Pol Hist* Nazi.

ne [n(ə)] (**n'** before vowel or mute h; used to form negative verb with **pas, jamais, que etc**) *adv* **1** (+ **pas**) not; **elle ne boit pas** she does not *ou* doesn't drink; **il n'ose (pas)** he doesn't dare; **n'importe** it doesn't matter. **2** (*with* **craindre, avoir peur** *etc*) **je crains qu'il ne parte** I'm afraid he'll leave.

né [ne] *a* born; **il est né** he was born; **née Dupont** née Dupont.

néanmoins [neɑ̃mwɛ] *adv* nevertheless, nonetheless.

néant [neɑ̃] *nm* nothingness, void; (*sur un formulaire*) = none.

nébuleux, -euse [nebylø, -øz] *a* hazy, nebulous.

nécessaire [neseser] *a* necessary; (*inéluctable*) inevitable; — *nm* **le n.** (*biens*) the necessities; **le strict n.** the bare necessities; **n. de couture** sewing box, workbox; **n. de toilette** sponge bag, dressing case; **faire le n.** to do what's necessary *ou* the necessary. ◆**né-**

cessairement *adv* necessarily; (*échouer etc*) inevitably. ◆**nécessité** *nf* necessity. ◆**nécessiter** *vt* to necessitate, require. ◆**nécessiteux, -euse** *a* needy.

nécrologie [nekrɔlɔʒi] *nf* obituary.

nectarine [nektarin] *nf* (*fruit*) nectarine.

néerlandais, -aise [neerlɑ̃dɛ, -ɛz] *a* Dutch; — *nmf* Dutchman, Dutchwoman; — *nm* (*langue*) Dutch.

nef [nɛf] *nf* (*d'église*) nave.

néfaste [nefast] *a* (*influence etc*) harmful (**à** to).

négatif, -ive [negatif, -iv] *a* negative; — *nm* *Phot* negative; — *nf* **répondre par la négative** to answer in the negative. ◆**négation** *nf* negation, denial (**de** of); *Gram* negation; (*mot*) negative.

négligeable [negliʒabl] *a* negligible.

négligent [negliʒɑ̃] *a* negligent, careless. ◆**négligemment** [-amɑ̃] *adv* negligently, carelessly. ◆**négligence** *nf* negligence, carelessness; (*faute*) (careless) error.

néglig/er [negliʒe] *vt* (*personne, conseil, travail etc*) to neglect; **n. de faire** to neglect to do; — **se n.** *vpr* (*négliger sa tenue ou sa santé*) to neglect oneself. ◆**-é** *a* (*tenue*) untidy, neglected; (*travail*) careless; — *nm* (*de tenue*) untidiness; (*vêtement*) negligee.

négoci/er [negɔsje] *vti* *Fin Pol* to negotiate. ◆**-ant, -ante** *nmf* merchant, trader. ◆**-able** *a* *Fin* negotiable. ◆**négociateur, -trice** *nmf* negotiator. ◆**négociation** *nf* negotiation.

nègre [nɛgr] **1** *a* (*art, sculpture etc*) Negro. **2** *nm* (*écrivain*) ghost writer.

neige [nɛʒ] *nf* snow; **n. fondue** sleet; **n. carbonique** dry ice. ◆**neiger** *v imp* to snow. ◆**neigeux, -euse** *a* snowy.

nénuphar [nenyfar] *nm* water lily.

néo [neo] *préf* neo-.

néon [neɔ̃] *nm* (*gaz*) neon; **au n.** (*éclairage etc*) neon-.

néophyte [neofit] *nmf* novice.

néo-zélandais, -aise [neozelɑ̃dɛ, -ɛz] *a* (*peuple etc*) New Zealand-; — *nmf* New Zealander.

nerf [nɛr] *nm* *Anat* nerve; **avoir du n.** (*vigueur*) *Fam* to have guts; **du n.!**, **un peu de n.!** buck up!; **ça me porte ou me tape sur les nerfs** it gets on my nerves; **être sur les nerfs** *Fig* to be keyed up *ou* het up. ◆**nerveux, -euse** *a* nervous; (*centre, cellule*) nerve-. ◆**nervosité** *nf* nervousness.

nervure [nɛrvyr] *nf* (*de feuille*) vein.

nescafé [nɛskafe] *nm* instant coffee.

n'est-ce pas? [nɛspɑ] *adv* isn't he?, don't

you? *etc*; **il fait beau, n'est-ce pas?** the weather's fine, isn't it?

net, nette [nɛt] **1** *a* (*conscience, idée, image, refus*) clear; (*coupure, linge*) clean; (*soigné*) neat; (*copie*) fair; – *adv* (*s'arrêter*) short, dead; (*tuer*) outright; (*parler*) plainly; (*refuser*) flat(ly); (*casser, couper*) clean. **2** *a* (*poids, prix etc*) Com net(t). ◆**nettement** *adv* clearly, plainly; (*sensiblement*) markedly. ◆**netteté** *nf* clearness; (*de travail*) neatness.

nettoyer [netwaje] *vt* to clean (up); (*plaie*) to cleanse, clean (up); (*vider, ruiner*) *Fam* to clean out. ◆**nettoiement** *nm* cleaning; **service du n.** refuse ou *Am* garbage collection. ◆**nettoyage** *nm* cleaning; **n. à sec** dry cleaning.

neuf¹, neuve [nœf, nœv] *a* new; **quoi de n.?** what's new(s)?; – *nm* **il y a du n.** there's been something new; **remettre à n.** to make as good as new.

neuf² [nœf] *a & nm* ([nœv] before **heures & ans**) nine. ◆**neuvième** *a & nmf* ninth.

neurasthénique [nørastenik] *a* depressed.

neutre [nøtr] **1** *a* (*pays, personne etc*) neutral; – *nm El* neutral. **2** *a & nm Gram* neuter. ◆**neutraliser** *vt* to neutralize. ◆**neutralité** *nf* neutrality.

neveu, -x [nəvø] *nm* nephew.

névralgie [nevralʒi] *nf* headache; *Méd* neuralgia. ◆**névralgique** *a* **centre n.** *Fig* nerve centre.

névrose [nevroz] *nf* neurosis. ◆**névrosé, -ée** *a & nmf* neurotic.

nez [ne] *nm* nose; **n. à n.** face to face (**avec** with); **au n. de qn** (*rire etc*) in s.o.'s face; **mettre le n. dehors** *Fam* to stick one's nose outside.

ni [ni] *conj* **ni . . . ni** (+ *ne*) neither . . . nor; **il n'a ni faim ni soif** he's neither hungry nor thirsty; **sans manger ni boire** without eating or drinking; **ni l'un(e) ni l'autre** neither (of them).

niais, -aise [njɛ, -ɛz] *a* silly, simple; – *nmf* simpleton. ◆**niaiserie** *nf* silliness; *pl* (*paroles*) nonsense.

niche [niʃ] *nf* (*de chien*) kennel; (*cavité*) niche, recess.

nich/er [niʃe] *vi* (*oiseau*) to nest; (*loger*) *Fam* to hang out; – **se n.** *vpr* (*oiseau*) to nest; (*se cacher*) to hide oneself. ◆**-ée** *nf* (*oiseaux, enfants*) brood; (*chiens*) litter.

nickel [nikɛl] *nm* (*métal*) nickel.

nicotine [nikɔtin] *nf* nicotine.

nid [ni] *nm* nest; **n. de poules** *Aut* pothole.

nièce [njɛs] *nf* niece.

nième [ɛnjɛm] *a* nth.

nier [nje] *vt* to deny (**que** that); – *vi Jur* to deny the charge.

nigaud, -aude [nigo, -od] *a* silly; – *nmf* silly fool.

Nigéria [niʒerja] *nm ou f* Nigeria.

n'importe [nɛ̃pɔrt] *voir* **importer 1**.

nippon, -one *ou* **-onne** [nipɔ̃, -ɔn] *a* Japanese.

niveau, -x [nivo] *nm* (*hauteur*) level; (*degré, compétence*) standard, level; **n. de vie** standard of living; **n. à bulle (d'air)** spirit level; **au n. de qn** (*élève etc*) up to s.o.'s standard. ◆**niveler** *vt* (*surface*) to level; (*fortunes etc*) to even (up).

noble [nɔbl] *a* noble; – *nmf* nobleman, noblewoman. ◆**noblement** *adv* nobly. ◆**noblesse** *nf* (*caractère, classe*) nobility.

noce(s) [nɔs] *nf(pl)* wedding; **faire la noce** *Fam* to have a good time, make merry; **noces d'argent/d'or** silver/golden wedding. ◆**noceur, -euse** *nmf Fam* fast liver, reveller.

nocif, -ive [nɔsif, -iv] *a* harmful. ◆**nocivité** *nf* harmfulness.

noctambule [nɔktɑ̃byl] *nmf* (*personne*) night bird *ou* prowler. ◆**nocturne** *a* nocturnal, night-; – *nm* (*de magasins etc*) late night opening; (**match en**) **n.** *Sp* floodlit match, *Am* night game.

Noël [nɔɛl] *nm* Christmas; **le père N.** Father Christmas, Santa Claus.

nœud [nø] *nm* **1** knot; (*ruban*) bow; **le n. du problème/etc** the crux of the problem/etc; **n. coulant** noose, slipknot. **n. papillon** bow tie. **2** (*mesure*) *Nau* knot.

noir, noire [nwar] *a* black; (*nuit, lunettes etc*) dark; (*idées*) gloomy; (*âme, crime*) vile; (*misère*) dire; **roman n.** thriller; **film n.** film noir; **il fait n.** it's dark; – *nm* (*couleur*) black; (*obscurité*) dark; **N.** (*homme*) black; **vendre au n.** to sell on the black market; – *nf Mus* crotchet, *Am* quarter note; **Noire** (*femme*) black. ◆**noirceur** *nf* blackness; (*d'une action etc*) vileness. ◆**noircir** *vt* to blacken; – *vi*, – **se n.** *vpr* to turn black.

noisette [nwazɛt] *nf* hazelnut. ◆**noisetier** *nm* hazel (tree).

noix [nwa] *nf* (*du noyer*) walnut; **n. de coco** coconut; **n. du Brésil** Brazil nut; **n. de beurre** knob of butter; **à la n.** *Fam* trashy, awful.

nom [nɔ̃] *nm* name; *Gram* noun; **n. de famille** surname; **n. de jeune fille** maiden name; **n. propre** *Gram* proper noun; **au n. de qn** on s.o.'s behalf; **sans n.** (*anonyme*) nameless; (*vil*) vile; **n. d'un chien!** *Fam* oh hell!

nomade [nɔmad] *a* nomadic; – *nmf* nomad.

nombre [nɔ̃br] *nm* number; **ils sont au** *ou* **du n. de** (*parmi*) they're among; **ils sont au n. de dix** there are ten of them; **elle est au n. de dix** she's one of; **le plus grand n. de** the majority of. ◆**nombreux, -euse** *a* (*amis, livres etc*) numerous; (*famille, collection etc*) large; **peu n.** few; **venir n.** to come in large numbers.

nombril [nɔ̃bri] *nm* navel.

nominal, -aux [nɔminal, -o] *a* nominal. ◆**nomination** *nf* appointment, nomination.

nommer [nɔme] *vt* (*appeler*) to name; **n. qn** (*désigner*) to appoint s.o. (**à un poste**/*etc* tó a post/*etc*); **n. qn président/lauréat** to nominate s.o. chairman/prizewinner; **—se n.** *vpr* (*s'appeler*) to be called. ◆**nommément** *adv* by name.

non [nɔ̃] *adv* & *nm inv* no; **n.!** no!; **tu viens ou n.?** are you coming or not?; **n. seulement** not only; **n. (pas) que** (+ *sub*) . . . not that . . . ; **c'est bien, n.?** *Fam* it's all right, isn't it?; **je crois que n.** I don't think so; **(ni) moi n.** plus neither do, am, can *etc* I; **une place n. réservée** an unreserved seat.

non- [nɔ̃] *préf* non-.

nonante [nɔnɑ̃t] *a* (*en Belgique, en Suisse*) ninety.

nonchalant [nɔ̃ʃalɑ̃] *a* nonchalant, apathetic. ◆**nonchalance** *nf* nonchalance, apathy.

non-conformiste [nɔ̃kɔ̃fɔrmist] *a* & *nmf* nonconformist.

non-fumeur, -euse [nɔ̃fymœr, -øz] *nmf* non-smoker.

non-sens [nɔ̃sɑ̃s] *nm inv* absurdity.

nord [nɔr] *nm* north; **au n. de** north of; **du n.** (*vent, direction*) northerly; (*ville*) northern; (*gens*) from *ou* in the north; **Amérique/Afrique/du N.** North America/Africa; **l'Europe du N.** Northern Europe; – *a inv* (*côte*) north(ern). ◆**n.-africain, -aine** *a* & *nmf* North African. ◆**n.-américain, -aine** *a* & *nmf* North American. ◆**n.-est** *nm* & *a inv* north-east. ◆**n.-ouest** *nm* & *a inv* north-west.

nordique [nɔrdik] *a* & *nmf* Scandinavian.

normal, -aux [nɔrmal, -o] *a* normal. ◆**normale** *nf* norm, normality; **au-dessus de la n.** above normal. ◆**normalement** *adv* normally. ◆**normaliser** *vt* (*uniformiser*) to standardize; (*relations etc*) to normalize.

normand, -ande [nɔrmɑ̃, -ɑ̃d] *a* & *nmf* Norman. ◆**Normandie** *nf* Normandy.

norme [nɔrm] *nf* norm.

Norvège [nɔrvɛʒ] *nf* Norway. ◆**norvégien, -ienne** *a* & *nmf* Norwegian; – *nm* (*langue*) Norwegian.

nos [no] *voir* **notre**.

nostalgie [nɔstalʒi] *nf* nostalgia. ◆**nostalgique** *a* nostalgic.

notable [nɔtabl] *a* (*fait etc*) notable; – *nm* (*personne*) notable. ◆**—ment** [-əmɑ̃] *adv* (*sensiblement*) notably.

notaire [nɔtɛr] *nm* solicitor, notary.

notamment [nɔtamɑ̃] *adv* notably.

note [nɔt] *nf* (*remarque etc*) & *Mus* note; (*chiffrée*) *Scol* mark, *Am* grade; (*compte, facture*) bill, *Am* check; **prendre n. de** to make a note of. ◆**noter** *vt* (*prendre note de*) to note; (*remarquer*) to note, notice; (*écrire*) to note down; (*devoir etc*) *Scol* to mark, *Am* grade; **être bien noté** (*personne*) to be highly rated.

notice [nɔtis] *nf* (*résumé, préface*) note; (*mode d'emploi*) instructions.

notifier [nɔtifje] *vt* **n. qch à qn** to notify s.o. of sth.

notion [nosjɔ̃] *nf* notion, idea; *pl* (*éléments*) rudiments.

notoire [nɔtwar] *a* (*criminel, bêtise*) notorious; (*fait*) well-known. ◆**notoriété** *nf* (*renom*) fame; (*fait*) general recognition.

notre, *pl* nos [nɔtr, no] *a poss* our. ◆**nôtre** *pron poss* **le** *ou* **la n., les nôtres** ours; – *nmpl* **les nôtres** (*parents etc*) our (own) people.

nouer [nwe] *vt* to tie, knot; (*amitié, conversation*) to strike up; **avoir la gorge nouée** to have a lump in one's throat. ◆**noueux, -euse** *a* (*bois*) knotty; (*doigts*) gnarled.

nougat [nuga] *nm* nougat.

nouille [nuj] *nf* (*idiot*) *Fam* drip.

nouilles [nuj] *nfpl* noodles.

nounours [nunurs] *nm* teddy bear.

nourrice [nuris] *nf* (*assistante maternelle*) child minder, nurse; (*qui allaite*) wet nurse; **mettre en n.** to put out to nurse.

nourr/ir [nurir] *vt* (*alimenter, faire vivre*) to feed; (*espoir etc*) *Fig* to nourish; (*esprit*) to enrich; **se n. de** to feed on; – *vi* (*aliment*) to be nourishing. ◆**—issant** *a* nourishing. ◆**nourriture** *nf* food.

nourrisson [nurisɔ̃] *nm* infant.

nous [nu] *pron* **1** (*sujet*) we; **n. sommes** we are. **2** (*complément direct*) us; **il n. connaît** he knows us. **3** (*indirect*) (to) us; **il n. l'a donné** he gave it to us, he gave us it. **4** (*réfléchi*) ourselves; **n. n. lavons** we wash ourselves. **5** (*réciproque*) each other;

n. n. **détestons** we hate each other. ◆**n.-mêmes** *pron* ourselves.

nouveau or **nouvel** *before vowel or mute h),* **nouvelle**[1], *pl* **nouveaux, nouvelles** [nuvo, nuvɛl] *a* new; – *nmf Scol* new boy, new girl; – *nm* **du n.** something new; **de n., à n.** again. ◆**n.-né, -ée** *a* & *nmf* new-born (baby). ◆**n.-venu** *nm,* ◆**nouvelle-venue** *nf* newcomer. ◆**nouveauté** *nf* newness, novelty; *pl (livres)* new books; *(disques)* new releases; *(vêtements)* new fashions; **une n.** *(objet)* a novelty.

nouvelle[2] [nuvɛl] *nf* **1 nouvelle(s)** news; **une n.** a piece of news. **2** *Littér* short story.

Nouvelle-Zélande [nuvɛlzelɑ̃d] *nf* New Zealand.

novateur, -trice [nɔvatœr, -tris] *nmf* innovator.

novembre [nɔvɑ̃br] *nm* November.

novice [nɔvis] *nmf* novice; – *a* inexperienced.

noyau, -x [nwajo] *nm (de fruit)* stone, *Am* pit; *(d'atome, de cellule)* nucleus; *(groupe)* group; **un n. d'opposants** a hard core of opponents.

noyaut/er [nwajote] *vt Pol* to infiltrate. ◆**—age** *nm* infiltration.

noy/er[1] [nwaje] *vt (personne etc)* to drown; *(terres)* to flood; – **se n.** *vpr* to drown; *(se suicider)* to drown oneself; **se n. dans le détail** to get bogged down in details. ◆**—é, -ée** *nmf (mort)* drowned person; – *a* **être n.** *(perdu) Fig* to be out of one's depth. ◆**noyade** *nf* drowning.

noyer[2] [nwaje] *nm (arbre)* walnut tree.

nu [ny] *a (personne, vérité)* naked; *(mains, chambre)* bare; **tout nu** (stark) naked, (in the) nude; **voir à l'œil nu** to see with the naked eye; **mettre à nu** *(exposer)* to lay bare; **se mettre nu** to strip off; **tête nue, nu-tête** bare-headed; – *nm (femme, homme, œuvre)* nude.

nuage [nɥaʒ] *nm* cloud; **un n. de lait** *Fig* a dash of milk. ◆**nuageux, -euse** *a (ciel)* cloudy.

nuance [nɥɑ̃s] *nf (de sens)* nuance; *(de couleurs)* shade, nuance; *(de regret)* tinge, nuance. ◆**nuanc/er** *vt (teintes)* to blend,

shade; *(pensée)* to qualify. ◆**—é** *a (jugement)* qualified.

nucléaire [nykleɛr] *a* nuclear.

nudisme [nydism] *nm* nudism. ◆**nudiste** *nmf* nudist. ◆**nudité** *nf* nudity, nakedness; *(de mur etc)* bareness.

nuée [nɥe] *nf* **une n. de** *(foule)* a host of; *(groupe compact)* a cloud of.

nues [ny] *nfpl* **porter qn aux n.** to praise s.o. to the skies.

nuire* [nɥir] *vi* **n. à** *(personne, intérêts etc)* to harm. ◆**nuisible** *a* harmful.

nuit [nɥi] *nf* night; *(obscurité)* dark(ness); **il fait n.** it's dark; **avant la n.** before nightfall; **la n.** *(se promener etc)* at night; **cette n.** *(aujourd'hui)* tonight; *(hier)* last night. ◆**nuitée** *nf* overnight stay *(in hotel etc).*

nul, nulle [nyl] **1** *a (risque etc)* non-existent, nil; *(médiocre)* useless, hopeless; *(non valable) Jur* null (and void); **faire match n.** *Sp* to tie, draw. **2** *a (aucun)* no; **de nulle importance** of no importance; **sans n. doute** without any doubt; **nulle part** nowhere; – *pron m (aucun)* no one. ◆**nullard, -arde** *nmf Fam* useless person. ◆**nullement** *adv* not at all. ◆**nullité** *nf (d'un élève etc)* uselessness; *(personne)* useless person.

numéraire [nymerɛr] *nm* cash, currency.

numéral, -aux [nymeral, -o] *a* & *nm* numeral. ◆**numérique** *a* numerical; *(montre etc)* digital.

numéro [nymero] *nm* number; *(de journal)* issue, number; *(au cirque)* act; **un n. de danse/de chant** a dance/song number; **quel n.!** *(personne) Fam* what a character!; **n. vert** *Tél* = Freefone®, = *Am* tollfree number. ◆**numérot/er** *vt (pages, sièges)* to number. ◆**—age** *nm* numbering.

nu-pieds [nypje] *nmpl* open sandals.

nuptial, -aux [nypsjal, -o] *a (chambre)* bridal; *(anneau, cérémonie)* wedding-.

nuque [nyk] *nf* back ou nape of the neck.

nurse [nœrs] *nf* nanny, (children's) nurse.

nutritif, -ive [nytritif, -iv] *a* nutritious, nutritive. ◆**nutrition** *nf* nutrition.

nylon [nilɔ̃] *nm (fibre)* nylon.

nymphe [nɛ̃f] *nf* nymph. ◆**nymphomane** *nf Péj* nymphomaniac.

O

O, o [o] *nm* O, o.

oasis [ɔazis] *nf* oasis.

obédience [ɔbedjɑ̃s] *nf Pol* allegiance.

obé/ir [ɔbeir] *vi* to obey; **o. à qn/qch** to obey s.o./sth; **être obéi** to be obeyed. ◆**—issant** *a* obedient. ◆**obéissance** *nf* obedience (à to).

obélisque [ɔbelisk] *nm* (*monument*) obelisk.

obèse [ɔbɛz] *a* & *nmf* obese (person). ◆**obésité** *nf* obesity.

objecter [ɔbʒɛkte] *vt* (*prétexte*) to put forward, plead; **o. que** to object that; **on lui objecta son jeune âge** they objected that he *ou* she was too young. ◆**objecteur** *nm* **o. de conscience** conscientious objector. ◆**objection** *nf* objection.

objectif, -ive [ɔbʒɛktif, -iv] **1** *a* (*opinion etc*) objective. **2** *nm* (*but*) objective; *Phot* lens. ◆**objectivement** *adv* objectively. ◆**objectivité** *nf* objectivity.

objet [ɔbʒɛ] *nm* (*chose, sujet, but*) object; (*de toilette*) article; **faire l'o. de** (*étude, critiques etc*) to be the subject of; (*soins, surveillance*) to be given, receive; **objets trouvés** (*bureau*) lost property, *Am* lost and found.

obligation [ɔbligasjɔ̃] *nf* (*devoir, lieu, nécessité*) obligation; *Fin* bond. ◆**obligatoire** *a* compulsory, obligatory; (*inévitable*) *Fam* inevitable. ◆**obligatoirement** *adv* (*fatalement*) inevitably; **tu dois o. le faire** you have to do it.

oblig/er [ɔbliʒe] *vt* **1** (*contraindre*) to compel, oblige (à faire to do); (*engager*) to bind; **être obligé de faire** to have to do, be compelled *ou* obliged to do. **2** (*rendre service à*) to oblige; **être obligé à qn de qch** to be obliged to s.o. for sth. ◆**—eant** *a* obliging, kind. ◆**—é** *a* (*obligatoire*) necessary; (*fatal*) *Fam* inevitable. ◆**obligeamment** [-amɑ̃] *adv* obligingly. ◆**obligeance** *nf* kindness.

oblique [ɔblik] *a* oblique; **regard o.** sidelong glance; **en o.** at an (oblique) angle. ◆**obliquer** *vi* (*véhicule etc*) to turn off.

oblitérer [ɔblitere] *vt* (*timbre*) to cancel; (*billet, carte*) to stamp; **timbre oblitéré** (*non neuf*) used stamp. ◆**oblitération** *nf* cancellation; stamping.

oblong, -ongue [ɔblɔ̃, -ɔ̃g] *a* oblong.

obnubilé [ɔbnybile] *a* (*obsédé*) obsessed (par with).

obscène [ɔpsɛn] *a* obscene. ◆**obscénité** *nf* obscenity.

obscur [ɔpskyr] *a* (*noir*) dark; (*peu clair, inconnu, humble*) obscure. ◆**obscurcir** *vt* (*chambre etc*) to darken; (*rendre peu intelligible*) to obscure (*text, ideas etc*); **— s'o.** *vpr* (*ciel*) to cloud over, darken; (*vue*) to become dim. ◆**obscurément** *adv* obscurely. ◆**obscurité** *nf* dark(ness); (*de texte, d'acteur etc*) obscurity.

obsédé/er [ɔpsede] *vt* to obsess, haunt. ◆**—ant** *a* haunting, obsessive. ◆**—é, -ée** *nmf* maniac (de for); **o. sexuel** sex maniac.

obsèques [ɔpsɛk] *nfpl* funeral.

obséquieux, -euse [ɔpsekjø, -øz] *a* obsequious.

observer [ɔpsɛrve] *vt* (*regarder*) to observe, watch; (*remarquer, respecter*) to observe; **faire o. qch à qn** (*signaler*) to point sth out to s.o. ◆**observateur, -trice** *a* observant; **— *nmf*** observer. ◆**observation** *nf* (*examen, remarque*) observation; (*reproche*) (critical) remark, rebuke; (*de règle etc*) observance; **en o.** (*malade*) under observation. ◆**observatoire** *nm* observatory; (*colline etc*) *Fig* & *Mil* observation post.

obsession [ɔpsesjɔ̃] *nf* obsession. ◆**obsessif, -ive** (*peur etc*) obsessive. ◆**obsessionnel, -elle** *a Psy* obsessive.

obstacle [ɔpstakl] *nm* obstacle; **faire o. à** to stand in the way of.

obstétrique [ɔpstetrik] *nf Méd* obstetrics.

obstin/er (s') [sɔpstine] *vpr* to be obstinate *ou* persistent; **s'o. à faire** to persist in doing. ◆**—é** *a* stubborn, obstinate, persistent. ◆**obstination** *nf* stubbornness, obstinacy, persistence.

obstruction [ɔpstryksjɔ̃] *nf Méd Pol Sp* obstruction; **faire de l'o.** *Pol Sp* to be obstructive. ◆**obstruer** *vt* to obstruct.

obtempérer [ɔptɑ̃pere] *vi* to obey an injunction; **o. à** to obey.

obtenir* [ɔptənir] *vt* to get, obtain, secure. ◆**obtention** *nf* obtaining, getting.

obturer [ɔptyre] *vt* (*trou etc*) to stop *ou* close up. ◆**obturateur** *nm Phot* shutter; *Tech* valve.

obtus [ɔpty] *a* (*angle, esprit*) obtuse.

obus [ɔby] nm Mil shell.

occasion [ɔkazjɔ̃] nf 1 (chance) opportunity, chance (**de faire** to do); (circonstance) occasion; **à l'o.** on occasion, when the occasion arises; **à l'o. de** on the occasion of. 2 Com (marché avantageux) bargain; (objet non neuf) second-hand buy; **d'o.** second-hand, used. ◆**occasionner** vt to cause; **o. qch à qn** to cause s.o. sth.

occident [ɔksidɑ̃] nm **l'O.** Pol the West. ◆**occidental, -aux** a Géog Pol western; – nmpl **les occidentaux** Pol Westerners. ◆**occidentalisé** a Pol Westernized.

occulte [ɔkylt] a occult.

occup/er [ɔkype] vt (maison, pays, usine etc) to occupy; (place, temps) to take up, occupy; (poste) to hold, occupy; **o. qn** (absorber) to occupy s.o., keep s.o. busy; (ouvrier etc) to employ s.o.; – **s'o.** vpr to keep (oneself) busy (**à faire** doing); **s'o. de** (affaire, problème etc) to deal with; (politique) to be engaged in; **s'o. de qn** (malade etc) to take care of s.o.; (client) to see to s.o., deal with s.o.; **ne t'en occupe pas!** (ne t'en fais pas) don't worry!; (ne t'en mêle pas) mind your own business! ◆**-ant, -ante** a (armée) occupying; – nmf (habitant) occupant; – nm Mil forces of occupation, occupier. ◆**-é** a busy (**à faire** doing); (place, maison etc) occupied; (ligne) Tél engaged, Am busy; (taxi) hired. ◆**occupation** nf (activité, travail etc) occupation; **l'o. de** (action) the occupation of.

occurrence [ɔkyrɑ̃s] nf Ling occurrence; **en l'o.** in the circumstances, as it happens ou happened.

océan [ɔseɑ̃] nm ocean. ◆**océanique** a oceanic.

ocre [ɔkr] nm & a inv (couleur) ochre.

octave [ɔktav] nf Mus octave.

octobre [ɔktɔbr] nm October.

octogénaire [ɔktɔʒenɛr] nmf octogenarian.

octogone [ɔktɔgɔn] nm octagon. ◆**octogonal, -aux** a octagonal.

octroi [ɔktrwa] nm Litt granting. ◆**octroyer** vt Litt to grant (**à** to).

oculaire [ɔkylɛr] a **témoin o.** eyewitness; **globe o.** eyeball. ◆**oculiste** nmf eye specialist.

ode [ɔd] nf (poème) ode.

odeur [ɔdœr] nf smell; (de fleur) scent. ◆**odorant** a sweet-smelling. ◆**odorat** nm sense of smell.

odieux, -euse [ɔdjø, -øz] a odious, obnoxious.

œcuménique [ekymenik] a Rel (o)ecumenical.

œil, pl **yeux** [œj, jø] nm eye; **sous mes yeux** before my very eyes; **lever/baisser les yeux** to look up/down; **fermer l'o.** (dormir) to shut one's eyes; **fermer les yeux sur** to turn a blind eye to; **ouvre l'o.!** keep your eyes open!; **coup d'o.** (regard) glance, look; **jeter un coup d'o. sur** to (have a) look ou glance at; **à vue d'o.** visibly; **faire les gros yeux à** to scowl at; **avoir à l'o.** (surveiller) to keep an eye on; **à l'o.** (gratuitement) Fam free; **faire de l'o. à** Fam to make eyes at; **o. au beurre noir** Fig black eye; **mon o.!** Fam (incrédulité) my foot!; (refus) no way!, no chance!

œillade [œjad] nf (clin d'œil) wink.

œillères [œjɛr] nfpl (de cheval) & Fig blinkers, Am blinders.

œillet [œjɛ] nm 1 Bot carnation. 2 (trou de ceinture) eyelet.

œuf, pl **œufs** [œf, ø] nm egg; pl (de poisson) (hard) roe; **o. sur le plat** fried egg; **étouffer qch dans l'o.** Fig to nip ou stifle sth in the bud.

œuvre [œvr] nf (travail, acte, livre etc) work; **o.** (de charité) (organisation) charity; **l'o. de** (production artistique etc) the works of; **mettre en o.** (employer) to make use of; **mettre tout en o.** to do everything possible (**pour faire** to do). ◆**œuvrer** vi Litt to work.

offense [ɔfɑ̃s] nf insult; Rel transgression. ◆**offens/er** vt to offend; **s'o. de** to take offence at. ◆**-ant** a offensive.

offensif, -ive [ɔfɑ̃sif, -iv] a offensive; – nf (attaque) offensive; (du froid) onslaught.

offert [ɔfɛr] voir **offrir**.

office [ɔfis] 1 nm (fonction) office; (bureau) office, bureau; **d'o.** (être promu etc) automatically; **faire o. de** to serve as; **ses bons offices** (service) one's good offices. 2 nm Rel service. 3 nm ou f (pièce pour provisions) pantry.

officiel, -ielle [ɔfisjɛl] a (acte etc) official; – nm (personnage) official. ◆**officiellement** adv officially. ◆**officieux, -euse** a unofficial.

officier [ɔfisje] 1 vi Rel to officiate. 2 nm (dans l'armée etc) officer.

offre [ɔfr] nf offer; (aux enchères) bid; **l'o. et la demande** Écon supply and demand; **offres d'emploi** Journ situations vacant. ◆**offrande** nf offering.

offr/ir [ɔfrir] vt (proposer, présenter) to offer (**de faire** to do); (donner en cadeau) to give; (démission) to tender, offer; **je lui ai offert de le loger** I offered to put him up; – **s'o.** vpr (cadeau etc) to treat oneself to; (se *proposer*) to offer oneself (**comme** as); **s'o. à faire** to offer *ou* volunteer to do; **s'o. (aux yeux)** (*vue etc*) to present itself. ◆**—ant au plus o.** to the highest bidder.

offusquer [ɔfyske] *vt* to offend, shock; **s'o. de** to take offence at.

ogive [ɔʒiv] *nf* (*de fusée*) nose cone; **o. nucléaire** nuclear warhead.

ogre [ɔgr] *nm* ogre.

oh! [o] *int* oh!, o!

ohé! [ɔe] *int* hey (there)!

oie [wa] *nf* goose.

oignon [ɔɲɔ̃] *nm* (*légume*) onion; (*de tulipe, lis etc*) bulb; **occupe-toi de tes oignons!** *Fam* mind your own business!

oiseau, -x [wazo] *nm* bird; **à vol d'o.** as the crow flies; **drôle d'o.** (*individu*) *Péj* odd fish, *Am* oddball; **o. rare** (*personne étonnante*) *Iron* rare bird, perfect gem.

oiseux, -euse [wazø, -øz] *a* (*futile*) idle, vain.

oisif, -ive [wazif, -iv] *a* (*inactif*) idle; — *nmf* idler. ◆**oisiveté** *nf* idleness.

oléoduc [ɔleɔdyk] *nm* oil pipeline.

olive [ɔliv] *nf* (*fruit*) olive; **huile d'o.** olive oil; — *a inv* (*couleur*) (**vert**) **o.** olive (green). ◆**olivier** *nm* (*arbre*) olive tree.

olympique [ɔlɛ̃pik] *a* (*jeux, record etc*) Olympic.

ombilical, -aux [ɔ̃bilikal, -o] *a* (*cordon*) umbilical.

ombrage [ɔ̃braʒ] *nm* **1** (*ombre*) shade. **2 prendre o. de** (*jalousie, dépit*) to take umbrage at. ◆**ombrager** *vt* to give shade to. ◆**—é** *a* shady. ◆**ombrageux, -euse** *a* (*caractère, personne*) touchy.

ombre [ɔ̃br] *nf* (*d'arbre etc*) shade; (*de personne, objet*) shadow; **l'o. d'un doute** *Fig* the shadow of a doubt; **l'o. de** (*remords, reproche etc*) the trace of; **30° à l'o.** 30° in the shade; **dans l'o.** (*comploter, travailler etc*) in secret.

ombrelle [ɔ̃brɛl] *nf* sunshade, parasol.

omelette [ɔmlɛt] *nf* omelet(te); **o. au fromage**/*etc* cheese/*etc* omelet(te).

omettre* [ɔmɛtr] *vt* to omit (**de faire** to do). ◆**omission** *nf* omission.

omni- [ɔmni] *préf* omni-. ◆**omnipotent** *a* omnipotent.

omnibus [ɔmnibys] *a* & *nm* (**train**) **o.** slow train (*stopping at all stations*).

omoplate [ɔmɔplat] *nf* shoulder blade.

on [ɔ̃] (*sometimes* **l'on** [lɔ̃]) *pron* (*les gens*) they, people; (*nous*) we, one; (*vous*) you, one; **on dit** they say, people say, it is said; **on frappe** (*quelqu'un*) someone's knocking;

on me l'a donné it was given to me, I was given it.

once [ɔ̃s] *nf* (*mesure*) & *Fig* ounce.

oncle [ɔ̃kl] *nm* uncle.

onctueux, -euse [ɔ̃ktɥø, -øz] *a* (*liquide, crème*) creamy; (*manières, paroles*) *Fig* smooth.

onde [ɔ̃d] *nf* *Phys Rad* wave; **grandes ondes** long wave; **ondes courtes/moyennes** short/medium wave; **sur les ondes** (*sur l'antenne*) on the radio.

ondée [ɔ̃de] *nf* (*pluie*) (sudden) shower.

on-dit [ɔ̃di] *nm inv* rumour, hearsay.

ondoyer [ɔ̃dwaje] *vi* to undulate. ◆**ondulation** *nf* undulation; (*de cheveux*) wave. ◆**onduler** *vi* to undulate; (*cheveux*) to be wavy. ◆**—é** *a* wavy.

onéreux, -euse [ɔnerø, -øz] *a* costly.

ongle [ɔ̃gl] *nm* (finger) nail.

onglet [ɔ̃glɛ] *nm* (*entaille de canif etc*) (nail) groove.

ont [ɔ̃] *voir* **avoir**.

ONU [ɔny] *nf abrév* (*Organisation des nations unies*) UN.

onyx [ɔniks] *nm* (*pierre précieuse*) onyx.

onze [ɔ̃z] *a* & *nm* eleven. ◆**onzième** *a* & *nmf* eleventh.

opale [ɔpal] *nf* (*pierre*) opal.

opaque [ɔpak] *a* opaque. ◆**opacité** *nf* opacity.

opéra [ɔpera] *nm* (*ouvrage, art*) opera; (*édifice*) opera house. ◆**opérette** *nf* operetta.

opér/er [ɔpere] **1** *vt* (*exécuter*) to carry out; (*choix*) to make; (*—y*) (*agir*) to work, act; (*procéder*) to proceed; — **s'o.** *vpr* (*se produire*) to take place. **2** *vt* (*personne, organe*) *Méd* to operate on (**de** for); (*tumeur*) to remove; **cela peut s'o.** this can be removed; **se faire o.** to have an operation; — *vi* (*chirurgien*) to operate. ◆**—ant** *a* (*efficace*) operative. ◆**—é, -ée** *nmf* *Méd* patient (*operated on*). ◆**opérateur, -trice** *nmf* (*de prise de vues*) *Cin* cameraman; (*sur machine*) operator. ◆**opération** *nf* (*acte*) & *Méd Mil Math etc* operation; *Fin* deal. ◆**opérationnel, -elle** *a* operational. ◆**opératoire** *a* *Méd* operative; **bloc o.** operating *ou* surgical wing.

opiner [ɔpine] *vi* (**o. de la tête** *ou* **du chef**) to nod assent.

opiniâtre [ɔpinjɑtr] *a* stubborn, obstinate. ◆**opiniâtreté** *nf* stubbornness, obstinacy.

opinion [ɔpinjɔ̃] *nf* opinion (**sur** about, on).

opium [ɔpjɔm] *nm* opium.

opportun [ɔpɔrtœ̃] *a* opportune, timely. ◆**opportunément** *adv* opportunely.

◆**opportunisme** *nm* opportunism. ◆**opportunité** *nf* timeliness.

oppos/er [ɔpoze] *vt* (*argument, résistance*) to put up (à against); (*équipes, rivaux*) to bring together, set against each other; (*objets*) to place opposite each other; (*couleurs*) to contrast; **o. qch à qch** (*objet*) to place sth opposite sth; **qn à qn** to set s.o. against s.o.; **match qui oppose ...** match between ...; **– s'o.** (*couleurs*) to contrast; (*équipes*) to confront each other; **s'o. à** (*mesure, personne etc*) to oppose, be opposed to; **je m'y oppose** I'm opposed to it, I oppose. ◆**–ant, -ante** opposing; – *nmf* opponent. ◆**–é** *a* (*direction etc*) opposite; (*intérêts, équipe*) opposing; (*opinions*) opposite, opposing; (*couleurs*) contrasting; **être o. à** to be opposed to; – *nm* **l'o.** the opposite (**de** of); **à l'o.** (*côté*) on the opposite side (**de** from, to); **à l'o. de** (*contrairement à*) contrary to. ◆**opposition** *nf* opposition; **faire o. à** to oppose; **par o. à** as opposed to.

oppress/er [ɔprese] *vt* (*gêner*) to oppress. ◆**–ant** *a* oppressive. ◆**–eur** *nm* Pol oppressor. ◆**oppressive, -ive** *a* (*loi etc*) oppressive. ◆**oppression** *nf* oppression. ◆**opprim/er** *vt* (*tyranniser*) to oppress. ◆**–és** *nmpl* les o. the oppressed.

opter [ɔpte] *vi* **o. pour** to opt for.

opticien, -ienne [ɔptisjɛ̃, -jɛn] *nmf* optician.

optimisme [ɔptimism] *nm* optimism. ◆**optimiste** *a* optimistic; – *nmf* optimist.

optimum [ɔptimɔm] *nm* & *a* optimum; **la température o.** the optimum temperature. ◆**optimal, -aux** *a* optimal.

option [ɔpsjɔ̃] *nf* (*choix*) option; (*chose*) optional extra.

optique [ɔptik] *a* (*verre*) optical; – *nf* optics; (*aspect*) Fig perspective; **d'o.** (*illusion, instrument etc*) optical.

opulent [ɔpylɑ̃] *a* opulent. ◆**opulence** *nf* opulence.

or [ɔr] **1** *nm* gold; **en or** (*chaîne etc*) gold-; **d'or** (*cheveux, âge, règle*) golden; (*cœur*) of gold; **mine d'or** Géol goldmine; (*fortune*) Fig goldmine; **affaire en or** (*achat*) bargain; (*commerce*) Fig goldmine; **or noir** (*pétrole*) Fig black gold. **2** *conj* (*alors, cependant*) now, well.

oracle [ɔrakl] *nm* oracle.

orage [ɔraʒ] *nm* (*thunder*)storm. ◆**orageux, -euse** *a* stormy.

oraison [ɔrɛzɔ̃] *nf* prayer; **o. funèbre** funeral oration.

oral, -aux [ɔral, -o] *a* oral; – *nm* (*examen*) Scol oral.

orange [ɔrɑ̃ʒ] *nf* (*fruit*) orange; **o. pressée** (fresh) orange juice; – *a* & *nm inv* (*couleur*) orange. ◆**orangé** *a* & *nm* (*couleur*) orange. ◆**orangeade** *nf* orangeade. ◆**oranger** *nm* orange tree.

orang-outan(g) [ɔrɑ̃utɑ̃] *nm* (*pl* **orangs-outan(g)s**) orang-outang.

orateur [ɔratœr] *nm* speaker, orator.

orbite [ɔrbit] *nf* (*d'astre etc*) & Fig orbit; (*d'œil*) socket; **mettre sur o.** (*fusée etc*) to put into orbit.

orchestre [ɔrkɛstr] *nm* (*classique*) orchestra; (*moderne*) band; (*places*) Th stalls, Am orchestra. ◆**orchestrer** *vt* (*organiser*) & Mus to orchestrate.

orchidée [ɔrkide] *nf* orchid.

ordinaire [ɔrdinɛr] *a* (*habituel, normal*) ordinary, Am regular; (*médiocre*) ordinary, average; **d'o., à l'o.** usually; **comme d'o., comme à l'o.** as usual; **de l'essence o.** two-star (petrol), Am regular. ◆**–ment** *adv* usually.

ordinal, -aux [ɔrdinal, -o] *a* (*nombre*) ordinal.

ordinateur [ɔrdinatœr] *nm* computer.

ordination [ɔrdinasjɔ̃] *nf* Rel ordination.

ordonnance [ɔrdɔnɑ̃s] *nf* **1** (*de médecin*) prescription. **2** (*décret*) Jur order, ruling. **3** (*disposition*) arrangement. **4** (*soldat*) orderly.

ordonn/er [ɔrdɔne] *vt* **1** (*enjoindre*) to order (**que** (+ *sub*) that); **o. à qn de faire** to order s.o. to do. **2** (*agencer*) to arrange, order. **3** (*médicament etc*) to prescribe. **4** (*prêtre*) to ordain. ◆**–é** *a* (*personne, maison etc*) orderly.

ordre [ɔrdr] *nm* (*commandement, structure, association etc*) order; (*absence de désordre*) tidiness (*of room, person etc*); **en o.** (*chambre etc*) tidy; **mettre en o., mettre de l'o. dans** to tidy (up); **de premier o.** first-rate; **o.** (*public*) (law and) order; **par o. d'âge** in order of age; **à l'o. du jour** (*au programme*) on the agenda; (*d'actualité*) of topical interest; **les forces de l'o.** the police; **jusqu'à nouvel o.** until further notice; **de l'o. de** (*environ*) of the order of.

ordure [ɔrdyr] *nf* filth, muck; *pl* (*débris*) refuse, rubbish, Am garbage. ◆**ordurier, -ière** *a* (*plaisanterie etc*) lewd.

oreille [ɔrɛj] *nf* ear; **être tout oreilles** to be all ears; **faire la sourde o.** to turn a deaf ear; **casser les oreilles à qn** to deafen s.o.

oreiller [ɔreje] *nm* pillow.

oreillons [ɔrɛjɔ̃] *nmpl* Méd mumps.

ores (d') [dɔr] *adv* **d'ores et déjà** [dɔrzedeʒa] henceforth.

orfèvre [ɔrfɛvr] nm goldsmith, silversmith. ◆**orfèvrerie** nf (magasin) goldsmith's ou silversmith's shop; (objets) gold ou silver plate.

organe [ɔrgan] nm Anat & Fig organ; (porte-parole) mouthpiece. ◆**organique** a organic. ◆**organisme** nm **1** (corps) body; Anat Biol organism. **2** (bureaux etc) organization.

organisation [ɔrganizasjɔ̃] nf (arrangement, association) organization.

organis/er [ɔrganize] vt to organize; — **s'o.** vpr to organize oneself, get organized. ◆**—é** a (esprit, groupe etc) organized. ◆**organisateur, -trice** nmf organizer.

organiste [ɔrganist] nmf Mus organist.

orgasme [ɔrgasm] nm orgasm.

orge [ɔrʒ] nf barley.

orgie [ɔrʒi] nf orgy.

orgue [ɔrg] nm Mus organ; **o. de Barbarie** barrel organ; — nfpl organ; **grandes orgues** great organ.

orgueil [ɔrgœj] nm pride. ◆**orgueilleux, -euse** a proud.

orient [ɔrjɑ̃] nm l'O. the Orient, the East; **Moyen-O., Proche-O.** Middle East; **Extrême-O.** Far East. ◆**oriental, -ale, -aux** a eastern; (de l'Orient) oriental; — nmf oriental.

orient/er [ɔrjɑ̃te] vt (lampe, antenne etc) to position, direct; (voyageur, élève etc) to direct; (maison) to orientate, Am orient; — **s'o.** vpr to find one's bearings ou direction; **s'o. vers** (carrière etc) to move towards. ◆**—é** a (ouvrage, film etc) slanted. ◆**orientable** a (lampe etc) adjustable, flexible; (bras de machine) movable. ◆**orientation** nf direction; (action) positioning, directing; (de maison) aspect, orientation; (tendance) Pol Littér trend; **o. professionnelle** vocational guidance.

orifice [ɔrifis] nm opening, orifice.

originaire [ɔriʒinɛr] a **être o. de** (natif) to be a native of.

original, -ale, -aux [ɔriʒinal, -o] **1** a (idée, artiste, version etc) original; — nm (modèle) original. **2** a & nmf (bizarre) eccentric. ◆**originalité** nf originality; eccentricity.

origine [ɔriʒin] nf origin; **à l'o.** originally; **d'o.** (pneu etc) original; **pays d'o.** country of origin. ◆**originel, -elle** a (sens, péché, habitant etc) original.

orme [ɔrm] nm (arbre, bois) elm.

ornement [ɔrnəmɑ̃] nm ornament. ◆**ornemental, -aux** a ornamental. ◆**ornementation** nf ornamentation. ◆**ornementé** a

adorned, ornamented (de with). ◆**orn/er** vt to decorate, adorn (de with). ◆**—é** a (syle etc) ornate.

ornière [ɔrnjɛr] nf (sillon) & Fig rut.

orphelin, -ine [ɔrfəlɛ̃, -in] nmf orphan; — a orphaned. ◆**orphelinat** nm orphanage.

orteil [ɔrtɛj] nm toe; **gros o.** big toe.

orthodoxe [ɔrtɔdɔks] a orthodox; — nmpl **les orthodoxes** the orthodox. ◆**orthodoxie** nf orthodoxy.

orthographe [ɔrtɔgraf] nf spelling. ◆**orthographier** vt (mot) to spell.

orthopédie [ɔrtɔpedi] nf orthop(a)edics.

ortie [ɔrti] nf nettle.

os [ɔs, pl o ou ɔs] nm bone; **trempé jusqu'aux os** soaked to the skin; **tomber sur un os** (difficulté) Fam = ouvrier spécialisé.

OS [ɔɛs] abrév = ouvrier spécialisé.

oscar [ɔskar] nm Cin Oscar.

osciller [ɔsile] vi Tech to oscillate; (se balancer) to swing, sway; (hésiter) to waver; (varier) to fluctuate; (flamme) to flicker. ◆**oscillation** nf Tech oscillation; (de l'opinion) fluctuation.

oseille [ozɛj] nf **1** Bot Culin sorrel. **2** (argent) Arg dough.

oser [oze] vti to dare; **o. faire** to dare (to) do. ◆**—é** a bold, daring.

osier [ozje] nm (branches) wicker.

ossature [ɔsatyr] nf (du corps) frame; (de bâtiment) & Fig framework. ◆**osselets** nmpl (jeu) jacks, knucklebones. ◆**ossements** nmpl (de cadavres) bones. ◆**osseux, -euse** a (tissu) bone-; (maigre) bony.

ostensible [ɔstɑ̃sibl] a conspicuous.

ostentation [ɔstɑ̃tasjɔ̃] nf ostentation.

otage [ɔtaʒ] nm hostage; **prendre qn en o.** to take s.o. hostage.

OTAN [ɔtɑ̃] nf abrév (Organisation du traité de l'Atlantique Nord) NATO.

otarie [ɔtari] nf (animal) sea lion.

ôter [ote] vt to remove, take away (à qn from s.o.); (vêtement) to take off, remove; (déduire) to take (away); **ôte-toi de là!** Fam get out of the way!

otite [ɔtit] nf ear infection.

oto-rhino [ɔtorino] nmf Méd Fam ear, nose and throat specialist.

ou [u] conj or; **ou bien** or else; **ou elle ou moi** either her or me.

où [u] adv & pron where; **le jour où** the day when, the day on which; **la table où** the table on which; **l'état où** the condition in which; **par où?** which way?; **d'où?** where from?; **d'où ma surprise**/*etc* (*conséquence*) hence my surprise/*etc*; **le pays d'où** the country from which; **où qu'il soit** wherever he may be.

ouate [wat] *nf Méd* cotton wool, *Am* absorbent cotton.

oubli [ubli] *nm* (*défaut*) forgetfulness; **l'o. de qch** forgetting sth; **un o.** a lapse of memory; (*omission*) an oversight; **tomber dans l'o.** to fall into oblivion. ◆**oublier** *vt* to forget (**de faire** to do); (*faute, problème*) to overlook; — **s'o.** *vpr* (*traditions etc*) to be forgotten; (*personne*) *Fig* to forget oneself. ◆**oublieux, -euse** *a* forgetful (**de** of).

oubliettes [ublijɛt] *nfpl* (*de château*) dungeon.

ouest [wɛst] *nm* west; **à l'o. de** west of; **d'o.** (*vent*) west(erly); **de l'o.** western; **Allemagne de l'O.** West Germany; **l'Europe de l'O.** Western Europe; — *a inv* (*côte*) west(ern). ◆**o.-allemand, -ande** *a* & *nmf* West German.

ouf! [uf] *int* (*soulagement*) ah!, phew!

oui [wi] *adv* & *nm inv* yes; **o.!** yes!; **les o.** (*votes*) the ayes; **tu viens, o.?** come on, will you?; **je crois que o.** I think so; **si o.** if so. ◆**oui-dire** [widir] *nm inv* hearsay.

ouïe¹ [wi] *nf* hearing; **être tout o.** *Fam* to be all ears.

ouïe²! [uj] *int* ouch!

ouïes [wi] *nfpl* (*de poisson*) gills.

ouille! [uj] *int* ouch!

ouragan [uragã] *nm* hurricane.

ourler [urle] *vt* to hem. ◆**ourlet** *nm* hem.

ours [urs] *nm* bear; **o. blanc/gris** polar/grizzly bear.

oursin [ursɛ̃] *nm* (*animal*) sea urchin.

ouste! [ust] *int Fam* scram!

outil [uti] *nm* tool. ◆**outiller** *vt* to equip. ◆**-age** *nm* tools; (*d'une usine*) equipment.

outrage [utraʒ] *nm* insult (**à** to). ◆**outrager** *vt* to insult, offend. ◆**-eant** *a* insulting, offensive.

outrance [utrãs] *nf* (*excès*) excess; **à o.** (*travailler etc*) to excess; **guerre à o.** all-out war. ◆**outrancier, -ière** *a* excessive.

outre [utr] *prép* besides; — *adv* **en o.** besides, moreover; **o. mesure** inordinately; **passer o.** to take no notice (**à** of). ◆**o.-Manche**

adv across the Channel. ◆**o.-mer** *adv* overseas; **d'o.-mer** (*peuple*) overseas.

outrepasser [utrapase] *vt* (*limite etc*) to go beyond, exceed.

outr/er [utre] *vt* to exaggerate, overdo; **o. qn** (*indigner*) to outrage s.o. ◆**-é a** (*excessif*) exaggerated; (*révolté*) outraged.

outsider [awtsajdœr] *nm Sp* outsider.

ouvert [uvɛr] *voir* **ouvrir**; — *a* open; (*robinet, gaz etc*) on; **à bras ouverts** with open arms. ◆**ouvertement** *adv* openly. ◆**ouverture** *nf* opening; (*trou*) hole; (*avance*) & *Mus* overture; (*d'objectif*) *Phot* aperture; **o. d'esprit** open-mindedness.

ouvrable [uvrabl] *a* **jour o.** working day.

ouvrage [uvraʒ] *nm* (*travail, objet, livre*) work; (*couture*) (needle)work; **un o.** (*travail*) a piece of work. ◆**ouvragé** *a* (*bijou etc*) finely worked.

ouvreuse [uvrøz] *nf Cin* usherette.

ouvrier, -ière [uvrije, -jɛr] *nmf* worker; **o. agricole** farm labourer; **o. qualifié/spécialisé** skilled/unskilled worker; — *a* (*législation etc*) industrial; (*quartier, éducation*) working-class; **classe ouvrière** working class.

ouvrir* [uvrir] *vt* to open (up); (*gaz, radio etc*) to turn on, switch on; (*inaugurer*) to open; (*hostilités*) to begin; (*appétit*) to whet; (*liste, procession*) to head; — *vi* to open; (*ouvrir sa porte*) to open (up); — **s'o.** *vpr* (*porte, boîte etc*) to open (up); **s'o. la jambe** to cut one's leg open; **s'o. à qn** *Fig* to open one's heart to s.o. (**de qch** about sth). ◆**ouvre-boîtes** *nm inv* tin opener, *Am* can-opener. ◆**ouvre-bouteilles** *nm inv* bottle opener.

ovaire [ovɛr] *nm Anat* ovary.

ovale [oval] *a* & *nm* oval.

ovation [ovasjɔ̃] *nf* (*standing*) ovation.

OVNI [ovni] *nm abrév* (*objet volant non identifié*) UFO.

oxyde [ɔksid] *nm Ch* oxide; **o. de carbone** carbon monoxide. ◆**oxyder** *vt*, — **s'o.** *vpr* to oxidize.

oxygène [ɔksiʒɛn] *nm* oxygen; **à o.** (*masque, tente*) oxygen-. ◆**oxygén/er** *vt* (*cheveux*) to bleach; — **s'o.** *vpr Fam* to breathe *ou* get some fresh air. ◆**-ée** *af* **eau o.** (*hydrogen*) peroxide.

P

P, p [pe] *nm* P. p.

pachyderme [paʃidɛrm] *nm* elephant.

pacifier [pasifje] *vt* to pacify. ◆**pacifica-tion** *nf* pacification. ◆**pacifique 1** *a* (*non violent, non militaire*) peaceful; (*personne, peuple*) peace-loving. **2** *a* (*côte etc*) Pacific; **Océan P.** Pacific Ocean; — *nm* **le P.** the Pacific. ◆**pacifiste** *a & nmf* pacifist.

pack [pak] *nm* (*de lait etc*) carton.

pacotille [pakɔtij] *nf* (*camelote*) trash.

pacte [pakt] *nm* pact. ◆**pactiser** *vi* p. avec qn *Péj* to be in league with s.o.

paf! [paf] **1** *int* bang!, wallop! **2** *a inv* (*ivre*) *Fam* sozzled, plastered.

pagaie [page] *nf* paddle. ◆**pagayer** *vi* (*ramer*) to paddle.

pagaïe, pagaille [pagaj] *nf* (*désordre*) *Fam* mess, shambles; **en p.** *Fam* in a mess; **avoir des livres/etc en p.** *Fam* to have loads of books/*etc*.

paganisme [paganism] *nm* paganism.

page [paʒ] **1** *nf* (*de livre etc*) page; **à la p.** (*personne*) *Fig* up-to-date. **2** *nm* (*à la cour*) *Hist* page (boy).

pagne [paɲ] *nm* loincloth.

pagode [pagɔd] *nf* pagoda.

paie [pe] *nf* pay, wages. ◆**paiement** *nm* payment.

païen, -enne [pajɛ̃, -ɛn] *a & nmf* pagan, heathen.

paillasson [pajasɔ̃] *nm* (door)mat.

paille [paj] *nf* straw; (*pour boire*) (drinking) straw; **homme de p.** *Fig* stooge, man of straw; **tirer à la courte p.** to draw lots; **sur la p.** penniless; **feu de p.** *Fig* flash in the pan. ◆**paillasse** *nf* **1** (*matelas*) straw mattress. **2** (*d'un évier*) draining-board.

paillette [pajɛt] *nf* (*d'habit*) sequin; *pl* (*de lessive, savon*) flakes; (*d'or*) *Géol* gold dust.

pain [pɛ̃] *nm* bread; **un p.** a loaf (of bread); **p. grillé** toast; **p. complet** wholemeal bread; **p. d'épice** gingerbread; **petit p.** roll; **p. de savon/de cire** bar of soap/wax; **avoir du p. sur la planche** (*travail*) *Fig* to have a lot on one's plate.

pair [pɛr] **1** *a* (*numéro*) even. **2** *nm* (*personne*) peer; **hors (de) p.** unrivalled, without equal; **aller de p.** to go hand in hand (avec with); **au p.** (*étudiante etc*) au pair; **travailler au p.** to work as an au pair.

paire [pɛr] *nf* pair (de of).

paisible [pezibl] *a* (*vie etc*) peaceful; (*caractère, personne*) peaceable.

paître* [petr] *vi* to graze; **envoyer p.** *Fig* to send packing.

paix [pe] *nf* peace; (*traité*) *Pol* peace treaty; **en p.** in peace; (*avec sa conscience*) at peace (avec with); **avoir la p.** to have (some) peace and quiet.

Pakistan [pakistɑ̃] *nm* Pakistan. ◆**pakis-tanais, -aise** *a & nmf* Pakistani.

palabres [palabr] *nmpl* palaver.

palace [palas] *nm* luxury hotel.

palais [palɛ] *nm* **1** (*château*) palace; **P. de justice** law courts; **p. des sports** sports stadium *ou* centre. **2** *Anat* palate.

palan [palɑ̃] *nm* (*de navire etc*) hoist.

pâle [pɑl] *a* pale.

palet [palɛ] *nm* (*hockey sur glace*) puck.

paletot [palto] *nm* (knitted) cardigan.

palette [palɛt] *nf* **1** (*de peintre*) palette. **2** (*support pour marchandises*) pallet.

pâleur [pɑlœr] *nf* paleness, pallor. ◆**pâlir** *vi* to go *ou* turn pale (de with).

palier [palje] *nm* **1** (*d'escalier*) landing; **être voisins de p.** to live on the same floor. **2** (*niveau*) level; (*phase de stabilité*) plateau; **par paliers** (*étapes*) in stages.

palissade [palisad] *nf* fence (of stakes).

pallier [palje] *vt* (*difficultés etc*) to alleviate. ◆**palliatif** *nm* palliative.

palmarès [palmarɛs] *nm* prize list; (*des chansons*) hit-parade.

palme [palm] *nf* **1** palm (leaf); (*symbole*) *Fig* palm. **2** (*de nageur*) flipper. ◆**palmier** *nm* palm (tree).

palmé [palme] *a* (*patte, pied*) webbed.

palombe [palɔ̃b] *nf* wood pigeon.

pâlot, -otte [pɑlo, -ɔt] *a* pale.

palourde [palurd] *nf* (*mollusque*) clam.

palp/er [palpe] *vt* to feel, finger. ◆**—able** *a* tangible.

palpit/er [palpite] *vi* (*frémir*) to quiver; (*cœur*) to palpitate, throb. ◆**—ant** *a* (*film etc*) thrilling. ◆**palpitations** *nfpl* quivering; palpitations.

pâmer (se) [səpame] *vpr* **se p. de** (*joie etc*) to be paralysed *ou* ecstatic with.

pamphlet [pɑ̃flɛ] *nm* lampoon.

pamplemousse [pɑ̃pləmus] *nm* grapefruit.

pan [pɑ̃] **1** *nm* (*de chemise*) tail; (*de ciel*) patch; (*de mur*) section of wall. **2** *int* bang!

pan- [pɑ̃, pan] *préf* Pan-.

panacée [panase] *nf* panacea.

panache [panaʃ] *nm* (*plumet*) plume; **avoir du p.** (*fière allure*) to have panache; **un p. de fumée** a plume of smoke.

panaché [panaʃe] **1** *a* (*bigarré, hétéroclite*) motley. **2** *a* & *nm* (*demi*) **p.** shandy; **bière panachée** shandy.

pancarte [pɑ̃kart] *nf* sign, notice; (*de manifestant*) placard.

pancréas [pɑ̃kreas] *nm Anat* pancreas.

panda [pɑ̃da] *nm* (*animal*) panda.

pané [pane] *a Culin* breaded.

panier [panje] *nm* (*ustensile, contenu*) basket; **p. à salade** salad basket; (*voiture*) *Fam* police van, prison van. ◆**p.-repas** *nm* (*pl paniers-repas*) packed lunch.

panique [panik] *nf* panic; **pris de p.** panic-stricken; – *a* **peur p.** panic fear. ◆**paniqu/er** *vi* to panic. ◆**-é** *a* panic-stricken.

panne [pan] *nf* breakdown; **tomber en p.** to break down; **être en p.** to have broken down; **p. d'électricité** power cut, blackout; **avoir une p. sèche** to run out of petrol *ou Am* gas.

panneau, -x [pano] *nm* (*écriteau*) sign, notice, board; **p. (de signalisation)** traffic *ou* road sign; **p. (d'affichage)** (*publicité*) hoarding, *Am* billboard. **2** (*de porte etc*) panel. ◆**panonceau, -x** *nm* (*enseigne*) sign.

panoplie [panɔpli] *nf* **1** (*jouet*) outfit. **2** (*gamme, arsenal*) (wide) range, assortment.

panorama [panɔrama] *nm* panorama. ◆**panoramique** *a* panoramic.

panse [pɑ̃s] *nf Fam* paunch, belly. ◆**pansu** *a* potbellied.

pans/er [pɑ̃se] *vt* (*plaie, main etc*) to dress, bandage; (*personne*) to dress the wound(s) of, bandage (up); (*cheval*) to groom. ◆**-ement** *nm* (*bande*) bandage, dressing; **p. adhésif** sticking plaster, *Am* Band-Aid®.

pantalon [pɑ̃talɔ̃] *nm* (pair of) trousers *ou Am* pants; **deux pantalons** two pairs of trousers *ou Am* pants; **en p.** in trousers, *Am* in pants.

pantelant [pɑ̃tlɑ̃] *a* gasping.

panthère [pɑ̃tɛr] *nf* (*animal*) panther.

pantin [pɑ̃tɛ̃] *nm* (*jouet*) jumping jack; (*personne*) *Péj* puppet.

pantois [pɑ̃twa] *a* flabbergasted.

pantoufle [pɑ̃tufl] *nf* slipper. ◆**pantou-**

flard, -arde *nmf Fam* stay-at-home, *Am* homebody.

paon [pɑ̃] *nm* peacock.

papa [papa] *nm* dad(dy); **de p.** (*désuet*) *Péj* outdated; **fils à p.** *Péj* rich man's son, daddy's boy.

pape [pap] *nm* pope. ◆**papauté** *nf* papacy.

paperasse(s) [papras] *nf(pl)* *Péj* (official) papers. ◆**paperasserie** *nf Péj* (official) papers; (*procédure*) red tape.

papeterie [papetri] *nf* (*magasin*) stationer's shop; (*articles*) stationery; (*fabrique*) paper mill. ◆**papetier, -ière** *nf* stationer.

papi [papi] *nm Fam* grand(d)ad.

papier [papje] *nm* (*matière*) paper; **un p.** (*feuille*) a piece *ou* sheet of paper; (*formulaire*) a form; *Journ* an article; **en p.** (*sac etc*) paper-; **papiers (d'identité)** (identity) papers; **p. à lettres** writing paper; **p. du journal** (some) newspaper; **p. peint** wallpaper; **p. de verre** sandpaper.

papillon [papijɔ̃] *nm* **1** (*insecte*) butterfly; (*écrou*) butterfly nut, *Am* wing nut; **p. (de nuit)** moth. **2** (*contravention*) (parking) ticket.

papot/er [papote] *vi* to prattle. ◆**-age(s)** *nm(pl)* prattle.

paprika [paprika] *nm* (*poudre*) *Culin* paprika.

papy [papi] *nm Fam* grand(d)ad.

Pâque [pɑk] *nf* **la P.** *Rel* Passover.

paquebot [pakbo] *nm Nau* liner.

pâquerette [pakrɛt] *nf* daisy.

Pâques [pɑk] *nm* & *nfpl* Easter.

paquet [pakɛ] *nm* (*de sucre, bonbons etc*) packet; (*colis*) package; (*de cigarettes*) pack(et); (*de cartes*) pack.

par [par] *prép* **1** (*agent, manière, moyen*) by; **choisi/frappé/etc p.** chosen/hit/*etc* by; **erreur par mistake; **p. mer** by sea; **p. le train** by train; **p. la force/le travail/etc** by *ou* through force/work/*etc*; **apprendre p. un voisin** to learn from *ou* through a neighbour; **commencer/s'ouvrir p. qch** (*récit etc*) to begin/open with sth; **p. malchance** unfortunately. **2** (*lieu*) through; **p. la porte/le tunnel/etc** through *ou* by the door/tunnel/*etc*; **regarder/jeter p. la fenêtre** to look/throw out (of) the window; **p. les rues** through the streets; **p. ici/là** (*aller*) this/that way; (*habiter*) around here/there. **3** (*motif*) out of, from; **p. respect/pitié/etc** out of *ou* from respect/pity/*etc*. **4** (*temps*) on; **p. un jour d'hiver/etc** on a winter's day/*etc*; **p. le passé** in the past; **p. ce froid** in this cold. **5** (*distributif*) **dix fois p.** an ten times a *ou* per year; **deux p. deux** two by two; **p. deux fois** twice. **6** (*trop*) **p. trop aimable**/*etc* far too kind/*etc*.

para [para] *nm Fam* para(trooper).

para- [para] *préf* para-.

parabole [parabɔl] *nf* **1** (*récit*) parable. **2** *Math* parabola.

parachever [paraʃve] *vt* to perfect.

parachute [paraʃyt] *nf* parachute. ◆**parachuter** *vt* to parachute; (*nommer*) *Fam* to pitchfork (**à un poste** into a job). ◆**parachutisme** *nm* parachute jumping. ◆**parachutiste** *nmf* parachutist; *Mil* paratrooper.

parade [parad] *nf* **1** (*étalage*) show, parade; (*spectacle*) *& Mil* parade. **2** *Boxe Escrime* parry; (*riposte*) *Fig* reply. ◆**parader** *vi* to parade, show off.

paradis [paradi] *nm* paradise, heaven. ◆**paradisiaque** *a* (*endroit etc*) *Fig* heavenly.

paradoxe [paradɔks] *nm* paradox. ◆**paradoxalement** *adv* paradoxically.

parafe [paraf] *voir* **paraphe**. ◆**parafer** *voir* **parapher**.

paraffine [parafin] *nf* paraffin (wax).

parages [paraʒ] *nmpl* region, area (**de** of); **dans ces p.** in these parts.

paragraphe [paragraf] *nm* paragraph.

paraître [parɛtr] *vi* **1** (*se montrer*) to appear; (*sembler*) to seem, look, appear; – *v imp* **il paraît qu'il va partir** it appears *ou* seems (that) he's leaving. **2** *vi* (*livre*) to be published, come out; **faire p.** to bring out.

parallèle [paralɛl] **1** *a* (*comparable*) *& Math* parallel (**à** with, to); (*marché*) *Com* unofficial. **2** *nm* (*comparaison* *& Géog* parallel. ◆**—ment** *adv* **p. à** parallel to.

paralyser [paralize] *vt* to paralyse, *Am* paralyze. ◆**paralysie** *nf* paralysis. ◆**paralytique** *a & nmf* paralytic.

paramètre [parametr] *nm* parameter.

paranoïa [paranɔja] *nf* paranoia. ◆**paranoïaque** *a & nmf* paranoid.

parapet [parapɛ] *nm* parapet.

paraphe [paraf] *nm* initials, signature; (*traits*) flourish. ◆**parapher** *vt* to initial, sign.

paraphrase [parafraz] *nf* paraphrase. ◆**paraphraser** *vt* to paraphrase.

parapluie [paraplɥi] *nm* umbrella.

parasite [parazit] *nm* (*personne, organisme*) parasite; *pl Rad* interference; – *a* parasitic(al).

parasol [parasɔl] *nm* parasol, sunshade.

paratonnerre [paratɔnɛr] *nm* lightning conductor *ou Am* rod.

paravent [paravɑ̃] *nm* (folding) screen.

parc [park] *nm* **1** park; (*de château*) grounds. **2** (*de bébé*) (play) pen; (*à moutons, à bétail*) pen; **p. de stationnement** car park, *Am* parking lot; **p. à huîtres** oyster bed.

parcelle [parsɛl] *nf* fragment, particle; (*terrain*) plot; (*de vérité*) *Fig* grain.

parce que [parsk(ə)] *conj* because.

parchemin [parʃəmɛ̃] *nm* parchment.

parcimonie [parsimɔni] *nf* **avec p.** parsimoniously. ◆**parcimonieux, -euse** *a* parsimonious.

par-ci par-là [parsiparla] *adv* here, there and everywhere.

parcmètre [parkmɛtr] *nm* parking meter.

parcourir* [parkurir] *vt* (*région*) to travel through, tour, scour; (*distance*) to cover; (*texte*) to glance through. ◆**parcours** *nm* (*itinéraire*) route; (*de fleuve*) *& Sp* course; (*voyage*) trip, journey.

par-delà [pard(ə)la] *voir* **delà**.

par-derrière [parderjɛr] *voir* **derrière**.

par-dessous [pard(ə)su] *prép & adv* under(neath).

pardessus [pard(ə)sy] *nm* overcoat.

par-dessus [pard(ə)sy] *prép & adv* over (the top of); **p.-dessus tout** above all.

par-devant [pard(ə)vɑ̃] *voir* **devant**.

pardon [pardɔ̃] *nm* forgiveness, pardon; **p.?** (*pour demander*) excuse me?, *Am* pardon me?; **p.!** (*je le regrette*) sorry!; **demander p.** to apologize (**à** to). ◆**pardonn/er** *vt* to forgive; **p. qch à qn/à qn d'avoir fait qch** to forgive s.o. for sth/for doing sth. ◆**—able** *a* forgivable.

pare-balles [parbal] *a inv* **gilet p.-balles** bulletproof jacket *ou Am* vest.

pare-brise [parbriz] *nm inv Aut* windscreen, *Am* windshield.

pare-chocs [parʃɔk] *nm inv Aut* bumper.

pareil, -eille [parɛj] *a* similar; **p. à** the same as, similar to; **être pareils** to be the same, be similar *ou* alike; **un p. désordre**/*etc* such a mess/*etc*; **en p. cas** in such a case; – *nmf* (*personne*) equal; **rendre la pareille à qn** to treat s.o. the same way; **sans p.** unparalleled, unique; – *adv Fam* the same. ◆**pareillement** *adv* in the same way; (*aussi*) likewise.

parement [parmɑ̃] *nm* (*de pierre, de vêtement*) facing.

parent, -ente [parɑ̃, -ɑ̃t] *nmf* relation, relative; – *nmpl* (*père et mère*) parents; – *a* related (**de** to). ◆**parenté** *nf* (*rapport*) relationship, kinship.

parenthèse [parɑ̃tɛz] *nf* (*signe*) bracket, parenthesis; (*digression*) digression.

parer [pare] **1** vt (coup) to parry, ward off; — vi p. à to be prepared for. **2** vt (orner) to adorn (de with).

paresse [parɛs] nf laziness, idleness. ◆**paresser** vi to laze (about). ◆**paresseux, -euse** a lazy, idle; — nmf lazybones.

parfaire [parfɛr] vt to perfect. ◆**parfait** a perfect; p.! excellent!; — nm Gram perfect (tense). ◆**parfaitement** adv perfectly; (certainement) certainly.

parfois [parfwa] adv sometimes.

parfum [parfœ̃] nm (odeur) fragrance, scent; (goût) flavour; (liquide) perfume, scent. ◆**parfum/er** vt to perfume, scent; (glace, crème etc) to flavour (à with); — se p. vpr to put on perfume; (habituellement) to wear perfume. ◆—é a (savon, mouchoir) scented; p. au café/etc coffee-/etc flavoured. ◆**parfumerie** nf (magasin) perfume shop.

pari [pari] nm bet, wager; pl Sp betting, bets; p. mutuel urbain = the tote, Am pari-mutuel. ◆**parier** vti to bet (sur on, que that). ◆**parieur, -euse** nmf Sp better, punter.

Paris [pari] nm ou f Paris. ◆**parisien, -ienne** a (accent etc) Parisian, Paris-; — nmf Parisian.

parité [parite] nf parity.

parjure [parʒyr] nm perjury; — nmf perjurer. ◆**se parjurer** vpr to perjure oneself.

parka [parka] nm parka.

parking [parkiŋ] nm (lieu) car park, Am parking lot.

par-là [parla] adv voir **par-ci**.

parlement [parləmɑ̃] nm parliament. ◆**parlementaire** a parliamentary; — nmf member of parliament.

parlementer [parləmɑ̃te] vi to parley, negotiate.

parl/er [parle] vi to talk, speak (de about, à to); tu parles! Fam you must be joking!; sans p. de . . . not to mention . . . ; — vt (langue) to speak; p. affaires/etc to talk business/etc; — se p. vpr (langue) to be spoken; — nm speech; (régional) dialect. ◆—ant a (film) talking; (regard etc) eloquent. ◆—é a (langue) spoken.

parloir [parlwar] nm (de couvent, prison) visiting room.

parmi [parmi] prép among(st).

parodie [parɔdi] nf parody. ◆**parodier** vt to parody.

paroi [parwa] nf wall; (de maison) inside wall; (de rocher) (rock) face.

paroisse [parwas] nf parish. ◆**paroissial,**

-aux a (registre, activité etc) parish-. ◆**paroissien, -ienne** nmf parishioner.

parole [parɔl] nf (mot, promesse) word; (faculté, langage) speech; adresser la p. à to speak to; prendre la p. to speak, make a speech; demander la p. to ask to speak; perdre la p. to lose one's tongue.

paroxysme [parɔksism] nm (de douleur etc) height.

parpaing [parpɛ̃] nm concrete block, breezeblock.

parquer [parke] vt (bœufs) to pen; (gens) to herd together, confine; (véhicule) to park; — se p. vpr Aut to park.

parquet [parke] nm **1** (parquet) floor(ing). **2** Jur Public Prosecutor's office.

parrain [parɛ̃] nm Rel godfather; (répondant) sponsor. ◆**parrain/er** vt to sponsor. ◆—age nm sponsorship.

pars, part [par] voir **partir**.

parsemer [parsəme] vt to strew, dot (de with).

part[2] [par] nf (portion) share, part; prendre p. à (activité) to take part in; (la joie etc de qn) to share; de toutes parts from ou on all sides; de p. et d'autre on both sides; d'une p., . . . d'autre p. on the one hand, . . . on the other hand; d'autre p. (d'ailleurs) moreover; pour ma p. as far as I'm concerned; de la p. de (provenance) from; c'est de la p. de qui? Tél who's speaking?; faire p. de qch à qn to inform s.o. of sth; quelque p. somewhere; nulle p. nowhere; autre p. somewhere else; à p. (séparément) apart; (mettre, prendre) aside; (excepté) apart from; un cas/une place/etc à p. a separate ou special case/place/etc; membre à p. entière full member.

partage [partaʒ] nm dividing (up), division; (participation) sharing; (distribution) sharing out; (sort) Fig lot. ◆**partag/er** vt (repas, frais, joie etc) to share (avec with); (diviser) to divide (up); (distribuer) to share out; — se p. vpr (bénéfices etc) to share (between themselves etc); se p. entre to divide one's time between. ◆—é a (avis etc) divided; p. entre (sentiments) torn between.

partance (en) [ɑ̃partɑ̃s] adv (train etc) about to depart (pour for).

partant [partɑ̃] nm (coureur, cheval) Sp starter.

partenaire [partənɛr] nmf (époux etc) & Sp Pol partner.

parterre [partɛr] nm **1** (de jardin etc) flower bed. **2** Th stalls, Am orchestra.

parti [parti] nm Pol party; (époux) match; prendre un p. to make a decision, follow a course; **prendre p. pour** to side with; **tirer p. de** to turn to (good) account; **p. pris** (*préjugé*) prejudice; **être de p. pris** to be prejudiced (**contre** against).

partial, -aux [parsjal, -o] *a* biased. **◆partialité** *nf* bias.

participe [partisip] *nm* Gram participle.

particip/er [partisipe] *vi* **p. à** (*activité, jeu etc*) to take part in, participate in; (*frais, joie etc*) to share (in). **◆-ant, -ante** *nmf* participant. **◆participation** *nf* participation; sharing; (*d'un acteur*) appearance, collaboration; **p. (aux frais)** (*contribution*) share (in the expenses).

particule [partikyl] *nf* particle.

particulier, -ière [partikylje, -jɛr] *a* (*spécial, spécifique*) particular; (*privé*) private; (*bizarre*) peculiar; **p. à** peculiar to; **en p.** (*surtout*) in particular; (*à part*) in private; — *nm* private individual *ou* citizen. **◆particularité** *nf* peculiarity. **◆particulièrement** *adv* particularly; **tout p.** especially.

partie [parti] *nf* part; (*de cartes, de tennis etc*) game; (*de chasse, de plaisir*) & *Jur* party; (*métier*) line, field; **en p.** partly, in part; **en grande p.** mainly; **faire p. de** to be a part of; (*adhérer à*) to belong to; (*comité*) to be on. **◆partiel, -ielle** *a* partial; — *nm* (*examen*) **p.** *Univ* term exam. **◆partiellement** *adv* partially.

part/ir [partir] *vi* (*aux être*) (*aller, disparaître*) to go; (*s'en aller*) to leave, go (off); (*se mettre en route*) to set off; (*s'éloigner*) to go (away); (*moteur*) to start; (*fusil, coup de feu*) to go off; (*flèche*) to shoot off; (*bouton*) to come off; (*tache*) to come out; **p. de** (*commencer par*) to start (off) with; **ça part du cœur** it comes from the heart; **p. bien** to get off to a good start; **à p. de** (*date, prix*) from. **◆—i** *a* **il a bien p.** off to a good start.

partisan [partizã] *nm* follower, supporter; *Mil* partisan; — *a* (*esprit*) *Péj* partisan; **être p. de qch/de faire** to be in favour of sth/of doing.

partition [partisjɔ̃] *nf* Mus score.

partout [partu] *adv* everywhere; **p. où tu vas *ou* iras** everywhere *ou* wherever you go; **p. sur la table**/*etc* all over the table/*etc*.

paru [pary] *voir* **paraître**. **◆parution** *nf* (*de livre etc*) publication.

parure [paryr] *nf* (*toilette*) finery; (*bijoux*) jewellery.

parven/ir [parvǝnir] *vi* (*aux être*) **p. à** (*lieu*) to reach; (*fortune, ses fins*) to achieve; **p. à faire** to manage to do. **◆—u, -ue** *nmf* *Péj* upstart.

parvis [parvi] *nm* square (*in front of church etc*).

pas ¹ [pɑ] *adv* (*négatif*) not; (**ne**) . . . **p.** not; **je ne sais p.** I do not *ou* don't know; **p. de pain**/**de café**/*etc* no bread/coffee/*etc*; **p. encore** not yet; **p. du tout** not at all.

pas ² [pɑ] *nm* **1** step, pace; (*allure*) pace; (*bruit*) footstep; (*trace*) footprint; **à deux p.** (**de**) close by; **revenir sur ses p.** to go back on one's tracks; **au p.** at a walking pace; **rouler au p.** (*véhicule*) to go dead slow(ly); **au p.** (*cadence*) in step; **faire les cent p.** to walk up and down; **faux p.** stumble; (*faute*) *Fig* blunder; **le p. de la porte** the doorstep. **2** (*de vis*) thread. **3** *Géog* straits; **le p. de Calais** the Straits of Dover.

pascal [paskal] *a* (*semaine, messe etc*) Easter-.

passable [pɑsabl] *a* acceptable, tolerable; **mention p.** *Scol Univ* pass. **◆—ment** [-amɑ̃] *adv* acceptably; (*beaucoup*) quite a lot.

passage [pɑsaʒ] *nm* (*action*) passing, passage; (*traversée*) *Nau* crossing; (*extrait*) passage; (*couloir*) passage(way); (*droit*) right of way; (*venue*) arrival; (*chemin*) path; **p. clouté** *ou* **pour piétons** (pedestrian) crossing; **obstruer le p.** to block the way; **p. souterrain** subway, *Am* underpass; **p. à niveau** level crossing, *Am* grade crossing; **'p. interdit'** 'no thoroughfare'; **'cédez le p.'** *Aut* 'give way', *Am* 'yield'; **être de p.** to be passing through (**à Paris**/*etc* Paris/*etc*); **hôte de p.** passing guest. **◆passager, -ère 1** *nmf* passenger; **p. clandestin** stowaway. **2** *a* (*de courte durée*) passing, temporary. **◆passagèrement** *adv* temporarily.

passant, -ante [pɑsã, -ãt] **1** *a* (*rue*) busy; — *nmf* passer-by. **2** *nm* (*de ceinture etc*) loop.

passe [pɑs] *nf* *Sp* pass; **mot de p.** password; **en p. de faire** on the road to doing; **une mauvaise p.** *Fig* a bad patch.

passe-montagne [pɑsmɔ̃taɲ] *nm* balaclava.

passe-partout [pɑspartu] *nm inv* (*clé*) master key; — *a inv* (*compliment, phrase*) all-purpose.

passe-passe [pɑspɑs] *nm inv* **tour de p.-passe** conjuring trick.

passe-plat [pɑspla] *nm* service hatch.

passeport [pɑspɔr] *nm* passport.

passer [pɑse] *vi* (*aux être ou avoir*) (*aller, venir*) to pass (**à** to); (*facteur, laitier*) to come; (*temps*) to pass (by), go by; (*courant*) to flow; (*film, programme*) to be shown, be on; (*loi*) to be passed; (*douleur, mode*) to pass; (*couleur*) to fade; **p. devant** (*maison etc*) to go past *ou* by, pass (by); **p. à** *ou* **par Paris** to pass through Paris; **p. à la radio** to come *ou* go on the radio; **p. à l'ennemi/à la caisse** to go over to the enemy/the cash desk; **laisser p.** (*personne, lumière*) to let in *ou* through; (*occasion*) to let slip; **p. prendre** to pick up, fetch; **p. voir qn** to drop in on s.o.; **p. pour** (*riche etc*) to be taken for; **faire p. qn pour** to pass s.o. off as; **p. sur** (*détail etc*) to overlook, pass over; **p. capitaine/etc** to be promoted captain/*etc*; **p. en** (*seconde etc*) *Scol* to pass up into; *Aut* to change up to; **ça passe** (*c'est passable*) that'll do; **en passant** (*dire qch*) in passing; – *vt* (*aux avoir*) (*frontière etc*) to cross; (*maison etc*) to pass, go past; (*donner*) to pass, hand (**à** to); (*mettre*) to put; (*omettre*) to overlook; (*temps*) to spend, pass (**à faire** doing); (*disque*) to play, put on; (*film, programme*) to show, put on; (*loi, motion*) to pass; (*chemise*) to slip on; (*examen*) to take, sit (for); (*thé*) to strain; (*café*) to filter; (*commande*) to place; (*accord*) to conclude; (*colère*) to vent (**sur** on); (*limites*) to go beyond; (*visite médicale*) to go through; **p.** (**son tour**) to pass; **p. qch à qn** (*caprice etc*) to grant s.o. sth; (*pardonner*) to excuse s.o. sth; **je vous passe . . .** *Tél* I'm putting you through to . . . ; **p. un coup d'éponge/etc à qch** to go over sth with a sponge/*etc*; **— se p.** (*se produire*) to take place, happen; (*douleur*) to pass, go (away); **se p. de** to do *ou* go without; **se p. de commentaires** to need no comment; **ça s'est bien passé** it went off all right. **◆passé 1** *a* (*temps etc*) past; (*couleur*) faded; **la semaine passée** last week; **dix heures passées** after *ou* gone ten (o'clock); **être passé** (*personne*) to have been (and gone); (*orage*) to be over; **avoir vingt ans passés** to be over twenty; – *nm* (*temps, vie passée*) past; *Gram* past (tense). **2** *prép* after; **p. huit heures** after eight (o'clock).

passerelle [pasrɛl] *nf* (*pont*) footbridge; (*voie d'accès*) *Nau Av* gangway.

passe-temps [pastɑ̃] *nm inv* pastime.

passeur, -euse [pasœr, -øz] *nmf* **1** *Nau* ferryman, ferrywoman. **2** (*contrebandier*) smuggler.

passible [pasibl] *a* **p. de** (*peine*) *Jur* liable to.

passif, -ive [pasif, -iv] **1** *a* (*rôle, personne etc*) passive; – *nm Gram* passive. **2** *nm Com* liabilities. **◆passivité** *nf* passiveness, passivity.

passion [pasjɔ̃] *nf* passion; **avoir la p. des**

voitures/d'écrire/*etc* to have a passion *ou* a great love for cars/writing/*etc*. **◆passionnel, -elle** *a* (*crime*) of passion. **◆passionner** *vt* to thrill, fascinate; **se p. pour** to have a passion for. **◆–ant** *a* thrilling. **◆–é, -ée** *a* passionate; **p. de qch** passionately fond of sth; – *nmf* fan (**de** of). **◆–ément** *adv* passionately.

passoire [paswar] *nf* (*pour liquides*) sieve (**à thé**) strainer; (*à légumes*) colander.

pastel [pastɛl] *nm* pastel; **au p.** (*dessin*) pastel-; – *a inv* (*ton*) pastel-.

pastèque [pastɛk] *nf* watermelon.

pasteur [pastœr] *nm Rel* pastor.

pasteurisé [pastœrize] *a* (*lait, beurre etc*) pasteurized.

pastiche [pastiʃ] *nm* pastiche.

pastille [pastij] *nf* pastille, lozenge.

pastis [pastis] *nm* aniseed liqueur, pastis.

pastoral, -aux [pastoral, -o] *a* pastoral.

patate [patat] *nf Fam* spud, potato.

patatras! [patatra] *int* crash!

pataud [pato] *a* clumsy, lumpish.

patauger [patoʒe] *vi* (*marcher*) to wade (*in the mud etc*); (*barboter*) to splash about; (*s'empêtrer*) *Fig* to flounder. **◆pataugeoire** *nf* paddling pool.

patchwork [patʃwœrk] *nm* patchwork.

pâte [pɑt] *nf* (*substance*) paste; (*à pain, à gâteau*) dough; (*à tarte*) pastry; **pâtes (alimentaires)** pasta; **p. à modeler** plasticine® modelling clay; **p. à frire** batter; **p. dentifrice** toothpaste.

pâté [pate] *nm* **1** (*charcuterie*) pâté; **p. (en croûte)** meat pie. **2 p. (de sable)** sand castle; **p. de maisons** block of houses. **3** (*tache d'encre*) (ink) blot.

pâtée [pate] *nf* (*pour chien, volaille etc*) mash.

patelin [patlɛ̃] *nm Fam* village.

patent [patɑ̃] *a* patent, obvious.

patère [patɛr] *nf* (*coat*) peg.

paternel, -elle [patɛrnɛl] *a* (*amour etc*) fatherly, paternal; (*parenté, réprimande*) paternal. **◆paternité** *nf* (*état*) paternity, fatherhood; (*de livre*) authorship.

pâteux, -euse [patø, -øz] *a* (*substance*) doughy, pasty; (*style*) woolly; **avoir la bouche** *ou* **la langue pâteuse** (*après s'être enivré*) to have a mouth full of cotton wool *ou Am* cotton.

pathétique [patetik] *a* moving; – *nm* pathos.

pathologie [patɔlɔʒi] *nf* pathology. **◆pathologique** *a* pathological.

patient, -ente [pasjɑ̃, -ɑ̃t] **1** *a* patient. **2** *nmf Méd* patient. **◆patiemment** [-amɑ̃] *adv* patiently. ◆**patience** nf patience; **prendre p.** to have patience; **perdre p.** to lose patience. ◆**patienter** vi to wait (patiently).

patin [patɛ̃] nm skate; (pour le parquet) cloth pad (used for walking); **p. à glace/à roulettes** ice/roller skate. ◆**patin/er** vi Sp to skate; (véhicule, embrayage) to slip. ◆**-age** nm Sp skating; **p. artistique** figure skating. ◆**-eur, -euse** nmf Sp skater. ◆**patinoire** nf (piste) & Fig skating rink, ice rink.

patine [patin] nf patina.

patio [patjo] nm patio.

pâtir [pɑtir] vi **p. de** to suffer from.

pâtisserie [pɑtisri] nf pastry, cake; (magasin) cake shop; (art) cake ou pastry making. ◆**pâtissier, -ière** nmf pastrycook and cake shop owner.

patois [patwa] nm Ling patois.

patraque [patrak] a (malade) Fam under the weather.

patriarche [patrijarʃ] nm patriarch.

patrie [patri] nf (native) country; (ville) birth place. ◆**patriote** nmf patriot; – a (personne) patriotic. ◆**patriotique** a (chant etc) patriotic. ◆**patriotisme** nm patriotism.

patrimoine [patrimwan] nm (biens) & Fig heritage.

patron, -onne [patrɔ̃, -ɔn] 1 nmf (chef) employer, boss; (propriétaire) owner (de qn); (gérant) manager, manageress; (de bar) landlord, landlady. 2 nmf Rel patron saint. 3 nm (modèle de papier) Tex pattern. ◆**patronage** nm 1 (protection) patronage. 2 (centre) youth club. ◆**patronal, -aux** a (syndicat etc) employers'. ◆**patronat** nm employers. ◆**patronner** vt to sponsor.

patrouille [patruj] nf patrol. ◆**patrouill/er** vi to patrol. ◆**-eur** nm (navire) patrol boat.

patte [pat] nf 1 (membre) leg; (de chat, chien) paw; (main) Fam hand; **à quatre pattes** on all fours. 2 (de poche) flap; (languette) tongue.

pattes [pat] nfpl (favoris) sideboards, Am sideburns.

pâture [pɑtyr] nf (nourriture) food; (intellectuelle) Fig fodder. ◆**pâturage** nm pasture.

paume [pom] nf (de main) palm.

paum/er [pome] vt Fam to lose; **un coin ou trou paumé** (sans attrait) a dump. ◆**-é, -ée** nmf (malheureux) Fam down-and-out, loser.

paupière [popjɛr] nf eyelid.

pause [poz] nf (arrêt) break; (dans le discours etc) pause.

pauvre [povr] a poor; (terre) impoverished, poor; **p. en** (calories etc) low in; (ressources etc) low on; – nmf (indigent, malheureux) poor man, poor woman; **les pauvres** the poor. ◆**pauvrement** adv poorly. ◆**pauvreté** nf (besoin) poverty; (insuffisance) poorness.

pavaner (se) [səpavane] vpr to strut (about).

pav/er [pave] vt to pave. ◆**-é** nm un **p.** a paving stone; (rond, de vieille chaussée) a cobblestone; **sur le p.** Fig on the streets. ◆**-age** nm (travail, revêtement) paving.

pavillon [pavijɔ̃] nm 1 (maison) house; (de chasse) lodge; (d'hôpital) ward; (d'exposition) pavilion. 2 (drapeau) flag.

pavoiser [pavwaze] vt to deck out with flags; – vi (exulter) Fig to rejoice.

pavot [pavo] nm (cultivé) poppy.

pay/er [peje] vt (personne, somme) to pay; (service, objet, faute) to pay for; (récompenser) to repay; **p. qch à qn** (offrir en cadeau) Fam to treat s.o. to sth; **p. qn pour faire** to pay s.o. to do ou for doing; – vi (personne, métier, crime) to pay; **se p. qch** (s'acheter) Fam to treat oneself to sth; **se p. la tête de qn** Fam to make fun of s.o. ◆**-ant** [pejɑ̃] a (hôte, spectateur) who pays, paying; (place, entrée) that one has to pay for; (rentable) worthwhile. ◆**payable** a payable. ◆**paye** nf pay, wages. ◆**payement** nm payment.

pays [pei] nm country; (région) region; (village) village; **p. des rêves/du soleil** land of dreams/sun; **du p.** (vin, gens etc) local.

paysage [peizaʒ] nm landscape, scenery.

paysan, -anne [peizɑ̃, -an] nmf (small) farmer; (rustre) Péj peasant; – a country-; (monde) farming.

Pays-Bas [peiba] nmpl **les P.-Bas** the Netherlands.

PCV [peseve] abrév (paiement contre vérification) **téléphoner en PCV** to reverse the charges, Am call collect.

PDG [pedeʒe] abrév = **président directeur général.**

péage [peaʒ] nm (droit) toll; (lieu) tollgate.

peau, -x [po] nf skin; (de fruit) peel, skin; (cuir) hide, skin; (fourrure) pelt; **dans la p. de qn** Fig in s.o.'s shoes; **faire p. neuve** Fig to turn over a new leaf. ◆**P.-Rouge** nmf (pl **Peaux-Rouges**) (Red) Indian.

pêche¹ [pɛʃ] nf (activité) fishing; (poissons) catch; **p. (à la ligne)** angling; **aller à la p.** to go fishing. ◆**pêcher¹** vi to fish; – vt (chercher à prendre) to fish for; (attraper) to catch; (*dénicher*) *Fam* to dig up. ◆**pêcheur** *nm* fisherman; angler.

pêche² [pɛʃ] *nf* (*fruit*) peach. ◆**pêcher²** *nm* (*arbre*) peach tree.

péché [peʃe] *nm* sin. ◆**péch/er** *vi* to sin; **p. par orgueil**/*etc* to be too proud/*etc*. ◆**—eur, -eresse** *nmf* sinner.

pectoraux [pɛktɔro] *nmpl* (*muscles*) chest muscles.

pécule [pekyl] *nm* **un p.** (*économies*) (some) savings, a nest egg.

pécuniaire [pekynjɛr] *a* monetary.

pédagogie [pedagɔʒi] *nf* (*science*) education, teaching methods. ◆**pédagogique** *a* educational. ◆**pédagogue** *nmf* teacher.

pédale [pedal] *nf* **1** pedal; **p. de frein** footbrake (pedal). **2** (*homosexuel*) *Péj Fam* pansy, queer. ◆**pédaler** *vi* to pedal.

pédalo [pedalo] *nm* pedal boat, pedalo.

pédant, -ante [pedɑ̃, -ɑ̃t] *nmf* pedant; – *a* pedantic. ◆**pédantisme** *nm* pedantry.

pédé [pede] *nm* (*homosexuel*) *Péj Fam* queer.

pédiatre [pedjatr] *nmf Méd* p(a)ediatrician. ◆**pédicure** [pedikyr] *nmf* chiropodist.

pedigree [pedigre] *nm* (*de chien, cheval etc*) pedigree.

pègre [pɛgr] *nf* **la p.** (*criminal*) underworld.

peigne [pɛɲ] *nm* comb; **passer au p. fin** *Fig* to go through with a fine toothcomb; **un coup de p.** (*action*) a comb. ◆**peigner** *vt* (*cheveux*) to comb; **p. qn** to comb s.o.'s hair; **– se p.** *vpr* to comb one's hair.

peignoir [pɛɲwar] *nm* dressing gown, *Am* bathrobe; **p. (de bain)** bathrobe.

peinard [penar] *a Arg* quiet (and easy).

peindre⁹ [pɛ̃dr] *vt* to paint; (*décrire*) *Fig* to depict, paint; **p. en bleu**/*etc* to paint blue/*etc*; – *vi* to paint.

peine [pen] *nf* **1** (*châtiment*) punishment; **p. de mort** death penalty *ou* sentence; **p. de prison** prison sentence; **'défense d'entrer sous p. d'amende'** 'trespassers will be fined'. **2** (*chagrin*) sorrow, grief; **avoir de la p.** to be upset *ou* sad; **faire de la p. à** to upset, cause pain *ou* sorrow to. **3** (*effort, difficulté*) trouble; **se donner de la p.** *ou* **beaucoup de p.** to go to a lot of trouble (**pour faire** to do); **avec p.** with difficulty; **ça vaut la p. d'attendre**/*etc* it's worth (while) waiting/*etc*; **ce n'est pas** *ou* **ça ne vaut pas la p.** it's not worth while *ou* worth it *ou* worth bothering. ◆**peiner 1** *vt* to upset, grieve. **2** *vi* to labour, struggle.

peine (à) [apɛn] *adv* hardly, scarcely.

peintre [pɛ̃tr] *nm* painter; **p. (en bâtiment)** (house) painter, (painter and) decorator. ◆**peinture** *nf* (*tableau, activité*) painting; (*couleur*) paint; **'p. fraîche'** 'wet paint'. ◆**peinturlurer** *vt Fam* to daub with colour; **se p. (le visage)** to paint one's face.

péjoratif, -ive [peʒɔratif, -iv] *a* pejorative, derogatory.

pékinois [pekinwa] *nm* (*chien*) pekin(g)ese.

pelage [pəlaʒ] *nm* (*d'animal*) coat, fur.

pelé [pəle] *a* bare.

pêle-mêle [pɛlmɛl] *adv* in disorder.

peler [pəle] *vt* (*fruit*) to peel; **se p. facilement** (*fruit*) to peel easily; – *vi* (*peau bronzée*) to peel.

pèlerin [pɛlrɛ̃] *nm* pilgrim. ◆**pèlerinage** *nm* pilgrimage.

pèlerine [pɛlrin] *nf* (*manteau*) cape.

pélican [pelikɑ̃] *nm* (*oiseau*) pelican.

pelisse [pəlis] *nf* fur-lined coat.

pelle [pɛl] *nf* shovel; (*d'enfant*) spade; **p. à poussière** dustpan; **ramasser** *ou* **prendre une p.** (*tomber*) *Fam* to come a cropper, *Am* take a spill; **à la p.** (*argent etc*) *Fam* galore. ◆**pelletée** *nf* shovelful. ◆**pelleteuse** *nf Tech* mechanical shovel, excavator.

pellicule [pelikyl] *nf Phot* film; (*couche*) film, layer; *pl Méd* dandruff.

pelote [pəlɔt] *nf* (*de laine*) ball; (*à épingles*) pincushion; **p. (basque)** *Sp* pelota.

peloter [pəlɔte] *vt* (*palper*) *Péj Fam* to paw.

peloton [pəlɔtɔ̃] *nm* **1** (*coureurs*) *Sp* pack, main body. **2** *Mil* squad; **p. d'exécution** firing squad. **3** (*de ficelle*) ball.

pelotonner (se) [səplɔtɔne] *vpr* to curl up (into a ball).

pelouse [pluz] *nf* lawn; *Sp* enclosure.

peluche [plyʃ] *nf* (*tissu*) plush; *pl* (*flocons*) fluff, lint; **une p.** (*flocon*) a bit of fluff *ou* lint; **jouet en p.** soft toy; **chien**/*etc* **en p.** (*jouet*) furry dog/*etc*; **ours en p.** teddy bear. ◆**pelucher** *vi* to get fluffy *ou* linty. ◆**pelucheux, -euse** *a* fluffy, linty.

pelure [plyr] *nf* (*épluchure*) peeling; **une p.** a (piece of) peeling.

pénal, -aux [penal, -o] *a* (*droit, code etc*) penal. ◆**pénalisation** *nf Sp* penalty. ◆**pénaliser** *vt Sp Jur* to penalize (**pour** for). ◆**pénalité** *nf Jur Rugby* penalty.

penalty, pl -ties [penalti, -iz] *nm Fb* penalty.

penaud [pəno] *a* sheepish.

penchant [pɑ̃ʃɑ̃] *nm* (*goût*) liking (**pour** for); (*tendance*) inclination (**à qch** towards sth).

pench/er [pɑ̃ʃe] *vt* (*objet*) to tilt; (*tête*) to lean; – *vi* (*arbre etc*) to lean (over); **p. pour** *Fig* to be inclined towards; **– se p.** *vpr* to lean (forward); **se p. par** (*fenêtre*) to lean out of; **se p. sur** (*problème etc*) to examine. **◆—é** a leaning.

pendaison [pɑ̃dɛzɔ̃] *nf* hanging.

pendant¹ [pɑ̃dɑ̃] *prép* (*au cours de*) during; **p. la nuit** during the night; **p. deux mois** (*pour une période de*) for two months; **p. que** while, whilst.

pendentif [pɑ̃dɑ̃tif] *nm* (*collier*) pendant.

penderie [pɑ̃dri] *nf* wardrobe.

pend/re [pɑ̃dr] *vti* to hang (**à** from); — **se p.** *vpr* (*se tuer*) to hang oneself; (*se suspendre*) to hang (**à** from). **◆—ant²** 1 a hanging; (*langue*) hanging out; (*joues*) sagging; (*question*) *Fig* pending. 2 *nm* **p. d'oreille** drop earring. 3 *nm* **le p. de** the companion piece to. **◆—u, -ue** a (*objet*) hanging (**à** from); — *nmf* hanged man, hanged woman.

pendule [pɑ̃dyl] 1 *nf* clock. 2 *nm* (*balancier*) & *Fig* pendulum. **◆pendulette** *nf* small clock.

pénétr/er [penetre] *vi* **p. dans** to enter; (*profondément*) to penetrate (into); — *vt* (*substance, mystère etc*) to penetrate; **se p. de** (*idée*) to become convinced of. **◆—ant** a (*esprit, froid etc*) penetrating, keen. **◆pénétration** *nf* penetration.

pénible [penibl] a (*difficile*) difficult; (*douloureux*) painful, distressing; (*ennuyeux*) tiresome; (*agaçant*) annoying. **◆—ment** [-əmɑ̃] *adv* with difficulty; (*avec douleur*) painfully.

péniche [penis] *nf* barge; **p. de débarquement** *Mil* landing craft.

pénicilline [penisilin] *nf* penicillin.

péninsule [penɛ̃syl] *nf* peninsula. **◆péninsulaire** a peninsular.

pénis [penis] *nm* penis.

pénitence [penitɑ̃s] *nf* (*punition*) punishment; (*peine*) *Rel* penance; (*regret*) penitence. **◆pénitent, -ente** *nmf Rel* penitent.

pénitencier [penitɑ̃sje] *nm* prison. **◆pénitentiaire** a (*régime etc*) prison.

pénombre [penɔ̃br] *nf* half-light, darkness.

pensée [pɑ̃se] *nf* 1 thought. 2 (*fleur*) pansy. **◆pens/er** *vi* to think (**à** of, about); **p. à qch/à faire qch** (*ne pas oublier*) to remember sth/to do sth; **p. à tout** (*prévoir*) to think of everything; **penses-tu!** you must be joking!, not at all!; (*concevoir*) to think out; (*imaginer*) to imagine ou think; **je pensais rester** I thought I'd stay; **je pense réussir** (*espoir*) I hope to succeed; **que pensez-vous de . . . ?** what do you think of ou about . . . ?; **p. du bien de** to think highly of. **◆—ant** a **bien p.** *Péj* or-

thodox. **◆—eur** *nm* thinker. **◆pensif, -ive** a thoughtful, pensive.

pension [pɑ̃sjɔ̃] *nf* 1 boarding school; (*somme, repas*) board; **être en p.** to board, be a boarder (**chez** with); **p. (de famille)** guesthouse, boarding house; **p. complète** full board. 2 (*allocation*) pension; **p. alimentaire** maintenance allowance. **◆pensionnaire** *nmf* (*élève*) boarder; (*d'hôtel*) resident; (*de famille*) lodger. **◆pensionnat** *nm* boarding school; (*élèves*) boarders. **◆pensionné, -ée** *nmf* pensioner.

pentagone [pɛ̃tagɔn] *nm* **le P.** *Am Pol* the Pentagon.

pentathlon [pɛ̃tatlɔ̃] *nm Sp* pentathlon.

pente [pɑ̃t] *nf* slope; **être en p.** to slope, be sloping.

Pentecôte [pɑ̃tkot] *nf* Whitsun, *Am* Pentecost.

pénurie [penyri] *nf* scarcity, shortage (**de** of).

pépère [pepɛr] 1 *nm Fam* grand(d)ad. 2 a (*tranquille*) *Fam* quiet (and easy).

pépier [pepje] *vi* (*oiseau*) to cheep, chirp.

pépin [pepɛ̃] *nm* 1 **de** (*fruit*) pip, *Am* pit. 2 (*ennui*) *Fam* hitch, bother. 3 (*parapluie*) *Fam* brolly.

pépinière [pepinjɛr] *nf Bot* nursery.

pépite [pepit] *nf* (*gold*) nugget.

péquenaud, -aude [pɛkno, -od] *nmf Péj Arg* peasant, bumpkin.

perçant [pɛrsɑ̃] a (*cri, froid*) piercing; (*yeux*) sharp, keen.

percée [pɛrse] *nf* (*dans une forêt*) opening; (*avance technologique, attaque militaire*) breakthrough.

perce-neige [pɛrsənɛʒ] *nm ou f inv Bot* snowdrop.

perce-oreille [pɛrsɔrɛj] *nm* (*insecte*) earwig.

percepteur [pɛrsɛptœr] *nm* tax collector. **◆perceptible** a perceptible (**à** to), noticeable. **◆perception** *nf* 1 (*bureau*) tax office; (*d'impôt*) collection. 2 (*sensation*) perception.

perc/er [pɛrse] *vt* (*trouer*) to pierce; (*avec perceuse*) to drill (a hole in); (*trou, ouverture*) to make, drill; (*mystère etc*) to uncover; **p. une dent** (*bébé*) to cut a tooth; — *vi* (*soleil, ennemi, sentiment*) to break ou come through; (*abcès*) to burst. **◆—euse** *nf* drill.

percevoir* [pɛrsəvwar] *vt* 1 (*sensation*) to perceive; (*son*) to hear. 2 (*impôt*) to collect.

perche [pɛrʃ] *nf* 1 (*bâton*) pole; **saut à la p.** pole-vaulting. 2 (*poisson*) perch.

perch/er [pɛrʃe] *vi* (*oiseau*) to perch; (*volailles*) to roost; (*loger*) *Fam* to hang out; —

vt (*placer*) *Fam* to perch; **— se p.** *vpr* (*oiseau, personne*) to perch. **◆—é** *a* perched. **◆perchoir** *nm* perch; (*de volailles*) roost.

percolateur [pɛrkɔlatœr] *nm* (*de restaurant*) percolator.

percussion [pɛrkysjɔ̃] *nf Mus* percussion.

percutant [pɛrkytɑ̃] *a Fig* powerful.

percuter [pɛrkyte] *vt* (*véhicule*) to crash into; **—** *vi* **p. contre** to crash into.

perd/re [pɛrdr] *vt* to lose; (*gaspiller*) to waste; (*ruiner*) to ruin; (*habitude*) to get out of; **p. de vue** to lose sight of; **—** *vi* to lose; (*récipient, tuyau*) to leak; **j'y perds** I lose out, I lose on the deal; **— se p.** *vpr* (*s'égarer*) to get lost; (*dans les détails*) to lose oneself; (*disparaître*) to disappear; **je m'y perds** I'm too confused. **◆—ant, -ante** *a* (*billet*) losing; **—** *nmf* loser. **◆—u** *a* lost; wasted; (*malade*) finished; (*lieu*) isolated, in the middle of nowhere; **à ses moments perdus** in one's spare time; **une balle perdue** a stray bullet; **c'est du temps p.** it's a waste of time. **◆perdition (en)** *adv* (*navire*) in distress.

perdrix [pɛrdri] *nf* partridge. **◆perdreau, -x** *nm* young partridge.

père [pɛr] *nm* father; **Dupont p.** Dupont senior; **le p. Jean** *Fam* old John.

péremptoire [perɑ̃ptwar] *a* peremptory.

perfection [pɛrfɛksjɔ̃] *nf* perfection. **◆perfection/er** *vt* to improve, perfect; **se p. en anglais/etc** to improve one's English/*etc.* **◆—é** *a* (*machine etc*) advanced. **◆—ement** *nm* improvement (*de in, par rapport à on*); **cours de p.** advanced *ou* refresher course. **◆perfectionniste** *nmf* perfectionist.

perfide [pɛrfid] *a Litt* treacherous, perfidious. **◆perfidie** *nf Litt* treachery.

perforer [pɛrfɔre] *vt* (*pneu, intestin etc*) to perforate; (*billet, carte*) to punch; **carte perforée** punch card. **◆perforateur** *nm* (*appareil*) drill. **◆perforation** *nf* perforation; (*trou*) punched hole. **◆perforatrice** *nf* (*pour cartes*) *Tech* (card) punch. **◆perforeuse** *nf* (paper) punch.

performance [pɛrfɔrmɑ̃s] *nf* (*d'athlète, de machine etc*) performance. **◆performant** *a* (highly) efficient.

péricliter [periklite] *vi* to go to rack and ruin.

péril [peril] *nm* peril; **à tes risques et périls** at your own risk. **◆périlleux, -euse** *a* perilous; **saut p.** somersault (*in mid air*).

périm/er [perime] *vi*, **— se p.** *vpr* laisser (**se**) **p.** (*billet*) to allow to expire. **◆—é** *a* expired; (*désuet*) outdated.

périmètre [perimɛtr] *nm* perimeter.

période [perjɔd] *nf* period. **◆périodique** *a* periodic; **—** *nm* (*revue*) periodical.

péripétie [peripesi] *nf* (unexpected) event.

périphérie [periferi] *nf* (*limite*) periphery; (*banlieue*) outskirts. **◆périphérique** *a* (*quartier*) outlying, peripheral; **—** *nm* (**boulevard**) *a* (motorway) ring road, *Am* beltway.

périphrase [perifraz] *nf* circumlocution.

périple [peripl] *nm* trip, tour.

pér/ir [perir] *vi* to perish, die. **◆—issable** *a* (*denrée*) perishable.

périscope [periskɔp] *nm* periscope.

perle [pɛrl] *nf* (*bijou*) pearl; (*de bois, verre etc*) bead; (*personne*) *Fig* gem, pearl; (*erreur*) *Iron* howler, gem. **◆perler** *vi* (*sueur*) to form beads; **grève perlée** go-slow, *Am* slow-down strike.

permanent, -ente [pɛrmanɑ̃, -ɑ̃t] **1** *a* permanent; (*spectacle*) *Cin* continuous; (*comité*) standing. **2** *nf* (*coiffure*) perm. **◆permanence** *nf* permanence; (*service, bureau*) duty office; (*salle*) *Scol* study room; **être de p.** to be on duty; **en p.** permanently.

perméable [pɛrmeabl] *a* permeable.

permettre* [pɛrmɛtr] *vt* to allow, permit; **p. à qn de faire** (*permission, possibilité*) to allow *ou* permit s.o. to do; **permettez!** excuse me!; **vous permettez?** may I?; **se p. de faire** to allow oneself to do, take the liberty to do; **se p. qch** (*se payer*) to afford sth. **◆permis** *a* allowed, permitted; **—** *nm* (*autorisation*) permit, licence; **p. de conduire** (*carte*) driving licence, *Am* driver's license; **p. de travail** work permit. **◆permission** *nf* permission; (*congé*) *Mil* leave; **demander la p.** to ask (for) permission (**de faire** to do).

permuter [pɛrmyte] *vt* to change round *ou* over, permutate. **◆permutation** *nf* permutation.

pernicieux, -euse [pɛrnisjø, -øz] *a* (*nocif*) & *Méd* pernicious.

pérorer [perɔre] *vi Péj* to speechify.

Pérou [peru] *nm* Peru.

perpendiculaire [pɛrpɑ̃dikylɛr] *a* & *nf* perpendicular (**à** to).

perpétrer [pɛrpetre] *vt* (*crime*) to perpetrate.

perpétuel, -elle [pɛrpetɥɛl] *a* perpetual; (*fonction, rente*) for life. **◆perpétuelle-ment** *adv* perpetually. **◆perpétuer** *vt* to perpetuate. ◆**perpétuité (à)** *adv* in perpetuity; (*condamné*) for life.

perplexe [pɛrplɛks] *a* perplexed, puzzled. ◆**perplexité** *nf* perplexity.

perquisition [pɛrkizisjɔ̃] *nf* (house) search (*by police*). ◆**perquisitionner** *vti* to search.

perron [pɛrɔ̃] *nm* (front) steps.

perroquet [pɛrɔkɛ] *nm* parrot.

perruche [pɛryʃ] *nf* budgerigar, *Am* parakeet.

perruque [pɛryk] *nf* wig.

persan [pɛrsɑ̃] *a* (*langue, tapis, chat*) Persian; – *nm* (*langue*) Persian.

persécut/er [pɛrsekyte] *vt* (*tourmenter*) to persecute; (*importuner*) to harass. ◆**persécuteur, -trice** *nmf* persecutor. ◆**persécution** *nf* persecution.

persévér/er [pɛrsevere] *vi* to persevere (*dans* in). ◆**-ant** *a* persevering. ◆**persévérance** *nf* perseverance.

persienne [pɛrsjɛn] *nf* (outside) shutter.

persil [pɛrsi] *nm* parsley.

persist/er [pɛrsiste] *vi* to persist (**à faire** in doing). ◆**-ant** *a* persistent; **à feuilles persistantes** (*arbre etc*) evergreen. ◆**persistance** *nf* persistence.

personnage [pɛrsɔnaʒ] *nm* (*célébrité*) (important) person; *Th Littér* character.

personnaliser [pɛrsɔnalize] *vt* to personalize; (*voiture*) to customize.

personnalité [pɛrsɔnalite] *nf* (*individualité, personnage*) personality.

personne [pɛrsɔn] **1** *nf* person; *pl* people; **grande p.** grown-up, adult; **jolie p.** pretty girl *ou* woman; **en p.** in person. **2** *pron* (*négatif*) nobody, no one; **ne . . . p.** nobody, no one; **je ne vois p.** I don't see anybody *ou* anyone; **mieux que p.** better than anybody *ou* anyone.

personnel, -elle [pɛrsɔnɛl] **1** *a* personal; (*joueur, jeu*) individualistic. **2** *nm* staff, personnel. ◆**personnellement** *adv* personally.

personnifier [pɛrsɔnifje] *vt* to personify. ◆**personnification** *nf* personification.

perspective [pɛrspɛktiv] *nf* (*art*) perspective; (*point de vue*) *Fig* viewpoint, perspective; (*de paysage etc*) view; (*possibilité, espérance*) prospect; **en p.** *Fig* in view, in prospect.

perspicace [pɛrspikas] *a* shrewd. ◆**perspicacité** *nf* shrewdness.

persuader [pɛrsɥade] *vt* to persuade (**qn de faire** s.o. to do); **se p.** to be convinced. ◆**persuasif, -ive** *a* persuasive.

◆**persuasion** *nf* persuasion; (*croyance*) conviction.

perte [pɛrt] *nf* loss; (*gaspillage*) waste (**de temps/d'argent** of time/money); (*ruine*) ruin; **à p. de vue** as far as the eye can see; **vendre à p.** to sell at a loss.

pertinent [pɛrtinɑ̃] *a* relevant, pertinent. ◆**pertinence** *nf* relevance.

perturb/er [pɛrtyrbe] *vt* (*trafic, cérémonie etc*) to disrupt; (*ordre public, personne*) to disturb. ◆**-é a** (*troublé*) *Fam* perturbed. ◆**perturbateur, -trice** *a* (*élément*) disruptive; – *nmf* trouble-maker. ◆**perturbation** *nf* disruption; (*crise*) upheaval.

péruvien, -ienne [peryvjɛ̃, -jɛn] *a & nmf* Peruvian.

pervenche [pɛrvɑ̃ʃ] *nf Bot* periwinkle.

pervers [pɛrvɛr] *a* wicked, perverse; (*dépravé*) perverted. ◆**perversion** *nf* perversion. ◆**perversité** *nf* perversity. ◆**pervert/ir** *vt* to pervert. ◆**-i, -ie** *nmf* pervert.

pesant [pəzɑ̃] *a* heavy, weighty; – *nm* **valoir son p. d'or** to be worth one's weight in gold. ◆**pesamment** *adv* heavily. ◆**pesanteur** *nf* heaviness; (*force*) *Phys* gravity.

pes/er [pəze] *vt* to weigh; – *vi* to weigh; **p. lourd** to be heavy; (*argument etc*) *Fig* to carry (a lot of) weight; **p. sur** (*appuyer*) to bear down upon; (*influer*) to bear upon; **p. sur qn** (*menace*) to hang over s.o.; **p. sur l'estomac** to lie (heavily) on the stomach. ◆**-ée** *nf* weighing; *Boxe* weigh-in; (*effort*) pressure. ◆**-age** *nm* weighing. ◆**pèse-bébé** *nm* (*baby*) scales. ◆**pèse-personne** *nm* (bathroom) scales.

pessimisme [pesimism] *nm* pessimism. ◆**pessimiste** *a* pessimistic; – *nmf* pessimist.

peste [pɛst] *nf Méd* plague; (*personne, enfant*) *Fig* pest.

pester [pɛste] *vi* to curse; **p. contre qch/qn** to curse sth/s.o.

pestilentiel, -ielle [pɛstilɑ̃sjɛl] *a* fetid, stinking.

pétale [petal] *nm* petal.

pétanque [petɑ̃k] *nf* (*jeu*) bowls.

pétarades [petarad] *nfpl* (*de moto etc*) backfiring. ◆**pétarader** *vi* to backfire.

pétard [petar] *nm* (*explosif*) firecracker, banger.

péter [pete] *vi Fam* (*éclater*) to go bang *ou* pop; (*se rompre*) to snap.

pétill/er [petije] *vi* (*eau, champagne*) to sparkle, fizz; (*bois, feu*) to crackle; (*yeux*) to sparkle. ◆**-ant** *a* (*eau, vin, regard*) sparkling.

petit, -ite [p(ə)ti, -it] *a* small, little; (*de taille*) short; (*bruit, espoir, coup*) slight; (*jeune*) young, small; (*mesquin, insignifiant*) petty; **tout p.** tiny; **un bon p. travail** a nice little job; **un p. Français** a (little) French boy; — *nmf* (little) boy, (little) girl; (*personne*) small person; *Scol* junior; *pl* (*d'animal*) young; (*de chien*) pups, young; (*de chat*) kittens, young; — *adv* **p. à p.** little by little. ◆**p.-bourgeois** *a Péj* middle-class. ◆**p.-suisse** *nm* soft cheese (*for dessert*). ◆**petitement** *adv* (*chichement*) shabbily, poorly. ◆**petitesse** *nf* (*de taille*) smallness; (*mesquinerie*) pettiness.

petit-fils [p(ə)tifis] *nm* (*pl* petits-fils) grandson, grandchild. ◆**petite-fille** *nf* (*pl* petites-filles) granddaughter, grandchild. ◆**petits-enfants** *nmpl* grandchildren.

pétition [petisjɔ̃] *nf* petition.

pétrifier [petrifje] *vt* (*de peur, d'émoi etc*) to petrify.

pétrin [petrɛ̃] *nm* (*situation*) *Fam* fix; **dans le p.** in a fix.

pétrir [petrir] *vt* to knead.

pétrole [petrɔl] *nm* oil, petroleum; **p. (lampant)** paraffin, *Am* kerosene; **nappe de p.** (*sur la mer*) oil slick. ◆**pétrolier, -ière** *a* (*industrie*) oil-; — *nm* (*navire*) oil tanker. ◆**pétrolifère** *a* **gisement p.** oil field.

pétulant [petylɑ̃] *a* exuberant.

pétunia [petynja] *nm Bot* petunia.

peu [pø] *adv* (*lire, manger etc*) not much, little; **elle mange p.** she doesn't eat much, she eats little; **un p.** (*lire, surpris etc*) a little, a bit; **p. de sel/de temps/etc** not much salt/time/*etc*, little salt/time/*etc*; **un p. de fromage/etc** a little cheese/*etc*, a bit of cheese/*etc*; **le p. de fromage que j'ai** the little cheese I have; **p. de gens/de livres/etc** few people/books/*etc*, not many people/books/*etc*; **p. sont** . . . few are . . . ; **un (tout) petit p.** a (tiny) little bit; **p. intéressant/souvent/etc** not very interesting/often/*etc*; **p. de chose** not much; **p. à p.** gradually, little by little; **à p. près** more or less; **p. après/avant** shortly after/before.

peuplade [pœplad] *nf* tribe.

peuple [pœpl] *nm* (*nation, masse*) people; **les gens du p.** the common people. ◆**peupl/er** *vt* to populate, people. ◆**-é** *a* (*quartier etc*) populated (**with**).

peuplier [pøplije] *nm* (*arbre, bois*) poplar.

peur [pœr] *nf* fear; **avoir p.** to be afraid ou frightened ou scared (**de** of); **faire p. à** to frighten ou scare; **de p. que** (+ *sub*) for fear that; **de p. de faire** for fear of doing.

◆**peureux, -euse** *a* fearful, easily frightened.

peut, peux [pø] *voir* **pouvoir 1.**

peut-être [pøtɛtr] *adv* perhaps, maybe; **p.-être qu'il viendra** perhaps ou maybe he'll come.

phallique [falik] *a* phallic. ◆**phallocrate** *nm Péj* male chauvinist.

phare [far] *nm Nau* lighthouse; *Aut* headlight, headlamp; **rouler pleins phares** *Aut* to drive on full headlights; **faire un appel de phares** *Aut* to flash one's lights.

pharmacie [farmasi] *nf* chemist's shop, *Am* drugstore; (*science*) pharmacy; (*armoire*) medicine cabinet. ◆**pharmaceutique** *a* pharmaceutical. ◆**pharmacien, -ienne** *nmf* chemist, pharmacist, *Am* druggist.

pharynx [farɛ̃ks] *nm Anat* pharynx.

phase [faz] *nf* phase.

phénomène [fenɔmɛn] *nm* phenomenon; (*personne*) *Fam* eccentric. ◆**phénoménal, -aux** *a* phenomenal.

philanthrope [filɑ̃trɔp] *nmf* philanthropist. ◆**philanthropique** *a* philanthropic.

philatélie [filateli] *nf* philately, stamp collecting. ◆**philatélique** *a* philatelic. ◆**philatéliste** *nmf* philatelist, stamp collector.

philharmonique [filarmɔnik] *a* philharmonic.

Philippines [filipin] *nfpl* **les P.** the Philippines.

philosophe [filɔzɔf] *nmf* philosopher; — *a* (*sage, résigné*) philosophical. ◆**philosopher** *vi* to philosophize (**sur** about). ◆**philosophie** *nf* philosophy. ◆**philosophique** *a* philosophical.

phobie [fɔbi] *nf* phobia.

phonétique [fɔnetik] *a* phonetic; — *nf* phonetics.

phonographe [fɔnɔgraf] *nm* gramophone, *Am* phonograph.

phoque [fɔk] *nm* (*animal marin*) seal.

phosphate [fɔsfat] *nm Ch* phosphate.

phosphore [fɔsfɔr] *nm Ch* phosphorus.

photo [fɔto] *nf* photo; (*art*) photography; **prendre une p., prendre en p.** to take a photo of; — *a inv* **appareil p.** camera. ◆**photocopie** *nf* photocopy. ◆**photocopier** *vt* to photocopy. ◆**photocopieur** *nm,* ◆**photocopieuse** *nf* (*machine*) photocopier. ◆**photogénique** *a* photogenic. ◆**photographe** *nmf* photographer. ◆**photographie** *nf* (*art*) photography; (*image*) photograph. ◆**photographier** *vt* to photograph. ◆**photographique** *a* photographic. ◆**photomaton**® *nm* (*appareil*) photo booth.

phrase [fraz] *nf* (*mots*) sentence.

physicien, -ienne [fizisjɛ̃, -jɛn] *nmf* physicist.

physiologie [fizjɔlɔʒi] *nf* physiology. ◆**physiologique** *a* physiological.

physionomie [fizjɔnɔmi] *nf* face.

physique [fizik] **1** *a* physical; – *nm* (*corps, aspect*) physique; **au p.** physically. **2** *nf* (*science*) physics. ◆**-ment** *adv* physically.

piaffer [pjafe] *vi* (*cheval*) to stamp; **p. d'impatience** *Fig* to fidget impatiently.

piailler [pjaje] *vi* (*oiseau*) to cheep; (*enfant*) *Fam* to squeal.

piano [pjano] *nm* piano; **p. droit/à queue** upright/grand piano. ◆**pianiste** *nmf* pianist.

piaule [pjol] *nf* (*chambre*) *Arg* room, pad.

pic [pik] *nm* **1** (*cime*) peak. **2** (*outil*) pick(axe); **p. à glace** ice pick. **3** (*oiseau*) woodpecker.

pic (à) [apik] *adv* (*verticalement*) sheer; **couler à p.** to sink to the bottom; **arriver à p.** *Fig* to arrive in the nick of time.

pichet [piʃɛ] *nm* jug, pitcher.

pickpocket [pikpɔkɛt] *nm* pickpocket.

pick-up [pikœp] *nm inv* (*camionnette*) pick-up truck.

picorer [pikɔre] *vti* to peck.

picoter [pikɔte] *vt* (*yeux*) to make smart; (*jambes*) to make tingle; **les yeux me picotent** my eyes are smarting.

pie [pi] **1** *nf* (*oiseau*) magpie. **2** *a inv* (*couleur*) piebald.

pièce [pjɛs] *nf* **1** (*de maison etc*) room. **2** (*morceau, objet etc*) piece; (*de pantalon*) patch; (*écrit*) & *Jur* document; **p. (de monnaie)** coin; **p. (de théâtre)** play; **p. (d'artillerie)** gun; **p. d'identité** proof of identity, identity card; **p. d'eau** pool, pond; **pièces détachées** *ou* **de rechange** (*de véhicule etc*) spare parts; **cinq dollars/etc (la) p.** five dollars/etc each; **travailler à la p.** to do piecework.

pied [pje] *nm* foot; (*de meuble*) leg; (*de verre, lampe*) base; *Phot* stand; **un p. de salade** a head of lettuce; **à p.** on foot; **aller à p.** to walk, go on foot; **au p. de** at the foot *ou* bottom of; **au p. de la lettre** *Fig* literally; **avoir p.** (*nageur*) to have a footing, touch the bottom; **coup de p.** kick; **donner un coup de p.** to kick (**à qn** s.o.); **sur p.** (*debout, levé*) up and about; **sur ses pieds** (*malade guéri*) up and about; **sur un p. d'égalité** on an equal footing; **comme un p.** (*mal*) *Fam* dreadfully; **faire un p. de nez** to thumb

one's nose (**à** at); **mettre sur p.** (*projet*) to set up. ◆**p.-noir** *nmf* (*pl* **pieds-noirs**) Algerian Frenchman *ou* Frenchwoman.

piédestal, -aux [pjedɛstal, -o] *nm* pedestal.

piège [pjɛʒ] *nm* (*pour animal*) & *Fig* trap. ◆**piéger** *vt* (*animal*) to trap; (*voiture etc*) to booby-trap; **engin piégé** booby trap; **lettre/colis/voiture piégé(e)** letter/parcel/car bomb.

pierre [pjɛr] *nf* stone; (*précieuse*) gem, stone; **p. à briquet** flint; **geler à p. fendre** to freeze (rock) hard. ◆**pierreries** *nfpl* gems, precious stones. ◆**pierreux, -euse** *a* stony.

piété [pjete] *nf* piety.

piétiner [pjetine] *vt* (*fouler aux pieds*) to trample (on); – *vi* to stamp (one's feet); (*marcher sur place*) to mark time; (*ne pas avancer*) *Fig* to make no headway.

piéton¹ [pjetɔ̃] *nm* pedestrian. ◆**piéton²**, **-onne** *a*, ◆**piétonnier, -ière** *a* (*rue etc*) pedestrian.

piètre [pjɛtr] *a* wretched, poor.

pieu, -x [pjø] *nm* **1** (*piquet*) post, stake. **2** (*lit*) *Fam* bed.

pieuvre [pjœvr] *nf* octopus.

pieux, -euse [pjø, -øz] *a* pious.

pif [pif] *nm* (*nez*) *Fam* nose. ◆**pifomètre (au)** *adv* (*sans calcul*) *Fam* at a rough guess.

pigeon [piʒɔ̃] *nm* pigeon; (*personne*) *Fam* dupe; **p. voyageur** carrier pigeon. ◆**pigeonner** *vt* (*voler*) *Fam* to rip off.

piger [piʒe] *vti* *Fam* to understand.

pigment [pigmɑ̃] *nm* pigment.

pignon [piɲɔ̃] *nm* (*de maison etc*) gable.

pile [pil] **1** *nf* *Él* battery; (*atomique*) pile; **radio à piles** battery radio. **2** *nf* (*tas*) pile; **en p. in a pile. 3** *nf* (*de pont*) pier. **4** *nf* **p. (ou face)?** heads (or tails)?; **jouer à p. ou face** to toss up. **5** *adv* **s'arrêter p.** to stop short *ou* dead; **à deux heures p.** on the dot of two.

piler [pile] **1** *vt* (*amandes*) to grind; (*ail*) to crush. **2** *vi* (*en voiture*) to stop dead. ◆**pilonner** *vt* *Mil* to bombard, shell.

pilier [pilje] *nm* pillar.

pilon [pilɔ̃] *nm* (*de poulet*) drumstick.

piller [pije] *vti* to loot, pillage. ◆**pillage** *nm* looting, pillage. ◆**pillard, -arde** *nmf* looter.

pilori [pilɔri] *nm* **mettre au p.** *Fig* to pillory.

pilote [pilɔt] *nm* *Av Nau* pilot; (*de voiture, char*) driver; (*guide*) *Fig* guide; – *a* **usine(-)/projet(-)p.** pilot factory/plan. ◆**pilot/er** *vt* *Av* to fly, pilot; *Nau* to pilot; **p. qn** to show s.o. around. ◆**-age** *nm* piloting; **école de p.** flying school; **poste de p.** cockpit.

pilotis [pilɔti] *nm* (*pieux*) *Archit* piles.

pilule [pilyl] *nf* pill; **prendre la p.** (*femme*) to be on the pill; **se mettre à/arrêter la p.** to go on/off the pill.

piment [pimã] *nm* pimento, pepper. ◆**pimenté** *a* *Culin* & *Fig* spicy.

pimpant [pɛ̃pɑ̃] *a* pretty, spruce.

pin [pɛ̃] *nm* (*bois, arbre*) pine; **pomme de p.** pine cone.

pinailler [pinaje] *vi* *Fam* to quibble, split hairs.

pinard [pinar] *nm* (*vin*) *Fam* wine.

pince [pɛ̃s] *nf* (*outil*) pliers; *Méd* forceps; (*de cycliste*) clip; (*levier*) crowbar; *pl* (*de crabe*) pincers; **p. (à linge)** (*clothes*) peg *ou* *Am* pin; **p. (à épiler)** tweezers; **p. (à sucre)** sugar tongs; **p. à cheveux** hairgrip. ◆**pinc/er** *vt* to pinch; (*corde*) *Mus* to pluck; **p. qn** (*arrêter*) *Jur* to nab s.o., pinch s.o.; **se p. le doigt** to get one's finger caught (**dans** in). ◆**-é** *a* (*air*) stiff, constrained. ◆**-ée** *nf* (*de sel etc*) pinch (**de** of). ◆**pincettes** *nfpl* (*fire*) tongs; (*d'horloger*) tweezers. ◆**pinçon** *nm* pinch (mark).

pinceau, -x [pɛ̃so] *nm* (*paint*)brush.

pince-sans-rire [pɛ̃sɑ̃rir] *nm inv* person of dry humour.

pinède [pinɛd] *nf* pine forest.

pingouin [pɛ̃gwɛ̃] *nm* auk, penguin.

ping-pong [piŋpɔ̃g] *nm* ping-pong.

pingre [pɛ̃gr] *a* stingy; — *nmf* skinflint.

pinson [pɛ̃sɔ̃] *nm* (*oiseau*) chaffinch.

pintade [pɛ̃tad] *nf* guinea fowl.

pin-up [pinœp] *nf inv* (*fille*) pinup.

pioche [pjɔʃ] *nf* pick(axe). ◆**piocher** *vti* (*creuser*) to dig (with a pick).

pion [pjɔ̃] *nm* **1** (*au jeu de dames*) piece; *Échecs* & *Fig* pawn. **2** *Scol* master (in charge of discipline).

pionnier [pjɔnje] *nm* pioneer.

pipe [pip] *nf* (*de fumeur*) pipe; **fumer la p.** to smoke a pipe.

pipeau, -x [pipo] *nm* (*flûte*) pipe.

pipe-line [piplin] *nm* pipeline.

pipi [pipi] *nm* **faire p.** *Fam* to go for a pee.

pique [pik] **1** *nm* (*couleur*) *Cartes* spades. **2** *nf* (*arme*) pike. **3** *nf* (*allusion*) cutting remark.

pique-assiette [pikasjɛt] *nmf inv* scrounger.

pique-nique [piknik] *nm* picnic. ◆**pique-niquer** *vi* to picnic.

piqu/er [pike] *vt* (*entamer, percer*) to prick; (*langue, yeux*) to sting; (*curiosité*) to rouse; (*coudre*) to (machine-)stitch; (*édredon, couvre-lit*) to quilt; (*crise de nerfs*) to have;

(*maladie*) to get; **p. qn** (*abeille*) to sting s.o.; (*serpent*) to bite s.o.; *Méd* to give s.o. an injection; **p. qch dans** (*enfoncer*) to stick into; **p. qn** (*arrêter*) *Jur* *Fam* to nab s.o., pinch s.o.; **p. qch** (*voler*) *Fam* to pinch sth; **p. une colère** to fly into a rage; **p. une tête** to plunge headlong; — *vi* (*avion*) to dive; (*moutarde etc*) to be hot; — **se p.** *vpr* to prick oneself; **se p. de faire qch** to pride oneself on being able to do sth. ◆**-ant** *a* (*épine*) prickly; (*froid*) biting; (*sauce, goût*) pungent, piquant; (*mot*) cutting; (*détail*) spicy; — *nm Bot* prickle, thorn; (*d'animal*) spine, prickle. ◆**-é** *a* (*meuble*) worm-eaten; (*fou*) *Fam* crazy; — *nm* *Av* (nose)dive; **descente en p.** *Av* nosedive. ◆**-eur, -euse** *nmf* (*sur machine à coudre*) machinist. ◆**piqûre** *nf* (*d'épingle*) prick; (*d'abeille*) sting; (*de serpent*) bite; (*trou*) hole; *Méd* injection; (*point*) stitch.

piquet [pikɛ] *nm* **1** (*pieu*) stake, picket; (*de tente*) peg. **2 p. (de grève)** picket (line), strike picket. **3 au p.** *Scol* in the corner.

piqueté [pikte] *a* **p.** **de** dotted with.

pirate [pirat] *nm* pirate; **p. de l'air** hijacker; — *a* (*radio, bateau*) pirate-. ◆**piraterie** *nf* piracy; (*acte*) act of piracy; **p. aérienne** hijacking.

pire [pir] *a* worse (**que** than); **le p. moment/résultat/etc** the worst moment/result/*etc*; — *nmf* **le** ***ou*** **la p.** the worst (one); **le p. de tout** the worst (thing) of all; **au p.** at (the very) worst; **s'attendre au p.** to expect the (very) worst.

pirogue [pirɔg] *nf* canoe, dugout.

pis [pi] *nm* **1** (*de vache*) udder. **2** *a inv* & *adv* *Litt* worse; **de mal en p.** from bad to worse; — *nm* **le p.** *Litt* the worst.

pis-aller [pizale] *nm inv* (*personne, solution*) stopgap.

piscine [pisin] *nf* swimming pool.

pissenlit [pisɑ̃li] *nm* dandelion.

pistache [pistaʃ] *nf* (*fruit, parfum*) pistachio.

piste [pist] *nf* (*trace de personne ou d'animal*) track, trail; *Sp* track, racetrack; (*de magnétophone*) track; *Av* runway; (*de cirque*) ring; (*de patinage*) rink; (*pour chevaux*) racecourse, racetrack; **p. cyclable** cycle track, *Am* bicycle path; **p. de danse** dance floor; **p. de ski** ski run; **tour de p.** *Sp* lap.

pistolet [pistɔlɛ] *nm* gun, pistol; (*de peintre*) spray gun.

piston [pistɔ̃] *nm* **1** *Aut* piston. **2 avoir du p.** (*appui*) to have connections. ◆**pistonner** *vt* (*appuyer*) to pull strings for.

pitié [pitje] *nf* pity; **j'ai p. de lui, il me fait p.** I pity him, I feel sorry for him. ◆**piteux, -euse** *a Iron* pitiful. ◆**pitoyable** [pitwajabl] *a* pitiful.

piton [pitɔ̃] *nm* **1** (*à crochet*) hook. **2** *Géog* peak.

pitre [pitr] *nm* clown. ◆**pitrerie(s)** *nf(pl)* clowning.

pittoresque [pitɔresk] *a* picturesque.

pivert [piver] *nm* (*oiseau*) woodpecker.

pivoine [pivwan] *nf Bot* peony.

pivot [pivo] *nm* pivot; (*personne*) *Fig* linchpin, mainspring. ◆**pivoter** *vi* (*personne*) to swing round; (*fauteuil*) to swivel; (*porte*) to revolve.

pizza [pidza] *nf* pizza. ◆**pizzeria** *nf* pizza parlour.

placage [plakaʒ] *nm* (*revêtement*) facing; (*en bois*) veneer.

placard [plakar] *nm* **1** (*armoire*) cupboard, *Am* closet. **2** (*pancarte*) poster. ◆**placarder** *vt* (*affiche*) to post (up); (*mur*) to cover with posters.

place [plas] *nf* (*endroit, rang*) & *Sp* place; (*occupée par qn ou qch*) room; (*lieu public*) square; (*siège*) seat, place; (*prix d'un trajet*) *Aut* fare; (*emploi*) job, position; **p. (forte)** *Mil* fortress; (*de parking*) (parking) space; **p. financière** (*money*) market; **à la p.** (*échange*) instead of (*de*); **à votre p.** in your place; **sur p.** on the spot; **en p.** (*objet*) in place; **ne pas tenir en p.** to be unable to keep still; **mettre en p.** to install, set up; **faire p. à** to give way to; **changer qch de p.** to move sth. ◆**plac/er** [plase] *vt* (*mettre*) to put, place; (*situer*) to place, position; (*invité, spectateur*) to seat; (*argent*) to invest, place (*dans* in); (*vendre*) to place, sell; **p. un mot** to get a word in edgeways *ou Am* edgewise; **— se p.** *vpr* (*personne*) to take up a position, place oneself; (*objet*) to be put *ou* placed; (*cheval, coureur*) to be placed; **se p. troisième/etc** *Sp* to come *ou* be third/*etc*. ◆**-é** *a* (*objet*) & *Sp* placed; **bien/mal p. pour faire** in a good/bad position to do; **les gens haut placés** people in high places. ◆**-ement** *nm* (*d'argent*) investment.

placide [plasid] *a* placid.

plafond [plafɔ̃] *nm* ceiling. ◆**plafonnier** *nm Aut* roof light.

plage [plaʒ] *nf* **1** beach; (*ville*) (seaside) resort. **2** (*sur disque*) track. **3** **p. arrière** *Aut* parcel shelf.

plagiat [plaʒja] *nm* plagiarism. ◆**plagier** *vt* to plagiarize.

plaid [plɛd] *nm* travelling rug.

plaider [plede] *vti Jur* to plead. ◆**plaideur,**

-euse *nmf* litigant. ◆**plaidoirie** *nf Jur* speech (for the defence). ◆**plaidoyer** *nm* plea.

plaie [plɛ] *nf* (*blessure*) wound; (*coupure*) cut; (*corvée, personne*) *Fig* nuisance.

plaignant, -ante [plɛɲɑ̃, -ɑ̃t] *nmf Jur* plaintiff.

plaindre* [plɛ̃dr] **1** *vt* to feel sorry for, pity. **2 se p.** *vpr* (*protester*) to complain (*de* about, *que* that); **se p. de** (*maux de tête etc*) to complain of *ou* about. ◆**plainte** *nf* complaint; (*cri*) moan, groan. ◆**plaintif, -ive** *a* sorrowful, plaintive.

plaine [plɛn] *nf Géog* plain.

plaire* [plɛr] *vi* & *v imp* **p.** to please; **elle lui plaît** he likes her, she pleases him; **ça me plaît** I like it; **il me plaît de faire** I like doing; **s'il vous** *ou* **te plaît** please; **— se p.** *vpr* (*à Paris etc*) to like *ou* enjoy it; (*l'un à l'autre*) to like each other.

plaisance [plɛzɑ̃s] *nf* **bateau de p.** pleasure boat; **navigation de p.** yachting.

plaisant [plɛzɑ̃] *a* (*drôle*) amusing; (*agréable*) pleasing; *— nm* **mauvais p.** *Péj* joker. ◆**plaisanter** *vi* to joke, jest; **p. avec qch** to trifle with sth; *— vt* to tease. ◆**plaisanterie** *nf* joke, jest; (*bagatelle*) trifle; **par p.** for a joke. ◆**plaisantin** *nm Péj* joker.

plaisir [plezir] *nm* pleasure; **faire p. à** to please; **faites-moi le p. de . . .** would you be good enough to . . . ; **pour le p.** for fun, for the fun of it; **au p. (de vous revoir)** see you again sometime.

plan [plɑ̃] *nm* **1** (*projet, dessin*) plan; (*de ville*) plan, map; (*niveau*) *Géom* plane; **au premier p.** in the foreground; **gros p.** *Phot Cin* close-up; **sur le p. politique/*etc*** from the political/*etc* viewpoint, politically/*etc*; **de premier p.** (*question etc*) major; **p. d'eau** stretch of water; **laisser en p.** (*abandonner*) to ditch. **2** *a* (*plat*) even, flat.

planche [plɑ̃ʃ] *nf* **1** board, plank; **p. à repasser/à dessin** ironing/drawing board; **p. (à roulettes)** skateboard; **p. (de surf)** surfboard; **p. (à voile)** sailboard; **faire de la p. (à voile)** to go windsurfing; **faire la p.** to float on one's back. **2** (*illustration*) plate. **3** (*de légumes*) bed, plot.

plancher [plɑ̃ʃe] *nm* floor.

plan/er [plane] *vi* (*oiseau*) to glide, hover; (*avion*) to glide; **p. sur qn** (*mystère, danger*) to hang over s.o.; **vol plané** glide. ◆**-eur** *nm* (*avion*) glider.

planète [planɛt] *nf* planet. ◆**planétaire** *a* planetary. ◆**planétarium** *nm* planetarium.

planifier [planifje] *vt Écon* to plan. ◆**pla-**

nification nf Écon planning. ◆**planning** nm (industriel, commercial) planning; **p** familial family planning.

planque [plɑ̃k] nf 1 (travail) Fam cushy job. **2** (lieu) Fam hideout. ◆**planquer** vt, − se **p.** vpr Fam to hide.

plant [plɑ̃] nm (plante) seedling; (de légumes etc) bed.

plante [plɑ̃t] nf 1 Bot plant; **p. d'appartement** house plant; **jardin des plantes** botanical gardens. **2 p. des pieds** sole (of the foot). ◆**plant/er** vt (arbre, plante etc) to plant; (clou, couteau) to drive in; (tente, drapeau, échelle) to put up; (mettre) to put (sur on, contre against); (regard) to fix (sur on); **p. là qn** to leave s.o. standing; **se p. devant** to plant oneself in front of. ◆**−é** a (immobile) standing; **bien p.** (personne) sturdy. ◆**plantation** nf (action) planting; (terrain) bed; (de café, d'arbres etc) plantation. ◆**planteur** nm plantation owner.

planton [plɑ̃tɔ̃] nm Mil orderly.

plantureux, -euse [plɑ̃tyrø, -øz] a (repas etc) abundant.

plaque [plak] nf plate; (de verre, métal) sheet; (de verglas) sheet; (de marbre) slab; (de chocolat) bar; (commémorative) plaque; (tache) Méd blotch; **p. chauffante** Culin hotplate; **p. tournante** (carrefour) Fig centre; **p. minéralogique, p. d'immatriculation** Aut number ou Am license plate; **p. dentaire** (dental) plaque.

plaqu/er [plake] vt (métal, bijou) to plate; (bois) to veneer; (cheveux) to plaster (down); Rugby to tackle; (aplatir) to flatten (contre against); (abandonner) Fam to give (sth) up; **p. qn** Fam to ditch s.o.; **se p. contre** to flatten oneself against. ◆**−é** a (bijou) plated; **p. or** gold-plated; − nm **p. or** gold plate. ◆**−age** nm Rugby tackle.

plasma [plasma] nm Méd plasma.

plastic [plastik] nm plastic explosive. ◆**plastiquer** vt to blow up.

plastique [plastik] a (art, substance) plastic; **matière p.** plastic; − nm (matière) plastic; **en p.** (bouteille etc) plastic.

plastron [plastrɔ̃] nm shirtfront.

plat [pla] **1** a flat; (mer) calm, smooth; (fade) flat, dull; **à fond p.** flat-bottomed; **à p. ventre** flat on one's face; **à p.** (pneu, batterie) flat; (déprimé, épuisé) Fam low; **poser à p.** to put ou lay (sth) down flat; **tomber à p.** to fall down flat; **assiette plate** dinner plate; **calme p.** dead calm; − nm (de la main) flat. **2** nm (récipient, mets) dish; (partie du repas) course; **'p. du jour'** (au restaurant) 'today's special'.

platane [platan] nm plane tree.

plateau, -x [plato] nm (pour servir) tray; (de balance) pan; (de tourne-disque) turntable; (plate-forme) Cin TV set; Th stage; Géog plateau; **p. à fromages** cheeseboard.

plate-bande [platbɑ̃d] nf (pl plates-bandes) flower bed.

plate-forme [platform] nf (pl plates-formes) platform; **p.-forme pétrolière** oil rig.

platine [platin] **1** nm (métal) platinum. **2** nf (d'électrophone) deck. ◆**platiné** a (cheveux) platinum, platinum-blond(e).

platitude [platityd] nf platitude.

plâtre [plɑtr] nm (matière) plaster; **un p.** Méd a plaster cast; **dans le p.** Méd in plaster; **les plâtres** (d'une maison etc) the plasterwork; **p. à mouler** plaster of Paris. ◆**plâtr/er** vt (mur) to plaster; (membre) to put in plaster. ◆**−age** nm plastering. ◆**plâtrier** nm plasterer.

plausible [plozibl] a plausible.

plébiscite [plebisit] nm plebiscite.

plein [plɛ̃] a (rempli, complet) full; (paroi) solid; (ivre) Fam tight; **p. de** full of; **en pleine mer** on the open sea; **en p. visage/etc** right in the middle of the face/etc; **en p. jour** in broad daylight; − prép & adv **des billes p. les poches** pockets full of marbles; **du chocolat p. la figure** chocolate all over one's face; **p. de lettres/d'argent/etc** (beaucoup de) Fam lots of letters/money/etc; **à p.** (travailler) to full capacity; − nm **faire le p.** Aut to fill up (the tank); **battre son p.** (fête) to be in full swing. ◆**pleinement** adv fully.

pléonasme [pleɔnasm] nm (expression) redundancy.

pléthore [pletɔr] nf plethora.

pleurer [plœre] vi to cry, weep (sur over); − vt (regretter) to mourn (for). ◆**pleureur** a **saule p.** weeping willow. ◆**pleurnicher** vi to snivel, grizzle. ◆**pleurs (en)** adv in tears.

pleurésie [plœrezi] nf Méd pleurisy.

pleuvoir* [pløvwar] v imp to rain; **il pleut** it's raining; − vi (coups etc) to rain down (sur on).

pli [pli] nm 1 (de papier etc) fold; (de jupe, robe) pleat; (de pantalon, de bouche) crease; (de bras) bend; (faux) p. crease; **mise en plis** (coiffure) set. **2** (enveloppe) Com envelope, letter; **sous p. séparé** under separate cover. **3** Cartes trick. **4** (habitude) habit; **prendre le p. de faire** to get into the habit of doing. ◆**pli/er** vt to fold; (courber) to bend; **p. qn à** to submit s.o. to; − vi (branche) to bend; − **se p.** vpr (lit, chaise *etc*) to fold (up); **se p.** à to submit to, give in to. ◆**–ant** *a* (*chaise etc*) folding; (*parapluie*) telescopic; – *nm* folding stool. ◆**–able** *a* pliable. ◆**–age** *nm* (*manière*) fold; (*action*) folding.

plinthe [plɛ̃t] *nf* skirting board, *Am* base-board.

pliss/er [plise] *vt* (*jupe, robe*) to pleat; (*froisser*) to crease; (*lèvres*) to pucker; (*front*) to wrinkle, crease; (*yeux*) to screw up. ◆**–é** *nm* pleating, pleats.

plomb [plɔ̃] *nm* (*métal*) lead; (*fusible*) *Él* fuse; (*poids pour rideau etc*) lead weight; *pl* (*de chasse*) lead shot, buckshot; **de p.** (*tuyau etc*) lead-; (*sommeil*) *Fig* heavy; (*soleil*) blazing; (*ciel*) leaden. ◆**plomb/er** *vt* (*dent*) to fill; (*colis*) to seal (with lead). ◆**–é** *a* (*teint*) leaden. ◆**–age** *nm* (*de dent*) filling.

plombier [plɔ̃bje] *nm* plumber. ◆**plomberie** *nf* (*métier, installations*) plumbing.

plong/er [plɔ̃ʒe] *vi* (*personne, avion etc*) to dive, plunge; (*route, regard*) *Fig* to plunge; – *vt* (*mettre, enfoncer*) to plunge, thrust (*dans into*); **se p. dans** (*lecture etc*) to immerse oneself in. ◆**–eant** *a* (*décolleté*) plunging; (*vue*) bird's-eye. ◆**–é** *a* **dans** (*lecture etc*) immersed *ou* deep in. ◆**–ée** *nf* diving; (*de sous-marin*) submersion; **en p.** (*sous-marin*) submerged. ◆**plongeoir** *nm* diving board. ◆**plongeon** *nm* dive. ◆**plongeur, –euse** *nmf* diver; (*employé de restaurant*) dishwasher.

plouf [pluf] *nm & int* splash.

ployer [plwaje] *vti* to bend.

plu [ply] *voir* **plaire, pleuvoir**.

pluie [plɥi] *nf* rain; **une p.** (*averse*) & *Fig* a shower; **sous la p.** in the rain.

plume [plym] *nf* **1** (*d'oiseau*) feather. **2** (*pour écrire*) *Hist* quill (pen); (*pointe en acier*) (pen) nib; **stylo à p.** (fountain) pen; **vivre de sa p.** *Fig* to live by one's pen. ◆**plumage** *nm* plumage. ◆**plumeau, –x** *nm* feather duster. ◆**plumer** *vt* (*volaille*) to pluck; **p. qn** (*voler*) *Fig* to fleece s.o. ◆**plumet** *nm* plume. ◆**plumier** *nm* pencil box, pen box.

plupart (la) [laplypar] *nf* most; **la p. des cas**/*etc* most cases/*etc*; **la p. du temps** most of the time; **la p. d'entre eux** most of them; **pour la p.** mostly.

pluriel, –ielle [plyrjɛl] *a & nm Gram* plural; **au p.** (*nom*) plural, in the plural.

plus¹ [ply] ([plyz] *before vowel*, [plys] *in end position*) **1** *adv comparatif* (*travailler etc*) more (**que** than); **p. d'un kilo/de dix**/*etc* (*quantité, nombre*) more than a kilo/ten/

etc; **p. de thé**/*etc* (*davantage*) more tea/*etc*; **p. beau/rapidement**/*etc* more beautiful/rapidly/*etc* (**que** than); **p. tard** later; **p. petit** smaller; **de p. en p.** more and more; **de p. en p. vite** quicker and quicker; **p. il crie p. il s'enroue** the more he shouts the more hoarse he gets; **p. ou moins** more or less; **en p.** in addition (**de** to); **de p.** more (**que** than); (*en outre*) moreover; **les enfants** (*âgés*) **de p. de dix** ans children over ten; **j'ai dix ans de p. qu'elle** I'm ten years older than she is; **il est p. de cinq heures** it's after five (*o'clock*). **2** *adv superlatif* **le p.** (*travailler etc*) (the) most; **le p. beau**/*etc* the most beautiful/*etc*; (*de deux*) the more beautiful/*etc*; **le p. grand**/*etc* the biggest/*etc*; the bigger/*etc*; **le p. de livres** (*the*) most books; **j'en ai le p.** I have (the) most; (**tout**) **au p.** at (the very) most.

plus² [ply] *adv de négation* **p. de** (*pain, argent etc*) no more; **il n'a p. de pain** he has no more bread, he doesn't have any more bread; **tu n'es p. jeune** you're no longer young, you're not young any more *ou* any longer; **elle ne le fait p.** she no longer does it, she doesn't do it any more *ou* any longer; **je ne le reverrai p.** I won't see him again.

plus³ [plys] *prép* plus; **deux p. deux font quatre** two plus two are four; **il fait p. deux** (*degrés*) it's two degrees above freezing; – *nm* **le signe p.** the plus sign.

plusieurs [plyzjœr] *a & pron* several.

plus-value [plyvaly] *nf* (*bénéfice*) profit.

plutonium [plytɔnjɔm] *nm* plutonium.

plutôt [plyto] *adv* rather (**que** than).

pluvieux, –euse [plyvjø, –øz] *a* rainy, wet.

PMU [peɛmy] *abrév = pari mutuel urbain.*

pneu [pnø] *nm* (*pl –s*) **1** (*de roue*) tyre, *Am* tire. **2** (*lettre*) express letter. ◆**pneumatique** *a* **1** (*à matelas etc*) inflatable; **marteau p.** pneumatic drill. **2** *nm* = **pneu.**

pneumonie [pnømɔni] *nf* pneumonia.

poche [pɔʃ] *nf* pocket; (*de kangourou etc*) pouch; (*sac en papier etc*) bag; *pl* (*sous les yeux*) bags; **livre de p.** paperback; **faire des poches** (*pantalon*) to be baggy; **j'ai un franc en p.** I have one franc on me. ◆**pochette** *nf* (*sac*) bag, envelope; (*d'allumettes*) book; (*de disque*) sleeve, jacket; (*mouchoir*) pocket handkerchief; (*sac à main*) (clutch) bag.

poch/er [pɔʃe] *vt* **1 p. l'œil à qn** to give s.o. a black eye. **2** (*œufs*) to poach. ◆**–é** *a* **œil p.** black eye.

podium [pɔdjɔm] *nm Sp* rostrum, podium.

poêle [pwal] **1** *nm* stove. **2** *nf* **p.** (à frire) frying pan.

poème [pɔɛm] *nm* poem. ◆**poésie** *nf* poetry; **une p.** (*poème*) a piece of poetry. ◆**poète** *nm* poet; – *a* **femme p.** poetess. ◆**poétique** *a* poetic.

pognon [pɔɲɔ̃] *nm* (*argent*) *Fam* dough.

poids [pwa] *nm* weight; **au p.** by weight; **de p.** (*influent*) influential; **poids lourd** (heavy) lorry *ou Am* truck; **lancer le p.** *Sp* to put *ou* hurl the shot.

poignant [pwaɲɑ̃] *a* (*souvenir etc*) poignant.

poignard [pwaɲar] *nm* dagger; **coup de p.** stab. ◆**poignarder** *vt* to stab.

poigne [pwaɲ] *nf* (*étreinte*) grip.

poignée [pwaɲe] *nf* (*quantité*) handful (**de** of); (*de porte, casserole etc*) handle; (*d'épée*) hilt; **p. de main** handshake; **donner une p. de main à** to shake hands with.

poignet [pwaɲɛ] *nm* wrist; (*de chemise*) cuff.

poil [pwal] *nm* hair; (*pelage*) coat, fur; (*de brosse*) bristle; *pl* (*de tapis*) pile; (*d'étoffe*) nap; **à p.** (*nu*) *Arg* (stark) naked; **au p.** (*travail etc*) *Arg* top-rate; **de bon/mauvais p.** *Fam* in a good/bad mood; **de tout p.** *Fam* of all kinds. ◆**poilu** *a* hairy.

poinçon [pwɛ̃sɔ̃] *nm* (*outil*) awl, bradawl; (*marque de bijou etc*) hallmark. ◆**poinçonner** *vt* (*bijou*) to hallmark; (*billet*) to punch. ◆**poinçonneuse** *nf* (*machine*) punch.

poindre [pwɛ̃dr] *vi* (*jour*) *Litt* to dawn.

poing [pwɛ̃] *nm* fist; **coup de p.** punch.

point¹ [pwɛ̃] *nm* (*lieu, question, degré, score etc*) point; (*sur i, à l'horizon etc*) dot; (*tache*) spot; (*note*) *Scol* mark; (*de couture*) stitch; **sur le p. de faire** about to do, on the point of doing; **p. (final)** full stop, period; **p. d'exclamation** exclamation mark *ou Am* point; **p. d'interrogation** question mark; **p. de vue** point of view, viewpoint; (*endroit*) viewing point; **à p. (nommé)** (*arriver etc*) at the right moment; **à p.** (*rôti etc*) medium (cooked); (*steak*) medium rare; **mal en p.** in bad shape; **mettre au p.** *Phot* to focus; *Aut* to tune; (*technique etc*) to elaborate, perfect; (*éclaircir*) *Fig* to clarify, clear up; **mise au p.** focusing; tuning, tune-up; elaboration; *Fig* clarification; **faire le p.** *Fig* to take stock, sum up; **p. mort** *Aut* neutral; **au p. mort** *Fig* at a standstill; **p. noir** *Aut* (*accident*) black spot; **p. du jour** daybreak; **p. de côté** (*douleur*) stitch (in one's side). ◆**p.-virgule** *nm* (*pl* points-virgules) semicolon.

point² [pwɛ̃] *adv Litt* = **pas**¹.

pointe [pwɛ̃t] *nf* (*extrémité*) point, tip; (*pour grille*) spike; (*clou*) nail; *Géog* headland; (*maximum*) *Fig* peak; **une p. de** (*soupçon, nuance*) a touch of; **sur la p. des pieds** on

tiptoe; **en p.** pointed; **de p.** (*technique etc*) latest, most advanced; **à la p. de** (*progrès etc*) *Fig* in *ou* at the forefront of.

point/er [pwɛ̃te] **1** *vt* (*cocher*) to tick (off), *Am* check (off). **2** *vt* (*braquer, diriger*) to point (**sur, vers** at). **3** *vti* (*employé*) to clock in, (*à la sortie*) to clock out; – **se p.** *vpr* (*arriver*) *Fam* to show up. **4** *vt* (*bourgeon etc*) to appear; **p. vers** to point upwards towards. ◆**–age** *nm* (*de personnel*) clocking in; clocking out.

pointillé [pwɛ̃tije] *nm* dotted line; – *a* dotted.

pointilleux, -euse [pwɛ̃tijø, -øz] *a* fussy, particular.

pointu [pwɛ̃ty] *a* (*en pointe*) pointed; (*voix*) shrill.

pointure [pwɛ̃tyr] *nf* (*de chaussure, gant*) size.

poire [pwar] *nf* **1** (*fruit*) pear. **2** (*figure*) *Fam* mug. **3** (*personne*) *Fam* sucker. ◆**poirier** *nm* pear tree.

poireau, -x [pwaro] *nm* leek.

poireauter [pwarote] *vi* (*attendre*) *Fam* to kick one's heels.

pois [pwa] *nm* (*légume*) pea; (*dessin*) (polka) dot; **petits p.** (garden) peas; **p. chiche** chickpea; **à p.** (*vêtement*) spotted, dotted.

poison [pwazɔ̃] *nm* (*substance*) poison.

poisse [pwas] *nf Fam* bad luck.

poisseux, -euse [pwasø, -øz] *a* sticky.

poisson [pwasɔ̃] *nm* fish; **p. rouge** goldfish; **les Poissons** (*signe*) Pisces. ◆**poissonnerie** *nf* fish shop. ◆**poissonnier, -ière** *nmf* fishmonger.

poitrine [pwatrin] *nf Anat* chest; (*seins*) breast, bosom; (*de veau, mouton*) *Culin* breast.

poivre [pwavr] *nm* pepper. ◆**poivr/er** *vt* to pepper. ◆**–é** *a Culin* peppery; (*plaisanterie*) *Fig* spicy. ◆**poivrier** *nm Bot* pepper plant; (*ustensile*) pepperpot. ◆**poivrière** *nf* pepperpot.

poivron [pwavrɔ̃] *nm* pepper, capsicum.

poivrot, -ote [pwavro, -ɔt] *nmf Fam* drunk(ard).

poker [pɔkɛr] *nm Cartes* poker.

polar [pɔlar] *nm* (*roman*) *Fam* whodunit.

polariser [pɔlarize] *vt* to polarize.

pôle [pol] *nm Géog* pole; **p. Nord/Sud** North/South Pole. ◆**polaire** *a* polar.

polémique [pɔlemik] *a* controversial, polemical; – *nf* controversy, polemic.

poli [pɔli] **1** *a* (*courtois*) polite (**avec** to, with). **2** *a* (*lisse, brillant*) polished; – *nm* (*aspect*) polish. ◆**—ment** *adv* politely.

police [pɔlis] *nf* **1** police; **faire** *ou* **assurer la**

p. to maintain order (**dans** in); **p. secours** emergency services; **p. mondaine** *ou* **des mœurs** = vice squad. **2 p. (d'assurance)** (insurance) policy. **◆policier** *a* (*enquête, état*) police-; **roman p.** detective novel; – *nm* policeman, detective.

polichinelle [poliʃinɛl] *nf* secret de p. open secret.

polio [poljo] *nf* (*maladie*) polio; – *nmf* (*personne*) polio victim. **◆poliomyélite** *nf* poliomyelitis.

polir [poliʀ] *vt* (*substance dure, style*) to polish.

polisson, -onne [polisɔ̃, -ɔn] *a* naughty; – *nmf* rascal.

politesse [polites] *nf* politeness; **une p.** (*parole*) a polite word; (*action*) an act of politeness.

politique [politik] *a* political; **homme p.** politician; – *nf* (*science, activité*) politics; (*mesures, manières de gouverner*) Pol policies; **une p.** (*tactique*) a policy. **◆politicien, -ienne** *nmf Péj* politician. **◆politiser** *vt* to politicize.

pollen [polɛn] *nm* pollen.

polluer [polɥe] *vt* to pollute. **◆polluant** *nm* pollutant. **◆pollution** *nf* pollution.

polo [polo] *nm* **1** (*chemise*) sweat shirt. **2** *Sp* polo.

polochon [poloʃɔ̃] *nm* (*traversin*) *Fam* bolster.

Pologne [polɔɲ] *nf* Poland. **◆polonais, -aise** *a* Polish; – *nmf* Pole; – *nm* (*langue*) Polish.

poltron, -onne [poltrɔ̃, -ɔn] *a* cowardly; – *nmf* coward.

polycopi/er [polikopje] *vt* to mimeograph, duplicate. **◆-é** *nm Univ* mimeographed copy (*of lecture etc*).

polyester [poliɛstɛr] *nm* polyester.

Polynésie [polinezi] *nf* Polynesia.

polyvalent [polivalɑ̃] *a* (*rôle*) multi-purpose, varied; (*professeur, ouvrier*) all-round; **école polyvalente, lycée p.** comprehensive school.

pommade [pomad] *nf* ointment.

pomme [pom] *nf* **1** apple; **p. d'Adam** *Anat* Adam's apple. **2** (*d'arrosoir*) rose. **3 p. de terre** (*pl* **pommes de terre**) potato; **pommes vapeur** steamed potatoes; **pommes frites** chips, *Am* French fries; **pommes chips** potato crisps *ou Am* chips. **◆pommier** *nm* apple tree.

pommette [pomet] *nf* cheekbone.

pompe [pɔ̃p] **1** *nf* pump; **p. à essence** petrol *ou Am* gas station; **p. à incendie** fire engine; **coup de p.** *Fam* tired feeling. **2** *nf* (*chaussure*) *Fam* shoe. **3** *nf* (*en gymnastique*)

press-up, *Am* push-up. **4** *nfpl* **pompes funèbres** undertaker's; **entrepreneur des pompes funèbres** undertaker. **5** *nf* **p. anti-sèche** *Scol* crib. **6** *nf* (*splendeur*) pomp. **◆pomper** *vt* to pump; (*évacuer*) to pump out (**de** of); (*absorber*) to soak up; (*épuiser*) *Fam* to tire out; – *vi* to pump. **◆pompeux, -euse** *a* pompous. **◆pompier 1** *nm* fireman; **voiture des pompiers** fire engine. **2** *a* (*emphatique*) pompous. **◆pompiste** *nmf Aut* pump attendant.

pompon [pɔ̃pɔ̃] *nm* (*ornement*) pompon.

pomponner [pɔ̃pɔne] *vt* to doll up.

ponce [pɔ̃s] *nf* (*pierre*) **p.** pumice (stone). **◆poncer** *vt* to rub down, sand. **◆ponceuse** *nf* (*machine*) sander.

ponctuation [pɔ̃ktɥasjɔ̃] *nf* punctuation. **◆ponctuer** *vt* to punctuate (**de** with).

ponctuel, -elle [pɔ̃ktɥɛl] *a* (*à l'heure*) punctual; (*unique*) *Fig* one-off, *Am* one-of-a-kind. **◆ponctualité** *nf* punctuality.

pondéré [pɔ̃dere] *a* level-headed. **◆pondération** *nf* level-headedness.

pondre [pɔ̃dr] *vt* (*œuf*) to lay; (*livre, discours*) *Péj Fam* to produce; – *vi* (*poule*) to lay.

poney [pone] *nm* pony.

pont [pɔ̃] *nm* bridge; (*de bateau*) deck; **p. (de graissage)** *Aut* ramp; **faire le p.** *Fig* to take the intervening day(s) off (*between two holidays*); **p. aérien** airlift. **◆p.-levis** *nm* (*pl* **ponts-levis**) drawbridge.

ponte [pɔ̃t] **1** *nf* (*d'œufs*) laying. **2** *nm* (*personne*) *Fam* bigwig.

pontife [pɔ̃tif] *nm* **1** (*souverain*) **p.** pope. **2** (*ponte*) *Fam* bigshot. **◆pontifical, -aux** *a* papal, pontifical.

pop [pop] *nm & a inv Mus* pop.

popote [popot] *nf* (*cuisine*) *Fam* cooking.

populace [popylas] *nf Péj* rabble.

populaire [popylɛr] *a* (*personne, tradition, gouvernement etc*) popular; (*quartier, milieu*) lower-class; (*expression*) colloquial; (*art*) folk-. **◆populariser** *vt* to popularize. **◆popularité** *nf* popularity (**auprès de** with).

population [popylasjɔ̃] *nf* population. **◆populeux, -euse** *a* populous, crowded.

porc [pɔr] *nm* pig; (*viande*) pork; (*personne*) *Péj* swine.

porcelaine [pɔrsalɛn] *nf* china, porcelain.

porc-épic [pɔrkepik] *nm* (*pl* **porcs-épics**) (*animal*) porcupine.

porche [pɔrʃ] *nm* porch.

porcherie [pɔrʃəri] *nf* pigsty.

pore [pɔr] *nm* pore. **◆poreux, -euse** *a* porous.

pornographie [pɔrnɔgrafi] *nf* pornography. ◆**pornographique** *a* (*Fam* **porno**) pornographic.

port [pɔr] *nm* **1** port, harbour; **arriver à bon p.** to arrive safely. **2** (*d'armes*) carrying; (*de barbe*) wearing; (*prix*) carriage, postage; (*attitude*) bearing.

portable [pɔrtabl] *a* (*robe etc*) wearable; (*portatif*) portable.

portail [pɔrtaj] *nm* (*de cathédrale etc*) portal.

portant [pɔrtɑ̃] **à bien p.** in good health.

portatif, -ive [pɔrtatif, -iv] *a* portable.

porte [pɔrt] *nf* door, doorway; (*de jardin*) gate; (*passage*) gateway; (*de ville*) entrance, *Hist* gate; **p. (d'embarquement)** *Av* (departure) gate; **Alger, p. de ... Al-**giers, gateway to ...; **p. d'entrée** front door; **mettre à la p.** (*jeter dehors*) to throw out; (*renvoyer*) to sack. ◆**p.-fenêtre** *nf* (*pl* **portes-fenêtres**) French window.

porte-à-faux [pɔrtafo] *nm inv* **en p.-à-faux** (*en déséquilibre*) unstable.

porte-avions [pɔrtavjɔ̃] *nm inv* aircraft carrier. ◆**p.-bagages** *nm inv* luggage rack. ◆**p.-bébé** *nm* (*nacelle*) carrycot, *Am* baby basket; (*kangourou®*) baby sling. ◆**p.-bonheur** *nm inv* (*fétiche*) (lucky) charm. ◆**p.-cartes** *nm inv* card holder *ou* case. ◆**p.-clés** *nm inv* key ring. ◆**p.-documents** *nm inv* briefcase. ◆**p.-drapeau, -x** *nm Mil* standard bearer. ◆**p.-jarretelles** *nm inv* suspender *ou Am* garter belt. ◆**p.-monnaie** *nm inv* purse. ◆**p.-parapluie** *nm inv* umbrella stand. ◆**p.-plume** *nm inv* pen (*for dipping in ink*). ◆**p.-revues** *nm inv* newspaper rack. ◆**p.-savon** *nm* soapdish. ◆**p.-serviettes** *nm inv* towel rail. ◆**p.-voix** *nm inv* megaphone.

portée [pɔrte] *nf* **1** (*de fusil etc*) range; **à la p. de qn** within reach of s.o.; (*richesse, plaisir etc*) *Fig* within s.o.'s grasp; **à p. de la main** within (easy) reach; **à p. de voix** within earshot; **hors de p.** out of reach. **2** (*animaux*) litter. **3** (*importance, effet*) significance, import. **4** *Mus* stave.

portefeuille [pɔrtəfœj] *nm* wallet; *Pol Com* portfolio.

portemanteau, -x [pɔrtmɑ̃to] *nm* (*sur pied*) hatstand; (*barre*) hat *ou* coat peg.

porte-parole [pɔrtparɔl] *nm inv* (*homme*) spokesman; (*femme*) spokeswoman (**de** for, of).

port/er [pɔrte] *vt* to carry; (*vêtement, lunettes, barbe etc*) to wear; (*trace, responsabilité, fruits etc*) to bear; (*regard*) to cast; (*attaque*) to make (**contre** against); (*coup*) to strike; (*sentiment*) to have (**à** for); (*inscrire*) to enter, write down; **p. qch à** (*amener*) to bring *ou* take sth to; **p. qn à faire** (*pousser*) to lead *ou* prompt s.o. to do; **p. bonheur/malheur** to bring good/bad luck; **se faire p. malade** to report sick; – *vi* (*voix*) to carry; (*canon*) to fire; (*vue*) to extend; **p. (juste)** (*coup*) to hit the mark; (*mot, reproche*) to hit home; **p. sur** (*reposer sur*) to rest on; (*concerner*) to bear on; (*accent*) to fall on; (*heurter*) to strike; – **se p.** *vpr* (*vêtement*) to be worn; **se p. bien/mal** to be well/ill; **comment te portes-tu?** how are you?; **se p. candidat** to stand as a candidate. ◆**—ant à bien p.** in good health. ◆**—é à p. à croire/etc** inclined to believe/etc; **p. sur qch** fond of sth. ◆**—eur, -euse** *nm Rail* porter; – *nmf Méd* carrier; (*de nouvelles, chèque*) bearer; **mère porteuse** surrogate mother.

portier [pɔrtje] *nm* doorkeeper, porter. ◆**portière** *nf* (*de véhicule, train*) door. ◆**portillon** *nm* gate.

portion [pɔrsjɔ̃] *nf* (*part, partie*) portion; (*de nourriture*) helping, portion.

portique [pɔrtik] *nm* **1** *Archit* portico. **2** (*de balançoire etc*) crossbar, frame.

porto [pɔrto] *nm* (*vin*) port.

portrait [pɔrtrɛ] *nm* portrait; **être le p. de** (*son père etc*) to be the image of; **faire un p.** to paint *ou* draw a portrait (**de** of); **p. en pied** full-length portrait. ◆**p.-robot** *nm* (*pl* **portraits-robots**) identikit (picture), photofit.

portuaire [pɔrtɥer] *a* (*installations etc*) harbour-.

Portugal [pɔrtygal] *nm* Portugal. ◆**portugais, -aise** *a* & *nmf* Portuguese; – *nm* (*langue*) Portuguese.

pose [poz] *nf* **1** (*installation*) putting up; putting in; laying. **2** (*attitude de modèle, affectation*) pose; (*temps*) *Phot* exposure. ◆**pos/er** *vt* to put (down); (*papier peint, rideaux*) to put up; (*sonnette, chauffage*) to put in; (*mine, moquette, fondations*) to lay; (*question*) to ask (**à qn** s.o.); (*principe, conditions*) to lay down; **p. sa candidature** to apply, put in one's application (**à** for); **pose la question de ...** it poses the question of ...; – *vi* (*modèle etc*) to pose (**pour** for); – **se p.** *vpr* (*oiseau, avion*) to land; (*problème, question*) to arise; **se p. sur** (*yeux*) to fix on; **se p. en chef/etc** to set oneself up as *ou* pose as a leader/etc; **la question se pose!** this question should be asked! ◆**—é** *a* (*calme*) calm, staid.

◆**—ément** adv calmly. ◆**—eur, -euse** nmf Péj poseur.

positif, -ive [pozitif, -iv] a positive. ◆**positivement** adv positively.

position [pozisjɔ̃] nf (attitude, emplacement, opinion etc) position; **prendre p.** Fig to take a stand (**contre** against); **prise de p.** stand.

posologie [pozolɔʒi] nf (de médicament) dosage.

posséder [posede] vt to possess; (maison etc) to own, possess; (bien connaître) to master. ◆**possesseur** nm possessor; owner. ◆**possessif, -ive** a (personne, adjectif etc) possessive; – nm Gram possessive. ◆**possession** nf possession; **en p.** de in possession of; **prendre p. de** to take possession of.

possible [posibl] a possible (à **faire** to do); **il (nous) est p. de le faire** it is possible (for us) to do it; **il est p. que** (+ sub) it is possible that; **si p.** if possible; **le plus tôt/etc p.** as soon/etc as possible; **autant que p.** as much ou as many as possible; – nm **faire son p.** to do one's utmost (**pour faire** to do); **dans la mesure du p.** as far as possible. ◆**possibilité** nf possibility.

post- [post] préf post-.

postdater [postdate] vt to postdate.

poste [post] 1 nf (service) post, mail; (local) post office; (Administration) bureau de p. post office; **Postes (et Télécommunications)** (administration) Post Office; **par la p.** by post, by mail; **par avion** airmail; **mettre à la p.** to post, mail. 2 nm (lieu, emploi) post; **p. de secours** first aid post; **p. de police** police station; **p. d'essence** petrol ou Am gas station; **p. d'incendie** fire hydrant; **p. d'aiguillage** signal box ou Am tower. 3 nm (appareil) Rad TV set; Tél extension (number). ◆**postal, -aux** a postal; **boîte postale** PO Box; **code p.** postcode, Am zip code. ◆**poster 1** vt (lettre) to post, mail. 2 vt (placer) Mil to post s.o. ◆**poster 3** [poster] nm poster.

postérieur [posterjœr] a (document etc) later; **p. à** after. 2 nm (derrière) Fam posterior.

postérité [posterite] nf posterity.

posthume [postym] a posthumous; **à titre p.** posthumously.

postiche [postiʃ] a false.

postier, -ière [postje, -jɛr] nmf postal worker.

postillonner [postijɔne] vi to sputter.

post-scriptum [postskriptɔm] nm inv postscript.

postul/er [postyle] vt 1 (emploi) to apply for. 2 (poser) Math to postulate. ◆**—ant, -ante** nmf applicant.

posture [postyr] nf posture.

pot [po] nm 1 pot; (à confiture) jar, pot; (à lait) jug; (à bière) mug; (de crème, yaourt) carton; **p. de chambre** chamber pot; **p. de fleurs** flower pot; **prendre un p.** (verre) Fam to have a drink. 2 (chance) Fam luck; **avoir du p.** to be lucky.

potable [potabl] a drinkable; (passable) Fam tolerable; **'eau p.'** 'drinking water'.

potage [potaʒ] nm soup.

potager, -ère [potaʒe, -ɛr] a (jardin) vegetable-; **plante potagère** vegetable; – nm vegetable garden.

potasser [potase] vt (examen) to cram for; – vi to cram.

pot-au-feu [potofø] nm inv (plat) beef stew.

pot-de-vin [podvɛ̃] nm (pl **pots-de-vin**) bribe.

pote [pot] nm (ami) Fam pal, buddy.

poteau, -x [poto] nm post; (télégraphique) pole; **p. d'arrivée** Sp winning post.

potelé [potle] a plump, chubby.

potence [potɑ̃s] nf (gibet) gallows.

potentiel, -ielle [potɑ̃sjɛl] a & nm potential.

poterie [potri] nf (art) pottery; **une p.** a piece of pottery; **des poteries** (objets) pottery. ◆**potier** nm potter.

potin [potɛ̃] 1 nmpl (cancans) gossip. 2 nm (bruit) Fam row.

potion [posjɔ̃] nf potion.

potiron [potirɔ̃] nm pumpkin.

pot-pourri [popuri] nm (pl **pots-pourris**) Mus medley.

pou, -x [pu] nm louse; **poux** lice.

poubelle [pubɛl] nf dustbin, Am garbage can.

pouce [pus] nm 1 thumb; **un coup de p.** Fam a helping hand. 2 (mesure) Hist & Fig inch.

poudre [pudr] nf powder; **p.** (à canon) (explosif) gunpowder; **en p.** (lait) powdered; (chocolat) drinking; **sucre en p.** castor ou caster sugar. ◆**poudrer** vt to powder; – **se p.** (femme) to powder one's nose. ◆**poudreux, -euse** a powdery, dusty. ◆**poudrier** nm (powder) compact. ◆**poudrière** nf powder magazine; (région) Fig powder keg.

pouf [puf] 1 int thump! 2 nm (siège) pouf(fe).

pouffer [pufe] vi **p.** (de rire) to burst out laughing, guffaw.

pouilleux, -euse [pujø, -øz] a (sordide) miserable; (mendiant) lousy.

poulain [pulɛ̃] nm (cheval) foal; **le p. de qn** Fig s.o.'s protégé.

poule [pul] *nf* 1 hen. *Culin* fowl; **être p. mouillée** (*lâche*) to be chicken; **oui, ma p.!** *Fam* yes, my pet! 2 (*femme*) *Péj* tart. ◆**poulailler** *nm* 1 (hen) coop. 2 *Th Fam* the gods, the gallery. ◆**poulet** *nm* 1 (*poule, coq*) *Culin* chicken. 2 (*policier*) *Fam* cop.

pouliche [pulif] *nf* (*jument*) filly.

poulie [puli] *nf* pulley.

poulpe [pulp] *nm* octopus.

pouls [pu] *nm Méd* pulse.

poumon [pum3] *nm* lung; **à pleins poumons** (*respirer*) deeply; (*crier*) loudly; **p. d'acier** iron lung.

poupe [pup] *nf Nau* stern, poop.

poupée [pupe] *nf* doll.

poupin [pupɛ̃] *a* **à visage p.** baby face.

poupon [pup3] *nm* (*bébé*) baby; (*poupée*) doll.

pour [pur] 1 *prép* for; **p. toi/moi/etc** for you/me/etc; **faites-le p. lui** do it for him, do it for his sake; **partir p.** (*Paris etc*) to leave for; **elle va partir p. cinq ans** she's leaving for five years; **p. femme/base/etc** as a wife/basis/etc; **p. moi, p. ma part** (*quant à moi*) as for me; **dix p. cent** ten per cent; **gentil p.** kind to; **elle est p.** she's in favour; **p. faire** (in order) to do, so as to do; **p. que tu saches** so (that) you may know; **p. quoi faire?** what for?; **trop petit/poli/etc** **p. faire** too small/polite/etc to do; **assez grand/etc** **p. faire** big enough to do; **p. cela** for that reason; **jour p. jour/heure p. heure** to the day/hour; **p. intelligent/etc qu'il soit** however clever/etc he may be; **ce n'est pas p. me plaire** it doesn't exactly please me; **acheter p. cinq francs de bonbons** to buy five francs' worth of sweets. 2 *nm* **le p. et le contre** the pros and cons.

pourboire [purbwar] *nm* (*argent*) tip.

pourcentage [pursɑ̃taʒ] *nm* percentage.

pourchasser [purfase] *vt* to pursue.

pourparlers [purparle] *nmpl* negotiations, talks.

pourpre [purpr] *a & nm* purple.

pourquoi [purkwa] *adv & conj* why; **p. pas?** why not?; – *nm inv* reason (**de** for); **le p. et le comment** the whys and wherefores.

pourra, pourrait [pura, pure] *voir* **pouvoir 1**.

pourrir [purir] *vi,* – **se p.** *vpr* to rot; – *vt* to rot; **p. qn** to corrupt s.o. ◆**pourri** *a* (*fruit, temps, personne etc*) rotten. ◆**pourriture** *nf* rot, rottenness; (*personne*) *Péj* swine.

poursuite [pursɥit] 1 *nf* chase, pursuit; (*du bonheur, de créancier*) pursuit (**de** of); (*continuation*) continuation; **se mettre à la p. de** to go in pursuit of. 2 *nfpl Jur* legal proceed-

ings (**contre** against). ◆**poursuiv/re°** 1 *vt* (*courir après*) to chase, pursue; (*harceler, relancer*) to hound, pursue; (*obséder*) to haunt; (*but, idéal etc*) to pursue. 2 *vt Jur* (*au criminel*) to prosecute s.o.; (*au civil*) to sue s.o. 3 *vt* (*lecture, voyage etc*) to continue (with), carry on (with), pursue; – *vi,* – **se p.** *vpr* to continue, go on. ◆**-ant, -ante** *nmf* pursuer.

pourtant [purtɑ̃] *adv* yet, nevertheless.

pourtour [purtur] *nm* perimeter.

pourvoir° [purvwar] *vt* to provide (**de** with); **être pourvu de** to have, be provided with; – *vi* **p. à** (*besoins etc*) to provide for. ◆**pourvoyeur, -euse** *nmf* supplier.

pourvu que [purvyk(ə)] *conj* (*condition*) provided *ou* providing (that); **p. qu'elle soit là** (*souhait*) I only hope (that) she's there.

pousse [pus] *nf* 1 (*bourgeon*) shoot, sprout. 2 (*croissance*) growth.

pousse-café [puskafe] *nm inv* after-dinner liqueur.

pouss/er [puse] 1 *vt* to push; (*du coude*) to nudge, poke; (*véhicule, machine*) to drive hard; (*recherches*) to pursue; (*cri*) to utter; (*soupir*) to heave; **p. qn à faire** to urge s.o. to do; **p. qn à bout** to push s.o. to his limits; **p. trop loin** (*gentillesse etc*) to carry too far; **p. à la perfection** to bring to perfection; – *vi* to push; **p. jusqu'à Paris/etc** to push on as far as Paris/etc; – **se p.** *vpr* (*se déplacer*) to move up *ou* over. 2 *vi* (*croître*) to grow; **faire p.** (*plante, barbe etc*) to grow. ◆**-é a** (*travail, études*) advanced. ◆**-ée** *nf* (*pression*) pressure; (*coup*) push; (*d'ennemi*) thrust, push; (*de fièvre etc*) outbreak; (*de l'inflation*) upsurge. ◆**poussette** *nf* pushchair, *Am* stroller; **p. canne** (baby) buggy, *Am* (collapsible) stroller; **p. de marché** shopping trolley *ou Am* cart. ◆**poussoir** *nm* (push) button.

poussière [pusjɛr] *nf* dust; **dix francs et des poussières** *Fam* a bit over ten francs. ◆**poussiéreux, -euse** *a* dusty.

poussif, -ive [pusif, -iv] *a* short-winded, puffing.

poussin [pusɛ̃] *nm* (*poulet*) chick.

poutre [putr] *nf* (*en bois*) beam; (*en acier*) girder. ◆**poutrelle** *nf* girder.

pouvoir° [puvwar] 1 *v aux* (*capacité*) to be able, can; (*permission, éventualité*) may, can; **je peux deviner** I can guess, I'm able to guess; **tu peux entrer** you may *ou* can come in; **il peut être malade** he may *ou* might be ill; **elle pourrait/pouvait venir** she might/could come; **j'ai pu l'obtenir** I managed to get it; **j'aurais pu l'obtenir** I could have got it *ou Am* gotten it; **je n'en peux plus** I'm utterly exhausted; – *v imp* **il peut neiger** it may snow; — **se p.** *vpr* **il se peut qu'elle parte** (it's possible that) she might leave. **2** *nm* (*capacité, autorité*) power; (*procuration*) power of attorney; **les pouvoirs publics** the authorities; **au p.** *Pol* in power; **en son p.** in one's power (**de faire** to do).

poux [pu] *voir* **pou.**

pragmatique [pragmatik] *a* pragmatic.

praire [prɛr] *nf* (*mollusque*) clam.

prairie [preri] *nf* meadow.

praline [pralin] *nf* sugared almond. ◆**praliné** *a* (*glace*) praline-flavoured.

praticable [pratikabl] *a* (*projet, chemin*) practicable.

praticien, -ienne [pratisjɛ̃, -jɛn] *nmf* practitioner.

pratique [pratik] **1** *a* (*connaissance, personne, instrument etc*) practical. **2** *nf* (*exercice, procédé*) practice; (*expérience*) practical experience; **la p. de la natation/du golf/***etc* swimming/golfing/*etc*; **mettre en p.** to put into practice; **en p.** (*en réalité*) in practice. ◆**pratiqu/er** *vt* (*art etc*) to practise; (*football*) to play, practise; (*trou, route*) to make; (*opération*) to carry out; **p. la natation** to go swimming; — *vi* to practise. ◆**-ant, -ante** *a Rel* practising; — *nmf* churchgoer.

pratiquement [pratikmɑ̃] *adv* (*presque*) practically; (*en réalité*) in practice.

pré [pre] *nm* meadow.

pré- [pre] *préf* pre-.

préalable [prealabl] *a* previous, preliminary; **p. à** prior to; – *nm* precondition, prerequisite; **au p.** beforehand. ◆**-ment** [-əmɑ̃] *adv* beforehand.

préambule [preɑ̃byl] *nm* (*de loi*) preamble; *Fig* prelude (**à** to).

préau, -x [preo] *nm Scol* covered playground.

préavis [preavi] *nm* (*de congé etc*) (advance) notice (**de** of).

précaire [prekɛr] *a* precarious.

précaution [prekosjɔ̃] *nf* (*mesure*) precaution; (*prudence*) caution; **par p.** as a precaution. ◆**précautionneux, -euse** *a* cautious.

précédent, -ente [presedɑ̃, -ɑ̃t] **1** *a* previous, preceding, earlier; – *nmf* previous one. **2** *nm* **un p.** (*fait, exemple*) a precedent; **sans p.** unprecedented. ◆**précédemment** [-amɑ̃] *adv* previously. ◆**précéder** *vti* to precede; **faire p. qch de qch** to precede sth by sth.

précepte [presɛpt] *nm* precept.

précepteur, -trice [preseptœr, -tris] *nmf* (*private*) tutor.

prêcher [preʃe] *vti* to preach; **p. qn** *Rel &* *Fig* to preach to s.o.

précieux, -euse [presjø, -øz] *a* precious.

précipice [presipis] *nm* abyss, chasm.

précipit/er [presipite] *vt* (*jeter*) to throw, hurl; (*plonger*) to plunge (**dans** into); (*hâter*) to hasten; — **se p.** *vpr* (*se jeter*) to throw *ou* hurl oneself; (*foncer*) to rush (**à, sur** on to); '(*s'accélérer*) to speed up. ◆**-é** *a* hasty. ◆**précipitamment** *adv* hastily. ◆**précipitation 1** *nf* haste. **2** *nfpl* (*pluie*) precipitation.

précis [presi] **1** *a* precise; (*idée, mécanisme*) accurate, precise; **à deux heures précises** at two o'clock sharp *ou* precisely. **2** *nm* (*résumé*) summary; (*manuel*) handbook. ◆**précisément** *adv* precisely. ◆**préciser** *vt* to specify (**que** that); — **se p.** *vpr* to become clear(er). ◆**précision** *nf* precision; accuracy; (*détail*) detail; (*explication*) explanation.

précoce [prekɔs] *a* (*fruit, mariage, mort etc*) early; (*personne*) precocious. ◆**précocité** *nf* precociousness; earliness.

préconçu [prekɔ̃sy] *a* preconceived.

préconiser [prekɔnize] *vt* to advocate (**que** that).

précurseur [prekyrsœr] *nm* forerunner, precursor; – *a* **un signe p. de qch** a sign heralding sth.

prédécesseur [predesesœr] *nm* predecessor.

prédestiné [predɛstine] *a* fated, predestined (**à faire** to do).

prédicateur [predikatœr] *nm* preacher.

prédilection [predilɛksjɔ̃] *nf* (special) liking; **de p.** favourite.

prédire [predir] *vt* to predict (**que** that). ◆**prédiction** *nf* prediction.

prédisposer [predispoze] *vt* to predispose (**à qch** to sth, **à faire** to do). ◆**prédisposition** *nf* predisposition.

prédomin/er [predomine] *vi* to predominate. ◆**-ant** *a* predominant. ◆**prédominance** *nf* predominance.

préfabriqué [prefabrike] *a* prefabricated.

préface [prefas] *nf* preface. ◆**préfacer** *vt* to preface.

préfér/er [prefere] *vt* to prefer (**à** to); **p. faire** to prefer to do. ◆**-é, -ée** *a & nmf* favourite. ◆**-able** *a* preferable (**à** to). ◆**préférence** *nf* preference; **de p.** preferably; **de p. à** in preference to. ◆**préférentiel, -ielle** *a* preferential.

préfet [prefɛ] *nm* prefect, *chief administrator in a department*; **p. de police** prefect of police, *Paris chief of police*. ◆**préfecture** *nf* prefecture; **p. de police** Paris police headquarters.

préfixe [prefiks] *nm* prefix.

préhistoire [preistwar] *nf* prehistory. ◆**préhistorique** *a* prehistoric.

préjudice [preʒydis] *nm* Jur prejudice, harm; **porter p. à** to prejudice, harm. ◆**préjudiciable** *a* prejudicial (à to).

préjugé [preʒyʒe] *nm* (*parti pris*) prejudice; **avoir un p.** *ou* **des préjugés** to be prejudiced (**contre** against).

prélasser (se) [səprelase] *vpr* to loll (about), lounge (about).

prélat [prela] *nm* Rel prelate.

prélever [prelve] *vt* (*échantillon*) to take (**sur** from); (*somme*) to deduct (**sur** from). ◆**prélèvement** *nm* taking; deduction; **p. de sang** blood sample; **p. automatique** Fin standing order.

préliminaire [preliminɛr] *a* preliminary; −*nmpl* preliminaries.

prélude [prelyd] *nm* prelude (à to).

prématuré [prematyre] *a* premature; − *nm* (*bébé*) premature baby. ◆**—ment** *adv* prematurely, too soon.

préméditer [premedite] *vt* to premeditate. ◆**préméditation** *nf* Jur premeditation.

premier, -ière [prəmje, -jɛr] *a* first; (*enfance*) early; (*page*) Journ front; first; (*qualité, nécessité, importance*) prime; (*état*) original; (*notion, cause*) basic; (*danseuse, rôle*) leading; (*inférieur*) bottom; (*supérieur*) top; **nombre p.** Math prime number; **le p. rang** the front *ou* first row; **à la première occasion** at the earliest opportunity; **P. ministre** Prime Minister, Premier; − *nmf* first (one); **arriver le p.** *ou* **en p.** to arrive first; **être le p. de la classe** to be (at) the top of the class; − *nm* (*date*) first; (*étage*) first *ou* Am second floor; **le p. de l'an** New Year's Day; − *nf* Th Cin première; Rail first class; Scol = sixth form, Am = twelfth grade; Aut first (gear); (*événement historique*) first. ◆**premier-né** *nm*, ◆**première-née** *nf* first-born (child). ◆**premièrement** *adv* firstly.

prémisse [premis] *nf* premiss.

prémonition [premonisjɔ̃] *nf* premonition.

prémunir [premynir] *vt* to safeguard (**contre** against).

prénatal, *mpl* -als [prenatal] *a* antenatal, Am prenatal.

prendre* [prɑ̃dr] *vt* to take (**à qn** from s.o.); (*attraper*) to catch; (*voyager par*) to take, travel by; (*acheter*) to get; (*douche, bain*) to take, have; (*repas*) to have; (*nouvelles*) to get; (*temps, heure*) to take (up); (*pensionnaire*) to take (in); (*ton, air*) to put on; (*engager*) to take (s.o.) on; (*chercher*) to pick up; **p. qn pour** (*un autre*) to (mis)take s.o. for; (*considérer*) to take s.o. for; **p. qn** (*doute etc*) to seize s.o.; **p. feu** to catch fire; **p. de la place** to take up room; **p. du poids/de la vitesse** to put on weight/speed; **à tout p.** on the whole; **qu'est-ce qui te prend?** what's got *ou* Am gotten into you?; − *vi* (*feu*) to catch; (*gelée, ciment*) to set; (*greffe, vaccin*) to take; (*mode*) to catch on; − **se p.** (*objet*) to be taken; (*s'accrocher*) to get caught; (*eau*) to freeze; **se p. pour un génie/etc** to think one is a genius/*etc*; **s'y p.** to go *ou* set about it; **s'en p. à** (*critiquer, attaquer*) to attack; (*accuser*) to blame; **se p. à faire** to begin to do. ◆**prenant** *a* (*travail, film etc*) engrossing; (*voix*) engaging. ◆**preneur, -euse** *nmf* taker, buyer.

prénom [prenɔ̃] *nm* first name. ◆**prénommer** *vt* to name; **il se prénomme Louis** his first name is Louis.

préoccuper [preɔkype] *vt* (*inquiéter*) to worry; (*absorber*) to preoccupy; **se p. de** to be worried about; to be preoccupied about. ◆**—ant** *a* worrying. ◆**—é** *a* worried. ◆**préoccupation** *nf* worry; (*idée, problème*) preoccupation.

préparer [prepare] *vt* to prepare; (*repas etc*) to get ready, prepare; (*examen*) to study for, prepare (for); **p. qch à qn** to prepare sth for s.o.; **p. qn à** (*examen*) to prepare s.o. *ou* coach s.o. for; − **se p.** *vpr* to get (oneself) ready, prepare oneself (**à qch** for sth); (*orage*) to brew, threaten. ◆**préparatifs** *nmpl* preparations (**de** for). ◆**préparation** *nf* preparation. ◆**préparatoire** *a* preparatory.

prépondérant [prepɔ̃derɑ̃] *a* dominant. ◆**prépondérance** *nf* dominance.

préposer [prepoze] *vt* **p. qn à** to put s.o. in charge of. ◆**—é, -ée** *nmf* employee; (*facteur*) postman, postwoman.

préposition [prepozisjɔ̃] *nf* preposition.

préretraite [prerətrɛt] *nf* early retirement.

prérogative [prerogativ] *nf* prerogative.

près [prɛ] *adv* **p. de qn/qch** near (to), close; **p. de deux ans/etc** (*presque*) nearly two years/*etc*; **p. de partir/etc** about to leave/*etc*; **tout p.** nearby (**de qn/qch** s.o./sth), close by (**de qn/qch** s.o./sth); **de p.** (*lire, examiner, suivre*) closely; **à peu de chose p.** almost; **à cela p.** except for that; **voici le**

chiffre à un franc p. here is the figure give or take a franc; **calculer au franc p.** to calculate to the nearest franc.

présage [prezaӡ] nm omen, foreboding.
◆**présager** vt to forebode.

presbyte [prɛsbit] a & nmf long-sighted (person). ◆**presbytie** [-bisi] nf long-sightedness.

presbytère [prɛsbitɛr] nm Rel presbytery.

préscolaire [preskɔlɛr] a (âge etc) pre-school.

prescrire* [prɛskrir] vt to prescribe.
◆**prescription** nf (instruction) & Jur prescription.

préséance [preseɑ̃s] nf precedence (**sur** over).

présent¹ [prezɑ̃] 1 a (non absent) present; **les personnes présentes** those present. 2 a (actuel) present; – nm (temps) present; Gram present (tense); **à p.** now, at present; **dès à p.** as from now. ◆**présence** nf presence; (à l'école, au bureau etc) attendance (**à** at); **feuille de p.** attendance sheet; **faire acte de p.** to put in an appearance; **en p.** (personnes) face to face; **en p. de** in the presence of; **p. d'esprit** presence of mind.

présent² [prezɑ̃] nm (cadeau) present.

présent/er [prezɑ̃te] vt (offrir, exposer, animer etc) to present; (montrer) to show, present; **p. qn à qn** to introduce ou present s.o. to s.o.; **– se p.** vpr to introduce ou present oneself (**à** to); (chez qn) to show up; (occasion etc) to arise; **se p. à** (examen) to sit for; (élections) to stand in ou at, run in; (emploi) to apply for; (autorités) to report to; **ça se présente bien** it looks promising. ◆**–able** a presentable. ◆**présentateur, -trice** nmf TV announcer, presenter. ◆**présentation** nf presentation; introduction. ◆**présentoir** nm (étagère) (display) stand.

préserver [prezɛrve] vt to protect, preserve (**de** from). ◆**préservatif** nm sheath, condom. ◆**préservation** nf protection, preservation.

présidence [prezidɑ̃s] nf (de nation) presidency; (de firme etc) chairmanship. ◆**président, -ente** nmf (de nation) president; (de réunion, firme) chairman, chairwoman; **p. directeur général** chairman and managing director, Am chief executive officer.
◆**présidentiel, -ielle** a presidential.

présider [prezide] vt (réunion) to preside at ou over, chair; – vi to preside.

présomption [prezɔ̃psjɔ̃] nf (conjecture, suffisance) presumption.

présomptueux, -euse [prezɔ̃ptɥø, -øz] a presumptuous.

presque [prɛsk(ə)] adv almost, nearly; **p. jamais/rien** hardly ever/anything.

presqu'île [prɛskil] nf peninsula.

presse [prɛs] nf (journaux, appareil) press; Typ (printing) press; **de p.** (conférence, agence) press-.

presse-citron [prɛssitrɔ̃] nm inv lemon squeezer. ◆**p.-papiers** nm inv paperweight. ◆**p.-purée** nm inv (potato) masher.

pressentir* [prɛsɑ̃tir] vt (deviner) to sense (**que** that). ◆**pressentiment** nm foreboding, presentiment.

press/er [prɛse] vt (serrer) to squeeze, press; (bouton) to press; (fruit) to squeeze; (départ etc) to hasten; **p. qn** to hurry s.o. (**de** faire to do); (assaillir) to harass s.o. (**de** questions with questions); **p. le pas** to speed up; – vi (temps) to press; (affaire) to be pressing ou urgent; **rien ne presse** there's no hurry; **– se p.** vpr (se grouper) to crowd, swarm; (se serrer) to squeeze (together); (se hâter) to hurry (**de** faire to do); **presse-toi (de partir)** hurry up (and go).
◆**–ant** a pressing, urgent. ◆**–é** a (personne) in a hurry; (air) hurried; (travail) pressing, urgent. ◆**pressing** [-iŋ] nm (magasin) dry cleaner's. ◆**pressoir** nm (wine) press.

pression [prɛsjɔ̃] nf pressure; **faire p. sur qn** to put pressure on s.o., pressurize s.o.; **bière (à la) p.** draught beer; – nm (bouton-)p. press-stud, Am snap.

pressuriser [presyrize] vt Av to pressurize.

prestance [prɛstɑ̃s] nf (imposing) presence.

prestation [prɛstasjɔ̃] nf 1 (allocation) allowance, benefit. 2 (performance) performance.

prestidigitateur, -trice [prɛstidiӡitatœr, -tris] nmf conjurer. ◆**prestidigitation** nf conjuring.

prestige [prɛstiӡ] nm prestige.
◆**prestigieux, -euse** a prestigious.

presto [prɛsto] Fam voir **illico.**

présumer [prezyme] vt to presume (**que** that).

présupposer [presypoze] vt to presuppose (**que** that).

prêt¹ [prɛ] a (préparé, disposé) ready (**à** faire to do, **à** qch for sth). ◆**p.-à-porter** [prɛtaporte] nm inv ready-to-wear clothes.

prêt² [prɛ] nm (emprunt) loan. ◆**p.-logement** nm (pl **prêts-logement**) mortgage.

prétend/re [pretɑ̃dr] vt to claim (**que** that); (vouloir) to intend (**faire** to do); **p.**

être/savoir to claim to be/to know; **elle se prétend riche** she claims to be rich; – *vi* p. à (*titre etc*) to lay claim to. ◆—**ant** *nm* (*amoureux*) suitor. ◆—**u** *a* so-called. ◆—**ument** *adv* supposedly.

prétentieux, -euse [pretɑ̃sjø, -øz] *a & nmf* pretentious (person). ◆**prétention** *nf* (*vanité*) pretension; (*revendication, ambition*) claim.

prêt/er [prete] *vt* (*argent, objet*) to lend (à to); (*aide, concours*) to give (à to); (*attribuer*) to attribute (à to); **p. attention** (à to) to pay attention (à to); **p. serment** to take an oath; – *vi* **p. à** (*phrase etc*) to lend itself to; **se p. à** (*consentir à*) to agree to; (*sujet etc*) to lend itself to. ◆—**eur, -euse** *nmf* (*d'argent*) lender; **p. sur gages** pawnbroker.

prétexte [pretɛkst] *nm* pretext, excuse; **sous p. de/que** on the pretext of/that. ◆**prétexter** *vt* to plead (que that).

prêtre [prɛtr] *nm* priest; **grand p.** high priest.

preuve [prœv] *nf* proof, evidence; **faire p. de** to show; **faire ses preuves** (*personne*) to prove oneself; (*méthode*) to prove itself.

prévaloir [prevalwar] *vi* to prevail (**contre** against, **sur** over).

prévenant [prevnɑ̃] *a* considerate. ◆**prévenance(s)** *nf(pl)* (*gentillesse*) consideration.

préven/ir* [prevnir] *vt* 1 (*avertir*) to warn (que that); (*aviser*) to tell, inform (que that). 2 (*désir, question*) to anticipate; (*malheur*) to avert. ◆—**u, -ue** 1 *nmf Jur* defendant, accused. 2 *a* prejudiced (**contre** against). ◆**préventif, -ive** *a* preventive. ◆**prévention** *nf* 1 prevention; **p. routière** road safety. 2 (*opinion*) prejudice.

prévoir* [prevwar] *vt* (*anticiper*) to foresee (que that); (*prédire*) forecast (que that); (*temps*) *Mét* to forecast; (*projeter, organiser*) to plan (for); (*réserver, préparer*) to allow, provide. ◆—**u** *a* (*conditions*) laid down; **un repas est p.** a meal is provided; **au moment p.** at the appointed time; **comme p.** as planned, as expected; **p. pour** (*véhicule, appareil etc*) designed for. ◆**prévisible** *a* foreseeable. ◆**prévision** *nf* (*opinion*) & *Mét* forecast; **en p.** in expectation of.

prévoyant [prevwajɑ̃] *a* (*personne*) provident. ◆**prévoyance** *nf* foresight; **société de p.** provident society.

prier [prije] 1 *vi Rel* to pray; – *vt* **p.** Dieu **pour qu'il nous accorde qch** to pray (to God) for sth. 2 *vt* **p. qn de faire** to ask *ou* request s.o. to do; (*implorer*) to beg s.o. to do; **je vous en prie** (*faites donc, allez-y*)

please; (*en réponse à 'merci'*) don't mention it; **je vous prie** please; **se faire p.** to wait to be asked. ◆**prière** *nf Rel* prayer; (*demande*) request; **p. de répondre**/*etc* please answer/*etc*.

primaire [primɛr] *a* primary.

prime [prim] 1 *nf* (*d'employé*) bonus; (*d'État*) subsidy; (*cadeau*) *Com* free gift; **p. (d'assurance)** (insurance) premium. 2 *a* **de p. abord** at the very first glance.

primé [prime] *a* (*animal*) prize-winning.

primer [prime] *vi* to excel, prevail; – *vt* to prevail over.

primeurs [primœr] *nfpl* early fruit and vegetables.

primevère [primvɛr] *nf* (*à fleurs jaunes*) primrose.

primitif, -ive [primitif, -iv] *a* (*art, société etc*) primitive; (*état, sens*) original; – *nm* (*artiste*) primitive. ◆**primitivement** *adv* originally.

primo [primo] *adv* first(ly).

primordial, -aux [primɔrdjal, -o] *a* vital (**de faire** to do).

prince [prɛ̃s] *nm* prince. ◆**princesse** *nf* princess. ◆**princier, -ière** *a* princely. ◆**principauté** *nf* principality.

principal, -aux [prɛ̃sipal, -o] *a* main, chief, principal; – *nm* (*de collège*) *Scol* principal; **le p.** (*essentiel*) the main *ou* chief thing. ◆—**ement** *adv* mainly.

principe [prɛ̃sip] *nm* principle; **par p.** on principle; **en p.** theoretically, in principle; (*normalement*) as a rule.

printemps [prɛ̃tɑ̃] *nm* (*saison*) spring. ◆**printanier, -ière** *a* (*temps etc*) spring-, spring-like.

priorité [priorite] *nf* priority; **la p.** *Aut* the right of way; **la p. à droite** *Aut* right of way to traffic coming from the right; **'cédez la p.'** *Aut* 'give way', *Am* 'yield'; **en p.** as a matter of priority. ◆**prioritaire** *a* (*industrie etc*) priority-; **être p.** to have priority, *Aut* to have the right of way.

pris [pri] *voir* **prendre**; – *a* (*place*) taken; (*crème, ciment*) set; (*eau*) frozen; (*gorge*) infected; (*nez*) congested; **être (très) p.** (*occupé*) to be (very) busy; **p. de** (*peur, panique*) stricken with.

prise [priz] *nf voir* **prendre**; (*manière d'empoigner*) grip, hold; (*de ville*) capture, taking; (*objet saisi*) catch; (*de tabac*) pinch; **p. (de courant)** *Él* (*mâle*) plug; (*femelle*) socket; **p. multiple** *Él* adaptor; **p. d'air** air vent; **p. de conscience** awareness; **p. de contact** first meeting; **p. de position** *Fig* stand; **p. de sang** blood test; **p. de**

de son (sound) recording; **p. de vue(s)** *Cin Phot* (*action*) shooting; (*résultat*) shot; **aux prises** avec at grips with.

priser [prize] **1** *vt* tabac à **p**. snuff; – *vi* to take snuff. **2** *vt* (*estimer*) to prize.

prisme [prism] *nm* prism.

prison [prizɔ̃] *nf* prison, jail, gaol; (*réclusion*) imprisonment; **mettre en p**. to imprison, put in prison. ◆**prisonnier, -ière** *nmf* prisoner; **faire qn p**. to take s.o. prisoner.

privé [prive] a private; **en p**. (*seul à seul*) in private; – *nm* **dans le p**. in private life; *Com Fam* in the private sector.

priver [prive] *vt* to deprive (**de** of); **se p. de** to deprive oneself of, do without. ◆**privation** *nf* deprivation (**de** of); *pl* (*sacrifices*) hardships.

privilège [privilɛʒ] *nm* privilege. ◆**privilégié, -ée** *a* & *nmf* privileged (person).

prix [pri] *nm* **1** (*d'un objet, du succès etc*) price; **à tout p**. at all costs; **à aucun p**. on no account; **hors (de) p**. exorbitant; **attacher du p. à** to attach importance to; **menu à p. fixe** set price menu. **2** (*récompense*) prize.

pro- [pro] *préf* pro-.

probable [prɔabl] *a* probable, likely; **peu p**. unlikely. ◆**probabilité** *nf* probability, likelihood; **selon toute p**. in all probability. ◆**probablement** *adv* probably.

probant [prɔbɑ̃] *a* conclusive.

probité [prɔbite] *nf* (*honnêteté*) integrity.

problème [prɔblɛm] *nm* problem. ◆**problématique** *a* doubtful, problematic.

procéd/er [prɔsede] *vi* (*agir*) to proceed; (*se conduire*) to behave; **p. à** (*enquête etc*) to carry out. ◆**-é** *nm* process; (*conduite*) behaviour. ◆**procédure** *nf* procedure; *Jur* proceedings.

procès [prɔsɛ] *nm* (*criminel*) trial; (*civil*) lawsuit; **faire un p. à** to take s.o. to court.

processeur [prɔsɛsœr] *nm* (*d'ordinateur*) processor.

procession [prɔsesjɔ̃] *nf* procession.

processus [prɔsesys] *nm* process.

procès-verbal, -aux [prɔsɛverbal, -o] *nm* (*de réunion*) minutes; (*constat*) *Jur* report; (*contravention*) fine, ticket.

prochain, -aine [prɔʃɛ̃, -ɛn] **1** *a* next; (*avenir*) near; (*parent*) close; (*mort, arrivée*) impending; (*mariage*) forthcoming; **un jour p**. one day soon; – *nf* **à la prochaine!** *Fam* see you soon!; **à la prochaine** (*station*) at the next stop. **2** *nm* (*semblable*) fellow (man). ◆**prochainement** *adv* shortly, soon.

proche [prɔʃ] *a* (*espace*) near, close; (*temps*)

close (at hand); (*parent, ami*) close; (*avenir*) near; **p. de** near (to), close to; **une maison/etc** **p**. a house/*etc* nearby *ou* close by; – *nmpl* close relations.

proclamer [prɔklame] *vt* to proclaim, declare (que that); **p. roi** to proclaim king. ◆**proclamation** *nf* proclamation, declaration.

procréer [prɔkree] *vt* to procreate. ◆**procréation** *nf* procreation.

procuration [prɔkyrasjɔ̃] *nf* power of attorney; **par p**. (*voter*) by proxy.

procurer [prɔkyre] *vt* **p. qch à qn** (*personne*) to obtain sth for s.o.; (*occasion etc*) to afford s.o. sth; **se p. qch** to obtain sth.

procureur [prɔkyrœr] *nm* = *Br* public prosecutor, = *Am* district attorney.

prodige [prɔdiʒ] *nm* (*miracle*) wonder; (*personne*) prodigy. ◆**prodigieux, -euse** *a* prodigious, extraordinary.

prodigue [prɔdig] *a* (*dépensier*) wasteful, prodigal. ◆**prodiguer** *vt* to lavish (**à qn** on s.o.).

production [prɔdyksjɔ̃] *nf* production; (*de la terre*) yield. ◆**producteur, -trice** *nmf Com Cin* producer; – *a* producing; **pays p. de pétrole** oil-producing country. ◆**productif, -ive** *a* (*terre, réunion etc*) productive. ◆**productivité** *nf* productivity.

produire* [prɔdyir] **1** *vt* (*fabriquer, présenter etc*) to produce; (*causer*) to bring about, produce. **2 se p**. *vpr* (*événement etc*) to happen, occur. ◆**produit** *nm* (*article etc*) product; (*pour la vaisselle*) liquid; (*d'une vente, d'une collecte*) proceeds; *pl* (*de la terre*) produce; **p. (chimique)** chemical; **p. de beauté** cosmetic.

proéminent [prɔeminɑ̃] *a* prominent.

prof [prɔf] *nm Fam* = **professeur**.

profane [prɔfan] **1** *nmf* lay person. **2** *a* (*art etc*) secular.

profaner [prɔfane] *vt* to profane, desecrate. ◆**profanation** *nf* profanation, desecration.

proférer [prɔfere] *vt* to utter.

professer [prɔfese] *vt* to profess (que that).

professeur [prɔfesœr] *nm* teacher; *Univ* lecturer, *Am* professor; (*titulaire d'une chaire*) *Univ* professor.

profession [prɔfesjɔ̃] *nf* **1** occupation, vocation; (*libérale*) profession; (*manuelle*) trade; **de p**. (*chanteur etc*) professional, by profession. **2 p. de foi** *Fig* declaration of principles. ◆**professionnel, -elle** *a* professional; (*école*) vocational, trade-; – *nmf* (*non amateur*) professional.

profil [prɔfil] *nm* (*de personne, objet*) profile;

de p. in profile. ◆**profiler** vt to outline, profile; — **se p.** vpr to be outlined ou profiled (sur against).

profit [prɔfi] nm profit; (avantage) advantage, profit; **vendre à p.** to sell at a profit; **tirer p. de** to benefit by, profit by; **au p. de** for the benefit of. ◆**profitable** a profitable (à to). ◆**profiter** vi p. **de** to take advantage of; **p. à qn** to profit s.o.; **p. (bien)** (enfant) Fam to thrive. ◆**profiteur, -euse** nmf Péj profiteer.

profond [prɔfɔ̃] a deep; (esprit, joie, erreur etc) profound, great; (cause) underlying; **p. de deux mètres** two metres deep; – adv (pénétrer etc) deep; – nm **au plus p. de** in the depths of. ◆**profondément** adv deeply; (dormir) soundly; (triste, souhaiter) profoundly; (extrêmement) thoroughly. ◆**profondeur** nf depth; profoundness; pl depths (de of); **en p.** (étudier etc) in depth; **à six mètres de p.** at a depth of six metres.

profusion [prɔfyzjɔ̃] nf profusion; **à p.** in profusion.

progéniture [prɔʒenityr] nf Hum offspring.

progiciel [prɔʒisjɛl] nm (pour ordinateur) (software) package.

programme [prɔgram] nm programme, Am program; (d'une matière) Scol syllabus; (d'ordinateur) program; **p. (d'études)** (d'une école) curriculum. ◆**programmation** nf programming. ◆**programmer** vt Cin Rad TV to programme, Am program; (ordinateur) to program. ◆**programmeur, -euse** nmf (computer) programmer.

progrès [prɔgrɛ] nm & nmpl progress; **faire des p.** to make (good) progress. ◆**progresser** vi to progress. ◆**progressif, -ive** a progressive. ◆**progression** nf progression. ◆**progressiste** a & nmf Pol progressive. ◆**progressivement** adv progressively, gradually.

prohiber [prɔibe] vt to prohibit, forbid. ◆**prohibitif, -ive** a prohibitive. ◆**prohibition** nf prohibition.

proie [prwa] nf prey; **être en p. à** to be (a) prey to, be tortured by.

projecteur [prɔʒɛktœr] nm (de monument) floodlight; (de prison) & Mil searchlight; Th spot(light); Cin projector.

projectile [prɔʒɛktil] nm missile.

projet [prɔʒɛ] nm plan; (ébauche) draft; (entreprise, étude) project.

projeter [prɔʒte] vt 1 (lancer) to hurl, eject. 2 (film, ombre) to project; (lumière) to flash. 3 (voyage, fête etc) to plan; **p. de faire** to plan to do. ◆**projection** nf (lancement,

hurling, projection; (de film, d'ombre) projection; (séance) showing.

prolétaire [prɔleter] nmf proletarian. ◆**prolétariat** nm proletariat. ◆**prolétarien, -ienne** a proletarian.

proliférer [prɔlifere] vi to proliferate. ◆**prolifération** nf proliferation.

prolifique [prɔlifik] a prolific.

prolixe [prɔliks] a verbose, wordy.

prologue [prɔlɔg] nm prologue (de, à to).

prolonger [prɔlɔ̃ʒe] vt to prolong, extend; — **se p.** vpr (séance, rue, effet) to continue. ◆**prolongateur** nm (rallonge) El extension cord. ◆**prolongation** nf extension; pl Fb extra time. ◆**prolongement** nm extension.

promenade [prɔmnad] nf (à pied) walk; (en voiture) ride, drive; (en vélo, à cheval) ride; (action) Sp walking; (lieu) walk, promenade; **faire une p.** = **se promener**. ◆**promener** vt to take for a walk ou ride; (visiteur) to take ou show around; **p. qch sur** qch (main, regard) to run sth over sth; **envoyer p.** Fam to send packing; — **se p.** vpr (à pied) to (go for a) walk; (en voiture) to (go for a) ride ou drive. ◆**promeneur, -euse** nmf walker, stroller.

promesse [prɔmɛs] nf promise. ◆**promett/re** vt to promise (qch à qn sth to s.o.); **p. de faire** to promise to do; **c'est promis** it's a promise; – vi **p. (beaucoup)** Fig to be promising; **se p. qch** to promise oneself sth; **se p. de faire** to resolve to do. ◆**—eur, -euse** a promising.

promontoire [prɔmɔ̃twar] nm Géog headland.

promoteur [prɔmɔtœr] nm **p. (immobilier)** property developer.

promotion [prɔmosjɔ̃] nf 1 promotion; **en p.** Com on (special) offer. 2 (candidats) Univ year. ◆**promouvoir** vt (personne, produit etc) to promote; **être promu** (employé) to be promoted (à to).

prompt [prɔ̃] a swift, prompt, quick. ◆**promptitude** nf swiftness, promptness.

promulguer [prɔmylge] vt to promulgate.

prôner [prone] vt (vanter) to extol; (préconiser) to advocate.

pronom [prɔnɔ̃] nm Gram pronoun. ◆**pronominal, -aux** a pronominal.

prononc/er [prɔnɔ̃se] vt (articuler) to pronounce; (dire) to utter; (discours) to deliver; (jugement) Jur to pronounce, pass; – vi Jur Ling to pronounce; — **se p.** vpr (mot) to be pronounced; (personne) to reach a decision (sur about, on); **se p. pour** to come out in favour of. ◆**—é** a (visible) pronounced, marked. ◆**prononciation** *nf* pronunciation.

pronostic [pronostik] *nm* (*prévision*) & *Sp* forecast. ◆**pronostiquer** *vt* to forecast.

propagande [propagɑ̃d] *nf* propaganda. ◆**propagandiste** *nmf* propagandist.

propager [propaʒe] *vt*, **— se p.** *vpr* to spread. ◆**propagation** *nf* spread(ing).

propension [propɑ̃sjɔ̃] *nf* propensity (**à qch** for sth, **à faire** to do).

prophète [profɛt] *nm* prophet. ◆**prophétie** [-fesi] *nf* prophecy. ◆**prophétique** *a* prophetic. ◆**prophétiser** *vti* to prophesy.

propice [propis] *a* favourable (**à to**).

proportion [proporsjɔ̃] *nf* proportion; *Math* ratio; **en p. de** in proportion to; **hors de p.** out of proportion (**avec to**). ◆**proportionnel, -elle** *a* proportional (**à to**). ◆**proportionn/er** *vt* to proportion (**à to**). ◆**—é** *a* proportionate (**à to**); **bien p.** well *ou* nicely proportioned.

propos [propo] **1** *nmpl* (*paroles*) remarks, utterances. **2** *nm* (*intention*) purpose. **3** *nm* (*sujet*) subject; **à p. de** about; **à p. de rien** for no reason; **à tout p.** for no reason, at every turn. **4** *adv* **à p.** (*arriver etc*) at the right time; **à p.!** by the way!; **juger à p. de faire** to consider it fit to do.

proposer [propoze] *vt* (*suggérer*) to suggest, propose (**qch à qn** sth to s.o., **que** (+ *sub*) that); (*offrir*) to offer (**qch à qn** s.o. sth, **de faire** to do); (*candidat*) to put forward, propose; **je te propose de rester** I suggest (that) you stay; **se p. pour faire** to offer to do; **se p. de faire** to propose *ou* mean to do. ◆**proposition** *nf* suggestion, proposal; (*de paix*) proposal, (*affirmation*) proposition; *Gram* clause.

propre[1] [propr] *a* clean; (*soigné*) neat; (*honnête*) decent; **— nm** mettre qch au p. to make a fair copy of sth. ◆**proprement**[1] *adv* (*avec propreté*) cleanly; (*avec netteté*) neatly; (*comme il faut*) decently. ◆**propreté** *nf* cleanliness; (*netteté*) neatness.

propre[2] [propr] *a* (*à soi*) own; **mon p.** argent my own money; **ses propres mots** his very *ou* his own words. **2** *a* (*qui convient*) right, proper; **p. à** (*attribut, coutume etc*) peculiar to; (*approprié*) well-suited to; **p. à faire** likely to do; **sens p.** literal meaning; **nom p.** proper noun; **— nm le p. de** (*qualité*) the distinctive quality of; **au p.** (*au sens propre*) literally. ◆**proprement**[2] *adv* (*strictement*) strictly; **à p. parler** strictly speaking; **le village/etc p. dit** the village/etc proper *ou* itself.

propriété [proprijete] *nf* **1** (*bien*) property;

(*droit*) ownership, property. **2** (*qualité*) property. **3** (*de mot*) suitability. ◆**propriétaire** *nmf* owner; (*d'hôtel*) proprietor, owner; (*qui loue*) landlord, landlady; **p. foncier** landowner.

propulser [propylse] *vt* (*faire avancer, projeter*) to propel. ◆**propulsion** *nf* propulsion.

prosaïque [prozaik] *a* prosaic, pedestrian.

proscrire* [proskrir] *vt* to proscribe, banish. ◆**proscrit, -ite** *nmf* (*personne*) exile. ◆**proscription** *nf* banishment.

prose [proz] *nf* prose.

prospecter [prospɛkte] *vt* (*sol*) to prospect; (*pétrole*) to prospect for; (*région*) *Com* to canvass. ◆**prospecteur, -trice** *nmf* prospector. ◆**prospection** *nf* prospecting; *Com* canvassing.

prospectus [prospɛktys] *nm* leaflet, prospectus.

prospère [prosper] *a* (*florissant*) thriving, prosperous; (*riche*) prosperous. ◆**prospérer** *vi* to thrive, flourish, prosper. ◆**prospérité** *nf* prosperity.

prostate [prostat] *nf Anat* prostate (gland).

prostern/er (se) [səprosterne] *vpr* to prostrate oneself (**devant** before). ◆**—é** *a* prostrate. ◆**—ement** *nm* prostration.

prostituer (se) [prostitɥe] *vt* to prostitute; **— se p.** *vpr* to prostitute oneself. ◆**prostituée** *nf* prostitute. ◆**prostitution** *nf* prostitution.

prostré [prostre] *a* (*accablé*) prostrate. ◆**prostration** *nf* prostration.

protagoniste [protagonist] *nmf* protagonist.

protecteur, -trice [protɛktœr, -tris] *nmf* protector; (*mécène*) patron; **— a** (*geste etc*) & *Écon* protective; (*ton, air*) *Péj* patronizing. ◆**protection** *nf* protection; (*mécénat*) patronage; **de p.** (*écran etc*) protective. ◆**protectionnisme** *nm Écon* protectionism.

protég/er [proteʒe] *vt* to protect (**de** from, **contre** against); (*appuyer*) *Fig* to patronize; **— se p.** *vpr* to protect oneself. ◆**—é** *nm* protégé. ◆**—ée** *nf* protégée. ◆**protège-cahier** *nm* exercise book cover.

protéine [protein] *nf* protein.

protestant, -ante [protɛstɑ̃, -ɑ̃t] *a* & *nmf* Protestant. ◆**protestantisme** *nm* Protestantism.

protester [protɛste] *vi* to protest (**contre** against); **p. de** (*son innocence etc*) to protest; **— vt** to protest (**que** that). ◆**protestation** *nf* protest (**contre** against); *pl* (*d'amitié*) protestations (**de** of).

prothèse [prɔtɛz] nf **(appareil de)** p. *(membre)* artificial limb; *(dents)* false teeth.

protocole [prɔtɔkɔl] nm protocol.

prototype [prɔtɔtip] nm prototype.

protubérance [prɔtyberɑ̃s] nf protuberance. ◆**protubérant** a *(yeux)* bulging; *(menton)* protruding.

proue [pru] nf Nau prow, bow(s).

prouesse [prues] nf feat, exploit.

prouver [pruve] vt to prove **(que** that).

Provence [prɔvɑ̃s] nf Provence. ◆**provençal, -ale, -aux** a & nmf Provençal.

provenir* [prɔvnir] vi p. **de** to come from. ◆**provenance** nf origin; **en** p. **de** from.

proverbe [prɔvɛrb] nm proverb. ◆**proverbial, -aux** a proverbial.

providence [prɔvidɑ̃s] nf providence. ◆**providentiel, -ielle** a providential.

province [prɔvɛ̃s] nf province; **la** p. the provinces; **en** p. in the provinces; **de** p. *(ville etc)* provincial. ◆**provincial, -ale, -aux** a & nmf provincial.

proviseur [prɔvizœr] nm *(de lycée)* headmaster.

provision [prɔvizjɔ̃] nf **1** *(réserve)* supply, stock; pl *(achats)* shopping; *(vivres)* provisions: **panier/sac à provisions** shopping basket/bag. **2** *(acompte)* advance payment; **chèque sans** p. dud cheque.

provisoire [prɔvizwar] a temporary, provisional. ◆**—ment** adv temporarily, provisionally.

provoquer [prɔvɔke] vt **1** *(causer)* to bring about, provoke; *(désir)* to arouse. **2** *(défier)* to provoke *(s.o.).* ◆**provocant** a provocative. ◆**provocateur** nm troublemaker. ◆**provocation** nf provocation.

proxénète [prɔksenɛt] nm pimp.

proximité [prɔksimite] nf closeness, proximity; **à** p. close by; **à** p. **de** close to.

prude [pryd] a prudish; – nf prude.

prudent [prydɑ̃] a *(circonspect)* cautious, careful; *(sage)* sensible. ◆**prudemment** [-amɑ̃] adv cautiously, carefully; *(sagement)* sensibly. ◆**prudence** nf caution, care, prudence; *(sagesse)* wisdom; **par** p. as a precaution.

prune [pryn] nf *(fruit)* plum. ◆**pruneau, -x** nm prune. ◆**prunelle** nf **1** *(fruit)* sloe. **2** *(de l'œil)* pupil. ◆**prunier** nm plum tree.

P.-S. [pees] abrév *(post-scriptum)* PS.

psaume [psom] nm psalm.

pseudo- [psødo] préf pseudo-.

pseudonyme [psødɔnim] nm pseudonym.

psychanalyse [psikanaliz] nf psychoanalysis. ◆**psychanalyste** nmf psychoanalyst.

psychiatre [psikjatr] nmf psychiatrist. ◆**psychiatrie** nf psychiatry. ◆**psychiatrique** a psychiatric.

psychique [psiʃik] a mental, psychic.

psycho [psiko] préf psycho-.

psychologie [psikɔlɔʒi] nf psychology. ◆**psychologique** a psychological. ◆**psychologue** nmf psychologist.

psychose [psikoz] nf psychosis.

PTT [petete] nfpl *(Postes, Télégraphes, Téléphones)* Post Office, = GPO.

pu [py] voir **pouvoir 1.**

puant [pɥɑ̃] a stinking. ◆**puanteur** nf stink, stench.

pub [pyb] nf Fam *(réclame)* advertising; *(annonce)* ad.

puberté [pybɛrte] nf puberty.

public, -ique [pyblik] a public; **dette publique** national debt; – nm public; *(de spectacle)* audience; **le grand** p. the general public; **en** p. in public. ◆**publiquement** adv publicly.

publication [pyblikasjɔ̃] nf *(action, livre etc)* publication. ◆**publier** vt to publish.

publicité [pyblisite] nf publicity **(pour** for); *(réclame)* advertising, publicity; *(annonce)* advertisement; Rad TV commercial. ◆**publicitaire** a *(agence, film)* publicity-, advertising-.

puce [pys] nf **1** flea; **le marché aux puces, les puces** the flea market. **2** *(d'un ordinateur)* chip, microchip.

puceron [pysrɔ̃] nm greenfly.

pudeur [pydœr] nf *(sense of)* modesty; **attentat à la** p. Jur indecency. ◆**pudibond** a prudish. ◆**pudique** a modest.

puer [pɥe] vi to stink; – vt to stink of.

puériculture [pɥerikyltyr] nf infant care, child care. ◆**puéricultrice** nf children's nurse.

puéril [pɥeril] a puerile. ◆**puérilité** nf puerility.

puis [pɥi] adv then; **et** p. **quoi?** and so what?

puiser [pɥize] vt to draw, take **(dans** from); – vi p. **dans** to dip into.

puisque [pɥisk(ə)] conj since, as.

puissant [pɥisɑ̃] a powerful. ◆**puissamment** adv powerfully. ◆**puissance** nf *(force, nation)* & Math Tech power; **en** p. *(talent, danger etc)* potential.

puits [pɥi] nm well; *(de mine)* shaft.

pull(-over) [pyl(ɔvɛr)] nm pullover, sweater.

pulluler [pylyle] vi Péj to swarm.

pulmonaire [pylmɔnɛr] a *(congestion, maladie)* of the lungs, lung-.

pulpe [pylp] *nf* (*de fruits*) pulp.

pulsation [pylsasjɔ̃] *nf* (*heart*)beat.

pulvériser [pylverize] *vt* (*broyer*) & *Fig* to pulverize; (*liquide*) to spray. ◆**pulvérisateur** *nm* spray, atomizer. ◆**pulvérisation** *nf* (*de liquide*) spraying.

punaise [pynez] *nf* 1 (*insecte*) bug. 2 (*clou*) drawing pin, *Am* thumbtack. ◆**punaiser** *vt* (*fixer*) to pin (up).

punch [pɔ̃ʃ] *nm* 1 (*boisson*) punch. 2 [pœnʃ] (*énergie*) punch.

punir [pynir] *vt* to punish. ◆**punissable** *a* punishable (de by). ◆**punition** *nf* punishment.

pupille [pypij] 1 *nf* (*de l'œil*) pupil. 2 *nmf* (*enfant sous tutelle*) ward.

pupitre [pypitr] *nm* (*d'écolier*) desk; (*d'orateur*) lectern; **p. à musique** music stand.

pur [pyr] *a* pure; (*alcool*) neat, straight. ◆**purement** *adv* purely. ◆**pureté** *nf* purity.

purée [pyre] *nf* purée; **p. (de pommes de terre)** mashed potatoes, mash.

purgatoire [pyrgatwar] *nm* purgatory.

purge [pyrʒ] *nf* *Pol Méd* purge.

purger [pyrʒe] *vt* 1 (*conduite*) *Tech* to drain, clear. 2 (*peine*) *Jur* to serve.

purifier [pyrifje] *vt* to purify. ◆**purification** *nf* purification.

purin [pyrɛ̃] *nm* liquid manure.

puriste [pyrist] *nmf Gram* purist.

puritain, -aine [pyritɛ̃, -ɛn] *a* & *nmf* puritan.

pur-sang [pyrsɑ̃] *nm inv* (*cheval*) thoroughbred.

pus [¹] [py] *nm* (*liquide*) pus, matter.

pus [²] [py] *voir* **pouvoir** 1.

putain [pytɛ̃] *nf Péj Fam* whore.

putois [pytwa] *nm* (*animal*) polecat.

putréfier [pytrefje] *vt*, **— se p.** *vpr* to putrefy. ◆**putréfaction** *nf* putrefaction.

puzzle [pœzl] *nm* (jigsaw) puzzle, jigsaw.

p.-v. [peve] *nm inv* (*procès-verbal*) (traffic) fine.

PVC [pevese] *nm* (*plastique*) PVC.

pygmée [pigme] *nm* pygmy.

pyjama [piʒama] *nm* pyjamas, *Am* pajamas; **un p.** a pair of pyjamas *ou Am* pajamas; **de p.** (*veste, pantalon*) pyjama-, *Am* pajama-.

pylône [pilon] *nm* pylon.

pyramide [piramid] *nf* pyramid.

Pyrénées [pirene] *nfpl* **les P.** the Pyrenees.

pyromane [piroman] *nmf* arsonist, firebug.

python [pitɔ̃] *nm* (*serpent*) python.

Q

Q, q [ky] *nm* Q, q.

QI [kyi] *nm inv abrév* (*quotient intellectuel*) IQ.

qu' [k] *voir* **que**.

quadrill/er [kadrije] *vt* (*troupes, police*) to be positioned throughout, comb, cover (*town etc*). ◆**-é** *a* (*papier*) squared. ◆**-age** *nm* (*lignes*) squares.

quadrupède [k(w)adryped] *nm* quadruped.

quadruple [k(w)adrypl] *a* **q. de** fourfold; — *nm* **le q. de** four times as much as. ◆**quadrupl/er** *vti* to quadruple. ◆**-és, -ées** *nmfpl* (*enfants*) quadruplets, quads.

quai [ke] *nm Nau* quay; (*pour marchandises*) wharf; (*de fleuve*) embankment, bank; *Rail* platform.

qualification [kalifikasjɔ̃] *nf* 1 description. 2 (*action*) *Sp* qualifying, qualification. ◆**qualificatif** *nm* (*mot*) term. ◆**qualifi/er** 1 *vt* (*décrire*) to describe (de as); **se faire q. de menteur**/*etc* to be called a liar/*etc*. 2 *vt* (*rendre apte*) & *Sp* to qualify

(pour qch for sth, pour faire to do); — se q. *vpr Sp* to qualify (pour for). 3 *vt Gram* to qualify. ◆**-é** *a* qualified (pour faire to do); (*ouvrier, main-d'œuvre*) skilled.

qualité [kalite] *nf* quality; (*condition sociale etc*) occupation, status; **produit**/*etc* de high-quality product/*etc*; **en sa q. de** in one's capacity as. ◆**qualitatif, -ive** *a* qualitative.

quand [kɑ̃] *conj* & *adv* when; **q. je viendrai** when I come; **c'est pour q.** (*réunion, mariage*) when is it?; **q. bien même vous le feriez** even if you did it; **q. même** all the same.

quant (à) [kɑ̃ta] *prép* as for.

quantité [kɑ̃tite] *nf* quantity; **une q., des quantités** (*beaucoup*) a lot (de of); **en q.** (*abondamment*) in plenty. ◆**quantifier** *vt* to quantify. ◆**quantitatif, -ive** *a* quantitative.

quarante [karɑ̃t] *a* & *nm* forty. ◆**quarantaine** *nf* 1 **une q. (de)** (*nombre*) (about) forty; **avoir la q.** (âge) to be about forty. **2** Méd quarantine; **mettre en q.** Méd to quarantine; Fig to send to Coventry, Am give the silent treatment to. ◆**quarantième** a & nmf fortieth.

quart [kar] nm **1** quarter; **q.** (de litre) quarter litre, quarter of a litre; **q. d'heure** quarter of an hour; **un mauvais q. d'heure** Fig a trying time; **une heure et q.** an hour and a quarter; **il est une heure et q.** it's a quarter past ou Am after one; **une heure moins le q.** a quarter to one. **2** Nau watch; **de q.** on watch.

quartette [kwartɛt] nm (jazz) quartet(te).

quartier [kartje] nm **1** neighbourhood, district; (chinois etc) quarter; **de q.** (cinéma etc) local; **les gens du q.** the local people. **2** nm (de pomme, lune) quarter; (d'orange) segment. **3** nm(pl) **quartier(s)** Mil quarters; **q. général** headquarters.

quartz [kwarts] nm quartz; **montre/etc à q.** quartz watch/etc.

quasi [kazi] adv almost. ◆**quasi-** préf near; **q.-obscurité** near darkness. ◆**quasiment** adv almost.

quatorze [katɔrz] a & nm fourteen. ◆**quatorzième** a & nmf fourteenth.

quatre [katr] a & nm four; **se mettre en q.** to go out of one's way (**pour faire** to do); **son q. heures** (goûter) one's afternoon snack; **un de ces q.** Fam some day soon. ◆**quatrième** a & nmf fourth. ◆**quatrièmement** adv fourthly.

quatre-vingt(s) [katrəvɛ̃] a & nm eighty; **q.-vingts ans** eighty years; **q.-vingt-un** eighty-one. ◆**q.-vingt-dix** a & nm ninety.

quatuor [kwatɥɔr] nm Mus quartet(te).

que [k(ə)] (**qu'** before a vowel or mute h) **1** conj that; **je pense qu'elle restera** I think (that) she'll stay; **qu'elle vienne ou non** whether she comes or not; **qu'il s'en aille!** let him leave! ; **ça fait un an q. je suis là** I've been here for a year; **ça fait un an q. je suis parti** I left a year ago. **2** (ne) . . . q. only; **tu n'as qu'un franc** you only have one franc. **3** (comparaison) than; (avec aussi, même, tel, autant) as; **plus/moins âgé q. lui** older/younger than him; **aussi sage/etc q.** as wise/etc as; **le même q.** the same as. **4** adv (ce) **qu'il est bête!** (comme) how silly he is!; **q. de gens!** (combien) what a lot of people! **5** pron rel (chose) that, which; (personne) that, whom; (temps) when; **le livre q. j'ai** the book (that ou which) I have; **l'ami q. j'ai** the friend (that ou whom) I have; **un jour/mois/etc q.** one day/month/etc when. **6** pron interrogatif what; **q. fait-il?,**

qu'est-ce qu'il fait? what is he doing?; **qu'est-ce qui est dans ta poche?** what's in your pocket?; **q. préférez-vous?** which do you prefer?

Québec [kebɛk] nm le Q. Quebec.

quel, quelle [kɛl] **1** a interrogatif what, which; (qui) who; **q. livre/acteur?** what ou which book/actor?; **q. livre/acteur préférez-vous?** which ou what book/actor do you prefer?; **q. est cet homme?** who is that man?; **je sais q. est ton but** I know what your aim is; **q. qu'il soit** (chose) whatever it may be; (personne) whoever it ou he may be; — pron interrogatif which (one); **q. est le meilleur?** which (one) is the best? **2** a exclamatif **q. idiot!** what a fool!; **q. joli bébé!** what a pretty baby!

quelconque [kɛlkɔ̃k] a **1** any, some (or other); **une raison q.** any reason (whatever ou at all), some reason (or other). **2** (banal) ordinary.

quelque [kɛlk(ə)] **1** a some; **q. jour** some day; **quelques femmes** a few women, some women; **les quelques amies qu'elle a** the few friends she has. **2** adv (environ) about, some; **et q.** Fam and a bit; **q. grand qu'il soit** however tall he may be; **q. numéro qu'elle choisisse** whichever number she chooses; **q. peu** somewhat. **3** pron **q. chose** something; (interrogation) anything, something; **il a q. chose** Fig there's something the matter with him; **q. chose d'autre** something else; **q. chose de grand/etc** something big/etc. **4** adv **q. part** somewhere; (interrogation) anywhere, somewhere.

quelquefois [kɛlkəfwa] adv sometimes.

quelques-uns, -unes [kɛlkəzœ̃, -yn] pron pl some.

quelqu'un [kɛlkœ̃] pron someone, somebody; (interrogation) anyone, anybody, someone, somebody; **q. d'intelligent/etc** someone clever/etc.

quémander [kemɑ̃de] vt to beg for.

qu'en-dira-t-on [kɑ̃diratɔ̃] nm inv (propos) gossip.

quenelle [kənɛl] nf Culin quenelle, fish ou meat roll.

querelle [kərɛl] nf quarrel, dispute. ◆**se quereller** vpr to quarrel. ◆**querelleur, -euse** a quarrelsome.

question [kɛstjɔ̃] nf question; (affaire, problème) matter, issue, question; **il est q. de** it's a matter ou question of (**faire** doing); (on projette de) there's some question of (**faire** doing); **il n'en est pas q.** there's no question of it, it's out of the question; **en q.** in question; **hors de q.** out of the question;

(re)mettre en q. to (call in) question. ◆**questionner** vt to question (sur about).

quête [kɛt] nf 1 (collecte) collection. 2 (recherche) quest (de for); en q. de in quest ou search of. ◆**quêter** vt to seek, beg for; – vi to collect money.

queue [kø] nf 1 (d'animal) tail; (de fleur) stalk, stem; (de fruit) stalk; (de poêle) handle; (de comète) trail; (de robe) train; (de cortège, train) rear; q. de cheval (coiffure) ponytail; faire une q. de poisson Aut to cut in (à qn in front of s.o.); à la q. (de classe) at the bottom of; à la q. leu leu (marcher) in single file. 2 (file) queue, Am line; faire la q. to queue up, Am line up. 3 (de billard) cue. ◆**q.-de-pie** nf (pl queues-de-pie) (habit) tails.

qui [ki] pron (personne) who, that; (interrogatif) who; (après prép) whom; (chose) which, that; l'homme q. the man who ou that; la maison q. the house which ou that; q.? who?; q. (est-ce q.) est là? who's there?; q. désirez-vous voir?, q. est-ce que vous désirez voir? who(m) do you want to see?; sans q. without whom; la femme de q. je parle the woman I'm talking about ou about whom I'm talking; l'ami sur l'aide de q. je compte the friend on whose help I rely; q. que vous soyez whoever you are, whoever you may be; q. que ce soit anyone (at all); à q. est ce livre? whose book is this?

quiche [kiʃ] nf (tarte) quiche.

quiconque [kikɔ̃k] pron (celui qui) whoever; (n'importe qui) anyone.

quignon [kiɲɔ̃] nm chunk (of bread).

quille [kij] nf 1 (de navire) keel. 2 (de jeu) skittle; pl (jeu) skittles, ninepins. 3 (jambe) Fam leg.

quincaillier, -ière [kɛ̃kaje, -jɛr] nmf hardware dealer, ironmonger. ◆**quincaillerie** nf hardware; (magasin) hardware shop.

quinine [kinin] nf Méd quinine.

quinquennal, -aux [kɛ̃kenal, -o] a (plan) five-year.

quinte [kɛ̃t] nf Méd coughing fit.

quintessence [kɛ̃tesɑ̃s] nf quintessence.

quintette [kɛ̃tɛt] nm Mus quintet(te).

quintuple [kɛ̃typl] a q. de fivefold; – nm le q. de five times as much as. ◆**quintupl/er** vti to increase fivefold. ◆**-és, -ées** nmfpl (enfants) quintuplets, quins.

quinze [kɛ̃z] a & nm fifteen; q. jours two weeks, fortnight. ◆**quinzaine** nf une q. (de) (nombre) (about) fifteen; q. (de jours) two weeks, fortnight. ◆**quinzième** a & nmf fifteenth.

quiproquo [kiprɔko] nm misunderstanding.

quittance [kitɑ̃s] nf receipt.

quitte [kit] a quits, even (envers with); q. à faire even if it means doing; en être q. pour une amende/etc to (be lucky enough to) get off with a fine/etc.

quitter [kite] vt to leave; (ôter) to take off; – vi ne quittez pas! Tél hold the line!, hold on!; – se q. vpr (se séparer) to part.

qui-vive (sur le) [syrləkiviv] adv on the alert.

quoi [kwa] pron what; (après prép) which; à q. penses-tu? what are you thinking about?; après q. after which; ce à q. je m'attendais what I was expecting; de q. manger/etc (assez) enough to eat/etc; de q. couper/écrire/etc (instrument) something to cut/write/etc with; q. que je dise whatever I say; q. que ce soit anything (at all); q. qu'il en soit be that as it may; il n'y a pas de q.! (en réponse à 'merci') don't mention it!; q.? what?; c'est un idiot, q.! (non traduit) Fam he's a fool!

quoique [kwak(ə)] conj (+ sub) (al)though.

quolibet [kɔlibɛ] nm Litt gibe.

quorum [k(w)ɔrɔm] nm quorum.

quota [k(w)ɔta] nm quota.

quote-part [kɔtpar] nf (pl quotes-parts) share.

quotidien, -ienne [kɔtidjɛ̃, -jɛn] a (journalier) daily; (banal) everyday; – nm daily (paper). ◆**quotidiennement** adv daily.

quotient [kɔsjɑ̃] nm quotient.

R

R, r [ɛr] nm R, r.

rabâch/er [rabɑʃe] vt to repeat endlessly; – vi to repeat oneself ◆**-age** nm endless repetition.

rabais [rabɛ] nm (price) reduction, discount; au r. (acheter) cheap, at a reduction.

rabaisser [rabese] vt (dénigrer) to belittle, humble; r. à (ravaler) to reduce to.

rabat-joie [rabaʒwa] nm inv killjoy.

rabattre° [rabatr] vt (baisser) to put ou pull down; (refermer) to close (down); (replier) to fold down ou over; (déduire) to take off; **en r.** (prétentieux) Fig to climb down (from one's high horse); **— se r.** vpr (se refermer) to close; (après avoir doublé) Aut to cut in (**devant** in front of); **r. sur** Fig to fall back on.

rabbin [rabĕ] nm rabbi; **grand r.** chief rabbi.

rabibocher [rabibɔʃe] vt (réconcilier) Fam to patch it up between; **— se r.** vpr Fam to patch it up.

rabiot [rabjo] nm (surplus) Fam extra (helping); **faire du r.** Fam to work extra time.

râblé [rable] a stocky, thickset.

rabot [rabo] nm (outil) plane. **◆raboter** vt to plane.

raboteux, -euse [rabotø, -øz] a uneven, rough.

rabougri [rabugri] a (personne, plante) stunted.

rabrouer [rabrue] vt to snub, rebuff.

racaille [rakɑj] nf rabble, riffraff.

raccommod/er [rakɔmɔde] vt 1 to mend; (chaussette) to darn. 2 vt (réconcilier) Fam to reconcile; **— se r.** vpr Fam to make it up (**avec** with). **◆—age** nm mending; darning.

raccompagner [rakɔ̃paɲe] vt to see ou take back (home); **r. à la porte** to see to the door, see out.

raccord [rakɔr] nm (dispositif) connection; (de papier peint) join; **r. (de peinture)** touch-up. **◆raccord/er** vt **— se r.** vpr to connect (up), join (up) (**à** with, to). **◆—ement** nm (action, résultat) connection.

raccourc/ir [rakursir] vt to shorten; **— vi** to get shorter; (au lavage) to shrink. **◆—i** 1 (chemin) short cut. 2 **en r.** (histoire etc) in a nutshell.

raccroc (par) [parrakro] adv by a (lucky) chance.

raccrocher [rakroʃe] vt to hang back up; (récepteur) Tél to put down; (relier) to connect (**à** with, to); (client) to accost; **se r. à** to hold on to, cling to; (se rapporter à) to link (up) with; **— vi** Tél to hang up, ring off.

race [ras] nf (groupe ethnique) race; (animale) breed; (famille) stock; (engeance) Péj breed; **de r.** (chien) pedigree-; (cheval) thoroughbred. **◆racé** a (chien) pedigree-; (cheval) thoroughbred; (personne) distinguished. **◆racial, -aux** a racial. **◆racisme** nm racism, racialism. **◆raciste** a & nmf racist, racialist.

rachat [raʃa] nm Com repurchase; (de firme)

take-over; Rel redemption. **◆racheter** vt to buy back; (objet d'occasion) to buy; (nouvel article) to buy another; (firme) to take over, buy out; (pécheur, dette) to redeem; (compenser) to make up for; **r. des chaussettes/du pain**/etc to buy (some) more socks/bread/etc; **— se r.** vpr to make amends, redeem oneself.

racine [rasin] nf (de plante, personne etc) & Math root; **prendre r.** (plante) & Fig to take root.

racket [raket] nm (association) racket; (activité) racketeering.

raclée [rakle] nf Fam hiding, thrashing.

racler [rakle] vt to scrape; (enlever) to scrape off; **se r. la gorge** to clear one's throat. **◆raclette** nf scraper; (à vitres) squeegee. **◆racloir** nm scraper. **◆raclures** nfpl (déchets) scrapings.

racol/er [rakole] vt (prostituée) to solicit (s.o.); (vendeur etc) to tout for (s.o.), solicit (s.o.). **◆—age** nm soliciting; touting. **◆—eur, -euse** nmf tout.

raconter [rakɔ̃te] vt (histoire) to tell, relate; (décrire) to describe; **r. qch à qn** (vacances etc) to tell s.o. about sth; **r. à qn que** to tell s.o. that, say to s.o. that. **◆racontars** nmpl gossip, stories.

racornir [rakɔrnir] vt to harden; **— se r.** vpr to get hard.

radar [radar] nm radar; **contrôle r.** (pour véhicules etc) radar control. **◆radariste** nmf radar operator.

rade [rad] nf 1 Nau (natural) harbour. 2 **laisser en r.** to leave stranded, abandon; **rester en r.** to be left behind.

radeau, -x [rado] nm raft.

radiateur [radjatœr] nm (à eau) & Aut radiator; (électrique, à gaz) heater.

radiation [radjasjɔ̃] nf 1 Phys radiation. 2 (suppression) removal (**de** from).

radical, -ale, -aux [radikal, -o] a radical; — nm Ling stem; — nmf Pol radical.

radier [radje] vt to strike ou cross off (**de** from).

radieux, -euse [radjø, -øz] a (personne, visage) radiant, beaming; (soleil) brilliant; (temps) glorious.

radin, -ine [radĕ, -in] a Fam stingy; — nmf Fam skinflint.

radio [radjo] nf 1 radio; (poste) radio (set); **à la r.** on the radio. 2 nf (photo) Méd X-ray; **passer** ou **faire une r.** to be X-rayed, have an X-ray. 3 nm (opérateur) radio operator. **◆radioactif, -ive** a radioactive. **◆radioactivité** nf radioactivity. **◆radiodiffuser** vt to broadcast (on the radio). **◆radio-**

diffusion *nf* broadcasting. ◆**radiographie** *nf* (*photo*) X-ray; (*technique*) radiography. ◆**radiographier** *vt* to X-ray. ◆**radiologie** *nf* Méd radiology. ◆**radiologue** *nmf* (*technicien*) radiographer; (*médecin*) radiologist. ◆**radiophonique** *a* (*programme*) radio-. ◆**radiotélévisé** *a* broadcast on radio and television.

radis [radi] *nm* radish; **r. noir** horseradish.

radot/er [radɔte] *vi* to drivel (on), ramble (on). ◆**—age** *nm* (*propos*) drivel.

radouc/ir (se) [səraduksir] *vpr* to calm down; (*temps*) to become milder. ◆**—issement** *nm* **r. (du temps)** milder weather.

rafale [rafal] *nf* (*vent*) gust, squall; (*de mitrailleuse*) burst; (*de balles*) hail.

raffermir [rafɛrmir] *vt* to strengthen; (*muscles etc*) to tone up; — **se r.** *vpr* to become stronger.

raffin/er [rafine] *vt* (*pétrole, sucre, manières*) to refine. ◆**—é** *a* refined. ◆**—age** *nm* (*du pétrole, sucre*) refining. ◆**—ement** *nm* (*de personne*) refinement. ◆**raffinerie** *nf* refinery.

raffoler [rafɔle] *vi* **r. de** (*aimer*) to be very fond of, be mad ou wild about.

raffut [rafy] *nm* Fam din, row.

rafiot [rafjo] *nm* (*bateau*) Péj (old) tub.

rafistoler [rafistɔle] *vt* Fam to patch up.

rafle [rafl] *nf* (*police*) raid.

rafler [rafle] *vt* (*enlever*) Fam to swipe, make off with.

rafraîch/ir [rafreʃir] *vt* to cool (down); (*remettre à neuf*) to brighten up; (*mémoire, personne*) to refresh; — *vi* **mettre à r.** Culin to chill; — **se r.** *vpr* (*boire*) to refresh oneself; (*se laver*) to freshen (oneself) up; (*temps*) to get cooler. ◆**—issant** *a* refreshing. ◆**—issement** *nm* **1** (*de température*) cooling. **2** (*boisson*) cold drink; *pl* (*fruits, glaces etc*) refreshments.

ragaillardir [ragajardir] *vt* to buck up.

rage [raʒ] *nf* **1** (*colère*) rage; **r. de dents** violent toothache; **faire r.** (*incendie, tempête*) to rage. **2** (*maladie*) rabies. ◆**rager** *vi* (*personne*) Fam to rage, fume. ◆**rageant** *a* Fam infuriating. ◆**rageur, -euse** *a* bad-tempered, furious.

ragots [rago] *nmpl* Fam gossip.

ragoût [ragu] *nm* Culin stew.

ragoûtant [ragutã] *a* **peu r.** (*mets, personne*) unsavoury.

raid [rɛd] *nm* (*incursion, attaque*) Mil Av raid.

raide [rɛd] *a* (*rigide, guindé*) stiff; (*côte*) steep; (*cheveux*) straight; (*corde etc*) tight; **c'est r.!** (*exagéré*) Fam it's a bit stiff ou

much!; — *adv* (*grimper*) steeply; **tomber r. mort** to drop dead. ◆**raideur** *nf* stiffness; steepness. ◆**raidillon** *nm* (*pente*) short steep rise. ◆**raidir** *vt*, — **se r.** *vpr* to stiffen; (*corde*) to tighten; (*position*) to harden; **se r.** contre Fig to steel oneself against.

raie [rɛ] *nf* **1** (*trait*) line; (*de tissu, zèbre*) stripe; (*de cheveux*) parting, *Am* part. **2** (*poisson*) skate, ray.

rail [raj] *nm* (*barre*) rail; **le r.** (*transport*) rail.

railler [raje] *vt* to mock, make fun of. ◆**raillerie** *nf* gibe, mocking remark. ◆**railleur, -euse** *a* mocking.

rainure [renyr] *nf* groove.

raisin [rɛzɛ̃] *nm* **raisin(s)** grapes; **grain de r.** grape; **manger du r.** *ou* **des raisins** to eat grapes.

raison [rɛzɔ̃] *nf* **1** (*faculté, motif*) reason; **entendre r.** to listen to reason; **la r.** pour **laquelle je . . .** the reason (why *ou* that) I . . . ; **pour raisons de famille/de santé/etc** for family/health/etc reasons; **en r. de** (*cause*) on account of; **à r. de** (*proportion*) at the rate of; **avoir r. de qn/de qch** to get the better of s.o./sth; **mariage de r.** marriage of convenience; **à plus forte r.** all the more so; **r. de plus** all the more reason (**pour faire to do, for doing**). **2** **avoir r.** to be right (**de faire to do, in doing**); **donner r. à qn** to agree with s.o.; (*événement etc*) to prove s.o. right; **avec r.** rightly. ◆**raisonnable** *a* reasonable. ◆**raisonnablement** *adv* reasonably.

raisonn/er [rɛzɔne] *vi* (*penser*) to reason; (*discuter*) to argue; — *vt* **r. qn** to reason with s.o. ◆**—é** *a* (*projet*) well-thought-out. ◆**—ement** *nm* (*faculté, activité*) reasoning; (*propositions*) argument. ◆**—eur, -euse** *a* Péj argumentative; — *nmf* Péj arguer.

rajeun/ir [raʒœnir] *vt* to make (feel *ou* look) younger; (*personnel*) to infuse new blood into; (*moderniser*) to modernize, update; (*personne âgée*) Méd to rejuvenate; — *vi* to get *ou* feel *ou* look younger. ◆**—issant** *a* Méd rejuvenating. ◆**—issement** *nm* Méd rejuvenation; **le r. de la population** the population getting younger.

rajout [raʒu] *nm* addition. ◆**rajouter** *vt* to add (à to); **en r.** Fig to overdo it.

rajuster [raʒyste] *vt* (*mécanisme*) to readjust; (*lunettes, vêtements*) to straighten, adjust; (*cheveux*) to rearrange; — **se r.** *vpr* to straighten ou tidy oneself up.

râle [rɑl] *nm* (*de blessé*) groan; (*de mourant*) death rattle. ◆**râler** *vi* (*blessé*) to groan; (*mourant*) to give the death rattle; (*protes-*

er) *Fam* to grouse, moan. ◆**râleur, -euse** *nmf Fam* grouser, moaner.

ralent/ir [ralɑ̃tir] *vti*, — **se r.** *vpr* to slow down. ◆**—i** *nm Cin TV* slow motion; **au r.** (*filmer, travailler*) in slow motion; (*vivre*) at a slower pace; **tourner au r.** (*moteur, usine*) to idle, tick over, *Am* turn over.

rallier [ralje] *vt* (*rassembler*) to rally; (*rejoindre*) to rejoin; **r. qn à** (*convertir*) to win s.o. over to; — **se r.** *vpr* (*se regrouper*) to rally; **se r. à** (*point de vue*) to come over *ou* round to.

rallonge [ralɔ̃ʒ] *nf* (*de table*) extension; (*fil électrique*) extension (lead); **une r. (de)** (*supplément*) *Fam* (some) extra. ◆**rallonger** *vti* to lengthen.

rallumer [ralyme] *vt* to light again, relight; (*lampe*) to switch on again; (*conflit, haine*) to rekindle; — **se r.** *vpr* (*guerre, incendie*) to flare up again.

rallye [rali] *nm Sp Aut* rally.

ramage [ramaʒ] **1** *nm* (*d'oiseaux*) song, warbling. **2** *nmpl* (*dessin*) foliage.

ramass/er [ramase] **1** *vt* (*prendre par terre, réunir*) to pick up; (*ordures, copies*) to collect, pick up; (*fruits, coquillages*) to gather; (*rhume, amende*) *Fam* to pick up, get; **r. une bûche** *ou* **une pelle** *Fam* to come a cropper, *Am* take a spill. **2 se r.** *vpr* (*se pelotonner*) to curl up. ◆**—é** *a* (*trapu*) squat, stocky; (*recroquevillé*) huddled; (*concis*) compact. ◆**—age** *nm* picking up; collection; gathering; **r. scolaire** school bus service.

ramassis [ramasi] *nm* **r. de** (*voyous etc*) *Péj* bunch of.

rambarde [rɑ̃bard] *nf* guardrail.

rame [ram] *nf* **1** (*aviron*) oar. **2** (*de métro*) train. **3** (*de papier*) ream. ◆**ramer** *vi* to row. ◆**rameur, -euse** *nmf* rower.

rameau, -x [ramo] *nm* branch; **les Rameaux** *Rel* Palm Sunday.

ramener [ramne] *vt* to bring *ou* take back; (*paix, calme, ordre etc*) to restore, bring back; (*remettre en place*) to put back; **r. à** (*réduire à*) to reduce to; **r. à la vie** to bring back to life; — **se r.** *vpr* (*arriver*) *Fam* to turn up; **se r. à** (*problème etc*) to boil down to.

ramier [ramje] *nm* (**pigeon**) **r.** wood pigeon.

ramification [ramifikasjɔ̃] *nf* ramification.

ramoll/ir [ramɔlir] *vt*, — **se r.** *vpr* to soften. ◆**—i** *a* soft; (*personne*) soft-headed.

ramon/er [ramɔne] *vt* (*cheminée*) to sweep. ◆**—age** *nm* (chimney) sweeping. ◆**—eur** *nm* (chimney)sweep.

rampe [rɑ̃p] *nf* **1** (*pente*) ramp, slope; **r. de lancement** (*de fusées etc*) launch(ing) pad. **2** (*d'escalier*) banister(s). **3** (*projecteurs*) *Th* footlights.

ramper [rɑ̃pe] *vi* to crawl; (*plante*) to creep; **r. devant** *Fig* to cringe *ou* crawl to.

rancard [rɑ̃kar] *nm Fam* (*rendez-vous*) date; (*renseignement*) tip.

rancart [rɑ̃kar] *nm* **mettre au r.** *Fam* to throw out, scrap.

rance [rɑ̃s] *a* rancid. ◆**rancir** *vi* to turn rancid.

ranch [rɑ̃tʃ] *nm* ranch.

rancœur [rɑ̃kœr] *nf* rancour, resentment.

rançon [rɑ̃sɔ̃] *nf* ransom; **la r. de** (*inconvénient*) the price of (*success, fame etc*). ◆**rançonner** *vt* to hold to ransom.

rancune [rɑ̃kyn] *nf* grudge; **garder à qn** to bear s.o. a grudge; **sans r.!** no hard feelings! ◆**rancunier, -ière** *a* vindictive, resentful.

randonnée [rɑ̃dɔne] *nf* (*à pied*) walk, hike; (*en voiture*) drive, ride; (*en vélo*) ride.

rang [rɑ̃] *nm* (*rangée*) row, line; (*condition, grade, classement*) rank; **les rangs** (*hommes*) *Mil* the ranks (de of); **les rangs de ses ennemis** (*nombre*) *Fig* the ranks of his enemies; **se mettre en rang(s)** to line up (*par trois/etc* in threes/*etc*); **par r. de** in order of. ◆**rangée** *nf* row, line.

rang/er [rɑ̃ʒe] *vt* (*papiers, vaisselle etc*) to put away; (*chambre etc*) to tidy (up); (*chiffres, mots*) to arrange; (*voiture*) to park; **r. parmi** (*auteur etc*) to rank among; — **se r.** *vpr* (*élèves etc*) to line up; (*s'écarter*) to stand aside; (*voiture*) to pull over; (*s'assagir*) to settle down; **se r. à** (*avis de qn*) to fall in with. ◆**—é** *a* (*chambre etc*) tidy; (*personne*) steady; (*bataille*) pitched. ◆**—ement** *nm* putting away; (*de chambre etc*) tidying (up); (*espace*) storage space.

ranimer [ranime] *vt* (*réanimer, revigorer*) to revive; (*encourager*) to spur on; (*feu, querelle*) to rekindle.

rapace [rapas] **1** *a* (*avide*) grasping. **2** *nm* (*oiseau*) bird of prey.

rapatrier [rapatrije] *vt* to repatriate. ◆**rapatriement** *nm* repatriation.

râpe [rɑp] *nf Culin* grater; shredder; (*lime*) rasp. ◆**râp/er** *vt* (*fromage*) to grate; (*carottes etc*) to shred, (*finement*) to grate; (*bois*) to rasp. ◆**—é 1** *a* (*fromage*) grated; — *nm* grated cheese. **2** *a* (*vêtement*) threadbare.

rapetisser [raptise] *vt* to make (look) smaller; (*vêtement*) to shorten; — *vi* to get smaller; (*au lavage*) to shrink; (*jours*) to get shorter.

râpeux, -euse [rɑpø, -øz] *a* rough.

raphia [rafja] *nm* raffia.

rapide [rapid] *a* fast, quick, rapid; *(pente)* steep; — *nm (train)* express (train); *(de fleuve)* rapid. ◆—**ment** *adv* fast, quickly, rapidly. ◆**rapidité** *nf* speed, rapidity.

rapiécer [rapjese] *vt* to patch (up).

rappel [rapɛl] *nm (de diplomate etc)* recall; *(évocation, souvenir)* reminder; *(paiement)* back pay; *pl Th* curtain calls; **(vaccination de) r.** *Méd* booster; **r. à l'ordre** call to order. ◆**rappeler** *vt (pour faire revenir)* & *Tél* to call back; *(diplomate, souvenir)* to recall; **r. qch à qn** *(redire)* to remind s.o. of sth; — *vi Tél* to call back; — **se r.** *vpr (histoire, personne etc)* to remember, recall, recollect.

rappliquer [raplike] *vi (arriver) Fam* to show up.

rapport [rapɔr] *nm* **1** *(lien)* connection; link; *pl (entre personnes)* relations; **rapports (sexuels)** (sexual) intercourse; **par r. à** compared to *ou* with; *(envers)* towards; **se mettre en r. avec qn** to get in touch with s.o.; **en r. avec** in keeping with; **sous le r. de** from the point of view of. **2** *(revenu) Com* return, yield. **3** *(récit)* report. ◆**rapporter 1** *(ramener)* to bring back *ou* take back; *(ajouter)* to add; — *vi (chien)* to retrieve. **2** *vt (récit)* to report; *(mot célèbre)* to repeat; — *vi (moucharder) Fam* to tell tales. **3** *vt (profit) Com* to bring in, yield; — *vi (investissement) Com* to bring in a good return. **4** **se r.** *à (rattacher)* to relate sth to; **se r. à** to relate to, be connected with; **s'en r. à** to rely on. ◆**rapporteur, -euse 1** *nmf (mouchard)* telltale. **2** *nm Jur* reporter. **3** *nm Géom* protractor.

rapproch/er [raprɔʃe] *vt* to bring closer (**de** to); *(chaise)* to pull up (**de** to); *(réconcilier)* to bring together; *(réunir)* to join; *(comparer)* to compare; — **se r.** *vpr* to come *ou* get closer (**de** to); *(se réconcilier)* to come together, be reconciled; *(ressembler)* to be close (**de** to). ◆—**é** *a* close, near; *(yeux)* close-set; *(fréquent)* frequent. ◆—**ement** *nm (réconciliation)* reconciliation; *(rapport)* connection; *(comparaison)* comparison.

rapt [rapt] *nm (d'enfant)* abduction.

raquette [rakɛt] *nf (de tennis)* racket; *(de ping-pong)* bat.

rare [rar] *a* rare; *(argent, main-d'œuvre etc)* scarce; *(barbe, herbe)* sparse; **il est r. que** (+ *sub*) it's seldom *ou* rare that. ◆**se raréfier** *vpr (denrées etc)* to get scarce. ◆—**rarement** *adv* rarely, seldom. ◆**rareté** *nf* rarity; scarcity; **une r.** *(objet)* a rarity.

ras [rɑ] *a (cheveux)* close-cropped; *(herbe, poil)* short; *(mesure)* full; **en rase campagne**

in (the) open country; **à r.** very close to; **à r. bord** *(remplir)* to the brim; **en avoir r. le bol** *Fam* to be fed up (**de** with); **pull (au) r. du cou** *ou* **à col r.** crew-neck(ed) pullover; — *adv* short.

ras/er [rɑze] **1** *vt (menton, personne)* to shave; *(barbe, moustache)* to shave off; — **se r.** *vpr* to (have a) shave. **2** *vt (démolir)* to raze, knock down. **3** *vt (frôler)* to skim, brush. **4** *vt (ennuyer) Fam* to bore. ◆—**ant** *a Fam* boring. ◆—**é** *a* **bien r.** clean-shaven; **mal r.** unshaven. ◆—**age** *nm* shaving. ◆—**eur, -euse** *nm Fam* bore. ◆**rasoir 1** *nm* shaver. **2** *a inv Fam* boring.

rassasier [rasazje] *vt* to satisfy; **être rassasié** to have had enough (**de** of).

rassembl/er [rasɑ̃ble] *vt* to gather (together), assemble; *(courage)* to summon up, muster; — **se r.** *vpr* to gather, assemble. ◆**rassemblement** *nm (action, gens)* gathering.

rasseoir* **(se)** [səraswar] *vpr* to sit down again.

rassis, *f* **rassie** [rasi] *a (pain, brioche etc)* stale. ◆**rassir** *vti* to turn stale.

rassur/er [rasyre] *vt* to reassure; **rassure-toi** set your mind at rest, don't worry. ◆—**ant** *a (nouvelle)* reassuring, comforting.

rat [ra] *nm* rat; **r. de bibliothèque** *Fig* bookworm.

ratatiner **(se)** [səratatine] *vpr* to shrivel (up); *(vieillard)* to become wizened.

rate [rat] *nf Anat* spleen.

râteau, -x [rato] *nm (outil)* rake.

râtelier [ratəlje] *nm* **1** *(support pour outils, armes etc)* rack. **2** *(dentier) Fam* set of false teeth.

rat/er [rate] *vt (bus, cible, occasion etc)* to miss; *(gâcher)* to spoil, ruin; *(vie)* to waste; *(examen)* to fail; — *vi (projet etc)* to fail; *(pistolet)* to misfire. ◆—**é, -ée 1** *nmf (personne)* failure. **2** *nmpl* **avoir des ratés** *Aut* to backfire. ◆—**age** *nm (échec) Fam* failure.

ratifier [ratifje] *vt* to ratify. ◆**ratification** *nf* ratification.

ration [rasjɔ̃] *nf* ration; **r. de** *Fig* share of. ◆**rationn/er** *vt (vivres, personne)* to ration. ◆—**ement** *nm* rationing.

rationaliser [rasjɔnalize] *vt* to rationalize. ◆**rationalisation** *nf* rationalization.

rationnel, -elle [rasjɔnɛl] *a (pensée, méthode)* rational.

ratisser [ratise] *vt* **1** *(allée etc)* to rake; *(feuilles etc)* to rake up. **2** *(fouiller)* to comb. **3 r. qn** *(au jeu) Fam* to clean s.o. out.

raton [ratɔ̃] *nm* **r. laveur** rac(c)oon.

rattach/er [rataʃe] *vt* to tie up again; *(in-*

corporer, joindre) to join (à to); (*idée, question*) to link (à to); **r. qn** à (*son pays etc*) to bind s.o. to; **se r.** à to be linked to. ◆—**ement** *nm* (*annexion*) joining (à to).

rattrap/er [ratrape] *vt* to catch; (*prisonnier etc*) to recapture; (*erreur, temps perdu*) to make up for; **r. qn** (*rejoindre*) to catch up with s.o., catch s.o. up; — **se r.** *vpr* to catch up; (*se dédommager, prendre une compensation*) to make up for it; **se r.** à (*branche etc*) to catch hold of. ◆—**age** *nm cours de r. Scol* remedial classes; **r. des prix/salaires** adjustment of prices/wages (*to the cost of living*).

rature [ratyr] *nf* deletion. ◆**raturer** *vt* to delete, cross out.

rauque [rok] *a* (*voix*) hoarse, raucous.

ravages [rava3] *nmpl* devastation; (*de la maladie, du temps*) havoc; **faire des r.** to wreak havoc. ◆**ravager** *vt* to devastate, ravage.

raval/er [ravale] *vt* **1** (*façade etc*) to clean (and restore). **2** (*salive, sanglots*) to swallow. **3** (*avilir*) *Litt* to lower. ◆—**ement** *nm* (*de façade etc*) cleaning (and restoration).

ravi [ravi] *a* delighted (**de** with, **de faire** to do).

ravier [ravje] *nm* hors-d'œuvre dish.

ravigoter [ravigote] *vt* *Fam* to buck up.

ravin [ravɛ̃] *nm* ravine, gully.

ravioli [ravjɔli] *nmpl* ravioli.

rav/ir [ravir] *vt* **1** to delight; **à r.** (*chanter etc*) delightfully. **2** (*emporter*) to snatch (à from). ◆—**issant** *a* delightful, lovely. ◆**ravisseur, -euse** *nmf* kidnapper.

raviser (se) [səravize] *vpr* to change one's mind.

ravitaill/er [ravitaje] *vt* to provide with supplies, supply; (*avion*) to refuel; — **se r.** *vpr* to stock up (with supplies). ◆—**ement** *nm* supplying; refuelling; (*denrées*) supplies; **aller au r.** (*faire des courses*) *Fam* to stock up, get stocks in.

raviver [ravive] *vt* (*feu, sentiment*) to revive; (*couleurs*) to brighten up.

ray/er [reje] *vt* (*érafler*) to scratch; (*mot etc*) to cross out; **r. qn de** (*liste*) to cross ou strike s.o. off. ◆—**é** *a* scratched; (*tissu*) striped; (*papier*) lined, ruled. ◆**rayure** *nf* scratch; (*bande*) stripe; **à rayures** striped.

rayon [rejɔ̃] *nm* **1** (*de lumière, soleil etc*) *Phys* ray; (*de cercle*) radius; (*de roue*) spoke; (*d'espoir*) *Fig* ray; **r. X** X-ray; **r. d'action** range; **dans un r. de** within a radius of. **2** (*planche*) shelf; (*de magasin*) department. **3** (*de ruche*) honeycomb. ◆**rayonnage** *nm* shelving, shelves.

rayonn/er [rejone] *vi* to radiate; (*dans une région*) to travel around (*from a central base*); **r. de joie** to beam with joy. ◆—**ant** *a* (*visage etc*) radiant, beaming (**de** with). ◆—**ement** *nm* (*éclat*) radiance; (*influence*) influence; (*radiation*) radiation.

raz-de-marée [rɑdmare] *nm inv* tidal wave; (*bouleversement*) *Fig* upheaval; **r.-de-marée électoral** landslide.

razzia [ra(d)zja] *nf* **faire une r. sur** (*tout enlever sur*) *Fam* to raid.

ré- [r(ə)] *préf* re-.

re- [re] *préf* re-.

réabonn/er (se) [səreabɔne] *vpr* to renew one's subscription (à to). ◆—**ement** *nm* renewal of subscription.

réacteur [reaktœr] *nm* (*d'avion*) jet engine; (*nucléaire*) reactor.

réaction [reaksjɔ̃] *nf* reaction; **r. en chaîne** chain reaction; **avion à r.** jet (aircraft); **moteur à r.** jet engine. ◆**réactionnaire** *a* & *nmf* reactionary.

réadapter [readapte] *vt*, — **se r.** *vpr* to readjust (à to). ◆**réadaptation** *nf* readjustment.

réaffirmer [reafirme] *vt* to reaffirm.

réagir [reaʒir] *vi* to react (**contre** against, **à** to); (*se secouer*) *Fig* to shake oneself out of it.

réalis/er [realize] *vt* (*projet etc*) to carry out, realize; (*ambition, rêve*) to fulfil; (*achat, bénéfice, vente*) to make; (*film*) to direct; (*capital*) *Com* to realize; (*se rendre compte*) to realize (**que** that); — **se r.** *vpr* (*vœu*) to come true; (*projet*) to be carried out; (*personne*) to fulfil oneself. ◆—**able** *a* (*plan*) workable; (*rêve*) attainable. ◆**réalisateur, -trice** *nmf* *Cin* *TV* director. ◆**réalisation** *nf* realization; (*de rêve*) fulfilment; *Cin* *TV* direction; (*œuvre*) achievement.

réalisme [realism] *nm* realism. ◆**réaliste** *a* realistic; – *nmf* realist.

réalité [realite] *nf* reality; **en r.** in (actual) fact, in reality.

réanimer [reanime] *vt* *Méd* to resuscitate. ◆**réanimation** *nf* resuscitation; (**service de**) **r.** intensive care unit.

réapparaître [reaparɛtr] *vi* to reappear. ◆**réapparition** *nf* reappearance.

réarmer [rearme] *vt* (*fusil etc*) to reload; — *vi*, — **se r.** *vpr* (*pays*) to rearm. ◆**réarmement** *nm* rearmament.

rébarbatif, -ive [rebarbatif, -iv] *a* forbidding, off-putting.

rebâtir [r(ə)bɑtir] *vt* to rebuild.

rebattu [r(ə)baty] *a* (*sujet*) hackneyed.

rebelle [rəbɛl] *a* rebellious; *(troupes)* rebel-; *(fièvre)* stubborn; *(mèche)* unruly; **r. à** resistant to; *– nmf* rebel. ◆**se rebeller** *vpr* to rebel *(contre* against*)*. ◆**rébellion** *nf* rebellion.

rebiffer (se) [sərəbife] *vpr Fam* to rebel.

rebond [rəbɔ̃] *nm* bounce; *(par ricochet)* rebound. ◆**rebondir** *vi* to bounce; to rebound; *(faire)* **r.** *(affaire, discussion etc)* to get going again. ◆**rebondissement** *nm* new development *(de* in*)*.

rebondi [rəbɔ̃di] *a* chubby, rounded.

rebord [rəbɔr] *nm* edge; *(de plat etc)* rim; *(de vêtement)* hem; **r. de (la) fenêtre** windowsill, window ledge.

reboucher [rəbuʃe] *vt (flacon)* to put the top back on.

rebours (à) [arəbur] *adv* the wrong way.

rebrousse-poil (à) [arbruspwal] *adv* prendre qn à **r.-poil** *Fig* to rub s.o. up the wrong way.

rebrousser [rəbruse] *vt* **r. chemin** to turn back.

rebuffade [rəbyfad] *nf Litt* rebuff.

rébus [rebys] *nm inv (jeu)* rebus.

rebut [rəby] *nm* mettre au **r.** to throw out, scrap; **le r. de la société** *Péj* the dregs of society.

rebut/er [rəbyte] *vt (décourager)* to put off; *(choquer)* to repel. ◆**—ant** *a* offputting; *(choquant)* repellent.

récalcitrant [rekalsitrɑ̃] *a* recalcitrant.

recaler [rəkale] *vt* **r. qn** *Scol Fam* to fail s.o., flunk s.o.; **se faire r.** *Scol Fam* to fail, flunk.

récapituler [rekapityle] *vti* to recapitulate. ◆**récapitulation** *nf* recapitulation.

recel [rəsɛl] *nm* receiving stolen goods, fencing; harbouring. ◆**receler** *vt (mystère, secret etc)* to contain; *(objet volé)* to receive; *(malfaiteur)* to harbour. ◆**receleur, -euse** *nmf* receiver *(of stolen goods)*, fence.

recens/er [rəsɑ̃se] *vt (population)* to take a census of; *(inventorier)* to make an inventory of. ◆**—ement** *nm* census; inventory.

récent [resɑ̃] *a* recent. ◆**récemment** [-amɑ̃] *adv* recently.

récépissé [resepise] *nm (reçu)* receipt.

récepteur [reseptœr] *nm Tél Rad* receiver. ◆**réceptif, -ive** *a* receptive *(à* to*)*. ◆**réception** *nf (accueil, soirée) & Rad* reception; *(de lettre etc) Com* receipt; *(d'hôtel etc)* reception *(desk)*. ◆**réceptionniste** *nmf* receptionist.

récession [resesjɔ̃] *nf Écon* recession.

recette [rəsɛt] *nf* **1** *Culin & Fig* recipe. **2**

(argent, bénéfice) takings; *(bureau)* tax office; **recettes** *(rentrées) Com* receipts; **faire r.** *Fig* to be a success.

recev/oir* [rəsəvwar] *vt* to receive; *(obtenir)* to get; receive; *(accueillir)* to welcome; *(accepter)* to accept; **être reçu (à)** *(examen)* to pass; **être reçu premier** to come first; *– vi* to receive guests *ou* visitors *ou Méd* patients. ◆**—able** *a (excuse etc)* admissible. ◆**—eur, -euse** *nmf (d'autobus)* (bus) conductor, (bus) conductress; *(des impôts)* tax collector; *(des postes)* postmaster, postmistress.

rechange (de) [dərəʃɑ̃ʒ] *a (pièce, outil etc)* spare; *(solution etc)* alternative; **vêtements/chaussures de r.** a change of clothes/shoes.

rechapé [rəʃape] *a* pneu **r.** retread.

réchapper [reʃape] *vi* **r. de** *ou* **à** *(accident etc)* to come through.

recharge [rəʃarʒ] *nf (de stylo etc)* refill. ◆**recharger** *vt (camion, fusil)* to reload; *(briquet, stylo etc)* to refill; *(batterie etc)* to recharge.

réchaud [reʃo] *nm (portable)* stove.

réchauff/er [reʃofe] *vt (personne, aliment etc)* to warm up; *– se r. vpr* to warm oneself up; *(temps)* to get warmer. ◆*—é nm* du **r.** *Fig Péj* old hat. ◆**—ement** *nm (de température)* rise *(de* in*)*.

rêche [rɛʃ] *a* rough, harsh.

recherche [rəʃɛrʃ] *nf* **1** search, quest *(de* for*)*; **à la r. de** in search of. **2 la r., les recherches** *(scientifique etc)* research *(sur* on, into*)*; **faire des recherches** to research; *(enquête)* to make investigations. **3** *(raffinement)* studied elegance, *Péj* affectation. ◆**recherch/er** *vt* to search *ou* hunt for; *(cause, faveur, perfection)* to seek. ◆*—é a* **1** *(très demandé)* in great demand; *(rare)* much sought-after; **r. pour meurtre** wanted for murder. **2** *(élégant)* elegant; *Péj* affected.

rechigner [rəʃiɲe] *vi (renâcler)* to jib *(à* **qch** at sth, **à faire** at doing*)*.

rechute [rəʃyt] *nf Méd* relapse. ◆**rechuter** *vi Méd* to (have a) relapse.

récidive [residiv] *nf Jur* further offence; *Méd* recurrence *(de* of*)*. ◆**récidiver** *vi Jur* to commit a further offence; *(maladie)* to recur. ◆**récidiviste** *nmf Jur* further offender.

récif [resif] *nm* reef.

récipient [resipjɑ̃] *nm* container, receptacle.

réciproque [resiprɔk] *a* mutual, reciprocal; *– nf (inverse)* opposite; **rendre la r. à qn** to get even with s.o. ◆**réciprocité** *nf* reciprocity. ◆**réciproquement** *adv* (*l'un l'autre*) each other; **et r.** and vice versa.

récit [resi] *nm* (*compte rendu*) account; (*histoire*) story.

récitai, *pl* **-ais** [resital] *nm Mus* recital.

réciter [resite] *vt* to recite. ◆**récitation** *nf* recitation.

réclame [reklam] *nf* advertising; (*annonce*) advertisement; **en r.** *Com* on (special) offer; **– a** *inv* **prix r.** (special) offer price; **vente r.** (bargain) sale.

réclamer [reklame] *vt* (*demander, nécessiter*) to demand, call for; (*revendiquer*) to claim; **– vi** to complain; **se r. de qn** to invoke s.o.'s authority. ◆**réclamation** *nf* complaint; *pl* (*bureau*) complaints department.

reclasser [r(ə)klɑse] *vt* (*fiches etc*) to reclassify.

reclus, -use [rəkly, -yz] *a* (*vie*) cloistered; **– nmf** recluse.

réclusion [reklyzjɔ̃] *nf* imprisonment (with hard labour); **r. à perpétuité** life imprisonment.

recoiffer (se) [sər(ə)kwafe] *vpr* (*se peigner*) to do *ou* comb one's hair.

recoin [rəkwɛ̃] *nm* nook, recess.

recoller [r(ə)kɔle] *vt* (*objet cassé*) to stick together again; (*enveloppe*) to stick back down.

récolte [rekɔlt] *nf* (*action*) harvest; (*produits*) crop, harvest; (*collection*) *Fig* crop. ◆**récolter** *vt* to harvest, gather (in); (*recueillir*) *Fig* to collect, gather; (*coups*) *Fam* to get.

recommand/er [r(ə)kɔmɑ̃de] **1** *vt* (*appuyer, conseiller*) to recommend; **r. à qn de faire** to recommend s.o. to do. **2** *vt* (*lettre etc*) to register. **3** *v r.* **à** (*âme*) to commend to. **4 se r.** *vpr* **se r. de qn** to invoke s.o.'s authority. ◆**–é** *nm* **en r.** (*envoyer*) by registered post. ◆**–able** **a peu r.** not very commendable. ◆**recommandation** *nf* **1** (*appui, conseil, louange*) recommendation. **2** (*de lettre etc*) registration.

recommenc/er [r(ə)kɔmɑ̃se] *vti* to start *ou* begin again. ◆**–ement** *nm* (*reprise*) renewal (**de** of).

récompense [rekɔ̃pɑ̃s] *nf* reward (**de** for); (*prix*) award; **en r. de** in return for. ◆**récompenser** *vt* to reward (**de, pour** for).

réconcilier [rekɔ̃silje] *vt* to reconcile; **– se r.** *vpr* to become reconciled, make it up (**avec** with). ◆**réconciliation** *nf* reconciliation.

reconduire* [r(ə)kɔ̃dɥir] *vt* **1 r. qn** to see *ou* take s.o. back; (*à la porte*) to show s.o. out. **2** (*mesures etc*) to renew. ◆**reconduction** *nf* renewal.

réconfort [rekɔ̃fɔr] *nm* comfort. ◆**réconfort/er** *vt* to comfort; (*revigorer*) to fortify. ◆**–ant** *a* comforting; (*boisson etc*) fortifying.

reconnaissant [r(ə)kɔnɛsɑ̃] *a* grateful, thankful (**à qn de qch** to s.o. for sth). ◆**reconnaissance**[1] *nf* (*gratitude*) gratitude.

reconnaître* [r(ə)kɔnɛtr] *vt* to recognize (**à qch** by sth); (*admettre*) to acknowledge, admit (**que** that); (*terrain*) *Mil* to reconnoitre; **être reconnu coupable** to be found guilty; **– se r.** *vpr* (*s'orienter*) to find one's bearings; **se r. coupable** to admit one's guilt. ◆**reconnu** *a* (*chef, fait*) acknowledged, recognized. ◆**reconnaissable** *a* recognizable (**à qch** by sth). ◆**reconnaissance**[2] *nf* recognition; (*aveu*) acknowledgement; *Mil* reconnaissance; **r. de dette** IOU.

reconsidérer [r(ə)kɔ̃sidere] *vt* to reconsider.

reconstituant [r(ə)kɔ̃stitɥɑ̃] *adj* (*aliment, régime*) restorative.

reconstituer [r(ə)kɔ̃stitɥe] *vt* (*armée, parti*) to reconstitute; (*crime, quartier*) to reconstruct; (*faits*) to piece together; (*fortune*) to build up again. ◆**reconstitution** *nf* reconstitution; reconstruction.

reconstruire* [r(ə)kɔ̃strɥir] *vt* (*ville, fortune*) to rebuild. ◆**reconstruction** *nf* rebuilding.

reconvertir [r(ə)kɔ̃vertir] **1** *vt* (*bâtiment etc*) to reconvert. **2 se r.** *vpr* to take up a new form of employment. ◆**reconversion** *nf* reconversion.

recopier [r(ə)kɔpje] *vt* to copy out.

record [r(ə)kɔr] *nm & a inv Sp* record.

recoucher (se) [sər(ə)kuʃe] *vpr* to go back to bed.

recoudre* [r(ə)kudr] *vt* (*bouton*) to sew back on.

recoup/er [r(ə)kupe] *vt* (*témoignage etc*) to tally with, confirm; **– se r.** *vpr* to tally, match *ou* tie up. ◆**–ement** *nm* crosscheck(ing).

recourbé [r(ə)kurbe] *a* curved; (*nez*) hooked.

recours [r(ə)kur] *nm* recourse (**à** to); *Jur* appeal; **avoir r. à** to resort to; (*personne*) to turn to; **notre dernier r.** our last resort. ◆**recourir*** *vi* **r. à** to resort to; (*personne*) to turn to.

recouvrer [r(ə)kuvre] vt (argent, santé) to recover.

recouvrir* [r(ə)kuvrir] vt (livre, meuble, sol etc) to cover; (de nouveau) to recover; (cacher) Fig to conceal, mask.

récréation [rekreasjɔ̃] nf recreation; (temps) Scol break, playtime.

récriminer [rekrimine] vi to complain bitterly (contre about). ◆**récrimination** nf (bitter) complaint.

récrire [rekrir] vt (lettre etc) to rewrite.

recroqueviller (se) [sər(ə)krɔkvije] vpr (papier, personne etc) to curl up.

recrudescence [rəkrydesɑ̃s] nf new outbreak (de of).

recrue [rəkry] nf recruit. ◆**recruter** vt to recruit. ◆**—ement** nm recruitment.

rectangle [rɛktɑ̃gl] nm rectangle. ◆**rectangulaire** a rectangular.

rectifier [rɛktifje] vt (erreur etc) to correct, rectify; (ajuster) to adjust. ◆**rectificatif** nm (document) amendment, correction. ◆**rectification** nf correction, rectification.

recto [rɛkto] nm front (of the page).

reçu [r(ə)sy] voir recevoir; — a (usages etc) accepted; (idée) conventional, received; (candidat) successful; — nm (écrit) Com receipt.

recueil [r(ə)kœj] nm (ouvrage) collection (de of).

recueill/ir* [r(ə)kœjir] 1 vt to collect, gather; (suffrages) to win, get; (prendre chez soi) to take in. 2 **se r.** vpr to meditate; (devant un monument) to stand in silence. ◆**—i** (air) meditative. ◆**—ement** nm meditation.

recul [r(ə)kyl] nm (d'armée, de négociateur, de maladie) retreat; (éloignement) distance; (déclin) decline; (mouvement de) r. (de véhicule) backward movement; **avoir un mouvement de r.** (personne) to recoil; **phare de r.** Aut reversing light. ◆**reculade** nf Péj retreat. ◆**reculer** vi to move ou step back; Aut to reverse; (armée) to retreat; (épidémie, glacier) to recede, retreat; (renoncer) to back down, retreat; (diminuer) to decline; **r. devant** Fig to recoil ou shrink from; — vt to move ou push back; (différer) to postpone. ◆**—é** a (endroit, temps) remote.

reculons (à) [arkylɔ̃] adv backwards.

récupérer [rekypere] vt to recover, get back; (ferraille etc) to salvage; (heures) to make up; (mouvement, personne etc) Pol Péj to take over, convert; — vi to recuperate, recover. ◆**récupération** nf recovery; salvage; recuperation.

récurer [rekyre] vt (casserole etc) to scour; **poudre à r.** scouring powder.

récuser [rekyze] vt to challenge; — **se r.** vpr to decline to give an opinion.

recycl/er [r(ə)sikle] vt (reconvertir) to retrain (s.o.); (matériaux) to recycle; — **se r.** vpr to retrain. ◆**—age** nm retraining; recycling.

rédacteur, -trice [redaktœr, -tris] nmf writer; (de chronique) Journ editor; (de dictionnaire etc) compiler; **r. en chef** Journ editor(-in-chief). ◆**rédaction** nf (action) writing; (de contrat) drawing up; (devoir) Scol essay, composition; (rédacteurs) Journ editorial staff; (bureaux) Journ editorial offices.

reddition [redisjɔ̃] nf surrender.

redemander [rədmɑ̃de] vt (pain etc) to ask for more; **r. qch à qn** to ask s.o. for sth back.

rédemption [redɑ̃psjɔ̃] nf Rel redemption.

redescendre [r(ə)desɑ̃dr] vi (aux être) to come ou go back down; — vt (aux avoir) (objet) to bring ou take back down.

redevable [rədvabl] a **être r. de qch à qn** (argent) to owe s.o. sth; Fig to be indebted to s.o. for sth.

redevance [rədvɑ̃s] nf (taxe) TV licence fee; Tél rental charge.

redevenir* [rədvənir] vi (aux être) to become again.

rédiger [rediʒe] vt to write; (contrat) to draw up; (dictionnaire etc) to compile.

redire [r(ə)dir] 1 vt to repeat. 2 vi **avoir ou trouver à r. à qch** to find fault with sth. ◆**redite** nf (pointless) repetition.

redondant [r(ə)dɔ̃dɑ̃] a (style) redundant.

redonner [r(ə)dɔne] vt to give back; (de nouveau) to give more.

redoubl/er [r(ə)duble] vti 1 to increase; **r. de patience/etc** to be much more patient/etc; **à coups redoublés** (frapper) harder and harder. 2 **r. (une classe)** Scol to repeat a year ou Am a grade. ◆**—ant, -ante** nmf pupil repeating a year ou Am a grade. ◆**—ement** nm increase (de in); repeating a year ou Am a grade.

redout/er [r(ə)dute] vt to dread (de faire doing). ◆**—able** a formidable, fearsome.

redress/er [r(ə)drese] vt to straighten (out); (économie, mât, situation, tort) to right; — **se r.** vpr (se mettre assis) to sit up; (debout) to stand up; (pays, situation etc) to right itself. ◆**—ement** [-ɛsmɑ̃] nm (essor) recovery.

réduction [redyksjɔ̃] nf reduction (**de** in); **en r.** (copie, modèle etc) small-scale.

réduire* [redɥir] vt to reduce (**à** to, **de** by); **r. qn à** (contraindre à) to reduce s.o. to (silence, inaction etc); **se r. à** (se ramener à) to come down to, amount to; **se r. en cendres**/etc to be reduced to ashes/etc; – vi (**faire**) **r.** (sauce) to reduce, boil down. ◆**réduit 1** a (prix, vitesse) reduced; (moyens) limited; (à petite échelle) small-scale. **2** nm (pièce) Péj cubbyhole; (recoin) recess.

réécrire [reekrir] vt (texte) to rewrite.

rééduquer [reedyke] vt (membre) Méd to re-educate; **r. qn** to rehabilitate s.o., re-educate s.o. ◆**rééducation** nf re-education; rehabilitation.

réel, -elle [reɛl] a a real; **le r.** reality. ◆**réellement** adv really.

réélire [reelir] vt to re-elect.

réexpédier [reɛkspedje] vt (lettre etc) to forward; (à l'envoyeur) to return.

refaire* [r(ə)fɛr] vt to do again, redo; (erreur, voyage) to make again; (réparer) to do up, redo; (duper) Fam to take in. ◆**réfection** nf repair(ing).

réfectoire [refɛktwar] nm refectory.

référendum [referɑ̃dɔm] nm referendum.

référer [refere] vi **en r. à** to refer the matter to; – **se r.** vpr **se r. à** to refer to. ◆**référence** nf reference.

refermer [r(ə)fɛrme] vt, – **se r.** vpr to close ou shut (again).

refiler [r(ə)file] vt (donner) Fam to palm off (**à** on).

réfléch/ir [refleʃir] **1** vt (image) to reflect; – **se r.** vpr to be reflected. **2** vi (penser) to think (**à, sur** about); – vt **r. que** to realize that. ◆**–i** a (personne) thoughtful, reflective; (action, décision) carefully thought-out; (verbe) Gram reflexive. ◆**réflecteur** nm reflector. ◆**réflexion** nf **1** (de lumière etc) reflection. **2** (méditation) thought, reflection; (remarque) remark; **à la r., r. faite** on second thoughts ou Am thought, on reflection.

reflet [r(ə)flɛ] nm (image) & Fig reflection; (lumière) glint; (couleur) tint. ◆**refléter** vt (image, sentiment etc) to reflect; – **se r.** vpr to be reflected.

réflexe [reflɛks] nm & a reflex.

refluer [r(ə)flye] vi (eaux) to ebb, flow back; (foule) to surge back. ◆**reflux** nm ebb; backward surge.

réforme nf **1** (changement) reform. **2** (de soldat) discharge. ◆**réformateur, -trice** nmf reformer. ◆**réformer 1** vt to reform;

– **se r.** vpr to mend one's ways. **2** vt (soldat) to invalid out, discharge.

refoul/er [r(ə)fule] vt to force ou drive back; (sentiment) to repress; (larmes) to hold back. ◆**–é** a (personne) Psy repressed. ◆**–ement** nm Psy repression.

réfractaire [refraktɛr] a **r. à** resistant to.

refrain [r(ə)frɛ̃] nm (de chanson) refrain, chorus; (rengaine) Fig tune.

refréner [r(ə)frene] vt to curb, check.

réfrigér/er [refriʒere] vt to refrigerate. ◆**–ant** a (accueil, air) Fam icy. ◆**réfrigérateur** nm refrigerator. ◆**réfrigération** nf refrigeration.

refroid/ir [r(ə)frwadir] vt to cool (down); (décourager) Fig to put off; (ardeur) to dampen, cool; – vi to get cold, cool down; – **se r.** vpr Méd to catch cold; (temps) to get cold; (ardeur) to cool (off). ◆**–issement** nm cooling; (rhume) chill; **r. de la température** fall in the temperature.

refuge [r(ə)fyʒ] nm refuge; (pour piétons) (traffic) island; (de montagne) (mountain) hut. ◆**se réfugi/er** vpr to take refuge. ◆**–é, -ée** nmf refugee.

refus [r(ə)fy] nm refusal; **ce n'est pas de r.** Fam I won't say no. ◆**refuser** vt to refuse (**qch à qn** s.o. sth, **de faire** to do); (offre, invitation) to turn down, refuse; (client) to turn away, refuse; (candidat) to fail; – **se r.** vpr (plaisir etc) to deny oneself; **se r. à** (évidence etc) to refuse to accept, reject; **se r. à croire**/etc to refuse to believe/etc.

réfuter [refyte] vt to refute.

regagner [r(ə)gaɲe] vt (récupérer) to regain; (revenir à) to get back to. ◆**regain** nm **r. de** (retour) renewal of.

régal, pl **-als** [regal] nm treat. ◆**régaler** vt to treat to a delicious meal; **r. de** to treat to; – **se r.** vpr to have a delicious meal.

regard nm **1** (coup d'œil, expression) look; (fixe) stare, gaze; **chercher du r.** to look (a)round for; **attirer les regards** to attract attention; **jeter un r. sur** to glance at. **2** **au r. de** in regard to; **en r. de** compared with. ◆**regard/er** vt to look at; (fixement) to stare at, gaze at; (observer) to watch; (considérer) to consider, regard (**comme** as); **r. qn faire** to watch s.o. do; – vi to look; to stare, gaze; to watch; **r. à** (dépense, qualité etc) to pay attention to; **r. vers** (maison etc) to face; – **se r.** vpr (personnes) to look at each other. **2** vt (concerner) to concern. ◆**–ant** a (économe) careful (with money).

régates [regat] nfpl regatta.

régence [reʒɑ̃s] nf regency.

régénérer [reʒenere] vt to regenerate.

régenter [reʒɑ̃te] vt to rule over.

régie [reʒi] nf (entreprise) state-owned company; Th stage management; Cin TV production department.

regimber [r(ə)ʒɛ̃be] vi to balk (**contre** at).

régime [reʒim] nm 1 system; Pol régime. 2 Méd diet; **se mettre au r.** to go on a diet; **suivre un r.** to be on a diet. 3 (de moteur) speed; **à ce r.** Fig at this rate. 4 (de bananes, dattes) bunch.

régiment [reʒimɑ̃] nm Mil regiment; **un r. de** (quantité) Fig a host of.

région [reʒjɔ̃] nf region, area. ◆**régional, -aux** a regional.

régir [reʒir] vt (déterminer) to govern.

régisseur [reʒisœr] nm (de propriété) steward; Th stage manager; Cin assistant director.

registre [reʒistr] nm register.

règle [rɛgl] 1 nf (principe) rule; **en r.** (papiers d'identité etc) in order; **être/se mettre en r. avec qn** to be/put oneself right with s.o.; **en r. générale** a (as a general) rule. 2 nf (instrument) ruler; **r. à calcul** slide rule. 3 nfpl (menstruation) period.

règlement [rɛgləmɑ̃] nm 1 (arrêté) regulation; (règles) regulations. 2 (de conflit, problème etc) settling; (paiement) payment; **r. de comptes** Fig (violent) settling of scores. ◆**réglementaire** a in accordance with the regulations; (tenue) Mil regulation-. ◆**réglementation** nf 1 (action) regulation. 2 (règles) regulations. ◆**réglementer** vt to regulate.

régler [regle] 1 vt (conflit, problème etc) to settle; (mécanisme) to regulate, adjust; (moteur) to tune; (papier) to rule; **se r. sur qn** to model oneself on. 2 vti (payer) to pay; **r. qn** to settle up with s.o.; **r. son compte à** Fig to settle old scores with. ◆**réglé** a (vie) ordered; (papier) ruled. ◆**réglable** a (siège etc) adjustable. ◆**réglage** nm adjustment; (de moteur) tuning.

réglisse [reglis] nf liquorice, Am licorice.

règne [rɛɲ] nm reign; (animal, minéral, végétal) kingdom. ◆**régner** vi to reign; (prédominer) to prevail; **faire r. l'ordre** to maintain (law and) order.

regorger [r(ə)gɔrʒe] vi **r. de** to be overflowing with.

régresser [regrese] vi to regress. ◆**régression** nf regression; **en r.** on the decline.

regret [r(ə)grɛ] nm regret; **à r.** with regret; **avoir le r. ou être au r. de faire** to be sorry to do. ◆**regretter** vt to regret; **r. qn** to miss s.o.; **je regrette** I'm sorry; **r. que** (+ sub) to

be sorry that, regret that. ◆**—able** a regrettable.

regrouper [r(ə)grupe] vt, **— se r.** vpr to gather together.

régulariser [regylarize] vt (situation) to regularize.

régulation [regylasjɔ̃] nf (action) regulation.

régulier, -ière [regylje, -jɛr] a regular; (progrès, vie, vitesse) steady; (légal) legal; (honnête) honest. ◆**régularité** nf regularity; steadiness; legality. ◆**régulièrement** adv regularly; (normalement) normally.

réhabiliter [reabilite] vt (dans l'estime public-que) to rehabilitate.

réhabituer (se) [səreabitɥe] vpr **se r. à qch/à faire qch** to get used to sth/to doing sth again.

rehausser [rəose] vt to raise; (faire valoir) to enhance.

réimpression [reɛ̃presjɔ̃] nf (livre) reprint.

rein [rɛ̃] nm kidney; **pl** (dos) (small of the) back; **r. artificiel** Méd kidney machine.

reine [rɛn] nf queen.

reine-claude [rɛnklod] nf greengage.

réintégrer [reɛ̃tegre] vt 1 (fonctionnaire etc) to reinstate. 2 (lieu) to return to. ◆**réintégration** nf reinstatement.

réitérer [reitere] vt to repeat.

rejaillir [r(ə)ʒajir] vi to spurt (up ou out); **r. sur** Fig to rebound on.

rejet [r(ə)ʒɛ] nm 1 (refus) & Méd rejection. 2 Bot shoot. ◆**rejeter** vt to throw back; (épave) to cast up; (vomir) to bring up; (refuser) & Méd to reject; **r. une erreur/etc sur qn** to put the blame for a mistake/etc on s.o.

rejeton [rəʒtɔ̃] nm (enfant) Fam kid.

rejoindre [r(ə)ʒwɛ̃dr] vt (famille, régiment) to rejoin, get ou go back to; (lieu) to get back to; (route, rue) to join; **r. qn** to join ou meet s.o.; (rattraper) to catch up with s.o.; **— se r.** vpr (personnes) to meet; (routes, rues) to join, meet.

réjou/ir [reʒwir] vt to delight; **— se r.** vpr to be delighted (**de** at, about; **de faire** to do). ◆**—i** a (air) joyful. ◆**—issant** a cheering. ◆**réjouissance** nf rejoicing; **pl** festivities, rejoicings.

relâche [r(ə)laʃ] nf Th Cin (temporary) closure; **faire r.** (théâtre, cinéma) to close; (bateau) to put in (**dans un port** at a port); **sans r.** without a break.

relâch/er [r(ə)laʃe] 1 vt to slacken; (discipline, étreinte) to relax; **r. qn** to release s.o.; **— se r.** vpr to slacken; (discipline) to get lax. 2 vi (bateau) to put in. ◆**—é** a lax.

◆—ement *nm* (*de corde etc*) slackness; (*de discipline*) slackening.

relais [r(ə)lε] *nm* El Rad TV relay; (*course de*) r. Sp relay (race); **r. routier** transport café, *Am* truck stop (*café*); **prendre le r.** to take over (**de** from).

relance [r(ə)lɑ̃s] *nf* (*reprise*) revival. ◆**relancer** *vt* to throw back; (*moteur*) to restart; (*industrie etc*) to put back on its feet; **r. qn** (*solliciter*) to pester s.o.

relater [r(ə)late] *vt* to relate (**que** that).

relatif, -ive [r(ə)latif, -iv] *a* relative (**à** to). ◆**relativement** *adv* relatively; **r. à** compared to, relative to.

relation [r(ə)lɑsjɔ̃] *nf* (*rapport*) relation(ship); (*ami*) acquaintance; **avoir des relations** (*amis influents*) to have connections; **entrer/être en relations avec** to come into/be in contact with; **relations internationales/***etc* international/*etc* relations.

relax(e) [rəlaks] *a Fam* relaxed, informal.

relaxer (se) [sər(ə)lakse] *vpr* to relax. ◆**relaxation** *nf* relaxation.

relayer [r(ə)leje] *vt* to relieve, take over from; (*émission*) to relay; **— se r.** *vpr* to take (it in) turns (**pour faire** to do); Sp to take over from one another.

reléguer [r(ə)lege] *vt* to relegate (**à** to).

relent [rɑlɑ̃] *nm* stench, smell.

relève [r(ə)lεv] *nf* (*remplacement*) relief; **prendre la r.** to take over (**de** from).

relev/er [ralve] *vt* to raise; (*ramasser*) to pick up; (*chaise etc*) to put up straight; (*personne tombée*) to help up; (*col*) to turn up; (*manches*) to roll up; (*copier*) to note down; (*traces*) to find; (*relayer*) to relieve; (*rehausser*) to enhance; (*sauce*) to season; (*faute*) to pick up ou point out; (*compteur*) to read; (*défi*) to accept; (*économie, pays*) to put back on its feet; (*mur*) to rebuild; **r. qn de** (*fonctions*) to relieve s.o. of; **— vi** **r. de** (*dépendre de*) to come under; (*maladie*) to get over; **— se r.** *vpr* (*personne*) to get up; **se r. de** (*malheur*) to recover from; (*ruines*) to rise from. ◆**—é** *nm* list; (*de dépenses*) statement; (*de compteur*) reading; **r. de compte** (*bank*) statement. ◆**relèvement** *nm* (*d'économie, de pays*) recovery.

relief [raljεf] **1** *nm* (*forme, ouvrage*) relief; **en r.** (*cinéma*) three-D; (*livre*) pop-up; **mettre en r.** *Fig* to highlight. **2** *nmpl* (*de repas*) remains.

relier [ralje] *vt* to link, connect (**à** to); (*ensemble*) to link (together); (*livre*) to bind.

religion [r(ə)liʒjɔ̃] *nf* religion; (*foi*) faith. ◆**religieux, -euse** **1** *a* religious; **mariage**

r. church wedding; **–** *nm* monk; **–** *nf* nun. **2** *nf* Culin cream bun.

reliquat [r(ə)lika] *nm* (*de dette etc*) remainder.

relique [r(ə)lik] *nf* relic.

relire* [r(ə)lir] *vt* to reread.

reliure [raljyr] *nf* (*couverture de livre*) binding; (*art*) bookbinding.

reluire [r(ə)lɥir] *vi* to shine, gleam; **faire r.** (*polir*) to shine (up). ◆**reluisant** *a* shiny; **peu r.** *Fig* far from brilliant.

reluquer [r(ə)lyke] *vt Fig* to eye (up).

remâcher [r(ə)mɑʃe] *vt Fig* to brood over.

remanier [r(ə)manje] *vt* (*texte*) to revise; (*ministère*) to reshuffle. ◆**remaniement** *nm* revision; reshuffle.

remarier (se) [sər(ə)marje] *vpr* to remarry.

remarque [r(ə)mark] *nf* (*mot*) remark, (*annotation*) note; **je lui en ai fait la r.** I remarked on it to him *ou* her. ◆**remarquable** *a* remarkable (**par** for). ◆**remarquablement** *adv* remarkably. ◆**remarquer** *vt* **1** (*apercevoir*) to notice (**que** that); **faire r.** to point out (**à** to, **que** that); **se faire r.** to attract attention; **remarque!** mind (you)! **2** (*dire*) to remark (**que** that).

rembarrer [rɑ̃bare] *vt* to rebuff, snub.

remblai [rɑ̃blε] *nm* (*terres*) embankment. ◆**remblayer** *vt* (*route*) to bank up; (*trou*) to fill in.

rembourr/er [rɑ̃bure] *vt* (*matelas etc*) to stuff, pad; (*vêtement*) to pad. ◆—**age** *nm* (*action, matière*) stuffing; padding.

rembourser [rɑ̃burse] *vt* to pay back, repay; (*billet*) to refund. ◆**remboursement** *nm* repayment; refund; **envoi contre r.** cash on delivery.

remède [r(ə)mεd] *nm* remedy, cure; (*médicament*) medicine. ◆**remédier** *vt* **r. à** to remedy.

remémorer (se) [sər(ə)memore] *vpr* (*histoire etc*) to recollect, recall.

remercier [r(ə)mεrsje] *vt* **1** to thank (**de qch, pour qch,** for sth); **je vous remercie d'être venu** thank you for coming; **je vous remercie** (*non merci*) no thank you. **2** (*congédier*) to dismiss. ◆**remerciements** *nmpl* thanks.

remettre* [r(ə)mεtr] *vt* to put back, replace; (*vêtement*) to put back on; (*donner*) to hand over (**à** to); (*restituer*) to give back (**à** to); (*démission, devoir*) to hand in; (*différer*) to postpone (**à** until); (*ajouter*) to add more ou another; (*peine*) *Jur* to remit; (*guérir*) to restore to health; **se remettre** to recover, remember; **r. en cause** *ou* **question** to call into question; **r. en état** to repair; **r. ça** *Fam* start again; **se r. à** (*activité*) to go back to; **se r. à faire** to start to do again; **se r. de** (*chagrin, maladie*) to recover from, get over; **s'en r. à** to rely on. ◆**remise** *nf* (*de lettre etc*) delivery; (*de peine*) *Jur* remission; (*ajournement*) postponement; **r. en cause** *ou* **question** calling into question; **r. en état** recovering; **2** (*rabais*) discount. **3** (*local*) shed; *Aut* garage. ◆**remiser** *vt* to put away.

réminiscences [reminisɑ̃s] *nfpl* (vague) recollections, reminiscences.

rémission [remisjɔ̃] *nf Jur Rel Méd* remission; **sans r.** (*travailler etc*) relentlessly.

remmener [rɑ̃mne] *vt* to take back.

remonte-pente [r(ə)mɔ̃tpɑ̃t] *nm* ski lift.

remont/er [r(ə)mɔ̃te] *vi* (*aux être*) to come *ou* go back up; (*niveau, prix*) to rise again, go back up; (*dans le temps*) to go back (à to); **r. dans** (*voiture*) to go *ou* get back in(to); (*bus, train*) to go *ou* get back on(to); **r. sur** (*cheval, vélo*) to remount; ─ *vt* (*aux avoir*) (*escalier, pente*) to come *ou* go back up; (*porter*) to bring *ou* take back up; (*montre*) to wind up; (*relever*) to raise; (*col*) to turn up; (*objet démonté*) to reassemble; (*garde-robe etc*) to restock; **r. qn** (*ragaillardir*) to buck s.o. up; **r. le moral à qn** to cheer s.o. up. ◆**─ant** (*boisson*) fortifying; ─ *nm Méd* tonic. ◆**─ée** *nf* **1** (*de pente etc*) ascent; (*d'eau, de prix*) rise. **2 r. mécanique** ski lift. ◆**remontoir** *nm* (*de mécanisme, montre*) winder.

remontrance [r(ə)mɔ̃trɑ̃s] *nf* reprimand; **faire des remontrances à** to reprimand, remonstrate with.

remontrer [r(ə)mɔ̃tre] *vi* **en r. à qn** to prove one's superiority over s.o.

remords [r(ə)mɔr] *nm & nmpl* remorse; **avoir des r.** to feel remorse.

remorque [r(ə)mɔrk] *nf Aut* trailer; (**câble de**) **r.** towrope; **prendre en r.** to tow; **en r.** on tow. ◆**remorquer** *vt* (*voiture, bateau*) to tow. ◆**remorqueur** *nm* tug(boat).

remous [r(ə)mu] *nm* eddy; (*de foule*) bustle; (*agitation*) *Fig* turmoil.

rempart [rɑ̃par] *nm* rampart.

remplacer [rɑ̃plase] *vt* to replace (**par** with, by); (*succéder à*) to take over from; (*temporairement*) to stand in for. ◆**remplaçant, -ante** *nmf* (*personne*) replacement; (*enseignant*) supply teacher; *Sp* reserve. ◆**remplacement** *nm* (*action*) replacement; **assurer le r. de qn** to stand in for s.o.; **en r. de** in place of.

rempl/ir [rɑ̃plir] *vt* to fill (up) (**de** with); (*fiche etc*) to fill in *ou* out; (*condition, de-*

voir, tâche) to fulfil; (*fonctions*) to perform; ─ **se r.** *vpr* to fill (up). ◆**─i** *a* full (**de** of). ◆**remplissage** *nm* filling; (*verbiage*) *Péj* padding.

remporter [rɑ̃pɔrte] *vt* **1** (*objet*) to take back. **2** (*prix, victoire*) to win; (*succès*) to achieve.

remu/er [r(ə)mɥe] *vt* (*déplacer, émouvoir*) to move; (*café etc*) to stir; (*terre*) to turn over; (*salade*) to toss; ─ *vi* to move; (*gigoter*) to fidget; (*se rebeller*) to stir; ─ **se r.** *vpr* to move; (*se démener*) to exert oneself. ◆**─ant** *a* (*enfant*) restless, fidgety. ◆**remue-ménage** *nm inv* commotion.

rémunérer [remynere] *vt* (*personne*) to pay; (*travail*) to pay for. ◆**rémunérateur, -trice** *a* remunerative. ◆**rémunération** *nf* payment (**de** for).

renâcler [r(ə)nakle] *vi* **1** (*cheval*) to snort. **2 r. à** to jib at, balk at.

renaître* [r(ə)nɛtr] *vi* (*fleur*) to grow again; (*espoir, industrie*) to revive. ◆**renaissance** *nf* rebirth, renaissance.

renard [r(ə)nar] *nm* fox.

renchérir [rɑ̃ʃerir] *vi* **r. sur** *qn ou* **sur ce que qn dit/etc** to go further than s.o. in what one says/*etc.*

rencontre [rɑ̃kɔ̃tr] *nf* meeting; (*inattendue*) & *Mil* encounter; *Sp* match, *Am* game; (*de routes*) junction; **aller à la r. de** to go to meet. ◆**rencontrer** *vt* to meet; (*difficultés*) to come up against, encounter; (*trouver*) to come across, find; (*heurter*) to hit; (*équipe*) *Sp* to play; ─ **se r.** *vpr* to meet.

rendez-vous [rɑ̃devu] *nm inv* appointment; (*d'amoureux*) date; (*lieu*) meeting place; **donner r.-vous à qn, prendre r.-vous avec qn** to make an appointment with s.o.

rendormir* (**se**) [sɑ̃rdɔrmir] *vpr* to go back to sleep.

rend/re [rɑ̃dr] *vt* (*restituer*) to give back, return; (*hommage*) to pay; (*invitation*) to return; (*santé*) to restore; (*monnaie, son*) to give; (*justice*) to dispense; (*jugement*) to pronounce, give; (*armes*) to surrender; (*exprimer, traduire*) to render; (*vomir*) to bring up; **r. célèbre/plus grand/possible/***etc* to make famous/bigger/possible/*etc*; ─ *vi* (*arbre, terre*) to yield; (*vomir*) to be sick; ─ **se r.** *vpr* (*capituler*) to surrender (à to); (*aller*) to go (à to); **se r. à** (*évidence, ordres*) to submit to; **se r. malade/utile/***etc* to make oneself ill/useful/*etc.* ◆**─u** *a* (*fatigué*) exhausted; **être r.** (*arrivé*) to have arrived. ◆**rendement** *nm Agr Fin* yield; (*de personne, machine*) output.

renégat, -ate [renega, -at] *nmf* renegade.

rênes [rɛn] *nfpl* reins.

renferm/er [rɑ̃fɛrme] *vt* to contain; **— se r.** *vpr* **se r. (en soi-même)** to withdraw into oneself. ◆**—é** *a* (*personne*) withdrawn. **2** *nm* **sentir le r.** (*chambre etc*) to smell stuffy.

renflé [rɑ̃fle] *a* bulging. ◆**renflement** *nm* bulge.

renflouer [rɑ̃flue] *vt* (*navire*) & *Com* to refloat.

renfoncement [rɑ̃fɔ̃smɑ̃] *nm* recess; **dans le r. d'une porte** in a doorway.

renforcer [rɑ̃fɔrse] *vt* to reinforce, strengthen. ◆**renforcement** *nm* reinforcement, strengthening. ◆**renfort** *nm* **des renforts** *Mil* reinforcements; **de r.** (*armée, personnel*) back-up; **à grand r. de** *Fig* with a great deal of.

renfrogn/er (se) [sərɑ̃frɔɲe] *vpr* to scowl. ◆**—é** *a* scowling, sullen.

rengaine [rɑ̃gɛn] *nf* **la même r.** *Fig Péj* the same old song *ou* story.

rengorger (se) [sərɑ̃gɔrʒe] *vpr* to give oneself airs.

renier [rənje] *vt* (*ami, pays etc*) to disown; (*foi, opinion*) to renounce. ◆**reniement** *nm* disowning; renunciation.

renifler [r(ə)nifle] *vti* to sniff. ◆**reniflement** *nm* sniff.

renne [rɛn] *nm* reindeer.

renom [rənɔ̃] *nm* renown; (*réputation*) reputation (**de** for). ◆**renommé** *a* famous, renowned (**pour** for). ◆**renommée** *nf* fame, renown; (*réputation*) reputation.

renoncer [r(ə)nɔ̃se] *vi* **r. à** to give up, abandon; **r. à faire** to give up (the idea of) doing. ◆**renoncement** *nm*, ◆**renonciation** *nf* renunciation (**à** of).

renouer [rənwe] **1** *vt* (*lacet etc*) to retie. **2** *vt* (*reprendre*) to renew; **—** *vi* **r. avec qch** (*mode, tradition etc*) to revive sth; **r. avec qn** to take up with s.o. again.

renouveau, -x [r(ə)nuvo] *nm* revival.

renouveler [r(ə)nuvle] *vt* to renew; (*action, erreur, question*) to repeat; **— se r.** *vpr* (*incident*) to recur, happen again; (*cellules, sang*) to be renewed. ◆**renouvelable** *a* renewable. ◆**renouvellement** *nm* renewal.

rénover [renɔve] *vt* (*institution, méthode*) to reform; (*édifice, meuble etc*) to renovate. ◆**rénovation** *nf* reform; renovation.

renseign/er [rɑ̃sɛɲe] *vt* to inform, give information to (**sur** about); **— se r.** *vpr* to inquire, make inquiries, find out (**sur** about). ◆**—ement** *nm* (*piece of*) information; *pl* information; *Tél* directory inquiries, *Am* information; *Mil* intelligence; **prendre** *ou* **demander des reseignements** to make inquiries.

rentable [rɑ̃tabl] *a* profitable. ◆**rentabilité** *nf* profitability.

rente [rɑ̃t] *nf* (*private*) income; (*pension*) pension; **avoir des rentes** to have private means. ◆**rentier, -ière** *nmf* person of private means.

rentr/er [rɑ̃tre] *vi* (*aux* **être**) to go *ou* come back, return; (*chez soi*) to go *ou* come (back) home; (*entrer*) to go *ou* come in; (*entrer de nouveau*) to go *ou* come back in; (*école*) to start again; (*argent*) to come in; **r. dans** (*entrer dans*) to go *ou* come into; (*entrer de nouveau dans*) to go *ou* come back into; (*famille, pays*) to return to; (*ses frais*) to get back; (*catégorie*) to come under; (*heurter*) to crash into; (*s'emboîter dans*) to fit into; **r. (en classe)** to start (school) again; **je lui suis rentré dedans** (*frapper*) *Fam* I laid into him *ou* her; **—** *vt* (*aux* **avoir**) to bring *ou* take in; (*voiture*) to put away; (*chemise*) to tuck in; (*griffes*) to draw in. ◆**—é** *a* (*colère*) suppressed; (*yeux*) sunken. ◆**—ée** *nf* **1** (*retour*) return; (*de parlement*) reassembly; (*d'acteur*) comeback; **r.** (**des classes**) beginning of term *ou* of the school year. **2** (*des foins etc*) bringing in; (*d'impôt*) collection; *pl* (*argent*) receipts.

renverse (à la) [alɑ̃rvɛrs] *adv* (*tomber*) backwards, on one's back.

renvers/er [rɑ̃vɛrse] *vt* (*mettre à l'envers*) to turn upside down; (*faire tomber*) to knock over *ou* down; (*piéton*) to knock down, run over; (*liquide*) to spill, knock over; (*courant, ordre*) to reverse; (*gouvernement*) to overturn, overthrow; (*projet*) to upset; (*tête*) to tip back; **— se r.** *vpr* (*en arrière*) to lean back; (*bouteille, vase etc*) to fall over. ◆**—ant** *a* (*nouvelle etc*) astounding. ◆**—ement** *nm* (*d'ordre, de situation*) reversal; (*de gouvernement*) overthrow.

renvoi [rɑ̃vwa] *nm* **1** return; dismissal; expulsion; postponement; (*dans un livre*) reference. **2** (*rot*) belch, burp. ◆**renvoyer***° *vt* to send back, return; (*importun*) to send away; (*employé*) to dismiss; (*élève*) to expel; (*balle etc*) to throw back; (*ajourner*) to postpone (**à** until); (*lumière, image etc*) to reflect; **r. qn à** (*adresser à*) to refer s.o. to.

réorganiser [reɔrganize] *vt* to reorganize.

réouverture [reuvertyr] *nf* reopening.

repaire [r(ə)pɛr] *nm* den.

repaître (se) [sərəpɛtr] *vpr* **se r. de** (*sang*) *Fig* to wallow in.

répand/re [repɑ̃dr] *vt* (*liquide*) to spill;

(*idées, joie, nouvelle*) to spread; (*fumée, odeur*) to give off; (*chargement, lumière, larmes, sang*) to shed; (*gravillons etc*) to scatter; (*dons*) to lavish; **— se r.** *vpr* (*nouvelle, peur etc*) to spread; (*liquide*) to spill; se r. **dans** (*fumée, odeur*) to spread through; se r. **en louanges**/*etc* to pour forth praise/*etc.* **—u** *a* (*opinion, usage*) widespread; (*épars*) scattered.

reparaître [r(ə)parɛtr] *vi* to reappear.

réparer [repare] *vt* to repair, mend; (*forces, santé*) to restore; (*faute*) to make amends for; (*perte*) to make good; (*oubli*) to put right. **◆réparable** *a* (*montre etc*) repairable. **◆réparateur, -trice** *nmf* repairer; — *a* (*sommeil*) refreshing. **◆réparation** *nf* repairing; (*compensation*) amends, compensation (**de** for); *pl Mil Hist* reparations; **en r.** under repair.

reparler [r(ə)parle] *vi* **r. de** to talk about again.

repartie [reparti] *nf* (*réponse vive*) repartee.

repartir* [r(ə)partir] *vi* (*aux être*) to set off again; (*s'en retourner*) to go back; (*reprendre*) to start again; **r. à** *ou* **de zéro** to go back to square one.

répartir [repartir] *vt* to distribute; (*partager*) to share (out); (*classer*) to divide (up); (*étaler dans le temps*) to spread (out) (**sur** over). **◆répartition** *nf* distribution; sharing; division.

repas [r(ə)pɑ] *nm* meal; **prendre un r.** to have *ou* eat a meal.

repass/er [r(ə)pase] **1** *vi* to come *ou* go back; — *vt* (*traverser*) to go back over; (*examen*) to resit; (*leçon, rôle*) to go over; (*film*) to show again; (*maladie, travail*) to pass on (**à** to). **2** *vt* (*linge*) to iron. **3** *vt* (*couteau*) to sharpen. **◆—age** *nm* ironing.

repêcher [r(ə)pɛʃe] *vt* to fish out; (*candidat*) *Fam* to allow to pass.

repenser [r(ə)pɑ̃se] *vt* to rethink.

repentir [r(ə)pɑ̃tir] *nm* repentance. **◆se repentir*** *vpr Rel* to repent (**de** of); se r. **de** (*regretter*) to regret, be sorry for. **◆repentant** *a*, **◆repenti** *a* repentant.

répercuter [reperkyte] *vt* (*son*) to echo; — se r. *vpr* to echo, reverberate; se r. **sur** *Fig* to have repercussions on. **◆répercussion** *nf* repercussion.

repère [r(ə)pɛr] *nm* (*guide*) mark; (*jalon*) marker; **point de r.** (*espace, temps*) landmark, point of reference. **◆repérer** *vt* to locate; (*personnne*) *Fam* to spot; **— se r.** *vpr* to get one's bearings.

répertoire [repɛrtwar] *nm* **1** index; (*carnet*) indexed notebook; **r. d'adresses** address

book. **2** *Th* repertoire. **◆répertorier** *vt* to index.

répéter [repete] *vti* to repeat; *Th* to rehearse; **— se r.** *vpr* (*radoter*) to repeat oneself; (*se reproduire*) to repeat itself. **◆répétitif, -ive** *a* repetitive. **◆répétition** *nf* repetition; *Th* rehearsal. **r. générale** *Th* (final) dress rehearsal.

repiquer [r(ə)pike] *vt* **1** (*plante*) to plant out. **2** (*disque*) to tape, record (on tape).

répit [repi] *nm* rest, respite; **sans r.** ceaselessly.

replacer [r(ə)plase] *vt* to replace, put back.

repli [r(ə)pli] *nm* fold; withdrawal; *pl* (**de** *l'âme*) recesses. **◆replier 1** *vt* to fold (up); (*siège*) to fold up; (*couteau, couverture*) to fold back; (*ailes, jambes*) to tuck in; **— se r.** *vpr* (*siège*) to fold up; (*couteau, couverture*) to fold back. **2** *vt*, **— se r.** *vpr Mil* to withdraw; **se r. sur soi-même** to withdraw into oneself.

réplique [replik] *nf* **1** (*réponse*) reply; (*riposte*) retort; *Th* lines; **pas de r.!** no answering back! **sans r.** (*argument*) irrefutable. **2** (*copie*) replica. **◆répliquer** *vt* to reply (**que** that); (*riposter*) to retort (**que** that); — *vi* (*être impertinent*) to answer back.

répond/re [repɔ̃dr] *vi* to answer, reply; (*être impertinent*) to answer back; (*réagir*) to respond (**à** to); **r. à qn** to answer s.o., reply to s.o.; (*avec impertinence*) to answer s.o. back; **r. à** (*lettre, objection, question*) to answer, reply to; (*salut*) to return; (*besoin*) to meet, answer; (*correspondre à*) to correspond to; **r. de** (*garantir*) to answer for (*s.o., sth*); — *vt* (*remarque etc*) to answer *ou* reply with; **r. que** to answer *ou* reply that. **◆—ant, -ante 1** *nmf* guarantor. **2** *nm* **avoir du r.** to have money behind one. **◆—eur** *nm Tél* answering machine. **◆réponse** *nf* answer, reply; (*réaction*) response (**à** to); **en r. à** in answer *ou* reply *ou* response to.

reporter¹ [r(ə)pɔrte] *vt* to take back; (*différer*) to postpone, put off (**à** until); (*transcrire, transférer*) to transfer (**sur** to); (*somme*) *Com* to carry forward (**sur** to); se r. à (*texte etc*) to refer to; (*en esprit*) to go think back to. **◆report** *nm* postponement; transfer; *Com* carrying forward. **◆reportage** *nm* (*news*) report, article; (*en direct*) commentary; (*métier*) reporting.

reporter² [r(ə)pɔrtɛr] *nm* reporter.

repos [r(ə)po] *nm* rest; (*tranquillité*) peace (and quiet); (*de l'esprit*) peace of mind; **r.!** *Mil* at ease! **jour de r.** day off; **de tout r.** (*situation etc*) safe. **◆repos/er 1** *vt* (*objet*) to put back down; (*problème, question*) to raise again. **2** *vt* (*délasser*) to rest, relax; **r. sa tête sur** (*appuyer*) to rest one's head on; – *vi* (*être enterré ou étendu*) to rest, lie; **r. sur** (*bâtiment*) to be built on; (*théorie etc*) to be based on, rest on; **laisser r.** (*vin*) to allow to settle; – **se r.** *vpr* to rest; **se r. sur qn** to rely on s.o. ◆**-ant** a relaxing, restful. ◆**-é** a rested, fresh.

repouss/er [r(ə)puse] **1** *vt* to push back; (*écarter*) to push away; (*attaque, ennemi*) to repulse; (*importun etc*) to turn away, repulse; (*dégoûter*) to repel; (*décliner*) to reject; (*différer*) to put off, postpone. **2** *vi* (*cheveux, feuilles*) to grow again. ◆**-ant** a repulsive, repellent.

répréhensible [repreãsibl] a reprehensible, blameworthy.

reprendre* [r(ə)prãdr] *vt* (*objet*) to take back; (*évadé, ville*) to recapture; (*passer prendre*) to pick up again; (*souffle*) to get back; (*activité*) to resume, take up again; (*texte*) to go back over; (*vêtement*) to alter; (*histoire, refrain*) to take up; (*pièce*) Th to put on again; (*blâmer*) to admonish; (*corriger*) to correct; **r. de la viande/un œuf/***etc* to take (some) more meat/another egg/*etc*; **r. ses esprits** to come round; **r. des forces** to recover one's strength; – *vi* (*plante*) to take again; (*recommencer*) to resume, start (up) again; (*affaires*) to pick up; (*dire*) to go on, continue; – **se r.** *vpr* (*se ressaisir*) to take a hold on oneself; (*se corriger*) to correct oneself; **s'y r. à deux/plusieurs fois** to have another go/several goes (at it).

représailles [r(ə)prezaj] *nfpl* reprisals, retaliation.

représent/er [r(ə)prezãte] *vt* to represent; (*jouer*) Th to perform; – **se r.** *vpr* (*s'imaginer*) to imagine. ◆**-ant, -ante** *nmf* representative; **r. de commerce** (travelling) salesman *ou* saleswoman, sales representative. ◆**représentatif, -ive** a representative (**de** of). ◆**représentation** *nf* representation; Th performance.

répression [represjã] *nf* suppression, repression; (*mesures de contrôle*) Pol repression. ◆**répressif, -ive** a repressive. ◆**réprimer** *vt* (*sentiment, révolte etc*) to suppress, repress.

réprimande [reprimãd] *nf* reprimand. ◆**réprimander** *vt* to reprimand.

repris [r(ə)pri] *nm* **r. de justice** hardened criminal.

reprise [r(ə)priz] *nf* (*de ville*) Mil recapture; (*recommencement*) resumption; (*de pièce de théâtre, de coutume*) revival; Rad TV repeat; (*de tissu*) mend, repair; Boxe round;

(*essor*) Com recovery, revival; (*d'un locataire*) money for fittings; (*de marchandise*) taking back; (*pour nouvel achat*) part exchange, trade-in; *pl* Aut acceleration; **à plusieurs reprises** on several occasions. ◆**repriser** *vt* (*chaussette etc*) to mend, darn.

réprobation [reprɔbasjã] *nf* disapproval. ◆**réprobateur, -trice** a disapproving.

reproche [r(ə)prɔʃ] *nm* reproach; **faire des reproches à qn** to reproach s.o.; **sans r.** beyond reproach. ◆**reprocher** *vt* **r. qch à qn** to reproach *ou* blame s.o. for sth; **r. qch à qch** to have sth against sth; **n'avoir rien à se r.** to have nothing to reproach *ou* blame oneself for.

reproduire* [r(ə)prɔdɥir] **1** *vt* (*son, modèle etc*) to reproduce; – **se r.** *vpr* Biol Bot to reproduce. **2 se r.** *vpr* (*incident etc*) to happen again, recur. ◆**reproducteur, -trice** a reproductive. ◆**reproduction** *nf* (*de son etc*) & Biol Bot reproduction.

réprouver [repruve] *vt* to disapprove of, condemn.

reptile [reptil] *nm* reptile.

repu [rəpy] a (*rassasié*) satiated.

république [repyblik] *nf* republic. ◆**républicain, -aine** a & *nmf* republican.

répudier [repydje] *vt* to repudiate.

répugnant [repynã] a repugnant, loathsome. ◆**répugnance** *nf* repugnance, loathing (**pour** for); (*manque d'enthousiasme*) reluctance. ◆**répugner** *vi* **r. à qn** to be repugnant to s.o.; **r. à faire** to be loath to do.

répulsion [repylsjã] *nf* repulsion.

réputation [repytasjã] *nf* reputation; **avoir la r. d'être franc** to have a reputation for frankness *ou* for being frank. ◆**réputé** a (*célèbre*) renowned (**pour** for); **r. pour être** (*considéré comme*) reputed to be.

requérir [rakerir] *vt* (*nécessiter*) to demand, require; (*peine*) Jur to call for. ◆**requête** *nf* request; Jur petition. ◆**requis** a required, requisite.

requiem [rekɥijem] *nm inv* requiem.

requin [r(ə)kɛ̃] *nm* (*poisson*) & Fig shark.

réquisition [rekizisjã] *nf* requisition. ◆**réquisitionner** *vt* to requisition, commandeer.

réquisitoire [rekizitwar] *nm* (*critique*) indictment (**contre** of).

rescapé, -ée [reskape] a surviving; – *nmf* survivor.

rescousse (à la) [alareskus] *adv* to the rescue.

réseau, -x [rezo] *nm* network; r. d'espionnage spy ring *ou* network.

réserve [rezεrv] *nf* **1** (*restriction, doute*) reservation; (*réticence*) reserve; **sans r.** (*admiration etc*) unqualified; **sous r. de** subject to; **sous toutes réserves** without guarantee. **2** (*provision*) reserve; (*entrepôt*) storeroom; (*de bibliothèque*) stacks; **la r.** *Mil* the reserve; **les réserves** (*soldats*) the reserves; **en r.** in reserve. **3** (*de chasse, pêche*) preserve; (*indienne*) reservation; **r. naturelle** nature reserve.

réserv/er [rezεrve] *vt* to reserve; (*garder*) to keep, save; (*marchandises*) to put aside (à for); (*place, table*) to book, reserve; (*sort, surprise etc*) to hold in store (à for); **se r. pour** to save oneself for; **se r. de faire** to reserve the right to do. ◆**—é** *a* (*personne, place*) reserved; (*prudent*) guarded. ◆**réservation** *nf* reservation, booking. ◆**réservoir** *nm* (*lac*) reservoir; (*citerne, cuve*) tank; **r. d'essence** *Aut* petrol *ou Am* gas tank.

résidence [rezidɑ̃s] *nf* residence; **r. secondaire** second home; **r. universitaire** hall of residence. ◆**résident, -ente** *nmf* (*foreign*) resident. ◆**résidentiel, -ielle** *a* (*quartier*) residential. ◆**résider** *vi* to reside, be resident (à, en, dans in); **r. dans** (*consister dans*) to lie in.

résidu [rezidy] *nm* residue.

résigner (se) [səreziɲe] *vpr* to resign oneself (à qch to sth, à faire to doing). ◆**résignation** *nf* resignation.

résilier [rezilje] *vt* (*contrat*) to terminate. ◆**résiliation** *nf* termination.

résille [rezij] *nf* (*pour cheveux*) hairnet.

résine [rezin] *nf* resin.

résistance [rezistɑ̃s] *nf* resistance (à to); (*conducteur*) *Él* (heating) element; **plat de r.** main dish. ◆**résist/er** *vi* **r. à** to resist; (*chaleur, fatigue, souffrance*) to withstand; (*examen*) to stand up to. ◆**—ant, -ante** *a* tough, strong; **r. à la chaleur** heat-resistant; **r. au choc** shockproof; – *nmf* *Mil Hist* Resistance fighter.

résolu [rezɔly] *voir* **résoudre**; – *a* resolute, determined; **r. à faire** resolved *ou* determined to do. ◆**—ment** *adv* resolutely. ◆**résolution** *nf* (*décision*) resolution; (*fermeté*) determination.

résonance [rezɔnɑ̃s] *nf* resonance.

résonner [rezɔne] *vi* to resound (de with); (*salle, voix*) to echo.

résorber [rezɔrbe] *vt* (*chômage*) to reduce; (*excédent*) to absorb; – **se r.** *vpr* to be re-

duced; to be absorbed. ◆**résorption** *nf* reduction; absorption.

résoudre* [rezudr] *vt* (*problème*) to solve; (*difficulté*) to resolve; **r. de faire** to decide *ou* resolve to do; **se r. à faire** to decide *ou* resolve to do; (*se résigner*) to bring oneself to do.

respect [rεspε] *nm* respect (**pour, de** for); **mes respects à** my regards *ou* respects to; **tenir qn en r.** to hold s.o. in check. ◆**respectabilité** *nf* respectability. ◆**respectable** *a* (*honorable, important*) respectable. ◆**respecter** *vt* to respect; **qui se respecte** self-respecting. ◆**respectueux, -euse** *a* respectful (**envers** to, of). ◆**respectif, -ive** [rεspεktif, -iv] *a* respective. ◆**respectivement** *adv* respectively.

respirer [rεspire] *vi* to breathe; (*reprendre haleine*) to get one's breath (back); (*être soulagé*) to breathe again; – *vt* to breathe (in); (*exprimer*) *Fig* to exude. ◆**respiration** *nf* breathing; (*haleine*) breath; **r. artificielle** *Méd* artificial respiration. ◆**respiratoire** *a* breathing-, respiratory.

resplend/ir [rεsplɑ̃dir] *vi* to shine; (*visage*) to glow (de with). ◆**—issant** *a* radiant.

responsable [rεspɔ̃sabl] *a* responsible (**de** qch for sth, **devant qn** to s.o.); – *nmf* (*chef*) person in charge; (*dans une organisation*) official; (*coupable*) person responsible (**de** for). ◆**responsabilité** *nf* responsibility; (*légale*) liability.

resquiller [rεskije] *vi* (*au cinéma, dans le métro etc*) to avoid paying; (*sans attendre*) to jump the queue, *Am* cut in (line).

ressaisir (se) [sər(ə)sezir] *vpr* to pull oneself together.

ressasser [r(ə)sase] *vt* (*ruminer*) to keep going over; (*répéter*) to keep trotting out.

ressemblance [r(ə)sɑ̃blɑ̃s] *nf* resemblance, likeness. ◆**ressembl/er** *vi* **r. à** to resemble, look *ou* be like; **cela ne lui ressemble pas** (*ce n'est pas son genre*) that's not like him *ou* her; – **se r.** *vpr* to look *ou* be alike. ◆**—ant** *a* **portrait r.** good likeness.

ressentiment [r(ə)sɑ̃timɑ̃] *nm* resentment.

ressentir* [r(ə)sɑ̃tir] *vt* to feel; **se r. de** to feel *ou* show the effects of.

resserre [r(ə)sεr] *nf* storeroom; (*remise*) shed.

resserrer [r(ə)sεre] *vt* (*nœud, boulon etc*) to tighten; (*contracter*) to close (up), contract; (*liens*) *Fig* to strengthen; – **se r.** *vpr* to tighten; (*amitié*) to become closer; (*se contracter*) to close (up), contract; (*route etc*) to narrow.

resservir [r(ə)sεrvir] **1** *vi* (*outil etc*) to come

in useful (again). **2 se r.** *vpr* **se r. de** (*plat etc*) to have another helping of.

ressort [r(ə)sɔr] *nm* **1** *Tech* spring. **2** (*énergie*) spirit. **3 du r. de** within the competence of; **en dernier r.** (*décider etc*) in the last resort, as a last resort.

ressortir¹* [r(ə)sɔrtir] *vi* (*aux être*) **1** to go *ou* come back out. **2** (*se voir*) to stand out; **faire r.** to bring out; **il ressort de** (*résulte*) it emerges from.

ressortir² [r(ə)sɔrtir] *vi* (*conjugated like finir*) **r. à** to fall within the scope of.

ressortissant, -ante [r(ə)sɔrtisɑ̃, -ɑ̃t] *nmf* (*citoyen*) national.

ressource [r(ə)surs] **1** *nfpl* (*moyens*) resources; (*argent*) means, resources. **2** *nf* (*recours*) recourse; (*possibilité*) possibility (**de faire** of doing); **dernière r.** last resort.

ressusciter [resysite] *vi* to rise from the dead; (*malade, pays*) to recover, revive; – *vt* (*mort*) to raise; (*malade, mode*) to revive.

restaurant [rɛstɔrɑ̃] *nm* restaurant.

restaurer [rɛstɔre] **1** *vt* (*réparer, rétablir*) to restore. **2 se r.** *vpr* to (have sth to) eat. ◆**restaurateur, -trice** *nmf* **1** (*de tableaux*) restorer. **2** (*hôtelier, hôtelière*) restaurant owner. ◆**restauration** *nf* **1** restoration. **2** (*hôtellerie*) catering.

reste [rɛst] *nm* rest, remainder (**de** *of*); *Math* remainder; *pl* remains (**de** *of*); (*de repas*) leftovers; **un r. de fromage**/*etc* some left-over cheese/*etc*; **au r., du r.** moreover, besides.

rester [rɛste] *vi* (*aux être*) to stay, remain; (*calme, jeune etc*) to keep, stay, remain; (*subsister*) to remain, be left; **il reste du pain**/*etc* there's some bread/*etc* left (over); **il me reste une minute**/*etc* I have one minute/*etc* left; **l'argent qui lui reste** the money he *ou* she has left; **reste à savoir** it remains to be seen; **il me reste deux choses à faire** I still have two things to do; **il me reste à vous remercier** it remains for me to thank you; **en r.** to stop at; **restons-en là** let's leave it at that. ◆**restant** *a* remaining; **poste restante** poste restante, *Am* general delivery; – *nm* **le r.** the rest, the remainder; **un r. de viande**/*etc* some left-over meat/*etc*.

restituer [rɛstitɥe] *vt* **1** (*rendre*) to return, restore (**à** *to*). **2** (*son*) to reproduce; (*énergie*) to release. ◆**restitution** *nf* return.

restreindre° [rɛstrɛ̃dr] *vt* to restrict, limit (**à** *to*); – **se r.** *vpr* to decrease; (*faire des économies*) to cut back *ou* down. ◆**restreint** *a* limited, restricted (**à** *to*). ◆**restrictif, -ive**

a restrictive. ◆**restriction** *nf* restriction; **sans r.** unreservedly.

résultat [rezylta] *nm* result; (*conséquence*) outcome, result; **avoir qch pour r.** to result in sth. ◆**résulter** *vi* **r. de** to result from.

résum/er [rezyme] *vt* to summarize; (*récapituler*) to sum up; – **se r.** *vpr* (*orateur etc*) to sum up; **se r. à** (*se réduire à*) to boil down to. ◆**-é** *nm* summary; **en r.** in short; (*en récapitulant*) to sum up.

resurrection [rezyrɛksjɔ̃] *nf* resurrection.

rétabl/ir [retablir] *vt* to restore; (*fait, vérité*) to re-establish; (*malade*) to restore to health; (*employé*) to reinstate; – **se r.** *vpr* to be restored; (*malade*) to recover. ◆**-issement** *nm* restoring; re-establishment; *Méd* recovery.

retaper [r(ə)tape] *vt* (*maison, voiture etc*) to do up; (*lit*) to straighten; (*malade*) *Fam* to buck up.

retard [r(ə)tar] *nm* lateness; (*sur un programme etc*) delay; (*infériorité*) backwardness; **en r.** late; (*retardé*) backward; **en r. dans qch** behind in sth; **en r. sur qn/qch** behind s.o./sth; **rattraper** *ou* **combler son r.** to catch up; **avoir du r.** to be late; (*sur un programme*) to be behind (schedule); (*montre*) to be slow; **avoir une heure de r.** to be an hour late; **prendre du r.** (*montre*) to lose (time); **sans r.** without delay. ◆**retardataire** *a* (*arrivant*) late; **enfant r.** *Méd* slow learner; – *nmf* latecomer. ◆**retardement** **à r.** delayed-action; **bombe à r.** time bomb.

retard/er [r(ə)tarde] *vt* to delay; (*départ, montre*) to put back; **r. qn** (*dans une activité*) to put s.o. behind; – *vi* (*montre*) to be slow; **r. de cinq minutes** to be five minutes slow; **r. (sur son temps)** (*personne*) to be behind the times. ◆**-é, -ée** *a* (*enfant*) backward; – *nmf* backward child.

retenir° [rətnir] *vt* (*empêcher d'agir, contenir*) to hold back; (*attention, souffle*) to hold; (*réserver*) to book; (*se souvenir de*) to remember; (*fixer*) to hold (in place), secure; (*déduire*) to take off; (*candidature, proposition*) to accept; (*chiffre*) *Math* to carry; (*chaleur, odeur*) to retain; (*invité, suspect etc*) to detain, keep; **r. qn prisonnier** to keep *ou* hold s.o. prisoner; **r. qn de faire** to stop s.o. (from) doing; – **se r.** *vpr* (*se contenir*) to restrain oneself; **se r. de faire** to stop oneself (from) doing; **se r. à** to cling to. ◆**retenue** *nf* **1** (*modération*) restraint. **2** (*de salaire*) deduction, stoppage; (*chiffre*) *Math* figure carried over. **3** *Scol* detention; **en r.** in detention.

retent/ir [r(ə)tɑ̃tir] *vi* to ring (out) (**de** with). ◆**—issant** *a* resounding; (*scandale*) major. ◆**—issement** *nm* (*effet*) effect; **avoir un grand r.** (*film etc*) to create a stir.

réticent [retisɑ̃] *a* (*réservé*) reticent; (*hésitant*) reluctant. ◆**réticence** *nf* reticence; reluctance.

rétine [retin] *nf Anat* retina.

retir/er [r(ə)tire] *vt* to withdraw; (*sortir*) to take out; (*ôter*) to take off; (*éloigner*) to take away; (*reprendre*) to pick up; (*offre, plainte*) to take back, withdraw; **r. qch à qn** (*permis etc*) to take sth away from s.o.; **r. qch de** (*gagner*) to derive sth from; **— se r.** *vpr* to withdraw, retire (**de** from); (*mer*) to ebb. ◆**—é** *a* (*lieu, vie*) secluded.

retomb/er [r(ə)tɔ̃be] *vi* to fall; (*de nouveau*) to fall again; (*pendre*) to hang (down); (*après un saut etc*) to land; (*intérêt*) to slacken; **r. dans** (*erreur, situation*) to fall on sink back into; **r. sur qn** (*frais, responsabilité*) to fall on s.o. ◆**retombées** *nfpl* (*radioactives*) fallout.

rétorquer [retɔrke] *vt* **r. que** to retort that.

retors [rətɔr] *a* wily, crafty.

rétorsion [retɔrsjɔ̃] *nf Pol* retaliation; **mesure de r.** reprisal.

retouche [r(ə)tuʃ] *nf* touching up; alteration. ◆**retoucher** *vt* (*photo, tableau*) to touch up, retouch; (*texte, vêtement*) to alter.

retour [r(ə)tur] *nm* return; (*de fortune*) reversal; **être de r.** to be back (**de** from); **en r.** (*en échange*) in return; **par r.** (*du courrier*) by return (of post), *Am* by return mail; **à mon retour** when I get *ou* got back (**de** from); **r. en arrière** flashback; **r. de flamme** *Fig* backlash; **match r.** return match *ou Am* game.

retourn/er [r(ə)turne] *vt* (*aux avoir*) (*tableau etc*) to turn round; (*matelas, steak etc*) to turn over; (*foin, terre etc*) to turn; (*vêtement, sac etc*) to turn inside out; (*maison*) to turn upside down; (*compliment, lettre*) to return; **r. qn** (*bouleverser*) *Fam* to upset s.o., shake s.o.; **r. contre qn** (*argument*) to turn against s.o.; (*arme*) to turn on s.o.; **de quoi il retourne** what it's about; **— vi** (*aux être*) to go back, return; **— se r.** *vpr* (*pour regarder*) to turn round, look back; (*sur le dos*) to turn over *ou* round; (*dans son lit*) to toss and turn; (*voiture*) to overturn; **s'en r.** to go back; **se r. contre** *Fig* to turn against.

retracer [r(ə)trase] *vt* (*histoire etc*) to retrace.

rétracter [retrakte] *vt,* **— se r.** *vpr* to retract. ◆**rétractation** *nf* (*désaveu*) retraction.

retrait [r(ə)trɛ] *nm* withdrawal; (*de bagages, billets*) collection; (*de mer*) ebb(ing); **en r.** (*maison etc*) set back.

retraite [r(ə)trɛt] *nf* **1** (*d'employé*) retirement; (*pension*) (retirement) pension; (*refuge*) retreat, refuge; **r. anticipée** early retirement; **prendre sa r.** to retire; **à la r.** retired; **mettre à la r.** to pension off. **2** *Mil* retreat; **r. aux flambeaux** torchlight tattoo. ◆**retraité, -ée** *a* retired; **– nmf** senior citizen, (old age) pensioner.

retrancher [r(ə)trɑ̃ʃe] *vt* (*mot, passage etc*) to cut (**de** from); (*argent, quantité*) to deduct (**de** from). **2 se r.** *vpr* (*soldat, gangster etc*) to entrench oneself; **se r. dans/derrière** *Fig* to take refuge in/behind.

retransmettre [r(ə)trɑ̃smɛtr] *vt* to broadcast. ◆**retransmission** *nf* broadcast.

rétréc/ir [retresir] *vt* to narrow; (*vêtement*) to take in; **– vi, — se r.** *vpr* (*au lavage*) to shrink; (*rue etc*) to narrow. ◆**—i** *a* (*esprit, rue*) narrow.

rétribuer [retribɥe] *vt* to pay, remunerate; (*travail*) to pay for. ◆**rétribution** *nf* payment, remuneration.

rétro [retro] *a inv* (*mode etc*) which harks back to the past, retro.

rétro- [retro] *préf* retro-. ◆**rétroactif, -ive** *a* retroactive.

rétrograde [retrɔgrad] *a* retrograde. ◆**rétrograder** *vi* (*reculer*) to move back; (*civilisation etc*) to go backwards; *Aut* to change down; **– vt** (*fonctionnaire, officier*) to demote.

rétrospectif, -ive [retrospɛktif, -iv] *a* (*sentiment etc*) retrospective; **– nf** (*de films, tableaux*) retrospective. ◆**rétrospectivement** *adv* in retrospect.

retrouss/er [r(ə)truse] *vt* (*jupe etc*) to hitch *ou* tuck up; (*manches*) to roll up ◆**—é** *a* (*nez*) snub, turned-up.

retrouver [r(ə)truve] *vt* to find (again); (*rejoindre*) to meet (again); (*forces, santé*) to regain; (*découvrir*) to rediscover; (*se rappeler*) to recall; **— se r.** *vpr* (*chose*) to be found (again); (*se trouver*) to find oneself (back); (*se rencontrer*) to meet (again); **s'y r.** (*s'orienter*) to find one's bearings *ou* way. ◆**retrouvailles** *nfpl* reunion.

réunion [reynjɔ̃] *nf* (*séance*) meeting; (*d'objets*) collection, gathering; (*d'éléments divers*) combination; (*jonction*) joining. ◆**réunir** *vt* to collect, gather; (*relier*) to join; (*convoquer*) to call together, assemble; (*rapprocher*) to bring together; (*qua-*

lités, tendances) to combine. ◆**réunis** *apl* (*éléments*) combined.

réus/ir [reysir] *vi* to succeed, be successful (*à faire* in doing); (*plante*) to thrive; **r. à** (*examen*) to pass; **r. à qn** to work (out) well for s.o.; (*aliment, climat*) to agree with s.o.; — *vt* to make a success of; — **l** a successful. ◆**réussite** *nf* 1 success. 2 **faire des réussites** *Cartes* to play patience.

revaloir [r(ə)valwar] *vt* **je vous le revaudrai** (*en bien ou en mal*) I'll pay you back.

revaloriser [r(ə)valorize] *vt* (*salaire*) to raise. ◆**revalorisation** *nf* raising.

revanche [r(ə)vɑ̃ʃ] *nf* revenge; *Sp* return game; **en r.** on the other hand.

rêve [rɛv] *nm* dream; **faire un r.** to have a dream; **maison/voiture/etc de r.** dream house/car/etc. ◆**rêvasser** *vi* to daydream.

revêche [rəvɛʃ] *a* bad-tempered, surly.

réveil [revɛj] *nm* waking (up); *Fig* awakening; (*pendule*) alarm (clock). ◆**réveill/er** *vt* (*personne*) to wake (up); (*sentiment, souvenir*) *Fig* to revive, awaken; — **se r.** *vpr* to wake (up); *Fig* to revive, awaken. ◆—**é** a awake. ◆**réveille-matin** *nm inv* alarm clock.

réveillon [revɛjɔ̃] *nm* (*repas*) midnight supper (*on Christmas Eve or New Year's Eve*). ◆**réveillonner** *vi* to take part in a *réveillon*.

révéler [revele] *vt* to reveal (*que* that); — **se r.** to be revealed; **se r. facile/etc** to turn out to be easy/etc. ◆**révélateur, -trice** a revealing; **r. de** indicative of. ◆**révélation** *nf* revelation.

revenant [rəvnɑ̃] *nm* ghost.

revendiquer [r(ə)vɑ̃dike] *vt* to claim; (*exiger*) to demand. ◆**revendicatif, -ive** a (*mouvement etc*) protest-. ◆**revendication** *nf* claim; demand; (*action*) claiming; demanding.

revendre [r(ə)vɑ̃dr] *vt* to resell; **avoir** (**de**) **qch à r.** to have sth to spare. ◆**revendeur, -euse** *nmf* retailer; (*d'occasion*) second-hand dealer; **r.** (**de drogue**) drug pusher; **r. de billets** ticket tout. ◆**revente** *nf* resale.

revenir* [rəvnir] *vi* (*aux être*) to come back, return; (*date*) to come round again; (*mot*) to come *ou* crop up; (*coûter*) to cost (**à qn** s.o.); **r. à** (*activité, sujet*) to go back to, return to; (*se résumer à*) to boil down to; **r. à qn** (*forces, mémoire*) to come back to s.o., return to s.o.; (*honneur*) to fall to s.o.; **r. à soi** to come to *ou* round; **r. de** (*maladie, surprise*) to get over; **r. sur** (*décision, promesse*) to go back on; (*passé, question*)

to go back over; **r. sur ses pas** to retrace one's steps; **faire r.** (*aliment*) to brown.

revenu [rəvny] *nm* income (**de** from); (*d'un État*) revenue (**de** from); **déclaration de revenus** tax return.

rêv/er [rɛve] *vi* to dream (**de** of, **de faire** of doing); — *vt* to dream (*que* that); (*désirer*) to dream of. ◆—**é** a ideal.

réverbération [reverberɑsjɔ̃] *nf* (*de lumière*) reflection; (*de son*) reverberation.

révérence [reverɑ̃s] *nf* reverence; (*salut d'homme*) bow; (*salut de femme*) curts(e)y; **faire une r.** to bow; to curts(e)y. ◆**révérer** *vt* to revere.

révérend, -ende [reverɑ̃, -ɑ̃d] a & *nm Rel* reverend.

rêverie [rɛvri] *nf* daydream; (*activité*) daydreaming.

revers [r(ə)vɛr] *nm* (*côté*) reverse; *Tennis* backhand; (*de veste*) lapel; (*de pantalon*) turn-up, *Am* cuff; (*d'étoffe*) wrong side; (*coup du sort*) setback, reverse; **r. de main** (*coup*) backhander; **le r. de la médaille** *Fig* the other side of the coin.

réversible [reversibl] a reversible.

revient [rəvjɛ̃] *nm* **prix de r.** cost price.

revigorer [r(ə)vigore] *vt* (*personne*) to revive.

revirement [r(ə)virmɑ̃] *nm* (*changement*) about-turn, *Am* about-face; (*de situation, d'opinion, de politique*) reversal.

réviser [revize] *vt* (*notes, texte*) to revise; (*jugement, règlement etc*) to review; (*machine, voiture*) to overhaul, service. ◆**révision** *nf* revision; review; overhaul, service.

revivre* [r(ə)vivr] *vi* to live again; **faire r.** to revive; — *vt* (*incident etc*) to relive.

révocation [revokɑsjɔ̃] *nf* 1 (*de contrat etc*) revocation. 2 (*de fonctionnaire*) dismissal.

revoici [r(ə)vwasi] *prép* **me r.** here I am again.

revoilà [r(ə)vwala] *prép* **la r.** there she is again.

revoir* [r(ə)vwar] *vt* to see (again); (*texte*) to revise; **au r.** goodbye.

révolte [revolt] *nf* revolt. ◆**révolt/er** *vt* to revolt, incense. **2 se r.** *vpr* to revolt, rebel (**contre** against). ◆—**ant** a (*honteux*) revolting. ◆—**é, -ée** *nmf* rebel.

révolu [revɔly] a (époque) past; **avoir trente ans révolus** to be over thirty (years of age).

révolution [revɔlysjɔ̃] nf (changement, rotation) revolution. ◆**révolutionnaire** a & nmf revolutionary. ◆**révolutionner** vt to revolutionize; (émouvoir) Fig to shake up.

revolver [revɔlvɛr] nm revolver, gun.

révoquer [revɔke] vt **1** (contrat etc) to revoke. **2** (fonctionnaire) to dismiss.

revue [r(ə)vy] nf **1** (examen) & Mil review; **passer en r.** to review. **2** (de music-hall) variety show. **3** (magazine) magazine; (spécialisée) journal.

rez-de-chaussée [redʃose] nm inv ground floor, Am first floor.

rhabiller (se) [sərabije] vpr to get dressed again.

rhapsodie [rapsɔdi] nf rhapsody.

rhétorique [retɔrik] nf rhetoric.

Rhin [rɛ̃] nm le R. the Rhine.

rhinocéros [rinɔserɔs] nm rhinoceros.

rhododendron [rɔdɔdɛ̃drɔ̃] nm rhododendron.

rhubarbe [rybarb] nf rhubarb.

rhum [rɔm] nm rum.

rhumatisme [rymatism] nm Méd rheumatism; **avoir des rhumatismes** to have rheumatism. ◆**rhumatisant, -ante** a & nmf rheumatic. ◆**rhumatismal, -aux** a (douleur) rheumatic.

rhume [rym] nm cold; **r. de cerveau** head cold; **r. des foins** hay fever.

riant [rjɑ̃] a cheerful, smiling.

ricaner [rikane] vi (sarcastiquement) to snigger; (bêtement) to giggle.

riche [riʃ] a rich; (personne, pays) rich, wealthy; **r. en** (minérai, vitamines etc) rich in; – nmf rich ou wealthy person; **les riches** the rich. ◆**-ment** (vêtu, illustré etc) richly. ◆**richesse** nf wealth; (d'étoffe, de son, vocabulaire) richness; pl (trésor) riches; (ressources) wealth.

ricin [risɛ̃] nm **huile de r.** castor oil.

ricocher [rikɔʃe] vi to ricochet, rebound. ◆**ricochet** nm ricochet, rebound; **par r.** Fig as an indirect result.

rictus [riktys] nm grin, grimace.

ride [rid] nf wrinkle; ripple. ◆**rider** vt (visage) to wrinkle; (eau) to ripple; – **se r.** vpr to wrinkle.

rideau, -x [rido] nm curtain; (métallique) shutter; (écran) Fig screen (de of); **le r. de fer** Pol the Iron Curtain.

ridicule [ridikyl] a ridiculous, ludicrous; – nm (moquerie) ridicule; (défaut) absurdity; (de situation etc) ridiculousness; **tourner en r.** to ridicule. ◆**ridiculiser** vt to ridicule.

rien [rjɛ̃] pron nothing; **il ne sait r.** he knows nothing, he doesn't know anything; **r. du tout** nothing at all; **r. d'autre/de bon/**etc nothing else/good/etc; **r. de tel** nothing like it; **de r.!** (je vous en prie) don't mention it! (ça ne fait r.) it doesn't matter; **en moins de r.** (vite) in no time; **trois fois r.** (chose insignifiante) next to nothing; **pour r.** (à bas prix) for next to nothing; **il n'en est r.** (ce n'est pas vrai) nothing of the kind; **r. que** only, just; – nm trifle, (mere) nothing; **un r. de** a hint ou touch of; **en un r. de temps** (vite) in no time; **un r. trop petit/**etc just a bit too small/etc.

rieur, -euse [rijœr, -øz] a cheerful.

rifard [rifar] nm Fam brolly, umbrella.

rigide [riʒid] a rigid; (carton, muscle) stiff; (personne) Fig inflexible; (éducation) strict. ◆**rigidité** nf rigidity; stiffness; inflexibility; strictness.

rigole [rigɔl] nf (conduit) channel; (filet d'eau) rivulet.

rigoler [rigɔle] vi Fam to laugh; (s'amuser) to have fun ou a laugh; (plaisanter) to joke (avec about). ◆**rigolade** nf Fam fun; (chose ridicule) joke, farce; **prendre qch à la r.** to make a joke out of sth. ◆**rigolo, -ote** a Fam funny; – nmf Fam joker.

rigueur [rigœr] nf rigour; harshness; strictness; (précision) precision; **être de r.** to be the rule; **à la r.** if absolutely necessary, at ou Am a pinch; **tenir r. à qn de qch** Fig to hold sth against s.o. ◆**rigoureux, -euse** a rigorous; (climat, punition) harsh; (personne, morale, sens) strict.

rillettes [rijɛt] nfpl potted minced pork.

rime [rim] nf rhyme. ◆**rimer** vi to rhyme (avec with); **ça ne rime à rien** it makes no sense.

rincer [rɛ̃se] vt to rinse (out). ◆**rinçage** nm rinsing; (opération) rinse.

ring [riŋ] nm (boxing) ring.

ringard [rɛ̃gar] a (démodé) Fam unfashionable, fuddy-duddy.

ripaille [ripaj] nf Fam feast.

riposte [ripɔst] nf (réponse) retort; (attaque) counter(attack). ◆**riposter** vi to retort; **r. à** (attaque) to counter; (insulte) to reply to; – vt r. que to retort that.

rire [rir] vi to laugh (de at); (s'amuser) to have a good time; (plaisanter) to joke; **faire qch pour r.** to do sth for a laugh ou a joke; **se r. de qch** to laugh sth off; – nm laugh; pl laughter; **le r.** (activité) laughter. ◆**risée** nf mockery; **être la r. de** to be the laughing stock of. ◆**risible** a laughable.

ris [ri] nm **r. de veau** Culin (calf) sweetbread.

risque [risk] *nm* risk; **r. du métier** occupational hazard; **au r. de qch/de faire** at the risk of sth/of doing; **à vos risques et périls** at your own risk; **assurance tous risques** comprehensive insurance. ◆**risquer** *vt* to risk; (*question, regard*) to venture, hazard; **r. de faire** to stand a good chance of doing; **se r. à faire** to dare to do; **se r. dans** to venture into. ◆**risqué** *a* risky; (*plaisanterie*) daring, risqué.

ristourne [risturn] *nf* discount.

rite [rit] *nm* rite; (*habitude*) *Fig* ritual. ◆**rituel, -elle** *a* & *nm* ritual.

rivage [rivaʒ] *nm* shore.

rival, -ale, -aux [rival, -o] *a* & *nmf* rival. ◆**rivaliser** *vi* to compete (**avec** with, **de** in). ◆**rivalité** *nf* rivalry.

rive [riv] *nf* (*de fleuve*) bank; (*de lac*) shore.

rivé [rive] *a* **r. à** (*chaise etc*) *Fig* riveted to; **r. sur** *Fig* riveted on. ◆**rivet** *nm* (*tige*) rivet. ◆**riveter** *vt* to rivet (together).

riverain, -aine [rivrɛ̃, -ɛn] *a* riverside; lakeside; -- *nmf* riverside resident; (*de lac*) lakeside resident; (*de rue*) resident.

rivière [rivjɛr] *nf* river.

rixe [riks] *nf* brawl, scuffle.

riz [ri] *nm* rice; **r. au lait** rice pudding. ◆**rizière** *nf* paddy (field), ricefield.

RN *abrév* = route nationale.

robe [rɔb] *nf* (*de femme*) dress; (*d'ecclésiastique, de juge*) robe; (*de professeur*) gown; (*pelage*) coat; **r. de soirée** ou **du soir** evening dress ou gown; **r. de grossesse/de mariée** maternity/wedding dress; **r. de chambre** dressing gown; **r. chasuble** pinafore (dress).

robinet [rɔbinɛ] *nm* tap, *Am* faucet; **eau du r.** tap water.

robot [rɔbo] *nm* robot; **r. ménager** food processor, liquidizer.

robuste [rɔbyst] *a* robust. ◆**robustesse** *nf* robustness.

roc [rɔk] *nm* rock.

rocaille [rɔkaj] *nf* (*terrain*) rocky ground; (*de jardin*) rockery. ◆**rocailleux, -euse** *a* rocky, stony; (*voix*) harsh.

rocambolesque [rɔkãbɔlɛsk] *a* (*aventure etc*) fantastic.

roche [rɔʃ] *nf*, **rocher** [rɔʃe] *nm* (*bloc, substance*) rock. ◆**rocheux, -euse** *a* rocky.

rock [rɔk] *nm* (*musique*) rock; -- *a inv* (*chanteur etc*) rock.

rod/er [rɔde] *vt* (*moteur, voiture*) to run in, *Am* break in; **être rodé** (*personne*) *Fig* to have got ou *Am* gotten the hang of things. ◆**--age** *nm* running in, *Am* breaking in.

rôd/er [rode] *vi* to roam (about); (*suspect*) to prowl (about). ◆**--eur, -euse** *nmf* prowler.

rogne [rɔɲ] *nf Fam* anger; **en r.** in a temper.

rogner [rɔɲe] *vt* to trim, clip; (*réduire*) to cut; -- *vi* **r. sur** (*réduire*) to cut down on. ◆**rognures** *nfpl* clippings, trimmings.

rognon [rɔɲ̃] *nm Culin* kidney.

roi [rwa] *nm* king; **fête** ou **jour des rois** Twelfth Night.

roitelet [rwatlɛ] *nm* (*oiseau*) wren.

rôle [rol] *nm* role, part; **à tour de r.** in turn.

romain, -aine [rɔmɛ̃, -ɛn] 1 *a* & *nmf* Roman. 2 *nf* (*laitue*) cos (lettuce), *Am* romaine.

roman [rɔmã] 1 *nm* novel; (*histoire*) *Fig* story; **r.-fleuve** *Saga*; (*langue*) Romance; *Archit* Romanesque. ◆**romancé** *a* (*histoire*) fictional. ◆**romancier, -ière** *nmf* novelist.

romanesque [rɔmanɛsk] *a* romantic; (*incroyable*) fantastic.

romanichel, -elle [rɔmaniʃɛl] *nmf* gipsy.

romantique [rɔmãtik] *a* romantic. ◆**romantisme** *nm* romanticism.

romarin [rɔmarɛ̃] *nm Bot Culin* rosemary.

romp/re [rɔpr] *vt* to break; (*pourparlers, relations*) to break off; (*digue*) to burst; -- *vi* to break (*Fig* **avec** with); to burst; (*fiancés*) to break it off; -- **se r.** *vpr* to break; to burst. ◆**--u** *a* 1 (*fatigué*) exhausted. 2 **r. à** (*expérimenté*) experienced in.

romsteck [rɔmstɛk] *nm* rump steak.

ronces [rɔs] *nfpl* (*branches*) brambles.

ronchonner [rɔ̃ʃɔne] *vi Fam* to grouse, grumble.

rond [rɔ̃] *a* round; (*gras*) plump; (*honnête*) straight; (*ivre*) *Fam* tight; **dix francs tout r.** ten francs exactly; -- *adv* **tourner r.** (*machine etc*) to run smoothly; -- *nm* (*objet*) ring; (*cercle*) circle; (*tranche*) slice; *pl* (*argent*) *Fam* money; **r. de serviette** napkin ring; **en r.** (*s'asseoir etc*) in a ring ou circle; **tourner en r.** (*toupie etc*) & *Fig* to go round and round. ◆**r.-de-cuir** *nm* (*pl* **ronds-de-cuir**) *Péj* pen pusher. ◆**r.-point** *nm* (*pl* **ronds-points**) *Aut* roundabout, *Am* traffic circle. ◆**ronde** *nf* (*tour de surveillance*) round; (*de policier*) beat; (*danse*) round (dance); (*note*) *Mus* semibreve, *Am* whole note; **à la r.** around; (*boire*) in turn. ◆**rondelet, -ette** *a* chubby; (*somme*) *Fig* tidy. ◆**rondelle** *nf* (*tranche*) slice; *Tech* washer. ◆**rondement** *adv* (*efficacement*) briskly; (*franchement*) straight. ◆**rondeur** *nf* roundness; (*du corps*) plumpness. ◆**rondin** *nm* log.

ronéotyper [rɔneotipe] *vt* to duplicate, roneo.

ronflant [rɔ̃flɑ̃] *a* (*langage etc*) *Péj* high-flown; (*feu*) roaring.

ronfler [rɔ̃fle] *vi* to snore; (*moteur*) to hum. ◆**ronflement** *nm* snore, snoring; hum(ming).

rong/er [rɔ̃ʒe] *vt* to gnaw (at); (*ver, mer, rouille*) to eat into (*sth*); (*chagrin, maladie*) to consume s.o.; **se r. les ongles** to bite one's nails; **se r. les sangs** (*s'inquiéter*) to worry oneself sick. ◆**-eur** *nm* (*animal*) rodent.

ronron [rɔ̃rɔ̃] *nm*, **ronronnement** [rɔ̃rɔnmɑ̃] *nm* purr(ing). ◆**ronronner** *vi* to purr.

roquette [rɔkɛt] *nf Mil* rocket.

rosbif [rɔsbif] *nm* **du r.** (*rôti*) roast beef; (*à rôtir*) roasting beef; **un r.** a joint of roast ou roasting beef.

rose [roz] **1** *nf* (*fleur*) rose. **2** *a* (*couleur*) pink; (*situation, teint*) rosy; **—** *nm* pink. ◆**rosé** *a* pinkish; **&** **—** *a & nm* (*vin*) rosé. ◆**rosette** *nf* (*d'un officier*) rosette; (*nœud*) bow. ◆**rosier** *nm* rose bush.

roseau, -x [rozo] *nm* (*plante*) reed.

rosée [roze] *nf* dew.

rosse [rɔs] *a & nf* nasty (person).

ross/er [rɔse] *vt Fam* to thrash. ◆**-ée** *nf Fam* thrashing.

rossignol [rɔsiɲɔl] *nm* **1** (*oiseau*) nightingale. **2** (*crochet*) picklock.

rot [ro] *nm Fam* burp, belch. ◆**roter** *vi Fam* to burp, belch.

rotation [rɔtasjɔ̃] *nf* rotation; (*de stock*) turnover. ◆**rotatif, -ive** *a* rotary; **—** *nf* rotary press.

rotin [rɔtɛ̃] *nm* rattan, cane.

rôt/ir [rotir] *vti*, **— se r.** *vpr* to roast; **faire r.** to roast. ◆**-i** *nm* **du r.** roasting meat; (*cuit*) roast meat; **un r.** a joint; **r. de bœuf/de porc** (joint of) roast beef/pork. ◆**rôtissoire** *nf* (roasting) spit.

rotule [rɔtyl] *nf* kneecap.

roturier, -ière [rɔtyrje, -jɛr] *nmf* commoner.

rouage [rwaʒ] *nm* (*de montre etc*) (working) part; (*d'organisation etc*) *Fig* cog.

roublard [rublar] *a* wily, foxy.

rouble [rubl] *nm* (*monnaie*) r(o)uble.

roucouler [rukule] *vi* (*oiseau, amoureux*) to coo.

roue [ru] *nf* wheel; **r.** (*dentée*) cog(wheel); **faire la r.** (*paon*) to spread its tail; (*se pavaner*) *Fig* to strut; **faire r. libre** *Aut* to freewheel.

roué, -ée [rwe] *a & nmf* sly ou calculating (person).

rouer [rwe] *vt* **r. qn de coups** to beat s.o. black and blue.

rouet [rwe] *nm* spinning wheel.

rouge [ruʒ] *a* (*fer*) red-hot; **—** *nm* (*couleur*) red; (*vin*) *Fam* red wine; **r.** (*à lèvres*) lipstick; **r.** (*à joues*) rouge; **le feu est au r.** *Aut* (the) traffic lights are red; **—** *nmf* (*personne*) *Pol* Red. ◆**r.-gorge** *nm* (*pl* **rouges-gorges**) robin. ◆**rougeâtre** *a* reddish. ◆**rougeaud** *a* red-faced. ◆**rougeoyer** *vi* to glow (red). ◆**rougeur** *nf* redness; (*due à la gêne ou à la honte*) blush(ing); *pl Méd* red spots ou blotches. ◆**rougir** *vti* to redden, turn red; **—** *vi* (*de gêne, de honte*) to blush (**de** with); (*de colère, de joie*) to flush (**de** with).

rougeole [ruʒɔl] *nf* measles.

rouget [ruʒɛ] *nm* (*poisson*) mullet.

rouille [ruj] *nf* rust; **—** *a inv* (*couleur*) rust(-coloured). ◆**rouill/er** *vi* to rust; **— se r.** *vpr* to rust; (*esprit, sportif etc*) *Fig* to get rusty. ◆**-é** *a* rusty.

roul/er [rule] *vt* to roll; (*brouette, meuble*) to wheel, push; (*crêpe, ficelle, manches etc*) to roll up; **r. qn** (*duper*) *Fam* to cheat s.o.; **—** *vi* to roll; (*train, voiture*) to go, travel; (*conducteur*) to drive; **r. sur** (*conversation*) to turn on; **ça roule!** *Fam* everything's fine!; **— se r.** *vpr* to roll; **se r. dans** (*couverture etc*) to roll oneself (up) in. ◆**-ant** *a* (*escalier, trottoir*) moving; (*meuble*) on wheels. ◆**-é** *nm* (*gâteau*) Swiss roll. ◆**rouleau, -x** *nm* (*outil, vague*) roller; (*de papier, pellicule etc*) roll; **r. à pâtisserie** rolling pin; **r. compresseur** steamroller. ◆**roulement** *nm* (*bruit*) rumbling, rumble; (*de tambour, de tonnerre, d'yeux*) roll; (*ordre*) rotation; **par r.** in rotation; **r. à billes** *Tech* ball bearing. ◆**roulette** *nf* (*de meuble*) castor; (*de dentiste*) drill; (*jeu*) roulette. ◆**roulis** *nm* (*de navire*) roll(ing).

roulotte [rulɔt] *nf* (*de gitan*) caravan.

Roumanie [rumani] *nf* Romania. ◆**roumain, -aine** *a & nmf* Romanian; **—** *nm* (*langue*) Romanian.

round [rawnd, rund] *nm Boxe* round.

roupiller [rupije] *vi Fam* to kip, sleep.

rouquin, -ine [rukɛ̃, -in] *a Fam* red-haired; **—** *nmf Fam* redhead.

rouspét/er [ruspete] *vi Fam* to grumble, complain. ◆**-eur, -euse** *nmf* grumbler.

rousse [rus] *voir* **roux**.

rousseur [rusœr] *nf* redness; **tache de r.** freckle. ◆**roussir** *vt* (*brûler*) to singe, scorch; **—** *vi* (*feuilles*) to turn brown; **faire r.** *Culin* to brown.

route [rut] *nf* road (**de** to); (*itinéraire*) way,

route; (*aérienne, maritime*) route; (*chemin*) *Fig* path, way; **r. nationale/départementale** main/secondary road; **grande r., grand-r.** main road; **code de la r.** Highway Code; **en r.** on the way, en route; **en r.!** let's go!; **par la r.** by road; **sur la bonne r.** *Fig* on the right track; **mettre en r.** (*voiture etc*) to start (up); **se mettre en r.** to set out (pour for); **une heure de r.** *Aut* an hour's drive; **bonne r.!** *Aut* have a good trip! ◆**routier, -ière** a (*carte etc*) road-; − *nm* (*camionneur*) (long distance) lorry *ou Am* truck driver; (*restaurant*) transport café, *Am* truck stop.

routine [rutin] *nf* routine; **de r.** (*contrôle etc*) routine-. ◆**routinier, -ière** a (*travail etc*) routine-; (*personne*) addicted to routine.

rouvrir* [ruvrir] *vti*, **− se r.** *vpr* to reopen.

roux, rousse [ru, rus] a (*cheveux*) red, ginger; (*personne*) red-haired; − *nmf* redhead.

royal, -aux [rwajal, -o] a royal; (*cadeau, festin etc*) fit for a king; (*salaire*) princely. ◆**royalement** adv (*traiter*) royally. ◆**royaliste** a & *nmf* royalist. ◆**royaume** *nm* kingdom. ◆**Royaume-Uni** *nm* United Kingdom. ◆**royauté** *nf* (*monarchie*) monarchy.

ruade [rɥad] *nf* (*d'âne etc*) kick.

ruban [rybɑ̃] *nm* ribbon; (*d'acier, de chapeau*) band; **r. adhésif** adhesive *ou* sticky tape.

rubéole [rybeɔl] *nf* German measles, rubella.

rubis [rybi] *nm* (*pierre*) ruby; (*de montre*) jewel.

rubrique [rybrik] *nf* (*article*) *Journ* column; (*catégorie, titre*) heading.

ruche [ryʃ] *nf* (bee)hive.

rude [ryd] a (*grossier*) crude; (*rêche*) rough; (*pénible*) tough; (*hiver, voix*) harsh; (*remarquable*) *Fam* tremendous. ◆**−ment** adv (*parler, traiter*) harshly; (*frapper, tomber*) hard; (*très*) *Fam* awfully. ◆**rudesse** *nf* harshness. ◆**rudoyer** *vt* to treat harshly.

rudiments [rydimɑ̃] *nmpl* rudiments. ◆**rudimentaire** a rudimentary.

rue [ry] *nf* street; **être à la r.** (*sans domicile*) to be on the streets. ◆**ruelle** *nf* alley(way).

ruer [rɥe] **1** *vi* (*cheval*) to kick (out). **2 se r.** *vpr* (*foncer*) to rush, fling oneself (**sur** at). ◆**ruée**, *nf* rush.

rugby [rygbi] *nm* rugby. ◆**rugbyman**, *pl* **-men** [rygbiman, -men] *nm* rugby player.

rug/ir [ryʒir] *vi* to roar. ◆**−issement** *nm* roar.

rugueux, -euse [rygø, -øz] a rough. ◆**rugosité** *nf* roughness; *pl* (*aspérités*) roughness.

ruine [rɥin] *nf* (*décombres*) & *Fig* ruin; (*édifice*) in ruins; **tomber en r.** to fall into ruin. ◆**ruiner** *vt* to ruin; **− se r.** *vpr* (*en dépensant*) to ruin oneself. ◆**ruineux, -euse** a (*goûts, projet*) ruinously expensive; (*dépense*) ruinous.

ruisseau, -x [rɥiso] *nm* stream; (*caniveau*) gutter. ◆**ruisseler** *vi* to stream (de with).

rumeur [rymœr] *nf* (*protestation*) clamour; (*murmure*) murmur; (*nouvelle*) rumour.

ruminer [rymine] *vt* (*méditer*) to ponder on, ruminate over.

rumsteak [rɔmstɛk] *nm* rump steak.

rupture [ryptyr] *nf* break(ing); (*de fiançailles, relations*) breaking off; (*de pourparlers*) breakdown (**de** in); (*brouille*) break up, split; (*de contrat*) breach; (*d'organe*) *Méd* rupture.

rural, -aux [ryral, -o] a rural, country-; − *nmpl* country people.

ruse [ryz] *nf* (*subterfuge*) trick; **la r.** (*habileté*) cunning; (*fourberie*) trickery. ◆**rusé, -ée** a & *nmf* crafty *ou* cunning (person). ◆**ruser** *vi* to resort to trickery.

Russie [rysi] *nf* Russia. ◆**russe** a & *nmf* Russian; − *nm* (*langue*) Russian.

rustique [rystik] a (*meuble*) rustic.

rustre [rystr] *nm* lout, churl.

rutabaga [rytabaga] *nm* (*racine*) swede, *Am* rutabaga.

rutilant [rytilɑ̃] a gleaming, glittering.

rythme [ritm] *nm* rhythm; (*de travail*) rate, tempo; (*de la vie*) pace; **au r. de trois par jour** at a *ou* the rate of three a day. ◆**rythmé** a, ◆**rythmique** a rhythmic(al).

S

S, s [ɛs] *nm* S, s.

s' [s] *voir* **se, si.**

sa [sa] *voir* **son**².

SA *abrév* (*société anonyme*) *Com* plc, *Am* Inc.

sabbat [saba] *nm* (Jewish) Sabbath.

◆**sabbatique** a (année etc) Univ sabbatical.

sable [sabl] nm sand; **sables mouvants** quicksand(s). ◆**sabler** vt (route) to sand. ◆**sableux, -euse** a (eau) sandy. ◆**sablier** nm hourglass; Culin egg timer. ◆**sablière** nf (carrière) sandpit. ◆**sablonneux, -euse** a (terrain) sandy.

sablé [sable] nm shortbread biscuit ou Am cookie.

saborder [saborde] vt (navire) to scuttle; (entreprise) Fig to shut down.

sabot [sabo] nm 1 (de cheval etc) hoof. 2 (chaussure) clog. 3 (de frein) Aut shoe; s. (de Denver) Aut (wheel) clamp.

sabot/er [sabote] vt (bâcler) to botch. ◆**-age** nm sabotage; **un s.** an act of sabotage. ◆**-eur, -euse** nmf saboteur.

sabre [sabr] nm sabre, sword.

sabrer [sabre] vt (élève, candidat) Fam to give a thoroughly bad mark to.

sac [sak] nm 1 bag; (grand et en toile) sack; **s.** (à main) handbag; **s.** à dos rucksack. 2 **mettre à s.** (ville) Mil to sack.

saccade [sakad] nf jerk, jolt; **par saccades** jerkily, in fits and starts. ◆**saccadé** (geste, style) jerky.

saccager [sakaʒe] vt (ville, région) Mil to sack; (bouleverser) Fig to turn upside down.

saccharine [sakarin] nf saccharin.

sacerdoce [saserdɔs] nm (fonction) Rel priesthood; Fig vocation.

sachet [saʃɛ] nm (small) bag; (de lavande etc) sachet; **s. de thé** teabag.

sacoche [sakɔʃ] nf bag; (de vélo, moto) saddlebag; Scol satchel.

sacquer [sake] vt Fam (renvoyer) to sack; (élève) to give a thoroughly bad mark to.

sacre [sakr] nm (d'évêque) consecration; (de roi) coronation. ◆**sacrer** vt (évêque) to consecrate; (roi) to crown.

sacré [sakre] a (saint) sacred; (maudit) Fam damned. ◆**-ment** adv Fam (très) damn(ed); (beaucoup) a hell of a lot.

sacrement [sakrəmã] nm Rel sacrament.

sacrifice [sakrifis] nm sacrifice. ◆**sacrifier** vt to sacrifice (à to, pour for); — vi s. à (mode etc) to pander to; — **se s.** vpr to sacrifice oneself (à to, pour for).

sacrilège [sakrilɛʒ] nm sacrilege; — a sacrilegious.

sacristie [sakristi] nf vestry.

sacro-saint [sakrosɛ̃] a Iron sacrosanct.

sadisme [sadism] nm sadism. ◆**sadique** a sadistic; — nmf sadist.

safari [safari] nm safari; **faire un s.** to be ou go on safari.

safran [safrã] nm saffron.

sagace [sagas] a shrewd, sagacious.

sage [saʒ] a wise; (enfant) well-behaved, good; (modéré) moderate; — nm wise man, sage. ◆**sagement** adv wisely; (avec calme) quietly. ◆**sagesse** nf wisdom; good behaviour; moderation.

sage-femme [saʒfam] nf (pl sages-femmes) midwife.

Sagittaire [saʒiter] nm le S. (signe) Sagittarius.

Sahara [saara] nm le S. the Sahara (desert).

saign/er [seɲe] vti to bleed. ◆**-ant** [seɲã] a (viande) Culin rare, underdone. ◆**-ée** nf 1 Méd bleeding, blood-letting; (perte) Fig heavy loss. 2 la s. du bras Anat the bend of the arm. ◆**saignement** nm bleeding; **s. de nez** nosebleed.

saillant [sajã] a projecting, jutting out; (trait etc) Fig salient. ◆**saillie** nf projection; **en s., faisant s.** projecting.

sain [sɛ̃] a healthy; (moralement) sane; (jugement) sound; (nourriture) wholesome, healthy; **s. et sauf** safe and sound, unhurt. ◆**sainement** adv (vivre) healthily; (raisonner) sanely.

saindoux [sɛ̃du] nm lard.

saint, sainte [sɛ̃, sɛ̃t] a holy; (personne) saintly; as **Jean Saint John**; **sainte nitouche** Iron little innocent; **la Sainte Vierge** the Blessed Virgin; — nmf saint. ◆**s.-bernard** nm (chien) St Bernard. ◆**S.-Esprit** nm Holy Spirit. ◆**S.-Siège** nm Holy See. ◆**S.-Sylvestre** nf New Year's Eve.

sais [sɛ] voir savoir.

saisie [sezi] nf Jur seizure; **s. de données** data capture ou entry.

sais/ir [sezir] 1 vt to grab (hold of), seize; (occasion) & Jur to seize; (comprendre) to understand, grasp; (frapper) Fig to strike; **se s. de** to grab (hold of), seize. 2 vt (viande) Culin to fry briskly. ◆**-l** a **s. de** (joie, peur etc) overcome by. ◆**-issant** (film etc) gripping; (contraste, ressemblance) striking. ◆**-issement** nm (émotion) shock.

saison [sɛzɔ̃] nf season; **en/hors s.** in/out of season; **en pleine ou haute s.** in (the) high season; **en basse s.** in the low season. ◆**saisonnier, -ière** a seasonal.

sait [sɛ] voir savoir.

salade [salad] nf 1 (laitue) lettuce; **s.** (verte) (green) salad; **s. de fruits/de tomates/etc** fruit/tomato/etc salad. 2 nf (désordre) Fam mess. 3 nfpl (mensonges) Fam stories, nonsense. ◆**saladier** nm salad bowl.

salaire [salɛr] nm wage(s), salary.

salaison [salɛzɔ̃] nf Culin salting; pl (denrées) salt(ed) meat ou fish.

salamandre [salamɑ̃dr] nf (animal) salamander.

salami [salami] nm Culin salami.

salarial, -aux [salarjal, -o] a (accord etc) wage-. ◆**salarié, -ée** a wage-earning; — nmf wage earner.

salaud [salo] nm Arg Péj bastard, swine.

sale [sal] a dirty; (dégoûtant) filthy; (mauvais) nasty; (couleur) dingy. ◆**salement** adv (se conduire, manger) disgustingly. ◆**saleté** nf dirtiness; filthiness; (crasse) dirt, filth; (action) dirty trick; (camelote) Fam rubbish, junk; pl (détritus) mess, dirt; (obscénités) filth. ◆**salir** vt to (make) dirty; (réputation) Fig to sully, tarnish; — se s. vpr to get dirty. ◆**salissant** a (métier) dirty, messy; (étoffe) easily dirtied. ◆**salissure** nf (tache) dirty mark.

sal/er [sale] vt Culin to salt. ◆**-é-a 1** (eau) salt-; (saveur) salty; (denrées) salted; (grivois) Fig spicy. **2** (excessif) Fam steep. ◆**salière** nf saltcellar.

salive [saliv] nf saliva. ◆**saliver** vi to salivate.

salle [sal] nf room; (très grande, publique) hall; Th auditorium; (d'hôpital) ward; (public) Th house, audience; **s. à manger** dining room; **s. d'eau** washroom, shower room; **s. d'exposition** Com showroom; **s. de jeux** (pour enfants) games room; (avec machines à sous) amusement arcade; **s. d'opération** Méd operating theatre.

salon [salɔ̃] nm sitting room, lounge; (exposition) show; **s. de beauté/de coiffure** beauty/hairdressing salon; **s. de thé** tearoom(s).

salope [salɔp] nf (femme) Arg Péj bitch, cow. ◆**saloperie** nf Arg (action) dirty trick; (camelote) rubbish, junk; **des saloperies** (propos) filth. ◆**salopette** [salɔpɛt] nf dungarees; (d'ouvrier) overalls.

salsifis [salsifi] nm Bot Culin salsify.

saltimbanque [saltɛ̃bɑ̃k] nmf (travelling) acrobat.

salubre [salybr] a healthy, salubrious. ◆**salubrité** nf healthiness; **s. publique** public health.

saluer [salɥe] vt to greet; (en partant) to take one's leave; (de la main) to wave to; (de la tête) to nod to; Mil to salute; **s. qn comme** Fig to hail s.o. as. ◆**salut 1** nm greeting; wave; nod; Mil salute; — int Fam hello!, hi!; (au revoir) bye! **2** nm (de peuple

etc) salvation; (sauvegarde) safety. ◆**salutation** nf greeting.

salutaire [salytɛr] a salutary.

salve [salv] nf salvo.

samedi [samdi] nm Saturday.

SAMU [samy] nm abrév (service d'assistance médicale d'urgence) emergency medical service.

sanatorium [sanatɔrjɔm] nm sanatorium.

sanctifier [sɑ̃ktifje] vt to sanctify.

sanction [sɑ̃ksjɔ̃] nf (approbation, peine) sanction. ◆**sanctionner** vt (confirmer, approuver) to sanction; (punir) to punish.

sanctuaire [sɑ̃ktɥɛr] nm Rel sanctuary.

sandale [sɑ̃dal] nf sandal.

sandwich [sɑ̃dwitʃ] nm sandwich.

sang [sɑ̃] nm blood; **coup de s.** Méd stroke. ◆**sanglant** a bloody; (critique, reproche) scathing. ◆**sanguin, -ine 1** a (vaisseau etc) blood-; (tempérament) full-blooded. **2** nf (fruit) blood orange. ◆**sanguinaire** a blood-thirsty.

sang-froid [sɑ̃frwa] nm self-control, calm; **avec s.-froid** calmly; **de s.-froid** (tuer) in cold blood.

sangle [sɑ̃gl] nf (de selle, parachute) strap.

sanglier [sɑ̃glije] nm wild boar.

sanglot [sɑ̃glo] nm sob. ◆**sangloter** vi to sob.

sangsue [sɑ̃sy] nf leech.

sanitaire [sanitɛr] a health-; (conditions) sanitary; (personnel) medical; (appareils etc) bathroom-, sanitary.

sans [sɑ̃] prép without; **s. faire** without doing; **ça va s. dire** that goes without saying; **s. qu'il le sache** without him ou his knowing; **s. cela, s. quoi** otherwise; **s. plus** (but) no more than that; **s. exception/faute** without exception/fail; **s. importance/travail** unimportant/unemployed; **s. argent/manches** penniless/sleeveless. ◆**s.-abri** nmf inv homeless person; **les s.-abri** the homeless. ◆**s.-gêne** a inv inconsiderate; — nm inv inconsiderateness. ◆**s.-travail** nmf inv unemployed person.

santé [sɑ̃te] nf health; **en bonne/mauvaise s.** in good/bad health, well/not well; (à votre) **s.!** (en trinquant) your health!, cheers!; **maison de s.** nursing home.

saoul [su] = **soûl**.

saper [sape] vt to undermine.

sapeur-pompier [sapœrpɔ̃pje] nm (pl sapeurs-pompiers) fireman.

saphir [safir] nm (pierre) sapphire; (d'électrophone) sapphire, stylus.

sapin [sapɛ̃] nm (arbre, bois) fir; **s. de Noël** Christmas tree.

sarbacane [sarbakan] nf (jouet) pea-shooter.

sarcasme [sarkasm] nm sarcasm; **un s.** a piece of sarcasm. ◆**sarcastique** a sarcastic.

sarcler [sarkle] vt (jardin etc) to weed.

Sardaigne [sardɛɲ] nf Sardinia.

sardine [sardin] nf sardine.

sardonique [sardɔnik] a sardonic.

SARL abrév (société à responsabilité limitée) Ltd, Am Inc.

sarment [sarmã] nm vine shoot.

sarrasin [sarazɛ̃] nm buckwheat.

sas [sa(s)] nm (pièce étanche) Nau Av airlock.

Satan [satã] nm Satan. ◆**satané** a (maudit) blasted. ◆**satanique** a satanic.

satellite [satelit] nm satellite; **pays s.** Pol satellite (country).

satiété [sasjete] nf **à s.** (boire, manger) one's fill; (répéter) ad nauseam.

satin [satɛ̃] nm satin. ◆**satiné** a satiny, silky.

satire [satir] nf satire (contre on). ◆**satirique** a satiric(al).

satisfaction [satisfaksjɔ̃] nf satisfaction. ◆**satisfaire**° vt to satisfy; – vi **s. à** (conditions, engagement etc) to fulfil. ◆**satisfaisant** a (acceptable) satisfactory. ◆**satisfait** a satisfied, content (de with).

saturer [satyre] vt to saturate (de with). ◆**saturation** [satyratœr] nm (de radiateur) humidifier.

satyre [satir] nm Fam sex fiend.

sauce [sos] nf sauce; (jus de viande) gravy; **s. tomate** tomato sauce. ◆**saucière** nf sauce boat; gravy boat.

saucisse [sosis] nf sausage. ◆**saucisson** nm (cold) sausage.

sauf¹ [sof] prép except (que that); **s. avis contraire** unless you hear otherwise; **s. erreur** barring error.

sauf², sauve [sof, sov] a (honneur) intact, saved; **avoir la vie sauve** to be unharmed. ◆**sauf-conduit** nm (document) safe-conduct.

sauge [soʒ] nf Bot Culin sage.

saugrenu [sogrəny] a preposterous.

saule [sol] nm willow; **s. pleureur** weeping willow.

saumâtre [somatr] a (eau) briny, brackish.

saumon [somɔ̃] nm salmon; – a inv (couleur) salmon (pink).

saumure [somyr] nf (pickling) brine.

sauna [sona] nm sauna.

saupoudrer [sopudre] vt (couvrir) to sprinkle (de with).

saur [sɔr] am **hareng s.** smoked herring, kipper.

saut [so] nm jump, leap; **faire un s.** to jump, leap; **faire un s. chez qn** (visite) to pop round to s.o.; **au s. du lit** on getting out of bed; **s. à la corde** skipping, Am jumping rope. ◆**sauter** vi to jump, leap; (bombe) to go off, explode; (poudrière etc) to go up, blow up; (fusible) to blow; (se détacher) to come off; **faire s.** (détruire) to blow up; (arracher) to tear off; (casser) to break; (renvoyer) Fam to get rid of, fire; (fusible) to blow; (mot, classe, repas) to skip. ◆**saute-mouton** nm (jeu) leapfrog. ◆**sautiller** vi to hop. ◆**sautoir** nm Sp jumping area.

sauté [sote] a & nm Culin sauté. ◆**sauteuse** nf (shallow) pan.

sauterelle [sotrel] nf grasshopper.

sautes [sot] nfpl (d'humeur, de température) sudden changes (de in).

sauvage [sovaʒ] a (primitif, cruel) savage; (farouche) unsociable, shy; (illégal) unauthorized; – nmf unsociable person; (brute) savage. ◆**sauvagerie** nf unsociability; (cruauté) savagery.

sauve [sov] a voir **sauf²**.

sauvegarde [sovgard] nf safeguard (contre against). ◆**sauvegarder** vt to safeguard.

sauver [sove] 1 vt to save; (d'un danger) to rescue (de from); (matériel) to salvage; **s. la vie à qn** to save s.o.'s life. 2 **se s.** vpr (s'enfuir) to run away ou off; (partir) Fam to get off, go. ◆**sauve-qui-peut** nm inv stampede. ◆**sauvetage** nm rescue; canot de s. lifeboat; ceinture de s. life belt; radeau de s. life raft. ◆**sauveteur** nm rescuer. ◆**sauveur** nm saviour.

sauvette (à la) [alasovet] adv vendre à la s. to hawk illicitly (on the streets).

savant [savã] a learned, scholarly; (manœuvre etc) masterly, clever; – nm scientist. ◆**savamment** adv learnedly; (avec habileté) cleverly, skilfully.

savate [savat] nf old shoe ou slipper.

saveur [savœr] nf (goût) flavour; (piment) Fig savour.

savoir° [savwar] vt to know; (nouvelle) to know, have heard; **j'ai su la nouvelle** I heard ou got to know the news; **s. lire/ nager/etc** (pouvoir) to know how to read/swim/etc; **faire s. à qn que** to inform ou tell s.o. that; **à s.** (c'est-à-dire) that is, namely; **je ne saurais pas** I could not, I cannot; **(pas) que je sache** (not) as far as I know; **je n'en sais rien** I have no idea, I don't know; **en s. long sur** to know a lot about; **un je ne sais quoi** a something or other; — *nm* (*culture*) learning, knowledge. ◆**s.-faire** *nm inv* know-how, ability. ◆**s.-vivre** *nm inv* good manners.

savon [savɔ̃] *nm* **1** soap; (*morceau*) bar of soap. **2 passer un s. à qn** (*réprimander*) *Fam* to give s.o. a dressing-down *ou* a talking-to. ◆**savonner** *vt* to soap. ◆**savonnette** *nf* bar of soap. ◆**savonneux, -euse** *a* soapy.

savourer [savure] *vt* to savour, relish. ◆**savoureux, -euse** *a* tasty; (*histoire etc*) *Fig* juicy.

saxophone [saksɔfɔn] *nm* saxophone.

sbire [sbir] *nm* (*homme de main*) *Péj* henchman.

scabreux, -euse [skabrø, -øz] *a* obscene.

scalpel [skalpɛl] *nm* scalpel.

scandale [skɑ̃dal] *nm* scandal; (*tapage*) uproar; **faire s.** (*livre etc*) to scandalize people; **faire un s.** to make a scene. ◆**scandaleux, -euse** *a* scandalous, outrageous. ◆**scandaleusement** *adv* outrageously. ◆**scandaliser** *vt* to scandalize, shock; — **se s.** *vpr* to be shocked *ou* scandalized (**de by, que** (+ *sub*) that).

scander [skɑ̃de] *vt* (*vers*) to scan; (*slogan*) to chant.

Scandinavie [skɑ̃dinavi] *nf* Scandinavia. ◆**scandinave** *a* & *nmf* Scandinavian.

scanner [skanɛr] *nm* (*appareil*) *Méd* scanner.

scaphandre [skafɑ̃dr] *nm* (*de plongeur*) diving suit; (*de cosmonaute*) spacesuit; **s. autonome** aqualung. ◆**scaphandrier** *nm* diver.

scarabée [skarabe] *nm* beetle.

scarlatine [skarlatin] *nf* scarlet fever.

scarole [skarɔl] *nf* endive.

sceau, -x [so] *nm* (*cachet, cire*) seal. ◆**scell/er** *vt* **1** (*document etc*) to seal. **2** (*fixer*) *Tech* to cement. ◆**—és** *nmpl* (*cachets de cire*) seals.

scélérat, -ate [selera, -at] *nmf* scoundrel.

scel-o-frais® [selɔfrɛ] *nm* clingfilm, *Am* plastic wrap.

scénario [senarjo] *nm* (*déroulement*) *Fig* scenario; (*esquisse*) *Cin* scenario; (*dialogues etc*) screenplay. ◆**scénariste** *nmf* *Cin* scriptwriter.

scène [sɛn] *nf* **1** *Th* scene; (*estrade, art*) stage; (*action*) action; **mettre en s.** (*pièce, film*) to direct. **2** (*dispute*) scene; **faire une s.** (à qn) to make *ou* create a scene; **s. de ménage** domestic quarrel.

scepticisme [sɛptism] *nm* scepticism, *Am* skepticism. ◆**sceptique** *a* sceptical, *Am* skeptical; — *nmf* sceptic, *Am* skeptic.

scheik [ʃɛk] *nm* sheikh.

schéma [ʃema] *nm* diagram; *Fig* outline. ◆**schématique** *a* diagrammatic; (*succinct*) *Péj* sketchy. ◆**schématiser** *vt* to represent diagrammatically; (*simplifier*) *Péj* to oversimplify.

schizophrène [skizɔfrɛn] *a* & *nmf* schizophrenic.

sciatique [sjatik] *nf Méd* sciatica.

scie [si] *nf* (*outil*) saw. ◆**scier** *vt* to saw. ◆**scierie** *nf* sawmill.

sciemment [sjamɑ̃] *adv* knowingly.

science [sjɑ̃s] *nf* science; (*savoir*) knowledge; (*habileté*) skill; **sciences humaines** social science(s); **étudier les sciences** to study science. ◆**s.-fiction** *nf* science fiction. ◆**scientifique** *a* scientific; — *nmf* scientist.

scinder [sɛ̃de] *vt*, — **se s.** *vpr* to divide, split.

scintill/er [sɛ̃tije] *vi* to sparkle, glitter; (*étoiles*) to twinkle. ◆**—ement** *nm* sparkling; twinkling.

scission [sisjɔ̃] *nf* (*de parti etc*) split (**de** in).

sciure [sjyr] *nf* sawdust.

sclérose [skleroz] *nf Méd* sclerosis; *Fig* ossification; **s. en plaques** multiple sclerosis. ◆**sclérosé** *a* (*société etc*) *Fig* ossified.

scolaire [skɔlɛr] *a* school-. ◆**scolariser** *vt* (*pays*) to provide with schools; (*enfant*) to send to school, put in school. ◆**scolarité** *nf* schooling.

scooter [skuter] *nm* (motor) scooter.

score [skɔr] *nm Sp* score.

scories [skɔri] *nfpl* (*résidu*) slag.

scorpion [skɔrpjɔ̃] *nm* scorpion; **le S.** (*signe*) Scorpio.

scotch [skɔtʃ] *nm* **1** (*boisson*) Scotch, whisky. **2**® (*ruban adhésif*) sellotape®, *Am* scotch (tape)®. ◆**scotcher** *vt* to sellotape, *Am* to tape.

scout [skut] *a* & *nm* scout. ◆**scoutisme** *nm* scout movement, scouting.

script [skript] *nm* (*écriture*) printing.

scrupule [skrypyl] *nm* scruple; **sans scrupules** unscrupulous; (*agir*) unscrupulously. ◆**scrupuleux, -euse** *a* scrupulous. ◆**scrupuleusement** *adv* scrupulously.

scruter [skryte] *vt* to examine, scrutinize.

scrutin [skrytɛ̃] *nm* (*vote*) ballot; (*opérations électorales*) poll(ing).

sculpter [skylte] *vt* to sculpt(ure), carve.

◆**sculpteur** *nm* sculptor. ◆**sculptural, -aux** *a* (*beauté*) statuesque. ◆**sculpture** *nf* (*art, œuvre*) sculpture; **s. sur bois** woodcarving.

se [s(ə)] (**s'** *before vowel or mute h*) *pron* **1** (*complément direct*) himself; (*sujet femelle*) herself; (*non humain*) itself; (*indéfini*) oneself; *pl* themselves; **il se lave** he washes himself. **2** (*indirect*) to himself; to herself; to itself; to oneself; **il se dit** he says to himself; **elle se dit** she says to herself. **3** (*réciproque*) each other, (to) one another; **ils s'aiment** they love each other *ou* one another; **ils** *ou* **elles se parlent** they speak to each other *ou* one another. **4** (*passif*) **ça se fait** that is done; **ça se vend bien** it sells well. **5** (*possessif*) **il se lave les mains** he washes his hands.

séance [seɑ̃s] *nf* **1** (*d'assemblée etc*) session, sitting; (*de travail etc*) session; **s. (de pose)** (*chez un peintre*) sitting. **2** *Cin Th* show, performance. **3 s. tenante** at once.

séant [seɑ̃] **1** *a* (*convenable*) seemly, proper. **2** *nm* **se mettre sur son s.** to sit up.

seau, -x [so] *nm* bucket, pail.

sec, sèche [sɛk, sɛʃ] *a* dry; (*fruits, légumes*) dried; (*ton*) curt, harsh; (*maigre*) spare; (*cœur*) *Fig* hard; **coup s. sharp** blow, tap; **bruit s.** (*rupture*) snap; – *adv* (*frapper, pleuvoir*) hard; (*boire*) neat, straight; – *nm* **à s.** dried up, dry; (*sans argent*) *Fam* broke; **au s.** in a dry place. ◆**séch/er** *vti* to dry; – **se s.** *vpr* to dry oneself. **2** *vt* (*cours*) *Scol Fam* to skip; – *vi* (*ignorer*) *Scol Fam* to be stumped. ◆**—age** *nm* drying. ◆**sécheresse** *nf* dryness; (*de ton*) curtness; *Mét* drought. ◆**séchoir** *nm* (*appareil*) drier; **s. à linge** clotheshorse.

sécateur [sekatœr] *nm* pruning shears, secateurs.

sécession [sesesjɔ̃] *nf* secession; **faire s.** to secede.

sèche [sɛʃ] *voir* **sec.** ◆**sèche-cheveux** *nm inv* hair drier. ◆**sèche-linge** *nm inv* tumble drier.

second, -onde [səgɔ̃, -ɔ̃d] *a & nmf* second; **de seconde main** second-hand; – *nm* (*adjoint*) second in command; (*étage*) second floor, *Am* third floor; – *nf Rail* second class; *Scol* = fifth form, *Am* = eleventh grade; (*vitesse*) *Aut* second (gear). ◆**secondaire** *a* secondary.

seconde[2] [səgɔ̃d] *nf* (*instant*) second.

seconder [səgɔ̃de] *vt* to assist.

secouer [s(ə)kwe] *vt* to shake; (*paresse, poussière*) to shake off; **s. qn** (*maladie, nouvelle etc*) to shake s.o. up; **s. qch de qch**

(*enlever*) to shake sth out of sth; – **se s.** *vpr* (*faire un effort*) *Fam* to shake oneself out of it.

secour/ir [skurir] *vt* to assist, help. ◆**—able** *a* (*personne*) helpful. ◆**secourisme** *nm* first aid. ◆**secouriste** *nmf* first-aid worker.

secours [s(ə)kur] *nm* assistance, help; (*aux indigents*) aid, relief; **le s., les s.** *Mil* relief; (*premiers*) **s.** *Méd* first aid; **au s.!** help!; **porter s. à qn** to give s.o. assistance *ou* help; **de s.** (*sortie*) emergency-; (*équipe*) rescue-; (*roue*) spare.

secousse [s(ə)kus] *nf* jolt, jerk; (*psychologique*) shock; *Géol* tremor.

secret, -ète [sakrɛ, -ɛt] *a* secret; (*cachottier*) secretive; – *nm* secret; (*discrétion*) secrecy; **en s.** in secret, secretly; **dans le s.** (*au courant*) in on the secret.

secrétaire [səkretɛr] **1** *nmf* secretary; **s. d'État** Secretary of State; **s. de mairie** town clerk; **s. de rédaction** subeditor. **2** *nm* (*meuble*) writing desk. ◆**secrétariat** *nm* (*bureau*) secretary's office; (*d'organisation internationale*) secretariat; (*métier*) secretarial work; **de s.** (*école, travail*) secretarial.

sécréter [sekrete] *vt Méd Biol* to secrete. ◆**sécrétion** *nf* secretion.

secte [sɛkt] *nf* sect. ◆**sectaire** *a & nmf Péj* sectarian.

secteur [sektœr] *nm Mil Com* sector; (*de ville*) district; (*domaine*) *Fig* area; (*de réseau*) *Él* supply area; (*ligne*) *Él* mains.

section [sɛksjɔ̃] *nf* section; (*de ligne d'autobus*) fare stage; *Mil* platoon. ◆**sectionner** *vt* to divide (into sections); (*artère, doigt*) to sever.

séculaire [sekylɛr] *a* (*tradition etc*) age-old.

secundo [s(ə)gɔ̃do] *adv* secondly.

sécurité [sekyrite] *nf* (*tranquillité*) security; (*matérielle*) safety; **s. routière** road safety; **s. sociale** = social services *ou* security; **de s.** (*dispositif, ceinture, marge etc*) safety-; **en s.** secure; safe. ◆**sécuriser** *vt* to reassure, make feel (emotionally) secure.

sédatif [sedatif] *nm* sedative.

sédentaire [sedɑ̃tɛr] *a* sedentary.

sédiment [sedimɑ̃] *nm* sediment.

séditieux, -euse [sedisjø, -øz] *a* seditious. ◆**sédition** *nf* sedition.

séduire* [seduir] *vt* to charm, attract; (*plaire à*) to appeal to; (*abuser de*) to seduce. ◆**séduisant** *a* attractive. ◆**séducteur, -trice** *a* seductive; – *nmf* seducer. ◆**séduction** *nf* attraction.

segment [segmɑ̃] *nm* segment.

ségrégation [segregasjɔ̃] *nf* segregation.

seiche [sɛʃ] nf cuttlefish.

seigle [sɛgl] nm rye.

seigneur [sɛɲœr] nm Hist lord; S. Rel Lord.

sein [sɛ̃] nm (mamelle, poitrine) breast; Fig bosom; **bout de s.** nipple; **au s. de** (parti etc) within; (bonheur etc) in the midst of.

Seine [sɛn] nf la S. the Seine.

séisme [seism] nm earthquake.

seize [sɛz] a & nm sixteen. ◆**seizième** a & nmf sixteenth.

séjour [seʒur] nm stay; (salle de) s. living room. ◆**séjourner** vi to stay.

sel [sɛl] nm salt; (piquant) Fig spice; (humour) wit; pl Méd (smelling) salts; **sels de bain** bath salts.

sélect [selɛkt] a Fam select.

sélectif, -ive [selɛktif, -iv] a selective. ◆**sélection** nf selection. ◆**sélectionner** vt to select.

self(-service) [sɛlf(sɛrvis)] nm self-service restaurant ou shop.

selle [sɛl] 1 nf (de cheval) saddle. 2 nfpl les **selles** Méd bowel movements, stools. ◆**seller** vt (cheval) to saddle.

sellette [selɛt] nf sur la s. (personne) under examination, in the hot seat.

selon [s(ə)lɔ̃] prép according to (que whether); **c'est s.** Fam it (all) depends.

Seltz (eau de) [odsɛls] nf soda (water).

semailles [s(ə)mɑj] nfpl (travail) sowing; (période) seedtime.

semaine [s(ə)mɛn] nf week; **en s.** (opposé à week-end) in the week.

sémantique [semɑ̃tik] a semantic; – nf semantics.

sémaphore [semafɔr] nm (appareil) Rail Nau semaphore.

semblable [sɑ̃blabl] a similar (à to); **être semblables** to be alike ou similar; **de semblables propos**/etc (tels) such remarks/etc; – nm fellow (creature); **toi et tes semblables** you and your kind.

semblant [sɑ̃blɑ̃] nm **faire s.** to pretend (**de faire** to do); **un s. de** a semblance of.

sembler [sɑ̃ble] vi to seem (à to); **il (me) semble vieux** he seems ou looks old (to me); **s. être/faire** to seem to be/to do; – v imp **il semble que** (+ sub ou indic) it seems that, it looks as if; **il me semble que** it seems to me that, I think that.

semelle [s(ə)mɛl] nf (de chaussure) sole; (intérieure) insole.

semer [s(ə)me] vt 1 (graines) to sow; (jeter) Fig to strew; (répandre) to spread; **semé de** Fig strewn with, dotted with. 2 (concurrent, poursuivant) to shake off. ◆**semence** nf

seed; (clou) tack. ◆**semeur, -euse** nmf sower (**de** of).

semestre [s(ə)mɛstr] nm half-year; Univ semester. ◆**semestriel, -ielle** a half-yearly.

semi- [səmi] préf semi-.

séminaire [seminɛr] nm 1 Univ seminar. 2 Rel seminary.

semi-remorque [səmirəmɔrk] nm (camion) articulated lorry, Am semi(trailer).

semis [s(ə)mi] nm sowing; (terrain) seedbed; (plant) seedling.

sémite [semit] a Semitic; – nmf Semite. ◆**sémitique** a (langue) Semitic.

semonce [səmɔ̃s] nf reprimand; **coup de s.** Nau warning shot.

semoule [s(ə)mul] nf semolina.

sempiternel, -elle [sɑ̃piternɛl] a endless, ceaseless.

sénat [sena] nm Pol senate. ◆**sénateur** nm Pol senator.

sénile [senil] a senile. ◆**sénilité** nf senility.

sens [sɑ̃s] nm 1 (faculté, raison) sense; (signification) meaning, sense; **à mon s.** to my mind; **s. commun** commonsense; **s. de l'humour** sense of humour; **ça n'a pas de s.** that doesn't make sense. 2 (direction) direction; **s. giratoire** Aut roundabout, Am traffic circle, rotary; **s. interdit** ou **unique** (rue) one-way street; 's. interdit' 'no entry'; **à s. unique** (rue) one-way; **s. dessus dessous** [sɑ̃dsydsu] upside down; **dans le s./le s. inverse des aiguilles d'une montre** clockwise/anticlockwise, Am counterclockwise.

sensation [sɑ̃sasjɔ̃] nf sensation, feeling; **faire s.** to cause ou create a sensation; **à s.** (film etc) Péj sensational. ◆**sensationnel, -elle** a Fig sensational.

sensé [sɑ̃se] a sensible.

sensible [sɑ̃sibl] a sensitive (à to); (douloureux) tender, sore; (perceptible) perceptible; (progrès etc) appreciable. ◆**sensiblement** adv (notablement) appreciably; (à peu près) more or less. ◆**sensibiliser** vt s. qn à (problème etc) to make s.o. alive to ou aware of. ◆**sensibilité** nf sensitivity.

sensoriel, -ielle [sɑ̃sɔrjɛl] a sensory.

sensuel, -elle [sɑ̃sɥɛl] a (sexuel) sensual; (musique, couleur etc) sensuous. ◆**sensualité** nf sensuality; sensuousness.

sentence [sɑ̃tɑ̃s] nf 1 Jur sentence. 2 (maxime) maxim.

senteur [sɑ̃tœr] nf (odeur) scent.

sentier [sɑ̃tje] nm path.

sentiment [sɑ̃timɑ̃] nm feeling; **avoir le s. de** (apprécier) to be aware of; **faire du s.** to be sentimental. ◆**sentimental, -aux** a sentimental; (*amoureux*) love-. ◆**sentimenta-lité** *nf* sentimentality.

sentinelle [sɑ̃tinɛl] *nf* sentry.

sentir* [sɑ̃tir] *vt* to feel; (*odeur*) to smell; (*goût*) to taste; (*racisme etc*) to smack of; (*connaître*) to sense, be conscious of; **le moisi/le parfum**/*etc* to smell musty/of perfume/*etc*; **s. le poisson**/*etc* (*avoir le goût de*) to taste of fish/*etc*; **je ne peux pas le s.** (*supporter*) *Fam* I can't bear ou stand him; **se faire s.** (*effet etc*) to make itself felt; **se s. fatigué/humilié**/*etc* to feel tired/humiliated/*etc*; – *vi* to smell.

séparation [separasjɔ̃] *nf* separation; (*en deux*) division, split; (*départ*) parting. ◆**séparer** *vt* to separate (*de* from); (*diviser en deux*) to divide, split (up); (*cheveux*) to part; — **se s.** *vpr* (*se quitter*) to part; (*adversaires, époux*) to separate; (*assemblée, cortège*) to disperse, break up; (*se détacher*) to split off; **se s. de** (*objet aimé, chien etc*) to part with. ◆**séparé** *a* (*distinct*) separate; (*époux*) separated (*de* from). ◆**séparément** *adv* separately.

sept [sɛt] *a & nm* seven. ◆**septième** *a & nmf* seventh; **un s.** a seventh.

septante [sɛptɑ̃t] *a & nm* (*en Belgique, Suisse*) seventy.

septembre [sɛptɑ̃br] *nm* September.

septennat [sɛptena] *nm Pol* seven-year term (of office).

septentrional, -aux [sɛptɑ̃trijɔnal, -o] *a* northern.

sépulcre [sepylkr] *nm Rel* sepulchre.

sépulture [sepyltyr] *nf* burial; (*lieu*) burial place.

séquelles [sekɛl] *nfpl* (*de maladie etc*) after-effects; (*de guerre*) aftermath.

séquence [sekɑ̃s] *nf Mus Cartes Cin* sequence.

séquestrer [sekɛstre] *vt* to confine (illegally), lock up.

sera, serait [s(ə)ra, s(ə)rɛ] *voir* être.

serein [sərɛ̃] *a* serene. ◆**sérénité** *nf* serenity.

sérénade [serenad] *nf* serenade.

sergent [sɛrʒɑ̃] *nm Mil* sergeant.

série [seri] *nf* series; (*ensemble*) set; **s. noire** *Fig* string ou series of disasters; **de s.** (*article etc*) standard; **fabrication en s.** mass production; **fins de s.** *Com* oddments; **hors s.** *Fig* outstanding.

sérieux, -euse [serjø, -øz] *a* (*personne, maladie, doute etc*) serious; (*de bonne foi*) genuine, serious; (*digne de foi, fiable*) reliable; (*bénéfices*) substantial; **de sérieuses chances de . . .** a good chance of . . . ; –

nm seriousness; (*fiabilité*) reliability; **prendre au s.** to take seriously; **garder son s.** to keep a straight face; **manquer de s.** (*travailleur*) to lack application. ◆**sérieusement** *adv* seriously; (*travailler*) conscientiously.

serin [s(ə)rɛ̃] *nm* canary.

seriner [s(ə)rine] *vt* **s. qch à qn** to repeat sth to s.o. over and over again.

seringue [s(ə)rɛ̃g] *nf* syringe.

serment [sɛrmɑ̃] *nm* (*affirmation solennelle*) oath; (*promesse*) pledge; **prêter s.** to take an oath; **faire le s. de faire** to swear to do; **sous s.** *Jur* on ou under oath.

sermon [sɛrmɔ̃] *nm Rel* sermon; (*discours*) *Péj* lecture. ◆**sermonner** *vt* (*faire la morale à*) to lecture.

serpe [sɛrp] *nf* bill(hook).

serpent [sɛrpɑ̃] *nm* snake; **s. à sonnette** rattlesnake.

serpenter [sɛrpɑ̃te] *vi* (*sentier etc*) to meander.

serpentin [sɛrpɑ̃tɛ̃] *nm* (*ruban*) streamer.

serpillière [sɛrpijɛr] *nf* floor cloth.

serre [sɛr] **1** *nf* greenhouse. **2** *nfpl* (*d'oiseau*) claws, talons.

serre-livres [sɛrlivr] *nm inv* bookend. ◆**s.-tête** *nm inv* (*bandeau*) headband.

serr/er [sere] *vt* (*saisir, tenir*) to grip, clasp; (*presser*) to squeeze, press; (*corde, nœud, vis*) to tighten; (*poing*) to clench; (*taille*) to hug; (*pieds*) to pinch; (*frein*) to apply, put on; (*rapprocher*) to close up; (*rangs*) *Mil* to close; **s. la main à** to shake hands with; **s. les dents** *Fig* to grit one's teeth; **s. qn** (*embrasser*) to hug s.o.; (*vêtement*) to be too tight for s.o.; **s. qn de près** (*talonner*) to be close behind s.o.; – *vi* **s. à droite** *Aut* to keep (to the) right; — **se s.** *vpr* (*se rapprocher*) to squeeze up ou together; **se s. contre** to squeeze up against. ◆**-é** *a* (*budget, nœud, vêtement*) tight; (*gens*) packed (together); (*mailles, lutte*) close; (*rangs*) serried; (*dense*) dense, thick; (*cœur*) *Fig* heavy; **avoir la gorge serrée** *Fig* to have a lump in one's throat.

serrure [seryr] *nf* lock. ◆**serrurier** *nm* locksmith.

sertir [sertir] *vt* (*diamant etc*) to set.

sérum [serɔm] *nm* serum.

servante [sɛrvɑ̃t] *nf* (*maid*)servant.

serveur, -euse [sɛrvœr, -øz] *nmf* waiter, waitress; (*au bar*) barman, barmaid.

serviable [sɛrvjabl] *a* helpful, obliging. ◆**serviabilité** *nf* helpfulness.

service [sɛrvis] *nm* service; (*fonction, travail*) duty; (*pourboire*) service (charge); (*département*) *Com* department; *Tennis* serve, service; **un s.** (*aide*) a favour; **rendre s.** to be of service (**à qn** to s.o.), help (**à qn** s.o.); **rendre un mauvais s. à qn** to do s.o. a disservice; **ça pourrait rendre s.** *Fam* that might come in useful; **s. (non) compris** service (not) included; **s. après-vente** *Com* aftersales (service); **s. d'ordre** (*policiers*) police; **être de s.** to be on duty; **s. à café/à thé** coffee/tea service *ou* set; **à votre s.!** at your service!

serviette [sɛrvjɛt] *nf* **1** towel; **s. de bain/de toilette** bath/hand towel; **s. hygiénique** sanitary towel; **s. (de table)** serviette, napkin. **2** (*sac*) briefcase.

servile [sɛrvil] *a* (*imitation*) slavish. ◆**servilité** *nf* servility; slavishness.

servir° [sɛrvir] **1** *vt* to serve (**qch à qn** s.o. with sth, sth to s.o.); (*convive*) to wait on; — *vi* to serve; — **se s.** *vpr* (*à table*) to help oneself (**de** to). **2** *vi* (*être utile*) to be useful, serve; **s. à qch/à faire** (*objet*) to be used for sth/to do *ou* for doing *etc*; **ça ne sert à rien** it's useless, it's no good *ou* use (**de faire** doing); **à quoi ça sert de protester/***etc* what's the use *ou* good of protesting/*etc*; **s. de qch** (*objet*) to be used for sth, serve as sth; **ça me sert à faire/de qch** it's used for *ou* for doing/as sth; **s. à qn de guide/***etc* to act as a guide/*etc* to s.o. **3 se s.** *vpr* **se s. de** (*utiliser*) to use.

serviteur [sɛrvitœr] *nm* servant. ◆**servitude** *nf* (*esclavage*) servitude; (*contrainte*) *Fig* constraint.

ses [se] *voir* **son²**.

session [sesjɔ̃] *nf* session.

set [sɛt] *nm* **1** *Tennis* set. **2 s. (de table)** (*napperon*) place mat.

seuil [sœj] *nm* doorstep; (*entrée*) doorway; (*limite*) *Fig* threshold; **au s. de** *Fig* on the threshold of.

seul, seule [sœl] *a* **1** (*sans compagnie*) alone; **tout s.** all alone, by oneself, on one's own; **se sentir s.** to feel lonely *ou* alone; — *adv* (*tout*) **s.** (*agir, vivre*) by oneself, alone, on one's own; (*parler*) to oneself; **s. à s.** (*parler*) in private. **2** *a* (*unique*) only; **la seule femme/***etc* the only *ou* sole woman/*etc*; **un s. chat/***etc* only one cat/*etc*; **une seule fois** only once; **pas un s. livre/***etc* not a single book/*etc*; **seuls les garçons** ... only the boys ...; **les garçons seuls** ... only the boys ...; — *nmf* **la s., le seul** the only one; **un s., une seule** only one, one only; **pas un s.** not (a single) one. ◆**seulement** *adv* only; **non s.** ... **mais** ... not only ... but (also) ...; **pas s.** (*même*) not even; **sans s. faire** without even doing.

sève [sɛv] *nf* *Bot* & *Fig* sap.

sévère [sever] *a* severe; (*parents, professeur*) strict. ◆**—ment** *adv* severely; (*élever*) strictly. ◆**sévérité** *nf* severity; strictness.

sévices [sevis] *nmpl* brutality.

sévir [sevir] *vi* (*fléau*) *Fig* to rage; **s. contre** to deal severely with.

sevrer [səvre] *vt* (*enfant*) to wean; **s. de** (*priver*) *Fig* to deprive of.

sexe [sɛks] *nm* (*catégorie, sexualité*) sex; (*organes*) genitals; **l'autre s.** the opposite sex. ◆**sexiste** *a* & *nmf* sexist. ◆**sexualité** *nf* sexuality. ◆**sexuel, -elle** *a* sexual; (*éducation, acte etc*) sex-.

sextuor [sɛkstɥɔr] *nm* sextet.

seyant [sejɑ̃] *a* (*vêtement*) becoming.

shampooing [ʃɑ̃pwɛ̃] *nm* shampoo; **s. colorant** rinse; **faire un s. à qn** to shampoo s.o.'s hair.

shérif [ʃerif] *nm* sheriff.

shooter [ʃute] *vti Fb* to shoot.

short [ʃɔrt] *nm* (pair of) shorts.

si [si] **1** (= **s'** [s] *before* **il, ils**) *conj* if; **s'il vient** if he comes; **si j'étais roi** if I were *ou* was king; **je me demande si** I wonder whether *ou* if; **si on restait?** (*suggestion*) what if we stayed?; **si je dis ça, c'est que** ... I say this because ...; **si ce n'est** (*sinon*) if not; **si oui** if so. **2** *adv* (*tellement*) so; **pas si riche que toi/que tu crois** not as rich as you/as you think; **un si bon dîner** such a good dinner; **si grand qu'il soit** however big he may be; **si bien que** with the result that. **3** *adv* (*après négative*) yes; **tu ne viens pas? – si!** you're not coming? – yes (I am!)

siamois [sjamwa] *a* Siamese; **frères s., sœurs siamoises** Siamese twins.

Sicile [sisil] *nf* Sicily.

SIDA [sida] *nm Méd* AIDS. ◆**sidéen, -enne** *nmf* AIDS sufferer.

sidérer [sidere] *vt Fam* to flabbergast.

sidérurgie [sideryrʒi] *nf* iron and steel industry.

siècle [sjɛkl] *nm* century; (*époque*) age.

siège [sjɛʒ] *nm* **1** seat; (*meuble, centre*) & *Pol* seat; (*d'autorité, de parti*) headquarters; **s. (social)** (*d'entreprise*) head office. **2** *Mil* siege; **mettre le s. devant** to lay siege to. ◆**siéger** *vi Pol* to sit.

sien, sienne [sjɛ̃, sjɛn] *pron poss* **le s., la sienne**, **les sien(ne)s** his; (*de femme*) hers; (*de chose*) its; **les deux siens** his *ou* her two; — *nmpl* **les siens** (*amis etc*) one's (own) people.

sieste [sjɛst] *nf* siesta; **faire la s.** to have *ou* take a nap.

siffler [sifle] *vi* to whistle; (*avec un sifflet*) to

blow one's whistle; (gaz, serpent) to hiss; (en respirant) to wheeze; – vt (chanson) to whistle; (chien) to whistle to; (faute, fin de match) Sp to blow one's whistle for; (acteur, pièce) to boo; (boisson) Fam to knock back. ◆sifflement nm whistling, whistle; hiss(ing). ◆sifflet nm (instrument) whistle; pl Th booing, boos; (coup de) s. (son) whistle. ◆siffloter vti to whistle.

sigle [sigl] nm (initiales) abbreviation; (prononcé comme un mot) acronym.

signal, -aux [sinal, -o] nm signal; s. d'alarme Rail communication cord; signaux routiers road signs. ◆signal/er 1 vt (faire remarquer) to point out (à qn to s.o., que that); (annoncer, indiquer) to indicate, signal; (dénoncer à la police etc) to report (à to). 2 se s. vpr se s. par to distinguish oneself by. ◆—ement nm (de personne) description, particulars. ◆signalisation nf signalling; Aut signposting; s. (routière) (signaux) road signs.

signature [sinatyr] nf signature; (action) signing. ◆signataire nmf signatory.◆signer 1 vt to sign. 2 se s. vpr Rel to cross oneself.

signe [sin] nm (indice) sign, indication; s. particulier/de ponctuation distinguishing/punctuation mark; faire s. à qn (geste) to motion to ou beckon s.o. (de faire to do); (contacter) to get in touch with s.o.; faire s. que oui to nod (one's head); faire s. que non to shake one's head.

signet [sine] nm bookmark.

signification [sinifikasjɔ̃] nf meaning. ◆significatif, -ive a significant, meaningful; s. de indicative of. ◆signifier vt to mean, signify (que that); s. qch à qn (faire connaître) to make sth known to s.o., signify sth to s.o.

silence [silɑ̃s] nm silence; Mus rest; en s. in silence; garder le s. to keep quiet ou silent (sur about). ◆silencieux, -euse 1 a silent. 2 nm Aut silencer, Am muffler; (d'arme) silencer. ◆silencieusement adv silently.

silex [sileks] nm (roche) flint.

silhouette [silwɛt] nf outline; (en noir) silhouette; (ligne du corps) figure.

silicium [silisjɔm] nm silicon. ◆silicone nf silicone.

sillage [sijaʒ] nm (de bateau) wake; dans le s. de Fig in the wake of.

sillon [sijɔ̃] nm furrow; (de disque) groove.

sillonner [sijɔne] vt (traverser) to cross; (en tous sens) to criss-cross.

silo [silo] nm silo.

simagrées [simagre] nfpl airs (and graces); (cérémonies) fuss.

similaire [similɛr] a similar. ◆similitude nf similarity.

similicuir [similikɥir] nm imitation leather.

simple [sɛ̃pl] a simple; (non multiple) single; (employé, particulier) ordinary; – nmf s. d'esprit simpleton; – nm Tennis singles. ◆simplement adv simply. ◆simplet, -ette a (personne) a bit simple. ◆simplicité nf simplicity. ◆simplification nf simplification. ◆simplifier vt to simplify. ◆simpliste a simplistic.

simulacre [simylakr] nm un s. de Péj a pretence of.

simuler [simyle] vt to simulate; (feindre) to feign. ◆simulateur, -trice 1 nmf (hypocrite) shammer; (tire-au-flanc) & Mil malingerer. 2 nm (appareil) simulator. ◆simulation nf simulation; feigning.

simultané [simyltane] a simultaneous. ◆—ment adv simultaneously.

sincère [sɛ̃sɛr] a sincere. ◆sincèrement adv sincerely. ◆sincérité nf sincerity.

sinécure [sinekyr] nf sinecure.

singe [sɛ̃ʒ] nm monkey, ape. ◆singer vt (imiter) to ape, mimic. ◆singeries nfpl antics, clowning.

singulariser (se) [səsɛ̃gylarize] vpr to draw attention to oneself.

singulier, -ière [sɛ̃gylje, -jɛr] 1 a peculiar, odd. 2 a & nm Gram singular. ◆singularité nf peculiarity. ◆singulièrement adv (notamment) particularly; (beaucoup) extremely.

sinistre [sinistr] 1 a (effrayant) sinister. 2 nm disaster; (incendie) fire; (dommage) Jur damage. ◆sinistré, -ée a (population, région) disaster-stricken; – nmf disaster victim.

sinon [sinɔ̃] conj (autrement) otherwise, or else; (sauf) except (que that); (si ce n'est) if not.

sinueux, -euse [sinɥø, -øz] a winding. ◆sinuosités nfpl twists (and turns).

sinus [sinys] nm inv Anat sinus.

siphon [sifɔ̃] nm siphon; (d'évier) trap, U-bend.

sirène [siren] nf 1 (d'usine etc) siren. 2 (femme) mermaid.

sirop [siro] nm syrup; (à diluer, boisson) (fruit) cordial; s. contre la toux cough mixture ou syrup.

siroter [sirɔte] vt Fam to sip (at).

sis [si] a Jur situated.

sismique [sismik] a seismic; **secousse s.** earth tremor.

site [sit] nm (endroit) site; (environnement) setting; (pittoresque) beauty spot; **s. (touristique)** (monument etc) place of interest.

sitôt [sito] adv **s. que** as soon as; **s. levée, elle partit** as soon as she was up, she left; **s. après** immediately after; **pas de s.** not for some time.

situation [situasjɔ̃] nf situation, position; (emploi) position; **s. de famille** marital status. ◆**situ/er** vt to situate, locate; **— se s.** vpr (se trouver) to be situated. ◆**-é** a (maison etc) situated.

six [sis] ([si] before consonant, [siz] before vowel) a & nm six. ◆**sixième** a & nmf sixth; **un s.** a sixth.

sketch [skɛtʃ] nm (pl **sketches**) Th sketch.

ski [ski] nm (objet) ski; (sport) skiing; **faire du s.** to ski; **s. nautique** water skiing. ◆**ski/er** vi to ski. ◆**-eur, -euse** nmf skier.

slalom [slalɔm] nm Sp slalom.

slave [slav] a Slav; (langue) Slavonic; **— nmf** Slav.

slip [slip] nm (d'homme) briefs, (under)pants; (de femme) panties, knickers; **s. de bain** (swimming) trunks; (d'un bikini) briefs.

slogan [slɔgɑ̃] nm slogan.

SMIC [smik] nm abrév (salaire minimum interprofessionnel de croissance) minimum wage.

smoking [smɔkiŋ] nm (veston, costume) dinner jacket, Am tuxedo.

snack(-bar) [snak(bar)] nm snack bar.

SNCF [ɛsɛnseɛf] nf abrév (Société nationale des Chemins de fer français) French railways.

snob [snɔb] nmf snob; **— a** snobbish. ◆**snober** vt **s. qn** to snub s.o. ◆**snobisme** nm snobbery.

sobre [sɔbr] a sober. ◆**sobriété** nf sobriety.

sobriquet [sɔbrikɛ] nm nickname.

sociable [sɔsjabl] a sociable. ◆**sociabilité** nf sociability.

social, -aux [sɔsjal, -o] a social. ◆**socialisme** nm socialism. ◆**socialiste** a & nmf socialist.

société [sɔsjete] nf society; (compagnie) & Com company; **s. anonyme** Com (public) limited company, Am incorporated company. ◆**sociétaire** nmf (d'une association) member.

sociologie [sɔsjɔlɔʒi] nf sociology.

◆**sociologique** a sociological. ◆**sociologue** nmf sociologist.

socle [sɔkl] nm (de statue, colonne) plinth, pedestal; (de lampe) base.

socquette [sɔkɛt] nf ankle sock.

soda [sɔda] nm (à l'orange etc) fizzy drink, Am soda (pop).

sœur [sœr] nf sister; Rel nun, sister.

sofa [sɔfa] nm sofa, settee.

soi [swa] pron oneself; **chacun pour s.** every man for himself; **en s.** in itself; **cela va de s.** it's self-evident (que that); **amour/conscience de s.** self-love/-awareness. ◆**s.-même** pron oneself.

soi-disant [swadizɑ̃] a inv so-called; **— adv** supposedly.

soie [swa] nf **1** silk. **2** (de porc etc) bristle. ◆**soierie** nf (tissu) silk.

soif [swaf] nf thirst; (Fig de for); **avoir s.** to be thirsty; **donner s. à qn** to make s.o. thirsty.

soign/er [swaɲe] vt to look after, take care of; (malade) to tend, nurse; (maladie) to treat; (détails, présentation, travail) to take care over; **se faire s.** to have (medical) treatment; **— se s.** vpr to take care of oneself, look after oneself. ◆**-é** a (personne) well-groomed; (vêtement) neat, tidy; (travail) careful. ◆**soigneux, -euse** a careful (de with); (propre) tidy, neat. ◆**soigneusement** adv carefully.

soin [swɛ̃] nm care; (ordre) tidiness, neatness; pl care; Méd treatment; **avoir** ou **prendre s. de qch/de faire** to take care of sth/to do; **les premiers soins** first aid; **soins de beauté** beauty care ou treatment; **aux bons soins de** (sur lettre) care of, c/o; **avec s.** carefully, with care.

soir [swar] nm evening; **le s.** (chaque soir) in the evening; **à neuf heures du s.** at nine in the evening; **du s.** (repas, robe etc) evening-. ◆**soirée** nf evening; (réunion) party; **s. dansante** dance.

soit 1 [swa] voir **être**. **2** [swa] conj (à savoir) that is (to say); **s. ... s. ...** either ... or ... **3** [swat] adv (oui) very well.

soixante [swasɑ̃t] a & nm sixty. ◆**soixantaine** nf **une s. (de)** (nombre) (about) sixty; **avoir la s.** (âge) to be about sixty. ◆**soixante-dix** a & nm seventy. ◆**soixante-dixième** a & nmf seventieth. ◆**soixantième** a & nmf sixtieth.

soja [sɔʒa] nm (plante) soya; **graine de s.** soya bean; **germes** ou **pousses de s.** bean-sprouts.

sol [sɔl] nm ground; (plancher) floor; (matière, territoire) soil.

solaire [sɔlɛr] *a* solar; (*chaleur, rayons*) sun's; (*crème, filtre*) sun-; (*lotion, huile*) suntan-.

soldat [sɔlda] *nm* soldier; **simple s.** private.

solde [sɔld] **1** *nm* (*de compte, à payer*) balance. **2** *nm* **en s.** (*acheter*) at sale price, *Am* on sale; *pl* (*marchandises*) sale goods; (*vente*) (clearance) sale(s). **3** *nf Mil* pay; **à la s. de** *Fig Péj* in s.o.'s pay. ◆**sold/er 1** *vt* (*articles*) to sell off, clear. **2** *vt* (*compte*) to pay the balance of. **3 se s.** *vpr* **se s. par** (*un échec, une défaite etc*) to end in. ◆**—é a** (*article*) reduced. ◆**solderie** *nf* discount *ou* reject shop.

sole [sɔl] *nf* (*poisson*) sole.

soleil [sɔlɛj] *nm* sun; (*chaleur, lumière*) sunshine; (*fleur*) sunflower; **au s.** in the sun; **il fait (du) s.** it's sunny, the sun's shining; **prendre un bain de s.** to sunbathe; **coup de s.** *Méd* sunburn.

solennel, -elle [sɔlanɛl] *a* solemn. ◆**solennellement** *adv* solemnly. ◆**solennité** [-anite] *nf* solemnity.

solex ® [sɔlɛks] *nm* moped.

solfège [sɔlfɛʒ] *nm* rudiments of music.

solidaire [sɔlidɛr] *a* **être s.** (*ouvriers etc*) to be as one, show solidarity (**de** with); (*pièce de machine*) to be interdependent (**de** with). ◆**solidairement** *adv* jointly. ◆**se solidariser** *vpr* to show solidarity (**avec** with). ◆**solidarité** *nf* solidarity; (*d'éléments*) interdependence.

solide [sɔlid] *a* (*voiture, nourriture, caractère etc*) & *Ch* solid; (*argument, qualité, raison*) sound; (*vigoureux*) robust; – *nm Ch* solid. ◆**solidement** *adv* solidly. ◆**se solidifier** *vpr* to solidify. ◆**solidité** *nf* solidity; (*d'argument etc*) soundness.

soliste [sɔlist] *nmf Mus* soloist.

solitaire [sɔlitɛr] *a* solitary; – *nmf* loner; (*ermite*) recluse, hermit; **en s.** on one's own. ◆**solitude** *nf* solitude.

solive [sɔliv] *nf* joist, beam.

solliciter [sɔlisite] *vt* (*audience, emploi etc*) to seek; (*tenter*) to tempt, entice; **s.** *qn* (*faire appel à*) to appeal to s.o. (**de faire** to do); **être (très) sollicité** (*personne*) to be in (great) demand. ◆**sollicitation** *nf* (*demande*) appeal; (*tentation*) temptation.

sollicitude [sɔlisityd] *nf* solicitude, concern.

solo [sɔlo] *a inv* & *nm Mus* solo.

solstice [sɔlstis] *nm* solstice.

soluble [sɔlybl] *a* (*substance, problème*) soluble; (*café*) instant coffee. ◆**solution** *nf* (*d'un problème etc*) & *Ch* solution (**de** to).

solvable [sɔlvabl] *a Fin* solvent. ◆**solvabilité** *nf Fin* solvency.

solvant [sɔlvã] *nm Ch* solvent.

sombre [sɔ̃br] *a* dark; (*triste*) sombre, gloomy; **il fait s.** it's dark.

sombrer [sɔ̃bre] *vi* (*bateau*) to sink, founder; **s. dans** (*folie, sommeil etc*) to sink into.

sommaire [sɔmɛr] *a* summary; (*repas, tenue*) scant; – *nm* summary, synopsis.

sommation [sɔmasjɔ̃] *nf Jur* summons; (*de sentinelle etc*) warning.

somme [sɔm] **1** *nf* sum; **faire la s. de** to add up; **en s., s. toute** in short. **2** *nm* (*sommeil*) nap; **faire un s.** to have *ou* take a nap.

sommeil [sɔmɛj] *nm* sleep; (*envie de dormir*) sleepiness, drowsiness; **avoir s.** to be *ou* feel sleepy *ou* drowsy. ◆**sommeiller** *vi* to doze; (*faculté, qualité*) *Fig* to slumber.

sommelier [sɔməlje] *nm* wine waiter.

sommer [sɔme] *vt* **s. qn de faire** (*enjoindre*) & *Jur* to summon s.o. to.

sommes [sɔm] *voir* **être**.

sommet [sɔmɛ] *nm* top; (*de montagne*) summit, top; (*de la gloire etc*) *Fig* height, summit; **conférence au s.** summit (conference).

sommier [sɔmje] *nm* (*de lit*) base; **s. à ressorts** spring base.

sommité [sɔmite] *nf* leading light, top person (**de** in).

somnambule [sɔmnɑ̃byl] *nmf* sleepwalker; **être s.** to sleepwalk. ◆**somnambulisme** *nm* sleepwalking.

somnifère [sɔmnifɛr] *nm* sleeping pill.

somnolence [sɔmnɔlɑ̃s] *nf* drowsiness, sleepiness. ◆**somnolent** *a* drowsy, sleepy. ◆**somnoler** *vi* to doze, drowse.

somptueux, -euse [sɔ̃ptɥø, -øz] *a* sumptuous, magnificent. ◆**somptuosité** *nf* sumptuousness, magnificence.

son¹ [sɔ̃] *nm* **1** (*bruit*) sound. **2** (*de grains*) bran.

son², sa, *pl* **ses** [sɔ̃, sa, se] (*sa becomes* **son** [sɔ̃n] *before a vowel or mute h*) *a poss* his; (*de femme*) her; (*de chose*) its; (*indéfini*) one's; **son père** his *ou* her *ou* one's father; **sa durée** its duration.

sonate [sɔnat] *nf Mus* sonata.

sonde [sɔ̃d] *nf Géol* drill; *Nau* sounding line; *Méd* probe; (*pour l'alimentation*) (feeding) tube; **s. spatiale** *Av* space probe. ◆**sondage** *nm* sounding; drilling; (*forage*) drilling; **s. (d'opinion)** opinion poll. ◆**sonder** *vt* (*rivière etc*) to sound; (*terrain*) to drill; *Av* & *Méd* to probe; (*personne, l'opinion*) *Fig* to sound out.

songe [sɔ̃ʒ] *nm* dream.

song/er [sɔ̃ʒe] *vi* **s. à qch/à faire** to think of sth/of doing; – *vt* **s. que** to consider *ou* think that. ◆—**eur, -euse** *a* thoughtful, pensive.

sonner [sɔne] *vi* to ring; (*cor, cloches etc*) to sound; *midi a sonné* it has struck twelve; — *vt* to ring; (*domestique*) to ring for; (*cor etc*) to sound; (*l'heure*) to strike; (*assommer*) to knock out. ◆**sonnantes** *afpl* **à cinq/etc heures s.** on the stroke of five/*etc* o'clock. ◆**sonné** *a* **1 trois/etc heures sonnées** gone *ou* past three/*etc* o'clock. **2** (*fou*) crazy. ◆**sonnerie** *nf* (*son*) ring(ing); (*de cor etc*) sound; (*appareil*) bell. ◆**sonnette** *nf* bell; **s. d'alarme** alarm (bell); **coup de s.** ring.

sonnet [sɔne] *nm* (*poème*) sonnet.

sonore [sɔnɔr] *a* (*rire*) loud; (*salle, voix*) resonant; (*effet, film, ondes etc*) sound-. ◆**sonorisation** *nf* (*matériel*) sound equipment *ou* system. ◆**sonoriser** *vt* (*film*) to add sound to; (*salle*) to wire for sound. ◆**sonorité** *nf* (*de salle*) acoustics, resonance; (*de violon etc*) tone.

sont [sɔ̃] *voir* **être**.

sophistiqué [sɔfistike] *a* sophisticated.

soporifique [sɔpɔrifik] *a* (*médicament, discours etc*) soporific.

soprano [sɔprano] *nmf* (*personne*) *Mus* soprano; — *nm* (*voix*) soprano.

sorbet [sɔrbɛ] *nm* *Culin* water ice, sorbet.

sorcellerie [sɔrselri] *nf* witchcraft, sorcery. ◆**sorcier** *nm* sorcerer. ◆**sorcière** *nf* witch; **chasse aux sorcières** *Pol* witch-hunt.

sordide [sɔrdid] *a* (*acte, affaire etc*) sordid; (*maison etc*) squalid.

sornettes [sɔrnɛt] *nfpl* (*propos*) *Péj* twaddle.

sort [sɔr] *nm* **1** (*destin, hasard*) fate; (*condition*) lot. **2** (*maléfice*) spell.

sorte [sɔrt] *nf* sort, kind (**de** of); **en quelque s.** as it were, in a way; **de (telle) s. que** so that, in such a way that; **de la s.** (*de cette façon*) in that way; **faire en s. que** (+ *sub*) to see to it that.

sortie [sɔrti] *nf* **1** departure, exit; (*de scène*) exit; (*promenade*) walk; (*porte*) exit, way out; (*de livre, modèle*) *Com* appearance; (*de disque, film*) release; (*d'ordinateur*) output; *pl* (*argent*) outgoings; **à la s. de l'école** (*moment*) when school comes out; **l'heure de la s. de qn** the time at which s.o. leaves; **première s.** (*de convalescent etc*) first time out. **2 s. de bain** (*peignoir*) bathrobe.

sortilège [sɔrtilɛʒ] *nm* (*magic*) spell.

sort/ir [sɔrtir] *vi* (*aux* **être**) to go out, leave; (*venir*) to come out; (*pour s'amuser*) to go out; (*film, modèle, bourgeon etc*) to come out; (*numéro gagnant*) to come up; **s. de** (*endroit*) to leave; (*sujet*) to stray from;

(*université*) to be a graduate of; (*famille, milieu*) to come from; (*légalité, limites*) to go beyond; (*compétence*) to be outside; (*gonds, rails*) to come off; **s. de l'ordinaire** to be out of the ordinary; **s. de table** to leave the table; (*plante, fondations*) to come up; **s. indemne** to escape unhurt (**de** from); — *vt* (*aux* **avoir**) to take out (**de** of); (*film, modèle, livre etc*) *Com* to bring out; (*dire*) *Fam* to come out with; (*expulser*) *Fam* to throw out; **s'en s., s. d'affaire** to pull *ou* come through, get out of trouble. ◆—**ant** *a* (*numéro*) winning; (*député etc*) *Pol* outgoing. ◆—**able** *a* (*personne*) presentable.

sosie [sɔzi] *nm* (*de personne*) double.

sot, sotte [so, sɔt] *a* foolish; — *nmf* fool. ◆**sottement** *adv* foolishly. ◆**sottise** *nf* foolishness; (*action, parole*) foolish thing; *pl* (*injures*) *Fam* insults; **faire des sottises** (*enfant*) to be naughty, misbehave.

sou [su] *nm* **sous** (*argent*) money; **elle n'a pas un** *ou* **le s.** she doesn't have a penny, she's penniless; **pas un s.** (*de bon sens etc*) not an ounce of; **appareil** *ou* **machine à sous** fruit machine, one-armed bandit.

soubresaut [subrɔso] *nm* (*sursaut*) (sudden) start.

souche [suʃ] *nf* (*d'arbre*) stump; (*de carnet*) stub, counterfoil; (*famille, de vigne*) stock.

souci [susi] *nm* (*inquiétude*) worry, concern; (*préoccupation*) concern; **se faire du s.** to be worried, worry; **ça lui donne du s.** it worries him *ou* her. ◆**se soucier** *vpr* **se s. de** to be concerned *ou* worried about. ◆**soucieux, -euse** *a* concerned, worried (**de qch** about sth); **s. de plaire**/*etc* anxious to please/*etc*.

soucoupe [sukup] *nf* saucer; **s. volante** flying saucer.

soudain [sudɛ̃] *a* sudden; — *adv* suddenly. ◆**soudainement** *adv* suddenly. ◆**soudaineté** *nf* suddenness.

Soudan [sudɑ̃] *nm* Sudan.

soude [sud] *nf* *Ch* soda; **cristaux de s.** washing soda.

souder [sude] *vt* to solder; (*par soudure autogène*) to weld; (*groupes etc*) *Fig* to unite (*closely*); — **se s.** *vpr* (*os*) to knit (together). ◆**soudure** *nf* soldering; (*métal*) solder; **s.** (*autogène*) welding.

soudoyer [sudwaje] *vt* to bribe.

souffle [sufl] *nm* puff, blow; (*haleine*) breath; (*respiration*) breathing; (*de bombe etc*) blast; (*inspiration*) *Fig* inspiration; **s.** (**d'air**) breath of air. ◆**souffler** *vi* to blow; (*haleter*) to puff; **laisser s. qn** (*reprendre haleine*) to let s.o. get his breath back; — *vt* *(bougie)* to blow out; *(fumée, poussière, verre)* to blow; *(par une explosion)* to blow down, blast; *(chuchoter)* to whisper; *(voler)* Fam to pinch (à from); *(étonner)* Fam to stagger; s. son rôle à qn Th to prompt s.o.; ne pas s. mot not to breathe a word. ◆soufflet nm 1 *(instrument)* bellows. 2 *(gifle)* Litt slap. ◆souffleur, -euse nmf Th prompter.

soufflé [sufle] nm Culin soufflé.

souffrance [sufrɑ̃s] nf 1 suffering. 2 en s. *(colis etc)* unclaimed; *(affaire)* in abeyance. souffreteux, -euse [sufrətø, -øz] a sickly.

souffr/ir* [sufrir] vi to suffer; s. de to suffer from; *(gorge, pieds etc)* to have trouble with; faire s. qn *(physiquement)* to hurt s.o.; *(moralement)* to make s.o. suffer, hurt s.o. 2 vt *(endurer)* to suffer; je ne peux pas le s. I can't bear him. 3 vt *(exception)* to admit of. ◆—ant a unwell.

soufre [sufr] nm sulphur, Am sulfur.

souhait [swe] nm wish; à vos souhaits! *(après un éternuement)* bless you!; à s. perfectly. ◆souhait/er vt *(bonheur etc)* to wish for; *(qch à qn)* to wish s.o. sth; s. faire to hope to do; s. que (+ sub) to hope that. ◆—able a desirable.

souiller [suje] vt to soil, dirty; *(déshonorer)* Fig to sully.

soûl [su] 1 a drunk. 2 nm tout son s. *(boire etc)* to one's heart's content. ◆soûler vt to make drunk; — se s. vpr to get drunk.

soulager [sulaʒe] vt to relieve (de of). ◆soulagement nm relief.

soulever [sulve] vt to raise, lift (up); *(l'opinion, le peuple)* to stir up; *(poussière, question)* to raise; *(sentiment)* to arouse; cela me soulève le cœur it makes me feel sick, it turns my stomach; — se s. vpr *(malade etc)* to lift oneself (up); *(se révolter)* to rise (up). ◆soulèvement nm *(révolte)* (up)rising.

soulier [sulje] nm shoe.

souligner [suliɲe] vt *(d'un trait)* to underline; *(accentuer, faire remarquer)* to emphasize, underline; s. que to emphasize that.

soumettre* [sumɛtr] vt 1 *(pays, rebelles)* to subjugate, subdue; s. à *(assujettir)* to subject to; — se s. vpr to submit (à to). 2 vt *(présenter)* to submit (à to). ◆soumis a *(docile)* submissive; s. à subject to. ◆soumission nf 1 submission; *(docilité)* submissiveness. 2 *(offre)* Com tender.

soupape [supap] nf valve.

soupçon [supsɔ̃] nm suspicion; un s. de *(quantité)* Fig a hint ou touch of. ◆soupçonner vt to suspect *(de of, d'avoir fait of

doing, que that).* ◆soupçonneux, -euse a suspicious.

soupe [sup] nf soup. ◆soupière nf *(soup)* tureen.

soupente [supɑ̃t] nf *(sous le toit)* loft.

souper [supe] nm supper; — vi to have supper.

soupeser [supəze] vt *(objet dans la main)* to feel the weight of; *(arguments etc)* Fig to weigh up.

soupir [supir] nm sigh. ◆soupir/er vi to sigh; s. après to yearn for. ◆—ant nm *(amoureux)* suitor.

soupirail, -aux [supiraj, -o] nm basement window.

souple [supl] a *(personne, esprit, règlement)* flexible; *(cuir, membre, corps)* supple. ◆souplesse nf flexibility; suppleness.

source [surs] nf 1 *(point d'eau)* spring; eau de s. spring water; prendre sa s. *(rivière)* to rise (à at, dans in). 2 *(origine)* source; de s. sûre on good authority.

sourcil [sursi] nm eyebrow. ◆sourciller vi ne pas s. Fig not to bat an eyelid.

sourd, sourde [sur, surd] 1 a deaf *(Fig à to)*; — nmf deaf person. 2 a *(bruit, douleur)* dull; *(caché)* secret. ◆sourd-muet *(pl sourds-muets)*, ◆sourde-muette *(pl sourdes-muettes)* a deaf and dumb; — nmf deaf mute.

sourdine [surdin] nf *(dispositif)* Mus mute; en s. Fig quietly, secretly.

souricière [surisjɛr] nf mousetrap; Fig trap.

sourire* [surir] vi to smile (à at); s. à qn *(fortune)* to smile on s.o.; — nm smile; faire un s. à qn to give s.o. a smile.

souris [suri] nf mouse.

sournois [surnwa] a sly, underhand. ◆sournoisement adv slyly. ◆sournoiserie nf slyness.

sous [su] prép *(position)* under(neath), beneath; *(rang)* under; s. la pluie in the rain; s. cet angle from that angle ou point of view; s. le nom de under the name of; s. Charles X under Charles X; s. peu *(bientôt)* shortly.

sous- [su] préf *(subordination, subdivision)* sub-; *(insuffisance)* under-.

sous-alimenté [suzalimɑ̃te] a undernourished. ◆sous-alimentation nf undernourishment.

sous-bois [subwa] nm undergrowth.

sous-chef [suʃɛf] nmf second-in-command.

souscrire* [suskrir] vi s. à *(payer, approuver)* to subscribe to. ◆souscription nf subscription.

sous-développé [sudevlɔpe] *a* (*pays*) underdeveloped.

sous-directeur, -trice [sudirɛktœr, -tris] *nmf* assistant manager, assistant manageress.

sous-entend/re [suzɑ̃tɑ̃dr] *vt* to imply. ◆**-u** *nm* insinuation.

sous-estimer [suzɛstime] *vt* to underestimate.

sous-jacent [suʒasɑ̃] *a* underlying.

sous-louer [sulwe] *vt* (*appartement*) to sublet.

sous-main [sumɛ̃] *nm inv* desk pad.

sous-marin [sumarɛ̃] *a* underwater; **plongée sous-marine** skin diving; − *nm* submarine.

sous-officier [suzɔfisje] *nm* noncommissioned officer.

sous-payer [supeje] *vt* (*ouvrier etc*) to underpay.

sous-produit [suprɔdɥi] *nm* by-product.

soussigné, -ée [susiɲe] *a & nmf* undersigned; **je s. I** the undersigned.

sous-sol [susɔl] *nm* basement; *Géol* subsoil.

sous-titre [sutitr] *nm* subtitle. ◆**sous-titrer** *vt* (*film*) to subtitle.

soustraire* [sustrɛr] *vt* to remove; *Math* to subtract, take away (**de** from); **s. qn à** (*danger etc*) to shield *ou* protect s.o. from; **se s. à** to escape from; (*devoir, obligation*) to avoid. ◆**soustraction** *nf Math* subtraction.

sous-trait/er [sutrete] *vi Com* to subcontract. ◆**-ant** *nm* subcontractor.

sous-verre [suvɛr] *nm inv* (*encadrement*) (frameless) glass mount.

sous-vêtement [suvɛtmɑ̃] *nm* undergarment; *pl* underwear.

soutane [sutan] *nf* (*de prêtre*) cassock.

soute [sut] *nf* (*magasin*) Nau hold.

souten/ir* [sutnir] *vt* to support, hold up; (*droits, opinion*) to uphold, maintain; (*candidat etc*) to back, support; (*malade*) to sustain; (*effort, intérêt*) to sustain, keep up; (*thèse*) to defend; (*résister à*) to withstand; **s. que** to maintain that; − **se s.** *vpr* (*blessé etc*) to hold oneself up; (*se maintenir, durer*) to be sustained. ◆**-u** *a* (*attention, effort*) sustained; (*style*) lofty. ◆**soutien** *nm* support; (*personne*) supporter; **s. de famille** breadwinner. ◆**soutien-gorge** *nm* (*pl* soutiens-gorge) bra.

souterrain [sutɛrɛ̃] *a* underground; − *nm* underground passage.

soutirer [sutire] *vt* **s. qch à qn** to extract *ou* get sth from s.o.

souvenir [suvnir] *nm* memory, recollection;

(*objet*) memento; (*cadeau*) keepsake; (*pour touristes*) souvenir; **en s. de** in memory of; **mon bon s. à** (give) my regards to. ◆**se souvenir*** *vpr* **se s. de** to remember, recall; **se s. que** to remember *ou* recall that.

souvent [suvɑ̃] *adv* often; **peu s.** seldom; **le plus s.** more often than not, most often.

souverain, -aine [suvrɛ̃, -ɛn] *a* sovereign; (*extrême*) *Péj* supreme; − *nmf* sovereign. ◆**souveraineté** *nf* sovereignty.

soviétique [sɔvjetik] *a* Soviet; **l'Union s.** the Soviet Union; − *nmf* Soviet citizen.

soyeux, -euse [swajø, -øz] *a* silky.

spacieux, -euse [spasjø, -øz] *a* spacious, roomy.

spaghetti(s) [spageti] *nmpl* spaghetti.

sparadrap [sparadra] *nm Méd* sticking plaster, *Am* adhesive tape.

spasme [spasm] *nm* spasm. ◆**spasmodique** *a* spasmodic.

spatial, -aux [spasjal, -o] *a* (*vol etc*) space-; **engin s.** spaceship, spacecraft.

spatule [spatyl] *nf* spatula.

speaker [spikœr] *nm*, **speakerine** [spikrin] *nf Rad TV* announcer.

spécial, -aux [spesjal, -o] *a* special; (*bizarre*) peculiar. ◆**spécialement** *adv* especially, particularly; (*exprès*) specially.

spécialiser (se) [səspesjalize] *vpr* to specialize (**dans** in). ◆**spécialisation** *nf* specialization. ◆**spécialiste** *nmf* specialist. ◆**spécialité** *nf* speciality, *Am* specialty.

spécifier [spesifje] *vt* to specify (**que** that).

spécifique [spesifik] *a Phys Ch* specific.

spécimen [spesimɛn] *nm* specimen; (*livre etc*) specimen copy.

spectacle [spɛktakl] *nm* **1** (*vue*) spectacle, sight; **se donner en s.** *Péj* to make an exhibition of oneself. **2** (*représentation*) show; **le s.** (*industrie*) show business. ◆**spectateur, -trice** *nmf Sp* spectator; (*témoin*) onlooker, witness; *pl Th Cin* audience.

spectaculaire [spɛktakylɛr] *a* spectacular.

spectre [spɛktr] *nm* **1** (*fantôme*) spectre, ghost. **2** (*solaire*) spectrum.

spéculer [spekyle] *vi Fin Phil* to speculate; **s. sur** (*tabler sur*) to bank *ou* rely on. ◆**spéculateur, -trice** *nmf* speculator. ◆**spéculatif, -ive** *a Fin Phil* speculative. ◆**spéculation** *nf Fin Phil* speculation.

spéléologie [speleɔlɔʒi] *nf* (*activité*) potholing, caving, *Am* spelunking. ◆**spéléologue** *nmf* potholer, *Am* spelunker.

sperme [spɛrm] *nm* sperm, semen.

sphère [sfɛr] *nf* (*boule, domaine*) sphere. ◆**sphérique** *a* spherical.

sphinx [sfɛ̃ks] *nm* sphinx.

spirale [spiral] *nf* spiral.

spirite [spirit] *nmf* spiritualist. ◆**spiritisme** *nm* spiritualism.

spirituel, -elle [spirityɛl] *a* 1 (*amusant*) witty. 2 (*pouvoir, vie etc*) spiritual.

spiritueux [spirityø] *nmpl* (*boissons*) spirits.

splendide [splɑ̃did] *a* (*merveilleux, riche, beau*) splendid. ◆**splendeur** *nf* splendour.

spongieux, -euse [spɔ̃ʒjø, -øz] *a* spongy.

spontané [spɔ̃tane] *a* spontaneous. ◆**spontanéité** *nf* spontaneity. ◆**spontanément** *adv* spontaneously.

sporadique [sporadik] *a* sporadic.

sport [spɔr] *nm* sport; **faire du s.** to play sport *ou* *Am* sports; **(de) s.** (*chaussures, vêtements*) casual; **voiture/veste de s.** sports car/jacket. ◆**sportif, -ive** *a* (*attitude, personne*) sporting; (*association, journal, résultats*) sports, sporting; (*allure*) athletic; — *nm* sportsman, sportsman. ◆**sportivité** *nf* (*esprit*) sportsmanship.

spot [spɔt] *nm* 1 (*lampe*) spot(light). 2 **s.** (*publicitaire*) *Rad TV* commercial.

sprint [sprint] *nm Sp* sprint. ◆**sprint/er** *vi* to sprint; — *nm* [-œr] sprinter. ◆**-euse** *nf* sprinter.

square [skwar] *nm* public garden.

squelette [skəlɛt] *nm* skeleton. ◆**squelettique** *a* (*personne, maigreur*) skeleton-like; (*exposé*) sketchy.

stable [stabl] *a* stable. ◆**stabilisateur** *nm* stabilizer. ◆**stabiliser** *vt* to stabilize; — **se s.** *vpr* to stabilize. ◆**stabilité** *nf* stability.

stade [stad] *nm* 1 *Sp* stadium. 2 (*phase*) stage.

stage [staʒ] *nm* training period; (*cours*) (training) course. ◆**stagiaire** *a* & *nmf* trainee.

stagner [stagne] *vi* to stagnate. ◆**stagnant** *a* stagnant. ◆**stagnation** *nf* stagnation.

stalle [stal] *nf* (*box*) & *Rel* stall.

stand [stɑ̃d] *nm* (*d'exposition etc*) stand, stall; **s. de ravitaillement** *Sp* pit; **s. de tir** (*de foire*) shooting range; *Mil* firing range.

standard [stɑ̃dar] *nm* 1 *Tél* switchboard. 2 *a inv* (*modèle etc*) standard. ◆**standardiser** *vt* to standardize. ◆**standardiste** *nmf* (switchboard) operator.

standing [stɑ̃diŋ] *nm* standing, status; **de (grand) s.** (*immeuble*) luxury-.

starter [starter] *nm* 1 *Aut* choke. 2 *Sp* starter.

station [stasjɔ̃] *nf* (*de métro, d'observation etc*) & *Rad* station; (*de ski etc*) resort; (*d'autobus*) stop; **s. de taxis** taxi rank, *Am*

taxi stand; **s. debout** standing (position); **s. (thermale)** spa. ◆**s.-service** *nf* (*pl* stations-service*) *Aut* service station.

stationnaire [stasjɔnɛr] *vi a* stationary.

stationn/er [stasjɔne] *vi* (*se garer*) to park; (*être garé*) to be parked. ◆**—ement** *nm* parking.

statique [statik] *a* static.

statistique [statistik] *nf* (*donnée*) statistic; **la s.** (*techniques*) statistics; — *a* statistical.

statue [staty] *nf* statue. ◆**statuette** *nf* statuette.

statuer [statɥe] *vi* **s./sur** *Jur* to rule on.

statu quo [statykwo] *nm inv* status quo.

stature [statyr] *nf* stature.

statut [staty] *nm* 1 (*position*) status. 2 *pl* (*règles*) statutes. ◆**statutaire** *a* statutory.

steak [stɛk] *nm* steak.

stencil [stɛnsil] *nm* stencil.

sténo [steno] *nf* (*personne*) stenographer; (*sténographie*) shorthand, stenography; **prendre en s.** to take down in shorthand. ◆**sténodactylo** *nf* shorthand typist, *Am* stenographer. ◆**sténographie** *nf* shorthand, stenography.

stéréo [stereo] *nf* stereo; — *a inv* (*disque etc*) stereo. ◆**stéréophonique** *a* stereophonic.

stéréotype [stereotip] *nm* stereotype. ◆**stéréotypé** *a* stereotyped.

stérile [steril] *a* sterile; (*terre*) barren. ◆**stérilisation** *nf* sterilization. ◆**stériliser** *vt* to sterilize. ◆**stérilité** *nf* sterility; (*de terre*) barrenness.

stérilet [sterilɛ] *nm* IUD, coil.

stéthoscope [stetoskɔp] *nm* stethoscope.

steward [stiwart] *nm Av Nau* steward.

stigmate [stigmat] *nm Fig* mark, stigma (**de** of). ◆**stigmatiser** *vt* (*dénoncer*) to stigmatize.

stimul/er [stimyle] *vt* to stimulate. ◆**—ant** *nm Fig* stimulus; *Méd* stimulant. ◆**stimulateur** *nm* **s. cardiaque** pacemaker. ◆**stimulation** *nf* stimulation.

stimulus [stimylys] *nm* (*pl* stimuli [-li]) (*physiologique*) stimulus.

stipuler [stipyle] *vt* to stipulate (**que** that). ◆**stipulation** *nf* stipulation.

stock [stɔk] *nm Com* & *Fig* stock (**de** of). ◆**stock/er** *vt* to (keep in) stock. ◆**—age** *nm* stocking.

stoïque [stɔik] *a* stoic(al). ◆**stoïcisme** *nm* stoicism.

stop [stɔp] **1** *int* stop; — *nm* (*panneau*) *Aut* stop sign; (*feu arrière*) *Aut* brake light. **2** *nm* **faire du s.** *Fam* to hitchhike. ◆**stopp/er** **1** *vti* to stop. **2** *vt* (*vêtement*) to mend (invisibly). ◆—**age** nm (invisible) mending.

store [stɔr] nm blind, Am (window) shade; (de magasin) awning.

strabisme [strabism] nm squint.

strapontin [strapɔ̃tɛ̃] nm tip-up seat.

stratagème [strataʒɛm] nm stratagem, ploy.

stratège [strateʒ] nm strategist. ◆**stratégie** nf strategy. ◆**stratégique** a strategic.

stress [strɛs] nm inv Méd Psy stress. ◆**stressant** a stressful. ◆**stressé** a under stress.

strict [strikt] a strict; (langue, tenue, vérité) plain; (droit) basic; **le s. minimum/nécessaire** the bare minimum/necessities. ◆**strictement** adv strictly; (vêtu) plainly.

strident [stridɑ̃] a strident, shrill.

strie [stri] nf streak; (sillon) groove. ◆**strier** vt to streak.

strip-tease [striptiz] nm striptease. ◆**strip-teaseuse** nf stripper.

strophe [strɔf] nf stanza, verse.

structure [stryktyr] nf structure. ◆**structural, -aux** a structural. ◆**structurer** vt to structure.

stuc [styk] nm stucco.

studieux, -euse [stydjø, -øz] a studious; (vacances etc) devoted to study.

studio [stydjo] nm (de peintre) & Cin TV studio; (logement) studio flat ou Am apartment.

stupéfait [stypefɛ] a amazed, astounded (de at, by). ◆**stupéfaction** nf amazement. ◆**stupéfi/er** vt to amaze, astound. ◆—**ant 1** a amazing, astounding. **2** nm drug, narcotic. ◆**stupeur** nf **1** (étonnement) amazement. **2** (inertie) stupor.

stupide [stypid] a stupid. ◆**stupidement** adv stupidly. ◆**stupidité** nf stupidity; (action, parole) stupid thing.

style [stil] nm style; **de s.** (meuble) period-. ◆**stylisé** a stylized. ◆**styliste** nmf (de mode etc) designer. ◆**stylistique** a stylistic.

stylé [stile] a well-trained.

stylo [stilo] nm pen; **s. à bille** ballpoint (pen), biro®; **s. à encre** fountain pen.

su [sy] voir savoir.

suave [sɥav] a (odeur, voix) sweet.

subalterne [sybaltɛrn] a & nmf subordinate.

subconscient [sypkɔ̃sjɑ̃] a & nm subconscious.

subdiviser [sybdivize] vt to subdivide (en into). ◆**subdivision** nf subdivision.

subir [sybir] vt to undergo; (conséquences, défaite, perte, tortures) to suffer; (influence) to be under; **s. qn** (supporter) Fam to put up with s.o.

subit [sybi] a sudden. ◆**subitement** adv suddenly.

subjectif, -ive [sybʒɛktif, -iv] a subjective. ◆**subjectivement** adv subjectively. ◆**subjectivité** nf subjectivity.

subjonctif [sybʒɔ̃ktif] nm Gram subjunctive.

subjuguer [sybʒyge] vt to subjugate; (envoûter) to captivate.

sublime [syblim] a & nm sublime.

sublimer [syblime] vt Psy to sublimate.

submerger [sybmɛrʒe] vt to submerge; (envahir) Fig to overwhelm; **submergé de** (travail etc) overwhelmed with; **submergé par** (ennemi, foule) swamped by. ◆**submersible** nm submarine.

subordonn/er [sybɔrdɔne] vt to subordinate (à to). ◆—**é, -ée** a subordinate (à to); **être s. à** (dépendre de) to depend on; — nmf subordinate. ◆**subordination** nf subordination.

subreptice [sybrɛptis] a surreptitious.

subside [sypsid] nm grant, subsidy.

subsidiaire [sybsidjɛr] a subsidiary; **question s.** (de concours) deciding question.

subsister [sybziste] vi (rester) to remain; (vivre) to get by, subsist; (doutes, souvenirs etc) to linger (on), subsist. ◆**subsistance** nf subsistence.

substance [sypstɑ̃s] nf substance; **en s.** Fig in essence. ◆**substantiel, -ielle** a substantial.

substantif [sypstɑ̃tif] nm Gram noun, substantive.

substituer [sypstitɥe] vt to substitute (à for); **se s. à qn** to take the place of s.o., substitute for s.o.; (représenter) to substitute for s.o. ◆**substitution** nf substitution.

subterfuge [sypterfyʒ] nm subterfuge.

subtil [syptil] a subtle. ◆**subtilité** nf subtlety.

subtiliser [syptilize] vt (dérober) Fam to make off with.

subvenir* [sybvənir] vi **s. à** (besoins, frais) to meet.

subvention [sybvɑ̃sjɔ̃] nf subsidy. ◆**subventionner** vt to subsidize.

subversif, -ive [sybvɛrsif, -iv] a subversive. ◆**subversion** nf subversion.

suc [syk] nm (gastrique, de fruit) juice; (de plante) sap.

succédané [syksedane] *nm* substitute (*de* for).

succéder [syksede] *vi* s. à qn to succeed s.o.; s. à qch to follow sth, come after sth; **— se s.** *vpr* to succeed one another; to follow one another. **◆successeur** *nm* successor. **◆successif, -ive** *a* successive. **◆successivement** *adv* successively. **◆succession** *nf* 1 succession (*de* of, à to); **prendre la s. de qn** to succeed s.o. 2 (*patrimoine*) *Jur* inheritance, estate.

succès [sykse] *nm* success; s. de librairie (*livre*) best-seller; **avoir du s.** to be successful, be a success; à s. (*auteur, film etc*) successful; **avec s.** successfully.

succinct [syksɛ̃] *a* succinct, brief.

succion [sy(k)sjɔ̃] *nf* suction.

succomber [sykɔ̃be] *vi* 1 (*mourir*) to die. 2 s. à (*céder à*) to succumb to, give in to.

succulent [sykylɑ̃] *a* succulent.

succursale [sykyrsal] *nf Com* branch; **magasin à succursales multiples** chain *ou* multiple store.

sucer [syse] *vt* to suck. **◆sucette** *nf* lollipop; (*tétine*) dummy, comforter, *Am* pacifier.

sucre [sykr] *nm* sugar; (*morceau*) sugar lump; s. cristallisé granulated sugar; s. en morceaux lump sugar; s. en poudre, semoule *Am* finely ground sugar; s. d'orge barley sugar. **◆sucr/er** *vt* to sugar, sweeten. **◆-é** *a* sweet, sugary; (*artificiellement*) sweetened; (*douceureux*) *Fig* sugary, syrupy. **◆sucrerie** 1 *(usine)* sugar refinery. 2 *nfpl* (*bonbons*) sweets, *Am* candy. **◆sucrier, -ière** *a* (*industrie*) sugar-; *— nm* (*récipient*) sugar bowl.

sud [syd] *nm* south; **au s. de** south of; **du s.** (*vent, direction*) southerly; (*ville*) southern; (*gens*) from *ou* in the south; **Amérique/Afrique du S.** South America/Africa; **l'Europe du S.** Southern Europe; — *a inv* (*côte*) south(ern). **◆s.-africain, -aine** *a* & *nmf* South African. **◆s.-américain, -aine** *a* & *nmf* South American. **◆s.-est** *nm* & *a inv* south-east. **◆s.-ouest** *nm* & *a inv* south-west.

Suède [suɛd] *nf* Sweden. **◆suédois, -oise** *a* Swedish; *— nmf* Swede; *— nm* (*langue*) Swedish.

suer [sue] *vi* (*personne, mur etc*) to sweat; **faire s. qn** *Fam* to get on s.o.'s nerves; **se faire s.** *Fam* to be bored stiff; *— vt* (*sang etc*) to sweat. **◆sueur** *nf* sweat; (*tout*) en s. sweating.

suffire° [syfir] *vi* to be enough *ou* sufficient, suffice (à for); **ça suffit!** that's enough!; **il**

suffit de faire one only has to do; **il suffit d'une goutte/etc pour faire** a drop/*etc* is enough to do; **il ne me suffit pas de faire** I'm not satisfied with doing; **— se s.** *vpr* **se s. (à soi-même)** to be self-sufficient. **◆suffisant** *a* 1 sufficient, adequate. 2 (*vaniteux*) conceited. **◆suffisamment** *adv* sufficiently; **s. de** sufficient, enough. **◆suffisance** *nf* (*vanité*) conceit.

suffixe [syfiks] *nm Gram* suffix.

suffoquer [syfɔke] *vti* to choke, suffocate. **◆suffocant** *a* stifling, suffocating. **◆suffocation** *nf* suffocation; (*sensation*) feeling of suffocation.

suffrage [syfraʒ] *nm Pol* (*voix*) vote; (*droit*) suffrage.

suggérer [sygʒere] *vt* (*proposer*) to suggest (*de faire* doing, *que* (+ *sub*) that); (*évoquer*) to suggest. **◆suggestif, -ive** *a* suggestive. **◆suggestion** *nf* suggestion.

suicide [suisid] *nm* suicide. **◆suicidaire** *a* suicidal. **◆se suicid/er** *vpr* to commit suicide. **◆-é, -ée** *nmf* suicide (victim).

suie [sui] *nf* soot.

suif [suif] *nm* tallow.

suinter [suɛ̃te] *vi* to ooze, seep. **◆suintement** *nm* oozing, seeping.

suis [sui] *voir* être, suivre.

Suisse [suis] *nf* Switzerland. **◆suisse** *a* & *nmf* Swiss. **◆Suissesse** *nf* Swiss (woman *ou* girl).

suite [suit] *nf* (*reste*) rest; (*continuation*) continuation; (*de film, roman*) sequel; (*série*) series, sequence; (*appartement, escorte*) & *Mus* suite; (*cohérence*) order; *pl* (*résultats*) consequences; (*séquelles*) effects; **attendre la s.** to wait and see what happens next; **donner s. à** (*demande etc*) to follow up; **faire s. (à)** to follow; **prendre la s. de qn** to take over from s.o.; **par la s.** afterwards; **par s. de** as a result of; **à la s.** one after another; **à la s. de** (*derrière*) behind; (*événement, maladie etc*) as a result of; **de s.** in succession.

suiv/re° [suivr] *vt* to follow; (*accompagner*) to go with, accompany; (*classe*) *Scol* to attend, go to; (*malade*) to treat; **s. (des yeux ou du regard)** to watch; **s. son chemin** to go on one's way; **se s.** to follow each other; *— vi* to follow; **faire s.** (*courrier*) to forward; **'à s.'** 'to be continued'; **comme suit** as follows. **◆-ant¹, -ante** *a* next, following; (*ci-après*) following; *— nmf* next (one); **au s.!** next!, the next person! **◆-ant²** *prép* (*selon*) according to. **◆-i** *a* (*régulier*) regular, steady; (*cohérent*) coherent; (*article*

Com regularly on sale; **peu/très s.** (*cours*) poorly/well attended.

sujet¹, -ette [syʒɛ, -ɛt] *a* **s. à** (*maladie etc*) subject *ou* liable to; – *nmf* (*personne*) Pol subject.

sujet² [syʒɛ] *nm* **1** (*question*) & Gram subject; (*d'examen*) question; **au s. de** about; **à quel s.?** about what? **2** (*raison*) cause; **avoir s. de faire** to have (good) cause *ou* (good) reason to do. **3** *nm* (*individu*) subject; **un mauvais s.** (*garçon*) a rotten egg.

sulfurique [sylfyrik] *a* (*acide*) sulphuric, *Am* sulfuric.

sultan [syltã] *nm* sultan.

summum [sɔmɔm] *nm* (*comble*) Fig height.

super [sypɛr] **1** *a* (*bon*) Fam great. **2** *nm* (*supercarburant*) Fam four-star (petrol), *Am* premium *ou* hi-test gas.

superbe [sypɛrb] *a* superb.

supercarburant [sypɛrkarbyrã] *nm* high-octane petrol *ou* *Am* gasoline.

supercherie [sypɛrʃəri] *nf* deception.

superficie [sypɛrfisi] *nf* surface; (*dimensions*) area. ◆**superficiel, -ielle** *a* superficial. ◆**superficiellement** *adv* superficially.

superflu [sypɛrfly] *a* superfluous.

super-grand [sypɛrgrã] *nm* Pol Fam superpower.

supérieur, -eure [sypɛrjœr] *a* (*étages, partie etc*) upper; (*qualité, air, ton*) superior; (*études*) higher; **à l'étage s.** on the floor above; **s. à** (*meilleur que*) superior to, better than; (*plus grand que*) above, greater than; – *nmf* superior. ◆**supériorité** *nf* superiority.

superlatif, -ive [sypɛrlatif, -iv] *a* & *nm* Gram superlative.

supermarché [sypɛrmarʃe] *nm* supermarket.

superposer [sypɛrpoze] *vt* (*objets*) to put on top of each other; (*images etc*) to superimpose.

superproduction [sypɛrprɔdyksjɔ̃] *nf* (*film*) blockbuster.

superpuissance [sypɛrpɥisãs] *nf* Pol superpower.

supersonique [sypɛrsɔnik] *a* supersonic.

superstitieux, -euse [sypɛrstisjø, -øz] *a* superstitious. ◆**superstition** *nf* superstition.

superviser [sypɛrvize] *vt* to supervise.

supplanter [syplãte] *vt* to take the place of.

supplé/er [syplee] *vt* (*remplacer*) to replace; (*compenser*) to make up for; – *vi* **s. à** (*compenser*) to make up for. ◆—**ant, -ante**

a & *nmf* (*personne*) substitute, replacement; (*professeur*) **s.** supply teacher.

supplément [syplemã] *nm* (*argent*) extra charge, supplement; (*de livre, revue*) supplement; **en s.** extra; **un s. de** (*information, travail etc*) extra, additional. ◆**supplémentaire** *a* extra, additional.

supplice [syplis] *nm* torture; **au s.** Fig on the rack. ◆**supplicier** *vt* to torture.

suppli/er [syplije] *vt* **s. qn de faire** to beg *ou* implore s.o. to do; **je vous en supplie!** I beg *ou* implore you! ◆—**ant, -ante** (*regard etc*) imploring. ◆**supplication** *nf* plea, entreaty.

support [sypɔr] *nm* **1** support; (*d'instrument etc*) stand. **2** (*moyen*) Fig medium; **s. audio-visuel** audio-visual aid.

support/er¹ [sypɔrte] *vt* to bear, endure; (*frais*) to bear; (*affront etc*) to suffer; (*résister à*) to withstand; (*soutenir*) to support. ◆—**able** *a* bearable; (*excusable, passable*) tolerable.

supporter² [sypɔrter] *nm* Sp supporter.

supposer [sypoze] *vt* to suppose, assume (*que that*); (*impliquer*) to imply (*que that*); **à s.** *ou* **en supposant que** (+ *sub*) supposing (that). ◆**supposition** *nf* supposition, assumption.

suppositoire [sypozitwar] *nm* Méd suppository.

supprimer [syprime] *vt* to remove, get rid of; (*institution, loi*) to abolish; (*journal etc*) to suppress; (*mot, passage*) to cut, delete; (*train etc*) to cancel; (*tuer*) to do away with; **s. qch à qn** to take sth away from s.o. ◆**suppression** *nf* removal; abolition; suppression; cutting; cancellation.

suprématie [sypremasi] *nf* supremacy. ◆**suprême** *a* supreme.

sur [syr] *prép* on, upon; (*par-dessus*) over; (*au sujet de*) on, about; **s. les trois heures** at about three o'clock; **six s. dix** six out of ten; **un jour s. deux** every other day; **coup s. coup** blow after *ou* upon blow; **six s. mètres s. dix** six metres by ten; **mettre/monter/etc s.** to put/climb/etc on (to); **aller/tourner/etc s.** to go/turn/etc towards; **s. ce** after which, and then; (*maintenant*) and now.

sur- [syr] *préf* over-.

sûr [syr] *a* sure, certain (**de** of, **que** that); (*digne de confiance*) reliable; (*avenir*) secure; (*lieu*) safe; (*main*) steady; (*goût*) unerring; (*jugement*) sound; **s. de soi** self-assured; **bien s.!** of course!

surabondant [syrabɔ̃dã] *a* over-abundant.

suranné [syrane] *a* outmoded.

surboum [syrbum] *nf* Fam party.

surcharge [syrʃarʒ] nf **1** overloading; (poids) extra load; **s. de travail** extra work; **en s.** (passagers etc) extra. **2** (correction de texte etc) alteration; (de timbre-poste) surcharge. ◆**surcharger** vt (voiture, personne etc) to overload (**de** with).

surchauffer [syrʃofe] vt to overheat.

surchoix [syrʃwa] a inv Com top-quality.

surclasser [syrklase] vt to outclass.

surcroît [syrkrwa] nm increase (**de** in); **de s., par s.** in addition.

surdité [syrdite] nf deafness.

surdoué, -ée [syrdwe] nmf child who has a genius-level IQ.

surélever [syrelve] vt to raise (the height of).

sûrement [syrmã] adv certainly; (sans danger) safely.

surenchère [syrãʃɛr] nf Com higher bid; **s. électorale** Fig bidding for votes. ◆**surenchérir** vi to bid higher (**sur** than).

surestimer [syrɛstime] vt to overestimate; (peinture etc) to overvalue.

sûreté [syrte] nf safety; (de l'état) security; (garantie) surety; (de geste) sureness; (de jugement) soundness; **être en s.** to be safe; **mettre en s.** to put in a safe place; **de s.** (épingle, soupape etc) safety-.

surexcité [syrɛksite] a overexcited.

surf [sœrf] nm Sp surfing; **faire du s.** to surf, go surfing.

surface [syrfas] nf surface; (dimensions) (surface) area; **faire s.** (sous-marin etc) to surface; **magasin à grande s.** hypermarket.

surfait [syrfɛ] a overrated.

surgelé [syrʒəle] a (deep-)frozen; −. nmpl (deep-)frozen foods.

surgir [syrʒir] vi to appear suddenly (**de** from); (conflit, problème) to arise.

surhomme [syrɔm] nm superman. ◆**surhumain** a superhuman.

sur-le-champ [syrləʃã] adv immediately.

surlendemain [syrlãdmɛ̃] nm **le s.** two days later; **le s. de** two days after.

surmen/er [syrmane] vt, − **se s.** vpr to overwork. ◆**-age** nm overwork.

surmonter [syrmɔ̃te] vt **1** (obstacle, peur etc) to overcome, get over. **2** (être placé sur) to be on top of, top.

surnager [syrnaʒe] vi to float.

surnaturel, -elle [syrnatyrɛl] a & nm supernatural.

surnom [syrnɔ̃] nm nickname. ◆**surnommer** vt to nickname.

surnombre [syrnɔ̃br] nm **en s.** too many; **je suis en s.** I am one too many.

surpasser [syrpase] vt to surpass (**en** in); − **se s.** vpr to surpass oneself.

surpeuplé [syrpœple] a overpopulated.

surplomb [syrplɔ̃] nm **en s.** overhanging. ◆**surplomber** vti to overhang.

surplus [syrply] nm surplus; pl Com surplus (stock).

surprendre* [syrprãdr] vt (étonner, prendre sur le fait) to surprise; (secret) to discover; (conversation) to overhear; **se s. à faire** to find oneself doing. ◆**surprenant** a surprising. ◆**surpris** a surprised (**de** at, **que** (+ sub) that). ◆**surprise** nf surprise. ◆**surprise-partie** nf (pl **surprises-parties**) party.

surréaliste [syrealist] a (bizarre) Fam surrealistic.

sursaut [syrso] nm (sudden) start ou jump; **en s.** with a start; **s. de** (énergie etc) burst of. ◆**sursauter** vi to start, jump.

sursis [syrsi] nm Mil deferment; (répit) Fig reprieve; **un an (de prison) avec s.** a one-year suspended sentence.

surtaxe [syrtaks] nf surcharge.

surtout [syrtu] adv especially; (avant tout) above all; **s. pas** certainly not; **s. que** especially as ou since.

surveill/er [syrveje] vt (garder) to watch, keep an eye on; (épier) to watch; (contrôler) to supervise; **s. son langage/sa santé** Fig to watch one's language/health; − **se s.** vpr to watch oneself. ◆**-ant, -ante** nmf (de lycée) supervisor (in charge of discipline); (de prison) warder; (de chantier) supervisor; **s. de plage** lifeguard. ◆**surveillance** nf watch (**sur** over); (de travaux, d'ouvriers) supervision; (de la police) surveillance, observation.

survenir* [syrvənir] vi to occur; (personne) to turn up.

survêtement [syrvɛtmã] nm Sp tracksuit.

survie [syrvi] nf survival. ◆**surviv/re*** [vt] to survive (**à qch** sth); **s. à qn** to outlive s.o., survive s.o. ◆**-ant, -ante** nmf survivor. ◆**survivance** nf (chose) survival, relic.

survol [syrvɔl] nm **le s. de** flying over; (question) Fig the overview of. ◆**survoler** vt (en avion) to fly over; (question) to go over (quickly).

survolté [syrvɔlte] a (surexcité) worked up.

susceptible [sysɛptibl] a **1** (ombrageux) touchy, sensitive. **2 s. de** (interprétations etc) open to; **s. de faire** likely ou liable to do; (capable) able to do. ◆**susceptibilité** nf touchiness, sensitiveness.

susciter [sysite] vt (sentiment) to arouse; (ennuis, obstacles etc) to create.

suspect, -ecte [syspɛ(kt), -ɛkt] *a* suspicious, suspect; **s. de** suspected of; – *nmf* suspect. **◆suspecter** *vt* to suspect (**de qch** of sth, **de faire** of doing); (*bonne foi etc*) to question, suspect, doubt.

suspend/re [syspɑ̃dr] *vt* **1** (*destituer, différer, interrompre*) to suspend. **2** (*fixer*) to hang (up) (**à** on); **se s. à** to hang from. **◆—u** *a s.* à hanging from; **pont s.** suspension bridge. **◆suspension** *nf* **1** (*d'hostilités, d'employé etc*) & *Aut* suspension; **points de s.** *Gram* dots, suspension points. **2** (*lustre*) hanging lamp.

suspens (en) [ɑ̃syspɑ̃] *adv* **1** (*affaire, travail*) in abeyance. **2** (*dans l'incertitude*) in suspense.

suspense [syspɛns] *nm* suspense; **film à s.** thriller, suspense film.

suspicion [syspisjɔ̃] *nf* suspicion.

susurrer [sysyre] *vti* to murmur.

suture [sytyr] *nf Méd* stitching; **point de s.** stitch. **◆suturer** *vt* to stitch up.

svelte [svɛlt] *a* slender. **◆sveltesse** *nf* slenderness.

SVP *abrév* (*s'il vous plaît*) please.

syllabe [silab] *nf* syllable.

symbole [sɛ̃bɔl] *nm* symbol. **◆symbolique** *a* symbolic; (*salaire*) nominal. **◆symboliser** *vt* to symbolize. **◆symbolisme** *nm* symbolism.

symétrie [simetri] *nf* symmetry. **◆symétrique** *a* symmetrical.

sympa [sɛ̃pa] *a inv Fam* = **sympathique**.

sympathie [sɛ̃pati] *nf* liking, affection; (*affinité*) affinity; (*condoléances*) sympathy; **avoir de la s. pour qn** to be fond of s.o. **◆sympathique** *a* nice, pleasant; (*accueil, geste*) friendly. **◆sympathis/er** *vi* to get

on well (**avec** with). **◆—ant, -ante** *nmf Pol* sympathizer.

symphonie [sɛ̃fɔni] *nf* symphony. **◆symphonique** *a* symphonic; (*orchestre*) symphony-.

symposium [sɛ̃pozjɔm] *nm* symposium.

symptôme [sɛ̃ptom] *nm* symptom. **◆symptomatique** *a* symptomatic (**de** of).

synagogue [sinagɔg] *nf* synagogue.

synchroniser [sɛ̃krɔnize] *vt* to synchronize.

syncope [sɛ̃kɔp] *nf Méd* blackout; **tomber en s.** to black out.

syndicat [sɛ̃dika] *nm* **1** (*d'employés, d'ouvriers*) (trade) union; (*de patrons etc*) association. **2 s. d'initiative** tourist (information) office. **◆syndical, -aux** *a* (*réunion etc*) (trade) union-. **◆syndicalisme** *nm* trade unionism. **◆syndicaliste** *nmf* trade unionist; – *a* (trade) union-. **◆syndiqu/er** *vt* to unionize; — **se s.** *vpr* (*adhérer*) to join a (trade) union. **◆—é, -ée** *nmf* (trade) union member.

syndrome [sɛ̃drom] *nm Méd & Fig* syndrome.

synode [sinɔd] *nm Rel* synod.

synonyme [sinɔnim] *a* synonymous (**de** with); – *nm* synonym.

syntaxe [sɛ̃taks] *nf Gram* syntax.

synthèse [sɛ̃tɛz] *nf* synthesis. **◆synthétique** *a* synthetic.

syphilis [sifilis] *nf* syphilis.

Syrie [siri] *nf* Syria. **◆syrien, -ienne** *a* & *nmf* Syrian.

système [sistɛm] *nm* (*structure, réseau etc*) & *Anat* system; **le s. D** *Fam* resourcefulness. **◆systématique** *a* systematic; (*soutien*) unconditional. **◆systématiquement** *adv* systematically.

T

T, t [te] *nm* T, t.

t' [t] *voir* **te.**

ta [ta] *voir* **ton** [1].

tabac [taba] **1** *nm* tobacco; (*magasin*) tobacconist's (shop), *Am* tobacco store; **t. (à priser)** snuff. **2** *nm* **passer à t.** to beat up; **passage à t.** beating up. **3** *a inv* (*couleur*) buff. **◆tabatière** *nf* (*boîte*) snuffbox.

tabasser [tabase] *vt Fam* to beat up.

table [tabl] *nf* **1** (*meuble*) table; (*nourriture*) fare; **t. de jeu/de nuit/d'opération** card/bedside/operating table; **t. basse** coffee

table; **t. à repasser** ironing board; **t. roulante** (tea) trolley, *Am* (serving) cart; **mettre/débarrasser la t.** to lay *ou* set/clear the table; **être à t.** to be sitting at the table; **à t.!** (food's) ready!; **faire t. rase** *Fig* to make a clean sweep (**de** of); **mettre sur t. d'écoute** (*téléphone*) to tap. **2** (*liste*) table; **t. des matières** table of contents.

tableau, -x [tablo] *nm* **1** (*peinture*) picture, painting; (*image, description*) picture; *Th* scene; **t. de maître** (*peinture*) old master. **2** (*panneau*) board; *Rail* train-indicator;

(liste) list; *(graphique)* chart; **t. (noir)** (black)board; **t. d'affichage** notice board, *Am* bulletin board; **t. de bord** *Aut* dashboard; **t. de contrôle** *Tech* control panel.

tabler [table] *vi* **t. sur** to count ou rely on.

tablette [tablet] *nf (d'armoire, de lavabo)* shelf; *(de cheminée)* mantelpiece; *(de chocolat)* bar, slab.

tablier [tablije] *nm* **1** *(vêtement)* apron; *(d'écolier)* smock; **rendre son t.** *(démissionner)* to give notice. **2** *(de pont)* roadway.

tabou [tabu] *a & nm* taboo.

tabouret [taburɛ] *nm* stool.

tabulateur [tabylatœr] *nm (de machine à écrire etc)* tabulator.

tac [tak] *nm* **répondre du t. au t.** to give tit for tat.

tache [taʃ] *nf* spot, mark; *(salissure)* stain; **faire t.** *(détonner)* Péj to jar, stand out; **faire t. d'huile** Fig to spread. ◆**tacher** *vt* & **se t.** *vpr (tissu etc)* to stain; – *vi (vin etc)* to stain. ◆**tacheté** a speckled, spotted.

tâche [taʃ] *nf* task, job; **travailler à la t.** to do piecework.

tâcher [taʃe] *vi* **t. de faire** to try ou endeavour to do.

tâcheron [taʃrɔ̃] *nm* drudge.

tacite [tasit] *a* tacit. ◆**—ment** *adv* tacitly.

taciturne [tasityrn] *a* taciturn.

tacot [tako] *nm (voiture)* Fam (old) wreck, banger.

tact [takt] *nm* tact.

tactile [taktil] *a* tactile.

tactique [taktik] *a* tactical; – *nf* **la t.** tactics; **une t.** a tactic.

Tahiti [taiti] *nm* Tahiti. ◆**tahitien, -ienne** [taisjɛ̃, -jɛn] *a* nmf Tahitian.

taie [tɛ] *nf* **t. d'oreiller** pillowcase, pillowslip.

taillade [tajad] *nf* gash, slash. ◆**taillader** *vt* to gash, slash.

taille¹ [taj] *nf* **1** *(stature)* height; *(dimension, mesure commerciale)* size; **de haute t.** *(personne)* tall; **de petite t.** short; **de t. moyenne** *(objet, personne)* medium-sized; **être de t. à faire** Fig to be capable of doing; **de t.** *(erreur, objet)* Fam enormous. **2** *Anat* waist; **tour de t.** waist measurement.

taille² [taj] *nf* cutting; cutting out; trimming; pruning; *(forme)* cut. ◆**taill/er¹** *vt* to cut; *(vêtement)* to cut out; *(haie, barbe)* to trim; *(arbre)* to prune; *(crayon)* to sharpen. **2 se t.** *vpr (partir)* Fam to clear off. ◆**—é** *a* **t. en athlète/etc** built like an athlete/etc; **t. pour faire** Fig cut out for doing.

taille-crayon(s) [tajkrɛjɔ̃] *nm inv* pencil-sharpener. ◆**t.-haies** *nm inv* (garden) shears; *(électrique)* hedge trimmer.

tailleur [tajœr] *nm* **1** *(personne)* tailor. **2** *(costume féminin)* suit.

taillis [taji] *nm* copse, coppice.

tain [tɛ̃] *nm (de glace)* silvering; **glace sans t.** two-way mirror.

taire* [tɛr] *vt* to say nothing about; – *vi* **faire t. qn** to silence s.o. – **se t.** *vpr (rester silencieux)* to keep quiet *(sur qch* about sth); *(cesser de parler)* to fall silent, shut up; **tais-toi!** be ou keep quiet!, shut up!

talc [talk] *nm* talcum powder.

talent [talɑ̃] *nm* talent; **avoir du t. pour** to have a talent for. ◆**talentueux, -euse** *a* talented.

taler [tale] *vt* to bruise.

talion [taljɔ̃] *nm* **la loi du t.** *(vengeance)* an eye for an eye.

talisman [talismɑ̃] *nm* talisman.

talkie-walkie [talkiwalki] *nm (poste)* walkie-talkie.

taloche [talɔʃ] *nf (gifle)* Fam clout, smack.

talon [talɔ̃] *nm* **1** heel; **(chaussures à) talons hauts** high heels, high-heeled shoes. **2** *(de chèque, carnet)* stub, counterfoil; *(bout de pain)* crust; *(de jambon)* heel. ◆**talonner** *vt (fugitif etc)* to follow on the heels of; *(ballon)* Rugby to heel; *(harceler)* Fig to hound, dog.

talus [taly] *nm* slope, embankment.

tambour [tɑ̃bur] *nm* **1** *(de machine etc)* & *Mus* drum; *(personne)* drummer. **2** *(porte)* revolving door. ◆**tambourin** *nm* tambourine. ◆**tambouriner** *vi (avec les doigts etc)* to drum *(sur* on).

tamis [tami] *nm* sieve. ◆**tamiser** *vt* to sift; *(lumière)* to filter, subdue.

Tamise [tamiz] *nf* **la T.** the Thames.

tampon [tɑ̃pɔ̃] *nm* **1** *(bouchon)* plug, stopper; *(d'ouate)* wad, pad; *Méd* swab; **t. hygiénique** *ou* **périodique** tampon; **t. à récurer** scouring pad. **2** *(de train etc)* & Fig buffer; **état t.** buffer state. **3** *(marque, instrument)* stamp; **t. buvard** blotter; **t. encreur** ink(ing) pad. ◆**tamponner/1** *vt (visage etc)* to dab; *(plaie)* to swab. **2** *vt (train, voiture)* to crash into; – **se t.** *vpr* to crash into each other. **3** *vt (lettre, document)* to stamp. ◆**—euses** *afpl* **autos t.** dodgems, bumper cars.

tam-tam [tamtam] *nm (tambour)* tom-tom.

tandem [tɑ̃dɛm] *nm* **1** *(bicyclette)* tandem. **2** *(duo)* Fig duo, pair; **en t.** *(travailler etc)* in tandem.

tandis que [tɑ̃di(s)ə] *conj (pendant que)* while; *(contraste)* whereas, while.

tangent [tɑ̃ʒɑ̃] *a* **1** *Géom* tangential *(à* to).

2 (*juste*) *Fam* touch and go, close. ◆**tangente** *nf Géom* tangent.

tangible [tɑ̃ʒibl] *a* tangible.

tango [tɑ̃go] *nm* tango.

tang/uer [tɑ̃ge] *vi* (*bateau, avion*) to pitch. ◆**—age** *nm* pitching.

tanière [tanjɛr] *nf* den, lair.

tank [tɑ̃k] *nm Mil* tank.

tanker [tɑ̃kɛr] *nm* (*navire*) tanker.

tann/er [tane] *vt* (*cuir*) to tan. ◆**—é** *a* (*visage*) weather-beaten, tanned.

tant [tɑ̃] *adv* so much (*que* that); **t. de** (*pain, temps etc*) so much (*que* that); (*gens, choses etc*) so many (*que* that); **t. de fois** so often, so many times; **t. que** (*autant que*) as much as; (*aussi fort que*) as hard as; (*aussi longtemps que*) as long as; **en t. que** (*considéré comme*) as; **t. mieux!** good!, I'm glad!; **t. pis!** too bad!, pity!; **t. soit peu** (*even*) remotely *ou* slightly; **un t.** soit peu somewhat; **t. s'en faut** far from it; **t. bien que mal** more or less, so-so.

tante [tɑ̃t] *nf* aunt.

tantinet [tɑ̃tinɛ] *nm & adv* **un t.** a tiny bit (of).

tantôt [tɑ̃to] *adv* **1 t....t.** sometimes... sometimes, now... now. **2** (*cet après-midi*) this afternoon.

taon [tɑ̃] *nm* horsefly, gadfly.

tapage [tapaʒ] *nm* din, uproar. ◆**tapageur, -euse** *a* **1** (*bruyant*) rowdy. **2** (*criard*) flashy.

tape [tap] *nf* slap. ◆**tap/er** *vt* (*enfant, cuisse*) to slap; (*table*) to bang; **t. qn** (*emprunter de l'argent à qn*) *Fam* to touch s.o., tap s.o. (*de for*); — *vi* (*soleil*) to beat down; **t. sur qch** to bang on sth; **t. à la porte** to bang on the door; **t. sur qn** (*critiquer*) *Fam* to run s.o. down, knock s.o.; **t. sur les nerfs de qn** *Fam* to get on s.o.'s nerves; **t. dans** (*provisions etc*) to dig into; **t. du pied** to stamp one's foot; **t. dans l'œil à qn** *Fam* to take s.o.'s fancy; — **se t.** *vpr* (*travail*) *Fam* to do, take on; (*repas, vin*) *Fam* to put away. **2** *vti* (*écrire à la machine*) to type. ◆**—ant** à midi t. at twelve sharp; à huit heures tapant(es) at eight sharp. ◆**—eur, -euse** *Fam* person who borrows money.

tape-à-l'œil [tapalœj] *a inv* flashy, gaudy.

tapée [tape] *nf* une **t. de** *Fam* a load of.

tapioca [tapjɔka] *nm* tapioca.

tapir (se) [sətapir] *vpr* to crouch (down). ◆**tapi** *a* crouching, crouched.

tapis [tapi] *nm* carpet; **t. de bain** bathmat; **t. roulant** (*pour marchandises*) conveyor belt; (*pour personnes*) moving pavement *ou* Am

sidewalk; **t. de sol** groundsheet; **t. de table** table cover; **envoyer qn au t.** (*abattre*) to floor s.o.; **mettre sur le t.** (*sujet*) to bring up for discussion. ◆**t.-brosse** *nm* doormat.

tapisser [tapise] *vt* (*mur*) to (wall)paper; to hang with tapestry; (*recouvrir*) *Fig* to cover. ◆**tapisserie** *nf* (*tenture*) tapestry; (*papier peint*) wallpaper. ◆**tapissier, -ière** *nmf* (*qui pose des tissus etc*) upholsterer; **t.(-décorateur)** interior decorator.

tapoter [tapɔte] *vt* to tap; (*joue*) to pat; — *vi* **t. sur** to tap (on).

taquin, -ine [takɛ̃, -in] *a* (*fond of*) teasing; — *nmf* tease(r). ◆**taquiner** *vt* to tease; (*inquiéter, agacer*) to bother. ◆**taquinerie(s)** *nf(pl)* teasing.

tarabiscoté [tarabiskɔte] *a* over-elaborate.

tarabuster [tarabyste] *vt* (*idée etc*) to trouble (*s.o.*).

tard [tar] *adv* late; **plus t.** later (on); **au plus t.** at the latest; **sur le t.** late in life. ◆**tarder** *vi* (*lettre, saison*) to be a long time coming; **t. à faire** to take one's time doing; (*différer*) to delay (*in*) doing; **ne tardez pas** (*agissez tout de suite*) don't delay; **elle ne va pas t.** she won't be long; **sans t.** without delay; **il me tarde de faire** I long to do. ◆**tardif, -ive** *a* late; (*regrets*) belated. ◆**tardivement** *adv* late.

tare [tar] *nf* **1** (*poids*) tare. **2** (*défaut*) *Fig* defect. ◆**taré** *a* (*corrompu*) corrupt; *Méd* defective; (*fou*) *Fam* mad, idiotic.

targuer (se) [sətarge] *vpr* **se t. de qch/de faire** to boast about sth/about doing.

tarif [tarif] *nm* (*prix*) rate; *Aut Rail* fare; (*tableau*) price list, tariff. ◆**tarification** *nf* (*price*) fixing.

tarir [tarir] *vti*, — **se t.** *vpr* (*fleuve etc*) *Fig* to dry up; **ne pas t. d'éloges sur qn** to rave about s.o.

tartare [tartar] *a* **sauce t.** tartar sauce.

tarte [tart] **1** *nf* tart, flan, *Am* (*open*) pie. **2** *a inv Fam* (*sot*) silly; (*laid*) ugly. ◆**tartelette** *nf* (*small*) tart.

tartine [tartin] *nf* slice of bread; **t. de beurre/de confiture** slice of bread and butter/jam. ◆**tartiner** *vt* (*beurre*) to spread; **fromage à t.** cheese spread.

tartre [tartr] *nm* (*de bouilloire*) scale, fur; (*de dents*) tartar.

tas [tɑ] *nm* pile, heap; **un ou des t. de** (*beaucoup*) *Fam* lots of; **mettre en t.** to pile *ou* heap up; **former qn sur le t.** (*au travail*) to train s.o. on the job.

tasse [tɑs] *nf* cup; **t. à café** coffee cup; **t. à thé** teacup; **boire la t.** *Fam* to swallow a mouthful (*when swimming*).

tasser [tase] *vt* to pack, squeeze (**dans** into); (*terre*) to pack down; **un café**/*etc* **bien tassé** (*fort*) a good strong coffee/*etc*; — **se t.** *vpr* (*se voûter*) to become bowed; (*se serrer*) to squeeze up; (*sol*) to sink, collapse; **ça va se t.** (*s'arranger*) *Fam* things will pan out (all right).

tâter [tate] *vt* to feel; (*sonder*) *Fig* to sound out; — *vi* **t. de** (*métier, prison*) to have a taste of, experience; — **se t.** *vpr* (*hésiter*) to be in *ou* of two minds. ◆**tâtonn/er** *vi* to grope about, feel one's way. ◆—**ement** *nm* par **t.** (*procéder*) by trial and error. ◆**tâtons (à)** *adv* **avancer à t.** to feel one's way (along); **chercher à t.** to grope for.

tatillon, -onne [tatijɔ̃, -ɔn] *a* finicky.

tatou/er [tatwe] *vt* (*corps, dessin*) to tattoo. ◆—**age** *nm* (*dessin*) tattoo; (*action*) tattooing.

taudis [todi] *nm* slum, hovel.

taule [tol] *nf* (*prison*) *Fam* nick, jug, *Am* can.

taupe [top] *nf* (*animal, espion*) mole. ◆**taupinière** *nf* molehill.

taureau, -x [tɔro] *nm* bull; **le T.** (*signe*) Taurus. ◆**tauromachie** *nf* bull-fighting.

taux [to] *nm* rate; **t. d'alcool/de cholestérol**/*etc* alcohol/cholesterol/*etc* level.

taverne [tavɛrn] *nf* tavern.

taxe [taks] *nf* (*prix*) official price; (*impôt*) tax; (*douanière*) duty; **t. de séjour** tourist tax; **t. à la valeur ajoutée** value-added tax. ◆**taxation** *nf* fixing of the price (**de** of); taxation (**de** of). ◆**taxer** *vt* **1** (*produit*) to fix the price of; (*objet de luxe etc*) to tax. **2 t. qn** to accuse s.o. of.

taxi [taksi] *nm* taxi.

taxiphone [taksifɔn] *nm* pay phone.

Tchécoslovaquie [tʃekɔslɔvaki] *nf* Czechoslovakia. ◆**tchèque** *a & nmf* Czech; — *nm* (*langue*) Czech.

te [t(ə)] (**t'** *before vowel or mute h*) *pron* **1** (*complément direct*) you; **je te vois** I see you. **2** (*indirect*) (to) you; **il te parle** he speaks to you; **elle te l'a dit** she told you. **3** (*réfléchi*) yourself; **tu te laves** you wash yourself.

technicien, -ienne [tɛknisjɛ̃, -jɛn] *nmf* technician. ◆**technique** *a* technical; — *nf* technique. ◆**techniquement** *adv* technically. ◆**technocrate** *nm* technocrat. ◆**technologie** *nf* technology. ◆**technologique** *a* technological.

teck [tɛk] *nm* (*bois*) teak.

teckel [tekɛl] *nm* (*chien*) dachshund.

tee-shirt [tiʃœrt] *nm* tee-shirt.

teindre [tɛdr] *vt* to dye; — **se t.** *vpr* to dye one's hair. ◆**teinture** *nf* dyeing; (*produit*) dye. ◆**teinturerie** *nf* (*boutique*) (dry) cleaner's. ◆**teinturier, -ière** *nmf* dry cleaner.

teint [tɛ̃] *nm* **1** (*de visage*) complexion. **2 bon ou grand t.** (*tissu*) colourfast; **bon t.** (*catholique etc*) *Fig* staunch.

teinte [tɛ̃t] *nf* shade, tint; **une t. de** (*dose*) *Fig* a tinge of. ◆**teinter** *vt* to tint; (*bois*) to stain; **se t. de** (*remarque, ciel*) *Fig* to be tinged with.

tel, telle [tɛl] *a* such; **un t. homme/livre**/*etc* such a man/book/*etc*; **un t. intérêt**/*etc* such interest/*etc*; **de tels mots**/*etc* such words/*etc*; **t. que** such as, like; **t. que je l'ai laissé** just as I left it; **laissez-le t. quel** leave it just as it is; **en tant que t., comme t.** as such; **t. ou t.** such and such; **rien de t. que ...** (*there's*) nothing like ...; **rien de t.** nothing like it; **Monsieur Un t.** Mr So-and-so; **t. père t. fils** like father like son.

télé [tele] *nf* (*téléviseur*) *Fam* TV, telly; **à la t.** on TV, on the telly; **regarder la t.** to watch TV *ou* the telly.

télé- [tele] *préf* tele-.

télébenne [teleben] *nf*, **télécabine** [telekabin] *nf* (*cabine, système*) cable car.

télécommande [telekɔmɑ̃d] *nf* remote control. ◆**télécommander** *vt* to operate by remote control.

télécommunications [telekɔmynikasjɔ̃] *nfpl* telecommunications.

téléfilm [telefilm] *nm* TV film.

télégramme [telegram] *nm* telegram.

télégraphe [telegraf] *nm* telegraph. ◆**télégraphie** *nf* telegraphy. ◆**télégraphier** *vt* (*message*) to wire, cable (**que** that). ◆**télégraphique** *a* (*fil, poteau*) telegraph-; (*style*) *Fig* telegraphic. ◆**télégraphiste** *nm* (*messager*) telegraph boy.

téléguid/er [telegide] *vt* to radio-control. ◆—**age** *nm* radio-control.

télématique [telematik] *nf* telematics, computer communications.

télépathie [telepati] *nf* telepathy.

téléphérique [teleferik] *nm* (*système*) cable car, cableway.

téléphone [telefɔn] *nm* (tele)phone; **coup de t.** (phone) call; **passer un coup de t. à qn** to give s.o. a call *ou* a ring; **au t.** on the (tele)phone; **avoir le t.** to be on the (tele)phone; **par le t. arabe** *Fig* on the grapevine. ◆**téléphoner** *vt* (*nouvelle etc*) to (tele)phone (**à** to); — *vi* to (tele)phone; **t. à qn** to (tele)phone s.o., call s.o. (up). ◆**téléphonique** *a* (*appel etc*) (tele)phone-. ◆**téléphoniste** *nmf* operator, telephonist.

télescope [telɛskɔp] *nm* telescope. ◆**télescopique** *a* telescopic.

télescop/er [telɛskɔpe] *vt Aut Rail* to smash into; **se t.** to smash into each other. ◆**—age** *nm* smash.

téléscripteur [teleskriptœr] *nm* (*appareil*) teleprinter.

télésiège [telesjɛʒ] *nm* chair lift.

téléski [teleski] *nm* ski tow.

téléspectateur, -trice [telespɛktatœr, -tris] *nmf* (television) viewer.

téléviser [televize] *vt* to televise; **journal télévisé** television news. ◆**téléviseur** *nm* television (set). ◆**télévision** *nf* television; **à la t.** on (the) television; **regarder la t.** to watch (the) television; **de t.** (*programme etc*) television-.

télex [telɛks] *nm* (*service, message*) telex.

telle [tɛl] *voir* **tel.**

tellement [tɛlmɑ̃] *adv* (*si*) so; (*tant*) so much; **t. grand/etc que** so big/etc that; **crier/etc t. que** to shout/etc so much that; **t. de** (*travail etc*) so much; (*soucis etc*) so many; **personne ne peut le supporter, il est bavard** nobody can stand him, he's so talkative; **tu aimes ça? - pas t.** do you like it? - not much ou not really.

téméraire [temerɛr] *a* rash, reckless. ◆**témérité** *nf* rashness, recklessness.

témoign/er [temwaɲe] **1** *vi Jur* to testify (**contre** against); **t. de qch** (*personne, attitude etc*) to testify to sth; — *vt* **t. que** *Jur* to testify that. **2** *vt* (*gratitude etc*) to show (**à qn** to) s.o.). ◆**—age** *nm* **1** testimony, evidence; (*récit*) account; **faux t.** (*délit*) *Jur* perjury. **2** (*d'affection etc*) *Fig* token, sign (**de** of); **en t. de** as a token ou sign of.

témoin [temwɛ̃] **1** *nm* witness; **t. oculaire** eyewitness; **être t. de** (*accident etc*) to witness; — *a* **appartement t.** show flat ou *Am* apartment. **2** *nm Sp* baton.

tempe [tɑ̃p] *nf Anat* temple.

tempérament [tɑ̃peramɑ̃] *nm* **1** (*caractère*) temperament; (*physique*) constitution. **2** **acheter à t.** to buy on hire purchase ou *Am* on the installment plan.

tempérance [tɑ̃perɑ̃s] *nf* temperance.

température [tɑ̃peratyr] *nf* temperature; **avoir** ou **faire de la t.** *Méd* to have a temperature.

tempér/er [tɑ̃pere] *vt Litt* to temper. ◆**—é** *a* (*climat, zone*) temperate.

tempête [tɑ̃pɛt] *nf* storm; **t. de neige** snowstorm, blizzard.

tempêter [tɑ̃pete] *vi* (*crier*) to storm, rage (**contre** against).

temple [tɑ̃pl] *nm Rel* temple; (*protestant*) church.

tempo [tɛmpo] *nm* tempo.

temporaire [tɑ̃pɔrɛr] *a* temporary. ◆**—ment** *adv* temporarily.

temporel, -elle [tɑ̃pɔrɛl] *a* temporal.

temporiser [tɑ̃pɔrize] *vi* to procrastinate, play for time.

temps¹ [tɑ̃] *nm* (*durée, période, moment*) time; *Gram* tense; (*étape*) stage; **t. d'arrêt** pause, break; **en t. de guerre** in time of war, in wartime; **avoir/trouver le t.** to have/find (the) time (**de faire** to do); **il est t.** it's time (**de faire** to do); **il était t.!** it was about time (too)!; **pendant un t.** for a while ou time; **ces derniers t.** lately; **de t. en t.** [dətɑ̃zɑ̃tɑ̃], **de t. à autre** [dətɑ̃zaotr] from time to time, now and again; **en t. utile** [ɑ̃tɑ̃zytil] in good ou due time; **en même t.** at the same time (**que** as); **à t.** (*arriver*) in time; **à plein t.** (*travailler etc*) full-time; **à t. partiel** (*travailler etc*) part-time; **dans le t.** (*autrefois*) once, at one time; **avec le t.** (*à la longue*) in time; **tout le t.** all the time; **du t. de** in the time of; **de mon t.** in my time; **à quatre t.** (*moteur*) four-stroke.

temps² [tɑ̃] *nm* (*atmosphérique*) weather; **il fait beau/mauvais t.** the weather's fine/bad; **quel t. fait-il?** what's the weather like?

tenable [tənabl] *a* bearable.

tenace [tənas] *a* stubborn, tenacious. ◆**ténacité** *nf* stubbornness, tenacity.

tenailler [tənaje] *vt* (*faim, remords*) to rack, torture (*s.o.*).

tenailles [tənaj] *nfpl* (*outil*) pincers.

tenancier, -ière [tənɑ̃sje, -jɛr] *nmf* (*d'hôtel etc*) manager, manageress.

tenant, -ante [tənɑ̃, -ɑ̃t] *nmf* (*de titre*) *Sp* holder. **2** *nm* (*partisan*) supporter (**de** of).

tenants [tənɑ̃] *nmpl* **les t. et les aboutissants** (*d'une question etc*) the ins and outs (**de** of).

tendance [tɑ̃dɑ̃s] *nf* (*penchant*) tendency; (*évolution*) trend (**à** towards); **avoir t. à faire** to have a tendency to do, tend to do.

tendancieux, -euse [tɑ̃dɑ̃sjø, -øz] *a Péj* tendentious.

tendeur [tɑ̃dœr] *nm* (*pour arrimer des bagages*) elastic strap.

tendon [tɑ̃dɔ̃] *nm Anat* tendon, sinew.

tend/re¹ [tɑ̃dr] **1** *vt* to stretch; (*main*) to hold out (**à qn** to s.o.); (*bras, jambe*) to stretch out; (*cou*) to strain, crane; (*muscle*) to tense, flex; (*arc*) to bend; (*piège*) to lay, set; (*filet*) to spread; (*tapisserie*) to hang; **t. qch à qn** to hold out sth to s.o.; **t. l'oreille** *Fig* to prick up one's ears; **— se t.** *vpr* (*rap-*

ports) to become strained. **2** *vi* **t** **à qch/à faire** to tend towards sth/to do. **◆—u** *a* (*corde*) tight, taut; (*personne, situation*) tense; (*rapports*) strained; (*main*) outstretched.

tendre² [tɑ̃dr] *a* **1** (*viande*) tender; (*peau*) delicate, tender; (*bois, couleur*) soft. **2** (*affectueux*) loving, tender. **◆—ment** [-əmɑ̃] *adv* lovingly, tenderly. **◆tendresse** *nf* (*affection*) affection, tenderness. **◆tendreté** *nf* (*de viande*) tenderness.

ténèbres [tenɛbr] *nfpl* darkness, gloom. **◆ténébreux, -euse** *a* dark, gloomy; (*mystérieux*) mysterious.

teneur [tənœr] *nf* (*de lettre etc*) content; **t. en alcool/*etc*** alcohol/*etc* content (**de** of).

tenir* [tənir] *vt* (*à la main etc*) to hold; (*pari, promesse*) to keep; (*hôtel*) to run, keep; (*comptes*) Com to keep; (*propos*) to utter; (*rôle*) to play; **t. propre/chaud/*etc*** to keep clean/hot/*etc*; **je le tiens!** (*je l'ai attrapé*) I've got him!; **je tiens de** (*fait etc*) I get it from; (*caractère héréditaire*) I get it from; **t. pour** to regard as; **t. sa droite** *Aut* to keep to the right; **t. la route** (*voiture*) to hold the road; **– vi** (*nœud etc*) to hold; (*coiffure, neige*) to last, hold; (*offre*) to stand; (*résister*) to hold out; **t. à** (*personne, jouet etc*) to be attached to, be fond of; (*la vie*) to value; (*provenir*) to stem from; **t. à faire** to be anxious to do; **t. dans qch** (*être contenu*) to fit into sth; **t. de qn** to take after s.o.; **tenez!** (*prenez*) here (you are)!; **tiens!** (*surprise*) hey!, well!; **– v imp** **il ne tient qu'à vous** it's up to you (**de faire** to do); **– se t.** *vpr* (*rester*) to keep, remain; (*avoir lieu*) to be held; **se t.** (**debout**) to stand (up); **se t. droit** to stand up *ou* sit up straight; **se t. par la main** to hold hands; **se t. à** to hold on to; **se t. bien** to behave oneself; **tout se tient** *Fig* it all hangs together; **s'en t. à** (*se limiter à*) to stick to; **savoir à quoi s'en t.** to know what's what.

tennis [tenis] *nm* tennis; (*terrain*) (tennis) court; **t. de table** table tennis; **– nfpl** (*chaussures*) plimsolls, pumps, *Am* sneakers.

ténor [tenɔr] *nm* *Mus* tenor.

tension [tɑ̃sjɔ̃] *nf* tension; **t. (artérielle)** blood pressure; **t. d'esprit** concentration; **avoir de la t.** *Méd* to have high blood pressure.

tentacule [tɑ̃takyl] *nm* tentacle.

tente [tɑ̃t] *nf* tent.

tenter¹ [tɑ̃te] *vt* (*essayer*) to try; **t. de faire** to try *ou* attempt to do. **◆tentative** *nf* attempt; **t. de suicide** suicide attempt.

tent/er² [tɑ̃te] *vt* (*allécher*) to tempt; **tenté de faire** tempted to do. **◆—ant** *a* tempting. **◆tentation** *nf* temptation.

tenture [tɑ̃tyr] *nf* (wall) hanging; (*de porte*) drape, curtain.

tenu [təny] *voir* **tenir**; **– a t. de faire** obliged to do; **bien/mal t.** (*maison etc*) well/badly kept.

ténu [teny] *a* (*fil etc*) fine; (*soupçon, différence*) tenuous; (*voix*) thin.

tenue [təny] *nf* **1** (*vêtements*) clothes, outfit; (*aspect*) appearance; **t. de combat** *Mil* combat dress; **t. de soirée** (*smoking*) evening dress. **2** (*conduite*) (good) behaviour; (*maintien*) posture; **manquer de t.** to lack (good) manners. **3** (*de maison, hôtel*) running; (*de comptes*) *Com* keeping. **4 t. de route** *Aut* road-holding.

ter [tɛr] *a* **4 t.** (*numéro*) 4B.

térébenthine [terebɑ̃tin] *nf* turpentine.

tergal® [tɛrgal] *nm* Terylene®, *Am* Dacron®.

tergiverser [tɛrʒivɛrse] *vi* to procrastinate.

terme [tɛrm] *nm* **1** (*mot*) term. **2** (*loyer*) rent; (*jour*) rent day; (*période*) rental period. **3** (*date limite*) time (limit), date; (*fin*) end; **mettre un t. à** to put an end to; **à court/long t.** (*projet etc*) short-/long-term; **être né avant/à t.** to be born prematurely/at (full) term. **4 moyen t.** (*solution*) middle course. **5 en bons/mauvais termes** on good/bad terms (**avec qn** with s.o.).

terminer [tɛrmine] *vt* (*achever*) to finish, complete; (*lettre, phrase, débat, soirée*) to end; **– se t.** *vpr* to end (**par** with, **en** in). **◆terminaison** *nf* *Gram* ending. **◆terminal, -aux** *a* final; (*phase*) *Méd* terminal; **– a & nf** (*classe*) **terminale** *Scol* = sixth form, *Am* = twelfth grade. **2** *nm* (*d'ordinateur, pétrolier*) terminal.

terminologie [tɛrminɔlɔʒi] *nf* terminology.

terminus [tɛrminys] *nm* terminus.

termite [tɛrmit] *nm* (*insecte*) termite.

terne [tɛrn] *a* (*couleur, journée etc*) dull, drab; (*personne*) dull. **◆ternir** *vt* (*métal, réputation*) to tarnish; (*miroir, meuble*) to dull; **– se t.** *vpr* (*métal*) to tarnish.

terrain [tɛrɛ̃] *nm* (*sol*) & *Fig* ground; (*étendue*) land; *Mil Géol* terrain; (*à bâtir*) plot, site; **un t. a piece of** land; **t. d'aviation** airfield; **t. de camping** campsite; **t. de football/rugby** football/rugby pitch; **t. de golf** golf course; **t. de jeu** playground; **t. de sport** sports ground, playing field; **t. vague** waste ground, *Am* vacant lot; **céder/gagner/perdre du t.** *Mil* & *Fig* to give/

lose ground; **tout t., tous terrains** (véhicule) all-purpose.

terrasse [teras] nf **1** terrace; (toit) terrace (roof). **2** (de café) pavement ou Am sidewalk area; **à la t.** outside.

terrassement [tɛrasmɑ̃] nm (travail) excavation.

terrasser [tɛrase] vt (adversaire) to floor, knock down; (accabler) Fig to overcome.

terrassier [tɛrasje] nm labourer, navvy.

terre [tɛr] nf (matière) earth; (sol) ground; (opposé à mer, étendue) land; pl (domaine) land, estate; Él earth, Am ground; **la t.** (le monde) the earth; **la T.** (planète) Earth; **à ou par t.** (poser, tomber) to the ground; **par t.** (assis, couché) on the ground; **aller à t.** Nau to go ashore; **sous t.** underground; **t. cuite** (baked) clay, earthenware; **en t. cuite** (poterie) clay-. ◆**t.-à-terre** a inv down-to-earth. ◆**t.-plein** nm (terre) platform; (au milieu de la route) central reservation, Am median strip. ◆**terrestre** a (vie, joies) earthly; (animaux, transport) land-; **la surface t.** the earth's surface; **globe t.** (terrestrial) globe. ◆**terreux, -euse** a (goût) earthy; (sale) grubby; (couleur) dull; (teint) ashen. ◆**terrien, -ienne** a land-owning; **propriétaire t.** landowner; – nmf (habitant de la terre) earth dweller, earthling.

terreau [tɛro] nm compost.

terrer (se) [sətɛre] vpr (fugitif, animal) to hide, go to ground ou earth.

terreur [tɛrœr] nf terror; **t. de** fear of. ◆**terrible** a terrible; (formidable) Fam terrific. ◆**terriblement** adv (extrêmement) terribly. ◆**terrifier** vt to terrify. ◆**—ant** a terrifying; (extraordinaire) incredible.

terrier [tɛrje] nm **1** (de lapin etc) burrow. **2** (chien) terrier.

terrine [tɛrin] nf (récipient) Culin terrine; (pâté) pâté.

territoire [tɛritwar] nm territory. ◆**territorial, -aux** a territorial.

terroir [tɛrwar] nm (sol) soil; (région) region; **du t.** (accent etc) rural.

terroriser [tɛrɔrize] vt to terrorize. ◆**terrorisme** nm terrorism. ◆**terroriste** a & nmf terrorist.

tertiaire [tɛrsjɛr] a tertiary.

tertre [tɛrtr] nm hillock, mound.

tes [te] voir **ton¹**.

tesson [tɛsõ] nm **t. de bouteille** piece of broken bottle.

test [tɛst] nm test. ◆**tester** vt (élève, produit) to test.

testament [tɛstamɑ̃] nm **1** Jur will; (œuvre)

Fig testament. **2** Ancien/Nouveau T. Rel Old/New Testament.

testicule [tɛstikyl] nm Anat testicle.

tétanos [tetanos] nm Méd tetanus.

têtard [tɛtar] nm tadpole.

tête [tɛt] nf head; (figure) face; (cheveux) (head of) hair; (cerveau) brain; (cime) top; (de clou, cortège, lit) head; (de page, liste) top, head; (coup) Fb header; **t. nucléaire** nuclear warhead; **tenir t.** à (s'opposer à) to stand up to; **t. nue** bare-headed; **tu n'as pas de t.!** you're a scatterbrain!; **faire la t.** (bouder) to sulk; **faire une t.** Fb to head the ball; **avoir/faire une drôle de t.** to have/give a funny look; **perdre la t.** Fig to lose one's head; **tomber la t. la première** to fall headlong ou head first; **calculer qch de t.** to work sth out in one's head; **se mettre dans la t. de faire** to get it into one's head to do; **à t. reposée** at one's leisure; **à la t. de** (entreprise, parti) at the head of; (classe) Scol at the top of; **de la t. aux pieds** from head ou top to toe; **en t.** Sp in the lead. ◆**t.-à-queue** nm inv faire un t.-à-queue Aut to spin right round. ◆**t.-à-tête** adv (en) t.-à-tête (seul) in private, alone together; – nm inv tête-à-tête. ◆**t.-bêche** adv head to tail.

tét/er [tete] vt (lait, biberon etc) to suck; **t. sa mère** (bébé) to suck, feed; – vi donner à t. **à** to feed, suckle. ◆**–ée** nf (de bébé) feed. ◆**tétine** nf **1** (de biberon) teat, Am nipple; (sucette) dummy, Am pacifier. **2** (de vache) udder. ◆**téton** nm Fam breast.

têtu [tety] a stubborn, obstinate.

texte [tɛkst] nm text; Th lines, text; (de devoir) Scol subject; (morceau choisi) Littér passage. ◆**textuel, -elle** a (traduction) literal.

textile [tɛkstil] a & nm textile.

texture [tɛkstyr] nf texture.

TGV [tezeve] abrév = train à grande vitesse.

Thaïlande [tailɑ̃d] nf Thailand. ◆**thaïlandais, -aise** a & nmf Thai.

thé [te] nm (boisson, réunion) tea. ◆**théière** nf teapot.

théâtre [teatr] nm (art, lieu) theatre; (œuvres) drama; (d'un crime) Fig scene; (des opérations) Mil theatre; **faire du t.** to act. ◆**théâtral, -aux** a theatrical.

thème [tɛm] nm theme; (traduction) Scol translation, prose.

théologie [teɔlɔʒi] nf theology. ◆**théologien** nm theologian. ◆**théologique** a theological.

théorème [teɔrɛm] nm theorem.

théorie [teɔri] nf theory; **en t.** in theory.

◆**théoricien, -ienne** *nmf* theorist, theoretician. ◆**théorique** *a* theoretical. ◆**théoriquement** *adv* theoretically.

thérapeutique [terapøtik] *a* therapeutic; − *nf (traitement)* therapy. ◆**thérapie** *nf* Psy therapy.

thermal, -aux [termal, -o] *a* **station thermale** spa; **eaux thermales** hot springs.

thermique [termik] *a (énergie, unité)* thermal.

thermomètre [termɔmɛtr] *nm* thermometer.

thermonucléaire [termɔnykleɛr] *a* thermonuclear.

thermos® [termɔs] *nm ou f* Thermos (flask)®, vacuum flask.

thermostat [termɔsta] *nm* thermostat.

thèse [tɛz] *nf (proposition, ouvrage)* thesis.

thon [tɔ̃] *nm* tuna (fish).

thorax [tɔraks] *nm Anat* thorax.

thym [tɛ̃] *nm Bot Culin* thyme.

thyroïde [tirɔid] *a & nf Anat* thyroid.

tibia [tibja] *nm* shin bone, tibia.

tic [tik] *nm (contraction)* tic, twitch; *(manie)* Fig mannerism.

ticket [tikɛ] *nm* ticket; **t. de quai** Rail platform ticket.

tic(-)tac [tiktak] *int & nm inv* tick-tock.

tiède [tjɛd] *a (luke)warm*, tepid; *(vent)* mild; *(accueil, partisan)* half-hearted. ◆**tiédeur** *nf (luke)warmness*, tepidness; mildness; half-heartedness. ◆**tiédir** *vt* to cool (down); *(chauffer)* to warm (up); − *vi* to cool (down); to warm up.

tien, tienne [tjɛ̃, tjɛn] *pron poss* **le t., la tienne, les tien(ne)s** yours; **les deux tiens** your two; − *nmpl* **les tiens** *(amis etc)* your (own) people.

tiens, tient [tjɛ̃] *voir* tenir.

tiercé [tjɛrse] *nm (pari)* place betting *(on horses)*; **gagner au t.** to win on the races.

tiers, tierce [tjɛr, tjɛrs] *a* third; − *nm (fraction)* third; *(personne)* third party; **assurance au t.** third-party insurance. ◆**T.-Monde** *nm* Third World.

tige [tiʒ] *nf (de plante)* stem, stalk; *(de botte)* leg; *(barre)* rod.

tignasse [tiɲas] *nf* mop (of hair).

tigre [tigr] *nm* tiger. ◆**tigresse** *nf* tigress.

tigré [tigre] *a (tacheté)* spotted; *(rayé)* striped.

tilleul [tijœl] *nm* lime (tree), linden (tree); *(infusion)* lime (blossom) tea.

timbale [tɛ̃bal] *nf* **1** *(gobelet)* (metal) tumbler. **2** Mus kettledrum.

timbre [tɛ̃br] *nm* **1** *(marque, tampon, vignette)* stamp; *(cachet de la poste)* post-

mark. **2** *(sonnette)* bell. **3** *(d'instrument, de voix)* tone (quality). ◆**t.-poste** *nm (pl timbres-poste)* (postage) stamp. ◆**timbr/er** *vt (affranchir)* to stamp *(letter)*; *(marquer)* to stamp *(document)*. ◆**−é** *a* **1** *(voix)* sonorous. **2** *(fou)* Fam crazy.

timide [timid] *a (gêné)* shy, timid; *(timoré)* timid. ◆**−ment** *adv* shyly; timidly. ◆**timidité** *nf* shyness; timidity.

timonier [timɔnje] *nm Nau* helmsman.

timoré [timɔre] *a* timorous, fearful.

tintamarre [tɛ̃tamar] *nm* din, racket.

tint/er [tɛ̃te] *vi (cloche)* to ring, toll; *(clés, monnaie)* to jingle; *(verres)* to chink. ◆**−ement(s)** *nm(pl)* ringing; jingling; chinking.

tique [tik] *nf (insecte)* tick.

tiquer [tike] *vi (personne)* to wince.

tir [tir] *nm (sport)* shooting; *(action)* firing, shooting; *(feu, rafale)* fire; Fb shot; **t. (forain), (stand de) t.** shooting *ou* rifle range; **t. à l'arc** archery; **ligne de t.** line of fire.

tirade [tirad] *nf* Th & Fig monologue.

tiraill/er [tiraje] **1** *vt* to pull (away) at; *(harceler)* Fig to pester, plague; **tiraillé entre** *(possibilités etc)* torn between. **2** *vi (au fusil)* to shoot wildly. ◆**−ement** *nm* **1** *(conflit)* conflict *(entre* between). **2** *(crampe)* Méd cramp.

tire [tir] *nf* **vol à la t.** Fam pickpocketing.

tire-au-flanc [tiroflɑ̃] *nm inv (paresseux)* shirker. ◆**t.-bouchon** *nm* corkscrew. ◆**t.-d'aile (à)** *adv* swiftly.

tirelire [tirlir] *nf* moneybox, Am coin bank.

tir/er [tire] *vt* to pull; *(langue)* to stick out; *(trait, conclusion, rideaux)* to draw; *(chapeau)* to raise; *(balle, canon)* to fire, shoot; *(gibier)* to shoot; Typ Phot to print; **t. de** *(sortir)* to take *ou* pull *ou* draw out of; *(obtenir)* to get from; *(nom, origine)* to derive from; *(produit)* to extract from; **t. qn de** *(danger, lit)* to get s.o. out of; − *vi* to pull *(sur* on, at); *(faire feu)* to fire, shoot *(sur* at); Fb to shoot; *(cheminée)* to draw; **t. sur** *(couleur)* to verge on; **t. au sort** to draw lots; **t. à sa fin** to draw to a close; − **se t.** *vpr (partir)* Fam to beat it; **se t. de** *(problème, travail)* to cope with; *(danger, situation)* to get out of; **se t. d'affaire** to get out of trouble; **s'en t.** Fam *(en réchapper)* to come *ou* pull through; *(réussir)* to get along. ◆**−é** *a (traits, visage)* drawn; **t. par les cheveux** Fig far-fetched. ◆**−age** *nm* **1** *(action)* Typ Phot printing; *(édition)* edition; *(quantité)* (print) run; *(de journal)* circulation. **2** *(de loterie)* draw; **t. au sort**

drawing of lots. **3** (de cheminée) draught. ◆**-eur** nm gunman; **t. d'élite** marksman; **un bon/mauvais t.** a good/bad shot. ◆**-euse de t.** fortune-teller.

tiret [tirɛ] nm (trait) dash.

tiroir [tirwar] nm (de commode etc) drawer. ◆**t.-caisse** nm (pl tiroirs-caisses) (cash) till.

tisane [tizan] nf herb(al) tea.

tison [tizɔ̃] nm (fire)brand, ember. ◆**tisonner** vt (feu) to poke. ◆**tisonnier** nm poker.

tiss/er [tise] vt to weave. ◆**-age** nm (action) weaving. ◆**tisserand, -ande** nmf weaver.

tissu [tisy] nm fabric, material, cloth; Biol tissue; **un t. de** (mensonges etc) a web of; **le t.** social the fabric of society, the social fabric; **du t.-éponge** (terry) towelling.

titre [titr] nm (nom, qualité) title; Com bond; (diplôme) qualification; pl (droits) claims (à to); (gros) t. Journ headline; **t. de propriété** title deed; **t. de transport** ticket; **à quel t.?** (pour quelle raison) on what grounds?; **à ce t.** (en cette qualité) as such; (pour cette raison) therefore; **à aucun t.** on no account; **au même t.** in the same way (que as); **à t. d'exemple/d'ami** as an example/friend; **à t. exceptionnel** exceptionally; **à t. privé** in a private capacity; **à juste t.** rightly. ◆**titr/er** vt (film) to title; Journ to run as a headline. ◆**-é-a** (personne) titled. ◆**titulaire** a (professeur) staff-, full; **être t. de** (permis etc) to be the holder of; (poste) to hold; – nmf (de permis, poste) holder (de of). ◆**titulariser** vt (fonctionnaire) to give tenure to.

tituber [titybe] vi to reel, stagger.

toast [tost] nm **1** (pain grillé) piece ou slice of toast. **2** (allocution) toast; **porter un t. à** to drink (a toast) to.

toboggan [tɔbɔgɑ̃] nm **1** (pente) slide; (traîneau) toboggan. **2** Aut flyover, Am overpass.

toc [tɔk] **1** int **t. t.!** knock knock! **2** nm du t. (camelote) rubbish, trash; **en t.** (bijou) imitation-.

tocsin [tɔksɛ̃] nm alarm (bell).

tohu-bohu [tɔybɔy] nm (bruit) hubbub, commotion; (confusion) hurly-burly.

toi [twa] pron **1** (complément) you; **c'est t.** it's you; **avec t.** with you. **2** (sujet) you; **t., tu peux** you may. **3** (réfléchi) assieds-t. (yourself) down; **dépêche-t.** hurry up. ◆**t.-même** pron yourself.

toile [twal] nf **1** cloth; (à voile) canvas; (à draps) linen; **une t.** a piece of cloth ou canvas ou linen; **t. de jute** hessian; **drap de t.** linen sheet; **t. de fond** Th & Fig backcloth. **2** (tableau) canvas, painting. **3** **t. d'araignée** cobweb, (spider's) web.

toilette [twalɛt] nf (action) wash(ing); (vêtements) outfit, clothes; **articles de t.** toiletries; **cabinet de t.** washroom; **eau/savon/trousse de t.** toilet water/soap/bag; **table de t.** dressing table; **faire sa t.** to wash (and dress); **les toilettes** (W-C) the toilet(s); **aller aux toilettes** to go to the toilet.

toiser [twaze] vt to eye scornfully.

toison [twazɔ̃] nf (de mouton) fleece.

toit [twa] nm roof; **t. ouvrant** Aut sunroof. ◆**toiture** nf roof(ing).

tôle [tol] nf la t. sheet metal; **une t.** a steel ou metal sheet; **t. ondulée** corrugated iron.

tolér/er [tɔlere] vt (permettre) to tolerate, allow; (supporter) to tolerate, bear; (à la douane) to allow. ◆**-ant** a tolerant (à l'égard de of). ◆**-able** a tolerable. ◆**tolérance** nf tolerance; (à la douane) allowance.

tollé [tɔle] nm outcry.

tomate [tɔmat] nf tomato; **sauce t.** tomato sauce.

tombe [tɔ̃b] nf grave; (avec monument) tomb. ◆**tombale** af pierre t. gravestone, tombstone. ◆**tombeau, -x** nm tomb.

tomb/er [tɔ̃be] vi (aux être) to fall; (température) to drop, fall; (vent) to drop (off); (cheveux, robe) to hang down; **t. malade** to fall ill; **t. (par terre)** to fall (down); **faire t.** (personne) to knock over; (gouvernement, prix) to bring down; **laisser t.** (objet) to drop; (personne, projet etc) Fig to drop, give up; **tu m'as laissé t. hier** Fig you let me down yesterday; **se laisser t. dans un fauteuil** to drop into an armchair; **tu tombes bien/mal** Fig you've come at the right/wrong time; **t. de fatigue** ou **de sommeil** to be ready to drop; **t. un lundi** to fall on a Monday; **t. sur** (trouver) to come across. ◆**-ée-nf t. de la nuit** nightfall.

tombereau, -x [tɔ̃bro] nm (charrette) tip cart.

tombola [tɔ̃bɔla] nf raffle.

tome [tom] nm (livre) volume.

ton¹, ta, pl tes [tɔ̃, ta, te] (ta becomes ton [tɔ̃n] before a vowel or mute h) a poss your; **t. père** your father; **ta mère** your mother; **ton ami(e)** your friend.

ton² [tɔ̃] nm (de couleur) shade, tone; (gamme) Mus key; (hauteur de son) & Ling pitch; **de bon t.** (goût) in good taste; **donner le t.** Fig to set the tone. ◆**tonalité** nf (de *radio etc*) tone; *Tél* dialling tone, *Am* dial tone.

tond/re [tɔ̃dr] *vt* **1** (*mouton*) to shear; (*cheveux*) to clip, crop; (*gazon*) to mow. **2 t. qn** (*escroquer*) *Fam* to fleece s.o. ◆**-euse** *nf* shears; (*à cheveux*) clippers; **t. (à gazon)** (lawn)mower.

tonifi/er [tɔnifje] *vt* (*muscles, peau*) to tone up; (*esprit, personne*) to invigorate. ◆**-ant** *a* (*activité, climat etc*) invigorating.

tonique [tɔnik] **1** *a* (*accent*) *Ling* tonic. **2** *a* (*froid, effet, vin*) tonic, invigorating; – *nm* *Méd* tonic.

tonitruant [tɔnitryɑ̃] *a* (*voix*) *Fam* booming.

tonnage [tɔnaʒ] *nm* *Nau* tonnage.

tonne [tɔn] *nf* (*poids*) metric ton, tonne; **des tonnes de** (*beaucoup*) *Fam* tons of.

tonneau, -x [tɔno] *nm* **1** (*récipient*) barrel, cask. **2** (*manœuvre*) *Av* roll; **faire un t.** *Aut* to roll over. **3** (*poids*) *Nau* ton. ◆**tonnelet** *nm* keg.

tonnelle [tɔnɛl] *nf* arbour, bower.

tonner [tɔne] *vi* (*canons*) to thunder; (*crier*) *Fig* to thunder, rage (**contre** against); – *v imp* **il tonne** it's thundering. ◆**tonnerre** *nm* thunder; **coup de t.** thunderclap; *Fig* bombshell, thunderbolt; **du t.** (*excellent*) *Fam* terrific.

tonte [tɔ̃t] *nf* (*de moutons*) shearing; (*de gazon*) mowing.

tonton [tɔ̃tɔ̃] *nm* *Fam* uncle.

tonus [tɔnys] *nm* (*énergie*) energy, vitality.

top [tɔp] *nm* (*signal sonore*) *Rad* stroke.

topaze [tɔpaz] *nf* (*pierre*) topaz.

topinambour [tɔpinɑ̃bur] *nm* Jerusalem artichoke.

topo [tɔpo] *nm* (*exposé*) *Fam* talk, speech.

topographie [tɔpɔɡrafi] *nf* topography.

toque [tɔk] *nf* (*de fourrure*) fur hat; (*de juge, jockey*) cap; (*de cuisinier*) hat.

toqu/er (se) [sətɔke] *vpr* **se t. de qn** *Fam* to become infatuated with s.o. ◆**-é** *a* (*fou*) *Fam* crazy. ◆**toquade** *nf* *Fam* (*pour qch*) craze (**pour** for); (*pour qn*) infatuation (**pour** with).

torche [tɔrʃ] *nf* (*flambeau*) torch; **t. électrique** torch, *Am* flashlight.

torcher [tɔrʃe] *vt* **1** (*travail*) to skimp. **2** (*essuyer*) *Fam* to wipe.

torchon [tɔrʃɔ̃] *nm* (*à vaisselle*) tea towel, *Am* dish towel; (*de ménage*) duster, cloth.

tord/re [tɔrdr] *vt* to twist; (*linge, cou*) to wring; (*barre*) to bend; **se t. la cheville/le pied/le dos** to twist *ou* sprain one's ankle/foot/back; – **se t.** *vpr* to twist; (*barre*) to bend; **se t. de douleur** to writhe with pain; **se t. (de rire)** to split one's sides

(laughing). ◆**-ant** *a* (*drôle*) *Fam* hilarious. ◆**-u** *a* twisted; (*esprit*) warped.

tornade [tɔrnad] *nf* tornado.

torpeur [tɔrpœr] *nf* lethargy, torpor.

torpille [tɔrpij] *nf* torpedo. ◆**torpill/er** *vt* *Mil* & *Fig* to torpedo. ◆**-eur** *nm* torpedo boat.

torréfier [tɔrefje] *vt* (*café*) to roast.

torrent [tɔrɑ̃] *nm* (*ruisseau*) torrent; **un t. de** (*injures, larmes*) a flood of; **il pleut à torrents** it's pouring (down). ◆**torrentiel, -ielle** *a* (*pluie*) torrential.

torride [tɔrid] *a* (*chaleur etc*) torrid, scorching.

torsade [tɔrsad] *nf* (*de cheveux*) twist, coil. ◆**torsader** *vt* to twist (together).

torse [tɔrs] *nm* *Anat* chest; (*statue*) torso.

torsion [tɔrsjɔ̃] *nf* twisting; *Phys Tech* torsion.

tort [tɔr] *nm* (*dommage*) wrong; (*défaut*) fault; **avoir t.** to be wrong (**de faire** to do, in doing); **tu as t. de fumer!** you shouldn't smoke!; **être dans son t.** *ou* **en t.** to be in the wrong; **donner t. à qn** (*accuser*) to blame s.o.; (*faits etc*) to prove s.o. wrong; **faire du t. à qn** to harm *ou* wrong s.o.; **à t.** wrongly; **à t. et à travers** wildly, indiscriminately; **à t. ou à raison** rightly or wrongly.

torticolis [tɔrtikɔli] *nm* stiff neck.

tortill/er [tɔrtije] *vt* to twist, twirl; (*moustache*) to twirl; (*tripoter*) to twiddle with; – **se t.** *vpr* (*ver, personne*) to wriggle; (*en dansant, des hanches*) to wiggle. ◆**-ement** *nm* wriggling, wiggling.

tortionnaire [tɔrsjɔnɛr] *nm* torturer.

tortue [tɔrty] *nf* tortoise; (*marine*) turtle; **quelle t.!** *Fig* what a slowcoach *ou* *Am* slowpoke!

tortueux, -euse [tɔrtɥø, -øz] *a* tortuous.

torture [tɔrtyr] *nf* torture. ◆**torturer** *vt* to torture; **se t. les méninges** to rack one's brains.

tôt [to] *adv* early; **au plus t.** at the earliest; **le plus t. possible** as soon as possible; **t. ou tard** sooner or later; **je n'étais pas plus t. sorti que ...** no sooner had I gone out than ....

total, -aux [tɔtal, -o] *a* & *nm* total; **au t.** all in all, in total; (*somme toute*) all in all. ◆**totalement** *adv* totally, completely. ◆**totaliser** *vt* to total. ◆**totalité** *nf* entirety; **la t. de** all of; **en t.** entirely, totally.

totalitaire [tɔtalitɛr] *a* *Pol* totalitarian.

toubib [tubib] *nm* (*médecin*) *Fam* doctor.

touche [tuʃ] *nf* (*de peintre*) touch; *Pêche* bite; (*clavier*) key; **une t. de** (*un peu de*) a touch *ou* hint of; **(ligne de) t.** Fb Rugby touchline.

touche-à-tout [tuʃatu] **1** *a & nmf inv (qui touche)* meddlesome (person). **2** *nmf inv (qui se disperse)* dabbler.

touch/er [tuʃe] *vt* to touch; *(paie)* to draw; *(chèque)* to cash; *(cible)* to hit; *(émouvoir)* to touch, move; *(concerner)* to affect; **t. qn** *(contacter)* to get in touch with s.o., reach s.o.; – *vi* **à** to touch; *(sujet)* to touch on; *(but, fin)* to approach; – **se t.** *vpr (lignes etc)* to touch; – *nm (sens)* touch; **au t.** to the touch. ◆—**ant** *a (émouvant)* touching, moving.

touffe [tuf] *nf (de cheveux, d'herbe)* tuft; *(de plantes)* cluster. ◆**touffu** *a (barbe, haie)* thick, bushy; *(livre)* Fig heavy.

toujours [tuʒur] *adv* always; *(encore)* still; **pour t.** for ever; **essaie t.!** *(quand même)* try anyhow!; **t. est-il que ...** the fact remains that ....

toupet [tupɛ] *nm (audace)* Fam cheek, nerve.

toupie [tupi] *nf (spinning)* top.

tour¹ [tur] *nf* **1** Archit tower; *(immeuble)* tower block, high-rise. **2** Échecs rook, castle.

tour² [tur] *nm* **1** *(mouvement, ordre, tournure)* turn; *(artifice)* trick; *(excursion)* trip, outing; *(à pied)* stroll, walk; *(en voiture)* drive; **t. (de phrase)** turn of phrase; **t. (de piste)** *Sp* lap; **t. de cartes** card trick; **t. d'horizon** survey; **t. de poitrine/etc** chest/ *etc* measurement *ou* size; **de dix mètres t.** ten metres round; **faire le t. de** to go round; *(question, situation)* to review; **faire un t.** *(à pied)* to go for a stroll *ou* walk; *(en voiture)* to go for a drive; *(voyage)* to go on a trip; **faire** *ou* **jouer un t. à qn** to play a trick on s.o.; **c'est mon t.** it's my turn; **à qui le tour?** whose turn (is it)?; **à son t.** in (one's) turn; **t. de rôle** in turn; **t. à t.** in turn, by turns. **2** *Tech* lathe; *(de potier)* wheel.

tourbe [turb] *nf* peat. ◆**tourbière** *nf* peat bog.

tourbillon [turbijɔ̃] *nm (de vent)* whirlwind; *(d'eau)* whirlpool; *(de neige, sable)* eddy; *(tournoiement)* Fig whirl, swirl. ◆**tourbillonner** *vi* to whirl, swirl; to eddy.

tourelle [turɛl] *nf* turret.

tourisme [turism] *nm* tourism; **faire du t.** to do some sightseeing *ou* touring; **agence/office de t.** tourist agency/office. ◆**touriste** *nmf* tourist. ◆**touristique** *a (guide, menu etc)* tourist-; **route t, circuit t.** scenic route.

tourment [turmɑ̃] *nm* torment. ◆**tour-**

ment/er *vt* to torment; – **se t.** *vpr* to worry (oneself). ◆—**é** *a (mer, vie)* turbulent, stormy; *(sol)* rough, uneven; *(expression, visage)* anguished.

tourmente [turmɑ̃t] *nf (troubles)* turmoil.

tourne-disque [turnədisk] *nm* record player.

tournée [turne] *nf* **1** *(de livreur etc)* round; *(théâtrale)* tour; **faire la t. de** to make the rounds of, go round. **2** *(de boissons)* round.

tourn/er [turne] *vt* to turn; *(film)* to shoot, make; *(difficulté)* to get round; **t. en ridicule** to ridicule; – *vi* to turn; *(tête, toupie)* to spin; *(Terre)* to revolve, turn; *(moteur)* to run, go; *(usine)* to run; *(lait, viande)* to go off; *Cin* to shoot; **t. autour de** *(objet)* to go round; *(maison, personne)* to hang around; *(question)* to centre on; **t. bien/mal** *(évoluer)* to turn out well/badly; **t. au froid** *(temps)* to turn cold; **t. à l'aigre** *(ton, conversation etc)* to turn nasty *ou* sour; **t. de l'œil** *Fam* to faint; – **se t.** *vpr* to turn *(vers* to, towards). ◆—**ant 1** *a* **pont t.** swing bridge. **2** *nm (virage)* bend, turning; *(moment)* Fig turning point. ◆—**age** *nm* Cin shooting, filming. ◆—**eur** *nm (ouvrier)* turner. ◆**tournoyer** *vi* to spin slowly, whirl. ◆**tournure** *nf (expression)* turn of phrase; **t. d'esprit** way of thinking; **t. des événements** turn of events; **prendre t.** *(forme)* to take shape.

tournesol [turnəsɔl] *nm* sunflower.

tournevis [turnəvis] *nm* screwdriver.

tourniquet [turnikɛ] *nm* **1** *(barrière)* turnstile. **2** *(pour arroser)* sprinkler.

tournoi [turnwa] *nm Sp & Hist* tournament.

tourte [turt] *nf* pie.

tourterelle [turtərɛl] *nf* turtledove.

Toussaint [tusɛ̃] *nf* All Saints' Day.

tousser [tuse] *vi* to cough.

tout, toute, *pl* **tous, toutes** [tu, tut, tu, tut] **1** *a* all; **tous les livres/etc** all the books/etc; **t. l'argent/le village/etc** the whole (of the) money/village/etc, all the money/village/ etc; **toute la nuit** all night, the whole (of the) night; **tous (les) deux** both; **tous (les) trois** all three; **t. un problème** quite a problem. **2** *a (chaque)* every, each; *(n'importe quel)* any; **tous les ans**/jours/etc every *ou* each year/day/etc; **tous les deux/trois mois**/etc every second/third month/etc; **tous les cinq mètres** every five metres; **t. homme** [tutɔm] every *ou* any man; **à toute heure** at any time. **3** *pron pl* **(tous** = [tus]) all; **ils sont tous là, tous sont là** they're all there. **4** *pron m sing* **tout** everything;

dépenser t. to spend everything, spend it all; **t. ce que** everything that, all that; **en t.** (au total) in all. **2** adv (très) very; **t. petit** very small; **t. neuf** brand new; **t. simplement** quite simply; **t. seul** all alone; **t. droit** straight ahead; **t. autour** all around, right round; **t. au début** right at the beginning; **le t. premier** the very first; **t. au moins/plus** at the very least/most; **t. en chantant/etc** while singing/etc; **t. rusé qu'il est** however sly he may be; **t. à coup** suddenly, all of a sudden; **t. à fait** completely, quite; **t. de même** all the same; (indignation) really!; **t. de suite** at once. **6** nm le t. everything, the lot; **un t.** a whole; **le t. est** (l'important) the main thing is (que that, de faire to do); **pas du t.** not at all; **rien du t.** nothing at all; **du t. au t.** (changer) entirely, completely. ◆**t.-puissant, toute-puissante** a all-powerful.

tout-à-l'égout [tutalegu] nm inv mains drainage.

toutefois [tutfwa] adv nevertheless, however.

toutou [tutu] nm (chien) Fam doggie.

toux [tu] nf cough.

toxicomane [toksikoman] nmf drug addict. ◆**toxicomanie** nf drug addiction. ◆**toxine** nf toxin. ◆**toxique** a toxic.

trac [trak] nm le t. (peur) the jitters; (de candidat) exam nerves; Th stage fright.

tracas [traka] nm worry. ◆**tracasser** vt, — **se t.** vpr to worry. ◆**tracasseries** nfpl annoyances. ◆**tracassier, -ière** a irksome.

trace [tras] nf (quantité, tache, vestige) trace; (marque) mark; (de fugitif etc) trail; (de bête, de pneus) tracks; **traces de pas** footprints; **suivre les traces de qn** Fig to follow in s.o.'s footsteps.

trac/er [trase] vt (dessiner) to draw; (écrire) to trace; **t. une route** to open up a route; (frayer) to open up a route. ◆**—é** nm (plan) layout; (ligne) line.

trachée [trafe] nf Anat windpipe.

tract [trakt] nm leaflet.

tractations [traktɑsjɔ̃] nfpl Péj dealings.

tracter [trakte] vt (caravane etc) to tow. ◆**tracteur** nm (véhicule) tractor.

traction [traksjɔ̃] nf Tech traction; Sp pull-up; **t. arrière/avant** Aut rear-/front-wheel drive.

tradition [tradisjɔ̃] nf tradition. ◆**traditionnel, -elle** a traditional.

traduire* [traduir] vt **1** to translate (de from, en into); (exprimer) Fig to express. **2** **t. qn en justice** to bring s.o. before the courts. ◆**traducteur, -trice** nmf translator. ◆**traduction** nf translation. ◆**traduisible** a translatable.

trafic [trafik] nm **1** Aut Rail etc traffic. **2** Com Péj traffic, trade; **faire du t.** to traffic, trade; **faire le t. de** to traffic in, trade in. ◆**trafiqu/er** vi to traffic, trade. **2** vt (produit) Fam to tamper with. ◆**—ant, -ante** nmf trafficker, dealer; **t. d'armes/de drogue** arms/drug trafficker or dealer.

tragédie [traʒedi] nf Th & Fig tragedy. ◆**tragique** a tragic. ◆**tragiquement** adv tragically.

trahir [trair] vt to betray; (secret etc) to betray, give away; (forces) to fail (s.o.); — **se t.** vpr to give oneself away, betray oneself. ◆**trahison** nf betrayal; (crime) Pol treason.

train [trɛ̃] nm **1** (locomotive, transport, jouet) train; **t. à grande vitesse** high-speed train; **t. couchettes** sleeper; **t. auto-couchettes** (car) sleeper. **2** **en t.** (forme) on form; **se mettre en t.** to get (oneself) into shape. **3** **être en t. de faire** to be (busy) doing; **mettre qch en t.** to get sth going, start sth off. **4** (allure) pace; **t. de vie** life style. **5** (de pneus) set; (de péniches, remorques) string. **6** **t. d'atterrissage** Av undercarriage.

traîne [trɛn] nf (de robe) train. **2** **à la t.** (en arrière) lagging behind.

traîneau, -x [trɛno] nm sledge, sleigh, Am sled.

traînée [trene] nf **1** (de substance) trail, streak; (bande) streak; **se répandre comme une t. de poudre** (vite) to spread like wildfire. **2** (prostituée) Arg tart.

traîner [trene] vt to drag; (mots) to drawl; (faire) **t. en longueur** (faire durer) to drag out; — vi (jouets, papiers etc) to lie around; (subsister) to linger on; (s'attarder) to lag behind, dawdle; (errer) to hang around; **t.** (par terre) (robe etc) to trail (on the ground); **t. (en longueur)** (durer) to drag on; — **se t.** vpr (avancer) to drag oneself (along); (par terre) to crawl; (durer) to drag on. ◆**traînant** a (voix) drawling. ◆**traînailler** vi Fam = **traînasser**. ◆**traînard, -arde** nmf slowcoach, Am slowpoke. ◆**traînasser** vi Fam to dawdle; (errer) to hang around.

train-train [trɛ̃trɛ̃] nm routine.

traire* [trer] vt (vache) to milk.

trait [trɛ] nm **1** line; (en dessinant) stroke; (caractéristique) feature, trait; pl (du visage) features; **t. d'union** hyphen; (intermédiaire) Fig link; **d'un t.** (boire) in one gulp, in one go; **à grands traits** in outline; **t. de** (*esprit, génie*) flash of; (*bravoure*) act of; **avoir t. à** (*se rapporter à*) to relate to. **2 cheval de t.** draught horse.

traite [trɛt] *nf* **1** (*de vache*) milking. **2** Com bill, draft. **3 d'une** (*seule*) **t.** (*sans interruption*) in one go. **4 t. des Noirs** slave trade; **t. des blanches** white slave trade.

traité [trete] *nm* **1** Pol treaty. **2** (*ouvrage*) treatise (**sur** on).

trait/er [trete] *vt* (*se comporter envers*) & *Méd* to treat; (*problème, sujet*) to deal with; (*marché*) Com to negotiate; (*matériau, produit*) to treat, process; **t. qn de lâche**/*etc* to call s.o. a coward/*etc*; — *vi* to negotiate, deal (**avec** with); **t. de** (*sujet*) to deal with. ◆—**ant** [-ɛtɑ̃] *a* médecin t. regular doctor. ◆—**ement** [-ɛtmɑ̃] *nm* **1** treatment; **mauvais traitements** rough treatment; **t. de données/de texte** data/word processing; **machine à t. de texte** word processor. **2** (*gains*) salary.

traiteur [trɛtœr] *nm* (*fournisseur*) caterer; **chez le t.** (*magasin*) at the delicatessen.

traître [trɛtr] *nm* traitor; **en t.** treacherously; — *a* (*dangereux*) treacherous; **être t. à** to be a traitor to. ◆**traîtrise** *nf* treachery.

trajectoire [traʒɛktwar] *nf* path, trajectory.

trajet [traʒɛ] *nm* journey, trip; (*distance*) distance; (*itinéraire*) route.

trame [tram] *nf* **1** (*de récit etc*) framework. **2** (*de tissu*) weft.

tramer [trame] *vt* (*évasion etc*) to plot; (*complot*) to hatch.

trampoline [trɑ̃polin] *nm* trampoline.

tram(way) [tram(wɛ)] *nm* tram, *Am* streetcar.

tranche [trɑ̃ʃ] *nf* (*morceau coupé*) slice; (*bord*) edge; (*partie*) portion; (*de salaire, impôts*) bracket; **t. d'âge** age bracket.

tranchée [trɑ̃ʃe] *nf* trench.

tranch/er [trɑ̃ʃe] **1** *vt* to cut. **2** *vt* (*difficulté, question*) to settle; — *vi* (*décider*) to decide. **3** *vi* (*contraster*) to contrast (**avec, sur** with). ◆—**ant 1** *a* (*couteau*) sharp; — *nm* (*cutting*) edge. **2** *a* (*péremptoire*) trenchant, cutting. ◆—**é** *a* (*couleurs*) distinct; (*opinion*) clear-cut.

tranquille [trɑ̃kil] *a* quiet; (*mer*) calm, still; (*conscience*) clear; (*esprit*) easy; (*certain*) *Fam* confident; **je suis t.** (*rassuré*) my mind is at rest; **soyez t.** don't worry; **laisser t.** to leave **be** ou alone. ◆**tranquillement** *adv* calmly. ◆**tranquillis/er** *vt* to reassure; **tranquillisez-vous** set your mind at rest. ◆—**ant** *nm Méd* tranquillizer. ◆**tranquil-**

lité *nf* (peace and) quiet; (*d'esprit*) peace of mind.

trans- [trɑ̃z, trɑ̃s] *préf* trans-.

transaction [trɑ̃zaksjɔ̃] *nf* **1** (*compromis*) compromise. **2** Com transaction.

transatlantique [trɑ̃zatlɑ̃tik] *a* transatlantic; — *nm* (*paquebot*) transatlantic liner; (*chaise*) deckchair.

transcend/er [trɑ̃sɑ̃de] *vt* to transcend. ◆—**ant** *a* transcendent.

transcrire* [trɑ̃skrir] *vt* to transcribe. ◆**transcription** *nf* transcription; (*document*) transcript.

transe [trɑ̃s] *nf* **en t.** (*mystique*) in a trance; (*excité*) very exited.

transférer [trɑ̃sfere] *vt* to transfer (**à** to). ◆**transfert** *nm* transfer.

transfigurer [trɑ̃sfigyre] *vt* to transform, transfigure.

transformer [trɑ̃sfɔrme] *vt* to transform, change; (*maison, matière première*) to convert; (*robe etc*) to alter; (*essai*) Rugby to convert; **t. en** to turn into; — **se t.** *vpr* to change, be transformed (**en** into). ◆**transformateur** *nm* Él transformer. ◆**transformation** *nf* transformation, change; conversion.

transfuge [trɑ̃sfyʒ] *nm* Mil renegade; — *nmf* Pol renegade.

transfusion [trɑ̃sfyzjɔ̃] *nf* **t.** (**sanguine**) (blood) transfusion.

transgresser [trɑ̃sgrese] *vt* (*loi, ordre*) to disobey.

transi [trɑ̃zi] *a* (*personne*) numb with cold; **t. de peur** paralysed by fear.

transiger [trɑ̃ziʒe] *vi* to compromise.

transistor [trɑ̃zistɔr] *nm* (*dispositif, poste*) transistor. ◆**transistorisé** *a* (*téléviseur etc*) transistorized.

transit [trɑ̃zit] *nm* transit; **en t.** in transit. ◆**transiter** *vt* (*faire*) **t.** to send in transit; — *vi* to be in transit.

transitif, -ive [trɑ̃zitif, -iv] *a* Gram transitive.

transition [trɑ̃zisjɔ̃] *nf* transition. ◆**transitoire** *a* (*qui passe*) transient; (*provisoire*) transitional.

transmettre* [trɑ̃smɛtr] *vt* (*héritage, message etc*) to pass on (**à** to); Phys Tech to transmit; Rad TV to broadcast, transmit. ◆**transmetteur** *nm* (*appareil*) transmitter, transmitting device. ◆**transmission** *nf* transmission; passing on.

transparaître* [trɑ̃sparɛtr] *vi* to show (through).

transparent [trɑ̃sparɑ̃] *a* transparent. ◆**transparence** *nf* transparency.

transpercer [trɑ̃sperse] *vt* to pierce, go through.

transpirer [trɑ̃spire] *vi* (*suer*) to perspire; (*information*) *Fig* to leak out. ◆**transpiration** *nf* perspiration.

transplanter [trɑ̃splɑ̃te] *vt* (*organe, plante etc*) to transplant. ◆**transplantation** *nf* transplantation; (*greffe*) *Méd* transplant.

transport [trɑ̃spɔr] *nm* 1 (*action*) transport, transportation (*de* of); (*moyens*) transport; **moyen de t.** means of transport; **transports en commun** public transport. 2 (*émotion*) *Litt* rapture. ◆**transporter** 1 *vt* (*véhicule, train*) to transport, convey; (*à la main*) to carry, take; **t. d'urgence à l'hôpital** to rush to hospital; — **se t.** *vpr* (*aller*) to take oneself (à to). 2 *vt Litt* to enrapture. ◆**transporteur** *nm* **t.** (*routier*) haulier, *Am* trucker.

transposer [trɑ̃spoze] *vt* to transpose. ◆**transposition** *nf* transposition.

transvaser [trɑ̃svɑze] *vt* (*vin*) to decant.

transversal, -aux [trɑ̃sversal, -o] *a* (*barre, rue etc*) cross-, transverse.

trapèze [trapɛz] *nm* (*au cirque*) trapeze. ◆**trapéziste** *nmf* trapeze artist.

trappe [trap] *nf* (*dans le plancher*) trap door.

trappeur [trapœr] *nm* (*chasseur*) trapper.

trapu [trapy] *a* 1 (*personne*) stocky, thickset. 2 (*problème etc*) *Fam* tough.

traquenard [traknar] *nm* trap.

traquer [trake] *vt* to track *ou* hunt (down).

traumatis/er [tromatize] *vt* to traumatize. ◆**-ant** *a* traumatic. ◆**traumatisme** *nm* (*choc*) trauma.

travail, -aux [travaj, -o] *nm* (*activité, lieu*) work; (*emploi, tâche*) job; (*façonnage*) working (**de** of); (*ouvrage, étude*) work, publication; *Écon Méd* labour; *pl* work; (*dans la rue*) roadworks; (*aménagement*) alterations; **travaux forcés** hard labour; **travaux ménagers** housework; **travaux pratiques** *Scol Univ* practical work; **travaux publics** public works; **t. au noir** moonlighting; **en t.** (*femme*) *Méd* in labour.

travaill/er [travaje] 1 *vi* to work (à **qch** at *ou* on sth); — *vt* (*discipline, rôle, style*) to work on; (*façonner*) to work; (*inquiéter*) to worry; **t. la terre** to work the land. 2 *vi* (*bois*) to warp. ◆**-é** *a* (*style*) elaborate. ◆**-eur, -euse** *a* hard-working; — *nmf* worker. ◆**travailliste** *a Pol* Labour-; — *nmf Pol* member of the Labour party.

travers [traver] 1 *prép* & *adv* **à t.** through; **en t.** (**de**) across. 2 *adv* **de t.** (*chapeau, nez etc*) crooked; (*comprendre*) badly; (*regarder*) askance; **aller de t.** *Fig* to go wrong; **j'ai avalé de t.** it went down the wrong way. 3 *nm* (*défaut*) failing.

traverse [travers] *nf* 1 *Rail* sleeper, *Am* tie. 2 **chemin de t.** short cut.

travers/er [traverse] *vt* to cross, go across; (*foule, période, mur*) to go through. ◆**-ée** *nf* (*action, trajet*) crossing.

traversin [traversɛ̃] *nm* (*coussin*) bolster.

travest/ir [travestir] *vt* to disguise; (*pensée, vérité*) to misrepresent. ◆**-i** *nm Th* female impersonator; (*homosexuel*) transvestite. ◆**-issement** *nm* disguise; misrepresentation.

trébucher [trebyʃe] *vi* to stumble (**sur** over); **faire t.** to trip (up).

trèfle [trɛfl] *nm* 1 (*plante*) clover. 2 (*couleur*) *Cartes* clubs.

treille [trɛj] *nf* climbing vine.

treillis [treji] *nm* 1 lattice(work); (*en métal*) wire mesh. 2 (*tenue militaire*) combat uniform.

treize [trez] *a* & *nm inv* thirteen. ◆**treizième** *a* & *nmf* thirteenth.

tréma [trema] *nm Gram* di(a)eresis.

trembl/er [trɑ̃ble] *vi* to tremble, shake; (*de froid, peur*) to tremble (**de** with); (*flamme, lumière*) to flicker; (*voix*) to tremble, quaver; (*avoir peur*) to be afraid (**que** (+ *sub*) that, **de faire** to do); **t. pour qn** to fear for s.o. ◆**-ement** *nm* (*action, frisson*) trembling; **t. de terre** earthquake. ◆**trembloter** *vi* to quiver.

trémousser (se) [sətremuse] *vpr* to wriggle (about).

trempe [trɑ̃p] *nf* (*caractère*) stamp; **un homme de sa t.** a man of his stamp.

tremper [trɑ̃pe] 1 *vt* to soak, drench; (*plonger*) to dip (**dans** into); — *vi* to soak; **faire t.** to soak; — **se t.** *vpr* (*se baigner*) to take a dip. 2 *vt* (*acier*) to temper. 3 *vi* (*participer*) *Péj* to be mixed up in. ◆**trempette** *nf* **faire t.** (*se baigner*) to take a dip.

tremplin [trɑ̃plɛ̃] *nm Natation* & *Fig* springboard.

trente [trɑ̃t] *a* & *nm* thirty; **un t.-trois tours** (*disque*) an LP. ◆**trentaine** *nf* **une t.** (**de**) (*nombre*) about thirty; **avoir la t.** (*âge*) to be about thirty. ◆**trentième** *a* & *nmf* thirtieth.

trépidant [trepidɑ̃] *a* (*vie etc*) hectic.

trépied [trepje] *nm* tripod.

trépigner [trepiɲe] *vi* to stamp (one's feet).

très [trɛ] *adv* (*[trɛz] before vowel or mute h*) very; **t. aimé/critiqué/etc** much liked/criticized/etc.

trésor [trezɔr] *nm* treasure; **le T.** (*public*)

(*service*) public revenue (department); (*finances*) public funds; **des trésors de** Fig a treasure house of. ◆**trésorerie** *nf* (*bureaux d'un club etc*) accounts department; (*capitaux*) funds; (*gestion*) accounting. ◆**trésorier, -ière** *nmf* treasurer.

tressaill/ir [tresajir] *vi* (*sursauter*) to jump, start; (*frémir*) to shake, quiver; (*de joie, peur*) to tremble (**de** with). ◆**—ement** *nm* start; quiver; trembling.

tressauter [tresote] *vi* (*sursauter*) to start, jump.

tresse [tres] *nf* (*cordon*) braid; (*cheveux*) plait, *Am* braid. ◆**tresser** *vt* to braid; to plait.

tréteau, -x [treto] *nm* trestle.

treuil [trœj] *nm* winch, windlass.

trêve [trev] *nf* Mil truce; (*répit*) Fig respite. **t. de** no more of.

tri [tri] *nm* sorting (out); **faire le t. de** to sort (out); (**centre de t.** (*des postes*) sorting office. ◆**triage** *nm* sorting (out).

triangle [trijɑ̃gl] *nm* triangle. ◆**triangulaire** *a* triangular.

tribord [tribɔr] *nm* Nau Av starboard.

tribu [triby] *nf* tribe. ◆**tribal, -aux** *a* tribal.

tribulations [tribylɑsjɔ̃] *nfpl* tribulations.

tribunal, -aux [tribynal, -o] *nm* Jur court; (*militaire*) tribunal.

tribune [tribyn] *nf* **1** (*de salle publique etc*) gallery; (*de stade*) (grand)stand; (*d'orateur*) rostrum. **2 t. libre** (*dans un journal*) open forum.

tribut [triby] *nm* tribute (**à** to).

tributaire [tribyter] *a* **t. de** Fig dependent on.

tricher [triʃe] *vi* to cheat. ◆**tricherie** *nf* cheating, trickery; **une t.** a piece of trickery. ◆**tricheur, -euse** *nmf* cheat, *Am* cheater.

tricolore [trikɔlɔr] *a* **1** (*cocarde etc*) red, white and blue; **le drapeau/l'équipe t.** the French flag/team. **2 feu t.** traffic lights.

tricot [triko] *nm* (*activité, ouvrage*) knitting; (*chandail*) jumper, sweater; **un t.** (*ouvrage*) a piece of knitting; **en t.** knitted; **t. de corps** vest, *Am* undershirt. ◆**tricoter** *vti* to knit.

tricycle [trisikl] *nm* tricycle.

trier [trije] *vt* (*séparer*) to sort (out); (*choisir*) to pick *ou* sort out.

trilogie [trilɔʒi] *nf* trilogy.

trimbal(l)er [trɛ̃bale] *vt* Fam to cart about, drag around; — **se t.** *vpr* Fam to trail around.

trimer [trime] *vi* Fam to slave (away), toil.

trimestre [trimɛstr] *nm* (*période*) Com quarter; *Scol* term. ◆**trimestriel, -ielle** *a* (*revue*) quarterly; (*bulletin*) *Scol* end-of-term.

tringle [trɛ̃gl] *nf* rail, rod; **t. à rideaux** curtain rail *ou* rod.

Trinité [trinite] *nf* **la T.** (*fête*) Trinity; (*dogme*) the Trinity.

trinquer [trɛ̃ke] *vi* to chink glasses; **t. à** to drink to.

trio [trijo] *nm* (*groupe*) & Mus trio.

triomphe [trijɔ̃f] *nm* triumph (**sur** over); **porter qn en t.** to carry s.o. shoulder-high. ◆**triomphal, -aux** *a* triumphal. ◆**triomph/er** *vi* to triumph (**de** over); (*jubiler*) to be jubilant. ◆**—ant** *a* triumphant.

tripes [trip] *nfpl* (*intestins*) Fam guts; Culin tripe. ◆**tripier, -ière** *nmf* tripe butcher.

triple [tripl] *a* treble, triple; — *nm* **le t.** three times as much (**de** as). ◆**tripl/er** *vti* to treble, triple. ◆**—és, -ées** *nmfpl* (*enfants*) triplets.

tripot [tripo] *nm* (*café etc*) Péj gambling den.

tripoter [tripɔte] *vt* to fiddle about *ou* mess about with; — *vi* to fiddle *ou* mess about.

trique [trik] *nf* cudgel, stick.

triste [trist] *a* sad; (*couleur, temps, rue*) gloomy, dreary; (*lamentable*) unfortunate, sorry. ◆**tristement** *adv* sadly. ◆**tristesse** *nf* sadness; gloom, dreariness.

triturer [trityre] *vt* (*manipuler*) to manipulate.

trivial, -aux [trivjal, -o] *a* coarse, vulgar. ◆**trivialité** *nf* coarseness, vulgarity.

troc [trɔk] *nm* exchange, barter.

troène [trɔɛn] *nm* (*arbuste*) privet.

trognon [trɔɲɔ̃] *nm* (*de pomme, poire*) core; (*de chou*) stump.

trois [trwɑ] *a* & *nm* three. ◆**troisième** *a* & *nmf* third. ◆**troisièmement** *adv* thirdly.

trolley(bus) [trɔlɛ(bys)] *nm* trolley(bus).

trombe [trɔ̃b] *nf* **t. d'eau** (*pluie*) rainstorm, downpour; **en t.** (*entrer etc*) Fig like a whirlwind.

trombone [trɔ̃bɔn] *nm* **1** Mus trombone. **2** (*agrafe*) paper clip.

trompe [trɔ̃p] *nf* **1** (*d'éléphant*) trunk; (*d'insecte*) proboscis. **2** Mus horn.

tromper [trɔ̃pe] *vt* to deceive, mislead; (*escroquer*) to cheat; (*échapper à*) to elude; (*être infidèle à*) to be unfaithful to; — **se t.** *vpr* to be mistaken, make a mistake; **se t. de route/de train/etc** to take the wrong road/train/etc; **se t. de date/de jour/etc** to get the date/day/etc wrong. ◆**tromperie** *nf* deceit, deception. ◆**trompeur, -euse** *a* (*apparences etc*) deceptive, misleading; (*personne*) deceitful.

trompette [trɔ̃pɛt] *nf* trumpet. ◆**trompettiste** *nmf* trumpet player.

tronc [trɔ̃] nm **1** Bot Anat trunk. **2** Rel collection box.

tronçon [trɔ̃sɔ̃] nm section. ◆**tronçonn/er** vt to cut (into sections). ◆**-euse** nf chain saw.

trône [tron] nm throne. ◆**trôner** vi (vase, personne etc) Fig to occupy the place of honour.

tronquer [trɔ̃ke] vt to truncate; (texte etc) to curtail.

trop [tro] adv too; too much; **t. dur/loin/etc** too hard/far/etc; **t. fatigué** too tired, overtired; **boire/lire/etc t.** to drink/read/etc too much; **t. de sel/etc** (quantité) too much salt/etc; **t. de gens/etc** (nombre) too many people/etc; **du fromage/etc de ou en t.** (quantité) too much cheese/etc; **des œufs/etc de t.** (nombre) too many eggs/etc; **un franc/verre/etc de t.** ou **en t.** one franc/glass/etc too many; **se sentir de t.** Fig to feel in the way.

trophée [trɔfe] nm trophy.

tropique [trɔpik] nm tropic. ◆**tropical, -aux** a tropical.

trop-plein [tropplɛ̃] nm (dispositif, liquide) overflow; (surabondance) Fig excess.

troquer [trɔke] vt to exchange (**contre** for).

trot [tro] nm trot; **aller au t.** to trot; **au t.** (sans traîner) Fam at the double. ◆**trott/er** [trɔte] vi (cheval) to trot; (personne) Fig to scurry (along). ◆**-eur** nm (de montre) second hand.

trotteuse [trɔtøz] nf (de montre) second hand.

trottiner [trɔtine] vi (personne) to patter (along).

trottinette [trɔtinɛt] nf (jouet) scooter.

trottoir [trɔtwar] nm pavement, Am sidewalk; **t. roulant** moving walkway, travolator.

trou [tru] nm hole; (d'aiguille) eye; (manque) Fig gap (**dans** in); (village) Péj hole, dump; **t. d'homme** (ouverture) manhole; **t. de** (la) **serrure** keyhole; **t. de** (**la**) **mémoire** Fig lapse (of memory).

trouble [trubl] **1** a (liquide) cloudy; (image) blurred; (affaire) shady; **voir t.** to see blurred. **2** nm (émoi, émotion) agitation; (désarroi) distress; (désordre) confusion; pl Méd trouble; (révolte) disturbances, troubles. ◆**troubl/er** vt to disturb; (liquide) to make cloudy; (projet) to upset; (esprit) to unsettle; (vue) to blur; (inquiéter) to trouble; — **se t.** vpr (liquide) to become cloudy; (candidat etc) to become flustered. ◆**-ant** a (détail etc) disquieting. ◆**trouble-fête** nmf inv killjoy, spoilsport.

trou/er [true] vt to make a hole ou holes in;

(silence, ténèbres) to cut through. ◆**-ée** nf gap; (brèche) Mil breach.

trouille [truj] nf **avoir la t.** Fam to have the jitters, be scared. ◆**trouillard** a (poltron) Fam chicken.

troupe [trup] nf Mil troop; (groupe) group; Th company, troupe; **la t., les troupes** (armée) the troops.

troupeau, -x [trupo] nm (de vaches) & Fig Péj herd; (de moutons, d'oies) flock.

trousse [trus] **1** nf (étui) case, kit; (d'écolier) pencil case; **t. à outils** toolkit; **t. à pharmacie** first-aid kit. **2** nfpl **aux trousses de qn** Fig on s.o.'s heels.

trousseau, -x [truso] nm **1** (de clés) bunch. **2** (de mariée) trousseau.

trouver [truve] vt to find; **aller/venir t. qn** to go/come and see s.o.; **je trouve que** (je pense que) I think that; **comment la trouvez-vous?** what do you think of her?; — **se t.** vpr to be; (être situé) to be situated; (se sentir) to feel; (dans une situation) to find oneself; **se t. mal** (s'évanouir) to faint; **il se trouve que** it happens that. ◆**trouvaille** nf (lucky) find.

truand [tryɑ̃] nm crook.

truc [tryk] nm **1** (astuce) trick; (moyen) way; **avoir/trouver le t.** to have/get the knack (**pour faire** of doing). **2** (chose) Fam thing. ◆**-age** nm = **truquage**.

truchement [tryʃmɑ̃] nm **par le t. de qn** through the intermediary of s.o.

truculent [trykylɑ̃] a (langage, personnage) colourful.

truelle [tryɛl] nf trowel.

truffe [tryf] nf **1** (champignon) truffle. **2** (de chien) nose.

truff/er [tryfe] vt (remplir) to stuff (**de** with). ◆**-é** a (pâté etc) Culin with truffles.

truie [trɥi] nf (animal) sow.

truite [trɥit] nf trout.

truqu/er [tryke] vt (photo etc) to fake; (élections, match) to rig, fix. ◆**-é** a (photo etc) fake-; (élections, match) rigged, fixed; (scène) Cin trick-. ◆**-age** nm Cin (special) effect; (action) faking; rigging.

trust [trœst] nm Com (cartel) trust; (entreprise) corporation.

tsar [dzar] nm tsar, czar.

TSF [teɛsɛf] nf abrév (télégraphie sans fil) wireless, radio.

tsigane [tsigan] a & nmf (Hungarian) gipsy.

TSVP [teɛsvepe] abrév (tournez s'il vous plaît) PTO.

TTC [tetese] abrév (toutes taxes comprises) inclusive of tax.

tu [ty] pron you (familiar form of address).

tu² [ty] *voir* taire.

tuba [tyba] *nm* **1** *Mus* tuba. **2** *Sp* snorkel.

tube [tyb] *nm* **1** tube; (*de canalisation*) pipe. **2** (*chanson, disque*) *Fam* hit. ◆**tubulaire** *a* tubular.

tuberculeux, -euse [tybɛrkylø, -øz] *a* tubercular; **être t.** to have tuberculosis *ou* TB. ◆**tuberculose** *nf* tuberculosis, TB.

tue-mouches [tymuʃ] *a inv* **papier t.-mouches** flypaper. ◆**t.-tête (à)** *adv* at the top of one's voice.

tu/er [tɥe] *vt* to kill; (*d'un coup de feu*) to shoot (dead), kill; (*épuiser*) *Fig* to wear out; **— se t.** *vpr* to kill oneself; to shoot oneself; (*dans un accident*) to be killed; **se t. à faire** *Fig* to wear oneself out doing. ◆**—ant** *a* (*fatigant*) exhausting. ◆**tuerie** *nf* slaughter. ◆**tueur, -euse** *nmf* killer.

tuile [tɥil] *nf* **1** tile. **2** (*malchance*) *Fam* (stroke of) bad luck.

tulipe [tylip] *nf* tulip.

tuméfié [tymefje] *a* swollen.

tumeur [tymœr] *nf* tumour, growth.

tumulte [tymylt] *nm* commotion; (*désordre*) turmoil. ◆**tumultueux, -euse** *a* turbulent.

tunique [tynik] *nf* tunic.

Tunisie [tynizi] *nf* Tunisia. ◆**tunisien, -ienne** *a & nmf* Tunisian.

tunnel [tynɛl] *nm* tunnel.

turban [tyrbɑ̃] *nm* turban.

turbine [tyrbin] *nf* turbine.

turbulences [tyrbylɑ̃s] *nfpl* *Phys Av* turbulence.

turbulent [tyrbylɑ̃] *a* (*enfant etc*) boisterous, turbulent.

turfiste [tyrfist] *nmf* racegoer, punter.

Turquie [tyrki] *nf* Turkey. ◆**turc, turque** *a* Turkish; *— nmf* Turk; *— nm* (*langue*) Turkish.

turquoise [tyrkwaz] *a inv* turquoise.

tuteur, -trice [tytœr, -tris] **1** *nmf* *Jur* guardian. **2** *nm* (*bâton*) stake, prop. ◆**tutelle** *nf* *Jur* guardianship; *Fig* protection.

tutoyer [tytwaje] *vt* to address familiarly (*using tu*). ◆**tutoiement** *nm* familiar address, use of *tu*.

tutu [tyty] *nm* ballet skirt, tutu.

tuyau, -x [tɥijo] *nm* **1** pipe; **t. d'arrosage** hose(pipe); **t. de cheminée** flue; **t. d'échappement** *Aut* exhaust (pipe). **2** (*renseignement*) *Fam* tip. ◆**tuyauter** *vt* **t. qn** (*conseiller*) *Fam* to give s.o. a tip. ◆**tuyauterie** *nf* (*tuyaux*) piping.

TVA [tevea] *nf abrév* (*taxe à la valeur ajoutée*) VAT.

tympan [tɛ̃pɑ̃] *nm* eardrum.

type [tip] *nm* (*modèle*) type; (*traits*) features; (*individu*) *Fam* fellow, guy, bloke; **le t. même de** *Fig* the very model of; *— a inv* (*professeur etc*) typical. ◆**typique** *a* typical (*de of*). ◆**typiquement** *adv* typically.

typhoïde [tifɔid] *nf* *Méd* typhoid (fever).

typhon [tif3] *nm* *Mét* typhoon.

typographe [tipɔgraf] *nmf* typographer. ◆**typographie** *nf* typography, printing. ◆**typographique** *a* typographical, printing-.

tyran [tirɑ̃] *nm* tyrant. ◆**tyrannie** *nf* tyranny. ◆**tyrannique** *a* tyrannical. ◆**tyranniser** *vt* to tyrannize.

tzigane [dzigan] *a & nmf* (Hungarian) gipsy.

U

U, u [y] *nm* U, u.

ulcère [ylsɛr] *nm* ulcer, sore.

ulcérer [ylsere] *vt* (*blesser, irriter*) to embitter.

ultérieur [ylterjœr] *a* later. ◆**—ement** *adv* later.

ultimatum [yltimatɔm] *nm* ultimatum.

ultime [yltim] *a* final, last.

ultra- [yltra] *préf* ultra-. ◆**u.-secret, -ète** *a* (*document*) top-secret.

ultramoderne [yltramɔdɛrn] *a* ultramodern.

ultraviolet, -ette [yltravjɔlɛ, -ɛt] *a* ultraviolet.

un, une [œ̃, yn] **1** *art indéf* a, (*devant voyelle*) an; **une page** a page; **un ange** an angel. **2** *a* one; **la page un** page one; **un kilo** one kilo; **un type** (*un quelconque*) some *ou* a fellow. **3** *pron & nmf* one; **l'un one**; **les uns** some; **le numéro un** number one; **j'en ai un** I have one; **l'un d'eux** one of them; **la une** *Journ* page one.

unanime [ynanim] *a* unanimous. ◆**unanimité** *nf* unanimity; **à l'u.** unanimously.

uni [yni] *a* united; (*famille etc*) close; (*surface*) smooth; (*couleur, étoffe*) plain.

unième [ynjɛm] *a* (*après un numéral*) (-)first; **trente et u.** thirty-first; **cent u.** hundred and first.

unifier [ynifje] *vt* to unify. ◆**unification** *nf* unification.

uniforme [yniform] **1** *a* (*régulier*) uniform. **2** *nm* (*vêtement*) uniform. ◆**uniformément** *adv* uniformly. ◆**uniformiser** *vt* to standardize. ◆**uniformité** *nf* uniformity.

unijambiste [yniʒãbist] *a & nmf* one-legged (man *ou* woman).

unilatéral, -aux [ynilateral, -o] *a* unilateral; (*stationnement*) on one side of the road only.

union [ynjɔ̃] *nf* union; (*association*) association; (*entente*) unity. ◆**unir** *vt* to unite, join (together); **u. la force au courage/etc** to combine strength with courage/*etc*; **— s'u.** *vpr* to unite; (*se marier*) to be joined together; (*se joindre*) to join (together).

unique [ynik] *a* **1** (*fille, fils*) only; (*espoir, souci etc*) only, sole; (*prix, salaire, voie*) single, one; **son seul et u. souci** his *ou* her one and only worry. **2** (*incomparable*) unique. ◆**uniquement** *adv* only, solely.

unisexe [yniseks] *a inv* (*vêtements etc*) unisex.

unisson (à l') [alynisɔ̃] *adv* in unison (de with).

unité [ynite] *nf* (*élément, grandeur*) & *Mil* unit; (*cohésion, harmonie*) unity. ◆**unitaire** *a* (*prix*) per unit.

univers [yniver] *nm* universe.

universel, -elle [yniversel] *a* universal. ◆**universellement** *adv* universally. ◆**universalité** *nf* universality.

université [yniversite] *nf* university; **à l'u.** at university. ◆**universitaire** *a* university-; *– nmf* academic.

uranium [yranjɔm] *nm* uranium.

urbain [yrbɛ̃] *a* urban, town-, city-. ◆**urbaniser** *vt* to urbanize, build up. ◆**urbanisme** *nm* town planning, *Am* city planning. ◆**urbaniste** *nmf* town planner, *Am* city planner.

urgent [yrʒã] *a* urgent, pressing. ◆**urgence** *nf* (*cas*) emergency; (*de décision, tâche etc*) urgency; **d'u.** (*mesures etc*) emergency-; **état d'u.** *Pol* state of emergency; **faire qch d'u.** to do sth urgently.

urine [yrin] *nf* urine. ◆**uriner** *vi* to urinate. ◆**urinoir** *nm* (public) urinal.

urne [yrn] *nf* **1** (*électorale*) ballot box; **aller aux urnes** to go to the polls. **2** (*vase*) urn.

URSS [yrs] *nf abrév* (Union des Républiques Socialistes Soviétiques) USSR.

usage [yzaʒ] *nm* use; *Ling* usage; (*habitude*) custom; **faire u. de** to make use of; **faire de l'u.** (*vêtement etc*) to wear well; **d'u.** (*habituel*) customary; **à l'u. de** for (the use of); **hors d'u.** no longer usable. ◆**usagé** *a* worn; (*d'occasion*) used. ◆**usager** *nm* user. ◆**us/er** *vt* (*vêtement, personne*) to wear out; (*consommer*) to use (up); (*santé*) to ruin; *– vi* **u. de** to use; *– s'u.* *vpr* (*tissu, machine*) to wear out; (*personne*) to wear oneself out. ◆**—é** *a* (*tissu etc*) worn (out); (*sujet etc*) well-worn; (*personne*) worn out.

usine [yzin] *nf* factory; (*à gaz, de métallurgie*) works.

usiner [yzine] *vt* (*pièce*) *Tech* to machine.

usité [yzite] *a* commonly used.

ustensile [ystãsil] *nm* utensil.

usuel, -elle [yzɥɛl] *a* everyday, ordinary; *– nmpl* (*livres*) reference books.

usure [yzyr] *nf* (*détérioration*) wear (and tear); **avoir qn à l'u.** *Fig* to wear s.o. down (in the end).

usurier, -ière [yzyrje, -jɛr] *nmf* usurer.

usurper [yzyrpe] *vt* to usurp.

utérus [yterys] *nm Anat* womb, uterus.

utile [ytil] *a* useful (à to). ◆**utilement** *adv* usefully.

utiliser [ytilize] *vt* to use, utilize. ◆**utilisable** *a* usable. ◆**utilisateur, -trice** *nmf* user. ◆**utilisation** *nf* use. ◆**utilité** *nf* use(fulness); **d'une grande u.** very useful.

utilitaire [ytiliter] *a* utilitarian; (*véhicule*) utility-.

utopie [ytɔpi] *nf* (*idéal*) utopia; (*projet, idée*) utopian plan *ou* idea. ◆**utopique** *a* utopian.

V

V, v [ve] *nm* V, v.

va [va] *voir* **aller 1**.

vacances [vakãs] *nfpl* holiday(s), *Am* vacation; **en v.** on holiday, *Am* on vacation; **prendre ses v.** to take one's holiday(s) *ou* *Am* vacation; **les grandes v.** the summer

holidays *ou Am* vacation. ◆**vacancier,
-ière** *nmf* holidaymaker, *Am* vacationer.

vacant [vakā] *a* vacant. ◆**vacance** *nf*
(*poste*) vacancy.

vacarme [vakarm] *nm* din, uproar.

vaccin [vaksɛ̃] *nm* vaccine; **faire un v. à** to
vaccinate. ◆**vaccination** *nf* vaccination.
◆**vacciner** *vt* to vaccinate.

vache [vaʃ] **1** *nf* cow; **v. laitière** dairy cow. **2**
nf (**peau de**) **v.** (*personne*) *Fam* swine; – *a*
(*méchant*) *Fam* nasty. ◆**vachement** *adv*
Fam (*très*) damned; (*beaucoup*) a hell of a
lot. ◆**vacherie** *nf* *Fam* (*action, parole*)
nasty thing; (*caractère*) nastiness.

vaciller [vasije] *vi* to sway, wobble;
(*flamme, lumière*) to flicker; (*jugement,
mémoire etc*) to falter, waver. ◆**—ant** *a*
(*démarche, mémoire*) shaky; (*lumière etc*)
flickering.

vadrouille [vadruj] *nf* **en v.** *Fam* roaming *ou*
wandering about. ◆**vadrouiller** *vi* *Fam* to
roam *ou* wander about.

va-et-vient [vaevjɛ̃] *nm inv* (*mouvement*)
movement to and fro; (*de personnes*) comings and goings.

vagabond, -onde [vagabɔ̃, -ɔ̃d] *a* wandering; – *nmf* (*clochard*) vagrant, tramp.
◆**vagabond/er** *vi* to roam *ou* wander
about; (*pensée*) to wander. ◆**—age** *nm*
wandering; *Jur* vagrancy.

vagin [vaʒɛ̃] *nm* vagina.

vagir [vaʒir] *vi* (*bébé*) to cry, wail.

vague [vag] **1** *a* vague; (*regard*) vacant;
(*souvenir*) dim, vague; – *nm* vagueness;
regarder dans le v. to gaze into space, gaze
vacantly; **rester dans le v.** (*être évasif*) to
keep it vague. **2** *nf* (*de mer*) & *Fig* wave; **v.
de chaleur** heat wave; **v. de froid** cold snap
ou spell; **v. de fond** (*dans l'opinion*) *Fig* tidal
wave. ◆**vaguement** *adv* vaguely.

vaillant [vajā] *a* brave, valiant; (*vigoureux*)
healthy. ◆**vaillamment** *adv* bravely, val-
iantly. ◆**vaillance** *nf* bravery.

vain [vɛ̃] *a* **1** (*futile*) vain, futile; (*mots,
promesse*) empty; **en v.** in vain, vainly. **2**
(*vaniteux*) vain. ◆**vainement** *adv* in vain,
vainly.

vaincre [vɛ̃kr] *vt* to defeat, beat;
(*surmonter*) to overcome. ◆**—u, -ue** *nm*
defeated man *ou* woman; *Sp* loser. ◆**vainqueur** *nm* victor; *Sp* winner; – *am* victorious.

vaisseau, -x [vɛso] *nm* **1** *Anat Bot* vessel. **2**
(*bateau*) ship, vessel; **v. spatial** spaceship.

vaisselle [vɛsɛl] *nf* crockery; (*à laver*) washing-up; **faire la v.** to do the washing-up, do
ou wash the dishes.

val, *pl* **vals** *ou* **vaux** [val, vo] *nm* valley.

valable [valabl] *a* (*billet, motif etc*) valid;
(*remarquable, rentable*) *Fam* worthwhile.

valet [valɛ] *nm* **1** *Cartes* jack. **2** **v.** (**de chambre**) valet, manservant; **v. de ferme** farm-
hand.

valeur [valœr] *nf* value; (*mérite*) worth;
(*poids*) importance, weight; *pl* (*titres*) *Com*
stocks and shares; **la v. de** (*quantité*) the
equivalent of; **avoir de la v.** to be valuable;
mettre en v. (*faire ressortir*) to highlight; **de
v.** (*personne*) of merit, able; **objets de v.**
valuables.

valide [valid] *a* **1** (*personne*) fit, able-
bodied; (*population*) able-bodied. **2** (*billet
etc*) valid. ◆**valider** *vt* to validate. ◆**validité** *nf* validity.

valise [valiz] *nf* (suit)case; **v. diplomatique**
diplomatic bag *ou Am* pouch; **faire ses valises** to pack (one's bags).

vallée [vale] *nf* valley. ◆**vallon** *nm* (small)
valley. ◆**vallonné** *a* (*région etc*) undulating.

valoir° [valwar] *vi* to be worth; (*s'appliquer*)
to apply (**pour** to); **v. mille francs/cher/etc**
to be worth a thousand francs/a lot/*etc*; **un
vélo vaut bien une auto** a bicycle is as good
as a car; **il vaut mieux rester** it's better to
stay; **il vaut mieux que j'attende** I'd better
wait; **ça ne vaut rien** it's worthless, it's no
good; **ça vaut le coup** *Fam ou* **la peine** it's
worthwhile (**de faire** doing); **faire v.** (*faire
ressortir*) to highlight, set off; (*argument*) to
put forward; (*droit*) to assert; – *vt* **v. qch à
qn** to bring *ou* get s.o. sth; – **se v.** *vpr
(objets, personnes)* to be as good as each
other; **ça se vaut** *Fam* it's all the same.

valse [vals] *nf* waltz. ◆**valser** *vi* to waltz.

valve [valv] *nf* (*clapet*) valve. ◆**valvule** *nf*
(*du cœur*) valve.

vampire [vɑ̃pir] *nm* vampire.

vandale [vɑ̃dal] *nmf* vandal. ◆**vandalisme** *nm* vandalism.

vanille [vanij] *nf* vanilla; **glace/etc à la v.**
vanilla ice cream/*etc.* ◆**vanillé** *a* vanil-
la-flavoured.

vanité [vanite] *nf* vanity. ◆**vaniteux,
-euse** *a* vain, conceited.

vanne [van] *nf* **1** (*d'écluse*) sluice (gate),
floodgate. **2** (*remarque*) *Fam* dig, jibe.

vanné [vane] *a* (*fatigué*) *Fam* dead beat.

vannerie [vanri] *nf* (*fabrication, objets*) bas-
ketwork, basketry.

vantail, -aux [vɑ̃taj, -o] *nm* (*de porte*) leaf.

vanter [vɑ̃te] *vt* to praise; – **se v.** *vpr* to
boast, brag (**de** about, of). ◆**vantard,
-arde** *a* boastful; – *nmf* boaster, braggart.

◆**vantardise** *nf* boastfulness; (*propos*) boast.

va-nu-pieds [vanypje] *nmf inv* tramp, beggar.

vapeur [vapœr] *nf* (*brume, émanation*) vapour; *v.* (**d'eau**) steam; **cuire à la v.** to steam; **bateau à v.** steamship. ◆**vaporeux, -euse** *a* hazy, misty; (*tissu*) translucent, diaphanous.

vaporiser [vaporize] *vt* to spray. ◆**vaporisateur** *nm* (*appareil*) spray.

vaquer [vake] *vi* **v. à** to attend to.

varappe [varap] *nf* rock-climbing.

varech [varɛk] *nm* wrack, seaweed.

vareuse [varøz] *nf* (*d'uniforme*) tunic.

varicelle [varisɛl] *nf* chicken pox.

varices [varis] *nfpl* varicose veins.

vari/er [varje] *vti* to vary (**de** from). ◆**—é** *a* (*diversifié*) varied; (*divers*) various. ◆**—able** *a* variable; (*humeur, temps*) changeable. ◆**variante** *nf* variant. ◆**variation** *nf* variation. ◆**variété** *nf* variety; **spectacle de variétés** *Th* variety show.

variole [varjɔl] *nf* smallpox.

vas [va] *voir* **aller 1**.

vase [vaz] **1** *nm* vase. **2** *nf* (*boue*) silt, mud.

vaseline [vazlin] *nf* Vaseline®.

vaseux, -euse [vazø, -øz] *a* **1** (*boueux*) silty, muddy. **2** (*fatigué*) off colour. **3** (*idées etc*) woolly, hazy.

vasistas [vazistas] *nm* (*dans une porte ou une fenêtre*) hinged panel.

vaste [vast] *a* vast, huge.

Vatican [vatikã] *nm* Vatican.

va-tout [vatu] *nm* **jouer son v.-tout** to stake one's all.

vaudeville [vodvil] *nm* *Th* light comedy.

vau-l'eau (à) [avolo] *adv* **aller à v.-l'eau** to go to rack and ruin.

vaurien, -ienne [vorjɛ̃, -jɛn] *nmf* good-for-nothing.

vautour [votur] *nm* vulture.

vautrer (se) [səvotre] *vpr* to sprawl; **se v. dans** (*boue, vice*) to wallow in.

va-vite (à la) [alavavit] *adv Fam* in a hurry.

veau, -x [vo] *nm* (*animal*) calf; (*viande*) veal; (*cuir*) calf(skin).

vécu [veky] *voir* **vivre**; — *a* (*histoire etc*) real(-life), true.

vedette [vədɛt] *nf* **1** *Cin Th* star; **avoir la v.** (*artiste*) to head the bill; **en v.** (*personne*) in the limelight; (*objet*) in a prominent position. **2** (*canot*) motor boat, launch.

végétal, -aux [veʒetal, -o] *a* (*huile, règne*) vegetable-; — *nm* plant. ◆**végétarien,**

-ienne *a & nmf* vegetarian. ◆**végétation 1** *nf* vegetation. **2** *nfpl Méd* adenoids.

végéter [veʒete] *vi* (*personne*) *Péj* to vegetate.

véhément [veemã] *a* vehement. ◆**véhémence** *nf* vehemence.

véhicule [veikyl] *nm* vehicle. ◆**véhiculer** *vt* to convey.

veille [vɛj] *nf* **1 la v. (de)** (*jour précédent*) the day before; **à la v. de** (*événement*) on the eve of; **la v. de Noël** Christmas Eve. **2** (*état*) wakefulness; *pl* vigils.

veill/er [veje] *vi* to stay up *ou* awake; (*sentinelle etc*) to be on watch; **v. à qch** to attend to sth, see to sth; **v. à ce que** (+ *sub*) to make sure that; **v. sur qn** to watch over s.o.; — *vt* (*malade*) to sit with, watch over. ◆**—ée** *nf* (*soirée*) evening; (*réunion*) evening get-together; (*mortuaire*) vigil. ◆**—eur** *nm* **v. de nuit** night watchman. ◆**—euse** *nf* (*lampe*) night light; (*de voiture*) sidelight; (*de réchaud*) pilot light.

veine [vɛn] *nf* **1** *Anat Bot Géol* vein. **2** (*chance*) *Fam* luck; **avoir de la v.** to be lucky; **une v.** a piece *ou* stroke of luck. ◆**veinard, -arde** *nmf Fam* lucky devil; — *a Fam* lucky.

vêler [vele] *vi* (*vache*) to calve.

vélin [velɛ̃] *nm* (*papier, peau*) vellum.

velléité [veleite] *nf* vague desire.

vélo [velo] *nm* bike, bicycle; (*activité*) cycling; **faire du v.** to cycle, go cycling. ◆**vélodrome** *nm Sp* velodrome, cycle track. ◆**vélomoteur** *nm* (lightweight) motorcycle.

velours [v(ə)lur] *nm* velvet; **v. côtelé** corduroy, cord. ◆**velouté** *a* soft, velvety; (*au goût*) mellow, smooth; — *nm* smoothness; **v. d'asperges**/*etc* (*potage*) cream of asparagus/*etc* soup.

velu [vəly] *a* hairy.

venaison [vənɛzɔ̃] *nf* venison.

vénal, -aux [venal, -o] *a* mercenary, venal.

vendange(s) [vãdãʒ] *nf*(*pl*) grape harvest, vintage. ◆**vendanger** *vi* to pick the grapes. ◆**vendangeur, -euse** *nmf* grape-picker.

vendetta [vãdeta] *nf* vendetta.

vend/re [vãdr] *vt* to sell; **v. qch à qn** to sell s.o. sth, sell sth to s.o.; **v. qn** (*trahir*) to sell s.o. out; **à v.** (*maison etc*) for sale; — **se v.** *vpr* to be sold; **ça se vend bien** it sells well. ◆**—eur, -euse** *nmf* (*de magasin*) sales *ou* shop assistant, *Am* sales clerk; (*marchand*) salesman, saleswoman; *Jur* vendor, seller.

vendredi [vãdrədi] *nm* Friday; **V. saint** Good Friday.

vénéneux, -euse [venenø, -øz] *a* poisonous.

vénérable [venerabl] *a* venerable. ◆**vénérer** *vt* to venerate.

vénérien, -ienne [venerjɛ̃, -jɛn] *a Méd* venereal.

venger [vɑ̃ʒe] *vt* to avenge; — **se v.** *vpr* to take (one's) revenge, avenge oneself (**de qn** on s.o., **de qch** for sth). ◆**vengeance** *nf* revenge, vengeance. ◆**vengeur, -eresse** *a* vengeful; — *nmf* avenger.

venin [vanɛ̃] *nm* (*substance*) & *Fig* venom. ◆**venimeux, -euse** *a* poisonous, venomous; (*haineux*) *Fig* venomous.

venir° [v(ə)nir] *vi* (*aux* **être**) to come (**de** from); **v. faire** to come to do; **viens me voir** come and *ou* to see me; **je viens/venais d'arriver** I've/I'd just arrived; **en v. à** (*conclusion etc*) to come to; **où veux-tu en v.?** what are you driving *ou* getting at?; **d'où vient que...?** how is it that...?; **s'il venait à faire** (*éventualité*) if he happened to do; **les jours/etc qui viennent** the coming days/etc; **une idée m'est venue** an idea occurred to me; **faire v.** to send for, get.

vent [vɑ̃] *nm* wind; **il fait** *ou* **il y a du v.** it's windy; **coup de v.** gust of wind; **avoir v. de** (*connaissance de*) to get wind of; **dans le v.** (*à la mode*) *Fam* trendy, with it.

vente [vɑ̃t] *nf* sale; **v.** (**aux enchères**) auction (sale); **v. de charité** bazaar, charity sale; **en v.** (*disponible*) on sale; **point de v.** sales *ou* retail outlet; **prix de v.** selling price; **salle des ventes** auction room.

ventilateur [vɑ̃tilatœr] *nm* (*électrique*) & *Aut* fan; (*dans un mur*) ventilator. ◆**ventilation** *nf* ventilation. ◆**ventiler** *vt* to ventilate.

ventouse [vɑ̃tuz] *nf* (*pour fixer*) suction grip; **à v.** (*crochet, flèchette etc*) suction-.

ventre [vɑ̃tr] *nm* belly, stomach; (*utérus*) womb; (*de cruche etc*) bulge; **avoir/prendre du v.** to have/get a paunch; **à plat v.** flat on one's face. ◆**ventru** *a* (*personne*) pot-bellied; (*objet*) bulging.

ventriloque [vɑ̃trilɔk] *nmf* ventriloquist.

venu, -ue[1] [v(ə)ny] *voir* **venir**; — *nmf* **nouveau v., nouvelle venue** newcomer; **premier v.** anyone; — *a* **bien v.** (*à propos*) timely; **mal v.** untimely; **être bien/mal v. de faire** to have good grounds/no grounds for doing.

venue[2] [v(ə)ny] *nf* (*arrivée*) coming.

vêpres [vɛpr] *nfpl Rel* vespers.

ver [vɛr] *nm* worm; (*larve*) grub; (*de fruits, fromage etc*) maggot; **v. luisant** glow-worm;

v. à soie silkworm; **v. solitaire** tapeworm; **v. de terre** earthworm.

véracité [verasite] *nf* truthfulness, veracity.

véranda [verɑ̃da] *nf* veranda(h).

verbe [vɛrb] *nm Gram* verb. ◆**verbal, -aux** *a* (*promesse, expression etc*) verbal.

verbeux, -euse [vɛrbø, -øz] *a* verbose. ◆**verbiage** *nm* verbiage.

verdâtre [vɛrdɑtr] *a* greenish.

verdeur [vɛrdœr] *nf* (*de fruit, vin*) tartness; (*de vieillard*) sprightliness; (*de langage*) crudeness.

verdict [vɛrdikt] *nm* verdict.

verdir [vɛrdir] *vti* to turn green. ◆**verdoyant** *a* green, verdant. ◆**verdure** *nf* (*arbres etc*) greenery.

véreux, -euse [verø, -øz] *a* (*fruit etc*) wormy, maggoty; (*malhonnête*) *Fig* dubious, shady.

verge [vɛrʒ] *nf Anat* penis.

verger [vɛrʒe] *nm* orchard.

vergetures [vɛrʒətyr] *nfpl* stretch marks.

verglas [vɛrɡla] *nm* (black) ice, *Am* sleet. ◆**verglacé** *a* (*route*) icy.

vergogne (sans) [sɑ̃vɛrgɔɲ] *a* shameless; — *adv* shamelessly.

véridique [veridik] *a* truthful.

vérifier [verifje] *vt* to check, verify; (*confirmer*) to confirm; (*comptes*) to audit. ◆**vérifiable** *a* verifiable. ◆**vérification** *nf* verification; confirmation; audit(ing).

vérité [verite] *nf* truth; (*de personnage, tableau etc*) trueness to life; (*sincérité*) sincerity; **en v.** in fact. ◆**véritable** *a* true, real; (*non imité*) real, genuine; (*exactement nommé*) veritable, real. ◆**véritablement** *adv* really.

vermeil, -eille [vɛrmɛj] *a* bright red, vermilion.

vermicelle(s) [vɛrmisɛl] *nm(pl) Culin* vermicelli.

vermine [vɛrmin] *nf* (*insectes, racaille*) vermine.

vermoulu [vɛrmuly] *a* worm-eaten.

vermouth [vɛrmut] *nm* vermouth.

verni [vɛrni] *a* (*chanceux*) *Fam* lucky.

vernir [vɛrnir] *vt* to varnish; (*poterie*) to glaze. ◆**vernis** *nm* varnish; glaze; (*apparence*) *Fig* veneer; **v. à ongles** nail polish *ou* varnish. ◆**vernissage** *nm* (*d'exposition de peinture*) first day. ◆**vernisser** *vt* (*poterie*) to glaze.

verra, verrait [vɛra, vɛrɛ] *voir* **voir**.

verre [vɛr] *nm* (*substance, récipient*) glass; **boire** *ou* **prendre un v.** to have a drink; **v. à bière/à vin** beer/wine glass; **v. de contact**

contact lens. ◆**verrerie** *nf* (*objets*) glass-ware. ◆**verrière** *nf* (*toit*) glass roof.

verrou [veru] *nm* bolt; **fermer au v.** to bolt; **sous les verrous** behind bars. ◆**verrouiller** *vt* to bolt.

verrue [very] *nf* wart.

vers[1] [vɛr] *prép* (*direction*) towards, toward; (*approximation*) around, about.

vers[2] [vɛr] *nm* (*d'un poème*) line; *pl* (*poésie*) verse.

versant [vɛrsɑ̃] *nm* slope, side.

versatile [vɛrsatil] *a* fickle, volatile.

verse (à) [avɛrs] *adv* in torrents; **pleuvoir à v.** to pour (down).

versé [vɛrse] *a* **v. dans** (well-)versed in.

Verseau [vɛrso] *nm* le **V.** (*signe*) Aquarius.

vers/er [vɛrse] **1** *vt* to pour; (*larmes, sang*) to shed. **2** *vt* (*argent*) to pay. **3** *vti* (*basculer*) to overturn. ◆**—ement** *nm* payment. ◆**—eur** *a* **bec v.** spout.

verset [vɛrse] *nm Rel* verse.

version [vɛrsjɔ̃] *nf* version; (*traduction*) *Scol* translation, unseen.

verso [vɛrso] *nm* back (of the page); **'voir au v.'** 'see overleaf.'

vert [vɛr] *a* green; (*pas mûr*) unripe; (*vin*) young; (*vieillard*) *Fig* sprightly; – *nm* green.

vert-de-gris [vɛrdəgri] *nm inv* verdigris.

vertèbre [vɛrtɛbr] *nf* vertebra.

vertement [vɛrtəmɑ̃] *adv* (*réprimander etc*) sharply.

vertical, -ale, -aux [vɛrtikal, -o] *a & nf* vertical; **à la verticale** vertically. ◆**verticalement** *adv* vertically.

vertige [vɛrtiʒ] *nm* (*feeling of*) dizziness *ou* giddiness; (*peur de tomber dans le vide*) vertigo; *pl* dizzy spells; **avoir le v.** to feel dizzy *ou* giddy. ◆**vertigineux, -euse** *a* (*hauteur*) giddy, dizzy; (*très grand*) *Fig* staggering.

vertu [vɛrty] *nf* virtue; **en v. de** in accordance with. ◆**vertueux, -euse** *a* virtuous.

verve [vɛrv] *nf* (*d'orateur etc*) brilliance.

verveine [vɛrvɛn] *nf* (*plante*) verbena.

vésicule [vezikyl] *nf* **v. biliaire** gall bladder.

vessie [vesi] *nf* bladder.

veste [vɛst] *nf* jacket, coat.

vestiaire [vɛstjɛr] *nm* cloakroom, *Am* locker room; (*meuble métallique*) locker.

vestibule [vɛstibyl] *nm* (entrance) hall.

vestiges [vɛstiʒ] *nmpl* (*restes, ruines*) remains; (*traces*) traces, vestiges.

vestimentaire [vɛstimɑ̃tɛr] *a* (*dépense*) clothing; (*détail*) of dress.

veston [vɛstɔ̃] *nm* (suit) jacket.

vêtement [vɛtmɑ̃] *nm* garment, article of

clothing; *pl* clothes; **du v.** (*industrie, commerce*) clothing-; **vêtements de sport** sportswear.

vétéran [veterɑ̃] *nm* veteran.

vétérinaire [veteriner] *a* veterinary; – *nmf* vet, veterinary surgeon, *Am* veterinarian.

vétille [vetij] *nf* trifle, triviality.

vêt/ir* [vetir] *vt*, – **se v.** *vpr* to dress. ◆**—u** *a* dressed (**de** in).

veto [veto] *nm inv* veto; **mettre** *ou* **opposer son v. à** to veto.

vétuste [vetyst] *a* dilapidated.

veuf, veuve [vœf, vœv] *a* widowed; – *nm* widower; – *nf* widow.

veuille [vœj] *voir* **vouloir.**

veule [vøl] *a* feeble. ◆**veulerie** *nf* feebleness.

veut, veux [vø] *voir* **vouloir.**

vex/er [vɛkse] *vt* to upset, hurt; – **se v.** *vpr* to be *ou* get upset (**de** at). ◆**—ant** *a* hurtful; (*contrariant*) annoying. ◆**vexation** *nf* humiliation.

viable [vjabl] *a* (*enfant, entreprise etc*) viable. ◆**viabilité** *nf* viability.

viaduc [vjadyk] *nm* viaduct.

viager, -ère [vjaʒe, -ɛr] *a* **rente viagère** life annuity; – *nm* life annuity.

viande [vjɑ̃d] *nf* meat.

vibrer [vibre] *vi* to vibrate; (*être ému*) to thrill (**de** with); **faire v.** (*auditoire etc*) to thrill. ◆**vibrant** *a* (*émouvant*) emotional; (*voix, son*) resonant, vibrant. ◆**vibration** *nf* vibration. ◆**vibromasseur** *nm* (*appareil*) vibrator.

vicaire [vikɛr] *nm* curate.

vice [vis] *nm* vice; (*défectuosité*) defect.

vice- [vis] *préf* vice-.

vice versa [vis(e)vɛrsa] *adv* vice versa.

vicier [visje] *vt* to taint, pollute.

vicieux, -euse [visjø, -øz] **1** *a* depraved; – *nmf* pervert. **2** *a* **cercle v.** vicious circle.

vicinal, -aux [visinal, -o] *a* **chemin v.** byroad, minor road.

vicissitudes [visisityd] *nfpl* vicissitudes.

vicomte [vikɔ̃t] *nm* viscount. ◆**vicomtesse** *nf* viscountess.

victime [viktim] *nf* victim; (*d'un accident*) casualty; **être v. de** to be the victim of.

victoire [viktwar] *nf* victory; *Sp* win. ◆**victorieux, -euse** *a* victorious; (*équipe*) winning.

victuailles [viktɥaj] *nfpl* provisions.

vidange [vidɑ̃ʒ] *nf* emptying, draining; *Aut* oil change; (*dispositif*) waste outlet. ◆**vidanger** *vt* to empty, drain.

vide [vid] *a* empty; – *nm* emptiness, void; (*absence d'air*) vacuum; (*gouffre etc*) drop;

(*trou, manque*) gap; **regarder dans le v.** to stare into space; **emballé sous v.** vacuum-packed; **v.** empty.

vidéo [video] *a inv* video. ◆**vidéocassette** *nf* video (cassette).

vide-ordures [vidɔrdyr] *nm inv* (refuse) chute. ◆**vide-poches** *nm inv Aut* glove compartment.

vid/er [vide] *vt* to empty; (*lieu*) to vacate; (*poisson, volaille*) Culin to gut; (*querelle*) to settle; **v. qn** Fam (*chasser*) to throw s.o. out; (*épuiser*) to tire s.o. out; **— se v.** *vpr* to empty. ◆**—é -e** *a* (*fatigué*) Fam exhausted. ◆**—eur** *nm* (*de boîte de nuit*) bouncer.

vie [vi] *nf* life; (*durée*) lifetime; **coût de la v.** cost of living; **gagner sa v.** to earn one's living ou livelihood; **en v.** living; **à v., pour la v.** for life; **donner la v. à** to give birth to; **avoir la v. dure** (*préjugés etc*) to die hard; **jamais de la v.!** not on your life!, never!

vieill/ir [vjejir] *vi* to grow old; (*changer*) to age; (*théorie, mot*) to become old-fashioned; **— vt v. qn** (*vêtement etc*) to age s.o. ◆**—i** *a* (*démodé*) old-fashioned. ◆**—issant** *a* ageing. ◆**—issement** *nm* ageing.

viens, vient [vjɛ̃] *voir* venir.

vierge [vjɛrʒ] *nf* virgin; **la V.** (*signe*) Virgo; **– a** (*femme, neige etc*) virgin; (*feuille de papier, film*) blank; **être v.** (*femme, homme*) to be a virgin.

Viêt-nam [vjɛtnam] *nm* Vietnam. ◆**vietnamien, -ienne** *a & nmf* Vietnamese.

vieux (*or* **vieil** before vowel or mute *h*), **vieille**, *pl* **vieux, vieilles** [vjø, vjɛj] *a* old; **être v. jeu** (*a inv*) to be old-fashioned; **v. garçon** bachelor; **vieille fille** *Péj* old maid; **– nm** old man; *pl* old people; **mon v.** (*mon cher*) Fam old boy, old man; **– nf** old woman; **ma vieille** (*ma chère*) Fam old girl. ◆**vieillard** *nm* old man; *pl* old people. ◆**vieillerie** *nf* (*objet*) old thing; (*idée*) old idea. ◆**vieillesse** *nf* old age. ◆**vieillot** *a* antiquated.

vif, vive [vif, viv] *a* (*enfant, mouvement*) lively; (*alerte*) quick, sharp; (*intelligence, intérêt, vent*) keen; (*couleur, lumière*) bright; (*froid*) biting; (*pas*) quick, brisk; (*impression, imagination, style*) vivid; (*parole*) sharp; (*regret, satisfaction, succès etc*) great; (*coléreux*) quick-tempered; **brûler/ enterrer qn v.** to burn/bury s.o. alive; **– nm le v. du sujet** the heart of the matter; **à v.** (*plaie*) open; **piqué au v.** (*vexé*) cut to the quick.

vigie [viʒi] *nf* (*matelot*) lookout; (*poste*) lookout post.

vigilant [viʒilā] *a* vigilant. ◆**vigilance** *nf* vigilance.

vigile [viʒil] *nm* (*gardien*) watchman; (*de nuit*) night watchman.

vigne [viɲ] *nf* (*plante*) vine; (*plantation*) vineyard. ◆**vigneron, -onne** *nmf* wine grower. ◆**vignoble** *nm* vineyard; (*région*) vineyards.

vignette [viɲɛt] *nf* Aut road tax sticker; (*de médicament*) price label (*for reimbursement by Social Security*).

vigueur [vigœr] *nf* vigour; **entrer/être en v.** (*loi*) to come into/be in force. ◆**vigoureux, -euse** *a* (*personne, style etc*) vigorous; (*bras*) sturdy.

vilain [vilɛ̃] *a* (*laid*) ugly; (*mauvais*) nasty; (*enfant*) naughty.

villa [villa] *nf* (detached) house.

village [vilaʒ] *nm* village. ◆**villageois, -oise** *a* village-; **– nmf** villager.

ville [vil] *nf* town; (*grande*) city; **aller/être en v.** to go into/be in town; **v. d'eaux** spa (town).

villégiature [villeʒjatyr] *nf* **lieu de v.** (holiday) resort.

vin [vɛ̃] *nm* wine; **v. ordinaire** *ou* **de table** table wine; **v. d'honneur** reception (*in honour of s.o.*). ◆**vinicole** *a* (*région*) wine-growing; (*industrie*) wine-.

vinaigre [vinɛgr] *nm* vinegar. ◆**vinaigré** *a* seasoned with vinegar. ◆**vinaigrette** *nf* (*sauce*) vinaigrette, French dressing, *Am* Italian dressing.

vindicatif, -ive [vɛ̃dikatif, -iv] *a* vindictive.

vingt [vɛ̃] ([vɛ̃t] before vowel or mute *h* and in numbers 22–29) *a & nm* twenty; **v. et un** twenty-one. ◆**vingtaine** *nf* **une v. (de)** (*nombre*) about twenty; **avoir la v.** (*âge*) to be about twenty. ◆**vingtième** *a & nmf* twentieth.

vinyle [vinil] *nm* vinyl.

viol [vjɔl] *nm* rape; (*de loi, lieu*) violation. ◆**violation** *nf* violation. ◆**violenter** *vt* to rape. ◆**violer** *vt* (*femme*) to rape; (*loi, lieu*) to violate. ◆**violeur** *nm* rapist.

violent [vjɔlā] *a* violent; (*remède*) drastic. ◆**violemment** [-amā] *adv* violently. ◆**violence** *nf* violence; (*acte*) act of violence.

violet, -ette [vjɔlɛ, -ɛt] **1** *a & nm* (*couleur*) purple, violet. **2** *nf* (*fleur*) violet. ◆**violacé** *a* purplish.

violon [vjɔlɔ̃] *nm* violin. ◆**violoncelle** *nm* cello. ◆**violoncelliste** *nmf* cellist. ◆**violoniste** *nmf* violinist.

vipère [viper] *nf* viper, adder.

virage [viraʒ] *nm* (*de route*) bend; (*de véhicule*) turn; (*revirement*) Fig change of course. ◆**vir/er 1** *vi* to turn, veer; (*sur soi*) to turn round; **v. au bleu**/*etc* to turn blue/*etc*. **2** *vt* (*expulser*) *Fam* to throw out. **3** *vt* (*somme*) *Fin* to transfer (à to). ◆**—ement** *nm Fin* (bank *ou* credit) transfer.

virée [vire] *nf Fam* trip, outing.

virevolter [virvɔlte] *vi* to spin round.

virginité [virʒinite] *nf* virginity.

virgule [virgyl] *nf Gram* comma; *Math* (decimal) point; **2 v. 5** 2 point 5.

viril [viril] *a* virile, manly; (*attribut*, *force*) male. ◆**virilité** *nf* virility, manliness.

virtuel, -elle [virtɥɛl] *a* potential.

virtuose [virtɥoz] *nmf* virtuoso. ◆**virtuosité** *nf* virtuosity.

virulent [virylɑ̃] *a* virulent. ◆**virulence** *nf* virulence.

virus [virys] *nm* virus.

vis¹ [vi] *voir* **vivre**, **voir**.

vis² [vis] *nf* screw.

visa [viza] *nm* (*timbre*) stamp, stamped signature; (*de passeport*) visa; **v. de censure** (*d'un film*) certificate.

visage [vizaʒ] *nm* face.

vis-à-vis [vizavi] *prép* **v.-à-vis de** opposite; (*à l'égard de*) with respect to; (*envers*) towards; (*comparé à*) compared to; – *nm inv* (*personne*) person opposite; (*bois*, *maison etc*) opposite view.

viscères [viser] *nmpl* intestines. ◆**viscéral, -aux** *a* (*haine etc*) *Fig* deeply felt.

viscosité [viskozite] *nf* viscosity.

viser [vize] **1** *vi* to aim (à at); **v. à faire** to aim to do; – *vt* (*cible*) to aim at; (*concerner*) to be aimed at. **2** *vt* (*passeport*, *document*) to stamp. ◆**visées** *nfpl* (*desseins*) *Fig* aims; **avoir des visées sur** to have designs on. ◆**viseur** *nm Phot* viewfinder; (*d'arme*) sight.

visible [vizibl] *a* visible. ◆**visiblement** *adv* visibly. ◆**visibilité** *nf* visibility.

visière [vizjer] *nf* (*de casquette*) peak; (*en plastique etc*) eyeshade; (*de casque*) visor.

vision [vizjɔ̃] *nf* (*conception*, *image*) vision; (*sens*) (eye)sight, vision; **avoir des visions** *Fam* to be seeing things. ◆**visionnaire** *a* & *nmf* visionary. ◆**visionner** *vt Cin* to view. ◆**visionneuse** *nf* (*pour diapositives*) viewer.

visite [vizit] *nf* visit; (*personne*) visitor; (*examen*) inspection; **rendre v. à**, **faire une v. à** to visit; **v. (à domicile)** *Méd* call, visit; **v. (médicale)** medical examination; **v. guidée** guided tour; **de v.** (*carte*, *heures*) visiting-. ◆**visiter** *vt* to visit; (*examiner*) to inspect. ◆**visiteur, -euse** *nmf* visitor.

vison [vizɔ̃] *nm* mink.

visqueux, -euse [viskø, -øz] *a* viscous; (*surface*) sticky; (*répugnant*) *Fig* slimy.

visser [vise] *vt* to screw on.

visuel, -elle [vizɥɛl] *a* visual.

vit [vi] *voir* **vivre**, **voir**.

vital, -aux [vital, -o] *a* vital. ◆**vitalité** *nf* vitality.

vitamine [vitamin] *nf* vitamin. ◆**vitaminé** *a* (*biscuits etc*) vitamin-enriched.

vite [vit] *adv* quickly, fast; (*tôt*) soon; **v.!** quick(ly)! ◆**vitesse** *nf* speed; (*régime*) *Aut* gear; **boîte de vitesses** gearbox; **à toute v.** at top *ou* full speed; **v. de pointe** top speed; **en v.** quickly.

viticole [vitikɔl] *a* (*région*) wine-growing; (*industrie*) wine-. ◆**viticulteur** *nm* wine grower. ◆**viticulture** *nf* wine growing.

vitre [vitr] *nf* (window)pane; (*de véhicule*) window. ◆**vitrage** *nm* (*vitres*) windows. ◆**vitrail, -aux** *nm* stained-glass window. ◆**vitré** *a* glass-, glazed. ◆**vitreux, -euse** *a* (*regard*, *yeux*) *Fig* glassy. ◆**vitrier** *nm* glazier.

vitrine [vitrin] *nf* (*de magasin*) (shop) window; (*meuble*) showcase, display cabinet.

vitriol [vitrijɔl] *nm Ch & Fig* vitriol.

vivable [vivabl] *a* (*personne*) easy to live with; (*endroit*) fit to live in.

vivace [vivas] *a* (*plante*) perennial; (*haine*) *Fig* inveterate.

vivacité [vivasite] *nf* liveliness; (*de l'air*, *d'émotion*) keenness; (*agilité*) quickness; (*de couleur*, *d'impression*, *de style*) vividness; (*emportement*) petulance; **v. d'esprit** quick-wittedness.

vivant [vivɑ̃] *a* (*en vie*) alive, living; (*être*, *matière*, *preuve*) living; (*conversation*, *enfant*, *récit*, *rue*) lively; **langue vivante** modern language; – *nm* **de son v.** in one's lifetime; **bon v.** jovial fellow; **les vivants** the living.

vivats [viva] *nmpl* cheers.

vive¹ [viv] *voir* **vif**.

vive² [viv] *int* **v. le roi**/*etc*! long live the king/*etc*!; **v. les vacances!** hurray for the holidays!

vivement [vivmɑ̃] *adv* quickly, briskly; (*répliquer*) sharply; (*sentir*) keenly; (*regretter*) deeply; **v. demain!** roll on tomorrow! I can hardly wait for tomorrow!; **v. que** (+ *sub*) I'll be glad when.

vivier [vivje] *nm* fish pond.

vivifier [vivifje] *vt* to invigorate.

vivisection [vivisɛksjɔ̃] *nf* vivisection.

vivre* [vivr] **1** *vi* to live; **elle vit encore** she's still alive *ou* living; **faire v.** (*famille etc*) to support; **v. vieux** to live to be old; **difficile/facile à v.** hard/easy to get on with; **manière de v.** way of life; **v. de** (*fruits etc*) to live on; (*travail etc*) to live by; **avoir de quoi v.** to have enough to live on; **vivent les vacances!** hurray for the holidays!; — *vt* (*vie*) to live; (*aventure, époque*) to live through; (*éprouver*) to experience. **2** *nmpl* food, supplies. ◆**vivoter** *vi* to jog along, get by.

vlan! [vlã] *int* bang!, wham!

vocable [vɔkabl] *nm* term, word.

vocabulaire [vɔkabylɛr] *nm* vocabulary.

vocal, -aux [vɔkal, -o] *a* (*cordes, musique*) vocal.

vocation [vɔkasjɔ̃] *nf* vocation, calling.

vociférer [vɔsifere] *vti* to shout angrily. ◆**vocifération** *nf* angry shout.

vodka [vɔdka] *nf* vodka.

vœu, -x [vø] *nm* (*souhait*) wish; (*promesse*) vow; **faire le v. de faire** (to make) a vow to do; **tous mes vœux!** (my) best wishes!

vogue [vɔg] *nf* fashion, vogue; **en v.** in fashion, in vogue.

voici [vwasi] *prép* here is, this is; *pl* here are, these are; **me v.** here I am; **me v. triste** I'm sad now; **v. dix ans** ten years ago; **v. dix ans que** it's ten years since.

voie [vwa] *nf* (*route*) road; (*rails*) track, line; (*partie de route*) lane; (*chemin*) way; (*moyen*) means, way; (*de communication*) line; (*diplomatique*) channels; (*quai*) *Rail* platform; **en v. de** in the process of; **en v. de développement** (*pays*) developing; **v. publique** public highway; **v. navigable** waterway; **v. sans issue** cul-de-sac, dead end; **préparer la v.** *Fig* to pave the way; **sur la** (**bonne**) **v.** on the right track.

voilà [vwala] *prép* there is, that is; *pl* there are, those are; **les v.** there they are; **v., j'arrive!** all right, I'm coming!; **le v. parti** he has left now; **v. dix ans** ten years ago; **v. dix ans que** it's ten years since.

voile¹ [vwal] *nm* (*étoffe qui cache, coiffure etc*) & *Fig* veil. ◆**voilage** *nm* net curtain. ◆**voil/er¹** *vt* (*visage, vérité etc*) to veil; — **se v.** *vpr* (*personne*) to wear a veil; (*ciel, regard*) to cloud over; ◆**—é** *a* (*femme, allusion*) veiled; (*terne*) dull; (*photo*) hazy.

voile² [vwal] *nf* (*de bateau*) sail; (*activité*) sailing; **bateau à voiles** sailing boat, *Am* sailboat; **faire de la v.** to sail, go sailing. ◆**voilier** *nm* sailing ship; (*de plaisance*) sailing boat, *Am* sailboat. ◆**voilure** *nf Nau* sails.

voiler² [vwale] *vt,* — **se v.** *vpr* (*roue*) to buckle.

voir* [vwar] *vti* to see; **faire** *ou* **laisser v. qch** to show sth; **fais v.** let me see, show me; **qn faire** to see s.o. do *ou* doing; **voyons!** (*sois raisonnable*) come on!; **y v. clair** (*comprendre*) to see clearly; **je ne peux pas la v.** (*supporter*) *Fam* I can't stand (the sight of) her; **v. venir** (*attendre*) to wait and see; **on verra bien** (*attendons*) we'll see; **ça n'a rien à v. avec** that's got nothing to do with; — **se v.** *vpr* to see oneself; (*se fréquenter*) to see each other; (*objet, attitude etc*) to be seen; (*reprise, tache*) to show; **ça se voit** that's obvious.

voire [vwar] *adv* indeed.

voirie [vwari] *nf* (*enlèvement des ordures*) refuse collection; (*routes*) public highways.

voisin, -ine [vwazɛ̃, -in] *a* (*pays, village etc*) neighbouring; (*maison, pièce*) next (**de** to); (*idée, état etc*) similar (**de** to); — *nmf* neighbour. ◆**voisinage** *nm* (*quartier, voisins*) neighbourhood; (*proximité*) proximity. ◆**voisiner** *vi* **v. avec** to be side by side with.

voiture [vwatyr] *nf Aut* car; *Rail* carriage, coach, *Am* car; (*charrette*) cart; **v.** (**à cheval**) (horse-drawn) carriage; **v. de course/ de tourisme** racing/private car; **v. d'enfant** pram, *Am* baby carriage; **en v.!** *Rail* all aboard!

voix [vwa] *nf* voice; (*suffrage*) vote; **à v. basse** in a whisper; **à portée de v.** within earshot; **avoir v. au chapitre** *Fig* to have a say.

vol [vɔl] *nm* **1** (*d'avion, d'oiseau*) flight; (*groupe d'oiseaux*) flock, flight; **v. libre** hang gliding; **v. à voile** gliding. **2** (*délit*) theft; (*hold-up*) robbery; **v. à l'étalage** shoplifting; **c'est du v.!** (*trop cher*) it's daylight robbery!

volage [vɔlaʒ] *a* flighty, fickle.

volaille [vɔlaj] *nf* **la v.** (*oiseaux*) poultry; **une v.** (*oiseau*) a fowl. ◆**volailler** *nm* poulterer.

volatile [vɔlatil] *nm* (*oiseau domestique*) fowl.

volatiliser (se) [səvɔlatilize] *vpr* (*disparaître*) to vanish (into thin air).

vol-au-vent [vɔlovã] *nm inv Culin* vol-au-vent.

volcan [vɔlkã] *nm* volcano. ◆**volcanique** *a* volcanic.

voler [vɔle] **1** *vi* (*oiseau, avion etc*) to fly; (*courir*) *Fig* to rush; **v.** (*dérober*) to steal (**à** from); **v. qn** to rob s.o.; — *vi* to steal. ◆**volant 1** *a* (*tapis etc*) flying; **feuille volante** loose sheet. **2** *nm Aut* (steering) wheel; (*objet*) *Sp* shuttlecock; (*de jupe*) flounce. ◆**volée** *nf* flight; (*groupe d'oiseaux*) flock, flight; (*de coups, flèches etc*) volley; (*suite de*

coups) thrashing; **lancer à toute v.** to throw as hard as one can; **sonner à toute v.** to peal *ou* ring out. ◆**voleter** *vi* to flutter.
◆**voleur, -euse** *nmf* thief; **au v.!** stop thief!; – *a* thieving.

volet [vɔlɛ] *nm* **1** (*de fenêtre*) shutter. **2** (*de programme, reportage etc*) section, part.

volière [vɔljɛr] *nf* aviary.

volley(-ball) [vɔlɛ(bol)] *nm* volleyball. ◆**volleyeur, -euse** *nmf* volleyball player.

volonté [vɔlɔ̃te] *nf* (*faculté, intention*) will; (*désir*) wish; *Phil Psy* free will; **elle a de la v.** she has willpower; **bonne v.** goodwill; **mauvaise v.** ill will; **à v.** at will; (*quantité*) as much as desired. ◆**volontaire** *a* (*délibéré, qui agit librement*) voluntary; (*opiniâtre*) wilful, *Am* willful; – *nmf* volunteer. ◆**volontairement** *adv* voluntarily; (*exprès*) deliberately. ◆**volontiers** [-tje] *adv* willingly, gladly; (*habituellement*) readily; **v.!** (*oui*) I'd love to!

volt [vɔlt] *nm* *Él* volt. ◆**voltage** *nm* voltage. ◆**volte-face** [vɔltafas] *nf inv* about turn, *Am* about face; **faire v.-face** to turn round. ◆**voltige** [vɔltiʒ] *nf* acrobatics. ◆**voltiger** [vɔltiʒe] *vi* to flutter.

volubile [vɔlybil] *a* (*bavard*) loquacious, voluble.

volume [vɔlym] *nm* (*capacité, intensité, tome*) volume. ◆**volumineux, -euse** *a* bulky, voluminous.

volupté [vɔlypte] *nf* sensual pleasure. ◆**voluptueux, -euse** *a* voluptuous.

vom/ir [vɔmir] *vt* to vomit, bring up; (*exécrer*) *Fig* to loathe; – *vi* to vomit, be sick. ◆**—i** *nm* *Fam* vomit. ◆**—issement** *nm* (*action*) vomiting. ◆**vomitif, -ive** *a* *Fam* nauseating.

vont [vɔ̃] *voir* **aller 1**.

vorace [vɔras] *a* (*appétit, lecteur etc*) voracious.

vos [vo] *voir* **votre**.

vote [vɔt] *nm* (*action*) vote, voting; (*suffrage*) vote; (*de loi*) passing; **bureau de v.** polling station. ◆**voter** *vi* to vote; – *vt* (*loi*) to pass; (*crédits*) to vote. ◆**votant, -ante** *nmf* voter.

votre, *pl* **vos** [vɔtr, vo] *a poss* your. ◆**vôtre** *pron poss* **le** *ou* **la v., les vôtres** yours; **à la v.!** (*toast*) cheers!; – *nmpl* **les vôtres** (*parents etc*) your (own) people.

vouer [vwe] *vt* (*promettre*) to vow (à to); (*consacrer*) to dedicate (à to); (*condamner*) to doom (à to); **se v. à** to dedicate oneself to.

vouloir* [vulwar] *vt* to want (**faire** to do); **je veux qu'il parte** I want him to go; **v. dire** to

mean (**que** that); **je voudrais rester** I'd like to stay; **je voudrais un pain** I'd like a loaf of bread; **voulez-vous me suivre** will you follow me; **si tu veux** *ou* **si on veut** if you wish; **en v. à qn d'avoir fait qch** to hold it against s.o. for doing sth; **l'usage veut que . . .** (*+ sub*) custom requires that . . . ; **v. du bien à qn** to wish s.o. well; **je veux bien** I don't mind (**faire** doing); **que voulez-vous!** (*résignation*) what can you expect!; **sans le v.** unintentionally; **ça ne veut pas bouger** it won't move; **ne pas v. de qch/de qn** not to want sth/s.o.; **veuillez attendre** kindly wait. ◆**voulu** *a* (*requis*) required; (*délibéré*) deliberate, intentional.

vous [vu] *pron* **1** (*sujet, complément direct*) you; **v. êtes** you are; **il v. connaît** he knows you. **2** (*complément indirect*) (to) you; **il v. l'a donné** he gave it to you, he gave you it. **3** (*réfléchi*) yourself, *pl* yourselves; **v. v. lavez** you wash yourself, you wash yourselves. **4** (*réciproque*) each other; **v. v. aimez** you love each other. ◆**v.-même** *pron* yourself. ◆**v.-mêmes** *pron pl* yourselves.

voûte [vut] *nf* (*plafond*) vault; (*porche*) arch(way). ◆**voûté** *a* (*personne*) bent, stooped.

vouvoyer [vuvwaje] *vt* to address formally (*using vous*).

voyage [vwajaʒ] *nm* trip, journey; (*par mer*) voyage; **aimer les voyages** to like travelling; **faire un v., partir en v.** to go on a trip; **être en v.** to be (away) travelling; **de v.** (*compagnon etc*) travelling; **bon v.!** have a pleasant trip!; **v. de noces** honeymoon; **v. organisé** (*package*) tour. ◆**voyager** *vi* to travel. ◆**voyageur, -euse** *nmf* traveller; (*passager*) passenger; **v. de commerce** commercial traveller. ◆**voyagiste** *nm* tour operator.

voyant [vwajɑ̃] **1** *a* gaudy, loud. **2** *nm* (*signal*) (*warning*) light; (*d'appareil électrique*) pilot light.

voyante [vwajɑ̃t] *nf* clairvoyant.

voyelle [vwajɛl] *nf* vowel.

voyeur, -euse [vwajœr, -øz] *nmf* peeping Tom, voyeur.

voyou [vwaju] *nm* hooligan, hoodlum.

vrac (en) [ɑ̃vrak] *adv* (*en désordre*) haphazardly; (*au poids*) loose, unpackaged.

vrai [vrɛ] *a* true; (*réel*) real; (*authentique*) genuine; – *adv* dire **v.** to tell the truth (à what one says); – *nm* (*vérité*) truth. ◆**—ment** *adv* really.

vraisemblable [vrɛsɑ̃blabl] *a* (*probable*) likely, probable; (*plausible*) plausible. ◆**vraisemblablement** *adv* probably.

◆**vraisemblance** nf likelihood; plausibility.

vrille [vrij] nf **1** (outil) gimlet. **2** Av (tail)spin.

vromb/ir [vrɔ̃bir] vi to hum. ◆—**issement** nm hum(ming).

vu [vy] **1** voir **voir**; **– a bien vu** well thought of; **mal vu** frowned upon. **2** prép in view of; **vu que** seeing that.

vue [vy] nf (spectacle) sight; (sens) (eye)sight; (panorama, photo, idée) view; **en v.** (proche) in sight; (en évidence) on view; (personne) Fig in the public eye; **avoir en v.** to have in mind; **à v.** (tirer) on sight; (payable) at sight; **à première v.** at first sight; **de v.** (connaître) by sight; **en v. de faire** with a view to doing.

vulgaire [vylgɛr] a (grossier) vulgar, coarse; (ordinaire) common. ◆—**ment** adv vulgarly, coarsely; (appeler) commonly. ◆**vulgariser** vt to popularize. ◆**vulgarité** nf vulgarity, coarseness.

vulnérable [vylnerabl] a vulnerable. ◆**vulnérabilité** nf vulnerability.

W

W, w [dubləve] nm W, w.

wagon [vagɔ̃] nm Rail (de voyageurs) carriage, coach, Am car; (de marchandises) wag(g)on, truck, Am freight car. ◆**w.-lit** nm (pl wagons-lits) sleeping car, sleeper. ◆**w.-restaurant** nm (pl wagons-restaurants) dining car, diner. ◆**wagonnet** nm (small) wagon ou truck.

wallon, -onne [walɔ̃, -ɔn] a & nmf Walloon.

waters [water] nmpl toilet.

watt [wat] nm Él watt.

w-c [(dubla)vese] nmpl toilet.

week-end [wikɛnd] nm weekend.

western [wɛstɛrn] nm Cin western.

whisky, pl **-ies** [wiski] nm whisky, Am whiskey.

X

X, x [iks] nm X, x; **rayon X** X-ray.

xénophobe [ksenɔfɔb] a xenophobic; – nmf xenophobe. ◆**xénophobie** nf xenophobia.

xérès [gzerɛs] nm sherry.

xylophone [ksilɔfɔn] nm xylophone.

Y

Y, y¹ [igrɛk] nm Y, y.

y² [i] **1** adv there; (dedans) in it; pl in them; (dessus) on it; pl on them; **elle y vivra** she'll live there; **j'y entrai** I entered (it); **allons-y** let's go; **j'y suis!** (je comprends) now I get it!; **je n'y suis pour rien** I have nothing to do with it, that's nothing to do with me. **2** pron (= à cela) **j'y pense** I think of it; **je m'y attendais** I was expecting it; **ça y est!** that's it!

yacht [jɔt] nm yacht.

yaourt [jaur(t)] nm yog(h)urt.

yeux [jø] voir **œil**.

yiddish [(j)idiʃ] nm & a Yiddish.

yoga [jɔga] nm yoga.

yog(h)ourt [jɔgur(t)] voir **yaourt**.

Yougoslavie [jugoslavi] nf Yugoslavia. ◆**yougoslave** a & nmf Yugoslav(ian).

yo-yo [jojo] nm inv yoyo.

Z

Z, z [zɛd] *nm* Z, z.
zèbre [zɛbr] *nm* zebra. ◆**zébré** *a* striped, streaked (**de** with).
zèle [zɛl] *nm* zeal; **faire du z.** to overdo it. ◆**zélé** *a* zealous.
zénith [zenit] *nm* zenith.
zéro [zero] *nm* (*chiffre*) nought, zero; (*dans un numéro*) 0 [əʊ]; (*température*) zero; (*rien*) nothing; (*personne*) *Fig* nobody, nonentity; **deux buts à z.** *Fb* two nil, *Am* two zero; **partir de z.** to start from scratch.
zeste [zɛst] *nm* **un z. de citron** (a piece of) lemon peel.
zézayer [zezeje] *vi* to lisp.
zibeline [ziblin] *nf* (*animal*) sable.

zigzag [zigzag] *nm* zigzag; **en z.** (*route etc*) zigzag(ging); ◆**zigzaguer** *vi* to zigzag.
zinc [zɛ̃g] *nm* (*métal*) zinc; (*comptoir*) *Fam* bar.
zizanie [zizani] *nf* discord.
zodiaque [zɔdjak] *nm* zodiac.
zona [zona] *nm Méd* shingles.
zone [zon] *nf* zone, area; (*domaine*) *Fig* sphere; (*faubourgs misérables*) shanty town; **z. bleue** restricted parking zone; **z. industrielle** trading estate, *Am* industrial park.
zoo [zo(o)] *nm* zoo. ◆**zoologie** [zɔɔlɔʒi] *nf* zoology. ◆**zoologique** *a* zoological; **jardin** *ou* **parc z.** zoo.
zoom [zum] *nm* (*objectif*) zoom lens.
zut! [zyt] *int Fam* bother!, heck!

French verb conjugations

REGULAR VERBS

		-ER Verbs	-IR Verbs	-RE Verbs
Infinitive		*donner*	*finir*	*vendre*
1	Present	je donne	je finis	je vends
		tu donnes	tu finis	tu vends
		il donne	il finit	il vend
		nous donnons	nous finissons	nous vendons
		vous donnez	vous finissez	vous vendez
		ils donnent	ils finissent	ils vendent
2	Imperfect	je donnais	je finissais	je vendais
		tu donnais	tu finissais	tu vendais
		il donnait	il finissait	il vendait
		nous donnions	nous finissions	nous vendions
		vous donniez	vous finissiez	vous vendiez
		ils donnaient	ils finissaient	ils vendaient
3	Past historic	je donnai	je finis	je vendis
		tu donnas	tu finis	tu vendis
		il donna	il finit	il vendit
		nous donnâmes	nous finîmes	nous vendîmes
		vous donnâtes	vous finîtes	vous vendîtes
		ils donnèrent	ils finirent	ils vendirent
4	Future	je donnerai	je finirai	je vendrai
		tu donneras	tu finiras	tu vendras
		il donnera	il finira	il vendra
		nous donnerons	nous finirons	nous vendrons
		vous donnerez	vous finirez	vous vendrez
		ils donneront	ils finiront	ils vendront
5	Subjunctive	je donne	je finisse	je vende
		tu donnes	tu finisses	tu vendes
		il donne	il finisse	il vende
		nous donnions	nous finissions	nous vendions
		vous donniez	vous finissiez	vous vendiez
		ils donnent	ils finissent	ils vendent
6	Imperative	donne	'inis	vends
		donnons	finissons	vendons
		donnez	finissez	vendez
7	Present participle	donnant	finissant	vendant
8	Past participle	donné	fini	vendu

SPELLING ANOMALIES OF -ER VERBS

Verbs in **-ger** (e.g. **manger**) take an extra e before endings beginning with **o** or **a**: *Present* je mange, nous mangeons; *Imperfect* je mangeais, nous mangions; *Past historic* je mangeai, nous mangeâmes; *Present participle* mangeant. Verbs in **-cer** (e.g. **commencer**) change **c** to **ç** before endings beginning with **o** or **a**: *Present* je commence, nous commençons; *Imperfect* je commençais, nous commencions; *Past historic* je commençai, nous commençâmes; *Present participle* commençant. Verbs containing mute **e** in their

(i)

penultimate syllable fall into two groups. In the first (e.g. **mener, peser, lever**), **e** becomes **è** before an unpronounced syllable in the present and subjunctive, and in the future and conditional tenses (e.g. je mène, ils mèneront). The second group contains most verbs ending in **-eler** and **-eter** (e.g. **appeler, jeter**). These verbs change **l** to **ll** before an unpronounced syllable (e.g. j'appelle, ils appelleront; je jette, ils jetteront). However, the following verbs in **-eler** and **-eter** fall into the first group in which **e** changes to **è** before mute **e** (e.g. je modèle, ils modèleront; j'achète, ils achèteront). **celer, ciseler, démanteler, geler, marteler, modeler, peler; acheter, crocheter, fureter, haleter.** Derived verbs (e.g. **dégeler, racheter**) are conjugated in the same way. Verbs containing **é** acute in their penultimate syllable change **é** before to **è** before the unpronounced endings of the present and subjunctive only (e.g. je cède but je céderai). Verbs in **-yer** (e.g. **essuyer**) change **y** to **i** before an unpronounced syllable in the present and subjunctive, and in the future and conditional tenses (e.g. j'essuie, ils essuieront). In verbs in **-ayer** (e.g. **balayer**), **y** may be retained before mute **e** (e.g. je balaie or balaye, ils balaieront or balayeront).

IRREGULAR VERBS

Listed below are those verbs considered to be the most useful. Forms and tenses not given are fully derivable. Note that the endings of the past historic fall into three categories, the 'a' and 'i' categories shown at *donner*, and at *finir* and *vendre*, and the 'u' category which has the following endings: -us, -ut, -ûmes, -ûtes, -urent. Most of the verbs listed below form their past historic with 'u'. The imperfect may usually be formed by adding -ais, -ait, -ions, -iez, -aient to the stem of the first person plural of the present tense. e.g. 'je buvais' etc may be derived from 'nous buvons' (stem 'buv-' and ending '-ons'); similarly, the present participle may generally be formed by substituting -ant for -ons (e.g. buvant). The future may usually be formed by adding -ai, -as, -a, -ons, -ez, -ont to the infinitive or to an infinitive without final 'e' where the ending is -re (e.g. conduire). The imperative usually has the same forms as the second persons singular and plural and first person plural of the present tense.

1 = Present   2 = Imperfect   3 = Past historic   4 = Future
5 = Subjunctive   6 = Imperative   7 = Present participle
8 = Past participle   n = nous   v = vous   †verbs conjugated with **être** only.

abattre	*like* **battre**
absoudre	1 j'absous, n absolvons 2 j'absolvais
	3 j'absolus (*rarely used*) 5 j'absolve 7 absolvant
	8 absous, absoute
†s'abstenir	*like* **tenir**
abstraire	1 j'abstrais, n abstrayons 2 j'abstrayais 3 *none* 5 j'abstraie
	7 abstrayant 8 abstrait
accourir	*like* **courir**
accroître	*like* **croître** *except* 8 accru
accueillir	*like* **cueillir**
acquérir	1 j'acquiers, n acquérons 2 j'acquérais 3 j'acquis
	4 j'acquerrai 5 j'acquière 7 acquérant 8 acquis
adjoindre	*like* **atteindre**
admettre	*like* **mettre**
†aller	1 je vais, tu vas, il va, n allons, v allez, ils vont 4 j'irai
	5 j'aille, nous allions, ils aillent 6 va, allons, allez (*but note* vas-y)
apercevoir	*like* **recevoir**
apparaître	*like* **connaître**
appartenir	*like* **tenir**
apprendre	*like* **prendre**
asseoir	1 j'assieds, n asseyons, ils asseyent 2 j'asseyais 3 j'assis
	4 j'assiérai 5 j'asseye 7 asseyant 8 assis

astreindre	*like* **atteindre**
atteindre	1 j'atteins, n atteignons, ils atteignent 2 j'atteignais
	3 j'atteignis 4 j'atteindrai 5 j'atteigne 7 atteignant
	8 atteint
avoir	1 j'ai, tu as, il a, n avons, v avez, ils ont 2 j'avais 3 j'eus
	4 j'aurai 5 j'aie, il ait, n ayons, ils aient 6 aie, ayons, ayez
	7 ayant 8 eu
battre	1 je bats, n battons 5 je batte
boire	1 je bois, n buvons, ils boivent 2 je buvais 3 je bus
	5 je boive, n buvions 7 buvant 8 bu
bouillir	1 je bous, n bouillons, ils bouillent 2 je bouillais
	3 *not used* 5 je bouille 7 bouillant
braire	(*defective*) 1 il brait, ils braient 4 il braira, ils brairont
combattre	*like* **battre**
commettre	*like* **mettre**
comparaître	*like* **connaître**
comprendre	*like* **prendre**
compromettre	*like* **mettre**
concevoir	*like* **recevoir**
conclure	1 je conclus, n concluons, ils concluent 5 je conclue
concourir	*like* **courir**
conduire	1 je conduis, n conduisons 3 je conduisis 5 je conduise
	8 conduit
connaître	1 je connais, il connaît, n connaissons 3 je connus
	5 je connaisse 7 connaissant 8 connu
conquérir	*like* **acquérir**
consentir	*like* **mentir**
construire	*like* **conduire**
contenir	*like* **tenir**
contraindre	*like* **atteindre**
contredire	*like* **dire** *except* 1 v contredisez
convaincre	*like* **vaincre**
convenir	*like* **tenir**
corrompre	*like* **rompre**
coudre	1 je couds, n cousons, ils cousent 3 je cousis 5 je couse
	7 cousant 8 cousu
courir	1 je cours, n courons 3 je courus 4 je courrai 5 je coure
	8 couru
couvrir	1 je couvre, n couvrons 2 je couvrais 5 je couvre 8 couvert
craindre	*like* **atteindre**
croire	1 je crois, n croyons, ils croient 2 je croyais 3 je crus
	5 je croie, n croyions 7 croyant 8 cru
croître	1 je crois, il croît, n croissons 2 je croissais 3 je crûs
	5 je croisse 7 croissant 8 crû, crue
cueillir	1 je cueille, n cueillons 2 je cueillais 4 je cueillerai
	5 je cueille 7 cueillant
cuire	1 je cuis, n cuisons 2 je cuisais 3 je cuisis 5 je cuise
	7 cuisant 8 cuit
débattre	*like* **battre**
décevoir	*like* **recevoir**
découvrir	*like* **couvrir**
décrire	*like* **écrire**
décroître	*like* **croître** *except* 8 décru
déduire	*like* **conduire**
défaillir	1 je défaille, n défaillons 2 je défaillais 3 je défaillis
	5 je défaille 7 défaillant 8 défailli

défaire	*like* faire
dépeindre	*like* atteindre
déplaire	*like* plaire
déteindre	*like* atteindre
détenir	*like* tenir
détruire	*like* conduire
†devenir	*like* tenir
devoir	1 je dois, n devons, ils doivent 2 je devais 3 je dus 4 je devrai 5 je doive, n devions 6 *not used* 7 devant 8 dû, due, *pl* dus, dues
dire	1 je dis, n disons, v dites 2 je disais 3 je dis 5 je dise 7 disant 8 dit
disparaître	*like* connaître
dissoudre	*like* absoudre
distraire	*like* abstraire
dormir	*like* mentir
†échoir	(*defective*) 1 il échoit 3 il échut, ils échurent 4 il échoira 7 échéant 8 échu
écrire	1 j'écris, n écrivons 2 j'écrivais 3 j'écrivis 5 j'écrive 7 écrivant 8 écrit
élire	*like* lire
émettre	*like* mettre
émouvoir	*like* mouvoir *except* 8 ému
encourir	*like* courir
endormir	*like* mentir
enduire	*like* conduire
enfreindre	*like* atteindre
†s'enfuir	*like* fuir
†s'ensuivre	*like* suivre (*but third person only*)
entreprendre	*like* prendre
entretenir	*like* tenir
entrevoir	*like* voir
entrouvrir	*like* couvrir
envoyer	4 j'enverrai
†s'éprendre	*like* prendre
éteindre	*like* atteindre
être	1 je suis, tu es, il est, n sommes, v êtes, ils sont 2 j'étais 3 je fus 4 je serai 5 je sois, n soyons, ils soient 6 sois, soyons, soyez 7 étant 8 été
exclure	*like* conclure
extraire	*like* abstraire
faillir	(*defective*) 3 je faillis 4 je faillirai 8 failli
faire	1 je fais, n faisons, v faites, ils font 2 je faisais 3 je fis 4 je ferai 5 je fasse 7 faisant 8 fait
falloir	(*impersonal*) 1 il faut 2 il fallait 3 il fallut 4 il faudra 5 il faille 6 *none* 7 *none* 8 fallu
feindre	*like* atteindre
foutre	1 je fous, n foutons 2 je foutais 3 *none* 5 je foute 7 foutant 8 foutu
frire	(*defective*) 1 je fris, tu fris, il frit 4 je frirai (*rare*) 6 fris (*rare*) 8 frit (*for other persons and tenses use* faire frire)
fuir	1 je fuis, n fuyons, ils fuient 2 je fuyais 3 je fuis 5 je fuie 7 fuyant 8 fui
haïr	1 je hais, il hait, n haïssons
inclure	*like* conclure
induire	*like* conduire
inscrire	*like* écrire

instruire	*like* conduire
interdire	*like* dire *except* 1 v interdisez
interrompre	*like* rompre
intervenir	*like* tenir
introduire	*like* conduire
joindre	*like* atteindre
lire	1 je lis, n lisons 2 je lisais 3 je lus 5 je lise 7 lisant 8 lu
luire	*like* nuire
maintenir	*like* tenir
maudire	1 je maudis, n maudissons 2 je maudissais 3 je maudis 4 je maudirai 5 je maudisse 7 maudissant 8 maudit
méconnaître	*like* connaître
médire	*like* dire *except* 1 v médisez
mentir	1 je mens, n mentons 2 je mentais 5 je mente 7 mentant
mettre	1 je mets, n mettons 2 je mettais 3 je mis 5 je mette 7 mettant 8 mis
moudre	1 je mouds, n moulons 2 je moulais 3 je moulus 5 je moule 7 moulant 8 moulu
†mourir	1 je meurs, n mourons, ils meurent 2 je mourais 3 je mourus 4 je mourrai 5 je meure, n mourions 7 mourant 8 mort
mouvoir	1 je meus, n mouvons, ils meuvent 2 je mouvais 3 je mus *(rare)* 4 je mouvrai 5 je meuve, n mouvions 8 mû, mue, *pl* mus, mues
†naître	1 je nais, il naît, n naissons 2 je naissais 3 je naquis 4 je naîtrai 5 je naisse 7 naissant 8 né
nuire	1 je nuis, n nuisons 2 je nuisais 3 je nuisis 5 je nuise 7 nuisant 8 nui
obtenir	*like* tenir
offrir	*like* couvrir
omettre	*like* mettre
ouvrir	*like* couvrir
paître	*(defective)* 1 il paît 2 il paissait 3 *none* 4 il paîtra 5 il paisse 7 paissant 8 *none*
paraître	*like* connaître
parcourir	*like* courir
†partir	*like* mentir
†parvenir	*like* tenir
peindre	*like* atteindre
percevoir	*like* recevoir
permettre	*like* mettre
plaindre	*like* atteindre
plaire	1 je plais, n plaisons 2 je plaisais 3 je plus 5 je plaise 7 plaisant 8 plu
pleuvoir	*(impersonal)* 1 il pleut 2 il pleuvait 3 il plut 4 il pleuvra 5 il pleuve 6 *none* 7 pleuvant 8 plu
poursuivre	*like* suivre
pourvoir	*like* voir *except* 4 je pourvoirai
pouvoir	1 je peux *or* je puis, tu peux, il peut, n pouvons, ils peuvent 2 je pouvais 3 je pus 4 je pourrai 5 je puisse 6 *not used* 7 pouvant 8 pu
prédire	*like* dire *except* 1 v prédisez
prendre	1 je prends, n prenons, ils prennent 2 je prenais 3 je pris 5 je prenne 7 prenant 8 pris
prescrire	*like* écrire
pressentir	*like* mentir

prévenir	*like* tenir
prévoir	*like* voir *except* 4 je prévoirai
produire	*like* conduire
promettre	*like* mettre
promouvoir	*like* mouvoir *except* 8 promu
proscrire	*like* écrire
†provenir	*like* tenir
rabattre	*like* battre
rasseoir	*like* asseoir
recevoir	1 je reçois, n recevons, ils reçoivent 2 je recevais 3 je reçus 4 je recevrai 5 je reçoive, n recevions, ils reçoivent 7 recevant 8 reçu
reconnaître	*like* connaître
reconduire	*like* conduire
reconstruire	*like* conduire
recoudre	*like* coudre
recourir	*like* courir
recouvrir	*like* couvrir
recueillir	*like* cueillir
†redevenir	*like* tenir
redire	*like* dire
réduire	*like* conduire
refaire	*like* faire
rejoindre	*like* atteindre
relire	*like* lire
remettre	*like* mettre
†renaître	*like* naître
rendormir	*like* mentir
renvoyer	*like* envoyer
†repartir	*like* mentir
repentir	*like* mentir
reprendre	*like* prendre
reproduire	*like* conduire
résoudre	1 je résous, n résolvons 2 je résolvais 3 je résolus 5 je résolve 7 résolvant 8 résolu
ressentir	*like* mentir
ressortir	*like* mentir
restreindre	*like* atteindre
retenir	*like* tenir
†revenir	*like* tenir
revêtir	*like* vêtir
revivre	*like* vivre
revoir	*like* voir
rire	1 je ris, n rions 2 je riais 3 je ris 5 je rie, n riions 7 riant 8 ri
rompre	*regular except* 1 il rompt
rouvrir	*like* couvrir
satisfaire	*like* faire
savoir	1 je sais, n savons, ils savent 2 je savais 3 je sus 4 je saurai 5 je sache 6 sache, sachons, sachez 7 sachant 8 su
séduire	*like* conduire
sentir	*like* mentir
servir	*like* mentir
sortir	*like* mentir
souffrir	*like* couvrir
soumettre	*like* mettre
sourire	*like* rire

souscrire	*like* **écrire**
soustraire	*like* **abstraire**
soutenir	*like* **tenir**
†se souvenir	*like* **tenir**
subvenir	*like* **tenir**
suffire	1 je suffis, n suffisons 2 je suffisais 3 je suffis 5 je suffise 7 suffisant 8 suffi
suivre	1 je suis, n suivons 2 je suivais 3 je suivis 5 je suive 7 suivant 8 suivi
surprendre	*like* **prendre**
†survenir	*like* **tenir**
survivre	*like* **vivre**
taire	1 je tais, n taisons 2 je taisais 3 je tus 5 je taise 7 taisant 8 tu
teindre	*like* **atteindre**
tenir	1 je tiens, n tenons, ils tiennent 2 je tenais 3 je tins, tu tins, il tint, n tînmes, v tîntes, ils tinrent 4 je tiendrai 5 je tienne 7 tenant 8 tenu
traduire	*like* **conduire**
traire	*like* **abstraire**
transcrire	*like* **écrire**
transmettre	*like* **mettre**
transparaître	*like* **connaître**
tressaillir	*like* **défaillir**
vaincre	1 je vaincs, il vainc, n vainquons 2 je vainquais 3 je vainquis 5 je vainque 7 vainquant 8 vaincu
valoir	1 je vaux, n valons 2 je valais 3 je valus 4 je vaudrai 5 je vaille 6 *not used* 7 valant 8 valu
†venir	*like* **tenir**
vêtir	1 je vêts, n vêtons 2 je vêtais 5 je vête 7 vêtant 8 vêtu
vivre	1 je vis, n vivons 2 je vivais 3 je vécus 5 je vive 7 vivant 8 vécu
voir	1 je vois, n voyons 2 je voyais 3 je vis 4 je verrai 5 je voie, n voyions 7 voyant 8 vu
vouloir	1 je veux, n voulons, ils veulent 2 je voulais 3 je voulus 4 je voudrai 5 je veuille 6 veuille, veuillons, veuillez 7 voulant 8 voulu.

Verbes anglais irréguliers

Infinitif	Prétérit	Participe passé
arise	arose	arisen
be	was, were	been
bear	bore	borne
beat	beat	beaten
become	became	become
begin	began	begun
bend	bent	bent
bet	bet, betted	bet, betted
bid	bade, bid	bidden, bid
bind	bound	bound
bite	bit	bitten
bleed	bled	bled
blow	blew	blown
break	broke	broken
breed	bred	bred

bring	brought	brought
broadcast	broadcast	broadcast
build	built	built
burn	burnt, burned	burnt, burned
burst	burst	burst
buy	bought	bought
cast	cast	cast
catch	caught	caught
choose	chose	chosen
cling	clung	clung
come	came	come
cost	cost	cost
creep	crept	crept
cut	cut	cut
deal	dealt	dealt
dig	dug	dug
dive	dived, *Am* dove	dived
do	did	done
draw	drew	drawn
dream	dreamed, dreamt	dreamed, dreamt
drink	drank	drunk
drive	drove	driven
dwell	dwelt	dwelt
eat	ate [et, *Am* eɪt]	eaten
fall	fell	fallen
feed	fed	fed
feel	felt	felt
fight	fought	fought
find	found	found
fling	flung	flung
fly	flew	flown
forbid	forbad(e)	forbidden
forecast	forecast	forecast
foresee	foresaw	foreseen
forget	forgot	forgotten
forgive	forgave	forgiven
forsake	forsook (*rare*)	forsaken
freeze	froze	frozen
get	got	got, *Am* gotten
give	gave	given
go	went	gone
grind	ground	ground
grow	grew	grown
hang	hung, hanged	hung, hanged
have	had	had
hear	heard	heard
hide	hid	hidden
hit	hit	hit
hold	held	held
hurt	hurt	hurt
keep	kept	kept
kneel	knelt, kneeled	knelt, kneeled
know	knew	known
lay	laid	laid
lead	led	led
lean	leant, leaned	leant, leaned
leap	leapt, leaped	leapt, leaped

learn	learnt, learned	learnt, learned
leave	left	left
lend	lent	lent
let	let	let
lie	lay	lain
light	lit, lighted	lit, lighted
lose	lost	lost
make	made	made
mean	meant	meant
meet	met	met
mislay	mislaid	mislaid
mislead	misled	misled
misunderstand	misunderstood	misunderstood
mow	mowed	mown, mowed
overcome	overcame	overcome
pay	paid	paid
put	put	put
quit	quit, quitted	quit, quitted
read	read [red]	read [red]
rid	rid	rid
ride	rode	ridden
ring	rang	rung
rise	rose	risen
run	ran	run
saw	sawed	sawn, sawed
say	said	said
see	saw	seen
seek	sought	sought
sell	sold	sold
send	sent	sent
set	set	set
sew	sewed	sewn, sewed
shake	shook	shaken
shed	shed	shed
shine	shone ([ʃɒn, Am ʃəʊn])	shone ([ʃɒn, Am ʃəʊn])
shoot	shot	shot
show	showed	shown, showed
shrink	shrank	shrunk, shrunken
shut	shut	shut
sing	sang	sung
sink	sank	sunk
sit	sat	sat
sleep	slept	slept
slide	slid	slid
sling	slung	slung
slit	slit	slit
smell	smelt, smelled	smelt, smelled
sow	sowed	sown, sowed
speak	spoke	spoken
speed	sped, speeded	sped, speeded
spell	spelt, spelled	spelt, spelled
spend	spent	spent
spill	spilt, spilled	spilt, spilled
spin	spun	spun
spit	spat, spit	spat, spit
split	split	split
spoil	spoilt, spoiled	spoilt, spoiled

spread	spread	spread
spring	sprang	sprung
stand	stood	stood
steal	stole	stolen
stick	stuck	stuck
sting	stung	stung
stink	stank, stunk	stunk
stride	strode	stridden (*rare*)
strike	struck	struck
string	strung	strung
strive	strove	striven
swear	swore	sworn
sweep	swept	swept
swell	swelled	swollen, swelled
swim	swam	swum
swing	swung	swung
take	took	taken
teach	taught	taught
tear	tore	torn
tell	told	told
think	thought	thought
throw	threw	thrown
thrust	thrust	thrust
tread	trod	trodden
undergo	underwent	undergone
understand	understood	understood
undertake	undertook	undertaken
upset	upset	upset
wake	woke	woken
wear	wore	worn
weave	wove	woven
weep	wept	wept
win	won	won
wind	wound	wound
withdraw	withdrew	withdrawn
withhold	withheld	withheld
withstand	withstood	withstood
wring	wrung	wrung
write	wrote	written

Numerals

Cardinal numbers

Les nombres

Les nombres cardinaux

nought	0	zéro
one	1	un
two	2	deux
three	3	trois
four	4	quatre
five	5	cinq
six	6	six
seven	7	sept
eight	8	huit
nine	9	neuf
ten	10	dix

eleven	11	onze
twelve	12	douze
thirteen	13	treize
fourteen	14	quatorze
fifteen	15	quinze
sixteen	16	seize
seventeen	17	dix-sept
eighteen	18	dix-huit
nineteen	19	dix-neuf
twenty	20	vingt
twenty-one	21	vingt et un
twenty-two	22	vingt-deux
thirty	30	trente
forty	40	quarante
fifty	50	cinquante
sixty	60	soixante
seventy	70	soixante-dix
seventy-five	75	soixante-quinze
eighty	80	quatre-vingts
eighty-one	81	quatre-vingt-un
ninety	90	quatre-vingt-dix
ninety-one	91	quatre-vingt-onze
a *or* one hundred	100	cent
a hundred and one	101	cent un
a hundred and two	102	cent deux
a hundred and fifty	150	cent cinquante
two hundred	200	deux cents
two hundred and one	201	deux cent un
two hundred and two	202	deux cent deux
a *or* one thousand	1,000 (1 000)	mille
a thousand and one	1,001 (1 001)	mille un
a thousand and two	1,002 (1 002)	mille deux
two thousand	2,000 (2 000)	deux mille
a *or* one million	1,000,000 (1 000 000)	un million

Ordinal numbers   Les nombres ordinaux

first	1st	1er	premier
second	2nd	2e	deuxième
third	3rd	3e	troisième
fourth	4th	4e	quatrième
fifth	5th	5e	cinquième
sixth	6th	6e	sixième
seventh	7th	7e	septième
eighth	8th	8e	huitième
ninth	9th	9e	neuvième
tenth	10th	10e	dixième
eleventh	11th	11e	onzième
twelfth	12th	12e	douzième
thirteenth	13th	13e	treizième
fourteenth	14th	14e	quatorzième
fifteenth	15th	15e	quinzième
twentieth	20th	20e	vingtième
twenty-first	21st	21e	vingt et unième
twenty-second	22nd	22e	vingt deuxième
thirtieth	30th	30e	trentième

three (times) out of ten	*trois (fois) sur dix*
ten at a time, in *or* by tens, ten by ten	*dix par dix, dix à dix*
the ten of us/you, we ten/you ten	*nous dix/vous dix*
all ten of them *or* us *or* you	*tous les dix, toutes les dix*
there are ten of us/them	*nous sommes dix/elles sont dix*
(between) the ten of them	*à eux dix, à elles dix*
ten of them came/were living together	*ils sont venus/ils vivaient à dix*
page ten	*page dix*
Charles the Tenth	*Charles Dix*
to live at number ten	*habiter au (numéro) dix*
to be the tenth to arrive/to leave	*arriver/partir le dixième*
to come tenth, be tenth *(in a race)*	*arriver dixième, être dixième*
it's the tenth (today)	*nous sommes le dix (aujourd'hui)*
the tenth of May, May the tenth, *Am* May tenth	*le dix mai*
to arrive/be paid/*etc* on the tenth	*arriver/être payé/etc le dix*
to arrive/be paid/*etc* on the tenth of May *or* on May the tenth *or Am* on May tenth	*arriver/être payé/etc le dix mai*
by the tenth, before the tenth	*avant le dix, pour le dix*
it's ten (o'clock)	*il est dix heures*
it's half past ten	*il est dix heures et demie*
ten past ten, *Am* ten after ten	*dix heures dix*
ten to ten	*dix heures moins dix*
by ten (o'clock), before ten (o'clock)	*pour dix heures, avant dix heures*
to be ten (years old)	*avoir dix ans*
a child of ten, a ten-year-old (child)	*un enfant de dix ans*

Days and months   Les jours et les mois

Monday *lundi*; Tuesday *mardi*; Wednesday *mercredi*; Thursday *jeudi*; Friday *vendredi*; Saturday *samedi*; Sunday *dimanche*

January *janvier*; February *février*; March *mars*; April *avril*; May *mai*; June *juin*; July *juillet*; August *août*; September *septembre*; October *octobre*; November *novembre*; December *décembre*

Examples of usage   Exemples d'emplois

on Monday (*e.g.* he arrives on Monday)	*lundi (par exemple il arrive lundi)*
(on) Mondays	*le lundi*
see you on Monday!	*à lundi!*
by Monday, before Monday	*avant lundi, pour lundi*
Monday morning/evening	*lundi matin/soir*
a week/two weeks on Monday, *Am* a week/two weeks from Monday	*lundi en huit/en quinze*
it's Monday (today)	*nous sommes (aujourd'hui) lundi*
Monday the tenth of May, Monday May the tenth, *Am* Monday May tenth	*(le) lundi dix mai*
on Monday the tenth of May, on Monday May the tenth *or Am* May tenth	*le lundi dix mai*
tomorrow is Tuesday	*demain c'est mardi*
in May	*en mai, au mois de mai*
every May, each May	*tous les ans en mai, chaque année en mai*
by May, before May	*avant mai, pour mai*

A

A, a [eɪ] n A, a m; 5A (number) 5 bis; A1 (dinner etc) Fam super, superbe; **to go from A to B** aller du point A au point B.

a [ə, stressed eɪ] (before vowel or mute h an [ən, stressed æn]) indef art **1** un, une; **a man** un homme; **an apple** une pomme. **2** (= def art in Fr) (art omitted in Fr) he's a doctor il est médecin; **Caen, a town in Normandy** Caen, ville de Normandie; **what a man!** quel homme! **4** (a certain) **a Mr Smith** un certain M. Smith. **5** (time) **twice a month** deux fois par mois. **6** (some) **to make a noise/a fuss** faire du bruit/des histoires.

aback [ə'bæk] adv **taken a.** déconcerté.

abandon [ə'bændən] **1** vt abandonner. **2** n (freedom of manner) laisser-aller m, abandon m. **◆—ment** n abandon m.

abase [ə'beɪs] vt **to a. oneself** s'humilier, s'abaisser.

abashed [ə'bæʃt] a confus, gêné.

abate [ə'beɪt] vi (of storm, pain) se calmer; (of flood) baisser; – vt diminuer, réduire. **◆—ment** n diminution f, réduction f.

abbey ['æbɪ] n abbaye f.

abbot ['æbət] n abbé m. **◆abbess** n abbesse f.

abbreviate [ə'briːvɪeɪt] vt abréger. **◆abbrevi'ation** n abréviation f.

abdicate ['æbdɪkeɪt] vti abdiquer. **◆abdi-'cation** n abdication f.

abdomen ['æbdəmən] n abdomen m. **◆ab'dominal** a abdominal.

abduct [æb'dʌkt] vt Jur enlever. **◆abduction** n enlèvement m, rapt m.

aberration [æbə'reɪʃ(ə)n] n (folly, lapse) aberration f.

abet [ə'bet] vt (-tt-) **to aid and a. s.o.** Jur être le complice de qn.

abeyance [ə'beɪəns] n **in a.** (matter) en suspens.

abhor [əb'hɔːr] vt (-rr-) avoir horreur de, exécrer. **◆abhorrent** a exécrable. **◆abhorrence** n horreur f.

abide [ə'baɪd] **1** vi **to a. by** (promise etc) rester fidèle à. **2** vt supporter; **I can't a. him** je ne peux pas le supporter.

ability [ə'bɪlɪtɪ] n capacité f (**to do** pour faire), aptitude f (**to do** à faire); **to the best of my a.** de mon mieux.

abject ['æbdʒekt] a abject; **a. poverty** la misère.

ablaze [ə'bleɪz] a en feu; **a. with** (light) resplendissant de; (anger) enflammé de.

able ['eɪb(ə)l] a (-er, -est) capable, compétent; **to be a. to do** être capable de faire, pouvoir faire; **to be a. to swim/drive** savoir nager/conduire. **◆a.-'bodied** a robuste. **◆ably** adv habilement.

ablutions [ə'bluːʃ(ə)nz] npl ablutions fpl.

abnormal [æb'nɔːm(ə)l] a anormal. **◆abnor'mality** n anomalie f; (of body) difformité f. **◆abnormally** adv Fig exceptionnellement.

aboard [ə'bɔːd] adv Nau à bord; **all a.** Rail en voiture; – prep **a. the ship** à bord du navire; **a. the train** dans le train.

abode [ə'bəʊd] n (house) Lit demeure f; Jur domicile m.

abolish [ə'bɒlɪʃ] vt supprimer, abolir. **◆abo'lition** n suppression f, abolition f.

abominable [ə'bɒmɪnəb(ə)l] a abominable. **◆abomi'nation** n abomination f.

aboriginal [æbə'rɪdʒən(ə)l] a & n aborigène (m). **◆aborigines** npl aborigènes mpl.

abort [ə'bɔːt] vt Med faire avorter; (space flight, computer program) abandonner; – vi Med & Fig avorter. **◆abortion** n avortement m; **to have an a.** se faire avorter. **◆abortive** a (plan etc) manqué, avorté.

abound [ə'baʊnd] vi abonder (**in, with** en).

about [ə'baʊt] adv **1** (approximately) à peu près, environ; (at) **a. two o'clock** vers deux heures. **2** (here and there) çà et là, ici et là; (ideas, flu) Fig dans l'air; (rumour) en circulation; **to look a.** regarder autour; **to follow a.** suivre partout; **to bustle a.** s'affairer; **there are lots a.** il en existe beaucoup; (out and) **a.** (after illness) sur pied, guéri; (up and) **a.** (out of bed) levé, debout; **a turn, a. face** Mil demi-tour m; Fig volte-face f inv; – prep **1** (around) **a. the garden** autour du jardin; **a. the streets** par or dans les rues. **2** (near to) **a. here** par ici. **3** (concerning) au sujet de; **to talk a.** parler de; **a book a.** un livre sur; **what's it (all) a.?** de quoi s'agit-il?; **while you're a. it** pendant que vous y êtes; **what** or **how a. me?** et moi alors?; **what** or **how a. a drink?** que dirais-tu de prendre un verre? **4** (+ *inf*) **a. to do** sur le point de faire; **I was a. to say** j'étais sur le point de dire, j'allais dire.

above [ə'bʌv] *adv* au-dessus; (*in book*) ci-dessus; **from a.** d'en haut; **floor a.** étage *m* supérieur *ou* du dessus; – *prep* au-dessus de; **a. all** par-dessus tout, surtout; **a. the bridge** (*on river*) en amont du pont; **he's a. me** (*in rank*) c'est mon supérieur; **a. lying** incapable de mentir; **a. asking** trop fier pour demander. ◆**a.-'mentioned** *a* susmentionné. ◆**aboveboard** *a* ouvert, honnête; – *adv* sans tricherie, cartes sur table.

abrasion [ə'breɪʒ(ə)n] *n* frottement *m*; *Med* écorchure *f*. ◆**abrasive** *a* (*substance*) abrasif; (*rough*) *Fig* rude, dur; (*irritating*) agaçant; – *n* abrasif *m*.

abreast [ə'brest] *adv* côte à côte, de front; **four a.** par rangs de quatre; **to keep a.** of *or* **with** se tenir au courant de.

abridge [ə'brɪdʒ] *vt* (*book etc*) abréger. ◆**abridg(e)ment** *n* abrégement *m* (of de); (*abridged version*) abrégé *m*.

abroad [ə'brɔːd] *adv* **1** (*in* or *to a foreign country*) à l'étranger; **from a.** de l'étranger. **2** (*over a wide area*) de tous côtés; **rumour a.** bruit *m* qui court.

abrogate ['æbrəgeɪt] *vt* abroger.

abrupt [ə'brʌpt] *a* (*sudden*) brusque; (*person*) brusque, abrupt; (*slope*, *style*) abrupt. ◆**-ly** *adv* (*suddenly*) brusquement; (*rudely*) avec brusquerie.

abscess ['æbses] *n* abcès *m*.

abscond [əb'skɒnd] *vi* *Jur* s'enfuir.

absence ['æbsəns] *n* absence *f*; **in the a. of sth** à défaut de qch, faute de qch; **a. of mind** distraction *f*.

absent ['æbsənt] *a* absent (**from** de); (*look*) distrait; – [æb'sent] *vt* **to a. oneself** s'absenter. ◆**a.-'minded** *a* distrait. ◆**a.-'mindedness** *n* distraction *f*. ◆**absen'tee** *n* absent, -ente *mf*. ◆**absen'teeism** *n* absentéisme *m*.

absolute ['æbsəluːt] *a* absolu; (*proof etc*) indiscutable; (*coward etc*) parfait, véritable. ◆**-ly** *adv* absolument; (*forbidden*) formellement.

absolve [əb'zɒlv] *vt* *Rel Jur* absoudre; **to a. from** (*vow*) libérer de. ◆**absolution** [æbsə'luːʃ(ə)n] *n* absolution *f*.

absorb [əb'zɔːb] *vt* absorber; (*shock*) amortir; **to become absorbed in** (*work*) s'absorber dans. ◆**-ing** *a* (*work*)

absorbant; (*book*, *film*) prenant. ◆**absorbent** *a* & *n* absorbant (*m*); **a. cotton** *Am* coton *m* hydrophile. ◆**absorber** *n* **shock a.** *Aut* amortisseur *m*. ◆**absorption** *n* absorption *f*.

abstain [əb'steɪn] *vi* s'abstenir (**from** de). ◆**abstemious** *a* sobre, frugal. ◆**abstention** *n* abstention *f*. ◆**'abstinence** *n* abstinence *f*.

abstract ['æbstrækt] **1** *a* & *n* abstrait (*m*). **2** *n* (*summary*) résumé *m*. **3** [əb'strækt] *vt* (*remove*) retirer; (*notion*) abstraire. ◆**ab'straction** *n* (*idea*) abstraction *f*; (*absent-mindedness*) distraction *f*.

abstruse [əb'struːs] *a* obscur.

absurd [əb'sɜːd] *a* absurde, ridicule. ◆**absurdity** *n* absurdité *f*. ◆**absurdly** *adv* absurdement.

abundant [ə'bʌndənt] *a* abondant. ◆**abundance** *n* abondance *f*. ◆**abundantly** *adv* **a. clear** tout à fait clair.

abuse [ə'bjuːs] *n* (*abusing*) abus *m* (of de); (*curses*) injures *fpl*; – [ə'bjuːz] *vt* (*misuse*) abuser de; (*malign*) dire du mal de; (*insult*) injurier. ◆**abusive** [ə'bjuːsɪv] *a* injurieux.

abysmal [ə'bɪzm(ə)l] *a* (*bad*) *Fam* désastreux, exécrable.

abyss [ə'bɪs] *n* abîme *m*.

acacia [ə'keɪʃə] *n* (*tree*) acacia *m*.

academic [ækə'demɪk] *a* universitaire; (*scholarly*) érudit, intellectuel; (*issue etc*) *Pej* théorique; (*style*, *art*) académique; – *n* (*teacher*) *Univ* universitaire *mf*.

academy [ə'kædəmɪ] *n* (*society*) académie *f*; *Mil Mus* école *f*. ◆**acade'mician** *n* académicien, -ienne *mf*.

accede [ək'siːd] *vi* **to a. to** (*request*, *throne*, *position*) accéder à.

accelerate [ək'seləreɪt] *vt* accélérer; – *vi* s'accélérer; *Aut* accélérer. ◆**acceleration** *n* accélération *f*. ◆**accelerator** *n* *Aut* accélérateur *m*.

accent ['æksənt] *n* accent *m*; – [æk'sent] *vt* accentuer. ◆**accentuate** [æk'sentʃʊeɪt] *vt* accentuer.

accept [ək'sept] *vt* accepter. ◆**-ed** *a* (*opinion etc*) reçu, admis. ◆**acceptable** *a* (*worth accepting*, *tolerable*) acceptable. ◆**acceptance** *n* acceptation *f*; (*approval*, *favour*) accueil *m* favorable.

access ['ækses] *n* accès *m* (**to sth** à qch, **to s.o.** auprès de qn). ◆**ac'cessible** *a* accessible.

accession [æk'seʃ(ə)n] *n* accession *f* (**to** à); (*increase*) augmentation *f*; (*sth added*) nouvelle acquisition *f*.

accessory [əkˈsesərɪ] **1** n (*person*) Jur complice mf. **2** npl (*objects*) accessoires mpl.

accident [ˈæksɪdənt] n accident m; **by a.** (*by chance*) par accident; (*unintentionally*) accidentellement, sans le vouloir. ◆**a.-prone** a prédisposé aux accidents. ◆**acci'dental** a accidentel, fortuit. ◆**acci'dentally** adv accidentellement, par mégarde; (*by chance*) par accident.

acclaim [əˈkleɪm] vt acclamer; **to a. king** proclamer roi. ◆**accla'mation** n acclamation(s) f(pl), louange(s) f(pl).

acclimate [ˈæklɪmeɪt] vti Am = **acclimatize**. ◆**a'cclimatize** vt acclimater; – vi s'acclimater. ◆**accli'mation** n Am, ◆**acclimati'zation** n acclimatisation f.

accolade [ˈækəleɪd] n (*praise*) Fig louange f.

accommodat/e [əˈkɒmədeɪt] vt (*of house*) loger, recevoir; (*have room for*) avoir de la place pour (mettre); (*adapt*) adapter (to à); (*supply*) fournir (**s.o. with sth** qch à qn); (*oblige*) rendre service à; (*reconcile*) concilier; **to a. oneself to** s'accomoder à. ◆**-ing** a accommodant, obligeant. ◆**accommo'dation** n **1** (*lodging*) logement m; (*rented room or rooms*) chambre(s) f(pl); pl (*in hotel*) Am chambre(s) f(pl). **2** (*compromise*) compromis m, accommodement m.

accompany [əˈkʌmpənɪ] vt accompagner. ◆**accompaniment** n accompagnement m. ◆**accompanist** n Mus accompagnateur, -trice mf.

accomplice [əˈkʌmplɪs] n complice mf.

accomplish [əˈkʌmplɪʃ] vt (*task, duty*) accomplir; (*aim*) réaliser. ◆**-ed** a accompli. ◆**-ment** n accomplissement m; (*of aim*) réalisation f; (*thing achieved*) réalisation f; pl (*skills*) talents mpl.

accord [əˈkɔːd] **1** n accord m; **of my own a.** volontairement, de mon plein gré; – vi concorder. **2** vt (*grant*) accorder. ◆**accordance** n **in a. with** conformément à.

according to [əˈkɔːdɪŋtuː] prep selon, d'après, suivant. ◆**accordingly** adv en conséquence.

accordion [əˈkɔːdɪən] n accordéon m.

accost [əˈkɒst] vt accoster, aborder.

account [əˈkaʊnt] **1** n Com compte m; pl comptabilité f, comptes mpl; **accounts department** comptabilité f; **to take into a.** tenir compte de; **ten pounds on a.** un acompte de dix livres; **of some a.** d'une certaine importance; **on a. of** à cause de; **on**

no a. en aucun cas. **2** n (*report*) compte rendu m, récit m; (*explanation*) explication f; **by all accounts** au dire de tous; **to give a good a. of oneself** s'en tirer à son avantage; – vi **to a. for** (*explain*) expliquer; (*give reckoning of*) rendre compte de. **3** vt **to a. oneself lucky/***etc* (*consider*) se considérer heureux/*etc*. ◆**accountable** a responsable (**for, to** devant); (*explainable*) explicable.

accountant [əˈkaʊntənt] n comptable mf. ◆**accountancy** n comptabilité f.

accoutrements [əˈkuːtrəmənts] (Am **accouterments** [əˈkuːtəmənts]) npl équipement m.

accredit [əˈkredɪt] vt (*ambassador*) accréditer; **to a. s.o. with sth** attribuer qch à qn.

accrue [əˈkruː] vi (*of interest*) Fin s'accumuler; **to a. to** (*of advantage etc*) revenir à.

accumulate [əˈkjuːmjʊleɪt] vt accumuler, amasser; – vi s'accumuler. ◆**accumu'lation** n accumulation f; (*mass*) amas m. ◆**accumulator** n El accumulateur m.

accurate [ˈækjʊrət] a exact, précis. ◆**accuracy** n exactitude f, précision f. ◆**accurately** adv avec précision.

accursed [əˈkɜːsɪd] a maudit, exécrable.

accus/e [əˈkjuːz] vt accuser (**of de**). ◆**-ed** n **the a.** Jur l'inculpé, -ée mf, l'accusé, -ée mf. ◆**-ing** a accusateur. ◆**accu'sation** n accusation f.

accustom [əˈkʌstəm] vt habituer, accoutumer. ◆**-ed** a habitué (**to sth** à qch, **to doing** à faire); **to get a. to** s'habituer à, s'accoutumer à.

ace [eɪs] n (*card, person*) as m.

acetate [ˈæsɪteɪt] n acétate m.

acetic [əˈsiːtɪk] a acétique.

ache [eɪk] n douleur f, mal m; **to have an a. in one's arm** avoir mal au bras; – vi faire mal; **my head aches** ma tête me fait mal; **it makes my heart a.** cela me serre le cœur; **to be aching to do** brûler de faire. ◆**aching** a douloureux.

achieve [əˈtʃiːv] vt accomplir, réaliser; (*success, aim*) atteindre; (*victory*) remporter. ◆**-ment** n accomplissement m, réalisation f (**of** de); (*feat*) réalisation f, exploit m.

acid [ˈæsɪd] a & n acide (m). ◆**a'cidity** n acidité f.

acknowledge [əkˈnɒlɪdʒ] vt reconnaître (**as** pour); (*greeting*) répondre à; **to a.** (*receipt of*) accuser réception de; **to a. defeat** s'avouer vaincu. ◆**-ment** n reconnaissance f, (*of letter*) accusé m de réception; (*receipt*) reçu m, récépissé m.

acme ['ækmɪ] n sommet m, comble m.

acne ['æknɪ] n acné f.

acorn ['eɪkɔːn] n Bot gland m.

acoustic [əˈkuːstɪk] a acoustique; – npl acoustique f.

acquaint [əˈkweɪnt] vt to a. s.o. with sth informer qn de qch; **to be acquainted with** (person) connaître; (fact) savoir; **we are acquainted** on se connaît. ◆**acquaintance** n (person, knowledge) connaissance f.

acquiesce [ækwɪˈes] vi acquiescer (**in** à). ◆**acquiescence** n acquiescement m.

acquire [əˈkwaɪər] vt acquérir; (taste) prendre (**for** à); (friends) se faire; **aquired taste** goût m qui s'acquiert. ◆**acqui'sition** n acquisition f. ◆**acquisitive** a avide, cupide.

acquit [əˈkwɪt] vt (-tt-) **to a. s.o. of a crime** acquitter qn. ◆**acquittal** n acquittement m.

acre ['eɪkər] n acre f (= 0,4 hectare). ◆**acreage** n superficie f.

acrid ['ækrɪd] a (smell, manner etc) âcre.

acrimonious [ækrɪˈməʊnɪəs] a acerbe.

acrobat ['ækrəbæt] n acrobate mf. ◆**acro'batic** a acrobatique; – npl acrobatie(s) f(pl).

acronym ['ækrənɪm] n sigle m.

across [əˈkrɒs] adv & prep (from side to side (of)) d'un côté à l'autre (de); (on the other side (of)) de l'autre côté (de); (crossways) en travers (de); **to be a kilometre/etc a.** (wide) avoir un kilomètre/etc de large; **to walk or go a.** (street etc) traverser; **to come a.** (person) rencontrer (par hasard), tomber sur; (thing) trouver (par hasard); **to get sth a. to s.o.** faire comprendre qch à qn.

acrostic [əˈkrɒstɪk] n acrostiche m.

acrylic [əˈkrɪlɪk] a & n acrylique (m).

act [ækt] **1** n (deed) acte m; **a. of** (parliament) loi f; **caught in the a.** pris sur le fait; **a. of walking** action f de marcher; **an a. of folly** une folie. **2** n (of play) Th acte m; (turn) Th numéro m; **in on the a.** Fam dans le coup; **to put on an a.** Fam jouer la comédie; – vt (part) Th jouer; **to a. the fool** faire l'idiot; – vi Th Cin jouer; (pretend) jouer la comédie. **3** vi (do sth, behave) agir; (function) fonctionner; **to a. as** (secretary etc) faire office de; (of object) servir de; **to a.** (up)on (affect) agir sur; (advice) suivre; **to a. on behalf of** représenter; **to a. 'up** (of person, machine) Fam faire des siennes. ◆**—ing 1** a (manager etc) intérimaire, provisoire. **2** n (of play) représentation f; (actor's art) jeu m; (career) théâtre m.

action ['ækʃ(ə)n] n action f; Mil combat m; Jur procès m, action f; **to take a.** prendre des mesures; **to put into a.** (plan) exécuter; **out of a.** hors d'usage, hors (de) service; (person) hors de combat; **killed in a.** mort au champ d'honneur; **to take industrial a.** se mettre en grève.

active ['æktɪv] a actif; (interest) vif; (volcano) en activité. ◆**activate** vt Ch activer; (mechanism) actionner. ◆**activist** n activiste mf. ◆**ac'tivity** n activité f; (in street) mouvement m.

actor ['æktər] n acteur m. ◆**actress** n actrice f.

actual ['æktʃʊəl] a réel, véritable; (example) concret; **the a. book** le livre même; **in a. fact** en réalité, effectivement. ◆**—ly** adv (truly) réellement; (in fact) en réalité, en fait.

actuary ['æktʃʊərɪ] n actuaire mf.

actuate ['æktʃʊeɪt] vt (person) animer; (machine) actionner.

acumen ['ækjʊmen, Am əˈkjuːmən] n perspicacité f, finesse f.

acupuncture ['ækjʊpʌŋktʃər] n acupuncture f.

acute [əˈkjuːt] a aigu (anxiety, emotion) vif, profond; (observer) perspicace; (shortage) grave. ◆**—ly** adv (to suffer, feel) vivement, profondément. ◆**—ness** n acuité f.

ad [æd] n Fam pub f; (private, in newspaper) annonce f; **small ad** petite annonce.

AD [eɪˈdiː] abbr (anno Domini) après Jésus-Christ.

adage ['ædɪdʒ] n adage m.

Adam ['ædəm] n **A.'s apple** pomme f d'Adam.

adamant ['ædəmənt] a inflexible.

adapt [əˈdæpt] vt adapter (**to** à); **to a.** (oneself) s'adapter; – (person) capable de s'adapter, adaptable. ◆**adaptable** a ◆**adaptor** n (device) adaptateur m; (plug) prise f multiple. ◆**adap'tation** n adaptation f.

add [æd] vt ajouter (**to** à, **that** que); **to a.** (up or together) (total) additionner; **to a. in** include; – vi **to a. to** (increase) augmenter; **to a. up to** (total) s'élever à; (mean) signifier; **it all adds up** Fam ça s'explique. ◆**a'ddendum,** pl **-da** n supplément m. ◆**adding machine** n machine f à calculer. ◆**a'ddition** n addition f; augmentation f; **in a.** de plus; **in a. to** en plus de. ◆**a'dditional** a supplémentaire. ◆**a'dditionally** adv de plus. ◆**additive** n additif m.

adder ['ædər] n vipère f.

addict ['ædɪkt] n intoxiqué, -ée mf; **jazz/sport a.** fanatique mf du jazz/du sport; **drug a.** drogué, -ée mf. ◆**a'ddicted a to be a. to** (study, drink) s'adonner à; (music) se passionner pour; (to have the habit of) avoir la manie de; **a. to cigarettes** drogué par la cigarette. ◆**a'ddiction** n (habit) manie f; (dependency) Med dépendance f; **drug a.** toxicomanie f. ◆**a'ddictive** a qui crée une dépendance.

address [ə'dres, Am 'ædres] n (on letter etc) adresse f; (speech) allocution f; **form of a.** formule f de politesse; – [ə'dres] vt (person) s'adresser à; (audience) parler devant; (words, speech) adresser (**to** à); (letter) mettre l'adresse sur; **to a. to s.o.** (send, intend for) adresser à qn. ◆**addressee** [ædre'siː] n destinataire mf.

adenoids ['ædɪnɔɪdz] npl végétations fpl (adénoïdes).

adept ['ædept, Am ə'dept] a expert (**in, at** à).

adequate ['ædɪkwət] a (quantity) suffisant; (acceptable) convenable; (person, performance) compétent. ◆**adequacy** n (of person) compétence f; **to doubt the a. of sth** douter que qch soit suffisant. ◆**adequately** adv suffisamment; convenablement.

adhere [əd'hɪər] vi **to a. to** adhérer à; (decision) s'en tenir à; (rule) respecter. ◆**adherence** n, ◆**adhesion** n (grip) adhérence f; (support) Fig adhésion f. ◆**adhesive** a & n adhésif (m).

ad infinitum [ædɪnfɪ'naɪtəm] adv à l'infini.

adjacent [ə'dʒeɪsənt] a (house, angle etc) adjacent (**to** à).

adjective ['ædʒɪktɪv] n adjectif m.

adjoin [ə'dʒɔɪn] vt avoisiner. ◆**—ing** a avoisinant, voisin.

adjourn [ə'dʒɜːn] vt (postpone) adjourner; (session) lever, suspendre; – vi lever la séance; **to a. to** (go) passer à. ◆**—ment** n ajournement m; suspension f (de séance), levée f de séance.

adjudicate [ə'dʒuːdɪkeɪt] vti juger. ◆**adjudi'cation** n jugement m. ◆**adjudicator** n juge m, arbitre m.

adjust [ə'dʒʌst] vt Tech régler, ajuster; (prices) (r)ajuster; (arrange) arranger; **to a.** (**oneself**) **to** s'adapter à. ◆**—able** a réglable. ◆**—ment** n Tech réglage m; (of person) adaptation f; (of prices) (r)ajustement m.

ad-lib [æd'lɪb] vi (-bb-) improviser; – a (joke etc) improvisé.

administer [əd'mɪnɪstər] **1** vt (manage, dispense) administrer (**to** à). **2** vi **to a. to**

pourvoir à. ◆**admini'stration** n administration f; (ministry) gouvernement m. ◆**administrative** a administratif. ◆**administrator** n administrateur, -trice mf.

admiral ['ædmərəl] n amiral m.

admir/e [əd'maɪər] vt admirer. ◆**—ing** a admiratif. ◆**—er** n admirateur, -trice mf. ◆**admirable** a admirable. ◆**admi'ration** n admiration f.

admit [əd'mɪt] vt (-tt-) (let in) laisser entrer; (accept) admettre; (acknowledge) reconnaître, avouer; – vi **to a. to sth** (confess) avouer qch; **to a. of** permettre. ◆**admittedly** adv c'est vrai (que). ◆**admissible** a admissible. ◆**admission** n (entry to theatre etc) entrée f (**to** à, de); (to club, school) admission f; (acknowledgement) aveu m; **a. (charge)** (prix m d')entrée f. ◆**admittance** n entrée f; **'no a.'** 'entrée interdite'.

admonish [əd'mɒnɪʃ] vt (reprove) réprimander; (warn) avertir.

ado [ə'duː] n without further a. sans (faire) plus de façons.

adolescent [ædə'lesənt] n adolescent, -ente mf. ◆**adolescence** n adolescence f.

adopt [ə'dɒpt] vt (child, method, attitude etc) adopter; (candidate) Pol choisir. ◆**—ed** a (child) adoptif; (country) d'adoption. ◆**adoption** n adoption f. ◆**adoptive** a (parent) adoptif.

adore [ə'dɔːr] vt adorer; **he adores being flattered** il adore qu'on le flatte. ◆**adorable** a adorable. ◆**ado'ration** n adoration f.

adorn [ə'dɔːn] vt (room, book) orner; (person, dress) parer. ◆**—ment** n ornement m; parure f.

adrenalin(e) [ə'drenəlɪn] n adrénaline f.

Adriatic [eɪdrɪ'ætɪk] n the A. l'Adriatique f.

adrift [ə'drɪft] a & adv Nau à la dérive; **to come a.** (of rope, collar etc) se détacher; **to turn s.o. a.** Fig abandonner qn à son sort.

adroit [ə'drɔɪt] a adroit, habile.

adulation [ædjʊ'leɪʃ(ə)n] n adulation f.

adult ['ædʌlt] a & n adulte (mf). ◆**adulthood** n âge m adulte.

adulterate [ə'dʌltəreɪt] vt (food) altérer.

adultery [ə'dʌltərɪ] n adultère m. ◆**adulterous** a adultère.

advanc/e [əd'vɑːns] n (movement, money) avance f; (of science) progrès mpl; pl (of friendship, love) avances fpl; **in a.** à l'avance, d'avance; (to arrive) en avance; **in a. of s.o.** avant qn; – a (payment) anticipé; **a. booking** réservation f; **a. guard** avant-garde f; – vt (put forward, lend) avancer; (*science, work*) faire avancer; – *vi* (*go forward, progress*) avancer; (*towards s.o.*) s'avancer, avancer. ◆**-ed** *a* avancé; (*studies*) supérieur; *a.* **in years** âgé. ◆**-ement** *n* (*progress, promotion*) avancement *m*.

advantage [ədˈvɑːntɪdʒ] *n* avantage *m* (**over** sur); **to take a. of** profiter de; (*person*) tromper, exploiter; (*woman*) séduire; **to show** (**off**) **to a.** faire valoir. ◆**advan'tageous** *a* avantageux (**to, pour**), profitable.

advent [ˈædvent] *n* arrivée *f*, avènement *m*; **A.** *Rel* l'Avent *m*.

adventure [ədˈventʃər] *n* aventure *f*; – *a* (*film etc*) d'aventures. ◆**adventurer** *n* aventurier, -ière *mf*. ◆**adventurous** *a* aventureux.

adverb [ˈædvɜːb] *n* adverbe *m*.

adversary [ˈædvəsərɪ] *n* adversaire *mf*.

adverse [ˈædvɜːs] *a* hostile, défavorable. ◆**ad'versity** *n* adversité *f*.

advert [ˈædvɜːt] *n* *Fam* pub *f*; (*private, in newspaper*) annonce *f*.

advertis/e [ˈædvətaɪz] *vt* (*goods*) faire de la publicité pour; (*make known*) annoncer; – *vi* faire de la publicité; **to a.** (**for s.o.**) mettre une annonce (pour chercher qn). ◆**-er** *n* annonceur *m*. ◆**-ement** [ədˈvɜːtɪsmənt, *Am* ædvəˈtaɪzmənt] *n* publicité *f*; (*private or classified in newspaper*) annonce *f*; (*poster*) affiche *f*; **classified a.** petite annonce; **the advertisements** *TV* la publicité.

advice [ədˈvaɪs] *n* conseil(s) *m(pl)*; *Com* avis *m*; **a piece of a.** un conseil.

advis/e [ədˈvaɪz] *vt* (*counsel*) conseiller; (*recommend*) recommander; (*notify*) informer; **to a. s.o. to do** déconseiller à qn de faire; **to a. against** déconseiller. ◆**-ed** *a* **well-a.** (*action*) prudent. ◆**-able** *a* (*wise*) prudent (**to do de faire**); (*advisable*) à conseiller. ◆**-edly** [-ɪdlɪ] *adv* après réflexion. ◆**-er** *n* conseiller, -ère *mf*. ◆**advisory** *a* consultatif.

advocate 1 [ˈædvəkət] *n* (*of cause*) défenseur *m*, avocat, -ate *mf*; *Jur* avocat *m*. **2** [ˈædvəkeɪt] *vt* préconiser, recommander.

aegis [ˈiːdʒɪs] *n* **under the a. of** sous l'égide de.

aeon [ˈiːən] *n* éternité *f*.

aerial [ˈeərɪəl] *n* antenne *f*; – *a* aérien.

aerobatics [eərəˈbætɪks] *npl* acrobatie *f* aérienne. ◆**ae'robics** *npl* aérobic *f*. ◆**'aerodrome** *n* aérodrome *m*. ◆**aero'dynamic** *a* aérodynamique. ◆**aero'nautics** *npl* aéronautique *f*. ◆**'aeroplane**

n avion *m*. ◆**'aerosol** *n* aérosol *m*. ◆**'aerospace** *a* (*industry*) aérospatial.

aesthetic [iːsˈθetɪk, *Am* esˈθetɪk] *a* esthétique.

afar [əˈfɑːr] *adv* **from a.** de loin.

affable [ˈæfəb(ə)l] *a* affable, aimable.

affair [əˈfeər] *n* (*matter, concern*) affaire *f*; (*love*) **a.** liaison *f*; **state of affairs** état *m* de choses.

affect [əˈfekt] *vt* (*move, feign*) affecter; (*concern*) toucher, affecter; (*harm*) nuire à; (*be fond of*) affectionner. ◆**-ed** *a* (*manner*) affecté; (*by disease*) atteint. ◆**affec'tation** *n* affectation *f*.

affection [əˈfekʃ(ə)n] *n* affection *f* (**for** pour). ◆**affectionate** *a* affectueux, aimant. ◆**affectionately** *adv* affectueusement.

affiliate [əˈfɪlɪeɪt] *vt* affilier; **to be affiliated** s'affilier (**to** à); **affiliated company** filiale *f*. ◆**affili'ation** *n* affiliation *f*; *pl* (*political*) attaches *fpl*.

affinity [əˈfɪnɪtɪ] *n* affinité *f*.

affirm [əˈfɜːm] *vt* affirmer. ◆**affir'mation** *n* affirmation *f*. ◆**affirmative** *a* affirmatif; – *n*.

affix [əˈfɪks] *vt* apposer.

afflict [əˈflɪkt] *vt* affliger (**with** de). ◆**affliction** *n* (*misery*) affliction *f*; (*disorder*) infirmité *f*.

affluent [ˈæfluənt] *a* riche; **a. society** société *f* d'abondance. ◆**affluence** *n* richesse *f*.

afford [əˈfɔːd] *vt* **1** (*pay for*) avoir les moyens d'acheter, pouvoir se payer; (*time*) pouvoir trouver; **I can a. to wait** je peux me permettre d'attendre. **2** (*provide*) fournir, donner; **to s.o. sth** fournir qch à qn.

affray [əˈfreɪ] *n* *Jur* rixe *f*, bagarre *f*.

affront [əˈfrʌnt] *n* affront *m*; – *vt* faire un affront à.

Afghanistan [æfˈgænɪstæn] *n* Afghanistan *m*. ◆**'Afghan** *a & n* afghan, -ane (*mf*).

afield [əˈfiːld] *adv* **further a.** plus loin; **too far a.** trop loin.

afloat [əˈfləʊt] *adv* (*ship, swimmer, business*) à flot; (*awash*) submergé; **life a.** la vie sur l'eau.

afoot [əˈfʊt] *adv* **there's sth a.** il se trame qch; **there's a plan a. to** on prépare un projet pour.

aforementioned [əˈfɔːmenʃ(ə)nd] *a* susmentionné.

afraid [əˈfreɪd] *a* **to be a.** avoir peur (**of, to** de; **that** que); **to make s.o. afraid** faire peur à qn; **he's a.** (**that**) **she may be ill** il a peur qu'elle (ne) soit malade; **I'm a.** **he's out** (*I regret to say*) je regrette, il est sorti.

afresh [ə'freʃ] *adv* de nouveau.

Africa ['æfrɪkə] *n* Afrique *f.* ◆**African** *a & n* africain, -aine *(mf).*

after ['ɑːftər] *adv* après; **the month a.** le mois suivant, le mois d'après; – *prep* après; **a. all** après tout; **a. eating** après avoir mangé; **day a. day** jour après jour; **page a. page** page sur page; **time a. time** bien des fois; **a. you!** je vous en prie!; **ten a. four** *Am* quatre heures dix; **to be a. sth/s.o.** *(seek)* chercher qch/qn; – *conj* après que; **a. he saw you** après qu'il l'a vu. ◆**aftercare** *n Med* soins *mpl* postopératoires; *Jur* surveillance *f.* ◆**aftereffects** *npl* suites *fpl*, séquelles *fpl.* ◆**afterlife** *n* vie *f* future. ◆**aftermath** [-mɑːθ] *n* suites *fpl.* ◆**after'noon** *n* après-midi *m or f inv*; **in the a.** l'après-midi; **good a.!** *(hello)* bonjour!; *(goodbye)* au revoir! ◆**after'noons** *adv Am* l'après-midi. ◆**aftersales (service)** *n* service *m* après-vente. ◆**aftershave (lotion)** *n* lotion *f* après-rasage. ◆**aftertaste** *n* arrière-goût *m.* ◆**afterthought** *n* réflexion *f* après coup. ◆**afterward(s)** *adv* après, plus tard.

afters ['ɑːftəz] *npl Fam* dessert *m.*

again [ə'gen, ə'geɪn] *adv* de nouveau, encore une fois; *(furthermore)* en outre; **to do a.** refaire; **to go down/up** a. redescendre/remonter; **never a.** plus jamais; **half as much a.** moitié plus; **a. and a., time and (time) a.** maintes fois; **what's his name a.?** comment s'appelle-t-il déjà?

against [ə'genst, ə'geɪnst] *prep* contre; **to go** *or* **be a.** s'opposer à; **a law a.** drinking une loi qui interdit de boire; **his age is a.** him son âge lui est défavorable; **a. a background of** sur (un) fond de; **a. the light** à contre-jour; **the law illégal; a. the rules** interdit, contraire aux règlements.

age [eɪdʒ] *n* *(lifespan, period)* âge *m*; *(old)* vieillesse *f*; **the Middle Ages** le moyen âge; **what a. are you?, what's your a.?** quel âge as-tu?; **five years of a.** âgé de cinq ans; **to be of a.** être majeur; **under a.** trop jeune, mineur; **to wait (for) ages** *Fam* attendre une éternité; **a. group** tranche *f* d'âge; *-vt (pres p ag(e)ing)* vieillir. ◆**a.-old** *a* séculaire. ◆**aged** *a* [eɪdʒd] **a. ten** âgé de dix ans; ['eɪdʒɪd] vieux, âgé; **the a.** les personnes *fpl* âgées. ◆**ageless** *a* toujours jeune.

agenda [ə'dʒendə] *n* ordre *m* du jour.

agent ['eɪdʒənt] *n* agent *m*; *(dealer)* concessionnaire *mf.* ◆**agency** *n* **1** *(office)* agence *f.* **2 through the a. of s.o.** par l'intermédiaire de qn.

agglomeration [əglɒmə'reɪʃ(ə)n] *n* agglomération *f.*

aggravate ['ægrəveɪt] *vt* *(make worse)* aggraver; **to a. s.o.** *Fam* exaspérer qn. ◆**aggra'vation** *n* aggravation *f*; *Fam* exaspération *f*; *(bother) Fam* ennui(s) *m(pl).*

aggregate ['ægrɪgət] *a* global; – *n* *(total)* ensemble *m.*

aggression [ə'greʃ(ə)n] *n* agression *f.* ◆**aggressive** *a* agressif. ◆**aggressiveness** *n* agressivité *f.* ◆**aggressor** *n* agresseur *m.*

aggrieved [ə'griːvd] *a* *(offended)* blessé, froissé; *(tone)* peiné.

aghast [ə'gɑːst] *a* consterné, horrifié.

agile ['ædʒaɪl, *Am* 'ædʒ(ə)l] *a* agile. ◆**a'gility** *n* agilité *f.*

agitate ['ædʒɪteɪt] *vt* *(worry, shake)* agiter; – *vi* **to a. for** *Pol* faire campagne pour. ◆**agi'tation** *n* *(anxiety, unrest)* agitation *f.* ◆**agitator** *n* agitateur, -trice *mf.*

aglow [ə'gləʊ] *a* **to be a.** briller *(with de).*

agnostic [æg'nɒstɪk] *a & n* agnostique *(mf).*

ago [ə'gəʊ] *adv* **a year a.** il y a un an; **how long a.?** il y a combien de temps (de cela)?; **as long a. as 1800** dès 1800.

agog [ə'gɒg] *a* *(excited)* en émoi; *(eager)* impatient.

agony ['ægənɪ] *n* *(pain)* douleur *f* atroce; *(anguish)* angoisse *f*; **to be in a.** souffrir horriblement; **a. column** *Journ* courrier *m* du cœur. ◆**agonize** *vi* se faire beaucoup de souci. ◆**agonized** *a* *(look)* angoissé; *(cry)* de douleur. ◆**agonizing** *a* *(pain)* atroce; *(situation)* angoissant.

agree [ə'griː] *vi* *(come to terms)* se mettre d'accord, s'accorder; *(be in agreement)* être d'accord, s'accorder *(with* avec); *(of facts, dates etc)* concorder; *Gram* s'accorder; **to a. upon** *(decide)* convenir de; **to a. to sth/to doing** consentir à qch/à faire; **it doesn't a. with me** *(food, climate)* ça ne me réussit pas; – *vt* *(figures)* faire concorder; *(accounts)* Com approuver; **to a. to do** accepter de faire; **to a. that** *(admit)* admettre que. ◆**agreed** *a* *(time, place)* convenu; **we are a.** nous sommes d'accord; **a.!** entendu! ◆**agreeable** *a* **1** *(pleasant)* agréable. **2 to be a.** *(agree)* être d'accord; **to be a. to sth** consentir à qch. ◆**agreement** *n* accord *m*; *Pol Com* convention *f*, accord *m*; **in a. with** d'accord avec.

agriculture ['ægrɪkʌltʃər] *n* agriculture *f.* ◆**agri'cultural** *a* agricole.

aground [ə'graʊnd] *adv* **to run a.** *Nau* (s')échouer.

ah! [ɑː] *int* ah!

ahead [əˈhed] *adv* (*in space*) en avant; (*leading*) en tête; (*in the future*) dans l'avenir; *a.* (*of time or of schedule*) en avance (sur l'horaire); **one hour/etc a.** une heure/*etc* d'avance (of sur); *a.* of (*space*) devant; (*time, progress*) en avance sur; **to go a.** (*advance*) avancer; (*continue*) continuer; (*start*) commencer; **go a.!** allez-y!; **to go a. with** (*task*) poursuivre; **to get a.** prendre de l'avance; (*succeed*) réussir; **to think a.** penser à l'avenir; **straight a.** tout droit.

aid [eid] *n* (*help*) aide *f*; (*apparatus*) support *m*, moyen *m*; **with the a.** of (*a stick etc*) à l'aide de; **in a.** of (*charity etc*) en avance (for; **what's this in a.** of? *Fam* quel est le but de tout ça?, ça sert à quoi?; — *vt* aider (**to do à** faire).

aide [eid] *n Pol* aide *mf*.

AIDS [eidz] *n Med* SIDA *m*.

ail [eil] *vt* **what ails you?** de quoi souffrez-vous? ◆—**ing** *a* souffrant, malade. ◆—**ment** *n* maladie *f*.

aim [eim] *n* but *m*; **to take a.** viser; **with the a.** of dans le but de; — *vt* (*gun*) braquer, diriger (**at** sur); (*lamp*) diriger (**at** vers); (*stone*) lancer (**at** à, vers); (*blow, remark*) décocher (**at** à); — *vi* viser; **to a. at s.o.** viser qn; **to a. to do** or **at doing** avoir l'intention de faire. ◆—**less** *a*, ◆—**lessly** *adv* sans but.

air [eər] **1** *n* air *m*; **in the open a.** en plein air; **by a.** (*to travel*) en or par avion; (*letter, freight*) par avion; **to be** or **go on the a.** (*person*) passer à l'antenne; (*programme*) être diffusé; (**up) in the a.** (*to throw*) en l'air; (*plan*) incertain, en l'air; **there's sth in the a.** *Fig* il se prépare qch; — *a* (*raid, force etc*) aérien; **a. force/hostess** armée *f*/hôtesse *f* de l'air; **a. terminal** aérogare *f*; — *vt* (*room*) aérer; (*views*) exposer; **airing cupboard** armoire *f* sèche-linge. **2** *n* (*appearance, tune*) air *m*; **to put on airs** se donner des airs; **with an a.** of sadness/*etc* d'un air triste/*etc*.

airborne [ˈeəbɔːn] *a* en (cours de) vol; (*troops*) aéroporté; **to become a.** (*of aircraft*) décoller. ◆**airbridge** *n* pont *m* aérien. ◆**air-conditioned** *a* climatisé. ◆**air-conditioner** *n* climatiseur *m*. ◆**aircraft** *n inv* avion(s) *m(pl)*; **a. carrier** porte-avions *m inv*. ◆**aircrew** *n Av* équipage *m*. ◆**airfield** *n* terrain *m* d'aviation. ◆**airgun** *n* carabine *f* à air comprimé. ◆**airletter** *n* aérogramme *m*. ◆**airlift** *n* pont *m* aérien; — *vt* transporter par avion. ◆**airline** *n* ligne *f* aérienne. ◆**airliner** *n*

avion *m* de ligne. ◆**airlock** *n* (*chamber*) *Nau Av* sas *m*; (*in pipe*) bouchon *m*. ◆**airmail** *n* poste *f* aérienne; **by a.** par avion. ◆**airman** *n* (*pl* -men) aviateur *m*. ◆**airplane** *n Am* avion *m*. ◆**airpocket** *n* trou *m* d'air. ◆**airport** *n* aéroport *m*. ◆**airship** *n* dirigeable *m*. ◆**airsickness** *n* mal *m* de l'air. ◆**airstrip** *n* terrain *m* d'atterrissage. ◆**airtight** *a* hermétique. ◆**airway** *n* (*route*) couloir *m* aérien. ◆**airworthy** *a* en état de navigation.

airy [ˈeəri] *a* (-ier, -iest) (*room*) bien aéré; (*promise*) vain; (*step*) léger. ◆**a.-fairy** *a Fam* farfelu. ◆**airily** *adv* (*not seriously*) d'un ton léger.

aisle [ail] *n* couloir *m*; (*of church*) nef *f* latérale.

aitch [eitʃ] *n* (*letter*) h *m*.

ajar [əˈdʒɑːr] *a* & *adv* (*door*) entrouvert.

akin [əˈkin] *a* apparenté (à).

alabaster [ˈæləbɑːstər] *n* albâtre *m*.

alacrity [əˈlækriti] *n* empressement *m*.

à la mode [ælæˈməʊd] *a Culin Am* avec de la crème glacée.

alarm [əˈlɑːm] *n* (*warning, fear*) alarme *f*; (*apparatus*) sonnerie *f* (d'alarme); **false a.** fausse alerte *f*; **a.** (*clock*) réveil *m*, réveille-matin *m inv*; — *vt* (*frighten*) alarmer. ◆**alarmist** *n* alarmiste *mf*.

alas [əˈlæs] *int* hélas!

albatross [ˈælbətrɒs] *n* albatros *m*.

albeit [ɔːlˈbiːit] *conj Lit* quoique.

albino [ælˈbiːnəʊ, *Am* ælˈbaɪnəʊ] *n* (*pl* -os) albinos *m*.

album [ˈælbəm] *n* (*book, record*) album *m*.

alchemy [ˈælkəmi] *n* alchimie *f*. ◆**alchemist** *n* alchimiste *m*.

alcohol [ˈælkəhɒl] *n* alcool *m*. ◆**alco'holic** *a* (*person*) alcoolique; (*drink*) alcoolisé; — *n* (*person*) alcoolique *mf*. ◆**alcoholism** *n* alcoolisme *m*.

alcove [ˈælkəʊv] *n* alcôve *f*.

alderman [ˈɔːldəmən] *n* (*pl* -men) conseiller, -ère *mf* municipal(e).

ale [eil] *n* bière *f*.

alert [əˈlɜːt] *a* (*watchful*) vigilant; (*sharp, awake*) éveillé; — *n* alerte *f*; **on the a.** sur le qui-vive; — *vt* alerter. ◆—**ness** *n* vigilance *f*.

alfalfa [ælˈfælfə] *n Am* luzerne *f*.

algebra [ˈældʒibrə] *n* algèbre *f*. ◆**alge'braic** *a* algébrique.

Algeria [ælˈdʒiəriə] *n* Algérie *f*. ◆**Algerian** *a* & *n* algérien, -ienne (*mf*).

alias [ˈeiliəs] *adv* alias; — *n* nom *m* d'emprunt.

alibi [ˈælibai] *n* alibi *m*.

alien ['eɪlɪən] a étranger (**to** à); – n étranger, -ère mf. ◆**alienate** vt aliéner; **to a. s.o.** (make unfriendly) s'aliéner qn.

alight [ə'laɪt] **1** a (fire) allumé; (building) en feu; (face) éclairé; **to set a.** mettre le feu à. **2** vi descendre (**from** de); (of bird) se poser.

align [ə'laɪn] vt aligner. ◆**–ment** n alignement m.

alike [ə'laɪk] **1** a (people, things) semblables, pareils; **to look** or **be a.** se ressembler. **2** adv de la même manière; **summer and winter a.** été comme hiver.

alimony ['ælɪmənɪ, Am 'ælɪməunɪ] n Jur pension f alimentaire.

alive [ə'laɪv] a vivant, en vie; **to a. to** conscient de; **a. with** grouillant de; **burnt a.** brûlé vif; **anyone a.** n'importe qui; **to keep a.** (custom, memory) entretenir, perpétuer; **a. and kicking** Fam plein de vie; **look a.!** Fam active-toi!

all [ɔːl] a tout, toute, pl tous, toutes; **a. day** toute la journée; **a. (the) men** tous les hommes; **with a. speed** à toute vitesse; **for a. her wealth** malgré toute sa fortune; – pron tous mpl, toutes fpl; (everything) tout; **a. will die** tous mourront; **my sisters are a. here** toutes mes sœurs sont ici; **he ate it a., he ate a. of it** il a tout mangé; **(that) he has** tout ce qu'il a; **a. in a.** tout prendre; **in a., a. told** en tout; **a. but impossible**/etc presque impossible/etc; **anything at a.** quoi que ce soit; **if he comes at a.** s'il vient effectivement; **if there's any wind at a.** s'il y a le moindre vent; **not at a.** pas du tout; (after 'thank you') il n'y a pas de quoi; **a. of us** nous tous; **take a. of it** prends (le) tout; – adv tout; **a. alone** tout seul; **a. bad** entièrement mauvais; **a. over** (everywhere) partout; (finished) fini; **a. right** (très) bien; **he's a. right** (not harmed) il est sain et sauf; (healthy) il va bien; **a. too soon** bien trop tôt; **six a.** Fb six buts partout; **a. there** Fam éveillé, intelligent; **not a. there** Fam simple d'esprit; **a. in** Fam épuisé; **a.-in price** prix global; – n my a. tout ce que j'ai. ◆**a.-'clear** n Mil fin f d'alerte. ◆**a.-night** a (party) qui dure toute la nuit; (shop) ouvert toute la nuit. ◆**a.-out** a (effort) violent; (war, strike) tous azimuts. ◆**a.-'powerful** a tout-puissant. ◆**a.-purpose** a (tool) universel. ◆**a.-round** a complet. ◆**a.-'rounder** n personne f qui fait de tout. ◆**a.-time** a (record) jamais atteint; **to reach an a.-time low/high** arriver au point le plus bas/le plus haut.

allay [ə'leɪ] vt calmer, apaiser.

alleg/e [ə'ledʒ] vt prétendre. ◆**–ed** a

(so-called) prétendu; (author, culprit) présumé; **he is a. to be** on prétend qu'il est. ◆**–edly** [-ɪdlɪ] adv d'après ce qu'on dit. ◆**alle'gation** n allégation f.

allegiance [ə'liːdʒəns] n fidélité f (**to** à).

allegory ['ælɪgərɪ, Am 'æləgɔːrɪ] n allégorie f. ◆**alle'gorical** a allégorique.

allergy ['ælədʒɪ] n allergie f. ◆**a'llergic** a allergique (**to** à).

alleviate [ə'liːvɪeɪt] vt alléger.

alley ['ælɪ] n (in park) allée f; **blind a.** impasse f; **that's up my a.** Fam c'est mon truc. ◆**alleyway** n ruelle f.

alliance [ə'laɪəns] n alliance f.

allied ['ælaɪd] a (country) allié; (matters) connexe.

alligator ['ælɪgeɪtər] n alligator m.

allocate ['æləkeɪt] vt (assign) attribuer, allouer (**to** à); (distribute) répartir. ◆**allo'cation** n attribution f.

allot [ə'lɒt] vt (-tt-) (assign) attribuer; (distribute) répartir. ◆**–ment** n attribution f; (share) partage m; (land) lopin m de terre (loué pour la culture).

allow [ə'lau] **1** vt permettre; (grant) accorder; (a request) accéder à; (deduct) Com déduire; (add) Com ajouter; **to a. s.o. to do** permettre à qn de faire, autoriser qn à faire; **a. me!** permettez-(moi)!; **not allowed** interdit; **you're not allowed to go on** vous interdit de partir. **2** vi **to a. for** tenir compte de. ◆**–able** a (acceptable) admissible; (expense) déductible.

allowance [ə'lauəns] n allocation f; (for travel, housing, food) indemnité f; (for duty-free goods) tolérance f; (tax-free amount) abattement m; **to make allowance(s) for** (person) être indulgent envers; (thing) tenir compte de.

alloy ['ælɔɪ] n alliage m.

allude [ə'luːd] vi **to a. to** faire allusion à. ◆**allusion** n allusion f.

allure [ə'luər] vt attirer.

ally ['ælaɪ] n allié, -ée mf; – [ə'laɪ] vt (country, person) allier.

almanac ['ɔːlmənæk] n almanach m.

almighty [ɔːl'maɪtɪ] **1** a tout-puissant; **the A.** le Tout-Puissant. **2** a (great) Fam terrible, formidable.

almond ['ɑːmənd] n amande f.

almost ['ɔːlməust] adv presque; **he a. fell**/etc il a failli tomber/etc.

alms [ɑːmz] npl aumône f.

alone [ə'ləun] a & adv seul; **an expert a. can ...** seul un expert peut ...; **I did it (all) a.** je l'ai fait à moi (tout) seul, je l'ai fait (tout)

seul; **to leave** or **let a.** (person) laisser tranquille or en paix; (thing) ne pas toucher à.
along [ə'lɒŋ] prep (all) a. (tout) le long de; **to go** or **walk a.** (street) passer par; **a. here** par ici; **a. with** avec; − adv all a. d'un bout à l'autre; (time) dès le début; **come a.!** venez!; **move a.!** avancez!
alongside [əlɒŋ'saɪd] prep & adv à côté (de); **to come a.** Nau accoster; **a. the kerb** le long du trottoir.
aloof [ə'luːf] a distant; − adv à distance; **to keep a.** garder ses distances (**from** par rapport à). ◆**−ness** n réserve f.
aloud [ə'laʊd] adv à haute voix.
alphabet ['ælfəbet] n alphabet m. ◆**alpha-'betical** a alphabétique.
Alps [ælps] npl the A. les Alpes fpl. ◆**alpine** a (club, range etc) alpin; (scenery) alpestre.
already [ɔːl'redɪ] adv déjà.
alright [ɔːl'raɪt] adv Fam = **all right.**
Alsatian [æl'seɪʃ(ə)n] n (dog) berger m allemand, chien-loup m.
also ['ɔːlsəʊ] adv aussi, également. ◆**a.-ran** n (person) Fig perdant, -ante nm.
altar ['ɔːltər] n autel m.
alter ['ɔːltər] vt changer, modifier; (clothing) retoucher; − vi changer. ◆**alte'ration** n changement m, modification f; retouche f.
altercation [ɔːltə'keɪʃ(ə)n] n altercation f.
alternat/e [ɔːl'tɜːnɪt] a alterné; **on a. days** tous les deux jours; **a. laughter and tears** des rires et des larmes qui se succèdent; − ['ɔːltəneɪt] vi alterner (**with** avec); −vt faire alterner. ◆**−ing** a (current) El alternatif. ◆**−ely** adv alternativement. ◆**alter-'nation** n alternance f.
alternative [ɔːl'tɜːnətɪv] a **an a. way**/etc une autre façon/etc; **a. answers**/etc d'autres réponses/etc (différentes); − n (choice) alternative f. ◆**−ly** adv comme alternative; **or a.** (or else) ou bien.
although [ɔːl'ðəʊ] adv bien que, quoique (+ sub).
altitude ['æltɪtjuːd] n altitude f.
altogether [ɔːltə'geðər] adv (completely) tout à fait; (on the whole) somme toute; **how much a.?** combien en tout?
aluminium [ælju'mɪnjəm] (Am **aluminum** [ə'luːmɪnəm]) n aluminium m.
alumnus, pl **-ni** [ə'lʌmnəs, -naɪ] n Am ancien(ne) élève mf, ancien(ne) étudiant, -ante mf.
always ['ɔːlweɪz] adv toujours; **he's a. criticizing** il est toujours à critiquer.
am [æm, unstressed əm] see **be.**
a.m. [eɪ'em] adv du matin.

amalgam [ə'mælgəm] n amalgame m. ◆**a'malgamate** vt amalgamer; (society) Com fusionner; − vi s'amalgamer; fusionner.
amass [ə'mæs] vt (riches) amasser.
amateur [ə'mætər] n amateur m; − a (interest, sports) d'amateur; **a. painter**/etc peintre/etc amateur. ◆**amateurish** a (work) Pej d'amateur; (person) Pej maladroit, malhabile. ◆**amateurism** n amateurisme m.
amaz/e [ə'meɪz] vt stupéfier, étonner. ◆**−ed** a stupéfait (**at sth** de qch), étonné (**at sth** par or de qch); **a. at seeing**/etc stupéfait or étonné de voir/etc. ◆**−ing** a stupéfiant; Fam extraordinaire. ◆**−ingly** adv extraordinairement; (miraculously) par miracle. ◆**amazement** n stupéfaction f.
ambassador [æm'bæsədər] n ambassadeur m; (woman) ambassadrice f.
amber ['æmbər] n ambre m; **a. (light)** Aut (feu m) orange m.
ambidextrous [æmbɪ'dekstrəs] a ambidextre.
ambiguous [æm'bɪgjʊəs] a ambigu. ◆**ambi'guity** n ambiguïté f.
ambition [æm'bɪʃ(ə)n] n ambition f. ◆**ambitious** a ambitieux.
ambivalent [æm'bɪvələnt] a ambigu, équivoque.
amble ['æmb(ə)l] vi marcher d'un pas tranquille.
ambulance ['æmbjʊləns] n ambulance f; **a. man** ambulancier m.
ambush ['æmbʊʃ] n guet-apens m, embuscade f; − vt prendre en embuscade.
amen [ɑː'men, eɪ'men] int amen.
amenable [ə'miːnəb(ə)l] a docile; **a. to** (responsive to) sensible à; **a. to reason** raisonnable.
amend [ə'mend] vt (text) modifier; (conduct) corriger; Pol amender. ◆**−ment** n Pol amendement m.
amends [ə'mendz] npl **to make a. for** réparer; **to make a.** réparer son erreur.
amenities [ə'miːnɪtɪz, Am ə'menɪtɪz] npl (pleasant things) agréments mpl; (of sports club etc) équipement m; (of town) aménagements mpl.
America [ə'merɪkə] n Amérique f; **North/South A.** Amérique du Nord/du Sud. ◆**American** a & n américain, -aine (mf). ◆**Americanism** n américanisme m.
amethyst ['æmɪθɪst] n améthyste f.
amiable ['eɪmɪəb(ə)l] a aimable.
amicab/le ['æmɪkəb(ə)l] a amical. ◆**−ly** adv amicalement; Jur à l'amiable.

amid(st) [ə'mɪd(st)] *prep* au milieu de, parmi.

amiss [ə'mɪs] *adv & a* mal (à propos); **sth is a.** (*wrong*) qch ne va pas; **that wouldn't come a.** ça ne ferait pas de mal; **to take a.** prendre en mauvaise part.

ammonia [ə'məunjə] *n* (*gas*) ammoniac *m*; (*liquid*) ammoniaque *f*.

ammunition [æmju'nɪʃ(ə)n] *n* munitions *fpl*.

amnesia [æm'niːzjə] *n* amnésie *f*.

amnesty ['æmnəstɪ] *n* amnistie *f*.

amok [ə'mɒk] *adv* **to run a.** se déchaîner, s'emballer.

among(st) [ə'mʌŋ(st)] *prep* parmi, entre; **a. themselves/friends** entre eux/amis; **a. the French/***etc* (*group*) chez les Français/*etc*; **a. the crowd** dans *or* parmi la foule.

amoral [eɪ'mɒrəl] *a* amoral.

amorous ['æmərəs] *a* amoureux.

amount [ə'maʊnt] **1** *n* quantité *f*; (*sum of money*) somme *f*; (*total of bill etc*) montant *m*; (*scope, size*) importance *f*. **2** *vi* **to a.** **to** s'élever à; (*mean*) Fig signifier; **it amounts to the same thing** ça revient au même.

amp(ere) ['æmp(eər)] *n* El ampère *m*.

amphibian [æm'fɪbɪən] *n & a* amphibie (*m*). **◆amphibious** *a* amphibie.

amphitheatre ['æmfɪθɪətər] *n* amphithéâtre *m*.

ample ['æmp(ə)l] *a* (*roomy*) ample; (*enough*) largement assez de; (*reasons, means*) solides; **you have a. time** tu as largement le temps. **◆amply** *adv* largement, amplement.

amplify ['æmplɪfaɪ] *vt* amplifier. **◆amplifier** *n* El amplificateur *m*.

amputate ['æmpjʊteɪt] *vt* amputer. **◆ampu'tation** *n* amputation *f*.

amuck [ə'mʌk] *adv see* amok.

amulet ['æmjʊlɪt] *n* amulette *f*.

amus/e [ə'mjuːz] *vt* amuser, divertir; **to keep s.o. amused** amuser qn. **◆−ing** *a* amusant. **◆−ement** *n* amusement *m*, divertissement *m*; (*pastime*) distraction *f*; **a. arcade** salle *f* de jeux.

an [æn, *unstressed* ən] *see* a.

anachronism [ə'nækrənɪz(ə)m] *n* anachronisme *m*.

an(a)emia [ə'niːmɪə] *n* anémie *f*. **◆an(a)emic** *a* anémique.

an(a)esthesia [ænɪs'θiːzɪə] *n* anesthésie *f*. **◆an(a)esthetic** [ænɪs'θetɪk] *n* (*substance*) anesthésique *m*; **under the a.** sous anesthésie; **general/local a.** anesthésie *f* générale/locale. **◆an(a)esthetize** [ə'niːsθɪtaɪz] *vt* anesthésier.

anagram ['ænəgræm] *n* anagramme *f*.

analogy [ə'nælədʒɪ] *n* analogie *f*. **◆analogous** *a* analogue (**to** à).

analyse ['ænəlaɪz] *vt* analyser. **◆analysis**, *pl* **-yses** [ə'næləsɪs, -ɪsiːz] *n* analyse *f*. **◆analyst** *n* analyste *mf*. **◆ana'lytical** *a* analytique.

anarchy ['ænəkɪ] *n* anarchie *f*. **◆a'narchic** *a* anarchique. **◆anarchist** *n* anarchiste *mf*.

anathema [ə'næθəmə] *n* Rel anathème *m*; **it is (an) a. to me** j'ai une sainte horreur de cela.

anatomy [ə'nætəmɪ] *n* anatomie *f*. **◆ana'tomical** *a* anatomique.

ancestor ['ænsestər] *n* ancêtre *m*. **◆an'cestral** *a* ancestral. **◆ancestry** *n* (*lineage*) ascendance *f*; (*ancestors*) ancêtres *mpl*.

anchor ['æŋkər] *n* ancre *f*; **to weigh a.** lever l'ancre; − *vt* (*ship*) mettre à l'ancre; − *vi* jeter l'ancre, mouiller. **◆−ed** *a* à l'ancre. **◆−age** *n* mouillage *m*.

anchovy ['æntʃəvɪ, *Am* æn'tʃəʊvɪ] *n* anchois *m*.

ancient ['eɪnʃənt] *a* ancien; (*pre-medieval*) antique; (*person*) Hum vétuste.

ancillary [æn'sɪlərɪ] *a* auxiliaire.

and [ænd, *unstressed* ən(d)] *conj* et; **a knife a. fork** un couteau et une fourchette; **two hundred a. two** deux cent deux; **better a. better** de mieux en mieux; **go a. see** va voir.

anecdote ['ænɪkdəʊt] *n* anecdote *f*.

anemone [ə'nemənɪ] *n* anémone *f*.

anew [ə'njuː] *adv* Lit de *or* à nouveau.

angel ['eɪndʒəl] *n* ange *m*. **◆an'gelic** *a* angélique.

anger ['æŋgər] *n* colère *f*; **in a., out of a.** sous le coup de la colère; − *vt* mettre en colère, fâcher.

angl/e ['æŋg(ə)l] **1** *n* angle *m*; **at an a.** en biais. **2** *vi* (*to fish*) pêcher à la ligne; **to a. for** Fig quêter. **◆−er** *n* pêcheur, -euse *mf* à la ligne. **◆−ing** *n* pêche *f* à la ligne.

Anglican ['æŋglɪkən] *a & n* anglican, -ane (*mf*).

anglicism ['æŋglɪsɪz(ə)m] *n* anglicisme *m*.

Anglo- ['æŋgləʊ] *pref* anglo-. **◆Anglo-'Saxon** *a & n* anglo-saxon, -onne (*mf*).

angora [æŋ'gɔːrə] *n* (*wool*) angora *m*.

angry ['æŋgrɪ] *a* (**-ier, -iest**) (*person, look*) fâché; (*letter*) indigné; **to get a.** se fâcher, se mettre en colère (**with** contre). **◆angrily** *adv* en colère; (*to speak*) avec colère.

anguish ['æŋgwɪʃ] *n* angoisse *f*. **◆−ed** *a* angoissé.

angular ['æŋgjʊlər] *a* (*face*) anguleux.

animal ['ænɪməl] *a* animal; – *n* animal *m*, bête *f*.

animate ['ænɪmeɪt] *vt* animer; **to become animated** s'animer; – [-'ænɪmət] *a* (*alive*) animé. ◆**ani'mation** *n* animation *f*.

animosity [ænɪ'mɒsɪtɪ] *n* animosité *f*.

aniseed ['ænɪsiːd] *n* Culin anis *m*.

ankle ['æŋk(ə)l] *n* cheville *f*; **a. sock** socquette *f*.

annals ['æn(ə)lz] *npl* annales *fpl*.

annex [ə'neks] *vt* annexer.

annex(e) ['æneks] *n* (*building*) annexe *f*. ◆**annex'ation** *n* annexion *f*.

annihilate [ə'naɪəleɪt] *vt* anéantir, annihiler. ◆**annihi'lation** *n* anéantissement *m*.

anniversary [ænɪ'vɜːsərɪ] *n* (*of event*) anniversaire *m*, commémoration *f*.

annotate ['ænəteɪt] *vt* annoter. ◆**anno-'tation** *n* annotation *f*.

announc/e [ə'naʊns] *vt* annoncer; (*birth, marriage*) faire part de. ◆**-ement** *n* annonce *f*; (*of birth, marriage*) avis *m*; (*private letter*) faire-part *m inv*. ◆**-er** *n* TV speaker *m*, speakerine *f*.

annoy [ə'nɔɪ] *vt* (*inconvenience*) ennuyer, gêner; (*irritate*) agacer, contrarier. ◆**-ed** *a* contrarié, fâché; **to get a.** se fâcher (**with** contre). ◆**-ing** *a* ennuyeux, contrariant. ◆**annoyance** *n* contrariété *f*, ennui *m*.

annual ['ænjʊəl] *a* annuel; – *n* (*book*) annuaire *m*. ◆**-ly** *adv* annuellement.

annuity [ə'njuːɪtɪ] *n* (*of retired person*) pension *f* viagère.

annul [ə'nʌl] *vt* (-ll-) annuler. ◆**-ment** *n* annulation *f*.

anoint [ə'nɔɪnt] *vt* oindre (**with** de). ◆**-ed** *a* oint.

anomalous [ə'nɒmələs] *a* anormal. ◆**anomaly** *n* anomalie *f*.

anon [ə'nɒn] *adv* Hum tout à l'heure.

anonymous [ə'nɒnɪməs] *a* anonyme; **to remain a.** garder l'anonymat. ◆**ano-'nymity** *n* anonymat *m*.

anorak ['ænəræk] *n* anorak *m*.

anorexia [ænə'reksɪə] *n* anorexie *f*.

another [ə'nʌðər] *a & pron* un(e) autre; **a. man** un autre homme; **a. month** (*additional*) encore un mois, un autre mois; **a. ten** encore dix; **one a.** l'un(e) l'autre, *pl* les un(e)s les autres; **they love one a.** ils s'aiment (l'un l'autre).

answer ['ɑːnsər] *n* réponse *f*; (*to problem*) solution *f* (**to** de); (*reason*) explication *f*; – *vt* (*person, question, phone etc*) répondre à; (*word*) répondre; (*problem*) résoudre; (*prayer, wish*) exaucer; **to a. the bell** *or* **the door** ouvrir la porte; – *vi* répondre; **to a.**

back répliquer, répondre; **to a. for** (*s.o., sth*) répondre de. ◆**-able** *a* responsable (**for** sth de qch, **to s.o.** devant qn).

ant [ænt] *n* fourmi *f*. ◆**anthill** *n* fourmilière *f*.

antagonism [æn'tægənɪz(ə)m] *n* antagonisme *m*; (*hostility*) hostilité *f*. ◆**antagonist** *n* antagoniste *mf*. ◆**antago'nistic** *a* antagoniste; (*hostile*) hostile. ◆**antagonize** *vt* provoquer (l'hostilité de).

antarctic [æn'tɑːktɪk] *a* antarctique; – *n* **the A.** l'Antarctique *m*.

antecedent [æntɪ'siːd(ə)nt] *n* antécédent *m*.

antechamber ['æntɪtʃeɪmbər] *n* antichambre *f*.

antedate ['æntɪdeɪt] *vt* (*letter*) antidater.

antelope ['æntɪləʊp] *n* antilope *f*.

antenatal [æntɪ'neɪt(ə)l] *a* prénatal.

antenna [æn'tenə], *pl* -ae [æn'teniː, -iː] *n* (*of insect etc*) antenne *f*.

antenna² [æn'tenə] *n* (*pl* -as) (*aerial*) Am antenne *f*.

anteroom ['æntɪrʊm] *n* antichambre *f*.

anthem ['ænθəm] *n* national **a.** hymne *m* national.

anthology [æn'θɒlədʒɪ] *n* anthologie *f*.

anthropology [ænθrə'pɒlədʒɪ] *n* anthropologie *f*.

anti- ['æntɪ, Am 'æntaɪ] *pref* anti-; **to be a. sth** Fam être contre qch. ◆**anti'aircraft** *a* antiaérien. ◆**antibi'otic** *a & n* antibiotique (*m*). ◆**antibody** *n* anticorps *m*. ◆**anti'climax** *n* chute *f* dans l'ordinaire; (*let-down*) déception *f*. ◆**anti'clockwise** *adv* dans le sens inverse des aiguilles d'une montre. ◆**anti'cyclone** *n* anticyclone *m*. ◆**antidote** *n* antidote *m*. ◆**antifreeze** *n* Aut antigel *m*. ◆**anti'histamine** *n* Med antihistaminique *m*. ◆**anti'perspirant** *n* antisudoral *m*. ◆**anti-Se'mitic** *a* antisémite. ◆**anti-'Semitism** *n* antisémitisme *m*. ◆**anti'septic** *a & n* antiseptique (*m*). ◆**anti'social** *a* (*misfit*) asocial; (*measure, principles*) antisocial; (*unsociable*) insociable.

anticipate [æn'tɪsɪpeɪt] *vt* (*foresee*) prévoir; (*forestall*) devancer; (*expect*) s'attendre à; (*the future*) anticiper sur. ◆**antici'pation** *n* prévision *f*; (*expectation*) attente *f*; **in a. of** en prévision de, dans l'attente de; **in a.** (*to thank s.o., pay etc*) d'avance.

antics ['æntɪks] *npl* bouffonneries *fpl*.

antipathy [æn'tɪpəθɪ] *n* antipathie *f*.

antipodes [æn'tɪpədiːz] *npl* antipodes *mpl*.

antiquarian [æntɪ'kweərɪən] *a* **a. bookseller**

libraire *mf* spécialisé(e) dans le livre ancien.

antiquated ['æntɪkweɪtɪd] *a* vieilli; (*person*) vieux jeu *inv*.

antique [æn'tiːk] *a* (*furniture etc*) ancien; (*of Greek etc antiquity*) antique; **a. dealer** antiquaire *mf*; **a. shop** magasin *m* d'antiquités; – *n* objet *m* ancien *or* d'époque, antiquité *f*. ◆**antiquity** *n* (*period etc*) antiquité *f*.

antithesis, *pl* **-eses** [æn'tɪθəsɪs, -ɪsiːz] *n* antithèse *f*.

antler ['æntlər] *n* (*tine*) andouiller *m*; *pl* bois *mpl*.

antonym ['æntənɪm] *n* antonyme *m*.

Antwerp ['æntwɜːp] *n* Anvers *m or f*.

anus ['eɪnəs] *n* anus *m*.

anvil ['ænvɪl] *n* enclume *f*.

anxiety [æŋ'zaɪətɪ] *n* (*worry*) inquiétude *f* (**about** au sujet de); (*fear*) anxiété *f*; (*eagerness*) impatience *f* (**for** de).

anxious ['æŋkʃəs] *a* (*worried*) inquiet (**about** de, pour); (*troubled*) anxieux; (*causing worry*) inquiétant; (*eager*) impatient (**to do** de faire); **I'm a. (that) he should go** je tiens beaucoup à ce qu'il parte. ◆**-ly** *adv* avec inquiétude; (*to wait etc*) impatiemment.

any ['enɪ] *a* **1** (*interrogative*) du, de la, des; **have you a. milk/tickets?** avez-vous du lait/des billets?; **is there a. man (at all) who** . . . ? y a-t-il un homme (quelconque) qui . . . ? **2** (*negative*) de; (*not any at all*) aucun; **he hasn't a. milk/tickets** il n'a pas de lait/de billets; **there isn't a. proof** il n'y a aucune preuve. **3** (*no matter which*) n'importe quel. **4** (*every*) tout; **at a. hour** à toute heure; **in a. case, at a. rate** de toute façon; – *pron* **1** (*no matter which one*) n'importe lequel; (*somebody*) quelqu'un; **if a. of you** si l'un d'entre vous, si quelqu'un parmi vous; **more than a.** plus qu'aucun. **2** (*quantity*) en; **have you a.?** en as-tu?; **I don't see a.** je n'en vois pas; – *adv* (*usually not translated*) (*not*) **a. further/happier/etc** (pas) plus loin/plus heureux/*etc*; **I don't see her a. more** je ne la vois plus; **a. more tea?** (*a little*) encore du thé?, encore un peu de thé?; **a. better?** (un peu) mieux?

anybody ['enɪbɒdɪ] *pron* **1** (*somebody*) quelqu'un; **do you see a.?** vois-tu quelqu'un?; **more than a.** plus qu'aucun. **2** (*negative*) personne; **he doesn't know a.** il ne connaît personne. **3** (*no matter who*) n'importe qui; **a. would think that . . .** on croirait que . . . .

anyhow ['enɪhaʊ] *adv* (*at any rate*) de toute façon; (*badly*) n'importe comment; **to**

leave sth a. (*in confusion*) laisser qch sens dessus dessous.

anyone ['enɪwʌn] *pron* = anybody.

anyplace ['enɪpleɪs] *adv Am* = anywhere.

anything ['enɪθɪŋ] *pron* **1** (*something*) quelque chose; **can you see a.?** voyez-vous quelque chose? **2** (*negative*) rien; **he doesn't do a.** il ne fait rien; **without a. sens** rien. **3** (*everything*) tout; **a. you like** (tout) ce que tu veux; **like a.** (*to work etc*) *Fam* comme un fou. **4** (*no matter what*) **a. (at all)** n'importe quoi.

anyway ['enɪweɪ] *adv* (*at any rate*) de toute façon.

anywhere ['enɪweər] *adv* **1** (*no matter where*) n'importe où. **2** (*everywhere*) partout; **a. you go** partout où vous allez, où que vous alliez; **a. you like** là où tu veux. **3** (*somewhere*) quelque part; **is he going a.?** va-t-il quelque part? **4** (*negative*) nulle part; **he doesn't go a.** il ne va nulle part; **without a. to put it** sans un endroit où le mettre.

apace [ə'peɪs] *adv* rapidement.

apart [ə'pɑːt] *adv* (*to or at one side*) à part; **to tear a.** (*to pieces*) mettre en pièces; **we kept them a.** (*separate*) on les tenait séparés; **with legs (wide) a.** les jambes écartées; **they are a metre a.** ils se trouvent à un mètre l'un de l'autre; **a. from** (*except for*) à part; **to take a.** démonter; **to come a.** (*of two objects*) se séparer; (*of knot etc*) se défaire; **to tell a.** distinguer entre; **worlds a.** (*very different*) diamétralement opposé.

apartheid [ə'pɑːteɪt] *n* apartheid *m*.

apartment [ə'pɑːtmənt] *n* (*flat*) *Am* appartement *m*; (*room*) chambre *f*; **a. house** *Am* immeuble *m* (d'habitation).

apathy ['æpəθɪ] *n* apathie *f*. ◆**apa'thetic** *a* apathique.

ape [eɪp] *n* singe; – *vt* (*imitate*) singer.

aperitif [ə'perətiːf] *n* apéritif *m*.

aperture ['æpətʃʊər] *n* ouverture *f*.

apex ['eɪpeks] *n Geom & Fig* sommet *m*.

aphorism ['æfərɪz(ə)m] *n* aphorisme *m*.

aphrodisiac [æfrə'dɪzɪæk] *a & n* aphrodisiaque (*m*).

apiece [ə'piːs] *adv* chacun; **a pound a.** une livre (la) pièce *or* chacun.

apish ['eɪpɪʃ] *a* simiesque; (*imitative*) imitateur.

apocalypse [ə'pɒkəlɪps] *n* apocalypse *f*. ◆**apoca'lyptic** *a* apocalyptique.

apocryphal [ə'pɒkrɪfəl] *a* apocryphe.

apogee ['æpədʒiː] *n* apogée *m*.

apologetic [əpɒlə'dʒetɪk] *a* (*letter*) plein d'excuses; **to be a. about** s'excuser de. ◆**apologetically** *adv* en s'excusant.

apology [ə'pɒlədʒɪ] n excuses fpl; **an a.** for a dinner Fam Pej un dîner minable. ◆**apologist** n apologiste mf. ◆**apologize** vi s'excuser (for de); **to a. to s.o.** faire ses excuses à qn (for pour).

apoplexy ['æpəpleksɪ] n apoplexie f. ◆**apo'plectic** a & n apoplectique (mf).

apostle [ə'pɒs(ə)l] n apôtre m.

apostrophe [ə'pɒstrəfɪ] n apostrophe f.

appal [ə'pɔːl] (Am **appall**) vt (-ll-) épouvanter. ◆**appalling** a épouvantable.

apparatus [æpə'reɪtəs, Am -'rætəs] n (equipment, organization) appareil m; (in gym) agrès mpl.

apparel [ə'pærəl] n habit m, habillement m.

apparent [ə'pærənt] a (obvious, seeming) apparent; **it's a. that** il est évident que. ◆**-ly** adv apparemment.

apparition [æpə'rɪʃ(ə)n] n apparition f.

appeal [ə'piːl] n (call) appel m; (entreaty) supplication f; (charm) attrait m; (interest) intérêt m; Jur appel m; − vt to a. to (s.o., s.o.'s kindness) faire appel à; to a. to s.o. (attract) plaire à qn, séduire qn; (interest) intéresser qn; **to a. to s.o. for sth** demander qch à qn; **to a. to s.o. to do** supplier qn de faire; − vi Jur faire appel. ◆**—ing** a (begging) suppliant; (attractive) séduisant.

appear [ə'pɪər] vi (become visible) apparaître; (present oneself) se présenter; (seem, be published) paraître; (act) Th jouer; Jur comparaître; **it appears that** (it seems) il semble que (+ sub or indic); (it is rumoured) il paraîtrait que (+ indic). ◆**appearance** n (act) apparition f; (look) apparence f, aspect m; (of book) parution f; **to put in an a.** faire acte de présence.

appease [ə'piːz] vt apaiser; (curiosity) satisfaire.

append [ə'pend] vt joindre, ajouter (to à). ◆**—age** n Anat appendice m.

appendix, pl **-ixes** or **-ices** [ə'pendɪks, -ɪksɪz, -ɪsiːz] n (of book) & Anat appendice m. ◆**appendicitis** [əpendɪ'saɪtɪs] n appendicite f.

appertain [æpə'teɪn] vi to a. to se rapporter à.

appetite ['æpɪtaɪt] n appétit m; **to take away s.o.'s a.** couper l'appétit à qn. ◆**appetizer** n (drink) apéritif m; (food) amuse-gueule m inv. ◆**appetizing** a appétissant.

applaud [ə'plɔːd] vt (clap) applaudir; (approve of) approuver, applaudir à; − vi applaudir. ◆**applause** n applaudissements mpl.

apple ['æp(ə)l] n pomme f; **stewed apples, a. sauce** compote f de pommes; **eating/**

cooking a. pomme f à couteau/à cuire; **a. pie** tarte f aux pommes; **a. core** trognon m de pomme; **a. tree** pommier m.

appliance [ə'plaɪəns] n appareil m.

apply [ə'plaɪ] **1** vt (put, carry out etc) appliquer; (brake) Aut appuyer sur; **to a. oneself to** s'appliquer à. **2** vi (be relevant) s'appliquer (to à); **to a.** (for job) poser sa candidature à, postuler; **to a. to s.o.** (ask) s'adresser à qn (for pour). ◆**applied** a (maths etc) appliqué. ◆**applicable** a applicable (to à). ◆**'applicant** n candidat, -ate mf (for à). ◆**appli'cation** n application f; (request) demande f; (for job) candidature f; (for membership) demande f d'adhésion or d'inscription; **a. (form)** (job) formulaire m de candidature; (club) formulaire m d'inscription or d'adhésion.

appoint [ə'pɔɪnt] vt (person) nommer (**to sth** à qch, **to do** pour faire); (time, place) fixer; **at the appointed time** à l'heure dite; **well-appointed** bien équipé. ◆**—ment** n nomination f; (meeting) rendez-vous m inv; (post) place f, situation f.

apportion [ə'pɔːʃ(ə)n] vt répartir.

apposite ['æpəzɪt] a juste, à propos.

appraise [ə'preɪz] vt évaluer. ◆**appraisal** n évaluation f.

appreciate [ə'priːʃɪeɪt] **1** vt (enjoy, value, assess) apprécier; (understand) comprendre; (be grateful for) être reconnaissant de. **2** vi prendre de la valeur. ◆**appreciable** a appréciable, sensible. ◆**appreci'ation** n **1** (judgement) appréciation f; (gratitude) reconnaissance f. **2** (rise in value) plus-value f. ◆**appreciative** a (grateful) reconnaissant (of de); (laudatory) élogieux; **to be a. of** (enjoy) apprécier.

apprehend [æprɪ'hend] vt (seize, arrest) appréhender. ◆**apprehension** n (fear) appréhension f. ◆**apprehensive** a inquiet (about de, au sujet de); **to be a. of** redouter.

apprentice [ə'prentɪs] n apprenti, -ie mf; − vt mettre en apprentissage (**to** chez). ◆**apprenticeship** n apprentissage m.

approach [ə'prəʊtʃ] vt (draw near to) s'approcher de (qn, feu, porte etc); (age, result, town) approcher de; (subject) aborder; (accost) aborder (qn); **to a. s.o. about** parler à qn de; − vi (of person, vehicle) s'approcher; (of date etc) approcher; − n approche f; (method) façon f de s'y prendre; (path) voie f d'accès m; **a. to** (question) manière f d'aborder; **to make approaches to** faire des avances

◆—**able** *a* (*place*) accessible; (*person*) abordable.

appropriate 1 [ə'prəupriət] *a* (*place, tools, clothes etc*) approprié, adéquat; (*remark, time*) opportun; **a. to** or **for** propre à, approprié à. **2** [ə'prəuprieit] *vt* (*set aside*) affecter; (*steal*) s'approprier. ◆—**ly** *adv* convenablement.

approv/e [ə'pruːv] *vt* approuver; **to a. of sth** approuver qch; **I don't a. of him** il ne me plaît pas, je ne l'apprécie pas; **I a. of his going** je trouve bon qu'il y aille; **I a. of her having accepted** je l'approuve de l'avoir accepté. ◆—**ing** *a* approbateur. ◆—**ingly** *adv* d'un air approbateur. ◆**approval** *n* approbation *f*; **on a.** (*goods*) *Com* à l'essai.

approximate [ə'prɒksimət] *a* approximatif; − [ə'prɒksimeit] *vi* **to a. to** se rapprocher de. ◆—**ly** *adv* à peu près, approximativement. ◆**approxi'mation** *n* approximation *f*.

apricot ['eiprikɒt] *n* abricot *m*.

April ['eiprəl] *n* avril *m*; **to make an A. fool of** faire un poisson d'avril à.

apron ['eiprən] *n* (*garment*) tablier *m*.

apse [æps] *n* (*of church*) abside *f*.

apt [æpt] *a* (*suitable*) convenable; (*remark, reply*) juste; (*word, name*) bien choisi; (*student*) doué, intelligent; **to be a. to** avoir tendance à; **a. at sth** habile à qch. ◆**aptitude** *n* aptitude *f* (**for** à, **pour**). ◆**aptly** *adv* convenablement; **a. named** qui porte bien son nom.

aqualung ['ækwəlʌŋ] *n* scaphandre *m* autonome.

aquarium [ə'kweəriəm] *n* aquarium *m*.

Aquarius [ə'kweəriəs] *n* (*sign*) le Verseau.

aquatic [ə'kwætik] *a* (*plant etc*) aquatique; (*sport*) nautique.

aqueduct ['ækwidʌkt] *n* aqueduc *m*.

aquiline ['ækwilain] *a* (*nose, profile*) aquilin.

Arab ['ærəb] *a & n* arabe (*mf*). ◆**Arabian** [ə'reibiən] *a* arabe. ◆**Arabic** *a & n* (*language*) arabe (*m*); **A. numerals** chiffres *mpl* arabes.

arabesque [ærə'besk] *n* (*decoration*) arabesque *f*.

arable ['ærəb(ə)l] *a* (*land*) arable.

arbiter ['aːbitər] *n* arbitre *m*. ◆**arbitrate** *vti* arbitrer. ◆**arbi'tration** *n* arbitrage *m*; **to go to a.** soumettre la question à l'arbitrage. ◆**arbitrator** *n* (*in dispute*) médiateur, -trice *mf*.

arbitrary ['aːbitrəri] *a* arbitraire.

arbour ['aːbər] *n* tonnelle *f*, charmille *f*.

arc [aːk] *n* (*of circle*) arc *m*.

arcade [aː'keid] *n* (*market*) passage *m* couvert.

arch [aːtʃ] *n* (*of bridge*) arche *f*; *Archit* voûte *f*, arc *m*; (*of foot*) cambrure *f*; − *vt* (*one's back etc*) arquer, courber. ◆**archway** *n* passage *m* voûté, voûte *f*.

arch- [aːtʃ] *pref* (*villain etc*) achevé; **a. enemy** ennemi *m* numéro un.

arch(a)eology [aːki'ɒlədʒi] *n* archéologie *f*. ◆**arch(a)eologist** *n* archéologue *mf*.

archaic [aː'keiik] *a* archaïque.

archangel ['aːkeindʒəl] *n* archange *m*.

archbishop [aːtʃ'biʃəp] *n* archevêque *m*.

archer ['aːtʃər] *n* archer *m*. ◆**archery** *n* tir *m* à l'arc.

archetype ['aːkitaip] *n* archétype *m*.

archipelago [aːki'peləgəu] *n* (*pl* -**oes** *or* -**os**) archipel *m*.

architect ['aːkitekt] *n* architecte *m*. ◆**architecture** *n* architecture *f*.

archives ['aːkaivz] *npl* archives *fpl*. ◆**archivist** *n* archiviste *mf*.

arctic ['aːktik] *a* arctique; (*weather*) polaire, glacial; − **the A.** l'Arctique *m*.

ardent ['aːdənt] *a* ardent. ◆—**ly** *adv* ardemment. ◆**ardour** *n* ardeur *f*.

arduous ['aːdjuəs] *a* ardu.

are [aːr] *see* **be**.

area ['eəriə] *n* *Math* superficie *f*; *Geog* région *f*; (*of town*) quartier *m*; *Mil* zone *f*; (*domain*) *Fig* domaine *m*, secteur *m*, terrain *m*; **built-up a.** agglomération *f*; **parking a.** aire *f* de stationnement; **a. code** *Tel Am* indicatif *m*.

arena [ə'riːnə] *n* *Hist & Fig* arène *f*.

Argentina [aːdʒən'tiːnə] *n* Argentine *f*. ◆**Argentine** ['aːdʒəntain] *a & n*, ◆**Argentinian** *a & n* argentin, -ine (*mf*).

argu/e ['aːgjuː] *vi* (*quarrel*) se disputer (**with** avec, **about** au sujet de); (*reason*) raisonner (**with** avec, **about** sur); **to a. in favour of** plaider pour; − *vt* (*matter*) discuter; **to a. that** (*maintain*) soutenir que. ◆—**able** ['aːgjuəb(ə)l] *a* discutable. ◆—**ably** *adv* on pourrait soutenir que. ◆—**ment** *n* (*quarrel*) dispute *f*; (*reasoning*) argument *m*; (*debate*) discussion *f*; **to have an a.** se disputer. ◆**argu'mentative** *a* raisonneur.

aria ['aːriə] *n* *Mus* air *m* (d'opéra).

arid ['ærid] *a* aride.

Aries ['eəriːz] *n* (*sign*) le Bélier.

arise [ə'raiz] *vi* (*pt* **arose**, *pp* **arisen**) (*of problem, opportunity etc*) se présenter; (*of cry, objection*) s'élever; (*result*) résulter (**from** de); (*get up*) *Lit* se lever.

aristocracy [æri'stɒkrəsi] *n* aristocratie *f*. ◆**aristocrat** ['æristəkræt, *Am* ə'ristəkræt] *n* aristocrate *mf*. ◆aristo'cratic *a* aristocratique.

arithmetic [ə'rɪθmətɪk] *n* arithmétique *f*.

ark [ɑːk] *n* Noah's a. l'arche *f* de Noé.

arm [ɑːm] **1** *n* bras *m*; **a. in a.** bras dessus bras dessous; **with open arms** à bras ouverts. **2** *n* (weapon) arme *f*; **arms race** course *f* aux armements; − *vt* armer (with de). ◆armament *n* armement *m*. ◆armband *n* brassard *m*. ◆armchair *n* fauteuil *m*. ◆armful *n* brassée *f*. ◆armhole *n* emmanchure *f*. ◆armpit *n* aisselle *f*. ◆armrest *n* accoudoir *m*.

armadillo [ɑːmə'dɪləʊ] *n* (pl -os) tatou *m*.

armistice ['ɑːmɪstɪs] *n* armistice *m*.

armour ['ɑːmər] *n* (of knight etc) armure *f*; (of tank etc) blindage *m*. ◆armoured *a*, ◆armour-plated *a* blindé. ◆armoury *n* arsenal *m*.

army ['ɑːmɪ] *n* armée *f*; − *a* (uniform etc) militaire; **to join the a.** s'engager; **regular a.** armée *f* active.

aroma [ə'rəʊmə] *n* arôme *m*. ◆aro'matic *a* aromatique.

arose [ə'rəʊz] see **arise**.

around [ə'raʊnd] *prep* autour de; (approximately) environ, autour de; **to go a. the world** faire le tour du monde; − *adv* autour; all a. tout autour; **to follow a.** suivre partout; **to rush a.** courir çà et là; **a. here** par ici; **he's still a.** il est encore là; **there's a lot of flu a.** il y a pas mal de grippes dans l'air; **up and a.** (after illness) Am sur pied, guéri.

arouse [ə'raʊz] *vt* éveiller, susciter; (sexually) exciter; **to a. from sleep** tirer du sommeil.

arrange [ə'reɪndʒ] *vt* arranger; (time, meeting) fixer; **it was arranged that** il était convenu que; **to a. to do** s'arranger pour faire. ◆—ment *n* (layout, agreement) arrangement *m*; *pl* (preparations) préparatifs *mpl*; (plans) projets *mpl*; **to make arrangements to** s'arranger pour.

array [ə'reɪ] *n* (display) étalage *m*. ◆arrayed *a* (dressed) Lit (re)vêtu (in de).

arrears [ə'rɪəz] *npl* (payment) arriéré *m*; **to be in a.** avoir des arriérés.

arrest [ə'rest] *vt* arrêter; − *n* Jur arrestation *f*; **under a.** en état d'arrestation; **cardiac a.** arrêt *m* du cœur. ◆—ing *a* (striking) Fig frappant.

arrive [ə'raɪv] *vi* arriver. ◆arrival *n* arrivée *f*; **new a.** nouveau venu *m*, nouvelle venue *f*; (baby) nouveau-né, -ée *mf*.

arrogant ['ærəgənt] *a* arrogant. ◆arrogance *n* arrogance *f*. ◆arrogantly *adv* avec arrogance.

arrow ['ærəʊ] *n* flèche *f*.

arsenal ['ɑːsən(ə)l] *n* arsenal *m*.

arsenic ['ɑːsnɪk] *n* arsenic *m*.

arson ['ɑːs(ə)n] *n* incendie *m* volontaire. ◆arsonist *n* incendiaire *mf*.

art [ɑːt] *n* art *m*; (cunning) artifice *m*; **work of a.** œuvre *f* d'art; **fine arts** beaux-arts *mpl*; **faculty of arts** Univ faculté *f* des lettres; **a. school** école *f* des beaux-arts.

artefact ['ɑːtɪfækt] *n* objet *m* fabriqué.

artery ['ɑːtərɪ] *n* Anat Aut artère *f*. ◆ar'terial *a* Anat artériel; **a. road** route *f* principale.

artful ['ɑːtfəl] *a* rusé, astucieux. ◆—ly *adv* astucieusement.

arthritis [ɑː'θraɪtɪs] *n* arthrite *f*.

artichoke ['ɑːtɪtʃəʊk] *n* (globe) a. artichaut *m*; **Jerusalem a.** topinambour *m*.

article ['ɑːtɪk(ə)l] *n* (object, clause) & Journ Gram article *m*; **a. of clothing** vêtement *m*; **articles of value** objets *mpl* de valeur; **leading a.** Journ éditorial *m*.

articulat/e [ɑː'tɪkjʊlət] *a* (sound) net, distinct; (person) qui s'exprime clairement; − [ɑː'tɪkjʊleɪt] *vti* (speak) articuler. ◆—ed *a* **a. lorry** semi-remorque *m*. ◆articu'lation *n* articulation *f*.

artifact ['ɑːtɪfækt] *n* objet *m* fabriqué.

artifice ['ɑːtɪfɪs] *n* artifice *m*.

artificial [ɑːtɪ'fɪʃ(ə)l] *a* artificiel. ◆artifici'ality *n* caractère *m* artificiel. ◆artificially *adv* artificiellement.

artillery [ɑː'tɪlərɪ] *n* artillerie *f*.

artisan ['ɑːtɪzæn] *n* artisan *m*.

artist ['ɑːtɪst] *n* (actor, painter etc) artiste *mf*. ◆artiste [ɑː'tiːst] *n* Th Mus artiste *m*. ◆ar'tistic *a* (sense, treasure) artistique; (person) artiste. ◆artistry *n* art *m*.

artless ['ɑːtləs] *a* naturel, naïf.

arty ['ɑːtɪ] *a* Pej du genre artiste.

as [æz, unstressed əz] *adv & conj* **1** (manner etc) comme; **as you like** comme tu veux; **such as** comme, tel que; **as much or as hard as I can** (au)tant que je peux; **as it is** (this being the case) les choses étant ainsi; (to leave sth) comme ça, tel quel; **it's late as it is** il est déjà tard; **as if, as though** comme si. **2** (comparison) **as tall as you** aussi grand que vous; **is he as tall as you?** est-il aussi or si grand que vous?; **as white as a sheet** blanc comme un linge; **as much or as hard as you** autant que vous; **the same as** le même que; **twice as big as** deux fois plus grand que. **3** (concessive) **(as) clever as he is** si or aussi intelligent qu'il soit. **4** (capacity) **as a**

teacher comme professeur, en tant que or en qualité de professeur; **to act as a father** agir en père. **5** (reason) puisque, comme; **as it's late** puisqu'il est tard, comme il est tard. **6** (time) **as I left** comme je partais; **as one grows older** à mesure que l'on vieillit; **as he slept** pendant qu'il dormait; **one day as ... un jour que ...** ; **as from, as** of (time) à partir de. **7** (concerning) **as for that, as to that** quant à cela. **8** (+ inf) so as to de manière à; **so stupid as to** assez bête pour.

asbestos [æs'bestəs] n amiante f.

ascend [ə'send] vi monter; – vt (throne) monter sur; (stairs) monter; (mountain) faire l'ascension de. ◆**ascent** n ascension f (of de); (slope) côte f.

ascertain [æsə'teɪn] vt (discover) découvrir; (check) s'assurer de.

ascetic [ə'setɪk] a ascétique; – n ascète mf.

ascribe [ə'skraɪb] vt attribuer (to à).

ash [æʃ] n **1** (of cigarette etc) cendre f; **A. Wednesday** mercredi m des Cendres. **2** (tree) frêne m. ◆**ashen** (a pale grey) cendré; (face) pâle. ◆**ashcan** n Am poubelle f. ◆**ashtray** n cendrier m.

ashamed [ə'ʃeɪmd] a honteux; **to be a. of** avoir honte de; **to be a. (of oneself)** avoir honte.

ashore [ə'ʃɔːr] adv **to go a.** débarquer; **to put s.o. a.** débarquer qn.

Asia ['eɪʃə] n Asie f. ◆**Asian** a asiatique; – n Asiatique m, Asiate mf.

aside [ə'saɪd] **1** adv de côté; **to draw a.** (curtain) écarter; **to take or draw s.o. a.** prendre qn à part; **to step a.** s'écarter; **a. from** en dehors de. **2** n Th aparté m.

asinine ['æsɪnaɪn] a stupide, idiot.

ask [ɑːsk] vt demander; (a question) poser; (invite) inviter; **to a. s.o. (for) sth** demander qch à qn; **to a. s.o. to do** demander à qn de faire; – vi demander; **to a. for sth/s.o.** demander qch/qn; **to a. for sth back** redemander qch; **to a. about sth** se renseigner sur qch; **to a. after or about s.o.** demander des nouvelles de qn; **to a. s.o. about** interroger qn sur; **asking price** prix m demandé.

askance [ə'skɑːns] adv **to look a.** at regarder avec méfiance.

askew [ə'skjuː] adv de biais, de travers.

aslant [ə'slɑːnt] adv de travers.

asleep [ə'sliːp] a endormi; (arm, leg) engourdi; **to be a.** dormir; **to fall a.** s'endormir.

asp [æsp] n (snake) aspic m.

asparagus [ə'spærəgəs] n (plant) asperge f; (shoots) Culin asperges fpl.

aspect ['æspekt] n aspect m; (of house) orientation f.

aspersions [ə'spɜːʃ(ə)nz] npl **to cast a. on** dénigrer.

asphalt ['æsfælt, Am 'æsfɔːlt] n asphalte m; – vt asphalter.

asphyxia [əs'fɪksɪə] n asphyxie f. ◆**asphyxiate** vt asphyxier. ◆**asphyxi- 'ation** n asphyxie f.

aspire [ə'spaɪər] vi **to a. to** aspirer à. ◆**aspi- 'ration** n aspiration f.

aspirin ['æsprɪn] n aspirine f.

ass [æs] n (animal) âne m; (person) Fam imbécile mf, âne m; **she-a.** ânesse f.

assail [ə'seɪl] vt assaillir (with de). ◆**assai- lant** n agresseur m.

assassin [ə'sæsɪn] n Pol assassin m. ◆**assassinate** vt Pol assassiner. ◆**assassi'nation** n Pol assassinat m.

assault [ə'sɔːlt] n Mil assaut m; Jur agres- sion f; – vt Jur agresser; (woman) violenter.

assemble [ə'semb(ə)l] vt (objects, ideas) assembler; (people) rassembler; (machine) monter; – vi se rassembler. ◆**assembly** n (meeting) assemblée f; Tech montage m, assemblage m; Sch rassemblement m; **a. line** (in factory) chaîne f de montage.

assent [ə'sent] n assentiment m; – vi consentir (to à).

assert [ə'sɜːt] vt affirmer (that que); (rights) revendiquer; **to a. oneself** s'affirmer. ◆**assertion** n affirmation f; revendication f. ◆**assertive** a affirmatif; Pej autoritaire.

assess [ə'ses] vt (estimate, evaluate) évaluer; (decide amount of) fixer le montant de; (person) juger. ◆—**ment** n évaluation f; jugement m. ◆**assessor** n (valuer) expert m.

asset ['æset] n atout m, avantage m; pl Com biens mpl, avoir m.

assiduous [ə'sɪdjuəs] a assidu.

assign [ə'saɪn] vt (allocate) assigner; (day etc) fixer; (appoint) nommer (to à). ◆—**ment** n (task) mission f; Sch devoirs mpl.

assimilate [ə'sɪmɪleɪt] vt assimiler; – vi s'assimiler. ◆**assimi'lation** n assimila- tion f.

assist [ə'sɪst] vti aider (in doing, to do à faire). ◆**assistance** n aide f; **to be of a.** to s.o. aider qn. ◆**assistant** n assistant, -ante mf; (in shop) vendeur, -euse mf; – a adjoint.

assizes [ə'saɪzɪz] npl Jur assises fpl.

associate [ə'səʊʃɪeɪt] vt associer (with à, avec); – vi **to a. with s.o.** fréquenter qn; **to**

a. (oneself) with (in business venture) s'associer à or avec; – [ə'səʊʃɪət] n a associé, -ée (mf). ◆associ'ation n association f; pl (memories) souvenirs mpl.

assort/ed [ə'sɔːtɪd] a (different) variés; (foods) assortis; well-a. bien assorti. ◆—ment n assortiment m.

assuage [ə'sweɪdʒ] vt apaiser, adoucir.

assum/e [ə'sjuːm] vt 1 (take on) prendre; (responsibility, role) assumer; (attitude, name) adopter. 2 (suppose) présumer (that que). ◆—ed a (feigned) faux; a. name nom m d'emprunt. ◆assumption n (supposition) supposition f.

assur/e [ə'ʃʊər] vt assurer. ◆—edly [-ɪdlɪ] adv assurément. ◆assurance n assurance f.

asterisk ['æstərɪsk] n astérisque m.

astern [ə'stɜːn] adv Nau à l'arrière.

asthma ['æsmə] n asthme m. ◆asth'matic a & n asthmatique (mf).

astir [ə'stɜːr] a (excited) en émoi; (out of bed) debout.

astonish [ə'stɒnɪʃ] vt étonner; to be astonished s'étonner (at de qch). ◆—ing a étonnant. ◆—ingly adv étonnamment. ◆—ment n étonnement m.

astound [ə'staʊnd] vt stupéfier, étonner. ◆—ing a stupéfiant.

astray [ə'streɪ] adv to go a. s'égarer; to lead a. égarer.

astride [ə'straɪd] adv à califourchon; – prep à cheval sur.

astringent [ə'strɪndʒənt] a (harsh) sévère.

astrology [ə'strɒlədʒɪ] n astrologie f. ◆astrologer n astrologue mf.

astronaut ['æstrənɔːt] n astronaute mf.

astronomy [ə'strɒnəmɪ] n astronomie f. ◆astronomer n astronome m. ◆astro'nomical a astronomique.

astute [ə'stjuːt] a (crafty) rusé; (clever) astucieux.

asunder [ə'sʌndər] adv (to pieces) en pièces; (in two) en deux.

asylum [ə'saɪləm] n asile m; lunatic a. Pej maison f de fous, asile m d'aliénés.

at [æt, unstressed ət] prep 1 à; at the end à la fin; at work au travail; at six (o'clock) à six heures. 2 chez; at the doctor's chez le médecin; at home chez soi, à la maison. ◆at-home n réception f. 3 en; at sea en mer; at war en guerre; good at (geography etc) fort en. 4 contre; angry at fâché contre. 5 sur; to shoot at tirer sur; at my request sur ma demande. 6 de; to laugh at rire de; surprised at surpris de. 7 (au)près de; at the window (au)près de la fenêtre. 8 par; to

come in at the door entrer par la porte; six at a time six par six. 9 at night la nuit; to look at regarder; not at all pas du tout; (after 'thank you') pas de quoi!; nothing at all rien du tout; to be (hard) at it être très occupé, travailler dur; he's always (on) at me Fam il est toujours après moi.

ate [et, Am eɪt] see eat.

atheism ['eɪθɪɪz(ə)m] n athéisme m. ◆atheist n athée m.

Athens ['æθɪnz] n Athènes m or f.

athlete ['æθliːt] n athlète mf; a.'s foot Med mycose f. ◆ath'letic a athlétique; a. meeting réunion f sportive. ◆ath'letics npl athlétisme m.

atishoo! [ə'tɪʃuː] (Am atchoo [ə'tʃuː]) int atchoum!

Atlantic [ət'læntɪk] a atlantique; – n the A. l'Atlantique m.

atlas ['ætləs] n atlas m.

atmosphere ['ætməsfɪər] n atmosphère f. ◆atmos'pheric a atmosphérique.

atom ['ætəm] n atome m; a. bomb bombe f atomique. ◆a'tomic a atomique. ◆atomizer n atomiseur m.

atone [ə'təʊn] vi to a. for expier. ◆—ment n expiation f (for de).

atrocious [ə'trəʊʃəs] a atroce. ◆atrocity n atrocité f.

atrophy ['ætrəfɪ] vi s'atrophier.

attach [ə'tætʃ] vt attacher (to à); (document) joindre (to à); attached to (fond of) attaché à. ◆—ment n (affection) attachement m; (fastener) attache f; (tool) accessoire m.

attaché [ə'tæʃeɪ] n 1 Pol attaché, -ée mf. 2 a. case attaché-case m.

attack [ə'tæk] n Mil Med & Fig attaque f; (of fever) accès m; (on s.o.'s life) attentat m; heart a. crise f cardiaque; – vt attaquer; (problem, plan) s'attaquer à; – vi attaquer. ◆—er n agresseur m.

attain [ə'teɪn] vt parvenir à, atteindre, réaliser. ◆—able a accessible. ◆—ment n (of ambition, aim etc) réalisation f (of de); pl (skills) talents mpl.

attempt [ə'tempt] n tentative f; to make an a. to essayer or tenter de; a. on (record) tentative pour battre; a. on s.o.'s life attentat m contre qn; – vt tenter; (task) entreprendre; to a. to do essayer or tenter de faire; attempted murder tentative de meurtre.

attend [ə'tend] vt (match etc) assister à; (course) suivre; (school, church) aller à; (wait on, serve) servir; (escort) accompagner; (patient) soigner; – vi assister; to a. to (pay attention to) prêter attention à;

(take care of) s'occuper de. ◆—ed *a* well-a. *(course)* très suivi; *(meeting)* où il y a du monde. ◆**attendance** *n* présence *f* (at à); *(people)* assistance *f*; **school a.** scolarité *f*; **in a.** de service. ◆**attendant 1** *n* employé, -ée *mf*; *(in museum)* gardien, -ienne *mf*; *pl (of prince, king etc)* suite *f*. **2 a** *(fact)* concomitant.

attention [ə'tenʃ(ə)n] *n* attention *f*; **to pay a.** prêter *or* faire attention (to à); **a.!** *Mil* garde-à-vous!; **to stand at a.** *Mil* être au garde-à-vous; **a. to detail** minutie *f*. ◆**attentive** *a (heedful)* attentif (to à); *(thoughtful)* attentionné (to pour). ◆**attentively** *adv* avec attention, attentivement.

attenuate [ə'tenjueɪt] *vt* atténuer.

attest [ə'test] *vti* **to a. (to)** témoigner de.

attic ['ætɪk] *n* grenier *m*.

attire [ə'taɪər] *n Lit* vêtements *mpl*.

attitude ['ætɪtjuːd] *n* attitude *f*.

attorney [ə'tɜːnɪ] *n (lawyer)* Am avocat *m*; **district a.** Am = procureur *m* (de la République).

attract [ə'trækt] *vt* attirer. ◆**attraction** *n* attraction *f*; *(charm, appeal)* attrait *m*. ◆**attractive** *a (price etc)* intéressant; *(girl)* belle, jolie; *(boy)* beau; *(manners)* attrayant.

attribute 1 ['ætrɪbjuːt] *n (quality)* attribut *m*. **2** [ə'trɪbjuːt] *vt (ascribe)* attribuer (to à). ◆—**able** *a* attribuable (to à).

attrition [ə'trɪʃ(ə)n] *n* **war of a.** guerre *f* d'usure.

attuned [ə'tjuːnd] *a* **a. to** *(of ideas, trends etc)* en accord avec; *(used to)* habitué à.

atypical [eɪ'tɪpɪk(ə)l] *a* peu typique.

aubergine ['əʊbəʒiːn] *n* aubergine *f*.

auburn ['ɔːbən] *a (hair)* châtain roux.

auction ['ɔːkʃən] *n* vente *f* (aux enchères); — *vt* **to a. (off)** vendre (aux enchères). ◆**auctio'neer** *n* commissaire-priseur *m*, adjudicateur, -trice *mf*.

audacious [ɔː'deɪʃəs] *a* audacieux. ◆**audacity** *n* audace *f*.

audib/le ['ɔːdɪb(ə)l] *a* perceptible, audible. ◆—**ly** *adv* distinctement.

audience ['ɔːdɪəns] *n* assistance *f*, public *m*; *(of speaker, musician)* auditoire *m*; *Th Cin* spectateurs *mpl*; *Rad* auditeurs *mpl*; *(interview)* audience *f*.

audio ['ɔːdɪəʊ] *a (cassette, system etc)* audio *inv.* ◆**audiotypist** *n* dactylo *f* au magnétophone, audiotypiste *mf.* ◆**audio-'visual** *a* audio-visuel.

audit ['ɔːdɪt] *vt (accounts)* vérifier; — *n* vérifi-

cation *f* *(des comptes).* ◆**auditor** *n* commissaire *m* aux comptes.

audition [ɔː'dɪʃ(ə)n] *n* audition *f*; — *vti* auditionner.

auditorium [ɔːdɪ'tɔːrɪəm] *n* salle *f (de spectacle, concert etc).*

augment [ɔːg'ment] *vt* augmenter (**with, by** de).

augur ['ɔːgər] *vt* présager; — *vi* **to a. well** être de bon augure.

august [ɔː'gʌst] *a* auguste.

August ['ɔːgəst] *n* août *m*.

aunt [ɑːnt] *n* tante *f*. ◆**auntie** *or* **aunty** *n Fam* tata *f*.

au pair [əʊ'peər] *adv* au pair; — *n* **au p. (girl)** jeune fille *f* au pair.

aura ['ɔːrə] *n* émanation *f*, aura *f*; *(of place)* atmosphère *f*.

auspices ['ɔːspɪsɪz] *npl* auspices *mpl.*

auspicious [ɔː'spɪʃəs] *a* favorable.

austere [ɔː'stɪər] *a* austère. ◆**austerity** *n* austérité *f*.

Australia [ɒ'streɪlɪə] *n* Australie *f.* ◆**Australian** *a & n* australien, -ienne *(mf).*

Austria ['ɒstrɪə] *n* Autriche *f.* ◆**Austrian** *a & n* autrichien, -ienne *(mf).*

authentic [ɔː'θentɪk] *a* authentique. ◆**authenticate** *vt* authentifier. ◆**authen'ticity** *n* authenticité *f.*

author ['ɔːθər] *n* auteur *m.* ◆**authoress** *n* femme *f* auteur. ◆**authorship** *n (of book etc)* paternité *f.*

authority [ɔː'θɒrɪtɪ] *n* autorité *f*; *(permission)* autorisation *f* (**to do** de faire); **to be in a.** *(in charge)* être responsable. ◆**authori'tarian** *a & n* autoritaire *(mf).* ◆**authori'tative** *a (report)* autorisé; *(tone, person)* autoritaire.

authorize ['ɔːθəraɪz] *vt* autoriser (**to do** à faire). ◆**authori'zation** *n* autorisation *f.*

autistic [ɔː'tɪstɪk] *a* autiste, autistique.

autobiography [ɔːtəbaɪ'ɒgrəfɪ] *n* autobiographie *f.*

autocrat ['ɔːtəkræt] *n* autocrate *m.* ◆**auto'cratic** *a* autocratique.

autograph ['ɔːtəgrɑːf] *n* autographe *m*; — *vt* dédicacer (**for** à).

automat ['ɔːtəmæt] *n Am* cafétéria *f* à distributeurs automatiques.

automate ['ɔːtəmeɪt] *vt* automatiser. ◆**auto'mation** *n* automatisation *f*, automation *f.*

automatic [ɔːtə'mætɪk] *a* automatique. ◆**automatically** *adv* automatiquement.

automaton [ɔː'tɒmətən] *n* automate *m.*

automobile [ɔːtəmə'biːl] *n Am* auto(mobile) *f.*

autonomous [ɔː'tɒnəməs] a autonome. ◆**autonomy** n autonomie f.

autopsy ['ɔːtɒpsɪ] n autopsie f.

autumn ['ɔːtəm] n automne m. ◆**autumnal** [ɔː'tʌmnəl] a automnal.

auxiliary [ɔːg'zɪljərɪ] a & n auxiliaire (mf); a. (verbe) (verbe m) auxiliaire m.

avail [ə'veɪl] **1** vt to a. oneself of profiter de, tirer parti de. **2** n to no a. en vain; of no a. inutile.

available [ə'veɪləb(ə)l] a (thing, means etc) disponible; (person) libre, disponible; (valid) valable; a. to all (goal etc) accessible à tous. ◆**availa'bility** n disponibilité f; validité f; accessibilité f.

avalanche ['ævəlɑːnʃ] n avalanche f.

avarice ['ævərɪs] n avarice f. ◆**ava'ricious** a avare.

avenge [ə'vendʒ] vt venger; to a. oneself se venger (on de).

avenue ['ævənjuː] n avenue f; (way to a result) Fig voie f.

average ['ævərɪdʒ] n moyenne f; on a. en moyenne; – a moyen; – vt (do) faire en moyenne; (reach) atteindre la moyenne de; (figures) faire la moyenne de.

averse [ə'vɜːs] a to be a. to doing répugner à faire. ◆**aversion** n (dislike) aversion f, répugnance f.

avert [ə'vɜːt] vt (prevent) éviter; (turn away) détourner (from de).

aviary ['eɪvɪərɪ] n volière f.

aviation [eɪvɪ'eɪʃ(ə)n] n aviation f. ◆**'aviator** n aviateur, -trice mf.

avid ['ævɪd] a avide (for de).

avocado [ævə'kɑːdəʊ] n (pl -os) a. (pear) avocat m.

avoid [ə'vɔɪd] vt éviter; to a. doing éviter de faire. ◆**-able** a évitable. ◆**avoidance** n his a. of (danger etc) son désir m d'éviter; tax a. évasion f fiscale.

avowed [ə'vaʊd] a (enemy) déclaré, avoué.

await [ə'weɪt] vt attendre.

awake [ə'weɪk] vi (pt awoke, pp awoken) s'éveiller; – vt (person, hope etc) éveiller; – a réveillé, éveillé; (wide-)a. éveillé; to keep s.o. a. empêcher qn de dormir, tenir qn éveillé; he's (still) a. il ne dort pas (encore); a. to (conscious of) conscient de. ◆**awaken 1** vti = awake. **2** vt to a. s.o. to sth faire prendre conscience de qch à qn. ◆**awakening** n réveil m.

award [ə'wɔːd] vt (money) attribuer; (prize) décerner, attribuer; (damages) accorder; – n (prize) prix m, récompense f; (scholarship) bourse f.

aware [ə'weər] a avisé, informé; a. of (conscious) conscient de; (informed) au courant de; to become a. of prendre conscience de. ◆**-ness** n conscience f.

awash [ə'wɒʃ] a inondé (with de).

away [ə'weɪ] adv **1** (distant) loin; (far) a. au loin, très loin; **5 km a.** à 5 km (de distance). **2** (absent) parti, absent; a. with you! va-t-en!; to drive a. partir (en voiture); to look a. détourner les yeux; to work/talk/etc a. travailler/parler/etc sans relâche; to fade/melt a. disparaître/fondre complètement. **3** to play a. Sp jouer à l'extérieur.

awe [ɔː] n crainte f (mêlée de respect); to be in a. of s.o. éprouver de la crainte envers qn. ◆**a.-inspiring** a, ◆**awesome** a (impressive) imposant; (frightening) effrayant.

awful ['ɔːfəl] a (terrible) affreux; (terrifying) épouvantable; (ill) malade; an a. lot of Fam un nombre incroyable de; I feel a. (about it) j'ai vraiment honte. ◆**-ly** adv affreusement; (very) Fam terriblement; thanks a. merci infiniment.

awhile [ə'waɪl] adv quelque temps; (to stay, wait) un peu.

awkward ['ɔːkwəd] a **1** (clumsy) maladroit; (age) ingrat. **2** (difficult) difficile; (cumbersome) gênant; (tool) peu commode; (time) inopportun; (silence) gêné. ◆**-ly** adv maladroitement; (speak) d'un ton gêné; (placed) à un endroit difficile. ◆**-ness** n maladresse f; difficulté f; (discomfort) gêne f.

awning ['ɔːnɪŋ] n auvent m; (over shop) store m; (glass canopy) marquise f.

awoke(n) [ə'wəʊk(ən)] see awake.

awry [ə'raɪ] adv to go a. (of plan etc) mal tourner.

axe [æks] (Am **ax**) n hache f; (reduction) Fig coupe f sombre; – vt réduire; (eliminate) supprimer.

axiom ['æksɪəm] n axiome m.

axis, pl **axes** ['æksɪs, 'æksiːz] n axe m.

axle ['æks(ə)l] n essieu m.

ay(e) [aɪ] **1** adv oui. **2** n the ayes (votes) les voix fpl pour.

azalea [ə'zeɪlɪə] n (plant) azalée f.

B

B, b [biː] n B, b m; **2B** (number) 2 ter.
BA abbr = Bachelor of Arts.
babble ['bæb(ə)l] vi (of baby, stream) gazouiller; (mumble) bredouiller; – vt **to b. (out)** bredouiller; – n inv gazouillement m, gazouillis m; (of voices) rumeur f.
babe [beib] n **1** petit(e) enfant mf, bébé m. **2** (girl) Sl pépée f.
baboon [bə'buːn] n babouin m.
baby ['beibi] **1** n bébé m; – a (clothes etc) de bébé. **b. boy** petit garçon m. **b. girl** petite fille f; **b. carriage** Am voiture f d'enfant; **b. sling** kangourou® m, porte-bébé m; **b. tiger/etc** bébé-tigre/etc m; **b. face** visage m poupin. **2** n Sl (girl) pépée f; (girlfriend) copine f. **3** vt Fam dorloter. ◆**b.-batterer** n bourreau m d'enfants. ◆**b.-minder** n gardien, -ienne mf d'enfants. ◆**b.-sit** vi (pt & pp -sat, pres p -sitting) garder les enfants, faire du baby-sitting. ◆**b.-sitter** n baby-sitter mf. ◆**b.-snatching** n rapt m d'enfant. ◆**b.-walker** n trotteur m, youpala® m.
babyish ['beibiɪʃ] a Pej de bébé; (puerile) enfantin.
bachelor ['bætʃələr] n **1** célibataire m; **b. flat** garçonnière f. **2 B. of Arts/of Science** licencié -ée mf ès lettres/ès sciences.
back [bæk] n (of person, animal) dos m; (of chair) dossier m; (of hand) revers m; (of house) derrière m, arrière m; (of room) fond m; (of page) verso m, (of fabric) envers m; Fb arrière m; **at the b. of** (book) à la fin de; (car) à l'arrière de; **at the b. of one's mind** derrière la tête; **b. to front** devant derrière, à l'envers; **to get s.o.'s b. up** Fam irriter qn; **in b. of** Am derrière; – a arrière inv, de derrière; (taxes) arriéré; **b. door** porte f de derrière; **b. room** pièce f du fond; **b. end** (of bus) arrière m; **b. street** rue f écartée; **b. number** vieux numéro m; **b. pay** rappel m de salaire; **b. tooth** molaire f; – adv en arrière; **far b.** loin derrière; **far b. in the past** à une époque reculée; **to stand b.** être en retrait (from par rapport à); **to go b. and forth** aller et venir; **to come b.** revenir; **he's b.** il est de retour, il est rentré ou revenu; **a month b.** il y a un mois; **the trip there and b.** le voyage aller et retour; – vt Com financer; (horse etc) parier sur, jouer;

(car) faire reculer; (wall) renforcer; **to b. s.o (up)** (support) appuyer qn; – vi (move backwards) reculer; **to b. down** se dégonfler; **to b. out** (withdraw) se retirer; Aut sortir en marche arrière; **to b. on to** (of window etc) donner par derrière sur; **to b. up** Aut faire marche arrière. ◆**-ing** n (aid) soutien m; (material) support m, renfort m. ◆**-er** n (supporter) partisan m, Sp parieur, -euse mf; Fin bailleur m de fonds.
backache ['bækeɪk] n mal m aux reins. ◆**back'bencher** n Pol membre m sans portefeuille. ◆**backbiting** n médisance f. ◆**backbreaking** a éreintant. ◆**backcloth** n toile f de fond. ◆**backchat** n impertinence f. ◆**back'date** vt (cheque) antidater. ◆**back'handed** a (compliment) équivoque. ◆**backhander** n revers m; (bribe) Fam pot-de-vin m. ◆**backrest** n dossier m. ◆**backside** n (buttocks) Fam derrière m. ◆**back'stage** adv dans les coulisses. ◆**backstroke** n Sp dos m crawlé. ◆**backtrack** vi rebrousser chemin. ◆**backup** n appui m; (tailback) Am embouteillage m; **b. lights** Aut feux mpl de recul. ◆**backwater** n (place) trou m perdu. ◆**backwoods** npl forêts f vierges. ◆**back'yard** n arrière-cour f; Am jardin m (à l'arrière d'une maison).
backbone ['bækbəʊn] n colonne f vertébrale; (of fish) grande arête f; (main support) pivot m.
backfire [bæk'faɪər] vi Aut pétarader; (of plot etc) Fig échouer.
backgammon ['bækgæmən] n trictrac m.
background ['bækgraʊnd] n fond m, arrière-plan m; (events) Fig antécédents mpl; (education) formation f; (environment) milieu m; (conditions) Pol climat m, contexte m; **to keep s.o. in the b.** tenir qn à l'écart; **b. music** musique f de fond.
backlash ['bæklæʃ] n choc m en retour, retour m de flamme.
backlog ['bæklɒg] n (of work) arriéré m.
backward ['bækwəd] a (glance etc) en arrière; (retarded) arriéré; **b. in doing** lent à faire; – adv = backwards. ◆**-ness** n (of country etc) retard m. ◆**backwards** adv en arrière; (to walk) à reculons; (to fall) à la

renverse; **to move b.** reculer; **to go b. and forwards** aller et venir.

bacon ['beɪkən] *n* lard *m*; (*in rashers*) bacon *m*; **b. and eggs** œufs *mpl* au jambon.

bacteria [bæk'tɪərɪə] *npl* bactéries *fpl*.

bad [bæd] *a* (**worse, worst**) mauvais; (*wicked*) méchant; (*sad*) triste; (*accident, wound etc*) grave; (*tooth*) carié; (*arm, leg*) malade; (*pain*) violent; (*air*) vicié; **b. language** gros mots *mpl*; **it's b. that ...** ce n'est pas bien de penser que ...; **to feel b.** Med se sentir mal; **I feel b. about it** ça m'a chagriné; **things are b.** ça va mal; **she's not b.!** elle n'est pas mal!; **to go** se gâter; (*of milk*) tourner; **in a b. way** mal en point; (*ill*) très mal; (*in trouble*) dans le pétrin; **too b.!** tant pis! ◆**b.-'mannered** *a* mal élevé. ◆**b.-'tempered** *a* grincheux. ◆**badly** *adv* (*hurt*) grièvement; (*affected/shaken*) très touché/bouleversé; **to be b. mistaken** se tromper lourdement; **b. off** dans la gène; **to be b. off for** manquer de; **to want b.** avoir grande envie de.

badge [bædʒ] *n* insigne *m*; (*of postman etc*) plaque *f*; (*bearing slogan or joke*) badge *m*.

badger ['bædʒər] **1** *n* (*animal*) blaireau *m*. **2** *vt* importuner.

badminton ['bædmɪntən] *n* badminton *m*.

baffle ['bæf(ə)l] *vt* (*person*) déconcerter, dérouter.

bag [bæg] **1** *n* sac *m*; *pl* (*luggage*) valises *fpl*, bagages *mpl*; (*under the eyes*) poches *fpl*; **bags of** Fam (*lots of*) beaucoup de; **an old b.** une vieille taupe; **in the b.** Fam dans la poche. **2** *vt* (*-gg-*) (*take, steal*) Fam piquer, s'adjuger; (*animal*) Sp tuer.

baggage ['bægɪdʒ] *n* bagages *mpl*; Mil équipement *m*; **b. car** Am fourgon *m*; **b. room** Am consigne *f*.

baggy ['bægɪ] *a* (*-ier, -iest*) (*clothing*) trop ample; (*trousers*) faisant des poches.

bagpipes ['bægpaɪps] *npl* cornemuse *f*.

Bahamas [bə'hɑːməz] *npl* **the B.** les Bahamas *fpl*.

bail [beɪl] **1** *n* Jur caution *f*; **on b.** en liberté provisoire; — *vt* **to b. (out)** fournir une caution pour; **to b. out** (*ship*) écoper; (*person, company*) Fig tirer d'embarras. **2** *vi* **to b. out** Am Av sauter (en parachute).

bailiff ['beɪlɪf] *n* Jur huissier *m*; (*of landowner*) régisseur *m*.

bait [beɪt] **1** *n* amorce *f*, appât *m*; — *vt* (*fishing hook*) amorcer. **2** *vt* (*annoy*) asticoter, tourmenter.

baize [beɪz] *n* **green b.** (*on card table etc*) tapis *m* vert.

bak/e [beɪk] *vt* (faire) cuire (au four); — *vi* (*of cook*) faire de la pâtisserie *or* du pain; (*of cake etc*) cuire (au four); **we're** *or* **it's baking (hot)** Fam on cuit. ◆**-ed** *a* (*potatoes*) au four; **b. beans** haricots *mpl* blancs (à la tomate). ◆**-ing** *n* cuisson *f*; **b. powder** levure *f* (chimique). ◆**-er** *n* boulanger, -ère *mf*. ◆**bakery** *n* boulangerie *f*.

balaclava [bælə'klɑːvə] *n* **b. (helmet)** passe-montagne *m*.

balance ['bæləns] *n* (*scales*) & Econ Pol Com balance *f*; (*equilibrium*) équilibre *m*; (*of account*) Com solde *m*; (*remainder*) reste *m*; **to strike a b.** trouver le juste milieu; **sense of b.** sens *m* de la mesure; **in the b.** incertain; **on b.** à tout prendre; **b. sheet** bilan *m*; — *vt* tenir *or* mettre en équilibre (**on** sur); (*budget, account*) équilibrer; (*compare*) mettre en balance, peser; **b. (out)** (*compensate for*) compenser; **to b. (oneself)** se tenir en équilibre; — *vi* (*of accounts*) être en équilibre, s'équilibrer.

balcony ['bælkənɪ] *n* balcon *m*.

bald [bɔːld] *a* (**-er, -est**) chauve; (*statement*) brutal; (*tyre*) lisse; **b. patch** *or* **spot** tonsure *f*. ◆**b.-'headed** *a* chauve. ◆**balding** *a* **to be b.** perdre ses cheveux. ◆**baldness** *n* calvitie *f*.

balderdash ['bɔːldədæʃ] *n* balivernes *fpl*.

bale [beɪl] **1** *n* (*of cotton etc*) balle *f*. **2** *vi* **to b. out** Av sauter (en parachute).

baleful ['beɪlfʊl] *a* sinistre, funeste.

balk [bɔːk] *vi* reculer (**at** devant), regimber (**at** contre).

ball [bɔːl] *n* balle *f*; (*inflated*) Fb Rugby etc ballon *m*; Billiards bille *f*; (*of string, wool*) pelote *f*; (*sphere*) boule *f*; (*of meat or fish*) Culin boulette *f*; **on the b.** (*alert*) Fam éveillé; **he's on the b.** (*efficient, knowledgeable*) Fam il connaît son affaire, il est au point; **b. bearing** roulement *m* à billes; **b. game** Am partie *f* de baseball; **it's a whole new b. game** *or* **a different b. game** Am Fig c'est une tout autre affaire. ◆**ballcock** *n* robinet *m* à flotteur. ◆**ballpoint** *n* stylo *m* à bille.

ball² [bɔːl] *n* (*dance*) bal *m*. ◆**ballroom** *n* salle *f* de danse.

ballad ['bæləd] *n* Liter ballade *f*; Mus romance *f*.

ballast ['bæləst] *n* lest *m*; — *vt* lester.

ballet ['bæleɪ] *n* ballet *m*. ◆**balle'rina** *n* ballerine *f*.

ballistic [bə'lɪstɪk] *a* **b. missile** engin *m* balistique.

balloon [bə'luːn] *n* ballon *m*; Met ballon-sonde *m*.

ballot ['bælət] *n* (*voting*) scrutin *m*; **b. (paper)** bulletin *m* de vote; **b. box** urne *f*; – *vt* (*members*) consulter (par un scrutin).

ballyhoo [bælɪ'huː] *n Fam* battage *m* (publicitaire).

balm [bɑːm] *n* (*liquid, comfort*) baume *m*. ◆**balmy** *a* (*-ier, -iest*) **1** (*air*) *Lit* embaumé. **2** (*crazy*) *Fam* dingue, timbré.

baloney [bə'ləʊnɪ] *n Sl* foutaises *fpl*.

Baltic ['bɔːltɪk] *n* the **B.** la Baltique.

balustrade ['bæləstreɪd] *n* balustrade *f*.

bamboo [bæm'buː] *n* bambou *m*.

bamboozle [bæm'buːz(ə)l] *vt* (*cheat*) *Fam* embobiner.

ban [bæn] *n* interdiction *f*; – *vt* (*-nn-*) interdire; **to b. from** (*club etc*) exclure de; **to ban s.o. from doing** interdire à qn de faire.

banal [bə'nɑːl, *Am* 'beɪn(ə)l] *a* banal. ◆**ba'nality** *n* banalité *f*.

banana [bə'nɑːmə] *n* banane *f*.

band [bænd] *n* **1** (*strip*) bande *f*; (*of hat*) ruban *m*; **rubber** *or* **elastic b.** élastique *m*. **2** (*group*) bande *f*; *Mus* (*petit*) orchestre *m*; *Mil* fanfare *f*; – *vi* **to b. together** former une bande, se grouper. ◆**bandstand** *n* kiosque *m* à musique. ◆**bandwagon** *n* **to jump on the B.** *Fig* suivre le mouvement.

bandage ['bændɪdʒ] *n* (*strip*) bande *f*; (*for wound*) pansement *m*; (*for holding in place*) bandage *m*; – *vt* **to b. (up)** (*arm, leg*) bander; (*wound*) mettre un pansement sur.

Band-Aid® ['bændeɪd] *n* pansement *m* adhésif.

bandit ['bændɪt] *n* bandit *m*. ◆**banditry** *n* banditisme *m*.

bandy ['bændɪ] **1** *a* (*-ier, -iest*) (*person*) bancal; (*legs*) arqué. ◆**b.-'legged** *a* bancal. **2** *vt* **to b. about** (*story etc*) faire circuler, propager.

bane [beɪn] *n Lit* fléau *m*. ◆**baneful** *a* funeste.

bang [bæŋ] **1** *n* (*hit, noise*) coup *m* (violent); (*of gun etc*) détonation *f*; (*of door*) claquement *m*; – *vt* cogner, frapper; (*door*) (faire) claquer; **to b. one's head** se cogner la tête; – *vi* cogner, frapper; (*of door*) claquer; (*of gun*) détoner; (*of firework*) éclater; **to b. down** (*lid*) rabattre (violemment); **to b. into sth** heurter qch; – *int* vlan!, pan!; **to go (off) b.** éclater. **2** *adv* (*exactly*) *Fam* exactement; **b. in the middle** en plein milieu; **b. on six** à six heures tapantes.

banger ['bæŋər] *n* **1** *Culin Fam* saucisse *f*. **2** (*firecracker*) pétard *m*. **3** old **b.** (*car*) *Fam* tacot *m*, guimbarde *f*.

bangle ['bæŋg(ə)l] *n* bracelet *m* (rigide).

bangs [bæŋz] *npl* (*of hair*) *Am* frange *f*.

banish ['bænɪʃ] *vt* bannir.

banister ['bænɪstər] *n* banister(s) rampe *f* (d'escalier).

banjo ['bændʒəʊ] *n* (*pl* -*os or* -*oes*) banjo *m*.

bank [bæŋk] **1** *n* (*of river*) bord *m*, rive *f*; (*raised*) berge *f*; (*of earth*) talus *m*; (*of sand*) banc *m*; **the Left B.** (*in Paris*) la Rive gauche; – *vt* **to b. (up)** (*earth etc*) amonceler; (*fire*) couvrir. **2** *n Com* banque *f*; **b. account** compte *m* en banque; **b. card** carte *f* d'identité bancaire; **b. holiday** jour *m* férié; **b. note** billet *m* de banque; **b. rate** taux *m* d'escompte; – *vt* (*money*) mettre en banque; – *vi* avoir un compte en banque (**with à**). **3** *vi Av* virer. **4** *vi* **to b. on s.o./sth** (*rely on*) compter sur qn/qch. ◆—**ing** *a* bancaire; – *n* (*activity, profession*) la banque. ◆—**er** *n* banquier *m*.

bankrupt ['bæŋkrʌpt] *a* **to go b.** faire faillite; **b. of** (*ideas*) *Fig* dénué de; – *vt* mettre en faillite. ◆**bankruptcy** *n* faillite *f*.

banner ['bænər] *n* (*at rallies etc*) banderole *f*; (*flag*) *and Fig* bannière *f*.

banns [bænz] *npl* bans *mpl*.

banquet ['bæŋkwɪt] *n* banquet *m*.

banter ['bæntər] *vti* plaisanter; – *n* plaisanterie *f*. ◆—**ing** *a* (*smile, air*) plaisantin.

baptism ['bæptɪzəm] *n* baptême *m*. ◆**baptize** *vt* baptiser.

bar [bɑːr] **1** *n* barre *f*; (*of chocolate*) tablette *f*; (*on window*) *& Jur* barreau *m*; **b. of soap** savonnette *f*; **behind bars** *Jur* sous les verrous; **to be a b. to** *Fig* faire obstacle à. **2** *n* (*pub*) bar *m*; (*counter*) comptoir *m*. **3** *n* (*group of notes*) *Mus* mesure *f*. **4** *vt* (*-rr-*) (*way etc*) bloquer, barrer; (*window*) griller. **5** *vt* (*prohibit*) interdire (**s.o. from doing** à qn de faire); (*exclude*) exclure (**from à**). **6** *prep* sauf. ◆**barmaid** *n* serveuse *f* de bar. ◆**barman** *n*, ◆**bartender** *n* barman *m*.

Barbados [bɑː'beɪdɒs] *n* Barbade *f*.

barbarian [bɑː'beərɪən] *n* barbare *mf*. ◆**barbaric** *a* barbare. ◆**barbarity** *n* barbarie *f*.

barbecue ['bɑːbɪkjuː] *n* barbecue *m*; – *vt* griller (au barbecue).

barbed [bɑːbd] *a* **b. wire** fil *m* de fer barbelé; (*fence*) barbelés *mpl*.

barber ['bɑːbər] *n* coiffeur *m* (*pour hommes*).

barbiturate [bɑː'bɪtjʊrət] *n* barbiturique *m*.

bare [beər] *a* (*-er, -est*) nu; (*tree, hill etc*) dénudé; (*cupboard*) vide; (*mere*) simple; **the b. necessities** le strict nécessaire; **with his b. hands** à mains nues; – *vt* mettre à nu.

◆—**ness** n (*of person*) nudité f.
◆**bareback** adv **to ride b.** monter à cru.
◆**barefaced** a (*lie*) éhonté. ◆**barefoot**
adv nu-pieds; – a aux pieds nus. ◆**bare-**
'**headed** a & adv nu-tête inv.

barely ['beəlı] adv (*scarcely*) à peine, tout
juste.

bargain ['bɑːgɪn] n (*deal*) marché m, affaire
f; **a (good) b.** (*cheap buy*) une occasion, une
bonne affaire; **it's a b.!** (*agreed*) c'est
entendu!; **into the b.** par-dessus le marché;
b. price prix m exceptionnel; **b. counter**
rayon m des soldes; – vi (*negotiate*)
négocier; (*haggle*) marchander; **to b. for** or
on sth Fig s'attendre à qch. ◆—**ing** n
négociations fpl; marchandage m.

barge [bɑːdʒ] **1** n chaland m, péniche f. **2** vi
to b. in (*enter a room*) faire irruption;
(*interrupt*) interrompre; **to b. into** (*hit*) se
cogner contre.

baritone ['bærɪtəʊn] n (*voice, singer*)
baryton m.

bark [bɑːk] **1** n (*of tree*) écorce f. **2** vi (*of dog
etc*) aboyer; – n aboiement f. ◆—**ing** n
aboiements mpl.

barley ['bɑːlɪ] n orge f; **b. sugar** sucre m
d'orge.

barmy ['bɑːmɪ] a (*-ier, -iest*) Fam dingue,
timbré.

barn [bɑːn] n (*for crops etc*) grange f; (*for
horses*) écurie f; (*for cattle*) étable f.
◆**barnyard** n basse-cour f.

barometer [bə'rɒmɪtər] n baromètre m.

baron ['bærən] n baron m; (*industrialist*) Fig
magnat m. ◆**baroness** n baronne f.

baroque [bə'rɒk, Am bə'rəʊk] a & n Archit
Mus etc baroque (m).

barracks ['bærəks] npl caserne f.

barrage ['bærɑːʒ, Am bə'rɑːʒ] n (*barrier*)
barrage m; **a b. of** (*questions etc*) un feu
roulant de.

barrel ['bærəl] n **1** (*cask*) tonneau m; (*of oil*)
baril m. **2** (*of gun*) canon m. **3 b. organ**
orgue m de Barbarie.

barren ['bærən] a stérile; (*style*) Fig aride.

barrette [bə'ret] n (*hair slide*) Am barrette f.

barricade [bærɪ'keɪd] n barricade f; – vt
barricader; **to b. oneself (in)** se barricader.

barrier ['bærɪər] n barrière f; Fig obstacle m,
barrière f; (*ticket*) b. Rail portillon m;
sound b. mur m du son.

barring ['bɑːrɪŋ] prep sauf, excepté.

barrister ['bærɪstər] n avocat m.

barrow ['bærəʊ] n charrette f or voiture f à
bras; (*wheelbarrow*) brouette f.

barter ['bɑːtər] vt troquer, échanger (**for**
contre); – n troc m, échange m.

base [beɪs] **1** n (*bottom, main ingredient*)
base f; (*of tree, lamp*) pied m. **2** n Mil base f.
3 vt baser, fonder (**on** sur); **based in** or **on
London** basé à Londres. **4** a (*dishonourable*)
bas, ignoble; (*metal*) vil. ◆—**less** a sans
fondement. ◆—**ness** n bassesse f.
◆**baseball** n base-ball m. ◆**baseboard**
n Am plinthe f.

basement ['beɪsmənt] n sous-sol m.

bash [bæʃ] n Fam (*bang*) coup m; **to have a
b.** (*try*) essayer un coup; – vt (*hit*) Fam
cogner; **to b. (about)** (*ill-treat*) malmener;
to b. s.o. up tabasser qn; **to b. in** or **down**
(*door etc*) défoncer. ◆—**ing** n (*thrashing*)
Fam raclée f.

bashful ['bæʃfəl] a timide.

basic ['beɪsɪk] a fondamental; (*pay etc*) de
base; – n **the basics** l'essentiel m.
◆—**ally** [-klɪ] adv au fond.

basil ['bæzɪ(ə)l] n Bot Culin basilic m.

basilica [bə'zɪlɪkə] n basilique f.

basin ['beɪs(ə)n] n bassin m, bassine f (*for
soup, food*) bol m; (*of river*) bassin m;
(*portable washbasin*) cuvette f; (*sink*)
lavabo m.

basis, pl **-ses** ['beɪsɪs, -siːz] n base f; **on the
b. of** d'après; **on that b.** dans ces conditions; **on a weekly/etc basis** chaque
semaine/etc.

bask [bɑːsk] vi se chauffer.

basket ['bɑːskɪt] n panier m; (*for bread,
laundry, litter*) corbeille f. ◆**basketball** n
basket(-ball) m.

Basque [bæsk] a & n basque (mf).

bass¹ [beɪs] n Mus basse f; – a (*note, voice*)
bas.

bass² [bæs] n (*sea fish*) bar m; (*fresh-water*)
perche f.

bassinet [bæsɪ'net] n (*cradle*) Am couffin m.

bastard ['bɑːstəd] **1** n & a bâtard, -arde
(mf). **2** n Pej Sl salaud m, salope f.

baste [beɪst] vt **1** (*fabric*) bâtir. **2** Culin
arroser.

bastion ['bæstɪən] n bastion m.

bat [bæt] **1** n (*animal*) chauve-souris f. **2** n
Cricket batte f; Table Tennis raquette f; **off
my own b.** de ma propre initiative; – vt
(*-tt-*) (*ball*) frapper. **3** vt **she didn't b. an
eyelid** elle n'a pas sourcillé.

batch [bætʃ] n (*of people*) groupe m; (*of
letters*) paquet m; (*of books*) lot m; (*of
loaves*) fournée f; (*of papers*) liasse f.

bated ['beɪtɪd] a **with b. breath** en retenant
son souffle.

bath [bɑːθ] n (pl **-s** [bɑːðz]) bain m; (*tub*)
baignoire f; **swimming baths** piscine f; – vt
baigner; – vi prendre un bain.

◆**bathrobe** n peignoir m (de bain); Am robe f de chambre. ◆**bathroom** n salle f de bain(s); (toilet) Am toilettes fpl. ◆**bathtub** n baignoire f.

bath/e ['beɪð] vt baigner; (wound) laver; – vi se baigner; Am prendre un bain; – n bain m (de mer), baignade f. ◆**–ing** n baignade(s) f(pl); **b. costume** or **suit** maillot m de bain.

baton ['bætən, Am bə'tɒn] n Mus Mil bâton m; (truncheon) matraque f.

battalion [bə'tæljən] n bataillon m.

batter ['bætər] **1** n pâte f à frire. **2** vt battre, frapper; (baby) martyriser; (town) to **b. down** (door) défoncer. ◆**–ed** a (car, hat) cabossé; (house) délabré; (face) meurtri; (wife) battu. ◆**–ing** n to take a b. Fig souffrir beaucoup.

battery ['bætərɪ] n Mil Aut Agr batterie f; (in radio etc) pile f.

battle ['bæt(ə)l] n bataille f; (struggle) lutte f; that's half the b. Fam c'est ça le secret de la victoire; **b. dress** tenue f de campagne; – vi se battre, lutter. ◆**battlefield** n champ m de bataille. ◆**battleship** n cuirassé m.

battlements ['bæt(ə)lmənts] npl (indentations) créneaux mpl; (wall) remparts mpl.

batty ['bætɪ] a (-ier, -iest) Sl dingue, toqué.

baulk [bɔːk] vi reculer (at devant), regimber (at contre).

bawdy ['bɔːdɪ] a (-ier, -iest) paillard, grossier.

bawl [bɔːl] vti to **b. (out)** beugler, brailler; to **b. s.o. out** Am Sl engueuler qn.

bay [beɪ] **1** n Geog Archit baie f. **2** n Bot laurier m. **3** n (for loading etc) aire f. **4** n (of dog) aboiement m; at **b.** aux abois; to **hold at b.** tenir à distance; – vi aboyer. **5** a (horse) bai.

bayonet ['beɪənɪt] n baïonnette f.

bazaar [bə'zɑːr] n (market, shop) bazar m; (charity sale) vente f de charité.

bazooka [bə'zuːkə] n bazooka m.

BC [biː'siː] abbr (before Christ) avant Jésus-Christ.

be [biː] vi (pres t **am, are, is;** pt **was, were;** pp **been;** pres p **being**) **1** être; **it is green/small** c'est vert/petit; **she's a doctor** elle est médecin; **he's an Englishman** c'est un Anglais; **it's 3 (o'clock)** il est trois heures; **it's the sixth of May** c'est or nous sommes le six mai. **2** avoir; to **be hot/right/lucky** avoir chaud/raison/de la chance; **my feet are cold** j'ai froid aux pieds; **he's 20** (age) il a 20 ans; to **be 2 metres high** avoir 2 mètres de haut; to **be 6 feet tall** mesurer 1,80 m. **3** (health) aller; **how are you?** comment vas-tu? **4** (place, situation) se trouver, être; **she's in York** elle se trouve or elle est à York. **5** (exist) être; **the best painter there is** le meilleur peintre qui soit; **leave me be** laissez-moi (tranquille); **that may be** cela se peut. **6** (go, come) **I've been to see her** je suis allé or j'ai été la voir; **he's (already) been** il est (déjà) venu. **7** (weather) & Math faire; **it's fine** il fait beau; **2 and 2 are 4** 2 et 2 font 4. **8** (cost) coûter, faire; **it's 20 pence** ça coûte 20 pence; **how much is it?** ça fait combien?, c'est combien? **9** (auxiliary) **I am/was doing** je fais/faisais; **I'm listening to the radio** (in the process of) je suis en train d'écouter la radio; **she's been there some time** elle est là depuis longtemps; **he was killed** il a été tué, on l'a tué; **I've been waiting (for)** two hours j'attends depuis deux heures; **it is said** on dit; **to be pitied** à plaindre; **isn't it?, aren't you?** etc n'est-ce pas?, non? **I am!, he is!** etc oui! **10** (+ inf) **he is to come** (must) il doit venir; **he's shortly to go** (intends to) il va bientôt partir. **11** there is or are il y a; (pointing) voilà; **here is** or **are** voici.

beach [biːtʃ] n plage f. ◆**beachcomber** n (person) ramasseur, -euse mf d'épaves.

beacon ['biːkən] n Nau Av balise f; (lighthouse) phare m.

bead [biːd] n (small sphere, drop of liquid) perle f; (of rosary) grain m; (of sweat) goutte f; (string of) **beads** collier m.

beak [biːk] n bec m.

beaker ['biːkər] n gobelet m.

beam [biːm] **1** n (of wood) poutre f. **2** n (of light) rayon m; (of headlight, torch) faisceau m (lumineux); – vi rayonner; (of person) Fig sourire largement. **3** vt Rad diffuser. ◆**–ing** a (radiant) radieux.

bean [biːn] n haricot m; (of coffee) grain m; (broad) b. fève f; to **be full of beans** Fam déborder d'entrain. ◆**beanshoots** npl, ◆**beansprouts** npl germes mpl de soja.

bear¹ [beər] n (animal) ours m.

bear² [beər] vt (pt **bore,** pp **borne**) (carry, show) porter; (endure) supporter; (resemblance) offrir; (comparison) soutenir; (responsibility) assumer; (child) donner naissance à; to **b. in mind** tenir compte de; to **b. out** corroborer; – vi to **b. left/etc** (turn) tourner à gauche/etc; to **b. north/etc** (go) aller en direction du nord/etc; to **b. (up)on** (relate to) se rapporter à; to **b. heavily on** (of burden) Fig peser sur; to **b. with** être indulgent envers, être patient avec; to **bring to b.** (one's energies) consacrer (on à);

(*pressure*) exercer (**on** sur); **to b. up** ne pas se décourager, tenir le coup; **b. up!** du courage! ◆**—ing** *n* (*posture, conduct*) maintien *m*; (*relationship, relevance*) relation *f* (**on** avec); *Nau Av* position *f*; **to get one's bearings** s'orienter. ◆**—able** *a* supportable. ◆**—er** *n* porteur, -euse *mf*.

beard [biəd] *n* barbe *f.* ◆**bearded** *a* barbu.

beast [biːst] *n* bête *f*, animal *m*; (*person*) *Pej* brute *f.* ◆**beastly** *a Fam* (*bad*) vilain, infect; (*spiteful*) méchant; *– adv Fam* terriblement.

beat [biːt] *n* (*of heart, drum*) battement *m*; (*of policeman*) ronde *f*; *Mus* mesure *f*, rythme *m*; *– vt* (*pt* **beat**, *pp* **beaten**) battre; (*defeat*) vaincre, battre; **to b. a drum** battre du tambour; **that beats me** ça me dépasse; **to b. s.o. to it** devancer qn; **b. it!** *Sl* fichez le camp!; **to b. back** *or* **off** repousser; **to b. down** (*price*) faire baisser; **to b. in** *or* **down** (*door*) défoncer; **to b. out** (*rhythm*) marquer; (*tune*) jouer; **to b. s.o. up** tabasser qn; *– vi* battre; (*at door*) frapper (**at** à); **to b. about** *or* **around the bush** *Fam* tourner autour du pot; **to b. down** (*of rain*) tomber à verse; (*of sun*) taper. ◆**—ing** *n* (*blows, defeat*) raclée *f.* ◆**—er** *n* (*for eggs*) batteur *m.*

beauty ['bjuːti] *n* (*quality, woman*) beauté *f*; **it's a b.!** c'est une merveille!; **the b. of it is ...** le plus beau, c'est que ...; **b. parlour** institut *m* de beauté; **b. spot** (*on skin*) grain *m* de beauté; (*in countryside*) site *m* pittoresque. ◆**beau'tician** *n* esthéticienne *f.* ◆**beautiful** *a* (très) beau; (*superb*) merveilleux. ◆**beautifully** *adv* merveilleusement.

beaver ['biːvər] *n* castor *m*; *– vi* **to b. away** travailler dur (**at** sth à qch).

because [bi'kɒz] *conj* parce que; **b. of** à cause de.

beck [bek] *n* **at s.o.'s b. and call** aux ordres de qn.

beckon ['bekən] *vti* **to b. (to) s.o.** faire signe à qn (**to do** de faire).

becom/e [bi'kʌm] **1** *vi* (*pt* **became**, *pp* **become**) devenir; **to b. a painter** devenir peintre; **to b. thin** maigrir; **to b. worried** commencer à s'inquiéter; **what has b. of her?** qu'est-elle devenue? **2** *vt* **that hat becomes her** ce chapeau lui sied *or* lui va. ◆**—ing** *a* (*clothes*) seyant; (*modesty*) bienséant.

bed [bed] *n* lit *m*; *Geol* couche *f*; (*of vegetables*) carré *m*; (*of sea*) fond *m*; (*flower bed*) parterre *m*; **to go to b.** (aller) se coucher; **in b.** couché; **to get out of b.** se lever; **b. and**

breakfast (*in hotel etc*) chambre *f* avec petit déjeuner; **b. settee** (*canapé m*) convertible *m*; **air b.** matelas *m* pneumatique; *– vt* (**-dd-**) **to b. (out)** (*plant*) repiquer; *– vi* **to b. down** se coucher. ◆**bedding** *n* literie *f.* ◆**bedbug** *n* punaise *f.* ◆**bedclothes** *npl* couvertures *fpl* et draps *mpl.* ◆**bedridden** *a* alité. ◆**bedroom** *n* chambre *f* à coucher. ◆**bedside** *n* chevet *m*; *– a* (*lamp, book, table*) de chevet. ◆**bed'sitter** *n*, *Fam* ◆**bedsit** *n* chambre *f* meublée. ◆**bedspread** *n* dessus-de-lit *m inv.* ◆**bedtime** *n* heure *f* du coucher.

bedeck [bi'dek] *vt* orner (**with** de).

bedevil [bi'dev(ə)l] *vt* (**-ll-**, *Am* **-l-**) (*plague*) tourmenter; (*confuse*) embrouiller; **bedevilled by** (*problems etc*) perturbé par, empoisonné par.

bedlam ['bedləm] *n* (*noise*) *Fam* chahut *m.*

bedraggled [bi'dræg(ə)ld] *a* (*clothes, person*) débraillé.

bee [biː] *n* abeille *f.* ◆**beehive** *n* ruche *f.* ◆**beekeeping** *n* apiculture *f.* ◆**beeline** *n* **to make a b.** for aller droit vers.

beech [biːtʃ] *n* (*tree, wood*) hêtre *m.*

beef [biːf] **1** *n* bœuf *m.* **2** *vi* (*complain*) *Sl* rouspéter. ◆**beefburger** *n* hamburger *m.* ◆**beefy** *a* (**-ier, -iest**) *Fam* musclé, costaud.

beer [biər] *n* bière *f*; **b. glass** chope *f.* ◆**beery** *a* (*room, person*) qui sent la bière.

beet [biːt] *n* betterave *f* (à sucre); *Am* = **beetroot.** ◆**beetroot** *n* betterave *f* (potagère).

beetle [biːt(ə)l] **1** *n* cafard *m*, scarabée *m.* **2** *vi* **to b. off** *Fam* se sauver.

befall [bi'fɔːl] *vt* (*pt* **befell**, *pp* **befallen**) arriver à.

befit [bi'fit] *vt* (**-tt-**) convenir à.

before [bi'fɔːr] *adv* avant; (*already*) déjà; (*in front*) devant; **the month b.** le mois d'avant *or* précédent; **the day b.** la veille; **I've never done it b.** je ne l'ai jamais (encore) fait; *– prep* (*time*) avant; (*place*) devant; **the year b. last** il y a deux ans; *– conj* avant que (+ ne + *sub*), avant de (+ *inf*); **b. he goes** avant qu'il (ne) parte; **b. going** avant de partir. ◆**beforehand** *adv* à l'avance, avant.

befriend [bi'frend] *vt* offrir son amitié à, aider.

befuddled [bi'fʌd(ə)ld] *a* (*drunk*) ivre.

beg [beg] *vt* (**-gg-**) **to b. (for)** solliciter, demander; (*bread, money*) mendier; **to b. s.o. to do** prier *or* supplier qn de faire; **I b. to** je me permets de; **to b. the question** esquiver la question; *– vi* mendier;

(*entreat*) supplier; **to go begging** (*of food, articles*) ne pas trouver d'amateurs. ◆**beggar** *n* mendiant, -ante *mf*; (*person*) **SI** individu *m*; **lucky b.** veinard, -arde *mf*. ◆**beggarly** *a* misérable.

beget [br'get] *vt* (*pt* **begot**, *pp* **begotten**, *pres p* **begetting**) engendrer.

begin [br'gin] *vt* (*pt* **began**, *pp* **begun**, *pres p* **beginning**) commencer; (*fashion, campaign*) lancer; (*bottle, sandwich*) entamer; (*conversation*) engager; **to b. doing** *or* **to do** commencer *or* se mettre à faire; – *vi* commencer (**with** par, **by doing** par faire); **to b. on sth** commencer qch; **beginning from** à partir de; **to b. with** (*first*) d'abord. ◆—**ning** *n* commencement *m*, début *m*. ◆—**ner** *n* débutant, -ante *mf*.

begrudge [br'grʌdʒ] *vt* (*give unwillingly*) donner à contrecœur; (*envy*) envier (**s.o. sth** qch à qn); (*reproach*) reprocher (**s.o. sth** qch à qn); **to b. doing** faire à contrecœur.

behalf [br'hɑːf] *n* **on b. of** pour, au nom de, de la part de; (*in the interest of*) en faveur de, pour.

behave [br'heɪv] *vi* se conduire; (*of machine*) fonctionner; **to b. (oneself)** se tenir bien; (*of child*) être sage. ◆**behaviour** *n* conduite *f*, comportement *m*; **to be on one's best b.** se conduire de son mieux.

behead [br'hed] *vt* décapiter.

behest [br'hest] *n Lit* ordre *m*.

behind [br'haɪnd] **1** *prep* derrière; (*more backward than, late according to*) en retard sur; – *adv* derrière; (*late*) en retard (**with**, in dans). **2** *n* (*buttocks*) *Fam* derrière *m*. ◆**behindhand** *adv* en retard.

beholden [br'həʊldən] *a* redevable (**to** à, **for** de).

beige [beɪʒ] *a & n* beige (*m*).

being [biːɪŋ] *n* (*person, life*) être *m*; **to come into b.** naître, être créé.

belated [br'leɪtɪd] *a* tardif.

belch [beltʃ] **1** *vi* (*of person*) faire un renvoi, éructer; – *n* renvoi *m*. **2** *vt* **to b.** (**out**) (*smoke*) vomir.

beleaguered [br'liːgəd] *a* (*besieged*) assiégé.

belfry ['belfrɪ] *n* beffroi *m*, clocher *m*.

Belgium ['beldʒəm] *n* Belgique *f*. ◆**Belgian** ['beldʒən] *a & n* belge (*mf*).

belie [br'laɪ] *vt* démentir.

belief [br'liːf] *n* (*believing, thing believed*) croyance *f* (**in s.o.** en qn, **in sth** à *or* en qch); (*trust*) confiance *f*, foi *f*; (*faith*) *Rel* foi *f* (in en).

believ/e [br'liːv] *vti* croire (**in sth** à qch, **in God/s.o.** en Dieu/qn); **I b. so** je crois que oui; **I b. I'm right** je crois avoir raison, to **b.**

in doing croire qu'il faut faire; **he doesn't b. in smoking** il désapprouve que l'on fume. ◆—**able** *a* croyable. ◆—**er** *n* croyant, -ante *mf*; **b. in** (*supporter*) partisan, -ane *mf* de.

belittle [br'lɪt(ə)l] *vt* déprécier.

bell [bel] *n* cloche *f*; (*small*) clochette *f*; (*in phone*) sonnerie *f*; (*on door, bicycle*) sonnette *f*; (*on dog*) grelot *m*. ◆**bellboy**, ◆**bellhop** *n Am* groom *m*.

belle [bel] *n* (*woman*) beauté *f*, belle *f*.

belligerent [br'lɪdʒərənt] *a & n* belligérant, -ante (*mf*).

bellow ['beləʊ] *vi* beugler, mugir.

bellows ['beləʊz] *npl* (*pair of*) b. soufflet *m*.

belly ['belɪ] *n* ventre *m*; **b. button SI** nombril *m*. ◆**bellyache** *n* mal *m* au ventre; – *vi* rouspéter. ◆**bellyful** *n* **to have a b.** *SI* en avoir plein le dos.

belong [br'lɒŋ] *vi* appartenir (**to** à); **to b. to** (*club*) être membre de; **the cup belongs here** la tasse se range ici. ◆—**ings** *npl* affaires *fpl*.

beloved [br'lʌvɪd] *a & n* bien-aimé, -ée (*mf*).

below [br'ləʊ] *prep* (*lower than*) au-dessous de; (*under*) sous, au-dessous de; (*unworthy of*) *Fig* indigne de; – *adv* en dessous; **see b.** (*in book etc*) voir ci-dessous.

belt [belt] **1** *n* ceinture *f*; (*area*) zone *f*, région *f*; *Tech* courroie *f*. **2** *vt* (*hit*) *SI* rosser. **3** *vi* **to b.** (**along**) (*rush*) *SI* filer à toute allure; **b. up!** (*shut up*) *SI* boucle-la!

bemoan [br'məʊn] *vt* déplorer.

bench [bentʃ] *n* (*seat*) banc *m*; (*work table*) établi *m*, banc *m*; **the B.** *Jur* la magistrature (*assise*); (*court*) le tribunal.

bend [bend] *n* courbe *f*; (*in river, pipe*) coude *m*; (*in road*) *Aut* virage *m*; (*of arm, knee*) pli *m*; **round the b.** (*mad*) *SI* tordu; – *vt* (*pt & pp* **bent**) courber; (*leg, arm*) plier; (*direct*) diriger; **to b. the rules** faire une entorse au règlement; – *vi* (*of branch*) plier, être courbé; (*of road*) tourner; **to b.** (**down**) se courber; **to b.** (**over** *or* **forward**) se pencher; **to b. to** (*s.o.'s will*) se soumettre à.

beneath [br'niːθ] *prep* au-dessous de, sous; (*unworthy of*) indigne de; – *adv* (au-)dessous.

benediction [benr'dɪkʃ(ə)n] *n* bénédiction *f*.

benefactor ['benɪfæktər] *n* bienfaiteur *m*. ◆**benefactress** *n* bienfaitrice *f*.

beneficial [benr'fɪʃəl] *a* bénéfique.

beneficiary [benr'fɪʃərɪ] *n* bénéficiaire *mf*.

benefit ['benɪfɪt] *n* (*advantage*) avantage *m*; (*money*) allocation *f*; *pl* (*of science, education etc*) bienfaits *mpl*; **to s.o.'s b.** dans l'intérêt de qn; **for your (own) b.** pour vous, pour votre bien; **to be of b.** faire du bien (**to** à); **to give s.o. the b. of the doubt** accorder à qn le bénéfice du doute; **b. concert**/*etc* concert/*etc* de bienfaisance; – *vt* faire du bien à; (*be useful to*) profiter à; – *vi* gagner (**from doing** à faire); **you'll b. from** *or* **by the rest** le repos vous fera du bien.

Benelux ['benɪlʌks] *n* Bénélux *m*.

benevolent [bɪ'nevələnt] *a* bienveillant.
◆**benevolence** *n* bienveillance *f*.

benign [bɪ'naɪn] *a* bienveillant, bénin; (*climate*) doux; (*tumour*) bénin.

bent [bent] **1** *a* (*nail, mind*) tordu; (*dishonest*) *Sl* corrompu; **b. on doing** résolu à faire. **2** *n* (*talent*) aptitude *f* (**for** pour); (*inclination, liking*) penchant *m*, goût *m* (**for** pour).

bequeath [bɪ'kwiːð] *vt* léguer (**to** à).
◆**bequest** *n* legs *m*.

bereaved [bɪ'riːvd] *a* endeuillé; – *n* **the b.** la famille, la femme *etc* du disparu.
◆**bereavement** *n* deuil *m*.

bereft [bɪ'reft] *a* **b. of** dénué de.

beret ['bereɪ, *Am* bə'reɪ] *n* béret *m*.

berk [bɜːk] *n* *Sl* imbécile *mf*.

Bermuda [bə'mjuːdə] *n* Bermudes *fpl*.

berry ['berɪ] *n* baie *f*.

berserk [bə'zɜːk] *a* **to go b.** devenir fou, se déchaîner.

berth [bɜːθ] *n* (*in ship, train*) couchette *f*; (*anchorage*) mouillage *m*; – *vi* (*of ship*) mouiller.

beseech [bɪ'siːtʃ] *vt* (*pt & pp* besought *or* beseeched) *Lit* implorer (**to do** de faire).

beset [bɪ'set] *vt* (*pt & pp* beset, *pres p* besetting) assaillir (*qn*); **b. with obstacles**/*etc* semé *or* hérissé d'obstacles/*etc*.

beside [bɪ'saɪd] *prep* à côté de; **that's b. the point** ça n'a rien à voir; **b. oneself** (*angry, excited*) hors de soi.

besides [bɪ'saɪdz] *prep* (*in addition to*) en plus de; (*except*) excepté; **there are ten of us b.** Paul nous sommes dix sans compter Paul; – *adv* (*in addition*) de plus; (*moreover*) d'ailleurs.

besiege [bɪ'siːdʒ] *vt* (*of soldiers, crowd*) assiéger; (*annoy*) *Fig* assaillir (**with** de).

besotted [bɪ'sɒtɪd] *a* (*drunk*) abruti; **b. with** (*infatuated*) entiché de.

bespatter [bɪ'spætər] *vt* éclabousser (**with** de).

bespectacled [bɪ'spektɪk(ə)ld] *a* à lunettes.

bespoke [bɪ'spəʊk] *a* (*tailor*) à façon.

best [best] *a* meilleur; **the b. page in the book** la meilleure page du livre; **the b. part of** (*most*) la plus grande partie de; **the b. thing is to** le mieux; **b. man** (*at wedding*) témoin *m*, garçon *m* d'honneur; – *n* **the b.** (one) le

meilleur, la meilleure; **it's for the b.** c'est pour le mieux; **at b.** au mieux; **to do one's b.** faire de son mieux; **to look one's b., be at one's b.** être à son avantage; **to the b. of my knowledge** autant que je sache; **to make the b. of** (*accept*) s'accommoder de; **to get the b. of it** avoir le dessus; **in one's Sunday b.** endimanché; **all the b.!** portez-vous bien!; (*in letter*) amicalement; – *adv* (**the**) **b.** (*to play etc*) le mieux; **the b. loved** le plus aimé; **to think it b.** to juger prudent de.
◆**b.-'seller** *n* (*book*) best-seller *m*.

bestow [bɪ'stəʊ] *vt* accorder, conférer (**on** à).

bet [bet] *n* pari *m*; – *vti* (*pt & pp* bet *or* betted, *pres p* betting) parier (**on** sur, **that** que); **you b.!** *Fam* (*of course*) tu parles!
◆**betting** *n* pari(s) *m*(*pl*); **b. shop** *or* **office** bureau *m* du pari mutuel.

betoken [bɪ'təʊkən] *vt* *Lit* annoncer.

betray [bɪ'treɪ] *vt* trahir; **to b. to s.o.** (*give away to*) livrer à qn. ◆**betrayal** *n* (*disloyalty*) trahison *f*; (*disclosure*) révélation *f*.

better ['betər] *a* meilleur (**than** que); **she's** (**much**) **b.** *Med* elle va (bien) mieux; **he's b. than** (*at games*) il joue mieux que; (*at maths etc*) il est plus fort que; **that's b.** c'est mieux; **to get b.** (*recover*) se remettre; (*improve*) s'améliorer; **it's b. to go** il vaut mieux partir; **the b. part of** (*most*) la plus grande partie de; – *adv* mieux; **I had b. go** il vaut mieux que je parte; **so much the b.**, **all the b.** tant mieux (**for** pour); – *n* **to get the b. of s.o.** l'emporter sur qn; **change for the b.** amélioration *f*; **one's betters** ses supérieurs *mpl*; – *vt* (*improve*) améliorer; (*outdo*) dépasser; **to b. oneself** améliorer sa condition. ◆**—ment** *n* amélioration *f*.

between [bɪ'twiːn] *prep* entre; **we did it b.** (**the two**) **of us** nous l'avons fait à nous deux; **b. you and me** entre nous; **in b.** entre; – *adv* au milieu, entre les deux; (*time*) dans l'intervalle.

bevel ['bevəl] *n* (*edge*) biseau *m*.

beverage ['bevərɪdʒ] *n* boisson *f*.

bevy ['bevɪ] *n* (*of girls*) essaim *m*, bande *f*.

beware [bɪ'weər] *vi* **to b. of** (*s.o., sth*) se méfier de, prendre garde à; **b.!** méfiez-vous!, prenez garde!; **b. of falling**/*etc* prenez garde de (ne pas) tomber/*etc*; **'b. of the trains'** 'attention aux trains'.

bewilder [bɪ'wɪldər] *vt* dérouter, rendre perplexe. ◆**—ment** *n* confusion *f*.

bewitch [bɪ'wɪtʃ] *vt* enchanter. ◆**—ing** *a* enchanteur.

beyond [bɪ'jɒnd] *prep* (*further than*) au-delà

de; (reach, doubt) hors de; (except) sauf; **b. a year**/etc (longer than) plus d'un an/etc; **b. belief** incroyable; **b. his** or **her means** au-dessus de ses moyens; **it's b. me** ça me dépasse; – adv (further) au-delà.

bias ['baɪəs] **1** n penchant m (**towards** pour); (prejudice) préjugé m, parti pris m; – vt (**-ss-** or **-s-**) influencer. **2** n cut on the **b.** (fabric) coupé dans le biais. ◆**bias(s)ed** a partial; **to be b. against** avoir des préjugés contre.

bib [bɪb] n (baby's) bavoir m.

bible ['baɪb(ə)l] n bible f; **the B.** la Bible. ◆**biblical** ['bɪblɪk(ə)l] a biblique.

bibliography [bɪblɪ'ɒgrəfɪ] n bibliographie f.

bicarbonate [baɪ'kɑːbənət] n bicarbonate m.

bicentenary [baɪsen'tiːnərɪ] n, ◆**bicentennial** n bicentenaire m.

biceps ['baɪseps] n Anat biceps m.

bicker ['bɪkər] vi se chamailler. ◆**-ing** n chamailleries fpl.

bicycle ['baɪsɪk(ə)l] n bicyclette f; – vi faire de la bicyclette.

bid[1] [bɪd] vt (pt & pp bid, pres p bidding) offrir, faire une offre de; – vi faire une offre (**for** pour); **to b. for** Fig tenter d'obtenir; – n (at auction) offre f, enchère f; (tender) Com soumission f; (attempt) tentative f. ◆**-ding**[1] n enchères fpl. ◆**-der** n enchérisseur m; soumissionnaire mf; **to the highest b.** au plus offrant.

bid[2] [bɪd] vt (pt bade [bæd], pp bidden or bid, pres p bidding) (command) commander (s.o. to do à qn de faire); (say) dire. ◆**-ding**[2] n ordre(s) m(pl).

bide [baɪd] vt **to b. one's time** attendre le bon moment.

bier [bɪər] n (for coffin) brancards mpl.

bifocals [baɪ'fəʊkəlz] npl verres mpl à double foyer.

big [bɪg] a (**bigger, biggest**) grand, gros; (in age, generous) grand; (in bulk, amount) gros; **b. deal!** Am Fam (bon é) alors!; **b. mouth** Fam grande gueule f; **b. toe** gros orteil m; – adv **to do things b.** Fam faire grand; **to talk b.** fanfaronner. ◆**bighead** n, ◆**big-'headed** a Fam prétentieux, -euse (mf). ◆**big-'hearted** a généreux. ◆**big-shot** n, ◆**bigwig** n Fam gros bonnet m. ◆**big-time** a Fam important.

bigamy ['bɪgəmɪ] n bigamie f. ◆**bigamist** n bigame mf. ◆**bigamous** a bigame.

bigot ['bɪgət] n fanatique mf; Rel bigot, -ote mf. ◆**bigoted** a fanatique; Rel bigot.

bike [baɪk] n Fam vélo m; – vi Fam aller à vélo.

bikini [bɪ'kiːnɪ] n bikini m.

bilberry ['bɪlbərɪ] n myrtille f.

bile [baɪl] n bile f. ◆**bilious** ['bɪlɪəs] a bilieux.

bilge [bɪldʒ] n (nonsense) Sl foutaises fpl.

bilingual [baɪ'lɪŋgwəl] a bilingue.

bill [bɪl] **1** n (of bird) bec m. **2** n (invoice) facture f, note f; (in restaurant) addition f; (in hotel) note f; (draft) Com effet m; (of sale) acte m; (banknote) Am billet m; (law) Pol projet m de loi; (poster) affiche f; **b. of fare** menu m; **b. of rights** déclaration f des droits; – vt Th mettre à l'affiche, annoncer; **to b. s.o.** Com envoyer la facture à qn. ◆**billboard** n panneau m d'affichage. ◆**billfold** n Am portefeuille m.

billet ['bɪlɪt] vt Mil cantonner; – n cantonnement m.

billiard ['bɪljəd] a (table etc) de billard. ◆**billiards** npl (jeu m de) billard m.

billion ['bɪljən] n billion m; Am milliard m.

billow ['bɪləʊ] n flot m; – vi (of sea) se soulever; (of smoke) tourbillonner.

billy-goat ['bɪlɪgəʊt] n bouc m.

bimonthly [baɪ'mʌnθlɪ] a (fortnightly) bimensuel; (every two months) bimestriel.

bin [bɪn] n boîte f; (for bread) coffre m, huche f; (for litter) boîte f à ordures, poubelle f.

binary ['baɪnərɪ] a binaire.

bind [baɪnd] **1** vt (pt & pp bound) lier; (fasten) attacher, lier; (book) relier; (fabric, hem) border; **to b. s.o. to do** Jur obliger ou astreindre qn à faire. **2** n (bore) Fam plaie f. ◆**-ing-**[1] a (contract) irrévocable; – n bande f. **2** n (of book) reliure f. ◆**-er** n (for papers) classeur m.

binge [bɪndʒ] n **to go on a b.** Sl faire la bringue.

bingo ['bɪŋgəʊ] n loto m.

binoculars [bɪ'nɒkjʊləz] npl jumelles fpl.

biochemistry [baɪə'kemɪstrɪ] n biochimie f.

biodegradable [baɪəʊdɪ'greɪdəb(ə)l] a biodégradable.

biography [baɪ'ɒgrəfɪ] n biographie f. ◆**biographer** n biographe mf.

biology [baɪ'ɒlədʒɪ] n biologie f. ◆**bio-'logical** a biologique.

biped ['baɪped] n bipède m.

birch [bɜːtʃ] n **1** (tree) bouleau m. **2** (whip) verge f; – vt fouetter.

bird [bɜːd] n oiseau m; Sl (fowl) Culin volaille f; (girl) Sl poulette f, nana f; **b.'s-eye view**

perspective f à vol d'oiseau; *Fig* vue f d'ensemble. ◆**birdseed** n grains mpl de millet.

biro® ['baɪərəʊ] n (pl -os) stylo m à bille, bic® m.

birth [bɜːθ] n naissance f; **to give b. to** donner naissance à; **b. certificate** acte m de naissance; **b. control** limitation f des naissances. ◆**birthday** n anniversaire m; **happy b.!** bon anniversaire! ◆**birthplace** n lieu m de naissance; *(house)* maison f natale. ◆**birthrate** n (taux m de) natalité f. ◆**birthright** n droit m (qu'on a dès sa naissance), patrimoine m.

biscuit ['bɪskɪt] n biscuit m, gâteau m sec; *Am* petit pain m au lait.

bishop ['bɪʃəp] n évêque m; *(in chess)* fou m.

bison ['baɪs(ə)n] n inv bison m.

bit¹ [bɪt] n **1** morceau m; *(of string, time)* bout m; **a b.** (*a little*) un peu; **a tiny b.** un tout petit peu; **quite a b.** (*very*) très; *(much)* beaucoup; **not a b.** pas du tout; **a b. of** luck une chance; **b. by b.** petit à petit; **in bits (and pieces)** en morceaux; **to come to bits** se démonter. **2** (*coin*) pièce f. **3** (*of horse*) mors m. **4** (*of drill*) mèche f. **5** (*computer information*) bit m.

bit² [bɪt] *see* **bite**.

bitch [bɪtʃ] n **1** chienne f; *(woman)* *Pej Fam* garce f. **2** vi (*complain*) *Fam* râler. ◆**bitchy** a (*-ier, -iest*) *Fam* vache.

bit/e [baɪt] n (*wound*) morsure f; (*from insect*) piqûre f; *Fishing* touche f; (*mouthful*) bouchée f; (*of style etc*) *Fig* mordant m; **a b. to eat** un morceau à manger; — vti (*pt bit, pp bitten*) mordre; (*of insect*) piquer, mordre; **to b. one's nails** se ronger les ongles; **to b. on sth** mordre qch; **to b. off** arracher qch d'un coup de dent(s). ◆**-ing** a mordant; *(wind)* cinglant.

bitter ['bɪtər] **1** a (*person, taste, irony etc*) amer; (*cold, wind*) glacial, âpre; (*criticism*) acerbe; (*shock, fate*) cruel; (*conflict*) violent. **2** n bière f (pression). ◆**-ness** n amertume f; âpreté f; violence f. ◆**bitter-'sweet** a aigre-doux.

bivouac ['bɪvʊæk] n *Mil* bivouac m; — vi (*-ck-*) bivouaquer.

bizarre [bɪ'zɑːr] a bizarre.

blab [blæb] vi (*-bb-*) jaser. ◆**blabber** vi jaser. ◆**blabbermouth** n jaseur, -euse mf.

black [blæk] a (*-er, -est*) noir; **b. eye** œil m au beurre noir; **to give s.o. a b. eye** pocher l'œil à qn; **b. and blue** (*bruised*) couvert de bleus; **b. sheep** *Fig* brebis f galeuse; **b. ice** verglas m; **b. pudding** boudin m; — n (*colour*) noir m; (*Negro*) Noir, -e mf; —

noircir; *(refuse to deal with)* boycotter; — vi **to b. out** (*faint*) s'évanouir. ◆**blacken** vti noircir. ◆**blackish** a noirâtre. ◆**blackness** n noirceur f; (*of night*) obscurité f.

blackberry ['blækbərɪ] n mûre f. ◆**blackbird** n merle m. ◆**blackboard** n tableau m (noir). ◆**black'currant** n cassis m. ◆**blackleg** n (*strike breaker*) jaune m. ◆**blacklist** n liste f noire; — vt mettre sur la liste noire. ◆**blackmail** n chantage m; — vt faire chanter. ◆**blackmailer** n maître chanteur m. ◆**blackout** n panne f d'électricité; (*during war*) *Mil* black-out m; *Med* syncope f; (*news*) **b.** black-out m. ◆**blacksmith** n forgeron m.

blackguard ['blægɑːd, -gəd] n canaille f.

bladder ['blædər] n vessie f.

blade [bleɪd] n lame f; (*of grass*) brin m; (*of windscreen wiper*) caoutchouc m.

blame [bleɪm] vt accuser; (*censure*) blâmer; **to b. s.o. on s.o. or s.o. for sth** rejeter la responsabilité de qch sur qn; **to b. s.o. for sth** (*reproach*) reprocher qch à qn; **you're to b.** c'est ta faute; — n faute f; (*censure*) blâme m. ◆**-less** a irréprochable.

blanch [blɑːntʃ] vt (*vegetables*) blanchir; — vi (*turn pale with fear etc*) blêmir.

blancmange [blə'mɒnʒ] n blanc-manger m.

bland [blænd] a (*-er, -est*) doux; (*food*) fade.

blank [blæŋk] a (*paper, page*) blanc, vierge; (*cheque*) en blanc; (*look, mind*) vide; (*puzzled*) ébahi; (*refusal*) absolu; — a & n **b.** (*space*) blanc m; **b.** (*cartridge*) cartouche f à blanc; **my mind's a b.** j'ai la tête vide. ◆**blankly** adv sans expression.

blanket ['blæŋkɪt] **1** n couverture f; (*of snow etc*) *Fig* couche f; — vt (*cover*) *Fig* recouvrir. **2** a (*term etc*) général. ◆**-ing** n (*blankets*) couvertures fpl.

blare [bleər] n (*noise*) beuglement m; (*of trumpet*) sonnerie f; — vi **to b.** (*out*) (*of radio*) beugler; (*of music, car horn*) retentir.

blarney ['blɑːnɪ] n *Fam* boniment(s) m(pl).

blasé ['blɑːzeɪ] a blasé.

blaspheme [blæs'fiːm] vti blasphémer. ◆**'blasphemous** a blasphématoire; (*person*) blasphémateur. ◆**'blasphemy** n blasphème m.

blast [blɑːst] **1** n explosion f; (*air from explosion*) souffle m; (*of wind*) rafale f, coup m; (*of trumpet*) sonnerie f; **(at) full b.** (*loud*) à plein volume; (*fast*) à pleine vitesse; **b. furnace** haut fourneau m; — vt (*blow up*) faire sauter; (*hopes*) *Fig* détruire; **to b. s.o.** *Fam* réprimander qn. **2** int zut!;

merde! ◆—ed *a Fam* fichu. ◆**blast-off** *n* (*of spacecraft*) mise *f* à feu.

blatant ['bleɪtənt] *a* (*obvious*) flagrant, criant; (*shameless*) éhonté.

blaze/e [bleɪz] **1** *n* (*fire*) flamme *f*, feu *m*; (*conflagration*) incendie *m*; (*splendour*) Fig éclat *m*; **b. of light** torrent *m* de lumière; – *vi* (*of fire*) flamber; (*of sun, colour, eyes*) flamboyer. **2** *vt* **to b. a trail** marquer la voie. ◆—**ing** *a* (*burning*) en feu; (*sun*) brûlant; (*argument*) Fig violent.

blazer ['bleɪzər] *n* blazer *m*.

bleach [bliːtʃ] *n* décolorant *m*; (*household detergent*) eau *f* de Javel; – *vt* (*hair*) décolorer, oxygéner; (*linen*) blanchir.

bleak [bliːk] *a* (*-er, -est*) (*appearance, future etc*) morne; (*countryside*) désolé.

bleary ['blɪərɪ] *a* (*eyes*) troubles, voilés.

bleat [bliːt] *vi* bêler.

bleed [bliːd] *vti* (*pt & pp* **bled**) saigner; **to b. to death** perdre tout son sang. ◆—**ing** *a* (*wound*) saignant; (*bloody*) *Sl* foutu.

bleep [bliːp] *n* signal *m*, bip *m*; – *vt* appeler au bip-bip. ◆**bleeper** *n* bip-bip *m*.

blemish ['blemɪʃ] *n* (*fault*) défaut *m*; (*on fruit, reputation*) tache *f*; – *vt* (*reputation*) ternir.

blend [blend] *n* mélange *m*; – *vt* mélanger; – *vi* se mélanger; (*go together*) se marier (*with* avec). ◆—**er** *n Culin* mixer *m*.

bless [bles] *vt* bénir; **to be blessed with** avoir le bonheur de posséder; **b. you!** (*sneezing*) à vos souhaits! ◆—**ed** [-ɪd] *a* saint, béni; (*happy*) *Rel* bienheureux; (*blasted*) *Fam* fichu, sacré. ◆—**ing** *n* bénédiction *f*; (*divine favour*) grâce *f*; (*benefit*) bienfait *m*; **what a b. that . . .** quelle chance que . . . .

blew [bluː] *see* blow [1].

blight [blaɪt] *n* (*on plants*) rouille *f*; (*scourge*) Fig fléau *m*; **to be** *or* **cast a b. on** avoir une influence néfaste sur; **urban b.** (*area*) quartier *m* délabré; (*condition*) délabrement *m* (*de quartier*). ◆**blighter** *n Pej Fam* type *m*.

blimey! ['blaɪmɪ] *int Fam* zut!, mince!

blimp [blɪmp] *n* dirigeable *m*.

blind [blaɪnd] **1** *a* aveugle; **b. person** aveugle *mf*; **b. in one eye** borgne; **he's b. to** (*fault*) il ne voit pas; **to turn a b. eye to** fermer les yeux sur; **b. alley** impasse *f*; – *n* **the b.** les aveugles *mpl*; – *vt* aveugler. **2** *n* (*on window*) store *m*; (*deception*) feinte *f*. ◆—**ly** *adv* aveuglément. ◆—**ness** *n* cécité *f*; Fig aveuglement'*m*. ◆**blinkers** *npl* ◆**blinders** *npl* œillères *fpl*. ◆**blindfold** *n* bandeau *m*; – *vt* bander les yeux à; – *adv* les yeux bandés.

blink [blɪŋk] *vi* cligner des yeux; (*of eyes*)

cligner; (*of light*) clignoter; – *vt* **to b. one's eyes** cligner des yeux; – *n* clignement *m*; **on the b.** (*machine*) *Fam* détraqué. ◆**blinkers** *npl* (*for horse*) œillères *fpl*; (*indicators*) Aut clignotants *mpl*.

bliss [blɪs] *n* félicité *f*. ◆**blissful** *a* (*happy*) très joyeux; (*wonderful*) merveilleux. ◆**blissfully** *adv* (*happy, unaware*) parfaitement.

blister ['blɪstər] *n* (*on skin*) ampoule *f*; – *vi* se couvrir d'ampoules.

blithe [blaɪð] *a* joyeux.

blitz [blɪts] *n* (*attack*) Av raid *m* éclair; (*bombing*) bombardement *m* aérien; Fig Fam offensive *f*; – *vt* bombarder.

blizzard ['blɪzəd] *n* tempête *f* de neige.

bloat [bləʊt] *vt* gonfler.

bloater ['bləʊtər] *n* hareng *m* saur.

blob [blɒb] *n* (*of water*) (grosse) goutte *f*; (*of ink, colour*) tache *f*.

bloc [blɒk] *n Pol* bloc *m*.

block [blɒk] **1** *n* (*of stone etc*) bloc *m*; (*of buildings*) pâté *m* (de maisons); (*in pipe*) obstruction *f*; (*mental*) blocage *m*; **b. of flats** immeuble *m*; **a b. away** Am une rue plus loin; **school b.** groupe *m* scolaire; **b. capitals** *or* **letters** majuscules *fpl*. **2** *vt* (*obstruct*) boucher, bloquer; (*pipe*) boucher, bloquer; (*one's view*) boucher; **to b. off** (*road*) barrer; (*light*) intercepter; **to b. up** (*pipe, hole*) bloquer. ◆**blo'ckade** *n* blocus *m*; – *vt* bloquer. ◆**blockage** *n* obstruction *f*. ◆**blockbuster** *n Cin* superproduction *f*, film *m* à grand spectacle. ◆**blockhead** *n* imbécile *mf*.

bloke [bləʊk] *n Fam* type *m*.

blond [blɒnd] *a & n* blond (*m*). ◆**blonde** *a & n* blonde (*f*).

blood [blʌd] *n* sang *m*; – *a* (*group, orange etc*) sanguin; (*donor, bath etc*) de sang; (*poisoning etc*) du sang. **b. pressure** tension *f* (artérielle); **high b. pressure** (hyper)tension *f*. ◆**bloodcurdling** *a* à vous tourner le sang. ◆**bloodhound** *n* (*dog, detective*) limier *m*. ◆**bloodletting** *n* saignée *f*. ◆**bloodshed** *n* effusion *f* de sang. ◆**bloodshot** *a* (*eye*) injecté de sang. ◆**bloodsucker** *n* (*insect, person*) sangsue *f*. ◆**bloodthirsty** *a* sanguinaire.

bloody ['blʌdɪ] **1** *a* (*-ier, -iest*) sanglant. **2** *a* (*blasted*) *Fam* sacré; – *adv Fam* vachement. ◆**b.-'minded** *a* hargneux, pas commode.

bloom [bluːm] *n* fleur *f*; **in b.** en fleur(s); – *vi* fleurir; (*of person*) Fig s'épanouir. ◆—**ing**

a **1** (*in bloom*) en fleur(s); (*thriving*) florissant. **2** (*blinking*) *Fam* fichu.

bloomer ['blu:mər] *n Fam* (*mistake*) gaffe *f*.

blossom ['blɒsəm] *n* fleur(s) *f(pl)*; – *vi* fleurir; **to b.** (**out**) (*of person*) s'épanouir; **to b.** (**out**) **into** devenir.

blot [blɒt] *n* tache *f*; – *vt* (-**tt**-) tacher; (*dry*) sécher; **to b.** (**out**) (*word*) rayer; (*memory*) effacer. ◆**blotting** *a* **b. paper** (papier *m*) buvard *m*. ◆**blotter** *n* buvard *m*.

blotch [blɒtʃ] *n* tache *f*. ◆**blotchy** *a* (-**ier**, -**iest**) couvert de taches; (*face*) marbré.

blouse [blauz, *Am* blaus] *n* chemisier *m*.

blow[1] [bləu] *vt* (*pt* **blew**, *pp* **blown**) (*of wind*) pousser (*un navire etc*), chasser (*la pluie etc*); (*smoke, glass*) souffler; (*bubbles*) faire; (*trumpet*) souffler dans; (*fuse*) faire sauter; (*kiss*) envoyer (**to** à); (*money*) *Fam* claquer; **to b. one's nose** se moucher; **to b. a whistle** siffler; **to b. away** (*of wind*) emporter; **to b. down** (*chimney etc*) faire tomber; **to b. off** (*hat etc*) emporter; (*arm*) arracher; **to b. out** (*candle*) souffler; (*cheeks*) gonfler; **to b. up** (*building etc*) faire sauter; (*tyre*) gonfler; (*photo*) agrandir; – *vi* (*of wind, person*) souffler; (*of papers etc*) s'éparpiller; **b.!** *Fam* zut!; **to b. down** (*fall*) tomber; **to b. off** or **away** s'envoler; **to b. out** (*of light*) s'éteindre; **to b. over** (*pass*) passer; **to b. up** (*explode*) exploser. ◆**—er** *n* (*telephone*) *Fam* bigophone *m*. ◆**blow-dry** *n* brushing *m*. ◆**blowlamp** *n* chalumeau *m*. ◆**blowout** *n* (*of tyre*) éclatement *m*; (*meal*) *Sl* gueuleton *m*. ◆**blowtorch** *n Am* chalumeau *m*. ◆**blow-up** *n Phot* agrandissement *m*.

blow[2] [bləu] *n* coup *m*; **to come to blows** en venir aux mains.

blowy ['bləui] *a* **it's b.** *Fam* il y a du vent.

blowzy ['blauzi] *a* **b. woman** (*slovenly*) *Fam* femme *f* débraillée.

blubber ['blʌbər] *n* graisse *f* (de baleine).

bludgeon ['blʌdʒən] *n* gourdin *m*; – *vt* matraquer.

blue [blu:] *a* (**bluer, bluest**) bleu; **to feel b.** *Fam* avoir le cafard; **b. film** *Fam* film *m* porno; – *n* bleu *m*; **the blues** (*depression*) *Fam* le cafard; *Mus* le blues. ◆**bluebell** *n* jacinthe *f* des bois. ◆**blueberry** *n* airelle *f*. ◆**bluebottle** *n* mouche *f* à viande. ◆**blueprint** *n Fig* plan *m* (de travail).

bluff [blʌf] *a* (*a person*) brusque, direct. **2** *vti* bluffer; – *n* bluff *m*.

blunder ['blʌndər] *n* (*mistake*) bévue *f*, gaffe *f*; – *vi* faire une bévue. **2** (*move awkwardly*) avancer à tâtons. ◆**—ing** *a* maladroit; – *n* maladresse *f*.

blunt [blʌnt] *a* (-**er**, -**est**) (*edge*) émoussé; (*pencil*) épointé; (*person*) brusque; (*speech*) franc; – *vt* émousser; épointer. ◆**—ly** *adv* carrément. ◆**—ness** *n Fig* brusquerie *f*; (*of speech*) franchise *f*.

blur [blɜ:r] *n* tache *f* floue, contour *m* imprécis; – *vt* (-**rr**-) estomper, rendre flou; (*judgment*) *Fig* troubler. ◆**blurred** *a* (*image*) flou, estompé.

blurb [blɜ:b] *n Fam* résumé *m* publicitaire, laïus *m*.

blurt [blɜ:t] *vt* **to b.** (**out**) laisser échapper, lâcher.

blush [blʌʃ] *vi* rougir (**at, with** de); – *n* rougeur *f*; **with a b.** en rougissant.

bluster ['blʌstər] *vi* (*of person*) tempêter; (*of wind*) faire rage. ◆**blustery** *a* (*weather*) de grand vent, à bourrasques.

boa ['bəuə] *n* (*snake*) boa *m*.

boar [bɔ:r] *n* (*wild*) **b.** sanglier *m*.

board[1] [bɔ:d] **1** *n* (*piece of wood*) planche *f*; (*for notices, games etc*) tableau *m*; (*cardboard*) carton *m*; (*committee*) conseil *m*, commission *f*; **b.** (**of directors**) conseil *m* d'administration; **on b.** *Nau Av* à bord (**de**); **B. of Trade** *Br Pol* ministère *m* du Commerce; **across the b.** (*pay rise*) général; **to go by the b.** (*of plan*) être abandonné. **2** *vt Nau Av* monter à bord de; (*bus, train*) monter dans; **to b. up** (*door*) boucher. ◆**—ing** *n Nau Av* embarquement *m*. ◆**boardwalk** *n Am* promenade *f*.

board[2] [bɔ:d] *n* (*food*) pension *f*; **b. and lodging, bed and b.** (*chambre f avec*) pension *f*; – *vi* (*lodge*) être en pension (**with** chez); **boarding house** pension *f* (de famille); **boarding school** pensionnat *m*. ◆**—er** *n* pensionnaire *mf*.

boast [bəust] *vi* se vanter (**about, of** de); – *vt* se glorifier de; **to b. that one can do** ... se vanter de (pouvoir) faire ...; – *n* vantardise *f*. ◆**—ing** *n* vantardise *f*. ◆**boastful** *a* vantard. ◆**boastfully** *adv* en se vantant.

boat [bəut] *n* bateau *m*; (*small*) barque *f*, canot *m*; (*liner*) paquebot *m*; **in the same b.** *Fig* logé à la même enseigne; **b. race** course *f* d'aviron. ◆**—ing** *n* canotage *m*; **b. trip** excursion *f* en bateau.

boatswain ['bəus(ə)n] *n* maître *m* d'équipage.

bob [bɒb] *vi* (-**bb**-) **to b.** (**up and down**) (*on water*) danser sur l'eau.

bobbin ['bɒbin] *n* bobine *f*.

bobby ['bɒbi] *n* **1** (*policeman*) *Fam* flic *m*, agent *m*. **2 b. pin** *Am* pince *f* à cheveux.

bode [bəʊd] *vi* **to b. well/ill** être de bon/mauvais augure.

bodice ['bɒdɪs] *n* corsage *m*.

body ['bɒdɪ] *n* corps *m*; (*of vehicle*) carrosserie *f*; (*quantity*) masse *f*; (*institution*) organisme *m*; **the main b. of** le gros de. **b. building** culturisme *m*. ◆**bodily** *a* physique; (*need*) matériel; – *adv* physiquement; (*as a whole*) tout entier. ◆**bodyguard** *n* garde du corps, gorille *m*. ◆**bodywork** *n* carrosserie *f*.

boffin ['bɒfɪn] *n Fam* chercheur, -euse *mf* scientifique.

bog [bɒg] *n* marécage *m*; – *vt* **to get bogged down** s'enliser. ◆**boggy** *a* (-ier, -iest) marécageux.

bogey ['bəʊgɪ] *n* spectre *m*; **b. man** croque-mitaine *m*.

boggle ['bɒg(ə)l] *vi* **the mind boggles** cela confond l'imagination.

bogus ['bəʊgəs] *a* faux.

bohemian [bəʊ'hiːmɪən] *a & n* (*artist etc*) bohème (*mf*).

boil [bɔɪl] **1** *n Med* furoncle *m*, clou *m*. **2** *vi* bouillir; **to b. away** (*until dry*) s'évaporer; (*on and on*) bouillir sans arrêt; **to b. down to** *Fig* se ramener à; **to b. over** (*of milk, emotions etc*) déborder; – *vt* **to b. (up)** faire bouillir; – *n* **to be on the b., come to the b.** bouillir; **to bring to the b.** amener à ébullition. ◆**-ed** *a* (*beef*) bouilli; (*potato*) (cuit) à l'eau; **b. egg** œuf *m* à la coque. ◆**-ing** *n* ébullition *f*; **at b. point** à ébullition; – *a & adv* **b. (hot)** bouillant; **it's b. (hot)** (*weather*) il fait une chaleur infernale. ◆**-er** *n* chaudière *f*; **b. suit** bleu *m* (de travail).

boisterous ['bɔɪstərəs] *a* (*noisy*) tapageur; (*child*) turbulent; (*meeting*) houleux.

bold [bəʊld] *a* (-er, -est) hardi; **b. type** caractères *mpl* gras. ◆**-ness** *n* hardiesse *f*.

Bolivia [bə'lɪvɪə] *n* Bolivie *f*. ◆**Bolivian** *a & n* bolivien, -ienne (*mf*).

bollard ['bɒləd, 'bɒlɑːd] *n Aut* borne *f*.

boloney [bə'ləʊnɪ] *n Sl* foutaises *fpl*.

bolster ['bəʊlstər] **1** *n* (*pillow*) traversin *m*, polochon *m*. **2** *vt* **to b. (up)** (*support*) soutenir.

bolt [bəʊlt] **1** *n* (*on door etc*) verrou *m*; (*for nut*) boulon *m*; – *vt* (*door*) verrouiller. **2** *n* (*dash*) fuite *f*, ruée *f*; – *vi* (*dash*) se précipiter; (*flee*) détaler; (*of horse*) s'emballer. **3** *n* **b. (of lightning)** éclair *m*. **4** *vt* (*food*) engloutir. **5** *adv* **b. upright** tout droit.

bomb [bɒm] *n* bombe *f*; **letter b.** lettre *f* piégée; **b. disposal** désamorçage *m*; – *vt* bombarder. ◆**-ing** *n* bombardement *m*.

◆**-er** *n* (*aircraft*) bombardier *m*; (*terrorist*) plastiqueur *m*. ◆**bombshell** *n* **to come as a b.** tomber comme une bombe. ◆**bombsite** *n* terrain *m* vague, lieu *m* bombardé.

bombard [bɒm'bɑːd] *vt* bombarder (**with** de). ◆**-ment** *n* bombardement *m*.

bona fide [bəʊnə'faɪdɪ, *Am* -'faɪd] *a* sérieux, de bonne foi.

bonanza [bə'nænzə] *n Fig* mine *f* d'or.

bond [bɒnd] **1** *n* (*agreement, promise*) engagement *m*; (*link*) lien *m*; *Com* bon *m*, obligation *f*; (*adhesion*) adhérence *f*. **2** *vt* (*goods*) entreposer.

bondage ['bɒndɪdʒ] *n* esclavage *m*.

bone [bəʊn] **1** *n* os *m*; (*of fish*) arête *f*; **b. of contention** pomme *f* de discorde; **b. china** porcelaine *f* tendre; – *vt* (*meat etc*) désosser. **2** *vi* **to b. up on** (*subject*) *Am Fam* bûcher. ◆**bony** *a* (-ier, -iest) (*thin*) osseux, maigre; (*fish*) plein d'arêtes.

bone-dry [bəʊn'draɪ] *a* tout à fait sec. ◆**b.-idle** *a* paresseux comme une couleuvre.

bonfire ['bɒnfaɪər] *n* (*for celebration*) feu *m* de joie; (*for dead leaves*) feu *m* (de jardin).

bonkers ['bɒŋkəz] *a* (*crazy*) *Fam* dingue.

bonnet ['bɒnɪt] *n* (*hat*) bonnet *m*; *Aut* capot *m*.

bonus ['bəʊnəs] *n* prime *f*; **no claims b.** *Aut* bonus *m*.

boo [buː] **1** *int* hou! **2** *vti* huer; – *npl* huées *fpl*.

boob [buːb] *n* (*mistake*) gaffe *f*; – *vi Sl* gaffer.

booby-trap ['buːbɪtræp] *n* engin *m* piégé; – *vt* (-pp-) piéger.

book [bʊk] *n* livre *m*; (*of tickets*) carnet *m*; (*record*) registre *m*; *pl* (*accounts*) comptes *mpl*; (*excercise*) **b.** cahier *m*. **2** *vt* **to b. (up)** (*seat etc*) réserver, retenir; **to b. s.o.** *Jur* donner un procès-verbal à qn; **to b. (down)** inscrire; (*fully*) **booked up** (*hotel, concert*) complet; (*person*) pris; – *vi* **to b. (up)** réserver des places; **to b. in** (*in hotel*) signer le registre. ◆**-ing** *n* réservation *f*; **b. clerk** guichetier, -ière *mf*; **b. office** bureau *m* de location, guichet *m*. ◆**-able** *a* (*seat*) qu'on peut réserver. ◆**bookish** *a* (*word, theory*) livresque; (*person*) studieux.

bookbinding ['bʊkbaɪndɪŋ] *n* reliure *f*. ◆**bookcase** *n* bibliothèque *f*. ◆**bookend** *n* serre-livres *m inv*. ◆**bookkeeper** *n* comptable *mf*. ◆**bookkeeping** *n* comptabilité *f*. ◆**booklet** *n* brochure *f*. ◆**book-lover** *n* bibliophile *mf*. ◆**bookmaker** *n* bookmaker *m*. ◆**bookmark** *n* marque f. ◆**bookseller** n libraire mf. ◆**bookshelf** n rayon m. ◆**bookshop** n, Am ◆**bookstore** n librairie f. ◆**bookstall** n kiosque m (à journaux). ◆**bookworm** n rat m de bibliothèque.

boom [buːm] **1** vi (of thunder, gun etc) gronder; – n grondement m; sonic b. bang m. **2** n Econ expansion f, essor m, boom m.

boomerang ['buːməraŋ] n boomerang m.

boon [buːn] n aubaine f, avantage m.

boor [buə] n rustre m. ◆**boorish** a rustre.

boost [buːst] vt (push) donner une poussée à; (increase) augmenter; (product) faire de la réclame pour; (economy) stimuler; (morale) remonter; – n to give a b. to = to boost. ◆**—er** n b. (injection) piqûre f de rappel.

boot [buːt] **1** n (shoe) botte f; (ankle) b. bottillon m; (knee) b. bottine f; to get the b. Fam être mis à la porte; b. polish cirage m; – vt (kick) donner un coup ou des coups de pied à; to b. out mettre à la porte. **2** n Aut coffre m. **3** n to b. en plus. ◆**bootblack** n cireur m. ◆**boo'tee** n (of baby) chausson m.

booth [buːð, buːθ] n Tel cabine f; (at fair) baraque f.

booty ['buːtɪ] n (stolen goods) butin m.

booz/e [buːz] n Fam alcool m, boisson(s) f(pl); (drinking bout) beuverie f; – vi to booze boire (beaucoup). ◆**—er** n Fam (person) buveur, -euse mf; (place) bistrot m.

border ['bɔːdə] n (of country) & Fig frontière f; (edge) bord m; (of garden etc) bordure f; – a (town) frontière inv; (incident) de frontière; – vt (street) border; to b. (on) (country) toucher à; to b. (up)on (resemble) être voisin de. ◆**borderland** n pays m frontière. ◆**borderline** n frontière f; b. case cas m limite.

bor·e¹ [bɔː] **1** vt (weary) ennuyer; to be bored s'ennuyer; – n (person) raseur, -euse mf; (thing) ennui m. **2** vt Tech forer, creuser; (hole) percer; – vi forer, to b. of gun) calibre m. ◆**—ing** a ennuyeux. ◆**boredom** n ennui m.

bore² [bɔː] see bear².

born [bɔːn] a né; to be b. naître; he was b. il est né.

borne [bɔːn] see bear².

borough ['bʌrə] n (town) municipalité f; (part of town) arrondissement m.

borrow ['bɒrəʊ] vt emprunter (from à). ◆**—ing** n emprunt m.

Borstal ['bɔːst(ə)l] n maison f d'éducation surveillée.

bosom ['buzəm] n (chest) & Fig sein m; b. friend ami, -ie mf intime.

boss [bɒs] n Fam patron, -onne mf, chef m; – vt Fam diriger; to b. s.o. around ou about régenter qn. ◆**bossy** a (-ier, -iest) Fam autoritaire.

boss-eyed ['bɒsaɪd] a to be b.-eyed loucher.

bosun ['bəʊs(ə)n] n maître m d'équipage.

botany ['bɒtənɪ] n botanique f. ◆**bo'tanical** a botanique. ◆**botanist** n botaniste mf.

botch [bɒtʃ] vt to b. (up) (spoil) bâcler; (repair) rafistoler.

both [bəʊθ] a les deux, l'un(e) et l'autre; – pron tous ou toutes (les) deux, l'un(e) et l'autre; b. of us nous deux; b. of them (at the same time) à la fois; b. you and I vous et moi.

bother ['bɒðə] vt (annoy, worry) ennuyer; (disturb) déranger; (pester) importuner; **I can't be bothered!** je n'en ai pas envie!, ça m'embête!; – vi to b. about (worry about) se préoccuper de; (deal with) s'occuper de; to b. doing ou to do se donner la peine de faire; – n (trouble) ennui m; (effort) peine f; (inconvenience) dérangement m; (oh) b.! zut alors!

bottle ['bɒt(ə)l] n bouteille f; (small) flacon m; (wide-mouthed) bocal m; (for baby) biberon m; (hot-water) b. bouillotte f; b. opener ouvre-bouteilles m inv; – vt mettre en bouteille; to b. up (feeling) contenir. ◆**b.-feed** vt (pt & pp -fed) nourrir au biberon. ◆**bottleneck** n (in road) goulot m d'étranglement; (traffic holdup) bouchon m.

bottom ['bɒtəm] n (of sea, box, etc) fond m; (of page, hill etc) bas m; (of table) bout m; (buttocks) Fam derrière m; (of class) Fam dernier m; – a (part, shelf) inférieur, du bas; b. floor rez-de-chaussée m; to be (at the) b. of the class être le dernier de la classe; – a (part, shelf) inférieur, du bas; b. floor rez-de-chaussée m; b. gear première vitesse f. ◆**—less** a insondable.

bough [baʊ] n Lit rameau m.

bought [bɔːt] see buy.

boulder ['bəʊldə] n rocher m.

boulevard ['buːləvɑːd] n boulevard m.

bounc/e [baʊns] **1** vi (of ball) rebondir; (of person) faire des bonds; to b. into bondir dans; – vt faire rebondir; – n (re)bond m. **2** vi (of cheque) Fam être sans provision, être en bois. ◆**—ing** a (baby) robuste. ◆**—er** n Fam (doorman) videur m.

bound¹ [baʊnd] **1** a b. to do (obliged) obligé de faire; (certain) sûr de faire; **it's b. to happen** ça arrivera sûrement; **to be b. for**

être en route pour. **2** *n* (*leap*) bond *m*; – *vi* bondir.

bound² [baʊnd] *see* bind 1; – *a* b. up with (*connected*) lié à.

bounds [baʊndz] *npl* limites *fpl*; **out of b.** (*place*) interdit. ◆**boundary** *n* limite *f*. ◆**bounded** *a* b. by limité par. ◆**boundless** *a* sans bornes.

bountiful ['baʊntɪfʊl] *a* généreux.

bounty ['baʊntɪ] *n* (*reward*) prime *f*.

bouquet [buː'keɪ] *n* (*of flowers, wine*) bouquet *m*.

bourbon ['bɜːbən] *n* (*whisky*) *Am* bourbon *m*.

bout [baʊt] *n* période *f*; *Med* accès *m*, crise *f*; *Boxing* combat *m*; (*session*) séance *f*.

boutique [buː'tiːk] *n* boutique *f* (de mode).

bow¹ [baʊ] *n* (*weapon*) arc *m*; *Mus* archet *m*; (*knot*) nœud *m*; **b. tie** nœud *m* papillon. ◆**b.-'legged** *a* aux jambes arquées.

bow² [baʊ] **1** *n* révérence *f*; (*nod*) salut *m*; – *vt* courber, incliner; – *vi* s'incliner (**to** devant); (*nod*) incliner la tête; **to b. down** (*submit*) s'incliner. **2** *n* *Nau* proue *f*.

bowels ['baʊəlz] *npl* intestins *mpl*; (*of earth*) *Fig* entrailles *fpl*.

bowl [bəʊl] **1** *n* (*for food*) bol *m*; (*basin*) & *Geog* cuvette *f*; (*for sugar*) sucrier *m*; (*for salad*) saladier *m*; (*for fruit*) corbeille *f*, coupe *f*. **2** *Sp* boules *fpl*. **3** *vi Cricket* lancer la balle; **to b. along** *Aut* rouler vite; – *vt* (*ball*) *Cricket* servir; **to b. s.o. over** (*knock down*) renverser qn; (*astound*) bouleverser qn. ◆**-ing** *n* (tenpin) b. bowling *m*; **b. alley** bowling *m*. ◆**-er¹** *n Cricket* lanceur, -euse *mf*.

bowler² ['bəʊlər] *n* (*hat*) (chapeau *m*) melon *m*.

box [bɒks] **1** *n* boîte *f*; (*large*) caisse *f*; (*of cardboard*) carton *m*; *Th* loge *f*; *Jur* barre *f*, banc *m*; (*for horse*) box *m*; *TV* *Fam* télé *f*; **b. office** bureau *m* de location, guichet *m*; **b. room** (*lumber room*) débarras *m*; (*bedroom*) petite chambre *f* (carrée); – *vt* **to b. (up)** mettre en boîte; **to b. in** (*enclose*) enfermer. **2** *vti Boxing* boxer; **to b. s.o.'s ears** gifler qn. ◆**-ing** *n* **1** boxe *f*; **b. ring** ring *m*. **2** **B. Day** le lendemain de Noël. ◆**-er** *n* boxeur *m*. ◆**boxcar** *n Rail Am* wagon *m* couvert. ◆**boxwood** *n* buis *m*.

boy [bɔɪ] *n* garçon *m*; **English b.** jeune Anglais *m*; **old b.** *Sch* ancien élève *m*; **yes, old b.!** oui, mon vieux!; **the boys** (*pals*) *Fam* les copains *mpl*; **my dear b.** mon cher ami; **oh b.!** *Am* mon Dieu! ◆**boyfriend** *n* petit ami *m*. ◆**boyhood** *n* enfance *f*. ◆**boyish** *a* de garçon; *Pej* puéril.

boycott ['bɔɪkɒt] *vt* boycotter; – *n* boycottage *m*.

bra [brɑː] *n* soutien-gorge *m*.

brac/e [breɪs] *n* (*for fastening*) attache *f*; (*dental*) appareil *m*; *pl* (*trouser straps*) bretelles *fpl*; – *vt* (*fix*) attacher; (*press*) appuyer; **to b. oneself for** (*news, shock*) se préparer à. ◆**-ing** *a* (*air etc*) fortifiant.

bracelet ['breɪslɪt] *n* bracelet *m*.

bracken ['brækən] *n* fougère *f*.

bracket ['brækɪt] *n Tech* support *m*, tasseau *m*; (*round sign*) parenthèse *f*; (*square*) *Typ* crochet *m*; *Fig* groupe *m*, tranche *f*; – *vt* mettre entre parenthèses *or* crochets; **to b. together** *Fig* mettre dans le même groupe.

bradawl ['brædɔːl] *n* poinçon *m*.

brag [bræg] *vi* (-gg-) se vanter (**about, of** de). ◆**-ging** *n* vantardise *f*. ◆**braggart** *n* vantard, -arde *m*.

braid [breɪd] *vt* (*hair*) tresser; (*trim*) galonner; – *n* tresse *f*; galon *m*.

Braille [breɪl] *n* braille *m*.

brain [breɪn] *n* cerveau *m*; (*of bird etc*) & *Pej* cervelle *f*; – *a* (*operation, death*) cérébral; – *vt Fam* assommer; **to have brains** (*sense*) avoir de l'intelligence; **b. drain** fuite *f* des cerveaux. ◆**brainchild** *n* invention *f* personnelle. ◆**brainstorm** *n Psy Fig* aberration *f*; *Am* idée *f* géniale. ◆**brainwash** *vt* faire un lavage de cerveau à. ◆**brainwave** *n* idée *f* géniale.

brainy ['breɪnɪ] *a* (-ier, -iest) *Fam* intelligent.

braise [breɪz] *vt Culin* braiser.

brak/e [breɪk] *vi* freiner; – *n* frein *m*; **b. light** *Aut* stop *m*. ◆**-ing** *n* freinage *m*.

bramble ['bræmb(ə)l] *n* ronce *f*.

bran [bræn] *n Bot* son *m*.

branch [brɑːntʃ] *n* branche *f*; (*of road*) embranchement *m*; (*of store etc*) succursale *f*; **b. office** succursale *f*; – *vi* **to b. off** (*of road*) bifurquer; **to b. out** (*of family, tree*) se ramifier; *Fig* étendre ses activités.

brand [brænd] *n* (*trademark, stigma & on cattle*) marque *f*; – *vt* (*mark*) marquer; (*stigmatize*) flétrir; **to be branded as** avoir la réputation de.

brandish ['brændɪʃ] *vt* brandir.

brand-new [brænd'njuː] *a* tout neuf, flambant neuf.

brandy ['brændɪ] *n* cognac *m*; (*made with pears etc*) eau-de-vie *f*.

brash [bræʃ] *a* effronté, fougueux.

brass [brɑːs] *n* cuivre *m*; (*instruments*) *Mus* cuivres *mpl*; **the top b.** (*officers, executives*) *Fam* les huiles *fpl*; **b. band** fanfare *f*.

brassiere ['bræzɪər, *Am* brə'zɪər] *n* soutien-gorge *m*.

brat [bræt] *n Pej* môme *mf*, gosse *mf*; (*badly behaved*) galopin *m*.

bravado [brə'vɑːdəʊ] *n* bravade *f*.

brave [breɪv] *a* (**-er, -est**) courageux, brave; – *n* (*Red Indian*) guerrier *m* (indien), brave *m*; – *vt* braver. ◆**bravery** *n* courage *m*.

bravo! ['brɑːvəʊ] *int* bravo!

brawl [brɔːl] *n* (*fight*) bagarre *f*; – *vi* se bagarrer. ◆**-ing** *a* bagarreur.

brawn [brɔːn] *n* muscles *mpl*. ◆**brawny** *a* (**-ier, -iest**) musclé.

bray [breɪ] *vi* (*of ass*) braire.

brazen ['breɪz(ə)n] *a* (*shameless*) effronté; – *vt* to b. it out payer d'audace, faire front.

Brazil [brə'zɪl] *n* Brésil *m*. ◆**Brazilian** *a & n* brésilien, -ienne (*mf*).

breach [briːtʃ] **1** *n* violation *f*, infraction *f*; (*of contract*) rupture *f*; (*of trust*) abus *m*; – *vt* (*law, code*) violer. **2** *n* (*gap*) brèche *f*; – *vt* (*wall etc*) ouvrir une brèche dans.

bread [bred] *n inv* pain *m*; (*money*) *Sl* blé *m*, fric *m*; loaf of b. pain *m*; (slice *or* piece of) b. and butter tartine *f*; b. and butter (*job*) *Fig* gagne-pain *m*. ◆**breadbin** *n, Am* ◆**breadbox** *n* coffre *m* à pain. ◆**breadboard** *n* planche *f* à pain. ◆**breadcrumb** *n* miette *f* (de pain); *pl Culin* chapelure *f*. ◆**breadline** *n* on the b. indigent. ◆**breadwinner** *n* soutien *m* de famille.

breadth [bretθ] *n* largeur *f*.

break [breɪk] *vt* (*pt* broke, *pp* broken) casser; (*into pieces*) briser; (*silence, vow etc*) rompre; (*strike, heart, ice etc*) briser; (*record*) *Sp* battre; (*law*) violer; (*one's word*) manquer à; (*journey*) interrompre; (*sound barrier*) franchir; (*a fall*) amortir; (*news*) révéler (to à); to b. (*oneself*) of (*habit*) se débarrasser de; to b. open (*safe*) percer; to b. new ground innover; – *vi* (*se*) casser; se briser; se rompre; (*of voice*) s'altérer, (*of boy's voice*) muer; (*of weather*) se gâter; (*of news*) éclater; (*of day*) se lever; (*of wave*) déferler; to b. free se libérer; to b. loose s'échapper; to b. with s.o. rompre avec qn; – *n* cassure *f*; (*in relationship, continuity etc*) rupture *f*; (*in journey*) interruption *f*; (*rest*) repos *m*; (*for tea*) pause *f*; *Sch* récréation *f*; (*change*) Met changement *m*; a lucky b. *Fam* une chance. ◆**-ing** *a* b. point Tech point *m* de rupture; at b. point (*patience*) à bout; (*person*) sur le point de craquer, à bout. ◆**-able** *a* cassable. ◆**-age** *n* casse *f*; *pl* (*things broken*) la casse. ◆**-er** *n* (*wave*) brisant *m*; (*dealer*)

Aut casseur *m*. ■ to b. away *vi* se détacher; – *vt* détacher. ◆**breakaway** *a* (*group*) dissident; (*resistance*) briser; (*analyse*) analyser; – *vi Aut Tech* tomber en panne; (*of negotiations etc*) échouer; (*collapse*) s'effondrer. ◆**breakdown** *n* panne *f*; analyse *f*; (*in talks*) rupture *f*; (*nervous*) dépression *f*; – *a* (*service*) *Aut* de dépannage; b. lorry dépanneuse *f*; to b. in *vi* interrompre; *vt* (*door*) enfoncer; (*of burglar*) entrer par effraction; – *vt* (*door*) enfoncer; (*horse*) dresser; (*vehicle*) *Am* roder. ◆**break-in** *n* cambriolage *m*; to b. into *vt* (*safe*) forcer; (*start*) entamer; to b. off *vt* détacher; (*relations*) rompre; – *vi* se détacher; (*stop*) s'arrêter; to b. off with rompre avec; to b. out *vi* éclater; (*escape*) s'échapper; to b. out in (*pimples*) avoir une poussée de; to b. through *vi* (*of sun*) & *Mil* percer; – *vt* (*defences*) percer. ◆**breakthrough** *n Fig* percée *f*, découverte *f*; to b. up *vt* mettre en morceaux; (*marriage*) briser; (*fight*) mettre fin à; – *vi* (*end*) prendre fin; (*of group*) se disperser; (*of marriage*) se briser; *Sch* partir en vacances. ◆**breakup** *n* fin *f*; (*in friendship, marriage*) rupture *f*.

breakfast ['brekfəst] *n* petit déjeuner *m*.

breakwater ['breɪkwɔːtər] *n* brise-lames *m inv*.

breast [brest] *n* sein *m*; (*chest*) poitrine *f*. ◆**b.-feed** *vt* (*pt & pp* -fed) allaiter. ◆**breaststroke** *n* (*swimming*) brasse *f*.

breath [breθ] *n* haleine *f*, souffle *m*; (*of air*) souffle *m*; under one's b. tout bas; one's last b. son dernier soupir; out of b. à bout de souffle; to get a b. of air prendre l'air; to take a deep b. respirer profondément. ◆**breathalyser®** *n* alcootest® *m*. ◆**breathless** *a* haletant. ◆**breathtaking** *a* sensationnel.

breath/e [briːð] *vti* respirer; to b. in aspirer; to b. out expirer; to b. air into sth souffler dans qch; – *vt* (a sigh) pousser; (a word) dire. ◆**-ing** *n* respiration *f*; b. space moment *m* de repos. ◆**-er** *n Fam* moment *m* de repos; to go for a b. sortir prendre l'air.

bred [bred] *see* breed 1; – *a* well-b. bien élevé.

breeches ['briːtʃɪz] *npl* culotte *f*.

breed [briːd] **1** *vt* (*pt & pp* bred) (*animals*) élever; (*cause*) *Fig* engendrer; – *vi* (*of animals*) se reproduire. **2** *n* race *f*, espèce *f*. ◆**-ing** *n* élevage *m*; reproduction *f*; *Fig* éducation *f*. ◆**-er** *n* éleveur, -euse *mf*.

breeze [briːz] *n* brise *f*. ◆**breezy** *a* (**-ier,**

-iest) 1 (*weather, day*) frais, venteux. **2** (*cheerful*) jovial; (*relaxed*) décontracté.

breezeblock ['briːzblɒk] *n* parpaing *m*, briquette *f*.

brevity ['brevɪtɪ] *n* brièveté *f*.

brew [bruː] *vt* (*beer*) brasser; (*trouble, plot*) préparer; **to b. tea** préparer du thé; (*infuse*) (faire) infuser du thé; – *vi* (*of beer*) fermenter; (*of tea*) infuser; (*of storm, trouble*) se préparer; – *n* (*drink*) breuvage *m*; (*of tea*) infusion *f*. **◆—er** *n* brasseur *m*. **◆brewery** *n* brasserie *f*.

bribe [braɪb] *n* pot-de-vin *m*; – *vt* soudoyer, corrompre. **◆bribery** *n* corruption *f*.

brick [brɪk] *n* brique *f*; (*child's*) cube *m*; **to drop a b.** *Fam* faire une gaffe; – *vt* **to b. up** (*gap, door*) murer. **◆bricklayer** *n* maçon *m*. **◆brickwork** *n* ouvrage *m* en briques; (*bricks*) briques *fpl*.

bridal ['braɪd(ə)l] *a* (*ceremony*) nuptial; **b. gown** robe *f* de mariée.

bride [braɪd] *n* mariée *f*; **the b. and groom** les mariés *mpl*. **◆bridegroom** *n* marié *m*. **◆bridesmaid** *n* demoiselle *f* d'honneur.

bridge [brɪdʒ] **1** *n* pont *m*; (*on ship*) passerelle *f*; (*of nose*) arête *f*; (*false tooth*) bridge *m*; – *vt* **to b. a gap** combler une lacune. **2** *n* Cards bridge *m*.

bridle ['braɪd(ə)l] *n* (*for horse*) bride *f*; – *vt* (*horse, instinct etc*) brider; **b. path** allée *f* cavalière.

brief [briːf] **1** *a* (**-er, -est**) bref; **in b.** en résumé. **2** *n* *Jur* dossier *m*; (*instructions*) *Mil Pol* instructions *fpl*; *Fig* tâche *f*, fonctions *fpl*; – *vt* donner des instructions à; (*inform*) mettre au courant (**on** de). **3** *npl* (*underpants*) slip *m*. **◆—ing** *n* *Mil Pol* instructions *fpl*; *Av* briefing *m*. **◆—ly** *adv* (*quickly*) en vitesse; (*to say*) brièvement.

brigade [brɪ'geɪd] *n* brigade *f*. **◆briga'dier** *n* général *m* de brigade.

bright [braɪt] *a* (**-er, -est**) brillant, vif; (*weather, room*) clair; (*clever*) intelligent; (*happy*) joyeux; (*future*) brillant, prometteur; (*idea*) génial; **b. interval** *Met* éclaircie *f*; – *adv* **b. and early** (*to get up*) de bonne heure. **◆—ly** *adv* brillamment. **◆—ness** *n* éclat *m*; (*of person*) intelligence *f*. **◆brighten** *vt* (*room*) égayer; – *vi* **to b. (up)** (*of weather*) s'éclaircir; (*of face*) s'éclairer.

brilliant ['brɪljənt] *a* (*light*) éclatant; (*very clever*) brillant. **◆brilliance** *n* éclat *m*; (*of person*) grande intelligence *f*.

brim [brɪm] *n* bord *m*; – *vi* (**-mm-**) **to b. over** déborder (**with** de).

brine [braɪn] *n* *Culin* saumure *f*.

bring [brɪŋ] *vt* (*pt & pp* brought) (*person, vehicle etc*) amener; (*thing*) apporter; (*to cause*) amener; (*action*) *Jur* intenter; **to b. along** *or* **over** *or* **round** amener; apporter; **to b. back** ramener; rapporter; (*memories*) rappeler; **to b. sth up/down** monter/descendre qch; **to b. sth in/out** rentrer/sortir qch; **to b. sth** (*to perfection, a peak etc*) porter qch à; **to b. to an end** mettre fin à; **to b. to mind** rappeler; **to b. sth on oneself** s'attirer qch; **to b. oneself to do** se résoudre à faire; **to b. about** provoquer, amener; **to b. down** (*overthrow*) faire tomber; (*reduce*) réduire; (*shoot down*) abattre; **to b. forward** (*in time or space*) avancer; (*witness*) produire; **to b. in** (*person*) faire entrer *or* rentrer; (*introduce*) introduire; (*income*) *Com* rapporter; **to b. off** (*task*) mener à bien; **to b. out** (*person*) faire sortir; (*meaning*) faire ressortir; (*book*) publier; (*product*) lancer; **to b. over** (*to convert to*) convertir à; **to b. round** *Med* ranimer; (*convert*) convertir (**to** à); **to b. s.o. to** *Med* ranimer qn; **to b. together** mettre en contact; (*reconcile*) réconcilier; **to b. up** (*child etc*) élever; (*question*) soulever; (*subject*) mentionner; (*vomit*) vomir.

brink [brɪŋk] *n* bord *m*.

brisk [brɪsk] *a* (**-er, -est**) vif; (*trade*) actif; **at a b. pace** d'un bon pas. **◆—ly** *adv* vivement; (*to walk*) d'un bon pas. **◆—ness** *n* vivacité *f*.

bristl/e ['brɪs(ə)l] *n* poil *m*; – *vi* se hérisser. **◆—ing** *a* **b. with** (*difficulties*) hérissé de.

Britain ['brɪt(ə)n] *n* Grande-Bretagne *f*. **◆British** *a* britannique; – *n* **the B.** les Britanniques *mpl*. **◆Briton** *n* Britannique *mf*.

Brittany ['brɪtənɪ] *n* Bretagne *f*.

brittle ['brɪt(ə)l] *a* cassant, fragile.

broach [brəʊtʃ] *vt* (*topic*) entamer.

broad[1] [brɔːd] *a* (**-er, -est**) (*wide*) large; (*outline*) grand, général; (*accent*) prononcé; **in b. daylight** au grand jour; **b. bean** fève *f*; **b. jump** *Sp Am* saut *m* en longueur. **◆b.-minded** *a* à l'esprit large. **◆b.-shouldered** *a* large d'épaules. **◆broaden** *vt* élargir; – *vi* s'élargir. **◆broadly** *adv* **b. (speaking)** en gros, grosso modo.

broad[2] [brɔːd] *n* (*woman*) *Am Sl* nana *f*.

broadcast ['brɔːdkɑːst] *vt* (*pt & pp* broadcast) *Rad & Fig* diffuser; *TV* téléviser; – *vi* (*of station*) émettre; (*of person*) parler à la radio *or* à la télévision; (*of programme*) diffusé, (*radio*)diffusé; télévisé; – *n* émission *f*. **◆—ing** *n* radiodiffusion *f*; télévision *f*.

broccoli ['brɒkəlı] n inv brocoli m.

brochure ['brəʊʃər] n brochure f, dépliant m.

brogue [brəʊg] n Ling accent m irlandais.

broil [brɔɪl] vti griller. ◆—**er** n poulet m (à rôtir); (apparatus) gril m.

broke [brəʊk] **1** see break. **2** a (penniless) fauché. ◆**broken** see break; – a (ground) accidenté; (spirit) abattu; (man, voice, line) brisé; **b. English** mauvais anglais m; **b. home** foyer m brisé. ◆**broken-'down** a (machine etc) (tout) déglingué, détraqué.

brolly ['brɒlı] n (umbrella) Fam pépin m.

bronchitis [brɒŋ'kaɪtɪs] n bronchite f.

bronze [brɒnz] n bronze m; – a (statue etc) en bronze.

brooch [brəʊtʃ] n (ornament) broche f.

brood [bruːd] **1** n couvée f, nichée f; – vi (of bird) couver. **2** vi méditer tristement (**over**, on sur); **to b. over** (a plan) ruminer. ◆**broody** a (-ier, -iest) (person) maussade, rêveur; (woman) Fam qui a envie d'avoir un enfant.

brook [brʊk] **1** n ruisseau m. **2** vt souffrir, tolérer.

broom [bruːm] n **1** (for sweeping) balai m. **2** Bot genêt m. ◆**broomstick** n manche m à balai.

Bros abbr (Brothers) Frères mpl.

broth [brɒθ] n bouillon m.

brothel ['brɒθ(ə)l] n maison f close, bordel m.

brother ['brʌðər] n frère m. ◆**b.-in-law** n (pl **brothers-in-law**) beau-frère m. ◆**brotherhood** n fraternité f. ◆**brotherly** a fraternel.

brow [braʊ] n (forehead) front m; (of hill) sommet m.

browbeat ['braʊbiːt] vt (pt -beat, pp -beaten) intimider.

brown [braʊn] a (-er, -est) brun; (reddish) marron; (hair) châtain; (tanned) bronzé; – n brun m; marron m; – vt brunir; Culin faire dorer; **to be browned off** Fam en avoir marre. ◆**brownish** a brunâtre.

Brownie ['braʊnɪ] n **1** (girl scout) jeannette f. **2 b.** Culin Am petit gâteau m au chocolat.

browse [braʊz] vi (in shop) regarder; (in bookshop) feuilleter les livres; (of animal) brouter; **to b. through** (book) feuilleter.

bruis/e [bruːz] vt contusionner, meurtrir; (fruit, heart) meurtrir; – n bleu m, contusion f. ◆—**ed** a couvert de bleus.

brunch [brʌntʃ] n repas m mixte (petit déjeuner pris comme déjeuner).

brunette [bruː'net] n brunette f.

brunt [brʌnt] n **to bear the b. of** (attack etc) subir le plus gros de.

brush [brʌʃ] n brosse f; (for shaving) blaireau m; (little broom) balayette f; (action) coup m de brosse; (fight) accrochage m; – vt (teeth, hair etc) brosser; (clothes) donner un coup de brosse à; **to b. aside** écarter; **to b. away** or **off** enlever; **to b. up (on)** (language) se remettre à; – vi **to b. against** effleurer. ◆**b.-off** n Fam to give s.o. **the b.-off** envoyer promener qn. ◆**b.-up** n coup m de brosse. ◆**brushwood** n broussailles fpl.

brusque [bruːsk] a brusque.

Brussels ['brʌs(ə)lz] n Bruxelles m or f; **B. sprouts** choux mpl de Bruxelles.

brutal ['bruːt(ə)l] a brutal. ◆**bru'tality** n brutalité f.

brute [bruːt] n (animal, person) brute f; – a **by b. force** par la force.

BSc, Am **BS** abbr = Bachelor of Science.

bubble ['bʌb(ə)l] n (of air, soap etc) bulle f (in boiling liquid) bouillon m; **b. and squeak** Fam friture f de purée et de viande réchauffées; **b. bath** bain m moussant; **b. gum** chewing-gum m; – vi bouillonner; **to b. over** déborder (**with** de). ◆**bubbly** n Hum Fam champagne m.

buck [bʌk] **1** n Am Fam dollar m. **2** n (animal) mâle m. **3** vt **to b. up** remonter le moral à; – vi **to b. up** prendre courage; (hurry) se grouiller. ◆**buckshot** n inv du gros plomb m. ◆**buck'tooth** n (pl -teeth) dent f saillante.

bucket ['bʌkɪt] n seau m.

buckle ['bʌk(ə)l] **1** n boucle f; – vt boucler. **2** vti (warp) voiler, gauchir. **3** vi **to b. down to** (task) s'atteler à.

bud [bʌd] n (of tree) bourgeon m; (of flower) bouton m; – vi (-dd-) bourgeonner; pousser des boutons. ◆**budding** a (talent) naissant; (doctor etc) en herbe.

Buddhist ['bʊdɪst] a & n bouddhiste (mf).

buddy ['bʌdɪ] n Am Fam copain m, pote m.

budge [bʌdʒ] vi bouger; – vt faire bouger.

budgerigar ['bʌdʒərɪgɑːr] n perruche f.

budget ['bʌdʒɪt] n budget m; – vi dresser un budget; **to b. for** inscrire au budget. ◆**budgetary** a budgétaire.

budgie ['bʌdʒɪ] n Fam perruche f.

buff [bʌf] **1** a **b.(-coloured)** chamois inv. **2** n jazz/etc **b.** Fam fana(tique) mf du jazz/etc. **3** n **in the b.** Fam tout nu.

buffalo ['bʌfələʊ] n (pl -oes or -o) buffle m; (American) **b.** bison m.

buffer ['bʌfər] n (on train) tampon m; (at end of track) butoir m; **b. state** état m tampon.

buffet 1 ['bʌfɪt] *vt* frapper; (*of waves*) battre; (*of wind, rain*) cingler (*qn*). **2** ['bufeɪ] *n* (*table, meal, café*) buffet *m*; **cold b.** viandes *fpl* froides.

buffoon [bə'fuːn] *n* bouffon *m*.

bug 1 [bʌg] **1** *n* punaise *f*; (*any insect*) *Fam* bestiole *f*; *Med Fam* microbe *m*, virus *m*; **the travel b.** (*urge*) le désir de voyager. **2** *n Fam* (*in machine*) défaut *m*; (*in computer program*) erreur *f*. **3** *n* (*apparatus*) *Fam* micro *m*; – *vt* (-gg-) (*room*) *Fam* installer des micros dans.

bug 2 [bʌg] *vt* (-gg-) (*annoy*) *Am Fam* embêter.

bugbear ['bʌgbeər] *n* (*worry*) cauchemar *m*.

buggy ['bʌgɪ] *n* (*baby*) **b.** (*pushchair*) poussette *f*; (*folding*) poussette-canne *f*; (*pram*) *Am* landau *m*.

bugle ['bjuːg(ə)l] *n* clairon *m*. ◆**bugler** *n* (*person*) clairon *m*.

build [bɪld] **1** *n* (*of person*) carrure *f*. **2** *vt* (*pt & pp* built) (*house, town*) construire, bâtir; **to b. in** (*cupboard etc*) encastrer; – *vi* bâtir, construire. ◆**built-in** *a* (*cupboard etc*) encastré; (*element of machine etc*) incorporé; (*innate*) *Fig* inné. **3 to b. up** *vt* (*reputation*) bâtir; (*increase*) augmenter; (*accumulate*) accumuler; (*business*) monter; (*speed, one's strength*) prendre; – *vi* augmenter, monter; s'accumuler. ◆**build-up** *n* montée *f*; accumulation *f*; *Mil* concentration *f*; *Journ* publicité *f*. ◆**built-up** *a* urbanisé; **b.-up area** agglomération *f*.

builder ['bɪldər] *n* maçon *m*; (*contractor*) entrepreneur *m*; (*of cars etc*) constructeur *m*; (*labourer*) ouvrier *m*.

building ['bɪldɪŋ] *n* bâtiment *m*; (*flats, offices*) immeuble *m*; (*action*) construction *f*; **b. society** caisse *f* d'épargne-logement, = société *f* de crédit immobilier.

bulb [bʌlb] *n Bot* bulbe *m*, oignon *m*; *El* ampoule *f*. ◆**bulbous** *a* bulbeux.

Bulgaria [bʌl'geərɪə] *n* Bulgarie *f*. ◆**Bulgarian** *a* & *n* bulgare (*mf*).

bulge [bʌldʒ] *vi* **to b.** (**out**) se renfler, bomber; (*of eyes*) sortir de la tête; – *n* renflement *m*; (*increase*) *Fam* augmentation *f*. ◆**-ing** *a* renflé, bombé; (*eyes*) protubérant; (*bag*) gonflé (**with** de).

bulk [bʌlk] *n inv* grosseur *f*, volume *m*; **the b. of** (*most*) la majeure partie de; **in b.** (*to buy, sell*) en gros. ◆**bulky** *a* (-ier, -iest) gros, volumineux.

bull [bul] *n* **1** taureau *m*. **2** (*nonsense*) *Fam* foutaises *fpl*. ◆**bullfight** *n* corrida *f*.

◆**bullfighter** *n* matador *m*. ◆**bullring** *n* arène *f*.

bulldog ['buldɒg] *n* bouledogue *m*; **b. clip** pince *f* (à dessin).

bulldoz/e ['buldəuz] *vt* passer au bulldozer. ◆**-er** *n* bulldozer *m*, bouteur *m*.

bullet ['bulɪt] *n* balle *f*. ◆**bulletproof** *a* (*jacket, Am vest*) pare-balles *inv*; (*car*) blindé.

bulletin ['bulətɪn] *n* bulletin *m*.

bullion ['buljən] *n* or *m* or argent *m* en lingots.

bullock ['bulək] *n* bœuf *m*.

bull's-eye ['bulzaɪ] *n* (*of target*) centre *m*; **to hit the b.-eye** faire mouche.

bully ['bulɪ] *n* (*grosse*) brute *f*, tyran *m*; – *vt* brutaliser; (*persecute*) tyranniser; **to b. into doing** forcer à faire.

bulwark ['bulwək] *n* rempart *m*.

bum [bʌm] **1** *n* (*loafer*) *Am Fam* clochard *m*; – *vi* (-mm-) **to b.** (**around**) se balader. **2** *vt* (-mm-) **to b. sth off s.o.** (*cadge*) *Am Fam* taper qn de qch. **3** *n* (*buttocks*) *Fam* derrière *m*.

bumblebee ['bʌmb(ə)lbiː] *n* bourdon *m*.

bumf [bʌmf] *n Pej Sl* paperasses *fpl*.

bump [bʌmp] *vt* (*of car etc*) heurter; **to b. one's head/knee** se cogner la tête/le genou; **to b. into** se cogner contre; (*of car*) rentrer dans; (*meet*) *Fam* tomber sur; **to b. off** (*kill*) *Sl* liquider; **to b. up** *Fam* augmenter; – *vi* **to b. along** (*on rough road*) *Aut* cahoter; – *n* (*impact*) choc *m*; (*jerk*) cahot *m*; (*on road, body*) bosse *f*. ◆**-er** *n* (*of car etc*) pare-chocs *m inv*; – *a* (*a crop etc*) exceptionnel; **b. cars** autos *fpl* tamponneuses. ◆**bumpy** *a* (-ier, -iest) (*road, ride*) cahoteux.

bumpkin ['bʌmpkɪn] *n* rustre *m*.

bumptious ['bʌmpʃəs] *a* prétentieux.

bun [bʌn] *n* **1** *Culin* petit pain *m* au lait. **2** (*of hair*) chignon *m*.

bunch [bʌntʃ] *n* (*of flowers*) bouquet *m*; (*of keys*) trousseau *m*; (*of bananas*) régime *m*; (*of people*) bande *f*; **b. of grapes** grappe *f* de raisin; **a b. of** (*mass*) *Fam* un tas de.

bundle ['bʌnd(ə)l] **1** *n* paquet *m*; (*of papers*) liasse *f*; (*of firewood*) fagot *m*. **2** *vt* (*put*) fourrer; (*push*) pousser (**into** dans); **to b.** (**up**) mettre en paquet; **to b. s.o. off** expédier qn; – *vi* **to b.** (**oneself**) **up** se couvrir (bien).

bung [bʌŋ] **1** *n* (*stopper*) bonde *f*; – *vt* **to b. up** (*stop up*) boucher. **2** *vt* (*toss*) *Fam* balancer, jeter.

bungalow ['bʌŋgələu] *n* bungalow *m*.

bungl/e ['bʌŋg(ə)l] *vt* gâcher; – *vi* travailler

mal. ◆—ing n gâchis m; — a (clumsy) maladroit.

bunion ['bʌnjən] n (on toe) oignon m.

bunk [bʌŋk] n 1 Rail Nau couchette f; b. beds lits mpl superposés. 2 Sl = bunkum. ◆**bunkum** n Sl foutaises fpl.

bunker ['bʌŋkər] n Mil Golf bunker m; (coalstore in garden) soute f.

bunny ['bʌnɪ] n Fam Jeannot m lapin.

buoy [bɔɪ] n bouée f; — vt to b. up (support) Fig soutenir.

buoyant ['bɔɪənt] a Fig gai, optimiste; (market) Fin ferme.

burden ['bɜːd(ə)n] n fardeau m; (of tax) poids m; — vt charger, accabler (with de).

bureau, pl -eaux ['bjuərəu, -əuz] n (office) bureau m; (desk) secrétaire m. ◆**bureaucracy** [bjuə'rɒkrəsɪ] n bureaucratie f. ◆**bureaucrat** ['bjuərəkræt] n bureaucrate mf.

burger ['bɜːgər] n Fam hamburger m.

burglar ['bɜːglər] n cambrioleur, -euse mf; b. alarm sonnerie f d'alarme. ◆**burglarize** vt Am cambrioler. ◆**burglary** n cambriolage m. ◆**burgle** vt cambrioler.

burial ['berɪəl] n enterrement m; — a (service) funèbre; b. ground cimetière m.

burlap ['bɜːlæp] n (sacking) Am toile f à sac.

burlesque [bɜː'lesk] n parodie f; Th Am revue f.

burly ['bɜːlɪ] a (-ier, -iest) costaud.

Burma ['bɜːmə] n Birmanie f. ◆**Bur'mese** a & n birman, -ane (mf).

burn [bɜːn] n brûlure f; — vt (pt & pp burned or burnt) brûler; to b. down or off or up brûler; burnt alive brûlé vif; — vi brûler; to b. down (of house) brûler (complètement), être réduit en cendres; to b. out (of fire) s'éteindre; (of fuse) sauter. ◆—ing a en feu; (fire) allumé; (topic, fever etc) Fig brûlant; — n smell of b. odeur f de brûlé. ◆—er n (of stove) brûleur m.

burp [bɜːp] n Fam rot m; — vi Fam roter.

burrow ['bʌrəu] n (hole) terrier m; — vti creuser.

bursar ['bɜːsər] n (in school) intendant, -ante mf.

bursary ['bɜːsərɪ] n (grant) bourse f.

burst [bɜːst] n éclatement m, explosion f; (of laughter) éclat m; (of applause) salve f; (of thunder) coup m; (surge) élan m; (fit) accès m; (burst water pipe) Fam tuyau m crevé; — vi (pt & pp burst) (of bomb etc) éclater; (of bubble, tyre, cloud etc) crever; to b. into (room) faire irruption dans; to b. into tears fondre en larmes; to b. into flames prendre feu, s'embraser; to b. open s'ouvrir avec

force; to b. out laughing éclater de rire; — vt crever, faire éclater; (rupture) rompre; to b. open ouvrir avec force. ◆—ing a (full) plein à craquer (with de); b. with (joy) débordant de; to be b. to do mourir d'envie de faire.

bury ['berɪ] vt (dead person) enterrer; (hide) enfouir; (plunge, absorb) plonger.

bus [bʌs] n (auto)bus m; (long-distance) (auto)car m; — a (driver, ticket etc) d'autobus; d'autocar; b. shelter abribus m; b. station gare f routière; b. stop arrêt m d'autobus; — vt (-ss-) (children) transporter (en bus) à l'école. ◆**bussing** n Sch ramassage m scolaire.

bush [buʃ] n buisson m; (of hair) tignasse f; the b. (land) la brousse. ◆**bushy** a (-ier, -iest) (hair, tail etc) broussailleux.

bushed [buʃt] a (tired) Fam éreinté.

business ['bɪznɪs] n affaires fpl, commerce m; (shop) commerce m; (task, concern, matter) affaire f; the textile b. le textile; big b. Fam les grosses entreprises fpl commerciales; on b. (to travel) pour affaires; it's your b. to ... c'est à vous de ...; you have no b. to ... vous n'avez pas le droit de ...; that's none of your b.! ça ne vous regarde pas!; to mean b. Fam ne pas plaisanter; — a commercial; (meeting, trip) d'affaires; b. hours (office) heures fpl de travail; (shop) heures fpl d'ouverture. ◆**businesslike** a sérieux, pratique. ◆**businessman** n (pl -men) homme m d'affaires. ◆**businesswoman** n (pl -women) femme f d'affaires.

busker ['bʌskər] n musicien, -ienne mf des rues.

bust [bʌst] n 1 (sculpture) buste m; (woman's breasts) poitrine f. 2 a (broken) Fam fichu; to go b. (bankrupt) faire faillite; — vt (pt & pp bust or busted) Fam = to burst & to break. ◆**b.-up** n Fam (quarrel) engueulade f; (breakup) rupture f.

bustle ['bʌs(ə)l] vi to b. (about) s'affairer; — n activité f, branle-bas m. ◆—ing a (street) bruyant.

bus/y ['bɪzɪ] a (-ier, -iest) occupé (doing à faire); (active) actif; (day) chargé; (street) animé; (line) Tel Am occupé; to be b. doing (in the process of) être en train de faire; — vt to b. oneself s'occuper (with à qch, doing à faire). ◆—ily adv activement. ◆**busybody** n to be a b. faire la mouche du coche.

but [bʌt, unstressed bət] 1 conj mais. 2 prep (except) sauf; b. for that sans cela; b. for him sans lui; no one b. you personne d'autre que toi. **3** *adv* (*only*) ne . . . que, seulement.

butane ['bjuːteɪn] *n* (*gas*) butane *m*.

butcher ['butʃər] *n* boucher *m*; **b.'s shop** boucherie *f*. – *vt* (*people*) massacrer; (*animal*) abattre. ◆**butchery** *n* massacre *m* (of de).

butler ['bʌtlər] *n* maître *m* d'hôtel.

butt [bʌt] **1** *n* (*of cigarette*) mégot *m*; (*of gun*) crosse *f*; (*buttocks*) *Am Fam* derrière *m*; **b. for ridicule** objet *m* de risée. **2** *vi* **to b.** interrompre, intervenir.

butter ['bʌtər] *n* beurre *m*; **b. bean** haricot *m* blanc; **b. dish** beurrier *m*; – *vt* beurrer; **to b. s.o. up** *Fam* flatter qn. ◆**buttercup** *n* bouton-d'or *m*. ◆**buttermilk** *n* lait *m* de beurre.

butterfly ['bʌtəflaɪ] *n* papillon *m*; **to have butterflies** *Fam* avoir le trac; **b. stroke** *Swimming* brasse *f* papillon.

buttock ['bʌtək] *n* fesse *f*.

button ['bʌtən] *n* bouton *m*; – *vt* **to b. (up)** boutonner; – *vi* **to b. up** (*of garment*) se boutonner. ◆**buttonhole 1** *n* boutonnière *f*; (*flower*) fleur *f*. **2** *vt* (*person*) *Fam* accrocher.

buttress ['bʌtrɪs] *n Archit* contrefort *m*; *Fig* soutien *m*; **flying b.** arc-boutant *m*; – *vt* (*support*) *Archit & Fig* soutenir.

buxom ['bʌksəm] *a* (*woman*) bien en chair.

buy [baɪ] *vt* (*pt & pp* bought) acheter (**from s.o.** à qn, **for s.o.** à *or* pour qn); (*story etc*) *Am Fam* avaler, croire; **to b. back** racheter; **to b. over** (*bribe*) corrompre; **to b. up** acheter en bloc; – *n* **a good b.** une bonne affaire. ◆**-er** *n* acheteur, -euse *mf*.

buzz [bʌz] **1** *vi* bourdonner; **to b. off** *Fam* décamper; – *n* bourdonnement *m*. **2** *vt* (*building etc*) *Av* raser. **3** *vt* **to b. s.o.** *Tel*

appeler qn; – *n Tel Fam* coup *m* de fil. ◆**-er** *n* interphone *m*; (*of bell, clock*) sonnerie *f*; (*hooter*) sirène *f*.

by [baɪ] *prep* **1** (*agent, manner*) par; **hit/chosen/etc by** frappé/choisi/*etc* par; **surrounded/followed/etc by** entouré/suivi/*etc* de; **by doing** en faisant; **by sea** par mer; **by mistake** par erreur; **by car** en voiture; **by bicycle** à bicyclette; **by moonlight** au clair de lune; **one by one** un à un; **day by day** de jour en jour; **by sight/day/far** de vue/jour/loin; **by the door** (*through*) par la porte; (**all**) **by oneself** tout seul. **2** (*next to*) à côté de; (*near*) près de; **by the lake/sea** au bord du lac/de la mer; **to pass by the bank** passer devant la banque. **3** (*before in time*) avant; **by Monday** avant lundi, d'ici lundi; **by now** à cette heure-ci, déjà; **by yesterday** (dès) hier. **4** (*amount, measurement*) à; **by the kilo** au kilo; **taller by a metre** plus grand d'un mètre; **paid by the hour** payé à l'heure. **5** (*according to*) d'après; – *adv* **close by** tout près; **to go by, pass by** passer; **to put by** mettre de côté; **by and by** bientôt; **by and large** en gros. ◆**by-election** *n* élection *f* partielle. ◆**by-law** *n* arrêté *m*; (*of organization*) *Am* statut *m*. ◆**by-product** *n* sous-produit *m*. ◆**by-road** *n* chemin *m* de traverse.

bye(-bye)! [baɪ('baɪ)] *int Fam* salut!, au revoir!

bygone ['baɪgɒn] *a* **in b. days** jadis.

bypass ['baɪpɑːs] *n* déviation *f* (routière), dérivation *f*; – *vt* contourner; (*ignore*) *Fig* éviter de passer par.

bystander ['baɪstændər] *n* spectateur, -trice *mf*; (*in street*) badaud, -aude *mf*.

byword ['baɪwɜːd] *n* **a b. for** *Pej* un synonyme de.

C

C, c [siː] *n* C, c *m*.

c *abbr* = cent.

cab [kæb] *n* taxi *m*; (*horse-drawn*) *Hist* fiacre *m*; (*of train driver etc*) cabine *f*. ◆**cabby** *n Fam* (*chauffeur m de*) taxi *m*; *Hist* cocher *m*.

cabaret ['kæbəreɪ] *n* (*show*) spectacle *m*; (*place*) cabaret *m*.

cabbage ['kæbɪdʒ] *n* chou *m*.

cabin ['kæbɪn] *n Nau Rail* cabine *f*; (*hut*) cabane *f*, case *f*; **c. boy** mousse *m*.

cabinet ['kæbɪnɪt] **1** *n* (*cupboard*) armoire *f*; (*for display*) vitrine *f*; (*filing*) **c.** classeur *m* (de bureau). **2** *n Pol* cabinet *m*; – *a* ministériel; **c. minister** ministre *m*. ◆**c.-maker** *n* ébéniste *m*.

cable ['keɪb(ə)l] *n* câble *m*; **c. car** (*with overhead cable*) téléphérique *m*; *Rail* funiculaire *m*; **c. television** la télévision par câble; **to have the c.** *Fam* avoir le câble; – *vt* (*message etc*) câbler (**to** à).

caboose [kə'buːs] n Rail Am fourgon m (de queue).

cache [kæʃ] n (place) cachette f; **an arms' c.** des armes cachées, une cache d'armes.

cachet ['kæʃeɪ] n (mark, character etc) cachet m.

cackle ['kæk(ə)l] vi (of hen) caqueter; (laugh) glousser; – n caquet m; gloussement m.

cacophony [kə'kɒfənɪ] n cacophonie f.

cactus ['kæktəs], pl -**ti** or -**tuses** [kæktəs, -taɪ, -təsɪz] n cactus m.

cad [kæd] n Old-fashioned Pej goujat m.

cadaverous [kə'dævərəs] a cadavérique.

caddie ['kædɪ] n Golf caddie m.

caddy ['kædɪ] n (tea) c. boîte f à thé.

cadence ['keɪdəns] n Mus cadence f.

cadet [kə'det] n Mil élève m officier.

cadge [kædʒ] vi (beg) Pej quémander; – vt (meal) se faire payer (**off s.o.** par qn); **to c. money from** or **off s.o.** taper qn.

Caesarean [sɪ'zeərɪən] n c. (**section**) Med césarienne f.

café ['kæfeɪ] n café(-restaurant) m. ◆**cafeteria** [kæfɪ'tɪərɪə] n cafétéria f.

caffeine ['kæfiːn] n caféine f.

cage [keɪdʒ] n cage f; – vt **to c. (up)** mettre en cage.

cagey ['keɪdʒɪ] a Fam peu communicatif (**about** à l'égard de).

cahoots [kə'huːts] n in c. Sl de mèche, en cheville (**with** avec).

cajole [kə'dʒəʊl] vt amadouer, enjôler.

cak/e [keɪk] **1** n gâteau m; (small) pâtisserie f; c. **of soap** savonnette f. **2** vi (harden) durcir; – vt (cover) couvrir (**with** de). ◆**-ed** a (mud) séché.

calamine ['kæləmaɪn] n c. (**lotion**) lotion f apaisante (à la calamine).

calamity [kə'læmɪtɪ] n calamité f. ◆**calamitous** a désastreux.

calcium ['kælsɪəm] n calcium m.

calculat/e ['kælkjʊleɪt] vti calculer; **to c. that** Fam supposer que; **to c. on** compter sur. ◆**-ing** a (shrewd) calculateur. ◆**calcu'lation** n calcul m. ◆**calculator** n (desk computer) calculatrice f; (pocket) c. calculatrice f (de poche). ◆**calculus** n Math Med calcul m.

calendar ['kælɪndər] n calendrier m; (directory) annuaire m.

calf [kɑːf] n (pl **calves**) **1** (animal) veau m. **2** Anat mollet m.

calibre ['kælɪbər] n calibre m. ◆**calibrate** vt calibrer.

calico ['kælɪkəʊ] n (pl -**oes** or -**os**) (fabric) calicot m; (printed) Am indienne f.

call [kɔːl] n appel m; (shout) cri m; (vocation) vocation f; (visit) visite f; (telephone) c. communication f, appel m téléphonique; **to make a c.** Tel téléphoner (**to** à); **on c.** de garde; **no c. to do** aucune raison de faire; **there's no c. for that article** Com cet article n'est pas très demandé; c. **box** cabine f (téléphonique); – vt appeler; (wake up) réveiller; (person to meeting) convoquer (**to** à); (attention) attirer (**to** sur); (truce) demander; (consider) considérer; **he's called David** il s'appelle David; **to c. a meeting** convoquer une assemblée; **to c. s.o. a liar**/etc qualifier or traiter qn de menteur/etc; **to c. into question** mettre en question; **let's c. it a day** Fam on va s'arrêter là, ça suffit; **to c. sth (out)** (shout) crier qch; – vi appeler; **to c. (out)** (cry out) crier; **to c.** (in or round or by or over) (visit) passer. ■ **to c. back** vti rappeler; **to c. for** vt (require) demander; (summon) demander; (collect) passer prendre; **to c. in** vt faire venir or entrer; (police) appeler; (recall) rappeler, faire rentrer; – vi **to c. in on s.o.** passer chez qn. ◆**call-in** a (programme) Rad à ligne ouverte; **to c. off** vt (cancel) annuler; (dog) rappeler; **to c. out** vt (doctor) appeler; (workers) donner une consigne de grève à; – vi **to c. out for** demander à haute voix; **to c. up** vt Mil Tel appeler; (memories) évoquer. ◆**call-up** n Mil appel m, mobilisation f; **to c. (up)on** vi (visit) passer voir, passer chez; (invoke) invoquer; **to c. (up)on s.o. to do** inviter qn à faire; (urge) sommer qn de faire. ◆**calling** n vocation f. ◆**call card** Am carte f de visite. ◆**caller** n visiteur, -euse mf; Tel correspondant, -ante mf.

calligraphy [kə'lɪgrəfɪ] n calligraphie f.

callous ['kæləs] a **1** cruel, insensible. **2** (skin) calleux. ◆**callus** n durillon m, cal m.

callow ['kæləʊ] a inexpérimenté.

calm [kɑːm] a (-er, -est) calme, tranquille; **keep c.!** (don't panic) du calme!; – n calme m; – vt **to c. (down)** calmer; – vi **to c. down** se calmer. ◆**-ly** adv calmement. ◆**-ness** n calme m.

calorie ['kælərɪ] n calorie f.

calumny ['kæləmnɪ] n calomnie f.

calvary ['kælvərɪ] n Rel calvaire m.

calve [kɑːv] vi (of cow) vêler.

camber ['kæmbər] n (in road) bombement m.

came [keɪm] see come.

camel ['kæməl] n chameau m.

camellia [kə'miːlɪə] n Bot camélia m.

cameo ['kæmɪəʊ] n camée m.

camera ['kæmrə] n appareil(-photo) m; TV Cin caméra f. ◆**cameraman** n (pl -men) caméraman m.

camomile ['kæməmaɪl] n Bot camomille f.

camouflage ['kæməflɑːʒ] n camouflage m; - vt camoufler.

camp¹ [kæmp] n camp m, campement m; c. bed lit m de camp; - vi to c. (out) camper. ◆**-ing** n Sp camping m; c. site terrain m de) camping m. ◆**-er** n (person) campeur, -euse mf; (vehicle) camping-car m. ◆**campfire** n feu m de camp. ◆**camp-site** n camping m.

camp² [kæmp] a (affected) affecté, exagéré (de façon à provoquer le rire).

campaign [kæm'peɪn] n Pol Mil Journ etc campagne f; - vi faire campagne. ◆**-er** n militant, -ante mf (for pour).

campus ['kæmpəs] n Univ campus m.

can¹ [kæn, unstressed kən] v aux (pres t can; pt could) (be able to) pouvoir; (know how to) savoir; if I c. si je peux; she c. swim elle sait nager; if I could swim si je savais nager; he could do it tomorrow il pourrait le faire demain; he couldn't help me il ne pouvait pas m'aider; he could have done it il aurait pu le faire; you could be wrong (possibility) tu as peut-être tort; he can't be old (probability) il ne doit pas être vieux; c. I come in? (permission) puis-je entrer?; you can't or c. not come tu ne peux pas venir; I c. see je vois.

can² [kæn] n (for water etc) bidon m; (tin for food) boîte f; - vt (-nn-) mettre en boîte. ◆**canned** a en boîte, en conserve; c. food conserves fpl. ◆**can-opener** n ouvre-boîtes m inv.

Canada ['kænədə] n Canada m. ◆**Canadian** [kə'neɪdɪən] a & n canadien, -ienne (mf).

canal [kə'næl] n canal m.

canary [kə'neərɪ] n canari m, serin m.

cancan ['kænkæn] n french-cancan m.

cancel ['kænsəl] vt (-ll-, Am -l-) annuler; (goods, taxi, appointment) décommander; (word, paragraph etc) biffer; (train) supprimer; (stamp) oblitérer; to c. a ticket (with date) composter un billet; (punch) poinçonner un billet; to c. each other out s'annuler. ◆**cance'llation** n annulation f; suppression f; oblitération f.

cancer ['kænsər] n cancer m; C. (sign) le Cancer; c. patient cancéreux, -euse mf. ◆**cancerous** a cancéreux.

candelabra [kændɪ'lɑːbrə] n candélabre m.

candid ['kændɪd] a franc, sincère. ◆**candour** n franchise f, sincérité f.

candidate ['kændɪdeɪt] n candidat, -ate mf. ◆**candidacy** n, ◆**candidature** n candidature f.

candle ['kænd(ə)l] n bougie f; (tallow) chandelle f; Rel cierge m; c. grease suif m. ◆**candlelight** n by c. à la (lueur d'une) bougie; to have dinner by c. dîner aux chandelles. ◆**candlestick** n bougeoir m; (tall) chandelier m.

candy ['kændɪ] n Am bonbon(s) m(pl); (sugar) sucre candi; c. store Am confiserie f. ◆**candied** a (fruit) confit, glacé. ◆**candyfloss** n barbe f à papa.

cane [keɪn] n canne f; (for basket) rotin m; Sch baguette f; - vt (punish) Sch fouetter.

canine ['keɪnaɪn] 1 a canin. 2 n (tooth) canine f.

canister ['kænɪstər] n boîte f (en métal).

canker ['kæŋkər] n (in disease) & Fig chancre m.

cannabis ['kænəbɪs] n (plant) chanvre m indien; (drug) haschisch m.

cannibal ['kænɪbəl] n & a cannibale (mf).

cannon ['kænən] n (pl -s or inv) canon m. ◆**cannonball** n boulet m (de canon).

cannot ['kænɒt] = can not.

canny ['kænɪ] a (-ier, -iest) rusé, malin.

canoe [kə'nuː] n canoë m, kayak m; - vi faire du canoë ou du kayak. ◆**-ing** n to go c. Sp faire du canoë ou du kayak. ◆**canoeist** n canoëiste mf.

canon ['kænən] n (law) canon m; (clergyman) chanoine m. ◆**canonize** vt Rel canoniser.

canopy ['kænəpɪ] n (over bed, altar etc) dais m; (hood of pram) capote f; (awning) auvent m; (made of glass) marquise f; (of sky) Fig voûte f.

cant [kænt] n (jargon) jargon m.

can't [kɑːnt] = can not.

cantaloup(e) ['kæntəluːp, Am -ləʊp] n (melon) cantaloup m.

cantankerous [kæn'tæŋkərəs] a grincheux, acariâtre.

cantata [kæn'tɑːtə] n Mus cantate f.

canteen [kæn'tiːn] n (place) cantine f; (flask) gourde f; c. of cutlery ménagère f.

canter ['kæntər] n petit galop m; - vi aller au petit galop.

cantor ['kæntɔːr] n Rel chantre m, maître m de chapelle.

canvas ['kænvəs] n (grosse) toile f; (for embroidery) canevas m.

canvass ['kænvəs] vt (an area) faire du démarchage dans; (opinions) sonder; to c.

s.o. *Pol* solliciter des voix de qn; *Com* solliciter des commandes de qn. ◆**-ing** *n Com* démarchage *m*, prospection *f*; *Pol* démarchage *m* (électoral). ◆**-er** *n Pol* agent *m* électoral; *Com* démarcheur, -euse *mf*.

canyon ['kænjən] *n* cañon *m*, canyon *m*.

cap ¹ [kæp] *n* **1** (*hat*) casquette *f*; (*for shower etc*) & *Nau* bonnet *m*; *Mil* képi *m*. **2** (*of bottle, tube, valve*) bouchon *m*; (*of milk or beer bottle*) capsule *f*; (*of pen*) capuchon *m*. **3** (*of child's gun*) amorce *f*, capsule *f*. **4** (**Dutch**) **c.** (*contraceptive*) diaphragme *m*.

cap ² [kæp] *vt* (-pp-) (*outdo*) surpasser; **to c. it all** pour combler; **capped with** (*covered*) coiffé de.

capable ['keipəb(ə)l] *a* (*a person*) capable (**of** sth de qch, **of doing** de faire), compétent; **c. of** (*thing*) susceptible de. ◆**ca'bility** *n* capacité *f*. ◆**capably** *adv* avec compétence.

capacity [kə'pæsiti] *n* (*of container*) capacité *f*, contenance *f*; (*ability*) aptitude *f*, capacité *f*; (*output*) rendement *m*; **in my c. as** en ma qualité de; **in an advisory/etc c.** à titre consultatif/*etc*; **filled to c.** absolument plein, comble; **c. audience** salle *f* comble.

cape [keip] *n* **1** (*cloak*) cape *f*; (*of cyclist*) pèlerine *f*. **2** *Geog* cap *m*; **C. Town** Le Cap.

caper ['keipər] **1** *vi* (*jump about*) gambader. **2** *n* (*activity*) *Sl* affaire *f*; (*prank*) *Fam* farce *f*; (*trip*) *Fam* virée *f*. **3** *n Bot Culin* câpre *f*.

capital ['kæpitəl] **1** *a* (*punishment, letter, importance*) capital; – *n* **c.** (*city*) capitale *f*; **c.** (**letter**) majuscule *f*, capitale *f*. **2** *n* (*money*) capital *m*, capitaux *mpl*. ◆**capitalism** *n* capitalisme *m*. ◆**capitalist** *a* & *n* capitaliste (*mf*). ◆**capitalize** *vi* **to c. on** tirer parti de.

capitulate [kə'pitʃuleit] *vi* capituler. ◆**capitu'lation** *n* capitulation *f*.

caprice [kə'priːs] *n* caprice *m*. ◆**capricious** [kə'prifəs] *a* capricieux.

Capricorn ['kæprikɔːn] *n* (*sign*) le Capricorne.

capsize [kæp'saiz] *vi Nau* chavirer; – *vt* (*faire*) chavirer.

capsule ['kæpsəl, 'kæpsjuːl] *n* (*medicine, of spaceship etc*) capsule *f*.

captain ['kæptin] *n* capitaine *m*; – *vt Nau* commander; *Sp* être le capitaine de.

caption ['kæpʃ(ə)n] *n Cin Journ* sous-titre *m*; (*under illustration*) légende *f*.

captivate ['kæptiveit] *vt* captiver.

captive ['kæptiv] *n* captif, -ive *mf*, prisonnier, -ière *m*. ◆**cap'tivity** *n* captivité *f*.

capture ['kæptʃər] *n* capture *f*; – *vt* (*person, animal*) prendre, capturer; (*town*) prendre; (*attention*) capter; (*represent in words, on film etc*) rendre, reproduire.

car [kɑːr] *n* voiture *f*, auto(mobile) *f*; *Rail* wagon *m*; – *a* (*industry*) automobile; **c. ferry** ferry-boat *m*; **c. park** parking *m*; **c. radio** autoradio *m*; **c. wash** (*action*) lavage *m* automatique; (*machine*) lave-auto *m*. ◆**carfare** *n Am* frais *mpl* de voyage. ◆**carport** *n* auvent *m* (pour voiture). ◆**carsick** *a* **to be c.** être malade en voiture.

carafe [kə'ræf] *n* carafe *f*.

caramel ['kærəməl] *n* (*flavouring, toffee*) caramel *m*.

carat ['kærət] *n* carat *m*.

caravan ['kærəvæn] *n* (*in desert*) & *Aut* caravane *f*; (*horse-drawn*) roulotte *f*; **c. site** camping *m* pour caravanes.

caraway ['kærəwei] *n Bot Culin* cumin *m*, carvi *m*.

carbohydrates [kɑːbəu'haidreits] *npl* (*in diet*) féculents *mpl*.

carbon ['kɑːbən] *n* carbone *m*; **c. copy** double *m* (au carbone); *Fig* réplique *f*, double *m*; **c. paper** (papier *m*) carbone *m*.

carbuncle ['kɑːbʌŋk(ə)l] *n Med* furoncle *m*, clou *m*.

carburettor [kɑːbju'retər] (*Am* **carburetor** ['kɑːbəreitər]) *n* carburateur *m*.

carcass ['kɑːkəs] *n* (*body, framework*) carcasse *f*.

carcinogenic [kɑːsinə'dʒenik] *a* cancérigène.

card [kɑːd] *n* carte *f*; (*cardboard*) carton *m*; (*index*) **c.** fiche *f*; **c. index** fichier *m*; **c. table** table *f* de jeu; **to play cards** jouer aux cartes; **on** or *Am* **in the cards** *Fam* très vraisemblable; **to get one's cards** (*be dismissed*) *Fam* être renvoyé. ◆**cardboard** *n* carton *m*. ◆**cardsharp** *n* tricheur, -euse *mf*.

cardiac ['kɑːdiæk] *a* cardiaque.

cardigan ['kɑːdigən] *n* cardigan *m*, gilet *m*.

cardinal ['kɑːdin(ə)l] **1** *a* (*number etc*) cardinal. **2** *n* (*priest*) cardinal *m*.

care [keər] **1** *vi* **to c. about** (*feel concern about*) se soucier de, s'intéresser à; **I don't c.** ça m'est égal; **I couldn't c. less** *Fam* je m'en fiche; **who cares?** qu'est-ce que ça fait? **2** *vi* (*like*) aimer, vouloir; **would you c. to try?** voulez-vous essayer?, aimeriez-vous essayer?; **I don't c. for it** (*music etc*) je n'aime pas tellement ça; **to c. for** (*a drink, a change etc*) avoir envie de; **to c. about** or **for s.o.** avoir de la sympathie pour qn; **to c. for**

(*look after*) s'occuper de; (*sick person*) soigner. **3** *n* (*application, heed*) soin(s) *m*(*pl*), attention *f*; (*charge, protection*) garde *f*, soin *m*; (*anxiety*) souci *m*; **to take c. not to do** faire attention à ne pas faire; **take c. to put** everything back veillez à tout ranger; **to take c. of** s'occuper de; **to take c. of itself** (*of matter*) s'arranger; **to take c. of oneself** (*manage*) se débrouiller; (*keep healthy*) faire attention à sa santé. ◆**carefree** *a* insouciant. ◆**caretaker** *n* gardien, -ienne *mf*, concierge *mf*.

career [kə'rɪər] **1** *n* carrière *f*; – *a* (*diplomat etc*) de carrière. **2** *vi* **to c. along** aller à toute vitesse.

careful ['keəf(ə)l] *a* (*diligent*) soigneux (*about, of* de); (*cautious*) prudent; (*with money*) regardant; **to be c. of** or **with** (*heed*) faire attention à. ◆**–ly** *adv* avec soin; prudemment. ◆**careless** *a* négligent; (*thoughtless*) irréfléchi; (*inattentive*) inattentif (*of* à). ◆**carelessness** *n* négligence *f*, manque *m* de soin.

caress [kə'res] *n* caresse *f*; – *vt* (*stroke*) caresser; (*kiss*) embrasser.

cargo ['kɑːgəʊ] *n* (*pl* **-oes**, *Am* **-os**) cargaison *f*; **c. boat** cargo *m*.

Caribbean [kærɪ'biːən, *Am* kə'rɪbɪən] *a* caraïbe; – *the* **C.** (**Islands**) les Antilles *fpl*.

caricature ['kærɪkətʃʊər] *n* caricature *f*; – *vt* caricaturer.

caring ['keərɪŋ] *a* (*loving*) aimant; (*understanding*) compréhensif; – *n* affection *f*.

carnage ['kɑːnɪdʒ] *n* carnage *m*.

carnal ['kɑːnəl] *a* charnel, sexuel.

carnation [kɑː'neɪʃən] *n* œillet *m*.

carnival ['kɑːnɪvəl] *n* carnaval *m*.

carnivore ['kɑːnɪvɔːr] *n* carnivore *m*. ◆**carnivorous** *a* carnivore.

carol ['kærəl] *n* chant *m* (de Noël).

carouse [kə'raʊz] *vi* faire la fête.

carp [kɑːp] **1** *n* (*fish*) carpe *f*. **2** *vi* critiquer; **to c.** at critiquer.

carpenter ['kɑːpɪntər] *n* (*for house building*) charpentier *m*; (*light woodwork*) menuisier *m*. ◆**carpentry** *n* charpenterie *f*, menuiserie *f*.

carpet ['kɑːpɪt] *n* tapis *m*; (*fitted*) moquette *f*; **c. sweeper** balai *m* mécanique; – *vt* recouvrir d'un tapis or d'une moquette, (*of snow etc*) *Fig* tapisser. ◆**–ing** *n* (*carpets*) tapis *mpl*; moquette *f*.

carriage ['kærɪdʒ] *n* (*horse-drawn*) voiture *f*, équipage *m*; *Rail* voiture *f*; *Com* transport *m*; (*bearing of person*) port *m*; (*of typewriter*) chariot *m*; **c. paid** port payé. ◆**carriageway** *n* (*of road*) chaussée *f*.

carrier ['kærɪər] *n* *Com* entreprise *f* de transports; *Med* porteur, -euse *mf*; **c.** (**bag**) sac *m* (en plastique); **c. pigeon** pigeon *m* voyageur.

carrion ['kærɪən] *n* charogne *f*.

carrot ['kærət] *n* carotte *f*.

carry ['kærɪ] *vt* porter; (*goods*) transporter; (*by wind*) emporter; (*involve*) comporter; (*interest*) *Com* produire; (*extend*) faire passer; (*win*) remporter; (*authority*) avoir; (*child*) *Med* attendre; (*motion*) *Pol* faire passer, voter; (*sell*) stocker; *Math* retenir; **to c. too far** pousser trop loin; **to c. oneself** se comporter; – *vi* (*of sound*) porter. ■ **to c. away** *vt* emporter; *Fig* transporter; **to be** or **get carried away** (*excited*) s'emballer; **to c. back** *vt* (*thing*) rapporter; (*person*) ramener; (*in thought*) reporter; **to c. off** *vt* emporter; (*kidnap*) enlever; (*prize*) remporter; **to c. it off** réussir; **to c. on** *vt* continuer; (*conduct*) diriger, mener; (*sustain*) soutenir; – *vi* continuer (*doing à* faire); (*behave*) *Pej* se conduire (mal); (*complain*) se plaindre; **to c. on with** sth continuer qch; **to c. on about** (*talk*) causer de. ◆**carryings-'on** *npl Pej* activités *fpl*; (*behaviour*) *Pej* façons *fpl*; **to c. out** (*plan etc*) exécuter, réaliser; (*repair etc*) effectuer; (*duty*) accomplir; (*meal*) *Am* emporter; **to c. through** (*plan etc*) mener à bonne fin.

carryall ['kærɪɔːl] *n* *Am* fourre-tout *m inv*. ◆**carrycot** *n* (nacelle *f*) porte-bébé *m*.

cart [kɑːt] **1** *n* charrette *f*; (*handcart*) voiture *f* à bras. **2** *vt* (*goods, people*) transporter; **to c.** (**around**) *Fam* trimbal(l)er; **to c. away** emporter. ◆**carthorse** *n* cheval *m* de trait.

cartel [kɑː'tel] *n* *Econ Pol* cartel *m*.

cartilage ['kɑːtɪlɪdʒ] *n* cartilage *m*.

carton ['kɑːtən] *n* (*box*) carton *m*; (*of milk, fruit juice etc*) brick *m*, pack *m*; (*of cigarettes*) cartouche *f*; (*of cream*) pot *m*.

cartoon [kɑː'tuːn] *n* *Journ* dessin *m* (humoristique); *Cin* dessin *m* animé; (*strip*) **c.** bande *f* dessinée. ◆**cartoonist** *n* *Journ* dessinateur, -trice *mf* (humoristique).

cartridge ['kɑːtrɪdʒ] *n* (*of firearm, pen, camera, tape deck*) cartouche *f*; (*of record player*) cellule *f*; **c. belt** cartouchière *f*.

carve [kɑːv] *vt* (*cut*) tailler (*out of* dans); (*sculpt*) sculpter; (*initials etc*) graver; **to c.** (**up**) (*meat*) découper; **to c. up** (*country*) dépecer, morceler; **to c. out for oneself** (*career etc*) se tailler qch. ◆**–ing** *n* (*wood*) **c.** sculpture *f* (sur bois).

cascade [kæs'keɪd] *n* (*of rocks*) chute *f*; (*of*

blows) déluge *m*; (*of lace*) flot *m*; — *vi* tomber; (*hang*) pendre.

case [keɪs] *n* **1** (*instance*) & *Med* cas *m*; *Jur* affaire *f*; *Phil* arguments *mpl*; **in any c.** en tout cas; **if it rains** en cas où il pleuvrait; **in c. of** en cas de; **(just) in c.** à tout hasard. **2** (*bag*) valise *f*; (*crate*) caisse *f*; (*for pen, glasses, camera, violin, cigarettes*) étui *m*; (*for jewels*) coffret *m*. ◆**casing** *n* (*covering*) enveloppe *f*.

cash [kæʃ] *n* argent *m*; **to pay (in) c.** (*not by cheque*) payer en espèces *or* en liquide; **to pay c. (down)** payer comptant; **c. price** prix *m* (au) comptant; **c. box** caisse *f*; **c. desk** caisse *f*; **c. register** caisse *f* enregistreuse; — *vt* (*banknote*) changer; **to cash a cheque** (*of person*) encaisser un chèque; (*of bank*) payer un chèque; **to c. in on** *Fam* profiter de. ◆**ca'shier 1** *n* caissier, -ière *mf*. **2** *vt* (*dismiss*) *Mil* casser.

cashew ['kæʃu] *n* (*nut*) cajou *m*.

cashmere ['kæʃmɪər] *n* cachemire *m*.

casino [kə'siːnəu] *n* (*pl -os*) casino *m*.

cask [kɑːsk] *n* fût *m*, tonneau *m*. ◆**casket** *n* (*box*) coffret *m*; (*coffin*) cercueil *m*.

casserole ['kæsərəul] *n* (*covered dish*) cocotte *f*; (*stew*) ragoût *m* en cocotte.

cassette [kə'set] *n* cassette *f*; *Phot* cartouche *f*; **c. player** lecteur *m* de cassettes; **c. recorder** magnétophone *m* à cassettes.

cassock ['kæsək] *n* soutane *f*.

cast [kɑːst] **1** *n Th* acteurs *mpl*; (*list*) *Th* distribution *f*; (*mould*) moulage *m*; (*of dice*) coup *m*; *Med* plâtre *m*; (*squint*) léger strabisme *m*; **c. of mind** tournure *f* d'esprit. **2** *vt* (*pt & pp* **cast**) (*throw*) jeter; (*light, shadow*) projeter; (*blame*) rejeter; (*glance*) jeter; (*doubt*) exprimer; (*lose*) perdre; (*metal*) couler; (*role*) *Th* distribuer; (*actor*) donner un rôle à; **to c. one's mind back** se reporter en arrière; **to c. a vote** voter; **to c. aside** rejeter; **to c. off** (*chains etc*) se libérer de; (*shed, lose*) se dépouiller de; *Fig* abandonner. **3** *vi* **to c. off** *Nau* appareiller. **4** *n* **c. iron** fonte *f*. ◆**c.-'iron** *a* (*pan etc*) en fonte; (*will etc*) *Fig* de fer, solide.

castaway ['kɑːstəweɪ] *n* naufragé, -ée *mf*.

caste [kɑːst] *n* caste *f*.

caster ['kɑːstər] *n* (*wheel*) roulette *f*; **c. sugar** sucre *m* en poudre.

castle ['kɑːs(ə)l] *n* château *m*; (*in chess*) tour *f*.

castoffs ['kɑːstɒfs] *npl* vieux vêtements *mpl*.

castor ['kɑːstər] *n* (*wheel*) roulette *f*; **c. oil** huile *f* de ricin; **c. sugar** sucre *m* en poudre.

castrate [kæ'streɪt] *vt* châtrer. ◆**castration** *n* castration *f*.

casual ['kæʒjuəl] *a* (*meeting*) fortuit; (*remark*) fait en passant; (*stroll*) sans but; (*offhand*) désinvolte, insouciant; (*work*) irrégulier; **c. clothes** vêtements *mpl* sport; **a c. acquaintance** quelqu'un que l'on connaît un peu. ◆**-ly** *adv* par hasard; (*informally*) avec désinvolture; (*to remark*) en passant.

casualty ['kæʒjuəltɪ] *n* (*dead*) mort *m*, morte *f*; (*wounded*) blessé, -ée *mf*; (*accident victim*) accidenté, -ée *mf*; **casualties** morts et blessés *mpl*; *Mil* pertes *fpl*; **c. department** *Med* service *m* des accidentés.

cat [kæt] *n* chat *m*, chatte *f*; **c. burglar** monte-en-l'air *m inv*; **c.'s eyes®** cataphotes® *mpl*, clous *mpl*. ◆**catcall** *n* sifflet *m*, huée *f*.

cataclysm ['kætəklɪzəm] *n* cataclysme *m*.

catalogue ['kætəlɒg] (*Am* **catalog**) *n* catalogue *m*; — *vt* cataloguer.

catalyst ['kætəlɪst] *n Ch* & *Fig* catalyseur *m*.

catapult ['kætəpʌlt] *n* lance-pierres *m inv*; *Hist Av* catapulte *f*; — *vt* catapulter.

cataract ['kætərækt] *n* (*waterfall*) & *Med* cataracte *f*.

catarrh [kə'tɑːr] *n* catarrhe *m*, rhume *m*.

catastrophe [kə'tæstrəfɪ] *n* catastrophe *f*. ◆**cata'strophic** *a* catastrophique.

catch [kætʃ] *vt* (*pt & pp* **caught**) (*ball, thief, illness etc*) attraper; (*grab*) prendre, saisir; (*surprise*) (sur)prendre; (*understand*) saisir; (*train etc*) attraper; (*réussir à*) prendre; (*attention*) attirer; (*of nail etc*) accrocher; (*finger etc*) se prendre (*in dans*); **to c. sight of** apercevoir; **to c. fire** prendre feu; **to c. s.o. (in)** *Fam* trouver qn (chez soi); **to c. one's breath** (*rest a while*) reprendre haleine; (*stop breathing*) retenir son souffle; **I didn't c. the train/etc** j'ai manqué le train/etc; **to c. s.o. out** prendre qn en défaut; **to c. s.o. up** rattraper qn; — *vi* (*of fire*) prendre; **her skirt (got) caught in the door** sa jupe s'est prise *or* coincée dans la porte; **to c. on** prendre, devenir populaire; (*understand*) saisir; **to c. up** se rattraper; **to c. up with s.o.** rattraper qn. — *n* capture *f*, prise *f*; (*trick, snare*) piège *m*; (*on door*) loquet *m*. ◆**-ing** *a* contagieux. ◆**catchphrase**, ◆**catchword** *n* slogan *m*.

catchy ['kætʃɪ] *a* (*-ier, -iest*) (*tune*) *Fam* facile à retenir.

catechism ['kætɪkɪzəm] *n Rel* catéchisme *m*.

category ['kætɪgərɪ] *n* catégorie *f*. ◆**cate-**

'gorical a catégorique. ◆categorize vt classer (par catégories).

cater ['keɪtər] vi s'occuper de la nourriture; to c. for or to (need, taste) satisfaire; (readership) Journ s'adresser à. ◆—ing n restauration f. ◆—er n traiteur m.

caterpillar ['kætəpɪlər] n chenille f.

catgut ['kætgʌt] n (cord) boyau m.

cathedral [kə'θiːdrəl] n cathédrale f.

catholic ['kæθlɪk] 1 a & n C. catholique (mf). 2 a (taste) universel; (view) libéral. ◆Ca'tholicism n catholicisme m.

cattle ['kætl] npl bétail m, bestiaux mpl.

catty ['kætɪ] a (-ier, -iest) Fam rosse, méchant.

caucus ['kɔːkəs] n Pol Am comité m électoral.

caught [kɔːt] see catch.

cauldron ['kɔːldrən] n chaudron m.

cauliflower ['kɒlɪflaʊər] n chou-fleur m.

cause [kɔːz] n cause f; (reason) raison f; c. for complaint sujet m de plainte; — vt causer, occasionner; (trouble) créer, causer (for à); to c. sth to move/etc faire bouger/etc qch.

causeway ['kɔːzweɪ] n chaussée f.

caustic ['kɔːstɪk] a (remark, substance) caustique.

cauterize ['kɔːtəraɪz] vt Med cautériser.

caution ['kɔːʃ(ə)n] n (care) prudence f, précaution f; (warning) avertissement m; — vt (warn) avertir; to c. s.o. against sth mettre qn en garde contre qch. ◆cautionary a (tale) moral. ◆cautious a prudent, circonspect. ◆cautiously adv prudemment.

cavalcade ['kævəlkeɪd] n (procession) cavalcade f.

cavalier [kævə'lɪər] 1 a (selfish) cavalier. 2 n (horseman, knight) Hist cavalier m.

cavalry ['kævəlrɪ] n cavalerie f.

cave [keɪv] 1 n caverne f, grotte f. 2 vi to c. in (fall in) s'effondrer. ◆caveman n (pl -men) homme m des cavernes. ◆cavern ['kævən] n caverne f.

caviar(e) ['kævɪɑːr] n caviar m.

cavity ['kævɪtɪ] n cavité f.

cavort [kə'vɔːt] vi Fam cabrioler; to c. naked/etc se balader tout nu/etc.

cease [siːs] vti cesser (doing à faire). ◆c.-fire n cessez-le-feu m inv. ◆ceaseless a incessant. ◆ceaselessly adv sans cesse.

cedar ['siːdər] n (tree, wood) cèdre m.

cedilla [sɪ'dɪlə] n Gram cédille f.

ceiling ['siːlɪŋ] n (of room, on wages etc) plafond m.

celebrat/e ['selɪbreɪt] vt (event) fêter; (mass, s.o.'s merits etc) célébrer; — vi faire la fête; we should c. (that)! il faut fêter ça! ◆—ed a célèbre. ◆cele'bration n fête f; the c. of (marriage etc) la célébration de. ◆ce'lebrity n (person) célébrité f.

celery ['selərɪ] n céleri m.

celibate ['selɪbət] a (abstaining from sex) célibataire; (monk etc) abstinent. ◆celibacy n (of young person etc) célibat m; (of monk etc) abstinence f.

cell [sel] n cellule f; El élément m. ◆cellular a cellulaire; c. blanket couverture f en cellular.

cellar ['selər] n cave f.

cello ['tʃeləʊ] n (pl -os) violoncelle m. ◆cellist n violoncelliste mf.

cellophane® ['seləfeɪn] n cellophane® f.

celluloid ['seljʊlɔɪd] n celluloïd m.

cellulose ['seljʊləʊs] n cellulose f.

Celsius ['selsɪəs] a Celsius inv.

Celt [kelt] n Celte mf. ◆Celtic a celtique, celte.

cement [sɪ'ment] n ciment m; c. mixer bétonnière f; — vt cimenter.

cemetery ['semɪtrɪ, Am 'semətərɪ] n cimetière m.

cenotaph ['senətɑːf] n cénotaphe m.

censor ['sensər] n censeur m; — vt (film etc) censurer. ◆censorship n censure f.

censure ['senʃər] vt blâmer; Pol censurer; — n blâme m; c. motion, vote of c. motion f de censure.

census ['sensəs] n recensement m.

cent [sent] n (coin) cent m; per c. pour cent.

centenary [sen'tiːnərɪ, Am sen'tenərɪ] n centenaire m.

centigrade ['sentɪgreɪd] a centigrade.

centimetre ['sentɪmiːtər] n centimètre m.

centipede ['sentɪpiːd] n mille-pattes m inv.

centre ['sentər] n centre m; c. forward Fb avant-centre m; — vt centrer; — vi to c. on (of thoughts) se concentrer sur; (of question) tourner autour de. ◆central a central. ◆centralize vt centraliser. ◆centrifugal [sen'trɪfjʊgəl] a centrifuge.

century ['sentʃərɪ] n siècle m; (score) Sp cent points mpl.

ceramic [sə'ræmɪk] a (tile etc) de or en céramique; — npl (objects) céramiques fpl; (art) céramique f.

cereal ['sɪərɪəl] n céréale f.

cerebral ['serɪbrəl, Am sə'riːbrəl] a cérébral.

ceremony ['serɪmənɪ] n (event) cérémonie f; to stand on c. faire des cérémonies or des façons. ◆cere'monial a de cérémonie; —

n cérémonial *m*. ◆**cere'monious** *a* cérémonieux.

certain ['sɜːtən] *a* (*particular, some*) certain; (*sure*) sûr, certain; **she's c. to come, she'll come for c.** c'est certain *or* sûr qu'elle viendra; **I'm not c. what to do** je ne sais pas très bien ce qu'il faut faire; **to be c. of sth/that** être certain de qch/que; **for c.** (*to say, know*) avec certitude; **be c. to go!** vas-y sans faute!; **to make c. of** (*fact*) s'assurer de; (*seat etc*) s'assurer. ◆**-ly** *adv* certainement; (*yes*) bien sûr; (*without fail*) sans faute; (*without any doubt*) sans aucun doute. ◆**certainty** *n* certitude *f*.

certificate [sə'tɪfɪkɪt] *n* certificat *m*; *Univ* diplôme *m*.

certify ['sɜːtɪfaɪ] *vt* certifier; **to c. (insane)** déclarer dément; – *vi* **to c. to sth** attester qch.

cervix ['sɜːvɪks] *n* col *m* de l'utérus.

cesspool ['sespuːl] *n* fosse *f* d'aisances; *Fig* cloaque *f*.

chafe [tʃeɪf] *vt* (*skin*) *Lit* frotter.

chaff [tʃæf] *vt* (*tease*) taquiner.

chaffinch ['tʃæfɪntʃ] *n* (*bird*) pinson *m*.

chagrin ['ʃægrɪn, *Am* ʃə'grɪn] *n* contrariété *f*; – *vt* contrarier.

chain [tʃeɪn] *n* (*of rings, mountains*) chaîne *f*; (*of ideas, events*) enchaînement *m*, suite *f*; (*of lavatory*) chasse *f* d'eau; **c. reaction** réaction *f* en chaîne; **to be a c.-smoker, to c.-smoke** fumer cigarette sur cigarette, fumer comme un pompier; **c. saw** tronçonneuse *f*; **c. store** magasin *m* à succursales multiples; – *vt* **to c. (down)** enchaîner; **to c. (up)** (*dog*) mettre à l'attache.

chair [tʃeər] *n* chaise *f*; (*armchair*) fauteuil *m*; *Univ* chaire *f*; **the c.** (*office*) la présidence; **c. lift** télésiège *m*; – *vt* (*meeting*) présider. ◆**chairman** *n* (*pl* **-men**) président, -ente *mf*. ◆**chairmanship** *n* présidence *f*.

chalet ['ʃæleɪ] *n* chalet *m*.

chalk [tʃɔːk] *n* craie *f*; **not by a long c.** loin de là, tant s'en faut; – *vt* marquer *or* écrire à la craie; **to c. up** (*success*) *Fig* remporter. ◆**chalky** *a* (**-ier, -iest**) crayeux.

challeng/e ['tʃælɪndʒ] *n* défi *m*; (*task*) gageure *f*; *Mil* sommation *f*; **c. for** (*bid*) tentative *f* d'obtenir; – *vt* défier (s.o. to do qn de faire); (*dispute*) contester; **to c. s.o. to a game** inviter qn à jouer; **to c. s.o. to a duel** provoquer qn en duel. ◆**-ing** *a* (*job*) exigeant; (*book*) stimulant. ◆**-er** *n* *Sp* challenger *m*.

chamber ['tʃeɪmbər] *n* chambre *f*; (*of judge*) cabinet *m*; – *a* (**-ier, -iest**) (*music, orchestra*) de cham-

bre; **c. pot** pot *m* de chambre. ◆**chambermaid** *n* femme *f* de chambre.

chameleon [kə'miːliən] *n* (*reptile*) caméléon *m*.

chamois ['ʃæmɪ] *n* **c. (leather)** peau *f* de chamois.

champagne [ʃæm'peɪn] *n* champagne *m*.

champion ['tʃæmpiən] *n* champion, -onne *mf*; **c. skier** champion, -onne du ski; – *vt* (*support*) se faire le champion de. ◆**championship** *n* *Sp* championnat *m*.

chance [tʃɑːns] *n* (*luck*) hasard *m*; (*possibility*) chances *fpl*, possibilité *f*; (*opportunity*) occasion *f*; (*risk*) risque *m*; **by c.** par hasard; **by any c.** (*possibly*) par hasard; **on the off c. (that)** you could help me au cas où tu pourrais m'aider; – *a* (*remark*) fait au hasard; (*occurrence*) accidentel; – *vt* **to c. doing** prendre le risque de faire; **to c. to find/etc** trouver/etc par hasard; **to c. it** risquer le coup; – *v imp* **it chanced that** (*happened*) il s'est trouvé que.

chancel ['tʃɑːnsəl] *n* (*in church*) chœur *m*.

chancellor ['tʃɑːnsələr] *n* *Pol Jur* chancelier *m*. ◆**chancellery** *n* chancellerie *f*.

chandelier [ʃændə'lɪər] *n* lustre *m*.

chang/e [tʃeɪndʒ] *n* changement *m*; (*money*) monnaie *f*; **for a c.** pour changer; **it makes a c. from** ça change de; **to have a c. of heart** changer d'avis; **a c. of clothes** des vêtements de rechange; – *vt* (*modify*) changer; (*exchange*) échanger (for contre); (*money*) changer; (*transform*) transformer (into en); **to c. trains/one's skirt/etc** changer de train/de jupe/etc; **to c. gear** *Aut* changer de vitesse; **to c. the subject** changer de sujet; – *vi* (*alter*) changer; (*change clothes*) se changer; **to c. over** passer. ◆**-ing** *n* (*of guard*) relève *f*; **c. room** vestiaire *m*. ◆**changeable** *a* (*weather, mood etc*) changeant, variable. ◆**changeless** *a* immuable. ◆**changeover** *n* passage *m* (from de, to à).

channel ['tʃæn(ə)l] *n* (*navigable*) chenal *m*; *TV* chaîne *f*, canal *m*; (*groove*) rainure *f*; *Fig* direction *f*; **through the c.** of par le canal de; **the C.** *Geog* la Manche; **the C. Islands** les îles anglo-normandes; – *vt* (**-ll-**, *Am* **-l-**) (*energies, crowd etc*) canaliser (into vers).

chant [tʃɑːnt] *n* (*of demonstrators*) chant *m* scandé; *Rel* psalmodie *f*; – *vt* (*slogan*) scander; – *vi* scander des slogans.

chaos ['keɪɒs] *n* chaos *m*. ◆**cha'otic** *a* chaotique.

chap [tʃæp] **1** *n* (*fellow*) *Fam* type *m*; **old c.!**

mon vieux! **2** *n* (*on skin*) gerçure *f*; − *vi* (**-pp-**) se gercer; − *vt* gercer.

chapel ['tʃæp(ə)l] *n* chapelle *f*; (*non-conformist church*) temple *m*.

chaperon(e) ['ʃæpərəʊn] *n* chaperon *m*; − *vt* chaperonner.

chaplain ['tʃæplɪn] *n* aumônier *m*.

chapter ['tʃæptər] *n* chapitre *m*.

char [tʃɑːr] **1** *vt* (**-rr-**) (*convert to carbon*) carboniser; (*scorch*) brûler légèrement. **2** *n* *Fam* femme *f* de ménage; − *vi* to go **charring** *Fam* faire des ménages. **3** *n* (*tea*) *Sl* thé *m*.

character ['kærɪktər] *n* (*of person, place etc*) & *Typ* caractère *m*; (*in book, film*) personnage *m*; (*strange person*) numéro *m*; *Th* actor acteur *m* de genre. ◆**characte-'ristic** *a* & *n* caractéristique (*f*). ◆**characte'ristically** *adv* typiquement. ◆**characterize** *vt* caractériser.

charade [ʃəˈrɑːd] *n* (*game*) charade *f* (mimée); (*travesty*) parodie *f*, comédie *f*.

charcoal ['tʃɑːkəʊl] *n* charbon *m* (de bois); (*crayon*) fusain *m*, charbon *m*.

charge [tʃɑːdʒ] *n* (*in battle*) *Mil* charge *f*; *Jur* accusation *f*; (*cost*) prix *m*; (*responsibility*) responsabilité *f*, charge *f*; (*care*) garde *f*; *pl* (*expenses*) frais *mpl*; there's a c. (for it) c'est payant; free of c. gratuit; extra c. supplément *m*; to take c. of prendre en charge; to be in c. of (*child etc*) avoir la garde de; (*office etc*) être responsable de; the person in c. ou le responsable; who's in c. here? qui commande ici?; − *vt* *Mil* El charger; *Jur* accuser, inculper; to c. s.o. *Com* faire payer qn; to c. (up) to *Com* mettre sur le compte de; how much do you c.? combien demandez-vous?; − *vi* (*rush*) se précipiter; c.! *Mil* chargez! ◆**-able** *a* to aux frais de. ◆**charger** *n* (*for battery*) chargeur *m*.

chariot ['tʃærɪət] *n* *Mil* char *m*.

charisma [kəˈrɪzmə] *n* magnétisme *m*.

charity ['tʃærɪtɪ] *n* (*kindness, alms*) charité *f*; (*society*) fondation *f* ou œuvre *f* charitable; to give to c. faire la charité. ◆**charitable** *a* charitable.

charlady ['tʃɑːleɪdɪ] *n* femme *f* de ménage.

charlatan ['ʃɑːlətən] *n* charlatan *m*.

charm [tʃɑːm] *n* (*attractiveness, spell*) charme *m*; (*trinket*) amulette *f*; − *vt* charmer. ◆**-ing** *a* charmant. ◆**-ingly** *adv* d'une façon charmante.

chart [tʃɑːt] *n* (*map*) carte *f*; (*graph*) graphique *m*, tableau *m*; (*pop*) charts hit-parade *m*; **flow c.** organigramme *m*; −

vt (*route*) porter sur la carte; (*figures*) faire le graphique de; (*of graph*) montrer.

charter ['tʃɑːtər] *n* (*document*) charte *f*; (*aircraft*) charter *m*; **the c. of** (*hiring*) l'affrètement *m* de; **flight charter** *m*; − *vt* (*aircraft etc*) affréter. ◆**-ed accoun-tant** expert-comptable *m*.

charwoman ['tʃɑːwʊmən] *n* (*pl* **-women**) femme *f* de ménage.

chary ['tʃeərɪ] *a* (**-ier, -iest**) (*cautious*) prudent.

chase [tʃeɪs] *n* poursuite *f*, chasse *f*; to give c. se lancer à la poursuite (to de); − *vt* poursuivre; to c. away or off chasser; to c. sth up *Fam* essayer d'obtenir qch, rechercher qch; − *vi* to c. after courir après.

chasm ['kæzəm] *n* abîme *m*, gouffre *m*.

chassis ['ʃæsɪ, *Am* 'tʃæsɪ] *n* *Aut* châssis *m*.

chaste [tʃeɪst] *a* chaste. ◆**chastity** *n* chasteté *f*.

chasten ['tʃeɪs(ə)n] *vt* (*punish*) châtier; (*cause to improve*) faire se corriger, assagir. ◆**-ing** *a* (*experience*) instructif.

chastise [tʃæˈstaɪz] *vt* punir.

chat [tʃæt] *n* causette *f*; to have a c. bavarder; − *vi* (**-tt-**) causer, bavarder; − *vt* to c. up *Fam* baratiner, draguer. ◆**chatty** *a* (**-ier, -iest**) (*person*) bavard; (*style*) familier; (*text*) plein de bavardages.

chatter ['tʃætər] *vi* bavarder; (*of birds, monkeys*) jacasser; **his teeth are chattering** il claque des dents; − *n* bavardage *m*; jacassement *m*. ◆**chatterbox** *n* bavard, -arde *mf*.

chauffeur ['ʃəʊfər] *n* chauffeur *m* (de maître).

chauvinist ['ʃəʊvɪnɪst] *n* & *a* chauvin, -ine (*mf*); **male c.** *Pej* phallocrate *m*.

cheap [tʃiːp] *a* (**-er, -est**) bon marché *inv*, pas cher; (*rate etc*) réduit; (*worthless*) sans valeur; (*superficial*) facile; (*mean, petty*) mesquin; **cheaper** moins cher, meilleur marché; − *adv* (*to buy*) (à) bon marché, au rabais; (*to feel*) humilié; *vt* Fig déprécier. ◆**cheaply** *adv* (à) bon marché. ◆**cheapen** *vt* Fig humilier. ◆**cheapness** *n* bas prix *m*; Fig mesquinerie *f*.

cheat [tʃiːt] *vt* (*deceive*) tromper; (*defraud*) frauder; to c. s.o. out of sth escroquer qch à qn; to c. on (*wife, husband*) faire une infidélité ou des infidélités à; − *vi* tricher; (*defraud*) frauder; − *n* (*at games etc*) tricheur, -euse *mf*; (*crook*) escroc *m*. ◆**-ing** *n* (*deceit*) tromperie *f*; (*trickery*) tricherie *f*. ◆**-er** *n* *Am* = **cheat**.

check[1] [tʃek] *vt* (*examine*) vérifier; (*inspect*) contrôler; (*tick*) cocher, pointer; (*stop*) arrêter, enrayer; *(restrain)* contenir, maîtriser; *(rebuke)* réprimander; *(baggage)* Am mettre à la consigne; **to c. in** *(luggage)* Av enregistrer; **to c. sth out** confirmer qch; – *vi* vérifier; **to c. in** *(at hotel etc)* signer le registre; *(arrive at hotel)* arriver; *(at airport)* se présenter (à l'enregistrement), enregistrer ses bagages; **to c. on sth** vérifier qch; **to c. out** *(at hotel etc)* régler sa note; **to c. up** se renseigner; – *n* vérification *f*; contrôle *m*; *(halt)* arrêt *m*; Chess échec *m*; *(curb)* frein *m*; *(tick)* = croix *f*; *(receipt)* Am reçu *m*; *(bill in restaurant)* Am addition *f*; *(cheque)* Am chèque *m*. ◆**c.-in** *n* Av enregistremen. *m* (des bagages). ◆**checking account** *n* Am compte *m* courant. ◆**checkmate** *n* Chess échec et mat *m*. ◆**checkout** *n* *(in supermarket)* caisse *f*. ◆**checkpoint** *n* contrôle *m*. ◆**checkroom** *n* Am vestiaire *m*; *(left-luggage office)* Am consigne *f*. ◆**checkup** *n* bilan *m* de santé.

check [tʃek] *n (pattern)* carreaux *mpl*; – *a* à carreaux. ◆**checked** *a* à carreaux.

checkered ['tʃekəd] *a* Am = **chequered**.

checkers ['tʃekəz] *npl* Am jeu *m* de dames.

cheddar ['tʃedər] *n (cheese)* cheddar *m*.

cheek [tʃiːk] *n* joue *f*; *(impudence)* Fig culot *m*. ◆**cheekbone** *n* pommette *f*. ◆**cheeky** *a* (-ier, -iest) *(person, reply etc)* effronté.

cheep [tʃiːp] *vi (of bird)* piauler.

cheer [tʃiər] *n* cheers *(shouts)* acclamations *fpl*; **cheers!** Fam à votre santé! – *vt (applaud)* acclamer; **to c. on** encourager; **to c. (up)** donner du courage à; *(amuse)* égayer; – *vi* applaudir; **to c. up** prendre courage; s'égayer; **c. up!** (du) courage! ◆**—ing** *n (shouts)* acclamations *fpl*; – *a (encouraging)* réjouissant.

cheer [tʃiər] *n (gaiety)* joie *f*; good c. *(food)* la bonne chère. ◆**cheerful** *a* gai. ◆**cheerfully** *adv* gaiement. ◆**cheerless** *a* morne.

cheerio! [tʃiəri'əʊ] *int* salut!, au revoir!

cheese [tʃiːz] *n* fromage *m*. ◆**cheeseburger** *n* cheeseburger *m*. ◆**cheesecake** *n* tarte *f* au fromage blanc. ◆**cheesed** *a* **to be c. (off)** Fam en avoir marre (with de). ◆**cheesy** *a* (-ier, -iest) *(shabby, bad)* Am Fam miteux.

cheetah ['tʃiːtə] *n* guépard *m*.

chef [ʃef] *n* Culin chef *m*.

chemistry ['kemɪstrɪ] *n* chimie *f*. ◆**chemical** *a* chimique; – *n* produit *m* chimique. ◆**chemist** *n (dispensing)* pharmacien,

-ienne *mf*; *(scientist)* chimiste *mf*; **chemist('s)** *(shop)* pharmacie *f*.

cheque [tʃek] *n* chèque *m*. ◆**chequebook** *n* carnet *m* de chèques.

chequered ['tʃekəd] *a (pattern)* à carreaux; *(career etc)* qui connaît des hauts et des bas.

cherish ['tʃerɪʃ] *vt (person)* chérir; *(hope)* nourrir, caresser.

cherry ['tʃerɪ] *n* cerise *f*; – *a* cerise *inv*; **c. brandy** cherry *m*.

chess [tʃes] *n* échecs *mpl*. ◆**chessboard** *n* échiquier *m*.

chest [tʃest] *n* **1** Anat poitrine *f*. **2** *(box)* coffre *m*; **c. of drawers** commode *f*.

chestnut ['tʃesnʌt] *n* châtaigne *f*, marron *m*; – *a (hair)* châtain; **c. tree** châtaignier *m*.

chew [tʃuː] *vt* **to c. (up)** mâcher; **to c. over** Fig ruminer; – *vi* mastiquer; **chewing gum** chewing-gum *m*.

chick [tʃik] *n* poussin *m*; *(girl)* Fam nana *f*. ◆**chicken 1** *n* poulet *m*; *(poultry)* volaille *f*; **it's c. feed** Fam c'est deux fois rien, c'est une bagatelle. **2** *a* Fam froussard; – *vi* **to c. out** Fam se dégonfler. ◆**chickenpox** *n* varicelle *f*.

chickpea ['tʃikpiː] *n* pois *m* chiche.

chicory ['tʃikərɪ] *n (in coffee etc)* chicorée *f*; *(for salad)* endive *f*.

chide [tʃaɪd] *vt* gronder.

chief [tʃiːf] *n* chef *m*; *(boss)* Fam patron *m*, chef *m*; **in c.** *(commander, editor)* en chef; – *a (main, highest in rank)* principal. ◆**—ly** *adv* principalement, surtout. ◆**chieftain** *n (of clan etc)* chef *m*.

chilblain ['tʃilbleɪn] *n* engelure *f*.

child, *pl* **children** [tʃaɪld, 'tʃɪldrən] *n* enfant *mf*; **c. care** *or* **welfare** protection *f* de l'enfance; **child's play** Fig jeu *m* d'enfant; **c. minder** gardien, -ienne *mf* d'enfants. ◆**childbearing** *n (act)* accouchement *m*; *(motherhood)* maternité *f*. ◆**childbirth** *n* accouchement *m*, couches *fpl*. ◆**childhood** *n* enfance *f*. ◆**childish** *a* puéril, enfantin. ◆**childishness** *n* puérilité *f*. ◆**childlike** *a* naïf, innocent.

chill [tʃil] *n* froid *m*; *(coldness in feelings)* froideur *f*; Med refroidissement *m*; **to catch a c.** prendre froid; – *vt (wine, melon)* faire rafraîchir; *(meat, food)* réfrigérer; **to c. s.o.** *(with fear, cold etc)* faire frissonner qn (with de); **to be chilled to the bone** être transi. ◆**—ed** *a (wine)* frais. ◆**chilly** *a* (-ier, -iest) froid; *(sensitive to cold)* frileux; **it's c.** il fait (un peu) froid.

chilli ['tʃili] *n (pl* -ies*)* piment *m* (de Cayenne).

chime [tʃaɪm] vi (of bell) carillonner; (of clock) sonner; **to c. in** (interrupt) interrompre; – n carillon m; sonnerie f.

chimney [ˈtʃɪmnɪ] n cheminée f. ◆**chimneypot** n tuyau m de cheminée. ◆**chimneysweep** n ramoneur m.

chimpanzee [tʃɪmpænˈzɪ] n chimpanzé m.

chin [tʃɪn] n menton m.

china [ˈtʃaɪnə] n inv porcelaine f; – a en porcelaine. ◆**chinaware** n (objects) porcelaine f.

China [ˈtʃaɪnə] n Chine f. ◆**Chi'nese** n & a chinois, -oise (mf); – n (language) chinois m.

chink [tʃɪŋk] **1** n (slit) fente f. **2** vi tinter; – vt faire tinter; – n tintement m.

chip [tʃɪp] vt (-pp-) (cup etc) ébrécher; (table etc) écorner; (paint) écailler; (cut) tailler; – vi to c. in Fam contribuer; – n (splinter) éclat m; (break) ébréchure f, écornure f; (microchip) puce f; (counter) jeton m; pl (French fries) frites fpl; (crisps) Am chips mpl. ◆**chipboard** n (bois m) aggloméré m. ◆**chippings** npl road or loose c. gravillons mpl.

chiropodist [kɪˈrɒpədɪst] n pédicure mf.

chirp [tʃɜːp] vi (of bird) pépier; – n pépiement m.

chirpy [ˈtʃɜːpɪ] a (-ier, -iest) gai, plein d'entrain.

chisel [ˈtʃɪz(ə)l] n ciseau m; – vt (-ll-, Am -l-) ciseler.

chit [tʃɪt] n (paper) note f, billet m.

chitchat [ˈtʃɪttʃæt] n bavardage m.

chivalry [ˈʃɪvəlrɪ] n (practices etc) chevalerie f; (courtesy) galanterie f. ◆**chivalrous** a (man) galant.

chives [tʃaɪvz] npl ciboulette f.

chloride [ˈklɔːraɪd] n chlorure m. ◆**chlorine** n chlore m. ◆**chloroform** n chloroforme m.

choc-ice [ˈtʃɒkaɪs] n (ice cream) esquimau m.

chock [tʃɒk] n (wedge) cale f; – vt caler. **chock-a-block** [tʃɒkəˈblɒk] a, ◆**c.-'full** a Fam archiplein.

chocolate [ˈtʃɒklɪt] n chocolat m; **milk c.** chocolat au lait; **plain** or Am **bittersweet c.** chocolat à croquer; – a (cake) au chocolat; (colour) chocolat inv.

choice [tʃɔɪs] n choix m; **from c., out of c.** de son propre choix; – a (goods) de choix.

choir [ˈkwaɪər] n chœur m. ◆**choirboy** n jeune choriste m.

chok/e [tʃəʊk] **1** vt (person) étrangler, étouffer; (pipe) boucher, engorger; **to c. back** (sobs etc) étouffer; – vi s'étrangler;

étouffer; **to c. on** (fish bone etc) s'étrangler avec. **2** n Aut starter m. ◆**–er** n (scarf) foulard m; (necklace) collier m (de chien).

cholera [ˈkɒlərə] n choléra m.

cholesterol [kəˈlestərɒl] n cholestérol m.

choose [tʃuːz] vt (pt chose, pp chosen) choisir (to do de faire); **to c. to do** (decide) juger bon de faire; – vi choisir; as I/you/etc c. comme il me/vous/etc plaît. ◆**choos(e)y** a (-sier, -siest) difficile (about sur).

chop [tʃɒp] **1** n (of lamb, pork) côtelette f; **to lick one's chops** Fig s'en lécher les babines; **to get the c.** Sl être flanqué à la porte. **2** vt (-pp-) couper (à la hache); (food) hacher; **to c. down** (tree) abattre; **to c. off** trancher; **to c. up** hacher. **3** vti (-pp-) **to c. and change** changer constamment d'idées, de projets etc. ◆**chopper** n hachoir m; Sl hélicoptère m. ◆**choppy** a (sea) agité.

chopsticks [ˈtʃɒpstɪks] npl Culin baguettes fpl.

choral [ˈkɔːrəl] a choral; **c. society** chorale f. ◆**chorister** [ˈkɒrɪstər] n choriste mf.

chord [kɔːd] n Mus accord m.

chore [tʃɔːr] n travail m (routinier); (unpleasant) corvée f; pl (domestic) travaux mpl du ménage.

choreographer [kɒrɪˈɒɡrəfər] n chorégraphe m. ◆**choreography** n chorégraphie f.

chortle [ˈtʃɔːt(ə)l] vi glousser; – n gloussement m.

chorus [ˈkɔːrəs] n chœur m; (dancers) Th troupe f; (of song) refrain m; **c. girl** girl f.

chose, chosen [tʃəʊz, ˈtʃəʊz(ə)n] see choose.

chowder [ˈtʃaʊdər] n Am soupe f aux poissons.

Christ [kraɪst] n Christ m. ◆**Christian** [ˈkrɪstʃən] a & n chrétien, -ienne (mf); **C. name** prénom m. ◆**Christi'anity** n christianisme m.

christen [ˈkrɪs(ə)n] vt (name) & Rel baptiser. ◆**–ing** n baptême m.

Christmas [ˈkrɪsməs] n Noël m; **at C.** (time) à (la) Noël; **Merry C.** Joyeux Noël; **Father C.** le père Noël; – a (tree, card, day, party etc) de Noël; **C. box** étrennes fpl.

chrome [krəʊm] n, ◆**chromium** n chrome m.

chromosome [ˈkrəʊməsəʊm] n chromosome m.

chronic [ˈkrɒnɪk] a (disease, state etc) chronique; (bad) Sl atroce.

chronicle [ˈkrɒnɪk(ə)l] n chronique f; – vt faire la chronique de.

chronology [krə'nɒlədʒɪ] *n* chronologie *f*.
◆**chrono'logical** *a* chronologique.

chronometer [krə'nɒmɪtər] *n* chronomètre *m*.

chrysanthemum [krɪ'sænθəməm] *n* chrysanthème *m*.

chubby ['tʃʌbɪ] *a* (-ier, -iest) (*body*) dodu; (*cheeks*) rebondi. ◆**c.-'cheeked** *a* joufflu.

chuck [tʃʌk] *vt Fam* jeter, lancer; **to c. (in)** or **(up)** (*give up*) *Fam* laisser tomber; **to c. away** *Fam* balancer; (*money*) gaspiller; **to c. out** *Fam* balancer.

chuckle ['tʃʌk(ə)l] *vi* glousser, rire; – *n* gloussement *m*.

chuffed [tʃʌft] *a Sl* bien content; (*displeased*) *Iron Sl* pas heureux.

chug [tʃʌg] *vi* (**-gg-**) **to c. along** (*of vehicle*) avancer lentement (*en faisant teuf-teuf*).

chum [tʃʌm] *n Fam* copain *m*. ◆**chummy** *a* (-ier, -iest) *Fam* amical; **c. with** copain avec.

chump [tʃʌmp] *n* (*fool*) crétin, -ine *mf*.

chunk [tʃʌŋk] *n* (gros) morceau *m*. ◆**chunky** *a* (-ier, -iest) (*person*) *Fam* trapu; (*coat, material etc*) de grosse laine.

church [tʃɜːtʃ] *n* église *f*; (*service*) office *m*; (*Catholic*) messe *f*; **c. hall** salle *f* paroissiale. ◆**churchgoer** *n* pratiquant, -ante *mf*. ◆**churchyard** *n* cimetière *m*.

churlish ['tʃɜːlɪʃ] *a* (*rude*) grossier; (*bad-tempered*) hargneux.

churn [tʃɜːn] **1** *n* (*for making butter*) baratte *f*; (*milk can*) bidon *m*. **2** *vt* **to c. out** *Pej* produire (*en série*).

chute [ʃuːt] *n* glissière *f*; (*in playground, pool*) toboggan *m*; (*for refuse*) vide-ordures *m inv*.

chutney ['tʃʌtnɪ] *n* condiment *m* épicé (*à base de fruits*).

cider ['saɪdər] *n* cidre *m*.

cigar [sɪ'gɑːr] *n* cigare *m*. ◆**ciga'rette** *n* cigarette *f*; **c. end** mégot *m*; **c. holder** fume-cigarette *m inv*; **c. lighter** briquet *m*.

cinch [sɪntʃ] *n* **it's a c.** *Fam* (*easy*) c'est facile; (*sure*) c'est (sûr et) certain.

cinder ['sɪndər] *n* cendre *f*; **c. track** *Sp* cendrée *f*.

Cinderella [sɪndə'relə] *n Liter* Cendrillon *f*; *Fig* parent *m* pauvre.

cine-camera ['sɪnɪkæmrə] *n* caméra *f*.

cinema ['sɪnəmə] *n* cinéma *m*. ◆**cinemagoer** *n* cinéphile *mf*. ◆**cinemascope** *n* cinémascope *m*.

cinnamon ['sɪnəmən] *n Bot Culin* cannelle *f*.

cipher ['saɪfər] *n* (*code, number*) chiffre *m*; (*zero, person*) *Fig* zéro *m*.

circle ['sɜːk(ə)l] *n* (*shape, group, range etc*)

cercle *m*; (*around eyes*) cerne *m*; *Th* balcon *m*; *pl* (*milieux*) milieux *mpl*; – *vt* (*move round*) faire le tour de; (*word etc*) entourer d'un cercle; – *vi* (*of aircraft, bird*) décrire des cercles. ◆**circular** *a* circulaire; – *n* (*letter*) circulaire *f*; (*advertisement*) prospectus *m*. ◆**circulate** *vi* circuler; – *vt* faire circuler. ◆**circu'lation** *n* circulation *f*; *Journ* tirage *m*; **in c.** (*person*) *Fam* dans le circuit.

circuit ['sɜːkɪt] *n* circuit *m*; *Jur Th* tournée *f*; **c. breaker** *El* disjoncteur *m*. ◆**circuitous** [sɜː'kjuːɪtəs] *a* (*route, means*) indirect. ◆**circuitry** *n El* circuits *mpl*.

circumcised ['sɜːkəmsaɪzd] *a* circoncis. ◆**circum'cision** *n* circoncision *f*.

circumference [sɜː'kʌmfərəns] *n* circonférence *f*.

circumflex ['sɜːkəmfleks] *n* circonflexe *m*.

circumscribe ['sɜːkəmskraɪb] *vt* circonscrire.

circumspect ['sɜːkəmspekt] *a* circonspect.

circumstance ['sɜːkəmstæns] *n* circonstance *f*; *pl Com* situation *f* financière; **in** or **under no circumstances** en aucun cas. ◆**circum'stantial** (*evidence*) *Jur* indirect.

circus ['sɜːkəs] *n Th Hist* cirque *m*.

cirrhosis [sɪ'rəʊsɪs] *n Med* cirrhose *f*.

cistern ['sɪstən] *n* (*in house*) réservoir *m* (d'eau).

citadel ['sɪtəd(ə)l] *n* citadelle *f*.

cite [saɪt] *vt* citer. ◆**citation** [saɪ'teɪʃ(ə)n] *n* citation *f*.

citizen ['sɪtɪz(ə)n] *n Pol Jur* citoyen, -enne *mf*; (*of town*) habitant, -ante *mf*; **Citizens' Band** *Rad* la CB. ◆**citizenship** *n* citoyenneté *f*.

citrus ['sɪtrəs] *a* **c. fruit(s)** agrumes *mpl*.

city ['sɪtɪ] *n* (grande) ville *f*, cité *f*; **c. dweller** citadin, -ine *mf*; **c. centre** centre-ville *m inv*; **c. hall** *Am* hôtel *m* de ville; **c. page** *Journ* rubrique *f* financière.

civic ['sɪvɪk] *a* (*duty*) civique; (*centre*) administratif; (*authorities*) municipal; – *npl* (*social science*) instruction *f* civique.

civil ['sɪv(ə)l] *a* **1** (*rights, war, marriage etc*) civil; **c. defence** défense *f* passive; **c. servant** fonctionnaire *mf*; **c. service** fonction *f* publique. **2** (*polite*) civil. ◆**ci'vilian** *a & n* civil, -ile (*mf*). ◆**ci'vility** *n* civilité *f*.

civilize ['sɪvɪlaɪz] *vt* civiliser. ◆**civili'zation** *n* civilisation *f*.

civvies ['sɪvɪz] *npl* **in c.** *Sl* (habillé) en civil.

clad [klæd] *a* vêtu (**in de**).

claim [kleɪm] *vt* (*one's due etc*) revendiquer, réclamer; (*require*) réclamer; **to c. that**

(*assert*) prétendre que; – *n* (*demand*) prétention *f*, revendication *f*; (*statement*) affirmation *f*; (*complaint*) réclamation *f*; (*right*) droit *m*; (*land*) concession *f*; (*insurance*) **c.** demande *f* d'indemnité; **to lay c. to** prétendre à. ◆**claimant** *n* allocataire *mf*.

clairvoyant [klɛəˈvɔɪənt] *n* voyant, -ante *mf*.

clam [klæm] *n* (*shellfish*) praire *f*.

clamber [ˈklæmbər] *vi* **to c. (up)** grimper; **to c. up** (*stairs*) grimper; (*mountain*) gravir.

clammy [ˈklæmɪ] *a* (*hands etc*) moite (et froid).

clamour [ˈklæmər] *n* clameur *f*; – *vi* vociférer (**against** contre); **to c. for** demander à grands cris.

clamp [klæmp] *n* crampon *m*; *Carp* serre-joint(s) *m*; (*wheel*) **c.** *Aut* sabot *m* (de Denver); – *vt* serrer; – *vi* **to c. down** *Fam* sévir (**on** contre). ◆**clampdown** *n* (*limitation*) *Fam* coup *m* d'arrêt, restriction *f*.

clan [klæn] *n* clan *m*.

clandestine [klænˈdestɪn] *a* clandestin.

clang [klæŋ] *n* son *m* métallique. ◆**clanger** *n* *Sl* gaffe *f*; **to drop a c.** faire une gaffe.

clap [klæp] **1** *vti* (*-pp-*) (*applaud*) applaudir; **to c. one's hands** battre des mains; – *n* battement *m* (des mains); (*on back*) tape *f*; (*of thunder*) coup *m*. **2** *vt* (*-pp-*) (*put*) *Fam* fourrer. ◆**clapped-'out** *a* (*car, person*) *Sl* crevé. ◆**clapping** *n* applaudissements *mpl*. ◆**claptrap** *n* (*nonsense*) *Fam* boniment *m*.

claret [ˈklærət] *n* (*wine*) bordeaux *m* rouge.

clarify [ˈklærɪfaɪ] *vt* clarifier. ◆**clarification** *n* clarification *f*.

clarinet [klærɪˈnet] *n* clarinette *f*.

clarity [ˈklærətɪ] *n* (*of water, expression etc*) clarté *f*.

clash [klæʃ] *vi* (*of plates, pans*) s'entrechoquer; (*of interests, armies*) se heurter; (*of colours*) jurer (**with** avec); (*of people*) se bagarrer; (*coincide*) tomber en même temps (**with** que); – *n* (*noise, of armies*) choc *m*, heurt *m*; (*of interests*) conflit *m*; (*of events*) coïncidence *f*.

clasp [klɑːsp] *vt* (*hold*) serrer; **to c. one's hands** joindre les mains; – *n* (*fastener*) fermoir *m*; (*of belt*) boucle *f*.

class [klɑːs] *n* classe *f*; (*lesson*) cours *m*; (*grade*) *Univ* mention *f*; **the c. of 1987** *Am* la promotion de 1987; – *vt* classer. ◆**classmate** *n* camarade *mf* de classe. ◆**classroom** *n* (*salle f de*) classe *f*.

classic [ˈklæsɪk] *a* classique; – *n* (*writer, work etc*) classique *m*; **to study classics**

étudier les humanités *fpl*. ◆**classical** *a* classique. ◆**classicism** *n* classicisme *m*.

classif/y [ˈklæsɪfaɪ] *vt* classer, classifier. ◆**-ied** *a* (*information*) secret. ◆**classification** *n* classification *f*.

classy [ˈklɑːsɪ] *a* (*-ier, -iest*) *Fam* chic *inv*.

clatter [ˈklætər] *n* bruit *m*, fracas *m*.

clause [klɔːz] *n* *Jur* clause *f*; *Gram* proposition *f*.

claustrophobia [klɔːstrəˈfəʊbɪə] *n* claustrophobie *f*. ◆**claustrophobic** *a* claustrophobe.

claw [klɔː] *n* (*of cat, sparrow etc*) griffe *f*; (*of eagle*) serre *f*; (*of lobster*) pince *f*; – *vt* (*scratch*) griffer; **to c. back** (*money etc*) *Pej Fam* repiquer, récupérer.

clay [kleɪ] *n* argile *f*.

clean [kliːn] *a* (*-er, -est*) propre; (*clear-cut*) net; (*fair*) *Sp* (*joke*) non paillard; (*record*) *Jur* vierge; **to c. living** vie *f* saine; **to make a c. breast of it** tout avouer; – *adv* (*utterly*) complètement, carrément; **to break c.** se casser net; **to cut c.** couper net; – *n* **to give sth a c.** nettoyer qch.; – *vt* nettoyer; (*wash*) laver; (*wipe*) essuyer; **to c. one's teeth** se brosser *or* se laver les dents; **to c. out** nettoyer; (*empty*) *Fig* vider; **to c. up** nettoyer; (*reform*) *Fig* épurer; – *vi* **to c. (up)** faire le nettoyage. ◆**-ing** *n* nettoyage *m*; (*housework*) ménage *m*; **c. woman** femme *f* de ménage. ◆**-er** *n* (*woman*) femme *f* de ménage; (*dry*) **c.** teinturier, -ière *mf*. ◆**-ly** *adv* (*to break, cut*) net. ◆**-ness** *n* propreté *f*. ◆**clean-'cut** *a* net. ◆**clean-'living** *a* honnête, chaste. ◆**clean-'shaven** *a* rasé (de près). ◆**clean-up** *n* *Fig* épuration *f*.

cleanliness [ˈklenlɪnɪs] *n* propreté *f*.

cleans/e [klenz] *vt* nettoyer; (*soul, person etc*) *Fig* purifier. ◆**-ing** *a* **c. cream** crème *f* démaquillante. ◆**-er** *n* (*cream, lotion*) démaquillant *m*.

clear [klɪər] *a* (*-er, -est*) (*water, sound etc*) clair; (*glass*) transparent; (*outline, photo*) net, clair; (*mind*) lucide; (*road*) libre, dégagé; (*profit*) net; (*obvious*) évident, clair; (*certain*) certain; (*complete*) entier; **to be c. of** (*free of*) être libre de; (*out of*) être hors de; **to make oneself c.** se faire comprendre; **c. conscience** conscience *f* nette *or* tranquille; – *adv* (*quite*) complètement; **c. of** (*away from*) à l'écart de; **to keep** *or* **steer c. of** se tenir à l'écart de; **to get c. of** (*away from*) s'éloigner de; – *vt* (*path, place, table*) débarrasser, dégager; (*land*) défricher; (*fence*) franchir (sans toucher); (*obstacle*) éviter; (*person*) *Jur* disculper;

(*cheque*) compenser; (*goods, debts*) liquider; (*through customs*) dédouaner; (*for security etc*) autoriser; **to c. s.o. of** (*suspicion*) laver qn de; **to c. one's throat** s'éclaircir la gorge; – *vi* **to c. (up)** (*of weather*) s'éclaircir; (*of fog*) se dissiper; ■ **to c. away** *vt* (*remove*) enlever; – *vi* (*of fog*) se dissiper; **to c. off** *vi* (*leave*) *Fam* filer; – *vt* (*table*) débarrasser; **to c. out** *vt* (*empty*) vider; (*clean*) nettoyer; (*remove*) enlever; **to c. up** (*mystery etc*) éclaircir; – *vti* (*tidy*) ranger. ◆**-ing** *n* (*in woods*) clairière *f.* ◆**-ly** *adv* clairement; (*to understand*) bien, clairement; (*obviously*) évidemment. ◆**-ness** *n* (*o*) *sound*) clarté *f*, netteté *f*; (*of mind*) lucidité *f.* ◆**clearance** *n* (*sale*) soldes *mpl*; (*space*) espace *m*; (*permission*) autorisation *f*; (*of cheque*) compensation *f.* ◆**clear-'cut** *a* net. ◆**clear-'headed** *a* lucide.

clearway ['klɪəweɪ] *n* route *f* à stationnement interdit.

cleavage ['kliːvɪdʒ] *n* (*split*) clivage *m*; (*of woman*) *Fam* naissance *f* des seins.

cleft [kleft] *a* (*palate*) fendu; (*stick*) fourchu; – *n* fissure *f.*

clement ['klemənt] *a* clément. ◆**clemency** *n* clémence *f.*

clementine ['klemən'tiːn] *n* clémentine *f.*

clench [klentʃ] *vt* (*press*) serrer.

clergy ['klɜːdʒi] *n* clergé *m.* ◆**clergyman** *n* (*pl* **-men**) ecclésiastique *m.*

cleric ['klerɪk] *n* *Rel* clerc *m.* ◆**clerical** *a* (*job*) d'employé; (*work*) de bureau; (*error*) d'écriture; *Rel* clérical.

clerk [klɑːk, *Am* klɜːk] *n* employé, -ée *mf* (de bureau); *Jur* clerc *m*; (*in store*) *Am* vendeur, -euse *mf*; **c. of the court** *Jur* greffier *m.*

clever ['klevər] *a* (**-er, -est**) intelligent; (*smart, shrewd*) astucieux; (*skilful*) habile (**at sth** à qch, **at doing** à faire); (*ingenious*) ingénieux; (*gifted*) doué; **c. at** (*English etc*) fort en; **c. with one's hands** habile *or* adroit de ses mains. ◆**-ly** *adv* intelligemment; habilement. ◆**-ness** *n* intelligence *f*; astuce *f*; habileté *f.*

cliché ['kliːʃeɪ] *n* (*idea*) cliché *m.*

click [klɪk] **1** *n* déclic *m*, bruit *m* sec; – *vi* faire un déclic; (*of lovers etc*) *Fam* se plaire du premier coup; **it clicked** (*I realized*) *Fam* j'ai compris tout à coup. **2** *vt* **to c. one's heels** *Mil* claquer des talons.

client ['klaɪənt] *n* client, -ente *mf.* ◆**clientele** [kliːɑːn'tel] *n* clientèle *f.*

cliff [klɪf] *n* falaise *f.*

climate ['klaɪmɪt] *n* *Met* & *Fig* climat *m.* ◆**cli'matic** *a* climatique.

climax ['klaɪmæks] *n* point *m* culminant; (*sexual*) orgasme *m*; – *vi* atteindre son point culminant.

climb [klaɪm] *vt* **to c. (up)** (*steps*) monter, gravir; (*hill, mountain*) gravir, faire l'ascension de; (*tree, ladder*) monter à, grimper à; **to c. (over)** (*wall*) escalader; **to c. down (from)** descendre de; – *vi* **to c. (up)** monter; (*of plant*) grimper; **to c. down** descendre; (*back down*) *Fig* en rabattre; – *n* montée *f.* ◆**-ing** *n* montée *f*; (*mountain*) c. alpinisme *m.* ◆**-er** *n* grimpeur, -euse *mf*; *Sp* alpiniste *mf*; *Bot* plante *f* grimpante; **social c.** arriviste *mf.*

clinch [klɪntʃ] *vt* (*deal, bargain*) conclure; (*argument*) consolider.

cling [klɪŋ] *vi* (*pt* & *pp* **clung**) se cramponner, s'accrocher (**to** à); (*stick*) adhérer (**to** à). ◆**-ing** *a* (*clothes*) collant. ◆**clingfilm** *n* scel-o-frais®*m*, film *m* étirable.

clinic ['klɪnɪk] *n* (*private*) clinique *f*; (*health centre*) centre *m* médical. ◆**clinical** *a* *Med* clinique; *Fig* scientifique, objectif.

clink [klɪŋk] *vi* tinter; – *vt* faire tinter; – *n* tintement *m.*

clip [klɪp] **1** *vt* (**-pp-**) (*cut*) couper; (*sheep*) tondre; (*hedge*) tailler; (*ticket*) poinçonner; **to c. sth out of** (*newspaper etc*) découper qch dans. **2** *n* (*for paper*) attache *f*, trombone *m*; (*for brooch, of cyclist, for hair*) pince *f*; – *vt* (**-pp-**) **to c. (on)** attacher. **3** *n* (*of film*) extrait *m*; (*blow*) *Fam* taloche *f.* ◆**clipping** *n* *Journ* coupure *f.* ◆**clippers** *npl* (*for hair*) tondeuse *f*; (*for nails*) pince *f* à ongles; (*pocket-sized, for finger nails*) coupe-ongles *m inv.*

clique [kliːk] *n* *Pej* clique *f.* ◆**cliquey** *a* *Pej* exclusif.

cloak [kləʊk] *n* (*grande*) cape *f*; *Fig* manteau *m*; **c. and dagger** (*film etc*) d'espionnage. ◆**cloakroom** *n* vestiaire *m*; (*for luggage*) *Rail* consigne *f*; (*lavatory*) toilettes *fpl.*

clobber ['klɒbər] **1** *vt* (*hit*) *Sl* rosser. **2** *n* (*clothes*) *Sl* affaires *fpl.*

clock [klɒk] *n* (*large*) horloge *f*; (*small*) pendule *f*; *Aut* compteur *m*; **against the c.** *Fig* contre la montre; **round the c.** *Fig* vingt-quatre heures sur vingt-quatre; **tower c.** clocher *m*; – *vt Sp* chronométrer; **to c. up** (*miles*) *Aut Fam* faire; – *vi* **to c. in** *or* **out** (*of worker*) pointer. ◆**clockwise** *adv* dans le sens des aiguilles d'une montre. ◆**clockwork** *a* mécanique; *Fig* régulier

4

– n **to go like c.** aller comme sur des roulettes.

clod [klɒd] n 1 (of earth) motte f. 2 (oaf) Fam balourd, -ourde mf.

clog [klɒg] 1 n (shoe) sabot m. 2 vt (-gg-) to c. (up) (obstruct) boucher.

cloister ['klɔɪstər] n cloître m; – vt cloîtrer.

close[1] [kləʊs] a (-er, -est) (place, relative etc) proche (**to** de); (collaboration, resemblance, connection) étroit; (friend etc) intime; (order, contest) serré; (study) rigoureux; (atmosphere) Met lourd; (vowel) fermé; **to c.** (near) près de, proche de; **to tears** au bord des larmes; **to have a c. shave** or **call** l'échapper belle; – adv **c. (by)**, **c. at hand** (tout) près; **c. to** près de; **c. behind** juste derrière; **c. to** (almost) Fam bien près de; **c. together** (to stand) serrés; **to follow c.** suivre de près; – n (enclosed area) enceinte f. ◆**c.-'cropped** a (hair) (coupé) ras. ◆**c.-'knit** a très uni. ◆**c.-up** n gros plan m.

close[2] [kləʊz] n fin f, conclusion f; **to bring to a c.** mettre fin à; **to draw to a c.** tirer à sa fin; – vt fermer; (discussion) terminer, clore; (opening) boucher; (road) barrer; (gap) réduire; (deal) conclure; **to c. the meeting** lever la séance; **to c. ranks** serrer les rangs; **to c. in** (enclose) entourer; **to c. up** fermer; – vi fermer; (end) (se) terminer; **to c. up** (of shop) se fermer; (of wound) se refermer; **to c. in** (approach) approcher; **to c. in on s.o.** se rapprocher de qn. ■ **to c. down** vti (close for good) fermer (définitivement); – vi TV terminer les émissions. ◆**c.-down** n fermeture f (définitive); TV fin f (des émissions). ◆**closing** n fermeture f; (of session) clôture f; – a final; **c. time** heure f de fermeture. ◆**closure** ['kləʊʒər] n fermeture f.

closely ['kləʊslɪ] adv (to link, guard) étroitement; (to follow) de près; (to listen) attentivement; **c. contested** très disputé; **to hold s.o. c.** tenir qn contre soi. ◆**closeness** n proximité f; (of collaboration etc) étroitesse f; (of friendship) intimité f; (of weather) lourdeur f.

closet ['klɒzɪt] n (cupboard) Am placard m; (wardrobe) Am penderie f.

clot [klɒt] 1 n (of blood) caillot m; – vt (-tt-) (blood) coaguler; – vi (of blood) se coaguler. 2 n (person) Fam imbécile mf.

cloth [klɒθ] n tissu m, étoffe f; (of linen) toile f; (of wool) drap m; (for dusting) chiffon m; (for dishes) torchon m; (tablecloth) nappe f.

cloth/e [kləʊð] vt habiller, vêtir (**in** de).

◆**-ing** n habillement m; (clothes) vêtements mpl; **an article of c.** un vêtement.

clothes [kləʊðz] npl vêtements mpl; **to put one's c. on** s'habiller; **c. shop** magasin m d'habillement; **c. brush** brosse f à habits; **c. peg**, Am **c. pin** pince f à linge; **c. line** corde f à linge.

cloud [klaʊd] n nuage m; (of arrows, insects) Fig nuée f; – vt (mind, issue) obscurcir; (window) embuer; – vi **to c. (over)** (of sky) se couvrir. ◆**cloudburst** n averse f. ◆**cloudy** a (-ier, -iest) (weather) couvert, nuageux; (liquid) trouble.

clout [klaʊt] 1 n (blow) Fam taloche f; – vt Fam flanquer une taloche à, talocher. 2 n Pol Fam influence f, pouvoir m.

clove [kləʊv] n clou m de girofle; **c. of garlic** gousse f d'ail.

clover ['kləʊvər] n trèfle m.

clown [klaʊn] n clown m; – vi **to c. (around)** faire le clown.

cloying ['klɔɪɪŋ] a écœurant.

club [klʌb] 1 n (weapon) matraque f, massue f; (golf) club m; – vt (-bb-) matraquer. 2 n (society) club m, cercle m; – vi (-bb-) **to c. together** se cotiser (**to buy** pour acheter). 3 n & npl Cards trèfle m. ◆**clubhouse** n pavillon m.

clubfoot ['klʌbfʊt] n pied m bot. ◆**club-'footed** a pied bot inv.

cluck [klʌk] vi (of hen) glousser.

clue [kluː] n indice m; (of crossword) définition f; (to mystery) clef f; **I don't have a c.** Fam je n'en ai pas la moindre idée. ◆**clueless** a Fam stupide.

clump [klʌmp] n (of flowers, trees) massif m.

clumsy ['klʌmzɪ] a (-ier, -iest) maladroit; (shape) lourd; (tool) peu commode. ◆**clumsily** adv maladroitement. ◆**clumsiness** n maladresse f.

clung [klʌŋ] see cling.

cluster ['klʌstər] n groupe m; (of flowers) grappe f; (of stars) amas m; – vi se grouper.

clutch [klʌtʃ] 1 n (hold tight) étreindre; (cling to) se cramponner à; (grasp) saisir; – vi **to c. at** essayer de saisir; – n étreinte f. 2 n (apparatus) Aut embrayage m; (pedal) pédale f d'embrayage. 3 npl **s.o.'s clutches** (power) les griffes fpl de qn.

clutter ['klʌtər] n (objects) fouillis m, désordre m; – vt **to c. (up)** encombrer (**with** de).

cm abbr (centimetre) cm.

co- [kəʊ] pref co-.

Co abbr (company) Cie.

coach [kəʊtʃ] 1 n (horse-drawn) carrosse m; Rail voiture f, wagon m; Aut autocar m. 2 n (person) Sch répétiteur, -trice mf; Sp entraîneur *m*; – *vt* (*pupil*) donner des leçons (particulières) à; (*sportsman etc*) entraîner; (*for* **c.s.o. for** (*exam*) préparer qn à. ◆**coachman** *n* (*pl* **-men**) cocher *m*.

coagulate [kəʊˈægjʊleɪt] *vi* (*of blood*) se coaguler; – *vt* coaguler.

coal [kəʊl] *n* charbon *m*; *Geol* houille *f*; – *a* (*basin etc*) houiller; (*merchant, fire*) de charbon; (*cellar, bucket*) à charbon. ◆**coalfield** *n* bassin *m* houiller. ◆**coalmine** *n* mine *f* de charbon.

coalition [kəʊəˈlɪʃ(ə)n] *n* coalition *f*.

coarse [kɔːs] *a* (**-er, -est**) (*person, manners*) grossier, vulgaire; (*surface*) rude; (*fabric*) grossier; (*salt*) gros; (*accent*) commun, vulgaire. ◆**—ness** *n* grossièreté *f*, vulgarité *f*.

coast [kəʊst] **1** *n* côte *f*. **2** *vi* **to c.** (**down** or **along**) (*of vehicle etc*) descendre en roue libre. ◆**c.s.o. for** (*exam*) **coastal** *a* côtier. ◆**coaster** *n* (*ship*) caboteur *m*; (*for glass etc*) dessous *m* de verre, rond *m*. ◆**coastguard** *n* (*person*) garde *m* maritime, garde-côte *m*. ◆**coastline** *n* littoral *m*.

coat [kəʊt] *n* manteau *m*; (*overcoat*) pardessus *m*; (*jacket*) veste *f*; (*of animal*) pelage *m*; (*of paint*) couche *f*; **c. of arms** blason *m*, armoiries *fpl*; **c. hanger** cintre *m*; – *vt* couvrir, enduire (**with de**); (*with chocolate*) enrober (**with de**). ◆**—ed** *a* **c. tongue** langue *f* chargée. ◆**—ing** *n* couche *f*.

coax [kəʊks] *vt* amadouer, cajoler; **to c.s.o. to do** or **into doing** amadouer qn pour qu'il fasse. ◆**—ing** *n* cajoleries *fpl*.

cob [kɒb] *n* **corn on the c.** épi *m* de maïs.

cobble [ˈkɒb(ə)l] *n* pavé *m*; – *vt* **to c. together** (*text etc*) *Fam* bricoler. ◆**cobbled** *a* pavé. ◆**cobblestone** *n* pavé *m*.

cobbler [ˈkɒblər] *n* cordonnier *m*.

cobra [ˈkəʊbrə] *n* (*snake*) cobra *m*.

cobweb [ˈkɒbweb] *n* toile *f* d'araignée.

cocaine [kəʊˈkeɪn] *n* cocaïne *f*.

cock [kɒk] **1** *n* (*rooster*) coq *m*; (*male bird*) (*oiseau m*) mâle *m*. **2** *vt* (*gun*) armer; **to c.** (**up**) (*ears*) dresser. ◆**c.-a-doodle-doo** *n* & *int* cocorico *m*. ◆**c.-and-'bull story** *n* histoire *f* à dormir debout.

cockatoo [kɒkəˈtuː] *n* (*bird*) cacatoès *m*.

cocker [ˈkɒkər] *n* **c.** (**spaniel**) cocker *m*.

cockerel [ˈkɒkərəl] *n* jeune coq *m*, coquelet *m*.

cock-eyed [kɒkˈaɪd] *a Fam* **1** (*cross-eyed*) bigleux. **2** (*crooked*) de travers. **3** (*crazy*) absurde, stupide.

cockle [ˈkɒk(ə)l] *n* (*shellfish*) coque *f*.

cockney [ˈkɒknɪ] *a* & *n* cockney (*mf*).

cockpit [ˈkɒkpɪt] *n Av* poste *m* de pilotage.

cockroach [ˈkɒkrəʊtʃ] *n* (*beetle*) cafard *m*.

cocksure [kɒkˈʃʊər] *a Fam* trop sûr de soi.

cocktail [ˈkɒkteɪl] *n* (*drink*) cocktail *m*; (*fruit*) **c.** macédoine *f* (de fruits); **c. party** cocktail *m*; **prawn c.** crevettes *fpl* à la mayonnaise.

cocky [ˈkɒkɪ] *a* (**-ier, -iest**) *Fam* trop sûr de soi, arrogant.

cocoa [ˈkəʊkəʊ] *n* cacao *m*.

coconut [ˈkəʊkənʌt] *n* noix *f* de coco; **c. palm** cocotier *m*.

cocoon [kəˈkuːn] *n* cocon *m*.

cod [kɒd] *n* morue *f*; (*fresh*) cabillaud *m*. ◆**c.-liver 'oil** *n* huile *f* de foie de morue.

COD [siːəʊˈdiː] *abbr* (*cash on delivery*) livraison *f* contre remboursement.

coddle [ˈkɒd(ə)l] *vt* dorloter.

cod/e [kəʊd] *n* code *m*; – *vt* coder. ◆**—ing** *n* codage *m*. ◆**codify** *vt* codifier.

co-educational [kəʊedjʊˈkeɪʃən(ə)l] *a* (*school, teaching*) mixte.

coefficient [kəʊɪˈfɪʃənt] *n Math* coefficient *m*.

coerce [kəʊˈɜːs] *vt* contraindre. ◆**coercion** *n* contrainte *f*.

coexist [kəʊɪɡˈzɪst] *vi* coexister. ◆**coexistence** *n* coexistence *f*.

coffee [ˈkɒfɪ] *n* café *m*; **white c.** café *m* au lait; (*ordered in restaurant etc*) (café *m*) crème *m*; **black c.** café *m* noir, café nature; **c. bar, c. house** café *m*, cafétéria *f*; **c. break** pause-café *f*; **c. table** table *f* basse. ◆**coffeepot** *n* cafetière *f*.

coffers [ˈkɒfəz] *npl* (*funds*) coffres *mpl*.

coffin [ˈkɒfɪn] *n* cercueil *m*.

cog [kɒg] *n Tech* dent *f*; (*person*) *Fig* rouage *m*.

cogent [ˈkəʊdʒənt] *a* (*reason, argument*) puissant, convaincant.

cogitate [ˈkɒdʒɪteɪt] *vi Iron* cogiter.

cognac [ˈkɒnjæk] *n* cognac *m*.

cohabit [kəʊˈhæbɪt] *vi* (*of unmarried people*) vivre en concubinage.

coherent [kəʊˈhɪərənt] *a* cohérent; (*speech*) compréhensible. ◆**cohesion** *n* cohésion *f*. ◆**cohesive** *a* cohésif.

cohort [ˈkəʊhɔːt] *n* (*group*) cohorte *f*.

coil [kɔɪl] *n* (*of wire etc*) rouleau *m*; *El* bobine *f*; (*contraceptive*) stérilet *m*; – *vt* (*rope, hair*) enrouler; – *vi* (*of snake etc*) s'enrouler.

coin [kɔɪn] *n* pièce *f* (de monnaie); (*currency*) monnaie *f*; – *vt* (*money*) frapper; (*word*) *Fig* inventer, forger; **to c. a phrase** pour ainsi dire. ◆**c.-operated** *a* automatique. ◆**coinage** n (coins) monnaie f; Fig invention f.

coincide [kəʊn'saɪd] vi coïncider (with avec). ◆**co'incidence** n coïncidence f. ◆**coinci'dental** a fortuit; **it's c.** c'est une coïncidence.

coke [kəʊk] n **1** (fuel) coke m. **2** (Coca-Cola®) coca m.

colander ['kʌləndər] n (for vegetables etc) passoire f.

cold [kəʊld] n froid m; Med rhume m; **to catch c.** prendre froid; **out in the c.** Fig abandonné, en carafe; – a (-er, -est) froid; **to be** or **feel c.** (of person) avoir froid; **my hands are c.** j'ai les mains froides; **it's c.** (of weather) il fait froid; **to get c.** (of weather) se refroidir; (of food) refroidir; **to get c. feet** Fam se dégonfler; **in c. blood** de sang-froid; **c. cream** crème f de beauté; **c. meats,** Am **c. cuts** Culin assiette f anglaise. ◆**c.-'blooded** a (person) cruel, insensible; (act) de sang-froid. ◆**c.-'shoulder** vt snober. ◆**coldly** adv avec froideur. ◆**coldness** n froideur f.

coleslaw ['kəʊlslɔː] n salade f de chou cru.

colic ['kɒlɪk] n coliques fpl.

collaborate [kə'læbəreɪt] vi collaborer (on à). ◆**collabo'ration** n collaboration f. ◆**collaborator** n collaborateur, -trice mf.

collage ['kɒlɑːʒ] n (picture) collage m.

collapse [kə'læps] vi (fall) s'effondrer, s'écrouler; (of government) tomber; (faint) Med se trouver mal; – n effondrement m, écroulement m; (of government) chute f. ◆**collapsible** a (chair etc) pliant.

collar ['kɒlər] n (on garment) col m; (of dog) collier m; **to seize by the c.** saisir au collet; – vt Fam saisir (qn) au collet; Fig Fam retenir (qn); (take, steal) Sl piquer. ◆**collarbone** n clavicule f.

collate [kə'leɪt] vt collationner, comparer (with avec).

colleague ['kɒliːg] n collègue mf, confrère m.

collect [kə'lekt] vt (pick up) ramasser; (gather) rassembler, recueillir; (taxes) percevoir; (rent, money) encaisser; (stamps etc as hobby) collectionner; (fetch, call for) (passer) prendre; – vi (of dust) s'accumuler; (of people) se rassembler; **to c. for** (in street, church) quêter pour; – adv **to call** or **phone c.** Am téléphoner en PCV. ◆**collection** [kə'lekʃ(ə)n] n ramassage m; (of taxes) perception f; (of objects) collection f; (of poems etc) recueil m; (of money in church etc) quête f; (of mail) levée f. ◆**collective** a collectif. ◆**collectively** adv

collectivement. ◆**collector** n (of stamps etc) collectionneur, -euse mf.

college ['kɒlɪdʒ] n Pol Rel Sch collège m; (university) université f; Mus conservatoire m; **teachers' training c.** école f normale; **art c.** école f des beaux-arts; **agricultural c.** institut m d'agronomie, lycée m agricole.

collide [kə'laɪd] vi entrer en collision (with avec), se heurter (with à). ◆**collision** n collision f; Fig conflit m, collision f.

colliery ['kɒlɪərɪ] n houillère f.

colloquial [kə'ləʊkwɪəl] a (word etc) familier. ◆**colloquialism** n expression f familière.

collusion [kə'luːʒ(ə)n] n collusion f.

collywobbles ['kɒlɪwɒb(ə)lz] npl **to have the c.** (feel nervous) Fam avoir la frousse.

cologne [kə'ləʊn] n eau f de Cologne.

colon ['kəʊlən] n **1** Gram deux-points m inv. **2** Anat côlon m.

colonel ['kɜːn(ə)l] n colonel m.

colony ['kɒlənɪ] n colonie f. ◆**colonial** [kə'ləʊnɪəl] a colonial. ◆**coloni'zation** n colonisation f. ◆**colonize** vt coloniser.

colossal [kə'lɒs(ə)l] a colossal.

colour ['kʌlər] n couleur f; – a (photo, television) en couleurs; (television set) couleur inv; (problem) racial; **c. supplement** Journ supplément m illustré; **off c.** (not well) mal fichu; (improper) scabreux; – vt colorer; **to c. (in)** (drawing) colorier. ◆**-ed** a (person, pencil) de couleur; (glass, water) coloré. ◆**-ing** n coloration f; (with crayons) coloriage m; (hue, effect) coloris m; (matter) colorant m. ◆**colour-blind** a daltonien. ◆**colourful** a (crowd, story) coloré; (person) pittoresque.

colt [kəʊlt] n (horse) poulain m.

column ['kɒləm] n colonne f. ◆**columnist** n Journ chroniqueur m; **gossip c.** échotier, -ière mf.

coma ['kəʊmə] n coma m; **in a c.** dans le coma.

comb [kəʊm] n peigne m; – vt peigner; (search) Fig ratisser; **to c. one's hair** se peigner; **to c. out** (hair) démêler.

combat ['kɒmbæt] n combat m; – vti combattre (for pour). ◆**'combatant** n combattant, -ante mf.

combin/e [kəm'baɪn] vt unir, joindre (with à); (elements, sounds) combiner; (qualities, efforts) allier, joindre; – vi s'unir; everything combined to . . . tout s'est ligué pour . . . . ◆**-ed** a (effort) conjugué; (forces) réunies; **c. wealth**/etc (put together) richesses/etc fpl réunies; **c. forces** Mil forces fpl alliées. ◆**combi'nation** n combinaison f; (of *qualities*) réunion *f*; (*of events*) concours *m*; **in c. with** en association avec.

combine² ['kɒmbaɪn] *n* Com cartel *m*; **c. harvester** *Agr* moissonneuse-batteuse *f*.

combustion [kəm'bʌstʃ(ə)n] *n* combustion *f*.

come [kʌm] *vi* (*pt* **came**, *pp* **come**) venir (*from* de, *to* à); (*arrive*) arriver; (*happen*) arriver; **c. and see me** viens me voir; **I've just c. from** venir de; **to c. for** venir chercher; **to c. home** rentrer; **coming!** j'arrive!; **c. now!** voyons!; **c. as a surprise (to)** surprendre; **to c. near or close to doing** faillir faire; **to c. on page 2** se trouver à la page 2; **nothing came of it** ça n'a abouti à rien; **to c. to** (*understand etc*) en venir à; (*a decision*) parvenir à; **to c. to an end** toucher à sa fin; **to c. true** se réaliser; **c. May/etc** *Fam* en mai/*etc*; **the life to c.** la vie future; **how c. that . . . ?** *Fam* comment se fait-il que . . . ? ∎ **to c. about** *vi* (*happen*) se faire, arriver; **to c. across** *vi* (*of speech*) faire de l'effet; (*of feelings*) se montrer; – *vt* (*thing, person*) tomber sur; **to c. along** *vi* venir (*with* avec); (*progress*) avancer; **c. along!** allons!; **to c. at** (*attack*) attaquer; **to c. away** *vi* (*leave, come off*) partir; **to c. back** *vi* revenir; (*return home*) rentrer. ◆**comeback** *n* retour *m*; *Th* Pol rentrée *f*; (*retort*) réplique *f*; **to c. by** *vt* (*obtain*) obtenir; (*find*) trouver; **to c. down** *vi* descendre; (*of rain, price*) tomber. ◆**comedown** *n* *Fam* humiliation *f*; **to c. forward** *vi* (*make oneself known, volunteer*) se présenter; **to c. forward** offrir, suggérer; **to c. in** *vi* entrer; (*of tide*) monter; (*of train, athlete*) arriver; *Pol* arriver au pouvoir; (*of clothes*) devenir la mode, se faire beaucoup; (*of money*) rentrer; **c. in for** recevoir; **to c. into** (*money*) hériter de; **to c. off** *vi* se détacher, partir; (*succeed*) réussir; (*happen*) avoir lieu; (*fare, manage*) s'en tirer; – *vt* (*fall from*) tomber de; (*get down from*) descendre de; **to c. on** *vi* (*follow*) suivre; (*progress*) avancer; (*start*) commencer; (*arrive*) arriver; (*of play*) être joué; **c. on!** allez!; **to c. out** *vi* sortir; (*of sun, book*) paraître; (*of stain*) s'enlever, partir; (*of secret*) être révélé; (*of photo*) réussir; **to c. out** (**on strike**) se mettre en grève; **to c. over** *vi* (*visit*) venir, passer; **to c. over funny or peculiar** se trouver mal; – *vt* (*take hold of*) saisir (*qn*), prendre (*qn*); **to c. round** *vi* (*visit*) venir, passer; (*recur*) revenir; (*regain consciousness*) revenir à soi; **to c. through** *vi* (*survive*) s'en tirer; – *vt* se tirer indemne de; **to c. to** (*regain consciousness*) revenir

à soi; (*amount to*) Com revenir à, faire; **to c. under** *vi* être classé sous; (*s.o.'s influence*) tomber sous; **to c. up** *vi* (*rise*) monter; (*of plant*) sortir; (*of question, job*) se présenter; **to c. up against** (*wall, problem*) se heurter à; **to c. up to** (*reach*) arriver jusqu'à; (*one's hopes*) répondre à; **to c. up with** (*idea, money*) trouver; **to c. upon** (*book, reference etc*) tomber sur. ◆**coming** *a* (*future*) à venir; – *n* Rel avènement *m*; **comings and goings** allées *fpl* et venues.

comedy ['kɒmɪdɪ] *n* comédie *f*. ◆**co'median** *n* (acteur *m*) comique *m*, actrice *f* comique.

comet ['kɒmɪt] *n* comète *f*.

comeuppance [kʌm'ʌpəns] *n* **he got his c.** *Pej* *Fam* il n'a eu que ce qu'il mérite.

comfort ['kʌmfət] *n* confort *m*; (*consolation*) réconfort *m*, consolation *f*; (*peace of mind*) tranquillité *f* d'esprit; **to like one's comforts** aimer ses aises *fpl*; **c. station** *Am* toilettes *fpl*; – *vt* consoler; (*cheer*) réconforter. ◆**-able** *a* (*chair, house etc*) confortable; (*rich*) aisé; **he's c.**, (*in chair etc*) il est à l'aise, il est bien; **make yourself c.** mets-toi à l'aise. ◆**-ably** *adv* **c. off** (*rich*) à l'aise. ◆**-er** *n* (*baby's dummy*) sucette *f*; (*quilt*) *Am* édredon *m*. ◆**comfy** *a* (**-ier, -iest**) (*chair etc*) *Fam* confortable; **I'm c.** je suis bien.

comic ['kɒmɪk] *a* comique; – *n* (*actor*) comique *m*; (*actress*) actrice *f* comique; (*magazine*) illustré *m*; **c. strip** bande *f* dessinée. ◆**comical** *a* comique, drôle.

comma ['kɒmə] *n* Gram virgule *f*.

command [kə'mɑːnd] *vt* (*order*) commander (**s.o. to do** à qn de faire); (*control, dominate*) commander (*régiment, vallée etc*); (*be able to use*) disposer de; (*respect*) imposer (*from* à); (*require*) exiger; – *vi* commander; – *n* ordre *m*; (*power*) commandement *m*; (*troops*) troupes *fpl*; (*mastery*) maîtrise *f* (**of** de); **at one's c.** (*disposal*) à sa disposition; **to be in c.** (**of**) (*ship, army etc*) commander; (*situation*) être maître (de). ◆**-ing** *a* (*authoritative*) imposant; (*position*) dominant; **c. officer** commandant *m*. ◆**-er** *n* chef *m*; *Mil* commandant *m*. ◆**-ment** *n* Rel commandement *m*.

commandant ['kɒmənd mænt] *m* Mil commandant *m* (*d'un camp etc*). ◆**comman'deer** *vt* réquisitionner.

commando [kə'mɑːndəʊ] *n* (*pl* -**os** or -**oes**) Mil commando *m*.

commemorate [kə'meməreɪt] *vt* commémorer. ◆**commemo'ration** *n* commémoration f. ◆**commemorative** a commémoratif.

commence [kə'mens] vti commencer (doing à faire). ◆**—ment** n commencement m; Univ Am remise f des diplômes.

commend [kə'mend] vt (praise) louer; (recommend) recommander; (entrust) confier (to à). ◆**—able** a louable. ◆**commen'dation** n éloge m.

commensurate [kə'menʃərət] a proportionné (to, with à).

comment ['kɒment] n commentaire m, remarque f; – vi faire des commentaires or des remarques (on sur); to c. on (text, event, news item) commenter; to c. that remarquer que. ◆**commentary** n commentaire m; (live) c. TV Rad reportage m. ◆**commentate** vi TV Rad faire un reportage (on sur). ◆**commentator** n TV Rad reporter m, commentateur, -trice m f.

commerce ['kɒmɜːs] n commerce m. ◆**co'mmercial 1** a commercial; (street) commerçant; (traveller) de commerce. 2 n (advertisement) TV publicité f; the **commercials** TV la publicité. ◆**co'mmercialize** vt (event) Pej transformer en une affaire de gros sous.

commiserate [kə'mɪzəreɪt] vi to c. with s.o. s'apitoyer sur (le sort de) qn. ◆**commise'ration** n commisération f.

commission [kə'mɪʃ(ə)n] n (fee, group) commission f; (order for work) commande f; out of c. hors service; to get one's c. être nommé officier; – vt (artist) passer une commande à; (book) commander; Mil nommer (qn) officier; to c. to do charger de faire. ◆**commissio'naire** n (in hotel etc) commissionnaire m. ◆**commissioner** n Pol commissaire m; (police) c. préfet m (de police).

commit [kə'mɪt] vt (-tt-) (crime) commettre; (entrust) confier (to à); to c. suicide se suicider; to c. to prison incarcérer; to c. oneself s'engager (to à); (compromise oneself) se compromettre. ◆**—ment** n obligation f; (promise) engagement m.

committee [kə'mɪtɪ] n comité m.

commodity [kə'mɒdɪtɪ] n produit m, article m.

common ['kɒmən] 1 a (-er, -est) (shared, vulgar) commun; (frequent) courant, fréquent, commun; the c. man l'homme m du commun; in c. (shared) en commun (with avec); to have nothing in c. n'avoir rien de commun (with avec); in c. with (like) comme; c. law droit m coutumier; c.

Market Marché m commun; c. room salle f commune; c. or garden ordinaire. 2 n (land) terrain m communal; House of Commons Pol Chambre f des Communes; the Commons Pol les Communes fpl. ◆**—er** n roturier, -ière mf. ◆**—ly** adv (generally) communément; (vulgarly) d'une façon commune. ◆**—ness** n fréquence f; (vulgarity) vulgarité f. ◆**commonplace** a banal; – n banalité f. ◆**common'sense** n sens m commun; – a sensé.

Commonwealth ['kɒmənwelθ] n the C. le Commonwealth.

commotion [kə'məʊʃ(ə)n] n agitation f.

communal [kə'mjuːn(ə)l] a (of the community) communautaire; (shared) commun. ◆**—ly** adv en commun; (to live) en communauté.

commune 1 ['kɒmjuːn] n (district) commune f; (group) communauté f. 2 [kə'mjuːn] vi Rel & Fig communier (with avec). ◆**co'mmunion** n communion f; (Holy) C. communion f.

communicate [kə'mjuːnɪkeɪt] vt communiquer; (illness) transmettre; – vi (of person, rooms etc) communiquer. ◆**communi'cation** n communication f; c. cord Rail signal m d'alarme. ◆**communicative** a communicatif. ◆**communiqué** n Pol communiqué m.

communism ['kɒmjunɪz(ə)m] n communisme m. ◆**communist** a & n communiste (mf).

community [kə'mjuːnɪtɪ] n communauté f; – a (rights, life etc) communautaire; the student c. les étudiants mpl; c. centre centre m socio-culturel; c. worker animateur, -trice mf socio-culturel(le).

commut/e [kə'mjuːt] 1 vt Jur commuer (to en). 2 vi (travel) faire la navette (to work pour se rendre à son travail). ◆**—ing** n trajets mpl journaliers. ◆**—er** n banlieusard, -arde mf; c. train train m de banlieue.

compact 1 [kəm'pækt] a (car, crowd, substance) compact; (style) condensé; c. disc ['kɒmpækt] disque m compact. 2 ['kɒmpækt] n (for face powder) poudrier m.

companion [kəm'pænjən] n (person) compagnon m, compagne f; (handbook) manuel m. ◆**companionship** n camaraderie f.

company ['kʌmpənɪ] n (fellowship, firm) compagnie f; (guests) invités, hôtes mpl; to keep s.o. c. tenir compagnie à qn; to keep good c. avoir de bonnes fréquentations; he's good c. c'est un bon compagnon.

compar/e [kəm'peər] *vt* comparer; **compared to** *or* **with** en comparaison de; – *vi* être comparable, se comparer (**with** à). ◆**-able** ['kɒmpərəb(ə)l] *a* comparable. ◆**comparative** *a* comparatif; (*relative*) relatif. ◆**comparatively** *adv* relativement. ◆**comparison** *n* comparaison *f* (**between** entre; **with** à, avec).

compartment [kəm'pɑːtmənt] *n* compartiment *m*. ◆**compart'mentalize** *vt* compartimenter.

compass ['kʌmpəs] *n* **1** (*for navigation*) boussole *f*; *Nau* compas *m*; (*range*) Fig portée *f*. **2** (*for measuring etc*) *Am* compas *m*; (**pair of**) **compasses** compas *m*.

compassion [kəm'pæʃ(ə)n] *n* compassion *f*. ◆**compassionate** *a* compatissant; **on c. grounds** pour raisons de famille.

compatible [kəm'pætɪb(ə)l] *a* compatible. ◆**compati'bility** *n* compatibilité *f*.

compatriot [kəm'pætrɪət, kəm'peɪtrɪət] *n* compatriote *mf*.

compel [kəm'pel] *vt* (**-ll-**) contraindre (**to do** à faire); (*respect etc*) imposer (**from** à); **compelled to do** contraint de faire. ◆**compelling** *a* irrésistible.

compendium [kəm'pendɪəm] *n* abrégé *m*.

compensate ['kɒmpenseɪt] *vt* **to c. s.o.** (*with payment, recompense*) dédommager qn (**for** de); **to c. for sth** (*make up for*) compenser qch; – *vi* compenser. ◆**compen'sation** *n* (*financial*) dédommagement *m*; (*consolation*) compensation *f*; **in c. for** en compensation de.

compère ['kɒmpeər] *n* TV Rad animateur, -trice *mf*, présentateur, -trice *mf*; – *vt* (*a show*) animer, présenter.

compete [kəm'piːt] *vi* prendre part (**in** à), concourir (**in** à); (*vie*) rivaliser (**with** avec); *Com* faire concurrence (**with** à); **to c. for** (*prize etc*) concourir pour; **to c. in a rally** courir dans un rallye.

competent ['kɒmpɪtənt] *a* (*capable*) compétent (**to do** pour faire); (*sufficient*) suffisant. ◆**-ly** *adv* avec compétence. ◆**competence** *n* compétence *f*.

competition [kɒmpə'tɪʃ(ə)n] *n* (*rivalry*) compétition *f*, concurrence *f*; **a c.** (*contest*) un concours; *Sp* une compétition. ◆**com'petitive** *a* (*price, market*) compétitif; (*selection*) par concours; (*person*) aimant la compétition; **c. exam(ination)** concours *m*. ◆**com'petitor** *n* concurrent, -ente *mf*.

compil/e [kəm'paɪl] *vt* (*dictionary*) rédiger; (*list*) dresser; (*documents*) compiler. ◆**-er** *n* rédacteur, -trice *mf*.

complacent [kəm'pleɪsənt] *a* content de

soi. ◆**complacence** *n*, ◆**complacency** *n* autosatisfaction *f*, contentement *m* de soi.

complain [kəm'pleɪn] *vi* se plaindre (**of, about** de; **that** que). ◆**complaint** *n* plainte *f*; *Com* réclamation *f*; *Med* maladie *f*; (**cause for**) **c.** sujet *m* de plainte.

complement ['kɒmplɪmənt] *n* complément *m*; – ['kɒmplɪment] *vt* compléter. ◆**comple'mentary** *a* complémentaire.

complete [kəm'pliːt] *a* (*total*) complet; (*finished*) achevé; (*downright*) Pej parfait; – *vt* (*add sth more*) compléter; (*finish*) achever; (*a form*) remplir. ◆**-ly** *adv* complètement, réalisation *f*. ◆**completion** *n* achèvement *m*, réalisation *f*.

complex ['kɒmpleks] **1** *a* complexe. **2** *n* (*feeling, buildings*) complexe *m*; **housing c.** grand ensemble *m*. ◆**com'plexity** *n* complexité *f*.

complexion [kəm'plekʃ(ə)n] *n* (*of the face*) teint *m*; Fig caractère *m*.

compliance [kəm'plaɪəns] *n* (*agreement*) conformité *f* (**with** avec).

complicat/e ['kɒmplɪkeɪt] *vt* compliquer. ◆**-ed** *a* compliqué. ◆**compli'cation** *n* complication *f*.

complicity [kəm'plɪsɪtɪ] *n* complicité *f*.

compliment ['kɒmplɪmənt] *n* compliment *m*; *pl* (*of author*) hommages *mpl*; **compliments of the season** meilleurs vœux pour Noël et la nouvelle année; – ['kɒmplɪment] *vt* complimenter. ◆**compli'mentary** *a* **1** (*flattering*) flatteur. **2** (*free*) à titre gracieux; (*ticket*) de faveur.

comply [kəm'plaɪ] *vi* obéir (**with** à); (*request*) accéder à.

component [kəm'pəʊnənt] *a* (*part*) constituant; – *n* (*chemical, electronic*) composant *m*; *Tech* pièce *f*; (*element*) Fig composante *f*.

compos/e [kəm'pəʊz] *vt* composer; **to c. oneself** se calmer. ◆**-ed** *a* calme. ◆**-er** *n* Mus compositeur, -trice *mf*. ◆**compo-'sition** *n* Mus Liter Ch composition *f*; Sch rédaction *f*. ◆**composure** *n* calme *m*, sang-froid *m*.

compost ['kɒmpɒst, *Am* 'kɒmpəʊst] *n* compost *m*.

compound 1 ['kɒmpaʊnd] *n* (*substance, word*) composé *m*; (*area*) enclos *m*; – *a* Ch composé; (*sentence, number*) complexe. **2** [kəm'paʊnd] *vt* Ch composer; (*increase*) Fig aggraver.

comprehend [kɒmprɪ'hend] *vt* comprendre. ◆**comprehensible** *a* compréhensible. ◆**comprehension** *n* compréhension

f. ◆**comprehensive** *a* complet; (*knowledge*) étendu; (*view, measure*) d'ensemble; (*insurance*) tous-risques *inv*; – *a & n* **c. (school)** = collège *m* d'enseignement secondaire.

compress [kəm'pres] *vt* comprimer; (*ideas etc*) *Fig* condenser. ◆**compression** *n* compression *f*; condensation *f*.

comprise [kəm'praiz] *vt* comprendre, englober.

compromise ['kɒmprəmaiz] *vt* compromettre; – *vi* accepter un compromis; – *n* compromis *m*; – *a* (*solution*) de compromis.

compulsion [kəm'pʌlʃ(ə)n] *n* contrainte *f*. ◆**compulsive** *a* (*behaviour*) *Psy* compulsif; (*smoker, gambler*) invétéré; **c. liar** mythomane *mf*.

compulsory [kəm'pʌlsəri] *a* obligatoire.

compunction [kəm'pʌŋkʃ(ə)n] *n* scrupule *m*.

comput/e [kəm'pjuːt] *vt* calculer. ◆**—ing** *n* informatique *f*. ◆**computer** *n* ordinateur *m*; – *a* (*system*) d'informatique; (*course*) d'informatique; **c. operator** opérateur, -trice *mf* sur ordinateur; **c. science** informatique *f*; **c. scientist** informaticien, -ienne *mf*. ◆**computerize** *vt* informatiser.

comrade ['kɒmreid] *n* camarade *mf*. ◆**comradeship** *n* camaraderie *f*.

con [kɒn] *vt* (-**nn**-) *Sl* rouler, escroquer; **to be conned** se faire avoir *or* rouler; – *n Sl* escroquerie *f*; **c. man** escroc *m*.

concave ['kɒnkeiv] *a* concave.

conceal [kən'siːl] *vt* (*hide*) dissimuler (**from** s.o., à qn); (*plan etc*) tenir secret. ◆**—ment** *n* dissimulation *f*.

concede [kən'siːd] *vt* concéder (**to** à, **that** que); – *vi* céder.

conceit [kən'siːt] *n* vanité *f*. ◆**conceited** *a* vaniteux. ◆**conceitedly** *adv* avec vanité.

conceiv/e [kən'siːv] *vt* (*idea, child etc*) concevoir; – *vi* (*of woman*) concevoir; **to c. of** concevoir. ◆**—able** *a* concevable, envisageable. ◆**—ably** *adv* yes, *c'est concevable.

concentrate ['kɒnsəntreit] *vt* concentrer; – *vi* se concentrer (**on** sur); **to c. on doing** s'appliquer à faire; – *n* concentré *m*. ◆**concen'tration** *n* concentration *f*; **c. camp** camp *m* de concentration.

concentric [kən'sentrik] *a* concentrique.

concept ['kɒnsept] *n* concept *m*. ◆**con'ception** *n* (*idea*) & *Med* conception *f*.

concern [kən'sɜːn] *vt* concerner; **to c. oneself with, be concerned with** s'occuper de; **to be concerned about** s'inquiéter de; –

n (*matter*) affaire *f*; (*anxiety*) inquiétude *f*; (*share*) *Com* intérêt(s) *m(pl)* (**in** dans); (*business*) **c.** entreprise *f*. ◆**—ed** *a* (*anxious*) inquiet; **the department c.** le service compétent; **the main person c.** le principal intéressé. ◆**—ing** *prep* en ce qui concerne.

concert ['kɒnsət] *n* concert *m*; **in c.** (*together*) de concert (**with** avec). ◆**c.-goer** *n* habitué, -ée *mf* des concerts. ◆**con'certed** *a* (*effort*) concerté.

concertina [kɒnsə'tiːnə] *n* concertina *m*; **c. crash** *Aut* carambolage *m*.

concession [kən'seʃ(ə)n] *n* concession *f* (**to** à).

conciliate [kən'silieit] *vt* **to c. s.o.** (*win over*) se concilier qn; (*soothe*) apaiser qn. ◆**concili'ation** *n* conciliation *f*; apaisement *m*. ◆**conciliatory** [kən'siliətəri, *Am* -tɔːri] *a* conciliant.

concise [kən'sais] *a* concis. ◆**—ly** *adv* avec concision. ◆**—ness** *n*, ◆**concision** *n* concision *f*.

conclud/e [kən'kluːd] *vt* (*end, settle*) conclure; **to c. that** (*infer*) conclure que; – *vi* (*of event etc*) se terminer (**with** par); (*of speaker*) conclure. ◆**—ing** *a* final. ◆**conclusion** *n* conclusion *f*; **in c.** pour conclure. ◆**conclusive** *a* concluant. ◆**conclusively** *adv* de manière concluante.

concoct [kən'kɒkt] *vt* *Culin Pej* concocter, confectionner; (*scheme*) *Fig* combiner. ◆**concoction** *n* (*substance*) *Pej* mixture *f*; (*act*) confection *f*; *Fig* combinaison *f*.

concord ['kɒŋkɔːd] *n* concorde *f*.

concourse ['kɒŋkɔːs] *n* (*hall*) *Am* hall *m*; *Rail* hall *m*, salle *f* des pas perdus.

concrete ['kɒŋkriːt] **1** *a* (*real, positive*) concret. **2** *n* béton *m*; – *a* en béton; **c. mixer** bétonnière *f*, bétonneuse *f*.

concur [kən'kɜːr] *vi* (-**rr**-) **1** (*agree*) être d'accord (**with** avec). **2** **to c. to** (*contribute*) concourir à.

concurrent [kən'kʌrənt] *a* simultané. ◆**—ly** *adv* simultanément.

concussion [kən'kʌʃ(ə)n] *n* *Med* commotion *f* (cérébrale).

condemn [kən'dem] *vt* condamner; (*building*) déclarer inhabitable. ◆**condem-'nation** *n* condamnation *f*.

condense [kən'dens] *vt* condenser; – *vi* se condenser. ◆**conden'sation** *n* condensation *f* (**of** de); (*mist*) buée *f*.

condescend [kɒndi'send] *vi* condescendre (**to do** à faire). ◆**condescension** *n* condescendance *f*.

condiment ['kɒndimənt] *n* condiment *m*.

condition [kəndiʃ(ə)n] **1** n (stipulation, circumstance, rank) condition f; (state) état m, condition f; **on c. that one does** à condition de faire, à condition que l'on fasse; **in/out of c.** en bonne/mauvaise forme. **2** vt (action etc) déterminer, conditionner; to c. s.o. Psy conditionner qn (**into doing** à faire). ◆**conditional** a conditionnel; **to be c. upon** dépendre de. ◆**conditioner** n (hair) n après-shampooing m.

condo ['kɒndəʊ] n abbr (pl **-os**) Am = **condominium.**

condolences [kən'dəʊlənsɪz] npl condoléances fpl.

condom ['kɒndəm] n préservatif m, capote f (anglaise).

condominium [kɒndə'mɪnɪəm] n Am (building) (immeuble m en) copropriété f; (apartment) appartement m dans une copropriété.

condone [kən'dəʊn] vt (forgive) pardonner; (overlook) fermer les yeux sur.

conducive [kən'djuːsɪv] a c. **to** favorable à.

conduct ['kɒndʌkt] n (behaviour, directing) conduite f; – [kən'dʌkt] vt (lead) conduire, mener; (orchestra) diriger; (electricity etc) conduire; to c. oneself se conduire. ◆**-ed** a (visit) guidé; c. **tour** excursion f accompagnée. ◆**conductor** n Mus chef m d'orchestre; (on bus) receveur m; Rail Am chef m de train; (metal, cable etc) conducteur m. ◆**conductress** n (on bus) receveuse f.

cone [kəʊn] n cône m; (of ice cream) cornet m; (paper) c. cornet m (de papier); **traffic c.** cône m de chantier.

confectioner [kən'fekʃənər] n (of sweets) confiseur, -euse mf; (of cakes) pâtissier, -ière mf. ◆**confectionery** n (sweets) confiserie f; (cakes) pâtisserie f.

confederate [kən'fedərət] a confédéré; – n (accomplice) complice mf, acolyte m. ◆**confederacy** n, ◆**confede'ration** n confédération f.

confer [kən'fɜːr] **1** vt (**-rr-**) (grant) conférer (**on** à); (degree) Univ remettre. **2** vi (**-rr-**) (talk together) se consulter. ◆**conference** ['kɒnfərəns] n conférence f; (scientific etc) congrès m.

confess [kən'fes] **1** vt avouer, confesser (that que, **to** à); – vi avouer; **to c. to** (crime etc) avouer, confesser. **2** vt Rel confesser; – vi se confesser. ◆**confession** n aveu m, confession f; Rel confession f. ◆**confessional** n Rel confessionnal m.

confetti [kən'fetɪ] n confettis mpl.

confide [kən'faɪd] vt confier (**to** à, that que);

– vi **to c. in** (talk to) se confier à. ◆**'confidant, -ante** [-ænt] n confident, -ente mf. ◆**'confidence** n (trust) confiance f; (secret) confidence f; (self-)c. confiance f en soi; **in c.** en confidence; **motion of no c.** Pol motion f de censure; **c. trick** escroquerie f; **c. trickster** escroc m. ◆**'confident** a sûr, assuré; (self-)c. sûr de soi. ◆**confi'dential** a confidentiel; (secretary) particulier. ◆**confi'dentially** adv en confidence. ◆**'confidently** adv avec confiance.

configuration [kənfɪgjʊ'reɪʃ(ə)n] n configuration f.

confine [kən'faɪn] vt enfermer, confiner (**to, in** dans); (limit) limiter (**to** à); **to c. oneself to doing** se limiter à faire. ◆**-ed** a (atmosphere) confiné; (space) réduit; **c. to bed** obligé de garder le lit. ◆**-ement** n Med couches fpl; Jur emprisonnement m. ◆**'confines** npl limites fpl, confins mpl.

confirm [kən'fɜːm] vt confirmer (that que); (strengthen) raffermir. ◆**-ed** a (bachelor) endurci; (smoker, habit) invétéré. ◆**confir'mation** n confirmation f; raffermissement m.

confiscate ['kɒnfɪskeɪt] vt confisquer (**from s.o.** à qn). ◆**confis'cation** n confiscation f.

conflagration [kɒnflə'greɪʃ(ə)n] n (grand) incendie m, brasier m.

conflict ['kɒnflɪkt] n conflit m; – [kən'flɪkt] vi être en contradiction, être incompatible (**with** avec); (of dates, events, TV programmes) tomber en même temps (**with** que). ◆**-ing** a (views, theories etc) contradictoires; (dates) incompatibles.

confluence ['kɒnflʊəns] n (of rivers) confluent m.

conform [kən'fɔːm] vi se conformer (**to, with** à); (of ideas etc) être en conformité. ◆**conformist** a & n conformiste (mf). ◆**conformity** n (likeness) conformité f; Pej conformisme m.

confound [kən'faʊnd] vt confondre; **c. him!** que le diable l'emporte! ◆**-ed** a (damned) Fam sacré.

confront [kən'frʌnt] vt (danger) affronter; (problems) faire face à; **to c. s.o.** (be face to face with) se trouver en face de qn; (oppose) s'opposer à qn; **to c. s.o. with** (person) confronter qn avec; (thing) mettre qn en présence de. ◆**confron'tation** n confrontation f.

confus/e [kən'fjuːz] vt (perplex) confondre; (muddle) embrouiller; **to c. with** (mistake for) confondre avec. ◆**-ed** a (situation, *noises etc*) confus; **to be c.** (*of person*) s'y perdre; **to get c.** s'embrouiller. ◆**—ing** *a* difficile à comprendre, déroutant. ◆**con-fusion** *n* confusion *f*; **in c.** en désordre.

congeal [kən'dʒiːl] *vt* figer; — *vi* (*se*) figer.

congenial [kən'dʒiːnɪəl] *a* sympathique.

congenital [kən'dʒenɪtəl] *a* congénital.

congested [kən'dʒestɪd] *a* (*street*) encombré; (*town*) surpeuplé; Med congestionné. ◆**congestion** *n* (*traffic*) encombrement(s) *m(pl)*; (*overcrowding*) surpeuplement *m*; Med congestion *f*.

Congo ['kɒŋgəʊ] *n* Congo *m*.

congratulate [kən'grætjʊleɪt] *vt* féliciter (s.o. on sth de qch). ◆**congratu-'lations** *npl* félicitations *fpl* (on pour). ◆**congratu-'latory** *a* (*telegram etc*) de félicitations.

congregate ['kɒŋgrɪgeɪt] *vi* se rassembler. ◆**congre'gation** *n* (*worshippers*) assemblée *f*, fidèles *mfpl*.

congress ['kɒŋgres] *n* congrès *m*; **C.** Pol Am le Congrès. ◆**Congressman** *n* (*pl* **-men**) Am membre *m* du Congrès. ◆**Con-'gressional** *a* Am du Congrès.

conic(al) ['kɒnɪk(ə)l] *a* conique.

conifer ['kɒnɪfər] *n* (*tree*) conifère *m*.

conjecture [kən'dʒektʃər] *n* conjecture *f*; — *vt* conjecturer; — *vi* faire des conjectures. ◆**conjectural** *a* conjectural.

conjugal ['kɒndʒʊgəl] *a* conjugal.

conjugate ['kɒndʒʊgeɪt] *vt* (*verb*) conjuguer. ◆**conju'gation** *n* Gram conjugaison *f*.

conjunction [kən'dʒʌŋkʃ(ə)n] *n* Gram conjonction *f*; **in c. with** conjointement avec.

conjur/e ['kʌndʒər] *vt* **to c. (up)** (*by magic*) faire apparaître; **to c. up** (*memories etc*) Fig évoquer. ◆**—ing** *n* prestidigitation *f*. ◆**—er** *n* prestidigitateur, -trice *mf*.

conk [kɒŋk] **1** *n* (*nose*) Sl pif *m*. **2** *vi* **to c. out** (*break down*) Fam claquer, tomber en panne.

conker ['kɒŋkər] *n* (*horse-chestnut fruit*) Fam marron *m* (d'Inde).

connect [kə'nekt] *vt* relier (**with, to** à); (*telephone, stove etc*) brancher; **to c. with** Tel mettre en communication avec; (*in memory*) associer avec; — *vi* (*be connected*) être relié; **to c. with** (*of train, bus*) assurer la correspondance avec. ◆**—ed** *a* (*facts etc*) lié, connexe; (*speech*) suivi; **to be c. with** (*have dealings with*) être lié à; (*have to do with, relate to*) avoir rapport à; (*by marriage*) être allié à. ◆**connection** *n* (*link*) rapport *m*, relation *f* (**with** avec);

(*train, bus etc*) correspondance *f*; (*phone call*) communication *f*; (*between pipes etc*) Tech raccord *m*; *pl* (*contacts*) relations *fpl*; **in c. with** à propos de.

connive [kə'naɪv] *vi* **to c.** at fermer les yeux sur; **to c. to do** se mettre de connivence pour faire (**with** avec); **to c. together** agir en complicité. ◆**connivance** *n* connivence *f*.

connoisseur [kɒnə'sɜːr] *n* connaisseur *m*.

connotation [kɒnə'teɪʃ(ə)n] *n* connotation *f*.

conquer ['kɒŋkər] *vt* (*country, freedom etc*) conquérir; (*enemy, habit*) vaincre. ◆**—ing** *a* victorieux. ◆**conqueror** *n* conquérant, -ante *mf*, vainqueur *m*. ◆**conquest** *n* conquête *f*.

cons [kɒnz] *npl* **the pros and (the) c.** le pour et le contre.

conscience ['kɒnʃəns] *n* conscience *f*. ◆**c.-stricken** *a* pris de remords.

conscientious [kɒnʃɪ'enʃəs] *a* consciencieux; **c. objector** objecteur *m* de conscience. ◆**—ness** *n* application *f*, sérieux *m*.

conscious ['kɒnʃəs] *a* conscient (**of sth** de qch); (*intentional*) délibéré; Med conscient; **to be c. of doing** avoir conscience de faire. ◆**—ly** *adv* (*knowingly*) consciemment. ◆**—ness** *n* conscience *f* (**of** de); Med connaissance *f*.

conscript ['kɒnskrɪpt] *n* Mil conscrit *m*; — [kən'skrɪpt] *vt* enrôler (par conscription). ◆**con'scription** *n* conscription *f*.

consecrate ['kɒnsɪkreɪt] *vt* (*church etc*) Rel consacrer. ◆**conse'cration** *n* consécration *f*.

consecutive [kən'sekjʊtɪv] *a* consécutif. ◆**—ly** *adv* consécutivement.

consensus [kən'sensəs] *n* consensus *m*, accord *m* (général).

consent [kən'sent] *vi* consentir (**to** à); — *n* consentement *m*; **by common c.** de l'aveu de tous; **by mutual c.** d'un commun accord.

consequence ['kɒnsɪkwəns] *n* (*result*) conséquence *f*; (*importance*) importance *f*, conséquence *f*. ◆**consequently** *adv* par conséquent.

conservative [kən'sɜːvətɪv] **1** *a* (*estimate*) modeste; (*view*) traditionnel. **2** *a* & *n* **C.** Pol conservateur, -trice (*mf*). ◆**conserv-ism** *n* (*in behaviour*) & Pol Rel conservatisme *m*.

conservatoire [kən'sɜːvətwɑːr] *n* Mus conservatoire *m*.

conservatory [kən'sɜːvətrɪ] *n* (*greenhouse*) serre *f*.

conserve [kən'sɜːv] *vt* préserver, conserver;

(*one's strength*) ménager; **to c. energy** faire des économies d'énergie. ◆**conser-'vation** *n* (*energy-saving*) économies *fpl* d'énergie; (*of nature*) protection *f* de l'environnement; *Phys* conservation *f*.

consider [kən'sɪdər] *vt* considérer; (*take into account*) tenir compte de; **I'll c. it** j'y réfléchirai; **to c.** doing envisager de faire; **to c. that** estimer *or* considérer que; **he's** *or* **she's being considered (for the job)** sa candidature est à l'étude; **all things considered** en fin de compte. ◆**—ing** *prep* étant donné, vu. ◆**—able** *a* (*large*) considérable; (*much*) beaucoup de. ◆**—ably** *adv* beaucoup, considérablement. ◆**conside-'ration** *n* (*thought, thoughtfulness, reason*) considération *f*; **under c.** à l'étude; **out of c. for** par égard pour; **to take into c.** prendre en considération.

considerate [kən'sɪdərət] *a* plein d'égards (**to** pour), attentionné (**to** à l'égard de).

consign [kən'saɪn] *vt* (*send*) expédier; (*give, entrust*) confier (**to** à). ◆**—ment** *n* (*act*) expédition *f*; (*goods*) arrivage *m*.

consist [kən'sɪst] *vi* consister (**of** en, **in** dans, **in** doing à faire).

consistent [kən'sɪstənt] *a* logique, conséquent; (*coherent*) cohérent; (*friend*) fidèle; **c. with** compatible avec, conforme à. ◆**—ly** *adv* (*logically*) avec logique; (*always*) constamment. ◆**consistency** *n* logique *f*; cohérence *f*. **2** (*of liquid etc*) consistance *f*.

console[1] [kən'səʊl] *vt* consoler. ◆**conso-'lation** *n* consolation *f*; **c. prize** prix *m* de consolation.

console[2] ['kɒnsəʊl] *n* (*control desk*) *Tech* console *f*.

consolidate [kən'sɒlɪdeɪt] *vt* consolider; – *vi* se consolider. ◆**consoli'dation** *n* consolidation *f*.

consonant ['kɒnsənənt] *n* consonne *f*.

consort **1** ['kɒnsɔːt] *n* époux *m*, épouse *f*; **prince c.** prince *m* consort. **2** [kən'sɔːt] *vi* **to c. with** *Pej* fréquenter.

consortium [kən'sɔːtɪəm] *n* *Com* consortium *m*.

conspicuous [kən'spɪkjʊəs] *a* visible, en évidence; (*striking*) remarquable, manifeste; (*showy*) voyant; **to be c. by one's absence** briller par son absence; **to make oneself c.** se faire remarquer. ◆**—ly** *adv* visiblement.

conspire [kən'spaɪər] **1** *vi* (*plot*) conspirer (**against** contre); **to c. to do** comploter de faire. **2** *vt* **to c. to do** (*of events*) conspirer à faire. ◆**conspiracy** *n* conspiration *f*.

constable ['kʌnstəb(ə)l] *n* (*police*) **c. agent** *m* (de police). ◆**con'stabulary** *n* la police.

constant ['kɒnstənt] *a* (*frequent*) incessant; (*unchanging*) constant; (*faithful*) fidèle. ◆**constancy** *n* constance *f*. ◆**constantly** *adv* constamment, sans cesse.

constellation [kɒnstə'leɪʃ(ə)n] *n* constellation *f*.

consternation [kɒnstə'neɪʃ(ə)n] *n* consternation *f*.

constipate ['kɒnstɪpeɪt] *vt* constiper. ◆**consti'pation** *n* constipation *f*.

constituent [kən'stɪtjʊənt] **1** *a* (*element etc*) constituant, constitutif. **2** *n* *Pol* électeur, -trice *mf*. ◆**constituency** *n* circonscription *f* électorale; (*voters*) électeurs *mpl*.

constitute ['kɒnstɪtjuːt] *vt* constituer. ◆**consti'tution** *n* (*of person etc*) & *Pol* constitution *f*. ◆**consti'tutional** *a* *Pol* constitutionnel.

constrain [kən'streɪn] *vt* contraindre.

constrict [kən'strɪkt] *vt* (*tighten, narrow*) resserrer; (*movement*) gêner. ◆**con-'striction** *n* resserrement *n*.

construct [kən'strʌkt] *vt* construire. ◆**con-struction** *n* construction *f*; **under c.** en construction. ◆**constructive** *a* constructif.

construe [kən'struː] *vt* interpréter, comprendre.

consul ['kɒnsəl] *n* consul *m*. ◆**consular** *a* consulaire. ◆**consulate** *n* consulat *m*.

consult [kən'sʌlt] *vt* consulter; – *vi* **to c. with** discuter avec, conférer avec. ◆**—ing** *a* (*room*) *Med* de consultation; (*physician*) consultant. ◆**consultancy** *n* **c.** (*firm*) *Com* cabinet *m* d'experts-conseils; **c. fee** honoraires *mpl* de conseils. ◆**consultant** *n* conseiller, -ère *mf*; *Med* spécialiste *mf*; (*financial, legal*) conseil *m*, expert-conseil *m*; – *a* (*engineer etc*) consultant. ◆**consul'tation** *n* consultation *f*. ◆**con-sultative** *a* consultatif.

consum/e [kən'sjuːm] *vt* (*food, supplies etc*) consommer; (*of fire, grief, hate*) consumer. ◆**—ing** *a* (*ambition*) brûlant. ◆**—er** *n* consommateur, -trice *mf*; **c. goods/society** biens *mpl*/société *f* de consommation. ◆**con'sumption** *n* consommation *f* (**of** de).

consummate ['kɒnsəmət] *a* (*perfect*) consommé.

contact ['kɒntækt] *n* contact *m*; (*person*) relation *f*; **in c. with** en contact avec; **c. lenses** lentilles *fpl or* verres *mpl* de contact; – *vt* se mettre en contact avec, contacter.

contagious [kən'teɪdʒəs] *a* contagieux.
contain [kən'teɪn] *vt* (*enclose, hold back*) contenir; **to c. oneself** se contenir. **◆—er** *n* récipient *m*; (*for transporting freight*) conteneur *m*, container *m*.
contaminate [kən'tæmɪneɪt] *vt* contaminer. **◆contami'nation** *n* contamination *f*.
contemplate ['kɒntəmpleɪt] *vt* (*look at*) contempler; (*consider*) envisager (**doing** faire). **◆contem'plation** *n* contemplation *f*; **in c. of** en prévision de.
contemporary [kən'tempərərɪ] *a* contemporain (**with** de); – *n* (*person*) contemporain, -aine *mf*.
contempt [kən'tempt] *n* mépris *m*; **to hold in c.** mépriser. **◆contemptible** *a* méprisable. **◆contemptuous** *a* dédaigneux (**of** de).
contend [kən'tend] **1** *vi* **to c. with** (*problem*) faire face à; (*person*) avoir affaire à; (*compete*) rivaliser avec; (*struggle*) se battre avec. **2** *vt* **to c. that** (*claim*) soutenir que. **◆—er** *n* concurrent, -ente *mf*. **◆contention** *n* **1** (*argument*) dispute *f*. **2** (*claim*) affirmation *f*. **◆contentious** *a* (*issue*) litigieux.
content[1] [kən'tent] *a* satisfait (**with** de); **he's c. to do it** ne demande pas mieux que de faire. **◆—ed** *a* satisfait. **◆—ment** *n* contentement *m*.
content[2] ['kɒntent] *n* (*of text, film etc*) contenu *m*; *pl* (*of container*) contenu *m*; (*table of*) **contents** (*of book*) table *f* des matières; **alcoholic/iron**/*etc* **c.** teneur *f* en alcool/fer/*etc*.
contest [kən'test] *vt* (*dispute*) contester; (*fight for*) disputer; – ['kɒntest] *n* (*competition*) concours *m*; (*fight*) lutte *f*; *Boxing* combat *m*. **◆con'testant** *n* concurrent, -ente *mf*; (*in fight*) adversaire *mf*.
context ['kɒntekst] *n* contexte *m*.
continent ['kɒntɪnənt] *n* continent *m*; **the C.** l'Europe *f* (continentale). **◆conti'nental** *a* continental; européen; **c. breakfast** petit déjeuner *m* à la française.
contingent [kən'tɪndʒənt] **1** *a* (*accidental*) contingent; **to be c. upon** dépendre de. **2** *nm* *Mil* contingent *m*. **◆contingency** *n* éventualité *f*; **c. plan** plan *m* d'urgence.
continu/e [kən'tɪnjuː] *vt* continuer (**to do** or **doing** à or de faire); (*resume*) reprendre; **to c. (with)** (*work, speech etc*) poursuivre, continuer; – *vi* continuer; (*resume*) reprendre; **to c. in** (*job*) garder. **◆—ed** *a* (*interest, attention etc*) soutenu, assidu; (*presence*) continu(el); **to be c.** (*of story*) à suivre. **◆continual** *a* continuel. **◆continually**

adv continuellement. **◆continuance** *n* continuation *f*. **◆continu'ation** *n* continuation *f*; (*resumption*) reprise *f*; (*new episode*) suite *f*. **◆continuity** [kɒntɪ'njuːɪtɪ] *n* continuité *f*. **◆continuous** *a* continu; **c. performance** *Cin* spectacle *m* permanent. **◆continuously** *adv* sans interruption.
contort [kən'tɔːt] *vt* (*twist*) tordre; **to c. oneself** se contorsionner. **◆contortion** *n* contorsion *f*. **◆contortionist** *n* (*acrobat*) contorsionniste *mf*.
contour ['kɒntʊə] *n* contour *m*.
contraband ['kɒntrəbænd] *n* contrebande *f*.
contraception [kɒntrə'sepʃ(ə)n] *n* contraception *f*. **◆contraceptive** *a* & *n* contraceptif (*m*).
contract 1 ['kɒntrækt] *n* contrat *m*; **c. work** travail *m* en sous-traitance; – *vi* **to c. out** (*of agreement etc*) se dégager de. **2** [kən'trækt] *vt* (*habit, debt, muscle etc*) contracter; – *vi* (*of heart etc*) se contracter. **◆con'traction** *n* (*of muscle, word*) contraction *f*. **◆con'tractor** *n* entrepreneur *m*.
contradict [kɒntrə'dɪkt] *vt* contredire; (*belie*) démentir. **◆contradiction** *n* contradiction *f*. **◆contradictory** *a* contradictoire.
contralto [kən'træltəʊ] *n* (*pl* -os) contralto *m*.
contraption [kən'træpʃ(ə)n] *n* *Fam* machin *m*, engin *m*.
contrary 1 ['kɒntrərɪ] *a* contraire (**to** à); – *adv* **c. to** contrairement à; – *n* contraire *m*; **on the c.** au contraire; **unless you, I** *etc* **hear to the c.** sauf avis contraire; **she said nothing to the c.** elle n'a rien dit contre. **2** [kən'treərɪ] *a* (*obstinate*) entêté, difficile.
contrast 1 ['kɒntrɑːst] *n* contraste *m*; **in c. to** par opposition à. **2** [kən'trɑːst] *vi* contraster (**with** avec); – *vt* faire contraster, mettre en contraste. **◆—ing** *a* (*colours etc*) opposés.
contravene [kɒntrə'viːn] *vt* (*law*) enfreindre. **◆contravention** *n* **in c. of** en contravention de.
contribute [kən'trɪbjuːt] *vt* donner, fournir (**to** à); (*article*) écrire (**to** pour); **to c. money to** contribuer à, verser de l'argent à; – *vi* **to c.** contribuer à; (*publication*) collaborer à. **◆contri'bution** *n* contribution *f*; (*to pension fund etc*) cotisation(s) *f*(*pl*); *Journ* article *m*. **◆contributor** *n* *Journ* collaborateur, -trice *mf*; (*of money*) donateur, -trice *mf*. **◆contributory** *a* **a c. factor** un facteur qui a contribué (**in** à).
contrite [kən'traɪt] *a* contrit. **◆contrition** *n* contrition *f*.
contriv/e [kən'traɪv] *vt* inventer; **to c. to do**

trouver moyen de faire. ◆—ed a artificiel. ◆**contrivance** n (device) dispositif m; (scheme) invention f.

control [kən'trəʊl] vt (-ll-) (business, organization) diriger; (traffic) régler; (prices, quality) contrôler; (emotion, reaction) maîtriser, contrôler; (disease) enrayer; (situation) être maître de; **to c. oneself** se contrôler; – n (authority) autorité f (over sur); (of traffic) réglementation f; (of prices etc) contrôle m; (of emotion) maîtrise f; pl (of train etc) commandes fpl; (knobs) TV Rad boutons mpl; **the c. of** (fires etc) la lutte contre; (self-)c. le contrôle de soi-même; **to keep s.o. under c.** tenir qn; **everything is under c.** tout est en ordre; **in c. of** maître de; **to lose c. of** (situation, vehicle) perdre le contrôle de; **out of c.** (situation, crowd) difficilement maîtrisable; **c. tower** Av tour f de contrôle. ◆**controller** n air traffic c. aiguilleur m du ciel.

controversy ['kɒntrəvɜːsɪ] n controverse f. ◆**contro'versial** a (book, author) contesté, discuté; (doubtful) discutable.

conundrum [kə'nʌndrəm] n devinette f, énigme f; (mystery) énigme f.

conurbation [kɒnɜː'beɪʃ(ə)n] n agglomération f, conurbation f.

convalesce [kɒnvə'les] vi être en convalescence. ◆**convalescence** n convalescence f. ◆**convalescent** n convalescent, -ente mf; **c. home** maison f de convalescence.

convector [kən'vektər] n radiateur m à convection.

convene [kən'viːn] vt convoquer; – vi se réunir.

convenient [kən'viːnɪənt] a commode, pratique; (well-situated) bien situé (for the shops/etc par rapport aux magasins/etc); (moment) convenable, opportun; **to be c. (for)** (suit) convenir (à). ◆—**ly** adv (to arrive) à propos; **c. situated** bien situé. ◆**convenience** n commodité f; (comfort) confort m; (advantage) avantage m; **to** or **at one's c.** à sa convenance; **c. food(s)** plats mpl or aliments mpl minute; (public) **conveniences** toilettes fpl.

convent ['kɒnvənt] n couvent m.

convention [kən'venʃ(ə)n] n (agreement) & Am Pol convention f; (custom) usage m, convention f; (meeting) Pol assemblée f. ◆**conventional** a conventionnel.

converg/e [kən'vɜːdʒ] vi converger. ◆—**ing** a convergent. ◆**convergence** n convergence f.

conversant [kən'vɜːsənt] a **to be c. with**

(custom etc) connaître; (fact) savoir; (car etc) s'y connaître en.

conversation [kɒnvə'seɪʃ(ə)n] n conversation f. ◆**conversational** a (tone) de la conversation; (person) loquace. ◆**conversationalist** n causeur, -euse mf.

converse 1 [kən'vɜːs] vi s'entretenir (with avec). **2** ['kɒnvɜːs] a & n inverse (m). ◆**con'versely** adv inversement.

convert [kən'vɜːt] vt (change) convertir (into en); (building) aménager (into en); **to c. s.o.** convertir qn (to à); – ['kɒnvɜːt] n converti, -ie mf. ◆**con'version** n conversion f; aménagement m. ◆**con'vertible** a convertible; – n (car) (voiture f) décapotable f.

convex ['kɒnveks] a convexe.

convey [kən'veɪ] vt (goods, people) transporter; (sound, message, order) transmettre; (idea) communiquer; (evoke) évoquer; (water etc through pipes) amener. ◆**conveyance** n transport m; Aut véhicule m. ◆**conveyor** n **c. belt** tapis m roulant.

convict ['kɒnvɪkt] n forçat m; – [kən'vɪkt] vt déclarer coupable, condamner. ◆**con'viction** n Jur condamnation f; (belief) conviction f; **to carry c.** (of argument etc) être convaincant.

convinc/e [kən'vɪns] vt convaincre, persuader. ◆—**ing** a convaincant. ◆—**ingly** adv de façon convaincante.

convivial [kən'vɪvɪəl] a joyeux, gai; (person) bon vivant.

convoke [kən'vəʊk] vt (meeting etc) convoquer.

convoluted [kɒnvə'luːtɪd] a (argument, style) compliqué, tarabiscoté.

convoy ['kɒnvɔɪ] n (ships, cars, people) convoi m.

convulse [kən'vʌls] vt bouleverser, ébranler; (face) convulser. ◆**convulsion** n convulsion f. ◆**convulsive** a convulsif.

coo [kuː] vi (of dove) roucouler.

cook [kʊk] vt (faire) cuire; (accounts) Fam truquer; **to c. up** Fam inventer; – vi (of food) cuire; (of person) faire la cuisine; **what's cooking?** Fam qu'est-ce qui se passe?; – n (person) cuisinier, -ière mf. ◆—**ing** n cuisine f; **c. apple** pomme f à cuire. ◆—**er** n (stove) cuisinière f; (apple) pomme f à cuire. ◆**cookbook** n livre m de cuisine. ◆**cookery** n cuisine f; **c. book** livre m de cuisine.

cookie ['kʊkɪ] n Am biscuit m, gâteau m sec.

cool [kuːl] a (-er, -est) (weather, place etc) frais; (manner, person) calme; (reception etc) froid; (impertinent) Fam effronté; **I feel**

c. j'ai (un peu) froid; **a c. drink** une boisson fraîche; **a c. £50** la coquette somme de 50 livres; – *n* (*of evening*) fraîcheur *f*; **to keep (in the) c.** tenir au frais; **to keep/lose one's c.** garder/perdre son sang-froid; – *vi* **to c. (down)** refroidir, rafraîchir; – *vi* **to c. (down** *or* **off)** (*of enthusiasm*) se refroidir; (*of anger, angry person*) se calmer; (*of hot liquid*) refroidir; **to c. off** (*refresh oneself by drinking, bathing etc*) se rafraîchir; **to c. off towards s.o.** se refroidir envers qn. **◆—ing** *n* (*of air, passion etc*) refroidissement *m*. **◆—er** *n* (*for food*) glacière *f*. **◆—ly** *adv* calmement; (*to welcome*) froidement; (*boldly*) effrontément. **◆—ness** *n* fraîcheur *f*; (*unfriendliness*) froideur *f*. **◆cool-'headed** *a* calme.

coop [ku:p] **1** *n* (*for chickens*) poulailler *m*. **2** *vt* **to c. up** (*person*) enfermer.

co-op ['kəʊɒp] *n Am* appartement *m* en copropriété.

co-operate [kəʊˈɒpəreɪt] *vi* coopérer (**in** à, **with** avec). **◆co-ope'ration** *n* coopération *f*. **◆co-operative** *a* coopératif; – *n* coopérative *f*.

co-opt [kəʊˈɒpt] *vt* coopter.

co-ordinate [kəʊˈɔːdɪneɪt] *vt* coordonner. **◆co-ordinates** [kəʊˈɔːdɪnəts] *npl Math* coordonnés *fpl*; (*clothes*) coordonnés *mpl*. **◆co-ordi'nation** *n* coordination *f*.

cop [kɒp] **1** *n* (*policeman*) *Fam* flic *m*. **2** (**-pp-**) (*catch*) *Sl* piquer. **3** *vi* (**-pp-**) **to c. out** *Sl* se défiler, éviter ses responsabilités.

cope [kəʊp] *vi* **to c. with** s'occuper de; (*problem*) faire face à; (**to be able**) **to c.** (*savoir*) se débrouiller.

co-pilot ['kəʊpaɪlət] *n* copilote *m*.

copious ['kəʊpɪəs] *a* copieux.

copper ['kɒpər] *n* **1** cuivre *m*; *pl* (*coins*) petite monnaie *f*. **2** (*policeman*) *Fam* flic *m*.

coppice ['kɒpɪs], **◆copse** [kɒps] *n* taillis *m*.

copulate ['kɒpjʊleɪt] *vi* s'accoupler. **◆copu'lation** *n* copulation *f*.

copy ['kɒpɪ] *n* copie *f*; (*of book etc*) exemplaire *m*; *Phot* épreuve *f*; – *vti* copier; – *vt* **to c. out** *or* **down** (re)copier. **◆copyright** *n* copyright *m*.

coral ['kɒrəl] *n* corail *m*; **c. reef** récif *m* de corail.

cord [kɔːd] **1** *n* (*of curtain, pyjamas etc*) cordon *m*; *El* cordon *m* électrique; **vocal cords** cordes *fpl* vocales. **2** *npl Fam* velours *m*, pantalon *m* en velours (côtelé).

cordial ['kɔːdɪəl] **1** *a* (*friendly*) cordial. **2** *n* (*fruit*) *a* c. sirop *m*.

cordon ['kɔːdən] *n* cordon *m*; – *vt* **to c. off** (*place*) boucler, interdire l'accès à.

corduroy ['kɔːdərɔɪ] *n* (*fabric*) velours *m* côtelé; *pl* pantalon *m* en velours (côtelé), velours *m*.

core [kɔːr] *n* (*of fruit*) trognon *m*; (*of problem*) cœur *m*; (*group of people*) & *Geol* El noyau *m*; – *vt* (*apple*) vider. **◆corer** *n* vide-pomme *m*.

cork [kɔːk] *n* liège *m*; (*for bottle*) bouchon *m*; – *vt* **to c. (up)** (*bottle*) boucher. **◆cork-screw** *n* tire-bouchon *m*.

corn [kɔːn] *n* **1** (*wheat*) blé *m*; (*maize*) *Am* maïs *m*; (*seed*) grain *m*; **c. on the cob** épi *m* de maïs. **2** (*hard skin*) cor *m*. **◆corned** *a* **c. beef** corned-beef *m*, singe *m*. **◆corn-flakes** *npl* céréales *fpl*. **◆cornflour** *n* farine *f* de maïs, maïzena® *f*. **◆corn-flower** *n* bleuet *m*. **◆cornstarch** *n Am* = cornflour.

cornea ['kɔːnɪə] *n Anat* cornée *f*.

corner ['kɔːnər] **1** *n* (*of street, room*) coin *m*, angle *m*; (*bend in road*) virage *m*; *Fb* corner *m*; **in a (tight) c.** dans une situation difficile. **2** *vt* (*animal, enemy etc*) acculer; (*person in corridor etc*) *Fig* coincer, accrocher; (*market*) *Com* accaparer; – *vi Aut* prendre un virage. **◆cornerstone** *n* pierre *f* angulaire.

cornet ['kɔːnɪt] *n* (*of ice cream etc*) & *Mus* cornet *m*.

Cornwall ['kɔːnwəl] *n* Cornouailles *fpl*. **◆Cornish** *a* de Cornouailles.

corny ['kɔːnɪ] *a* (**-ier, -iest**) (*joke etc*) rebattu.

corollary [kəˈrɒlərɪ, *Am* ˈkɒrələrɪ] *n* corollaire *m*.

coronary ['kɒrənərɪ] *n Med* infarctus *m*.

coronation [kɒrəˈneɪʃ(ə)n] *n* couronnement *m*, sacre *m*.

coroner ['kɒrənər] *n Jur* coroner *m*.

corporal ['kɔːpərəl] **1** *n Mil* caporal(-chef) *m*. **2** *a* **c. punishment** châtiment *m* corporel.

corporation [kɔːpəˈreɪʃ(ə)n] *n* (*business*) société *f* commerciale; (*of town*) conseil *m* municipal. **◆'corporate** *a* collectif; **c. body** corps *m* constitué.

corps [kɔːr, *pl* kɔːz] *n Mil Pol* corps *m*.

corpse [kɔːps] *n* cadavre *m*.

corpulent ['kɔːpjʊlənt] *a* corpulent. **◆corpulence** *n* corpulence *f*.

corpus ['kɔːpəs] *n Ling* corpus *m*.

corpuscle ['kɔːpʌs(ə)l] *n Med* globule *m*.

corral [kəˈræl] *n Am* corral *m*.

correct [kəˈrekt] *a* (*right, accurate*) exact, correct; (*proper*) correct; **he's c.** il a raison; – *vt* corriger. **◆—ly** *adv* correctement.

◆—ness n (accuracy, propriety) correction f. ◆correction n correction f. ◆corrective a (act, measure) rectificatif.

correlate ['korəleit] vi correspondre (with à); – vt faire correspondre. ◆corre'lation n corrélation f.

correspond [kori'spond] vi 1 (agree, be similar) correspondre (to à, with avec). 2 (by letter) correspondre (with avec). ◆—ing a (matching) correspondant; (similar) semblable. ◆correspondence n correspondance f; c. course cours m par correspondance. ◆correspondent n correspondant, -ante mf; Journ envoyé, -ée mf.

corridor ['koridor] n couloir m, corridor m.

corroborate [kə'robəreit] vt corroborer.

corrode [kə'rəud] vt ronger, corroder; – vi se corroder. ◆corrosion n corrosion f. ◆corrosive a corrosif.

corrugated ['korəgeitid] a (cardboard) ondulé; c. iron tôle f ondulée.

corrupt [kə'rʌpt] vt corrompre; – a corrompu. ◆corruption n corruption f.

corset ['kɔːsit] n (boned) corset m; (elasticated) gaine f.

Corsica ['kɔːsikə] n Corse f.

cos [kɒs] n c. (lettuce) (laitue f) romaine f.

cosh [kɒʃ] n matraque f; – vt matraquer.

cosiness ['kəuzinəs] n intimité f, confort m.

cosmetic [kɒz'metik] n produit m de beauté; – a esthétique, Fig superficiel.

cosmopolitan [kɒzmə'pɒlitən] a & n cosmopolite (mf).

cosmos ['kɒzmɒs] n cosmos m. ◆cosmic a cosmique. ◆cosmonaut n cosmonaute mf.

Cossack ['kɒsæk] n cosaque m.

cosset ['kɒsit] vt choyer.

cost [kɒst] vti (pt & pp cost) coûter; how much does it c.? ça coûte or ça vaut combien?; to c. the earth Fam coûter les yeux de la tête; – n coût m, prix m; at great c. à grands frais; to my c. à mes dépens; at any c., at all costs à tout prix; at c. price au prix coûtant. ◆c.-effective a rentable. ◆costly a (-ier, -iest) (expensive) coûteux; (valuable) précieux.

co-star ['kəustɑː] n Cin Th partenaire mf.

costume ['kɒstjuːm] n costume m; (woman's suit) tailleur m; (swimming) c. maillot m (de bain); c. jewellery bijoux mpl de fantaisie.

cosy ['kəuzi] a (-ier, -iest) douillet, intime; make yourself (nice and) c. mets-toi à l'aise; we're c. on est bien ici. 2 n (tea) c. couvre-théière m.

cot [kɒt] n lit m d'enfant; (camp bed) Am lit m de camp.

cottage ['kɒtidʒ] n petite maison f de campagne; (thatched) c. chaumière f; c. cheese fromage m blanc (maigre); c. industry travail m à domicile (activité artisanale).

cotton ['kɒtən] n coton m; (yarn) fil m (de coton); absorbent c. Am, c. wool coton m hydrophile, ouate f; c. candy Am barbe f à papa. 2 vi to c. on (to) Sl piger.

couch [kautʃ] 1 n canapé m. 2 vt (express) formuler.

couchette [kuːˈʃet] n Rail couchette f.

cough [kɒf] n toux f; c. mixture sirop m contre la toux; – vi tousser; to c. up (blood) cracher. 2 vt to c. up (money) Sl cracher; – vi to c. up Sl payer, casquer.

could [kud, unstressed kəd] see can[1].

couldn't ['kud(ə)nt] = could not.

council ['kauns(ə)l] n conseil m; c. flat/house appartement m/maison f loué(e) à la municipalité, HLM m or f. ◆councillor n conseiller, -ère mf; (town) c. conseiller m municipal.

counsel ['kaunsəl] n (advice) conseil m; Jur avocat, -ate mf; – vt (-ll-, Am -l-) conseiller (s.o. to do à qn de faire). ◆counsellor n conseiller, -ère mf.

count[1] [kaunt] vt (find number of, include) compter; (deem) considérer; not counting Paul sans compter Paul; to c. in (include) inclure; to c. out exclure; (money) compter; – vi (calculate, be important) compter; to c. against s.o. être un désavantage pour qn, jouer contre qn; to c. on s.o. (rely on) compter sur qn; to c. on doing compter faire; – n compte m; Jur chef m (d'accusation); he's lost c. of the books he has il ne sait plus combien il a de livres. ◆countdown n compte m à rebours.

count[2] [kaunt] n (title) comte m.

countenance ['kauntinəns] 1 n (face) mine f, expression f. 2 vt (allow) tolérer; (approve) approuver.

counter ['kauntər] 1 n (in shop, bar etc) comptoir m; (in bank etc) guichet m; under the c. Fig clandestinement, au marché noir; over the c. (to obtain medicine) sans ordonnance. 2 n (in games) jeton m. 3 n Tech compteur m. 4 adv c. to à l'encontre de. 5 vt (plan) contrarier; (insult) riposter à; (blow) parer; – vi riposter (with par).

counter- ['kauntər] pref contre-.

counterattack ['kauntərətæk] n contre-attaque f; – vti contre-attaquer.

counterbalance ['kauntəbæləns] n contre-poids m; – vt contrebalancer.

counterclockwise [kauntə'klɒkwaɪz] *a* & *adv Am* dans le sens inverse des aiguilles d'une montre.

counterfeit ['kauntəfɪt] *a* faux; – *n* contrefaçon *f*, faux *m*; – *vt* contrefaire.

counterfoil ['kauntəfɔɪl] *n* souche *f*.

counterpart ['kauntəpɑːt] *n* (*thing*) équivalent *m*; (*person*) homologue *mf*.

counterpoint ['kauntəpɔɪnt] *n Mus* contrepoint *m*.

counterproductive [kauntəprə'dʌktɪv] *a* (*action*) inefficace, qui produit l'effet contraire.

countersign ['kauntəsaɪn] *vt* contresigner.

countess ['kauntɪs] *n* comtesse *f*.

countless ['kauntləs] *a* innombrable.

countrified ['kʌntrɪfaɪd] *a* rustique.

country ['kʌntrɪ] *n* pays *m*; (*region*) région *f*, pays *m*; (*homeland*) patrie *f*; (*opposed to town*) campagne *f*; – *a* (*house etc*) de campagne; **c. dancing** la danse folklorique. ◆**countryman** *n* (*pl* -**men**) (*fellow*) *n* compatriote *m*. ◆**countryside** *n* campagne *f*.

county ['kauntɪ] *n* comté *m*; **c. seat** *Am*, **c. town** chef-lieu *m*.

coup [kuː, *pl* kuːz] *n Pol* coup *m* d'État.

couple ['kʌp(ə)l] **1** *n* (*of people, animals*) couple *m*; **a c.** (*of*) deux ou trois; (*a few*) quelques. **2** *vt* (*connect*) accoupler. **3** *vi* (*mate*) s'accoupler.

coupon ['kuːpɒn] *n* (*voucher*) bon *m*; (*ticket*) coupon *m*.

courage ['kʌrɪdʒ] *n* courage *m*. ◆**courageous** [kə'reɪdʒəs] *a* courageux.

courgette [kuə'ʒet] *n* courgette *f*.

courier ['kurɪər] *n* (*for tourists*) guide *m*; (*messenger*) messager *m*; **c. service** service *m* de messagerie.

course [kɔːs] **1** *n* (*duration, movement*) cours *m*; (*of ship*) route *f*; (*of river*) cours *m*; (*way*) Fig route *f*, chemin *m*; (*means*) moyen *m*; **c.** (*of action*) ligne *f* de conduite; (*option*) parti *m*; **your best c. is to** ... le mieux c'est de ...; **as a matter of c.** normalement; **in** (**the**) **c. of time** avec le temps, à la longue; **in due c.** en temps utile. **2** *n Sch Univ* cours *m*; **c. of lectures** série *f* de conférences; (*of treatment*) *Med* traitement *m*. **3** *n Culin* plat *m*; **first c.** entrée *f*. **4** *n* (*racecourse*) champ *m* de courses; (*golf*) **c.** terrain *m* de golf). **5** *adv* **of c.!** bien sûr!, mais oui!; **of c. not!** bien sûr que non!

court [kɔːt] **1** *n* (*of monarch*) cour *f*; *Jur* cour *f*, tribunal *m*; *Tennis* court *m*; **c. of enquiry** commission *f* d'enquête; **high c.** cour *f* suprême; **to take to c.** poursuivre en justice; **c. shoe** escarpin *m*. **2** *vt* (*woman*) faire la cour à; (*danger, support*) rechercher. ◆**—ing** *a* (*couple*) d'amoureux; **they are c.** ils sortent ensemble. ◆**courthouse** *n* palais *m* de justice. ◆**courtier** *n Hist* courtisan *m*. ◆**courtroom** *n* salle *f* du tribunal. ◆**courtship** *n* (*act, period of time*) cour *f*. ◆**courtyard** *n* cour *f*.

courteous ['kɜːtɪəs] *a* poli, courtois. ◆**courtesy** *n* politesse *f*, courtoisie *f*.

court-martial [kɔːt'mɑːʃəl] *n* conseil *m* de guerre; – *vt* (-**ll**-) faire passer en conseil de guerre.

cousin ['kʌz(ə)n] *n* cousin, -ine *mf*.

cove [kəuv] *n* (*bay*) *Geog* anse *f*.

covenant ['kʌvənənt] *n Jur* convention *f*; *Rel* alliance *f*.

Coventry ['kɒvəntrɪ] *n* **to send s.o. to C.** *Fig* mettre qn en quarantaine.

cover ['kʌvər] *n* (*lid*) couvercle *m*; (*of book*) & *Fin* couverture *f*; (*for furniture, typewriter*) housse *f*; (*bedspread*) dessus-de-lit *m*; **the covers** (*blankets*) les couvertures *fpl*; **to take c.** se mettre à l'abri; **c. charge** (*in restaurant*) couvert *m*; **c. note** certificat *m* provisoire d'assurance; **under separate c.** (*letter*) sous pli séparé; – *vt* couvrir; (*protect*) protéger, couvrir; (*distance*) parcourir, couvrir; (*include*) englober, recouvrir; (*treat*) traiter; (*event*) *Journ TV Rad* couvrir, faire le reportage de; (*aim gun at*) tenir en joue; (*insure*) assurer; **to c. over** recouvrir; **to c. up** recouvrir; (*truth, tracks*) dissimuler; (*scandal*) étouffer, camoufler; – *vi* **to c. up** (*oneself*) se couvrir; **to c. up for s.o.** couvrir qn. ◆**c.-up** *n* tentative *f* pour étouffer *or* camoufler une affaire. ◆**covering** *n* (*wrapping*) enveloppe *f*; (*layer*) couche *f*; **c. letter** lettre *f* jointe (à *un document*).

coveralls ['kʌvərɔːlz] *npl Am* bleus *mpl* de travail.

covert ['kəuvət, 'kʌvət] *a* secret.

covet ['kʌvɪt] *vt* convoiter. ◆**covetous** *a* avide.

cow [kau] **1** *n* vache *f*; (*of elephant etc*) femelle *f*; (*nasty woman*) *Fam* chameau *m*. **2** *vt* (*person*) intimider. ◆**cowboy** *n* cow-boy *m*. ◆**cowhand** *n* vacher, -ère *m*. ◆**cowshed** *n* étable *f*.

coward ['kauəd] *n* lâche *mf*. ◆**—ly** *a* lâche. ◆**cowardice** *n* lâcheté *f*.

cower ['kauər] *vi* (*crouch*) se tapir; (*with fear*) *Fig* reculer (par peur).

cowslip ['kauslɪp] *n Bot* coucou *m*.

cox [kɒks] vt Nau barrer; — n barreur, -euse mf.

coy [kɔɪ] a (-er, -est) qui fait son ou sa timide. ◆**coyness** n timidité f feinte.

coyote [kaɪˈəʊtɪ] n (wolf) Am coyote m.

cozy [ˈkəʊzɪ] Am = cosy.

crab [kræb] 1 n crabe m. 2 n c. **apple** pomme f sauvage. 3 vi (-bb-) (complain) Fam rouspéter. ◆**crabbed** a (person) grincheux.

crack¹ [kræk] n (fissure) fente f; (in glass etc) fêlure f; (in skin) crevasse f; (snapping noise) craquement m; (of whip) claquement m; (blow) coup m; (joke) Fam plaisanterie f (at aux dépens de); **to have a c. at doing** Fam essayer de faire; **at the c. of dawn** au point du jour; — vt (glass, ice) fêler; (nut) casser; (ground, skin) crevasser; (whip) faire claquer; (joke) lancer; (problem) résoudre; (code) déchiffrer; (safe) percer; **it's not as hard as it's cracked up to be** ce n'est pas aussi dur qu'on le dit; — vi se fêler; se crevasser; (of branch, wood) craquer; **to get cracking** (get to work) Fam s'y mettre; (hurry) Fam se grouiller; **to c. down on** sévir contre; **to c. up** (mentally) Fam craquer. ◆**c.-up** n dépression f nerveuse; (crash) Am Fam accident m. ◆**cracked** a (crazy) Fam fou. ◆**cracker** n 1 (cake) biscuit m (salé). 2 (firework) pétard m; **Christmas c.** diablotin m. 3 **she's a c.** Fam elle est sensationnelle. ◆**crackers** a (mad) Sl cinglé. ◆**crackpot** a Fam fou; — n fou m, folle f.

crack² [kræk] a (first-rate) de premier ordre; **c. shot** tireur m d'élite.

crackle [ˈkræk(ə)l] vi crépiter; (of sth frying) Culin grésiller; — n crépitement m; grésillement m.

cradle [ˈkreɪd(ə)l] n berceau m; — vt bercer.

craft [krɑːft] 1 n (skill) art m; (job) métier m (artisanal); — vt façonner. 2 n (cunning) ruse f. 3 n inv (boat) bateau m. ◆**craftsman** n (pl -men) artisan m. ◆**craftsmanship** n (skill) art m; **a piece of c.** un beau travail, une belle pièce. ◆**crafty** a (-ier, -iest) astucieux, Pej rusé.

crag [kræg] n rocher m à pic. ◆**craggy** a (rock) à pic; (face) rude.

cram [kræm] vt (-mm-) **to c. into** (force) fourrer dans; **to c. with** (fill) bourrer de; — vi **to c. into** (of people) s'entasser dans; **to c.** (for an exam) bachoter.

cramp [kræmp] n Med crampe f (in à). ◆**cramped** a (in a room or one's clothes) à l'étroit; **in c. conditions** à l'étroit.

cranberry [ˈkrænbərɪ] n Bot canneberge f.

crane [kreɪn] 1 n (bird) & Tech grue f. 2 vt **to c. one's neck** tendre le cou.

crank [kræŋk] 1 n (person) Fam excentrique mf; (fanatic) fanatique mf. 2 n (handle) Tech manivelle f; — vt **to c. (up)** (vehicle) faire démarrer à la manivelle. ◆**cranky** a (-ier, -iest) excentrique; (bad-tempered) Am grincheux.

crannies [ˈkrænɪz] npl **nooks and c.** coins et recoins mpl.

craps [kræps] n **to shoot c.** Am jouer aux dés.

crash [kræʃ] n accident m; (of firm) faillite f; (noise) fracas m; (of thunder) coup m; **c. course/diet** cours m/régime m intensif; **c. helmet** casque m (anti-choc); **c. landing** atterrissage m en catastrophe; — int (of fallen object) patatras!; — vt (car) avoir un accident avec; **to c. one's car into** faire rentrer sa voiture dans; — vi Aut Av s'écraser; **to c. into** rentrer dans; **the cars crashed (into each other)** les voitures se sont percutées or carambolées; **to c. (down)** tomber; (break) se casser; (of roof) s'effondrer. ◆**c.-land** vi atterrir en catastrophe.

crass [kræs] a grossier; (stupidity) crasse.

crate [kreɪt] n caisse f, cageot m.

crater [ˈkreɪtər] n cratère m; (bomb) c. entonnoir m.

cravat [krəˈvæt] n foulard m (autour du cou).

crav/e [kreɪv] vt **to c. (for)** éprouver un grand besoin de; (mercy) implorer. ◆**—ing** n désir m, grand besoin m (for de).

craven [ˈkreɪvən] a Pej lâche.

crawl [krɔːl] vi ramper; (of child) se traîner (à quatre pattes); Aut avancer au pas; **to be crawling with** grouiller de; — n Swimming crawl m; **to move at a c.** Aut avancer au pas.

crayfish [ˈkreɪfɪʃ] n inv écrevisse f.

crayon [ˈkreɪən] n crayon m, pastel m.

craze [kreɪz] n manie f (for de), engouement m (for pour). ◆**crazed** a affolé.

crazy [ˈkreɪzɪ] a (-ier, -iest) fou; **c. about sth** fana de qch; **c. about s.o.** fou de qn; **c. paving** dallage m irrégulier. ◆**craziness** n folie f.

creak [kriːk] vi (of hinge) grincer; (of timber) craquer. ◆**creaky** a grinçant; qui craque.

cream [kriːm] n crème f; (élite) Fig crème f, gratin m; — a (a cake) à la crème; **c.(-coloured)** crème inv; **c. cheese** fromage m blanc; — vt (milk) écrémer; **to c. off** Fig écrémer. ◆**creamy** a (-ier, -iest) crémeux.

crease [kriːs] vt froisser, plisser; — vi se froisser; — n pli m; (accidental) (faux) pli m. ◆**c.-resistant** a infroissable.

create [kri:'eɪt] vt créer; (impression, noise) faire. ◆**creation** n création f. ◆**creative** a créateur, créatif. ◆**creativeness** n créativité f. ◆**crea'tivity** n créativité f. ◆**creator** n créateur, -trice mf.

creature [kri:tʃər] n animal m, bête f; (person) créature f; one's c. comforts ses aises fpl.

crèche [kreʃ] n (nursery) crèche f; (manger) Rel Am crèche f.

credence [kri:dəns] n to give or lend c. to ajouter foi à.

credentials [kri'denʃəlz] npl références fpl; (identity) pièces fpl d'identité; (of diplomat) lettres fpl de créance.

credible [kredɪb(ə)l] a croyable; (politician, information) crédible. ◆**credi'bility** n crédibilité f.

credit [kredɪt] n (influence, belief) & Fin crédit m; (merit) mérite m; Univ unité f de valeur; pl Cin générique m; to give c. to (person) Fin faire crédit à; Fig reconnaître le mérite de; (statement) ajouter foi à; to be a c. to faire honneur à; on c. à crédit; in c. (account) créditeur; to one's c. Fig à son actif; – a (balance) créditeur; c. card carte f de crédit; c. facilities facilités fpl de paiement; – vt (believe) croire; Fin créditer (s.o. with sth qn de qch); to c. s.o. with (qualities) attribuer à qn. ◆**creditable** a honorable. ◆**creditor** n créancier, -ière mf. ◆**creditworthy** a solvable.

credulous [kredjuləs] a crédule.

creed [kri:d] n credo m.

creek [kri:k] n (bay) crique f; (stream) Am ruisseau m; up the c. (in trouble) Sl dans le pétrin.

creep [kri:p] 1 vi (pt & pp crept) ramper; (silently) se glisser (furtivement); (slowly) avancer lentement; it makes my flesh c. ça me donne la chair de poule. 2 n (person) Sl salaud m; it gives me the creeps Fam ça me fait froid dans le dos. ◆**creepy** a (-ier, -iest) Fam terrifiant; (nasty) Fam vilain. ◆**creepy-'crawly** n Fam, Am ◆**creepy-crawler** n Fam bestiole f.

cremate [kri'meɪt] vt incinérer. ◆**cremation** n crémation f. ◆**crema'torium** n crématorium m. ◆**'crematory** n Am crématorium m.

Creole [kri:əʊl] n créole mf; Ling créole m.

crêpe [kreɪp] n (fabric) crêpe m; c. (rubber) crêpe m; c. paper papier m crêpon.

crept [krept] see creep 1.

crescendo [kri'ʃendəʊ] n (pl -os) crescendo m inv.

crescent [kres(ə)nt] n croissant m; (street) Fig rue f (en demi-lune).

cress [kres] n cresson m.

crest [krest] n (of bird, wave, mountain) crête f; (of hill) sommet m; (on seal, letters etc) armoiries fpl.

Crete [kri:t] n Crète f.

cretin [kretɪn, Am kri:t(ə)n] n crétin, -ine mf. ◆**cretinous** a crétin.

crevasse [kri'væs] n (in ice) Geol crevasse f.

crevice [krevɪs] n (crack) crevasse f, fente f.

crew [kru:] n Nau Av équipage m; (gang) équipe f; c. cut (coupe f en) brosse f. ◆**c.-neck(ed)** a à col ras.

crib [krɪb] 1 n (cradle) berceau m; (cot) Am lit m d'enfant; Rel crèche f. 2 n (copy) plagiat m; Sch traduction f; (list of answers) Sch pompe f anti-sèche; – vti (-bb-) copier.

crick [krɪk] n c. in the neck torticolis m; c. in the back tour m de reins.

cricket [krɪkɪt] n 1 (game) cricket m. 2 (insect) grillon m. ◆**cricketer** n joueur, -euse mf de cricket.

crikey! [kraɪkɪ] int Sl zut (alors!)

crime [kraɪm] n crime m; (not serious) délit m; (criminal practice) criminalité f. ◆**criminal** a & n criminel, -elle (mf).

crimson [krɪmz(ə)n] a & n cramoisi (m).

cring/e [krɪndʒ] vi reculer (from devant); Fig s'humilier (to, before devant). ◆**—ing** a Fig servile.

crinkle [krɪŋk(ə)l] vt froisser; – vi se froisser; – n froncé m. ◆**crinkly** a froissé; (hair) frisé.

cripple [krɪp(ə)l] n (lame) estropié, -ée mf; (disabled) infirme mf; – vt estropier; (disable) rendre infirme; (nation etc) Fig paralyser. ◆**—ed** a estropié; infirme; (ship) désemparé; c. with (rheumatism, pains) perclus de. ◆**—ing** a (tax) écrasant.

crisis, pl **-ses** [kraɪsɪs, -si:z] n crise f.

crisp [krɪsp] 1 a (-er, -est) (biscuit) croustillant; (apple etc) croquant; (snow) craquant; (air, style) vif. 2 npl (potato) crisps (pommes fpl) chips mpl. ◆**crispbread** n pain m suédois.

criss-cross [krɪskrɒs] a (lines) entrecroisés; (muddled) enchevêtrés; – vi s'entrecroiser; – vt sillonner (en tous sens).

criterion, pl **-ia** [kraɪ'tɪərɪən, -ɪə] n critère m.

critic [krɪtɪk] n critique m. ◆**critical** a critique. ◆**critically** adv (to examine etc) en critique; (harshly) sévèrement; (ill) gravement. ◆**criticism** n critique f. ◆**criticize** vti critiquer. ◆**cri'tique** n (essay etc) critique f.

croak [krəuk] vi (of frog) croasser; – n croassement m.

crochet ['krəuʃeɪ] vt faire au crochet; – vi faire du crochet; – n (travail m au) crochet m; **c. hook** crochet m.

crock [krɒk] n a c., an (old) c. Fam (person) un croulant; (car) un tacot.

crockery ['krɒkərɪ] n (cups etc) vaisselle f.

crocodile ['krɒkədaɪl] n crocodile m.

crocus ['krəukəs] n crocus m.

crony ['krəunɪ] n Pej Fam copain m, copine f.

crook [kruk] n 1 (thief) escroc m. 2 (shepherd's stick) houlette f.

crooked ['krukɪd] a courbé; (path) tortueux; (hat, picture) de travers; (deal, person) malhonnête; – adv de travers. ◆**-ly** adv de travers.

croon [kruːn] vti chanter (à voix basse).

crop [krɒp] n 1 (harvest) récolte f; (produce) culture f; (of questions etc) Fig série f; (of people) groupe m. 2 vt (-pp-) (hair) couper (ras); – n c. of hair chevelure f. 3 vi (-pp-) to c. up se présenter, survenir. ◆**cropper** n to come a c. Sl (fall) ramasser une pelle; (fail) échouer.

croquet ['krəukeɪ] n (game) croquet m.

croquette [krəu'ket] n Culin croquette f.

cross[1] [krɒs] n 1 croix f; a c. between (animal) un croisement entre or de. 2 vt traverser; (threshold, barrier) franchir; (legs, animals) croiser; (thwart) contrecarrer; (cheque) barrer; to c. off or out rayer; it never crossed my mind that ... il ne m'est pas venu à l'esprit que ... ; crossed lines Tel lignes fpl embrouillées; – vi (of paths) se croiser; to c. (over) traverser. ◆**-ing** n Nau traversée f; (pedestrian) passage m clouté. ◆**cross-breed** n métis, -isse mf, hybride m. ◆**c.-'country** a à travers champs; **c.-country race** cross-(country) m. ◆**c.-exami'nation** n contre-interrogatoire m. ◆**c.-e'xamine** vt interroger. ◆**c.-eyed** a qui louche. ◆**c.-'legged** a & adv les jambes croisées. ◆**c.-'purposes** npl to be at c.-purposes se comprendre mal. ◆**c.-'reference** n renvoi m. ◆**c.-section** n coupe f transversale; Fig échantillon m.

cross[2] [krɒs] a (angry) fâché (with contre). ◆**-ly** adv d'un air fâché.

crossbow ['krɒsbəu] n arbalète f.

crosscheck [krɒs'tʃek] n contre-épreuve f; – vt vérifier.

crossfire ['krɒsfaɪər] n feux mpl croisés.

crossroads ['krɒsrəudz] n carrefour m.

crosswalk ['krɒswɔːk] n Am passage m clouté.

crossword ['krɒswɜːd] n c. (puzzle) mots mpl croisés.

crotch [krɒtʃ] n (of garment) entre-jambes m inv.

crotchet ['krɒtʃɪt] n Mus noire f.

crotchety ['krɒtʃɪtɪ] a grincheux.

crouch [krautʃ] vi to c. (down) s'accroupir, se tapir. ◆**-ing** a accroupi, tapi.

croupier ['kruːpɪər] n (in casino) croupier m.

crow [krəu] 1 n corbeau m, corneille f; **as the c. flies** à vol d'oiseau; **c.'s nest** Nau nid m de pie. 2 vi (of cock) chanter; (boast) Fig se vanter (about de). ◆**crowbar** n levier m.

crowd [kraud] n foule f; (particular group) bande f; (of things) Fam masse f; **quite a c.** beaucoup de monde; – vi to c. into (of people) s'entasser dans; to c. round s.o. se presser autour de qn; to c. together se serrer; – vt (fill) remplir; to c. into (of people) entasser dans; **don't c. me!** Fam ne me bouscule pas! ◆**-ed** a plein (with de); (train etc) bondé, plein; (city) encombré; **it's very c.!** il y a beaucoup de monde!

crown [kraun] n (of king, tooth) couronne f; (of head, hill) sommet m; **c. court** cour f d'assises; **C. jewels**, joyaux mpl de la Couronne; – vt couronner. ◆**-ing** a (glory etc) suprême; **c. achievement** couronnement m.

crucial ['kruːʃəl] a crucial.

crucify ['kruːsɪfaɪ] vt crucifier. ◆**crucifix** ['kruːsɪfɪks] n crucifix m. ◆**cruci'fixion** n crucifixion f.

crude [kruːd] a (-er, -est) (oil, fact) brut; (manners, person) grossier; (language, light) cru; (painting, work) rudimentaire. ◆**-ly** adv (to say, order etc) crûment. ◆**-ness** n grossièreté f; crudité f; état m rudimentaire.

cruel [kruəl] a (crueller, cruellest) cruel. ◆**cruelty** n cruauté f; **an act of c.** une cruauté.

cruet ['kruːɪt] n c. (stand) salière f, poivrière f et huilier m.

cruis/e [kruːz] vi Nau croiser; Aut rouler; Av voler; (of taxi) marauder; (of tourists) faire une croisière; – n croisière f; **to go on a c.** croisière; **c. speed** Nau Av & Fig vitesse f de croisière. ◆**-ing** a c. speed Nau Av & Fig vitesse f de croisière. ◆**-er** n Nau croiseur m.

crumb [krʌm] n miette f; (of comfort) Fig brin m; **crumbs!** Hum Fam zut!

crumble ['krʌmb(ə)l] vt (bread) émietter; – vi (collapse) s'effondrer; to c. (away) (in small pieces) s'émietter; Fig s'effriter. ◆**crumbly** a friable.

crummy ['krʌmɪ] a (-ier, -iest) Fam moche, minable.

crumpet ['krʌmpɪt] *n Culin* petite crêpe *f* grillée *(servie beurrée)*.

crumple ['krʌmp(ə)l] *vt* froisser; – *vi* se froisser.

crunch [krʌntʃ] **1** *vt (food)* croquer; – *vi (of snow)* craquer. **2** *n* the c. *Fam* le moment critique. ◆**crunchy** *a* (-ier, -iest) *(apple etc)* croquant.

crusade [kruː'seɪd] *n Hist & Fig* croisade *f*; – *vi* faire une croisade. ◆**crusader** *n Hist* croisé *m*; *Fig* militant, -ante *mf*.

crush [krʌʃ] **1** *n (crowd)* cohue *f*; *(rush)* bousculade *f*; to have a c. on s.o. *Fam* avoir le béguin pour qn. **2** *vt* écraser; *(hope)* détruire; *(clothes)* froisser; *(cram)* entasser **(into** dans). ◆**-ing** *a (defeat)* écrasant.

crust [krʌst] *n* croûte *f*. ◆**crusty** *a* (-ier, -iest) *(bread)* croustillant.

crutch [krʌtʃ] *n* **1** *Med* béquille *f*. **2** *(crotch)* entre-jambes *m inv*.

crux [krʌks] *n* the c. of *(problem, matter)* le nœud de.

cry [kraɪ] *n (shout)* cri *m*; to have a c. *Fam* pleurer; – *vi (weep)* pleurer; *(shout out)* pousser un cri, crier; *(exclaim)* s'écrier; to c. **(out)** for demander (à grands cris); to be crying out for avoir grand besoin de; to c. off *(withdraw)* abandonner; to c. off **(sth)** se désintéresser (de qch); to c. over pleurer (sur); – *vt (shout)* crier. ◆**-ing** *a (need etc)* très grand; **a c. shame** une véritable honte; – *n* cris *mpl*; *(weeping)* pleurs *mpl*.

crypt [krɪpt] *n* crypte *f*.

cryptic ['krɪptɪk] *a* secret, énigmatique.

crystal ['krɪst(ə)l] *n* cristal *m*. ◆**c.-'clear** *a (water, sound)* cristallin; *Fig* clair comme le jour *or* l'eau de roche. ◆**crystallize** *vt* cristalliser; – *vi (se)* cristalliser.

cub [kʌb] *n* **1** *(of animal)* petit *m*. **2** *(scout)* louveteau *m*.

Cuba ['kjuːbə] *n* Cuba *m*. ◆**Cuban** *a & n* cubain, -aine *(mf)*.

cubbyhole ['kʌbɪhəʊl] *n* cagibi *m*.

cube [kjuːb] *n* cube *m*; *(of meat etc)* dé *m*. ◆**cubic** *a (shape)* cubique; *(metre etc)* cube; **c. capacity** volume *m*; *Aut* cylindrée *f*.

cubicle ['kjuːbɪk(ə)l] *n (for changing)* cabine *f*; *(in hospital)* box *m*.

cuckoo ['kʊkuː] **1** *n (bird)* coucou *m*; **c. clock** coucou *m*. **2** *a (stupid) Sl* cinglé.

cucumber ['kjuːkʌmbər] *n* concombre *m*.

cuddle ['kʌd(ə)l] *vt (hug)* serrer (dans ses bras); *(caress)* câliner; – *vi (of lovers)* se serrer; to **(kiss and) c.** s'embrasser; to **c. up to** *(huddle)* se serrer *or* se blottir contre; –

caresse *f*. ◆**cuddly** *a* (-ier, -iest) *a* câlin, caressant; *(toy)* doux, en peluche.

cudgel ['kʌdʒəl] *n* trique *f*, gourdin *m*.

cue [kjuː] *n* **1** *Th* réplique *f*; *(signal)* signal *m*. **2** *(billiard)* **c.** queue *f* (de billard).

cuff [kʌf] *n* **1** *(of shirt etc)* poignet *m*, manchette *f*; *(of trousers) Am* revers *m*; **off the c.** *Fig* impromptu; **c. link** bouton *m* de manchette. **2** *vt (strike)* gifler.

cul-de-sac ['kʌldəsæk] *n* impasse *f*, cul-de-sac *m*.

culinary ['kʌlɪnərɪ] *a* culinaire.

cull [kʌl] *vt* choisir; *(animals)* abattre sélectivement.

culminat/e ['kʌlmɪneɪt] *vi* to c. **in** finir par. ◆**culmi'nation** *n* point *m* culminant.

culprit ['kʌlprɪt] *n* coupable *mf*.

cult [kʌlt] *n* culte *m*.

cultivat/e ['kʌltɪveɪt] *vt (land, mind etc)* cultiver. ◆**-ed** *a* cultivé. ◆**culti'vation** *n* culture *f*; **land** *or* **fields under c.** cultures *fpl*.

culture ['kʌltʃər] *n* culture *f*. ◆**cultural** *a* culturel. ◆**cultured** *a* cultivé.

cumbersome ['kʌmbəsəm] *a* encombrant.

cumulative ['kjuːmjʊlətɪv] *a* cumulatif; **c. effect** *(long-term)* effet *m or* résultat *m* à long terme.

cunning ['kʌnɪŋ] *a* astucieux; *Pej* rusé; – *n* astuce *f*; ruse *f*. ◆**-ly** *adv* avec astuce; avec ruse.

cup [kʌp] *n* tasse *f*; *(goblet, prize)* coupe *f*; **that's my c. of tea** *Fam* c'est à mon goût; **c. final** *Fb* finale *f* de la coupe. ◆**c.-tie** *n Fb* match *m* éliminatoire. ◆**cupful** *n* tasse *f*.

cupboard ['kʌbəd] *n* armoire *f*; *(built-in)* placard *m*.

Cupid ['kjuːpɪd] *n* Cupidon *m*.

cupola ['kjuːpələ] *n Archit* coupole *f*.

cuppa ['kʌpə] *n Fam* tasse *f* de thé.

curate ['kjʊərɪt] *n* vicaire *m*.

curator [kjʊə'reɪtər] *n (of museum)* conservateur *m*.

curb [kɜːb] *n* **1** *(kerb) Am* bord *m* du trottoir. **2** *vt (feelings)* refréner, freiner; *(ambitions)* modérer; *(expenses)* limiter; – *n* frein *m*; **to put a c. on** mettre un frein à.

curdle ['kɜːd(ə)l] *vt* cailler; – *vi* se cailler; *(of blood) Fig* se figer.

curds [kɜːdz] *npl* lait *m* caillé. ◆**curd cheese** *n* fromage *m* blanc *(maigre)*.

cure [kjʊər] **1** *vt* guérir (**of** de); *(poverty) Fig* éliminer; – *n* remède *m* **(for** contre); *(recovery)* guérison *f*; **rest c.** cure *f* de repos. **2** *vt Culin (meat)* fumer; *(salt)* saler; *(dry)* sécher. ◆**curable** *a* guérissable, curable. ◆**curative** *a* curatif.

curfew ['kɜːfjuː] *n* couvre-feu *m*.

curio ['kjuǝriǝu] n (pl -os) bibelot m, curiosité f.

curious ['kjuǝriǝs] a (odd) curieux; (inquisitive) curieux (about de); **c. to know** curieux de savoir. ◆-**ly** adv (oddly) curieusement. ◆**curi'osity** n curiosité f.

curl [kɜːl] **1** vti (hair) boucler, friser; – n boucle f; (of smoke) Fig spirale f. **2** vi to **c. up** (shrivel) se racornir; **to c. oneself up** (into a ball) se pelotonner. ◆-**er** n bigoudi m. ◆**curly** a (-ier, -iest) bouclé, frisé.

currant ['kʌrǝnt] n (fruit) groseille f; (dried grape) raisin m de Corinthe.

currency ['kʌrǝnsɪ] n (money) monnaie f; (acceptance) Fig cours m; **(foreign) c.** devises fpl (étrangères).

current ['kʌrǝnt] **1** a (fashion, trend etc) actuel; (opinion, use, phrase) courant; (year, month) en cours, courant; **c. affairs** questions fpl d'actualité; **c. events** actualité f; **the c. issue** (of magazine etc) le dernier numéro. **2** n (of river, air) & El courant m. ◆-**ly** adv actuellement, à présent.

curriculum, pl -**la** [kǝ'rɪkjʊlǝm, -lǝ] n programme m (scolaire); **c. (vitae)** curriculum (vitae) m inv.

curry ['kʌrɪ] **1** n Culin curry m, cari m. **2** vt to **c. favour with** s'insinuer dans les bonnes grâces de.

curs/e [kɜːs] n malédiction f; (swearword) juron m; (bane) Fig fléau m; – vt maudire; **cursed with** (blindness etc) affligé de; – vi (swear) jurer. ◆-**ed** [-ɪd] a Fam maudit.

cursor ['kɜːsǝr] n (on computer screen) curseur m.

cursory ['kɜːsǝrɪ] a (trop) rapide, superficiel.

curt [kɜːt] a brusque. ◆-**ly** adv d'un ton brusque. ◆-**ness** n brusquerie f.

curtail [kɜː'teɪl] vt écourter, raccourcir; (expenses) réduire. ◆-**ment** n raccourcissement m; réduction f.

curtain ['kɜːt(ǝ)n] n rideau m; **c. call** Th rappel m.

curts(e)y ['kɜːtsɪ] n révérence f; – vi faire une révérence.

curve [kɜːv] n courbe f; (in road) Am virage m; pl (of woman) Fam rondeurs fpl; – vt courber; – vi se courber; (of road) tourner, faire une courbe.

cushion ['kʊʃǝn] n coussin m; – vt (shock) Fig amortir. ◆**cushioned** a (seat) rembourré; **c. against** Fig protégé contre.

cushy ['kʊʃɪ] a (-ier, -iest) (job, life) Fam pépère, facile.

custard ['kʌstǝd] n crème f anglaise; (when set) crème f renversée.

custodian [kʌ'stǝudɪǝn] n gardien, -ienne mf.

custody ['kʌstǝdɪ] n (care) garde f; **to take into c.** Jur mettre en détention préventive. ◆**cu'stodial** a **c. sentence** peine f de prison.

custom ['kʌstǝm] n coutume f; (patronage) Com clientèle f. ◆**customary** a habituel, coutumier; **it is c.** to il est d'usage de. ◆**custom-built** a, ◆**customized** a (car etc) (fait) sur commande.

customer ['kʌstǝmǝr] n client, -ente mf; Pej individu m.

customs ['kʌstǝmz] n & npl **(the) c.** la douane; (duties) droits mpl de douane; **c. officer** douanier m; **c. union** union f douanière.

cut [kʌt] n coupure f; (stroke) coup m; (of clothes, hair) coupe f; (in salary) réduction f; (of meat) morceau m; – vt (pt & pp **cut**, pres p **cutting**) couper; (meat) découper; (glass, tree) tailler; (record) graver; (hay) faucher; (profits, prices etc) réduire; (tooth) percer; (corner) Aut prendre à la corde; **to c. open** ouvrir (au couteau etc); **to c. short** (visit) abréger; – vi (of person, scissors) couper; (of material) se couper; **to c. into** (cake) entamer. ■ **to c. away** vt (remove) enlever; **to c. back (on)** vti réduire. ◆**cutback** n réduction f; **to c. down** vt (tree) abattre; **to c. down (on)** vti réduire; **to c. in** vi interrompre; Aut faire une queue de poisson (on s.o. à qn); **to c. off** vt couper; (isolate) isoler; **to c. out** vi (of engine) Aut caler; – vt (article) découper; (garment) tailler; (remove) enlever; (leave out, get rid of) Fam supprimer; **to c. out drinking** (stop) Fam s'arrêter de boire; **c. it out!** Fam ça suffit!; **c. out to be a doctor**/etc fait pour être médecin/etc. ◆**cutout** n (picture) découpage m; El coupe-circuit m inv; **to c. up** vt couper (en morceaux); (meat) découper; **c. up about** démoralisé par. ◆**cutting** n coupe f; (of diamond) taille f; (article) Journ coupure f; (plant) bouture f; Cin montage m; – a (wind, word) cinglant; **c. edge** tranchant m.

cute [kjuːt] a (-er, -est) Fam (pretty) mignon; (shrewd) astucieux.

cuticle ['kjuːtɪk(ǝ)l] n petites peaux fpl (de l'ongle).

cutlery ['kʌtlǝrɪ] n couverts mpl.

cutlet ['kʌtlɪt] n (of veal etc) côtelette f.

cut-price [kʌt'praɪs] a à prix réduit.

cutthroat ['kʌtθrǝut] n assassin m; – a (competition) impitoyable.

cv [si:'vi:] *n abbr* curriculum (vitae) *m inv.*

cyanide ['saɪənaɪd] *n* cyanure *m.*

cybernetics [saɪbə'netɪks] *n* cybernétique *f.*

cycle ['saɪk(ə)l] **1** *n* bicyclette *f*, vélo *m*; – *a* (*path, track*) cyclable; (*race*) cycliste; – *vi* aller à bicyclette (**to** à); *Sp* faire de la bicyclette. **2** *n* (*series, period*) cycle *m.* ◆**cycling** *n* cyclisme *m*; – *a* (*champion*) cycliste. ◆**cyclist** *n* cycliste *mf.* ◆**cyclic(al)** ['sɪklɪk(ə)l] *a* cyclique.

cyclone ['saɪkləun] *n* cyclone *m.*

cylinder ['sɪlɪndər] *n* cylindre *m.* ◆**cy-'lindrical** *a* cylindrique.

cymbal ['sɪmbəl] *n* cymbale *f.*

cynic ['sɪnɪk] *n* cynique *mf.* ◆**cynical** *a* cynique. ◆**cynicism** *n* cynisme *m.*

cypress ['saɪprəs] *n* (*tree*) cyprès *m.*

Cyprus ['saɪprəs] *n* Chypre *f.* ◆**Cypriot** ['sɪprɪət] *a & n* cypriote (*mf*).

cyst [sɪst] *n Med* kyste *m.*

czar [zɑːr] *n* tsar *m.*

Czech [tʃek] *a & n* tchèque (*mf*). ◆**Czecho'slovak** *a & n* tchécoslovaque (*mf*). ◆**Czechoslo'vakia** *n* Tchécoslovaquie *f.* ◆**Czechoslo'vakian** *a & n* tchécoslovaque (*mf*).

D

D, d [diː] *n* D, d *m.* ◆**D.-day** *n* le jour J.

dab [dæb] *n* a d. of un petit peu de; – *vt* (**-bb-**) (*wound, brow etc*) tamponner; **to d. sth on sth** appliquer qch (à petits coups) sur qch.

dabble ['dæb(ə)l] *vi* to d. in s'occuper or se mêler un peu de.

dad [dæd] *n Fam* papa *m.* ◆**daddy** *n Fam* papa *m*; **d. longlegs** (*cranefly*) tipule *f*; (*spider*) *Am* faucheur *m.*

daffodil ['dæfədɪl] *n* jonquille *f.*

daft [dɑːft] *a* (**-er, -est**) *Fam* idiot, bête.

dagger ['dægər] *n* poignard *m*; **at daggers drawn** à couteaux tirés (**with** avec).

dahlia ['deɪljə, *Am* 'dæljə] *n* dahlia *m.*

daily ['deɪlɪ] *a* quotidien, journalier; (*wage*) journalier; – *adv* quotidiennement; – *n* d. (**paper**) quotidien *m*; **d.** (**help**) (*cleaning woman*) femme *f* de ménage.

dainty ['deɪntɪ] *a* (**-ier, -iest**) délicat; (*pretty*) mignon; (*tasteful*) élégant. ◆**daintily** *adv* délicatement; élégamment.

dairy ['deərɪ] *n* (*on farm*) laiterie *f*; (*shop*) crémerie *f*; – *a* (*produce, cow etc*) laitier. ◆**dairyman** *n* (*pl* **-men**) (*dealer*) laitier *m.* ◆**dairywoman** *n* (*pl* **-women**) laitière *f.*

daisy ['deɪzɪ] *n* pâquerette *f.*

dale [deɪl] *n Geog Lit* vallée *f.*

dally ['dælɪ] *vi* musarder, lanterner.

dam [dæm] *n* (*wall*) barrage *m*; – *vt* (**-mm-**) (*river*) barrer.

damag/e ['dæmɪdʒ] *n* dégâts *mpl*, dommages *mpl*; (*harm*) *Fig* préjudice *m*; *pl Jur* dommages-intérêts *mpl*; – *vt* (*spoil*) abîmer; (*material object*) endommager, abîmer; (*harm*) *Fig* nuire à. ◆**—ing** *a* préjudiciable (**to** à).

dame [deɪm] *n Lit* dame *f*; *Am Sl* nana *f*, fille *f.*

damn [dæm] *vt* (*condemn, doom*) condamner; *Rel* damner; (*curse*) maudire; **d. him!** *Fam* qu'il aille au diable!; – *int* d. (**it**)! *Fam* zut!, merde!; – *a* d. Fam sacrément; **d. all** rien du tout. ◆**—ed 1** *a* (*soul*) damné. **2** *Fam* – damné *a & adv.* ◆**—ing** *a* (*evidence etc*) accablant. ◆**dam'nation** *n* damnation *f.*

damp [dæmp] *a* (**-er, -est**) humide; (*skin*) moite; – *n* humidité *f.* ◆**damp(en)** *vt* humecter; **to d.** (**down**) (*zeal*) refroidir; (*ambition*) étouffer. ◆**damper** *n* to put a d. on jeter un froid sur. ◆**dampness** *n* humidité *f.*

damsel ['dæmzəl] *n Lit & Hum* demoiselle *f.*

damson ['dæmzən] *n* prune *f* de Damas.

danc/e [dɑːns] *n* danse *f*; (*social event*) bal *m*; **d. hall** dancing *m*; – *vi* danser; **to d. for joy** sauter de joie; – *vt* (*polka etc*) danser. ◆**—ing** *n* danse *f*; **d. partner** cavalier, -ière *mf.* ◆**—er** *n* danseur, -euse *mf.*

dandelion ['dændɪlaɪən] *n* pissenlit *m.*

dandruff ['dændrʌf] *n* pellicules *fpl.*

dandy ['dændɪ] **1** *n* dandy *m.* **2** *a* (*very good*) *Am Fam* formidable.

Dane [deɪn] *n* Danois, -oise *mf.*

danger ['deɪndʒər] *n* (*peril*) danger *m* (**to** pour); (*risk*) risque *m*; **in d.** en danger; **in d. of** (*threatened by*) menacé de; **to be in d. of falling**/*etc* risquer de tomber/*etc*; **on the d. list** *Med* dans un état critique; **d. signal** signal *m* d'alarme; **d. zone** zone *f* dangereuse. ◆**dangerous** *a* (*place, illness,*

person etc) dangereux (**to** pour).
◆**dangerously** *adv* dangereusement; (*ill*) gravement.

dangle ['dæŋg(ə)l] *vt* balancer; (*prospect*) *Fig* faire miroiter (**before s.o.** aux yeux de qn); – *vi* (*hang*) pendre; (*swing*) se balancer.

Danish ['deɪnɪʃ] *a* danois; – *n* (*language*) danois *m*.

dank [dæŋk] *a* (**-er, -est**) humide (et froid).

dapper ['dæpər] *a* pimpant, fringant.

dappled ['dæp(ə)ld] *a* pommelé, tacheté.

dar/e [deər] *vt* oser (**do faire**); **she d. not come** elle n'ose pas venir; **he doesn't d. (to) go** il n'ose pas y aller; **if you d. (to)** si tu l'oses, si tu oses le faire; **I d. say he tried** il a sans doute essayé, je suppose qu'il a essayé; **to d. s.o. to do** défier qn de faire. ◆**-ing** *a* audacieux; – *n* audace *f*. ◆**daredevil** *n* casse-cou *m inv*, risque-tout *m inv*.

dark [dɑːk] *a* (**-er, -est**) obscur, noir, sombre; (*colour*) foncé, sombre; (*skin*) brun, foncé; (*hair*) brun, noir, foncé; (*eyes*) foncé; (*gloomy*) sombre; **it's d.** il fait nuit or noir; **to keep sth d.** tenir qch secret; **d. glasses** lunettes *fpl* noires; – *n* noir *m*, obscurité *f*; **after d.** après la tombée de la nuit; **to keep s.o. in the d.** laisser qn dans l'ignorance (**about** de). ◆**d.-'haired** *a* aux cheveux bruns. ◆**d.-'skinned** *a* brun; (*race*) de couleur. ◆**darken** *vt* assombrir, obscurcir; (*colour*) foncer; – *vi* s'assombrir; (*of colour*) foncer. ◆**darkness** *n* obscurité *f*, noir *m*.

darkroom ['dɑːkruːm] *n Phot* chambre *f* noire.

darling ['dɑːlɪŋ] *n* (*favourite*) chouchou, -oute *mf*; (**my) d.** (mon) chéri, (ma) chérie; **he's a d.** c'est un amour; **be a d.!** sois un ange!; – *a* chéri; (*delightful*) *Fam* adorable.

darn [dɑːn] **1** *vt* (*socks*) repriser. **2** *int* **d. it!** bon sang! ◆**-ing** *n* reprise *f*; – *a* (*needle, wool*) à repriser.

dart [dɑːt] **1** *vi* se précipiter, s'élancer (**for** vers); – *n* **to make a d.** se précipiter (**for** vers). **2** *n Sp* fléchette *f; pl* (*game*) fléchettes *fpl*. ◆**dartboard** *n Sp* cible *f*.

dash [dæʃ] **1** *n* (*run, rush*) ruée *f*; **to make a d.** se précipiter (**for** vers); – *vi* se précipiter; (*of waves*) se briser (**against** contre); **to d. off** or **away** partir or filer en vitesse; – *vt* jeter (avec force); (*shatter*) briser; **d. (it)!** *Fam* zut!; **to d. off** (*letter*) faire en vitesse. **2** *n* **a d.** of un (petit) peu de; **a d. of milk** une goutte or un nuage de lait. **3** *n* (*stroke*) trait

m; Typ tiret *m*. ◆**-ing** *a* (*person*) sémillant.

dashboard ['dæʃbɔːd] *n Aut* tableau *m* de bord.

data ['deɪtə] *npl* données *fpl*; **d. processing** informatique *f*.

date¹ [deɪt] *n* date *f*; (**on coin**) millésime *m*; (*meeting*) *Fam* rendez-vous *m inv*; (*person*) *Fam* copain, -ine *mf* (*avec qui on a un rendez-vous*); **up to d.** moderne; (*information*) à jour; (*well-informed*) au courant (**on** de); **out of d.** (*old-fashioned*) démodé; (*expired*) périmé; **to d.** à ce jour, jusqu'ici; **d. stamp** (*object*) (tampon *m*) dateur *m*; (*mark*) cachet *m*; – *vt* (*letter etc*) dater; (*girl, boy*) *Fam* sortir avec; – *vi* (*become out of date*) dater; **to d. back to, to d. from** dater de. ◆**dated** *a* démodé.

date² [deɪt] *n Bot* datte *f*.

datebook ['deɪtbʊk] *n Am* agenda *m*.

daub [dɔːb] *vt* barbouiller (**with** de).

daughter ['dɔːtər] *n* fille *f*. ◆**d.-in-law** *n* (*pl* **daughters-in-law**) belle-fille *f*, bru *f*.

daunt [dɔːnt] *vt* décourager, rebuter. ◆**-less** *a* intrépide.

dawdl/e ['dɔːd(ə)l] *vi* traîner, lambiner. ◆**-er** *n* traînard, -arde *mf*.

dawn [dɔːn] *n* aube *f*, aurore *f*; – *vi* (**of day**) poindre; (**of new era, idea**) naître, voir le jour; **it dawned upon him that ...** il lui est venu à l'esprit que ... ◆**-ing** *n* naissant.

day [deɪ] *n* jour *m*; (**working period, whole day long**) journée *f; pl* (*period*) époque *f*, temps *mpl*; **all d. (long)** toute la journée; **what d. is it?** quel jour sommes-nous?; **the following** or **next d.** le lendemain; **the d. before** la veille; **the d. before yesterday** avant-hier; **the d. after tomorrow** après-demain; **to the d.** jour pour jour; **d. boarder** demi-pensionnaire *mf*; **d. nursery** crèche *f*; **d. return** *Rail* aller et retour *m* (*pour une journée*); **d. tripper** excursionniste *mf*. ◆**d.-to-'d.** *a* journalier; **on a d.-to-day basis** (*every day*) journellement. ◆**daybreak** *n* point *m* du jour. ◆**daydream** *n* rêverie *f*; – *vi* rêvasser. ◆**daylight** *n* (lumière *f* du) jour *m*; (*dawn*) point *m* du jour; **it's d.** il fait jour. ◆**daytime** *n* journée *f*.

daze [deɪz] *vt* (**with drugs etc**) hébéter; (**by blow**) étourdir; – *n* **in a d.** étourdi, hébété.

dazzle ['dæz(ə)l] *vt* éblouir; – *n* éblouissement *m*.

deacon ['diːkən] *n Rel* diacre *m*.

dead [ded] *a* mort; (*numb*) engourdi; (*party etc*) qui manque de vie, mortel; (*telephone*) sans tonalité; **in (the) d. centre** au beau milieu; **to be a d. loss** (*person*) *Fam* n'être bon à rien; **it's a d. loss** *Fam* ça ne vaut rien; **d. silence** un silence de mort; **a d. stop** un arrêt complet; **d. end** (*street*) & *Fig* impasse *f*; **a d.-end job** un travail sans avenir; – *adv* (*completely*) absolument; (*very*) très; **d. beat** *Fam* éreinté; **d. drunk** *Fam* ivre mort; **to stop d.** s'arrêter net; – *n* **the d.** les morts *mpl*; **in the d. of** (*night, winter*) au cœur de. ◆**—ly** *a* (**-ier, -iest**) (*enemy, silence, paleness*) mortel; (*weapon*) meurtrier; **d. sins** péchés *mpl* capitaux; – *adv* mortellement. ◆**deadbeat** *n Am Fam* parasite *m*. ◆**deadline** *n* date *f* limite; (*hour*) heure *f* limite. ◆**deadlock** *n Fig* impasse *f*. ◆**deadpan** *a* (*face*) figé, impassible.

deaden ['ded(ə)n] *vt* (*shock*) amortir; (*pain*) calmer; (*feeling*) émousser.

deaf [def] *a* sourd (**to** à); **d. and dumb** sourd-muet; **d. in one ear** sourd d'une oreille; – *n* **the d.** les sourds *mpl*. ◆**d.-aid** *n* audiophone *m*, prothèse *f* auditive. ◆**deafen** *vt* assourdir. ◆**deafness** *n* surdité *f*.

deal¹ [diːl] **1** *n* **a good** *or* **great d.** beaucoup (**of** de). **2** *n Com* marché *m*, affaire *f*; *Cards* donne *f*; **fair d.** traitement *m or* arrangement *m* équitable; **it's a d.** d'accord; **big d.!** *Iron* la belle affaire! **3** *vt* (*pt* & *pp* **dealt** [delt]) (*blow*) porter; **to d. (out)** (*cards*) donner; (*money*) distribuer. **4** *vi* (*trade*) traiter (**with** s.o. avec qn); **to d. in** faire le commerce de; **to d. with** (*take care of*) s'occuper de; (*concern*) traiter de, parler de; **I can d. with him** (*handle*) je sais m'y prendre avec lui. ◆**—ings** *npl* relations *fpl* (**with** avec); *Com* transactions *fpl*. ◆**—er** *n* marchand, -ande *mf* (**in** de); (*agent*) dépositaire *mf*; (*for cars*) concessionnaire *mf*; (*in drugs*) *Sl* revendeur, -euse *mf* de drogues; *Cards* donneur, -euse *mf*.

deal² [diːl] *n* (*wood*) sapin *m*.

dean [diːn] *n Rel Univ* doyen *m*.

dear [diər] *a* (**-er, -est**) (*loved, precious, expensive*) cher; (*price*) élevé; **D. Sir** (*in letter*) *Com* Monsieur; **D. Uncle** (*mon*) cher oncle; **oh d.!** oh là là!, oh mon Dieu!; – *n* (*my*) **d.** (*darling*) (mon) chéri, (ma) chérie; (*friend*) mon cher, ma chère; **she's a d.** c'est un amour; **be a d.!** sois un ange!; – *adv* (*to cost, pay*) cher. ◆**—ly** *adv* tendrement; (*very much*) beaucoup; **to pay d. for sth** payer qch cher.

dearth [dɜːθ] *n* manque *m*, pénurie *f*.

death [deθ] *n* mort *f*; **to put to d.** mettre à mort; **to be bored to d.** s'ennuyer à mourir;

to be burnt to d. mourir carbonisé; **to be sick to d.** en avoir vraiment marre; **many deaths** (*people killed*) de nombreux morts *mpl*; – *a* (*march*) funèbre; (*mask*) mortuaire; **d. certificate** acte *m* de décès; **d. duty** droits *mpl* de succession; **d. penalty** *or* **sentence** peine *f* de mort; **d. rate** mortalité *f*; **it's a d. trap** il y a danger de mort. ◆**deathbed** *n* lit *m* de mort. ◆**death-blow** *n* coup *m* mortel. ◆**deathly** *a* mortel, de mort; – *adv* **d. pale** d'une pâleur mortelle.

debar [drˈbɑːr] *vt* (**-rr-**) exclure; **to d. from** doing interdire de faire.

debase [drˈbeɪs] *vt* (*person*) avilir; (*reputation, talents*) galvauder; (*coinage*) altérer.

debate [drˈbeɪt] *vti* discuter; **to d. (with oneself) whether to leave/etc** se demander si on doit partir/etc; – *n* débat *m*, discussion *f*. ◆**—able** *a* discutable, contestable.

debauch [drˈbɔːtʃ] *vt* corrompre, débaucher. ◆**debauchery** *n* débauche *f*.

debilitate [drˈbɪlɪteɪt] *vt* débiliter. ◆**debility** *n* faiblesse *f*, débilité *f*.

debit ['debɪt] *n* débit *m*; **in d.** (*account*) débiteur; – *a* (*balance*) *Fin* débiteur; – *vt* débiter (**s.o. with sth** qn de qch).

debonair [debəˈneər] *a* jovial; (*charming*) charmant; (*polite*) poli.

debris ['debriː] *n* débris *mpl*.

debt [det] *n* dette *f*; **to be in d.** avoir des dettes; **to be £50 in d.** devoir 50 livres; **to run** *or* **get into d.** faire des dettes. ◆**debtor** *n* débiteur, -trice *mf*.

debunk [diːˈbʌŋk] *vt Fam* démystifier.

debut ['debjuː] *n Th* début *m*.

decade ['dekeɪd] *n* décennie *f*.

decadent ['dekədənt] *a* décadent. ◆**decadence** *n* décadence *f*.

decaffeinated [diːˈkæfɪneɪtɪd] *a* décaféiné.

decal ['diːkæl] *n Am* décalcomanie *f*.

decant [drˈkænt] *vt* (*wine*) décanter. ◆**—er** *n* carafe *f*.

decapitate [drˈkæpɪteɪt] *vt* décapiter.

decathlon [drˈkæθlon] *n Sp* décathlon *m*.

decay [drˈkeɪ] *vi* (*go bad*) se gâter; (*rot*) pourrir; (*of tooth*) se carier, se gâter; (*of building*) tomber en ruine; (*decline*) *Fig* décliner; – *n* pourriture *f*; *Archit* délabrement *m*; (*of tooth*) carie(s) *f(pl)*; (*of nation*) décadence *f*; **to fall into d.** (*of building*) tomber en ruine. ◆**—ing** *a* (*meat, fruit etc*) pourrissant.

deceased [drˈsiːst] *a* décédé; – *n* **the d.** le défunt, la défunte; *pl* les défunt(e)s.

deceit [drˈsiːt] *n* tromperie *f*. ◆**deceitful** *a*

trompeur. ◆**deceitfully** adv avec duplicité.

deceive [dɪ'siːv] vti tromper; **to d. oneself** se faire des illusions.

December [dɪ'sembər] n décembre m.

decent ['diːsənt] a (respectable) convenable, décent; (good) Fam bon; (kind) Fam gentil; **that was d. (of you)** c'était chic de ta part. ◆**decency** n décence f; (kindness) Fam gentillesse f. ◆**decently** adv décemment.

decentralize [diː'sentrəlaɪz] vt décentraliser. ◆**decentrali'zation** n décentralisation f.

deception [dɪ'sepʃ(ə)n] n tromperie f. ◆**deceptive** a trompeur.

decibel ['desɪbel] n décibel m.

decid/e [dɪ'saɪd] vt (question etc) régler, décider; (s.o.'s career, fate etc) décider de; **to d. to do** décider de faire; **to d. that** décider que; **to d. s.o. to do** décider qn à faire; – vi (make decisions) décider; (make up one's mind) se décider (on doing à faire); **to d. on sth** décider de qch, se décider à qch; (choose) se décider pour qch. ◆**-ed** a (firm) décidé, résolu; (clear) net. ◆**-edly** adv résolument; nettement. ◆**-ing** a (factor etc) décisif.

decimal ['desɪml] a décimal; **d. point** virgule f; – n décimale f. ◆**decimali'zation** n décimalisation f.

decimate ['desɪmeɪt] vt décimer.

decipher [dɪ'saɪfər] vt déchiffrer.

decision [dɪ'sɪʒ(ə)n] n décision f. ◆**decisive** [dɪ'saɪsɪv] a (defeat, tone etc) décisif; (victory) net, incontestable. ◆**decisively** adv (to state) avec décision; (to win) nettement, incontestablement.

deck [dek] **1** n Nau pont m; **top d.** (of bus) impériale f. **2** n d. **of cards** jeu m de cartes. **3** n (of record player) platine f. **4** vt **to d. (out)** (adorn) orner. ◆**deckchair** n chaise f longue.

declare [dɪ'kleər] vt déclarer (that que); (verdict, result) proclamer. ◆**decla'ration** n déclaration f; proclamation f.

declin/e [dɪ'klaɪn] **1** vi (deteriorate) décliner; (of birthrate, price etc) baisser; **to d. in importance** perdre de l'importance; – n déclin m; (fall) baisse f. **2** vt refuser, décliner; **to d. to do** refuser de faire. ◆**-ing** a one's d. years ses dernières années.

decode [diː'kəʊd] vt (message) décoder.

decompose [diːkəm'pəʊz] vt décomposer; – vi se décomposer. ◆**decompo'sition** n décomposition f.

decompression [diːkəm'preʃ(ə)n] n décompression f.

decontaminate [diːkən'tæmɪneɪt] vt décontaminer.

decor ['deɪkɔːr] n décor m.

decorat/e ['dekəreɪt] vt (cake, house, soldier) décorer (with de); (paint etc) peindre (et tapisser); (hat, skirt etc) orner (with de). ◆**-ing** n interior d. décoration f d'intérieurs. ◆**deco'ration** n décoration f. ◆**decorative** a décoratif. ◆**decorator** n (house painter and) peintre m décorateur; (interior) d. ensemblier m, décorateur, -trice mf.

decorum [dɪ'kɔːrəm] n bienséances fpl.

decoy ['diːkɔɪ] n (artificial bird) appeau m; (police) d. policier m en civil.

decreas/e [dɪ'kriːs] vti diminuer; – ['diːkriːs] n diminution f (in de). ◆**-ing** a (number etc) décroissant. ◆**-ingly** adv de moins en moins.

decree [dɪ'kriː] n Pol Rel décret m; Jur jugement m; (municipal) arrêté m; – vt (pt & pp decreed) décréter.

decrepit [dɪ'krepɪt] a (building) en ruine; (person) décrépit.

decry [dɪ'kraɪ] vt décrier.

dedicat/e ['dedɪkeɪt] vt (devote) consacrer (to à); (book) dédier (to à); **to d. oneself to** se consacrer à. ◆**dedi'cation** n (in book) dédicace f; (devotion) dévouement m.

deduce [dɪ'djuːs] vt (conclude) déduire (from de, that que).

deduct [dɪ'dʌkt] vt (subtract) déduire, retrancher (from de); (from wage, account) prélever (from sur). ◆**deductible** a à déduire (from de); (expenses) déductible. ◆**deduction** n (inference) & Com déduction f.

deed [diːd] n action f, acte m; (feat) exploit m; Jur acte m (notarié).

deem [diːm] vt juger, estimer.

deep [diːp] a (-er, -est) profond; (snow) épais; (voice) grave; (note) Mus bas; (person) insondable; **to be six metres/etc d.** avoir six mètres/etc de profondeur; **d. in thought** absorbé or plongé dans ses pensées; **the d. end** (in swimming pool) le grand bain; **d. red** rouge foncé; – adv (to breathe) profondément; **d. into the night** tard dans la nuit; – n the d. l'océan m. ◆**-ly** adv (grateful, to regret etc) profondément. ◆**deep-'freeze** vt surgeler; – n congélateur m. ◆**d.-'fryer** n friteuse f. ◆**d.-'rooted** a, ◆**d.-'seated** a bien ancré, profond. ◆**d.-'set** a (eyes) enfoncés.

deepen ['diːpən] vt approfondir; (increase) augmenter; – vi devenir plus profond; (of mystery) s'épaissir. ◆—ing a grandissant.

deer [dɪər] n inv cerf m.

deface [dɪ'feɪs] vt (damage) dégrader; (daub) barbouiller.

defamation [defə'meɪʃ(ə)n] n diffamation f. ◆de'famatory a diffamatoire.

default [dɪ'fɔːlt] n by d. Jur par défaut; to win by d. gagner par forfait; – vi faire défaut; to d. on one's payments Fin être en rupture de paiement.

defeat [dɪ'fiːt] vt battre, vaincre; (plan) faire échouer; – n défaite f; (of plan) échec m. ◆defeatism n défaitisme m.

defect 1 [ˈdiːfekt] n défaut m. **2** [dɪ'fekt] vi Pol déserter, faire défection; to d. to (the West, the enemy) passer à. ◆de'fection n défection f. ◆de'fective a défectueux; Med déficient. ◆de'fector n transfuge mf.

defence [dɪ'fens] (Am **defense**) n défense f; the body's defences la défense de l'organisme (against contre); in his d. Jur à sa décharge, pour le défendre. ◆defenceless a sans défense. ◆defensible a défendable. ◆defensive a défensif; – n on the d. sur la défensive.

defend [dɪ'fend] vt défendre. ◆defendant n (accused) Jur prévenu, -ue mf. ◆defender n défenseur m; (of title) Sp détenteur, -trice mf.

defer [dɪ'fɜːr] **1** vt (-rr-) (postpone) différer, reporter. **2** vi (-rr-) to d. to (yield) déférer à. ◆—ment n report m.

deference ['defərəns] n déférence f. ◆defe'rential a déférent, plein de déférence.

defiant [dɪ'faɪənt] a (tone etc) de défi; (person) rebelle. ◆defiance n (resistance) défi m (of à); in d. of (contempt) au mépris de. ◆defiantly adv d'un air de défi.

deficient [dɪ'fɪʃənt] a insuffisant; Med déficient; to be d. in manquer de. ◆deficiency n manque m; (flaw) défaut m; Med carence f; (mental) déficience f.

deficit ['defɪsɪt] n déficit m.

defile [dɪ'faɪl] vt souiller, salir.

define [dɪ'faɪn] vt définir. ◆defi'nition n définition f.

definite ['defɪnɪt] a (date, plan) précis, déterminé; (obvious) net, évident; (firm) ferme; (certain) certain; d. article Gram article m défini. ◆—ly adv certainement; (appreciably) nettement; (to say) catégoriquement.

definitive [dɪ'fɪnɪtɪv] a définitif.

deflate [dɪ'fleɪt] vt (tyre) dégonfler. ◆deflation n dégonflement m; Econ déflation f.

deflect [dɪ'flekt] vt faire dévier; – vi dévier.

deform [dɪ'fɔːm] vt déformer. ◆—ed a (body) difforme. ◆deformity n difformité f.

defraud [dɪ'frɔːd] vt (customs, State etc) frauder; to d. s.o. of sth escroquer qch à qn.

defray [dɪ'freɪ] vt (expenses) payer.

defrost [dɪ'frɒst] vt (fridge) dégivrer; (food) décongeler.

deft [deft] a adroit (with de). ◆—ness n adresse f.

defunct [dɪ'fʌŋkt] a défunt.

defuse [dɪ'fjuːz] vt (bomb, conflict) désamorcer.

defy [dɪ'faɪ] vt (person, death etc) défier; (effort, description) résister à; to d. s.o. to do défier qn de faire.

degenerate [dɪ'dʒenəreɪt] vi dégénérer (into en); – [dɪ'dʒenərət] a & n dégénéré, -ée (mf). ◆degene'ration n dégénérescence f.

degrade [dɪ'greɪd] vt dégrader. ◆degradation [degrə'deɪʃ(ə)n] n Mil Ch dégradation f; (of person) déchéance f.

degree [dɪ'griː] n **1** degré m; not in the slightest d. pas du tout; to such a d. à tel point (that que). **2** Univ diplôme m; (Bachelor's) licence f; (Master's) maîtrise f; (PhD) doctorat m.

dehumanize [diː'hjuːmənaɪz] vt déshumaniser.

dehydrate [diːhaɪ'dreɪt] vt déshydrater.

de-ice [diː'aɪs] vt Av Aut dégivrer.

deign [deɪn] vt daigner (to do faire).

deity ['diːɪtɪ] n dieu m.

dejected [dɪ'dʒektɪd] a abattu, découragé. ◆dejection n abattement m.

dekko ['dekəʊ] n Sl coup m d'œil.

delay [dɪ'leɪ] vt retarder; (payment) différer; – vi (be slow) tarder (doing à faire); (linger) s'attarder; – n (lateness) retard m; (waiting period) délai m; without d. sans tarder. ◆delayed-'action a (bomb) à retardement. ◆delaying a d. tactics moyens mpl dilatoires.

delectable [dɪ'lektəb(ə)l] a délectable.

delegate 1 ['delɪgeɪt] vt déléguer (to à). **2** ['delɪgət] n délégué, -ée mf. ◆dele'gation n délégation f.

delete [dɪ'liːt] vt rayer, supprimer. ◆deletion n (thing deleted) rature f; (act) suppression f.

deleterious [delɪ'tɪərɪəs] a néfaste.

deliberate¹ [dɪ'lɪbəreɪt] vi délibérer; – vt délibérer sur.

deliberate² [dɪ'lɪbərət] a (intentional) délibéré; (cautious) réfléchi; (slow) mesuré.

◆—ly adv (intentionally) exprès, délibérément; (to walk) avec mesure. ◆deliberation n délibération f.

delicate ['delɪkət] a délicat. ◆delicacy n délicatesse f; Culin mets m délicat, gourmandise f. ◆delicately adv délicatement. ◆delica'tessen n (shop) épicerie f fine, traiteur m.

delicious [dɪ'lɪʃəs] a délicieux.

delight [dɪ'laɪt] n délice m, grand plaisir m, joie f; pl (pleasures, things) délices fpl; to be the d. of faire les délices de; to take d. in sth/in doing se délecter de qch/à faire; − vt réjouir; − vi se délecter (in doing à faire). ◆—ed a ravi, enchanté (with sth de qch, to do de faire, that que). ◆delightful a charmant; (meal, perfume, sensation) délicieux. ◆delightfully adv avec beaucoup de charme; (wonderfully) merveilleusement.

delineate [dɪ'lɪnɪeɪt] vt (outline) esquisser; (portray) décrire.

delinquent [dɪ'lɪŋkwənt] a & n délinquant, -ante (mf). ◆delinquency n délinquance f.

delirious [dɪ'lɪərɪəs] a délirant; to be d. avoir le délire, délirer. ◆delirium n Med délire m.

deliver [dɪ'lɪvər] vt 1 (goods, milk etc) livrer; (letters) distribuer; (hand over) remettre (to à). 2 (rescue) délivrer (from de). 3 (give birth to) mettre au monde, accoucher de; to d. a woman('s baby) accoucher une femme. 4 (speech) prononcer; (ultimatum, warning) lancer; (blow) porter. ◆deliverance n délivrance f. ◆delivery n 1 livraison f; distribution f; remise f 2 Med accouchement m. 3 (speaking) débit m. ◆deliveryman n (pl -men) livreur m.

delta ['deltə] n (of river) delta m.

delude [dɪ'luːd] vt tromper; to d. oneself se faire des illusions. ◆delusion n illusion f; Psy aberration f mentale.

deluge ['delju:dʒ] n (of water, questions etc) déluge m; − vt inonder (with de).

de luxe [də'lʌks] a de luxe.

delve [delv] vi to d. into (question, past) fouiller; (books) fouiller dans.

demagogue ['deməgɒg] n démagogue mf.

demand [dɪ'mɑːnd] vt exiger (sth from s.o. qch de qn); réclamer (sth from s.o. qch à qn); (rights, more pay) revendiquer; to d. that exiger que; to d. to know insister pour savoir; − n exigence f; (claim) revendication f, réclamation f; (request f) & Econ demande f; in great d. très demandé; to

make demands on s.o. exiger beaucoup de qn. ◆—ing a exigeant.

demarcation [diːmɑːˈkeɪʃ(ə)n] n démarcation f.

demean [dɪ'miːn] vt to d. oneself s'abaisser, s'avilir.

demeanour [dɪ'miːnər] n (behaviour) comportement m.

demented [dɪ'mentɪd] a dément.

demerara [demə'reərə] n d. (sugar) cassonade f, sucre m roux.

demise [dɪ'maɪz] n (death) décès m; Fig disparition f.

demo ['deməu] n (pl -os) (demonstration) Fam manif f.

demobilize [diːˈməubɪlaɪz] vt démobiliser.

democracy [dɪ'mɒkrəsɪ] n démocratie f. ◆democrat ['deməkræt] n démocrate mf. ◆demo'cratic a démocratique; (person) démocrate.

demography [dɪ'mɒgrəfɪ] n démographie f.

demolish [dɪ'mɒlɪʃ] vt démolir. ◆demo-'lition n démolition f.

demon ['diːmən] n démon m.

demonstrate ['demənstreɪt] vt démontrer; (machine) faire une démonstration de; − vi Pol manifester. ◆demon'stration n démonstration f; Pol manifestation f. ◆de'monstrative a démonstratif. ◆demonstrator n Pol manifestant, -ante mf; (in shop etc) démonstrateur, -trice mf.

demoralize [dɪ'mɒrəlaɪz] vt démoraliser.

demote [dɪ'məut] vt rétrograder.

demure [dɪ'mjuər] a sage, réservé.

den [den] n antre m, tanière f.

denationalize [diːˈnæʃ(ə)nəlaɪz] vt dénationaliser.

denial [dɪ'naɪəl] n (of truth etc) dénégation f; (of rumour) démenti m; (of authority) rejet m; to issue a d. publier un démenti.

denigrate ['denɪgreɪt] vt dénigrer.

denim ['denɪm] n (toile f de) coton m; pl (jeans) blue-jean m.

denizen ['denɪz(ə)n] n habitant, -ante mf.

Denmark ['denmɑːk] n Danemark m.

denomination [dɪnɒmɪ'neɪʃ(ə)n] n confession f, religion f; (sect) secte m; (of coin, banknote) valeur f; Math unité f. ◆denominational a (school) confessionnel.

denote [dɪ'nəut] vt dénoter.

denounce [dɪ'nauns] vt (person, injustice etc) dénoncer (to à); to d. s.o. as a spy/etc accuser qn publiquement d'être un espion/etc. ◆denunci'ation n dénonciation f; accusation f publique.

dense [dens] a (-er, -est) dense; (stupid)

Fam lourd, bête. ◆**—ly** *adv* **d. popu-lated**/*etc* très peuplé/*etc*. ◆**density** *n* densité *f*.

dent [dent] *n* (*in metal*) bosselure *f*; (*in car*) bosse *f*, gnon *m*; **full of dents** (*car*) cabossé; **to make a d. in one's savings** taper dans ses économies; – *vt* cabosser, bosseler.

dental ['dent(ə)l] *a* dentaire; **d. surgeon** chirurgien *m* dentiste. ◆**dentist** *n* dentiste *mf*. ◆**dentistry** *n* médecine *f* dentaire; **school of d.** école *f* dentaire. ◆**dentures** *npl* dentier *m*.

deny [dɪ'naɪ] *vt* nier (*doing* avoir fait, *that* que); (*rumour*) démentir; (*authority*) rejeter; (*disown*) renier; **to d. s.o. sth** refuser qch à qn.

deodorant [diː'əʊdərənt] *n* déodorant *m*.

depart [dɪ'pɑːt] *vi* partir; (*deviate*) s'écarter (*from* de); – *vt* **to d. this world** quitter ce monde. ◆**—ed** *a* & *n* (*dead*) défunt, -unte (*mf*). ◆**departure** *n* départ *m*; **a d. from** (*custom, rule*) un écart par rapport à, une entorse à; **to be a new d. for** constituer une nouvelle voie pour.

department [dɪ'pɑːtmənt] *n* département *m*; (*in office*) service *m*; (*in shop*) rayon *m*; *Univ* section *f*, département *m*; **that's your d.** (*sphere*) c'est ton rayon; **d. store** grand magasin *m*. ◆**depart'mental** *a* **d. manager** (*office*) chef *m* de service; (*shop*) chef *m* de rayon.

depend [dɪ'pend] *vi* dépendre (**on, upon** de); **to d.** (**up)on** (*rely on*) compter sur (**for sth** pour qch); **you can d. on it!** tu peux en être sûr! ◆**—able** *a* (*person, information etc*) sûr; (*machine*) fiable, sûr. ◆**dependant** *n* personne *f* à charge. ◆**dependence** *n* dépendance *f*. ◆**dependency** *n* (*country*) dépendance *f*. ◆**dependent** *a* dépendant (**on, upon** de); (*relative*) à charge; **to be d.** (**up)on** dépendre de.

depict [dɪ'pɪkt] *vt* (*describe*) dépeindre; (*pictorially*) représenter. ◆**depiction** *n* peinture *f*; représentation *f*.

deplete [dɪ'pliːt] *vt* (*use up*) épuiser; (*reduce*) réduire. ◆**depletion** *n* épuisement *m*; réduction *f*.

deplor/e [dɪ'plɔː] *vt* déplorer. ◆**—able** *a* déplorable.

deploy [dɪ'plɔɪ] *vt* (*troops etc*) déployer.

depopulate [diː'pɒpjʊleɪt] *vt* dépeupler. ◆**depopu'lation** *n* dépeuplement *m*.

deport [dɪ'pɔːt] *vt* *Pol Jur* expulser; (*to concentration camp etc*) *Hist* déporter. ◆**depor'tation** *n* expulsion *f*; déportation *f*.

deportment [dɪ'pɔːtmənt] *n* maintien *m*.

depose [dɪ'pəʊz] *vt* (*king etc*) déposer.

deposit [dɪ'pɒzɪt] *vt* (*object, money etc*) déposer; – *n* (*in bank, wine*) & *Ch* dépôt *m*; (*part payment*) acompte *m*; (*against damage*) caution *f*; (*on bottle*) consigne *f*; **d. account** *Fin* compte *m* d'épargne. ◆**—or** *n* déposant, -ante *mf*, épargnant, -ante *mf*.

depot ['depəʊ, *Am* 'diːpəʊ] *n* dépôt *m*; (*station*) *Rail Am* gare *f*; (*bus*) **d.** *Am* gare *f* routière.

deprave [dɪ'preɪv] *vt* dépraver. ◆**depravity** *n* dépravation *f*.

deprecate ['deprɪkeɪt] *vt* désapprouver.

depreciate [dɪ'priːʃɪeɪt] *vt* (*reduce in value*) déprécier; – *vi* se déprécier. ◆**depreci-'ation** *n* dépréciation *f*.

depress [dɪ'pres] *vt* (*discourage*) déprimer; (*push down*) appuyer sur. ◆**—ed** *a* déprimé; (*in decline*) en déclin; (*in crisis*) en crise; **to get d.** se décourager. ◆**depression** *n* dépression *f*.

depriv/e [dɪ'praɪv] *vt* priver (**of** de). ◆**—ed** *a* (*child etc*) déshérité. ◆**depri'vation** *n* privation *f*; (*loss*) perte *f*.

depth [depθ] *n* profondeur *f*; (*of snow*) épaisseur *f*; (*of interest*) intensité *f*; **in the depths of** (*forest, despair*) au plus profond de; (*winter*) au cœur de; **to get out of one's d.** *Fig* perdre pied, nager; **in d.** en profondeur.

deputize ['depjʊtaɪz] *vi* assurer l'intérim (**for** de); – *vt* députer (**s.o. to do** qn pour faire). ◆**depu'tation** *n* députation *f*. ◆**deputy** *n* (*replacement*) suppléant, -ante *mf*; (*assistant*) adjoint, -ointe *mf*; **d.** (*sheriff*) *Am* shérif *m* adjoint; **d. chairman** vice-président, -ente *mf*.

derailed [dɪ'reɪld] *a* **to be d.** (*of train*) dérailler. ◆**derailment** *n* déraillement *m*.

deranged [dɪ'reɪndʒd] *a* (*person, mind*) dérangé.

derelict ['derɪlɪkt] *a* à l'abandon, aban-donné.

deride [dɪ'raɪd] *vt* tourner en dérision. ◆**derision** *n* dérision *f*. ◆**derisive** *a* (*laughter etc*) moqueur; (*amount*) dérisoire. ◆**derisory** *a* dérisoire.

derive [dɪ'raɪv] *vt* **to d. from** (*pleasure, profit etc*) *Ling* tirer de; **to be derived from** dériver de, provenir de; – *vi* **to d. from** dériver de. ◆**deri'vation** *n* *Ling* dériva-tion *f*. ◆**derivative** *a* & *n* *Ling Ch* dérivé (*m*).

dermatology [dɜːmə'tɒlədʒɪ] *n* dermato-logie *f*.

derogatory [dɪ'rɒgət(ə)rɪ] *a* (*word*) péjora-tif; (*remark*) désobligeant (**to** pour).

derrick ['derɪk] n (over oil well) derrick m.

derv [dɜːv] n gazole m, gas-oil m.

descend [dɪ'send] vi descendre (**from** de); (of rain) tomber; **to d. upon** (attack) faire une descente sur, tomber sur; (of tourists) envahir; – vt (stairs) descendre; **to be descended from** descendre de. ◆**—ing** a (order) décroissant. ◆**descendant** n descendant, -ante mf. ◆**descent** n **1** descente f, (into crime) chute f. **2** (ancestry) souche f, origine f.

describe [dɪ'skraɪb] vt décrire. ◆**description** n description f; (on passport) signalement m; **of every d.** de toutes sortes. ◆**descriptive** a descriptif.

desecrate ['desɪkreɪt] vt profaner. ◆**desecration** n profanation f.

desegregate [diː'segrɪgeɪt] vt supprimer la ségrégation raciale dans. ◆**desegregation** n déségrégation f.

desert¹ ['dezət] n désert m; – a désertique; **d. island** île f déserte.

desert² [dɪ'zɜːt] vt déserter, abandonner; **to d. s.o.** (of luck etc) abandonner qn; – vi Mil déserter. ◆**—ed** a (place) désert. ◆**—er** n Mil déserteur m. ◆**desertion** n désertion f; (by spouse) abandon m (du domicile conjugal).

deserts [dɪ'zɜːts] n **one's just d.** ce qu'on mérite.

deserv/e [dɪ'zɜːv] vt mériter (**to do** de faire). ◆**—ing** a (person) méritant; (act, cause) louable, méritoire; **d. of** digne de. ◆**—edly** [-ɪdlɪ] adv à juste titre.

desiccated ['desɪkeɪtɪd] a (des)séché.

design [dɪ'zaɪn] vt (car, furniture etc) dessiner; (dress) créer, dessiner; (devise) concevoir (**for s.o.** pour qn, **to do** pour faire); **well designed** bien conçu; – n (aim) dessein m, intention f; (sketch) plan m, dessin m; (of dress, car) modèle m; (planning) conception f, création f; (pattern) motif m, dessin m; **industrial d.** dessin m industriel; **by d.** intentionnellement; **to have designs on** avoir des desseins sur. ◆**—er** n dessinateur, -trice mf; **d. clothes** vêtements mpl griffés.

designate ['dezɪgneɪt] vt désigner. ◆**designation** n désignation f.

desir/e [dɪ'zaɪər] n désir m; **I've no d.** to je n'ai aucune envie de; – vt désirer (**to do** faire). ◆**—able** a désirable; **d. property/etc** (in advertising) (très) belle propriété/etc.

desk [desk] n Sch pupitre m; (in office) bureau m; (in shop) caisse f; (reception) **d.** réception f; **the news d.** Journ le service des

informations; – a (job) de bureau; **d. clerk** (in hotel) Am réceptionniste mf.

desolate ['desələt] a (deserted) désolé; (in ruins) dévasté; (dreary, bleak) morne, triste. ◆**desolation** n (ruin) dévastation f; (emptiness) solitude f.

despair [dɪ'speər] n désespoir m; **to drive s.o. to d.** désespérer qn; **in d.** au désespoir; – vi désespérer (**of s.o.** de qn, **of doing** de faire). ◆**—ing** a désespéré. ◆**'desperate** a désespéré; (criminal) capable de tout; (serious) grave; **to be d. for** (money, love etc) avoir désespérément besoin de; (a cigarette, baby etc) mourir d'envie d'avoir. ◆**'desperately** adv (ill) gravement; (in love) éperdument. ◆**despe'ration** n désespoir m; **in d.** (as a last resort) en désespoir de cause.

despatch [dɪ'spætʃ] see **dispatch**.

desperado [despə'raːdəʊ] n (pl -oes or -os) criminel m.

despise [dɪ'spaɪz] vt mépriser. ◆**despicable** a ignoble, méprisable.

despite [dɪ'spaɪt] prep malgré.

despondent [dɪ'spɒndənt] a découragé. ◆**despondency** n découragement m.

despot ['despɒt] n despote m. ◆**despotism** n despotisme m.

dessert [dɪ'zɜːt] n dessert m. ◆**dessertspoon** n cuiller f à dessert.

destabilize [diː'steɪbəlaɪz] vt déstabiliser.

destination [destɪ'neɪʃ(ə)n] n destination f.

destine [dɪ'stɪn] vt destiner (**for** à, **to do** à faire); **it was destined to happen** ça devait arriver. ◆**destiny** n destin m; (fate of individual) destinée f.

destitute ['destɪtjuːt] a (poor) indigent; **d. of** (lacking in) dénué de. ◆**desti'tution** n dénuement m.

destroy [dɪ'strɔɪ] vt détruire; (horse etc) abattre. ◆**—er** n (person) destructeur, -trice mf; (ship) contre-torpilleur m. ◆**destruction** n destruction f. ◆**destructive** a (person, war) destructeur; (power) destructif.

detach [dɪ'tætʃ] vt détacher (**from** de). ◆**—ed** a (indifferent) détaché; (view) désintéressé; **d. house** maison f individuelle. ◆**—able** a (lining) amovible. ◆**—ment** n (attitude) & Mil détachement m; **the d. of** (action) la séparation de.

detail [dittel, Am di'teil] n **1** détail m; **in d.** en détail; – vt raconter ou exposer en détail or par le menu, détailler. **2** Mil détacher (**to do** pour faire); – n détachement m. ◆**—ed** a (account etc) détaillé.

detain [dɪ'teɪn] vt retenir; (imprison) détenir.

◆detai'nee n Pol Jur détenu, -ue mf.
◆detention n Jur détention f; Sch retenue f.

detect [dɪ'tekt] vt découvrir; (perceive) distinguer; (identify) identifier; (mine) détecter; (illness) dépister. ◆detection n découverte f; identification f; détection f; dépistage m. ◆detector n détecteur m.

detective [dɪ'tektɪv] n agent m de la Sûreté, policier m (en civil); (private) détective m; – a (film etc) policier; d. story roman m policier; d. constable = inspecteur m de police.

deter [dɪ'tɜːr] vt (-rr-) to d. s.o. dissuader ou décourager qn (from doing de faire, from sth de qch).

detergent [dɪ'tɜːdʒənt] n détergent m.

deteriorate [dɪ'tɪərɪəreɪt] vi se détériorer; (of morals) dégénérer. ◆deterio'ration n détérioration f; dégénérescence f.

determin/e [dɪ'tɜːmɪn] vt déterminer; (price) fixer; to d. s.o. décider qn à faire; to d. that décider que; to d. to do se déterminer à faire. ◆–ed a (look, quantity) déterminé; to do or on doing décidé à faire; I'm d. she'll succeed je suis bien décidé à ce qu'elle réussisse.

deterrent [dɪ'terənt, Am dɪ'tɜːrənt] n Mil force f de dissuasion; to be a d. Fig être dissuasif.

detest [dɪ'test] vt détester (doing faire). ◆–able a détestable.

detonate ['detəneɪt] vt faire détoner ou exploser; – vi détoner. ◆deto'nation n détonation f. ◆detonator n détonateur m.

detour ['diːtuər] n détour m.

detract [dɪ'trækt] vi to d. from (make less) diminuer. ◆detractor n détracteur, -trice mf.

detriment ['detrɪmənt] n détriment m. ◆detri'mental a préjudiciable (to à).

devalue [diː'væljuː] vt (money) & Fig dévaluer. ◆devalu'ation n dévaluation f.

devastat/e ['devəsteɪt] vt (lay waste) dévaster; (opponent) anéantir; (person) Fig foudroyer. ◆–ing a (storm etc) dévastateur; (overwhelming) confondant, accablant; (charm) irrésistible.

develop [dɪ'veləp] vt développer; (area, land) mettre en valeur; (habit, illness) contracter; (talent) manifester; Phot développer; to d. a liking for prendre goût à; – vi se développer; (of event) se produire; to d. into devenir. ◆–ing a (country) en voie de développement; – n Phot développement m. ◆–er n (property) d. promoteur m (de construction).

◆–ment n développement m; (of land) mise f en valeur; (housing) d. lotissement m; (large) grand ensemble m; a (new) d. (in situation) un fait nouveau.

deviate ['diːvɪeɪt] vi dévier (from de); to d. from the norm s'écarter de la norme. ◆deviant a anormal. ◆devi'ation n déviation f.

device [dɪ'vaɪs] n dispositif m, engin m; (scheme) stratagème m; left to one's own devices livré à soi-même.

devil ['dev(ə)l] n diable m; a or the d. of a problem Fam un problème épouvantable; a or the d. of a noise Fam un bruit infernal; I had a or the d. of a job Fam j'ai eu un mal fou (doing, to do à faire); what/where/why the d.? Fam que/où/pourquoi diable?; like the d. (to run etc) comme un fou. ◆devilish a diabolique. ◆devilry n (mischief) diablerie f.

devious ['diːvɪəs] a (mind, behaviour) tortueux; he's d. il a l'esprit tortueux. ◆–ness n (of person) esprit m tortueux.

devise [dɪ'vaɪz] vt (plan) combiner; (plot) tramer; (invent) inventer.

devitalize [diː'vaɪtəlaɪz] vt rendre exsangue, affaiblir.

devoid [dɪ'vɔɪd] a d. of dénué ou dépourvu de; (guilt) exempt de.

devolution [diːvə'luːʃ(ə)n] n Pol décentralisation f; the d. of (power) la délégation de.

devolve [dɪ'vɒlv] vi to d. upon incomber à.

devot/e [dɪ'vəʊt] vt consacrer (to à). ◆–ed a dévoué; (admirer) fervent. ◆–edly adv avec dévouement. ◆devo'tee n Sp Mus passionné, -ée mf. ◆devotion n dévouement m; (religious) dévotion f; pl (prayers) dévotions fpl.

devour [dɪ'vaʊər] vt (eat, engulf, read etc) dévorer.

devout [dɪ'vaʊt] a dévot, pieux; (supporter, prayer) fervent.

dew [djuː] n rosée f. ◆dewdrop n goutte f de rosée.

dext(e)rous ['dekst(ə)rəs] a adroit, habile. ◆dex'terity n adresse f, dextérité f.

diabetes [daɪə'biːtiːz] n Med diabète m. ◆diabetic a n diabétique (mf).

diabolical [daɪə'bɒlɪk(ə)l] a diabolique; (bad) épouvantable.

diadem ['daɪədem] n diadème m.

diagnosis, pl -oses [daɪəg'nəʊsɪs, -əʊsiːz] n diagnostic m. ◆'diagnose vt diagnostiquer.

diagonal [daɪ'æg(ə)nl] n diagonale f; – n (line) diagonale f. ◆–ly adv en diagonale.

diagram ['daɪəgræm] n schéma m,

diagramme *m*; *Geom* figure *f*. ◆**dia-gra'mmatic** *a* schématique.

dial [daɪəl] *n* cadran *m*; – *vt* (**-ll-**, *Am* **-l-**) (*number*) *Tel* faire, composer; (*person*) appeler; **to d. s.o. direct** appeler qn par l'automatique; **d. tone** *Am* tonalité *f*. ◆**dialling** *a* **d. code** indicatif *m*; **d. tone** tonalité *f*.

dialect ['daɪəlekt] *n* (*regional*) dialecte *m*; (*rural*) patois *m*.

dialogue ['daɪəlɒg] (*Am* **dialog**) *n* dialogue *m*.

dialysis, *pl* **-yses** [daɪ'ælɪsɪs, -ɪsiːz] *n* *Med* dialyse *f*.

diameter [daɪ'æmɪtər] *n* diamètre *m*. ◆**dia-'metrically** *adv* (*opposed*) diamétralement.

diamond ['daɪəmənd] **1** *n* (*stone*) diamant *m*; (*shape*) losange *m*; (*baseball*) **d.** *Am* terrain *m* (de baseball). ◆**d. necklace** *etc* rivière *f*/*etc* de diamants. **2** *n* & *npl* *Cards* carreau *m*.

diaper ['daɪəpər] *n* (*for baby*) *Am* couche *f*.

diaphragm ['daɪəfræm] *n* diaphragme *m*.

diarrh(o)ea [daɪə'rɪə] *n* diarrhée *f*.

diary ['daɪərɪ] *n* (*calendar*) agenda *m*; (*private*) journal *m* (intime).

dice [daɪs] *n inv* dé *m* (à jouer); – *vt* *Culin* couper en dés.

dicey ['daɪsɪ] *a* (**-ier**, **-iest**) *Fam* risqué.

dichotomy [daɪ'kɒtəmɪ] *n* dichotomie *f*.

dickens ['dɪkɪnz] *n* **where/what/the d.?** *Fam* où/pourquoi/que diable?

dictate [dɪk'teɪt] *vt* dicter (**to** à); – *vi* dicter; **to d. to s.o.** (*order around*) régenter qn. ◆**dictation** *n* dictée *f*. ◆**'dictaphone**® *n* dictaphone® *m*.

dictates ['dɪkteɪts] *npl* préceptes *mpl*; **the d. of conscience** la voix de la conscience.

dictator [dɪk'teɪtər] *n* dictateur *m*. ◆**dicta-'torial** *a* dictatorial. ◆**dictatorship** *n* dictature *f*.

diction ['dɪk(ʃə)n] *n* langage *m*; (*way of speaking*) diction *f*.

dictionary ['dɪkʃənərɪ] *n* dictionnaire *m*.

dictum ['dɪktəm] *n* dicton *m*.

did [dɪd] *see* **do**.

diddle ['dɪd(ə)l] *vt* *Sl* rouler; **to d. s.o. out of sth** carotter qch à qn; **to get diddled out of sth** se faire refaire de qch.

die [daɪ] **1** *vi* (*pt* & *pp* **died**, *pres p* **dying**) mourir (**of, from** de); **to be dying to do** mourir d'envie de faire; **to be dying for sth** *Fam* avoir une envie folle de qch; **to d. away** (*of noise*) mourir; **to d. down** (*of fire*) mourir; (*of storm*) se calmer; **to d. off** mourir (les uns après les autres); **to d. out** (*of custom*) mourir. **2** *n* (*in engraving*) coin

m; *Tech* matrice *f*; **the d. is cast** *Fig* les dés sont jetés.

diehard ['daɪhɑːd] *n* réactionnaire *mf*.

diesel ['diːzəl] *a* & *n* **d.** (**engine**) (moteur *m*) diesel *m*; **d.** (**oil**) gazole *m*.

diet ['daɪət] *n* (*for slimming etc*) régime *m*; (*usual food*) alimentation *f*; **to go on a d.** faire un régime; – *vi* suivre un régime. ◆**dietary** *a* diététique; **d. fibre** fibre(s) *f*(*pl*) alimentaire(s). ◆**die'tician** *n* diététicien, -ienne *mf*.

differ ['dɪfər] *vi* différer (**from** de); (*disagree*) ne pas être d'accord (**from** avec). ◆**differ-ence** *n* différence *f* (**in** de); (*in age, weight etc*) écart *m*, différence *f*; **d.** (**of opinion**) différend *m*; **it makes no d.** ça n'a pas d'importance; **it makes no d. to me** ça m'est égal; **to make a d. in** sth changer qch. ◆**different** *a* différent (**from, to** de); (*another*) autre; (*various*) différents, divers. ◆**diffe-'rential** *a* différentiel; – *npl* *Econ* écarts *mpl* salariaux. ◆**diffe'rentiate** *vt* différencier (**from** de); – *vi* **to d.** (**between**) faire la différence entre. ◆**differently** *adv* différemment (**from, to** de), autrement (**from, to** que).

difficult ['dɪfɪkəlt] *a* difficile (**to do** à faire); **it's d. for us to . . .** il nous est difficile de . . . ; **the d. thing is to . . .** le plus difficile est de . . . ◆**difficulty** *n* difficulté *f*; **to have d. doing** avoir du mal à faire; **to be in d.** avoir des difficultés; **d. with** des ennuis *mpl* avec.

diffident ['dɪfɪdənt] *a* (*person*) qui manque d'assurance; (*smile, tone*) mal assuré. ◆**diffidence** *n* manque *m* d'assurance.

diffuse [dɪ'fjuːz] *vt* (*spread*) diffuser; – [dɪ'fjuːs] *a* (*spread out, wordy*) diffus. ◆**diffusion** *n* diffusion *f*.

dig [dɪg] *vt* (*pt* & *pp* **dug**, *pres p* **digging**) (*ground*) bêcher; (*hole, grave etc*) creuser; (*understand*) *Sl* piger; (*appreciate*) *Sl* aimer; **to d. sth into** (*thrust*) enfoncer qch dans; **to d. out** (*animal, fact*) déterrer; (*accident victim*) dégager; (*find*) *Fam* dénicher; **to d. up** (*weed*) déterrer; (*earth*) retourner; (*street*) piocher; – *vi* creuser; (*of pig*) fouiller; **to d. (oneself) in** *Mil* se retrancher; **to d. in** (*eat*) *Fam* manger; **to d. into** (*s.o.'s past*) fouiller dans; (*meal*) *Fam* attaquer; – *n* (*with spade*) coup *m* de bêche; (*push*) coup *m* de poing *or* de coude; (*remark*) *Fam* coup *m* de griffe. ◆**digger** *n* (*machine*) pelleteuse *f*.

digest [daɪ'dʒest] *vti* digérer; – ['daɪdʒest] *n* *Journ* condensé *m*. ◆**digestible** *a* digeste.

◆**digestion** n digestion f. ◆**digestive** a digestif.

digit ['dɪdʒɪt] n (number) chiffre m. ◆**digital** a (watch, keyboard etc) numérique.

dignified ['dɪgnɪfaɪd] a digne, qui a de la dignité. ◆**dignify** vt donner de la dignité à; **to d. with the name of** honorer du nom de. ◆**dignitary** n dignitaire m. ◆**dignity** n dignité f.

digress [daɪ'gres] vi faire une digression; **to d. from** s'écarter de. ◆**digression** n digression f.

digs [dɪgz] npl Fam chambre f (meublée), logement m.

dilapidated [dɪ'læpɪdeɪtɪd] a (house) délabré. ◆**dilapi'dation** n délabrement m.

dilate [daɪ'leɪt] vt dilater; — vi se dilater. ◆**dilation** n dilatation f.

dilemma [daɪ'lemə] n dilemme m.

dilettante [dɪlɪ'tæntɪ] n dilettante mf.

diligent ['dɪlɪdʒənt] a assidu, appliqué; **to be d. in doing sth** faire qch avec zèle. ◆**diligence** n zèle m, assiduité f.

dilly-dally [dɪlɪ'dælɪ] vi Fam (dawdle) lambiner, lanterner; (hesitate) tergiverser.

dilute [daɪ'luːt] vt diluer; — a dilué.

dim [dɪm] a (dimmer, dimmest) (feeble) faible; (colour) terne; (room) sombre; (memory, outline) vague; (person) stupide; — vt (-mm-) (light) baisser, réduire; (glory) ternir; (memory) estomper. ◆**—ly** adv faiblement; (vaguely) vaguement. ◆**—ness** n faiblesse f; (of memory etc) vague m; (of room) pénombre f. ◆**dimwit** n idiot, -ote mf. ◆**dim'witted** a idiot.

dime [daɪm] n (US & Can coin) (pièce f de) dix cents mpl; **a d. store** = un Prisunic®, un Monoprix®.

dimension [daɪ'menʃ(ə)n] n dimension f; (extent) Fig étendue f. ◆**dimensional** a **two-d.** à deux dimensions.

diminish [dɪ'mɪnɪʃ] vti diminuer. ◆**—ing** a qui diminue.

diminutive [dɪ'mɪnjʊtɪv] **1** a (tiny) minuscule. **2** a & n Gram diminutif (m).

dimple ['dɪmp(ə)l] n fossette f. ◆**dimpled** a (chin, cheek) à fossettes.

din [dɪn] **1** n (noise) vacarme m. **2** vt (-nn-) **to d. into s.o. that** rabâcher à qn que.

dine [daɪn] vi dîner (off, on de); **to d. out** dîner en ville. ◆**—ing** a **d. car** Rail wagon-restaurant m; **d. room** salle f à manger. ◆**—er** n dîneur, -euse mf; Rail wagon-restaurant m; (short-order restaurant) Am petit restaurant m.

ding(dong)! ['dɪŋ(dɒŋ)] int (of bell) dring!, ding (dong)!

dinghy ['dɪŋgɪ] n petit canot m, youyou m; (rubber) d. canot m pneumatique.

dingy ['dɪndʒɪ] a (-ier, -iest) (dirty) malpropre; (colour) terne. ◆**dinginess** n malpropreté f.

dinner ['dɪnər] n (evening meal) dîner m; (lunch) déjeuner m; (for dog, cat) pâtée f; **to have d.** dîner; **to have s.o. to d.** avoir qn à dîner; **d. dance** dîner-dansant m; **d. jacket** smoking m; **d. party** dîner m (à la maison); **d. plate** grande assiette f; **d. service, d. set** service m de table.

dinosaur ['daɪnəsɔːr] n dinosaure m.

dint [dɪnt] n **by d. of** à force de.

diocese ['daɪəsɪs] n Rel diocèse m.

dip [dɪp] n (-pp-) plonger; (into liquid) tremper, plonger; **to d. one's headlights** se mettre en code; — vi (of sun etc) baisser; (of road) plonger; **to d. into** (pocket, savings) puiser dans; (book) feuilleter; — n (in road) déclivité f; **to go for a d.** faire trempette.

diphtheria [dɪp'θɪərɪə] n diphtérie f.

diphthong ['dɪfθɒŋ] n Ling diphtongue f.

diploma [dɪ'pləʊmə] n diplôme m.

diplomacy [dɪ'pləʊməsɪ] n (tact) & Pol diplomatie f. ◆**'diplomat** n diplomate mf. ◆**diplo'matic** a diplomatique; **to be d.** (tactful) Fig être diplomate.

dipper ['dɪpər] n **the big d.** (at fairground) les montagnes fpl russes.

dire ['daɪər] a affreux; (poverty, need) extrême.

direct [daɪ'rekt] **1** a (result, flight, person etc) direct; (danger) immédiat; — adv directement. **2** vt (work, one's steps, one's attention) diriger; (letter, remark) adresser (**to** à); (efforts) orienter (**to, towards** vers); (film) réaliser; (play) mettre en scène; **to d. s.o. to** (place) indiquer à qn le chemin de; **to d. s.o. to do** charger qn de faire. ◆**direction** n direction f, sens m; (management) direction f; (of film) réalisation f; (of play) mise f en scène; pl (orders) indications fpl; **directions (for use)** mode m d'emploi; **in the opposite d.** en sens inverse. ◆**directive** [dɪ'rektɪv] n directive f. ◆**directly** adv (without detour) directement; (at once) tout de suite; (to speak) franchement; — conj Fam aussitôt que. ◆**directness** n (of reply) franchise f. ◆**director** n directeur, -trice mf; (of film) réalisateur, -trice mf; (of play) metteur m en scène. ◆**directorship** n Com poste m de directeur.

directory [daɪ'rektərɪ] n Tel annuaire m; (of

streets) guide *m*; (*of addresses*) répertoire *m*; **d. enquiries** *Tel* renseignements *mpl*.

dirge [dɜːdʒ] *n* chant *m* funèbre.

dirt [dɜːt] *n* saleté *f*; (*filth*) ordure *f*; (*mud*) boue *f*; (*earth*) terre *f*; (*talk*) *Fig* obscénité(s) *f(pl)*; **d. cheap** *Fam* très bon marché; **d. road** chemin *m* de terre; **d. track** *Sp* cendrée *f*. ◆**dirty** *a* (*-ier, -iest*) sale; (*job*) salissant; (*obscene, unpleasant*) sale; (*word*) grossier, obscène; **to get d.** se salir; **to get sth d.** salir qch; **a d. joke** une histoire cochonne; **a d. trick** un sale tour; **a d. old man** un vieux cochon; (*fight*) déloyalement; – *vt* salir; (*machine*) encrasser; – *vi* se salir.

disabl/e [dɪˈseɪb(ə)l] *vt* rendre infirme; (*maim*) mutiler. ◆**-ed** *a* infirme, handicapé; (*maimed*) mutilé; – *n* **the d.** les infirmes *mpl*, les handicapés *mpl*. ◆**disa-'bility** *n* infirmité *f*; *Fig* désavantage *m*.

disadvantage [dɪsədˈvɑːntɪdʒ] *n* désavantage *m*; – *vt* désavantager.

disaffected [dɪsəˈfektɪd] *a* mécontent. ◆**disaffection** *n* désaffection *f* (**for** pour).

disagree [dɪsəˈɡriː] *vi* ne pas être d'accord, être en désaccord (**with** avec); (*of figures*) ne pas concorder; **to d. with** (*of food etc*) ne pas réussir à. ◆**-able** *a* désagréable. ◆**-ment** *n* désaccord *m*; (*quarrel*) différend *m*.

disallow [dɪsəˈlaʊ] *vt* rejeter.

disappear [dɪsəˈpɪər] *vi* disparaître. ◆**disappearance** *n* disparition *f*.

disappoint [dɪsəˈpɔɪnt] *vt* décevoir; **I'm disappointed with it** ça m'a déçu. ◆**-ing** *a* décevant. ◆**-ment** *n* déception *f*.

disapprov/e [dɪsəˈpruːv] *vi* **to d.** of s.o./sth désapprouver qn/qch; **I d.** je suis contre. ◆**-ing** *a* (*look etc*) désapprobateur. ◆**disapproval** *n* désapprobation *f*.

disarm [dɪsˈɑːm] *vti* désarmer. ◆**disarmament** *n* désarmement *m*.

disarray [dɪsəˈreɪ] *n* (*disorder*) désordre *m*; (*distress*) désarroi *m*.

disaster [dɪˈzɑːstər] *n* désastre *m*, catastrophe *f*; **d. area** région *f* sinistrée. ◆**d.-stricken** *a* sinistré. ◆**disastrous** *a* désastreux.

disband [dɪsˈbænd] *vt* disperser; – *vi* se disperser.

disbelief [dɪsbəˈliːf] *n* incrédulité *f*.

disc [dɪsk] (*Am* **disk**) *n* disque *m*; **identity d.** plaque *f* d'identité; **d. jockey** animateur, -trice *mf* (de variétés etc), disc-jockey *m*.

discard [dɪsˈkɑːd] *vt* (*get rid of*) se débarrasser de; (*plan, hope etc*) *Fig* abandonner.

discern [dɪˈsɜːn] *vt* discerner. ◆**-ing** *a*

(*person*) averti, sagace. ◆**-ible** *a* perceptible. ◆**-ment** *n* discernement *m*.

discharge [dɪsˈtʃɑːdʒ] *vt* (*gun, accused person*) décharger; (*liquid*) déverser; (*patient, employee*) renvoyer; (*soldier*) libérer; (*unfit soldier*) réformer; (*one's duty*) accomplir; – *vi* (*of wound*) suppurer; – ['dɪstʃɑːdʒ] *n* (*of gun*) & *El* décharge *f*; (*of liquid*) & *Med* écoulement *m*; (*dismissal*) renvoi *m*; (*freeing*) libération *f*; (*of unfit soldier*) réforme *f*.

disciple [dɪˈsaɪp(ə)l] *n* disciple *m*.

discipline [ˈdɪsɪplɪn] *n* (*behaviour, subject*) discipline *f*; – *vt* (*control*) discipliner; (*punish*) punir. ◆**disci'plinarian** *n* partisan, -ane *mf* de la discipline; **to be a (strict) d.** être très à cheval sur la discipline. ◆**disci'plinary** *a* disciplinaire.

disclaim [dɪsˈkleɪm] *vt* désavouer; (*responsibility*) (dè)nier.

disclose [dɪsˈkləʊz] *vt* révéler, divulguer. ◆**disclosure** *n* révélation *f*.

disco [ˈdɪskəʊ] *n* (*pl* -os) *Fam* disco(thèque) *f*.

discolour [dɪsˈkʌlər] *vt* décolorer; (*teeth*) jaunir; – *vi* se décolorer; jaunir. ◆**disco(u)ration** *n* décoloration *f*; jaunissement *m*.

discomfort [dɪsˈkʌmfət] *n* (*physical, mental*) malaise *m*, gêne *f*; (*hardship*) inconvénient *m*.

disconcert [dɪskənˈsɜːt] *vt* déconcerter.

disconnect [dɪskəˈnekt] *vt* (*unfasten etc*) détacher; (*unplug*) débrancher; (*wires*) *El* déconnecter; (*gas, telephone etc*) couper. ◆**-ed** *a* (*speech*) décousu.

discontent [dɪskənˈtent] *n* mécontentement *m*. ◆**discontented** *a* mécontent.

discontinu/e [dɪskənˈtɪnjuː] *vt* cesser, interrompre. ◆**-ed** *a* (*article*) *Com* qui ne se fait plus.

discord [ˈdɪskɔːd] *n* discorde *f*; *Mus* dissonance *f*.

discotheque [ˈdɪskətek] *n* (*club*) discothèque *f*.

discount 1 [ˈdɪskaʊnt] *n* (*on article*) remise *f*; (*on account paid early*) escompte *m*; **at a d.** (*to buy, sell*) au rabais; **d. store** solderie *f*. **2** [dɪsˈkaʊnt] *vt* (*story etc*) ne pas tenir compte de.

discourage [dɪsˈkʌrɪdʒ] *vt* décourager; **to get discouraged** se décourager. ◆**-ment** *n* découragement *m*.

discourse [ˈdɪskɔːs] *n* discours *m*.

discourteous [dɪsˈkɜːtɪəs] *a* impoli, discourtois. ◆**discourtesy** *n* impolitesse *f*.

discover [dɪsˈkʌvər] *vt* découvrir. ◆**discovery** *n* découverte *f*.

discredit [dis'kredit] vt (cast slur on) discréditer; (refuse to believe) ne pas croire; – n discrédit m. ◆-able a indigne.

discreet [dis'kri:t] a (careful) prudent, avisé; (unassuming, reserved etc) discret. ◆discretion n prudence f; discrétion f; I'll use my own d. je ferai comme bon me semblera. ◆discretionary a discrétionnaire.

discrepancy [dis'krepənsi] n divergence f, contradiction f (between entre).

discreet/e [dis'kri:t] vi to d. between distinguer entre; to d. against établir une discrimination contre; – vt to d. sth/s.o. from distinguer qch/qn de. ◆-ing a (person) averti, sagace; (ear) fin. ◆discrimi'nation n (judgement) discernement m; (distinction) distinction f; (partiality) discrimination f. ◆discriminatory [-ətəri] a discriminatoire.

discus ['diskəs] n Sp disque m.

discuss [dis'kʌs] vt (talk about) discuter de; (examine in detail) discuter. ◆discussion n discussion f; under d. (matter etc) en question, en discussion.

disdain [dis'dein] vt dédaigner; – n dédain m. ◆disdainful a dédaigneux; to be d. of dédaigner.

disease [di'zi:z] n maladie f. ◆diseased a malade.

disembark [disim'ba:k] vti débarquer. ◆disembar'kation n débarquement n.

disembodied [disim'bodid] a désincarné.

disembowel [disim'bauəl] vt (-ll-, Am -l-) éventrer.

disenchant [disin'tʃa:nt] vt désenchanter. ◆-ment n désenchantement m.

disengage [disin'geidʒ] vt (object) dégager; (troops) désengager.

disentangle [disin'tæŋg(ə)l] vt démêler; to d. oneself from se dégager de.

disfavour [dis'feivər] n défaveur f.

disfigure [dis'figər] vt défigurer. ◆-ment n défigurement n.

disgorge [dis'gɔ:dʒ] vt (food) vomir.

disgrac/e [dis'greis] n (shame) honte f (to à); (disfavour) disgrâce f; – vt déshonorer, faire honte à. ◆-ed a (politician etc) disgracié. ◆disgraceful a honteux (of s.o. de la part de qn). ◆disgracefully adv honteusement.

disgruntled [dis'grʌnt(ə)ld] a mécontent.

disguise [dis'gaiz] vt déguiser (as en); – n déguisement m. in d. déguisé.

disgust [dis'gʌst] n dégoût m (for, at, with de); in d. dégoûté; – vt dégoûter, écœurer. ◆-ed a dégoûté (at, by, with de); to be d. with s.o. (annoyed) être fâché contre qn; d.

to hear that ... indigné d'apprendre que .... ◆-ing a dégoûtant, écœurant. ◆-ingly adv d'une façon dégoûtante.

dish [diʃ] 1 n (container) plat m; (food) mets m, plat m; the dishes la vaisselle; she's a (real) d. Sl c'est un beau brin de fille. 2 vt to d. out distribuer; to d. out or up (food) servir. ◆dishcloth n (for washing) lavette f; (for drying) torchon m. ◆dishpan n Am bassine f (à vaisselle). ◆dishwasher n lave-vaisselle m inv.

disharmony [dis'ha:məni] n désaccord m; Mus dissonance f.

dishearten [dis'ha:t(ə)n] vt décourager.

dishevelled [di'ʃevəld] a hirsute, échevelé.

dishonest [dis'ɒnist] a malhonnête; (insincere) de mauvaise foi. ◆dishonesty n malhonnêteté f; mauvaise foi f.

dishonour [dis'ɒnər] n déshonneur m; – vt déshonorer; (cheque) refuser d'honorer. ◆-able a peu honorable. ◆-ably adv avec déshonneur.

dishy [diʃi] a (-ier, -iest) (woman, man) Sl beau, sexy, qui a du chien.

disillusion [disi'lu:ʒ(ə)n] vt désillusionner; – n désillusion f. ◆-ment n désillusion f.

disincentive [disin'sentiv] n mesure f dissuasive; to be a d. to s.o. décourager qn; it's a d. to work/invest/etc cela n'encourage pas à travailler/investir/etc.

disinclined [disin'klaind] a peu disposé (to à). ◆disincli'nation n répugnance f.

disinfect [disin'fekt] vt désinfecter. ◆disinfectant a & n désinfectant (m). ◆disinfection n désinfection f.

disinherit [disin'herit] vt déshériter.

disintegrate [dis'intigreit] vi se désintégrer; – vt désintégrer. ◆disinte'gration n désintégration f.

disinterested [dis'intristid] a (impartial) désintéressé; (uninterested) Fam indifférent (in à).

disjointed [dis'dʒɔintid] a décousu.

disk [disk] n 1 Am = disc. 2 (magnetic) d. (of computer) disque m (magnétique).

dislike [dis'laik] vt ne pas aimer (doing faire); he doesn't d. it ça ne lui déplaît pas; – n aversion f (for, of pour); to take a d. to (person, thing) prendre en grippe; our likes and dislikes nos goûts et dégoûts mpl.

dislocate [dis'ləkeit] vt (limb) disloquer; Fig désorganiser. ◆dislo'cation n dislocation f.

dislodge [dis'lɒdʒ] vt faire bouger, déplacer; (enemy) déloger.

disloyal [dis'lɔiəl] a déloyal. ◆disloyalty n déloyauté f.

dismal ['dɪzməl] a morne, triste. ◆—**ly** adv (to fail, behave) lamentablement.

dismantle [dɪs'mænt(ə)l] vt (machine etc) démonter; (organization) démanteler.

dismay [dɪs'meɪ] vt consterner; – n consternation f.

dismember [dɪs'membər] vt (country etc) démembrer.

dismiss [dɪs'mɪs] vt congédier, renvoyer (from de); (official) destituer; (appeal) Jur rejeter; (thought etc) Fig écarter; **d.!** Mil rompez!; (class) **d.!** Sch vous pouvez partir. ◆**dismissal** n renvoi m; destitution f.

dismount [dɪs'maʊnt] vi descendre (from de); – vt (rider) démonter, désarçonner.

disobey [dɪsə'beɪ] vt désobéir à; – vi désobéir. ◆**disobedience** n désobéissance f. ◆**disobedient** a désobéissant.

disorder [dɪs'ɔːdər] n (confusion) désordre m; (riots) désordres mpl; **disorder(s)** Med troubles mpl. ◆**disorderly** a (meeting etc) désordonné.

disorganize [dɪs'ɔːɡənaɪz] vt désorganiser.

disorientate [dɪs'ɔːrɪənteɪt] (Am **disorient** [dɪs'ɔːrɪənt]) vt désorienter.

disown [dɪs'əʊn] vt désavouer, renier.

disparag/e [dɪs'pærɪdʒ] vt dénigrer. ◆—**ing** a peu flatteur.

disparate ['dɪspərət] a disparate. ◆**disparity** n disparité f (between entre, de).

dispassionate [dɪs'pæʃənət] a (unemotional) calme; (not biased) impartial.

dispatch [dɪs'pætʃ] vt (letter, work) expédier; (troops, messenger) envoyer; – n expédition f (of de); (troops, messenger) Journ Mil dépêche f; **d. rider** Mil etc courrier m.

dispel [dɪs'pel] vt (-ll-) dissiper.

dispensary [dɪs'pensərɪ] n (in hospital) pharmacie f; (in chemist's shop) officine f.

dispense [dɪs'pens] **1** vt (give out) distribuer; (justice) administrer; (medicine) préparer. **2** vi to **d. with** (do without) se passer de; to **d. with the need for** rendre superflu. ◆**dispen'sation** n distribution f; **special d.** (exemption) dérogation f. ◆**dispenser** n (device) distributeur m; **cash d.** distributeur m de billets.

disperse [dɪs'pɜːs] vt disperser; – vi se disperser. ◆**dispersal** n, ◆**dispersion** n dispersion f.

dispirited [dɪ'spɪrɪtɪd] a découragé.

displace [dɪs'pleɪs] vt (bone, furniture, refugees) déplacer; (replace) supplanter.

display [dɪs'pleɪ] vt montrer; (notice, electronic data etc) afficher; (painting, goods) exposer; (courage etc) faire preuve de; – n (in shop) étalage m; (of force) déploiement m; (of anger etc) manifestation f; (of paintings) exposition f; (of luxury) étalage m; Mil parade f; (of electronic data) affichage m; **d.** (unit) (of computer) moniteur m; on **d.** exposé; **air d.** fête f aéronautique.

displeas/e [dɪs'pliːz] vt déplaire à. ◆—**ed** a mécontent (with de). ◆—**ing** a désagréable. ◆**displeasure** n mécontentement m.

dispos/e [dɪs'pəʊz] vt disposer (s.o. to do qn à faire); – vi to **d. of** (get rid of) se débarrasser de; (one's time, money) disposer de; (sell) vendre; (matter) expédier, liquider; (kill) liquider. ◆—**ed** a disposé (to do à faire); **well-d.-towards** bien disposé envers. ◆—**able** a (plate etc) à jeter, jetable; (income) disponible. ◆**disposal** n (sale) vente f; (of waste) évacuation f; **at the d. of** à la disposition de. ◆**dispo'sition** n (placing) disposition f; (character) naturel m; (readiness) inclination f.

dispossess [dɪspə'zes] vt déposséder (of de).

disproportion [dɪsprə'pɔːʃ(ə)n] n disproportion f. ◆**disproportionate** a disproportionné.

disprove [dɪs'pruːv] vt réfuter.

dispute [dɪ'spjuːt] n discussion f; (quarrel) dispute f; Pol conflit m; Jur litige m; **beyond d.** incontestable; **in d.** (matter) en litige; (territory) contesté; – vt (claim etc) contester; (discuss) discuter.

disqualify [dɪs'kwɒlɪfaɪ] vt (make unfit) rendre inapte (from à); Sp disqualifier; to **d.** from driving retirer le permis à. ◆**disqualifi'cation** n Sp disqualification f.

disquiet [dɪs'kwaɪət] n inquiétude f; – vt inquiéter.

disregard [dɪsrɪ'ɡaːd] vt ne tenir aucun compte de; – n indifférence f (for à); (law) désobéissance f (for à).

disrepair [dɪsrɪ'peər] n (in a state of) **d.** en mauvais état.

disreputable [dɪs'repjʊtəb(ə)l] a peu recommandable; (behaviour) honteux.

disrepute [dɪsrɪ'pjuːt] n discrédit m; **to bring into d.** jeter le discrédit sur.

disrespect [dɪsrɪ'spekt] n manque m de respect. ◆**disrespectful** a irrespectueux (to envers).

disrupt [dɪs'rʌpt] vt perturber; (communications) interrompre; (plan) déranger. ◆**disruption** n perturbation f; interruption f;

dérangement *m.* ◆**disruptive** *a* (*element etc*) perturbateur.

dissatisfied [dɪ'sætɪsfaɪd] *a* mécontent (**with** de). ◆**dissatis'faction** *n* mécontentement *m.*

dissect [daɪ'sekt] *vt* disséquer. ◆**dissection** *n* dissection *f.*

disseminate [dɪ'semɪneɪt] *vt* disséminer.

dissension [dɪ'senʃ(ə)n] *n* dissension *f.*

dissent [dɪ'sent] *vi* différer (d'opinion) (**from sth** à l'égard de qch); – *n* dissentiment *m.* ◆**-ing** *a* dissident.

dissertation [dɪsə'teɪʃ(ə)n] *n Univ* mémoire *m.*

dissident ['dɪsɪdənt] *a & n* dissident, -ente (*mf*). ◆**dissidence** *n* dissidence *f.*

dissimilar [dɪ'sɪmɪlər] *a* dissemblable (**to** à).

dissipate ['dɪsɪpeɪt] *vt* dissiper; (*energy*) gaspiller. ◆**dissi'pation** *n* dissipation *f*; gaspillage *m.*

dissociate [dɪ'səʊʃɪeɪt] *vt* dissocier (**from** de).

dissolute ['dɪsəluːt] *a* (*life, person*) dissolu.

dissolve [dɪ'zɒlv] *vt* dissoudre; – *vi* se dissoudre. ◆**disso'lution** *n* dissolution *f.*

dissuade [dɪ'sweɪd] *vt* dissuader (**from doing** de faire); **to d. s.o. from sth** détourner qn de qch. ◆**dissuasion** *n* dissuasion *f.*

distance ['dɪstəns] *n* distance *f*; **in the d.** au loin; **from a d.** de loin; **at a d.** à quelque distance; **it's within walking d.** on peut y aller à pied; **to keep one's d.** garder ses distances. ◆**distant** *a* éloigné, lointain; (*relative*) éloigné; (*reserved*) distant; **5 km d. from** à une distance de 5 km de. ◆**distantly** *adv* **we're d. related** nous sommes parents éloignés.

distaste [dɪs'teɪst] *n* aversion *f* (**for** pour). ◆**distasteful** *a* désagréable, déplaisant.

distemper [dɪs'tempər] **1** *n* (*paint*) badigeon *m*; – *vt* badigeonner. **2** *n* (*in dogs*) maladie *f.*

distend [dɪs'tend] *vt* distendre; – *vi* se distendre.

distil [dɪs'tɪl] *vt* (**-ll-**) distiller. ◆**distillation** *n* distillation *f.* ◆**distillery** *n* distillerie *f.*

distinct [dɪs'tɪŋkt] *a* **1** (*voice, light etc*) distinct; (*definite, marked*) net, marqué; (*promise*) formel. **2** (*different*) distinct (**from** de). ◆**distinction** *n* distinction *f*; *Univ* mention *f* très bien; **of d.** (*singer, writer etc*) de marque. ◆**distinctive** *a* distinctif. ◆**distinctively** *adv* distinctement; (*to stipulate, forbid*) formellement; (*noticeably*) nettement, sensiblement; **d. possible** tout à fait possible.

distinguish [dɪs'tɪŋgwɪʃ] *vti* distinguer (**from** de, **between** entre); **to d. oneself** se distinguer (**as** en tant que). ◆**-ed** *a* distingué. ◆**-ing** *a* **d. mark** signe *m* particulier; (*discernible*) visible.

distort [dɪs'tɔːt] *vt* déformer. ◆**-ed** *a* (*false*) faux. ◆**distortion** *n El Med* distorsion *f*; (*of truth*) déformation *f.*

distract [dɪs'trækt] *vt* distraire (**from** de). ◆**-ed** *a* (*troubled*) préoccupé; (*mad with worry*) éperdu. ◆**-ing** *a* (*noise etc*) gênant. ◆**distraction** *n* (*lack of attention, amusement*) distraction *f*; **to drive to d.** rendre fou.

distraught [dɪs'trɔːt] *a* éperdu, affolé.

distress [dɪs'tres] *n* (*pain*) douleur *f*; (*anguish*) chagrin *m*; (*misfortune, danger*) détresse *f*; **in d.** (*ship, soul*) en détresse; **in (great) d.** (*poverty*) dans la détresse; – *vt* affliger, peiner. ◆**-ing** *a* affligeant, pénible.

distribute [dɪs'trɪbjuːt] *vt* distribuer; (*spread evenly*) répartir. ◆**distri'bution** *n* distribution *f*; répartition *f.* ◆**distributor** *n Aut Cin* distributeur *m*; (*of goods*) *Com* concessionnaire *mf.*

district ['dɪstrɪkt] *n* région *f*; (*of town*) quartier *m*; (*administrative*) arrondissement *m*; **d. attorney** *Am* = procureur *m* (de la République); **d. nurse** infirmière *f* visiteuse.

distrust [dɪs'trʌst] *vt* se méfier de; – *n* méfiance *f* (**of** de). ◆**distrustful** *a* méfiant; **to be d. of** se méfier de.

disturb [dɪs'tɜːb] *vt* (*sleep, water*) troubler; (*papers, belongings*) déranger; **to d. s.o.** (*bother*) déranger qn; (*alarm, worry*) troubler qn. ◆**-ed** *a* (*person etc*) *Psy* troublé. ◆**-ing** *a* (*worrying*) inquiétant; (*annoying, irksome*) gênant. ◆**disturbance** *n* (*noise*) tapage *m*; *pl Pol* troubles *mpl.*

disunity [dɪs'juːnɪtɪ] *n* désunion *f.*

disuse [dɪs'juːs] *n* **to fall into d.** tomber en désuétude. ◆**disused** [-'juːzd] *a* désaffecté.

ditch [dɪtʃ] **1** *n* fossé *m.* **2** *vt Fam* se débarrasser de.

dither ['dɪðər] *vi Fam* hésiter, tergiverser; **to d. (around)** (*waste time*) tourner en rond.

ditto ['dɪtəʊ] *adv* idem.

divan [dɪ'væn] *n* divan *m.*

div/e [daɪv] **1** *vi* (*pt* **dived**, *Am* **dove** [dəʊv]) plonger; (*rush*) se précipiter, se jeter; **to d. for** (*pearls*) pêcher; – *n* plongeon *m*; (*of submarine*) plongée *f*; (*of aircraft*) piqué *m.* **2** *n* (*bar, club*) *Pej* boui-boui *m.* ◆**-ing** *n* (*underwater*) plongée *f* sous-marine; **d. suit** scaphandre *m*; **d. board** plongeoir *m.* ◆**—er** *n* plongeur, -euse *mf*; (*in suit*) scaphandrier *m.*

diverge [daɪ'vɜːdʒ] *vi* diverger (**from** de). ◆**divergence** *n* divergence *f.* ◆**divergent** *a* divergent.

diverse [daɪ'vɜːs] *a* divers. ◆**diversify** *vt* diversifier; – *vi Econ* se diversifier. ◆**diversity** *n* diversité *f.*

divert [daɪ'vɜːt] *vt* détourner (**from** de); (*traffic*) dévier; (*aircraft*) dérouter; (*amuse*) divertir. ◆**diversion** *n Aut* déviation *f*; (*amusement*) divertissement *m*; *Mil* diversion *f.*

divest [daɪ'vest] *vt* **to d. of** (*power, rights*) priver de.

divid/e [dɪ'vaɪd] *vt* diviser (**into** en); **to d.** (**off**) **from** séparer de; **to d. up** (*money*) partager; **to d. one's time between** partager son temps entre; – *vi* se diviser. ◆**—ed** *a* (*opinion*) partagé. ◆**—ing** *a* **d. line** ligne *f* de démarcation.

dividend ['dɪvɪdend] *n Math Fin* dividende *m.*

divine [dɪ'vaɪn] *a* divin. ◆**divinity** *n* (*quality, deity*) divinité *f*; (*study*) théologie *f.*

division [dɪ'vɪʒ(ə)n] *n* division *f*; (*dividing object*) séparation *f.* ◆**divisible** *a* divisible. ◆**divisive** [-'vaɪsɪv] *a* qui sème la zizanie.

divorc/e [dɪ'vɔːs] *n* divorce *m*; – *vt* (*spouse*) divorcer d'avec; *Fig* séparer; – *vi* divorcer. ◆**—ed** *a* divorcé (**from** d'avec); **to get d.** divorcer. ◆**divorcee** [dɪvɔː'siː, *Am* dɪvɔːr'seɪ] *n* divorcé, -ée *mf.*

divulge [daɪ'vʌldʒ] *vt* divulguer.

DIY [diːaɪ'waɪ] *n abbr* (*do-it-yourself*) bricolage *m.*

dizzy ['dɪzɪ] *a* (*-ier, -iest*) (*heights*) vertigineux; **to feel d.** avoir le vertige; **to make s.o.** (**feel**) **d.** donner le vertige à qn. ◆**dizziness** *n* vertige *m.*

DJ [diː'dʒeɪ] *abbr* = disc jockey.

do [duː] **1** *v aux* (*3rd person sing pres t* **does**; *pt* **did**; *pp* **done**; *pres p* **doing**) **do you know?** savez-vous?, est-ce que vous savez?; **I do not** *or* **don't see** je ne vois pas; **he did say so** (*emphasis*) il l'a bien dit; **do stay** reste donc; **you know him, don't you?** tu le connais, n'est-ce pas?; **better than I do** mieux que je ne le fais; **neither do I** moi non plus; **so do I** moi aussi; **oh, does he?** (*surprise*) ah oui?; **don't!** non! **2** *vt* faire; **to do nothing but sleep** ne faire que dormir; **what does she do?** (*in general*), **what is she doing?** (*now*) qu'est-ce qu'elle fait?, que

fait-elle?; **what have you done (with)** . . . ? qu'as-tu fait (de) . . . ?; **well done** (*congratulations*) bravo!; *Culin* bien cuit; **it's over and done (with)** c'est fini; **that'll do me** (*suit*) ça fera mon affaire; **I've been done** (*cheated*) *Fam* je me suis fait avoir; **I'll do you!** *Fam* je t'aurai!; **to do s.o. out of sth** escroquer qch à qn; **he's hard done by** on le traite durement; **I'm done (in)** (*tired*) *Sl* je suis claqué *or* vanné; **he's done for** *Fam* il est fichu; **to do in** (*kill*) *Sl* supprimer; **to do out** (*clean*) nettoyer; **to do over** (*redecorate*) refaire; **to do up** (*coat, button*) boutonner; (*zip*) fermer; (*house*) refaire; (*goods*) emballer; **do yourself up (well!)** (*wrap up*) couvre-toi (bien)! **3** *vi* (*get along*) aller, marcher; (*suit*) faire l'affaire, convenir; (*be enough*) suffire; (*finish*) finir; **how do you do?** (*introduction*) enchanté; (*greeting*) bonjour; **he did well** *or* **right to leave** il a bien fait de partir; **do as I do** fais comme moi; **to make do** se débrouiller; **to do away with sth/s.o.** supprimer qch/qn; **I could do with** (*need, want*) j'aimerais bien (avoir *or* prendre); **to do without sth/s.o.** se passer de qch/qn; **to have to do with** (*relate to*) avoir à voir avec; (*concern*) concerner; **anything doing?** *Fam* est-ce qu'il se passe quelque chose? **4** *n* (*pl* **dos** *or* **do's**) (*party*) soirée *f*, fête *f*; **the do's and don'ts** ce qu'il faut faire ou pas faire.

docile ['dəʊsaɪl] *a* docile.

dock [dɒk] **1** *n Nau* dock *m*; – *vi* (*in port*) relâcher; (*at quayside*) se mettre à quai; (*of spacecraft*) s'arrimer. **2** *n Jur* banc *m* des accusés. **3** *vt* (*wages*) rogner; **to d. sth from** (*wages*) retenir qch sur. ◆**—er** *n* docker *m.* ◆**dockyard** *n* chantier *m* naval.

docket ['dɒkɪt] *n* fiche *f*, bordereau *m.*

doctor ['dɒktər] **1** *n Med* médecin *m*, docteur *m*; *Univ* docteur *m.* **2** *vt* (*text, food*) altérer; (*cat*) *Fam* châtrer. ◆**doctorate** *n* doctorat *m* (**in ès, en**).

doctrine ['dɒktrɪn] *n* doctrine *f.* ◆**doctri'naire** *a* & *n Pej* doctrinaire (*mf*).

document ['dɒkjʊmənt] *n* document *m*; – ['dɒkjʊment] *vt* (*inform*) documenter; (*report in detail*) *TV Journ* accorder une large place à. ◆**docu'mentary** *a* & *n* documentaire (*m*).

doddering ['dɒdərɪŋ] *a* (*senile*) gâteux; (*shaky*) branlant.

dodge [dɒdʒ] *vt* (*question, acquaintance etc*) esquiver; (*pursuer*) échapper à; (*tax*) éviter de payer; – *vi* faire un saut (de côté); **to d. out of sight** s'esquiver; **to d. through**

(*crowd*) se faufiler dans; – *n* mouvement *m* de côté; (*trick*) truc *m*, tour *m*.

dodgems ['dɒdʒəmz] *npl* autos *fpl* tamponneuses.

dodgy ['dɒdʒɪ] *a* (-ier, -iest) *Fam* (*tricky*) délicat; (*dubious*) douteux; (*unreliable*) peu sûr.

doe [dəʊ] *n* (*deer*) biche *f*.

doer ['duːər] *n Fam* personne *f* dynamique.

does [dʌz] *see* do.

dog [dɒg] **1** *n* chien *m*; (*person*) *Pej* type *m*; **d. biscuit** biscuit *m* or croquette *f* pour chien; **d. collar** *Fam* col *m* de pasteur; **d. days** canicule *f*. **2** *vt* (-gg-) (*follow*) poursuivre. ◆**d.-eared** *a* (*page etc*) écorné. ◆**d.-'tired** *a Fam* claqué, crevé. ◆**doggy** *n Fam* toutou *m*; **d. bag** (*in restaurant*) *Am* petit sac *m* pour emporter les restes.

dogged ['dɒgɪd] *a* obstiné. ◆**—ly** *adv* obstinément.

dogma ['dɒgmə] *n* dogme *m*. ◆**dog'matic** *a* dogmatique. ◆**dogmatism** *n* dogmatisme *m*.

dogsbody ['dɒgzbɒdɪ] *n Pej* factotum *m*, sous-fifre *m*.

doily ['dɔɪlɪ] *n* napperon *m*.

doing ['duːɪŋ] *n* that's your d. c'est toi qui as fait ça; **doings** *Fam* affaires *fpl*, occupations *fpl*.

do-it-yourself [duːɪtjɔːˈself] *n* bricolage *m*; – *a* (*store*, *book*) de bricolage.

doldrums ['dɒldrəmz] *npl* **to be in the d.** (*of person*) avoir le cafard; (*of business*) être en plein marasme.

dole [dəʊl] *n* **d.** (*money*) allocation *f* de chômage; **to go on the d.** s'inscrire au chômage. **2** *vt* **to d. out** distribuer au compte-gouttes.

doleful ['dəʊlfʊl] *a* morne, triste.

doll [dɒl] **1** *n* poupée *f*; (*girl*) *Fam* nana *f*; **doll's house**, *Am* **dollhouse** maison *f* de poupée. **2** *vt* **to d. up** *Fam* bichonner.

dollar ['dɒlər] *n* dollar *m*.

dollop ['dɒləp] *n* (*of food*) gros morceau *m*.

dolphin ['dɒlfɪn] *n* (*sea animal*) dauphin *m*.

domain [dəʊˈmeɪn] *n* (*land*, *sphere*) domaine *m*.

dome [dəʊm] *n* dôme *m*, coupole *f*.

domestic [dəˈmestɪk] *a* familial, domestique; (*animal*) domestique; (*trade*, *flight*) intérieur; (*product*) national; **d. science** arts *mpl* ménagers; **d. servant** domestique *mf*. ◆**domesticated** *a* habitué à la vie du foyer; (*animal*) domestiqué.

domicile ['dɒmɪsaɪl] *n* domicile *m*.

dominant ['dɒmɪnənt] *a* dominant;

(*person*) dominateur. ◆**dominance** *n* prédominance *f*. ◆**dominate** *vti* dominer. ◆**domi'nation** *n* domination *f*. ◆**domi-'neering** *a* dominateur.

dominion [dəˈmɪnjən] *n* domination *f*; (*land*) territoire *m*; *Br Pol* dominion *m*.

domino ['dɒmɪnəʊ] *n* (*pl* **-oes**) domino *m*; *pl* (*game*) dominos *mpl*.

don [dɒn] **1** *n Br Univ* professeur *m*. **2** *vt* (-nn-) revêtir.

donate [dəʊˈneɪt] *vt* faire don de; (*blood*) donner; – *vi* donner. ◆**donation** *n* don *m*.

done [dʌn] *see* do.

donkey ['dɒŋkɪ] *n* âne *m*; **for d.'s years** *Fam* depuis belle lurette, depuis un siècle; **d. work** travail *m* ingrat.

donor ['dəʊnər] *n* (*of blood*, *organ*) donneur, -euse *mf*.

doodle ['duːd(ə)l] *vi* griffonner.

doom [duːm] *n* ruine *f*; (*fate*) destin *m*; (*gloom*) *Fam* tristesse *f*; – *vt* condamner, destiner (**to** à); **to be doomed** (**to failure**) être voué à l'échec.

door [dɔːr] *n* porte *f*; (*of vehicle*, *train*) portière *f*, porte *f*; **out of doors** dehors; **d.-to-door salesman** démarcheur *m*. ◆**doorbell** *n* sonnette *f*. ◆**doorknob** *n* poignée *f* de porte. ◆**doorknocker** *n* marteau *m*. ◆**doorman** *n* (*pl* **-men**) (*of hotel etc*) portier *m*, concierge *m*. ◆**doormat** *n* paillasson *m*. ◆**doorstep** *n* seuil *m*. ◆**doorstop(per)** *n* butoir *m* (de porte). ◆**doorway** *n* **in the d.** dans l'encadrement de la porte.

dope [dəʊp] **1** *n Fam* drogue *f*; (*for horse*, *athlete*) doping *m*; – *vt* doper. **2** *n* (*information*) *Fam* tuyaux *mpl*. **3** *n* (*idiot*) *Fam* imbécile *mf*. ◆**dopey** *a* (-ier, -iest) *Fam* (*stupid*) abruti; (*sleepy*) endormi; (*drugged*) drogué, camé.

dormant ['dɔːmənt] *a* (*volcano*, *matter*) en sommeil; (*passion*) endormi.

dormer ['dɔːmər] *n* **d.** (**window**) lucarne *f*.

dormitory ['dɔːmɪtrɪ, *Am* 'dɔːmɪtɔːrɪ] *n* dortoir *m*; *Am* résidence *f* (universitaire).

dormouse, *pl* **-mice** ['dɔːmaʊs, -maɪs] *n* loir *m*.

dos/e [dəʊs] *n* dose *f*; (*of hard work*) *Fig* période *f*; (*of illness*) attaque *f*; – *vt* **to d. oneself** (**up**) se bourrer de médicaments. ◆**—age** *n* (*amount*) dose *f*.

dosshouse ['dɒshaʊs] *n Sl* asile *m* (de nuit).

dossier ['dɒsɪeɪ] *n* (*papers*) dossier *m*.

dot [dɒt] *n* point *m*; **polka d.** pois *m*; **on the d.** *Fam* à l'heure pile; – *vt* (-tt-) (*an i*) mettre un point sur. ◆**dotted** a d. line pointillé m; d. with parsemé de.

dot/e ['dəʊt] vt to d. on être gaga de. ◆**—ing** a affectueux; her d. husband/father son mari/père qui lui passe tout.

dotty ['dɒtɪ] a (-ier, -iest) Fam cinglé, toqué.

double ['dʌb(ə)l] a double; a d. bed un grand lit; a d. room une chambre pour deux personnes; d. 's' deux 's'; d. six deux fois six; d. three four two (phone number) trente-trois quarante-deux; – adv deux fois; (to fold) en deux; he earns d. what I earn il gagne le double de moi or deux fois plus que moi; to see d. voir double; – n double m; (person) double m, sosie m; (stand-in) Cin doublure f; on or at the d. au pas de course; – vt doubler; to d. back or over replier; – vi doubler; to d. back (of person) revenir en arrière; to d. up (with pain, laughter) être plié en deux. ◆**d.-'barrelled** a (gun) à deux canons; (name) à rallonges. ◆**d.-'bass** n Mus contrebasse f. ◆**d.-'breasted** a (jacket) croisé. ◆**d.-'cross** vt tromper. ◆**d.-'dealing** n double jeu m. ◆**d.-decker (bus)** n autobus m à impériale. ◆**d.-'door** n porte f à deux battants. ◆**d.-'dutch** n Fam baragouin m. ◆**d.-'glazing** n (window) double vitrage m, double(s) fenêtre(s) f(pl). ◆**d.-'parking** n stationnement m en double file. ◆**d.-'quick** adv en vitesse.

doubly ['dʌblɪ] adv doublement.

doubt [daʊt] n doute m; to be in d. about avoir des doutes sur; I have no d. about it je n'en doute pas; no d. (probably) sans doute; in d. (result, career etc) dans la balance; – vt douter de; to d. whether or that or if douter que (+ sub). ◆**doubtful** a douteux; to be d. about sth avoir des doutes sur qch; it's d. whether or that il est douteux que (+ sub). ◆**doubtless** adv sans doute.

dough [dəʊ] n pâte f; (money) Fam fric m, blé m. ◆**doughnut** n beignet m (rond).

dour ['dʊər] a austère.

douse [daʊs] vt arroser, tremper; (light) Fam éteindre.

dove¹ [dʌv] n colombe f. ◆**dovecote** [-kɒt] n colombier m.

dove² [dəʊv] Am see dive 1.

Dover ['dəʊvər] n Douvres m or f.

dovetail ['dʌvteɪl] **1** n Carp queue f d'aronde. **2** vi (fit) Fig concorder.

dowdy ['daʊdɪ] a (-ier, -iest) peu élégant, sans chic.

down¹ [daʊn] adv en bas; (to the ground) par terre, à terre; (of sun) couché; (of blind, temperature) baissé; (out of bed) descendu; (of tyre) dégonflé, (worn) usé; (in writing) inscrit; (lie) d.! (to dog) couché!; to come or go d. descendre; to come d. from (place) arriver de; to fall d. tomber (par terre); d. there or here en bas; d. with traitors/etc! à bas les traîtres/etc!; d. with (the) flu grippé; to feel d. (depressed) Fam avoir le cafard; d. to (in series, numbers, dates etc) jusqu'à; d. payment acompte m; d. at heel, Am d. at the heels miteux; – prep (at bottom of) en bas de; (from top to bottom of) du haut en bas de; (along) le long de; to go (hill etc) descendre; to live d. the street habiter plus loin dans la rue; – vt (shoot down) abattre; (knock down) terrasser; to d. a drink vider un verre. ◆**down-and-'out** a sur le pavé; – n clochard, -arde mf. ◆**downbeat** a (gloomy) Fam pessimiste. ◆**downcast** a découragé. ◆**downfall** n chute f. ◆**downgrade** vt (job etc) déclasser; (person) rétrograder. ◆**down'hearted** a découragé. ◆**down'hill** adv en pente; to go d. descendre; Fig être sur le déclin. ◆**downmarket** a Com bas de gamme. ◆**downpour** n averse f, pluie f torrentielle. ◆**downright** a (rogue etc) véritable; (refusal etc) catégorique; a d. nerve or cheek un sacré culot; – adv (rude etc) franchement. ◆**'downstairs** a (room, neighbours) d'en bas; (on the ground floor) du rez-de-chaussée; – [daʊn'steəz] adv en bas; au rez-de-chaussée; to come or go d. descendre l'escalier. ◆**down'stream** adv en aval. ◆**down-to-'earth** a terre-à-terre inv. ◆**down'town** adv en ville; d. Chicago/etc le centre de Chicago/etc. ◆**downtrodden** a opprimé. ◆**downward** a vers le bas; (path) qui descend; (trend) à la baisse. ◆**downward(s)** adv vers le bas.

down² [daʊn] n (on bird, person etc) duvet m.

downs [daʊnz] npl collines fpl.

dowry ['daʊrɪ] n dot f.

doze [dəʊz] n petit somme m; – vi sommeiller; to d. off s'assoupir. ◆**dozy** a (-ier, -iest) assoupi; (silly) Fam bête, gourde.

dozen ['dʌz(ə)n] n douzaine f; a d. (eggs, books etc) une douzaine de; dozens of Fig des dizaines de.

Dr abbr (Doctor) Docteur.

drab [dræb] a terne; (weather) gris. ◆**—ness** n caractère m terne; (of weather) grisaille f.

draconian [drə'kəʊnɪən] a draconien.

draft [drɑːft] **1** n (outline) ébauche f; (of letter etc) brouillon m; (bill) Com traite f; – vt to d. (out) (sketch out) faire le brouillon de; (write out) rédiger. **2** n Mil Am conscription f; (men) contingent m; – vt (conscript) appeler (sous les drapeaux). **3** n Am = **draught.**

draftsman ['drɑːftsmən] n = **draughtsman.**

drag [dræg] vt (-gg-) traîner, tirer; (river) draguer; **to d. sth from s.o.** (confession etc) arracher qch à qn; **to d. along** (en)traîner; **to d. s.o. away from** arracher qn à; **to d. s.o. into** entraîner qn dans; – vi traîner; **to d. on or out** (last a long time) se prolonger; – n Fam (tedium) corvée f; (person) raseur, -euse mf; (on cigarette) bouffée f (on de); **in d.** (clothing) en travesti.

dragon ['drægən] n dragon m. ◆**dragonfly** n libellule f.

drain [dreɪn] n (sewer) égout m; (pipe, channel) canal m; (outside house) puisard m; (in street) bouche f d'égout; **it's (gone) down the d.** (wasted) Fam c'est fichu; **to be a d.** on (resources, patience) épuiser; – vt (land) drainer; (glass, tank) vider; (vegetables) égoutter; (resources) épuiser; **to d. (off)** (liquid) faire écouler; **to d. of** (deprive of) priver de; – vi **to d. (off)** (of liquid) s'écouler; **to d. away** (of strength) s'épuiser; **draining board** paillasse f. ◆**-age** n (act) drainage m; (sewers) système m d'égouts. ◆**-er** n (board) paillasse f; (rack, basket) égouttoir m. ◆**drainboard** n Am paillasse f. ◆**drainpipe** n tuyau m d'évacuation.

drake [dreɪk] n canard m (mâle).

dram [dræm] n (drink) Fam goutte f.

drama ['drɑːmə] n (event) drame m; (dramatic art) théâtre m. ◆**d. critic** critique m dramatique. ◆**dra'matic** a dramatique; (very great, striking) spectaculaire. ◆**dra-'matically** adv (to change, drop etc) de façon spectaculaire. ◆**dra'matics** n théâtre m. ◆**dramatist** ['dræmətɪst] n dramaturge m. ◆**dramatize** vt (exaggerate) dramatiser; (novel etc) adapter (pour la scène or l'écran).

drank [dræŋk] see **drink.**

drap/e [dreɪp] vt draper (with de); (wall) tapisser (de tentures); – npl tentures fpl; (heavy curtains) Am rideaux mpl. ◆**-er** n marchand, -ande mf de nouveautés.

drastic ['dræstɪk] a radical, sévère; (reduction) massif. ◆**drastically** adv radicalement.

draught [drɑːft] n courant m d'air; (for fire) tirage m; pl (game) dames fpl; – a (horse) de trait; (beer) (à la) pression. **d. excluder**

bourrelet m (de porte, de fenêtre). ◆**draughtboard** n damier m. ◆**draughty** a (-ier, -iest) (room) plein de courants d'air.

draughtsman ['drɑːftsmən] n (pl -men) dessinateur, -trice mf (industriel(le) or technique).

draw[1] [drɔː] n (of lottery) tirage m au sort; Sp match m nul; (attraction) attraction f; – vt (pt **drew,** pp **drawn**) (pull) tirer; (pass) passer (over sur, into dans); (prize) gagner; (applause) provoquer; (money from bank) retirer (from, out of de); (salary) toucher; (attract) attirer; (well-water, comfort) puiser (from dans); **to d. a smile** faire sourire (from s.o. qn); **to d. a bath** faire couler un bain; **to d. sth to a close** mettre fin à qch; **to d. a match** Sp faire match nul; **to d. in** (claws) rentrer; – vi (of tea, coffee) infuser; **to d. near (to)** s'approcher (de); (of time) approcher (de); **to d. to a close** tirer à sa fin; **to d. aside** (step aside) s'écarter; **to d. away** (go away) s'éloigner; **to d. back** (recoil) reculer; **to d. in** (of days) diminuer; **to d. on** (of time) s'avancer; **to d. up** (of vehicle) s'arrêter. ◆**drawback** n inconvénient m. ◆**drawbridge** n pont-levis m.

draw[2] [drɔː] vt (pt **drew,** pp **drawn**) (picture) dessiner; (circle) tracer; (parallel, distinction) Fig faire (between entre); – vi (as artist) dessiner. ◆**-ing** n dessin m; **d. board** planche f à dessin; **d. pin** punaise f; **d. room** salon m.

drawer [drɔːr] **1** n (in furniture) tiroir m. **2** npl (women's knickers) culotte f.

drawl [drɔːl] vi parler d'une voix traînante; – n voix f traînante.

drawn [drɔːn] see **draw**[1,2]; – a (face) tiré, crispé; **d. match** or **game** match m nul.

dread [dred] vt redouter (doing de faire); – n crainte f, terreur f. ◆**dreadful** a épouvantable; (child) insupportable; (ill) malade; **I feel d. (about it)** j'ai vraiment honte. ◆**dreadfully** adv terriblement; **to be** or **feel d. sorry** regretter infiniment.

dream [driːm] vti (pt & pp **dreamed** or **dreamt** [dremt]) rêver; (imagine) songer (of à, that que); **I wouldn't d. of it!** (il n'en est pas question!; **to d. sth up** imaginer qch; – n rêve m; (wonderful thing or person) Fam merveille f; **to have a d.** faire un rêve (about de); **to have dreams of** rêver de; **a d. house/etc** une maison/etc de rêve; **a d.**

world un monde imaginaire. ◆**—er** n rêveur, -euse mf. ◆**dreamy** a (-ier, -iest) rêveur.

dreary ['drɪərɪ] a (-ier, -iest) (gloomy) morne; (monotonous) monotone; (boring) ennuyeux.

dredg/e [dredʒ] vt (river etc) draguer; — n drague f. ◆**—er** n 1 (ship) dragueur m. 2 Culin saupoudreuse f.

dregs [dregz] npl **the d.** (in liquid, of society) la lie.

drench [drentʃ] vt tremper; **to get drenched** se faire tremper (jusqu'aux os).

dress [dres] 1 n (woman's garment) robe f; (style of dressing) tenue f; **d. circle** Th (premier) balcon m; **d. designer** dessinateur, -trice mf de mode; (well-known) couturier m; **d. rehearsal** (répétition f) générale f; **d. shirt** chemise f de soirée. 2 vt (clothe) habiller; (adorn) orner; (salad) assaisonner; (wound) panser; (skins, chicken) préparer; **to get dressed** s'habiller; **dressed for tennis/etc** en tenue de tennis/etc; — vi s'habiller; **to d. up** (smartly) bien s'habiller; (in disguise) se déguiser (as en). ◆**—ing** n Med pansement m; (seasoning) Culin assaisonnement m; **to give s.o. a d.-down** passer un savon à qn; **d. gown** robe f de chambre; (of boxer) peignoir m; **d. room** Th loge f; **d. table** coiffeuse f. ◆**—er** n 1 (furniture) vaisselier m; Am coiffeuse f. 2 **she's a good d.** elle s'habille toujours bien. ◆**dressmaker** n couturière f. ◆**dressmaking** n couture f.

dressy ['dresɪ] a (-ier, -iest) (smart) chic inv; (too) habillé.

drew [druː] see **draw** [1,2].

dribble ['drɪb(ə)l] vi (of baby) baver; (of liquid) tomber goutte à goutte; Sp dribbler; — vt laisser tomber goutte à goutte; (ball) Sp dribbler.

dribs [drɪbz] npl **in d. and drabs** par petites quantités; (to arrive) par petits groupes.

dried [draɪd] a (fruit) sec; (milk) en poudre; (flowers) séché.

drier ['draɪər] n = **dryer**.

drift [drɪft] vi être emporté par le vent or le courant; (of ship) dériver; Fig aller à la dérive; (of snow) s'amonceler; **to d. about** (aimlessly) se promener sans but, traînailler; **to d. apart** (of husband and wife) devenir des étrangers l'un pour l'autre; **to d. into/towards** glisser dans/vers; — n mouvement m; (direction) sens m; (of events) cours m; (of snow) amoncellement m, congère f; (meaning) sens m général.

◆**—er** n (aimless person) paumé, -ée mf. ◆**driftwood** n bois m flotté.

drill [drɪl] 1 n (tool) perceuse f; (bit) mèche f; (for rock) foreuse f; (for tooth) fraise f; (pneumatic) marteau m pneumatique; — vt percer; (tooth) fraiser; (oil well) forer; — vi **to d. for oil** faire de la recherche pétrolière. 2 n Mil Sch exercice(s) m(pl); (procedure) Fig marche f à suivre; — vi faire l'exercice; — vt faire faire l'exercice à.

drink [drɪŋk] n boisson f; (glass of sth) verre m; **to give s.o. a d.** donner (quelque chose) à boire à qn; — vt (pt **drank**, pp **drunk**) boire; **to d. oneself to death** se tuer à force de boire; **to d. down** or **up** boire; — vi boire (out of dans); **to d. up** finir son verre; **to d. to** boire à la santé de. ◆**—ing** a (water) potable; (song) à boire; **d. bout** beuverie f; **d. fountain** fontaine f publique, borne-fontaine f; **d. trough** abreuvoir m. ◆**—able** a (fit for drinking) potable; (palatable) buvable. ◆**—er** n buveur, -euse mf.

drip [drɪp] vi (-pp-) dégouliner, dégoutter; (of washing, vegetables) s'égoutter; (of tap) fuir; — vt (paint etc) laisser couler; — n (drop) goutte f; (sound) bruit m (de goutte); (fool) Fam nouille f. ◆**d.-dry** a (shirt etc) sans repassage. ◆**dripping** n (Am **drippings**) Culin graisse f; — a & adv **d.** (**wet**) dégoulinant.

driv/e [draɪv] n promenade f en voiture; (energy) énergie f; Psy instinct m; Pol campagne f; (road to private house) allée f; **an hour's d.** une heure de voiture; **left-hand d.** Aut (vehicle m à) conduite f à gauche; **front-wheel d.** Aut traction f avant; — vt (pt **drove**, pp **driven**) (vehicle, train, passenger) conduire; (machine) actionner; **to d.** (away or out) (chase away) chasser; **to d. s.o. to do** pousser qn à faire; **to d. to despair** réduire au désespoir; **to d. crazy** rendre fou; **to d. the rain/smoke against** (of wind) rabattre la pluie/fumée contre; **to d. back** (enemy etc) repousser; (passenger) Aut ramener (en voiture); **to d. in** (thrust) enfoncer; **to d. s.o. hard** surmener qn; **he drives a Ford** il a une Ford; — vi (drive a car) conduire; **to d. along** (go, run) Aut rouler; **to d. on the left** rouler à gauche; **to d. away** or **off** Aut partir; **to d. back** Aut revenir; **to d. on** Aut continuer; **to d. to** Aut aller (en voiture) à; **to d. up** Aut arriver; **what are you driving at?** Fig où veux-tu en venir? ◆**—ing** 1 n conduite f; **d. lesson** leçon f de conduite; **d. licence**, **d. test** permis m de conduire; **d. school** auto-école

f. **2** a (*forceful*) d. force force f agissante; d. rain pluie f battante. ◆—er n (*of car*) conducteur, -trice mf; (*of taxi, lorry*) chauffeur m, conducteur, -trice mf; (*train*) d. mécanicien m; she's a good d. elle conduit bien; driver's license Am permis m de conduire.

drivel ['drɪv(ə)l] vi (**-ll-**, Am **-l-**) radoter; – n radotage m.

drizzle ['drɪz(ə)l] n bruine f, crachin m; – vi bruiner. ◆**drizzly** a (*weather*) de bruine; it's d. il bruine.

droll [drəʊl] a drôle, comique.

dromedary ['drɒmədərɪ, Am 'drɒmɪderɪ] n dromadaire m.

drone [drəʊn] **1** n (*bee*) abeille f mâle. **2** n (*hum*) bourdonnement m; (*purr*) ronronnement m; Fig débit m monotone; – vi (*of bee*) bourdonner; (*of engine*) ronronner; to d. (on) Fig parler d'une voix monotone.

drool [druːl] vi (*slaver*) baver; Fig radoter; to d. over Fig s'extasier devant.

droop [druːp] vi (*of head*) pencher; (*of eyelid*) tomber; (*of flower*) se faner.

drop [drɒp] **1** n (*of liquid*) goutte f. **2** n (*fall*) baisse f, chute f (**in** de); (*slope*) descente f; (*distance of fall*) hauteur f (de chute); (*jump*) Av saut m; – vt (**-pp-**) laisser tomber; (*price, voice*) baisser; (*bomb*) larguer; (*passenger, goods*) Aut déposer; Nau débarquer; (*letter*) envoyer (**to** à); (*put*) mettre; (*omit*) omettre; (*remark*) laisser échapper; (*get rid of*) supprimer; (*habit*) abandonner; (*team member*) Sp écarter; to d. s.o. off Aut déposer qn; to d. a line écrire un petit mot (**to** à); to d. a hint faire une allusion; to d. a hint that laisser entendre que; to d. one's h's ne pas aspirer les h; to d. a word in s.o.'s ear glisser un mot à l'oreille de qn; – vi (*fall*) tomber; (*of person*) (se laisser) tomber; (*of price*) baisser; (*of conversation*) tomber; he's ready to d. Fam il tombe de fatigue; let it d.! Fam laisse tomber!; to d. across or in passer (chez qn); to d. away (*diminish*) diminuer; to d. back or behind rester en arrière, se laisser distancer; to d. off (*fall asleep*) s'endormir; (*fall off*) tomber; (*of interest, sales etc*) diminuer. ◆d.-off n (*decrease*) diminution f (**in** de); to d. out (*fall out*) tomber; (*withdraw*) se retirer; (*socially*) se mettre en marge de la société; Sch Univ laisser tomber ses études. ◆d.-out n marginal, -ale mf; Univ étudiant, -ante mf qui abandonne ses études. ◆**droppings** npl (*of animal*) crottes fpl; (*of bird*) fiente f.

dross [drɒs] n déchets mpl.

drought [draʊt] n sécheresse f.

drove [drəʊv] see drive.

droves [drəʊvz] npl (*of people*) foules fpl; in d. en foule.

drown [draʊn] vi se noyer; – vt noyer; to d. oneself, be drowned se noyer; to d. one's sorrows noyer son chagrin; – n (*death*) noyade f. ◆—ing a qui se noie; – n (*death*) noyade f.

drowse [draʊz] vi somnoler. ◆**drowsy** a (**-ier**, **-iest**) somnolent; to feel d. avoir sommeil; to make s.o. (feel) d. assoupir qn. ◆—ily adv d'un air somnolent. ◆—iness n somnolence f.

drubbing ['drʌbɪŋ] n (*beating*) raclée f.

drudge [drʌdʒ] n bête f de somme, esclave mf du travail; – vi trimer. ◆**drudgery** n corvée(s) f(pl), travail m ingrat.

drug [drʌg] n Med médicament m, drogue f; (*narcotic*) stupéfiant m, drogue f; Fig drogue f; drugs (*dope in general*) la drogue; to be on drugs, take drugs se droguer; d. addict drogué, -ée mf; d. addiction toxicomanie f; d. taking usage m de la drogue; – vt (**-gg-**) droguer; (*drink*) mêler un somnifère à. ◆**druggist** n Am pharmacien, -ienne mf, droguiste mf. ◆**drugstore** n Am drugstore m.

drum [drʌm] n Mus tambour m; (*for oil*) bidon m; the big d. Mus la grosse caisse; the drums Mus la batterie; – vi (**-mm-**) Mil battre du tambour; (*with fingers*) tambouriner; – vt to d. sth into s.o. Fig rabâcher qch à qn; to d. up (*support, interest*) susciter; to d. up business or custom attirer les clients. ◆**drummer** n (*joueur, -euse mf de*) tambour m; (*in pop or jazz group*) batteur m. ◆**drumstick** n Mus baguette f de tambour; (*of chicken*) pilon m, cuisse f.

drunk [drʌŋk] see drink; – a ivre; d. with Fig ivre de; to get d. s'enivrer; – n ivrogne mf, pochard, -arde mf. ◆**drunkard** n ivrogne mf. ◆**drunken** a (*quarrel*) d'ivrogne; (*person*) ivrogne; (*driver*) ivre; d. driving conduite f en état d'ivresse. ◆**drunkenness** n (*state*) ivresse f; (*habit*) ivrognerie f.

dry [draɪ] a (**drier**, **driest**) sec (f. *well, river*) à sec; (*day*) sans pluie; (*toast*) sans beurre; (*wit*) caustique; (*subject, book*) aride; on d. land sur la terre ferme; to keep sth d. tenir qch au sec; to wipe d. essuyer; to run d. se tarir; to feel or be d. Fam avoir soif; d. dock cale f sèche; d. goods store Am magasin m de nouveautés; – vt sécher; (*dishes etc*) essuyer; to d. off or up sécher; – vi sécher; to d. off sécher; to d. up sécher; (*run dry*) se tarir; d. up! Fam tais-toi! ◆—ing n séchage m; essuyage m. ◆—er n (*for hair,* *clothes*) séchoir *m*; (*helmet-style for hair*) casque *m*. **◆—ness** *n* sécheresse *f*; (*of wit*) causticité *f*; (*of book etc*) aridité *f*. **◆dry-'clean** *vt* nettoyer à sec. **◆dry-'cleaner** *n* teinturier, -ière *mf*.

dual ['djuːəl] *a* double; **d. carriageway** route *f* à deux voies (séparées). **◆du'ality** *n* dualité *f*.

dub [dʌb] *vt* (**-bb-**) **1** (*film*) doubler. **2** (*nickname*) surnommer. **◆dubbing** *n* Cin doublage *m*.

dubious ['djuːbɪəs] *a* (*offer, person etc*) douteux; **I'm d.** about going or whether to go je me demande si je dois y aller; **to be d.** about sth douter de qch.

duchess ['dʌtʃɪs] *n* duchesse *f*. **◆duchy** *n* duché *m*.

duck [dʌk] *n* **1** canard *m*. **2** *vi* se baisser (vivement); — *vt* (*head*) baisser; **to d. s.o.** plonger qn dans l'eau. **◆—ing** *n* bain *m* forcé. **◆duckling** *n* caneton *m*.

duct [dʌkt] *n* Anat Tech conduit *m*.

dud [dʌd] *a* Fam (*bomb*) non éclaté; (*coin*) faux; (*cheque*) en bois; (*watch etc*) qui ne marche pas; — *n* (*person*) zéro *m*, type *m* nul.

dude [duːd] *n* Am Fam dandy *m*; **d. ranch** ranch(-hôtel) *m*.

due¹ [djuː] *a* (*money, sum*) dû (to à); (*rent, bill*) à payer; (*respect*) qu'on doit (to à); (*fitting*) qui convient; **to be d.** to échoir, il doit arriver, il est attendu; **I'm d. there** je dois être là-bas; **in d. course** (*at proper time*) en temps utile; (*finally*) à la longue; **d. to** (*attributable to*) dû à; (*because of*) à cause de; (*thanks to*) grâce à; — *n* dû *m*; *pl* (*of club*) cotisation *f*; (*official charges*) droits *mpl*; **to give s.o. his d.** admettre que qn a raison.

due² [djuː] *adv* (tout) droit; **d. north/south** plein nord/sud.

duel ['djuːəl] *n* duel *m*; — *vi* (**-ll-**, *Am* **-l-**) se battre en duel.

duet [djuː'et] *n* duo *m*.

duffel, duffle ['dʌf(ə)l] *a* **d. bag** sac *m* de marin; **d. coat** duffel-coat *m*.

dug [dʌg] *see* **dig**. **◆dugout** *n* **1** Mil abri *m* souterrain. **2** (*canoe*) pirogue *f*.

duke [djuːk] *n* duc *m*.

dull [dʌl] *a* (**-er, -est**) (*boring*) ennuyeux; (*colour, character*) terne; (*weather*) maussade; (*mind*) lourd, borné; (*sound, ache*) sourd; (*edge, blade*) émoussé; (*hearing, sight*) faible; — *vt* (*senses*) émousser; (*sound, pain*) amortir; (*colour*) ternir;

(*mind*) engourdir. **◆—ness** *n* (*of mind*) lourdeur *f* d'esprit; (*tedium*) monotonie *f*; (*of colour*) manque *m* d'éclat.

duly ['djuːlɪ] *adv* (*properly*) comme il convient (*convenant etc*); (*in fact*) en effet; (*in due time*) en temps utile.

dumb [dʌm] *a* (**-er, -est**) muet; (*stupid*) Fam idiot, bête. **◆—ness** *n* mutisme *m*; bêtise *f*. **◆dumbbell** *n* (*weight*) haltère *m*. **◆dumb'waiter** *n* (*lift for food*) monte-plats *m inv*.

dumbfound [dʌm'faʊnd] *vt* sidérer, ahurir.

dummy ['dʌmɪ] *n* **1** (*of baby*) sucette *f*; (*of dressmaker*) mannequin *m*; (*of book*) maquette *f*; (*of ventriloquist*) pantin *m*; (*fool*) Fam idiot, -ote *mf*. **2** *a* factice, faux; **d. run** (*on car etc*) essai *m*.

dump [dʌmp] *vt* (*rubbish*) déposer; **to d.** (**down**) déposer; **to d. s.o.** (*ditch*) Fam plaquer qn; — *n* (*for refuse*) décharge *f*; Mil dépôt *m*; (*dirty or dull town*) Fam trou *m*; (*house, slum*) Fam baraque *f*; (*rubbish*) Mil tas *m* d'ordures; (*place*) dépôt *m* d'ordures, décharge *f*; **to be** (**down**) **in the dumps** Fam avoir le cafard; **d. truck = dumper.** **◆—er** *n* **d.** (**truck**) camion *m* à benne basculante.

dumpling ['dʌmplɪŋ] *n* Culin boulette *f* (de pâte).

dumpy ['dʌmpɪ] *a* (**-ier, -iest**) (*person*) boulot, gros et court.

dunce [dʌns] *n* cancre *m*, âne *m*.

dune [djuːn] *n* dune *f*.

dung [dʌŋ] *n* crotte *f*; (*of cattle*) bouse *f*; (*manure*) fumier *m*.

dungarees [dʌŋgə'riːz] *npl* (*of child, workman*) salopette *f*; (*jeans*) Am jean *m*.

dungeon ['dʌndʒən] *n* cachot *m*.

dunk [dʌŋk] *vt* (*bread, biscuit etc*) tremper.

dupe [djuːp] *vt* duper; — *n* dupe *f*.

duplex ['djuːpleks] *n* (*apartment*) Am duplex *m*.

duplicate ['djuːplɪkeɪt] *vt* (*key, map*) faire un double de; (*on machine*) polycopier; — ['djuːplɪkət] *n* double *m*; **in d.** en deux exemplaires; **a d. copy/etc** une copie/*etc* en double; **a d. key** un double de la clef. **◆dupli'cation** *n* (*on machine*) polycopie *f*; (*of effort*) répétition *f*. **◆duplicator** *n* duplicateur *m*.

duplicity [djuː'plɪsɪtɪ] *n* duplicité *f*.

durable ['djuərəb(ə)l] *a* (*shoes etc*) résistant; (*friendship, love*) durable. **◆dura'bility** *n* résistance *f*; durabilité *f*.

duration [djuə'reɪʃ(ə)n] *n* durée *f*.

duress [djuə'res] *n* **under d.** sous la contrainte.

during ['djuərɪŋ] *prep* pendant, durant.

dusk [dʌsk] n (twilight) crépuscule m.

dusky ['dʌski] a (-ier, -iest) (complexion) foncé.

dust [dʌst] n poussière f; **d. cover** (for furniture) housse f; (for book) jaquette f; **d. jacket** jaquette f; – vt épousseter; (sprinkle) saupoudrer (with de). ◆**—er** n chiffon m. ◆**dustbin** n poubelle f. ◆**dustcart** n camion-benne m. ◆**dustman** n (pl **-men**) éboueur m, boueux m. ◆**dustpan** n petite pelle f (à poussière).

dusty ['dʌsti] a (-ier, -iest) poussiéreux.

Dutch [dʌtʃ] a néerlandais, hollandais; **D. cheese** hollande m; **to go D.** partager les frais (with avec); – n (language) hollandais m. ◆**Dutchman** n (pl **-men**) Hollandais m. ◆**Dutchwoman** n (pl **-women**) Hollandaise f.

duty ['djuːti] n devoir m; (tax) droit m; pl (responsibilities) fonctions fpl; **on d.** Mil de service; (doctor etc) de garde; Sch de permanence; **off d.** libre. ◆**d.-'free** a (goods, shop) hors-taxe inv. ◆**dutiful** a respectueux, obéissant; (worker) consciencieux.

dwarf [dwɔːf] n nain m, naine f; – vt (of building, person etc) rapetisser, écraser.

dwell [dwel] vi (pt & pp **dwelt**) demeurer; **to d. (up)on** (think about) penser sans cesse à; (speak about) parler sans cesse de, s'étendre sur; (insist on) appuyer sur. ◆**—ing** n habitation f. ◆**—er** n habitant, -ante m.

dwindl/e ['dwind(ə)l] vi diminuer (peu à peu). ◆**—ing** a (interest etc) décroissant.

dye [dai] n teinture f; – vt teindre; **to d. green/etc** teindre en vert/etc. ◆**dyeing** n teinture f; (industry) teinturerie f. ◆**dyer** n teinturier, -ière m.

dying ['daiiŋ] see **die 1**; – a mourant, moribond; (custom) qui se perd; (day, words) dernier; – n (death) mort f.

dyke [daik] n (wall) digue f; (ditch) fossé m.

dynamic [dai'næmik] a dynamique. ◆**'dynamism** n dynamisme m.

dynamite ['dainəmait] n dynamite f; – vt dynamiter.

dynamo ['dainəməu] n (pl **-os**) dynamo f.

dynasty ['dinəsti, Am 'dainəsti] n dynastie f.

dysentery ['disəntri] n Med dysenterie f.

dyslexic [dis'leksik] a & n dyslexique (mf).

E

E, e [iː] n E, e m.

each [iːtʃ] a chaque; – pron chacun, -une; **e. one** chacun, -une; **e. other** l'un(e) l'autre, pl les un(e)s les autres; **to see e. other** se voir (l'un(e) l'autre); **e. of us** chacun, -une d'entre nous.

eager ['iːgər] a impatient (**to do** de faire); (enthusiastic) ardent, passionné; **to be e. for** désirer vivement; **e. for** (money) avide de; **e. to help** empressé (à aider); **to be e. to do** (want) avoir envie de faire. ◆**—ly** adv (to await) avec impatience; (to work, serve) avec empressement. ◆**—ness** n impatience f (**to do** de faire); (zeal) empressement m (**to do** à faire); (greed) avidité f.

eagle ['iːg(ə)l] n aigle m. ◆**e.-'eyed** a au regard d'aigle.

ear [iər] n oreille f; **all ears** Fam tout ouïe; **up to one's ears in work** débordé de travail; **to play it by e.** Fam agir selon la situation; **thick e.** Fam gifle f. ◆**earache** n mal m d'oreille. ◆**eardrum** n tympan m. ◆**earmuffs** npl serre-tête m inv (pour protéger les oreilles), protège-oreilles m inv. ◆**earphones** npl casque m. ◆**earpiece** n écouteur m. ◆**earplug** n (to keep out noise) boule f Quiès®. ◆**earring** n boucle f d'oreille. ◆**earshot** n **within e.** à portée de voix. ◆**ear-splitting** a assourdissant.

ear² [iər] n (of corn) épi m.

earl [ɜːl] n comte m.

early ['ɜːli] a (-ier, -iest) (first) premier; (fruit, season) précoce; (death) prématuré; (age) jeune; (painting, work) de jeunesse; (reply) rapide; (return, retirement) anticipé; (ancient) ancien; **it's e.** (looking at time) il est tôt; (referring to appointment etc) c'est tôt; **it's too e. to get up/etc** il est trop tôt pour se lever/etc; **to be e.** (ahead of time) arriver de bonne heure or tôt, être en avance; (in getting up) être matinal; **in e. times** jadis; **in e. summer** au début de l'été; **one's e. life** sa jeunesse; – adv tôt, de bonne heure; (ahead of time) en avance; (to die) prématurément; **as e. as possible** le plus tôt possible; **earlier (on)** plus tôt; **at**

the earliest au plus tôt; **as e. as yesterday** déjà hier. ◆**e.-'warning system** *n* dispositif *m* de première alerte.

earmark ['ɪəmɑːk] *vt* (*funds*) assigner (**for** à).

earn [ɜːn] *vt* gagner; (*interest*) *Fin* rapporter. ◆**—ings** (*wages*) rémunérations *fpl*; (*profits*) bénéfices *mpl*.

earnest ['ɜːnɪst] *a* sérieux; (*sincere*) sincère; *– n* in **e.** sérieusement; **it's raining in e.** il pleut pour de bon; **he's in e.** il est sérieux. ◆**—ness** *n* sérieux *m*; sincérité *f*.

earth [ɜːθ] *n* (*world, ground*) terre *f*; *El* terre *f*, masse *f*; **to e.** tomber à or par terre; **nothing/nobody on e.** rien/personne au monde; **where/what on e.?** où/que diable? ◆**earthy** *a* terreux; (*person*) *Fig* terre-à-terre *inv.* ◆**earthquake** *n* tremblement *m* de terre. ◆**earthworks** *npl* (*excavations*) terrassements *mpl.* ◆**earthworm** *n* ver *m* de terre.

earthenware ['ɜːθənweər] *n* faïence *f*; *– a* en faïence.

earwig ['ɪəwɪg] *n* (*insect*) perce-oreille *m*.

ease [iːz] **1** *n* (*physical*) bien-être *m*; (*mental*) tranquillité *f*; (*facility*) facilité *f*; (*ill*) **at e.** (*in situation*) (mal) à l'aise; **at e.** (*of mind*) tranquille; (**stand**) **at e.!** *Mil* repos!; **with e.** facilement. **2** *vt* (*pain*) soulager; (*mind*) calmer; (*tension*) diminuer; (*loosen*) relâcher; **to e. off/along** enlever/déplacer doucement; **to e. oneself through** se glisser par; *– vi* **to e.** (**off** or **up**) (*of situation*) se détendre; (*of pressure*) diminuer; (*of demand*) baisser; (*of pain*) se calmer; (*not work so hard*) se relâcher. ◆**easily** *adv* facilement. **e. the best/**etc de loin le meilleur/etc; **that could e. be** ça pourrait bien être. ◆**easiness** *n* aisance *f*.

easel ['iːz(ə)l] *n* chevalet *m*.

east [iːst] *n* est *m*; **Middle/Far E.** Moyen-/Extrême-Orient *m*; *– a* (*coast*) est *inv*; (*wind*) d'est; **E. Africa** Afrique *f* de l'Est; *– adv* à l'est, vers l'est. ◆**eastbound** *a* (*carriageway*) est *inv*; (*traffic*) en direction de l'est. ◆**easterly** *a* (*point*) est *inv*; (*direction*) de l'est; (*wind*) d'est. ◆**eastern** *a* (*coast*) est *inv*; **E. France** l'Est *m* de la France; **E. Europe** Europe *f* de l'Est. ◆**easterner** *n* habitant, -ante *mf* de l'Est. ◆**eastward(s)** *a & adv* vers l'est.

Easter ['iːstər] *n* Pâques *m sing* or *fpl*; **E. week** semaine *f* pascale; **Happy E.!** joyeuses Pâques!

easy ['iːzɪ] *a* (*-ier, -iest*) facile; (*manners*) naturel; (*life*) tranquille; (*pace*) modéré; **to feel e.** in one's mind être tranquille; **to be an e. first** *Sp* être bon premier; **I'm e.** *Fam* ça m'est égal; **e.** chair fauteuil *m* (rembourré); *– adv* doucement; **go e. on** (*sugar etc*) vas-y doucement or mollo avec; (*person*) ne sois pas trop dur avec or envers; **take it e.** (*rest*) repose-toi; (*work less*) ne te fatigue pas; (*calm down*) calme-toi; (*go slow*) ne te presse pas. ◆**easy'going** *a* (*carefree*) insouciant; (*easy to get on with*) traitable.

eat [iːt] *vt* (*pt* ate [et, *Am* eɪt], *pp* eaten ['iːt(ə)n]) manger; (*breakfast, lunch*) (*one's words*) *Fig* ravaler; **to e. breakfast** or **lunch** déjeuner; (*meal*) prendre; (*one's words*) *Fig* ravaler; **what's eating you?** *Sl* qu'est-ce qui te tracasse?; **to e. up** (*finish*) finir; **eaten up with** (*envy*) dévoré de; *– vi* manger; **to e. into** (*of acid*) ronger; **to e. out** (*lunch*) déjeuner dehors; (*dinner*) dîner dehors. ◆**—ing** *a* **e.** apple pomme *f* à couteau; **e. place** restaurant *m*. ◆**—able** *a* mangeable. ◆**—er** *n* big **e.** gros mangeur *m*, grosse mangeuse *f*.

eau de Cologne [əʊdəkə'ləʊn] *n* eau *f* de Cologne.

eaves [iːvz] *npl* avant-toit *m*. ◆**eavesdrop** *vt* (**-pp-**) **to e.** (**on**) écouter (de façon indiscrète). ◆**eavesdropper** *n* oreille *f* indiscrète.

ebb [eb] *n* reflux *m*; **e. and flow** le flux et le reflux; **e. tide** marée *f* descendante; **at a low e.** *Fig* très bas; *– vi* refluer; **to e.** (**away**) (*of strength etc*) *Fig* décliner.

ebony ['ebənɪ] *n* (*wood*) ébène *f*.

ebullient [ɪ'bʌlɪənt] *a* exubérant.

eccentric [ɪk'sentrɪk] *a & n* excentrique (*mf*). ◆**eccen'tricity** *n* excentricité *f*.

ecclesiastic [ɪkliːzɪ'æstɪk] *a & n* ecclésiastique (*m*). ◆**ecclesiastical** *a* ecclésiastique.

echelon ['eʃəlɒn] *n* (*of organization*) échelon *m*.

echo ['ekəʊ] *n* (*pl* **-oes**) écho *m*; *– vt* (*sound*) répercuter; (*repeat*) *Fig* répéter; *– vi* the **explosion/**etc **echoed** l'écho de l'explosion/etc se répercuta; **to e. with the sound of** résonner de l'écho de.

éclair [eɪ'kleər] *n* (*cake*) éclair *m*.

eclectic [ɪ'klektɪk] *a* éclectique.

eclipse [ɪ'klɪps] *n* (*of sun etc*) & *Fig* éclipse *f*; *– vt* éclipser.

ecology [ɪ'kɒlədʒɪ] *n* écologie *f*. ◆**eco-'logical** *a* écologique.

economic [iːkə'nɒmɪk] *a* économique; ◆**economical** *a* (*profitable*) rentable.

économique; (*thrifty*) économe. ◆**economically** *adv* économiquement. ◆**economics** *n* (science *f*) économique *f*; (*profitability*) aspect *m* financier.

economy ['ɪkɒnəmɪ] *n* (*saving, system, thrift*) économie *f*; **e. class** *Av* classe *f* touriste. ◆**economist** *n* économiste *mf*. ◆**economize** *vti* économiser (**on** sur).

ecstasy ['ɛkstəsɪ] *n* extase *f*. ◆**ec'static** *a* extasié; **to be e. about** s'extasier sur. ◆**ec'statically** *adv* avec extase.

ecumenical [iːkjuːˈmɛnɪk(ə)l] *a* œcuménique.

eczema ['ɛksɪmə] *n Med* eczéma *m*.

eddy ['ɛdɪ] *n* tourbillon *m*, remous *m*.

edg/e [ɛdʒ] *n* bord *m*; (*of forest*) lisière *f*; (*of town*) abords *mpl*; (*of page*) marge *f*; (*of knife etc*) tranchant *m*, fil *m*; **on e.** (*person*) énervé; (*nerves*) tendu; **to set s.o.'s teeth on e.** (*irritate s.o.*) crisper qn, faire grincer les dents à qn; **to have the e. or a slight e.** *Fig* être légèrement supérieur (**over, on** à); – *vt* (*clothing etc*) border (**with** de); – *vti* **to e.** (**oneself**) **into** (*move*) se glisser dans; **to e.** (**oneself**) **forward** avancer doucement. ◆**—ing** *n* (*border*) bordure *f*. ◆**edgeways** *adv* de côté; **to get a word in e.** *Fam* placer un mot.

edgy ['ɛdʒɪ] *a* (-**ier**, -**iest**) énervé. ◆**edginess** *n* nervosité *f*.

edible ['ɛdɪb(ə)l] *a* (*mushroom, berry etc*) comestible; (*meal, food*) mangeable.

edict ['iːdɪkt] *n* décret *m*; *Hist* édit *m*.

edifice ['ɛdɪfɪs] *n* (*building, organization*) édifice *m*.

edify ['ɛdɪfaɪ] *vt* (*improve the mind of*) édifier.

Edinburgh ['ɛdɪnb(ə)rə] *n* Édimbourg *m or f*.

edit ['ɛdɪt] *vt* (*newspaper etc*) diriger; (*article etc*) mettre au point; (*film*) monter; (*annotate*) éditer; (*compile*) rédiger; **to e.** (**out**) (*cut out*) couper. ◆**editor** *n* (*of review*) directeur, -trice *mf*; (*compiler*) rédacteur, -trice *mf*; *TV Rad* réalisateur, -trice *mf*; **sports e.** *Journ* rédacteur *m* sportif, rédactrice *f* sportive; **the e. (in chief)** (*of newspaper*) le rédacteur *m* en chef. ◆**edi'torial** *a* de la rédaction; **e. staff** rédaction *f*; – *n* éditorial *m*.

edition [ɪ'dɪʃ(ə)n] *n* édition *f*.

educat/e ['ɛdjʊkeɪt] *vt* (*family, children*) éduquer; (*pupil*) instruire; (*mind*) former, éduquer; **to be educated at** faire ses études à. ◆**—ed** *a* (*voice*) cultivé; (**well-**)**e.** (*person*) instruit. ◆**edu'cation** *n* éducation *f*; (*teaching*) instruction *f*, enseigne-

ment *m*; (*training*) formation *f*; (*subject*) *Univ* pédagogie *f*. ◆**edu'cational** *a* (*establishment*) d'enseignement; (*method*) pédagogique; (*game*) éducatif; (*supplies*) scolaire. ◆**edu'cationally** *adv* du point de vue de l'éducation. ◆**educator** *n* éducateur, -trice *mf*.

EEC [iːiːˈsiː] *n abbr* (*European Economic Community*) CEE *f*.

eel [iːl] *n* anguille *f*.

eerie ['ɪərɪ] *a* (-**ier**, -**iest**) sinistre, étrange.

efface [ɪ'feɪs] *vt* effacer.

effect [ɪ'fɛkt] **1** *n* (*result, impression*) effet *m* (**on** sur); *pl* (*goods*) biens *mpl*; **to no e.** en vain; **in e.** en fait; **to put into e.** mettre en application, faire entrer en vigueur; **to come into e., take e.** entrer en vigueur; **to take e.** (*of drug etc*) agir; **to have an e.** (*of medicine etc*) faire de l'effet; **to have no e.** rester sans effet; **to this e.** (*in this meaning*) dans ce sens; **to the e. that** (*saying that*) comme quoi. **2** *vt* (*carry out*) effectuer, réaliser.

effective [ɪ'fɛktɪv] *a* (*efficient*) efficace; (*actual*) effectif; (*striking*) frappant; **to become e.** (*of law*) prendre effet. ◆**—ly** *adv* efficacement; (*in effect*) effectivement. ◆**—ness** *n* efficacité *f*; (*quality*) effet *m* frappant.

effeminate [ɪ'fɛmɪnət] *a* efféminé.

effervescent [ɛfə'vɛs(ə)nt] *a* (*mixture, youth*) effervescent; (*drink*) gazeux. ◆**effervesce** *vi* (*of drink*) pétiller. ◆**effervescence** *n* (*excitement*) & *Ch* effervescence *f*; pétillement *m*.

effete [ɪ'fiːt] *a* (*feeble*) mou, faible; (*decadent*) décadent.

efficient [ɪ'fɪʃ(ə)nt] *a* (*method*) efficace; (*person*) compétent, efficace; (*organization*) efficace, performant; (*machine*) performant, à haut rendement. ◆**efficiency** *n* efficacité *f*; compétence *f*; performances *fpl*. ◆**efficiently** *adv* efficacement; avec compétence; **to work e.** (*of machine*) bien fonctionner.

effigy ['ɛfɪdʒɪ] *n* effigie *f*.

effort ['ɛfət] *n* effort *m*; **to make an e.** faire un effort (**to pour**); **it isn't worth the e.** ça ne or n'en vaut pas la peine; **his** *or* **her latest e.** *Fam* ses dernières tentatives. ◆**—less** *a* (*victory etc*) facile. ◆**—lessly** *adv* facilement, sans effort.

effrontery [ɪ'frʌntərɪ] *n* effronterie *f*.

effusive [ɪ'fjuːsɪv] *a* (*person*) expansif; (*thanks, excuses*) sans fin. ◆**—ly** *adv* avec effusion.

e.g. [ˌiːˈdʒiː] *abbr* (*exempli gratia*) par exemple.

egalitarian [ɪɡælɪˈteərɪən] *a* (*society etc*) égalitaire.

egg [eg] *n* œuf *m*; **e. timer** sablier *m*; **e. whisk** fouet *m* (à œufs). ◆**eggcup** *n* coquetier *m*. ◆**egghead** *n Pej* intellectuel, -elle *mf*. ◆**eggplant** *n* aubergine *f*. ◆**eggshell** *n* coquille *f*.

egg [eg] *vt* **to e. on** (*encourage*) inciter (**to do** à faire).

ego [ˈiːɡəʊ] *n* (*pl* -**os**) **the e.** *Psy* le moi. ◆**ego'centric** *a* égocentrique. ◆**egoism** *n* égoïsme *m*. ◆**egoist** *n* égoïste *mf*. ◆**ego'istic(al)** *a* égoïste. ◆**egotism** *n* égotisme *m*.

Egypt [ˈiːdʒɪpt] *n* Égypte *f*. ◆**E'gyptian** *a* & *n* égyptien, -ienne (*mf*).

eh? [eɪ] *int Fam* hein?

eiderdown [ˈaɪdədaʊn] *n* édredon *m*.

eight [eɪt] *a* & *n* huit (*m*). ◆**eigh'teen** *a* & *n* dix-huit (*m*). ◆**eigh'teenth** *a* & *n* dix-huitième (*mf*). ◆**eighth** *a* & *n* huitième (*mf*); **an e.** un huitième. ◆**eighth** *a* & *n* quatre-vingtième (*mf*). ◆**eighty** *a* & *n* quatre-vingts (*m*); **e.-one** quatre-vingt-un.

Eire [ˈeərə] *n* République *f* d'Irlande.

either [ˈaɪðər] **1** *a* & *pron* (*one or other*) l'un(e) ou l'autre; (*with negative*) ni l'un(e) ni l'autre; (*each*) chaque; **on e. side of** de chaque côté, des deux côtés. **2** *adv* she can't swim e. elle ne sait pas nager non plus; **I don't e.** (ni) moi non plus; **not so far off e.** (*moreover*) pas si loin d'ailleurs. **3** *conj* e. ... or ou (bien) ... ou (bien), soit ... soit; (*with negative*) ni ... ni.

eject [ɪˈdʒekt] *vt* expulser; *Tech* éjecter. ◆**ejector** *a* **e. seat** *Av* siège *m* éjectable.

eke [iːk] *vt* **to e. out** (*income etc*) faire durer; **to e. out a living** gagner (difficilement) sa vie.

elaborate [ɪˈlæbərət] *a* compliqué, détaillé; (*preparation*) minutieux; (*style*) recherché; (*meal*) raffiné; — [ɪˈlæbəreɪt] *vt* (*theory etc*) élaborer; — *vi* entrer dans les détails (**on** de). ◆—**ly** *adv* (*to plan*) minutieusement; (*to decorate*) avec recherche. ◆**elabo-'ration** *n* élaboration *f*.

elapse [ɪˈlæps] *vi* s'écouler.

elastic [ɪˈlæstɪk] *a* (*object, character*) élastique; **e. band** élastique *m*; — *n* (*fabric*) élastique *m*. ◆**ela'sticity** *n* élasticité *f*.

elated [ɪˈleɪtɪd] *a* transporté de joie. ◆**ela-tion** *n* exaltation *f*.

elbow [ˈelbəʊ] *n* coude *m*; **e. grease** *Fam* huile *f* de coude; **to have enough e. room**

avoir assez de place; — *vt* **to e. one's way** frayer un chemin (à coups de coude) (**through** à travers).

elder [ˈeldər] *a* & *n* (*of two people*) aîné, -ée (*mf*). ◆**elderly** *a* assez âgé, entre deux âges. ◆**eldest** *a* & *n* aîné, -ée (*mf*); **his** *or* **her e.** brother l'aîné de ses frères.

elder [ˈeldər] *n* (*tree*) sureau *m*.

elect [ɪˈlekt] *vt Pol* élire (**to** à); **to e. to do** choisir de faire; — *a* **the president**/*etc* **e.** le président/*etc* désigné. ◆**election** *n* élection *f*; **general e.** élections *fpl* législatives; — **(campaign)** électoral; (**day, results**) du scrutin, des élections. ◆**electio'neering** *n* campagne *f* électorale. ◆**elective** *a* (*course*) *Am* facultatif. ◆**electoral** *a* électoral. ◆**electorate** *n* électorat *m*.

electric [ɪˈlektrɪk] *a* électrique; **e. blanket** couverture *f* chauffante; **e. shock** décharge *f* électrique; **e. shock treatment** électrochoc *m*. ◆**electrical** *a* électrique; **e. engineer** ingénieur *m* électricien. ◆**elec'trician** *n* électricien *m*. ◆**elec'tricity** *n* électricité *f*. ◆**electrify** *vt Rail* électrifier; (*excite*) *Fig* électriser. ◆**electrocute** *vt* électrocuter.

electrode [ɪˈlektrəʊd] *n El* électrode *f*.

electron [ɪˈlektron] *n* électron *m*; — *a* (*microscope*) électronique. ◆**elec'tronic** *a* électronique. ◆**elec'tronics** *n* électronique *f*.

elegant [ˈelɪɡənt] *a* élégant. ◆**elegance** *n* élégance *f*. ◆**elegantly** *adv* avec élégance, élégamment.

elegy [ˈelədʒɪ] *n* élégie *f*.

element [ˈelɪmənt] *n* (*component, environment*) élément *m*; (*of heater*) résistance *f*; **an e. of truth** un grain *or* une part de vérité; **the human/chance e.** le facteur humain/chance; **in one's e.** dans son élément. ◆**ele'mental** *a* élémentaire. ◆**ele'mentary** *a* élémentaire; (*school*) *Am* primaire; **e. courtesy** la courtoisie la plus élémentaire.

elephant [ˈelɪfənt] *n* éléphant *m*. ◆**ele-phantine** [elɪˈfæntaɪn] *a* (*large*) éléphantesque; (*clumsy*) gauche.

elevate [ˈelɪveɪt] *vt* élever (**to** à). ◆**ele-'vation** *n* élévation *f* (**of** de); (*height*) altitude *f*. ◆**elevator** *n Am* ascenseur *m*.

eleven [ɪˈlev(ə)n] *a* & *n* onze (*m*). ◆**elevenses** [ɪˈlev(ə)nzɪz] *n Fam* pause-café *f* (*vers onze heures du matin*). ◆**eleventh** *a* & *n* onzième (*mf*).

elf [elf] *n* (*pl* **elves**) lutin *m*.

elicit [ɪˈlɪsɪt] *vt* tirer, obtenir (**from** de).

elide [ɪˈlaɪd] *vt Ling* élider. ◆**elision** *n* élision *f*.

eligible ['elɪdʒəb(ə)l] *a* (*for post etc*) admissible (**for** à); (*for political office*) éligible (**for** à); **to be e. for** (*entitled to*) avoir droit à; **an e. young man** (*suitable as husband*) un beau parti. ◆**eligi'bility** *n* admissibilité *f*; *Pol* éligibilité *f*.

eliminate [ɪ'lɪmɪneɪt] *vt* éliminer (**from** de). ◆**elimi'nation** *n* élimination *f*.

elite [eɪ'liːt] *n* élite *f* (**of** de).

elk [elk] *n* (*animal*) élan *m*.

ellipse [ɪ'lɪps] *n Geom* ellipse *f*. ◆**elliptical** *a* elliptique.

elm [elm] *n* (*tree, wood*) orme *m*.

elocution [elə'kjuːʃ(ə)n] *n* élocution *f*.

elongate ['iːlɒŋgeɪt] *vt* allonger. ◆**elon'gation** *n* allongement *m*.

elope [ɪ'ləʊp] *vi* (*of lovers*) s'enfuir (**with** avec). ◆**—ment** *n* fugue *f* (amoureuse).

eloquent ['eləkwənt] *a* éloquent. ◆**eloquence** *n* éloquence *f*.

else [els] *adv* d'autre; **someone e.** quelqu'un d'autre; **everybody e.** tout le monde à part moi, vous *etc*, tous les autres; **nobody/nothing e.** personne/rien d'autre; **something e.** autre chose; **something** *or* **anything e.?** encore quelque chose? **somewhere e.** ailleurs, autre part; **who e.?** qui encore?, qui d'autre? **how e.?** de quelle autre façon?; **or e.** ou bien, sinon. ◆**elsewhere** *adv* ailleurs; **e. in the town** dans une autre partie de la ville.

elucidate [ɪ'luːsɪdeɪt] *vt* élucider.

elude [ɪ'luːd] *vt* (*enemy*) échapper à; (*question*) éluder; (*obligation*) se dérober à; (*blow*) esquiver. ◆**elusive** *a* (*enemy, aims*) insaisissable; (*reply*) évasif.

emaciated [ɪ'meɪsɪeɪtɪd] *a* émacié.

emanate ['eməneɪt] *vi* émaner (**from** de).

emancipate [ɪ'mænsɪpeɪt] *vt* (*women*) émanciper. ◆**emanci'pation** *n* émancipation *f*.

embalm [ɪm'bɑːm] *vt* (*dead body*) embaumer.

embankment [ɪm'bæŋkmənt] *n* (*of path etc*) talus *m*; (*of river*) berge *f*.

embargo [ɪm'bɑːgəʊ] *n* (*pl* -oes) embargo *m*.

embark [ɪm'bɑːk] *vt* embarquer; – *vi* (s')embarquer; **to e. on** (*start*) commencer, entamer; (*launch into*) se lancer dans, s'embarquer dans. ◆**embar'kation** *n* embarquement *m*.

embarrass [ɪm'bærəs] *vt* embarrasser, gêner. ◆**—ing** *a* (*question etc*) embarrassant. ◆**—ment** *n* embarras *m*, gêne *f*; (*financial*) embarras *mpl*.

embassy ['embəsɪ] *n* ambassade *f*.

embattled [ɪm'bæt(ə)ld] *a* (*political party, person etc*) assiégé de toutes parts; (*attitude*) belliqueux.

embedded [ɪm'bedɪd] *a* (*stick, bullet*) enfoncé; (*jewel*) & *Ling* enchâssé; (*in one's memory*) gravé; (*in stone*) scellé.

embellish [ɪm'belɪʃ] *vt* embellir. ◆**—ment** *n* embellissement *m*.

embers ['embəz] *npl* braise *f*, charbons *mpl* ardents.

embezzl/e [ɪm'bez(ə)l] *vt* (*money*) détourner. ◆**—ement** *n* détournement *m* de fonds. ◆**—er** *n* escroc *m*, voleur *m*.

embitter [ɪm'bɪtər] *vt* (*person*) aigrir; (*situation*) envenimer.

emblem ['embləm] *n* emblème *m*.

embody [ɪm'bɒdɪ] *vt* (*express*) exprimer; (*represent*) incarner; (*include*) réunir. ◆**embodiment** *n* incarnation *f* (**of** de).

emboss [ɪm'bɒs] *vt* (*metal*) emboutir; (*paper*) gaufrer, emboutir. ◆**—ed** *a* en relief.

embrace [ɪm'breɪs] *vt* étreindre, embrasser; (*include, adopt*) embrasser; – *vi* s'étreindre, s'embrasser; – *n* étreinte *f*.

embroider [ɪm'brɔɪdər] *vt* (*cloth*) broder; (*story, facts*) *Fig* enjoliver. ◆**embroidery** *n* broderie *f*.

embroil [ɪm'brɔɪl] *vt* **to e. s.o. in** mêler qn à.

embryo ['embrɪəʊ] *n* (*pl* -os) embryon *m*. ◆**embry'onic** *a Med* & *Fig* embryonnaire.

emcee [em'siː] *n Am* présentateur, -trice *mf*.

emend [ɪ'mend] *vt* (*text*) corriger.

emerald ['emərəld] *n* émeraude *f*.

emerge [ɪ'mɜːdʒ] *vi* apparaître (**from** de); (*from hole etc*) sortir; (*of truth, from water*) émerger; (*of nation*) naître; **it emerges that** il apparaît que. ◆**emergence** *n* apparition *f*.

emergency [ɪ'mɜːdʒənsɪ] *n* (*case*) urgence *f*; (*crisis*) crise *f*; (*contingency*) éventualité *f*; **in an e.** en cas d'urgence; – *a* (*measure etc*) d'urgence; (*exit, brake*) de secours; (*ward, services*) *Med* des urgences; **e. landing** atterrissage *m* forcé; **e. powers** *Pol* pouvoirs *mpl* extraordinaires.

emery ['emərɪ] *a* **e. cloth** toile *f* (d')émeri.

emigrant ['emɪgrənt] *n* émigrant, émigré. ◆**emigrate** *vi* émigrer. ◆**emi'gration** *n* émigration *f*.

eminent ['emɪnənt] *a* éminent. ◆**eminence** *n* distinction *f*; **his E.** *Rel* son Éminence *f*. ◆**eminently** *adv* hautement, remarquablement.

emissary ['emɪsərɪ] *n* émissaire *m*.

emit [ɪ'mɪt] *vt* (-tt-) (*light, heat etc*) émettre;

(*smell*) dègager. ◆**emission** n émission f; dégagement m.

emotion [ɪ'məʊʃ(ə)n] n (*strength of feeling*) émotion f; (*joy, love etc*) sentiment m. ◆**emotional** a (*person, reaction*) émotif; (*story, speech*) émouvant; (*moment*) d'émotion intense; (*state*) Psy émotionnel. ◆**emotionally** adv (*to say*) avec émotion; **to be e. unstable** avoir des troubles émotifs. ◆**emotive** a (*person*) émotif; (*word*) affectif; **an e. issue** une question sensible.

emperor ['empərər] n empereur m.

emphasize ['emfəsaɪz] vt souligner (*that* que); (*word, fact*) appuyer or insister sur, souligner. ◆**emphasis** n Ling accent m (tonique); (*insistence*) insistance f; **to lay** or **put e. on** mettre l'accent sur. ◆**em'phatic** a (*person, refusal*) catégorique; (*forceful*) énergique; **to be e. about** insister sur. ◆**em'phatically** adv catégoriquement; énergiquement; **e. no!** absolument pas!

empire ['empaɪər] n empire m.

empirical [em'pɪrɪk(ə)l] a empirique. ◆**empiricism** n empirisme m.

employ [ɪm'plɔɪ] vt (*person, means*) employer; – n **in the e. of** employé par. ◆**employee** [ɪm'plɔɪiː, emplɔɪ'iː] n employé, -ée mf. ◆**employer** n patron, -onne mf. ◆**employment** n emploi m; **place of e.** lieu m de travail; **in the e. of** employé par; **e. agency** bureau m de placement.

empower [ɪm'paʊər] vt autoriser (**to do** à faire).

empress ['emprɪs] n impératrice f.

empt/y ['empti] a (**-ier, -iest**) vide; (*threat, promise etc*) vain; (*stomach*) creux; **on an e. stomach** à jeun; **to return/etc e.-handed** revenir/etc les mains vides; – npl (*bottles*) bouteilles fpl vides; – vt **to e.** (**out**) (*box, pocket, liquid etc*) vider; (*vehicle*) décharger; (*objects in box etc*) sortir (**from, out of** de); – vi se vider; (*of river*) se jeter (**into** dans). ◆**-iness** n vide m.

emulate ['emjʊleɪt] vt imiter. ◆**emu'lation** n émulation f.

emulsion [ɪ'mʌlʃ(ə)n] n (*paint*) peinture f (mate); Phot émulsion f.

enable [ɪ'neɪb(ə)l] vt **to e. s.o. to do** permettre à qn de faire.

enact [ɪn'ækt] vt (*law*) promulguer; (*part of play*) jouer.

enamel [ɪ'næm(ə)l] n émail m; – a en émail; – vt (**-ll-, Am -l-**) émailler.

enamoured [ɪn'æməd] a **e. of** (*thing*) séduit par; (*person*) amoureux de.

encamp [ɪn'kæmp] vi camper. ◆**-ment** n campement m.

encapsulate [ɪn'kæpsjʊleɪt] vt Fig résumer.

encase [ɪn'keɪs] vt recouvrir (**in** de).

enchant [ɪn'tʃɑːnt] vt enchanter. ◆**-ing** a enchanteur. ◆**-ment** n enchantement m.

encircle [ɪn'sɜːk(ə)l] vt entourer; Mil encercler. ◆**-ment** n encerclement m.

enclave ['enkleɪv] n enclave f.

enclos/e [ɪn'kləʊz] vt (*send with letter*) joindre (**in, with** à); (*fence off*) clôturer; **to e. with** (*a fence, wall*) entourer de. ◆**-ed** a (*space*) clos; (*cheque etc*) ci-joint; (*market*) couvert. ◆**enclosure** n Com pièce f jointe; (*fence, place*) enceinte f.

encompass [ɪn'kʌmpəs] vt (*surround*) entourer; (*include*) inclure.

encore ['ɒŋkɔː] int & n bis (m); – vt bisser.

encounter [ɪn'kaʊntər] vt rencontrer; – n rencontre f.

encourage [ɪn'kʌrɪdʒ] vt encourager (**to do** à faire). ◆**-ment** n encouragement m.

encroach [ɪn'krəʊtʃ] vi empiéter (**on, upon** sur); **to e. on the land/** (*of sea*) gagner du terrain. ◆**-ment** n empiétement m.

encumber [ɪn'kʌmbər] vt encombrer (**with** de). ◆**encum'brance** n embarras m.

encyclical [ɪn'sɪklɪk(ə)l] n Rel encyclique f.

encyclop(a)edia [ɪnsaɪklə'piːdɪə] n encyclopédie f. ◆**encyclop(a)edic** a encyclopédique.

end [end] n (*of street, object etc*) bout m, extrémité f; (*of time, meeting, book etc*) fin f; (*purpose*) fin f, but m; **at an e.** (*discussion etc*) fini; (*period*) écoulé; (*patience*) à bout; **in the e.** à la fin; **to come to an e.** prendre fin; **to put an e. to, bring to an e.** mettre fin à; **there's no e. to it** ça n'en finit plus; **no e. of** Fam beaucoup de; **six days on e.** six jours d'affilée; **for days on e.** pendant des jours (et des jours); (**standing**) **on e.** (*box etc*) debout; (*hair*) hérissé; – a (*row, house*) dernier; **e. product** Com produit m fini; Fig résultat m; – vt finir, terminer, achever (**with** par); (*rumour, speculation*) mettre fin à; – vi finir, se terminer, s'achever; **to e. in failure** se solder par un échec; **to e. in a point** finir en pointe; **to e. up doing** finir par faire; **to e. up in** (*London etc*) se retrouver à; **he ended up in prison/a doctor** il a fini en prison/par devenir médecin.

endanger [ɪn'deɪndʒər] vt mettre en danger.

endear [ɪn'dɪər] vt faire aimer or apprécier (**to** de); **that's what endears him to me** c'est cela qui me plaît en lui. ◆**-ing** a attachant, sympathique. ◆**-ment** n

endeavour [in'devər] vi s'efforcer (to do faire); – n effort m (to do pour faire).

ending ['endiŋ] n fin f; (outcome) issue f; *Ling* terminaison f. ◆**endless** a (speech, series etc) interminable; (patience) infini; (countless) innombrable. ◆**endlessly** adv interminablement.

endive ['endiv, *Am* 'endaiv] n *Bot* Culin (curly) chicorée f; (smooth) endive f.

endorse [in'dɔːs] vt (cheque etc) endosser; (action) approuver; (claim) appuyer. ◆**-ment** n (on driving licence) contravention f.

endow [in'dau] vt (institution) doter (with de); (chair, hospital bed) fonder; **endowed with** (person) *Fig* doté de. ◆**-ment** n dotation f; fondation f.

endur/e [in'djuər] **1** vt (bear) supporter (doing de faire). **2** vi (last) durer. ◆**-ing** a durable. ◆**-able** a supportable. ◆**endurance** n endurance f, résistance f.

enemy ['enəmi] n ennemi, -ie mf; – a (army, tank etc) ennemi.

energy ['enədʒi] n énergie f; – a (crisis, resources etc) énergétique. ◆**ener'getic** a énergique; **to feel e.** se sentir en pleine forme. ◆**ener'getically** adv énergiquement.

enforc/e [in'fɔːs] vt (law) faire respecter; (discipline) imposer (on à). ◆**-ed** a (rest, silence etc) forcé.

engag/e [in'geidʒ] vt (take on) engager, prendre; **to e. s.o. in conversation** engager la conversation avec qn; **to e. the clutch** *Aut* embrayer; – vi **to e.** (in) (launch into) se lancer dans; (be involved in) être mêlé à. ◆**-ed** a **1** (person, toilet) & *Tel* occupé; **e. in doing** occupé à faire; **to be e. in business/etc** être dans les affaires/etc. **2** (betrothed) fiancé; **to get e.** se fiancer. ◆**-ing** a (smile) engageant. ◆**-ement** n (agreement to marry) fiançailles fpl; (meeting) rendez-vous m inv; (undertaking) engagement m; **to have a prior e.** (be busy) être déjà pris, ne pas être libre; **e. ring** bague f de fiançailles.

engender [in'dʒendər] vt (produce) engendrer.

engine ['endʒin] n *Aut* moteur m; *Rail* locomotive f; *Nau* machine f; **e. driver** mécanicien m.

engineer [endʒi'niər] **1** n ingénieur m; (repairer) dépanneur m; *Rail Am* mécanicien m; **civil e.** ingénieur m des travaux publics; **mechanical e.** ingénieur

mécanicien. **2** vt (arrange secretly) machiner. ◆**-ing** n ingénierie f; (civil) **e.** génie m civil, travaux mpl publics; (mechanical) **e.** mécanique f; **e. factory** atelier m de construction mécanique.

England ['iŋglənd] n Angleterre f. ◆**English** a anglais; **the E. Channel** la Manche; **the E.** les Anglais mpl; – n (language) anglais m. ◆**Englishman** n (pl -men) Anglais m. ◆**English-speaking** a anglophone. ◆**Englishwoman** n (pl -women) Anglaise f.

engrav/e [in'greiv] vt graver. ◆**-ing** n gravure f. ◆**-er** n graveur m.

engrossed [in'graust] a **e. in** absorbé (in par).

engulf [in'gʌlf] vt engloutir.

enhance [in'haːns] vt (beauty etc) rehausser; (value) augmenter.

enigma [i'nigmə] n énigme f. ◆**enig'matic** a énigmatique.

enjoy [in'dʒɔi] vt aimer (doing faire); (meal) apprécier; (income, standard of living etc) jouir de; **to e. the evening** passer une bonne soirée; **to e. oneself** s'amuser; **to e. being in London/etc** se plaire à Londres/etc. ◆**-able** a agréable. ◆**-ably** adv agréablement. ◆**-ment** n plaisir m.

enlarge [in'laːdʒ] vt agrandir; – vi s'agrandir; **to e.** (up)on (say more about) s'étendre sur. ◆**-ment** n agrandissement m.

enlighten [in'lait(ə)n] vt éclairer (s.o. on or about sth qn sur qch). ◆**-ing** a instructif. ◆**-ment** n (explanations) éclaircissements mpl; **an age of e.** une époque éclairée.

enlist [in'list] vi (in the army etc) s'engager; – vt (recruit) engager; (supporter) recruter; (support) obtenir. ◆**-ment** n engagement m; recrutement m.

enliven [in'laiv(ə)n] vt (meeting, people etc) égayer, animer.

enmeshed [in'meʃt] a empêtré (in dans).

enmity ['enmiti] n inimitié f (between entre).

enormous [i'nɔːməs] a énorme; (explosion) terrible; (success) fou. ◆**enormity** n (vastness, extent) énormité f; (atrocity) atrocité f. ◆**enormously** adv (very much) énormément; (very) extrêmement.

enough [i'nʌf] a & n assez (de); **e. time/ cups/etc** assez de temps/de tasses/etc; **to have e. to live on** avoir de quoi vivre; **to have e. to drink** avoir assez à boire; **to have had e. of** *Pej* en avoir assez de; **it's e. for me to see that . . .** il me suffit de voir que . . . ; **that's e.** ça suffit, c'est assez; – adv assez, suffisamment (**to** pour); **strangely e., he left** chose curieuse, il est parti.

enquire [ɪn'kwaɪər] vi = **inquire**.

enquiry [ɪn'kwaɪərɪ] n = **inquiry**.

enrage [ɪn'reɪdʒ] vt mettre en rage.

enrapture [ɪn'ræptʃər] vt ravir.

enrich [ɪn'rɪtʃ] vt enrichir; (soil) fertiliser. ◆—**ment** n enrichissement m.

enrol [ɪn'rəʊl] (Am **enroll**) vi (-ll-) s'inscrire (**in, for** à); – vt inscrire. ◆—**ment** n inscription f; (people enrolled) effectif m.

ensconced [ɪn'skɒnst] a bien installé (**in** dans).

ensemble [ɒn'sɒmb(ə)l] n (clothes) & Mus ensemble m.

ensign ['ensən] n (flag) pavillon m; (rank) Am Nau enseigne m de vaisseau.

enslave [ɪn'sleɪv] vt asservir.

ensu/e [ɪn'sjuː] vi s'ensuivre. ◆—**ing** a (day, year etc) suivant; (event) qui s'ensuit.

ensure [ɪn'ʃʊər] vt assurer; **to e. that** (make sure) s'assurer que.

entail [ɪn'teɪl] vt (imply, involve) entraîner, impliquer.

entangle [ɪn'tæŋg(ə)l] vt emmêler, enchevêtrer; **to get entangled** s'empêtrer. ◆—**ment** n enchevêtrement m; **an e. with** (police) des démêlés mpl avec.

enter ['entər] vt (room, vehicle, army etc) entrer dans; (road) s'engager dans; (university) s'inscrire à; (write down) inscrire (**in** dans, **on** sur); (in ledger) porter (**in** sur); **to e. s.o. for** (exam) présenter qn à; **to e. a painting/etc in** (competition) présenter un tableau/etc à; **it didn't e. my head** ça ne m'est pas venu à l'esprit (that que); – vi entrer; **to e. for** (race, exam) s'inscrire pour; **to e. into** (plans) entrer dans; (conversation, relations) entrer en; **you don't e. into it** tu n'y es pour rien; **to e. into or upon** (career) entrer dans; (negotiations) entamer; (agreement) conclure.

enterpris/e ['entəpraɪz] n (undertaking, firm) entreprise f; (spirit) Fig initiative f. ◆—**ing** a (person) plein d'initiative; (attempt) hardi.

entertain [entə'teɪn] vt amuser, distraire; (guest) recevoir; (idea, possibility) envisager; (hope) chérir; **to e. s.o. to a meal** recevoir qn à dîner; – vi (receive guests) recevoir. ◆—**ing** a amusant. ◆—**er** n artiste mf. ◆—**ment** n amusement m, distraction f; (show) spectacle m.

enthral(l) [ɪn'θrɔːl] vt (-ll-) (delight) captiver.

enthuse [ɪn'θjuːz] vi **to e. over** Fam s'emballer pour. ◆**enthusiasm** n enthousiasme m. ◆**enthusiast** n enthousiaste

mf; **jazz/etc e.** passionné, -ée mf du jazz/etc. ◆**enthusi'astic** a enthousiaste; (golfer etc) passionné; **to be e. about** (hobby) être passionné de; **he was e. about** or **over** (gift etc) il a été emballé par; **to get e.** s'emballer (**about** pour). ◆**enthusi-'astically** adv avec enthousiasme.

entic/e [ɪn'taɪs] vt attirer (par la ruse); **to e. to do** entraîner (par la ruse) à faire. ◆—**ing** a séduisant, alléchant. ◆—**ement** n (bait) attrait m.

entire [ɪn'taɪər] a entier. ◆—**ly** adv tout à fait, entièrement. ◆**entirety** [ɪn'taɪərətɪ] n intégralité f; **in its e.** en entier.

entitl/e [ɪn'taɪt(ə)l] vt **to e. s.o. to do** donner à qn le droit de faire; **to e. s.o. to sth** donner à qn (le) droit à qch; **this entitles me to believe that ...** ça m'autorise à croire que ... . ◆—**ed** a (book) intitulé; **to be e. to do** avoir le droit de faire; **to be e. to sth** avoir droit à qch. ◆—**ement** n one's **e.** son dû.

entity ['entɪtɪ] n entité f.

entourage ['ɒntʊrɑːʒ] n entourage m.

entrails ['entreɪlz] npl entrailles fpl.

entrance 1 ['entrəns] n entrée f (**to** de); (to university etc) admission f (**to** à); **e. examination** examen m d'entrée. **2** [ɪn'trɑːns] vt Fig transporter, ravir.

entrant ['entrənt] n (in race) concurrent, -ente mf; (for exam) candidat, -ate mf.

entreat [ɪn'triːt] vt supplier, implorer (**to do** de faire). ◆**entreaty** n supplication f.

entrée ['ɒntreɪ] n Culin entrée f; (main dish) Am plat m principal.

entrench [ɪn'trentʃ] vt **to e. oneself** Mil & Fig se retrancher.

entrust [ɪn'trʌst] vt confier (**to** à); **to e. s.o. with sth** confier qch à qn.

entry ['entrɪ] n (way in, action) entrée f; (in ledger) écriture f; (term in dictionary or logbook) entrée f; (competitor) Sp concurrent, -ente mf; (thing to be judged in competition) objet m (or œuvre f or projet m) soumis à un jury; **e. form** feuille f d'inscription; **'no e.'** (on door etc) 'entrée interdite'; (road sign) 'sens interdit'.

entwine [ɪn'twaɪn] vt entrelacer.

enumerate [ɪ'njuːməreɪt] vt énumérer. ◆**enume'ration** n énumération f.

enunciate [ɪ'nʌnsɪeɪt] vt (word) articuler; (theory) énoncer. ◆**enunci'ation** n articulation f; énonciation f.

envelop [ɪn'veləp] vt envelopper (**in** fog/mystery/etc de brouillard/mystère/etc).

envelope ['envələʊp] n enveloppe f.

envious ['envɪəs] a envieux (**of sth** de qch);

e. of s.o. jaloux de qn. ◆**enviable** a enviable. ◆**enviously** adv avec envie.

environment [ɪn'vaɪərənmənt] n milieu m; (cultural, natural) environnement m. ◆**environ'mental** a du milieu; de l'environnement. ◆**environ'mentalist** n écologiste mf.

envisage [ɪn'vɪzɪdʒ] vt (imagine) envisager; (foresee) prévoir.

envision [ɪn'vɪʒ(ə)n] vt Am = envisage.

envoy ['envɔɪ] n Pol envoyé, -ée mf.

envy ['envɪ] n envie f; – vt envier (s.o. sth qch à qn).

ephemeral [ɪ'femərəl] a éphémère.

epic ['epɪk] a épique; – n épopée f; (screen) e. film m à grand spectacle.

epidemic [epɪ'demɪk] n épidémie f; – a épidémique.

epilepsy ['epɪlepsɪ] n épilepsie f. ◆**epi'leptic** a & n épileptique (mf).

epilogue ['epɪlɒg] n épilogue m.

episode ['epɪsəʊd] n épisode m. ◆**epi'sodic** [epɪ'sɒdɪk] a épisodique.

epistle [ɪ'pɪs(ə)l] n épître f.

epitaph ['epɪtɑːf] n épitaphe f.

epithet ['epɪθet] n épithète f.

epitome [ɪ'pɪtəmɪ] n the e. of l'exemple même de, l'incarnation de. ◆**epitomize** vt incarner.

epoch ['iːpɒk] n époque f. ◆**e.-making** a (event) qui fait date.

equal ['iːkwəl] a égal (to à); with e. hostility avec la même hostilité; on an e. footing sur un pied d'égalité (with avec); to be e. to (task, situation) Fig à la hauteur de; – n égal, -ale mf; to treat s.o. as an e. traiter qn en égal or d'égal à égal; he doesn't have his e. il n'a pas son pareil; – vt (-ll-, Am -l-) égaler (in beauty/etc en beauté/etc); equals sign Math signe m d'égalité. ◆**e'quality** n égalité f. ◆**equalize** vt égaliser; – vi Sp égaliser. ◆**equally** adv (to an equal degree, also) également; (to divide) en parts égales; he's e. stupid (just as) il est tout aussi bête.

equanimity [ekwə'nɪmɪtɪ] n égalité f d'humeur.

equate [ɪ'kweɪt] vt mettre sur le même pied (with que), assimiler (with à).

equation [ɪ'kweɪʒ(ə)n] n Math équation f.

equator [ɪ'kweɪtər] n équateur m; at or on the e. sous l'équateur. ◆**equatorial** [ekwə-'tɔːrɪəl] a équatorial.

equestrian [ɪ'kwestrɪən] a équestre.

equilibrium [iːkwɪ'lɪbrɪəm] n équilibre m.

equinox ['iːkwɪnɒks] n équinoxe m.

equip [ɪ'kwɪp] vt (-pp-) équiper (with de);

(well-)equipped with pourvu de; (well-)equipped to do compétent pour faire. ◆**—ment** n équipement m, matériel m.

equity ['ekwɪtɪ] n (fairness) équité f; pl Com actions fpl. ◆**equitable** a équitable.

equivalent [ɪ'kwɪvələnt] a & n équivalent (m). ◆**equivalence** n équivalence f.

equivocal [ɪ'kwɪvək(ə)l] a équivoque.

era ['ɪərə, Am 'erə] n époque f; (historical, geological) ère f.

eradicate [ɪ'rædɪkeɪt] vt supprimer; (evil, prejudice) extirper.

erase [ɪ'reɪz, Am ɪ'reɪs] vt effacer. ◆**eraser** n (rubber) gomme f. ◆**erasure** n rature f.

erect [ɪ'rekt] 1 a (upright) (bien) droit. 2 vt (build) construire; (statue, monument) ériger; (scaffolding) monter; (tent) dresser. ◆**erection** n construction f; érection f; montage m; dressage m.

ermine ['ɜːmɪn] n (animal, fur) hermine f.

erode [ɪ'rəʊd] vt éroder; (confidence etc) Fig miner, ronger. ◆**erosion** n érosion f.

erotic [ɪ'rɒtɪk] a érotique. ◆**eroticism** n érotisme m.

err [ɜːr] vi (be wrong) se tromper; (sin) pécher.

errand ['erənd] n commission f, course f; e. boy garçon m de courses.

erratic [ɪ'rætɪk] a (conduct etc) irrégulier; (person) lunatique.

error ['erər] n (mistake) erreur f, faute f; (wrongdoing) erreur f; in e. par erreur. ◆**erroneous** [ɪ'rəʊnɪəs] a erroné.

erudite ['erudaɪt, Am 'erjudaɪt] a érudit, savant. ◆**eru'dition** n érudition f.

erupt [ɪ'rʌpt] vi (of volcano) entrer en éruption; (of pimples) apparaître; (of war, violence) éclater. ◆**eruption** n (of volcano, pimples, anger) éruption f (of de); (of violence) flambée f.

escalate ['eskəleɪt] vi (of war, violence) s'intensifier; (of prices) monter en flèche; – vt intensifier. ◆**esca'lation** n escalade f.

escalator ['eskəleɪtər] n escalier m roulant.

escapade ['eskəpeɪd] n (prank) frasque f.

escape [ɪ'skeɪp] vi (of gas, animal etc) s'échapper; (of prisoner) s'évader, s'échapper; to e. from (person) échapper à; (place, object) s'échapper de; escaped prisoner évadé, -ée mf; – vt (death) échapper à; (punishment) éviter; that name escapes me ce nom m'échappe; to e. notice passer inaperçu; – n (of gas etc) fuite f; (of person) évasion f, fuite f; to have a lucky or narrow e. l'échapper belle. ◆**escapism** n évasion f (hors de la réalité). ◆**escapist** a (film etc) d'évasion.

eschew [ɪ'stʃuɪ] vt éviter, fuir.

escort ['eskɔɪt] n Mil Nau escorte f; (of woman) cavalier m; – [ɪ'skɔɪt] vt escorter.

Eskimo ['eskɪməʊ] n (pl -os) Esquimau, -aude mf; – a esquimau.

esoteric [esəʊ'terɪk] a obscur, ésotérique.

especial [ɪ'speʃəl] a particulier. ◆—**ly** adv (in particular) particulièrement; (for particular purpose) (tout) exprès; **e. as** d'autant plus que.

espionage ['espɪənɑɪʒ] n espionnage m.

esplanade ['espləneɪd] n esplanade f.

espouse [ɪ'spaʊz] vt (a cause) épouser.

espresso [e'spresəʊ] n (pl -os) (café m) express m.

Esq ['skwaɪər] abbr (esquire) **J. Smith Esq** (on envelope) Monsieur J. Smith.

essay ['eseɪ] n (attempt) & Liter essai m; Sch rédaction f; Univ dissertation f.

essence ['esəns] n Phil Ch essence f; Culin extrait m, essence f; (main point) essentiel m (of de); **in e.** essentiellement.

essential [ɪ'senʃ(ə)l] a (principal) essentiel; (necessary) indispensable, essentiel; **it's e. that** il est indispensable que (+ sub); – npl **the essentials** l'essentiel m (of de); (of grammar) les éléments mpl. ◆—**ly** adv essentiellement.

establish [ɪ'stæblɪʃ] vt établir; (state, society) fonder. ◆—**ed** a (well-)e. (firm) solide; (fact) reconnu; (reputation) établi; **she's (well-)e.** elle a une réputation établie. ◆—**ment** n (institution, firm) établissement m; **the e. of** l'établissement de, la fondation de; **the E.** les classes fpl dirigeantes.

estate [ɪ'steɪt] n (land) terre(s) f(pl), propriété f; (possessions) Jur fortune f; (of deceased person) succession f; housing e. lotissement m; (workers') cité f (ouvrière); **industrial e.** complexe m industriel; **e. agency** agence f immobilière; **e. agent** agent m immobilier; **e. car** break m; **e. tax** Am droits mpl de succession.

esteem [ɪ'stiɪm] vt estimer; **highly esteemed** très estimé; – n estime f.

esthetic [es'θetɪk] a Am esthétique.

estimate ['estɪmeɪt] vt (value) estimer, évaluer; (consider) estimer (that que); – ['estɪmət] n (assessment) évaluation f, estimation f; (judgement) évaluation f; (price for work to be done) devis m; **rough e.** chiffre m approximatif. ◆**esti'mation** n jugement m; (esteem) estime f; **in my e.** à mon avis.

estranged [ɪ'streɪndʒd] a **to become e.** (of couple) se séparer.

estuary ['estjʊərɪ] n estuaire m.

etc [et'setərə] adv etc.

etch [etʃ] vti graver à l'eau forte. ◆—**ing** n (picture) eau-forte f.

eternal [ɪ'tɜɪn(ə)l] a éternel. ◆**eternally** adv éternellement. ◆**eternity** n éternité f.

ether ['iɪθər] n éther m. ◆**e'thereal** a éthéré.

ethic ['eθɪk] n éthique f. ◆**ethics** n (moral standards) moralité f; (study) Phil éthique f. ◆**ethical** a moral, éthique.

Ethiopia [iɪθɪ'əʊpɪə] n Éthiopie f. ◆**Ethiopian** a & n éthiopien, -ienne (mf).

ethnic ['eθnɪk] a ethnique.

ethos ['iɪθɒs] n génie m.

etiquette ['etɪket] n (rules) bienséances fpl; (diplomatic) e. protocole m, étiquette f; **professional e.** déontologie f.

etymology [etɪ'mɒlədʒɪ] n étymologie f.

eucalyptus [juɪkə'lɪptəs] n (tree) eucalyptus m.

eulogy ['juɪlədʒɪ] n panégyrique m, éloge m.

euphemism ['juɪfəmɪz(ə)m] n euphémisme m.

euphoria [juɪ'fɔɪrɪə] n euphorie f. ◆**euphoric** a euphorique.

Euro- ['jʊərəʊ] pref euro-.

Europe ['jʊərəp] n Europe f. ◆**Euro'pean** a & n européen, -éenne (mf).

euthanasia [juɪθə'neɪzɪə] n euthanasie f.

evacuate [ɪ'vækjʊeɪt] vt évacuer. ◆**evacu-'ation** n évacuation f.

evade [ɪ'veɪd] vt éviter, esquiver; (pursuer, tax) échapper à; (law, question) éluder.

evaluate [ɪ'væljʊeɪt] vt évaluer (at à). ◆**evalu'ation** n évaluation f.

evangelical [iɪvæn'dʒelɪk(ə)l] a Rel évangélique.

evaporat/e [ɪ'væpəreɪt] vi s'évaporer; (of hopes) s'évanouir. ◆—**ed** a **e. milk** lait m concentré. ◆**evapo'ration** n évaporation f.

evasion [ɪ'veɪʒ(ə)n] n **e. of** (pursuer etc) fuite f devant; (question) esquive f de; **tax e.** évasion f fiscale. ◆**evasive** a évasif.

eve [iɪv] n **the e. of** la veille de.

even ['iɪv(ə)n] 1 a (flat) uni, égal, lisse; (equal) égal; (regular) régulier; (number) pair; **to get e. with** se venger de; **I'll get e. with him (for that)** je lui revaudrai ça; **we're e.** (quits) nous sommes quittes; (in score) nous sommes à égalité; **to break e.** Fin s'y retrouver; – vt **to e.** (out or up) égaliser. **2** adv même; **e. better/more** encore mieux/plus; **e. if** or **though** même si; **e.** so quand même. ◆—**ly** adv de manière égale; (regularly) régulièrement. ◆—**ness** n (of *surface, temper*) égalité f; (*of movement etc*) régularité f. ◆**even-'tempered** a de caractère égal.

evening ['iːvnɪŋ] n soir m; (*duration of evening, event*) soirée f; **in the e.,** Am **evenings** le soir; **at seven in the e.** à sept heures du soir; **every Tuesday e.** tous les mardis soir; **all e.** (long) toute la soirée; **e.** (*newspaper etc*) du soir; **e. performance** Th soirée f; **e. dress** tenue f de soirée; (*of woman*) robe f du soir or de soirée.

event [ɪ'vent] n évènement m; Sp épreuve f; **in the e.** of death en cas de décès; **in any e.** en tout cas; **after the e.** après coup. ◆**eventful** a (*journey etc*) mouvementé; (*occasion*) mémorable.

eventual [ɪ'ventʃuəl] a final, définitif. ◆**eventu'ality** n éventualité f. ◆**eventually** adv finalement, à la fin; (*some day or other*) un jour ou l'autre; (*after all*) en fin de compte.

ever ['evər] adv jamais; **has he e. seen it?** l'a-t-il jamais vu?; **more than e.** plus que jamais; **nothing e.** jamais rien; **hardly e.** presque jamais; **e. ready** toujours prêt; **the first e.** le tout premier; **e. since** (*that event etc*) depuis; **e. since then** depuis lors, dès lors; **for e.** (*for always*) pour toujours; (*continually*) sans cesse; **the best son e.** le meilleur fils du monde; **e. so sorry/happy/etc** Fam vraiment désolé/heureux/etc; **thank you e. so much** Fam merci mille fois; **it's e. such a pity** Fam c'est vraiment dommage; **why e. not?** pourquoi cela donc? ◆**evergreen** n arbre m à feuilles persistantes. ◆**ever'lasting** a éternel. ◆**ever'more** adv **for e.** à (tout) jamais.

every ['evrɪ] a chaque; **e. child** chaque enfant, tous les enfants; **e. time** chaque fois (**that** que); **e. one** chacun; **e. single one** tous (sans exception); **to have e. confidence in** avoir pleine confiance en; **e. second** or **other day** tous les deux jours; **her e. gesture** ses moindres gestes; **e. bit as big** tout aussi grand (**as** que); **e. so often,** **e. now and then** de temps en temps. ◆**everybody** pron tout le monde; **e. in turn** chacun à son tour. ◆**everyday** a (*happening, life etc*) de tous les jours; (*banal*) banal; **in e. use** d'usage courant. ◆**everyone** pron = **everybody**. ◆**everyplace** adv Am = **everywhere**. ◆**everything** pron tout; **e. I have** tout ce que j'ai. ◆**everywhere** adv partout; **e. she goes** où qu'elle aille, partout où elle va.

evict [ɪ'vɪkt] vt expulser (**from** de). ◆**eviction** n expulsion f.

evidence ['evɪdəns] n (*proof*) preuve(s) f(pl); (*testimony*) témoignage m; (*obviousness*) évidence f; **to give e.** témoigner (**against** contre); **e.** (*of wear etc*) des signes mpl de; **in e.** (*noticeable*) (bien) en vue. ◆**evident** a évident (**that** que); **it is e. from . . .** il apparaît de . . . (**that** que). ◆**evidently** adv (*obviously*) évidemment; (*apparently*) apparemment.

evil ['iːv(ə)l] a (*spell, influence, person*) malfaisant; (*deed, advice, system*) mauvais; (*consequence*) funeste; **–** n mal m; **to speak e.** dire du mal (**about,** of de).

evince [ɪ'vɪns] vt manifester.

evoke [ɪ'vəuk] vt (*recall, conjure up*) évoquer; (*admiration*) susciter. ◆**evocative** a évocateur.

evolution [iːvə'luːʃ(ə)n] n évolution f. ◆**evolve** vi (*of society, idea etc*) évoluer; (*of plan*) se développer; **–** vt (*system etc*) développer.

ewe [juː] n brebis f.

ex [eks] n (*former spouse*) Fam ex mf.

ex- [eks] pref ex-; **ex-wife** ex-femme f.

exacerbate [ɪk'sæsəbeɪt] vt (*pain*) exacerber.

exact [ɪg'zækt] 1 a (*accurate, precise etc*) exact; **to be** (**more**) **e. about** préciser. 2 vt (*demand*) exiger (**from** de); (*money*) extorquer (**from** à). ◆**–ing** a exigeant. ◆**–ly** adv exactement; **it's e. 5 o'clock** il est 5 heures juste. ◆**–ness** n exactitude f.

exaggerate [ɪg'zædʒəreɪt] vt exagérer; (*in one's own mind*) s'exagérer; **–** vi exagérer. ◆**exagge'ration** n exagération f.

exalt [ɪg'zɔːlt] vt (*praise*) exalter. ◆**–ed** a (*position, rank*) élevé. ◆**exal'tation** n exaltation f.

exam [ɪg'zæm] n Univ Sch Fam examen m.

examine [ɪg'zæmɪn] vt examiner; (*accounts, luggage*) vérifier; (*passport*) contrôler; (*orally*) interroger (*témoin,* élève). ◆**exami'nation** n (*inspection*) & Univ Sch examen m; (*of accounts etc*) vérification f; (*of passport*) contrôle m; **class e.** Sch composition f. ◆**examiner** n Sch examinateur, -trice mf.

example [ɪg'zɑːmp(ə)l] n exemple m; **for e.** par exemple; **to set a good/bad e.** donner le bon/mauvais exemple (**to** à); **to make an e. of** punir pour l'exemple.

exasperate [ɪg'zɑːspəreɪt] vt exaspérer; **to get exasperated** s'exaspérer (**at** de). ◆**exaspe'ration** n exaspération f.

excavate ['ekskəveɪt] vt (*dig*) creuser; (*for relics etc*) fouiller; (*uncover*) déterrer. ◆**exca'vation** n Tech creusement m; (*archeological*) fouille f.

exceed [ık'siːd] vt dépasser, excéder.
◆—**ingly** adv extrêmement.

excel [ık'sel] vi (-ll-) exceller (**in** sth en qch, **in doing** à faire); − vt surpasser.

Excellency ['eksələnsı] n (title) Excellence f.

excellent ['eksələnt] a excellent. ◆**excellence** n excellence f. ◆**excellently** adv parfaitement, admirablement.

except [ık'sept] prep sauf, excepté; **e. for** à part; **e. that** à part le fait que, sauf que; **e. if** sauf si; **to do nothing e.** wait ne rien faire sinon attendre; − vt excepter. ◆**exception** n exception f; **with the e. of** à l'exception de; **to take e. to** (object to) désapprouver; (be hurt by) s'offenser de. ◆**exceptional** a exceptionnel. ◆**exceptionally** adv exceptionnellement.

excerpt ['eksɜːpt] n (from film, book etc) extrait m.

excess ['ekses] n excès m; (surplus) Com excédent m; **one's excesses** un excès mpl; **to e.** à l'excès; **an e. of** (details) un luxe de; − a (weight etc) excédentaire, en trop; **e. fare** supplément m (de billet); **e. luggage** excédent m de bagages. ◆**ex'cessive** a excessif. ◆**ex'cessively** adv (too, too much) excessivement; (very) extrêmement.

exchange [ıks'tʃeındʒ] vt (addresses, blows etc) échanger (**for** contre); − n échange m; Fin change m; (telephone) central m (téléphonique); **in e.** en échange (**for** de).

Exchequer [ıks'tʃekər] n Chancellor **of the E.** = ministre m des Finances.

excise ['eksaız] n taxe f (**on** sur).

excit/e [ık'saıt] vt (agitate, provoke, stimulate) exciter; (enthuse) passionner, exciter. ◆—**ed** a exciter; (laughter) énervé; **to get e.** (nervous, angry, enthusiastic) s'exciter; **to be e. about** (new car, news) se réjouir de; **to be e. about the holidays** être surexcité à l'idée de partir en vacances. ◆—**ing** a (book, adventure) passionnant. ◆—**able** a excitable. ◆—**edly** adv avec agitation; (to wait, jump about) dans un état de surexcitation. ◆—**ement** n agitation f, excitation f, fièvre f; (emotion) vive émotion f; (adventure) aventure f; **great e.** surexcitation f.

exclaim [ık'skleım] vti s'exclamer, s'écrier (that que). ◆**excla'mation** n exclamation f; **e. mark** or Am **point** point m d'exclamation.

exclude [ık'skluːd] vt exclure (**from** de); (name from list) écarter (**from** de). ◆**exclusion** n exclusion f. ◆**exclusive** a (right, interest, design) exclusif; (club, group) fermé; (interview) en exclusivité; **e.**

of wine/etc vin/etc non compris. ◆**exclusively** adv exclusivement.

excommunicate [ekskə'mjuːnıkeıt] vt excommunier.

excrement ['ekskrəmənt] n excrément(s) m(pl).

excruciating [ık'skruːʃıeıtıŋ] a insupportable, atroce.

excursion [ık'skɜːʃ(ə)n] n excursion f.

excuse [ık'skjuːz] vt (justify, forgive) excuser (s.o. **for doing** qn d'avoir fait, qn de faire); (exempt) dispenser (**from** de); **e. me for asking** permettez-moi de demander; **e. me!** excusez-moi!, pardon!; **you're excused** tu peux t'en aller or sortir; − [ık'skjuːs] n excuse f; **it was an e. for** cela a servi de prétexte à.

ex-directory [eksdaı'rektərı] a Tel sur la liste rouge.

execute ['eksıkjuːt] vt (criminal, order, plan etc) exécuter. ◆**exe'cution** n exécution f. ◆**exe'cutioner** n bourreau m.

executive [ıg'zekjʊtıv] a (power) exécutif; (ability) d'exécution; (job) de cadre; (car, plane) de direction; − n (person) cadre m; (board, committee) bureau m; **the e.** Pol l'exécutif m; (senior) e. cadre m supérieur; **junior e.** jeune cadre m; **business e.** directeur m commercial.

exemplary [ıg'zemplərı] a exemplaire. ◆**exemplify** vt illustrer.

exempt [ıg'zempt] a exempt (**from** de); − vt exempter (**from** de). ◆**exemption** n exemption f.

exercise ['eksəsaız] n (of power etc) & Sch Sp Mil exercice m; pl Univ Am cérémonies fpl; **e. book** cahier m; − vt exercer; (troops) faire faire l'exercice à; (dog, horse etc) promener; (tact, judgement etc) faire preuve de; (rights) faire valoir, exercer; − vi (take exercise) prendre de l'exercice.

exert [ıg'zɜːt] vt exercer; (force) employer; **to e. oneself** (physically) se dépenser; **he never exerts himself** (takes the trouble) il ne se fatigue jamais; **to e. oneself to do** (try hard) s'efforcer de faire. ◆**exertion** n effort m; (of force) emploi m.

exhale [eks'heıl] vt (breathe out) expirer; (give off) exhaler; − vi expirer.

exhaust [ıg'zɔːst] 1 vt (use up, tire) épuiser; **to become exhausted** s'épuiser. 2 n **e.** (**pipe**) Aut pot m or tuyau m d'échappement. ◆—**ing** a épuisant. ◆**exhaustion** n épuisement m. ◆**exhaustive** a (study etc) complet; (research) approfondi.

exhibit [ıg'zıbıt] vt (put on display) exposer; (ticket, courage etc) montrer; − n objet m exposé; *Jur* pièce *f* à conviction. ◆exhi**bition** *n* exposition *f*; **an e. of** (*display*) une démonstration de; **to make an e. of oneself** se donner en spectacle. ◆exhi'bitionist *n* exhibitionniste *mf*. ◆exhibitor *n* exposant, -ante *mf*.

exhilarate [ɪgˈzɪləreɪt] *vt* stimuler; (*of air*) vivifier; (*elate*) rendre fou de joie. ◆exhila'ration *n* liesse *f*, joie *f*.

exhort [ɪgˈzɔːt] *vt* exhorter (**to do** à faire, **to sth** à qch).

exhume [eksˈhjuːm] *vt* exhumer.

exile [ˈeɡzaɪl] *vt* exiler; – *n* (*absence*) exil *m*; (*person*) exilé, -ée *mf*.

exist [ɪgˈzɪst] *vi* exister; (*live*) vivre (on de); (**to continue**) to e. subsister; **the notion exists that** . . . il existe une notion selon laquelle . . . . ◆**-ing** *a* (*law*) existant; (*circumstances*) actuel. ◆existence *n* existence *f*; **to come into e.** être créé; **to be in e.** exister. ◆exi'stentialism *n* existentialisme *m*.

exit [ˈeksɪt, ˈeɡzɪt] *n* (*action*) sortie *f*; (*door, window*) sortie *f*, issue *f*; – *vi* Th sortir.

exodus [ˈeksədəs] *n inv* exode *m*.

exonerate [ɪgˈzɒnəreɪt] *vt* (*from blame*) disculper (from de).

exorbitant [ɪgˈzɔːbɪtənt] *a* exorbitant. ◆**-ly** *adv* démesurément.

exorcize [ˈeksɔːsaɪz] *vt* exorciser. ◆exorcism *n* exorcisme *m*.

exotic [ɪgˈzɒtɪk] *a* exotique.

expand [ɪkˈspænd] *vt* (*one's fortune, knowledge etc*) étendre; (*trade, ideas*) développer; (*production*) augmenter; (*gas, metal*) dilater; – *vi* s'étendre; se développer; augmenter; se dilater; **to e. on** développer ses idées sur; (*fast or rapidly*) **expanding sector/etc** Com secteur/*etc* en (pleine) expansion. ◆expansion *n* Com Phys Pol expansion *f*; développement *m*; augmentation *f*. ◆expansionism *n* expansionnisme *m*.

expanse [ɪkˈspæns] *n* étendue *f*.

expansive [ɪkˈspænsɪv] *a* expansif. ◆**-ly** *adv* avec effusion.

expatriate [ekˈspætrɪət, *Am* eksˈpeɪtrɪət] *a & n* expatrié, -ée (*mf*).

expect [ɪkˈspekt] *vt* (*anticipate*) s'attendre à, attendre, escompter; (*think*) penser (that que); (*suppose*) supposer (that que); (*await*) attendre; **to e. sth from** s.o./sth attendre qch de qn/qch; **to e. to do** compter faire; **to e. that** (*anticipate*) s'attendre à ce que (+ *sub*); **I e. you to come** (*want*) je te demande de venir; **it was expected** c'était prévu (that que); **she's expecting a baby** elle attend un bébé. ◆expectancy *n* attente *f*; **life e.** espérance *f* de vie. ◆expectant *a* (*crowd*) qui attend; **e. mother** future mère *f*. ◆expec'tation *n* attente *f*; **to come up to s.o.'s expectations** répondre à l'attente de qn.

expedient [ɪkˈspiːdɪənt] *a* avantageux; (*suitable*) opportun; – *n* (*resource*) expédient *m*.

expedite [ˈekspədaɪt] *vt* (*hasten*) accélérer; (*task*) exécuter.

expedition [ekspɪˈdɪʃ(ə)n] *n* expédition *f*.

expel [ɪkˈspel] *vt* (-ll-) expulser (from de); (*from school*) renvoyer; (*enemy*) chasser.

expend [ɪkˈspend] *vt* (*energy, money*) dépenser; (*resources*) épuiser. ◆**-able** *a* (*object*) remplaçable; (*soldiers*) sacrifiable. ◆expenditure *n* (*money spent*) dépenses *fpl*; **an e. of** (*time, money*) une dépense de.

expense [ɪkˈspens] *n* frais *mpl*, dépense *f*; *pl* Fin frais *mpl*; **business/travelling expenses** frais *mpl* généraux/de déplacement; **to go to some e.** faire des frais; **at s.o.'s e.** aux dépens de qn; **an** *or* **one's e. account** une *or* sa note de frais (*professionnels*).

expensive [ɪkˈspensɪv] *a* (*goods etc*) cher, coûteux; (*hotel etc*) cher; (*tastes*) dispendieux; **to be e.** coûter cher; **an e. mistake** une faute qui coûte cher. ◆**-ly** *adv* à grands frais.

experienc/e [ɪkˈspɪərɪəns] *n* (*knowledge, skill, event*) expérience *f*; **from** *or* **by e.** par expérience; **he's had e. of** (*work etc*) il a déjà fait; (*grief etc*) il a déjà éprouvé; **I've had e. of driving** j'ai déjà conduit; **terrible experiences** de rudes épreuves *fpl*; **unforgettable e.** moment *m* inoubliable; – *vt* (*undergo*) connaître, subir; (*remorse, difficulty*) éprouver; (*joy*) ressentir. ◆**-ed** *a* (*person*) expérimenté; (*eye, ear*) exercé; **to be e. in** s'y connaître en (matière de).

experiment [ɪkˈsperɪmənt] *n* expérience *f*; – [ɪkˈsperɪment] *vi* faire une expérience *or* des expériences; **to e. with sth** *Phys Ch* expérimenter qch. ◆experi'mental *a* expérimental; **e. period** période *f* d'expérimentation.

expert [ˈekspɜːt] *n* expert *m* (on, in de), spécialiste *mf* (on, in de); – *a* expert (in sth en qch, in *or* at doing à faire); (*advice*) d'un expert, d'expert; (*eye*) connaisseur; **e. touch** doigté *m*, grande habileté *f*. ◆exper'tise *n* compétence *f* (in en). ◆expertly *adv* habilement.

expiate [ˈekspɪeɪt] *vt* (*sins*) expier.

expir/e [ɪkˈspaɪər] *vi* expirer. ◆**-ed** *a*

(ticket, passport etc) périmé. ◆**expl'ration** *n Am.* ◆**expiry** *n* expiration *f.*

explain [ɪkˈspleɪn] *vt* expliquer (to à, that que); *(reasons)* exposer; *(mystery)* éclaircir; e. yourself! explique-toi!; to e. away justifier. ◆**-able** *a* explicable. ◆**expla-'nation** *n* explication *f.* ◆**explanatory** *a* explicatif.

expletive [ɪkˈspliːtɪv, *Am* ˈeksplɪtɪv] *n (oath)* juron *m.*

explicit [ɪkˈsplɪsɪt] *a* explicite. ◆**-ly** *adv* explicitement.

explode [ɪkˈspləʊd] *vi* exploser; to e. with laughter *Fig* éclater de rire; – *vt* faire exploser; *(theory) Fig* démythifier, discréditer.

exploit 1 [ɪkˈsplɔɪt] *vt (person, land etc)* exploiter. **2** [ˈeksplɔɪt] *n (feat)* exploit *m.* ◆**exploi'tation** *n* exploitation *f.*

explore [ɪkˈsplɔːr] *vt* explorer; *(possibilities)* examiner. ◆**explo'ration** *n* exploration *f.* ◆**exploratory** *a* d'exploration; e. operation *Med* sondage *m.* ◆**explorer** *n* explorateur, -trice *mf.*

explosion [ɪkˈspləʊʒ(ə)n] *n* explosion *f.* ◆**explosive** *a (weapon, question)* explosif; *(mixture, gas)* détonant; – *n* explosif *m.*

exponent [ɪkˈspəʊnənt] *n (of opinion, theory etc)* interprète *m (of* de).

export [ˈekspɔːt] *n* exportation *f*; – *a (goods etc)* d'exportation; – [ɪkˈspɔːt] *vt* exporter (to vers, from de). ◆**expor'tation** *n* exportation *f.* ◆**ex'porter** *n* exportateur, -trice *mf; (country)* pays *m* exportateur.

expose [ɪkˈspəʊz] *vt (leave uncovered, describe)* & *Phot* exposer; *(wire)* dénuder; *(plot, scandal etc)* révéler, dévoiler; *(crook etc)* démasquer; to e. to *(subject to)* exposer à; to e. oneself *Jur* commettre un attentat à la pudeur. ◆**expo'sition** *n* exposition *f.* ◆**exposure** *n* exposition *f* (to à); *(of plot etc)* révélation *f; (of house etc)* exposition *f; Phot* pose *f;* to die of e. mourir de froid.

expound [ɪkˈspaʊnd] *vt (theory etc)* exposer.

express [ɪkˈspres] **1** *vt* exprimer; *(proposition)* énoncer; to e. oneself s'exprimer. **2** *a (order)* exprès, formel; *(intention)* exprès; *(purpose)* seul; *(letter, delivery)* exprès *inv; (train)* rapide, express *inv;* – *adv (to send)* par exprès; – *n (train)* rapide *m,* express *m inv.* ◆**expression** *n (phrase, look etc)* expression *f; (of gratitude, affection etc)* un témoignage de. ◆**expressive** *a* expressif. ◆**expressly** *adv* expressément. ◆**expressway** *n Am* autoroute *f.*

expulsion [ɪkˈspʌlʃ(ə)n] *n* expulsion *f; (from school)* renvoi *m.*

expurgate [ˈekspɜːgeɪt] *vt* expurger.

exquisite [ɪkˈskwɪzɪt] *a* exquis. ◆**-ly** *adv* d'une façon exquise.

ex-serviceman [eksˈsɜːvɪsmən] *n (pl -men)* ancien combattant *m.*

extant [ekˈstænt, ekˈstænt] *a* existant.

extend [ɪkˈstend] *vt (arm, business)* étendre; *(line, visit, meeting)* prolonger (by de); *(hand)* tendre (to s.o. à qn); *(house)* agrandir; *(knowledge)* élargir; *(time limit)* reculer; *(help, thanks)* offrir (to à); to e. an invitation to faire une invitation à; – *vi (of wall, plain etc)* s'étendre (to jusqu'à); *(in time)* se prolonger; to e. to s.o. *(of joy etc)* gagner qn. ◆**extension** *n (in space)* prolongement *m; (in time)* prolongation *f; (of powers, measure, meaning, strike)* extension *f; (for table, wire)* rallonge *f; (to building)* agrandissement(s) *m(pl); (of telephone)* appareil *m* supplémentaire; *(of office telephone)* poste *m;* an e. (of time) un délai. ◆**extensive** *a* étendu, vaste; *(repairs, damage)* important; *(use)* courant. ◆**extensively** *adv (very much)* beaucoup, considérablement; e. used largement répandu.

extent [ɪkˈstent] *n (scope)* étendue *f; (size)* importance *f; (degree)* mesure *f;* to a large/certain e. dans une large/certaine mesure; to such an e. that à tel point que.

extenuating [ɪkˈstenjʊeɪtɪŋ] *a* e. circumstances circonstances *fpl* atténuantes.

exterior [ɪkˈstɪərɪər] *a* & *n* extérieur *(m).*

exterminate [ɪkˈstɜːmɪneɪt] *vt (people etc)* exterminer; *(disease)* supprimer; *(evil)* extirper. ◆**extermi'nation** *n* extermination *f;* suppression *f.*

external [ekˈstɜːn(ə)l] *a (influence, trade etc)* extérieur; for e. use *(medicine)* à usage externe; e. affairs *Pol* affaires *fpl* étrangères. ◆**-ly** *adv* extérieurement.

extinct [ɪkˈstɪŋkt] *a (volcano, love)* éteint; *(species, animal)* disparu. ◆**extinction** *n* extinction *f;* disparition *f.*

extinguish [ɪkˈstɪŋgwɪʃ] *vt* éteindre. ◆**-er** *n* (fire) e. extincteur *m.*

extol [ɪkˈstəʊl] *vt* (-ll-) exalter, louer.

extort [ɪkˈstɔːt] *vt (money)* extorquer (from à); *(consent)* arracher (from à). ◆**extortion** *n Jur* extorsion *f* de fonds); it's *(sheer)* e.! c'est du vol! ◆**extortionate** *a* exorbitant.

extra [ˈekstrə] *a (additional)* supplémentaire; one e. glass un verre *de or* en plus, encore un verre; (any) e. bread?

encore du pain?; **to be e.** (*spare*) être en trop; (*cost more*) être en supplément; (*of postage*) être en sus; **wine is 3 francs e.** il y a un supplément de 3F pour le vin; **e. care** un soin tout particulier; **e. charge** or **portion** supplément *m*; **e. time** Fb prolongation *f*; – *adv* **e.** big/*etc* plus grand/*etc* que d'habitude; – *n* (*perk*) à-côté *m*; Cin Th figurant, -ante *mf*; *pl* (*expenses*) frais *mpl* supplémentaires; **an optional e.** (*for car etc*) un accessoire en option.

extra- ['ekstrə] *pref* extra-. ◆**e.-'dry** *a* (*champagne*) brut. ◆**e.-'fine** *a* extra-fin. ◆**e.-'strong** *a* extra-fort.

extract [ik'strækt] *vt* extraire (**from** de); (*tooth*) arracher, extraire; (*promise*) arracher, soutirer (**from** à); (*money*) soutirer (**from** à); – ['ekstrækt] *n* (*of book etc*) & Culin Ch extrait *m*. ◆**ex'traction** *n* extraction *f*; arrachement *m*; (*descent*) origine *f*.

extra-curricular [ekstrəkə'rikjulər] *a* (*activities etc*) en dehors des heures de cours, extrascolaire.

extradite ['ekstrədait] *vt* extrader. ◆**extra-'dition** *n* extradition *f*.

extramarital [ekstrə'mærit(ə)l] *a* en dehors du mariage, extra-conjugal.

extramural [ekstrə'mjuərəl] *a* (*studies*) hors faculté.

extraneous [ik'streiniəs] *a* (*detail etc*) accessoire.

extraordinary [ik'strɔːdən(ə)ri] *a* (*strange, exceptional*) extraordinaire.

extra-special [ekstrə'spefəl] *a* (*occasion*) très spécial; (*care*) tout particulier.

extravagant [ik'strævəgənt] *a* (*behaviour, idea etc*) extravagant; (*claim*) exagéré; (*wasteful with money*) dépensier, prodigue. ◆**extravagance** *n* extravagance *f*; prodigalité *f*; (*thing bought*) folle dépense *f*.

extravaganza [ikstrævə'gænzə] *n* Mus Liter & Fig fantaisie *f*.

extreme [ik'striːm] *a* (*exceptional, furthest*) extrême; (*danger, poverty*) très grand; (*praise*) outré; **at the e. end** à l'extrémité; **of**

e. importance de première importance; **– n** (*furthest degree*) extrême *m*; **to carry** or **take to extremes** pousser à l'extrême; **extremes of temperature** températures *fpl* extrêmes; **extremes of climate** excès *mpl* du climat. ◆**extremely** *adv* extrêmement. ◆**extremist** *a* & *n* extrémiste (*mf*). ◆**extremity** [ik'stremiti] *n* extrémité *f*.

extricate ['ekstrikeit] *vt* dégager (**from** de); **to e. oneself from** (*difficulty*) se tirer de.

extrovert ['ekstrəvɜːt] *n* extraverti, -ie *mf*.

exuberant [ig'z(j)uːbərənt] *a* exubérant. ◆**exuberance** *n* exubérance *f*.

exude [ig'zjuːd] *vt* (*charm, honesty etc*) Fig respirer.

exultation [egzʌl'teiʃ(ə)n] *n* exultation *f*.

eye[1] [ai] *n* œil *m* (*pl* yeux); **before my very eyes** sous mes yeux; **to be all eyes** être tout yeux; **as far as the e. can see** à perte de vue; **up to one's eyes in debt** endetté jusqu'au cou; **up to one's eyes in work** débordé de travail; **to have an e. on** (*house, car*) avoir en vue; **to keep an e. on** surveiller; **to make eyes at** Fam faire de l'œil à; **to lay** or **set eyes on** voir, apercevoir; **to take one's eyes off** s.o./sth quitter qn/qch des yeux; **to catch the e.** attirer l'œil, accrocher le regard; **keep an e. out!, keep your eyes open!** ouvre l'œil!, sois vigilant!; **we don't see e. to e.** nous n'avons pas le même point de vue; **e. shadow** fard *m* à paupières; **to be an e.-opener for** s.o. Fam être une révélation pour qn. ◆**eyeball** *n* globe *m* oculaire. ◆**eyebrow** *n* sourcil *m*. ◆**eye-catching** *a* (*title etc*) accrocheur. ◆**eyeglass** *n* monocle *m*. ◆**eyeglasses** *npl* (*spectacles*) Am lunettes *fpl*. ◆**eyelash** *n* cil *m*. ◆**eyelid** *n* paupière *f*. ◆**eyeliner** *n* eye-liner *m*. ◆**eyesight** *n* vue *f*. ◆**eyesore** *n* (*building etc*) horreur *f*. ◆**eyestrain** *n* **to have e.** avoir les yeux qui tirent. ◆**eyewash** *n* (*nonsense*) Fam sottises *fpl*. ◆**eyewitness** *n* témoin *m* oculaire.

eye[2] [ai] *vt* reluquer, regarder.

F

F, f [ef] *n* F, f *m*.

fable ['feib(ə)l] *n* fable *f*.

fabric ['fæbrik] *n* (*cloth*) tissu *m*, étoffe *f*; (*of building*) structure *f*; **the f. of society** le tissu

social.

fabricate ['fæbrikeit] *vt* (*invent, make*) fabriquer. ◆**fabri'cation** *n* fabrication *f*.

fabulous ['fæbjʊləs] a (incredible, legendary) fabuleux; (wonderful) Fam formidable.

façade [fə'sɑːd] n Archit & Fig façade f.

face [feɪs] n visage m, figure f; (expression) mine f; (of clock) cadran m; (of building) façade f; (of cliff) paroi f; (of the earth) surface f; **she laughed in my f.** elle m'a ri au nez; **to show one's f.** se montrer; **f. down(wards)** (person) face contre terre; (thing) tourné à l'envers; **f. to f.** face à face; **in the f. of** devant; (despite) en dépit de; **to save/lose f.** sauver/perdre la face; **to make or pull faces** faire des grimaces; **to tell s.o. sth to his f.** dire qch à qn tout cru; **f. powder** poudre f de riz; **f. value** (of stamp etc) valeur f; **to take sth at f. value** prendre qch au pied de la lettre; - vt (danger, enemy etc) faire face à; (accept) accepter; (look in the face) regarder (qn) bien en face; **to f., be facing** (be opposite) être en face de; (of window etc) donner sur; **faced with** (prospect, problem) face à, devant; (defeat) menacé par; (bill) contraint à payer; **he can't f. leaving** il n'a pas le courage de partir; - vi (of house) être orienté (north/etc au nord/etc); (of person) se tourner (towards vers); **to f. up to** (danger) faire face à; (fact) accepter; **about f.! Am Mil** demi-tour! ◆**facecloth** n gant m de toilette. ◆**facelift** n Med lifting m; (of building) ravalement m.

faceless ['feɪsləs] a anonyme.

facet ['fæsɪt] n (of problem, diamond etc) facette f.

facetious [fə'siːʃəs] a (person) facétieux; (remark) plaisant.

facial ['feɪʃ(ə)l] a du visage; Med facial; - n soin m du visage.

facile ['fæsaɪl, Am 'fæs(ə)l] a facile, superficiel.

facilitate [fə'sɪlɪteɪt] vt faciliter. ◆**facility** n (ease) facilité f; pl (possibilities) facilités fpl; (for sports) équipements mpl; (in harbour, airport etc) installations fpl; (means) moyens mpl, ressources fpl; **special facilities** (conditions) conditions fpl spéciales (for pour).

facing ['feɪsɪŋ] n (of dress etc) parement m.

fact [fækt] n fait m; **as a matter of f.,** in f. en fait; **the facts of life** les choses fpl de la vie; **is that a f.?** c'est vrai?; **f. and fiction** le réel et l'imaginaire.

faction ['fækʃ(ə)n] n (group) Pol faction f.

factor ['fæktər] n (element) facteur m.

factory ['fækt(ə)rɪ] n (large) usine f; (small)

fabrique f; **arms/porcelain f.** manufacture f d'armes/de porcelaine.

factual ['fæktʃʊəl] a objectif, basé sur les faits, factuel; (error) de fait.

faculty ['fækəltɪ] n (aptitude) & Univ faculté f.

fad [fæd] n (personal habit) marotte f; (fashion) folie f, mode f (for de).

fade [feɪd] vi (of flower) se faner; (of light) baisser; (of colour) passer; (of fabric) se décolorer; **to f. (away)** (of memory, smile) s'effacer; (of sound) s'affaiblir; (of person) dépérir; - vt (fabric) décolorer.

fag [fæg] n **1** (cigarette) Fam clope m, tige f; **f. end** mégot m. **2** (male homosexual) Am Sl pédé m.

fagged [fægd] a **f. (out)** (tired) Sl claqué.

faggot ['fægət] n **1** Culin boulette f (de viande). **2** (male homosexual) Am Sl pédé m.

fail [feɪl] vi (of person, plan etc) échouer; (of business) faire faillite; (of light, health, sight) baisser; (of memory, strength) défaillir; (of brakes) Aut lâcher; (run short) manquer; (of gas, electricity) être coupé; (of engine) tomber en panne; **to f. in** (one's duty) manquer à; (exam) échouer à; - vt (exam) échouer à; (candidate) refuser, recaler; **to f. s.o.** (let down) laisser tomber qn, décevoir qn; (of words) manquer à qn, faire défaut à qn; **to f. to do** (omit) manquer de faire; (not be able) ne pas arriver à faire; **I f. to see** je ne vois pas; — **without f.** à coup sûr, sans faute. ◆**-ed** a (attempt, poet) manqué. ◆**-ing** n (fault) défaut m; — prep à défaut de; **f. this, f. that** à défaut. ◆**failure** n échec m; (of business) faillite f; (of engine, machine) panne f; (of gas etc) coupure f, panne f; (person) raté, -ée mf; **f. to do** (inability) incapacité f de faire; **her f. to leave** le fait qu'elle n'est pas partie; **to end in f.** se solder par un échec; **heart f.** arrêt m du cœur.

faint [feɪnt] **1** a (-er, -est) (sound, voice) faible; (colour) pâle; (idea) vague; **I haven't the faintest idea** je n'en ai pas la moindre idée. **2** a Med défaillant (with de); **to feel f.** se trouver mal, défaillir; — vi s'évanouir (from de); **fainting fit** évanouissement m. ◆**-ly** adv (weakly) faiblement; (slightly) légèrement. ◆**-ness** n légèreté f; faiblesse f. ◆**faint-'hearted** a timoré, timide.

fair [feər] n foire f; (for charity) fête f; (funfair) fête f foraine; (larger) parc m d'attractions. ◆**fairground** n champ m de foire.

fair² [feər] **1** *a* (-er, -est) (*equitable*) juste, équitable; (*game, fight*) loyal; **f. (and square)** honnête(ment); **f. play** fair-play *m inv*; **that's not f. play!** ce n'est pas du jeu!; **that's not f. to him** ce n'est pas juste pour lui; **f. enough!** très bien!; — *adv* (*to play*) loyalement. **2** *a* (*rather good*) passable, assez bon; (*amount, warning*) raisonnable; **a f. amount (of)** pas mal (de); **f. copy** copie *f* au propre. **3** *a* (*wind*) favorable; (*weather*) beau. **◆-ly** *adv* **1** (*to treat*) équitablement; (*to get*) loyalement. **2** (*rather*) assez, plutôt; **f. sure** presque sûr. **◆-ness¹** *n* justice *f*; (*of decision*) équité *f*; **in all f.** en toute justice. **◆fair-'minded** *a* impartial. **◆fair-'sized** *a* assez grand.

fair³ [feər] *n* (*hair, texture*) blond; (*complexion, skin*) clair. **◆-ness²** *n* (*of hair*) blond *m*; (*of skin*) blancheur *f*. **◆fair-'haired** *a* blond. **◆fair-'skinned** *a* à la peau claire.

fairy ['feəri] *n* fée *f*; **f. lights** guirlande *f* multicolore; **f. tale** conte *m* de fées.

faith [feiθ] *n* foi *f*; **to have f. in s.o.** avoir confiance en qn; **to put one's f. in** (*justice, medicine etc*) se fier à; **in good/bad f.** de bonne/mauvaise foi; **f. healer** guérisseur, -euse *mf*. **◆faithful** *a* fidèle. **◆faithfully** *adv* fidèlement; **yours f.** (*in letter*) Com veuillez agréer l'expression de mes salutations distinguées. **◆faithfulness** *n* fidélité *f*. **◆faithless** *a* déloyal, infidèle.

fake [feik] *n* (*painting, document etc*) faux *m*; (*person*) imposteur *m*; — *vt* (*document, signature etc*) falsifier, maquiller; (*election*) truquer; **f. death** faire semblant d'être mort; — *vi* (*pretend*) faire semblant; — *a* faux; (*elections*) truqué.

falcon ['fɔːlkən] *n* faucon *m*.

fall [fɔːl] *n* chute *f*; (*in price, demand etc*) baisse *f*; *pl* (*waterfall*) chutes *fpl* (d'eau); **the f.** *Am* l'automne *m*; — *vi* (*pt* **fell**, *pp* **fallen**) tomber; (*of building*) s'effondrer; **her face fell** Fig son visage se rembrunit; **to f. into** tomber dans; (*habit*) Fig prendre; **to f. off a bicycle/etc** tomber d'une bicyclette/etc; **to f. off** or **down a ladder** tomber (en bas) d'une échelle; **to fall on s.o.** (*of onus*) retomber sur qn; **to f. on a Monday/etc** (*of event*) tomber un lundi/etc; **to f. over sth** tomber en butant contre qch; **to f. short of** (*expectation*) ne pas répondre à; **to f. short of being** être loin d'être; **to f. victim** devenir victime (to de); **to f. asleep** s'endormir; **to f. ill** tomber malade; **to f. due** échoir. ■ **to f. apart** (*of mechanism*) tomber en morceaux; Fig se désagréger; **to f. away** (*come off*) se

détacher, tomber; (*of numbers*) diminuer; **to f. back on** (*as last resort*) se rabattre sur; **to f. behind** rester en arrière; (*in work*) prendre du retard; **to f. down** tomber; (*of building*) s'effondrer; **to f. for** Fam (*person*) tomber amoureux de; (*trick*) se laisser prendre à; **to f. in** (*collapse*) s'écrouler; **to f. in with** (*tally with*) cadrer avec; (*agree to*) accepter; **to f. off** (*come off*) se détacher, tomber; (*of numbers*) diminuer. **◆falling-'off** *n* diminution *f*; **to f. out with** (*quarrel with*) se brouiller avec; **to f. over** tomber; (*of table, vase*) se renverser; **to f. through** (*of plan*) tomber à l'eau, échouer. **◆fallen** *a* tombé; (*angel, woman*) déchu; **f. leaf** feuille *f* morte. **◆fallout** *n* (*radioactive*) retombées *fpl*.

fallacious [fə'leiʃəs] *a* faux. **◆fallacy** ['fæləsi] *n* erreur *f*; Phil faux raisonnement *m*.

fallible ['fæləb(ə)l] *a* faillible.

fallow ['fæləu] *a* (*land*) en jachère.

false [fɔːls] *a* faux; **a f. bottom** un double fond. **◆falsehood** *n* mensonge *m*; **truth and f.** le vrai et le faux. **◆falseness** *n* fausseté *f*. **◆falsify** *vt* falsifier.

falter ['fɔːltər] *vi* (*of step, resolution*) chanceler; (*of voice, speaker*) hésiter; (*of courage*) vaciller.

fame [feim] *n* renommée *f*; (*glory*) gloire *f*. **◆famed** *a* renommé.

familiar [fə'miljər] *a* (*task, atmosphere etc*) familier; (*event*) habituel; **f. with s.o.** (*too friendly*) familier avec qn; **to be f. with** (*know*) connaître; **I'm f. with her voice** je connais bien sa voix, sa voix m'est familière; **to make oneself f. with** se familiariser avec; **he looks f. (to me)** je l'ai déjà vu (quelque part). **◆famili'arity** *n* familiarité *f* (**with** avec); (*of event, sight etc*) caractère *m* familier. **◆familiarize** *vt* familiariser (**with** avec); **to f. oneself with** se familiariser avec.

family ['fæmili] *n* famille *f*; — *a* (*name, doctor etc*) de famille; (*planning, problem*) familial; (*tree*) généalogique; **f. man** père *m* de famille.

famine ['fæmin] *n* famine *f*.

famished ['fæmiʃt] *a* affamé.

famous ['feiməs] *a* célèbre (**for** par, pour). **◆-ly** *adv* (*very well*) Fam rudement bien.

fan [fæn] **1** *n* (*hand-held*) éventail *m*; (*mechanical*) ventilateur *m*; **f. heater** radiateur *m* soufflant; — *vt* (-**nn**-) (*person etc*) éventer; (*fire, quarrel*) attiser. **2** *n* (*of person*) admirateur, -trice *mf*, fan *m*; Sp supporter *m*; **to be a jazz/sports f.** être passionné *or* mordu de jazz/de sport.

fanatic [fə'nætik] *n* fanatique *mf*. ◆**fanatical** *a* fanatique. ◆**fanaticism** *n* fanatisme *m*.

fancy ['fænsɪ] **1** *n* (*whim, imagination*) fantaisie *f*; (*liking*) goût *m*; **to take a f. to s.o.** se prendre d'affection pour qn; **I took a f. to it,** it took my f. j'en ai eu envie; **when the f. takes me** quand ça me chante; **– a** (*hat, button etc*) fantaisie *inv*; (*idea*) fantaisiste; (*price*) exorbitant; (*car*) de luxe; (*house, restaurant*) chic; **f. dress** (*costume*) travesti *m*; **f.-dress ball** bal *m* masqué. **2** *vt* (*imagine*) se figurer (**that** que); (*think*) croire (**that** que); (*want*) avoir envie de; (*like*) aimer; **f. that!** tiens (donc)!; **he fancies her** *Fam* elle lui plaît; **to f. oneself** as se prendre pour; **she fancies herself!** elle se prend pour qn! ◆**fancier** *n* **horse/***etc* **f.** amateur *m* de chevaux/*etc*. ◆**fanciful** *a* fantaisiste.

fanfare ['fænfeər] *n* (*of trumpets*) fanfare *f*.

fang [fæŋ] *n* (*of dog etc*) croc *m*; (*of snake*) crochet *m*.

fantastic [fæn'tæstɪk] *a* fantastique; **a f. idea** (*absurd*) une idée aberrante.

fantasy ['fæntəsɪ] *n* (*imagination*) fantaisie *f*; *Psy* fantasme *m*. ◆**fantasize** *vi* fantasmer (**about** sur).

far [fɑːr] *adv* (**farther** *or* **further, farthest** *or* **furthest**) (*distance*) loin; **f. bigger/more expensive/***etc* (*much*) beaucoup plus grand/plus cher/*etc* (**than** que); **f. more** beaucoup plus; **f. advanced** très avancé; **how f. is it to . . . ?** combien y a-t-il d'ici à . . . ?; **is it f. to . . . ?** sommes-nous, suis-je *etc* loin de . . . ?; **how f. are you going?** jusqu'où vas-tu?; **how f. has he got with?** (*plans, work etc*) où en est-il de?; **so f.** (*time*) jusqu'ici; (*place*) jusque-là; **as f. as** (*place*) jusqu'à; **as f.** *or* **so f. as I know** autant que je sache; **as f.** *or* **so f. as I'm concerned** en ce qui me concerne; **as f. back as 1820** dès 1820; **f. from doing** loin de faire; **f. from it!** loin de là!; **f. away** *or* **off** au loin; **to be (too) f. away** être (trop) loin (**from** de); **f. and wide** partout; **by f.** de loin; **f. into the night** très avant dans la nuit; **– a** (*side, end*) autre; **it's a f. cry from** on est loin de. ◆**faraway** *a* lointain; (*look*) distrait, dans le vague. ◆**far-'fetched** *a* forcé, exagéré. ◆**f.-'flung** *a* (*widespread*) vaste. ◆**f.-'off** *a* lointain. ◆**f.-'reaching** *a* de grande portée. ◆**f.-'sighted** *a* clairvoyant.

farce [fɑːs] *n* farce *f*. ◆**farcical** *a* grotesque, ridicule.

fare [feər] **1** *n* (*price*) prix *m* du billet; (*ticket*) billet *m*; (*taxi passenger*) client, -ente *mf*. **2** *n* (*food*) chère *f*, nourriture *f*; **prison f.** régime *m* de prison; **bill of f.** menu *m*. **3** *vi* (*manage*) se débrouiller; **how did he f.?** comment ça s'est passé (pour elle)?

farewell [feə'wel] *n* & *int* adieu (*m*); **– a** (*party etc*) d'adieu.

farm [fɑːm] *n* ferme *f*; **– a** (*worker, produce etc*) agricole; **f. land** terres *fpl* cultivées; **–** *vt* cultiver; **–** *vi* être agriculteur. ◆**–ing** *n* agriculture *f*; (*breeding*) élevage *m*; **dairy f.** industrie *f* laitière. ◆**–er** *n* fermier, -ière *mf*, agriculteur *m*. ◆**farmhand** *n* ouvrier, -ière *mf* agricole. ◆**farmhouse** *n* ferme *f*. ◆**farmyard** *n* basse-cour *f*.

farther ['fɑːðər] *adv* plus loin; **nothing is f. from** (*my mind, the truth etc*) rien n'est plus éloigné de; **f. forward** plus avancé; **to get f. away** s'éloigner; **– a** (*end*) autre. ◆**farthest** *a* le plus éloigné; **–** *adv* le plus loin.

fascinate ['fæsɪneɪt] *vt* fasciner. ◆**fasci-** **'nation** *n* fascination *f*.

fascism ['fæʃɪz(ə)m] *n* fascisme *m*. ◆**fas-** **cist** *a* & *n* fasciste (*mf*).

fashion ['fæʃ(ə)n] **1** *n* (*style in clothes etc*) mode *f*; **in f.** à la mode; **out of f.** démodé; **f. designer** (grand) couturier *m*; **f. house** maison *f* de couture; **f. show** présentation *f* de collections. **2** *n* (*manner*) façon *f*; (*custom*) habitude *f*; **after a f.** tant bien que mal, plus au moins. **3** *vt* (*make*) façonner. ◆**–able** *a* à la mode; (*place*) chic *inv*; **it's f.** **to do** il est de bon ton de faire. ◆**–ably** *adv* (*dressed etc*) à la mode.

fast [fɑːst] **1** *a* (-**er, -est**) rapide; **to be f.** (*of clock*) avancer (**by** de); **f. colour** couleur *f* grand teint *inv*; **f. living** vie *f* dissolue; **–** *adv* (*quickly*) vite; (*firmly*) ferme, bien; **how f.?** à quelle vitesse?; **f. asleep** profondément endormi. **2** *vi* (*go without food*) jeûner; **–** *n* jeûne *m*.

fasten ['fɑːs(ə)n] *vt* attacher (**to** à); (*door, window*) fermer (**to** à); **to f. down** *or* **up** attacher; **–** *vi* (*of dress etc*) s'attacher; (*of door, window*) se fermer. ◆**–er** *n*, ◆**–ing** *n* (*clip*) attache *f*; (*of garment*) fermeture *f*; (*of bag*) fermoir *m*; (*hook*) agrafe *f*.

fastidious [fə'stɪdɪəs] *a* difficile (à contenter), exigeant.

fat [fæt] **1** *n* graisse *f*; (*on meat*) gras *m*; **vegetable f.** huile *f* végétale. **2** *a* (**fatter, fattest**) gras; (*cheek, salary, volume*) gros; **to get f.** grossir; **that's a f. lot of good** *or* **use!** *Iron*

Fam ça va vraiment servir (à quelque chose)! ◆**fathead** *n* imbécile *mf*.

fatal ['feɪt(ə)l] *a* mortel; (*error, blow etc*) *Fig* fatal. ◆**—ly** *adv* (*wounded*) mortellement.

fatality [fə'tælɪtɪ] *n* **1** (*person killed*) victime *f*. **2** (*of event*) fatalité *f*.

fate [feɪt] *n* destin *m*, sort *m*; **one's f.** son sort. ◆**fated** *a* **f. to do** destiné à faire; **our meeting/his death/etc was f.** notre rencontre/sa mort/*etc* devait arriver. ◆**fateful** *a* (*important*) fatal, décisif; (*prophetic*) fatidique; (*disastrous*) néfaste.

father ['fɑːðər] *n* père *m*; — *vt* engendrer; (*idea*) *Fig* inventer. ◆**f.-in-law** *n* (*pl* **fathers-in-law**) beau-père *m*. ◆**fatherhood** *n* paternité *f*. ◆**fatherland** *n* patrie *f*. ◆**fatherly** *a* paternel.

fathom ['fæðəm] **1** *n Nau* brasse *f* (= 1,8 *m*). **2** *vt* **f. (out)** (*understand*) comprendre.

fatigue [fə'tiːg] **1** *n* fatigue *f*; — *vt* fatiguer. **2** *n* **f.** (*duty*) *Mil* corvée *f*.

fatness ['fætnɪs] *n* corpulence *f*. ◆**fatten** *vt* engraisser. ◆**fattening** *a* qui fait grossir. ◆**fatty** *a* (**-ier, -iest**) (*food*) gras; (*tissue*) *Med* adipeux; — *n* (*person*) *Fam* gros lard *m*.

fatuous ['fætʃuəs] *a* stupide.

faucet ['fɔːsɪt] *n* (*tap*) *Am* robinet *m*.

fault [fɔːlt] *n* (*blame*) faute *f*; (*failing, defect*) défaut *m*; (*mistake*) erreur *f*; *Geol* faille *f*; **to find f. (with)** critiquer; **it's f. c'est sa faute**, il est fautif; **his** *or* **her memory is at f.** sa mémoire lui fait défaut; — *vt* **to find f. with s.o./sth** trouver des défauts chez qn/à qch. ◆**f.-finding** *a* critique, chicanier. ◆**faultless** *a* irréprochable. ◆**faulty** *a* (**-ier, -iest**) défectueux.

fauna ['fɔːnə] *n* (*animals*) faune *f*.

favour ['feɪvər] *n* (*approval, advantage*) faveur *f*; (*act of kindness*) service *m*; **to do s.o. a f.** rendre service à qn; **in f.** (*person*) bien vu; (*fashion*) en vogue; **it's in her f. to do** elle a intérêt à faire; **in f. of** (*for the sake of*) au profit de, en faveur de; **to be in f. of** (*support*) être pour, être partisan de; (*prefer*) préférer; — *vt* (*encourage*) favoriser; (*support*) être partisan de; (*prefer*) préférer; **he favoured me with a visit** il a eu la gentillesse de me rendre visite. ◆**—able** *a* favorable (**to** à). ◆**favourite** *a* favori, préféré; — *n* favori, -ite *mf*. ◆**favouritism** *n* favoritisme *m*.

fawn [fɔːn] **1** *n* (*deer*) faon *m*; — *a* & *n* (*colour*) fauve (*m*). **2** *vi* **to f. (up)on** flatter, flagorner.

fear [fɪər] *n* crainte *f*, peur *f*; **for f. of** de peur de; **for f. that** de peur que (+ *ne* + *sub*);

there's no f. of his going il ne risque pas d'y aller; **there are fears (that) he might leave** on craint qu'il ne parte; — *vt* craindre; **I f. (that) he might leave** je crains qu'il ne parte; **to f. for** (*one's life etc*) craindre pour. ◆**fearful** *a* (*frightful*) affreux; (*timid*) peureux. ◆**fearless** *a* intrépide. ◆**fearlessness** *n* intrépidité *f*. ◆**fearsome** *a* redoutable.

feasible ['fiːzəb(ə)l] *a* (*practicable*) faisable; (*theory, explanation etc*) plausible. ◆**feasi'bility** *n* possibilité *f* (**of doing** de faire); plausibilité *f*.

feast [fiːst] *n* festin *m*, banquet *m*; *Rel* fête *f*; — *vi* banqueter; **to f. on** (*cakes etc*) se régaler de.

feat [fiːt] *n* exploit *m*, tour *m* de force; **f. of skill** tour *m* d'adresse.

feather ['feðər] **1** *n* plume *f*; **f. duster** plumeau *m*. **2** *vt* **to f. one's nest** (*enrich oneself*) faire sa pelote.

feature ['fiːtʃər] **1** *n* (*of face, person*) trait *m*; (*of thing, place, machine*) caractéristique *f*; (*article*) article *m* de fond; (*film*) grand film *m*; **to be a regular f.** (*in newspaper*) paraître régulièrement (**as** comme); *Journ Cin* présenter; **a film featuring Chaplin** un film avec Charlot en vedette; — *vi* (*appear*) figurer (**in** dans).

February ['februərɪ] *n* février *m*.

fed [fed] *see* **feed**; — *a* **to be f. up** *Fam* en avoir marre (**with** de).

federal ['fedərəl] *a* fédéral. ◆**federate** *vt* fédérer. ◆**fede'ration** *n* fédération *f*.

fee [fiː] *n* (*price*) prix *m*; (*sum*) somme *f*; **fee's** (*professional*) honoraires *mpl*; (*of artist*) cachet *m*; (*for registration*) droits *mpl*; **tuition fees** frais *mpl* de scolarité; **entrance f.** droit *m* d'entrée; **membership fee('s)** cotisation *f*; **f.-paying school** école *f* privée.

feeble ['fiːb(ə)l] *a* (**-er, -est**) faible; (*excuse*) pauvre. ◆**f.-'minded** *a* imbécile.

feed [fiːd] *n* (*food*) nourriture *f*; (*baby's breast feed*) tétée *f*; (*baby's bottle feed*) biberon *m*; — *vt* (*pt* & *pp* **fed**) donner à manger à, nourrir; (*breast-feed*) allaiter (*un bébé*); (*bottle-feed*) donner le biberon à (*un bébé*); (*machine*) *Fig* alimenter; — *vi* (*eat*) manger; **to f. on** se nourrir de. ◆**—ing** *n* alimentation *f*. ◆**feedback** *n* réaction(s) *f(pl)*.

feel [fiːl] *n* (*touch*) toucher *m*; (*sensation*) sensation *f*; — *vt* (*pt* & *pp* **felt**) (*be aware of*) sentir; (*experience*) éprouver, ressentir; (*touch*) tâter, palper; (*think*) avoir l'impression (**that** que); **to f. one's way**

avancer à tâtons; – vi (tired, old etc) se sentir; **to f. (about)** (grope) tâtonner; (in pocket etc) fouiller; **it feels hard** c'est dur (au toucher); **I f. sure** je suis sûr (that que); **I f. hot/sleepy/hungry** j'ai chaud/sommeil/faim; **she feels better** elle va mieux; **to f. like** (want) avoir envie de; **to f. as if** avoir l'impression que; **it feels like cotton** on dirait du coton; **what do you f. about...?** que pensez-vous de...?; **I f. bad about it** ça m'ennuie, ça me fait de la peine; **what does it f. like?** quelle impression ça te fait?; **to f. for** (look for) chercher; (pity) éprouver de la pitié pour; **to f. up to doing** être (assez) en forme pour faire. ◆**–ing** n (emotion, impression) sentiment m; (physical) sensation f; **to f.** (person) de la sympathie pour; (music) une appréciation de; **bad f.** animosité f. ◆**–er** n (of snail etc) antenne f; **to put out a f.** Fig lancer un ballon d'essai.

feet [fiːt] see **foot** [1].

feign [feɪn] vt feindre, simuler.

feint [feɪnt] n Mil Boxing feinte f.

feisty ['faɪstɪ] a (-ier, -iest) (lively) Am Fam plein d'entrain.

felicitous [fə'lɪsɪtəs] a heureux.

feline ['fiːlaɪn] a félin.

fell [fel] 1 see **fall**. 2 vt (tree etc) abattre.

fellow ['feləʊ] n 1 (man, boy) garçon m, type m; an old f., un vieux; **poor f.!** pauvre malheureux! 2 (comrade) compagnon m, compagne f; **f. being** or **man** semblable m; **f. countryman** or **f. countrywoman** compatriote mf; **f. passenger** compagnon m de voyage, compagne f de voyage. 3 (of society) membre m. ◆**fellowship** n camaraderie f; (group) association f; (membership) qualité f de membre; (grant) bourse f universitaire.

felony ['felənɪ] n crime m.

felt [1] [felt] see **feel**.

felt [2] [felt] n feutre m; **f.-tip(ped) pen** crayon m feutre.

female ['fiːmeɪl] a (animal etc) femelle; (quality, name, voice etc) féminin; (vote) des femmes; **f. student** étudiante f; – n (woman) femme f; (animal) femelle f.

feminine ['femɪnɪn] a féminin. ◆**femi'ninity** n féminité f. ◆**feminist** a & n féministe (mf).

fenc/e [fens] 1 n barrière f, clôture f; Sp obstacle m; – vt **to f. (in)** clôturer. 2 vi (with sword) faire de l'escrime. 3 n (criminal) Fam receleur, -euse mf. ◆**–ing** n Sp escrime f.

fend [fend] 1 vi **to f. for oneself** se débrouil-

ler. 2 vt **to f. off** (blow etc) parer, éviter. ◆**–er** n 1 (for fire) garde-feu m inv. 2 (on car) Am aile f.

fennel ['fen(ə)l] n Bot Culin fenouil m.

ferment ['fɜːment] n ferment m; Fig effervescence f; – [fə'ment] vi fermenter. ◆**fermen'tation** n fermentation f.

fern [fɜːn] n fougère f.

ferocious [fə'rəʊʃəs] a féroce. ◆**ferocity** n férocité f.

ferret ['ferɪt] n (animal) furet m; – vi **to f. about** (pry) fureter; – vt **to f. out** dénicher.

Ferris wheel ['ferɪswiːl] n (at funfair) grande roue f.

ferry ['ferɪ] n ferry-boat m; (small, for river) bac m; – vt transporter.

fertile ['fɜːtaɪl, Am 'fɜːt(ə)l] a (land, imagination) fertile; (person, creature) fécond. ◆**fer'tility** n fertilité f; fécondité f. ◆**fertilize** vt (land) fertiliser; (egg, animal etc) féconder. ◆**fertilizer** n engrais m.

fervent ['fɜːv(ə)nt] a fervent. ◆**fervour** n ferveur f.

fester ['festər] vi (of wound) suppurer; (of anger etc) Fig couver.

festival ['festɪv(ə)l] n Mus Cin festival m; Rel fête f. ◆**festive** a (atmosphere, clothes) de fête; (mood) joyeux; **f. season** période f des fêtes. ◆**fe'stivities** npl réjouissances fpl, festivités fpl.

festoon [fe'stuːn] vt **to f. with** orner de.

fetch [fetʃ] vt 1 (person) amener; (object) apporter; **to (go and) f.** aller chercher; **to f. in** rentrer; **to f. out** sortir. 2 (be sold for) rapporter (ten pounds/etc dix livres/etc); (price) atteindre. ◆**–ing** a (smile etc) charmant, séduisant.

fête [feɪt] n fête f; – vt fêter.

fetid ['fetɪd] a fétide.

fetish ['fetɪʃ] n (magical object) fétiche m; **to make a f. of** Fig être obsédé par.

fetter ['fetər] vt (hinder) entraver.

fettle ['fet(ə)l] n **in fine f.** en pleine forme.

fetus ['fiːtəs] n Am fœtus m.

feud [fjuːd] n querelle f, dissension f.

feudal ['fjuːd(ə)l] a féodal.

fever ['fiːvər] n fièvre f; **to have a f.** (temperature) avoir de la fièvre. ◆**feverish** a (person, activity) fiévreux.

few [fjuː] a & pron peu (de); **f. towns/etc** peu de villes/etc; **a f. towns/etc** quelques villes/etc; **f. of them** peu d'entre eux; **a f.** quelques-un(e)s (of de); **a f. of us** quelques-uns d'entre nous; **one of the f. books** l'un des rares livres; **quite a f.**, **a good f.** bon nombre (de); **a f. more books/etc** encore quelques livres/etc; **f. and far between** rares (et espacés); **f. came** peu sont venus; **to be f.** être peu nombreux; **every f. days** tous les trois ou quatre jours. ◆**fewer** *a & pron* moins (de) (**than** que); **to be f.** être moins nombreux (**than** que); **no f. than** pas moins de. ◆**fewest** *a & pron* le moins (de).

fiancé(e) [fɪˈɒnseɪ] *n* fiancé, -ée *mf*.

fiasco [fɪˈæskəʊ] *n* (*pl* -os, *Am* -oes) fiasco *m*.

fib [fɪb] *n Fam* blague *f*, bobard *m*; – *vi* (-bb-) *Fam* raconter des blagues. ◆**fibber** *n Fam* blagueur, -euse *mf*.

fibre [ˈfaɪbər] *n* fibre *f*; *Fig* caractère *m*. ◆**fibreglass** *n* fibre *f* de verre.

fickle [ˈfɪk(ə)l] *a* inconstant.

fiction [ˈfɪkʃ(ə)n] *n* fiction *f*; (*works of*) *f.* romans *mpl*. ◆**fictional**, ◆**fic'titious** *a* fictif.

fiddle [ˈfɪd(ə)l] **1** *n* (*violin*) *Fam* violon *m*; – *vi Fam* jouer du violon. **2** *vi Fam* **to f. about** (*waste time*) traînailler, glandouiller; **to f. (about) with** (*watch, pen etc*) tripoter; (*cars etc*) bricoler. **3** *n* (*dishonesty*) *Fam* combine *f*, fraude *f*; – *vi* (*swindle*) *Fam* faire de la fraude; – *vt* (*accounts etc*) *Fam* falsifier. ◆**-ing** *a* (*petty*) insignifiant. ◆**-er** *n* **1** *Fam* joueur, -euse *mf* de violon. **2** (*swindler*) *Fam* combinard, -arde *mf*. ◆**fiddly** *a* (*task*) délicat.

fidelity [fɪˈdelɪtɪ] *n* fidélité *f* (**to** à).

fidget [ˈfɪdʒɪt] *vi* **to f. (about)** gigoter, se trémousser; **to f. (about) with** tripoter; – *n* personne *f* qui ne tient pas en place. ◆**fidgety** *a* agité, remuant.

field [fiːld] *n* champ *m*; *Sp* terrain *m*; (*sphere*) domaine *m*; **to have a f. day** (*a good day*) s'en donner à cœur joie; **f. glasses** jumelles *fpl*; **f. marshal** maréchal *m*.

fiend [fiːnd] *n* démon *m*; **a jazz/etc f.** *Fam* un(e) passionné, -ée de jazz/etc; (*sex*) **f.** *Fam* satyre *m*. ◆**fiendish** *a* diabolique.

fierce [fɪəs] *a* (-er, -est) féroce; (*wind, attack*) furieux. ◆**-ness** *n* férocité *f*; fureur *f*.

fiery [ˈfaɪərɪ] *a* (-ier, -iest) (*person, speech*) fougueux; (*sun, eyes*) ardent.

fiesta [fɪˈestə] *n* fiesta *f*.

fifteen [fɪfˈtiːn] *a & n* quinze (*m*). ◆**fifteenth** *a & n* quinzième (*mf*). ◆**fifth** *a & n* cinquième (*mf*); **a f.** un cinquième. ◆**'fiftieth** *a & n* cinquantième (*mf*). ◆**'fifty** *a & n* cinquante (*m*).

fig [fɪg] *n* figue *f*; **f. tree** figuier *m*.

fight [faɪt] *n* bagarre *f*, rixe *f*; *Mil Boxing* combat *m*; (*struggle*) lutte *f*; (*quarrel*) dispute *f*; (*spirit*) combativité *f*; **to put up a (good) f.** bien se défendre; – *vi* (*pt & pp*

fought) se battre (**against** contre); *Mil* se battre, combattre; (*struggle*) lutter; (*quarrel*) se disputer; **to f. back** se défendre; **to f. over sth** se disputer qch; – *vt* se battre avec (s.o. qn); (*evil*) lutter contre, combattre; **to f. a battle** livrer bataille; **to f. back** (*tears*) refouler; **to f. off** (*attacker, attack*) repousser; (*illness*) lutter contre; **to f. it out** se bagarrer. ◆**-ing** *n Mil* combat(s) *m(pl)*; – *a* (*person*) combatif; (*troops*) de combat. ◆**-er** *n* combattant, -ante *mf*; *Boxing* boxeur *m*; *Fig* battant *m*, lutteur, -euse *mf*; (*aircraft*) chasseur *m*.

figment [ˈfɪgmənt] *n* **a f. of one's imagination** une création de son esprit.

figurative [ˈfɪgjʊrətɪv] *a* (*meaning*) figuré; (*art*) figuratif. ◆**-ly** *adv* au figuré.

figure [ˈfɪgər, *Am* ˈfɪgjər] *n* **1** (*numeral*) chiffre *m*; (*price*) prix *m*; *pl* (*arithmetic*) calcul *m*. **2** (*shape*) forme *f*; (*outlined shape*) silhouette *f*; (*of woman*) ligne *f*; **she has a nice f.** elle est bien faite. **3** (*diagram*) & *Liter* figure *f*; **a f. of speech** une figure de rhétorique; *Fig* une façon de parler; **f. of eight**, *Am* **f. eight** huit *m*; **f. skating** patinage *m* artistique. **4** (*important person*) figure *f*, personnage *m*. ◆**figurehead** *n Nau* figure *f* de proue; (*person*) *Fig* potiche *f*.

figure [ˈfɪgər, *Am* ˈfɪgjər] **1** *vt* (*imagine*) (s')imaginer; (*guess*) penser (**that** que); **to f. out** arriver à comprendre; (*problem*) résoudre; – *vi* (*make sense*) s'expliquer; **to f. on doing** *Am* compter faire. **2** *vi* (*appear*) figurer (**on** sur).

filament [ˈfɪləmənt] *n* filament *m*.

filch [fɪltʃ] *vt* (*steal*) voler (**from** à).

file [faɪl] *n* **1** (*tool*) lime *f*; – *vt* **to f. (down)** limer. **2** *n* (*folder, information*) dossier *m*; (*loose-leaf*) classeur *m*; (*for card index, computer data*) fichier *m*; – *vt* (*claim, application*) déposer; **to f. (away)** classer. **3** *n* **in single f.** en file; – *vi* **to f. in/out** entrer/sortir à la queue leu leu; **to f. past** (*coffin etc*) défiler devant. ◆**-ing 1** *a* **f. clerk** documentaliste *mf*; **f. cabinet** classeur *m*. **2** *npl* (*particles*) limaille *f*.

fill [fɪl] *vt* remplir (**with** de); (*tooth*) plomber; (*sail*) gonfler; (*need*) répondre à; **to f. in** (*form*) remplir; (*hole*) combler; (*door*) condamner; **to f. s.o. in on** *Fam* mettre qn au courant de; **to f. up** (*glass etc*) remplir; **to f. up or out** (*form*) remplir; – *vi* **to f. (up)** se remplir; **to f. out** (*get fatter*) grossir. **se** remplmmer; **to f. up** *Aut* faire le plein; – **to eat one's f.** manger à sa faim; **to have had one's f. of** *Pej* en avoir assez de. ◆**-ing** *a* (*meal etc*) substantiel, nourrissant; – *n* (*in tooth*) plombage *m*; *Culin* garniture *f*; **f. station** poste *m* d'essence. ◆**—er** *n* (*for cracks in wood*) mastic *m*.

fillet ['fɪlɪt, *Am* fɪ'leɪ] *n* *Culin* filet *m*; – *vt* (*pt & pp Am* fɪ'leɪd) (*fish*) découper en filets; (*meat*) désosser.

fillip ['fɪlɪp] *n* (*stimulus*) coup *m* de fouet.

filly ['fɪlɪ] *n* (*horse*) pouliche *f*.

film [fɪlm] *n* film *m*; (*layer*) & *Phot* pellicule *f*; – *a* (*festival*) du film; (*studio, technician, critic*) de cinéma; **f. fan** *or* **buff** cinéphile *mf*; **f. library** cinémathèque *f*; **f. star** vedette *f* (de cinéma); – *vt* filmer.

filter ['fɪltər] *n* filtre *m*; (*traffic sign*) flèche *f*; **f. lane** *Aut* couloir *m* (pour tourner); **f. tip** (bout *m*) filtre *m*; **f.-tipped cigarette** cigarette *f* (à bout) filtre; – *vt* filtrer; – *vi* filtrer (**through** sth à travers qch); **to f. through** filtrer.

filth [fɪlθ] *n* saleté *f*; (*obscenities*) *Fig* saletés *fpl*. ◆**filthy** *a* (**-ier, -iest**) (*hands etc*) sale; (*language*) obscène; (*habit*) dégoûtant; **f. weather** un temps infect, un sale temps.

fin [fɪn] *n* (*of fish, seal*) nageoire *f*; (*of shark*) aileron *m*.

final ['faɪn(ə)l] *a* dernier; (*decision*) définitif; (*cause*) final; – *n* *Sp* finale *f*; *pl Univ* examens *mpl* de dernière année. ◆**finalist** *n* *Sp* finaliste *mf*. ◆**finalize** *vt* (*plan*) mettre au point; (*date*) fixer (définitivement). ◆**finally** *adv* (*lastly*) enfin, en dernier lieu; (*eventually*) finalement, enfin; (*once and for all*) définitivement.

finale [fɪ'nɑːlɪ] *n* *Mus* finale *m*.

finance ['faɪnæns] *n* finance *f*; – *a* (*company, page*) financier; – *vt* financer. ◆**fi'nancial** *a* financier; **f. year** année *f* budgétaire. ◆**fi'nancially** *adv* financièrement. ◆**fi'nancier** *n* (grand) financier *m*.

find [faɪnd] *n* (*discovery*) trouvaille *f*; – *vt* (*pt & pp* **found**) trouver; (*sth or s.o. lost*) retrouver; (*difficulty*) éprouver, trouver (**in doing** à faire); **I f.** that je trouve que; **£20 all found** 20 livres logé et nourri; **to f. s.o. guilty** *Jur* prononcer qn coupable; **to f. one's feet** (*settle in*) s'adapter; **to f. oneself** (*to be*) se trouver. ■ **to f. out** *vt* (*information etc*) découvrir; (*person*) démasquer; – *vi* (*enquire*) se renseigner (**about** sur); **to f. out about** (*discover*) découvrir. ◆**—ings** *npl* conclusions *fpl*.

fine¹ [faɪn] *n* (*money*) amende *f*; *Aut* contravention *f*; – *vt* **to f. s.o.** (**£10/**etc) infliger une amende (de dix livres/etc) à qn.

fine² [faɪn] **1** *a* (**-er, -est**) (*thin, small, not coarse*) fin; (*gold*) pur; (*feeling*) délicat;

(*distinction*) subtil; – *adv* (*to cut, write*) menu. **2** *a* (**-er, -est**) (*beautiful*) beau; (*good*) bon; (*excellent*) excellent; **to be f.** (*in good health*) aller bien; – *adv* (*well*) très bien. ◆**—ly** *adv* (*dressed*) magnifiquement; (*chopped*) menu; (*embroidered, ground*) finement.

finery ['faɪnərɪ] *n* (*clothes*) parure *f*, belle toilette *f*.

finesse [fɪ'nes] *n* (*skill, tact*) doigté *m*; (*refinement*) finesse *f*.

finger ['fɪŋgər] *n* doigt *m*; **little f.** auriculaire *m*, petit doigt *m*; **middle f.** majeur *m*; **f. mark** trace *f* de doigt; – *vt* toucher (des doigts), palper. ◆**—ing** *n* *Mus* doigté *m*. ◆**fingernail** *n* ongle *m*. ◆**fingerprint** *n* empreinte *f* digitale. ◆**fingerstall** *n* doigtier *m*. ◆**fingertip** *n* bout *m* du doigt.

finicky ['fɪnɪkɪ] *a* (*precise*) méticuleux; (*difficult*) difficile (**about** sur).

finish ['fɪnɪʃ] *n* (*end*) fin *f*; *Sp* arrivée *f*; (*of article, car etc*) finition *f*; **paint with a matt f.** peinture *f* mate; – *vt* **to f.** (**off** *or* **up**) finir, terminer; **to f. doing** finir de faire; **to f. s.o. off** (*kill*) achever qn; – *vi* (*of meeting etc*) finir, se terminer; (*of person*) finir, terminer; **to f. first** terminer premier; (*in race*) arriver premier; **to have finished with** (*object*) ne plus avoir besoin de; (*situation, person*) en avoir fini avec; **to f. off** *or* **up** (*of person*) finir, terminer; **to f. up in** (*end up in*) se retrouver à; **to f. up doing** finir par faire; **finishing school** institution *f* pour jeunes filles; **finishing touch** touche *f* finale. ◆**—ed** *a* (*ended, done for*) fini.

finite ['faɪnaɪt] *a* fini.

Finland ['fɪnlənd] *n* Finlande *f*. ◆**Finn** *n* Finlandais, -aise *mf*, Finnois, -oise *mf*. ◆**Finnish** *a* finlandais, finnois; – *n* (*language*) finnois *m*.

fir [fɜːr] *n* (*tree, wood*) sapin *m*.

fire¹ ['faɪər] *n* feu *m*; (*accidental*) incendie *m*; (*electric*) radiateur *m*; **on f.** en feu; (**there's a**) **f.!** au feu!; **f.!** *Mil* feu!; **f. alarm** avertisseur *m* d'incendie; **f. brigade**, *Am* **f. department** pompiers *mpl*; **f. engine** (*vehicle*) voiture *f* de pompiers; (*machine*) pompe *f* à incendie; **f. escape** escalier *m* de secours; **f. station** caserne *f* de pompiers. ◆**firearm** *n* arme *f* à feu. ◆**firebug** *n* pyromane *mf*. ◆**firecracker** *n* *Am* pétard *m*. ◆**fireguard** *n* garde-feu *m inv*. ◆**fireman** *n* (*pl* **-men**) (sapeur-)pompier *m*. ◆**fireplace** *n* cheminée *f*. ◆**fireproof** *a* (*door*) ignifugé, anti-incendie. ◆**fireside** *n* coin *m* du feu; **f. chair** fauteuil *m*. ◆**firewood** *n* bois *m* de chauffage.

◆**firework** n feu m d'artifice; **a f. display, fireworks,** un feu d'artifice.

fire [ˈfaɪər] vt (cannon) tirer; (pottery) cuire; (imagination) enflammer; **to f. a gun** tirer un coup de fusil; **to f. questions at** bombarder de questions; **to f. s.o.** (dismiss) Fam renvoyer qn; – vi tirer (at sur); **f. away!** Fam vas-y, parle!; **firing squad** peloton m d'exécution; **in** or **Am on the firing line** en butte aux attaques.

firm [fɜːm] **1** n Com maison f, firme f. **2** a (-er, -est) (earth, decision etc) ferme; (strict) ferme (with avec); (faith) solide; (character) résolu. ◆**-ly** adv fermement; (to speak) d'une voix ferme. ◆**-ness** n fermeté f; (of faith) solidité f.

first [fɜːst] a premier; **I'll do it f. thing in the morning** je le ferai dès le matin, sans faute; **f. cousin** cousin, -ine mf germain(e); – adv d'abord, premièrement; (for the first time) pour la première fois; **f. of all** tout d'abord; **at f.** d'abord; **to come f.** (in race) arriver premier; (in exam) être le premier; – n premier, -ière mf; Univ = licence f avec mention très bien; **from the f.** dès le début; **f. aid** premiers soins mpl or secours mpl; (gear) Aut première f. ◆**f.-'class** a (ticket etc) de première (classe); (mail) ordinaire; – adv (to travel) en première. ◆**f.-'hand** a & adv de première main; **to have (had) f.-hand experience of** avoir fait l'expérience personnelle de. ◆**f.-'rate** a excellent. ◆**firstly** adv premièrement.

fiscal [ˈfɪsk(ə)l] a fiscal.

fish [fɪʃ] n (pl inv or -es [-ɪz]) poisson m; **f. market** marché m aux poissons; **f. bone** arête f; **f. bowl** bocal m; **f. fingers,** Am **f. sticks** Culin bâtonnets mpl de poisson; **f. shop** poissonnerie f; – vi pêcher; **to f. for** (salmon etc) pêcher; (compliment etc) Fig chercher; – vt **to f. out** (from water) repêcher; (from pocket etc) Fig sortir. ◆**-ing** n pêche f; **to go f.** aller à la pêche; **f. net** (of fisherman) filet m (de pêche); (of angler) épuisette f; **f. rod** canne f à pêche. ◆**fisherman** n (pl -men) pêcheur m. ◆**fishmonger** n poissonnier, -ière mf. ◆**fishy** a (-ier, -iest) (smell) de poisson; Fig Pej louche.

fission [ˈfɪʃ(ə)n] n Phys fission f.

fissure [ˈfɪʃər] n fissure f.

fist [fɪst] n poing m. ◆**fistful** n poignée f.

fit¹ [fɪt] **1** a (fitter, fittest) (suited) propre, bon (for à); (fitting) convenable; (worthy) digne (for de); (able) capable (for de, to do de faire); (healthy) en bonne santé; **f. to eat** bon à manger, mangeable; **to see f. to do**

juger à propos de faire; **as you see f.** comme bon vous semble; **f. to drop** Fam prêt à tomber; **to keep f.** se maintenir en forme. **2** vt (-tt-) (of coat etc) aller (bien) à (qn); (of dress etc) être à la taille de (qn); (match) répondre à; (equal) égaler; (in s.o.'s mind) graver (in dans); (conduct fraudulently) Am préparer, faire; (in s.o.'s mind) graver (in dans); **to f. sth (on) to** (put) poser qch sur qch; (adjust) adapter qch à qch; (fix) fixer qch à qch; **to f. (out** or **up) with** (house, ship etc) équiper de; **to f. (in)** (window) poser; **to f. in** (object) faire entrer; (patient, customer) prendre; **to f. (in) the lock** (of key) aller dans la serrure; – vi (of clothes) aller (bien) (à qn); **this shirt fits** (the correct size) cette chemise me va; **to f. (in)** (go in) entrer, aller; (of facts, plans) s'accorder, cadrer (with avec); **he doesn't f. in** il ne peut pas s'intégrer; – n **a good f.** (dress etc) à la bonne taille; **a close** or **tight f.** ajusté. ◆**fitted** a (cupboard) encastré; (garment) ajusté; **f. carpet** moquette f; **f. (kitchen) units** éléments mpl de cuisine. ◆**fitting 1** a (suitable) convenable. **2** n (of clothes) essayage m; **f. room** salon m d'essayage; (booth) cabine f d'essayage. **3** npl (in house etc) installations fpl. ◆**fitment** n (furniture) meuble m encastré; (accessory) Tech accessoire m. ◆**fitness** n (of remark etc) à-propos m; (for job) aptitudes fpl (for pour); Med santé f. ◆**fitter** n Tech monteur, -euse mf.

fit² [fɪt] n Med & Fig accès m, crise f; **in fits and starts** par à-coups. ◆**fitful** a (sleep) agité.

five [faɪv] a & n cinq (m). ◆**fiver** n Fam billet m de cinq livres.

fix [fɪks] **1** vt (make firm, decide) fixer; (tie with rope) attacher; (mend) réparer; (deal with) arranger; (prepare, cook) Am préparer, faire; (in s.o.'s mind) graver (in dans); (conduct fraudulently) Am truquer; (bribe) Fam acheter; (hopes, ambitions) mettre (on en); **to f. s.o.** (punish) Fam régler son compte à qn; **to f. (on)** (lid etc) mettre en place; **to f. up** arranger; **to f. s.o. up with sth** (job etc) procurer qch à qn. **2** n Av Nau position f; (injection) Sl piqûre f; **in a f.** Fam dans le pétrin. ◆**-ed** a (idea, price etc) fixe; (resolution) inébranlable; **how's he f. for . . . ?** Fam (cash etc) a-t-il assez de . . . ?; (tomorrow etc) est-ce qu'il fait pour . . . ? ◆**fixings** npl Culin Am garniture f. ◆**fix'ation** n fixation f. ◆**fixer** n (schemer) Fam combinard, -arde mf. ◆**fixture 1** n Sp match m (prévu). **2** npl (in house) meubles mpl fixes, installations fpl.

fizz [fɪz] vi (of champagne) pétiller. (of gas) siffler. ◆**fizzy** a (-ier, -iest) pétillant.

fizzle ['fɪz(ə)l] vi (hiss) siffler; (of liquid) pétiller; **to f. out** (of firework) rater, faire long feu; (of plan) Fig tomber à l'eau; (of custom) disparaître.

flabbergasted ['flæbəgɑːstɪd] a Fam sidéré.

flabby ['flæbɪ] a (-ier, -iest) (skin, character, person) mou, flasque.

flag [flæg] **1** n drapeau m; Nau pavillon m; (for charity) insigne m; **f. stop** Am arrêt m facultatif; — vt (-gg-) **to f. down** (taxi) faire signe à. **2** vi (-gg-) (of plant) dépérir; (of conversation) languir; (of worker) fléchir. ◆**flagpole** n mât m.

flagrant ['fleɪgrənt] a flagrant.

flagstone ['flægstəun] n dalle f.

flair [fleər] n (intuition) flair m; **to have a f. for** (natural talent) avoir un don pour.

flake [fleɪk] n (of snow etc) flocon m; (of metal, soap) paillette f; — vi **to f. (off)** (of paint) s'écailler. ◆**flaky** a **f. pastry** pâte f feuilletée.

flamboyant [flæm'bɔɪənt] a (person, manner) extravagant.

flam/e [fleɪm] n flamme f; **to go up in flames** s'enflammer; — vi **to f. (up)** (of fire, house) flamber. ◆**-ing** a **1** (sun) flamboyant. **2** (damn) Fam fichu.

flamingo [flə'mɪŋgəʊ] n (pl -os or -oes) (bird) flamant m.

flammable ['flæməb(ə)l] a inflammable.

flan [flæn] n tarte f.

flank [flæŋk] n flanc m; — vt flanquer (with de).

flannel ['flæn(ə)l] n (cloth) flanelle f; (face) f. gant m de toilette, carré-éponge m. ◆**flanne'lette** n pilou m, finette f.

flap [flæp] **1** vi (-pp-) (of wings, sail, shutter etc) battre; — vt **to f. its wings** (of bird) battre des ailes; — n battement m. **2** n (of pocket, envelope) rabat m; (of table) abattant m; (of door) battant m.

flare [fleər] n (light) éclat m; Mil fusée f éclairante; (for runway) balise f; — vi (blaze) flamber; (shine) briller; **to f. up** (of fire) s'enflammer; (of region) Fig s'embraser; (of war) éclater; (get angry) s'emporter. ◆**f.-up** n (of violence, anger) flambée f; (of region) embrasement m. ◆**flared** a (skirt) évasé; (trousers) à pattes d'éléphant.

flash [flæʃ] n (of light) éclat m; (of anger, genius) éclair m; Phot flash m; **f. of lightning** éclair m; **news f.** flash m; **in a f.** en un clin d'œil; — vi (shine) briller; (on and off) clignoter; **to f. past** (rush) Fig passer comme un éclair; — vt (aim) diriger (**on, at** sur); (a light) projeter; (a glance) jeter; **to f. (around)** (flaunt) étaler; **to f. one's head-lights** faire un appel de phares. ◆**flashback** n retour m en arrière. ◆**flashlight** n lampe f électrique or de poche; Phot flash m.

flashy ['flæʃɪ] a (-ier, -iest) a voyant, tape-à-l'œil inv.

flask [flɑːsk] n thermos® m or f inv; Ch flacon m; (phial) fiole f.

flat¹ [flæt] a (flatter, flattest) plat; (tyre, battery) à plat; (nose) aplati; (beer) éventé; (refusal) net; (rate, fare) fixe; (voice) Mus faux; (razed to the ground) rasé; **to put sth (down)** f. mettre qch à plat; **f. (on one's face)** à plat ventre; **to fall f.** Fig tomber à plat; **to be f.-footed** avoir les pieds plats; — adv (to say) carrément; (to sing) faux; **f. broke** Fam complètement fauché; **in two minutes f.** en deux minutes pile; **f. out** (to work) d'arrache-pied; (to run) à toute vitesse; — n (of hand) plat m; (puncture) Aut crevaison f; Mus bémol m. ◆**-ly** adv (to deny etc) catégoriquement. ◆**-ness** n (of surface) égalité f. ◆**flatten** vt (crops) coucher; (town) raser; **to f. (out)** (metal etc) aplatir.

flat² [flæt] n (rooms) appartement m.

flatter ['flætər] vt flatter; (of clothes) avantager (qn). ◆**-ing** a flatteur; (clothes) avantageux. ◆**-er** n flatteur, -euse mf. ◆**flattery** n flatterie f.

flatulence ['flætjʊləns] n **to have f.** avoir des gaz.

flaunt [flɔːnt] vt (show off) faire étalage de; (defy) Am narguer, défier.

flautist ['flɔːtɪst] n flûtiste mf.

flavour ['fleɪvər] n (taste) goût m, saveur f; (of ice cream, sweet etc) parfum m; — vt (food) assaisonner; (sauce) relever; (ice cream etc) parfumer (with à). ◆**-ing** n assaisonnement m; (in cake) parfum m.

flaw [flɔː] n défaut m. ◆**flawed** a imparfait. ◆**flawless** a parfait.

flax [flæks] n lin m. ◆**flaxen** a de lin.

flay [fleɪ] vt (animal) écorcher; (criticize) Fig éreinter.

flea [fliː] n puce f; **f. market** marché m aux puces. ◆**fleapit** n Fam cinéma m miteux.

fleck [flek] n (mark) petite tache f.

fledgling ['fledʒlɪŋ] n (novice) blanc-bec m.

flee [fliː] vi (pt & pp **fled**) fuir, s'enfuir, se sauver; — vt (place) s'enfuir de; (danger etc) fuir.

fleece [fliːs] **1** n (sheep's coat) toison f. **2** vt (rob) voler.

fleet [fliːt] n (of ships) flotte f; **a f. of cars** un parc automobile.

fleeting ['fliːtɪŋ] a (visit, moment) bref; (beauty) éphémère.

Flemish ['flemɪʃ] a flamand; – n (language) flamand m.

flesh [fleʃ] n chair f; **her (own) f. and blood** la chair de sa chair; **in the f.** en chair et en os; **f. wound** blessure f superficielle. ◆**fleshy** a (-ier, -iest) charnu.

flew [fluː] see **fly** [2].

flex [fleks] **1** vt (limb) fléchir; (muscle) faire jouer, bander. **2** n (wire) film (souple); (for telephone) cordon m.

flexible ['fleksɪb(ə)l] a flexible, souple. ◆**flexi'bility** n flexibilité f.

flick [flɪk] vt donner un petit coup à; **to f. off** (remove) enlever (d'une chiquenaude); – vi **to f. over** or **through** (pages) feuilleter; – n petit coup m; (with finger) chiquenaude f; **f. knife** couteau m à cran d'arrêt.

flicker ['flɪkər] vi (of flame, light) vaciller; (of needle) osciller; – n vacillement m; **f. of light** lueur f.

flier ['flaɪər] n **1** (person) aviateur, -trice mf. **2** (handbill) Am prospectus m, Pol tract m.

flies [flaɪz] npl (on trousers) braguette f.

flight [flaɪt] n (of bird, aircraft etc) vol m; (of bullet) trajectoire f; (of imagination) élan f; (floor, storey) étage m; **f. of stairs** escalier m; **f. deck** cabine f de pilotage. **2** (fleeing) fuite f (from de); **to take f.** prendre la fuite.

flighty ['flaɪtɪ] a (-ier, -iest) inconstant, volage.

flimsy ['flɪmzɪ] a (-ier, -iest) (cloth, structure etc) (trop) léger or mince; (excuse) mince, frivole.

flinch [flɪntʃ] vi (with pain) tressaillir; **to f. from** (duty etc) se dérober à; **without flinching** (complaining) sans broncher.

fling [flɪŋ] **1** vt (pt & pp flung) jeter, lancer; **to f. open** (door etc) ouvrir brutalement. **2** n **to have one's** or **a f.** (indulge oneself) s'en donner à cœur joie.

flint [flɪnt] n silex m; (for cigarette lighter) pierre f.

flip [flɪp] **1** vt (-pp-) (with finger) donner une chiquenaude à; – vi **to f. through** (book etc) feuilleter; – n chiquenaude f; **the f. side** (of record) la face deux. **2** a (cheeky) Am Fam effronté.

flip-flops ['flɪpflɒps] npl tongs fpl.

flippant ['flɪpənt] a irrévérencieux; (off-hand) désinvolte.

flipper ['flɪpər] n (of seal) nageoire f; (of swimmer) palme f.

flipping ['flɪpɪŋ] a Fam sacré; – adv Fam sacrément, bougrement.

flirt [flɜːt] vi flirter (with avec); – n flirteur, -euse mf. ◆**flir'tation** n flirt m. ◆**flir'tatious** a flirteur.

flit [flɪt] vi (-tt-) (fly) voltiger; **to f. in and out** (of person) Fig entrer et sortir (rapidement).

float [fləʊt] n Fishing flotteur m; (in parade) char m; – vi flotter (on sur); **to f. down the river** descendre la rivière; – vt (boat, currency) faire flotter; (loan) Com émettre. ◆**—ing** a (wood, debt etc) flottant; (population) instable; (voters) indécis.

flock [flɒk] n (of sheep etc) troupeau m; (of birds) volée f; Rel Hum ouailles fpl; (of tourists etc) foule f; – vi venir en foule; **to f. round s.o.** s'attrouper autour de qn.

floe [fləʊ] n (ice) f. banquise f.

flog [flɒg] vt (-gg-) **1** (beat) flageller. **2** (sell) Sl vendre. ◆**flogging** n flagellation f.

flood [flʌd] n inondation f; (of letters, tears etc) Fig flot m, déluge m, torrent m; – vt (field etc) inonder (with de); (river) faire déborder; **to f. (out)** (house) inonder; – vi (of building) être inondé; (of river) déborder; (of people, money) affluer; **to f. into** (of tourists etc) envahir. ◆**—ing** n inondation f. ◆**floodgate** n (in water) vanne f.

floodlight ['flʌdlaɪt] n projecteur m; – vt (pt & pp floodlit) illuminer; **floodlit match** Sp (match m en) nocturne m.

floor [flɔːr] n **1** (ground) sol m; (wooden etc in building) plancher m; (storey) étage m; (dance) f. piste f (de danse); **on the f.** par terre; **first f.** premier étage m; (ground floor) Am rez-de-chaussée m inv; **f. polish** encaustique f; **f. show** spectacle m (de cabaret). **2** vt (knock down) terrasser; (puzzle) stupéfier. ◆**floorboard** n planche f.

flop [flɒp] **1** vi (-pp-) **to f. down** (collapse) s'effondrer; **to f. about** s'agiter mollement. **2** vi (-pp-) Fam échouer; (of play, film etc) faire un four; – n Fam échec m, fiasco m; Th Cin four m.

floppy ['flɒpɪ] a (-ier, -iest) (soft) mou; (clothes) (trop) large; (ears) pendant; **f. disk** (of computer) disquette f.

flora ['flɔːrə] n (plants) flore f. ◆**floral** a floral; (material) à fleurs.

florid ['florɪd] a (style) fleuri; (complexion) rougeaud, fleuri.

florist ['florɪst] n fleuriste mf.

floss [flɒs] n (dental) fil m (de soie) dentaire.

flotilla [flə'tɪlə] n Nau flottille f.

flounce [flauns] n (*frill on dress etc*) volant m.

flounder ['flaundər] **1** vi (*in water etc*) patauger (avec effort); se débattre; (*in speech*) hésiter, patauger. **2** n (*fish*) carrelet m.

flour [flauər] n farine f.

flourish ['flʌriʃ] **1** vi (*of person, business, plant etc*) prospérer; (*of the arts*) fleurir. **2** vt (*wave*) brandir. **3** n (*decoration*) fioriture f; Mus fanfare f. ◆—**ing** a prospère, florissant.

flout [flaut] vt narguer, braver.

flow [fləu] vi couler; (*of current*) El circuler; (*of hair, clothes*) flotter; (*of traffic*) s'écouler; **to f. in** (*of people, money*) affluer; **to f. back** refluer; **to f. into the sea** se jeter dans la mer; – n (*of river*) courant m; (*of tide*) flux m; (*of blood*) & El circulation f; (*of traffic, liquid*) écoulement m; (*of words*) Fig flot m. ◆—**ing** a (*movement*) gracieux; (*style*) coulant; (*beard*) flottant.

flower ['flauər] n fleur f; **f. bed** plate-bande f; **f. shop** (*boutique f de*) fleuriste mf; **f. show** floralies fpl; – vi fleurir. ◆—**ed** a (*dress*) à fleurs. ◆—**ing** n floraison f; – a (*in bloom*) en fleurs; (*with flowers*) à fleurs. ◆**flowery** a (*style etc*) fleuri; (*material*) à fleurs.

flown [fləun] *see* fly².

flu [flu:] n (*influenza*) Fam grippe f.

fluctuate ['flʌktʃueit] vi varier. ◆**fluctu'ation(s)** n(pl) (*in prices etc*) fluctuations fpl (in de).

flue [flu:] n (*of chimney*) conduit m.

fluent ['flu:ənt] a (*style*) aisé; **to be f., be a f. speaker** s'exprimer avec facilité; **he's f. in Russian, his Russian is f.** il parle couramment le russe. ◆**fluency** n facilité f. ◆**fluently** adv avec facilité; (*to speak*) Ling couramment.

fluff [flʌf] **1** n (*down*) duvet m; (*of material*) peluche(s) f(pl); (*on floor*) moutons mpl. **2** vt (*bungle*) Fam rater. ◆**fluffy** a (-**ier**, -**iest**) (*bird etc*) duveteux; (*material*) pelucheux; (*toy*) en peluche; (*hair*) bouffant.

fluid ['flu:id] a fluide; (*plans*) flexible, non arrêté; – n fluide m, liquide m.

fluke [flu:k] n Fam coup m de chance; **by a f.** par raccroc.

flummox ['flʌməks] vt Fam désorienter, dérouter.

flung [flʌŋ] *see* fling.

flunk [flʌŋk] vi (*in exam*) Am Fam être collé; – vt Am Fam (*pupil*) coller; (*exam*) être collé à; (*school*) laisser tomber.

flunk(e)y ['flʌŋki] n Pej larbin m.

fluorescent [fluə'res(ə)nt] a fluorescent.

fluoride ['fluəraid] n (*in water, toothpaste*) fluor m.

flurry ['flʌri] n **1** (*of activity*) poussée f. **2** (*of snow*) rafale f.

flush [flʌʃ] **1** n (*of blood*) flux m; (*blush*) rougeur f; (*of youth, beauty*) éclat m; (*of victory*) ivresse f; – vi (*blush*) rougir. **2** vt (**f. out**) (*clean*) nettoyer à grande eau; **to f. the pan** or **the toilet** tirer la chasse d'eau; **to f. s.o. out** (*chase away*) faire sortir qn (from de). **3** a (*level*) de niveau (**with** de); **f. (with money)** Fam bourré de fric. ◆—**ed** a (*cheeks etc*) rouge; **f. with** (*success*) ivre de.

flute [flu:t] n flûte f. ◆**flutist** n Am flûtiste mf.

flutter ['flʌtər] **1** vi voltiger; (*of wing*) battre; (*of flag*) flotter (mollement); (*of heart*) palpiter; **to f. about** (*of person*) papillonner; – vt **to f. its wings** battre des ailes. **2** n (*bet*) Fam pari m.

flux [flʌks] n changement m continuel.

fly¹ [flai] n (*insect*) mouche f; **f. swatter** (*instrument*) tapette f. ◆**flypaper** n papier m tue-mouches.

fly² [flai] vi (pt **flew**, pp **flown**) (*of bird, aircraft etc*) voler; (*of passenger*) aller en avion; (*of time*) passer vite; (*of flag*) flotter; (*flee*) fuir; **to f. away** or **off** s'envoler; **to f. out** Av partir en avion; (*from room*) sortir à toute vitesse; **I must f.!** il faut que je file!; **to f. at s.o.** (*attack*) sauter sur qn; – vt (*aircraft*) piloter; (*passengers*) transporter (par avion); (*airline*) voyager par; (*flag*) arborer; (*kite*) faire voler; **to f. the French flag** battre pavillon français; **to f. across** or **over** survoler. ◆—**ing** n (*flight*) vol m; (*air travel*) aviation f; **to like f.** aimer l'avion; – a (*personnel, saucer etc*) volant; (*visit*) éclair inv; **with f. colours** (*to succeed*) haut la main; **a f. start** un très bon départ; **f. time** (*length*) Av durée f du vol; **ten hours'/etc f. time** dix heures/etc de vol. ◆—**er** n = **flier**. ◆**flyby** n Av Am défilé m aérien. ◆**fly-by-night** a (*firm*) véreux. ◆**flyover** n (*bridge*) toboggan m. ◆**flypast** n Av défilé m aérien.

fly³ [flai] n (*on trousers*) braguette f.

foal [fəul] n poulain m.

foam [fəum] n (*on sea, mouth*) écume f; (*on beer*) mousse f; **f. rubber** caoutchouc m mousse; **f. (rubber) mattress/etc** matelas m/etc mousse; – vi (*of sea, mouth*) écumer; (*of beer, soap*) mousser.

fob [fɒb] vt (-bb-) to f. sth off on s.o., f. s.o. off with sth, refiler qch à qn.

focal ['fəʊk(ə)l] a focal; f. point point m central. ◆**focus** n foyer m; (of attention, interest) centre m; in f. au point; − vt Phot mettre au point; (light) faire converger; (efforts, attention) concentrer (on sur); − vi (converge) converger (on sur); to f. (one's eyes) on fixer les yeux sur; to f. on (direct one's attention to) se concentrer sur.

fodder ['fɒdər] n fourrage m.

foe [fəʊ] n ennemi, -ie mf.

foetus ['fiːtəs] n fœtus m.

fog [fɒg] n brouillard m, brume f; − vt (-gg-) (issue) Fig embrouiller. ◆**fogbound** a bloqué par le brouillard. ◆**foghorn** n corne f de brume; (voice) Pej voix f tonitruante. ◆**foglamp** n (phare m) anti-brouillard m. ◆**foggy** a (-ier, -iest) (day) de brouillard; it's f. il fait du brouillard; f. weather brouillard m; she hasn't the foggiest (idea) Fam elle n'en a pas la moindre idée.

fog(e)y ['fəʊgɪ] n old f. vieille baderne f.

foible ['fɔɪb(ə)l] n petit défaut m.

foil [fɔɪl] 1 n feuille f de métal; Culin papier m alu(minium). 2 n (contrasting person) repoussoir m. 3 vt (plans etc) déjouer.

foist [fɔɪst] vt to f. sth on s.o. (fob off) refiler qch à qn; to f. oneself on s.o. s'imposer à qn.

fold[1] [fəʊld] n pli m; − vt plier; (wrap) envelopper (in dans); to f. away or down or up plier; to f. back or over replier; to f. one's arms (se) croiser les bras; − vi (of chair etc) se plier; (of business) Fam s'écrouler; to f. away or down or up (of chair etc) se plier; to f. back or over (of blanket etc) se replier. ◆**-ing** a (chair etc) pliant. ◆**-er** n (file holder) chemise f; (pamphlet) dépliant m.

fold[2] [fəʊld] n (for sheep) parc m à moutons; Rel Fig bercail m.

-fold [fəʊld] suffix tenfold a par dix; − adv dix fois.

foliage ['fəʊlɪɪdʒ] n feuillage m.

folk [fəʊk] 1 n gens mpl or fpl; pl gens mpl or fpl; (parents) Fam parents mpl; hello folks! Fam salut tout le monde!; old f. like it les vieux l'apprécient. 2 a (dance etc) folklorique; f. music (contemporary) (musique f) folk m. ◆**folklore** n folklore m.

follow ['fɒləʊ] vt suivre; (career) poursuivre; followed by suivi de; to f. suit Fig en faire autant; to f. s.o. around suivre qn partout; to f. through (idea etc) poursuivre jusqu'au bout; to f. up (suggestion, case) suivre; (advantage) exploiter; (letter) donner suite à; (remark) faire suivre (with de); − vi to f. (on) suivre; it follows that il s'ensuit que; that doesn't f. ce n'est pas logique. ◆**-ing 1** a suivant; − prep à la suite de. 2 n (supporters) partisans mpl; to have a large f. avoir de nombreux partisans; (of serial, fashion) être très suivi. ◆**-er** n partisan m. ◆**follow-up** n suite f; (letter) rappel m.

folly ['fɒlɪ] n folie f, sottise f.

foment [fəʊ'ment] vt (revolt etc) fomenter.

fond [fɒnd] a (-er, -est) (loving) tendre, affectueux; (doting) indulgent; (wish, ambition) naïf; to be (very) f. of aimer (beaucoup). ◆**-ly** adv tendrement. ◆**-ness** n (for things) prédilection f (for pour); (for people) affection f (for pour).

fondle ['fɒnd(ə)l] vt caresser.

food [fuːd] n nourriture f; (particular substance) aliment m; (cooking) cuisine f; (for cats, pigs) pâtée f; (for plants) engrais m; pl (foodstuffs) aliments mpl; − a (needs etc) alimentaire; a fast f. shop un fast-food; f. poisoning intoxication f alimentaire; f. value valeur f nutritive. ◆**foodstuffs** npl denrées fpl or produits mpl alimentaires.

fool [fuːl] n imbécile mf, idiot, -ote mf; (you) silly f.! espèce d'imbécile!; to make a f. of (ridicule) ridiculiser; (trick) duper; to be enough to do être assez stupide pour faire; to play the f. faire l'imbécile; − vt (trick) duper; − vi to f. (about or around) faire l'imbécile; (waste time) perdre son temps; to f. around (make love) Am Fam faire l'amour (with avec). ◆**foolish** a bête, idiot. ◆**foolishly** adv bêtement. ◆**foolishness** n bêtise f, sottise f. ◆**foolproof** a (scheme etc) infaillible.

foolhardy ['fuːlhɑːdɪ] a téméraire. ◆**foolhardiness** n témérité f.

foot[1], pl **feet** [fʊt, fiːt] n pied m; (of animal) patte f; (measure) pied m (= 30,48 cm); at the f. of (page, stairs) au bas de; (table) au bout de; on f. à pied; on one's feet (standing) debout; (recovered) Med sur pied; f. brake Aut frein m au plancher; f.-and-mouth disease fièvre f aphteuse. ◆**footbridge** n passerelle f. ◆**foothills** npl contreforts mpl. ◆**foothold** n prise f (de pied); Fig position f; to gain a f. prendre pied. ◆**footlights** npl Th rampe f. ◆**footloose** a libre de toute attache. ◆**footman** n (pl -men) valet m de pied. ◆**footmark** n empreinte f (de pied). ◆**footnote** n note f au bas de la page; Fig post-scriptum m. ◆**footpath** n sentier m; (at roadside) chemin m (piétonnier). ◆**footstep** n pas m; **to follow in s.o.'s footsteps** suivre les traces de qn. ◆**footwear** n chaussures fpl.

foot² [fut] vt (bill) payer.

football ['futbɔːl] n (game) football m; (ball) ballon m. ◆**footballer** n joueur, -euse mf de football.

footing ['futiŋ] n prise f (de pied), Fig position f; **on a war f.** sur le pied de guerre; **on an equal f.** sur un pied d'égalité.

for [fɔr, unstressed fər] **1** prep pour; (in exchange for) contre; (for a distance of) pendant; (in spite of) malgré; **f. you/me/**etc pour toi/moi/etc; **what f.?** pourquoi?; **what's it f.?** ça sert à quoi?; **f. example** par exemple; **f. love** par amour; **f. sale** à vendre; **to swim f.** (towards) nager vers; **a train f.** un train à destination de ou en direction de; **the road f. London** la route (en direction) de Londres; **fit f. eating** bon à manger; **eager f.** avide de; **to look f.** chercher; **to come f. dinner** venir dîner; **to sell f. £7** vendre sept livres; **what's the Russian f. 'book'?** comment dit-on 'livre' en russe?; **but f. her** sans elle; **he was away f. a month** (throughout) il a été absent pendant un mois; **he won't be back f. a month** il ne sera pas de retour avant un mois; **he's been here f. a month** (he's still here) il est ici depuis un mois; **I haven't seen him f. ten years** voilà dix ans que je ne l'ai vu; **it's easy f. her to do it** il lui est facile de le faire; **it's f. you to say** c'est à toi de dire; **f. that to be done** pour que ça soit fait. **2** conj (because) car.

forage ['fɒridʒ] vi **to f. (about)** fourrager (for pour trouver).

foray ['fɒrei] n incursion f.

forbearance [fɔ'beərəns] n patience f.

forbid [fə'bid] vt (pt forbade(e), pp forbidden, pres p forbidding) interdire, défendre (s.o. to do à qn de faire); **to s.o. sth** interdire ou défendre qch à qn. ◆**forbidden** a (fruit etc) défendu; **she is f. to leave** il lui est interdit de partir. ◆**forbidding** a menaçant, sinistre.

force [fɔːs] n force f; **the (armed) forces** Mil les forces armées; **by (sheer) f.** de force; **in f.** (rule) en vigueur; (in great numbers) en grand nombre, en force; – vt contraindre, forcer (to do à faire); (impose) imposer (on à); (push) pousser; (lock) forcer; (confession) arracher (from à); **to f. back** (enemy etc) faire reculer; (repress) refouler; **to f. down** (aircraft) forcer à atterrir; **to f. out**

faire sortir de force. ◆**forced** a forcé (**to do** de faire); **a f. smile** un sourire forcé. ◆**force-feed** vt (pt & pp -fed) nourrir de force. ◆**forceful** a énergique, puissant. ◆**forcefully** adv avec force, énergiquement. ◆**forcible** a de force; (forceful) énergique. ◆**forcibly** adv (by force) de force.

forceps ['fɔːseps] n forceps m.

ford [fɔːd] n gué m; – vt (river etc) passer à gué.

fore [fɔːr] n **to come to the f.** se mettre en évidence.

forearm ['fɔːrɑːm] n avant-bras m inv.

forebod/e [fɔ'bəʊd] vt (be a warning of) présager. ◆**—ing** n (feeling) pressentiment m.

forecast ['fɔːkɑːst] vt (pt & pp forecast) prévoir; – n prévision f; Met prévisions fpl; Sp pronostic m.

forecourt ['fɔːkɔːt] n avant-cour f; (of filling station) aire f (de service), devant m.

forefathers ['fɔːfɑːðəz] npl aïeux mpl.

forefinger ['fɔːfiŋgər] n index m.

forefront ['fɔːfrʌnt] n **in the f. of** au premier rang de.

forego [fɔ'gəʊ] vt (pp foregone) renoncer à. ◆**foregone** a **it's a f. conclusion** c'est couru d'avance.

foregoing [fɔ'gəʊiŋ] a précédent.

foreground ['fɔːgraʊnd] n premier plan m.

forehead ['fɒrid, 'fɔːhed] n (brow) front m.

foreign ['fɒrin] a étranger; (trade) extérieur; (travel, correspondent) à l'étranger; (produce) de l'étranger; **F. Minister** ministre m des Affaires étrangères. ◆**foreigner** n étranger, -ère mf.

foreman ['fɔːmən] n (pl -men) (worker) contremaître m; (of jury) président m.

foremost ['fɔːməust] **1** a principal. **2** adv **first and f.** tout d'abord.

forensic [fə'rensik] a (medicine) légal; (laboratory) médico-légal.

forerunner ['fɔːrʌnər] n précurseur m.

foresee [fɔː'siː] vt (pt foresaw, pp foreseen) prévoir. ◆**—able** a prévisible.

foreshadow [fɔː'ʃædəʊ] vt présager.

foresight ['fɔːsait] n prévoyance f.

forest ['fɒrist] n forêt f. ◆**forester** n (garde m) forestier m.

forestall [fɔː'stɔːl] vt devancer.

foretaste ['fɔːteist] n avant-goût m.

foretell [fɔː'tel] vt (pt & pp foretold) prédire.

forethought ['fɔːθɔːt] n prévoyance f.

forever [fə'revər] adv (for always) pour toujours; (continually) sans cesse.

forewarn [fɔː'wɔːn] vt avertir.

foreword ['fɔːwɜːd] *n* avant-propos *m inv.*

forfeit ['fɔːfit] *vt* (*lose*) perdre; – *n* (*penalty*) peine *f;* (*in game*) gage *m.*

forg/e [fɔːdʒ] **1** *vt* (*signature, money*) contrefaire; (*document*) falsifier. **2** *vt* (*friendship, bond*) forger. **3** *vi* to f. ahead (*progress*) aller de l'avant. **4** *vt* (*metal*) forger; – *n* forge *f.* ◆**—er** *n* (*of banknotes etc*) faussaire *m.* ◆**forgery** *n* faux *m,* contrefaçon *f.*

forget [fə'get] *vt* (*pt* forgot, *pp* forgotten, *pres p* forgetting) oublier (to do, de faire); f. it! *Fam* (*when thanked*) pas de quoi!; (*it doesn't matter*) peu importe!; to f. oneself s'oublier; – *vi* oublier; to f. about oublier. ◆**f.-me-not** *n Bot* myosotis *m.* ◆**forgetful** *a* to be f. (of) oublier, être oublieux (de). ◆**forgetfulness** *n* manque *m* de mémoire; (*carelessness*) négligence *f;* in a moment of f. dans un moment d'oubli.

forgiv/e [fə'gɪv] *vt* (*pt* forgave, *pp* forgiven) pardonner (s.o. sth qch à qn). ◆**—ing** *a* indulgent. ◆**forgiveness** *n* pardon *m;* (*compassion*) clémence *f.*

forgo [fɔː'gəʊ] *vt* (*pp* forgone) renoncer à.

fork [fɔːk] **1** *n* (*for eating*) fourchette *f;* (*for garden etc*) fourche *f.* **2** *vi* (*of road*) bifurquer; to f. left (*in vehicle*) prendre à gauche; – *n* bifurcation *f,* fourche *f.* **3** *vt* to f. out (*money*) *Fam* allonger; – *vi* to f. out (*pay*) *Fam* casquer. ◆**—ed** *a* fourchu. ◆**forklift truck** *n* chariot *m* élévateur.

forlorn [fə'lɔːn] *a* (*forsaken*) abandonné; (*unhappy*) triste, affligé.

form [fɔːm] *n* (*shape, type, style*) forme *f;* (*document*) formulaire *m; Sch* classe *f;* it's good f. c'est ce qui se fait; in the f. of en forme de; a f. of speech une façon de parler; on f., in good f. en (pleine) forme; – *vt* (*group, character etc*) former; (*clay*) façonner; (*habit*) contracter; (*an opinion*) se former; (*constitute*) constituer, former; to f. part of faire partie de; – *vi* (*appear*) se former. ◆**for'mation** *n* formation *f.* ◆**formative** *a* formateur.

formal ['fɔːm(ə)l] *a* (*person, tone etc*) cérémonieux; (*stuffy*) *Pej* compassé; (*official*) officiel; (*in due form*) en bonne et due forme; (*denial, structure, logic*) formel; (*resemblance*) extérieur; f. dress tenue *f* or habit *m* de cérémonie; f. education éducation *f* scolaire. ◆**for'mality** *n* cérémonie *f;* (*requirement*) formalité *f.* ◆**formally** *adv* (*to declare etc*) officiellement; f. dressed en tenue de cérémonie.

format ['fɔːmæt] *n* format *m.*

former ['fɔːmər] **1** *a* (*previous*) ancien; (*situ-*

ation) antérieur; her f. husband son ex-mari *m;* in f. days autrefois. **2** *a* (*of two*) premier; – *pron* the f. celui-là, celle-là, le premier, la première. ◆**—ly** *adv* autrefois.

formidable ['fɔːmidəb(ə)l] *a* effroyable, terrible.

formula ['fɔːmjʊlə] *n* **1** (*pl* -as *or* -ae [-iː]) formule *f.* **2** (*pl* -as) (*baby's feed*) *Am* mélange *m* lacté. ◆**formulate** *vt* formuler. ◆**formu'lation** *n* formulation *f.*

forsake [fə'seɪk] *vt* (*pt* forsook, *pp* forsaken) abandonner.

fort [fɔːt] *n Hist Mil* fort *m;* to hold the f. (*in s.o.'s absence*) *Fam* prendre la relève.

forte ['fɔːteɪ, *Am* fɔːt] *n* (*strong point*) fort *m.*

forth [fɔːθ] *adv* en avant; from this day f. désormais; and so f. et ainsi de suite.

forthcoming [fɔːθ'kʌmɪŋ] *a* **1** (*event*) à venir; (*book, film*) qui va sortir; my f. book mon prochain livre. **2** (*available*) disponible. **3** (*open*) communicatif; (*helpful*) serviable.

forthright ['fɔːθraɪt] *a* direct, franc.

forthwith [fɔːθ'wɪθ] *adv* sur-le-champ.

fortieth ['fɔːtɪəθ] *a & n* quarantième (*mf*).

fortify ['fɔːtɪfaɪ] *vt* (*strengthen*) fortifier; to f. s.o. (*of food, drink*) réconforter qn, remonter qn. ◆**fortifi'cation** *n* fortification *f.*

fortitude ['fɔːtɪtjuːd] *n* courage *m* (moral).

fortnight ['fɔːtnaɪt] *n* quinze jours *mpl,* quinzaine *f.* ◆**—ly** *adv* bimensuel; – *adv* tous les quinze jours.

fortress ['fɔːtrɪs] *n* forteresse *f.*

fortuitous [fɔː'tjuːɪtəs] *a* fortuit.

fortunate ['fɔːtʃənət] *a* (*choice, event etc*) heureux; to be f. (*of person*) avoir de la chance; it's f. (for her) that c'est heureux (pour elle) que. ◆**—ly** *adv* heureusement.

forty ['fɔːtɪ] *a & n* quarante (*m*).

forum ['fɔːrəm] *n* forum *m.*

forward ['fɔːwəd] *adv* forward(s) en avant; to go f. avancer; from this time f. désormais; – *a* (*movement*) en avant; (*gears*) *Aut* avant *inv;* (*child*) *Fig* précoce; (*pert*) effronté; – *n Fb* avant *m;* – *vt* (*letter*) faire suivre; (*goods*) expédier. ◆**—ness** *n* précocité *f;* effronterie *f.* ◆**forward-looking** *a* tourné vers l'avenir.

fossil ['fɒs(ə)l] *n & a* fossile (*m*).

foster ['fɒstər] **1** vt encourager; (hope) nourrir. **2** vt (child) élever; – a (child, family) adoptif.

fought [fɔːt] see fight.

foul [faʊl] **1** a (-er, -est) infect; (air) vicié; (breath) fétide; (language) grossier; (action, place) immonde; **to be f.-mouthed** un langage grossier. **2** n Sp coup m irrégulier; Fb faute f; – a f. **play** Sp jeu m irrégulier; Jur acte m criminel. **3** vt **to f. (up)** salir; (air) vicier; (drain) encrasser; **to f. up** (life, plans) Fam gâcher. ◆**f.-up** n (in system) Fam raté m.

found¹ [faʊnd] see find.

found² [faʊnd] vt (town, opinion etc) fonder (on sur). ◆**—er¹** n fondateur, -trice mf. ◆**foun'dation** n fondation f; (basis) Fig base f; fondement m; **without f.** sans fondement; **f. cream** fond m de teint.

founder² ['faʊndər] vi (of ship) sombrer.

foundry ['faʊndrɪ] n fonderie f.

fountain ['faʊntɪn] n fontaine f; **f. pen** stylo(-plume) m.

four [fɔːr] a & n quatre (m); **on all fours** à quatre pattes; **the Big F.** Pol les quatre Grands; **f.-letter word** = mot m de cinq lettres. ◆**fourfold** a quadruple; – adv au quadruple. ◆**foursome** n deux couples mpl. ◆**four'teen** a & n quatorze (m). ◆**fourth** a & n quatrième (mf).

fowl [faʊl] n (hens) volaille f; **a f.** une volaille.

fox [fɒks] **1** n renard m. **2** vt (puzzle) mystifier; (trick) tromper. ◆**foxy** a (sly) rusé, futé.

foxglove ['fɒksglʌv] n Bot digitale f.

foyer ['fɔɪeɪ] n Th foyer m; (in hotel) hall m.

fraction ['frækʃ(ə)n] n fraction f. ◆**fractionally** adv un tout petit peu.

fractious ['frækʃəs] a grincheux.

fracture ['fræktʃər] n fracture f; – vt fracturer; **to f. one's leg/etc** se fracturer la jambe/etc; – vi se fracturer.

fragile ['frædʒaɪl, Am 'frædʒ(ə)l] a fragile. ◆**fra'gility** n fragilité f.

fragment ['frægmənt] n fragment m, morceau m. ◆**frag'mented**, ◆**fragmentary** a fragmentaire.

fragrant ['freɪɡrənt] a parfumé. ◆**fragrance** n parfum m.

frail [freɪl] a (-er, -est) (person) frêle, fragile; (hope, health) fragile. ◆**frailty** n fragilité f.

frame [freɪm] **1** n (of person, building) charpente f; (of picture, bicycle) cadre m; (of window, car) châssis m; (of spectacles) monture f; **f. of mind** humeur f; – vt (picture) encadrer; (proposals etc) Fig

formuler. **2** vt **to f. s.o.** Fam monter un coup contre qn. ◆**f.-up** n Fam coup m monté. ◆**framework** n structure f; (with)in the f. of (context) dans le cadre de.

franc [fræŋk] n franc m.

France [frɑːns] n France f.

franchise ['fræntʃaɪz] n **1** Pol droit m de vote. **2** (right to sell product) Com franchise f.

Franco- ['fræŋkəʊ] pref franco-.

frank [fræŋk] **1** a (-er, -est) (honest) franc. **2** vt (letter) affranchir. ◆**—ly** adv franchement. ◆**—ness** n franchise f.

frankfurter ['fræŋkfɜːtər] n saucisse f de Francfort.

frantic ['fræntɪk] a (activity, shout) frénétique; (rush, desire) effréné; (person) hors de soi; **f. with joy** fou de joie. ◆**frantically** adv comme un fou.

fraternal [frə'tɜːn(ə)l] a fraternel. ◆**fraternity** n (bond) fraternité f; (society) & Univ Am confrérie f. ◆**fraternize** ['frætənaɪz] vi fraterniser (with avec).

fraud [frɔːd] n **1** Jur fraude f. **2** (person) imposteur m. ◆**fraudulent** a frauduleux.

fraught [frɔːt] a (with plein de, chargé de; **to be f.** (of situation) être tendu; (of person) Fam être contrarié.

fray [freɪ] **1** vt (garment) effilocher; (rope) user; – vi s'effilocher; s'user. **2** n (fight) rixe f. ◆**—ed** a (nerves) Fig tendu.

freak [friːk] n (person) phénomène m, monstre m; **a jazz/etc f.** Fam un(e) fana de jazz/etc; – a (result, weather etc) anormal. ◆**freakish** a anormal.

freckle ['frek(ə)l] n tache f de rousseur. ◆**freckled** a couvert de taches de rousseur.

free [friː] a (freer, freest) (at liberty, not occupied) libre; (gratis) gratuit; (lavish) généreux (with de); **to get f.** se libérer; **f. to do** libre de faire; **to let s.o. go f.** relâcher qn; **f. of charge** gratuit; **f. of** (without) sans; **f. of s.o.** (rid of) débarrassé de qn; **to have a f. hand** Fig avoir carte blanche (**to do** pour faire); **f. and easy** décontracté; **f. trade** libre-échange m; **f. speech** liberté f d'expression; **f. kick** Fb coup m franc; **f.-range egg** œuf m de ferme; – adv **f. (of charge)** gratuitement; – vt (pt & pp **freed**) (prisoner etc) libérer; (trapped person, road) dégager; (country) affranchir, libérer; (untie) détacher. ◆**Freefone** Tel = numéro m vert. ◆**free-for-'all** n mêlée f générale. ◆**freehold** n propriété f foncière libre. ◆**freelance** a indépendant; – n collaborateur, -trice mf indépendant(e). ◆**freeloader** n (*sponger*) Am parasite m. ◆**Freemason** n franc-maçon m. ◆**Freemasonry** n franc-maçonnerie f. ◆**freestyle** n Swimming nage f libre. ◆**free'thinker** n libre penseur, -euse mf. ◆**freeway** n Am autoroute f.

freedom ['friːdəm] n liberté f; f. from (*worry*, *responsibility*) absence f de.

freely ['friːli] adv (*to speak*, *circulate* etc) librement; (*to give*) libéralement.

freez/e [friːz] vi (*pt* froze, *pp* frozen) geler; (*of smile*) Fig se figer; Culin se congeler; to f. to death mourir de froid; to f. up or over geler; (*of windscreen*) se givrer; − vt Culin congeler, surgeler; (*credits*, *river*) geler; (*prices*, *wages*) bloquer; **frozen food** surgelés mpl; − n Met gel m; (*of prices*, *wages*) blocage m. ◆**−ing** a (*weather* etc) glacial; (*hands*, *person*) gelé; **it's f.** on gèle; − n below f. au-dessous de zéro. ◆**−er** n (*deep-freeze*) congélateur m; (*in fridge*) freezer m.

freight [freɪt] n (*goods*, *price*) fret m; (*transport*) transport m; **f. train** Am train m de marchandises; − vt (*ship*) affréter. ◆**−er** n (*ship*) cargo m.

French [frentʃ] a français; (*teacher*) de français; (*embassy*) de France; **F. fries** Am frites fpl; **the F.** les Français mpl; − n (*language*) français m. ◆**Frenchman** n (*pl* -men) Français m. ◆**French-speaking** a francophone. ◆**Frenchwoman** n (*pl* -women) Française f.

frenzy ['frenzi] n frénésie f. ◆**frenzied** a (*shouts* etc) frénétique; (*person*) effréné; (*attack*) violent.

fresco ['freskəu] n (*pl* -oes or -os) fresque f.

fresh [freʃ] a (-er, -est) frais; (*new*) nouveau; (*impudent*) Fam culotté; **to get some f. air** prendre le frais; **f. water** eau f douce. **2** adv **f.** from fraîchement arrivé de; **f. out of**, **f. from** (*university*) frais émoulu de. ◆**freshen 1** vi (*of wind*) fraîchir. **2** vi to **f. up** faire un brin de toilette; − vt to **f. up** (*house* etc) retaper; to **f. s.o. up** (*of bath*) rafraîchir qn. ◆**freshener** n air f. désodorisant m. ◆**freshman** n (*pl* -men) étudiant, -ante mf de première année. ◆**freshness** n fraîcheur f; (*cheek*) Fam culot m.

fret [fret] vi (-tt-) (*worry*) se faire du souci, s'en faire; (*of baby*) pleurer. ◆**fretful** a (*baby* etc) grognon.

friar ['fraɪər] n frère m, moine m.

friction ['frɪkʃ(ə)n] n friction f.

Friday ['fraɪdɪ] n vendredi m.

fridge [frɪdʒ] n Fam frigo m.

fried [fraɪd] *pt* & *pp* of **fry 1**; − a (*fish* etc) frit; **f. egg** œuf m sur le plat. ◆**frier** n (*pan*) friteuse f.

friend [frend] n ami, -ie mf; (*from school*, *work*) camarade mf; **to be friends with** être ami avec; **to make friends** se lier (*with* avec). ◆**friendly** a (-ier, -iest) amical; (*child*, *animal*) gentil, affectueux; (*kind*) gentil; **some f. advice** un conseil d'ami; **to be f. with** être ami avec. ◆**friendship** n amitié f.

frieze [friːz] n Archit frise f.

frigate ['frɪgət] n (*ship*) frégate f.

fright [fraɪt] n peur f; (*person*, *hat* etc) Fig Fam horreur f; **to have a f.** avoir peur; **to give s.o. a f.** faire peur à qn. ◆**frighten** vt effrayer, faire peur à; to **f. away** or **off** (*animal*) effaroucher; (*person*) chasser. ◆**frightened** a effrayé; **to be f.** avoir peur (*of* de). ◆**frightening** a effrayant. ◆**frightful** a affreux. ◆**frightfully** adv (*ugly*, *late*) affreusement; (*kind*, *glad*) terriblement.

frigid ['frɪdʒɪd] a (*air*, *greeting* etc) froid; Psy frigide.

frill [frɪl] n Tex volant m; *pl* (*fuss*) Fig manières fpl, chichis mpl; (*useless embellishments*) fioritures fpl, superflu m; **no frills** (*spartan*) spartiate.

fringe [frɪndʒ] **1** n (*of hair*, *clothes* etc) frange f. **2** n (*of forest*) lisière f; **on the fringe(s) of society** en marge de la société; − a (*group*, *theatre*) marginal; **f. benefits** avantages mpl divers.

frisk [frɪsk] **1** vt (*search*) fouiller (au corps). **2** vi **f.** (*about*) gambader. ◆**frisky** a (-ier, -iest) a vif.

fritter ['frɪtər] **1** vt to **f. away** (*waste*) gaspiller. **2** n Culin beignet m.

frivolous ['frɪvələs] a frivole. ◆**fri'volity** n frivolité f.

frizzy ['frɪzɪ] a (*hair*) crépu.

fro [frəu] adv to go **to and f.** aller et venir.

frock [frɒk] n (*dress*) robe f; (*of monk*) froc m.

frog [frɒg] n grenouille f; **a f. in one's throat** Fig un chat dans la gorge. ◆**frogman** n (*pl* -men) homme-grenouille m.

frolic ['frɒlɪk] vi (*pt* & *pp* frolicked) to **f.** (*about*) gambader; − npl (*capers*) ébats mpl; (*pranks*) gamineries fpl.

from [frɒm, *unstressed* frəm] prep **1** de; **a letter f.** une lettre de; **to suffer f.** souffrir de;

where are you f.? d'où êtes-vous?; **a train f.** un train en provenance de; **to be ten metres (away)** the house être à dix mètres de la maison. **2** (*time onwards*) à partir de, dès, depuis; **f. today (on),** as **f. today** à partir d'aujourd'hui; dès aujourd'hui; **f. her childhood** dès *ou* depuis son enfance. **3** (*numbers, prices onwards*) à partir de; **f. five francs** à partir de cinq francs. **4** (*away from*) à; **to take/hide/borrow f.** prendre/cacher/emprunter à. **5** (*out of*) dans; sur; **to take f.** (*box*) prendre dans; (*table*) prendre sur; **to drink f. a cup/***etc* boire dans une tasse/*etc*; **to drink f. the bottle** boire à la bouteille. **6** (*according to*) d'après; **f. what I saw** d'après ce que j'ai vu. **7** (*cause*) par; **f. conviction/habit/***etc* par conviction/habitude/*etc.* **8** (*on the part of, on behalf of*) de la part de; **tell her f. me** dis-lui de ma part.

front [frʌnt] *n* (*of garment, building*) devant *m*; (*of boat, car*) avant *m*; (*of crowd*) premier rang *m*; (*of book*) début *m*; *Mil Pol Met* front *m*; (*of beach*) front *m* de mer; (*appearance*) *Fig* façade *f*; **in f. (of)** devant; **in f.** (*ahead*) en avant; *Sp* en tête; **in the f.** (*of vehicle*) à l'avant; (*of house*) devant; − *a* (*tooth etc*) de devant; (*part, wheel, car seat*) avant *inv*; (*row, page*) premier; (*view*) de face; **f. door** porte *f* d'entrée; **f. line** *Mil* front *m*; **f. room** (*lounge*) salon *m*; **f. runner** *Fig* favori, -ite *mf*; **f.-wheel drive** (*on vehicle*) traction *f* avant; − *vi* to **f. on to** (*of windows etc*) donner sur. ◆**frontage** *n* façade *f*. ◆**frontal** (*attack*) de front.

frontier ['frʌntɪər] *n* frontière *f*; − *a* (*town, post*) frontière *inv*.

frost [frɒst] *n* gel *m*, gelée *f*; (*frozen drops on glass, grass etc*) gelée *f* blanche, givre *m*; − *vi* to **f. up** (*of windscreen etc*) se givrer. ◆**frostbite** *n* gelure *f*. ◆**frostbitten** *a* gelé. ◆**frosty** *a* (-ier, -iest) glacial; (*window*) givré; **it's f.** il gèle.

frosted ['frɒstɪd] *a* (*glass*) dépoli.

frosting ['frɒstɪŋ] *n* (*icing*) *Culin* glaçage *m*.

froth [frɒθ] *n* mousse *f*; − *vi* mousser. ◆**frothy** *a* (-ier, -iest) (*beer etc*) mousseux.

frown [fraʊn] *n* froncement *m* de sourcils; − *vi* froncer les sourcils; **to f. (up)on** *Fig* désapprouver.

froze, frozen [frəʊz, 'frəʊz(ə)n] *see* freeze.

frugal ['fruːg(ə)l] *a* (*meal*) frugal; (*thrifty*) parcimonieux. ◆**-ly** *adv* parcimonieusement.

fruit [fruːt] *n* fruit *m*; (*some*) **f.** (*one item*) un fruit; (*more than one*) des fruits; − *a*

(*basket*) à fruits; (*drink*) aux fruits; (*salad*) de fruits; **f. tree** arbre *m* fruitier. ◆**fruitcake** *n* cake *m*. ◆**fruiterer** *n* fruitier, -ière *mf*. ◆**fruitful** *a* (*meeting, career etc*) fructueux, fécond. ◆**fruitless** *a* stérile. ◆**fruity** *a* (-ier, -iest) *a* fruité, de fruit; (*joke*) *Fig Fam* corsé.

fruition [fruːˈɪʃ(ə)n] *n* to **come to f.** se réaliser.

frumpish ['frʌmpɪʃ] *a*, **frumpy** ['frʌmpɪ] *a Fam* (mal) fagoté.

frustrat/e [frʌˈstreɪt] *vt* (*person*) frustrer; (*plans*) faire échouer. ◆**-ed** *a* (*mentally, sexually*) frustré; (*effort*) vain. ◆**-ing** *a* irritant. ◆**fru'stration** *n* frustration *f*; (*disappointment*) déception *f*.

fry [fraɪ] **1** *vt* (faire) frire; − *vi* frire. **2** *n* small **f.** menu fretin *m*. ◆**-ing** *n* friture *f*; **f. pan** poêle *f* (à frire). ◆**-er** *n* (*pan*) friteuse *f*.

ft *abbr* (*measure*) = **foot, feet.**

fuddled ['fʌd(ə)ld] *a* (*drunk*) gris; (*confused*) embrouillé.

fuddy-duddy ['fʌdɪdʌdɪ] *n* **he's an old f.-duddy** *Fam* il est vieux jeu.

fudge [fʌdʒ] **1** *n* (*sweet*) caramel *m* mou. **2** *vt* to **f. the issue** refuser d'aborder le problème.

fuel [fjʊəl] *n* combustible *m*; *Aut* carburant *m*; **f.** (*oil*) mazout *m*; − *vt* (-ll-, *Am* -l-) (*stove*) alimenter; (*ship*) ravitailler (en combustible); (*s.o.'s anger*) attiser.

fugitive ['fjuːdʒɪtɪv] *n* fugitif, -ive *mf*.

fugue [fjuːg] *n Mus* fugue *f*.

fulfil, *Am* **fulfill** [fʊlˈfɪl] *vt* (-ll-) (*ambition, dream*) accomplir, réaliser; (*condition, duty*) remplir; (*desire*) satisfaire; **to f. oneself** s'épanouir. ◆**fulfilling** *a* satisfaisant. ◆**fulfilment**, *Am* ◆**fulfillment** *n* accomplissement *m*, réalisation *f*; (*feeling*) satisfaction *f*.

full [fʊl] *a* (-er, -est) plein (de); (*bus, theatre, meal*) complet; (*life, day*) (bien) rempli; (*skirt*) ample; (*hour*) entier; (*member*) à part entière; **f. price** le prix fort; **to pay (the) f. fare** payer plein tarif; **to be f. (up)** (*of person*) *Culin* n'avoir plus faim; (*of hotel*) être complet; **the f. facts** tous les faits; **at f. speed** à toute vitesse; **f. name** (*on form*) nom et prénom; **f. stop** *Gram* point *m*; − *adv* to **know f. well** savoir fort bien; **f. in the face** (*to hit etc*) en pleine figure; − *n* **in f.** (*text*) intégral; (*to publish, read*) intégralement; (*to write one's name*) en toutes lettres; **to the f.** (*completely*) tout à fait. ◆**fullness** *n* (*of details*) abondance f; (of dress) ampleur f. ◆**fully** adv entièrement; (at least) au moins.

full-back ['fulbæk] n Fb arrière m. ◆**f.-'grown** a adulte; (foetus) arrivé à terme. ◆**f.-'length** a (film) de long métrage; (portrait) en pied; (dress) long. ◆**f.-'scale** a (model etc) grandeur nature inv; (operation etc) Fig de grande envergure. ◆**f.-'sized** a (model) grandeur nature inv. ◆**f.-'time** a & adv à plein temps.

fully-fledged, Am **full-fledged** [ful(i)'fledʒd] a (engineer etc) diplômé; (member) à part entière. ◆**f.-formed** a (baby etc) formé. ◆**f.-grown** a = **full-grown**.

fulsome ['fulsəm] a (praise etc) excessif.

fumble ['fʌmb(ə)l] vi to f. (about) (grope) tâtonner; (search) fouiller (for pour trouver); to f. (about) with tripoter.

fume [fjum] vi (give off fumes) fumer; (of person) rager; – npl émanations fpl; (from car exhaust) gaz m inv.

fumigate ['fjumɪgeɪt] vt désinfecter (par fumigation).

fun [fʌn] n amusement m; to be (good) f. être très amusant; to have (some) f. s'amuser; to make f. of, poke f. at se moquer de; for f., for the f. of it pour le plaisir.

function ['fʌŋkʃ(ə)n] 1 n (role, duty) & Math fonction f; (meeting) réunion f; (ceremony) cérémonie f (publique). 2 vi (work) fonctionner. ◆**functional** a fonctionnel.

fund [fʌnd] n (for pension, relief etc) Fin caisse f; (of knowledge etc) Fig fond m; pl (money resources) fonds mpl; (for special purpose) crédits mpl; – vt (with money) fournir des fonds or des crédits à.

fundamental [fʌndə'ment(ə)l] a fondamental; – npl principes mpl essentiels.

funeral ['fjunərəl] n enterrement m; (grandiose) funérailles fpl; – a (service, march) funèbre; (expenses, parlour) funéraire. ◆**funfair** ['fʌnfeər] n fête f foraine; (larger) parc m d'attractions.

fungus, pl **-gi** ['fʌŋgəs, -gaɪ] n Bot champignon m; (mould) moisissure f.

funicular [fjuˈnɪkjʊlər] n funiculaire m.

funk [fʌŋk] n to be in a f. (afraid) Fam avoir la frousse; (depressed, sulking) Am Fam faire la gueule.

funnel ['fʌn(ə)l] n 1 (of ship) cheminée f. 2 (tube for pouring) entonnoir m.

funny ['fʌnɪ] a (-ier, -iest) (amusing) drôle; (strange) bizarre; a f. idea une drôle d'idée; there's some f. business going on il y a quelque chose de louche; to feel f. ne pas se

sentir très bien. ◆**funnily** adv drôlement; bizarrement; f. **enough** . . . chose bizarre

fur [fɜr] 1 n (of animal) poil m, pelage m; (for wearing etc) fourrure f. 2 n (in kettle) dépôt m (de tartre); – vi (-rr-) to f. (up) s'entartrer.

furious ['fjʊərɪəs] a (violent, angry) furieux (with, at contre); (pace, speed) fou. ◆**-ly** adv furieusement; (to drive, rush) à une allure folle.

furnace ['fɜnɪs] n (forge) fourneau m; (room etc) Fig fournaise f.

furnish ['fɜnɪʃ] vt 1 (room) meubler. 2 (supply) fournir (s.o. with sth qch à qn). ◆**-ings** npl ameublement m.

furniture ['fɜnɪtʃər] n meubles mpl; a piece of f. un meuble.

furrier ['fʌrɪər] n fourreur m.

furrow ['fʌrəʊ] n (on brow) & Agr sillon m.

furry ['fɜrɪ] a (animal) à poil; (toy) en peluche.

further ['fɜðər] 1 adv & a = farther. 2 adv (more) davantage, plus; (besides) en outre; – a (additional) supplémentaire; (education) post-scolaire; f. details de plus amples détails; a f. case/etc un autre cas/etc; without f. delay sans plus attendre. 3 vt (cause, research etc) promouvoir. ◆**furthermore** adv en outre. ◆**furthest** a & adv = **farthest**.

furtive ['fɜtɪv] a furtif.

fury ['fjʊərɪ] n (violence, anger) fureur f.

fuse [fjuz] 1 vti (metal) Tech fondre; Fig fusionner. 2 vt to f. the lights etc faire sauter les plombs; – vi the lights etc have fused les plombs ont sauté; – n (wire) El fusible m, plomb m. 3 n (of bomb) amorce f. ◆**fused** a (plug) El avec fusible incorporé. ◆**fusion** n (union) & Phys Biol fusion f.

fuselage ['fjuzɪlɑːʒ] n Av fuselage m.

fuss [fʌs] n façons fpl, histoires fpl, chichis mpl; (noise) agitation f; **what a (lot of) f.!** quelle histoire!; to kick up or make a f. faire des histoires; to make a f. of être aux petits soins pour; – vi faire des chichis; (worry) se tracasser (about pour); (rush about) s'agiter; to f. over s.o. être aux petits soins pour qn. ◆**fusspot**, Am **fussbudget** n Fam enquiquineur, -euse mf. ◆**fussy** a (-ier, -iest) méticuleux; (difficult) difficile (about sur).

fusty ['fʌstɪ] a (-ier, -iest) (smell) de renfermé.

futile ['fjutaɪl, Am 'fjuːt(ə)l] a futile, vain. ◆**fu'tility** n futilité f.

future ['fjuːtʃər] n avenir m; Gram futur m; **in f.** (from now on) à l'avenir; **in the f.** (one day) un jour (futur); – a futur, à venir; (date) ultérieur.

fuzz [fʌz] n **1** (down) Fam duvet m. **2 the f.** (police) Sl les flics mpl. ◆**fuzzy** a (-ier, -iest) (hair) crépu; (picture, idea) flou.

G

G, g [dʒiː] n G, g m. ◆**G.-string** n (cloth) cache-sexe m inv.

gab [gæb] n to have the gift of the g. Fam avoir du bagou(t).

gabardine [gæbə'diːn] n (material, coat) gabardine f.

gabble ['gæb(ə)l] vi (chatter) jacasser; (indistinctly) bredouiller; – n baragouin m.

gable ['geɪb(ə)l] n Archit pignon m.

gad [gæd] vi (-dd-) to g. about se balader, vadrouiller.

gadget ['gædʒɪt] n gadget m.

Gaelic ['geɪlɪk, 'gælɪk] a & n gaélique (m).

gaffe [gæf] n (blunder) gaffe f, bévue f.

gag [gæg] **1** n (over mouth) bâillon m; – vt (-gg-) (victim, press etc) bâillonner. **2** n (joke) plaisanterie f; Cin Th gag m. **3** vi (-gg-) (choke) Am s'étouffer (on sur).

gaggle ['gæg(ə)l] n (of geese) troupeau m.

gaiety ['geɪətɪ] n gaieté f; (of colour) éclat m. ◆**gaily** adv gaiement.

gain [geɪn] vt (obtain, win) gagner; (objective) atteindre; (experience, reputation) acquérir; (popularity) gagner en; to g. speed/weight prendre de la vitesse/du poids; – vi (of watch) avancer; to g. in strength gagner en force; to g. on (catch up with) rattraper; – n (increase) augmentation f (in de); (profit) Com bénéfice m, gain m; Fig avantage m. ◆**gainful** a profitable; (employment) rémunéré.

gainsay [geɪn'seɪ] vt (pt & pp gainsaid [-sed]) (person) contredire; (facts) nier.

gait [geɪt] n (walk) démarche f.

gala ['gɑːlə, 'geɪlə] n gala m, fête f; **swimming g.** concours m de natation.

galaxy ['gæləksɪ] n galaxie f.

gale [geɪl] n grand vent m, rafale f (de vent).

gall [gɔːl] **1** n Med bile f; (bitterness) Fig fiel m; (cheek) Fam effronterie f; **g. bladder** vésicule f biliaire. **2** vt (vex) blesser, froisser.

gallant ['gælənt] a (brave) courageux; (splendid) magnifique; (chivalrous) galant. ◆**gallantry** n (bravery) courage m.

galleon ['gælɪən] n (ship) Hist galion m.

gallery ['gælərɪ] n (room etc) galerie f; (for public, press) tribune f; **art g.** (private) galerie f d'art; (public) musée m d'art.

galley ['gælɪ] n (ship) Hist galère f; (kitchen) Nau Av cuisine f.

Gallic ['gælɪk] a (French) français. ◆**gallicism** n (word etc) gallicisme m.

gallivant ['gælɪvænt] vi to g. (about) Fam courir, vadrouiller.

gallon ['gælən] n gallon m (Br = 4,5 litres, Am = 3,8 litres).

gallop ['gæləp] n galop m; – vi galoper; to g. away (rush) Fig partir au galop or en vitesse; ◆**-ing** a (inflation etc) Fig galopant.

gallows ['gæləʊz] npl potence f.

gallstone ['gɔːlstəʊn] n Med calcul m biliaire.

galore [gə'lɔːr] adv à gogo, en abondance.

galoshes [gə'lɒʃɪz] npl (shoes) caoutchoucs mpl.

galvanize ['gælvənaɪz] vt (metal) & Fig galvaniser.

gambit ['gæmbɪt] n opening g. Fig manœuvre f stratégique.

gambl/e ['gæmb(ə)l] vi jouer (on sur, with avec); to g. on (count on) miser sur; – vt (wager) jouer; to g. (away) (lose) perdre (au jeu); – n (bet) & Fig coup m risqué. ◆**-ing** n jeu m. ◆**-er** n joueur, -euse mf.

game [geɪm] **1** n (of football, cricket etc) match m; (of tennis, chess, cards) partie f; **to have a g. of** jouer un match de; faire une partie de; **games** Sch Sch sport; **games teacher** professeur m d'éducation physique. **2** n (animals, birds) gibier m; **to be fair g. for** Fig être une proie idéale pour. **3** a (brave) courageux; **g. for** (willing) prêt à. **4** a (leg) estropié; **to have a g. leg** être boiteux. ◆**gamekeeper** n garde-chasse m.

gammon ['gæmən] n (ham) jambon m fumé.

gammy ['gæmɪ] a Fam = game 4.

gamut ['gæmət] n Mus & Fig gamme f.

gang [gæŋ] n bande f; (of workers) équipe f; (of crooks) gang m; – vi to g. up on or

against se liguer contre. ◆**gangster** n gangster m.

gangling ['gæŋglɪŋ] a dégingandé.

gangrene ['gæŋgriːn] n gangrène f.

gangway ['gæŋweɪ] n passage m; (in train) couloir m; (in bus, cinema, theatre) allée f; (footbridge) Av Nau passerelle f. g.! dégagez!

gaol [dʒeɪl] n & vt = **jail**.

gap [gæp] n (empty space) trou m, vide m; (breach) trou m; (in time) intervalle m; (in knowledge) lacune f; the g. between (divergence) l'écart m entre.

gap/e [geɪp] vi (stare) rester or être bouche bée; to g. at regarder bouche bée. ◆**-ing** a (chasm, wound) béant.

garage ['gæra(ɪ)dʒ, 'gærɪdʒ, Am gə'rɑːʒ] n garage m; — vt mettre au garage.

garb [gɑːb] n (clothes) costume m.

garbage ['gɑːbɪdʒ] n ordures fpl; g. can Am poubelle f; g. collector or man Am éboueur m; g. truck Am camion-benne m.

garble ['gɑːb(ə)l] vt (words etc) déformer, embrouiller.

garden ['gɑːd(ə)n] n jardin m; the gardens (park) le parc; g. centre (store) jardinerie f; (nursery) pépinière f; g. party garden-party f; g. produce produits mpl maraîchers; — vi to be gardening jardiner. ◆**-ing** n jardinage m. ◆**-er** n jardinier, -ière mf.

gargle ['gɑːg(ə)l] vi se gargariser; — n gargarisme m.

gargoyle ['gɑːgɔɪl] n Archit gargouille f.

garish ['geərɪʃ, Am 'gæərɪʃ] a voyant, criard.

garland ['gɑːlənd] n guirlande f.

garlic ['gɑːlɪk] n ail m; g. sausage saucisson m à l'ail.

garment ['gɑːmənt] n vêtement m.

garnish ['gɑːnɪʃ] vt garnir (with de); — n garniture f.

garret ['gærət] n mansarde f.

garrison ['gærɪsən] n Mil garnison f.

garrulous ['gærələs] a (talkative) loquace.

garter ['gɑːtər] n (round leg) jarretière f; (attached to belt) Am jarretelle f; (for men) fixe-chaussette f.

gas [gæs] 1 n gaz m inv; (gasoline) Am essence f; Med Fam anesthésie f au masque; — a (meter, mask, chamber) à gaz; (pipe) de gaz; (industry) du gaz; (heating) au gaz; g. fire or heater appareil m de chauffage à gaz; g. station Am poste m d'essence; g. stove (portable) réchaud m à gaz; (large) cuisinière f à gaz; — vt (-ss-) (poison) asphyxier; Mil gazer. 2 vi (-ss-) (talk) Fam bavarder; — n for a g. (fun) Am Fam pour rire. ◆**gasbag** n Fam commère

f. ◆**gasman** n (pl -men) employé m du gaz. ◆**gasoline** n Am essence f. ◆**gasworks** n usine f à gaz.

gash [gæʃ] n entaille f; — vt entailler.

gasp [gɑːsp] 1 vi to g. (for breath) haleter; — n halètement m. 2 vi to g. with or in surprise/etc avoir le souffle coupé de surprise/etc; — vt (say gasping) hoqueter; — n a g. of surprise/etc un hoquet de surprise/etc.

gassy ['gæsɪ] a (-ier, -iest) (drink) gazeux.

gastric ['gæstrɪk] a (juices, ulcer) gastrique. ◆**ga'stronomy** n gastronomie f.

gate [geɪt] n (of castle, airport etc) porte f; (at level crossing, field etc) barrière f; (metal) grille f; (in Paris Metro) portillon m. ◆**gateway** n the g. to success/etc le chemin du succès/etc.

gâteau, pl **-eaux** ['gætəʊ, -əʊz] n Culin gros gâteau m à la crème.

gatecrash ['geɪtkræʃ] vti to g. (a party) s'inviter de force (à une réception).

gather ['gæðər] vt (people, objects) rassembler; (pick up) ramasser; (flowers) cueillir; (information) recueillir; (understand) comprendre; (skirt, material) froncer; I g. that … (infer) je crois comprendre que …; to g. speed prendre de la vitesse; to g. in (crops, harvest) rentrer; (essays, exam papers) ramasser; to g. up (strength) rassembler; (papers) ramasser; — vi (of people) se rassembler, s'assembler, s'amasser; (of clouds) se former; (of dust) s'accumuler; to g. round s'approcher; to g. round s.o. entourer qn. ◆**-ing** n (group) réunion f.

gaudy ['gɔːdɪ] a (-ier, -iest) voyant, criard.

gauge [geɪdʒ] n (instrument) jauge f, indicateur m; Rail écartement m; to be a g. of sth Fig permettre de jauger qch; — vt (measure) mesurer; (estimate) évaluer, jauger.

gaunt [gɔːnt] a (thin) décharné.

gauntlet ['gɔːntlɪt] n gant m; to run the g. of Fig essuyer (le feu de).

gauze [gɔːz] n (fabric) gaze f.

gave [geɪv] see **give**.

gawk [gɔːk] vi to g. (at) regarder bouche bée.

gawp [gɔːp] vi = **gawk**.

gay [geɪ] a (-er, -est) 1 (cheerful) gai, joyeux; (colour) vif, gai. 2 Fam homo(sexuel), gay inv.

gaze [geɪz] n regard m (fixe); — vi regarder; to g. at regarder (fixement).

gazelle [gə'zel] n (animal) gazelle f.

gazette [gə'zet] n journal m officiel.

GB [dʒiːˈbiː] abbr (Great Britain) Grande-Bretagne f.

GCSE [dʒiːsiːesˈiː] abbr (General Certificate of Secondary Education) = baccalauréat m.

gear [gɪər] **1** n matériel m, équipement m; (belongings) affaires fpl; (clothes) Fam vêtements mpl (à la mode); (toothed wheels) Tech engrenage m; (speed) Aut vitesse f; **in g.** Aut en prise; **not in g.** Aut au point mort; **g. lever,** Am **g. shift** levier m de (changement de) vitesse. **2** vt (adapt) adapter (**to** à); **geared (up) to** do prêt à faire; **to g. oneself up for** se préparer pour. ◆**gearbox** n boîte f de vitesses.

gee! [dʒiː] int Am Fam ça alors!

geese [giːs] see **goose**.

geezer [ˈgiːzər] n Hum Sl type m.

Geiger counter [ˈgaɪɡəkaʊntər] n compteur m Geiger.

gel [dʒel] n (substance) gel m.

gelatin(e) [ˈdʒelətiːn, Am -tən] n gélatine f.

gelignite [ˈdʒelɪɡnaɪt] n dynamite f (au nitrate de soude).

gem [dʒem] n pierre f précieuse; (person or thing of value) Fig perle f; (error) Iron perle f.

Gemini [ˈdʒemɪnaɪ] n (sign) les Gémeaux mpl.

gen [dʒen] n (information) Sl coordonnées fpl; − vi (**-nn-**) **to g. up on** Sl se rancarder sur.

gender [ˈdʒendər] n Gram genre m; (of person) sexe m.

gene [dʒiːn] n Biol gène m.

genealogy [dʒiːnɪˈælədʒɪ] n généalogie f.

general [ˈdʒenərəl] **1** a général; **in g.** en général; **the g. public** le (grand) public; **for g. use** à l'usage du public; **g. favourite** aimé or apprécié de tous; **g. delivery** Am poste f restante; **to be g.** (widespread) être très répandu. **2** n (officer) Mil général m. ◆**gene'rality** n généralité f. ◆**generali-'zation** n généralisation f. ◆**generalize** vti généraliser; **g. speaking** en général, généralement parlant.

generate [ˈdʒenəreɪt] vt (heat) produire; (fear, hope etc) & Ling engendrer. ◆**gene-'ration** n génération f; **the g. of** (heat) la production de; **g. gap** conflit m des générations. ◆**generator** n El groupe m électrogène, générateur f.

generous [ˈdʒenərəs] a généreux (with de); (helping, meal etc) copieux. ◆**gene'rosity** n générosité f. ◆**generously** adv généreusement; (to serve s.o.) copieusement.

genesis [ˈdʒenəsɪs] n genèse f.

genetic [dʒɪˈnetɪk] a génétique. ◆**genetics** n génétique f.

Geneva [dʒɪˈniːvə] n Genève m or f.

genial [ˈdʒiːnɪəl] a (kind) affable; (cheerful) jovial.

genie [ˈdʒiːnɪ] n (goblin) génie m.

genital [ˈdʒenɪt(ə)l] a génital; − npl organes mpl génitaux.

genius [ˈdʒiːnɪəs] n (ability, person) génie m; **to have a g. for doing/for sth** avoir le génie pour faire/de qch.

genocide [ˈdʒenəsaɪd] n génocide m.

gent [dʒent] n Fam monsieur m; **gents' shoes** Com chaussures fpl pour hommes; **the gents** Fam les toilettes fpl (pour hommes).

genteel [dʒenˈtiːl] a Iron distingué.

gentle [ˈdʒent(ə)l] a (**-er, -est**) (person, sound, slope etc) doux; (hint, reminder) discret; (touch) léger; (pace) mesuré; (exercise, progress) modéré; (birth) noble. ◆**gentleman** n (pl **-men**) monsieur m (well-bred) gentleman m, monsieur m bien élevé. ◆**gentlemanly** a distingué, bien élevé. ◆**gentleness** n douceur f. ◆**gently** adv doucement; (to remind) discrètement; (smoothly) en douceur.

genuine [ˈdʒenjʊɪn] a (authentic) véritable, authentique; (sincere) sincère, vrai. ◆**—ly** adv authentiquement; sincèrement. ◆**—ness** n authenticité f; sincérité f.

geography [dʒɪˈɒɡrəfɪ] n géographie f. ◆**geo'graphical** a géographique.

geology [dʒɪˈɒlədʒɪ] n géologie f. ◆**geo-'logical** a géologique. ◆**geologist** n géologue mf.

geometry [dʒɪˈɒmɪtrɪ] n géométrie f. ◆**geo'metric(al)** a géométrique.

geranium [dʒɪˈreɪnɪəm] n Bot géranium m.

geriatric [dʒerɪˈætrɪk] a (hospital) du troisième âge; **g. ward** service m de gériatrie.

germ [dʒɜːm] n Biol & Fig germe m; Med microbe m; **g. warfare** guerre f bactériologique.

German [ˈdʒɜːmən] a & n allemand, -ande (mf); **G. measles** Med rubéole f; **G. shepherd** (dog) Am berger m allemand; − n (language) allemand m. ◆**Ger'manic** a germanique.

Germany [ˈdʒɜːmənɪ] n Allemagne f; **West G.** Allemagne de l'Ouest.

germinate [ˈdʒɜːmɪneɪt] vi Bot & Fig germer.

gestation [dʒeˈsteɪʃ(ə)n] n gestation f.

gesture [ˈdʒestʃər] n geste m; − vi **to g. to**

s.o. to do faire signe à qn de faire.
◆ge'sticulate vi gesticuler.

get [get] 1 vt (pt & pp got, Am gotten, pres
p getting) (obtain) obtenir, avoir; (find)
trouver; (buy) acheter, prendre; (receive)
recevoir, avoir; (catch) attraper, prendre;
(seize) prendre, saisir; (fetch) aller
chercher (qn, qch); (put) mettre; (derive)
tirer (from de); (understand) comprendre,
saisir; (prepare) préparer; (lead) mener;
(target) atteindre, avoir; (reputation) se
faire; (annoy) Fam ennuyer; I have got, Am
I have gotten j'ai; to g. s.o. to do sth faire
faire qch à qn; to g. sth built/etc faire
construire/etc qch; to g. things going or
started faire démarrer les choses. 2 vi (go)
aller; (arrive) arriver (to à); (become)
devenir, se faire; to g. caught/run over/etc
se faire prendre/écraser/etc; to g. married
se marier; to g. dressed/washed
s'habiller/se laver; where have you got or
Am gotten to? où en es-tu?; you've got to
stay (must) tu dois rester; to g. to do
(succeed in doing) parvenir à faire; to g.
working se mettre à travailler. ■ to g. about
or (a)round vi se déplacer; (of news)
circuler; (of person) faire traverser;
(message) communi-
quer; – vi traverser; (of speaker) se
faire comprendre (to de); to g. across to s.o.
that faire comprendre à qn que; to g. along
vi (leave) se sauver; (manage) se débrouiller; (progress) avancer; (be on good terms)
s'entendre (with avec); to g. at vt (reach)
parvenir à, atteindre; (taunt) s'en prendre
à; what is he getting at? où veut-il en
venir?; to g. away vi (leave) partir, s'en
aller; (escape) s'échapper; there's no
getting away from it il faut le reconnaître,
c'est comme ça. ◆getaway n (escape)
fuite f; to g. back vi (recover) récupérer;
(replace) remettre; – vi (return) revenir,
retourner; to g. back at, g. one's own back
at (punish) se venger de; g. back! (move
back) reculez!; to g. by vi (pass) passer;
(manage) se débrouiller; to g. down vi (go
down) descendre (from de); – vt (bring
down) descendre (from de); (write) noter;
(depress) Fam déprimer; to g. down to
(task, work etc) se mettre à; to g. in vt (bicycle,
washing etc) rentrer; (buy) acheter;
(summon) faire venir; to g. in a car/etc
monter dans une voiture/etc; – vi (enter)
entrer; (come home) rentrer; (enter vehicle
or train) monter; (of plane, train) arriver;
(of candidate) Pol être élu; to g. into vt
entrer dans; (vehicle, train) monter dans;

(habit) prendre; to g. into bed/a rage se
mettre au lit/en colère; to g. into trouble
avoir des ennuis; to g. off vi (leave) partir;
(from vehicle or train) descendre (from de);
(escape) s'en tirer; (finish work) sortir; (be
acquitted) Jur être acquitté; – vt (remove)
enlever; (despatch) expédier; Jur faire
acquitter (qn, qch); to g. off (from) a chair se
lever d'une chaise; to g. off doing Fam se
dispenser de faire; to g. on vt (shoes,
clothes) mettre; (bus, train) monter dans; –
vi (progress) marcher, avancer; (continue)
continuer; (succeed) réussir; (enter bus or
train) monter; (be on good terms)
s'entendre (with avec); how are you getting
on? comment ça va?; to g. on to s.o. (telephone) toucher qn, contacter qn; to g. on
with (task) continuer; to g. out vi sortir;
(from vehicle or train) descendre (from, of
de); to g. out of (obligation) échapper à;
(trouble) se tirer de; (habit) perdre; – vt
(remove) enlever; (bring out) sortir (qch),
faire sortir (qn); to g. over vt (road) traverser; (obstacle) surmonter; (fence)
franchir; (illness) se remettre de; (surprise)
revenir de; (ideas) communiquer; let's g. it
over with finissons-en; – vi (cross) traverser; to g. round vt (obstacle) contourner;
(person) entortiller; – vi to g. round to
doing en venir à faire; to g. through vi
(pass) passer; (finish) finir; (pass exam)
être reçu; to g. through to s.o. faire
comprendre de qn; (on the telephone)
contacter qn; – vt (hole etc) passer par;
(task, meal) venir à bout de; (exam) être
reçu à; g. me through to your boss (on the
telephone) passe-moi ton patron; to g.
together vi (of people) se rassembler.
◆g.-together n réunion f; to g. up vi (rise)
se lever (from de); to g. up to (in book) en
arriver à; (mischief, trouble etc) faire; – vt
(ladder, stairs etc) monter; (party, group)
organiser; to g. sth up (bring up) monter
qch. ◆g.-up n (clothes) Fam accoutrement
m.

geyser ['gizər] n 1 (water heater)
chauffe-eau m inv. 2 Geol geyser m.

Ghana ['gɑːnə] n Ghana m.

ghastly ['gɑːstlɪ] a (-ier, -iest) (pale) blème,
pâle; (horrible) affreux.

gherkin ['gɜːkɪn] n cornichon m.

ghetto ['getəʊ] n (pl -os) ghetto m.

ghost [gəʊst] n fantôme m; not the g. of a
chance pas l'ombre d'une chance; – a
(story) de fantômes; (ship) fantôme; (town)
mort. ◆-ly a spectral.

ghoulish ['guːlɪʃ] a morbide.

giant ['dʒaɪənt] *n* géant *m*; – *a* géant, gigantesque; (*steps*) de géant; (*packet etc*) Com géant.

gibberish ['dʒɪbərɪʃ] *n* baragouin *m*.

gibe [dʒaɪb] *vi* railler; **to g. at** railler; – *n* raillerie *f*.

giblets ['dʒɪblɪts] *npl* (*of fowl*) abats *mpl*.

giddy ['gɪdɪ] *a* (**-ier, -iest**) (*heights*) vertigineux; **to feel g.** avoir le vertige; **to make g.** donner le vertige à. ◆**giddiness** *n* vertige *m*.

gift ['gɪft] *n* cadeau *m*; (*talent*) & *Jur* don *m*; **g. voucher** chèque-cadeau *m*. ◆**gifted** *a* doué (**with de, for** pour). ◆**giftwrapped** *a* en paquet-cadeau.

gig [gɪg] *n Mus Fam* engagement *m*, séance *f*.

gigantic [dʒaɪˈgæntɪk] *a* gigantesque.

giggle ['gɪg(ə)l] *vi* rire (sottement); – *n* petit rire *m* sot; **to have the giggles** avoir le fou rire.

gild [gɪld] *vt* dorer. ◆**gilt** *a* doré; – *n* dorure *f*.

gills [gɪlz] *npl* (*of fish*) ouïes *fpl*.

gimmick ['gɪmɪk] *n* (*trick, object*) truc *m*.

gin [dʒɪn] *n* (*drink*) gin *m*.

ginger ['dʒɪndʒər] **1** *a* (*hair*) roux. **2** *n Bot Culin* gingembre *m*; **g. beer** boisson *f* gazeuse au gingembre. ◆**gingerbread** *n* pain *m* d'épice.

gingerly ['dʒɪndʒəlɪ] *adv* avec précaution.

gipsy ['dʒɪpsɪ] *n* bohémien, -ienne *mf*; (*Central European*) Tsigane *mf*; – *a* (*music*) tsigane.

giraffe [dʒɪˈrɑːf, dʒɪˈræf] *n* girafe *f*.

girder ['gɜːdər] *n* (*metal beam*) poutre *f*.

girdle ['gɜːd(ə)l] *n* (*belt*) ceinture *f*; (*corset*) gaine *f*.

girl ['gɜːl] *n* (jeune) fille *f*; (*daughter*) fille *f*; (*servant*) bonne *f*; (*sweetheart*) *Fam* petite amie *f*; **English g.** jeune Anglaise *f*; **g. guide** éclaireuse *f*. ◆**girlfriend** *n* amie *f*; (*of boy*) petite amie *f*. ◆**girlish** *a* de (jeune) fille.

girth [gɜːθ] *n* (*measure*) circonférence *f*; (*of waist*) tour *m*.

gist [dʒɪst] *n* **to get the g. of** comprendre l'essentiel de.

give [gɪv] *vt* (*pt* gave, *pp* given) donner (**to** à); (*help, support*) prêter; (*gesture, pleasure*) faire; (*a sigh*) pousser; (*a look*) jeter; (*a blow*) porter; **g. me York 234** passez-moi le 234 à York; **she doesn't g. a damn** *Fam* elle s'en fiche; **to g. way** (*yield, break*) céder (**to** à); (*collapse*) s'effondrer; (*car*) laisser la priorité (**to** à); – *n* (*in fabric etc*) élasticité *f*. ■ **to g. away** *vt* (*prize*) distribuer; (*money*) donner; (*facts*) révéler; (*betray*) trahir (*qn*);

to g. back *vt* (*return*) rendre; **to g. in** *vi* (*surrender*) céder (**to** à); – *vt* (*hand in*) remettre; **to g. off** *vt* (*smell, heat*) dégager; **to g. out** *vt* distribuer; – *vi* (*of supplies, patience*) s'épuiser; (*of engine*) rendre l'âme; **to g. over** *vt* (*devote*) donner, consacrer (**to** à); **to g. oneself over to** s'adonner à; – *vi* **g. over!** (*stop*) *Fam* arrête!; **to g. up** *vi* abandonner, renoncer; – *vt* abandonner, renoncer à; (*seat*) céder (**to** à); (*prisoner*) livrer (**to** à); (*patient*) condamner; **to g. up smoking** cesser de fumer. ◆**given** *a* (*fixed*) donné, convenu; **to be g. to doing** (*prone to do*) avoir l'habitude de faire; **g. your age** (*in view of*) étant donné votre âge; **g. that** étant donné que. ◆**giver** *n* donateur, -trice *mf*.

glacier ['glæsɪə, 'gleɪsjər] *n* glacier *m*.

glad [glæd] *a* (*person*) content (**of, about** de). ◆**gladden** *vt* réjouir. ◆**gladly** *adv* (*willingly*) volontiers.

glade [gleɪd] *n* clairière *f*.

gladiolus, *pl* **-i** [glædɪˈəʊləs, -aɪ] *n Bot* glaïeul *m*.

glamour ['glæmər] *n* (*charm*) enchantement *m*; (*splendour*) éclat *m*. ◆**glamorize** *vt* montrer sous un jour séduisant. ◆**glamorous** *a* séduisant.

glance [glɑːns] **1** *n* coup *m* d'œil; – *vi* jeter un coup d'œil (**at** à, sur). **2** *vt* **to g. off sth** (*of bullet*) ricocher sur qch.

gland [glænd] *n* glande *f*. ◆**glandular** *a* **g. fever** *Med* mononucléose *f* infectieuse.

glar/e ['gleər] *vi* **to g. at s.o.** foudroyer qn (du regard); – *n* regard *m* furieux. **2** *vi* (*of sun*) briller d'un éclat aveuglant; – *n* éclat *m* aveuglant. ◆**—ing** *a* (*sun*) aveuglant; (*eyes*) furieux; (*injustice*) flagrant; **a g. mistake** une faute énorme.

glass [glɑːs] *n* verre *m*; (*mirror*) miroir *m*, glace *f*; *pl* (*spectacles*) lunettes *fpl*; **a pane of g.** une vitre, un carreau; – *a* (*door*) vitré; (*industry*) du verre. ◆**glassful** *n* (*plein*) verre *m*.

glaze [gleɪz] *vt* (*door*) vitrer; (*pottery*) vernisser; (*paper*) glacer; – *n* (*on pottery*) vernis *m*; (*on paper*) glacé *m*. ◆**glazier** *n* vitrier *m*.

gleam [gliːm] *n* lueur *f*; – *vi* (re)luire.

glean [gliːn] *vt* (*grain, information etc*) glaner.

glee [gliː] *n* joie *f*. ◆**gleeful** *a* joyeux.

glen [glen] *n* vallon *m*.

glib [glɪb] *a* (*person*) qui a la parole facile; (*speech*) facile, peu sincère. ◆**—ly** *adv* (*to say*) peu sincèrement.

glid/e [glaɪd] *vi* glisser; (*of vehicle*) avancer

silencieusement; *(of aircraft, bird)* planer.
◆—ing *n Av Sp* vol m à voile. **◆—er** *n Av*
planeur m.

glimmer ['glɪmər] *vi* luire (faiblement); – *n*
(light, of hope etc) (faible) lueur *f.*

glimpse [glɪmps] *n* aperçu m; **to catch** *or* **get**
a g. *of* entrevoir.

glint [glɪnt] *vi (shine with flashes)* briller; – *n*
éclair m; *(in eye)* étincelle *f.*

glisten ['glɪs(ə)n] *vi (of wet surface)* briller;
(of water) miroiter.

glitter ['glɪtər] *vi* scintiller, briller; – *n* scintillement m.

gloat [gləʊt] *vi* jubiler *(over à la vue de).*

globe [gləʊb] *n* globe m. **◆global** *a*
(comprehensive) global; *(universal)* universel, mondial.

gloom [glum] *n (darkness)* obscurité *f;*
(sadness) Fig tristesse *f.* **◆gloomy** *a* (*-ier,*
-iest) (dark, dismal) sombre, triste; *(sad)*
Fig triste; *(pessimistic)* pessimiste.

glory ['glɔːrɪ] *n* gloire *f;* **in all one's g.**
Fam dans toute sa splendeur; **to be in one's g.**
(very happy) Fam être à son affaire; – *vi* **to**
g. in se glorifier de. **◆glorify** *vt (praise)*
glorifier; **it's a glorified barn**/etc ce n'est
guère plus qu'une grange/etc. **◆glorious**
a (full of glory) glorieux; *(splendid, enjoya-*
ble) magnifique.

gloss [glɒs] **1** *n (shine)* brillant m; **g. paint**
peinture *f* brillante; **g. finish** brillant m. **2**
n (note) glose *f,* commentaire m. **3** *vt* **to g.**
over *(minimize)* glisser sur; *(conceal)*
dissimuler. **◆glossy** *a (-ier, -iest) (shine)*
brillant; *(paper)* glacé; *(magazine)* de luxe.

glossary ['glɒsərɪ] *n* glossaire m.

glove [glʌv] *n* gant m; **g. compartment** *Aut*
(shelf) vide-poches m *inv; (enclosed)* boîte *f*
à gants. **◆gloved** *a* **g. hand** une main
gantée.

glow [gləʊ] *vi (of sky, fire)* rougeoyer; *(of*
lamp) luire; *(of eyes, person) Fig* rayonner
(with de); – *n* rougeoiement m; *(of colour)*
éclat m; *(of lamp)* lueur *f.* **◆—ing** *a*
(account, terms etc) très favorable, enthousiaste. **◆glow-worm** *n* ver m luisant.

glucose ['glukəʊs] *n* glucose m.

glue [glu] *n* colle *f;* – *vt* coller *(to, on à).*
◆glued *a* **g. to** *(eyes) Fam* fixés *or* rivés
sur; **to be g. to** *(television) Fam* être cloué
devant.

glum [glʌm] *a (glummer, glummest)* triste.

glut [glʌt] *vt (-tt-) (overfill)* rassasier;
(market) Com surcharger *(with de);* – *n (of*
produce, oil etc) Com surplus m *(of de).*

glutton ['glʌt(ə)n] *n* glouton, -onne *mf;* **g.**
for work bourreau m de travail; **g. for**

punishment masochiste *mf.* **◆gluttony** *n*
gloutonnerie *f.*

glycerin(e) ['glɪsərɪn] *n* glycérine *f.*

GMT [dʒiːem'tiː] *abbr (Greenwich Mean*
Time) GMT.

gnarled [nɑːld] *a* noueux.

gnash [næʃ] *vt* **to g. one's teeth** grincer des
dents.

gnat [næt] *n (insect)* cousin m.

gnaw [nɔː] *vti* **to g. (at)** ronger.

gnome [nəʊm] *n (little man)* gnome m.

go [gəʊ] **1** *vi (3rd person sing pres t* **goes;** *pt*
went; *pp* **gone;** *pres p* **going)** aller *(to* à, *from*
de); *(depart)* partir, s'en aller; *(disappear)*
disparaître; *(be sold)* se vendre; *(function)*
marcher, fonctionner; *(progress)* aller,
marcher; *(become)* devenir; *(be)* être; *(of*
time) passer; *(of hearing, strength)* baisser;
(of rope) céder; *(of fuse)* sauter; *(of mate-*
rial) s'user; **to go well/badly** *(of event)* se
passer bien/mal; **she's going to do** *(is about*
to, intends to) elle va faire; **it's all gone**
(finished) il n'y en a plus; **to go and get**
(fetch) aller chercher; **to go and see** aller
voir; **to go riding/sailing/on a trip**/etc faire
du cheval/de la voile/un voyage/etc; **to let**
go of *(release)* lâcher; **to go** *(to doctor, tunnel etc)*
aller voir; **to get things going** faire démar-
rer les choses; **is there any beer going?**
(available) y a-t-il de la bière? **it goes to**
show that... ça sert à montrer que...;
two hours/etc **to go** *(still left)* encore deux
heures/etc. **2** *n (pl* **goes)** *(energy)* dynamisme m; *(attempt)* coup m; **to have a go at**
(doing) *sth* essayer de (faire) qch; **at one go**
d'un seul coup; **on the go** en mouvement,
actif; **to make a go of** *(make a success of)*
réussir. ■ **to go about** *or* **(a)round** *vt* se
déplacer; *(of news, rumour)* circuler; **to go**
about *(one's duties etc)* s'occuper de; **to**
know how to go about it savoir s'y prendre;
to go across *vt* traverser; – *vi (cross)* traverser; *(go) aller (to* à); **to go across to**
s.o.('s) faire un saut chez qn; **to go after** *vt*
(follow) suivre; *(job)* viser; **to go against** *vt*
(of result) être défavorable à; *(s.o.'s wishes)*
aller contre; *(harm)* nuire à; **to go ahead**
avancer, aller de l'avant; **to go ahead with**
(plan etc) poursuivre; **go ahead!** allez-y! **◆go-**
ahead *a* dynamique; – *n* **to get the**
go-ahead avoir le feu vert; **to go along** *vi*
aller, avancer; **to go along with** *(agree)* être
d'accord avec; **to go away** *vi* partir, s'en
aller; **to go back** *vi* retourner, revenir; *(in*
time) remonter; *(retreat, step back)* reculer;
to go back on *(promise)* revenir sur; **to go**
by *vi* passer; – *vt (act according to)* se

fonder sur; (*judge from*) juger d'après; (*instruction*) suivre; **to go down** *vi* descendre; (*fall down*) tomber; (*of ship*) couler; (*of sun*) se coucher; (*of storm*) s'apaiser; (*of temperature, price etc*) baisser; (*of tyre*) se dégonfler; (*of speech etc*) être bien reçu; **to go down well** (*of exam*) se passer bien; **to go down with** (*illness*) attraper; – *vt* **to go down the stairs/street** descendre l'escalier/la rue; **to go for** *vt* (*fetch*) aller chercher; (*attack*) attaquer; (*like*) *Fam* aimer beaucoup; **to go forward(s)** *vi* avancer; **to go in** *vi* (r)entrer; (*of sun*) se cacher; **to go in for** (*exam*) se présenter à; (*hobby, sport*) faire; (*career*) entrer dans; (*like*) *Fam* aimer beaucoup; – *vt* **to go in a room/***etc* entrer dans une pièce/*etc*; **to go into** *vt* (*room etc*) entrer dans; (*question*) examiner; **to go off** *vi* (*leave*) partir; (*of bad*) se gâter; (*of effect*) passer; (*of alarm*) se déclencher; (*of event*) se passer; – *vt* (*one's food*) perdre le goût de; **to go on** *vi* continuer (doing à faire); (*travel*) poursuivre sa route; (*happen*) se passer; (*last*) durer; (*of time*) passer; **to go on at** (*nag*) *Fam* s'en prendre à; **to go on about** *Fam* parler sans cesse de; **to go out** *vi* sortir; (*of light, fire*) s'éteindre; (*of tide*) descendre; (*of newspaper, product*) être distribué (to à); (*depart*) partir; **to go out to work** travailler (au dehors); **to go over** *vi* (*go*) aller (to à); (*cross over*) traverser; (*to enemy*) passer (to à); – *vt* examiner; (*speech*) revoir; (*in one's mind*) repasser; (*touch up*) retoucher; (*overhaul*) réviser (*véhicule, montre*); **to go round** *vi* (*turn*) tourner; (*make a detour*) faire le tour; (*be sufficient*) suffire; **to go round to s.o.('s)** passer chez qn, faire un saut chez qn; **enough to go round** assez pour tout le monde; – *vt* **to go round a corner** tourner un coin; **to go through** *vi* passer; (*of deal*) être conclu; – *vt* (*undergo, endure*) subir; (*examine*) examiner; (*search*) fouiller; (*spend*) dépenser; (*wear out*) user; (*perform*) accomplir; **to go through with** (*carry out*) réaliser, aller jusqu'au bout de; **to go under** *vi* (*of ship, person, firm*) couler; **to go up** *vi* monter; (*explode*) sauter; – *vt* **to go up the stairs/street** monter l'escalier/la rue; **to go without** *vi* se passer de.

goad [gəud] *n* aiguillon *m*; – *vt* **to g. (on)** aiguillonner.

goal [gəul] *n* but *m*. ◆**goalkeeper** *n* Fb gardien *m* de but, goal *m*. ◆**goalpost** *n* Fb poteau *m* de but.

goat [gəut] *n* chèvre *f*; **to get s.o.'s g.** *Fam*

énerver qn. ◆**goa'tee** *n* (*beard*) barbiche *f*.

gobble ['gɒb(ə)l] *vt* **to g. (up)** engloutir.

go-between ['gəubitwiːn] *n* intermédiaire *mf*.

goblet ['gɒblit] *n* verre *m* à pied.

goblin ['gɒblin] *n* (*evil spirit*) lutin *m*.

god [gɒd] *n* dieu *m*; **G.** Dieu *m*; **the gods** *Th Fam* le poulailler. ◆**g.-fearing** *a* croyant. ◆**g.-forsaken** *a* (*place*) perdu, misérable. ◆**goddess** *n* déesse *f*. ◆**godly** *a* dévot. ◆**godchild** *n* (*pl* **-children**) filleul, -eule *mf*. ◆**goddaughter** *n* filleule *f*. ◆**godfather** *n* parrain *m*. ◆**godmother** *n* marraine *f*. ◆**godson** *n* filleul *m*.

goddam(n) ['gɒdæm] *a Am Fam* foutu.

godsend ['gɒdsend] *n* aubaine *f*.

goes [gəuz] *see go* 1.

goggle ['gɒg(ə)l] **1** *vi* **to g. at** regarder en roulant de gros yeux. **2** *npl* (*spectacles*) lunettes *fpl* (protectrices). ◆**g.-'eyed** *a* aux yeux saillants.

going ['gəuiŋ] **1** *n* (*departure*) départ *m*; (*speed*) allure *f*; (*conditions*) conditions *fpl*; **it's hard g.** c'est difficile. **2** *a* **the g. price** le prix pratiqué (for pour); **a g. concern** une entreprise qui marche bien. ◆**goings-'on** *npl Pej* activités *fpl*.

go-kart ['gəukɑːt] *n Sp* kart *m*.

gold [gəuld] *n* or *m*; – *a* (*watch etc*) en or; (*coin, dust*) d'or. ◆**golden** *a* (*made of gold*) d'or; (*in colour*) doré, d'or; (*opportunity*) excellent. ◆**goldmine** *n* mine *f* d'or. ◆**gold-'plated** *a* plaqué or. ◆**goldsmith** *n* orfèvre *m*.

goldfinch ['gəuldfintʃ] *n* (*bird*) chardonneret *m*.

goldfish ['gəuldfiʃ] *n* poisson *m* rouge.

golf [gɒlf] *n* golf *m*. ◆**golfer** *n* golfeur, -euse *mf*.

golly! ['gɒli] *int* (by) **g.!** *Fam* mince (alors)!

gondola ['gɒndələ] *n* (*boat*) gondole *f*. ◆**gondo'lier** *n* gondolier *m*.

gone [gɒn] *see go* 1; – *a* **it's g. two** *Fam* il est plus de deux heures. ◆**goner** *n* **to be a g.** *Sl* être fichu.

gong [gɒŋ] *n* gong *m*.

good [gud] *a* (**better**, **best**) bon; (*kind*) gentil; (*weather*) beau; (*pleasant*) bon, agréable; (*well-behaved*) sage; **be g. enough to . . .** ayez la gentillesse de . . . ; **my g. friend** mon cher ami; **a g. chap** *or* **fellow** un brave type; **g. and strong** bien fort; **a g. (long) walk** une bonne promenade; **very g.!** (*all right*) très bien!; **that's g. of you** c'est gentil de ta part; **to feel g.** se sentir bien;

that isn't g. enough (bad) ça ne va pas; (not sufficient) ça ne suffit pas; **it's g. for us** ça nous fait du bien; **g. at** (French etc) Sch bon or fort en; **to be g. with** (children) savoir s'y prendre avec; **it's a g. thing (that)**... heureusement que... ; **a g. many, a g. deal (of)** beaucoup; **as g. as** (almost) pratiquement; **g. afternoon**, g. **morning** bonjour; (on leaving someone) au revoir; **g. evening** bonsoir; **g. night** bonsoir; (before going to bed) bonne nuit; **to make g.** vi (succeed) réussir; − vt (loss) compenser; (damage) réparer; **G. Friday** Vendredi m Saint; − n (virtue) bien m; **for her g.** pour son bien; **there's some g. in him** il a du bon; **it's no g. crying/shouting/etc** ça ne sert à rien de pleurer/crier/etc; **that's no g.** (worthless) ça ne vaut rien; (bad) ça ne va pas; **what's the g.?** à quoi bon? **for g.** (to leave, give up etc) pour de bon. ◆**g.-for-nothing** a & n propre à rien (mf). ◆**g.-'humoured** a de bonne humeur. ◆**g.-'looking** a beau. ◆**goodness** n bonté f; **my g.!** mon Dieu! ◆**good'will** n bonne volonté f; (zeal) zèle m.

goodbye [gud'bai] int & n au revoir (m inv).

goodly ['gudli] a (size, number) grand.

goods [gudz] npl marchandises fpl; (articles for sale) articles mpl.

gooey ['gu:i] a Fam gluant, poisseux.

goof [gu:f] vi **to g. (up)** (blunder) Am faire une gaffe.

goon [gu:n] n Fam idiot, -ote mf.

goose, pl **geese** [gu:s, gi:s] n oie f; **g. pimples** or **bumps** chair f de poule. ◆**gooseflesh** n chair f de poule.

gooseberry ['guzbəri, Am 'gu:sbəri] n groseille f à maquereau.

gorge [gɔ:dʒ] 1 n (ravine) gorge f. 2 vt (food) engloutir; **to g. oneself** s'empiffrer (on de).

gorgeous ['gɔ:dʒəs] a magnifique.

gorilla [gə'rilə] n gorille m.

gormless ['gɔ:mləs] a Fam stupide.

gorse [gɔ:s] n inv ajonc(s) m(pl).

gory ['gɔ:ri] a (-ier, -iest) (bloody) sanglant; (details) Fig horrible.

gosh! [gɒʃ] int Fam mince (alors)!

go-slow [gəu'sləu] n (strike) grève f perlée.

gospel ['gɒspəl] n évangile m.

gossip ['gɒsip] n (talk) bavardage(s) m(pl); (malicious) cancan(s) m(pl); (person) commère f; **g. column** Journ échos mpl; − vi bavarder; (maliciously) cancaner. ◆**—ing** n Fam graffiti mpl. ◆**—gossipy** a bavard, cancanier.

got, Am **gotten** [gɒt, 'gɒt(ə)n] see **get**.

Gothic ['gɒθik] a & n gothique m.

gouge [gaudʒ] vt **to g. out** (eye) crever.

goulash ['gu:læʃ] n Culin goulasch f.

gourmet ['guəmei] n gourmet m.

gout [gaut] n Med goutte f.

govern ['gʌvən] vt (rule) gouverner; (city) administrer; (business) gérer; (emotion) maîtriser, gouverner; (influence) déterminer; − vi Pol gouverner; **governing body** conseil m d'administration. ◆**governess** n gouvernante f. ◆**government** n gouvernement m; (local) administration f; − a (department, policy etc) gouvernemental; (loan) d'État. ◆**govern'mental** a gouvernemental. ◆**governor** n gouverneur m; (of school) administrateur, -trice mf; (of prison) directeur, -trice mf.

gown [gaun] n (dress) robe f; (of judge, lecturer) toge f.

GP [dʒi:'pi:] n abbr (general practitioner) (médecin m) généraliste m.

GPO [dʒi:pi:'əu] abbr (General Post Office) = PTT fpl.

grab [græb] vt (-bb-) **to g. (hold of)** saisir, agripper; **to g. sth from s.o.** arracher qch à qn.

grace [greis] 1 n (charm, goodwill etc) Rel grâce f; (extension of time) délai m de grâce; **to say g.** dire le bénédicité. 2 vt (adorn) orner; (honour) honorer (with de). ◆**graceful** a gracieux. ◆**gracious** a (kind) aimable, gracieux (to envers); (elegant) élégant; **good g.!** Fam bonté divine!

gradation [grə'dei(ə)n, Am grei'dei(ə)n] n gradation f.

grade [greid] n catégorie f; Mil Math grade m; (of milk) qualité f; (of eggs) calibre m; (level) niveau m; (mark) Sch Univ note f; (class) Am Sch classe f; **g. school** Am école f primaire; **g. crossing** Am passage m à niveau; − vt (classify) classer; (colours etc) graduer; (paper) Sch Univ noter.

gradient ['greidiənt] n (slope) inclinaison f.

gradual ['grædʒuəl] a progressif, graduel; (slope) doux. ◆**—ly** adv progressivement, peu à peu.

graduat/e ['grædʒueit] vi Univ obtenir son diplôme; Am Sch obtenir son baccalauréat; **to g. from** sortir de; − vt (mark with degrees) graduer; − ['grædʒuət] n diplômé, -ée mf, licencié, -ée mf. ◆**—ed** a (tube etc) gradué; **to be g.** Am Sch Univ = **to graduate** vi. ◆**gradu'ation** n Univ remise f des diplômes.

graffiti [grə'fi:ti] npl graffiti mpl.

graft [grɑ:ft] n Med Bot greffe f; − vt greffer (on to à).

grain [grein] n (seed, particle) grain m;

(*seeds*) grain(s) *m(pl)*; (*in cloth*) fil *m*; (*in wood*) fibre *f*; (*in leather, paper*) grain *m*; (*of truth*) *Fig* once *f*.

gram(me) [græm] *n* gramme *m*.

grammar ['græmər] *n* grammaire *f*; **g. school** lycée *m*. ◆**gra'mmatical** *a* grammatical.

gramophone ['græməfəʊn] *n* phonographe *m*.

granary ['grænəri] *n Agr* grenier *m*; **g. loaf** pain *m* complet.

grand [grænd] **1** *a* (*-er, -est*) magnifique, grand; (*style*) grandiose; (*concert, duke*) grand; (*piano*) à queue; (*wonderful*) *Fam* magnifique. **2** *n inv Am Sl* mille dollars *mpl*; *Br Sl* mille livres *fpl*. ◆**grandeur** ['grændʒər] *n* magnificence *f*; (*of person, country*) grandeur *f*.

grandchild ['græntʃaɪld] *n* (*pl* -children) petit(e)-enfant *mf*. ◆**grand(d)ad** *n Fam* pépé *m*, papi *m*. ◆**granddaughter** *n* petite-fille *f*. ◆**grandfather** *n* grand-père *m*. ◆**grandmother** *n* grand-mère *f*. ◆**grandparents** *npl* grands-parents *mpl*. ◆**grandson** *n* petit-fils *m*.

grandstand ['grændstænd] *n Sp* tribune *f*.

grange [greɪndʒ] *n* (*house*) manoir *m*.

granite ['grænɪt] *n* granit(e) *m*.

granny ['grænɪ] *n Fam* mamie *f*.

grant [grɑːnt] **1** *vt* accorder (**to** à); (*request*) accéder à; (*prayer*) exaucer; (*admit*) admettre (**that** que); **to take for granted** (*event*) considérer comme allant de soi; (*person*) considérer comme faisant partie du décor; **I take (it) for granted that ...** je présume que... **2** *n* subvention *f*, allocation *f*; *Univ* bourse *f*.

granule ['grænjuːl] *n* granule *m*. ◆**granulated** *a* **g. sugar** sucre *m* cristallisé.

grape [greɪp] *n* grain *m* de raisin; *pl* le raisin, les raisins *mpl*; **to eat grapes** manger du raisin *or* des raisins; **g. harvest** vendange *f*. ◆**grapefruit** *n* pamplemousse *m*. ◆**grapevine** *n* **on the g.** *Fig* par le téléphone arabe.

graph [græf, grɑːf] *n* graphique *m*, courbe *f*; **g. paper** papier *m* millimétré.

graphic ['græfɪk] *a* graphique; (*description*) *Fig* explicite, vivant. ◆**graphically** *adv* (*to describe*) explicitement.

grapple ['græp(ə)l] *vi* **to g. with** (*person, problem etc*) se colleter avec.

grasp [grɑːsp] *vt* (*seize, understand*) saisir; – *n* (*firm hold*) prise *f*; (*understanding*) compréhension *f*; (*knowledge*) connaissance *f*; **to have a strong g.** (*strength of hand*) avoir de la poigne; **within s.o.'s g.**

(*reach*) à la portée de qn. ◆**-ing** *a* (*greedy*) rapace.

grass [grɑːs] *n* herbe *f*; (*lawn*) gazon *m*; **the g. roots** *Pol* la base. ◆**grasshopper** *n* sauterelle *f*. ◆**grassland** *n* prairie *f*. ◆**grassy** *a* herbeux.

grat/e [greɪt] **1** *n* (*for fireplace*) grille *f* de foyer. **2** *vt Culin* râper. **3** *vi* (*of sound*) grincer (**on** sur); **to g. on the ears** écorcher les oreilles; **to g. on s.o.'s nerves** taper sur les nerfs de qn. ◆**-ing 1** *a* (*sound*) grinçant; *Fig* irritant. **2** *n* (*bars*) grille *f*. ◆**-er** *n Culin* râpe *f*.

grateful ['greɪtfʊl] *a* reconnaissant (**to** à, **for** de); (*words, letter*) de remerciement; (*friend, attitude*) plein de remerciement; **I'm g. (to you) for your help** je vous suis reconnaissant de votre aide; **I'd be g. if you'd be quieter** j'aimerais bien que tu fasses moins de bruit; **g. thanks** mes sincères remerciements. ◆**-ly** *adv* avec reconnaissance.

gratify ['grætɪfaɪ] *vt* (*whim*) satisfaire; **to g. s.o.** faire plaisir à qn. ◆**-ied** *a* très content (**with** *or* **at sth** de qch, **to do** de faire). ◆**-ying** *a* très satisfaisant; **it's g. to ... ça** fait plaisir de ... ◆**gratifi'cation** *n* satisfaction *f*.

gratis ['grætɪs, 'greɪtɪs] *adv* gratis.

gratitude ['grætɪtjuːd] *n* reconnaissance *f*, gratitude *f* (**for** de).

gratuitous [grə'tjuːɪtəs] *a* (*act etc*) gratuit.

gratuity [grə'tjuːɪtɪ] *n* (*tip*) pourboire *m*.

grave¹ [greɪv] *n* tombe *f*; **g. digger** fossoyeur *m*. ◆**gravestone** *n* pierre *f* tombale. ◆**graveyard** *n* cimetière *m*; **auto g.** *Am Fam* cimetière *m* de voitures.

grave² [greɪv] *a* (*-er, -est*) (*serious*) grave. ◆**-ly** *adv* gravement; (*concerned, displeased*) extrêmement.

gravel ['græv(ə)l] *n* gravier *m*.

gravitate ['græviteɪt] *vi* **to g. towards** (*be drawn towards*) être attiré vers; (*move towards*) se diriger vers. ◆**gravi'tation** *n* gravitation *f*.

gravity ['grævɪtɪ] *n* **1** (*seriousness*) gravité *f*. **2** *Phys* pesanteur *f*, gravité *f*.

gravy ['greɪvɪ] *n* jus *m* de viande.

gray [greɪ] *Am* = **grey**.

graze [greɪz] **1** *vi* (*of cattle*) paître. **2** *vt* (*scrape*) écorcher; (*touch lightly*) frôler, effleurer; – *n* (*wound*) écorchure *f*.

grease [griːs] *n* graisse *f*; – *vt* graisser. ◆**greaseproof** *a & n* **g. (paper)** papier *m* sulfurisé. ◆**greasy** *a* (*-ier, -iest*) graisseux; (*hair*) gras; (*road*) glissant.

great [greɪt] *a* (*-er, -est*) grand; (*effort, heat,*

parcel) gros, grand; (*excellent*) magnifique, merveilleux; **g. at** (*English, tennis etc*) doué pour; **a g. deal** *or* **number (of)**, **a g. many** beaucoup (de); **a g. opinion of** une haute opinion de; **a very g. age** un âge très avancé; **the greatest team**/*etc* (*best*) la meilleure équipe/*etc*; **Greater London** le grand Londres. ◆**g.-'grandfather** *n* arrière-grand-père *m*. ◆**g.-'grandmother** *n* arrière-grand-mère *f*. ◆**greatly** *adv* (*much*) beaucoup; (*very*) très, bien; **I g. prefer** je préfère de beaucoup. ◆**greatness** *n* (*in size, importance*) grandeur *f*; (*in degree*) intensité *f*.

Great Britain [greɪt'brɪt(ə)n] *n* Grande-Bretagne *f*.

Greece [griːs] *n* Grèce *f*. ◆**Greek** *a* grec; – *n* Grec *m*, Grecque *f*; (*language*) grec *m*.

greed [griːd] *n* avidité *f* (**for**, de); (*for food*) gourmandise *f*. ◆**greed/y** *a* (**-ier**, **-iest**) avide (**for**, de); (*for food*) glouton, gourmand. ◆**-ily** *adv* avidement; (*to eat*) gloutonnement. ◆**-iness** *n* = **greed**.

green [griːn] *a* (**-er**, **-est**) vert; (*pale*) blême, vert; (*immature*) Fig inexpérimenté, naïf; **to turn** *or* **go g.** verdir; **the g. light** Fig le (feu) vert; **to have g. fingers** *or* Am **a g. thumb** avoir la main verte; **g. with envy** Fig vert de jalousie; – *n* (*colour*) vert *m*; (*lawn*) pelouse *f*; (*village square*) place *f* gazonnée; *pl* Culin légumes *mpl* verts. ◆**greenery** *n* (*plants, leaves*) verdure *f*. ◆**greenfly** *n* puceron *m* (*des plantes*). ◆**greengrocer** *n* marchand, -ande *mf* de légumes. ◆**greenhouse** *n* serre *f*. ◆**greenish** *a* verdâtre. ◆**greenness** *n* (*colour*) vert *m*; (*greenery*) verdure *f*.

greengage ['griːngeɪdʒ] *n* (*plum*) reine-claude *f*.

Greenland ['griːnlənd] *n* Groenland *m*.

greet [griːt] *vt* saluer, accueillir; **to g. s.o.** (*of sight*) s'offrir aux regards de qn. ◆**-ing** *n* salutation *f*; (*welcome*) accueil *m*; *pl* (*for birthday, festival*) vœux *mpl*; **send my greetings to...** envoie mon bon souvenir à...; **greetings card** carte *f* de vœux.

gregarious [grɪ'geərɪəs] *a* (*person*) sociable; (*instinct*) grégaire.

gremlin ['gremlɪn] *n* Fam petit diable *m*.

grenade [grə'neɪd] *n* (*bomb*) grenade *f*.

grew [gruː] *see* **grow**.

grey [greɪ] *a* (**-er**, **-est**) gris; (*outlook*) Fig sombre; **to be going g.** grisonner; – *vi* **to be greying** être grisonnant *f*. ◆**g.-'haired** *a* aux cheveux gris. ◆**greyhound** *n* lévrier *m*. ◆**greyish** *a* grisâtre.

grid [grɪd] *n* (*grating*) grille *f*; (*system*) El réseau *m*; Culin gril *m*. ◆**gridiron** *n* Culin gril *m*.

griddle ['grɪd(ə)l] *n* (*on stove*) plaque *f* à griller.

grief [griːf] *n* chagrin *m*, douleur *f*; **to come to g.** avoir des ennuis; (*of driver, pilot etc*) avoir un accident; (*of plan*) échouer; **good g.!** ciel! bon sang!

grieve [griːv] *vt* peiner, affliger; – *vi* s'affliger (**over**, de); **to g. for s.o.** pleurer qn. ◆**grievance** *n* grief *m*; *pl* (*complaints*) doléances *fpl*.

grievous ['griːvəs] *a* (*serious*) très grave.

grill [grɪl] **1** *n* (*utensil*) gril *m*; (*dish*) grillade *f*; – *vti* griller. **2** *vt* (*question*) Fam cuisiner.

grille [grɪl] *n* (*metal bars*) grille *f*; (*radiator*) **g.** Aut calandre *f*.

grim [grɪm] *a* (**grimmer**, **grimmest**) sinistre; (*face*) sévère; (*truth*) brutal; (*bad*) Fam (*plutôt*) affreux; **a g. determination** une volonté inflexible. ◆**-ly** *adv* (*to look at*) sévèrement.

grimace ['grɪməs] *n* grimace *f*; – *vi* grimacer.

grime [graɪm] *n* saleté *f*. ◆**grimy** *a* (**-ier**, **-iest**) sale.

grin [grɪn] *vi* (**-nn-**) avoir un large sourire; (*with pain*) avoir un rictus; – *n* large sourire *m*; rictus *m*.

grind [graɪnd] **1** *vt* (*pt & pp* **ground**) moudre; (*blade, tool*) aiguiser; (*handle*) tourner; (*oppress*) Fig écraser; **to g. one's teeth** grincer des dents; – *vi* **to g. to a halt** s'arrêter (*progressivement*). **2** *n* Fam corvée *f*, travail *m* long et monotone. ◆**-ing** *a* **g. poverty** la misère noire. ◆**-er** *n* **coffee g.** moulin *m* à café.

grip [grɪp] *vt* (**-pp-**) (*seize*) saisir; (*hold*) serré; (*of story*) Fig empoigner (**qn**); **to g. the road** (*of tyres*) adhérer à la route; – *vi* (*of brakes*) mordre; – *n* (*hold*) prise *f*; (*hand clasp*) poigne *f*; **get a g. on yourself!** secoue-toi!; **to get to grips with** (*problem*) s'attaquer à; **in the g. of** en proie à. ◆**gripping** *a* (*book, film etc*) prenant.

gripe [graɪp] *vi* (*complain*) Sl rouspéter.

grisly ['grɪzlɪ] *a* (*gruesome*) horrible.

gristle ['grɪs(ə)l] *n* Culin cartilage *m*.

grit [grɪt] **1** *n* (*sand*) sable *m*; (*gravel*) gravillon *m*; – *vt* (**-tt-**) (*road*) sabler. **2** *n* (*pluck*) Fam cran *m*. **3** *vt* (**-tt-**) **to g. one's teeth** serrer les dents.

grizzle ['grɪz(ə)l] *vi* Fam pleurnicher. ◆**grizzly** *a* **1** (*child*) Fam pleurnicheur. **2** (*bear*) gris.

groan [grəʊn] *vi* (*with pain*) gémir;

(*complain*) grogner, gémir; – *n* gémissement *m*; grognement *m*.

grocer ['grəʊsər] *n* épicier, -ière *mf*; **grocer's (shop)** épicerie *f*. ◆**grocery** *n* (*shop*) épicerie *f*; *pl* (*food*) épicerie *f*.

grog [grɒg] *n* (*drink*) grog *m*.

groggy ['grɒgɪ] *a* (**-ier, -iest**) (*weak*) faible; (*shaky on one's feet*) pas solide sur les jambes.

groin [grɔɪn] *n Anat* aine *f*.

groom [gruːm] **1** *n* (*bridegroom*) marié *m*. **2** *n* (*for horses*) lad *m*; – *vt* (*horse*) panser; to g. s.o. for (*job*) *Fig* préparer qn pour; **well groomed** (*person*) très soigné.

groove [gruːv] *n* (*for sliding door etc*) rainure *f*; (*in record*) sillon *m*.

grope [grəʊp] *vi* to g. (**about**) tâtonner; to g. for chercher à tâtons.

gross [grəʊs] **1** *a* (**-er, -est**) (*coarse*) grossier; (*error*) gros, grossier; (*injustice*) flagrant. **2** *a* (*weight, income*) *Com* brut; – *vt* faire une recette brute de. **3** *n* (*number*) grosse *f*. ◆**-ly** *adv* grossièrement; (*very*) énormément, extrêmement.

grotesque [grəʊˈtesk] *a* (*ludicrous, strange*) grotesque; (*frightening*) monstrueux.

grotto ['grɒtəʊ] *n* (*pl* **-oes** *or* **-os**) grotte *f*.

grotty ['grɒtɪ] *a* (**-ier, -iest**) *Fam* affreux, moche.

ground¹ [graʊnd] **1** *n* terre *f*, sol *m*; (*area for camping, football etc*) & *Fig* terrain *m*; (*estate*) terres *fpl*; (*earth*) El *Am* terre *f*, masse *f*; (*background*) fond *m*; *pl* (*reasons*) raisons *fpl*, motifs *mpl*; (*gardens*) parc *m*; **on the** g. (*lying etc*) par terre; **to lose** g. perdre du terrain; g. **floor** rez-de-chaussée *m inv*; g. **frost** gelée *f* blanche. **2** *vt* (*aircraft*) bloquer *or* retenir au sol. ◆**-ing** *n* connaissances *fpl* (de fond) (**in** en). ◆**groundless** *a* sans fondement. ◆**groundnut** *n* arachide *f*. ◆**ground-sheet** *n* tapis *m* de sol. ◆**groundswell** *n* lame *f* de fond. ◆**groundwork** *n* préparation *f*.

ground² [graʊnd] *see* **grind** 1; – *a* (*coffee*) moulu; – *npl* (*coffee*) **grounds** marc *m* (de café).

group [gruːp] *n* groupe *m*; – *vt* to g. (**together**) grouper; – *vi* se grouper. ◆**-ing** *n* (*group*) groupe *m*.

grouse [graʊs] **1** *n inv* (*bird*) coq *m* de bruyère. **2** *vi* (*complain*) *Fam* rouspéter.

grove [grəʊv] *n* bocage *m*.

grovel ['grɒv(ə)l] *vi* (**-ll-**, *Am* **-l-**) *Pej* ramper, s'aplatir (**to s.o.** devant qn).

grow [grəʊ] *vi* (*pt* **grew**, *pp* **grown**) (*of person*) grandir; (*of plant, hair*) pousser;

(*increase*) augmenter, grandir, croître; (*expand*) s'agrandir; to g. **fat(ter)** grossir; to g. **to like** finir par aimer; to g. **into** devenir; to g. **on s.o.** (*of book, music etc*) plaire progressivement à qn; to g. **out of** (*one's clothes*) devenir trop grand pour; (*a habit*) perdre; to g. **up** devenir adulte; **when I g. up** quand je serai grand; – *vt* (*plant, crops*) cultiver, faire pousser; (*beard, hair*) laisser pousser. ◆**-ed-** *a* (*child*) qui grandit; (*number*) grandissant. ◆**grown** *a* (*full-grown*) adulte. ◆**grown-up** *n* grande personne *f*, adulte *mf*; – *a* (*ideas etc*) d'adulte. ◆**grower** *n* (*person*) cultivateur, -trice *mf*.

growl [graʊl] *vi* grogner (**at** contre); – *n* grognement *m*.

growth [grəʊθ] *n* croissance *f*; (*increase*) augmentation *f* (**in** de); (*of hair*) pousse *f*; (*beard*) barbe *f*; *Med* tumeur *f* (**on** à).

grub [grʌb] *n* (*food*) *Fam* bouffe *f*.

grubby ['grʌbɪ] *a* (**-ier, -iest**) sale.

grudg/e [grʌdʒ] **1** *vt* (*give*) donner à contrecœur; (*reproach*) reprocher (**s.o. sth** qch à qn); to g. **doing** faire à contrecœur. **2** *n* rancune *f*; **to have a** g. **against** en vouloir à. ◆**-ingly** *adv* (*to give etc*) à contrecœur.

gruelling, *Am* **grueling** ['gruːəlɪŋ] *a* (*day, detail etc*) éprouvant, atroce.

gruesome ['gruːsəm] *a* horrible.

gruff [grʌf] *a* (**-er, -est**) (*voice, person*) bourru.

grumble ['grʌmb(ə)l] *vi* (*complain*) grogner (**about, at** contre), se plaindre (**about, at** de).

grumpy ['grʌmpɪ] *a* (**-ier, -iest**) grincheux.

grunt [grʌnt] *vti* grogner; – *n* grognement *m*.

guarantee [gærənˈtiː] *n* garantie *f*; – *vt* garantir (**against** contre); (*vouch for*) se porter garant de; to g. (**s.o.**) **that** certifier *or* garantir (à qn) que. ◆**guarantor** *n* garant, -ante *mf*.

guard [gɑːd] *n* (*vigilance, group of soldiers etc*) garde *f*; (*individual person*) garde *m*; *Rail* chef *m* de train; **to keep a** g. **on** surveiller; **under** g. sous surveillance; **on one's** g. sur ses gardes; **to catch s.o. off his** g. prendre qn au dépourvu; **on** g. (*duty*) de garde; **to stand** g. monter la garde; – *vt* (*protect*) protéger (**against** contre); (*watch over*) surveiller, garder; to g. **against** (*protect oneself*) se prémunir contre; (*prevent*) empêcher; to g. **against doing** se garder de faire. ◆**-ed-** *a* (*cautious*) prudent.

◆**guardian** n gardien, -ienne mf; (of child) Jur tuteur, -trice mf.

guerrilla [gə'rɪlə] n (person) guérillero m; g. **warfare** guérilla f.

guess [ges] n conjecture f; (intuition) intuition f; (estimate) estimation f; **to make a g.** (essayer de) deviner; **an educated or informed g.** une conjecture fondée; **at a g.** au jugé, à vue de nez; – vt deviner (that que); (estimate) estimer; (suppose) Am supposer (that que); (think) Am croire (that que); – vi deviner; **I g. (so)** Am je suppose; je crois. ◆**guesswork** n hypothèse f; **by g.** au jugé.

guest [gest] n invité, -ée mf; (in hotel) client, -ente mf; (at meal) convive mf; – a (speaker, singer etc) invité. ◆**guesthouse** n pension f de famille. ◆**guestroom** n chambre f d'ami.

guffaw [gə'fɔː] vi rire bruyamment.

guidance ['gaɪdəns] n (advice) conseils mpl.

guid/e [gaɪd] n (person, book etc) guide m; (indication) indication f; (girl) g. éclaireuse f; **g. dog** chien m d'aveugle; **g. book** guide m; – vt (lead) guider. ◆**-ed** a (missile, rocket) téléguidé; **g. tour** visite f guidée. ◆**-ing** a (principle) directeur. ◆**guidelines** npl lignes fpl directrices, indications fpl à suivre.

guild [gɪld] n association f; Hist corporation f.

guile [gaɪl] n (deceit) ruse f.

guillotine ['gɪlətiːn] n guillotine f; (for paper) massicot m.

guilt [gɪlt] n culpabilité f. ◆**guilty** a (-ier, -iest) coupable; **g. person** coupable mf; **to find s.o. g.** déclarer qn coupable.

guinea pig ['gɪnɪpɪg] n (animal) & Fig cobaye m.

guise [gaɪz] n **under the g. of** sous l'apparence de.

guitar [gɪ'tɑːr] n guitare f. ◆**guitarist** n guitariste mf.

gulf [gʌlf] n (in sea) golfe m; (chasm) gouffre m; **a g. between** Fig un abîme entre.

gull [gʌl] n (bird) mouette f.

gullet ['gʌlɪt] n gosier m.

gullible ['gʌlɪb(ə)l] a crédule.

gully ['gʌlɪ] n (valley) ravine f; (drain) rigole f.

gulp [gʌlp] **1** vt **to g. (down)** avaler (vite); – n (of drink) gorgée f, lampée f; **in** or **at one**

g. d'une seule gorgée. **2** vi (with emotion) avoir la gorge serrée; – n serrement m de gorge.

gum [gʌm] n Anat gencive f. ◆**gumboil** n abcès m (dentaire).

gum [gʌm] **1** n (glue from tree) gomme f; (any glue) colle f; – vt (-mm-) coller. **2** n (for chewing) chewing-gum m.

gumption ['gʌmpʃ(ə)n] n Fam (courage) initiative f; (commonsense) jugeote f.

gun [gʌn] n pistolet m, revolver m; (cannon) canon m; – vt (-nn-) **to g. down** abattre. ◆**gunfight** n échange m de coups de feu. ◆**gunfire** n coups mpl de feu; Mil tir m d'artillerie. ◆**gunman** n (pl -men) bandit m armé. ◆**gunner** n Mil artilleur m. ◆**gunpoint** n **at g.** sous la menace d'un pistolet or d'une arme. ◆**gunpowder** n poudre f à canon. ◆**gunshot** n coup m de feu; **g. wound** blessure f par balle.

gurgle ['gɜːg(ə)l] vi (of water) glouglouter; – n glouglou m.

guru ['gʊruː] n (leader) Fam gourou m.

gush [gʌʃ] vi jaillir (out of de); – n jaillissement m.

gust [gʌst] n (of smoke) bouffée f; **g. (of wind)** rafale f (de vent). ◆**gusty** a (-ier, -iest) (weather) venteux; (day) de vent.

gusto ['gʌstəʊ] n **with g.** avec entrain.

gut [gʌt] **1** n Anat intestin m; (catgut) boyau m; pl Fam (innards) ventre m, tripes fpl; (pluck) cran m, tripes fpl; **he hates your guts** Fam il ne peut pas te sentir. **2** vt (-tt-) (of fire) dévaster.

gutter ['gʌtər] n (on roof) gouttière f; (in street) caniveau m.

guttural ['gʌtərəl] a guttural.

guy [gaɪ] n (fellow) Fam type m.

guzzle ['gʌz(ə)l] vi (eat) bâfrer; – vt (eat) engloutir; (drink) siffler.

gym [dʒɪm] n gym(nastique) f; (gymnasium) gymnase m; **g. shoes** tennis fpl. ◆**gym'nasium** n gymnase m. ◆**gymnast** n gymnaste m/f. ◆**gym'nastics** n gymnastique f.

gynaecology, Am **gynecology** [gaɪn-ɪ'kɒlədʒɪ] n gynécologie f. ◆**gynae-cologist** n, Am **gynecologist** n gynécologue mf.

gypsy ['dʒɪpsɪ] = **gipsy.**

gyrate [dʒaɪ'reɪt] vi tournoyer.

H

H, h [eɪtʃ] n H, h m; **H bomb** bombe f H.

haberdasher ['hæbədæʃər] n mercier, -ière mf; (men's outfitter) Am chemisier m. ◆**haberdashery** n mercerie f; Am chemiserie f.

habit ['hæbɪt] n 1 habitude f; **to be in/get into the h. of doing** avoir/prendre l'habitude de faire; **to make a h. of doing** avoir pour habitude de faire. 2 (addiction) Med accoutumance f; **a h.-forming drug** une drogue qui crée une accoutumance. 3 (costume) Rel habit m. ◆**ha'bitual** a habituel; (smoker, drinker etc) invétéré. ◆**ha'bitually** adv habituellement.

habitable ['hæbɪtəb(ə)l] a habitable. ◆**habitat** n (of animal, plant) habitat m. ◆**habi'tation** n habitation f; **fit for h.** habitable.

hack [hæk] 1 vt (cut) tailler, hacher. 2 n (old horse) rosse f; (hired) cheval m de louage; h. (writer) Pej écrivaillon m.

hackney ['hæknɪ] a h. **carriage** Hist fiacre m. ◆**hackneyed** a (saying) rebattu, banal.

had [hæd] see have.

haddock ['hædək] n (fish) aiglefin m; **smoked h.** haddock m.

haemorrhage ['hemərɪdʒ] n Med hémorragie f.

haemorrhoids ['hemərɔɪdz] npl hémorroïdes fpl.

hag [hæg] n (woman) Pej (vieille) sorcière f.

haggard ['hægəd] a (person, face) hâve, émacié.

haggl/e ['hæg(ə)l] vi marchander; **to h. over** (thing) marchander; (price) débattre, discuter. ◆**—ing** n marchandage m.

Hague (The) [ðə'heɪg] n La Haye.

ha-ha! [hɑː'hɑː] int (laughter) ha, ha!

hail ¹ [heɪl] n Met & Fig grêle f; – v imp Met grêler; **it's hailing** il grêle. ◆**hailstone** n grêlon m.

hail ² [heɪl] 1 vt (greet) saluer; (taxi) héler. 2 vi **to h. from** (of person) être originaire de; (of ship etc) être en provenance de.

hair [heər] n (on head) cheveux mpl; (on body, of animal) poils mpl; (a h., single strand) un cheveu; (on body, of animal) un poil; **by a hair's breadth** de justesse; **long-/red-/etc haired** aux cheveux longs/roux/etc; h.

cream brillantine f; **h. dryer** sèche-cheveux m inv; **h. spray** (bombe f de) laque f. ◆**hairbrush** n brosse f à cheveux. ◆**haircut** n coupe f de cheveux; **to have a h.** se faire couper les cheveux. ◆**hairdo** n (pl -dos) Fam coiffure f. ◆**hairdresser** n coiffeur, -euse mf. ◆**hairgrip** n pince f à cheveux. ◆**hairnet** n résille f. ◆**hairpiece** n postiche m. ◆**hairpin** n épingle f à cheveux; **h. bend** Aut virage m en épingle à cheveux. ◆**hair-raising** a à faire dresser les cheveux sur la tête. ◆**hair-splitting** n ergotage m. ◆**hairstyle** n coiffure f.

hairy ['heərɪ] a (-ier, -iest) (person, animal, body) poilu; (unpleasant, frightening) Fam effroyable.

hake [heɪk] n (fish) colin m.

hale [heɪl] a **h. and hearty** vigoureux.

half [hɑːf] n (pl halves) moitié f, demi, -ie mf; (of match) Sp mi-temps f; **h. (of) the apple/etc** la moitié de la pomme/etc; **ten and a h.** dix et demi; **ten and a h. weeks** dix semaines et demie; **to cut in h.** couper en deux; **to go halves with** partager les frais avec; – a demi; **h. a day, a h.-day** une demi-journée; **at h. price** à moitié prix; **h. man h. beast** mi-homme mi-bête; **h. sleeves** manches fpl mi-longues; – a (dressed, full etc) à demi, à moitié; (almost) presque; **h. asleep** à moitié endormi; **h. past one** une heure et demie; **he isn't h. lazy/etc** Fam il est rudement paresseux/etc; **h. as much as** moitié moins que; **h. as much again** moitié plus.

half-back ['hɑːfbæk] n Fb demi m. ◆**h.-'baked** a (idea) Fam à la manque, à la noix. ◆**h.-breed** n, ◆**h.-caste** n Pej métis, -isse mf. ◆**h.-(a-)'dozen** n demi-douzaine f. ◆**h.-'hearted** a (person, manner) peu enthousiaste; (effort) timide. ◆**h.-'hour** n demi-heure f. ◆**h.-light** n demi-jour m. ◆**h.-'mast** a **h.-mast** (flag) en berne. ◆**h.-'open** a entrouvert. ◆**h.-'term** n Sch petites vacances fpl, congé m de demi-trimestre. ◆**h.-'time** n Sp mi-temps f. ◆**half'way** adv (between places) à mi-chemin (between entre); **to fill/etc h.** remplir/etc à moitié; **h. through**

(*book*) à la moitié de. ◆**h.-wit** *n*, ◆**h.-'witted** *a* imbécile (*mf*).

halibut ['hælɪbət] *n* (*fish*) flétan *m*.

hall [hɔːl] *n* (*room*) salle *f*; (*house entrance*) entrée *f*, vestibule *m*; (*of hotel*) hall *m*; (*mansion*) manoir *m*; (*for meals*) *Univ* réfectoire *m*; **h. of residence** *Univ* pavillon *m* universitaire; **halls of residence** cité *f* universitaire; **lecture h.** *Univ* amphithéâtre *m*. ◆**hallmark** *n* (*on silver or gold*) poinçon *m*; *Fig* sceau *m*. ◆**hallstand** *n* portemanteau *m*. ◆**hallway** *n* entrée *f*, vestibule *m*.

hallelujah [hælɪ'luːjə] *n* & *int* alléluia (*m*).

hallo! ['hæləʊ] *int* (*greeting*) bonjour!; *Tel* allô!; (*surprise*) tiens!

hallow ['hæləʊ] *vt* sanctifier.

Hallowe'en [hæləʊ'iːn] *n* la veille de la Toussaint.

hallucination [həluːsɪ'neɪʃ(ə)n] *n* hallucination *f*.

halo ['heɪləʊ] *n* (*pl* -oes *or* -os) auréole *f*, halo *m*.

halt [hɔːlt] *n* halte *f*; **to call a h.** to mettre fin à; **to come to a h.** s'arrêter; − *vi* faire halte; − *int Mil* halte! ◆**−ing** *a* (*voice*) hésitant.

halve [hɑːv] *vt* (*time, expense*) réduire de moitié; (*cake, number etc*) diviser en deux.

ham [hæm] *n* **1** jambon *m*; **h. and eggs** œufs *mpl* au jambon. **2** (*actor*) *Th Pej* cabotin, -ine *mf*. ◆**h.-'fisted** *a Fam* maladroit.

hamburger ['hæmbɜːgər] *n* hamburger *m*.

hamlet ['hæmlɪt] *n* hameau *m*.

hammer ['hæmər] *n* marteau *m*; − *vt* (*metal, table*) marteler; (*nail*) enfoncer (*into* dans); (*defeat*) *Fam* battre à plate(s) couture(s); (*criticize*) *Fam* démolir; **to h. out** (*agreement*) mettre au point; − *vi* frapper (au marteau). ◆**−ing** *n* (*defeat*) *Fam* raclée *f*, défaite *f*.

hammock ['hæmək] *n* hamac *m*.

hamper ['hæmpər] **1** *vt* gêner. **2** *n* (*basket*) panier *m*; (*laundry basket*) *Am* panier *m* à linge.

hamster ['hæmstər] *n* hamster *m*.

hand [hænd] *n* **1** main *f*; **to hold in one's h.** tenir à la main; **by h.** (*to deliver etc*) à la main; **at or to h.** (*within reach*) sous la main, à portée de la main; (*close*) **at h.** (*person etc*) tout près; (*day etc*) proche; **in h.** (*situation*) bien en main; (*matter*) en question; (*money*) disponible; **on h.** (*ready for use*) disponible; **to have s.o. on one's hands** *Fig* avoir qn sur les bras; **on the right h.** du côté droit (*of* de); **on the one h. . . .** d'une part . . . ; **on the other h. . . .** d'autre part . . . ; **hands up!** (*in attack*) haut les

mains!; *Sch* levez la main!; **hands off!** pas touche!, bas les pattes!; **my hands are full** *Fig* je suis très occupé; **to give s.o. a** (*helping*) **h.** donner un coup de main à qn; **to get out of h.** (*of person*) devenir impossible; (*of situation*) devenir incontrôlable; **to h.** la main dans la main; **h. in h.** with (*together with*) *Fig* de pair avec; **at first h.** de première main; **to win hands down** gagner haut la main; − a (*luggage etc*) à main. **2** (*worker*) ouvrier, -ière *mf*; (*of clock*) aiguille *f*; *Cards* jeu *m*; (*writing*) écriture *f*. ◆**handbag** *n* sac *m* à main. ◆**handbook** *n* (*manual*) manuel *m*; (*guide*) guide *m*. ◆**handbrake** *n* frein *m* à main. ◆**handbrush** *n* balayette *f*. ◆**handcuff** *vt* passer les menottes à. ◆**handcuffs** *npl* menottes *fpl*. ◆**hand'made** *a* fait à la main. ◆**hand'picked** *a Fig* trié sur le volet. ◆**handrail** *n* (*on stairs*) rampe *f*. ◆**handshake** *n* poignée *f* de main. ◆**handwriting** *n* écriture *f*. ◆**hand'written** *a* écrit à la main.

hand² [hænd] *vt* (*give*) donner (**to** à); **to h. down** (*bring down*) descendre; (*knowledge, heirloom*) transmettre (**to** à); **to h. in** remettre; **to h. out** distribuer; **to h. over** remettre; (*power*) transmettre; **to h. round** (*cakes*) passer. ◆**handout** *n* (*leaflet*) prospectus *m*; (*money*) aumône *f*.

handful ['hændfʊl] *n* (*bunch, group*) poignée *f*; (*quite*) **a h.** (*difficult*) *Fig* difficile.

handicap ['hændɪkæp] *n* (*disadvantage*) & *Sp* handicap *m*; − *vt* (**-pp-**) handicaper. ◆**handicapped** *a* (*disabled*) handicapé.

handicraft ['hændɪkrɑːft] *n* artisanat *m* d'art. ◆**handiwork** *n* artisanat *m* d'art; (*action*) *Fig* ouvrage *m*.

handkerchief ['hæŋkətʃɪf] *n* (*pl* **-fs**) mouchoir *m*; (*for neck*) foulard *m*.

handle ['hænd(ə)l] **1** *n* (*of door*) poignée *f*; (*of knife*) manche *m*; (*of bucket*) anse *f*; (*of saucepan*) queue *f*; (*of pump*) bras *m*. **2** *vt* (*manipulate*) manier; (*touch*) toucher à; (*ship, vehicle*) manœuvrer; (*deal with*) s'occuper de; (*difficult child etc*) s'y prendre avec; − *vi* **to h. well** (*of machine*) être facile à manier.

handlebars ['hænd(ə)lbɑːz] *npl* guidon *m*.

handsome ['hænsəm] *a* (*person, building etc*) beau; (*gift*) généreux; (*profit, sum*) considérable. ◆**−ly** *adv* (*generously*) généreusement.

handy ['hændɪ] *a* (**-ier, -iest**) (*convenient, practical*) commode, pratique; (*skilful*) habile (**at doing** à faire); (*useful*) utile; (*near*) proche, accessible; **to come in h.** se

révéler utile; **to keep h.** avoir sous la main.
◆**handyman** n (pl **-men**) (DIY enthusiast) bricoleur m.

hang¹ [hæŋ] 1 vt (pt & pp **hung**) suspendre (on, from à); (on hook) accrocher (on, from à); (wallpaper) poser; (-) (let dangle) laisser pendre (from, out of de); **to h.** (decorate with) orner de; **to h. out** (washing) étendre; (flag) arborer; **to h. up** (picture etc) accrocher; – vi (dangle) pendre; (of threat) planer; (of fog, smoke) flotter; **to h. about** (loiter) traîner, rôder; (wait) Fam attendre; **to h. down** (hang) pendre; (of hair) tomber; **to h. on** (hold out) résister; (wait) Fam attendre; **to h. on to** (cling to) ne pas lâcher; (keep) garder; **to h. out** (of tongue, shirt) pendre; (live) Sl crécher; **to h. together** (of facts) se tenir; (of plan) tenir debout; **to h. up** Tel raccrocher. 2 n **to get the h. of sth** Fam arriver à comprendre qch; **to get the h. of doing** Fam trouver le truc pour faire. ◆**-ing¹** n suspension f; – a suspendu (from à); (leg, arm) pendant; **h. on** (wall) accroché à.
◆**hang-glider** n delta-plane® m.
◆**hang-gliding** n vol m libre. ◆**hangnail** n petites peaux fpl. ◆**hangover** n Fam gueule f de bois. ◆**hangup** n Fam complexe m.

hang² [hæŋ] vt (pt & pp **hanged**) (criminal) pendre (for pour); – vi (of criminal) se pendu. ◆**-ing²** n Jur pendaison f.
◆**hangman** n (pl **-men**) bourreau m.

hangar ['hæŋər] n Av hangar m.

hanger ['hæŋər] n (coat) **h.** cintre m.
◆**hanger-'on** n (pl **hangers-on**) (person) Pej parasite m.

hanker ['hæŋkər] vi **to h. after** or **for** avoir envie de. ◆**-ing** n (forte) envie f, (vif) désir m.

hankie, hanky ['hæŋkɪ] n Fam mouchoir m.

hanky-panky [hæŋkɪ'pæŋkɪ] n inv (deceit) manigances fpl, magouilles fpl; (sexual behaviour) papouilles fpl, pelotage m.

haphazard [hæp'hæzəd] a au hasard, au petit bonheur; (selection, arrangement) aléatoire. ◆**-ly** adv au hasard.

hapless ['hæplɪs] a Lit infortuné.

happen ['hæpən] vi arriver, se passer, se produire; **to h. to s.o./sth** arriver à qn/qch; **it (so) happens that** I know, I h. to know il se trouve que je le sais; **do you h. to have . . . ?** est-ce que par hasard vous avez . . . ?; **whatever happens** quoi qu'il arrive. ◆**-ing** n évènement m.

happy ['hæpɪ] a (-ier, -iest) heureux (**to do**

de faire, **about sth** de qch); **I'm not** (too or very) **h. about** (doing) **it** ça ne me plaît pas beaucoup (de le faire); **H. New Year!** bonne année!; **H. Christmas!** joyeux Noël!
◆**h.-go-'lucky** a insouciant. ◆**happily** adv (contentedly) tranquillement; (joyously) joyeusement; (fortunately) heureusement. ◆**happiness** n bonheur m.

harass ['hærəs, Am hə'ræs] vt harceler.
◆**-ment** n harcèlement m.

harbour ['hɑːbər] 1 n port m. 2 vt (shelter) héberger; (criminal) cacher, abriter; (fear, secret) nourrir.

hard [hɑːd] a (-er, -est) (not soft, severe) dur; (difficult) difficile, dur; (study) assidu; (fact) brutal; (drink) alcoolisé; (water) calcaire; **h. drinker/worker** gros buveur m/travailleur m; **a h. frost** une forte gelée; **to be h. on** or **to s.o.** être dur avec qn; **to find it h. to sleep**/etc avoir du mal à dormir/etc; **h. labour** Jur travaux mpl forcés; **h. cash** espèces fpl; **h. core** (group) noyau m; **h. of hearing** malentendant; **h. up** (broke) Fam fauché; **to be h. up for** manquer de; – adv (-er, -est) (to work) dur; (to pull) fort; (to hit, freeze) dur, fort; (to study) assidûment; (to think) sérieusement; (to rain) à verse; (badly) mal; **h. by** tout près; **h. done by** traité injustement.
◆**hard-and-fast** [hɑːdən(d)'fɑːst] a (rule) strict. ◆**'hardback** n livre m relié.
◆**'hardboard** n Isorel® m. ◆**hard-'boiled** a (egg) dur. ◆**hard-'core** a (rigid) Pej inflexible. ◆**hard-'headed** a réaliste. ◆**hard'wearing** a résistant.
◆**hard-'working** a travailleur.

harden ['hɑːd(ə)n] vti durcir; **to h. oneself to** s'endurcir à. ◆**-ed** a (criminal) endurci.

hardly ['hɑːdlɪ] adv à peine; **he h. talks** il parle à peine, il ne parle guère; **h. ever** presque jamais.

hardness ['hɑːdnɪs] n dureté f.

hardship ['hɑːdʃɪp] n (ordeal) épreuve(s) f(pl); (deprivation) privation(s) f(pl).

hardware ['hɑːdweər] n inv quincaillerie f; (of computer) & Mil matériel m.

hardy ['hɑːdɪ] a (-ier, -iest) (person, plant) résistant.

hare [heər] n lièvre m. ◆**h.-brained** a (person) écervelé; (scheme) insensé.

harem [hɑː'riːm] n harem m.

hark [hɑːk] vi Lit écouter; **h. back to** (subject etc) Fam revenir sur.

harm [hɑːm] n (hurt) mal m; (prejudice) tort m; **he means** (us) **no h.** il ne nous veut pas de mal; **she'll come to no h.** il ne lui arrivera rien; – vt (hurt) faire du mal à; (prejudice) (a person) desservir.

nuire à, faire du tort à; *(object)* endommager, abîmer. ◆**harmful** *a* nuisible. ◆**harmless** *a (person, treatment)* inoffensif; *(hobby, act)* innocent; *(gas, fumes etc)* qui n'est pas nuisible, inoffensif.

harmonica [hɑːˈmɒnɪkə] *n* harmonica *m*.

harmony [ˈhɑːmənɪ] *n* harmonie *f*. ◆**har'monic** *a & n* *Mus* harmonique *(m)*. ◆**har'monious** *a* harmonieux. ◆**har'monium** *n* *Mus* harmonium *m*. ◆**harmonize** *vt* harmoniser; – *vi* s'harmoniser.

harness [ˈhɑːnɪs] *n (for horse, baby)* harnais *m*; – *vt (horse)* harnacher; *(energy etc) Fig* exploiter.

harp [hɑːp] **1** *n Mus* harpe *f*. **2** *vt* to h. on *(about)* sth *Fam* rabâcher qch. ◆**harpist** *n* harpiste *mf*.

harpoon [hɑːˈpuːn] *n* harpon *m*; – *vt (whale)* harponner.

harpsichord [ˈhɑːpsɪkɔːd] *n* *Mus* clavecin *m*.

harrowing [ˈhærəʊɪŋ] *a (tale, memory)* poignant; *(cry, sight)* déchirant.

harsh [hɑːʃ] *a (-er, -est) (severe)* dur, sévère; *(sound, taste)* âpre; *(surface)* rugueux; *(fabric)* rêche. ◆**—ly** *adv* durement, sévèrement. ◆**—ness** *n* dureté *f*, sévérité *f*; âpreté *f*, rugosité *f*.

harvest [ˈhɑːvɪst] *n* moisson *f*, récolte *f*; *(of people, objects) Fig* ribambelle *f*; – *vt* moissonner, récolter.

has [hæz] *see* **have**. ◆**has-been** *n Fam* personne *f* finie.

hash [hæʃ] **1** *n Culin* hachis *m*; – *vt* to h. (up) hacher. **2** *n (mess) Fam* gâchis *m*. **3** *n (hashish) Sl* hasch *m*, H *m*.

hashish [ˈhæʃiːʃ] *n* haschisch *m*.

hassle [ˈhæs(ə)l] *n Fam (trouble)* histoires *fpl*; *(bother)* mal *m*, peine *f*.

haste [heɪst] *n* hâte *f*; in h. à la hâte; to make h. se hâter. ◆**hasten** *vi* se hâter *(to do* faire*)*; – *vt* hâter. ◆**hasty** *a (-ier, -iest) (sudden)* précipité; *(visit)* rapide; *(decision, work)* hâtif. ◆**hastily** *adv (quickly)* en hâte; *(too quickly)* hâtivement.

hat [hæt] *n* chapeau *m*; that's old h. *Fam (old-fashioned)* c'est vieux jeu; *(stale)* c'est vieux comme les rues; to score *or* get a h. trick *Sp* réussir trois coups consécutifs.

hatch [hætʃ] **1** *vi (of chick, egg)* éclore; – *vt* faire éclore; *(plot) Fig* tramer. **2** *n (in kitchen wall)* passe-plats *m inv*.

hatchback [ˈhætʃbæk] *n (door)* hayon *m*; *(car)* trois-portes *f inv*, cinq-portes *f inv*.

hatchet [ˈhætʃɪt] *n* hachette *f*.

hate [heɪt] *vt* détester, haïr; to h. doing *or* to

do détester faire; I h. to say it ça me gêne de le dire; – *n* haine *f*; pet h. *Fam* bête *f* noire. ◆**hateful** *a* haïssable. ◆**hatred** *n* haine *f*.

haughty [ˈhɔːtɪ] *a (-ier, -iest)* hautain. ◆**haughtily** *adv* avec hauteur.

haul [hɔːl] **1** *vt (pull)* tirer, traîner; *(goods)* camionner. **2** *n (fish)* prise *f*; *(of thief)* butin *m*; a long h. *(trip)* un long voyage. ◆**haulage** *n* camionnage *m*. ◆**hauler** *n Am,* ◆**haulier** *n* transporteur *m* routier.

haunt [hɔːnt] **1** *vt* hanter. **2** *n* endroit *m* favori; *(of criminal)* repaire *m*. ◆**—ing** *a (music, memory)* obsédant.

have [hæv] **1** *(3rd person sing pres t* has; *pt & pp* had; *pres p* having*)* *vt* avoir; *(get)* recevoir, avoir; *(meal, shower etc)* prendre; he has got, he has il a; to h. a walk/dream/*etc* faire une promenade/un rêve/*etc*; to h. a drink prendre *or* boire un verre; to h. a wash se laver; to h. a holiday *(spend)* passer des vacances; will you h. . . . ? *(a cake, some tea etc)* est-ce que tu veux . . . ?; to let s.o. h. sth donner qch à qn; to h. it from s.o. that tenir de qn que; he had me by the hair il me tenait par les cheveux; I won't h. this *(allow)* je ne tolérerai pas ça; you've had it! *Fam* tu es fichu!; to h. on *(clothes)* porter; to have sth on *(be busy)* être pris; to h. s.o. over inviter qn chez soi. **2** *v aux* avoir; *(with* monter, sortir *etc &* pronominal *verbs)* être; to h. decided/been avoir décidé/été; to h. gone être allé; to h. cut oneself s'être coupé; I've just done it je viens de le faire; to h. to do *(must)* devoir faire; I've got to go, I h. to go je dois partir, il me faut *or* il faut que je parte; I don't h. to go je ne suis pas obligé de partir; to h. sth done *(get sth done)* faire faire qch; he's had his suitcase brought up il a fait monter sa valise; I've had my car stolen on m'a volé mon auto; she's had her hair cut elle s'est fait couper les cheveux; I've been doing it for months je le fais depuis des mois; haven't I?, hasn't she? *etc* n'est-ce pas?; no I haven't! non!; yes I h.! si!; after he had eaten, he left après avoir mangé, il partit. **3** *npl* the haves and (the) have-nots les riches *mpl* et les pauvres *mpl*.

haven [ˈheɪv(ə)n] *n* refuge *m*, havre *m*.

haversack [ˈhævəsæk] *n (shoulder bag)* musette *f*.

havoc [ˈhævək] *n* ravages *mpl*.

hawk [hɔːk] **1** *n (bird) & Pol* faucon *m*. **2** *vt (goods)* colporter. ◆**—er** *n* colporteur, -euse *mf*.

hawthorn [ˈhɔːθɔːn] *n* aubépine *f*.

hay [heɪ] n foin m; **h. fever** rhume m des foins. ◆**haystack** n meule f de foin.

haywire ['heɪwaɪər] a **to go h.** (of machine) se détraquer; (of scheme, plan) mal tourner.

hazard ['hæzəd] n risque m; **health h.** risque m pour la santé; **it's a fire h.** ça risque de provoquer un incendie; − vt (guess, remark etc) hasarder, risquer. ◆**hazardous** a hasardeux.

haze [heɪz] n brume f; **in a h.** (person) Fig dans le brouillard. ◆**hazy** a (-ier, -iest) (weather) brumeux; (sun) voilé; (photo, idea) flou; **I'm h. about my plans** je ne suis pas sûr de mes projets.

hazel ['heɪz(ə)l] n (bush) noisetier m; − a (eyes) noisette inv. ◆**hazelnut** n noisette f.

he [hiː] pron il; (stressed) lui; **he wants it** il le veut; **he's a happy man** c'est un homme heureux; **if I were he** si j'étais lui; **he and I** lui et moi; − n mâle m; **he-bear** ours m mâle.

head [hed] **1** n (of person, hammer etc) tête f; (of page) haut m; (of arrow) pointe f; (of beer) mousse f; (leader) chef m; (subject heading) rubrique f; **h. of hair** chevelure f; **h. cold** rhume m de cerveau; **it didn't enter my h.** ça ne m'est pas venu à l'esprit (**that** que); **to take it into one's h. to do** se mettre en tête de faire; **the h. Sch** = **the headmaster**; = **the headmistress**; **to shout one's h. off** Fam crier à tue-tête; **to have a good h. for business** avoir le sens des affaires; **at the h. of** (in charge of) à la tête de; **at the h. of the table** au haut bout de la table; **at the h. of the list** en tête de liste; **it's above my h.** ça me dépasse; **to keep one's h.** garder son sang-froid; **to go off one's h.** devenir fou; **it's coming to a h.** (of situation) ça devient critique; **heads or tails?** pile ou face? **per h., a h.** (each) par personne. **2** a principal, (gardener) en chef; **h. waiter** maître m d'hôtel; **h. start** une grosse avance. **3** vt (group, firm) être à la tête de; (list, poll) être en tête de; (vehicle) diriger (**towards** vers); **to h. the ball** Fb faire une tête; **to h.** (person) détourner son chemin; (prevent) empêcher; **to be headed for** Am = **to h. for**; − vi **to h. for, be heading for** (place) se diriger vers; (ruin etc) Fig aller à. ◆**-ed** a (paper) à en-tête. ◆**-ing** n (of chapter, page etc) titre m; (of subject) rubrique f; (printed on letter etc) en-tête m. ◆**-er** n Fb coup m de tête.

headache ['hedeɪk] n mal m de tête; (difficulty, person) Fig problème m. ◆**head-dress** n (ornamental) coiffe f.

◆**headlamp** n, ◆**headlight** n Aut phare m. ◆**headline** n (of newspaper) manchette f; pl (gros) titres mpl; Rad TV (grands) titres mpl. ◆**headlong** adv (to fall) la tête la première; (to rush) tête baissée. ◆**headmaster** n Sch directeur m; (of lycée) proviseur m. ◆**headmistress** n Sch directrice f; (of lycée) proviseur m. ◆**head-'on** adv & a (to collide, collision) de plein fouet. ◆**headphones** npl casque m (à écouteurs). ◆**headquarters** npl Com Pol siège m (central); Mil quartier m général. ◆**headrest** n appuie-tête m inv. ◆**headscarf** n (pl -scarves) foulard m. ◆**headstrong** a têtu. ◆**headway** n progrès mpl.

heady ['hedɪ] a (-ier, -iest) (wine etc) capiteux; (action, speech) emporté.

heal [hiːl] vi **to h. (up)** (of wound) se cicatriser; − vt (wound) cicatriser, guérir; (person, sorrow) guérir. ◆**-er** n guérisseur, -euse mf.

health [helθ] n santé f; **h. food** aliment m naturel; **h. food shop** or Am **store** magasin m diététique; **h. resort** station f climatique; **the H. Service** = **la Sécurité Sociale**. ◆**healthful** a (climate) sain. ◆**healthy** a (-ier, -iest) (person) en bonne santé, sain; (food, attitude etc) sain; (appetite) bon, robuste.

heap [hiːp] n tas m; **heaps of** Fam des tas de; **to have heaps of time** Fam avoir largement le temps; − vt entasser, empiler; **to h. on s.o.** (gifts, praise) couvrir qn de; (work) accabler qn de. ◆**-ed** a **h. spoonful** grosse cuillerée f. ◆**-ing** a **h. spoonful** Am grosse cuillerée f.

hear [hɪər] vt (pt & pp **heard** [hɜːd]) entendre; (listen to) écouter; (learn) apprendre (**that** que); **I heard him coming** je l'ai entendu venir; **to h. it said that** entendre dire que; **have you heard the news?** connais-tu la nouvelle?; **I've heard that ...** on m'a dit que ..., j'ai appris que ...; **to h. out** écouter jusqu'au bout; **h., h.!** bravo!; − vi entendre; (get news) recevoir or avoir des nouvelles (**from** de); **I've heard of** or **about him** j'ai entendu parler de lui; **she wouldn't h. of it** elle ne voulait pas en entendre parler; **I wouldn't h. of it!** pas question! ◆**-ing** n (sense) ouïe f; Jur audition f; **h. aid** appareil m auditif. ◆**hearsay** n ouï-dire m inv.

hearse [hɜːs] n corbillard m.

heart [hɑːt] n cœur m; pl Cards cœur m; (off) **by h.** par cœur; **to lose h.** perdre courage; **to one's h.'s content** tout son

saoul *or* content; **at h.** au fond; **his h. is
on it** il le veut à tout prix, il y tient; **his h. is
set on doing it** il veut le faire à tout prix, il
tient à le faire; **h. disease** maladie *f* de
cœur; **h. attack** crise *f* cardiaque.
◆**heartache** *n* chagrin *m.* ◆**heartbeat** *n*
battement *m* de cœur. ◆**heartbreaking** *a*
navrant. ◆**heartbroken** *a* navré, au cœur
brisé. ◆**heartburn** *n Med* brûlures *fpl*
d'estomac. ◆**heartthrob** *n* (*man*) *Fam*
idole *f.*

hearten ['hɑːt(ə)n] *vt* encourager. ◆**—ing** *a*
encourageant.

hearth [hɑːθ] *n* foyer *m.*

hearty ['hɑːtɪ] *a* (*-ier, -iest*) (*meal, appetite*)
gros. ◆**heartily** *adv* (*to eat*) avec appétit;
(*to laugh*) de tout son cœur; (*absolutely*)
absolument.

heat [hiːt] **1** *n* chaleur *f*; (*of oven*) température *f*; (*heating*) chauffage *m*; **in the h. of**
(*argument etc*) dans le feu de; (*the day*) au
plus chaud de; **at low h., on a low h.** *Culin* à
feu doux; **h. wave** vague *f* de chaleur; — *vti*
to h. (up) chauffer. **2** *n* (*in race, competition*)
éliminatoire *f*; **it was a dead h.** ils sont
arrivés ex aequo. ◆**—ed** *a* (*swimming
pool*) chauffé; (*argument*) passionné.
◆**—edly** *adv* avec passion. ◆**—ing** *n*
chauffage *m.* ◆**—er** *n* radiateur *m*, appareil
m de chauffage; **water h.** chauffe-eau *m inv.*

heath [hiːθ] *n* (*place, land*) lande *f.*

heathen ['hiːð(ə)n] *a & n* païen, -enne (*mf*).

heather ['heðər] *n* (*plant*) bruyère *f.*

heave [hiːv] *vt* (*lift*) soulever; (*pull*) tirer;
(*drag*) traîner; (*throw*) *Fam* lancer; (*a sigh*)
pousser; — *vi* (*of stomach, chest*) se
soulever; (*retch*) *Fam* avoir des
haut-le-cœur; — *n* (*effort*) effort *m* (*pour
soulever etc*).

heaven ['hev(ə)n] *n* ciel *m*, paradis *m*; **h.
knows when** *Fam* Dieu sait quand; **good
heavens!** *Fam* mon Dieu!; **it was h.** *Fam*
c'était divin. ◆**—ly** *a* céleste; (*pleasing*)
Fam divin.

heavy ['hevɪ] *a* (*-ier, -iest*) lourd; (*weight etc*)
lourd, pesant; (*work, cold etc*) gros; (*blow*)
violent; (*concentration, rain*) fort; (*traffic*)
dense; (*smoker, drinker*) grand; (*film, text*)
difficile; **a h. day** une journée chargée; **h.
casualties** de nombreuses victimes; **to be h.
on petrol** *or* **Am gas** *Aut* consommer
beaucoup; **it's going** c'est difficile.
◆**heavily** *adv* (*to walk, tax etc*) lourdement; (*to breathe*) péniblement; (*to smoke,
drink*) beaucoup; (*underlined*) fortement;
(*involved*) très; **to rain h.** pleuvoir à verse.
◆**heaviness** *n* pesanteur *f*, lourdeur *f.*

◆**heavyweight** *n Boxing* poids *m* lourd;
Fig personnage *m* important.

Hebrew ['hiːbruː] *a* hébreu (*m only*),
hébraïque; — *n* (*language*) hébreu *m.*

heck [hek] *int Fam* zut!; — *n* = **hell in**
expressions.

heckl/e ['hek(ə)l] *vt* interpeller, interrompre. ◆**—ing** *n* interpellations *fpl.* ◆**—er** *n*
interpellateur, -trice *mf.*

hectic ['hektɪk] *a* (*activity*) fiévreux;
(*period*) très agité; (*trip*) mouvementé; **h.
life** vie *f* trépidante.

hedge [hedʒ] **1** *n Bot* haie *f.* **2** *vi* (*answer
evasively*) ne pas se mouiller, éviter de se
compromettre. ◆**hedgerow** *n Bot* haie *f.*

hedgehog ['hedʒhɒg] *n* (*animal*) hérisson
m.

heed [hiːd] *vt* faire attention à; — *n* **to pay h.**
to faire attention à. ◆**—less** *a* **h. of**
(*danger etc*) inattentif à.

heel [hiːl] *n* **1** talon *m*; **down at h., Am down
at the heels** (*shabby*) miteux; **h. bar** cordonnerie *f* express; (*on sign*) 'talon minute'. **2**
(*person*) *Am Fam* salaud *m.*

hefty ['heftɪ] *a* (*-ier, -iest*) (*large, heavy*) gros;
(*person*) costaud.

heifer ['hefər] *n* (*cow*) génisse *f.*

height [haɪt] *n* hauteur *f*; (*of person*) taille *f*;
(*of mountain*) altitude *f*; **the h. of** (*glory,
success, fame*) le sommet de, l'apogée *m* de;
(*folly, pain*) le comble de; **at the h. of**
(*summer, storm*) au cœur de. ◆**heighten**
vt (*raise*) rehausser; (*tension, interest*) *Fig*
augmenter.

heinous ['heɪnəs] *a* (*crime etc*) atroce.

heir [eər] *n* héritier *m.* ◆**heiress** *n* héritière
f. ◆**heirloom** *n* héritage *m*, bijou *m or*
meuble *m* de famille.

heist [haɪst] *n Am Sl* hold-up *m inv.*

held [held] *see* **hold.**

helicopter ['helɪkɒptər] *n* hélicoptère *m.*
◆**heliport** *n* héliport *m.*

hell [hel] *n* enfer *m*; **a h. of a lot** (*very much*)
Fam énormément, vachement; **a h. of a lot
of** (*very many, very much*) *Fam* énormément de; **a h. of a nice guy** *Fam* un type
super; **what the h. are you doing?** *Fam*
qu'est-ce que tu fous?; **to h. with him** *Fam*
qu'il aille se faire voir; **h.!** *Fam* zut!; **to be
h.-bent on** *Fam* être acharné à. ◆**hellish** *a*
diabolique.

hello! [hə'ləʊ] *int* = **hallo.**

helm [helm] *n Nau* barre *f.*

helmet ['helmɪt] *n* casque *m.*

help [help] *n* aide *f*, secours *m*; (*cleaning
woman*) femme *f* de ménage; (*office or shop
workers*) employés, -ées *mfpl*; **with the h. of**

(*stick etc*) à l'aide de; **to cry** *or* **shout for h.** crier au secours; **h.!** au secours!; – *vt* aider (**do, to do** à faire); **to h. s.o. to soup**/*etc* (*serve*) servir du potage/*etc* à qn; **to h. out** aider; **to h. up** aider à monter; **to h. oneself** se servir (**to** de); **I can't h. laughing**/*etc* je ne peux m'empêcher de rire/*etc*; **he can't h. being blind**/*etc* ce n'est pas sa faute s'il est aveugle/*etc*; **it can't be helped** on n'y peut rien; – *vi* to h. (**out**) aider. ◆—**ing** *n* (*serving*) portion *f*. ◆—**er** *n* assistant, -ante *mf*. ◆**helpful** *a* (*useful*) utile; (*obliging*) serviable. ◆**helpless** *a* (*powerless*) impuissant; (*baby*) désarmé; (*disabled*) impotent. ◆**helplessly** *adv* (**to struggle**) en vain.

helter-skelter [heltə'skeltər] **1** *adv* à la débandade. **2** *n* (*slide*) toboggan *m*.

hem [hem] *n* ourlet *m*; – *vt* (**-mm-**) (*garment*) ourler; **to h. in** *Fig* enfermer, cerner.

hemisphere ['hemisfiər] *n* hémisphère *m*.

hemorrhage ['hemərid3] *n Med* hémorragie *f*.

hemorrhoids ['hemərɔidz] *npl* hémorroïdes *fpl*.

hemp [hemp] *n* chanvre *m*.

hen [hen] *n* poule *f*; **h. bird** oiseau *m* femelle. ◆**henpecked** *a* (*husband*) harcelé *or* dominé par sa femme.

hence [hens] *adv* **1** (*therefore*) d'où. **2** (*from now*) **ten years**/*etc* **h.** d'ici dix ans/*etc*. ◆**henceforth** *adv* désormais.

henchman ['hentʃmən] *n* (*pl* **-men**) *Pej* acolyte *m*.

hepatitis [hepə'taitis] *n* hépatite *f*.

her [hɜːr] **1** *pron* la, l'; (*after prep etc*) elle; (**to**) **h.** (*indirect*) lui; **I see h.** je la vois; **I saw h.** je l'ai vue; **I give** (**to**) **h.** je lui donne; **with h.** avec elle. **2** *poss a* son, sa, *pl* ses.

herald ['herəld] *vt* annoncer.

heraldry ['herəldri] *n* héraldique *f*.

herb [hɜːb, *Am* ɜːb] *n* herbe *f*; *pl Culin* fines herbes *fpl*. ◆**herbal** *a* **h. tea** infusion *f* (d'herbes).

Hercules ['hɜːkjuliːz] *n* (*strong man*) hercule *m*.

herd [hɜːd] *n* troupeau *m*; – *vti* **to h. together** (*se*) rassembler (en troupeau).

here [hiər] **1** *adv* **1** ici; (*then*) alors; **h. is, h. are** voici; **h. he is** le voici; **h. she is** la voici; **this man h.** cet homme-ci; **I won't be h. tomorrow** je ne serai pas là demain; **h. and there** çà et là; **h. you are!** (*take this*) tenez!; **h.'s to you!** (*toast*) à la tienne! **2** *int* (*calling s.o.'s attention*) holà!, écoutez!; (*giving s.o. sth*) tenez! ◆**herea'bouts** *adv* par ici. ◆**here-**

'**after** *adv* après; (*in book*) ci-après. ◆**here'by** *adv* (*to declare*) par le présent acte. ◆**here'with** *adv* (*with letter*) *Com* ci-joint.

heredity [hi'rediti] *n* hérédité *f*. ◆**heredi-tary** *a* héréditaire.

heresy ['herəsi] *n* hérésie *f*. ◆**heretic** *n* hérétique *mf*. ◆**he'retical** *a* hérétique.

heritage ['heritidʒ] *n* héritage *m*.

hermetically [hɜː'metikli] *adv* hermétiquement.

hermit ['hɜːmit] *n* solitaire *mf*, ermite *m*.

hernia ['hɜːniə] *n Med* hernie *f*.

hero ['hiərəu] *n* (*pl* **-oes**) héros *m*. ◆**he'roic** *a* héroïque. ◆**he'roics** *npl Pej* grandiloquence *f*. ◆**heroine** ['herəuin] *n* héroïne *f*. ◆**heroism** ['herəuiz(ə)m] *n* héroïsme *m*.

heroin ['herəuin] *n* (*drug*) héroïne *f*.

heron ['herən] *n* (*bird*) héron *m*.

herring ['herin] *n* hareng *m*; **a red h.** *Fig* une diversion.

hers [hɜːz] *poss pron* le sien, la sienne, *pl* les sien(ne)s; **this hat is h.** ce chapeau est à elle *or* est le sien; **a friend of h.** une amie à elle. ◆**her'self** *pron* elle-même; (*reflexive*) se, s'; (*after prep*) elle; **she cut h.** elle s'est coupée; **she thinks of h.** elle pense à elle.

hesitate ['heziteit] *vi* hésiter (**over, about** sur; **to do** à faire). ◆**hesitant** *a* hésitant. ◆**hesitantly** *adv* avec hésitation. ◆**hesi-'tation** *n* hésitation *f*.

hessian ['hesiən] *n* toile *f* de jute.

heterogeneous [het(ə)rəu'dʒiːniəs] *a* hétérogène.

het up [het'ʌp] *a Fam* énervé.

hew [hjuː] *vt* (*pp* **hewn** *or* **hewed**) tailler.

hexagon ['heksəgən] *n* hexagone *m*. ◆**hex-'agonal** *a* hexagonal.

hey! [hei] *int* hé!, holà!

heyday ['heidei] *n* (*of person*) apogée *m*, zénith *m*; (*of thing*) âge *m* d'or.

hi! [hai] *int Am Fam* salut!

hiatus [hai'eitəs] *n* (*gap*) hiatus *m*.

hibernate ['haibəneit] *vi* hiberner. ◆**hiber-'nation** *n* hibernation *f*.

hiccough, hiccup ['hikʌp] *n* hoquet *m*; (**the**) **hiccoughs** *or* **hiccups** le hoquet; – *vi* hoqueter.

hick [hik] *n* (*peasant*) *Am Sl Pej* plouc *mf*.

hide¹ [haid] *vt* (*pt* **hid**, *pp* **hidden**) cacher, dissimuler (**from** à); – *vi* **to h.** (**away** *or* **out**) se cacher (**from** de). ◆**h.-and-'seek** *n* cache-cache *m inv*. ◆**h.-out** *n* cachette *f*. ◆**hiding** *n* **1** **to go into h.** se cacher; **h. place** cachette *f*. **2** **a good h.** (*thrashing*) *Fam* une bonne volée *or* correction.

hide [haɪd] n (skin) peau f.

hideous ['hɪdɪəs] a horrible; (person, sight, crime) hideux. ◆-**ly** adv (badly, very) horriblement.

hierarchy ['haɪərɑːkɪ] n hiérarchie f.

hi-fi ['haɪfaɪ] n hi-fi f inv; (system) chaîne f hi-fi; – a hi-fi inv.

high [haɪ] a (-er, -est) haut; (speed) grand; (price) élevé; (fever) fort, gros; (colour, complexion) vif; (idea, number) grand, élevé; (meat, game) faisandé; (on drugs) Fam défoncé; **to be five metres h.** être haut de cinq mètres, avoir cinq mètres de haut; **it is h. time that** il est grand temps que (+ sub); **h. jump** Sp saut m en hauteur; **h. noon** plein midi m; **h. priest** grand prêtre m; **h. school** Am = collège m d'enseignement secondaire; **h. spirits** entrain m; **h. spot** (of visit, day) point m culminant; (of show) clou m; **h. street** grand-rue f; **h. summer** le cœur de l'été; **h. table** table f d'honneur; **h. and mighty** arrogant; **to leave s.o. h. and dry** Fam laisser qn en plan; – adv h. (up) (to fly, throw etc) haut; **to aim h.** viser haut; – n on **h.** en haut; **a new h., an all-time h.** (peak) Fig un nouveau record. ◆-**er** a supérieur (than à). ◆-**ly** adv hautement, fortement; (interesting) très; (paid) très bien; (to recommend) chaudement; **to speak h. of** dire beaucoup de bien de; **h. strung** nerveux. ◆-**ness** n H. (title) Altesse f.

highbrow ['haɪbraʊ] a & n intellectuel, -elle (mf).

high-chair ['haɪtʃeər] n chaise f haute. ◆**h.-'class** a (service) de premier ordre; (building) de luxe; (person) raffiné. ◆**h.-'flown** a (language) ampoulé. ◆**h.-'handed** a tyrannique. ◆**h.-'minded** a à l'âme noble. ◆**h.-'pitched** a (sound) aigu. ◆**h.-'powered** a (person) très dynamique. ◆**h.-rise** a **h.-rise flats** tour f. ◆**h.-'speed** a ultra-rapide. ◆**h.-'strung** a Am nerveux. ◆**h.-'up** a (person) haut placé.

highlands ['haɪləndz] npl régions fpl montagneuses.

highlight ['haɪlaɪt] n (of visit, day) point m culminant; (of show) clou m; (in hair) reflet m; – vt souligner.

highroad ['haɪrəʊd] n grand-route f.

highway ['haɪweɪ] n grande route f; Am autoroute f; **public h.** voie f publique; **h. code** code m de la route.

hijack ['haɪdʒæk] vt (aircraft, vehicle) détourner; – n détournement m. ◆-**ing** n (air piracy) piraterie f aérienne; (hijack)

détournement m. ◆-**er** n Av pirate m de l'air.

hik/e [haɪk] **1** n excursion f à pied; – vi marcher à pied. **2** vt (price) Am Fam augmenter; – n Fam hausse f. ◆-**er** n excursionniste mf.

hilarious [hɪ'leərɪəs] a (funny) désopilant.

hill [hɪl] n colline f; (small) coteau m; (slope) pente f. ◆**hillbilly** n Am Fam péquenaud, -aude mf. ◆**hillside** n coteau m; **on the h.** à flanc de coteau. ◆**hilly** a (-ier, -iest) accidenté.

hilt [hɪlt] n (of sword) poignée f; **to the h.** Fig au maximum.

him [hɪm] pron le, l'; (after prep etc) lui; (to) **h.** (indirect) lui; **I see h.** je le vois; **I saw h.** je l'ai vu; **I give** (to) **h.** je lui donne; **with h.** avec lui. ◆**him'self** pron lui-même; (reflexive) se, s'; (after prep) lui; **he cut h.** il s'est coupé; **he thinks of h.** il pense à lui.

hind [haɪnd] a de derrière, postérieur. ◆**hindquarters** npl arrière-train m.

hinder ['hɪndər] vt (obstruct) gêner; (prevent) empêcher (**from doing** de faire). ◆**hindrance** n gêne f.

hindsight ['haɪndsaɪt] n **with h.** rétrospectivement.

Hindu ['hɪnduː] a & n hindou, -oue (mf).

hing/e [hɪndʒ] **1** n (of box, stamp) charnière f; (of door) gond m, charnière f. **2** vi **to h. on** (depend on) dépendre de. ◆-**ed** a à charnière(s).

hint [hɪnt] n indication f; (insinuation) allusion f; (trace) trace f; pl (advice) conseils mpl; **to drop a h.** faire une allusion; – vt laisser entendre (**that** que); – vi **to h. at** faire allusion à.

hip [hɪp] n Anat hanche f.

hippie ['hɪpɪ] n hippie mf.

hippopotamus [hɪpə'pɒtəməs] n hippopotame m.

hire ['haɪər] vt (vehicle etc) louer; (person) engager; **to h. out** donner en location, louer; – n location f; (of boat, horse) louage m; **for h.** à louer; **on h.** en location; **h. purchase** vente f à crédit, location-vente f; **on h. purchase** à crédit.

his [hɪz] **1** poss a son, sa, pl ses. **2** poss pron le sien, la sienne, pl les sien(ne)s; **this hat is h.** ce chapeau est à lui or est le sien; **a friend of h.** un ami à lui.

Hispanic [hɪs'pænɪk] a & n Am hispano-américain, -aine (mf).

hiss [hɪs] vti siffler; – n sifflement m; pl Th sifflets mpl. ◆-**ing** n sifflement(s) m(pl).

history ['hɪstərɪ] n (study, events) histoire f; **it will make h.** or **go down in h.** ça va faire date; **your medical h.** vos antécédents médicaux. ◆**hi'storian** n historien, -ienne mf. ◆**hi'storic(al)** a historique.

histrionic [hɪstrɪ'ɒnɪk] a Pej théâtral; – npl attitudes fpl théâtrales.

hit [hɪt] vti (pt & pp hit, pres p hitting) (strike) frapper; (knock against) & Aut heurter; (reach) atteindre; (affect) toucher, affecter; (find) trouver, rencontrer; **to h. the head-lines** Fam faire les gros titres; **to h. back** rendre coup pour coup; (verbally, militarily etc) riposter; **to h. it off** Fam s'entendre bien (with avec); **to h. out (at)** Fam attaquer; **to h. (up)on** (find) tomber sur; – n (blow) coup m; (success) coup m réussi; Th succès m; **h. (song)** chanson f à succès; **to make a h. with** Fam avoir un succès avec; **h.-and-run driver** chauffard m (qui prend la fuite). ◆**h.-or-'miss** a (chancy, random) aléatoire.

hitch [hɪtʃ] 1 n (snag) anicroche f, os m, problème m. 2 vt (fasten) accrocher (to à). 3 vti **to h.** (a lift or a ride) Fam faire du stop (to jusqu'à). ◆**hitchhike** vi faire de l'auto-stop (to jusqu'à). ◆**hitchhiking** n auto-stop m. ◆**hitchhiker** n auto-stoppeur, -euse mf.

hitherto [hɪðə'tuː] adv jusqu'ici.

hive [haɪv] 1 n ruche f. 2 vt **to h. off** (industry) dénationaliser.

hoard [hɔːd] n réserve f; (of money) trésor m; – vt amasser. ◆**—ing** n (fence) panneau m d'affichage.

hoarfrost ['hɔːfrɒst] n givre m.

hoarse [hɔːs] a (-er, -est) (person, voice) enroué. ◆**—ness** n enrouement m.

hoax [həʊks] n canular m; – vt faire un canular à, mystifier.

hob [hɒb] n (on stove) plaque f chauffante.

hobble ['hɒb(ə)l] vi (walk) clopiner.

hobby ['hɒbɪ] n passe-temps m inv; **my h.** mon passe-temps favori. ◆**hobbyhorse** n (favourite subject) dada m.

hobnob ['hɒbnɒb] vi (-bb-) **to h. with** frayer avec.

hobo ['həʊbəʊ] n (pl -oes or -os) Am vaga-bond m.

hock [hɒk] vt (pawn) Fam mettre au clou; – n in h. Fam au clou.

hockey ['hɒkɪ] n hockey m; **ice h.** hockey sur glace.

hocus-pocus [həʊkəs'pəʊkəs] n (talk) charabia m; (deception) tromperie f.

hodgepodge ['hɒdʒpɒdʒ] n fatras m.

hoe [həʊ] n binette f, houe f; – vt biner.

hog [hɒg] 1 n (pig) cochon m, porc m; **road h.** Fig chauffard m. 2 n **to go the whole h.** Fam aller jusqu'au bout. 3 vt (-gg-) Fam monopoliser, garder pour soi.

hoist [hɔɪst] vt hisser; – n Tech palan m.

hold [həʊld] n (grip) prise f; (of ship) cale f; (of aircraft) soute f; **to get h. of** (grab) saisir; (contact) joindre; (find) trouver; **to get a h. of oneself** se maîtriser; – vt (pt & pp held) (breath, interest, heat, atten-tion) retenir; (a post) occuper; (a record) détenir; (weight) supporter; (possess) posséder; (contain) contenir; (maintain, believe) maintenir (that que); (ceremony, mass) célébrer; (keep) garder; **to h. hands** se tenir par la main; **to h. one's own** se débrouiller; (of sick person) se maintenir; **h. the line!** Tel ne quittez pas!; **h. it!** (stay still) ne bouge pas!; **to be held** (of event) avoir lieu; **to h. back** (crowd, tears) contenir; (hide) cacher (from à); **to h. down** (job) occuper; (keep) garder; (person on ground) maintenir au sol; **to h. in** (stomach) rentrer; **to h. off** (enemy) tenir à distance; **to h. on** (keep in place) tenir en place (son chapeau etc); **to h. out** (offer) offrir; (arm) étendre; **to h. over** (postpone) remettre; **to h. together** (nation, group) assurer l'union de; **to h. up** (raise) lever; (support) soutenir; (delay) retarder; (bank) attaquer (à main armée); – vi (of nail, rope) tenir; (of weather) se maintenir; **to h. (good)** (of argu-ment) valoir (for pour); **to h. forth** (talk) Pej disserter; **if the rain holds off** s'il ne pleut pas; **to h. on** (endure) tenir bon; (wait) attendre; **h. on!** Tel ne quittez pas!; **to h. onto** (cling to) tenir bien; (keep) garder; **h. on (tight)!** tenez bon!; **to h. out** (resist) résister; (last) durer. ◆**holdall** n (bag) fourre-tout m inv. ◆**holdup** n (attack) hold-up m inv; (traffic jam) bouchon m; (delay) retard m.

holder ['həʊldər] n (of post, passport) titu-laire mf; (of record, card) détenteur, -trice mf; (container) support m.

holdings ['həʊldɪŋz] npl Fin possessions fpl.

hole [həʊl] n trou m; (town etc) Fam bled m, trou m; (room) Fam baraque f; – vt trouer; – vi **to h. up** (hide) Fam se terrer.

holiday ['hɒlɪdeɪ] n (rest) vacances fpl; holi-day(s) (from work, school etc) vacances fpl; **a h.** (day off) un congé; **a (public or bank) h.,** Am a legal h. un jour férié; **on h.** en vacances; **holidays with pay** congés mpl payés; – a (camp, clothes etc) de vacances; **in h. mood** d'humeur folâtre. ◆**holiday-maker** n vacancier, -ière m.

holiness ['həʊlɪnəs] n sainteté f.

Holland ['hɒlənd] n Hollande f.

hollow ['hɒləʊ] *a* creux; (*victory*) faux; (*promise*) vain; – *n* creux *m*; – *vt* to h. out creuser.

holly ['hɒlɪ] *n* houx *m*.

holocaust ['hɒləkɔːst] *n* (*massacre*) holocauste *m*.

holster ['həʊlstər] *n* étui *m* de revolver.

holy ['həʊlɪ] *a* (**-ier, -iest**) saint; (*bread, water*) bénit; (*ground*) sacré.

homage ['hɒmɪdʒ] *n* hommage *m*.

home[1] [həʊm] *n* maison *f*; (*country*) pays *m* (natal); (*for soldiers*) foyer *m*; (**at**) **h.** à la maison, chez soi; **to feel at h.** se sentir à l'aise; **to play at h.** *Fb* jouer à domicile; **far from h.** loin de chez soi; **a broken h.** un foyer désuni; **a good h.** une bonne famille; **to make one's h.** in s'installer à *or* en; **my h. is here** j'habite ici; – *adv* à la maison, chez soi; **to go** *or* **come h.** rentrer; **to be h.** être rentré; **to drive h.** ramener (*qn* en voiture); (*nail*) enfoncer; **to bring sth h. to s.o.** *Fig* faire voir qch à qn; – *a* (*life, pleasures etc*) de famille; *Pol* national; (*cooking, help*) familial; (*visit, match*) à domicile; **h. economics** économie *f* domestique; **h. town** (*birth place*) ville *f* natale; **h. rule** *Pol* autonomie *f*; **H. Office** = ministère *m* de l'Intérieur; **H. Secretary** = ministre *m* de l'Intérieur. ◆**homecoming** *n* retour *m* au foyer. ◆**home'grown** *a Bot* du jardin; *Pol* du pays. ◆**homeland** *n* patrie *f*. ◆**homeloving** *a* casanier. ◆**home'made** *a* (fait à la) maison *inv*. ◆**homework** *n Sch* devoir(s) *m(pl)*.

home[2] [həʊm] *vi* **to h. in on** se diriger automatiquement sur.

homeless ['həʊmlɪs] *a* sans abri; – *n* **the h.** les sans-abri *m inv*.

homely ['həʊmlɪ] *a* (**-ier, -iest**) (*simple*) simple; (*comfortable*) accueillant; (*ugly*) *Am* laid.

homesick ['həʊmsɪk] *a* nostalgique; **to be h.** avoir le mal du pays. ◆**-ness** *n* nostalgie *f*, mal *m* du pays.

homeward ['həʊmwəd] *a* (*trip*) de retour; – *adv* **h. bound** sur le chemin de retour.

homey ['həʊmɪ] *a* (**-ier, -iest**) *Am Fam* accueillant.

homicide ['hɒmɪsaɪd] *n* homicide *m*.

homily ['hɒmɪlɪ] *n* homélie *f*.

homogeneous [həʊmə'dʒiːnɪəs] *a* homogène.

homosexual [həʊmə'seksʊəl] *a* & *n* homosexuel, -elle (*mf*). ◆**homosexu-'ality** *n* homosexualité *f*.

honest ['ɒnɪst] *a* honnête; (*frank*) franc (*with* avec); (*profit, money*) honnêtement

gagné; **the h. truth** la pure vérité; **to be** (*quite*) **h**.... pour être franc.... ◆**honesty** *n* honnêteté *f*; franchise *f*; (*of report, text*) exactitude *f*.

honey ['hʌnɪ] *n* miel *m*; (*person*) *Fam* chéri, -ie *mf*. ◆**honeycomb** *n* rayon *m* de miel. ◆**honeymoon** *n* (*member*) lune *f* de miel; (*trip*) voyage *m* de noces. ◆**honeysuckle** *n Bot* chèvrefeuille *f*.

honk [hɒŋk] *vi Aut* klaxonner; – *n* coup *m* de klaxon®.

honour ['ɒnər] *n* honneur *m*; **in h. of** en l'honneur de; **an honours degree** *Univ* = une licence; – *vt* honorer (**with** de). ◆**honorary** *a* (*member*) honoraire; (*title*) honorifique. ◆**honourable** *a* honorable.

hood [hʊd] *n* **1** capuchon *m*; (*mask of robber*) cagoule *f*; (*soft car or pram roof*) capote *f*; (*bonnet*) *Aut Am* capot *m*; (*above stove*) hotte *f*. **2** (*hoodlum*) *Am Sl* gangster *m*. ◆**hooded** *a* (*person*) encapuchonné; (*coat*) à capuchon.

hoodlum ['hʊdləm] *n Fam* (*hooligan*) voyou *m*; (*gangster*) gangster *m*.

hoodwink ['hʊdwɪŋk] *vt* tromper, duper.

hoof, *pl* **-fs, -ves** [huːf, -fs, -vz] (*Am* [huf, -fs, huvz]) *n* sabot *m*.

hoo-ha ['huːhɑː] *n Fam* tumulte *m*.

hook [hʊk] *n* crochet *m*; (*on clothes*) agrafe *f*; *Fishing* hameçon *m*; **off the h.** (*phone*) décroché; **to let** *or* **get s.o. off the h.** tirer qn d'affaire; – *vt* **to h.** (**on** *or* **up**) accrocher (**to** à). ◆**-ed** *a* (*nose, beak*) recourbé, crochu; (*end, object*) recourbé; **h. on** *Fam* (*chess etc*) enragé de; (*person*) entiché de; **to be h. on drugs** *Fam* ne plus pouvoir se passer de la drogue. ◆**-er** *n Am Sl* prostituée *f*.

hook(e)y ['hʊkɪ] *n* **to play h.** *Am Fam* faire l'école buissonnière.

hooligan ['huːlɪgən] *n* vandale *m*, voyou *m*. ◆**hooliganism** *n* vandalisme *m*.

hoop [huːp] *n* cerceau *m*; (*of barrel*) cercle *m*.

hoot [huːt] **1** *vi Aut* klaxonner; (*of train*) siffler; (*of owl*) hululer; – *n Aut* coup *m* de klaxon®. **2** *vti* (*jeer*) huer; – *n* huée *f*. ◆**-er** *n Aut* klaxon®-*m*; (*of factory*) sirène *f*.

hoover® ['huːvər] *n* aspirateur *m*; – *vt Fam* passer à l'aspirateur.

hop [hɒp] *vi* (**-pp-**) (*of person*) sauter (à cloche-pied); (*of bird*) sautiller. **h. in!** (*in car*) montez!; **to h. on a bus** monter dans un autobus; **to h. on a plane** attraper un vol; – *vt* **h. it!** *Fam* fiche le camp!; – *n* (*leap*) saut *m*; *Av* étape *f*.

hope [həʊp] *n* espoir *m*, espérance *f*; – *vi*

espérer; **to h.** for (desire) espérer; (expect) attendre; **I h. so/not** j'espère que oui/non; – vt espérer (**to do** faire, **that** que). ◆**hopeful** a (person) optimiste, plein d'espoir; (promising) prometteur; (encouraging) encourageant; **to be h.** that avoir bon espoir que. ◆**hopefully** adv avec optimisme; (one hopes) on espère (que). ◆**hopeless** a désespéré, sans espoir; (useless, bad) nul; (liar) invétéré. ◆**hopelessly** adv sans espoir; (extremely) complètement; (in love) éperdument.

hops [hɒps] npl Bot houblon m.

hopscotch ['hɒpskɒtʃ] n (game) marelle f.

horde [hɔːd] n horde f, foule f.

horizon [hə'raɪz(ə)n] n horizon m; **on the h.** à l'horizon.

horizontal [hɒrɪ'zɒnt(ə)l] a horizontal. ◆**—ly** adv horizontalement.

hormone ['hɔːməʊn] n hormone f.

horn [hɔːn] n 1 n (of animal) corne f; Mus cor m; Aut klaxon® m. 2 vi **to h.** in Am Fam dire son mot, interrompre.

hornet ['hɔːnɪt] n (insect) frelon m.

horoscope ['hɒrəskəʊp] n horoscope m.

horror ['hɒrər] n horreur f; (little h.) (child) Fam petit monstre m; – a (film etc) d'épouvante, d'horreur. ◆**ho'rrendous** a horrible. ◆**horrible** a horrible, affreux. ◆**horribly** adv horriblement. ◆**horrid** a horrible; (child) épouvantable, méchant. ◆**ho'rrific** a horrible, horrifiant. ◆**horrify** vt horrifier.

hors-d'œuvre [ɔː'dɜːv] n hors-d'œuvre m inv.

horse [hɔːs] n 1 cheval m; **to go h.** riding faire du cheval; **h. show** concours m hippique. 2 h. chestnut marron m (d'Inde). ◆**horseback** n **on h.** à cheval. ◆**horseman** n (pl -men) cavalier m. ◆**horseplay** n jeux mpl brutaux. ◆**horsepower** n cheval m (vapeur). ◆**horseracing** n courses fpl. ◆**horseradish** n radis m noir, raifort m. ◆**horseshoe** n fer m à cheval. ◆**horsewoman** n (pl -women) cavalière f.

horticulture ['hɔːtɪkʌltʃər] n horticulture f. ◆**horti'cultural** a horticole.

hose [həʊz] n (tube) tuyau m; – vt (garden etc) arroser. ◆**hosepipe** n tuyau m.

hosiery ['həʊzɪərɪ, Am 'həʊʒərɪ] n bonneterie f.

hospice ['hɒspɪs] n (for dying people) hospice m (pour incurables).

hospitable [hɒ'spɪtəb(ə)l] a hospitalier. ◆**hospitably** adv avec hospitalité. ◆**hospi'tality** n hospitalité f.

hospital ['hɒspɪt(ə)l] n hôpital m; **in h.,** Am

in the h. à l'hôpital; – a (bed etc) d'hôpital; (staff, services) hospitalier. ◆**hospitalize** vt hospitaliser.

host [həʊst] n 1 (man who receives guests) hôte m **2 a h.** of (many) une foule de. 3 Rel hostie f. ◆**hostess** n (in house, aircraft, nightclub) hôtesse f.

hostage ['hɒstɪdʒ] n otage m; **to take s.o. h.** prendre qn en otage.

hostel ['hɒst(ə)l] n foyer m; **youth h.** auberge f de jeunesse.

hostile ['hɒstaɪl, Am 'hɒst(ə)l] a hostile (to, towards à). ◆**ho'stility** n hostilité f (to, towards envers); pl Mil hostilités fpl.

hot[1] [hɒt] a (**hotter, hottest**) chaud; (spice) fort; (temperament) passionné; (news) Fam dernier; (favourite) Sp grand; **to be or feel h.** avoir chaud; **it's h.** il fait chaud; **not so h. at** (good at) Fam pas très calé en; **not so h.** (bad) Fam pas fameux; **h. dog** (sausage) hot-dog m. ◆**hotbed** n Pej foyer m (of de). ◆**hot-'blooded** a ardent. ◆**hothead** n tête f brûlée. ◆**hot'headed** a impétueux. ◆**hothouse** n serre f (chaude). ◆**hotplate** n chauffe-plats m inv; (on stove) plaque f chauffante. ◆**hot-'tempered** a emporté. ◆**hot-'water bottle** n bouillotte f.

hot[2] [hɒt] vi (**-tt-**) **to h.** up (increase) s'intensifier; (become dangerous or excited) chauffer.

hotchpotch ['hɒtʃpɒtʃ] n fatras m.

hotel [həʊ'tel] n hôtel m; – a (industry) hôtelier. ◆**hotelier** [həʊ'telɪər] n hôtelier, -ière mf.

hotly ['hɒtlɪ] adv passionnément.

hound [haʊnd] n 1 (dog) chien m courant. 2 vt (pursue) poursuivre avec acharnement; (worry) harceler.

hour ['aʊər] n heure f; **half an h.,** a half-hour une demi-heure; **a quarter of an h.** un quart d'heure; **paid ten francs an h.** payé dix francs (de) l'heure; **ten miles an h.** dix miles à l'heure; **open all hours** ouvert à toute heure; **h. hand** (of watch, clock) petite aiguille f. ◆**—ly** a (rate, pay) horaire; **an h. bus/train**/etc un bus/train/etc toutes les heures; – adv toutes les heures; **h. paid, paid h.** payé à l'heure.

house[1], pl **-ses** [haʊs, -zɪz] n maison f; (audience) Th salle f, auditoire m; (performance) Th séance f; **the H.** Pol la Chambre; **the Houses of Parliament** le Parlement; **at or to my h.** chez moi; **on the h.** (free of charge) aux frais de la maison; **h. prices** prix mpl immobiliers. ◆**housebound** a confiné chez soi.

breaking n Jur cambriolage m. ◆**house-broken** a (dog etc) Am propre. ◆**household** n ménage m, maison f, famille f; **h. duties** soins mpl du ménage; **a h. name** un nom très connu. ◆**householder** n (owner) propriétaire m; (family head) chef m de famille. ◆**housekeeper** n (employee) gouvernante f; (housewife) ménagère f. ◆**housekeeping** n ménage m. ◆**houseman** n (pl -men) interne mf (des hôpitaux). ◆**houseproud** a qui s'occupe méticuleusement de sa maison. ◆**housetrained** a (dog etc) propre. ◆**housewarming** n & a **to have a h.-warming (party)** pendre la crémaillère. ◆**housewife** n (pl -wives) ménagère f. ◆**housework** n (travaux mpl de) ménage m.

hous/e² [hauz] vt loger, (of building) abriter; **it is housed in** (kept) on le garde dans. ◆**—ing** n logement m; (houses) logements mpl; — a (crisis etc) du logement.

hovel ['hɒv(ə)l] n (slum) taudis m.

hover ['hɒvər] vi (of bird, aircraft, danger etc) planer; (of person) rôder, traîner. ◆**hovercraft** n aéroglisseur m.

how [hau] adv comment; **h.'s that?, h. so?, h. come?** Fam comment ça?; **h. kind!** comme c'est gentil!; **h. do you do?** (greeting) bonjour; **h. long/high is . . . ?** quelle est la longueur/hauteur de . . . ?; **h. much?, h. many?** combien?; **h. much time/etc?** combien de temps/etc?; **h. many apples/etc?** combien de pommes/etc?; **h. about a walk?** si on faisait une promenade?; **h. about some coffee?** (si on prenait) du café?; **h. about me?** et moi?

howdy! ['haudi] int Am Fam salut!

however [hau'evər] 1 adv **h. big he may be** quelque or si grand qu'il soit; **h. she may do it** de quelque manière qu'elle le fasse; **h. that may be** quoi qu'il en soit. 2 conj cependant.

howl [haul] vi hurler; (of baby) brailler; (of wind) mugir; — n hurlement m; braillement m; mugissement m; (of laughter) éclat m.

howler ['haulər] n (mistake) Fam gaffe f.

HP [eitʃ'pi:] abbr = **hire purchase**.

hp abbr (horsepower) CV.

HQ [eitʃ'kju:] abbr = **headquarters**.

hub [hʌb] n (of wheel) moyeu m; Fig centre m. ◆**hubcap** n Aut enjoliveur m.

hubbub ['hʌbʌb] n vacarme m.

huckleberry ['hʌk(ə)lbəri] n Bot Am myrtille f.

huddle ['hʌd(ə)l] vi **to h. (together)** se blottir (les uns contre les autres).

hue [hju:] n (colour) teinte f.

huff [hʌf] n **in a h.** (offended) Fam fâché.

hug [hʌg] vt (-gg-) (person) serrer dans ses bras, étreindre; **to h. the kerb/coast** (stay near) serrer le trottoir/la côte; — n (embrace) étreinte f.

huge [hju:dʒ] a énorme. ◆**—ly** adv énormément. ◆**—ness** n énormité f.

hulk [hʌlk] n (person) lourdaud, -aude mf.

hull [hʌl] n (of ship) coque f.

hullabaloo [hʌləbə'lu:] n Fam (noise) vacarme m; (fuss) histoire(s) f(pl).

hullo! [hʌ'ləu] int = **hallo**.

hum [hʌm] vi (-mm-) (of insect) bourdonner; (of person) fredonner; (of top, radio) ronfler; (of engine) vrombir; — vt (tune) fredonner; — n (of insect) bourdonnement m.

human ['hju:mən] a humain; **h. being** être m humain; — npl humains mpl. ◆**hu'mane** a (kind) humain. ◆**hu'manely** adv humainement. ◆**humani'tarian** a & n humanitaire (mf). ◆**hu'manity** n (human beings, kindness) humanité f. ◆**humanly** adv (possible etc) humainement.

humble ['hʌmb(ə)l] a humble; — vt humilier. ◆**humbly** adv humblement.

humbug ['hʌmbʌg] n (talk) fumisterie f; (person) fumiste mf.

humdrum ['hʌmdrʌm] a monotone.

humid ['hju:mid] a humide. ◆**hu'midify** vt humidifier. ◆**hu'midity** n humidité f.

humiliate [hju:'milieit] vt humilier. ◆**humili'ation** n humiliation f. ◆**humility** n humilité f.

humour ['hju:mər] 1 n (fun) humour m; (temper) humeur f; **to have a sense of h.** avoir le sens de l'humour; **in a good h.** de bonne humeur. 2 vt **to h. s.o.** faire plaisir à qn, ménager qn. ◆**humorist** n humoriste mf. ◆**humorous** a (book etc) humoristique; (person) plein d'humour. ◆**humorously** adv avec humour.

hump [hʌmp] 1 n (lump, mound) bosse f; — vt (one's back) voûter. 2 n **to have the h.** Fam (depression) avoir le cafard; (bad temper) être en rogne. ◆**humpback** a **h. bridge** Aut pont m en dos d'âne.

hunch [hʌntʃ] 1 vt (one's shoulders) voûter. 2 n (idea) Fam intuition f, idée f. ◆**hunchback** n bossu, -ue mf.

hundred ['hʌndrəd] a & n cent (m); **a h. pages** cent pages; **two h. pages** deux cents pages; **hundreds of** des centaines de.

◆**hundredfold** a centuple; – adv au centuple. ◆**hundredth** a & n centième (mf). ◆**hundredweight** n 112 livres (= 50,8 kg); Am 100 livres (= 45,3 kg).

hung [hʌŋ] see hang¹.

Hungary ['hʌŋgərɪ] n Hongrie f. ◆**Hungarian** a & n hongrois, -oise (mf); – n (language) hongrois m.

hunger ['hʌŋgər] n faim f. ◆**hungry** a (-ier, -iest) to be or feel h. avoir faim; to go h. souffrir de la faim; **to make h.** donner faim à; h. for (news etc) avide de. ◆**hungrily** adv avidement.

hunk [hʌŋk] n (gros) morceau m.

hunt [hʌnt] n Sp chasse f; (search) recherche f (for de); – vt Sp chasser; (pursue) poursuivre; (seek) chercher; **to h. down** (fugitive etc) traquer; **to h. out** (information etc) dénicher; – vi Sp chasser; **to h. for sth** (re)chercher qch. ◆**-ing** n Sp chasse f. ◆**-er** n (person) chasseur m.

hurdle ['hɜːd(ə)l] n (fence) Sp haie f; (obstacle) Fig obstacle m.

hurl [hɜːl] vt (throw) jeter, lancer; (abuse) lancer; **to h. oneself at s.o.** se ruer sur qn.

hurly-burly ['hɜːlɪbɜːlɪ] n tumulte m.

hurray! [hʊ'reɪ] int hourra!

hurricane ['hʌrɪkən, Am 'hʌrɪkeɪn] n ouragan m.

hurry ['hʌrɪ] n hâte f; **in a h.** à la hâte, en hâte; **to be in a h.** être pressé; **to be in a h. to do** avoir hâte de faire; **there's no h.** rien ne presse; – vi se dépêcher, se presser (to do de faire); **to h. out** sortir à la hâte; **to h. along** or **on** or **up** se dépêcher; – vt (person) bousculer, presser; (pace) presser; **to h. one's meal** manger à toute vitesse; **to h. s.o. out** faire sortir qn à la hâte. ◆**hurried** a (steps, decision etc) précipité; (travail) fait à la hâte; (visit) éclair inv; **to be h.** (in a hurry) être pressé.

hurt [hɜːt] vt (pt & pp hurt) (physically) faire du mal à, blesser; (emotionally) faire de la peine à; (offend) blesser; (prejudice, damage) nuire à; **to h. s.o.'s feelings** blesser qn; **his arm hurts (him)** son bras lui fait mal; – vi faire mal; – n mal m; – a (injured) blessé. ◆**hurtful** a (remark) blessant.

hurtle ['hɜːt(ə)l] vi **to h. along** aller à toute vitesse; **to h. down** dégringoler.

husband ['hʌzbənd] n mari m.

hush [hʌʃ] int chut!; – n silence m; – vt (person) faire taire; (baby) calmer; **to h. up** (scandal) Fig étouffer. ◆**-ed** a (voice)

étouffé; (silence) profond. ◆**hush-hush** a Fam ultra-secret.

husk [hʌsk] n (of rice, grain) enveloppe f.

husky ['hʌskɪ] a (-ier, -iest) (voice) enroué, voilé.

hussy ['hʌsɪ] n Pej friponne f, coquine f.

hustings ['hʌstɪŋz] npl campagne f électorale, élections fpl.

hustle ['hʌs(ə)l] 1 vt (shove, rush) bousculer (qn); – vi (work busily) Am se démener (to get sth pour avoir qch). 2 n h. and bustle agitation f, activité f, tourbillon m.

hut [hʌt] n cabane f, hutte f.

hutch [hʌtʃ] n (for rabbit) clapier m.

hyacinth ['haɪəsɪnθ] n jacinthe f.

hybrid ['haɪbrɪd] a & n hybride (m).

hydrangea [haɪ'dreɪndʒə] n (shrub) hortensia m.

hydrant ['haɪdrənt] n (fire) h. bouche f d'incendie.

hydraulic [haɪ'drɔːlɪk] a hydraulique.

hydroelectric [haɪdrəʊ'lektrɪk] a hydro-électrique.

hydrogen ['haɪdrədʒən] n Ch hydrogène m.

hyena [haɪ'iːnə] n (animal) hyène f.

hygiene ['haɪdʒiːn] n hygiène f. ◆**hy'gienic** a hygiénique.

hymn [hɪm] n Rel cantique m, hymne m.

hyper- ['haɪpər] pref hyper-.

hypermarket ['haɪpəmɑːkɪt] n hypermarché m.

hyphen ['haɪf(ə)n] n trait m d'union. ◆**hyphenat/e** vt mettre un trait d'union à. ◆**-ed** a (word) à trait d'union.

hypnosis [hɪp'nəʊsɪs] n hypnose f. ◆**hypnotic** a hypnotique. ◆**hypnotism** ['hɪpnətɪzəm] n hypnotisme m. ◆**'hypnotist** n hypnotiseur m. ◆**'hypnotize** vt hypnotiser.

hypochondriac [haɪpə'kɒndrɪæk] n malade mf imaginaire.

hypocrisy [hɪ'pɒkrɪsɪ] n hypocrisie f. ◆**'hypocrite** n hypocrite mf. ◆**hypo'critical** a hypocrite.

hypodermic [haɪpə'dɜːmɪk] a hypodermique.

hypothesis, pl **-eses** [haɪ'pɒθɪsɪs, -ɪsiːz] n hypothèse f. ◆**hypo'thetical** a hypothétique.

hysteria [hɪ'stɪərɪə] n hystérie f. ◆**hysterical** a hystérique; (funny) Fam désopilant; **to be** or **become h.** (wildly upset) avoir une crise de nerfs. ◆**hysterically** adv (to cry) sans pouvoir s'arrêter; **to laugh h.** rire aux larmes. ◆**hysterics** npl (tears etc) crise f de nerfs; (laughter) crise f de rire.

I

I, i [aɪ] n I, i m.

I [aɪ] pron je, j'; (stressed) moi; **I want je veux; she and I** elle et moi.

ice¹ [aɪs] n glace f; (on road) verglas m; **i. (cream)** glace f; black i. (on road) verglas m; **i. cube** glaçon m; – vt **to i. (over)** (of lake) geler; (of windscreen) givrer. ◆—**ed** a (tea) glacé. ◆**iceberg** n iceberg m. ◆**icebox** n (box) & Fig glacière f; Am réfrigérateur m. ◆**ice-'cold** a glacial; (drink) glacé. ◆**ice-skating** n patinage m (sur glace). ◆**icicle** n glaçon m.

ice² [aɪs] vt (cake) glacer. ◆—**ing** n (on cake etc) glaçage m.

Iceland ['aɪslənd] n Islande f. ◆**Ice'landic** a islandais.

icon ['aɪkɒn] n Rel icône f.

icy ['aɪsɪ] a (-ier, -iest) (water, hands, room) glacé; (manner, weather) glacial; (road etc) verglacé.

idea [aɪ'dɪə] n idée f (of d); **I have an i. that ...** j'ai l'impression que ...; **that's my i. of rest** c'est ce que j'appelle du repos; **that's the i.!** Fam c'est ça!; **not the slightest or foggiest i.** pas la moindre idée.

ideal [aɪ'dɪəl] a idéal; – n (aspiration) idéal m; pl (spiritual etc) idéal m. ◆**idealism** n idéalisme m. ◆**idealist** n idéaliste mf. ◆**idea'listic** a idéaliste. ◆**idealize** vt idéaliser. ◆**ideally** adv idéalement; **i. we should stay** l'idéal, ce serait de rester or que nous restions.

identical [aɪ'dentɪk(ə)l] a identique (**to**, with à). ◆**identifi'cation** n identification f; **I have (some) i.** j'ai une pièce d'identité. ◆**identify** vt identifier; **to i. (oneself) with** s'identifier avec. ◆**identikit** n portrait-robot m. ◆**identity** n identité f; **i. card** carte f d'identité.

ideology [aɪdɪ'ɒlədʒɪ] n idéologie f. ◆**ideo-'logical** a idéologique.

idiom ['ɪdɪəm] n expression f idiomatique; (language) idiome m. ◆**idio'matic** a idiomatique.

idiosyncrasy [ɪdɪə'sɪŋkrəsɪ] n particularité f.

idiot ['ɪdɪət] n idiot, -ote mf. ◆**idiocy** n idiotie f. ◆**idi'otic** a idiot, bête. ◆**idi'otically** adv idiotement.

idle ['aɪd(ə)l] a (unoccupied) désœuvré, oisif; (lazy) paresseux; (unemployed) en chômage; (moment) de loisir; (machine) au repos; (promise) vain; (pleasure, question) futile; (rumour) sans fondement; – vi (laze about) paresser; (of machine, engine) tourner au ralenti; – vt **to i. away** (time) gaspiller. ◆—**ness** n oisiveté f; (laziness) paresse f. ◆**idler** n paresseux, -euse mf. ◆**idly** adv paresseusement; (to suggest, say) négligemment.

idol ['aɪd(ə)l] n idole f. ◆**idolize** vt idolâtrer.

idyllic [aɪ'dɪlɪk] a idyllique.

i.e. [aɪ'i:] abbr (id est) c'est-à-dire.

if [ɪf] conj si; **if he comes** s'il vient; **even if** même si; **if so** dans ce cas, si c'est le cas; **if not for pleasure** sinon pour le plaisir; **if only I were rich** si seulement j'étais riche; **if only to look** ne serait-ce que pour regarder; **as if** comme si; **as if nothing had happened** comme si de rien n'était; **as if to say** comme pour dire; **if necessary** s'il le faut.

igloo ['ɪglu:] n igloo m.

ignite [ɪg'naɪt] vt mettre le feu à; – vi prendre feu. ◆**ignition** n Aut allumage m; **to switch on the i.** mettre le contact.

ignominious [ɪgnə'mɪnɪəs] a déshonorant, ignominieux.

ignoramus [ɪgnə'reɪməs] n ignare mf.

ignorance ['ɪgnərəns] n ignorance f (**of** de). ◆**ignorant** a ignorant (**of** de). ◆**ignorantly** adv par ignorance.

ignore [ɪg'nɔ:r] vt ne prêter aucune attention à, ne tenir aucun compte de; (duty) méconnaître; (pretend not to recognize) faire semblant de ne pas reconnaître.

ilk [ɪlk] n **of that i.** (kind) de cet acabit.

ill [ɪl] a (sick) malade; (bad) mauvais; **ill will** malveillance f; – npl (misfortunes) maux mpl, malheurs mpl; – adv mal; **to speak i. of** dire du mal de. ◆**ill-ad'vised** a malavisé, peu judicieux. ◆**ill-'fated** a malheureux. ◆**ill-'gotten** a mal acquis. ◆**ill-in'formed** a mal renseigné. ◆**ill-'mannered** a mal élevé. ◆**ill-'natured** a (mean, unkind) désagréable. ◆**ill-'timed** a inopportun. ◆**ill-'treat** vt maltraiter.

illegal [ɪ'li:g(ə)l] a illégal. ◆**ille'gality** n illégalité f.

illegible [ɪ'ledʒəb(ə)l] a illisible.

illegitimate [ɪlɪ'dʒɪtɪmət] a (child, claim) illégitime. ◆**illegitimacy** n illégitimité f.

illicit [ɪ'lɪsɪt] a illicite.

illiterate [ɪ'lɪtərət] a & n illettré, -ée (mf), analphabète (mf). ◆**illiteracy** n analphabétisme m.

illness [ɪlnɪs] n maladie f.

illogical [ɪ'lɒdʒɪk(ə)l] a illogique.

illuminate [ɪ'luːmɪneɪt] vt (street, question etc) éclairer; (monument etc for special occasion) illuminer. ◆**illumi'nation** n éclairage m; illumination f.

illusion [ɪ'luːʒ(ə)n] n illusion f (about sur); **I'm not under any i.** je ne me fais aucune illusion (about sur, quant à). ◆**illusory** a, ◆**illusive** a, illusoire.

illustrate [ɪləstreɪt] vt (with pictures, examples) illustrer (with de). ◆**illu'stration** n illustration f. ◆**i'llustrative** a (example) explicatif.

illustrious [ɪ'lʌstrɪəs] a illustre.

image [ɪmɪdʒ] n image f; (public) i. (of firm etc) image de marque; **he's the (living or spitting or very) i. of his brother** c'est (tout) le portrait de son frère. ◆**imagery** n images fpl.

imagin/e [ɪ'mædʒɪn] vt (picture to oneself) (s')imaginer, se figurer (that que); (suppose) imaginer (that que)... i. that... imaginez que...; **you're imagining (things)!** tu te fais des illusions! ◆**-ings** npl (dreams) imaginations fpl. ◆**-able** a imaginable; **the worst thing i.** le pire que l'on puisse imaginer. ◆**imaginary** a imaginaire. ◆**imagi'nation** n imagination f. ◆**imaginative** a plein d'imagination, imaginatif.

imbalance [ɪm'bæləns] n déséquilibre m.

imbecile [ɪmbəsiːl, Am ɪmbəs(ə)l] a & n imbécile (mf). ◆**imbe'cility** n imbécillité f.

imbibe [ɪm'baɪb] vt absorber.

imbued [ɪm'bjuːd] a i. with (ideas) imprégné de; (feelings) pénétré de, imbu de.

imitate [ɪmɪteɪt] vt imiter. ◆**imi'tation** n imitation f; – a (jewels) artificiel; **i. leather** imitation f cuir. ◆**imitative** a imitateur. ◆**imitator** n imitateur, -trice mf.

immaculate [ɪ'mækjʊlət] a (person, appearance, shirt etc) impeccable.

immaterial [ɪmə'tɪərɪəl] a peu important (to pour).

immature [ɪmə'tʃʊər] a (fruit) vert; (animal) jeune; (person) qui manque de maturité.

immeasurable [ɪ'meʒərəb(ə)l] a incommensurable.

immediate [ɪ'miːdɪət] a immédiat. ◆**immediacy** n caractère m immédiat. ◆**immediately** adv (at once) tout de suite, immédiatement; (to concern, affect) directement; – conj (as soon as) dès que.

immense [ɪ'mens] a immense. ◆**immensely** adv (rich etc) immensément; **to enjoy oneself i.** s'amuser énormément. ◆**immensity** n immensité f.

immerse [ɪ'mɜːs] vt plonger, immerger; **immersed in work** plongé dans le travail. ◆**immersion** n immersion f; **i. heater** chauffe-eau m inv électrique.

immigrate [ɪmɪgreɪt] vi immigrer. ◆**immigrant** n immigrant, -ante mf; (long-established) immigré, -ée mf; – a immigré. ◆**immi'gration** n immigration f.

imminent [ɪmɪnənt] a imminent. ◆**imminence** n imminence f.

immobile [ɪ'məʊbaɪl, Am ɪ'məʊb(ə)l] a immobile. ◆**immo'bility** n immobilité f. ◆**immobilize** vt immobiliser.

immoderate [ɪ'mɒdərət] a immodéré.

immodest [ɪ'mɒdɪst] a impudique.

immoral [ɪ'mɒrəl] a immoral. ◆**immo'rality** n immoralité f.

immortal [ɪ'mɔːt(ə)l] a immortel. ◆**immor'tality** n immortalité f. ◆**immortalize** vt immortaliser.

immune [ɪ'mjuːn] a Med & Fig immunisé (to, from contre). ◆**immunity** n immunité f. ◆**immunize** vt immuniser (against contre).

immutable [ɪ'mjuːtəb(ə)l] a immuable.

imp [ɪmp] n diablotin m, lutin m.

impact [ɪmpækt] n impact m (on sur).

impair [ɪm'peər] vt détériorer; (hearing, health) abîmer.

impale [ɪm'peɪl] vt empaler.

impart [ɪm'pɑːt] vt communiquer (to à).

impartial [ɪm'pɑːʃ(ə)l] a impartial. ◆**imparti'ality** n impartialité f.

impassable [ɪm'pɑːsəb(ə)l] a (road) impraticable; (river) infranchissable.

impasse [ɪempɑːs, Am ɪmpæs] n (situation) impasse f.

impassioned [ɪm'pæʃ(ə)nd] a (speech etc) enflammé, passionné.

impassive [ɪm'pæsɪv] a impassible. ◆**-ness** n impassibilité f.

impatient [ɪm'peɪʃ(ə)nt] a impatient (to do de faire); **i. of or with** intolérant à l'égard de. ◆**impatience** n impatience f. ◆**impatiently** adv impatiemment.

impeccab/le [ɪm'pekəb(ə)l] a impeccable. ◆**-ly** adv impeccablement.

impecunious [impi'kju:niəs] *a Hum* sans le sou, impécunieux.

impede [im'pi:d] *vt* (*hamper*) gêner; **to i. s.o. from doing** (*prevent*) empêcher qn de faire.

impediment [im'pedimənt] *n* obstacle *m*; (*of speech*) défaut *m* d'élocution.

impel [im'pel] *vt* (-ll-) (*drive*) pousser; (*force*) obliger (**to do** à faire).

impending [im'pendiŋ] *a* imminent.

impenetrable [im'penitrəb(ə)l] *a* (*forest, mystery etc*) impénétrable.

imperative [im'perətiv] *a* (*need, tone*) impérieux; (*necessary*) essentiel; **it is i. that you come** il faut absolument que *or* il est indispensable que tu viennes; – *n Gram* impératif *m*.

imperceptible [impə'septəb(ə)l] *a* imperceptible (**to** à).

imperfect [im'pɜ:fikt] **1** *a* imparfait; (*goods*) défectueux. **2** *n* (*tense*) *Gram* imparfait *m*. ◆**imper'fection** *n* imperfection *f*.

imperial [im'piəriəl] *a* impérial; (*majestic*) majestueux; (*measure*) *Br* légal. ◆**imperialism** *n* impérialisme *m*.

imperil [im'peril] *vt* (-ll-, *Am* -l-) mettre en péril.

imperious [im'piəriəs] *a* impérieux.

impersonal [im'pɜ:sən(ə)l] *a* impersonnel.

impersonate [im'pɜ:səneit] *vt* (*mimic*) imiter; (*pretend to be*) se faire passer pour. ◆**imperso'nation** *n* imitation *f*. ◆**impersonator** *n* imitateur, -trice *mf*.

impertinent [im'pɜ:tinənt] *a* impertinent (**to** envers). ◆**impertinence** *n* impertinence *f*. ◆**impertinently** *adv* avec impertinence.

impervious [im'pɜ:viəs] *a* imperméable (**to** à).

impetuous [im'petjuəs] *a* impétueux. ◆**impetu'osity** *n* impétuosité *f*.

impetus [im'petəs] *n* impulsion *f*.

impinge [im'pindʒ] *vi* **to i. on** (*affect*) affecter; (*encroach on*) empiéter sur.

impish [im'piʃ] *a* (*naughty*) espiègle.

implacable [im'plækəb(ə)l] *a* implacable.

implant [im'plɑ:nt] *vt* (*ideas*) inculquer (**in** à).

implement¹ [im'plimənt] *n* (*tool*) instrument *m*; (*utensil*) *Culin* ustensile *m*; *pl Agr* matériel *m*.

implement² ['impliment] *vt* (*carry out*) mettre en œuvre, exécuter. ◆**implemen'tation** *n* mise *f* en œuvre, exécution *f*.

implicate ['implikeit] *vt* impliquer (**in** dans). ◆**impli'cation** *n* (*consequence, involvement*) implication *f*; (*innuendo*) insinuation *f*; (*impact*) portée *f*; **by i.** implicitement.

implicit [im'plisit] *a* (*implied*) implicite;

(*belief, obedience etc*) absolu. ◆**—ly** *adv* implicitement.

implore [im'plɔ:r] *vt* implorer (**s.o. to do** qn de faire).

imply [im'plai] *vt* (*assume*) impliquer, supposer (**that** que); (*suggest*) laisser entendre (**that** que); (*insinuate*) *Pej* insinuer (**that** que). ◆**implied** *a* implicite.

impolite [impə'lait] *a* impoli. ◆**—ness** *n* impolitesse *f*.

import 1 [im'pɔ:t] *vt* (*goods etc*) importer (**from** de); – ['impɔ:t] *n* (*object, action*) importation *f*. **2** ['impɔ:t] *n* (*meaning*) sens *m*. ◆**im'porter** *n* importateur, -trice *mf*.

importance [im'pɔ:təns] *n* importance *f*; **to be of i.** avoir de l'importance; **of no i.** sans importance. ◆**important** *a* (*significant*) important. ◆**importantly** *adv* **more i.** ce qui est plus important.

impose [im'pəuz] *vt* imposer (**on** à); (*fine, punishment*) infliger (**on** à); **to i. (oneself) on s.o.** s'imposer à qn; – *vi* s'imposer. ◆**impo'sition** *n* imposition *f* (**of** de); (*inconvenience*) dérangement *m*.

impossible [im'pɒsəb(ə)l] *a* impossible (**to do** à faire); **it is i. (for us) to do** il (nous) est impossible de faire; **it is i. that** il est impossible que (+ *sub*); **to make it i. for s.o. to do** mettre qn dans l'impossibilité de faire; – *n* **to do the i.** faire l'impossible. ◆**impossi'bility** *n* impossibilité *f*. ◆**impossibly** *adv* (*late, hard*) incroyablement.

impostor [im'pɒstər] *n* imposteur *m*.

impotent ['impətənt] *a Med* impuissant. ◆**impotence** *n Med* impuissance *f*.

impound [im'paund] *vt* (*of police*) saisir, confisquer; (*vehicle*) emmener à la fourrière.

impoverish [im'pɒvəriʃ] *vt* appauvrir.

impracticable [im'præktikəb(ə)l] *a* irréalisable, impraticable.

impractical [im'præktik(ə)l] *a* peu réaliste.

imprecise [impri'sais] *a* imprécis.

impregnable [im'pregnəb(ə)l] *a Mil* imprenable; (*argument*) *Fig* inattaquable.

impregnate ['impregneit] *vt* (*imbue*) imprégner (**with** de); (*fertilize*) féconder.

impresario [impri'sa:riəu] *n* (*pl* -os) impresario *m*.

impress [im'pres] *vt* impressionner (*qn*); (*mark*) imprimer; **to i. sth on s.o.** faire comprendre qch à qn. ◆**impression** *n* impression *f*; **to be under** *or* **have the i.** that avoir l'impression que; **to make a good i. on s.o.** faire une bonne impression à qn. ◆**impressionable** *a* (*person*) impressionnable; *(age)* où l'on est impressionnable. **◆impressive** *a* impressionnant.

imprint [ɪm'prɪnt] *vt* imprimer; – ['ɪmprɪnt] *n* empreinte *f*.

imprison [ɪm'prɪz(ə)n] *vt* emprisonner. **◆-ment** *n* emprisonnement *m*; **life i.** la prison à vie.

improbable [ɪm'prɒbəb(ə)l] *a* improbable; *(story, excuse)* invraisemblable. **◆improba'bility** *n* improbabilité *f*; invraisemblance *f*.

impromptu [ɪm'prɒmptjuː] *a* & *adv* impromptu.

improper [ɪm'prɒpər] *a (indecent)* inconvenant, indécent; *(wrong)* incorrect. **◆impropriety** [ɪmprə'praɪətɪ] *n* inconvenance *f*; *(wrong use)* Ling impropriété *f*.

improve [ɪm'pruːv] *vt* améliorer; *(mind)* cultiver, développer; **to i. one's English** se perfectionner en anglais; **to i. s.o.'s looks** embellir qn; **to i. oneself** se cultiver; – *vi* s'améliorer; *(of business)* aller de mieux en mieux, reprendre; **to i. on** *(do better than)* faire mieux que. **◆-ment** *n* amélioration *f*; *(of mind)* développement *m*; *(progress)* progrès *m(pl)*; **there has been some** *or* **an i.** il y a du mieux.

improvise ['ɪmprəvaɪz] *vti* improviser. **◆improvi'sation** *n* improvisation *f*.

impudent ['ɪmpjʊdənt] *a* impudent. **◆impudence** *n* impudence *f*.

impulse ['ɪmpʌls] *n* impulsion *f*; **on i.** sur un coup de tête. **◆im'pulsive** *a (person, act)* impulsif, irréfléchi; *(remark)* irréfléchi. **◆im'pulsively** *adv* de manière impulsive.

impunity [ɪm'pjuːnɪtɪ] *n* **with i.** impunément.

impure [ɪm'pjʊər] *a* impur. **◆impurity** *n* impureté *f*.

in [ɪn] *prep* **1** dans; **in the box/the school/***etc* dans la boîte/l'école/*etc*; **in an hour('s time)** dans une heure; **in so far as** dans la mesure où. **2** à; **in school** à l'école; **in the garden** dans le jardin, au jardin; **in Paris** à Paris; **in the USA** aux USA; **in Portugal** au Portugal; **in fashion** à la mode; **in pencil** au crayon; **in my opinion** mon avis. **3** en; **in summer/secret/French** en été/secret/français; **in Spain** en Espagne; **in May** en mai, au mois de mai; **in season** en saison; **in an hour** *(during the period of an hour)* en une heure; **in doing** en faisant; **dressed in black** habillé en noir; **in all** en tout. **4** de; **in a soft voice** d'une voix douce; **the best in the class** le meilleur de la classe. **5 in the rain** sous la pluie; **in the morning** le matin; **he hasn't done it in years** ça fait des années qu'il ne l'a pas fait; **in an hour** *(at the end of an hour)* au bout d'une heure; **one in ten** un sur dix; **in thousands** par milliers; **in here** ici; **in there** là-dedans. **6** *adv* **to be in** *(home)* être là, être à la maison; *(of train)* être arrivé; *(in fashion)* être en vogue; *(in season)* être en saison; *(in power)* Pol être au pouvoir; **day in day out** jour après jour; **in on** *(a secret)* au courant de; **we're in for some rain/trouble/***etc* on va avoir de la pluie/des ennuis/*etc*; **it's the thing** Fam c'est dans le vent. **7** *npl* **the ins and outs of** les moindres détails de.

inability [ɪnə'bɪlɪtɪ] *n* incapacité *f* **(to do** faire).

inaccessible [ɪnæk'sesəb(ə)l] *a* inaccessible.

inaccurate [ɪn'ækjʊrət] *a* inexact. **◆inaccuracy** *n* inexactitude *f*.

inaction [ɪn'ækʃ(ə)n] *n* inaction *f*.

inactive [ɪn'æktɪv] *a* inactif; *(mind)* inerte. **◆inac'tivity** *n* inactivité *f*, inaction *f*.

inadequate [ɪn'ædɪkwət] *a (quantity)* insuffisant; *(person)* pas à la hauteur, insuffisant; *(work)* médiocre. **◆inadequacy** *n* insuffisance *f*. **◆inadequately** *adv* insuffisamment.

inadmissible [ɪnəd'mɪsəb(ə)l] *a* inadmissible.

inadvertently [ɪnəd'vɜːtntlɪ] *adv* par inadvertance.

inadvisable [ɪnəd'vaɪzəb(ə)l] *a (action)* à déconseiller; **it is i.** to il est déconseillé de.

inane [ɪ'neɪn] *a (absurd)* inepte.

inanimate [ɪn'ænɪmət] *a* inanimé.

inappropriate [ɪnə'prəʊprɪət] *a (unsuitable)* peu approprié, inadéquat; *(untimely)* inopportun.

inarticulate [ɪnɑː'tɪkjʊlət] *a (person)* incapable de s'exprimer; *(sound)* inarticulé.

inasmuch as [ɪnəz'mʌtʃəz] *adv (because)* vu que; *(to the extent that)* en ce sens que.

inattentive [ɪnə'tentɪv] *a* inattentif **(to** à).

inaudible [ɪn'ɔːdəb(ə)l] *a* inaudible.

inaugural [ɪ'nɔːgjʊrəl] *a* inaugural. **◆inaugurate** *vt (policy, building)* inaugurer; *(official)* installer (dans ses fonctions). **◆inaugu'ration** *n* inauguration *f*; investiture *f*.

inauspicious [ɪnɔː'spɪʃəs] *a* peu propice.

inborn [ɪn'bɔːn] *a* inné.

inbred [ɪn'bred] *a (quality etc)* inné.

Inc *abbr (Incorporated)* Am Com SA, SARL.

incalculable [ɪn'kælkjʊləb(ə)l] *a* incalculable.

incandescent [ɪnkæn'des(ə)nt] *a* incandescent.

incapable [ɪn'keɪpəb(ə)l] *a* incapable **(of**

doing de faire; **i. of** (*pity etc*) inaccessible à.

incapacitate [ɪnkə'pæsɪteɪt] *vt Med* rendre incapable (*de travailler etc*). ◆**incapacity** *n* (*inability*) incapacité *f*.

incarcerate [ɪn'kɑːsəreɪt] *vt* incarcérer. ◆**incarce'ration** *n* incarcération *f*.

incarnate [ɪn'kɑːnət] *a* incarné; – [ɪn'kɑːneɪt] *vt* incarner. ◆**incar'nation** *n* incarnation *f*.

incendiary [ɪn'sendɪərɪ] *a* (*bomb*) incendiaire.

incense 1 [ɪn'sens] *vt* mettre en colère. **2** ['ɪnsens] *n* (*substance*) encens *m*.

incentive [ɪn'sentɪv] *n* encouragement *m*, motivation *f*; **to give s.o. an i. to work**/*etc* encourager qn à travailler/*etc*.

inception [ɪn'sepʃ(ə)n] *n* début *m*.

incessant [ɪn'ses(ə)nt] *a* incessant. ◆**-ly** *adv* sans cesse.

incest ['ɪnsest] *n* inceste *m*. ◆**in'cestuous** *a* incestueux.

inch [ɪntʃ] *n* pouce *m* (= 2,54 *cm*); (*loosely*) *Fig* centimètre *m*; **within an i. of** (*success*) à deux doigts de; **i. by i.** petit à petit; – *vti* to **i. (one's way) forward** avancer petit à petit.

incidence ['ɪnsɪdəns] *n* fréquence *f*.

incident ['ɪnsɪdənt] *n* incident *m*; (*in book, film etc*) épisode *m*.

incidental [ɪnsɪ'dent(ə)l] *a* accessoire, secondaire; (*music*) de fond; **i. expenses** frais *mpl* accessoires. ◆**-ly** *adv* accessoirement; (*by the way*) à propos.

incinerate [ɪn'sɪnəreɪt] *vt* (*refuse, leaves etc*) incinérer. ◆**incinerator** *n* incinérateur *m*.

incipient [ɪn'sɪpɪənt] *a* naissant.

incision [ɪn'sɪʒ(ə)n] *n* incision *f*.

incisive [ɪn'saɪsɪv] *a* incisif.

incisor [ɪn'saɪzər] *n* (*tooth*) incisive *f*.

incite [ɪn'saɪt] *vt* inciter (**to do** à faire). ◆**-ment** *n* incitation *f* (**to do** à faire).

incline 1 [ɪn'klaɪn] *vt* (*tilt, bend*) incliner; **to i. s.o. to do** incliner qn à faire; **to be inclined to do** (*feel a wish to*) être enclin à faire; (*tend to*) avoir tendance à faire; – *vi* to **i. or be inclined towards** (*indulgence etc*) incliner à. **2** ['ɪnklaɪn] *n* (*slope*) inclinaison *f*. ◆**incli'nation** *n* inclination *f*; **to have no i. to do** n'avoir aucune envie de faire.

includ/e [ɪn'kluːd] *vt* (*contain*) comprendre, englober; (*refer to*) s'appliquer à; **my invitation includes you** mon invitation s'adresse aussi à vous; **to be included** être compris; (*on list*) être inclus. ◆**-ing** *prep* y compris; **i. service** service *m* compris. ◆**inclusion** *n* inclusion *f*. ◆**inclusive** *a* inclus; **from the fourth to the tenth of May**

i. du quatre jusqu'au dix mai inclus(ivement); **to be i. of** comprendre; **i. charge** prix *m* global.

incognito [ɪnkɒg'niːtəʊ] *adv* incognito.

incoherent [ɪnkəʊ'hɪərənt] *a* incohérent. ◆**-ly** *adv* sans cohérence.

income ['ɪnkʌm] *n* revenu *m*; **private i.** rentes *fpl*; **i. tax** impôt *m* sur le revenu.

incoming ['ɪnkʌmɪŋ] *a* (*tenant, president*) nouveau; **i. tide** marée *f* montante; **i. calls** *Tel* appels *mpl* de l'extérieur.

incommunicado [ɪnkəmjuːnɪ'kɑːdəʊ] *a* (*tenu*) au secret.

incomparable [ɪn'kɒmpərəb(ə)l] *a* incomparable.

incompatible [ɪnkəm'pætəb(ə)l] *a* incompatible (**with** avec). ◆**incompati'bility** *n* incompatibilité *f*.

incompetent [ɪn'kɒmpɪtənt] *a* incompétent. ◆**incompetence** *n* incompétence *f*.

incomplete [ɪnkəm'pliːt] *a* incomplet.

incomprehensible [ɪnkɒmprɪ'hensəb(ə)l] *a* incompréhensible.

inconceivable [ɪnkən'siːvəb(ə)l] *a* inconcevable.

inconclusive [ɪnkən'kluːsɪv] *a* peu concluant.

incongruous [ɪn'kɒŋɡrʊəs] *a* (*building, colours*) qui jure(nt) (**with** avec); (*remark, attitude*) incongru; (*absurd*) absurde.

inconsequential [ɪnkɒnsɪ'kwenʃ(ə)l] *a* sans importance.

inconsiderate [ɪnkən'sɪdərət] *a* (*action, remark*) irréfléchi, inconsidéré; **to be i.** (*of person*) manquer d'égards (**towards** envers).

inconsistent [ɪnkən'sɪstənt] *a* inconséquent, incohérent; (*reports etc at variance*) contradictoires; **i. with** incompatible avec. ◆**inconsistency** *n* inconséquence *f*, incohérence *f*.

inconsolable [ɪnkən'səʊləb(ə)l] *a* inconsolable.

inconspicuous [ɪnkən'spɪkjʊəs] *a* peu en évidence, qui passe inaperçu. ◆**-ly** *adv* discrètement.

incontinent [ɪn'kɒntɪnənt] *a* incontinent.

inconvenient [ɪnkən'viːnɪənt] *a* (*room, situation*) incommode; (*time*) inopportun; **it's i. (for me) to...** ça me dérange de...; **that's very i.** c'est très gênant. ◆**inconvenience** *n* (*bother*) dérangement *m*; (*disadvantage*) inconvénient *m*; – *vt* déranger, gêner.

incorporate [ɪn'kɔːpəreɪt] *vt* (*introduce*) incorporer (**into** dans); (*contain*) contenir;

incorporated society *Am* société *f* anonyme, société *f* à responsabilité limitée.

incorrect [ɪnkəˈrekt] *a* incorrect, inexact; you're i. vous avez tort.

incorrigible [ɪnˈkɒrɪdʒəb(ə)l] *a* incorrigible.

incorruptible [ɪnkəˈrʌptəb(ə)l] *a* incorruptible.

increas/e [ɪnˈkriːs] *vi* augmenter; (*of effort, noise*) s'intensifier; **to i. in weight** prendre du poids; – *vt* augmenter; intensifier; – ['ɪnkriːs] *n* augmentation *f* (**in**, of de); intensification *f* (**in**, of de); **on the i.** en hausse. ◆**—ing** *a* (*amount etc*) croissant. ◆**—ingly** *adv* de plus en plus.

incredib/le [ɪnˈkredəb(ə)l] *a* incroyable. ◆**—ly** *adv* incroyablement.

incredulous [ɪnˈkredjʊləs] *a* incrédule. ◆**incre'dulity** *n* incrédulité *f*.

increment ['ɪŋkrəmənt]] *n* augmentation *f*.

incriminat/e [ɪnˈkrɪmɪneɪt] *vt* incriminer. ◆**—ing** *a* compromettant.

incubate ['ɪŋkjubeɪt] *vt* (*eggs*) couver. ◆**incu'bation** *n* incubation *f*. ◆**incubator** *n* (*for baby, eggs*) couveuse *f*.

inculcate ['ɪnkʌlkeɪt] *vt* inculquer (**in** à).

incumbent [ɪnˈkʌmbənt] *a* **it is i. upon him or her** to il lui incombe de; – *n Rel Pol* titulaire *mf*.

incur [ɪnˈkɜːr] *vt* (**-rr-**) (*debt*) contracter; (*expenses*) faire; (*criticism, danger*) s'attirer.

incurable [ɪnˈkjʊərəb(ə)l] *a* incurable.

incursion [ɪnˈkɜːʃ(ə)n] *n* incursion *f* (**into** dans).

indebted [ɪnˈdetɪd] *a* **i. to s.o. for sth/for doing sth** redevable à qn de qch/d'avoir fait qch. ◆**—ness** *n* dette *f*.

indecent [ɪnˈdiːs(ə)nt] *a* (*offensive*) indécent; (*unsuitable*) peu approprié. ◆**indecency** *n* indécence *f*; (*crime*) *Jur* outrage *m* à la pudeur. ◆**indecently** *adv* indécemment.

indecisive [ɪndɪˈsaɪsɪv] *a* (*person, answer*) indécis. ◆**indecision** *n*, ◆**indecisiveness** *n* indécision *f*.

indeed [ɪnˈdiːd] *adv* en effet; **very good/etc i.** vraiment très bon/etc; **yes i.!** bien sûr!; **thank you very much i.!** merci mille fois!

indefensible [ɪndɪˈfensəb(ə)l] *a* indéfendable.

indefinable [ɪndɪˈfaɪnəb(ə)l] *a* indéfinissable.

indefinite [ɪnˈdefɪnət] *a* (*feeling, duration etc*) indéfini; (*plan*) mal déterminé. ◆**—ly** *adv* indéfiniment.

indelible [ɪnˈdeləb(ə)l] *a* (*ink, memory*) indélébile; **i. pencil** crayon *m* à marquer.

indelicate [ɪnˈdelɪkət] *a* (*coarse*) indélicat.

indemnify [ɪnˈdemnɪfaɪ] *vt* indemniser (**for** de). ◆**indemnity** *n* indemnité *f*.

indented [ɪnˈdentɪd] *a* (*edge*) dentelé, découpé; (*line*) *Typ* renfoncé. ◆**inden'tation** *n* denteiure *f*, découpure *f*; *Typ* renfoncement *m*.

independent [ɪndɪˈpendənt] *a* indépendant (**of** de); (*opinions, reports*) de sources différentes. ◆**independence** *n* indépendance *f*. ◆**independently** *adv* de façon indépendante; **i. of** indépendamment de.

indescribable [ɪndɪˈskraɪbəb(ə)l] *a* indescriptible.

indestructible [ɪndɪˈstrʌktəb(ə)l] *a* indestructible.

indeterminate [ɪndɪˈtɜːmɪnət] *a* indéterminé.

index ['ɪndeks] *n* (*in book etc*) index *m*; (*in library*) catalogue *m*; (*number, sign*) indice *m*; **i. card** fiche *f*; **i. finger** index *m*; – *vt* (*classify*) classer. ◆**i.-'linked** *a Econ* indexé (**to** sur).

India ['ɪndɪə] *n* Inde *f*. ◆**Indian** *a & n* indien, -ienne (*mf*).

indicate ['ɪndɪkeɪt] *vt* indiquer (**that** que); **I was indicating right** *Aut* j'avais mis mon clignotant droit. ◆**indi'cation** *n* (*sign*) indice *m*, indication *f*; (*idea*) idée *f*. ◆**in'dicative** *a* indicatif (**of** de); – *n* (*mood*) *Gram* indicatif *m*. ◆**indicator** *n* (*instrument*) indicateur *m*; (*sign*) indication *f* (**of** de); *Aut* clignotant *m*; (*display board*) tableau *m* (indicateur).

indict [ɪnˈdaɪt] *vt* inculper (**for** de). ◆**—ment** *n* inculpation *f*.

Indies ['ɪndɪz] *npl* **the West I.** les Antilles *fpl*.

indifferent [ɪnˈdɪf(ə)rənt] *a* indifférent (**to** à); (*mediocre*) *Pej* médiocre. ◆**indifference** *n* indifférence *f* (**to** à). ◆**indifferently** *adv* indifféremment.

indigenous [ɪnˈdɪdʒɪnəs] *a* indigène.

indigestion [ɪndɪˈdʒestʃ(ə)n] *n* dyspepsie *f*; (**an attack of**) **i.** une indigestion, une crise de foie. ◆**indigestible** *a* indigeste.

indignant [ɪnˈdɪgnənt] *a* indigné (**at** de, **with** contre); **to become i.** s'indigner. ◆**indignantly** *adv* avec indignation. ◆**indig'nation** *n* indignation *f*.

indignity [ɪnˈdɪgnɪtɪ] *n* indignité *f*.

indigo ['ɪndɪgəʊ] *n* & *a* (*colour*) indigo *m* & *a inv*.

indirect [ɪndaɪˈrekt] *a* indirect. ◆**—ly** *adv* indirectement.

indiscreet [ɪndɪˈskriːt] *a* indiscret. ◆**indiscretion** *n* indiscrétion *f*.

indiscriminate [ɪndɪˈskrɪmɪnət] *a* (*person*)

qui manque de discernement; (*random*) fait, donné *etc* au hasard. ◆**―ly** *adv* (*at random*) au hasard; (*without discrimination*) sans discernement.

indispensable [ɪndɪ'spensəb(ə)l] *a* indispensable (**to** à).

indisposed [ɪndɪ'spəʊzd] *a* (*unwell*) indisposé. ◆**indispo'sition** *n* indisposition *f*.

indisputable [ɪndɪ'spjuːtəb(ə)l] *a* incontestable.

indistinct [ɪndɪ'stɪŋkt] *a* indistinct.

indistinguishable [ɪndɪ'stɪŋɡwɪʃəb(ə)l] *a* indifférenciable (**from** de).

individual [ɪndɪ'vɪdʒʊəl] *a* individuel; (*unusual, striking*) singulier, particulier; ― *n* (*person*) individu *m*. ◆**individualist** *n* individualiste *mf*. ◆**individua'listic** *a* individualiste. ◆**individu'ality** *n* (*distinctiveness*) individualité *f*. ◆**individually** *adv* (*separately*) individuellement; (*unusually*) de façon (très) personnelle.

indivisible [ɪndɪ'vɪzəb(ə)l] *a* indivisible.

Indo-China [ɪndəʊ'tʃaɪnə] *n* Indochine *f*.

indoctrinate [ɪn'dɒktrɪneɪt] *vt Pej* endoctriner. ◆**indoctri'nation** *n* endoctrinement *m*.

indolent ['ɪndələnt] *a* indolent. ◆**indolence** *n* indolence *f*.

indomitable [ɪn'dɒmɪtəb(ə)l] *a* (*will, energy*) indomptable.

Indonesia [ɪndəʊ'niːʒə] *n* Indonésie *f*.

indoor ['ɪndɔːr] *a* (*games, shoes etc*) d'intérieur; (*swimming pool etc*) couvert. ◆**in'doors** *adv* à l'intérieur; **to go** *or* **come i.** rentrer.

induce [ɪn'djuːs] *vt* (*persuade*) persuader (**to do** de faire); (*cause*) provoquer; **to i. labour** *Med* déclencher le travail. ◆**―ment** *n* encouragement *m* (**to do** à faire).

indulge [ɪn'dʌldʒ] *vt* (*s.o.'s desires*) satisfaire; (*child etc*) gâter, tout passer à; **to i. oneself** se gâter; ― *vi* **to i. in** (*action*) s'adonner à; (*ice cream etc*) se permettre. ◆**indulgence** *n* indulgence *f*. ◆**indulgent** *a* indulgent (**to** envers, **with** avec).

industrial [ɪn'dʌstrɪəl] *a* industriel; (*conflict, legislation*) du travail; **i. action** action *f* revendicative; **i. park** *Am* complexe *m* industriel. ◆**industrialist** *n* industriel, -ielle *mf*. ◆**industrialized** *a* industrialisé.

industrious [ɪn'dʌstrɪəs] *a* travailleur.

industry ['ɪndəstrɪ] *n* industrie *f*; (*hard work*) application *f*.

inedible [ɪn'edəb(ə)l] *a* immangeable.

ineffective [ɪnɪ'fektɪv] *a* (*measure etc*) sans effet, inefficace; (*person*) incapable. ◆**―ness** *n* inefficacité *f*.

ineffectual [ɪnɪ'fektʃʊəl] *a* (*measure etc*) inefficace; (*person*) incompétent.

inefficient [ɪnɪ'fɪʃ(ə)nt] *a* (*person, measure etc*) inefficace; (*machine*) peu performant. ◆**inefficiency** *n* inefficacité *f*.

ineligible [ɪn'elɪdʒəb(ə)l] *a* (*candidate*) inéligible; **to be i. for** ne pas avoir droit à.

inept [ɪ'nept] *a* (*foolish*) inepte; (*unskilled*) peu habile (**at sth** à qch); (*incompetent*) incapable, inapte. ◆**ineptitude** *n* (*incapacity*) inaptitude *f*.

inequality [ɪnɪ'kwɒlɪtɪ] *n* inégalité *f*.

inert [ɪ'nɜːt] *a* inerte. ◆**inertia** [ɪ'nɜːʃə] *n* inertie *f*.

inescapable [ɪnɪ'skeɪpəb(ə)l] *a* inéluctable.

inevitable [ɪn'evɪtəb(ə)l] *a* inévitable. ◆**inevitably** *adv* inévitablement.

inexcusable [ɪnɪk'skjuːzəb(ə)l] *a* inexcusable.

inexhaustible [ɪnɪɡ'zɔːstəb(ə)l] *a* inépuisable.

inexorable [ɪn'eksərəb(ə)l] *a* inexorable.

inexpensive [ɪnɪk'spensɪv] *a* bon marché *inv*.

inexperience [ɪnɪk'spɪərɪəns] *n* inexpérience *f*. ◆**inexperienced** *a* inexpérimenté.

inexplicable [ɪnɪk'splɪkəb(ə)l] *a* inexplicable.

inexpressible [ɪnɪk'spresəb(ə)l] *a* inexprimable.

inextricable [ɪnɪk'strɪkəb(ə)l] *a* inextricable.

infallible [ɪn'fæləb(ə)l] *a* infaillible. ◆**infalli'bility** *n* infaillibilité *f*.

infamous ['ɪnfəməs] *a* (*evil*) infâme. ◆**infamy** *n* infamie *f*.

infant ['ɪnfənt] *n* (*child*) petit(e) enfant *mf*; (*baby*) nourrisson *m*; **i. school** classes *fpl* préparatoires. ◆**infancy** *n* petite enfance *f*; **to be in its i.** (*of art, technique etc*) en être à ses premiers balbutiements. ◆**infantile** *a* (*illness, reaction etc*) infantile.

infantry ['ɪnfəntrɪ] *n* infanterie *f*.

infatuated [ɪn'fætjʊeɪtɪd] *a* amoureux; **i. with** (*person*) amoureux ou engoué de; (*sport etc*) engoué de. ◆**infatu'ation** *n* engouement *m* (**for, with** pour).

infect [ɪn'fekt] *vt* (*contaminate*) *Med* infecter; **to become infected** s'infecter; **to i. s.o. with sth** communiquer qch à qn. ◆**infection** *n* infection *f*. ◆**infectious** *a* (*disease*) infectieux, contagieux; (*person, laughter etc*) contagieux.

infer [ɪn'fɜːr] *vt* (**-rr-**) déduire (**from** de, **that** que). ◆**'inference** *n* déduction *f*, conclusion *f*.

inferior [ɪn'fɪərɪər] a inférieur (**to** à); (*goods, work*) de qualité inférieure; – n (*person*) Pej inférieur, -eure mf. ◆**inferi'ority** n infériorité f.

infernal [ɪn'fɜːn(ə)l] a infernal. ◆-**ly** adv Fam épouvantablement.

inferno [ɪn'fɜːnəʊ] n (pl -os) (*blaze*) brasier m, incendie m; (*hell*) enfer m.

infertile [ɪn'fɜːtaɪl, Am ɪn'fɜːt(ə)l] a (*person, land*) stérile.

infest [ɪn'fest] vt infester (**with** de).

infidelity [ɪnfɪ'delɪtɪ] n infidélité f.

infighting ['ɪnfaɪtɪŋ] n (*within group*) luttes fpl intestines.

infiltrate ['ɪnfɪltreɪt] vi s'infiltrer (**into** dans); – vt (*group etc*) s'infiltrer dans. ◆**infil'tration** n infiltration f; Pol noyautage m.

infinite ['ɪnfɪnɪt] a & n infini (m). ◆**infinitely** adv infiniment. ◆**in'finity** n Math Phot infini m; **to i.** Math à l'infini.

infinitive [ɪn'fɪnɪtɪv] n Gram infinitif m.

infirm [ɪn'fɜːm] a infirme. ◆**infirmary** n (*sickbay*) infirmerie f; (*hospital*) hôpital m. ◆**infirmity** n (*disability*) infirmité f.

inflame [ɪn'fleɪm] vt enflammer. ◆**inflammable** a inflammable. ◆**infla'mmation** n Med inflammation f. ◆**inflammatory** a (*remark*) incendiaire.

inflate [ɪn'fleɪt] vt (*tyre, prices etc*) gonfler. ◆**inflatable** a gonflable. ◆**inflation** n Econ inflation f. ◆**inflationary** a Econ inflationniste.

inflection [ɪn'flekʃ(ə)n] n Gram flexion f; (*of voice*) inflexion f.

inflexible [ɪn'fleksəb(ə)l] a inflexible.

inflexion [ɪn'flekʃ(ə)n] n = inflection.

inflict [ɪn'flɪkt] vt infliger (**on** à); (*wound*) occasionner (on à).

influence ['ɪnflʊəns] n influence f; **under the i.** of (*anger, drugs*) sous l'effet de; **the i. of drink** or **alcohol** Jur en état d'ébriété; – vt influencer. ◆**influ'ential** a influent.

influenza [ɪnflʊ'enzə] n Med grippe f.

influx ['ɪnflʌks] n flot m, afflux m.

info ['ɪnfəʊ] n Sl tuyaux mpl, renseignements mpl (on sur).

inform [ɪn'fɔːm] vt informer (**of** de, **that** que); – vi **to i. on** dénoncer. ◆-**ed** a informé; **to keep s.o. i.** of tenir au courant de. ◆**informant** n informateur, -trice mf. ◆**informative** a instructif. ◆**informer** n (*police*) **i.** indicateur, -trice mf.

informal [ɪn'fɔːm(ə)l] a (*without fuss*) simple, sans façon; (*occasion*) dénué de formalité; (*tone, expression*) familier; (*announcement*) officieux; (*meeting*) non-officiel. ◆**infor-**

'mality n simplicité f; (*of tone etc*) familiarité f. ◆**informally** adv (*without fuss*) sans cérémonie; (*to meet*) officieusement; (*to dress*) simplement.

information [ɪnfə'meɪʃ(ə)n] n (*facts*) renseignements mpl (**about, on** sur); (*knowledge*) & Math information f; **a piece of i.** un renseignement, une information; **to get some i.** se renseigner.

infrared [ɪnfrə'red] a infrarouge.

infrequent [ɪn'friːkwənt] a peu fréquent.

infringe [ɪn'frɪndʒ] vt (*rule*) contrevenir à; – vi **to i. upon** (*encroach on*) empiéter sur. ◆-**ment** n infraction f (**of** à).

infuriate [ɪn'fjʊərɪeɪt] vt exaspérer. ◆-**ing** a exaspérant.

infuse [ɪn'fjuːz] vt (*tea*) (faire) infuser. ◆**infusion** n infusion f.

ingenious [ɪn'dʒiːnɪəs] a ingénieux. ◆**inge'nuity** n ingéniosité f.

ingot ['ɪŋgət] n lingot m.

ingrained [ɪn'greɪnd] a (*prejudice*) enraciné; **i. dirt** crasse f.

ingratiat/e [ɪn'greɪʃɪeɪt] vt **to i. oneself with** s'insinuer dans les bonnes grâces de. ◆-**ing** a (*person, smile*) insinuant.

ingratitude [ɪn'grætɪtjuːd] n ingratitude f.

ingredient [ɪn'griːdɪənt] n ingrédient m.

ingrown [ɪn'grəʊn] a (*nail*) incarné.

inhabit [ɪn'hæbɪt] vt habiter. ◆-**able** a habitable. ◆**inhabitant** n habitant, -ante mf.

inhale [ɪn'heɪl] vt aspirer; **to i. the smoke** (*of smoker*) avaler la fumée. ◆**inha'lation** n inhalation f. ◆**inhaler** n Med inhalateur m.

inherent [ɪn'hɪərənt] a inhérent (**in** à). ◆-**ly** adv intrinsèquement, en soi.

inherit [ɪn'herɪt] vt hériter (de); (*title*) succéder à. ◆**inheritance** n héritage m; (*process*) Jur succession f; (*cultural*) patrimoine m.

inhibit [ɪn'hɪbɪt] vt (*hinder*) gêner; (*control*) maîtriser; (*prevent*) empêcher (**from** de); **to be inhibited** être inhibé, avoir des inhibitions. ◆**inhi'bition** n inhibition f.

inhospitable [ɪnhɒ'spɪtəb(ə)l] a inhospitalier.

inhuman [ɪn'hjuːmən] a (*not human, cruel*) inhumain. ◆**inhu'mane** a (*not kind*) inhumain. ◆**inhu'manity** n brutalité f, cruauté f.

inimitable [ɪ'nɪmɪtəb(ə)l] a inimitable.

iniquitous [ɪ'nɪkwɪtəs] a inique. ◆**iniquity** n iniquité f.

initial [ɪ'nɪʃ(ə)l] a initial, premier; – n (*letter*) initiale f; (*signature*) paraphe m; –

vt (-ll-, Am -l-) parapher. ◆—ly adv initialement, au début.

initiate ['ɪnʃɪeɪt] vt (reforms) amorcer; (schemes) inaugurer; **to i. s.o. into** initier qn à; **the initiated** les initiés mpl. ◆**initi'ation** n amorce f; inauguration f; initiation f. ◆**initiator** n initiateur, -trice mf.

initiative ['ɪnʃətɪv] n initiative f.

inject [ɪn'dʒekt] vt injecter (into); (new life etc) Fig insuffler (into à). ◆**injection** n Med injection f, piqûre f.

injunction [ɪn'dʒʌŋk(ə)n] n Jur ordonnance f.

injur/e ['ɪndʒər] vt (physically) blesser; (prejudice, damage) nuire à; (one's chances) compromettre; **to i. one's foot**/etc se blesser au pied/etc. ◆—**ed** a blessé; — n **the i.** les blessés mpl. ◆**injury** n (to flesh) blessure f; (fracture) fracture f; (sprain) foulure f; (bruise) contusion f; (wrong) Fig préjudice m.

injurious [ɪn'dʒʊərɪəs] a préjudiciable (to à).

injustice [ɪn'dʒʌstɪs] n injustice f.

ink [ɪŋk] n encre f; **Indian i.** encre f de Chine. ◆**inkpot** n, ◆**inkwell** n encrier m. ◆**inky** a couvert d'encre.

inkling ['ɪŋklɪŋ] n (petite) idée f; **to have some** or **an i. of sth** soupçonner qch, avoir une (petite) idée de qch.

inlaid [ɪn'leɪd] a (marble etc) incrusté (with de); (wood) marqueté.

inland ['ɪnlənd, 'ɪnlænd] a intérieur; — n (intérieur; **I. Revenue** le fisc; — [ɪn'lænd] adv à l'intérieur (des terres).

in-laws ['ɪnlɔːz] npl belle-famille f.

inlet ['ɪnlet] n (of sea) crique f; **i. pipe** tuyau m d'arrivée.

inmate ['ɪnmeɪt] n résident, -ente mf; (of asylum) interné, -ée mf; (of prison) détenu, -ue mf.

inmost ['ɪnməʊst] a le plus profond.

inn [ɪn] n auberge f. ◆**innkeeper** n aubergiste mf.

innards ['ɪnədz] npl Fam entrailles fpl.

innate ['ɪneɪt] a inné.

inner ['ɪnər] a intérieur; (ear) interne; (feelings) intime, profond; **the i. city** le cœur de la ville; **an i. circle** (group of people) un cercle restreint; **the i. circle** le saint des saints; **i. tube** (of tyre) chambre f à air. ◆**innermost** a le plus profond.

inning ['ɪnɪŋ] n Baseball tour m de batte. ◆**innings** n inv Cricket tour m de batte; **a good i.** Fig une vie longue.

innocent ['ɪnəs(ə)nt] a innocent. ◆**inno-**

cence n innocence f. ◆**innocently** adv innocemment.

innocuous [ɪ'nɒkjʊəs] a inoffensif.

innovate ['ɪnəveɪt] vi innover. ◆**inno-'vation** n innovation f. ◆**innovator** n innovateur, -trice mf.

innuendo [ɪnjʊ'endəʊ] n (pl -oes or -os) insinuation f.

innumerable [ɪ'njuːmərəb(ə)l] a innombrable.

inoculate [ɪ'nɒkjʊleɪt] vt vacciner (against contre). ◆**inocu'lation** n inoculation f.

inoffensive [ɪnə'fensɪv] a inoffensif.

inoperative [ɪn'ɒprətɪv] a (without effect) inopérant.

inopportune [ɪn'ɒpətjuːn] a inopportun.

inordinate [ɪ'nɔːdɪnət] a excessif. ◆—**ly** adv excessivement.

in-patient ['ɪnpeɪʃ(ə)nt] n malade mf hospitalisé(e).

input ['ɪnpʊt] n (computer operation) entrée f; (data) données fpl; (current) El énergie f.

inquest ['ɪnkwest] n enquête f.

inquir/e [ɪn'kwaɪər] vi se renseigner (about sur); **to i. after** s'informer de; **to i. into** examiner, faire une enquête sur; — vt demander; **to i. how to get to** demander le chemin de. ◆—**ing** a (mind, look) curieux. ◆**inquiry** n (question) question f; (request for information) demande f de renseignements; (information) renseignements mpl; Jur enquête f; **to make inquiries** demander des renseignements; (of police) enquêter.

inquisitive [ɪn'kwɪzɪtɪv] a curieux. ◆**inquisitively** adv avec curiosité. ◆**inqui'sition** n (inquiry) & Rel inquisition f.

inroads ['ɪnrəʊdz] npl (attacks) incursions fpl (into dans); **to make i. into** (start on) Fig entamer.

insane [ɪn'seɪn] a fou, dément. ◆**insanely** adv comme un fou. ◆**insanity** n folie f, démence f.

insanitary [ɪn'sænɪt(ə)rɪ] a insalubre.

insatiable [ɪn'seɪʃəb(ə)l] a insatiable.

inscribe [ɪn'skraɪb] vt inscrire; (book) dédicacer (to à). ◆**inscription** n inscription f; dédicace f.

inscrutable [ɪn'skruːtəb(ə)l] a impénétrable.

insect ['ɪnsekt] n insecte m; — a (powder, spray) insecticide m. **i. repellant** crème f anti-insecte. ◆**in'secticide** n insecticide m.

insecure [ɪnsɪ'kjʊər] a (not fixed) peu solide; (furniture, ladder) branlant, bancal; (window) mal fermé; (uncertain) incertain;

(*unsafe*) peu sûr; (*person*) qui manque d'assurance. ◆**insecurity** n (*of person, situation*) insécurité f.

insemination [ɪnsemɪ'neɪʃ(ə)n] n Med insémination f.

insensible [ɪn'sensəb(ə)l] a Med inconscient.

insensitive [ɪn'sensɪtɪv] a insensible (**to** à). ◆**insen'tivity** n insensibilité f.

inseparable [ɪn'sep(ə)rəb(ə)l] a inséparable (**from** de).

insert [ɪn'sɜːt] vt insérer (**in, into** dans). ◆**insertion** n insertion f.

inshore ['ɪnʃɔːr] a côtier.

inside [ɪn'saɪd] adv dedans, à l'intérieur; **come i.!** entrez!; – prep à l'intérieur de, dans; (*time*) en moins de; – n dedans m, intérieur m; pl (*stomach*) Fam ventre m; **on the i.** à l'intérieur (**of** de); **i. out** (*coat, socks etc*) à l'envers; (*to know, study etc*) à fond; **to turn everything i. out** Fig tout chambouler; – a intérieur; (*information*) obtenu à la source; **the i. lane** Aut la voie de gauche, Am la voie de droite.

insidious [ɪn'sɪdɪəs] a insidieux.

insight ['ɪnsaɪt] n perspicacité f; **to give an i. into** (*s.o.'s character*) permettre de comprendre, éclairer; (*question*) donner un aperçu de.

insignia [ɪn'sɪgnɪə] npl (*of important person*) insignes mpl.

insignificant [ɪnsɪg'nɪfɪkənt] a insignifiant. ◆**insignificance** n insignifiance f.

insincere [ɪnsɪn'sɪər] a peu sincère. ◆**insincerity** n manque m de sincérité.

insinuate [ɪn'sɪnjʊeɪt] vt **1** Pej insinuer (**that** que). **2 to i. oneself into** s'insinuer dans. ◆**insinu'ation** n insinuation f.

insipid [ɪn'sɪpɪd] a insipide.

insist [ɪn'sɪst] vi insister (**on doing** pour faire); **to i. on sth** (*demand*) exiger qch; (*assert*) affirmer qch; – vt (*order*) insister (**that** pour que); (*declare firmly*) affirmer (**that** que); **I i. that you come or on your coming** j'insiste pour que tu viennes. ◆**insistence** n insistance f; **her i. on seeing me** l'insistance qu'elle met à vouloir me voir. ◆**insistent** a insistant; **I was i.** (**about it**) j'ai été pressant. ◆**insistently** adv avec insistance.

insolent ['ɪnsələnt] a insolent. ◆**insolence** n insolence f. ◆**insolently** adv insolemment.

insoluble [ɪn'sɒljʊb(ə)l] a insoluble.

insolvent [ɪn'sɒlvənt] a Fin insolvable.

insomnia [ɪn'sɒmnɪə] n insomnie f. ◆**insomniac** n insomniaque m/f.

insomuch as [ɪnsəʊ'mʌtʃəz] adv = **inasmuch as.**

inspect [ɪn'spekt] vt inspecter; (*tickets*) contrôler; (*troops*) passer en revue. ◆**inspection** n inspection f; contrôle m; revue f. ◆**inspector** n inspecteur, -trice mf; (*on bus*) contrôleur, -euse mf.

inspire [ɪn'spaɪər] vt inspirer (**s.o. with sth** qch à qn); **to be inspired to do** avoir l'inspiration de faire. ◆**–ed** a inspiré. ◆**–ing** a qui inspire. ◆**inspi'ration** n inspiration f; (*person*) source f d'inspiration.

instability [ɪnstə'bɪlɪtɪ] n instabilité f.

install [ɪn'stɔːl] vt installer. ◆**insta'llation** n installation f.

instalment [ɪn'stɔːlmənt] (Am **installment**) n (*of money*) acompte m, versement m (partiel); (*of serial*) épisode m; (*of publication*) fascicule m; **to buy on the i. plan** Am acheter à crédit.

instance ['ɪnstəns] n (*example*) exemple m; (*case*) cas m; (*occasion*) circonstance f; **for i. par exemple**; **in the first i.** en premier lieu.

instant ['ɪnstənt] a immédiat; **i. coffee** café m soluble or instantané, nescafé® m; **of the 3rd i.** (*in letter*) Com du 3 courant; – n (*moment*) instant m; **this (very) i.** (*at once*) à l'instant; **the i. that** (*as soon as*) dès que. ◆**instan'taneous** a instantané. ◆**instantly** adv immédiatement.

instead [ɪn'sted] adv (*as alternative*) au lieu de cela, plutôt; **i. of sth** au lieu de qch, à la place de qch; **i.** (**of him or her**) à sa place.

instep ['ɪnstep] n (*of foot*) cou-de-pied m; (*of shoe*) cambrure f.

instigate ['ɪnstɪgeɪt] vt provoquer. ◆**insti'gation** n instigation f. ◆**instigator** n instigateur, -trice mf.

instil [ɪn'stɪl] vt (**-ll-**) (*idea*) inculquer (**into** à); (*courage*) insuffler (**into** à).

instinct ['ɪnstɪŋkt] n instinct m; **by i.** d'instinct. ◆**in'stinctive** a instinctif. ◆**in'stinctively** adv instinctivement.

institute ['ɪnstɪtjuːt] **1** vt (*rule, practice*) instituer; (*inquiry, proceedings*) Jur entamer, intenter. **2** n Institut m. ◆**insti'tution** n (*custom, private or charitable organization etc*) institution f; (*school, hospital*) établissement m; (*home*) Med asile m. ◆**insti'tutional** a institutionnel.

instruct [ɪn'strʌkt] vt (*teach*) enseigner (**s.o. in sth** qch à qn); **to i. s.o. about sth** (*inform*) instruire qn de qch; **to i. s.o. to do** (*order*) charger qn de faire. ◆**instruction** n (*teaching*) instruction f; pl (*orders*) instructions fpl; **instructions** (**for use**) mode m

d'emploi. ◆**instructive** a instructif.
◆**instructor** n professeur m; Sp moniteur, -trice mf; Mil instructeur m; Univ Am maître-assistant, -ante mf; **driving i.** moniteur, -trice mf de conduite.

instrument ['ɪnstrəmənt] n instrument m.
◆**instru'mental** a Mus instrumental; **to be i. in sth/in doing sth** contribuer à qch/à faire qch. ◆**instru'mentalist** n Mus instrumentaliste mf. ◆**instrumen'tation** n Mus orchestration f.

insubordinate [ɪnsəˈbɔːdɪnət] a insubordiné. ◆**insubordi'nation** n insubordination f.

insubstantial [ɪnsəbˈstænʃ(ə)l] a (argument, evidence) peu solide.

insufferable [ɪnˈsʌf(ə)rəb(ə)l] a intolérable.

insufficient [ɪnsəˈfɪʃənt] a insuffisant. ◆**-ly** adv insuffisamment.

insular ['ɪnsjʊlər] a (climate) insulaire; (views) Pej étroit, borné.

insulate ['ɪnsjʊleɪt] vt (against cold etc) & El isoler; (against sound) insonoriser; **to i. s.o. from** Fig protéger qn de; **insulating tape** chatterton m. ◆**insu'lation** n isolation f; insonorisation f; (material) isolant m.

insulin ['ɪnsjʊlɪn] n Med insuline f.

insult [ɪnˈsʌlt] vt insulter; – ['ɪnsʌlt] n insulte f (to à).

insuperable [ɪnˈsuːp(ə)rəb(ə)l] a insurmontable.

insure [ɪnˈʃʊər] vt 1 (protect against damage etc) assurer (**against** contre). 2 Am = ensure. ◆**insurance** n assurance f; **i. company** compagnie f d'assurances; **i. policy** police f d'assurance.

insurgent [ɪnˈsɜːdʒənt] a & n insurgé, -ée (mf).

insurmountable [ɪnsəˈmaʊntəb(ə)l] a insurmontable.

insurrection [ɪnsəˈrekʃ(ə)n] n insurrection f.

intact [ɪnˈtækt] a intact.

intake ['ɪnteɪk] n (of food) consommation f; Sch Univ admissions fpl; Tech admission f.

intangible [ɪnˈtændʒəb(ə)l] a intangible.

integral ['ɪntɪɡrəl] a intégral; **to be an i. part of** faire partie intégrante de.

integrate ['ɪntɪɡreɪt] vt intégrer (**into** dans); – vi s'intégrer (**into** dans); (racially) **integrated** (school etc) Am où se pratique la déségrégation raciale. ◆**integration** n intégration f; (racial) **i.** déségrégation f raciale.

integrity [ɪnˈteɡrɪti] n intégrité f.

intellect ['ɪntɪlekt] n (faculty) intellect m, intelligence f; (cleverness, person) intelli-

gence f. ◆**inte'llectual** a & n intellectuel, -elle (mf).

intelligence [ɪnˈtelɪdʒəns] n intelligence f; Mil renseignements mpl. ◆**intelligent** a intelligent. ◆**intelligently** adv intelligemment. ◆**intelli'gentsia** n intelligentsia f.

intelligible [ɪnˈtelɪdʒəb(ə)l] a intelligible. ◆**intelligi'bility** n intelligibilité f.

intemperance [ɪnˈtempərəns] n intempérance f.

intend [ɪnˈtend] vt (gift, remark etc) destiner (**for** à); **to i. to do** avoir l'intention de faire; **I i. you to stay** mon intention est que vous restiez. ◆**-ed** a (deliberate) intentionnel, voulu; (planned) projeté; **i. to be** (meant) destiné à être. ◆**intention** n intention f (of doing de faire). ◆**intentional** a intentionnel; **it wasn't i.** ce n'était pas fait exprès. ◆**intentionally** adv intentionnellement, exprès.

intense [ɪnˈtens] a intense; (interest) vif; (person) passionné. ◆**intensely** adv intensément; Fig extrêmement. ◆**intensifi'cation** n intensification f. ◆**intensify** vt intensifier; – vi s'intensifier. ◆**intensity** n intensité f. ◆**intensive** a intensif; **in i. care** Med en réanimation.

intent [ɪnˈtent] 1 a (look) attentif; **i. on** (task) absorbé par; **i. on doing** résolu à faire. 2 n intention f; **to all intents and purposes** en fait, essentiellement.

inter [ɪnˈtɜːr] vt (-rr-) enterrer.

inter- [ɪntə(r)] pref inter-.

interact [ɪntərˈækt] vi (of ideas etc) être interdépendants; (of people) agir conjointement; Ch interagir. ◆**interaction** n interaction f.

intercede [ɪntəˈsiːd] vi intercéder (**with** auprès de).

intercept [ɪntəˈsept] vt intercepter. ◆**interception** n interception f.

interchange ['ɪntətʃeɪndʒ] n Aut échangeur m. ◆**inter'changeable** a interchangeable.

intercom ['ɪntəkɒm] n interphone m.

interconnect/ed [ɪntəkəˈnektɪd] a (facts etc) liés. ◆**-ing** a **i. rooms** pièces fpl communicantes.

intercontinental [ɪntəkɒntɪˈnent(ə)l] a intercontinental.

intercourse ['ɪntəkɔːs] n (sexual, social) rapports mpl.

interdependent [ɪntədɪˈpendənt] a interdépendant; (parts of machine) solidaire.

interest ['ɪnt(ə)rɪst, 'ɪntrəst] n intérêt m; Fin intérêts mpl; **an i. in** (stake) Com des intérêts dans; **his or her i. is** (hobby etc) ce qui l'intéresse c'est; **to take an i.** in s'intéresser à; **to be of i.** to s.o. intéresser qn; – *vt* intéresser. **◆—ed** *a (involved)* intéressé; *(look)* d'intérêt; **to seem i.** sembler intéressé (in par); **to be i.** in sth/s.o. s'intéresser à qch/qn; **I'm i.** in doing ça m'intéresse de faire; **are you i.?** ça vous intéresse? **◆—ing** *a* intéressant. **◆—ingly** *adv* **i.** (enough), she ... curieusement, elle ....

interface ['ɪntəfeɪs] *n Tech* interface *f*.

interfer/e [ɪntəˈfɪər] *vi* se mêler des affaires d'autrui; **to i.** in s'ingérer dans; **to i. with** *(upset)* déranger; *(touch)* toucher (à). **◆—ing** *a (person)* importun. **◆interference** *n* ingérence *f*; *Rad* parasites *mpl*.

interim ['ɪntərɪm] *n* intérim *m*; **in the i.** pendant l'intérim; – *a (measure etc)* provisoire; *(post)* intérimaire.

interior [ɪnˈtɪərɪər] *a* intérieur; – *n* intérieur *m*; **Department of the I.** *Am* ministère *m* de l'Intérieur.

interjection [ɪntəˈdʒekʃ(ə)n] *n* interjection *f*.

interlock [ɪntəˈlɒk] *vi Tech* s'emboîter.

interloper [ɪn'tələupər] *n* intrus, -use *mf*.

interlude ['ɪntəluːd] *n* intervalle *m*; *Th* intermède *m*; *Mus TV* interlude *m*.

intermarry [ɪntəˈmærɪ] *vi* se marier (entre eux). **◆intermarriage** *n* mariage *m* (entre personnes de races etc différentes).

intermediary [ɪntəˈmiːdɪərɪ] *a & n* intermédiaire (*mf*).

intermediate [ɪntəˈmiːdɪət] *a* intermédiaire; *(course)* *Sch* moyen.

interminable [ɪnˈtɜːmɪnəb(ə)l] *a* interminable.

intermingle [ɪntəˈmɪŋɡ(ə)l] *vi* se mélanger.

intermission [ɪntəˈmɪʃ(ə)n] *n Cin Th* entracte *m*.

intermittent [ɪntəˈmɪtənt] *a* intermittent. **◆—ly** *adv* par intermittence.

intern 1 [ɪnˈtɜːn] *vt Pol* interner. **2** ['ɪntɜːn] *n Med Am* interne *mf* (des hôpitaux). **◆inter'nee** *n* interné, -ée *mf*. **◆in'ternment** *n Pol* internement *m*.

internal [ɪnˈtɜːn(ə)l] *a* interne; *(policy, flight)* intérieur; **i.´ combustion engine** moteur *m* à explosion; **the I. Revenue Service** *Am* le fisc. **◆—ly** *adv* intérieurement.

international [ɪntəˈnæʃ(ə)nəl] *a* international; *(fame, reputation)* mondial; – *n (match)* rencontre *f* internationale; *(player)* international *m*. **◆—ly** *adv* *(renowned etc)* mondialement.

interplanetary [ɪntəˈplænɪt(ə)rɪ] *a* interplanétaire.

interplay ['ɪntəpleɪ] *n* interaction *f*, jeu *m*.

interpolate [ɪnˈtɜːpəleɪt] *vt* interpoler.

interpret [ɪnˈtɜːprɪt] *vt* interpréter; – *vi Ling* faire l'interprète. **◆interpre'tation** *n* interprétation *f*. **◆interpreter** *n* interprète *mf*.

interrelated [ɪntərɪˈleɪtɪd] *a* en corrélation. **◆interrelation** *n* corrélation *f*.

interrogate [ɪnˈterəɡeɪt] *vt (question closely)* interroger. **◆interro'gation** *n* interrogation *f*; *Jur* interrogatoire *m*. **◆interrogator** *n (questioner)* interrogateur, -trice *mf*.

interrogative [ɪntəˈrɒɡətɪv] *a & n Gram* interrogatif (*m*).

interrupt [ɪntəˈrʌpt] *vt* interrompre. **◆interruption** *n* interruption *f*.

intersect [ɪntəˈsekt] *vt* couper; – *vi* s'entrecouper, se couper. **◆intersection** *n (crossroads)* croisement *m*; *(of lines etc)* intersection *f*.

intersperse [ɪntəˈspɜːs] *vt* parsemer (with de).

intertwine [ɪntəˈtwaɪn] *vt* entrelacer.

interval ['ɪntəv(ə)l] *n* intervalle *m*; *Th* entracte *m*; **at intervals** *(time)* de temps à autre; *(space)* par intervalles; **bright intervals** *Met* éclaircies *fpl*.

intervene [ɪntəˈviːn] *vi* intervenir; *(of event)* survenir; **ten years intervened** dix années s'écoulèrent; **if nothing intervenes** s'il n'arrive rien entre-temps. **◆intervention** *n* intervention *f*.

interview ['ɪntəvjuː] *n* entrevue *f*, entretien *m* (with avec); *Journ TV* interview *f*; **to call for (an) i.** convoquer; – *vt* avoir une entrevue avec; *Journ TV* interviewer. **◆—er** *n Journ TV* interviewer *m*; *Com Pol* enquêteur, -euse *mf*.

intestine [ɪnˈtestɪn] *n* intestin *m*.

intimate¹ ['ɪntɪmət] *a* intime; *(friendship)* profond; *(knowledge, analysis)* approfondi. **◆intimacy** *n* intimité *f*. **◆intimately** *adv* intimement.

intimate² ['ɪntɪmeɪt] *vt (hint)* suggérer (that que). **◆inti'mation** *n (announcement)* annonce *f*; *(hint)* suggestion *f*; *(sign)* indication *f*.

intimidate [ɪnˈtɪmɪdeɪt] *vt* intimider. **◆intimi'dation** *n* intimidation *f*.

into ['ɪntuː, *unstressed* 'ɪntə] *prep* **1** dans; **to put i.** mettre dans; **to go i.** *(room, detail)* entrer dans. **2** en; **to translate i.** traduire en; **to change i.** transformer *ou* changer en; **to go i. town** aller en ville; **i. pieces** *(to break etc)* en morceaux. **3** **to be i. yoga**/*etc Fam* être à fond dans le yoga/*etc*.

intolerable [ɪnˈtɒlərəb(ə)l] *a* intolérable

(that que (+ *sub*)). ◆**intolerably** *adv* insupportablement. ◆**intolerance** *n* intolérance *f*. ◆**intolerant** *a* intolérant (**of** de). ◆**intolerantly** *adv* avec intolérance.

intonation [ɪntə'neɪʃ(ə)n] *n Ling* intonation *f*.

intoxicate [ɪn'tɒksɪkeɪt] *vt* enivrer. ◆**intoxicated** *a* ivre. ◆**intoxi'cation** *n* ivresse *f*.

intra- ['ɪntrə] *pref* intra-.

intransigent [ɪn'trænsɪdʒənt] *a* intransigeant. ◆**intransigence** *n* intransigeance *f*.

intransitive [ɪn'trænsɪtɪv] *a* & *n Gram* intransitif (*m*).

intravenous [ɪntrə'viːnəs] *a Med* intraveineux.

intrepid [ɪn'trepɪd] *a* intrépide.

intricate ['ɪntrɪkət] *a* complexe, compliqué. ◆**intricacy** *n* complexité *f*. ◆**intricately** *adv* de façon complexe.

intrigu/e 1 ['ɪntriːg] *vt* (*interest*) intriguer; **I'm intrigued to know** . . . je suis curieux de savoir . . . **2** ['ɪntriːg] *n* (*plot*) intrigue *f*. ◆**-ing** *a* (*news etc*) curieux.

intrinsic [ɪn'trɪnsɪk] *a* intrinsèque. ◆**intrinsically** *adv* intrinsèquement.

introduce [ɪntrə'djuːs] *vt* (*insert, bring in*) introduire (**into** dans); (*programme, subject*) présenter; **to i. s.o. to s.o.** présenter qn à qn; **to i. s.o. to** Dickens/geography/*etc* faire découvrir Dickens/la géographie/*etc* à qn. ◆**introduction** *n* introduction *f*; présentation *f*; (*book title*) initiation *f*; **her i. to** (*life abroad etc*) son premier contact avec. ◆**introductory** *a* (*words*) d'introduction; (*speech*) de présentation; (*course*) d'initiation.

introspective [ɪntrə'spektɪv] *a* introspectif. ◆**introspection** *n* introspection *f*.

introvert ['ɪntrəvɜːt] *n* introverti, -ie *mf*.

intrude [ɪn'truːd] *vi* (*of person*) s'imposer (**on** s.o. à qn), déranger (**on** s.o. qn); **to i. on** (*s.o.'s time etc*) abuser de. ◆**intruder** *n* intrus, -use *mf*. ◆**intrusion** *n* intrusion *f* (**into** dans); **forgive my i.** pardonnez-moi de vous avoir dérangé.

intuition [ɪntjuː'ɪʃ(ə)n] *n* intuition *f*. ◆**in'tuitive** *a* intuitif.

inundate ['ɪnʌndeɪt] *vt* inonder (**with** de); **inundated with work** submergé de travail. ◆**inun'dation** *n* inondation *f*.

invad/e [ɪn'veɪd] *vt* envahir; (*privacy*) violer. ◆**-er** *n* envahisseur, -euse *mf*.

invalid 1 ['ɪnvəliːd] *a* & *n* malade (*mf*); (*through injury*) infirme (*mf*); **i. car** voiture *f* d'infirme.

invalid 2 [ɪn'vælɪd] *a* non valable. ◆**invalidate** *vt* invalider, annuler.

invaluable [ɪn'væljʊəb(ə)l] *a* (*help etc*) inestimable.

invariab/le [ɪn'veərɪəb(ə)l] *a* invariable. ◆**-ly** *adv* invariablement.

invasion [ɪn'veɪʒ(ə)n] *n* invasion *f*; **i. of s.o.'s privacy** intrusion *f* dans la vie privée de qn.

invective [ɪn'vektɪv] *n* invective *f*.

inveigh [ɪn'veɪ] *vi* **to i. against** invectiver contre.

inveigle [ɪn'veɪg(ə)l] *vt* **to i. s.o. into doing** amener qn à faire par la ruse.

invent [ɪn'vent] *vt* inventer. ◆**invention** *n* invention *f*. ◆**inventive** *a* inventif. ◆**inventiveness** *n* esprit *m* d'invention. ◆**inventor** *n* inventeur, -trice *mf*.

inventory ['ɪnvənt(ə)rɪ] *n* inventaire *m*.

inverse [ɪn'vɜːs] *a* & *n Math* inverse (*m*).

invert [ɪn'vɜːt] *vt* intervertir; **inverted commas** guillemets *mpl*. ◆**inversion** *n* intervension *f*; *Gram Anat etc* inversion *f*.

invest [ɪn'vest] *vt* (*funds*) investir (**in** dans); (*money*) placer, investir; (*time, effort*) consacrer (**in** à); **to i. s.o. with** (*endow*) investir qn de; − *vi* **to i. in** (*project*) placer son argent dans; (*firm*) investir dans; (*house, radio etc*) *Fig* se payer. ◆**investiture** *n* (*of bishop etc*) investiture *f*. ◆**investment** *n* investissement *m*, placement *m*. ◆**investor** *n* (*in shares*) actionnaire *mf*; (*saver*) épargnant, -ante *mf*.

investigate [ɪn'vestɪgeɪt] *vt* (*examine*) examiner, étudier; (*crime*) enquêter sur. ◆**investi'gation** *n* examen *m*, étude *f*; (*by police*) enquête *f* (**of** sur); (*inquiry*) enquête *f*, investigation *f*. ◆**investigator** *n* (*detective*) enquêteur, -euse *mf*.

inveterate [ɪn'vetərət] *a* invétéré.

invidious [ɪn'vɪdɪəs] *a* qui suscite la jalousie; (*hurtful*) blessant; (*odious*) odieux.

invigilate [ɪn'vɪdʒɪleɪt] *vi* être de surveillance (**à un examen**). ◆**invigilator** *n* surveillant, -ante *mf*.

invigorate [ɪn'vɪgəreɪt] *vt* revigorer. ◆**-ing** *a* stimulant.

invincible [ɪn'vɪnsɪb(ə)l] *a* invincible.

invisible [ɪn'vɪzɪb(ə)l] *a* invisible; **i. ink** encre *f* sympathique.

invit/e [ɪn'vaɪt] *vt* inviter (**to do** à faire); (*ask for*) demander; (*lead to, give occasion for*) appeler; (*trouble*) chercher; **to i. out** inviter (à sortir); **to i. over** inviter (à venir); − ['ɪnvaɪt] *n Fam* invitation *f*. ◆**-ing** *a* engageant, invitant; (*food*) appétissant. ◆**invi'tation** *n* invitation *f*.

invoice ['ɪnvɔɪs] *n* facture *f*; − *vt* facturer.

invoke [ɪn'vəʊk] vt invoquer.

involuntar/y [ɪn'vɒləntərɪ] a involontaire. ◆**-ily** adv involontairement.

involv/e [ɪn'vɒlv] vt (include) mêler (qn) (in à), impliquer (qn) (in dans); (associate) associer (qn) (in à); (entail) entraîner; **to i. oneself, get involved** (commit oneself) s'engager (in dans); **to i. s.o. in expense** entraîner qn à des dépenses; **the job involves going abroad** le poste nécessite des déplacements à l'étranger. ◆**-ed** a (complicated) compliqué; **the factors/etc i.** (at stake) les facteurs/etc en jeu; **the person i.** la personne en question; **i. with s.o.** mêlé aux affaires de qn; **personally i.** concerné; **emotionally i.** with amoureux de; **to become i.** (of police) intervenir. ◆**-ement** n participation f (in à), implication f (in dans); (commitment) engagement m (in dans); (problem) difficulté f; **emotional i.** liaison f.

invulnerable [ɪn'vʌlnərəb(ə)l] a invulnérable.

inward ['ɪnwəd] a & adv (movement, to move) vers l'intérieur. – a (inner) intérieur. ◆**i.-looking** a replié sur soi. ◆**inwardly** adv (inside) à l'intérieur; (to laugh, curse etc) intérieurement. ◆**inwards** adv vers l'intérieur.

iodine ['aɪədiːn, Am 'aɪədaɪn] n Med teinture f d'iode.

iota [aɪ'əʊtə] n (of truth etc) grain m; (in text) iota m.

IOU [aɪəʊ'juː] n abbr (I owe you) reconnaissance f de dette.

IQ [aɪ'kjuː] n abbr (intelligence quotient) QI m inv.

Iran [ɪ'rɑːn] n Iran m. ◆**Iranian** [ɪ'reɪnɪən] a & n iranien, -ienne (mf).

Iraq [ɪ'rɑːk] n Irak m. ◆**Iraqi** a & n irakien, -ienne (mf).

irascible [ɪ'ræsəb(ə)l] a irascible.

ire ['aɪər] n Lit courroux m. ◆**i'rate** a furieux.

Ireland ['aɪələnd] n Irlande f. ◆**Irish** a irlandais; – n (language) irlandais m. ◆**Irishman** n (pl -men) Irlandais m. ◆**Irishwoman** n (pl -women) Irlandaise f.

iris ['aɪərɪs] n Anat Bot iris m.

irk [ɜːk] vt ennuyer. ◆**irksome** a ennuyeux.

iron ['aɪən] n fer m; (for clothes) fer m (à repasser); **old i., scrap i.** ferraille f; **i. and steel industry** sidérurgie f; **the I. Curtain** Pol le rideau de fer; – vt (clothes) repasser; **to i. out** (difficulties) Fig aplanir. ◆**-ing** n repassage m; **i. board** planche f à repasser. ◆**ironmonger** n quincaillier m. ◆**iron-**

mongery n quincaillerie f. ◆**ironwork** n ferronnerie f.

irony ['aɪərənɪ] n ironie f. ◆**i'ronic(al)** a ironique.

irradiate [ɪ'reɪdɪeɪt] vt irradier.

irrational [ɪ'ræʃən(ə)l] a (act) irrationnel; (fear) irraisonné; (person) peu rationnel, illogique.

irreconcilable [ɪrekən'saɪləb(ə)l] a irréconciliable, inconciliable; (views, laws etc) inconciliable.

irrefutable [ɪrɪ'fjuːtəb(ə)l] a irréfutable.

irregular [ɪ'regjʊlər] a irrégulier. ◆**irregu'larity** n irrégularité f.

irrelevant [ɪ'reləvənt] a (remark) non pertinent; (course) peu utile; **i. to** sans rapport avec; **that's i.** ça n'a rien à voir. ◆**irrelevance** n manque m de rapport.

irreparable [ɪ'rep(ə)rəb(ə)l] a (harm, loss) irréparable.

irreplaceable [ɪrɪ'pleɪsəb(ə)l] a irremplaçable.

irrepressible [ɪrɪ'presəb(ə)l] a (laughter etc) irrépressible.

irresistible [ɪrɪ'zɪstəb(ə)l] a (person, charm etc) irrésistible.

irresolute [ɪ'rezəluːt] a irrésolu, indécis.

irrespective of [ɪrɪ'spektɪvəv] prep sans tenir compte de.

irresponsible [ɪrɪ'spɒnsəb(ə)l] a (act) irréfléchi; (person) irresponsable.

irretrievable [ɪrɪ'triːvəb(ə)l] a irréparable.

irreverent [ɪ'revərənt] a irrévérencieux.

irreversible [ɪrɪ'vɜːsəb(ə)l] a (process) irréversible; (decision) irrévocable.

irrevocable [ɪ'revəkəb(ə)l] a irrévocable.

irrigate ['ɪrɪgeɪt] vt irriguer. ◆**irri'gation** n irrigation f.

irritat/e ['ɪrɪteɪt] vt irriter. ◆**-ing** a irritant. ◆**irritable** a (easily annoyed) irritable. ◆**irritant** a irritant m. ◆**irri'tation** n (anger) & Med irritation f.

is [ɪz] see be.

Islam ['ɪzlɑːm] n islam m. ◆**Islamic** [ɪz'læmɪk] a islamique.

island ['aɪlənd] n île f; **traffic i.** refuge m; – a insulaire. ◆**islander** n insulaire mf. ◆**isle** [aɪl] n île f; **the British Isles** les îles Britanniques.

isolate ['aɪsəleɪt] vt isoler (from de). ◆**isolated** a (remote, unique) isolé. ◆**iso'lation** n isolement m; **in i.** isolément.

Israel ['ɪzreɪl] n Israël m. ◆**Is'raeli** a & n israélien, -ienne (mf).

issue ['ɪʃuː] vt (book etc) publier; (an order) donner; (tickets) distribuer; (passport) délivrer; (stamps, banknotes) émettre;

(*warning*) lancer; (*supply*) fournir (**with** de, **to** à); – *vi* to i. **from** (*of smell*) se dégager de; (*stem from*) provenir de; – *n* (*matter*) question *f*; (*problem*) problème *m*; (*outcome*) résultat *m*; (*of text*) publication *f*; (*of stamps etc*) émission *f*; (*newspaper*) numéro *m*; **at** i. (*at stake*) en cause; **to make an** i. **of** faire toute une affaire de.

isthmus ['ismas] *n* Geog isthme *m*.

it [ɪt] *pron* **1** (*subject*) il, elle; (*object*) le, la, l'; (**to**) **it** (*indirect object*) lui; **it bites** (*dog*) il mord; **I've done it** je l'ai fait. **2** (*impersonal*) il; **it's snowing** il neige; **it's hot** il fait chaud. **3** (*non specific*) ce, cela, ça; **it's good** c'est bon; **it was pleasant** c'était agréable; **who is it?** qui est-ce?; **that's it!** (*I agree*) c'est ça!; (*it's done*) ça y est!; **to consider it wise to do** juger prudent de faire; **it was Paul who . . .** c'est Paul qui . . .; **she's got it in her to succeed** elle est capable de réussir; **to have it in for s.o.** en vouloir à qn. **4 of** it, **from** it, **about** it *etc*; **in** it, **to** it, **at** it y; **on** it dessus; **under** it dessous.

italic [ɪ'tælɪk] *a* Typ italique; – *npl* italique *m*.

Italy ['ɪtəlɪ] *n* Italie *f*. ◆**I'talian** *a* & *n* italien, -ienne (*mf*); – *n* (*language*) italien *m*.

itch [ɪtʃ] *n* démangeaison(s) *f*(*pl*); **to have an** i. **to do** avoir une envie folle de faire; – *vi* démanger; **his arm itches** son bras le *or* lui démange; **I'm itching to do** Fig ça me démange de faire. ◆**-ing** *n* démangeaison(s) *f*(*pl*). ◆**itchy** *a* an i. **hand** une main qui me démange.

item ['aɪtəm] *n* Com Journ article *m*; (*matter*) question *f*; (*on entertainment programme*) numéro *m*; **a news** i. une information. ◆**itemize** *vt* détailler.

itinerant [aɪ'tɪnərənt] *a* (*musician, actor*) ambulant; (*judge, preacher*) itinérant.

itinerary [aɪ'tɪnərərɪ] *n* itinéraire *m*.

its [ɪts] *poss a* son, sa, *pl* ses. ◆**it'self** *pron* lui-même, elle-même; (*reflexive*) se, s'; **goodness** i. la bonté même; **by** i. tout seul.

IUD [aɪju'diː] *n abbr* (*intrauterine device*) stérilet *m*.

ivory ['aɪvərɪ] *n* ivoire *m*.

ivy ['aɪvɪ] *n* lierre *m*.

J

J, j [dʒeɪ] *n* J, j *m*.

jab [dʒæb] *vt* (**-bb-**) (*thrust*) enfoncer (**into** dans); (*prick*) piquer (*qn*) (**with sth** du bout de qch); – *n* coup *m* (sec); (*injection*) Med Fam piqûre *f*.

jabber ['dʒæbər] *vi* bavarder, jaser; – *vt* bredouiller. ◆**-ing** *n* bavardage *m*.

jack [dʒæk] **1** *n* Aut cric *m*; – *vt* to i. **up** soulever (*avec un cric*); (*price*) Fig augmenter. **2** *n* Cards valet *m*. **3** *vt* to j. **(in)** (*job etc*) Fam plaquer. **4** *n* j. **of all trades** homme *m* à tout faire. ◆**j.-in-the-box** *n* diable *m* (à ressort).

jackal ['dʒæk(ə)l] *n* (*animal*) chacal *m*.

jackass ['dʒækæs] *n* (*fool*) idiot, -ote *mf*.

jackdaw ['dʒækdɔː] *n* (*bird*) choucas *m*.

jacket ['dʒækɪt] *n* (*short coat*) veste *f*; (*of man's suit*) veston *m*; (*of woman*) veste *f*, jaquette *f*; (*bulletproof*) gilet *m*; (*dust*) j. (*of book*) jaquette *f*; **in their jackets** (*potatoes*) en robe des champs.

jack-knife ['dʒæknaɪf] **1** *n* couteau *m* de poche. **2** *vi* (*of lorry, truck*) se mettre en travers de la route.

jackpot ['dʒækpɒt] *n* gros lot *m*.

jacks [dʒæks] *npl* (*jeu m* d')osselets *mpl*.

jacuzzi [dʒə'kuːzɪ] *n* (*bath, pool*) jacousi *m*.

jade [dʒeɪd] *n* **1** (*stone*) jade *m*. **2** (*horse*) rosse *f*, canasson *m*.

jaded ['dʒeɪdɪd] *a* blasé.

jagged ['dʒægɪd] *a* déchiqueté.

jaguar ['dʒægjuər] *n* (*animal*) jaguar *m*.

jail [dʒeɪl] *n* prison *f*; – *vt* emprisonner (**for** theft/*etc* pour vol/*etc*); **j. for life** condamner à perpétuité. ◆**jailbreak** *n* évasion *f* (de prison). ◆**jailer** *n* geôlier, -ière *mf*.

jalopy [dʒə'lɒpɪ] *n* (*car*) Fam vieux tacot *m*.

jam[1] [dʒæm] *n* Culin confiture *f*. ◆**jamjar** *n* pot *m* à confiture.

jam[2] [dʒæm] **1** *n* (*traffic*) j. embouteillage *m*; **in a** j. (*trouble*) Fig Fam dans le pétrin. **2** *vt* (**-mm-**) (*squeeze, make stuck*) coincer, bloquer; (*gun*) enrayer; (*street, corridor etc*) encombrer; (*building*) envahir; Rad brouiller; **to** j. **sth into** (*pack, cram*) (en)tasser qch dans; (*thrust, put*) enfoncer *or* fourrer qch dans; **to** j. **on** (*brakes*) bloquer; – *vi* (*get stuck*) se coincer, se bloquer; (*of gun*) s'enrayer; **to** j. **into** (*of crowd*) s'entasser dans. ◆**jammed** a (machine etc) coincé, bloqué; (street etc) encombré. ◆**jam-'packed** a (hall etc) bourré de monde.

Jamaica [dʒə'meɪkə] n Jamaïque f.

jangl/e ['dʒæŋg(ə)l] vi cliqueter; − n cliquetis m. ◆**−ing** a (noise) discordant.

janitor ['dʒænɪtər] n concierge m.

January ['dʒænjʊərɪ] n janvier m.

Japan [dʒə'pæn] n Japon m. ◆**Japa'nese** a & n japonais, -aise (mf); − n (language) japonais m.

jar [dʒɑːr] 1 n (vessel) pot m; (large, glass) bocal m. 2 n (jolt) choc m; − vt (-rr-) (shake) ébranler. 3 vi (-rr-) (of noise) grincer; (of note) Mus détonner; (of colours, words) jurer (with avec); to j. on (s.o.'s nerves) porter sur; (s.o.'s ears) écorcher. ◆**jarring** a (note) discordant.

jargon ['dʒɑːgən] n jargon m.

jasmine ['dʒæzmɪn] n Bot jasmin m.

jaundice ['dʒɔːndɪs] n Med jaunisse f. ◆**jaundiced** a (bitter) Fig aigri; to take a j. view of voir d'un mauvais œil.

jaunt [dʒɔːnt] n (journey) balade f.

jaunt/y ['dʒɔːntɪ] a (-ier, -iest) (carefree) insouciant; (cheerful, lively) allègre; (hat etc) coquet, chic. ◆**−ily** adv avec insouciance; allègrement.

javelin ['dʒævlɪn] n javelot m.

jaw [dʒɔː] 1 n Anat mâchoire f. 2 vi (talk) Pej Fam papoter; − n to have a j. Pej Fam tailler une bavette.

jay [dʒeɪ] n (bird) geai m.

jaywalker ['dʒeɪwɔːkər] n piéton m imprudent.

jazz [dʒæz] n jazz m; − vt to j. up Fam (music) jazzifier; (enliven) animer; (clothes, room) égayer.

jealous ['dʒeləs] a jaloux (of de). ◆**jealousy** n jalousie f.

jeans [dʒiːnz] npl (blue-)jean m.

jeep [dʒiːp] n jeep f.

jeer [dʒɪər] vti to j. (at) (mock) railler; (boo) huer; − n raillerie f; pl (boos) huées fpl. ◆**−ing** a railleur; − n railleries fpl; (of crowd) huées fpl.

jell [dʒel] vi (of ideas etc) Fam prendre tournure.

jello® ['dʒeləʊ] n inv Culin Am gelée f. ◆**jellied** a Culin en gelée. ◆**jelly** n Culin gelée f. ◆**jellyfish** n méduse f.

jeopardy ['dʒepədɪ] n danger m, péril m. ◆**jeopardize** vt mettre en danger ou en péril.

jerk [dʒɜːk] 1 vt donner une secousse à (pour tirer, pousser etc); − n secousse f, saccade f. 2 n (person) Pej Fam pauvre type m;

(stupid) j. crétin, -ine mf. ◆**jerk/y** a (-ier, -iest) 1 saccadé. 2 (stupid) Am Fam stupide, bête. ◆**−ily** adv par saccades.

jersey ['dʒɜːzɪ] n (cloth) jersey m; (garment) & Fb maillot m.

Jersey ['dʒɜːzɪ] n Jersey f.

jest [dʒest] n plaisanterie f; in j. pour rire; − vi plaisanter. ◆**−er** n Hist bouffon m.

Jesus ['dʒiːzəs] n Jésus m; J. Christ Jésus-Christ m.

jet [dʒet] 1 n (of liquid, steam etc) jet m. 2 n Av avion m à réaction; − a (engine) à réaction; j. lag fatigue f (due au décalage horaire). ◆**jet-lagged** n Fam qui souffre du décalage horaire.

jet-black [dʒet'blæk] a noir comme (du) jais, (noir) de jais.

jettison ['dʒetɪs(ə)n] vt Nau jeter à la mer; (fuel) Av larguer; Fig abandonner.

jetty ['dʒetɪ] n jetée f; (landing-place) embarcadère m.

Jew [dʒuː] n (man) Juif m; (woman) Juive f. ◆**Jewess** n Juive f. ◆**Jewish** a juif.

jewel ['dʒuːəl] n bijou m; (in watch) rubis m. ◆**jewelled** a orné de bijoux. ◆**jeweller** n bijoutier, -ière mf. ◆**jewellery** n, Am ◆**jewelry** n bijoux mpl.

jib [dʒɪb] vi (-bb-) regimber (at devant); to j. at doing se refuser à faire.

jibe [dʒaɪb] vi & n = gibe.

jiffy ['dʒɪfɪ] n Fam instant m.

jig [dʒɪg] n (dance, music) gigue f.

jigsaw ['dʒɪgsɔː] n j. (puzzle) puzzle m.

jilt [dʒɪlt] vt (lover) laisser tomber.

jingle ['dʒɪŋg(ə)l] vi (of keys, bell etc) tinter; − vt faire tinter; − n tintement m.

jinx [dʒɪŋks] n (person, object) porte-malheur m inv; (spell, curse) (mauvais) sort m, poisse f.

jitters ['dʒɪtəz] npl to have the j. Fam avoir la frousse. ◆**jittery** a to be j. Fam avoir la frousse.

job [dʒɒb] n (task) travail m; (post) poste m, situation f; (crime) Fam coup m; to have a j. doing or to do (much trouble) avoir du mal à faire; to have the j. of doing (unpleasant task) être obligé de faire; (for a living etc) être chargé de faire; it's a good j. (that) Fam heureusement que; that's just the j. Fam c'est juste ce qu'il faut; out of a j. au chômage. ◆**jobcentre** n agence f nationale pour l'emploi. ◆**jobless** a au chômage.

jockey ['dʒɒkɪ] n jockey m; − vi to j. for (position, job) manœuvrer pour obtenir.

jocular ['dʒɒkjʊlər] a jovial, amusant.

jog [dʒɒg] 1 n (jolt) secousse f; (nudge) coup

m de coude; — *vt* (**-gg-**) (*shake*) secouer; (*elbow*) pousser; (*memory*) Fig rafraîchir. **3** *vi* (**-gg-**) **to j. along** (*of vehicle*) cahoter; (*of work*) aller tant bien que mal; (*of person*) faire son petit bonhomme de chemin. **3** *vi* (**-gg-**) Sp faire du jogging. ◆**jogging** *n* Sp jogging *m*.

john [dʒɒn] *n* (*toilet*) Am Sl cabinets *mpl*.

join [dʒɔɪn] **1** *vt* (*unite*) joindre, réunir; (*link*) relier; (*wires, pipes*) raccorder; (*catch up with, meet*) rejoindre qn; (*associate oneself with, go with*) se joindre à qn (**in** doing pour faire); **to j. the sea** (*of river*) rejoindre la mer; **to j. hands** se donner la main; **to j. together** or **up** (*objects*) joindre; — *vi* (*of roads, rivers etc*) se rejoindre; **to j. (together** or **up)** (*of objects*) se joindre (**with** à); **to j. in** participer; **to j. in a game** prendre part à un jeu; — *n* raccord *m*, joint *m*. **2** *vt* (*become a member of*) s'inscrire à (*club, parti*); (*army*) s'engager dans; (*queue, line*) se mettre à; — *vi* (*become a member*) devenir membre; **to j. up** *Mil* s'engager.

joiner [dʒɔɪnər] *n* menuisier *m*.

joint [dʒɔɪnt] **1** *n* Anat articulation *f*; Culin rôti *m*; Tech joint *m*; **out of j.** Med démis. **2** *n* (*nightclub etc*) Sl boîte *f*. **3** *a* (*account, statement etc*) commun; (*effort*) conjugué; **j. author** coauteur *m*. ◆**-ly** *adv* conjointement.

jok/e [dʒəʊk] *n* plaisanterie *f*; (*trick*) tour *m*; **it's no j.** (*it's unpleasant*) ce n'est pas drôle (**doing** de faire); — *vi* plaisanter (**about** sur). ◆**-er** *n* plaisantin *m*; (*fellow*) Fam type *m*; Cards joker *m*. ◆**-ingly** *adv* en plaisantant.

jolly [dʒɒlɪ] **1** *a* (**-ier, -iest**) (*happy*) gai; (*drunk*) Fam éméché. **2** *adv* (*very*) Fam rudement. ◆**jollifi'cation** *n* (*merry-making*) réjouissances *fpl*. ◆**jollity** *n* jovialité *f*; (*merry-making*) réjouissances *fpl*.

jolt [dʒəʊlt] *vt* **to j. s.o.** (*of vehicle*) cahoter qn; (*shake*) Fig secouer qn; — *vi* **to j. (along)** (*of vehicle*) cahoter; — *n* cahot *m*, secousse *f*; (*shock*) Fig secousse *f*.

Jordan [dʒɔːd(ə)n] *n* Jordanie *f*.

jostle [dʒɒs(ə)l] *vt* **to j.** (*push*) bousculer; — *vi* (*push each other*) se bousculer (**for** pour obtenir); **don't j.!** ne bousculez pas!

jot [dʒɒt] *vt* (**-tt-**) **to j. down** noter. ◆**jotter** *n* (*notepad*) bloc-notes *m*.

journal [dʒɜːn(ə)l] *n* (*periodical*) revue *f*, journal *m*. ◆**journa'lese** *n* jargon *m* journalistique. ◆**journalism** *n* journalisme *m*. ◆**journalist** *n* journaliste *mf*.

journey [dʒɜːnɪ] *n* (*trip*) voyage *m*;

(*distance*) trajet *m*; **to go on a j.** partir en voyage; — *vi* voyager.

jovial [dʒəʊvɪəl] *a* jovial.

joy [dʒɔɪ] *n* joie *f*; *pl* (*of countryside, motherhood etc*) plaisirs *mpl* (**of** de). ◆**joyful** *a*, ◆**joyous** *a* joyeux. ◆**joyride** *n* virée *f* (*dans une voiture volée*).

joystick [dʒɔɪstɪk] *n* (*of aircraft, computer*) manche *m* à balai.

JP [dʒeɪ'piː] *abbr* = Justice of the Peace.

jubilant [dʒuːbɪlənt] *a* **to be j.** jubiler. ◆**jubi'lation** *n* jubilation *f*.

jubilee [dʒuːbɪliː] *n* (*golden*) jubilé *m*.

Judaism [dʒuːdeɪɪz(ə)m] *n* judaïsme *m*.

judder [dʒʌdər] *vi* (*shake*) vibrer; — *n* vibration *f*.

judg/e [dʒʌdʒ] *n* juge *m*; — *vti* juger; **judging by** en juger par. ◆**-(e)ment** *n* jugement *m*.

judicial [dʒuː'dɪʃ(ə)l] *a* judiciaire. ◆**judiciary** *n* magistrature *f*. ◆**judicious** *a* judicieux.

judo [dʒuːdəʊ] *n* judo *m*.

jug [dʒʌg] *n* cruche *f*; (*for milk*) pot *m*.

juggernaut [dʒʌgənɔːt] *n* (*truck*) poids *m* lourd, mastodonte *m*.

juggl/e [dʒʌg(ə)l] *vi* jongler; — *vt* jongler avec. ◆**-er** *n* jongleur, -euse *mf*.

Jugoslavia [juːgəʊ'slɑːvɪə] *n* Yougoslavie *f*. ◆**Jugoslav** *a* & *n* yougoslave (*mf*).

juice [dʒuːs] *n* jus *m*; (*in stomach*) suc *m*. ◆**juicy** *a* (**-ier, -iest**) (*fruit*) juteux; (*meat*) succulent; (*story*) Fam savoureux.

jukebox [dʒuːkbɒks] *n* juke-box *m*.

July [dʒuː'laɪ] *n* juillet *m*.

jumble [dʒʌmb(ə)l] *vt* **to j. (up)** (*objects, facts etc*) brouiller, mélanger; — *n* fouillis *m*; **j. sale** (*used clothes etc*) vente *f* de charité.

jumbo [dʒʌmbəʊ] *a* géant; — *a* & *n* (*pl* **-os**) **j. (jet)** jumbo-jet *m*, gros-porteur *m*.

jump [dʒʌmp] *n* (*leap*) saut *m*, bond *m*; (*start*) sursaut *m*; (*increase*) hausse *f*; — *vi* sauter (**at** sur); (*start*) sursauter; (*of price, heart*) faire un bond; **to j. about** sautiller; **to j. across sth** traverser qch d'un bond; **to j. to conclusions** tirer des conclusions hâtives; **j. in** or **on!** Aut montez!; **to j. on** (*bus*) sauter dans; **to j. off** or **out** sauter de; **to j. off sth, to j. out of sth** sauter de qch; **to j. out of the window** sauter par la fenêtre; **to j. up** se lever d'un bond; — *vt* sauter; **to j. the lights** Aut griller un feu rouge; **to j. the rails** (*of train*) dérailler; **to j. the queue** resquiller.

jumper [dʒʌmpər] *n* pull-(over) *m*; (*dress*) Am robe *f* chasuble.

jumpy [dʒʌmpɪ] *a* (**-ier, -iest**) nerveux.

junction ['dʒʌŋkʃ(ə)n] n (*joining*) jonction f; (*crossroads*) carrefour m.

juncture ['dʒʌŋktʃər] n **at this j.** (*critical point in time*) en ce moment même.

June [dʒuːn] n juin m.

jungle ['dʒʌŋg(ə)l] n jungle f.

junior ['dʒuːnɪər] a (*younger*) plus jeune; (*in rank, status etc*) subalterne; (*teacher, doctor*) jeune; **to be j. to s.o.** be **s.o.'s j.** être plus jeune que qn; (*in rank, status*) être au-dessous de qn; **Smith j.** Smith fils or junior; **j. school** école f primaire; **j. high school** Am = collège m d'enseignement secondaire; n cadet, -ette mf; Sch petit, -ite mf, petit(e) élève mf; Sp junior mf, cadet, -ette mf.

junk [dʒʌŋk] 1 n (*objects*) bric-à-brac m inv; (*metal*) ferraille f; (*goods*) Pej camelote f; (*film, book etc*) Pej idiotie f; (*nonsense*) idioties fpl; **j. shop** (boutique f de) brocanteur m. 2 vt (*get rid of*) Am Fam balancer.

junkie ['dʒʌŋkɪ] n Fam drogué, -ée mf.

junta ['dʒʌntə] n Pol junte f.

jurisdiction [dʒʊərɪs'dɪkʃ(ə)n] n juridiction f.

jury ['dʒʊərɪ] n (*in competition*) & Jur jury m. ◆**juror** n juré m.

just [dʒʌst] 1 adv (*exactly, slightly*) juste; (*only*) juste, seulement; (*simply*) (tout) simplement; **it's j. as I thought** c'est bien ce que je pensais; **j. at that time** à cet instant

même; **she has/had j. left** elle vient/venait de partir; **I've j. come from** j'arrive de; **I'm j. coming!** j'arrive!; **he'll (only) j. catch the bus** il aura son bus de justesse; **he j. missed it** il l'a manqué de peu; **j. as big/light/etc** tout aussi grand/léger/etc (as que); **j. listen!** écoute donc!; **j. a moment!** un instant!; **j. over ten** un peu plus de dix; **j. one** un(e) seul(e) (de); **j. about** (*approximately*) à peu près; (*almost*) presque; **j. about to do** sur le point de faire. 2 a (*fair*) juste (to envers). ◆**-ly** adv avec justice. ◆**-ness** n (*of cause etc*) justice f.

justice ['dʒʌstɪs] n justice f; (*judge*) juge m; **to do j. to** (*meal*) faire honneur à; **it doesn't do you j.** (*hat, photo*) cela ne vous avantage pas; (*attitude*) cela ne vous fait pas honneur; **J. of the Peace** juge m de paix.

justify ['dʒʌstɪfaɪ] vt justifier; **to be justified in doing** (*have right*) être en droit de faire; (*have reason*) avoir toutes les bonnes raisons de faire. ◆**justi'fiable** a justifiable. ◆**justi'fiably** adv légitimement. ◆**justifi'cation** n justification f.

jut [dʒʌt] vi (-tt-) to **j. out** faire saillie; **to j. out over sth** (*overhang*) surplomber qch.

jute [dʒuːt] n (*fibre*) jute m.

juvenile ['dʒuːvənaɪl] n adolescent, -ente mf; - a (*court, book etc*) pour enfants; (*delinquent*) jeune; (*behaviour*) Pej puéril. ◆**juxtapose** [dʒʌkstə'pəʊz] vt juxtaposer. ◆**juxtapo'sition** n juxtaposition f.

K

K, k [keɪ] n K, k m.

kaleidoscope [kə'laɪdəskəʊp] n kaléidoscope m.

kangaroo [kæŋgə'ruː] n kangourou m.

kaput [kə'pʊt] a (*broken, ruined*) Sl fichu.

karate [kə'rɑːtɪ] n Sp karaté m.

keel [kiːl] n Nau quille f; – vi to k. over (*of boat*) chavirer.

keen [kiːn] a (*edge, appetite*) aiguisé; (*interest, feeling*) vif; (*mind*) pénétrant; (*wind*) coupant, piquant; (*enthusiastic*) enthousiaste; **a k. sportsman** un passionné de sport; **to be k. to do** or **on doing** tenir (beaucoup) à faire; **to be k. on** (*music, sport etc*) être passionné de; **he is k. on her/the idea** elle/l'idée lui plaît beaucoup. ◆**-ly** adv (*to work etc*) avec enthousiasme; (*to feel, interest*) vivement. ◆**-ness** n (*to*

enthousiasme m; (*of mind*) pénétration f; (*of interest*) intensité f; **k. to do** empressement m à faire.

keep[1] [kiːp] vt (pt & pp kept) garder; (*shop, car*) avoir; (*diary, promise*) tenir; (*family*) entretenir; (*rule*) observer, respecter; (*feast day*) célébrer; (*birthday*) fêter; (*detain, delay*) retenir; (*put*) mettre; **to k. (on) doing** (*continue*) continuer à faire; **to k. clean** tenir or garder propre; **to k. from** (*conceal*) cacher à; **to k. s.o. from doing** (*prevent*) empêcher qn de faire; **to k. s.o. waiting/working** faire attendre/travailler qn; **to k. sth going** (*engine, machine*) laisser qch en marche; **to k. s.o. in whisky/etc** fournir qn en whisky/etc; **to k. an appointment** se rendre à un rendez-vous; **to k. back** (*withhold, delay*) retenir; (*conceal*) cacher (from à); **to k. down** (*control*) maîtriser; (*restrict*) limiter; (*costs, price*) maintenir bas; **to k. in** empêcher de sortir; (*pupil*) *Sch* consigner; **to k. off** *or* **away** (*person*) éloigner (**from** de); **'k. off the grass'** 'ne pas marcher sur les pelouses'; **k. your hands off!** n'y touche(z) pas!; **to k. on** (*hat, employee*) garder; **to k. out** empêcher d'entrer; **to k. up** (*continue, maintain*) continuer (**doing sth** à faire qch); (*road, building*) entretenir; – *vi* (*continue*) continuer; (*remain*) rester; (*of food*) se garder, se conserver; **how is he keeping?** comment va-t-il?; **to k. still** rester *or* se tenir tranquille; **to k. from doing** (*refrain*) s'abstenir de faire; **to k. going** (*continue*) continuer; **to k. at it** (*keep doing it*) continuer à le faire; **to k. away** *or* **off** *or* **back** (*not go near*) ne pas s'approcher (**from** de); **if the rain keeps off** s'il ne pleut pas; **to k. on at s.o.** harceler qn; **to k. out** rester en dehors (**of** de); **to k. to** (*subject, path*) ne pas s'écarter de; (*room*) garder; **to k. to the left** tenir la gauche; **to k. to oneself** se tenir à l'écart; **to k. up** (*continue*) continuer; (*follow*) suivre; **to k. up with s.o** (*follow*) suivre qn; (*in quality of work etc*) se maintenir à la hauteur de qn; – *n* (*food*) subsistance *f*; **to have one's k.** être logé et nourri; **for keeps** *Fam* pour toujours. ◆**–ing** *n* (*care*) garde *f*; **in k. with** en rapport avec. ◆**–er** *n* gardien, -ienne *mf*.

keep² [kiːp] *n* (*tower*) *Hist* donjon *m*.

keepsake ['kiːpseɪk] *n* (*object*) souvenir *m*.

keg [keg] *n* tonnelet *m*.

kennel ['ken(ə)l] *n* niche *f*; (*for boarding*) chenil *m*.

Kenya ['kiːnjə, 'kenjə] *n* Kenya *m*.

kept [kept] *see* keep¹; – *a* **a well** *or* **nicely k.** (*house etc*) bien tenu.

kerb [kɜːb] *n* bord du trottoir.

kernel ['kɜːn(ə)l] *n* (*of nut*) amande *f*.

kerosene ['kerəsiːn] *n* (*aviation fuel*) kérosène *m*; (*paraffin*) *Am* pétrole *m* (lampant).

ketchup ['ketʃəp] *n* (*sauce*) ketchup *m*.

kettle ['ket(ə)l] *n* bouilloire *f*; **the k. is boiling** l'eau bout.

key [kiː] *n* clef *f*, clé *f*; (*of piano, typewriter, computer*) touche *f*; – *a* (*industry, post etc*) clef (*f inv*), clé (*f inv*); **k. man** pivot *m*; **k. ring** porte-clefs *m inv*. ◆**keyboard** *n* clavier *m*. ◆**keyhole** *n* trou *m* de (la) serrure. ◆**keynote** *n* (*of speech*) note *f* dominante. ◆**keystone** *n* (*of policy etc*) clef *f*; *Archit* clef *f* de voûte.

keyed [kiːd] *a* **to be k. up** avoir les nerfs tendus.

khaki ['kɑːkɪ] *a* & *n* kaki *a inv* & *m*.

kibbutz [kɪ'buts] *n* kibboutz *m*.

kick [kɪk] *n* coup *m* de pied; (*of horse*) ruade *f*; (*thrill*) *Fam* plaisir *m*; **to get a k. out of doing** (*thrill*) *Fam* prendre un malin plaisir à faire; **for kicks** *Pej Fam* pour le plaisir; – *vt* donner un coup de pied à; (*of horse*) lancer une ruade à; **to k. back** (*ball*) renvoyer (*du pied*); **to k. down** *or* **in** démolir à coups de pied; **to k. out** (*eject*) *Fam* flanquer dehors; **to k. up** (*fuss, row*) *Fam* faire; – *vi* donner des coups de pied; (*of horse*) ruer; **to k. off** *Fb* donner le coup d'envoi; (*start*) *Fam* démarrer. ◆**k.-off** *n Fb* coup *m* d'envoi.

kid [kɪd] *n* 1 (*goat*) chevreau *m*. 2 *n* (*child*) *Fam* gosse *mf*; **his** *or* **her k. brother** *Am Fam* son petit frère. 3 *vti* (**-dd-**) (*joke, tease*) *Fam* blaguer; **to k. oneself** se faire des illusions.

kidnap ['kɪdnæp] *vt* (**-pp-**) kidnapper. ◆**kidnapping** *n* enlèvement *m*. ◆**kidnapper** *n* kidnappeur, -euse *mf*.

kidney ['kɪdnɪ] *n Anat* rein *m*; *Culin* rognon *m*; **on a k. machine** sous rein artificiel; **k. bean** haricot *m* rouge.

kill [kɪl] *vt* tuer; (*bill*) *Pol* repousser, faire échouer; (*chances*) détruire; (*rumour*) étouffer; (*story*) *Fam* supprimer; (*engine*) *Fam* arrêter; **my feet are killing me** *Fam* je ne sens plus mes pieds, j'ai les pieds en compote; **to k. off** (*person etc*) & *Fig* détruire; – *vi* tuer; – *n* mise *f* à mort; (*prey*) animaux *mpl* tués. ◆**–ing** 1 *n* (*of person*) meurtre *m*; (*of group*) massacre *m*; (*of animal*) mise *f* à mort; **to make a k.** *Fin* réussir un beau coup. 2 *a* (*tiring*) *Fam* tuant. ◆**–er** *n* tueur, -euse *mf*. ◆**killjoy** *n* rabat-joie *m inv*.

kiln [kɪln] *n* (*for pottery*) four *m*.

kilo ['kiːləʊ] *n* (*pl* **-os**) kilo *m*. ◆**kilogramme** ['kɪləʊgræm] *n* kilogramme *m*.

kilometre [kɪ'lɒmɪtər] *n* kilomètre *m*.

kilowatt ['kɪləʊwɒt] *n* kilowatt *m*.

kilt [kɪlt] *n* kilt *m*.

kimono [kɪ'məʊnəʊ] *n* (*pl* **-os**) kimono *m*.

kin [kɪn] *n* (*relatives*) parents *mpl*; **one's next of k.** son plus proche parent.

kind [kaɪnd] 1 *n* (*sort, type*) genre *m*; **a k. of** une sorte *or* une espèce de; **to pay in k.** payer en nature; **what k. of drink/etc is it?** qu'est-ce que c'est comme boisson/*etc*?; **that's the k. of man he is** il est comme ça; **nothing of the k.!** absolument pas!; **k. of worried/sad/etc** (*somewhat*) plutôt inquiet/triste/*etc*; **k. of fascinated** (*as if*) *Fam* comme fasciné; **it's the only one of its k.,** **it's one of a k.** c'est unique en son genre; **we are**

two of a k. nous nous ressemblons. **2** a (-er, -est) (helpful, pleasant) gentil (to avec, pour), bon (to pour); **that's k.** of you c'est gentil or aimable à vous. ◆**k.-'hearted** a qui a bon cœur. ◆**kindly** adv avec bonté; **k. wait/***etc* ayez la bonté d'attendre/*etc*; **not to take k.** to sth ne pas apprécier qch; – a (person) bienveillant. ◆**kindness** n bonté f, gentillesse f.

kindergarten ['kɪndəgɑːt(ə)n] n jardin m d'enfants.

kindle ['kɪnd(ə)l] vt allumer; – vi s'allumer.

kindred ['kɪndrɪd] n (relationship) parenté f; (relatives) parents mpl; **k. spirit** semblable mf, âme f sœur.

king [kɪŋ] n roi m. ◆**k.-size(d)** a géant; (cigarette) long. ◆**kingdom** n royaume m; **animal/plant k.** règne m animal/végétal. ◆**kingly** a royal.

kingfisher ['kɪŋfɪʃər] n (bird) martin-pêcheur m.

kink [kɪŋk] n (in rope) entortillement m.

kinky ['kɪŋkɪ] a (-ier, -iest) (person) Psy Pej vicieux; (clothes etc) bizarre.

kinship ['kɪnʃɪp] n parenté f.

kiosk ['kiːɒsk] n kiosque m; (telephone) k. cabine f (téléphonique).

kip [kɪp] vi (-pp-) (sleep) Sl roupiller.

kipper ['kɪpər] n (herring) kipper m.

kiss [kɪs] n baiser m, bise f; **the k. of life** Med le bouche-à-bouche; – vt (person) embrasser; **k. s.o.'s hand** baiser la main de qn; – vi s'embrasser.

kit [kɪt] n équipement m, matériel m; (set of articles) trousse f; **gym k.** (belongings) affaires fpl de gym; **tool k.** trousse f à outils; **(do-it-yourself) k.** kit m; **in k. form** en kit; **k. bag** sac m (de soldat etc); – vt (-tt-) **to k. out** équiper (with de).

kitchen ['kɪtʃɪn] n cuisine f; **k. cabinet** buffet m de cuisine; **k. garden** jardin m potager; **k. sink** évier m. ◆**kitche'nette** n kitchenette f, coin-cuisine m.

kite [kaɪt] n (toy) cerf-volant m.

kith [kɪθ] n **k. and kin** amis mpl et parents mpl.

kitten ['kɪt(ə)n] n chaton m, petit chat m.

kitty ['kɪtɪ] n (fund) cagnotte f.

km abbr (kilometre) km.

knack [næk] n (skill) coup m (de main), truc m (of doing pour faire); **to have a** or **the k. of doing** (aptitude, tendency) avoir le don de faire.

knackered ['nækəd] a (tired) Sl vanné.

knapsack ['næpsæk] n sac m à dos.

knead [niːd] vt (dough) pétrir.

knee [niː] n genou m; **to go down on one's**

knees se mettre à genoux; **k. pad** Sp genouillère f. ◆**kneecap** n Anat rotule f. ◆**knees-up** n Sl soirée f dansante, sauterie f.

kneel [niːl] vi (pt & pp knelt or kneeled) **to k. (down)** s'agenouiller; **to be kneeling (down)** être à genoux.

knell [nel] n glas m.

knew [njuː] see **know**.

knickers ['nɪkəz] npl (woman's undergarment) culotte f, slip m.

knick-knack ['nɪknæk] n babiole f.

knife [naɪf] n (pl knives) couteau m; (penknife) canif m; – vt poignarder.

knight [naɪt] n Hist & Br Pol chevalier m; Chess cavalier m; – vt (of monarch) Br Pol faire (qn) chevalier. ◆**knighthood** n titre m de chevalier.

knit [nɪt] vt (-tt-) tricoter; **to k. together** Fig souder; **to k. one's brow** froncer les sourcils; – vi tricoter; **to k. (together)** (of bones) se souder. ◆**knitting** n tricot m; **k. needle** aiguille f à tricoter. ◆**knitwear** n tricots mpl.

knob [nɒb] n (on door etc) bouton m; (on stick) pommeau m; (of butter) noix f.

knock [nɒk] vt (strike) frapper; (collide with) heurter; (criticize) Fam critiquer; **to k. one's head on** se cogner la tête contre; **to k. senseless** (stun) assommer; **to k. to the ground** jeter à terre; **to k. about** (ill-treat) malmener; **to k. back** (drink, glass etc) Fam s'envoyer (derrière la cravate), siffler; **to k. down** (vase, pedestrian etc) renverser; (house, tree, wall etc) abattre; (price) baisser, casser; **to k. in** (nail) enfoncer; **to k. off** (person, object) faire tomber (from de); (do quickly) Fam expédier; (steal) Fam piquer; **to k. £5 off** (the price) baisser le prix de cinq livres, faire cinq livres sur le prix; **to k. out** (stun) assommer; (beat in competition) éliminer; **to k. oneself out** (tire) Fam s'esquinter (doing à faire); **to k. over** (pedestrian, vase etc) renverser; **to k. up** (meal) Fam préparer à la hâte; – vi (strike) frapper; **to k. against** or **into** (bump into) heurter; **to k. about** (travel) Fam bourlinguer; (lie around, stand around) traîner; **to k. off** (stop work) Fam s'arrêter de travailler; – n (blow) coup m; (collision) heurt m; **there's a k. at the door** quelqu'un frappe; **I heard a k.** j'ai entendu frapper. ◆**knockdown** n **k. price** prix m imbattable. ◆**knock-'kneed** a cagneux. ◆**knock-out** n Boxing knock-out m; **to be a k.-out** (of person, film etc) Fam être formidable.

knocker ['nɒkər] n (for door) marteau m.

knot [nɒt] **1** n (in rope etc) nœud m; – vt (-tt-) nouer. **2** n (unit of speed) Nau nœud m. ◆**knotty** a (-ier, -iest) (wood etc) noueux; (problem) Fig épineux.

know [nəʊ] vt (pt **knew**, pp **known**) (facts, language etc) savoir; (person, place etc) connaître; (recognize) reconnaître (by à); **to k. that** savoir que; **to k. how to do** savoir faire; **for all I k.** (autant) que je sache; **I'll let you k.** je te le ferai savoir; **I'll have you k. that . . .** sachez que . . . ; **to k. (a lot) about** (person, event) s'y connaître en; (cars, sewing etc) s'y connaître en; **I've never known him to complain** je ne l'ai jamais vu se plaindre; **to get to k. (about)** sth apprendre qch; **to get to k. s.o.** (meet) faire la connaissance de qn; – vi savoir; **I k.** je (le) sais; **I wouldn't k., I k. nothing about it** je n'en sais rien; **I k. about that** je sais ça, je suis au courant; **to k. of** (have heard of) avoir entendu parler de; **do you k. of?** (a good tailor etc) connais-tu?; **you (should) k. better than to do that** tu es trop intelligent pour faire ça; **you should have known better** tu aurais dû réfléchir; – n **in the k.** Fam au courant. ◆**-ing** a (smile, look) entendu. ◆**-ingly** adv (consciously) sciemment. ◆**known** a (fact, danger) reconnu; **a k. expert** un expert reconnu; **well k.** (bien) connu (that que); **she is k. to be . . .** on sait qu'elle est . . . . ◆**know-all** n, Am ◆**know-it-all** n je-sais-tout mf inv. ◆**know-how** n (skill) compétence f (to do pour faire), savoir-faire m inv.

knowledge ['nɒlɪdʒ] n connaissance f (of de); (learning) connaissances fpl, savoir m; **to (the best of) my k.** à ma connaissance; **without the k. of** à l'insu de; **to have no k. of** ignorer; **general k.** culture f générale. ◆**knowledgeable** a bien informé (about sur).

knuckle ['nʌk(ə)l] **1** n articulation f du doigt. **2** vi **to k. down to** (task) Fam s'atteler à; **to k. under** céder.

Koran [kə'rɑːn] n Rel Coran m.

kosher ['kəʊʃər] a Rel kascher inv.

kowtow [kaʊ'taʊ] vi se prosterner (to devant).

kudos ['kjuːdɒs] n (glory) gloire f.

L

L, l [el] L, l m.

lab [læb] n Fam labo m. ◆**laboratory** [lə'bɒrət(ə)rɪ, Am 'læbrətərɪ] n laboratoire m; **language l.** laboratoire m de langues.

label ['leɪb(ə)l] n étiquette f; – vt (-ll-, Am -l-) (goods, person) étiqueter (as comme).

laborious [lə'bɔːrɪəs] a laborieux.

labour ['leɪbər] n (work, childbirth) travail m; (workers) main-d'œuvre f; L. Br Pol les travaillistes mpl; **in l.** Med au travail; – a (market, situation) du travail; (conflict, dispute) ouvrier; (relations) ouvriers-patronat inv; **l. force** main-d'œuvre f; **l. union** Am syndicat m; – vi (toil) peiner; – vt **to l. a point** insister sur un point. ◆-ed a (style) laborieux. ◆-er n (on roads etc) manœuvre m; Agr ouvrier m agricole.

laburnum [lə'bɜːnəm] n Bot cytise f.

labyrinth ['læbɪrɪnθ] n labyrinthe m.

lace [leɪs] **1** n (cloth) dentelle f. **2** n (of shoe) lacet m; – vt **to l. (up)** (tie up) lacer. **3** vt (drink) additionner, arroser (with de).

lacerate ['læsəreɪt] vt (flesh etc) lacérer.

lack [læk] n manque m; **for l. of** à défaut de; – vt manquer de; – vi **to be lacking** manquer (in, for de).

lackey ['lækɪ] n Hist & Fig laquais m.

laconic [lə'kɒnɪk] a laconique.

lacquer ['lækər] n laque f; – vt laquer.

lad [læd] n gars m, garçon m; **when I was a l.** quand j'étais gosse.

ladder ['lædər] n échelle f; (in stocking) maille f filée; – vti (stocking) filer.

laden ['leɪd(ə)n] a chargé (with de).

ladle ['leɪd(ə)l] n louche f.

lady ['leɪdɪ] n dame f; **a young l.** une jeune fille; (married) une jeune femme; **the l. of the house** la maîtresse de maison; **Ladies and Gentlemen!** Mesdames, Mesdemoiselles, Messieurs!; **l. doctor** femme f médecin; **l. friend** amie f; **ladies' room** Fig toilettes fpl. ◆**l.-in-'waiting** n (pl ladies-in-waiting) dame f d'honneur. ◆**ladybird** n, Am ◆**ladybug** n coccinelle f. ◆**ladylike** a (manner) distingué; **she's (very) l.** elle est très grande dame.

lag [læg] **1** vi (-gg-) **to l. behind** (in progress, work) avoir du retard; (dawdle) traîner; **to l. behind s.o.** avoir du retard sur qn; – n

time l. (*between events*) décalage *m*; (*between countries*) décalage *m* horaire. **2** *vt* (*-gg-*) (*pipe*) calorifuger.

lager ['lɑːgər] *n* bière *f* blonde.

lagoon [lə'guːn] *n* lagune *f*; (*small, coral*) lagon *m*.

laid [leɪd] *see* lay². ◆**l.-'back** *a Fam* relax.

lain [leɪn] *see* lie¹.

lair [leər] *n* tanière *f*.

laity ['leɪtɪ] *n* the l. les laïcs *mpl*.

lake [leɪk] *n* lac *m*.

lamb [læm] *n* agneau *m*. ◆**lambswool** *n* laine *f* d'agneau.

lame [leɪm] *a* (*-er*, *-est*) (*person, argument*) boiteux; (*excuse*) piètre; **to be l.** boiter. ◆**-ness** *n Med* claudication *f*; (*of excuse*) *Fig* faiblesse *f*.

lament [lə'ment] *n* lamentation *f*; – *vt* **to l.** (*over*) se lamenter sur. ◆**lamentable** *a* lamentable. ◆**lamen'tation** *n* lamentation *f*.

laminated ['læmɪneɪtɪd] *a* (*metal*) laminé.

lamp [læmp] *n* lampe *f*; (*bulb*) ampoule *f*; *Aut* feu *m*. ◆**lamppost** *n* réverbère *m*. ◆**lampshade** *n* abat-jour *m inv*.

lance [lɑːns] **1** *n* (*weapon*) lance *f*. **2** *vt Med* inciser.

land [lænd] **1** *n* terre *f*; (*country*) pays *m*; (*plot of*) l. terrain *m*; **on dry l.** sur la terre ferme; **no man's l.** *Mil & Fig* no man's land *m inv*; – *a* (*flora, transport etc*) terrestre; (*reform, law*) agraire; (*owner, tax*) foncier. **2** *vi* (*of aircraft*) atterrir, se poser; (*of ship*) mouiller, relâcher; (*of passengers*) débarquer; (*of bomb etc*) (re)tomber; **to l. up** (*end up*) se retrouver; – *vt* (*passengers, cargo*) débarquer; (*aircraft*) poser; (*blow*) *Fig* flanquer (**on** a); (*job, prize etc*) *Fam* décrocher; **to l. s.o. in trouble** *Fam* mettre-qn dans le pétrin; **to be landed with** *Fam* (*person*) avoir sur les bras; (*fine*) ramasser, écoper de. ◆**-ed** *a* (*owning land*) terrien. ◆**-ing** *n* **1** *Av* atterrissage *m*; *Nau* débarquement *m*; **forced l.** atterrissage *m* forcé; **stage débarcadère** *m*. **2** *n* (*at top of stairs*) palier *m*; (*floor*) étage *m*. ◆**landlady** *n* logeuse *f*, propriétaire *f*. ◆**landlocked** *a* sans accès à la mer. ◆**landlord** *n* propriétaire *m*; (*of pub*) patron *m*. ◆**landmark** *n* point *m* de repère. ◆**landslide** *n Geol* glissement *m* de terrain, éboulement *m*; *Pol* raz-de-marée *m inv* électoral.

landscape ['lændskeɪp] *n* paysage *m*.

lane [leɪn] *n* (*in country*) chemin *m*; (*in town*) ruelle *f*; (*division of road*) voie *f*; (*line of traffic*) file *f*; *Av Nau Sp* couloir *m*; **bus l.** couloir *m* (*réservé aux autobus*).

language ['læŋgwɪdʒ] *n* (*faculty, style*) langage *m*; (*national tongue*) langue *f*; **computer l.** langage *m* machine; – *a* (*laboratory*) de langues; (*teacher, studies*) de langue(s).

languid ['læŋgwɪd] *a* languissant. ◆**languish** *vi* languir (**for, after** après).

lank [læŋk] *a* (*hair*) plat et terne.

lanky ['læŋkɪ] *a* (*-ier, -iest*) dégingandé.

lantern ['læntən] *n* lanterne *f*; **Chinese l.** lampion *m*.

lap [læp] **1** *n* (*of person*) genoux *mpl*; **the l. of luxury** le plus grand luxe. **2** *n Sp* tour *m* (de piste). **3** *vt* (*-pp-*) **to l. up** (*drink*) laper; (*like very much*) *Fam* adorer; (*believe*) *Fam* gober; – *vi* (*of waves*) clapoter. **4** *vi* (*-pp-*) **to l. over** (*overlap*) se chevaucher.

lapel [lə'pel] *n* (*of jacket etc*) revers *m*.

lapse [læps] **1** *n* (*fault*) faute *f*; (*weakness*) défaillance *f*; **a l. of memory** un trou de mémoire; **a l. in behaviour** un écart de conduite; – *vi* (*err*) commettre une faute; **to l. into** retomber dans. **2** *n* (*interval*) intervalle *m*; **a l. of time** un intervalle (**between** entre). **3** *vi* (*expire*) se périmer, expirer; (*of subscription*) prendre fin.

larceny ['lɑːsənɪ] *n* vol *m* simple.

lard [lɑːd] *n* saindoux *m*.

larder ['lɑːdər] *n* (*cupboard*) garde-manger *m inv*.

large [lɑːdʒ] *a* (*-er, -est*) (*in size or extent*) grand; (*in volume, bulkiness*) gros; (*quantity*) grand, important; **to become** *or* **grow** *or* **get l.** grossir, grandir; **to a l. extent** en grande mesure; **at l.** (*of prisoner, animal*) en liberté; (*as a whole*) en général; **by and l.** dans l'ensemble, généralement. ◆**l.-scale** *a* (*reform*) (fait) sur une grande échelle. ◆**largely** *adv* (*to a great extent*) en grande mesure. ◆**largeness** *n* grandeur *f*; grosseur *f*.

largesse [lɑː'ʒes] *n* largesse *f*.

lark [lɑːk] **1** *n* (*bird*) alouette *f*. **2** *n* (*joke*) *Fam* rigolade *f*, blague *f*; – *vi* **to l. about** s'amuser.

larva, pl -vae ['lɑːvə, -viː] *n* (*of insect*) larve *f*.

larynx ['lærɪŋks] *n Anat* larynx *m*. ◆**laryn-'gitis** *n Med* laryngite *f*.

lascivious [lə'sɪvɪəs] *a* lascif.

laser ['leɪzər] *n* laser *m*.

lash¹ [læʃ] *n* (*with whip*) coup *m* de fouet; (*tie*) attacher (**to** à); **the dog lashed its tail** le chien donna un coup de queue; – *vi* **to l. out** (*spend wildly*) *Fam* claquer son argent; **to l. out at** envoyer des coups à; (*abuse*) *Fig* invectiver; (*criticize*) *Fig* fustiger. ◆–ings *npl* l. of *Culin Fam* des masses de. ◆l. une montagne de.

lash² [læʃ] *n* (*eyelash*) cil *m*.

lass [læs] *n* jeune fille *f*.

lassitude [ˈlæsɪtjuːd] *n* lassitude *f*.

lasso [læˈsuː] *n* (*pl* -os) lasso *m*; – *vt* attraper au lasso.

last¹ [lɑːst] *a* dernier; the l. ten lines les dix dernières lignes; the l. but one avant-dernier; l. night (*evening*) hier soir; (*during night*) cette nuit; the day before l. avant-hier; – *adv* (*lastly*) en dernier lieu, enfin; (*on the last occasion*) (pour) la dernière fois; to leave l. sortir le dernier *or* en dernier; – *n* (*person, object*) dernier, -ière *mf*; (*end*) fin *f*; the l. of the beer/*etc* (*remainder*) le reste de la bière/*etc*; at (long) l. enfin. ◆l.-ditch *a* désespéré. ◆l.-minute *a* de dernière minute. ◆lastly *adv* en dernier lieu, enfin.

last² [lɑːst] *vi* durer; to l. (out) (*endure, resist*) tenir; (*of money, supplies*) durer; it lasted me ten years ça m'a duré *or* fait dix ans. ◆–ing *a* durable.

latch [lætʃ] **1** *n* loquet *m*; the door is on the l. la porte n'est pas fermée à clef. **2** *vi* to l. on to *Fam* (*grab*) s'accrocher à; (*understand*) saisir.

late¹ [leɪt] *a* (-er, -est) (*not on time*) en retard (for à); (*former*) ancien; (*meal, fruit, season, hour*) tardif; (*stage*) avancé; (*edition*) dernier; to be l. (*of person, train etc*) être en retard, avoir du retard; to be (in) coming arriver en retard; he's an hour l. il a une heure de retard; to make s.o. l. mettre qn en retard; it's l. il est tard; Easter/*etc* is l. Pâques/*etc* est en retard; in l. June/*etc* fin juin/*etc*; a later edition/*etc* (*more recent*) une édition/*etc* plus récente; the latest edition/*etc* (*last*) la dernière édition/*etc*; in later life plus tard dans la vie; to take a later train prendre un train plus tard; at a later date à une date ultérieure; the latest date la date limite; at the latest au plus tard; of l. dernièrement; – *adv* (*in the day, season etc*) tard; (*not on time*) en retard; it's getting l. il se fait tard; later (on) plus tard; not *or* no later than plus tard que. ◆latecomer *n* retardataire *mf*. ◆lately *adv* dernièrement. ◆lateness *n* (*of person, train etc*) retard *m*; constant l. des retards continuels; the l. of the hour l'heure tardive.

late² [leɪt] *a* the l. Mr Smith/*etc* (*deceased*) feu Monsieur Smith/*etc*; our l. friend notre regretté ami.

latent [ˈleɪtənt] *a* latent.

lateral [ˈlætərəl] *a* latéral.

lathe [leɪð] *n Tech* tour *m*.

lather [ˈlɑːðər] *n* mousse *f*; – *vt* savonner; – *vi* mousser.

Latin [ˈlætɪn] *a & n* latin, -ine *mf*; L. America Amérique *f* latine; L. American d'Amérique latine; – *n* (*person*) Latin, -ine *mf*; (*language*) latin *m*.

latitude [ˈlætɪtjuːd] *n Geog & Fig* latitude *f*.

latrines [ləˈtriːnz] *npl* latrines *fpl*.

latter [ˈlætər] *a* (*later, last-named*) dernier; (*second*) deuxième; – *n* dernier, -ière *mf*; second, -onde *mf*. ◆–ly *adv* dernièrement; (*late in life*) sur le tard.

lattice [ˈlætɪs] *n* treillis *m*.

laudable [ˈlɔːdəb(ə)l] *a* louable.

laugh [lɑːf] *n* rire *m*; to have a good l. bien rire; – *vi* rire (at, about de); to l. to oneself rire en soi-même; – *vt* to l. off tourner en plaisanterie. ◆–ing *a* riant; it's no l. matter il n'y a pas de quoi rire; to be the l.-stock of être la risée de. ◆–able *a* ridicule. ◆laughter *n* rire(s) *m*(*pl*); to roar with l. rire aux éclats.

launch [lɔːntʃ] **1** *n* (*motor boat*) vedette *f*; (*pleasure boat*) bateau *m* de plaisance. **2** *vt* (*rocket, boat, fashion etc*) lancer; – *vi* to l. (out) into (*begin*) se lancer dans; – *n* lancement *m*. ◆–ing *n* lancement *m*.

launder [ˈlɔːndər] *vt* (*clothes*) blanchir; (*money from drugs etc*) *Fig* blanchir. ◆–ing *n* blanchissage *m*. ◆launde'rette *n*, *Am* 'laundromat *n* laverie *f* automatique. ◆laundry *n* (*place*) blanchisserie *f*; (*clothes*) linge *m*.

laurel [ˈlɒrəl] *n Bot* laurier *m*.

lava [ˈlɑːvə] *n Geol* lave *f*.

lavatory [ˈlævətrɪ] *n* cabinets *mpl*.

lavender [ˈlævɪndər] *n* lavande *f*.

lavish [ˈlævɪʃ] *a* prodigue (with de); (*helping, meal*) généreux; (*decor, house etc*) somptueux; (*expenditure*) excessif; – *vt* prodiguer (sth on s.o. qch à qn). ◆–ly *adv* (*to give*) généreusement; (*to furnish*) somptueusement.

law [lɔː] *n* (*rule, rules*) loi *f*; (*study, profession, system*) droit *m*; court of l., l. court cour *f* de justice; l. and order ordre public. ◆l.-abiding *a* respectueux des lois. ◆lawful *a* (*action*) légal; (*child, wife etc*) légitime. ◆lawfully *adv* légalement. ◆lawless *a* (*country*) anarchique. ◆lawlessness *n* anarchie *f*. ◆lawsuit *n* procès *m*.

lawn [lɔːn] *n* pelouse *f*, gazon *m*; l. mower tondeuse *f* (à gazon); l. tennis tennis *m* (sur gazon).

lawyer [ˈlɔːjər] *n* (*in court*) avocat *m*; (*author,* *legal expert*) juriste *m*; (*for wills, sales*) notaire *m*.

lax [læks] *a* (*person*) négligent; (*discipline, behaviour*) relâché; **to be l. in doing** faire avec négligence. ◆**laxity** *n*, ◆**laxness** *n* négligence *f*; relâchement *m*.

laxative [ˈlæksətɪv] *n & a Med* laxatif (*m*).

lay[1] [leɪ] *a* (*non-religious*) laïque; (*non-specialized*) d'un profane; **l. person** profane *mf*. ◆**layman** *n* (*pl* -**men**) (*non-specialist*) profane *mf*.

lay[2] [leɪ] *pt & pp laid* 1 *vt* (*put down, place*) poser; (*table*) mettre; (*blanket*) étendre (**over** sur); (*trap*) tendre; (*money*) miser (**on** sur); (*accusation*) porter; (*ghost*) exorciser; **to l. a bet** parier; **to l. bare** mettre à nu; **to l. waste** ravager; **to l. s.o. open to** exposer qn à; **to l. one's hands on** mettre la main sur; **to l. a hand** *or* **a finger on s.o.** lever la main sur qn; **to l. down** (*arms*) déposer; (*condition*) (im)poser; **to l. down the law** faire la loi (**to** à); **to l. s.o. off** (*worker*) licencier qn; **to l. on** (*install*) mettre, installer; (*supply*) fournir; **to l. it on** (*thick*) *Fam* y aller un peu fort; **to l. out** (*garden*) dessiner; (*house*) concevoir; (*prepare*) préparer; (*display*) disposer; (*money*) *Fam* dépenser (**on** pour); **to be laid up** (*in bed*) *Med* être alité; − *vi* **to l. into** *Fam* attaquer; **to l. off** (*stop*) *Fam* arrêter; **to l. off s.o.** (*leave alone*) *Fam* laisser qn tranquille; **l. off!** (*don't touch*) *Fam* pas touche!; **to l. out** *Fam* payer. 2 *vt* (*egg*) pondre; − *vi* (*of bird etc*) pondre. ◆**layabout** *n Fam* fainéant, -ante *mf*. ◆**lay-by** *n* (*pl* -**bys**) *Aut* aire *f* de stationnement *or* de repos. ◆**lay-off** *n* (*of worker*) licenciement *m*. **layout** *n* disposition *f*; *Typ* mise *f* en pages. ◆**lay-over** *n Am* halte *f*.

lay[3] [leɪ] *see* **lie**[1].

layer [ˈleɪər] *n* couche *f*.

laze [leɪz] *vi* **to l.** (**about** *or* **around**) paresser. ◆**lazy** *a* (-**ier**, -**iest**) (*person etc*) paresseux; (*holiday*) passé à ne rien faire. ◆**lazybones** *n Fam* paresseux, -euse *mf*.

lb *abbr* (*libra*) = **pound** (*weight*).

lead[1] [liːd] *vt* (*pt & pp* **led**) (*conduct*) mener, conduire (**to** à); (*team, government etc*) diriger; (*regiment*) commander; (*life*) mener; **to l. s.o. in/out/etc** faire entrer/sortir/*etc* qn; **to l. s.o. to do** (*induce*) amener qn à faire; **to l. the way** montrer le chemin; **to l. the world** tenir le premier rang mondial; **easily led** influençable; **to l. away** *or* **off** emmener; **to l. back** ramener; **to l. on** (*tease*) faire marcher; − *vi* (*of street etc*) mener, conduire (**to** à); (*in match*) mener;

(*in race*) être en tête; (*go ahead*) aller devant; **to l. to** (*result in*) aboutir à; (*cause*) causer, amener; **to l. up to** (*of street*) conduire à, mener à; (*precede*) précéder; (*approach gradually*) en venir à; − *n* (*distance or time ahead*) *Sp* avance *f* (**over** sur); (*example*) exemple *m*, initiative *f*; (*clue*) piste *f*, indice *m*; (*star part*) *Th* rôle *m* principal; (*leash*) laisse *f*; (*wire*) *El* fil *m*; **to take the l.** *Sp* prendre la tête; **to be in the l.** (*in race*) être en tête; (*in match*) mener. ◆**leading** *a* (*main*) principal; (*important*) important; (*front*) de tête; **l. author** l'auteur principal *or* le plus important; **a l. figure** un personnage marquant; **the l. lady** *Cin* la vedette féminine; **l. article** *Journ* éditorial *m*. ◆**leader** *n* chef *m*; *Pol* dirigeant, -ante *mf*; (*of strike, riot*) meneur, -euse *mf*; (*guide*) guide *m*; (*article*) *Journ* éditorial *m*. ◆**leadership** *n* direction *f*; (*qualities*) qualités *fpl* de chef; (*leaders*) *Pol* dirigeants *mpl*.

lead[2] [led] *n* (*metal*) plomb *m*; (*of pencil*) mine *f*; **l. pencil** crayon *m* à mine de plomb. ◆**leaden** *a* (*sky*) de plomb.

leaf [liːf] 1 *n* (*pl* **leaves**) *Bot* feuille *f*; (*of book*) feuillet *m*; (*of table*) rallonge *f*. 2 *vi* **to l. through** (*book*) feuilleter. ◆**leaflet** *n* prospectus *m*; (*containing instructions*) notice *f*. ◆**leafy** *a* (-**ier**, -**iest**) (*tree*) feuillu.

league [liːg] *n* 1 (*alliance*) ligue *f*; *Sp* championnat *m*; **in l. with** *Pej* de connivence avec. 2 (*measure*) *Hist* lieue *f*.

leak [liːk] *n* (*in pipe, information etc*) fuite *f*; (*in boat*) voie *f* d'eau; − *vi* (*of liquid, pipe, tap etc*) fuir; (*of ship*) faire eau; **to l. out** (*of information*) *Fig* être divulgué; − *vt* (*liquid*) répandre; (*information*) *Fig* divulguer. ◆-**age** *n* fuite *f*; (*amount lost*) perte *f*. ◆**leaky** *a* (-**ier**, -**iest**) (*kettle etc*) qui fuit.

lean[1] [liːn] *a* (-**er**, -**est**) (*thin*) maigre; (*year*) difficile. ◆-**ness** *n* maigreur *f*.

lean[2] [liːn] *vi* (*pt & pp* **leaned** *or* **leant** [lent]) (*of object*) pencher; (*of person*) se pencher; **to l. against/on** (*of person*) s'appuyer contre/sur; **to l. back against** s'adosser à; **to l. on s.o.** (*influence*) *Fam* faire pression sur qn (**to do** pour faire); **to l. forward** *or* **over** (*of person*) se pencher (en avant); **to l. over** (*of object*) pencher; − *vt* appuyer (*against* contre); **to l. one's head on/out of** pencher la tête sur/par. ◆-**ing**[1] *a* **l. against** (*resting*) appuyé contre. 2 *npl* tendances *fpl* (**towards** à). ◆**lean-to** *n* (*pl* -**tos**) (*building*) appentis *m*.

leap [liːp] *n* (*jump*) bond *m*, saut *m*; (*change, increase etc*) *Fig* bond *m*; **l. year** année *f* bissextile; **in leaps and bounds** à pas de géant; – vi (pt & pp **leaped** or **leapt** [lɛpt]) bondir, sauter; (of flames) jaillir; (of profits) faire un bond; **to l. to one's feet, l. up** se lever d'un bond. ◆**leapfrog** n saute-mouton m inv.

learn [lɜːn] vt (pt & pp **learned** or **learnt**) apprendre (**that** que); **to l. (how) to do** apprendre à faire; – vi apprendre; **to l. about** (study) étudier; (hear about) apprendre. ◆**-ed** [-ɪd] a savant. ◆**-ing** n érudition f, savoir m; (of language) apprentissage m (**of** de). ◆**-er** n débutant, -ante mf.

lease [liːs] n Jur bail m; **a new l. of life** or Am **on life** un regain de vie, une nouvelle vie; – vt (house etc) louer à bail. ◆**leasehold** n propriété f louée à bail.

leash [liːʃ] n laisse f; **on a l.** en laisse.

least [liːst] a (**the l.** (smallest amount of) le moins de; (slightest) le or la moindre; **he has** (the) **l. talent** il a le moins de talent (of all de tous); **the l. effort/noise/**etc le moindre effort/bruit/etc; – n **the l.** le moins; **at l.** (with quantity) au moins; **at l.** that's what she says ou moins c'est ce qu'elle dit; **not in the l.** pas du tout; – adv **the l.** (to work, eat etc) le moins; (with adjective) le or la moins; **l. of all** (especially not) surtout pas.

leather [ˈlɛðər] n cuir m; (wash) **l.** peau f de chamois.

leave [liːv] 1 n (holiday) congé m; (consent) & Mil permission f; **l. of absence** congé m exceptionnel; **to take** (one's) **l.** prendre congé de. 2 vt (pt & pp **left**) (allow to remain, forget) laisser; (depart from) quitter; (room) sortir de, quitter; **to l. the table** sortir de table; **to l. s.o. in charge of s.o./sth** laisser à la garde de qn/qch; **to l. sth with s.o.** (entrust, give) laisser qch à qn; **to be left** (over) rester; **there's no hope/bread/**etc **left** il ne reste plus d'espoir/de pain/etc; **l. it to me!** laisse-moi faire!; **I'll l. it** (up) **to you** je m'en remets à toi; **to l. go** (of) (release) lâcher; **to l. behind** laisser; (surpass) dépasser; (in race) Sp distancer; **to l. off** (lid) ne pas (re)mettre; **to l. off doing** (stop) Fam arrêter de faire; **to l. on** (hat, gloves) garder; **to l. out** (forget) omettre; (exclude) exclure; – vi (depart) partir (**from** de, **for** pour); **to l. off** (stop) Fam s'arrêter. ◆**leavings** npl restes mpl.

Lebanon [ˈlɛbənən] n Liban m. ◆**Lebanese** a & n libanais, -aise (mf).

lecher [ˈlɛtʃər] n débauché m. ◆**lecherous** a lubrique, luxurieux.

lectern [ˈlɛktən] n (for giving speeches) pupitre m; Rel lutrin m.

lecture [ˈlɛktʃər] 1 n (public speech) conférence f; (as part of series) Univ cours m (magistral); – vi faire une conférence or un cours; **l l. in chemistry** je suis professeur de chimie. 2 vt (scold) Fig faire la morale à, sermonner; – n (scolding) sermon m. ◆**lecturer** n conférencier, -ière mf; Univ enseignant, -ante mf. ◆**lectureship** n poste m à l'université.

led [lɛd] see **lead**[1].

ledge [lɛdʒ] n rebord m; (on mountain) saillie f.

ledger [ˈlɛdʒər] n Com registre m, grand livre m.

leech [liːtʃ] n (worm, person) sangsue f.

leek [liːk] n poireau m.

leer [lɪər] vi **to l. (at)** lorgner; – n regard m sournois.

leeway [ˈliːweɪ] n (freedom) liberté f d'action; (safety margin) marge f de sécurité.

left[1] [lɛft] see **leave** 2; – a **l.** luggage office consigne f. ◆**leftovers** npl restes mpl.

left[2] [lɛft] a (side, hand etc) gauche; – adv à gauche; – n gauche f; **on** or **to the l.** à gauche (**of** de). ◆**l.-hand** a à or de gauche; **on the l.-hand side** à gauche (**of** de). ◆**l.-'handed** a (person) gaucher. ◆**l.-wing** a Pol de gauche. ◆**leftist** n & a Pol gauchiste (mf).

leg [lɛg] n jambe f; (of bird, dog etc) patte f; (of lamb) Culin gigot m; (of chicken) Culin cuisse f; (of table) pied m; (of journey) étape f; **to pull s.o.'s l.** (make fun of) mettre en boîte; **on its last legs** (machine etc) Fam prêt à claquer; **to be on one's last legs** Fam avoir un pied dans la tombe. ◆**l.-room** n place f pour les jambes. ◆**leggy** a (-ier, -iest) (person) aux longues jambes, tout en jambes.

legacy [ˈlɛgəsɪ] n Jur & Fig legs m.

legal [ˈliːg(ə)l] a (lawful) légal; (mind, affairs, adviser) juridique; (aid, error) judiciaire; **l. expert** juriste m; **l. proceedings** procès m. ◆**le'gality** n légalité f. ◆**legalize** vt légaliser. ◆**legally** adv légalement.

legation [lɪˈgeɪʃ(ə)n] n Pol légation f.

legend [ˈlɛdʒənd] n (story, inscription etc) légende f. ◆**legendary** a légendaire.

leggings [ˈlɛgɪnz] npl jambières fpl.

legible [ˈlɛdʒəb(ə)l] a lisible. ◆**legi'bility** n lisibilité f. ◆**legibly** adv lisiblement.

legion [ˈliːdʒən] n Mil & Fig légion f. ◆**legis-**

legislate [ˈlɛdʒɪsleɪt] vi légiférer; – **legis-**

'lation n (laws) législation f; (action) élaboration f des lois; (piece of) l. loi f. ◆**legislative** a législatif.

legitimate [lɪ'dʒɪtɪmət] a (reason, child etc) légitime. ◆**legitimacy** n légitimité f.

legless [legləs] a (drunk) Fam (complètement) bourré.

leisure ['leʒər, Am 'liːʒər] n l. (time) loisirs mpl; l. activities loisirs mpl; moment of l. moment m de loisir; at (one's) l. à tête reposée. ◆**-ly** a (walk, occupation) peu fatigant; (meal, life) calme; at a l. pace, in a l. way sans se presser.

lemon ['lemən] n citron m; l. drink, l. squash citronnade f; l. tea thé m au citron. ◆**lemo'nade** n (fizzy) limonade f; (still) Am citronnade f.

lend [lend] vt (pt & pp lent) prêter (to à); (charm, colour etc) Fig donner à (to à); to l. credence to ajouter foi à. ◆**-ing** n prêt m. ◆**-er** n prêteur, -euse mf.

length [leŋθ] n longueur f; (section of pipe etc) morceau m; (of road) tronçon m; (of cloth) métrage m; (of horse, swimming pool) Sp longueur f; (duration) durée f; l. of time temps m; at l. (at last) enfin; at (great) l. (in detail) dans le détail; (for a long time) longuement; to go to great lengths se donner beaucoup de mal (to do pour faire). ◆**lengthen** vt allonger; (in time) prolonger. ◆**lengthwise** adv dans le sens de la longueur. ◆**lengthy** a (-ier, -iest) long.

lenient ['liːnɪənt] a indulgent (to envers). ◆**leniency** n indulgence f. ◆**leniently** adv avec indulgence.

lens [lenz] n lentille f; (in spectacles) verre m; Phot objectif m.

Lent [lent] n Rel Carême m.

lentil ['lent(ə)l] n Bot Culin lentille f.

leopard ['lepəd] n léopard m.

leotard ['liːətɑːd] n collant m (de danse).

leper ['lepər] n lépreux, -euse mf. ◆**leprosy** n lèpre f.

lesbian ['lezbɪən] n & a lesbienne (f).

lesion ['liːʒ(ə)n] n Med lésion f.

less [les] a & n moins (de) (than que); l. time/etc moins de temps/etc; she has l. (than you) elle en a moins (que toi); l. than a kilo/ten/etc (with quantity, number) moins d'un kilo/de dix/etc; – adv (to sleep, know etc) moins (than que); l. (often) moins souvent; l. and l. de moins en moins; one l. un(e) de moins; – prep moins; l. six francs moins six francs. ◆**lessen** vti diminuer. ◆**lessening** n diminution f. ◆**lesser** a moindre; – n the l. of le or la moindre de.

-less [ləs] suffix sans; **childless** sans enfants.

lesson ['les(ə)n] n leçon f; an English l. une leçon or un cours d'anglais; I have lessons now j'ai cours maintenant.

lest [lest] conj Lit de peur que (+ ne + sub).

let¹ [let] vt (pt & pp let, pres p letting) (allow) laisser (s.o. do qn faire); to l. s.o. have sth donner qch à qn; to l. s.o. away (allow to leave) laisser partir; to l. s.o. down (lower) baisser; (hair) dénouer; (dress) rallonger; (tyre) dégonfler; Fig décevoir qn; don't l. me down je compte sur toi; the car l. me down la voiture est tombée en panne. ◆**letdown** n déception f; to l. in (person, dog) faire entrer; (noise, light) laisser entrer; to l. in the clutch Aut embrayer; to l. s.o. in on Fig mettre qn au courant de; to l. oneself in for (expense) se laisser entraîner à; (trouble) s'attirer; to l. off (bomb) faire éclater; (firework, gun) faire partir; to l. s.o. off (disappoint) (not punish) ne pas punir qn; (clear) Jur disculper qn; to be l. off with (a fine etc) s'en tirer avec; to l. s.o. off doing dispenser qn de faire; to l. on that Fam (admit) avouer que; (reveal) dire que; to l. out (let or leave out) (prisoner) relâcher; (cry, secret) laisser échapper; (skirt) élargir; to l. s.o. out (of the house) ouvrir la porte à qn; to l. out the clutch Aut débrayer; – vi not to l. on Fam ne rien dire, garder la bouche cousue; to l. up (of rain, person etc) s'arrêter. ◆**letup** n arrêt m, répit m. **2** v aux l. us eat/go/etc, l.'s eat/go/etc mangeons/partons/etc; l.'s go for a stroll allons nous promener; l. him come qu'il vienne.

let² [let] vt (pt & pp let, pres p letting) to l. (off or out) (house, room etc) louer. ◆**letting** n (renting) location f.

lethal ['liːθ(ə)l] a mortel; (weapon) meurtrier.

lethargy ['leθədʒɪ] n léthargie f. ◆**le'thargic** a léthargique.

letter ['letər] n (missive, character) lettre f; man of letters homme m de lettres; l. bomb lettre f piégée; l. writer correspondant, -ante mf. ◆**letterbox** n boîte f aux or à lettres. ◆**letterhead** n en-tête m. ◆**lettering** n (letters) lettres fpl; (on tomb) inscription f.

lettuce ['letɪs] n laitue f, salade f.

leuk(a)emia [luː'kiːmɪə] n leucémie f.

level ['lev(ə)l] **1** n niveau m; on the l. (speed) en palier; – a (surface) plat, uni; (object on surface) horizontal; (spoonful) ras; (equal in score) à égalité (with avec); (in height) au même niveau, à la même hauteur (with que); **l. crossing** Rail passage m à niveau; − vt (surface, differences) niveler, aplanir; (plane down) raboter; (building) raser; (gun) braquer; (accusation) lancer (at contre); − vi to **l. off** or **out** (stabilize) Fig se stabiliser. **2** n on the **l.** Fam (honest) honnête, franc; (frankly) honnêtement, franchement; − vi (-ll-, Am -l-) to talk Fam être franc avec. ◆**l.-'headed** a équilibré.

lever ['liːvər, Am 'levər] n levier m. ◆**leverage** n (power) influence f.

levity ['leviti] n légèreté f.

levy ['levi] vt (tax, troops) lever; − n (tax) impôt m.

lewd [luːd] a (-er, -est) obscène.

liable ['laɪəb(ə)l] a **l.** to (dizziness etc) sujet à; (fine, tax) passible de; **he's l. to do** il est susceptible de faire, il pourrait faire; **l. for** (responsible) responsable de. ◆**lia'bility** n responsabilité f (for de); (disadvantage) handicap m; pl (debts) dettes fpl.

liaise [lɪ'eɪz] vi travailler en liaison (with avec). ◆**liaison** n (association) & Mil liaison f.

liar ['laɪər] n menteur, -euse mf.

libel ['laɪb(ə)l] vt (-ll-, Am -l-) diffamer (par écrit); − n diffamation f.

liberal ['lɪbərəl] a (open-minded) & Pol libéral; (generous) généreux (with de); − n Pol libéral, -ale mf. ◆**liberalism** n libéralisme m.

liberate ['lɪbəreɪt] vt libérer. ◆**libe'ration** n libération f. ◆**liberator** n libérateur, -trice mf.

liberty ['lɪbətɪ] n liberté f; **at l. to do** libre de faire; **what a l.!** (cheek) Fam quel culot!; to **take liberties with s.o.** se permettre des familiarités avec qn.

Libra ['liːbrə] n (sign) la Balance.

library ['laɪbrərɪ] n bibliothèque f. ◆**li'brarian** n bibliothécaire mf.

libretto [lɪ'bretəʊ] n (pl -os) Mus livret m.

Libya ['lɪbɪə] n Libye f. ◆**Libyan** a & n libyen, -enne (mf).

lice [laɪs] see **louse**.

licence, Am **license** ['laɪsəns] n **1** permis m, autorisation f; (for driving) permis m; Com licence f; **pilot's l.** brevet m de pilote; **l. fee** Rad TV redevance f; **l. plate/number** Aut plaque f/numéro m d'immatriculation. **2** (freedom) licence f.

license ['laɪsəns] vt accorder une licence à, autoriser; **licensed premises** établissement m qui a une licence de débit de boissons.

licit ['lɪsɪt] a licite.

lick [lɪk] vt lécher; (defeat) Fam écraser; (beat physically) Fam rosser; **to be licked** (by problem etc) Fam être dépassé; − n coup m de langue; **a l. of paint** un coup de peinture. ◆**-ing** n Fam (defeat) déculottée f; (beating) rossée f.

licorice ['lɪkərɪʃ, -rɪs] n Am réglisse f.

lid [lɪd] n **1** (of box etc) couvercle m. **2** (of eye) paupière f.

lido ['liːdəʊ] n (pl -os) piscine f (découverte).

lie [laɪ] vi (pt lay, pp lain, pres p lying) (in flat position) s'allonger, s'étendre; (remain) rester; (be) être; (in grave) reposer; **to be lying** (on the grass etc) être allongé ou étendu; **he lay asleep** il dormait; **here lies** (on tomb) ci-gît; **the problem lies in** le problème réside dans; **to l. heavy on** (of meal etc) & Fig peser sur; **to l. low** (hide) se cacher; (be inconspicuous) se faire tout petit; **to l. about** or **around** (of objects, person) traîner; **to l. down, to have a l.-down** s'allonger, se coucher; **lying down** (resting) allongé, couché; **to l. in, to have a l.-in** Fam faire la grasse matinée.

lie [laɪ] vi (pt & pp lied, pres p lying) (tell lies) mentir; − n mensonge m; **to give the l. to** (show as untrue) démentir.

lieu [luː] n **in l.** au lieu de.

lieutenant [lef'tenənt, Am lu'tenənt] n lieutenant m.

life [laɪf] n (pl lives) vie f; (of battery, machine) durée f (de vie); **to come to l.** (of street, party etc) s'animer; **at your time of l.** à ton âge; **loss of l.** perte f en vies humaines; **true to l.** conforme à la réalité; **to take one's (own) l.** se donner la mort; **bird l.** les oiseaux mpl; − a (cycle, style) de vie; (belt, raft) de sauvetage; (force) vital; **l. annuity** rente f viagère; **l. insurance** assurance-vie f; **l. blood** Fig âme f; **l. insurance** assurance f; **l. jacket** gilet m de sauvetage; **l. peer** pair m à vie. ◆**lifeboat** n canot m de sauvetage. ◆**lifebuoy** n bouée f de sauvetage. ◆**lifeguard** n maître-nageur m-sauveteur. ◆**lifeless** a sans vie. ◆**lifelike** a qui semble vivant. ◆**lifelong** a de toute sa vie; (friend) de toujours. ◆**lifesaving** n sauvetage m. ◆**lifesize(d)** a grandeur nature inv. ◆**lifetime** n vie f; Fig éternité f; **in my l.** de mon vivant; **a once-in-a-l. experience**/etc l'expérience/etc de votre vie.

lift [lɪft] vt lever; (sth heavy) soulever; (ban, siege) Fig lever; (idea etc) Fig voler, prendre (from à); **to l. down** or **off** (take down) descendre (from de); **to l. out** (take out) sortir; **to l. up** (arm, eyes) lever; (object) (sou)lever; – vi (of fog) se lever; **to l. off** (of space vehicle) décoller; – n (elevator) ascenseur m; **to give s.o. a l.** emmener ou accompagner qn (en voiture) (to à). ◆**l.-off** n Av décollage m.

ligament ['lɪɡəmənt] n ligament m.

light¹ [laɪt] **1** n lumière f; (daylight) jour m, lumière f; (on vehicle) feu m, (headlight) phare m; **by the l. of** à la lumière de; **in the l. of** (considering) à la lumière de; **in that l.** Fig sous ce jour ou cet éclairage; **against the l.** à contre-jour; **to bring to l.** mettre en lumière; **to come to l.** être découvert; **to throw l. on** (matter) éclaircir; **do you have a l.?** (for cigarette) est-ce que vous avez du feu?; **to set l. to** mettre le feu à; **leading l.** (person) Fig phare m, sommité f, lumière f; **l. bulb** ampoule f (électrique); – vt (pt & pp lit or lighted) (candle etc) allumer; (match) gratter; **to l. (up)** (room) éclairer; – vi **to l. up** (of window) s'éclairer. **2** a (bright, not dark) clair; a **l. green jacket** une veste vert clair. ◆**-ing** n El éclairage m; **the l.** of (candle etc) l'allumage m de. ◆**lighten¹** vt (light up) éclairer; (colour, hair) éclaircir. ◆**lighter** n (for cigarettes etc) briquet m; Culin allume-gaz m inv. ◆**lighthouse** n phare m. ◆**lightness¹** n clarté f.

light² [laɪt] a (in weight, quantity, strength etc) léger; (task) facile; **l. rain** pluie f fine; **to travel l.** voyager avec peu de bagages. ◆**l.-'fingered** a chapardeur. ◆**l.-'headed** a (giddy, foolish) étourdi. ◆**l.-'hearted** a gai. ◆**lighten²** vt (a load) alléger. ◆**lightly** adv légèrement. ◆**lightness²** n légèreté f.

light³ [laɪt] vi (pt & pp lit or lighted) **to l. upon** trouver par hasard.

lightning ['laɪtnɪŋ] n Met (light) éclair m; (charge) foudre f; (flash of) **l.** éclair m; – a (speed) foudroyant; (visit) éclair inv; **l. conductor** paratonnerre m.

lightweight ['laɪtweɪt] a (cloth etc) léger; (not serious) peu sérieux, léger.

like¹ [laɪk] a (alike) semblable, pareil; – prep comme; **l. this** comme ça; **what's it l.?** (physically, as character) comment est-il?; **to be** or **look l.** ressembler à; **what was the book l.?** comment a-t-on trouvé le livre?; **I have one l. it** j'en ai un pareil; – adv nothing **l. as big** etc loin d'être aussi grand/etc; – conj (as) Fam comme; **it's l. I say** c'est comme je vous le dis; – n ... and the l. ... et ainsi de suite; **the l. of which we shan't see again** comme on n'en reverra plus; **the likes of you** des gens de ton acabit.

lik/e² [laɪk] vt aimer (bien) (to do, doing faire); **I l. him** il l'aime bien, il me plaît; **she likes it here** elle se plaît ici; **I l. best** préférer; **I'd l. to come** (want) je voudrais (bien) ou j'aimerais (bien) venir; **I'd l. a kilo of apples** je voudrais un kilo de pommes; **would you l. a cigar?** voulez-vous un cigare?; **if you l.** si vous voulez; **(how) would you l. to come?** ça te plairait ou te dirait de venir?; – npl **one's likes** nos goûts mpl. ◆**-ing** n **a l. for** (person) de la sympathie pour; (thing) du goût pour; **to my l.** à mon goût. ◆**likeable** a sympathique.

likely ['laɪklɪ] a (-ier, -iest) (event, result etc) probable; (excuse) vraisemblable; (place) propice; (candidate) prometteur; **a l. excuse!** Iron belle excuse!; **it's l. (that) she'll come** il est probable qu'elle viendra; **he's l. to come** il viendra probablement; **he's not l. to come** il ne risque pas de venir; – adv **very l.** très probablement; **not l.!** pas question! ◆**likelihood** n probabilité f; **there's little l. that** il y a peu de chances que (+ sub).

liken ['laɪkən] vt comparer (to à). ◆**likeness** ['laɪknɪs] n ressemblance f; **a family l.** un air de famille; **it's a good l.** c'est très ressemblant.

likewise ['laɪkwaɪz] adv (similarly) de même, pareillement.

lilac ['laɪlək] n lilas m; – a (colour) lilas inv.

Lilo® ['laɪləʊ] n (pl -os) matelas m pneumatique.

lilt [lɪlt] n Mus cadence f.

lily ['lɪlɪ] n lis m, lys m; **l. of the valley** muguet m.

limb [lɪm] n Anat membre m; **to be out on a l.** Fig être le seul de son opinion.

limber ['lɪmbər] vi **to l. up** faire des exercices d'assouplissement.

limbo (in) [ɪn'lɪmbəʊ] adv (uncertain, waiting) dans l'expectative.

lime [laɪm] n **1** (tree) tilleul m. **2** (substance) chaux f. **3** (fruit) lime f, citron m vert; **l. juice** jus m de citron vert.

limelight ['laɪmlaɪt] n **in the l.** (glare of publicity) en vedette.

limit ['lɪmɪt] n limite f; (restriction) limitation f (of de); **that's the l.!** Fam c'est le comble!; **within limits** dans une certaine limite; – vt limiter (to à); **to l. oneself to doing** se borner à faire. ◆**-ed** a (restricted) limité; (mind) borné; (edition) à tirage limité; **l. company** Com société f à responsabilité limitée; **(public) l. company** (with shareholders) société f anonyme; **to a**

l. degree jusqu'à un certain point. ◆**limi'tation** n limitation f. ◆**limitless** a illimité.

limousine [lɪməˈziːn] n (car) limousine f; (airport etc shuttle) Am voiture-navette f.

limp [lɪmp] **1** vi (of person) boiter; (of vehicle etc) Fig avancer tant bien que mal; **to have a l.** boiter. **2** a (-er, -est) (soft) mou; (flabby) flasque; (person, hat) avachi.

limpid [ˈlɪmpɪd] a (liquid) Lit limpide.

linchpin [ˈlɪntʃpɪn] n (person) pivot m.

linctus [ˈlɪŋktəs] n Med sirop m (contre la toux).

line¹ [laɪn] n ligne f; (stroke) trait m, ligne f; (of poem) vers m; (wrinkle) ride f; (track) voie f; (rope) corde f; (row) rangée f, ligne f; (of vehicles) file f; (queue) Am file f, queue f; (family) lignée f; (business) métier m, rayon m; (article) Com article m; **one's lines** (of actor) son texte m; **on the l.** Tel (speaking) au téléphone; (at other end of line) au bout du fil; **to be on the l.** (at risk) être en danger; **hold the l.!** Tel ne quittez pas!; **the hot l.** Tel le téléphone rouge; **to stand in l.** Am faire la queue; **to step** or **get out of l.** Fig refuser de se conformer; (misbehave) faire une incartade; **out of l. with** (ideas etc) en désaccord avec; **in l. with** (contrast) he's in l. for (promotion etc) il doit recevoir; **to take a hard l.** adopter une attitude ferme; **along the same lines** (to work, think) de la même façon; **sth along those lines** qch dans ce genre-là; **to drop a l.** Fam envoyer un mot (to à); **where do we draw the l.?** où fixer les limites?; - vt (paper) régler; (face) rider; **to l. the street** (of trees) border la rue; (of people) faire la haie le long de la rue; **to l. up** (children, objects) aligner; (arrange) organiser; (get ready) préparer; **to have sth lined up** (in mind) avoir en vue; - vi **to l. up** s'aligner; (queue) Am faire la queue. ◆**l.-up** n (row) file f; Pol front m; TV programme(s) m(pl).

line² [laɪn] vt (clothes) doubler; (pockets) Fig se remplir. ◆**lining** n (of clothes) doublure f; (of brakes) garniture f.

lineage [ˈlɪnɪdʒ] n lignée f.

linear [ˈlɪnɪər] a linéaire.

linen [ˈlɪnɪn] n (sheets etc) linge m; (material) (toile f de) lin m, fil m.

liner [ˈlaɪnər] n **1** (ship) paquebot m. **2** (dust)bin l. sac à poubelle.

linesman [ˈlaɪnzmən] n (pl -men) Fb etc juge m de touche.

linger [ˈlɪŋɡər] vi **to l. (on)** (of person) s'attarder; (of smell, memory) persister; (of doubt) subsister. ◆**-ing** a (death) lent.

lingo [ˈlɪŋɡəʊ] n (pl -os) Hum Fam jargon m.

linguist [ˈlɪŋɡwɪst] n linguiste mf. ◆**lin'guistic** a linguistique. ◆**lin'guistics** n linguistique f.

liniment [ˈlɪnɪmənt] n onguent m, pommade f.

link [lɪŋk] vt (connect) relier (to à); (relate, associate) lier (to à); **to l. up** Tel relier; - vi **to l. up** (of roads) se rejoindre; - n (connection) lien m; (of chain) maillon m; (by road, rail) liaison f. ◆**l.-up** n TV Rad liaison f; (of spacecraft) jonction f.

lino [ˈlaɪnəʊ] n lino m. ◆**linoleum** [lɪˈnəʊlɪəm] n linoléum m.

linseed [ˈlɪnsiːd] n **l. oil** huile f de lin.

lint [lɪnt] n Med tissu m ouaté; (fluff) peluche(s) f(pl).

lion [ˈlaɪən] n lion m; **l. cub** lionceau m. ◆**lioness** n lionne f.

lip [lɪp] n Anat lèvre f; (rim) bord m; (cheek) Sl culot m. ◆**l.-read** vi (pt & pp -read [red]) lire sur les lèvres. ◆**lipstick** n (material) rouge m à lèvres; (stick) tube m de rouge.

liqueur [lɪˈkjʊər] n liqueur f.

liquid [ˈlɪkwɪd] n & a liquide (m). ◆**liquefy** vt liquéfier; - vi se liquéfier. ◆**liquidizer** n Culin (for fruit juices) centrifugeuse f; (for purées etc) robot m, moulinette f.

liquidate [ˈlɪkwɪdeɪt] vt (debt, person) liquider. ◆**liqui'dation** n liquidation f.

liquor [ˈlɪkər] n alcool m, spiritueux m; **l. store** Am magasin m de vins et de spiritueux.

liquorice [ˈlɪkərɪs, -rɪʃ] n réglisse f.

lira [ˈlɪərə] n, pl **lire** [ˈlɪəreɪ] (currency) lire f.

lisp [lɪsp] vi zézayer; - n le sa vie l. zézayer.

list [lɪst] n **1** - vt (one's possessions etc) faire la liste de; (names) mettre sur la liste; (enumerate) énumérer; (catalogue) cataloguer. **2** vi (of ship) gîter. ◆**-ed** a (monument) classé.

listen [ˈlɪsən] vi écouter; **to l. to** écouter; **to l. (out) for** (telephone, person etc) tendre l'oreille pour, guetter; **to l. in (to)** Rad écouter. ◆**-ing** n écoute f (to de). ◆**-er** n Rad auditeur, -trice mf; **to be a good l.** (pay attention) savoir écouter.

listless [ˈlɪstləs] a apathique, indolent. ◆**-ness** n apathie f.

lit [lɪt] see **light¹ 1**.

litany [ˈlɪtənɪ] n Rel litanies fpl.

literal [ˈlɪtərəl] a littéral; (not exaggerated) réel. ◆**-ly** adv littéralement; (really) réellement; **he took it l.** il l'a pris au pied de la lettre.

literate [ˈlɪtərət] a qui sait lire et écrire;

highly l. (*person*) très instruit. ◆**literacy** *n* capacité *f* de lire et d'écrire; (*of country*) degré *m* d'alphabétisation.

literature ['lɪt(ə)rɪtʃər] *n* littérature *f*; (*pamphlets etc*) documentation *f*. ◆**literary** *a* littéraire.

lithe [laɪð] *a* agile, souple.

litigation [lɪtɪ'geɪʃ(ə)n] *n* Jur litige *m*.

litre ['liːtər] *n* litre *m*.

litter ['lɪtər] **1** *n* (*rubbish*) détritus *m*; (*papers*) papiers *mpl*; (*bedding for animals*) litière *f*; (*confusion*) Fig fouillis *m*; **l. basket** *or* **bin** boîte *f* à ordures; – *vt* **to l.** (**with papers** *or* **rubbish**) (*street etc*) laisser traîner des papiers *or* des détritus dans; **a street littered with** une rue jonchée de. **2** *n* (*young animals*) portée *f*.

little ['lɪt(ə)l] **1** *a* (*small*) petit; **the l. ones** les petits. **2** *a* & *n* (*not much*) peu (de); **l. time/money/etc** peu de temps/d'argent/*etc*; **I've l.** il m'en reste peu; **she eats l.** elle mange peu; **to have l. to say** avoir peu de chose à dire; **as l. as possible** le moins possible; **a l. money/time/etc** (*some*) un peu d'argent/de temps/*etc*; **I have a l.** (*some*) j'en ai un peu; **the l. that I have** le peu que j'ai; – *adv* (*somewhat, rather*) peu; **a l. heavy/etc** un peu lourd/*etc*; **to work/etc a l.** travailler/*etc* un peu; **it's l. better** (*hardly*) ce n'est guère mieux; **l. by l.** peu à peu.

liturgy ['lɪtədʒɪ] *n* liturgie *f*.

live¹ [lɪv] *vi* (*reside*) habiter, vivre; **where do you l.?** où habitez-vous?; **to l. in Paris** habiter (à) Paris; – *vt* **to l. off** *or* **on** (*eat*) vivre de, (*sponge on*) Pej vivre aux crochets *or* aux dépens de (*qn*); **to l. on** (*of memory etc*) survivre, se perpétuer; **to l. through** (*experience*) vivre; (*survive*) survivre à; **to l. up to** (*one's principles*) vivre selon; (*s.o.'s expectations*) se montrer à la hauteur de; – *vt* (*life*) vivre, mener; (*one's faith etc*) vivre pleinement; **to l. down** faire oublier (avec le temps); **to l. it up** Fam mener la grande vie.

live² [laɪv] **1** *a* (*alive, lively*) vivant; (*coal*) ardent; (*bomb*) non explosé; (*ammunition*) réel, de combat; (*wire*) El sous tension; (*switch*) El mal isolé; (*plugged in*) El branché; **a real l. king/etc** un roi/etc en chair et en os. **2** *a* & *adv* Rad TV en direct; **a l. broadcast** une émission en direct; **a l. audience** le *or* un public; **a l. recording** un enregistrement public.

livelihood ['laɪvlɪhʊd] *n* moyens *mpl* de subsistance; **my l.** mon gagne-pain; **to earn one's** *or* **a l.** gagner sa vie.

livel/y ['laɪvlɪ] *a* (**-ier, -iest**) (*person, style*)

vif, vivant; (*street, story*) vivant; (*interest, mind, colour*) vif; (*day*) mouvementé; (*forceful*) vigoureux; (*conversation, discussion*) animé. ◆**-iness** *n* vivacité *f*.

liven ['laɪv(ə)n] *vt* **to l. up** (*person*) égayer; (*party*) animer; – *vi* **to l. up** (*of person, party*) s'animer.

liver ['lɪvər] *n* foie *m*.

livery ['lɪvərɪ] *n* (*uniform*) livrée *f*.

livestock ['laɪvstɒk] *n* bétail *m*.

livid ['lɪvɪd] *a* (*blue-grey*) livide; (*angry*) Fig furieux; **l. with cold** blême de froid.

living ['lɪvɪŋ] **1** *a* (*alive*) vivant; **not a l. soul** (*nobody*) personne, pas âme qui vive; **within l. memory** de mémoire d'homme; **l. or dead** mort ou vif; **the l. vivants** *mpl*. **2** *n* (*livelihood*) vie *f*; **to make a** *or* **one's l.** gagner sa vie; **to work for a l.** travailler pour vivre; **the cost of l.** le coût de la vie; – *a* (*standard, conditions*) de vie; (*wage*) qui permet de vivre; **l. room** salle *f* de séjour.

lizard ['lɪzəd] *n* lézard *m*.

llama ['lɑːmə] *n* (*animal*) lama *m*.

load [ləʊd] *n* (*object carried, burden*) charge *f*; (*freight*) chargement *m*, charge *f*; (*strain, weight*) poids *m*; **a l. of, loads of** (*people, money etc*) Fam un tas de, énormément de; **to take a l. off s.o.'s mind** ôter un grand poids à qn; – *vt* charger; **to l. down** *or* **up** (*with*) charger (with de); – *vi* **to l.** (**up**) charger la voiture, le navire *etc*. ◆**-ed** *a* (*gun, vehicle etc*) chargé; (*dice*) pipé; (*rich*) Fam plein aux as; **a l. question** une question piège; **l.** (**down**) **with** (*debts*) accablé de.

loaf [ləʊf] **1** *n* (*pl* **loaves**) pain *m*; French **l. baguette** *f*. **2** *vi* **to l.** (**about**) fainéanter. ◆**-er** *n* fainéant, -ante *mf*.

loam [ləʊm] *n* (*soil*) terreau *m*.

loan [ləʊn] *n* (*money lent*) prêt *m*; (*money borrowed*) emprunt *m*; **on l. from** prêté par; (*out*) **on l.** (*book*) sorti; **may I have the l. of . . . ?** puis-je emprunter . . . ?; – *vt* (*lend*) prêter (**to** à).

loath [ləʊθ] *a* **l. to do** Lit peu disposé à faire.

loath/e [ləʊð] *vt* détester (**doing** faire). ◆**-ing** *n* dégoût *m*. ◆**loathsome** *a* détestable.

lobby ['lɒbɪ] **1** *n* (*of hotel*) vestibule *m*, hall *m*; Th foyer *m*. **2** *n* Pol groupe *m* de pression, lobby *m*; – *vt* faire pression sur.

lobe [ləʊb] *n* Anat lobe *m*.

lobster ['lɒbstər] *n* homard *m*; (*spiny*) langouste *f*.

local ['ləʊk(ə)l] **1** *a* local; (*of the neighbourhood*) du *or* de quartier; (*regional*) du pays; **are you l.?** êtes-vous du coin *or* d'ici?; **the doctor is l.** le médecin est tout près d'ici; **a l. phone call** (*within town*) une communication urbaine; – *n* (*pub*) *Fam* bistrot *m* du coin, pub *m*; **she's a l.** elle est du coin; **the locals** (*people*) les gens du coin. ◆**lo'cality** *n* (*neighbourhood*) environs *mpl*; (*region*) région *f*; (*place*) lieu *m*; (*site*) emplacement *m*. ◆**localize** *vt* (*confine*) localiser. ◆**locally** *adv* dans les environs, dans le coin; (*around here*) par ici; (*in precise place*) localement.

locate [ləʊˈkeɪt] *vt* (*find*) repérer; (*pain, noise, leak*) localiser; (*situate*) situer; (*build*) construire. ◆**location** *n* (*site*) emplacement *m*; (*act*) repérage *m*, localisation *f*; **on l.** Cin en extérieur.

lock [lɒk] **1** *vt* **to l.** (**up**) fermer à clef; **to l. the wheels** *Aut* bloquer les roues; **to l. s.o. in** enfermer qn; **to l. s.o. in sth** enfermer qn dans qch; **to l. s.o. out** (*accidentally*) enfermer qn dehors; **to l. away** *or* **up** (*prisoner*) enfermer; (*jewels etc*) mettre sous clef, enfermer; – *vi* **to l.** (**up**) fermer à clef; – *n* (*on door, chest etc*) serrure *f*; (*of gun*) cran *m* de sûreté; (*turning circle*) *Aut* rayon *m* de braquage; (**anti-theft**) *l.* *Aut* antivol *m*; **under l. and key** sous clef. **2** *n* (*on canal*) écluse *f*. **3** *n* (*of hair*) mèche *f*. ◆**locker** *n* casier *m*; (*for luggage*) *Rail* casier *m* de consigne automatique; (*for clothes*) vestiaire *m* (métallique); **l. room** *Sp Am* vestiaire *m*. ◆**lockout** *n* (*industrial*) lock-out *m inv*. ◆**locksmith** *n* serrurier *m*.

locket [ˈlɒkɪt] *n* (*jewel*) médaillon *m*.

loco [ˈləʊkəʊ] *a Sl* cinglé, fou.

locomotion [ləʊkəˈməʊʃ(ə)n] *n* locomotion *f*. ◆**locomotive** *n* locomotive *f*.

locum [ˈləʊkəm] *n* (*doctor*) remplaçant, -ante *mf*.

locust [ˈləʊkəst] *n* criquet *m*, sauterelle *f*.

lodge [lɒdʒ] **1** *vt* (*person*) loger; (*valuables*) déposer (**with** chez); **to l. a complaint** porter plainte; – *vi* (*of bullet*) se loger (**in** dans); **to be lodging** (*accommodated*) être logé (**with** chez). **2** *n* (*house*) pavillon *m* de gardien *or* de chasse; (*porter*) loge *f*. ◆**–ing** *n* (*accommodation*) logement *m*; *pl* (*flat*) logement *m*; (*room*) chambre *f*; **in lodgings** en meublé. ◆**–er** *n* (*room and meals*) pensionnaire *mf*; (*room only*) locataire *mf*.

loft [lɒft] *n* (*attic*) grenier *m*.

loft/y [ˈlɒftɪ] *a* (**-ier, -iest**) (*high, noble*) élevé; (*haughty*) hautain. ◆**–iness** *n* hauteur *f*.

log [lɒg] **1** *n* (*tree trunk*) rondin *m*; (*for fire*) bûche *f*, rondin *m*; **l. fire** feu *m* de bois. **2** *vt* (**-gg-**) (*facts*) noter; **to l.** (**up**) (*distance*) faire, couvrir. ◆**logbook** *n* Nau Av journal *m* de bord.

logarithm [ˈlɒgərɪðm] *n* logarithme *m*.

loggerheads (at) [ætˈlɒgəhedz] *adv* en désaccord (**with** avec).

logic [ˈlɒdʒɪk] *n* logique *f*. ◆**logical** *a* logique. ◆**logically** *adv* logiquement.

logistics [ləˈdʒɪstɪks] *n* logistique *f*.

logo [ˈləʊgəʊ] *n* (*pl* **-os**) logo *m*.

loin [lɔɪn] *n* (*meat*) filet *m*.

loins [lɔɪnz] *npl* Anat reins *mpl*.

loiter [ˈlɔɪtər] *vi* traîner.

loll [lɒl] *vi* (*in armchair etc*) se prélasser.

lollipop [ˈlɒlɪpɒp] *n* (*sweet on stick*) sucette *f*; (*ice on stick*) esquimau *m*. ◆**lolly** *n Fam* sucette *f*; (*money*) *Sl* fric *m*; (**ice**) **l.** *Fam* esquimau *m*.

London [ˈlʌndən] *n* Londres *m* *or* *f*; – *a* (*taxi etc*) londonien, -ienne. ◆**Londoner** *n* Londonien, -ienne *mf*.

lone [ləʊn] *a* solitaire; **l. wolf** *Fig* solitaire *mf*. ◆**loneliness** *n* solitude *f*. ◆**lonely** *a* (**-ier, -iest**) (*road, house, life etc*) solitaire; (*person*) seul, solitaire. ◆**loner** *n* solitaire *mf*. ◆**lonesome** *a* solitaire.

long[1] [lɒŋ] **1** *a* (**-er, -est**) long; **to be ten metres l.** être long de dix mètres, avoir dix mètres de long; **to be six weeks l.** durer six semaines; **how l. is ...?** quelle est la longueur de ...?; (*time*) quelle est la durée de ...?; **a l. time** longtemps; **in the l. run** à la longue; **a l. face** une grimace; **a l. memory** une bonne mémoire; **l. jump** *Sp* saut *m* en longueur. **2** *adv* (*a long time*) longtemps; **l. before** longtemps avant; **has he been here l.?** il y a longtemps qu'il est ici?, il est ici depuis longtemps?; **how l.** (*ago*)? (il y a) combien de temps?; **not l. ago** il y a peu de temps; **before l.** sous *or* avant peu; **no longer** ne plus; **she no longer swims** elle ne nage plus; **a bit longer** (*to wait etc*) encore un peu; **I won't be l.** je n'en ai pas pour longtemps; **at the longest** (tout) au plus; **all summer l.** tout l'été; **l. live the queen/etc** vive la reine/etc; **as l. as, so l. as** (*provided that*) pourvu que (+ *sub*); **as l. as I live** tant que je vivrai.

long[2] [lɒŋ] *vi* **to l. for sth** avoir très envie de qch; **to l. for s.o.** languir après qn; **to l. to do** avoir très envie de faire. ◆**–ing** *n* désir *m*, envie *f*.

long-distance [lɒŋˈdɪstəns] *a* (*race*) de fond; (*phone call*) interurbain; (*flight*) long-courrier. ◆**long-drawn-'out** *a* interminable. ◆**long'haired** *a* aux cheveux longs. ◆**longhand** *n* écriture *f* normale. ◆**long-'playing** *a* **l.-playing record** 33 tours *m inv*. ◆**long-'range** *a* (*forecast*) à long terme. ◆**long'sighted** *a* – *Med* presbyte. ◆**long'standing** a de longue date. ◆**long'suffering** a très patient. ◆**long-term** a à long terme. ◆**long-winded** a (speech, speaker) verbeux.

longevity [lɒn'dʒevɪtɪ] n longévité f.

longitude ['lɒndʒɪtjuːd] n longitude f.

longways ['lɒŋweɪz] adv en longueur.

loo [luː] n (toilet) Fam cabinets mpl.

look [luk] n regard m; (appearance) air m, allure f; (good) looks la beauté, un beau physique; **to have a l. (at)** jeter un coup d'œil (à), regarder; **to have a l. (for)** chercher; **to have a l. (a)round** regarder; (walk) faire un tour; **let me have a l.** fais voir; **I like the l. of him** il me fait bonne impression, il me plaît; – vti regarder; **to l. s.o. in the face** regarder qn dans les yeux; **to l. tired/happy/etc** (seem) sembler or avoir l'air fatigué/heureux/etc, avoir l'air fatigué/etc; **to l. pretty/ugly** (be) être joli/laid; **to l. one's age** faire son âge; **l. here!** dites donc!; **you l. like or as if you're tired** tu as l'air fatigué, on dirait que tu es fatigué; **it looks like or as if she won't leave** elle n'a pas l'air de vouloir partir; **it looks like it!** c'est probable!; **to l. like a child** avoir l'air d'un enfant; **to l. like an apple** avoir l'air d'être une pomme; **you l. like my brother** (resemble) tu ressembles à mon frère; **it looks like rain** (to me) il me semble or on dirait qu'il va pleuvoir; **what does he l. like?** (describe him) comment est-il?; **to l. well or good** (of person) avoir bonne mine; **you l. good in that** (clothes) ce chapeau/etc te va très bien; **that looks bad** (action etc) ça fait mauvais effet. ■ **to l. after** vt (deal with) s'occuper de; (patient, hair) soigner; (keep safely) garder (for s.o. pour qn); **to l. after oneself** (keep healthy) faire bien attention à soi; **I can l. after myself** (cope) je suis assez grand pour me débrouiller; **to l. around** vt (visit) visiter; – vi (have a look) regarder; (walk round) faire un tour; **to l. at** vt regarder; (consider) considérer, voir; (check) vérifier; **to l. away** vi détourner les yeux; **to l. back** vi regarder derrière soi; (in time) regarder en arrière; **to l. down** vi baisser les yeux; (from height) regarder en bas; **to l. down on** (consider scornfully) mépriser, regarder de haut; **to l. for** (seek) chercher; **to l. forward to** vt (event) attendre avec impatience; **to l. in** vi regarder (à l'intérieur); **to l. in on s.o.** Fam passer voir qn; **to l. into** vt (examine) examiner; (find out about) se renseigner sur; **to l. on** vi regarder; – vt (consider) considérer, voir; **to l. out** vi (be careful) faire attention (for à); **to l. out for** (seek)

chercher; (watch) guetter; **to l. (out) on to** (of window, house etc) donner sur; **to l. over or through** vt (examine fully) examiner, regarder de près; (briefly) parcourir; (region, town) parcourir, visiter; **to l. round** vt (visit) visiter; – vi (have a look) regarder; (walk round) faire un tour; (look back) se retourner; **to l. round for** (seek) chercher; **to l. up** vi (of person) lever les yeux; (into the air or sky) regarder en l'air; (improve) s'améliorer; **to l. up to s.o.** Fig respecter qn; – vt (word) chercher; **to l. s.o. up** (visit) passer voir qn. ◆**-looking** suffix pleasant-/tired-/etc à l'air agréable/fatigué/etc. ◆**-looking-glass** n glace f, miroir m.

lookout ['lukaut] n (soldier) guetteur m; (sailor) vigie f; **l. (post)** poste m de guet; (on ship) vigie f; **to be on the l.** faire le guet; **to be on the l. for** guetter.

loom [luːm] 1 vi **to l. (up)** (of mountain etc) apparaître indistinctement; Fig paraître imminent. 2 n Tex métier m à tisser.

loony ['luːnɪ] n & a Sl imbécile mf.

loop [luːp] n (in river etc) & Av boucle f; (contraceptive device) stérilet m; – vt **to l. the loop** Av boucler la boucle. ◆**loophole** n (in rules) point m faible, lacune f; (way out) échappatoire f.

loose [luːs] a (-er, -est) (screw, belt, knot) desserré; (tooth, stone) branlant; (page) détaché; (animal) libre, (set loose) lâché; (clothes) flottant; (hair) dénoué; (flesh) flasque; (wording, translation) approximatif, vague; (link) vague; (discipline) relâché; (articles) Com en vrac; (cheese, tea etc) Com au poids; (woman) Pej facile; **l. change** petite monnaie f; **l. covers** housses fpl; **l. living** vie f dissolue; **to get l.** (of dog, page) se détacher; **to set or turn l.** (dog etc) libérer, lâcher; **he's at a l. end** or Am at l. ends il ne sait pas trop quoi faire; – n on the l. (prisoner etc) en liberté; – vt (animal) lâcher. ◆**loosely** adv (to hang) lâchement; (to hold, tie) sans serrer; (to translate) librement; (to link) vaguement. ◆**loosen** vt (knot, belt, screw) desserrer; (rope) détendre; (grip) relâcher; – vi **to l. up** Sp faire des exercices d'assouplissement. ◆**looseness** n (of screw, machine parts) jeu m.

loot [luːt] n butin m; (money) Sl fric m; – vt piller. ◆**-ing** n pillage m. ◆**-er** n pillard, -arde mf.

lop [lɒp] vt (-pp-) **to l. (off)** couper.

lop-sided [lɒp'saɪdd] a (crooked) de travers; **to walk l.-sided** (limp) se déhancher.

loquacious [ləʊ'kweɪʃəs] a loquace.

lord [lɔːd] *n* seigneur *m*; (*title*) *Br* lord *m*; **good L.!** *Fam* bon sang!; **oh L.!** *Fam* mince!; **the House of Lords** *Pol* la Chambre des Lords; – *vt* **to l. it over s.o.** dominer qn. ◆**lordly** *a* digne d'un grand seigneur; (*arrogant*) hautain. ◆**lordship** *n* **Your L.** (*to judge*) Monsieur le juge.

lore [lɔːr] *n* traditions *fpl*.

lorry ['lɒrɪ] *n* camion *m*; (*heavy*) poids *m* lourd; **l. driver** camionneur *m*; **long-distance l. driver** routier *m*.

lose* [luːz] *vt* (*pt & pp* **lost**) perdre; **to get lost** (*of person*) se perdre; **the ticket/etc got lost** on a perdu le billet/*etc*; **get lost!** *Fam* fiche le camp!; **to l. s.o. sth** faire perdre qch à qn; **to l. interest in** se désintéresser de; **I've lost my bearings** je suis désorienté; **the clock loses six minutes a day** la pendule retarde de six minutes par jour; **to l. one's life** trouver la mort (*in* dans); – *vi* perdre; **to l. out** être perdant; **to l. to** *Sp* être battu par. ◆**-ing** *a* perdant; **a l. battle** *Fig* une bataille perdue d'avance. ◆**-er** *n* perdant, -ante *mf*; (*failure in life*) *Fam* paumé, -ée *mf*; **to be a good l.** être bon et beau joueur.

loss [lɒs] *n* perte *f*; **at a l.** (*confused*) perplexe; **to sell at a l.** *Com* vendre à perte; **at a l. to do** incapable de faire. ◆**lost** *a* perdu; **l. property**, *Am* **l. and found** objets *mpl* trouvés.

lot¹ [lɒt] *n* **1** (*destiny*) sort *m*; (*batch, land*) lot *m*; **to draw lots** tirer au sort; **parking l.** *Am* parking *m*; **a bad l.** (*person*) *Fam* un mauvais sujet. **2 the l.** (*everything*) (le) tout; **the l. of you** vous tous; **a l. of, lots of** beaucoup de; **a l.** beaucoup; **quite a l.** pas mal (*of* de); **such a l.** tellement (*of* de), tant (*of* de); **what a l. of flowers/water/etc!** que de fleurs/d'eau/*etc*!; **what a l.!** quelle quantité!; **what a l. of flowers/etc you have!** que vous avez (beaucoup) de fleurs/*etc*!

lotion ['ləʊʃ(ə)n] *n* lotion *f*.

lottery ['lɒtərɪ] *n* loterie *f*.

lotto ['lɒtəʊ] *n* (*game*) loto *m*.

loud [laʊd] *a* (**-er**, **-est**) bruyant; (*voice, radio*) fort; (*noise, cry*) grand; (*gaudy*) voyant; – *adv* (*to shout etc*) fort; **out l.** tout haut. ◆**-ly** *adv* (*to speak, laugh etc*) bruyamment, fort; (*to shout*) fort. ◆**-ness** *n* (*of voice etc*) force *f*; (*noise*) bruit *m*. ◆**loud'hailer** *n* mégaphone *m*. ◆**loudmouth** *n* (*person*) *Fam* grande gueule *f*. ◆**loud'speaker** *n* haut-parleur *m*; (*of hi-fi unit*) enceinte *f*.

lounge [laʊndʒ] **1** *n* salon *m*; **l. suit** complet *m* veston. **2** *vi* (*loll*) se prélasser; **to l. about** (*idle*) paresser; (*stroll*) flâner.

louse, *pl* **lice** [laʊs, laɪs] **1** *n* (*insect*) pou *m*. **2** *n* (*person*) *Pej Sl* salaud *m*. **3** *vt* **to l. up** (*mess up*) *Sl* gâcher.

lousy ['laʊzɪ] *a* (**-ier**, **-iest**) (*bad*) *Fam* infect; **l. with** (*crammed, loaded*) *Sl* bourré de.

lout [laʊt] *n* rustre *m*. ◆**loutish** *a* (*attitude*) de rustre.

love [lʌv] *n* amour *m*; *Tennis* zéro *m*; **in l.** amoureux (*with* de); **they're in l.** ils s'aiment; **art is his** *or* **her l.** l'art est sa passion; **yes, my l.** oui mon amour; – *vt* aimer; (*like very much*) adorer, aimer (beaucoup) (**to do, doing** faire); **give him** *or* **her my l.** (*greeting*) dis-lui bien des choses de ma part; **l. affair** liaison *f* (amoureuse). ◆**-ing** *a* affectueux, aimant. ◆**-able** *a* adorable. ◆**-er** *n* (*man*) amant *m*; (*woman*) maîtresse *f*; **a l. of** (*art, music etc*) un amateur de; **a l. of nature** un amoureux de la nature. ◆**lovesick** *a* amoureux.

lovely ['lʌvlɪ] *a* (**-ier**, **-iest**) (*pleasing*) agréable, bon; (*excellent*) excellent; (*pretty*) joli; (*charming*) charmant; (*kind*) gentil; **the weather's l.** il fait beau; **l. to see you!** je suis ravi de te voir; **l. and hot/dry/etc** bien chaud/sec/*etc*.

low¹ [ləʊ] *a* (**-er**, **-est**) bas; (*speed, income, intelligence*) faible; (*opinion, quality*) mauvais; **she's l. on** (*money etc*) elle n'a plus beaucoup de; **to feel l.** (*depressed*) être déprimé; **in a l. voice** à voix basse; **lower** inférieur; – *adv* (**-er**, **-est**) bas; **to turn (down) l.** mettre plus bas; **to run l.** (*of supplies*) s'épuiser; – *n* *Met* dépression *f*; **to reach a new l.** *or* **an all-time l.** (*of prices etc*) atteindre leur niveau le plus bas. ◆**low-'calorie** *a* (*diet*) à basses calories. ◆**low-'cost** *a* bon marché *inv*. ◆**low-cut** *a* décolleté. ◆**low-down** *a* méprisable. ◆**lowdown** *n* (*facts*) *Fam* tuyaux *mpl*. ◆**low-'fat** *a* (*milk*) écrémé; (*cheese*) de régime. ◆**low-'key** *a* (*discreet*) discret. ◆**lowland(s)** *n* plaine *f*. ◆**low-level** *a* bas. ◆**low-paid** *a* mal payé. ◆**low-'salt** *a* (*food*) à faible teneur en sel.

low² [ləʊ] *vi* (*of cattle*) meugler.

lower ['ləʊər] *vt* baisser; **to l. s.o./sth** (*by rope*) descendre qn/qch; **to l. oneself** *Fig* s'abaisser. ◆**-ing** *n* (*drop*) baisse *f*.

lowly ['ləʊlɪ] *a* (**-ier**, **-iest**) humble.

loyal ['lɔɪəl] *a* loyal (**to** envers), fidèle (**to** à). ◆**loyalty** *n* loyauté *f*, fidélité *f*.

lozenge ['lɒzɪndʒ] *n* (*sweet*) *Med* pastille *f*; (*shape*) *Geom* losange *m*.

LP [el'piː] *abbr* = **long-playing record**.

L-plates ['elplets] *npl Aut* plaques *fpl* d'apprenti conducteur.

Ltd *abbr* (Limited) *Com* SARL.

lubricate ['lu:brɪkeɪt] *vt* lubrifier; *Aut* graisser. **◆lubricant** *n* lubrifiant *m*. **◆lubri'cation** *n Aut* graissage *m*.

lucid ['lu:sɪd] *a* lucide. **◆lu'cidity** *n* lucidité *f*.

luck [lʌk] *n* (chance) chance *f*; (good fortune) (bonne) chance *f*, bonheur *m*; (fate) hasard *m*, fortune *f*; **bad l.** malchance *f*, malheur *m*; **hard l.!**, **tough l.!** pas de chance!; **worse l.** (unfortunately) malheureusement. **◆luckily** *adv* heureusement. **◆lucky** *a* (-ier, -iest) (person) chanceux, heureux; (guess, event) heureux; **to be l.** (of person) avoir de la chance (**to do** de faire); **I've had a l. day** j'ai eu de la chance aujourd'hui; **l. charm** porte-bonheur *m inv*; **l. number/etc** chiffre *m/etc* porte-bonheur; **how l.!** quelle chance!

lucrative ['lu:krətɪv] *a* lucratif.

ludicrous ['lu:dɪkrəs] *a* ridicule.

ludo ['lu:dəʊ] *n* jeu *m* des petits chevaux.

lug [lʌg] *vt* (-gg-) (pull) traîner; **to l. around** trimbaler.

luggage ['lʌgɪdʒ] *n* bagages *mpl*.

lugubrious [lu:'gu:brɪəs] *a* lugubre.

lukewarm ['lu:kwɔ:m] *a* tiède.

lull [lʌl] **1** *n* arrêt *m*; (in storm) accalmie *f*. **2** *vt* (-ll-) apaiser; **to l. to sleep** endormir.

lullaby ['lʌləbaɪ] *n* berceuse *f*.

lumbago [lʌm'beɪgəʊ] *n* lumbago *m*.

lumber[1] ['lʌmbər] *n* (timber) bois *m* de charpente; (junk) bric-à-brac *m inv*. **◆lumberjack** *n Am Can* bûcheron *m*. **◆lumberjacket** *n* blouson *m*. **◆lumber-room** *n* débarras *m*.

lumber[2] ['lʌmbər] *vt* **to l. s.o. with sth/s.o.** *Fam* coller qch/qn à qn; **he got lumbered with the chore** il s'est appuyé la corvée.

luminous ['lu:mɪnəs] *a* (dial etc) lumineux.

lump [lʌmp] *n* morceau *m*; (in soup) grumeau *m*; (bump) bosse *f*; (swelling) *Med* grosseur *f*; **l. sum** somme *f* forfaitaire; – *vt* **to l. together** réunir; *Fig Pej* mettre dans le même sac. **◆lumpy** *a* (-ier, -iest) (soup etc) grumeleux; (surface) bosselé.

lunar ['lu:nər] *a* lunaire.

lunatic ['lu:nətɪk] *a* fou, dément; – *n* fou *m*, folle *f*. **◆lunacy** *n* folie *f*, démence *f*.

lunch [lʌntʃ] *n* déjeuner *m*; **to have l.** déjeuner; **l. break**, **l. hour**, **l. time** heure *f* du déjeuner; – *vi* déjeuner (**on**, **off** de). **◆luncheon** *n* déjeuner *m*; **l. meat** mortadelle *f*, saucisson *m*; **l. voucher** chèque-déjeuner *m*.

lung [lʌŋ] *n* poumon *m*; **l. cancer** cancer *m* du poumon.

lunge [lʌndʒ] *n* coup *m* en avant; – *vi* **to l.** at s.o. se ruer sur qn.

lurch [lɜ:tʃ] **1** *vi* (of person) tituber; (of ship) faire une embardée. **2** *n* **to leave s.o. in the l.** *Fam* laisser qn en plan, laisser tomber qn.

lure [ljʊər] *vt* attirer (par la ruse) (**into** dans); – *n* (attraction) attrait *m*.

lurid ['ljʊərɪd] *a* (horrifying) horrible, affreux; (sensational) à sensation; (gaudy) voyant; (colour, sunset) sanglant.

lurk [lɜ:k] *vi* (hide) se cacher (**in** dans); (prowl) rôder; (of suspicion, fear etc) persister.

luscious ['lʌʃəs] *a* (food etc) appétissant.

lush [lʌʃ] **1** *a* (vegetation) luxuriant; (wealthy) *Fam* opulent. **2** *n Am Sl* ivrogne *mf*.

lust [lʌst] *n* (for person, object) convoitise *f* (**for** de); (for power, knowledge) soif *f* (**for** de); – *vi* **to l. after** (object, person) convoiter; (power, knowledge) avoir soif de.

lustre ['lʌstər] *n* (gloss) lustre *m*.

lusty ['lʌstɪ] *a* (-ier, -iest) vigoureux.

lute [lu:t] *n Mus* luth *m*.

Luxembourg ['lʌksəmbɜ:g] *n* Luxembourg *m*.

luxuriant [lʌg'ʒʊərɪənt] *a* luxuriant. **◆luxuriate** *vi* (laze about) paresser (**in** bed/etc au lit/etc).

luxury ['lʌkʃərɪ] *n* luxe *m*; – *a* (goods, flat etc) de luxe. **◆luxurious** [lʌg'ʒʊərɪəs] *a* luxueux.

lying ['laɪɪŋ] see **lie**[1,2]; – *n* le mensonge; – *a* (account) mensonger; (person) menteur.

lynch [lɪntʃ] *vt* lyncher. **◆—ing** *n* lynchage *m*.

lynx [lɪŋks] *n* (animal) lynx *m*.

lyre ['laɪər] *n Mus Hist* lyre *f*.

lyric ['lɪrɪk] *a* lyrique; – *npl* (of song) paroles *fpl*. **◆lyrical** *a* (effusive) lyrique. **◆lyricism** *n* lyrisme *m*.

M

M, m [em] *n* M, *m* m.

m *abbr* **1** (*metre*) mètre *m*. **2** (*mile*) mile *m*.

MA *abbr* = **Master of Arts.**

ma'am [mæm] *n* madame *f*.

mac [mæk] *n* (*raincoat*) *Fam* imper *m*.

macabre [mə'kɑːbrə] *a* macabre.

macaroni [mækə'rəʊnɪ] *n* macaroni(s) *m(pl)*.

macaroon [mækə'ruːn] *n* (*cake*) macaron *m*.

mace [meɪs] *n* (*staff, rod*) masse *f*.

Machiavellian [mækɪə'velɪən] *a* machiavélique.

machination [mækɪ'neɪʃ(ə)n] *n* machination *f*.

machine [mə'ʃiːn] *n* (*apparatus, car, system etc*) machine *f*. ◆**machinegun** *n* mitrailleuse *f*; – *vt* (**-nn-**) mitrailler. ◆**machinery** *n* (*machines*) machines *fpl*; (*works*) mécanisme *m*; *Fig* rouages *mpl*. ◆**machinist** *n* (*on sewing machine*) piqueur, -euse *mf*.

macho ['mætʃəʊ] *n* (*pl* **-os**) macho *m*; – *a* (*attitude etc*) macho (*f inv*).

mackerel ['mækrəl] *n inv* (*fish*) maquereau *m*.

mackintosh ['mækɪntɒʃ] *n* imperméable *m*.

mad [mæd] *a* (**madder, maddest**) fou; (*dog*) enragé; (*bull*) furieux; **m. (at)** (*angry*) *Fam* furieux (contre); **to be m.** (**keen**) **on** *Fam* (*person*) être fou de; (*films etc*) se passionner or s'emballer pour; **to drive m.** rendre fou; (*irritate*) énerver; **he drove me m. to go** *Fam* il m'a cassé les pieds pour que j'y aille; **like m.** comme un fou. ◆**maddening** *a* exaspérant. ◆**madhouse** *n Fam* maison *f* de fous. ◆**madly** *adv* (*in love, to spend money etc*) follement; (*desperately*) désespérément. ◆**madman** *n* (*pl* **-men**) fou *m*. ◆**madness** *n* folie *f*.

Madagascar [mædə'gæskər] *n* Madagascar *f*.

madam ['mædəm] *n* (*married*) madame *f*; (*unmarried*) mademoiselle *f*.

made [meɪd] *see* **make.**

Madeira [mə'dɪərə] *n* (*wine*) madère *m*.

madonna [mə'dɒnə] *n Rel* madone *f*.

maestro ['maɪstrəʊ] *n* (*pl* **-os**) *Mus* maestro *m*.

Mafia ['mæfɪə] *n* maf(f)ia *f*.

magazine [mægə'ziːn] *n* (*periodical*) magazine *m*, revue *f*; (*of gun, camera*) magasin *m*.

maggot ['mægət] *n* ver *m*, asticot *m*. ◆**maggoty** *a* véreux.

magic ['mædʒɪk] *n* magie *f*; – *a* (*word, wand*) magique. ◆**magical** *a* (*evening etc*) magique. ◆**ma'gician** *n* magicien, -ienne *mf*.

magistrate ['mædʒɪstreɪt] *n* magistrat *m*.

magnanimous [mæg'nænɪməs] *a* magnanime.

magnate ['mægneɪt] *n* (*tycoon*) magnat *m*.

magnesium [mæg'niːzɪəm] *n* magnésium *m*.

magnet ['mægnɪt] *n* aimant *m*. ◆**mag'netic** *a* magnétique. ◆**magnetism** *n* magnétisme *m*. ◆**magnetize** *vt* magnétiser.

magnificent [mæg'nɪfɪsənt] *a* magnifique. ◆**magnificence** *n* magnificence *f*. ◆**magnificently** *adv* magnifiquement.

magnify ['mægnɪfaɪ] *vt* (*image*) & *Fig* grossir; (*sound*) amplifier; **magnifying glass** loupe *f*. ◆**magnifi'cation** *n* grossissement *m*; amplification *f*; (*of image*) grossissement *m*; amplification *f*; ampleur *f*.

magnitude ['mægnɪtjuːd] *n* ampleur *f*.

magnolia [mæg'nəʊlɪə] *n* (*tree*) magnolia *m*.

magpie ['mægpaɪ] *n* (*bird*) pie *f*.

mahogany [mə'hɒgənɪ] *n* acajou *m*.

maid [meɪd] *n* (*servant*) bonne *f*; **old m.** *Pej* vieille fille *f*. ◆**maiden** *n Old-fashioned* jeune fille *f*; – *a* (*speech etc*) premier; (*flight*) inaugural; **m. name** nom *m* de jeune fille. ◆**maidenly** *a* virginal.

mail [meɪl] *n* (*system*) poste *f*; (*letters*) courrier *m*; – *a* (*van, bag etc*) postal; **m. order** vente *f* par correspondance; – *vt* mettre à la poste; **mailing list** liste *f* d'adresses. ◆**mailbox** *n Am* boîte *f* à or aux lettres. ◆**mailman** *n* (*pl* **-men**) *Am* facteur *m*.

maim [meɪm] *vt* mutiler, estropier.

main [meɪn] **1** *a* principal; **the m. thing is to** . . . l'essentiel est de . . . ; **m. line** *Rail* grande ligne *f*; **m. road** grande route *f*; **in the m.** (*mostly*) en gros, dans l'ensemble. **2** *n* **water/gas m.** conduite *f* d'eau/de gaz; **the mains** *El* le secteur; **a mains radio** une radio secteur. ◆**-ly** *adv* principalement, surtout. ◆**mainland** *n* continent *m*. ◆**main-**

stay n (of family etc) soutien m; (of organization, policy) pilier m. ◆**mainstream** n tendance f dominante.

maintain [meɪnˈteɪn] vt (continue, assert) maintenir (that que); (vehicle, family etc) entretenir; (silence) garder. ◆**maintenance** n (of vehicle, road etc) entretien m; (of prices, order, position etc) maintien m; (alimony) pension f alimentaire.

malsonette [mæzɔˈnet] n duplex m.

maize [meɪz] n (cereal) maïs m.

majesty [ˈmædʒɪstɪ] n majesté f; Your M. (title) Votre Majesté. ◆**maˈjestic** a majestueux.

major [ˈmeɪdʒər] 1 a (main, great) & Mus majeur; a m. road une grande route. 2 n Mil commandant m. 3 n (subject) Univ Am dominante f; – vi to m. in se spécialiser en. ◆**majoˈrette** n (drum) m. majorette f.

Majorca [məˈjɔːkə] n Majorque f.

majority [məˈdʒɒrɪtɪ] n majorité f (of de); in the or a m. en majorité, majoritaire; the m. of people la plupart des gens; – a (vote etc) majoritaire.

make [meɪk] vt (pt & pp made) faire; (tool, vehicle etc) fabriquer; (decision) prendre; (friends, wage) se faire; (points) Sp marquer; (destination) arriver à; to m. happy/tired/etc rendre heureux/fatigué/etc; he made ten francs on it Com ça lui a rapporté dix francs; she made the train (did not miss) elle a eu le train; to m. s.o. do sth faire faire qch à qn, obliger qn à faire qch; to m. oneself heard se faire entendre; to m. oneself at home se mettre à l'aise; to m. ready préparer; to m. yellow jaunir; she made him her husband elle en a fait son mari; to m. do (manage) se débrouiller (with avec); to m. do with (be satisfied with) se contenter de; to m. it (arrive) arriver; (succeed) réussir; (say) dire; I m. it five o'clock j'ai cinq heures; what do you m. of it? qu'en penses-tu?; I can't m. anything of it je n'y comprends rien; to m. a living gagner sa vie; you're made (for life) ton avenir est assuré; to m. believe (pretend) faire semblant (that one is d'être); (n) it's m.-believe (story etc) c'est pure invention; to live in a world of m.-believe se bercer d'illusions; – vi to m. as if to (appear to) faire mine de; to m. for (go towards) aller vers; – n (brand) marque f; of French/etc m. de fabrication française/etc. ■ to m. off vi (run away) se sauver; to m. out vt (see) distinguer; (understand) comprendre; (decipher) déchiffrer; (draw up) faire (chèque, liste); (claim) prétendre (that que);

you made me out to be silly tu m'as fait passer pour un idiot; – vi (manage) Fam se débrouiller; to m. over vt (transfer) céder; (change) transformer (into en); to m. up vt (story) inventer; (put together) faire (collection, liste, etc); (prepare) préparer; (form) former, composer; (loss) compenser; (quantity) compléter; (quarrel) régler; (one's face) maquiller; to m. (of friends) se réconcilier; to m. up for (loss, damage, fault) compenser; (lost time, mistake) rattraper. ◆**m.-up** n (of object etc) constitution f; (of person) caractère m; (for face) maquillage m. ◆**making** n (manufacture) fabrication f; (of dress) confection f; history in the m. l'histoire en train de se faire; the makings of les éléments mpl (essentiels) de; to have the makings of a pianist/etc avoir l'étoffe d'un pianiste/etc. ◆**maker** n Com fabricant m. ◆**makeshift** n expédient m; – a (arrangement etc) de fortune, provisoire.

maladjusted [mæləˈdʒʌstɪd] a inadapté.

malaise [mæˈleɪz] n malaise m.

malaria [məˈleərɪə] n malaria f.

Malaysia [məˈleɪzɪə] n Malaisie f.

male [meɪl] a Biol Bot etc mâle; (clothes, sex) masculin; – n (man, animal) mâle m.

malevolent [məˈlevələnt] a malveillant. ◆**malevolence** n malveillance f.

malfunction [mælˈfʌŋkʃ(ə)n] n mauvais fonctionnement m; – vi fonctionner mal.

malice [ˈmælɪs] n méchanceté f; to bear s.o. m. vouloir du mal à qn. ◆**maˈlicious** a malveillant. ◆**maˈliciously** adv avec malveillance.

malign [məˈlaɪn] vt (slander) calomnier.

malignant [məˈlɪgnənt] a (person etc) malfaisant; m. tumour Med tumeur f maligne. ◆**maˈlignancy** n Med malignité f.

malingerer [məˈlɪŋgərər] n (pretending illness) simulateur, -euse mf.

mall [mɔːl] n (shopping) m. (covered) galerie f marchande; (street) rue f piétonnière.

malleable [ˈmælɪəb(ə)l] a malléable.

mallet [ˈmælɪt] n (tool) maillet m.

malnutrition [mælnjuˈtrɪʃ(ə)n] n malnutrition f, sous-alimentation f.

malpractice [mælˈpræktɪs] n Med Jur faute f professionnelle.

malt [mɔːlt] n malt m.

Malta [ˈmɔːltə] n Malte f. ◆**Malˈtese** a & n maltais, -aise (mf).

mammal [ˈmæm(ə)l] n mammifère m.

mammoth [ˈmæməθ] a (large) immense; – n (extinct animal) mammouth m.

man [mæn] n (pl **men** [men]) homme m;
(player) Sp joueur m; (chess piece) pièce f;
a golf m. (enthusiast) un amateur de golf;
he's a Bristol m. (by birth) il est de Bristol;
to be m. and wife être mari et femme; **my
old m.** Fam (father) mon père; (husband)
mon homme; **yes old m.!** Fam mon
vieux!; **the m. in the street** l'homme de la
rue; – vt (-nn-) (ship) pourvoir d'un équipage; (fortress) armer; (guns) servir; (be on
duty at) être de service à; **manned spacecraft** engin m spatial habité. ◆**manhood**
n (period) âge m d'homme. ◆**manhunt** n
chasse f à l'homme. ◆**manlike** a (quality)
d'homme viril. ◆**manly** a (-ier, -iest) viril.
◆**man-'made** a artificiel; (fibre) synthétique. ◆**manservant** n (pl **menservants**)
domestique m. ◆**man-to-'man** a & adv
d'homme à homme.

manacle ['mænɪk(ə)l] n menotte f.

manag/e ['mænɪdʒ] vt (run) diriger; (affairs
etc) Com gérer; (handle) manier; (task)
Fam prendre; (eat) Fam manger; (contribute) Fam donner; **to m. to do** (succeed)
réussir or arriver à (faire); (contrive) se
débrouiller pour faire; **I'll m. it** j'y
arriverai; – vi (succeed) y arriver; (make
do) se débrouiller (with avec); **to m. without
sth** se passer de qch. ◆**-ing** a **m. director**
directeur m général; **the m. director** le
PDG. ◆**-eable** a (parcel, person etc)
maniable; (feasible) faisable. ◆**-ement** n
direction f; (of property etc) gestion f;
(executive staff) cadres mpl. ◆**-er** n
directeur m; (of shop, café) gérant m; (business) m. (of actor, boxer etc) manager m.
◆**manage'ress** n directrice f; gérante f.
◆**manag'erial** [mænə'dʒɪərɪəl] a directo-
rial; **the m. class** or **staff** les cadres mpl.

mandarin ['mændərɪn] **1** n (high-ranking
official) haut fonctionnaire m; (in political
party) bonze m; (in university) Pej mandarin m. **2** a & n **m.** (orange) mandarine f.

mandate ['mændeɪt] n mandat m.
◆**mandatory** a obligatoire.

mane [meɪn] n crinière f.

maneuver [mə'nuːvər] n & vti Am =
manoeuvre.

mangle ['mæŋg(ə)l] **1** n (for wringing)
essoreuse f; – vt (clothes) essorer. **2** vt
(damage) mutiler.

mango ['mæŋgəʊ] n (pl -oes or -os) (fruit)
mangue f.

mangy ['meɪndʒɪ] a (animal) galeux.

manhandle [mæn'hænd(ə)l] vt maltraiter.

manhole ['mænhəʊl] n trou m d'homme; **m.
cover** plaque f d'égout.

mania ['meɪnɪə] n manie f. ◆**maniac** n fou
m, folle f; Psy Med maniaque mf; **sex m.**
obsédé m sexuel.

manicure ['mænɪkjʊər] n soin m des mains;
– vt (person) manucurer; (s.o.'s nails) faire.
◆**manicurist** n manucure mf.

manifest ['mænɪfest] **1** a (plain) manifeste.
2 vt (show) manifester.

manifesto [mænɪ'festəʊ] n (pl -os or -oes)
Pol manifeste m.

manifold ['mænɪfəʊld] a multiple.

manipulate [mə'nɪpjʊleɪt] vt manœuvrer;
(facts, electors etc) Pej manipuler.
◆**manipu'lation** n manœuvre f; Pej
manipulation f (of de).

mankind [mæn'kaɪnd] n (humanity) le genre
humain.

manner ['mænər] n (way) manière f; (behaviour) attitude f, comportement m; pl
(social habits) manières fpl; **in this m.** (like
this) de cette manière; **all m. of** toutes
sortes de. ◆**mannered** a (affected)
manière; **well-/bad-m.** bien/mal élevé.
◆**mannerism** n Pej tic m.

manoeuvre [mə'nuːvər] n manœuvre f; –
vti manœuvrer. ◆**manoeuvra'bility** n (of
vehicle etc) maniabilité f.

manor ['mænər] n m. (house) manoir m.

manpower ['mænpaʊər] n (labour)
main-d'œuvre f; Mil effectifs mpl; (effort)
force f.

mansion ['mænʃ(ə)n] n hôtel m particulier;
(in country) manoir m.

manslaughter ['mænslɔːtər] n Jur homicide
m involontaire.

mantelpiece ['mænt(ə)lpiːs] n (shelf)
cheminée f.

mantle ['mænt(ə)l] n (cloak) cape f.

manual ['mænjʊəl] **1** a (work etc) manuel. **2**
n (book) manuel m.

manufactur/e [mænjʊ'fæktʃər] vt fabriquer; – n fabrication f. ◆**-er** n fabricant,
-ante f.

manure [mə'njʊər] n fumier m, engrais m.

manuscript ['mænjʊskrɪpt] n manuscrit m.

many ['menɪ] a & n beaucoup (de); **m. things**
beaucoup de choses; **m. came** beaucoup
sont venus; **very m., a good** or **great m.** un
très grand nombre (de); **(a good or great)
m. of** un (très) grand nombre de; **m. of**
them un grand nombre d'entre eux; **m.
times, a time** bien des fois; **m. kinds**
toutes sortes (of de); **how m.?** combien
(de)?; **too m.** trop (de); **one m.** de trop;
there are too m. of them ils sont trop
nombreux; **so m.** tant (de); **as m. books/etc**

map   500   Marxism

as autant de livres/*etc* que; **as m. as** (*up to*) jusqu'à.

map [mæp] *n* (*of country etc*) carte *f*; (*plan*) plan *m*; – *vt* (-**pp**-) faire la carte *or* le plan de; **to m. out** (*road*) faire le tracé de; (*one's day etc*) Fig organiser.

maple ['meɪp(ə)l] *n* (*tree, wood*) érable *m*.

mar [mɑːr] *vt* (-**rr**-) gâter.

marathon ['mærəθən] *n* marathon *m*.

maraud [mə'rɔːd] *vi* piller. ◆—**ing** *a* pillard. ◆—**er** *n* pillard, -arde *mf*.

marble ['mɑːb(ə)l] *n* (*substance*) marbre *m*; (*toy ball*) bille *f*.

march [mɑːtʃ] *n* Mil marche *f*; – *vi* Mil marcher (au pas); **to m. in/out**/*etc* Fig entrer/sortir/*etc* d'un pas décidé; **to m. past** défiler; – *vt* **to m. s.o. off** *or* **away** emmener qn. ◆**m.-past** *n* défilé *m*.

March [mɑːtʃ] *n* mars *m*.

mare [meər] *n* jument *f*.

margarine [mɑːdʒə'riːn] *n* margarine *f*.

margin ['mɑːdʒɪn] *n* (*of page etc*) marge *f*; **by a narrow m.** (*to win*) de justesse. ◆**marginal** *a* marginal; **m. seat** Pol siège *m* disputé. ◆**marginally** *adv* très légèrement.

marguerite [mɑːɡə'riːt] *n* (*daisy*) marguerite *f*.

marigold ['mærɪɡəʊld] *n* (*flower*) souci *m*.

marijuana [mærɪ'wɑːnə] *n* marijuana *f*.

marina [mə'riːnə] *n* marina *f*.

marinate ['mærɪneɪt] *vti* Culin mariner.

marine [mə'riːn] **1** *a* (*life, flora etc*) marin. **2** *n* (*soldier*) fusilier *m* marin, *Am* marine *m*.

marionette [mærɪə'net] *n* marionnette *f*.

marital ['mærɪt(ə)l] *a* matrimonial; (*relations*) conjugal; **m. status** situation *f* de famille.

maritime ['mærɪtaɪm] *a* (*province, climate etc*) maritime.

marjoram ['mɑːdʒərəm] *n* (*spice*) marjolaine *f*.

mark¹ [mɑːk] *n* (*symbol*) marque *f*; (*stain, trace*) trace *f*, tache *f*, marque *f*; (*token, sign*) Fig signe *m*; (*for exercise etc*) Sch note *f*; (*target*) but *m*; (*model*) Tech série *f*; **to make one's m.** Fig s'imposer; **up to the m.** (*person, work*) à la hauteur; – *vt* marquer; (*exam etc*) Sch corriger, noter; (*pay attention to*) faire attention à; **to m. time** Mil marquer le pas; Fig piétiner; **m. you . . . !** remarque que . . . !; **to m. down** (*price*) baisser; **to m. off** (*separate*) séparer; (*on list*) cocher; **to m. out** (*area*) délimiter; **to m. s.o. out for** désigner qn pour; **to m. up** (*increase*) augmenter. ◆—**ed** *a* (*noticeable*) marqué. ◆—**edly** [-ɪdlɪ] *adv* visiblement.

◆—**ing(s)** *n(pl)* (*on animal etc*) marques *fpl*; (*on road*) signalisation *f* horizontale. ◆—**er** *n* (*flag etc*) marque *f*; (*pen*) feutre *m*, marqueur *m*.

mark² [mɑːk] *n* (*currency*) mark *m*.

market ['mɑːkɪt] *n* marché *m*; **on the open m.** en vente libre; **on the black m.** au marché noir; **the Common M.** le Marché commun; **m. value** valeur *f* marchande; **m. price** prix *m* courant; **m. gardener** maraîcher, -ère *mf*; – *vt* (*sell*) vendre; (*launch*) commercialiser. ◆—**ing** *n* marketing *m*, vente *f*. ◆—**able** *a* vendable.

marksman ['mɑːksmən] *n* (*pl* -**men**) tireur *m* d'élite.

marmalade ['mɑːməleɪd] *n* confiture *f* d'oranges.

maroon [mə'ruːn] *a* (*colour*) bordeaux *inv*.

marooned [mə'ruːnd] *a* abandonné; (*in snowstorm etc*) bloqué (by par).

marquee [mɑːkiː] *n* (*for concerts, garden parties etc*) chapiteau *m*; (*awning*) *Am* marquise *f*.

marquis ['mɑːkwɪs] *n* marquis *m*.

marrow ['mærəʊ] *n* **1** (*of bone*) moelle *f*. **2** (*vegetable*) courge *f*.

marr/y ['mærɪ] *vt* épouser, se marier avec; **to m. (off)** (*of priest etc*) marier; – *vi* se marier. ◆—**ied** *a* marié; (*life, state*) conjugal; **m. name** nom *m* de femme mariée; **to get m.** se marier. ◆**marriage** *n* mariage *m*; **to be related by m.** to être parent *m* par alliance (*bond*) conjugal; (*certificate*) de mariage; **m. bureau** agence *f* matrimoniale. ◆**marriageable** *a* en état de se marier.

marsh [mɑːʃ] *n* marais *m*, marécage *m*. ◆**marshland** *n* marécages *mpl*. ◆**marsh-'mallow** *n* Bot Culin guimauve *f*.

marshal ['mɑːʃ(ə)l] **1** *n* (*in army*) maréchal *m*; (*in airforce*) général *m*; (*at public event*) membre *m* du service d'ordre; Jur Am shérif *m*; – *vt* (-**ll**-, *Am* -**l**-) (*gather*) rassembler; (*lead*) mener cérémonieusement.

martial ['mɑːʃ(ə)l] *a* martial; **m. law** loi *f* martiale.

Martian ['mɑːʃ(ə)n] *n* & *a* martien, -ienne (*mf*).

martyr ['mɑːtər] *n* martyr, -yre *mf*; – *vt* Rel martyriser. ◆**martyrdom** *n* martyre *m*.

marvel ['mɑːv(ə)l] *n* (*wonder*) merveille *f*; (*miracle*) miracle *m*; – *vi* (-**ll**-, *Am* -**l**-) s'émerveiller (**at** de); – *vt* **to m. that** s'étonner de ce que (+ *sub or indic*). ◆**marvellous** *a* merveilleux.

Marxism ['mɑːksɪz(ə)m] *n* marxisme *m*. ◆**Marxist** *a* & *n* marxiste (*mf*).

marzipan ['mɑːzɪpæn] n pâte f d'amandes.

mascara [mæ'skɑːrə] n mascara m.

mascot ['mæskɒt] n mascotte f.

masculine ['mæskjʊlɪn] a masculin.
◆**mascu'linity** n masculinité f.

mash [mæʃ] n (for poultry etc) pâtée f; (potatoes) Culin purée f; − vt to m. (up) (crush) & Culin écraser; **mashed potatoes** purée f (de pommes de terre).

mask [mɑːsk] n masque m; − vt (cover, hide) masquer (**from** à).

masochism ['mæsəkɪz(ə)m] n masochisme m. ◆**masochist** n masochiste mf. ◆**maso'chistic** a masochiste.

mason ['meɪs(ə)n] n maçon m. ◆**masonry** n maçonnerie f.

masquerade [mɑːskə'reɪd] n (gathering, disguise) mascarade f; − vi to m. as se faire passer pour.

mass¹ [mæs] n masse f; a m. of (many) une multitude de; (pile) un tas de, une masse de; **to be a m. of bruises** Fam être couvert de bleus; **masses of** Fam des masses de; **the masses** (people) les masses fpl; − a (education) des masses; (culture, demonstration) de masse; (protests, departure) en masse; (production) en série, en masse; (hysteria) collectif; **m. grave** fosse f commune; **the media** mass media mpl; − vi (of troops, people) se masser. ◆**m.-pro'duce** vt fabriquer en série.

mass² [mæs] n Rel messe f.

massacre ['mæsəkər] n massacre m; − vt massacrer.

massage ['mæsɑːʒ] n massage m; − vt masser. ◆**ma'sseur** n masseur m.
◆**ma'sseuse** n masseuse f.

massive ['mæsɪv] a (solid) massif; (huge) énorme, considérable. ◆**-ly** adv (to increase, reduce etc) considérablement.

mast [mɑːst] n Nau mât m; Rad TV pylône m.

master ['mɑːstər] n maître m; (in secondary school) professeur m; a m.'s degree une maîtrise (**in** de); **M. of Arts/Science** (person) Univ Maître m ès lettres/sciences; **m. of ceremonies** (presenter) Am animateur, -trice mf; **m. card** carte f maîtresse; **m. stroke** coup m de maître; **key** passe-partout m inv; **old m.** (painting) tableau m de maître; **I'm my own m.** je ne dépends que de moi; − vt (control) maîtriser; (subject, situation) dominer; **she has mastered Latin** elle possède le latin.
◆**masterly** a magistral. ◆**mastery** n maîtrise f (**of** de).

mastermind ['mɑːstəmaɪnd] n (person) cerveau m; − vt organiser.

masterpiece ['mɑːstəpiːs] n chef-d'œuvre m.

mastic ['mæstɪk] n mastic m (silicone).

masturbate ['mæstəbeɪt] vi se masturber. ◆**mastur'bation** n masturbation f.

mat [mæt] **1** n tapis m, natte f; (at door) paillasson m; (**table**) m. (of fabric) napperon m; (hard) dessous-de-plat m inv; (**place**) m. set m (de table). **2** a (paint, paper) mat.

match¹ [mætʃ] n allumette f; **book of matches** pochette f d'allumettes. ◆**matchbox** n boîte f à allumettes. ◆**matchstick** n allumette f.

match² [mætʃ] n (game) Sp match m; (equal) égal, -ale mf; (marriage) mariage m; **to be a good m.** (of colours, people etc) être bien assortis; **he's a good m.** (man to marry) c'est un bon parti; − vt (of clothes) aller (bien) avec; **to m. (up to)** (equal) égaler; **to m. (up)** (plates etc) assortir; **to be well-matched** (of colours, people etc) être (bien) assortis, aller (bien) ensemble; − vi (go with each other) être assortis, aller (bien) ensemble. ◆**-ing** a (dress etc) assorti.

mate [meɪt] **1** n (friend) camarade mf; (of animal) mâle m, femelle f; (**builder's/electrician's**/etc m. aide-maçon/-électricien/etc m. **2** vi (of animals) s'accoupler (**with** avec). **3** n Chess mat m; − vt faire ou mettre mat.

material [mə'tɪərɪəl] **1** a matériel; (important) important. **2** n (substance) matière f; (cloth) tissu m; (for book) matériaux mpl; **material(s)** (equipment) matériel m; **building material(s)** matériaux mpl de construction. ◆**materialism** n matérialisme m.
◆**materialist** n matérialiste mf.
◆**materia'listic** a matérialiste. ◆**materialize** vi se matérialiser. ◆**materially** adv matériellement; (well-off etc) sur le plan matériel.

maternal [mə'tɜːn(ə)l] a maternel.
◆**maternity** n maternité f; **m. hospital, m. unit** maternité f; − a (clothes) de grossesse; (allowance, leave) de maternité.

mathematical [mæθə'mætɪk(ə)l] a mathématique; **to have a m. brain** être doué pour les maths. ◆**mathema'tician** n mathématicien, -ienne mf. ◆**mathematics** n mathématiques fpl. − **maths** n, Am **math** n Fam maths fpl.

matinée ['mætɪneɪ] n Th matinée f.

matriculation [mətrɪkjʊ'leɪʃ(ə)n] n Univ inscription f.

matrimony ['mætrɪmənɪ] n mariage m. ◆**matri'monial** a matrimonial.

matrix, pl **-ices** ['meɪtrɪks, -ɪsɪz] n Tech matrice f.

matron ['meɪtrən] n Lit mère f de famille, dame f âgée; (nurse) infirmière f (en) chef. ◆**matronly** a (air etc) de mère de famille; (mature) mûr; (portly) corpulent.

matt [mæt] a (paint, paper) mat.

matted ['mætɪd] a **m. hair** cheveux mpl emmêlés.

matter¹ ['mætər] n matière f; (affair) affaire f, question f; (thing) chose f; **no m.!** (no importance) peu importe!; **no m. what she does** quoi qu'elle fasse; **no m. where you go** où que tu ailles; **no m. who you are** qui que vous soyez; **no m. when** quel que soit le moment; **what's the m.?** qu'est-ce qu'il y a?; **what's the m. with you?** qu'est-ce que tu as?; **there's sth the m.** il y a qch qui ne va pas; **there's sth the m. with my leg** j'ai qch à la jambe; **there's nothing the m. with him** il n'a rien; — vi (be important) importer (to à); **it doesn't m. if/when/who/etc** peu importe si/quand/qui/etc; **it doesn't m.!** ça ne fait rien!, peu importe! ◆**m.-of-'fact** a (person, manner) terre à terre; (voice) neutre.

matter² ['mætər] n (pus) Med pus m.

matting ['mætɪŋ] n (material) nattage m; **a piece of m.**, **some m.** une natte.

mattress ['mætrɪs] n matelas m.

mature [mə'tjʊər] a mûr; (cheese) fait; — vt (person, plan) (faire) mûrir; — vi mûrir; (of cheese) se faire. ◆**maturity** n maturité f.

maul [mɔːl] vt (of animal) mutiler; (of person) Fig malmener.

mausoleum [mɔːsə'lɪəm] n mausolée m.

mauve [məʊv] a & n (colour) mauve (m).

maverick ['mævərɪk] n & a Pol dissident, -ente (mf).

mawkish ['mɔːkɪʃ] a d'une sensiblerie excessive, mièvre.

maxim ['mæksɪm] n maxime f.

maximum ['mæksɪməm] n (pl **-ima** [-ɪmə] or **-imums**) maximum m; — a maximum (f inv), maximal. ◆**maximize** vt porter au maximum.

may [meɪ] v aux (pt **might**) **1** (possibility) he m. come il peut arriver; he might come il pourrait arriver; **I m. or might be wrong** il se peut que je me trompe, je me trompe peut-être; **you m. or might have** tu aurais pu; **I m. or might have forgotten** it je l'ai peut-être oublié; **we m. or might as well go**

nous ferions aussi bien de partir; **she fears I m.** or **might get lost** elle a peur que je ne me perde. **2** (permission) **m. I stay?** puis-je rester?; **m. I?** vous permettez?; **you m.** go tu peux partir. **3** (wish) **m. you be happy** (que tu) sois heureux. ◆**maybe** adv peut-être.

May [meɪ] n mai m.

mayhem ['meɪhem] n (chaos) pagaïe f; (havoc) ravages mpl.

mayonnaise [meɪə'neɪz] n mayonnaise f.

mayor [meər] n (man, woman) maire m. ◆**mayoress** n femme f du maire.

maze [meɪz] n labyrinthe m.

MC [em'siː] abbr = **master of ceremonies**.

me [miː] pron me, m'; (after prep etc) moi; (to) me (indirect) me, m'; **she knows me** elle me connaît; **he helps me** il m'aide; **he gives (to) me** il me donne; **with me** avec moi.

meadow ['medəʊ] n pré m, prairie f.

meagre ['miːgər] a maigre.

meal [miːl] n **1** (food) repas m. **2** (flour) farine f.

mealy-mouthed [miːlɪ'maʊðd] a mielleux.

mean¹ [miːn] vt (pt & pp **meant** [ment]) (signify) vouloir dire, signifier; (destine) destiner (for à); (entail) entraîner; (represent) représenter; (refer to) faire allusion à; **to m. to do** (intend) avoir l'intention de faire, vouloir faire; **I m. it, I m. what I say** je suis sérieux; **to m. sth to s.o.** (matter) avoir de l'importance pour qn; **it means sth to me** (name, face) ça me dit qch; **I didn't m. to!** je ne l'ai pas fait exprès!; **you were meant to come** vous étiez censé venir. ◆**-ing** n sens m, signification f. ◆**meaningful** a significatif. ◆**meaningless** a qui n'a pas de sens; (absurd) Fig insensé.

mean² [miːn] a (-er, -est) (stingy) avare, mesquin; (petty) mesquin; (nasty) méchant; (inferior) misérable. ◆**-ness** n (greed) avarice f; (nastiness) méchanceté f.

mean³ [miːn] a (distance) moyen; — n (middle position) milieu m; (average) Math moyenne f; **the happy m.** le juste milieu.

meander [mɪ'ændər] vi (of river) faire des méandres.

means [miːnz] n(pl) (method) moyen(s) m(pl) (**to do**, of doing faire); (wealth) moyens mpl; **by m. of** (stick etc) au moyen de; (work, concentration) à force de; **by all m.!** très certainement!; **by no m.** nullement; **independent** or **private m.** fortune f personnelle.

meant [ment] see **mean¹**.

meantime ['miːntaɪm] adv & n (in the) m. entre-temps. ◆**meanwhile** adv entre-temps.

measles ['miːz(ə)lz] n rougeole f.

measly ['miːzlɪ] a (contemptible) Fam minable.

measur/e ['meʒər] n mesure f; (ruler) règle f; **made to m.** fait sur mesure; – vt mesurer; (strength etc) Fig estimer, mesurer; (adjust, adapt) adapter (**to** à); **to m. up** mesurer; – vi **to m. up to** être à la hauteur de. ◆**-ed** a (careful) mesuré. ◆**-ement** n (of chest, waist etc) tour m; pl (dimensions) mesures fpl; **your hip m.** ton tour de hanches.

meat [miːt] n viande f; (of crab, lobster etc) chair f; Fig substance f; **m. diet** régime m carné. ◆**meaty** a (**-ier, -iest**) (fleshy) charnu; (flavour) de viande; Fig substantiel.

mechanic [mɪ'kænɪk] n mécanicien, -ienne mf. ◆**mechanical** a mécanique; (reply etc) Fig machinal. ◆**mechanics** n (science) mécanique f; pl (workings) mécanisme m. ◆'**mechanism** n mécanisme m. ◆'**mechanize** vt mécaniser.

medal ['med(ə)l] n médaille f. ◆**me-'dallion** n (ornament, jewel) médaillon m. ◆**medallist** n médaillé, -ée mf; **to be a gold/silver m.** Sp être médaille d'or/d'argent.

meddle ['med(ə)l] vi (interfere) se mêler (**in** de); (tamper) toucher (**with** à). ◆**meddlesome** a qui se mêle de tout.

media ['miːdɪə] npl **1** (the (mass) m. les médias mpl. **2** see **medium**.

mediaeval [medɪ'iːv(ə)l] a médiéval.

median ['miːdɪən] a **m. strip** Aut Am bande f médiane.

mediate ['miːdɪeɪt] vi servir d'intermédiaire (**between** entre). ◆**medi'ation** n médiation f. ◆**mediator** n médiateur, -trice f.

medical ['medɪk(ə)l] a médical; (school, studies) de médecine; (student) en médecine; – n (in school, army) visite f médicale; (private) examen m médical. ◆**medicated** a (shampoo) médical. ◆**medi'cation** n médicaments mpl. ◆**me'dicinal** a médicinal. ◆**medicine** n médecine f; (substance) médicament m; **m. cabinet, m. chest** pharmacie f.

medieval [medɪ'iːv(ə)l] a médiéval.

mediocre [miːdɪ'əʊkər] a médiocre. ◆**mediocrity** n médiocrité f.

meditate ['medɪteɪt] vi méditer (**on** sur). ◆**medi'tation** n méditation f. ◆**meditative** a méditatif.

Mediterranean [medɪtə'reɪnɪən] a méditerranéen; – n **the M.** la Méditerranée.

medium ['miːdɪəm] **1** a (average, middle) moyen. **2** n (pl **media** ['miːdɪə]) Phys véhicule m; Biol milieu m; (for conveying data or publicity) support m; **through the m. of** par l'intermédiaire de; **the happy m.** le juste milieu. **3** n (person) médium m. ◆**m.-sized** a à moyen, de taille moyenne.

medley ['medlɪ] n mélange m; Mus pot-pourri m.

meek [miːk] a (**-er, -est**) doux.

meet [miːt] vt (pt & pp **met**) (encounter) rencontrer; (see again, join) retrouver; (pass in street, road etc) croiser; (fetch) (aller or venir) chercher; (wait for) attendre; (debt, enemy, danger) faire face à; (need) combler; **to arrange to m. s.o.** donner rendez-vous à qn; – vi (of people, teams, rivers, looks) se rencontrer; (of people by arrangement) se retrouver; (be introduced) se connaître; (of society) se réunir; (of trains, vehicles) se croiser; **to m. up with** rencontrer; (by arrangement) retrouver; **to m. up** se rencontrer; se retrouver; **to m. with** (accident, problem) avoir; (loss, refusal) essuyer; (obstacle, difficulty) rencontrer; **to m. with s.o.** Am rencontrer qn; retrouver qn; – n Sp Am réunion f; **to make a m. with** Fam donner rendez-vous à. ◆**-ing** n (gathering) (large) assemblée f; (between two people) rencontre f, (prearranged) rendez-vous m inv; **in a m.** en conférence.

megalomania [megələʊ'meɪnɪə] n mégalomanie f. ◆**megalomaniac** n mégalomane mf.

megaphone ['megəfəʊn] n porte-voix m inv.

melancholy ['melənkəlɪ] n mélancolie f; – a mélancolique.

mellow ['meləʊ] a (**-er, -est**) (fruit) mûr; (colour, voice, wine) moelleux; (character) mûri par l'expérience; – vi (of person) s'adoucir.

melodrama ['melədrɑːmə] n mélodrame m. ◆**melodra'matic** a mélodramatique.

melody ['melədɪ] n mélodie f. ◆**me'lodic** a mélodique. ◆**me'lodious** a mélodieux.

melon ['melən] n (fruit) melon m.

melt [melt] vi fondre; **to m. into** (merge) Fig se fondre dans; – vt (faire) fondre; **to m. down** (metal object) fondre; **melting point** point m de fusion; **melting pot** Fig creuset m.

member ['membər] n membre m; **M. of Parliament** député m. ◆**membership** n adhésion f (**of** à); (number) nombre m de(s) membres; (members) membres mpl; **m. (fee)** cotisation f.

membrane ['membreɪn] n membrane f.

memento [mə'mentəʊ] n (pl -os or -oes) (object) souvenir m.

memo ['meməʊ] n (pl -os) note f; **m. pad** bloc-notes m. ◆**memo'randum** n note f; Pol Com mémorandum m.

memoirs ['memwɑːz] npl (essays) mémoires mpl.

memory ['memərɪ] n mémoire f; (recollection) souvenir m; **to the** or **in m. of** à la mémoire de. ◆**memorable** a mémorable. ◆**me'morial** (plaque etc) commémoratif; – n monument m, mémorial m. ◆**memorize** vt apprendre par cœur.

men [men] see **man**. ◆**menfolk** n Fam hommes mpl.

menac/e ['menɪs] n danger m; (nuisance) Fam plaie f; (threat) menace f; – vt menacer. ◆**—ingly** adv (to say) d'un ton menaçant; (to do) d'une manière menaçante.

menagerie [mɪ'nædʒərɪ] n ménagerie f.

mend [mend] vt (repair) réparer; (clothes) raccommoder; **to m. one's ways** se corriger, s'amender; – n raccommodage m; **to be on the m.** (after illness) aller mieux.

menial ['miːnɪəl] a inférieur.

meningitis [menɪn'dʒaɪtɪs] n Med méningite f.

menopause ['menəpɔːz] n ménopause f.

menstruation [menstrʊ'eɪʃ(ə)n] n menstruation f.

mental ['ment(ə)l] a mental; (hospital) psychiatrique; (mad) Sl fou; **m. strain** tension f nerveuse. ◆**men'tality** n mentalité f. ◆**mentally** adv mentalement; **he's m. handicapped** c'est un handicapé mental; **she's m. ill** c'est une malade mentale.

mention ['menʃ(ə)n] vt mentionner, faire mention de; **not to m.** . . . sans parler de . . . , sans compter . . . ; **don't m. it!** il n'y a pas de quoi!; **no savings/etc worth mentioning** pratiquement pas d'économies/etc; – n mention f.

mentor ['mentɔː] n (adviser) mentor m.

menu ['menjuː] n menu m.

mercantile ['mɜːkəntaɪl] a (activity etc) commercial; (ship) marchand; (nation) commerçant.

mercenary ['mɜːsɪnərɪ] a n mercenaire (m).

merchandise ['mɜːtʃəndaɪz] n (articles) marchandises fpl; (total stock) marchandise f.

merchant ['mɜːtʃ(ə)nt] n (trader) Fin négociant, -ante mf; (retail) **m.** commerçant m (en détail); **wine m.** négociant, -ante mf en vins; (shopkeeper) marchand m de

vins; – a (vessel, navy) marchand; (seaman) de la marine marchande; **m. bank** banque f de commerce.

mercury ['mɜːkjʊrɪ] n mercure m.

mercy ['mɜːsɪ] n pitié f; Rel miséricorde f; **to beg for m.** demander grâce; **at the m. of** à la merci de; **it's a m. that** . . . (stroke of luck) c'est une chance que . . . ◆**merciful** a miséricordieux. ◆**mercifully** adv (fortunately) Fam heureusement. ◆**merciless** a impitoyable.

mere [mɪə] a simple; (only) ne . . . que; **she's a m. child** ce n'est qu'une enfant; **it's a m. kilometre** ça ne fait qu'un kilomètre; **by m. chance** par pur hasard; **the m. sight of her** or **him** sa seule vue. ◆**—ly** adv (tout) simplement.

merg/e [mɜːdʒ] vi (blend) se mêler (with à); (of roads) se (re)joindre; (of firms) Com fusionner; – vt (unify) Pol unifier; Com fusionner. ◆**—er** n Com fusion f.

meridian [mə'rɪdɪən] n méridien m.

meringue [mə'ræŋ] n (cake) meringue f.

merit ['merɪt] n mérite m; **on its merits** (to consider sth etc) objectivement; – vt mériter.

mermaid ['mɜːmeɪd] n (woman) sirène f.

merry ['merɪ] a (-ier, -iest) gai; (drunk) Fam éméché. ◆**m.-go-round** n (at funfair etc) manège m. ◆**m.-making** n réjouissances fpl. ◆**merrily** adv gaiement. ◆**merriment** n gaieté f, rires mpl.

mesh [meʃ] n (of net etc) maille f; (fabric) tissu m à mailles; (of intrigue etc) Fig réseau m; (of circumstances) Fig engrenage m; **wire m.** grillage m.

mesmerize ['mezməraɪz] vt hypnotiser.

mess[1] [mes] n **1** (confusion) désordre m, pagaïe f; (muddle) gâchis m; (dirt) saleté f; **in a m.** en désordre; (trouble) Fam dans le pétrin; (pitiful state) dans un triste état; **to make a m. of** (spoil) gâcher. **2** vt **to m. s.o. about** (bother, treat badly) Fam déranger qn, embêter qn; **to m. up** (spoil) gâcher; (dirty) salir; (room) mettre en désordre; – vi **to m. about** (have fun, idle) s'amuser; (play the fool) faire l'idiot; **to m. about with** (fiddle with) s'amuser avec. ◆**m.-up** n (disorder) Fam gâchis m. ◆**messy** a (-ier, -iest) (untidy) en désordre; (dirty) sale; (confused) Fig embrouillé, confus.

mess[2] [mes] n Mil mess m inv.

message ['mesɪdʒ] n message m. ◆**messenger** n messager, -ère mf; (in office, hotel) coursier, -ière mf.

Messiah [mɪ'saɪə] n Messie m.

Messrs ['mesəz] *npl* M. Brown Messieurs *or* MM Brown.

met [met] *see* meet.

metal ['met(ə)l] *n* métal *m*. ◆**me'tallic** *a* métallique; (*paint*) métallisé. ◆**metal-work** *n* (*objects*) ferronnerie *f*; (*study, craft*) travail *m* des métaux.

metamorphosis, *pl* **-oses** [metə'mɔ:fəsɪs, -sɪːz] *n* métamorphose *f*.

metaphor ['metəfər] *n* métaphore *f*. ◆**met-a'phorical** *a* métaphorique.

metaphysical [metə'fɪzɪk(ə)l] *a* métaphysique.

mete [miːt] *vt* to m. out (*justice*) rendre; (*punishment*) infliger.

meteor ['miːtɪər] *n* météore *m*. ◆**mete'oric** *a* m. rise *Fig* ascension *f* fulgurante. ◆**meteorite** *n* météorite *m*.

meteorological [miːtɪərə'lɒdʒɪk(ə)l] *a* météorologique. ◆**meteo'rology** *n* météorologie *f*.

meter ['miːtər] *n* (*device*) compteur *m*; (*parking*) m. parcmètre *m*; m. maid *Aut Fam* contractuelle *f*.

method ['meθəd] *n* méthode *f*. ◆**me'thodical** *a* méthodique.

Methodist ['meθədɪst] *a* & *n Rel* méthodiste (*mf*).

methylated ['meθɪleɪtɪd] *a* m. spirit(s) alcool *m* à brûler. ◆**meths** *n Fam* = **methylated spirits**.

meticulous [mɪ'tɪkjʊləs] *a* méticuleux. ◆**-ness** *n* soin *m* méticuleux.

metre ['miːtər] *n* mètre *m*. ◆**metric** ['metrɪk] *a* métrique.

metropolis [mə'trɒpəlɪs] *n* (*chief city*) métropole *f*. ◆**metro'politan** *a* métropolitain.

mettle ['met(ə)l] *n* courage *m*, fougue *f*.

mew [mjuː] *vi* (*of cat*) miauler.

mews [mjuːz] *n* (*street*) ruelle *f*; m. flat appartement *m* chic (*aménagé dans une ancienne écurie*).

Mexico ['meksɪkəʊ] *n* Mexique *m*. ◆**Mexican** *a* & *n* mexicain, -aine (*mf*).

mezzanine ['mezənɪn] *n* m. (floor) entresol *m*.

miaow [miː'aʊ] *vi* (*of cat*) miauler; – *n* miaulement *m*; – *int* miaou.

mice [maɪs] *see* mouse.

mickey ['mɪkɪ] *n* to take the m. out of s.o. *Sl* charrier qn.

micro- ['maɪkrəʊ] *pref* micro-.

microbe ['maɪkrəʊb] *n* microbe *m*.

microchip ['maɪkrəʊtʃɪp] *n* puce *f*.

microcosm ['maɪkrəʊkɒz(ə)m] *n* microcosme *m*.

microfilm ['maɪkrəʊfɪlm] *n* microfilm *m*.

microphone ['maɪkrəfəʊn] *n* microphone *m*.

microscope ['maɪkrəskəʊp] *n* microscope *m*. ◆**micro'scopic** *a* microscopique.

microwave ['maɪkrəʊweɪv] *n* micro-onde *f*; m. oven four *m* à micro-ondes.

mid [mɪd] *a* (in) m.-June (à) la mi-juin; (in) m. morning au milieu de la matinée; in m. air en plein ciel; to be in one's m.-twenties avoir environ vingt-cinq ans.

midday [mɪd'deɪ] *n* midi *m*; – *a* de midi.

middle ['mɪd(ə)l] *n* milieu *m*; (*waist*) *Fam* taille *f*; (right) in the m. of au (beau) milieu de; in the m. of work en plein travail; in the m. of saying/working/*etc* en train de dire/travailler/*etc*; – *a* (*central*) du milieu; (*class, ear, quality*) moyen; (*name*) deuxième. ◆**m.-'aged** *a* d'un certain âge. ◆**m.-'class** *a* bourgeois. ◆**m.-of-the-'road** *a* (*politics, views*) modéré; (*music, tastes*) sage.

middling ['mɪdlɪŋ] *a* moyen, passable.

midge [mɪdʒ] *n* (*fly*) moucheron *m*.

midget ['mɪdʒɪt] *n* nain *m*, naine *f*; – *a* minuscule.

Midlands ['mɪdləndz] *npl* the M. les comtés *mpl* du centre de l'Angleterre.

midnight ['mɪdnaɪt] *n* minuit *m*.

midriff ['mɪdrɪf] *n* *Anat* diaphragme *m*; (*belly*) *Fam* ventre *m*.

midst [mɪdst] *n* in the m. of (*middle*) au milieu de; in our/their m. parmi nous/eux.

midsummer [mɪd'sʌmər] *n* milieu *m* de l'été; (*solstice*) solstice *m* d'été. ◆**mid-winter** *n* milieu *m* de l'hiver; solstice *m* d'hiver.

midterm ['mɪdtɜːm] *a* m. holidays *Sch* petites vacances *fpl*.

midway [mɪd'weɪ] *a* & *adv* à mi-chemin.

midweek [mɪd'wiːk] *n* milieu *m* de la semaine.

midwife ['mɪdwaɪf] *n* (*pl* **-wives**) sage-femme *f*.

might [maɪt] **1** *see* may. **2** *n* (*strength*) force *f*. ◆**mighty** *a* (**-ier, -iest**) puissant; (*ocean*) vaste; (*very great*) *Fam* sacré; – *adv* (*very*) *Fam* rudement.

migraine ['miːɡreɪn, 'maɪɡreɪn] *n* *Med* migraine *f*.

migrate [maɪ'ɡreɪt] *vi* émigrer. ◆**'migrant** *a* & *n* m. (worker) migrant, -ante (*mf*). ◆**migration** *n* migration *f*.

mike [maɪk] *n* *Fam* micro *m*.

mild [maɪld] *a* (**-er, -est**) (*person, weather, taste etc*) doux; (*beer, punishment*) léger; (*medicine, illness*) bénin. ◆**-ly** *adv* doucement; (*slightly*) légèrement; **to put it m.** pour ne pas dire plus. ◆**—ness** n douceur f; légèreté f; caractère m bénin.

mildew ['mɪldjuː] n (*on cheese etc*) moisissure f.

mile [maɪl] n mile m, mille m (= 1,6 km); pl (*loosely*) = kilomètres mpl; **to walk for miles** marcher pendant des kilomètres; **miles better** (*much*) Fam bien mieux. ◆**mileage** n — kilométrage m; (*per gallon*) consommation f aux cent kilomètres. ◆**milestone** n — borne f kilométrique; Fig jalon m.

militant ['mɪlɪtənt] a & n militant, -ante (mf). ◆**military** a militaire; — the **m.** (*soldiers*) les militaires mpl; (*army*) l'armée f. ◆**militate** vi (*of arguments etc*) militer (**in favour of pour**).

militia [mə'lɪʃə] n milice f. ◆**militiaman** n (pl **-men**) milicien m.

milk [mɪlk] n lait m; evaporated m. lait concentré; – a (*chocolate*) au lait; (*bottle, can*) à lait; (*diet*) lacté; (*produce*) laitier; m. **float** voiture f de laitier; m. **shake** milk-shake m; – vt (*cow*) traire; (*extract*) Fig soutirer (**s.o. of sth** qch à qn); (*exploit*) Fig exploiter. ◆**—ing** n traite f. ◆**milkman** n (pl **-men**) laitier m. ◆**milky** a (**-ier**, **-iest**) (*diet*) lacté; (*coffee, tea*) au lait; (*colour*) laiteux; **the M. Way** la Voie lactée.

mill [mɪl] n **1** moulin m; (*factory*) usine f; **cotton m.** filature f de coton; **paper m.** papeterie f; – vt (*grind*) moudre. **2** vi **to m. around** (*of crowd*) grouiller. ◆**miller** n meunier, -ière mf. ◆**millstone** n (*burden*) boulet m (**round one's neck** qu'on traîne).

millennium, pl **-nia** [mɪ'lenɪəm, -nɪə] n millénaire m.

millet ['mɪlɪt] n Bot millet m.

milli- [mɪlɪ] pref milli-.

millimetre ['mɪlɪmiːtər] n millimètre m.

million ['mɪljən] n million m; **a m.** men/etc un million d'hommes/etc; **two m.** deux millions. ◆**millio'naire** n millionnaire mf. ◆**millionth** a & n millionième (mf).

mime [maɪm] n (*actor*) mime mf; (*art*) mime m; – vti mimer.

mimeograph® ['mɪmɪəgræf] vt polycopier.

mimic ['mɪmɪk] vt (**-ck-**) imiter; – n imitateur, -trice mf. ◆**mimicking** n, ◆**mimicry** n imitation f.

mimosa [mɪ'məuzə] n Bot mimosa m.

minaret [mɪnə'ret] n (*of mosque*) minaret m.

mince [mɪns] n (*meat*) hachis m (de viande); Am = **mincemeat**; – vt hacher; **not to m. matters** or **one's words** ne pas mâcher ses

mots. ◆**mincemeat** n (*dried fruit*) mélange m de fruits secs. ◆**mincer** n (*machine*) hachoir m.

mind [maɪnd] **1** n esprit m; (*sanity*) raison f; (*memory*) mémoire f; (*opinion*) avis m, idée f; (*thought*) pensée f; (*head*) tête f; **to change one's m.** changer d'avis; **to my m.** à mon avis; **in two minds** (*undecided*) irrésolu; **to make up one's m.** se décider; **to be on s.o.'s m.** (*worry*) préoccuper qn; **out of one's m.** (*mad*) fou; **to bring to m.** (*recall*) rappeler; **to bear** or **keep in m.** (*remember*) se souvenir de; **to have in m.** (*person, plan*) avoir en vue; **to have a good m. to do** avoir bien envie de faire. **2** vti (*heed*) faire attention à; (*look after*) garder, s'occuper de; (*noise, dirt etc*) être gêné par; (*one's language*) surveiller; **m. you don't fall** (*beware*) prends garde de ne pas tomber; **m. you do it** n'oublie pas de le faire; **do you m. if?** (*I smoke etc*) ça vous gêne si?; (*I leave, help etc*) ça ne vous fait rien si?; **I don't m. the sun** le soleil ne me gêne pas, je ne suis pas gêné par le soleil; **I don't m.** (*care*) ça m'est égal; **I wouldn't m. a cup of tea** (*would like*) j'aimerais bien une tasse de thé; **I m. that . . .** ça m'ennuie or me gêne que . . . ; **never m.!** (*it doesn't matter*) ça ne fait rien!, tant pis!; (*don't worry*) ne vous en faites pas! **m.** (**out!**) (*watch out*) attention!; **m. you . . .** remarquez (que) . . . ; **m. your own business!**, never you **m.!** mêlez-vous de ce qui vous regarde! ◆**—ed** suffix **fair-m.** a impartial; **like-m.** a de même opinion. ◆**—er** n (*for children*) gardien, -ienne mf, (*nurse*) nourrice f; (*bodyguard*) Fam gorille m. ◆**mind-boggling** a stupéfiant, qui confond l'imagination. ◆**mindful** a m. **of sth/doing** attentif à qch/à faire. ◆**mindless** a stupide.

mine¹ [maɪn] poss pron le mien, la mienne, pl les mien(ne)s; **this hat is m.** ce chapeau est à moi or est le mien; **a friend of m.** un ami à moi.

min/e² [maɪn] n **1** (*for coal, gold etc*) & Fig mine f; – vt **to m. (for)** (*coal etc*) extraire. **2** (*explosive*) mine f; – vt (*beach, bridge etc*) miner. ◆**—ing** n exploitation f minière; – a (*industry*) minier. ◆**—er** n mineur m.

mineral ['mɪnərəl] a & n minéral (m).

mingle ['mɪŋg(ə)l] vi se mêler (**with** à); **to m. with** (*socially*) fréquenter.

mingy ['mɪndʒɪ] a (**-ier**, **-iest**) (*mean*) Fam radin.

mini- [mɪnɪ] pref mini-.

miniature ['mɪnɪtʃər] n miniature f; – a (*train etc*) miniature inv; (*tiny*) minuscule.

minibus ['mɪnɪbʌs] *n* minibus *m*. ◆**minicab** *n* (radio-)taxi *m*.

minim ['mɪnɪm] *n Mus* blanche *f*.

minimum ['mɪnɪməm] *n* (*pl* -**ima** [-ɪmə] or -**imums**) minimum *m*; – *a* minimum (*f inv*), minimal. ◆**minimal** *a* minimal. ◆**minimize** *vt* minimiser.

minister ['mɪnɪstər] *n Pol Rel* ministre *m*. ◆**mini'sterial** *a* ministériel. ◆**ministry** *n* ministère *m*.

mink [mɪŋk] *n* (*animal, fur*) vison *m*.

minor ['maɪnər] *a* (*small*) *Jur Mus* mineur; (*detail, operation*) petit; – *n Jur* mineur, -eure *mf*.

Minorca [mɪ'nɔːkə] *n* Minorque *f*.

minority [maɪ'nɒrɪtɪ] *n* minorité *f*; **in the** or **a m.** en minorité, minoritaire; – *a* minoritaire.

mint [mɪnt] **1** *n* (*place*) Hôtel *m* de la Monnaie; **a m.** (*of money*) Fig une petite fortune; – *vt* (*money*) frapper; – *a* (*stamp*) neuf; **in m. condition** à l'état neuf. **2** *n Bot Culin* menthe *f*; (*sweet*) pastille *f* de menthe; – *a* à la menthe.

minus ['maɪnəs] *prep Math* moins; (*without*) Fam sans; **it's m. ten (degrees)** il fait moins dix (degrés); – *n m.* (*sign*) (signe *m*) moins *m*.

minute[1] ['mɪnɪt] **1** *n* minute *f*; **this (very) m.** (*now*) à la minute; **any m. (now)** d'une minute à l'autre; **m. hand** (*of clock*) grande aiguille *f*. **2** *npl* (*of meeting*) procès-verbal *m*.

minute[2] [maɪ'njuːt] *a* (*tiny*) minuscule; (*careful, exact*) minutieux.

minx [mɪŋks] *n* (*girl*) Pej diablesse *f*, chipie *f*.

miracle ['mɪrək(ə)l] *n* miracle *m*. ◆**mi'raculous** *a* miraculeux.

mirage ['mɪrɑːʒ] *n* mirage *m*.

mire [maɪər] *n Lit* fange *f*.

mirror ['mɪrər] *n* miroir *m*, glace *f*; Fig miroir *m*; (**rear view**) **m.** Aut rétroviseur *m*; – *vt* refléter.

mirth [mɜːθ] *n Lit* gaieté *f*, hilarité *f*.

misadventure [mɪsəd'ventʃər] *n* mésaventure *f*.

misanthropist [mɪ'zænθrəpɪst] *n* misanthrope *m*.

misapprehend [mɪsæprɪ'hend] *vt* mal comprendre. ◆**misapprehension** *n* malentendu *m*.

misappropriate [mɪsə'prəuprɪeɪt] *vt* (*money*) détourner.

misbehave [mɪsbɪ'heɪv] *vi* se conduire mal; (*of child*) faire des sottises.

miscalculate [mɪs'kælkjuleɪt] *vt* mal

calculer; – *vi* Fig se tromper. ◆**miscalcu-'lation** *n* erreur *f* de calcul.

miscarriage [mɪs'kærɪdʒ] *n* **to have a m.** Med faire une fausse couche; **m. of justice** erreur *f* judiciaire. ◆**miscarry** *vi* Med faire une fausse couche; (*of plan*) Fig échouer.

miscellaneous [mɪsɪ'leɪnɪəs] *a* divers.

mischief ['mɪstʃɪf] *n* espièglerie *f*; (*maliciousness*) méchanceté *f*; **to get into m.** faire des bêtises; **full of m.** = mischievous; **to make m. for** (*trouble*) créer des ennuis à; **to do s.o. a m.** (*harm*) faire mal à qn; **a little m.** (*child*) un petit démon. ◆**mischievous** *a* (*playful, naughty*) espiègle, malicieux; (*malicious*) méchant.

misconception [mɪskən'sepʃ(ə)n] *n* idée *f* fausse.

misconduct [mɪs'kɒndʌkt] *n* mauvaise conduite *f*; Com mauvaise gestion *f*.

misconstrue [mɪskən'struː] *vt* mal interpréter.

misdeed [mɪs'diːd] *n* méfait *m*.

misdemeanor [mɪsdɪ'miːnər] *n Jur* délit *m*.

misdirect [mɪsdɪ'rekt] *vt* (*letter*) mal adresser; (*energies*) mal diriger; (*person*) mal renseigner.

miser ['maɪzər] *n* avare *mf*. ◆**—ly** *a* avare.

misery ['mɪzərɪ] *n* (*suffering*) souffrances *fpl*; (*sadness*) tristesse *f*; (*sad person*) Fam grincheux, -euse *mf*; *pl* (*troubles*) misères *fpl*; **his life is a m.** il est malheureux. ◆**miserable** *a* (*wretched*) misérable; (*unhappy*) malheureux; (*awful*) affreux; (*derisory*) dérisoire. ◆**miserably** *adv* misérablement; (*to fail*) lamentablement.

misfire [mɪs'faɪər] *vi* (*of engine*) avoir des ratés; (*of plan*) Fig rater.

misfit ['mɪsfɪt] *n Pej* inadapté, -ée *mf*.

misfortune [mɪs'fɔːtʃuːn] *n* malheur *m*, infortune *f*.

misgivings [mɪs'gɪvɪŋz] *npl* (*doubts*) doutes *mpl*; (*fears*) craintes *fpl*.

misguided [mɪs'gaɪdɪd] *a* (*action etc*) imprudent; **to be m.** (*of person*) se tromper.

mishandle [mɪs'hænd(ə)l] *vt* (*affair, situation*) traiter avec maladresse; (*person*) s'y prendre mal avec.

mishap ['mɪshæp] *n* (*accident*) mésaventure *f*; (*hitch*) contretemps *m*.

misinform [mɪsɪn'fɔːm] *vt* mal renseigner.

misinterpret [mɪsɪn'tɜːprɪt] *vt* mal interpréter.

misjudge [mɪs'dʒʌdʒ] *vt* (*person, distance etc*) mal juger.

mislay [mɪs'leɪ] *vt* (*pt* & *pp* mislaid) égarer.

mislead [mɪs'liːd] *vt* (*pt* & *pp* misled) tromper. ◆**—ing** *a* trompeur.

mismanage [mɪs'mænɪdʒ] *vt* mal administrer. ◆—ment *n* mauvaise administration *f*.

misnomer [mɪs'nəumər] *n* (*name*) nom *m* or terme *m* impropre.

misogynist [mɪ'sɒdʒɪnɪst] *n* misogyne *mf*.

misplace [mɪs'pleɪs] *vt* (*trust etc*) mal placer; (*lose*) égarer. ◆—ed *a* (*remark etc*) déplacé.

misprint [mɪsprɪnt] *n* faute *f* d'impression, coquille *f*.

mispronounce [mɪsprə'nauns] *vt* mal prononcer.

misquote [mɪs'kwəut] *vt* citer inexactement.

misrepresent [mɪsreprɪ'zent] *vt* présenter sous un faux jour.

miss[1] [mɪs] *vt* (*train, target, opportunity etc*) manquer, rater; (*not see*) ne pas voir; (*not understand*) ne pas comprendre; (*one's youth, deceased person etc*) regretter; (*sth just lost*) remarquer l'absence de; **he misses Paris/her** Paris/elle lui manque; **I m. you** tu me manques; **don't m. seeing this play** (*don't fail to*) ne manque pas de voir cette pièce; **to m. out** (*omit*) sauter; – *vi* manquer, rater; **to m. out** (*lose a chance*) rater l'occasion; **to m. out on** (*opportunity etc*) rater, laisser passer; – *n* coup *m* manqué; **that was** *or* **we had a near m.** on l'a échappé belle; **I'll give it a m.** *Fam* (*not go*) je n'y irai pas; (*not take or drink or eat*) je n'en prendrai pas. ◆—ing *a* (*absent*) absent; (*in war, after disaster*) disparu; (*object*) manquant; **there are two cups/students m.** il manque deux tasses/deux étudiants.

miss[2] [mɪs] *n* mademoiselle *f*; **Miss Brown** Mademoiselle or Mlle Brown.

misshapen [mɪs'ʃeɪp(ə)n] *a* difforme.

missile ['mɪsaɪl, *Am* 'mɪs(ə)l] *n* (*rocket*) *Mil* missile *m*; (*object thrown*) projectile *m*.

mission ['mɪʃ(ə)n] *n* mission *f*. ◆**missionary** *n* missionnaire *m*.

missive ['mɪsɪv] *n* (*letter*) missive *f*.

misspell [mɪs'spel] *vt* (*pt & pp* **-ed** *or* **misspelt**) mal écrire.

mist [mɪst] *n* (*fog*) brume *f*; (*on glass*) buée *f*; – *vi* **to m. over** *or* **up** s'embuer.

mistake [mɪ'steɪk] *n* erreur *f*, faute *f*; **to make a m.** se tromper, faire (une) erreur; **by m.** par erreur; – *vt* (*pt* **mistook**, *pp* **mistaken**) (*meaning, intention etc*) se tromper sur; **to m. the date/place/etc** se tromper de date/de lieu/*etc*; **you can't m.**, **there's no mistaking** (*his face, my car etc*) il est impossible de ne pas reconnaître; **to m.**

s.o./sth for prendre qn/qch pour. ◆**mistaken** *a* (*idea etc*) erroné; **to be m.** se tromper. ◆**mistakenly** *adv* par erreur.

mister ['mɪstər] *n Fam* monsieur *m*.

mistletoe ['mɪs(ə)ltəu] *n Bot* gui *m*.

mistreat [mɪs'tri:t] *vt* maltraiter.

mistress ['mɪstrɪs] *n* maîtresse *f*; (*in secondary school*) professeur *m*.

mistrust [mɪs'trʌst] *n* méfiance *f*; – *vt* se méfier de. ◆**mistrustful** *a* méfiant.

misty ['mɪstɪ] *a* (-**ier**, -**iest**) (*foggy*) brumeux; (*glass*) embué.

misunderstand [mɪsʌndə'stænd] *vt* (*pt & pp* -**stood**) mal comprendre. ◆**misunderstanding** *n* (*disagreement*) malentendu *m*; (*mistake*) erreur *f*. ◆**misunderstood** *a* (*person*) incompris.

misuse [mɪs'ju:z] *vt* (*word, tool*) mal employer; (*power etc*) abuser de; – [mɪs'ju:s] *n* (*of word*) emploi *m* abusif; (*of tool*) usage *m* abusif; (*of power etc*) abus *m*.

mite [maɪt] *n* 1 (*insect*) mite *f*. 2 (*poor*) **m.** (*child*) (pauvre) petit, -ite *mf*. 3 **a m.** (*somewhat*) *Fam* un petit peu.

mitigate ['mɪtɪgeɪt] *vt* atténuer.

mitt(en) [mɪt, 'mɪt(ə)n] *n* (*glove*) moufle *f*.

mix [mɪks] *vt* mélanger, mêler; (*cement, cake*) préparer; (*salad*) remuer; – *vi* se mélanger; (*perplex*) embrouiller (qn); (*confuse, mistake*) confondre (**with** avec); **to be mixed up with s.o.** (*involved*) être mêlé aux affaires de qn; **to m. up in** (*involve*) mêler à; – *vi* se mêler; (*of colours*) s'allier; **to m. with** (*socially*) fréquenter; **she doesn't m. (in)** elle n'est pas sociable; – *n* (*mixture*) mélange *m*. ◆—**ed** *a* (*school, marriage*) mixte; (*society*) mêlé; (*feelings*) mitigés, mêlés; (*results*) divers; (*nuts, chocolates etc*) assortis; **to be (all) m. up** (*of person*) être désorienté; (*of facts, account etc*) être embrouillé. ◆—**ing** *n* mélange *m*. ◆—**er** *n* *Culin El* mixe(u)r *m*; (*for mortar*) *Tech* malaxeur *m*; **to be a good m.** (*of person*) être sociable. ◆**mixture** *n* mélange *m*; (*for cough*) sirop *m*. ◆**mix-up** *n Fam* confusion *f*.

mm *abbr* (*millimetre*) mm.

moan [məun] *vi* (*groan*) gémir; (*complain*) se plaindre (**to** à, **about** de, **that** que); – *n* gémissement *m*; plainte *f*.

moat [məut] *n* douve(s) *f(pl)*.

mob [mɒb] *n* (*crowd*) cohue *f*, foule *f*; (*gang*) bande *f*; **the m.** (*masses*) la populace; (*Mafia*) *Am Sl* la mafia; – *vt* (-**bb**-) assiéger. ◆**mobster** *n Am Sl* gangster *m*.

mobile ['məubaɪl, *Am* 'məub(ə)l] *a* mobile; (*having a car etc*) *Fam* motorisé; **m. home**

mobil-home *m*; **m. library** bibliobus *m*; – *n* (*Am* ['məubi:l]) (*ornament*) mobile *m*. ◆**mo'bility** *n* mobilité *f*. ◆**mobili'zation** *n* mobilisation *f*. ◆**mobilize** *vti* mobiliser.

moccasin ['mɒkəsɪn] *n* (*shoe*) mocassin *m*.

mocha ['məukə] *n* (*coffee*) moka *m*.

mock [mɒk] **1** *vt* se moquer de; (*mimic*) singer; – *vi* se moquer (**at de**). **2** *a* (*false*) simulé; (*exam*) blanc. ◆**—ing** *n* moquerie *f*; – *a* moqueur. ◆**mockery** *n* (*act*) moquerie *f*; (*parody*) parodie *f*; **to make a m. of** tourner en ridicule.

mock-up ['mɒkʌp] *n* (*model*) maquette *f*.

mod cons [mɒd'kɒnz] *abbr Fam* = **modern conveniences.**

mode [məud] *n* (*manner, way*) mode *m*; (*fashion, vogue*) mode *f*.

model ['mɒd(ə)l] *n* (*example, person etc*) modèle *m*; (*fashion*) **m.** mannequin *m*; (*scale*) **m.** maquette *f*; – *a* (*behaviour, factory etc*) modèle; (*car, plane*) modèle réduit *inv*; **m. railway** train *m* miniature; – *vt* modeler (**on** sur); (*hats*) présenter (les modèles de); – *vi* (*for fashion*) être mannequin; (*pose for artist*) poser. ◆**modelling** *n* (*of statues etc*) modelage *m*.

moderate¹ ['mɒdərət] *a* modéré; (*in speech*) mesuré; (*result*) passable; – *n Pol* modéré, -ée *mf*. ◆**—ly** *adv* (*in moderation*) modérément; (*averagely*) moyennement.

moderate² ['mɒdəreɪt] *vt* (*diminish, tone down*) modérer. ◆**mode'ration** *n* modération *f*; **in m.** avec modération.

modern ['mɒd(ə)n] *a* moderne; **m. languages** langues *fpl* vivantes; **m. conveniences** tout le confort moderne. ◆**modernism** *n* modernisme *m*. ◆**moderni'zation** *n* modernisation *f*. ◆**modernize** *vt* moderniser.

modest ['mɒdɪst] *a* modeste. ◆**modesty** *n* (*quality*) modestie *f*; (*moderation*) modération *f*; (*of salary etc*) modicité *f*.

modicum ['mɒdɪkəm] *n* **a m. of** un soupçon de, un petit peu de.

modify ['mɒdɪfaɪ] *vt* (*alter*) modifier; (*tone down*) modérer. ◆**modifi'cation** *n* modification *f*.

modulate ['mɒdjuleɪt] *vt* moduler. ◆**modu'lation** *n* modulation *f*.

module ['mɒdju:l] *n* module *m*.

mogul ['məug(ə)l] *n* magnat *m*, manitou *m*.

mohair ['məuheə] *n* mohair *m*.

moist [mɔɪst] *a* (**-er, -est**) humide; (*clammy, sticky*) moite. ◆**moisten** *vt* humecter. ◆**moisture** *n* humidité *f*; (*on glass*) buée *f*.

◆**moisturiz/e** *vt* (*skin*) hydrater. ◆**—er** *n* (*cream*) crème *f* hydratante.

molar ['məulə] *n* (*tooth*) molaire *f*.

molasses [mə'læsɪz] *n* (*treacle*) *Am* mélasse *f*.

mold [məuld] *Am* = **mould.**

mole [məul] *n* **1** (*on skin*) grain *m* de beauté. **2** (*animal, spy*) taupe *f*.

molecule ['mɒlɪkju:l] *n* molécule *f*.

molest [mə'lest] *vt* (*annoy*) importuner; (*child, woman*) *Jur* attenter à la pudeur de.

mollusc ['mɒləsk] *n* mollusque *m*.

mollycoddle ['mɒlɪkɒd(ə)l] *vt* dorloter.

molt [məult] *Am* = **moult.**

molten ['məult(ə)n] *a* (*metal*) en fusion.

mom [mɒm] *n Am Fam* maman *f*.

moment ['məumənt] *n* moment *m*, instant *m*; **this (very) m.** (*now*) à l'instant; **the m. she leaves** dès qu'elle partira; **any m. (now)** d'un moment ou d'un instant à l'autre. ◆**momentarily** (*Am* [məumən'terɪlɪ]) *adv* (*temporarily*) momentanément; (*soon*) *Am* tout à l'heure. ◆**momentary** *a* momentané.

momentous [məu'mentəs] *a* important.

momentum [məu'mentəm] *n* (*speed*) élan *m*; **to gather** or **gain m.** (*of ideas etc*) *Fig* gagner du terrain.

mommy ['mɒmɪ] *n Am Fam* maman *f*.

Monaco ['mɒnəkəu] *n* Monaco *f*.

monarch ['mɒnək] *n* monarque *m*. ◆**monarchy** *n* monarchie *f*.

monastery ['mɒnəst(ə)rɪ] *n* monastère *m*.

Monday ['mʌndɪ] *n* lundi *m*.

monetary ['mʌnɪt(ə)rɪ] *a* monétaire.

money ['mʌnɪ] *n* argent *m*; **paper m.** papier-monnaie *m*, billets *mpl*; **to get one's m.'s worth** en avoir pour son argent; **he gets** or **earns good m.** il gagne bien (sa vie); **to be in the m.** *Fam* rouler sur l'or; **m. order** mandat *m*. ◆**moneybags** *n Pej Fam* richard, -arde *mf*. ◆**moneybox** *n* tirelire *f*. ◆**moneychanger** *n* changeur *m*. ◆**moneylender** *n* prêteur, -euse *mf* sur gages. ◆**moneymaking** *a* lucratif. ◆**money-spinner** *n* (*source of wealth*) *Fam* mine *f* d'or.

mongol ['mɒŋg(ə)l] *n & a Med* mongolien, -ienne (*mf*).

mongrel ['mʌŋgrəl] *n* (*dog*) bâtard *m*.

monitor ['mɒnɪtə] **1** *n* (*pupil*) chef *m* de classe. **2** *n* (*screen*) *Tech* moniteur *m*. **3** *vt* (*a broadcast*) *Rad* écouter; (*check*) *Fig* contrôler.

monk [mʌŋk] *n* moine *m*, religieux *m*.

monkey ['mʌŋkɪ] *n* singe *m*; **little m.** (*child*) *Fam* polisson, -onne *mf*; **m. business** *Fam*

singeries *fpl*; − *vi* **to m. about** *Fam* faire l'idiot.
mono ['mɒnəʊ] *a* (*record etc*) mono *inv*.
mono- ['mɒnəʊ] *pref* mono-.
monocle ['mɒnək(ə)l] *n* monocle *m*.
monogram ['mɒnəgræm] *n* monogramme *m*.
monologue ['mɒnəlɒg] *n* monologue *m*.
monopoly [mə'nɒpəlɪ] *n* monopole *m*. ◆**monopolize** *vt* monopoliser.
monosyllable ['mɒnəsɪləb(ə)l] *n* monosyllabe *m*. ◆**monosyllabic** *a* monosyllabique.
monotone ['mɒnətəʊn] *n* **in a m.** sur un ton monocorde.
monotony [mə'nɒtənɪ] *n* monotonie *f*. ◆**monotonous** *a* monotone.
monsoon [mɒn'su:n] *n* (*wind, rain*) mousson *f*.
monster ['mɒnstər] *n* monstre *m*. ◆**monstrosity** *n* (*horror*) monstruosité *f*. ◆**monstrous** *a* (*abominable, enormous*) monstrueux.
month [mʌnθ] *n* mois *m*. ◆**monthly** *a* mensuel; **m. payment** mensualité *f*; − *n* (*periodical*) mensuel *m*; − *adv* (*every month*) mensuellement.
Montreal [mɒntrɪ'ɔːl] *n* Montréal *m or f*.
monument ['mɒnjʊmənt] *n* monument *m*. ◆**monu'mental** *a* monumental; **m. mason** marbrier *m*.
moo [mu:] *vi* meugler; − *n* meuglement *m*.
mooch [mu:tʃ] *vi* **to m. around** *Fam* flâner. **2** *vt* **to m. sth off s.o.** (*cadge*) *Am Sl* taper qch à qn.
mood [mu:d] *n* (*of person*) humeur *f*; (*of country*) état *m* d'esprit; *Gram* mode *m*; **in a good/bad m.** de bonne/mauvaise humeur; **to be in the m. to do** or **for doing** être d'humeur à faire, avoir envie de faire. ◆**moody** *a* (**-ier, -iest**) (*changeable*) d'humeur changeante; (*bad-tempered*) de mauvaise humeur.
moon [mu:n] *n* lune *f*; **once in a blue m.** (*rarely*) *Fam* tous les trente-six du mois; **over the m.** (*delighted*) *Fam* ravi (**about** de). ◆**moonlight** **1** *n* clair *m* de lune. **2** *vi Fam* travailler au noir. ◆**moonshine** *n* (*talk*) *Fam* balivernes *fpl*.
moor [mʊər] **1** *vt Nau* amarrer; − *vi* mouiller. **2** *n* (*open land*) lande *f*. ◆**-ings** *npl Nau* (*ropes etc*) amarres *fpl*; (*place*) mouillage *m*.
moose [mu:s] *n inv* (*animal*) orignac *m*, élan *m*.
moot [mu:t] **1** *a* (*point*) discutable. **2** *vt* (*question*) soulever, suggérer.

mop [mɒp] **1** *n* balai *m* (à laver), balai *m* éponge; **dish m.** lavette *f*; **m. of hair** tignasse *f*. **2** *vt* (**-pp-**) **to m. (up)** (*wipe*) essuyer; **to m. one's brow** s'essuyer le front.
mope [məʊp] *vi* **to m. (about)** être déprimé, avoir le cafard.
moped ['məʊped] *n* cyclomoteur *m*, mobylette® *f*.
moral ['mɒrəl] *a* moral; − *n* (*of story etc*) morale *f*; *pl* (*standards*) moralité *f*, morale *f*. ◆**morale** [mə'rɑːl, *Am* mə'ræl] *n* moral *m*. ◆**moralist** *n* moraliste *mf*. ◆**mo'rality** *n* (*morals*) moralité *f*. ◆**moralize** *vi* moraliser. ◆**morally** *adv* moralement.
morass [mə'ræs] *n* (*land*) marais *m*; (*mess*) *Fig* bourbier *m*.
moratorium [mɒrə'tɔːrɪəm] *n* moratoire *m*.
morbid ['mɔːbɪd] *a* morbide.
more [mɔːr] *a & n* plus (de) (**than** que); (*other*) d'autres; **m. cars/etc** plus de voitures/*etc*; **he has m.** (**than you**) il en a plus (que toi); **a few m. months** encore quelques mois, quelques mois de plus; (*some*) **m. tea/etc** encore du thé/*etc*; (*some*) **m. details** d'autres détails; **m. than a kilo/ten/etc** (*with quantity, number*) plus d'un kilo/de dix/*etc*; − *adv* (*tired, rapidly etc*) plus (**than** que); **m. and m.** de plus en plus; **m.** or **less** plus ou moins; **the m.** he shouts **the m.** hoarse he gets plus il crie plus il s'enroue; **she hasn't any m.** elle n'en a plus. ◆**mo'reover** *adv* de plus, d'ailleurs.
moreish ['mɔːrɪʃ] *a Fam* qui a un goût de revenez-y.
mores ['mɔːreɪz] *npl* mœurs *fpl*.
morgue [mɔːg] *n* (*mortuary*) morgue *f*.
moribund ['mɒrɪbʌnd] *a* moribond.
morning ['mɔːnɪŋ] *n* matin *m*; (*duration of morning*) matinée *f*; **in the m.** (*every morning*) le matin; (*during the morning*) pendant la matinée; (*tomorrow*) demain matin; **at seven in the m.** à sept heures du matin; **every Tuesday m.** tous les mardis matin; **in the early m.** au petit matin; − *a* du matin, matinal. ◆**mornings** *adv Am* le matin.
Morocco [mə'rɒkəʊ] *n* Maroc *m*. ◆**Moroccan** *a & n* marocain, -aine (*mf*).
moron ['mɔːrɒn] *n* crétin, -ine *mf*.
morose [mə'rəʊs] *a* morose.
morphine ['mɔːfiːn] *n* morphine *f*.
Morse [mɔːs] *n & a* **M. (code)** morse *m*.
morsel ['mɔːs(ə)l] *n* (*of food*) petite bouchée *f*.
mortal ['mɔːt(ə)l] *a & n* mortel, -elle (*mf*). ◆**mor'tality** *n* (*death rate*) mortalité *f*.
mortar ['mɔːtər] *n* mortier *m*.

mortgage ['mɔːgɪdʒ] n prêt-logement m; – vt (house, future) hypothéquer.

mortician [mɔː'tɪʃ(ə)n] n Am entrepreneur m de pompes funèbres.

mortify ['mɔːtɪfaɪ] vt mortifier.

mortuary ['mɔːtʃʊərɪ] n morgue f.

mosaic [məʊ'zeɪɪk] n mosaïque f.

Moscow ['mɒskəʊ, Am 'mɒskaʊ] n Moscou m or f.

Moses ['məʊzɪz] a M. basket couffin m.

Moslem ['mɒzlɪm] a & n musulman, -ane (mf).

mosque [mɒsk] n mosquée f.

mosquito [mɒ'skiːtəʊ] n (pl -oes) moustique m; m. net moustiquaire f.

moss [mɒs] n Bot mousse f. ◆**mossy** a moussu.

most [məʊst] a & n the m. (greatest in amount etc) le plus (de); I have (the) m. books j'ai le plus de livres; I have (the) m. j'en ai le plus; m. (of the) books/etc la plupart des livres/etc; m. of the cake/etc la plus grande partie du gâteau/etc; m. of them la plupart d'entre eux; m. of it la plus grande partie; at (the very) m. tout au plus; to make the m. of profiter (au maximum) de; – adv (le) plus; (very) fort, très; the m. beautiful le plus beau, la plus belle (in, of de); to talk (the) m. parler le plus; m. of all (especially) surtout. ◆-**ly** adv surtout, pour la plupart.

motel [məʊ'tel] n motel m.

moth [mɒθ] n papillon m de nuit; (clothes) m. mite f. ◆**m.-eaten** a mité. ◆**mothball** n boule f de naphtaline.

mother ['mʌðər] n mère f; M.'s Day la fête des Mères; m. **tongue** langue f maternelle; – vt (care for) materner. ◆**motherhood** n maternité f. ◆**motherly** a maternel. **mother-in-law** ['mʌðərɪnlɔː] n (pl mothers-in-law) belle-mère f. ◆**m.-of-pearl** n (substance) nacre f. ◆**m.-to-be** n (pl mothers-to-be) future mère f.

motion ['məʊʃ(ə)n] n mouvement m; Pol motion f; m. **picture** film m; – vti to m. (to) s.o. to do faire signe à qn de faire. ◆-**less** a immobile.

motive ['məʊtɪv] n motif m (for, of de); Jur mobile m (for de); – a (power, decision etc) moteur. ◆**motivate** vt (person, decision etc) motiver. ◆**moti'vation** n motivation f; (incentive) encouragement m.

motley ['mɒtlɪ] a (coloured) bigarré; (collection) hétéroclite.

motor ['məʊtər] n (engine) moteur m; (car) Fam auto f; – a (industry, vehicle etc) automobile; (accident) d'auto; m. **boat** canot m automobile; m. **mechanic** mécanicien-auto

m; m. **mower** tondeuse f à moteur; – vi (drive) rouler en auto. ◆-**ing** n Sp automobilisme m; **school of m.** auto-école f. ◆**motorbike** n Fam moto f. ◆**motorcade** n cortège m (officiel) (de voitures). ◆**motorcar** n automobile f. ◆**motorcycle** n moto f, motocyclette f. ◆**motorcyclist** n motocycliste m f. ◆**motorist** n automobiliste mf. ◆**motorized** a motorisé. ◆**motorway** n autoroute f.

mottled ['mɒt(ə)ld] a tacheté.

motto ['mɒtəʊ] n (pl -oes) devise f.

mould [məʊld] **1** n (shape) moule m; – vt (clay etc) mouler; (statue, character) modeler. **2** n (growth, mildew) moisissure f. ◆**mouldy** a (-ier, -iest) moisi; to go m. moisir.

moult [məʊlt] vi muer. ◆-**ing** n mue f.

mound [maʊnd] n (of earth) tertre m; (pile) Fig monceau m.

mount [maʊnt] **1** n (mountain) Lit mont m. **2** n (horse) monture f; (frame for photo or slide) cadre m; (stamp hinge) charnière f; – vt (horse, hill, jewel, photo, demonstration etc) monter; (ladder, tree etc) monter sur, grimper à; (stamp) coller (dans un album); – vi to m. (up) (on horse) se mettre en selle. **3** vi (increase) monter; to m. up (add up) chiffrer (to à); (accumulate) s'accumuler.

mountain ['maʊntɪn] n montagne f; – a (people, life) montagnard. ◆**mountaineer** n alpiniste mf. ◆**mountaineering** n alpinisme m. ◆**mountainous** a montagneux.

mourn [mɔːn] vti to m. (for) pleurer. ◆-**ing** n deuil m; in m. en deuil. ◆-**er** n parent, -ente mf or ami, -ie mf du défunt or de la défunte. ◆**mournful** a triste.

mouse, pl **mice** [maʊs, maɪs] n souris f. ◆**mousetrap** n souricière f.

mousse [muːs] n Culin mousse f.

moustache [mə'stɑːʃ, Am 'mʌstæʃ] n moustache f.

mousy ['maʊsɪ] a (-ier, -iest) (hair) Pej châtain terne; (shy) timide.

mouth [maʊθ] n (pl -s [maʊðz]) bouche f; (of dog, lion etc) gueule f; (of river) embouchure f; (of cave, harbour) entrée f; – [maʊð] vt Pej dire. ◆**mouthful** n (of food) bouchée f; (of liquid) gorgée f. ◆**mouthorgan** n harmonica m. ◆**mouthpiece** n Mus embouchure f; (spokesman) Fig porte-parole m inv. ◆**mouthwash** n bain m de bouche. ◆**mouth-watering** a appétissant.

mov/e [muːv] n mouvement m; (change of

house etc) déménagement *m*; (*change of job*) changement *m* d'emploi; (*transfer of employee*) mutation *f*; (*in game*) coup *m*, (*one's turn*) tour *m*; (*act*) Fig démarche *f*; (*step*) pas *m*; (*attempt*) tentative *f*; **to make a m.** (*leave*) se préparer à partir; (*act*) Fig passer à l'action; **to get a m. on** Fam se dépêcher; **on the m.** en marche; – *vt* déplacer, remuer, bouger; (*arm, leg*) remuer; (*crowd*) faire partir; (*put*) mettre; (*transport*) transporter; (*piece in game*) jouer; (*propose*) Pol proposer; **to m. s.o.** (*incite*) pousser qn (*to do* à faire); (*emotionally*) émouvoir qn; (*transfer in job*) muter qn; **to m. house** déménager; **to m. sth back** reculer qch; **to m. sth down** descendre qch; **to m. sth forward** avancer qch; **to m. sth over** pousser qch; – *vi* bouger, remuer; (*go*) aller (**to** à); (*pass*) passer (**to** à); (*leave*) partir; (*change seats*) changer de place; (*progress*) avancer; (*act*) agir; (*play*) jouer; **to m.** (**out**) (*of house etc*) déménager; **to m. to** (*a new region etc*) aller habiter; **to m. about** se déplacer; (*fidget*) remuer; **to m. along** *or* **forward** *or* **on** avancer; **to m. away** *or* **off** (*go away*) s'éloigner; **to m. back** (*withdraw*) reculer; (*return*) retourner; **to m. in** (*to house*) emménager; **to m. into** (*house*) emménager dans; **m. on!** circulez!; **to m. over** *or* **up** se pousser. ◆**—ing** *a* en mouvement; (*part*) Tech mobile; (*stairs*) mécanique; (*touching*) émouvant. ◆**move(able)** *a* mobile. ◆**movement** *n* (*action, group etc*) & *Mus* mouvement *n*.

movie ['mu:vı] *n* Fam film *m*; **the movies** (*cinema*) le cinéma; **m. camera** caméra *f*. ◆**moviegoer** *n* cinéphile *mf*.

mow [məʊ] *vt* (*pp* **mown** *or* **mowed**) (*field*) faucher; **to m. the lawn** tondre le gazon; **to m. down** (*kill etc*) Fig faucher. ◆**—er** *n* (*lawn*) m. tondeuse *f* (à gazon).

MP [em'pi:] *n abbr* (*Member of Parliament*) député *m*.

Mrs ['mısız] *n* (*married woman*) **Mrs Brown** Madame *or* Mme Brown.

Ms [mız] *n* (*married or unmarried woman*) **Ms Brown** Madame *or* Mme Brown.

MSc, *Am* **MS** *abbr* = **Master of Science.**

much [mʌtʃ] *a & n* beaucoup (de); **not m. time/money/etc** pas beaucoup de temps/d'argent/*etc*; **not m.** pas beaucoup; **m. of** (*a good deal of*) une bonne partie de; **as m. as** (*to do, know etc*) autant que; **as m. wine/etc** as autant de vin/*etc* que; **as m. as you like** autant que tu veux; **twice as m.** deux fois plus (de); **how m.?** combien (de)?; **too m.**

trop (de); **so m.** tant (de), tellement (de); **I know/I shall do this m.** je sais/je ferai ceci (du moins); **this m. wine** ça de vin; **it's not m. of a garden** ce n'est pas merveilleux comme jardin; **m. the same** presque le même; – *adv* very **m.** beaucoup; **not** (**very**) **m.** pas beaucoup; **she doesn't say very m.** elle ne dit pas grand-chose.

muck [mʌk] **1** *n* (*manure*) fumier *m*; (*filth*) Fig saleté *f*. **2** *vi* **to m. about** (*have fun, idle*) s'amuser; (*play the fool*) faire l'idiot; **to m. about with** Fam (*fiddle with*) s'amuser avec; (*alter*) changer (*texte etc*); **to m. in** (*join in*) Fam participer, contribuer; – *vt* **to m. s.o. about** Fam embêter qn, déranger qn; **to m. up** (*spoil*) Fam gâcher, ruiner. ◆**m.-up** *n* Fam gâchis *m*. ◆**mucky** *a* (**-ier, -iest**) sale.

mucus ['mju:kəs] *n* mucosités *fpl*.

mud [mʌd] *n* boue *f*. ◆**muddy** *a* (**-ier, -iest**) (*water*) boueux; (*hands etc*) couvert de boue. ◆**mudguard** *n* garde-boue *m inv*.

muddle ['mʌd(ə)l] *n* (*mess*) désordre *m*; (*mix-up*) confusion *f*; **in a m.** (*room etc*) sens dessus dessous, en désordre; (*person*) désorienté; (*mind, ideas*) embrouillé; – *vt* (*person, facts etc*) embrouiller; (*papers*) mélanger; – *vi* **to m. through** Fam se débrouiller tant bien que mal.

muff [mʌf] *n* (*for hands*) manchon *m*.

muffin ['mʌfɪn] *n* petit pain *m* brioché.

muffl/e ['mʌf(ə)l] *vt* (*noise*) assourdir. ◆**—ed** *a* (*noise*) sourd. ◆**—er** *n* (*scarf*) cache-col *m inv*; *Aut Am* silencieux *m*.

mug [mʌg] **1** *n* grande tasse *f*; (*of metal or plastic*) gobelet *m*; (*beer*) **m.** chope *f*. **2** *n* (*face*) Sl gueule *f*; **m. shot** Fam photo *f* d'identité). **3** *n* (*fool*) Fam naïs, -aise *mf*. **4** *vt* (**-gg-**) (*attack*) agresser. ◆**mugger** *n* agresseur *m*. ◆**mugging** *n* agression *f*.

muggy ['mʌgı] *a* (**-ier, -iest**) (*weather*) lourd.

mulberry ['mʌlbərı] *n* (*fruit*) mûre *f*.

mule [mju:l] *n* (*male*) mulet *m*; (*female*) mule *f*.

mull [mʌl] **1** *vt* (*wine*) chauffer. **2** *vi* **to m. over** (*think over*) ruminer.

mullet ['mʌlɪt] *n* (*fish*) mulet *m*; (**red**) **m.** rouget *m*.

multi- ['mʌltı] *pref* multi-.

multicoloured ['mʌltıkʌləd] *a* multicolore.

multifarious [mʌltı'feərıəs] *a* divers.

multimillionaire [mʌltımıljə'neər] *n* milliardaire *mf*.

multinational [mʌltı'næʃ(ə)nəl] *n* multinationale *f*.

multiple [ˈmʌltɪp(ə)l] *a* multiple; – *n Math* multiple *m*. ◆**multipli'cation** *n* multiplication *f*. ◆**mul'tiplicity** *n* multiplicité *f*. ◆**multiply** [-plaɪ] *vt* multiplier; – *vi* (*reproduce*) se multiplier.

multistorey [mʌltɪˈstɔːrɪ] (*Am* **multistoried**) *a* à étages.

multitude [ˈmʌltɪtjuːd] *n* multitude *f*.

mum [mʌm] **1** *n Fam* maman *f*. **2** *a* **to keep m.** garder le silence.

mumble [ˈmʌmb(ə)l] *vti* marmotter.

mumbo-jumbo [mʌmbəʊˈdʒʌmbəʊ] *n* (*words*) charabia *m*.

mummy [ˈmʌmɪ] *n* **1** *Fam* maman *f*. **2** (*body*) momie *f*.

mumps [mʌmps] *n* oreillons *mpl*.

munch [mʌntʃ] *vti* (*chew*) mastiquer; **to m. (on)** (*eat*) *Fam* bouffer.

mundane [mʌnˈdeɪn] *a* banal.

municipal [mjuːˈnɪsɪp(ə)l] *a* municipal. ◆**munici'pality** *n* municipalité *f*.

munitions [mjuːˈnɪʃ(ə)nz] *npl* munitions *fpl*.

mural [ˈmjʊərəl] *a* mural; – *n* fresque *f*, peinture *f* murale.

murder [ˈmɜːdər] *n* meurtre *m*, assassinat *m*; **it's m.** (*dreadful*) *Fam* c'est affreux; – *vt* (*kill*) assassiner; (*spoil*) *Fig* massacrer. ◆**–er** *n* meurtrier, -ière *mf*, assassin *m*. ◆**murderous** *a* meurtrier.

murky [ˈmɜːkɪ] *a* (*-ier, -iest*) obscur; (*water, business, past*) trouble; (*weather*) nuageux.

murmur [ˈmɜːmər] *n* murmure *m*; (*of traffic*) bourdonnement *m*; – *vti* murmurer.

muscle [ˈmʌs(ə)l] *n* muscle *m*; – *vi* **to m. in on** (*group*) *Sl* s'introduire par la force à. ◆**muscular** *a* (*tissue etc*) musculaire; (*brawny*) musclé.

muse [mjuːz] *vi* méditer (**on** sur).

museum [mjuːˈzɪəm] *n* musée *m*.

mush [mʌʃ] *n* (*soft mass*) bouillie *f*; *Fig* sentimentalité *f*. ◆**mushy** *a* (*-ier, -iest*) (*food etc*) en bouillie; *Fig* sentimental.

mushroom [ˈmʌʃrʊm] **1** *n* champignon *m*. **2** *vi* (*grow*) pousser comme des champignons; (*spread*) se multiplier.

music [ˈmjuːzɪk] *n* musique *f*; **m. centre** chaîne *f* stéréo compacte; **m. critic** critique *m* musical; **m. hall** music-hall *m*; **m. lover** mélomane *mf*; **canned m.** musique *f* (de fond) enregistrée. ◆**musical** *a* musical; (*instrument*) de musique; **to be (very) m.** être (très) musicien; – *n* (*film, play*)

comédie *f* musicale. ◆**mu'sician** *n* musicien, -ienne *mf*.

musk [mʌsk] *n* (*scent*) musc *m*.

Muslim [ˈmʊzlɪm] *a & n* musulman, -ane (*mf*).

muslin [ˈmʌzlɪn] *n* (*cotton*) mousseline *f*.

mussel [ˈmʌs(ə)l] *n* (*mollusc*) moule *f*.

must [mʌst] *v aux* **1** (*necessity*) **you m.** obey tu dois obéir, il faut que tu obéisses. **2** (*certainty*) **she m. be clever** elle doit être intelligente; **I m. have seen it** j'ai dû le voir; – *n*: **this is a m.** ceci est (absolument) indispensable.

mustache [ˈmʌstɑːʃ] *n Am* moustache *f*.

mustard [ˈmʌstəd] *n* moutarde *f*.

muster [ˈmʌstər] *vt* (*gather*) rassembler; (*sum*) réunir; – *vi* se rassembler.

musty [ˈmʌstɪ] *a* (*-ier, -iest*) (*smell*) de moisi; **it smells m., it's m.** ça sent le moisi.

mutation [mjuːˈteɪʃ(ə)n] *n Biol* mutation *f*.

mut/e [mjuːt] *a* (*silent*) & *Gram* muet; – *vt* (*sound, colour*) assourdir. ◆**–ed** *a* (*criticism*) voilé.

mutilate [ˈmjuːtɪleɪt] *vt* mutiler. ◆**muti'lation** *n* mutilation *f*.

mutiny [ˈmjuːtɪnɪ] *n* mutinerie *f*; – *vi* se mutiner. ◆**mutinous** *a* (*troops*) mutiné.

mutter [ˈmʌtər] *vti* marmonner.

mutton [ˈmʌt(ə)n] *n* (*meat*) mouton *m*.

mutual [ˈmjuːtʃʊəl] *a* (*help, love etc*) mutuel, réciproque; (*common, shared*) commun; **m. fund** *Fin Am* fonds *m* commun de placement. ◆**–ly** *adv* mutuellement.

muzzle [ˈmʌz(ə)l] *n* (*snout*) museau *m*; (*device*) muselière *f*; (*of gun*) gueule *f*; – *vt* (*animal, press etc*) museler.

my [maɪ] *poss a* mon, ma, *pl* mes. ◆**my'self** *pron* moi-même; (*reflexive*) me, m'; (*after prep*) moi; **I wash m.** je me lave; **I think of m.** je pense à moi.

mystery [ˈmɪstərɪ] *n* mystère *m*. ◆**my'sterious** *a* mystérieux.

mystic [ˈmɪstɪk] *a & n* mystique (*mf*). ◆**mystical** *a* mystique. ◆**mysticism** *n* mysticisme *m*. ◆**my'stique** *n* (*mystery, power*) mystique *f* (of de).

mystify [ˈmɪstɪfaɪ] *vt* (*bewilder*) laisser perplexe; (*fool*) mystifier. ◆**mystifi'cation** *n* (*bewilderment*) perplexité *f*.

myth [mɪθ] *n* mythe *m*. ◆**mythical** *a* mythique. ◆**mytho'logical** *a* mythologique. ◆**my'thology** *n* mythologie *f*.

N

N, n [en] n N, n m; **the nth time** la énième fois.

nab [næb] vt (-bb-) (catch, arrest) Fam épingler.

nag [næg] vti (-gg-) (criticize) critiquer; **to n. (at) s.o.** (pester) harceler or embêter qn (**to do** pour qu'il fasse). ◆**nagging** a (doubt, headache) qui subsiste; ◆ n critiques fpl.

nail [neɪl] 1 n (of finger, toe) ongle m; – a (polish, file etc) à ongles. 2 n (metal) clou m; – vt clouer; **to n. s.o.** (nab) Fam épingler qn; **to n. down** (lid etc) clouer.

naïve [naɪ'iːv] a naïf. ◆**naïveté** n naïveté f.

naked ['neɪkɪd] a (person) (tout) nu; (eye, flame) nu; **to see with the n. eye** voir à l'œil nu. ◆**—ness** n nudité f.

name [neɪm] 1 n nom m; (reputation) Fig réputation f; **my n. is . . .** je m'appelle . . .; **in the n. of** au nom de; **to put one's name down for** (school, course) s'inscrire à; (job, house) demander, faire une demande pour avoir; **to call s.o. names** injurier qn; **first n., given n.** prénom m; **to n.** m de famille; **a good/bad n.** Fig une bonne/mauvaise réputation; **n. plate** plaque f; – vt nommer; (ship, street) baptiser; (designate) désigner, nommer; (date, price) fixer; **he was named after or Am for . . .** il a reçu le nom de . . . ◆**—less** a sans nom, anonyme. ◆**—ly** adv (that is) à savoir. ◆**namesake** n (person) homonyme m.

nanny ['nænɪ] n nurse f, bonne f d'enfants; (grandmother) Fam mamie f.

nanny-goat ['nænɪɡəʊt] n chèvre f.

nap [næp] n (sleep) petit somme m; **to have or take a n.** faire un petit somme; (after lunch) faire la sieste; – vi (-pp-) **to be napping** sommeiller; **to catch napping** Fig prendre au dépourvu.

nape [neɪp] n (of the neck) nuque f.

napkin ['næpkɪn] n (at table) serviette f; (for baby) couche f. ◆**nappy** n (for baby) couche f. ◆**nappy-liner** n protège-couche m.

narcotic [nɑːˈkɒtɪk] a & n narcotique (m).

narrate [nəˈreɪt] vt raconter. ◆**narration** n. ◆**'narrative** n (story) récit m, narration f; (art, act) narration f. ◆**narrator** n narrateur, -trice f.

narrow ['nærəʊ] a (-er, -est) étroit; (major-

ity) faible, petit; – vi (of path) se rétrécir; **to n. down** (of choice etc) se limiter (**to** à); – vt **to n. (down)** (limit) limiter. ◆**—ly** adv (to miss etc) de justesse; (strictly) strictement; **he n. escaped or missed being killed**/etc il a failli être tué/etc. ◆**—ness** n étroitesse f.

narrow-minded [nærəʊˈmaɪndɪd] a borné. ◆**—ness** n étroitesse f (d'esprit).

nasal ['neɪz(ə)l] a nasal; (voice) nasillard.

nasty ['nɑːstɪ] a (-ier, -iest) (bad) mauvais, vilain; (spiteful) méchant, désagréable (**to, towards** avec); **a n. mess or muddle** un gâchis. ◆**nastily** adv (to act) méchamment; (to rain) horriblement. ◆**nastiness** n (malice) méchanceté f; **the n. of the weather/taste**/etc le mauvais temps/goût/etc.

nation ['neɪʃ(ə)n] n nation f; **the United Nations** les Nations Unies. ◆**n.-wide** a & adv dans le pays (tout) entier. ◆**national** a national; **n. anthem** hymne m national; **N. Health Service** = Sécurité f Sociale; **n. insurance** = assurances fpl sociales; – n (citizen) ressortissant, -ante mf. ◆**nationalist** n nationaliste mf. ◆**nationa'listic** a Pej nationaliste. ◆**natio'nality** n nationalité f. ◆**nationalize** vt nationaliser. ◆**nationally** adv (to travel, be known etc) dans le pays (tout) entier.

native ['neɪtɪv] a (country) natal; (habits, costume) du pays; (tribe, plant) indigène; (charm, ability) inné; **n. language** langue f maternelle; **to be an English n. speaker** parler l'anglais comme langue maternelle; – n (person) autochtone mf, (non-European in colony) indigène mf; **to be a n. of** être originaire or natif de.

nativity [nəˈtɪvɪtɪ] n Rel nativité f.

NATO ['neɪtəʊ] n abbr (North Atlantic Treaty Organization) OTAN f.

natter ['nætər] vi Fam bavarder; – n Fam **to have a n.** bavarder.

natural ['nætʃ(ə)rəl] a naturel; (actor, gardener etc) né; – n **to be a n. for** (job etc) Fam être celui qu'il faut pour, être fait pour. ◆**naturalist** n naturaliste mf. ◆**naturally** adv (as normal, of course) naturellement; (by nature) de nature; (with naturalness) avec naturel. ◆**naturalness** n naturel m.

naturalize ['nætʃ(ə)rəlaɪz] vt (person) Pol naturaliser. ◆**naturali'zation** n naturalisation f.

nature ['neɪtʃər] n (natural world, basic quality) nature f; (disposition) naturel m; **by n.** de nature; **n. study** sciences fpl naturelles.

naught [nɔːt] n **1** Math zéro m. **2** (nothing) Lit rien m.

naught/y ['nɔːtɪ] a (-ier, -iest) (child) vilain, malicieux; (joke, story) osé, grivois. ◆**—ily** adv (to behave) mal; (to say) avec malice. ◆**—iness** n mauvaise conduite f.

nausea ['nɔːzɪə] n nausée f. ◆**nauseate** vt écœurer. ◆**nauseous** a (smell etc) nauséabond; **to feel n.** Am (sick) avoir envie de vomir; (disgusted) Fig être écœuré.

nautical ['nɔːtɪk(ə)l] a nautique.

naval ['neɪv(ə)l] a naval; (power, hospital) maritime; (officer) de marine.

nave [neɪv] n (of church) nef f.

navel ['neɪv(ə)l] n Anat nombril m.

navigate ['nævɪgeɪt] vi naviguer; — vt (boat) diriger, piloter; (river) naviguer sur. ◆**navigable** a (river) navigable; (seaworthy) en état de naviguer. ◆**navi'gation** n navigation f. ◆**navigator** n Av navigateur m.

navvy ['nævɪ] n (labourer) terrassier m.

navy ['neɪvɪ] n marine f; — a **n. (blue)** bleu marine inv.

Nazi ['nɑːtsɪ] a & n Pol Hist nazi, -ie (mf).

near [nɪər] adv (-er, -est) près; quite n., n. at hand tout près; **to draw n.** (s')approcher (to de); (of date) approcher; **to come n. to being killed/etc** faillir être tué/etc; **n. enough** (more or less) Fam plus ou moins; — prep (-er, -est) **n. (to)** près de; **n. the bed** près du lit; **n.** (to) **victory/death** frôler la victoire/la mort; **the end** vers la fin; **to come n. s.o.** s'approcher de qn; — a (-er, -est) proche; (likeness) fidèle; **the nearest hospital** l'hôpital le plus proche; **the nearest way** la route la plus directe; **in the n. future** dans un avenir proche; **to the nearest franc** (to calculate) à un franc près; (to round up or down) au franc supérieur ou inférieur; — **n. side** Aut côté m gauche, Am côté m droit; — vt (approach) approcher de; **nearing completion** près d'être achevé. ◆**near·by** adv tout près; — ['nɪəbaɪ] a proche. ◆**nearness** n (in space, time) proximité f.

nearly ['nɪəlɪ] adv presque, près; **(very) n. fell** elle a failli tomber; **not n. as clever/etc** as loin d'être aussi intelligent/etc que.

neat [niːt] a (-er, -est) (clothes, work) soigné, propre, net; (room) ordonné, bien rangé; (style) élégant; (pretty) Fam joli, beau; (pleasant) Fam agréable; **to drink one's whisky/etc n.** prendre son whisky/etc sec. ◆**—ly** adv avec soin; (skilfully) habilement. ◆**—ness** n netteté f; (of room) ordre m.

necessary ['nesɪs(ə)rɪ] a nécessaire; **it's n. to do it** il est nécessaire de faire, il faut faire; **to make it n. for s.o.** to do mettre qn dans la nécessité de faire; **to do what's n.** or **the n.** Fam faire le nécessaire (for pour); — npl **the necessaries** (food etc) l'indispensable m. ◆**nece'ssarily** adv nécessairement.

necessity [nɪ'sesɪtɪ] n (obligation, need) nécessité f; (poverty) indigence f; **there's no n.** for you to do that tu n'es pas obligé de faire cela; **of n.** nécessairement; **to be a n.** être indispensable; **the (bare) necessities** le (strict) nécessaire. ◆**necessitate** vt nécessiter.

neck [nek] n Anat cou m; (of dress, horse) encolure f; (of bottle) col m; **low n.** (of dress) décolleté m; **n. and n.** Sp à égalité. ◆**necklace** n collier m. ◆**neckline** n encolure f. ◆**necktie** n cravate f.

neck² [nek] vi (kiss etc) Fam se peloter.

nectarine ['nektərɪn] n (fruit) nectarine f, brugnon m.

née [neɪ] adv **n.** Dupont née Dupont.

need [niːd] n **1** n (necessity, want, poverty) besoin m; **in n.** dans le besoin; **to be in n. of** avoir besoin de; **there's no n. (for you) to do** tu n'as pas besoin de faire; **if n. be** si besoin est, s'il le faut; — vt avoir besoin de; **you n. it** tu en as besoin, il te le faut; **it needs an army to do, an army is needed to do** il faut une armée pour faire; **this sport needs patience** ce sport demande de la patience; **her hair needs cutting** il faut qu'elle se fasse couper les cheveux. **2** v aux **n. he wait?** est-il obligé d'attendre?, a-t-il besoin d'attendre?; **I needn't have rushed** ce n'était pas la peine de me presser; **I n. hardly say that . . .** je n'ai guère besoin de dire que . . . . ◆**needless** a inutile. ◆**needlessly** adv inutilement. ◆**needy** a (-ier, -iest) nécessiteux.

needle ['niːd(ə)l] n **1** aiguille f; (of record player) saphir m. **2** vt (irritate) Fam agacer. ◆**needlework** n couture f, travaux mpl d'aiguille; (object) ouvrage m.

negate [nɪ'geɪt] vt (nullify) annuler; (deny) nier. ◆**negation** n (denial) & Gram négation f.

negative ['negətɪv] a négatif; — n Phot négatif m; (word) Gram négation f; (form)

Gram forme *f* négative; **to answer in the n.** répondre par la négative.

neglect [nɪ'glekt] *vt* (*person, health, work etc*) négliger; (*garden, car etc*) ne pas s'occuper de; (*duty*) manquer à; (*rule*) désobéir à, méconnaître; **to n. to do** négliger de faire; − *n* (*of person*) manque *m* de soins (*of* envers); (*of rule*) désobéissance *f* (**of** à); (*of duty*) manquement *m* (**of** à); (*carelessness*) négligence *f*; **in a state of n.** (*garden, house etc*) mal tenu. ◆**neglected** *a* (*appearance, person*) négligé; (*garden, house etc*) mal tenu; **to feel n.** sentir qu'on vous néglige. ◆**neglectful** *a* négligent; **to be n. of** négliger.

negligent ['neglɪdʒənt] *a* négligent. ◆**negligence** *n* négligence *f*. ◆**negligently** *adv* négligemment.

negligible ['neglɪdʒəb(ə)l] *a* négligeable.

negotiate [nɪ'gəuʃɪeɪt] **1** *vti Fin Pol* négocier. **2** *vt* (*fence, obstacle*) franchir; (*bend*) *Aut* négocier. ◆**negotiable** *a Fin* négociable. ◆**negoti'ation** *n* négociation *f*; **in n. with** en pourparlers avec. ◆**negotiator** *n* négociateur, -trice *mf*.

Negro ['niːgrəu] *n* (*pl* -**oes**) (**man**) Noir *m*; (**woman**) Noire *f*; − *a* noir; (*art, sculpture etc*) nègre. ◆**Negress** *n* Noire *f*.

neigh [neɪ] *vi* (*of horse*) hennir; − *n* hennissement *m*.

neighbour ['neɪbər] *n* voisin, -ine *mf*. ◆**neighbourhood** *n* (*neighbours*) voisinage *m*; (*district*) quartier *m*, voisinage *m*; (*region*) région *f*; **in the n. of ten pounds** dans les dix livres. ◆**neighbouring** *a* avoisinant. ◆**neighbourly** *a* (*feeling etc*) de bon voisinage, amical; **they're n.** (*people*) ils sont bons voisins.

neither ['naɪðər, *Am* 'niːðər] *adv* ni; **n. . . . nor** ni . . . ni; **you nor me** ni toi ni moi; **he n. sings nor dances** il ne chante ni ne danse; − *conj* (*not either*) non plus; **n. shall I go** je n'y irai pas non plus; **n. do I**, **n. can I** *etc* (ni) moi non plus; − *a* **n. boy (came)** aucun des deux garçons (n'est venu); **on n. side** ni d'un côté ni de l'autre; − *pron* **n. (of them)** ni l'un(e) ni l'autre, aucun(e) (des deux).

neo- ['niːəu] *pref* néo-.

neon ['niːɒn] *n* (*gas*) néon *m*; − *a* (*lighting etc*) au néon.

nephew ['nevjuː, 'nefjuː] *n* neveu *m*.

nepotism ['nepətɪz(ə)m] *n* népotisme *m*.

nerve [nɜːv] *n* nerf *m*; (*courage*) *Fig* courage *m* (**to do** de faire); (*confidence*) assurance *f*; (*calm*) sang-froid *m*; (*cheek*) *Fam* culot *m* (**to do** de faire); **you get on my nerves** *Fam*

tu me portes *or* me tapes sur les nerfs; **to have (an attack of) nerves** (*fear, anxiety*) avoir le trac; **a bundle** *or* **mass** *or* **bag of nerves** (*person*) *Fam* un paquet de nerfs; **to have bad nerves** être nerveux; − *a* (*cell, centre*) nerveux. ◆**n.-racking** *a* éprouvant pour les nerfs. ◆**nervous** *a* (*tense*) & *Anat* nerveux; (*worried*) inquiet (**about** de); **to be** *or* **feel n.** (*ill-at-ease*) se sentir mal à l'aise; (*before exam etc*) avoir le trac. ◆**nervously** *adv* nerveusement; (*worriedly*) avec inquiétude. ◆**nervousness** *n* nervosité *f*; (*fear*) trac *m*. ◆**nervy** *a* (-**ier**, -**iest**) *Fam* (*anxious*) nerveux; (*brash*) *Am* culotté.

nest [nest] *n* nid *m*; **n. egg** (*money saved*) pécule *m*; **n. of tables** table *f* gigogne; − *vi* (*of bird*) (se) nicher.

nestle ['nes(ə)l] *vi* se pelotonner (**up to** contre); **a village nestling in** (*forest, valley etc*) un village niché dans.

net [net] **1** *n* filet *m*; **n. curtain** voilage *m*; − *vt* (-**tt**-) (*fish*) prendre au filet. **2** *a* (*profit, weight etc*) net; − *vt* (-**tt**-) (*of person, firm etc*) gagner net; **this venture netted him** *or* **her . . .** cette entreprise lui a rapporté . . . . ◆**netting** *n* (*nets*) filets *mpl*; (*mesh*) mailles *fpl*; (*fabric*) voile *m*; (*wire*) n. treillis *m*.

Netherlands (the) [ðə'neðələndz] *npl* les Pays-Bas *mpl*.

nettle ['net(ə)l] *n Bot* ortie *f*.

network ['netwɜːk] *n* réseau *m*.

neurosis, *pl* -**oses** [njuə'rəusɪs, -əusiːz] *n* névrose *f*. ◆**neurotic** *a* & *n* névrosé, -ée (*mf*).

neuter ['njuːtər] **1** *a* & *n Gram* neutre (*m*). **2** *vt* (*cat etc*) châtrer.

neutral ['njuːtrəl] *a* neutre; (*policy*) de neutralité; − *n El* neutre *m*; **in n.** (*gear*) *Aut* au point mort. ◆**neu'trality** *n* neutralité *f*. ◆**neutralize** *vt* neutraliser.

never ['nevər] *adv* **1** (*not ever*) (ne) . . . jamais; **she n. lies** elle ne ment jamais; **n. in (all) my life** jamais de ma vie; **n.** *or* **hardly ever** jamais ou presque. **2** (*certainly not*) *Fam* **I n. did it** je ne l'ai pas fait. ◆**n.-'ending** *a* interminable.

nevertheless [nevəðə'les] *adv* néanmoins, quand même.

new [njuː] *a* (-**er**, -**est**) nouveau; (*brand-new*) neuf; **to be n. to** (*job*) être nouveau dans; (*city*) être un nouveau venu dans, être fraîchement installé dans; **a n. boy** *Sch* un nouveau; **what's n.?** *Fam* quoi de neuf?; **a n. glass/pen/etc** (*different*) un autre verre/stylo/*etc*; **to break n. ground** innover; **n. look** style *m* nouveau; **as good as**

n. comme neuf; **a n.-laid egg** un œuf du jour; **a n.-born baby** un nouveau-né, une nouveau-née. ◆**newcomer** n nouveau-venu m, nouvelle-venue f. ◆**new-'fangled** a Pej moderne. ◆**new-found** a nouveau. ◆**newly** adv (recently) nouvellement, fraîchement; **the n.-weds** les nouveaux mariés. ◆**newness** n (condition) état m neuf; (novelty) nouveauté f.

news [njuːz] n nouvelle(s) f(pl); Journ Rad TV informations fpl, actualités fpl; **sports/etc** n. (newspaper column) chronique f or rubrique f sportive/etc; **a piece of n.,** **some n.** une nouvelle; Journ Rad TV une information; **n. headlines** titres mpl de l'actualité; **n. flash** flash m. ◆**newsagent** n marchand, -ande mf de journaux. ◆**newsboy** n vendeur m de journaux. ◆**newscaster** n présentateur, -trice mf. ◆**newsletter** n (of club, group etc) bulletin m. ◆**newspaper** n journal m. ◆**newsreader** n présentateur, -trice mf. ◆**newsreel** n Cin actualités fpl. ◆**newsworthy** a digne de faire l'objet d'un reportage. ◆**newsy** a (-ier, -iest) Fam plein de nouvelles.

newt [njuːt] n (animal) triton m.

New Zealand [njuːˈziːlənd] n Nouvelle-Zélande f; – a néo-zélandais. ◆**New Zealander** n Néo-Zélandais, -aise mf.

next [nekst] a prochain; (room, house) d'à-côté, voisin; (following) suivant; **n.** **month** (in the future) le mois prochain; **he returned the n. month** (in the past) il revint le mois suivant; **the n. day** le lendemain; **the n. morning** le lendemain matin; **within the n. ten days** d'ici à dix jours, dans un délai de dix jours; **(by) this time n. week** d'ici (à) la semaine prochaine; **from one year to the n.** d'une année à l'autre; **you're n.** c'est ton tour; **n. (please)!** (au) suivant! **the n. thing to do is . . .** ce qu'il faut faire ensuite c'est . . . ; **the n. size (up)** la taille au-dessus; **to live/etc n. door** habiter/etc à côté (to de); **n.-door neighbour/room** voisin m/pièce f d'à-côté; – n (in series etc) suivant, -ante mf; – adv (afterwards) ensuite, après; (now) maintenant; **when you come n.** la prochaine fois que tu viendras; **the n. best solution** la seconde solution; – prep n. to (beside) à côté de; **n. to nothing** presque rien.

NHS [eneɪtʃˈes] abbr = National Health Service.

nib [nɪb] n (of pen) plume f, bec m.

nibble [ˈnɪb(ə)l] vti (eat) grignoter; (bite) mordiller.

nice [naɪs] a (-er, -est) (pleasant) agréable; (charming) charmant, gentil; (good) bon; (fine) beau; (pretty) joli; (kind) gentil (to avec); (respectable) bien inv; (subtle) délicat; **it's n. here** c'est bien ici; **n. and easy/warm/etc** (very) bien facile/chaud/etc. ◆**n.-'looking** a beau, joli. ◆**nicely** adv agréablement; (kindly) gentiment; (well) bien. ◆**niceties** [ˈnaɪsətɪz] npl (pleasant things) agréments mpl; (subtleties) subtilités fpl.

niche [niːʃ, nɪtʃ] n **1** (recess) niche f. **2** (job) (bonne) situation f; (direction) voie f; **to make a n. for oneself** faire son trou.

nick [nɪk] **1** n (on skin, wood) entaille f; (in blade, crockery) brèche f. **2** n (prison) Sl taule f; – vt (steal, arrest) Sl piquer. **3** n **in the n. of time** juste à temps; **in good n.** Sl en bon état.

nickel [ˈnɪk(ə)l] n (metal) nickel m; (coin) Am pièce f de cinq cents.

nickname [ˈnɪkneɪm] n (informal name) surnom m; (short form) diminutif m; – vt surnommer.

nicotine [ˈnɪkətiːn] n nicotine f.

niece [niːs] n nièce f.

nifty [ˈnɪftɪ] a (-ier, -iest) (stylish) chic inv; (skilful) habile; (fast) rapide.

Nigeria [naɪˈdʒɪərɪə] n Nigéria m or f. ◆**Nigerian** a & n nigérian, -ane (mf).

niggardly [ˈnɪgədlɪ] a (person) avare; (amount) mesquin.

niggling [ˈnɪglɪŋ] a (trifling) insignifiant; (irksome) irritant; (doubt) persistant.

night [naɪt] n nuit f; (evening) soir m; Th soirée f; **last n.** (evening) hier soir; (night) la nuit dernière; **to have an early/late n.** se coucher tôt/tard; **to have a good n.** (sleep well) bien dormir; **first n.** Th première f; – a (work etc) de nuit; (life) nocturne; **n.** **school** cours mpl du soir; **n. watchman** veilleur m de nuit. ◆**nightcap** n (drink) boisson f (alcoolisée ou chaude prise avant de se coucher). ◆**nightclub** n boîte f de nuit. ◆**nightdress** n, ◆**nightgown** n, Fam ◆**nightie** n (woman's) chemise f de nuit. ◆**nightfall** n at n. à la tombée de la nuit. ◆**nightlight** n veilleuse f. ◆**nighttime** n nuit f.

nightingale [ˈnaɪtɪŋgeɪl] n rossignol m.

nightly [ˈnaɪtlɪ] adv chaque nuit or soir; – a de chaque nuit or soir.

nil [nɪl] n (nothing) & Sp zéro m; **the** **risk/result/etc is n.** le risque/résultat/etc est nul.

nimble [ˈnɪmb(ə)l] a (-er, -est) agile.

nincompoop ['nɪŋkəmpuːp] *n Fam* imbécile *mf*.

nine [naɪn] *a & n* neuf (*m*). ◆**nine'teen** *a & n* dix-neuf (*m*). ◆**nine'teenth** *a & n* dix-neuvième (*mf*). ◆**ninetieth** *a & n* quatre-vingt-dixième (*mf*). ◆**ninety** *a & n* quatre-vingt-dix (*m*). ◆**ninth** *a & n* neuvième (*mf*); a n. un neuvième.

nip [nɪp] **1** *vt* (-pp-) (*pinch, bite*) pincer; **to n. in the bud** *Fig* étouffer dans l'œuf; — *n* pinçon *m*; **there's a n. in the air** ça pince. **2** *vi* (-pp-) (*dash*) *Fam* **to n. round** to s.o. courir or faire un saut chez qn; **to n. in/out** entrer/sortir en un instant.

nipper ['nɪpər] *n* (*child*) *Fam* gosse *mf*.

nipple ['nɪp(ə)l] *n* bout *m* de sein, mamelon *m*; (*teat on bottle*) *Am* tétine *f*.

nippy ['nɪpɪ] *a* **1** (-ier, -iest) (*chilly*) frais; **it's n.** (*weather*) ça pince. **2** **to be n.** (*about it*) (*quick*) *Fam* faire vite.

nit [nɪt] *n* **1** (*fool*) *Fam* idiot, -ote *mf*. **2** (*of louse*) lente *f*. ◆**nitwit** *n* (*fool*) *Fam* idiot, -ote *mf*.

nitrogen ['naɪtrədʒən] *n* azote *m*.

nitty-gritty ['nɪtɪ'grɪtɪ] *n* **to get down to the n.-gritty** *Fam* en venir au fond du problème.

no [nəʊ] *adv & n* non (*m inv*); **no! non!**; **no more than ten/a kilo**/*etc* pas plus de dix/d'un kilo/*etc*; **no more time**/*etc* plus de temps/*etc*; **I have no more time** je n'ai plus de temps; **no more than you** pas plus que vous; **you can do no better** tu ne peux pas faire mieux; **the noes** *Pol* les non; — *a* aucun(e); pas de; **I've (got) I have no idea** je n'ai aucune idée; **no child came** aucun enfant n'est venu; **I've (got) or I have no time**/*etc* je n'ai pas de temps/*etc*; **of no importance/value**/*etc* sans importance/ valeur/*etc*; **with no gloves**/*etc* on sans gants/*etc*; **there's no knowing . . . impossible de savoir . . . ; 'no smoking'** 'défense de fumer'; **no way!** *Am Fam* pas question!; **no one = nobody**.

noble ['nəʊb(ə)l] *a* (-er, -est) noble; (*building*) majestueux. ◆**nobleman** *n* (*pl* -men) noble *m*. ◆**noblewoman** *n* (*pl* -women) noble *f*. ◆**no'bility** *n* (*character, class*) noblesse *f*.

nobody ['nəʊbɒdɪ] *pron* (ne) . . . personne; **n. came** personne n'est venu; **he knows n.** il ne connaît personne; **n.!** personne!; — *n a* une nullité.

nocturnal [nɒk'tɜːn(ə)l] *a* nocturne.

nod [nɒd] **1** *vti* (-dd-) **to n.** (*one's head*) incliner la tête, faire un signe de tête; — *n*

inclination *f* or signe *m* de tête. **2** *vi* (-dd-) **to n. off** (*go to sleep*) s'assoupir.

noise [nɔɪz] *n* bruit *m*; (*of bell, drum*) son *m*; **to make a n.** faire du bruit. ◆**noisily** *adv* bruyamment. ◆**noisy** *a* (-ier, -iest) (*person, street etc*) bruyant.

nomad ['nəʊmæd] *n* nomade *mf*. ◆**no'madic** *a* nomade.

nominal ['nɒmɪn(ə)l] *a* (*value, fee etc*) nominal; (*head, ruler*) de nom.

nominate ['nɒmɪneɪt] *vt Pol* désigner, proposer (**for** comme candidat à); (*appoint*) désigner, nommer. ◆**nomi'nation** *n* désignation *f* or proposition *f* de candidat; (*appointment*) nomination *f*. ◆**nomi'nee** *n* (*candidate*) candidat *m*.

non- [nɒn] *pref* non-.

nonchalant ['nɒnʃələnt] *a* nonchalant.

noncommissioned [nɒnkə'mɪʃ(ə)nd] *a* **n. officer** *Mil* sous-officier *m*.

non-committal [nɒnkə'mɪt(ə)l] *a* (*answer, person*) évasif.

nonconformist [nɒnkən'fɔːmɪst] *a & n* non-conformiste (*mf*).

nondescript ['nɒndɪskrɪpt] *a* indéfinissable; *Pej* médiocre.

none [nʌn] *pron* aucun(e) *mf*; (*in filling a form*) néant; **n. of them** aucun d'eux; **she has n. (at all)** elle n'en a pas (du tout); **n. (at all) came** pas un(e) seul(e) n'est venu(e); **n. can tell** personne ne peut le dire; **n. of the cake**/*etc* pas une seule partie du gâteau/*etc*; **n. of the trees**/*etc* aucun arbre/*etc*, aucun des arbres/*etc*; **n. of it or this** rien (de ceci); — *adv* **n. too hot**/*etc* pas tellement chaud/*etc*; **he's n. the happier/wiser**/*etc* il n'en est pas plus heureux/sage/*etc*; **n. the less** néanmoins. ◆**none'less** *adv* néanmoins.

nonentity [nɒ'nentɪtɪ] *n* (*person*) nullité *f*.

non-existent [nɒnɪg'zɪstənt] *a* inexistant.

non-fiction [nɒn'fɪkʃ(ə)n] *n* littérature *f* non-romanesque; (*in library*) ouvrages *mpl* généraux.

non-flammable [nɒn'flæməb(ə)l] *a* ininflammable.

nonplus [nɒn'plʌs] *vt* (-ss-) dérouter.

nonsense ['nɒnsəns] *n* absurdités *fpl*; **that's n.** c'est absurde. ◆**non'sensical** *a* absurde.

non-smoker [nɒn'sməʊkər] *n* (*person*) non-fumeur, -euse *mf*; (*compartment*) *Rail* compartiment *m* non-fumeurs.

non-stick [nɒn'stɪk] *a* (*pan*) anti-adhésif, qui n'attache pas.

non-stop [nɒn'stɒp] *a* sans arrêt; (*train,*

flight) direct; − *adv* (*to work etc*) sans arrêt; (*to fly*) sans escale.

noodles ['nuːd(ə)lz] *npl* nouilles *fpl*; (*in soup*) vermicelle(s) *m*(*pl*).

nook [nʊk] *n* coin *m*; **in every n.** and cranny dans tous les coins (et recoins).

noon [nuːn] *n* midi *m*; **at n.** à midi; − *a* (*sun etc*) de midi.

noose [nuːs] *n* (*loop*) nœud *m* coulant; (*of hangman*) corde *f*.

nor [nɔːr] *conj* ni; **neither you n.** me ni toi ni moi; **she neither drinks n.** smokes elle ne fume ni ne boit; **n. do I, n. can I** *etc* (ni) moi non plus; **n. will I (go)** je n'y irai pas non plus.

norm [nɔːm] *n* norme *f*.

normal ['nɔːm(ə)l] *a* normal; − *n* **above n.** au-dessus de la normale. ◆**nor'mality** *n* normalité *f*. ◆**normalize** *vt* normaliser. ◆**normally** *adv* normalement.

Norman ['nɔːmən] *a* normand.

north [nɔːθ] *n* nord *m*; − *a* (*coast*) nord *inv*; (*wind*) du nord; **to be n. of** être au nord de; **N. America/Africa** Amérique *f*/Afrique *f* du Nord; **N. American** *a* & *n* nord-américain(e) (*mf*); − *adv* au nord, vers le nord. ◆**northbound** *a* (*carriageway*) nord *inv*; (*traffic*) en direction du nord. ◆**north-'east** *n* & *a* nord-est *m* & *a inv*. ◆**northerly** *a* (*point*) nord *inv*; (*direction, wind*) du nord. ◆**northern** *a* (*coast*) nord *inv*; (*town*) du nord; **N. France** le Nord de la France; **N. Europe** Europe *f* du Nord; **N. Ireland** Irlande *f* du Nord. ◆**northerner** *n* habitant, -ante *mf* du Nord. ◆**northward(s)** *a* & *adv* vers le nord. ◆**north-'west** *n* & *a* nord-ouest *m* & *a inv*.

Norway ['nɔːweɪ] *n* Norvège *f*. ◆**Nor'wegian** *a* & *n* norvégien, -ienne (*mf*); − *n* (*language*) norvégien *m*.

nose [nəʊz] *n* nez *m*; **her n.** is bleeding elle saigne du nez; **to turn one's n.** up *Fig* faire le dégoûté (**at** devant); − *vi* **to n. about** (*pry*) *Fam* fouiner. ◆**nosebleed** *n* saignement *m* de nez. ◆**nosedive** *n* *Av* piqué *m*; (*in prices*) chute *f*.

nos(e)y ['nəʊzɪ] *a* (**-ier, -iest**) fouineur, indiscret; **n.** parker fouineur, -euse *mf*.

nosh [nɒʃ] *vi* *Fam* (*eat heavily*) bouffer; (*nibble*) grignoter (entre les repas); − *n* (*food*) *Fam* bouffe *f*.

nostalgia [nɒ'stældʒə] *n* nostalgie *f*. ◆**nostalgic** *a* nostalgique.

nostril ['nɒstr(ə)l] *n* (*of person*) narine *f*; (*of horse*) naseau *m*.

not [nɒt] *adv* **1** (*ne*) . . . pas; **he's n.** there, he

isn't there il n'est pas là; **n. yet** pas encore; **why n.?** pourquoi pas?; **n.** one reply/*etc* pas une seule réponse/*etc*; **n. at all** pas du tout; (*after 'thank you'*) je vous en prie. **2 non; I think/hope n.** je pense?/j'espère que non; **n. guilty** non coupable; **isn't she?, don't you?** *etc* non?

notable ['nəʊtəb(ə)l] *a* (*remarkable*) notable; − *n* (*person*) notable *m*. ◆**notably** *adv* (*noticeably*) notablement; (*particularly*) notamment.

notary ['nəʊtərɪ] *n* notaire *m*.

notation [nəʊ'teɪʃ(ə)n] *n* notation *f*.

notch [nɒtʃ] **1** *n* (*in wood etc*) entaille *f*, encoche *f*; (*in belt, wheel*) cran *m*. **2** *vt* **to n. up** (*a score*) marquer; (*a victory*) enregistrer.

note [nəʊt] *n* (*written comment, tone etc*) & *Mus* note *f*; (*summary, preface*) notice *f*; (*banknote*) billet *m*; (*piano key*) touche *f*; (*message, letter*) petit mot *m*; **to take (a) n. of, make a n. of** prendre note de; **of n.** (*athlete, writer etc*) éminent; − *vt* (*take note of*) noter; (*notice*) remarquer, noter; **to n. down** noter. ◆**notebook** *n* carnet *m*; *Sch* cahier *m*; (*pad*) bloc-notes *m*. ◆**notepad** *n* bloc-notes *m*. ◆**notepaper** *n* papier *m* à lettres.

noted ['nəʊtɪd] *a* (*author etc*) éminent; **to be n.** for être connu pour.

noteworthy ['nəʊtwɜːðɪ] *a* notable.

nothing ['nʌθɪŋ] *pron* (*ne*) . . . rien; **he knows n.** il ne sait rien; **n.** to do/eat/*etc* rien à faire/manger/*etc*; **n.** big/*etc* rien de grand/*etc*; **n.** much pas grand-chose; **I've got n.** to do with it je n'y suis pour rien; **I can do n.** (about it) je n'y peux rien; **to come to n.** (*of effort etc*) ne rien donner; **there's n.** like it il n'y a rien de tel; **for n.** (*in vain, free of charge*) pour rien; − *adv* **to look n.** like s.o. ne ressembler nullement à qn; **n.** like as large/*etc* loin d'être aussi grand/*etc*; − *n* **a** (*mere*) **n.** (*person*) une nullité; (*thing*) un rien. ◆**-ness** *n* (*void*) néant *m*.

notice ['nəʊtɪs] *n* (*notification*) avis *m*; *Journ* annonce *f*; (*sign*) pancarte *f*, écriteau *m*; (*poster*) affiche *f*; (*review of film etc*) critique *f*; (*attention*) attention *f*; (*knowledge*) connaissance *f*; (*advance*) **n.** (*of departure etc*) préavis *m*; **n.** (*to quit*), **n.** (*of dismissal*) congé *m*; **to give (in) one's n.** (*resignation*) donner sa démission; **to give s.o. n. of** (*inform of*) avertir qn de; **to take n.** faire attention (**of** à); **to bring sth to s.o.'s n.** porter qch à la connaissance de qn; **until further n.** jusqu'à nouvel ordre; **at short n.** à bref délai; **n. board** tableau *m* d'affichage; – *vt* (*perceive*) remarquer (*qn*); (*fact, trick, danger*) s'apercevoir de, remarquer; **I n. that** je m'aperçois que. ◆—**able** *a* visible, perceptible; **that's n.** ça se voit; **she's n.** elle se fait remarquer.

notify ['nǝutɪfaɪ] *vt* (*inform*) aviser (**s.o. of sth** qn de qch); (*announce*) notifier (**to** à). ◆**notifi'cation** *n* annonce *f*, avis *m*.

notion ['nǝuʃ(ǝ)n] **1** *n* (*thought*) idée *f*; (*awareness*) notion *f*; **some n. of** (*knowledge*) quelques notions de. **2** *npl* (*sewing articles*) *Am* mercerie *f*.

notorious [nǝu'tɔ:rɪǝs] *a* (*event, person etc*) tristement célèbre; (*stupidity, criminal*) notoire. ◆**notoriety** [-ǝ'raɪǝtɪ] *n* (triste) notoriété *f*.

notwithstanding [nɒtwɪð'stændɪŋ] *prep* malgré; – *adv* tout de même.

nougat ['nu:gɑ:, 'nʌgǝt] *n* nougat *m*.

nought [nɔ:t] *n* *Math* zéro *m*.

noun [naun] *n* *Gram* nom *m*.

nourish ['nʌrɪʃ] *vt* nourrir. ◆—**ing** *a* nourrissant. ◆—**ment** *n* nourriture *f*.

novel ['nɒv(ǝ)l] **1** *n* *Liter* roman *m*. **2** *a* (*new*) nouveau, original. ◆**novelist** *n* romancier, -ière *mf*. ◆**novelty** (*newness, object, idea*) nouveauté *f*.

November [nǝu'vembǝr] *n* novembre *m*.

novice ['nɒvɪs] *n* novice *mf* (**at** en).

now [nau] *adv* maintenant; **just n., right n.** en ce moment; **I saw her just n.** je l'ai vue à l'instant; **for n.** pour le moment; **even n.** encore maintenant; **from n. on** désormais, à partir de maintenant; **until n., up to n.** jusqu'ici; **before n.** avant; **n. and then** de temps à autre; **n. hot, n. cold** tantôt chaud, tantôt froid; **n.** (**then**)! bon!, alors!; (*telling s.o. off*) allons!; **it happened that . . .** ou **il advint que . . . ;** – *conj* **n.** (**that**) maintenant que. ◆**nowadays** *adv* aujourd'hui, de nos jours.

noway ['nǝuweɪ] *adv Am* nullement.

nowhere ['nǝuweǝr] *adv* nulle part; **n. else** nulle part ailleurs; **it's n. I know** ce n'est pas un endroit que je connais; **n. near the house** loin de la maison; **n. near enough** loin d'être assez.

nozzle ['nɒz(ǝ)l] *n* (*of hose*) jet *m*, lance *f* (à eau); (*of syringe, tube*) embout *m*.

nth [enθ] *a* nième.

nuance ['nju:ɑ:ns] *n* (*of meaning, colour etc*) nuance *f*.

nub [nʌb] *n* (*of problem*) cœur *m*.

nuclear ['nju:klɪǝr] *a* nucléaire; **n. scientist** spécialiste *mf* du nucléaire, atomiste *mf*.

nucleus, *pl* **-clei** ['nju:klɪǝs, -klaɪ] *n* noyau *m*.

nude [nju:d] *a* nu; – *n* (*female or male figure*) nu *m*; **in the n.** (tout) nu. ◆**nudism** *n* nudisme *m*, naturisme *m*. ◆**nudist** *n* nudiste *mf*, naturiste *mf*; – *a* (*camp*) de nudistes, de naturistes. ◆**nudity** *n* nudité *f*.

nudge [nʌdʒ] *vt* pousser du coude; – *n* coup *m* de coude.

nugget ['nʌgɪt] *n* (*of gold etc*) pépite *f*.

nuisance ['nju:sǝns] *n* (*annoyance*) embêtement *m*; (*person*) peste *f*; **that's a n.** c'est embêtant; **he's being a n., he's making a n. of himself** il nous embête, il m'embête *etc*.

null [nʌl] *a* **n.** (**and void**) nul (et non avenu). ◆**nullify** *vt* infirmer.

numb [nʌm] *a* (*stiff*) engourdi; *Fig* paralysé; – *vt* engourdir; *Fig* paralyser.

number ['nʌmbǝr] *n* nombre *m*; (*of page, house, newspaper etc*) numéro *m*; **a dance/song n.** un numéro de danse/de chant; **a/any n. of** un certain/grand nombre de; **n. plate** (*of vehicle*) plaque *f* d'immatriculation; *vt* (*page etc*) numéroter; (*include, count*) compter; **they n. eight** ils sont au nombre de huit. ◆—**ing** *n* numérotage *m*.

numeral ['nju:m(ǝ)rǝl] *n* chiffre *m*; – *a* numéral. ◆**nu'merical** *a* numérique. ◆**numerous** *a* nombreux.

numerate ['nju:m(ǝ)rǝt] *a* (*person*) qui sait compter.

nun [nʌn] *n* religieuse *f*.

nurs/e [nɜ:s] **1** *n* infirmière *f*; (*nanny*) nurse *f*; (*male*) **n.** infirmier *m*. **2** *vt* (*look after*) soigner; (*cradle*) bercer; (*suckle*) nourrir; (*a grudge etc*) *Fig* nourrir; (*support, encourage*) *Fig* épauler (*qn*). ◆—**ing** *a* (*mother*) qui allaite; **the n. staff** le personnel infirmier; – *n* (*care*) soins *mpl*; (*job*) profession *f* d'infirmière ou d'infirmier; **n. home** clinique *f*. ◆**nursemaid** *n* bonne *f* d'enfants.

nursery ['nɜ:sǝrɪ] *n* (*room*) chambre *f* d'enfants; (*for plants, trees*) pépinière *f*; (**day**) **n.** (*school etc*) crèche *f*, garderie *f*; **n. rhyme** chanson *f* enfantine; **n. school** école *f* maternelle.

nurture ['nɜ:tʃǝr] *vt* (*educate*) éduquer.

nut¹ [nʌt] *n* (*fruit*) fruit *m* à coque; (*walnut*) noix *f*; (*hazelnut*) noisette *f*; (*peanut*) cacah(o)uète *f*; **Brazil/cashew n.** noix *f* du Brésil/de cajou. ◆**nutcracker(s)** *n* (*pl*) casse-noix *m inv*. ◆**nutshell** *n* coquille *f* de noix; **in a n.** *Fig* en un mot.

nut² [nʌt] *n* **1** (*for bolt*) *Tech* écrou *m*. **2**

(head) Sl caboche f. **3** *(person)* Sl cinglé, -ée mf; **to be nuts** Sl être cinglé. ◆**nutcase** n cinglé, -ée mf. ◆**nutty** a (-ier, -iest) Sl cinglé.

nutmeg ['nʌtmeg] n muscade f.

nutritious [nju:'trɪʃəs] a nutritif. ◆'nutri-

ent n élément m nutritif. ◆**nutrition** n nutrition f.

nylon ['naɪlɒn] n nylon m; pl *(stockings)* bas mpl nylon.

nymph [nɪmf] n nymphe f. ◆**nympho-'maniac** n Pej nymphomane f.

O

O, o [əʊ] n O, o m.

oaf [əʊf] n rustre m. ◆**oafish** a *(behaviour)* de rustre.

oak [əʊk] n *(tree, wood)* chêne m.

OAP [əʊer'pi:] n abbr *(old age pensioner)* retraité, -ée mf.

oar [ɔːr] n aviron m, rame f.

oasis, pl **oases** [əʊ'eɪsɪs, əʊ'eɪsiːz] n oasis f.

oath [əʊθ] n *(pl -s* [əʊðz]*) (promise)* serment m; *(profanity)* juron m; **to take an o.** to do faire le serment de faire.

oats [əʊts] npl avoine f. ◆**oatmeal** n flocons mpl d'avoine.

obedient [ə'biːdɪənt] a obéissant. ◆**obe-dience** n obéissance f (**to** à). ◆**obediently** adv docilement.

obelisk ['ɒbəlɪsk] n *(monument)* obélisque m.

obese [əʊ'biːs] a obèse. ◆**obesity** n obésité f.

obey [ə'beɪ] vt obéir à; **to be obeyed** être obéi; – vi obéir.

obituary [ə'bɪtjʊərɪ] n nécrologie f.

object[1] ['ɒbdʒɪkt] n *(thing)* objet m; *(aim)* but m, objet m; Gram complément m *(d'objet)*; **with the o.** of dans le but de; **that's no o.** *(no problem)* ça ne pose pas de problème; **price no o.** prix m indifférent.

object[2] [əb'dʒekt] vi **to o. to sth/s.o.** désapprouver qch/qn; **I o. to you(r) doing that** ça me gêne que tu fasses ça; **I o.!** je proteste!; **she didn't o. when ...** elle n'a fait aucune objection quand ...; – vt **to o. that** objecter que. ◆**objection** n objection f; **I've got no o.** ça ne me gêne pas, je n'y vois pas d'objection or d'inconvénient. ◆**objectionable** a très désagréable. ◆**objector** n opposant, -ante mf (**to** à); **conscientious o.** objecteur m de conscience.

objective [əb'dʒektɪv] **1** a *(opinion)* objectif. **2** n *(aim, target)* objectif m. ◆**objectively** adv objectivement. ◆**ob-jec'tivity** n objectivité f.

obligate ['ɒblɪgeɪt] vt contraindre (**to do** à faire). ◆**obli'gation** n obligation f; *(debt)* dette f; **under an o. to do** dans l'obligation de faire; **under an o. to s.o.** redevable à qn (**for** de). ◆**o'bligatory** a *(compulsory)* obligatoire; *(imposed by custom)* de rigueur.

oblig/e [ə'blaɪdʒ] vt **1** *(compel)* obliger (**s.o. to do** qn à faire); **obliged to do** obligé de faire. **2** *(help)* rendre service à, faire plaisir à; **obliged to s.o.** reconnaissant à qn *(for* de); **much obliged!** merci infiniment! ◆—**ing** a *(kind)* obligeant. ◆—**ingly** adv obligeamment.

oblique [ə'bliːk] a oblique; *(reference)* Fig indirect.

obliterate [ə'blɪtəreɪt] vt effacer. ◆**oblite-'ration** n effacement m.

oblivion [ə'blɪvɪən] n oubli m. ◆**oblivious** a inconscient (**to, of** de).

oblong ['ɒblɒŋ] a *(elongated)* oblong; *(rectangular)* rectangulaire; – n rectangle m.

obnoxious [əb'nɒkʃəs] a odieux; *(smell)* nauséabond.

oboe ['əʊbəʊ] n Mus hautbois m.

obscene [əb'siːn] a obscène. ◆**obscenity** n obscénité f.

obscure [əb'skjʊər] a *(reason, word, actor, life etc)* obscur; – vt *(hide)* cacher; *(confuse)* embrouiller, obscurcir. ◆**obscurely** adv obscurément. ◆**obscurity** n obscurité f.

obsequious [əb'siːkwɪəs] a obséquieux.

observe [əb'zɜːv] vt *(notice, watch, respect)* observer; *(say)* (faire) remarquer (**that** que); **to o. the speed limit** respecter la limitation de vitesse. ◆**observance** n *(of rule etc)* observation f. ◆**observant** a observateur. ◆**obser'vation** n *(observing, remark)* observation f; *(by police)* surveillance f; **under o.** *(hospital patient)* en observation. ◆**observatory** n observatoire m. ◆**observer** n observateur, -trice mf.

obsess [əb'ses] vt obséder. ◆**obsession** n obsession f; **to have an o. with** or **about** avoir l'obsession de. ◆**obsessive** a (memory, idea) obsédant; (fear) obsessif; (neurotic) Psy obsessionnel; **to be o. about** avoir l'obsession de.

obsolete ['ɒbsəliːt] a (out of date, superseded) désuet, dépassé; (ticket) périmé; (machinery) archaïque. ◆**obso'lescent** a quelque peu désuet; (word) vieilli.

obstacle ['ɒbstək(ə)l] n obstacle m.

obstetrics [əb'stetrɪks] n Med obstétrique f. ◆**obste'trician** n médecin m accoucheur.

obstinate ['ɒbstɪnət] a (person, resistance etc) obstiné, opiniâtre; (disease, pain) rebelle, opiniâtre. ◆**obstinacy** n obstination f. ◆**obstinately** adv obstinément.

obstreperous [əb'strepərəs] a turbulent.

obstruct [əb'strʌkt] vt (block) boucher; (hinder) entraver; (traffic) entraver, bloquer. ◆**obstruction** n (act, state) & Med Pol Sp obstruction f; (obstacle) obstacle m; (in pipe) bouchon m; (traffic jam) embouteillage m. ◆**obstructive** a to be o. faire de l'obstruction.

obtain [əb'teɪn] 1 vt obtenir. 2 vi (of practice etc) avoir cours. ◆—**able** a (available) disponible; (on sale) en vente.

obtrusive [əb'truːsɪv] a (person) importun; (building etc) trop en évidence.

obtuse [əb'tjuːs] a (angle, mind) obtus.

obviate ['ɒbvɪeɪt] vt (necessity) éviter.

obvious ['ɒbvɪəs] a évident; **he's the o. man to see** c'est évidemment l'homme qu'il faut voir. ◆—**ly** adv (evidently, of course) évidemment; (conspicuously) visiblement.

occasion [ə'keɪʒ(ə)n] 1 n (time, opportunity) occasion f; (event, ceremony) évènement m; **on the o. of** à l'occasion de; **on o.** à l'occasion; **on several occasions** à plusieurs reprises or occasions. 2 n (cause) raison f, occasion f; – vt occasionner. ◆**occa-sional** a (event) qui a lieu de temps en temps; (rain, showers) intermittent; **she drinks the o.** whisky elle boit un whisky de temps en temps. ◆**occasionally** adv de temps en temps; **very o.** très peu souvent, rarement.

occult [ə'kʌlt] a occulte.

occupy ['ɒkjʊpaɪ] vt (house, time, space, post etc) occuper; **to keep oneself occupied** s'occuper (doing à faire). ◆**occupant** n (inhabitant) occupant, -ante mf. ◆**occu-'pation** n (activity) occupation f; (job) emploi m; (trade) métier m; (profession)

profession f; **the o. of** (action) l'occupation f de; **fit for o.** (house) habitable. ◆**occu-'pational** a (hazard) du métier; (disease) du travail. ◆**occupier** n (of house) occupant, -ante mf; Mil occupant m.

occur [ə'kɜːr] vi (-rr-) (happen) avoir lieu; (be found) se rencontrer; (arise) se présenter; **it occurs to me that . . .** il me vient à l'esprit que . . . ; **the idea occurred to her to . . .** l'idée lui est venue de . . . ◆**occurrence** [ə'kʌrəns] n (event) évènement m; (existence) existence f; (of word) Ling occurrence f.

ocean ['əʊʃ(ə)n] n océan m. ◆**oce'anic** a océanique.

o'clock [ə'klɒk] adv (it's) three o'c./etc (il est) trois heures/etc.

octagon ['ɒktəgən] n octogone m. ◆**oc'tagonal** a octogonal.

octave ['ɒktɪv, 'ɒkteɪv] n Mus octave f.

October [ɒk'təʊbər] n octobre m.

octogenarian [ɒktəʊdʒɪneərɪən] n octogénaire mf.

octopus ['ɒktəpəs] n pieuvre f.

odd [ɒd] a 1 (strange) bizarre, curieux; **an o. size** une taille peu courante. 2 (number) impair. 3 (left over) **I have an o.** penny il me reste un penny; **a few o.** stamps quelques timbres (qui restent); **the o. man out, the o. one out** l'exception f; **sixty o.** soixante et quelques; **an o. glove/book/etc** un gant/livre/etc dépareillé. 4 (occasional) qu'on fait, voit etc de temps en temps; **to find the o. mistake** trouver de temps en temps une (petite) erreur; **at o. moments** de temps en temps; **o. jobs** (around house) menus travaux mpl; **o. job** man homme m à tout faire. ◆**oddity** n (person) personne f bizarre; (object) curiosité f; pl (of language, situation) bizarreries fpl. ◆**oddly** adv bizarrement; **o.** (enough), **he was . . .** chose curieuse, il était . . . ◆**oddment** n Com fin f de série. ◆**oddness** n bizarrerie f.

odds [ɒdz] npl 1 (in betting) cote f; (chances) chances fpl; **we have heavy o.** against us nous avons très peu de chances de réussir. 2 **it makes no o.** (no difference) Fam ça ne fait rien. 3 **at o.** (in disagreement) en désac-cord (with avec). 4 **o. and ends** des petites choses.

ode [əʊd] n (poem) ode f.

odious ['əʊdɪəs] a détestable, odieux.

odour ['əʊdər] n odeur f. ◆—**less** a inodore.

oecumenical [iːkjʊ'menɪk(ə)l] a Rel œcuménique.

of [əv, stressed ɒv] prep de; **of the table** de la

table; **of the boy** du garçon; **of the boys** des garçons; **of a book** d'un livre; **of it, of them** en; **she has a lot of it** *or* **of them** elle en a beaucoup; **a friend of his** un ami à lui; **there are ten of us** nous sommes dix; **that's nice of you** c'est gentil de ta part; **of no value/interest/***etc* sans valeur/intérêt/*etc*; **of late** ces derniers temps; **a man of fifty** un homme de cinquante ans; **the fifth of June** le cinq juin.

off [ɒf] **1** *adv* (*absent*) absent, parti; (*light, gas, radio etc*) éteint, fermé; (*tap*) fermé; (*switched off at mains*) coupé; (*detached*) détaché; (*removed*) enlevé; (*cancelled*) annulé; (*not fit to eat or drink*) mauvais; (*milk, meat*) tourné; **2 km o.** à 2 km (d'ici or de là), éloigné de 2 km; **to be** ou **go o.** (*leave*) partir; **where are you o. to?** où vas-tu?; **he has his hat o.** il a enlevé son chapeau; **with his, my** *etc* **gloves o.** sans gants; **a day o.** (*holiday*) un jour de congé; **I'm o. today, I have today o.** j'ai congé aujourd'hui; **the strike's o.** il n'y aura pas de grève, la grève est annulée; **5% o.** une réduction de 5%; **on and o.,** *or* **on and on** (*sometimes*) de temps à autre; **to be better o.** (*wealthier, in a better position*) être mieux. **2** *prep* (*from*) de; (*distant*) éloigné de; **to fall/***etc* **o. the wall/ladder/***etc* tomber/*etc* du mur/de l'échelle/*etc*; **to get o. the bus/***etc* descendre du bus/*etc*; **to take sth. o. the table/***etc* prendre qch sur la table/*etc*; **to eat o. a plate** manger dans une assiette; **to keep** *or* **stay o. the grass** ne pas marcher sur les pelouses; **she's o. her food** elle ne mange plus rien; **o. Dover/***etc* Nau au large de Douvres/*etc*; **o. limits** interdit; **the o. side** Aut le côté droit, Am le côté gauche. ◆**off'beat** *a* excentrique. ◆**off-'colour** *a* (*ill*) patraque; (*indecent*) scabreux. ◆**off'hand** *a* désinvolte; – *adv* impromptu. ◆**off'handedness** *n* désinvolture *f*. ◆**off-licence** *n* magasin *m* de vins et de spiritueux. ◆**off-'load** *vt* (*vehicle etc*) décharger; **to o.-load sth onto s.o.** (*task etc*) se décharger de qch sur qn. ◆**off-'peak** *a* (*crowds, traffic*) aux heures creuses; (*rate, price*) heures creuses *inv*; **o.-peak hours** heures *fpl* creuses. ◆**off-putting** *a* Fam rebutant. ◆**off'side** *a* **to be o.** Fb être hors jeu. ◆**off'stage** *a* & *adv* dans les coulisses. ◆**off-'white** *a* blanc cassé *inv*.

offal ['ɒf(ə)l] *n* Culin abats *mpl*.

offence [ə'fens] *n* Jur délit *m*; **to take o.** s'offenser (at de); **to give o.** offenser.

offend [ə'fend] *vt* froisser, offenser; (*eye*) Fig

choquer; **to be offended (at)** se froisser (de), s'offenser (de). ◆—**ing** *a* (*object, remark*) incriminé. ◆**offender** *n* Jur délinquant, -ante *mf*; (*habitual*) récidiviste *mf*.

offensive [ə'fensiv] **1** *a* (*unpleasant*) choquant, repoussant; (*insulting*) insultant, offensant; (*weapon*) offensif *f*. **2** *n* Mil offensive *f*.

offer ['ɒfər] *n* offre *f*; **on (special) o.** Com en promotion, en réclame; **o. of marriage** demande *f* en mariage; – *vt* offrir; (*opinion, remark*) proposer; **to o. to do** offrir *or* proposer de faire. ◆—**ing** *n* (*gift*) offrande *f*; (*act*) offre *f*; **peace o.** cadeau de réconciliation.

office ['ɒfis] *n* **1** bureau *m*; (*of doctor*) Am cabinet *m*; (*of lawyer*) étude *f*; **head o.** siège *m* central; **o. block** immeuble *m* de bureaux; **o. worker** employé, -ée *mf* de bureau. **2** (*post*) fonction *f*; (*duty*) fonctions *fpl*; **to be in o.** (*of party etc*) Pol être au pouvoir. **3** **one's good offices** (*help*) ses bons offices *mpl*.

officer ['ɒfisər] *n* (*in army, navy etc*) officier *m*; (*of company*) Com directeur, -trice *mf*; (*police*) **o.** agent *m* (de police).

official [ə'fiʃ(ə)l] *a* officiel; (*uniform*) règlementaire; – *n* (*person of authority*) officiel *m*; (*civil servant*) fonctionnaire *m*; (*employee*) employé, -ée *mf*. ◆**officialdom** *n* bureaucratie *f*. ◆**officially** *adv* officiellement. ◆**officiate** *vi* faire fonction d'officiel (at à); (*preside*) présider; Rel officier.

officious [ə'fiʃəs] *a* Pej empressé.

offing ['ɒfiŋ] *n* **in the o.** en perspective.

offset ['ɒfset, ɒf'set] *vt* (*pt & pp* offset, *pres p* offsetting) (*compensate for*) compenser; (*s.o.'s beauty etc by contrast*) faire ressortir.

offshoot ['ɒfʃuːt] *n* (*of firm*) ramification *f*; (*consequence*) conséquence *f*.

offshore ['ɒfʃɔːr] *a* (*industry, product*) pétrolier; (*painting, paints*) à l'huile; **o. lamp** lampe *f* à pétrole *or* à huile; **o. change** Aut vidange *f*; – *vt*

offspring ['ɒfsprɪŋ] *n* progéniture *f*.

often ['ɒf(ə)n] *adv* souvent; **how o.?** combien de fois?; **how o. do they run?** (*trains, buses etc*) il y en a tous les combien?; **once too o.** une fois de trop; **every so o.** de temps en temps.

ogle ['əʊg(ə)l] *vt* Pej reluquer.

ogre ['əʊgər] *n* ogre *m*.

oh! [əʊ] *int* oh!, ah!; (*pain*) aïe!; **oh yes?** ah oui?, ah bon?

oil [ɔɪl] *n* (*for machine, in cooking etc*) huile *f*; (*mineral*) pétrole *m*; (*fuel oil*) mazout *m*; **to paint in oils** faire de la peinture à l'huile; – *a* (*industry, product*) pétrolier; (*painting, paints*) à l'huile; **o. lamp** lampe *f* à pétrole *or* à huile; **o. change** Aut vidange *f*; – *vt*

graisser, huiler. ◆**oilcan** n burette f.
◆**oilfield** n gisement m pétrolifère. ◆**oil-
fired** a au mazout. ◆**oilskin(s)** n(pl)
(garment) cirè m. ◆**oily** a (-ier, -iest)
(substance, skin) huileux; (hands) graisseux; (food) gras.

ointment ['ɔɪntmənt] n pommade f.

OK [əʊ'keɪ] int (approval, exasperation) ça
va!; (agreement) d'accord!, entendu!, OK!;
– a (satisfactory) bien inv; (unharmed) sain
et sauf; (undamaged) intact; (without
worries) tranquille; it's OK now (fixed) ça
marche maintenant; I'm OK (healthy) je
vais bien; – adv (to work etc) bien; – vt (pt
& pp **OKed**, pres p **OKing**) approuver.

okay [əʊ'keɪ] = **OK**.

old [əʊld] a (-er, -est) vieux; (former)
ancien; how o. is he? quel âge a-t-il?; he's
ten years o. il a dix ans, il est âgé de dix
ans; he's older than il est plus âgé que; an
older son un fils aîné; the oldest son le fils
aîné; o. enough to do assez grand pour
faire; o. enough to marry/vote en âge de se
marier/de voter; an o. man un vieillard, un
vieil homme; an o. woman une vieille
(femme); to get or grow old(er) vieillir; o.
age vieillesse f; the O. Testament l'Ancien
Testament; the O. World l'Ancien Monde;
any o. how Fam n'importe comment; – n
the o. (people) les vieux mpl. ◆**o.-
'fashioned** a (customs etc) d'autrefois;
(idea, attitude) Pej vieux jeu inv; (person)
de la vieille école, Pej vieux jeu inv.
◆**o.-'timer** n (old man) Fam vieillard m.

olden ['əʊld(ə)n] a in o. days jadis.

olive ['ɒlɪv] n (fruit) olive f; – a o. (green)
(vert) olive inv; o. oil huile f d'olive; o. tree
olivier m.

Olympic [ə'lɪmpɪk] a olympique.

ombudsman ['ɒmbʊdzmən] n (pl -men)
Pol médiateur m.

omelet(te) ['ɒmlɪt] n omelette f; cheese/etc
o. omelette au fromage/etc.

omen ['əʊmən] n augure m. ◆**ominous** a
de mauvais augure; (tone) menaçant;
(noise) sinistre.

omit [əʊ'mɪt] vt (-tt-) omettre (to do de
faire). ◆**omission** n omission f.

omni- ['ɒmnɪ] prep omni-. ◆**om'nipotent**
a omnipotent.

on [ɒn] prep **1** (position) sur; on the chair sur
la chaise; to put on (to) mettre sur; to look
out on to donner sur. **2** (concerning, about)
sur; an article on un article sur; to speak or
talk on Dickens/etc parler sur Dickens/etc.
3 (manner, means) à; on foot à pied; on the
blackboard au tableau; on the radio à la

radio; on the train/plane/etc dans le
train/avion/etc; on holiday, Am on vacation en vacances; to be on (course) suivre;
(project) travailler à; (salary) toucher;
(team, committee) être membre de, faire
partie de; to keep or stay on (road, path etc)
suivre; it's on me! (I'll pay) Fam c'est moi
qui paie! **4** (time) on Monday lundi; on
Mondays le lundi; on May 3rd le 3 mai; on
the evening of May 3rd le 3 mai au soir; on
my arrival à mon arrivée. **5** (+ present
participle) en; on learning that... en
apprenant que...; on seeing this en
voyant ceci. **6** adv (ahead) en avant; (in
progress) en cours; (started) commencé;
(lid, brake) mis; (light, radio) allumé; (gas,
tap) ouvert; (machine) en marche; on (and
on) sans cesse; to play/etc on continuer à
jouer/etc; she has her hat on elle a mis or
elle porte son chapeau; he has sth/nothing
on il est habillé/tout nu; I've got sth on
(I'm busy) je suis pris; the strike's on la
grève aura lieu; what's on? TV qu'y a-t-il à
la télé? Cin Th qu'est-ce qu'on joue?;
there's a film on on passe un film; to be on
at s.o. (pester) Fam être après qn; I've been
on to him Tel je l'ai eu au bout du fil; to be
on to s.o. (of police etc) être sur la piste de
qn; from then on à partir de là.
◆**on-coming** a (vehicle) qui vient en sens
inverse. ◆**on-going** a (project) en cours.

once [wʌns] adv (on one occasion) une fois;
(formerly) autrefois; o. a month/etc une
fois par mois/etc; o. again, o. more encore
une fois; at o. (immediately) tout de suite;
all at o. (suddenly) tout à coup; (at the same
time) à la fois; o. and for all une fois pour
toutes; – conj une fois que. ◆**o.-over** n to
give sth the o.-over (quick look) Fam
regarder qch d'un coup d'œil.

one [wʌn] a **1** un, une; o. man un homme; o.
woman une femme; twenty-o. vingt-et-un.
2 (sole) seul; my o. (and only) mon seul
(et unique) but. **3** (same) même; in the o.
bus dans le même bus; – pron **1** un, une; do
you want o.? en veux-tu (un)?; he's o. of us
il est des nôtres; o. of them l'un d'eux, l'une
d'elles; a big/small/etc o. un grand/petit/
etc; this book is o. that I've read ce livre est
parmi ceux que j'ai lus; she's o. (a teacher,
gardener etc) elle l'est; this o. celui-ci,
celle-ci; that o. celui-là, celle-là; the o. who
or which celui or celle qui; it's Paul's o. Fam
c'est celui de Paul; it's o. my o. Fam c'est à
moi; another o. un(e) autre; I for o. pour
ma part. **2** (impersonal) on; o. knows on
sait; it helps o. ça nous or vous aide; one's

family sa famille. ◆one-'armed a (person) manchot. ◆one-'eyed a borgne. ◆one-'off a, Am one-of-a-'kind a Fam unique, exceptionnel. ◆one-'sided a (judgement etc) partial; (contest) inégal; (decision) unilatéral. ◆one-time a (former) ancien. ◆one-'way a (street) à sens unique; (traffic) en sens unique; (ticket) Am simple.

oneself [wʌn'self] pron soi-même; (reflexive) se, s'; to cut o. se couper.

onion ['ʌnjən] n oignon m.

onlooker ['ɒnlʊkər] n spectateur, -trice mf.

only ['əʊnlɪ] a seul; the o. house/etc la seule maison/etc; the o. one le seul, la seule; an o. son un fils unique; – adv seulement, ne . . que; I o. have ten, I have ten o. je n'en ai que dix, j'en ai dix seulement; if o. si seulement; not o. non seulement; I have o. just seen it je viens tout juste de le voir; o. he knows lui seul le sait; – conj (but) Fam seulement; o. I can't seulement je ne peux pas.

onset ['ɒnset] n (of disease) début m; (of old age) approche m.

onslaught ['ɒnslɔːt] n attaque f.

onto ['ɒntʊ] prep = on to.

onus ['əʊnəs] n inv the o. is on you/etc c'est votre/etc responsabilité (to do de faire).

onward(s) ['ɒnwəd(z)] adv en avant; from that time o. à partir de là.

onyx ['ɒnɪks] n (precious stone) onyx m.

ooze [uːz] vi to o. (out) suinter; – vt (blood etc) laisser couler.

opal ['əʊp(ə)l] n (precious stone) opale f.

opaque [əʊ'peɪk] a opaque; (unclear) Fig obscur.

open ['əʊpən] a ouvert; (site, view, road) dégagé; (car) décapoté, découvert; (meeting) public; (competition) ouvert à tous; (post) vacant; (attempt, envy) manifeste; (question) non résolu; (result) indécis; (ticket) Av open inv; wide o. grand ouvert; in the o. air en plein air; in (the) o. country en rase campagne; the o. spaces les grands espaces; it's o. to doubt c'est douteux; o. to (criticism, attack) exposé à; (ideas, suggestions) ouvert à; I've got an o. mind on it je n'ai pas d'opinion arrêtée là-dessus; to leave o. (date) ne pas préciser; – n (out) in the o. (outside) en plein air; to sleep (out) in the o. dormir à la belle étoile; to bring (out) into the o. (reveal) divulguer; – vt ouvrir; (conversation) entamer; (legs) écarter; to o. out or up ouvrir; – vi (of flower, eyes etc) s'ouvrir; (of shop, office etc) ouvrir; (of play) débuter; (of film) sortir; the door opens (is

opened) la porte s'ouvre; (can open) la porte ouvre; to o. on to (of window etc) donner sur; to o. out or up s'ouvrir; to o. out (widen) s'élargir; to o. up (open a or the door) ouvrir. ◆–ing n ouverture f; (of flower) éclosion f; (career prospect, trade outlet) débouché m; – a (time, speech) d'ouverture; o. night Th première f. ◆–ly adv (not secretly, frankly) ouvertement; (publicly) publiquement. ◆–ness n (frankness) franchise f; o. of mind ouverture f d'esprit.

open-air [əʊpən'eər] a (pool etc) en plein air. ◆o.-'heart a (operation) Med à cœur ouvert. ◆o.-'necked a (shirt) sans cravate. ◆o.-'plan a Archit sans cloisons.

opera ['ɒprə] n opéra m; o. glasses jumelles fpl de théâtre. ◆ope'ratic a d'opéra. ◆ope'retta n opérette f.

operat/e ['ɒpəreɪt] 1 vi (of machine etc) fonctionner; (proceed) opérer; – vt faire fonctionner; (business) gérer. 2 vi (of surgeon) opérer (on s.o. qn, for de). ◆–ing a o. costs frais mpl d'exploitation; to. theatre, Am o. room Med salle f d'opération; o. wing Med bloc m opératoire. ◆–ation n operation f (working) fonctionnement m; Med Mil Math etc opération f; in o. (machine) en service; (plan) Fig en vigueur. ◆ope-'rational a opérationnel. ◆operative a Med opératoire; (law, measure etc) en vigueur; – n ouvrier, -ière mf. ◆operator n Tel standardiste mf; (on machine) opérateur, -trice mf; (criminal) escroc mf; tour o. organisateur, -trice mf de voyages, voyagiste m.

opinion [ə'pɪnjən] n opinion f, avis m; in my o. à mon avis. ◆opinionated a dogmatique.

opium ['əʊpɪəm] n opium m.

opponent [ə'pəʊnənt] n adversaire mf.

opportune ['ɒpətjuːn] a opportun. ◆oppor'tunism n opportunisme m.

opportunity [ɒpə'tjuːnɪtɪ] n occasion f (to do de faire); pl (prospects) perspectives fpl; equal opportunities des chances fpl égales.

oppos/e [ə'pəʊz] vt (person, measure etc) s'opposer à; (law, motion) Pol faire opposition à. ◆–ed a opposé (to à); as o. to par opposition à. ◆–ing a (team, interests) opposé. ◆oppo'sition n opposition f (to à); the o. (rival camp) Fam l'adversaire m.

opposite ['ɒpəzɪt] a (side etc) opposé; (house) d'en face; one's o. number (counterpart) son homologue m; – adv en face; – prep o. (to) en face de; – n the o. le contraire, l'opposé m:

oppress [ə'pres] *vt* (*tyrannize*) opprimer; (*of heat, anguish*) oppresser; **the oppressed** les opprimés *mpl*. ◆**oppression** *n* oppression *f*. ◆**oppressive** *a* (*ruler etc*) oppressif; (*heat*) oppressant; (*régime*) tyrannique. ◆**oppressor** *n* oppresseur *m*.

opt [ɒpt] *vi* **to o. for** opter pour; **to o. to do** choisir de faire; **to o. out** *Fam* refuser de participer (*of* à). ◆**option** *n* option *f*; (*subject*) *Sch* matière *f* à option; **she has no o.** elle n'a pas le choix. ◆**optional** *a* facultatif; **o. extra** (*on car etc*) option *f*, accessoire *m* en option.

optical ['ɒptik(ə)l] *a* (*glass*) optique; (*illusion, instrument etc*) d'optique. ◆**opti'cian** *n* opticien, -ienne *mf*.

optimism ['ɒptimiz(ə)m] *n* optimisme *m*. ◆**optimist** *n* optimiste *mf*. ◆**opti'mistic** *a* optimiste. ◆**opti'mistically** *adv* avec optimisme.

optimum ['ɒptiməm] *a* & *n* optimum (*m*); **the o. temperature** la température optimum. ◆**optimal** *a* optimal.

opulent ['ɒpjʊlənt] *a* opulent. ◆**opulence** *n* opulence *f*.

or [ɔːr] *conj* ou; **one or two** un ou deux; **he doesn't drink or smoke** il ne boit ni ne fume; **ten or so** environ dix.

oracle ['ɒrək(ə)l] *n* oracle *m*.

oral ['ɔːrəl] *a* oral; – *n* (*examination*) *Sch* oral *m*.

orange ['ɒrindʒ] **1** *n* (*fruit*) orange *f*; – *a* (*drink*) à l'orange; **o. tree** oranger *m*. **2** *a* & *n* (*colour*) orange *a* & *m* *inv*. ◆**orangeade** *n* orangeade *f*.

orang-outang [ɔːræŋʊ'tæŋ] *n* orang-outan(g) *m*.

oration [ɔː'reiʃ(ə)n] *n* funeral **o.** oraison *f* funèbre.

oratory ['ɒrətəri] *n* (*words*) *Pej* rhétorique *f*.

orbit ['ɔːbit] *n* (*of planet etc*) & *Fig* orbite *f*; – *vt* (*sun etc*) graviter autour de.

orchard ['ɔːtʃəd] *n* verger *m*.

orchestra ['ɔːkistrə] *n* (*classical*) orchestre *m*. ◆**or'chestral** *a* (*music*) orchestral; (*concert*) symphonique. ◆**orchestrate** *vt* (*organize*) & *Mus* orchestrer.

orchid ['ɔːkid] *n* orchidée *f*.

ordain [ɔː'dein] *vt* (*priest*) ordonner; **to o. that** décréter que.

ordeal [ɔː'diːl] *n* épreuve *f*, supplice *m*.

order ['ɔːdər] *n* (*command, structure, association etc*) ordre *m*; (*purchase*) *Com* commande *f*; **in o.** (*drawer, room etc*) en ordre; (*passport etc*) en règle; **in** (*numerical*) **o.** dans l'ordre numérique; **in working o.** en état de marche; **in o. of age** par ordre

d'âge; **in o. to do** pour faire; **in o. that** pour que (+ *sub*); **it's in o. to smoke/etc** (*allowed*) il est permis de fumer/etc; **out of o.** (*machine*) en panne; (*telephone*) en dérangement; **to make** *or* **place an o.** *Com* passer une commande; **on o.** *Com* commandé; **money o.** mandat *m*; **postal o.** mandat *m* postal; – *vt* (*command*) ordonner (**s.o. to do** à qn de faire); (*meal, goods etc*) commander; (*taxi*) appeler; **to o. s.o. around** commander qn, régenter qn; – *vi* (*in café etc*) commander. ◆**—ly 1** *a* (*tidy*) ordonné; (*mind*) méthodique; (*crowd*) discipliné. **2** *n* *Mil* planton *m*; (*in hospital*) garçon *m* de salle.

ordinal ['ɔːdinəl] *a* (*number*) ordinal.

ordinary ['ɔːd(ə)nri] *a* (*usual*) ordinaire; (*average*) moyen; (*mediocre*) médiocre, ordinaire; **an o. individual** un simple particulier; **in o. use** d'usage courant; **in the o. course of events** en temps normal; **in the o. way** normalement; **it's out of the o.** ça sort de l'ordinaire.

ordination [ɔːdi'neiʃ(ə)n] *n* *Rel* ordination *f*.

ordnance ['ɔːdnəns] *n* (*guns*) *Mil* artillerie *f*.

ore [ɔːr] *n* minerai *m*.

organ ['ɔːgən] *n* **1** *Anat* & *Fig* organe *m*. **2** *Mus* orgue *m*, orgues *fpl*; **barrel o.** orgue *m* de Barbarie. ◆**organist** *n* organiste *mf*.

organic [ɔː'gænik] *a* organique. ◆**'organism** *n* organisme *m*.

organization [ɔːgənai'zeiʃ(ə)n] *n* (*arrangement, association*) organisation *f*.

organiz/e ['ɔːgənaiz] *vt* organiser. ◆**—ed** *a* (*mind, group etc*) organisé. ◆**—er** *n* organisateur, -trice *mf*.

orgasm ['ɔːgæz(ə)m] *n* orgasme *m*.

orgy ['ɔːdʒi] *n* orgie *f*.

orient ['ɔːrient] *vt* *Am* = orientate. ◆**orientate** *vt* orienter.

Orient ['ɔːrient] *n* **the O.** l'Orient *m*. ◆**ori'ental** *a* & *n* oriental, -ale (*mf*).

orifice ['ɒrifis] *n* orifice *m*.

origin ['ɒridʒin] *n* origine *f*.

original [ə'ridʒin(ə)l] *a* (*first*) premier, originel, primitif; (*novel, unusual*) original; (*sin*) originel; (*copy, version*) original; – *n* (*document etc*) original *m*. ◆**ori'ginality** *n* originalité *f*. ◆**originally** *adv* (*at first*) à l'origine; (*in a novel way*) originalement; **she comes o. from** elle est originaire de. ◆**originate** *vi* (*begin*) prendre naissance (**in** dans); **to o. from** (*of idea etc*) émaner de; (*of person*) être originaire de; – *vt* être l'auteur de. ◆**originator** *n* auteur *m*.

ornament ['ɔːnəmənt] *n* (*decoration*) ornement *m*; *pl* (*vases etc*) bibelots *mpl.* ◆**orna'mental** *a* ornemental. ◆**orna'men'tation** *n* ornementation *f.* ◆**or'nate** *a* (*style etc*) (très) orné. ◆**or'nately** *adv* (*decorated etc*) de façon surchargée, à outrance.

orphan ['ɔːf(ə)n] *n* orphelin, -ine *mf*; – *a* orphelin. ◆**orphaned** *a* orphelin; **he was o. by the accident** l'accident l'a rendu orphelin. ◆**orphanage** *n* orphelinat *m.*

orthodox ['ɔːθədɒks] *a* orthodoxe. ◆**orthodoxy** *n* orthodoxie *f.*

orthop(a)edics [ɔːθə'piːdɪks] *n* orthopédie *f.*

Oscar ['ɒskər] *n Cin* oscar *m.*

oscillate ['ɒsɪleɪt] *vi* osciller.

ostensibly [ɒ'stensɪblɪ] *adv* apparemment, en apparence.

ostentation [ɒsten'teɪʃ(ə)n] *n* ostentation *f.* ◆**ostentatious** *a* plein d'ostentation, prétentieux.

ostracism ['ɒstrəsɪz(ə)m] *n* ostracisme *m.* ◆**ostracize** *vt* proscrire, frapper d'ostracisme.

ostrich ['ɒstrɪtʃ] *n* autruche *f.*

other ['ʌðər] *a* autre; **o. people** d'autres; **the o. one** l'autre *mf*; **I have no o. gloves than these** je n'ai pas d'autres gants que ceux-ci; – *pron* autre; (*some*) **others** d'autres; **some do, others don't** les uns le font, les autres ne le font pas; **none o. than, no o. than** nul autre que; – *adv* **o. than** autrement que. ◆**otherwise** *adv* autrement; – *a* (*different*) (tout) autre.

otter ['ɒtər] *n* loutre *f.*

ouch! [aʊtʃ] *int* aïe!, ouille!

ought [ɔːt] *v aux* **1** (*obligation, desirability*) **you o. to leave** tu devrais partir; **I o. to have done it** j'aurais dû le faire; **he said he o. to stay** il a dit qu'il devait rester. **2** (*probability*) **it o. to be ready** ça devrait être prêt.

ounce [aʊns] *n* (*measure*) & *Fig* once *f* (= 28,35 g).

our [aʊər] *poss a* notre, *pl* nos. ◆**ours** *pron* le nôtre, la nôtre, *pl* les nôtres; **this book is o.** ce livre est à nous *or* est le nôtre; **a friend of o.** un ami à nous. ◆**our'selves** *pron* nous-mêmes; (*reflexive & after prep etc*) nous; **we wash o.** nous nous lavons.

oust [aʊst] *vt* évincer (**from** de).

out [aʊt] *adv* (*outside*) dehors; (*not at home etc*) sorti; (*light, fire*) éteint; (*news, secret etc*) connu, révélé; (*flower*) ouvert; (*book*) publié, sorti; (*finished*) fini; **to be** *or* **go o. a lot** sortir beaucoup; **he's o. in Italy** il est (parti) en Italie; **o. there** là-bas; **to have a**

day o. sortir pour la journée; **5 km o.** *Nau* à 5 km du rivage; **the sun's o.** il fait (du) soleil; **the tide's o.** la marée est basse; **you're o.** (*wrong*) tu t'es trompé; (*in game etc*) tu es éliminé (**of** de); **the trip** *or* **journey o.** l'aller *m*; **to be o.** to **win** être résolu à gagner; – *prep* **o. of** (*outside*) en dehors de; (*danger, breath, reach, water*) hors de; (*without*) sans; **o. of pity/love/***etc* par pitié/amour/*etc*; **to look/jump/***etc* **o.** (*window etc*) regarder/sauter/*etc* par; **to drink/take/copy o.** boire/prendre/copier dans; **made o. of** (*wood etc*) fait en; **to make sth o. of a box/rag/***etc* faire qch avec une boîte/un chiffon/*etc*; **a page o.** of une page de; **she's o. of town** elle n'est pas en ville; **5 km o. of** (*away from*) à 5 km de; **four o. of five** quatre sur cinq; **o. of the blue** de manière inattendue; **to feel o. of it** *or* **of things** se sentir hors du coup. ◆**'out-and-out** *a* (*cheat, liar etc*) achevé; (*believer*) à tout crin. ◆**o.-of-'date** *a* (*expired*) périmé; (*old-fashioned*) démodé. ◆**o.-of-'doors** *adv* dehors. ◆**o.-of-the-'way** *a* (*place*) écarté.

outbid [aʊt'bɪd] *vt* (*pt & pp* outbid, *pres p* outbidding) **to o. s.o.** (sur)enchérir sur qn.

outboard ['aʊtbɔːd] *a* **o. motor** *Nau* moteur *m* hors-bord *inv.*

outbreak ['aʊtbreɪk] *n* (*of war*) début *m*; (*of violence, pimples*) éruption *f*; (*of fever*) accès *m*; (*of hostilities*) ouverture *f.*

outbuilding ['aʊtbɪldɪŋ] *n* (*of mansion, farm*) dépendance *f.*

outburst ['aʊtbɜːst] *n* (*of anger, joy*) explosion *f*; (*of violence*) flambée *f*; (*of laughter*) éclat *m.*

outcast ['aʊtkɑːst] *n* (*social*) **o.** paria *m.*

outcome ['aʊtkʌm] *n* résultat *m*, issue *f.*

outcry ['aʊtkraɪ] *n* tollé *m.*

outdated [aʊt'deɪtɪd] *a* démodé.

outdistance [aʊt'dɪstəns] *vt* distancer.

outdo [aʊt'duː] *vt* (*pt* outdid, *pp* outdone) surpasser (**in** en).

outdoor ['aʊtdɔːr] *a* (*game*) de plein air; (*pool, life*) en plein air; **o. clothes** tenue *f* pour sortir. ◆**out'doors** *adv* dehors.

outer ['aʊtər] *a* extérieur; **o. space** l'espace *m* (cosmique); **the o. suburbs** la grande banlieue.

outfit ['aʊtfɪt] *n* équipement *m*; (*kit*) trousse *f*; (*toy*) panoplie *f* (*de pompier, cow-boy etc*); (*clothes*) costume *m*; (*for woman*) toilette *f*; (*group, gang*) *Fam* bande *f*; (*firm*) *Fam* boîte *f*; **sports/ski o.** tenue *f* de sport/de ski. ◆**outfitter** *n* chemisier *m.*

outgoing ['aʊtgəʊɪŋ] **1** *a* (*minister etc*)

sortant; (*mail, ship*) en partance. **2** *a* (*sociable*) liant, ouvert. **3** *npl* (*expenses*) dépenses *fpl*.

outgrow [aut'grau] *vt* (*pt* outgrew, *pp* outgrown) (*clothes*) devenir trop grand pour; (*habit*) perdre (en grandissant); **to o. s.o.** (*grow more than*) grandir plus vite que qn.

outhouse ['authaus] *n* (*of mansion, farm*) dépendance *f*; (*lavatory*) *Am* cabinets *mpl* extérieurs.

outing ['autɪŋ] *n* sortie *f*, excursion *f*.

outlandish [aut'lændɪʃ] *a* (*weird*) bizarre; (*barbaric*) barbare.

outlast [aut'lɑːst] *vt* durer plus longtemps que; (*survive*) survivre à.

outlaw ['autlɔː] *n* hors-la-loi *m inv*; – *vt* (*ban*) proscrire.

outlay ['autleɪ] *n* (*money*) dépense(s) *f(pl)*.

outlet ['autlet] *n* (*for liquid, of tunnel etc*) sortie *f*; **El** prise *f* de courant; (*for goods*) **Com** débouché *m*; (*for feelings, energy*) moyen *m* d'exprimer, exutoire *m*; **retail o.** Com point *m* de vente, magasin *m*.

outline ['autlaɪn] *n* (*shape*) contour *m*, profil *m*; (*rough*) **o.** (*of article, plan etc*) esquisse *f*; **the broad** *or* **general** *or* **main outline(s)** (*chief features*) les grandes lignes; – *vt* (*plan, situation*) décrire à grands traits, esquisser; (*book, speech*) résumer; **to be outlined against** (*of tree etc*) se profiler sur.

outlive [aut'lɪv] *vt* survivre à.

outlook ['autluk] *n inv* (*for future*) perspective(s) *f(pl)*; (*point of view*) perspective *f* (**on** sur), attitude *f* (**on** à l'égard de); **Met** prévisions *fpl*.

outlying ['autlaɪɪŋ] *a* (*remote*) isolé; (*neighbourhood*) périphérique.

outmoded [aut'məudɪd] *a* démodé.

outnumber [aut'nʌmbər] *vt* être plus nombreux que.

outpatient ['autpeɪʃ(ə)nt] *n* malade *mf* en consultation externe.

outpost ['autpəust] *n* avant-poste *m*.

output ['autput] *n* rendement *m*, production *f*; (*computer process*) sortie *f*; (*computer data*) donnée(s) *f(pl)* de sortie.

outrage ['autreɪdʒ] *n* atrocité *f*, crime *m*; (*indignity*) indignité *f*; (*scandal*) scandale *m*; (*indignation*) indignation *f*; **bomb o.** attentat *m* à la bombe; – *vt* (*morals*) outrager; **outraged by sth** indigné de qch.
◆**out'rageous** *a* (*atrocious*) atroce; (*shocking*) scandaleux; (*dress, hat etc*) grotesque.

outright [aut'raɪt] *adv* (*completely*) complètement; (*to say, tell*) franchement; (*to be*

killed) sur le coup; **to buy o.** (*for cash*) acheter au comptant; – [ˈautraɪt] *a* (*complete*) complet; (*lie, folly*) pur; (*refusal, rejection etc*) catégorique, net; (*winner*) incontesté.

outset ['autset] *n* **at the o.** au début; **from the o.** dès le départ.

outside [aut'saɪd] *adv* (au) dehors, à l'extérieur; **to go o.** sortir; – *prep* à l'extérieur de, en dehors de; (*beyond*) *Fig* en dehors de; **o. my room** *or* **door** à la porte de ma chambre; – *n* extérieur *m*, dehors *m*; – ['autsaɪd] *a* extérieur; (*bus or train seat etc*) côté couloir *inv*; (*maximum*) *Fig* maximum; **the o. lane** *Aut* la voie de droite, *Am* la voie de gauche; **an o. chance** une faible chance. ◆**out'sider** *n* (*stranger*) étranger, -ère *mf*; *Sp* outsider *m*.

outsize ['autsaɪz] *a* (*clothes*) grande taille *inv*.

outskirts ['autskɜːts] *npl* banlieue *f*.

outsmart [aut'smɑːt] *vt* être plus malin que.

outspoken [aut'spəuk(ə)n] *a* (*frank*) franc.

outstanding [aut'stændɪŋ] *a* remarquable, exceptionnel; (*problem, business*) non réglé, en suspens; (*debt*) impayé; **work o.** travail *m* à faire.

outstay [aut'steɪ] *vt* **to o. one's welcome** abuser de l'hospitalité de son hôte, s'incruster.

outstretched [aut'stretʃt] *a* (*arm*) tendu.

outstrip [aut'strɪp] *vt* (-pp-) devancer.

outward ['autwəd] *a* (*look, movement*) vers l'extérieur; (*sign, appearance*) extérieur; **o. journey** *or* **trip** aller *m*. ◆**outward(s)** *adv* vers l'extérieur.

outweigh [aut'weɪ] *vt* (*be more important than*) l'emporter sur.

outwit [aut'wɪt] *vt* (-tt-) être plus malin que.

oval ['əuv(ə)l] *a* & *n* ovale (*m*).

ovary ['əuvəri] *n* **Anat** ovaire *m*.

ovation [əu'veɪʃ(ə)n] *n* (*standing*) **o.** ovation *f*.

oven ['ʌv(ə)n] *n* four *m*; (*hot place*) *Fig* fournaise *f*; **o. glove** gant *m* isolant.

over ['əuvər] *prep* (*on*) sur; (*above*) au-dessus de; (*on the other side of*) de l'autre côté de; **bridge o. the river** pont *m* sur le fleuve; **to jump/look/etc o. sth** sauter/regarder/etc par-dessus qch; **to fall o. the balcony/etc** tomber du balcon/etc; **she fell o.** il elle en est tombée; **o. it** (*on*) dessus; (*above*) au-dessus; (*to jump etc*) par-dessus; **to criticize/etc o. sth** (*about*) critiquer/etc à propos de qch; **an advantage o.** un avantage sur or par rapport à; **o. the radio** (*on*) à la radio; **o. the phone** au télé-

phone; **o. the holidays** (*during*) pendant les vacances; **o. ten days** (*more than*) plus de dix jours; **men o.** sixty les hommes de plus de soixante ans; **o. and above** en plus de; **he's o. his flu** (*recovered from*) il est remis de sa grippe; **all o. Spain** (*everywhere in*) dans toute l'Espagne, partout en Espagne; **all o. the carpet** (*everywhere on*) partout sur le tapis; – *adv* (*above*) (par-)dessus; (*finished*) fini; (*danger*) passé; (*again*) encore; (*too*) trop; **jump o.!** sautez par-dessus!; **o. here** ici; **o. there** là-bas; **to be** *or* **come** *or* **go o.** (*visit*) passer; **he's o. in Italy** il est (parti) en Italie; **she's o. from Paris** elle est venue de Paris; **all o.** (*everywhere*) partout; **wet all o.** tout mouillé; **it's (all) o.!** (*finished*) c'est fini!; **she's o.** (*fallen*) elle est tombée; **a kilo o. o.** (*more*) un kilo ou plus; **I have ten o.** (*left*) il m'en reste dix; **there's some bread o.** il reste du pain; **o. and o. (again)** (*often*) à plusieurs reprises; **to start all o. (again)** recommencer à zéro; **o. pleased/etc** trop content/etc.
  ◆**o.-a'bundant** *a* surabondant. ◆**o.-de'veloped** *a* trop développé. ◆**o.-fa'miliar** *a* trop familier. ◆**o.-in'dulge** *vt* (*one's desires etc*) céder trop facilement à; (*person*) trop gâter. ◆**o.-sub'scribed** *a* (*course*) ayant trop d'inscrits.

overall 1 [əʊvər'ɔːl] *a* (*measurement, length, etc*) total; (*result, effort etc*) global; – *adv* globalement. **2** ['əʊvərɔːl] *n* blouse *f* (de travail); *pl* bleus *mpl* de travail.

overawe [əʊvər'ɔː] *vt* intimider.

overbalance [əʊvə'bæləns] *vi* basculer.

overbearing [əʊvə'beərɪŋ] *a* autoritaire.

overboard [əʊvə'bɔːd] *adv* à la mer.

overburden [əʊvə'bɜːd(ə)n] *vt* surcharger.

overcast [əʊvə'kɑːst] *a* (*sky*) couvert.

overcharge [əʊvə'tʃɑːdʒ] *vt* **to o. s.o. for sth** faire payer qch trop cher à qn.

overcoat ['əʊvəkəʊt] *n* pardessus *m*.

overcome [əʊvə'kʌm] *vt* (*pt* **overcame**, *pp* **overcome**) (*enemy, shyness etc*) vaincre; (*disgust, problem*) surmonter; **to be o. by** (*fatigue, grief*) être accablé par; (*fumes, temptation*) succomber à; **he was o. by emotion** l'émotion eut raison de lui.

overcrowded [əʊvə'kraʊdɪd] *a* (*house, country*) surpeuplé; (*bus, train*) bondé. ◆**overcrowding** *n* surpeuplement *m*.

overdo [əʊvə'duː] *vt* (*pt* **overdid**, *pp* **overdone**) exagérer; *Culin* cuire trop; **to o. it** (*exaggerate*) exagérer; (*work too much*) se surmener; *Iron* se fatiguer.

overdose ['əʊvədəʊs] *n* overdose *f*, dose *f* excessive (*de barbituriques etc*).

overdraft ['əʊvədrɑːft] *n* *Fin* découvert *m*. ◆**over'draw** *vt* (*pt* **overdrew**, *pp* **overdrawn**) (*account*) mettre à découvert.

overdress [əʊvə'dres] *vi* s'habiller avec trop de recherche.

overdue [əʊvə'djuː] *a* (*train etc*) en retard; (*debt*) arriéré; (*apology, thanks*) tardif.

overeat [əʊvər'iːt] *vi* manger trop.

overestimate [əʊvər'estɪmeɪt] *vt* surestimer.

overexcited [əʊvərɪk'saɪtɪd] *a* surexcité.

overfeed [əʊvə'fiːd] *vt* (*pt & pp* **overfed**) suralimenter.

overflow 1 ['əʊvəfləʊ] *n* (*outlet*) trop-plein *m*; (*of people, objects*) *Fig* excédent *m*. **2** [əʊvə'fləʊ] *vi* déborder (**with** de); **to be overflowing with** (*of town, shop, house etc*) regorger de (*visiteurs, livres etc*).

overgrown [əʊvə'grəʊn] *a* envahi par la végétation; **o. with** (*weeds etc*) envahi par; **you're an o. schoolgirl** *Fig Pej* tu as la mentalité d'une écolière.

overhang [əʊvə'hæŋ] *vi* (*pt & pp* **overhung**) faire saillie; – *vt* surplomber.

overhaul [əʊvə'hɔːl] *vt* (*vehicle, doctrine etc*) réviser; – ['əʊvəhɔːl] *n* révision *f*.

overhead [əʊvə'hed] *adv* au-dessus; – ['əʊvəhed] **1** *a* (*railway etc*) aérien. **2** *npl* (*expenses*) frais *mpl* généraux.

overhear [əʊvə'hɪər] *vt* (*pt & pp* **overheard**) surprendre, entendre.

overheat [əʊvə'hiːt] *vt* surchauffer; – *vi* (*of engine*) chauffer.

overjoyed [əʊvə'dʒɔɪd] *a* ravi, enchanté.

overland ['əʊvəlænd] *a & adv* par voie de terre.

overlap [əʊvə'læp] *vi* (*-pp-*) se chevaucher; – *vt* chevaucher; – ['əʊvəlæp] *n* chevauchement *m*.

overleaf [əʊvə'liːf] *adv* au verso.

overload [əʊvə'ləʊd] *vt* surcharger.

overlook [əʊvə'lʊk] *vt* **1** (*not notice*) ne pas remarquer; (*forget*) oublier; (*disregard, ignore*) passer sur. **2** (*of window, house etc*) donner sur; (*of tower, fort*) dominer.

overly ['əʊvəlɪ] *adv* excessivement.

overmuch [əʊvə'mʌtʃ] *adv* trop, excessivement.

overnight [əʊvə'naɪt] *adv* (*during the night*) (pendant) la nuit; (*all night*) toute la nuit; (*suddenly*) *Fig* du jour au lendemain; **to stay o.** passer la nuit; – ['əʊvənaɪt] *a* (*stay*) d'une nuit; (*clothes*) pour une nuit; (*trip*) de nuit.

overpass ['əʊvəpæs] *n* (*bridge*) *Am* toboggan *m*.

overpopulated [əuvə'pɒpjuleɪtɪd] *a* sur-peuplé.

overpower [əuvə'pauər] *vt* (*physically*) maîtriser; (*defeat*) vaincre; *Fig* accabler. ◆—**ing** *a* (*charm etc*) irrésistible; (*heat etc*) accablant.

overrat/e [əuvə'reɪt] *vt* surestimer. ◆—**ed** *a* surfait.

overreach [əuvə'riːtʃ] *vt* to o. oneself trop entreprendre.

overreact [əuvərɪ'ækt] *vi* réagir excessive-ment.

overrid/e [əuvə'raɪd] *vt* (*pt* overrode, *pp* overridden) (*invalidate*) annuler; (*take no notice of*) passer outre à; (*be more impor-tant than*) l'emporter sur. ◆—**ing** *a* (*passion*) prédominant; (*importance*) primordial.

overrule [əuvə'ruːl] *vt* (*reject*) rejeter.

overrun [əuvə'rʌn] *vt* (*pt* overran, *pp* over-run, *pres p* overrunning) **1** (*invade*) envahir. **2** (*go beyond*) aller au-delà de.

overseas [əuvə'siːz] *adv* (*Africa etc*) outre-mer; (*abroad*) à l'étranger; — ['əuvəsiːz] *a* (*visitor, market etc*) d'outre-mer; étranger; (*trade*) extérieur.

overse/e [əuvə'siː] *vt* (*pt* oversaw, *pp* over-seen) surveiller. ◆—**er** ['əuvəsɪər] *n* (*fore-man*) contremaître *m*.

overshadow [əuvə'ʃædəu] *vt* (*make less important*) éclipser; (*make gloomy*) assom-brir.

overshoot [əuvə'ʃuːt] *vt* (*pt & pp* overshot) (*of aircraft*) & *Fig* dépasser.

oversight ['əuvəsaɪt] *n* omission *f*, oubli *m*; (*mistake*) erreur *f*.

oversimplify [əuvə'sɪmplɪfaɪ] *vti* trop sim-plifier.

oversize(d) ['əuvəsaɪz(d)] *a* trop grand.

oversleep [əuvə'sliːp] *vi* (*pt & pp* overslept) dormir trop longtemps, oublier de se réveiller.

overspend [əuvə'spend] *vi* dépenser trop.

overstaffed [əuvə'stɑːft] *a* au personnel pléthorique.

overstay [əuvə'steɪ] *vt* to o. one's welcome abuser de l'hospitalité de son hôte, s'incruster.

overstep [əuvə'step] *vt* (**-pp-**) dépasser.

overt ['əuvɜːt] *a* manifeste.

overtake [əuvə'teɪk] *vt* (*pt* overtook, *pp* overtaken) dépasser; (*vehicle*) doubler, dépasser; **overtaken by** (*nightfall, storm*) surpris par; — *vi Aut* doubler, dépasser.

overtax [əuvə'tæks] *vt* **1** (*strength*) excéder; (*brain*) fatiguer. **2** (*taxpayer*) surimposer.

overthrow [əuvə'θrəu] *vt* (*pt* overthrew, *pp* overthrown) *Pol* renverser; — ['əuvəθrəu] *n* renversement *m*.

overtime ['əuvətaɪm] *n* heures *fpl* supplé-mentaires; — *adv* to work o. faire des heures supplémentaires.

overtones ['əuvətəunz] *npl Fig* note *f*, nuance *f* (of de).

overture ['əuvətjuər] *n Mus & Fig* ouver-ture *f*.

overturn [əuvə'tɜːn] *vt* (*chair, table etc*) renverser; (*car, boat*) retourner; (*decision etc*) *Fig* annuler; — *vi* (*of car, boat*) se retourner.

overweight [əuvə'weɪt] *a* to be o. (*of suitcase etc*) peser trop; (*of person*) avoir des kilos en trop.

overwhelm [əuvə'welm] *vt* (*of feelings, heat etc*) accabler; (*defeat*) écraser; (*amaze*) bouleverser. ◆—**ed** *a* (*with grief, work etc*) accablé de; (*with joy, kindness*) rempli de; (*offers*) submergé par; **o. by** (*kindness, gift etc*) vivement touché par. ◆—**ing** *a* (*heat, grief etc*) accablant; (*majority*) écrasant; (*desire*) irrésistible; (*impression*) dominant. ◆—**ingly** *adv* (*to vote, reject etc*) en masse; (*utterly*) carrément.

overwork [əuvə'wɜːk] *n* surmenage *m*; — *vi* se surmener; — *vt* surmener.

overwrought [əuvə'rɔːt] *a* (*tense*) tendu.

owe [əu] *vt* devoir (to à); **I'll o. it (to) you, I'll o. you (for) it** (*money*) je te le devrai; **to o. it to oneself to do** se devoir de faire. ◆—**owing 1** *a* (*money etc*) dû, qu'on doit. **2** *prep* **o. to** à cause de.

owl [aul] *n* hibou *m*.

own [əun] **1** *a* propre; **my o. house** ma propre maison; — *pron* **it's my (very) o.** c'est à moi (tout seul); **a house of his o.** sa propre maison, sa maison à lui; **(all) on one's o.** (*alone*) tout seul; **to get one's o. back** prendre sa revanche (**on** sur, **for** de); **to come into one's o.** (*fulfil oneself*) s'épanouir. **2** *vt* (*possess*) posséder; **who owns this ball/etc?** à qui appartient cette balle/etc? **3** *vi* to o. up (*confess*) avouer; **to o. up to sth** avouer qch. ◆—**owner** *n* propriétaire *mf*. ◆—**ownership** *n* posses-sion *f*; **home o.** accession *f* à la propriété; **public o.** *Econ* nationalisation *f*.

ox [ɒks], *pl* **oxen** [ɒks(ə)n] *n* bœuf *m*.

oxide ['ɒksaɪd] *n Ch* oxide *m*. ◆—**oxidize** *vi* s'oxyder; — *vt* oxyder.

oxygen ['ɒksɪdʒən] *n* oxygène *m*; — *a* (*mask, tent*) à oxygène.

oyster ['ɔɪstər] *n* huître *f*.

P

P, p [piː] n P, p m.

p [piː] abbr = **penny, pence.**

pa [paː] n (father) Fam papa m.

pace [peɪs] n (speed) pas m, allure f; (measure) pas m; **to keep p. with** (follow) suivre; (in work, progress) se maintenir à la hauteur de; – vi **to p. up and down** faire les cent pas; – vt (room etc) arpenter. ◆**pacemaker** n (device) stimulateur m cardiaque.

Pacific [pəˈsɪfɪk] a (coast etc) pacifique; – n **the P.** le Pacifique.

pacify [ˈpæsɪfaɪ] vt (country) pacifier; (calm, soothe) apaiser. ◆**pacifier** n (dummy) Am sucette f, tétine f. ◆**pacifist** n & a pacifiste (mf).

pack [pæk] **1** n (bundle, packet) paquet m; (bale) balle f; (of animal) charge f; (rucksack) sac m (à dos); Mil paquetage m; (of hounds, wolves) meute f; (of runners) Sp peloton m; (of thieves) bande f; (of cards) jeu m; (of lies) tissu m. **2** vt (fill) remplir (with de); (excessively) bourrer; (suitcase) faire; (object into box etc) emballer; (object into suitcase) mettre dans sa valise; (make into package) empaqueter; **to p. into** (cram) entasser dans; (put) mettre dans; **to p. away** (tidy away) ranger; **to p. off** (person Fam expédier; **to p. up** (put into box) emballer; (put into case) mettre dans sa valise; (give up) Fam laisser tomber; – vi (fill one's bags) faire ses valises; **to p. into** (of people) s'entasser dans; **to p. in or up** (of machine, vehicle) Fam tomber en panne; **to p. up** (stop) Fam s'arrêter; (leave) plier bagage. ◆**—ed** a (bus, cinema etc) bourré; **p. lunch** panier-repas m; **p. out** (crowded) Fam bourré. ◆**—ing** n (material, action) emballage m; **p. case** caisse f d'emballage.

package [ˈpækɪdʒ] n paquet m; (computer programs) progiciel m; **p. deal** Com contrat m global, train m de propositions; **p. tour** voyage m organisé; – vt emballer, empaqueter. ◆**—ing** n (material, action) emballage m.

packet [ˈpækɪt] n paquet m; (of sweets) sachet m, paquet m; **to make/cost a p.** Fam faire/coûter beaucoup d'argent.

pact [pækt] n pacte m.

pad [pæd] n (wad, plug) tampon m; (for writing, notes etc) bloc m; (on leg) Sp jambière f; (on knee) Sp genouillère f; (room) Sl piaule f; **launch(ing) p.** rampe f de lancement; **ink(ing) p.** tampon m encreur; – vt (-dd-) (stuff) rembourrer, matelasser; **to p. out** (speech, text) délayer. ◆**padding** n rembourrage m; (of speech, text) délayage m.

paddle [ˈpæd(ə)l] **1** vi (splash about) barboter; (dip one's feet) se mouiller les pieds; – n **to have a (little) p.** se mouiller les pieds. **2** n (pole) pagaie f; **p. boat, p. steamer** bateau m à roues; – vt **to p. a canoe** pagayer.

paddock [ˈpædək] n enclos m; (at racecourse) paddock m.

paddy [ˈpædɪ] n **p. (field)** rizière f.

padlock [ˈpædlɒk] n (on door etc) cadenas m; (on bicycle, moped) antivol m; – vt (door etc) cadenasser.

p(a)ediatrician [piːdɪəˈtrɪʃ(ə)n] n Med pédiatre mf.

pagan [ˈpeɪɡən] a & n païen, -enne (mf). ◆**paganism** n paganisme m.

page [peɪdʒ] **1** n (of book etc) page f. **2** n **p. (boy)** (in hotel etc) chasseur m; (at court) Hist page m; – vt **to p. s.o.** faire appeler qn.

pageant [ˈpædʒənt] n grand spectacle m historique. ◆**pageantry** n pompe f, apparat m.

pagoda [pəˈɡəʊdə] n pagode f.

paid [peɪd] see **pay**; – a (assassin etc) à gages; **to put p. to** (hopes, plans) anéantir; **to put p. to s.o.** (ruin) couler qn.

pail [peɪl] n seau m.

pain [peɪn] n (physical) douleur f; (grief) peine f; pl (efforts) efforts mpl; **to have a p. in one's arm** avoir mal or une douleur au bras; **to be in p.** souffrir; **to go to or take (great) pains to do** (exert oneself) se donner du mal à faire; **to go to or take (great) pains not to do** (be careful) prendre bien soin de ne pas faire; **to be a p. (in the neck)** (of person) Fam être casse-pieds; **to** (grieve) peiner. ◆**p.-killer** n analgésique m, calmant m. ◆**painful** a (illness, operation) douloureux; (arm, leg) qui fait mal, douloureux; (distressing) douloureux, pénible; (difficult) pénible; (bad) Fam

affreux. ◆**painless** *a* sans douleur; (*illness, operation*) indolore; (*easy*) *Fam* facile. ◆**painstaking** *a* (*person*) soigneux; (*work*) soigné.

paint [peɪnt] *n* peinture *f*; *pl* (*in box, tube*) couleurs *fpl*; – *vt* (*colour, describe*) peindre; **to p. blue**/*etc* peindre en bleu/*etc*; – *vi* peindre. ◆**—ing** *n* (*activity*) peinture *f*; (*picture*) tableau *m*, peinture *f*. ◆**—er** *n* peintre *m*. ◆**paintbrush** *n* pinceau *m*. ◆**paintwork** *n* peinture(s) *f(pl)*.

pair [peər] *n* paire *f*; (*man and woman*) couple *m*; **a p. of shorts** un short; **the p. of you** *Fam* vous deux; – *vi* **to p. off** (*of people*) former un couple; – *vt* (*marry*) marier.

pajama(s) [pəˈdʒɑːmə(z)] *a* & *npl Am* = pyjama(s).

Pakistan [pɑːkɪˈstɑːn] *n* Pakistan *m*. ◆**Pakistani** *a* & *n* pakistanais, -aise (*mf*).

pal [pæl] *n Fam* copain *m*, copine *f*; – *vi* (*-ll-*) **to p. up** devenir copains; **to p. up with** devenir copain avec.

palace [ˈpælɪs] *n* (*building*) palais *m*. ◆**palatial** [pəˈleɪʃ(ə)l] *a* comme un palais.

palatable [ˈpælətəb(ə)l] *a* (*food*) agréable; (*fact, idea etc*) acceptable.

palate [ˈpælɪt] *n Anat* palais *m*.

palaver [pəˈlɑːvər] *n Fam* (*fuss*) histoire(s) *f(pl)*; (*talk*) palabres *mpl*.

pale [peɪl] *a* (*-er, -est*) (*face, colour etc*) pâle; **p. ale** bière *f* blonde; – *vi* pâlir. ◆**—ness** *n* pâleur *f*.

palette [ˈpælɪt] *n* (*of artist*) palette *f*.

paling [ˈpeɪlɪŋ] *n* (*fence*) palissade *f*.

pall [pɔːl] **1** *vi* devenir insipide *ou* ennuyeux (*on s.o.*). **2** *n* (*of smoke*) voile *m*.

pallbearer [ˈpɔːlbeərər] *n* personne *f* qui aide à porter un cercueil.

pallid [ˈpælɪd] *a* pâle. ◆**pallor** *n* pâleur *f*.

pally [ˈpælɪ] *a* (*-ier, -iest*) *Fam* copain *am*, copine *af* (*with* avec).

palm [pɑːm] **1** *n* (*of hand*) paume *f*. **2** *n* (*symbol*) palme *f*; **p. (tree)** palmier *m*; (*leaf*) palme *f*; **P. Sunday** les Rameaux *mpl*. **3** *vt Fam* **to p. sth off** (*pass off*) refiler qch (**on s.o.** à); **to p. s.o. off** coller qch (**on s.o.** à); **to p. s.o. off on s.o.** coller qn à qn.

palmist [ˈpɑːmɪst] *n* chiromancien, -ienne *mf*. ◆**palmistry** *n* chiromancie *f*.

palpable [ˈpælpəb(ə)l] *a* (*obvious*) manifeste.

palpitate [ˈpælpɪteɪt] *vi* (*of heart*) palpiter. ◆**palpi'tation** *n* palpitation *f*.

paltry [ˈpɔːltrɪ] *a* (*-ier, -iest*) misérable, dérisoire.

pamper [ˈpæmpər] *vt* dorloter.

pamphlet [ˈpæmflɪt] *n* brochure *f*.

pan [pæn] **1** *n* casserole *f*; (*for frying*) poêle *f* (à frire); (*of lavatory*) cuvette *f*. **2** *vt* (*-nn-*) (*criticize*) *Fam* éreinter. **3** *vi* (*-nn-*) **to p. out** (*succeed*) *Fam* aboutir.

Pan- [pæn] *pref* pan-.

panacea [pænəˈsiːə] *n* panacée *f*.

panache [pəˈnæʃ] *n* (*showy manner*) panache *m*.

pancake [ˈpænkeɪk] *n* crêpe *f*.

pancreas [ˈpæŋkrɪəs] *n Anat* pancréas *m*.

panda [ˈpændə] *n* (*animal*) panda *m*; **P. car** = voiture *f* pie *inv* (de la police).

pandemonium [pændɪˈməʊnɪəm] *n* (*chaos*) chaos *m*; (*uproar*) tumulte *m*; (*place*) bazar *m*.

pander [ˈpændər] *vi* **to p. to** (*tastes, fashion etc*) sacrifier à; **to p. to s.o.** *or* **to s.o.'s desires** se plier aux désirs de qn.

pane [peɪn] *n* vitre *f*, carreau *m*.

panel [ˈpæn(ə)l] *n* **1** (*of door etc*) panneau *m*; (*control*) **p.** *Tech El* console *f*; (*instrument*) **p.** *Av Aut* tableau *m* de bord. **2** (*of judges*) jury *m*; (*of experts*) groupe *m*; (*of candidates*) équipe *f*; **a p. of guests** des invités; **a p. game** *TV Rad* un jeu par équipes. ◆**panelled** *a* (*room etc*) lambrissé. ◆**panelling** *n* lambris *m*. ◆**panellist** *n TV Rad* (*guest*) invité, -ée *mf*; (*expert*) expert *m*; (*candidate*) candidat, -ate *mf*.

pangs [pæŋz] *npl* **p. of conscience** remords *mpl* (de conscience); **p. of hunger/death** les affres *fpl* de la faim/de la mort.

panic [ˈpænɪk] *n* panique *f*; **to get into a p.** paniquer; – *vi* (*-ck-*) s'affoler, paniquer. ◆**p.-stricken** *a* affolé. ◆**panicky** *a Fam* qui s'affole facilement; **to get p.** s'affoler.

panorama [pænəˈrɑːmə] *n* panorama *m*. ◆**panoramic** *a* panoramique.

pansy [ˈpænzɪ] *n Bot* pensée *f*.

pant [pænt] *vi* (*gasp*) haleter.

panther [ˈpænθər] *n* (*animal*) panthère *f*.

panties [ˈpæntɪz] *npl* (*female underwear*) slip *m*.

pantomime [ˈpæntəmaɪm] *n* (*show*) spectacle *m* de Noël.

pantry [ˈpæntrɪ] *n* (*larder*) garde-manger *m inv*; (*storeroom in hotel etc*) office *m* or *f*.

pants [pænts] *npl* (*male underwear*) slip *m*; (*loose, long*) caleçon *m*; (*female underwear*) slip *m*; (*trousers*) *Am* pantalon *m*.

pantyhose [ˈpæntɪhəʊz] *n* (*tights*) *Am* collant(s) *m(pl)*.

papacy [ˈpeɪpəsɪ] *n* papauté *f*. ◆**papal** *a* papal.

paper [ˈpeɪpər] *n* papier *m*; (*newspaper*) journal *m*; (*wallpaper*) papier *m* peint;

(exam) épreuve f (écrite); (student's exercise) Sch copie f; (learned article) exposé m, communication f; **brown p.** papier m d'emballage; **to put down on p.** mettre par écrit; – a (bag etc) en papier; (cup, plate) en carton; **p. clip** trombone m inv; **p. knife** coupe-papier m inv; **p. mill** papeterie f; **p. shop** marchand m de journaux; – vt (room, wall) tapisser. ◆**paperback** n (book) livre m de poche. ◆**paperboy** n livreur m de journaux. ◆**paperweight** n presse-papiers m inv. ◆**paperwork** n Com écritures fpl; (red tape) Pej paperasserie f.

paprika ['pæprikə] n paprika m.

par [pɑːr] n **on a par** au même niveau (with que); **below p.** (unwell) Fam pas en forme.

para- ['pærə] pref para-.

parable ['pærəb(ə)l] n (story) parabole f.

parachute ['pærəʃuːt] n parachute f; **to drop by p.** (men, supplies) parachuter; – vi descendre en parachute; – vt parachuter. ◆**parachutist** n parachutiste mf.

parade [pə'reɪd] **1** n Mil (ceremony) parade f; (procession) défilé m; **fashion p.** défilé m de mode ou de mannequins; **p. ground** Mil terrain m de manœuvres; **to make a p.** of faire étalage de; – vi Mil défiler; **to p. about** (walk about) se balader; – vt faire étalage de. **2** n (street) avenue f.

paradise ['pærədaɪs] n paradis m.

paradox ['pærədɒks] n paradoxe m. ◆**para'doxically** adv paradoxalement.

paraffin ['pærəfɪn] n pétrole m (lampant); (wax) Am paraffine f; **p. lamp** lampe f à pétrole.

paragon ['pærəg(ə)n] n **p. of virtue** modèle m de vertu.

paragraph ['pærəgrɑːf] n paragraphe m; **'new p.'** 'à la ligne'.

parakeet ['pærəkiːt] n perruche f.

parallel ['pærəlel] a (comparable) & Math parallèle (with, to à); **to run p. to** or **with** être parallèle à; – n (comparison) & Geog parallèle m; (line) Math parallèle f; – vt être semblable à.

paralysis [pə'ræləsɪs] n paralysie f. ◆**'paralyse** vt (Am -lyze) paralyser. ◆**para'lytic** a & n paralytique (mf).

parameter [pə'ræmɪtər] n paramètre m.

paramount ['pærəmaʊnt] a **of p. importance** de la plus haute importance.

paranoia [pærə'nɔɪə] n paranoïa f. ◆**'paranoid** a & n paranoïaque (mf).

parapet ['pærəpɪt] n parapet m.

paraphernalia [pærəfə'neɪljə] n attirail m.

paraphrase ['pærəfreɪz] n paraphrase f; – vt paraphraser.

parasite ['pærəsaɪt] n (person, organism) parasite m.

parasol ['pærəsɒl] n (over table, on beach) parasol m; (lady's) ombrelle f.

paratrooper ['pærətruːpər] n Mil parachutiste m. ◆**paratroops** npl Mil parachutistes mpl.

parboil ['pɑːbɔɪl] vt Culin faire bouillir à demi.

parcel ['pɑːs(ə)l] **1** n colis m, paquet m; **to be part and p. of** faire partie intégrante de. **2** vt (-ll-, Am -l-) **to p. out** (divide) partager; **to p. up** faire un paquet de.

parch [pɑːtʃ] vt dessécher; **to be parched** (thirsty) être assoiffé; **to make parched** (thirsty) donner très soif à.

parchment ['pɑːtʃmənt] n parchemin m.

pardon ['pɑːd(ə)n] n pardon m; Jur grâce f; **general p.** amnistie f; **I beg your p.** (apologize) je vous prie de m'excuser; (not hearing) vous dites?; **p.?** (not hearing) comment?; **p. (me)!** (sorry) pardon! – vt pardonner (s.o. for sth qch à qn); **to p. s.o.** pardonner à qn; Jur gracier qn.

pare [peər] vt (trim) rogner; (peel) éplucher; **to p. down** Fig réduire, rogner.

parent ['peərənt] n père m, mère f; **one's parents** ses parents mpl, son père et sa mère; **p. firm, p. company** Com maison f mère. ◆**parentage** n (origin) origine f. ◆**pa'rental** a des parents, parental. ◆**parenthood** n paternité f, maternité f.

parenthesis, pl -eses [pə'renθəsɪs, -əsiːz] n parenthèse f.

Paris ['pærɪs] n Paris m. ◆**Parisian** [pə'rɪzɪən, Am pə'rɪʒən] a & n parisien, -ienne (mf).

parish ['pærɪʃ] n Rel paroisse f; (civil) commune f; – a (church, register) paroissial; **p. council** conseil m municipal. ◆**pa'rishioner** n paroissien, -ienne mf.

parity ['pærɪtɪ] n parité f.

park [pɑːk] **1** n (garden) parc m. **2** vt (vehicle) garer; (put) Fam mettre, poser; – vi Aut se garer; (remain parked) stationner. ◆**—ing** n stationnement m; **'no p.'** 'défense de stationner'; **p. bay** aire f de stationnement; **p. lot** Am parking m; **p. meter** parcmètre m; **p. place** endroit m pour se garer; **p. ticket** contravention f.

parka ['pɑːkə] n (coat) parka m.

parkway ['pɑːkweɪ] n Am avenue f.

parliament ['pɑːləmənt] n parlement m; P. Br Parlement m. ◆**parlia'mentary** a parlementaire. ◆**parlia'mentarian** n parlementaire mf (expérimenté(e)).

parlour ['pɑːlər] n (in mansion) (petit) salon

m; **ice-cream p.** *Am* salon *de* glaces; **p. game** jeu *m* de société.

parochial [pə'rəʊkɪəl] *a* (*mentality, quarrel*) *Pej* de clocher; (*person*) *Pej* provincial, borné; *Rel* paroissial.

parody ['pærədɪ] *n* parodie *f*; – *vt* parodier.

parole [pə'rəʊl] *n* **on p.** *Jur* en liberté conditionnelle.

parquet ['pɑːkeɪ] *n* **p.** (**floor**) parquet *m*.

parrot ['pærət] *n* perroquet *m*; **p. fashion** *Pej* comme un perroquet.

parry ['pærɪ] *vt* (*blow*) parer; (*question*) éluder; – *n Sp* parade *f*.

parsimonious [pɑːsɪ'məʊnɪəs] *a* parcimonieux. ◆**-ly** *adv* avec parcimonie.

parsley ['pɑːslɪ] *n* persil *m*.

parsnip ['pɑːsnɪp] *n* panais *m*.

parson ['pɑːs(ə)n] *n* pasteur *m*; **p.'s nose** (*of chicken*) croupion *m*.

part [pɑːt] **1** *n* partie *f*; (*of machine*) pièce *f*; (*of periodical*) livraison *f*; (*of serial*) épisode *m*; (*in play, film, activity*) rôle *m*; (*division*) *Culin* mesure *f*; (*in hair*) *Am* raie *f*; **to take p.** participer (**in** à); **to take s.o.'s p.** (*side*) prendre parti pour qn; **in p.** en partie; **for the most p.** dans l'ensemble; **to be a p. of** faire partie de; **on the p. of** (*on behalf of*) de la part de; **for my p.** pour ma part; **in these parts** dans ces parages; **p. exchange** reprise *f*; **to take in p. exchange** reprendre; **p. owner** copropriétaire *mf*; **p. payment** paiement *m* partiel; – *adv* en partie; **p. American** en partie américain. **2** *vt* (*separate*) séparer; (*crowd*) diviser; **to p. one's hair** se faire une raie; **to p. company with** (*leave*) quitter; – *vi* (*of friends etc*) se quitter; (*of married couple*) se séparer; **to p. with** (*get rid of*) se séparer de. ◆**-ing 1** *n* séparation *f*; – *a* (*gift, words*) d'adieu. **2** *n* (*in hair*) raie *f*.

partake [pɑː'teɪk] *vi* (*pt* **partook**, *pp* **partaken**) **to p. in** participer à; **to p. of** (*meal, food*) prendre, manger.

partial ['pɑːʃəl] *a* partiel; (*biased*) partial (**towards** envers); **to be p.** to (*fond of*) *Fam* avoir un faible pour. ◆**parti'ality** *n* (*bias*) partialité *f*; (*liking*) prédilection *f*.

participate [pɑː'tɪsɪpeɪt] *vi* participer (**in** à). ◆**participant** *n* participant, -ante *mf*. ◆**partici'pation** *n* participation *f*.

participle ['pɑːtɪsɪp(ə)l] *n* participe *m*.

particle ['pɑːtɪk(ə)l] *n* (*of atom, dust, name*) particule *f*; (*of truth*) grain *m*.

particular [pə'tɪkjʊlər] **1** *a* (*specific, special*) particulier; (*fastidious, fussy*) difficile (*about* sur); (*meticulous*) méticuleux; **this p. book** ce livre-ci en particulier; **in p.** en

particulier; **to be p. about** faire très attention à. **2** *n* (*detail*) détail *m*; **s.o.'s particulars** le nom et l'adresse de qn; (*description*) le signalement de qn. ◆**-ly** *adv* particulièrement.

partisan [pɑːtɪ'zæn, *Am* 'pɑːtɪz(ə)n] *n* partisan *m*.

partition [pɑː'tɪʃ(ə)n] **1** *n* (*of room*) cloison *f*; – *vt* **to p. off** cloisonner. **2** *n* (*of country*) *Pol* partition *f*, partage *m*; – *vt Pol* partager.

partly ['pɑːtlɪ] *adv* en partie; **p. English p. French** moitié anglais moitié français.

partner ['pɑːtnər] *n Com* associé, -ée *mf*; (*lover, spouse*) & *Sp Pol* partenaire *mf*; (*of racing driver etc*) coéquipier, -ière *mf*; (*dancing*) **p.** cavalier, -ière *mf*. ◆**partnership** *n* association *f*; **to take s.o. into p.** prendre comme associé(e); **in p. with** en association avec.

partridge ['pɑːtrɪdʒ] *n* perdrix *f*.

part-time [pɑːt'taɪm] *a* & *adv* à temps partiel; (*half-time*) à mi-temps.

party ['pɑːtɪ] *n* **1** (*group*) groupe *m*; *Pol* parti *m*; (*in contract, lawsuit*) *Jur* partie *f*; *Mil* détachement *m*; *Tel* correspondant, -ante *mf*; **rescue p.** équipe *f* de sauveteurs or de secours; **third p.** *Jur* tiers *m*; **innocent p.** innocent, -ente *mf*; **to be (a) p. to** (*crime*) être complice de; **p. line** *Tel* ligne *f* partagée; *Pol* ligne *f* du parti; **p. ticket** billet *m* collectif. **2** (*gathering*) réception *f*; (*informal*) surprise-partie *f*; (*for birthday*) fête *f*; **cocktail p.** cocktail *m*; **dinner p.** dîner *m*; **tea p.** thé *m*.

pass [pɑːs] **1** *n* (*entry permit*) laissez-passer *m inv*; (*free ticket*) *Th* billet *m* de faveur; (*season ticket*) carte *f* d'abonnement; (*over mountains*) *Geog* col *m*; *Fb* etc passe *f*; (*in exam*) mention *f* passable (**in French**/*etc* en français/*etc*); **to make a p. at** faire des avances à; **p. mark** (*in exam*) moyenne *f*, barre *f* d'admissibilité; **p. key** passe-partout *m inv*. **2** *vi* (*go, come, disappear*) passer (**to** à, **through** par); (*overtake*) *Aut* dépasser; (*in exam*) être reçu (**in French**/*etc* en français/*etc*); (*take place*) se passer; **that'll p.** (*be acceptable*) ça ira; **he can p. for thirty** on lui donnerait trente ans; **to p. along** or **through** passer; **to p. away** or **on** (*die*) mourir; **to p. by** passer (à côté); **to p. off** (*happen*) se passer; **to p. on to** (*move on to*) passer à; **to p. out** (*faint*) s'évanouir; – *vt* (*move, spend, give etc*) passer (**to** à); (*go past*) dépasser devant (*immeuble etc*); (*vehicle*) dépasser; (*exam*) être reçu à; (*candidate*) recevoir; (*judgement, opinion*) prononcer (**on** sur); (*remark*) faire; (*allow*) autoriser; (*bill, law*) *Pol* voter; **to p. (by)** s.o. (*in street*) croiser qn; **to p. by** (*building*) passer devant; **to p. oneself off as** se faire passer pour; **to p. sth off on** (*fob off on*) refiler qch à; **to p. on** (*message, title, illness etc*) transmettre (**to** à); **to p. out** *or* **round** (*hand out*) distribuer; **to p. over** (*ignore*) passer sur, oublier; **to p. round** (*cigarettes, sweets etc*) faire passer; **to p. up** (*chance etc*) laisser passer. **◆—ing** (*a vehicle etc*) qui passe; (*beauty*) passager; – *n* (*of visitor, vehicle etc*) passage *m*; (*of time*) écoulement *m*; (*death*) disparition *f*.

passable ['pɑːsəb(ə)l] *a* (*not bad*) passable; (*road*) praticable; (*river*) franchissable.

passage ['pæsɪdʒ] *n* (*passing, way through, of text, of speech etc*) passage *m*; (*of time*) écoulement *m*; (*corridor*) couloir *m*; *Nau* traversée *f*, passage *m*. **◆passageway** *n* (*way through*) passage *m*; (*corridor*) couloir *m*.

passbook ['pɑːsbʊk] *n* livret *m* de caisse d'épargne.

passenger ['pæsɪndʒər] *n* passager, -ère *mf*; *Rail* voyageur, -euse *mf*.

passer-by [pɑːsə'baɪ] *n* (*pl* passers-by) passant, -ante *mf*.

passion ['pæʃ(ə)n] *n* passion *f*; **to have a p. for** (*cars etc*) avoir la passion de, adorer. **◆passionate** *a* passionné. **◆passionately** *adv* passionnément.

passive ['pæsɪv] *a* (*not active*) passif; – *n* *Gram* passif *m*. **◆—ness** *n* passivité *f*.

Passover ['pɑːsəʊvər] *n* *Rel* Pâque *f*.

passport ['pɑːspɔːt] *n* passeport *m*.

password ['pɑːswɜːd] *n* mot *m* de passe.

past [pɑːst] **1** *n* (*time, history*) passé *m*; **in the p.** (*formerly*) dans le temps; **it's a thing of the p.** ça n'existe plus; – *a* (*gone by*) passé; (*former*) ancien; **these p. months** ces derniers mois; **that's all p.** c'est du passé; **in the p. tense** *Gram* au passé. **2** *prep* (*in front of*) devant; (*after*) après; (*further than*) plus loin que; (*too old for*) *Fig* trop vieux pour; **p. four o'clock** quatre heures passées, plus de quatre heures; **to be p. fifty** avoir cinquante ans passés; **it's p. belief** c'est incroyable; **I wouldn't put it p. him** ça ne m'étonnerait pas de lui, il en est bien capable; – *adv* devant; **to go p.** passer.

pasta ['pæstə] *n* *Culin* pâtes *fpl* (alimentaires).

paste [peɪst] **1** *n* (*of meat*) pâté *m*; (*of anchovy etc*) beurre *m*; (*dough*) pâte *f*. **2** *n* (*glue*) colle *f* (blanche); – *vt* coller; **to p. up** (*notice etc*) afficher.

pastel ['pæstəl, *Am* pæ'stel] *n* pastel *m*; – *a* (*shade*) pastel *inv*; (*drawing*) au pastel.

pasteurized ['pæstəraɪzd] *a* (*milk*) pasteurisé.

pastiche [pæ'stiːʃ] *n* pastiche *m*.

pastille ['pæstɪl, *Am* pæ'stiːl] *n* pastille *f*.

pastime ['pɑːstaɪm] *n* passe-temps *m* *inv*.

pastor ['pɑːstər] *n* *Rel* pasteur *m*. **◆pastoral** *a* pastoral.

pastry ['peɪstrɪ] *n* (*dough*) pâte *f*; (*cake*) pâtisserie *f*; **puff p.** pâte *f* feuilletée. **◆pastrycook** *n* pâtissier, -ière *mf*.

pasture ['pɑːstʃər] *n* pâturage *m*.

pasty ['peɪstɪ] *a* (*-ier, -iest*) (*complexion*) terreux. **2** ['pæstɪ] *n* *Culin* petit pâté *m* (en croûte).

pat [pæt] **1** *vt* (*-tt-*) (*cheek, table etc*) tapoter; (*animal*) caresser; – *n* petite tape; caresse *f*. **2** *adv* **to answer p.** avoir la réponse toute prête; **to know sth off p.** savoir qch sur le bout du doigt.

patch [pætʃ] *n* (*for clothes*) pièce *f*; (*over eye*) bandeau *m*; (*for bicycle tyre*) rustine® *f*; (*of colour*) tache *f*; (*of sky*) morceau *m*; (*of fog*) nappe *f*; (*of ice*) plaque *f*; **a cabbage/etc p.** un carré de choux/etc; **a bad p.** *Fig* une mauvaise passe; **not to be a p. on** (*not as good as*) *Fam* ne pas arriver à la cheville de; – *vt* **to p. (up)** (*clothing*) rapiécer; **to p. up** (*quarrel*) régler; (*marriage*) replâtrer. **◆patchwork** *n* patchwork *m*. **◆patchy** *a* (*-ier, -iest*) inégal.

patent 1 ['peɪtənt] *a* patent, manifeste; **p. leather** cuir *m* verni. **2** ['peɪtənt, 'pætənt] *n* brevet *m* (d'invention); – *vt* (faire) breveter. **◆—ly** *adv* manifestement.

paternal [pə'tɜːn(ə)l] *a* paternel. **◆paternity** *n* paternité *f*.

path [pɑːθ] *n* (*pl* -s [pɑːðz]) sentier *m*, chemin *m*; (*in park*) allée *f*; (*of river*) cours *m*; (*of bullet, planet*) trajectoire *f*. **◆pathway** *n* sentier *m*, chemin *m*.

pathetic [pə'θetɪk] *a* pitoyable.

pathology [pə'θɒlədʒɪ] *n* pathologie *f*. **◆patho'logical** *a* pathologique.

pathos ['peɪθɒs] *n* pathétique *m*.

patient 1 ['peɪʃ(ə)nt] *a* patient. **2** *n* (*in hospital*) malade *mf*, patient, -ente *mf*; (*on doctor's or dentist's list*) patient, -ente *mf*. **◆patience** *n* patience *f*; **to have p.** prendre patience; **to lose p.** perdre patience; **I have no p. with him** il m'impatiente; **to play p.** *Cards* faire des réussites. **◆patiently** *adv* patiemment.

patio ['pætɪəʊ] *n* (*pl* -os) patio *m*.

patriarch ['peɪtrɪɑːk] *n* patriarche *m*.

patriot ['pætrɪət, 'peɪtrɪət] *n* patriote *mf*.
◆**patri'otic** *a* (*views, speech etc*) patriotique; (*person*) patriote. ◆**patriotism** *n* patriotisme *m*.

patrol [pə'trəʊl] *n* patrouille *f*; **p. boat** patrouilleur *m*; **police p. car** voiture *f* de police; **p. wagon** *Am* fourgon *m* cellulaire; – *vi* (**-ll-**) patrouiller; – *vt* patrouiller dans. ◆**patrolman** *n* (*pl* **-men**) *Am* agent *m* de police; (*repair man*) *Aut* dépanneur *m*.

patron ['peɪtrən] *n* (*of artist*) protecteur, -trice *mf*; (*customer*) *Com* client, -ente *mf*; (*of cinema, theatre*) habitué, -ée *mf*; **p. saint** patron, -onne *mf*. ◆**patronage** *n* (*support*) patronage *m*; (*of the arts*) protection *f*; (*custom*) clientèle *f*. ◆**patroniz/e** ['pætrənaɪz, *Am* 'peɪtrənaɪz] *vt* 1 *Com* accorder sa clientèle à. 2 (*person*) *Pej* traiter avec condescendance. ◆**–ing** *a* condescendant.

patter ['pætər] 1 *n* (*of footsteps*) petit bruit *m*; (*of rain, hail*) crépitement *m*; – *vi* (*of rain, hail*) crépiter, tambouriner. 2 *n* (*talk*) baratin *m*.

pattern ['pæt(ə)n] *n* dessin *m*, motif *m*; (*paper model for garment*) patron *m*; (*fabric sample*) échantillon *m*; *Fig* modèle *m*; (*plan*) plan *m*; (*method*) formule *f*; (*of a crime*) scénario *m*. ◆**patterned** *a* (*dress, cloth*) à motifs.

paucity ['pɔːsɪtɪ] *n* pénurie *f*.

paunch [pɔːntʃ] *n* panse *f*, bedon *m*. ◆**paunchy** *a* (**-ier, -iest**) bedonnant.

pauper ['pɔːpər] *n* pauvre *mf*, indigent, -ente *mf*.

pause [pɔːz] *n* pause *f*; (*in conversation*) silence *m*; – *vi* (*stop*) faire une pause; (*hesitate*) hésiter.

pav/e [peɪv] *vt* paver; **to p. the way for** *Fig* ouvrir la voie à. ◆**–ing** *n* (*surface*) pavage *m*, dallage *m*; **p. stone** pavé *m*. ◆**pavement** *n* trottoir *m*; (*roadway*) *Am* chaussée *f*; (*stone*) pavé *m*.

pavilion [pə'vɪljən] *n* (*building*) pavillon *m*.

paw [pɔː] 1 *n* patte *f*; – *vt* (*of animal*) donner des coups de patte à. 2 *vt* (*touch improperly*) tripoter.

pawn [pɔːn] 1 *n* *Chess* pion *m*. 2 *vt* mettre en gage; – *n* **in p.** en gage. ◆**pawnbroker** *n* prêteur, -euse *mf* sur gages. ◆**pawnshop** *n* mont-de-piété *m*.

pay [peɪ] *n* salaire *m*; (*of workman*) paie *f*, salaire *m*; *Mil* solde *f*; (*of employee*) traitement *m*; **p. phone** téléphone *m* public; **p. day** jour *m* de paie; **p. slip** bulletin *m* or fiche *f* de paie; – *vt* (*pt & pp* **paid**) (*person, sum*) payer; (*deposit*) verser; (*yield*) *Com* rapporter; (*compli-* *ment, attention, visit*) faire; **to p. s.o. to do** or **for doing** payer qn pour faire; **to p. s.o. for sth** payer qch à qn; **to p. money into one's account** or **the bank** verser de l'argent sur son compte; **it pays (one) to be cautious on** a intérêt à être prudent; **to p. homage** or **tribute to** rendre hommage à; **I'll p. you back for this!** je te revaudrai ça!; **to p. in** (*cheque*) verser (to one's account **sur** son compte); **to p. off** (*debt, creditor etc*) rembourser; (*in instalments*) rembourser par acomptes; (*staff, worker*) licencier; **to p. off an old score** or **a grudge** *Fig* régler un vieux compte; **to p. out** (*spend*) dépenser; – *vi* **p. up** payer; **to p. for sth** payer qch; **to p. a lot (for)** payer cher; **to p. off** (*be successful*) être payant; **to p. up** payer. ◆**–ing** *a* (*guest*) payant; (*profitable*) rentable; **a cheque p. to** un chèque à l'ordre de. ◆**–able** *a* (*due*) payable; **a cheque p. to** un chèque à l'ordre de. ◆**–ment** *n* paiement *m*; (*of deposit*) versement *m*; (*reward*) récompense *f*; **on p. of 20 francs** moyennant 20 francs. ◆**payoff** *n* *Fam* (*reward*) récompense *f*; (*revenge*) règlement *m* de comptes. ◆**payroll** *n* **to be on the p. of** (*firm, factory*) être employé par; **to have twenty workers on the p.** employer vingt ouvriers.

pea [piː] *n* pois *m*; **garden** or **green peas** petits pois *mpl*; **p. soup** soupe *f* aux pois.

peace [piːs] *n* paix *f*; **p. of mind** tranquillité *f* d'esprit; **in p.** en paix; **at p.** en paix (**with** avec); **to have (some) p. and quiet** avoir la paix; **to disturb the p.** troubler l'ordre public; **to hold one's p.** garder le silence. ◆**p.-keeping** *a* (*force*) de maintien de la paix; (*measure*) de pacification. ◆**p.-loving** *a* pacifique. ◆**peaceable** *a* paisible, pacifique. ◆**peaceful** *a* paisible, calme; (*coexistence, purpose, demonstration*) pacifique. ◆**peacefulness** *n* paix *f*.

peach [piːtʃ] *n* (*fruit*) pêche *f*; (*tree*) pêcher *m*; – *a* (*colour*) pêche *inv*.

peacock ['piːkɒk] *n* paon *m*.

peak [piːk] *n* (*mountain top*) sommet *m*; (*mountain itself*) pic *m*; (*of cap*) visière *f*; (*of fame etc*) *Fig* sommet *m*, apogée *m*; **the traffic has reached** or **is at its p.** la circulation est à son maximum; – *a* (*hours, period*) de pointe; (*demand, production*) maximum; – *vi* (*of sales etc*) atteindre son maximum. ◆**peaked** *a* **p. cap** casquette *f*.

peaky ['piːkɪ] *a* (**-ier, -iest**) *Fam* (*ill*) patraque *f*; (*pale*) pâlot.

peal [piːl] 1 *n* (*of laughter*) éclat *m*; (*of thun-*

der) roulement m. **2** n p. of bells carillon m;
– vi to p. (out) (of bells) carillonner.

peanut ['piːnʌt] n cacah(o)uète f. (plant)
arachide f; to earn/etc peanuts (little
money) Fam gagner/etc des clopinettes.

pear [peər] n poire f; p. tree poirier m.

pearl [pɜːl] n perle f; (mother-of-pearl) nacre
f. ◆**pearly** a (-ier, -iest) (colour) nacré.

peasant ['pezənt] n & a paysan, -anne (mf).

peashooter ['piːʃuːtər] n sarbacane f.

peat [piːt] n tourbe f.

pebble ['peb(ə)l] n (stone) caillou m; (on
beach) galet m. ◆**pebbly** a (beach)
(couvert) de galets.

pecan [piːkæn] n (nut) Am pacane f.

peck [pek] vti to p. (at) (of bird) picorer (du
pain etc); (person) donner un coup de
bec à; to p. at one's food (of person) manger
du bout des dents; – n coup de bec;
(kiss) Fam bécot m.

peckish ['pekiʃ] a to be p. (hungry) Fam
avoir un petit creux.

peculiar [pi'kjuːliər] a (strange) bizarre;
(characteristic, special) particulier (to à).
◆**peculi'arity** n (feature) particularité f;
(oddity) bizarrerie f. ◆**peculiarly** adv
bizarrement; (specially) particulièrement.

pedal ['ped(ə)l] n pédale f; p. boat pédalo m;
– vi (-ll-, Am -l-) pédaler; (bicycle etc)
actionner les pédales de. ◆**pedalbin** n
poubelle f à pédale.

pedant ['pedənt] n pédant, -ante mf.
◆**pe'dantic** a pédant. ◆**pedantry** n
pédantisme m.

peddl/e ['ped(ə)l] vt colporter; (drugs) faire
le trafic de; – vi faire du colportage. ◆**-er**
n Am (door-to-door) colporteur, -euse mf;
(in street) camelot m; drug p. revendeur,
-euse mf de drogues.

pedestal ['pedɪst(ə)l] n Archit & Fig
piédestal m.

pedestrian [pi'destriən] **1** n piéton m; p.
crossing passage n pour piétons; p.
precinct zone f piétonnière. **2** a (speech,
style) prosaïque. ◆**pedestrianize** vt
(street etc) rendre piétonnier.

pedigree ['pedɪgriː] n (of dog, horse etc)
pedigree m; (of person) ascendance f; – a
(dog, horse etc) de race.

pedlar ['pedlər] n (door-to-door) colporteur,
-euse mf; (in street) camelot m.

pee [piː] n to go for a p. Fam faire pipi.

peek [piːk] n coup d'œil m (furtif); – vi jeter
un coup d'œil furtif (at à).

peel [piːl] n (of vegetable, fruit) pelure(s)
f(pl), épluchure(s) f(pl); (of orange skin)
écorce f; (in food, drink) zeste m; a piece of

p. une pelure, une épluchure; – vt (fruit,
vegetable) peler, éplucher; to keep one's
eyes peeled Fam être vigilant; to p. off
(label etc) décoller; – vi (of sunburnt skin)
peler; (of paint) s'écailler; to p. easily (of
fruit) se peler facilement. ◆**-ings** npl
pelures fpl, épluchures fpl. ◆**-er** n (knife
etc) éplucheur m.

peep [piːp] **1** n coup d'œil m (furtif); – vi to
p. (at) regarder furtivement; to p. out se
montrer; peeping Tom voyeur, -euse mf. **2**
vi (of bird) pépier. ◆**peephole** n judas m.

peer [piər] **1** n (equal) pair m, égal, -ale mf;
(noble) pair m. **2** vi to p. (at) regarder attentivement (comme pour mieux voir); to p.
into (darkness) scruter. ◆**peerage** n
(rank) pairie f.

peeved [piːvd] a Fam irrité.

peevish ['piːviʃ] a grincheux, irritable.

peg [peg] n **1** (wooden) Tech cheville f;
(metal) Tech fiche f; (for tent) piquet m;
(for clothes) pince f (à linge); (for coat, hat
etc) patère f; to buy off the peg acheter en
prêt-à-porter. **2** vt (-gg-) (prices) stabiliser.

pejorative [pi'dʒɒrətiv] a péjoratif.

pekin(g)ese [piːki'niːz] n (dog) pékinois m.

pelican ['pelikən] n (bird) pélican m.

pellet ['pelit] n (of paper etc) boulette f; (for
gun) (grain m de) plomb m.

pelt [pelt] **1** n (skin) peau f; (fur) fourrure f.
2 vt to p. s.o. with (stones etc) bombarder
de. **3** vi it's pelting (down) (raining) il pleut
à verse. **4** vi to p. along (run, dash) Fam
foncer, courir.

pelvis ['pelvis] n Anat bassin m.

pen [pen] n **1** (dipped in ink) porte-plume m
inv; (fountain pen) stylo m (à encre or à
plume); (ballpoint) stylo m à bille,
stylo(-)bille m; to live by one's p. Fig vivre
de sa plume; p. friend, p. pal correspondant, -ante mf; p. name pseudonyme m; p.
nib (bec m de) plume f; p. pusher Péj
gratte-papier m inv; – vt (-nn-) (write)
écrire. **2** n (enclosure for baby or sheep or
cattle) parc m.

penal ['piːn(ə)l] a (law, code etc) pénal;
(colony) pénitentiaire. ◆**penalize** vt Sp
Jur pénaliser (for pour); (handicap) désavantager.

penalty ['pen(ə)lti] n Jur peine f; (fine)
amende f; Sp pénalisation f; Fb penalty m;
Rugby pénalité f; to pay the p. Fig subir les
conséquences.

penance ['penəns] n pénitence f.

pence [pens] see penny.

pencil ['pens(ə)l] n crayon m; in p. au
crayon; p. box plumier m; p. sharpener

taille-crayon(s) *m inv*; – *vt* (**-ll-**, *Am* **-l-**) crayonner; **to p. in** *Fig* noter provisoirement.

pendant ['pendənt] *n* pendentif *m*; (*on earring, chandelier*) pendeloque *f*.

pending ['pendɪŋ] **1** *a* (*matter*) en suspens. **2** *prep* (*until*) en attendant.

pendulum ['pendjʊləm] *n* (*of clock*) balancier *m*, pendule *m*; *Fig* pendule *m*.

penetrat/e ['penɪtreɪt] *vt* (*substance, mystery etc*) percer; (*plan, secret etc*) découvrir; – *vti* to p. **into** (*forest, group etc*) pénétrer dans. ◆**–ing** *a* (*mind, cold etc*) pénétrant. ◆**pene'tration** *n* pénétration *f*.

penguin ['peŋgwɪn] *n* manchot *m*, pingouin *m*.

penicillin [penɪ'sɪlɪn] *n* pénicilline *f*.

peninsula [pə'nɪnsjʊlə] *n* presqu'île *f*, péninsule *f*. ◆**peninsular** *a* péninsulaire.

penis ['piːnɪs] *n* pénis *m*.

penitent ['penɪtənt] *a* & *n* pénitent, -ente (*mf*). ◆**penitence** *n* pénitence *f*.

penitentiary [penɪ'tenʃərɪ] *n Am* prison *f* (centrale).

penknife ['pennaɪf] *n* (*pl* **-knives**) canif *m*.

pennant ['penənt] *n* (*flag*) flamme *f*, banderole *f*.

penny ['penɪ] *n* **1** (*pl* **pennies**) (*coin*) penny *m*; *Am Can* cent *m*; **I don't have a p.** *Fig* je n'ai pas le sou. **2** (*pl* **pence** [pens]) (*value, currency*) penny *m*. ◆**p.-pinching** *a* (*miserly*) *Fam* avare. ◆**penniless** *a* sans le sou.

pension ['penʃ(ə)n] *n* pension *f*; **retirement p.** (*pension f de*) retraite *f*; (*private*) retraite *f* complémentaire; – *vt* **to p. off** mettre à la retraite. ◆**–able** *a* (*age*) de la retraite; (*job*) qui donne droit à une retraite. ◆**–er** *n* pensionné, -ée *mf*; (**old age**) **p.** retraité, -ée *mf*.

pensive ['pensɪv] *a* pensif.

pentagon ['pentəgən] *n* **the P.** *Am Pol* le Pentagone.

pentathlon [pen'tæθlən] *n Sp* pentathlon *m*.

Pentecost ['pentɪkɒst] *n* (*Whitsun*) *Am* Pentecôte *f*.

penthouse ['penthaʊs] *n* appartement *m* de luxe (*construit sur le toit d'un immeuble*).

pent-up [pent'ʌp] *a* (*feelings*) refoulé.

penultimate [pɪ'nʌltɪmət] *a* avant-dernier.

peony ['pɪənɪ] *n Bot* pivoine *f*.

people ['piːp(ə)l] *npl* (*in general*) gens *mpl or fpl*; (*specific persons*) personnes *fpl*; (*of region, town*) habitants *mpl*, gens *mpl or fpl*; **the p.** (*citizens*) *Pol* le peuple; **old p.** les personnes *fpl* âgées; **old people's home**

hospice *m* de vieillards; (*private*) maison *f* de retraite; **two p.** deux personnes; **English p.** les Anglais *mpl*, le peuple anglais; **a lot of p.** beaucoup de monde or de gens; **I think that . . .** on pense que . . . ; – *n* (*nation*) peuple *m*; – *vt* (*populate*) peupler (**with** de).

pep [pep] *n* entrain *m*; **p. talk** *Fam* petit laïus d'encouragement; – *vt* (**-pp-**) **to p. up** (*perk up*) ragaillardir.

pepper ['pepər] *n* poivre *m*; (*vegetable*) poivron *m*; – *vt* poivrer. ◆**peppercorn** *n* grain de poivre. ◆**peppermint** *n* (*plant*) menthe *f* poivrée; (*sweet*) pastille *f* de menthe. ◆**peppery** *a Culin* poivré.

per [pɜːr] *prep* par; **p. annum** par an; **p. head, p. person** par personne; **p. cent** pour cent; **50 pence p. kilo** 50 pence le kilo; **40 km p. hour** 40 km à l'heure. ◆**per'centage** *n* pourcentage *m*.

perceive [pə'siːv] *vt* (*see, hear*) percevoir; (*notice*) remarquer (**that** que). ◆**perceptible** *a* perceptible. ◆**perception** *n* perception *f* (**of** de); (*intuition*) intuition *f*. ◆**perceptive** *a* (*person*) perspicace; (*study, remark*) pénétrant.

perch [pɜːtʃ] **1** *n* perchoir *m*; – *vi* (*of bird*) (se) percher; (*of person*) *Fig* se percher, se jucher; – *vt* (*put*) percher. **2** *n* (*fish*) perche *f*.

percolate ['pɜːkəleɪt] *vi* (*of liquid*) filtrer, passer (**through** par); – *vt* (*coffee*) faire dans une cafetière; **percolated coffee** du vrai café. ◆**percolator** *n* cafetière *f*; (*in café or restaurant*) percolateur *m*.

percussion [pə'kʌʃ(ə)n] *n Mus* percussion *f*.

peremptory [pə'remptərɪ] *a* péremptoire.

perennial [pə'renɪəl] **1** *a* (*complaint, subject etc*) perpétuel. **2** *a* (*plant*) vivace; – *n* plante *f* vivace.

perfect ['pɜːfɪkt] *a* parfait; – *n* (*tense*) *Gram* parfait *m*; – [pə'fekt] *vt* (*book, piece of work etc*) parachever, parfaire; (*process, technique*) mettre au point; (*one's French etc*) parfaire ses connaissances en. ◆**per'fection** *n* perfection *f*; (*act*) parachèvement *m* (**of** de); **mise** *f* **au point** (**of** de); **to p. à la perfection.** ◆**per'fectionist** *n* perfectionniste *mf*. ◆**perfectly** *adv* parfaitement.

perfidious [pə'fɪdɪəs] *a Lit* perfide.

perforate ['pɜːfəreɪt] *vt* perforer. ◆**perfo'ration** *n* perforation *f*.

perform [pə'fɔːm] *vt* (*task, miracle*) accomplir; (*a function, one's duty*) remplir; (*rite*) célébrer; (*operation*) *Med* pratiquer (**on**

sur); (a play, symphony) jouer; (sonata) interpréter; – vi (play) jouer; (sing) chanter; (dance) danser; (of circus animal) faire un numéro; (function) fonctionner; (behave) se comporter; **you performed very well!** tu as très bien fait! ◆**-ing** a (animal) savant. ◆**performance** n 1 (show) Th représentation f, séance f; Cin Mus séance f. 2 (of athlete, machine etc) performance f; (of actor, musician etc) interprétation f; (circus act) numéro m; (fuss) Fam histoire(s) f(pl); **the p. of one's duties** l'exercice m de ses fonctions. ◆**performer** n interprète mf (of de); (entertainer) artiste mf.

perfume ['pɜːfjuːm] n parfum m; – [pə'fjuːm] vt parfumer.

perfunctory [pə'fʌŋktəri] a (action) superficiel; (smile etc) de commande.

perhaps [pə'hæps] adv peut-être; **p. not** peut-être que non.

peril ['perɪl] n péril m, danger m; **at your p.** à vos risques et péril. ◆**perilous** a périlleux.

perimeter [pə'rɪmɪtər] n périmètre m.

period ['pɪərɪəd] 1 n (length of time, moment in time) période f; (historical) époque f; (time limit) délai m; (lesson) Sch leçon f; (full stop) Gram point m; **in the p. of a month** en l'espace d'un mois; **I refuse, p.!** Am je refuse, un point c'est tout!; – a (furniture etc) (costume) d'époque; (costume) de l'époque. 2 n (menstruation) règles fpl. ◆**peri'odic** a périodique. ◆**peri'odical** n (magazine) périodique m. ◆**peri'odically** adv périodiquement.

periphery [pə'rɪfəri] n périphérie f. ◆**peripheral** a (question) sans rapport direct (**to** avec); (interest) accessoire; (neighbourhood) périphérique.

periscope ['perɪskəʊp] n périscope m.

perish ['perɪʃ] vi (die) périr; (of food, substance) se détériorer; **to be perished** or **perishing** (of person) Fam être frigorifié. ◆**-ing** a (cold, weather) Fam glacial. ◆**-able** a (food) périssable; – npl denrées fpl périssables.

perjure ['pɜːdʒər] vt **to p. oneself** se parjurer. ◆**perjurer** n (person) parjure mf. ◆**perjury** n parjure m; **to commit p.** se parjurer.

perk [pɜːk] 1 vi **to p. up** (buck up) se ragaillardir; – vt **to p. s.o. up** (buck up) ragaillardir; **to p. s.o. up** remonter qn, ragaillardir qn. 2 n (advantage) avantage m; (extra profit) à-côté m. ◆**perky** a (-ier, -iest) (cheerful) guilleret, plein d'entrain.

perm [pɜːm] n (of hair) permanente f; – vt **to**

have one's hair permed se faire faire une permanente.

permanent ['pɜːmənənt] a permanent; (address) fixe; **she's p. here** elle est ici à titre permanent. ◆**permanence** n permanence f. ◆**permanently** adv à titre permanent.

permeate ['pɜːmɪeɪt] vt (of ideas etc) se répandre dans; **to p. (through)** (of liquid etc) pénétrer. ◆**permeable** a perméable.

permit [pə'mɪt] vt (-tt-) permettre (**s.o. to do** à qn de faire); **weather permitting** si le temps le permet; – ['pɜːmɪt] n (licence) permis m; (entrance pass) laissez-passer m inv. ◆**per'missible** a permis. ◆**per'mission** n permission f, autorisation f (**to do** de faire); **to ask (for)/give p.** demander/donner la permission. ◆**per'missive** a (trop) tolérant, laxiste. ◆**per'missiveness** n laxisme m.

permutation [pɜːmjuː'teɪʃ(ə)n] n permutation f.

pernicious [pə'nɪʃəs] a (harmful) & Med pernicieux.

pernickety [pə'nɪkətɪ] a Fam (precise) pointilleux; (demanding) difficile (**about** sur).

peroxide [pə'rɒksaɪd] n (bleach) eau f oxygénée; – a (hair, blond) oxygéné.

perpendicular [pɜːpən'dɪkjʊlər] a & n perpendiculaire f.

perpetrate ['pɜːpɪtreɪt] vt (crime) perpétrer. ◆**perpetrator** n auteur m.

perpetual [pə'petʃʊəl] a perpétuel. ◆**perpetually** adv perpétuellement. ◆**perpetuate** vt perpétuer. ◆**perpetuity** [pɜːpɪ'tjuːɪtɪ] n perpétuité f.

perplex [pə'pleks] vt rendre perplexe, dérouter. ◆**-ed** a perplexe. ◆**-ing** a déroutant. ◆**perplexity** n perplexité f; (complexity) complexité f.

persecute ['pɜːsɪkjuːt] vt persécuter. ◆**perse'cution** n persécution f.

persevere [pɜːsɪ'vɪər] vi persévérer (**in** dans). ◆**-ing** a (persistent) persévérant. ◆**perseverance** n persévérance f.

Persian ['pɜːʃ(ə)n, 'pɜːʒ(ə)n] a (language, cat, carpet) persan; – n (language) persan m.

persist [pə'sɪst] vi persister (**in doing** à faire, **in sth** dans qch). ◆**persistence** n persistance f. ◆**persistent** a (fever, smell etc) persistant; (person) obstiné; (attempts, noise etc) continuel. ◆**persistently** adv (stubbornly) obstinément; (continually) continuellement.

person ['pɜːs(ə)n] n personne f; **in p.** en personne; **a p. to p. call** Tel une communi-

cation avec préavis. ◆**personable** a
avenant, qui présente bien.

personal ['pɜːsən(ə)l] a personnel; (*application*) en personne; (*hygiene, friend*) intime; (*life*) privé; (*indiscreet*) indiscret; **p. assistant, p. secretary** secrétaire m particulier, secrétaire f particulière. ◆**perso'nality** n (*character, famous person*) personnalité f; **a television p.** une vedette de la télévision. ◆**personalize** vt personnaliser. ◆**personally** adv personnellement; (*in person*) en personne.

personify [pə'sɒnɪfaɪ] vt personnifier. ◆**personifi'cation** n personnification f.

personnel [pɜːsə'nel] n (*staff*) personnel m; (*department*) service m du personnel.

perspective [pə'spektɪv] n (*artistic & viewpoint*) perspective f; (**in its true**) **p.** Fig sous son vrai jour.

perspire [pə'spaɪər] vi transpirer. ◆**perspi'ration** n transpiration f, sueur f.

persuade [pə'sweɪd] vt persuader (**s.o. to do** qn de faire). ◆**persuasion** n persuasion f; Rel religion f. ◆**persuasive** a (*person, argument etc*) persuasif. ◆**persuasively** adv de façon persuasive.

pert [pɜːt] a (*impertinent*) impertinent; (*lively*) gai, plein d'entrain; (*hat etc*) coquet, chic. ◆**—ly** adv impertinence.

pertain [pə'teɪn] vi **to p.** (*to relate*) se rapporter à; (*belong*) appartenir à.

pertinent ['pɜːtɪnənt] a pertinent. ◆**—ly** adv pertinemment.

perturb [pə'tɜːb] vt troubler, perturber.

Peru [pə'ruː] n Pérou m. ◆**Peruvian** a & n péruvien, -ienne (mf).

peruse [pə'ruːz] vt lire (attentivement); (*skim through*) parcourir. ◆**perusal** n lecture f.

pervade [pə'veɪd] vt se répandre dans. ◆**pervasive** a qui se répand partout, envahissant.

perverse [pə'vɜːs] a (*awkward*) contrariant; (*obstinate*) entêté; (*wicked*) pervers. ◆**perversion** n perversion f; (*of justice, truth*) travestissement m. ◆**perversity** n esprit m de contradiction; (*obstinacy*) entêtement m; (*wickedness*) perversité f.

pervert [pə'vɜːt] vt pervertir; (*mind*) corrompre; (*justice, truth*) travestir; ['pɜːvɜːt] n perverti, -ie mf.

pesky ['peskɪ] a (-ier, -iest) (*troublesome*) Am Fam embêtant.

pessimism ['pesɪmɪz(ə)m] n pessimisme m. ◆**pessimist** n pessimiste mf. ◆**pessi'mistic** a pessimiste. ◆**pessi'mistically** adv avec pessimisme.

pest [pest] n animal m or insecte m nuisible; (*person*) Fam casse-pieds mf inv, peste f. ◆**pesticide** n pesticide m.

pester ['pestər] vt (*harass*) harceler (**with questions** de questions); **to p. s.o. to do sth/for sth** harceler or tarabuster qn pour qu'il fasse qch/jusqu'à ce qu'il donne qch.

pet [pet] **1** n animal m (domestique); (*favourite person*) chouchou, -oute mf; **yes** (**my**) **p.** Fam oui mon chou; **to have** or **keep a p.** avoir un animal chez soi; – a (*dog etc*) domestique; (*tiger etc*) apprivoisé; (*favourite*) favori; **p. shop** magasin m d'animaux; **p. hate** bête f noire; **p. name** petit nom m (d'amitié); **p. subject** dada m. **2** vt (-**tt-**) (*fondle*) caresser; (*sexually*) Fam peloter; – vi Fam se peloter.

petal ['pet(ə)l] n pétale m.

peter ['piːtər] vi **to p. out** (*run out*) s'épuiser; (*dry up*) se tarir; (*die out*) mourir; (*disappear*) disparaître.

petite [pə'tiːt] a (*woman*) petite et mince, menue.

petition [pə'tɪʃ(ə)n] n (*signatures*) pétition f; (*request*) Jur requête f; **p. for divorce** demande f en divorce; – vt adresser une pétition or une requête à (**for sth** pour demander qch).

petrify ['petrɪfaɪ] vt (*frighten*) pétrifier de terreur.

petrol ['petrəl] n essence f; **I've run out of p.** je suis tombé en panne d'essence; **p. engine** moteur m à essence; **p. station** poste m d'essence, station-service f.

petroleum [pə'trəʊlɪəm] n pétrole m.

petticoat ['petɪkəʊt] n jupon m.

petty ['petɪ] a (-ier, -iest) (*small*) petit; (*trivial*) insignifiant, menu, petit; (*mean*) mesquin; **p. cash** Com petite caisse f, menue monnaie f. ◆**pettiness** n petitesse f; insignifiance f; mesquinerie f.

petulant ['petjʊlənt] a irritable. ◆**petulance** n irritabilité f.

petunia [pɪ'tjuːnɪə] n Bot pétunia m.

pew [pjuː] n banc m d'église; **take a p.!** Hum assieds-toi!

pewter ['pjuːtər] n étain m.

phallic ['fælɪk] a phallique.

phantom ['fæntəm] n fantôme m.

pharmacy ['fɑːməsɪ] n pharmacie f. ◆**pharmaceutical** [-'sjuːtɪk(ə)l] a pharmaceutique. ◆**pharmacist** n pharmacien, -ienne mf.

pharynx ['færɪŋks] n Anat pharynx m. ◆**pharyn'gitis** n Med pharyngite f.

phase [feɪz] n (*stage*) phase f; – vt **to p.**

in/out introduire/supprimer progressivement. ◆**phased** a (changes etc) progressif.

PhD [pi:eɪtʃ'di:] n abbr (Doctor of Philosophy) (degree) Univ doctorat m.

pheasant ['fezənt] n (bird) faisan m.

phenomenon, pl **-ena** [fɪ'nɒmɪnən, -ɪnə] n phénomène m. ◆**phenomenal** a phénoménal.

phew! [fju:] int (relief) ouf!

philanderer [fɪ'lændərər] n coureur m de jupons.

philanthropist [fɪ'lænθrəpɪst] n philanthrope mf. ◆**philan'thropic** a philanthropique.

philately [fɪ'lætəlɪ] n philatélie. ◆**phila'telic** a philatélique. ◆**philatelist** n philatéliste m.

philharmonic [fɪlə'mɒnɪk] a philharmonique.

Philippines ['fɪlɪpi:nz] npl the P. les Philippines fpl.

philistine ['fɪlɪstaɪn] n béotien, -ienne m, philistin m.

philosophy [fɪ'lɒsəfɪ] n philosophie f. ◆**philosopher** n philosophe mf. ◆**philo'sophical** a philosophique; (stoical, resigned) Fig philosophe. ◆**philo'sophically** adv (to say etc) avec philosophie. ◆**philosophize** vi philosopher.

phlegm [flem] n (in throat) glaires fpl; (calmness) Fig flegme m. ◆**phleg'matic** a flegmatique.

phobia ['fəʊbɪə] n phobie f.

phone [fəʊn] n téléphone m; **on the p.** (speaking here) au téléphone; (at other end) au bout du fil; **to be on the p.** (as subscriber) avoir le téléphone; **p. call** coup m de fil ou de téléphone; **to make a p. call** téléphoner (to à); **p. book** annuaire m; **p. box, p. booth** cabine f téléphonique; **p. number** numéro m de téléphone; – vt (message) téléphoner (to à); **to p. s.o. (up)** téléphoner à qn; – vi **to p. (up)** téléphoner; **to p. back** rappeler. ◆**phonecard** n télécarte f.

phonetic [fə'netɪk] a phonétique. ◆**phonetics** n (science) phonétique f.

phoney ['fəʊnɪ] a (-ier, -iest) Fam (jewels, writer etc) faux; (attack, firm) bidon inv; (attitude) fumiste; – n Fam (impostor) imposteur m; (joker, shirker) fumiste mf; it's a p. (jewel, coin etc) c'est du faux.

phonograph ['fəʊnəɡræf] n Am électrophone m.

phosphate ['fɒsfeɪt] n Ch phosphate m.

phosphorus ['fɒsfərəs] n Ch phosphore m.

photo ['fəʊtəʊ] n (pl **-os**) photo f; **to have one's p. taken** se faire photographier.

◆**photocopier** n (machine) photocopieur m. ◆**photocopy** n photocopie f; – vt photocopier. ◆**photo'genic** a photogénique. ◆**photograph** n photographie f; – vt photographier; – vi **to p. well** être photogénique. ◆**photographer** [fə'tɒɡrəfər] n photographe mf. ◆**photo'graphic** a photographique. ◆**photography** [fə'tɒɡrəfɪ] n (activity) photographie f. ◆**photostat®** = photocopy.

phras/e [freɪz] n (saying) expression f; (idiom) & Gram locution f; – vt (express) exprimer; (letter) rédiger. ◆**—ing** n (wording) termes mpl. ◆**phrasebook** n (for tourists) manuel m de conversation.

physical ['fɪzɪk(ə)l] a physique; (object, world) matériel; **p. examination** Med examen m médical; **p. education, p. training** éducation f physique. ◆**physically** adv physiquement; **p. impossible** matériellement impossible.

physician [fɪ'zɪʃ(ə)n] n médecin m.

physics ['fɪzɪks] n (science) physique f. ◆**physicist** n physicien, -ienne mf.

physiology [fɪzɪ'ɒlədʒɪ] n physiologie f. ◆**physio'logical** a physiologique.

physiotherapy [fɪzɪəʊ'θerəpɪ] n kinésithérapie f. ◆**physiotherapist** n kinésithérapeute mf.

physique [fɪ'zi:k] n (appearance) physique m; (constitution) constitution f.

piano [pɪ'ænəʊ] n (pl **-os**) piano m. ◆**'pianist** n pianiste mf.

piazza [pɪ'ætsə] n (square) place f; (covered) passage m couvert.

picayune [pɪkə'ju:n] a (petty) Am Fam mesquin.

pick [pɪk] n (choice) choix m; **the p. of** (best) le meilleur de; **the p. of the bunch** le dessus du panier; **to take one's p.** faire son choix, choisir; – vt (choose) choisir; (flower, fruit etc) cueillir; (hole) faire (in dans); (lock) crocheter; **to p. one's nose** se mettre les doigts dans le nez; **to p. one's teeth** se curer les dents; **to p. a fight** chercher la bagarre (with avec); **to p. holes in** Fig relever les défauts de; **to p. (off)** (remove) enlever; **to p. out** (choose) choisir; (identify) reconnaître, distinguer; **to p. up** (sth dropped) ramasser; (fallen person or chair) relever; (person into air, weight) soulever; (cold, money) Fig ramasser; (habit, accent, speed) prendre; (fetch, collect) passer prendre; (find) trouver; (baby) prendre dans ses bras; (programme etc) Rad capter; (survivor) recueillir; (arrest) arrêter, ramasser; (learn) apprendre; – vi **to p. and choose** choisir avec soin; **to p. on** (*nag*) harceler; (*blame*) accuser; **why p. on me?** pourquoi moi?; **to p. up** (*improve*) s'améliorer; (*of business, trade*) reprendre; *Med* aller mieux; (*resume*) continuer. ◆**-ing 1** n (*choosing*) choix m (**of** de); (*of flower, fruit etc*) cueillette f. **2** npl (*leftovers*) restes mpl; *Com* profits mpl. ◆**pick-me-up** n (*drink*) Fam remontant m. ◆**pick-up** n (*of record player*) (bras m de) pick-up m; (*person*) Pej Fam partenaire mf de rencontre; **p.-up (truck)** pick-up m.

pick(axe) (*Am* **-ax**) ['pɪk(æks)] n (*tool*) pioche f; **ice pick** pic m à glace.

picket ['pɪkɪt] **1** n (*striker*) gréviste mf; **p. (line)** piquet m (de grève); **–** vt (*factory*) installer des piquets de grève aux portes de. **2** n (*stake*) piquet m.

pickle ['pɪk(ə)l] **1** n (*brine*) saumure f; (*vinegar*) vinaigre m; pl (*vegetables*) pickles mpl; *Am* concombres mpl, cornichons mpl; **–** vt mariner. **2** n **in a p.** (*trouble*) Fam dans le pétrin.

pickpocket ['pɪkpɒkɪt] n (*thief*) pickpocket m.

picky ['pɪkɪ] a (**-ier, -iest**) (*choosey*) Am difficile.

picnic ['pɪknɪk] n pique-nique m; **–** vi (**-ck-**) pique-niquer.

pictorial [pɪk'tɔːrɪəl] a (*in pictures*) en images; (*periodical*) illustré.

picture ['pɪktʃər] **1** n image f; (*painting*) tableau m, peinture f; (*drawing*) dessin m; (*photo*) photo f; (*film*) film m; (*scene*) Fig tableau m; **the pictures** Cin le cinéma; **to put s.o. in the p.** Fig mettre au courant; **p. frame** cadre m. **2** vt (*imagine*) s'imaginer (**that** que); (*remember*) revoir; (*depict*) décrire.

picturesque [pɪktʃə'resk] a pittoresque.

piddling ['pɪdlɪŋ] a Pej dérisoire.

pidgin ['pɪdʒɪn] n **p. (English)** pidgin m.

pie [paɪ] n (*of meat, vegetable*) tourte f; (*of fruit*) tourte f, tourte f; (*compact filling*) pâté m en croûte; **cottage p.** hachis m Parmentier.

piebald ['paɪbɔːld] a pie inv.

piece [piːs] n morceau m; (*of bread, paper, chocolate, etc*) bout m, morceau m; (*of fabric, machine, game, artillery*) pièce f; (*coin*) pièce f; **bits and pieces** des petites choses; **in pieces** en morceaux, en pièces; **to smash to pieces** briser en morceaux; **to take to pieces** (*machine etc*) démonter; **to come to pieces** se démonter; **to go to pieces** (*of person*) Fig craquer; **a p.** of luck/news/etc une chance/nouvelle/etc; **in**

one p. (*object*) intact; (*person*) indemne; **–** vt **to p. together** (*facts*) reconstituer; (*one's life*) refaire. ◆**piecemeal** adv petit à petit; **–** a (*unsystematic*) peu méthodique. ◆**piecework** n travail m à la tâche or à la pièce.

pier [pɪər] n (*promenade*) jetée f; (*for landing*) appointement m.

pierc/e [pɪəs] vt percer; (*of cold, sword, bullet*) transpercer (qn). ◆**-ing** a (*voice, look etc*) perçant; (*wind etc*) glacial.

piety ['paɪətɪ] n piété f.

piffling ['pɪflɪŋ] a Fam insignifiant.

pig [pɪg] n cochon m, porc m; (*evil person*) Pej cochon m; (*glutton*) Pej goinfre m. ◆**piggish** a Pej (*dirty*) sale; (*greedy*) goinfre. ◆**piggy** a (*greedy*) Fam goinfre. ◆**piggybank** n tirelire f (*en forme de cochon*).

pigeon ['pɪdʒɪn] n pigeon m. ◆**pigeonhole** n casier m; **–** vt classer; (*shelve*) mettre en suspens.

piggyback ['pɪgɪbæk] n **to give s.o. a p.** porter qn sur le dos.

pigheaded [pɪg'hedɪd] a obstiné.

pigment ['pɪgmənt] n pigment m. ◆**pigmen'tation** n pigmentation f.

pigsty ['pɪgstaɪ] n porcherie f.

pigtail ['pɪgteɪl] n (*hair*) natte f.

pike [paɪk] n **1** (*fish*) brochet m. **2** (*weapon*) pique f.

pilchard ['pɪltʃəd] n pilchard m, sardine f.

pile¹ [paɪl] n pile f; (*fortune*) Fam fortune f; **piles of,** **a p. of** Fam beaucoup de, un tas de; **–** vt **to p. (up)** (*stack up*) empiler; **–** vi **to p. into** (*of people*) s'entasser dans; **to p. up** (*accumulate*) s'accumuler, s'amonceler. ◆**p.-up** n Aut collision f en chaîne, carambolage m.

pile² [paɪl] n (*of carpet*) poils mpl.

piles [paɪlz] npl Med hémorroïdes fpl.

pilfer ['pɪlfər] vt (*steal*) chaparder (**from s.o.** à qn). ◆**-ing**, ◆**-age** n chapardage m.

pilgrim ['pɪlgrɪm] n pèlerin m. ◆**pilgrimage** n pèlerinage m.

pill [pɪl] n pilule f; **to be on the p.** (*of woman*) prendre la pilule; **to go on/off the p.** se mettre à/arrêter la pilule.

pillage ['pɪlɪdʒ] vti piller; **–** n pillage m.

pillar ['pɪlər] n pilier m; (*of smoke*) Fig colonne f. ◆**p.-box** n boîte f à or aux lettres (*située sur le trottoir*).

pillion ['pɪljən] adv **to ride p.** (*on motorbike*) monter derrière.

pillory ['pɪlərɪ] vt (*ridicule, scorn*) mettre au pilori.

pillow ['pɪləʊ] n oreiller m. ◆**pillowcase** n, ◆**pillowslip** n taie f d'oreiller.

pilot ['paɪlət] 1 n (of aircraft, ship) pilote m; – vt piloter; – a p. light (on appliance) voyant m. 2 a (experimental) (-)pilote; p. scheme projet(-)pilote m.

pimento [pɪ'mentəʊ] n (pl -os) piment m.

pimp [pɪmp] n souteneur m.

pimple ['pɪmp(ə)l] n bouton m. ◆**pimply** a (-ier, iest) boutonneux.

pin [pɪn] n épingle f; (drawing pin) punaise f; Tech goupille f, fiche f; to have pins and needles Med Fam avoir des fourmis (in dans); p. money argent m de poche; – vt (-nn-) to p. (on) (attach) épingler (to sur, à); (to wall) punaiser (to, on à); to p. one's hopes on mettre tous ses espoirs dans; to p. on (to) s.o. (crime, action) accuser qn de; to p. down (immobilize) immobiliser; (fix) fixer; (enemy) clouer; to p. s.o. down Fig forcer qn à préciser ses idées; to p. up (notice) afficher. ◆**pincushion** n pelote f (à épingles). ◆**pinhead** n tête f d'épingle.

pinafore ['pɪnəfɔːr] n (apron) tablier m; (dress) robe f chasuble.

pinball ['pɪnbɔːl] n p. machine flipper m.

pincers ['pɪnsəz] npl tenailles fpl.

pinch [pɪntʃ] 1 n (mark) pinçon m; (of salt) pincée f; to give s.o. a p. pincer qn; at a p., Am in a p. (if necessary) au besoin; to feel the p. Fig souffrir (du manque d'argent etc); – vt pincer; – vi (of shoes) faire mal. 2 vt Fam (steal) piquer (from à); (arrest) pincer.

pine [paɪn] 1 n (tree, wood) pin m; p. forest pinède f. 2 vi to p. for désirer vivement (retrouver), languir après; to p. away dépérir.

pineapple ['paɪnæp(ə)l] n ananas m.

ping [pɪŋ] n bruit m métallique. ◆**pinger** n (on appliance) signal m sonore.

ping-pong ['pɪŋpɒŋ] n ping-pong m.

pink [pɪŋk] a & n (colour) rose (m).

pinkie ['pɪŋkɪ] n Am petit doigt m.

pinnacle ['pɪnək(ə)l] n (highest point) Fig apogée m.

pinpoint ['pɪnpɔɪnt] vt (locate) repérer; (define) définir.

pinstripe ['pɪnstraɪp] a (suit) rayé.

pint [paɪnt] n pinte f (Br = 0,57 litre, Am = 0,47 litre); a p. of beer = un demi.

pinup ['pɪnʌp] n (girl) pin-up f inv.

pioneer [paɪə'nɪər] n pionnier, -ière mf; – vt (research, study) entreprendre pour la première fois.

pious ['paɪəs] a (person, deed) pieux.

pip [pɪp] 1 n (of fruit) pépin m. 2 n (on

uniform) Mil galon m, sardine f. 3 npl the pips (sound) Tel le bip-bip.

pip/e [paɪp] 1 n (of smoker) pipe f; (instrument) Mus pipeau m; the pipes (bagpipes) Mus la cornemuse; (peace) p. calumet m de la paix; to smoke a p. fumer la pipe; p. cleaner cure-pipe m; p. dream chimère f; – vt (water etc) transporter par tuyaux or par canalisation; piped music musique f (de fond) enregistrée. 2 vi to p. down (shut up) Fam la boucler, se taire. ◆**-ing** (system of pipes) canalisations fpl, tuyaux mpl; length of p. tuyau m; – adv it's p. hot (soup etc) c'est très chaud. ◆**pipeline** n pipeline m; it's in the p. Fig c'est en route.

pirate ['paɪərət] n pirate m; – a (radio, ship) pirate. ◆**piracy** n piraterie f. ◆**pirated** a (book, record etc) pirate.

Pisces ['paɪsiːz] npl (sign) les Poissons mpl.

pistachio [pɪ'stæʃɪəʊ] n (pl -os) (fruit, flavour) pistache f.

pistol ['pɪst(ə)l] n pistolet m.

piston ['pɪst(ə)n] n Aut piston m.

pit [pɪt] 1 n (hole) trou m; (mine) mine f; (quarry) carrière f; (of stomach) creux m; Th orchestre m; Sp Aut stand m de ravitaillement. 2 vt (-tt-) to p. oneself or one's wits against se mesurer à. 3 n (stone of fruit) Am noyau m. ◆**pitted** a 1 (face) grêlé; p. with rust piqué de rouille. 2 (fruit) Am dénoyauté.

pitch¹ [pɪtʃ] 1 n Sp terrain m; (in market) place f. 2 n (degree) degré m; (of voice) hauteur f; Mus ton m. 3 vt (ball) lancer; (camp) établir; (tent) dresser; a pitched battle Mil une bataille rangée; Fig une belle bagarre. 4 vi (of ship) tanguer. 5 vi to p. in (cooperate) Fam se mettre de la partie; to p. into s.o. attaquer qn.

pitch² [pɪtʃ] n (tar) poix f. ◆**p.-'black** a, ◆**p.-'dark** a noir comme dans un four.

pitcher ['pɪtʃər] n cruche f, broc m.

pitchfork ['pɪtʃfɔːk] n fourche f (à foin).

pitfall ['pɪtfɔːl] n (trap) piège m.

pith [pɪθ] n (of orange) peau f blanche; (essence) Fig moelle f. ◆**pithy** a (-ier, -iest) (remark etc) piquant et concis.

pitiful ['pɪtɪfəl] a pitoyable. ◆**pitiless** a impitoyable.

pittance ['pɪtəns] n (income) revenu m or salaire m misérable; (sum) somme f dérisoire.

pitter-patter ['pɪtəpætər] n = patter 1.

pity ['pɪtɪ] n pitié f; (what) a p.! (quel) dommage!; it's a p. c'est dommage (that que (+ *sub*), **to do** de (faire); **to have** or **take p. on** avoir pitié de; – *vt* plaindre.

pivot ['pɪvət] *n* pivot m; – *vi* pivoter.

pixie ['pɪksɪ] *n* (*fairy*) lutin m.

pizza ['piːtsə] *n* pizza f.

placard ['plækɑːd] *n* (*notice*) affiche f.

placate [plə'keɪt, *Am* 'pleɪkeɪt] *vt* calmer.

place [pleɪs] *n* endroit m; (*specific*) lieu m; (*house*) maison f; (*premises*) locaux mpl; (*seat, position, rank*) place f; **in the first p.** (*firstly*) en premier lieu; **to take p.** (*happen*) avoir lieu; **p. of work** lieu m de travail; **market p.** (*square*) place f du marché; **at my p.**, **to my p.** *Fam* chez moi; **some p.** (*somewhere*) *Am* quelque part; **no p.** (*nowhere*) *Am* nulle part; **all over the p.** partout; **to lose one's p.** perdre sa place; (*in book etc*) perdre sa page; **p. setting** couvert m; **to lay three places** (*at the table*) mettre trois couverts; **to take the p. of** remplacer; **in p. of** à la place de; **out of p.** (*remark, object*) déplacé; (*person*) dépaysé; **p. mat** set m (de table); – *vt* (*put, situate, invest*) & *Sp* placer; (*an order*) *Com* passer (**with s.o.** à qn); (*remember, identify*) reconnaître. ◆**placing** *n* (*of money*) placement m.

placid ['plæsɪd] *a* placide.

plagiarize ['pleɪdʒəraɪz] *vt* plagier. ◆**plagiarism** *n* plagiat m.

plague [pleɪg] **1** *n* (*disease*) peste f; (*nuisance*) *Fam* plaie f. **2** *vt* (*harass, pester*) harceler (**with** de).

plaice [pleɪs] *n* (*fish*) carrelet m, plie f.

plaid [plæd] *n* (*fabric*) tissu m écossais.

plain[1] [pleɪn] **1** *a* (**-er, -est**) (*clear, obvious*) clair; (*outspoken*) franc; (*simple*) simple; (*not patterned*) uni; (*woman, man*) sans beauté; (*sheer*) pur; **in p. clothes** en civil; **to make it p. to s.o. that** faire comprendre à qn que; **p. speaking** franc-parler m; – *adv* (*tired etc*) tout bonnement. ◆**–ly** *adv* clairement, franchement. ◆**–ness** *n* clarté f; simplicité f; manque m de beauté.

plain[2] [pleɪn] *n Geog* plaine f.

plaintiff ['pleɪntɪf] *n Jur* plaignant, -ante mf.

plait [plæt] *n* tresse f, natte f; – *vt* tresser, natter.

plan [plæn] *n* projet m; (*elaborate*) plan m; (*of house, book etc*) & *Pol Econ* plan m; **the best p. would be to . . .** le mieux serait de . . . ; **according to p.** comme prévu; **to have no plans** (*be free*) n'avoir rien de prévu; **to change one's plans** (*decide differently*) changer d'idée; **master p.** stratégie f d'ensemble; – *vt* (**-nn-**) (*envisage, decide on*) prévoir, projeter; (*organize*) organiser;

(*prepare*) préparer; (*design*) concevoir; *Econ* planifier; **to p. to do** (*intend*) avoir l'intention de faire; **as planned** comme prévu; – *vi* faire des projets; **to p. for** (*rain, disaster*) prévoir. ◆**planning** *n Econ* planification f; (*industrial, commercial*) planning m; **family p.** planning m familial; **town p.** urbanisme m. ◆**planner** *n* **town p.** urbaniste mf.

plane [pleɪn] *n* **1** (*aircraft*) avion m. **2** *Carp* rabot m. **3** (*tree*) platane m. **4** (*level*) & *Fig* plan m.

planet ['plænɪt] *n* planète f. ◆**planetarium** *n* planétarium m. ◆**planetary** *a* planétaire.

plank [plæŋk] *n* planche f.

plant [plɑːnt] **1** *n* plante f; **house p.** plante d'appartement; – *vt* planter (**with** de); (*bomb*) *Fig* (dé)poser; **to p. sth on s.o.** (*hide*) cacher qch sur qn. **2** *n* (*machinery*) matériel m; (*fixtures*) installation f; (*factory*) usine f. ◆**plan'tation** *n* (*land, trees etc*) plantation f.

plaque [plæk] *n* **1** (*commemorative plate*) plaque f. **2** (*on teeth*) plaque f dentaire.

plasma ['plæzmə] *n Med* plasma m.

plaster ['plɑːstər] *n* (*substance*) plâtre m; (*sticking*) sparadrap m; **p. of Paris** plâtre m à mouler; **in p.** *Med* dans le plâtre; **p. cast** *Med* plâtre m; – *vt* plâtrer; **to p. down** (*hair*) plaquer; **to p. with** (*cover*) couvrir de. ◆**–er** *n* plâtrier m.

plastic ['plæstɪk] *a* (*substance, art*) plastique; (*object*) en plastique; **p. explosive** plastic m; **p. surgery** chirurgie f esthétique; – *n* plastique m, matière f plastique.

plasticine® ['plæstɪsiːn] *n* pâte f à modeler.

plate [pleɪt] *n* (*dish*) assiette f; (*metal sheet on door, on vehicle etc*) plaque f; (*book illustration*) gravure f; (*dental*) dentier m; **gold/silver p.** vaisselle f d'or/d'argent; **a lot on one's p.** (*work*) *Fig* du pain sur la planche; **p. glass** verre m à vitre; – *vt* (*jewellery, metal*) plaquer (**with** de). ◆**plateful** *n* assiettée f, assiette f.

plateau ['plætəʊ] *n Geog* (pl **-s** or **-x**) plateau m.

platform ['plætfɔːm] *n* estrade f; (*for speaker*) tribune f; (*on bus*) & *Pol Rail* quai m; **plate-forme** f; **p. shoes** chaussures fpl à semelles compensées.

platinum ['plætɪnəm] *n* (*metal*) platine m; – *a p.* or **p.-blond(e) hair** cheveux mpl platinés.

platitude ['plætɪtjuːd] *n* platitude f.

platonic [plə'tɒnɪk] *a* (*love etc*) platonique.

platoon [plə'tuːn] *n Mil* section f.

platter ['plætər] n Culin plat m.

plaudits ['plɔːdɪts] npl applaudissements mpl.

plausible ['plɔːzəb(ə)l] a (argument etc) plausible; (speaker etc) convaincant.

play [pleɪ] n (amusement, looseness) jeu m; Th pièce f (de théâtre), spectacle m; a p. on words un jeu de mots; to come into p. entrer en jeu; to call into p. faire entrer en jeu; — vt (card, part, tune etc) jouer; (game) jouer à; (instrument) jouer de; (match) disputer (with avec); (team, opponent) jouer contre; (record) passer; (radio) faire marcher; to p. ball with Fig coopérer avec; to p. the fool faire l'idiot; to p. a part in doing/in sth contribuer à faire/à qch; to p. it cool Fam garder son sang-froid; to p. back (tape) réécouter; to p. s.o. up Fam (of bad back etc) tracasser qn; (of child etc) faire enrager qn; — vi jouer (with avec, at à); (of record player, tape recorder) marcher; what are you playing at? Fam qu'est-ce que tu fais?; to p. about or around jouer, s'amuser; to p. on (piano etc) jouer de; (s.o.'s emotions etc) jouer sur; to p. up (of child, machine etc) Fam faire des siennes; to p. up to s.o. faire de la lèche à qn. ◆–ing n jeu m; p. card carte f à jouer; p. field terrain m de jeu. ◆–er n Sp joueur, -euse mf; Th acteur m, actrice f; clarinette/etc p. joueur, -euse mf de clarinette/etc; cassette p. lecteur m de cassettes.

play-act ['pleɪækt] vi jouer la comédie. ◆**playboy** n playboy m. ◆**playgoer** n amateur m de théâtre. ◆**playground** n Sch cour f de récréation. ◆**playgroup** n = playschool. ◆**playmate** n camarade mf. ◆**playpen** n parc m (pour enfants). ◆**playroom** n (in house) salle f de jeux. ◆**playschool** n garderie f (d'enfants). ◆**plaything** n (person) Fig jouet m. ◆**playtime** n Sch récréation f. ◆**playwright** n dramaturge mf.

playful ['pleɪfəl] a enjoué; (child) joueur. ◆–ly adv (to say) en badinant. ◆–ness n enjouement m.

plc [piːel'siː] abbr (public limited company) SA.

plea [pliː] n (request) appel m; (excuse) excuse f; to make a p. of guilty Jur plaider coupable. ◆**plead** vi Jur plaider; to p. with s.o. to do implorer qn de faire; to p. for (help etc) implorer; — vt Jur plaider; (as excuse) alléguer. ◆**pleading** n (requests) prières fpl.

pleasant ['plezənt] a agréable; (polite) aimable. ◆–ly adv agréablement. ◆—ness n (charm) charme m; (of person) amabilité f. ◆**pleasantries** npl (jokes) plaisanteries fpl; (polite remarks) civilités fpl.

pleas/e [pliːz] adv s'il vous plaît, s'il te plaît; p. sit down asseyez-vous, je vous prie; p. do! bien sûr!, je vous en prie!; 'no smoking p.' 'prière de ne pas fumer'; — vt plaire à; (satisfy) contenter; hard to p. difficile (à contenter), exigeant; p. yourself! comme tu veux!; — vi plaire; do as you p. fais comme tu veux; as much or as many as you p. autant qu'il vous plaira. ◆—ed a content (with de, that que (+ sub), to do de faire); p. to meet you! enchanté; I'd be p. to! avec plaisir! ◆—ing a agréable, plaisant.

pleasure ['pleʒər] n plaisir m; p. boat bateau m de plaisance. ◆**pleasurable** a très agréable.

pleat [pliːt] n (fold) pli m; — vt plisser.

plebiscite ['plebɪsɪt, -saɪt] n plébiscite m.

pledge [pledʒ] n 1 (promise) promesse f, engagement m (to do de faire); — vt promettre (to do de faire). 2 n (token, object) gage m; — vt (pawn) engager.

plenty ['plentɪ] n abondance f; in p. en abondance; p. of beaucoup de; that's p. (enough) c'est assez, ça suffit. ◆**plentiful** a abondant.

plethora ['pleθərə] n pléthore f.

pleurisy ['plʊərɪsɪ] n Med pleurésie f.

pliable ['plaɪəb(ə)l] a souple.

pliers ['plaɪəz] npl (tool) pince(s) f(pl).

plight [plaɪt] n (crisis) situation f critique; (sorry) p. triste situation f.

plimsoll ['plɪmsəʊl] n chaussure f de tennis, tennis f.

plinth [plɪnθ] n socle m.

plod [plɒd] vi (-dd-) to p. (along) avancer or travailler laborieusement; to p. through (book) lire laborieusement. ◆**plodding** a (slow) lent; (step) pesant. ◆**plodder** n (steady worker) bûcheur, -euse mf.

plonk [plɒŋk] n (thud) bruit sourd! 2 vt to p. (down) (drop) Fam poser (bruyamment). 3 n (wine) Pej Sl pinard m.

plot [plɒt] n 1 (conspiracy) complot m (against contre); Cin Th Liter intrigue f; — vti (-tt-) comploter (to do de faire). 2 n p. (of land) terrain m; (patch in garden) carré m de terre; building p. terrain m à bâtir. 3 vt (-tt-) to p. (out) déterminer; (graph, diagram) tracer; (one's position) relever. ◆**plotting** n (conspiracies) complots mpl.

plough [plaʊ] n charrue f; — vt labourer; to

p. back into (*money*) *Fig* réinvestir dans; – *vi* labourer; **to p. into** (*crash into*) percuter; **to p. through** (*snow etc*) avancer péniblement dans; (*fence, wall*) défoncer. ◆**ploughman** *n* (*pl* -men) laboureur *m*; **p.'s lunch** *Culin* assiette *f* composée (*de crudités et fromage*).

plow [plau] *Am* = **plough**.

ploy [plɔɪ] *n* stratagème *m*.

pluck [plʌk] *n* courage *m*; – *vt* **to p. up courage** s'armer de courage. **2** *vt* (*fowl*) plumer; (*eyebrows*) épiler; (*string*) *Mus* pincer; (*flower*) cueillir. ◆**plucky** *a* (-ier, -iest) courageux.

plug [plʌg] **1** *n* (*of cotton wool, wood etc*) tampon *m*, bouchon *m*; (*for sink or drainage*) bonde *f*; – *vt* (-gg-) **to p. (up)** (*stop up*) boucher. **2** *n* *El* fiche *f*, prise *f* (*mâle*); – *vt* (-gg-) **to p. in** brancher. **3** *n* *Aut* bougie *f*. **4** *n* (*publicity*) *Fam* battage *m* publicitaire; – *vt* (-gg-) *Fam* faire du battage publicitaire pour. **5** *vi* (-gg-) **to p. away** (*work*) *Fam* bosser (**at** à). ◆**plughole** *n* trou *m* (*du lavabo etc*), vidange *f*.

plum [plʌm] *n* prune *f*; **a p. job** *Fam* un travail en or, un bon fromage.

plumage ['pluːmɪdʒ] *n* plumage *m*.

plumb [plʌm] **1** *vt* (*probe, understand*) sonder. **2** *adv* (*crazy etc*) *Am Fam* complètement; **p. in the middle** en plein milieu. ◆**plumber** *n* plombier *m*. ◆**plumbing** *n* plomberie *f*.

plume [pluːm] *n* (*feather*) plume *f*; (*on hat etc*) plumet *m*; **a p. of smoke** un panache de fumée.

plummet ['plʌmɪt] *vi* (*of aircraft etc*) plonger; (*of prices*) dégringoler.

plump [plʌmp] **1** *a* (-er, -est) (*person*) grassouillet; (*arm, chicken*) dodu; (*cushion, cheek*) rebondi. **2** *vi* **to p. for** (*choose*) se décider pour, choisir. ◆**-ness** *n* rondeur *f*.

plunder ['plʌndər] *vt* piller; – *n* (*act*) pillage *m*; (*goods*) butin *m*.

plung/e [plʌndʒ] **1** *vt* (*thrust*) plonger (**into** dans); – *vi* (*dive*) plonger (**into** dans); (*fall*) tomber (**from** de); (*rush*) se lancer; – *n* (*dive*) plongeon *m*; (*fall*) chute *f*; **to take the p.** *Fig* se jeter à l'eau. ◆**-ing** *a* (*neckline*) plongeant. ◆**-er** *n* ventouse *f* (*pour déboucher un tuyau*), débouchoir *m*.

plural ['pluərəl] *a* (*form*) pluriel; (*noun*) au pluriel; – *n* pluriel *m*; **in the p.** au pluriel.

plus [plʌs] *prep* plus; – *a* (*factor etc*) & *El* positif; **twenty p.** vingt et quelques; – *n* **p.**

(*sign*) *Math* (signe *m*) plus *m*; **it's a p.** c'est un (avantage en) plus.

plush [plʌʃ] *a* (-er, -est) (*splendid*) somptueux.

plutonium [pluː'təʊnɪəm] *n* plutonium *m*.

ply [plaɪ] **1** *vt* (*trade*) exercer; (*oar, tool*) *Lit* manier. **2** *vi* **to p. between** (*travel*) faire la navette entre. **3** *vt* **to p. s.o. with** (*whisky etc*) faire boire continuellement à qn; (*questions*) bombarder qn de.

p.m. [piː'em] *adv* (*afternoon*) de l'après-midi; (*evening*) du soir.

PM [piː'em] *n abbr* (*Prime Minister*) Premier ministre *m*.

pneumatic [njuː'mætɪk] *a* **p. drill** marteau-piqueur *m*, marteau *m* pneumatique.

pneumonia [njuː'məʊnɪə] *n* pneumonie *f*.

poach [pəʊtʃ] **1** *vt* (*egg*) pocher. **2** *vi* (*hunt, steal*) braconner; – *vt* (*employee from rival firm*) débaucher, piquer. ◆**-ing** *n* braconnage *m*. ◆**-er** *n* **1** (*person*) braconnier *m*. **2** (*egg*) pocheuse *f*.

PO Box [piːəʊ'bɒks] *abbr* (*Post Office Box*) BP.

pocket ['pɒkɪt] *n* poche *f*; (*area*) *Fig* petite zone *f*; (*of resistance*) poche *f*, îlot *m*; **I'm $5 out of p.** j'ai perdu 5 dollars; – *a* (*money, book etc*) de poche; – *vt* (*gain, steal*) empocher. ◆**pocketbook** *n* (*notebook*) carnet *m*; (*woman's handbag*) *Am* sac *m* à main. ◆**pocketful** *n* **a p.** d'une pleine poche de.

pockmarked ['pɒkmɑːkt] *a* (*face*) grêlé.

pod [pɒd] *n* cosse *f*.

podgy ['pɒdʒɪ] *a* (-ier, -iest) (*arm etc*) dodu; (*person*) rondelet.

podium ['pəʊdɪəm] *n* podium *m*.

poem ['pəʊɪm] *n* poème *m*. ◆**poet** *n* poète *m*. ◆**po'etic** *a* poétique. ◆**poetry** *n* poésie *f*.

poignant ['pɔɪnjənt] *a* poignant.

point [pɔɪnt] **1** *n* (*of knife etc*) pointe *f*; *pl Rail* aiguillage *m*; (*power*) *El* prise *f* (*de courant*). **2** *n* (*dot, position, question, degree, score etc*) point *m*; (*decimal*) virgule *f*; (*meaning*) *Fig* sens *m*; (*importance*) intérêt *m*; (*remark*) remarque *f*; **p. of view** point *m* de vue; **at this p. in time** en ce moment; **on the p. of doing** sur le point de faire; **what's the p.?** à quoi bon? (*of waiting/etc* attendre/*etc*); **there's no p. (in) staying/etc** ça ne sert à rien de rester/*etc*; **that's not the p.** là n'est pas la question; **it's beside the p.** c'est à côté de la question; **to the p.** (*relevant*) pertinent; **to get to the p.!** au fait!; **to make a p. of doing** prendre garde de faire; **his good**

points ses qualités *fpl*; **his bad points** ses défauts *mpl*. **3** *vt* (*aim*) pointer (**at** sur); (*vehicle*) tourner (**towards** vers); **to p. the way** indiquer le chemin (**to** à); *Fig* montrer la voie (**to** à); **to p. one's finger at** indiquer du doit, pointer son doigt vers; **to p. out** (*show*) indiquer; (*mention*) signaler (**that** que); – *vi* **to p.** (**at** *or* **to** s.o.) indiquer (qn) du doigt; **to p. to, be pointing to** (*show*) indiquer; **to p. east** indiquer l'est; **to be pointing** (*of vehicle*) être tourné (**towards** vers); (*of gun*) être braqué (**at** sur). ◆**—ed** *a* pointu; (*beard*) en pointe; (*remark, criticism*) *Fig* pertinent; (*incisive*) mordant. ◆**—edly** *adv* (*to the point*) avec pertinence; (*incisively*) d'un ton mordant. ◆**—er** *n* (*on dial etc*) index *m*; (*advice*) conseil *m*; (*clue*) indice *m*; **to be a p. to** (*possible solution etc*) laisser entrevoir. ◆**—less** *a* inutile, futile. ◆**—lessly** *adv* inutilement.

point-blank [pɔint'blæŋk] *adv* & *a* (*to shoot, a shot*) à bout portant; (*to refuse, a refusal*) *Fig* (tout) net; (*to request, a request*) de but en blanc.

pois/e [pɔiz] *n* (*balance*) équilibre *m*; (*of body*) port *m*; (*grace*) grâce *f*; (*confidence*) assurance *f*, calme *m*; – *vi* tenir en équilibre. ◆**—ed** *a* en équilibre; (*hanging*) suspendu; (*composed*) calme; **p. to attack/etc** (*ready*) prêt à attaquer/*etc*.

poison ['pɔiz(ə)n] *n* poison *m*; (*of snake*) venin *m*; **p. gas** gaz *m* toxique; – *vt* empoisonner; **to p. s.o.'s mind** corrompre qn. ◆**poisoning** *n* empoisonnement *m*. ◆**poisonous** *a* (*fumes, substance*) toxique; (*snake*) venimeux; (*plant*) vénéneux.

pok/e [pəuk] *vt* (*push*) pousser (*avec un bâton etc*); (*touch*) toucher; (*fire*) tisonner; **to p. sth into** (*put, thrust*) fourrer *or* enfoncer qch dans; **to p. one's finger at** pointer son doigt vers; **to p. one's nose into** fourrer le nez dans; **to p. a hole in** faire un trou dans; **to p. one's head out of the window** passer la tête par la fenêtre; **to p. out s.o.'s eye** crever œil à qn; – *vi* pousser; **to p. about** *or* **around in** fouiner dans; – *n* (*jab*) (petit) coup *m*; (*shove*) poussée *f*, coup *m*. ◆**—er** *n* **1** (*for fire*) tisonnier *m*. **2** *Cards* poker *m*.

poky ['pəuki] *a* (**-ier, -iest**) (*small*) exigu et misérable, rikiki; (*slow*) *Am* lent.

Poland ['pəulənd] *n* Pologne *f*. ◆**Pole** *n* Polonais, -aise *mf*.

polarize ['pəulərɑiz] *vt* polariser.

pole [pəul] *n* **1** (*rod*) perche *f*; (*fixed*) poteau *m*; (*for flag*) mât *m*. **2** *Geog* pôle *m*;

North/South P. pôle Nord/Sud. ◆**polar** *a* polaire; **p. bear** ours *m* blanc.

polemic [pə'lemik] *n* polémique *f*. ◆**polemical** *a* polémique.

police [pə'lis] *n* police *f*; **more** *or* **extra p.** des renforts *mpl* de police; – *a* (*inquiry etc*) de la police; (*state, dog*) policier; **p. cadet** agent *m* de police stagiaire; **p. car** voiture *f* de police; **p. force** police *f*; – *vt* (*city etc*) maintenir l'ordre *or* la paix dans; (*frontier*) contrôler. ◆**policeman** *n* (*pl* **-men**) agent *m* de police. ◆**policewoman** *n* (*pl* **-women**) femme-agent *f*.

policy ['pɔlisi] *n* **1** *Pol Econ etc* politique *f*; (*individual course of action*) règle *f*, façon *f* d'agir; *pl* (*ways of governing*) *Pol* politique *f*; **matter of p.** question *f* de principe. **2** (*insurance*) **p.** police *f* (d'assurance); **p. holder** assuré, -ée *mf*.

polio(myelitis) ['pəuliəu(mɑiə'lɑitis)] *n* polio(myélite) *f*; **p. victim** polio *mf*.

polish ['pɔliʃ] *vt* (*floor, table, shoes etc*) cirer; (*metal*) astiquer; (*rough surface*) polir; (*manners*) *Fig* raffiner; (*style*) *Fig* polir; **to p. up** (*one's French etc*) travailler; **to p. off** (*food, work etc*) *Fam* liquider, finir (en vitesse); – *n* (*for shoes*) cirage *m*; (*for floor, furniture*) cire *f*; (*shine*) vernis *m*; *Fig* raffinement *m*; (*nail*) **p.** vernis *m* (à ongles); **to give sth a p.** faire briller qch.

Polish ['pəuliʃ] *a* polonais; – *n* (*language*) polonais *m*.

polite [pə'lɑit] *a* (**-er, -est**) poli (**to, with** avec); **in p. society** dans la bonne société. ◆**—ly** *adv* poliment. ◆**—ness** *n* politesse *f*.

political [pə'litik(ə)l] *a* politique. ◆**politician** *n* homme *m* *or* femme *f* politique. ◆**politicize** *vt* politiser. ◆**politics** *n* politique *f*.

polka ['pɔlkə, *Am* 'pəulkə] *n* (*dance*) polka *f*; **p. dot** pois *m*.

poll [pəul] *n* (*voting*) scrutin *m*, élection *f*; (*vote*) vote *m*; (*turnout*) participation *f* électorale; (*list*) liste *f* électorale; **to go to the polls** aller aux urnes; (*opinion*) **p.** sondage *m* (d'opinion); **50% of the p.** 50% des votants; – *vt* (*votes*) obtenir; (*people*) sonder l'opinion de. ◆**—ing** *n* (*election*) élections *fpl*; **p. booth** isoloir *m*; **p. station** bureau *m* de vote.

pollen ['pɔlən] *n* pollen *m*.

pollute [pə'luit] *vt* polluer. ◆**pollutant** *n* polluant *m*. ◆**pollution** *n* pollution *f*.

polo ['pəuləu] *n* *Sp* polo *m*; **p. neck** (*sweater, neckline*) col *m* roulé.

polyester [pɔli'estər] *n* polyester *m*.

Polynesia [pɒlɪ'niːʒə] n Polynésie f.

polytechnic [pɒlɪ'teknɪk] n institut m universitaire de technologie.

polythene ['pɒlɪθiːn] n polyéthylène m; **p. bag** sac m en plastique.

pomegranate ['pɒmɪgrænɪt] n (fruit) grenade f.

pomp [pɒmp] n pompe f. ◆**pom'posity** n emphase f, solennité f. ◆**pompous** a pompeux.

pompon ['pɒmpɒn] n (ornament) pompon m.

pond [pɒnd] n étang m; (stagnant) mare f; (artificial) bassin m.

ponder ['pɒndər] vt to **p. (over)** réfléchir à; – vi réfléchir.

ponderous ['pɒndərəs] a (heavy, slow) pesant.

pong [pɒŋ] n Sl mauvaise odeur f; – vi (stink) Sl schlinguer.

pontificate [pɒn'tɪfɪkeɪt] vi (speak) Pej pontifier (about sur).

pony ['pəʊnɪ] n poney m. ◆**ponytail** n (hair) queue f de cheval.

poodle ['puːd(ə)l] n caniche m.

poof [puf] n (homosexual) Pej Sl pédé m.

pooh! [puː] int bah!; (bad smell) ça pue!

pooh-pooh [puː'puː] vt (scorn) dédaigner; (dismiss) se moquer de.

pool [puːl] 1 n (puddle) flaque f; (of blood) mare f; (pond) étang m; (for swimming) piscine f. 2 n (of experience, talent) réservoir m; (of advisers etc) équipe f; (of typists) Com pool m; (kitty) cagnotte f; (football) **pools** prognostics mpl (sur les matchs de football); – vt (share) mettre en commun; (combine) unir. 3 n Sp billard m américain.

pooped [puːpt] a (exhausted) Am Fam vanné, crevé.

poor [pʊər] a (-er, -est) (not rich, deserving pity) pauvre; (bad) mauvais; (inferior) médiocre; (meagre) maigre; (weak) faible; **p. thing!** le or la pauvre!; – n **the p.** les pauvres mpl. ◆**-ly** 1 adv (badly) mal; (clothed, furnished) pauvrement. 2 a (ill) malade.

pop¹ [pɒp] 1 int pan! – n (noise) bruit m sec; to go **p.** faire pan; (of champagne bottle) faire pop; – vt (-pp-) (balloon etc) crever; (bottle top, button) faire sauter; – vi (burst) crever; (come off) sauter; (of ears) se déboucher. 2 vt Fam mettre; – vi Fam to **p. in** (go in) entrer (en passant); to **p. off** (leave) partir; to **p. out** sortir (un instant); to **p. over** or **round** faire un saut (to chez); to **p. up** (of person) surgir, réapparaître; (of question etc) surgir.

◆**p.-'eyed** a aux yeux exorbités. ◆**p.-up book** n livre m en relief.

pop² [pɒp] 1 n (music) pop m; – a (concert, singer etc) pop inv. 2 n (father) Am Fam papa m. 3 n (soda) **p.** (drink) Am soda m.

popcorn ['pɒpkɔːn] n pop-corn m.

pope [pəʊp] n pape m; **p.'s nose** (of chicken) croupion m.

poplar ['pɒplər] n (tree, wood) peuplier m.

poppy ['pɒpɪ] n (cultivated) pavot m; (red, wild) coquelicot m.

poppycock ['pɒpɪkɒk] n Fam fadaises fpl.

popsicle® ['pɒpsɪk(ə)l] n (ice lolly) Am esquimau m.

popular ['pɒpjʊlər] a (a person, song, vote, science etc) populaire; (fashionable) à la mode; to be **p. with** plaire beaucoup à. ◆**popu'larity** n popularité f (with auprès de). ◆**popularize** vt populariser; (science, knowledge) vulgariser. ◆**popularly** adv communément.

populat/e ['pɒpjʊleɪt] vt peupler. ◆**-ed** a peuplé (with de). ◆**popu'lation** n population f. ◆**populous** a (crowded) populeux.

porcelain ['pɔːsəlɪn] n porcelaine f.

porch [pɔːtʃ] n porche m; (veranda) Am véranda f.

porcupine ['pɔːkjupaɪn] n (animal) porc-épic m.

pore [pɔːr] 1 n (of skin) pore m. 2 vi to **p. over** (book, question etc) etudier de près. ◆**porous** a poreux.

pork [pɔːk] n (meat) porc m; **p. butcher** charcutier, -ière mf.

pornography [pɔː'nɒgrəfɪ] n (Fam porn) pornographie f. ◆**porno'graphic** a pornographique, porno (f inv).

porpoise ['pɔːpəs] n (sea animal) marsouin m.

porridge ['pɒrɪdʒ] n porridge m; **p. oats** flocons mpl d'avoine.

port [pɔːt] 1 n (harbour) port m; **p. of call** escale f; – a (authorities, installations etc) portuaire. 2 n **p. (side)** (left) Nau Av bâbord m; – a de bâbord. 3 n (wine) porto m.

portable ['pɔːtəb(ə)l] a portatif, portable.

portal ['pɔːt(ə)l] n portail m.

porter ['pɔːtər] n (for luggage) porteur m; (doorman) portier m; (caretaker) concierge m, (of public building) gardien, -ienne mf.

portfolio [pɔːt'fəʊlɪəʊ] n (pl -os) Com Pol portefeuille m.

porthole ['pɔːthəʊl] n Nau Av hublot m.

portico ['pɔːtɪkəʊ] n (pl -oes or -os) Archit portique m; (of house) porche m.

portion ['pɔːʃ(ə)n] n (share, helping) portion

f; (of train, book etc) partie f; – vt **to p. out**
répartir.

portly ['pɔːtlɪ] a (-ier, -iest) corpulent.

portrait ['pɔːtrɪt, 'pɔːtreɪt] n portrait m; **p.
painter** portraitiste mf.

portray [pɔː'treɪ] vt (describe) représenter.
◆**portrayal** n portrait m, représentation f.

Portugal ['pɔːtjug(ə)l] n Portugal. ◆**Portu-
'guese** a & n inv portugais, -aise (mf); – n
(language) portugais m.

pose [pəʊz] **1** n (in art or photography) &
Fig pose f; – vi (of model etc) poser (for
pour); **to p. as a lawyer**/etc se faire passer
pour un avocat/etc. **2** vt (question) poser.
◆**poser** n **1** (question) Fam colle f. **2** =
poseur. ◆**poseur** [-'zɜːr] n Pej poseur,
-euse mf.

posh [pɒʃ] a Pej Fam (smart) chic inv;
(snobbish) snob (f inv).

position [pə'zɪʃ(ə)n] n (place, posture, opinion etc) position f; (of building, town)
emplacement m, position f; (job, circumstances) situation f; (customer window in
bank etc) guichet m; **in a p. to do** en mesure
or en position de faire; **in a good p. to do**
bien placé pour faire; **in p.** en place, en
position; – vt (camera, machine etc) mettre
en position; (put) placer.

positive ['pɒzɪtɪv] a (test) positif m; (order)
catégorique; (progress, change) réel; (tone)
assuré; (sure) sûr, certain (of de, that que);
a p. genius Fam un vrai génie. ◆–**ly** adv
(for certain) & El positivement; (undenia-
bly) indéniablement; (completely) complètement; (categorically) catégoriquement.

possess [pə'zes] vt posséder. ◆**possession** n possession f; **in p.** of en possession
de; **to take p. of** prendre possession de.
◆**possessive** a (adjective, person etc)
possessif; – n Gram possessif m. ◆**possessor** n possesseur m.

possible ['pɒsəb(ə)l] a possible (**to do** à
faire); **it is p. (for us) to do it** il (nous) est
possible de le faire; **it is p. that** il est possible que (+ sub); **as far as p.** dans la mesure
du possible; **if p.** si possible; **as much or as
many as p.** autant que possible; – n (person, object) Fam choix m possible.
◆possi'bility n possibilité f; **some p.** of
quelques chances fpl de; **there's some p.
that** il est (tout juste) possible que (+ sub);
she has possibilities elle promet; **it's a
distinct p.** c'est bien possible. ◆**possibly**
adv **1** (with can, could etc) **if you p. can** si
cela t'est possible; **to do all one p. can** faire
tout son possible (**to do** pour faire); **he**

cannot p. stay il ne peut absolument pas
rester. **2** (perhaps) peut-être.

post¹ [pəʊst] n **1** (postal system) poste f;
(letters) courrier m; **by p.** par la poste; **to
catch/miss the p.** avoir/manquer la levée;
– a (bag, code etc) postal; **p. office** (bureau
m de) poste f; **P. Office** (administration)
(service m des) postes fpl; – vt (put in
postbox) poster, mettre à la poste; (send)
envoyer; **to keep s.o. posted** Fig tenir qn au
courant. ◆**postage** n tarif m (postal),
tarifs mpl (postaux) (**to** pour); **p. stamp**
timbre-poste m. ◆**postal** a (district etc)
postal; (inquiries) par la poste; (clerk) des
postes; (vote) par correspondance.
◆**postbox** n boîte f à or aux lettres.
◆**postcard** n carte f postale. ◆**postcode**
n code m postal. ◆**post-'free** adv,
◆**post'paid** adv franco.

post² [pəʊst] n (job, place) & Mil poste m;
– vt (sentry, guard) poster; (employee)
affecter (**to** à). ◆–**ing** n (appointment)
affectation f.

post³ [pəʊst] n (pole) poteau m; (of bed,
door) montant m; **finishing or winning p.** Sp
poteau m d'arrivée; – vt **to p. (up)** (notice
etc) afficher.

post- [pəʊst] pref post-; **p.-1800** après 1800.

postdate [pəʊst'deɪt] vt postdater.

poster ['pəʊstər] n affiche f; (for decoration)
poster m.

posterior [pɒ'stɪərɪər] n (buttocks) Hum
postérieur m.

posterity [pɒ'sterɪtɪ] n postérité f.

postgraduate [pəʊst'grædʒuət] a (studies
etc) Univ de troisième cycle; – n étudiant,
-ante mf de troisième cycle.

posthumous ['pɒstjuməs] a posthume.
◆–**ly** adv à titre posthume.

postman ['pəʊstmən] n (pl -men) facteur m.
◆**postmark** n cachet m de la poste; – vt
oblitérer. ◆**postmaster** n receveur m (des
postes).

post-mortem [pəʊst'mɔːtəm] n **p.-mortem**
(examination) autopsie f (**on** de).

postpone [pəʊs'pəʊn] vt remettre (**for** de),
renvoyer (à plus tard). ◆–**ment** n remise
f, renvoi m.

postscript ['pəʊstskrɪpt] n post-scriptum m
inv.

postulate ['pɒstjuleɪt] vt postuler.

posture ['pɒstʃər] n posture f; Fig attitude
f; – vi (for effect) Pej poser.

postwar ['pəʊstwɔːr] a d'après-guerre.

posy ['pəʊzɪ] n petit bouquet m (de fleurs).

pot [pɒt] n **1** pot m; (for cooking) marmite f;
pots and pans casseroles fpl; **jam p.** pot m à

confiture; **to take p. luck** tenter sa chance; (*with food*) manger à la fortune du pot; **to go to p.** Fam aller à la ruine; **gone to p.** (*person, plans etc*) Fam fichu; – *vt* (**-tt-**) mettre en pot. **2** *n* (*marijuana*) Sl marie-jeanne *f*; (*hashish*) Sl haschisch *m*. ◆**potted** *a* **1** (*plant*) en pot; (*jam, meat*) en bocaux. **2** (*version etc*) abrégé, condensé.

potato [pə'teɪtəʊ] *n* (*pl* **-oes**) pomme *f* de terre; **p. peeler** (*knife*) couteau *m* à éplucher, éplucheur *m*; **p. crisps**, *Am* **p. chips** pommes *fpl* chips.

potbelly ['pɒtbelɪ] *n* bedaine *f*. ◆**potbellied** *a* ventru.

potent ['pəʊtənt] *a* puissant; (*drink*) fort; (*man*) viril. ◆**potency** *n* puissance *f*; (*of man*) virilité *f*.

potential [pə'tenʃ(ə)l] *a* (*danger, resources*) potentiel; (*client, sales*) éventuel; (*leader, hero etc*) en puissance; – *n* potentiel *m*; *Fig* (*perspectives of future*) d'avenir *m*; **to have p.** avoir de l'avenir. ◆**potenti'ality** *n* potentialité *f*; *pl Fig* (*perspectives fpl* d'avenir *m*. ◆**potentially** *adv* potentiellement.

pothole ['pɒthəʊl] *n* (*in road*) nid *m* de poules; (*in rock*) gouffre *m*; (*cave*) caverne *f*. ◆**potholing** *n* spéléologie *f*.

potion ['pəʊʃ(ə)n] *n* breuvage *m* magique; *Med* potion *f*.

potshot ['pɒtʃɒt] *n* **to take a p.** faire un carton (**at** sur).

potter ['pɒtər] **1** *n* (*person*) potier *m*. **2** *vi* **to p.** (**about**) bricoler. ◆**pottery** *n* (*art*) poterie *f*; (*objects*) poteries *fpl*; **a piece of p.** une poterie.

potty ['pɒtɪ] *a* **1** (**-ier, -iest**) (*mad*) Fam toqué. **2** *n* (*for baby*) pot *m* (de bébé).

pouch [paʊtʃ] *n* petit sac *m*; (*of kangaroo, under eyes*) poche *f*; (*for tobacco*) blague *f*.

pouf(fe) [puːf] *n* (*seat*) pouf *m*.

poultice ['pəʊltɪs] *n* *Med* cataplasme *m*.

poultry ['pəʊltrɪ] *n* volaille *f*. ◆**poulterer** *n* volailler *m*.

pounce [paʊns] *vi* (*leap*) bondir, sauter (**on** sur); **to p. on** (*idea*) *Fig* sauter sur; – *n* bond *m*.

pound [paʊnd] **1** *n* (*weight*) livre *f* (= 453,6 grammes); **p. (sterling)** livre *f* (sterling). **2** *n* (*for cars, dogs*) fourrière *f*. **3** *vt* (*spices, nuts etc*) piler; (*meat*) attendrir; (*bombard*) *Mil* pilonner; **to p. (on)** (*thump*) *Fig* taper sur, marteler; (*of sea*) battre; – *vi* (*of heart*) battre à tout rompre; (*walk heavily*) marcher à pas pesants.

pour [pɔːr] *vt* (*liquid*) verser; (*wax*) couler; **to p. money into** investir beaucoup d'argent

dans; **to p. away** or **off** (*empty*) vider; **to p. out** verser; (*empty*) vider; (*feelings*) épancher (**to** devant); – *vi* **to p. (out)** (*of liquid*) couler or sortir à flots; **to p. in** (*of liquid, sunshine*) entrer à flots; (*of people, money*) *Fig* affluer; **to p. out** (*of people*) sortir en masse (**from** de); (*of smoke*) s'échapper (**from** de); **it's pouring (down)** il pleut à verse; **pouring rain** pluie *f* torrentielle.

pout [paʊt] *vti* **to p. one's lips** faire la moue; – *n* moue *f*.

poverty ['pɒvətɪ] *n* pauvreté *f*; (**grinding** or **extreme**) **p.** misère *f*. ◆**p.-stricken** *a* (*person*) indigent; (*conditions*) misérable.

powder ['paʊdər] *n* poudre *f*; **p. keg** (*place*) *Fig* poudrière *f*; **p. puff** houppette *f*; **p. room** toilettes *fpl* (*pour dames*); – *vt* (*hair, skin*) poudrer; **to p. one's face** or **nose** se poudrer. ◆**-ed** *a* (*milk, eggs*) en poudre. ◆**powdery** *a* (*snow*) poudreux; (*face*) couvert de poudre.

power ['paʊər] *n* (*ability, authority*) pouvoir *m*; (*strength, nation*) & *Math Tech* puissance *f*; (*energy*) *Phys Tech* énergie *f*; (*current*) *El* courant *m*; **he's a p. within the firm** c'est un homme de poids au sein de l'entreprise; **in p.** *Pol* au pouvoir; **in one's p.** en son pouvoir; **the p. of speech** la faculté de la parole; **p. cut** coupure *f* de courant; **p. station**, *Am* **p. plant** *El* centrale *f* (électrique); – *vt* **to be powered by** être actionné or propulsé par; (*gas, oil etc*) fonctionnant à. ◆**powerful** *a* puissant. ◆**powerfully** *adv* puissamment. ◆**powerless** *a* impuissant (**to do** à faire).

practicable ['præktɪkəb(ə)l] *a* (*project, road etc*) praticable.

practical ['præktɪk(ə)l] *a* (*knowledge, person, tool etc*) pratique; **p. joke** farce *f*. ◆**practi'cality** *n* (*of scheme etc*) aspect *m* pratique; (*of person*) sens *m* pratique; (*detail*) détail *m* pratique.

practically ['præktɪk(ə)lɪ] *adv* (*almost*) pratiquement.

practice ['præktɪs] *n* (*exercise, proceeding*) pratique *f*; (*habit*) habitude *f*; *Sp* entraînement *m*; (*rehearsal*) répétition *f*; (*of profession*) exercice *m* (**of** de); (*clients*) clientèle *f*; **to put into p.** mettre en pratique; **in p.** (*in reality*) en pratique; **to be in p.** (*have skill etc*) être en forme; (*of doctor, lawyer*) exercer; **to be in general p.** (*of doctor*) faire de la médecine générale; **to be out of p.** avoir perdu la pratique. ◆**practis/e** *vt* (*put into practice*) pratiquer; (*medicine, law etc*) exercer; (*flute,* piano etc) s'exercer à; (language) (s'exercer à) parler (on avec); (work at) travailler; (do) faire; – vi Mus Sp s'exercer; (of doctor, lawyer) exercer; – vt Am = practice. ◆–ed a (experienced) chevronné; (ear, eye) exercé. ◆–ing a Rel pratiquant; (doctor, lawyer) exerçant.

practitioner [præk'tɪʃ(ə)nər] n praticien, -ienne mf; **general p.** (médecin m) généraliste m.

pragmatic [præg'mætɪk] a pragmatique.

prairie(s) ['preərɪ(z)] n(pl) (in North America) Prairies fpl.

praise [preɪz] vt louer (for sth de qch); **to p. s.o. for doing** or **having done** louer qn d'avoir fait; – n louange(s) f(pl), éloge(s) m(pl); **in p. of** à la louange de. ◆**praiseworthy** a digne d'éloges.

pram [præm] n landau m, voiture f d'enfant.

prance [prɑːns] vi **to p. about** (of dancer etc) caracoler; (strut) se pavaner; (go about) Fam se balader.

prank [præŋk] n (trick) farce f, tour m; (escape) frasque f.

prattle ['præt(ə)l] vi jacasser.

prawn [prɔːn] n crevette f(rose), bouquet m.

pray [preɪ] vt Lit prier (that + sub); **s.o. to do** prier qn de faire); – vi Rel prier; **to p.** (**to God**) **for sth** prier Dieu pour qu'il nous accorde qch. ◆**prayer** [preər] n prière f.

pre- [priː] pref **p.-1800** avant 1800.

preach [priːtʃ] vti (sermon) faire; **to p. to s.o.** Rel & Fig prêcher qn. ◆–ing n prédication f. ◆–er n prédicateur m.

preamble [priː'æmb(ə)l] n préambule m.

prearrange [priːə'reɪndʒ] vt arranger à l'avance.

precarious [prɪ'keərɪəs] a précaire.

precaution [prɪ'kɔːʃ(ə)n] n précaution f (of doing de faire); **as a p.** par précaution.

precede [prɪ'siːd] vti précéder; **to p. sth by sth** faire précéder qch de qch. ◆–ing a précédent.

precedence ['presɪdəns] n (in rank) préséance f; (importance) priorité f; **to take p. over** avoir la préséance sur; avoir la priorité sur. ◆**precedent** n précédent m.

precept ['priːsept] n précept m.

precinct ['priːsɪŋkt] n (of convent etc) enceinte f; (boundary) limite f; (in town) Am Pol circonscription f; (for shopping) zone f (piétonnière).

precious ['preʃəs] 1 a précieux; **her p. little bike** Iron son cher petit vélo. 2 adv **p. few, p. little** Fam très peu (de).

precipice ['presɪpɪs] n (sheer face) Geog à-pic m inv; (chasm) Fig précipice m.

precipitate [prɪ'sɪpɪteɪt] vt (hasten, throw) & Ch précipiter; (trouble, reaction etc) provoquer, déclencher. ◆**precipi'tation** n (haste) & Ch précipitation f; (rainfall) précipitations fpl.

précis ['preɪsiː, pl 'preɪsiːz] n inv précis m.

precise [prɪ'saɪs] a précis; (person) minutieux. ◆–ly adv (accurately, exactly) précisément; **at 3 o'clock p.** à 3 heures précises; **p. nothing** absolument rien. ◆**precision** n précision f.

preclude [prɪ'kluːd] vt (prevent) empêcher (from doing de faire); (possibility) exclure.

precocious [prɪ'kəʊʃəs] a (child etc) précoce. ◆–ness n précocité f.

preconceived [priːkən'siːvd] a préconçu. ◆**preconception** n préconception f.

precondition [priːkən'dɪʃ(ə)n] n préalable m.

precursor [priː'kɜːsər] n précurseur m.

predate [priː'deɪt] vt (precede) précéder; (cheque etc) antidater.

predator ['predətər] n (animal) prédateur m. ◆**predatory** a (animal, person) rapace.

predecessor ['priːdɪsesər] n prédécesseur m.

predicament [prɪ'dɪkəmənt] n situation f fâcheuse.

predict [prɪ'dɪkt] vt prédire. ◆**predictable** a prévisible. ◆**prediction** n prédiction f.

predispose [priːdɪ'spəʊz] vt prédisposer (to do à faire). ◆**predispo'sition** n prédisposition f.

predominant [prɪ'dɒmɪnənt] a prédominant. ◆**predominance** n prédominance f. ◆**predominantly** adv (almost all) pour la plupart, en majorité. ◆**predominate** vi prédominer (over sur).

preeminent [priː'emɪnənt] a prééminent.

preempt [priː'empt] vt (decision, plans etc) devancer.

preen [priːn] vt (feathers) lisser; **she's preening herself** Fig elle se bichonne.

prefab ['priːfæb] n Fam maison f préfabriquée. ◆**pre'fabricate** vt préfabriquer.

preface ['prefɪs] n préface f; – vt (speech etc) faire précéder (with de).

prefect ['priːfekt] n Sch élève mf chargé(e) de la discipline; (French official) préfet m.

prefer [prɪ'fɜːr] vt (-rr-) préférer (to à), aimer mieux (to que); **to p. to do** préférer faire, aimer mieux faire; **to p. charges** Jur porter plainte (against contre). ◆**preferable** a préférable (to à). ◆**preferably** adv de préférence. ◆**preference** n préférence f (for pour); **in p. to** de préférence à. ◆**prefe'rential** a préférentiel.

prefix ['priːfɪks] *n* préfixe *m*.

pregnant ['pregnənt] *a* (*woman*) enceinte; (*animal*) pleine; **five months p.** enceinte de cinq mois. ◆**pregnancy** *n* (*of woman*) grossesse *f*.

prehistoric [priːhɪ'stɒrɪk] *a* préhistorique.

prejudge [priː'dʒʌdʒ] *vt* (*question*) préjuger de; (*person*) juger d'avance.

prejudic/e ['predʒədɪs] *n* (*bias*) préjugé *m*, parti *m* pris; (*attitude*) préjugés *mpl*; *Jur* préjudice *m*; – *vt* (*person*) prévenir (*against* contre); (*success, chances etc*) porter préjudice à, nuire à. ◆**—ed** *a* (*idea*) partial; **she's p.** elle a des préjugés ou un préjugé (*against* contre); (*on an issue*) elle est de parti pris. ◆**preju'dicial** *a* *Jur* préjudiciable.

preliminary [prɪ'lɪmɪnərɪ] *a* (*initial*) initial; (*speech, inquiry, exam*) préliminaire; – *npl* préliminaires *mpl*.

prelude ['preljuːd] *n* prélude *m*; – *vt* préluder à.

premarital [priː'mærɪt(ə)l] *a* avant le mariage.

premature ['premətʃuər, *Am* priːmə'tʃuər] *a* prématuré. ◆**—ly** *adv* prématurément; (*born*) avant terme.

premeditate [priː'medɪteɪt] *vt* préméditer. ◆**premedi'tation** *n* préméditation *f*.

premier ['premɪər, *Am* prɪ'mɪər] *n* Premier ministre *m*.

première ['premɪeər, *Am* prɪ'mjeər] *n* *Th Cin* première *f*.

premise ['premɪs] *n* *Phil* prémisse *f*.

premises ['premɪsɪz] *npl* locaux *mpl*; **on the p.** sur les lieux; **off the p.** hors des lieux.

premium ['priːmɪəm] *n* *Fin* prime *f*; (*insurance*) **p.** prime *f* (d'assurance); **to be at a p.** (*rare*) être (une) denrée rare, faire prime; **p. bond** bon *m* à lots.

premonition [premə'nɪʃ(ə)n, *Am* priːmə-'nɪʃ(ə)n] *n* prémonition *f*, pressentiment *m*.

prenatal [priː'neɪt(ə)l] *a* *Am* prénatal.

preoccupy [priː'ɒkjupaɪ] *vt* (*worry*) préoccuper (*with* de). ◆**preoccu'pation** *n* préoccupation *f*; **a p. with** (*money etc*) une obsession de.

prep [prep] *a* **p. school** école *f* primaire privée; *Am* école *f* secondaire privée; – *n* (*homework*) *Sch* devoirs *mpl*.

prepaid [priː'peɪd] *a* (*reply*) payé.

prepar/e [prɪ'peər] *vt* préparer (*sth for s.o.* qch à qn, *s.o. for sth* qn à qch); **to p.** to do se préparer à faire; – *vi* **to p. for** (*journey, occasion*) faire ses préparatifs pour; (*get dressed up for*) se préparer pour; (*exam*) préparer. ◆**—ed** *a* (*ready*) prêt, disposé (**to**

do à faire); **to be p. for** (*expect*) s'attendre à. ◆**prepa'ration** *n* préparation *f*; *pl* préparatifs *mpl* (**for** de). ◆**pre'paratory** *a* préparatoire; **p. school = prep school.**

preposition [prepə'zɪʃ(ə)n] *n* préposition *f*.

prepossessing [priːpə'zesɪŋ] *a* avenant, sympathique.

preposterous [prɪ'pɒstərəs] *a* absurde.

prerecorded [priːrɪ'kɔːdɪd] *a* (*message etc*) enregistré à l'avance; **p. broadcast** *Rad TV* émission *f* en différé.

prerequisite [priː'rekwɪzɪt] *n* (*condition f*) préalable *m*.

prerogative [prɪ'rɒgətɪv] *n* prérogative *f*.

Presbyterian [prezbɪ'tɪərɪən] *a & n* *Rel* presbytérien, -ienne (*mf*).

preschool ['priːskuːl] *a* (*age etc*) préscolaire.

prescrib/e [prɪ'skraɪb] *vt* prescrire. ◆**—ed** *a* (*textbook*) (inscrit) au programme. ◆**prescription** *n* (*order*) prescription *f*; *Med* ordonnance *f*; **on p.** sur ordonnance.

presence ['prezns] *n* présence *f*; **in the p. of** en présence de; **p. of mind** présence *f* d'esprit.

present[1] ['preznt] **1** *a* (*not absent*) présent (**at** à, **in** dans); **those p.** les personnes présentes. **2** *a* (*year, state etc*) présent, actuel; (*being considered*) présent; (*job, house etc*) actuel; – *n* (*time*) présent *m*; **for the p.** pour le moment; **at p.** à présent. **3** *n* (*gift*) cadeau *m*. ◆**—ly** *adv* (*soon*) tout à l'heure; (*now*) à présent. ◆**present-'day** *a* actuel.

present[2] [prɪ'zent] *vt* (*show, introduce, compère etc*) présenter (**to** à); (*concert etc*) donner; (*proof*) fournir; **to p. s.o. with** (*gift*) offrir à qn; (*prize*) remettre à qn. ◆**—able** *a* présentable. ◆**—er** *n* présentateur, -trice *mf*. ◆**presen'tation** *n* présentation *f*; (*of prize*) remise *f*.

preserve [prɪ'zɜːv] **1** *vt* (*keep, maintain*) conserver; (*fruit etc*) *Culin* mettre en conserve; **to p. from** (*protect*) préserver de. **2** *n* (*sphere*) domaine *m*. **3** *n & npl* (*fruit etc*) *Culin* confiture *f*. ◆**preser'vation** *n* conservation *f*. ◆**preservative** *n* (*in food*) agent *m* de conservation. ◆**preserver** *n* **life p.** *Am* gilet *m* de sauvetage.

preside [prɪ'zaɪd] *vi* présider; **to p. over** *or* **at** (*meeting*) présider.

president ['prezɪdənt] *n* président, -ente *mf*. ◆**presidency** *n* présidence *f*. ◆**presi'dential** *a* présidentiel.

press[1] [pres] **1** *n* (*newspapers*) presse *f*; (*printing firm*) imprimerie *f*; (*printing*) **p.** presse *f*; – *a* (*conference etc*) de presse. **2** *n* (*machine for trousers, gluing etc*) presse *f*; (*for making wine*) pressoir *m*.

press² [pres] *vt* (*button, doorbell etc*) appuyer sur; (*tube, lemon, creditor*) presser; (*hand*) serrer; (*clothes*) repasser; (*demand, insist on*) insister sur; (*claim*) renouveler; **to p. s.o. to do** (*urge*) engager qn de faire; **to p. down** (*button etc*) appuyer sur; **to p. charges** *Jur* engager des poursuites (**against** contre); – *vi* (*with finger*) appuyer (**on** sur); (*of weight*) faire pression (**on** sur); (*of time*) presser; **to p. for sth** faire des démarches pour obtenir qch; (*insist*) insister pour obtenir qch; **to p. on** (*continue*) continuer (**with sth** qch); – *n* **to give sth a p.** (*trousers etc*) repasser qch. ◆**—ed** *a* (*hard*) **p.** (*busy*) débordé; **to be hard p.** (*in difficulties*) être en difficultés; **to be** (*hard*) **p. for** (*time, money*) être à court de. ◆**—ing 1** *a* (*urgent*) pressant. **2** *n* (*ironing*) repassage *m*.

pressgang ['presgæn] *vt* **to p. s.o.** faire pression sur qn (**into doing** pour qu'il fasse). ◆**press-stud** *n* (bouton-)pression *m*. ◆**press-up** *n Sp* pompe *f*.

pressure ['preʃər] *n* pression *f*; **the p. of work** le surmenage; **p. cooker** cocotte-minute *f*; **p. group** groupe *m* de pression; **under p.** (*duress*) sous la contrainte; (*hurriedly, forcibly*) sous pression; – *vt* **to p. s.o.** faire pression sur qn (**into doing** pour qu'il fasse). ◆**pressurize** *vt Av* pressuriser; **to p. s.o.** faire pression sur qn (**into doing** pour qu'il fasse).

prestige [pre'sti:ʒ] *n* prestige *m*. ◆**prestigious** [*Am* -'sti:dʒəs] *a* prestigieux.

presume [pri'zjuːm] *vt* (*suppose*) présumer (**that** que); **to p. to do** se permettre de faire. ◆**presumably** *adv* (*you'll come etc*) je présume que. ◆**presumption** *n* (*supposition, bold attitude*) présomption *f*. ◆**presumptuous** *a* présomptueux.

presuppose [pri:sə'pəuz] *vt* présupposer (**that** que).

pretence [pri'tens] *n* feinte *f*; (*claim, affectation*) prétention *f*; (*pretext*) prétexte *m*; **to make a p. of sth/of doing** feindre qch/de faire; **on** *or* **under false pretences** sous des prétextes fallacieux. ◆**pretend** *vt* (*make believe*) faire semblant (**to do** de faire, **that** que); (*claim, maintain*) prétendre (**to do** de faire, **that** que); – *vi* faire semblant; **to p.** (*throne, title*) prétendre à.

pretension [pri'tenʃ(ə)n] *n* (*claim, vanity*) prétention *f*; ◆**pre'tentious** *a* prétentieux.

pretext ['pri:tekst] *n* prétexte *m*; **on the p. of/that** sous prétexte de/que.

pretty ['priti] **1** *a* (**-ier, -iest**) joli. **2** *adv Fam* (*rather, quite*) assez; **p. well, p. much, p. nearly** (*almost*) pratiquement, à peu de chose près.

prevail [pri'veil] *vi* (*be prevalent*) prédominer; (*win*) prévaloir (**against** contre); **to p. (up)on s.o.** (*persuade*) persuader qn (**to do** de faire). ◆**—ing** *a* (*most common*) courant; (*most important*) prédominant; (*situation*) actuel; (*wind*) dominant. ◆**prevalence** *n* fréquence *f*; (*predominance*) prédominance *f*. ◆**prevalent** ['prevələnt] *a* courant, répandu.

prevaricate [pri'værikeit] *vi* user de faux-fuyants.

prevent [pri'vent] *vt* empêcher (**from doing** de faire). ◆**preventable** *a* évitable. ◆**prevention** *n* prévention *f*. ◆**preventive** *a* préventif.

preview ['pri:vju:] *n* (*of film, painting*) avant-première *f*; (*survey*) Fig aperçu *m*.

previous ['pri:viəs] *a* précédent, antérieur; (*experience*) préalable; **she's had a p. job** elle a déjà eu un emploi; **p. to** avant. ◆**—ly** *adv* avant, précédemment.

prewar ['pri:wɔ:r] *a* d'avant-guerre.

prey [prei] *n* proie *f*; **to be** (**a**) **p.** to être en proie à; **bird of p.** rapace *m*, oiseau *m* de proie; – *vi* **to p. on** faire sa proie de; **to p. on s.o.** *or* **s.o.'s mind** *Fig* tracasser qn.

price [prais] *n* (*of object, success etc*) prix *m*; **to pay a high p. for sth** payer cher qch; *Fig* payer chèrement qch; **he wouldn't do it at any p.** il ne le ferait à aucun prix; – *a* (*control, war, rise etc*) des prix; **p. list** tarif *m*; – *vt* mettre un prix à; **it's priced at £5** ça coûte cinq livres. ◆**priceless** *a* (*jewel, help etc*) inestimable; (*amusing*) *Fam* impayable. ◆**pricey** *a* (**-ier, -iest**) *Fam* coûteux.

prick [prik] *vt* piquer (**with** avec); (*burst*) crever; **to p. up one's ears** dresser l'oreille; – *n* (*act, mark, pain*) piqûre *f*.

prickle ['prik(ə)l] *n* (*of animal*) piquant *m*; (*of plant*) épine *f*, piquant *m*. ◆**prickly** *a* (**-ier, -iest**) (*plant*) épineux; (*animal*) hérissé; (*subject*) *Fig* épineux; (*person*) *Fig* irritable.

pride [praid] *n* (*satisfaction*) fierté *f*; (*self-esteem*) amour-propre *m*, orgueil *m*; (*arrogance*) orgueil *m*; **to take p. in** (*person, work etc*) être fier de; (*look after*) prendre soin de; **to take p. in doing** mettre (toute) sa fierté à faire; **to be s.o.'s p. and joy** être la fierté de qn; **to have p. of place** avoir la place d'honneur; – *vt* **to p. oneself on** s'enorgueillir de.

priest [priːst] *n* prêtre *m*. ◆**priesthood** *n* (*function*) sacerdoce *m*. ◆**priestly** *a* sacerdotal.

prig [prig] *n* hypocrite *mf*, pharisien, -ienne *mf*. ◆**priggish** *a* hypocrite, suffisant.

prim [prim] *a* (**primmer, primmest**) p. (**and proper**) (*affected*) guindé; (*seemly*) convenable; (*neat*) impeccable.

primacy ['praiməsi] *n* primauté *f*.

primary ['praiməri] *a* (*Sch Sol Geol etc*) primaire; (*main, basic*) principal, premier; **of p. importance** de première importance; – *n* (*election*) *Am* primaire *f*. ◆**primarily** [*Am* prai'merili] *adv* essentiellement.

prime [praim] **1** *a* (*reason etc*) principal; (*importance*) primordial; (*quality, number*) premier; (*meat*) de premier choix; (*example, condition*) excellent, parfait; **P. Minister** Premier ministre *m*. **2** *n* **the p. of life** la force de l'âge. **3** *vt* (*gun, pump*) amorcer; (*surface*) apprêter. ◆**primer** *n* **1** (*book*) *Sch* premier livre *m*. **2** (*paint*) apprêt *m*.

primeval [prai'miːv(ə)l] *a* primitif.

primitive ['primitiv] *a* (*art, society, conditions etc*) primitif; –**ly** *adv* (*to live*) dans des conditions primitives.

primrose ['primrəuz] *n* *Bot* primevère *f* (jaune).

prince [prins] *n* prince *m*. ◆**princely** *a* princier. ◆**prin'cess** *n* princesse *f*. ◆**princi'pality** *n* principauté *f*.

principal ['prinsip(ə)l] **1** *a* (*main*) principal. **2** *n* (*of school*) directeur, -trice *mf*. ◆–**ly** *adv* principalement.

principle ['prinsip(ə)l] *n* principe *m*; **in p.** en principe; **on p.** par principe.

print [print] *n* (*of finger, foot etc*) empreinte *f*; (*letters*) caractères *mpl*; (*engraving*) estampe *f*, gravure *f*; (*fabric, textile design*) imprimé *m*; *Phot* épreuve *f*; (*ink*) encre *m*; **in p.** (*book*) disponible (en librairie); **out of p.** (*book*) épuisé; – *vt* Typ imprimer; Phot tirer; (*write*) écrire en caractères d'imprimerie; **to p. 100 copies of** (*book etc*) tirer à 100 exemplaires; **to p. out** (*of computer*) imprimer. ◆–**ed** *a* imprimé; **p. matter** *or* **papers** imprimés *mpl*; **to have a book p.** publier un livre. ◆–**ing** *n* (*action*) Typ impression *f*; (*technique, art*) imprimerie *f*; Phot tirage *m*; **p. press** Typ presse *f*. ◆–**able** *a* **not p.** (*word etc*) *Fig* obscène. ◆–**er** *n* (*person*) imprimeur *m*; (*of computer*) imprimante *f*. ◆**print-out** *n* (*of computer*) sortie *f* sur imprimante.

prior ['praiər] *a* précédent, antérieur; (*expe-*

rience) préalable; **p. to sth/to doing** avant qch/de faire.

priority [prai'ɒriti] *n* priorité *f* (**over** sur).

priory ['praiəri] *n* Rel prieuré *m*.

prise [praiz] *vt* **to p. open/off** (*box, lid*) ouvrir/enlever (en faisant levier).

prism ['priz(ə)m] *n* prisme *m*.

prison ['priz(ə)n] *n* prison *f*; **in p.** en prison; – *a* (*system, life etc*) pénitentiaire; (*camp*) de prisonniers; **p. officer** gardien, -ienne *mf* de prison. ◆**prisoner** *n* prisonnier, -ière *mf*; **to take s.o. p.** faire qn prisonnier.

prissy ['prisi] *a* (**-ier, -iest**) bégueule.

pristine ['pristiːn] *a* (*condition*) parfait; (*primitive*) primitif.

privacy ['praivəsi, 'privəsi] *n* intimité *f*, solitude *f*; (*quiet place*) coin *m* retiré; (*secrecy*) secret *m*; **to give s.o. some p.** laisser qn seul. ◆**private 1** *a* (*lesson, car etc*) particulier; (*confidential*) confidentiel; (*personal*) personnel; (*wedding etc*) intime; **a p. citizen** un simple particulier; **p. detective, p. investigator,** *Fam* **p. eye** détective *m* privé; **p. parts** parties *fpl* génitales; **p. place** coin *m* retiré; **p. tutor** précepteur *m*; **to be a very p. person** aimer la solitude; – *n* **in p.** (*not publicly*) en privé; (*ceremony*) dans l'intimité. **2** *n* Mil (*simple*) soldat *m*. ◆**privately** *adv* en privé; (*inwardly*) intérieurement; (*personally*) à titre personnel; (*to marry, dine etc*) dans l'intimité; **p. owned** appartenant à un particulier.

privet ['privit] *n* (*bush*) troène *m*.

privilege ['privilidʒ] *n* privilège *m*. ◆**privileged** *a* privilégié; **to be p. to do** avoir le privilège de faire.

privy ['privi] *a* **p. to** (*knowledge etc*) au courant de.

prize[1] [praiz] *n* prix *m*; (*in lottery*) lot *m*; **the first p.** (*in lottery*) le gros lot; – *a* (*essay, animal etc*) primé; **a p. fool**/*etc Fig Hum* un parfait idiot/*etc*. ◆**p.-giving** *n* distribution *f* des prix. ◆**p.-winner** *n* lauréat, -ate *mf*; (*in lottery*) gagnant, -ante *mf*. ◆**p.-winning** *a* (*essay, animal etc*) primé; (*ticket*) gagnant.

priz/e[2] [praiz] *vt* (*value*) priser. ◆–**ed** *a* (*possession etc*) précieux.

prize[3] [praiz] *vt* = **prise**.

pro [prəu] *n* (*professional*) *Fam* pro *mf*.

pro- [prəu] *pref* pro-.

probable ['prɒbəb(ə)l] *a* probable (**that** que); (*plausible*) vraisemblable. ◆**probability** *n* probabilité *f*; **in all p.** selon toute probabilité. ◆**probably** *adv* probablement, vraisemblablement.

probation [prə'beiʃ(ə)n] *n* **on p.** *Jur* en

liberté surveillée, sous contrôle judiciaire; (*in job*) à l'essai; **p. officer** responsable *mf* des délinquants mis en liberté surveillée. ◆**probationary** *a* (*period*) d'essai, *Jur* de liberté surveillée.

prob/e [prəʊb] *n* (*device*) sonde *f*; *Journ* enquête *f* (**into** dans); – *vt* (*investigate* & *Med* sonder; (*examine*) examiner; – *vi* (*investigate*) faire des recherches; *Pej* fouiner; **to p. into** (*origins etc*) sonder. ◆**—ing** *a* (*question etc*) pénétrant.

problem ['prɒbləm] *n* problème *m*; **he's got a drug/a drink p.** c'est un drogué/un alcoolique; **you've got a smoking p.** tu fumes beaucoup trop; **no p.!** *Am Fam* pas de problème!; **to have a p. doing** avoir du mal à faire; – *a* (*child*) difficile, caractériel. ◆**proble'matic** *a* problématique; **it's p. whether** il est douteux que (+ *sub*).

procedure [prə'siːdʒər] *n* procédure *f*.

proceed [prə'siːd] *vi* (*go*) avancer, aller; (*act*) procéder; (*continue*) continuer; (*of debate*) se poursuivre; **to p. to** (*next question etc*) passer à; **to p. with** (*task etc*) continuer; **to p. to do** (*start*) se mettre à faire. ◆**—ing** *n* (*course of action*) procédé *m*; *pl* (*events*) événements *mpl*; (*meeting*) séance *f*; (*discussions*) débats *mpl*; (*minutes*) actes *mpl*; **to take (legal) proceedings** intenter un procès (**against** contre).

proceeds ['prəʊsiːdz] *npl* (*profits*) produit *m*, bénéfices *mpl*.

process ['prəʊses] **1** *n* (*operation, action*) processus *m*; (*method*) procédé *m* (**for** or **of doing** pour faire); **in p.** (*work etc*) en cours; **in the p. of doing** en train de faire. **2** *vt* (*food, data etc*) traiter; (*examine*) examiner; *Phot* développer; **processed cheese** fromage *m* fondu. ◆**—ing** *n* traitement *m*; *Phot* développement *m*; **data** or **information p.** informatique *f*. ◆**processor** *n* (*in computer*) processeur *m*; **food p.** robot *m* (*ménager*); **word p.** machine *f* de traitement de texte.

procession [prə'sɛʃ(ə)n] *n* cortège *m*, défilé *m*.

proclaim [prə'kleɪm] *vt* proclamer (**that** que); **to p. king** proclamer roi. ◆**procla'mation** *n* proclamation *f*.

procrastinate [prə'kræstɪneɪt] *vi* temporiser, tergiverser.

procreate ['prəʊkrɪeɪt] *vt* procréer. ◆**procre'ation** *n* procréation *f*.

procure [prə'kjʊər] *vt* obtenir; **to p. sth** (**for oneself**) se procurer qch; **to p. sth for s.o.** procurer qch à qn.

prod [prɒd] *vti* (-dd-) **to p. (at)** pousser (*du*

coude, avec un bâton etc); **to p. s.o. into doing** *Fig* pousser qn à faire; – *n* (*petit*) coup *m*; (*shove*) poussée *f*.

prodigal ['prɒdɪg(ə)l] *a* (*son etc*) prodigue.

prodigious [prə'dɪdʒəs] *a* prodigieux.

prodigy ['prɒdɪdʒɪ] *n* prodige *m*; **infant p., child p.** enfant *mf* prodige.

produce [prə'djuːs] *vt* (*manufacture, yield etc*) produire; (*bring out, show*) sortir (*pistolet, mouchoir etc*); (*passport, proof*) présenter; (*profit*) rapporter; (*cause*) provoquer, produire; (*publish*) publier; (*play*) *Th TV* mettre en scène; (*film*) *Cin* produire; *Rad* réaliser; (*baby*) donner naissance à; **oil-producing country** pays *m* producteur de pétrole; – *vi* (*of factory etc*) produire; (*of farmer*) produire; – *n* (*agricultural etc*) produits *mpl*. ◆**pro'ducer** *n* (*of goods*) & *Cin* producteur *m*; *Th TV* metteur *m* en scène; *Rad* réalisateur, -trice *mf*.

product ['prɒdʌkt] *n* produit *m*.

production [prə'dʌkʃ(ə)n] *n* production *f*; *Th TV* mise *f* en scène; *Rad* réalisation *f*; **to work on the p. line** travailler à la chaîne. ◆**productive** *a* (*land, meeting, efforts*) productif. ◆**produc'tivity** *n* productivité *f*.

profane [prə'feɪn] *a* (*sacrilegious*) sacrilège; (*secular*) profane; – *vt* (*dishonour*) profaner. ◆**profanities** *npl* (*oaths*) blasphèmes *mpl*.

profess [prə'fes] *vt* professer; **to p. to be** prétendre être. ◆**—ed** *a* (*anarchist etc*) déclaré.

profession [prə'feʃ(ə)n] *n* profession *f*; **by p.** de profession. ◆**professional** *a* professionnel; (*man, woman*) qui exerce une profession libérale; (*army*) de métier; (*diplomat*) de carrière; (*piece of work*) de professionnel; – *n* professionnel, -elle *mf*; (*executive, lawyer etc*) membre *m* des professions libérales. ◆**professionalism** *n* professionnalisme *m*. ◆**professionally** *adv* professionnellement; (*to perform, play*) en professionnel; (*to meet s.o.*) dans le cadre de son travail.

professor [prə'fesər] *n Univ* professeur *m* (*titulaire d'une chaire*). ◆**profe'ssorial** *a* professoral.

proffer ['prɒfər] *vt* offrir.

proficient [prə'fɪʃ(ə)nt] *a* compétent (**in** en). ◆**proficiency** *n* compétence *f*.

profile ['prəʊfaɪl] *n* (*of person, object*) profil *m*; **in p.** de profil; **to keep a low p.** *Fig* garder un profil bas. ◆**profiled** *a* **to be p. against** se profiler sur.

profit ['prɒfɪt] *n* profit *m*, bénéfice *m*; **to sell**

at a p. vendre à profit; **p. margin** marge *f* bénéficiaire; **p. motive** recherche *f* du profit; **– vi to p. by** on from tirer profit de. **◆p.-making** *a* à but lucratif. **◆profita-'bility** *n Com* rentabilité *f*. **◆profitable** *a Com* rentable; (*worthwhile*) *Fig* rentable, profitable. **◆profitably** *adv* avec profit. **◆profi'teer** *n Pej* profiteur, -euse *mf*; **– vi** *Pej* faire des profits malhonnêtes.

profound [prəˈfaʊnd] *a* (*silence, remark etc*) profond. **◆profoundly** *adv* profondément. **◆profundity** *n* profondeur *f*.

profuse [prəˈfjuːs] *a* abondant; **p. in** (*praise etc*) prodigue de. **◆profusely** *adv* (*to flow, grow*) à profusion; (*to bleed*) abondamment; (*to thank*) avec effusion; **to apologize p.** se répandre en excuses. **◆profusion** *n* profusion *f*; **in p.** à profusion.

progeny [ˈprɒdʒɪnɪ] *n* progéniture *f*.

program[1] [ˈprəʊɡræm] *n* (*of computer*) programme *m*; **– vt** (**-mm-**) (*computer*) programmer. **◆programming** *n* programmation *f*. **◆programmer** *n* (*computer*) *p.* programmeur, -euse *mf*.

programme, *Am* **program**[2] [ˈprəʊɡræm] *n* programme *m*; (*broadcast*) émission *f*; **– vt** (*arrange*) programmer.

progress [ˈprəʊɡres] *n* progrès *m* (*pl*); **to make (good) p.** faire des progrès; (*in walking, driving etc*) bien avancer; **in p.** en cours; **–** [prəˈɡres] *vi* (*advance, improve*) progresser; (*of story, meeting*) se dérouler. **◆pro'gression** *n* progression *f*. **◆pro-'gressive** *a* (*gradual*) progressif; (*party*) *Pol* progressiste; (*firm, ideas*) moderniste. **◆pro'gressively** *adv* progressivement.

prohibit [prəˈhɪbɪt] *vt* interdire (**s.o. from doing** à qn de faire); **we're prohibited from leaving**/*etc* il nous est interdit de partir/*etc*. **◆prohi'bition** *n* prohibition *f*. **◆prohibitive** *a* (*price, measure etc*) prohibitif.

project **1** [ˈprɒdʒekt] *n* (*plan*) projet *m* (**for** sth pour qch; **to do, for doing** pour faire); (*undertaking*) entreprise *f*; (*study*) étude *f*; (*housing*) **p.** (*for workers*) *Am* cité *f* (ouvrière). **2** [prəˈdʒekt] *vt* (*throw, show etc*) projeter; **– vi** (*jut out*) faire saillie. **◆-ed** *a* (*planned*) prévu. **◆pro'jection** *n* projection *f*; (*projecting object*) saillie *f*. **◆pro'jectionist** *n Cin* projectionniste *mf*. **◆pro'jector** *n Cin* projecteur *m*.

proletarian [prəʊləˈteərɪən] *n* prolétaire *mf*; **–** *a* (*class*) prolétarien; (*outlook*) de prolétaire. **◆proletariat** *n* prolétariat *m*.

proliferate [prəˈlɪfəreɪt] *vi* proliférer. **◆prolife'ration** *n* prolifération *f*.

prolific [prəˈlɪfɪk] *a* prolifique.

prologue [ˈprəʊlɒɡ] *n* prologue *m* (**to** de, à).

prolong [prəˈlɒŋ] *vt* prolonger.

promenade [prɒməˈnɑːd] *n* (*place, walk*) promenade *f*; (*gallery*) *Th* promenoir *m*.

prominent [ˈprɒmɪnənt] *a* (*nose*) proéminent; (*chin, tooth*) saillant; (*striking*) *Fig* frappant, remarquable; (*role*) majeur; (*politician*) marquant; (*conspicuous*) (bien) en vue. **◆prominence** *n* (*importance*) importance *f*. **◆prominently** *adv* (*displayed, placed*) bien en vue.

promiscuous [prəˈmɪskjʊəs] *a* (*person*) de mœurs faciles; (*behaviour*) immoral. **◆promi'scuity** *n* liberté *f* de mœurs; immoralité *f*.

promis/e [ˈprɒmɪs] *n* promesse *f*; **to show great p., be full of p.** (*hope*) être très prometteur; **– vt** promettre (**s.o. sth, sth to s.o.** qch à qn; **to do** de faire; **that** que); **– vi I p.!** je te le promets! **p.? promis?** **◆–ing** *a* (*start etc*) prometteur; (*person*) qui promet; **that looks p.** ça s'annonce bien.

promote [prəˈməʊt] *vt* (*product, research*) promouvoir; (*good health, awareness*) favoriser; **to p. s.o.** promouvoir qn (**to** à); **promoted (to) manager/general**/*etc* promu directeur/général/*etc*. **◆promoter** *n Sp* organisateur, -trice *mf*; (*instigator*) promoteur, -trice *mf*. **◆promotion** *n* (*of person*) avancement *n*, promotion *f*; (*of sales, research etc*) promotion *f*.

prompt [prɒmpt] **1** *a* (*speedy*) rapide; (*punctual*) à l'heure, ponctuel; **p. to act** prompt à agir; **– adv** **at 8 o'clock** à 8 heures pile. **2** *vt* (*urge*) inciter, pousser (**to do** à faire); (*cause*) provoquer. **3** *vt* (*person*) *Th* souffler (son rôle) à. **◆–ing** *n* (*urging*) incitation *f*. **◆–er** *n Th* souffleur, -euse *mf*. **◆–ness** *n* rapidité *f*; (*readiness to act*) promptitude *f*.

prone [prəʊn] *a* **1** **p. to sth** (*liable*) prédisposé à qch; **to be p. to do** avoir tendance à faire. **2** (*lying flat*) sur le ventre.

prong [prɒŋ] *n* (*of fork*) dent *f*.

pronoun [ˈprəʊnaʊn] *n Gram* pronom *m*. **◆pro'nominal** *a* pronominal.

pronounce [prəˈnaʊns] *vt* (*articulate, declare*) prononcer; **– vi** (*articulate*) prononcer; (*give judgment*) se prononcer (**on** sur). **◆pronouncement** *n* déclaration *f*. **◆pronunci'ation** *n* prononciation *f*.

pronto [ˈprɒntəʊ] *adv* (*at once*) *Fam* illico.

proof [pruːf] *n* **1** (*evidence*) preuve *f*; (*of book, photo*) épreuve *f*; (*of drink*) teneur *f* en alcool. **2** *a* **p. against** (*material*) à l'épreuve de (*feu, acide etc*). ◆**proof-reader** *n* Typ correcteur, -trice *mf*.

prop [prop] **1** *n* Archit support *m*, étai *m*; (*for clothes line*) perche *f*; (*person*) Fig soutien *m*; – *vt* (-**pp-**) **to p. up** (*ladder etc*) appuyer (**against** contre); (*one's head*) caler; (*wall*) étayer; (*help*) Fig soutenir. **2** *n* **prop(s)** Th accessoire(s) *m(pl)*.

propaganda [propə'gændə] *n* propagande *f*. ◆**propagandist** *n* propagandiste *mf*.

propagate ['propəgeɪt] *vt* propager; – *vi* se propager.

propel [prə'pel] *vt* (-**ll-**) (*drive, hurl*) propulser. ◆**propeller** *n* Av Nau hélice *f*.

propensity [prə'pensɪtɪ] *n* propension *f* (**for** sth à qch, **to do** à faire).

proper ['propər] *a* (*suitable, seemly*) convenable; (*correct*) correct; (*right*) bon; (*real, downright*) véritable; (*noun, meaning*) propre; **in the p. way** comme il faut; **the** village/*etc* **p.** le village/*etc* proprement dit. ◆**-ly** *adv* comme il faut, convenablement, correctement; (*completely*) Fam vraiment; **very p.** (*quite rightly*) à juste titre.

property ['propətɪ] **1** *n* (*building etc*) propriété *f*; (*possessions*) biens *mpl*, propriété *f*; – *a* (*crisis, market etc*) immobilier; (*owner, tax*) foncier. **2** *n* (*of substance etc*) propriété *f*. ◆**propertied** *a* possédant.

prophecy ['profɪsɪ] *n* prophétie *f*. ◆**prophesy** [-ɪsaɪ] *vti* prophétiser; **to p. that** prédire que.

prophet ['profɪt] *n* prophète *m*. ◆**prophetic** *a* prophétique.

proponent [prə'pəʊnənt] *n* (*of cause etc*) défenseur *m*, partisan, -ane *mf*.

proportion [prə'pɔ:ʃ(ə)n] *n* (*ratio*) proportion *f*; (*portion*) partie *f*; (*amount*) pourcentage *m*; *pl* (*size*) proportions *fpl*; **in p.** en proportion (**to** de); **out of p.** hors de proportion (**to** avec); – *vt* proportionner (**to** à); **well** *or* **nicely proportioned** bien proportionné. ◆**proportional** *a*, ◆**proportionate** *a* proportionnel (**to** à).

propose [prə'pəʊz] *vt* (*suggest*) proposer (**to** à, **that** que (+ *sub*)); **to p. to do, p. doing** (*intend*) se proposer de faire; – *vi* faire une demande (en mariage) (**to** à). ◆**proposal** *n* proposition *f*; (*of marriage*) demande *f* (en mariage). ◆**proposition** *n* proposition *f*; (*matter*) Fig affaire *f*.

propound [prə'paʊnd] *vt* proposer.

proprietor [prə'praɪətər] *n* propriétaire *mf*. ◆**proprietary** *a* (*article*) Com de marque déposée; **p. name** marque *f* déposée.

propriety [prə'praɪətɪ] *n* (*behaviour*) bienséance *f*; (*of conduct, remark*) justesse *f*.

propulsion [prə'pʌlʃ(ə)n] *n* propulsion *f*.

pros [prəʊz] *npl* **the p. and cons** le pour et le contre.

prosaic [prəʊ'zeɪɪk] *a* prosaïque.

proscribe [prəʊ'skraɪb] *vt* proscrire.

prose [prəʊz] *n* prose *f*; (*translation*) Sch thème *m*.

prosecute ['prosɪkju:t] *vt* poursuivre (en justice) (**for stealing**/*etc* pour vol/*etc*). ◆**prose'cution** *n* Jur poursuites *fpl*; **the p.** (*lawyers*) = le ministère public. ◆**prosecutor** *n* (**public**) **p.** Jur procureur *m*.

prospect¹ ['prospekt] *n* (*idea, outlook*) perspective *f* (**of doing** de faire); (*possibility*) possibilité *f* (**of sth** de qch); (*future*) **prospects** perspectives *fpl* d'avenir; **it has prospects** c'est prometteur; **she has prospects** elle a de l'avenir. ◆**pro'spective** *a* (*possible*) éventuel; (*future*) futur.

prospect² [prə'spekt] *vt* (*land*) prospecter; – *vi* **to p. for** (*gold etc*) chercher. ◆**-ing** *n* prospection *f*. ◆**prospector** *n* prospecteur, -trice *mf*.

prospectus [prə'spektəs] *n* (*publicity leaflet*) prospectus *m*; Univ guide *m* (de l'étudiant).

prosper ['prospər] *vi* prospérer. ◆**pro'sperity** *n* prospérité *f*. ◆**prosperous** *a* (*thriving*) prospère; (*wealthy*) riche, prospère.

prostate ['prosteɪt] *n* **p. (gland)** Anat prostate *f*.

prostitute ['prostɪtju:t] *n* (*woman*) prostituée *f*; – *vt* prostituer. ◆**prosti'tution** *n* prostitution *f*.

prostrate ['prostreɪt] *a* (*prone*) sur le ventre; (*worshipper*) prosterné; (*submissive*) soumis; (*exhausted*) prostré; – [pro'streɪt] *vt* **to p. oneself** se prosterner (**before** devant).

protagonist [prəʊ'tægənɪst] *n* protagoniste *mf*.

protect [prə'tekt] *vt* protéger (**from** de, **against** contre); (*interests*) sauvegarder. ◆**protection** *n* protection *f*. ◆**protective** *a* (*tone etc*) & Econ protecteur; (*screen, clothes etc*) de protection. ◆**protector** *n* protecteur, -trice *mf*.

protein ['prəʊti:n] *n* protéine *f*.

protest ['prəʊtest] *n* protestation *f* (**against** contre); **under p.** contre son gré; – [prə'test] *vt* protester (**that** que); (*one's innocence*) protester de; – *vi* protester (**against** contre); (*in the streets etc*) Pol contester. ◆**-er** *n* Pol contestataire *mf*.

Protestant ['protɪstənt] *a* & *n* protestant,

-ante (*mf*). ◆**Protestantism** *n* protestantisme *m*.

protocol ['prəutəkɒl] *n* protocole *m*.

prototype ['prəutəutaɪp] *n* prototype *m*.

protract [prə'trækt] *vt* prolonger.

protractor [prə'træktər] *n* (*instrument*) *Geom* rapporteur *m*.

protrud/e [prə'truːd] *vi* dépasser; (*of balcony, cliff etc*) faire saillie; (*of tooth*) avancer. ◆**—ing** *a* saillant; (*of tooth*) qui avance.

proud [praʊd] *a* (**-er, -est**) (*honoured, pleased*) fier (**of** de, **to do** de faire); (*arrogant*) orgueilleux. ◆**-ly** *adv* fièrement; orgueilleusement.

prove [pruːv] *vt* prouver (**that** que); **to p.** oneself faire ses preuves; **–** *vi* **to p.** (**to be**) difficult/*etc* s'avérer difficile/*etc*. ◆**proven** *a* (*method etc*) éprouvé.

proverb ['prɒvɜːb] *n* proverbe *m*. ◆**proverbial** *a* proverbial.

provid/e [prə'vaɪd] *vt* fournir (s.o. **with sth** qch à qn); (*give*) donner, offrir (**to** à); **to p. s.o. with** (*equip*) pourvoir qn de. **to p. that** *Jur* stipuler que; **–** *vi* **to p. for s.o.** (*s.o.'s needs*) pourvoir aux besoins de qn; (*s.o.'s future*) assurer l'avenir de qn; **to p. for sth** (*make allowance for*) prévoir qch. ◆**-ed** *conj* **p.** (**that**) pourvu que (+ *sub*). ◆**-ing** *conj* **p.** (**that**) pourvu que (+ *sub*).

providence ['prɒvɪdəns] *n* providence *f*.

provident ['prɒvɪdənt] *a* (*society*) de prévoyance; (*person*) prévoyant.

province ['prɒvɪns] *n* province *f*; *Fig* domaine *m*, compétence *f*; **the provinces** la province; **in the provinces** en province. ◆**pro'vincial** *a* & *n* provincial, -ale (*mf*).

provision [prə'vɪʒ(ə)n] *n* (*supply*) provision *f*; (*clause*) disposition *f*; **the p. of** (*supplying*) la fourniture de; **to make p. for** = **provide for.**

provisional [prə'vɪʒən(ə)l] *a* provisoire. ◆**-ly** *adv* provisoirement.

proviso [prə'vaɪzəu] *n* (*pl* **-os**) stipulation *f*.

provok/e [prə'vəuk] *vt* (*rouse, challenge*) provoquer (**to do, into doing** à faire); (*annoy*) agacer; (*cause*) provoquer (*accident, reaction etc*). ◆**-ing** *a* (*annoying*) agaçant. ◆**provo'cation** *n* provocation *f*. ◆**provocative** *a* (*person, remark etc*) provocant; (*thought-provoking*) qui donne à penser.

prow [praʊ] *n* Nau proue *f*.

prowess ['praʊɪs] *n* (*bravery*) courage *m*; (*skill*) talent *m*.

prowl [praʊl] *vi* **to p.** (**around**) rôder; **–** *n* **to**

be on the p. rôder. ◆**-er** *n* rôdeur, -euse *mf*.

proximity [prɒk'sɪmɪtɪ] *n* proximité *f*.

proxy ['prɒksɪ] *n* **by p.** par procuration.

prude [pruːd] *n* prude *f*. ◆**prudery** *n* pruderie *f*. ◆**prudish** *a* prude.

prudent ['pruːdənt] *a* prudent. ◆**prudence** *n* prudence *f*. ◆**prudently** *adv* prudemment.

prun/e [pruːn] **1** *n* (*dried plum*) pruneau *m*. **2** *vt* (*cut*) *Bot* tailler, élaguer; (*speech etc*) *Fig* élaguer. ◆**-ing** *n* *Bot* taille *f*.

pry [praɪ] **1** *vi* être indiscret; **to p. into** (*meddle*) se mêler de; (*s.o.'s reasons etc*) chercher à découvrir. **2** *vt* **to p. open** *Am* forcer (en faisant levier). ◆**-ing** *a* indiscret.

PS [piː'es] *abbr* (*postscript*) P.-S.

psalm [sɑːm] *n* psaume *m*.

pseud [sjuːd] *n* *Fam* bêcheur, -euse *mf*.

pseudo- ['sjuːdəu] *pref* pseudo-.

pseudonym ['sjuːdənɪm] *n* pseudonyme *m*.

psychiatry [saɪ'kaɪətrɪ] *n* psychiatrie *f*. ◆**psychi'atric** *a* psychiatrique. ◆**psychiatrist** *n* psychiatre *mf*.

psychic ['saɪkɪk] *a* (*méta*)psychique; **I'm not p.** *Fam* je ne suis pas devin; **–** *n* (*person*) médium *m*.

psycho- ['saɪkəu] *pref* psycho-. ◆**psychoa'nalysis** *n* psychanalyse *f*. ◆**psycho-'analyst** *n* psychanalyste *mf*.

psychology [saɪ'kɒlədʒɪ] *n* psychologie *f*. ◆**psycho'logical** *a* psychologique. ◆**psychologist** *n* psychologue *mf*.

psychopath ['saɪkəupæθ] *n* psychopathe *mf*.

psychosis, *pl* **-oses** [saɪ'kəusɪs, -əusiːz] *n* psychose *f*.

PTO [piːtiː'əu] *abbr* (*please turn over*) TSVP.

pub [pʌb] *n* pub *m*.

puberty ['pjuːbətɪ] *n* puberté *f*.

public ['pʌblɪk] *a* public; (*baths, library*) municipal; **to make a p. protest** protester publiquement; **in the p. eye** très en vue; **p. building** édifice *m* public; **p. company** société *f* par actions; **p. corporation** société *f* nationalisée; **p. figure** personnalité *f* connue; **p. house** pub *m*; **p. life** les affaires *fpl* publiques; **to be p.-spirited** avoir le sens civique; **–** *n* public *m*; **in p.** en public; **a member of the p.** un simple particulier; **the sporting**/*etc* **p.** les amateurs *mpl* de sport/*etc*. ◆**-ly** *adv* publiquement; **p. owned** (*nationalized*) *Com* nationalisé.

publican ['pʌblɪk(ə)n] *n* patron, -onne *mf* d'un pub.

publication [pʌblɪˈkeɪʃ(ə)n] n (*publishing, book etc*) publication f.

publicity [pʌbˈlɪsɪtɪ] n publicité f. ◆**'publicize** vt rendre public; (*advertise*) Com faire de la publicité pour.

publish [ˈpʌblɪʃ] vt publier; (*book*) éditer, publier; **to p. s.o.** éditer qn; '**published weekly**' 'paraît toutes les semaines'. ◆**-ing** n publication f (of de); (*profession*) édition f. ◆**-er** n éditeur, -trice mf.

puck [pʌk] n (*in ice hockey*) palet m.

pucker [ˈpʌkər] vt ou **to p. (up)** (*brow, lips*) plisser; — vi **to p. (up)** se plisser.

pudding [ˈpʊdɪŋ] n dessert m, gâteau m; (*plum*) pudding m; **rice p.** riz au lait.

puddle [ˈpʌd(ə)l] n flaque f (d'eau).

pudgy [ˈpʌdʒɪ] a (-ier, -iest) = **podgy**.

puerile [ˈpjʊəraɪl] a puérile.

puff [pʌf] n (of smoke) bouffée f; (of wind, air) bouffée f, souffle m; **to have run out of p.** Fam être à bout de souffle; — vi (blow, pant) souffler; **to p. at** (cigar) tirer sur; — vt (smoke etc) souffler (**into** dans); **to p. out** (cheeks etc) gonfler. ◆**puffy** a (-ier, -iest) (swollen) gonflé.

puke [pjuːk] vi (vomit) Sl dégueuler.

pukka [ˈpʌkə] a Fam authentique.

pull [pʊl] n (attraction) attraction f; (force) force f; (influence) influence f; **to give sth a p.** tirer qch; — vt (draw, tug) tirer; (tooth) arracher; (stopper) enlever; (trigger) appuyer sur; (muscle) se claquer; **to p. apart** ou **to bits** ou **to pieces** mettre en pièces; **to p. a face** faire la moue; **to (get s.o. to) p. strings** Fig faire pistonner; — vi (tug) tirer; (go, move) aller; **to p. at** ou **on** tirer (sur). ▪ **to p. along** vt (drag) traîner (**to** jusqu'à); **to p. away** vt (move) éloigner; (snatch) arracher (**from** à); — vi Aut démarrer; **to p. away from** s'éloigner de; **to p. back** vi (withdraw) Mil se retirer; — vt retirer; (curtains) ouvrir; **to p. down** vt (lower) baisser; (knock down) faire tomber; (demolish) démolir, abattre; **to p. in** vt (rope) ramener; (drag into room etc) faire entrer; (stomach) rentrer; (crowd) attirer; — vi (arrive) Aut arriver; (stop) Aut se garer; **to p. into the station** (of train) entrer en gare; **to p. off** vt enlever; (plan, deal) Fig mener à bien; **to p. it off** Fig réussir son coup; **to p. on** vt (boots etc) mettre; **to p. out** vt (extract) arracher (**from** à); (remove) enlever (**from** de); (from pocket, bag etc) tirer, sortir (**from** de); (troops) retirer; — vi (depart) Aut démarrer; (move out) Aut déboîter; **to p. out of** (negotiations etc) se retirer de; **to p. over** vt (drag) traîner (**to** jusqu'à); (knock down) faire tomber; — vi Aut se ranger (sur le côté); **to p. round** vi Med se remettre; **to p. through** vi se tirer; **to p. oneself together** vt se ressaisir; **to p. up** vt (socks, bucket etc) remonter; (haul up) hisser; (uproot) arracher; (stop) arrêter; — vi Aut s'arrêter. ◆**p.-up** n Sp traction f.

pulley [ˈpʊlɪ] n poulie f.

pullout [ˈpʊlaʊt] n (in newspaper etc) supplément m détachable.

pullover [ˈpʊləʊvər] n pull-(over) m.

pulp [pʌlp] n (of fruit etc) pulpe f; (for paper) pâte f à papier; **in a p.** Fig en bouillie.

pulpit [ˈpʊlpɪt] n Rel chaire f.

pulsate [pʌlˈseɪt] vi produire des pulsations, battre. ◆**pulsation** n (heartbeat etc) pulsation f.

pulse [pʌls] n Med pouls m.

pulverize [ˈpʌlvəraɪz] vt (grind, defeat) pulvériser.

pumice [ˈpʌmɪs] n **p. (stone)** pierre f ponce.

pump [pʌmp] 1 n pompe f; (petrol) **p. attendant** pompiste mf; — vt pomper; (blood) Med faire circuler; (money) Fig injecter (**into** dans); **to p. s.o. (for information)** tirer les vers du nez à qn; **to p. in** refouler (à l'aide d'une pompe); **to p. out** pomper (of de); **to p. air into, to p.** (tyre) gonfler; — vi pomper; (of heart) battre. 2 n (for dancing) escarpin m; (plimsoll) tennis f.

pumpkin [ˈpʌmpkɪn] n potiron m.

pun [pʌn] n calembour m.

punch[1] [pʌntʃ] n (blow) coup m de poing; (force) Fig punch m; **to pack a p.** Boxing & Fig avoir du punch; **p. line** (of joke) astuce f finale; — vt (person) donner un coup de poing à; (ball etc) frapper d'un coup de poing. ◆**p.-up** n Fam bagarre f.

punch[2] [pʌntʃ] 1 n (for tickets) poinçonneuse f; (for paper) perforeuse f; **p. card** carte f perforée; — vt (ticket) poinçonner, (with date) composter; (card, paper) perforer; **to p. a hole in** faire un trou dans. 2 n (drink) punch m.

punctilious [pʌŋkˈtɪlɪəs] a pointilleux.

punctual [ˈpʌŋktʃʊəl] a (arriving on time) à l'heure; (regularly on time) ponctuel, exact. ◆**punctu'ality** n ponctualité f, exactitude f. ◆**punctually** adv à l'heure; (habitually) ponctuellement.

punctuate [ˈpʌŋktʃʊeɪt] vt ponctuer (**with** de). ◆**punctu'ation** n ponctuation f; **p. mark** signe m de ponctuation.

puncture [ˈpʌŋktʃər] n (in tyre) crevaison f;

to have a p. crever; – *vt* (*burst*) crever; (*pierce*) piquer; – *vi* (*of tyre*) crever.

pundit ['pʌndɪt] *n* expert *m*, ponte *m*.

pungent ['pʌndʒənt] *a* âcre, piquant. ◆**pungency** *n* âcreté *f*.

punish ['pʌnɪʃ] *vt* punir (**for sth** de qch, **for doing** *or* **having done** pour avoir fait); (*treat roughly*) Fig malmener. ◆**-ing** *n* punition *f*; – *a* (*tiring*) éreintant. ◆**-able** *a* punissable (**by de**). ◆**-ment** *n* punition *f*, châtiment *m*; **capital p.** peine *f* capitale; **to take a** (**lot of**) **p.** (*damage*) Fig en encaisser.

punitive ['pjuːnɪtɪv] *a* (*measure etc*) punitif.

punk [pʌŋk] **1** *n* (*music*) punk *m*; (*fan*) punk *mf*; – **a p. rocker** *inv.* **2** *n* (*hoodlum*) *Am Fam* voyou *m*.

punt [pʌnt] **1** *n* barque *f* (à fond plat). **2** *vi* (*bet*) *Fam* parier. ◆**-ing** *n* canotage *m*. ◆**-er** *n* **1** (*gambler*) parieur, -euse *mf.* **2** (*customer*) *Sl* client, -ente *mf.*

puny ['pjuːnɪ] *a* (**-ier, -iest**) (*sickly*) chétif; (*small*) petit; (*effort*) faible.

pup ['pʌp] *n* (*dog*) chiot *m*.

pupil ['pjuːp(ə)l] *n* **1** (*person*) élève *mf.* **2** (*of eye*) pupille *f.*

puppet ['pʌpɪt] *n* marionnette *f*; – *a* (*government, leader*) fantoche *m*.

puppy ['pʌpɪ] *n* (*dog*) chiot *m.*

purchas/e ['pɜːtʃɪs] *n* (*bought article, buying*) achat *m*; – *vt* acheter (**from s.o.** à qn, **for s.o.** à *or* pour qn). ◆**-er** *n* acheteur, -euse *mf.*

pure [pjʊər] *a* (**-er, -est**) pur. ◆**purely** *adv* purement. ◆**purifi'cation** *n* purification *f.* ◆**purify** *vt* purifier. ◆**purity** *n* pureté *f.*

purée ['pjʊəreɪ] *n* purée *f.*

purgatory ['pɜːgətrɪ] *n* purgatoire *m.*

purge [pɜːdʒ] *n* Pol Med purge *f*; – *vt* (*rid*) purger (**of** de); (*group*) Pol épurer.

purist ['pjʊərɪst] *n* puriste *mf.*

puritan ['pjʊərɪt(ə)n] *n* & *a* puritain, -aine (*mf*). ◆**puri'tanical** *a* puritain.

purl [pɜːl] *n* (*knitting stitch*) maille *f* à l'envers.

purple ['pɜːp(ə)l] *a* & *n* violet (*m*); **to go p.** (*with anger*) devenir pourpre; (*with shame*) devenir cramoisi.

purport [pɜː'pɔːt] *vt* **to p. to be** (*claim*) prétendre être.

purpose ['pɜːpəs] *n* **1** (*aim*) but *m*; **for this p.** dans ce but; **on p.** exprès; **to no p.** inutile-ment; **to serve no p.** ne servir à rien; **for (the) purposes of** pour les besoins de. **2** (*determination, will*) résolution *f*; **to have a sense of p.** être résolu. ◆**p.-'built** *a* construit spécialement. ◆**purposeful** *a* (*determined*) résolu. ◆**purposefully** *adv*

dans un but précis; (*resolutely*) résolument. ◆**purposely** *adv* exprès.

purr [pɜːr] *vi* ronronner; – *n* ronron(nement) *m.*

purse [pɜːs] **1** *n* (*for coins*) porte-monnaie *m inv*; (*handbag*) *Am* sac *m* à main. **2** *vt* **to p. one's lips** pincer les lèvres.

purser ['pɜːsər] *n* Nau commissaire *m* du bord.

pursue [pə'sjuː] *vt* (*chase, hound, seek, continue*) poursuivre; (*fame, pleasure*) rechercher; (*course of action*) suivre. ◆**pursuer** *n* poursuivant, -ante *mf.* ◆**pursuit** *n* (*of person, glory etc*) poursuite *f*; (*activity, pastime*) occupation *f*; **to go in p. of** se mettre à la poursuite de.

purveyor [pə'veɪər] *n* Com fournisseur *m.*

pus [pʌs] *n* pus *m.*

push [pʊʃ] *n* (*shove*) poussée *f*; (*energy*) Fig dynamisme *m*; (*help*) coup *m* de pouce; (*campaign*) campagne *f*; **to give s.o./sth a p.** pousser qn/qch; **to give s.o. the p.** (*dismiss*) *Fam* flanquer qn à la porte; – *vt* (*get s.o. to do*) pousser (**to,** *as far as* jusqu'à); (*product*) Com pousser la vente de; (*drugs*) *Fam* revendre; **to p.** (**down**) (*button*) appuyer sur; (*lever*) abaisser; **to p. (forward)** (*views etc*) mettre en avant; **to p. sth into/between** (*thrust*) enfoncer *or* fourrer qch dans/entre; **to p. s.o. into doing** (*urge*) pousser qn à faire; **to p. sth off the table** faire tomber qch de la table (**en le poussant**); **to p. s.o. off a cliff** pousser qn du haut d'une falaise; **to be pushing forty/etc** *Fam* friser la quaran-taine/etc; – *vi* pousser; **to p. for** faire pres-sion pour obtenir. ■ **to p. about** *or* **around** *vt* (*bully*) *Fam* marcher sur les pieds à; **to p. aside** *vt* (*person, objection etc*) écarter; **to p. away** *or* **back** *vt* repousser; (*curtains*) ouvrir; **to p. in** *vi* (*in queue*) *Fam* resquiller; **to p. off** *vi* (*leave*) *Fam* filer; **p. off!** *Fam* fiche le camp!; **to p. on** *vi* continuer (**with sth** qch); (*in journey*) poursuivre sa route; **to p. over** *vt* (*topple*) renverser; **to p. through** *vt* (*law*) faire adopter; – *vti* **to p. through** (**one's way**) through se frayer un chemin (**a crowd/etc** à travers une foule/etc); **to p. up** *vt* (*lever etc*) relever; (*increase*) *Fam* augmenter, relever. ◆**pushed** *a* **to be p.** (**for time**) (*rushed, busy*) être très bousculé. ◆**pusher** *n* (*of drugs*) revendeur, -euse *mf* (*de drogue*).

pushbike ['pʊʃbaɪk] *n* Fam vélo *m.* ◆**push-button** *n* poussoir *m*; – *a* (*radio etc*) à poussoir. ◆**pushchair** *n* poussette *f* (*pliante*). ◆**pushover** *n* **to be a p.** (*easy*)

Fam être facile, être du gâteau. ◆**push-up** *n Sp Am* pompe *f.*

pushy ['puʃɪ] *a* (-ier, -iest) *Pej* entreprenant; (*in job*) arriviste.

puss(y) ['pus(ɪ)] *n* (*cat*) minet *m*, minou *m.*

put [put] *vt* (*pt & pp* put, *pres p* putting) mettre; (*savings, money*) placer (**into** dans); (*pressure, mark*) faire (**on** sur); (*problem, argument*) présenter (**to** à); (*question*) poser (**to** à); (*say*) dire; (*estimate*) évaluer (**at** à); **to p. it bluntly** pour parler franc. ■ **to p. across** *vt* (*idea etc*) communiquer (**to** à); **to p. away** *vt* (*in its place*) ranger (*livre, voiture etc*); **to p. s.o. away** (*criminal*) mettre qn en prison; (*insane person*) enfermer qn; **to p. back** *vt* remettre; (*receiver*) *Tel* raccrocher; (*progress, clock*) retarder; **to p. by** *vt* (*money*) mettre de côté; **to p. down** *vt* (*on floor, table etc*) poser; (*passenger*) déposer; (*deposit*) *Fin* verser; (*revolt*) réprimer; (*write down*) inscrire; (*assign*) attribuer (**to** à); (*kill*) faire piquer (*chien etc*); **to p. forward** *vt* (*argument, clock, meeting*) avancer; (*opinion*) exprimer; (*candidate*) proposer (**for** à); **to p. in** *vt* (*insert*) introduire; (*add*) ajouter; (*present*) présenter; (*request, application*) faire; (*enrol*) inscrire (**for** à); (*spend*) passer (*une heure etc*) (**doing** à faire); – *vi* **to p. in for** (*job etc*) faire une demande de; **to p. in at** (*of ship etc*) faire escale à; **to p. off** *vt* (*postpone*) renvoyer (à plus tard); (*passenger*) déposer; (*gas, radio*) fermer; (*dismay*) déconcerter; **to p. s.o. off** (*dissuade*) dissuader qn (**doing** de faire); **to p. s.o. off** (*disgust*) dégoûter qn (**sth** de qch); **to p. s.o. off doing** (*disgust*) ôter à qn l'envie de faire; **to p. on** *vt* (*clothes, shoe etc*) mettre; (*weight, accent*) prendre; (*film*) jouer; (*gas, radio*) mettre, allumer; (*record, cassette*) passer; (*clock*) avancer; **to p. s.o. on** (*tease*) *Am* faire marcher qn; **she p. me on to you** elle m'a donné votre adresse; **p. me on to him!** *Tel* passez-le-moi!; **to p. out** *vt* (*take*

outside) sortir; (*arm, leg*) étendre; (*hand*) tendre; (*tongue*) tirer; (*gas, light*) éteindre, fermer; (*inconvenience*) déranger; (*upset*) déconcerter; (*issue*) publier; (*dislocate*) démettre; **to p. through** *vt Tel* passer (**to** à); **to p. together** *vt* (*assemble*) assembler; (*compose*) composer; (*prepare*) préparer; (*collection*) réunir; **to p. up** *vt* (*lodge*) descendre (**at a hotel** dans un hôtel); **to p. up with** (*tolerate*) supporter; – *vt* (*lift*) lever; (*window*) remonter; (*tent, statue, barrier, ladder*) dresser; (*flag*) hisser; (*building*) construire; (*umbrella*) ouvrir; (*picture, poster*) mettre; (*price, sales, numbers*) augmenter; (*resistance, plea, suggestion*) offrir; (*candidate*) proposer (**for** à); (*guest*) loger; **p.-up job** *Fam* coup m monté. ◆**p.-you-up** *n* canapé-lit *m*, convertible *m.*

putrid ['pjutrɪd] *a* putride. ◆**putrify** *vi* se putréfier.

putt [pʌt] *n Golf* putt *m.* ◆**putting** *n Golf* putting *m;* **p. green** green *m.*

putter ['pʌtər] *vi* **to p. around** *Am* bricoler.

putty ['pʌtɪ] *n* (*pour fixer une vitre*) mastic *m.*

puzzl/e ['pʌz(ə)l] *n* mystère *m*, énigme *f;* (*game*) casse-tête *m inv;* (*jigsaw*) puzzle *m;* – *vt* laisser perplexe; **to p. out why/when/** *etc* essayer de comprendre pourquoi/quand/*etc;* – *vi* **to p. over** (*problem, event*) se creuser la tête sur. ◆**—ed** *a* perplexe. ◆**—ing** *a* mystérieux, surprenant.

PVC [piːviːsiː] *n* (*plastic*) PVC *m.*

pygmy ['pɪgmɪ] *n* pygmée *m.*

pyjama [pɪ'dʒɑːmə] *a* (*jacket etc*) de pyjama. ◆**pyjamas** *npl* pyjama *m;* **a pair of p.** un pyjama.

pylon ['paɪlən] *n* pylône *m.*

pyramid ['pɪrəmɪd] *n* pyramide *f.*

Pyrenees [pɪrə'niːz] *npl* **the P.** les Pyrénées *fpl.*

python ['paɪθən] *n* (*snake*) python *m.*

Q

Q, q [kjuː] *n* Q, q *m.*

quack [kwæk] **1** *n* (*of duck*) coin-coin *m inv.* **2** *a & n* **q.** (*doctor*) charlatan *m.*

quad(rangle) ['kwɒd(ræŋg(ə)l)] *n* (*of college*) cour *f.*

quadruped ['kwɒdruped] *n* quadrupède *m.*

quadruple [kwɒ'druːp(ə)l] *vt* quadrupler.

quadruplets [kwɒ'druːplɪts] (*Fam* **quads** [kwɒdz]) *npl* quadruplés, -ées *mfpl.*

quaff [kwɒf] *vt* (*drink*) avaler.

quagmire ['kwægmaɪər] *n* bourbier *m.*

quail [kweɪl] *n* (*bird*) caille *f.*

quaint [kweɪnt] a (-er, -est) (*picturesque*) pittoresque; (*antiquated*) vieillot; (*odd*) bizarre. ◆**-ness** n pittoresque m; caractère m vieillot; bizarrerie f.

quake [kweɪk] vi trembler (**with** de); – n Fam tremblement m de terre.

Quaker ['kweɪkər] n quaker, -eresse mf.

qualification [kwɒlɪfɪˈkeɪʃ(ə)n] n 1 (*competence*) compétence f (**for** pour, **to do** pour faire); (*diploma*) diplôme m; pl (*requirements*) conditions fpl requises. 2 (*reservation*) réserve f.

qualify ['kwɒlɪfaɪ] 1 vt (*make competent*) & Sp qualifier (**for sth** pour qch, **to do** pour faire); – vi obtenir son diplôme (**as a doctor**/etc de médecin/etc); Sp se qualifier (**for** pour); to q. **for** (*post*) remplir les conditions requises pour. 2 vt (*modify*) faire des réserves à; (*opinion*) nuancer; Gram qualifier. ◆**qualified** a (*able*) qualifié (**to do** pour faire); (*doctor* etc) diplômé; (*success*) limité; (*opinion*) nuancé; (*support*) conditionnel. ◆**qualifying** a (*exam*) d'entrée; **q. round** Sp (*épreuve* f) éliminatoire f.

quality ['kwɒlɪtɪ] n qualité f; – a (*product*) de qualité. ◆**qualitative** a qualitatif.

qualms [kwɑːmz] npl (*scruples*) scruples mpl; (*anxieties*) inquiétudes fpl.

quandary ['kwɒndrɪ] n in a q. bien embarrassé; **to be in a q. about what to do** ne pas savoir quoi faire.

quantity ['kwɒntɪtɪ] n quantité f; in q. (*to purchase* etc) en grande(s) quantité(s). ◆**quantify** vt quantifier. ◆**quantitative** a quantitatif.

quarantine ['kwɒrəntiːn] n Med quarantaine f; – vt mettre en quarantaine.

quarrel ['kwɒrəl] n querelle f, dispute f; **to pick a q.** chercher querelle (**with s.o.** à qn); – vi (**-ll-**, Am **-l-**) se disputer, se quereller (**with** avec); **to q. with sth** se trouver à redire à qch. ◆**quarrelling** n, Am ◆**quarreling** n (*quarrels*) querelles fpl. ◆**quarrelsome** a querelleur.

quarry ['kwɒrɪ] n 1 (*excavation*) carrière f. 2 (*prey*) proie f.

quart [kwɔːt] n litre m (*mesure approximative*) (Br = 1,14 litres, Am = 0,95 litre).

quarter ['kwɔːtər] n 1 quart m; (*of year*) trimestre m; (*money*) Am Can quart m de dollar; (*of moon, fruit*) quartier m; **to divide into quarters** diviser en quatre; **q. (of a) pound** quart m de livre; **a q. past nine**, Am **a q. after nine** neuf heures et quart; **a q. to nine** neuf heures moins le quart; **from all quarters** de toutes parts. 2 n (*district*)

quartier m; pl (*circles*) milieux mpl; (*living*) **quarters** logement(s) m (pl); Mil quartier(s) m(pl); – vt (*troops*) Mil cantonner. ◆**-ly** a trimestriel; – adv trimestriellement; – n publication f trimestrielle.

quarterfinal [kwɔːtəˈfaɪn(ə)l] n Sp quart m de finale.

quartet(te) [kwɔːˈtet] n Mus quatuor m; (*jazz*) quartette m.

quartz [kwɔːts] n quartz m; – a (*clock* etc) à quartz.

quash [kwɒʃ] vt (*rebellion* etc) réprimer; (*verdict*) Jur casser.

quaver ['kweɪvər] 1 vi chevroter; – n chevrotement m. 2 n Mus croche f.

quay [kiː] n Nau quai m. ◆**quayside** n on the q. sur les quais.

queas/y ['kwiːzɪ] a (-ier, -iest) to feel or be q. avoir mal au cœur, avoir mal au cœur. ◆**-iness** n mal m au cœur.

Quebec [kwɪˈbek] n le Québec.

queen [kwiːn] n reine f; Chess Cards dame f; the q. mother la reine mère.

queer ['kwɪər] a (-er, -est) (*odd*) bizarre; (*dubious*) louche; (*ill*) Fam patraque; – n (*homosexual*) Pej Fam pédé m.

quell [kwel] vt (*revolt* etc) réprimer.

quench [kwentʃ] vt (*fire*) éteindre; **to q. one's thirst** se désaltérer.

querulous ['kweruləs] a (*complaining*) grognon.

query ['kwɪərɪ] n question f; (*doubt*) doute m; – vt mettre en question.

quest [kwest] n quête f (**for** de); **in q. of** en quête de.

question ['kwestʃ(ə)n] n question f; **there's some q. of it** il en est question; **there's no q. of it, it's out of the q.** il n'en est pas question, c'est hors de question; **without q.** incontestable(ment); **in q.** en question, dont il s'agit; – vt interroger (**about** sur); (*doubt*) mettre en question; **to q. whether** douter que (+ sub). ◆**-ing** a (*look* etc) interrogateur; – n interrogation f. ◆**-able** a douteux. ◆**questio'nnaire** n questionnaire m.

queue [kjuː] n (*of people*) queue f; (*of cars*) file f; **to stand in a q., form a q.** faire la queue; – vi **to q. (up)** faire la queue.

quibbl/e ['kwɪb(ə)l] vi ergoter, discuter (**over** sur). ◆**-ing** n ergotage m.

quiche [kiːʃ] n (*tart*) quiche f.

quick [kwɪk] 1 a (-er, -est) rapide; **q. to react** prompt à réagir; **to be q.** faire vite; **to have a q. shave/meal**/etc se raser/manger/etc en vitesse; **to be a q. worker** travailler vite; – *adv* (**-er, -est**) vite; **as q. as a flash** en un clin d'œil. **2 n to cut to the q.** blesser au vif. ◆**q.-'tempered** *a* irascible. ◆**q.-'witted** *a* à l'esprit vif. ◆**quicken** *vt* accélérer; – *vi* s'accélérer. ◆**quickie** *n* (*drink*) *Fam* pot *m* (*pris en vitesse*). ◆**quickly** *adv* vite. ◆**quicksands** *npl* sables *mpl* mouvants.

quid [kwɪd] *n inv Fam* livre *f* (sterling).

quiet [kwaɪət] *a* (**-er, -est**) (*silent, still, peaceful*) tranquille, calme; (*machine, vehicle, temperament*) silencieux; (*gentle*) doux; (*voice*) bas, doux; (*sound*) léger, doux; (*private*) intime; (*colour*) discret; **to be or keep q.** (*shut up*) se taire; (*make no noise*) ne pas faire de bruit; **q.!** silence!; **to keep q. about sth, keep sth q.** ne pas parler de qch; **on the q.** (*secretly*) *Fam* en cachette; – *vt* = **quieten.** ◆**quieten** *vti* **to q. (down)** (*se*) calmer. ◆**quietly** *adv* tranquillement; (*gently, not loudly*) doucement; (*silently*) silencieusement; (*secretly*) en cachette; (*discreetly*) discrètement. ◆**quietness** *n* tranquillité *f*.

quill [kwɪl] *n* (*pen*) plume *f* (d'oie).

quilt [kwɪlt] *n* édredon *m*; (*continental*) **q.** couette *f*; – *vt* (*stitch*) piquer; (*pad*) matelasser.

quintessence [kwɪn'tesəns] *n* quintessence *f*.

quintet(te) [kwɪn'tet] *n* quintette *m*.

quintuplets [kwɪn'tjuːplɪts] (*Fam* **quins** [kwɪnz]) *npl* quintuplés, -ées *mfpl*.

quip [kwɪp] *n* (*remark*) boutade *f*; – *vi* (**-pp-**) faire des boutades; – *vt* dire sur le ton de la boutade.

quirk [kwɜːk] *n* bizarrerie *f*; (*of fate*) caprice *m*.

quit [kwɪt] *vt* (*pt & pp* **quit** *or* **quitted**, *pres p* **quitting**) (*leave*) quitter; **to q. doing** arrêter de faire; – *vi* (*give up*) abandonner; (*resign*) démissionner.

quite [kwaɪt] *adv* (*entirely*) tout à fait; (*really*) vraiment; (*rather*) assez; **q. another matter** une tout autre affaire *or* question; **q. a genius** un véritable génie; **q. good** (*not bad*) pas mal (du tout); **q. (so)!** exactement!; **q. a lot** pas mal (of **de**); **q. a (long) time ago** il y a pas mal de temps.

quits [kwɪts] *a* quitte (**with** envers); **to call it q.** en rester là.

quiver [kwɪvər] *vi* frémir (**with** de); (*of voice*) trembler, frémir; (*of flame*) vaciller, trembler.

quiz [kwɪz] *n* (*pl* **quizzes**) (*riddle*) devinette *f*; (*test*) test *m*; **q. (programme)** *TV Rad* jeu(-concours) *m*; – *vt* (**-zz-**) questionner. ◆**quizmaster** *n TV Rad* animateur, -trice *mf*.

quizzical [kwɪzɪk(ə)l] *a* (*mocking*) narquois; (*perplexed*) perplexe.

quorum [kwɔːrəm] *n* quorum *m*.

quota [kwəʊtə] *n* quota *m*.

quote [kwəʊt] *vt* citer; (*reference number*) *Com* rappeler; (*price*) indiquer; (*price on Stock Exchange*) coter; – *vi* **to q. from** (*author, book*) citer; – *n Fam* = **quotation**; **in quotes** entre guillemets. ◆**quo'tation** *n* citation *f*; (*estimate*) *Com* devis *m*; (*on Stock Exchange*) cote *f*; **q. marks** guillemets *mpl*; **in q. marks** entre guillemets.

quotient [kwəʊʃ(ə)nt] *n* quotient *m*.

R

R, r [ɑːr] *n* R, r *m*.

rabbi [ˈræbaɪ] *n* rabbin *m*; **chief r.** grand rabbin.

rabbit [ˈræbɪt] *n* lapin *m*.

rabble [ˈræb(ə)l] *n* (*crowd*) cohue *f*; **the r.** *Pej* la populace.

rabies [ˈreɪbiːz] *n Med* rage *f.* ◆**rabid** [ˈræbɪd] *a* (*dog*) enragé; (*person*) *Fig* fanatique.

raccoon [rəˈkuːn] *n* (*animal*) raton *m* laveur.

rac/e¹ [reɪs] *n Sp & Fig* course *f*; – *vt*

(*horse*) faire courir; (*engine*) emballer; **to r.** (**against** *or* **with**) **s.o.** faire une course avec qn; – *vi* (*run*) courir; (*of engine*) s'emballer; (*of pulse*) battre à tout rompre. ◆**—ing** *n* courses *fpl*; – *a* (*car, bicycle etc*) de course; **r. driver** coureur *m* automobile. ◆**racecourse** *n* champ *m* de courses. ◆**racegoer** *n* turfiste *m.* ◆**racehorse** *n* cheval *m* de course. ◆**racetrack** *n* piste *f*; (*for horses*) *Am* champ *m* de courses.

race² [reɪs] *n* (*group*) race *f*; – *a* (*prejudice etc*) racial; **r. relations** rapports *mpl* entre

les races. ◆**racial** a racial. ◆**racialism** n
racisme m. ◆**racism** n racisme m.
◆**racist** a & n raciste (mf).

rack [ræk] n **1** (shelf) étagère f; (for bottles
etc) casier m; (for drying dishes) égouttoir
m; (luggage) r. (on bicycle) porte-bagages
m inv; (on bus, train etc) filet m à bagages;
(roof) r. (of car) galerie f. **2** vt to r. one's
brains se creuser la cervelle. **3** n to go to r.
and ruin (of person) aller à la ruine; (of
building) tomber en ruine; (of health) se
délabrer.

racket [ˈrækɪt] n **1** (for tennis etc) raquette f.
2 (din) vacarme m. **3** (crime) racket m;
(scheme) combine f; the drug(s) r. le trafic
m de (la) drogue. ◆**racke'teer** n racket-
teur m. ◆**racke'teering** n racket m.

racoon [rəˈkuːn] n (animal) raton m laveur.

racy [ˈreɪsɪ] a (-ier, -iest) piquant; (suggestive) osé.

radar [ˈreɪdɑːr] n radar m; – a (control, trap
etc) radar inv. **r. operator** radariste mf.

radiant [ˈreɪdɪənt] a (person) rayonnant
(with de), radieux. ◆**radiance** n éclat m,
rayonnement m. ◆**radiantly** adv (to shine)
avec éclat; **r. happy** rayonnant de joie.

radiate [ˈreɪdɪeɪt] vt (emit) dégager; (joy) Fig
rayonner de; – vi (of heat, lines) rayonner
(from de). ◆**radia'tion** n (of heat etc)
rayonnement m (of de); (radioactivity)
Phys radiation f; (rays) irradiation f; r.
sickness mal m des rayons.

radiator [ˈreɪdɪeɪtər] n radiateur m.

radical [ˈrædɪk(ə)l] a radical; – n (person)
Pol radical, -ale mf.

radio [ˈreɪdɪəʊ] n (pl -os) radio f; on the r. à
la radio; **car r.** autoradio m; **r. set** poste m
(de) radio; **r. operator** radio m; **r. wave**
onde f hertzienne; – vt (message) transmettre (par radio) (to à); to r. s.o. appeler
qn par radio. ◆**r.-con'trolled** a radio-
guidé. ◆**radio'active** a radioactif. ◆**ra-
dioac'tivity** n radioactivité f.

radiographer [reɪdɪˈɒɡrəfər] n (technician)
radiologue mf. ◆**radiography** n radiographie f. ◆**radiologist** n (doctor) radiologue mf. ◆**radiology** n radiologie f.

radish [ˈrædɪʃ] n radis m.

radius [ˈreɪdɪəs], pl **-dii** [-dɪaɪ], -diɪ] n (of circle)
rayon m; **within a r. of** dans un rayon de.

RAF [ɑːreɪˈef] n abbr (Royal Air Force) armée
f de l'air (britannique).

raffia [ˈræfɪə] n raphia m.

raffle [ˈræf(ə)l] n tombola f.

raft [rɑːft] n (boat) radeau m.

rafter [ˈrɑːftər] n (beam) chevron m.

rag [ræg] n **1** (old garment) loque f, haillon

m; (for dusting etc) chiffon m; **in rags**
(clothes) en loques; (person) en haillons;
r.-and-bone man chiffonnier m. **2** (newspaper) torchon m. **3** (procession) Univ
carnaval m (au profit d'œuvres de charité).
◆**ragged** [ˈrægɪd] a (clothes) en loques;
(person) en haillons; (edge) irrégulier.
◆**ragman** n (pl -men) chiffonnier m.

ragamuffin [ˈrægəmʌfɪn] n va-nu-pieds m
inv.

rag/e [reɪdʒ] n rage f; (of sea) furie f; **to fly
into a r.** se mettre en rage; **to be all the r.** (of
fashion etc) faire fureur; – vi (be angry)
rager; (of storm, battle) faire rage. ◆**—ing**
a (storm, fever) violent; **a r. fire** un grand
incendie; **in a r. temper** furieux.

raid [reɪd] n Mil raid m; (by police) descente
f; (by thieves) hold-up m; **air r.** raid m
aérien, attaque f aérienne; – vt faire un
raid or une descente or un hold-up dans;
Av attaquer; (larder, fridge etc) Fam dévaliser. ◆**raider** n (criminal) malfaiteur m;
pl Mil commando m.

rail [reɪl] n **1** (for train) rail m; **by r.** (to
travel) par le train; (to send) par chemin de
fer; **to go off the rails** (of train) dérailler; –
a ferroviaire; (strike) des cheminots. **2** n
(rod on balcony) balustrade f; (on stairs, for
spotlight) rampe f; (for curtain) tringle f;
(towel) r. porte-serviettes m inv. ◆**railing**
n (of balcony) balustrade f; pl (fence) grille
f. ◆**railroad** n Am = railway; **r. track** voie
f ferrée. ◆**railway** n (system) chemin de
fer; (track) voie f ferrée; – a (ticket) de
chemin de fer; (network) ferroviaire; **r. line**
(route) ligne f de chemin de fer; (track) voie
f ferrée; **r. station** gare f. ◆**railwayman** n
(pl -men) cheminot m.

rain [reɪn] n pluie f; **in the r.** sous la pluie; **I'll
give you a r. check** (for invitation) Am Fam
j'accepterai volontiers à une date ultérieure; – vi il pleuvoir; **to r. (down)** (of blows,
bullets) pleuvoir; **it's raining** il pleut.
◆**rainbow** n arc-en-ciel m. ◆**raincoat** n
imper(méable) m. ◆**raindrop** n goutte f
de pluie. ◆**rainfall** n (shower) chute f de
pluie; (amount) précipitations fpl. ◆**rainstorm** n trombe f d'eau. ◆**rainwater** n eau
f de pluie. ◆**rainy** a (-ier, -iest) pluvieux;
the r. season la saison des pluies.

raise [reɪz] vt (lift) lever; (sth heavy)
(sou)lever; (child, animal, voice, statue)
élever; (crops) cultiver; (salary, price)
augmenter, relever; (temperature) faire
monter; (question, protest) soulever; (taxes,
blockade) lever; **to r. a smile/a laugh** (in
others) faire sourire/rire; **to r. s.o.'s hopes**

faire naître les espérances de qn; **to r. money** réunir des fonds; – *n* (*pay rise*) *Am* augmentation *f* (de salaire).

raisin ['reɪz(ə)n] *n* raison *m* sec.

rake [reɪk] *n* râteau *m*; – *vt* (*garden*) ratisser; (*search*) fouiller dans; **to r. (up)** (*leaves*) ramasser (avec un râteau); **to r. in** (*money*) *Fam* ramasser à la pelle; **to r. up** (*the past*) remuer. ◆**r.-off** *n Fam* pot-de-vin *m*, ristourne *f*.

rally ['rælɪ] *vt* (*unite, win over*) rallier (**to** à); (*one's strength*) *Fig* reprendre; – *vi* se rallier (**to** à); (*recover*) se remettre (**from** de); **to r. round** (*help*) venir en aide (**s.o.** à qn); – *n Mil* ralliement *m*; *Pol* rassemblement *m*; *Sp Aut* rallye *m*.

ram [ræm] **1** *n* (*animal*) bélier *m*. **2** *vt* (-mm-) (*ship*) heurter; (*vehicle*) emboutir; **to r. sth into** (*thrust*) enfoncer qch dans.

rambl/e ['ræmb(ə)l] **1** *n* (*hike*) randonnée *f*; – *vi* faire une randonnée or des randonnées. **2** *vi* **to r. on** (*talk*) *Pej* discourir. ◆**-ing** **1** *a* (*house*) construit sans plan; (*spread out*) vaste; (*rose etc*) grimpant. **2** *a* (*speech*) décousu; – *npl* divagations *fpl*. ◆**-er** *n* promeneur, -euse *mf*

ramification [ræmɪfɪˈkeɪʃ(ə)n] *n* ramification *f*.

ramp [ræmp] *n* (*slope*) rampe *f*; (*in garage*) *Tech* pont *m* (de graissage); *Av* passerelle *f*; **'r.'** *Aut* 'dénivellation'.

rampage ['ræmpeɪdʒ] *n* **to go on the r.** (*of crowd*) se déchaîner; (*loot*) se livrer au pillage.

rampant ['ræmpənt] *a* **to be r.** (*of crime, disease etc*) sévir.

rampart ['ræmpɑːt] *n* rempart *m*.

ramshackle ['ræmʃæk(ə)l] *a* délabré.

ran [ræn] *see* **run**.

ranch [rɑːntʃ] *n Am* ranch *m*; **r. house** maison *f* genre bungalow (sur sous-sol).

rancid ['rænsɪd] *a* rance.

rancour ['ræŋkər] *n* rancœur *f*.

random ['rændəm] *n* **at r.** au hasard; – *a* (*choice*) fait au hasard; (*sample*) prélevé au hasard; (*pattern*) irrégulier.

randy ['rændɪ] *a* (-ier, -iest) *Fam* sensuel, lascif.

rang [ræŋ] *see* **ring²**.

range [reɪndʒ] **1** *n* (*of gun, voice etc*) portée *f*; (*of aircraft, ship*) rayon *m* d'action; (*series*) gamme *f*; (*choice*) choix *m*; (*of prices*) éventail *m*; (*of voice*) *Mus* étendue *f*; (*of temperature*) variations *fpl*; (*sphere*) *Fig* champ *m*, étendue *f*; – *vi* (*vary*) varier; (*extend*) s'étendre; (*roam*) errer, rôder. **2** *n* (*of mountains*) chaîne *f*; (*grassland*) *Am*

prairie *f*. **3** *n* (*stove*) *Am* cuisinière *f*. **4** *n* (**shooting** or **rifle**) **r.** (*at funfair*) stand *m* de tir; (*outdoors*) champ *m* de tir.

ranger ['reɪndʒər] *n* (*forest*) **r.** *Am* garde *m* forestier.

rank [ræŋk] **1** *n* (*position, class*) rang *m*; (*grade*) *Mil* grade *m*, rang *m*; **the r. and file** (*workers etc*) *Pol* la base; **the ranks** (*men in army, numbers*) les rangs *mpl* (**of** de); **taxi r.** station *f* de taxi; – *vt* **to r. among** compter parmi. **2** *a* (-er, -est) (*smell*) fétide; (*vegetation*) luxuriant; *Fig* absolu.

rankle ['ræŋk(ə)l] *vi* **it rankles (with me)** je l'ai sur le cœur.

ransack ['rænsæk] *vt* (*search*) fouiller; (*plunder*) saccager.

ransom ['rænsəm] *n* rançon *f*; **to hold to r.** rançonner; – *vt* (*redeem*) racheter.

rant [rænt] *vi* **to r. (and rave)** tempêter (**at** contre).

rap [ræp] *n* petit coup *m* sec; – *vi* (-pp-) frapper (**at** à); – *vt* **to r. s.o. over the knuckles** taper sur les doigts de qn.

rapacious [rəˈpeɪʃəs] *a* (*greedy*) rapace.

rape [reɪp] *vt* violer; – *n* viol *m*. ◆**rapist** *n* violeur *m*.

rapid ['ræpɪd] **1** *a* rapide. **2** *n* & *npl* (*of river*) rapide(s) *m(pl)*. ◆**ra'pidity** *n* rapidité *f*. ◆**rapidly** *adv* rapidement.

rapport [ræˈpɔːr] *n* (*understanding*) rapport *m*.

rapt [ræpt] *a* (*attention*) profond.

rapture ['ræptʃər] *n* extase *f*; **to go into raptures** s'extasier (**about** sur). ◆**rapturous** *a* (*welcome, applause*) enthousiaste.

rare [reər] *a* (-er, -est) rare; (*meat*) *Culin* saignant; (*first-rate*) *Fam* fameux; **it's r. for her to do it** il est rare qu'elle le fasse. ◆**-ly** *adv* rarement. ◆**-ness** *n* rareté *f*. ◆**rarity** *n* (*quality, object*) rareté *f*.

rarefied ['reərɪfaɪd] *a* raréfié.

raring ['reərɪŋ] *a* **r. to start/etc** impatient de commencer/*etc*.

rascal ['rɑːsk(ə)l] *n* coquin, -ine *mf*. ◆**rascally** *a* (*child etc*) coquin; (*habit, trick etc*) de coquin.

rash [ræʃ] **1** *n Med* éruption *f*. **2** *a* (-er, -est) irréfléchi. ◆**-ly** *adv* sans réfléchir. ◆**-ness** *n* irréflexion *f*.

rasher ['ræʃər] *n* tranche *f* de lard.

rasp [rɑːsp] *n* (*file*) râpe *f*.

raspberry ['rɑːzbərɪ] *n* (*fruit*) framboise *f*; (*bush*) framboisier *m*.

rasping ['rɑːspɪŋ] *a* (*voice*) âpre.

rat [ræt] **1** *n* rat *m*; **r. poison** mort-aux-rats *f*; **the r. race** *Fig* la course au bifteck, la jungle. **2** *vi* (-tt-) **to r. on** (*desert*) lâcher;

(denounce) cafarder sur; (promise etc) manquer à.

rate [reɪt] 1 n (percentage, level) taux m; (speed) vitesse f; (price) tarif m; pl (on housing) impôts mpl locaux; insurance rates primes fpl d'assurance; r. of flow débit m; postage or postal r. tarif m postal; at the r. of à une vitesse de; (amount) à raison de; at this r. (slow speed) à ce train-là; at any r. en tout cas; the success r. (chances) les chances fpl de succès; (candidates) le pourcentage de reçus. 2 vt (evaluate) évaluer; (regard) considérer (as comme); (deserve) mériter; to r. highly apprécier (beaucoup); to be highly rated être très apprécié. ◆rateable a r. value valeur f locative nette. ◆ratepayer n contribuable mf.

rather ['rɑːðər] adv (preferably, fairly) plutôt; I'd r. stay j'aimerais mieux or je préférerais rester (than que); I'd r. you came je préférerais que vous veniez; r. than leave/etc plutôt que de partir/etc; r. more tired/etc un peu plus fatigué/etc (than que); it's nice c'est bien.

ratify ['rætɪfaɪ] vt ratifier. ◆ratifi'cation n ratification f.

rating ['reɪtɪŋ] n (classification) classement m; (wage etc level) indice m; credit r. Fin réputation f de solvabilité; the ratings TV l'indice m d'écoute.

ratio ['reɪʃɪəʊ] n (pl -os) proportion f.

ration ['ræʃ(ə)n, Am 'reɪʃ(ə)n] n ration f; pl (food) vivres mpl; − vt rationner; I was rationed to .. ma ration était ....

rational ['ræʃən(ə)l] a (method, thought etc) rationnel; (person) raisonnable. ◆rationalize vt (organize) rationaliser; (explain) justifier. ◆rationally adv raisonnablement.

rattle ['ræt(ə)l] 1 n (baby's toy) hochet m; (of sports fan) crécelle f. 2 n petit bruit m (sec); cliquetis m; crépitement m; − vi faire du bruit; (of bottles) cliqueter; (of gunfire) crépiter; (of window) trembler; − vt (shake) agiter; (window) faire trembler; (keys) faire cliqueter. 3 vt to r. s.o. (make nervous) Fam ébranler qn; to r. off (poem etc) Fam débiter (à toute vitesse). ◆rattlesnake n serpent m à sonnette.

ratty ['rætɪ] a (-ier, -iest) 1 (shabby) Am Fam minable. 2 to get r. (annoyed) Fam prendre la mouche.

raucous ['rɔːkəs] a rauque.

raunchy ['rɔːntʃɪ] a (-ier, -iest) (joke etc) Am Fam grivois.

ravage ['rævɪdʒ] vt ravager; − npl ravages mpl.

rav/e [reɪv] vi (talk nonsense) divaguer; (rage) tempêter (at contre); to r. about (enthuse) ne pas se lasser d'éloges sur; − a r. review Fam critique f dithyrambique. ◆−ing a to be r. mad être fou furieux; − npl (wild talk) divagations fpl.

raven ['reɪv(ə)n] n corbeau m.

ravenous ['rævənəs] a vorace; I'm r. Fam j'ai une faim de loup.

ravine [rə'viːn] n ravin m.

ravioli [rævɪ'əʊlɪ] n ravioli mpl.

ravish ['rævɪʃ] vt (rape) Lit violenter. ◆−ing a (beautiful) ravissant. ◆−ingly adv r. beautiful d'une beauté ravissante.

raw [rɔː] a (-er, -est) (vegetable etc) cru; (sugar) brut; (immature) inexpérimenté; (wound) à vif; (skin) écorché; (weather) rigoureux; r. edge bord m coupé; r. material matière f première; to get a r. deal Fam être mal traité.

Rawlplug® ['rɔːlplʌg] n cheville f, tampon m.

ray [reɪ] n (of light, sun etc) & Phys rayon m; (of hope) Fig lueur f.

raze [reɪz] vt to r. (to the ground) (destroy) raser.

razor ['reɪzər] n rasoir m.

re [riː] prep Com en référence à.

re- [riː] pref ré-, re-, r-.

reach [riːtʃ] vt (place, aim etc) atteindre, arriver à; (gain access to) accéder à; (of letter) parvenir à (qn); (contact) joindre (qn); to r. s.o. (over) sth (hand over) passer qch à qn; to r. out (one's arm) (é)tendre; − vi (extend) s'étendre (to à); (of voice) porter; to r. (out) (é)tendre le bras (for pour prendre); − n portée f; Boxing allonge f; within r. of à portée de; (near) à proximité de; within easy r. (object) à portée de main; (shops) facilement accessible.

react [rɪ'ækt] vi réagir. ◆reaction n réaction f. ◆reactionary a & n réactionnaire (mf).

reactor [rɪ'æktər] n réacteur m.

read [riːd] vt (pt & pp read [red]) lire; (study) Univ faire des études de; (meter) relever; (of instrument) indiquer; to r. back or over relire; to r. out lire (à haute voix); to r. through (skim) parcourir; to r. up (on) (study) étudier; − vi lire; to r. well (of degree) Univ préparer; − n to have a r. Fam faire un peu de lecture; this book's a

good r. *Fam* ce livre est agréable à lire. ◆**-ing** n lecture f; (of meter) relevé m; (by instrument) indication f; (variant) variante f; – a (room) de lecture; **r. matter** choses fpl à lire; **r. lamp** lampe f de bureau or de chevet. ◆**-able** a lisible. ◆**-er** n lecteur, -trice mf; (book) livre m de lecture. ◆**readership** n lecteurs mpl, public m.

readjust [riːəˈdʒʌst] vt (instrument) régler; (salary) réajuster; – vi se réadapter (**to** à). ◆**-ment** n réglage m; réajustement m; réadaptation f.

readily [ˈredɪlɪ] adv (willingly) volontiers; (easily) facilement. ◆**readiness** n empressement m (**to do** à faire); **in r. for** prêt pour.

ready [ˈredɪ] a (-ier, -iest) prêt (**to do** à faire, **for sth** à or pour qch); (quick) prompt (**to do** à faire); **to get sth r.** préparer qch; **to get r.** se préparer (**for sth** à qch, **to do** à faire); **r. cash, r. money** argent m liquide; – n **at the r.** tout prêt. ◆**r.-'cooked** a tout cuit. ◆**r.-'made** a tout fait; **r.-made clothes** prêt-à-porter m inv.

real [rɪəl] a vrai, véritable; (life, world etc) réel; **it's the r. thing** *Fam* c'est du vrai de vrai; **r. estate** Am immobilier m; – adv *Fam* vraiment; **r. stupid** vraiment bête; – n **for r.** *Fam* pour de vrai. ◆**realism** n réalisme m. ◆**realist** n réaliste mf. ◆**rea-'listic** a réaliste. ◆**rea'listically** adv avec réalisme.

reality [rɪˈælətɪ] n réalité f; **in r.** en réalité.

realize [ˈrɪəlaɪz] vt **1** (know) se rendre compte de, réaliser; (understand) comprendre (**that** que); – vi **to r. that** (know) se rendre compte que. **2** (carry out, convert into cash) réaliser; (price) atteindre. ◆**reali'zation** n **1** (prise f de) conscience f. **2** (of aim, assets) réalisation f.

really [ˈrɪəlɪ] adv vraiment; **is it r. true?** est-ce bien vrai?

realm [relm] n (kingdom) royaume m; (of dreams etc) Fig monde m.

realtor [ˈrɪəltər] n Am agent m immobilier.

reap [riːp] vt (field, crop) moissonner; Fig récolter.

reappear [riːəˈpɪər] vi réapparaître.

reappraisal [riːəˈpreɪz(ə)l] n réévaluation f.

rear [rɪər] **1** n (back part) arrière m; (of column) queue f; **in** or **at the r.** à l'arrière (of de); **from the r.** par derrière; – a arrière inv, de derrière; **r.-view mirror** rétroviseur m. **2** vt (family, animals etc) élever; (one's head) relever. **3** vi **to r. (up)** (of horse) se cabrer. ◆**rearguard** n arrière-garde f.

rearrange [riːəˈreɪndʒ] vt réarranger.

reason [ˈriːz(ə)n] n (cause, sense) raison f; **the r. for/why** or **that...** la raison de/pour laquelle...; **for no r.** sans raison; **that stands to r.** cela va sans dire, c'est logique; **within r.** avec modération; **to do everything within r.** to... faire tout ce qu'il est raisonnable de faire pour...; **to have every r. to believe/**etc avoir tout lieu de croire/etc; – vi raisonner; **to r. with s.o.** raisonner qn; – vt **to r. that** calculer que. ◆**-ing** n raisonnement m. ◆**-able** a raisonnable. ◆**-ably** adv raisonnablement; (fairly, rather) assez; **r. fit** en assez bonne forme.

reassur/e [riːəˈʃʊər] vt rassurer. ◆**-ing** a rassurant. ◆**reassurance** n réconfort m.

reawaken [riːəˈweɪk(ə)n] vt (interest etc) réveiller. ◆**-ing** n réveil m.

rebate [ˈriːbeɪt] n (discount on purchase) ristourne f; (refund) remboursement m (partiel).

rebel [ˈreb(ə)l] a & n rebelle (mf); – [rɪˈbel] vi (-ll-) se rebeller (**against** contre). ◆**re'bellion** n rébellion f. ◆**re'bellious** a rebelle.

rebirth [ˈriːbɜːθ] n renaissance f.

rebound [rɪˈbaʊnd] vi (of ball) rebondir; (of stone) ricocher; (of lies, action etc) Fig retomber (**on** sur); – [ˈriːbaʊnd] n rebond m; ricochet m; **on the r.** (to marry s.o. etc) par dépit.

rebuff [rɪˈbʌf] vt repousser; – n rebuffade f.

rebuild [riːˈbɪld] vt (pt & pp rebuilt) reconstruire.

rebuke [rɪˈbjuːk] vt réprimander; – n réprimande f.

rebuttal [rɪˈbʌt(ə)l] n réfutation f.

recalcitrant [rɪˈkælsɪtrənt] a récalcitrant.

recall [rɪˈkɔːl] vt (call back) rappeler; (remember) se rappeler (**that** que, **doing** avoir fait); **to r. sth to s.o.** rappeler qch à qn; – n rappel m; **beyond r.** irrévocable.

recant [rɪˈkænt] vi se rétracter.

recap [riːˈkæp] vti (-pp-) récapituler; – n récapitulation f. ◆**reca'pitulate** vti récapituler. ◆**recapitu'lation** n récapitulation f.

recapture [riːˈkæptʃər] vt (prisoner etc) reprendre; (rediscover) retrouver; (recreate) recréer; – n (of prisoner) arrestation f.

rece/de [rɪˈsiːd] vi (into the distance) s'éloigner; (of floods) baisser. ◆**-ing** a (forehead) fuyant; **his hair(line)** r. son front se dégarnit.

receipt [rɪˈsiːt] n (for payment) reçu m (**for** de); (for letter, parcel) récépissé m, accusé *m* de réception; *pl* (*takings*) recettes *fpl*; **to acknowledge r.** accuser réception (**of** de); **on r.** dès réception de.

receiv/e [rɪ'siːv] *vt* recevoir; (*stolen goods*) *Jur* receler. **◆—ing** *n Jur* recel *m*. **◆—er** *n Tel* combiné *m*; *Rad* récepteur *m*; (*of stolen goods*) *Jur* receleur, -euse *mf*; **to pick up** *or* **lift the r.** *Tel* décrocher.

recent ['riːsənt] *a* récent; **in r. months** ces mois-ci. **◆—ly** *adv* récemment; **as r. as** pas plus tard que.

receptacle [rɪ'septək(ə)l] *n* récipient *m*.

reception [rɪ'sep(ə)n] *n* (*receiving, welcome, party etc*) réception *f*; **r. desk** réception *f*; **r. room** salle *f* de séjour. **◆receptionist** *n* réceptionniste *mf*. **◆receptive** *a* réceptif (**to an idea/etc** à une idée/*etc*); **r. to s.o.** compréhensif envers qn.

recess [rɪ'ses, 'riːses] *n* **1** (*holiday*) vacances *fpl*; *Sch Am* récréation *f*. **2** (*alcove*) renfoncement *m*; (*nook*) *& Fig* recoin *m*.

recession [rɪ'se(ə)n] *n Econ* récession *f*.

recharge [riː'tʃɑːdʒ] *vt* (*battery*) recharger.

recipe ['resɪpɪ] *n Culin & Fig* recette *f* (**for** de).

recipient [rɪ'sɪpɪənt] *n* (*of award, honour*) récipiendaire *m*.

reciprocal [rɪ'sɪprək(ə)l] *a* réciproque. **◆reciprocate** *vt* (*compliment*) retourner; (*gesture*) faire à son tour; – *vi* (*do the same*) en faire autant.

recital [rɪ'saɪt(ə)l] *n Mus* récital *m*.

recite [rɪ'saɪt] *vt* (*poem etc*) réciter; (*list*) énumérer. **◆reci'tation** *n* récitation *f*.

reckless ['rekləs] *a* (*rash*) imprudent. **◆—ly** *adv* imprudemment.

reckon ['rek(ə)n] *vt* (*count*) compter; (*calculate*) calculer; (*consider*) considérer; (*think*) *Fam* penser (**that** que); – *vi* compter; calculer; **to r. with** (*take into account*) compter avec; (*deal with*) avoir affaire à; **to r. on/without** compter sur/sans; **to r. on doing** *Fam* compter *or* penser faire. **◆—ing** *n* calcul(s) *m(pl)*.

reclaim [rɪ'kleɪm] *vt* **1** (*land*) mettre en valeur; (*from sea*) assécher. **2** (*ask for back*) réclamer; (*luggage at airport*) récupérer.

reclin/e [rɪ'klaɪn] *vi* (*of person*) être allongé; (*of head*) être appuyé; – *vt* (*head*) appuyer (**on** sur). **◆—ing** *a* (*seat*) à dossier inclinable *or* réglable.

recluse [rɪ'kluːs] *n* reclus, -use *mf*.

recognize ['rekəgnaɪz] *vt* reconnaître (**by** à, **that** que). **◆recog'nition** *n* reconnaissance *f*; **to change beyond** *or* **out of all r.** devenir méconnaissable; **to gain r.** être

reconnu. **◆recognizable** *a* reconnaissable.

recoil [rɪ'kɔɪl] *vi* reculer (**from doing** à l'idée de faire).

recollect [rekə'lekt] *vt* se souvenir de; **to r. that** se souvenir que; – *vi* se souvenir. **◆recollection** *n* souvenir *m*.

recommend [rekə'mend] *vt* (*praise, support, advise*) recommander (**to** à, **for** pour); **to r. s.o. to do** recommander à qn de faire. **◆recommen'dation** *n* recommandation *f*.

recompense ['rekəmpens] *vt* (*reward*) récompenser; – *n* récompense *f*.

reconcile ['rekənsaɪl] *vt* (*person*) réconcilier (**with, to** avec); (*opinion*) concilier (**with** avec); **to r. oneself to sth** se résigner à qch. **◆reconcili'ation** *n* réconciliation *f*.

reconditioned [riːkən'dɪʃ(ə)nd] *a* (*engine*) refait (à neuf).

reconnaissance [rɪ'kɒnɪsəns] *n Mil* reconnaissance *f*. **◆reconnoitre** [rekə'nɔɪtər] *vt Mil* reconnaître.

reconsider [riːkən'sɪdər] *vt* reconsidérer; – *vi* revenir sur sa décision.

reconstruct [riːkən'strʌkt] *vt* (*crime*) reconstituer.

record 1 ['rekɔːd] *n* (*disc*) disque *m*; **r. library** discothèque *f*; **r. player** électrophone *m*. **2** *n Sp & Fig* record *m*; – *a* (*attendance, time etc*) record *inv*. **3** *n* (*report*) rapport *m*; (*register*) registre *m*; (*recording on tape etc*) enregistrement *m*; (*mention*) mention *f*; (*note*) note *f*; (*background*) antécédents *mpl*; (*case history*) dossier *m*; (*police*) **r.** casier *m* judiciaire; (*public*) **records** archives *fpl*; **to make** *or* **keep a r. of** noter; **on r.** (*fact, event*) attesté; **off the r.** à titre confidentiel; **their safety is on r.** leurs résultats *mpl* en matière de sécurité. **4** [rɪ'kɔːd] *vt* (*on tape etc, in register etc*) enregistrer; (*in diary*) noter; (*relate*) rapporter (**that** que); – *vi* (*on tape etc*) enregistrer. **◆—ed** *a* enregistré; (*prerecorded*) *TV* en différé; (*fact*) attesté; **letter sent (by) r. delivery** = lettre *f* avec avis de réception. **◆—ing** *n* enregistrement *m*. **◆—er** *n Mus* flûte *f* à bec; (*tape*) **r.** magnétophone *m*.

recount 1 [rɪ'kaʊnt] *vt* (*relate*) raconter. **2** ['riːkaʊnt] *n Pol* nouveau dépouillement *m* du scrutin.

recoup [rɪ'kuːp] *vt* (*loss*) récupérer.

recourse ['riːkɔːs] *n* recours *m*; **to have r. to** avoir recours à.

recover [rɪ'kʌvər] **1** *vt* (*get back*) retrouver, récupérer. **2** *vi* (*from shock etc*) se remettre; (*get better*) *Med* se remettre (**from** de); (*of* *economy, country*) se redresser; (*of currency*) remonter. ◆**recovery** *n 1 Econ* redressement *m.* **2 the r. of sth** (*getting back*) la récupération de qch.

recreate [riːkriˈeɪt] *vt* recréer.

recreation [rekriˈeɪʃ(ə)n] *n* récréation *f.* ◆**recreational** (*a activity etc*) de loisir.

recrimination [rikrimiˈneɪʃ(ə)n] *n Jur* contre-accusation *f.*

recruit [riˈkruːt] *n* recrue *f;* – *vt* recruter; **to r. s.o. to do** (*persuade*) *Fig* embaucher qn pour faire. ◆**—ment** *n* recrutement *m.*

rectangle [ˈrektæŋg(ə)l] *n* rectangle *m.* ◆**rec'tangular** *a* rectangulaire.

rectify [ˈrektɪfaɪ] *vt* rectifier. ◆**rectifi'cation** *n* rectification *f.*

rector [ˈrektər] *n Rel* curé *m; Univ* président *m.*

recuperate [riˈkuːpəreɪt] *vi* récupérer (ses forces); – *vt* récupérer.

recur [riˈkɜːr] *vi* (**-rr-**) (*of theme*) revenir; (*of event*) se reproduire; (*of illness*) réapparaître. ◆**recurrence** [riˈkʌrəns] *n* répétition *f;* (*of illness*) réapparition *f.* ◆**recurrent** *a* fréquent.

recycle [riːˈsaɪk(ə)l] *vt* (*material*) recycler.

red [red] *a* (**redder, reddest**) rouge; (*hair*) roux; **to turn** *or* **go r. rougir; r. light** (*traffic light*) feu *m* rouge; **R. Cross** Croix-Rouge *f;* **R. Indian** Peau-Rouge *mf;* – *n* (*colour*) rouge *m;* **R.** (*person*) *Pol* rouge *mf;* **in the r.** (*firm, account*) en déficit; (*person*) à découvert. ◆**r.-'faced** *a Fig* rouge de confusion. ◆**r.-'handed** *adv* **caught r.-handed** pris en flagrant délit. ◆**r.-'hot** *a* brûlant. ◆**redden** *vti* rougir. ◆**reddish** *a* rougeâtre; (*hair*) carotte. ◆**redness** *n* rougeur *f;* (*of hair*) rousseur *f.*

redcurrant [redˈkʌrənt] *n* groseille *f.*

redecorate [riːˈdekəreɪt] *vt* (*room etc*) refaire; – *vi* refaire la peinture et les papiers.

redeem [riˈdiːm] *vt* (*restore to favour, free, pay off*) racheter; (*convert into cash*) réaliser; **redeeming feature** point *m* favorable. ◆**redemption** *n* rachat *m;* réalisation *f; Rel* rédemption *f.*

redeploy [riːdɪˈplɔɪ] *vt* (*staff*) réorganiser; (*troops*) redéployer.

redhead [ˈredhed] *n* roux *m,* rousse *f.*

redirect [riːdaɪˈrekt] *vt* (*mail*) faire suivre.

redo [riːˈduː] *vt* (*pt* **redid,** *pp* **redone**) refaire.

redress [riˈdres] *n* **to seek r.** demander réparation (**for**).

reduce [riˈdjuːs] *vt* réduire (**to** à, **by** de); (*temperature*) faire baisser; **at a reduced**

price (*ticket*) à prix réduit; (*goods*) au rabais. ◆**reduction** *n* réduction *f;* (*of temperature*) baisse *f;* (*discount*) rabais *m.*

redundant [riˈdʌndənt] *a* (*not needed*) superflu, de trop; **to make r.** (*workers*) mettre en chômage, licencier. ◆**redundancy** *n* (*of workers*) licenciement *m; r.* **pay(ment)** indemnité *f* de licenciement.

re-echo [riːˈekəʊ] *vi* résonner; – *vt* (*sound*) répercuter; *Fig* répéter.

reed [riːd] *n 1 Bot* roseau *m.* **2** *Mus* anche *f;* – *a* (*instrument*) à anche.

re-educate [riːˈedjukeɪt] *vt* (*criminal, limb*) rééduquer.

reef [riːf] *n* récif *m,* écueil *m.*

reek [riːk] *vi* puer; **to r. of** (*smell*) & *Fig* puer; – *n* puanteur *f.*

reel [riːl] *n 1* (*of thread, film*) bobine *f;* (*film itself*) *Cin* bande *f;* (*of hose*) dévidoir *m;* (*for fishing line*) moulinet *m.* **2** *vi* (*stagger*) chanceler; (*of mind*) chavirer; (*of head*) tourner. **3** *vt* **to r. off** (*rattle off*) débiter (à toute vitesse).

re-elect [riːiˈlekt] *vt* réélire.

re-entry [riːˈentrɪ] *n* (*of spacecraft*) rentrée *f.*

re-establish [riːɪˈstæblɪʃ] *vt* rétablir.

ref [ref] *n Sp Fam* arbitre *m.*

refectory [riˈfektərɪ] *n* réfectoire *m.*

refer [riˈfɜːr] *vi* (**-rr-**) **to r. to** (*allude to*) faire allusion à; (*speak of*) parler de; (*apply to*) s'appliquer à; (*consult*) se reporter à; – *vt* **to r. sth to** (*submit*) soumettre qch à; **to r. s.o. to** (*office, article etc*) renvoyer qn à. ◆**refe'ree** *n Sp* arbitre *m;* (*for job etc*) répondant, -ante *mf;* – *vt Sp* arbitrer. ◆**'reference** *n* (*in book, recommendation*) référence *f;* (*allusion*) allusion *f* (**to** à); (*mention*) mention *f* (**to** de); (*connection*) rapport *m* (**to** avec); **in** *or* **with r. to** concernant; *Com* suite à; **terms of r.** (*of person, investigating body*) compétence *f;* (*of law*) étendue *f;* **r. book** livre *m* de référence.

referendum [refəˈrendəm] *n* référendum *m.*

refill [riːˈfɪl] *vt* remplir (à nouveau); (*lighter, pen etc*) recharger; – [ˈriːfɪl] *n* recharge *f;* **a r.** (*drink*) *Fam* un autre verre.

refine [riˈfaɪn] *vt* (*oil, sugar, manners*) raffiner; (*metal, ore*) affiner; (*technique, machine*) perfectionner; – *vi* **to r. upon** raffiner sur. ◆**refinement** *n* (*of person*) raffinement *m;* (*of sugar, oil*) raffinage *m;* (*of technique*) perfectionnement *m; pl* (*improvements*) *Tech* améliorations *fpl.* ◆**refinery** *n* raffinerie *f.*

refit [riːˈfɪt] *vt* (**-tt-**) (*ship*) remettre en état.

reflate [riːˈfleɪt] *vt* (*economy*) relancer.

reflect [rɪ'flekt] **1** vt (*light*) & Fig refléter; (*of mirror*) réfléchir, refléter; **to r. sth on s.o.** (*credit, honour*) faire rejaillir qch sur qn; — vi **to r. on s.o., be reflected on s.o.** (*rebound*) rejaillir sur qn. **2** vi (*think*) réfléchir (**on** à); — vt **to r. that** penser que. ◆**reflection** n **1** (*thought, criticism*) réflexion (**on** sur); **on r.** tout bien réfléchi. **2** (*image*) & Fig reflet m; (*reflecting*) réflexion f (**of** de). ◆**reflector** n réflecteur m. ◆**reflexion** n = **reflection**. ◆**reflexive** a (verb) Gram réfléchi.

reflex ['ri:fleks] n & a réflexe (m); **r. action** réflexe m.

refloat [ri:'fləʊt] vt (*ship*) & Com renflouer.

reform [rɪ'fɔːm] n réforme f; — vt réformer; (*person, conduct*) corriger; — vi (*of person*) se réformer. ◆**-er** n réformateur, -trice mf.

refrain [rɪ'freɪn] **1** vi s'abstenir (**from doing** de faire). **2** n Mus & Fig refrain m.

refresh [rɪ'freʃ] vt (*of bath, drink*) rafraîchir; (*of sleep, rest*) délasser; **to r. oneself** (*drink*) se rafraîchir; **to r. one's memory** se rafraîchir la mémoire. ◆**-ing** a rafraîchissant; (*sleep*) réparateur; (*pleasant*) agréable; (*original*) nouveau. ◆**-er** a (course) de recyclage. ◆**-ments** npl (*drinks*) rafraîchissements mpl; (*snacks*) collation f.

refrigerate [rɪ'frɪdʒəreɪt] vt réfrigérer. ◆**refrigerator** n réfrigérateur m.

refuel [ri:'fjʊəl] vi (**-ll-**, Am **-l-**) Av se ravitailler; — vt Av ravitailler.

refuge ['refju:dʒ] n refuge m; **to take r.** se réfugier (**in** dans). ◆**refu'gee** n réfugié, -ée mf.

refund [rɪ'fʌnd] vt rembourser; — ['ri:fʌnd] n remboursement m.

refurbish [ri:'fɜːbɪʃ] vt remettre à neuf.

refuse¹ [rɪ'fju:z] vt refuser (**s.o. sth** qch à qn, **to do** de faire); — vi refuser. ◆**refusal** n refus m.

refuse² ['refju:s] n (*rubbish*) ordures fpl, détritus m; (*waste materials*) déchets mpl; **r. collector** éboueur m; **r. dump** dépôt m d'ordures.

refute [rɪ'fju:t] vt réfuter.

regain [rɪ'geɪn] vt (*favour, lost ground*) regagner; (*strength*) récupérer, retrouver, reprendre; (*health, sight*) retrouver; (*consciousness*) reprendre.

regal ['ri:g(ə)l] a royal, majestueux.

regalia [rɪ'geɪlɪə] npl insignes mpl (royaux).

regard [rɪ'gɑːd] vt (*consider*) considérer, regarder; (*concern*) regarder; **as regards** en ce qui concerne; — n considération f (**for** pour); **to have (a) great r. for** avoir de l'estime pour; **without r. to** sans égard

pour; **with r. to** en ce qui concerne; **to give** or **send one's regards to** (*greetings*) faire ses hommages à. ◆**-ing** prep en ce qui concerne. ◆**-less 1** a r. of sans tenir compte de. **2** adv (all the same) Fam quand même.

regatta [rɪ'gætə] n régates fpl.

regency ['ri:dʒənsɪ] n régence f.

regenerate [rɪ'dʒenəreɪt] vt régénérer.

reggae ['regeɪ] n (*music*) reggae m; — a (*group etc*) reggae inv.

régime [reɪ'ʒi:m] n Pol régime m.

regiment ['redʒɪmənt] n régiment m. ◆**regi'mental** a régimentaire, du régiment. ◆**regimen'tation** n discipline f excessive.

region ['ri:dʒ(ə)n] n région f; **in the r. of** (*about*) Fig environ; **in the r. of £500** dans les 500 livres. ◆**regional** a régional.

register ['redʒɪstər] n registre m; Sch cahier m d'appel; **electoral r.** liste f électorale; — vt (*record, note*) enregistrer; (*birth, death*) déclarer; (*vehicle*) immatriculer; (*express*) exprimer; (*indicate*) indiquer; (*letter*) recommander; (*realize*) Fam réaliser; — vi (*enrol*) s'inscrire; (*in hotel*) signer le registre; **it hasn't registered (with me)** Fam je n'ai pas encore réalisé ça. ◆**-ed** a (*member*) inscrit; (*letter*) recommandé; **r. trademark** marque f déposée. ◆**regi'strar** n officier m de l'état civil; Univ secrétaire m général. ◆**regi'stration** n enregistrement m; (*enrolment*) inscription f; **r. (number)** Aut numéro m d'immatriculation; **r. document** Aut = carte f grise. ◆**registry** a & n **r. (office)** bureau m de l'état civil.

regress [rɪ'gres] vi régresser.

regret [rɪ'gret] vt (**-tt-**) regretter (**doing, to do** de faire; **that** que (+ sub)); **I r. to hear that** … je suis désolé d'apprendre que …; — n regret m. ◆**regretfully** adv **r., I** … à mon grand regret, je … . ◆**regrettable** a regrettable (**that** que (+ sub)). ◆**regrettably** adv malheureusement; (*poor, ill etc*) fâcheusement.

regroup [ri:'gru:p] vi se regrouper; — vt regrouper.

regular ['regjʊlər] a (*steady, even*) régulier; (*surface*) uni; (*usual*) habituel; (*price, size*) normal; (*reader, listener*) fidèle; (*staff*) permanent; (*fool, slave etc*) Fam vrai; **a r. guy** Am Fam un chic type; — n (*in bar etc*) habitué, -ée mf; Mil régulier m. ◆**regu'larity** n régularité f. ◆**regularly** adv régulièrement.

regulate ['regjʊleɪt] vt régler. ◆**regu-**

'**lation 1** n (*rule*) règlement m; – a (*uniform etc*) règlementaire. **2** n (*regulating*) réglage m.

rehabilitate [riːhəˈbɪlɪteɪt] vt (*in public esteem*) réhabiliter; (*wounded soldier etc*) réadapter.

rehash [riːˈhæʃ] vt (*text*) Pej remanier; Culin réchauffer; – [ˈriːhæʃ] n a r. Culin & Fig du réchauffé.

rehearse [rɪˈhɜːs] vt Th répéter; (*prepare*) Fig préparer; – vi Th répéter. ◆**rehearsal** n Th répétition f.

reign [reɪn] n règne m; **in** or **during the r. of** sous le règne de; – vi régner (**over** sur).

reimburse [riːɪmˈbɜːs] vt rembourser (**for** de). ◆—**ment** n remboursement m.

rein [reɪn] n **reins** rênes fpl; **to give free r. to** Fig donner libre cours à.

reindeer [ˈreɪndɪər] n inv renne m.

reinforce [riːɪnˈfɔːs] vt renforcer (**with** de); **reinforced concrete** béton m armé. ◆—**ment** n renforcement m (**of** de); pl Mil renforts mpl.

reinstate [riːɪnˈsteɪt] vt réintégrer. ◆—**ment** n réintégration f.

reissue [riːˈɪʃuː] vt (*book*) rééditer.

reiterate [riːˈɪtəreɪt] vt (*say again*) réitérer.

reject [rɪˈdʒekt] vt (*refuse to accept*) rejeter; (*as useless*) refuser; – [ˈriːdʒekt] n Com article m de rebut; – a (*article*) de deuxième choix; **r. shop** solderie f. ◆**re'jection** n rejet m; (*of candidate etc*) refus m.

rejoic/e [rɪˈdʒɔɪs] vi se réjouir (**over** or **at sth** de qch, **in doing** de faire). ◆—**ing(s)** n(pl) réjouissance(s) f(pl).

rejoin [rɪˈdʒɔɪn] **1** vt (*join up with*) rejoindre. **2** vi (*retort*) répliquer.

rejuvenate [rɪˈdʒuːvəneɪt] vt rajeunir.

rekindle [riːˈkɪnd(ə)l] vt rallumer.

relapse [rɪˈlæps] n Med rechute f; – vi Med rechuter; **to r. into** Fig retomber dans.

relat/e [rɪˈleɪt] **1** vt (*narrate*) raconter (**that** que); (*report*) rapporter (**that** que). **2** vt (*connect*) établir un rapport entre (*faits etc*); **to r. sth to** (*link*) rattacher qch à; – vi **to r. to** (*apply to*) se rapporter à; (*get on with*) communiquer or s'entendre avec. ◆—**ed** a (*linked*) lié (**to** à); (*languages, styles*) apparentés; **to be r. to** (*by family*) être parent de.

relation [rɪˈleɪʃ(ə)n] n (*relative*) parent, -ente mf; (*relationship*) rapport m, relation f (**between** entre, **with** avec); **what r. are you to him?** quel est ton lien de parenté avec lui?; **international/etc relations** relations fpl internationales/etc. ◆**relationship** n (*kinship*) lien(s) m(pl) de parenté; (*rela-*

tions) relations fpl, rapports mpl; (*connection*) rapport m; **in r. to** relativement à.

relative [ˈrelətɪv] n (*person*) parent, -ente mf; – a relatif (**to** à); (*respective*) respectif; **r. to** (*compared to*) relativement à; **to be r. to** (*depend on*) être fonction de. ◆**relatively** adv relativement.

relax [rɪˈlæks] **1** vt (*person, mind*) détendre; – vi se détendre; **r.!** (*calm down*) Fam du calme! **2** vt (*grip, pressure etc*) relâcher; (*restrictions, principles, control*) assouplir. ◆—**ed** a (*person, atmosphere*) décontracté, détendu. ◆—**ing** a (*bath etc*) délassant. ◆**rela'xation** n **1** (*rest, recreation*) détente f; (*of body*) décontraction f. **2** (*of grip etc*) relâchement m; (*of restrictions etc*) assouplissement m.

relay [ˈriːleɪ] n relais m; **r. race** course f de relais; – vt (*message etc*) Rad retransmettre, Fig transmettre (**to** à).

release [rɪˈliːs] vt (*free*) libérer (**from** de); (*bomb, s.o.'s hand*) lâcher; (*spring*) déclencher; (*brake*) desserrer; (*film, record*) sortir; (*news, facts*) publier; (*smoke, trapped person*) dégager; (*tension*) éliminer; – n libération f; (*of film, book*) sortie f (**of** de); (*record*) nouveau disque m; (*film*) nouveau film m; (*relief*) Psy délivrance f, Psy défoulement m; **press r.** communiqué m de presse; **to be on general r.** (*of film*) passer dans toutes les salles.

relegate [ˈreləgeɪt] vt reléguer (**to** à).

relent [rɪˈlent] vi (*be swayed*) se laisser fléchir; (*change one's mind*) revenir sur sa décision. ◆—**less** a implacable.

relevant [ˈreləvənt] a (*apt*) pertinent (**to** à); (*fitting*) approprié; (*useful*) utile; (*significant*) important; **that's not r.** ça n'a rien à voir. ◆**relevance** n pertinence f (**to** à); (*significance*) intérêt m; (*connection*) rapport m (**to** avec).

reliable [rɪˈlaɪəb(ə)l] a (*person, information, firm*) sérieux, sûr, fiable; (*machine*) fiable. ◆**relia'bility** n (*of person*) sérieux m, fiabilité f; (*of machine, information, firm*) fiabilité f. ◆**reliably** adv **to be r. informed that** apprendre de source sûre que.

reliance [rɪˈlaɪəns] n (*trust*) confiance f (**on** en); (*dependence*) dépendance f (**on** de). ◆**reliant** a **to be r. on** (*dependent*) dépendre de; (*trusting*) avoir confiance en.

relic [ˈrelɪk] n relique f; pl (*of the past*) vestiges mpl.

relief [rɪˈliːf] n (*from pain etc*) soulagement m (**from** à); (*help, supplies*) secours m; (*in art*) & Geog relief m; **tax r.** dégrèvement m; **to be on r.** Am recevoir l'aide sociale; – a *(train etc)* supplémentaire; *(work etc)* de secours; **r. road** route f de délestage. ◆**relieve** vt *(pain etc)* soulager; *(boredom)* dissiper; *(situation)* remédier à; *(take over from)* relayer *(qn)*; *(help)* secourir, soulager; **to r. s.o. of** *(rid)* débarrasser qn de; **to r. s.o. of his post** relever qn de ses fonctions; **to r. congestion in** *Aut* décongestionner; **to r. oneself** *(go to the lavatory)* Hum Fam se soulager.

religion [rɪˈlɪdʒ(ə)n] n religion f. ◆**religious** a religieux; *(war, book)* de religion. ◆**religiously** adv religieusement.

relinquish [rɪˈlɪŋkwɪʃ] vt *(give up)* abandonner; *(let go)* lâcher.

relish [ˈrelɪʃ] n *(liking, taste)* goût m *(for* pour); *(pleasure)* plaisir m; *(seasoning)* assaisonnement m; **to eat with r.** manger de bon appétit; – vt *(food etc)* savourer; *(like)* aimer *(doing* faire).

relocate [riːləʊˈkeɪt] vi *(move to new place)* déménager; **to r. in** or **to** s'installer à.

reluctant [rɪˈlʌktənt] a *(greeting, gift, promise)* accordé à contrecœur; **to be r. to do** être peu disposé à faire; **a r. teacher** etc un professeur/etc malgré lui. ◆**reluctance** n répugnance f *(to do* à faire). ◆**reluctantly** adv à contrecœur.

rely [rɪˈlaɪ] vi **to r. on** *(count on)* compter sur; *(be dependent upon)* dépendre de.

remain [rɪˈmeɪn] **1** vi rester. **2** npl restes mpl; mortal **r.** dépouille f mortelle. ◆**-ing** a qui reste(nt). ◆**remainder** n **1** reste m; **the r.** *(remaining people)* les autres mfpl; **the r. of the girls** les autres filles. **2** *(book)* invendu m soldé.

remand [rɪˈmɑːnd] vt **to r. (in custody)** Jur placer en détention préventive; – n **on r.** en détention préventive.

remark [rɪˈmɑːk] n remarque f; – vt *(faire)* remarquer *(that* que); – vi **to r. on** faire des remarques sur. ◆**-able** a remarquable *(for* par). ◆**-ably** adv remarquablement.

remarry [riːˈmærɪ] vi se remarier.

remedial [rɪˈmiːdɪəl] a *(class)* Sch de rattrapage; *(measure)* de redressement; *(treatment)* Med thérapeutique.

remedy [ˈremɪdɪ] vt remédier à; – n remède m *(for* contre, à, de).

remember [rɪˈmembər] vt se souvenir de, se rappeler; *(commemorate)* commémorer; **to r. that/doing** se rappeler que/d'avoir fait; **to r. to do** *(not forget to do)* penser à faire; **r. me to him** or **her!** rappelle-moi à son bon souvenir!; – vi se souvenir, se rappeler. ◆**remembrance** n *(memory)* souvenir m; **in r. of** en souvenir de.

remind [rɪˈmaɪnd] vt rappeler *(s.o. of sth* qch à qn, *s.o. that* à qn que); **to r. s.o. to do** faire penser à qn à faire; **that** or **which reminds me!** à propos! ◆**-er** n *(of event & letter)* rappel m; *(note to do sth)* pense-bête m; **it's a r.** *(for him* or *her) that* . . . c'est pour lui rappeler que. . . .

reminisce [remɪˈnɪs] vi raconter or se rappeler ses souvenirs *(about* de). ◆**reminiscences** npl réminiscences fpl. ◆**reminiscent** a **r. of** qui rappelle.

remiss [rɪˈmɪs] a négligent.

remit [rɪˈmɪt] vt (-tt-) *(money)* envoyer. ◆**remission** n Jur remise f *(de peine)*; Med Rel rémission f. ◆**remittance** n *(sum)* paiement m.

remnant [ˈremnənt] n *(remaining part)* reste m; *(trace)* vestige m; *(of fabric)* coupon m; *(oddment)* fin f de série.

remodel [riːˈmɒd(ə)l] vt (-ll-, Am -l-) remodeler.

remonstrate [ˈremənstreɪt] vi **to r. with s.o.** faire des remontrances à qn.

remorse [rɪˈmɔːs] n remords m(pl) *(for* pour); **without r.** sans pitié. ◆**-less** a implacable. ◆**-lessly** adv *(to hit etc)* implacablement.

remote [rɪˈməʊt] a (-er, -est) **1** *(far-off)* lointain, éloigné; *(isolated)* isolé; *(aloof)* distant; **r. from** loin de; **r. control** télécommande f. **2** *(slight)* petit, vague; **not the remotest idea** pas la moindre idée. ◆**-ly** adv *(slightly)* vaguement, un peu; *(situated)* au loin; **not r. aware** etc nullement conscient/etc. ◆**-ness** n éloignement m; isolement m; Fig attitude f distante.

remould [ˈriːməʊld] n pneu m rechapé.

remove [rɪˈmuːv] vt *(clothes, stain etc)* enlever *(from s.o.* à qn, *from sth* de qch); *(withdraw)* retirer; *(lead away)* emmener *(to* à); *(furniture)* déménager; *(obstacle, threat, word)* supprimer; *(fear, doubt)* dissiper; *(employee)* renvoyer; **(far)** removed from loin de. ◆**removable** a *(lining etc)* amovible. ◆**removal** n enlèvement m; déménagement m; suppression f; **r. man** déménageur m; **r. van** camion m de déménagement. ◆**remover** n *(for make-up)* démaquillant m; *(for nail polish)* dissolvant m; *(for paint)* décapant m; *(for stains)* détachant m.

remunerate [rɪˈmjuːnəreɪt] vt rémunérer. ◆**remune'ration** n rémunération f.

renaissance [rəˈneɪsəns] n *(in art etc)* renaissance f.

rename [riːˈneɪm] vt *(street etc)* rebaptiser.

render [ˈrendər] vt *(give, make)* rendre; Mus

interpréter; *(help)* prêter. ◆**—ing** *n Mus* interprétation *f*; *(translation)* traduction *f*.
rendez-vous ['rɒndɪvuː, *pl* -vuːz] *n inv* rendez-vous *m inv*.
renegade ['renɪɡeɪd] *n* renégat, -ate *mf*.
reneg(u)e [rɪ'niːɡ] *vi* to **r. on** *(promise etc)* revenir sur.
renew [rɪ'njuː] *vt* renouveler; *(resume)* reprendre; *(library book)* renouveler le prêt de. ◆**—ed** *a (efforts)* renouvelés; *(attempt)* nouveau; **with r. vigour**/*etc* avec un regain de vigueur/*etc.* ◆**renewable** *a* renouvelable. ◆**renewal** *n* renouvellement *m*; *(resumption)* reprise *f*; *(of strength etc)* regain *m*.
renounce [rɪ'naʊns] *vt (give up)* renoncer à; *(disown)* renier.
renovate ['renəveɪt] *vt (house)* rénover, restaurer; *(painting)* restaurer. ◆**reno-'vation** *n* rénovation *f*; restauration *f*.
renown [rɪ'naʊn] *n* renommée *f*. ◆**renowned** *a* renommé (**for** pour).
rent [rent] *n* loyer *m*; *(of television)* (prix *m* de) location *f*; **r. collector** encaisseur *m* de loyers; – *vt* louer; **to r. out** louer; – *vi (of house etc)* se louer. ◆**r.-'free** *adv* sans payer de loyer; – *a* gratuit. ◆**rental** *n (of television)* (prix *m* de) location *f*; *(of telephone)* abonnement *m*.
renunciation [rɪnʌnsɪ'eɪʃ(ə)n] *n (giving up)* renonciation *f (of* à); *(disowning)* reniement *m (of* de).
reopen [riː'əʊpən] *vti* rouvrir. ◆**—ing** *n* réouverture *f*.
reorganize [riː'ɔːɡənaɪz] *vt* réorganiser.
rep [rep] *n Fam* représentant, -ante *mf* de commerce.
repaid [riː'peɪd] *see* repay.
repair [rɪ'peə(r)] *vt* réparer; – *n* réparation *f*; **beyond r.** irréparable; **in good/bad r.** en bon/mauvais état; **'road under r.'** *Aut* 'travaux'; **r. man** réparateur *m*; **r. woman** réparatrice *f*.
reparation [repə'reɪʃ(ə)n] *n* réparation *f (for* de); *pl Mil Hist* réparations *fpl*.
repartee [repɑː'tiː] *n (sharp reply)* repartie *f*.
repatriate [riː'pætrɪeɪt] *vt* rapatrier.
repay [riː'peɪ] *vt (pt & pp* repaid) *(pay back)* rembourser; *(kindness)* payer de retour; *(reward)* récompenser (**for** de). ◆**—ment** *n* remboursement *m*; récompense *f*.
repeal [rɪ'piːl] *vt (law)* abroger; – *n* abrogation *f*.
repeat [rɪ'piːt] *vt* répéter (**that** que); *(promise, threat)* réitérer; *(class)* Sch redoubler; **to r. oneself** *or* **itself** se répéter; – *vi* répéter; **to r. on s.o.** *(of food)* Fam revenir à

qn; – *n TV Rad* rediffusion *f*; – *a (performance)* deuxième. ◆**—ed** *a* répété; *(efforts)* renouvelés. ◆**—edly** *adv* à maintes reprises.
repel [rɪ'pel] *vt (-ll-)* repousser. ◆**repellent** *a* repoussant; **insect r.** insectifuge *m*.
repent [rɪ'pent] *vi* se repentir (**of** de). ◆**repentance** *n* repentir *m*. ◆**repentant** *a* repentant.
repercussion [riːpə'kʌʃ(ə)n] *n* répercussion *f*.
repertoire ['repətwɑː(r)] *n Th & Fig* répertoire *m*. ◆**repertory** *n Th & Fig* répertoire *m*; **r. (theatre)** théâtre *m* de répertoire.
repetition [repɪ'tɪʃ(ə)n] *n* répétition *f*. ◆**repetitious** *a*, ◆**re'petitive** *a (speech etc)* répétitif.
replace [rɪ'pleɪs] *vt (take the place of)* remplacer (**by, with** par); *(put back)* remettre, replacer; *(receiver)* Tel raccrocher. ◆**—ment** *n* remplacement *m (of* de); *(person)* remplaçant, -ante *mf*; *(machine part)* pièce *f* de rechange.
replay ['riːpleɪ] *n Sp* match *m* rejoué; **(instant** *or* **action) r.** *TV* répétition *f* immédiate (au ralenti).
replenish [rɪ'plenɪʃ] *vt (refill)* remplir (de nouveau) (**with** de); *(renew)* renouveler.
replete [rɪ'pliːt] *a* **r. with** rempli de; **r. (with food)** rassasié.
replica ['replɪkə] *n* copie *f* exacte.
reply [rɪ'plaɪ] *vti* répondre; – *n* réponse *f*; **in r.** en réponse (**to** à).
report [rɪ'pɔːt] *n (account)* rapport *m*; *(of meeting)* compte rendu *m*; *Journ TV Rad* reportage *m*; *Pol* enquête *f*; *Sch Met* bulletin *m*; *(rumour)* rumeur *f*; *(of gun)* détonation *f*; – *vt (give account of)* rapporter, rendre compte de; *(announce)* annoncer (**that** que); *(notify)* signaler (**to** à); *(denounce)* dénoncer (**to** à); *(event)* Journ faire un reportage sur; – *vi* faire un rapport *or* Journ un reportage (**on** sur); *(go)* se présenter (**to** à, **to s.o.** chez qn, **for work** au travail). ◆**—ed** *a (speech)* Gram indirect; **it is r. that** on dit que; **r. missing** porté disparu. ◆**—edly** *adv* à ce qu'on dit. ◆**—ing** *n Journ* reportage *m*. ◆**—er** *n* reporter *m*.
repose [rɪ'pəʊz] *n Lit* repos *m*.
repossess [riːpə'zes] *vt Jur* reprendre possession de.
reprehensible [reprɪ'hensəb(ə)l] *a* répréhensible.
represent [reprɪ'zent] *vt* représenter. ◆**represen'tation** *n* représentation *f*; *pl (complaints)* remontrances *fpl*. ◆**repre-**

sentative a représentatif (**of** de); – n représentant, -ante mf; Pol Am député m.

repress [rɪ'pres] vt réprimer; (feeling) refouler. ◆**repressive** a répressif.

reprieve [rɪ'priːv] n Jur sursis m; Fig répit m, sursis m; – vt accorder un sursis or Fig un répit à.

reprimand ['reprɪmɑːnd] n réprimande f; – vt réprimander.

reprint ['riːprɪnt] n (reissue) réimpression f; – vt réimprimer.

reprisal [rɪ'praɪz(ə)l] n reprisals représailles fpl; **in r.** en représailles de.

reproach [rɪ'prəʊtʃ] n (blame) reproche m; (shame) honte f; **beyond r.** sans reproche; – vt reprocher (**s.o. for sth** qch à qn). ◆**reproachful** a réprobateur. ◆**reproachfully** adv d'un ton or d'un air réprobateur.

reproduce [riːprə'djuːs] vt reproduire; – vi Biol Bot se reproduire. ◆**reproduction** n (of sound etc) & Biol Bot reproduction f. ◆**reproductive** a reproducteur.

reptile ['reptaɪl] n reptile m.

republic [rɪ'pʌblɪk] n république f. ◆**republican** a & n républicain, -aine (mf).

repudiate [rɪ'pjuːdɪeɪt] vt (offer) repousser; (accusation) rejeter; (spouse, idea) répudier.

repugnant [rɪ'pʌgnənt] a répugnant; **he's r. to me** il me répugne. ◆**repugnance** n répugnance f (**for** pour).

repulse [rɪ'pʌls] vt repousser. ◆**repulsion** n répulsion f. ◆**repulsive** a repoussant.

reputable ['repjʊtəb(ə)l] a de bonne réputation. ◆**re'pute** n réputation f; **of r.** de bonne réputation. ◆**re'puted** a réputé (**to be** pour être). ◆**re'putedly** adv à ce qu'on dit.

reputation [repjʊ'teɪʃ(ə)n] n réputation f; **to have a r. for frankness/etc** avoir la réputation d'être franc/etc.

request [rɪ'kwest] n demande f (**for** de); **on r.** sur demande; **on s.o.'s r.** à la demande de qn; **by popular r.** à la demande générale; **r. stop** (for bus) arrêt m facultatif; – vt demander (**from** or **of s.o.** à qn, **s.o. to do** à qn de faire).

requiem ['rekwɪəm] n requiem m inv.

requir/e [rɪ'kwaɪər] vt (necessitate) demander; (demand) exiger; (of person) avoir besoin de (qch, qn); (staff) rechercher; **to r. sth of s.o.** (order) exiger qch de qn; **to r. s.o. to do** exiger de qn qu'il fasse; (ask) demander à qn de faire; **if required** s'il le faut. ◆**–ed** a requis, exigé. ◆**–ement** n

(need) exigence f; (condition) condition f (requise).

requisite ['rekwɪzɪt] **1** a nécessaire. **2** n (for travel etc) article m; **toilet requisites** articles mpl or nécessaire m de toilette.

requisition [rekwɪ'zɪʃ(ə)n] vt réquisitionner; – n réquisition f.

reroute [riː'ruːt] vt (aircraft etc) dérouter.

rerun ['riːrʌn] n Cin reprise f; TV rediffusion f.

resale ['riːseɪl] n revente f.

resat [riː'sæt] see resit.

rescind [rɪ'sɪnd] vt Jur annuler; (law) abroger.

rescu/e ['reskjuː] vt (save) sauver; (set free) délivrer (**from** de); – n (action) sauvetage m (of person); (help, troops etc) secours mpl; **to go/etc to s.o.'s r.** aller/etc au secours de qn; **to the r.** à la rescousse; – a (team, operation) de sauvetage. ◆**–er** n sauveteur m.

research [rɪ'sɜːtʃ] n recherches fpl (**on, into** sur); **some r.** de la recherche; **a piece of r.** (work) un travail de recherche; – vi faire des recherches (**on, into** sur). ◆**–er** n chercheur, -euse mf.

resemble [rɪ'zembəl] vt ressembler à. ◆**resemblance** n ressemblance f (**to** avec).

resent [rɪ'zent] vt (anger) s'indigner de, ne pas aimer; (bitterness) éprouver de l'amertume à l'égard de; **I r. that** ça m'indigne. ◆**resentful** a **to be r.** éprouver de l'amertume. ◆**resentment** n amertume f, ressentiment m.

reserv/e [rɪ'zɜːv] **1** vt (room, decision etc) réserver; (right) se réserver; (one's strength) ménager; – n (reticence) réserve f. **2** n (stock, land) réserve f; **r.** (player) Sp remplaçant, -ante mf; **the r.** Mil la réserve; **the reserves** (troops) Mil les réserves fpl; **nature r.** réserve f naturelle; **in r.** en réserve; **r. tank** Av Aut réservoir m de secours. ◆**–ed** a (person, room) réservé. ◆**reser'vation** n **1** (doubt etc) réserve f; (booking) réservation f. **2** (land) Am réserve f; **central r.** (on road) terre-plein m.

reservoir ['rezəvwɑːr] n réservoir m.

resettle [riː'set(ə)l] vt (refugees) implanter.

reshape [riː'ʃeɪp] vt (industry etc) réorganiser.

reshuffle [riː'ʃʌf(ə)l] n (cabinet) **r.** Pol remaniement m (ministériel); – vt Pol remanier.

reside [rɪ'zaɪd] vi résider. ◆**'residence** n (home) résidence f; (of students) foyer m; **in r.** (doctor) sur place; (students on campus) sur le campus, (in halls of residence) rentrés. ◆**'resident** n habitant, -ante mf; (of hotel) pensionnaire mf; (foreigner) résident, -ente mf; – a résidant, qui habite sur place; (population) fixe; (correspondent) permanent; **to be r. in London** résider à Londres. ◆**resi'dential** a (neighbourhood) résidentiel.

residue ['rezɪdjuː] n résidu m. ◆**re'sidual** a résiduel.

resign [rɪ'zaɪn] vt (right, claim) abandonner; **to r. (from) one's job** démissionner; **to r. oneself to sth/to doing** se résigner à qch/à faire; – vi démissionner (from de). ◆**-ed** a résigné. ◆**resig'nation** n (from job) démission f; (attitude) résignation f.

resilient [rɪ'zɪlɪənt] a élastique; (person) Fig résistant. ◆**resilience** n élasticité f; Fig résistance f.

resin ['rezɪn] n résine f.

resist [rɪ'zɪst] vt (attack etc) résister à; **to r. doing sth** s'empêcher de faire qch; **she can't r. cakes** elle ne peut pas résister devant les gâteaux; **he can't r. her** (indulgence) il ne peut rien lui refuser; (charm) il ne peut pas résister à son charme; – vi résister. ◆**resistance** n résistance f (to à). ◆**resistant** a résistant (to à); **r. to** Med rebelle à.

resit [riː'sɪt] vt (pt & pp resat, pres p resitting) (exam) repasser.

resolute ['rezəluːt] a résolu. ◆**-ly** adv résolument. ◆**reso'lution** n résolution f.

resolve [rɪ'zɒlv] vt résoudre (**to do** de faire, **that** que); – n résolution f. ◆**-ed** a résolu (**to do** à faire).

resonant ['rezənənt] a (voice) résonnant; **to be r. with** résonner de. ◆**resonance** n résonance f.

resort [rɪ'zɔːt] **1** n (recourse) recours m (**to** à); **as a last r.** en dernier ressort; – vi **to r. to s.o.** avoir recours à qn; **to r. to doing** en venir à faire; **to r. to drink** se rabattre sur la boisson. **2** n (holiday) **r. station** f de vacances; **seaside/ski r.** station f balnéaire/de ski.

resound [rɪ'zaʊnd] vi résonner (**with** de); Fig avoir du retentissement. ◆**-ing** a (success, noise) retentissant.

resource [rɪ'sɔːs, rɪ'zɔːs] n (expedient, recourse) ressource f; pl (wealth etc) ressources fpl. ◆**resourceful** a (person, scheme) ingénieux. ◆**resourcefulness** n ingéniosité f, ressource f.

respect [rɪ'spekt] n respect m (**for** pour, de); (aspect) égard m; **in r. of, with r. to** en ce qui concerne; **with all due r.** sans vouloir vous vexer; – vt respecter. ◆**respecta'bility** n

respectabilité f. ◆**respectable** a (honourable, sizeable) respectable; (satisfying) honnête; (clothes, behaviour) convenable. ◆**respectably** adv (to dress etc) convenablement; (rather well) passablement. ◆**respectful** a respectueux (**to** envers, **of** de). ◆**respectfully** adv respectueusement.

respective [rɪ'spektɪv] a respectif. ◆**-ly** adv respectivement.

respiration [respɪ'reɪʃ(ə)n] n respiration f.

respite ['respaɪt] n répit m.

respond [rɪ'spɒnd] vi répondre (**to** à); **to r. to treatment** Med réagir positivement au traitement. ◆**response** n réponse f; **in p. to** en réponse à.

responsible [rɪ'spɒnsəb(ə)l] a responsable (**for** de, **to s.o.** devant qn); **who's r. for...?** qui est (le) responsable de...? ◆**responsi'bility** n responsabilité f. ◆**responsibly** adv de façon responsable.

responsive [rɪ'spɒnsɪv] a (reacting) **r.** réagit bien; (alert) éveillé; (attentive) qui fait attention; **r. to** (kindness) sensible à; (suggestion) réceptif à. ◆**-ness** n (bonne) réaction f.

rest¹ [rest] n (repose) repos m; (support) support m; **to have** or **take a r.** se reposer; **to set** or **put s.o.'s mind at r.** tranquilliser qn; **to come to r.** (of ball etc) s'immobiliser; (of bird, eyes) se poser (**on** sur); **r. home** maison f de repos; **r. room** Am toilettes fpl; – vi (relax) se reposer; (be buried) reposer; **to r. on** (of roof, argument) reposer sur; **I won't r. till** je n'aurai de repos que (+ sub); **to be resting on** (of hand etc) être posé sur; **a resting place** un lieu de repos; – vt (eyes etc) reposer; (horse etc) laisser reposer; (lean) poser, appuyer (**on** sur); (base) fonder. ◆**restful** a reposant.

rest² [rest] n (remainder) reste m (**of** de); **the r.** (others) les autres mfpl; **the r. of the men/etc** les autres hommes/etc; – vi (remain) **it rests with you to do** il vous incombe de faire; **r. assured** soyez assuré (**that** que).

restaurant ['restərɒnt] n restaurant m.

restitution [restɪ'tjuːʃ(ə)n] n (for damage) Jur réparation f; **to make r.** of restituer.

restive ['restɪv] a (person, horse) rétif.

restless ['restləs] a agité. ◆**-ly** adv avec agitation. ◆**-ness** n agitation f.

restore [rɪ'stɔːr] vt (give back) rendre (**to** à); (order, rights) Jur rétablir; (building, painting) restaurer; (to life or power) ramener (qn) (**to** à).

restrain [rɪ'streɪn] vt (person, emotions) retenir, maîtriser; (crowd) contenir; (limit) limiter; **to r. s.o. from doing** retenir qn de faire; **to r. oneself** se maîtriser. ◆**—ed** a (feelings) contenu; (tone) mesuré. ◆**restraint** n (moderation) retenue f, mesure f; (restriction) contrainte f.

restrict [rɪ'strɪkt] vt limiter, restreindre (**to** à). ◆**—ed** a (space, use) restreint; (sale) contrôlé. ◆**restriction** n restriction f, limitation f. ◆**restrictive** a restrictif.

result [rɪ'zʌlt] n (outcome, success) résultat m; **as a r. of** en conséquence; **as a r.** of par suite de; – vi résulter (**from** de); **to r. in** aboutir à.

resume [rɪ'zjuːm] vti (begin or take again) reprendre; **to r. doing** se remettre à faire. ◆**resumption** n reprise f.

résumé ['rezjumeɪ] n (summary) résumé m; Am curriculum vitae m inv.

resurface [riː'sɜːfɪs] vt (road) refaire le revêtement de.

resurgence [rɪ'sɜːdʒəns] n réapparition f.

resurrect [rezə'rekt] vt (custom, hero) Pej ressusciter. ◆**resurrection** n résurrection f.

resuscitate [rɪ'sʌsɪteɪt] vt Med réanimer.

retail ['riːteɪl] n (vente f au) détail m; – a (price, shop etc) de détail; – vi se vendre (au détail); – vt vendre (au détail), détailler; – adv (to sell) au détail. ◆**—er** n détaillant, -ante mf.

retain [rɪ'teɪn] vt (hold back, remember) retenir; (freshness, heat etc) conserver. ◆**retainer** n (fee) avance f, acompte m. ◆**retention** n (memory) mémoire f. ◆**retentive** a (memory) fidèle.

retaliate [rɪ'tælɪeɪt] vi riposter (**against s.o.** contre qn, **against an attack** à une attaque). ◆**retali'ation** n riposte f, représailles fpl; **in r. for** en représailles de.

retarded [rɪ'tɑːdɪd] a (mentally) r. arriéré.

retch [retʃ] vi avoir un or des haut-le-cœur.

rethink [riː'θɪŋk] vt (pt & pp rethought) repenser.

reticent ['retɪsənt] a réticent. ◆**reticence** n réticence f.

retina ['retɪnə] n Anat rétine f.

retir/e [rɪ'taɪər] vi 1 (from work) prendre sa retraite; – vt mettre à la retraite. 2 vi (withdraw) se retirer (**from** de, **to** à); (go to bed) aller se coucher. ◆**—ed** a (having stopped working) retraité. ◆**—ing** a 1 (age) de la retraite. 2 (reserved) réservé. ◆**retirement** n retraite f; **r. age** âge m de la retraite.

retort [rɪ'tɔːt] vt rétorquer; – n réplique f.

retrace [riː'treɪs] vt (past event) se

remémorer, reconstituer; **to r. one's steps** revenir sur ses pas, rebrousser chemin.

retract [rɪ'trækt] vt (statement etc) rétracter; – vi (of person) se rétracter. ◆**retraction** n (of statement) rétractation f.

retrain [riː'treɪn] vi se recycler; – vt recycler. ◆**—ing** n recyclage m.

retread [riː'tred] n pneu m rechapé.

retreat [rɪ'triːt] n (withdrawal) retraite f; (place) refuge m; – vi se retirer (**from** de); Mil battre en retraite.

retrial [riː'traɪəl] n Jur nouveau procès m.

retribution [retrɪ'bjuːʃ(ə)n] n châtiment m.

retrieve [rɪ'triːv] vt (recover) récupérer; (rescue) sauver (**from** de); (loss, error) réparer; (honour) rétablir. ◆**retrieval** n récupération f; **information r.** recherche f documentaire. ◆**retriever** n (dog) chien m d'arrêt.

retro- ['retrəʊ] pref rétro-. ◆**retro'active** a rétroactif.

retrograde ['retrəʊgreɪd] a rétrograde.

retrospect ['retrəspekt] **in r.** rétrospectivement. ◆**retro'spective 1** a (law, effect) rétroactif. **2** n (of film director, artist) rétrospective f.

return [rɪ'tɜːn] vi (come back) revenir; (go back) retourner; (go back home) rentrer; **to r. to** (subject) revenir à; – vt (give back) rendre; (put back) remettre; (bring back) & Fin rapporter; (send back) renvoyer; (greeting) répondre à; (candidate) Pol élire; – n retour m; (yield) Fin rapport m; pl (profits) Fin bénéfices mpl; **the r. to school** la rentrée (des classes); **r. (ticket)** (billet m d')aller et retour m; **tax r.** déclaration f de revenus; **many happy returns (of the day)!** bon anniversaire!; **in r.** (exchange) en échange (**for** de); – a (trip, flight etc) (de) retour; **r. match** match m retour. ◆**—able** a (bottle) consigné.

reunion [riː'juːnɪən] n réunion f. ◆**reu'nite** vt réunir.

rev [rev] n Aut Fam tour m; **r. counter** compte-tours m inv; – vt (-vv-) **to r. (up)** (engine) Fam faire ronfler.

revamp [riː'væmp] vt (method, play etc) Fam remanier.

reveal [rɪ'viːl] vt (make known) révéler (**that** que); (make visible) laisser voir. ◆**—ing** a (sign etc) révélateur.

revel ['rev(ə)l] vi (-ll-) faire la fête; **to r. in sth** se délecter de qch. ◆**revelling** n, ◆**revelry** n festivités fpl. ◆**reveller** n noceur, -euse mf.

revenge [rɪ'vendʒ] n vengeance f; Sp revanche f; **to have** or **get one's r.** se venger

(on s.o. de qn, on s.o. for sth de qch sur qn);
in r. pour se venger; – vt venger.

revenue ['revənju:] n revenu m.

reverberate [rɪ'vɜːbəreɪt] vi (of sound) se
répercuter.

revere [rɪ'vɪər] vt révérer. ◆**'reverence** n
révérence f. ◆**'reverend** a (father) Rel
révérend; – n R. Smith (Anglican) le révérend Smith; (Catholic) l'abbé m Smith;
(Jewish) le rabbin Smith. ◆**'reverent** a
respecteux.

reverse [rɪ'vɜːs] a contraire; (order, image)
inverse; r. side (of coin etc) revers m; (of
paper) verso m; – n contraire m; (of coin,
fabric etc) revers m; (of paper) verso m; in r.
(gear) Aut en marche arrière; – vt (situation) renverser; (order, policy) inverser;
(decision) annuler; (bucket etc) retourner;
to r. the charges Tel téléphoner en PCV; –
vti to r. (the car) faire marche arrière; to r.
in/out rentrer/sortir en marche arrière;
reversing light phare m de recul. ◆**reversal** n renversement m; (of policy, situation,
opinion) revirement m; (of fortune) revers
m. ◆**reversible** a (fabric etc) réversible.

revert [rɪ'vɜːt] vi to r. to revenir à.

review [rɪ'vjuː] 1 vt (troops, one's life) passer
en revue; (situation) réexaminer; (book)
faire la critique de; – n revue f; (of book)
critique f. 2 n (magazine) revue f. ◆**-er** n
critique m.

revile [rɪ'vaɪl] vt injurier.

revise [rɪ'vaɪz] vt (opinion, notes, text)
réviser; – vi (for exam) réviser (for pour).
◆**revision** n révision f.

revitalize [riː'vaɪt(ə)laɪz] vt revitaliser.

revive [rɪ'vaɪv] vt (unconscious person,
memory, conversation) ranimer; (dying
person) réanimer; (custom, plan, fashion)
ressusciter; (hope, interest) faire renaître; –
vi (of unconscious person, dying person)
reprendre
connaissance; (of country, dying person)
ressusciter; (of hope, interest) renaître.
◆**revival** n (of custom, business, play)
reprise f; (of country) essor m; (of faith,
fashion, theatre) renouveau m.

revoke [rɪ'vəʊk] vt (decision) annuler;
(contract) Jur révoquer.

revolt [rɪ'vəʊlt] n révolte f; – vt (disgust)
révolter; – vi (rebel) se révolter (against
contre). ◆**-ing** a dégoûtant; (injustice)
révoltant.

revolution [revə'luːʃ(ə)n] n révolution f.
◆**revolutionary** a & n révolutionnaire
(mf). ◆**revolutionize** vt révolutionner.

revolv/e [rɪ'vɒlv] vi tourner (**around** autour

de). ◆**-ing** a r. chair fauteuil m pivotant;
r. door(s) (porte f à) tambour m.

revolver [rɪ'vɒlvər] n revolver m.

revue [rɪ'vjuː] n (satirical) Th revue f.

revulsion [rɪ'vʌlʃ(ə)n] n 1 (disgust) dégoût
m. 2 (change) revirement m.

reward [rɪ'wɔːd] n récompense f (for de); –
vt récompenser (s.o. for sth qn de or pour
qch). ◆**-ing** a qui (en) vaut la peine;
(satisfying) satisfaisant; (financially)
rémunérateur.

rewind [riː'waɪnd] vt (pt & pp rewound)
(tape) réembobiner.

rewire [riː'waɪər] vt (house) refaire
l'installation électrique de.

rewrite [riː'raɪt] vt (pt rewrote, pp rewritten)
récrire; (edit) réécrire.

rhapsody ['ræpsədɪ] n rhapsodie f.

rhetoric ['retərɪk] n rhétorique f. ◆**rhe-
'torical** a (question) de pure forme.

rheumatism ['ruːmətɪz(ə)m] n Med rhumatisme m; to have r. avoir des rhumatismes. ◆**rheu'matic** a (pain) rhumatismal;
(person) rhumatisant.

rhinoceros [raɪ'nɒsərəs] n rhinocéros m.

rhubarb ['ruːbɑːb] n rhubarbe f.

rhyme [raɪm] n rime f; (poem) vers mpl; – vi
rimer.

rhythm ['rɪð(ə)m] n rythme m.
◆**rhythmic(al)** a rythmique.

rib [rɪb] n Anat côte f.

ribald ['rɪb(ə)ld] a Lit grivois.

ribbon ['rɪbən] n ruban m; to tear to ribbons
mettre en lambeaux.

rice [raɪs] n riz m. ◆**ricefield** n rizière f.

rich [rɪtʃ] a (-er, -est) riche (in en); (profits)
gros; – n the r. les riches mpl. ◆**riches** npl
richesses fpl. ◆**richly** adv (dressed, illustrated etc) richement; (deserved) amplement. ◆**richness** n richesse f.

rick [rɪk] vt to r. one's back se tordre le dos.

rickety ['rɪkɪtɪ] a (furniture) branlant.

ricochet ['rɪkəʃeɪ] vi ricocher; – n ricochet
m.

rid [rɪd] vt (pt & pp rid, pres p ridding) débarrasser (of de); to get r. of, r. oneself of se
débarrasser de. ◆**riddance** n good r.! Fam
bon débarras!

ridden ['rɪd(ə)n] see ride.

-ridden ['rɪd(ə)n] suffix debt-r. criblé de
dettes; disease-r. en proie à la maladie.

riddle ['rɪd(ə)l] 1 n (puzzle) énigme f. 2 vt
cribler (**with** de); **riddled with** (bullets, holes,
mistakes) criblé de; (criminals) plein de;
(corruption) en proie à.

rid/e [raɪd] n (on bicycle, by car etc) promenade f; (distance) trajet m; (in taxi) course

f; *(on merry-go-round)* tour *m*; **to go for a (car) r.** faire une promenade (en voiture); **to give s.o. a r.** *Aut* emmener qn en voiture; **to have a r. on** *(bicycle)* monter sur; **to take s.o. for a r.** *(deceive) Fam* mener qn en bateau; – *vi (pt* **rode**, *pp* **ridden)** aller (à bicyclette, à moto, à cheval *etc)* rouler; *(on horse) Sp* monter (à cheval); **to be riding in a car** être en voiture; **to r. up** *(of skirt)* remonter; – *vt (a particular horse)* monter; *(distance)* faire (à cheval *etc)*; **to r. a horse** *or* **horses** *(go riding) Sp* monter à cheval; **I was riding (on) a bike/donkey** j'étais à bicyclette/à dos d'âne; **to know how to r. a bike** savoir faire de la bicyclette; **to r. a bike** to aller à bicyclette **a; may I r. your bike?** puis-je monter sur ta bicyclette?; **to r. s.o.** *(annoy) Am Fam* harceler qn. ◆**─ing** *n (horse)* équitation *f*; **r. boots** bottes *fpl* de cheval. ◆**─er** *n* **1** *(on horse)* cavalier, -ière *mf*; *(cyclist)* cycliste *mf*. **2** *(to document) Jur* annexe *f*.

ridge [rɪdʒ] *n (of roof, mountain)* arête *f*, crête *f*.

ridicule ['rɪdɪkjuːl] *n* ridicule *m*; **to hold up to r.** tourner en ridicule; **object of r.** objet *m* de risée; – *vt* tourner en ridicule, ridiculiser. ◆**ri'diculous** *a* ridicule.

rife [raɪf] *a (widespread)* répandu.

riffraff ['rɪfræf] *n* racaille *f*.

rifle ['raɪf(ə)l] **1** *n* fusil *m*, carabine *f*. **2** *vt (drawers, pockets etc)* vider.

rift [rɪft] *n (crack)* fissure *f*; *(in party) Pol* scission *f*; *(disagreement)* désaccord *m*.

rig [rɪg] **1** *n* **(oil) r.** derrick *m*; *(at sea)* plate-forme *f* pétrolière. **2** *vt* (**-gg-**) *(result, election etc) Pej* truquer; **to r. up** *(equipment)* installer; *(meeting etc) Fam* arranger. **3** *vt* (**-gg-**) **to r. out** *(dress) Fam* habiller. ◆**r.-out** *n Fam* tenue *f*.

right¹ [raɪt] **1** *a (correct)* bon, exact, juste; *(fair)* juste; *(angle)* droit; **to be r.** *(of person)* avoir raison **(to do or de faire)**; **it's the r. road** c'est la bonne route, c'est bien la route; **the r. time** l'heure exacte; **the clock's r.** la pendule est à l'heure; **at the r. time** au bon moment; **he's the r. man** c'est l'homme qu'il faut; **the r. thing to do** la meilleure chose à faire; **it's not r. to steal** ce n'est pas bien de voler; **it doesn't look r.** ça ne va pas; **to put r.** *(error)* rectifier; *(fix)* arranger; **to put s.o. r.** *(inform)* éclairer qn, détromper qn; **r.!** bien!; **that's r.** c'est ça, c'est bien, c'est exact; – *adv (straight)* (tout) droit; *(completely)* tout à fait; *(correctly)* juste; *(well)* bien; **she did r.** elle a bien fait; **r. round** tout autour **(sth de qch)**;

r. behind juste derrière; **r. here** ici même; **r. away, r. now** tout de suite; **R. Honourable** *Pol* Très Honorable; – *n* **to be in the r.** avoir raison; **r. and wrong** le bien et le mal; – *vt (error, wrong, car)* redresser. **2 all r.** *a (satisfactory)* bien *inv*; *(unharmed)* sain et sauf; *(undamaged)* intact; *(without worries)* tranquille; **it's all r.** ça va; **it's all r. now** *(fixed)* ça marche maintenant; **I'm all r.** *(healthy)* je vais bien, ça va; – *adv (well)* bien; **all r.!, r. you are!** *(yes)* d'accord!; **I got your letter all r.** j'ai bien reçu ta lettre. ◆**rightly** *adv* bien, correctement; *(justifiably)* à juste titre; **r. or wrongly** à tort ou à raison.

right² [raɪt] *a (hand, side etc)* droit; – *adv* à droite; – *n* droite *f*; **on** *or* **to the r.** à droite **(of de)**. ◆**r.-hand** *a* à *or* de droite; **on the r.-hand side** à droite **(of de)**; **r.-hand man** bras *m* droit. ◆**r.-'handed** *a (person)* droitier. ◆**r.-wing** *a Pol* de droite.

right³ [raɪt] *n (claim, entitlement)* droit *m* **(to do de faire)**; **to have a r. to sth** avoir droit à qch; **he's famous in his own r.** il est lui-même célèbre; **r. of way** *Aut* priorité *f*; **human rights** les droits de l'homme.

righteous ['raɪtʃəs] *a (person)* vertueux; *(cause, indignation)* juste.

rightful ['raɪtfəl] *a* légitime. ◆**-ly** *adv* légitimement.

rigid ['rɪdʒɪd] *a* rigide. ◆**ri'gidity** *n* rigidité *f*. ◆**rigidly** *adv (opposed)* rigoureusement (**to** à).

rigmarole ['rɪgmərəʊl] *n (process)* procédure *f* compliquée.

rigour ['rɪgər] *n* rigueur *f*. ◆**rigorous** *a* rigoureux.

rile [raɪl] *vt (annoy) Fam* agacer.

rim [rɪm] *n (of cup etc)* bord *m*; *(of wheel)* jante *f*.

rind [raɪnd] *n (of cheese)* croûte *f*; *(of melon, lemon)* écorce *f*; *(of bacon)* couenne *f*.

ring¹ [rɪŋ] *n* anneau *m*; *(on finger)* anneau *m*, *(with stone)* bague *f*; *(of people, chairs)* cercle *m*; *(of smoke, for napkin)* rond *m*; *(gang)* bande *f*; *(at circus)* piste *f*; **Boxing r.** ring *m*; *(burner on stove)* brûleur *m*; **diamond r.** bague *f* de diamants; **to have rings under one's eyes** avoir les yeux cernés; **r. road** route *f* de ceinture; *(motorway)* périphérique *m*; – *vt* **to r. (round)** *(surround)* entourer **(with de)**; *(item on list etc)* entourer d'un cercle. ◆**ringleader** *n Pej (of gang)* chef *m* de bande; *(of rebellion etc)* meneur, -euse *mf*.

ring² [rɪŋ] *n (sound)* sonnerie *f*; **there's a r. on** sonne; **to give s.o. a r.** *(phone call)* passer un coup de fil à qn ; **a r. of** (truth) Fig l'accent m de; – vi (pt **rang**, pp **rung**) (of bell, person etc) sonner; (of sound, words) retentir; **to r. (up)** Tel téléphoner; **to r. back** Tel rappeler; **to r. for s.o.** sonner qn; **to r. off** Tel raccrocher; **to r.** (of bell) sonner; (of sound) retentir; – vt sonner; **to r. s.o. (up)** Tel téléphoner à qn; **to r. s.o. back** Tel rappeler qn; **to r. the bell** sonner; **to r. the doorbell** sonner à la porte; **that rings a bell** Fam ça me rappelle quelque chose; **to r. in** (the New Year) carillonner. ◆**—ing** a r. tone Tel tonalité f; – n (of bell) sonnerie f; **a r. in one's ears** un bourdonnement dans les oreilles.

ringlet ['rɪŋlɪt] n (curl) anglaise f.

rink [rɪŋk] n (ice-skating) patinoire f; (roller-skating) skating m.

rinse [rɪns] vt rincer; **to r. one's hands** se passer les mains à l'eau; (remove soap) se rincer les mains; **to r. out** rincer; – n rinçage m; (hair colouring) shampooing m colorant; **to give sth a r.** rincer qch.

riot ['raɪət] n (uprising) émeute f; (demonstration) manifestation f violente; **a r. of colour** Fig une orgie de couleurs; **to run r.** (of crowd) se déchaîner; **the r. police** = les CRS mpl; – vi (rise up) faire une émeute; (fight) se bagarrer. ◆**—ing** n émeutes fpl; bagarres fpl. ◆**—er** n émeutier, -ière mf; (demonstrator) manifestant, -ante mf violent(e). ◆**riotous** a (crowd etc) tapageur; **r. living** vie f dissolue.

rip [rɪp] vt (-pp-) déchirer; **to r. off or out** arracher; **to r. off** Fam (deceive) rouler; (steal) Am voler; **to r. up** déchirer; – vi (of fabric) se déchirer; – n déchirure f; **it's a r.-off** Fam c'est du vol organisé.

ripe [raɪp] a (-er, -est) mûr; (cheese) fait. ◆**ripen** vti mûrir. ◆**ripeness** n maturité f.

ripple ['rɪp(ə)l] n (on water) ride f; (of laughter) Fig cascade f; – vi (of water) se rider.

ris/e [raɪz] vi (pt **rose**, pp **risen**) (get up from chair or bed) se lever; (of temperature, balloon, price etc) monter, s'élever; (in society) s'élever; (of hope) grandir; (of sun, curtain, wind) se lever; (of dough) lever; **to r. in price** augmenter de prix; **to r. to the surface** remonter à la surface; **the river rises in . . .** le fleuve prend sa source dans . . . ; **to r. (up)** (rebel) se soulever (against contre); **to r. to power** accéder au pouvoir; **to r. from the dead** ressusciter; – n (of land, curtain) lever m; (in pressure, price etc) hausse f (**in** de); (in river) crue f; (of leader) Fig ascension f; (of industry, technology)

essor m; (to power) accession f; (slope in ground) éminence f; **(pay) r.** augmentation f (de salaire); **to give r. to** donner lieu à. ◆**—ing** n (of curtain) lever m; (of river) crue f; (revolt) soulèvement m; – a (sun) levant; (number) croissant; (tide) montant; (artist etc) d'avenir; **the r. generation** la nouvelle génération; **r. prices** la hausse des prix. ◆**—er** n early r. lève-tôt mf inv; late r. lève-tard mf inv.

risk [rɪsk] n risque m (of doing de faire); **at r.** (person) en danger; (job) menacé; **at your own r.** à tes risques et périls; – vt (one's life, an accident etc) risquer; **she won't r. leaving** (take the risk) elle ne risquera pas à partir; **let's r. it** risquons le coup. ◆**riskiness** n risques mpl. ◆**risky** a (-ier, -iest) (full of risk) risqué.

rissole ['rɪsəʊl] n Culin croquette f.

rite [raɪt] n rite m; **the last rites** Rel les derniers sacrements mpl. ◆**ritual** a & n rituel (m).

ritzy ['rɪtsɪ] a (-ier, -iest) Fam luxueux, classe f.

rival ['raɪv(ə)l] a (firm etc) rival; (forces, claim etc) opposé; – n rival, -ale mf; – vt (-ll-, Am -l-) (compete with) rivaliser avec (**in** de); (equal) égaler (**in** en). ◆**rivalry** n rivalité f (**between** entre).

river ['rɪvər] n (small) rivière f; (major, flowing into sea) Fig fleuve m; **the R. Thames** la Tamise; – a (port etc) fluvial; **r. bank** rive f. ◆**riverside** a & n (by the) r. au bord de l'eau.

rivet ['rɪvɪt] n (pin) rivet m; – vt riveter; (eyes) Fig fixer. ◆**—ing** a (story etc) fascinant.

Riviera [rɪvɪ'eərə] n the (French) R. la Côte d'Azur.

road [rəʊd] n route f (to qui va à); (small) chemin m; (in town) rue f; (roadway) chaussée f; (path) Fig voie f, chemin m, route f (to de); **the Paris r.** la route de Paris; **across or over the r.** (building etc) en face; **by r.** par la route; **get out of the r.!** ne reste pas sur la chaussée!; – a (map, safety) routier; (accident) de la route; (sense) de la conduite; **r. hog** Fam chauffard m; **r. sign** panneau m (routier or de signalisation); **r. works** travaux mpl. ◆**roadblock** n barrage m routier. ◆**roadside** a & n (by the) r. au bord de la route. ◆**roadway** n chaussée f. ◆**roadworthy** a (vehicle) en état de marche.

roam [rəʊm] vt parcourir; – vi errer, rôder; **to r. (about) the streets** (of child etc) traîner dans les rues.

roar [rɔːr] vi hurler; (of lion, wind, engine) rugir; (of thunder) gronder; **to r. with laughter** éclater de rire; **to r. past** (of truck etc) passer dans un bruit de tonnerre; — vt **to r. (out)** hurler; — n hurlement m; rugissement m; grondement m. ◆**—ing** n roar n; — a **a r. fire** une belle flambée; **a r. success** un succès fou; **to do a r. trade** vendre beaucoup (**in de**).

roast [rəust] vt rôtir; (coffee) griller; — vi (of meat) rôtir; **we're roasting here** Fam on rôtit ici; — n (meat) rôti m; — a (chicken etc) rôti; **r. beef** rosbif m.

rob [rɒb] vt (**-bb-**) (person) voler; (bank, house) dévaliser; **to r. s.o. of sth** voler qch à qn; (deprive) priver qn de qch. ◆**robber** n voleur, -euse mf. ◆**robbery** n vol m; **it's daylight r.!** c'est du vol organisé; **armed r.** vol m à main armée.

robe [rəub] n (of priest, judge etc) robe f; (dressing gown) peignoir m.

robin [ˈrɒbin] n (bird) rouge-gorge m.

robot [ˈrəubɒt] n robot m.

robust [rəuˈbʌst] a robuste.

rock¹ [rɒk] **1** vt (baby, boat) bercer, balancer; (cradle, branch) balancer; (violently) secouer; — vi (sway) se balancer; (of building, ground) trembler. **2** n Mus rock m. ◆**—ing** a (horse, chair) à bascule. ◆**rocky¹** a (-ier, -iest) (furniture etc) branlant.

rock² [rɒk] n (substance) roche f; (boulder, rock face) rocher m; (stone) Am pierre f; **a stick of r.** (sweet) un bâton de sucre d'orge; **r. face** paroi f rocheuse; **on the rocks** (whisky) avec des glaçons; (marriage) en pleine débâcle. ◆**r.-ˈbottom** n point m le plus bas; — a (prices) les plus bas, très bas. ◆**r.-climbing** n varappe f. ◆**rockery** n (in garden) rocaille f. ◆**rocky²** a (-ier, -iest) (road) cailouteux; (hill) rocheux.

rocket [ˈrɒkit] n fusée f; — vi (of prices) Fig monter en flèche.

rod [rɒd] n (wooden) baguette f; (metal) tige f; (of curtain) tringle f; (for fishing) canne f à pêche.

rode [rəud] see ride.

rodent [ˈrəudənt] n (animal) rongeur m.

rodeo [ˈrəudiəu] n (pl -os) Am rodéo m.

roe [rəu] n **1** (eggs) œufs mpl de poisson. **2** r. (deer) chevreuil m.

rogue [rəug] n (dishonest) crapule f; (mischievous) coquin, -ine mf. ◆**roguish** a (smile etc) coquin.

role [rəul] n rôle m.

roll [rəul] n (of paper, film etc) rouleau m; (of bread) petit pain m; (of fat, flesh) bourrelet

m; (of drum, thunder) roulement m; (of ship) roulis m; (list) liste f; **to have a r. call** faire l'appel; **r. neck** (neckline, sweater) col m roulé; — vi (of ball, ship etc) rouler; (of person, animal) se rouler; **to be rolling in money or in it** Fam rouler sur l'or; **r. on tonight!** Fam vivement ce soir!; **to r. in** Fam (flow in) affluer; (of person) s'amener; **to r. over** (many times) se rouler; (once) se retourner; **to r. up** (arrive) Fam s'amener; **to r. (up) into a ball** (of animal) se rouler en boule; — vt rouler; **to r. down** (blind) baisser; (slope) descendre (en roulant); **to r. on** (paint, stocking) mettre; **to r. out** (dough) étaler; **to r. up** (map, cloth) rouler; (sleeve, trousers) retrousser. ◆**—ing** a (ground, gait) onduleux; **r. pin** rouleau m à pâtisserie. ◆**—er** n (for hair, painting etc) rouleau m; **r. coaster** (at funfair) montagnes fpl russes. ◆**roller-skate** n patin m à roulettes; — vi faire du patin à roulettes.

rollicking [ˈrɒlikiŋ] a joyeux (et bruyant).

roly-poly [rəuliˈpəuli] a Fam grassouillet.

Roman [ˈrəumən] **1** a & n romain, -aine mf. **2 R. Catholic** a & n catholique (mf).

romance [rəuˈmæns] n **1** (story) histoire f ou roman m d'amour; (love) amour m; (affair) aventure f amoureuse; (charm) poésie f. **2** a **R. language** langue f romane. ◆**romantic** a (of love, tenderness etc) romantique; (fanciful, imaginary) romanesque; — n (person) romantique mf. ◆**romantically** adv (to behave) de façon romantique. ◆**romanticism** n romantisme m.

Romania [rəuˈmeiniə] n Roumanie f. ◆**Romanian** a & n roumain, -aine mf; — n (language) roumain m.

romp [rɒmp] vi s'ébattre (bruyamment); **to r. through** (exam) Fig avoir les doigts dans le nez; — n ébats mpl.

rompers [ˈrɒmpəz] npl (for baby) barboteuse f.

roof [ruːf] n (of building, vehicle) toit m; (of tunnel, cave) plafond m; **r. of the mouth** voûte f du palais; **r. rack** (of car) galerie f. ◆**—ing** n toiture f. ◆**rooftop** n toit m.

rook [ruk] n **1** (bird) corneille f. **2** Chess tour f.

rookie [ˈruki] n (new recruit) Mil Fam bleu m.

room [ruːm, rum] n **1** (in house etc) pièce f; (bedroom) chambre f; (large, public) salle f; **one's rooms** son appartement m; **in furnished rooms** en meublé; **men's r., ladies' r.** Am toilettes fpl. **2** (space) place f (for pour); (some) r. de la place; **there's r. for doubt** le doute est permis; **no r. for** doubt aucun doute possible. ◆**rooming house** n Am maison f de rapport. ◆**roommate** n camarade mf de chambre. ◆**roomy** a (-ier, -iest) spacieux; (clothes) ample.

roost [ruːst] vi (of bird) percher; – n perchoir m.

rooster [ˈruːstər] n coq m.

root [ruːt] **1** n (of plant, person etc) & Math racine f; Fig cause f, origine f; **to pull up by the root(s)** déraciner; **to take r.** (of plant) & Fig prendre racine; **to put down (new) roots** Fig s'enraciner; **r. cause** cause f première; – vt **r. out** (destroy) extirper. **2** vi (of plant cutting) s'enraciner; **to r. about for** fouiller pour trouver. **3** vi **r. for** (cheer, support) Fam encourager. ◆—**ed** a **deeply r.** bien enraciné (in dans); **r. to the spot** (immobile) cloué sur place. ◆—**less** a sans racines.

rope [rəʊp] n corde f; Nau cordage m; **to know the ropes** Fam être au courant; – vt (tie) lier; **to r. s.o. in** (force to help) Fam embrigader qn (**to do** pour faire); **to r. off** séparer (par une corde). ◆**r.-and-'tumble** n (fight) mêlée f; (of s.o.'s life) remue-ménage m. ◆**roughen** vt rendre rude. ◆**roughly¹** adv (not gently) rudement; (coarsely) grossièrement; (brutally) brutalement. ◆**roughness** n rudesse f, inégalité f; grossièreté f; brutalité f.

rosary [ˈrəʊzəri] n Rel chapelet m.

rose¹ [rəʊz] n **1** (flower) rose f; (colour) rose m; **r. bush** rosier m. **2** (of watering can) pomme f. ◆**ro'sette** n Sp cocarde f; (rose-shaped) rosette f. ◆**rosy** a (-ier, -iest) (pink) rose; (future) Fig rose in rose.

rose² [rəʊz] see rise.

rosé [ˈrəʊzeɪ] n (wine) rosé m.

rosemary [ˈrəʊzməri] n Bot Culin romarin m.

roster [ˈrɒstər] n (duty) r. liste f (de service).

rostrum [ˈrɒstrəm] n tribune f; Sp podium m.

rot [rɒt] n pourriture f; (nonsense) Fam inepties fpl; – vti (-tt-) **to r. (away)** pourrir.

rota [ˈrəʊtə] n liste f (de service).

rotate [rəʊˈteɪt] vi tourner; – vt faire tourner; (crops) alterner. ◆**'rotary** a rotatif; **r. airer** (washing line) séchoir m parapluie; – n (roundabout) Aut Am sens m giratoire. ◆**rotation** n rotation f; **in r.** à tour de rôle.

rote [rəʊt] n **by r.** machinalement.

rotten [ˈrɒt(ə)n] a (decayed, corrupt) pourri; (bad) Fam moche; (filthy) Fam sale; **to feel r.** (ill) être mal fichu. ◆**rottenness** n pourriture f. ◆**rotting** a (meat, fruit etc) qui pourrit.

rotund [rəʊˈtʌnd] a (round) rond; (plump) rondelet.

rouble [ˈruːb(ə)l] n (currency) rouble m.

rouge [ruːʒ] n rouge m (à joues).

rough¹ [rʌf] a (-er, -est) (surface, task, manners) rude; (ground) inégal, accidenté; (rocky) rocailleux; (plank, bark) rugueux; (sound) âpre, rude; (coarse) grossier; (brutal) brutal; (weather, neighbourhood) mauvais; (sea) agité; (justice) sommaire; (diamond) brut; **a r. child** (unruly) un enfant dur; **to feel r.** (ill) Fam être mal fichu; **r. and ready** (conditions, solution) grossier (mais adéquat); – adv **to sleep, live**) à la dure; (to play) brutalement; (of violent man) Fam voyou m; – vt **to r. it** Fam vivre à la dure; **to r. up** (hair) ébouriffer; (person) Fam malmener. ◆**r.-and-'tumble** n (fight) mêlée f; (of s.o.'s life) remue-ménage m. ◆**roughen** vt rendre rude. ◆**roughly¹** adv (not gently) rudement; (coarsely) grossièrement; (brutally) brutalement. ◆**roughness** n rudesse f, inégalité f; grossièreté f; brutalité f.

roughage [ˈrʌfɪdʒ] n (in food) fibres fpl (alimentaires).

rough² [rʌf] a (-er, -est) (calculation, figure, terms etc) approximatif; **r. copy, r. draft** brouillon m; **r. paper** du papier brouillon; **r. guess, r. estimate** approximation f; **a r. plan** l'ébauche f d'un projet; – vt **to r. out** (plan) ébaucher. ◆—**ly²** adv (approximately) à peu (de choses) près.

roulette [ruːˈlet] n roulette f.

round [raʊnd] **1** adv autour; **all r., right r.** tout autour; **to go r. to s.o.** passer chez qn; **to ask r.** inviter chez soi; **he'll be r.** il passera; **r. here** par ici; **the long way r.** le chemin le plus long; – prep autour de; **r. about** (house etc) autour de; (approximately) environ; **r. (about) midday** vers midi; **to go r.** (world) faire le tour de; (corner) tourner. **2** a (-er, -est) rond; **a r. trip** Am (voyage) aller et retour. **3** n (slice) Culin tranche f; Sp Mil manche f; (of golf) partie f; Boxing round m; (of talks) série f; (of drinks, visits) tournée f; **one's round(s)** (of milkman etc) sa tournée; (of doctor) ses visites fpl; (of policeman) sa ronde; **delivery r.** livraisons fpl, tournée f; **r. of applause** salve f d'applaudissements; **r. of ammunition** cartouche f, balle f; – vt **to turn a corner** (in car) prendre un virage; **to r. off** (finish) terminer; **to r. up** (gather) rassembler; (figure) arrondir au chiffre supérieur. ◆**r.-'shouldered** a voûté, aux épaules rondes. ◆**rounded** a arrondi. ◆**rounders** npl Sp sorte de baseball. ◆**roundness** n rondeur f. ◆**roundup** n (of criminals) rafle f.

roundabout ['raʊndəbaʊt] **1** *a* indirect, détourné. **2** *n* (*at funfair*) manège *m*; (*junction*) *Aut* rond-point *m* (à sens giratoire).

rous/e [raʊz] *vt* éveiller; **roused (to anger)** en colère; **to r. to action** inciter à agir. **◆-ing** *a* (*welcome*) enthousiaste; (*speech*) vibrant; (*music*) allègre.

rout [raʊt] *n* (*defeat*) déen déroute *f*; **- vt** mettre route.

route **1** [ruːt] *n* itinéraire *m*; (*of aircraft*) route *f*; **sea r.** route *f* maritime; **bus r.** ligne *f* d'autobus; **- vt** (*delivery round*) *Am* tournée de. **2** [raʊt] *n* (*delivery round*) *Am* tournée.

routine [ruːˈtiːn] *n* routine *f*; **one's daily r.** (*in office etc*) son travail journalier; **the daily r.** (*monotony*) le train-train quotidien; **- a** (*inquiry, work etc*) de routine; *Pej* de routine.

rov/e [raʊv] *vi* errer; **- vt** parcourir. **◆-ing** *a* (*life*) nomade; (*ambassador*) itinérant.

row **1** [raʊ] *n* (*line*) rang *m*, rangée *f*; (*of cars*) file *f*; **two days in a r.** deux jours de suite *or* d'affilée. **2** *vi* (*in boat*) ramer; **- vt** (*boat*) faire aller à la rame; (*person*) transporter en canot; **- n to go for a r.** canoter; **r. boat** *Am* bateau *m* à rames. **◆-ing** *n* canotage *m*; *Sp* aviron *m*; **r. boat** bateau *m* à rames.

row **2** [raʊ] *n Fam* (*noise*) vacarme *m*; (*quarrel*) querelle *f*; **- vi** *Fam* se quereller (**with** avec).

rowdy ['raʊdɪ] *a* (**-ier, -iest**) chahuteur (et brutal); **- n** (*person*) *Fam* voyou *m*.

royal ['rɔɪəl] *a* royal; **- npl the royals** *Fam* la famille royale. **◆royalist** *a* & *n* royaliste (*mf*). **◆royally** *adv* (*to treat*) royalement. **◆royalty 1** *n* (*persons*) personnages *mpl* royaux. **2** *npl* (*from book*) droits *mpl* d'auteur; (*on oil, from patent*) royalties *fpl*.

rub [rʌb] *vt* (**-bb-**) frotter; (*polish*) astiquer; **to r. shoulders with** *Fig* coudoyer, côtoyer; **to r. away** (*mark*) effacer; (*tears*) essuyer; **to r. down** (*person*) frictionner; (*wood, with sandpaper*) poncer; **to r. it in** *Pej Fam* retourner le couteau dans la plaie; **to r. off** *or* **out** (*mark*) effacer; **rubbing alcohol** *Am* alcool *m* à 90°; **- vi** frotter; **to r. off** (*of mark*) partir; (*of manners etc*) déteindre (**on s.o.** sur qn); **- n** (*massage*) friction *f*; **to give sth a r.** frotter qch; (*polish*) astiquer qch.

rubber ['rʌbər] *n* (*substance*) caoutchouc *m*; (*eraser*) gomme *f*; (*contraceptive*) *Am Sl* capote *f*; **r. stamp** tampon *m*. **◆r.-'stamp** *vt Pej* approuver (sans discuter). **◆rubbery** *a* caoutchouteux.

rubbish ['rʌbɪʃ] **1** *n* (*refuse*) ordures *fpl*; (*junk*) saleté(s) *f(pl)*; (*nonsense*) *Fig* absurdités *fpl*; **that's r.** (*absurd*) c'est absurde; (*worthless*) ça ne vaut rien; **r. bin** poubelle *f*; **r. dump** dépôt *m* d'ordures, décharge *f* (publique); (*in garden*) tas *m* d'ordures. **2** *vt* **r. s.o./sth** (*criticize*) *Fam* dénigrer qn/qch. **◆rubbishy** *a* (*book etc*) sans valeur; (*goods*) de mauvaise qualité.

rubble ['rʌb(ə)l] *n* décombres *mpl*.

ruble ['ruːb(ə)l] *n* (*currency*) rouble *m*.

ruby ['ruːbɪ] *n* (*gem*) rubis *m*.

rucksack ['rʌksæk] *n* sac *m* à dos.

ruckus ['rʌkəs] *n* (*uproar*) *Fam* chahut *m*.

rudder ['rʌdər] *n* gouvernail *m*.

ruddy ['rʌdɪ] *a* (**-ier, -iest**) **1** (*complexion*) coloré. **2** (*bloody*) *Sl* fichu.

rude [ruːd] *a* (**-er, -est**) (*impolite*) impoli (**to** envers); (*coarse*) grossier; (*indecent*) indécent, obscène; (*shock*) violent. **◆-ly** *adv* impoliment; grossièrement. **◆-ness** *n* impolitesse *f*; grossièreté *f*.

rudiments ['ruːdɪmənts] *npl* rudiments *mpl*. **◆rudi'mentary** *a* rudimentaire.

ruffian ['rʌfɪən] *n* voyou *m*.

ruffle ['rʌf(ə)l] **1** *vt* (*hair*) ébouriffer; (*water*) troubler; **to r. s.o.** (*offend*) froisser qn. **2** *n* (*frill*) ruche *f*.

rug [rʌg] *n* carpette *f*, petit tapis *m*; (*over knees*) plaid *m*; (*bedside*) descente *f* de lit.

rugby ['rʌgbɪ] *n* **r.** (*football*) rugby *m*. **◆rugger** *n Fam* rugby *m*.

rugged ['rʌgɪd] *a* (*surface*) rugueux, rude; (*terrain, coast*) accidenté; (*person, features, manners*) rude; (*determination*) *Fig* farouche.

ruin ['ruːɪn] *n* (*destruction, rubble, building etc*) ruine *f*; **in ruins** (*building*) en ruine; **- vt** (*health, country, person etc*) ruiner; (*clothes*) abîmer; (*spoil*) gâter. **◆-ed** *a* (*person, country etc*) ruiné; (*building*) en ruine. **◆ruinous** *a* ruineux.

rul/e [ruːl] **1** *n* (*principle*) règle *f*; (*regulation*) règlement *m*; (*custom*) coutume *f*; (*authority*) autorité *f*; *Pol* gouvernement *m*; **against the rules** contraire à la règle; **as a** (**general**) **r.** en règle générale; **it's the** *or* **a r. that** il est de règle que (+ *sub*); **- vt** (*country*) *Pol* gouverner; (*decide*) *Jur Sp* décider (**that** que); **to r. s.o.** (*dominate*) mener qn; **to r. out** (*exclude*) exclure; **- vi** (*of monarch*) régner (**over** sur); (*of judge*) statuer (**against** contre, **on** sur). **2** *n* (*for measuring*) règle *f*. **◆-ed** *a* (*paper*) réglé, ligné. **◆-ing** *a* (*passion*) dominant;

(*class*) dirigeant; (*party*) *Pol* au pouvoir; – *n Jur Sp* décision *f.* ◆**ruler n 1** (*of country*) *Pol* dirigeant, -ante *mf*; (*sovereign*) souverain, -aine *mf.* **2** (*measure*) règle *f.*

rum [rʌm] *n* rhum *m.*

Rumania [ruːˈmeɪnɪə] *see* **Romania.**

rumble [ˈrʌmb(ə)l] *vi* (*of train, thunder, gun*) gronder; (*of stomach*) gargouiller; – *n* grondement *m*; gargouillement *m.*

ruminate [ˈruːmɪneɪt] *vi* to r. over (*scheme etc*) ruminer.

rummage [ˈrʌmɪdʒ] *vi* to r. (**about**) farfouiller; **r. sale** (*used clothes etc*) *Am* vente *f* de charité.

rumour [ˈruːmər] *n* rumeur *f*, bruit *m.* ◆**rumoured** *a* **it is r. that** on dit que.

rump [rʌmp] *n* (*of horse*) croupe *f*; (*of fowl*) croupion *m*; **r. steak** rumsteck *m.*

rumple [ˈrʌmp(ə)l] *vt* (*clothes*) chiffonner.

run [rʌn] *n* (*running*) course *f*; (*outing*) tour *m*; (*journey*) parcours *m*, trajet *m*; (*series*) série *f*; (*period*) période *f*; *Cards* suite *f*; (*rush*) ruée *f* (**on** sur); (*trend*) tendance *f*; (*for skiing*) piste *f*; (*in cricket*) point *m*; **to go for a r.** courir, faire une course à pied; **on the r.** (*prisoner etc*) en fuite; **to have the r. of** (*house etc*) avoir à sa disposition; **in the long r.** avec le temps, à la longue; **the runs** *Med Fam* la diarrhée; – *vi* (*pt* **ran**, *pp* **run**, *pres p* **running**) courir; (*flee*) fuir; (*of curtain*) glisser; (*of river, nose, pen, tap*) couler; (*of colour in washing*) déteindre; (*of ink*) baver; (*melt*) fondre; (*of play, film*) se jouer; (*of contract*) être valide; (*last*) durer; (*pass*) passer; (*function*) marcher; (*tick over*) *Aut* tourner; (*of stocking*) filer; **to r. down/in/out** (*enter, leave*) descendre/entrer/*etc* en courant; **to r. for president** être candidat à la présidence; **to r. with blood** ruisseler de sang; **to r. between** (*of bus*) faire le service entre; **to go running** *Sp* faire du jogging; **the road runs to ...** la route va à ...; **the river runs into the sea** le fleuve se jette dans la mer; **it runs into a hundred pounds** ça va chercher dans les cent livres; **it runs in the family** ça tient de famille; – *vt* (*race, risk*) courir; (*horse*) faire courir; (*temperature, errand*) faire; (*blockade*) forcer; (*machine*) faire fonctionner; (*engine*) *Aut* faire tourner; (*drive*) *Aut* conduire; (*furniture, goods*) transporter (**to** à); (*business, country etc*) diriger; (*courses, events*) organiser; (*film, play*) présenter; (*house*) tenir; (*article*) publier (**on** sur); (*bath*) faire couler; **to r. one's hand over** passer la main sur; **to r. one's eye over** jeter un coup d'œil à sur; **to r. its course** (*of illness etc*) suivre son

cours; **to r. 5 km** *Sp* faire 5 km de course à pied; **to r. a car** avoir une voiture. ■ **to r. about** *vi* courir çà et là; (*gallivant*) se balader; **to r. across** *vt* (*meet*) tomber sur; **to r. along** *vi* **r. along!** filez!; **to r. away** *vi* (*flee*) s'enfuir, se sauver (**from** de); **to r. back** *vt* (*person*) *Aut* ramener (**to** à); **to r. down** *vt* (*pedestrian*) *Aut* renverser; (*belittle*) dénigrer; (*restrict*) limiter peu à peu. ◆**r.-down** *a* (*weak, tired*) *Med* à plat; (*district etc*) miteux; **to r. in** *vt* (*vehicle*) roder; **to r. s.o. in** *Jur Fam* arrêter qn; **to r. into** *vt* (*meet*) tomber sur; (*crash into*) *Aut* percuter; **to r. into debt** s'endetter; **to r. off** *vt* (*print*) tirer; – *vi* (*flee*) s'enfuir; **to r. out** *vi* (*of stocks*) s'épuiser; (*of lease*) expirer; (*of time*) manquer; **to r. out of** (*time, money*) manquer de; **we've run out of coffee** on n'a plus de café; – *vt* **to r. s.o. out of** (*chase*) chasser qn de; **to r. over** *vi* (*of liquid*) déborder; – *vt* (*kill pedestrian*) *Aut* écraser; (*knock down pedestrian*) *Aut* renverser; (*notes, text*) revoir; **to r. round** *vt* (*surround*) entourer; **to r. through** *vt* (*recap*) revoir; **to r. up** *vt* (*bill, debts*) laisser s'accumuler. ◆**r.-up** *n* **the r.-up to** (*elections etc*) la période qui précède. ◆**running** *n* course *f*; (*of machine*) fonctionnement *m*; (*of firm, country*) direction *f*; **to be in/out of the r.** être/ne plus être dans la course; – *a* (*commentary*) suivi; (*battle*) continuel; **r. water** eau *f* courante; **six days/***etc* **r.** six jours/*etc* de suite; **r. costs** (*of factory*) frais *mpl* d'exploitation; (*of car*) dépenses *fpl* courantes. ◆**runner** *n Sp etc* coureur *m*; **r. bean** haricot *m* (grimpant). ◆**runner-'up** *n Sp* second, -onde *mf.* ◆**runny** *a* (-**ier**, -**iest**) *a* liquide; (*nose*) qui coule.

runaway [ˈrʌnəweɪ] *n* fugitif, -ive *mf*; – *a* (*car, horse*) emballé; (*lorry*) fou; (*wedding*) clandestin; (*victory*) qu'on remporte haut la main; (*inflation*) galopant.

rung¹ [rʌŋ] *n* (*of ladder*) barreau *m.*

rung² [rʌŋ] *see* **ring².**

run-of-the-mill [rʌnəvðəˈmɪl] *a* ordinaire.

runway [ˈrʌnweɪ] *n Av* piste *f.*

rupture [ˈrʌptʃər] *n Med* hernie *f*; **the r. of** (*breaking*) la rupture de; – *vt* rompre; **to r. oneself** se donner une hernie.

rural [ˈrʊərəl] *a* rural.

ruse [ruːz] *n* (*trick*) ruse *f.*

rush¹ [rʌʃ] *n* (*to move fast, throw oneself*) se précipiter, se ruer (**at** sur, **towards** vers); (*of blood*) affluer (**to** à); (*hurry*) se dépêcher (**to do** de faire); (*of vehicle*) foncer; **to r. out** partir en vitesse; – *vt* (*attack*) *Mil* foncer sur; **to r. s.o.** bousculer qn; **to r. s.o. to hospital** transporter qn d'urgence à l'hôpital; **to r. (through) sth** (*job, meal, order etc*) faire, manger, envoyer *etc* qch en vitesse; **to be rushed into** (*decision, answer etc*) être forcé à prendre, donner *etc*; – *n* ruée *f* (**for** vers, **on** sur); (*confusion*) bousculade *f*; (*hurry*) hâte *f*; (*of orders*) avalanche *f*; **to be in a r.** être pressé (**to do** de faire); **to leave/etc in a r.** partir/*etc* en vitesse; **the gold r.** la ruée vers l'or; **the r. hour** l'heure *f* d'affluence; **a r. job** un travail d'urgence.

rush² [rʌʃ] *n* (*plant*) jonc *m*.

rusk [rʌsk] *n* biscotte *f*.

russet [ˈrʌsɪt] *a* roux, roussâtre.

Russia [ˈrʌʃə] *n* Russie *f*. ◆**Russian** *a & n* russe (*mf*); – *n* (*language*) russe *m*.

rust [rʌst] *n* rouille *f*; – *vi* (se) rouiller. ◆**rustproof** *a* inoxydable. ◆**rusty** *a* (**-ier, -iest**) (*metal, athlete, memory etc*) rouillé.

rustic [ˈrʌstɪk] *a* rustique.

rustle [ˈrʌs(ə)l] **1** *vi* (*of leaves*) bruire; (*of skirt*) froufrouter; – *n* bruissement *m*; frou-frou *m*. **2** *vt* **to r. up** *Fam* (*prepare*) préparer; (*find*) trouver.

rut [rʌt] *n* ornière *f*; **to be in a r.** *Fig* être encroûté.

rutabaga [ruːtəˈbeɪgə] *n* (*swede*) *Am* rutabaga *m*.

ruthless [ˈruːθləs] *a* (*attack, person etc*) impitoyable, cruel; (*in taking decisions*) très ferme. ◆**—ness** *n* cruauté *f*.

rye [raɪ] *n* seigle *m*; **r. bread** pain *m* de

S

S, s [es] *n* S, s *m*.

Sabbath [ˈsæbəθ] *n* (*Jewish*) sabbat *m*; (*Christian*) dimanche *m*. ◆**sa'bbatical** *a* (*year etc*) *Univ* sabbatique.

sabotage [ˈsæbətɑːʒ] *n* sabotage *m*; – *vt* saboter. ◆**saboteur** [-ˈtɜːr] *n* saboteur, -euse *mf*.

sabre [ˈseɪbər] *n* (*sword*) sabre *m*.

saccharin [ˈsækərɪn] *n* saccharine *f*.

sachet [ˈsæʃeɪ] *n* (*of lavender etc*) sachet *m*; (*of shampoo*) dosette *f*.

sack [sæk] **1** *n* (*bag*) sac *m*. **2** *vt* (*dismiss*) *Fam* virer, renvoyer; – *n Fam* **to get the s.** se faire virer; **to give s.o. the s.** virer qn. **3** *vt* (*town etc*) saccager, mettre à sac. ◆**—ing** *n* **1** (*cloth*) toile *f* à sac. **2** (*dismissal*) *Fam* renvoi *m*.

sacrament [ˈsækrəmənt] *n Rel* sacrement *m*.

sacred [ˈseɪkrɪd] *a* (*holy*) sacré.

sacrifice [ˈsækrɪfaɪs] *n* sacrifice *m*; – *vt* sacrifier (**to** à, **for sth/s.o.** pour qch/qn).

sacrilege [ˈsækrɪlɪdʒ] *n* sacrilège *m*. ◆**sacri'legious** *a* sacrilège.

sacrosanct [ˈsækrəʊsæŋkt] *a Iron* sacro-saint.

sad [sæd] *a* (**sadder, saddest**) triste. ◆**sadden** *vt* attrister. ◆**sadly** *adv* tristement; (*unfortunately*) malheureusement; (*very*) très. ◆**sadness** *n* tristesse *f*.

saddle [ˈsæd(ə)l] *n* selle *f*; **to be in the s.** (*in*

control) *Fig* tenir les rênes; – *vt* (*horse*) seller; **to s.o. with** (*chore, person*) *Fam* coller à qn.

sadism [ˈseɪdɪz(ə)m] *n* sadisme *m*. ◆**sadist** *n* sadique *mf*. ◆**sa'distic** *a* sadique.

sae [eseiˈi:] *abbr* = stamped addressed envelope.

safari [səˈfɑːrɪ] *n* safari *m*; **to be** or **go on s.** faire un safari.

safe¹ [seɪf] *a* (**-er, -est**) (*person*) en sécurité; (*equipment, toy, animal*) sans danger; (*place, investment, method*) sûr; (*bridge, ladder*) solide; (*prudent*) prudent; (*winner*) assuré, garanti; **s. (and sound)** sain et sauf; **it's s. to go out** on peut sortir sans danger; **the safest thing (to do) is . . .** le plus sûr est de . . .; **s. from** à l'abri de; **to be on the s. side** pour plus de sûreté; **in s. hands** en mains sûres; **s. journey!** bon voyage! ◆**s.-'conduct** *n* sauf-conduit *m*. ◆**safe-keeping** *n* **for s.** à garder en sécurité. ◆**safely** *adv* (*without mishap*) sans accident; (*securely*) en sûreté; (*without risk*) sans risque, sans danger. ◆**safety** *n* sécurité *f*; (*solidity*) solidité *f*; (*salvation*) salut *m*; – *a* (*belt, device, screen, margin*) de sécurité; (*pin, razor, chain, valve*) de sûreté; **s. precaution** mesure *f* de sécurité.

safe² [seɪf] *n* (*for money etc*) coffre-fort *m*.

safeguard [ˈseɪfgɑːd] *n* sauvegarde *f* (**against** contre); – *vt* sauvegarder.

saffron ['sæfrən] *n* safran *m*.

sag [sæg] *vi* (**-gg-**) (*of roof, ground*) s'affaisser; (*of cheeks*) pendre; (*of prices, knees*) fléchir. ◆**sagging** *a* (*roof, breasts*) affaissé.

saga ['sɑːɡə] *n Liter* saga *f*; (*bad sequence of events*) *Fig* feuilleton *m*.

sage [seɪdʒ] *n* **1** *Bot Culin* sauge *f*. **2** (*wise man*) sage *m*.

Sagittarius [sædʒɪ'teərɪəs] *n* (*sign*) le Sagittaire.

sago ['seɪɡəʊ] *n* (*cereal*) sagou *m*.

Sahara [sə'hɑːrə] *n* the S. (*desert*) le Sahara.

said [sed] *see* **say**.

sail [seɪl] *vi* (*navigate*) naviguer; (*leave*) partir; *Sp* faire de la voile; (*glide*) *Fig* glisser; **to s. into port** entrer au port; **to s. round** (*world, island etc*) faire le tour de en bateau; **to s. through** (*exam etc*) *Fig* réussir haut la main; – *vt* (*boat*) piloter; (*seas*) parcourir; – *n* voile *f*; (*trip*) tour *m* en bateau; **to set s.** (*of boat*) partir (**for** à destination de). ◆**–ing** *n* navigation *f*; *Sp* voile *f*; (*departure*) départ *m*; (*crossing*) traversée *f*; **s. boat** voilier *m*. ◆**sailboard** *n* planche *f* (à voile). ◆**sailboat** *n Am* voilier *m*. ◆**sailor** *n* marin *m*, matelot *m*.

saint [seɪnt] *n* saint, sainte *f*; **S. John** Jean; **s.'s day** *Rel* fête *f* (de saint). ◆**saintly** *a* (**-ier, -iest**) saint.

sake [seɪk] *n* **for my/your s.** pour moi/toi; **for your father's s.** pour (l'amour de) ton père; (**just**) **for the s. of eating**/*etc* simplement pour manger/*etc*; **for heaven's or God's s.** pour l'amour de Dieu.

salacious [sə'leɪʃəs] *a* obscène.

salad ['sæləd] *n* (*dish of vegetables, fruit etc*) salade *f*; **s. bowl** saladier *m*; **s. cream** mayonnaise *f*; **s. dressing** vinaigrette *f*.

salamander ['sæləmændər] *n* (*lizard*) salamandre *f*.

salami [sə'lɑːmɪ] *n* salami *m*.

salary ['sælərɪ] *n* (*professional*) traitement *m*; (*wage*) salaire *m*. ◆**salaried** *a* (*person*) qui perçoit un traitement.

sale [seɪl] *n* vente *f*; **sale(s)** (*at reduced prices*) *Com* soldes *mpl*; **in a** *or* **the s.**, *Am* **on s.** (*cheaply*) en solde; **on s.** (*available*) en vente; (**up**) **for s.** à vendre; **to put up for s.** mettre en vente; **sales check** *or* **slip** *Am* reçu *m*. ◆**saleable** *a Com* vendable. ◆**salesclerk** *n Am* vendeur, -euse *mf*. ◆**salesman** *n* (*pl* **-men**) (*in shop*) vendeur *m*; (*travelling*) représentant *m* de commerce). ◆**saleswoman** *n* (*pl* **-women**) vendeuse *f*; représentante *f* de commerce).

salient ['seɪlɪənt] *a* (*point, fact*) marquant.

saliva [sə'laɪvə] *n* salive *f*. ◆**salivate** *vi* saliver.

sallow ['sæləʊ] *a* (**-er, -est**) jaunâtre.

sally ['sælɪ] *n Mil* sortie *f*; – *vi* **to s. forth** *Fig* sortir allègrement.

salmon ['sæmən] *n* saumon *m*.

salmonella [sælmə'nelə] *n* (*poisoning*) salmonellose *f*.

salon ['sælɒn] *n* **beauty/hairdressing s.** salon *m* de beauté/de coiffure.

saloon [sə'luːn] *n Nau* salon *m*; (*car*) berline *f*; (*bar*) *Am* bar *m*; **s. bar** (*of pub*) salle *f* chic.

salt [sɔːlt] *n* sel *m*; **bath salts** sels *mpl* de bain; – *a* (*water, beef etc*) salé; (*mine*) de sel; **s. free** sans sel; – *vt* saler. ◆**saltcellar**, *Am* ◆**saltshaker** *n* salière *f*. ◆**salty** *a* (**-ier, -iest**) *a* salé.

salubrious [sə'luːbrɪəs] *a* salubre.

salutary ['sæljʊtərɪ] *a* salutaire.

salute [sə'luːt] *n Mil* (*of guns*) salve *f*; – *vt* (*greet*) & *Mil* saluer; – *vi Mil* faire un salut.

salvage ['sælvɪdʒ] *n* sauvetage *m* (**of** de); récupération *f* (**of** de); (*saved goods*) objets *mpl* sauvés; – *vt* (*save*) sauver (**from** de); (*old iron etc to be used again*) récupérer.

salvation [sæl'veɪʃ(ə)n] *n* salut *m*.

same [seɪm] *a* même; **the** (**very**) **s. house as** (*exactement*) la même maison que; – *pron* **the s.** le même, la même; **the s.** (**thing**) la même chose; **it's all the s. to me** ça m'est égal; **all** *or* **just the s.** tout de même; **to do the s.** en faire autant. ◆**–ness** *n* identité *f*; *Pej* monotonie *f*.

sample ['sɑːmp(ə)l] *n* échantillon *m*; (*of blood*) prélèvement *m*; – *vt* (*wine, cheese etc*) déguster, goûter; (*product, recipe etc*) essayer; (*army life etc*) goûter de. ◆**–ing** *n* (*of wine*) dégustation *f*.

sanatorium [sænə'tɔːrɪəm] *n* sanatorium *m*.

sanctify ['sæŋktɪfaɪ] *vt* sanctifier. ◆**sanctity** *n* sainteté *f*. ◆**sanctuary** *n Rel* sanctuaire *m*; (*refuge*) & *Pol* asile *m*; (*for animals*) réserve *f*.

sanctimonious [sæŋktɪ'məʊnɪəs] *a* (*person, manner*) tartufe.

sanction ['sæŋkʃ(ə)n] *n* (*approval, punishment*) sanction *f*; – *vt* (*approve*) sanctionner.

sand [sænd] *n* sable *m*; **the sands** (*beach*) la plage; (*road*) sabler; **to s.** (**down**) (*wood etc*) poncer. ◆**sandbag** *n* sac *m* de sable. ◆**sandcastle** *n* château *m* de sable. ◆**sander** *n* (*machine*) ponceuse *f*. ◆**sandpaper** *n* papier *m* de verre; – *vt* poncer. ◆**sandstone** n (rock) grès m. ◆**sandy** a (-ier, -iest) (beach) de sable; (road, ground) sablonneux; (water) sableux. 2 (hair) blond roux inv.

sandal ['sænd(ə)l] n sandale f.

sandwich ['sænwɪdʒ] 1 n sandwich m; cheese/etc s. sandwich au fromage/etc. 2 vt to s. (in) (fit in) intercaler; sandwiched in between (cars etc) coincé entre.

sane [seɪn] a (-er, -est) (person) sain (d'esprit); (idea, attitude) raisonnable.

sang [sæŋ] see sing.

sanguine ['sæŋgwɪn] a (hopeful) optimiste.

sanitarium [sænɪ'teərɪəm] n Am sanatorium m.

sanitary ['sænɪtərɪ] a (fittings, conditions) sanitaire; (clean) hygiénique. ◆**sani'tation** n hygiène f (publique); (plumbing etc) installations fpl sanitaires.

sanity ['sænɪtɪ] n santé f mentale; (reason) raison f.

sank [sæŋk] see sink[2].

Santa Claus ['sæntəklɔːz] n le père Noël.

sap [sæp] 1 n Bot & Fig sève f. 2 vt (-pp-) (weaken) miner (énergie etc).

sapphire ['sæfaɪər] n (jewel, needle) saphir m.

sarcasm ['sɑːkæz(ə)m] n sarcasme m. ◆**sar'castic** a sarcastique.

sardine [sɑː'diːn] n sardine f.

Sardinia [sɑː'dɪnɪə] n Sardaigne f.

sardonic [sɑː'dɒnɪk] a sardonique.

sash [sæʃ] n 1 (on dress) ceinture f; (of mayor etc) écharpe f. 2 s. window fenêtre f à guillotine.

sat [sæt] see sit.

Satan ['seɪt(ə)n] n Satan m. ◆**sa'tanic** a satanique.

satchel ['sætʃ(ə)l] n cartable m.

satellite ['sætəlaɪt] n satellite m; s. (country) Pol pays m satellite.

satiate ['seɪʃɪeɪt] vt rassasier.

satin ['sætɪn] n satin m.

satire ['sætaɪər] n satire f (on contre). ◆**sa'tirical** a satirique. ◆**satirist** n écrivain m satirique. ◆**satirize** vt faire la satire de.

satisfaction [sætɪs'fækʃ(ə)n] n satisfaction f. ◆**satisfactory** a satisfaisant. ◆**satisfy** vt satisfaire; (persuade, convince) persuader (that que); (demand, condition) satisfaire à; to s. oneself as to/that s'assurer de/que; satisfied with satisfait de; — vi donner satisfaction. ◆**satisfying** a satisfaisant; (food, meal) substantiel.

satsuma [sæt'suːmə] n (fruit) mandarine f.

saturate ['sætʃəreɪt] vt (fill) saturer (with

de); (soak) tremper. ◆**satu'ration** n saturation f.

Saturday ['sætədɪ] n samedi m.

sauce [sɔːs] n 1 sauce f; tomato s. sauce tomate; s. boat saucière f. 2 (cheek) Fam toupet m. ◆**saucy** a (-ier, -iest) (cheeky) impertinent; (smart) Fam coquet.

saucepan ['sɔːspən] n casserole f.

saucer ['sɔːsər] n soucoupe f.

Saudi Arabia [saʊdɪə'reɪbɪə, Am sɔːdɪə'reɪbɪə] n Arabie f Séoudite.

sauna ['sɔːnə] n sauna m.

saunter ['sɔːntər] vi flâner.

sausage ['sɒsɪdʒ] n (cooked, for cooking) saucisse f; (precooked, dried) saucisson m.

sauté ['səʊteɪ] a Culin sauté.

savage ['sævɪdʒ] a (primitive) sauvage; (fierce) féroce; (brutal, cruel) brutal, sauvage; — n (brute) sauvage mf; — vt (of animal, critic etc) attaquer (férocement). ◆**savagery** n (cruelty) sauvagerie f.

save [seɪv] 1 vt sauver (from de); (keep) garder, réserver; (money, time) économiser, épargner; (stamps) collectionner; (prevent) empêcher (from de); (problems, trouble) éviter; that will s. him or her (the bother of) going ça lui évitera d'y aller; to s. up (money) économiser; — vi to s. (up) faire des économies (for sth, to buy sth pour (s')acheter qch); — n Fb arrêt m. 2 prep (except) sauf. ◆**—ing** n (of time, money) économie f, épargne f (of de); (rescue) sauvetage m; (thrifty habit) l'épargne f; pl (money) économies fpl; savings bank caisse f d'épargne. ◆**saviour** n sauveur m.

saveloy ['sævəlɔɪ] n cervelas m.

savour ['seɪvər] n (taste, interest) saveur f; — vt savourer. ◆**savoury** a (tasty) savoureux; (not sweet) Culin salé; not very s. (neighbourhood) Fig peu recommandable.

saw[1] [sɔː] n scie f; — vt (pt sawed, pp sawn or sawed) scier; to s. off scier; a sawn-off or Am sawed-off shotgun un fusil à canon scié. ◆**sawdust** n sciure f. ◆**sawmill** n scierie f.

saw[2] [sɔː] see see[1].

saxophone ['sæksəfəʊn] n saxophone m.

say [seɪ] vt (pt & pp said [sed]) dire (to à, that que); (prayer) faire, dire; (of dial etc) marquer; to s. again répéter; it is said that ... on dit que ... ; what do you s. to a walk? que dirais-tu d'une promenade?; (let's) s. tomorrow disons demain; to s. the least c'est le moins que l'on puisse dire; to s. nothing of ... sans parler de ... ; that's to s. c'est-à-dire; — vi dire; you don't s.!

Fam sans blague!; **I s.!** dites donc!; **s.!** *Am Fam* dis donc!; **– to have one's s.** dire ce que l'on a à dire, s'exprimer; **to have a lot of s.** avoir beaucoup d'influence; **to have no s.** ne pas avoir voix au chapitre (**in** pour). ◆**—ing** *n* proverbe *m*.

scab [skæb] *n* **1** *Med* croûte *f*. **2** (*blackleg*) *Fam* jaune *m*.

scaffold ['skæfəld] *n* échafaudage *m*; (*gallows*) échafaud *m*. ◆**—ing** *n* échafaudage *m*.

scald [skɔːld] *vt* (*burn, cleanse*) ébouillanter; (*sterilize*) stériliser; **– n** brûlure *f*.

scale [skeɪl] **1** *n* (*of map, wages etc*) échelle *f*; (*of numbers*) série *f*; *Mus* gamme *f*; **on a small/large s.** sur une petite/grande échelle; **– a** (*drawing*) à l'échelle; **s. model** modèle *m* réduit; **– vt to s. down** réduire (proportionnellement). **2** *n* (*on fish*) écaille *f*; (*dead skin*) *Med* squame *f*; (*on teeth*) tartre *m*; **– vt** (*teeth*) détartrer. **3** *vt* (*wall*) escalader.

scales [skeɪlz] *npl* (*for weighing*) balance *f*; (*bathroom*) **s.** pèse-personne *m*; (*baby*) **s.** pèse-bébé *m*.

scallion ['skæljən] *n* (*onion*) *Am* ciboule *f*.

scallop ['skɒləp] *n* coquille *f* Saint-Jacques.

scalp [skælp] *n* *Med* cuir *m* chevelu; **– vt** (*cut off too much hair from*) *Fig Hum* tondre (qn).

scalpel ['skælp(ə)l] *n* bistouri *m*, scalpel *m*.

scam [skæm] *n* (*swindle*) *Am Fam* escroquerie *f*.

scamp [skæmp] *n* coquin, -ine *mf*.

scamper ['skæmpər] *vi* **to s. off** *or* **away** détaler.

scampi ['skæmpɪ] *npl* gambas *fpl*.

scan [skæn] **1** *vt* (*-nn-*) (*look at briefly*) parcourir (des yeux); (*scrutinize*) scruter; (*poetry*) scander; (*of radar*) balayer. **2** *n* **to have a s.** (*of pregnant woman*) passer une échographie.

scandal ['skænd(ə)l] *n* (*disgrace*) scandale *m*; (*gossip*) médisances *fpl*; **to cause a s.** (*of film, book etc*) causer un scandale; (*of attitude, conduct*) faire (du) scandale. ◆**scandalize** *vt* scandaliser. ◆**scandalous** *a* scandaleux.

Scandinavia [skændɪ'neɪvɪə] *n* Scandinavie *f*. ◆**Scandinavian** *a & n* scandinave (*mf*).

scanner ['skænər] *n* (*device*) *Med* scanner *m*.

scant [skænt] *a* (*meal, amount*) insuffisant; **s. attention/regard** peu d'attention/de cas. ◆**scantily** *adv* insuffisamment; **s. dressed** à peine vêtu. ◆**scanty** *a* (*-ier, -iest*) insuffisant; (*bikini*) minuscule.

scapegoat ['skeɪpgəʊt] *n* bouc *m* émissaire.

scar [skɑːr] *n* cicatrice *f*; **– vt** (*-rr-*) marquer d'une cicatrice; *Fig* marquer.

scarce [skeəs] *a* (*-er, -est*) (*food, people, book etc*) rare; **to make oneself s.** se tenir à l'écart. ◆**scarcely** *adv* à peine. ◆**scarceness** *n*, ◆**scarcity** *n* (*shortage*) pénurie *f*; (*rarity*) rareté *f*.

scare [skeər] *n* peur *f*; **to give s.o. a s.** faire peur à qn; **bomb s.** alerte *f* à la bombe; **– vt** faire peur à; **to s. off** (*person*) faire fuir; (*animal*) effaroucher. ◆**scared** *a* effrayé; **to be s.** (*stiff*) avoir (très) peur. ◆**scarecrow** *n* épouvantail *m*. ◆**scaremonger** *n* alarmiste *mf*. ◆**scary** *a* (*-ier, -iest*) *Fam* qui fait peur.

scarf [skɑːf] *n* (*pl* **scarves**) (*long*) écharpe *f*; (*square, for women*) foulard *m*.

scarlet ['skɑːlət] *a* écarlate; **s. fever** scarlatine *f*.

scathing ['skeɪðɪŋ] *a* (*remark etc*) acerbe; **to be s.** about critiquer de façon acerbe.

scatter ['skætər] *vt* (*disperse*) disperser (*foule, nuages etc*); (*dot or throw about*) éparpiller; (*spread*) répandre; **– vi** (*of crowd*) se disperser. ◆**—ing** *n* **a s. of houses/etc** quelques maisons/etc dispersées. ◆**scatterbrain** *n* écervelé, -ée *mf*. ◆**scatty** *a* (*-ier, -iest*) *Fam* écervelé, farfelu.

scaveng/e ['skævɪndʒ] *vi* fouiller dans les ordures (**for** pour trouver). ◆**—er** *n Pej* clochard, -arde *mf* (qui fait les poubelles).

scenario [sɪ'nɑːrɪəʊ] *n* (*pl* -os) *Cin & Fig* scénario *m*.

scene [siːn] *n* (*setting, fuss*) *Th* scène *f*; (*of crime, accident etc*) lieu *m*; (*situation*) situation *f*; (*incident*) incident *m*; (*view*) vue *f*; **behind the scenes** *Th & Fig* dans les coulisses; **on the s.** sur les lieux; **to make** *or* **create a s.** faire une scène (à qn). ◆**scenery** *n* paysage *m*, décor *m*; *Th* décor(s) *m(pl)*. ◆**scenic** *a* (*beauty etc*) pittoresque.

scent [sent] *n* (*fragrance, perfume*) parfum *m*; (*animal's track*) *& Fig* piste *f*; **– vt** parfumer (**with** de); (*smell, sense*) flairer.

sceptic ['skeptɪk] *a & n* sceptique (*mf*). ◆**sceptical** *a* sceptique. ◆**scepticism** *n* scepticisme *m*.

sceptre ['septər] *n* sceptre *m*.

schedul/e ['ʃedjuːl, *Am* 'skedjuːl] *n* (*of work etc*) programme *m*; (*timetable*) horaire *m*; (*list*) liste *f*; **to be behind s.** (*of person, train*) avoir du retard; **to be on s.** (*on time*) être à l'heure; (*up to date*) être à jour; **ahead of s.** en avance; **according to s.** comme prévu; **–**

scheme 588 scout

scheme vt (plan) prévoir; (event) fixer le programme ou l'horaire de. ◆—**ed** a (planned) prévu; (service, flight) régulier; **she's s. to leave** at 8 elle doit partir à 8 h.

schem/e [skiːm] n plan m (**to do** pour faire); (idea) idée f; (dishonest trick) combine f, manœuvre f; (arrangement) arrangement m; — vi manœuvrer. ◆—**ing** a intrigant; — npl Pej machinations fpl. ◆—**er** n intrigant, -ante mf.

schizophrenic [skitsəʊ'frenik] a & n schizophrène (mf).

scholar ['skɒlər] n érudit, -ite mf; (specialist) spécialiste mf; (grant holder) boursier, -ière mf. ◆**scholarly** a érudit. ◆**scholarship** n érudition f; (grant) bourse f (d'études). ◆**scho'lastic** a scolaire.

school [skuːl] n école f; (teaching, lessons) classe f; Univ Am faculté f; (within university) institut m, département m; **in** or **at s.** à l'école; **secondary s.**, Am **high s.** collège m, lycée m; **public s.** école f privée; Am école publique; **s. of motoring** auto-école f; **summer s.** cours mpl d'été ou de vacances; – a (year, equipment etc) scolaire; (hours) de classe; **s. fees** frais mpl de scolarité. ◆—**ing** n (learning) instruction f; (attendance) scolarité f. ◆**schoolboy** n écolier m. ◆**schooldays** npl années fpl d'école. ◆**schoolgirl** n écolière f. ◆**schoolhouse** n école f. ◆**school-'leaver** n jeune mf qui a terminé ses études secondaires. ◆**schoolmaster** n (primary) instituteur m; (secondary) professeur m. ◆**schoolmate** n camarade mf de classe. ◆**schoolmistress** n institutrice f; professeur m. ◆**schoolteacher** n (primary) instituteur, -trice mf; (secondary) professeur m.

schooner ['skuːnər] n Nau goélette f.

science ['saɪəns] n science f; **to study s.** étudier les sciences; – a (subject) scientifique; (teacher) de sciences; **s. fiction** science-fiction f. ◆**scien'tific** a scientifique. ◆**scientist** n scientifique mf.

scintillating ['sɪntɪleɪtɪŋ] a (conversation, wit) brillant.

scissors ['sɪzəz] npl ciseaux mpl; **a pair of s.** une paire de ciseaux.

sclerosis [sklɪ'rəʊsɪs] n Med sclérose f; **multiple s.** sclérose en plaques.

scoff [skɒf] **1** vi **to s. at** se moquer de. **2** vti (eat) Fam bouffer.

scold [skəʊld] vt gronder, réprimander (**for doing** pour avoir fait). ◆—**ing** n réprimande f.

scone [skəʊn, skɒn] n petit pain m au lait.

scoop [skuːp] n (shovel) pelle f (à main);

(spoon-shaped) Culin cuiller f; Journ exclusivité f; **at one s.** d'un seul coup; – vt (prizes) rafler; **to s. out** (hollow out) (é)vider; **to s. up** ramasser (avec une pelle ou une cuiller).

scoot [skuːt] vi (rush, leave) Fam filer.

scooter ['skuːtər] n (child's) trottinette f; (motorcycle) scooter m.

scope [skəʊp] n (range) étendue f; (of mind) envergure f; (competence) compétence(s) f(pl); (limits) limites fpl; **for sth/for doing** (opportunity) des possibilités fpl de qch/de faire; **the s. of one's activity** le champ de ses activités.

scorch [skɔːtʃ] vt (linen, grass etc) roussir; – n s. (mark) brûlure f légère. ◆—**ing** a (day) torride; (sun, sand) brûlant. ◆—**er** n Fam journée f torride.

score¹ [skɔːr] n Sp score m; Cards marque f; Mus partition f; (of film) musique f; **a s. to settle** Fig un compte à régler; **on that s.** (in that respect) à cet égard; – vt (point, goal) marquer; (exam mark) avoir; (success) remporter; Mus orchestrer; – vi marquer un point ou un but; (keep score) marquer les points. ◆**scoreboard** n Sp tableau m d'affichage. ◆**scorer** n Sp marqueur m.

score² [skɔːr] n (twenty) vingt; **a s.** de une vingtaine; **scores of** Fig un grand nombre de.

score³ [skɔːr] vt (cut) rayer; (paper) marquer.

scorn [skɔːn] vt mépriser; – n mépris m. ◆**scornful** a méprisant; **to be s. of** mépriser. ◆**scornfully** adv avec mépris.

Scorpio ['skɔːpɪəʊ] n (sign) le Scorpion.

scorpion ['skɔːpɪən] n scorpion m.

Scot [skɒt] n Écossais, -aise mf. ◆**Scotland** n Écosse f. ◆**Scotsman** n (pl -men) Écossais m. ◆**Scotswoman** n (pl -women) Écossaise f. ◆**Scottish** a écossais.

scotch [skɒtʃ] **1** a **s. tape**® Am scotch® m. **2** vt (rumour) étouffer; (attempt) faire échouer.

Scotch [skɒtʃ] n (whisky) scotch m.

scot-free ['skɒt'friː] adv sans être puni.

scoundrel ['skaʊndr(ə)l] n vaurien m.

scour ['skaʊər] vt (pan) récurer; (streets etc) Fig parcourir (**for** à la recherche de). ◆—**er** n tampon m à récurer.

scourge [skɜːdʒ] n fléau m.

scout [skaʊt] **1** n (soldier) éclaireur m; (boy) **s.** scout m, éclaireur m; **girl s.** Am éclaireuse f; **s. camp** camp m scout. **2** vi to

s. round for (*look for*) chercher. ◆—**ing** n scoutisme m.

scowl [skaʊl] vi se renfrogner; **to s. at s.o.** regarder qn d'un air mauvais. ◆—**ing** a renfrogné.

scraggy ['skrægɪ] a (-**ier**, -**iest**) (*bony*) osseux, maigrichon; (*unkempt*) débraillé.

scram [skræm] vi (-**mm**-) Fam filer.

scramble ['skræmb(ə)l] **1** vi **to s. for** se ruer vers; **to s. up** (*climb*) grimper; **to s. through** traverser avec difficulté; – n ruée f (for vers). **2** vt (*egg, message*) brouiller.

scrap [skræp] **1** n (*piece*) petit morceau m (of de); (*of information, news*) fragment m; pl (*food*) restes mpl; **not a s. of** (*truth etc*) pas un brin de; **s. paper** (papier m) brouillon m. **2** n (*metal*) ferraille f; **to sell for s.** vendre à la casse; – a (*yard, heap*) de ferraille; **s. dealer, s. merchant** marchand m de ferraille; **s. iron** ferraille f; **on the s. heap** Fig au rebut; – vt (*unwanted object, idea, plan*) Fig mettre au rancart. **3** n (*fight*) Fam bagarre f. ◆**scrapbook** n album m (*pour collages etc*).

scrap/e [skreɪp] vt racler, gratter; (*skin*) Med érafler; **to s. away** or **off** (*mud etc*) racler; **to s. together** (*money, people*) réunir (difficilement); – vi **s. against** frotter contre; **to s. along** Fig se débrouiller; **to s. through** (*in exam*) réussir de justesse; – n raclement m; éraflure f; **to get into a s.** Fam s'attirer des ennuis. ◆—**ings** npl raclures fpl. ◆—**er** n racloir m.

scratch [skrætʃ] n (*mark, injury*) éraflure f; (*on glass*) rayure f; **to have a s.** (*scratch oneself*) Fam se gratter; **to start from s.** (re)partir de zéro; **to be/come up to s.** être/se montrer à la hauteur; – vt (*to relieve an itch*) gratter; (*skin, wall etc*) érafler; (*glass*) rayer; (*with claw*) griffer; (*one's name*) graver (on sur); – vi (*relieve an itch*) se gratter; (*of cat etc*) griffer; (*of pen*) gratter, accrocher.

scrawl [skrɔːl] vt gribouiller; – n gribouillis m.

scrawny ['skrɔːnɪ] a (-**ier**, -**iest**) (*bony*) osseux, maigrichon.

scream [skriːm] vti crier, hurler; **to s. at s.o.** crier après qn; **s. with pain**/etc hurler de douleur/etc; – n cri m (perçant).

screech [skriːtʃ] vi crier, hurler; (*of brakes*) hurler; – n cri m; hurlement m.

screen [skriːn] **1** n écran m; Fig masque m; (*folding*) s. paravent m. **2** vt (*hide*) cacher (from s.o. à qn); (*protect*) protéger (from de); (*a film*) projeter; (*visitors, documents*) filtrer; (*for cancer etc*) Med faire subir un test de dépistage à (qn) (for pour). ◆—**ing** n (*of film*) projection f; (*selection*) tri m; (*medical examination*) (test m de) dépistage m. ◆**screenplay** n Cin scénario m.

screw [skruː] n vis f; – vt visser (to à); **to s. down** or **on** visser; **to s. off** dévisser; (*paper*) chiffonner; (*eyes*) plisser; (*face*) Sl gâcher; **to s. one's face up** grimacer. ◆**screwball** n & a Am Fam cinglé, -ée (mf). ◆**screwdriver** n tournevis m. ◆**screwy** a (-**ier**, -**iest**) (*idea, person etc*) farfelu.

scribble ['skrɪb(ə)l] vti griffonner; – n griffonnage m.

scribe [skraɪb] n scribe m.

scrimmage ['skrɪmɪdʒ] n Fb Am mêlée f.

script [skrɪpt] n (*of film*) scénario m; (*of play*) texte m; (*in exam*) copie f. ◆**scriptwriter** n Cin scénariste mf, dialoguiste f; TV Rad dialoguiste mf.

Scripture ['skrɪptʃər] n Rel Écriture f (sainte).

scroll [skrəʊl] n rouleau m (de parchemin); (*book*) manuscrit m.

scrooge [skruːdʒ] n (*miser*) harpagon m.

scroung/e [skraʊndʒ] vt (*meal*) se faire payer (off or from s.o. par qn); (*steal*) piquer (off or from s.o. à qn); **to s. money off** or **from** taper; – vi vivre en parasite; (*beg*) quémander; **to s. around for** Pej chercher. ◆—**er** n parasite m.

scrub [skrʌb] **1** vt (-**bb**-) frotter, nettoyer (à la brosse); (*pan*) récurer; (*cancel*) Fig annuler; **to s. out** (*erase*) Fig effacer; – vi (*scrub floors*) frotter les planchers; **scrubbing brush** brosse f dure; – n **to give sth a s.** frotter qch; **s. brush** Am brosse f dure. **2** n (*land*) broussailles fpl.

scruff [skrʌf] n **1** **by the s. of the neck** par la peau du cou. **2** (*person*) Fam individu m débraillé. ◆**scruffy** a (-**ier**, -**iest**) (*untidy*) négligé; (*dirty*) malpropre.

scrum [skrʌm] n Rugby mêlée f.

scrumptious ['skrʌmpʃəs] a Fam super bon, succulent.

scruple ['skruːp(ə)l] n scrupule m. ◆**scrupulous** a scrupuleux. ◆**scrupulously** adv (*conscientiously*) scrupuleusement; (*completely*) absolument.

scrutinize ['skruːtɪnaɪz] vt scruter. ◆**scrutiny** n examen m minutieux.

scuba ['skjuːbə, Am 'skuːbə] n scaphandre m autonome; **s. diving** la plongée sous-marine.

scuff [skʌf] vt **to s. (up)** (*scrape*) érafler.

scuffle ['skʌf(ə)l] n bagarre f.

scullery ['skʌlərɪ] n arrière-cuisine f.

sculpt [skʌlpt] vti sculpter. ◆**sculptor** n sculpteur m. ◆**sculpture** n (art, object) sculpture f. – vti sculpter.

scum [skʌm] n 1 (on liquid) écume f. 2 Pej (people) racaille f; (person) salaud m; **the s. of** (society etc) la lie de.

scupper ['skʌpər] vt (plan) Fam saboter.

scurf [skɜːf] n pellicules fpl.

scurrilous ['skʌrɪləs] a (criticism, attack) haineux, violent et grossier.

scurry ['skʌrɪ] vi (rush) se précipiter, courir; **to s. off** décamper.

scuttle ['skʌt(ə)l] 1 vt (ship) saborder. 2 vi **to s. off** filer.

scythe [saɪð] n faux f.

sea [siː] n mer f; (out) **at s.** en mer; **by s.** par mer; **by** or **beside the s.** au bord de la mer; **to be all at s.** Fig nager complètement; – a (level, breeze) de la mer; (water, fish) de mer; (air, salt) marin; (battle, power) naval; (route) maritime; **s. bed, s. floor** fond m de la mer; **s. lion** (animal) otarie f. ◆**seaboard** n littoral m. ◆**seafarer** n marin m. ◆**seafood** n fruits mpl de mer. ◆**seafront** n front m de mer. ◆**seagull** n mouette f. ◆**seaman** n (pl -men) marin m. ◆**seaplane** n hydravion m. ◆**seaport** n port m de mer. ◆**seashell** n coquillage m. ◆**seashore** n bord m de la mer. ◆**seasick** a **to be s.** avoir le mal de mer. ◆**seasickness** n mal m de mer. ◆**seaside** n bord m de la mer; – a (town, holiday) au bord de la mer. ◆**seaway** n route f maritime. ◆**seaweed** n algue(s) f(pl). ◆**seaworthy** a (ship) en état de naviguer.

seal [siːl] n 1 (animal) phoque m. 2 n (mark, design) sceau m; (on letter) cachet m (de cire); (putty for sealing) joint m; – vt (document, container) sceller; (with wax) cacheter; (stick down) coller; (with putty) boucher; (s.o.'s fate) Fig décider de; **to s. off** (room etc) interdire l'accès de; **to s. off a house/district** (of police, troops) boucler une maison/un quartier.

seam [siːm] n (in cloth etc) couture f; (of coal, quartz etc) veine f.

seamy ['siːmɪ] a (-ier, -iest) **the s. side** le côté peu reluisant (of a).

séance ['seɪɑːns] n séance f de spiritisme.

search [sɜːtʃ] n (quest) recherche f (for); (of person, place) fouille f; **in s. of** à la recherche de; **s. party** équipe f de secours; – vt (person, place) fouiller (for pour trouver); (study) examiner (documents etc); **to s. (through) one's papers**/etc **for sth** chercher qch dans ses papiers/etc; – vi

chercher; **to s. for sth** chercher qch. ◆**-ing** a (look) pénétrant; (examination) minutieux. ◆**searchlight** n projecteur m.

season ['siːz(ə)n] 1 n saison f; **the festive s.** la période des fêtes; **in the peak s., in (the) high s.** en pleine or haute saison; **in the low** or **off s.** en basse saison; **a Truffaut s.** Cin une rétrospective Truffaut; **s. ticket** carte f d'abonnement. 2 vt (food) assaisonner; **highly seasoned** (dish) relevé. ◆**-ed** a (worker) expérimenté; (soldier) aguerri. ◆**-ing** n Culin assaisonnement m. ◆**seasonable** a (weather) de saison. ◆**seasonal** a saisonnier.

seat [siːt] n (for sitting, centre) & Pol siège m; (on train, bus) banquette f; Cin Th fauteuil m; (place) place f; (of trousers) fond m; **to take** or **have a s.** s'asseoir; **in the hot s.** (in difficult position) Fig sur la sellette; **s. belt** ceinture f de sécurité; – vt (at table) placer (qn); (on one's lap) asseoir (qn); **the room seats 50** la salle a 50 places (assises); **be seated!** asseyez-vous! ◆**-ed** a (sitting) assis. ◆**-ing** n (room) (seats) places fpl assises; **the s. arrangements** la disposition des places; **s. capacity** nombre m de places assises. ◆**-er** n **a two-s. (car)** voiture f à deux places.

secateurs [sekə'tɜːz] npl sécateur m.

secede [sɪ'siːd] vi faire sécession. ◆**secession** n sécession f.

secluded [sɪ'kluːdɪd] a (remote) isolé. ◆**seclusion** n solitude f.

second[1] ['sekənd] a deuxième, second; **every s. week** une semaine sur deux; **in s. (gear)** Aut en seconde; **s. to none** sans pareil; **s. in command** second m; Mil commandant m en second; – adv (to say) deuxièmement; **to come s.** Sp se classer deuxième; **the s. biggest** le deuxième en ordre de grandeur; **the s. richest country** le deuxième pays le plus riche; **my s. best** (choice) mon deuxième choix; – n (person, object) deuxième mf, second, -onde mf; **Louis the S.** Louis Deux; pl (goods) Com articles mpl de second choix; – vt (motion) appuyer. ◆**s.-'class** a (product) de qualité inférieure; (ticket) Rail de seconde (classe); (mail) non urgent. ◆**s.-'rate** a médiocre. ◆**secondly** adv deuxièmement.

second[2] ['sekənd] n (unit of time) seconde f; **s. hand** (of clock, watch) trotteuse f.

second[3] [sɪ'kɒnd] vt (employee) détacher (to à). ◆**-ment** n détachement m; **on s.** en (position de) détachement (to à).

secondary ['sekəndərɪ] a secondaire.

secondhand [sekənd'hænd] 1 a & adv (not

new) d'occasion. **2** a (*report, news*) de seconde main.

secret ['siːkrɪt] a secret; – n secret m; **in s. en secret; an open s.** le secret de Polichinelle. ◆**secrecy** n (*discretion, silence*) secret m; **in s.** en secret. ◆**secretive** a (*person*) cachottier; (*organization*) qui a le goût du secret; **to be s. about** faire un mystère de; (*organization*) être très discret sur. ◆**secretively** adv en catimini.

secretary ['sekrət(ə)rɪ] n secrétaire mf; **Foreign S.,** Am **S. of State** = ministre m des Affaires étrangères. ◆**secre'tarial** a (*work*) de secrétaire, de secrétariat; (*school*) de secrétariat. ◆**secre'tariat** n (*in international organization*) secrétariat m.

secrete [sɪ'kriːt] vt Med Biol sécréter. ◆**se'cretion** n sécrétion f.

sect [sekt] n secte f. ◆**sec'tarian** a & n Pej sectaire (mf).

section ['sekʃ(ə)n] n (*of road, book, wood etc*) section f; (*of town, country*) partie f; (*of machine, furniture*) élément m; (*department*) section f; (*in store*) rayon m; **the sports/etc s.** (*of newspaper*) la page des sports/etc; – vt **to s. off** (*separate*) séparer.

sector ['sektər] n secteur m.

secular ['sekjʊlər] a (*teaching etc*) laïque; (*music, art*) profane.

secure [sɪ'kjʊər] **1** a (*person, valuables*) en sûreté, en sécurité; (*in one's mind*) tranquille; (*place*) sûr; (*solid, firm*) solide; (*door, window*) bien fermé; (*certain*) assuré; **s. from** à l'abri de; (*emotionally*) s. sécurisé; – vt (*fasten*) attacher; (*window etc*) bien fermer; (*success, future etc*) assurer; **to s. against** protéger de. **2** vt (*obtain*) procurer (sth for s.o. qch à qn); **to s. sth** (*for oneself*) se procurer qch. ◆**securely** adv (*firmly*) solidement; (*safely*) en sûreté. ◆**security** n sécurité f; (*for loan, bail*) caution f; **s. firm** société f de surveillance; **s. guard** agent m de sécurité; (*transferring money*) convoyeur m de fonds.

sedan [sɪ'dæn] n (*saloon*) Aut Am berline f.

sedate [sɪ'deɪt] **1** a calme. **2** vt mettre sous calmants. ◆**sedation** n **under s.** sous calmants. ◆'**sedative** n calmant m.

sedentary ['sedəntərɪ] a sédentaire.

sediment ['sedɪmənt] n sédiment m.

sedition [sə'dɪʃ(ə)n] n sédition f. ◆**seditious** a séditieux.

seduce [sɪ'djuːs] vt séduire. ◆**seducer** n séducteur, -trice mf. ◆**seduction** n séduc-

tion f. ◆**seductive** a (*person, offer*) séduisant.

see[1] [siː] vti (pt saw, pp seen) voir; **we'll s. on verra (bien); I s.!** je vois!; **I s. clearly**) j'y vois clair; **I saw him run(ning)** je l'ai vu courir; **to s. reason** entendre raison; **to s. the joke** comprendre la plaisanterie; **s. who it is** va voir qui c'est; **s. you (later)!** à tout à l'heure!; **s. you (soon)!** à bientôt!; **to s. about** (*deal with*) s'occuper de; (*consider*) songer à; **to s. in the New Year** fêter la Nouvelle Année; **to s. s.o. off** accompagner qn (à la gare etc); **to s. s.o. out** raccompagner qn; **to s. through** (*task*) mener à bonne fin; **to s. s.o. through** (*be enough for*) suffire à qn; **to s. through s.o.** deviner le jeu de qn; **to s. through sth** s'occuper de; (*mend*) réparer; **to s. (to it) that** (*attend*) veiller à ce que (+ sub); (*check*) s'assurer que; **to s. s.o. to** (*accompany*) raccompagner qn à. ◆**s.-through** a (*dress etc*) transparent.

see[2] [siː] n (*of bishop*) siège m (épiscopal).

seed [siːd] n Agr graine f; (*in grape*) pépin m; (*source*) Fig germe m; Tennis tête f de série; **seed(s)** (*for sowing*) Agr graines fpl; **to go to s.** (*of lettuce etc*) monter en graine. ◆**seedbed** n Bot semis m; (*of rebellion etc*) Fig foyer m (of de). ◆**seedling** n (*plant*) semis m.

seedy ['siːdɪ] a (-ier, -iest) miteux. ◆**seediness** n aspect m miteux.

seeing ['siːɪŋ] conj **s.** (**that**) vu que.

seek [siːk] vt (pt & pp sought) chercher (**to do** à faire); (*ask for*) demander (**from** à); **to s.** (*after*) rechercher; **to s. out** aller trouver.

seem [siːm] vi sembler (**to do** faire); **it seems that . . .** (*impression*) il semble que . . . (+ sub or indic); (*rumour*) il paraît que . . . ; **it seems to me that . . .** il me semble que . . . ; **we s. to know each other** il me semble qu'on se connaît; **I can't s. to do it** je n'arrive pas à le faire. ◆**—ing** a apparent. ◆**—ingly** adv apparemment.

seemly ['siːmlɪ] a convenable.

seen [siːn] see see[1].

seep [siːp] vi (*ooze*) suinter; **to s. into** s'infiltrer dans. ◆**—age** n suintement m; infiltration(s) f(pl) (**into** dans); (*leak*) fuite f.

seesaw ['siːsɔː] n (*jeu m de*) bascule f.

seethe [siːð] vi **to s. with anger** bouillir de colère; **to s. with people** grouiller de monde.

segment ['segmənt] n segment m; (*of orange*) quartier m.

segregate ['segrɪgeɪt] vt séparer; (*racially*)

segregated (*school*) où se pratique la ségrégation raciale. ◆**segre'gation** *n* ségrégation *f*.

seize [siːz] **1** *vt* saisir; (*power, land*) s'emparer de; – *vi* to **s. on** (*offer etc*) saisir. **2** *vi* to **s. up** (*of engine*) (se) gripper. ◆**seizure** [-ʒər] *n* (*of goods etc*) saisie *f*; *Mil* prise *f*; *Med* crise *f*.

seldom ['seldəm] *adv* rarement.

select [sɪ'lekt] *vt* choisir (*from* parmi); (*candidates, players etc*) *Sp* sélectionner; – *a* (*chosen*) choisi; (*exclusive*) sélect, chic *inv*. ◆**selection** *n* sélection *f*. ◆**selective** *a* (*memory, recruitment etc*) sélectif; (*person*) qui opère un choix; (*choosey*) difficile.

self [self] *n* (*pl* **selves**) **the s.** *Phil* le moi; **he's back to his old s.** Fam il est redevenu lui-même. ◆**s.-a'ssurance** *n* assurance *f*. ◆**s.-a'ssured** *a* sûr de soi. ◆**s.-'catering** *a* où l'on fait la cuisine soi-même. ◆**s.-'centred** *a* égocentrique. ◆**s.-'cleaning** (*oven*) autonettoyant. ◆**s.-con'fessed** *a* (*liar*) de son propre aveu. ◆**s.-'confident** *a* sûr de soi. ◆**s.-'conscious** *a* gêné. ◆**s.-'consciousness** *n* gêne *f*. ◆**s.-con'tained** *a* (*flat*) indépendant. ◆**s.-con'trol** *n* maîtrise *f* de soi. ◆**s.-de'feating** *a* qui a un effet contraire à celui qui est recherché. ◆**s.-de'fence** *n Jur* légitime défense *f*. ◆**s.-de'nial** *n* abnégation *f*. ◆**s.-determi'nation** *n* autodétermination *f*. ◆**s.-'discipline** *n* autodiscipline *f*. ◆**s.-em'ployed** *a* qui travaille à son compte. ◆**s.-es'teem** *n* amour-propre *m*. ◆**s.-'evident** *a* évident, qui va de soi. ◆**s.-ex'planatory** *a* qui tombe sous le sens, qui se passe d'explication. ◆**s.-'governing** *a* autonome. ◆**s.-im'portant** *a* suffisant. ◆**s.-in'dulgent** *a* qui ne se refuse rien. ◆**s.-'interest** *n* intérêt *m* (personnel). ◆**s.-o'pinionated** *a* entêté. ◆**s.-'pity** *n* to feel s.-pity s'apitoyer sur son propre sort. ◆**s.-'portrait** *n* autoportrait *m*. ◆**s.-po'ssessed** *a* assuré. ◆**s.-raising** *or Am* **s.-rising 'flour** *n* farine *f* à levure. ◆**s.-re'liant** *a* indépendant. ◆**s.-re'spect** *n* amour-propre *m*. ◆**s.-re'specting** *a* qui se respecte. ◆**s.-'righteous** *a* pharisaïque. ◆**s.-'sacrifice** *n* abnégation *f*. ◆**s.-'satisfied** *a* content de soi. ◆**s.-'service** *n* & *a* libre-service (*m inv*). ◆**s.-'styled** *a* soi-disant. ◆**s.-su'fficient** *a* indépendant, qui a son indépendance. ◆**s.-sup-**

porting *a* financièrement indépendant. ◆**s.-'taught** *a* autodidacte.

selfish ['selfiʃ] *a* égoïste; (*motive*) intéressé. ◆**selfless** *a* désintéressé. ◆**selfishness** *n* égoïsme *m*.

selfsame ['selfseɪm] *a* même.

sell [sel] *vt* (*pt & pp* **sold**) vendre; (*idea etc*) *Fig* faire accepter; **she sold me it for twenty pounds** elle me l'a vendu vingt livres; **to s. back** revendre; **to s. off** liquider; **to have** *or* **be sold out** (*of cheese etc*) n'avoir plus de; **this book is sold out** ce livre est épuisé; – *vi* se vendre; (*of idea etc*) *Fig* être accepté; **to s. up** vendre sa maison; *Com* vendre son affaire; **selling price** prix *m* de vente. ◆**seller** *n* vendeur, -euse *mf*. ◆**sellout** *n* **1** (*betrayal*) trahison *f*. **2** **it was a s.** *Th Cin* on a joué à guichets fermés.

sellotape® ['seləteɪp] *n* scotch® *m*; – *vt* scotcher.

semantic [sɪ'mæntɪk] *a* sémantique. ◆**semantics** *n* sémantique *f*.

semaphore ['seməfɔːr] *n* (*device*) *Rail Nau* sémaphore *m*; (*system*) signaux *mpl* à bras.

semblance ['semblans] *n* semblant *m*.

semen ['siːmən] *n* sperme *m*.

semester [sɪ'mestər] *n Univ* semestre *m*.

semi- ['semɪ] *pref* demi-, semi-. ◆**semi-auto'matic** *a* semi-automatique. ◆**semibreve** [-briːv] *n Mus* ronde *f*. ◆**semicircle** *n* demi-cercle *m*. ◆**semi'circular** *a* semi-circulaire. ◆**semi'colon** *n* point-virgule *m*. ◆**semi-'conscious** *a* à demi conscient. ◆**semide'tached** *a* house maison *f* jumelle. ◆**semi'final** *n Sp* demi-finale *f*.

seminar ['semɪnɑːr] *n Univ* séminaire *m*.

seminary ['semɪnərɪ] *n Rel* séminaire *m*.

Semite ['siːmaɪt, *Am* 'semaɪt] *n* Sémite *mf*. ◆**Se'mitic** *a* sémite; (*language*) sémitique.

semolina [semə'liːnə] *n* semoule *f*.

senate ['senɪt] *n Pol* sénat *m*. ◆**senator** ['senətər] *n Pol* sénateur *m*.

send [send] *vt* (*pt & pp* **sent**) envoyer (**to** à); **to s. s.o. for sth/s.o.** envoyer qn chercher qch/qn; **to s. s.o. crazy** *or* **mad** rendre qn fou; **to s. s.o. packing** Fam envoyer promener qn; **to s. away** *or* **off** envoyer (**to** à); (*dismiss*) renvoyer; **to s. back** renvoyer; **to s. in** (*form*) envoyer; (*person*) faire entrer; **to s. on** (*letter, luggage*) faire suivre; **to s. out** (*invitation*) envoyer; (*heat*) émettre; (*from room etc*) faire sortir (qn); **to s. up** (*balloon, rocket*) lancer; (*price, luggage*) faire monter; (*mock*) *Fam* parodier; – *vi* **to s. away** *or* **off for** commander (par courrier); **to s. for** (doctor etc) faire venir, envoyer chercher; **to s. (out) for** (meal, groceries) envoyer chercher. ◆**s.-off** n to give s.o. a **s.-off** Fam faire des adieux chaleureux à qn. ◆**s.-up** n Fam parodie f. ◆**sender** n expéditeur, -trice mf.

senile ['siːnail] a gâteux, sénile. ◆**se'nility** n gâtisme m, sénilité f.

senior ['siːniər] a (older) plus âgé; (position, executive, rank) supérieur; (teacher, partner) principal; **to be s. to s.o., be s.o.'s s.** être plus âgé que qn; (in rank) être au-dessus de qn; **Brown s.** Brown père; – n (older person) aîné, -ée mf; Sch grand. -ande mf; Sch Univ Am étudiant, -ante mf de dernière année; Sp senior mf. ◆**seni'ority** n priorité f d'âge; (in service) ancienneté f; (in rank) supériorité f.

sensation [sen'seiʃ(ə)n] n sensation f. ◆**sensational** a (event) qui fait sensation; (newspaper, film) à sensation; (terrific) Fam sensationnel.

sense [sens] n (faculty, awareness, meaning) sens m; **a s. of hearing** (le sens de) l'ouïe f; **to have (good) s.** avoir du bon sens; **a s. of** (physical) une sensation de (chaleur etc); (mental) un sentiment de (honte etc); **a s. of humour/direction** le sens de l'humour/de l'orientation; **a s. of time** la notion de l'heure; **to bring s.o. to his senses** ramener qn à la raison; **to make s.** (of story, action etc) avoir du sens; **to make s. of** comprendre; – vt sentir (intuitivement) (that que); (have a foreboding of) pressentir. ◆**—less** a (stupid, meaningless) insensé; (unconscious) sans connaissance. ◆**—lessness** n stupidité f.

sensibility [sensi'biliti] n sensibilité f; pl (touchiness) susceptibilité f.

sensible ['sensəb(ə)l] a (wise) raisonnable, sensé; (clothes) pratique. ◆**sensibly** adv raisonnablement.

sensitive ['sensitiv] a (responsive, painful) sensible (**to** à); (delicate) délicat (peau, question etc); (touchy) susceptible (**about** à propos de). ◆**sensi'tivity** n sensibilité f; (touchiness) susceptibilité f.

sensory ['sensəri] a sensoriel.

sensual ['senʃʊəl] a (bodily, sexual) sensuel. ◆**sensu'ality** n sensualité f. ◆**sensuous** a (pleasing, refined) sensuel. ◆**sensuously** adv avec sensualité. ◆**sensuousness** n sensualité f.

sent [sent] see **send**.

sentence ['sentəns] **1** n Gram phrase f. **2** n Jur condamnation f; (punishment) peine f;

to pass s. prononcer une condamnation (**on s.o.** contre qn); **to serve a s.** purger une peine; – vt Jur prononcer une condamnation contre; **to s. to** condamner à.

sentiment ['sentimənt] n sentiment m. ◆**senti'mental** a sentimental. ◆**senti-men'tality** n sentimentalité f.

sentry ['sentri] n sentinelle f; **s. box** guérite f.

separate ['sepərət] a (distinct) séparé; (independent) indépendant; (different) différent; (individual) particulier; – ['sepəreit] vt séparer (**from** de); – vi se séparer (**from** de). ◆**separately** adv séparément. ◆**sepa-'ration** n séparation f.

separates ['sepərəts] npl (garments) coordonnés mpl.

September [sep'tembər] n septembre m.

septic ['septik] a (wound) infecté; **s. tank** fosse f septique.

sequel ['siːkw(ə)l] n suite f.

sequence ['siːkwəns] n (order) ordre m; (series) succession f; Mus Cards séquence f; **film s.** séquence de film; **in s.** dans l'ordre, successivement.

sequin ['siːkwin] n paillette f.

serenade [serə'neid] n sérénade f; – vt donner une or la sérénade à.

serene [sə'riːn] a serein. ◆**serenity** n sérénité f.

sergeant ['saːdʒənt] n Mil sergent m; (in police force) brigadier m.

serial ['siːriəl] n (story, film) feuilleton m; **s. number** (of banknote, TV set etc) numéro de série. ◆**serialize** vt publier en feuilleton; TV Rad adapter en feuilleton.

series ['siːriːz] n inv série f; (book collection) collection f.

serious ['siːriəs] a sérieux; (illness, mistake, tone) grave; (damage) important. ◆**—ly** adv sérieusement; (ill, damaged) gravement; **to take s.** prendre au sérieux. ◆**—ness** n sérieux m; (of illness etc) gravité f; (of damage) importance f; **in all s.** sérieusement.

sermon ['səːmən] n sermon m.

serpent ['səːpənt] n serpent m.

serrated [sə'reitid] a (knife) à dents (de scie).

serum ['siːrəm] n sérum m.

servant ['səːvənt] n (in house etc) domestique mf; (person who serves) serviteur m; **public s.** fonctionnaire f.

serve [səːv] vt servir (**to s.o.** à qn, **s.o. with sth** qch à qn); (of train, bus etc) desservir (un village, un quartier etc); (supply) El alimenter; (apprenticeship) faire; (summons) Jur remettre (**on** à); **it serves its**

purpose ça fait l'affaire; **(it) serves you right!** *Fam* ça t'apprendra!; **to s. up** *or* **out** servir; – *vi* servir (**as** de); **to s. on** (*jury, committee*) être membre de; **to s. to show**/*etc* servir à montrer/*etc*; – *n* Tennis service *m*.

servic/e ['sɜːvɪs] *n* (*serving*) & *Mil Rel Tennis* service *m*; (*machine or vehicle repair*) révision *f*; **to be of s. to** être utile à, rendre service à; **the (armed) services** les forces *fpl* armées; **s. (charge)** (*tip*) service *m*; **s. department** (*workshop*) atelier *m*; **s. area** (*on motorway*) aire *f* de service; **s. station** station-service *f*; – *vt* (*machine, vehicle*) réviser. ◆**serviceable** *a* (*usable*) utilisable; (*useful*) commode; (*durable*) solide. ◆**serviceman** *n* (*pl* **-men**) *n* militaire *m*.

serviette [sɜːvɪˈet] *n* serviette *f* (de table).

servile ['sɜːvaɪl] *a* servile.

session ['seʃ(ə)n] *n* séance *f*; *Jur Pol* session *f*, séance *f*; *Univ* année *f* *or* trimestre *m* universitaire; *Univ Am* semestre *m* universitaire.

set [set] **1** *n* (*of keys, needles, tools*) jeu *m*; (*of stamps, numbers*) série *f*; (*of people*) groupe *m*; (*of facts*) & *Math* ensemble *m*; (*of books*) collection *f*; (*of plates*) service *m*; (*of tyres*) train *m*; (*kit*) trousse *f*; (*stage*) *Th Cin* plateau *m*; (*scenery*) *Th Cin* décor *m*, scène *f*; (*hairstyle*) mise *f* en plis; *Tennis* set *m*; **television s.** téléviseur *m*; **radio s.** poste *m* de radio; **tea s.** service *m* à thé; **chess s.** (*box*) jeu *m* d'échecs; **a s. of teeth** une rangée de dents, une denture; **the skiing/racing s.** le monde du ski/des courses. **2** *a* (*time etc*) fixe; (*lunch*) à prix fixe; (*book etc*) *Sch* au programme; (*speech*) préparé à l'avance; (*in one's habits*) régulier; (*situated*) situé; **s. phrase** expression *f* consacrée; **a s. purpose** un but déterminé; **the s. menu** le plat du jour; **dead s. against** absolument opposé à; **s. on doing** résolu à faire; **to be s. on sth** vouloir qch à tout prix; **all s.** (*ready*) prêt (**to** do pour faire); **to be s. back from** (*of house etc*) être en retrait de (*route etc*). **3** *vt* (*pt* & *pp* **set**, *pres p* **setting**) (*put*) mettre, poser; (*date, limit etc*) fixer; (*record*) *Sp* établir; (*adjust*) *Tech* régler; (*arm etc in plaster*) *Med* plâtrer; (*task*) donner (**for** s.o. à qn); (*problem*) poser; (*diamond*) monter; (*precedent*) créer; **to have one's hair s.** se faire faire une mise en plis; **to s.** (*loose*) (*dog*) lâcher (**on** contre); **to s. off** (*bomb*) faire

down déposer; **to s. off** (*bomb*) faire exploser; (*activity, mechanism*) déclencher; (*complexion, beauty*) rehausser; **to s. out** (*display, explain*) exposer (**to** à); (*arrange*) disposer; **to s. up** (*furniture*) installer; (*statue, tent*) dresser; (*school*) fonder; (*government*) établir; (*business*) créer; (*inquiry*) ouvrir; **to s. s.o. up in business** lancer qn dans les affaires; – *vi* (*of sun*) se coucher; (*of jelly*) prendre; (*of bone*) se ressouder; **to s. about** (*job*) se mettre à; **to s. about doing** se mettre à faire; **to s. in** (*start*) commencer; (*arise*) surgir; **to s. off** *or* **out** (*leave*) partir; **to s. out to do do** entreprendre de faire; **to s. up in business** monter une affaire; **to s. upon** (*attack*) attaquer (*qn*). ◆**setting** *n* (*surroundings*) cadre *m*; (*of sun*) coucher *m*; (*of diamond*) monture *f*. ◆**setter** *n* chien *m* couchant.

setback ['setbæk] *n* revers *m*; *Med* rechute *f*.

setsquare ['setskweər] *n* *Math* équerre *f*.

settee [se'tiː] *n* canapé *m*.

settle ['set(ə)l] *vt* (*decide, arrange, pay*) régler; (*date*) fixer; (*place in position*) placer; (*person*) installer (*dans son lit etc*); (*nerves*) calmer; (*land*) coloniser; **let's things** arrangeons les choses; **that's (all) settled** (*decided*) c'est décidé; – *vi* (*live*) s'installer, s'établir; (*of dust*) se déposer; (*of bird*) se poser; (*of snow*) tenir; **to s. (down) into** (*armchair*) s'installer dans; (*job*) s'habituer à; **to s. (up) with s.o.** régler qn; **to s. for** se contenter de, accepter; **to s. down** (*in chair or house*) s'installer; (*of nerves*) se calmer; (*in one's lifestyle*) se ranger; (*marry*) se caser; **s. s. down to** (*get used to*) s'habituer à; (*work, task*) se mettre à. ◆**settled** *a* (*weather, period*) stable; (*habits*) régulier. ◆**settlement** *n* (*of account etc*) règlement *m*; (*agreement*) accord *m*; (*colony*) colonie *f*. ◆**settler** *n* colon *m*.

set-to [set'tuː] *n* (*quarrel*) *Fam* prise *f* de bec.

setup ['setʌp] *n* *Fam* situation *f*.

seven ['sev(ə)n] *a* & *n* sept (*m*). ◆**seven'teen** *a* & *n* dix-sept (*m*). ◆**seven'teenth** *a* & *n* dix-septième (*mf*). ◆**seventh** *a* & *n* septième (*mf*). ◆**seventieth** *a* & *n* soixante-dixième (*mf*). ◆**seventy** *a* & *n* soixante-dix (*m*); **s.-one** soixante et onze.

sever ['sevər] *vt* sectionner, couper; (*relations*) *Fig* rompre. ◆**severing** *n*, ◆**severance** *n* (*of relations*) rupture *f*.

several ['sev(ə)rəl] *a* & *pron* plusieurs (**of** d'entre).

severe [sə'vɪər] a (judge, tone etc) sévère; (winter, training) rigoureux; (test) dur; (injury) grave; (blow, pain) violent; (cold, frost) intense; (overwork) excessif; a s. cold Med un gros rhume; s. to or with s.o. sévère envers qn. ◆**severely** adv sévèrement; (wounded) gravement. ◆**se'verity** n sévérité f; rigueur f; gravité f; violence f.

sew [səu] vti (pt sewed, pp sewn [səun] or sewed) coudre; to s. on (button) (re)coudre; to s. up (tear) (re)coudre; **–ing** n couture f; s. machine machine f à coudre.

sewage ['su:ɪdʒ] n eaux fpl usées or d'égout. ◆**sewer** n égout m.

sewn [səun] see sew.

sex [seks] n (gender, sexuality) sexe m; (activity) relations fpl sexuelles; the opposite s. l'autre sexe; to have s. with coucher avec; – a (education, act etc) sexuel; s. maniac obsédé, -ée mf sexuel(le). ◆**sexist** a & n sexiste (mf). ◆**sexual** a sexuel. ◆**sexu'ality** n sexualité f. ◆**sexy** a (-ier, -iest) (book, garment, person) sexy inv; (aroused) qui a envie (de faire l'amour).

sextet [sek'stet] n sextuor m.

sh! [ʃ] int chut!

shabby ['ʃæbɪ] a (-ier, -iest) (town, room etc) miteux; (person) pauvrement vêtu; (mean) Fig mesquin. ◆**shabbily** adv (dressed) pauvrement. ◆**shabbiness** n aspect m miteux; mesquinerie f.

shack [ʃæk] **1** n cabane f. **2** vi to s. up with Pej Fam se coller avec.

shackles ['ʃæk(ə)lz] npl chaînes fpl.

shade [ʃeɪd] n ombre f; (of colour) ton m, nuance f; (of opinion, meaning) nuance f; (of lamp) abat-jour m inv; (blind) store m; in the s. à l'ombre; a s. faster/taller/etc (slightly) un rien plus vite/plus grand/etc; – vt (of tree) ombrager; (protect) abriter (from de); to s. in (drawing) ombrer. ◆**shady** a (-ier, -iest) (place) ombragé; (person etc) Fig louche.

shadow ['ʃædəu] **1** n ombre f. **2** a (cabinet) Pol fantôme. **3** vt to s. s.o. (follow) filer qn. ◆**shadowy** a (-ier, -iest) (form etc) obscur, vague.

shaft [ʃɑːft] n **1** (of tool) manche m; (in machine) arbre m; s. of light trait m de lumière. **2** (of mine) puits m; (of lift) cage f.

shaggy ['ʃægɪ] a (-ier, -iest) (hair, beard) broussailleux; (dog etc) à longs poils.

shake [ʃeɪk] vt (pt shook, pp shaken) (move up and down) secouer; (bottle) agiter; (belief, resolution etc) Fig ébranler; (upset) bouleverser, secouer; to s. the windows (of shock) ébranler les vitres; to s. one's head

(say no) secouer la tête; to s. hands with serrer la main à; we shook hands nous nous sommes serré la main; to s. off (dust etc) secouer; (cough, infection, person) Fig se débarrasser de; to s. s.o. up (disturb, rouse) secouer qn; to s. sth out of sth (remove) secouer qch de qch; s. yourself out of it! secoue-toi!; – vi trembler (with de); – n secousse f; to give sth a s. secouer qch; with a s. of his or her head en secouant la tête; in two shakes (soon) Fam dans une minute. ◆**s.-up** n Fig réorganisation f.

shaky ['ʃeɪkɪ] a (-ier, -iest) (trembling) tremblant; (ladder etc) branlant; (memory, health) chancelant; (on one's legs, in a language) mal assuré.

shall [ʃæl, unstressed ʃəl] v aux **1** (future) I s. come, I'll come je viendrai; we s. not come, we shan't come nous ne viendrons pas. **2** (question) s. I leave? veux-tu que je parte?; s. we leave? on part? **3** (order) he s. do it if I order it il devra le faire si je l'ordonne.

shallot [ʃə'lɒt] n (onion) échalote f.

shallow ['ʃæləu] a (-er, -est) peu profond; Fig Pej superficiel; – npl (of river) bas-fond m. ◆**-ness** n manque m de profondeur; Fig Pej caractère m superficiel.

sham [ʃæm] n (pretence) comédie f, feinte f; (person) imposteur m; (jewels) imitation f; – a (false) faux; (illness, emotion) feint; – vt (-mm-) feindre.

shambles ['ʃæmb(ə)lz] n désordre m, pagaïe f; to be a s. être en pagaïe; to make a s. of gâcher.

shame [ʃeɪm] n (feeling, disgrace) honte f; it's a s. c'est dommage (to do de faire); it's a s. that c'est dommage que (+ sub); what a s.! (quel) dommage!; to put to s. faire honte à; – vt (disgrace, make ashamed) faire honte à. ◆**shamefaced** a honteux; (bashful) timide. ◆**shameful** a honteux. ◆**shamefully** adv honteusement. ◆**shameless** a (brazen) effronté; (indecent) impudique.

shammy ['ʃæmɪ] n s. (leather) Fam peau f de chamois.

shampoo [ʃæm'puː] n shampooing m; – vt (carpet) shampooiner; to s. s.o.'s hair faire un shampooing à qn.

shandy ['ʃændɪ] n (beer) panaché m.

shan't [ʃɑːnt] = shall not.

shanty[1] n (hut) baraque f. ◆**shantytown** n bidonville f.

shanty[2] [ʃæntɪ] n sea s. chanson f de marins.

shap/e [ʃeɪp] n forme f; in (good) s. (fit) en forme; to be in good/bad s. (of vehicle, *house etc*) être en bon/mauvais état; (*of business*) marcher bien/mal; **to take s.** prendre forme; **in the s. of a pear** en forme de poire; − *vt* (*fashion*) façonner (**into** en); (*one's life*) *Fig* déterminer; − *vi* **to s. up** (*of plans*) prendre (bonne) tournure, s'annoncer bien; (*of pupil, wrongdoer*) s'y mettre, s'appliquer; (*of patient*) faire des progrès. ◆−**ed** *suffix* pear-s./etc en forme de poire/etc. ◆**shapeless** *a* informe. ◆**shapely** *a* (**-ier, -iest**) (*woman, legs*) bien tourné.

share [ʃeər] *n* part *f* (**of, in** de); (*in company*) *Fin* action *f*; **one's (fair) s.** sa part de; **to do one's (fair) s.** fournir sa part d'efforts; **stocks and shares** *Fin* valeurs *fpl* (boursières); − *vt* (*meal, joy, opinion etc*) partager (**with** avec); (*characteristic*) avoir en commun; **to s. out** (*distribute*) partager; − *vi* **to s. (in)** partager. ◆**shareholder** *n Fin* actionnaire *mf*.

shark [ʃɑːk] *n* (*fish*) & *Fig* requin *m*.

sharp [ʃɑːp] **1** *a* (**-er, -est**) (*knife, blade etc*) tranchant; (*pointed*) pointu; (*point, voice*) aigu; (*pace, mind*) vif; (*pain*) aigu, vif; (*change, bend*) brusque; (*taste*) piquant; (*words, wind, tone*) âpre; (*eyesight, cry*) perçant; (*distinct*) net; (*lawyer etc*) *Pej* peu scrupuleux; **s. practice** *Pej* procédé(s) *m(pl)* malhonnête(s); − *adv* (*to stop*) net; **five o'clock**/etc à cinq heures/etc pile; **right/left** tout de suite à droite/à gauche. **2** *n Mus* dièse *m*. ◆**sharpen** *vt* (*knife*) aiguiser; (*pencil*) tailler. ◆**sharpener** *n* (*for pencils*) taille-crayon(s) *m inv*; (*for blades*) aiguisoir *m*. ◆**sharply** *adv* (*suddenly*) brusquement; (*harshly*) vivement; (*clearly*) nettement. ◆**sharpness** *n* (*of blade*) tranchant *m*; (*of picture*) netteté *f*. ◆**sharpshooter** *n* tireur *m* d'élite.

shatter [ʃætər] *vt* (*smash*) fracasser; (*glass*) faire voler en éclats; (*career, health*) briser; (*person, hopes*) anéantir; − *vi* (*smash*) se fracasser; (*of glass*) voler en éclats. ◆−**ed** *a* (*exhausted*) anéanti. ◆−**ing** *a* (*defeat*) accablant; (*news, experience*) bouleversant.

shav/e [ʃeɪv] *vt* (*person, head*) raser; **to s. off one's beard**/etc se raser la barbe/etc; − *vi* se raser; − *n* **to have a s.** se raser, se faire la barbe; **to have a close s.** *Fig Fam* l'échapper belle. ◆−**ing** *n* rasage *m*; (*strip of wood*) copeau *m*; **s. brush** blaireau *m*; **s. cream, s. foam** crème *f* à raser. ◆**shaven** *a* rasé (de près). ◆**shaver** *n* rasoir *m* électrique.

shawl [ʃɔːl] *n* châle *m*.

she [ʃiː] *pron* elle; **s. wants** elle veut; **she's a**

happy woman c'est une femme heureuse; **if I were s.** si j'étais elle; − *n* femelle *f*; **s.-bear** ourse *f*.

sheaf [ʃiːf] *n* (*pl* **sheaves**) (*of corn*) gerbe *f*.

shear [ʃɪər] *vt* tondre; − *npl* cisaille(s) *f(pl)*; **pruning shears** sécateur *m*. ◆−**ing** *n* tonte *f*.

sheath [ʃiːθ] *n* (*pl* **-s** [ʃiːðz]) (*container*) gaine *f*, fourreau *m*; (*contraceptive*) préservatif *m*.

shed [ʃed] **1** *n* (*in garden etc*) remise *f*; (*for goods or machines*) hangar *m*. **2** *vt* (*pt & pp* **shed,** *pres p* **shedding**) (*lose*) perdre; (*tears, warmth etc*) répandre; (*get rid of*) se défaire de; (*clothes*) enlever; **to s. light on** *Fig* éclairer.

sheen [ʃiːn] *n* lustre *m*.

sheep [ʃiːp] *n inv* mouton *m*. ◆**sheepdog** *n* chien *m* de berger. ◆**sheepskin** *n* peau *f* de mouton.

sheepish [ʃiːpɪʃ] *a* penaud. ◆−**ly** *adv* d'un air penaud.

sheer [ʃɪər] **1** *a* (*luck, madness etc*) pur; (*impossibility etc*) absolu; **it's s. hard work** ça demande du travail; **by s. determination/hard work** à force de détermination/de travail. **2** *a* (*cliff*) à pic; − *adv* (*to rise*) à pic. **3** *a* (*fabric*) très fin.

sheet [ʃiːt] *n* (*on bed*) drap *m*; (*of paper, wood etc*) feuille *f*; (*of glass, ice*) plaque *f*; (*dust cover*) housse *f*; (*canvas*) bâche *f*; **s. metal** tôle *f*.

sheikh [ʃeɪk] *n* scheik *m*, cheik *m*.

shelf [ʃelf] *n* (*pl* **shelves**) rayon *m*, étagère *f*; (*in shop*) rayon *m*; (*on cliff*) saillie *f*; **to be (left) on the s.** (*not married*) *Fam* être toujours célibataire.

shell [ʃel] **1** *n* coquille *f*; (*of tortoise*) carapace *f*; (*seashell*) coquillage *m*; (*of peas*) cosse *f*; (*of building*) carcasse *f*; − *vt* (*peas*) écosser; (*nut, shrimp*) décortiquer. **2** *n* (*explosive*) *Mil* obus *m*; − *vt* (*town etc*) *Mil* bombarder. ◆−**ing** *n Mil* bombardement *m*. ◆**shellfish** *n inv Culin* (*oysters etc*) fruits *mpl* de mer.

shelter [ʃeltər] *n* (*place, protection*) abri *m*; **to take s.** se mettre à l'abri (**from** de); **to seek s.** chercher un abri; − *vt* abriter (**from** de); (*criminal*) protéger; − *vi* s'abriter. ◆−**ed** *a* (*place*) abrité; (*life*) très protégé.

shelve [ʃelv] *vt* (*postpone*) laisser en suspens.

shelving [ʃelvɪŋ] *n* (*shelves*) rayonnage(s) *m(pl)*; **s. unit** (*set of shelves*) étagère *f*.

shepherd [ʃepəd] **1** *n* berger *m*; **s.'s pie** hachis *m* Parmentier. **2** *vt* **to s. in** faire entrer; **to s. s.o. around** piloter qn. ◆**shepherdess** n bergère f.

sherbet ['ʃɜːbət] n (powder) poudre f acidulée; (water ice) Am sorbet m.

sheriff ['ʃerɪf] n Am shérif m.

sherry ['ʃerɪ] n xérès m, sherry m.

shh! [ʃ] int chut!

shield [ʃiːld] n bouclier m; (on coat of arms) écu m; (screen) Tech écran m; – vt protéger (**from** de).

shift [ʃɪft] n (change) changement m (of, **in** de); (period of work) poste m; (workers) équipe f; **gear s.** Aut Am levier m de vitesse; **s. work** travail m en équipe; – vt (move) déplacer, bouger; (limb) bouger; (employee) muter (**to** à); (scenery) Th changer; (blame) rejeter (on to à); **to s. places** changer de place; **to s. gear(s)** Aut Am changer de vitesse; – vi bouger; (of heavy object) se déplacer; (of views) changer; (pass) passer (**to** à); (go) aller (**to** à); **to s. to** (new town) déménager à; **to s. along** avancer; **to s. over** or **up** se pousser. ◆**-ing** a (views) changeant.

shiftless ['ʃɪftləs] a velléitaire, paresseux.

shifty ['ʃɪftɪ] a (**-ier**, **-iest**) (sly) sournois; (dubious) louche.

shilling ['ʃɪlɪŋ] n shilling m.

shilly-shally ['ʃɪlɪʃælɪ] vi hésiter, tergiverser.

shimmer ['ʃɪmər] vi chatoyer, miroiter; – n chatoiement m, miroitement m.

shin [ʃɪn] n tibia m; **s. pad** n Sp jambière f.

shindig ['ʃɪndɪg] n Fam réunion f bruyante.

shin/e [ʃaɪn] vi (pt & pp shone [ʃɒn, Am ʃəʊn]) briller; **to s. with** (happiness etc) rayonner de; – vt (polish) faire briller; **to s. a light** or **a torch** éclairer (**on** sth qch); – n éclat m; (on shoes, cloth) brillant m. ◆**-ing** a (bright, polished) brillant; **a shining example** of un bel exemple de. ◆**shiny** a (**-ier**, **-iest**) (bright, polished) brillant; (clothes, through wear) lustré.

shingle ['ʃɪŋg(ə)l] n (on beach) galets mpl; (on roof) bardeau m.

shingles ['ʃɪŋg(ə)lz] n Med zona m.

ship [ʃɪp] n navire m, bateau m; **by s.** en bateau; **s. owner** armateur m; – vt (**-pp-**) (send) expédier; (transport) transporter; (load up) embarquer (**on to** sur). ◆**-ping** n (traffic) navigation f; (ships) navires mpl; – a (agent) maritime; **s. line** compagnie f de navigation. ◆**shipbuilding** n construction f navale. ◆**shipmate** n camarade m de bord. ◆**shipment** n (goods) chargement m, cargaison f. ◆**shipshape** a & adv en ordre. ◆**shipwreck** n naufrage m. ◆**shipwrecked** a

naufragé; **to be s.** faire naufrage. ◆**shipyard** n chantier m naval.

shirk [ʃɜːk] vt (duty) se dérober à; (work) éviter de faire; – vi tirer au flanc. ◆**-er** n tire-au-flanc m inv.

shirt [ʃɜːt] n chemise f; (of woman) chemisier m. ◆**shirtfront** n plastron m. ◆**shirtsleeves** npl **in (one's) s.** en bras de chemise.

shiver ['ʃɪvər] vi frissonner (**with** de); – n frisson m.

shoal [ʃəʊl] n (of fish) banc m.

shock [ʃɒk] n (moral blow) choc m; (impact) & Med choc m; (of explosion) secousse f; (electric) **s.** décharge f (électrique) (**from** sth en touchant qch); **a feeling of s.** un sentiment d'horreur; **suffering from s., in a state of s.** en état de choc; **to come as a s. to s.o.** stupéfier qn; – a (tactics, wave) de choc; (effect, image etc) -choc inv; **s. absorber** amortisseur m; – vt (offend) choquer; (surprise) stupéfier; (disgust) dégoûter. ◆**-ing** a affreux; (outrageous) scandaleux; (indecent) choquant. ◆**-ingly** adv affreusement. ◆**-er** n **to be a s.** Fam être affreux or horrible. ◆**shockproof** a résistant au choc.

shoddy ['ʃɒdɪ] a (**-ier**, **-iest**) (goods etc) de mauvaise qualité. ◆**shoddily** adv (made, done) mal.

shoe [ʃuː] n chaussure f, soulier m; (for horse) fer m; (brake) s. Aut sabot m (de frein); **in your shoes** Fig à ta place; **s. polish** cirage m; – vt (pt & pp shod) (horse) ferrer. ◆**shoehorn** n chausse-pied m. ◆**shoelace** n lacet m. ◆**shoemaker** n fabricant m de chaussures; (cobbler) cordonnier m. ◆**shoestring** n **on a s.** Fig avec peu d'argent (en poche).

shone [ʃɒn, Am ʃəʊn] see shine.

shoo [ʃuː] vt **to s. (away)** chasser; – int ouste!

shook [ʃʊk] see shake.

shoot¹ [ʃuːt] vt (pt & pp shot) (kill) tuer (d'un coup de feu), abattre; (wound) blesser (d'un coup de feu); (execute) fusiller; (hunt) chasser; (gun) tirer un coup de; (bullet) tirer; (missile, glance, questions) lancer (**at** à); (film) tourner; (person) Phot prendre; **to s. down** (aircraft) abattre; – vi (with gun, bow etc) tirer (**at** sur); **to s. ahead/off** avancer/partir à toute vitesse; **to s. up** (grow) pousser vite; (rise, spurt) jaillir; (of price) monter en flèche. ◆**-ing** n (gunfire, execution) fusillade f; (shots) coups mpl de feu; (murder) meurtre m; (of *film*) tournage *m*; (*hunting*) chasse *f*. ◆**shoot-out** *n Fam* fusillade *f*.

shoot² [ʃuːt] *vi* (*on plant*) pousse *f*.

shop [ʃɒp] **1** *n* magasin *m*; (*small*) boutique *f*; (*workshop*) atelier *m*; **at the baker's s.** à la boulangerie, chez le boulanger; **s. assistant** vendeur, -euse *mf*; **s. floor** (*workers*) ouvriers *mpl*; **s. steward** délégué, -ée *mf* syndical(e); **s. window** vitrine *f*; – *vi* (**-pp-**) faire ses courses (**at** chez); **to s. around** comparer les prix. **2** *vt* (**-pp-**) **to s. s.o.** *Fam* dénoncer qn (**à la police** *etc*). ◆**shopping** *n* (*goods*) achats *mpl*; **to go s.** faire des courses; **to do one's s.** faire ses courses; – *a* (*street, district*) commerçant; (*bag*) à provisions; **s. centre** centre *m* commercial. ◆**shopper** *n* (*buyer*) acheteur, -euse *mf*; (*customer*) client, -ente *mf*; (*bag*) sac *m* à provisions.

shopkeeper [ˈʃɒpkiːpər] *n* commerçant, -ante *mf*. ◆**shoplifter** *n* voleur, -euse *mf* à l'étalage. ◆**shoplifting** *n* vol *m* à l'étalage. ◆**shopsoiled** *a*, *Am* ◆**shopworn** *a* abîmé.

shore [ʃɔːr] **1** *n* (*of sea, lake*) rivage *m*; (*coast*) côte *f*, bord *m* de (la) mer; (*beach*) plage *f*; **on s.** (*passenger*) *Nau* à terre. **2** *vt* **to s. up** (*prop up*) étayer.

shorn [ʃɔːn] *a* (*a head*) tondu; **s. of** (*stripped of*) *Lit* dénué de.

short [ʃɔːt] *a* (**-er, -est**) court; (*person, distance*) petit; (*syllable*) bref; (*curt, impatient*) brusque; **a s. time** *or* **while** il y a peu de temps; **s. cut** raccourci *m*; **to be s. of money/time** être à court d'argent/de temps; **we're s. of ten men** il nous manque dix hommes; **money/time is s.** l'argent/le temps manque; **not far s. of** pas loin de; **s. of** (*except*) sauf; **to be s. for** (*of name*) être l'abréviation *or* le diminutif de; **in s.** bref; **s. circuit** *El* court-circuit *m*; **s. list** liste *f* de candidats choisis; – *adv* **to cut s.** (*visit etc*) abréger; (*person*) couper la parole à; **to go** *or* **get** *or* **run s. of** manquer de; **to get** *or* **run s.** manquer; **to stop s.** s'arrêter net; – *El* court-circuit *m*; **(a pair of) shorts** un short.
◆**shorten** *vt* (*visit, time, dress etc*) raccourcir. ◆**shortly** *adv* (*soon*) bientôt; **s. after** peu après. ◆**shortness** *n* (*of person*) petitesse *f*; (*of hair, stick, legs*) manque *m* de longueur.

shortage [ˈʃɔːtɪdʒ] *n* manque *m*, pénurie *f*; (*crisis*) crise *f*.

shortbread [ˈʃɔːtbred] *n* sablé *m*. ◆**short-'change** *vt* (*buyer*) ne pas rendre juste à. ◆**short-'circuit** *vt El* & *Fig* court-circuiter. ◆**shortcoming** *n* défaut *m*.

◆**shortfall** *n* manque *m*. ◆**shorthand** *n* sténo *f*; **s. typist** sténodactylo *f*. ◆**short-'handed** *a* à court de personnel. ◆**short-'lived** *a* éphémère. ◆**short-'sighted** *a* myope; *Fig* imprévoyant. ◆**short-'sightedness** *n* myopie *f*; imprévoyance *f*. ◆**short-'sleeved** *a* à manches courtes. ◆**short-'staffed** *a* à court de personnel. ◆**short-'term** *a* à court terme.

shortening [ˈʃɔːt(ə)nɪŋ] *n Culin* matière *f* grasse.

shot [ʃɒt] *see* **shoot¹**; – *n* coup *m*; (*bullet*) balle *f*; *Cin Phot* prise *f* de vues; (*injection*) *Med* piqûre *f*; **a good s.** (*person*) un bon tireur; **to have a s. at (doing) sth** essayer de faire qch; **a long s.** (*attempt*) un coup à tenter; **big s.** *Fam* gros bonnet *m*; **like a s.** (*at once*) tout de suite; **to be s. of** (*rid of*) *Fam* être débarrassé de. ◆**shotgun** *n* fusil *m* de chasse.

should [ʃud, *unstressed* ʃəd] *v aux* **1** (= *ought to*) you s. do it vous devriez le faire; **I s. have stayed** j'aurais dû rester; **that s. be Pauline** ça doit être Pauline. **2** (= *would*) **I s. like to** j'aimerais bien; **it's strange she say no** il est étrange qu'elle dise non. **3** (*possibility*) **if he s. come** s'il vient; **s. I be free** si je suis libre.

shoulder [ˈʃəuldər] **1** *n* épaule *f*; **to have round shoulders** avoir le dos voûté, être voûté; (*hard*) **s.** (*of motorway*) accotement *m* stabilisé; **s. bag** sac *m* à bandoulière; **s. blade** omoplate *f*; **s.-length hair** cheveux *mpl* mi-longs. **2** *vt* (*responsibility*) endosser, assumer.

shout [ʃaut] *n* cri *m*; **to give s.o. a s.** appeler qn; – *vi* **to s. (out)** crier; **to s. to** *or* **at s.o.** to do crier à qn de faire; **to s. at s.o.** (*scold*) crier après qn; – *vt* **to s. (out)** (*insult etc*) crier; **to s. down** (*speaker*) huer. ◆**—ing** *n* (*shouts*) cris *mpl*.

shove [ʃʌv] *n* poussée *f*; **to give s. (to)** pousser; – *vt* pousser; (*put*) *Fam* fourrer; **to s. sth into** (*thrust*) enfoncer *or* fourrer qch dans; **to s. s.o. around** *Fam* régenter qn; – *vi* pousser; **to s. off** (*leave*) *Fam* ficher le camp, filer; **to s. over** (*move over*) *Fam* se pousser.

shovel [ˈʃʌv(ə)l] *n* pelle *f*; – *vt* (**-ll-**, *Am* **-l-**) (*grain etc*) pelleter; **to s. up** *or* **away** (*remove*) enlever à la pelle; **to s. sth into** (*thrust*) *Fam* fourrer qch dans.

show [ʃəu] *n* (*of joy, force*) démonstration *f* (*of* de); (*semblance*) semblant *m* (*of* de); (*ostentation*) parade *f*; (*sight*) & *Th* spectacle *m*; (*performance*) *Cin* séance *f*; (*exhibition*) exposition *f*; **the Boat/Motor S.** le

Salon de la Navigation/de l'Automobile; **horse s.** concours *m* hippique; **to give a good s.** *Sp Mus Th* jouer bien; **good s.!** bravo!; **(just) for s.** pour l'effet; **on s.** (*painting etc*) exposé; **s. business** le monde du spectacle; **s. flat** appartement *m* témoin; – *vt* (*pt* **showed,** *pp* **shown**) montrer (**to à, that** que); (*exhibit*) exposer; (*film*) passer, donner; (*indicate*) indiquer, montrer; **to s. s.o. to the door** reconduire qn; **it (just) goes to s. that . . .** ça (dé)montre (bien) que . . .; **I'll s. him or her!** *Fam* je lui apprendrai!; – *vi* (*be visible*) se voir; (*of film*) passer; **'now showing'** *Cin* 'à l'affiche' (**at à**). ■ **to s. (a)round** *vt* faire visiter; **he** *or* **she was shown (a)round the house** on lui a fait visiter la maison; **to s. in** *vt* faire entrer; **to s. off** *vt Pej* étaler; (*highlight*) faire valoir; – *vi Pej* crâner. ◆**s.-off** *n Pej* crâneur, -euse *mf*; **to s. out** *vt* (*visitor*) reconduire; **to s. up** *vt* (*fault*) faire ressortir; (*humiliate*) faire honte à; – *vi* ressortir (**against** sur); (*of error*) être visible; (*of person*) *Fam* arriver, s'amener. ◆**showing** *n* (*of film*) projection *f* (**of** de); (*performance*) *Cin* séance *f*; (*of team, player*) performance *f*.

showcase [ˈʃəʊkeɪs] *n* vitrine *f*. ◆**showdown** *n* confrontation *f*, conflit *m*. ◆**showgirl** *n* (*in chorus etc*) girl *f*. ◆**showjumping** *n Sp* jumping *m*. ◆**showmanship** *n* art *m* de la mise en scène. ◆**showpiece** *n* modèle *m* du genre. ◆**showroom** *n* (*for cars etc*) salle *f* d'exposition.

shower [ˈʃaʊər] *n* (*of rain*) averse *f*; (*of blows*) déluge *m*; (*bath*) douche *f*; (*party*) *Am* réception *f* (*pour la remise de cadeaux*); – *vt* **to s. s.o. with** (*gifts, abuse*) couvrir qn de. ◆**showery** *a* pluvieux.

shown [ʃəʊn] *see* show.

showy [ˈʃəʊɪ] *a* (-**ier,** -**iest**) (*colour, hat*) voyant; (*person*) prétentieux.

shrank [ʃræŋk] *see* shrink 1.

shrapnel [ˈʃræpn(ə)l] *n* éclats *mpl* d'obus.

shred [ʃred] *n* lambeau *m*; (*of truth*) *Fig* grain *m*; **not a s. of evidence** pas la moindre preuve; – *vt* (**-dd-**) mettre en lambeaux; (*cabbage, carrots*) râper. ◆**shredder** *n Culin* râpe *f*.

shrew [ʃruː] *n* (*woman*) *Pej* mégère *f*.

shrewd [ʃruːd] *a* (-**er,** -**est**) (*person, plan*) astucieux. ◆**-ly** *adv* astucieusement. ◆**-ness** *n* astuce *f*.

shriek [ʃriːk] *n* cri *m* (aigu); – *vti* crier; **to s. with pain/laughter** hurler de douleur/de rire.

shrift [ʃrɪft] *n* **to get short s.** être traité sans ménagement.

shrill [ʃrɪl] *a* (-**er,** -**est**) aigu, strident.

shrimp [ʃrɪmp] *n* crevette *f*; (*person*) *Pej* nabot, -ote *mf*; (*child*) *Pej* puce *f*.

shrine [ʃraɪn] *n* lieu *m* saint; (*tomb*) châsse *f*.

shrink [ʃrɪŋk] **1** *vi* (*pt* **shrank,** *pp* **shrunk** *or* **shrunken**) (*of clothes*) rétrécir; (*of aging person*) se tasser; (*of amount, audience etc*) diminuer; **to s. from** reculer devant (**doing** l'idée de faire); – *vt* rétrécir. **2** *n* (*person*) *Am Hum* psy(chiatre) *m*. ◆**—age** *n* rétrécissement *m*; diminution *f*.

shrivel [ˈʃrɪv(ə)l] *vi* (**-ll-,** *Am* **-l-**) **to s. (up)** se ratatiner; – *vt* **to s. (up)** ratatiner.

shroud [ʃraʊd] *n* linceul *m*; (*of mystery*) *Fig* voile *m*; – *vt* **shrouded in mist** enseveli *or* enveloppé sous la brume; **shrouded in mystery** enveloppé de mystère.

Shrove Tuesday [ʃrəʊvˈtjuːzdɪ] *n* Mardi *m* gras.

shrub [ʃrʌb] *n* arbrisseau *m*.

shrug [ʃrʌg] *vt* (**-gg-**) **to s. one's shoulders** hausser les épaules; **to s. off** (*dismiss*) écarter (dédaigneusement); – *n* haussement *m* d'épaules.

shrunk(en) [ˈʃrʌŋk(ən)] *see* shrink 1.

shudder [ˈʃʌdər] *vi* frémir (**with** de); (*of machine etc*) vibrer; – *n* frémissement *m*; vibration *f*.

shuffle [ˈʃʌf(ə)l] **1** *vti* **to s. (one's feet)** traîner les pieds. **2** *vt* (*cards*) battre.

shun [ʃʌn] *vt* (**-nn-**) fuir, éviter; **to s. doing** éviter de faire.

shunt [ʃʌnt] *vt* (*train, conversation*) aiguiller (**on to** sur); **we were shunted (to and fro)** *Fam* on nous a baladés (**from office to office/etc** de bureau en bureau/etc).

shush! [ʃʊʃ] *int* chut!

shut [ʃʌt] *vt* (*pt & pp* **shut,** *pp* **shutting**) fermer; **to s. one's finger in** (*door etc*) se prendre le doigt dans; **to s. away** *or* **in** (*lock away or in*) enfermer; **to s. down** fermer; **to s. off** fermer; (*engine*) arrêter; (*isolate*) isoler; **to s. out** (*light*) empêcher d'entrer; (*view*) boucher; (*exclude*) exclure (**of, from** de); **to s. s.o. out** (*lock out accidentally*) enfermer qn dehors; **to s. up** fermer; (*lock up*) enfermer (*personne, objet précieux etc*); (*silence*) *Fam* faire taire; – *vi* (*of door etc*) se fermer; (*of shop, museum etc*) fermer; **the door doesn't s.** la porte ne ferme pas; **to s. down** fermer (*définitivement*); **to s. up** (*be quiet*) *Fam* se taire. ◆**shutdown** *n* fermeture *f*.

shutter [ˈʃʌtər] *n* volet *m*; (*of camera*) obturateur *m*.

shuttle ['ʃʌt(ə)l] *n* (*bus, spacecraft etc*) navette *f*; **s. service** navette *f*; – *vi* faire la navette; – *vt* (*in vehicle etc*) transporter. ◆**shuttlecock** *n* (*in badminton*) volant *m*.

shy [ʃaɪ] *a* (**-er, -est**) timide; **to be s.** of doing avoir peur de faire; **to s. away** reculer (**from s.o.** devant qn, **from doing** à l'idée de faire). ◆**-ness** *n* timidité *f*.

Siamese [saɪə'miːz] *a* siamois; **S. twins** frères *mpl* siamois, sœurs *fpl* siamoises.

sibling ['sɪblɪŋ] *n* frère *m*, sœur *f*.

Sicily ['sɪsɪlɪ] *n* Sicile *f*.

sick [sɪk] *a* (**-er, -est**) (*ill*) malade; (*mind*) malsain; (*humour*) noir; (*cruel*) sadique; **to be s.** (*vomit*) vomir; **to be off** *or* **away s., be on s. leave** être en congé de maladie; **to feel s.** avoir mal au cœur; **to be s. (and tired) of** *Fam* en avoir marre de; **he makes me s.** *Fam* il m'écœure; – *n* **the s.** les malades *mpl*; – *vi* (*vomit*) *Fam* vomir; – *vt* **to s. sth up** *Fam* vomir qch. ◆**sickbay** *n* infirmerie *f*. ◆**sickbed** *n* lit *m* de malade. ◆**sickly** *a* (**-ier, -iest**) maladif; (*pale, faint*) pâle; (*taste*) écœurant. ◆**sickness** *n* maladie *f*; (*vomiting*) vomissement(s) *m(pl)*; **motion s.** *Aut* mal *m* de la route.

sicken ['sɪkən] **1** *vt* écœurer. **2** *vi* **to be sickening for** (*illness*) couver. ◆**-ing** *a* écœurant.

side [saɪd] *n* côté *m*; (*of hill, animal*) flanc *m*; (*of road, river*) bord *m*; (*of beef*) quartier *m*; (*of question*) aspect *m*; (*of character*) facette *f*, aspect *m*; *Sp* équipe *f*; *Pol* parti *m*; **the right s.** (*of fabric*) l'endroit *m*; **the wrong s.** (*of fabric*) l'envers *m*; **by the s. of** (*nearby*) à côté de; **at** *or* **by my s.** à côté de moi, à mes côtés; **s. by s.** l'un à côté de l'autre; **to move to one s.** s'écarter; **on this s. de** ce côté; **on the other s. de** l'autre côté; **the other s.** *TV Fam* l'autre chaîne *f*; **on the big**/*etc* **s.** *Fam* plutôt grand/*etc*; **to take sides with** se ranger du côté de; **on our s.** de notre côté, avec nous; **on the s.** *Fam* (*secretly*) en catimini; (*to make money*) en plus; – *a* (*lateral*) latéral; (*effect, issue*) secondaire; (*glance, view*) de côté; (*street*) transversal; – *vi* **to s. with** se ranger du côté de. ◆**-sided** *suffix* **ten-s.** à dix côtés. ◆**sideboard 1** *n* buffet *m*. **2** *npl* (*hair*) pattes *fpl*. ◆**sideburns** *npl* (*hair*) *Am* pattes *fpl*. ◆**sidecar** *n* side-car *m*. ◆**sidekick** *n* *Fam* associé, -ée *mf*. ◆**sidelight** *n* *Aut* feu *m* de position. ◆**sideline** *n* activité *f* secondaire. ◆**sidesaddle** *adv* (*to ride*) en amazone. ◆**sidestep** *vt* (**-pp-**) éviter. ◆**sidetrack** *vt* **to get sidetracked**

s'écarter du sujet. ◆**sidewalk** *n* *Am* trottoir *m*. ◆**sideways** *adv* & *a* de côté.

siding ['saɪdɪŋ] *n* *Rail* voie *f* de garage.

sidle ['saɪd(ə)l] *vi* **to s. up to s.o.** s'approcher furtivement de qn.

siege [siːdʒ] *n* *Mil* siège *m*.

siesta [sɪ'estə] *n* sieste *f*.

sieve [sɪv] *n* tamis *m*; (*for liquids*) *Culin* passoire *f*; – *vt* tamiser. ◆**sift** *vt* tamiser; **to s. out** (*truth*) *Fig* dégager; – *vi* **to s. through** (*papers etc*) examiner (à la loupe).

sigh [saɪ] *n* soupir *m*; – *vti* soupirer.

sight [saɪt] *n* vue *f*; (*spectacle*) spectacle *m*; (*on gun*) mire *f*; **to lose s. of** perdre de vue; **to catch s. of** apercevoir; **to come into s.** apparaître; **at first s.** à première vue; **by s.** de vue; **on** *or* **at s.** à vue; **in s.** (*target, end, date etc*) en vue; **keep out of s.!** ne te montre pas!; **he hates the s. of me** il ne peut pas me voir; **it's a lovely s.** c'est beau à voir; **the (tourist) sights** les attractions *fpl* touristiques; **to set one's sights on** (*job etc*) viser; **a s. longer**/*etc* *Fam* bien plus long/*etc*; (*land*) apercevoir. ◆**-ed** *a* qui voit. ◆**clairvoyant.** ◆**-ing** *n* **to make a s.** of voir. ◆**sightseer** *n* touriste *mf*. ◆**sightseeing** *n* tourisme *m*.

sightly ['saɪtlɪ] *a* **not very s.** laid.

sign [saɪn] **1** *n* signe *m*; (*notice*) panneau *m*; (*over shop, inn*) enseigne *f*; **no s. of** aucune trace de; **to use s. language** parler par signes. **2** *vt* (*put signature to*) signer; **to s. away** *or* **over** céder (**to** à); **to s. on** *or* **up** (*worker, soldier*) engager; – *vi* signer; **to s. for** (*letter*) signer le reçu de; **to s. in** signer le registre; **to s. off** dire au revoir; **to s. on** (*on the dole*) s'inscrire au chômage; **to s. on** *or* **up** (*of soldier, worker*) s'engager; (*for course*) s'inscrire. ◆**signpost** *n* poteau *m* indicateur; – *vt* flécher.

signal ['sɪgnəl] *n* signal *m*; **traffic signals** feux *mpl* de circulation; **s. box**, *Am* **s. tower** *Rail* poste *m* d'aiguillage; – *vt* (**-ll-**, *Am* **-l-**) (*message*) communiquer (**to** à); (*arrival etc*) signaler (**to** à); – *vi* faire des signaux; **to s. (to) s.o. to do** faire signe à qn de faire. ◆**signalman** *n* (*pl* **-men**) *Rail* aiguilleur *m*.

signature ['sɪgnətʃər] *n* signature *f*; **s. tune** indicatif *m* (*musical*). ◆**signatory** *n* signataire *mf*.

signet ring ['sɪgnɪtrɪŋ] *n* chevalière *f*.

significant [sɪg'nɪfɪkənt] *a* (*meaningful*) significatif; (*important, large*) important. ◆**significance** *n* (*meaning*) signification *f*; (*importance*) importance *f*. ◆**significantly** *adv* (*appreciably*) sensiblement; **s.,**

he . . . . fait significatif, il . . . . ◆**'signify** vt (mean) signifier (**that** que); (make known) indiquer, signifier (**to** à).

silence ['saɪləns] n silence m; **in s.** en silence; – vt faire taire. ◆**silencer** n (on car, gun) silencieux m. ◆**silent** a silencieux; (film, anger) muet; **to keep** or **be s.** garder le silence (**about** sur). ◆**silently** adv silencieusement.

silhouette [sɪluːˈet] n silhouette f. ◆**silhouetted** a **to be s. against** se profiler contre.

silicon ['sɪlɪkən] n silicium m; **s. chip** puce f de silicium. ◆**silicone** ['sɪlɪkəʊn] n silicone f.

silk [sɪlk] n soie f. ◆**silky** a (-ier, -iest) soyeux.

sill [sɪl] n (of window etc) rebord m.

silly ['sɪlɪ] a (-ier, -iest) idiot, bête; **to do sth s.** faire une bêtise; **s. fool**, Fam **s. billy** idiot, -ote mf; – adv (to act, behave) bêtement.

silo ['saɪləʊ] n (pl -os) silo m.

silt [sɪlt] n vase f.

silver ['sɪlvər] n argent m; (silverware) argenterie f; **£5 in s.** 5 livres en pièces d'argent; – a (spoon etc) en argent, d'argent; (hair, colour) argenté; **s. jubilee** vingt-cinquième anniversaire m (d'un événement); **s. paper** papier m d'argent; **s. plate** argenterie f. ◆**s.-'plated** a plaqué argent. ◆**silversmith** n orfèvre m. ◆**silverware** n argenterie f. ◆**silvery** a (colour) argenté.

similar ['sɪmɪlər] a semblable (**to** à). ◆**simi-'larity** n ressemblance f (**between** entre, **to** avec). ◆**similarly** adv de la même façon; (likewise) de même.

simile ['sɪmɪlɪ] n Liter comparaison f.

simmer ['sɪmər] vi Culin mijoter, cuire à feu doux; (of water) frémir; (of revolt, hatred etc) couver; **to s. with** (rage) bouillir de; **to s. down** (calm down) Fam se calmer; – vt faire cuire à feu doux; (water) laisser frémir.

simper ['sɪmpər] vi minauder.

simple ['sɪmp(ə)l] a (-er, -est) (plain, uncomplicated, basic etc) simple. ◆**s.-'minded** a simple d'esprit. ◆**s.-'mindedness** n simplicité f d'esprit. ◆**simpleton** n nigaud, -aude mf. ◆**sim'plicity** n simplicité f. ◆**simplifi'cation** n simplification f. ◆**simplify** vt simplifier. ◆**sim'plistic** a simpliste. ◆**simply** adv (plainly, merely) simplement; (absolutely) absolument.

simulate ['sɪmjʊleɪt] vt simuler.

simultaneous [sɪməlˈteɪnɪəs, Am saɪməl-

'teɪnɪəs] a simultané. ◆**-ly** adv simultanément.

sin [sɪn] n péché m; – vi (-nn-) pécher.

since [sɪns] **1** prep (in time) depuis; **s. my departure** depuis mon départ; – conj depuis que; **s. she's been here** depuis qu'elle est ici; **it's a year s. I saw him** ça fait un an que je ne l'ai pas vu; – adv (ever) s. depuis. **2** conj (because) puisque.

sincere [sɪnˈsɪər] a sincère. ◆**sincerely** adv sincèrement; **yours s.** (in letter) Com veuillez croire à mes sentiments dévoués. ◆**sin'cerity** n sincérité f.

sinew ['sɪnjuː] n Anat tendon m.

sinful ['sɪnfəl] a (guilt-provoking) coupable; (shocking) scandaleux; **he's a s.** c'est un pécheur; **that's s.** c'est un péché.

sing [sɪŋ] vti (pt **sang**, pp **sung**) chanter; **to s. up** chanter plus fort. ◆**-ing** n (of bird & musical technique) chant m; (way of singing) façon f de chanter; – a (lesson, teacher) de chant. ◆**-er** n chanteur, -euse mf.

singe [sɪndʒ] vt (cloth) roussir; (hair) brûler; **to s. s.o.'s hair** (at hairdresser's) faire un brûlage à qn.

single ['sɪŋg(ə)l] a (only one) seul; (room, bed) pour une personne; (unmarried) célibataire; **s. ticket** billet m simple; **every s. day** tous les jours sans exception; **s. party** Pol parti m unique; – n (ticket) aller m simple; (record) 45 tours m inv; pl Tennis simples mpl; **singles bar** bar m pour célibataires; – vt **to s. out** (choose) choisir. ◆**s.-'breasted** a (jacket) droit. ◆**s.-'decker** n (bus) autobus m sans impériale. ◆**s.-'handed** a sans aide. ◆**s.-'minded** a (person) résolu, qui n'a qu'une idée en tête. ◆**singly** adv (one by one) un à un.

singlet ['sɪŋglɪt] n (garment) maillot m de corps.

singsong ['sɪŋsɒŋ] n **to get together for a s.** se réunir pour chanter.

singular ['sɪŋgjʊlər] **1** a (unusual) singulier. **2** a Gram (form) singulier; (noun) au singulier; – n Gram singulier m; **in the s.** au singulier.

sinister ['sɪnɪstər] a sinistre.

sink¹ [sɪŋk] n (in kitchen) évier m; (washbasin) lavabo m.

sink² [sɪŋk] vi (pt **sank**, pp **sunk**) (of ship, person etc) couler; (of sun, price, water level) baisser; (collapse, subside) s'affaisser; **to s. (down) into** (mud etc) s'enfoncer dans; (armchair etc) s'affaler dans; **to s. in** (of ink etc) pénétrer; (of fact etc) Fam rentrer (dans le crâne); **has that sunk in?** *Fam* as-tu compris ça?; – *vt* (*ship*) couler; (*well*) creuser; **to s. into** (*thrust*) enfoncer dans; (*money*) *Com* investir dans; **a sinking feel-ing** un serrement de cœur.

sinner ['sɪnər] *n* pécheur *m*, pécheresse *f*.

sinuous ['sɪnjuəs] *a* sinueux.

sinus ['saɪnəs] *n Anat* sinus *m inv*.

sip [sɪp] *vi* (**-pp-**) boire à petites gorgées; – *n* (*mouthful*) petite gorgée *f*; (*drop*) goutte *f*.

siphon ['saɪfən] *n* siphon *m*; – *vt* **to s. off** (*petrol*) siphonner; (*money*) *Fig* détourner.

sir [sɜːr] *n* monsieur *m*; **S. Walter Raleigh** (*title*) sir Walter Raleigh.

siren ['saɪərən] *n* (*of factory etc*) sirène *f*.

sirloin ['sɜːlɔɪn] *n* (*steak*) faux-filet *m*; (*joint*) aloyau *m*.

sissy ['sɪsɪ] *n* (*boy, man*) *Fam* femmelette *f*.

sister ['sɪstər] *n* sœur *f*; (*nurse*) infirmière *f* en chef. ◆**s.-in-law** *n* (*pl* **sisters-in-law**) belle-sœur *f*. ◆**sisterly** *a* fraternel.

sit [sɪt] *vi* (*pt* & *pp* **sat**, *pres p* **sitting**) s'asseoir; (*for artist*) poser (**for** pour); (*remain*) rester; (*of assembly etc*) siéger, être en séance; **to be sitting** (*of person, cat etc*) être assis; (*of bird*) être perché; **she sat** *or* **was sitting reading** elle était assise à lire; **to s. around** (*do nothing*) ne rien faire; **to s. back** (*in chair*) se caler; (*rest*) se reposer; (*do nothing*) ne rien faire; **to s. down** s'asseoir; **s.-down strike** grève *f* sur le tas; **to s. in on** (*lecture etc*) assister à; **to s. on** (*jury etc*) être membre de; (*fact etc*) *Fam* garder pour soi; **to s. through** *or* **out** (*film etc*) rester jusqu'au bout de; **to s. up** (*straight*) s'asseoir (bien droit); **to s. up waiting for s.o.** (*at night*) ne pas se coucher en attendant qn; – *vt* (*exam*) se présenter à; **to s. (for)** (*exam*) se présenter à; **to s. out** (*event, dance*) ne pas prendre part à. ◆**sitting** *n* séance *f*; (*for one's portrait*) séance *f* de pose; (*in restaurant*) service *m*; – *a* (*committee etc*) en séance; **s. duck** *Fam* victime *f* facile; **s. tenant** locataire *mf* en possession des lieux. ◆**sitting-room** *n* salon *m*.

site [saɪt] *n* emplacement *m*; (*archaeological*) site *m*; (*building*) chantier *m*; (*launching*) aire *f* de lancement; – *vt* (*building*) placer.

sit-in ['sɪtɪn] *n Pol* sit-in *m inv*.

sitter ['sɪtər] *n* (*for child*) baby-sitter *mf*.

situate ['sɪtʃʊeɪt] *vt* situer; **to be situated** être situé. ◆**situ'ation** *n* situation *f*.

six [sɪks] *a* & *n* six (*m*). ◆**six'teen** *a* & *n* seize (*m*). ◆**six'teenth** *a* & *n* seizième (*mf*). ◆**sixth** *a* & *n* sixième (*mf*); (*lower*) s.

form *Sch* = classe *f* de première; (*upper*) s. form *Sch* = classe *f* terminale; **a s.** (*fraction*) un sixième. ◆**sixtieth** *a* & *n* soixan-tième (*mf*). ◆**sixty** *a* & *n* soixante (*m*).

size [saɪz] **1** *n* (*of person, animal, garment etc*) taille *f*; (*measurements*) dimensions *fpl*; (*of egg, packet*) grosseur *f*; (*of book*) gran-deur *f*, format *m*; (*of problem, town, damage*) importance *f*, étendue *f*; (*of sum*) montant *m*, importance *f*; (*of shoes, gloves*) pointure *f*; (*of shirt*) encolure *f*; **hip/chest s.** tour *m* de hanches/de poitrine; **it's the s. of** . . . c'est grand comme . . . **2** *n* (*glue*) colle *f*. **3** *vt* **to s. up** (*person*) jauger; (*situation*) évaluer. ◆**sizeable** *a* assez grand *or* gros.

sizzl/e ['sɪz(ə)l] *vi* grésiller. ◆**-ing** *a* **s.** (**hot**) brûlant.

skat/e[1] [skeɪt] *n* patin *m*; – *vi* patiner. ◆**-ing** *n* patinage *m*; **to go s.** faire du patinage; **s. rink** (*ice*) patinoire *f*; (*roller*) skating *m*. ◆**skateboard** *n* skateboard *m*. ◆**skater** *n* patineur, -euse *mf*.

skate[2] [skeɪt] *n* (*fish*) raie *f*.

skedaddle [skɪ'dæd(ə)l] *vi Fam* déguerpir.

skein [skeɪn] *n* (*of yarn*) écheveau *m*.

skeleton ['skelɪt(ə)n] *n* squelette *m*; – *a* (*crew, staff*) (réduit au) minimum; **s. key** passe-partout *m inv*.

skeptic ['skeptɪk] *Am* = **sceptic**.

sketch [sketʃ] *n* (*drawing*) croquis *m*, esquisse *f*; *Th* sketch *m*; **a rough s. of** (*plan*) *Fig* une esquisse de; – *vt* **to s.** (**out**) (*view, idea etc*) esquisser; **to s. in** (*details*) ajouter; – *vi* faire un *or* des croquis. ◆**sketchy** *a* (**-ier, -iest**) incomplet, superficiel.

skew [skjuː] *n* **on the s.** de travers.

skewer ['skjuːər] *n* (*for meat etc*) broche *f*; (*for kebab*) brochette *f*.

ski [skiː] *n* (*pl* **skis**) ski *m*; **s. lift** télésiège *m*; **s. pants** fuseau *m*; **s. run** piste *f* de ski; **s. tow** téléski *m*; – *vi* (*pt* **skied** [skiːd], *pres p* **skiing**) faire du ski. ◆**-ing** *n Sp* ski *m*; – *a* (*school, clothes*) de ski. ◆**-er** *n* skieur, -euse *mf*.

skid [skɪd] **1** *vi* (**-dd-**) *Aut* déraper; **to s. into** déraper et heurter; – *n* dérapage *m*. **2** **a s. row** *Am* quartier *m* de clochards *or* de squats.

skill [skɪl] *n* habileté *f*, adresse *f* (**at** à); (*technique*) technique *f*; **one's skills** (*aptitudes*) ses compétences *fpl*. ◆**skilful** *a*, *Am* ◆**skillful** *a* habile (**at doing** à faire, **at sth** à qch). ◆**skilled** *a* habile (**at doing** à faire, **at sth** à qch); (*worker*) qualifié; (*work*) de spécialiste, de professionnel.

skillet ['skɪlɪt] *n Am* poêle *f* (à frire).

skim [skɪm] **1** *vt* (**-mm-**) (*milk*) écrémer;

(*soup*) écumer. **2** *vti* (**-mm-**) to s. (over) (*surface*) effleurer; to s. through (*book*) parcourir.

skimp [skɪmp] *vi* (*on fabric, food etc*) lésiner (on sur). ◆**skimpy** *a* (**-ier, -iest**) (*clothes*) étriqué; (*meal*) insuffisant.

skin [skɪn] *n* peau *f*; he has thick s. *Fig* c'est un dur; s. diving plongée *f* sous-marine; s. test cuti-(réaction) *f*; – *vt* (**-nn-**) (*animal*) écorcher; (*fruit*) peler. ◆**s.-'deep** *a* superficiel. ◆**s.-'tight** *a* moulant, collant.

skinflint ['skɪnflɪnt] *n* avare *mf*.

skinhead ['skɪnhed] *n* skinhead *m*, jeune voyou *m*.

skinny ['skɪni] *a* (**-ier, -iest**) maigre.

skint [skɪnt] *a* (*penniless*) *Fam* fauché.

skip[1] [skɪp] **1** *vi* (**-pp-**) (*jump*) sauter; (*hop about*) sautiller; (*with rope*) sauter à la corde; to s. off (*leave*) *Fam* filer; skipping rope corde *f* à sauter; – *n* petit saut *m*. **2** *vt* (**-pp-**) (*omit, miss*) sauter; to s. classes sécher les cours; s. it! (*forget it*) *Fam* laisse tomber!

skip[2] [skɪp] *n* (*container for debris*) benne *f*.

skipper ['skɪpər] *n Nau Sp* capitaine *m*.

skirmish ['skɜːmɪʃ] *n* accrochage *m*.

skirt [skɜːt] **1** *n* jupe *f*. **2** *vt* to s. round contourner; skirting board (*on wall*) plinthe *f*.

skit [skɪt] *n Th* pièce *f* satirique; a s. on une parodie de.

skittle ['skɪt(ə)l] *n* quille *f*; *pl* (*game*) jeu *m* de quilles.

skiv/e [skaɪv] *vi* (*skirk*) *Fam* tirer au flanc; to s. off (*slip away*) *Fam* se défiler. ◆**-er** *n Fam* tire-au-flanc *m inv*.

skivvy [skɪvɪ] *n Pej Fam* bonne *f* à tout faire, bon(n)iche *f*.

skulk [skʌlk] *vi* rôder (furtivement).

skull [skʌl] *n* crâne *m*. ◆**skullcap** *n* calotte *f*.

skunk [skʌŋk] *n* (*animal*) mouffette *f*, (*person*) *Pej* salaud *m*.

sky [skaɪ] *n* ciel *m*. ◆**skydiving** *n* parachutisme *m* (en chute libre). ◆**sky-'high** *a* (*prices*) exorbitant. ◆**skylight** *n* lucarne *f*. ◆**skyline** *n* (*outline of buildings*) ligne *f* d'horizon. ◆**skyrocket** *vi* (*of prices*) *Fam* monter en flèche. ◆**skyscraper** *n* gratte-ciel *m inv*.

slab [slæb] *n* (*of concrete etc*) bloc *m*; (*thin, flat*) plaque *f*; (*of chocolate*) tablette *f*, plaque *f*; (*paving stone*) dalle *f*.

slack [slæk] *a* (**-er, -est**) (*knot, spring*) lâche; (*discipline, security*) relâché, lâche; (*trade, grip*) faible, mou; (*negligent*) négligent; (*worker, student*) peu sérieux; s. periods

(*weeks etc*) périodes *fpl* creuses; (*hours*) heures *fpl* creuses; to be s. (*of rope*) avoir du mou; – *vi* to s. off (*in effort*) se relâcher. ◆**slacken** *vi* to s. (off) (*in effort*) se relâcher; (*of production, speed, zeal*) diminuer; – *vt* to s. (off) (*rope*) relâcher; (*pace, effort*) ralentir. ◆**slacker** *n* (*person*) *Fam* flemmard, -arde *mf*. ◆**slackly** *adv* (*loosely*) lâchement. ◆**slackness** *n* négligence *f*; (*of discipline*) relâchement *m*; (*of rope*) mou *m*; *Com* stagnation *f*.

slacks [slæks] *npl* pantalon *m*.

slag [slæg] *n* (*immoral woman*) *Sl* salope *f*, traînée *f*.

slagheap ['slæghiːp] *n* terril *m*.

slake [sleɪk] *vt* (*thirst*) *Lit* étancher.

slalom ['slɑːləm] *n Sp* slalom *m*.

slam [slæm] **1** *vt* (**-mm-**) (*door, lid*) claquer; (*hit*) frapper violemment; to s. (down) (*put down*) poser violemment; to s. on the brakes écraser le frein, freiner à bloc; – *vi* (*of door*) claquer; – *n* claquement *m*. **2** *vt* (**-mm-**) (*criticize*) *Fam* critiquer (avec virulence).

slander ['slɑːndər] *n* diffamation *f*, calomnie *f*; – *vt* diffamer, calomnier.

slang [slæŋ] *n* argot *m*; – *a* (*word etc*) d'argot, argotique. ◆**slanging match** *n Fam* engueulade *f*.

slant [slɑːnt] *n* inclinaison *f*; (*point of view*) *Fig* angle *m* (on sur); (*bias*) *Fig* parti-pris *m*; on a s. penché; (*roof*) en pente; – *vi* (*of writing*) pencher; (*of roof*) être en pente; – *vt* (*writing*) faire pencher; (*news*) *Fig* présenter de façon partiale. ◆**-ed** *a*, ◆**-ing** *a* penché; (*roof*) en pente.

slap [slæp] **1** *n* tape *f*, claque *f*; (*on face*) gifle *f*; – *vt* (**-pp-**) donner une tape à; to s. s.o.'s face gifler qn; to s. s.o.'s bottom donner une fessée à qn. **2** *vt* (**-pp-**) (*put*) mettre, flanquer; to s. on (*apply*) appliquer à la va-vite; (*add*) ajouter. **3** *adv* s. in the middle *Fam* en plein milieu. ◆**slapdash** *a* (*person*) négligent; (*task*) fait à la va-vite; – *adv* à la va-vite. ◆**slaphappy** *a Fam* (*carefree*) insouciant; (*negligent*) négligent. ◆**slap-up 'meal** *n Fam* gueuleton *m*.

slapstick *a & n* s. (comedy) grosse farce *f*. ◆**slash** [slæʃ] **1** *vt* (*cut with blade*) entailler, taillader; (*sever*) trancher; – *n* entaille *f*, taillade *f*. **2** *vt* (*reduce*) réduire radicalement; (*prices*) *Com* écraser.

slat [slæt] *n* (*in blind*) lamelle *f*.

slate [sleɪt] **1** *n* ardoise *f*. **2** *vt* (*book etc*) *Fam* critiquer, démolir.

slaughter ['slɔːtər] *vt* (*people*) massacrer;

(*animal*) abattre; – *n* massacre *m*; abattage *m*. ◆**slaughterhouse** *n* abattoir *m*.

Slav [slɑːv] *a* & *n* slave (*mf*). ◆**Sla'vonic** *a* (*language*) slave.

slave [sleɪv] *n* esclave *mf*; **the s. trade** *Hist* la traite des noirs; **s. driver** *Fig Pej* négrier *m*; – *vi* **to s.** (**away**) se crever (au travail), bosser comme une bête; **to s. away doing** s'escrimer à faire. ◆**slavery** *n* esclavage *m*. ◆**slavish** *a* servile.

slaver [ˈslævər] *vi* (*dribble*) baver (**over** sur); – *n* bave *f*.

slay [sleɪ] *vt* (*pt* slew, *pp* slain) *Lit* tuer.

sleazy [ˈsliːzɪ] *a* (**-ier, -iest**) *Fam* sordide, immonde.

sledge [sledʒ] (*Am* **sled** [sled]) *n* luge *f*; (*horse-drawn*) traîneau *m*.

sledgehammer [ˈsledʒhæmər] *n* masse *f*.

sleek [sliːk] *a* (**-er, -est**) lisse, brillant; (*manner*) onctueux.

sleep [sliːp] *n* sommeil *m*; **to have a s., get some s.** dormir; **to send to s.** endormir; **to go or get to s.** s'endormir; **to get to s.** (*of arm, foot*) *Fam* s'engourdir; – *vi* (*pt* & *pp* slept) dormir; (*spend the night*) coucher; **s. tight or well!** dors bien!; **I'll s. on it** *Fig* je déciderai demain, la nuit portera conseil; – *vt* **this room sleeps six** on peut coucher or loger six personnes dans cette chambre; **to s. it off** *Fam* cuver son vin. ◆**-ing** (*asleep*) endormi; **s. bag** sac *m* de couchage; **s. car** wagon-lit *m*; **s. pill** somnifère *m*; **s. quarters** chambre(s) *f*(*pl*), dortoir *m*. ◆**sleeper** *n* **1** to be a **light/sound s.** avoir le sommeil léger/lourd. **2** *Rail* (*on track*) traverse *f*; (*berth*) couchette *f*; (*train*) train *m* couchettes. ◆**sleepiness** *n* torpeur *f*. ◆**sleepless** *a* (*hours*) sans sommeil; (*night*) d'insomnie. ◆**sleepwalker** *n* somnambule *mf*. ◆**sleepwalking** *n* somnambulisme *m*. ◆**sleepy** *a* (**-ier, -iest**) (*town, voice*) endormi; **to be s.** (*of person*) avoir sommeil.

sleet [sliːt] *n* neige *f* fondue; (*sheet of ice*) *Am* verglas *m*; – *vi* **it's sleeting** il tombe de la neige fondue.

sleeve [sliːv] *n* (*of shirt etc*) manche *f*; (*of record*) pochette *f*; **up one's s.** (*surprise, idea etc*) *Fig* en réserve; **long-/short-sleeved** à manches longues/courtes.

sleigh [sleɪ] *n* traîneau *m*.

sleight [slaɪt] *n* **s. of hand** prestidigitation *f*.

slender [ˈslendər] *a* (*person*) mince, svelte; (*neck, hand*) fin; (*feeble, small*) *Fig* faible.

slept [slept] *see* sleep.

sleuth [sluːθ] *n* (*detective*) *Hum* (fin) limier *m*.

slew [sluː] *n* **a s. of** *Am Fam* un tas de, une tapée de.

slice [slaɪs] *n* tranche *f*; (*portion*) *Fig* partie *f*, part *f*; – *vt* **to s.** (**up**) couper (en tranches); **to s. off** (*cut off*) couper.

slick [slɪk] *a* (**-er, -est**) (*glib*) qui a la parole facile; (*manner*) mielleux; (*cunning*) astucieux; (*smooth, slippery*) lisse. **2** *n* **oil s.** nappe *f* de pétrole; (*large*) marée *f* noire.

slide [slaɪd] *n* (*act*) glissade *f*; (*in value etc*) *Fig* (légère) baisse *f*; (*in playground*) toboggan *m*; (*on ice*) glissoire *f*; (*for hair*) barrette *f*; *Phot* diapositive *f*; (*of microscope*) lamelle *f*, lame *f*; **s. rule** règle *f* à calcul; – *vi* (*pt* & *pp* slid) glisser; **to s. into** (*room etc*) se glisser dans; – *vt* (*letter etc*) glisser (**into** dans); (*table etc*) faire glisser. ◆**-ing** (*door, panel*) à glissière; (*roof*) ouvrant; **s. scale** *Com* échelle *f* mobile

slight [slaɪt] **1** *a* (**-er, -est**) (*slim*) mince; (*frail*) frêle; (*intelligence*) faible; **the slightest thing** la moindre chose; **not in the slightest** pas le moins du monde. **2** *vt* (*offend*) offenser; (*ignore*) bouder; – *n* affront *m* (**on** à). ◆**-ly** *adv* légèrement, un peu; **s. built** fluet.

slim [slɪm] *a* (**slimmer, slimmest**) mince; – *vi* (**-mm-**) maigrir. ◆**slimming** *a* (*diet*) amaigrissant; (*food*) qui ne fait pas grossir. ◆**slimness** *n* minceur *f*.

slime [slaɪm] *n* boue *f* (visqueuse); (*of snail*) bave *f*. ◆**slimy** *a* (**-ier, -iest**) (*muddy*) boueux; (*sticky, smarmy*) visqueux.

sling [slɪŋ] **1** *n* (*weapon*) fronde *f*; (*toy*) lance-pierres *m inv*; (*for arm*) *Med* écharpe *f*; **in a s.** en écharpe. **2** *vt* (*pt* & *pp* slung) (*throw*) jeter, lancer; (*hang*) suspendre; **to s. away or out** (*throw out*) *Fam* balancer. ◆**slingshot** *n* *Am* lance-pierres *m inv*.

slip [slɪp] **1** *n* (*mistake*) erreur *f*; (*woman's undergarment*) combinaison *f*; (*of paper for filing*) fiche *f*; **a s. of paper** (*bit*) un bout de papier; **a s. (of the tongue)** un lapsus; **to give s.o. the s.** fausser compagnie à qn; **s. road** *Aut* bretelle *f*. **2** *vi* (**-pp-**) glisser; **to s. into** (*go, get*) se glisser dans; (*habit*) prendre; (*garment*) mettre; **to let s.** (*chance, oath, secret*) laisser échapper; **to s. through** (*crowd*) se faufiler parmi; **to s. along or over to** faire un saut chez; **to s. away** (*escape*) s'esquiver; **to s. back/in** retourner/entrer furtivement; **to s. out** sortir furtivement; (*pop out*) sortir (un instant); (*of secret*) s'éventer; **to s. past** (*guards*) passer sans être vu de; **to s. up** (*make a* *mistake*) *Fam* gaffer; − *vt* (*slide*) glisser (**to à**, **into** dans); **it slipped his** *or* **her notice** ça lui a échappé; **it slipped his** *or* **her mind** ça lui est sorti de l'esprit; **to s. off** (*garment etc*) enlever; **to s. on** (*garment etc*) mettre. ◆**s.-up** *n Fam* gaffe *f*, erreur *f*.

slipcover ['slɪpkʌvər] *n Am* housse *f*.

slipper ['slɪpər] *n* pantoufle *f*.

slippery ['slɪpərɪ] *a* glissant.

slipshod ['slɪpʃɒd] *a* (*negligent*) négligent; (*slovenly*) négligé.

slit [slɪt] *n* (*opening*) fente *f*; (*cut*) coupure *f*; − *vt* (*pt* & *pp* slit, *pres p* slitting) (*cut*) couper; (*tear*) déchirer; **to s. open** (*sack*) éventrer.

slither ['slɪðər] *vi* glisser; (*of snake*) se couler.

sliver ['slɪvər] *n* (*of apple etc*) lichette *f*; (*of wood*) éclat m.

slob [slɒb] *n Fam* malotru m, goujat m.

slobber ['slɒbər] *vi* (*of dog etc*) baver (**over** sur); − *n* bave *f*.

slog [slɒg] **1** *n a* (*hard*) **s.** (*effort*) un gros effort; (*work*) un travail dur; − *vi* (-**gg**-) **to s.** (**away**) bosser, trimer. **2** *vt* (-**gg**-) (*hit*) donner un grand coup à.

slogan ['sləʊgən] *n* slogan m.

slop [slɒp] *n* **slops** eaux *fpl* sales; − *vi* (-**pp**-) **to s.** (**over**) (*spill*) se répandre; − *vt* répandre.

slop/e [sləʊp] *n* pente *f*; (*of mountain*) flanc m; (*slant*) inclinaison *f*; − *vi* être en pente; (*of handwriting*) pencher; **to s. down** descendre en pente. ◆**-ing** *a* en pente; (*handwriting*) penché.

sloppy ['slɒpɪ] *a* (-**ier**, -**iest**) (*work*, *appearance*) négligé; (*person*) négligent; (*mawkish*) sentimental; (*wet*) détrempé; (*watery*) liquide.

slosh [slɒʃ] *vt* (*pour*) *Fam* répandre. ◆**-ed** *a* (*drunk*) *Fam* bourré.

slot [slɒt] *n* (*slit*) fente *f*; (*groove*) rainure *f*; (*in programme*) *Rad TV* créneau m; **s. machine** (*vending*) distributeur *m* automatique; (*gambling*) machine *f* à sous; − *vt* (-**tt**-) (*insert*) insérer (**into** dans); − *vi* s'insérer (**into** dans).

sloth [sləʊθ] *n Lit* paresse *f*.

slouch [slaʊtʃ] **1** *vi* ne pas se tenir droit; (*have stoop*) avoir le dos voûté; (*in chair*) se vautrer (**in** dans); **slouching over** (*desk etc*) penché sur; − *n* mauvaise tenue *f*; **with a s.** (*to walk*) en se tenant mal; le dos voûté. **2** *n Fam* (*person*) lourdaud m, -aude *mf*; (*lazy*) paresseux, -euse *mf*.

slovenly ['slʌvənlɪ] *a* négligé. ◆**slovenli-**

ness *n* (*of dress*) négligé m; (*carelessness*) négligence *f*.

slow [sləʊ] *a* (-**er**, -**est**) lent; (*business*) calme; (*party*, *event*) ennuyeux; (**at**) **a**) **s. speed** à vitesse réduite; **to be a s. walker** marcher lentement; **to be s.** (*of clock*, *watch*) retarder; **to be five minutes s.** retarder de cinq minutes; **to be s. to act** *or* **in acting** être lent à agir; **in motion** au ralenti; − *adv* lentement; − *vt* **to s. down** *or* **up** (*delay*) retarder; − *vi* **to s. down** *or* **up** ralentir. ◆**-ly** *adv* lentement; (*bit by bit*) peu à peu. ◆**-ness** *n* lenteur *f*.

slowcoach ['sləʊkəʊtʃ] *n Fam* lambin, -ine *mf*. ◆**slow-down** *n* ralentissement m; **s.-down** (*strike*) *Am* grève *f* perlée. ◆**slow-'moving** *a* (*vehicle etc*) lent. ◆**slowpoke** *n Am Fam* lambin, -ine *mf*.

sludge [slʌdʒ] *n* gadoue *f*.

slue [sluː] *n Am Fam* see **slew**.

slug [slʌg] **1** *n* (*mollusc*) limace *f*. **2** *n* (*bullet*) *Am Sl* pruneau m. **3** *vt* (-**gg**-) (*hit*) *Am Fam* frapper; − *n* coup m, marron m.

sluggish ['slʌgɪʃ] *a* lent, mou.

sluice [sluːs] *n* (*gate*) vanne *f*.

slum [slʌm] *n* (*house*) taudis m; **the slums** les quartiers *mpl* pauvres; − *a* (*district*) pauvre; − *vt* (-**mm**-) **to s. it** *Fam* manger de la vache enragée. ◆**slummy** *a* (-**ier**, -**iest**) sordide, pauvre.

slumber ['slʌmbər] *n Lit* sommeil m.

slump [slʌmp] *n* baisse *f* soudaine (**in** de); (*in prices*) effondrement m; *Econ* crise *f*; − *vi* (*decrease*) baisser; (*of prices*) s'effondrer; **to s. into** (*armchair etc*) s'affaisser dans.

slung [slʌŋ] *see* **sling 2**.

slur [slɜːr] **1** *vt* (-**rr**-) prononcer indistinctement; **to s. one's words** manger ses mots. **2** *n* **to cast a s. on** (*reputation etc*) porter atteinte à. ◆**slurred** *a* (*speech*) indistinct.

slush [slʌʃ] *n* (*snow*) neige *f* fondue; (*mud*) gadoue *f*. ◆**slushy** *a* (-**ier**, -**iest**) (*road*) couvert de neige fondue.

slut [slʌt] *n Pej* (*immoral*) salope *f*, traînée *f*; (*untidy*) souillon *f*.

sly [slaɪ] *a* (-**er**, -**est**) (*deceitful*) sournois; (*crafty*) rusé; − *n* **on the s.** en cachette. ◆**-ly** *adv* sournoisement; (*in secret*) en cachette.

smack [smæk] **1** *n* claque *f*; gifle *f*; fessée *f*; − *vt* donner une claque à; **to s. s.o.'s face** gifler qn; **to s. s.o.('s bottom)** donner une fessée à qn. **2** *adv* **s. in the middle** *Fam* en plein milieu. **3** *vi* **to s. of** (*be suggestive of*) avoir des relents de. ◆**-ing** *n* fessée *f*.

small [smɔːl] *a* (-**er**, -**est**) petit; **in the s. hours** au petit matin; **s. talk** menus propos mpl; – *adv* (*to cut, chop*) menu; – n the s. of the back le creux *m* des reins. ◆–ness *n* petitesse *f*. ◆smallholding *n* petite ferme *f*. ◆small-scale *a* Fig peu important. ◆small-time *a* (*crook, dealer etc*) petit, sans grande envergure.

smallpox ['smɔːlpɒks] *n* petite vérole *f*.

smarmy ['smɑːmɪ] *a* (-ier, -iest) Pej Fam visqueux, obséquieux.

smart[1] [smɑːt] *a* (-er, -est) (*in appearance*) élégant; (*astute*) astucieux; (*clever*) intelligent; (*quick*) rapide; s. aleck Fam je-sais-tout *mf inv*. ◆smarten *vt* to s. up (*room etc*) embellir; – *vti* to s. (*oneself*) up (*make oneself spruce*) se faire beau, s'arranger. ◆smartly *adv* élégamment; (*quickly*) en vitesse; (*astutely*) astucieusement. ◆smartness *n* élégance *f*.

smart[2] [smɑːt] *vi* (*sting*) brûler, faire mal.

smash [smæʃ] *vt* (*break*) briser; (*shatter*) fracasser; (*enemy*) écraser; (*record*) pulvériser; to s. s.o.'s face (in) Fam casser la gueule à qn; to s. down *or* in (*door*) fracasser; to s. up (*car*) esquinter; (*room*) démolir; – *vi* se briser; to s. into (*of car*) se fracasser contre; – *n* (*noise*) fracas *m*; (*blow*) coup *m*; (*accident*) collision *f*; s. hit Fam succès *m* fou. ◆s.-up *n* collision *f*.

smashing ['smæʃɪŋ] *a* (*wonderful*) Fam formidable. ◆smasher *n* to be a (real) s. Fam être formidable.

smattering ['smætərɪŋ] *n* a s. of (*French etc*) quelques notions *fpl* de.

smear [smɪər] *vt* (*coat*) enduire (with de); (*stain*) tacher (with de); (*smudge*) faire une trace sur; – *n* (*mark*) trace *f*; (*stain*) tache *f*; Med frottis *m*; a s. on (*attack*) Fig une atteinte à; s. campaign campagne *f* de diffamation.

smell [smel] *n* odeur *f*; (*sense of*) s. odorat *m*; – *vt* (*pt & pp* smelled *or* smelt) sentir; (*of animal*) flairer; – *vi* (*stink*) sentir (mauvais); (*have smell*) avoir une odeur; to s. of smoke/*etc* sentir la fumée/*etc*; smelling salts sels *mpl*. ◆smelly *a* (-ier, -iest) to be s. sentir (mauvais).

smelt[1] [smelt] *see* smell.

smelt[2] [smelt] *vt* (*ore*) fondre; smelting works fonderie *f*.

smidgen ['smɪdʒən] *n* a s. (*a little*) Am Fam un brin (of de).

smil/e [smaɪl] *n* sourire *m*; – *vi* sourire (at s.o. à qn, at sth de qch). ◆–ing *a* souriant.

smirk [smɜːk] *n* (*smug*) sourire *m* suffisant; (*scornful*) sourire *m* goguenard.

smith [smɪθ] *n* (*blacksmith*) forgeron *m*.

smithereens [smɪðə'riːnz] *npl* to smash to s. briser en mille morceaux.

smitten ['smɪt(ə)n] *a* s. with Hum (*desire, remorse*) pris de; (*in love with*) épris de.

smock [smɒk] *n* blouse *f*.

smog [smɒg] *n* brouillard *m* épais, smog *m*.

smoke [sməʊk] *n* fumée *f*; to have a s. fumer une cigarette *etc*; – *vt* (*cigarette, salmon etc*) fumer; to s. out (*room etc*) enfumer; – *vi* fumer; 'no smoking' 'défense de fumer'; smoking compartment Rail compartiment *m* fumeurs. ◆smokeless *a* s. fuel combustible *m* non polluant. ◆smoker *n* fumeur, -euse *mf*; Rail compartiment *m* fumeurs. ◆smoky *a* (-ier, -iest) (*air*) enfumé; (*wall*) noirci de fumée; it's s. here il y a de la fumée ici.

smooth [smuːð] *a* (-er, -est) (*surface, skin etc*) lisse; (*road*) à la surface égale; (*movement*) régulier, sans à-coups; (*flight*) agréable; (*cream, manners*) onctueux; (*person*) doucereux; (*sea*) calme; the s. running la bonne marche (of de); – *vt* to s. down *or* out lisser; to s. out *or* over (*problems etc*) Fig aplanir. ◆–ly *adv* (*to land, pass off*) en douceur. ◆–ness *n* aspect *m* lisse; (*of road*) surface *f* égale.

smother ['smʌðər] *vt* (*stifle*) étouffer; to s. with (*kisses etc*) Fig couvrir de.

smoulder ['sməʊldər] *vi* (*of fire, passion etc*) couver.

smudge [smʌdʒ] *n* tache *f*, bavure *f*; – *vt* (*paper etc*) faire des taches sur, salir.

smug [smʌg] *a* (smugger, smuggest) (*smile etc*) béat; (*person*) content de soi, suffisant. ◆–ly *adv* avec suffisance.

smuggl/e ['smʌg(ə)l] *vt* passer (en fraude); smuggled goods contrebande *f*. ◆–ing *n* contrebande *f*. ◆–er *n* contrebandier, -ière *mf*.

smut [smʌt] *n inv* (*obscenity*) saleté(s) *f(pl)*. ◆smutty *a* (-ier, -iest) (*joke etc*) cochon.

snack [snæk] *n* casse-croûte *m inv*; s. bar snack(-bar) *m*.

snafu [snæ'fuː] *n Sl* embrouillamini *m*.

snag [snæg] *n* 1 (*hitch*) inconvénient *m*, os *m*. 2 (*in cloth*) accroc *m*.

snail [sneɪl] *n* escargot *m*; at a s.'s pace comme une tortue.

snake [sneɪk] *n* (*reptile*) serpent *m*; – *vi* (*of river*) serpenter.

snap [snæp] 1 *vt* (-pp-) casser (avec un bruit sec); (*fingers, whip*) faire claquer; to s. up a bargain sauter sur une occasion; – *vi* se casser net; (*of whip*) claquer; (*of person*) Fig parler sèchement (à à); s. out of it! Fam secoue-toi!; – *n* claquement *m*, bruit *m sec*; *Phot* photo *f*; (*fastener*) *Am* bouton-pression *m*; **cold s.** Met coup *m* de froid. **2** *a* soudain, brusque; **to make a s. decision** décider sans réfléchir. ◆**snapshot** *n* photo *f*, instantané *m*.

snappy ['snæpɪ] *a* (**-ier, -iest**) (*pace*) vif; **make it s.!** *Fam* dépêche-toi!

snare [sneər] *n* piège *m*.

snarl [snɑːl] *vi* gronder (en montrant les dents); – *n* grondement *m*. ◆**s.-up** *n* *Aut Fam* embouteillage *m*.

snatch [snætʃ] *vt* saisir (*d'un geste vif*); (*some rest etc*) *Fig* (réussir à) prendre; **to s. sth from s.o.** arracher qch à qn; – *n* (*theft*) vol *m* (à l'arraché).

snatches ['snætʃɪz] *npl* (*bits*) fragments *mpl* (of).

snazzy ['snæzɪ] *a* (**-ier, -iest**) *Fam* (*flashy*) tapageur; (*smart*) élégant.

sneak [sniːk] **1** *vi* **to s. in/out** entrer/sortir furtivement; **to s. off** s'esquiver; – *a* (*attack, visit*) furtif. **2** *n* (*telltale*) *Sch Fam* rapporteur, -euse *mf*; – *vi* **to s. on** *Sch Fam* dénoncer. ◆**sneaking** *a* (*suspicion*) vague; (*desire*) secret. ◆**sneaky** *a* (**-ier, -iest**) (*sly*) *Fam* sournois.

sneaker ['sniːkər] *n* (*shoe*) tennis *f*.

sneer [snɪər] *n* ricanement *m*; – *vi* ricaner; **to s. at** se moquer de.

sneeze [sniːz] *n* éternuement *m*; – *vi* éternuer.

snicker ['snɪkər] *n* & *vi* *Am* = snigger.

snide [snaɪd] *a* (*remark etc*) sarcastique.

sniff [snɪf] *n* reniflement *m*; – *vt* renifler; (*of dog*) flairer, renifler; **to s. out** (*bargain*) *Fig* renifler; – *vi* **to s. (at)** renifler. ◆**sniffle** *vi* renifler; – *n* a **s., the sniffles** *Fam* un petit rhume.

snigger ['snɪgər] *n* (petit) ricanement *m*; – *vi* ricaner. ◆**-ing** *n* ricanement(s) *m(pl)*.

snip [snɪp] *n* (*piece*) petit bout *m* (coupé); (*bargain*) *Fam* bonne affaire *f*; **to make a s. couper**; – *vt* (**-pp-**) couper.

sniper ['snaɪpər] *n* *Mil* tireur *m* embusqué.

snippet ['snɪpɪt] *n* (*of conversation etc*) bribe *f*.

snivel ['snɪv(ə)l] *vi* (**-ll-**, *Am* **-l-**) pleurnicher. ◆**snivelling** *a* pleurnicheur.

snob [snɒb] *n* snob *mf*. ◆**snobbery** *n* snobisme *m*. ◆**snobbish** *a* snob *inv*.

snook [snuːk] *n* **to cock a s.** faire un pied de nez (at à).

snooker ['snuːkər] *n* snooker *m*, sorte de jeu de billard.

snoop [snuːp] *vi* fourrer son nez partout; **to s. on s.o.** (*spy on*) espionner qn.

snooty ['snuːtɪ] *a* (**-ier, -iest**) *Fam* snob *inv*.

snooze [snuːz] *n* petit somme *m*; – *vi* faire un petit somme.

snor/e [snɔːr] *vi* ronfler; – *n* ronflement *m*. ◆**-ing** *n* ronflement *m*.

snorkel ['snɔːk(ə)l] *n* *Sp Nau* tuba *m*.

snort [snɔːt] *vi* (*grunt*) grogner; (*sniff*) renifler; (*of horse*) renâcler; – *n* (*grunt*) grognement *m*.

snot [snɒt] *n* *Pej Fam* morve *f*. ◆**snotty** *a* (**-ier, -iest**) *Fam* (*nose*) qui coule; (*child*) morveux. ◆**snotty-nosed** *a* *Fam* morveux.

snout [snaʊt] *n* museau *m*.

snow [snəʊ] *n* neige *f*; – *vi* neiger; – *vt* **to be snowed in** être bloqué par la neige; **to be s. under with** (*work etc*) être submergé de. ◆**snowball** *n* boule *f* de neige; – *vi* (*increase*) faire boule de neige. ◆**snowbound** *a* bloqué par la neige. ◆**snow-capped** *a* (*mountain*) enneigé. ◆**snowdrift** *n* congère *f*. ◆**snowdrop** *n* *Bot* perce-neige *m or f inv*. ◆**snowfall** *n* chute *f* de neige. ◆**snowflake** *n* flocon *m* de neige. ◆**snowman** *n* (*pl* **-men**) bonhomme *m* de neige. ◆**snowmobile** *n* motoneige *f*. ◆**snowplough** *n*, *Am* ◆**snowplow** *n* chasse-neige *m inv*. ◆**snowstorm** *n* tempête *f* de neige. ◆**snowy** *a* (**-ier, -iest**) (*weather, hills, day etc*) neigeux.

snub [snʌb] **1** *n* rebuffade *f*; – *vt* (**-bb-**) (*offer etc*) rejeter; **to s. s.o.** snober qn. **2** *a* (*nose*) retroussé.

snuff [snʌf] **1** *n* tabac *m* à priser. **2** *vt* **to s. (out)** (*candle*) moucher. ◆**snuffbox** *n* tabatière *f*.

snuffle ['snʌf(ə)l] *vi* & *n* = sniffle.

snug [snʌg] *a* (**snugger, snuggest**) (*house etc*) confortable, douillet; (*garment*) bien ajusté; **we're s.** (*in chair etc*) on est bien; **s. in bed** bien au chaud dans son lit.

snuggle ['snʌg(ə)l] *vi* **to s. up to** se pelotonner contre.

so [səʊ] **1** *adv* (*to such a degree*) si, tellement (*that* que); (*thus*) ainsi, comme ça; **so that** (*purpose*) pour que (+ *sub*); (*result*) si bien que; **so as to do** pour faire; **I think so** je le pense, je pense que oui; **do so!** faites-le!; **if so** si oui; **is that so?** c'est vrai?; **so am I, so do I** *etc* moi aussi; **so much** (*to work etc*) tant, tellement (*that* que); (*money, time etc*) tant, tellement (*that* que); **so many** (*books etc*) tant *or* tellement de livres/*etc* (*that* que); **so very fast**/*etc* vraiment si vite/*etc*; **ten or so** environ dix; **so long!** *Fam* au revoir!; **and so on** et ainsi de suite. **2** *conj* (*therefore*) donc; (*in that case*) alors; so what? et alors? ◆**So-and-so** *n* Mr So-and-so Monsieur Un tel. ◆**so-'called** *a* soi-disant *inv*. ◆**so-so** *a Fam* comme ci comme ça.

soak [səʊk] *vt* (*drench*) tremper; (*washing, food*) faire tremper; **to s. up** absorber; — *vi* (*of washing etc*) tremper; **to s. in** (*of liquid*) s'infiltrer; — *vt* to **give sth a s.** faire tremper qch. ◆**—ed** *a* s. (**through**) trempé (jusqu'aux os). ◆**—ing** *a* & *adv* s. (**wet**) trempé; — *n* trempage *m*.

soap [səʊp] *n* savon *m*; s. **opera** téléroman *m*; s. **powder** lessive *f*; — *vt* savonner. ◆**soapflakes** *npl* savon *m* en paillettes. ◆**soapsuds** *npl* mousse *f* de savon. ◆**soapy** *a* (-**ier, -iest**) *a* savonneux.

soar [sɔːr] *vi* (*of bird etc*) s'élever; (*of price*) monter (en flèche); (*of hope*) *Fig* grandir.

sob [sɒb] *n* sanglot *m*; — *vi* (-**bb-**) sangloter. ◆**sobbing** *n* (*sobs*) sanglots *mpl*.

sober [ˈsəʊbər] **1** *a* **he's s.** (*not drunk*) il n'est pas ivre; — *vti* to **s. up** dessoûler. **2** *a* (*serious*) sérieux, sensé; (*meal, style*) sobre. ◆**—ly** *adv* sobrement.

soccer [ˈsɒkər] *n* football *m*.

sociable [ˈsəʊʃəb(ə)l] *a* (*a person*) sociable; (*evening*) amical. ◆**sociably** *adv* (*to act, reply*) aimablement.

social [ˈsəʊʃəl] *a* social; (*life, gathering*) mondain; s. **club** foyer *m*; s. **science(s)** sciences *fpl* humaines; s. **security** (*aid*) aide *f* sociale; (*retirement pension*) *Am* pension *f* de retraite; s. **services** = sécurité *f* sociale; s. **worker** assistant *m* social; — *n* (*gathering*) réunion *f* (amicale). ◆**socialism** *n* socialisme *m*. ◆**socialist** *a* & *n* socialiste (*mf*). ◆**socialite** *n* mondain, -aine *mf*. ◆**socialize** *vi* (*mix*) se mêler aux autres; (*talk*) bavarder (**with** avec.) ◆**socially** *adv* socialement; (*to meet s.o., behave*) en société.

society [səˈsaɪətɪ] *n* (*community, club, companionship etc*) société *f*; *Univ Sch* club *m*; – *a* (*a wedding etc*) mondain.

sociology [səʊsɪˈɒlədʒɪ] *n* sociologie *f*. ◆**socio'logical** *a* sociologique. ◆**sociologist** *n* sociologue *mf*.

sock [sɒk] **1** *n* chaussette *f*. **2** *vt* (*hit*) *Sl* flanquer un marron à.

socket [ˈsɒkɪt] *n* (*of bone*) cavité *f*; (*of eye*) orbite *f*; (*power point*) *El* prise *f* de courant; (*of lamp*) douille *f*.

sod [sɒd] *n* (*turf*) *Am* gazon *m*.

soda [ˈsəʊdə] *n* **1** *Ch* soude *f*; **washing s.** cristaux *mpl* de soude. **2** (*water*) eau *f* de Seltz; **s.** (**pop**) *Am* soda *m*.

sodden [ˈsɒd(ə)n] *a* (*ground*) détrempé.

sodium [ˈsəʊdɪəm] *n Ch* sodium *m*.

sofa [ˈsəʊfə] *n* canapé *m*, divan *m*; **s. bed** canapé-lit *m*.

soft [sɒft] *a* (-**er, -est**) (*smooth, gentle, supple*) doux; (*butter, ground, snow*) mou; (*wood, heart, paste, colour*) tendre; (*flabby*) flasque, mou; (*easy*) facile; (*indulgent*) indulgent; (*cowardly*) *Fam* poltron; (*stupid*) *Fam* ramolli; **it's too s.** (*radio etc*) ce n'est pas assez fort; **s. drink** boisson *f* non alcoolisée. ◆**s.-'boiled** *a* (*egg*) à la coque. ◆**soften** [ˈsɒf(ə)n] *vt* (*object*) ramollir; (*voice, pain, colour*) adoucir; — *vi* se ramollir; s'adoucir. ◆**softie** *n Fam* sentimental, -ale *mf*; (*weakling*) mauviette *f*. ◆**softly** *adv* doucement. ◆**softness** *n* douceur *f*; (*of butter, ground, snow*) mollesse *f*.

software [ˈsɒftweər] *n inv* (*of computer*) logiciel *m*.

soggy [ˈsɒgɪ] *a* (-**ier, -iest**) (*ground*) détrempé; (*biscuit, bread*) ramolli.

soil [sɔɪl] **1** *n* (*earth*) sol *m*, terre *f*. **2** *vt* (*dirty*) salir; — *vi* se salir.

solar [ˈsəʊlər] *a* solaire.

sold [səʊld] *see* **sell**.

solder [ˈsɒldər, *Am* ˈsɒdər] *vt* souder; — *n* soudure *f*.

soldier [ˈsəʊldʒər] **1** *n* soldat *m*, militaire *m*. **2** *vi* to **s. on** persévérer.

sole [səʊl] **1** *n* (*of shoe*) semelle *f*; (*of foot*) plante *f*; — *vt* ressemeler. **2** *a* (*only*) seul, unique; (*rights, representative*) *Com* exclusif. **3** *n* (*fish*) sole *f*. ◆**—ly** *adv* uniquement; **you're s. to blame** tu es seul coupable.

solemn [ˈsɒləm] *a* (*formal*) solennel; (*serious*) grave. ◆**so'lemnity** *n* solennité *f*; gravité *f*. ◆**solemnly** *adv* (*to promise*) solennellement; (*to say*) gravement.

solicit [səˈlɪsɪt] *vt* (*seek*) solliciter; — *vi* (*of prostitute*) racoler. ◆**solicitor** *n* (*for wills etc*) notaire *m*.

solid [ˈsɒlɪd] *a* (*car, character, meal etc*) & *Ch* solide; (*wall, line, ball*) plein; (*gold, rock*) massif; (*crowd, mass*) compact; **frozen s.** entièrement gelé; **ten days s.** dix jours d'affilée; — *n Ch* solide *m*; *pl Culin* aliments *mpl* solides. ◆**so'lidify** *vi* se solidifier. ◆**so'lidity** *n* solidité *f*. ◆**solidly** *adv* (*built etc*) solidement; (*to support, vote*) en masse.

solidarity [sɒlɪˈdærətɪ] *n* solidarité *f* (**with** avec.)

soliloquy [səˈlɪləkwɪ] *n* monologue *m*.

solitary [ˈsɒlɪtərɪ] *a* (*lonely, alone*) solitaire;

(only) seul; **s. confinement** *Jur* isolement *m* (cellulaire). ◆**solitude** *n* solitude *f*.

solo ['səʊləʊ] *n (pl -os) Mus* solo *m; – a solo inv; – a* *Mus* en solo; *(to fly)* en solitaire. ◆**soloist** *n Mus* soliste *(mf)*.

solstice ['sɒlstɪs] *n* solstice *m*.

soluble ['sɒljʊb(ə)l] *a (substance, problem)* soluble.

solution [sə'luːʃ(ə)n] *n (to problem etc)* & *Ch* solution *f* (to de).

solv/e [sɒlv] *vt (problem etc)* résoudre. ◆**-able** *a* soluble.

solvent ['sɒlvənt] **1** *a (financially)* solvable. **2** *n Ch* (dis)solvant *m*. ◆**solvency** *n Fin* solvabilité *f*.

sombre ['sɒmbər] *a* sombre, triste.

some [sʌm] *a* **1** *(amount, number)* **s. wine** du vin; **s. glue** de la colle; **s. water** de l'eau; **s. dogs** des chiens; **s. pretty flowers** de jolies fleurs. **2** *(unspecified)* un, une; **s. man** (or other) un homme (quelconque); **s. charm** *(a certain amount of)* un certain charme; **s. other way** quelque autre *or* un autre moyen; **that's s. book!** *Fam* ça, c'est un livre! **3** *(a few)* quelques, certains; *(a little)* un peu de; – *pron* **1** *(number)* quelques-un(e)s, certain(e)s (of de, d'entre). **2** *(a certain quantity)* en; **I want s.** j'en veux; **do you have s.?** en as-tu?; **s. of it is over** il en reste un peu *or* une partie; – *adv (about)* quelque; **s. ten years** quelque dix ans.

somebody ['sʌmbədɪ] *pron* = **someone**. ◆**someday** *adv* un jour. ◆**somehow** *adv (in some way)* d'une manière ou d'une autre; *(for some reason)* on ne sait pourquoi. ◆**someone** *pron* = **someone**; **at s.'s house** chez qn; **s. small/etc** quelqu'un de petit/*etc*. ◆**someplace** *adv Am* quelque part. ◆**something** *pron* quelque chose; **s. awful/etc** quelque chose d'affreux/*etc*; **s. of a liar/etc** un peu menteur/*etc*; – *adv* **she plays s. like...** elle joue un peu comme...; **it was s. awful** c'était vraiment affreux. ◆**sometime** **1** *adv* un jour; **s. in May/etc** au cours du mois de mai/*etc*; **s. before his departure** avant son départ. **2** *a (former)* ancien. ◆**sometimes** *adv* quelquefois, parfois. ◆**somewhat** *adv* quelque peu, assez. ◆**somewhere** *adv* quelque part; **s. about fifteen** *(approximately)* environ quinze.

somersault ['sʌməsɔːlt] *n* culbute *f; (in air)* saut *m* périlleux; – *vi* faire la *or* une culbute.

son [sʌn] *n* fils *m*. ◆**s.-in-law** *n (pl* **sons-in-law)** beau-fils *m*, gendre *m*.

sonar ['səʊnɑːr] *n* sonar *m*.

sonata [sə'nɑːtə] *n Mus* sonate *f*.

song [sɒŋ] *n* chanson *f; (of bird)* chant *m*. ◆**songbook** *n* recueil *m* de chansons.

sonic ['sɒnɪk] *a* **s. boom** bang *m* (supersonique).

sonnet ['sɒnɪt] *n (poem)* sonnet *m*.

soon [suːn] *adv* **(-er, -est)** *(in a short time)* bientôt; *(quickly)* vite; *(early)* tôt; **s. after** peu après; **as s. as she leaves** aussitôt qu'elle partira; **no sooner had he spoken than à peine avait-il parlé** que; **I'd sooner leave** je préférerais partir; **I'd just as s. leave** j'aimerais autant partir; **sooner or later** tôt ou tard.

soot [sʊt] *n* suie *f*. ◆**sooty** *a* **(-ier, -iest)** couvert de suie.

sooth/e [suːð] *vt (pain, nerves)* calmer; *Fig* rassurer. ◆**-ing** *a (ointment, words)* calmant.

sophisticated [sə'fɪstɪkeɪtɪd] *a (person, taste)* raffiné; *(machine, method, beauty)* sophistiqué.

sophomore ['sɒfəmɔːr] *n Am* étudiant, -ante *mf* de seconde année.

soporific [sɒpə'rɪfɪk] *a (substance, speech etc)* soporifique.

sopping ['sɒpɪŋ] *a & adv* **s. (wet)** trempé.

soppy ['sɒpɪ] *a* **(-ier, -iest)** *Fam (silly)* idiot, bête; *(sentimental)* sentimental.

soprano [sə'prɑːnəʊ] *n (pl -os) Mus (singer)* soprano *mf; (voice)* soprano *m*.

sorbet ['sɔːbeɪ] *n (water ice)* sorbet *m*.

sorcerer ['sɔːsərər] *n* sorcier *m*.

sordid ['sɔːdɪd] *a (act, street etc)* sordide.

sore [sɔːr] *a* **(-er, -est)** *(painful)* douloureux; *(angry) Am* fâché (at contre); **a s. point** *Fig* un sujet délicat; **she has a s. thumb** elle a mal au pouce; **he's still s.** *Med* il a encore mal; – *n Med* plaie *f*. ◆**-ly** *adv (tempted, regretted)* très; **s. needed** dont on a grand besoin. ◆**-ness** *n (pain)* douleur *f*.

sorrow ['sɒrəʊ] *n* chagrin *m*, peine *f*. ◆**sorrowful** *a* triste.

sorry ['sɒrɪ] *a* **(-ier, -iest)** *(sight, state etc)* triste; **to be s.** *(regret)* être désolé, regretter *(to do de faire)*; **I'm s. she can't come** je regrette qu'elle ne puisse pas venir; **I'm s. about the delay** je m'excuse pour ce retard; **s.!** pardon!; **to say s.** demander pardon (to à); **to feel** *or* **be s. for** plaindre.

sort [sɔːt] *n* **1** genre *m*, espèce *f*, sorte *f; **a s. of** une sorte *or* espèce de; **a good s.** *(person) Fam* un brave type; **s. of sad/etc** plutôt triste/*etc*. **2** *vt (letters)* trier; **s. out** *(classify, select)* trier; *(separate)* séparer *(from* de); *(arrange)* arranger; *(tidy)* ranger; *(problem)* régler; **to s. s.o. out** *(punish) Fam* faire voir à qn; – *vi* **to s. through** (*letters etc*) trier; **sorting office** centre *m* de tri. ◆**-er** *n* (*person*) trieur, -euse *mf*.

soufflé ['suːfleɪ] *n Culin* soufflé *m*.

sought [sɔːt] *see* seek.

soul [səʊl] *n* âme *f*; **not a living s.** (*nobody*) personne, pas âme qui vive; **a good s.** Fig un brave type; **s. mate** âme *f* sœur. ◆**s.-destroying** *a* abrutissant. ◆**s.-searching** *n* examen *m* de conscience.

sound[1] [saʊnd] *n* son *m*; (*noise*) bruit *m*; **I don't like the s. of it** ça ne me plaît pas du tout; – *a* (*wave, film*) sonore; (*engineer*) du son; **s. archives** phonothèque *f*; **s. barrier** mur *m* du son; **s. effects** bruitage *m*; – *vt* (*bell, alarm etc*) sonner; (*bugle*) sonner de; (*letter*) Gram prononcer; **to s. one's horn** Aut klaxonner; – *vi* retentir, sonner; (*seem*) sembler; **to s. like** sembler être; (*resemble*) ressembler à; **it sounds like** or **as if** il semble que (+ *sub* or *indic*); **to s. off about** Pej (*boast*) se vanter de; (*complain*) rouspéter à propos de. ◆**soundproof** *a* insonorisé; – *vt* insonoriser. ◆**soundtrack** *n* (*of film etc*) bande *f* sonore.

sound[2] [saʊnd] *a* (**-er, -est**) (*healthy*) sain; (*sturdy, reliable*) solide; (*instinct*) sûr; (*advice*) sensé; (*beating, sense*) bon; – *adv* **s. asleep** profondément endormi. ◆**-ly** *adv* (*asleep*) profondément; (*reasoned*) solidement; (*beaten*) complètement. ◆**-ness** *n* (*of mind*) santé *f*; (*of argument*) solidité *f*.

sound[3] [saʊnd] *vt* (*test, measure*) sonder; **to s. s.o. out** sonder qn (**about** sur).

soup [suːp] *n* soupe *f*, potage *m*; **in the s.** (*in trouble*) Fam dans le pétrin.

sour ['saʊər] *a* (**-er, -est**) aigre; **to turn s.** (*of wine*) s'aigrir; (*of milk*) tourner; (*of friendship*) se détériorer; (*of conversation*) tourner au vinaigre; – *vi* (*of temper*) s'aigrir.

source [sɔːs] *n* (*origin*) source *f*; **s. of energy** source d'énergie.

south [saʊθ] *n* sud *m*; – *a* (*coast*) sud *inv*; (*wind*) du sud; **to be s. of** être au sud de; **S. America/Africa** Amérique *f*/Afrique *f* du Sud; **S. American** *a* & *n* sud-américain, -aine (*mf*); **S. African** *a* & *n* sud-africain, -aine (*mf*); – *adv* au sud, vers le sud. ◆**southbound** *a* (*carriageway*) sud; (*traffic*) en direction du sud. ◆**south-'east** *n* & *a* sud-est *m* & *a inv*. ◆**southerly** ['sʌðəlɪ] *a* (*point*) sud *inv*; (*direction, wind*) du sud. ◆**southern** ['sʌðən] *a* (*town*) du sud; (*coast*) sud *inv*; **S. Italy** le Sud de

l'Italie; **S. Africa** Afrique *f* australe. ◆**southerner** ['sʌðənər] *n* habitant, -ante *mf* du Sud. ◆**southward(s)** *a* & *adv* vers le sud. ◆**south-'west** *n* & *a* sud-ouest *m* & *a inv*.

souvenir [suːvə'nɪər] *n* (*object*) souvenir *m*.

sovereign ['sɒvrɪn] *n* souverain, -aine *mf*; – *a* (*State, authority*) souverain; (*rights*) de souveraineté. ◆**sovereignty** *n* souveraineté *f*.

Soviet ['səʊvɪət] *a* soviétique; **the S. Union** l'Union *f* soviétique.

sow[1] [saʊ] *n* (*pig*) truie *f*.

sow[2] [səʊ] *vt* (*pt* sowed, *pp* sowed or sown) (*seeds, doubt etc*) semer; (*land*) ensemencer (**with** de).

soya ['sɔɪə] *n* **s. (bean)** graine *f* de soja. ◆**soybean** *n Am* graine *f* de soja.

sozzled ['sɒz(ə)ld] *a* (*drunk*) Sl bourré.

spa [spɑː] *n* (*town*) station *f* thermale; (*spring*) source *f* minérale.

space [speɪs] *n* (*gap, emptiness*) espace *m*; (*period*) période *f*; **blank s.** espace *m*, blanc *m*; (*outer*) **s.** l'espace (cosmique); **to take up s.** (*room*) prendre de la place; **in the s. of** en l'espace de; **s. heater** (*electric*) radiateur *m*; – *a* (*voyage etc*) spatial; – *vt* **to s.** **out** espacer; **double/single spacing** (*on typewriter*) double/simple interligne *m*. ◆**spaceman** *n* (*pl* -men) astronaute *m*. ◆**spaceship** *n*, ◆**spacecraft** *n inv* engin *m* spatial. ◆**spacesuit** *n* scaphandre *m* (de cosmonaute).

spacious ['speɪʃəs] *a* spacieux, grand. ◆**-ness** *n* grandeur *f*.

spade [speɪd] *n* **1** (*for garden*) bêche *f*; (*of child*) pelle *f*. **2** Cards pique *m*. ◆**spadework** *n* Fig travail *m* préparatoire; (*around problem or case*) débroussaillage *m*.

spaghetti [spə'getɪ] *n* spaghetti(s) *mpl*.

Spain [speɪn] *n* Espagne *f*.

span [spæn] *n* (*of arch*) portée *f*; (*of wings*) envergure *f*; (*of life*) Fig durée *f*; – *vt* (**-nn-**) (*of bridge etc*) enjamber (*rivière etc*); Fig couvrir, embrasser.

Spaniard ['spænjəd] *n* Espagnol, -ole *mf*. ◆**Spanish** *a* espagnol; – *n* (*language*) espagnol *m*. ◆**Spanish-A'merican** *a* hispano-américain.

spaniel ['spænjəl] *n* épagneul *m*.

spank [spæŋk] *vt* fesser, donner une fessée à; – *n* **to give s.o. a s.** fesser qn. ◆**-ing** *n* fessée *f*.

spanner ['spænər] *n* (*tool*) clé *f* (à écrous); **adjustable s.** clé *f* à molette.

spar/e[1] [speər] **1** *a* (*extra, surplus*) de or en

trop; (*clothes, tyre*) de rechange; (*wheel*) de secours; (*available*) disponible; (*bed, room*) d'ami; **s. time** loisirs *mpl*; – *n* s. (*part*) *Tech Aut* pièce *f* détachée. **2** *vt* (*do without*) se passer de; (*s.o.'s life*) épargner; (*efforts, s.o.'s feelings*) ménager; **to s. s.o.** (*not kill*) épargner qn; (*grief, details etc*) épargner à qn; (*time*) accorder à qn; (*money*) donner à qn; **I can't s. the time** je n'ai pas le temps; **five to s.** cinq de trop. ◆**–ing** *a* (*use*) modéré; **to be s. with** (*butter etc*) ménager.

spare² [spear] *a* (*lean*) maigre.

spark [spɑːk] **1** *n* étincelle *f*. **2** *vt* **to s. off** (*cause*) provoquer. ◆**spark(ing) plug** *n Aut* bougie *f*.

sparkl/e [spɑːk(ə)l] *vi* étinceler, scintiller; – *n* éclat *m*. ◆**–ing** *a* (*wine, water*) pétillant.

sparrow [spærəʊ] *n* moineau *m*.

sparse [spɑːs] *a* clairsemé. ◆**–ly** *adv* (*populated etc*) peu.

spartan [spɑːtən] *a* spartiate, austère.

spasm [spæzəm] *n* (*of muscle*) spasme *m*; (*of coughing etc*) *Fig* accès *m*. ◆**spas-'modic** *a* (*pain etc*) spasmodique; *Fig* irrégulier.

spastic [spæstɪk] *n* handicapé, -ée *mf* moteur.

spat [spæt] *see* spit 1.

spate [speɪt] *n* a s. of (*orders etc*) une avalanche de.

spatter [spætər] *vt* (*clothes, person etc*) éclabousser (with de); – *vi* to s. over s.o. (*of mud etc*) éclabousser qn.

spatula [spætjʊlə] *n* spatule *f*.

spawn [spɔːn] *n* (*of fish etc*) frai *m*; – *vi* frayer; – *vt* pondre; *Fig* engendrer.

speak [spiːk] *vi* (*pt* spoke, *pp* spoken) parler; (*formally, in assembly*) prendre la parole; **so to s.** pour ainsi dire; **that speaks for itself** c'est évident; **to s. well of** dire du bien de; **nothing to s. of** pas grand-chose; **Bob speaking** *Tel* Bob à l'appareil; **that's spoken for** c'est pris *or* réservé; **to s. out** *or* **up** (*boldly*) parler (franchement); **to s. up** (*more loudly*) parler plus fort; – *vt* (*language*) parler; (*say*) dire; **to s. one's mind** dire ce que l'on pense. ◆**–ing** *n* to be on s. terms with parler à; **English-/French-speaking** anglophone/francophone. ◆**–er** *n* (*public*) orateur *m*; (*in dialogue*) interlocuteur, -trice *mf*; (*loudspeaker*) *El* haut-parleur *m*; (*of hi-fi*) enceinte *f*; **to be a Spanish/a bad/etc s.** parler espagnol/mal/*etc*.

spear [spɪər] *n* lance *f*. ◆**spearhead** *vt*

(*attack*) être le fer de lance de; (*campaign*) mener.

spearmint [spɪəmɪnt] *n Bot* menthe *f* (verte); – *a* à la menthe; (*chewing-gum*) mentholé.

spec [spek] *n* on s. (*as a gamble*) *Fam* à tout hasard.

special [speʃ(ə)l] *a* spécial; (*care, attention*) (tout) particulier; (*measures*) *Pol* extraordinaire; (*favourite*) préféré; **by s. delivery** (*letter etc*) par exprès; – *n* **today's s.** (*in restaurant*) le plat du jour. ◆**specialist** *n* spécialiste *mf* (in de); – *a* (*dictionary, knowledge*) technique, spécialisé. ◆**speci'ality** *n* spécialité *f*. ◆**specialize** *vi* se spécialiser (in dans). ◆**specialized** *a* spécialisé. ◆**specially** *adv* (*specifically*) spécialement; (*on purpose*) (tout) spécialement. ◆**specialty** *n Am* spécialité *f*.

species [spiːʃiːz] *n inv* espèce *f*.

specific [spəˈsɪfɪk] *a* précis, explicite; *Phys Ch* spécifique. ◆**specifically** *adv* (*expressly*) expressément; (*exactly*) précisément.

specify [spesɪfaɪ] *vt* spécifier (that que). ◆**specifi'cation** *n* spécification*f*; *pl* (*of car, machine etc*) caractéristiques *fpl*.

specimen [spesɪmɪn] *n* (*example, person*) spécimen *m*; (*of blood*) prélèvement *m*; (*of urine*) échantillon *m*; **s. signature** spécimen *m* de signature; **s. copy** (*of book etc*) spécimen *m*.

specious [spiːʃəs] *a* spécieux.

speck [spek] *n* (*stain*) petite tache *f*; (*of dust*) grain *m*; (*dot*) point *m*.

speckled [spek(ə)ld] *a* tacheté.

specs [speks] *npl Fam* lunettes *fpl*.

spectacle [spektək(ə)l] **1** *n* (*sight*) spectacle *m*. **2** *npl* (*glasses*) lunettes *fpl*. ◆**spec-'tacular** *a* spectaculaire. ◆**spec'tator** *n Sp etc* spectateur, -trice *mf*.

spectre [spektər] *n* (*menacing image*) spectre *m* (of de).

spectrum, *pl* **-tra** [spektrəm, -trə] *n Phys* spectre *m*; (*range*) *Fig* gamme *f*.

speculate [spekjʊleɪt] *vi Fin Phil* spéculer; **to s. about** (*s.o.'s motives etc*) s'interroger sur; – *vt* to s. that (*guess*) conjecturer que. ◆**specu'lation** *n Fin Phil* spéculation *f*; (*guessing*) conjectures *fpl* (about sur). ◆**speculator** *n* spéculateur, -trice *mf*. ◆**speculative** *a Fin Phil* spéculatif; **that's s.** (*guesswork*) c'est (très) hypothétique.

sped [sped] *see* speed 1.

speech [spiːtʃ] *n* (*talk, address*) & *Gram* discours *m* (on sur); (*faculty*) parole *f*;

(diction) élocution *f*; *(of group)* langage *m*; **a short s.** une allocution *f*; **freedom of s.** liberté *f* d'expression; **part of s.** *Gram* catégorie *f* grammaticale. ◆**—less** *a* muet *(with de).*

speed [spiːd] **1** *n (rate of movement) f*; *(swiftness)* rapidité *f*; **s. limit** *Aut* limitation *f* de vitesse; – *vt (pt & pp* **sped) to s. up** accélérer; – *vi* **to s. up** *(of person)* aller plus vite; *(of pace)* s'accélérer; **to s. past** passer à toute vitesse *(sth* devant qch*).* **2** *vi (pt & pp* **speeded)** *(drive too fast)* aller trop vite. ◆**—ing** *n Jur* excès *m* de vitesse. ◆**speedboat** *n* vedette *f*. ◆**spee'dometer** *n Aut* compteur *m* (de vitesse). ◆**speedway** *n Sp* piste *f* de vitesse pour motos; *Sp Aut Am* autodrome *m*.

speed/y [spiːdɪ] *a* (**-ier, -iest**) rapide. ◆**—ily** *adv* rapidement.

spell[1] [spel] *n (magic)* charme *m*, sortilège *m*; *(curse)* sort *m*; *Fig* charme *m*; **under a s.** envoûté. ◆**spellbound** *a (audience etc)* captivé.

spell[2] [spel] *n (period)* (courte) période *f*; *(moment, while)* moment *m*; **s. of duty** tour *m* de service.

spell[3] [spel] *vt (pt & pp* **spelled** *or* **spelt)** *(write)* écrire; *(say aloud)* épeler; *(of letters)* former *(mot)*; *(mean) Fig* signifier; **to be able to s.** savoir l'orthographe; **how is it spelt?** comment cela s'écrit-il?; **to s. out** *(aloud)* épeler; *Fig* expliquer très clairement. ◆**—ing** *n* orthographe *f*.

spend [spend] **1** *vt (pt & pp* **spent)** *(money)* dépenser **(on** pour*)*; – *vi* dépenser. **2** *vt (pt & pp* **spent)** *(time, holiday etc)* passer **(on sth** sur qch, **doing à** faire*)*; *(energy, care etc)* consacrer **(on sth à** qch, **doing à** faire*)*. ◆**—ing** *n* dépenses *fpl*; – *a (money)* de poche. ◆**—er** *n* **to be a big s.** dépenser beaucoup. ◆**spendthrift** *n* **to be a s.** être dépensier.

spent [spent] *see* **spend**; – *a (used)* utilisé; *(energy)* épuisé.

sperm [spɜːm] *n (pl* **sperm** *or* **sperms)** sperme *m*.

spew [spjuː] *vt* vomir.

sphere [sfɪər] *n (of influence, action etc) & Geom Pol* sphère *f*; *(of music, poetry etc)* domaine *m*; **the social s.** le domaine social. ◆**spherical** [ˈsferɪk(ə)l] *a* sphérique.

sphinx [sfɪŋks] *n* sphinx *m*.

spice [spaɪs] *n Culin* épice *f*; *(interest etc) Fig* piment *m*; – *vt* épicer. ◆**spicy** *a* (**-ier, -iest**) épicé; *(story) Fig* pimenté.

spick-and-span [spɪkənˈspæn] *a (clean)* impeccable.

spider [ˈspaɪdər] *n* araignée *f*.

spiel [ʃpiːl] *n Fam* baratin *m*.

spike [spaɪk] *n (of metal)* pointe *f*; – *vt (pierce)* transpercer. ◆**spiky** *a* (**-ier, -iest**) *a* garni de pointes.

spill [spɪl] *vt (pt & pp* **spilled** *or* **spilt)** *(liquid)* répandre, renverser **(on, over** sur*)*; **to s. the beans** *Fam* vendre la mèche; – *vi* **to s. (out)** se répandre; **to s. over** déborder.

spin [spɪn] *n (motion)* tour *m*; *(car ride)* petit tour *m*; *(on washing machine)* essorage *m*; **s. dryer** essoreuse *f*; – *vt (pt & pp* **spun**, *pres p* **spinning)** *(web, yarn, wool etc)* filer **(into** en*)*; *(wheel, top)* faire tourner; *(washing)* essorer; *(story) Fig* débiter; **to s. out** *(speech etc)* faire durer; – *vi (of spinner, spider)* filer; **to s. (round)** *(of dancer, top, planet etc)* tourner; *(of head, room) Fig* tourner; *(of vehicle)* faire un tête-à-queue. ◆**spinning** *n (by hand)* filage *m*; *(process) Tech* filature *f*; **s. top** toupie *f*; **s. wheel** rouet *m*. ◆**spin-'dry** *vt* essorer. ◆**spin-off** *n* avantage *m* inattendu; *(of process, book etc)* dérivé *m*.

spinach [ˈspɪnɪdʒ] *n (plant)* épinard *m*; *(leaves) Culin* épinards *mpl*.

spindle [ˈspɪnd(ə)l] *n Tex* fuseau *m*. ◆**spindly** *a* (**-ier, -iest**) *(legs, arms)* grêle.

spine [spaɪn] *n Anat* colonne *f* vertébrale; *(spike of animal or plant)* épine *f*. ◆**spinal** *a (column)* vertébral; **s. cord** moelle *f* épinière. ◆**spineless** *a Fig* mou, faible.

spinster [ˈspɪnstər] *n* célibataire *f*; *Pej* vieille fille *f*.

spiral [ˈspaɪərəl] **1** *n* spirale *f*; – *a* en spirale; *(staircase)* en colimaçon. **2** *vi* (**-ll-**, *Am* **-l-**) *(of prices)* monter en flèche.

spire [ˈspaɪər] *n (of church)* flèche *f*.

spirit [ˈspɪrɪt] **1** *n (soul, ghost etc)* esprit *m*; *(courage) Fig* courage *m*, vigueur *f*; **s.** *(drink)* alcool *m*, spiritueux *mpl*; **spirit(s)** *(morale)* moral *m*; *Ch* alcool *m*; **in good spirits** de bonne humeur; **the right s.** l'attitude *f* qu'il faut; – *a (lamp)* à alcool; **s. level** niveau *m* à bulle (d'air). **2** *vt* **to s. away** *(person)* faire disparaître mystérieusement; *(steal) Hum* subtiliser. ◆**—ed** *a (person, remark)* fougueux; *(campaign)* vigoureux.

spiritual [ˈspɪrɪtʃuəl] *a Phil Rel* spirituel; – *n (Negro)* **s.** (negro-)spiritual *m*. ◆**spiritualism** *n* spiritisme *m*. ◆**spiritualist** *n* spirite *mf*.

spit [spɪt] **1** *n* crachat *m*; – *vt (pt & pp* **spat** *or* **spit**, *pres p* **spitting)** cracher; *(splutter) Fig* crépiter; – *vt* cracher; **to s. out** (re)cracher; **the spitting image of s.o.** le portrait (tout craché) de qn. **2** n (for meat) broche f.

spite ['spaɪt] **1** n in s. of malgré; in s. of the fact that (although) bien que (+ sub). **2** n (dislike) rancune f; – vt (annoy) contrarier. ◆**spiteful** a méchant. ◆**spitefully** adv méchamment.

spittle ['spɪt(ə)l] n salive f, crachat(s) m(pl).

splash [splæʃ] vt (spatter) éclabousser (with de, over sur); (spill) répandre; – vi (of mud, ink etc) faire des éclaboussures; (of waves) clapoter, déferler; to s. water over sth/s.o. éclabousser qch/qn; to s. (about) (in river, mud) patauger; (in bath) barboter; to s. out (spend money) Fam claquer de l'argent; – n (splashing) éclaboussement m; (of colour) Fig tache f; s. (mark) éclaboussure f; s.! plouf!

spleen [spliːn] n Anat rate f.

splendid ['splendɪd] a (wonderful, rich, beautiful) splendide. ◆**splendour** n splendeur f.

splint [splɪnt] n Med éclisse f.

splinter ['splɪntər] n (of wood etc) éclat m; (in finger) écharde f; **s. group** Pol groupe m dissident.

split [splɪt] n fente f; (tear) déchirure f; (of couple) rupture f; Pol scission f; to do the **splits** (in gymnastics) faire le grand écart; **one's s. (share)** Fam sa part; – a a **s. second** une fraction de seconde; – vt (pt & pp **split**, pres p **splitting**) (break apart) fendre; (tear) déchirer; to s. **(up)** (group) diviser; (money, work) partager (**between** entre); to s. **one's head open** s'ouvrir la tête; to s. **one's sides (laughing)** se tordre (de rire); to s. **hairs** Fig couper les cheveux en quatre; **s.-level apartment** duplex m; – vi se fendre; (tear) se déchirer; to s. **(up)** (of group) éclater; (of couple) rompre, se séparer; to s. **off** (become loose) se détacher (**from** de); to s. **up** (of crowd) se disperser. ◆**splitting** a (headache) atroce. ◆**split-up** n (of couple) rupture f.

splodge [splɒdʒ] n, **splotch** [splɒtʃ] n (mark) tache f.

splurge [splɜːdʒ] vi (spend money) Fam claquer de l'argent.

splutter ['splʌtər] vi (of sparks, fat) crépiter; (stammer) bredouiller.

spoil [spɔɪl] vt (pt & pp **spoilt** or **spoiled**) (pamper, make unpleasant or less good) gâter; (damage, ruin) abîmer; (pleasure, life) gâcher, gâter. ◆**spoilsport** n rabat-joie m inv.

spoils [spɔɪlz] npl (rewards) butin m.

spoke[1] [spəʊk] n (of wheel) rayon m.

spoke[2] [spəʊk] see speak. ◆**spoken** see speak; – a (language etc) parlé; **softly s.** (person) à la voix douce. ◆**spokesman** n (pl -men) porte-parole m inv (for, of de).

sponge [spʌndʒ] **1** n éponge f; **s. bag** trousse f de toilette; **s. cake** gâteau m de Savoie; – vt to s. **down/off** laver/enlever à l'éponge. **2** vi to s. **off** or **on s.o.** Fam vivre aux crochets de qn; – vt to s. **sth off** s.o. Fam taper qn de qch. ◆**sponger** n Fam parasite m. ◆**spongy** a (-ier, -iest) spongieux.

sponsor ['spɒnsər] n (of appeal, advertiser etc) personne f assurant le patronage (of de); (for membership) parrain m, marraine f; Jur garant, -ante mf; Sp sponsor m; – vt (appeal etc) patronner; (member, firm) parrainer. ◆**sponsorship** n patronage m; parrainage m.

spontaneous [spɒn'teɪnɪəs] a spontané. ◆**spontaneity** [spɒntə'neɪtɪ] n spontanéité f. ◆**spontaneously** adv spontanément.

spoof [spuːf] n Fam parodie f (on de).

spooky ['spuːkɪ] a (-ier, -iest) Fam qui donne le frisson.

spool [spuːl] n bobine f.

spoon [spuːn] n cuiller f. ◆**spoonfeed** vt (pt & pp **spoonfed**) (help) Fig mâcher le travail à. ◆**spoonful** n cuillerée f.

sporadic [spə'rædɪk] a sporadique; **s. fighting** échauffourées fpl. ◆**sporadically** adv sporadiquement.

sport [spɔːt] **1** n sport m; **a (good) s.** (person) Fam un chic type; to play **s.** or Am **sports** faire du sport; **sports club** club m sportif; **sports car/jacket** voiture f/veste f de sport; **sports results** résultats mpl sportifs. **2** vt (wear) arborer. ◆**-ing** a (conduct, attitude, person etc) sportif; **that's s. of you** Fig c'est chic de ta part. ◆**sportsman** n (pl -men) sportif m. ◆**sportsmanlike** a sportif. ◆**sportsmanship** n sportivité f. ◆**sportswear** n vêtements mpl de sport. ◆**sportswoman** n (pl -women) sportive f. ◆**sporty** a (-ier, -iest) sportif.

spot[1] [spɒt] n (stain, mark) tache f; (dot) point m; (polka dot) pois m; (pimple) bouton m; (place) endroit m, coin m; (act) Th numéro m; (drop) goutte f; **a s. of** (bit) Fam un peu de; **a soft s. for** un faible pour; **on the s.** sur place, sur les lieux; (at once) sur le coup; (in a tight) s. (difficulty) dans le pétrin; (accident) **black s.** Aut point m noir; **s. cash** argent m comptant; **s. check** contrôle m au hasard ou à l'improviste. ◆**spotless** a (clean) impeccable. ◆**spot-**

lessly adv s. clean impeccable. ◆**spotlight** n (lamp) Th projecteur m; (for photography etc) spot m; in the s. Th sous le feu des projecteurs. ◆**spot-'on** a Fam tout à fait exact. ◆**spotted** a (fur) tacheté; (dress etc) à pois; (stained) taché. ◆**spotty** a (-ier, -iest) **1** (face etc) boutonneux. **2** (patchy) Am inégal.

spot² [spɒt] vt (-tt-) (notice) apercevoir, remarquer.

spouse [spaʊs, spaʊz] n époux m, épouse f.

spout [spaʊt] **1** n (of jug etc) bec m; up the s. (hope etc) Sl foutu. **2** vi s. (out) jaillir. **3** vt (say) Pej débiter.

sprain [spreɪn] n entorse f, foulure f; to s. one's ankle/wrist se fouler la cheville/le poignet.

sprang [spræŋ] see **spring¹**.

sprawl [sprɔːl] vi (of town, person) s'étaler; to be sprawling être étalé; – n the urban s. les banlieues fpl tentaculaires. ◆**-ing** a (city) tentaculaire.

spray [spreɪ] **1** n (water drops) (nuage m de) gouttelettes fpl; (from sea) embruns mpl; (can, device) bombe f, vaporisateur m; hair s. laque f à cheveux; – vt (liquid, surface) vaporiser; (crops, plant) arroser, traiter; (car etc) peindre à la bombe. **2** n (of flowers) petit bouquet m.

spread [spred] vt (pt & pp spread) (stretch, open out) étendre; (legs, fingers) écarter; (strew) répandre, étaler (over sur); (paint, payment, cards, visits) étaler; (people) disperser; (fear, news) répandre; (illness) propager; to s. out étendre; écarter; étaler; – vi (of fire, town, fog) s'étendre; (of news, fear) se répandre; to s. out (of people) se disperser; – n (of fire, illness, ideas) propagation f; (of wealth) répartition f; (paste) Culin pâte f (à tartiner); (meal) festin m; cheese s. fromage m à tartiner. ◆**s.-'eagled** a bras et jambes écartés.

spree [spriː] n to go on a spending s. faire des achats extravagants.

sprig [sprɪg] n (branch of heather etc) brin m; (of parsley) bouquet m.

sprightl/y ['spraɪtlɪ] a (-ier, -iest) alerte. ◆**-iness** n vivacité f.

spring¹ [sprɪŋ] n (metal device) ressort m; (leap) bond m; – vi (pt sprang, pp sprung) (leap) bondir; to s. to mind venir à l'esprit; to s. into action passer à l'action; to s. from (stem from) provenir de; to s. up (appear) surgir; – vt (news) annoncer brusquement (on à); (surprise) faire (on à); to s. a leak (of boat) commencer à faire eau. ◆**spring-**

board n tremplin m. ◆**springy** a (-ier, -iest) élastique.

spring² [sprɪŋ] n (season) printemps m; in (the) s. au printemps; s. onion ciboule f. ◆**s.-'cleaning** n nettoyage m de printemps. ◆**springlike** a printanier. ◆**springtime** n printemps m.

spring³ [sprɪŋ] n (of water) source f; s. water eau f de source.

sprinkl/e ['sprɪŋk(ə)l] vt (sand etc) répandre (on, over sur); to s. with water, s. water on asperger d'eau, arroser; to s. with (sugar, salt, flour) saupoudrer de. ◆**-ing** n a s. of (a few) quelques. ◆**-er** n (in garden) arroseur m.

sprint [sprɪnt] n Sp sprint m; – vi sprinter. ◆**-er** n sprinter m, sprinteuse f.

sprite [spraɪt] n (fairy) lutin m.

sprout [spraʊt] **1** vi (of seed, bulb etc) germer, pousser; to s. up (grow) pousser vite; (appear) surgir; – vt (leaves) pousser; (beard) Fig laisser pousser. **2** n (Brussels) s. chou m de Bruxelles.

spruce [spruːs] a (-er, -est) (neat) pimpant, net; – vt to s. oneself up se faire beau.

sprung [sprʌŋ] see **spring¹**; – a (mattress, seat) à ressorts.

spry [spraɪ] a (spryer, spryest) (old person etc) alerte.

spud [spʌd] n (potato) Fam patate f.

spun [spʌn] see **spin**.

spur [spɜːr] n (of horse rider etc) éperon m; (stimulus) Fig aiguillon m; on the s. of the moment sur un coup de tête; – vt (-rr-) to s. (on) (urge on) éperonner.

spurious ['spjʊərɪəs] a faux.

spurn [spɜːn] vt rejeter (avec mépris).

spurt [spɜːt] vi (gush out) jaillir; (rush) foncer; to s. out jaillir; – n jaillissement m; (of energy) sursaut m; to put on a s. (rush) foncer.

spy [spaɪ] n espion, -onne mf; – a (story etc) d'espionnage; s. hole (peephole) judas m; s. ring réseau m d'espionnage; – vi espionner; to s. on s.o. espionner qn; – vt (notice) Lit apercevoir. ◆**-ing** n espionnage m.

squabbl/e ['skwɒb(ə)l] vi se chamailler (over à propos de); – n chamaillerie f. ◆**-ing** n chamailleries fpl.

squad [skwɒd] n (group) & Mil escouade f; (team) Sp équipe f; s. car voiture f de police.

squadron ['skwɒdrən] n Mil escadron m; Nau Av escadrille f.

squalid ['skwɒlɪd] a sordide. ◆**squalor** n conditions fpl sordides.

squall [skwɔːl] n (of wind) rafale f.

squander ['skwɒndər] vt (money, time etc) gaspiller (on en).

square ['skweər] n carré m; (on chessboard, graph paper) case f; (in town) place f; (drawing implement) Tech équerre f; **to be back to s. one** repartir à zéro; – a carré; (in order, settled) Fig en ordre; (honest) honnête; (meal) solide; **(all) s. (quits)** quitte (with envers); – vt (settle) mettre en ordre, régler; (arrange) arranger; Math carrer; (reconcile) faire cadrer; – vi (tally) cadrer (with avec); **to s. up to** faire face à. **◆-ly** adv (honestly) honnêtement; (exactly) tout à fait; **s. in the face** bien en face.

squash [skwɒʃ] **1** vt (crush) écraser; (squeeze) serrer; – n **lemon/orange s.** (concentrated) sirop m de citron/d'orange; (diluted) citronnade f/orangeade f. **2** n (game) squash m. **3** n (vegetable) Am courge f. **◆squashy** a (-ier, -iest) (soft) mou.

squat [skwɒt] **1** a (short and thick) trapu. **2** vi (-tt-) **to s. (down)** s'accroupir. **3** n (house) squat m. **◆squatting** a accroupi. **◆squatter** n squatter m.

squawk [skwɔːk] vi pousser des cris rauques; – n cri m rauque.

squeak [skwiːk] vi (of door) grincer; (of shoe) craquer; (of mouse) faire couic; – n grincement m; craquement m; couic m. **◆squeaky** a (-ier, -iest) (door) grinçant; (shoe) qui craque.

squeal [skwiːl] vi pousser des cris aigus; (of tyres) crisser; – n cri m aigu; crissement m. **2** vi **to s. on s.o.** (inform on) Fam balancer qn.

squeamish ['skwiːmɪʃ] a bien délicat, facilement dégoûté.

squeegee ['skwiːdʒiː] n raclette f (à vitres).

squeeze/e [skwiːz] vt (press) presser; (hand, arm) serrer; **to s. sth out of s.o.** (information) soutirer qch à qn; **to s. sth into** faire rentrer qch dans; **to s. (out)** (extract) exprimer (from de); – vi **to s. through/into/etc** (force oneself) se glisser par/dans/etc; **to s. in** trouver un peu de place; – n pression f; **to give sth a s.** presser qch; **it's a tight s.** il y a peu de place; **credit s.** Fin restrictions fpl de crédit. **◆-er** n lemon s. presse-citron m inv.

squelch [skweltʃ] **1** vi patauger (en faisant floc-floc). **2** vt (silence) Fam réduire au silence.

squid [skwɪd] n (mollusc) calmar m.

squiggle ['skwɪg(ə)l] n ligne f onduleuse, gribouillis m.

squint [skwɪnt] n Med strabisme m; **to have a s.** loucher; – vi loucher; (in the sunlight etc) plisser les yeux.

squire ['skwaɪər] n propriétaire m terrien.

squirm [skwɜːm] vi (wriggle) se tortiller; **to s. in pain** se tordre de douleur.

squirrel ['skwɪrəl, Am 'skwɜːrəl] n écureuil m.

squirt [skwɜːt] **1** vt (liquid) faire gicler; – vi gicler; – n giclée f, jet m. **2** n **little s.** (person) Fam petit morveux m.

stab [stæb] vt (-bb-) (with knife etc) poignarder; – n coup m (de couteau or de poignard). **◆stabbing** n **there was a s.** quelqu'un a été poignardé; – a (pain) lancinant.

stable [ˈsteɪb(ə)l] a (-er, -est) stable; **mentally s.** (person) bien équilibré. **◆stability** n stabilité f; **mental s.** équilibre m. **◆stabilize** vt stabiliser; – vi se stabiliser. **◆stabilizer** n stabilisateur m.

stable [ˈsteɪb(ə)l] n écurie f; **s. boy** lad m.

stack [stæk] **1** n (heap) tas m; **stacks of** (lots of) Fam un or des tas de; – vt **to s. (up)** entasser. **2** npl (in library) réserve f.

stadium [ˈsteɪdɪəm] n Sp stade m.

staff [stɑːf] **1** n personnel m; Sch professeurs mpl; Mil état-major m; **s. meeting** Sch Univ conseil m des professeurs; **s. room** Sch Univ salle f des professeurs; – vt pourvoir en personnel. **2** n (stick) Lit bâton m.

stag [stæg] n cerf m; **s. party** réunion f entre hommes.

stage [steɪdʒ] n (platform) Th scène f; **the s.** (profession) le théâtre; **on s.** sur (la) scène; **s. door** entrée f des artistes; **s. fright** le trac; – vt (play) Th monter; Fig organiser, effectuer; **it was staged** (not real) c'était un coup monté. **◆s.-hand** n machiniste m. **◆s.-manager** n régisseur m.

stage [steɪdʒ] n (phase) stade m, étape f; (of journey) étape f; (of track, road) section f; **in (easy) stages** par étapes; **at an early s.** au début.

stagecoach ['steɪdʒkəʊtʃ] n Hist diligence f.

stagger ['stægər] **1** vi (reel) chanceler. **2** vt (holidays etc) étaler, échelonner. **3** vt **to s.o.** (shock, amaze) stupéfier qn. **◆-ing** a stupéfiant.

stagnant ['stægnənt] a stagnant. **◆stag'nate** vi stagner. **◆stag'nation** n stagnation f.

staid [steɪd] a posé, sérieux.

stain [steɪn] **1** vt (mark, dirty) tacher (with

de); – n tache f. **2** vt (colour) teinter (du bois); **stained glass window** vitrail m; – n (colouring for wood) teinture f. ◆**-less** a (steel) inoxydable; **s.-steel knife/etc** couteau m/etc inoxydable.

stair [steər] n a s. (step) une marche; the **stairs** (staircase) l'escalier m; (carpet etc) d'escalier. ◆**staircase** n, ◆**stairway** n escalier m.

stake [steik] **1** n (post) pieu m; (for plant) tuteur m; Hist bûcher m; – vt to s. (out) (land) jalonner, délimiter; to s. one's claim to revendiquer. **2** n (betting) enjeu m; (investment) Fin investissement m; (interest) Fin intérêts mpl; at s. en jeu; – vt (bet) jouer (on sur).

stale [steil] a (-er, -est) (food) pas frais; (bread) rassis; (beer) éventé; (air) vicié; (smell) de renfermé; (news) Fig vieux; (joke) usé, vieux; (artist) manquant d'invention. ◆**-ness** n (of food) manque m de fraîcheur.

stalemate ['steilmeit] n Chess pat m; Fig impasse f.

stalk [stɔːk] **1** n (of plant) tige f, queue f; (of fruit) queue f. **2** vt (animal, criminal) traquer. **3** vi to s. (walk) partir avec raideur ou en marchant à grands pas.

stall [stɔːl] **1** n (in market) étal m, éventaire m; (for newspapers, flowers) kiosque m; (in stable) stalle f; the **stalls** Cin l'orchestre m. **2** vti Aut caler. **3** vi to s. (for time) chercher à gagner du temps.

stallion ['stæljən] n (horse) étalon m.

stalwart ['stɔːlwət] a (supporter) brave, fidèle; – n (follower) fidèle mf.

stamina ['stæminə] n vigueur f, résistance f.

stammer ['stæmər] vti bégayer; – n bégaiement m; to have a s. être bègue.

stamp [stæmp] **1** n (for postage, implement) timbre m; (mark) cachet m, timbre m; the s. of Fig la marque de; men of your s. les hommes de votre trempe; **s. collecting** philatélie f; – vt (mark) tamponner, timbrer; (letter) timbrer; (metal) estamper; to s. sth on sth (affix) apposer qch sur qch; to s. out (rebellion, evil) écraser; (disease) supprimer; **stamped addressed envelope** enveloppe f timbrée à votre adresse. **2** vti to s. (one's foot) taper ou frapper des pieds; **stamping ground** Fam lieu m favori.

stampede [stæm'piːd] n fuite f précipitée; (rush) ruée f; – vi fuir en désordre; (rush) se ruer.

stance [stɑːns] n position f.

stand [stænd] n (position) position f; (support) support m; (at exhibition) stand

m; (for spectators) Sp tribune f; (witness) s. Jur Am barre f; to make a s., take one's s. prendre position (against contre); **news/flower s.** (in street) kiosque m à journaux/à fleurs; **hat s.** porte-chapeaux m inv; **music s.** pupitre m à musique; – vt (pt & pp **stood**) (pain, journey, person etc) supporter; to s. (up) (put straight) mettre (debout); to s. s.o. sth (pay for) payer qch à qn; to s. a chance avoir une chance; to s. s.o. up Fam poser un lapin à qn; – vi être ou se tenir (debout); (rise) se lever; (remain) rester (debout); (be situated) se trouver; (be) être; (of object, argument) reposer (on sur); to leave to s. (liquid) laisser reposer; to s. to lose risquer de perdre; to s. around (in street etc) traîner; to s. aside s'écarter; to s. back reculer; to s. by (do nothing) rester là (sans rien faire); (be ready) être prêt (à partir ou à intervenir); (one's opinion) s'en tenir à; (friend etc) rester fidèle à; to s. down (withdraw) se désister; to s. for (represent) représenter; Pol être candidat à; (put up with) supporter; to s. in for (replace) remplacer; to s. out (be visible or conspicuous) ressortir (against sur); to s. over s.o. (watch closely) surveiller qn; to s. up (rise) se lever; to s. up for (defend) défendre; to s. up to (resist) résister à. ◆**-ing** a debout inv; (committee, offer, army) permanent; **s. room** places fpl debout; **s. joke** plaisanterie f classique; – n (reputation) réputation f; (social, professional) rang m; (financial) situation f; of six years' s. (duration) qui dure depuis six ans; of long s. de longue date. ◆**standby** n (pl -bys) on s. prêt à partir ou à intervenir; – a (battery etc) de réserve; (ticket) Av sans garantie. ◆**stand-in** n remplaçant, -ante mf (for de); Th doublure f (for de).

standard ['stændəd] **1** n (norm) norme f, critère m; (level) niveau m; (of weight, gold) étalon m; pl (morals) principes mpl; **s. of living** niveau m de vie; to be ou come up to s. (of person) être à la hauteur; (of work etc) être au niveau; – a (average) ordinaire, courant; (model, size) Com standard inv; (weight) étalon inv; (dictionary, book) classique; **s. lamp** lampadaire m. **2** n (flag) étendard m. ◆**standardize** vt standardiser.

stand-offish [stænd'ɒfiʃ] a (person) distant, froid.

standpoint ['stændpoint] n point m de vue.

standstill ['stændstil] n to bring to a s. immobiliser; to come to a s. s'immobiliser;

at a s. immobile; (*industry, negotiations*) paralysé.

stank [stæŋk] *see* **stink**.

stanza ['stænzə] *n* strophe *f*.

stapl/e ['steıp(ə)l] **1** *a* (*basic*) de base; **s. food** *or* **diet** nourriture *f* de base. **2** *n* (*for paper etc*) agrafe *f*; − *vt* agrafer. ◆**−er** *n* (*for paper etc*) agrafeuse *f*.

star [staːr] *n* étoile *f*; (*person*) *Cin* vedette *f*; **shooting** s. étoile *f* filante; **s. part** rôle *m* principal; **the Stars and Stripes, the S.-Spangled Banner** *Am* la bannière étoilée; **two-s.** (*petrol*) de l'ordinaire *m*; **four-s.** (*petrol*) du super; − *vi* (**-rr-**) (*of actor*) être la vedette (**in** de); − *vt* (*of film*) avoir pour vedette. ◆**stardom** *n* célébrité *f*. ◆**starfish** *n* étoile *f* de mer. ◆**starlit** *a* (*night*) étoilé.

starboard ['staːbəd] *n* Nau Av tribord *m*.

starch [staːtʃ] *n* (*for stiffening*) amidon *m*; *pl* (*foods*) féculents *mpl*; − *vt* amidonner. ◆**starchy** *a* (**-ier, -iest**) (*food*) féculent; (*formal*) Fig guindé.

stare [steər] *n* regard *m* (fixe); − *vi* **to s.** fixer (**du regard**); − *vt* **to s. s.o. in the face** dévisager qn.

stark [staːk] *a* (**-er, -est**) (*place*) désolé; (*austere*) austère; (*fact, reality*) brutal; **the s. truth** la vérité toute nue; − *adv* **s. naked** complètement nu. ◆**starkers** *a* *Sl* complètement nu, à poil.

starling ['staːlıŋ] *n* étourneau *m*.

starry ['staːrı] *a* (**-ier, -iest**) (*sky*) étoilé. ◆**s.-'eyed** *a* (*naïve*) ingénu, naïf.

start¹ [staːt] *n* commencement *m*, début *m*; (*of race*) départ *m*; (*lead*) *Sp* & *Fig* avance *f* (**on** sur); **to make a s.** commencer; **for a s.** pour commencer; **from the s.** dès le début; − *vt* commencer; (*bottle*) entamer, commencer; (*fashion*) lancer; **to s. a war** provoquer une guerre; **to s. a fire** (*in grate*) allumer un feu; (*accidentally*) provoquer un incendie; **to s. s.o.** (**off**) (*on career*) lancer qn dans; **to s.** (**up**) (*engine, vehicle*) mettre en marche; **to s. doing** *or* **to do** commencer *or* se mettre à faire; − *vi* commencer (**with sth** par qch, **by doing** par faire); **to s. on sth** commencer qch; **to s.** (**up**) commencer; (*of vehicle*) démarrer; **to s.** (**off** *or* **out**) (*leave*) partir (**for** pour); (*in job*) débuter; **to s. back** (*return*) repartir; **to s. with** (*firstly*) pour commencer. ◆**−ing** *n* (*point, line*) de départ; **s. post** *Sp* ligne *f* de départ; **s. from** à partir de. ◆**−er** *n* (*runner*) partant *m*; (*official*) *Sp* starter *m*; (*device*) *Aut* démarreur *m*; *pl* Culin

hors-d'œuvre *m inv*; **for starters** (*first*) pour commencer.

start² [staːt] *vi* (*be startled, jump*) sursauter; − *n* sursaut *m*; **to give s.o. a s.** faire sursauter qn.

startle ['staːt(ə)l] *vt* (*make jump*) faire sursauter; (*alarm*) Fig alarmer; (*surprise*) surprendre.

starve [staːv] *vi* (*die*) mourir de faim; (*suffer*) souffrir de la faim; **I'm starving** Fig je meurs de faim; − *vt* (*kill*) laisser mourir de faim; (*make suffer*) faire souffrir de la faim; (*deprive*) Fig priver (**of** de). ◆**star'vation** *n* faim *f*; − *a* (*wage, ration*) de famine; **on a s. diet** à la diète.

stash [stæʃ] *vt* **to s. away** (*hide*) cacher; (*save up*) mettre de côté.

state¹ [steıt] *n* **1** (*condition*) état *m*; (*pomp*) apparat *m*; **not in a** (**fit**) **s. to, in no** (**fit**) **s. to lie in s.** (*of body*) être exposé. **2** *n* **S.** (*nation etc*) État *m*; **the States** *Geog Fam* les États-Unis *mpl*; − *a* (*secret, document*) d'État; (*control, security*) de l'État; (*school, education*) public; **s. visit** voyage *m* officiel; **S. Department** *Pol Am* Département *m* d'État. ◆**stateless** *a* apatride; **s. person** apatride *mf*. ◆**state-'owned** *a* étatisé. ◆**statesman** *n* (*pl* **-men**) homme *m* d'État. ◆**statesmanship** *n* diplomatie *f*.

state² [steıt] *vt* déclarer (**that** que); (*opinion*) formuler; (*problem*) exposer; (*time, date*) fixer. ◆**statement** *n* déclaration *f*; *Jur* déposition *f*; **bank s., s. of account** *Fin* relevé *m* de compte.

stately ['steıtlı] *a* (**-ier, -iest**) majestueux; **s. home** château *m*.

static ['stætık] *a* statique; − *n* (*noise*) Rad parasites *mpl*.

station ['steıʃ(ə)n] *n* Rail gare *f*; (*underground*) station *f*; (*position*) & *Mil* poste *m*; (*social*) rang *m*; (*police*) commissariat *m* *or* poste *m* (de police); **space/observation/radio/etc.** station *f* spatiale/d'observation/de radio/*etc*; **bus** *or* **coach s.** gare *f* routière; **s. wagon** *Aut Am* break *m*; − *vt* (*position*) placer, poster. ◆**stationmaster** *n* Rail chef *m* de gare.

stationary ['steıʃən(ə)rı] *a* (*motionless*) stationnaire; (*vehicle*) à l'arrêt.

stationer ['steıʃ(ə)nər] *n* papetier, -ière *mf*; **s.'s** (**shop**) papeterie *f*. ◆**stationery** *n* (*paper*) papier *m*; (*articles*) papeterie *f*.

statistic [stə'tıstık] *n* (*fact*) statistique *f*; *pl* (*science*) la statistique. ◆**statistical** *a* statistique.

statue ['stætʃuː] n statue f. ◆**statu'esque** a (beauty etc) sculptural.

stature ['stætʃər] n stature f.

status ['steɪtəs] n (position) situation f; Jur statut m; (prestige) standing m, prestige m; **s. symbol** marque f de standing; **s. quo** statu quo m inv.

statute ['stætʃuːt] n (law) loi f; pl (of club, institution) statuts mpl. ◆**statutory** a (right etc) statutaire; **s. holiday** fête f légale.

staunch [stɔːntʃ] a (-er, -est) loyal, fidèle. ◆**-ly** adv loyalement.

stave [steɪv] n **1** to s. off (danger, disaster) conjurer; (hunger) tromper. **2** n Mus portée f.

stay [steɪ] **1** n (visit) séjour m; – vi (remain) rester; (reside) loger; (visit) séjourner; **to s. put** ne pas bouger; **to s. with** (plan, idea) ne pas lâcher; **to s. away** (keep one's distance) ne pas s'approcher (from de); **to s. away from** (school, meeting etc) ne pas aller à; **to s. in** (at home) rester à la maison; (of nail, tooth etc) tenir; **to s. out** (outside) rester dehors; (not come home) ne pas rentrer; **to s. out of sth** (not interfere in) ne pas se mêler de qch; (avoid) éviter qch; **to s. up** (at night) ne pas se coucher; (of fence etc) tenir; **to s. up late** se coucher tard; **staying power** endurance f. **2** vt (hunger) tromper. ◆**s.-at-home** n & a Pej casanier, -ière (mf).

St Bernard [sənt'bɜːnəd, Am seɪntbə'nɑːd] n (dog) saint-bernard m.

stead [sted] n **to stand s. in good s.** être bien utile à qn; **in s.o.'s s.** à la place de qn.

steadfast ['stedfɑːst] a (intention etc) ferme.

steady ['stedɪ] a (-er, -est) (firm, stable) stable; (hand) sûr, assuré; (progress, speed, demand) régulier, constant; (nerves) solide; (staid) sérieux; **a s. boyfriend** un petit ami; **s. (on one's feet)** solide sur ses jambes; – adv **to go s. with** Fam sortir avec; – vt (chair etc) maintenir (en place); (hand) assurer; (nerves) calmer; (wedge, prop up) caler; **to s. oneself** (stop oneself falling) reprendre son aplomb. ◆**steadily** adv (to walk) d'un pas assuré; (regularly) régulièrement; (gradually) progressivement; (continuously) sans arrêt. ◆**steadiness** n stabilité f; régularité f.

steak [steɪk] n steak m, bifteck m. ◆**steakhouse** n grill-(room) m.

steal¹ [stiːl] vti (pt stole, pp stolen) voler (from s.o. à qn).

steal² [stiːl] vi (pt stole, pp stolen) **to s. in/ out** entrer/sortir furtivement; **to s. off** n by s. furtivement. ◆**stealthy** a (-ier, -iest) furtif.

steam [stiːm] n vapeur f; (on glass) buée f; **to let off s.** (unwind) Fam se défouler, décompresser; **s. engine/iron** locomotive f/fer m à vapeur; – vt Culin cuire à la vapeur; **to get steamed up** (of glass) se couvrir de buée; Fig Fam s'énerver; – vi (of kettle etc) fumer; **to s. up** (of glass) se couvrir de buée. ◆**steamer** n, ◆**steamship** n (bateau m à) vapeur m; (liner) paquebot m. ◆**steamroller** n rouleau m compresseur. ◆**steamy** a (-ier, -iest) humide; (window) embué; (love affair etc) brûlant.

steel [stiːl] **1** n acier m; **s. industry** sidérurgie f. **2** vt **to s. oneself** s'endurcir (against contre). ◆**steelworks** n aciérie f.

steep [stiːp] **1** a (-er, -est) (stairs, slope etc) raide; (hill) escarpé; (price) Fig excessif. **2** vt (soak) tremper (in dans); **steeped in** Fig imprégné de. ◆**-ly** adv (to rise) en pente raide; (of prices) Fig excessivement.

steeple ['stiːp(ə)l] n clocher m.

steeplechase ['stiːp(ə)ltʃeɪs] n (race) steeple(-chase) m.

steer [stɪər] vt (vehicle, person) diriger, piloter; (ship) diriger, gouverner; – vi (of person) Nau tenir le gouvernail, gouverner; **to s. towards** faire route vers; **to s. clear of** éviter. ◆**-ing** n Aut direction f; **s. wheel** volant m.

stem [stem] **1** n (of plant etc) tige f; (of glass) pied m. **2** vt (-mm-) **to s. (the flow of)** (stop) arrêter, contenir. **3** vi (-mm-) **to s. from** provenir de.

stench [stentʃ] n puanteur f.

stencil ['stens(ə)l] n (metal, plastic) pochoir m; (paper, for typing) stencil m; – vt (-ll-, Am -l-) (notes etc) polycopier.

stenographer [stə'nɒɡrəfər] n Am sténodactylo f.

step [step] n (movement, sound) pas m; (stair) marche f; (on train, bus) marchepied m; (doorstep) pas m de la porte; (action) Fig mesure f; **(flight of) steps** (indoors) escalier m; (outdoors) perron m; **(pair of) steps** (ladder) escabeau m; **s. by s.** pas à pas; **to keep in s.** marcher au pas; **in s. with** Fig en accord avec; – vi (-pp-) (walk) marcher (on sur); **s. this way!** (venez) par ici!; **to s. aside** s'écarter; **to s. back** reculer; **to s. down** descendre (from de); (withdraw) Fig se down descendre; **to s. forward** faire un pas en avant; **to s. in** entrer; (intervene) Fig intervenir; **to s. into** (car etc) monter dans; **to s. off** (chair etc) descendre de; **to s. out of** (car etc) descendre de; **to s. over** (*obstacle*) enjamber; – *vt* **to s. up** (*increase*) augmenter, intensifier; (*speed up*) activer. ◆**step-ladder** *n* escabeau *m*. ◆**stepping-stone** *n Fig* tremplin *m* (**to** pour arriver à).

stepbrother ['stepbrʌðər] *n* demi-frère *m*. ◆**stepdaughter** *n* belle-fille *f*. ◆**step-father** *n* beau-père *m*. ◆**stepmother** *n* belle-mère *f*. ◆**stepsister** *n* demi-sœur *f*. ◆**stepson** *n* beau-fils *m*.

stereo ['steriəʊ] *n* (*pl* -**os**) (*sound*) stéréo(phonie) *f*; (*record player*) chaîne *f* (stéréo *inv*); – *a* (*record etc*) stéréo *inv*; (*broadcast*) en stéréo. ◆**stereo'phonic** *a* stéréophonique.

stereotype ['steriətaip] *n* stéréotype *m*. ◆**stereotyped** *a* stéréotypé.

sterile ['sterail, *Am* 'sterəl] *a* stérile. ◆**ste'rility** *n* stérilité *f*. ◆**sterili'zation** *n* stérilisation *f*. ◆**sterilize** *vt* stériliser.

sterling ['stɜːlɪŋ] *n* (*currency*) livre(s) *f*(*pl*) sterling *inv*; – *a* (*pound*) sterling *inv*; (*silver*) fin; (*quality, person*) *Fig* sûr.

stern [stɜːn] **1** *a* (-**er**, -**est**) sévère. **2** *n* (*of ship*) arrière *m*.

stethoscope ['steθəskəʊp] *n* stéthoscope *m*.

stetson ['stetsən] *n Am* chapeau *m* à larges bords.

stevedore ['stiːvədɔːr] *n* docker *m*.

stew [stjuː] *n* ragoût *m*; **in a s.** *Fig* dans le pétrin; – **s. pan, s. pot** cocotte *f*; – *vt* (*meat*) faire *or* cuire en ragoût; (*fruit*) faire cuire; **stewed fruit** compote *f*; – *vi* cuire. ◆—**ing** *a* (*pears etc*) à cuire.

steward ['stjuːəd] *n Av Nau* steward *m*; (*in college, club etc*) intendant *m* (*préposé au ravitaillement*); **shop s.** délégué, -ée *mf* syndical(e). ◆**stewar'dess** *n Av* hôtesse *f*.

stick¹ [stɪk] *n* (*piece of wood, chalk, dynamite*) bâton *m*; (*branch*) branche *f*; (*for walking*) canne *f*; **the sticks** *Pej Fam* la campagne, la cambrousse; **to give s.o. some s.** (*scold*) *Fam* engueuler qn.

stick² [stɪk] *vt* (*pt & pp* **stuck**) (*glue*) coller; (*put*) *Fam* mettre, planter; (*tolerate*) *Fam* supporter; **to s. sth into** (*thrust*) planter *or* enfoncer qch dans; **to s. down** (*envelope*) coller; (*put down*) *Fam* poser; **to s. on** (*stamp*) coller; (*hat etc*) mettre, planter; **to s. out** (*tongue*) tirer; (*head*) *Fam* sortir; **to s. it out** (*resist*) *Fam* tenir le coup; **to s. up** (*notice*) afficher; (*hand*) *Fam* lever; – *vi* coller, adhérer (**to** à); (*of food in pan*) attacher; (*remain*) *Fam* rester; (*of drawer etc*) être bloqué *or* coincé; **to s. by s.o.** rester fidèle à qn; **to s. to the facts** (*confine oneself to*) s'en tenir aux faits; **to s. around** *Fam*

rester dans les parages; **to s. out** (*of petticoat etc*) dépasser; (*of tooth*) avancer; **to s. up for** (*defend*) défendre; **sticking plaster** sparadrap *m*. ◆**sticker** *n* (*label*) autocollant *m*. ◆**stick-on** *a* (*label*) adhésif. ◆**stick-up** *n Fam* hold-up *m inv*.

stickler ['stɪklər] *n* **s. for** (*rules, discipline, details*) intransigeant sur.

sticky ['stɪkɪ] *a* (-**ier**, -**iest**) collant, poisseux; (*label*) adhésif; (*problem*) *Fig* difficile.

stiff [stɪf] *a* (-**er**, -**est**) raide; (*joint, leg etc*) ankylosé; (*brush, paste*) dur; (*person*) *Fig* froid, guindé; (*difficult*) difficile; (*price*) élevé; (*whisky*) bien tassé; **to have a s. neck** avoir le torticolis; **to be bored s.** *Fam* s'ennuyer à mourir; **frozen s.** *Fam* complètement gelé. ◆**stiffen** *vt* raidir; – *vi* se raidir. ◆**stiffly** *adv* (*coldly*) *Fig* froidement. ◆**stiffness** *n* raideur *f*; (*hardness*) dureté *f*.

stifle ['staif(ə)l] *vt* (*feeling, person etc*) étouffer; – *vi* **it's stifling** on étouffe.

stigma ['stɪgmə] *n* (*moral stain*) flétrissure *f*. ◆**stigmatize** *vt* (*denounce*) stigmatiser.

stile [stail] *n* (*between fields etc*) échalier *m*.

stiletto [stɪ'letəʊ] *a* **s. heel** talon *m* aiguille.

still¹ [stɪl] *adv* encore, toujours; (*even*) encore; (*nevertheless*) tout de même; **better s., s. better** encore mieux.

still² [stɪl] *a* (-**er**, -**est**) (*motionless*) immobile; (*calm*) calme, tranquille; (*drink*) non gazeux; **to keep** *or* **lie** *or* **stand s.** rester tranquille; **s. life** nature *f* morte; – *n* (*of night*) silence *m*; *Cin* photo *f*. ◆**stillborn** *a* mort-né. ◆**stillness** *n* immobilité *f*; calme *m*.

still³ [stɪl] *n* (*for making alcohol*) alambic *m*.

stilt [stɪlt] *n* (*pole*) échasse *f*.

stilted ['stɪltɪd] *a* guindé.

stimulate ['stɪmjʊleɪt] *vt* stimuler. ◆**stimulant** *n Med* stimulant *m*. ◆**stimu'lation** *n* stimulation *f*. ◆**stimulus, *pl* -li** [-laɪ] *n* (*encouragement*) stimulant *m*; (*physiological*) stimulus *m*.

sting [stɪŋ] *vt* (*pt & pp* **stung**) (*of insect, ointment, wind etc*) piquer; (*of remark*) *Fig* blesser; – *vi* piquer; – *n* piqûre *f*; (*insect's organ*) dard *m*. ◆—**ing** *a* (*pain, remark*) cuisant.

sting/y ['stɪndʒɪ] *a* (-**ier**, -**iest**) avare, mesquin; **s. with** (*money, praise*) avare *or* (*food, wine*) mesquin sur. ◆—**iness** *n* avarice *f*.

stink [stɪŋk] *n* puanteur *f*; **to cause** *or* **make a s.** (*trouble*) *Fam* faire du foin; – *vi* (*pt* **stank** *or* **stunk**, *pp* **stunk**) puer; (*of book, film etc*)

Fam être infect; **to s. of smoke**/*etc* empester la fumée/*etc*; – *vt* **to s. out** (*room etc*) empester. ◆**–er** *n Fam* (*person*) sale type *m*; (*question, task etc*) vacherie *f*.

stint [stɪnt] **1** *n* (*share*) part *f* de travail; (*period*) période *f* de travail. **2** *vi* **to s. on** lésiner sur.

stipend ['staɪpend] *n Rel* traitement *n*.

stipulate ['stɪpjuleɪt] *vt* stipuler (**that** que). ◆**stipu'lation** *n* stipulation *f*.

stir [stɜːr] *n* agitation *f*; **to give sth a s.** remuer qch; **to cause a s.** Fig faire du bruit; – *vt* (**-rr-**) (*coffee, leaves etc*) remuer; (*excite*) Fig exciter; (*incite*) inciter (**to do** à faire); **to s. oneself** (*make an effort*) se secouer; **to s. up** (*trouble*) provoquer; (*memory*) réveiller; – *vi* remuer, bouger. ◆**stirring** *a* (*speech etc*) excitant, émouvant.

stirrup ['stɪrəp] *n* étrier *m*.

stitch [stɪtʃ] *n* point *m*; (*in knitting*) maille *f*; *Med* point *m* de suture; **a s.** (*in one's side*) (*pain*) un point de côté; **to be in stitches** *Fam* se tordre (de rire); – *vt* **to s. (up)** (*sew up*) coudre; *Med* suturer.

stoat [stəʊt] *n* (*animal*) hermine *f*.

stock [stɒk] *n* (*supply*) provision *f*, stock *m*, réserve *f*; (*of knowledge, jokes*) fonds *m*, mine *f*; *Fin* valeurs *fpl*, titres *mpl*; (*descent, family*) souche *f*; (*soup*) bouillon *m*; (*cattle*) bétail *m*; **the stocks** *Hist* le pilori; **in s.** (*goods*) en magasin, disponible; **out of s.** (*goods*) épuisé, non disponible; **to take s.** *Fig* faire le point (**of** de); **s. reply**/**size** réponse *f*/taille *f* courante; **s. phrase** expression *f* toute faite; **the S. Exchange** *ou* **Market** la Bourse; – *vt* (*sell*) vendre; (*keep in store*) stocker; **to s. (up)** (*shop, larder*) approvisionner; **well-stocked** bien approvisionné; – *vi* **to s. up** s'approvisionner (**with de**, **en**). ◆**stockbroker** *n* agent *m* de change. ◆**stockcar** *n* stock-car *m*. ◆**stockholder** *n Fin* actionnaire *mf*. ◆**stockist** *n* dépositaire *m*, stockiste *m*. ◆**stockpile** *vt* stocker, amasser. ◆**stockroom** *n* réserve *f*, magasin *m*. ◆**stocktaking** *n Com* inventaire *m*.

stocking ['stɒkɪŋ] *n* (*garment*) bas *m*.

stocky ['stɒkɪ] *a* (**-ier, -iest**) trapu.

stodge [stɒdʒ] *n* (*food*) *Fam* étouffe-chrétien *m inv*. ◆**stodgy** *a* (**-ier, -iest**) *Fam* lourd, indigeste; (*person, style*) compassé.

stoic ['stəʊɪk] *a & n* stoïque (*mf*). ◆**stoical** *a* stoïque. ◆**stoicism** *n* stoïcisme *m*.

stok/e [stəʊk] *vt* (*fire*) entretenir; (*engine*) chauffer. ◆**–er** *n Rail* chauffeur *m*.

stole[1] [stəʊl] *n* (*shawl*) étole *f*.

stole[2], **stolen** [stəʊl, 'stəʊl(ə)n] *see* steal[1,2].

stolid ['stɒlɪd] *a* (*manner, person*) impassible.

stomach ['stʌmək] *n Anat* estomac *m*; (*abdomen*) ventre *m*; – *vt* (*put up with*) *Fig* supporter. ◆**stomachache** *n* mal *m* de ventre; **to have a s.** avoir mal au ventre.

stone [stəʊn] *n* pierre *f*; (*pebble*) caillou *m*; (*in fruit*) noyau *m*; (*in kidney*) *Med* calcul *m*; (*weight*) = 6,348 kg; **a stone's throw away** *Fig* à deux pas d'ici; – *vt* lancer des pierres sur, lapider; (*fruit*) dénoyauter. ◆**stonemason** *n* tailleur *m* de pierre, maçon *m*. ◆**stony** *a* **1** (**-ier, -iest**) (*path etc*) pierreux, caillouteux. **2 s. broke** (*penniless*) *Sl* fauché.

stone-   [stəʊn] *pref* complètement. ◆**s.-'broke** *a Am Sl* fauché. ◆**s.-'cold** *a* complètement froid. ◆**s.-'dead** *a* raide mort. ◆**s.-'deaf** *a* sourd comme un pot.

stoned [stəʊnd] *a* (*high on drugs*) *Fam* camé.

stooge [stuːdʒ] *n* (*actor*) comparse *mf*; (*flunkey*) *Pej* larbin *m*; (*dupe*) *Pej* pigeon *m*.

stood [stʊd] *see* stand.

stool [stuːl] *n* tabouret *m*.

stoop [stuːp] **1** *n* **to have a s.** être voûté; – *vi* se baisser; **to s. to doing**/**to sth** *Fig* s'abaisser à faire/à qch. **2** *n* (*in front of house*) *Am* perron *m*.

stop [stɒp] *n* (*place, halt*) arrêt *m*, halte *f*; *Av Nau* escale *f*; *Gram* point *m*; **bus s.** arrêt *m* d'autobus; **to put a s. to** mettre fin à; **to bring to a s.** arrêter; **to come to a s.** s'arrêter; **without a s.** sans arrêt; **s. light** (*on vehicle*) stop *m*; **s. sign** (*road sign*) stop *m*; – *vt* (**-pp-**) arrêter; (*end*) mettre fin à; (*prevent*) empêcher (**from doing** de faire); (*cheque*) faire opposition à; **to s. up** (*sink, pipe, leak etc*) boucher; – *vi* s'arrêter; (*of pain, conversation etc*) cesser; (*stay*) rester; **to s. eating**/*etc* s'arrêter de manger/*etc*; **to s. snowing**/*etc* cesser de neiger/*etc*; **to s. by** passer (**s.o.'s** chez qn); **to s. off** *ou* **over** (*on journey*) s'arrêter. ◆**stoppage** *n* arrêt *m*; (*in pay*) retenue *f*; (*in work*) arrêt *m* de travail; (*strike*) débrayage *m*; (*blockage*) obstruction *f*. ◆**stopper** *n* bouchon *m*.

stopcock ['stɒpkɒk] *n* robinet *m* d'arrêt. ◆**stopgap** *n* bouche-trou *m*; – *a* intérimaire. ◆**stopoff** *n*, ◆**stopover** *n* halte *f*. ◆**stopwatch** *n* chronomètre *m*.

store [stɔːr] n (supply) provision f; (of information, jokes etc) Fig fonds m; (depot, warehouse) entrepôt m; (shop) grand magasin m, Am magasin m; (computer memory) mémoire f; **to have sth in s. for s.o.** (surprise) réserver qch à qn; **to keep in s.** garder en réserve; **to set great s. by** attacher une grande importance à; – vt **to s. (up)** (in warehouse etc) emmagasiner; (for future use) mettre en réserve; **to s. (away)** (furniture) entreposer. ◆**storage** n emmagasinage m; (for future use) mise f en réserve; **s. space** or **room** espace m de rangement. ◆**storekeeper** n magasinier m; (shopkeeper) Am commerçant, -ante mf. ◆**storeroom** n réserve f.

storey [stɔːrɪ] n étage m.

stork [stɔːk] n cigogne f.

storm [stɔːm] 1 n (weather) & Fig tempête f; (thundershower) orage m; **s. cloud** nuage m orageux. 2 vt (attack) Mil prendre d'assaut. 3 vi **to s. out** (angrily) sortir comme une furie. ◆**stormy** a (-ier, -iest) (weather, meeting etc) orageux; (wind) d'orage.

story [stɔːrɪ] 1 n histoire f; (newspaper article) article m; **s. (line)** Cin Th intrigue f; **short s.** Liter nouvelle f, conte m; **fairy s.** conte m de fées. 2 (storey) Am étage m. ◆**storyteller** n conteur, -euse mf; (liar) Fam menteur, -euse mf.

stout [staʊt] 1 a (-er, -est) (person) gros, corpulent; (stick, volume) gros, épais; (shoes) solide. 2 n (beer) bière f brune. ◆**-ness** n grosseur f.

stove [stəʊv] n (for cooking) cuisinière f; (solid fuel) fourneau m; (small) réchaud m; (for heating) poêle m.

stow [staʊ] 1 vt (cargo) arrimer; **to s. away** (put away) ranger. 2 vi **to s. away** Nau voyager clandestinement. ◆**stowaway** n Nau passager, -ère mf clandestin(e).

straddle ['stræd(ə)l] vt (chair, fence) se mettre or être à califourchon sur; (step over, span) enjamber; (line in road) Aut chevaucher.

straggl/e ['stræg(ə)l] vi (stretch) s'étendre (en désordre); (trail) traîner (en désordre); **to s. in** entrer par petits groupes. ◆**-er** n traînard, -arde mf.

straight [streɪt] a (-er, -est) droit; (hair) raide; (route) direct; (tidy) en ordre; (frank) franc; (refusal) net; (actor, role) sérieux; **I want to get this s.** comprenons-nous bien; **to keep a s. face** garder son sérieux; **to put** or **set s.** (tidy) ranger; – n **the s.** Sp la ligne droite; – adv (to walk etc) droit; (directly) tout droit, directe-

ment; (to drink gin, whisky etc) sec; **s. away** (at once) tout de suite; **s. out, s. off** sans hésiter; **s. opposite** juste en face; **s. ahead** or **on** (to walk etc) tout droit; **s. ahead** (to look) droit devant soi. ◆**straighta'way** adv tout de suite. ◆**straighten** vt to **s. (up)** redresser; (tie, room) arranger; **to s. things out** Fig arranger les choses. ◆**straight-'forward** a (frank) franc; (easy) simple.

strain [streɪn] 1 n tension f; (tiredness) fatigue f; (stress) Med tension f nerveuse; (effort) effort m; – vt (rope, wire) tendre excessivement; (muscle) Med froisser; (ankle, wrist) fouler; (eyes) fatiguer; (voice) forcer; Fig mettre à l'épreuve; **to s. one's ears** (to hear) tendre l'oreille; **to s. oneself** (hurt oneself) se faire mal; (tire oneself) se fatiguer; – vi fournir un effort (**to do** pour faire). 2 vt (soup etc) passer; (vegetables) égoutter. 3 n (breed) lignée f; (of virus) souche f; (streak) tendance f. 4 npl Mus accents mpl (of de). ◆**-ed** a (relations) tendu; (laugh) forcé; (ankle, wrist) foulé. ◆**-er** n passoire f.

strait [streɪt] 1 n & npl Geog détroit m. 2 npl **in financial straits** dans l'embarras. ◆**straitjacket** n camisole f de force. ◆**strait'laced** a collet monté inv.

strand [strænd] n (of wool etc) brin m; (of hair) mèche f; (of story) Fig fil m.

stranded ['strændɪd] a (person, vehicle) en rade.

strange [streɪndʒ] a (-er, -est) (odd) étrange, bizarre; (unknown) inconnu; (new) nouveau; **to feel s.** (in a new place) se sentir dépaysé. ◆**strangely** adv étrangement; **s. (enough) she . . .** chose étrange, elle . . . . ◆**strangeness** n étrangeté f. ◆**stranger** n (unknown) inconnu, -ue mf; (outsider) étranger, -ère mf; **he's a s. here** il n'est pas d'ici; **she's a s. to me** elle m'est inconnue.

strangle ['stræŋg(ə)l] vt étrangler. ◆**strangler** n étrangleur, -euse mf. ◆**stranglehold** n emprise f totale (**on** sur).

strap [stræp] n courroie f, sangle f; (on dress) bretelle f; (on watch) bracelet m; (on sandal) lanière f; – vt (-pp-) **to s. (down** or **in)** attacher (avec une courroie).

strapping ['stræpɪŋ] a (well-built) robuste.

stratagem ['strætədʒəm] n stratagème m.

strategy ['strætədʒɪ] n stratégie f. ◆**stra-'tegic** a stratégique.

stratum, pl **-ta** ['strɑːtəm, -tə] n couche f.

straw [strɔː] n paille f; **a (drinking) s.** une paille; **that's the last s.!** c'est le comble!

strawberry ['strɔːbərɪ] n fraise f; – a

(flavour, ice cream) à la fraise; *(jam)* de fraises; *(tart)* aux fraises.

stray [streɪ] *a (lost)* perdu; **a s. car**/*etc* une voiture/*etc* isolée; **a few s. cars**/*etc* quelques rares voitures/*etc*; – *n* animal *m* perdu; – *vi* s'égarer; **to s. from** *(subject, path)* s'écarter de.

streak [striːk] *n (line)* raie *f*; *(of light)* filet *m*; *(of colour)* strie *f*; *(trace)* Fig trace *f*; *(tendency)* tendance *f*; **grey**/*etc* **streaks** *(in hair)* mèches *fpl* grises/*etc*; **a mad s.** une tendance à la folie; **my literary s.** ma fibre littéraire. ◆**streaked** *a (marked)* strié, zébré; *(stained)* taché (**with** de). ◆**streaky** *a* (**-ier, -iest**) strié; *(bacon)* pas trop maigre.

stream [striːm] *n (brook)* ruisseau *m*; *(current)* courant *m*; *(flow)* & Fig flot *m*; Sch classe *f* (de niveau); – *vi* ruisseler (**with** de); **to s. in** *(of sunlight, people etc)* Fig entrer à flots.

streamer [ˈstriːmər] *n (paper)* serpentin *m*; *(banner)* banderole *f*.

streamlin/e [ˈstriːmlaɪn] *vt (work, method etc)* rationaliser. ◆**-ed** *a (shape)* aérodynamique.

street [striːt] *n* rue *f*; **s. door** porte *f* d'entrée; **s. lamp, s. light** réverbère *m*; **s. map, s. plan** plan *m* des rues; **up my s.** Fig Fam dans mes cordes; **streets ahead** Fam très en avance (**of** sur). ◆**streetcar** *n (tram)* Am tramway *m*.

strength [streŋθ] *n* force *f*; *(health, energy)* forces *fpl*; *(of wood, fabric)* solidité *f*; **on the s. of** Fig en vertu de; **in full s.** au (grand) complet. ◆**strengthen** *vt (building, position etc)* renforcer, consolider; *(body, soul, limb)* fortifier.

strenuous [ˈstrenjuəs] *a (effort etc)* vigoureux, énergique; *(work)* ardu; *(active)* actif; *(tiring)* fatigant. ◆**-ly** *adv* énergiquement.

strep [strep] *a* **s. throat** Med Am angine *f*.

stress [stres] *n (pressure)* pression *f*; Med Psy tension *f (nerveuse)*, stress *m*; *(emphasis)* & Gram accent *m*; Tech tension *f*; **under s.** Med Psy sous pression, stressé; – *vt* insister sur; *(word)* accentuer; **to s. that** souligner que. ◆**stressful** *a* stressant.

stretch [stretʃ] *vt (rope, neck)* tendre; *(shoe, rubber)* étirer; *(meaning)* forcer; **to s. (out)** *(arm, leg)* étendre, allonger; **to s. (out) one's arm** *(reach out)* tendre le bras (**to** pour prendre); **to s. one's legs** Fig se dégourdir les jambes; **to s. oneself** Fig exiger un effort de qn; **to be (fully) stretched** *(of budget etc)* être tiré au maximum; **to s. out** *(visit)* prolonger; – *vi (of person, elastic)*

s'étirer; *(of influence etc)* s'étendre; **to s. (out)** *(of rope, plain)* s'étendre; – *n (area, duration)* étendue *f*; *(of road)* tronçon *m*, partie *f*; *(route, trip)* trajet *m*; **at a s.** d'une (seule) traite; **ten**/*etc* **hours at a s.** dix/*etc* heures d'affilée; **s. socks**/*etc* chaussettes *fpl*/*etc* extensibles; **s. nylon** nylon *m* stretch *inv*. ◆**stretchmarks** *npl (on body)* vergetures *fpl*.

stretcher [ˈstretʃər] *n* brancard *m*.

strew [struː] *vt (pt* strewed, *pp* strewed *or* strewn) *(scatter)* répandre; **strewn with** *(covered)* jonché de.

stricken [ˈstrɪk(ə)n] *a* **s. with** *(illness)* atteint de; *(panic)* frappé de.

strict [strɪkt] *a* (**-er, -est**) *(severe, absolute)* strict. ◆**-ly** *adv* strictement; **s. forbidden** formellement interdit. ◆**-ness** *n* sévérité *f*.

stride [straɪd] *n (grand)* pas *m*, enjambée *f*; **to make great strides** Fig faire de grands progrès; – *vi (pt* strode) **to s. across** *or* **over** enjamber; **to s. up and down a room** arpenter une pièce.

strident [ˈstraɪdənt] *a* strident.

strife [straɪf] *n inv* conflit(s) *m(pl)*.

strik/e [straɪk] **1** *n (attack)* Mil raid *m (aérien)*; *(of oil etc)* découverte *f*; – *vt (pt* & *pp* struck) *(hit, impress)* frapper; *(collide with)* heurter; *(beat)* battre; *(a blow)* donner; *(a match)* frotter; *(gold, problem)* trouver; *(coin)* frapper; *(of clock)* sonner; **to s. a bargain** conclure un accord; **to s. a balance** trouver l'équilibre; **to s. (off)** *(from list)* rayer *(from* de); **to be struck off** *(of doctor)* être radié; **it strikes me as/that il me semble être/que; how did it s. you?** quelle impression ça t'a fait?; **to s. down** *(of illness etc)* terrasser *(qn)*; **to s. up a friendship** lier amitié *(with* avec); – *vi* **to s. (at)** *(attack)* attaquer; **to s. back** *(retaliate)* riposter; **to s. out** donner des coups. **2** *n (of workers)* grève *f*; **to go (out) on s.** se mettre en grève *(for* pour obtenir, **against** pour protester contre); – *vi (pt* & *pp* struck) *(of workers)* faire grève. ◆**-ing** *a (impressive)* frappant. ◆**-ingly** *adv (beautiful etc)* extraordinairement. ◆**-er** *n* gréviste *mf*; Fb buteur *m*.

string [strɪŋ] *n* ficelle *f*; *(of anorak, apron)* cordon *m*; *(of violin, racket etc)* corde *f*; *(of pearls, beads)* rang *m*; *(of onions, insults)* chapelet *m*; *(of people, vehicles)* file *f*; *(of questions etc)* série *f*; **to pull strings** Fig faire jouer ses relations; – *a (instrument, quartet)* Mus à cordes; **s. bean** haricot *m* vert; – *vt (pt* & *pp* strung) *(beads)* enfiler; **to s. up**

(hang up) suspendre; − vi to s. along (with) Fam suivre. ◆−ed a (instrument) Mus à cordes. ◆stringy a (-ier, -iest) (meat etc) filandreux.

stringent ['strɪndʒ(ə)nt] a rigoureux. ◆stringency n rigueur f.

strip [strɪp] 1 n (piece) bande f; (of water) bras m; (thin) s. (of metal etc) lamelle f; landing s. piste f or terrain m d'atterrissage; s. cartoon, comic s. bande f dessinée. 2 vt (-pp-) (undress) déshabiller; (bed) défaire; (deprive) dépouiller (of de); to s. (down) (machine) démonter; to s. off (remove) enlever; − vi to s. (off) (undress) se déshabiller. ◆stripper n (woman) stripteaseuse f; (paint) s. décapant m. ◆strip-'tease n strip-tease m.

stripe [straɪp] n rayure f; Mil galon m. ◆striped a rayé (with de). ◆stripy a rayé.

strive [straɪv] vi (pt strove, pp striven) s'efforcer (to do de faire, for d'obtenir).

strode [strəud] see stride.

stroke [strəuk] n (movement) coup m; (of pen, genius) trait m; (of brush) touche f; (on clock) coup m; (caress) caresse f; Med coup m de sang; (swimming style) nage f; at a s. d'un coup; a s. of luck un coup de chance; you haven't done a s. (of work) tu n'as rien fait; heat s. (sunstroke) insolation f; four-s. engine moteur m à quatre temps; − vt (beard, cat etc) caresser.

stroll [strəul] n promenade f; − vi se promener, flâner; to s. in/etc entrer/etc sans se presser. ◆−ing a (musician etc) ambulant.

stroller ['strəulər] n (pushchair) Am poussette f.

strong [strɒŋ] a (-er, -est) fort; (shoes, nerves) solide; (interest) vif; (measures) énergique; (supporter) ardent; sixty s. au nombre de soixante; − adv to be going s. aller toujours bien. ◆−ly adv (to protest, defend) énergiquement; (to desire, advise, remind) fortement; (to feel) profondément; s. built solide. ◆strongarm a brutal. ◆strongbox n coffre-fort m. ◆stronghold n bastion m. ◆strong-'willed a résolu.

strove [strəuv] see strive.

struck [strʌk] see strike 1,2.

structure ['strʌktʃər] n structure f; (of building) armature f; (building itself) construction f. ◆structural a structural; (fault) Archit de construction.

struggle ['strʌg(ə)l] n (fight) lutte f (to do pour faire); (effort) effort m; to put up a s.

résister; to have a s. doing or to do avoir du mal à faire; − vi (fight) lutter, se battre (with avec); (resist) résister; (thrash about wildly) se débattre; to s. to do (try hard) s'efforcer de faire; to s. out of sortir péniblement de; to s. along or on se débrouiller; a struggling lawyer/etc un avocat/etc qui a du mal à débuter.

strum [strʌm] vt (-mm-) (guitar etc) gratter de.

strung [strʌŋ] see string; − a s. out (things, people) espacés; (washing) étendu.

strut [strʌt] 1 vi (-tt-) to s. (about or around) se pavaner. 2 n (support) Tech étai m.

stub [stʌb] 1 n (of pencil, cigarette etc) bout m; (counterfoil of cheque etc) talon m; − vt (-bb-) to s. out (cigarette) écraser. 2 vt (-bb-) to s. one's toe se cogner le doigt de pied (on, against contre).

stubble ['stʌb(ə)l] n barbe f de plusieurs jours.

stubborn ['stʌbən] a (person) entêté, opiniâtre; (cough, efforts, manner etc) opiniâtre. ◆−ly adv opiniâtrement. ◆−ness n entêtement m; opiniâtreté f.

stubby ['stʌbɪ] a (-ier, -iest) (finger etc) gros et court, épais; (person) trapu.

stuck [stʌk] see stick²; − a (caught, jammed) coincé; s. in bed/indoors cloué au lit/chez soi; to be s. (unable to do sth) ne pas savoir quoi faire; I'm s. (for an answer) je ne sais que répondre; to be s. with sth/s.o. se farcir qch/qn. ◆s.-'up a Fam prétentieux, snob inv.

stud [stʌd] n 1 (nail) clou m (à grosse tête; (for collar) bouton m de col. 2 (farm) haras m; (horses) écurie f; (stallion) étalon m; (virile man) Sl mâle m. ◆studded a (boots, tyres) clouté; s. with (covered) Fig constellé de, parsemé de.

student ['stju:dənt] n Univ étudiant, -ante mf; Sch Am élève mf; music/etc s. étudiant, -ante en musique/etc; − a (life, protest) étudiant; (restaurant, residence, grant) universitaire.

studio ['stju:dɪəu] n (pl -os) (of painter etc) & Cin TV studio m; s. flat or Am apartment studio m.

studious ['stju:dɪəs] a (person) studieux. ◆−ly adv (carefully) avec soin. ◆−ness n application f.

study ['stʌdɪ] n étude f; (office) bureau m; − vt (learn, observe) étudier; − vi étudier; to s. to be a doctor/etc faire des études pour devenir médecin/etc; to s. for (exam) préparer. ◆studied a (deliberate) étudié.

stuff [stʌf] 1 n (thing) truc m, chose f;

(*substance*) substance *f*; (*things*) trucs *mpl*, choses *fpl*; (*possessions*) affaires *fpl*; (*nonsense*) sottises *fpl*; **this s.'s good, it's good** s. c'est bon (ça). **2** *vt* (*chair, cushion etc*) rembourrer (**with** avec); (*animal*) empailler; (*cram, fill*) bourrer (**with** de); (*put, thrust*) fourrer (**into** dans); (*chicken etc*) Culin farcir; **to s. (up)** (*hole etc*) colmater; **my nose is stuffed (up)** j'ai le nez bouché. ◆—**ing** *n* (*padding*) bourre *f*; Culin farce *f*.

stuffy ['stʌfɪ] *a* (-ier, -iest) (*room etc*) mal aéré; (*formal*) Fig compassé; (*old-fashioned*) vieux jeu *inv*; **it smells s.** ça sent le renfermé.

stumble ['stʌmb(ə)l] *vi* trébucher (**over** sur, **against** contre); **to s. across** *or* **on** (*find*) tomber sur; **stumbling block** pierre *f* d'achoppement.

stump [stʌmp] *n* (*of tree*) souche *f*; (*of limb*) moignon *m*; (*of pencil*) bout *m*; Cricket piquet *m*.

stumped ['stʌmpt] *a* **to be s. by sth** (*baffled*) ne pas savoir que penser de qch.

stun [stʌn] *vt* (-nn-) (*daze*) étourdir; (*animal*) assommer; (*amaze*) Fig stupéfier. ◆**stunned** *a* Fig stupéfait (**by** par). ◆**stunning** *a* (*blow*) étourdissant; (*news*) stupéfiant; (*terrific*) Fam sensationnel.

stung [stʌŋ] *see* sting.

stunk [stʌŋk] *see* stink.

stunt [stʌnt] **1** *n* (*feat*) tour *m* (de force); Cin cascade *f*; (*ruse, trick*) truc *m*; **s. man** Cin cascadeur *m*; **s. woman** Cin cascadeuse *f*. **2** *vt* (*growth*) retarder. ◆—**ed** *a* (*person*) rabougri.

stupefy ['stju:pɪfaɪ] *vt* (*of drink etc*) abrutir; (*amaze*) Fig stupéfier.

stupendous [stju:'pendəs] *a* prodigieux.

stupid ['stju:pɪd] *a* stupide, bête; **a s.** thing une sottise; **s. fool, s. idiot** idiot, -ote *mf*. ◆**stu'pidity** *n* stupidité *f*. ◆**stupidly** *adv* stupidement, bêtement.

stupor ['stju:pər] *n* (*daze*) stupeur *f*.

sturdy ['stɜ:dɪ] *a* (-ier, -iest) (*person, shoe etc*) robuste. ◆**sturdiness** *n* robustesse *f*.

sturgeon ['stɜ:dʒ(ə)n] *n* (*fish*) esturgeon *m*.

stutter ['stʌtər] *n* bégaiement *m*; **to have a s.** être bègue; – *vi* bégayer.

sty [staɪ] *n* (*pigsty*) porcherie *f*.

sty(e) [staɪ] *n* (*on eye*) orgelet *m*.

style [staɪl] *n* style *m*; (*fashion*) mode *f*; (*design of dress etc*) modèle *m*; (*of hair*) coiffure *f*; (*sort*) genre *m*; **to have s.** avoir de la classe; **in s.** (*in superior manner*) de la meilleure façon possible; (*to live, travel*) dans le luxe; – *vt* (*design*) créer; **he styles**

himself . . . *Pej* il se fait appeler . . . ; **to s. s.o.'s hair** coiffer qn. ◆**styling** *n* (*cutting of hair*) coupe *f*. ◆**stylish** *a* chic, élégant. ◆**stylishly** *adv* élégamment. ◆**stylist** *n* (*hair*) coiffeur, -euse *mf*. ◆**sty'listic** *a* de style, stylistique. ◆**stylized** *a* stylisé.

stylus ['staɪləs] *n* (*of record player*) pointe *f* de lecture.

suave [swɑ:v] *a* (-er, -est) (*urbane*) courtois; *Pej* doucereux.

sub- [sʌb] *pref* sous-, sub-.

subconscious [sʌb'kɒnʃəs] *a* & *n* subconscient (*m*). ◆—**ly** *adv* inconsciemment.

subcontract [sʌbkən'trækt] *vt* sous-traiter. ◆**subcontractor** *n* sous-traitant *m*.

subdivide [sʌbdɪ'vaɪd] *vt* subdiviser (**into** en). ◆**subdivision** *n* subdivision *f*.

subdu/e [səb'dju:] *vt* (*country*) asservir; (*feelings*) maîtriser. ◆—**ed** *a* (*light*) atténué; (*voice*) bas; (*reaction*) faible; (*person*) qui manque d'entrain.

subheading ['sʌbhedɪŋ] *n* sous-titre *m*.

subject[1] ['sʌbdʒɪkt] *n* **1** (*matter*) & Gram sujet *m*; Sch Univ matière *f*; **s. matter** (*topic*) sujet *m*; (*content*) contenu *m*. **2** (*citizen*) ressortissant, -ante *mf*; (*of monarch, monarchy*) sujet, -ette *mf*; (*person etc in experiment*) sujet *m*.

subject[2] [səb'dʒekt] *a* (*tribe etc*) soumis; **to** (*prone to*) sujet à (*maladie etc*); (*ruled by*) soumis à (*loi, règle etc*); (*conditional upon*) sous réserve de; **prices are s. to change** les prix peuvent être modifiés; – [səb'dʒekt] *vt* soumettre (**to** à); (*expose*) exposer (**to** à). ◆**sub'jection** *n* soumission *f* (**to** à).

subjective [səb'dʒektɪv] *a* subjectif. ◆—**ly** *adv* subjectivement. ◆**subjec'tivity** *n* subjectivité *f*.

subjugate ['sʌbdʒʊgeɪt] *vt* subjuguer.

subjunctive [səb'dʒʌŋktɪv] *n* Gram subjonctif *m*.

sublet [sʌb'let] *vt* (*pt* & *pp* sublet, *pres p* subletting) sous-louer.

sublimate ['sʌblɪmeɪt] *vt* Psy sublimer.

sublime [sə'blaɪm] *a* sublime; (*indifference, stupidity*) suprême; – *n* sublime *m*.

submachine-gun [sʌbmə'ʃi:ngʌn] *n* mitraillette *f*.

submarine ['sʌbməri:n] *n* sous-marin *m*.

submerge [səb'mɜ:dʒ] *vt* (*flood, overwhelm*) submerger; (*immerse*) immerger (**in** dans); – *vi* (*of submarine*) s'immerger.

submit [səb'mɪt] *vt* (-tt-) soumettre (**to** à); **to s. that** *Jur* suggérer que; – *vi* se soumettre (**to** à). ◆**submission** *n* soumission *f* (**to** à). ◆**submissive** *a* soumis. ◆**submissively** *adv* avec soumission.

subnormal [sʌb'nɔːm(ə)l] *a* au-dessous de la normale; *(mentally)* arriéré.

subordinate [sə'bɔːdɪnət] *a* subalterne; *Gram* subordonné; − *n* subordonné, -ée *mf*; − [sə'bɔːdɪneɪt] *vt* subordonner (**to** à). ◆**subordi'nation** *n* subordination *f* (**to** à).

subpoena [səb'piːnə] *vt Jur* citer; − *n Jur* citation *f*.

subscribe [səb'skraɪb] *vt (money)* donner (**to** à); − *vi* cotiser; **to s. to** *(take out subscription)* s'abonner à *(journal etc)*; *(be a subscriber)* être abonné à *(journal etc)*; *(fund, idea)* souscrire à. ◆**subscriber** *n Journ Tel* abonné, -ée *mf*. ◆**subscription** *n (to newspaper etc)* abonnement *m*; *(to fund, idea)* & *Fin* souscription *f*; *(to club etc)* cotisation *f*.

subsequent ['sʌbsɪkwənt] *a* postérieur (**to** à); **our s.** problèmes que nous avons eus par la suite; **s. to** *(as a result of)* consécutif à. ◆**−ly** *adv* par la suite.

subservient [səb'sɜːvɪənt] *a* obséquieux; **to be s. to** *(a slave to)* être asservi à.

subside [səb'saɪd] *vi (of building, land)* s'affaisser; *(of wind, flood)* baisser. ◆**'subsidence** *n* affaissement *m*.

subsidiary [səb'sɪdɪərɪ] *a* accessoire; *(subject) Univ* secondaire; − *n (company) Com* filiale *f*.

subsidize ['sʌbsɪdaɪz] *vt* subventionner. ◆**subsidy** *n* subvention *f*.

subsist [səb'sɪst] *vi (of person, doubts etc)* subsister. ◆**subsistence** *n* subsistance *f*.

substance ['sʌbstəns] *n* substance *f*; *(firmness)* solidité *f*; **a man of s.** un homme riche. ◆**substantial** [səb'stænʃ(ə)l] *a* important, considérable; *(meal)* substantiel. ◆**sub'stantially** *adv* considérablement, beaucoup; **s. true**/*etc (to a great extent)* en grande partie vrai/*etc*; **s. different** très différent.

substandard [sʌb'stændəd] *a* de qualité inférieure.

substantiate [səb'stænʃɪeɪt] *vt* prouver, justifier.

substitute ['sʌbstɪtjuːt] *n (thing)* produit *m* de remplacement; *(person)* remplaçant, -ante *mf* (**for** de); **there's no s. for** . . . rien ne peut remplacer . . . ; − *vt* substituer *(for* à); − *vi* **to s. for** remplacer; *(deputize for in job)* se substituer à. ◆**substi'tution** *n* substitution *f*.

subtitle ['sʌbtaɪt(ə)l] *n* sous-titre *m*; − *vt* sous-titrer.

subtle ['sʌt(ə)l] *a* (**-er, -est**) subtil. ◆**sub-**

tlety *n* subtilité *f*. ◆**subtly** *adv* subtilement.

subtotal [sʌb'təʊt(ə)l] *n* total *m* partiel, sous-total *m*.

subtract [səb'trækt] *vt* soustraire (**from** de). ◆**subtraction** *n* soustraction *f*.

suburb ['sʌbɜːb] *n* banlieue *f*; **the suburbs** la banlieue; **in the suburbs** en banlieue. ◆**su'burban** *a (train)* de banlieue; *(accent)* de la banlieue. ◆**su'burbia** *n* la banlieue.

subversive [səb'vɜːsɪv] *a* subversif. ◆**subversion** *n* subversion *f*. ◆**subvert** *vt (system etc)* bouleverser; *(person)* corrompre.

subway ['sʌbweɪ] *n* passage *m* souterrain; *Rail Am* métro *m*.

succeed [sək'siːd] **1** *vi* réussir (**in doing** à faire, **in sth** dans qch). **2** *vt* **to s. s.o.** *(follow)* succéder à qn; − *vi* **to s. to the throne** succéder à la couronne. ◆**−ing** *a (in past)* suivant; *(in future)* futur; *(consecutive)* consécutif.

success [sək'ses] *n* succès *m*, réussite *f*; **to make a s. of sth** réussir qch; **he was a s.** il a eu du succès; **his** *or* **her s. in the exam** sa réussite à l'examen; **s. story** réussite *f* complète *or* exemplaire. ◆**successful** *a (venture etc)* couronné de succès, réussi; *(outcome)* heureux; *(firm)* prospère; *(candidate in exam)* admis, reçu; *(in election)* élu; *(writer, film etc)* à succès; **to be s.** réussir (**in dans, in an exam** à un examen, **in doing** à faire). ◆**successfully** *adv* avec succès.

succession [sək'seʃ(ə)n] *n* succession *f*; **in s.** successivement; **ten days in s.** dix jours consécutifs; **in rapid s.** coup sur coup. ◆**successive** *a* successif; **ten s. days** dix jours consécutifs. ◆**successor** *n* successeur *m* (**of, to** de).

succinct [sək'sɪŋkt] *a* succinct.

succulent ['sʌkjʊlənt] *a* succulent.

succumb [sə'kʌm] *vi (yield)* succomber (**to** à).

such [sʌtʃ] *a* tel; **s. a car**/*etc* une telle voiture/*etc*; **s. happiness**/*etc (so much)* tant *or* tellement de bonheur/*etc*; **there's no s. thing** ça n'existe pas; **I said no s. thing** je n'ai rien dit de tel; **s.** as comme, tel que; **and s.** tel ou tel; − *adv (so very)* si; *(in comparisons)* aussi; **s. a kind woman as you** une femme aussi gentille que vous; **s. long trips** de si longs voyages; **s. a large helping** une si grosse portion; − *pron* **happiness**/*etc* **as s.** le bonheur/*etc* en tant que tel; **s. was**

my idea telle était mon idée. ◆**suchlike** *n* . . . and s. *Fam* . . . et autres.

suck [sʌk] *vt* sucer; (*of baby*) téter (*lait, biberon etc*); **to s. (up)** (*with straw, pump*) aspirer; **to s. up** *or* **in** (*absorb*) absorber; – *vi* (*of baby*) téter; **to s. at** sucer. ◆**–er** *n* **1** (*fool*) *Fam* pigeon *m*, dupe *f*. **2** (*pad*) ventouse *f*.

suckle ['sʌk(ə)l] *vt* (*of woman*) allaiter; (*of baby*) téter.

suction ['sʌkʃ(ə)n] *n* succion *f*; **s. disc, s. pad** ventouse *f*.

Sudan [suː'dɑːn] *n* Soudan *m*.

sudden ['sʌd(ə)n] *a* soudain, subit; **all of a s.** tout à coup. ◆**–ly** *adv* subitement. ◆**–ness** *n* soudaineté *f*.

suds [sʌdz] *npl* mousse *f* de savon.

sue [suː] *vt* poursuivre (en justice); – *vi* engager des poursuites (judiciaires).

suede [sweɪd] *n* daim *m*; – *a* de daim.

suet ['suːɪt] *n* graisse *f* de rognon.

suffer ['sʌfər] *vi* souffrir (**from** de); **to s. from pimples/the flu** avoir des boutons/la grippe; **your work/etc will s.** ton travail/*etc* s'en ressentira; – *vt* (*attack, loss etc*) subir; (*pain*) ressentir; (*tolerate*) souffrir. ◆**–ing** *n* souffrance(s) *f(pl)*. ◆**–er** *n Med* malade *mf*; (*from misfortune*) victime *f*.

suffice [sə'faɪs] *vi* suffire.

sufficient [sə'fɪʃ(ə)nt] *a* (*quantity, number*) suffisant; **s. money/etc** (*enough*) suffisamment d'argent/*etc*; **to have s.** en avoir suffisamment. ◆**–ly** *adv* suffisamment.

suffix ['sʌfɪks] *n Gram* suffixe *m*.

suffocate ['sʌfəkeɪt] *vti* étouffer, suffoquer. ◆**suffo'cation** *n* (*of industry, mind etc*) & *Med* étouffement *m*, asphyxie *f*.

suffrage ['sʌfrɪdʒ] *n* (*right to vote*) *Pol* suffrage *m*.

suffused [sə'fjuːzd] *a* **s. with** (*light, tears*) baigné de.

sugar ['ʃʊgər] *n* sucre *m*; – *a* (*cane, tongs*) à sucre; (*industry*) sucrier; **s. bowl** sucrier *m*; – *vt* sucrer. ◆**sugary** *a* (*taste, tone*) sucré.

suggest [sə'dʒest] *vt* (*propose*) proposer, suggérer (**to** à, **that** que (+ *sub*)); (*evoke, imply*) suggérer; (*hint*) *Pej* insinuer. ◆**suggestion** *n* suggestion *f*, proposition *f*; (*evocation*) suggestion *f*; *Pej* insinuation *f*. ◆**suggestive** *a* suggestif; **to be s. of** suggérer.

suicide ['suːɪsaɪd] *n* suicide *m*; **to commit s.** se suicider. ◆**sui'cidal** *a* suicidaire.

suit [suːt] *n* **1** (*man's*) complet *m*, costume *m*; (*woman's*) tailleur *m*; (*of pilot, diver etc*) combinaison *f*. **2** (*lawsuit*) *Jur* procès *m*. **3** *n Cards* couleur *f*. **4** *vt* (*satisfy, be appropri-*

ate to) convenir à; (*of dress, colour etc*) aller (bien) à; (*adapt*) adapter (**to** à); **it suits me to stay** ça m'arrange de rester; **s. yourself!** comme tu voudras!; **suited to** (*made for*) fait pour; (*appropriate to*) approprié à; **well suited** (*couple etc*) bien assorti. ◆**suita'bility** *n* (*of remark etc*) à-propos *m*; (*of person*) aptitudes *fpl* (**for** pour); **I'm not sure of the s. of it** (*date etc*) je ne sais pas si ça convient. ◆**suitable** *a* qui convient (**for** à); (*dress, colour*) qui va (bien); (*example*) approprié; (*socially*) convenable. ◆**suitably** *adv* convenablement.

suitcase ['suːtkeɪs] *n* valise *f*.

suite [swiːt] *n* (*rooms*) suite *f*; (*furniture*) mobilier *m*; **bedroom s.** (*furniture*) chambre *f* à coucher.

suitor ['suːtər] *n* soupirant *m*.

sulfur ['sʌlfər] *n Am* soufre *m*.

sulk [sʌlk] *vi* bouder. ◆**sulky** *a* (**-ier, -iest**) boudeur.

sullen ['sʌlən] *a* maussade. ◆**–ly** *adv* d'un air maussade.

sully ['sʌlɪ] *vt Lit* souiller.

sulphur ['sʌlfər] *n* soufre *m*.

sultan ['sʌltən] *n* sultan *m*.

sultana [sʌl'tɑːnə] *n* raisin *m* de Smyrne.

sultry ['sʌltrɪ] *a* (**-ier, -iest**) (*heat*) étouffant; *Fig* sensuel.

sum [sʌm] **1** *n* (*amount, total*) somme *f*; *Math* calcul *m*; *pl* (*arithmetic*) le calcul; **s. total** résultat *m*. **2** *vt* (**-mm-**) **to s. up** (*facts etc*) récapituler, résumer; (*text*) résumer; (*situation*) évaluer; (*person*) jauger; – *vi* **to s. up** récapituler. ◆**summing-'up** *n* (*pl* **summings-up**) résumé *m*.

summarize ['sʌməraɪz] *vt* résumer. ◆**summary** *n* résumé *m*; – *a* (*brief*) sommaire.

summer ['sʌmər] *n* été *m*; **in (the) s.** en été; **Indian s.** été indien *or* de la Saint-Martin; – *a* d'été; **s. holidays** grandes vacances *fpl*. ◆**summerhouse** *n* pavillon *m* (*de jardin*). ◆**summertime** *n* été *m*; **in (the) s.** en été. ◆**summery** *a* (*weather etc*) estival; (*dress*) d'été.

summit ['sʌmɪt] *n* (*of mountain, power etc*) sommet *m*; **s. conference/meeting** *Pol* conférence *f*/rencontre *f* au sommet.

summon ['sʌmən] *vt* (*call*) appeler; (*meeting, s.o. to meeting*) convoquer (**to** à); **to s. s.o. to do** sommer qn de faire; **to s. up** (*courage, strength*) rassembler.

summons ['sʌmənz] *n Jur* assignation *f*; – *vt Jur* assigner.

sumptuous ['sʌmptʃʊəs] *a* somptueux. ◆**–ness** *n* somptuosité *f*.

sun [sʌn] *n* soleil *m*; **in the s.** au soleil; **the**

sun's shining il fait (du) soleil; – *a* (*cream, filter etc*) solaire; **s. lounge** solarium *m*; – *vt* (*-nn-*) **to s. oneself** se chauffer au soleil. ◆**sunbaked** *a* brûlé par le soleil. ◆**sunbathe** *vi* prendre un bain de soleil. ◆**sunbeam** *n* rayon *m* de soleil. ◆**sunburn** *n* (*tan*) bronzage *m*; *Med* coup *m* de soleil. ◆**sunburnt** *a* bronzé; *Med* brûlé par le soleil. ◆**sundial** *n* cadran *m* solaire. ◆**sundown** *n* coucher *m* du soleil. ◆**sundrenched** *a* brûlé par le soleil. ◆**sunflower** *n* tournesol *m*. ◆**sunglasses** *npl* lunettes *fpl* de soleil. ◆**sunlamp** *n* lampe *f* à rayons ultraviolets. ◆**sunlight** *n* (lumière *f* du) soleil *m*. ◆**sunlit** *a* ensoleillé. ◆**sunrise** *n* lever *m* du soleil. ◆**sunroof** *n* *Aut* toit *m* ouvrant. ◆**sunset** *n* coucher *m* du soleil. ◆**sunshade** *n* (*on table*) parasol *m*; (*portable*) ombrelle *f*. ◆**sunshine** *n* soleil *m*. ◆**sunstroke** *n* insolation *f*. ◆**suntan** *n* bronzage *m*; – *a* (*lotion, oil*) solaire. ◆**suntanned** *a* bronzé. ◆**sunup** *n* *Am* lever *m* du soleil.

sundae ['sʌndeɪ] *n* glace *f* aux fruits.

Sunday ['sʌndɪ] *n* dimanche *m*.

sundry ['sʌndrɪ] *a* divers; **all and s.** tout le monde; – *npl* Com **articles** *mpl* divers.

sung [sʌŋ] *see* **sing**.

sunk [sʌŋk] *see* **sink** ²; – **I'm s.** *Fam* je suis fichu. ◆**sunken** *a* (*rock etc*) submergé; (*eyes*) cave.

sunny ['sʌnɪ] *a* (*-ier, -iest*) ensoleillé; **it's s.** il fait (du) soleil; **s. period** *Met* éclaircie *f*.

super ['suːpər] *a* *Fam* sensationnel.

super- ['suːpər] *pref* super-.

superannuation [suːpərænjuˈeɪʃ(ə)n] *n* (*amount*) cotisations *fpl* (pour la) retraite.

superb [suːˈpɜːb] *a* superbe.

supercilious [suːpəˈsɪlɪəs] *a* hautain.

superficial [suːpəˈfɪʃ(ə)l] *a* superficiel. ◆**-ly** *adv* superficiellement.

superfluous [suːˈpɜːfluəs] *a* superflu.

superhuman [suːpəˈhjuːmən] *a* surhumain.

superimpose [suːpərɪmˈpəuz] *vt* superposer (**on** à).

superintendent [suːpərɪnˈtendənt] *n* directeur, -trice *mf*; (*police*) **s.** commissaire *m* (de police).

superior [suːˈpɪərɪər] *a* supérieur (**to** à); (*goods*) de qualité supérieure; – *n* (*person*) supérieur, -eure *mf*. ◆**superi'ority** *n* supériorité *f*.

superlative [suːˈpɜːlətɪv] *a* sans pareil; – *a* & *n* *Gram* superlatif (*m*).

superman ['suːpəmæn] *n* (*pl* **-men**) surhomme *m*.

supermarket ['suːpəmɑːkɪt] *n* supermarché *m*.

supernatural [suːpəˈnætʃ(ə)rəl] *a* & *n* surnaturel (*m*).

superpower ['suːpəpauər] *n* *Pol* superpuissance *f*.

supersede [suːpəˈsiːd] *vt* remplacer, supplanter.

supersonic [suːpəˈsɒnɪk] *a* supersonique.

superstition [suːpəˈstɪʃ(ə)n] *n* superstition *f*. ◆**superstitious** *a* superstitieux.

supertanker ['suːpətæŋkər] *n* pétrolier *m* géant.

supervise ['suːpəvaɪz] *vt* (*person, work*) surveiller; (*office, research*) diriger. ◆**super'vision** *n* surveillance *f*; direction *f*. ◆**supervisor** *n* surveillant, -ante *mf*; (*in office*) chef *m* de service; (*shop*) chef *m* de rayon. ◆**super'visory** *a* (*post*) de surveillant(e).

supper ['sʌpər] *n* dîner *m*; (*late-night*) souper *m*.

supple ['sʌp(ə)l] *a* souple. ◆**—ness** *n* souplesse *f*.

supplement *n* ['sʌplɪmənt] *n* (*addition*) & *Journ* supplément *m* (**to** à); – ['sʌplɪment] *vt* compléter; **to s. one's income** arrondir ses fins de mois. ◆**supple'mentary** *a* supplémentaire.

supply [səˈplaɪ] *vt* (*provide*) fournir; (*feed*) alimenter (**with** en); (*equip*) équiper, pourvoir (**with** de); **to s. a need** subvenir à un besoin; **to s. s.o. with sth, s. sth to s.o.** (*facts etc*) fournir qch à qn; – *n* (*stock*) provision *f*, réserve *f*; (*equipment*) matériel *m*; **the s. of** (*act*) la fourniture de; **the s. of gas/electricity** to l'alimentation *f* en gaz/électricité de; (*food*) **supplies** vivres *mpl*; (*office*) **supplies** fournitures *fpl* (de bureau); **s. and demand** l'offre *f* et la demande; **to be in short s.** manquer; – *a* (*ship, train*) ravitailleur; **s. teacher** suppléant, -ante *mf*. ◆**-ing** *n* (*provision*) fourniture *f*; (*feeding*) alimentation *f*. ◆**supplier** *n* Com fournisseur *m*.

support [səˈpɔːt] *vt* (*bear weight of*) supporter, supporter; (*help, encourage*) soutenir, appuyer; (*theory, idea*) appuyer; (*be in favour of*) être en faveur de; (*family, wife etc*) assurer la subsistance de; (*endure*) supporter; – *n* (*help, encouragement*) appui *m*, soutien *m*; *Tech* support *m*; **means of s.** moyens *mpl* de subsistance; **in s. of** en faveur de; (*evidence, theory*) à l'appui de. ◆**-ing** *a* (*role*) *Th* Cin secondaire; (*actor*) qui a un rôle secondaire. ◆**supporter** *n* partisan, -ane *mf*; *Fb* supporter *m*. ◆**supportive** *a* to be s. prêter son appui (**of,** to à).

suppos/e [sə'pəʊz] *vti* supposer (**that** que); **I'm supposed to work** *or* **be working** (*ought*) je suis censé travailler; **he's s. to be rich** on le dit riche; **I s. (so)** je pense; **I don't s. so, I s. not** je ne pense pas; **you're tired, I s.** vous êtes fatigué, je suppose; **s.** *or* **supposing we go** (*suggestion*) si nous partions; **s.** *or* **supposing (that) you're right** supposons que tu aies raison. ◆**—ed** *a* soi-disant. ◆**—edly** [-ɪdlɪ] *adv* soi-disant. ◆**supposi'tion** *n* supposition *f*.

suppository [sə'pɒzɪtərɪ] *n Med* suppositoire *m*.

suppress [sə'pres] *vt* (*put an end to*) supprimer; (*feelings*) réprimer; (*scandal, yawn etc*) étouffer. ◆**suppression** *n* suppression *f*; répression *f*. ◆**suppressor** *n El* dispositif *m* antiparasite.

supreme [suː'priːm] *a* suprême. ◆**supremacy** *n* suprématie *f* (**over** sur). **supremo** [suː'priːməʊ] *n* (*pl* **-os**) *Fam* grand chef *m*.

surcharge ['sɜːtʃɑːdʒ] *n* (*extra charge*) supplément *m*; (*on stamp*) surcharge *f*; (*tax*) surtaxe *f*.

sure [ʃʊə] *a* (**-er, -est**) sûr (**of** de, **that** que); **she's s. to accept** il est sûr qu'elle acceptera; **it's s. to snow** il va sûrement neiger; **to make s. of** s'assurer de; **for s.** à coup sûr, pour sûr; **s.!,** *Fam* **s. thing!** bien sûr!; **s. enough** (*in effect*) en effet; **it's s. cold** *Am* il fait vraiment froid; **be s. to do it!** ne manquez pas de le faire! ◆**surefire** *a* infaillible. ◆**surely** *adv* (*certainly*) sûrement; **s. he didn't refuse?** (*I think, I hope*) il n'a tout de même pas refusé.

surety ['ʃʊərətɪ] *n* caution *f*.

surf [sɜːf] *n* (*foam*) ressac *m*. ◆**surfboard** *n* planche *f* (de surf). ◆**surfing** *n Sp* surf *m*.

surface ['sɜːfɪs] *n* surface *f*; **s. area** superficie *f*; **s. mail** courrier *m* par voie(s) de surface; **on the s.** (*to all appearances*) *Fig* en apparence; — *vt* (*road*) revêtir; — *vi* (*of swimmer etc*) remonter à la surface; (*of ideas, person etc*) *Fam* apparaître.

surfeit ['sɜːfɪt] *n* (*excess*) excès *m* (**of** de).

surge [sɜːdʒ] *n* (*of sea, enthusiasm*) vague *f*; (*rise*) montée *f*; — *vi* (*of crowd, hatred*) déferler; (*rise*) monter; **to s. forward** se lancer en avant.

surgeon ['sɜːdʒ(ə)n] *n* chirurgien *m*. ◆**surgery** *n* (*science*) chirurgie *f*; (*doctor's office*) cabinet *m*; (*sitting period*) consultation *f*; **to undergo s.** subir une intervention.

◆**surgical** *a* chirurgical; (*appliance*) orthopédique; **s. spirit** alcool *m* à 90°.

surly ['sɜːlɪ] *a* (**-ier, -iest**) bourru. ◆**surliness** *n* air *m* bourru.

surmise [sə'maɪz] *vt* conjecturer (**that** que).

surmount [sə'maʊnt] *vt* (*overcome, be on top of*) surmonter.

surname ['sɜːneɪm] *n* nom *m* de famille.

surpass [sə'pɑːs] *vt* surpasser (**in** en).

surplus ['sɜːpləs] *n* surplus *m*; — *a* (*goods*) en surplus; **some s. material**/*etc* (*left over*) un surplus de tissu/*etc*; **s. stock** surplus *mpl*.

surpris/e [sə'praɪz] *n* surprise *f*; **to give s.o. a s.** faire une surprise à qn; **to take s.o. by s.** prendre qn au dépourvu; — *a* (*visit, result etc*) inattendu; — *vt* (*astonish*) étonner, surprendre; (*come upon*) surprendre. ◆**—ed** *a* surpris (**that** que (+ *sub*), **at sth** de qch, **at seeing**/*etc* de voir/*etc*); **I'm s. at his** *or* **her stupidity** sa bêtise m'étonne *or* me surprend. ◆**—ing** *a* surprenant. ◆**—ingly** *adv* étonnamment; **s. (enough) he...** chose étonnante, il...

surrealistic [sərɪə'lɪstɪk] *a* (*strange*) *Fig* surréaliste.

surrender [sə'rendər] **1** *vi* (*give oneself up*) se rendre (**to** à); **to s. to** (*police*) se livrer à; — *n Mil* reddition *f*, capitulation *f*. **2** *vt* (*hand over*) remettre, rendre (**to** à); (*right, claim*) renoncer à.

surreptitious [sʌrəp'tɪʃəs] *a* subreptice.

surrogate ['sʌrəgət] *n* substitut *m*; **s. mother** mère *f* porteuse.

surround [sə'raʊnd] *vt* entourer (**with** de); *Mil* encercler; **surrounded by** entouré de. ◆**—ing** *a* environnant. ◆**—ings** *npl* environs *mpl*; (*setting*) cadre *m*.

surveillance [sɜː'veɪləns] *n* (*of prisoner etc*) surveillance *f*.

survey [sə'veɪ] *vt* (*look at*) regarder; (*review*) passer en revue; (*house etc*) inspecter; (*land*) arpenter; — ['sɜːveɪ] *n* (*investigation*) enquête *f*; (*of house etc*) inspection *f*; (*of opinion*) sondage *m*; **a (general) s.** of une vue générale de. ◆**sur'veying** *n* arpentage *m*. ◆**sur'veyor** *n* (arpenteur *m*) géomètre *m*; (*of house etc*) expert *m*.

survive [sə'vaɪv] *vi* (*of person, custom etc*) survivre; — *vt* survivre à. ◆**survival** *n* (*act*) survie *f*; (*relic*) vestige *m*. ◆**survivor** *n* survivant, -ante *mf*.

susceptible [sə'septəb(ə)l] *a* (*sensitive*) sensible (**to** à); **s. to colds**/*etc* (*prone to*) prédisposé aux rhumes/*etc*. ◆**suscepti'bility** *n* sensibilité *f*; prédisposition *f*; *pl* susceptibilité *f*.

suspect ['sʌspekt] n & a suspect, -ecte (mf); – [sə'spekt] vt soupçonner (**that** que, of sth de qch, **of doing** d'avoir fait); (think questionable) suspecter, douter de; **yes, I s.** oui, j'imagine.

suspend [sə'spend] vt 1 (hang) suspendre (**from** à). 2 (stop, postpone, dismiss) suspendre; (passport etc) retirer (provisoirement); (pupil) Sch renvoyer; **suspended sentence** Jur condamnation f avec sursis. ◆**suspender** n (for stocking) jarretelle f; pl (braces) Am bretelles fpl; **s. belt** porte-jarretelles m inv. ◆**suspension** n 1 (stopping) suspension f; (of passport etc) retrait m (provisoire). 2 (of vehicle etc) suspension f; **s. bridge** pont m suspendu.

suspense [sə'spens] n attente f (angoissée); (in film, book etc) suspense m; **in s.** (person, matter) en suspens.

suspicion [sə'spiʃ(ə)n] n soupçon m; **to arouse s.** éveiller les soupçons; **with s.** (distrust) avec méfiance; **under s.** considéré comme suspect. ◆**suspicious** a (person) soupçonneux, méfiant; (behaviour) suspect; **s.(-looking)** (suspect) suspect; **to be s. of** or **about** (distrust) se méfier de. ◆**suspiciously** adv (to behave etc) d'une manière suspecte; (to consider etc) avec méfiance.

sustain [sə'stein] vt (effort, theory) soutenir; (weight) supporter; (with food) nourrir; (life) maintenir; (damage, attack) subir; (injury) recevoir. ◆**sustenance** n (food) nourriture f; (quality) valeur f nutritive.

swab [swɔb] n (pad) Med tampon m; (specimen) Med prélèvement m.

swagger ['swægər] vi (walk) parader; – n démarche f fanfaronne.

swallow 1 ['swɔləʊ] 1 vt avaler; **to s. down** or **up** avaler; **to s. up** Fig engloutir; – vi avaler. 2 n (bird) hirondelle f.

swam [swæm] see **swim**.

swamp [swɔmp] n marais m, marécage m; – vt (flood, overwhelm) submerger (**with** de). ◆**swampy** a (-ier, -iest) marécageux.

swan [swɔn] n cygne m.

swank [swæŋk] vi (show off) Fam crâner, fanfaronner.

swap [swɔp] n échange m; pl (stamps etc) doubles mpl; – vt (-pp-) échanger (**for** contre); **to s. seats** changer de place; – vi échanger.

swarm [swɔːm] n (of bees, people etc) essaim m; – vi (of streets, insects, people etc) fourmiller (**with** de); **to s. in** (of people) entrer en foule.

swarthy ['swɔːði] a (-ier, -iest) (dark) basané.

swastika ['swɒstɪkə] n (Nazi emblem) croix f gammée.

swat [swɔt] vt (-tt-) (fly etc) écraser.

sway [swei] vi se balancer, osciller; – vt balancer; Fig influencer; – n balancement m; Fig influence f.

swear [swɛər] vt (pt swore, pp sworn) jurer (**to do** faire, **that** que); **to s. an oath** prêter serment; **to s. s.o. to secrecy** faire jurer le silence à qn; **sworn enemies** ennemis mpl jurés; – vi (take an oath) jurer (**to sth** of qch); (curse) jurer, pester (**at** contre); **she swears by this lotion** elle ne jure que par cette lotion. ◆**swearword** n gros mot m, juron m.

sweat [swet] n sueur f; **s. shirt** sweat-shirt m; – vi (of person, wall etc) suer (**with** de); – vt **to s. out** (cold) Med se débarrasser de (en transpirant). ◆**sweater** n (garment) pull m. ◆**sweaty** a (-ier, -iest) (shirt etc) plein de sueur; (hand) moite; (person) (tout) en sueur, (tout) en nage.

swede [swiːd] n (vegetable) rutabaga m.

Swede [swiːd] n Suédois, -oise mf. ◆**Sweden** n Suède f. ◆**Swedish** a suédois; – n (language) suédois m.

sweep [swiːp] n coup m de balai; (movement) Fig (large) mouvement m; (curve) courbe f; **to make a clean s.** (removal) faire table rase (**of** de); (victory) remporter une victoire totale; – vt (pt & pp swept) (with broom) balayer; (chimney) ramoner; (river) draguer; **to s. away** or **out** or **up** balayer; **to s. away** or **along** (carry off) emporter; **to s. aside** (dismiss) écarter; – vi **to s. (up)** balayer; **to s. in** (of person) Fig entrer rapidement or majestueusement; **to s. through** (of fear etc) saisir (groupe etc); (of disease etc) ravager (pays etc). ◆**-ing** a (gesture) large; (change) radical; (statement) trop général. ◆**sweepstake** n (lottery) sweepstake m.

sweet [swiːt] a (-er, -est) (not sour) doux; (agreeable) agréable, doux; (tea, coffee etc) sucré; (person, house, kitchen) mignon, gentil; **to have a s. tooth** aimer les sucreries; **to be s.-smelling** sentir bon; **s. corn** maïs m; **s. pea** Bot pois m de senteur; **s. potato** patate f douce; **s. shop** confiserie f; **s. talk** Fam cajoleries fpl, douceurs fpl; – n (candy) bonbon m; (dessert) dessert m; **my s.!** (darling) mon ange! ◆**sweeten** vt (tea etc) sucrer; Fig adoucir. ◆**sweetener** n saccharine f. ◆**sweetie** n (darling) Fam chéri, -ie mf. ◆**sweetly** adv (kindly) genti-

ment; (softly) doucement. ◆**sweetness** n
douceur f; (taste) goût m sucré.

sweetbread ['swiːtbred] n ris m de veau or
d'agneau.

sweetheart ['swiːthɑːt] n (lover) ami, -ie mf;
my s.! (darling) mon ange!

swell [swel] **1** n (of sea) houle f. **2** a (very
good) Am Fam formidable. **3** vi (pt swelled,
pp swollen or swelled) se gonfler; (of river,
numbers) grossir; to s. (up) Med enfler,
gonfler; – vt (river, numbers) grossir.
◆**-ing** n Med enflure f.

swelter ['sweltər] vi étouffer. ◆**-ing** a
étouffant; it's s. on étouffe.

swept [swept] see **sweep**.

swerve [swɜːv] vi (while running etc) faire un
écart; (of vehicle) faire une embardée.

swift [swɪft] **1** a (-er, -est) rapide; s. to act
prompt à agir. **2** n (bird) martinet m.
◆**-ly** adv rapidement. ◆**-ness** n rapidité f.

swig [swɪg] n (of beer etc) lampée f.

swill [swɪl] vt to s. (out or down) laver (à
grande eau).

swim [swɪm] n baignade f; to go for a s. se
baigner, nager; – vi (pt swam, pp swum,
pres p swimming) nager; Sp faire de la natation; (of head, room) Fig tourner; to go
swimming aller nager; to s. away se sauver
(à la nage); – vt (river) traverser à la nage;
(length, crawl etc) nager. ◆**swimming** n
natation f; s. costume maillot m de bain; s.
pool, s. baths piscine f; s. trunks slip m or
caleçon m de bain. ◆**swimmer** n nageur,
-euse mf. ◆**swimsuit** n maillot m de bain.

swindl/e ['swɪnd(ə)l] n escroquerie f; – vt
escroquer; to s. s.o. out of money escroquer
de l'argent à qn. ◆**-er** n escroc m.

swine [swaɪn] n inv (person) Pej salaud m.

swing [swɪŋ] n (seat) balançoire f; (movement) balancement m; (of pendulum) oscillation f; (in opinion) revirement m;
(rhythm) rythme m; to be in full s. battre
son plein; to be in the s. of things Fam être
dans le bain; s. door porte f de salon; – vi
(pt & pp swung) (sway) se balancer; (of
pendulum) osciller; (turn) virer; to s. round
(turn suddenly) virer, tourner; (of person) se
retourner (vivement); (of vehicle in collision
etc) faire un tête-à-queue; to s. into action
passer à l'action; – vt (arms etc) balancer;
(axe) brandir; (influence) Fam influencer;
to s. round (car etc) faire tourner. ◆**-ing** a
Fam (trendy) dans le vent; (lively) plein de
vie; (music) entraînant.

swingeing ['swɪndʒɪŋ] a s. cuts des réduc-
tions fpl draconiennes.

swipe [swaɪp] vt Fam (hit) frapper dur;
(steal) piquer (from s.o. à qn); – n Fam
grand coup m.

swirl [swɜːl] n tourbillon m; – vi tourbillonner.

swish [swɪʃ] **1** a (posh) rupin, chic. **2** vi
(of whip etc) siffler; (of fabric) froufrouter;
– n sifflement m; froufrou m.

Swiss [swɪs] a suisse; – n inv Suisse m, Suis-
sesse f; the S. les Suisses mpl.

switch [swɪtʃ] n El bouton m (électrique),
interrupteur m; (change) changement m (in
de); (reversal) revirement m (in de); to s.
(money, employee etc) transférer (to à);
(affection, support) reporter (to sur, from
de); (exchange) échanger (for contre); to s.
buses/etc changer de bus/etc; to s. places
or seats changer de place; to s. off (lamp,
gas, radio etc) éteindre; (engine) arrêter; to
s. itself off (of heating etc) s'éteindre tout
seul; to s. on (lamp, gas, radio etc) mettre,
allumer; (engine) mettre en marche; – vi to
s. (over) to passer à; to s. off (switch off
light, radio etc) éteindre; to s. on (switch on
light, radio etc) allumer. ◆**switchback** n
(at funfair) montagnes fpl russes.
◆**switchblade** n Am couteau m à cran
d'arrêt. ◆**switchboard** n Tel standard m;
s. operator standardiste mf.

Switzerland ['swɪtsələnd] n Suisse f.

swivel ['swɪv(ə)l] vi (-ll-, Am -l-) to s. (round)
(of chair etc) pivoter; – a s. chair fauteuil m
pivotant.

swollen ['swəʊl(ə)n] see **swell** **3**; – a (leg etc)
enflé.

swoon [swuːn] vi Lit se pâmer.

swoop [swuːp] **1** vi to s. (down) on (of bird)
fondre sur. **2** n (of police) descente f; – vi
faire une descente (on dans).

swop [swɒp] n, vt & vi = **swap**.

sword [sɔːd] n épée f. ◆**swordfish** n
espadon m.

swore, sworn [swɔːr, swɔːn] see **swear**.

swot [swɒt] vti (-tt-) to s. (up) (study) Fam
potasser; to s. (up) for (exam), to s. up on
(subject) Fam potasser; – n Pej Fam
bûcheur, -euse mf.

swum [swʌm] see **swim**.

swung [swʌŋ] see **swing**.

sycamore ['sɪkəmɔːr] n (maple) sycomore
m; (plane) Am platane m.

sycophant ['sɪkəfænt] n flagorneur, -euse
mf.

syllable ['sɪləb(ə)l] n syllabe f.

syllabus ['sɪləbəs] n Sch Univ programme
m.

symbol ['sɪmb(ə)l] n symbole m. ◆**sym-**

'bolic a symbolique. ◆symbolism n symbolisme m. ◆symbolize vt symboliser.

symmetry ['sɪmɪtrɪ] n symétrie f. ◆sy'mmetrical a symétrique.

sympathy ['sɪmpəθɪ] n (pity) compassion f; (understanding) compréhension f; (condolences) condoléances fpl; (solidarity) solidarité f (for avec); to be in s. with (workers in dispute) être du côté de; (s.o.'s opinion etc) comprendre, être en accord avec. ◆sympa'thetic a (showing pity) compatissant; (understanding) compréhensif; s. to (favourable) bien disposé à l'égard de. ◆sympa'thetically adv avec compassion; avec compréhension. ◆sympathize vi I s. (with you) (pity) je compatis (à votre sort); (understanding) je vous comprends. ◆sympathizer n Pol sympathisant, -ante mf.

symphony ['sɪmfənɪ] n symphonie f; – a (orchestra, concert) symphonique. ◆sym'phonic a symphonique.

symposium [sɪm'pəʊzɪəm] n symposium m.

symptom ['sɪmptəm] n symptôme m. ◆sympto'matic a symptomatique (of de).

synagogue ['sɪnəgɒg] n synagogue f.

synchronize ['sɪŋkrənaɪz] vt synchroniser.

syndicate ['sɪndɪkət] n (of businessmen, criminals) syndicat m.

syndrome ['sɪndrəʊm] n Med & Fig syndrome m.

synod ['sɪnəd] n Rel synode m.

synonym ['sɪnənɪm] n synonyme m. ◆sy'nonymous a synonyme (with de).

synopsis, pl -opses [sɪ'nɒpsɪs, -ɒpsiːz] n résumé m, synopsis m; (of film) synopsis m.

syntax ['sɪntæks] n Gram syntaxe f.

synthesis, pl -theses ['sɪnθəsɪs, -θəsiːz] n synthèse f.

synthetic [sɪn'θetɪk] a synthétique.

syphilis ['sɪfɪlɪs] n syphilis f.

Syria ['sɪrɪə] n Syrie f. ◆Syrian a & n syrien, -ienne (mf).

syringe [sɪ'rɪndʒ] n seringue f.

syrup ['sɪrəp] n sirop m; (golden) s. (treacle) mélasse f (raffinée). ◆syrupy a sirupeux.

system ['sɪstəm] n (structure, plan, network etc) & Anat système m; (human body) organisme m; (order) méthode f; systems analyst analyste-programmeur mf. ◆syste'matic a systématique. ◆syste'matically adv systématiquement.

T

T, t [tiː] n T, t m. ◆T-junction n Aut intersection f en T. ◆T-shirt n tee-shirt m, T-shirt m.

ta! [tɑː] int Sl merci!

tab [tæb] n (label) étiquette f; (tongue) patte f; (loop) attache f; (bill) Am addition f; to keep tabs on Fam surveiller (de près).

tabby ['tæbɪ] a t. cat chat, chatte mf tigré(e).

table¹ ['teɪb(ə)l] n 1 (furniture) table f; bedside/card/operating t. table de nuit/de jeu/d'opération; to lay or set/clear the t. mettre/débarrasser la table; (sitting) at the t. à table; t. top dessus m de table. 2 (list) table f; t. of contents table des matières. ◆tablecloth n nappe f. ◆tablemat n (of fabric) napperon m; (hard) dessous-de-plat m inv. ◆tablespoon n = cuiller f à soupe. ◆tablespoonful n = cuillerée f à soupe.

table² ['teɪb(ə)l] vt (motion etc) Pol présenter; (postpone) Am ajourner.

tablet ['tæblɪt] n 1 (pill) Med comprimé m. 2 (inscribed stone) plaque f.

tabloid ['tæblɔɪd] n (newspaper) quotidien m populaire.

taboo [tə'buː] a & n tabou (m).

tabulator ['tæbjʊleɪtər] n (of typewriter) tabulateur m.

tacit ['tæsɪt] a tacite. ◆—ly adv tacitement.

taciturn ['tæsɪtɜːn] a taciturne.

tack [tæk] 1 n (nail) semence f; (thumbtack) Am punaise f; to get down to brass tacks Fig en venir aux faits; – vt to t. (down) clouer. 2 n (stitch) Tex point m de bâti; – vt to t. (down or on) bâtir; to t. on (add) Fig (r)ajouter. 3 vi (of ship) louvoyer; – n (course of action) Fig voie f.

tackle ['tæk(ə)l] 1 n (gear) matériel m, équipement m. 2 vt (task, problem etc) s'attaquer à; (thief etc) saisir; Sp plaquer; – n Sp plaquage m.

tacky ['tækɪ] a (-ier, -iest) 1 (wet, sticky) collant, pas sec. 2 (clothes, attitude etc) Am Fam moche.

tact [tækt] n tact m. ◆tactful a (remark etc) plein de tact, diplomatique; she's t. elle a du tact. ◆**tactfully** adv avec tact. ◆**tactless** a qui manque de tact. ◆**tactlessly** adv sans tact.

tactic ['tæktik] n a t. une tactique; **tactics** la tactique. ◆**tactical** a tactique.

tactile ['tæktail] a tactile.

tadpole ['tædpəʊl] n têtard m.

taffy ['tæfi] n (toffee) Am caramel m (dur).

tag [tæg] **1** n (label) étiquette f; (end piece) bout m; – vt (-gg-) to t. on (add) Fam rajouter (to à). **2** vi (-gg-) to t. along (follow) suivre.

Tahiti [tɑːˈhiːti] n Tahiti m.

tail [teil] **1** n (of animal) queue f; (of shirt) pan m; pl (outfit) habit m, queue-de-pie f; t. end fin f, bout m; **heads or tails?** pile ou face? **2** vt (follow) suivre, filer. **3** vi to t. off (lessen) diminuer. ◆**tailback** n (of traffic) bouchon m. ◆**tailcoat** n queue-de-pie f. ◆**taillight** n Aut Am feu m arrière m.

tailor ['teilər] n (person) tailleur m; – vt (garment) façonner; Fig adapter (to, to suit à). ◆**t.-'made** a fait sur mesure; **t.-made for** (specially designed) conçu pour; (suited) fait pour.

tainted ['teintid] a (air) pollué; (food) gâté; Fig souillé.

take [teik] vt (pt took, pp taken) prendre; (choice) faire; (prize) remporter; (exam) passer; (contain) contenir; Math soustraire (from de); (tolerate) supporter; (bring) apporter (qch to à), (person) amener (to à), (person by car) conduire (to à); (escort) accompagner (to à); (lead away) emmener; (of road) mener (qn); to t. sth to s.o. (ap)porter qch à qn; to t. s.o. (out) to (theatre etc) emmener qn à; to t. sth with one — emporter qch; to t. over or round or along (object) apporter; (person) amener; to t. s.o. home (on foot, by car etc) ramener qn; it takes an army/courage/etc (requires) il faut une armée/du courage/etc (to do pour faire); I took an hour to do it or over it j'ai mis une heure à le faire, ça m'a pris une heure pour le faire; I t. it that je présume que; – n Cin prise f de vue(s); – vi (of fire) prendre. ■ to t. after vt (be like) ressembler à; to t. apart vt (machine) démonter; to t. away vt (thing) emporter; (person) emmener; (remove) enlever (from à); Math soustraire (from de). ◆**t.-away** a (meal) à emporter; – n café m or restaurant m qui fait des plats à emporter; (meal) plat m à emporter; to t. back vt reprendre; (return) rapporter; (statement) retirer; to t. down vt (object) descendre; (notes) prendre; to t. in vt (chair, car etc) rentrer; (orphan) recueil-

lir; (skirt) reprendre; (include) englober; (distance) couvrir; (understand) comprendre; (deceive) Fam rouler; to t. off vt (remove) enlever; (train, bus) supprimer; (lead away) emmener; (mimic) imiter; Math déduire (from de); – vi (of aircraft) décoller. ◆**takeoff** n (of aircraft) décollage m; to t. on vt (work, employee, passenger, shape) prendre; to t. out vt (from pocket etc) sortir; (stain) enlever; (tooth) arracher; (licence, insurance) prendre; to t. it out on Fam passer sa colère sur. ◆**t.-out** a & n Am = t.-away; to t. over vt (be responsible for the running of) prendre la direction de; (overrun) envahir; (buy out) Com racheter (compagnie); to t. over s.o.'s job remplacer qn; – vi Mil Pol prendre le pouvoir; (relieve) prendre la relève (from de); (succeed) prendre la succession (from de). ◆**t.-over** n Com rachat m; Fin prise f de pouvoir; to t. round vt (distribute) distribuer; (visitor) faire visiter; to t. to vt to t. to doing se mettre à faire; I didn't t. to him/it il/ça ne m'a pas plu; to t. up vt (carry up) monter; (hem) raccourcir; (continue) reprendre; (occupy) prendre; (hobby) se mettre à; – vi to t. up with se lier avec. ◆**taken** a (seat) pris; (impressed) impressionné (with, by par); to be t. ill tomber malade. ◆**taking** n (capture) Mil prise f; pl (money) Com recette f.

talcum ['tælkəm] a t. powder talc m.

tale [teil] n (story) conte m; (account, report) récit m; (lie) histoire f; **to tell tales** rapporter (on sur).

talent ['tælənt] n talent m; (talented people) talents mpl; **to have a t. for** avoir du talent pour. ◆**talented** a doué, talentueux.

talk [tɔːk] n (words) propos mpl; (gossip) bavardage(s) m(pl); (conversation) conversation f (about à propos de); (interview) entretien m; (lecture) exposé m (on sur); (informal) causerie f (on sur); pl (negotiations) pourparlers mpl; **to have a t.** with parler avec; **there's t.** of on parle de; – vi parler (to à; with avec; about, of de); (chat) bavarder; to t. down to s.o. parler à qn comme à un inférieur; – vt (nonsense) dire; to t. politics parler politique; to t. s.o. into doing/out of doing persuader qn de faire/de ne pas faire; to t. over discuter (de); to t. round persuader qn. ◆**-ing** a (film) parlant; **to give s.o. a talking-to** Fam passer un savon à qn. ◆**talker** n causeur m, -euse mf; **she's a good t.** elle parle bien.

tall [tɔːl] a (-er, -est) (person) grand; (tree,

house etc) haut; **how t. are you?** combien mesures-tu?; **a t. story** *Fig* une histoire invraisemblable *or* à dormir debout. ◆**tallboy** *n* grande commode *f.* ◆**tallness** *n* (*of person*) grande taille *f*; (*of building etc*) hauteur *f.*

tally ['tælɪ] *vi* correspondre (**with** à).

tambourine [tæmbə'riːn] *n* tambourin *m.*

tame [teɪm] *a* (**-er, -est**) (*animal, bird*) apprivoisé; (*person*) *Fig* docile; (*book, play*) fade. – *vt* (*animal, bird*) apprivoiser; (*lion, passion*) dompter.

tamper ['tæmpər] *vi* **to t. with** (*lock, car etc*) toucher à; (*text*) altérer.

tampon ['tæmpɒn] *n* tampon *m* hygiénique.

tan [tæn] **1** *n* (*suntan*) bronzage *m*; – *vti* (**-nn-**) bronzer. **2** *a* (*colour*) marron clair *inv.* **3** *vt* (**-nn-**) (*hide*) tanner.

tandem ['tændəm] *n* **1** (*bicycle*) tandem *m.* **2 in t.** (*to work etc*) en tandem.

tang [tæŋ] *n* (*taste*) saveur *f* piquante; (*smell*) odeur *f* piquante. ◆**tangy** *a* (**-ier, -iest**) piquant.

tangerine [tændʒə'riːn] *n* mandarine *f.*

tangible ['tændʒəb(ə)l] *a* tangible.

tangl/e ['tæŋg(ə)l] *n* enchevêtrement *m*; **to get into a t.** (*of rope*) s'enchevêtrer; (*of hair*) s'emmêler; (*of person*) *Fig* se mettre dans une situation pas possible. ◆**—ed** *a* enchevêtré; (*hair*) emmêlé; **to get t.** = **to get into a tangle.**

tank [tæŋk] *n* **1** (*for storage of water, fuel etc*) réservoir *m*; (*vat*) cuve *f*; (*fish*) aquarium *m.* **2** (*vehicle*) *Mil* char *m*, tank *m.*

tankard ['tæŋkəd] *n* (*beer mug*) chope *f.*

tanker ['tæŋkər] *n* (*truck*) *Aut* camion-citerne *m*; (*oil*) t. (*ship*) pétrolier *m.*

tantalizing ['tæntəlaɪzɪŋ] *a* (*irrésistiblement*) tentant. ◆**—ly** *adv* d'une manière tentante.

tantamount ['tæntəmaʊnt] *a* **it's t. to** cela équivaut à.

tantrum ['tæntrəm] *n* accès *m* de colère.

tap [tæp] **1** *n* (*for water*) robinet *m*; **on t.** *Fig* disponible. **2** *vti* (**-pp-**) frapper légèrement, tapoter; – *n* petit coup *m*; **t. dancing** claquettes *fpl.* **3** *vt* (**-pp-**) (*phone*) placer sur table d'écoute. **4** *vt* (**-pp-**) (*resources*) exploiter.

tape [teɪp] **1** *n* ruban *m*; (*sticky*) **t.** ruban adhésif; **t. measure** mètre *m* à ruban; – *vt* (*stick*) coller (*avec du ruban adhésif*). **2** *n* (*for sound recording*) bande *f* (magnétique); (*video*) **t.** bande (*f*); **t. recorder** magnétophone *m*; – *vt* enregistrer.

taper ['teɪpər] **1** *vi* (*of fingers etc*) s'effiler; **to t. off** *Fig* diminuer. **2** *n* (*candle*) *Rel* cierge

m. ◆**—ed** *a*, ◆**—ing** *a* (*fingers*) fuselé; (*trousers*) à bas étroits.

tapestry ['tæpɪstrɪ] *n* tapisserie *f.*

tapioca [tæpɪ'əʊkə] *n* tapioca *m.*

tar [tɑːr] *n* goudron *m*; – *vt* (**-rr-**) goudronner.

tardy ['tɑːdɪ] *a* (**-ier, -iest**) (*belated*) tardif; (*slow*) lent.

target ['tɑːgɪt] *n* cible *f*, *Fig* objectif *m*; **t. date** date *f* fixée; – *vt* (*aim*) *Fig* destiner (**at** à); (*aim at*) *Fig* viser.

tariff ['tærɪf] *n* (*tax*) tarif *m* douanier; (*prices*) tarif *m.*

tarmac ['tɑːmæk] *n* macadam *m* (*goudronné*); (*runway*) piste *f.*

tarnish ['tɑːnɪʃ] *vt* ternir.

tarpaulin [tɑː'pɔːlɪn] *n* bâche *f* (goudronnée).

tarragon ['tærəgən] *n Bot Culin* estragon *m.*

tarry ['tærɪ] *vi* (*remain*) *Lit* rester.

tart [tɑːt] **1** *n* (*pie*) tarte *f.* **2** *a* (**-er, -est**) (*taste, remark*) aigre. **3** *n* (*prostitute*) *Pej Fam* poule *f.* **4** *vt* **to t. up** *Pej Fam* (*decorate*) embellir; (*dress*) attifer. ◆**—ness** *n* aigreur *f.*

tartan ['tɑːt(ə)n] *n* tartan *m*; – *a* écossais.

tartar ['tɑːtər] *n* **1** (*on teeth*) tartre *m.* **2 a t. sauce** sauce *f* tartare.

task [tɑːsk] *n* tâche *f*; **to take to t.** prendre à partie; **t. force** *Mil* détachement *m* spécial; *Pol* commission *f* spéciale.

tassel ['tæs(ə)l] *n* (*on clothes etc*) gland *m.*

taste [teɪst] *n* goût *m*; **to get a t. for** prendre goût à; **in good/bad t.** de bon/mauvais goût; **to have a t. of** goûter; goûter à; goûter de; – *vt* (*eat, enjoy*) goûter; (*try, sample*) goûter à; (*make out the taste of*) sentir (le goût de); (*experience*) goûter de; – *vi* **to t. of** *or* **like** avoir un goût de; **to t. delicious/etc** avoir un goût délicieux/*etc*; **how does it t.?** comment le trouves-tu?; – **a t. bud** papille *f* gustative. ◆**tasteful** *a* de bon goût. ◆**tastefully** *adv* avec goût. ◆**tasteless** *a* (*food etc*) sans goût; (*joke etc*) *Fig* de mauvais goût. ◆**tasty** *a* (**-ier, -iest**) savoureux.

tat [tæt] *see* **tit.**

ta-ta! [tæ'tɑː] *int Sl* au revoir!

tattered ['tætəd] *a* (*clothes*) en lambeaux; (*person*) déguenillé. ◆**tatters** *npl* **in t.** en lambeaux.

tattoo [tæ'tuː] *n* **1** (*pl* **-oos**) (*on body*) tatouage *m*; – *vt* tatouer. **2** *n* (*pl* **-oos**) *Mil* spectacle *m* militaire.

tatty ['tætɪ] *a* (**-ier, -iest**) (*clothes etc*) *Fam* miteux.

taught [tɔːt] *see* **teach.**

taunt [tɔːnt] *vt* railler; – *n* raillerie *f*.
◆**-ing.** *a* railleur.

Taurus ['tɔːrəs] *n* (*sign*) le Taureau.

taut [tɔːt] *a* (*rope, person etc*) tendu.

tavern ['tævən] *n* taverne *f*.

tawdry ['tɔːdrɪ] *a* (-**ier, -iest**) *Pej* tape-à-l'œil *inv*.

tawny ['tɔːnɪ] *a* (*colour*) fauve; (*port*) ambré.

tax¹ [tæks] *n* taxe *f*, impôt *m*; (*income*) t. impôts *mpl* (sur le revenu); – *a* fiscal; **t. collector** percepteur *m*; **t. relief** dégrèvement *m* (d'impôt); – *vt* (*person, goods*) imposer. ◆**taxable** *a* imposable. ◆**tax- 'ation** *n* (*act*) imposition *f*; (*taxes*) impôts *mpl*. ◆**tax-free** *a* exempt d'impôts. ◆**taxman** *n* (*pl* -**men**) *Fam* percepteur *m*. ◆**taxpayer** *n* contribuable *mf*.

tax² [tæks] *vt* (*patience etc*) mettre à l'épreuve; (*tire*) fatiguer. ◆**-ing** *a* (*journey etc*) éprouvant.

taxi ['tæksɪ] **1** *n* taxi *m*; **t. cab** taxi *m*; **t. rank,** *Am* **t. stand** station *f* de taxis. **2** *vi* (*of aircraft*) rouler au sol.

tea [tiː] *n* thé *m*; (*snack*) goûter *m*; **high t.** goûter *m* (dînatoire); **to have t.** prendre le thé; (*afternoon snack*) goûter; **t. break** pause-thé *f*; **t. chest** caisse *f* (à thé); **t. cloth** (*for drying dishes*) torchon *m*; **t. set** service *m* à thé; **t. towel** torchon *m*. ◆**teabag** *n* sachet *m* de thé. ◆**teacup** *n* tasse *f* à thé. ◆**tealeaf** *n* (*pl* -**leaves**) feuille *f* de thé. ◆**teapot** *n* théière *f*. ◆**tearoom** *n* salon *m* de thé. ◆**teaspoon** *n* petite cuiller *f*. ◆**teaspoonful** *n* cuillerée *f* à café. ◆**tea- time** *n* l'heure *f* du thé.

teach [tiːtʃ] *vt* (*pt & pp* **taught**) apprendre (s.o. sth qch à qn, that que); (*in school etc*) enseigner (s.o. sth qch à qn); **to t. s.o. (how) to do** apprendre à qn à faire; **t. to school** *Am* enseigner; **to t. oneself sth** apprendre qch tout seul; – *vi* enseigner. ◆**-ing** *n* enseignement *m*; – *a* (*staff*) enseignant; (*method, material*) pédagogique; **t. profes- sion** enseignement *m*; (*teachers*) enseignants *mpl*; **t. qualification** diplôme *m* permettant d'enseigner. ◆**-er** *n* profes- seur *m*; (*in primary school*) instituteur, -trice *mf*.

teak [tiːk] *n* (*wood*) teck *m*.

team [tiːm] *n Sp* équipe *f*; (*of oxen*) attelage *m*; **t. mate** coéquipier, -ière *mf*; – *vi* **to t. up** faire équipe (**with** avec). ◆**teamster** *n Am* routier *m*. ◆**teamwork** *n* collaboration *f*.

tear¹ [teə] *n* 1 *n* déchirure *f*; – *vt* (*pt* **tore**, *pp* **torn**) (*rip*) déchirer; (*snatch*) arracher (**from** s.o. à qn); **torn between** *Fig* tiraillé entre; **to t. down** (*house etc*) démolir; **to t. away or off**

or **out** (*forcefully*) arracher; (*stub, receipt, stamp etc*) détacher; **to t. up** déchirer; – *vi* (*of cloth etc*) se déchirer. **2** *vi* (*pt* **tore**, *pp* **torn**) (*rush*) aller à toute vitesse; **to t. along** (*of vehicle etc*) foncer.

tear² [tɪər] *n* larme *f*; **in tears** en larmes; **close to** or **near (to) tears** au bord des larmes. ◆**tearful** *a* (*eyes, voice*) lar- moyant; (*person*) en larmes. ◆**tearfully** *adv* en pleurant. ◆**teargas** *n* gaz *m* lacry- mogène.

tearaway ['teərəweɪ] *n Fam* petit voyou *m*.

teas/e [tiːz] *vt* taquiner; (*harshly*) tour- menter; – *n* (*person*) taquin, -ine *mf*. ◆**-ing** *a* (*remark etc*) taquin. ◆**-er** *n* **1** (*person*) taquin, -ine *mf*. **2** (*question*) *Fam* colle *f*.

teat [tiːt] *n* (*of bottle, animal*) tétine *f*.

technical ['teknɪk(ə)l] *a* technique. ◆**techni'cality** *n* (*detail*) détail *m* tech- nique. ◆**technically** *adv* techniquement; *Fig* théoriquement. ◆**tech'nician** *n* technicien, -ienne *mf*. ◆**tech'nique** *n* technique *f*. ◆**technocrat** *n* technocrate *m*. ◆**techno'logical** *a* technologique. ◆**tech'nology** *n* technologie *f*.

teddy ['tedɪ] *n* **t. (bear)** ours *m* (en peluche).

tedious ['tiːdɪəs] *a* fastidieux. ◆**tedious- ness** *n*. ◆**tedium** *n* ennui *m*.

teem [tiːm] *vi* **1** (*swarm*) grouiller (**with** de). **2 to t. (with rain)** pleuvoir à torrents. ◆**-ing** *a* **1** (*crowd, street etc*) grouillant. **2** **t. rain** pluie *f* torrentielle.

teenage ['tiːneɪdʒ] *a* (*person, behaviour*) adolescent; (*fashion*) pour adolescents. ◆**teenager** *n* adolescent, -ente *mf*. ◆**teens** *npl* **in one's t.** adolescent.

teeny (weeny) ['tiːnɪ(wiːnɪ)] *a* (*tiny*) *Fam* minuscule.

tee-shirt ['tiːʃɜːt] *n* tee-shirt *m*.

teeter ['tiːtər] *vi* chanceler.

teeth [tiːθ] *see* **tooth**. ◆**teeth/e** [tiːð] *vi* faire ses dents. ◆**-ing** *n* dentition *f*; **t. ring** anneau *m* de dentition; **t. troubles** *fpl* difficultés *fpl* de mise en route.

teetotal [tiː'təʊt(ə)l] *a*. ◆**teetotaller** *n* (*personne f*) qui ne boit pas d'alcool.

tele- ['telɪ] *pref* télé-.

telecommunications [telɪkəmjuːnɪ'keɪ- ʃ(ə)nz] *npl* télécommunications *fpl*.

telegram ['telɪgræm] *n* télégramme *m*.

telegraph ['telɪgrɑːf] *n* télégraphe *m*; – *a* (*wire etc*) télégraphique; **t. pole** poteau *m* télégraphique.

telepathy [tɪ'lepəθɪ] *n* télépathie *f*.

telephone ['telɪfəʊn] *n* téléphone *m*; **on the t.** (*speaking*) au téléphone; – *a* (*call, line etc*) téléphonique; (*directory*) du téléphone; (number) de téléphone; t. booth, t. box cabine f téléphonique; – vi téléphoner; – vt (message) téléphoner (to s.o.); to t. s.o. téléphoner à qn. ◆te'lephonist n téléphoniste mf.

teleprinter ['teliprintər] n télescripteur m.

telescope ['teliskəup] n télescope m. ◆tele'scopic a (pictures, aerial, umbrella) télescopique.

teletypewriter [teli'taipraitər] n Am télescripteur m.

televise ['telivaiz] vt téléviser. ◆television n télévision f; on (the) t. à la télévision; to watch (the) t. regarder la télévision; – a (programme etc) de télévision; (serial, report) télévisé.

telex ['teleks] n (service, message) télex m; – vt envoyer par télex.

tell [tel] vt (pt & pp told) dire (s.o. sth qch à qn, that que); (story) raconter; (future) prédire; (distinguish) distinguer (from de); (know) savoir; to s.o. to do dire à qn de faire; to know how to t. the time savoir lire l'heure; to t. the difference voir la différence (between entre); to t. off (scold) Fam gronder; – vi dire; (have an effect) avoir un effet; (know) savoir; to t. of or about sth parler de qch; to t. on s.o. Fam rapporter sur qn. ◆—ing a (smile, blow) révélateur; (blow) efficace. ◆telltale n Fam rapporteur, -euse mf.

teller ['telər] n (bank) t. caissier, -ière mf.

telly ['teli] n Fam télé f.

temerity [tə'meriti] n témérité f.

temp [temp] n (secretary etc) Fam intérimaire mf.

temper ['tempər] n 1 (mood, nature) humeur f; (anger) colère f; to lose one's t. se mettre en colère; in a bad t. de mauvaise humeur; to have a (bad or an awful) t. avoir un caractère de cochon. 2 vt (steel) tremper; Fig tempérer.

temperament ['temp(ə)rəmənt] n tempérament m. ◆tempera'mental a (person, machine etc) capricieux; (inborn) inné.

temperance ['temp(ə)rəns] n (in drink) tempérance f.

temperate ['tempərət] a (climate etc) tempéré.

temperature ['temp(ə)rətʃər] n température f; to have a t. Med avoir or faire de la température.

tempest ['tempist] n Lit tempête f. ◆tem'pestuous a (meeting etc) orageux.

template ['templət] n (of plastic, metal etc) Tex patron m; Math trace-courbes f inv.

temple ['temp(ə)l] n 1 Rel temple m. 2 Anat tempe f.

tempo ['tempəu] n (pl -os) tempo m.

temporal ['temp(ə)rəl] a temporel.

temporary ['temp(ə)rəri] a provisoire; (job, worker) temporaire; (secretary) intérimaire.

tempt [tempt] vt tempted; tempted to do faire; to t. s.o. to do persuader qn de faire. ◆—ing a tentant. ◆—ingly adv d'une manière tentante. ◆temp'tation n tentation f.

ten [ten] a & n dix (m). ◆tenfold a t. increase augmentation f par dix; – adv to increase t. (se) multiplier par dix.

tenable ['tenəb(ə)l] a (argument) défendable; (post) qui peut être occupé.

tenacious [tə'neiʃəs] a tenace. ◆tenacity n ténacité f.

tenant ['tenənt] n locataire nmf. ◆tenancy n (lease) location f; (period) occupation f.

tend [tend] 1 vt (look after) s'occuper de. 2 vi to t. to do avoir tendance à faire; to t. towards incliner vers. ◆tendency n tendance f (to do à faire).

tendentious [ten'denʃəs] a Pej tendancieux.

tender¹ ['tendər] a (delicate, soft, loving) tendre; (painful, sore) sensible. ◆—ly adv tendrement. ◆—ness n tendresse f; (soreness) sensibilité f; (of meat) tendreté f.

tender² ['tendər] 1 vt (offer) offrir; to t. one's resignation donner sa démission. 2 n to be legal t. (of money) avoir cours. 3 n (for services etc) Com soumission f (for pour).

tendon ['tendən] n Anat tendon m.

tenement ['tenəmənt] n immeuble m (de rapport) (Am dans un quartier pauvre).

tenet ['tenit] n principe m.

tenner ['tenər] n Fam billet m de dix livres.

tennis ['tenis] n tennis m; table t. tennis de table; t. court court m (de tennis), tennis m.

tenor ['tenər] n 1 (sense, course) sens m général. 2 Mus ténor m.

tenpin ['tenpin] a t. bowling bowling m. ◆tenpins n Am bowling m.

tense [tens] 1 a (-er, -est) (person, muscle, situation) tendu; – vt tendre, crisper; – vi to t. (up) (of person, face) se crisper. 2 n Gram temps m. ◆tenseness n tension f. ◆tension n tension f.

tent [tent] n tente f.

tentacle ['tentək(ə)l] n tentacule m.

tentative ['tentətiv] a (not definite) provisoire; (hesitant) timide. ◆—ly adv provisoirement; timidement.

tenterhooks ['tentəhuks] npl on t. (anxious) sur des charbons ardents.

tenth [tenθ] *a & n* dixième (*mf*); **a t.** un dixième.

tenuous ['tenjʊəs] *a* (*link, suspicion etc*) ténu.

tenure ['tenjər] *n* (*in job*) période *f* de jouissance; (*job security*) *Am* titularisation *f*.

tepid ['tepɪd] *a* (*liquid*) & *Fig* tiède.

term [tɜːm] *n* (*word, limit*) terme *m*; (*period*) période *f*; *Sch Univ* trimestre *m*; (*semester*) *Am* semestre *m*; *pl* (*conditions*) conditions *fpl*; (*prices*) *Com* prix *mpl*; **t.** (*of office*) *Pol* mandat *m*; **easy terms** *Fin* facilités *fpl* de paiement; **on good/bad terms** (**with s.o.** avec qn); **to be on close terms** être intime (**with** avec); **in terms of** (*speaking of*) sur le plan de; **in real terms** dans la pratique; **to come to terms with** (*person*) tomber d'accord avec; (*situation etc*) *Fig* faire face à; **in the long/short t.** à long/court terme; **at** (**full**) **t.** (*baby*) à terme; – *vt* (*name, call*) appeler.

terminal ['tɜːmɪn(ə)l] **1** *n* (*of computer*) terminal *m*; *El* borne *f*; (**air**) **t.** aérogare *f*; (**oil**) **t.** terminal *m* (pétrolier). **2** *a* (*patient, illness*) incurable; (*stage*) terminal. **◆-ly** *adv* **t. ill** (*patient*) incurable.

terminate ['tɜːmɪneɪt] *vt* mettre fin à; (*contract*) résilier; (*pregnancy*) interrompre; – *vi* se terminer. **◆termi'nation** *n* fin *f*; résiliation *f*; interruption *f*.

terminology [tɜːmɪ'nɒlədʒɪ] *n* terminologie *f*.

terminus ['tɜːmɪnəs] *n* terminus *m*.

termite ['tɜːmaɪt] *n* (*insect*) termite *m*.

terrace ['terɪs] *n* terrace *f*; (*houses*) maisons *fpl* en bande; **the terraces** *Sp* les gradins *mpl*. **◆terraced** *a* **t. house** maison *f* attenante aux maisons voisines.

terracota [terə'kɒtə] *n* terre *f* cuite.

terrain [tə'reɪn] *n* *Mil Geol* terrain *m*.

terrestrial [tə'restrɪəl] *a* terrestre.

terrible ['terəb(ə)l] *a* affreux, terrible. **◆terribly** *adv* (*badly*) affreusement; (*very*) terriblement.

terrier ['terɪər] *n* (*dog*) terrier *m*.

terrific [tə'rɪfɪk] *a* *Fam* (*extreme*) terrible; (*excellent*) formidable, terrible. **◆terrifically** *adv* *Fam* (*extremely*) terriblement; (*extremely well*) terriblement bien.

terrify ['terɪfaɪ] *vt* terrifier; **to be terrified of** avoir très peur de. **◆-ing** *a* terrifiant. **◆-ingly** *adv* épouvantablement.

territory ['terɪtərɪ] *n* territoire *m*. **◆terri'torial** *a* territorial.

terror ['terər] *n* terreur *f*; (*child*) *Fam* polisson, -onne *mf*. **◆terrorism** *n* terrorisme

m. **◆terrorist** *n & a* terroriste (*mf*). **◆terrorize** *vt* terroriser.

terry(cloth) ['terɪ(klɒθ)] *n* tissu-éponge *m*.

terse [tɜːs] *a* laconique.

tertiary ['tɜːʃərɪ] *a* tertiaire.

Terylene® ['terɪliːn] *n* tergal® *m*.

test [test] *vt* (*try*) essayer; (*examine*) examiner; (*analyse*) analyser; (*product, intelligence*) tester; (*pupil*) *Sch* faire subir une interrogation à; (*nerves, courage etc*) *Fig* éprouver; – *n* (*trial*) test *m*, essai *m*; examen *m*; analyse *f*; *Sch* interrogation *f*, test *m*; (*of courage etc*) *Fig* épreuve *f*; **driving t.** (*examen m du*) permis *m* de conduire; *a* (*pilot, flight*) d'essai; **t. case** *Jur* affaire-test *f*; **t. match** *Sp* match *m* international; **t. tube** éprouvette *f*; **t. tube baby** bébé *m* éprouvette.

testament ['testəmənt] *n* testament *m*; (*proof, tribute*) témoignage *m*; **Old/New T.** *Rel* Ancien/Nouveau Testament.

testicle ['testɪk(ə)l] *n* *Anat* testicule *m*.

testify ['testɪfaɪ] *vi* *Jur* témoigner (*against* contre); **to t. to sth** (*of person, event etc*) témoigner de qch; – *vt* **to t. that** *Jur* témoigner que. **◆testi'monial** *n* références *fpl*, recommandation *f*. **◆testimony** *n* témoignage *m*.

testy ['testɪ] *a* (*-ier, -iest*) irritable.

tetanus ['tetənəs] *n* *Med* tétanos *m*.

tête-à-tête [teɪtɑː'teɪt] *n* tête-à-tête *m inv*.

tether ['teðər] **1** *vt* (*fasten*) attacher. **2** *n* **at the end of one's t.** à bout de nerfs.

text [tekst] *n* texte *m*. **◆textbook** *n* manuel *m*.

textile ['tekstaɪl] *a & n* textile (*m*).

texture ['tekstʃər] *n* (*of fabric, cake etc*) texture *f*; (*of paper, wood*) grain *m*.

Thames [temz] *n* **the T.** la Tamise *f*.

than [ðæn, *stressed* ðæn] *conj* **1** que; **happier t.** plus heureux que; **he has more t. you** il en a plus que toi; **fewer oranges t. plums** moins d'oranges que de prunes. **2** (*with numbers*) de; **more t. six** plus de six.

thank [θæŋk] *vt* remercier (**for sth** de qch, **for doing** d'avoir fait); **t. you** merci (**for sth** pour *ou* de qch, **for doing** d'avoir fait); **no, t. you** (*non*) merci; **t. God, t. heavens, t. goodness** Dieu merci; – *npl* remerciements *mpl*; **thanks to** (*because of*) grâce à; (**many**) **thanks!** merci (beaucoup)! **◆thankful** *a* reconnaissant (**for** de); **t. that** bien heureux que (+ *sub*). **◆thankfully** *adv* (*gratefully*) avec reconnaissance; (*happily*) heureusement. **◆thankless** *a* ingrat. **◆Thanks-'giving** *n* **T.** (**day**) (*holiday*) *Am* jour *m* d'action de grâce(s).

that [ðət, *stressed* ðæt] **1** *conj* que; **to say t.** dire que. **2** *rel pron* (*subject*) qui; (*object*) que; **the boy t. left** le garçon qui est parti; **the book t. I read** le livre que j'ai lu; **the carpet t. I put it on** (*with prep*) le tapis sur lequel je l'ai mis; **the house t. she told me about** la maison dont elle m'a parlé; **the day/morning t. she arrived** le jour/matin où elle est arrivée. **3** *dem a* (*pl see* **those**) ce, (*before vowel or mute h*) cet, cette; (*opposed to 'this'*) ... + -là; **t. day** ce jour; **t. man** cet homme; **t. girl** cette fille; cette fille-là. **4** *dem pron* (*pl see* **those**) ça, cela; ce; **t.** (*one*) celui-là m, celle-là f; **give me t.** donne-moi ça *or* cela; **I prefer t.** (*one*) je préfère celui-là; **before t.** avant ça *or* cela; **t.'s right** c'est juste; **who's t.?** qui est-ce?; **t.'s the house** c'est la maison; (*pointing*) voilà la maison; **what do you mean by t.?** qu'entends-tu par là; **t. is** (*to say*) c'est-à-dire .... **5** *adv* (*so*) *Fam* si; **not t. good** pas si bon; **t. high** (*pointing*) haut comme ça; **t. much** (*to cost, earn etc*) (au)tant que ça.

thatch [θætʃ] *n* chaume *m*. ◆**thatched** *a* (*roof*) de chaume; **t. cottage** chaumière *f*.

thaw [θɔː] *n* dégel *m*; – *vi* dégeler; (*of snow*) fondre; **it's thawing** *Met* ça dégèle; **to t.** (*out*) (*of person*) *Fig* se dégeler; – *vt* (*ice*) dégeler, faire fondre; (*food*) faire dégeler; (*snow*) faire fondre.

the [ðə, *before vowel* ði, *stressed* ðiː] *def art* le, l', la, *pl* les; **t. roof** le toit; **t. man** l'homme; **t. moon** la lune; **t. orange** l'orange; **t. boxes** les boîtes; **the smallest** le plus petit; **of t., from t.** du, de l', de la, *pl* des; **to t., at t.** au, à l', à la, *pl* aux; **Elizabeth t. Second** Élisabeth deux; **all t. better** d'autant mieux.

theatre [ˈθɪətər] *n* (*place, art*) & *Mil* théâtre *m*. ◆**theatregoer** *n* amateur *m* de théâtre. ◆**the'atrical** *a* théâtral; **t. company** troupe *f* de théâtre.

theft [θeft] *n* vol *m*.

their [ðeər] *poss a* leur, *pl* leurs; **t. house** leur maison *f*. ◆**theirs** [ðeəz] *poss pron* le leur, la leur, *pl* les leurs; **this book is t.** ce livre est à eux *or* est le leur; **a friend of t.** un ami à eux.

them [ðəm, *stressed* ðem] *pron* les; (*after prep etc*) eux *mpl*, elles *fpl*; (*to*) **t.** (*indirect*) leur; **I see t.** je les vois; **I give** (**to**) **t.** je leur donne; **with t.** avec eux, avec elles; **ten of t.** dix d'entre eux, dix d'entre elles; **all of t.** tous, toutes. ◆**them'selves** *pron* eux-mêmes *mpl*, elles-mêmes *fpl*; (*reflexive*) se, s'; (*after prep etc*) eux *mpl*, elles *fpl*;

they wash t. ils se lavent, elles se lavent; **they think of t.** ils pensent à eux, elles pensent à elles.

theme [θiːm] *n* thème *m*; **t. song** *or* **tune** *Cin TV* chanson *f* principale.

then [ðen] **1** *adv* (*at that time*) alors, à ce moment-là; (*next*) ensuite, puis; **from t. on** dès lors; **before t.** avant cela; **until t.** jusque-là, jusqu'alors; – *a* **the t. mayor/etc** le maire/*etc* d'alors. **2** *conj* (*therefore*) donc, alors.

theology [θɪˈɒlədʒɪ] *n* théologie *f*. ◆**theo'logical** *a* théologique. ◆**theo'logian** *n* théologien *m*.

theorem [ˈθɪərəm] *n* théorème *m*.

theory [ˈθɪərɪ] *n* théorie *f*; **in t.** en théorie. ◆**theo'retical** *a* théorique. ◆**theo'retically** *adv* théoriquement. ◆**theorist** *n* théoricien, -ienne *mf*.

therapy [ˈθerəpɪ] *n* thérapeutique *f*. ◆**ther**-**a'peutic** *a* thérapeutique.

there [ðeər] *adv* là; (*down or over*) là-bas; **on t.** là-dessus; **she'll be t.** elle sera là, elle y sera; **t. is, t. are** il y a; (*pointing*) voilà; **t. he is** le voilà; **t. she is** la voilà; **t. they are** les voilà; **that man t.** cet homme-là; **t.** (*you are!*) (*take this*) tenez!; **t., (t.,) don't cry!** allons, allons, ne pleure pas! ◆**therea-** **'bout(s)** *adv* par là; (*in amount*) à peu près. ◆**there'after** *adv* après cela. ◆**thereby** *adv* de ce fait. ◆**therefore** *adv* donc. ◆**thereu'pon** *adv* sur ce.

thermal [ˈθɜːm(ə)l] *a* (*energy, unit*) thermique; (*springs*) thermal; (*underwear*) tribo-électrique, en thermolactyl®.

thermometer [θəˈmɒmɪtər] *n* thermomètre *m*.

thermonuclear [θɜːməʊˈnjuːklɪər] *a* thermonucléaire.

Thermos® [ˈθɜːməs] *n* **T. (flask)** thermos® *m or f*.

thermostat [ˈθɜːməstæt] *n* thermostat *m*.

thesaurus [θɪˈsɔːrəs] *n* dictionnaire *m* de synonymes.

these [ðiːz] **1** *dem a* (*sing see* **this**) ces; (*opposed to 'those'*) ... + -ci; **t. men** ces hommes; ces hommes-ci. **2** *dem pron* (*sing see* **this**) **t.** (*ones*) ceux-ci *mpl*, celles-ci *fpl*; **t. are my friends** ce sont mes amis.

thesis, *pl* **theses** [ˈθiːsɪs, ˈθiːsiːz] *n* thèse *f*.

they [ðeɪ] *pron* **1** ils *mpl*, elles *fpl*; (*stressed*) eux *mpl*, elles *fpl*; **t. go** ils vont, elles vont; **t. are doctors** ce sont des médecins. **2** (*people in general*) on; **t. say** on dit.

thick [θɪk] *a* (**-er, -est**) épais (*f* épaisse); (*stupid*) *Fam* lourd; **to be t.** (*of friends*) *Fam* être très liés; – *adv* (*to grow*) dru; (*to spread*) en couche épaisse; – *n* **in the t.** (*of battle etc*) au plus gros de. ◆**thicken** vt épaissir; – vi s'épaissir. ◆**thickly** adv (to grow, fall) dru; (to spread) en couche épaisse; (populated, wooded) très. ◆**thickness** n épaisseur f.

thicket ['θɪkɪt] n (trees) fourré m.

thickset [θɪk'set] a (person) trapu. ◆**thick-skinned** a (person) dur, peu sensible.

thief [θiːf] n (pl thieves) voleur, -euse mf. ◆**thiev/e** vti voler. ◆**—ing** n vol m.

thigh [θaɪ] n cuisse f. ◆**thighbone** n fémur m.

thimble ['θɪmb(ə)l] n dé m (à coudre).

thin [θɪn] a (thinner, thinnest) (slice, paper etc) mince; (person, leg) maigre, mince; (soup) peu épais; (hair, audience) clairsemé; (powder) fin; (excuse, profit) Fig maigre, mince; – adv (to spread) en couche mince; – vt (-nn-) to t. (down) (paint etc) délayer; – vi to t. out (of crowd, mist) s'éclaircir. ◆**—ly** adv (to spread) en couche mince; (populated, wooded) peu; (disguised) à peine. ◆**—ness** n minceur f; maigreur f.

thing [θɪŋ] n chose f; one's things (belongings, clothes) ses affaires fpl; it's a funny t. c'est drôle; poor little t.! pauvre petit!; that's (just) the t. voilà (exactement) ce qu'il faut; how are things? comment (ça) va?; Fam how's things? comment (ça) va?; I'll think things over j'y réfléchirai; for one t...., and for another t. d'abord ... et ensuite; tea things (set) service m à thé; (dishes) vaisselle f. ◆**thingummy** n Fam truc m, machin m.

think [θɪŋk] vi (pt & pp thought) penser (about, of à); to t. (carefully) réfléchir (about, of à); to t. of doing penser or songer à faire; to t. highly of, to t. a lot of penser beaucoup de bien de; she doesn't t. much of it ça ne lui dit pas grand-chose; to t. better of it se raviser; I can't t. of it je n'arrive pas à m'en souvenir; – vt (name that que); I t. so je pense or crois que oui; what do you t. of him? que penses-tu de lui?; I thought it difficult je l'ai trouvé difficile; to t. out or through (reply etc) réfléchir sérieusement à, peser; to t. over réfléchir à; to t. up (invent) inventer, avoir l'idée de; – n to have a t. Fam réfléchir (about à); – a t. tank comité m d'experts. ◆**—ing** a (person) intelligent; – n (opinion) opinion f; to my t. à mon avis. ◆**—er** n penseur, -euse mf.

thin-skinned [θɪn'skɪnd] a (person) susceptible.

third [θɜːd] a troisième; t. person or party tiers m; t.-party insurance assurance f au tiers m; **T. World** Tiers-Monde m; – n

troisième mf; a t. (fraction) un tiers; – adv (in race) troisième. ◆**—ly** adv troisièmement.

third-class [θɜːd'klɑːs] a de troisième classe. ◆**t.-rate** a (très) inférieur.

thirst [θɜːst] n soif f (for de). ◆**thirsty** a (-ier, -iest) a to be or feel t. avoir soif; to make t. donner soif à; t. for (power etc) Fig assoiffé de.

thirteen [θɜː'tiːn] a & n treize (m). ◆**thirteenth** a & n treizième (mf). ◆**'thirtieth** a & n trentième (mf). ◆**'thirty** a & n trente (m).

this [ðɪs] 1 dem a (pl see these) ce, cet (before vowel or mute h), cette; (opposed to 'that') ... + -ci; t. book ce livre-ci; t. photo cette photo; cette photo-ci. 2 dem pron (pl see these) ceci; ce; t. (one) celui-ci m, celle-ci f; give me t. donne-moi ceci; I prefer t. (one) je préfère celui-ci; before t. avant ceci; who's t.? qui est-ce?; t. is Paul c'est Paul; t. is the house voilà la maison. 3 adv (so) Fam si; t. high (pointing) haut comme ceci; t. far (until now) jusqu'ici.

thistle ['θɪs(ə)l] n chardon m.

thorn [θɔːn] n épine f. ◆**thorny** a (-ier, -iest) (bush, problem etc) épineux.

thorough ['θʌrə] a (painstaking, careful) minutieux, consciencieux; (knowledge, examination) approfondi; (rogue, liar) fieffé; (disaster) complet; to give sth a t. washing laver qch à fond. ◆**—ly** adv (completely) tout à fait; (painstakingly) avec minutie; (to know, clean, wash) à fond. ◆**—ness** n minutie f; (depth) profondeur f.

thoroughbred ['θʌrəbred] n (horse) pur-sang m inv.

thoroughfare ['θʌrəfeər] n (street) rue f; 'no t.' 'passage interdit'.

those [ðəʊz] 1 dem a (sing see that) ces; (opposed to 'these') ... + -là; t. men ces hommes; ces hommes-là. 2 dem pron (sing see that) t. (ones) ceux-là mpl, celles-là fpl; t. are my friends ce sont mes amis.

though [ðəʊ] 1 conj (even) t. bien que (+ sub); as t. comme si; strange t. it may seem si étrange que cela puisse paraître. 2 adv (nevertheless) cependant, quand même.

thought [θɔːt] see think; – n pensée f; (idea) idée f, pensée f; (careful) t. réflexion f; without (a) t. for sans penser à; on second thoughts changer d'avis; on second thoughts, Am on second t. à la réflexion. ◆**thoughtful** a (pensive) pensif; (serious) sérieux; (considerate, kind) gentil, prévenant. ◆**thoughtfully** adv (considerately) gentiment. ◆**thoughtfulness** n gentillesse f, prévenance f. ◆**thoughtless** a (towards others) désinvolte; (careless) étourdi. ◆**thoughtlessly** adv (carelessly) étourdiment; (inconsiderately) avec désinvolture.

thousand ['θaʊzənd] a & n mille a & m inv; a t. pages mille pages; two t. pages deux mille pages; thousands of ten milliers de.

thrash [θræʃ] 1 vt to t. s.o. rouer qn de coups; (defeat) écraser qn; to t. out (plan etc) élaborer (à force de discussions). 2 vi to t. about (struggle) se débattre. ◆—**ing** n (beating) correction f.

thread [θred] n (yarn) & Fig fil m; (of screw) pas m; — vt (needle, beads) enfiler; to t. one's way Fig se faufiler (through the crowd/etc dans la foule/etc). ◆**threadbare** a élimé, râpé.

threat [θret] n menace f (to à). ◆**threaten** vi menacer; — vt menacer (to do de faire, with sth de qch). ◆**threatening** a menaçant. ◆**threateningly** adv (to say) d'un ton menaçant.

three [θriː] a & n trois (m); t.-piece suite canapé m et deux fauteuils. ◆**threefold** a triple; — adv to **increase** t. tripler. ◆**three-'wheeler** n (tricycle) tricycle m; (car) voiture f à trois roues.

thresh [θreʃ] vt Agr battre.

threshold ['θreʃhəʊld] n seuil m.

threw [θruː] see throw.

thrift [θrɪft] n (virtue) économie f. ◆**thrifty** a (-ier, -iest) économe.

thrill [θrɪl] n émotion f, frisson m; to get a t. out of doing prendre plaisir à faire; — vt (delight) réjouir; (excite) faire frissonner. ◆—**ed** a ravi (with sth de qch, to do de faire). ◆—**ing** a passionnant. ◆—**er** n film m or roman m à suspense.

thriv/e [θraɪv] vi (of business, person, plant etc) prospérer; he or she thrives on hard work le travail lui profite. ◆—**ing** a prospère, florissant.

throat [θrəʊt] n gorge f; to have a sore t. avoir mal à la gorge. ◆**throaty** a (voice) rauque; (person) à la voix rauque.

throb [θrɒb] vi (-bb-) (of heart) palpiter; (of engine) vrombir; Fig vibrer; my finger is throbbing mon doigt me fait des élancements; — n palpitation f; vrombissement m; élancement m.

throes [θrəʊz] npl in the t. of au milieu de; (illness, crisis) en proie à; in the t. of doing en train de faire.

thrombosis [θrɒm'bəʊsɪs] n (coronary) Med infarctus m.

throne [θrəʊn] n trône m.

throng [θrɒŋ] n foule f; — vi (rush) affluer; — vt (street, station etc) se presser dans; **thronged with people** noir de monde.

throttle ['θrɒt(ə)l] 1 n Aut accélérateur m. 2 vt (strangle) étrangler.

through [θruː] prep (place) à travers; (time) pendant; (means) par; (thanks to) grâce à; to go or get t. (forest etc) traverser; (hole etc) passer par; t. the window/door par la fenêtre/porte; to speak t. one's nose parler du nez; Tuesday t. Saturday Am de mardi à samedi; — adv (across) to go t. (cross) traverser; (pass) passer; to let t. laisser passer; all or right t. (to the end) jusqu'au bout; French t. and t. français jusqu'au bout des ongles; to be t. (finished) Am Fam avoir fini; we're t. Am Fam c'est fini entre nous; I'm t. with the book Am Fam je n'ai plus besoin du livre; t. to or till jusqu'à; I'll put you t. (to him) Tel je vous le passe; — a (train, traffic, ticket) direct; 'no t. road' (no exit) 'voie sans issue'. ◆**through'out** prep t. the **neighbourhood**/etc dans tout le quartier/etc; t. the day/etc (time) pendant toute la journée/etc; — adv (everywhere) partout; (all the time) tout le temps. ◆**throughway** n Am autoroute f.

throw [θrəʊ] n (of stone etc) jet m; Sp lancer m; (of dice) coup m; (turn) tour m; — vt (pt threw, pp thrown) jeter (to, at à); (stone, ball) lancer, jeter; (hurl) projeter; (of horse) désarçonner (qn); (party, reception) donner; (baffle) Fam dérouter; to t. away (discard) jeter; (ruin, waste) Fig gâcher; to t. back (ball) renvoyer (to à); (one's head) rejeter en arrière; to t. in (include as extra) Fam donner en prime; to t. off (get rid of) se débarrasser de; to t. out (discard) jeter; (suggestion) repousser; (expel) mettre (qn) à la porte; (distort) fausser (calcul etc); to t. over abandonner; to t. up (job) Fam laisser tomber; — vi to t. up (vomit) Sl dégobiller. ◆**throwaway** a (disposable) à jeter, jetable.

thrush [θrʌʃ] n (bird) grive f.

thrust [θrʌst] n (push) poussée f; (stab) coup m; (of argument) poids m; (dynamism) allant m; — vt (pt & pp thrust) (push) pousser; (put) mettre (into dans); to t. sth into sth (stick, knife, pin) enfoncer qch dans qch; to t. sth/s.o. upon s.o. Fig imposer qch/qn à qn.

thud [θʌd] n bruit m sourd.

thug [θʌg] n voyou m.

thumb [θʌm] n pouce m; **with a t. index** (book) à onglets; – vt **to t. (through)** (book etc) feuilleter; **to t. a lift or a ride** Fam faire du stop. ◆**thumbtack** n Am punaise f.

thump [θʌmp] vt (person) frapper, cogner sur; (table) taper sur; **to t. one's head** (on door etc) se cogner la tête (on contre); – vi frapper, cogner (on sur); (of heart) battre à grands coups; – n (grand) coup m; (noise) bruit m sourd. ◆**-ing** a (huge, great) Fam énorme.

thunder [θʌndər] n tonnerre m; – vi (of weather, person, guns) tonner; **it's thundering** Met il tonne; **to t. past** passer (vite) dans un bruit de tonnerre. ◆**thunderbolt** n (event) Fig coup m de tonnerre. ◆**thunderclap** n coup m de tonnerre. ◆**thunderstorm** n orage m. ◆**thunderstruck** a abasourdi.

Thursday [θɜːzdi] n jeudi m.

thus [ðʌs] adv ainsi.

thwart [θwɔːt] vt (plan, person) contrecarrer.

thyme [taɪm] n Bot Culin thym m.

thyroid [θaɪrɔɪd] a & n Anat thyroïde (f).

tiara [tɪˈɑːrə] n (of woman) diadème m.

tic [tɪk] n (in face, limbs) tic m.

tick [tɪk] 1 n (of clock) tic-tac m; – vi faire tic-tac; **to t. over** (of engine, factory, business) tourner au ralenti. 2 n (on list) coche f, trait m; – vt **to t. (off)** cocher; **to t. off** (reprimand) Fam passer un savon à. 3 n (moment) Fam instant m. 4 n (insect) tique f. 5 adv **on t.** (on credit) Fam à crédit. ◆**-ing** n (of clock) tic-tac m; **to give s.o. a t.-off** Fam passer un savon à qn.

ticket [tɪkɪt] n billet m; (for tube, bus, cloakroom) ticket m; (for library) carte f; (fine) Aut Fam contravention f, contredanse f; Pol Am liste f; (price) étiquette f; **t. collector** contrôleur, -euse mf; **t. holder** personne f munie d'un billet; **t. office** guichet m.

tickle [tɪk(ə)l] vt chatouiller; (amuse) Fig amuser; – n chatouillement m. ◆**ticklish** a (person) chatouilleux; (fabric) qui chatouille; (problem) Fig délicat.

tidbit [tɪdbɪt] n (food) Am bon morceau m.

tiddlywinks [tɪdlɪwɪŋks] n jeu m de puce.

tide [taɪd] 1 n marée f; **against the t.** Nau & Fig à contre-courant; **the rising t. of** discontent le mécontentement grandissant. 2 vt **to t. s.o. over** (help out) dépanner qn. ◆**tidal** a (river) qui a une marée; **t. wave** raz-de-marée m inv; (in public opinion etc) Fig vague f de fond. ◆**tidemark** n Fig Hum ligne f de crasse.

tidings [taɪdɪŋz] npl Lit nouvelles fpl.

tidy [taɪdɪ] a (-ier, -iest) (place, toys etc) bien rangé; (clothes, looks) soigné; (methodical) ordonné; (amount, sum) Fam joli, bon; **to make t.** ranger; – vt **to t. (up or away)** ranger; **to t. oneself (up)** s'arranger; **to t. out** (cupboard etc) vider; – vi **to t. up** ranger. ◆**tidily** adv avec soin. ◆**tidiness** n (bon) ordre m; (of person) soin m.

tie [taɪ] n (string, strap) & Fig lien m, attache f; (necktie) cravate f; (sleeper) Rail Am traverse f; Sp égalité f de points; (match) match m nul; – vt (fasten) attacher, lier (to à); (a knot) faire (in à); (shoe) lacer; (link) lier (to à); **to t. down** attacher; **to t. s.o. down to** (date, place etc) obliger qn à accepter; **to t. up** attacher; (money) immobiliser; **to be tied up** (linked) être lié (with avec); (busy) Fam être occupé; – vi Sp finir à égalité de points; Fb faire match nul; (in race) être ex aequo; **to t. in with** (tally with) se rapporter à. ◆**t.-up** n (link) lien m; (traffic jam) Am Fam bouchon m.

tier [tɪər] n (seats) Sp Th gradin m; (of cake) étage m.

tiff [tɪf] n petite querelle f.

tiger [taɪgər] n tigre m. ◆**tigress** n tigresse f.

tight [taɪt] a (-er, -est) (rope etc) raide; (closely-fitting clothing) ajusté, (fitting too closely) (trop) étroit; (trop) serré; (drawer, lid) dur; (control) strict; (schedule, credit) serré; (drunk) Fam gris; (with money) Fam avare; **t. spot or corner** Fam une situation difficile; **it's a t. squeeze** il y a juste la place; – adv (to hold, shut, sleep) bien; (to squeeze) fort; **to sit t.** ne pas bouger. ◆**tighten** vt **to t. (up)** (rope) tendre; (bolt etc) (res)serrer; (security) Fig renforcer; – vi **to t. up on** se montrer plus strict à l'égard de. ◆**tightly** adv (to hold) bien; (to squeeze) fort; **t. knit** (close) très uni. ◆**tightness** n (of garment) étroitesse f; (of control) rigueur f; (of rope) tension f.

tight-fitting [taɪtfɪtɪŋ] a (garment) ajusté. ◆**tightfisted** a avare. ◆**tightrope** n corde f raide. ◆**tightwad** n (miser) Am Fam grippe-sou m.

tights [taɪts] npl (garment) collant m; (for dancer etc) justaucorps m.

til/e [taɪl] n (on roof) tuile f; (on wall or floor) carreau m; – vt (wall, floor) carreler. ◆**-ed** a (roof) de tuiles; (wall, floor) carrelé.

till [tɪl] **1** prep & conj = **until**. **2** n (for money) caisse f (enregistreuse). **3** vt (land) Agr cultiver.

tilt [tɪlt] *vti* pencher; – *n* inclinaison *f*; **(at) full t.** à toute vitesse.

timber ['tɪmbər] *n* bois *m* (de construction); *(trees)* arbres *mpl*; – *a* de *or* en bois. ◆**timberyard** *n* entrepôt *m* de bois.

time [taɪm] *n* temps *m*; *(point in time)* moment *m*; *(epoch)* époque *f*; *(on clock)* heure *f*; *(occasion)* fois *f*; *Mus* mesure *f*; **in (the course of) t., with (the passage of) t.** avec le temps; **some of the t.** *(not always)* une partie du temps; **most of the t.** la plupart du temps; **in a year's t.** dans un an; **a long t.** longtemps; **a short t.** peu de temps, un petit moment; **full-t.** à plein temps; **part-t.** à temps partiel; **to have a good or a nice t.** *(fun)* s'amuser (bien); **to have a hard t. doing** avoir du mal à faire; **t. off** du temps libre; **in no t. (at all)** en un rien de temps; **(just) in t.** *(to arrive)* à temps **(for sth** pour qch, **to do** pour faire); **in my t.** *(formerly)* de mon temps; **from t. to t.** de temps en temps; **what t. is it?** quelle heure est-il?; **the right or exact t.** l'heure *f* exacte; **on t.** à l'heure; **at the same t.** en même temps (as que); *(simultaneously)* à la fois; **for the t. being** pour le moment; **at the t.** à ce moment-là; **at the present t.** à l'heure actuelle; **at times** par moments, parfois; **at one t.** à un moment donné; **this t. tomorrow** demain à cette heure-ci; **(the) next t. you come** la prochaine fois que tu viendras; **(the) last t.** la dernière fois; **one at a t.** un à un; **t. and again** maintes fois; **ten times ten** dix fois dix; **t. bomb** bombe *f* à retardement; **t. lag** décalage *m*; **t. limit** délai *m*; **t. zone** fuseau *m* horaire; – *vt* *(sportsman, worker etc)* chronométrer; *(programme, operation)* minuter; *(choose the time of)* choisir le moment de; *(to plan)* prévoir. ◆**timing** *n* chronométrage *m*; minutage *m*; *(judgement of artist etc)* rythme *m*; **the t. of** *(time)* le moment choisi pour. ◆**time-consuming** *a* qui prend du temps. ◆**time-honoured** *a* consacré (par l'usage).

timeless ['taɪmləs] *a* éternel.

timely ['taɪmlɪ] *a* à propos. ◆**timeliness** *n* à-propos *m*.

timer ['taɪmər] *n Culin* minuteur *m*, compte-minutes *m inv*; *(sand-filled)* sablier *m*; *(on machine)* minuteur *m*; *(to control lighting)* minuterie *f*.

timetable ['taɪmteɪb(ə)l] *n* horaire *m*; *(in school)* emploi *m* du temps.

timid ['tɪmɪd] *a (shy)* timide; *(fearful)* timoré. ◆**-ly** *adv* timidement.

tin [tɪn] *n* étain *m*; *(tinplate)* fer-blanc *m*;

(can) boîte *f*; *(for baking)* moule *m*; **t. can** boîte *f* (en fer-blanc); **t. opener** ouvre-boîtes *m inv*; **t. soldier** soldat *m* de plomb. ◆**tinfoil** *n* papier *m* d'aluminium, papier alu. ◆**tinned** *a* en boîte. ◆**tin-plate** *n* fer-blanc *m*.

tinge [tɪndʒ] *n* teinte *f*. ◆**tinged** *a* **t. with** *(pink etc)* teinté de; *(jealousy etc) Fig* empreint de.

tingle ['tɪŋg(ə)l] *vi* picoter; **it's tingling** ça me picote. ◆**tingly** *a (feeling)* de picotement.

tinker ['tɪŋkər] *vi* **to t. (about with** bricoler.

tinkle ['tɪŋk(ə)l] *vi* tinter; – *n* tintement *m*; **to give s.o. a t.** *(phone s.o.) Fam* passer un coup de fil à qn.

tinny ['tɪnɪ] *a (-ier, -iest) (sound)* métallique; *(vehicle, machine)* de mauvaise qualité.

tinsel ['tɪns(ə)l] *n* clinquant *m*, guirlandes *fpl* de Noël.

tint [tɪnt] *n* teinte *f*; *(for hair)* shampooing *m* colorant; – *vt* *(paper, glass)* teinter.

tiny ['taɪnɪ] *a (-ier, -iest)* tout petit.

tip [tɪp] **1** *n (end)* bout *m*; *(pointed)* pointe *f*. **2** *n (money)* pourboire *m*; – *vt* *(-pp-)* donner un pourboire à. **3** *n (advice)* conseil *m*; *(information)* & *Sp* tuyau *m*; **to get a t.-off** se faire tuyauter; – *vt* *(-pp-)* **to t. a horse/etc** donner un cheval/etc gagnant; **to t. off** *(police)* prévenir. **4** *n (for rubbish)* décharge *f*; – *vt* *(-pp-)* **to t. (up or over)** *(tilt)* incliner, pencher; *(overturn)* faire basculer; **to t. (out)** *(liquid, load)* déverser **(into** dans); – *vi* **to t. (up or over)** *(tilt)* pencher; *(overturn)* basculer.

tipped [tɪpt] *a* **t. cigarette** cigarette *f* (à bout) filtre.

tipple ['tɪp(ə)l] *vi (drink) Fam* picoler.

tipsy ['tɪpsɪ] *a (-ier, -iest) (drunk)* gai, pompette.

tiptoe ['tɪptəʊ] *n* **on t.** sur la pointe des pieds; – *vi* marcher sur la pointe des pieds.

tiptop ['tɪptɒp] *a Fam* excellent.

tirade [taɪ'reɪd] *n* diatribe *f*.

tire[1] ['taɪər] *vt* fatiguer; **to t. out** *(exhaust)* épuiser; – *vi* se fatiguer. ◆**-ed** *a* fatigué; **to be t. of sth/s.o./doing** en avoir assez de qch/de qn/de faire; **to get t. of doing** se lasser de faire. ◆**-ing** *a* fatigant. ◆**tiredness** *n* fatigue *f*. ◆**tireless** *a* infatigable. ◆**tiresome** *a* ennuyeux.

tire[2] ['taɪər] *n Am* pneu *m*.

tissue ['tɪʃuː] *n Biol* tissu *m*; *(handkerchief)* mouchoir *m* en papier, kleenex® *m*; **t. (paper)** papier *m* de soie.

tit [tɪt] *n* **1** *(bird)* mésange *f*. **2** **to give t. for tat** rendre coup pour coup.

titbit ['tɪtbɪt] *n (food)* bon morceau *m*.

titillate ['tɪtɪleɪt] vt exciter.

titl/e ['taɪt(ə)l] n (name, claim) & Sp titre m; **t. deed** titre m de propriété; **t. role** Th Cin rôle m principal; – vt (film) intituler, titrer. ◆—**ed** a (person) titré.

titter ['tɪtər] vi rire bêtement.

tittle-tattle ['tɪt(ə)ltæt(ə)l] n Fam commérages mpl.

to [tə, stressed tuː] **1** prep à; (towards) vers; (of feelings, attitude) envers; (right up to) jusqu'à; (of) de; **give it to him** or **her** donne-le-lui; **to town** en ville; **to France** en France; **to Portugal** au Portugal; **to the butcher('s)**/etc chez le boucher/etc; **the road to** la route de; **the train to** le train pour; **well-disposed to** bien disposé envers; **kind to** gentil envers or avec or pour; **from bad to worse** de mal en pis; **ten to one** (proportion) dix contre un; **it's ten (minutes) to one** il est une heure moins dix; **one person to a room** une personne par chambre; **to say/to remember/**etc (with inf) dire/se souvenir/etc; **she tried to** elle a essayé; **wife/**etc-**to-be** future femme f/etc. **2** adv **to push to** (door) fermer; **to go** or **walk to and fro** aller et venir. ◆**to-do** [tə'duː] n (fuss) Fam histoire f.

toad [təʊd] n crapaud m.

toadstool ['təʊdstuːl] n champignon m (vénéneux).

toast [təʊst] **1** n Culin pain m grillé, toast m; – vt (bread) (faire) griller. **2** n (drink) toast m; – vt (person) porter un toast à; (success, event) arroser. ◆**toaster** n grille-pain m inv.

tobacco [tə'bækəʊ] n (pl -os) tabac m. ◆**tobacconist** n buraliste mf; **t., tobacconist's (shop)** (bureau m de) tabac m.

toboggan [tə'bɒgən] n luge f, toboggan m.

today [tə'deɪ] adv & n aujourd'hui (m).

toddle ['tɒd(ə)l] vi **to t. off** (leave) Hum Fam se sauver.

toddler ['tɒdlər] n petit(e) enfant mf.

toddy ['tɒdɪ] n (hot) **t.** grog m.

toe [təʊ] **1** n orteil m; **on one's toes** Fig vigilant. **2** vt **to t. the line** se conformer; **to t. the party line** respecter la ligne du parti. ◆**toenail** n ongle m du pied.

toffee ['tɒfɪ] n (sweet) caramel m (dur); **t. apple** pomme f d'amour.

together [tə'geðər] adv ensemble; (at the same time) en même temps; **t.** with avec. ◆—**ness** n (of group) camaraderie f; (of husband and wife) intimité f.

togs [tɒgz] npl (clothes) Sl nippes fpl.

toil [tɔɪl] n labeur m; – vi travailler dur.

toilet ['tɔɪlɪt] n (room) toilettes fpl, cabinets mpl; (bowl, seat) cuvette f or siège m des cabinets; **to go to the t.** aller aux toilettes; – a (articles) de toilette; **t. paper** papier m hygiénique; **t. roll** rouleau m de papier hygiénique; **t. water** (perfume) eau f de toilette. ◆**toiletries** npl articles mpl de toilette.

token ['təʊkən] n (symbol, sign) témoignage m; (metal disc) jeton m; (voucher) bon m; **gift t.** chèque-cadeau m; **book t.** chèque-livre m; **record t.** chèque-disque m; – a symbolique.

told [təʊld] see tell; – adv **all t.** (taken together) en tout.

tolerable ['tɒlərəb(ə)l] a (bearable) tolérable; (fairly good) passable. ◆**tolerably** adv (fairly, fairly well) passablement. ◆**tolerance** n tolérance f. ◆**tolerant** a tolérant (of à l'égard de). ◆**tolerantly** adv avec tolérance. ◆**tolerate** vt tolérer.

toll [təʊl] **1** n péage m; – a (road) à péage. **2** n **the death t.** le nombre de morts, le bilan en vies humaines; **to take a heavy t.** (of accident etc) faire beaucoup de victimes. **3** vi (of bell) sonner. ◆**tollfree** a **t. number** Tel Am numéro m vert.

tomato [tə'mɑːtəʊ, Am tə'meɪtəʊ] n (pl -oes) tomate f.

tomb [tuːm] n tombeau m. ◆**tombstone** n pierre f tombale.

tomboy ['tɒmbɔɪ] n̩ (girl) garçon m manqué.

tomcat ['tɒmkæt] n matou m.

tome [təʊm] n (book) tome m.

tomfoolery [tɒm'fuːlərɪ] n niaiserie(s) f(pl).

tomorrow [tə'mɒrəʊ] adv & n demain (m); **t. morning/evening** demain matin/soir; **the day after t.** après-demain.

ton [tʌn] n tonne f (Br = 1016 kg, Am = 907 kg); **metric t.** tonne f (= 1000 kg); **tons of** (lots of) Fam des tonnes de.

tone [təʊn] n ton m; (of radio, telephone) tonalité f; **in that t.** sur ce ton; **to set the t.** donner le ton; **she's t.-deaf** elle n'a pas d'oreille; – vt **to t.** down atténuer; **to t.** up (muscles, skin) tonifier; – vi **to t. in** s'harmoniser (with avec).

tongs [tɒŋz] npl pinces fpl; (for sugar) pince f; (curling) **t.** fer m à friser.

tongue [tʌŋ] n langue f; **t. in cheek** ironique(ment). ◆**t.-tied** a muet (et gêné).

tonic ['tɒnɪk] n & a tonique (m); **gin and t.** gin-tonic m.

tonight [tə'naɪt] adv & n (this evening) ce soir (m); (during the night) cette nuit (f).

tonne [tʌn] n (metric) tonne f. ◆**tonnage** n tonnage m.

tonsil ['tɒns(ə)l] n amygdale f. ◆**tonsi'l-**

lectomy n opération f des amygdales. ◆**tonsillitis** [tɒnsəˈlaɪtɪs] n **to have t.** avoir une angine.

too [tuː] adv **1** (excessively) trop; **t. tired to play** trop fatigué pour jouer; **t. hard to solve** trop difficile à résoudre; **it's only t. true** ce n'est que trop vrai. **2** (also) aussi; (moreover) en plus.

took [tʊk] see **take**.

tool [tuːl] n outil m; **t. bag, t. kit** trousse f à outils.

toot [tuːt] vti **to t. (the horn)** Aut klaxonner.

tooth, pl **teeth** [tuːθ, tiːθ] n dent f; **front t.** dent f de devant; **back t.** molaire f; **milk/wisdom t.** dent de lait/de sagesse; **t. decay** carie f dentaire; **to have a sweet t.** aimer les sucreries; **long in the t.** (old) Hum chenu, vieux. ◆**toothache** n mal m de dents. ◆**toothbrush** n brosse f à dents. ◆**toothcomb** n peigne m fin. ◆**toothpaste** n dentifrice m. ◆**toothpick** n cure-dent m.

top¹ [tɒp] n (of mountain, tower, tree) sommet m; (of wall, dress, ladder, page) haut m; (of box, table, surface) dessus m; (of list) tête f; (of water) surface f; (of car) toit m; (of bottle, tube) bouchon m; (bottle cap) capsule f; (of saucepan) couvercle m; (of pen) capuchon m; **pyjama t.** veste f de pyjama; **(at the) t. of the class** le premier de la classe; **on t. of** sur; (in addition to) Fig en plus de; **on t.** (in bus etc) en haut; **from t. to bottom** de fond en comble; **the big t.** (circus) le chapiteau; – a (drawer, shelf) du haut, premier; (step, layer, storey) dernier; (upper) supérieur; (in rank, exam) premier; (chief) principal; (best) meilleur; (great, distinguished) éminent; (maximum) maximum; **in t. gear** Aut en quatrième vitesse; **at t. speed** à toute vitesse; **t. hat** (chapeau m) haut-de-forme m. ◆**t.-'flight** a Fam excellent. ◆**t.-'heavy** a trop lourd du haut. ◆**t.-level** a (talks etc) au sommet. ◆**t.-'notch** a Fam excellent. ◆**t.-'ranking** a (official) haut placé. ◆**t.-'secret** a ultra-secret.

top² [tɒp] vt (-pp-) (exceed) dépasser; **to t. up** (glass etc) remplir (de nouveau); (coffee, oil etc) rajouter; **and to t. it all . . .** et pour comble . . . ; **topped with** Culin nappé de.

top³ [tɒp] n (toy) toupie f.

topaz [ˈtəʊpæz] n (gem) topaze f.

topic [ˈtɒpɪk] n sujet m. ◆**topical** a d'actualité. ◆**topi'cality** n actualité f.

topless [ˈtɒpləs] a (woman) aux seins nus.

topography [təˈpɒgrəfɪ] n topographie f.

topple [ˈtɒp(ə)l] vi **to t. (over)** tomber; – vt **to t. (over)** faire tomber.

topsy-turvy [tɒpsɪˈtɜːvɪ] a & adv sens dessus dessous.

torch [tɔːtʃ] n (burning) torche f, flambeau m; (electric) lampe f électrique. ◆**torchlight** n & a by t. à la lumière des flambeaux; **t. procession** retraite f aux flambeaux.

tore [tɔːr] see **tear¹**.

torment [tɔːˈment] vt (make suffer) tourmenter; (annoy) agacer; – [ˈtɔːment] n tourment m.

tornado [tɔːˈneɪdəʊ] n (pl -oes) tornade f.

torpedo [tɔːˈpiːdəʊ] n (pl -oes) torpille f; **t. boat** torpilleur m; – vt torpiller.

torrent [ˈtɒrənt] n torrent m. ◆**torrential** [təˈrenʃ(ə)l] a torrentiel.

torrid [ˈtɒrɪd] a (love affair etc) brûlant, passionné; (climate, weather) torride.

torso [ˈtɔːsəʊ] n (pl -os) torse m.

tortoise [ˈtɔːtəs] n tortue f. ◆**tortoiseshell** a (comb etc) en écaille; (spectacles) à monture d'écaille.

tortuous [ˈtɔːtjʊəs] a tortueux.

tortur/e [ˈtɔːtʃər] n torture f; – vt torturer. ◆**—er** n tortionnaire m.

Tory [ˈtɔːrɪ] n tory m; – a tory inv.

toss [tɒs] vt (throw) jeter, lancer (to à); **to s.o. (about)** (of boat, vehicle) ballotter qn, faire tressauter qn; **to t. a coin** jouer à pile ou à face; **to t. back** (one's head) rejeter en arrière; – vi **to t. (about), t. and turn** (in one's sleep etc) se tourner et se retourner; **we'll t. (up) for it, we'll t. up** on va jouer à pile ou à face; – vi **with a t. of the head** d'un mouvement brusque de la tête. ◆**t.-up** n **it's a t.-up whether he leaves or stays** Si il y a autant de chances pour qu'il parte ou pour qu'il reste.

tot [tɒt] **1** n (tiny) **t.** petit(e) enfant mf. **2** vt (-tt-) **to t. up** (total) Fam additionner.

total [ˈtəʊt(ə)l] a total; **the t. sales** le total des ventes; – n total m; **in t.** au total; – vt (-ll-, Am -l-) (of debt, invoice) s'élever à; **to t. (up)** (find the total of) totaliser; **that totals $9** ça fait neuf dollars en tout. ◆**—ly** adv totalement.

totalitarian [təʊtælɪˈteərɪən] a Pol totalitaire.

tote [təʊt] **1** n Sp Fam pari m mutuel. **2** vt (gun) porter.

totter [ˈtɒtər] vi chanceler.

touch [tʌtʃ] n (contact) contact m, toucher m; (sense) toucher m; (of painter) & Fb Rugby touche f; **a t. of** (small amount) un petit peu de, un soupçon de; **the finishing**

touches la dernière touche; **in t. with** (*person*) en contact avec; (*events*) au courant de; **to be out of t. with** ne plus être en contact avec; (*events*) ne plus être au courant de; **to get in t.** se mettre en contact (**with** avec); **we lost t.** on s'est perdu de vue; – *vt* toucher; (*lay a finger on, tamper with, eat*) toucher à; (*move emotionally*) toucher; (*equal*) Fig égaler; **to t. up** retoucher; **I don't t. the stuff** (*beer etc*) je n'en bois jamais; – *vi* (*of lines, ends etc*) se toucher; **don't t.!** n'y ou ne touche pas!; **he's always touching** c'est un touche-à-tout; **to t. down** (*of aircraft*) atterrir; **to t. on** (*subject*) toucher à. ◆—ed *a* (*emotionally*) touché (**by** de); (*crazy*) Fam cinglé. ◆—ing *a* (*story etc*) touchant. ◆touch-and-'go *a* (*uncertain*) Fam douteux. ◆touchdown *n Av* atterrissage *m*. ◆touchline *n Fb Rugby* (ligne *f* de) touche *f*.

touchy ['tʌtʃɪ] *a* (**-ier, -iest**) (*sensitive*) susceptible (**about** à propos de).

tough [tʌf] *a* (**-er, -est**) (*hard*) dur; (*meat, businessman*) coriace; (*sturdy*) solide; (*strong*) fort; (*relentless*) acharné; (*difficult*) difficile, dur; **t. guy** dur *m*; **t. luck!** Fam pas de chance!, quelle déveine!; – *n* (*tough guy*) Fam dur *m*. ◆toughen *vt* (*body, person*) endurcir; (*reinforce*) renforcer. ◆toughness *n* dureté *f*; solidité *f*; force *f*.

toupee ['tuːpeɪ] *n* postiche *m*.

tour [tuər] *n* (*journey*) voyage *m*; (*visit*) visite *f*; (*by artist, team etc*) tournée *f*; (*on bicycle, on foot*) randonnée *f*; **on t.** en voyage; en tournée; **a t. of** (*France*) un voyage en; une tournée en; une randonnée en; – *vt* visiter; (*of artist etc*) être en tournée ou dans *etc*. ◆—ing *n* tourisme *m*; **to go t.** faire du tourisme. ◆tourism *n* tourisme *m*. ◆tourist *n* touriste *mf*; – *a* touristique; (*class*) touriste *inv*; **t. office** syndicat *m* d'initiative. ◆touristy *a Pej Fam* (*trop*) touristique.

tournament ['tuənəmənt] *n Sp & Hist* tournoi *m*.

tousled ['tauzəld] *a* (*hair*) ébouriffé.

tout [taut] *vi* racoler; **to t. for** (*customers*) racoler; – *n* racoleur, -euse *mf*; **ticket t.** revendeur, -euse *mf* (en fraude) de billets.

tow [təu] *vt* (*car, boat*) remorquer; (*caravan, trailer*) tracter; **to t. away** (*vehicle*) Jur emmener à la fourrière; – *n* '**on t.**' 'en remorque'; **t. truck** (*breakdown lorry*) *Am* dépanneuse *f*. ◆towpath *n* chemin *m* de halage. ◆towrope *n* (câble *m* de) remorque *f*.

toward(s) [təˈwɔːd(z), *Am* tɔːd(z)] *prep* vers;

(*of feelings*) envers; **money t.** de l'argent pour (acheter).

towel ['tauəl] *n* serviette *f* (de toilette); (*for dishes*) torchon *m*; **t. rail** porte-serviettes *m inv*. ◆towelling *n*, *Am* ◆toweling *n* tissu-éponge *m*; (*kitchen*) **t.** *Am* essuie-tout *m inv*.

tower ['tauər] *n* tour *f*; **t. block** tour *f*, immeuble *m*; **ivory t.** Fig tour d'ivoire; – *vi* **to t. above** ou **over** dominer. ◆—ing *a* très haut.

town [taun] *n* ville *f*; **in t., (in)to t.** en ville; **out of t.** en province; **country t.** bourg *m*; **t. centre** centre-ville *m*; **t. clerk** secrétaire *mf* de mairie; **t. council** conseil *m* municipal; **t. hall** mairie *f*; **t. planner** urbaniste *mf*; **t. planning** urbanisme *m*. ◆township *n* (*in South Africa*) commune *f* (noire).

toxic ['tɒksɪk] *a* toxique. ◆toxin *n* toxine *f*.

toy [tɔɪ] *n* jouet *m*; **soft t.** (jouet *m* en) peluche *f*; – *a* (*gun*) d'enfant; (*house, car, train*) miniature; – *vi* **to t. with** jouer avec. ◆toyshop *n* magasin *m* de jouets.

trac/e [treɪs] *n* trace *f* (of de); **to vanish** ou **disappear without (a) t.** disparaître sans laisser de traces; – *vt* (*draw*) tracer; (*with tracing paper*) (dé)calquer; (*locate*) retrouver (la trace de), dépister; (*follow*) suivre (la piste de (**to** à); (*relate*) retracer; **to t. (back) to** (*one's family*) faire remonter jusqu'à. ◆—ing *n* (*drawing*) calque *m*; **t. paper** papier-calque *m inv*.

track [træk] *n* trace *f*, (*of bullet, rocket*) trajectoire *f*; (*of person, animal, tape recorder*) & *Sp* piste *f*; (*of record*) plage *f*; *Rail* voie *f*; (*path*) piste *f*, chemin *m*; *Sch Am* classe *f* (de niveau); **to keep t. of** suivre; **to lose t. of** (*friend*) perdre de vue; (*argument*) perdre le fil de; **to make tracks** Fam se sauver; **the right t.** la bonne voie ou piste; **t. event** *Sp* épreuve *f* sur piste; **t. record** (*of person, firm etc*) Fig antécédents *mpl*; – *vt* **to t. (down)** (*locate*) retrouver, dépister; (*pursue*) traquer. ◆—er *a* **t. dog** chien *m* policier. ◆tracksuit *n Sp* survêtement *m*.

tract [trækt] *n* (*stretch of land*) étendue *f*.

traction ['trækʃ(ə)n] *n Tech* traction *f*.

tractor ['træktər] *n* tracteur *m*.

trade [treɪd] *n* commerce *m*; (*job*) métier *m*; (*exchange*) échange *m*; – *a* (*fair, balance, route*) commercial; (*price*) de (demi-)gros; (*secret*) de fabrication; (*barrier*) douanier; **t. union** syndicat *m*; **t. unionist** syndicaliste *mf*; – *vi* faire du commerce (**with** avec); **to t. in** (*sugar etc*) faire le commerce de; – *vt* (*exchange*) échanger (**for** contre); **to t. sth in** (*old article*) faire reprendre qch. ◆t.-in *n*

Com reprise f. ◆t.-off n échange m.
◆trading n commerce m; – a (activity,
port etc) commercial; (nation) commerçant; t. estate zone f industrielle. ◆trader
n commerçant, -ante mf; (street) t.
vendeur, -euse mf de rue. ◆tradesman n
(pl -men) commerçant m.

trademark ['treidmɑːk] n marque f de
fabrique; (registered) t. marque déposée.

tradition [trə'dɪʃ(ə)n] n tradition f. ◆tra-
'ditional a traditionnel. ◆traditionally
adv traditionnellement.

traffic ['træfik] 1 n (on road) circulation f;
Av Nau Rail trafic m; busy or heavy t.
beaucoup de circulation; heavy t. (vehicles)
poids mpl lourds; t. circle Am rond-point
m; t. cone cône m de chantier; t. jam
embouteillage m; t. lights feux mpl (de
signalisation); (when red) feu m rouge; t.
sign panneau m de signalisation. 2 n (trade)
Pej trafic m (in de); – vi (-ck-) trafiquer (in
de). ◆trafficker n Pej trafiquant, -ante mf.

tragedy ['trædʒədɪ] n Th & Fig tragédie f.
◆tragic a tragique. ◆tragically adv
tragiquement.

trail [treɪl] n (of powder, smoke, blood etc)
traînée f; (track) piste f, trace f; (path)
sentier m; in its t. (wake) dans son sillage;
– vt (drag) traîner; (caravan) tracter;
(follow) suivre (la piste de); – vi (on the
ground etc) traîner; (of plant) ramper; to t.
behind (lag behind) traîner. ◆-er n 1 Aut
remorque f; Am caravane f. 2 Cin bande f
annonce.

train [treɪn] n (engine, transport, game)
train m; (underground) rame f; (procession)
Fig file f; (of events) suite f; (of dress) traîne
f; my t. of thought le fil de ma pensée; t. set
train m électrique. 2 vt (teach, develop)
former (to do à faire); Sp entraîner
(animal, child) dresser (to do à faire); (ear)
exercer; to t. oneself to do s'entraîner à
faire; to t. sth on (aim) braquer qch sur; –
vi recevoir une formation (as a doctor/etc
de médecin/etc); Sp s'entraîner. ◆-ed a
(having professional skill) qualifié; (nurse
etc) diplômé; (animal) dressé; (ear) exercé.
◆-ing n formation f; Sp entraînement m;
(of animal) dressage m; to be in t. Sp
s'entraîner; (teachers') t. college école f
normale. ◆trai'nee n & a stagiaire (mf).
◆trainer n (of athlete, racehorse)
entraîneur m; (of dog, lion etc) dresseur m;
(running shoe) jogging m, chaussure f de
sport.

traipse [treɪps] vi Fam (tiredly) traîner les
pieds; to t. (about) (wander) se balader.

trait [treɪt] n (of character) trait m.

traitor ['treɪtər] n traître m.

trajectory [trə'dʒektərɪ] n trajectoire f.

tram [træm] n tram(way) m.

tramp [træmp] 1 n (vagrant) clochard, -arde
mf; (woman) Pej Am traînée f. 2 vi (walk)
marcher d'un pas lourd; (hike) marcher à
pied; – vt (streets etc) parcourir; – n
(sound) pas lourds mpl; (hike) randonnée f.

trample ['træmp(ə)l] vti to t. sth (underfoot),
t. on sth piétiner qch.

trampoline ['træmpəliːn] n trampoline m.

trance [trɑːns] n (mystic) en transe.

tranquil ['træŋkwɪl] a tranquille. ◆tran-
'quillity n tranquillité f. ◆tranquillizer n
Med tranquillisant m.

trans- [trɑːns, trænz] pref trans-.

transact [træn'zækt] vt (business) traiter.
◆transaction n (in bank etc) opération f;
(on Stock Market) transaction f; the t. of
(business) la conduite de.

transatlantic [trænzət'læntɪk] a transatlantique.

transcend [træn'send] vt transcender.
◆transcendent a transcendant.

transcribe [træn'skraɪb] vt transcrire.
◆'transcript n (document) transcription f.
◆transcription n transcription f.

transfer [træns'fɜːr] vt (-rr-) (person, goods
etc) transférer (to à); (power) Pol faire
passer (to à); to t. the charges téléphoner
en PCV; – vi être transféré (to à); –
['trænsfɜːr] n transfert m (to à); (of power)
Pol passation f; (image) décalcomanie f;
bank or credit t. virement m (bancaire).
◆trans'ferable a not t. (on ticket) strictement personnel.

transform [træns'fɔːm] vt transformer (into
en). ◆transfor'mation n transformation
f. ◆transformer n El transformateur m.

transfusion [træns'fjuːʒ(ə)n] n (blood) t.
transfusion f (sanguine).

transient ['trænzɪənt] a (ephemeral) transitoire.

transistor [træn'zɪstər] n (device) transistor
m; t. (radio) transistor m.

transit ['trænzɪt] n in t. en transit.

transition [træn'zɪʃ(ə)n] n transition f.
◆transitional a de transition.

transitive ['trænzɪtɪv] a Gram transitif.

transitory ['trænzɪtərɪ] a transitoire.

translate [træns'leɪt] vt traduire (from de,
into en). ◆translation n traduction f;
(into mother tongue) Sch version f; (from
mother tongue) Sch thème m. ◆translator
n traducteur, -trice mf.

transmit [trænz'mɪt] vt (-tt-) (send, pass)

transmettre; – *vti* (*broadcast*) émettre.
◆**transmission** *n* transmission *f*; (*broadcast*) émission *f*. ◆**transmitter** *n* Rad TV émetteur *m*.

transparent [træns'pærənt] *a* transparent. ◆**transparency** *n*; (*slide*) Phot diapositive *f*.

transpire [træn'spaɪər] *vi* (*of secret etc*) s'ébruiter; (*happen*) Fam arriver; **it transpired that . . .** il s'est avéré que . . . .

transplant [træns'plɑːnt] *vt* (*plant*) transplanter; (*organ*) Med greffer, transplanter; – ['trænsplɑːnt] *n* Med greffe *f*, transplantation *f*.

transport [træn'spɔːt] *vt* transporter; – ['trænspɔːt] *n* transport *m*; **public t.** les transports en commun; **do you have t.?** es-tu motorisé?; **t. café** routier *m*. ◆**transpor'tation** *n* transport *m*.

transpose [træns'pəʊz] *vt* transposer.

transvestite [trænz'vestaɪt] *n* travesti *m*.

trap [træp] *n* piège *m*; (*mouth*) Pej Sl gueule *f*; **t. door** trappe *f*; – *vt* (-pp-) (*snare*) prendre (au piège); (*jam*, *corner*) coincer, bloquer; (*cut off by snow etc*) bloquer (by par); **to t. one's finger** se coincer le doigt. ◆**trapper** *n* (*hunter*) trappeur *m*.

trapeze [trə'piːz] *n* (*in circus*) trapèze *m*; **t. artist** trapéziste *mf*.

trappings [træpɪŋz] *npl* signes *mpl* extérieurs.

trash [træʃ] *n* (*nonsense*) sottises *fpl*; (*junk*) saleté(s) *f(pl)*; (*waste*) Am ordures *fpl*; (*riffraff*) Am racaille *f*. ◆**trashcan** *n* Am poubelle *f*. ◆**trashy** *a* (-ier, -iest) (*book etc*) moche, sans valeur; (*goods*) de camelote.

trauma ['trɔːmə, 'traʊmə] *n* (*shock*) traumatisme *m*. ◆**trau'matic** *a* traumatisant. ◆**traumatize** *vt* traumatiser.

travel ['trævəl] *vi* (-ll-, Am -l-) voyager; (*move*) aller, se déplacer; – *vt* (*country*, *distance*, *road*) parcourir; – *n* & *npl* voyages *mpl*; **on one's travels** en voyage; – *a* (*agency*, *book*) de voyages; **t. brochure** dépliant *m* touristique. ◆**travelled** *a* **to be well** or **widely t.** avoir beaucoup voyagé. ◆**travelling** *n* voyages *mpl*; – *a* (*bag etc*) de voyage; (*expenses*) de déplacement; (*circus*, *musician*) ambulant. ◆**traveller** *n* voyageur, -euse *mf*; **traveller's cheque,** Am **traveler's check** chèque *m* de voyage. ◆**travelogue** *n*, Am **travelog** *n* (*book*) récit *m* de voyages. ◆**travelsickness** *n* (*in car*) mal *m* de la route; (*in aircraft*) mal *m* de l'air.

travesty ['trævəstɪ] *n* parodie *f*.

travolator ['trævəleɪtər] *n* trottoir *m* roulant.

trawler ['trɔːlər] *n* (*ship*) chalutier *m*.

tray [treɪ] *n* plateau *m*; (*for office correspondence etc*) corbeille *f*.

treacherous ['tretʃ(ə)rəs] *a* (*person*, *action*, *road*, *journey etc*) traître. ◆**treacherously** *adv* traîtreusement; (*dangerously*) dangereusement. ◆**treachery** *n* traîtrise *f*.

treacle ['triːk(ə)l] *n* mélasse *f*.

tread [tred] *vi* (*pt* trod, *pp* trodden) (*walk*) marcher (*sur* on); (*proceed*) Fig avancer; – *vt* (*path*) parcourir; (*soil*) Fig fouler; **to t. sth into a carpet** étaler qch (avec les pieds) sur un tapis; – *n* (*step*) pas *m*; (*of tyre*) chape *f*. ◆**treadmill** *n* Pej Fig routine *f*.

treason ['triːz(ə)n] *n* trahison *f*.

treasure ['treʒər] *n* trésor *m*; **a real t.** (*person*) Fig une vraie perle; **t. hunt** chasse *f* au trésor; – *vt* (*value*) tenir à, priser; (*keep*) conserver (précieusement). ◆**treasurer** *n* trésorier, -ière *mf*. ◆**Treasury** *n* the **T.** Pol = le ministère des Finances.

treat [triːt] **1** *vt* (*person*, *product etc*) & Med traiter; (*consider*) considérer (*as* comme); **to t. with care** prendre soin de; **to t. s.o. to sth** offrir qch à qn. **2** *n* (*pleasure*) plaisir *m* (*special*); (*present*) cadeau-surprise *m*; (*meal*) régal *m*; **it was a t.** (*for me*) to do it ça m'a fait plaisir de le faire. ◆**treatment** *n* (*behaviour*) & Med traitement *m*; **his t. of her** la façon dont il la traite; **rough t.** mauvais traitements *mpl*.

treatise ['triːtɪz] *n* (*book*) traité *m* (*on* de).

treaty ['triːtɪ] *n* Pol traité *m*.

treble ['treb(ə)l] *a* triple; – *vti* tripler; – *n* le , triple; **it's t. the price** c'est le triple du prix.

tree [triː] *n* arbre *m*; **Christmas t.** sapin *m* de Noël; **family t.** arbre *m* généalogique. ◆**t.-lined** *a* bordé d'arbres. ◆**t.-top** *n* cime *f* (d'un arbre). ◆**t.-trunk** *n* tronc *m* d'arbre.

trek [trek] *vi* (-kk-) cheminer or voyager (*péniblement*); Sp marcher à pied; (*go*) Fam traîner; – *n* voyage *m* (pénible); Sp randonnée *f*; (*distance*) Fam tirée *f*.

trellis ['trelɪs] *n* treillage *m*.

tremble ['tremb(ə)l] *vi* trembler (*with* de). ◆**tremor** *n* tremblement *m*; (*earth*) **t.** secousse *f* (sismique).

tremendous [trə'mendəs] *a* (*huge*) énorme; (*dreadful*) terrible; (*wonderful*) formidable, terrible. ◆**-ly** *adv* terriblement.

trench [trentʃ] *n* tranchée *f*.

trend [trend] *n* tendance *f* (*towards* à); the **t.** (*fashion*) la mode; **to set a** or **the t.** donner le ton, lancer une *or* la mode. ◆**trendy** *a* (-ier, -iest) (*person, clothes, topic etc*) *Fam* à la mode, dans le vent.

trepidation [trepr'deɪʃ(ə)n] *n* inquiétude *f*.

trespass ['trespas] *vi* s'introduire sans autorisation (**on, upon** dans); '**no trespassing**' 'entrée interdite'.

tresses ['tresɪz] *npl Lit* chevelure *f*.

trestle ['tres(ə)l] *n* tréteau *m*.

trial ['traɪəl] *n Jur* procès *m*; (*test*) essai *m*; (*ordeal*) épreuve *f*; **t. of strength** épreuve de force; **to put** *or* **be on t., stand t.** passer en jugement; **to put s.o. on t.** juger qn; **by t. and error** par tâtonnements; – *a* (*period, flight etc*) d'essai; (*offer*) à l'essai; **t. run** (*of new product etc*) période *f* d'essai.

triangle ['traɪæŋg(ə)l] *n* triangle *m*; (*setsquare*) *Math Am* équerre *f*. ◆**triangular** *a* triangulaire.

tribe [traɪb] *n* tribu *f*. ◆**tribal** *a* tribal.

tribulations [trɪbju'leɪʃ(ə)nz] *npl* (**trials and**) **t.** tribulations *fpl*.

tribunal [traɪ'bjuːn(ə)l] *n* commission *f*, tribunal *m*; *Mil* tribunal *m*.

tributary ['trɪbjutərɪ] *n* affluent *m*.

tribute ['trɪbjuːt] *n* hommage *m*, tribut *m*; **to pay t.** rendre hommage à.

trick [trɪk] *n* (*joke, deception & of conjurer etc*) tour *m*; (*ruse*) astuce *f*; (*habit*) manie *f*; **to play a t. on s.o.** jouer un tour à qn; **card t.** tour *m* de cartes; **that will do the t.** *Fam* ça fera l'affaire; **t. photo** photo *f* truquée; **t. question** question-piège *f*; – *vt* (*deceive*) tromper, attraper; **to t. s.o. into doing sth** amener qn à faire qch par la ruse. ◆**trickery** *n* ruse *f*. ◆**tricky** *a* (-ier, -iest) (*problem etc*) difficile, délicat; (*person*) rusé.

trickle ['trɪk(ə)l] *n* (*of liquid*) filet *m*; **a t. of** (*letters, people etc*) *Fig* un petit nombre de; – *vi* (*flow*) dégouliner, couler (lentement); **to t. in** (*of letters, people etc*) *Fig* arriver en petit nombre.

tricycle ['traɪsɪk(ə)l] *n* tricycle *m*.

trier ['traɪər] *n* **to be a t.** être persévérant.

trifl/e ['traɪf(ə)l] *n* (*article, money*) bagatelle *f*; (*dessert*) diplomate *m*; – *adv* **a t. small/too much/***etc* un tantinet petit/trop/*etc*; – *vi* **to t. with** (*s.o.'s feelings*) jouer avec; (*person*) plaisanter avec. ◆**—ing** *a* insignifiant.

trigger ['trɪgər] *n* (*of gun*) gâchette *f*; – *vt* **to t. (off)** (*start, cause*) déclencher.

trilogy ['trɪlədʒɪ] *n* trilogie *f*.

trim [trɪm] **1** *a* (**trimmer, trimmest**) (*neat*) soigné, net; (*slim*) svelte; – *n* **in t.** (*fit*) en (bonne) forme. **2** *n* (*cut*) légère coupe *f*; (*haircut*) coupe *f* de rafraîchissement; *vt*

have a t. se faire rafraîchir les cheveux; – *vt* (-mm-) couper (légèrement); (*finger nail, edge*) rogner; (*hair*) rafraîchir. **3** *n* (*on garment*) garniture *f*; (*on car*) garnitures *fpl*; – *vt* (-mm-) **to t. with** (*lace etc*) orner de. ◆**trimmings** *npl* garniture(s) *f*(*pl*); (*extras*) *Fig* accessoires *mpl*.

Trinity ['trɪnɪtɪ] *n* **the T.** (*union*) *Rel* la Trinité.

trinket ['trɪŋkɪt] *n* colifichet *m*.

trio ['triːəʊ] *n* (*pl* -os) (*group*) & *Mus* trio *m*.

trip [trɪp] **1** *n* (*journey*) voyage *m*; (*outing*) excursion *f*; **to take a t. to** (*shops, place etc*) aller à. **2** *n* (*stumble*) faux pas *m*; – *vi* (-pp-) **to t.** (**over** *or* **up**) trébucher; **to t. over sth** trébucher contre qch; – *vt* **to t. s.o. up** faire trébucher qn. **3** *vi* (-pp-) (*walk gently*) marcher d'un pas léger. ◆**tripper** *n* **day t.** excursionniste *mf*.

tripe [traɪp] *n Culin* tripes *fpl*; (*nonsense*) *Fam* bêtises *fpl*.

triple ['trɪp(ə)l] *a* triple; – *vti* tripler. ◆**triplets** *npl* (*children*) triplés, -ées *mfpl*.

triplicate ['trɪplɪkət] *n* **in t.** en trois exemplaires.

tripod ['traɪpɒd] *n* trépied *m*.

trite [traɪt] *a* banal. ◆**—ness** *n* banalité *f*.

triumph ['traɪʌmf] *n* triomphe *m* (**over** sur); – *vi* triompher (**over** de). ◆**tri'umphal** *a* triomphal. ◆**tri'umphant** *a* (*team, army, gesture*) triomphant; (*success, welcome, return*) triomphal. ◆**tri'umphantly** *adv* triomphalement.

trivia ['trɪvɪə] *npl* vétilles *fpl*. ◆**trivial** *a* (*unimportant*) insignifiant; (*trite*) banal. ◆**trivi'ality** *n* insignifiance *f*; banalité *f*; *pl* banalités *fpl*.

trod, trodden [trɒd, 'trɒd(ə)n] *see* tread.

trolley ['trɒlɪ] *n* (*for luggage*) chariot *m*; (*for shopping*) poussette *f* (de marché); (*in supermarket*) caddie® *m*; (*trolleybus*) trolley *m*; (**tea**) **t.** table *f* roulante; (*for tea urn*) chariot *m*; **t.** (**car**) *Am* tramway *m*. ◆**trolleybus** *n* trolleybus *m*.

trombone [trɒm'bəʊn] *n Mus* trombone *m*.

troop [truːp] *n* bande *f*; *Mil* troupe *f*; **the troops** (*army, soldiers*) les troupes, la troupe; – *vi* **to t. in/out/***etc* entrer/sortir/*etc* en masse. ◆**—ing** *n* **the t. the colour** le salut du drapeau. ◆**—er** *n* (*state*) *Am* **t.** membre *m* de la police montée.

trophy ['trəʊfɪ] *n* trophée *m*.

tropic ['trɒpɪk] *n* tropique *m*. ◆**tropical** *a* tropical.

trot [trɒt] *n* (*of horse*) trot *m*; **on the t.** (*one after another*) *Fam* de suite; – *vi* (-tt-) trot-

ter; **to t. off** or **along** (*leave*) *Hum Fam* se
sauver; − *vt* **to t. out** (*say*) *Fam* débiter.

troubl/e ['trʌb(ə)l] *n* (*difficulty*) ennui(s)
m (*pl*); (*bother, effort*) peine *f*, mal *m*; **trou-
ble(s)** (*social unrest etc*) & *Med* troubles
mpl; **to be in t.** avoir des ennuis; to get into
t. s'attirer des ennuis (**with** avec); **the t.**
(**with you**) **is** ... l'ennui (avec toi) c'est que
... ; **to go to the t. of doing, take the t. to do**
se donner la peine *or* le mal de faire; **I
didn't put her to any t.** je ne l'ai pas
dérangée; **to find the t.** trouver le
problème; **a spot of t.** un petit problème; **a
t. spot** *Pol* un point chaud; − *vt* (*inconvenience*) déranger, ennuyer; (*worry, annoy*)
ennuyer; (*hurt*) faire mal à; (*grieve*) peiner;
to t. to do se donner la peine de faire; − *vi*
to t. (oneself) se déranger. **◆−ed** *a*
(*worried*) inquiet; (*period*) agité.
◆trouble-free *a* (*machine, vehicle*) qui
ne tombe jamais en panne, fiable.
◆troublemaker *n* fauteur *m* de troubles.
◆troubleshooter *n Tech* dépanneur *m*,
expert *m*; *Pol* conciliateur, -trice *mf*.

troublesome ['trʌb(ə)ls(ə)m] *a* ennuyeux,
gênant; (*leg etc*) qui fait mal.

trough [trɒf] *n* (*for drinking*) abreuvoir *m*;
(*for feeding*) auge *f*; **t. of low pressure** *Met*
dépression *f*.

trounce [traʊns] *vt* (*defeat*) écraser.

troupe [truːp] *n Th* troupe *f*.

trousers ['traʊzəz] *npl* pantalon *m*; **a pair of
t., some t.** un pantalon; (**short**) **t.** culottes
fpl courtes.

trousseau ['truːsəʊ] *n* (*of bride*) trousseau
m.

trout [traʊt] *n* truite *f*.

trowel ['traʊəl] *n* (*for cement or plaster*)
truelle *f*; (*for plants*) déplantoir *m*.

truant ['truːənt] *n* (*pupil, shirker*) absentéiste
mf; **to play t.** faire l'école buissonnière.
◆truancy *n Sch* absentéisme *m* scolaire.

truce [truːs] *n Mil* trêve *f*.

truck [trʌk] *n* **1** (*lorry*) camion *m*; *Rail*
wagon *m* plat; **t. driver** camionneur *m*;
(*long-distance*) routier *m*; **t. stop** (*restaurant*) routier *m*. **2** *Am* **t. farmer** *Am* maraîcher,
-ère *mf*. **◆trucker** *n Am* (*haulier*) transporteur *m* routier; (*driver*) camionneur *m*,
routier *m*.

truculent ['trʌkjʊlənt] *a* agressif.

trudge [trʌdʒ] *vi* marcher d'un pas pesant.

true [truː] *a* (**-er, -est**) vrai; (*accurate*) exact;
(*genuine*) vrai, véritable; **t.** to (*person,
promise etc*) fidèle à; **t. to life** conforme à la
réalité; **to come t.** se réaliser; **to hold t.** (*of
argument etc*) valoir (**for** pour); **too t.!** *Fam*

ah, ça oui! **◆truly** *adv* vraiment; (*faithfully*) fidèlement; **well and t.** bel et bien.

truffle ['trʌf(ə)l] *n* (*mushroom*) truffe *f*.

truism ['truːɪz(ə)m] *n* lapalissade *f*.

trump [trʌmp] **1** *n Cards* atout *m*; **t. card**
(*advantage*) *Fig* atout *m*. **2** *vt* **to t. up**
(*charge, reason*) inventer.

trumpet ['trʌmpɪt] *n* trompette *f*; **t. player**
trompettiste *mf*.

truncate [trʌŋ'keɪt] *vt* tronquer.

truncheon ['trʌntʃ(ə)n] *n* matraque *f*.

trundle ['trʌnd(ə)l] *vti* **to t. along** rouler
bruyamment.

trunk [trʌŋk] *n* (*of tree, body*) tronc *m*; (*of
elephant*) trompe *f*; (*case*) malle *f*; (*of vehicle*) *Am* coffre *m*; *pl* (*for swimming*) slip *m*
or caleçon *m* de bain; **t. call** *Tel* communication *f* interurbaine; **t. road** route *f*
nationale.

truss [trʌs] *vt* **to t. (up)** (*prisoner*) ligoter.

trust [trʌst] *n* (*faith*) confiance *f* (**in** en);
(*group*) *Fin* trust *m*; *Jur* fidéicommis *m*; **to
take on t.** accepter de confiance; − *vt*
(*person, judgement*) avoir confiance en, se
fier à; (*instinct, promise*) se fier à; **to t. s.o.
with sth, t. sth to s.o.** confier qch à qn; **to t.
s.o. to do** (*rely on, expect*) compter sur qn
pour faire; **I t. that** (*hope*) j'espère que; − *vi*
to t. in s.o. se fier à qn; **to t. to luck** *or*
chance se fier au hasard. **◆−ed** *a* (*friend,
method etc*) éprouvé. **◆−ing** *a* confiant.
◆trus'tee *n* (*of school*) administrateur
-trice *mf*. **◆trustworthy** *a* sûr, digne de
confiance.

truth [truːθ] *n* (*pl* **-s** [truːðz]) vérité *f*; **there's
some t. in** ... il y a du vrai dans ....
◆truthful *a* (*statement etc*) véridique, vrai;
(*person*) sincère. **◆truthfully** *adv* sincèrement.

try [traɪ] **1** *vt* essayer (**to do, doing** de faire);
(*s.o.'s patience etc*) mettre à l'épreuve; **to t.
one's hand at** s'essayer à; **to t. one's luck**
tenter sa chance; **to t. (out)** (*car, method
etc*) essayer; (*employee etc*) mettre à l'essai;
to t. on (*clothes, shoes*) essayer; − *vi* essayer
(**for sth** d'obtenir qch); **to t. hard** faire un
gros effort; **t. and come!** essaie de venir!; −
n (*attempt*) & *Rugby* essai *m*; **to have a t.**
essayer; **at the first t.** du premier coup. **2**
vt (*person*) *Jur* juger (**for theft** /etc pour
vol/etc). **◆−ing** *a* pénible, éprouvant.

tsar [zɑːr] *n* tsar *m*.

tub [tʌb] *n* (*for washing clothes etc*) baquet
m; (*bath*) baignoire *f*; (*for ice cream etc*)
pot *m*.

tuba ['tjuːbə] *n Mus* tuba *m*.

tubby ['tʌbɪ] *a* (**-ier, -iest**) *Fam* dodu.

tube [tjuːb] n tube m; Rail Fam métro m; (of tyre) chambre f à air. ◆**tubing** n (tubes) tubes mpl. ◆**tubular** a tubulaire.

tuberculosis [tjuːbɜːkjuˈləʊsɪs] n tuberculose f.

tuck [tʌk] **1** n (fold in garment) rempli m; − vt (put) mettre; **to t. away** ranger; (hide) cacher; **to t. in** (shirt) rentrer; (person in bed, a blanket) border; **to t. up** (skirt) remonter. **2** vi **to t. in** (eat) Fam manger; **to t. into** (meal) Fam attaquer; − **t. shop** Sch boutique f à provisions.

Tuesday [ˈtjuːzdɪ] n mardi m.

tuft [tʌft] n (of hair, grass) touffe f.

tug [tʌg] **1** vt (-gg-) (pull) tirer; − vi tirer (at, on sur); − n **to give sth a t.** tirer (sur) qch. **2** n (boat) remorqueur m.

tuition [tjuːˈɪʃ(ə)n] n (teaching) enseignement m; (lessons) leçons fpl; (fee) frais mpl de scolarité.

tulip [ˈtjuːlɪp] n tulipe f.

tumble [ˈtʌmb(ə)l] vi **to t. (over)** (fall) dégringoler; (backwards) tomber à la renverse; **to t. to sth** (understand) Sl réaliser qch; − n (fall) dégringolade f; **t. drier** sèche-linge m inv.

tumbledown [ˈtʌmb(ə)ldaʊn] a délabré.

tumbler [ˈtʌmblər] n (drinking glass) gobelet m.

tummy [ˈtʌmɪ] n Fam ventre m.

tumour [ˈtjuːmər] n tumeur f.

tumult [ˈtjuːmʌlt] n tumulte m. ◆**tuˈmultuous** a tumultueux.

tuna [ˈtjuːnə] n **t. (fish)** thon m.

tun/e [tjuːn] n (melody) air m; **to be** or **sing in t./out of t.** chanter juste/faux; **in t.** (instrument) accordé; **out of t.** (instrument) désaccordé; **in t. with** (harmony) Fig en accord avec; **to the t. of £50** d'un montant de 50 livres, dans les 50 livres; − vt **to t. (up)** Mus accorder; Aut régler; − vi **to t. in (to)** Rad TV se mettre à l'écoute (de), écouter. ◆**-ing** n Aut réglage m; **t. fork** Mus diapason m. ◆**tuneful** a mélodieux.

tunic [ˈtjuːnɪk] n tunique f.

Tunisia [tjuːˈnɪzɪə] n Tunisie f. ◆**Tunisian** a & n tunisien, -ienne (mf).

tunnel [ˈtʌn(ə)l] n tunnel m; (in mine) galerie f; − vi (-ll-, Am -l-) percer un tunnel (into dans).

turban [ˈtɜːbən] n turban m.

turbine [ˈtɜːbaɪn, Am ˈtɜːbɪn] n turbine f.

turbulence [ˈtɜːbjʊləns] n Phys Av turbulences fpl.

turbulent [ˈtɜːbjʊlənt] a (person etc) turbulent.

tureen [tjuːˈriːn, təˈriːn] n (soup) **t.** soupière f.

turf [tɜːf] **1** n (grass) gazon m; **the t.** Sp le turf; **t. accountant** bookmaker m. **2** vt **to t. out** (get rid of) Fam jeter dehors.

turgid [ˈtɜːdʒɪd] a (style, language) boursouflé.

turkey [ˈtɜːkɪ] n dindon m, dinde f; (as food) dinde f.

Turkey [ˈtɜːkɪ] n Turquie f. ◆**Turk** n Turc m, Turque f. ◆**Turkish** a turc; **T. delight** (sweet) loukoum m; − n (language) turc m.

turmoil [ˈtɜːmɔɪl] n confusion f, trouble m; **in t.** en ébullition.

turn [tɜːn] n (movement, action & in game etc) tour m; (in road) tournant m; (of events, mind) tournure f; Med crise f; (act) Th numéro m; **t. of phrase** tour m or tournure f (de phrase); **to take turns** se relayer; **in t.** à tour de rôle; **by turns** tour à tour; **in (one's) t.** à son tour; **it's your t. to play** c'est à toi de jouer; **to do s.o. a good t.** rendre service à qn; **the t. of the century** le début du siècle; − vt tourner; (mechanically) faire tourner; (mattress, pancake) retourner; **to t. s.o./sth into** (change) changer or transformer qn/qch en; **to t. sth red/yellow** rougir/jaunir qch; **to t. sth on s.o.** (aim) braquer qch sur qn; **she's turned twenty** elle a vingt ans passés; **it's turned seven** il est sept heures passées; **it turns my stomach** cela me soulève le cœur; − vi (of wheel, driver etc) tourner; (turn head or body) se (re)tourner (towards vers); (become) devenir; **to t. to** (question, adviser etc) se tourner vers; **to t. against** se retourner contre; **to t. into** (change) se changer or se transformer en. ■ **to t. around** vi (of person) se retourner; **to t. away** vt (avert) détourner (from de); (refuse) renvoyer (qn); − vi (stop facing) détourner les yeux, se détourner; **to t. back** vt (bed sheet, corner of page) replier; (person) renvoyer; (clock) reculer (to jusqu'à); − vi (return) retourner (sur ses pas); **to t. down** vt (fold down) rabattre; (gas, radio etc) baisser; (refuse) refuser (qn, offre etc); **to t. in** vt (hand in) rendre (to à); (prisoner etc) Fam livrer (à la police); − vi (go to bed) Fam se coucher; **to t. off** vt (light, radio etc) éteindre; (tap) fermer; (machine) arrêter; − vi (in vehicle) tourner; **to t. on** vt (light, radio etc) mettre, allumer; (tap) ouvrir; (machine) mettre en marche; **to t. on s.o.** (sexually) Fam exciter qn; − vi **to t. on s.o.** (attack) attaquer qn; **to t. out** vt (light) éteindre; (contents of box etc) vider (from de); (produce) produire; − vi (of crowds) venir; (happen) se passer; **it turns out that il**

s'avère que; **she turned out to be ...** elle s'est révélée être ... ; **to t. over** vt (page) tourner; – vi (of vehicle, person etc) se retourner; (of car engine) tourner au ralenti; **to t. round** vt (head, object) tourner; (vehicle) faire faire demi-tour à; – vi (of person) se retourner; **to t. up** vt (radio, light etc) mettre plus fort; (collar) remonter; (unearth, find) déterrer; **a turned-up nose** un nez retroussé; – vi (arrive) arriver; (be found) être (re)trouvé. ◆**turning** (street) petite rue f; (bend in road) tournant m; **t. circle** Aut rayon m de braquage; **t. point** (in time) tournant m. ◆**turner** n (workman) tourneur m.

turncoat ['tɜːnkəʊt] n renégat, -ate mf. ◆**turn-off** n (in road) embranchement m. ◆**turnout** n (people) assistance f; (at polls) participation f. ◆**turnover** n (money) Com chiffre m d'affaires; (of stock) Com rotation f; **staff t.** (starting and leaving) la rotation du personnel; **apple t.** chausson m (aux pommes). ◆**turnip** n (on trousers) revers m.

turnip ['tɜːnɪp] n navet m.

turnpike ['tɜːnpaɪk] n Am autoroute f à péage.

turnstile ['tɜːnstaɪl] n (gate) tourniquet m.

turntable ['tɜːnteɪb(ə)l] n (of record player) platine f.

turpentine ['tɜːpəntaɪn] (Fam **turps** [tɜːps]) n térébenthine f.

turquoise ['tɜːkwɔɪz] a turquoise inv.

turret ['tʌrɪt] n tourelle f.

turtle ['tɜːt(ə)l] n tortue f de mer; Am tortue f. ◆**turtleneck** a (sweater) à col roulé; – n col m roulé.

tusk [tʌsk] n (of elephant) défense f.

tussle ['tʌs(ə)l] n bagarre f.

tutor ['tjuːtər] n précepteur, -trice mf; Univ directeur, -trice mf d'études; Univ Am assistant, -ante mf; – vt donner des cours particuliers à. ◆**tu'torial** n Univ travaux mpl dirigés.

tut-tut! [tʌt'tʌt] int allons donc!

tuxedo [tʌk'siːdəʊ] n (pl -os) Am smoking m.

TV [tiː'viː] n télé f.

twaddle ['twɒd(ə)l] n fadaises fpl.

twang [twæŋ] n son m vibrant; (nasal) **t.** nasillement m; – vi (of wire etc) vibrer.

twee [twiː] a (fussy) maniéré.

tweed [twiːd] n tweed m.

tweezers ['twiːzəz] npl pince f (à épiler).

twelve [twelv] a & n douze (m). ◆**twelfth** a & n douzième (mf).

twenty ['twentɪ] a & n vingt (m). ◆**twentieth** a & n vingtième (mf).

twerp [twɜːp] n Sl crétin, -ine mf.

twice [twaɪs] adv deux fois; **t. as heavy/etc** deux fois plus lourd/etc; **t. a month/etc, t. monthly/etc** deux fois par mois/etc.

twiddle ['twɪd(ə)l] vti to t. (with) sth (pencil, knob etc) tripoter qch; **to t. one's thumbs** se tourner les pouces.

twig [twɪg] **1** n (of branch) brindille f. **2** vti (-gg-) (understand) Sl piger.

twilight ['twaɪlaɪt] n crépuscule m; – a crépusculaire.

twin [twɪn] n jumeau m, jumelle f; **identical t.** vrai jumeau; **t. brother** frère m jumeau; **t. beds** lits mpl jumeaux; **t. town** ville f jumelée; – vt (-nn-) (town) jumeler. ◆**twinning** n jumelage m.

twine [twaɪn] **1** n (string) ficelle f. **2** vi (twist) s'enlacer (round autour de).

twinge [twɪndʒ] n a t. (of pain) un élancement; **a t. of remorse** un pincement de remords.

twinkle ['twɪŋk(ə)l] vi (of star) scintiller; (of eye) pétiller; – n scintillement m; pétillement m.

twirl [twɜːl] vi tournoyer; – vt faire tournoyer; (moustache) tortiller.

twist [twɪst] vt (wine, arm etc) tordre; (roll round) enrouler; (weave together) entortiller; (knob) tourner; (truth etc) Fig déformer; **to t. s.o.'s arm** Fig forcer la main à qn; – vi (wind) s'entortiller (round sth autour de qch); (of road, river) serpenter; – n torsion f; (turn) tour m; (in rope) entortillement m; (bend in road) tournant m; (in story) coup m de théâtre; (in event) tournure f; (of lemon) zeste m; **a road full of twists** une route qui fait des zigzags. ◆**–ed** a (ankle, wire, mind) tordu. ◆**–er** n **tongue t.** mot m ou expression f imprononçable.

twit [twɪt] n Fam idiot, -ote mf.

twitch [twɪtʃ] **1** n (nervous) tic m; – vi (of person) avoir un tic; (of muscle) se convulser. **2** n (jerk) secousse f.

twitter ['twɪtər] vi (of bird) pépier.

two [tuː] a & n deux (m). ◆**t.-cycle** n Am = **t.-stroke.** ◆**t.-'faced** a Fig hypocrite. ◆**t.-'legged** a bipède. ◆**t.-piece** n (garment) deux-pièces m inv. ◆**t.-'seater** n Aut voiture f à deux places. ◆**t.-stroke** n **t.-stroke (engine)** deux-temps m inv. ◆**t.-way** a (traffic) dans les deux sens; **t.-way radio** émetteur-récepteur m.

twofold ['tuːfəʊld] a double; – adv to increase t. doubler.

twosome ['tuːsəm] n couple m.

tycoon [taɪ'kuːn] n magnat m.

type[1] [taɪp] n 1 (example, person) type m; (sort) genre m, sorte f, type m; **blood** t. groupe m sanguin. 2 (print) Typ caractères mpl; **in large** t. en gros caractères. ◆**typesetter** n compositeur, trice mf.

typ/e[2] vt (write) taper (à la machine). ◆**—ing** n dactylo(graphie) f; **a page of** t. une page dactylographiée; **t. error** faute f de frappe. ◆**typewriter** n machine f à écrire. ◆**typewritten** a dactylographié. ◆**typist** n dactylo f.

typhoid ['taɪfɔɪd] n **t. (fever)** Med typhoïde f.

typhoon [taɪ'fuːn] n Met typhon m.

typical ['tɪpɪk(ə)l] a typique (of de); (customary) habituel; **that's t. (of him)!** c'est bien lui! ◆**typically** adv typiquement; (as usual) comme d'habitude. ◆**typify** vt être typique de; (symbolize) représenter.

tyranny ['tɪrənɪ] n tyrannie f. ◆**tyrannical** [tɪ'rænɪk(ə)l] a tyrannique. ◆**tyrant** ['taɪərənt] n tyran m.

tyre ['taɪər] n pneu m.

U

U, u [juː] n U, u m. ◆**U-turn** n Aut demi-tour m; Fig Pej volte-face f inv.

ubiquitous [juː'bɪkwɪtəs] a omniprésent.

udder ['ʌdər] n (of cow etc) pis m.

ugh! [ɜː(h)] int pouah!

ugly ['ʌglɪ] a (-ier, -iest) laid, vilain. ◆**ugliness** n laideur f.

UK [juː'keɪ] abbr = United Kingdom.

ulcer ['ʌlsər] n ulcère m.

ulterior [ʌl'tɪərɪər] a **u. motive** arrière-pensée f.

ultimate ['ʌltɪmət] a (final, last) ultime; (definitive) définitif; (basic) fondamental; (authority) suprême. ◆**—ly** adv (finally) à la fin; (fundamentally) en fin de compte; (subsequently) à une date ultérieure.

ultimatum [ʌltɪ'meɪtəm] n ultimatum m.

ultra- ['ʌltrə] pref ultra-.

ultramodern [ʌltrə'mɒdən] a ultra-moderne.

ultraviolet [ʌltrə'vaɪələt] a ultraviolet.

umbilical [ʌm'bɪlɪk(ə)l] a **u. cord** cordon m ombilical.

umbrage ['ʌmbrɪdʒ] n **to take u.** se froisser (at de).

umbrella [ʌm'brelə] n parapluie m; **u. stand** porte-parapluies m inv.

umpire ['ʌmpaɪər] n Sp arbitre m; – vt arbitrer.

umpteen [ʌmp'tiːn] a (many) Fam je ne sais combien de. ◆**umpteenth** a Fam énième.

un- [ʌn] pref in-, peu, non, sans.

UN [juː'en] abbr = United Nations.

unabashed [ʌnə'bæʃt] a nullement déconcerté.

unabated [ʌnə'beɪtɪd] a aussi fort qu'avant.

unable [ʌn'eɪb(ə)l] a **to be u. to do** être incapable de faire; **he's u. to swim** il ne sait pas nager.

unabridged [ʌnə'brɪdʒd] a intégral.

unacceptable [ʌnək'septəb(ə)l] a inacceptable.

unaccompanied [ʌnə'kʌmpənɪd] a (person) non accompagné; (singing) sans accompagnement.

unaccountab/le [ʌnə'kaʊntəb(ə)l] a inexplicable. ◆**—ly** adv inexplicablement.

unaccounted [ʌnə'kaʊntɪd] a **to be (still) u. for** rester introuvable.

unaccustomed [ʌnə'kʌstəmd] a inaccoutumé; **to be u. to sth/to doing** ne pas être habitué à qch/à faire.

unadulterated [ʌnə'dʌltəreɪtɪd] a pur.

unaided [ʌn'eɪdɪd] a sans aide.

unanimity [juːnə'nɪmɪtɪ] n unanimité f. ◆**u'nanimous** a unanime. ◆**u'nanimously** adv à l'unanimité.

unappetizing [ʌn'æpɪtaɪzɪŋ] a peu appétissant.

unapproachable [ʌnə'prəʊtʃəb(ə)l] a (person) inabordable.

unarmed [ʌn'ɑːmd] a (person) non armé; (combat) à mains nues.

unashamed [ʌnə'ʃeɪmd] a éhonté; **she's u. about it** elle n'en a pas honte. ◆**—ly** [-ɪdlɪ] adv sans vergogne.

unassailable [ʌnə'seɪləb(ə)l] a (argument, reputation) inattaquable.

unassuming [ʌnə'sjuːmɪŋ] a modeste.

unattached [ʌnə'tætʃt] a (independent, not married) libre.

unattainable [ʌnə'teɪnəb(ə)l] a (goal, aim) inaccessible.

unattended [ʌnə'tendɪd] *a* sans surveillance.

unattractive [ʌnə'træktɪv] *a* (*idea, appearance etc*) peu attrayant; (*character*) peu sympathique; (*ugly*) laid.

unauthorized [ʌn'ɔːθəraɪzd] *a* non autorisé.

unavailable [ʌnə'veɪləb(ə)l] *a* (*person, funds*) indisponible; (*article*) Com épuisé.

unavoidab/le [ʌnə'vɔɪdəb(ə)l] *a* inévitable. ◆**-ly** *adv* inévitablement; (*delayed*) pour une raison indépendante de sa volonté.

unaware [ʌnə'weər] *a* to be u. of ignorer; to be u. that ignorer que. ◆**unawares** *adv* to catch s.o. u. prendre qn au dépourvu.

unbalanced [ʌn'bælənst] *a* (*mind, person*) déséquilibré.

unbearab/le [ʌn'beərəb(ə)l] *a* insupportable. ◆**-ly** *adv* insupportablement.

unbeatable [ʌn'biːtəb(ə)l] *a* imbattable. ◆**unbeaten** *a* (*player*) invaincu; (*record*) non battu.

unbeknown(st) [ʌnbɪ'nəʊn(st)] *a* u. to à l'insu de.

unbelievable [ʌnbɪ'liːvəb(ə)l] *a* incroyable. ◆**unbelieving** *a* incrédule.

unbend [ʌn'bend] *vi* (*pt & pp* unbent) (*relax*) se détendre. ◆**-ing** *a* inflexible.

unbias(s)ed [ʌn'baɪəst] *a* impartial.

unblock [ʌn'blɒk] *vt* (*sink etc*) déboucher.

unborn [ʌn'bɔːn] *a* (*child*) à naître.

unbounded [ʌn'baʊndɪd] *a* illimité.

unbreakable [ʌn'breɪkəb(ə)l] *a* incassable. ◆**unbroken** *a* (*continuous*) continu; (*intact*) intact; (*record*) non battu.

unbridled [ʌn'braɪd(ə)ld] *a* Fig débridé.

unburden [ʌn'bɜːd(ə)n] *vt* to u. oneself Fig s'épancher (to auprès de, avec).

unbutton [ʌn'bʌt(ə)n] *vt* déboutonner.

uncalled-for [ʌn'kɔːldfɔːr] *a* déplacé, injustifié.

uncanny [ʌn'kænɪ] *a* (-ier, -iest) étrange, mystérieux.

unceasing [ʌn'siːsɪŋ] *a* incessant. ◆**-ly** *adv* sans cesse.

unceremoniously [ʌnserɪ'məʊnɪəslɪ] *adv* (*to treat*) sans ménagement; (*to show out*) brusquement.

uncertain [ʌn'sɜːt(ə)n] *a* incertain (about, of de); it's or he's u. whether or that il n'est pas certain que (+ *sub*). ◆**uncertainty** *n* incertitude *f*.

unchanged [ʌn'tʃeɪndʒd] *a* inchangé. ◆**unchanging** *a* immuable.

uncharitable [ʌn'tʃærɪtəb(ə)l] *a* peu charitable.

unchecked [ʌn'tʃekt] *adv* sans opposition.

uncivil [ʌn'sɪv(ə)l] *a* impoli, incivil.

uncivilized [ʌn'sɪvɪlaɪzd] *a* barbare.

uncle [ʌŋk(ə)l] *n* oncle *m*.

unclear [ʌn'klɪər] *a* (*meaning*) qui n'est pas clair; (*result*) incertain; it's u. whether . . . on ne sait pas très bien si . . . .

uncomfortable [ʌn'kʌmftəb(ə)l] *a* (*house, chair etc*) inconfortable; (*heat, experience*) désagréable; (*feeling*) embarrassant; she is or feels u. (*uneasy*) elle est mal à l'aise.

uncommon [ʌn'kɒmən] *a* rare. ◆**-ly** *adv* (*very*) extraordinairement; not u. (*fairly often*) assez souvent.

uncommunicative [ʌnkə'mjuːnɪkətɪv] *a* peu communicatif.

uncomplicated [ʌn'kɒmplɪkeɪtɪd] *a* simple.

uncompromising [ʌn'kɒmprəmaɪzɪŋ] *a* intransigeant.

unconcerned [ʌnkən'sɜːnd] *a* (*not anxious*) imperturbable; (*indifferent*) indifférent (by, with à).

unconditional [ʌnkən'dɪʃ(ə)nəl] *a* inconditionnel; (*surrender*) sans condition.

unconfirmed [ʌnkən'fɜːmd] *a* non confirmé.

uncongenial [ʌnkən'dʒiːnɪəl] *a* peu agréable; (*person*) antipathique.

unconnected [ʌnkə'nektɪd] *a* (*events, facts etc*) sans rapport (with avec).

unconscious [ʌn'kɒnʃəs] *a* Med sans connaissance; (*desire*) inconscient; u. of (*unaware of*) inconscient de; – *n* Psy inconscient *m*. ◆**-ly** *adv* inconsciemment.

uncontrollable [ʌnkən'trəʊləb(ə)l] *a* (*emotion, laughter*) irrépressible.

unconventional [ʌnkən'venʃ(ə)nəl] *a* peu conventionnel.

unconvinced [ʌnkən'vɪnst] *a* to be or remain u. ne pas être convaincu (of de). ◆**unconvincing** *a* peu convaincant.

uncooperative [ʌnkəʊ'ɒp(ə)rətɪv] *a* peu coopératif.

uncork [ʌn'kɔːk] *vt* (*bottle*) déboucher.

uncouple [ʌn'kʌp(ə)l] *vt* (*carriages*) Rail dételer.

uncouth [ʌn'kuːθ] *a* grossier.

uncover [ʌn'kʌvər] *vt* (*saucepan, conspiracy etc*) découvrir.

unctuous ['ʌŋktʃʊəs] *a* (*insincere*) onctueux.

uncut [ʌn'kʌt] *a* (*film, play*) intégral; (*diamond*) brut.

undamaged [ʌn'dæmɪdʒd] *a* (*goods*) en bon état.

undaunted [ʌn'dɔːntɪd] *a* nullement découragé.

undecided [ʌndɪ'saɪdɪd] *a* (*person*) indécis

(about sur); **I'm u.** whether to do it or not je n'ai pas décidé si je le ferai ou non.

undefeated [ʌndɪˈfiːtɪd] a invaincu.

undeniable [ʌndɪˈnaɪəb(ə)l] a incontestable.

under [ˈʌndər] prep sous; (less than) moins de; (according to) selon; **children u. nine** les enfants de moins de or enfants au-dessous de neuf ans; **u. the circumstances** dans les circonstances; **u. there** là-dessous; **u. it** dessous; **u. (the command of) s.o.** sous les ordres de qn; **u. age** mineur; **u.** discussion/repair en discussion/réparation; **u. way** (in progress) en cours; (on the way) en route; **to be u. the impression that** avoir l'impression que; – adv au-dessous.

under- [ˈʌndər] pref sous-.

undercarriage [ˈʌndəkærɪdʒ] n (of aircraft) train m d'atterrissage.

undercharge [ʌndəˈtʃɑːdʒ] vt **I undercharged him (for it)** je ne (le) lui ai pas fait payer assez.

underclothes [ˈʌndəkləʊðz] npl sous-vêtements mpl.

undercoat [ˈʌndəkəʊt] n (of paint) couche f de fond.

undercooked [ʌndəˈkʊkt] a pas assez cuit.

undercover [ʌndəˈkʌvər] a (agent, operation) secret.

undercurrent [ˈʌndəkʌrənt] n (in sea) courant m (sous-marin); **an u. of** Fig un courant profond de.

undercut [ʌndəˈkʌt] vt (pt & pp undercut, pres p undercutting) Com vendre moins cher que.

underdeveloped [ʌndədɪˈveləpt] a (country) sous-développé.

underdog [ˈʌndədɒg] n (politically, socially) opprimé, -ée mf; (likely loser) perdant, -ante mf probable.

underdone [ʌndəˈdʌn] a Culin pas assez cuit; (steak) saignant.

underestimate [ʌndərˈestɪmeɪt] vt sous-estimer.

underfed [ʌndəˈfed] a sous-alimenté.

underfoot [ʌndəˈfʊt] adv sous les pieds.

undergo [ʌndəˈgəʊ] vt (pt underwent, pp undergone) subir.

undergraduate [ʌndəˈgrædʒuət] n étudiant, -ante mf (qui prépare une licence).

underground [ˈʌndəgraʊnd] a souterrain; (secret) Fig clandestin; (organization) Pol résistance f; – [ʌndəˈgraʊnd] adv sous terre; **to go u.** (of fugitive etc) Fig passer dans la clandestinité.

undergrowth [ˈʌndəgrəʊθ] n sous-bois m inv.

underhand [ʌndəˈhænd] a (dishonest) sournois.

underlie [ʌndəˈlaɪ] vt (pt underlay, pp underlain, pres p underlying) sous-tendre. ◆**underlying** a (basic) fondamental; (hidden) profond.

underline [ʌndəˈlaɪn] vt (text, idea etc) souligner.

undermanned [ʌndəˈmænd] a (office etc) à court de personnel.

undermine [ʌndəˈmaɪn] vt (building, strength, society etc) miner, saper.

underneath [ʌndəˈniːθ] prep sous; – adv (en) dessous; **the book u.** le livre d'en dessous; – n dessous m.

undernourished [ʌndəˈnʌrɪʃt] a sous-alimenté.

underpants [ˈʌndəpænts] npl (male underwear) slip m; (loose, long) caleçon m.

underpass [ˈʌndəpɑːs] n (for cars or pedestrians) passage m souterrain.

underpay [ʌndəˈpeɪ] vt sous-payer. ◆**underpaid** a sous-payé.

underpriced [ʌndəˈpraɪst] a **it's u.** le prix est trop bas, c'est bradé.

underprivileged [ʌndəˈprɪvɪlɪdʒd] a défavorisé.

underrate [ʌndəˈreɪt] vt sous-estimer.

undershirt [ˈʌndəʃɜːt] n Am tricot m or maillot m de corps.

underside [ˈʌndəsaɪd] n dessous m.

undersigned [ʌndəˈsaɪnd] a soussigné; **I the u.** je soussigné(e).

undersized [ʌndəˈsaɪzd] a trop petit.

underskirt [ˈʌndəskɜːt] n jupon m.

understaffed [ʌndəˈstɑːft] a à court de personnel.

understand [ʌndəˈstænd] vti (pt & pp understood) comprendre; **I u. that** je crois comprendre que, il paraît que; **I've been given to u. that** on m'a fait comprendre que. ◆**-ing** n (act, faculty) compréhension f; (agreement) accord m, entente f; (sympathy) entente f; **on the u. that** à condition que (+ sub); – a (person) compréhensif. ◆**understood** a (agreed) entendu; (implied) sous-entendu. ◆**understandable** a compréhensible. ◆**understandably** adv naturellement.

understatement [ˈʌndəsteɪtmənt] n euphémisme m.

understudy [ˈʌndəstʌdɪ] n Th doublure f.

undertake [ʌndəˈteɪk] vt (pt undertook, pp undertaken) (task) entreprendre; (responsibility) assumer; **to u. to do** se charger de faire. ◆**-ing** n (task) entreprise f; (prom-

undertaker ['ʌndəteɪkər] n entrepreneur m de pompes funèbres.

undertone ['ʌndətəʊn] n **in an u.** à mi-voix; **an u. of** (criticism, sadness etc) Fig une note de.

undervalue [ʌndə'væljuː] vt sous-évaluer; **it's undervalued at ten pounds** ça vaut plus que dix livres.

underwater [ʌndə'wɔːtər] a sous-marin; – adv sous l'eau.

underwear ['ʌndəweər] n sous-vêtements mpl.

underweight [ʌndə'weɪt] a (person) qui ne pèse pas assez; (goods) d'un poids insuffisant.

underworld ['ʌndəwɜːld] n the u. (criminals) le milieu, la pègre.

undesirable [ʌndɪ'zaɪərəb(ə)l] a peu souhaitable (that que (+ sub)); (person) indésirable; – n (person) indésirable mf.

undetected [ʌndɪ'tektɪd] a non découvert; **to go u.** passer inaperçu.

undies ['ʌndiz] npl (female underwear) Fam dessous mpl.

undignified [ʌn'dɪgnɪfaɪd] a qui manque de dignité.

undisciplined [ʌn'dɪsɪplɪnd] a indiscipliné.

undiscovered [ʌndɪ'skʌvəd] a **to remain u.** ne pas être découvert.

undisputed [ʌndɪ'spjuːtɪd] a incontesté.

undistinguished [ʌndɪ'stɪŋgwɪʃt] a médiocre.

undivided [ʌndɪ'vaɪdɪd] a **my u. attention** toute mon attention.

undo [ʌn'duː] vt (pt **undid**, pp **undone**) défaire; (bound person, hands) détacher, délier; (a wrong) réparer. ◆**-ing** n (downfall) perte f, ruine f. ◆**undone** a **to leave u.** (work etc) ne pas faire; **to come u.** (of knot etc) se défaire.

undoubted [ʌn'daʊtɪd] a indubitable. ◆**-ly** adv indubitablement.

undreamt-of [ʌn'dremtɒv] a insoupçonné.

undress [ʌn'dres] vi se déshabiller; – vt déshabiller; **to get undressed** se déshabiller.

undue [ʌn'djuː] a excessif. ◆**unduly** adv excessivement.

undulating ['ʌndjʊleɪtɪŋ] a (movement) onduleux; (countryside) vallonné.

undying [ʌn'daɪɪŋ] a éternel.

unearned [ʌn'ɜːnd] a **u. income** rentes fpl.

unearth [ʌn'ɜːθ] vt (from ground) déterrer; (discover) Fig dénicher, déterrer.

unearthly [ʌn'ɜːθlɪ] a sinistre, mystérieux; **u. hour** Fam heure f indue.

uneasy [ʌn'iːzɪ] a (peace, situation) précaire; (silence) gêné; **to be or feel u.** (ill at ease) être mal à l'aise, être gêné; (worried) être inquiet.

uneconomic(al) [ʌniːkə'nɒmɪk((ə)l)] a peu économique.

uneducated [ʌn'edʒʊkeɪtɪd] a (person) inculte; (accent) populaire.

unemployed [ʌnɪm'plɔɪd] a sans travail, en chômage; – n the u. les chômeurs mpl. ◆**unemployment** n chômage m.

unending [ʌn'endɪŋ] a interminable.

unenthusiastic [ʌnɪnθjuːzɪ'æstɪk] a peu enthousiaste.

unenviable [ʌn'envɪəb(ə)l] a peu enviable.

unequal [ʌn'iːkwəl] a inégal; **to be u. to** (task) ne pas être à la hauteur de. ◆**unequalled** a (incomparable) inégalé.

unequivocal [ʌnɪ'kwɪvək(ə)l] a sans équivoque.

unerring [ʌn'ɜːrɪŋ] a infaillible.

unethical [ʌn'eθɪk(ə)l] a immoral.

uneven [ʌn'iːv(ə)n] a inégal.

uneventful [ʌnɪ'ventfəl] a (journey, life etc) sans histoires.

unexceptionable [ʌnɪk'sepʃ(ə)nəb(ə)l] a irréprochable.

unexpected [ʌnɪk'spektɪd] a inattendu. ◆**-ly** adv à l'improviste; (suddenly) subitement; (unusually) exceptionnellement.

unexplained [ʌnɪk'spleɪnd] a inexplicable.

unfailing [ʌn'feɪlɪŋ] a (optimism, courage, support etc) inébranlable; (supply) inépuisable.

unfair [ʌn'feər] a injuste (to s.o. envers qn); (competition) déloyal. ◆**-ly** adv injustement. ◆**-ness** n injustice f.

unfaithful [ʌn'feɪθfəl] a infidèle (to à).

unfamiliar [ʌnfə'mɪlɪər] a inconnu, peu familier; **to be u. with** ne pas connaître.

unfashionable [ʌn'fæʃ(ə)nəb(ə)l] a (subject etc) démodé; (district etc) peu chic inv, ringard; **it's u. to do** il n'est pas de bon ton de faire.

unfasten [ʌn'fɑːs(ə)n] vt défaire.

unfavourable [ʌn'feɪv(ə)rəb(ə)l] a défavorable.

unfeeling [ʌn'fiːlɪŋ] a insensible.

unfinished [ʌn'fɪnɪʃt] a inachevé; **to have some u. business** avoir une affaire à régler.

unfit [ʌn'fɪt] a (unwell) mal fichu; (unsuited) inapte (for sth à qch, to do à faire); (unworthy) indigne (for sth de qch, to do de faire);

to be u. to do (*incapable*) ne pas être en état de faire.

unflagging [ʌn'flægɪŋ] *a* (*zeal*) inlassable; (*interest*) soutenu.

unflappable [ʌn'flæpəb(ə)l] *a Fam* imperturbable.

unflattering [ʌn'flæt(ə)rɪŋ] *a* peu flatteur.

unflinching [ʌn'flɪntʃɪŋ] *a* (*fearless*) intrépide.

unfold [ʌn'fəuld] *vt* déplier; (*wings*) déployer; (*ideas, plan*) *Fig* exposer; − *vi* (*of story, view*) se dérouler.

unforeseeable [ʌnfɔː'siːəb(ə)l] *a* imprévisible. ◆**unforeseen** *a* imprévu.

unforgettable [ʌnfə'getəb(ə)l] *a* inoubliable.

unforgivable [ʌnfə'gɪvəb(ə)l] *a* impardonnable.

unfortunate [ʌn'fɔːtʃ(ə)nət] *a* malheureux; (*event*) fâcheux; **you were u.** tu n'as pas eu de chance. ◆**-ly** *adv* malheureusement.

unfounded [ʌn'faundɪd] *a* (*rumour etc*) sans fondement.

unfriendly [ʌn'frendlɪ] *a* peu amical, froid. ◆**unfriendliness** *n* froideur *f*.

unfulfilled [ʌnful'fɪld] *a* (*desire*) insatisfait; (*plan*) non réalisé; (*condition*) non rempli.

unfurl [ʌn'fɜːl] *vt* (*flag etc*) déployer.

unfurnished [ʌn'fɜːnɪʃt] *a* non meublé.

ungainly [ʌn'geɪnlɪ] *a* (*clumsy*) gauche.

ungodly [ʌn'gɒdlɪ] *a* impie; **u. hour** *Fam* heure *f* indue.

ungrammatical [ʌngrə'mætɪk(ə)l] *a* non grammatical.

ungrateful [ʌn'greɪtfəl] *a* ingrat.

unguarded [ʌn'gɑːdɪd] *a* **in an u. moment** dans un moment d'inattention.

unhappy [ʌn'hæpɪ] *a* (**-ier, -iest**) (*sad*) malheureux, triste; (*worried*) inquiet; **u. with** (*not pleased*) mécontent de; **he's u. about doing it** ça le dérange de le faire. ◆**unhappily** *adv* (*unfortunately*) malheureusement. ◆**unhappiness** *n* tristesse *f*.

unharmed [ʌn'hɑːmd] *a* indemne, sain et sauf.

unhealthy [ʌn'helθɪ] *a* (**-ier, -iest**) (*person*) en mauvaise santé; (*climate, place, job*) malsain; (*lungs*) malade.

unheard-of [ʌn'hɜːdɒv] *a* (*unprecedented*) inouï.

unheeded [ʌn'hiːdɪd] *a* **it went u.** on n'en a pas tenu compte.

unhelpful [ʌn'helpfəl] *a* (*person*) peu obligeant *or* serviable; (*advice*) peu utile.

unhinge [ʌn'hɪndʒ] *vt* (*person, mind*) déséquilibrer.

unholy [ʌn'həulɪ] *a* (**-ier, -iest**) impie; (*din*) *Fam* de tous les diables.

unhook [ʌn'huk] *vt* (*picture, curtain*) décrocher; (*dress*) dégrafer.

unhoped-for [ʌn'həuptfɔːr] *a* inespéré.

unhurried [ʌn'hʌrɪd] *a* (*movement*) lent; (*stroll, journey*) fait sans hâte.

unhurt [ʌn'hɜːt] *a* indemne, sain et sauf.

unhygienic [ʌnhaɪ'dʒiːnɪk] *a* pas très hygiénique.

unicorn ['juːnɪkɔːn] *n* licorne *f*.

uniform ['juːnɪfɔːm] **1** *n* uniforme *m*. **2** *a* (*regular*) uniforme; (*temperature*) constant. ◆**uniformed** *a* en uniforme. ◆**uni'formity** *n* uniformité *f*. ◆**uniformly** *adv* uniformément.

unify ['juːnɪfaɪ] *vt* unifier. ◆**unifi'cation** *n* unification *f*.

unilateral [juːnɪ'læt(ə)rəl] *a* unilatéral.

unimaginable [ʌnɪ'mædʒɪnəb(ə)l] *a* inimaginable. ◆**unimaginative** *a* (*person, plan etc*) qui manque d'imagination.

unimpaired [ʌnɪm'peəd] *a* intact.

unimportant [ʌnɪm'pɔːtənt] *a* peu important.

uninhabitable [ʌnɪn'hæbɪtəb(ə)l] *a* inhabitable. ◆**uninhabited** *a* inhabité.

uninhibited [ʌnɪn'hɪbɪtɪd] *a* (*person*) sans complexes.

uninitiated [ʌnɪ'nɪʃɪeɪtɪd] *n* **the u.** les profanes *mpl*, les non-initiés.

uninjured [ʌn'ɪndʒəd] *a* indemne.

uninspiring [ʌnɪn'spaɪərɪŋ] *a* (*subject etc*) pas très inspirant.

unintelligible [ʌnɪn'telɪdʒəb(ə)l] *a* inintelligible.

unintentional [ʌnɪn'tenʃ(ə)nəl] *a* involontaire.

uninterested [ʌn'ɪntrɪstɪd] *a* indifférent (**in** à). ◆**uninteresting** *a* (*book etc*) inintéressant; (*person*) fastidieux.

uninterrupted [ʌnɪntə'rʌptɪd] *a* ininterrompu.

uninvited [ʌnɪn'vaɪtɪd] *a* (*to arrive*) sans invitation. ◆**uninviting** *a* peu attrayant.

union ['juːnɪən] *n* union *f*; (*trade union*) syndicat *m*; − *a* (*syndical*; (*trade*) u. member syndiqué, -ée *mf*; **U. Jack** drapeau *m* britannique. ◆**unionist** *n* **trade u.** syndicaliste *mf*. ◆**unionize** *vt* syndiquer.

unique [juː'niːk] *a* unique. ◆**-ly** *adv* exceptionnellement.

unisex ['juːnɪseks] *a* (*clothes etc*) unisexe *inv*.

unison ['juːnɪs(ə)n] *n* **in u.** à l'unisson (**with** de).

unit ['juːnɪt] *n* unité *f*; (*of furniture etc*) élément *m*; (*system*) bloc *m*; (*group, team*) groupe *m*; **u. trust** *Fin* fonds *m* commun de placement.

unite [ju:'naɪt] *vt* unir; (*country, party*) unifier; **United Kingdom** Royaume-Uni *m*; **United Nations** (Organisation *f* des) Nations unies *fpl*; **United States (of America)** États-Unis *mpl* (d'Amérique); − *vi* s'unir. ◆**unity** *n* (*cohesion*) unité *f*; (*harmony*) *Fig* harmonie *f*.

universal [ju:nɪ'vɜ:s(ə)l] *a* universel. ◆**-ly** *adv* universellement.

universe ['ju:nɪvɜ:s] *n* univers *m*.

university [ju:nɪ'vɜ:sɪtɪ] *n* université *f*; **at u.** à l'université; − *a* universitaire; (*student, teacher*) d'université.

unjust [ʌn'dʒʌst] *a* injuste.

unjustified [ʌn'dʒʌstɪfaɪd] *a* injustifié.

unkempt [ʌn'kempt] *a* (*appearance*) négligé; (*hair*) mal peigné.

unkind [ʌn'kaɪnd] *a* peu aimable (**to s.o.** avec qn); (*nasty*) méchant (**to s.o.** avec qn). ◆**-ly** *adv* méchamment.

unknowingly [ʌn'nəʊɪŋlɪ] *adv* inconsciemment.

unknown [ʌn'nəʊn] *a* inconnu; **u. to me, he'd left** il était parti, ce que j'ignorais; − *n* (*person*) inconnu, -ue *mf*; **the u. Phil** l'inconnu *m*; **u.** (*quantity*) *Math* & *Fig* inconnue *f*.

unlawful [ʌn'lɔ:fəl] *a* illégal.

unleaded [ʌn'ledɪd] *a* (*gasoline*) *Am* sans plomb.

unleash [ʌn'li:ʃ] *vt* (*force etc*) déchaîner.

unless [ʌn'les] *conj* à moins que; **u. she comes** à moins qu'elle ne vienne; **u. you work harder, you'll fail** à moins de travailler plus dur, vous échouerez.

unlike [ʌn'laɪk] *a* différent; − *prep* **u. me, she . . .** à la différence de moi ou contrairement à moi, elle . . . ; **he's very u. his father** il n'est pas du tout comme son père; **that's u. him** ça ne lui ressemble pas.

unlikely [ʌn'laɪklɪ] *a* improbable; (*implausible*) invraisemblable; **she's u. to win** il est peu probable qu'elle gagne. ◆**unlikelihood** *n* improbabilité *f*.

unlimited [ʌn'lɪmɪtɪd] *a* illimité.

unlisted [ʌn'lɪstɪd] *a* (*phone number*) *Am* qui ne figure pas à l'annuaire.

unload [ʌn'ləʊd] *vt* décharger.

unlock [ʌn'lɒk] *vt* ouvrir (*avec une clef*).

unlucky [ʌn'lʌkɪ] *a* (**-ier, -iest**) (*person*) malchanceux; (*colour, number etc*) qui porte malheur; **you're u.** tu n'as pas de chance. ◆**unluckily** *adv* malheureusement.

unmade [ʌn'meɪd] *a* (*bed*) défait.

unmanageable [ʌn'mænɪdʒəb(ə)l] *a* (*child*) difficile; (*hair*) difficile à coiffer; (*packet, size*) peu maniable.

unmanned [ʌn'mænd] *a* (*ship*) sans équipage; (*spacecraft*) inhabité.

unmarked [ʌn'mɑ:kt] *a* (*not blemished*) sans marque; **u. police car** voiture *f* banalisée.

unmarried [ʌn'mærɪd] *a* célibataire.

unmask [ʌn'mɑ:sk] *vt* démasquer.

unmentionable [ʌn'menʃ(ə)nəb(ə)l] *a* dont il ne faut pas parler; (*unpleasant*) innommable.

unmercifully [ʌn'mɜ:sɪf(ə)lɪ] *adv* sans pitié.

unmistakable [ʌnmɪ'steɪkəb(ə)l] *a* (*obvious*) indubitable; (*face, voice etc*) facilement reconnaissable.

unmitigated [ʌn'mɪtɪgeɪtɪd] *a* (*disaster*) absolu; (*folly*) pur.

unmoved [ʌn'mu:vd] *a* **to be u.** (*feel no emotion*) ne pas être ému (**by par**); (*be unconcerned*) être indifférent (**by à**).

unnatural [ʌn'nætʃ(ə)rəl] *a* (*not normal*) pas naturel; (*crime*) contre nature; (*affected*) qui manque de naturel. ◆**-ly** *adv* **not u.** naturellement.

unnecessary [ʌn'nesəs(ə)rɪ] *a* inutile; (*superfluous*) superflu.

unnerve [ʌn'nɜ:v] *vt* désarçonner, déconcerter.

unnoticed [ʌn'nəʊtɪst] *a* inaperçu.

unobstructed [ʌnəb'strʌktɪd] *a* (*road, view*) dégagé.

unobtainable [ʌnəb'teɪnəb(ə)l] *a* impossible à obtenir.

unobtrusive [ʌnəb'tru:sɪv] *a* discret.

unoccupied [ʌn'ɒkjʊpaɪd] *a* (*person, house*) inoccupé; (*seat*) libre.

unofficial [ʌnə'fɪʃ(ə)l] *a* officieux; (*visit*) privé; (*strike*) sauvage. ◆**-ly** *adv* à titre officieux.

unorthodox [ʌn'ɔ:θədɒks] *a* peu orthodoxe.

unpack [ʌn'pæk] *vt* (*case*) défaire; (*goods, belongings, contents*) déballer; **to u. a comb/etc from** sortir un peigne/etc de; − *vi* défaire sa valise; (*take out goods*) déballer.

unpaid [ʌn'peɪd] *a* (*bill, sum*) impayé; (*work, worker*) bénévole; (*leave*) non payé.

unpalatable [ʌn'pælətəb(ə)l] *a* désagréable, déplaisant.

unparalleled [ʌn'pærəleld] *a* sans égal.

unperturbed [ʌnpə'tɜ:bd] *a* nullement déconcerté.

unplanned [ʌn'plænd] *a* (*visit, baby etc*) imprévu.

unpleasant [ʌn'plezənt] *a* désagréable (**to s.o.** avec qn). ◆**-ness** *n* caractère *m* désagréable (**of** de); (*quarrel*) petite querelle *f*.

unplug [ʌnˈplʌg] *vt* (**-gg-**) *El* débrancher; (*unblock*) déboucher.

unpopular [ʌnˈpɒpjʊlər] *a* impopulaire; **to be u. with** ne pas plaire à.

unprecedented [ʌnˈpresɪdentɪd] *a* sans précédent.

unpredictable [ʌnprɪˈdɪktəb(ə)l] *a* imprévisible; (*weather*) indécis.

unprepared [ʌnprɪˈpeəd] *a* non préparé; (*speech*) improvisé; **to be u. for** (*not expect*) ne pas s'attendre à.

unprepossessing [ʌnpriːprəˈzesɪŋ] *a* peu avenant.

unpretentious [ʌnprɪˈtenʃəs] *a* sans prétention.

unprincipled [ʌnˈprɪnsɪp(ə)ld] *a* sans scrupules.

unprofessional [ʌnprəˈfeʃ(ə)nəl] *a* (*unethical*) contraire aux règles de sa profession.

unpublished [ʌnˈpʌblɪʃt] *a* (*text, writer*) inédit.

unpunished [ʌnˈpʌnɪʃt] *a* **to go u.** rester impuni.

unqualified [ʌnˈkwɒlɪfaɪd] *a* **1** (*teacher etc*) non diplômé; **he's u. to do** il n'est pas qualifié pour faire. **2** (*support*) sans réserve; (*success, rogue*) parfait.

unquestionable [ʌnˈkwestʃ(ə)nəb(ə)l] *a* incontestable. ◆**—ly** *adv* incontestablement.

unravel [ʌnˈræv(ə)l] *vt* (**-ll-**, *Am* **-l-**) (*threads etc*) démêler; (*mystery*) *Fig* éclaircir.

unreal [ʌnˈrɪəl] *a* irréel. ◆**unrea'listic** *a* peu réaliste.

unreasonable [ʌnˈriːz(ə)nəb(ə)l] *a* qui n'est pas raisonnable; (*price*) excessif.

unrecognizable [ʌnrekəgˈnaɪzəb(ə)l] *a* méconnaissable.

unrelated [ʌnrɪˈleɪtɪd] *a* (*facts etc*) sans rapport (**to** avec); **we're u.** il n'y a aucun lien de parenté entre nous.

unrelenting [ʌnrɪˈlentɪŋ] *a* (*person*) implacable; (*effort*) acharné.

unreliable [ʌnrɪˈlaɪəb(ə)l] *a* (*person*) peu sérieux, peu sûr; (*machine*) peu fiable.

unrelieved [ʌnrɪˈliːvd] *a* (*constant*) constant; (*colour*) uniforme.

unremarkable [ʌnrɪˈmɑːkəb(ə)l] *a* médiocre.

unrepeatable [ʌnrɪˈpiːtəb(ə)l] *a* (*offer*) unique.

unrepentant [ʌnrɪˈpentənt] *a* impénitent.

unreservedly [ʌnrɪˈzɜːvɪdlɪ] *adv* sans réserve.

unrest [ʌnˈrest] *n* troubles *mpl*, agitation *f*.

unrestricted [ʌnrɪˈstrɪktɪd] *a* illimité; (*access*) libre.

unrewarding [ʌnrɪˈwɔːdɪŋ] *a* ingrat; (*financially*) peu rémunérateur.

unripe [ʌnˈraɪp] *a* (*fruit*) vert, pas mûr.

unroll [ʌnˈrəʊl] *vt* dérouler; – *vi* se dérouler.

unruffled [ʌnˈrʌf(ə)ld] *a* (*person*) calme.

unruly [ʌnˈruːlɪ] *a* (**-ier, -iest**) indiscipliné.

unsafe [ʌnˈseɪf] *a* (*place, machine etc*) dangereux; (*person*) en danger.

unsaid [ʌnˈsed] *a* **to leave sth u.** passer qch sous silence.

unsaleable [ʌnˈseɪləb(ə)l] *a* invendable.

unsatisfactory [ʌnsætɪsˈfækt(ə)rɪ] *a* peu satisfaisant. ◆**un'satisfied** *a* insatisfait; **u. with** peu satisfait de.

unsavoury [ʌnˈseɪv(ə)rɪ] *a* (*person, place etc*) répugnant.

unscathed [ʌnˈskeɪðd] *a* indemne.

unscrew [ʌnˈskruː] *vt* dévisser.

unscrupulous [ʌnˈskruːpjʊləs] *a* (*person, act*) peu scrupuleux.

unseemly [ʌnˈsiːmlɪ] *a* inconvenant.

unseen [ʌnˈsiːn] **1** *a* inaperçu. **2** *n* (*translation*) *Sch* version *f*.

unselfish [ʌnˈselfɪʃ] *a* (*person, motive etc*) désintéressé.

unsettle [ʌnˈset(ə)l] *vt* (*person*) troubler. ◆**—ed** *a* (*weather, situation*) instable; (*in one's mind*) troublé; (*in a job*) mal à l'aise.

unshakeable [ʌnˈʃeɪkəb(ə)l] *a* (*person, faith*) inébranlable.

unshaven [ʌnˈʃeɪv(ə)n] *a* pas rasé.

unsightly [ʌnˈsaɪtlɪ] *a* laid, disgracieux.

unskilled [ʌnˈskɪld] *a* inexpert; (*work*) de manœuvre; **u. worker** manœuvre *m*, ouvrier, -ière *mf* non qualifié(e).

unsociable [ʌnˈsəʊʃəb(ə)l] *a* insociable.

unsocial [ʌnˈsəʊʃəl] *a* **to work u. hours** travailler en dehors des heures de bureau.

unsolved [ʌnˈsɒlvd] *a* (*problem*) non résolu; (*mystery*) inexpliqué; (*crime*) dont l'auteur n'est pas connu.

unsophisticated [ʌnsəˈfɪstɪkeɪtɪd] *a* simple.

unsound [ʌnˈsaʊnd] *a* (*construction etc*) peu solide; (*method*) peu sûr; (*decision*) peu judicieux; **he is of u. mind** il n'a pas toute sa raison.

unspeakable [ʌnˈspiːkəb(ə)l] *a* (*horrible*) innommable.

unspecified [ʌnˈspesɪfaɪd] *a* indéterminé.

unsporting [ʌnˈspɔːtɪŋ] *a* déloyal.

unstable [ʌnˈsteɪb(ə)l] *a* instable.

unsteady [ʌnˈstedɪ] *a* (*hand, voice, step etc*) mal assuré; (*table, ladder etc*) instable. ◆**unsteadily** *adv* (*to walk*) d'un pas mal assuré.

unstinting [ʌnˈstɪntɪŋ] a (generosity) sans bornes.

unstoppable [ʌnˈstɒpəb(ə)l] a qu'on ne peut (pas) arrêter.

unstuck [ʌnˈstʌk] a **to come u.** (of stamp etc) se décoller; (fail) Fam se planter.

unsuccessful [ʌnsəkˈsesfəl] a (attempt etc) infructueux; (outcome, candidate) malheureux; (application) non retenu; **to be u.** ne pas réussir (**in doing** à faire); (of book, artist) ne pas avoir de succès. ◆—**ly** adv en vain, sans succès.

unsuitable [ʌnˈsuːtəb(ə)l] a qui ne convient pas (**for** à); (example) peu approprié; (manners, clothes) peu convenable. ◆**unsuited** a **u. to** impropre à; **they're u.** ils ne sont pas compatibles.

unsure [ʌnˈʃʊər] a incertain (**of, about** de).

unsuspecting [ʌnsəˈspektɪŋ] a qui ne se doute de rien.

unswerving [ʌnˈswɜːvɪŋ] a (loyalty etc) inébranlable.

unsympathetic [ʌnsɪmpəˈθetɪk] a incompréhensif; **u. to** indifférent à.

untangle [ʌnˈtæŋg(ə)l] vt (rope etc) démêler.

untapped [ʌnˈtæpt] a inexploité.

untenable [ʌnˈtenəb(ə)l] a (position) intenable.

unthinkable [ʌnˈθɪŋkəb(ə)l] a impensable, inconcevable.

untidy [ʌnˈtaɪdɪ] a (**-ier, -iest**) (appearance, hair) peu soigné; (room) en désordre; (unmethodical) désordonné. ◆**untidily** adv sans soin.

untie [ʌnˈtaɪ] vt (person, hands) détacher; (knot, parcel) défaire.

until [ʌnˈtɪl] prep jusqu'à; **u. then** jusque-là; **not u. tomorrow/etc** (in the future) pas avant demain/etc; **I didn't come u. Monday** (in the past) je ne suis venu que lundi; — conj **u. she comes** jusqu'à ce qu'elle vienne, en attendant qu'elle vienne; **do nothing u. I come** (before) ne fais rien avant que j'arrive.

untimely [ʌnˈtaɪmlɪ] a inopportun; (death) prématuré.

untiring [ʌnˈtaɪə)rɪŋ] a infatigable.

untold [ʌnˈtəʊld] a (quantity, wealth) incalculable.

untoward [ʌntəˈwɔːd] a malencontreux.

untranslatable [ʌntrænˈsleɪtəb(ə)l] a intraduisible.

untroubled [ʌnˈtrʌb(ə)ld] a (calm) calme.

untrue [ʌnˈtruː] a faux. ◆**untruth** n contre-vérité f. ◆**untruthful** a (person) menteur; (statement) mensonger.

unused 1 [ʌnˈjuːzd] a (new) neuf; (not in

use) inutilisé. **2** [ʌnˈjuːst] a **u. to sth/to doing** peu habitué à qch/à faire.

unusual [ʌnˈjuːʒʊəl] a exceptionnel, rare; (strange) étrange. ◆—**ly** adv exceptionnellement.

unveil [ʌnˈveɪl] vt dévoiler. ◆—**ing** n (ceremony) inauguration f.

unwanted [ʌnˈwɒntɪd] a (useless) superflu, dont on n'a pas besoin; (child) non désiré.

unwarranted [ʌnˈwɒrəntɪd] a injustifié.

unwavering [ʌnˈweɪvərɪŋ] a (belief etc) inébranlable.

unwelcome [ʌnˈwelkəm] a (news, fact) fâcheux; (gift, visit) inopportun; (person) importun.

unwell [ʌnˈwel] a indisposé.

unwieldy [ʌnˈwiːldɪ] a (package etc) encombrant.

unwilling [ʌnˈwɪlɪŋ] a **he's u. to do** il ne neut pas faire, il est peu disposé à faire. ◆—**ly** adv à contrecœur.

unwind [ʌnˈwaɪnd] **1** vt (thread etc) dérouler; — vi se dérouler. **2** vi (relax) Fam décompresser.

unwise [ʌnˈwaɪz] a imprudent. ◆—**ly** adv imprudemment.

unwitting [ʌnˈwɪtɪŋ] a involontaire. ◆—**ly** adv involontairement.

unworkable [ʌnˈwɜːkəb(ə)l] a (idea etc) impraticable.

unworthy [ʌnˈwɜːðɪ] a indigne (**of** de).

unwrap [ʌnˈræp] vt (**-pp-**) ouvrir, défaire.

unwritten [ʌnˈrɪt(ə)n] a (agreement) verbal, tacite.

unyielding [ʌnˈjiːldɪŋ] a (person) inflexible.

unzip [ʌnˈzɪp] vt (**-pp-**) ouvrir (la fermeture éclair® de).

up [ʌp] adv en haut; (in the air) en l'air; (of sun, hand) levé; (out of bed) levé, debout; (of road) en travaux; (of building) construit; (finished) fini; **to come** or **go up** monter; **to be up** (of price, level etc) être monté (**by** de); **up there** là-haut; **up above** au-dessus; **up on** (roof etc) sur; **further** or **higher up** plus haut; **up to** (as far as) jusqu'à; (task) Fig à la hauteur de; **to be up to doing** (capable) être de taille à faire; (in a position to) être à même de faire; **it's up to you to do it** c'est à toi de le faire; **it's up to you ça dépend de toi;** **where are you up to?** (in book etc) où en es-tu?; **what are you up to?** Fam que fais-tu?; **what's up?** (what's the matter?) Fam qu'est-ce qu'il y a?; **time's up** c'est l'heure; **halfway up** (on hill etc) à mi-chemin; **to walk up and down** marcher de long en large; **to be well up in** (versed in) Fam s'y connaître en; **to be up against**

(confront) être confronté à; **up (with) the workers**/etc! *Fam* vive(nt) les travailleurs/etc!; – *prep* (a hill) en haut de; (a tree) dans; (a ladder) sur; **to go up** (hill, stairs) monter; **to live up the street** habiter plus loin dans la rue; – *npl* **to have ups and downs** avoir des hauts et des bas; – *vt* (**-pp-**) (increase) *Fam* augmenter.
◆**up-and-'coming** *a* plein d'avenir. ◆**upbeat** *a* (cheerful) *Am Fam* optimiste. ◆**upbringing** *n* éducation *f*. ◆**upcoming** *a Am* imminent. ◆**up'date** *vt* mettre à jour. ◆**up'grade** *vt* (job) revaloriser; (person) promouvoir. ◆**up'hill 1** *adv* **to go u.** monter. **2** [ˈʌphɪl] *a* (struggle, task) pénible. ◆**up'hold** *vt* (*pt* & *pp* **upheld**) maintenir. ◆**upkeep** *n* entretien *m*. ◆**uplift** [ʌpˈlɪft] *vt* élever; – [ˈʌplɪft] *n* élévation *f* spirituelle. ◆**upmarket** *a Com* haut de gamme. ◆**upright 1** *a* & *adv* (erect) droit; – *n* (post) montant *m*. **2** *a* (honest) droit. ◆**uprising** *n* insurrection *f*. ◆**up'root** *vt* (plant, person) déraciner. ◆**upside 'down** *adv* à l'envers; **to turn u. down** (room, plans etc) *Fig* chambouler. ◆**up'stairs** *adv* en haut; **to go u.** monter (l'escalier); – [ˈʌpsteəz] *a* (people, room) du dessus. ◆**up'stream** *adv* en amont. ◆**upsurge** *n* (of interest) recrudescence *f*; (of anger) accès *m*. ◆**uptake** *n* **to be quick on the u.** comprendre vite. ◆**up'tight** *a Fam* (tense) crispé; (angry) en colère. ◆**up-to-'date** *a* moderne; (information) à jour; (well-informed) au courant (**on** de). ◆**upturn** *n* (improvement) amélioration *f* (in de); (rise) hausse *f* (in de). ◆**up'turned** *a* (nose) retroussé. ◆**upward** *a* (movement) ascendant; (path) qui monte; (trend) à la hausse. ◆**upwards** *adv* vers le haut; **from five francs u.** à partir de cinq francs; **u. of fifty** cinquante et plus.

upheaval [ʌpˈhiːv(ə)l] *n* bouleversement *m*.

upholster [ʌpˈhəʊlstər] *vt* (pad) rembourrer; (cover) recouvrir. ◆**upholsterer** *n* tapissier *m*. ◆**upholstery** *n* (activity) réfection *f* de sièges; (in car) sièges *mpl*.

upon [əˈpɒn] *prep* sur.

upper [ˈʌpər] **1** *a* supérieur; **u. class** aristocratie *f*; **to have/get the u. hand** avoir/prendre le dessus. **2** *n* (of shoe) empeigne *f*, dessus *m*. ◆**u.-'class** *a* aristocratique. ◆**uppermost** *a* (highest) le plus haut; **to be u.** (on top) être en dessus.

uproar [ˈʌprɔːr] *n* tumulte *m*.

upset [ʌpˈset] *vt* (*pt* & *pp* **upset**, *pres p* **upsetting**) (knock over) renverser; (plans, stomach, routine etc) déranger; **to u. s.o.** (grieve)

peiner qn; (offend) vexer qn; (annoy) contrarier qn; – *a* vexé; contrarié; (stomach) dérangé; – [ˈʌpset] *n* (in plans etc) dérangement *m* (in de); (grief) peine *f*; **to have a stomach u.** avoir l'estomac dérangé.

upshot [ˈʌpʃɒt] *n* résultat *m*.

upstart [ˈʌpstɑːt] *n Pej* parvenu, -ue *mf*.

uranium [juˈreɪnɪəm] *n* uranium *m*.

urban [ˈɜːbən] *a* urbain. **urbane** [ɜːˈbeɪn] *a* courtois, urbain.

urchin [ˈɜːtʃɪn] *n* polisson, -onne *mf*.

urge [ɜːdʒ] *vt* **to u. s.o. to do** (advise) conseiller vivement à qn de faire; **to u.** (on) (person, team) encourager; – *n* forte envie *f*, besoin *m*.

urgency [ˈɜːdʒənsɪ] *n* urgence *f*; (of request, tone) insistance *f*. ◆**urgent** *a* urgent, pressant; (tone) insistant; (letter) urgent. ◆**urgently** *adv* d'urgence; (insistently) avec insistance.

urinal [juˈraɪn(ə)l] *n* urinoir *m*.

urine [ˈjʊə(ə)rɪn] *n* urine *f*. ◆**urinate** *vi* uriner.

urn [ɜːn] *n* urne *f*; (for coffee or tea) fontaine *f*.

us [əs, *stressed* ʌs] *pron* nous; **(to) us** (indirect) nous; **she sees us** elle nous voit; **he gives (to) us** il nous donne; **with us** avec nous; **all of us** nous tous; **let's** or **let us eat!** mangeons!

US [juːˈes] *abbr* = **United States**.

USA [juːesˈeɪ] *abbr* = **United States of America**.

usage [ˈjuːsɪdʒ] *n* (custom) & *Ling* usage *m*.

use [juːs] *n* usage *m*, emploi *m*; (way of using) emploi *m*; **to have the u. of** avoir l'usage de; **to make u. of** se servir de; **in u.** en usage; **out of u.** hors d'usage; **ready for u.** prêt à l'emploi; **to be of u.** servir, être utile; **it's no u. crying**/etc ça ne sert à rien de pleurer/etc; **what's the u. of worrying**/etc? à quoi bon s'inquiéter/etc?, à quoi ça sert de s'inquiéter/etc?; **I have no u. for** it je n'en ai pas l'usage, qu'est-ce que je ferais de ça?; **he's no u.** (hopeless) il est nul; – [juːz] *vt* se servir de, utiliser, employer (**as** comme; **to do, for doing** pour faire); **it's used to do** or **for doing** ça sert à faire; **it's used to as** ça sert de; **I u. it to clean** je m'en sers pour nettoyer, ça me sert à nettoyer; **to u. (up)** (fuel etc) consommer; (supplies) épuiser; (money) dépenser. ◆**used 1** [juːzd] *a* (second-hand) d'occasion; (stamp) oblitéré. **2** [juːst] *v* aux **I u. to do** avant, je faisais; – *a* **u. to sth/to doing** (accustomed) habitué à qch/à faire; **to get u. to** s'habituer à. ◆**useful** [ˈjuːsfəl] *a* utile; **to**

come in u. être utile; **to make oneself u.** se rendre utile. ◆**usefulness** n utilité f.
◆**useless** [ˈjuːsləs] a inutile; (*unusable*) inutilisable; (*person*) nul, incompétent.
◆**user** [ˈjuːzər] n (*of road, dictionary etc*) usager m; (*of machine*) utilisateur, -trice mf.

usher [ˈʌʃər] n (*in church or theatre*) placeur m; (*in law court*) huissier m; – vt **to u. in** faire entrer; (*period etc*) Fig inaugurer. ◆**ushe'rette** n f in ouvreuse f.

USSR [juːesesˈɑːr] n abbr (Union of Soviet Socialist Republics) URSS f.

usual [ˈjuːʒʊəl] a habituel, normal; **as u.** comme d'habitude; **it's her u.** practice c'est son habitude; – **the u.** (*food, excuse etc*) Fam la même chose que d'habitude. ◆**-ly** adv d'habitude.

usurer [ˈjuːʒʊrər] n usurier, -ière mf.

usurp [juːˈzɜːp] vt usurper.

utensil [juːˈtensəl] n ustensile m.

uterus [ˈjuːtərəs] n Anat utérus m.

utilitarian [juːtɪlɪˈteərɪən] a utilitaire.
◆**u'tility** n (*public*) u. service m public; – a (*goods vehicle*) utilitaire.

utilize [ˈjuːtɪlaɪz] vt utiliser. ◆**utili'zation** n utilisation f.

utmost [ˈʌtməʊst] a **the u.** ease/etc (*greatest*) la plus grande facilité/etc; **the u.** danger/limit/etc (*extreme*) un danger/une limite/etc extrême; – n **to do one's u.** faire tout son possible (**to do** pour faire).

utopia [juːˈtəʊpɪə] n (*perfect state*) utopie f. ◆**utopian** a utopique.

utter [ˈʌtər] 1 a complet, total; (*folly*) pur; (*idiot*) parfait; **it's u. nonsense** c'est complètement absurde. 2 vt (*say, express*) proférer; (*a cry, sigh*) pousser. ◆**utterance** n (*remark etc*) déclaration f; **to give u. to** exprimer. ◆**utterly** adv complètement.

V

V, v [viː] n V, v m. ◆**V.-neck(ed)** a (*pullover etc*) à col en V.

vacant [ˈveɪkənt] a (*post*) vacant; (*room, seat*) libre; (*look*) vague, dans le vide. ◆**vacancy** n (*post*) poste m vacant; (*room*) chambre f disponible; 'no vacancies' (*in hotel*) 'complet'. ◆**vacantly** adv **to gaze v.** regarder dans le vide.

vacate [vəˈkeɪt, Am ˈveɪkeɪt] vt quitter.

vacation [verˈkeɪʃ(ə)n] n Am vacances fpl; **on v.** en vacances. ◆**-er** n Am vacancier, -ière mf.

vaccinate [ˈvæksɪneɪt] vt vacciner. ◆**vacci'nation** n vaccination f. ◆**vaccine** [-iːn] n vaccin m.

vacillate [ˈvæsɪleɪt] vi (*hesitate*) hésiter.

vacuum [ˈvækjʊəm] n vide m; **v. cleaner** aspirateur m; **v. flask** thermos® m or f; – vt (*carpet etc*) passer à l'aspirateur. ◆**v.-packed** a emballé sous vide.

vagabond [ˈvægəbɒnd] n vagabond, -onde mf.

vagary [ˈveɪgərɪ] n caprice m.

vagina [vəˈdʒaɪnə] n vagin m.

vagrant [ˈveɪgrənt] n Jur vagabond, -onde mf.

vague [veɪg] a (-er, -est) vague; (*memory, outline, photo*) flou; **the vaguest idea** la moindre idée; **he was v. (about it)** il est resté vague. ◆**-ly** adv vaguement.

vain [veɪn] a (-er, -est) 1 (*attempt, hope*) vain; **in v.** en vain; **his or her efforts were in v.** ses efforts ont été inutiles. 2 (*conceited*) vaniteux. ◆**-ly** adv (*in vain*) vainement.

valentine [ˈvæləntaɪn] n (*card*) carte f de la Saint-Valentin.

valet [ˈvælɪt, ˈvæleɪ] n valet m de chambre.

valiant [ˈvælɪənt] a courageux. ◆**valour** n bravoure f.

valid [ˈvælɪd] a (*ticket, motive etc*) valable. ◆**validate** vt valider. ◆**va'lidity** n validité f; (*of argument*) justesse f.

valley [ˈvælɪ] n vallée f.

valuable [ˈvæljʊəb(ə)l] a (*object*) de (grande) valeur; (*help, time etc*) Fig précieux; – npl objets mpl de valeur.

value [ˈvæljuː] n valeur f; **to be of great/little v.** (*of object*) valoir cher/peu (cher); **it's good v.** c'est très avantageux; **v. added tax** taxe f à la valeur ajoutée; – vt (*appraise*) évaluer; (*appreciate*) attacher de la valeur à. ◆**valu'ation** n évaluation f; (*by expert*) expertise f. ◆**valuer** n expert m.

valve [vælv] n (*of machine*) soupape f; (*in radio*) lampe f; (*of tyre*) valve f; (*of heart*) valvule f.

vampire [ˈvæmpaɪər] n vampire m.

van [væn] n (*small*) camionnette f; (*large*) camion m; Rail fourgon m.

vandal [ˈvænd(ə)l] n vandale mf. ◆**vandal-**

ism n vandalisme m. ◆**vandalize** vt saccager, détériorer.

vanguard ['væŋgɑːd] n (of army, progress etc) avant-garde f.

vanilla [vəˈnɪlə] n vanille f; – a (ice cream) à la vanille.

vanish ['vænɪʃ] vi disparaître.

vanity ['vænɪtɪ] n vanité f; v. **case** vanity m inv.

vanquish ['væŋkwɪʃ] vt vaincre.

vantage point ['vɑːntɪdʒpɔɪnt] n (place, point of view) (bon) point m de vue.

vapour ['veɪpər] n vapeur f; (on glass) buée f.

variable ['veərɪəb(ə)l] a variable. ◆**variance** n at v. en désaccord (with avec). ◆**variant** a différent; – n variante f. ◆**vari'ation** n variation f.

varicose ['værɪkəʊs] a v. **veins** varices fpl.

variety [vəˈraɪətɪ] n 1 (diversity) variété f; a **v. of opinions/reasons/etc** (many) diverses opinions/raisons/etc; a **v. of** (articles) Com une gamme de. 2 Th variétés fpl; **v. show** spectacle m de variétés.

various ['veərɪəs] a divers. ◆–**ly** adv diversement.

varnish ['vɑːnɪʃ] vt vernir; – n vernis m.

vary ['veərɪ] vti varier (**from** de). ◆**varied** a varié. ◆**varying** a variable.

vase [vɑːz, Am veɪs] n vase m.

Vaseline® ['væsɪliːn] n vaseline f.

vast [vɑːst] a vaste, immense. ◆–**ly** adv (very) infiniment, extrêmement. ◆–**ness** n immensité f.

vat [væt] n cuve f.

VAT [viːeɪˈtiː, væt] n abbr (value added tax) TVA f.

Vatican ['vætɪkən] n Vatican m.

vaudeville ['vɔːdəvɪl] n Th Am variétés fpl.

vault [vɔːlt] n 1 (cellar) cave f; (tomb) caveau m; (in bank) chambre f forte, coffres mpl; (roof) voûte f. 2 vti (jump) sauter.

veal [viːl] n (meat) veau m.

veer [vɪər] vi (of wind) tourner; (of car, road) virer; **to v. off the road** quitter la route.

vegan ['viːgən] n végétaliste mf.

vegetable ['vedʒtəb(ə)l] n légume m; – a (kingdom, oil) végétal; **v. garden** (jardin m) potager m. ◆**vege'tarian** a & n végétarien, -ienne (mf). ◆**vege'tation** n végétation f.

vegetate ['vedʒteɪt] vi (of person) Pej végéter.

vehement ['viːəmənt] a (feeling, speech) véhément; (attack) violent. ◆–**ly** adv avec véhémence, violemment.

vehicle ['viːɪk(ə)l] n véhicule m; **heavy goods v.** (lorry) poids m lourd.

veil [veɪl] n (covering) & Fig voile m; – vt (face, truth etc) voiler.

vein [veɪn] n (in body or rock) veine f; (in leaf) nervure f; (mood) Fig esprit m.

vellum ['veləm] n (paper, skin) vélin m.

velocity [vəˈlɒsɪtɪ] n vélocité f.

velvet ['velvɪt] n velours m; – a de velours. ◆**velvety** a velouté.

vendetta [venˈdetə] n vendetta f.

vending machine ['vendɪŋməʃiːn] n distributeur m automatique.

vendor ['vendər] n vendeur, -euse mf.

veneer [vəˈnɪər] n (wood) placage m; (appearance) Fig vernis m.

venerable ['ven(ə)rəb(ə)l] a vénérable. ◆**venerate** vt vénérer.

venereal [vəˈnɪərɪəl] a (disease etc) vénérien.

venetian [vəˈniːʃ(ə)n] a **v. blind** store m vénitien.

vengeance ['vendʒəns] n vengeance f; **with a v.** (to work, study etc) furieusement; (to rain, catch up etc) pour de bon.

venison ['venɪs(ə)n] n venaison f.

venom ['venəm] n (substance) & Fig venin m. ◆**venomous** a (speech, snake etc) venimeux.

vent [vent] n 1 (hole) orifice m; (for air) bouche f d'aération; (in jacket) fente f. 2 **to give v. to** (feeling etc) donner libre cours à; – vt (anger) décharger (**on** sur).

ventilate ['ventɪleɪt] vt ventiler. ◆**venti'lation** n ventilation f. ◆**ventilator** n (in wall etc) ventilateur m.

ventriloquist [venˈtrɪləkwɪst] n ventriloque mf.

venture ['ventʃər] n entreprise f (risquée); **my v. into** mon incursion f dans; – vt (opinion, fortune) hasarder; **to v. to do** (dare) oser faire; – vi s'aventurer, se risquer (**into** dans).

venue ['venjuː] n lieu m de rencontre or de rendez-vous.

veranda(h) [vəˈrændə] n véranda f.

verb [vɜːb] n verbe m. ◆**verbal** a (promise, skill etc) verbal. ◆**verbatim** [vɜːˈbeɪtɪm] a & adv mot pour mot.

verbose [vɜːˈbəʊs] a (wordy) verbeux.

verdict ['vɜːdɪkt] n verdict m.

verdigris ['vɜːdɪgrɪs] n vert-de-gris m inv.

verge [vɜːdʒ] n (of road) accotement m, bord m; **on the v. of** Fig (ruin, tears etc) au bord de; (discovery) à la veille de; **on the v. of doing** sur le point de faire; – vi **to v. on** friser, frôler; (of colour) tirer sur.

verger ['vɜːdʒər] n Rel bedeau m.

verify ['verifai] vt vérifier. ◆**verifi'cation** n vérification f.

veritable ['veritəb(ə)l] a véritable.

vermicelli [vɜːmɪ'selɪ] n Culin vermicelle(s) m(pl).

vermin ['vɜːmɪn] n (animals) animaux mpl nuisibles; (insects, people) vermine f.

vermouth ['vɜːməθ] n vermouth m.

vernacular [və'nækjulər] n (of region) dialecte m.

versatile ['vɜːsətail, Am 'vɜːsət(ə)l] a (mind) souple; (material, tool, computer) polyvalent; **he's v.** il a des talents variés, il est polyvalent. ◆**versa'tility** n souplesse f; his v. la variété de ses talents.

verse [vɜːs] n (stanza) strophe f; (poetry) vers mpl; (of Bible) verset m.

versed [vɜːst] a (well) v. in versé dans.

version ['vɜːʃ(ə)n] n version f.

versus ['vɜːsəs] prep contre.

vertebra, pl **-ae** ['vɜːtɪbrə, -iː] n vertèbre f.

vertical ['vɜːtɪk(ə)l] a vertical; – n verticale f. ◆**-ly** adv verticalement.

vertigo ['vɜːtɪgəu] n (fear of falling) vertige m.

verve [vɜːv] n fougue f.

very ['verɪ] **1** adv très; **I'm v. hot** j'ai très chaud; **v. much** beaucoup; **the v. first** le tout premier; **at the v. least/most** tout au moins/plus; **at the v. latest** au plus tard. **2** a (actual) même; **his** or **her v. brother** son frère même; **at the v. end** (of play etc) tout à la fin; **to the v. end** jusqu'au bout.

vespers ['vespəz] npl Rel vêpres fpl.

vessel ['ves(ə)l] n Anat Bot Nau vaisseau m; (receptacle) récipient m.

vest [vest] n tricot m or maillot m de corps; (woman's) chemise f (américaine); (waistcoat) Am gilet m.

vested ['vestɪd] a **v. interests** Com droits mpl acquis; **she's got a v. interest in** Fig elle est directement intéressée dans.

vestige ['vestɪdʒ] n vestige m; **not a v. of** truth/good sense pas un grain de vérité/de bon sens.

vestry ['vestrɪ] n sacristie f.

vet [vet] n **1** n vétérinaire mf. **2** vt (-tt-) (document) examiner de près; (candidate) se renseigner à fond sur. ◆**veteri'narian** n Am vétérinaire mf. ◆**veterinary** a vétérinaire; **v. surgeon** vétérinaire mf.

veteran ['vet(ə)rən] n vétéran m; (war) v. ancien combattant m; – a v. golfer/etc golfeur/etc expérimenté.

veto ['viːtəu] n (pl -oes) (refusal) veto m inv; (power) droit m de veto; – vt mettre or opposer son veto à.

vex [veks] vt contrarier, fâcher; **vexed question** question f controversée.

via ['vaɪə] prep via, par.

viable ['vaɪəb(ə)l] a (baby, firm, plan etc) viable. ◆**via'bility** n viabilité f.

viaduct ['vaɪədʌkt] n viaduc m.

vibrate [vaɪ'breɪt] vi vibrer. ◆**'vibrant** a vibrant. ◆**vibration** n vibration f. ◆**vibrator** n vibromasseur m.

vicar ['vɪkər] n (in Church of England) pasteur m. ◆**vicarage** n presbytère m.

vicarious [vɪ'keəriəs] a (emotion) ressenti indirectement. ◆**-ly** adv (to experience) indirectement.

vice [vaɪs] n **1** (depravity) vice m; (fault) défaut m; **v. squad** brigade f des mœurs. **2** (tool) étau m.

vice- [vaɪs] pref vice-. ◆**v.-'chancellor** n Univ président m.

vice versa [vaɪs(ɪ)'vɜːsə] adv vice versa.

vicinity [və'sɪnɪtɪ] n environs mpl; **in the v. of** (place, amount) aux environs de.

vicious ['vɪʃəs] a (spiteful) méchant; (violent) brutal; **v. circle** cercle m vicieux. ◆**-ly** adv méchamment; brutalement. ◆**-ness** n méchanceté f; brutalité f.

vicissitudes [vɪ'sɪsɪtjuːdz] npl vicissitudes fpl.

victim ['vɪktɪm] n victime f; **to be the v. of** être victime de. ◆**victimize** vt persécuter. ◆**victimi'zation** n persécution f.

Victorian [vɪk'tɔːriən] a & n victorien, -ienne (mf).

victory ['vɪktərɪ] n victoire f. ◆**victor** n vainqueur m. ◆**vic'torious** a victorieux.

video ['vɪdɪəu] a video inv; – n v. (cassette) vidéocassette f; **v. (recorder)** magnétoscope m; **on v.** sur cassette; **to make a v. of** faire une cassette de; – vt (programme etc) enregistrer au magnétoscope. ◆**videotape** n bande f vidéo.

vie [vaɪ] vi (pres p vying) rivaliser (with avec).

Vietnam [vjet'næm, Am -'nɑːm] n Viêt-nam m. ◆**Vietna'mese** a & n vietnamien, -ienne (mf).

view [vjuː] n vue f; **to come into v.** apparaître; **in full v. of everyone** à la vue de tous; **in my v.** (opinion) à mon avis; **on v.** (exhibit) exposé; **in v. of** (considering) étant donné (the fact that que); **with a v. to doing** afin de faire; – vt (regard) considérer; (house) visiter. ◆**-er** n **1** TV téléspectateur, -trice mf. **2** (for slides) visionneuse f. ◆**viewfinder** n Phot viseur m. ◆**viewpoint** n point m de vue.

vigil ['vɪdʒɪl] n veille f; (over sick person or corpse) veillée f.

vigilant ['vɪdʒɪlənt] a vigilant. ◆**vigilance** n vigilance f.

vigilante [vɪdʒɪ'lænti] n Pej membre m d'une milice privée.

vigour ['vɪgər] n vigueur f. ◆**vigorous** a (person, speech etc) vigoureux.

vile [vaɪl] a (-er, -est) (base) infâme, vil; (unpleasant) abominable.

vilify ['vɪlɪfaɪ] vt diffamer.

villa ['vɪlə] n (in country) grande maison f de campagne.

village ['vɪlɪdʒ] n village m. ◆**villager** n villageois, -oise mf.

villain ['vɪlən] n scélérat, -ate mf; (in story or play) traître m. ◆**villainy** n infamie f.

vindicate ['vɪndɪkeɪt] vt justifier. ◆**vindication** n justification f.

vindictive [vɪn'dɪktɪv] a vindicatif, rancunier.

vine [vaɪn] n (grapevine) vigne f; **v. grower** viticulteur m. ◆**vineyard** ['vɪnjəd] n vignoble m.

vinegar ['vɪnɪgər] n vinaigre m.

vintage ['vɪntɪdʒ] **1** n (year) année f. **2** a (wine) de grand cru; (car) d'époque; (film) classique; (good) Fig bon; **v. Shaw**/etc du meilleur Shaw/etc.

vinyl ['vaɪn(ə)l] n vinyle m.

viola [vɪ'əʊlə] n (instrument) Mus alto m.

violate ['vaɪəleɪt] vt violer. ◆**violation** n violation f.

violence ['vaɪələns] n violence f. ◆**violent** a violent; **a v. dislike** une aversion vive. ◆**violently** adv violemment; **to be v. sick** (vomit) vomir.

violet ['vaɪələt] **1** a & n (colour) violet (m). **2** n (plant) violette f.

violin [vaɪə'lɪn] n violon m; — a (concerto etc) pour violon. ◆**violinist** n violoniste mf.

VIP [vi:aɪ'pi:] n abbr (very important person) personnage m de marque.

viper ['vaɪpər] n vipère f.

virgin ['vɜːdʒɪn] n vierge f; **to be a v.** (of woman, man) être vierge; − a (woman, snow etc) vierge. ◆**vir'ginity** n virginité f.

Virgo ['vɜːgəʊ] n (sign) la Vierge.

virile ['vɪraɪl, Am 'vɪrəl] a viril. ◆**vi'rility** n virilité f.

virtual ['vɜːtʃʊəl] a it was a v. failure/etc ce fut en fait un échec/etc. ◆**—ly** adv (in fact) en fait; (almost) pratiquement.

virtue ['vɜːtʃuː] n **1** (goodness, chastity) vertu f; (advantage) mérite m, avantage m. **2 by**

or **in v. of** en raison de. ◆**virtuous** a vertueux.

virtuoso, pl **-si** [vɜːtʃʊ'əʊsəʊ, -siː] n virtuose mf. ◆**virtuosity** [-'ɒsɪtɪ] n virtuosité f.

virulent ['vɪrʊlənt] a virulent. ◆**virulence** n virulence f.

virus ['vaɪ(ə)rəs] n virus m.

visa ['viːzə] n visa m.

vis-à-vis [viːzɑː'viː] prep vis-à-vis de.

viscount ['vaɪkaʊnt] n vicomte m. ◆**viscountess** n vicomtesse f.

viscous ['vɪskəs] a visqueux.

vise [vaɪs] n (tool) Am étau m.

visible ['vɪzəb(ə)l] a visible. ◆**visi'bility** n visibilité f. ◆**visibly** adv visiblement.

vision ['vɪʒ(ə)n] n vision f; **a man/a woman of v.** Fig un homme/une femme qui voit loin. ◆**visionary** a & n visionnaire (mf).

visit ['vɪzɪt] n (call, tour) visite f; (stay) séjour m; − vt (place) visiter; **to visit s.o.** (call on) rendre visite à qn; (stay with) faire un séjour chez qn; − vi être en visite (Am with chez). ◆**—ing** a (card, hours) de visite. ◆**visitor** n visiteur, -euse mf; (guest) invité, -ée mf; (in hotel) client, -ente mf.

visor ['vaɪzər] n (of helmet) visière f.

vista ['vɪstə] n (view of place etc) vue f; (of future) Fig perspective f.

visual ['vɪʒʊəl] a visuel; **v. aid** (in teaching) support m visuel. ◆**visualize** vt (imagine) se représenter; (foresee) envisager.

vital ['vaɪt(ə)l] a vital; **of v. importance** d'importance capitale; **v. statistics** (of woman) Fam mensurations fpl. ◆**—ly** adv extrêmement.

vitality [vaɪ'tælɪtɪ] n vitalité f.

vitamin ['vɪtəmɪn, Am 'vaɪtəmɪn] n vitamine f.

vitriol ['vɪtrɪəl] n Ch Fig vitriol m. ◆**vitri'olic** a (attack, speech etc) au vitriol.

vivacious [vɪ'veɪʃəs] a plein d'entrain.

vivid ['vɪvɪd] a (imagination, recollection etc) vif; (description) vivant. ◆**—ly** adv (to describe) de façon vivante; **to remember sth v.** avoir un vif souvenir de qch.

vivisection [vɪvɪ'sekʃ(ə)n] n vivisection f.

vocabulary [vəʊ'kæbjʊlərɪ] n vocabulaire m.

vocal ['vəʊk(ə)l] a (cords, music) vocal; (outspoken, noisy, critical) qui se fait entendre. ◆**vocalist** n chanteur, -euse mf.

vocation [vəʊ'keɪʃ(ə)n] n vocation f. ◆**vocational** a professionnel.

vociferous [və'sɪf(ə)rəs] a bruyant.

vodka ['vɒdkə] n vodka f.

vogue [vəʊg] n vogue f; **in v.** en vogue.

voice [vɔɪs] n voix f; **at the top of one's v.** à

tue-tête; – vt (feeling, opinion etc) formuler, exprimer.

void [vɔid] **1** n vide m; – a **v. of** (lacking in) dépourvu de. **2** a (not valid) Jur nul.

volatile ['vɒlǝtail, Am 'vɒlǝt(ǝ)l] a (person) versatile, changeant; (situation) explosif.

volcano [vɒl'keinǝu] n (pl -oes) volcan m. ◆**volcanic** [-'kænik] a volcanique.

volition [vǝ'liʃ(ǝ)n] n of one's own v. de son propre gré.

volley ['vɒli] n (of blows) volée f; (gunfire) salve f; (of insults) Fig bordée f. ◆**volleyball** n Sp volley(-ball) m.

volt [vǝult] n El volt m. ◆**voltage** n voltage m.

volume ['vɒljum] n (book, capacity, loudness) volume m. ◆**voluminous** [vǝ'lumɪnǝs] a volumineux.

voluntary ['vɒlǝnt(ǝ)ri] a volontaire; (unpaid) bénévole. ◆**voluntarily** [Am vɒlǝn'terili] adv volontairement; bénévolement. ◆**volun'teer** n volontaire mf; – vi se proposer (for sth pour qch, to do pour faire); Mil s'engager comme volontaire (for dans); – vt offrir (spontanément).

voluptuous [vǝ'lʌptʃuǝs] a voluptueux, sensuel.

vomit ['vɒmit] vti vomir; – n (matter) vomi m.

voracious [vǝ'reiʃǝs] a (appetite, reader etc) vorace.

vot/e [vǝut] n vote m; (right to vote) droit m de vote; **to win votes** gagner des voix; **v. of censure** or **no confidence** motion f de censure; **v. of thanks** discours m de remerciement; – vt (bill, funds etc) voter; (person) élire; – vi voter; **to v. Conservative** voter conservateur or pour les conservateurs. ◆**—ing** n vote m (of de); (polling) scrutin m. ◆**—er** n Pol électeur, -trice mf.

vouch [vautʃ] vi **to v. for** répondre de.

voucher ['vautʃǝr] n (for meals etc) bon m, chèque m.

vow [vau] n vœu m; – vt (obedience etc) jurer (to à); **to v. to do** jurer de faire, faire le vœu de faire.

vowel ['vauǝl] n voyelle f.

voyage ['vɔiidʒ] n voyage m (par mer).

vulgar ['vʌlgǝr] a vulgaire. ◆**vul'garity** n vulgarité f.

vulnerable ['vʌln(ǝ)rǝb(ǝ)l] a vulnérable. ◆**vulnera'bility** n vulnérabilité f.

vulture ['vʌltʃǝr] n vautour m.

W

W, w ['dʌb(ǝ)lju] n W, w m.

wacky ['wæki] a (-ier, -iest) Am Fam farfelu.

wad [wɒd] n (of banknotes, papers etc) liasse f; (of cotton wool, cloth) tampon m.

waddle ['wɒd(ǝ)l] vi se dandiner.

wade [weid] vi **to w. through** (mud, water etc) patauger dans; (book etc) Fig venir péniblement à bout de; **I'm wading through this book** j'avance péniblement dans ce livre.

wafer ['weifǝr] n (biscuit) gaufrette f; Rel hostie f.

waffle ['wɒf(ǝ)l] **1** n (talk) Fam verbiage m, blabla m; – vi Fam parler pour ne rien dire, blablater. **2** n (cake) gaufre f.

waft [wɒft] vi (of smell etc) flotter.

wag [wæg] **1** vt (-gg-) (tail, finger) agiter, remuer; – vi remuer; **tongues are wagging** Pej on en jase, les langues vont bon train. **2** n (joker) farceur, -euse mf.

wage [weidʒ] **1** n wage(s) salaire m, paie f; **w. claim** or **demand** revendication f salariale; **w. earner** salarié, -ée mf; (breadwin-

ner) soutien m de famille; **w. freeze** blocage m des salaires; **w. increase** or **rise** augmentation f de salaire. **2** vt (campaign) mener; **to w. war** faire la guerre (on à).

wager ['weidʒǝr] n pari m; – vt parier (that que).

waggle ['wæg(ǝ)l] vti remuer.

wag(g)on ['wægǝn] n (cart) chariot m; Rail wagon m (de marchandises); **on the w.** (abstinent) Fam au régime sec.

waif [weif] n enfant mf abandonné(e).

wail [weil] vi (cry out, complain) gémir; (of siren) hurler; – n gémissement m; (of siren) hurlement m.

waist [weist] n taille f; **stripped to the w.** nu jusqu'à la ceinture. ◆**waistband** n (of garment) ceinture f. ◆**waistcoat** ['weiskǝut] n gilet m. ◆**waistline** n taille f.

wait [weit] **1** n attente f; **to lie in w. (for)** guetter; – vi attendre; **to w. for s.o/sth** attendre qn/qch; **w. until I've gone, w. for me to go** attends que je sois parti; **to keep s.o. waiting** faire attendre qn; **w. and see!** attends voir!; **I can't w.**

to do it j'ai hâte de le faire; **to w. about (for)** attendre; **to w. behind** rester; **to w. up** veiller; **to w. up for s.o.** attendre le retour de qn avant de se coucher. **2** vi (serve) **to w. at table** servir à table; **to w. on s.o.** servir qn. ◆**—ing** n attente f; **'no w.'** Aut 'arrêt interdit'; – a w. **list/room** liste f/salle f d'attente. ◆**waiter** n garçon m (de café), serveur m; **w.!** garçon! ◆**waitress** n serveuse f; **w.!** mademoiselle!

waive [weɪv] vt renoncer à, abandonner.

wake[1] [weɪk] vi (pt **woke**, pp **woken**) **to w. (up)** se réveiller; **to w. up to** (fact etc) Fig prendre conscience de; – vt **to w. (up)** réveiller; **to spend one's waking hours** working/etc passer ses journées à travailler/etc. ◆**waken** vt éveiller, réveiller; – vi s'éveiller, se réveiller.

wake[2] [weɪk] n (of ship) & Fig sillage m; **in the w. of** Fig dans le sillage de, à la suite de.

Wales [weɪlz] n pays m de Galles.

walk [wɔːk] n promenade f; (short) (petit) tour m; (gait) démarche f; (pace) marche f, pas m; (path) allée f, chemin m; **to go for a w.** faire une promenade; (shorter) faire un (petit) tour; **to take for a w.** (child etc) emmener se promener; (baby, dog) promener; **five minutes' w. (away)** à cinq minutes à pied; **walks of life** Fig conditions sociales fpl; – vi marcher; (stroll) se promener; (go on foot) aller à pied; **w.!** (don't run) ne cours pas!; **to w. away or off** s'éloigner, partir (from de); **to w. away or off with** (steal) Fam faucher; **to w. in** entrer; **to w. into** (tree etc) rentrer dans; (trap) tomber dans; **to w. out** (leave) partir; (of workers) se mettre en grève; **to w. out on** s.o. (desert) Fam laisser tomber qn; **to w. over** (to go up to) s'approcher de; – vt (distance) faire à pied; (streets) (par)courir; (take for a walk) promener (bébé, chien); **to w. s.o. to** (station etc) accompagner qn à. ◆**—ing** n marche f (à pied); – a a w. **corpse/dictionary** (person) Fig un cadavre/dictionnaire ambulant; **at a w. pace** au pas; **w. stick** canne f. ◆**walker** n marcheur, -euse mf; (for pleasure) promeneur, -euse mf. ◆**walkout** n (strike) grève f surprise; (from meeting) départ m (en signe de protestation). ◆**walkover** n (in contest etc) victoire f facile. ◆**walkway** n **moving w.** trottoir m roulant.

walkie-talkie [wɔːkɪ'tɔːkɪ] n talkie-walkie m.

Walkman® ['wɔːkmən] n (pl **Walkmans**) baladeur m.

wall [wɔːl] n mur m; (of cabin, tunnel, stomach etc) paroi f; (of ice) Fig muraille f; (of smoke) Fig rideau m; **to go to the w.** (of firm) Fig faire faillite; – a mural; – vt **to w. up** (door etc) murer; **walled city** ville f fortifiée. ◆**wallflower** n Bot giroflée f; **to be a w.** (at dance) faire tapisserie. ◆**wallpaper** n papier m peint; – vt tapisser. ◆**wall-to-wall 'carpet(ing)** n moquette f.

wallet ['wɒlɪt] n portefeuille m.

wallop ['wɒləp] vt (hit) Fam taper sur; – n (blow) Fam grand coup m.

wallow ['wɒləʊ] vi **to w. in** (mud, vice etc) se vautrer dans.

wally ['wɒlɪ] n (idiot) Fam andouille f, imbécile mf.

walnut ['wɔːlnʌt] n (nut) noix f; (tree, wood) noyer m.

walrus ['wɔːlrəs] n (animal) morse m.

waltz [wɔːls, Am wɒlts] n valse f; – vi valser.

wan [wɒn] a (pale) Lit pâle.

wand [wɒnd] n baguette f (magique).

wander ['wɒndər] vi (of thoughts) vagabonder; **to w. (about or around)** (roam) errer, vagabonder; (stroll) flâner; **to w. from or off** (path, subject) s'écarter de; **to w. off** (go away) s'éloigner; **my mind's wandering** je suis distrait; – vt **to w. the streets** errer dans les rues. ◆**—ing** a (life, tribe) vagabond, nomade; – npl **wanderings** mpl. ◆**—er** n vagabond, -onde mf.

wane [weɪn] vi (of moon, fame, strength etc) décroître; – n **to be on the w.** décroître, être en déclin.

wangle ['wæŋg(ə)l] vt Fam (obtain) se débrouiller pour obtenir; (avoiding payment) carotter (from à).

want [wɒnt] vt vouloir (**to do** faire); (ask for) demander; (need) avoir besoin de; **I w. him to go** je veux qu'il parte; **you w. to try** (should) tu devrais essayer; **you're wanted on the phone** on vous demande au téléphone; – vi **not to w. for** (not lack) ne pas manquer de; – n (lack) manque m (de); (poverty) besoin m; **for w. of** par manque de; **for w. of money/time** faute d'argent/de temps; **for w. of anything better** faute de mieux; **your wants** (needs) tes besoins mpl. ◆**—ed** (a man, criminal) recherché par la police; **to feel w.** sentir qu'on vous aime. ◆**—ing** a (inadequate) insuffisant; **to be w.** manquer (**in** de).

wanton ['wɒntən] a (gratuitous) gratuit; (immoral) impudique.

war [wɔːr] n guerre f; **at w.** en guerre (**with** avec); **to go to w.** entrer en guerre (**with** avec); **to declare w.** déclarer la guerre (**on** à); – a (wound, criminal etc) de guerre; **w.**

memorial monument *m* aux morts.
◆**warfare** *n* guerre *f*. ◆**warhead** *n* (*of missile*) ogive *f*. ◆**warlike** *a* guerrier. ◆**warmonger** *n* fauteur *m* de guerre. ◆**warpath** *n* to be on the w. (*angry*) *Fam* être d'humeur massacrante. ◆**warring** *a* (*countries etc*) en guerre; (*ideologies etc*) Fig en conflit. ◆**warship** *n* navire *m* de guerre. ◆**wartime** *n* in w. en temps de guerre.

warble ['wɔːb(ə)l] *vi* (*of bird*) gazouiller.

ward¹ ['wɔːd] *n* 1 (*in hospital*) salle *f*. 2 (*child*) *Jur* pupille *mf*. 3 (*electoral division*) circonscription *f* électorale.

ward² ['wɔːd] *vt* to w. off (*blow, anger*) détourner; (*danger*) éviter.

warden ['wɔːd(ə)n] *n* (*of institution, Am of prison*) directeur, -trice *mf*; (*of park*) gardien, -ienne *mf*; **(traffic) w.** contractuel, -elle *mf*.

warder ['wɔːdər] *n* gardien *m* (de prison).

wardrobe ['wɔːdrəub] *n* (*cupboard*) penderie *f*; (*clothes*) garde-robe *f*.

warehouse, *pl* **-ses** ['weəhaus, -zɪz] *n* entrepôt *m*.

wares [weəz] *npl* marchandises *fpl*.

warily ['weərɪlɪ] *adv* avec précaution.

warm [wɔːm] *a* (-er, -est) chaud; (*iron, oven*) moyen; (*welcome, thanks etc*) chaleureux; **to be** *or* **feel w.** avoir chaud; **it's (nice and) w.** (*of weather*) il fait (agréablement) chaud; **to get w.** (*of person, room etc*) se réchauffer; (*of food, water*) chauffer; *– vt* **to w. (up)** (*person, food etc*) réchauffer; *– vi* **to w. up** (*of person, room, engine*) se réchauffer; (*of food, water*) chauffer; (*of discussion*) s'échauffer; **to w. to s.o.** *Fig* se prendre de sympathie pour qn. ◆**warm-'hearted** *a* chaleureux. ◆**warmly** *adv* (*to wrap up*) chaudement; (*to welcome, thank etc*) chaleureusement. ◆**warmth** *n* chaleur *f*.

warn [wɔːn] *vt* avertir, prévenir (that que); **to w. s.o. against** *or* **of** mettre qn en garde contre qch; **to w. s.o. against doing** conseiller à qn de ne pas faire. ◆**-ing** *n* avertissement *m*; (*advance notice*) (pré)avis *m*; *Mil* avis *m*; (*alarm*) alerte *f*; **without w.** sans prévenir; **a note** *or* **word of w.** une mise en garde; **w. light** (*on appliance etc*) voyant *m* lumineux; **hazard w. lights** *Aut* feux *mpl* de détresse.

warp [wɔːp] **1** *vt* (*wood etc*) voiler; (*judgment, person etc*) *Fig* pervertir; **a warped mind** un esprit tordu; **a warped account** un récit déformé; *– vi* se voiler. **2** *n* *Tex* chaîne *f*.

warrant ['wɒrənt] **1** *n* *Jur* mandat *m*; **a w. for**

your arrest un mandat d'arrêt contre vous. **2** *vt* (*justify*) justifier; **I w. you that …** (*declare confidently*) je t'assure que … . ◆**warranty** *n* *Com* garantie *f*.

warren ['wɒrən] *n* (*rabbit*) **w.** garenne *f*.

warrior ['wɒrɪər] *n* guerrier, -ière *mf*.

wart [wɔːt] *n* verrue *f*.

wary ['weərɪ] *a* (-ier, -iest) prudent; **to be w. of s.o./sth** se méfier de qn/qch; **to be w. of doing** hésiter beaucoup à faire.

was [wɒz, *stressed* wɒz] *see* be.

wash [wɒʃ] *n* (*clothes*) lessive *f*; (*of ship*) sillage *m*; **to have a w.** se laver; **to give sth a w.** laver qch; **to do the w.** faire la lessive; **in the w.** à la lessive; *– vt* laver; (*flow over*) baigner; **to w. one's hands** se laver les mains (Fig of sth de qch); **to w. away** (*of sea etc*) emporter (*qch, qn*); **to w. away** *or* **off** *or* **out** (*stain*) faire partir (en lavant); **to w. down** (*vehicle, deck*) laver à grande eau; (*food*) arroser (with de); **to w. out** (*bowl etc*) laver; *– vi* se laver; (*do the dishes*) faire la vaisselle; **to w. away** *or* **off** *or* **out** (*of stain*) partir (au lavage); **to w. up** (*do the dishes*) faire la vaisselle; (*have a wash*) *Am* se laver. ◆**washed-'out** *a* (*tired*) lessivé. ◆**washed-'up** *a* (all) **w.-up** (*person, plan*) *Sl* fichu. ◆**washable** *a* lavable. ◆**washbasin** *n* lavabo *m*. ◆**washcloth** *n* *Am* gant *m* de toilette. ◆**washout** *n* *Sl* (*event etc*) fiasco *m*; (*person*) nullité *f*. ◆**washroom** *n* *Am* toilettes *fpl*.

washer ['wɒʃər] *n* (*ring*) rondelle *f*, joint *m*.

washing ['wɒʃɪŋ] *n* (*act*) lavage *m*; (*clothes*) lessive *f*, linge *m*; **to do the w.** faire la lessive; **w. line** corde *f* à linge; **w. machine** machine *f* à laver; **w. powder** lessive *f*. ◆**w.-'up** *n* vaisselle *f*; **to do the w.-up** faire la vaisselle; **w.-up liquid** produit *m* pour la vaisselle.

wasp [wɒsp] *n* guêpe *f*.

wast/e [weɪst] *n* gaspillage *m*; (*of time*) perte *f*; (*rubbish*) déchets *mpl*; *pl* (*land*) étendue *f* déserte; **w. disposal unit** broyeur *m* d'ordures; *– a* **w. material** *or* **products** déchets *mpl*; **w. land** (*uncultivated*) terres *fpl* incultes; (*in town*) terrain *m* vague; **w. paper** vieux papiers *mpl*; **w. pipe** tuyau *m* d'évacuation; *– vt* (*money, food etc*) gaspiller; (*time, opportunity*) perdre; **to w. one's time on frivolities/etc** gaspiller son temps en frivolités/*etc*, perdre son temps à des frivolités/*etc*; **to w. one's life** gâcher sa vie; *– vi* **to w. away** dépérir. ◆**-ed** *a* (*effort*) inutile; (*body etc*) émacié. ◆**wastage** *n* gaspillage *m*; (*losses*) pertes *fpl*; **some w.** (*of goods, staff etc*) du déchet. ◆**wastebin**

(in kitchen) poubelle f. ◆**wastepaper basket** n corbeille f (à papier).
wasteful ['weistfəl] a (person) gaspilleur; (process) peu économique.

watch [wɒtʃ] **1** n (small clock) montre f. **2** n (over suspect, baby etc) surveillance f; Nau quart m; **to keep (a) w.** on or over surveiller; **to keep w.** faire le guet; **to be on the w. (for)** guetter; — vt regarder; (observe) observer; (suspect, baby etc) surveiller; (be careful of) faire attention à; — vi regarder; **to w. (out) for** (be on the lookout for) guetter; **to w. out** (take care) faire attention (for à); **w. out!** attention!; **to w. over** surveiller. ◆**watchdog** n chien m de garde. ◆**watchmaker** n horloger, -ère mf. ◆**watchman** n (pl -men) night w. veilleur m de nuit. ◆**watchstrap** n bracelet m de montre. ◆**watchtower** n tour f de guet.

watchful ['wɒtʃfəl] a vigilant.

water ['wɔːtər] n eau f; **by w.** en bateau; **under w.** (road, field etc) inondé; (to swim) sous l'eau; **at high w.** à marée haute; **it doesn't hold w.** (of theory etc) Fig ça ne tient pas debout; **in hot w.** Fig dans le pétrin; **w. cannon** lance f à eau; **w. ice** sorbet m; **w. lily** nénuphar m; **w. pistol** pistolet m à eau; **w. polo** Sp water-polo m; **w. power** énergie f hydraulique; **w. rates** eaux fpl; **w. skiing** ski m nautique; **w. tank** réservoir m d'eau; **w. tower** château m d'eau; — vt (plant etc) arroser; **to w. down** (wine etc) couper (d'eau); (text etc) édulcorer; — vi (of eyes) larmoyer; **it makes his** or **her mouth w.** ça lui fait venir l'eau à la bouche. ◆**—ing** n (of plant etc) arrosage m; **w. can** arrosoir m. ◆**watery** a (colour) délavé; (soup) Pej trop liquide; (eyes) larmoyant; **w. tea** or **coffee** de la lavasse.

watercolour ['wɔːtəkʌlər] n (picture) aquarelle f; (paint) couleur f pour aquarelle. ◆**watercress** n cresson m (de fontaine). ◆**waterfall** n chute f d'eau. ◆**waterhole** n (in desert) point m d'eau. ◆**waterline** n (on ship) ligne f de flottaison. ◆**waterlogged** a délavé. ◆**watermark** n (in paper) filigrane m. ◆**watermelon** n pastèque f. ◆**waterproof** a (material) imperméable. ◆**watershed** n (turning point) tournant m (décisif). ◆**watertight** a (container etc) étanche. ◆**waterway** n voie f navigable. ◆**waterworks** n (place) station f hydraulique.

watt [wɒt] n El watt m.

wave [weiv] n (of sea) & Fig vague f; (in hair) ondulation f; Rad onde f; (sign) signe m (de la main); **long/medium/short w.** Rad ondes fpl longues/moyennes/ courtes; — vi (with hand) faire signe (de la main); (of flag) flotter; **to w. to** (greet) saluer de la main; — vt (arm, flag etc) agiter; (hair) onduler; **to w. s.o. on** faire signe à qn d'avancer; **to w. aside** (objection etc) écarter. ◆**waveband** n Rad bande f de fréquence. ◆**wavelength** n Rad & Fig longueur f d'ondes.

waver ['weivər] vi (of flame, person etc) vaciller.

wavy ['weivi] a (-ier, -iest) (line) onduleux; (hair) ondulé.

wax [wæks] **1** n cire f; (for ski) fart m; — vt cirer; (ski) farter; (car) lustrer; — a (candle, doll etc) de cire; **w. paper** Culin Am papier m paraffiné. **2** vi (of moon) croître. **3** vi **to w. lyrical/merry** (become) se faire lyrique/gai. ◆**waxworks** npl (place) musée m de cire; (dummies) figures fpl de cire.

way [wei] **1** n (path, road) chemin m (to de); (direction) sens m, direction f; (distance) distance f; **all the w., the whole w.** (to eat etc) pendant tout le chemin; **this w.** par ici; **that way** (by that way); **which w.?** par où?; **to lose one's w.** se perdre; **I'm on my w.** (coming) j'arrive; (going) je pars; **he made his w. out/home** il est sorti/rentré; **the w. there** l'aller m; **the w. back** le retour; **the w. in** l'entrée f; **the w. out** la sortie; **a w. out of** (problem etc) Fig une solution à; **the w. is clear** Fig la voie est libre; **across the w.** en face; **on the w.** en route (to pour); **by w. of** (via) par; (as) Fig comme; **out of the w.** (isolated) isolé; **to go out of one's w. to do** se donner du mal pour faire; **by the w....** Fig à propos ...; **to be** or **stand in the w.** barrer le passage; **she's in my w.** (hindrance) Fig elle me gêne; **to get out of the w., make w.** s'écarter; **to give w.** céder; Aut céder le passage ou la priorité; **a long w. (away** or **off)** très loin; **it's the wrong w. up** c'est dans le mauvais sens; **do it the other w. round** fais le contraire; **to get under w.** (of campaign etc) démarrer; — adv (behind etc) très loin; **w. ahead** très en avance (of sur). **2** n (manner) façon f; (means) moyen m; (condition) état m; (habit) habitude f; (particular) égard m; **one's ways** (behaviour) ses manières fpl; **to get one's own w.** obtenir ce qu'on veut; **(in) this w.** de cette façon; **in a way** (to some extent) dans un certain sens; **w. of life** façon f de vivre, mode m de vie; **no w.!** (certainly not) Fam pas question! ◆**wayfarer** n voyageur, -euse mf. ◆**way-'out** a Fam extraordinaire. ◆**wayside** n by the w. au bord de la route.

waylay [weɪˈleɪ] vt (pt & pp **-laid**) (attack) attaquer par surprise; (stop) Fig arrêter au passage.

wayward ['weɪwəd] a rebelle, capricieux.

WC [dʌb(ə)ljuːˈsiː] n w-c mpl, waters mpl.

we [wiː] pron nous; **we go** nous allons; **we teachers** nous autres professeurs; **we never know** (indefinite) on ne sait jamais.

weak [wiːk] a (**-er, -est**) faible; (tea, coffee) léger; (health, stomach) fragile. ◆**w.-'willed** a faible. ◆**weaken** vt affaiblir; – vi faiblir. ◆**weakling** n (in body) mauviette f; (in character) faible mf. ◆**weakly** adv faiblement. ◆**weakness** n faiblesse f; (of health, stomach) fragilité f; (fault) point m faible; **a w. for** (liking) un faible pour.

weal [wiːl] n (wound on skin) marque f, zébrure f.

wealth [welθ] n (money, natural resources) richesse(s) f(pl); **a w. of** (abundance) Fig une profusion de. ◆**wealthy** a (**-ier, -iest**) riche; – n the w. les riches mpl.

wean [wiːn] vt (baby) sevrer.

weapon ['wepən] n arme f. ◆**weaponry** n armements mpl.

wear [weər] **1** vt (pt **wore**, pp **worn**) (have on body) porter; (look, smile) avoir; (put on) mettre; **to have nothing to w.** n'avoir rien à se mettre; – n **men's/sports w.** vêtements mpl pour hommes/de sport; **evening w.** tenue f de soirée. **2** vt (pt **wore**, pp **worn**) **to w.** (away or down or out) (material, patience etc) user; **to w. s.o. out** (exhaust) épuiser qn; **to w. oneself out** s'épuiser (doing à faire); – vi (last) faire de l'usage, durer; **to w.** (out) (of clothes etc) s'user; **to w. off** (of colour, pain etc) passer, disparaître; **to w. on** (of time) passer; **to w. out** (of patience) s'épuiser; – n (use) usage m; **w.** (and tear) usure f. ◆**-ing** a (tiring) épuisant. ◆**-er** n the w. of (hat, glasses etc) la personne qui porte.

weary ['wɪərɪ] a (**-ier, -iest**) (tired) fatigué, las (of doing de faire); (tiring) fatigant; (look, smile) las; – vi to w. of se lasser de. ◆**wearily** adv avec lassitude. ◆**weariness** n lassitude f.

weasel ['wiːz(ə)l] n belette f.

weather ['weðər] n temps m; what's the w. like? quel temps fait-il?; in (the) hot w. par temps chaud; under the w. (not well) Fig patraque; – a (chart etc) météorologique. w. forecast, w. report prévisions fpl météorologiques, météo f; w. vane girouette f; –

vt (storm, hurricane) essuyer; (crisis) Fig surmonter. ◆**weather-beaten** a (face, person) tanné, hâlé. ◆**weathercock** n girouette f. ◆**weatherman** n (pl **-men**) TV Rad Fam monsieur m météo.

weav/e [wiːv] vt (pt **wove**, pp **woven**) (cloth, plot) tisser; (basket, garland) tresser; – vi Tex tisser; **to w. in and out of** (crowd, cars etc) Fig se faufiler entre; – n (style) tissage m. ◆**-ing** n tissage m. ◆**-er** n tisserand, -ande mf.

web [web] n (of spider) toile f; (of lies) Fig tissu m. ◆**webbed** a (foot) palmé. ◆**webbing** n (in chair) sangles fpl.

wed [wed] vt (**-dd-**) (marry) épouser; (qualities etc) Fig allier (**to** à); – vi se marier. ◆**wedded** a (bliss, life) conjugal. ◆**wedding** n mariage m; **golden/silver w.** noces fpl d'or/d'argent; – a (cake) de noces; (anniversary, present) de mariage; (dress) de mariée; **his** or **her w. day** le jour de son mariage; **w. ring, Am w. band** alliance f. ◆**wedlock** n **born out of w.** illégitime.

wedge [wedʒ] n (for splitting) coin m; (under wheel, table etc) cale f; **w. heel** (of shoe) semelle f compensée; – vt (wheel, table etc) caler; (push) enfoncer (**into** dans); **wedged (in) between** (caught, trapped) coincé entre.

Wednesday ['wenzdɪ] n mercredi m.

wee [wiː] a (tiny) Fam tout petit.

weed [wiːd] n (plant) mauvaise herbe f; (weak person) Fam mauviette f; **w. killer** désherbant m; – vti désherber; – vt **to w. out** Fig éliminer (**from** de). ◆**weedy** a (**-ier, -iest**) (person) Fam maigre et chétif.

week [wiːk] n semaine f; the w. before last pas la semaine dernière, celle d'avant; the w. after next pas la semaine prochaine, celle d'après; tomorrow w., a w. tomorrow demain en huit. ◆**weekday** n jour m de semaine. ◆**week'end** n week-end m; at or on or over the w. ce week-end, pendant le week-end. ◆**weekly** a hebdomadaire; – adv toutes les semaines; – n (magazine) hebdomadaire m.

weep [wiːp] vi (pt pp **wept**) pleurer; (of wound) suinter; **to w. for s.o.** pleurer qn; – vt (tears) pleurer; **weeping willow** saule m pleureur.

weft [weft] n Tex trame f.

weigh [weɪ] vt peser; **to w. down** (with load etc) surcharger (**with** de); (bend) faire plier; **to w. up** (goods, chances etc) peser; – vi peser; **it's weighing on my mind** ça me tracasse; **to w. down on s.o.** (of worries etc) accabler qn. ◆**weighing-machine** n balance f.

weight [weɪt] n poids m; **to put on w.** grossir; **to lose w.** maigrir; **to carry w.** (of argument etc) Fig avoir du poids (**with** pour); **to pull one's w.** (do one's share) Fig faire sa part du travail; **w. lifter** haltérophile mf; **w. lifting** haltérophilie f; − vt **to w.** (**down**) (light object) maintenir avec un poids; **to w. down with** (overload) surcharger de. ◆**weightlessness** n apesanteur f. ◆**weighty** a (-ier, -iest) lourd; (argument, subject) Fig de poids.

weighting ['weɪtɪŋ] n (on salary) indemnité f de résidence.

weir [wɪər] n (across river) barrage m.

weird [wɪəd] a (-er, -est) (odd) bizarre; (eerie) mystérieux.

welcome ['welkəm] a (pleasant) agréable; (timely) opportun; **to be w.** (of person, people) être le bienvenu or la bienvenue or les bienvenu(e)s; **w.!** soyez le bienvenu or la bienvenue or les bienvenu(e)s!; **to make s.o.** (feel) **w.** faire bon accueil à qn; **you're w.!** (after 'thank you') il n'y a pas de quoi!; **w. to do** (free) libre de faire; **you're w. to** (take or use) **my bike** mon vélo est à ta disposition; **you're w. to it!** Iron grand bien vous fasse!; − n accueil m; **to extend a w. to** (greet) souhaiter la bienvenue à; − vt accueillir; (warmly) faire bon accueil à; (be glad of) se réjouir de; **I w. you!** je vous souhaite la bienvenue! ◆**welcoming** a (smile etc) accueillant; (speech, words) d'accueil.

weld [weld] vt **to w.** (**together**) souder; (groups etc) Fig unir; − n (joint) soudure f. ◆−**ing** n soudure f. ◆−**er** n soudeur m.

welfare ['welfeər] n (physical, material) bien-être m; (spiritual) santé f; (public aid) aide f sociale; **public w.** (good) le bien public; **the w. state** (in Great Britain) l'État-providence m; **w. work** assistance f sociale.

well[1] [wel] n (for water) puits m; (of stairs, lift) cage f; (oil) **w.** puits de pétrole. **2** vi **to w. up** (rise) monter.

well[2] [wel] adv (better, best) bien; **to do w.** (succeed) réussir; **you'd do w. to refuse** tu ferais bien de refuser; **w. done!** bravo!; **I, you, she** etc **might (just) as w. have left** it valait mieux partir, autant valait partir; **it's just as w. that** (lucky) heureusement que . . . ; **as w. (also)** aussi; **as w. as** plus bien que; **as w. as two cats, he has . . .** en plus de deux chats, il a . . . ; − a bien inv; **she's w.** (healthy) elle va bien; **not a w. man** un

homme malade; **to get w.** se remettre; **that's all very w., but . . .** tout ça c'est très joli, mais . . . ; − int eh bien!; **w., w.!** (surprise) tiens, tiens!; **enormous, w., quite big** énorme, enfin, assez grand.

well-behaved [welbɪ'heɪvd] a sage. ◆**w.-'being** n bien-être m. ◆**w.-'built** a (person, car) solide. ◆**w.-'founded** a bien fondé. ◆**w.-'heeled** a (rich) Fam nanti. ◆**w.-in'formed** a (person, newspaper) bien informé. ◆**w.-'known** a (bien) connu. ◆**w.-'meaning** a bien intentionné. ◆**w.-'nigh** adv presque. ◆**w.-'off** a aisé, riche. ◆**w.-'read** a instruit. ◆**w.-'spoken** a (person) qui a un accent cultivé, qui parle bien. ◆**w.-'thought-of** a hautement considéré. ◆**w.-'timed** a opportun. ◆**w.-to-'do** a aisé, riche. ◆**w.-'tried** a (method) éprouvé. ◆**w.-'trodden** a (path) battu. ◆**w.-'wishers** npl admirateurs, -trices mfpl. ◆**w.-'worn** a (clothes, carpet) usagé.

wellington ['welɪŋtən] n botte f de caoutchouc.

welsh [welʃ] vi **to w. on** (debt, promise) ne pas honorer.

Welsh [welʃ] a gallois; **W. rabbit** Culin toast m au fromage; − n (language) gallois m. ◆**Welshman** n (pl -men) Gallois m. ◆**Welshwoman** n (pl -women) Galloise f.

wench [wentʃ] n Hum jeune fille f.

wend [wend] vt **to w. one's way** s'acheminer (**to** vers).

went [went] see **go 1.**

wept [wept] see **weep.**

were [wər, stressed wɜr] see **be.**

werewolf ['weəwulf] n (pl -wolves) loup-garou m.

west [west] n ouest m; − a (coast) ouest inv; (wind) d'ouest; **W. Africa** Afrique f occidentale; **W. Indian** a & n antillais, -aise (mf); **the W. Indies** les Antilles fpl; − adv à l'ouest, vers l'ouest. ◆**westbound** a (carriageway) ouest inv; (traffic) en direction de l'ouest. ◆**westerly** a (point) ouest inv; (direction) de l'ouest; (wind) d'ouest. ◆**western** a (coast) ouest inv; (culture) Pol occidental; **W. Europe** Europe f de l'Ouest; − n (film) western m. ◆**westerner** n habitant, -ante mf de l'Ouest; Pol occidental, -ale mf. ◆**westernize** vt occidentaliser. ◆**westward(s)** a & adv vers l'ouest.

wet [wet] a (wetter, wettest) mouillé; (damp, rainy) humide; (day, month) de pluie; **w. paint/ink** peinture f/encre f fraîche; **w. through** trempé; **to get w.** se mouiller; **it's w.** (raining) il pleut; **he's w.** (weak-willed)

Fam c'est une lavette; **w. blanket** *Fig* rabat-joie *m inv*; **w. nurse** nourrice *f*; **w. suit** combinaison *f* de plongée; – *n* **the w.** (*rain*) la pluie; (*damp*) l'humidité *f*; – *vt* (**-tt-**) mouiller. ◆**-ness** *n* humidité *f*.

whack [wak] *n* (*blow*) grand coup *m*; – *vt* donner un grand coup à. ◆**-ed** *a* **w.** (**out**) (*tired*) *Fam* claqué. ◆**-ing** *a* (*big*) *Fam* énorme.

whale [weɪl] *n* baleine *f*. ◆**whaling** *n* pêche *f* à la baleine.

wham! [wæm] *int* vlan!

wharf [wɔːf] *n* (*pl* **wharfs** *or* **wharves**) (*for ships*) quai *m*.

what [wɒt] **1** *a* quel, quelle, *pl* quel(le)s; **w. book?** quel livre?; **w. one?** lequel, laquelle?; **w. a fool/etc!** quel idiot/etc!; **I know w. book it is** je sais quel livre c'est; **w.** (**little**) **she has** le peu qu'elle a. **2** *pron* (*in questions*) qu'est-ce qui, qu'est-ce que; (*object*) (qu'est-ce) que; (*after prep*) quoi; **w.'s happening?** qu'est-ce qui se passe?; **w. does he do?** qu'est-ce qu'il fait?, que fait-il?; **w. is it?** qu'est-ce que c'est?; **w.'s that book?** quel est ce livre?; **w.!** (*surprise*) quoi!, comment!; **w.'s it called?** comment ça s'appelle?; **w. for?** pourquoi?; **w. about me/etc?** et moi/etc?; **w. about leaving/etc?** si on partait/etc? **3** *pron* (*indirect, relative*) ce qui; (*object*) ce que; **I know w. will happen/w. she'll do** je sais ce qui arrivera/ce qu'elle fera; **w. happens is ...** ce qui arrive c'est que ...; **w. I need** ce dont j'ai besoin. ◆**what'ever** *a* **w.** (**the**) **mistake/etc** (*no matter what*) quelle que soit l'erreur/etc; **of w. size** de n'importe quelle taille; **no chance w.** pas la moindre chance; **nothing w.** rien du tout; – *pron* (*no matter what*) quoi que (+ *sub*); **w. happens** quoi qu'il arrive; **w. you do** quoi que tu fasses; **w. is important** tout ce qui est important; **w. you want** tout ce que tu veux. ◆**what's-it** *n* (*thing*) *Fam* machin *m*. ◆**whatso'ever** *a* & *pron* = **whatever.**

wheat [wiːt] *n* blé *m*, froment *m*. ◆**wheatgerm** *n* germes *mpl* de blé.

wheedle ['wiːd(ə)l] *vt* **to w. s.o.** enjôler qn (**into doing** *pour* qu'il fasse); **to w. sth out of s.o.** obtenir qch de qn par la flatterie.

wheel [wiːl] **1** *n* roue *f*; **at the w.** *Aut* au volant; *Nau* au gouvernail; – *vt* (*push*) pousser; – *vi* (*turn*) tourner. **2** *vi* **to w. and deal** *Fam* faire des combines. ◆**wheelbarrow** *n* brouette *f*. ◆**wheelchair** *n* fauteuil *m* roulant.

wheeze [wiːz] **1** *vi* respirer bruyamment. **2** *n*

(*scheme*) *Fam* combine *f*. ◆**wheezy** *a* (**-ier, -iest**) poussif.

whelk [welk] *n* (*mollusc*) buccin *m*.

when [wen] *adv* quand; – *conj* quand, lorsque; (*whereas*) alors que; **w. I finish, w. I've finished** quand j'aurai fini; **w. I saw him** *or* **w. I'd seen him, I left** après l'avoir vu, je suis parti; **the day/moment w.** le jour/moment où; **I talked about w. ...** j'ai parlé de l'époque où ... ◆**when'ever** *conj* (*at whatever time*) quand; (*each time that*) chaque fois que.

where [weər] *adv* où; **w. are you from?** d'où êtes-vous?; – *conj* où; (*whereas*) alors que; **that's w. you'll find it** c'est là que tu le trouveras; **I found it w. she'd left it** je l'ai trouvé là où elle l'avait laissé; **I went to w. he was** je suis allé à l'endroit où il était. ◆**whereabouts** *adv* où (*donc*); – *n* **his w.** l'endroit *m* où il est. ◆**where'as** *conj* alors que. ◆**where'by** *adv* par quoi. ◆**where'upon** *adv* sur quoi. ◆**wher'ever** *conj* **w. you go** (*everywhere*) partout où tu iras, où que tu ailles; **I'll go w. you like** (*anywhere*) j'irai (là) où vous voudrez.

whet [wet] *vt* (**-tt-**) (*appetite, desire etc*) aiguiser.

whether ['weðər] *conj* si; **I don't know w. to leave** je ne sais pas si je dois partir; **w. she does it or not** qu'elle le fasse ou non; **w. now or tomorrow** que ce soit maintenant ou demain; **it's doubtful w.** il est douteux que (+ *sub*).

which [wɪtʃ] **1** *a* (*in questions etc*) quel, quelle, *pl* quel(le)s; **w. hat?** quel chapeau?; **in w. case** auquel cas. **2** *rel pron* (*object*) que; (*after prep*) lequel, laquelle, *pl* lesquel(le)s; **the house w. is ...** la maison qui est ...; **the book w. I like** le livre que j'aime; **the film of w. ...** le film dont *or* duquel ...; **she's ill, w. is sad** elle est malade, ce qui est triste; **he lies, w. I don't like** il ment, ce que je n'aime pas; **after w.** (*whereupon*) après quoi. **3** *pron* **w.** (**one**) (*in questions*) lequel, laquelle, *pl* lesquel(le)s; **w.** (**one**) **of us?** lequel *or* laquelle d'entre nous?; **w.** (**ones**) **are the best of these books?** quels sont les meilleurs de ces livres? **4** *pron* **w.** (**one**) (*the one that*) celui qui, celle qui, *pl* ceux qui, celles qui; (*object*) celui *etc* que; **show me w.** (**one**) **is red** montrez-moi celui *or* celle qui est rouge; **I know w.** (**ones**) **you want** je sais ceux *or* celles que vous désirez. ◆**which'ever** *a* & *pron* **w.** (**one**) **book/etc** *or* **w. of the books/etc you buy** quel que soit le livre/etc que tu achètes; **take w. books** *or* **w. of the books interest you** prenez les livres qui vous intéressent; **take w. (one) you like** prends celui or celle que tu veux; **w. (ones) remain** ceux or celles qui restent.

whiff [wɪf] n (puff) bouffée f; (smell) odeur f.

while [waɪl] conj (when) pendant que; (although) bien que (+ sub); (as long as) tant que; (whereas) tandis que; **w. doing** (in the course of) en faisant; – n a w. un moment, quelque temps; **all the w.** tout le temps; – vt **to w. away** (time) passer. ◆**whilst** [waɪlst] conj = while.

whim [wɪm] n caprice m.

whimper ['wɪmpər] vi (of dog, person) gémir faiblement; (snivel) Pej pleurnicher; – n faible gémissement m; **without a w.** (complaint) Fig sans se plaindre.

whimsical ['wɪmzɪk(ə)l] a (look, idea) bizarre; (person) fantasque, capricieux.

whine [waɪn] vi gémir; (complain) Fig se plaindre; – n gémissement m; plainte f.

whip [wɪp] n fouet m; – vt (-pp-) (person, cream etc) fouetter; (defeat) Fam dérouiller; **to w. off** (take off) enlever brusquement; **to w. out** (from pocket etc) sortir brusquement (from de); **to w. up** (interest) susciter; (meal) Fam préparer rapidement; – vi (move) aller à toute vitesse; **to w. round to s.o.'s** faire un saut chez qn. ◆**whip-round** n Fam collecte f.

whirl [wɜːl] vi tourbillonner, tournoyer; – vt faire tourbillonner; – n tourbillon m. ◆**whirlpool** n tourbillon m; **w. bath** Am bain m à remous. ◆**whirlwind** n tourbillon m (de vent).

whirr [wɜːr] vi (of engine) vrombir; (of top) ronronner.

whisk [wɪsk] 1 Culin fouet m; – vt fouetter. 2 vt **to w. away** or **off** (tablecloth etc) enlever rapidement; (person) emmener rapidement; (chase away) chasser.

whiskers ['wɪskəz] npl (of animal) moustaches fpl; (beard) barbe f; (moustache) moustache f; (side) w. favoris mpl.

whisky, Am **whiskey** ['wɪskɪ] n whisky m.

whisper ['wɪspər] vti chuchoter; **w. to me!** chuchote à mon oreille!; – n chuchotement m; (rumour) Fig rumeur f, bruit m.

whistle ['wɪs(ə)l] n sifflement m; (object) sifflet m; **to blow** or **give a w.** siffler; – vti siffler; **to w. at** (girl) siffler; **to w. for** (dog, taxi) siffler.

Whit [wɪt] a **W. Sunday** dimanche m de Pentecôte.

white [waɪt] a (-er, -est) blanc; **to go** or **turn w.** blanchir; **w. coffee** café m au lait; **w. elephant** Fig objet m or projet m etc inutile;

w. lie pieux mensonge m; **w. man** blanc m; **w. woman** blanche f; – n (colour, of egg, of eye) blanc m; (person) blanc m, blanche f. ◆**white-collar 'worker** n employé, -ée mf de bureau. ◆**whiten** vti blanchir. ◆**whiteness** n blancheur f. ◆**whitewash** n (for walls etc) blanc m de chaux; – vt blanchir à la chaux; (person) Fig blanchir; (faults) justifier.

whiting ['waɪtɪŋ] n (fish) merlan m.

Whitsun ['wɪts(ə)n] n la Pentecôte.

whittle ['wɪt(ə)l] vt **to w. down** (wood) tailler; (price etc) Fig rogner.

whizz [wɪz] 1 vi (rush) aller à toute vitesse; **to w. past** passer à toute vitesse; **to w. through the air** fendre l'air. 2 a **w. kid** Fam petit prodige m.

who [huː] pron qui; **w. did it?** qui (est-ce qui) a fait ça?; **the woman w.** la femme qui; **w. did you see** tu as vu qui? ◆**who'ever** pron (no matter who) qui que ce soit qui; (object) qui que ce soit que; **w. has travelled** (anyone who) quiconque a or celui qui a voyagé; **you are** qui que vous soyez; **this man, w. he is** cet homme, quel qu'il soit; **w. did that?** qui donc a fait ça?

whodunit [huː'dʌnɪt] n (detective story) Fam polar m.

whole [həʊl] a entier (intact) intact; **the w. time** tout le temps; **the w. apple** toute la pomme, la pomme (tout) entière; **the w. truth** toute la vérité; **the w. world** le monde entier; **the w. lot** le tout; **to swallow sth w.** avaler qch tout rond; – n (unit) tout m; (total) totalité f; **the w. of the village** le village (tout) entier, tout le village; **the w. of the night** toute la nuit; **on the w., as a w.** dans l'ensemble. ◆**whole-'hearted** a, ◆**whole-'heartedly** adv sans réserve. ◆**wholemeal** a, Am ◆**wholewheat** a (bread) complet. ◆**wholly** adv entièrement.

wholesale ['həʊlseɪl] n Com gros m; – a (firm) de gros; (destruction etc) Fig en masse; – adv (in bulk) en gros; (to buy or sell one article) au prix de gros; (to destroy etc) Fig en masse. ◆**wholesaler** n grossiste mf.

wholesome ['həʊlsəm] a (food, climate etc) sain.

whom [huːm] pron (object) que; (in questions and after prep) qui; **w. did she see?** qui a-t-elle vu?; **the man w. you know** l'homme que tu connais; **with w.** avec qui; **of w.** dont.

whooping cough ['huːpɪŋkɒf] n coqueluche f.

whoops! [wups] *int (apology etc)* oups!

whopping ['wɒpɪŋ] *a (big) Fam* énorme. ◆**whopper** *n Fam* chose *f* énorme.

whore [hɔːr] *n (prostitute)* putain *f*.

whose [huːz] *poss pron & a* à qui, de qui; w. book is this?, w. is this book? à qui est ce livre?; w. daughter are you? de qui es-tu la fille?; **the woman w. book I have** la femme dont *or* de qui j'ai le livre; **the man w. mother I spoke to** l'homme à la mère de qui j'ai parlé.

why [waɪ] **1** *adv* pourquoi; w. not? pourquoi pas?; — *conj* **the reason w. they . . .** la raison pour laquelle ils . . . ; — *npl* **the whys and wherefores** le pourquoi et le comment. **2** *int (surprise)* eh bien!, tiens!

wick [wɪk] *n (of candle, lamp)* mèche *f*.

wicked ['wɪkɪd] *a (evil)* méchant, vilain; *(mischievous)* malicieux. ◆**—ly** *adv* méchamment; malicieusement. ◆**—ness** *n* méchanceté *f*.

wicker ['wɪkər] *n* osier *m*; — *a (chair etc)* en osier, d'osier. ◆**wickerwork** *n (objects)* vannerie *f*.

wicket ['wɪkɪt] *n (cricket stumps)* guichet *m*.

wide [waɪd] *a (-er, -est)* large; *(desert, ocean)* vaste; *(choice, knowledge, variety)* grand; **to be three metres w.** avoir trois mètres de large; — *adv (to fall, shoot)* loin du but; *(to open)* tout grand. ◆**wide-'awake** *a (alert, not sleeping)* éveillé. ◆**widely** *adv (to broadcast, spread)* largement; *(to travel)* beaucoup; w. different très différent; w. thought *or* believed that . . . on pense généralement que . . . . ◆**widen** *vt* élargir; — *vi* s'élargir. ◆**wideness** *n* largeur *f*.

widespread ['waɪdspred] *a (très)* répandu.

widow ['wɪdəu] *n* veuve *f*. ◆**widowed** *a (man)* veuf; *(woman)* veuve; **to be w.** *(become a widower or widow)* devenir veuf *or* veuve. ◆**widower** *n* veuf *m*.

width [wɪdθ] *n* largeur *f*.

wield [wiːld] *vt (handle)* manier; *(brandish)* brandir; *(power) Fig* exercer.

wife [waɪf] *n (pl* wives) femme *f*, épouse *f*.

wig [wɪg] *n* perruque *f*.

wiggle ['wɪg(ə)l] *vt* agiter; **to w. one's hips** tortiller des hanches; — *vi (of worm etc)* se tortiller; *(of tail)* remuer.

wild [waɪld] *a (-er, -est) (animal, flower, region etc)* sauvage; *(enthusiasm, sea)* déchaîné; *(idea, life)* fou; *(look)* farouche; *(angry)* furieux *(with* contre); w. with *(joy, anger etc)* fou de; **I'm not w. about it** *(plan etc) Fam* ça ne m'emballe pas; **to be w. about s.o.** *(very fond of)* être dingue de qn; **to grow w.** *(of plant)* pousser à l'état sau-

vage; **to run w.** *(of animals)* courir en liberté; *(of crowd)* se déchaîner; **the W. West** *Am* le Far West; — *npl* régions *fpl* sauvages. ◆**wildcat 'strike** *n* grève *f* sauvage. ◆**wild-'goose chase** *n* fausse piste *f*. ◆**wildlife** *n* animaux *mpl* sauvages, faune *f*.

wilderness ['wɪldənəs] *n* désert *m*.

wildly ['waɪldlɪ] *adv (madly)* follement; *(violently)* violemment.

wile [waɪl] *n* ruse *f*, artifice *m*.

wilful ['wɪlfəl] *a (Am* willful) *(intentional, obstinate)* volontaire. ◆**—ly** *adv* volontairement.

will[1] [wɪl] *v aux* **he will come, he'll come** *(future tense)* il viendra **(won't he?** n'est-ce pas?); **you will not come, you won't come** tu ne viendras pas **(will you?** n'est-ce pas?); w. **you have a tea?** veux-tu prendre un thé?; w. **you be quiet!** veux-tu te taire!; I w.! *(yes)* oui!; **it won't open** ça ne s'ouvre pas, ça ne veut pas s'ouvrir.

will[2] [wɪl] **1** *vt (wish, intend)* vouloir **(that** que (+ *sub*)); **to w. oneself to do** faire un effort de volonté pour faire; — *n* volonté *f*; **against one's w.** à contrecœur; **at w.** *(to depart etc)* quand on veut; *(to choose)* à volonté. **2** *n (legal document)* testament *m*. ◆**willpower** *n* volonté *f*.

willing ['wɪlɪŋ] *a (helper, worker)* de bonne volonté; *(help etc)* spontané; **to be w. to do** être disposé *or* prêt à faire, vouloir bien faire; — *n* **to show w.** faire preuve de bonne volonté. ◆**—ly** *adv (with pleasure)* volontiers; *(voluntarily)* volontairement. ◆**—ness** *n* bonne volonté *f*; **his** *or* **her w. to do** *(enthusiasm)* son empressement *m* à faire.

willow ['wɪləu] *n (tree, wood)* saule *m*. ◆**willowy** *a (person)* svelte.

willy-nilly [wɪlɪ'nɪlɪ] *adv* bon gré mal gré, de gré ou de force.

wilt [wɪlt] *vi (of plant)* dépérir; *(of enthusiasm etc) Fig* décliner.

wily ['waɪlɪ] *a (-ier, -iest)* rusé.

wimp [wɪmp] *n (weakling) Fam* mauviette *f*.

win [wɪn] *n (victory)* victoire *f*; — *vi (pt & pp* won, *pres p* winning) gagner; — *vt (money, race etc)* gagner; *(victory, prize)* remporter; *(fame)* acquérir; *(friends)* se faire; **to w. s.o. over** gagner qn **(to** à). ◆**winning** *a (number, horse etc)* gagnant; *(team)* victorieux; *(goal)* décisif; *(smile)* engageant; — *npl* gains *mpl*.

wince [wɪns] *vi (flinch)* tressaillir; *(pull a face)* grimacer; **without wincing** sans sourciller.

winch [wɪntʃ] n treuil m; – vt **to w. (up)** hisser au treuil.

wind [waɪnd] n vent m; (breath) souffle m; **to have w.** Med avoir des gaz; **to get w. of** Fig avoir vent de; **in the w.** Fig dans l'air; **w. instrument** Mus instrument m à vent; – vt **to w. s.o.** (of blow etc) couper le souffle à qn. ◆**windbreak** n (fence, trees) brise-vent m inv. ◆**windcheater** n Am **windbreaker** n blouson m, coupe-vent m inv. ◆**windfall** n (piece of fruit) fruit m abattu par le vent; (unexpected money) Fig aubaine f. ◆**windmill** n moulin m à vent. ◆**windpipe** n Anat trachée f. ◆**windscreen** n, Am **windshield** n Aut pare-brise m inv; **w. wiper** essuie-glace m inv. ◆**windsurfing** n **to go w.** faire de la planche à voile. ◆**windswept** a (street etc) balayé par les vents. ◆**windy** a (-ier, -iest) venteux, venté; **it's w.** (of weather) il y a du vent.

wind² [waɪnd] vt (pt & pp **wound**) (roll) enrouler; **to w. (up)** (clock) remonter; **to w. up** (meeting) terminer; (firm) liquider; – vi (of river, road) serpenter; **to w. down** (relax) se détendre; **to w. up** (end up) finir (doing par faire); **to w. up with** se retrouver avec qch. ◆**-ing** n (road etc) sinueux; (staircase) tournant. ◆**-er** n (of watch) remontoir m.

window [wɪndəʊ] n fenêtre f; (pane) vitre f, carreau m; (in vehicle or train) vitre f; (in shop) vitrine f; (counter) guichet m; **French w.** porte-fenêtre f; **w. box** jardinière f; **w. cleaner** or Am **washer** laveur, -euse mf de carreaux; **w. dresser** étalagiste mf; **w. ledge** = **windowsill**; **to go w. shopping** faire du lèche-vitrines. ◆**windowpane** n vitre f, carreau m. ◆**windowsill** n (inside) appui m de (la) fenêtre; (outside) rebord m de (la) fenêtre.

wine [waɪn] n vin m; – a (bottle, cask) à vin; **w. cellar** cave f (à vin); **w. grower** viticulteur m; **w. list** carte f des vins; **w. taster** dégustateur, -trice mf de vins; **w. tasting** dégustation f de vins; **w. waiter** sommelier m; – vt **to w. and dine s.o.** offrir à dîner et à boire à qn. ◆**wineglass** n verre m à vin. ◆**wine-growing** a viticole.

wing [wɪŋ] n aile f; **the wings** Th les coulisses fpl; **under one's w.** Fig sous son aile. ◆**winged** a ailé. ◆**winger** n Sp ailier m. ◆**wingspan** n envergure f.

wink [wɪŋk] vi faire un clin d'œil (at, to à); (of light) clignoter; – n clin m d'œil.

winkle [wɪŋk(ə)l] n (sea animal) bigorneau m.

winner [wɪnər] n (of contest etc) gagnant, -ante mf; (of argument, fight) vainqueur m; **that idea/etc is a w.** Fam c'est une idée/etc en or.

winter [wɪntər] n hiver m; – a d'hiver; **in (the) w.** en hiver. ◆**wintertime** n hiver m. ◆**wintry** a hivernal.

wipe [waɪp] vt essuyer; **to w. one's feet/hands** s'essuyer les pieds/les mains; **to w. away** or **off** or **up** (liquid) essuyer; **to w. out** (clean) essuyer; (erase) effacer; (destroy) anéantir; – vi **to w. up** (dry the dishes) essuyer la vaisselle; – n coup m de torchon or d'éponge. ◆**-er** n Aut essuie-glace m inv.

wir/e [waɪər] n fil m; (telegram) télégramme m; **w. netting** grillage m; – vt **to w. (up)** (house) El faire l'installation électrique de; **to w. s.o.** (telegraph) télégraphier à qn. ◆**-ing** n El installation f électrique. ◆**wirecutters** npl pince f coupante.

wireless [waɪələs] n (set) TSF f, radio f; **by w.** (to send a message) par sans-fil.

wiry [waɪərɪ] a (-ier, -iest) maigre et nerveux.

wisdom [wɪzdəm] n sagesse f.

wise [waɪz] a (-er, -est) (prudent) sage, prudent; (learned) savant; **to put s.o. w./be w. to** Fam mettre qn/être au courant de; **w. guy** Fam gros malin m. ◆**wisecrack** n Fam (joke) astuce f; (sarcastic remark) sarcasme m. ◆**wisely** adv prudemment.

-wise [waɪz] suffix (with regard to) **money/etc-wise** question argent/etc.

wish [wɪʃ] vt souhaiter, vouloir (to do faire); **I w. (that) you could help me/could have helped me** je voudrais que/j'aurais voulu que vous m'aidiez; **I w. I hadn't done that** je regrette d'avoir fait ça; **if you w.** si tu veux; **I w. you well** or **luck** je vous souhaite bonne chance; **I wished him** or **her** (a) **happy birthday** je lui ai souhaité bon anniversaire; **I w. I could** si seulement je pouvais; – vi **to w. for sth** souhaiter qch; – n (specific) souhait m, vœu m; (general) désir m; **the w. for sth/to do** le désir de qch/de faire; **best wishes** (on greeting card) meilleurs vœux mpl; (in letter) amitiés fpl, bien amicalement; **send him** or **her my best wishes** fais-lui mes amitiés. ◆**wishbone** n bréchet m. ◆**wishful** a **it's w. thinking (on your part)** tu te fais des illusions, tu prends tes désirs pour la réalité.

wishy-washy [wɪʃɪwɒʃɪ] a (taste, colour) fade.

wisp [wɪsp] n (of smoke) volute f; (of hair)

fine mèche f; **a (mere) w. of a girl** une fillette toute menue.

wisteria [wɪˈstɪərɪə] n Bot glycine f.

wistful [ˈwɪstfəl] a mélancolique et rêveur. ◆**-ly** adv avec mélancolie.

wit [wɪt] n **1** (humour) esprit m; (person) homme m or femme f d'esprit. **2 wit(s)** (intelligence) intelligence f (to do de faire); **to be at one's wits'** or **wit's end** ne plus savoir que faire.

witch [wɪtʃ] n sorcière f. ◆**witchcraft** n sorcellerie f. ◆**witch-hunt** n Pol chasse f aux sorcières.

with [wɪð] prep **1** avec; **come w. me** viens avec moi; **w. no hat** sans chapeau; **I'll be right w. you** je suis à vous dans une minute; **I'm w. you** (I understand) Fam je te suis; **w. it** (up-to-date) Fam dans le vent. **2** (at the house, flat etc) of) chez; **she's staying w. me** elle loge chez moi; **it's a habit w. me** c'est une habitude chez moi. **3** (cause) de; **to jump w. joy** sauter de joie. **4** (instrument, means) avec, de; **to write w. a pen** écrire avec un stylo; **to fill w.** remplir de; **satisfied w.** satisfait de; **w. my own eyes** de mes propres yeux. **5** (description) à; **w. blue eyes** aux yeux bleus. **6** (despite) malgré.

withdraw [wɪðˈdrɔː] vt (pt withdrew, pp withdrawn) retirer (from de); - vi se retirer (from de). ◆**withdrawn** a (person) renfermé. ◆**withdrawal** n retrait m; **to suffer from w. symptoms** (of drug addict etc) être en manque.

wither [ˈwɪðər] vi (of plant etc) se flétrir; - vt flétrir. ◆**-ed** a (limb) atrophié. ◆**-ing** a (look) foudroyant; (remark) cinglant.

withhold [wɪðˈhəʊld] vt (pt & pp withheld) (help, permission etc) refuser (from à); (decision) différer; (money) retenir (from de); (information etc) cacher (from à).

within [wɪˈðɪn] adv à l'intérieur; - prep (place, container etc) à l'intérieur de, dans; **w. a kilometre of** à moins d'un kilomètre de; **w. a month** (to return etc) avant un mois; (to finish sth) en moins d'un mois; (to pay) sous un mois; **w. my means** dans les limites de mes moyens; **w. sight** en vue.

without [wɪˈðaʊt] prep sans; **w. a tie**/etc sans cravate/etc; **w. doing** sans faire.

withstand [wɪðˈstænd] vt (pt & pp withstood) résister à.

witness [ˈwɪtnɪs] n (person) témoin m; (evidence) Jur témoignage m; **to bear w. to** témoigner de; - vt être (le) témoin de, voir; (document) signer (pour attester l'authenticité de).

witty [ˈwɪtɪ] a (-ier, -iest) spirituel. ◆**witti-**cism** n bon mot m, mot m d'esprit. ◆**witti-ness** n esprit m.

wives [waɪvz] see **wife.**

wizard [ˈwɪzəd] n magicien m; (genius) Fig génie m, as m.

wizened [ˈwɪz(ə)nd] a ratatiné.

wobble [ˈwɒb(ə)l] vi (of chair etc) branler, boiter; (of cyclist, pile etc) osciller; (of jelly, leg) trembler; (of wheel) tourner de façon irrégulière. ◆**wobbly** a (table etc) bancal, boiteux; **to be w. = to wobble.**

woe [wəʊ] n malheur m. ◆**woeful** a triste.

woke, woken [wəʊk, ˈwəʊk(ə)n] see **wake** [1].

wolf [wʊlf] **1** n (pl wolves) loup m; **w. whistle** sifflement m admiratif. **2** vt **to w. (down)** (food) engloutir.

woman, pl **women** [ˈwʊmən, ˈwɪmɪn] n femme f; **she's a London w.** c'est une Londonienne; **w. doctor** femme f médecin; **women drivers** les femmes fpl au volant; **w. friend** amie f; **w. teacher** professeur m femme; **women's** (attitudes, clothes etc) féminin. ◆**womanhood** n (quality) fémini-ité f; **to reach w.** devenir femme. ◆**womanizer** n Pej coureur m (de femmes or de jupons). ◆**womanly** a féminin.

womb [wuːm] n utérus m.

women [ˈwɪmɪn] see **woman.**

won [wʌn] see **win.**

wonder [ˈwʌndər] **1** n (marvel) merveille f, miracle m; (sense, feeling) émerveillement m; **in w.** (to watch etc) émerveillé; **(it's) no w.** ce n'est pas étonnant (that que (+ sub)); - vi (marvel) s'étonner (at de); - vt **I w. that** je or ça m'étonne que (+ sub). **2** vt (ask oneself) se demander (if si, why pourquoi); - vi (reflect) songer (about à). ◆**wonderful** a (excellent, astonishing) merveilleux. ◆**wonderfully** adv (beautiful, hot etc) merveilleusement; (to do, work etc) à merveille.

wonky [ˈwɒŋkɪ] a (-ier, -iest) Fam (table etc) bancal; (hat, picture) de travers.

won't [wəʊnt] = **will not.**

woo [wuː] vt (woman) faire la cour à, courtiser; (try to please) Fig chercher à plaire à.

wood [wʊd] n (material, forest) bois m. ◆**woodcut** n gravure f sur bois. ◆**wooded** a (valley etc) boisé. ◆**wooden** a de or en bois; (manner, dancer etc) Fig raide. ◆**woodland** n région f boisée. ◆**woodpecker** n (bird) pic m. ◆**wood-wind** n (instruments) Mus bois mpl. ◆**woodwork** n (craft, objects) menuiserie f. ◆**woodworm** n (larvae) vers mpl (du bois); **it has w.** c'est vermoulu. ◆**woody** a

(-ier, -iest) (*hill etc*) boisé; (*stem etc*) ligneux.

wool [wul] *n* laine *f*; – *a* de laine; (*industry*) lainier. ◆**woollen** *a* de laine; (*industry*) lainier; – *npl* (*garments*) lainages *mpl.* ◆**woolly** *a* (**-ier, -iest**) laineux; (*unclear*) *Fig* nébuleux; – *n* (*garment*) *Fam* lainage *m.*

word [wɜːd] *n* mot *m*; (*spoken*) parole *f*, mot *m*; (*promise*) parole *f*; (*command*) ordre *m*; *pl* (*of song etc*) paroles *fpl*; **by w. of mouth** de vive voix; **to have a w. with s.o.** (*speak to*) parler à qn; (*advise, lecture*) avoir un mot avec qn; **in other words** autrement dit; **I have no w. from** (*news*) je suis sans nouvelles de; **to send w. that . . .** faire savoir que . . . ; **to leave w. that . . .** dire que . . . ; **the last w. in** (*latest development*) le dernier cri en matière de; **w. processing** traitement *m* de texte; – *vt* (*express*) rédiger, formuler. ◆**wording** *n* termes *mpl.* ◆**wordy** *a* (**-ier, -iest**) verbeux.

wore [wɔːr] *see* **wear 1,2.**

work [wɜːk] *n* travail *m*; (*product*) & *Liter* œuvre *f*, ouvrage *m*; (*building or repair work*) travaux *mpl*; **to be at w.** travailler; **farm w.** travaux *mpl* agricoles; **out of w.** au *or* en chômage; **a day off w.** un jour de congé *or* de repos; **he's off w.** il n'est pas allé travailler; **the works** (*mechanism*) le mécanisme; **a gas works** (*factory*) une usine à gaz; **w. force** main-d'œuvre *f*; **a heavy w. load** beaucoup de travail; – *vi* travailler; (*of machine etc*) marcher, fonctionner; (*of drug*) agir; **to w. on** (*book etc*) travailler à; (*principle*) se baser sur; **to w. at** *or* **on sth** (*improve*) travailler qch; **to w. loose** (*of knot, screw*) se desserrer; (*of tooth*) se mettre à branler; **to w. towards** (*result, agreement, aim*) travailler à; **to w. out** (*succeed*) marcher; (*train*) *Sp* s'entraîner; **it works out at £5** ça fait cinq livres; **it works up to** (*climax*) ça tend vers; **to w. up to sth** (*in speech etc*) en venir à qch; – *vt* (*person*) faire travailler; (*machine*) faire marcher; (*mine*) exploiter; (*miracle*) faire; (*metal, wood etc*) travailler; **to get worked up** s'exciter; **to w. in** (*reference, bolt*) introduire; **to w. off** (*debt*) payer en travaillant; (*excess fat*) se débarrasser de par l'exercice; (*anger*) passer, assouvir; **to w. out** (*solve*) résoudre; (*calculate*) calculer; (*scheme, plan*) élaborer; **to w. up an appetite** s'ouvrir l'appétit; **to w. up enthusiasm** s'enthousiasmer; **to w. one's way up** (*rise socially etc*) faire du chemin. ◆**working** *a* (*day, clothes etc*) de travail; (*population*

actif; **Monday's a w. day** on travaille le lundi, lundi est un jour ouvré; **w. class** class *f* ouvrière; **in w. order** en état de marche; – *npl* (*mechanism*) mécanisme *m.* ◆**workable** *a* (*plan*) praticable. ◆**worker** *n* travailleur, -euse *mf*; (*manual*) ouvrier, -ière *mf*; (*employee, clerk*) employé, -ée *mf*; **blue-collar w.** col *m* bleu.

workaholic [wɜːkə'hɒlɪk] *n* *Fam* bourreau *m* de travail. ◆**workbench** *n* établi *m.* ◆**working-'class** *a* ouvrier. ◆**workman** *n* (*pl* **-men**) ouvrier *m.* ◆**workmanship** *n* maîtrise *f*, travail *m.* ◆**workmate** *n* camarade *mf* de travail. ◆**workout** *n* *Sp* (*séance f*) d'entraînement *m.* ◆**workroom** *n* salle *f* de travail. ◆**workshop** *n* atelier *m.* ◆**work-shy** *a* peu enclin au travail. ◆**work-to-'rule** *n* grève *f* du zèle.

world [wɜːld] *n* monde *m*; **all over the w.** dans le monde entier; **the richest/etc in the world** le *or* la plus riche/*etc* du monde; **a w. of** (*a lot of*) énormément de; **to think the w. of** penser énormément de bien de; **why in the w. . . . ?** pourquoi diable . . . ?; **out of this w.** (*wonderful*) *Fam* formidable; – *a* (*war etc*) mondial; (*champion, cup, record*) du monde. ◆**world-'famous** *a* de renommée mondiale. ◆**worldly** *a* (*pleasures*) de ce monde; (*person*) qui a l'expérience du monde. ◆**world'wide** *a* universel.

worm [wɜːm] **1** *n* ver *m.* **2** *vt* **to w. one's way into** s'insinuer dans; **to w. sth out of s.o.** soutirer qch à qn. ◆**worm-eaten** *a* (*wood*) vermoulu; (*fruit*) véreux.

worn [wɔːn] *see* **wear 1,2;** – *a* (*tyre etc*) usé. ◆**worn-'out** *a* (*object*) complètement usé; (*person*) épuisé.

worry [ˈwʌrɪ] *n* souci *m*; – *vi* s'inquiéter (**about sth** de qch, **about s.o.** pour qn); – *vt* inquiéter; **to be worried** être inquiet; **to be worried sick** se ronger les sangs. ◆**—ing** *a* (*news etc*) inquiétant. ◆**worrier** *n* anxieux, -euse *mf.* ◆**worryguts** *n*, *Am* ◆**worrywart** *n* *Fam* anxieux, -euse *mf.*

worse [wɜːs] *a* pire, plus mauvais (**than** que); **to get w.** se détériorer; **he's getting w.** (*in health*) il va de plus en plus mal; (*in behaviour*) il se conduit de plus en plus mal; – *adv* plus mal (**than** que); **I could do w.** je pourrais faire pire; **to hate/etc w. than** détester/*etc* plus que; **to be w. off** (*financially*) aller moins bien financièrement; – *n* **there's w.** (**to come**) il y a pire encore; **a change for the w.** une détérioration. ◆**worsen** *vti* empirer.

worship [ˈwɜːʃɪp] *n* culte *m*; **his W. the Mayor** Monsieur le Maire; – *vt* (**-pp-**)

(*person*) & *Rel* adorer; (*money etc*) *Pej* avoir le culte de; – *vi* faire ses dévotions (at à). ◆**worshipper** *n* adorateur, -trice *mf*; (*in church*) fidèle *mf*.

worst [wɜːst] *a* pire, plus mauvais; – *adv* (the) w. le plus mal; **to come off w.** (*in struggle etc*) avoir le dessous; – *n* **the w.** (one) (*object, person*) le *or* la pire, le *or* la plus mauvais(e); **the w. (thing) is that . . .** le pire c'est que . . . ; **at (the) w.** au pis aller; **at its w.** (*crisis*) au plus mauvais point *or* moment; **to get the w. of it** (*in struggle etc*) avoir le dessous; **the w. is yet to come** on n'a pas encore vu le pire.

worsted [ˈwustid] *n* laine *f* peignée.

worth [wɜːθ] *n* valeur *f*; **to buy 50 pence w. of chocolates** acheter pour cinquante pence de chocolats; – *a* **to be w.** valoir; **how much** *or* **what is it w.?** ça vaut combien?; **the film's w. seeing** le film vaut la peine *or* le coup d'être vu; **it's w. (one's) while** ça (en) vaut la peine *or* le coup; **it's w. (while) waiting** ça vaut la peine d'attendre. ◆**worthless** *a* qui ne vaut rien. ◆**worth'while** *a* (*book, film etc*) qui vaut la peine d'être lu, vu *etc*; (*activity*) qui (en) vaut la peine; (*contribution, plan*) valable; (*cause*) louable; (*satisfying*) qui donne des satisfactions.

worthy [ˈwɜːði] *a* (**-ier, -iest**) digne (of de); (*laudable*) louable; – *n* (*person*) notable *m*.

would [wud, *unstressed* wəd] *v aux* **I w. stay, I'd stay** (*conditional tense*) je resterais; **he w. have done it** il l'aurait fait; **w. you help me, please?** voudriez-vous m'aider, s'il vous plaît?; **w. you like some tea?** voudriez-vous (prendre) du thé?; **I w. see her every day** (*used to*) je la voyais chaque jour. ◆**would-be** *a* (*musician etc*) soi-disant.

wound[1] [wuːnd] *vt* (*hurt*) blesser; **the wounded** les blessés *mpl*; – *n* blessure *f*.

wound[2] [waund] *see* **wind**[2].

wove, woven [wauv, ˈwauv(ə)n] *see* **weave**.

wow! [wau] *int Fam* (c'est) formidable!

wrangle [ˈræŋg(ə)l] *n* dispute *f*; – *vi* se disputer.

wrap [ræp] *vt* (**-pp-**) **to w.** envelopper; **to w. (oneself) up** (*dress warmly*) se couvrir; **wrapped up in** (*engrossed*) *Fig* absorbé par; – *n* (*shawl*) châle *m*; (*cape*) pèlerine *f*; **plastic w.** *Am* scel-o-frais® *m*. ◆**wrapping** *n* (*action, material*) emballage *m*; **w. paper** papier *m* d'emballage. ◆**wrapper** *n* (*of sweet*) papier *m*; (*of book*) jaquette *f*.

wrath [rɒθ] *n Lit* courroux *m*.

wreak [riːk] *vt* **to w. vengeance** on se venger de; **to w. havoc** on ravager.

wreath [riːθ] *n* (*pl* **-s** [riːðz]) (*on head, for funeral*) couronne *f*.

wreck [rek] *n* (*ship*) épave *f*; (*sinking*) naufrage *m*; (*train etc*) train *m* etc accidenté; (*person*) épave *f* (humaine); **to be a nervous w.** être à bout de nerfs; – *vt* détruire; (*ship*) provoquer le naufrage de; (*career, hopes etc*) *Fig* briser, détruire. ◆**-age** *n* (*fragments*) débris *mpl.* ◆**-er** *n* (*breakdown truck*) *Am* dépanneuse *f*.

wren [ren] *n* (*bird*) roitelet *m*.

wrench [rentʃ] *vt* (*tug at*) tirer sur; (*twist*) tordre; **to w. sth from s.o.** arracher qch à qn; – *n* mouvement *m* de torsion; (*tool*) clé *f* (à écrous), *Am* clé *f* à mollette; (*distress*) *Fig* déchirement *m*.

wrest [rest] *vt* **to w. sth from s.o.** arracher qch à qn.

wrestl/e [ˈres(ə)l] *vi* lutter (**with s.o.** contre qn); **to w. with** (*problem etc*) *Fig* se débattre avec. ◆**-ing** *n Sp* lutte *f*; (**all-in**) *vi* catch *m.* ◆**-er** *n* lutteur, -euse *mf*; catcheur, -euse *mf*.

wretch [retʃ] *n* (*unfortunate person*) malheureux, -euse *mf*; (*rascal*) misérable *mf.* ◆**wretched** [-id] *a* (*poor, pitiful*) misérable; (*dreadful*) affreux; (*annoying*) maudit.

wriggle [ˈrɪg(ə)l] *vi* **to w.** (**about**) se tortiller; (*of fish*) frétiller; **to w. out of** (*difficulty, task etc*) esquiver; – *vt* (*fingers, toes*) tortiller.

wring [rɪŋ] *vt* (*pt & pp* **wrung**) (*neck*) tordre; **to w. (out)** (*clothes*) essorer; (*water*) faire sortir; **to w. sth out of s.o.** *Fig* arracher qch à qn; **wringing wet** (trempé) à tordre.

wrinkle [ˈrɪŋk(ə)l] *n* (*on skin*) ride *f*; (*in cloth or paper*) pli *m*; (*on skin*) rider; (*cloth, paper*) plisser; – *vi* se rider; faire des plis.

wrist [rist] *n* poignet *m.* ◆**wristwatch** *n* montre-bracelet *f*.

writ [rit] *n* acte *m* judiciaire; **to issue a w. against s.o.** assigner qn (en justice).

write [rait] *vti* (*pt* **wrote**, *pp* **written**) écrire; **to w. down** noter; **to w. off** (*debt*) passer aux profits et pertes; **to w. out** écrire; (*copy*) recopier; **to w. up** (*from notes*) rédiger; (*diary, notes*) mettre à jour; – *vi* écrire; **to w. away** *or* **off** *or* **up for** (*details etc*) écrire pour demander; **to w. back** répondre; **to w. in** *Rad TV* écrire (**for information**/*etc* pour demander des renseignements/*etc*). ◆**w.-off** *n* **a (complete) w.-off** (*car*) une véritable épave. ◆**w.-up** *n* (*report*) *Journ* compte rendu *m.* ◆**writing** *n* (*handwriting*) écriture *f*; (*literature*) littérature *f*; **to put (down) in w.** mettre par écrit; **some w.** (*on page*) quelque chose d'écrit; **his** *or* **her**

writing(s) (*works*) ses écrits *mpl*; **w. desk** secrétaire *m*; **w. pad** bloc *m* de papier à lettres; **w. paper** papier *m* à lettres. ◆**writer** *n* auteur *m* (of de); (*literary*) écrivain *m*.

writhe [raɪð] *vi* (in pain etc) se tordre.

written ['rɪt(ə)n] *see* write.

wrong [rɒŋ] *a* (*sum, idea etc*) faux, erroné; (*direction, time etc*) mauvais; (*unfair*) injuste; **to be w.** (of person) avoir tort (**to do** de faire); (*mistaken*) se tromper; **it's w. to swear/etc** (*morally*) c'est mal de jurer/etc; **it's the w. road** ce n'est pas la bonne route; **you're the w. man** (for job etc) tu n'es pas l'homme qu'il faut; **the clock's w.** la pendule n'est pas à l'heure; **something's w.** quelque chose ne va pas; **something's w. with the phone** le téléphone ne marche pas bien; **something's w. with her arm** elle a quelque chose au bras; **nothing's w.** tout va bien; **what's w. with you?** qu'est-ce qui ne va; **the w. way round** *or* **up** à l'envers; – *adv* mal; **to go w.** (*err*) se tromper; (of plan) mal tourner; (of vehicle, machine) tomber en panne; – *n* (*injustice*) injustice *f*; (*evil*) mal *m*; **to be in the w.** avoir tort; **right and w.** le bien et le mal; – *vt* faire (du) tort à. ◆**wrongdoer** *n* (*criminal*) malfaiteur *m*. ◆**wrongful** *a* injustifié; (*arrest*) arbitraire. ◆**wrongfully** *adv* à tort. ◆**wrongly** *adv* incorrectement; (to inform, translate) mal; (to suspect etc) à tort.

wrote [rəʊt] *see* write.

wrought [rɔːt] *a* **w. iron** fer *m* forgé. ◆**w.-'iron** *a* en fer forgé.

wrung [rʌŋ] *see* wring.

wry [raɪ] *a* (wryer, wryest) (*comment*) ironique; (*smile*) forcé; **to pull a w. face** grimacer.

X

X, x [eks] *n* X, x *m*. ◆**X-ray** *n* (*beam*) rayon *m* X; (*photo*) radio(graphie) *f*; **to have an X-ray** passer une radio; **X-ray examination** examen *m* radioscopique; – *vt* radiographier.

xenophobia [zenəˈfəʊbɪə] *n* xénophobie *f*.

Xerox® [ˈzɪərɒks] *n* photocopie *f*; – *vt* photocopier.

Xmas [ˈkrɪsməs] *n* Fam Noël *m*.

xylophone [ˈzaɪləfəʊn] *n* xylophone *m*.

Y

Y, y [waɪ] *n* Y, y *m*.

yacht [jɒt] *n* yacht *m*. ◆**—ing** *n* yachting *m*.

yank [jæŋk] *vt* Fam tirer d'un coup sec; **to y. off** *or* **out** arracher; – *n* coup *m* sec.

Yank(ee) [ˈjæŋk(ɪ)] *n* Fam Ricain, -aine *mf*, Pej Amerloque *mf*.

yap [jæp] *vi* (-pp-) (of dog) japper; (*jabber*) Fam jacasser.

yard [jɑːd] *n* **1** (of house etc) cour *f*; (for storage) dépôt *m*, chantier *m*; (*garden*) Am jardin *m* (à l'arrière de la maison); **builder's y.** chantier *m* de construction. **2** (*measure*) yard *m* (= 91,44 cm). ◆**yardstick** *n* (*criterion*) mesure *f*.

yarn [jɑːn] *n* **1** (*thread*) fil *m*. **2** (*tale*) Fam longue histoire *f*.

yawn [jɔːn] *vi* bâiller; – *n* bâillement *m*. ◆**—ing** *a* (gulf etc) béant.

yeah [jeə] *adv* (*yes*) Fam ouais.

year [jɪər] *n* an *m*, année *f*; (of wine) année *f*; **school/tax/etc y.** année *f* scolaire/fiscale/etc; **this y.** cette année; **in the y.** 1990 en (l'an) 1990; **he's ten years old** il a dix ans; **New Y.** Nouvel An, Nouvelle Année; **New Year's Day** le jour de l'An; **New Year's Eve** la Saint-Sylvestre. ◆**yearbook** *n* annuaire *m*. ◆**yearly** *a* annuel; – *adv* annuellement.

yearn [jɜːn] *vi* **to y. for s.o.** languir après qn; **to y. for sth** avoir très envie de qch; **to y. to do** avoir très envie de faire. ◆**—ing** *n* grande envie *f* (**for** de, **to do** de faire); (*nostalgia*) nostalgie *f*.

yeast [jiːst] *n* levure *f*.

yell [jel] *vti* **to y. (out)** hurler; **to y. at s.o.** (*scold*) crier après qn; – *n* hurlement *m*.

yellow ['jeləu] **1** *a* & *n* (*colour*) jaune (*m*); — *vi* jaunir. **2** *a* (*cowardly*) *Fam* froussard. ◆**yellowish** *a* jaunâtre.

yelp [jelp] *vi* (*of dog*) japper; — *n* jappement *m*.

yen [jen] *n* (*desire*) grande envie *f* (**for** de, **to** do de faire).

yes [jes] *adv* oui; (*contradicting negative question*) si; — *n* oui *m inv*.

yesterday ['jestədɪ] *adv* & *n* hier (*m*); **y. morning/evening** hier matin/soir; **the day before y.** avant-hier.

yet [jet] **1** *adv* encore; (*already*) déjà; **she hasn't come (as) y.** elle n'est pas encore venue; **has he come y.?** est-il déjà arrivé?; **the best y.** le meilleur jusqu'ici; **y. more complicated** (*even more*) encore plus compliqué; **not (just) y.** pas y. **while y.** pour l'instant. **2** *conj* (*nevertheless*) pourtant.

yew [juː] *n* (*tree, wood*) if *m*.

Yiddish ['jɪdɪʃ] *n* & *a* yiddish (*m*).

yield [jiːld] *n* rendement *m*; (*profit*) rapport *m*; — *vt* (*produce*) produire, rendre; (*profit*) rapporter; (*give up*) céder (**to** à); — *vi* (*surrender, give way*) céder (**to** à); (*of tree, land etc*) rendre; **'y.'** (*road sign*) *Am* 'cédez la priorité'.

yob(bo) ['jɒb(əʊ)] *n* (*pl* **yob(bo)s** *Sl* loubar(d) *m*.

yoga ['jəʊgə] *n* yoga *m*.

yog(h)urt ['jɒgət, *Am* 'jəʊgɜːt] *n* yaourt *m*.

yoke [jəʊk] *n* (*for oxen*) & *Fig* joug *m*.

yokel ['jəʊk(ə)l] *n Pej* plouc *m*.

yolk [jəʊk] *n* jaune *m* (d'œuf).

yonder ['jɒndər] *adv Lit* là-bas.

you [juː] *pron* **1** (*polite form singular*) vous; (*familiar form singular*) tu; (*polite and familiar form plural*) vous; (*object*) vous; te, t'; *pl* vous; (*after prep & stressed*) vous; toi; *pl* vous; **(to) y.** (*indirect*) vous; te, t'; *pl* vous; **y. are** vous êtes; tu es; **I see** je vous vois; je te vois; **I give it to y.** je vous le donne; je te le donne; **with y.** avec vous; avec toi; **y. teachers** vous autres professeurs; **y. idiot!** espèce d'imbécile! **2** (*indefinite*) on; (*object*) vous; te, t'; *pl* vous; **y. never know** on ne sait jamais.

young [jʌŋ] *a* (**-er, -est**) jeune; **my young(er) brother** mon (frère) cadet; **his** *or* **her youngest brother** le cadet de ses frères; **the youngest son** le cadet; — *n* (*of animals*) petits *mpl*; **the y.** (*people*) les jeunes *mpl*. ◆**young-looking** *a* qui a l'air jeune. ◆**youngster** *n* jeune *mf*.

your [jɔːr] *poss a* (*polite form singular, polite and familiar plural*) votre, *pl* vos; (*familiar form singular*) ton, ta, *pl* tes; (*one's*) son, sa, *pl* ses. ◆**yours** *poss pron* le vôtre, la vôtre, *pl* les vôtres; (*familiar singular*) le tien, la tienne, *pl* les tien(ne)s; **this book is y.** ce livre est à vous *or* est le vôtre; ce livre est à toi *or* est le tien; **a friend of y.** un ami à vous; un ami à toi. ◆**yourself** *pron* (*polite form*) vous-même; (*familiar form*) toi-même; (*reflexive*) vous; te, t'; (*after prep*) vous; toi; **you wash y.** vous vous lavez; tu te laves. ◆**yourselves** *pron pl* vous-mêmes; (*reflexive & after prep*) vous.

youth [juːθ] *n* (*pl* **-s** [juːðz]) (*age, young people*) jeunesse *f*; (*young man*) jeune *m*; **y. club** maison *f* des jeunes. ◆**youthful** *a* (*person*) jeune; (*quality, smile etc*) juvénile, jeune. ◆**youthfulness** *n* jeunesse *f*.

yoyo ['jəʊjəʊ] *n* (*pl* **-os**) yo-yo *m inv*.

yucky ['jʌkɪ] *a Sl* dégueulasse.

Yugoslav ['juːgəʊslɑːv] *a* & *n* yougoslave (*mf*). ◆**Yugoslavia** *n* Yougoslavie *f*.

yummy ['jʌmɪ] *a* (**-ier, -iest**) *Sl* délicieux.

yuppie ['jʌpɪ] *n* jeune cadre *m* ambitieux, jeune loup *m*, NAP *mf*.

Z

Z, z [zed, *Am* ziː] *n* Z, z *m*.

zany ['zeɪnɪ] *a* (**-ier, -iest**) farfelu.

zeal [ziːl] *n* zèle *m*. ◆**zealous** ['zeləs] *a* zélé. ◆**zealously** *adv* avec zèle.

zebra ['ziːbrə, 'zebrə] *n* zèbre *m*; **z. crossing** passage *m* pour piétons.

zenith ['zenɪθ] *n* zénith *m*.

zero ['zɪərəʊ] *n* (*pl* **-os**) zéro *m*; **z. hour** *Mil* & *Fig* l'heure H.

zest [zest] *n* **1** (*gusto*) entrain *m*; (*spice*) *Fig* piquant *m*; **z. for living** appétit *m* de vivre. **2** (*of lemon, orange*) zeste *m*.

zigzag ['zɪgzæg] *n* zigzag *m*; — *a* & *adv* en zigzag; — *vi* (**-gg-**) zigzaguer.

zinc [zɪŋk] *n* (*metal*) zinc *m*.

zip [zɪp] **1** *n* **z.** (*fastener*) fermeture *f* éclair®; — *vt* (**-pp-**) **to z. (up)** fermer (avec une fermeture éclair®). **2** *n* (*vigour*) *Fam* entrain *m*; − *vi* (**-pp-**) (*go quickly*) aller comme l'éclair. **3** *a* **z. code** *Am* code *m* postal. ◆**zipper** *n Am* fermeture *f* éclair®.

zit [zɪt] *n* (*pimple*) *Am Fam* bouton *m*.

zither ['zɪðər] *n* cithare *f*.

zodiac ['zəʊdɪæk] *n* zodiaque *m*.

zombie ['zɒmbɪ] *n* (*spiritless person*) *Fam* robot *m*, zombie *m*.

zone [zəʊn] *n* zone *f*; (*division of city*) secteur *m*.

zoo [zuː] *n* zoo *m*. ◆**zoological** [zuːə-'lɒdʒɪk(ə)l] *a* zoologique. ◆**zoology** [zuː-'ɒlədʒɪ] *n* zoologie *f*.

zoom [zuːm] **1** *vi* (*rush*) se précipiter; **to z. past** passer comme un éclair. **2** *n* **z. lens** zoom *m*; − *vi* **to z. in** *Cin* faire un zoom, zoomer (**on** sur).

zucchini [zuː'kiːnɪ] *n* (*pl* **-ni** *or* **-nis**) *Am* courgette *f*.

zwieback ['zwiːbæk] *n* (*rusk*) *Am* biscotte *f*.